Patents
and the
Federal Circuit

Fifth Edition

Patents
and the
Federal Circuit

Fifth Edition

Robert L. Harmon
www.ptoexpert.com

Retired Shareholder, Brinks Hofer Gilson & Lione

Islamorada, Florida
Chicago, Illinois
Oxford, Wisconsin

The Bureau of National Affairs, Inc., Washington, D.C.

Library of Congress Cataloging-in-Publication Data

Harmon, Robert L.
    Patents and the Federal Circuit / Robert L. Harmon. -- 5th ed.
        p. cm.
    Includes index.
    ISBN 1-57018-267-1
        1. Patent laws and legislation--United States. 2. Patent practice--United States. I. Title.

KF3114.H347 2001
346.7304'86--dc21   2001037779

Published by BNA Books
1231 25ᵗʰ Street NW, Washington, DC 20037

International Standard Book Number 1-57018-267-1
Printed in the United States of America

To Sue

Preface to the Fifth Edition

The Court of Appeals for the Federal Circuit continues to work, with vigor and skill, at its assigned task of increasing doctrinal stability in the patent field. This fifth edition covers all important Federal Circuit patent decisions handed down through the end of the year 2000. Included are all opinions reported by BNA through *United States Patents Quarterly (Second)*, Volume 55, and the court's remarkable *Festo* decision, which appears at 56 USPQ2d 1865 (November 29, 2000).

Three years ago, at the end of 1997, I retired from my active law firm practice at Chicago's Brinks Hofer Gilson & Lione. My intention is to continue to devote my time and attention to continuing maintenance and revision of this book, to consultation to my former firm, and to service as a special master and expert witness in patent infringement litigation.

Thanks are due the editors and staff at BNA, whose encouragement is always timely, and whose guidance is always necessary. They have made the production of this book truly painless for its author. I am also grateful for the assistance of my wife Sue.

Sue deserves more than just thanks. The first edition of this book was dedicated to Judge Arthur Smith of the predecessor Court of Customs and Patent Appeals, for whom I clerked in the period 1963–1965. It was the Judge who set me on the track. But it has been Sue who kept me there—a much more formidable task. It is only right, therefore, that I dedicate subsequent editions to her.

ROBERT L. HARMON

Islamorada
January 2001

Preface to the First Edition

The Court of Appeals for the Federal Circuit was created October 1, 1982, and was given exclusive jurisdiction over, among other things, appeals from final decisions of district courts in those cases where the district court's jurisdiction was based in whole or part on the patent provisions of 28 U.S.C. §1338. In simpler terms, practically speaking, the court was to have exclusive appellate jurisdiction in patent cases, and its job was to increase doctrinal stability in the field of patent law. *Chemical Eng'g Corp. v. Marlo, Inc.*, 754 F.2d 331, 222 USPQ 738 (Fed. Cir. 1984).

It would be chauvinistic in the extreme for this author to suggest that the court has in any way failed to do that job. Indeed, as the only appellate court dealing with the substantive law of patents, it could hardly fail. No, the only complaint on that score—if it may be called a complaint—is that the court may have attacked its job with perhaps a touch too much evangelical fervor. The result has been not opinions that are wrong, but language that goes too far, that is overbroad for the purpose.

Near the end of its second full year of existence, the court was taken to task gently by Senior Circuit Judge Nichols in a concurring opinion. What Judge Nichols had to say eloquently summarizes the present thoughts of the author of this book; three years later still:

> So I am taking issue about what we say, not what we do, and my position here is contrary to my more usual view that talk is cheap and the mere words chosen by an intermediate appellate judge are of little consequence. I think we are painting ourselves into corners by our eagerness to pronounce legal doctrines not immediately necessary to make our decisions, and the more important our words are, the more confining will be the corners into which we have painted ourselves. I further think that our exclusive jurisdiction, over certain areas of law, is not to be construed as a legislative direction to ignore the efforts of other courts to deal with the same problems, efforts exerted when over many years they shared the responsibility that is now ours. Not only are such efforts not to be ignored, but sporadic notice of them, when it occurs, is not to take the form of selecting decisions that happen to agree with our thinking, without regard to their place in the development of

the case law in that jurisdiction. "The life of the law is not logic but experience," and judicial experience is having to confront not just one case, but a series. As of right now, many other courts have had more continuous experience with patent validity issues than we have, at least as one body. Congress decreed that their conclusions should not bind us, but surely it did not require us to ignore them. Every court except, apparently, this one, knows the difference between being *bound* by the decision of another court, and being *aided* by study of the efforts of that other court to solve problems we must solve, if the aid is given only by providing examples to avoid.

Weiner v. Rollform, Inc., 744 F.2d 797, 223 USPQ 369 (Fed. Cir. 1984).

The very concept for this book grew from an early recognition that the Court of Appeals for the Federal Circuit would very likely be disinclined to pay much attention to the patent law precedents of any other court save its predecessors. This has proved to be so, and it is for that reason that the book concentrates, virtually exclusively, on Federal Circuit decisions. What other courts have to say about patent law these days is of little concern to the pragmatic practitioner. This is regrettable. Any time we reduce the number of educated, intelligent people of the caliber of federal appellate judges who are thinking and writing about a particular area of law, we are bound to lose some of the literature of that law.

As a lawyer with a large Chicago intellectual property firm, my time had been largely devoted, for some 20 years, to patent infringement litigation. I therefore greeted the creation of the Federal Circuit with mixed feelings, to say the least. I welcomed the prospect of doctrinal stability, but I dreaded the loss of healthy cross-fertilization of ideas that would no longer be forthcoming from the regional courts of appeals. Like it or not, however, it was clear that my partners and associates and I in our day-to-day practice simply had to be able to know, quickly and accurately, whether the Federal Circuit had confronted a given issue and, if so, what its views were.

Fortunately, the firm at that time was just in the beginning stages of a massive computerization—one that has resulted in virtually every lawyer having a personal computer in his or her office, and most with one at home as well. My own involvement in that project led me to the idea of creating my own Federal Circuit "database"—a sort of personalized digest of Federal Circuit decisions that could be accessed by computer. Thus I began, religiously, to read each opinion of the Federal Circuit as it was published in the weekly advance sheets and to create my own headnotes.

This database quickly became a useful research resource for the lawyers in my firm. In particular, it could, if used properly, ease the life of an associate, for whom the most frequently encountered work assignment, then and now, began with the words "see what the Federal Circuit has said about" such and such a subject. Just as quickly, however, I began to notice a somewhat unexpected phenomenon. The Federal Circuit appeared to be developing a significant and important body of case law much more rapidly than I had thought possible.

When I was a law clerk for Judge Arthur Smith at the predecessor Court of Customs and Patent Appeals, in the early 1960s, we heard 200 cases a year, but these produced no more than a dozen or so rulings that were of interest to anyone but the immediate parties. Now I was seeing a successor court producing only perhaps 80 or 100 published patent opinions a year, but fully a third or more of these were noteworthy in some respect.

In retrospect, two factors unique to this new court should have prepared me for this performance. First, it *was* a new court and naturally determined to make its mark. Second, and probably much more significant, the Federal Circuit, unlike the CCPA before it, was now looking at patent issues in the context of infringement litigation, resulting in a richer variety of questions and problems than even its other predecessor, the Court of Claims, had ever been exposed to.

Whatever the cause, the effect was clear: this court was developing precedent at a rate that was nothing short of amazing. The Federal Circuit database was accumulating week after week, kilobyte upon kilobyte—indeed, it was reaching *book-like* proportions. It dawned upon me, before the court was three years old, that perhaps this rate would produce sufficient material for a book in record time. And such has proved to be the case: this book reflects the work of a scant four and one-half years of judicial decision—barely 500 cited cases.

The next step was, in the words of a familiar patent statute, obvious: I had only to turn this computerized legal database into a book. You will, mercifully, be spared the details of this conversion process. Suffice it to say that this book may be one of the first in the legal field that was, almost entirely, written by a computer. The database was searched and sorted by computer. The outline was generated by computer. The data were retrieved and organized by computer and inserted into a textual format by a computerized word processor. The footnotes were generated, compiled, tabulated, and checked by computer. The index and case table were constructed by computer. The entire conglomeration was then rewritten, spell-checked, and edited, again using the ubiquitous computer. Finally, when the procreative acts reached term, the computer gave birth to a series of small diskettes, which were rushed to the publisher's own larger and perhaps more motherly computer, there to be incubated and transformed into the book you now have before you.

Looking back, I sometimes wonder where I, the putative author, fit into this creative scheme. I have concluded that it must have been, like any father, at the very beginning, when I read the cases and made the notes that reflected my own perception of what the Federal Circuit was doing about, and to, my beloved patent law. The rest was just busy work, organizing those perceptions into some coherent patterns that might possibly be useful to other practitioners. I hope that you will find them so.

The bulk of the book is devoted to substantive patent law, with emphasis on how those issues arise in infringement litigation. The final two chapters, however, consider in some detail the jurisdiction and judicial method of the Federal Circuit and, to a lesser extent, its general jurisprudence.

The Appendix comprises a statistical analysis of the court's validity and infringement holdings during its first five years of work.

Special thanks go to Cathy Scarriot, who supervised the preparation of the appendices, and to my secretaries, Sharon Stewart and Mary Morgan, who did everything they could to insulate me from the real world of clients and courts during the busy days of this project.

The dedication page is a reflection of how I came to the patent practice. The fact that this book exists at all is a reflection of the constant support and encouragement of my wife, Sue.

ROBERT L. HARMON

Chicago
1987

Summary Contents

IV—Remedies

V—The Patent Office

VI—The Federal Circuit

Detailed Table of Contents

II—Infringement

III—Ownership and Enforcement

IV.—Remedies

VI—The Federal Circuit

Glossary of Abbreviations

Certain phrases and terms are used in this book with sufficient frequency to warrant special abbreviations or acronyms, as follows:

CIP	continuation-in-part patent application
CCPA	United States Court of Customs and Patent Appeals
Commissioner or Director	Commissioner of Patents and Trademarks (now Director of the Patent and Trademark Office)
DOE	doctrine of equivalents
FRAP	Federal Rules of Appellate Procedure
FRCP	Federal Rules of Civil Procedure
FRE	Federal Rules of Evidence
ITC	United States International Trade Commission
JMOL	judgment as a matter of law (formerly JNOV)
JNOV	judgment notwithstanding the verdict
MPEP	Manual of Patent Examining Procedure
MPF	means-plus-function (under 35 U.S.C. §112¶6)
OG	Official Gazette of the United States Patent and Trademark Office
PHE	Prosecution history estoppel
PTO	United States Patent and Trademark Office
PTO Board or Board	Board of Patent Appeals and Interferences

Citations to various Titles of the United States Code are to the most recent enactment or amendment unless a date is given.

I

Patentability

1

Patents

§1.1 The Patent Grant

(a) A Property Right of Exclusion

The creator and builder of a device that is not patented or otherwise divulged to the public has certain common law rights that accompany ownership of tangible personal property. These include the right to possession of the idea and its physical embodiments, the right to limit disclosure to others, and the right to contract for the terms of use by others. The laws governing ownership and use of unpatented property and unpublished information derive from theories of property, adapted to achieve fairness in commercial relationships, and are rooted in the common law.[1] Thus, the act of invention itself vests an inventor with a common law or "natural" right to make, use, and sell that invention absent conflicting patent rights in others.[2] But the common law does not provide the right to exclude others, and absent the right to exclude that is granted by the patent statute, an inventor's recourse to the common law requires that the invention meet the criteria of secrecy as appropriate to the circumstances.[3] A patent on that invention is something more. A patent in effect enlarges the natural right, adding to it the right to exclude others from making, using, or selling the patented invention.[4]

Thus inventors possess the natural right to exploit their inventions—subject to the patent rights of others in a dominant patent—apart from any government grant. Patent rights do not depend upon the exercise of rights already in the patentee's possession. The patent laws provide that a patent confers the right to exclude others from exploiting an invention; it does not confer the right to exploit the invention already possessed by the inventor. As a consequence, in order to exercise the right to exclude others from exploiting an invention, the patentee need not have exercised its natural right to itself make, use, or sell the invention.[5]

A patent grants to the patentee the right to exclude others from making, using, or selling the patented invention throughout the United States for the statutory term of the patent.[6] The term of a

---

[1]*Lariscey v. United States*, 949 F.2d 1137, 20 USPQ2d 1845 (Fed. Cir. 1991). The law governing protection of trade secrets has developed in this common law context. There has evolved a complex of equitable and legal criteria designed to balance the protection of proprietary information against the public interest in the free flow of ideas. The foundation of trade secret law is intended to protect commercial information from competitors who do not know or use it. *Id.*

[2]*Arachnid, Inc. v. Merit Indus., Inc.*, 939 F.2d 1574, 19 USPQ2d 1513 (Fed. Cir. 1991). See also *Lariscey v. United States*, 949 F.2d 1137, 20 USPQ2d 1845 (Fed. Cir. 1991).

[3]*Lariscey v. United States*, 949 F.2d 1137, 20 USPQ2d 1845 (Fed. Cir. 1991).

[4]*Arachnid, Inc. v. Merit Indus., Inc.*, 939 F.2d 1574, 19 USPQ2d 1513 (Fed. Cir. 1991).

[5]*King Instr. Corp. v. Perego*, 65 F.3d 941, 36 USPQ2d 1129 (Fed. Cir. 1995).

[6]*Joy Techs., Inc. v. Flakt, Inc.*, 6 F.3d 770, 28 USPQ2d 1378 (Fed. Cir. 1993). A patent's territorial scope is the United States. 35 U.S.C. §271. There can be no infringement of a U.S. patent without some nexus to the United States. *Tieleman Food Equip., B.V. v. Stork Gamco,*

patent used to be 17 years.[7] The Uruguay Round Agreements Act amended the patent law to provide that U.S. patents expire 20 years after the date the patent application is filed; for patents in force on June 8, 1995, the patent term is the greater of 17 years from grant or 20 years from filing.[8] Because the rights flowing from a patent exist only for the term of the patent, there can be no infringement once the patent expires. An invention claimed in a patent passes into the public domain upon termination of the statutory term.[9] Indeed, in the case of an expired patent, the patent laws create a federal right to copy and use.[10]

It is beyond reasonable debate that patents are property,[11] but what kind? The statute also tells us that "patents shall have the

---

Inc., 56 F.3d 1373, 35 USPQ2d 1568 (Fed. Cir. 1995). Among the most important rights in the bundle of rights owned by a patent holder is the right to exclude others. This right is not limited to a particular situs, but exists anywhere the patent is recognized. A patent is a federally created property right, valid throughout the United States. Its legal situs would seem to be anywhere it is called into play. As an example, the right to exclude is violated at the situs where a sale occurs. Similarly, economic loss occurs to the patent holder at the place where the infringing sale is made because the patent owner loses business there, either in lost sales of competing products or loss of potential revenue through licensing or other arrangements. *Mars, Inc. v. Kabushiki-Kaisha Nippon Conlux*, 24 F.3d 1368, 30 USPQ2d 1621 (Fed. Cir. 1994). Patent infringement occurs where the allegedly infringing sales are made. *North Am. Philips Corp. v. American Vending Sales, Inc.*, 35 F.3d 1576, 32 USPQ2d 1203 (Fed. Cir. 1994).

[7]See *Atari Games Corp. v. Nintendo of Am., Inc.*, 897 F.2d 1572, 14 USPQ2d 1034, 1036 (Fed. Cir. 1990). The term is 14 years in the case of a design patent. 35 U.S.C. §173. It is obvious that a party cannot be held liable for infringement of a nonexistent patent. No damages are payable on products manufactured and sold before the patent issued. *Gustafson, Inc. v. Intersystems Indus. Prods., Inc.*, 897 F.2d 508, 13 USPQ2d 1972 (Fed. Cir. 1990). But what about use? Patent rights do not peter out as the end of the patent term is approached. *Atlas Powder Co. v. Ireco Chems.*, 773 F.2d 1230, 227 USPQ 289 (Fed. Cir. 1985). Nonetheless, the patent property is a wasting asset. *Continental Can Co. v. Monsanto Co.*, 948 F.2d 1264, 20 USPQ2d 1746 (Fed. Cir. 1991). Under certain circumstances the term of a patent may be extended pursuant to 35 U.S.C. §§155–156. See *Merck & Co. v. Kessler*, 80 F.3d 1543, 38 USPQ2d 1347 (Fed. Cir. 1996); *Telectronics Pacing Sys., Inc. v. Ventritex, Inc.*, 982 F.2d 1520, 25 USPQ2d 1196 (Fed. Cir. 1992); *Hoechst Aktiengesellschaft v. Quigg*, 917 F.2d 522, 16 USPQ2d 1549 (Fed. Cir. 1990); *Glaxo Oper. UK Ltd. v. Quigg*, 894 F.2d 392, 13 USPQ2d 1628 (Fed. Cir. 1990). Violations of patent rights are continuing events. *Genentech, Inc. v. Eli Lilly & Co.*, 998 F.2d 931, 27 USPQ2d 1241 (Fed. Cir. 1993). Patent infringement, both direct and by inducement, involves continuous infliction of injury upon the victim. *Beverly Hills Fan Co. v. Royal Sovereign Corp.*, 21 F.3d 1558, 30 USPQ2d 1001 (Fed. Cir. 1994).

[8]*Merck & Co. v. Kessler*, 80 F.3d 1543, 38 USPQ2d 1347 (Fed. Cir. 1996). The Act also creates a limited safe harbor for persons who commenced acts or made substantial investment toward commission of acts, before June 8, 1995, that become infringing because of the extension of the patent period. Patentees may not assert their traditional patent remedies for infringing acts committed by such persons during the so-called Delta period (between original expiration and extended expiration). In exchange, qualifying persons must pay an equitable remuneration to the patentee. *DuPont Merck Pharm. Co. v. Bristol-Meyers Squibb Co.*, 62 F.3d 1397, 35 USPQ2d 1718 (Fed. Cir. 1995). See 35 U.S.C. §154.

[9]*Kearns v. Chrysler Corp.*, 32 F.3d 1541, 31 USPQ2d 1746 (Fed. Cir. 1994).

[10]*Elmer v. ICC Fabricating, Inc.*, 67 F.3d 1571, 36 USPQ2d 1417 (Fed. Cir. 1995).

[11]*Patlex Corp. v. Mossinghoff*, 758 F.2d 594, 225 USPQ 243 (Fed. Cir. 1985). Patents and copyrights are distinct property rights, while trademarks are not. *Visa, U.S.A., Inc. v. Birmingham Trust Nat'l Bank*, 696 F.2d 1371, 216 USPQ 649 (Fed. Cir. 1982). Know-how, improvements, data, and information are, when subject to a confidential relationship, intellectual property in the eyes of the law and are protected in accordance with law. *Richardson v. Suzuki Motor Co.*, 868 F.2d 1226, 9 USPQ2d 1913 (Fed. Cir. 1989).

attributes of personal property,"[12] and so they do, in many respects. Certainly a patent is not strictly a "deed," a term normally used to describe an attribute of real property.[13] And yet patents are subject to principles of eminent domain,[14] and they may be mortgaged and their assignments recorded just like any piece of real estate.[15] Indeed, the claims of a patent are legal documents like the descriptions of lands by metes and bounds in a deed.[16]

In exploring and finally rejecting the notion that claim interpretation is analogous to contract interpretation, the court in its important *Markman*[17] decision had some interesting things to say about the nature of patents. In some ways, the contract analogy is appropriate, in that the inventor is required to make a full public disclosure, something that he or she is not otherwise obligated to do, in return for the property right of exclusion granted by the government (something that it is not otherwise obligated to do). But this analogy is not useful in the context of a patent infringement suit. Patents are not contracts per se and patent infringement actions have never been viewed as breach of contract actions. Patent infringement has often been described as a tort. The inventor sues a competitor for infringing upon the right to exclude. The competitor is never a party to the putative contract between the government and the inventor; nor does the competitor breach this contract by infringing. In the end, then, a patent is not a contract. Contracts are executory in nature—they contain promises that must be performed. Once a patent is issued, any purported exchange of promises between the applicant and the PTO has been fully executed. There is no discretion on the part of the PTO as to whether or not to grant the patent; if the statutory requirements are met, a patent is issued. Likewise, the other party to the transaction, the patentee, cannot "contract" with anyone other than the federal government to receive a right to exclude others from the invention.

Perhaps the only sensible way to view a patent is in terms of the rights it secures to its owner. Patent property rights, necessarily

---

[12]35 U.S.C. §261. See, e.g., *In re Etter*, 756 F.2d 852, 225 USPQ 1 (Fed. Cir. 1985). Property rights in an invention are by definition personal property. *Filmtec Corp. v. Allied-Signal Inc.*, 939 F.2d 1568, 19 USPQ2d 1508 (Fed. Cir. 1991).

[13]*In re Etter*, 756 F.2d 852, 225 USPQ 1 (Fed. Cir. 1985).

[14]*Patlex Corp. v. Mossinghoff*, 758 F.2d 594, 225 USPQ 243 (Fed. Cir. 1985).

[15]35 U.S.C. §261. A patent is, in effect, a bundle of rights that may be divided and assigned, or retained in whole or part. *Vaupel Textilmaschinen KG v. Meccanical Euro Italia S.P.A.*, 944 F.2d 870, 20 USPQ2d 1045 (Fed. Cir. 1991). Section 261 adopts the principle of the real property recording acts and provides that the bona fide purchaser for value cuts off the rights of a prior assignee who has failed to record the prior assignment in the PTO. *Filmtec Corp. v. Allied-Signal Inc.*, 939 F.2d 1568, 19 USPQ2d 1508 (Fed. Cir. 1991).

[16]*In re Vamco Mach., Inc.*, 752 F.2d 1564, 224 USPQ 617, 625 n.5 (Fed. Cir. 1985). See also *In re Warmerdam*, 33 F.3d 1354, 31 USPQ2d 1754 (Fed. Cir. 1994). A patent is a fully integrated written instrument. *Markman v. Westview Instr., Inc.*, 52 F.3d 967, 34 USPQ2d 1321 (Fed. Cir. 1995), *aff'd* 517 U.S. 370, 38 USPQ2d 1461 (1996).

[17]*Markman v. Westview Instr., Inc.*, 52 F.3d 967, 34 USPQ2d 1321 (Fed. Cir. 1995), *aff'd* 517 U.S. 370, 38 USPQ2d 1461 (1996).

including the right to license and exploit patents, fall squarely within both classical and judicial definitions of protectable property. Property has been defined as the collection of rules that are presently accepted as governing the exploitation and enjoyment of resources. This analysis is particularly apt with respect to patents.[18] Thus a patent represents the legal right to exclude others from making, using, selling, or offering to sell a patented invention in the United States, and from importing the invention into the United States.[19] The right to exclude recognized in a patent is but the essence of the concept of property,[20] all property.[21] A patent inhibits those who would compete with its owner by warning them not to practice the invention.[22] An act of infringement trespasses on the right to exclude.[23] Fundamentally, the right to exclude others is the very definition of property.[24] So viewed, the patent property right is certainly not inconsequential.[25]

The grant of a patent is the grant of the right to invoke the power of the state in order to exclude others from utilizing the patentee's discovery without his or her consent.[26] Once infringement is established, it is contrary to the laws of property—of which the patent law partakes—to deny the patentee's right to exclude others from use of that property. It is therefore the general rule that an injunction will issue when infringement has been adjudged, absent a sound reason for denying it.[27] But while the right to exclude is the essence of the

[18]*Patlex Corp. v. Mossinghoff,* 758 F.2d 594, 225 USPQ 243 (Fed. Cir. 1985).

[19]*Prima Tek II L.L.C. v. A-Roo Co.,* 222 F.3d 1372, 55 USPQ2d 1742 (Fed. Cir. 2000). See also *McCoy v. Mitsuboshi Cutlery, Inc.,* 67 F.3d 917, 36 USPQ2d 1289 (Fed. Cir. 1995); *Kimberly-Clark Corp. v. Procter & Gamble Distrib. Co.,* 973 F.2d 911, 23 USPQ2d 1921 (Fed. Cir. 1992); *Vaupel Textilmaschinen KG v. Meccanical Euro Italia S.P.A.,* 944 F.2d 870, 20 USPQ2d 1045 (Fed. Cir. 1991); *Standard Oil Co. v. American Cyanamid Co.,* 774 F.2d 448, 227 USPQ 293 (Fed. Cir. 1985).

[20]*Connell v. Sears, Roebuck & Co.,* 722 F.2d 1542, 220 USPQ 193 (Fed. Cir. 1983).

[21]*In re Etter,* 756 F.2d 852, 225 USPQ 1 (Fed. Cir. 1985).

[22]*Manildra Milling Corp. v. Ogilvie Mills, Inc.,* 76 F.3d 1178, 37 USPQ2d 1707 (Fed. Cir. 1996).

[23]*King Instr. Corp. v. Perego,* 65 F.3d 941, 36 USPQ2d 1129 (Fed. Cir. 1995).

[24]*Schenck, A.G. v. Nortron Corp.,* 713 F.2d 782, 218 USPQ 698 (Fed. Cir. 1983). Implicit in the right to exclude, however, is the ability to waive that right, i.e., to license activities that would otherwise be excluded, such as making, using, and selling the patented invention in the United States. *Prima Tek II L.L.C. v. A-Roo Co.,* 222 F.3d 1372, 55 USPQ2d 1742 (Fed. Cir. 2000).

[25]*In re Etter,* 756 F.2d 852, 225 USPQ 1 (Fed. Cir. 1985). Infringement of the patentee's right to exclude carries with it the potential for serious consequences. The infringer may be enjoined and required to pay increased damages, costs, and attorney fees. *Markman v. Westview Instr., Inc.,* 52 F.3d 967, 34 USPQ2d 1321 (Fed. Cir. 1995), *aff'd* 517 U.S. 370, 38 USPQ2d 1461 (1996).

[26]*Smith Int'l, Inc. v. Hughes Tool Co.,* 718 F.2d 1573, 219 USPQ 686 (Fed. Cir. 1983). The court certainly feels that damage to a patentee's intellectual property rights is more than mere financial loss. See *Cedars-Sinai Med. Ctr. v. Watkins,* 11 F.3d 1573, 29 USPQ2d 1188 (Fed. Cir. 1993). Where there are several patents at issue in litigation, each is a separate chose in action. *Stark v. Advanced Magnetics, Inc.,* 29 F.3d 1570, 31 USPQ2d 1290 (Fed. Cir. 1994). Separate patents describe separate and distinct inventions and it cannot be presumed that related patents rise and fall together. *Comair Rotron, Inc. v. Nippon Densan Corp.,* 49 F.3d 1535, 33 USPQ2d 1929 (Fed. Cir. 1995).

[27]*Richardson v. Suzuki Motor Co.,* 868 F.2d 1226, 9 USPQ2d 1913 (Fed. Cir. 1989).

concept of property, district courts are, nevertheless, given broad discretion under 35 U.S.C. §283 to determine whether the facts of a case warrant the grant of an injunction and to determine the scope of the injunction.[28]

A patent is a creature of statute, as is the right of a patentee to have a remedy for infringement of his or her patent. Suit must be brought on the patent, as ownership only of the invention gives no right to exclude, which is obtained only from the patent grant. In order to exercise that right, a plaintiff must necessarily have standing as comprehended by the patent statute.[29]

Although the government has consented to be sued in the Court of Federal Claims for reasonable and entire compensation for making or using a patented invention, it has not consented to invoke its own power to exclude itself from those acts. Thus, while an injunction against making, using, or selling the invention would, taken at face value, seem to include the right to prevent a manufacturer from selling the invention to the government, it does not because the statute says it does not. The patentee takes a patent from the United States subject to the government's eminent domain right to obtain and use what it needs.[30]

The complex question of state immunity from patent infringement suits is discussed in §18.4.

(b) Claims and the Concept of Domination

It is important to understand the limits of the right to exclude. The basic right concomitant to the patent grant is sometimes said to be the right of exclusivity.[31] But one must not make the mistake of supposing that a patent grants the right to use the patented subject matter.[32] Indeed, the federal patent laws do not create any affirmative right to make, use, or sell anything.[33] The patent laws say nothing

---

[28]*Joy Techs., Inc. v. Flakt, Inc.*, 6 F.3d 770, 28 USPQ2d 1378 (Fed. Cir. 1993). The purpose behind the injunction must be to prevent the violation of any right secured by the patent. It may not be punitive. *Id.* When the rights secured by a patent are no longer protectable by virtue of expiration or unenforceability, entitlement to injunctive relief becomes moot because such relief is no longer available. *Kearns v. Chrysler Corp.*, 32 F.3d 1541, 31 USPQ2d 1746 (Fed. Cir. 1994).

[29]*Arachnid, Inc. v. Merit Indus., Inc.*, 939 F.2d 1574, 19 USPQ2d 1513 (Fed. Cir. 1991). While it may be appropriate to speak loosely of patent infringement as a tort, more accurately the cause of action for infringement is created and defined by statute; 35 U.S.C. §271 does not speak generally of the tort of patent infringement, but specifically of a liability that arises upon the making, using, or selling of an infringing article. *North Am. Philips Corp. v. American Vending Sales, Inc.*, 35 F.3d 1576, 32 USPQ2d 1203 (Fed. Cir. 1994).

[30]*W.L. Gore & Assoc., Inc. v. Garlock, Inc.*, 842 F.2d 1275, 6 USPQ2d 1277 (Fed. Cir. 1988). Rights of patentees against the government are spelled out in 28 U.S.C. §1498. See §11.1.

[31]*Patlex Corp. v. Mossinghoff*, 758 F.2d 594, 225 USPQ 243 (Fed. Cir. 1985).

[32]*Studiengesellschaft Kohle v. Northern Petrochem. Co.*, 784 F.2d 351, 228 USPQ 837 (Fed. Cir. 1986).

[33]*Leatherman Tool Group Inc. v. Cooper Indus. Inc.*, 131 F.3d 1011, 44 USPQ2d 1837 (Fed. Cir. 1997).

about the right to copy or the right to use; they speak only in terms of the right to exclude.[34] A product may infringe more than one patent, and one may not be able to practice the invention protected by an improvement patent unless one is authorized under the basic patent.[35] This is the concept of "domination," which grows out of the fact that patents have claims, whereunder one patent has a broad or generic claim that reads on an invention defined by a narrower or more specific claim in another patent. The former dominates the latter because the more narrowly claimed invention cannot be practiced without infringing the broader claim. The broader claim embraces or encompasses the subject matter defined by the narrower claim.[36] That someone has a patent right to exclude others from making the invention claimed in his patent does not mean that his invention cannot infringe claims of another's patent broad enough to encompass, i.e., to "dominate," his invention.[37]

Thus, devices that have been modified to such an extent that the modification may be separately patented may nonetheless infringe the claims of a patent.[38] And although a license agreement may be couched in terms of the licensee being given the right to make, use, and sell a product, the agreement cannot convey that absolute right because not even the patentee is given that right. The patentee's right is merely one to exclude others from making, using, or selling the product, and both patentee and its licensee can be subject to suit under other patents for making, using, and selling the product.[39]

To understand the concept of domination, one must be familiar with the nature and function of patent claims. The statute requires that the written specification of a patent "shall conclude with one or more claims particularly pointing out and distinctly claiming the subject matter which the applicant regards as his invention."[40] It is

---

[34]*Interpart Corp. v. Italia,* 777 F.2d 678, 228 USPQ 124 (Fed. Cir. 1985).

[35]*Milliken Res. Corp. v. Dan River, Inc.,* 739 F.2d 587, 222 USPQ 571 (Fed. Cir. 1984).

[36]*In re Kaplan,* 789 F.2d 1574, 229 USPQ 678 (Fed. Cir. 1986). Dominating patents are not uncommon. *United States Steel Corp. v. Phillips Petroleum Co.,* 865 F.2d 1247, 9 USPQ2d 1461 (Fed. Cir. 1989).

[37]*Rolls-Royce Ltd. v. GTE Valeron Corp.,* 800 F.2d 1101, 231 USPQ 185 (Fed. Cir. 1986). That a product claimed in a later patent may be patentable does not mean that a person making, using, or selling that product cannot be guilty of infringing an earlier patent. *United States Steel Corp. v. Phillips Petroleum Co.,* 865 F.2d 1247, 9 USPQ2d 1461 (Fed. Cir. 1989).

[38]*Texas Instr., Inc. v. United States ITC,* 805 F.2d 1558, 231 USPQ 833 (Fed. Cir. 1986). A patent may issue on an improvement that infringes another's patent. *Water Techs. Corp. v. Calco, Ltd.,* 850 F.2d 660, 7 USPQ2d 1097 (Fed. Cir. 1988). The fact of separate patentability presents no legal or evidentiary presumption of noninfringement. *Hoechst Celanese Corp. v. BP Chem. Ltd.,* 78 F.3d 1575, 38 USPQ2d 1126 (Fed. Cir. 1996).

[39]*Spindelfabrik GmbH v. Schubert & Salzer,* 829 F.2d 1075, 4 USPQ2d 1044 (Fed. Cir. 1987). A patent license agreement is in essence nothing more than a promise by the licensor not to sue the licensee. *Id.*

[40]35 U.S.C. §112¶2. Under §112, it is clear that the specification of a patent consists of, and contains, both the claims and a written description of the invention. In present day usage, that statutory structure is not always adhered to. Thus, it is not uncommon for the claims and specification to be treated as distinct entities. *In re Dossel,* 115 F.3d 942, 42 USPQ2d 1881 (Fed. Cir. 1997).

axiomatic that the claims define the invention that an applicant believes is patentable.[41] The function of claims is to point out what the invention is in such a way as to distinguish it from what was previously known, i.e., the prior art, and to define the scope of protection afforded by the patent.[42] The claims of a patent are the sole measure of the patent grant. Once they issue in a particular form, the protected invention is, as a matter of law, that form.[43] The disclosure of a patent is in the public domain save as the claims forbid. The claims alone delimit the right to exclude; only they may be infringed.[44] Subject matter disclosed but not claimed in a patent is dedicated to the public.[45]

Thus, the scope of a patent's claims determines what infringes the patent,[46] and the sole effect of the grant of the property right to exclude others for a limited time from unauthorized use of a patented invention is to require that others avoid the claimed structure or process.[47] In view of this exclusionary function, it has been well said that the claims of a patent constitute one of the most difficult legal instruments to draw.[48] Indeed, a patent is both a technical and a legal document. While a judge is well equipped to interpret the legal aspects of the document, he or she must also interpret the technical aspects of the document, and its overall meaning, from the vantage point of one skilled in the art.[49]

---

[41]*In re Van Geuns,* 988 F.2d 1181, 26 USPQ2d 1057 (Fed. Cir. 1993).

[42]*In re Vamco Mach., Inc.,* 752 F.2d 1564, 224 USPQ 617 (Fed. Cir. 1985).

[43]*Bandag, Inc. v. Al Bolser's Tire Stores, Inc.,* 750 F.2d 903, 223 USPQ 982 (Fed. Cir. 1984). Although apparatus claims give patent protection covering all uses for the claimed apparatus, a patent owner cannot use the patent laws to proscribe use of another noninfringing apparatus to perform a method that is not claimed. *Augustine Med. Inc. v. Gaymar Indus. Inc.,* 181 F.3d 1291, 50 USPQ2d 1900 (Fed. Cir. 1999). The claims are the measure of the protected right. An essential purpose of patent examination is to fashion claims that are precise, clear, correct, and unambiguous. Only in this way can uncertainties of claim scope be removed, as much as possible, during the administrative process. *In re Zletz,* 893 F.2d 319, 13 USPQ2d 1320 (Fed. Cir. 1989).

[44]*Environmental Instr., Inc. v. Sutron Corp.,* 877 F.2d 1561, 11 USPQ2d 1132 (Fed. Cir. 1989). The language of the claims (plus equivalents of the claimed invention) defines the bounds of the patentee's exclusive rights. *Wiener v. NEC Elec., Inc.,* 102 F.3d 534, 41 USPQ2d 1023 (Fed. Cir. 1996).

[45]*Unique Concepts, Inc. v. Brown,* 939 F.2d 1558, 19 USPQ2d 1500, 1504 (Fed. Cir. 1991).

[46]*In re Benno,* 768 F.2d 1340, 226 USPQ 683 (Fed. Cir. 1985). The claims are no measure of what the patent discloses. Otherwise, Morse's telegraph patent claims, which were broad enough to cover a modern Telex machine, would also invalidate a Telex patent.

[47]*Panduit Corp. v. Dennison Mfg. Co.,* 810 F.2d 1561, 1 USPQ2d 1593 (Fed. Cir. 1987).

[48]*Laitram Corp. v. Cambridge Wire Cloth Co.,* 863 F.2d 855, 9 USPQ2d 1289 (Fed. Cir. 1988); *Slimfold Mfg. Co. v. Kinkead Indus., Inc.,* 810 F.2d 1113, 1 USPQ2d 1563 (Fed. Cir. 1987).

[49]*Pitney Bowes Inc. v. Hewlett-Packard Co.,* 182 F.3d 1298, 51 USPQ2d 1161, 1168 (Fed. Cir. 1999).

§1.2 Constitutional Source and Purpose

The patent right is created by a grant from the government.[50] Article I, section 8, clause 8 of the Constitution says that Congress shall have the power to "promote the Progress of Science and useful Arts, by securing for limited Times to Authors and Inventors the exclusive Right to their respective Writings and Discoveries." The power to grant patents to inventors is for the promotion of the useful arts, while the power to grant copyrights to authors is for the promotion of "Science," which had a much broader meaning in the 18th century than it does today.[51]

Thus, the statutory standard of patentability rests on a constitutional grant of power.[52] Rooted in the Constitution, it serves a very positive function in our system of competition, i.e., the encouragement of investment-based risk. By so doing, it encourages innovation and its fruits: new jobs and new industries, new consumer goods, and trade benefits.[53] The exclusive right, constitutionally derived, was for the national purpose of advancing the useful arts—the process today called technological innovation.[54]

The patent system encourages inventors to invent and disclose. Corporations don't invent; people do. Yet the patent system also encourages corporations and investors to risk investment in research, development, and marketing without which the public could not gain the full benefit of the patent system. The right to exclude conferred by a valid patent deserves the same respect when it is in the hands of an individual as when it is in the hands of a corporation. In assessing damages, emphasis on an individual inventor's lack of money and manufacturing capacity can tend to distinguish the respect due the patent rights of impecunious individual inventors from that due the patent rights of well-funded, well-lawyered, large manufacturing corporations. Any such distinction should be rejected as the disservice it is to the public interest in technological advancement.[55] Another of the benefits of the patent system is its so-called negative incentive to design around a competitor's products, even when they are patented, thus bringing a steady flow of innovations to the marketplace.[56]

---

[50]*In re Etter,* 756 F.2d 852, 225 USPQ 1 (Fed. Cir. 1985). Congress gave inventors the right to exclude others from making, using, or selling the invention, without the consent of the patent owner, for a period of time. *Atari Games Corp. v. Nintendo of Am., Inc.,* 897 F.2d 1572, 14 USPQ2d 1034 (Fed. Cir. 1990).

[51]*Constant v. Advanced Micro-Devices, Inc.,* 848 F.2d 1560, 7 USPQ2d 1057 (Fed. Cir. 1988).

[52]*Structural Rubber Prods. Co. v. Park Rubber Co.,* 749 F.2d 707, 223 USPQ 1264 (Fed. Cir. 1984). See also *Interpart Corp. v. Italia,* 777 F.2d 678, 228 USPQ 124 (Fed. Cir. 1985).

[53]*Loctite Corp. v. Ultraseal Ltd.,* 781 F.2d 861, 228 USPQ 90 (Fed. Cir. 1985); *Patlex Corp. v. Mossinghoff,* 758 F.2d 594, 225 USPQ 243 (Fed. Cir. 1985).

[54]*Paulik v. Rizkalla,* 760 F.2d 1270, 226 USPQ 224 (Fed. Cir. 1985).

[55]*Fromson v. Western Litho Plate & Supp. Co.,* 853 F.2d 1568, 7 USPQ2d 1606 (Fed. Cir. 1988).

[56]*Read Corp. v. Portec, Inc.,* 970 F.2d 816, 23 USPQ2d 1426 (Fed. Cir. 1992); *State Indus., Inc. v. A.O. Smith Corp.,* 751 F.2d 1226, 224 USPQ 418 (Fed. Cir. 1985).

The ability of the public successfully to design around—to use the patent disclosure to design a product or process that does not infringe, but like the claimed invention, is an improvement over the prior art—is one of the important public benefits that justify awarding the patent owner exclusive rights to his or her invention.[57]

It should not be supposed, however, that there are no public costs associated with the right to exclude. These include inflated prices (invariably absorbed by the consumer), which frequently accompany exclusive rights, and overinvestment. The patent system seeks to maintain an efficient balance between incentives to create and commercialize and the public costs engendered by these incentives.[58]

Though technology has burgeoned, the patent system is not limited to sophisticated technologies and powerful corporations. Nowhere in the statute or the Constitution is the patent system opened only to those who make complex inventions that are difficult for judges to understand and foreclosed to those who make less mysterious inventions a judge can grasp after hearing the inventor's explanation of his or her invention and the engineering principles he or she employed. The constitutional purpose is to encourage disclosure of patentable contributions to progress in the useful arts, all the useful arts, not just the esoteric. The statute requires utility, novelty, and nonobviousness, not complexity.[59]

The Patent and Copyright Clause of the Constitution speaks in terms of "securing" to inventors the exclusive right to their discoveries. But it is erroneous to argue that the word "securing" requires that a patent issued by the PTO be conclusively valid and unchallengeable. Since the adoption of the first patent act in 1790, Congress has permitted judicial review of the validity of patents. The courts, the interpreters of the meaning of the Constitution, have consistently construed the Patent and Copyright Clause to permit judicial review of patents. Public policy requires that only inventions that fully meet the statutory standards be entitled to patents. This policy is furthered when the validity of a patent, which was originally obtained in ex parte proceedings in the PTO, can be challenged in court. There may be debate as to the full meaning of "due process," and the courts have struggled to define its boundaries and requirements within the context of nonjudicial governmental action. However, it is unambiguously clear that federal judicial proceedings, with their extensive notice, opportunity to be heard, and procedural protections, satisfy the constitutional requirement of procedural due process required for the invalidation of a patent.[60]

---

[57]*Hilton Davis Chem. Co. v. Warner-Jenkinson Co.,* 62 F.3d 1512, 35 USPQ2d 1641 (Fed. Cir. 1995), *rev'd & rem'd* 520 U.S. 17, 41 USPQ2d 1865 (1997).

[58]*Cover v. Hydramatic Packing Co.,* 83 F.3d 1390, 38 USPQ2d 1783 (Fed. Cir. 1996).

[59]*Panduit Corp. v. Dennison Mfg. Co.,* 810 F.2d 1561, 1 USPQ2d 1593 (Fed. Cir. 1987).

[60]*Constant v. Advanced Micro-Devices, Inc.,* 848 F.2d 1560, 7 USPQ2d 1057 (Fed. Cir. 1988).

§1.3 Statutory Framework

The law must be the same for all patents and types of inventions. A level playing ground for the marketplace of ideas is as necessary for technological innovation as it is for politics and social policy.[61] Congress has attempted to deal with this need by creating a fairly complex framework of laws to regulate and govern our patent system. Although there are more than 30 statutory provisions touching upon various aspects of patents,[62] the bulk of the legislative implementation is found in the Patent Act of 1952, Title 35, United States Code. There are several fundamental concepts embodied in that statute that are essential to even a superficial understanding of substantive patent law. The matter of formally claiming the patented invention, and the related concept of domination, have already been discussed. The others are considered briefly below.

Combinations of old elements. The phrase "combination patent" is not found in the statute and there is no warrant for classification of patents as such.[63] It is simplistic and unrealistic to employ a separate test of patentability for combinations of old elements when the language of the 1952 Act provides no basis for either classifying patents into different types or for applying different treatment to different types of patents.[64] That an invention is a combination of known elements is not relevant in determining patentability.[65] Virtually all inventions are combinations of old, known elements, and most inventions employ known principles.[66] The fact that particular elements of a claim are present both in the prior art and in an accused device does not negate infringement of a claim consisting of a combination of elements.[67] Invention itself is the process of combining prior art in a nonobvious manner.[68]

Value of the invention. Disclosure of an invention found to have revolutionized an industry is but a classic example of the ideal working

---

[61]*Panduit Corp. v. Dennison Mfg. Co.*, 810 F.2d 1561, 1 USPQ2d 1593 (Fed. Cir. 1987).

[62]*Wyden v. Commissioner of Patents*, 807 F.2d 934, 231 USPQ 918 (Fed. Cir. 1986) (dissenting opinion of Markey, C.J.).

[63]*Stratoflex, Inc. v. Aeroquip Corp.*, 713 F.2d 1530, 218 USPQ 871 (Fed. Cir. 1983).

[64]*Raytheon Co. v. Roper Corp.*, 724 F.2d 951, 220 USPQ 592 (Fed. Cir. 1983).

[65]*Mac Corp. v. Williams Patent Crusher Co.*, 767 F.2d 882, 226 USPQ 515 (Fed. Cir. 1985). But the court has indicated that a mechanical combination in a crowded field is entitled only to a narrow scope of equivalents for infringement purposes. *Slimfold Mfg. Co. v. Kinkead Indus.*, 932 F.2d 1453, 18 USPQ2d 1842, 1846 (Fed. Cir. 1991).

[66]*Lindemann Maschinenfabrik v. American Hoist & Derrick Co.*, 730 F.2d 1452, 221 USPQ 481 (Fed. Cir. 1984).

[67]*Micro Chem., Inc. v. Great Plains Chem. Co.*, 103 F.3d 1538, 41 USPQ2d 1238 (Fed. Cir. 1997).

[68]*In re Rouffet*, 149 F.3d 1350, 47 USPQ2d 1453 (Fed. Cir. 1998).

of the patent system.[69] Under our economic and patent systems, valuation of the worth of an inventor's contribution is left to the public, not to the judiciary, in determining patentability. A judge is nowhere authorized to declare a patent invalid on his or her personal evaluation. Judges are not to decide whether they think a particular invention "ought" to be patented. Were it otherwise, a letter to the court would do, and trials, Title 35, and the PTO would all be unnecessary.[70]

A finding that an invention is an improvement is not a prerequisite to patentability. It is possible for an invention to be less effective than existing devices but nevertheless meet the statutory criteria for patentability.[71]

A patentee need produce no commercial device. Infringement is determined by comparison with the patentee's claimed invention, not with its marketed product.[72] If a patentee or licensee enjoys widespread sales, that too is but an example of the incentive of the patent system.[73]

It is the prior public knowledge—the "prior art"—by which patentability is tested. A patentee may set the metes and bounds of that which is sought to be patented, and it is not material whether the phenomena just outside those claimed limits are qualitatively different from that which is claimed. The patentee is not required to show that some technological discontinuity exists between the claimed invention and the subject matter just outside the claims, but only that the claimed subject matter would have been nonobvious in view of the prior art.[74] Nor is it a requirement that the inventor correctly set forth, or even know, how or why the invention works, so long as he or she teaches how to achieve the claimed result.[75]

Public domain. An invention claimed in a patent passes into the public domain upon termination of the patent's statutory term.[76] As implemented by the patent statute, the grant of the right to exclude carries the obligation to disclose the workings of the invention, thereby adding to the store of knowledge without diminishing the patent-supported incentive to innovate. But the obligation to disclose is not

---

[69]*Schenck, A.G. v. Nortron Corp.,* 713 F.2d 782, 218 USPQ 698 (Fed. Cir. 1983).

[70]*Panduit Corp. v. Dennison Mfg. Co.,* 810 F.2d 1561, 1 USPQ2d 1593 (Fed. Cir. 1987).

[71]*Custom Accessories, Inc. v. Jeffrey-Allan Indus., Inc.,* 807 F.2d 955, 1 USPQ2d 1196 (Fed. Cir. 1986).

[72]*Perkin-Elmer Corp. v. Computervision Corp.,* 732 F.2d 888, 221 USPQ 669 (Fed. Cir. 1984). An infringer is liable even when the patent owner puts out no product. *Avia Group Int'l, Inc. v. L.A. Gear Calif., Inc.,* 853 F.2d 1557, 7 USPQ2d 1548 (Fed. Cir. 1988).

[73]*Schenck, A.G. v. Nortron Corp.,* 713 F.2d 782, 218 USPQ 698 (Fed. Cir. 1983). The right to exclude others from a specific market, no matter how large or small that market, is an essential element of the patent right. Inventors with small markets are as entitled to exclusivity under the patent statute as are those with large markets. *Polymer Tech., Inc. v. Bridwell H.A.,* 103 F.3d 970, 41 USPQ2d 1185 (Fed. Cir. 1996).

[74]*Andrew Corp. v. Gabriel Elec., Inc.,* 847 F.2d 819, 6 USPQ2d 2010 (Fed. Cir. 1988).

[75]*Newman v. Quigg,* 877 F.2d 1575, 11 USPQ2d 1340 (Fed. Cir. 1989).

[76]*Kearns v. Chrysler Corp.,* 32 F.3d 1541, 31 USPQ2d 1746 (Fed. Cir. 1994).

the principal reason for a patent system; indeed, it is a rare invention that cannot be deciphered more readily from its commercial embodiment than from a printed patent. The reason for a patent system is to encourage innovation and its fruits.[77]

One way or the other, though, by disclosure or product, the innovation gets to the public and eventually becomes part of the public domain. Does the patentee remove anything from the public domain? Paramount among the patentability requirements is that which is sought to be patented must be new.[78] Thus the Federal Circuit has indicated that the real reason for denying patent rights is the basic principle that no patent should be granted that withdraws from the public domain technology already available to the public. Prior art is knowledge that is available, including what would be obvious from it, at a given time, to a person of ordinary skill in an art. Society, speaking through Congress, has said "thou shalt not take it away."[79]

Valid patent claims therefore do not remove existing knowledge from the public domain, for there was no such knowledge before it was disclosed in the inventor's patent. Nor do the claims restrict access to materials earlier available, for those materials remain available. The patent law is and has always been clear that, during the short life of a patent, all workers in the art remain perfectly free to employ and combine elements as they were before the patented invention. They need only avoid the inventor's novel combination and structure as claimed.[80]

There is nothing improper, illegal, or inequitable in filing a patent application for the purpose of obtaining a right to exclude a known competitor's product from the market; nor is it in any manner improper to amend or insert claims intended to cover a competitor's product that the applicant's attorney has learned about during the prosecution of a patent application. Any such amendment or insertion must comply with all statutes and regulations, of course, but if it does, its genesis in the marketplace is simply irrelevant and cannot of itself evidence deceitful intent.[81]

First to invent vs. first to file. The unique premise of the U.S. patent system is that it rewards the first to invent, not the first to file.[82] United States patent law embraces the principle that the patent right is granted to the first inventor rather than the first to file a

---

[77]*Paulik v. Rizkalla,* 760 F.2d 1270, 226 USPQ 224 (Fed. Cir. 1985).

[78]*In re Schoenwald,* 964 F.2d 1122, 22 USPQ2d 1671 (Fed. Cir. 1992).

[79]*Kimberly-Clark Corp. v. Johnson & Johnson,* 745 F.2d 1437, 223 USPQ 603 (Fed. Cir. 1984). For example, the printed publication bar of 35 U.S.C. §102(a) is grounded on the principle that once an invention is in the public domain, it is no longer patentable by anyone. *In re Hall,* 781 F.2d 897, 228 USPQ 453 (Fed. Cir. 1986).

[80]*Panduit Corp. v. Dennison Mfg. Co.,* 810 F.2d 1561, 1 USPQ2d 1593 (Fed. Cir. 1987).

[81]*Kingsdown Med. Cons, Ltd. v. Hollister, Inc.,* 863 F.2d 867, 9 USPQ2d 1384 (Fed. Cir. 1988).

[82]*Bruning v. Hirose,* 161 F.3d 681, 48 USPQ2d 1934 (Fed. Cir. 1998).

patent application. The law does not inquire as to the fits and starts by which an invention is made. Mere lapse of time will not prevent the inventor from receiving a patent.[83] Nonetheless, early public disclosure has been called a linchpin of the patent system. As between a prior inventor who benefits from a process by selling its product but suppresses, conceals, or otherwise keeps the process from the public and a later inventor who promptly files a patent application from which the public will gain a disclosure of the process, the law favors the latter.[84]

Thus, one of the principal policies of 35 U.S.C. §102(b) is to encourage early filing.[85] Yet rigid standards are especially unsuited to the on-sale provision of that statute where the policies underlying the bar, in effect, define it. Each case must be weighed in view of public policy. Policy favors prompt and widespread disclosure of inventions to the public, while giving the inventor a reasonable amount of time (one year, by statute) to determine whether a patent is worthwhile, but precluding attempts by the inventor or his or her assignee from commercially exploiting the invention more than a year before the application for patent is filed.[86]

Equivalents and claim scope. A claim in a patent provides the metes and bounds of the right the patent confers on the patentee to exclude others from making, using, or selling the protected invention. The words of a claim describe and point out the invention by a series of limiting words or phrases—"limitations."[87] A court may not disregard claim limitations and effectively rewrite the claims,[88] nor may it read narrow claim limitations into broader claims, whether to avoid invalidity or to escape infringement.[89] Without these fundamental rules, the court fears, the entire statutory and regulatory structure governing the drafting, submission, examination, allowance, and enforceability of claims would crumble.[90]

---

[83]*Paulik v. Rizkalla,* 760 F.2d 1270, 226 USPQ 224 (Fed. Cir. 1985). The sole exception to this principle resides in 35 U.S.C. §102(g) and the exigencies of the priority contest. Under §102(g), a distinction must be drawn between deliberate suppression or concealment of an invention, which is probably not curable by resumption of effort, and a legal inference of suppression or concealment based on "too long" a delay. The first probably results in an absolute forfeiture of the right to a patent, while the second can be cured. *Id.*

[84]*W.L. Gore & Assoc. v. Garlock, Inc.,* 721 F.2d 1540, 220 USPQ 303 (Fed. Cir. 1983).

[85]*J.A. LaPorte, Inc. v. Norfolk Dredging Co.,* 787 F.2d 1577, 229 USPQ 435 (Fed. Cir. 1986).

[86]*Western Mar. Elec., Inc. v. Furuno Elec. Co.,* 764 F.2d 840, 226 USPQ 334 (Fed. Cir. 1985).

[87]*Corning Glass Works v. Sumitomo Elec. U.S.A., Inc.,* 868 F.2d 1251, 9 USPQ2d 1962 (Fed. Cir. 1989).

[88]*Panduit Corp. v. Dennison Mfg. Co.,* 810 F.2d 1561, 1 USPQ2d 1593 (Fed. Cir. 1987). See also *Pennwalt Corp. v. Durand-Wayland, Inc.,* 833 F.2d 931, 4 USPQ2d 1737 (Fed. Cir. 1987). In a special concurring opinion, Judge Nies gives great weight—almost in a due process context—to the requirement that the public must be put on notice as to what is forbidden by a patent.

[89]*D.M.I., Inc. v. Deere & Co.,* 755 F.2d 1570, 225 USPQ 236 (Fed. Cir. 1985).

[90]*Panduit Corp. v. Dennison Mfg. Co.,* 810 F.2d 1561, 1 USPQ2d 1593, 1603 (Fed. Cir. 1987); *D.M.I., Inc. v. Deere & Co.,* 755 F.2d 1570, 225 USPQ 236 (Fed. Cir. 1985).

By the same token, the claimed invention is not to be limited to preferred embodiments or specific examples in the specification. The details of performing each step need not be included in the claims unless required to distinguish the claimed invention from the prior art or otherwise specifically point out and distinctly claim the invention. These principles are not unlimited in their application but simply reflect the equitable concept that claims should be read in a way that avoids enabling an infringer to practice a fraud on a patent.[91] To hold a patentee to the precise claim language in all cases could turn the patent grant into a hollow and useless thing.[92]

Thus the Federal Circuit is continually faced with a difficult dichotomy. On the one side rests the very important necessity of employing the clearest possible wording in preparing the specification and claims of a patent, one of the most difficult legal instruments to draw with accuracy. On the other lies the equally important necessity of determining infringement without the risk of injustice that may result from a blindered focus on words alone. The former concern recognizes a competitor's need for precise wording as an aid in avoiding infringement. The latter invokes the doctrine of equivalents. Requiring a look at all the words of a claim while resisting their tyranny, and requiring, because the claims measure the invention, a look at all claim limitations, the doctrine of equivalents, in a proper case, tempers unsparing logic and prevents an infringer from stealing the benefits of an invention. In that sense, the doctrine recognizes a fact of the real business world: words are not misappropriated—claimed inventions are.[93]

It is important to understand that claims are not "expanded" or "broadened" under the doctrine of equivalents. The doctrine, by definition, involves going beyond any permissible interpretation of the claim language to determine whether the accused product is "equivalent" to what is described by the claim language. Prior art is a limitation on the range of permissible equivalents, not because the accused product was in the public domain, and not because claims are construed narrowly to preserve their validity, but because a patentee should not be able to obtain by equivalents what could not lawfully have been obtained from the PTO by literal claims.[94]

Still, the determination of equivalency by its nature is inimical to the basic precept of patent law that the claims are the measure of the grant. The doctrine of equivalents, ubiquitous since its origin, exists solely for the equitable purpose of preventing an infringer from stealing the benefit of an invention. To achieve this purpose,

---

[91]*Texas Instr., Inc. v. United States ITC*, 805 F.2d 1558, 231 USPQ 833 (Fed. Cir. 1986).

[92]*Corning Glass Works v. Sumitomo Elec. U.S.A., Inc.*, 868 F.2d 1251, 9 USPQ2d 1962 (Fed. Cir. 1989).

[93]*Laitram Corp. v. Cambridge Wire Cloth Co.*, 863 F.2d 855, 9 USPQ2d 1289 (Fed. Cir. 1988).

[94]*Wilson Sporting Goods Co. v. David Geoffrey & Assoc.*, 904 F.2d 677, 14 USPQ2d 1942 (Fed. Cir. 1990).

equivalency is judicially determined by reviewing the content of the patent, the prior art, and the accused device, and essentially redefining the scope of the claims. This constitutes a deviation from the need of the public to know the precise legal limits of patent protection without recourse to judicial ruling. For the occasional pioneering invention, devoid of significant prior art, whose boundaries probe the policy behind the law, there are no immutable rules. But the incentive to innovation that flows from inventing around an adversely held patent must be preserved. To the extent that the doctrine of equivalents represents an exception to the requirement that the claims define the metes and bounds of the patent protection, the purpose of the rule is to serve the greater interest of justice.[95]

Thus, intentional designing around the claims of a patent is not by itself a wrong that must be compensated by invocation of the doctrine of equivalents. Designing around patents is, in fact, one of the ways in which the patent system works to the advantage of the public in promoting progress in the useful arts, its constitutional purpose. Inherent in our claim-based patent system is also the principle that the protected invention is what the claims say it is, and thus that infringement can be avoided by avoiding the language of the claims. It is only when the changes are so insubstantial as to result in a fraud on the patent that application of the equitable doctrine of equivalents becomes desirable.[96]

The term "claims" has been used in patent legislation since the Patent Act of 1836 to define the invention that an applicant believes is patentable. Since that time, the term has represented that portion of the specification that defines the patent owner's property rights in the invention. This concept of a claim is related to, but distinct from, the concept of infringement. Direct infringement consists of making, using, offering to sell, or selling the invention defined by the claims of a patent, without the authority of the patent owner. With respect to direct infringement, then, the claims define the patent owner's property rights whereas infringement is the act of trespassing upon those rights. The relationship between infringement and the claims becomes even more tenuous under the doctrine of equivalents, where a product is deemed to infringe the patentee's right to exclude even though the product does not fall within the scope of the patent's claims. In sum, the concept of a claim is different from the concept of infringement.[97]

---

[95]*Texas Instr., Inc. v. United States ITC,* 805 F.2d 1558, 231 USPQ 833 (Fed. Cir. 1986). A divided court, sitting in banc, held that an infringement analysis under the doctrine of equivalents must deal with each claimed element, rather than a less focused consideration of the invention as a whole. *Pennwalt Corp. v. Durand-Wayland, Inc.,* 833 F.2d 931, 4 USPQ2d 1737 (Fed. Cir. 1987). The Supreme Court recently embraced this view. *Warner-Jenkinson Co. v. Hilton Davis Chem. Co.,* 520 U.S. 17, 41 USPQ2d 1865 (1997). For a more detailed discussion of these important decisions, see §6.3(a)(ii).

[96]*Slimfold Mfg. Co. v. Kinkead Indus.,* 932 F.2d 1453, 18 USPQ2d 1842 (Fed. Cir. 1991).

[97]*Hoechst-Roussel Pharm., Inc. v. Lehman,* 109 F.3d 756, 42 USPQ2d 1220, 1223 (Fed. Cir. 1997).

§1.4 Associated Legal Concepts

(a) Copyright

The authority to grant copyrights to authors finds its source, like the power to grant patents, in Article I, section 8, clause 8 of the Constitution.[98] The Constitution sets forth the purpose of copyright protection as the promotion of the "Progress of Science," not the rewarding of authors.[99] The Copyright Act thus balances the interests of authors in the control and exploitation of their writings on the one hand, and society's competing interests in the free flow of ideas and information on the other hand. While providing exclusive rights to expression, the Act encourages others to build freely upon the ideas and information conveyed by a work. The author does not acquire exclusive rights to a literary work in its entirety. Under the Act, society is free to exploit facts, ideas, processes, or methods of operation in a copyrighted work. To protect processes or methods of operation, a creator must look to patent laws.[100]

In *Atari v. Nintendo*,[101] the court specifically applied these principles to computer programs encoded on semiconductor chips. The court reasoned that the Copyright Act of 1976, in general, protects original works of authorship fixed in any tangible medium of expression. Works of authorship include "literary works," which in turn embrace computer programs and instructions encoded on silicon chips. However, the copyright protection cannot extend to the methodology or processes adopted by the programmer, but only to the programmer's expression of his or her ideas. Thus a program must be separated into manageable components, and the court must filter out as unprotectable the ideas, expression necessarily incident to the ideas, expression already in the public domain, expression dictated by external factors (e.g., the computer's mechanical specifications, compatibility with other programs, and demands of the industry served by the program), and expression not original to the programmer. What remains is protectable expression.

The *Atari* court elaborated the differences between copyright and patent protection. Thus, patent and copyright laws protect distinct aspects of a computer program. Title 35 protects the process or method performed by a computer program; Title 17 protects the expression

[98]*Constant v. Advanced Micro-Devices, Inc.,* 848 F.2d 1560, 7 USPQ2d 1057 (Fed. Cir. 1988).

[99]*Atari Games Corp. v. Nintendo of Am., Inc.,* 975 F.2d 832, 24 USPQ2d 1015 (Fed. Cir. 1992). See also *Constant v. Advanced Micro-Devices, Inc.,* 848 F.2d 1560, 7 USPQ2d 1057 (Fed. Cir. 1988).

[100]*Atari Games Corp. v. Nintendo of Am., Inc.,* 975 F.2d 832, 24 USPQ2d 1015 (Fed. Cir. 1992).

[101]*Atari Games Corp. v. Nintendo of Am., Inc.,* 975 F.2d 832, 24 USPQ2d 1015 (Fed. Cir. 1992).

of that process or method. While Title 35 protects any novel, nonobvious, and useful process, Title 17 can protect a multitude of expressions that implement that process. If the patentable process is embodied inextricably in the line-by-line instructions of the computer program, however, then the process merges with the expression and precludes copyright protection.

The court went on to explain the fair use exception in the context of copyrighted software or firmware. An author cannot acquire patent-like protection by putting an idea, process, or method of operation in an unintelligible format and asserting copyright infringement against those who try to understand it. The Copyright Act permits an individual in rightful possession of a copy of a work to undertake necessary efforts to understand the work's ideas. Thus the fair use exception to copyright exclusivity permits reverse engineering object code to discern the unprotectable ideas in a computer program. It does not, however, justify extensive efforts to profit from replicating protected expression. Fair use reproductions of a computer program must not exceed what is necessary to understand the unprotected elements of the work.[102]

To prevail on a copyright infringement claim, the plaintiff must show ownership and copying of protectable expression. Copying can be shown by establishing that the defendant made literal copies or by establishing access and substantial similarity in protectable expression.[103] In copyright law, the principle of substantial similarity recognizes that the existence of differences between an accused and copyrighted work may not negate infringement if a material portion of the copyrighted work is appropriated. If the copied portion is qualitatively important, the finder of fact may properly find substantial similarity under copyright law.[104] A single copy is sufficient to support a claim of copyright infringement. Even for works warranting little copyright protection, verbatim copying is infringement.[105] Although attorney fees are generally awarded to a prevailing plaintiff under the Copyright Act, they may be denied in various situations, including (1) the presence of a complex or novel issue of law that the defendant litigates vigorously and in good faith, (2) the defendant's status as an innocent, rather than willful or knowing, infringer, (3) the plaintiff's prosecution of the case in bad faith, and (4) the defendant's good faith

---

[102]The accused infringer had improperly obtained the source code from the Copyright Office and used it to correct mistakes in object code that had been developed by reverse engineering. That reverse engineering, untainted by the purloined source code, would not have been infringement. But the access to the source code, coupled with substantial similarity in the end result, led the court to conclude that there was a substantial likelihood that infringement would be established at trial.

[103]*Atari Games Corp. v. Nintendo of Am., Inc.*, 975 F.2d 832, 24 USPQ2d 1015 (Fed. Cir. 1992).

[104]*Brooktree Corp. v. Advanced Micro Devices, Inc.*, 977 F.2d 1555, 24 USPQ2d 1401 (Fed. Cir. 1992).

[105]*Atari Games Corp. v. Nintendo of Am., Inc.*, 975 F.2d 832, 24 USPQ2d 1015 (Fed. Cir. 1992).

attempt to avoid infringement. Attorney fees decisions under the Act are reviewed under the abuse of discretion standard.[106]

Because copyrights are not within its exclusive jurisdictional grant, the Federal Circuit will not get many copyright cases. In those that do arrive there, it applies regional circuit law.[107] The court seems inclined to apply copyright law principles, where appropriate, to questions arising under the Semiconductor Chip Protection Act.[108]

(b) Antitrust

Nowhere in any statute is a patent described as a monopoly. That the property right conferred by the patent law, like other property rights, may be used in a scheme violative of antitrust law creates no conflict between those laws. The antitrust laws were enacted long after the patent laws and deal with appropriation of what should belong to others. A valid patent gives the public what it did not earlier have. It is an obfuscation to describe a patent as an exception to the general rule against monopolies.[109]

Consequently, the characterization of a patentee by the term "monopolist" is pejorative and should be avoided.[110] Indeed, the court disfavors the term monopoly because it is used in a different sense in patent and antitrust law. Because of its antitrust connotations and association with illegality in connection therewith, it often evokes negative reactions inappropriate to a dispassionate analysis of patent law problems.[111] Patent rights are not legal monopolies in the antitrust sense of the word. Not every patent is a monopoly, and not every patent confers market power.[112] The commercial advantage gained by new technology and its protection by patent do not convert the possessor thereof into a prohibited monopolist.[113] The mere procurement of a patent, whatever the conduct of the applicant in the procurement, cannot without more affect the welfare of the consumer and cannot in itself violate the antitrust laws. There is no relationship between the antitrust laws and a patent that is valid, properly procured, and enforced.[114]

---

[106]*Brooktree Corp. v. Advanced Micro Devices, Inc.,* 977 F.2d 1555, 24 USPQ2d 1401 (Fed. Cir. 1992).

[107]*Atari Games Corp. v. Nintendo of Am., Inc.,* 975 F.2d 832, 24 USPQ2d 1015 (Fed. Cir. 1992).

[108]*Brooktree Corp. v. Advanced Micro Devices, Inc.,* 977 F.2d 1555, 24 USPQ2d 1401 (Fed. Cir. 1992). The Semiconductor Chip Protection Act is discussed below in §2.2(d).

[109]*Schenck, A.G. v. Nortron Corp.,* 713 F.2d 782, 218 USPQ 698 (Fed. Cir. 1983).

[110]*Jamesbury Corp. v. Litton Indus. Prods., Inc.,* 756 F.2d 1556, 225 USPQ 253 (Fed. Cir. 1985).

[111]*In re Kaplan,* 789 F.2d 1574, 229 USPQ 678 (Fed. Cir. 1986).

[112]*Abbott Labs. v. Brennan,* 952 F.2d 1346, 21 USPQ2d 1192 (Fed. Cir. 1992); *Loctite Corp. v. Ultraseal Ltd.,* 781 F.2d 861, 228 USPQ 90 (Fed. Cir. 1985).

[113]*Abbott Labs. v. Brennan,* 952 F.2d 1346, 21 USPQ2d 1192 (Fed. Cir. 1992).

[114]*FMC Corp. v. Manitowoc Co.,* 835 F.2d 1411, 5 USPQ2d 1112 (Fed. Cir. 1987).

Thus, when the patented product is merely one of many products that actively compete on the market, few problems arise between the property rights of a patent owner and the antitrust laws. However, when the patented product is so successful that it creates its own economic market or consumes a large section of any existing market, the aims and objectives of the patent and antitrust laws may seem, at first glance, wholly at odds.[115]

But the enforceability of restrictions on the use of patented goods derives from the patent grant, which is, in classical terms of property, the right to exclude. This right to exclude may be waived in whole or in part. The conditions of such waiver are subject to patent, contract, antitrust, and any other applicable law, as well as equitable considerations such as are reflected in the law of patent misuse. As in other areas of commerce, private parties may contract as they choose, provided that no law is violated thereby. The concept of patent misuse arose to restrain practices that did not in themselves violate any law, but that drew anticompetitive strength from the patent right, and thus were deemed to be contrary to public policy. The policy purpose was to prevent a patentee from using the patent to obtain market benefit beyond that which inheres in the statutory patent right.[116]

Any patent owner has the right to exclude others and can enforce that right until such time as the patent is held invalid. Making threats of suit and bringing suit are well within the enforcement rights of a patentee, and such actions without more cannot be regarded as unfair competition, even if they take business away from the infringer.[117] The public purpose of the patent grant as an incentive to invention, investment, and disclosure is achieved solely by the statutory right to exclude.[118] On the other hand, the patentee may not take the property right granted by a patent and use it to extend power in the marketplace improperly, i.e., beyond the limits of what Congress intended to give in the patent laws. The fact that a patent is obtained does not wholly insulate the patent owner from the antitrust laws. When a patent owner uses patent rights not only as a shield to protect the invention, but as a sword to eviscerate competition unfairly, that owner may be found to have abused the grant and may become liable

---

[115]*Atari Games Corp. v. Nintendo of Am., Inc.*, 897 F.2d 1572, 14 USPQ2d 1034 (Fed. Cir. 1990).

[116]*Mallinckrodt, Inc. v. Medipart, Inc.*, 976 F.2d 700, 24 USPQ2d 1173 (Fed. Cir. 1992).

[117]*Concrete Unlimited Inc. v. Cementcraft, Inc.*, 776 F.2d 1537, 227 USPQ 784 (Fed. Cir. 1985). Congress has specifically granted patent owners the right to commence a civil suit in order to protect their inventions. *Atari Games Corp. v. Nintendo of Am., Inc.*, 897 F.2d 1572, 14 USPQ2d 1034 (Fed. Cir. 1990). Thus a patentee that has a good faith belief that its patents are being infringed violates no protected right when it so notifies infringers. *Mallinckrodt, Inc. v. Medipart, Inc.*, 976 F.2d 700, 24 USPQ2d 1173 (Fed. Cir. 1992). In our patent system, patent applications are secret, and patentees are authorized to sue "innocent" manufacturers immediately after their patents issue and without warning. To hold such patentees entitled to increased damages or attorney fees on the ground of willful infringement, however, would be to reward use of the patent system as a form of ambush. *Gustafson, Inc. v. Intersystems Indus. Prods., Inc.*, 897 F.2d 508, 13 USPQ2d 1972 (Fed. Cir. 1990).

[118]*Abbott Labs. v. Brennan*, 952 F.2d 1346, 21 USPQ2d 1192 (Fed. Cir. 1992).

for antitrust violations where sufficient power in the relevant market is present. Therefore, patent owners may incur antitrust liability for attempted enforcement of a patent known to be obtained through fraud, or known to be invalid, where a license of a patent compels the purchase of unpatented goods, or where there is an overall scheme to use the patent to violate the antitrust laws.[119]

In the end analysis, the treble damage threat of antitrust liability should not be used to thwart good faith efforts at patent enforcement. Because the patent system encourages innovation and its fruits, and because the underlying goal of the antitrust laws is to promote competition, the patent and antitrust laws are complementary.[120] The patent and antitrust laws serve the public in different ways, both of importance to the nation.[121]

(c) *Federal Preemption of State Action*

It is well established that a state court has authority to adjudicate patent questions so long as the action itself does not arise under the patent laws. This is so regardless of whether the state law claim is grounded in contract or tort.[122]

Pursuant to the Supremacy Clause, state causes of action are preempted if they stand as an obstacle to the accomplishment and execution of the full purposes and objectives of Congress in enacting a statute.[123] Thus, it has been settled that state law that conflicts with federal law is without effect. The Supreme Court has set forth two presumptions that guide the preemption analysis. First, it is presumed that Congress does not cavalierly preempt state law causes of action, for the States are independent sovereigns in our federal system. The historic police powers of the States were not to be superseded by a federal act unless that was the clear and manifest purpose

---

[119]*Atari Games Corp. v. Nintendo of Am., Inc.,* 897 F.2d 1572, 14 USPQ2d 1034 (Fed. Cir. 1990).

[120]*Loctite Corp. v. Ultraseal Ltd.,* 781 F.2d 861, 228 USPQ 90 (Fed. Cir. 1985). Both bodies of law are aimed at encouraging innovation, industry, and competition. *Atari Games Corp. v. Nintendo of Am., Inc.,* 897 F.2d 1572, 14 USPQ2d 1034 (Fed. Cir. 1990). By the same token, awards of increased damages and attorney fees should not be allowed to thwart efforts to challenge the validity of patents believed in good faith to be invalid. *Kloster Speedsteel AB v. Crucible Inc.,* 793 F.2d 1565, 230 USPQ 81 (Fed. Cir. 1986).

[121]*Intergraph Corp. v. Intel Corp.,* 195 F.3d 1346, 52 USPQ2d 1641, 1652 (Fed. Cir. 1999).

[122]*Dow Chem. Co. v. Exxon Corp.,* 139 F.3d 1470, 46 USPQ2d 1120 (Fed. Cir. 1998). Although a state court is without power to invalidate an issued patent, there is no limitation on the ability of a state court to decide the question of validity when properly raised in a state court proceeding. *Jacobs Wind Elec. Co. v. Florida Dep't of Transp.,* 919 F.2d 726, 16 USPQ2d 1972 (Fed. Cir. 1990). The potential effect of state court judgments on matters within the particular purview of the federal patent laws has not yet been clearly ruled on by the court. E.g., *Intermedics Infusaid Inc. v. Regents of Univ. of Minnesota,* 804 F.2d 129, 231 USPQ 653 (Fed. Cir. 1986).

[123]*Dow Chem. Co. v. Exxon Corp.,* 139 F.3d 1470, 46 USPQ2d 1120 (Fed. Cir. 1998). See also *Cover v. Hydramatic Packing Co.,* 83 F.3d 1390, 38 USPQ2d 1783 (Fed. Cir. 1996); *Interpart Corp. v. Italia,* 777 F.2d 678, 228 USPQ 124 (Fed. Cir. 1985).

of Congress, particularly when Congress is legislating in a field that the States have traditionally occupied. Second, preemption analysis is guided by the oft-repeated principle that the purpose of Congress is the ultimate touchstone.[124]

In determining whether a state statute is preempted, the Federal Circuit feels there is no crystal clear, distinctly marked formula. Nonetheless, the Supreme Court has set forth three grounds for preemption: (1) explicit preemption, whereby Congress explicitly provides for preemption of state law in the federal statute; (2) field preemption, wherein the scheme of federal regulation is so pervasive as to make reasonable the inference that Congress left no room for the States to supplement it; and (3) conflict preemption, where compliance with both federal and state regulation is a physical impossibility, or where state law stands as an obstacle to the accomplishment and execution of the full purposes and objectives of Congress.[125]

The patent grant is within the exclusive purview of federal law.[126] Inherent in our patent system is a tension between the desire to exploit freely the full potential of our inventive resources and the need to create an incentive to deploy those resources by granting the right to exclude to those who promote the progress of the useful arts. Where this balance between incentives and free exploitation of knowledge is clear, States may not intervene to provide protection to subject matter that is statutorily unprotected by the patent laws. On the other hand, States are free to regulate the use of intellectual property in any manner not inconsistent with federal law.[127]

Because federal patent law plainly does not provide for explicit preemption, there is no preemption on this ground. Field and conflict preemption rely on an implicit congressional intent to preempt. Under field preemption, state law is preempted when it regulates conduct in a field that Congress intends the federal government to occupy exclusively. Such an intent may be inferred from a scheme of federal regulation so pervasive as to make reasonable the inference that Congress left no room for the States to supplement it, or when congressional legislation touches a field in which the federal interest is so dominant that the federal system will be assumed to preclude enforcement of state laws on the same subject. Alternatively, state law is preempted to the extent that it actually conflicts with federal law.

---

[124]*Hunter Douglas Inc. v. Harmonic Design Inc.*, 153 F.3d 1318, 47 USPQ2d 1769 (Fed. Cir. 1998).

[125]*Cover v. Hydramatic Packing Co.*, 83 F.3d 1390, 38 USPQ2d 1783 (Fed. Cir. 1996). In this case, which involved Pennsylvania's version of the UCC, the court held that Congress did not, in writing 35 U.S.C. §287(a), explicitly preempt state commercial law. Nor is there field preemption, for Title 35 occupies the field of patent law, not commercial law. The question then became whether there is conflict preemption. In a decision that is probably closely limited to the complex facts of the case, the court held there to be no conflict preemption of that provision of the UCC that warrants freedom from liability for patent infringement except where a buyer furnishes specifications.

[126]*Abbott Labs. v. Brennan*, 952 F.2d 1346, 21 USPQ2d 1192 (Fed. Cir. 1992).

[127]*Cover v. Hydramatic Packing Co.*, 83 F.3d 1390, 38 USPQ2d 1783 (Fed. Cir. 1996).

Thus, there is conflict preemption when it is impossible for a private party to comply with both state and federal requirements, or when state law stands as an obstacle to the accomplishment and execution of the full purposes and objectives of Congress. Finally, the Supreme Court has recognized that these three categories of preemption are not rigidly distinct. For example, field preemption is a species of conflict preemption, for a state law that falls within a preempted field conflicts with Congress's intent (either express or plainly implied) to exclude state regulation.[128]

The copying of an article itself that is unprotected by the federal patent and copyright laws cannot be protected by state law.[129] While the patent laws provide the right to exclude others from making, using, or selling a claimed invention for a statutorily limited amount of time, if such rights could be but were not awarded under the patent laws, the States may not provide commensurate protection. Therefore, the patent laws do speak to the issue of the public's right to copy what is in the public domain, but only in the context of unfettering such protection or lack thereof from state interference.[130]

---

[128]*Hunter Douglas Inc. v. Harmonic Design Inc.,* 153 F.3d 1318, 47 USPQ2d 1769 (Fed. Cir. 1998).

[129]*Gemveto Jewelry Co. v. Jeff Cooper Inc.,* 800 F.2d 256, 230 USPQ 876 (Fed. Cir. 1986). For example, a state may not grant relief against copying of an unpatented design. *Litton Sys., Inc. v. Whirlpool Corp.,* 728 F.2d 1423, 221 USPQ 97 (Fed. Cir. 1984). In *Sears, Roebuck & Co. v. Stiffel Co.,* 376 U.S. 225, 140 USPQ 524 (1964), and *Compco Corp. v. Day-Brite Lighting, Inc.,* 376 U.S. 234, 140 USPQ 528 (1964), the Supreme Court held that a state may not give relief against copying of any unpatented industrial design. In *Sears* and *Compco* the copied design was the subject of an invalid patent. In *Litton,* the patent was valid but the copied design did not infringe it. In both situations, therefore, the copy was unpatented.

[130]*Leatherman Tool Group Inc. v. Cooper Indus. Inc.,* 131 F.3d 1011, 44 USPQ2d 1837 (Fed. Cir. 1997). In *Interpart Corp. v. Italia,* 777 F.2d 678, 228 USPQ 124 (Fed. Cir. 1985), the court held that a state statute that prohibits the making of a mold directly from a product does not clash with the federal patent laws. It does not give the creator of the product the right to exclude others from making, using, or selling the product. The public is free to copy the product in any other way it chooses. In *Bonito Boats, Inc. v. Thunder Craft Boats, Inc.,* 489 U.S. 141, 9 USPQ2d 1847 (1989), the Supreme Court struck down Florida's "direct molding" statute as preempted by the Supremacy Clause and, in so doing, criticized the reasoning and impliedly overruled the holding of the Federal Circuit in *Interpart.* The Federal Circuit feels that the *Sears* and *Compco* right to copy unpatented and uncopyrighted designs of articles of manufacture was positively reaffirmed in *Bonito Boats.* Accordingly, even distinctive product designs cannot be absolutely shielded from copying under §43(a) of the Lanham Act: likelihood of confusion must be shown. *L.A. Gear, Inc. v. Thom McAn Shoe Co.,* 988 F.2d 1117, 25 USPQ2d 1913 (Fed. Cir. 1993). The court recognizes that trademark or trade dress law may not be used to secure patent-like protection for useful product features. Patent law, not trade dress law, is the principal means for providing exclusive rights in useful product features. Extending trademark and trade dress law to protect functional features might create perpetual, patent-like rights in unpatented or unpatentable items. *Elmer v. ICC Fabricating, Inc.,* 67 F.3d 1571, 36 USPQ2d 1417 (Fed. Cir. 1995). A product feature is functional if it is essential to the use or purpose of the article or if it affects the cost or quality of the article, that is, if exclusive use of the feature would put competitors at a significant non-reputation-related disadvantage. But trade dress protection, under the Lanham Act or state law, does not depend on whether a patent has been obtained for the product or feature in question. To be sure, statements in a patent may provide evidence that the asserted trade dress is functional, and thus not entitled to legal protection. But the fact that a patent has been acquired does not convert what otherwise would have been protected trade dress into nonprotected matter. *Midwest Indus. Inc. v. Karavan Trailers Inc.,* 175 F.3d 1356, 50 USPQ2d 1672 (Fed. Cir. 1999).

But the Federal Circuit certainly feels that federal law does not preempt all state unfair competition law.[131] Whereas patent law is completely preempted by federal law, the law of unfair competition, despite some federal encroachment, remains largely free from federal exclusivity. The provisions of the federal patent law are not in pari materia with the state and federal provisions governing unfair competition.[132]

There is no reason to believe that the clear and manifest purpose of Congress was for federal patent law to occupy exclusively the field pertaining to state unfair competition law. Because of the lack of such congressional intent, in conjunction with the underlying presumption disfavoring preemption, there is no field preemption of state unfair competition claims that rely on a substantial question of federal patent law. State unfair competition law regulates conduct in a different field from federal patent law. Not only does this precedent show the substantial difference between the two fields, but it also demonstrates that the regulation of business affairs is traditionally a matter for state regulation. Hence, the presumption against preemption has greater force because of the States' long-standing governance of such affairs. That reinforced presumption instructs against field preemption. Thus, the Federal Circuit has adopted conflict preemption as the analytical tool for resolving state-federal tensions in unfair competition cases. For conflict preemption, it considers whether the state law actions frustrate the accomplishment and execution of the full purposes and objectives of Congress. To determine whether state law torts are in conflict with federal patent law and accordingly preempted, it assesses a defendant's allegedly tortious conduct. If a plaintiff bases its tort action on conduct that is protected or governed by federal patent law, then the plaintiff may not invoke the state law remedy, which must be preempted for conflict with federal patent law. Conversely, if the conduct is not so protected or governed, then the remedy is not preempted.[133]

Thus, the court has held that a state tort action for abuse of process cannot be invoked as a remedy for inequitable or other unsavory conduct of parties to proceedings in the PTO. Although certain traditional state law concerns may properly be raised when patent rights are litigated, the conduct of litigants in administrative proceedings before the PTO is not remediable by state action in tort, at least not unless it is shown that the entire federal agency action is a "sham." A contrary result would in effect create another forum for litigating issues arising from the administrative process or a new system of judicial overview of actions in the PTO. This would not harmonize

---

[131]*Gemveto Jewelry Co. v. Jeff Cooper Inc.*, 800 F.2d 256, 230 USPQ 876 (Fed. Cir. 1986). For example, state law may require those who copy to identify the source of their product. *Id.*

[132]*Mars, Inc. v. Kabushiki-Kaisha Nippon Conlux*, 24 F.3d 1368, 33 USPQ2d 1621 (Fed. Cir. 1994).

[133]*Hunter Douglas Inc. v. Harmonic Design Inc.*, 153 F.3d 1318, 45 USPQ2d 1769 (Fed. Cir. 1998).

with the traditional judicial disfavor of collateral attack, under the common law, on proceedings before the PTO. Thus, the federal administrative process of examining and issuing patents, including proceedings before the PTO's boards, is not subject to collateral review in terms of the common law tort of abuse of process. The PTO procedures themselves provide a remedy for any malfeasance on the part of litigants, and an additional state action would be an inappropriate collateral intrusion on the regulatory procedures of the PTO under the guise of a complaint sounding in tort. This would be contrary to the preemptive regulation of Congress in the area of patent law.[134]

Federal patent law bars the imposition of liability for conduct before the PTO unless the plaintiff can show that the patentholder's conduct amounted to fraud or rendered the patent application process a sham. Federal patent law also bars the imposition of liability for publicizing a patent in the marketplace unless the plaintiff can show that the patentholder acted in bad faith. These two precepts of federal patent law mandate that such conduct may not be the subject of state tort liability. Accordingly, in a case involving a patentholder's conduct in obtaining or publicizing its patent, if the plaintiff were to fail to allege that the defendant patentholder was guilty of fraudulent conduct before the PTO or bad faith in the publication of a patent, then the complaint would be dismissed for failure to state a claim upon which relief can be granted because of federal preemption. If the complaint were sufficient but the proof were not to show such conduct, then the claim would fail on the merits. Of course, neither fraud nor bad faith need be a required element of a state law tort for that cause of action to stave off preemption by federal patent law, because a plaintiff could prove fraud or bad faith for a tort that not only would be met by such a showing of proof, but also would be satisfied by less. Although to state and maintain a claim under a state law tort, a plaintiff may not be required to allege or prove that the patentholder perpetrated fraud before the PTO or acted in bad faith in the marketplace, to escape preemption, the plaintiff would need to allege and ultimately prove such conduct. To require less would impermissibly alter the balance between the competing purposes of federal patent law that Congress has prescribed.[135]

---

[134]*Abbott Labs. v. Brennan,* 952 F.2d 1346, 21 USPQ2d 1192 (Fed. Cir. 1992). Similarly, a claim under the New Jersey RICO statute predicated upon inequitable conduct is preempted by federal patent law. *Semiconductor Energy Lab. Co. v. Samsung Elec. Co.,* 204 F.3d 1368, 54 USPQ2d 1001 (Fed. Cir. 2000).

[135]*Hunter Douglas Inc. v. Harmonic Design Inc.,* 153 F.3d 1318, 47 USPQ2d 1769 (Fed. Cir. 1998). But see *Dow Chem. Co. v. Exxon Corp.,* 139 F.3d 1470, 46 USPQ2d 1120 (Fed. Cir. 1998). The torts of interference with actual or prospective business relationships require that the purportedly interfering communications or other conduct not be legally justified. However, where the conduct was giving notice of patent rights and the intent to enforce them, the question of legal justification raises considerations of federal law governing the giving of notice of patent rights. To the extent that conflict arises in the interaction between state commercial law and federal patent law, federal law must be applied. National uniformity, in confluence with the national scope of the patent grant and the general federal exclusivity in patent causes, requires that determination of the propriety of a patentee's actions in giving notice of its patent rights

In general, the patent laws will not preempt state law claims if they include additional elements not found in the federal patent law cause of action and if they are not an impermissible attempt to offer patent-like protection to subject matter addressed by federal law. Thus, a state law claim that the defendant attempted to dissuade others from taking a license from the plaintiff is not preempted. This claim, whether viewed as tortious interference or unfair competition, would require elements in addition to those involved in the patent law tort of inducement to infringe. Tortious interference protects business relationships. Unfair competition prevents unethical and oppressive business practices. Neither of these regimes purports to extend protection to the classes of invention protected by Title 35.[136] Similarly, state unfair competition claims alleging that a patentee made false representations of infringement and inability to design around are not preempted, provided the state law requires an element of bad faith.[137] A state law claim for fraudulent nondisclosure and unjust enrichment that was based upon nonjoinder of inventors was not preempted.[138] Where it is clear that the patent laws do not require disclosure of production secrets, such as dimensions and tolerances, there can be and is no conflict with state trade secrecy law, and thus no question of preemption.[139]

Different considerations underlie federal preemption of state laws dealing with unfair competition and state laws dealing with contracts. Enforcement of a contract does not restrict the actions of nonparties to the contract. The Supreme Court in *Aronson v. Quick Point*[140] spoke broadly on federal preemption of state contracts laws, and that decision binds all regional circuits. Thus the Federal Circuit looks to *Aronson* for guidance.[141]

---

is governed by federal statute and precedent and is not a matter of state tort law. *Mikohn Gaming Corp. v. Acres Gaming Inc.*, 165 F.3d 891, 49 USPQ2d 1308 (Fed. Cir. 1998).

[136]*Rodime PLC v. Seagate Tech. Inc.*, 174 F.3d 1294, 50 USPQ2d 1429 (Fed. Cir. 1999). A similar analysis applies to questions of preemption by the federal copyright laws. See *DSC Comm. Corp. v. Pulse Comm.*, 170 F.3d 1354, 50 USPQ2d 1001 (Fed. Cir. 1999).

[137]*Zenith Elec. Corp. v. Exzec Inc.*, 182 F.3d 1340, 51 USPQ2d 1337 (Fed. Cir. 1999). This case applied similar reasoning to the question of conflict between the patent laws and the Lanham Act.

[138]*University of Colorado Found. v. American Cyanamid Co.*, 196 F.3d 1366, 52 USPQ2d 1801 (Fed. Cir. 1999). The court did, however, hold that federal law preempts the use of a state law standard for determining inventorship with respect to a U.S. patent. The case therefore had to be remanded so that the district court could apply federal inventorship law.

[139]*Christianson v. Colt Indus. Oper. Corp.*, 822 F.2d 1544, 3 USPQ2d 1241 (Fed. Cir. 1987), *vacated on jurisdictional grounds*, 486 U.S. 800, 7 USPQ2d 1109 (1988). By the same token, nondisclosure of the trade secrets in patent applications is not inconsistent with the objectives of the patent system, and the patentee is not thereby extending its exclusionary rights in the patented invention. *Id.*

[140]*Aronson v. Quick Point Pencil Co.*, 440 U.S. 257, 201 USPQ 1 (1979).

[141]*Power Lift, Inc. v. Weatherford Nipple-Up Sys., Inc.*, 871 F.2d 1082, 10 USPQ2d 1464 (Fed. Cir. 1989). A state law dealing only with forfeiture of contract rights neither conflicts with nor obstructs the patent statute. *Id.* The court upheld an Oklahoma statute that provides relief from forfeiture provisions of contracts if the breaching party pays full compensation. Such a statute creates no uncertainty regarding a patentee's patent rights. Indeed, when equity

In its decision in *Universal Gym v. ERWA,*[142] the Federal Circuit gave its interpretation of several Supreme Court decisions dealing with preemption in the intellectual property field. Thus, *Sears* and *Compco*[143] held that the patent law bars the application of state unfair competition law to prohibit (or award damages for) the copying of an unpatented article. *Kewanee Oil*[144] held that the patent law does not preempt the application of state trade secret law and that such law can be applied to enjoin and grant damages for the use or disclosure of trade secrets obtained during employment. None of these cases, in the view of the Federal Circuit, presented any question about the compatibility with patent law of an agreement barring a company that was licensed to manufacture and sell another company's product from including any of the features and designs of the licensor's product in products the licensee manufactured after the license agreement was terminated.[145] The court pointed out that parties to a contract may limit their right to take action they previously had been free to take, and the *Sears/Compco* doctrine nullifies a private contract only if its enforcement would conflict with the patent law.[146]

In *Midwest v. Karavan,*[147] the court expressly overruled its prior contrary decisions, and held that it will apply its own law, rather than that of the regional circuit, when determining whether patent law preempts particular state law causes of action or conflicts with rights created by other federal laws.

(d) Foreign Patents and Patent Law

Participation in the U.S. patent system, as patentees and as licensees, is available to citizens and noncitizens alike.[148] But will the Federal Circuit open the U.S. judicial system to aliens or citizens for

---

dictates relief under the statute, the patentee's patent rights are nonetheless enforced, the licensee being forced to pay all royalties.

[142]*Universal Gym Equip., Inc. v. ERWA Exercise Equip. Ltd.,* 827 F.2d 1542, 4 USPQ2d 1035 (Fed. Cir. 1987).

[143]*Sears, Roebuck & Co. v. Stiffel Co.,* 376 U.S. 225, 140 USPQ 524 (1964), and *Compco Corp. v. Day-Brite Lighting, Inc.,* 376 U.S. 234, 140 USPQ 528 (1964).

[144]*Kewanee Oil Co. v. Bicron Corp.,* 416 U.S. 470, 181 USPQ 673 (1974). And *Lear, Inc. v. Adkins,* 395 U.S. 653, 162 USPQ 1 (1969), held that a licensee of a patent is not estopped from challenging the validity of the patent.

[145]*Universal Gym Equip., Inc. v. ERWA Exercise Equip. Ltd.,* 827 F.2d 1542, 4 USPQ2d 1035 (Fed. Cir. 1987).

[146]*Universal Gym Equip., Inc. v. ERWA Exercise Equip. Ltd.,* 827 F.2d 1542, 4 USPQ2d 1035 (Fed. Cir. 1987). It should be noted that the licensee had reverse engineered the licensor's product prior to entering into the agreement and could have sold copies had it chosen to do so. Instead, it contracted to sell the product under the licensor's trademark in return for payment of royalties. The posttermination obligation was not limited to confidential proprietary information, but any features and designs.

[147]*Midwest Indus. Inc. v. Karavan Trailers Inc.,* 175 F.3d 1356, 50 USPQ2d 1672 (Fed. Cir. 1999). See also *University of Colorado Found. v. American Cyanamid Co.,* 196 F.3d 1366, 52 USPQ2d 1801 (Fed. Cir. 1999).

[148]*Schenck, A.G. v. Nortron Corp.,* 713 F.2d 782, 218 USPQ 698 (Fed. Cir. 1983).

the purpose of enforcing their foreign patents? Perhaps not. The court said in one case that only a British court, applying British law, can determine validity and infringement of British patents.[149] And it has flatly held that a claim of infringement of a foreign patent is not a claim of unfair competition that can be joined with a U.S. patent infringement claim under 28 U.S.C. §1338(b). Nonetheless, it seemed to leave the door slightly ajar for district courts to exercise supplemental jurisdiction over such a claim, pursuant to 28 U.S.C. §1367(a), in an appropriate case.[150]

Certainly the court has cautioned that due regard must be given to differences in foreign patent law [151] and has held, in the face of an argument that the court should adopt the conclusion of a German tribunal, that the patent laws of the United States are the laws governing a determination of obviousness of a U.S. patent in a federal court.[152] The court recognizes that the theories and laws of patentability vary from country to country, as do the examination practices. Thus, caution is required when weighing the action of a foreign patent examiner in deciding whether the requirements of nonobviousness are met under U.S. law. International uniformity in theory and practice has not yet been achieved.[153]

United States courts must sometimes decide the status of foreign patent-like instruments in the context of whether the invention was "patented" in a foreign country within the meaning of 35 U.S.C. §102(a).[154]

§1.5　Presumption of Validity

(a)　General

A patent is born valid. It remains valid until a challenger proves it was stillborn or had birth defects, or it is no longer viable as an enforceable right.[155] That, the Federal Circuit has told us, time after

---

[149]*Stein Assoc., Inc. v. Heat & Control, Inc.*, 748 F.2d 653, 223 USPQ 1277 (Fed. Cir. 1984).

[150]*Mars, Inc. v. Kabushiki-Kaisha Nippon Conlux*, 24 F.3d 1368, 30 USPQ2d 1621 (Fed. Cir. 1994).

[151]*Lindemann Maschinenfabrik v. American Hoist & Derrick Co.*, 730 F.2d 1452, 221 USPQ 481 (Fed. Cir. 1984); *Caterpillar Tractor Co. v. Berco, S.P.A.*, 714 F.2d 1110, 219 USPQ 185 (Fed. Cir. 1983).

[152]*Medtronic, Inc. v. Daig Corp.*, 789 F.2d 903, 229 USPQ 664 (Fed. Cir. 1986). The argument was termed specious.

[153]*Heidelberger Druckmaschinen AG v. Hantscho Comm. Prods., Inc.*, 21 F.3d 1068, 30 USPQ2d 1377 (Fed. Cir. 1994).

[154]Thus the Federal Circuit has held that a German Geschmacksmuster, which is a design registration obtained by an applicant from the German government, is a foreign patent and constitutes prior art for purposes of §102(a). *In re Carlson*, 983 F.2d 1032, 25 USPQ2d 1207 (Fed. Cir. 1993).

[155]*Roper Corp. v. Litton Sys., Inc.*, 757 F.2d 1266, 225 USPQ 345, 347 (Fed. Cir. 1985). See also *Orthokinetics, Inc. v. Safety Travel Chairs, Inc.*, 806 F.2d 1565, 1 USPQ2d 1081 (Fed.

time, is the simple meaning of the statutory phrase "A patent shall be presumed valid."[156]

The presumption of validity under 35 U.S.C. §282 is a procedural device, not substantive law.[157] The presumption is one of law, not fact, and does not constitute "evidence" to be weighed against a challenger's evidence.[158] It simply places the burden of persuasion on the party challenging validity.[159] The decision maker is required to begin by accepting the proposition that the patent is valid and then looking to the challenger for proof to the contrary.[160]

In patent infringement litigation the burden never shifts.[161] While a patentee may have the burden of going forward with rebuttal evidence once a challenger has presented a prima facie case of invalidity, the presumption of validity remains intact and the ultimate burden of proving invalidity remains with the challenger throughout the litigation.[162] However, the court has not yet spoken clearly as to the precise standard of proof that the patentee must meet for rebuttal. It has stated, without much discussion, that once a challenger has made out a prima facie case of public use before the critical date, the patent owner must come forward with clear and convincing evidence to counter the prima facie case.[163] In cases of on-sale, it has not specified the standard of rebuttal proof required to establish experimental purpose.[164] And in a case involving a challenger's defense of prior invention, the court seemed to signal that the rebuttal standard of proving priority is by a preponderance rather than clear and convincing evidence.[165]

Cir. 1986); *Datascope Corp. v. SMEC, Inc.,* 776 F.2d 320, 227 USPQ 838 (Fed. Cir. 1985); *Panduit Corp. v. Dennison Mfg. Co.,* 774 F.2d 1082, 227 USPQ 337 (Fed. Cir. 1985).

[156]35 U.S.C. §282.

[157]*Fromson v. Advance Offset Plate, Inc.,* 755 F.2d 1549, 225 USPQ 26 (Fed. Cir. 1985); *Stratoflex, Inc. v. Aeroquip Corp.,* 713 F.2d 1530, 218 USPQ 871 (Fed. Cir. 1983). See text accompanying note 60 above. The fact that a movant obtains discovery from the patentee and uses it in a motion for summary judgment of invalidity does not deprive the patentee of the procedural advantage of the presumption of validity. *Constant v. Advanced Micro-Devices, Inc.,* 848 F.2d 1560, 7 USPQ2d 1057 (Fed. Cir. 1988).

[158]*Avia Group Int'l, Inc. v. L.A. Gear Calif., Inc.,* 853 F.2d 1557, 7 USPQ2d 1548 (Fed. Cir. 1988). See also *New England Braiding Co. v. A.W. Chesterton Co.,* 970 F.2d 878, 23 USPQ2d 1622 (Fed. Cir. 1992).

[159]E.g., *Smithkline Diagnostics, Inc. v. Helena Labs. Corp.,* 859 F.2d 878, 8 USPQ2d 1468 (Fed. Cir. 1988); *RCA Corp. v. Applied Digital Data Sys., Inc.,* 730 F.2d 1440, 221 USPQ 385 (Fed. Cir. 1984); *Stratoflex, Inc. v. Aeroquip Corp.,* 713 F.2d 1530, 218 USPQ 871 (Fed. Cir. 1983).

[160]*Lear Siegler, Inc. v. Aeroquip Corp.,* 733 F.2d 881, 221 USPQ 1025 (Fed. Cir. 1984).

[161]E.g., *RCA Corp. v. Applied Digital Data Sys., Inc.,* 730 F.2d 1440, 221 USPQ 385 (Fed. Cir. 1984); *American Hoist & Derrick Co. v. Sowa & Sons, Inc.,* 725 F.2d 1350, 220 USPQ 763 (Fed. Cir. 1984); *Stratoflex, Inc. v. Aeroquip Corp.,* 713 F.2d 1530, 218 USPQ 871 (Fed. Cir. 1983).

[162]*Innovative ScubaConcepts, Inc. v. Feder Indus., Inc.,* 26 F.3d 1112, 31 USPQ2d 1132 (Fed. Cir. 1994).

[163]*Tone Bros., Inc. v. Sysco Corp.,* 28 F.3d 1192, 31 USPQ2D 1321 (Fed. Cir. 1994). See also note 203 below.

[164]See note 203 below.

[165]*Innovative ScubaConcepts, Inc. v. Feder Indus., Inc.,* 26 F.3d 1112, 31 USPQ2D 1132 (Fed. Cir. 1994). The district court had held that where the challenger introduced evidence of an anticipating invention prior to the filing date, the burden shifted to the patentee to establish

The burden is "most formidable" when the party asserting invalidity relies only upon prior art that was considered by the PTO.[166] Beyond question, it is more difficult to satisfy the burden of persuasion where the party attacking the patent proffers the same prior art considered by the PTO examiner.[167] This is simply a reflection of an added burden of overcoming the deference that is due to a qualified government agency presumed to have properly done its job.[168] If references were in front of the examiner, it must be assumed that he or she reviewed them. There is a presumption that an earlier examination complied with the applicable statutes and regulations and that earlier examiners did their work correctly with respect to the prior art references at their disposal.[169]

The presumption of validity is based in part on the expertise of patent examiners presumed to have done their job; indeed, it may be viewed as a presumption of administrative correctness.[170] That job is typically discharged by one or more examiners who are assumed to have some expertise in interpreting the references and to be familiar from their work with the level of skill in the art, and whose duty it is to issue valid patents.[171]

It is certainly not the role of the court to start from scratch, as a surrogate examiner, to referee de novo a dispute on the validity

---

by clear and convincing evidence that it had both conceived and reduced to practice prior to the challenger's date. The Federal Circuit simply held that there was error in placing the ultimate burden of persuasion on the patentee; the only burden shift should be that of going forward with evidence. The court held that the patent owner had met its burden by introducing evidence of an actual reduction to practice prior to the challenger's invention and did not specifically address the need for an actual reduction to practice or the clear and convincing nature of the showing. The clear signal, however, is that the required showing is only by a preponderance.

[166]*Central Soya Co. v. Geo. A. Hormel & Co.,* 723 F.2d 1573, 220 USPQ 490 (Fed. Cir. 1983).

[167]E.g., *Bausch & Lomb, Inc. v. Barnes-Hind, Inc.,* 796 F.2d 443, 230 USPQ 416 (Fed. Cir. 1986); *Hughes Aircraft Co. v. United States,* 717 F.2d 1351, 219 USPQ 473 (Fed. Cir. 1983). The burden of showing invalidity is especially difficult when the prior art was before the examiner. *Hewlett-Packard Co. v. Bausch & Lomb, Inc.,* 909 F.2d 1464, 15 USPQ2d 1525 (Fed. Cir. 1990).

[168]*Kloster Speedsteel AB v. Crucible Inc.,* 793 F.2d 1565, 230 USPQ 81 (Fed. Cir. 1986); *American Hoist & Derrick Co. v. Sowa & Sons, Inc.,* 725 F.2d 1350, 220 USPQ 763 (Fed. Cir. 1984). It is presumed that public officials do their assigned jobs. *Northern Telecom, Inc. v. Datapoint Corp.,* 908 F.2d 931, 15 USPQ2d 1321 (Fed. Cir. 1990).

[169]*In re Portola Packaging, Inc.,* 110 F.3d 786, 42 USPQ2d 1295 (Fed. Cir. 1997). Though the examiner is indeed presumed to have done his or her job correctly, there is no support in the law for a presumption that the examiner will understand foreign languages such as Japanese or will request a costly complete translation of every submitted foreign language document, particularly in the absence of any reason to do so. Consequently, while the examiner's initials require that it be presumed that he or she considered a foreign language reference, this presumption extends only to the examiner's consideration of any translated portion and any concise statement of materiality submitted by the applicant. *Semiconductor Energy Lab. Co. v. Samsung Elec. Co.,* 204 F.3d 1368, 54 USPQ2d 1001 (Fed. Cir. 2000).

[170]*Brooktree Corp. v. Advanced Micro Devices, Inc.,* 977 F.2d 1555, 24 USPQ2d 1401 (Fed. Cir. 1992).

[171]*Bausch & Lomb, Inc. v. Barnes-Hind, Inc.,* 796 F.2d 443, 230 USPQ 416 (Fed. Cir. 1986); *American Hoist & Derrick Co. v. Sowa & Sons, Inc.,* 725 F.2d 1350, 220 USPQ 763 (Fed. Cir. 1984).

question. Such procedure would render the PTO unnecessary. Although courts are clearly not bound by the events in the PTO or its decisions, there is no point or value in, and no warrant for, proceeding as though nothing happened before suit except the naked issue of a patent.[172]

If the patent challenger's burden is more difficult when all it has to offer is the prior art that was before the PTO, it is reasonable to suppose the converse to be true. Certainly it can be said that where the accused infringer offers new prior art that is more pertinent than that which was available to the PTO, the burden is more easily carried.[173] In such a case, it is easier to rebut the presumption,[174] and the offering party is simply more likely to meet the burden of persuasion.[175]

It is futile, however, to argue one way or another whether the presumption of validity *applies* to art not cited by the PTO. Of course it does, and if the trial court commits more than rhetorical error in denying the patentee the benefit of the presumption, its judgment cannot stand.[176] The Federal Circuit insists that the presence of art more pertinent than that before the PTO does not weaken or destroy the presumption of validity.[177] At the same time, there is no legal authority for the view that the court must first determine that prior art in an evaluation of obviousness is more pertinent than the prior art considered by the PTO. Any relevant evidence, whether more or less pertinent, can be considered in an analysis of obviousness.[178] The

---

[172]*Panduit Corp. v. Dennison Mfg. Co.*, 774 F.2d 1082, 227 USPQ 337 (Fed. Cir. 1985). Where the PTO has considered a piece of prior art, and issued a patent notwithstanding that prior art, a court owes some deference to the PTO's decision. *Minnesota Min. & Mfg. Co. v. Johnson & Johnson Orthopaedics, Inc.*, 976 F.2d 1559, 24 USPQ2d 1321 (Fed. Cir. 1992).

[173]*EWP Corp. v. Reliance Universal Inc.*, 755 F.2d 898, 225 USPQ 20 (Fed. Cir. 1985); *Lindemann Maschinenfabrik v. American Hoist & Derrick Co.*, 730 F.2d 1452, 221 USPQ 481 (Fed. Cir. 1984); *RCA Corp. v. Applied Digital Data Sys., Inc.*, 730 F.2d 1440, 221 USPQ 385 (Fed. Cir. 1984).

[174]*Aktiebolaget Karlstads v. United States ITC*, 705 F.2d 1565, 217 USPQ 865 (Fed. Cir. 1983).

[175]*Ryco, Inc. v. Ag-Bag Corp.*, 857 F.2d 1418, 8 USPQ2d 1323 (Fed. Cir. 1988); *SSIH Equip. S.A. v. United States ITC*, 713 F.2d 746, 218 USPQ 678 (Fed. Cir. 1983). See also *Railroad Dynamics, Inc. v. A. Stucki Co.*, 727 F.2d 1506, 220 USPQ 929 (Fed. Cir. 1984).

[176]*Lear Siegler, Inc. v. Aeroquip Corp.*, 733 F.2d 881, 221 USPQ 1025 (Fed. Cir. 1984).

[177]*Alco Standard Corp. v. Tennessee Valley Auth.*, 808 F.2d 1490, 1 USPQ2d 1337 (Fed. Cir. 1986); *RCA Corp. v. Applied Digital Data Sys., Inc.*, 730 F.2d 1440, 221 USPQ 385 (Fed. Cir. 1984). It may at most require the patentee to come forward with countervailing evidence of validity. *Stratoflex, Inc. v. Aeroquip Corp.*, 713 F.2d 1530, 218 USPQ 871 (Fed. Cir. 1983). If the patent challenger introduces evidence that might lead to a conclusion of invalidity, a patentee would be well advised to introduce evidence sufficient to rebut that of the challenger. *Orthokinetics, Inc. v. Safety Travel Chairs, Inc.*, 806 F.2d 1565, 1 USPQ2d 1081 (Fed. Cir. 1986). The court has set aside, despite wide discretion in the district judge, a ruling that the presumption of validity was destroyed, as a sanction for attorney misconduct. *In re Mark Indus.*, 751 F.2d 1219, 224 USPQ 521 (Fed. Cir. 1984). The patent challenger's burden is not lessened by the introduction at trial of prior art not before the PTO during prosecution. *Gillette Co. v. S.C. Johnson & Son*, 919 F.2d 720, 16 USPQ2d 1923 (Fed. Cir. 1990).

[178]*Constant v. Advanced Micro-Devices, Inc.*, 848 F.2d 1560, 7 USPQ2d 1057 (Fed. Cir. 1988).

presentation of evidence that was not before the examiner does not change the presumption of validity, although the burden may be more or less easily carried because of the additional evidence.[179]

Nor does the presumption alter the burden of proof. One who challenges a patent must establish invalidity by clear and convincing evidence.[180] The court has made it clear that the proffer of more pertinent prior art than that before the PTO does not reduce this burden to a mere preponderance of the evidence.[181] Proof of facts offered to defeat the presumption of validity must always be by evidence that is clear and convincing,[182] and this applies to each fact upon which the ultimate conclusion of invalidity is based.[183] But it is the disputed facts underlying the legal conclusion of obviousness that must be established by clear and convincing evidence, not the ultimate legal conclusion of obviousness itself. Where a trial court is applying the legal test of obviousness to a set of established facts, it is not restricted by any quantum of proof or lofty standard.[184]

If new art facilitates meeting the challenger's burden, how does one identify art as "new" or "more pertinent"? The failure to cite specific prior art is not conclusive that the examiner did not consider it.[185] Nor can it be presumed, at least where fraud or other egregious conduct is concerned, that the PTO considered prior art if it was not cited.[186] The court feels it is pointless to argue about whether there is a presumption that the examiner considered and rejected art found in the same PTO classification, since the ultimate question is whether

---

[179]*Kahn v. General Motors Corp.*, 135 F.3d 1472, 45 USPQ2d 1608 (Fed. Cir. 1998).

[180]E.g., *Carella v. Starlight Archery & Pro Line Co.*, 804 F.2d 135, 231 USPQ 644 (Fed. Cir. 1986); *Bausch & Lomb, Inc. v. Barnes-Hind, Inc.*, 796 F.2d 443, 230 USPQ 416 (Fed. Cir. 1986); *Ashland Oil, Inc. v. Delta Resins & Refracs., Inc.*, 776 F.2d 281, 227 USPQ 657 (Fed. Cir. 1985); *Lindemann Maschinenfabrik v. American Hoist & Derrick Co.*, 730 F.2d 1452, 221 USPQ 481 (Fed. Cir. 1984). An attack on the validity of a patent requires proof of facts by clear and convincing evidence or its equivalent, by whatever form of words it may be expressed. The clear and convincing standard of proof is an intermediate standard that lies somewhere between proof beyond a reasonable doubt and a preponderance of the evidence. Although not susceptible to precise definition, clear and convincing evidence has been described as evidence that produces in the mind of the trier of fact an abiding conviction that the truth of the factual contentions is highly probable. *Buildex, Inc. v. Kason Indus., Inc.*, 849 F.2d 1461, 7 USPQ2d 1325 (Fed. Cir. 1988). But even under the clear and convincing standard, proof need not be airtight. The law requires persuasion, not perfection. *Id.*

[181]*Medtronic Inc. v. Intermedics, Inc.*, 799 F.2d 734, 230 USPQ 641 (Fed. Cir. 1986); *Jamesbury Corp. v. Litton Indus. Prods., Inc.*, 756 F.2d 1556, 225 USPQ 253 (Fed. Cir. 1985). See also *Alco Standard Corp. v. Tennessee Valley Auth.*, 808 F.2d 1490, 1 USPQ2d 1337 (Fed. Cir. 1986). The court passed the question the first time it was presented. See *Underwater Devices, Inc. v. Morrison-Knudsen Co.*, 717 F.2d 1380, 219 USPQ 569 (Fed. Cir. 1983).

[182]*Ryco, Inc. v. Ag-Bag Corp.*, 857 F.2d 1418, 8 USPQ2d 1323 (Fed. Cir. 1988); *Connell v. Sears, Roebuck & Co.*, 722 F.2d 1542, 220 USPQ 193 (Fed. Cir. 1983).

[183]*Ashland Oil, Inc. v. Delta Resins & Refracs., Inc.*, 776 F.2d 281, 227 USPQ 657 (Fed. Cir. 1985).

[184]*Newell Cos. v. Kenney Mfg. Co.*, 864 F.2d 757, 9 USPQ2d 1417 (Fed. Cir. 1988).

[185]*Lear Siegler, Inc. v. Aeroquip Corp.*, 733 F.2d 881, 221 USPQ 1025, 1029 (Fed. Cir. 1984).

[186]*Driscoll v. Cebalo*, 731 F.2d 878, 221 USPQ 745 (Fed. Cir. 1984). Any presumption that the examiner is aware of all the prior art in the classifications that he or she searched certainly does not apply in the fraud context.

it is more pertinent.[187] One thing seems clear: it is the burden of the challenger to show that art was not considered by the PTO, rather than the burden of the patentee to show that it was.[188]

The court summed up well when it said the presumption has no separate evidentiary value. It cautions the decision maker against a rush to conclude invalidity. Submission of additional art that is merely "pertinent" does not dispel that caution. It is difficult to imagine a patent lawsuit in which an accused infringer is unable to add some new "pertinent" art. The inescapable burden of persuasion on one who would prove invalidity, however, remains throughout the trial.[189]

(b) Specific Applications

In dealing with the statutory presumption of validity, the court has developed some fairly well-defined rules and has displayed a certain amount of impatience with lawyers and trial judges who cannot, for one reason or another, bring themselves to adhere strictly to those rules.[190]

Holdings of validity. Because a patent is born valid, it is not a required role of the court in a suit for patent infringement to declare patents valid. A suit brought only for a declaration that a patent is valid would be an anomaly, and a patentee who in an infringement suit asks the court to hold his or her patent valid states a redundancy and suggests a blurring of the burden assignment. Counsel for the patentee should not undertake the nonexistent initial burden of proving validity, but need only be prepared to rebut whatever case of invalidity may be made by the patent's challenger.[191] In this context, the court has critically observed that patentees historically "go first" with testimony on validity, on the empirically unproven premise that a favorable first impression of the merits of the invention will carry through to victory. Courts and alleged infringers have acquiesced in the practice. The resulting erroneous but clear impression that patentees bear a burden of proving validity has frequently resulted

---

[187]*Lindemann Maschinenfabrik v. American Hoist & Derrick Co.,* 730 F.2d 1452, 221 USPQ 481 (Fed. Cir. 1984). The court suggests that a good way to determine how the examiner feels on that question is to seek reexamination.

[188]*Richdel, Inc. v. Sunspool Corp.,* 714 F.2d 1573, 219 USPQ 8 (Fed. Cir. 1983). The court also seems to have indicated that the challenger has the burden of showing that its prior art is more pertinent than that considered by the judge in an earlier litigation. *Leinoff v. Louis Milona & Sons,* 726 F.2d 734, 220 USPQ 845 (Fed. Cir. 1984).

[189]*W.L. Gore & Assoc. v. Garlock, Inc.,* 721 F.2d 1540, 220 USPQ 303 (Fed. Cir. 1983).

[190]Here as elsewhere the court itself sometimes strays from its own well-marked path. How else can one explain a statement that recognition of, and due weight to, the presumption of validity is particularly important where the trial judge acknowledges that the obviousness question is close? *Loctite Corp. v. Ultraseal Ltd.,* 781 F.2d 861, 228 USPQ 90 (Fed. Cir. 1985). Is it not clear beyond question that the presumption must be recognized, and duly weighed, in all cases, close or not?

[191]*Panduit Corp. v. Dennison Mfg. Co.,* 774 F.2d 1082, 227 USPQ 337 (Fed. Cir. 1985).

in cluttered records, irrelevant detours, undue burdens on the judicial process, and unnecessary work for the trial court.[192]

Thus, in an infringement action, it is not part of a patent owner's initial burden of going forward with proof of its case to submit evidence supporting validity. Rather, the burden is first on a challenger to introduce evidence that raises the issue of invalidity. Further, a challenger must establish facts, by clear and convincing evidence, that persuasively lead to the conclusion of invalidity. A challenger's silence leaves untouched at this stage what the statute presumes, namely, that the patent is valid. Any argument that the patentee unfairly waited for rebuttal to present its evidence regarding validity clearly fails. The patentee has no obligation to introduce any evidence initially on validity.[193]

Consequently, it is not necessary that the district court hold a patent valid; it is only necessary that it hold that the patent challenger has failed to carry its burden.[194] If the burden of proving invalidity of a patent is not met, the appropriate conclusion is that the patent was not shown to be invalid. A patent should not be declared "valid" by a court because other challengers may be able to prove invalidity using different evidence.[195] A patent is not held "valid" for all purposes, but simply not invalid on the record before the court.[196]

Prior adjudications. Although the court has held that the presumption of validity is not augmented by an earlier adjudication that the patent is not invalid, it has indicated that prior litigation over the same patent should be given some weight, short of stare decisis effect.[197] In *Mendenhall v. Cedarapids*,[198] the court found no abuse of discretion in refusing to admit into evidence the opinion of another district court holding the patents infringed, enforceable, and not invalid in a suit against other infringers. Such a prior opinion must be given "weight," but only as precedent not evidence. The precedent would serve only as a "red flag warning" to inform the court that caution must be taken in reaching a contrary legal conclusion. But

---

[192]*Orthokinetics, Inc. v. Safety Travel Chairs, Inc.,* 806 F.2d 1565, 1 USPQ2d 1081, 1084 (Fed. Cir. 1986).

[193]*Avia Group Int'l, Inc. v. L.A. Gear Calif., Inc.,* 853 F.2d 1557, 7 USPQ2d 1548 (Fed. Cir. 1988).

[194]*Jones v. Hardy,* 727 F.2d 1524, 220 USPQ 1021 (Fed. Cir. 1984); *Environmental Designs, Ltd. v. Union Oil Co.,* 713 F.2d 693, 218 USPQ 865 (Fed. Cir. 1983). There is a stronger public interest in the elimination of invalid patents than in the affirmation of a patent as valid, at least in part because of the presumption of validity. *Nestier Corp. v. Menasha Corp.,* 739 F.2d 1576, 222 USPQ 747 (Fed. Cir. 1984).

[195]*Durango Assoc., Inc. v. Reflange, Inc.,* 843 F.2d 1349, 6 USPQ2d 1290 (Fed. Cir. 1988).

[196]*Stevenson v. Sears, Roebuck & Co.,* 713 F.2d 705, 218 USPQ 969 (Fed. Cir. 1983).

[197]*Allen Archery, Inc. v. Browning Mfg. Co.,* 819 F.2d 1087, 2 USPQ2d 1490 (Fed. Cir. 1987); *Shelcore, Inc. v. Durham Indus., Inc.,* 745 F.2d 621, 223 USPQ 584 (Fed. Cir. 1984). The fact that the validity of claims has previously been upheld in an earlier litigation is to be given weight in determining validity, though not stare decisis effect. *Gillette Co. v. S.C. Johnson & Son,* 919 F.2d 720, 16 USPQ2d 1923 (Fed. Cir. 1990).

[198]*Mendenhall v. Cedarapids, Inc.,* 5 F.3d 1556, 28 USPQ2d 1081 (Fed. Cir. 1993).

it is not evidence and should not be admitted as evidence for this purpose.[199] Nor can the opinion be given stare decisis effect. That different judgments can be reached, and must be affirmed, on essentially the same evidentiary record is a vagary of our justice system. As a matter of due process, each new defendant in a patent suit is entitled to makes its own defense.[200]

Particular issues. The burden placed on patent challengers by 35 U.S.C. §282 is not undue. There are many grounds for challenging a patent. Challengers often press them all; and challengers win if they establish only one.[201] The presumption of validity therefore goes to validity of the patent in relation to the patent statute as a whole, not just to nonobviousness under §103.[202] Validity encompasses three separate tests of patentability: novelty, utility, and nonobviousness. Thus, included within the presumption of validity is a presumption of novelty, a presumption of nonobviousness, and a presumption of utility, each of which is presumed to have been met.[203] The presumption of validity also includes a presumption that the patent complies

---

[199]In dissent, Judge Mayer expressed the view that the earlier opinion was very probative evidence for resolving the questions of fact and law present in the case. He felt that the proffering party had demonstrated a real need for the opinion for use in questioning the other side's patent law expert, who had not even read the prior opinion. It is also interesting to note that the prior judgment had eventually been affirmed by the Federal Circuit!

[200]The court went on to hold that the district court was not required, under the mantle of stare decisis, to admit the entire trial record of the earlier case into evidence, and certainly was not required to reach the same conclusion. It then turned to the question of whether the opinion itself was properly excludable under FRE 403. Although the prior litigation might be evidence of secondary considerations such as commercial success or copying, or might be relevant to willfulness, it might also carry too great a risk of prejudice to the jury—a risk that might not be alleviated by a cautionary instruction, which would require an unseemly explanation to the jury of why the current judge disagreed with the earlier judge on the law. One expects that this case will not be the Federal Circuit's final word on the subject. It is particularly interesting to note that the majority passed the question of whether the judgment, as opposed to the opinion, would have been admissible under FRE 403.

[201]*Railroad Dynamics, Inc. v. A. Stucki Co.,* 727 F.2d 1506, 220 USPQ 929 (Fed. Cir. 1984).

[202]*Hybritech Inc. v. Monoclonal Antibodies, Inc.,* 802 F.2d 1367, 231 USPQ 81 (Fed. Cir. 1986). It is error, however, to instruct a jury that the presumption of validity means that it is to be presumed that there were no irregularities during examination. *Magnivision, Inc. v. Bonneau Co.,* 115 F.3d 956, 42 USPQ2d 1925 (Fed. Cir. 1997). Recognition of laches as a defense to a patent does not affect the presumption of its validity. *A.C. Aukerman Co. v. R.L. Chaides Constr. Co.,* 960 F.2d 1020, 22 USPQ2d 1321 (Fed. Cir. 1992).

[203]*Structural Rubber Prods. Co. v. Park Rubber Co.,* 749 F.2d 707, 223 USPQ 1264 (Fed. Cir. 1984). See also *Raytheon Co. v. Roper Corp.,* 724 F.2d 951, 220 USPQ 592 (Fed. Cir. 1983) (utility). The law does not impose on the patentee the burden of establishing that the combined teachings of the individual prior art references would not have led one of skill to the invention. Where the party asserting invalidity must rely upon a combination of prior art references to establish invalidity, that party bears the burden of showing some teaching or suggestion in the references to support their use in combination. *Ashland Oil, Inc. v. Delta Resins & Refracs., Inc.,* 776 F.2d 281, 227 USPQ 657 (Fed. Cir. 1985). Apparently, once a prima facie case of on-sale is made out, it is incumbent upon the patent owner to come forward with evidence directed to showing an experimental purpose. Compare *Barmag Barmer Masch. AG v. Murata Mach., Ltd.,* 731 F.2d 831, 221 USPQ 561 (Fed. Cir. 1984), with *TP Labs., Inc. v. Professional Positioners, Inc.,* 724 F.2d 965, 220 USPQ 577 (Fed. Cir. 1984). Certainly a prima facie case of public use before the critical date requires the patentee to come forward with clear and convincing evidence to counter that showing. *Hycor Corp. v. Schlueter Co.,* 740 F.2d 1529, 222 USPQ 553 (Fed. Cir.

with §112.[204] A party asserting invalidity by reason of failure to comply with §112 bears no less a burden and no fewer responsibilities than any other patent challenger. It must show §112 invalidity by clear and convincing proof.[205] The presumption also applies to eligibility questions.[206]

The burden of showing misjoinder or nonjoinder of inventors is a heavy one and must be proved by clear and convincing evidence, both as to patent applications under 35 U.S.C. §116 and issued patents under §256. This rule rests on important policy considerations. The inventors as named in an issued patent are presumed to be correct. The temptation for persons who consulted with the inventor and provided him or her with materials and advice, to reconstruct, so as to further their own position, the extent of their contribution to the conception of the invention, is simply too great to permit a lower standard than clear and convincing evidence.[207]

Each claim of a patent is presumed valid independently of the validity of other claims.[208] It is therefore error for the trial court to

---

1984). On motion for summary judgment, once an alleged infringer has presented facts sufficient to establish a prima facie case of public use, it falls to the patent owner to come forward with some evidence to the contrary sufficient to raise a genuine issue of material fact. *Sinskey v. Pharmacia Ophthalmics, Inc.*, 982 F.2d 494, 25 USPQ2d 1290 (Fed. Cir. 1992).

[204]*National Recovery Tech. Inc. v. Magnetic Sep. Sys. Inc.*, 166 F.3d 1190, 49 USPQ2d 1671 (Fed. Cir. 1999).

[205]*Northern Telecom, Inc. v. Datapoint Corp.*, 908 F.2d 931, 15 USPQ2d 1321 (Fed. Cir. 1990); *Ralston Purina Co. v. Far-Mar-Co, Inc.*, 772 F.2d 1570, 227 USPQ 177 (Fed. Cir. 1985). Even where the patentee must have support in order to rely on a parent application's filing date, it is apparently the burden of the challenger to show lack of support. *Id.* It is also the burden of the challenger to make out a prima facie case of acquiescence in a §112 rejection, such as new matter, lack of best mode, or insufficient disclosure, if he or she intends to argue estoppel. *Pennwalt Corp. v. Akzona Inc.*, 740 F.2d 1573, 222 USPQ 833 (Fed. Cir. 1984). It is the burden of a patent challenger under 35 U.S.C. §112 to show by facts supported by clear and convincing evidence that the patent is not enabling. *United States v. Telectronics, Inc.*, 857 F.2d 778, 8 USPQ2d 1217 (Fed. Cir. 1988). There is a presumption that the PTO complies with its own rules, including those relating to review of the content of amendments filed by an applicant. A district court should not require more of an applicant than is required by the PTO. *Rite-Hite Corp. v. Kelley Co.*, 819 F.2d 1120, 2 USPQ2d 1915 (Fed. Cir. 1987). But while the PTO is presumed to have complied with all applicable rules, that presumption cannot overcome a clear statutory violation. *Baxter Int'l Inc. v. McGaw Inc.*, 149 F.3d 1321, 47 USPQ2d 1225 (Fed. Cir. 1998).

[206]*Arrhythmia Res. Tech., Inc. v. Corazonix Corp.*, 958 F.2d 1053, 22 USPQ2d 1033 (Fed. Cir. 1992).

[207]*Hess v. Advanced Cardiovascular Sys., Inc.*, 106 F.3d 976, 41 USPQ2d 1782 (Fed. Cir. 1997). See also *Ethicon Inc. v. United States Surgical Corp.*, 135 F.3d 1456, 45 USPQ2d 1545 (Fed. Cir. 1998); *Canon Computer Sys. Inc. v. NuKote Int'l Inc.*, 134 F.3d 1085, 45 USPQ2d 1355 (Fed. Cir. 1998); *Fina Oil & Chem. Co. v. Ewen*, 123 F.3d 1466, 43 USPQ2d 1935 (Fed. Cir. 1997).

[208]*Carroll Touch, Inc. v. Electro Mechanical Sys., Inc.*, 3 F.3d 404, 27 USPQ2D 1836 (Fed. Cir. 1993); *Miles Labs., Inc. v. Shandon, Inc.*, 997 F.2d 870, 27 USPQ2d 1123 (Fed. Cir. 1993); *Custom Accessories, Inc. v. Jeffrey-Allan Indus., Inc.*, 807 F.2d 955, 1 USPQ2d 1196 (Fed. Cir. 1986); *Bausch & Lomb, Inc. v. Barnes-Hind, Inc.*, 796 F.2d 443, 230 USPQ 416 (Fed. Cir. 1986); *Kloster Speedsteel AB v. Crucible Inc.*, 793 F.2d 1565, 230 USPQ 81 (Fed. Cir. 1986); *Loctite Corp. v. Ultraseal Ltd.*, 781 F.2d 861, 228 USPQ 90 (Fed. Cir. 1985); *Datascope Corp. v. SMEC, Inc.*, 776 F.2d 320, 227 USPQ 838 (Fed. Cir. 1985); *Shelcore, Inc. v. Durham Indus., Inc.*, 745 F.2d 621, 223 USPQ 584 (Fed. Cir. 1984); *Vandenberg v. Dairy Equip. Co.*, 740 F.2d 1560, 224 USPQ 195 (Fed. Cir. 1984); *Preemption Devices, Inc. v. Minnesota Min. & Mfg. Co.*, 732 F.2d

hold an entire patent invalid when fewer than all claims are in issue.[209] If a defendant wishes to show that a dependent claim is invalid, it must submit evidence directed to that claim.[210]

As part of its normal burden of proving infringement, the patentee bears the burden of showing that the range of equivalents it seeks will not ensnare the prior art. This does not undermine the presumption of validity of the actual patent claims, which will remain valid whether or not the patentee succeeds in persuading the court that it is entitled to the range of equivalents it seeks.[211]

The presumption of validity is the same for design patents as for utility patents.[212] In an appropriate case, even one involving a design patent, the presumption is a permissible basis for supporting a preliminary injunction.[213]

The court has observed that because patents are cloaked in a presumption of validity, a patent infringement suit is presumed to be brought in good faith.[214]

Particular proceedings. The presumption of validity does not increase the difficulty of showing an absence of factual issues on a motion for summary judgment.[215] Thus, once an accused infringer has established a prima facie case for overcoming the presumption of validity, the nonmovant patentee must submit evidence setting forth specific facts that raise a genuine issue for trial.[216] A patentee who moves for summary judgment that the patent is not invalid need not introduce any evidence due to the presumption of validity.[217]

903, 221 USPQ 841 (Fed. Cir. 1984); *Jones v. Hardy,* 727 F.2d 1524, 220 USPQ 1021 (Fed. Cir. 1984). Apparently this applies to double patenting challenges, as well. See *Ortho Pharm. Corp. v. Smith,* 959 F.2d 936, 22 USPQ2d 1119 (Fed. Cir. 1992).

[209]*Vandenberg v. Dairy Equip. Co.,* 740 F.2d 1560, 224 USPQ 195 (Fed. Cir. 1984). If a defendant does not counterclaim for invalidity of all claims, a judgment of invalidity encompassing all claims must be reversed where it appears that the validity of certain claims was not actually litigated. *Datascope Corp. v. SMEC, Inc.,* 776 F.2d 320, 227 USPQ 838 (Fed. Cir. 1985). It would be inappropriate for a district court to state in its judgment form that four patents were valid if only one claim of each were asserted and tried. In the absence of any indication that the four claims tried were stipulated to be representative, the district court should consider whether its judgment should be recast to limit it to the claims in suit. *Dow Chem. Co. v. American Cyanamid Co.,* 816 F.2d 617, 2 USPQ2d 1350 (Fed. Cir. 1987). However, where the parties stipulate to representative claims, a validity resolution for the representative claims applies to the other claims as well. *Miles Labs., Inc. v. Shandon, Inc.,* 997 F.2d 870, 27 USPQ2d 1123 (Fed. Cir. 1993).

[210]*Shelcore, Inc. v. Durham Indus., Inc.,* 745 F.2d 621, 223 USPQ 584, 586 (Fed. Cir. 1984).

[211]*Wilson Sporting Goods Co. v. David Geoffrey & Assoc.,* 904 F.2d 677, 14 USPQ2d 1942 (Fed. Cir. 1990).

[212]*Litton Sys., Inc. v. Whirlpool Corp.,* 728 F.2d 1423, 221 USPQ 97 (Fed. Cir. 1984). There is a statutory presumption that the design is not merely functional. *L.A. Gear, Inc. v. Thom McAn Shoe Co.,* 988 F.2d 1117, 25 USPQ2d 1913 (Fed. Cir. 1993).

[213]*Power Controls Corp. v. Hybrinetics, Inc.,* 806 F.2d 234, 231 USPQ 774 (Fed. Cir. 1986).

[214]*Atari Games Corp. v. Nintendo of Am., Inc.,* 897 F.2d 1572, 14 USPQ2d 1034 (Fed. Cir. 1990). Surely the court did not mean this to extend to the infringement question; one could bring a suit knowing there is no infringement and thereby incur antitrust liability.

[215]*D.L. Auld Co. v. Chroma Graphics Corp.,* 714 F.2d 1144, 219 USPQ 13 (Fed. Cir. 1983).

[216]*Cable Elec. Prods., Inc. v. Genmark, Inc.,* 770 F.2d 1015, 226 USPQ 881 (Fed. Cir. 1985).

[217]*Massey v. Del Labs., Inc.,* 118 F.3d 1568, 43 USPQ2d 1367 (Fed. Cir. 1997).

A patentee seeking preliminary injunctive relief cannot establish a likelihood of success on the merits of validity and enforceability simply by reliance upon the presumption of validity, at least where the accused infringer comes forward with some evidence of invalidity or unenforceability. The accused infringer does not have the same burden of clear and convincing proof that it will have at trial.[218] The presumption of validity is not evidence that can be weighed in determining the likelihood of success, and it does not relieve a patentee who moves for a preliminary injunction from carrying the normal burden of demonstrating that it will likely succeed on all disputed liability issues at trial.[219]

Where there is a jury verdict of validity, the question is not whether the patentee has introduced sufficiently substantial evidence to support the verdict, but whether the challenger's evidence so met the burden imposed by §282 that reasonable jurors could not have concluded that the challenger failed to overcome that burden.[220] When the verdict connotes invalidity, a properly instructed jury has necessarily determined that the challenger's evidence met the §282 burden.[221]

The concern of the U.S. ITC for public health and welfare and a competitive economy is not inimical to the public policy that undergirds §282. The presumption of validity assigns the burden of proof to the challenger and thus necessarily requires that there be a challenger. It is beyond cavil that a district court does not have authority to invalidate a patent at its own initiative if validity is not challenged by a party. Inasmuch as patent invalidity is a statutory defense, not a regulatory duty, the ITC has no authority to redetermine patent validity when no defense of validity has been raised.[222]

(c) PTO Proceedings

Ex parte prosecution. The presumption of validity does not operate in the PTO.[223] Patent applications are not entitled to the procedural advantages of §282. The standard of proof required properly to

---

[218]*Nutrition 21 v. United States*, 930 F.2d 867, 18 USPQ2d 1347 (Fed. Cir. 1991).

[219]*New England Braiding Co. v. A.W. Chesterton Co.*, 970 F.2d 878, 23 USPQ2d 1622 (Fed. Cir. 1992).

[220]*Perkin-Elmer Corp. v. Computervision Corp.*, 732 F.2d 888, 221 USPQ 669 (Fed. Cir. 1984). The precise question on motion for JNOV after a jury verdict of validity is whether the moving party's evidence is so clear and convincing that reasonable jurors could only conclude that the patent claims in issue were invalid. *Verdegaal Bros., Inc. v. Union Oil Co.*, 814 F.2d 628, 2 USPQ2d 1051 (Fed. Cir. 1987).

[221]*Railroad Dynamics, Inc. v. A. Stucki Co.*, 727 F.2d 1506, 220 USPQ 929 (Fed. Cir. 1984). The court may have effectively decided a very significant point with no discussion whatever. The jury deadlocked on a special interrogatory as to validity. The Federal Circuit reversed a JMOL of noninfringement, but when the successful patentee argued that the district court should have entered judgment in its favor, on the ground that the defendant had failed to meet its burden of proving invalidity by clear and convincing evidence, the court simply disagreed without discussion and remanded. *Baxter Healthcare Corp. v. Spectramed, Inc.*, 49 F.3d 1575, 34 USPQ2d 1120 (Fed. Cir. 1995).

[222]*Lannom Mfg. Co. v. United States ITC*, 799 F.2d 1572, 231 USPQ 32 (Fed. Cir. 1986).

[223]*In re Morris*, 127 F.3d 1048, 44 USPQ2d 1023 (Fed. Cir. 1997).

reject the claims of a patent application is necessarily lower than that required to invalidate patent claims. Other than issues of fraud or violation of the disclosure duty, which require clear and convincing evidence, the standard of proof that must be met by the PTO in making rejections is a preponderance of the evidence.[224] Moreover, the old premise that doubts as to patentability should be resolved in favor of the patent applicant is now defunct. That rule would cause the presumption of validity to lose its legitimacy.[225]

Prima facie unpatentability. In ex parte prosecution, the PTO has the initial burden of producing a factual basis for a rejection.[226] In other words, the PTO must establish a case of prima facie obviousness. Then the applicant is obliged to come forward with rebuttal, which is merely a showing of facts supporting the opposite conclusion.[227] The procedural devices of the examiner's prima facie case and the applicant's rebuttal were formed to allocate clearly the burdens of going forward and of persuasion as between the examiner and the applicant.[228]

This procedural device is not limited to obviousness. Once the PTO establishes a prima facie case of anticipation based on inherency, the burden shifts to the applicant to prove that the subject matter shown to be in the prior art does not possess the characteristic relied on by the PTO.[229] Similarly, the PTO bears the initial burden of showing prima facie that the claims sought to be patented are unpatentable because of inoperativeness.[230]

Reexamination and reissue. After reissue or reexamination, the challenger's burden of proof, as an evidentiary matter, is usually more difficult to sustain.[231] On the other hand, there is nothing untoward

---

[224]*In re Caveney,* 761 F.2d 671, 226 USPQ 1 (Fed. Cir. 1985).

[225]*In re Andersen,* 743 F.2d 1578, 223 USPQ 378 (Fed. Cir. 1984).

[226]*In re Piasecki,* 745 F.2d 1468, 223 USPQ 785 (Fed. Cir. 1984); *In re Gordon,* 733 F.2d 900 (Fed. Cir. 1984).

[227]*In re Piasecki,* 745 F.2d 1468, 223 USPQ 785 (Fed. Cir. 1984).

[228]*In re Johnson,* 747 F.2d 1456, 223 USPQ 1260 (Fed. Cir. 1984); *In re Piasecki,* 745 F.2d 1468, 223 USPQ 785 (Fed. Cir. 1984). In an unusual situation, the claims in a parent application had been rejected, the rejection affirmed by the PTO Board, and the Board decision affirmed by the CCPA. The applicant filed a continuation and introduced new evidence to overcome the finding of prima facie obviousness in the original application. The resultant patent was held invalid on summary judgment by the district court on grounds of collateral estoppel in view of the CCPA decision. On appeal the Federal Circuit held that the district court did not give proper weight to the presumption of validity. In order for the summary judgment to stand upon remand, the record must show conclusively that the new evidence was immaterial. *Applied Materials, Inc. v. Gemini Research Corp.,* 835 F.2d 279, 15 USPQ2d 1816 (Fed. Cir. 1987).

[229]*In re King,* 801 F.2d 1324, 231 USPQ 136 (Fed. Cir. 1986). It will not suffice merely to make an assertion that the inherent characteristic does not exist and challenge the PTO to prove the contrary by experiment or otherwise. The PTO is not equipped to perform such tasks.

[230]*Fregeau v. Mossinghoff,* 776 F.2d 1034, 227 USPQ 848 (Fed. Cir. 1985). Here the applicant conceded that, by the very nature of the invention itself, the PTO enjoyed a prima facie case, and the applicant had the burden of coming forward with countervailing evidence.

[231]*Kaufman Co. v. Lantech,* 807 F.2d 970, 1 USPQ2d 1202 (Fed. Cir. 1986); *Custom Accessories, Inc. v. Jeffrey-Allan Indus., Inc.,* 807 F.2d 955, 1 USPQ2d 1196 (Fed. Cir. 1986);

about the PTO upholding the validity of a reexamined patent that the district court later finds invalid. This is essentially what occurs when a court finds a patent invalid after the PTO has granted it. It is important to understand that the district court and the PTO can consider different evidence. Accordingly, different results between the two forums may be entirely reasonable.[232] Indeed, the Federal Circuit insists that each do its own separate analysis.[233]

But does the presumption of validity apply during the course of such proceedings? Clearly not.[234] It does not meet the statutory purpose of the presumption of administrative correctness to apply it to a procedure the purpose of which is the remedy of administrative error.[235] The presumption of validity is a rule of procedure placing the burden of persuasion on one who attacks a patent's validity. There is no such attacker in a reexamination, and hence no one on whom that burden may be placed. The examiner is not attacking the validity of a patent, but is conducting a subjective examination of claims in the light of prior art. Even where a third party requests reexamination, that party may be heard only on whether there is a substantial new question of patentability. In litigation, where a patentee cannot amend claims, or add new claims, the presumption has an important role to play. In reexamination, where claims can be amended and new claims added, and where no litigating adversary is present, that role and its rationale simply vanish.[236]

Windsurfing Int'l, Inc. v. AMF, Inc., 782 F.2d 995, 228 USPQ 562 (Fed. Cir. 1986); *American Hoist & Derrick Co. v. Sowa & Sons, Inc.,* 725 F.2d 1350, 220 USPQ 763 (Fed. Cir. 1984).

[232]*Ethicon v. Quigg,* 849 F.2d 1422, 7 USPQ2d 1152 (Fed. Cir. 1988).

[233]In *Greenwood v. Hattori Seiko Co.,* 900 F.2d 238, 14 USPQ2d 1474 (Fed. Cir. 1990), a reexamination request was filed after the patentee had sued for infringement. The examiner rejected the claims over certain prior art references but the patentee antedated those references and the examiner issued a reexamination certificate. The trial court then found that the patentee's showing of invention prior to the references was defective, and purported to "restore" the examiner's rejection. The Federal Circuit vacated and remanded on the ground that simply adopting the examiner's original position disregards the presumption of validity.

[234]*Patlex Corp. v. Mossinghoff,* 758 F.2d 594, 225 USPQ 243 (Fed. Cir. 1985); *In re Etter,* 756 F.2d 852, 225 USPQ 1 (Fed. Cir. 1985).

[235]*Patlex Corp. v. Mossinghoff,* 758 F.2d 594, 225 USPQ 243 (Fed. Cir. 1985).

[236]*In re Etter,* 756 F.2d 852, 225 USPQ 1, 6 (Fed. Cir. 1985). In a reexamination proceeding, there is no presumption of validity and the focus of the reexamination returns essentially to that of an initial examination, at which a preponderance of the evidence must show nonpatentability before the PTO may reject the claims of a patent application. The intent underlying reexamination is to start over in the PTO with respect to the limited examination areas involved, and to *reexamine* the claims, and to examine new or amended claims, as they would have been considered if they had been originally examined in light of all of the prior art of record. *Ethicon v. Quigg,* 849 F.2d 1422, 7 USPQ2d 1152 (Fed. Cir. 1988). But see *Hess v. Advanced Cardiovascular Sys., Inc.,* 106 F.3d 976, 41 USPQ2d 1782 (Fed. Cir. 1997).

2

Utility and Eligibility

§2.1 Introduction

Only certain matter qualifies to be the subject of a patent. First, only "inventions" may be patented. For many decades it was supposed that the word "invention" had an abstract qualitative meaning that in and of itself established an independent condition for patentability. This unfortunate byway is explored in detail in Chapter 4. The ascendance of the obviousness inquiry under 35 U.S.C. §103 has removed most of the substantive meaning from the word, and we can now be satisfied that "invention" is simply definitional. "Inventions" may be patentable, and patents cover "inventions." The statute is uncharacteristically terse here, stating only that the "term 'invention' means invention or discovery."[1]

Second, only certain inventions and discoveries are eligible for patent protection. Here the statute becomes more expansive. Section 101, titled "Inventions patentable," defines them as "any new and useful process, machine, manufacture, or composition of matter, or any new and useful improvement thereof."[2] Section 100(b) fills out the definition even more: "The term 'process' means process, art or method, and includes a new use of a known process, machine, manufacture, composition of matter, or material."[3] Despite the oft-quoted statement in the legislative history of the 1952 Patent Act that Congress intended statutory subject matter to include "anything under the sun that is made by man," Congress did not so mandate. It included in the subject matter that is eligible for patents only those things that qualify as any "process, machine, manufacture, or composition of matter" or improvement thereof, within the meaning of 35 U.S.C. §101.[4] Finally, look again at §101 and see that it requires that the process, machine, manufacture, or composition be "useful" in order to qualify for patent protection. Though this requirement of utility has lost much of its original significance, it does form the basis for exclusion of frivolous or inoperable inventions and also plays a role in assessing the patentability of chemical and pharmacological discoveries.

It may be useful to think of eligibility as a precondition for patentability, and of utility as one of the three fundamental conditions for patentability, together with novelty (Chapter 3) and nonobviousness (Chapter 4). This chapter will approach the concepts in that way and will also investigate the special considerations involved in the patenting of designs, and plants, each of which has its own underlying statutory premise.

---

[1] 35 U.S.C. §100(a).
[2] 35 U.S.C. §101.
[3] 35 U.S.C. §100(b).
[4] *In re Warmerdam*, 33 F.3d 1354, 31 USPQ2d 1754 (Fed. Cir. 1994).

§2.2 Patentable Subject Matter

Each statutory class of eligible subjects must be considered on its own footing.[5] There is no doubt that an inventor is entitled to claim his or her invention as he or she chooses in this regard, but a court must evaluate the claim as it finds it.[6] Whether a claim is directed to statutory subject matter is a question of law. Determination of that question may require findings of underlying facts specific to the particular subject matter and its mode of claiming, but if the material facts are undisputed, the Federal Circuit will undertake plenary review.[7] The presumption of validity applies to eligibility questions.[8]

As will be seen, sometimes the decision as to whether an invention should be claimed in the context of a product or a process can be crucial to ultimate patentability.

(a) Products

(i) General

The statute itself makes a new use of a known process or product eligible for patenting as a process.[9] Not so in the case of an old product produced by a new process or obtained from a new source.[10] It has even been said that the mere purification of a known material does not result in a product that is eligible for patenting.[11] Although it might have made sense a century ago to disqualify such inventions on grounds of eligibility, the proper approach in modern times is to analyze them in terms of novelty and unobviousness—an old product is unpatentable because it is old, not because it constitutes ineligible subject matter.

The eligible products identified in §101 are machines, manufactures, and compositions of matter. In general, those words have a meaning as broad as the human mind can range and have created little controversy.[12]

---

[5]*Loctite Corp. v. Ultraseal Ltd.*, 781 F.2d 861, 228 USPQ 90 (Fed. Cir. 1985).

[6]*In re Durden*, 763 F.2d 1406, 226 USPQ 359 (Fed. Cir. 1985).

[7]*Arrhythmia Res. Tech., Inc. v. Corazonix Corp.*, 958 F.2d 1053, 22 USPQ2d 1033 (Fed. Cir. 1992). Invalidity for failure to claim statutory subject matter under 35 U.S.C. §101 is a question of law that the court reviews without deference. *AT&T Corp. v. Excel Comm Inc.*, 172 F.3d 1352, 50 USPQ2d 1447 (Fed. Cir. 1999).

[8]*Arrhythmia Res. Tech., Inc. v. Corazonix Corp.*, 958 F.2d 1053, 22 USPQ2d 1033 (Fed. Cir. 1992).

[9]35 U.S.C. §100(b). See §2.2(b)(iv).

[10]*Cochrane v. Badische Anilin & Soda Fabrik*, 111 U.S. 293 (1884); *American Wood Paper Co. v. Fiber Disintegrating Co.*, 90 U.S. 566 (1874).

[11]*Risdon Locomotive Works v. Medart*, 158 U.S. 68 (1895); *American Wood Paper Co. v. Fiber Disintegrating Co.*, 90 U.S. 566 (1874).

[12]But see *American Fruit Growers, Inc. v. Brogdex Co.*, 283 U.S. 1, 8 USPQ 131 (1931), where the Court held that an orange having its skin impregnated with a chemical to resist mold damage was not a "manufacture." This decision is indefensible.

Printed matter. The patentability of printed matter is one notable exception. This question has caused great difficulty over the years, principally due to the notion that printed matter is an "abstraction" and thus not patentable as a manufacture. In view of hornbook law that abstractions, i.e., concepts, are not patentable,[13] it might have been thought that the Federal Circuit would likewise have difficulty with the issue. Previous CCPA decisions[14] had eased the way, however, and the court was able to handle the issue with relative clarity when it was presented in an early case. A printed matter rejection was said to stand on a "questionable legal and logical footing"; indeed, printed matter "may well constitute structural limitations upon which patentability can be predicated." Thus the court was willing to reverse an obviousness rejection of a claim covering an endless loop of paper with printed matter thereon (a series of digits related by an algorithm), where the only difference over the prior art was in the printed matter itself. Printed matter may not constitute patentable subject matter per se, but it must be considered as part of the claimed subject matter as a whole in pursuing the obviousness inquiry. Printed matter, if functionally related to other claim elements, is to be given patentable weight.[15]

This approach seems likely to establish a direction for the court in dealing with other potentially troublesome eligibility issues. Thus, despite Supreme Court dicta casting doubt on the eligibility of architectural designs and buildings,[16] and a direct holding against modified natural food products,[17] the Federal Circuit cannot be expected to be very receptive to such defenses or rejections.

Product-by-process. Although so-called product-by-process claims are certainly eligible for patent protection, an old product is not patentable even if produced by a new and unobvious process. As indicated above, the issue is really one of obviousness not eligibility. Thus, where a claimed product appears identical to one in the prior art,

---

[13]*RCA Corp. v. Applied Digital Data Sys., Inc.,* 730 F.2d 1440, 221 USPQ 385, 389 n.5 (Fed. Cir. 1984); see also *Texas Instr., Inc. v. United States ITC,* 805 F.2d 1558, 231 USPQ 833, 841 (Fed. Cir. 1986).

[14]E.g., *In re Miller,* 418 F.2d 1392, 164 USPQ 46 (CCPA 1969).

[15]*In re Gulack,* 703 F.2d 1381, 217 USPQ 401 (Fed. Cir. 1983). The PTO must consider all claim limitations when determining patentability of an invention over the prior art, and may not disregard claim limitations comprised of printed matter. Indeed, the PTO must establish, at least prima facie, that there is no new and nonobvious relationship between the data structure and the memory. *In re Lowry,* 32 F.3d 1579, 32 USPQ2d 1031 (Fed. Cir. 1994). In *Lowry* the claim was to a memory containing a certain data structure. The PTO Board treated the data structure as printed matter and found no new and unobvious relationship between the data structure and the memory. The Federal Circuit held that printed matter cases such as *Gulack* have no factual relevance where the invention as defined by the claims requires that the information be processed not by the mind but by a machine, the computer. Here the data structure was a physical entity that provided increased efficiency in computer operation and was not analogous to printed matter.

[16]*Fond du Lac County v. May,* 137 U.S. 395 (1890); *Jacobs v. Baker,* 74 U.S. 295 (1869).

[17]*American Fruit Growers, Inc. v. Brogdex Co.,* 283 U.S. 1, 8 USPQ 131 (1931).

albeit produced by a different process, the burden falls to the patent applicant to demonstrate patentably significant differences in the product.[18] In determining patentability of product-by-process claims, the product is construed as not limited by the process stated in the claims.[19] In deciding that a machine having a memory containing particular data could be eligible for patentability, the court observed that there is no requirement that a machine claim incorporating process steps must conform to the conventional definition of a product-by-process claim.[20]

(ii) Naturally Occurring Products

A product found in the identical state in nature is quite clearly unpatentable, presumably because it is not a "manufacture" and is therefore ineligible.[21] The Supreme Court took this reasoning a step too far, however, in a case involving inoculants of a bacterium genus. Previous inoculants had consisted of a single species because mixtures were thought to be mutually inhibiting. The patentee discovered mutually noninhibitive strains and obtained claims to multispecies mixtures. The Court observed that the noninhibition qualities were the work of nature not the inventor and held that "patents cannot issue for the discovery of the phenomena of nature."[22] The Court was clearly wrong, both in statement and result. The discovery of phenomena of nature, in applied form, is the rationale of the patent system. The multispecies mixtures of bacteria did not exist in nature and were not naturally occurring.

It might be suggested that here again novelty and obviousness would be better tests of patentability than a simple rule that natural

---

[18]*In re Marosi,* 710 F.2d 799, 218 USPQ 289 (Fed. Cir. 1983).

[19]*Scripps Clinic & Res. Found. v. Genentech, Inc.,* 927 F.2d 1565, 18 USPQ2d 1001 (Fed. Cir. 1991). Using the familiar principle that claims must be construed the same way for validity and for infringement, the court went on to hold that the correct reading of product-by-process claims for infringement purposes is that they are not limited to a product prepared by the process set forth in the claims. In a later decision, *Atlantic Thermoplastics Co. v. Faytex Corp.,* 970 F.2d 834, 23 USPQ2d 1481 (Fed. Cir. 1992), a panel of the court concluded that the *Scripps* panel had not fully considered prior Supreme Court precedent, and held to the contrary. As a result, it now appears that PTO patentability determinations will use the broad interpretation: i.e., a product-by-process claim cannot rely for patentability upon the process limitation. In litigation, however, the process will limit the claim for both infringement and validity. See note 5:336 and accompanying text.

[20]*In re Warmerdam,* 33 F.3d 1354, 31 USPQ2d 1754 (Fed. Cir. 1994). The court also remarked that it was not certain that the claim failed to conform to that definition, inasmuch as the storage of data in a memory physically alters the memory, and thus in some sense gives rise to a new memory.

[21]See, e.g., *In re Bergy,* 563 F.2d 1031, 195 USPQ 344 (CCPA 1977); *In re Mancy,* 499 F.2d 1289, 182 USPQ 303 (CCPA 1974). A synthetic composition identical to the natural is not patentable in the context of product claims. *Cochrane v. Badische Anilin & Soda Fabrik,* 111 U.S. 293 (1884). Nor is a more pure composition, unless the differences in purity have patentable significance in the obviousness inquiry. *In re Bergstrom,* 427 F.2d 1394, 166 USPQ 256 (CCPA 1970); *In re Cofer,* 354 F.2d 664, 148 USPQ 268 (CCPA 1966).

[22]*Funk Bros. Seed Co. v. Kalo Inoculant Co.,* 333 U.S. 127, 76 USPQ 280 (1948).

products are not "manufactures." Naturally occurring products, being old in nature, can hardly be said to be novel, much less unobvious. Caution is advised, however, for it is difficult as a matter of logic and common sense to attribute knowledge of a previously undiscovered and unsuspected natural product to the hypothetical person of skill in the art for prior art purposes.

One probably cannot get a product patent for discovering a new property of an old composition of matter, but the court walks a fine line here. It distinguishes between cases where property limitations need to be shown for anticipation and cases where no prior art showing of such limitations is necessary by characterizing the former type of case as one where "structure alone may be inadequate to define the invention, making it appropriate to define the invention in part by property limitations."[23]

(iii) Living Organisms

Living organisms are clearly patentable as manufactures or compositions of matter, where the inventor has a hand in their production and they possess characteristics different from those found in nature. Thus, a biologically pure culture of a naturally occurring microorganism is patentable,[24] as is a new microorganism produced by genetic engineering.[25] The PTO now considers nonnaturally occurring, nonhuman multicellular organisms, including animals, to be eligible for patenting.[26] Despite the Plant Patent Act and the Plant Variety Protection Act (see §2.5 below), seeds and seed-grown plants are patentable subject matter under §101.[27]

---

[23]*E.I. duPont & Co. v. Phillips Petroleum Co.*, 849 F.2d 1430, 7 USPQ2d 1129 (Fed. Cir. 1988). In *Titanium Metals Corp. v. Banner*, 778 F.2d 775, 227 USPQ 773 (Fed. Cir. 1985), which involved an alloy, once the alloy disclosed in the prior art reference was determined to possess the structural limitations of the claim, the burden shifted to the patentee to show that the alloy disclosed in the reference did not possess the claimed property. But in *Phillips Petroleum*, which involved a polymer, structure alone was insufficient, and the patentee was entitled to define the invention in terms of properties as well. Nonetheless, the court took pains to explain that the issue is not whether one can get a patent on the discovery of a new property of an old composition, but whether the claimed composition, as defined in part by various property parameters, is new.

[24]*In re Bergy*, 563 F.2d 1031, 195 USPQ 344 (CCPA 1977).

[25]*Diamond v. Chakrabarty*, 447 U.S. 303, 206 USPQ 193 (1980).

[26]In 1985 the PTO Board extended *Chakrabarty* (see note 25 above) to hold that man-made multicellular plants not found in nature were patentable, *Ex parte Hibberd*, 227 USPQ 443 (PTO Board 1985); and, later, that a genetically altered strain of polyploid oysters was eligible, *Ex parte Allen*, 2 USPQ2d 1425 (PTO Board 1987). Within days of *Allen*, the PTO issued a Notice stating that it "now considers non-naturally occurring, non-human multicellular organisms, including animals, to be patentable subject matter." In rejecting, for lack of standing, a challenge to this Notice by animal rights groups, the Federal Circuit held, with apparent approval, that it did no more than interpret decisional law. *Animal Legal Defense Fund v. Quigg*, 932 F.2d 920, 18 USPQ2d 920 (Fed. Cir. 1991).

[27]*Pioneer Hi-Bred Int'l Inc. v. J.E.M. Ag Supp. Inc.*, 200 F.3d 1374, 53 USPQ2d 1440 (Fed. Cir. 2000).

(b) Processes

(i) General

The Supreme Court has struggled with the definition of a process. Variously, a process is a mode of treatment of certain materials to produce a given result; it is an act, or a series of acts, performed upon a subject that is to be transformed or reduced to a different state or thing.[28] It is an act, or a mode of acting, to produce a useful result.[29] It is not limited to chemical action but can involve mechanical[30] and electrical operations.[31] The Federal Circuit has not burdened itself with definitional baggage. Simply, and broadly, a process is a manipulation according to an algorithm—doing something to or with something according to a schema.[32]

Concepts and ideas are not patentable, but methods employing those concepts and ideas may well be.[33] However, taking several abstract ideas and manipulating them together adds nothing to the basic equation.[34] Excluded from patentability is subject matter in the categories of laws of nature, physical phenomena, and abstract ideas. A mathematical formula may describe a law of nature, a scientific truth, or an abstract idea. But it also may be used to describe steps of a statutory method or elements of a statutory apparatus.[35] The line between patentable process and unpatentable principle does not always "shimmer with clarity,"[36] but it does seem clear that the application of a newly discovered law of nature or a newly developed mathematical formula to a known process can result in patentable subject matter.[37] And where claimed steps of correlating and combining can be performed by a machine as well as a person, those steps are not mere mental processes that render the claim unpatentable.[38] The determination whether a claimed method is an eligible process

---

[28]*Cochrane v. Deener,* 94 U.S. 780 (1877).

[29]*Tilghman v. Proctor,* 102 U.S. 707 (1881).

[30]*Expanded Metal Co. v. Bradford,* 214 U.S. 366 (1909).

[31]Compare *Dolbear v. American Bell Tel. Co.,* 126 U.S. 1 (1888), with *O'Reilly v. Morse,* 56 U.S. (15 How.) 62 (1854).

[32]*In re Durden,* 763 F.2d 1406, 226 USPQ 359 (Fed. Cir. 1985). In an interesting case, the court rejected an argument that claims directed to host cells used to produce recombinant erythropoietin should be treated as a special sort of "nontraditional" process claim. *Amgen, Inc. v. United States ITC,* 902 F.2d 1532, 14 USPQ2d 1734 (Fed. Cir. 1990).

[33]*RCA Corp. v. Applied Digital Data Sys., Inc.,* 730 F.2d 1440, 221 USPQ 385 (Fed. Cir. 1984); *Jones v. Hardy,* 727 F.2d 1524, 220 USPQ 1021 (Fed. Cir. 1984).

[34]*In re Warmerdam,* 33 F.3d 1354, 31 USPQ2d 1754 (Fed. Cir. 1994).

[35]*Arrhythmia Res. Tech., Inc. v. Corazonix Corp.,* 958 F.2d 1053, 22 USPQ2d 1033 (Fed. Cir. 1992).

[36]*Parker v. Flook,* 437 U.S. 584, 198 USPQ 193 (1978).

[37]*Diamond v. Diehr,* 450 U.S. 175, 209 USPQ 1 (1981).

[38]*Alco Standard Corp. v. Tennessee Valley Auth.,* 808 F.2d 1490, 1 USPQ2d 1337 (Fed. Cir. 1986).

within the meaning of 35 U.S.C. §101 is unaffected by the particular apparatus for carrying out the method.[39]

(ii) Algorithms and Software

The rapid computerization of America over the last two decades doubtless contributed to what has been an even more rapid change in the law of eligibility as it relates to computer software and mathematical algorithms. These products of human thought were long said to be ineligible subject matter for patents, while processes that use specially programmed digital computers and mathematical techniques as essential steps were regarded as patentable. How to tell one from the other was the subject of dozens of law review articles and many pages of thoughtful analysis by a leading commentator.[40] Any effort to duplicate that work is well beyond the scope of this treatise. Suffice, instead, to consider briefly a few cases that have pointed the direction for the Federal Circuit as it began to grapple with this problem.

In its 1972 *Benson* decision the Supreme Court held that a method for converting binary-coded decimal numerals into pure binary numerals, useful in programming digital computers, was ineligible for patenting as a process.[41] In a second case, the Court extended *Benson,* with the result that an unpatentable algorithm did not become eligible by the addition of conventional, postsolution applications as method steps. In other words, the unpatentable mathematical formula must be considered as part of the prior art.[42] Finally, in 1981 the Court was confronted with a process for curing rubber, in which an important step was the solution of a mathematical formula using a programmed digital computer. This process was held to be eligible,[43] apparently on the ground that the applicant was not seeking to patent the formula in the abstract or foreclose its use by others outside the context of the specific process claimed. In the preceding cases, it had appeared to the Court that the applicant was in reality attempting to patent a law of nature—a physical phenomenon or an abstract idea.

One seriously doubts whether the Supreme Court's distinction could be understood and applied on any but the most excruciating

---

[39]*In re Grams,* 888 F.2d 835, 12 USPQ2d 1824 (Fed. Cir. 1989).

[40]Chisum, *Patents* §1.03[6] (1985). In *Atari Games Corp. v. Nintendo of Am., Inc.,* 975 F.2d 832, 24 USPQ2d 1015 (Fed. Cir. 1992), the court compared and contrasted the protection available for software under both the patent laws and the copyright laws. Protection under the Semiconductor Chip Protection Act is discussed below in §2.2(d).

[41]*Gottschalk v. Benson,* 409 U.S. 63, 175 USPQ 673 (1972).

[42]*Parker v. Flook,* 437 U.S. 584, 198 USPQ 193 (1978).

[43]*Diamond v. Diehr,* 450 U.S. 175, 209 USPQ 1 (1981). The Supreme Court in *Diehr* placed the patentability of computer-aided inventions in the mainstream of the law. Thus the rule is that process steps or apparatus functions that entail computer-performed calculations, whether the calculations are described in mathematical symbols or in words, do not of themselves render a claim nonstatutory. *Arrhythmia Res. Tech., Inc. v. Corazonix Corp.,* 958 F.2d 1053, 22 USPQ2d 1033 (Fed. Cir. 1992).

case-by-case basis. The CCPA had already begun this work at the inception of the new court.[44] In the Federal Circuit's first pertinent decision the applicant was permitted to distinguish over the prior art on the basis of a particular sequence of digits on a physical band, where the derivation of that sequence was attributable solely to an algorithm.[45]

In re Grams[46] provided the court with its first real opportunity to examine the Supreme Court's *Benson*[47] decision. Despite statements by the high Court in later decisions[48] to the effect that "anything under the sun that is made by man" is patentable subject matter, and to the effect that Congress need not expressly authorize patentability in a new area, the Federal Circuit in *Grams* confirmed *Benson's* basic tenet that an algorithm cannot be the subject of a patent. The mere recital of an algorithm does not automatically render a claim nonstatutory. But the inclusion of a mathematical algorithm in a claim can render it nonstatutory if the claim in essence covers only the algorithm. Mathematical algorithms thus joined the list of nonpatentable subject matter not within the scope of 35 U.S.C. §101, including methods of doing business, naturally occurring phenomena, and laws of nature.[49]

In *Grams* the court reaffirmed the *Walter*[50] test that once a mathematical algorithm has been found, the claim as a whole must be further analyzed. If it appears that the algorithm is implemented in a specific manner to define structural relationships between the physical elements of the claim (in apparatus claims) or to refine or limit claim steps (in process claims), the claim (if otherwise statutory) passes muster under §101.[51] Under the Federal Circuit's more recent formulation of the *Walter* test, it is first determined whether a mathematical algorithm is recited directly or indirectly in the claim. If so, it is next determined whether the claimed invention as a whole is no more than the algorithm itself; that is, whether the claim is directed to a mathematical algorithm that is not applied to or limited by physical elements or process steps. Such claims are nonstatutory. However, when the mathematical algorithm is applied in one or more steps of an otherwise statutory process claim, or one or more elements

---

[44]E.g., *In re Meyer,* 688 F.2d 789, 215 USPQ 193 (CCPA 1982); *In re Abele,* 684 F.2d 902, 214 USPQ 682 (CCPA 1982); *In re Taner,* 681 F.2d 787, 214 USPQ 678 (CCPA 1982).

[45]*In re Gulack,* 703 F.2d 1381, 217 USPQ 401 (Fed. Cir. 1983).

[46]*In re Grams,* 888 F.2d 835, 12 USPQ2d 1824 (Fed. Cir. 1989).

[47]See note 41 above, and accompanying text.

[48]*Diamond v. Diehr,* 450 U.S. 175, 209 USPQ 1 (1981); *Diamond v. Chakrabarty,* 447 U.S. 303, 206 USPQ 193 (1980).

[49]*In re Grams,* 888 F.2d 835, 12 USPQ2d 1824 (Fed. Cir. 1989). It is of no moment that the algorithm is not expressed in terms of a mathematical formula. Words used in a claim operating on data to solve a problem can serve the same purpose as a formula. *Id.*

[50]*In re Walter,* 618 F.2d 758, 205 USPQ 397 (CCPA 1980).

[51]*In re Grams,* 888 F.2d 835, 12 USPQ2d 1824 (Fed. Cir. 1989). See also *In re Iwahashi,* 888 F.2d 1370, 12 USPQ2d 1908 (Fed. Cir. 1989).

of an otherwise statutory apparatus claim, the requirements of §101 are met.[52] Even more recently, the court proposed an alternative to the *Walter* test (or, as it is sometimes termed, the *Freeman-Walter-Abele* test). The difficulty is that there is no clear agreement as to what is a mathematical algorithm, which makes rather dicey the determination of whether the claim as a whole is no more than that. Thus, an alternative to creating *Walter's* arbitrary definitional terms that deviate from those used in the statute may lie simply in returning to the language of the statute and the basic principles enunciated by the Supreme Court, which may be summarized by saying that excluded from eligible subject matter are laws of nature, natural phenomena, and abstract ideas.[53]

Nonetheless, *Walter* is not the exclusive test. Satisfaction of *Walter* necessarily depicts statutory subject matter, but failure to meet the *Walter* test does not necessarily doom the claim, provided that the application of the algorithm is circumscribed by more than a field of use limitation or nonessential postsolution activity. If the algorithm operates on a claimed physical step, and if the claim without the algorithm would present statutory subject matter, even though inoperative or less useful, then the claim likewise presents statutory subject matter when the algorithm is included.[54] Where ideas are expressed in mathematical form, if a claim requires more than the manipulation of ideas, so that the process described in the claim produces something quite different, then the process might indeed describe statutory subject matter.[55]

The *Walter* test can be difficult to apply, in that it requires careful interpretation of each claim in light of its supporting disclosure to answer the critical question: What did the applicant invent? But the test is facilitated somewhat where the only physical step involves merely gathering data for the algorithm.[56] Indeed, a physical measure-

---

[52]*Arrhythmia Res. Tech., Inc. v. Corazonix Corp.*, 958 F.2d 1053, 22 USPQ2d 1033 (Fed. Cir. 1992).

[53]*In re Warmerdam*, 33 F.3d 1354, 31 USPQ2d 1754 (Fed. Cir. 1994).

[54]*In re Grams*, 888 F.2d 835, 12 USPQ2d 1824 (Fed. Cir. 1989). See also *Arrhythmia Res. Tech., Inc. v. Corazonix Corp.*, 958 F.2d 1053, 22 USPQ2d 1033 (Fed. Cir. 1992).

[55]*In re Warmerdam*, 33 F.3d 1354, 31 USPQ2d 1754 (Fed. Cir. 1994). Here the claimed method required two steps: locating a medial axis of an object and creating a bubble hierarchy on the axis. The preferred, and perhaps the only practical, embodiment involved steps that are essentially mathematical in nature. Nonetheless, the claim did not necessarily recite the solving of an algorithm. Despite this the court, eschewing the *Walter* test, simply found that the steps of "locating" and "creating" describe nothing more than the manipulation of mathematical constructs, the paradigmatic "abstract idea." The court also found ineligible a claim to a data structure generated by that method.

[56]*In re Grams*, 888 F.2d 835, 12 USPQ2d 1824 (Fed. Cir. 1989). The *Grams* decision stops short of holding that §101 precludes patentability in every case where the physical step of obtaining data for the algorithm is the only other significant element in algorithm-containing claims. It signals instead a case-by-case analysis. See also *In re Iwahashi*, 888 F.2d 1370, 12 USPQ2d 1908 (Fed. Cir. 1989), decided a few days later. The PTO argued that since all but one claim element were means plus function limitations, the claim would cover any and every means for performing the algorithm. The court rejected this on the ground that 35 U.S.C.

ment step is indistinguishable from a data measuring step and neither is sufficient, standing alone, to impart patentability to a claim.[57]

In *State Street Bank*,[58] the court signaled a readiness to abandon the *Freeman-Walter-Abele* test altogether. It held that the transformation of data, representing discrete dollar amounts, by a machine through a series of mathematical calculations into a final share price, constitutes a practical application of a mathematical algorithm, formula, or calculation, because it produces "a useful, concrete and tangible result"—a final share price momentarily fixed for recording and reporting purposes and even accepted and relied upon by regulatory authorities and in subsequent trades. The question of whether a claim encompasses statutory subject matter should not focus on which of the four categories of subject matter a claim is directed to—process, machine, manufacture, or composition of matter—but rather on the essential characteristics of the subject matter, in particular, its practical utility. In a subsequent case,[59] it took *State Street Bank* to its logical conclusion: a process that applies an algorithm to produce a useful, concrete, tangible result without preempting other uses of the mathematical principle falls within the scope of §101. A physical transformation or conversion of subject matter from one state into another is not invariably required; that is merely one example of how a mathematical algorithm may bring about a useful application. Nor are structural limitations necessary. It would seem that the test has boiled down to one of claimed utility.

Computer programs and programmed machines. With the foregoing decisional analysis of algorithm eligibility as a foundation, the court turned its attention to software. Acting in concert with the PTO, it has turned the law of eligibility, at least with respect to the patentability of computer programs, completely on its ear. Three decisions handed down in the summer of 1994 set the process in motion. In its *Lowry*[60] decision, the court approved a claim to a memory containing a certain data structure. And in *Warmerdam*,[61] it allowed a claim to a machine having a memory containing data representing a bubble hierarchy determined by the method of another claim that was thought to be ineligible because it involved simply a manipulation of abstract ideas. Most importantly, in *Alappat*[62] the court held that

---

§112 limits the coverage of such limitations to "equivalents" of the structure disclosed in the application.

[57]*In re Warmerdam*, 33 F.3d 1354, 31 USPQ2d 1754 (Fed. Cir. 1994).

[58]*State Street Bank & Trust Co. v. Signature Fin. Group Inc.*, 149 F.3d 1368, 47 USPQ2d 1596 (Fed. Cir. 1998).

[59]*AT&T Corp. v. Excel Comm Inc.*, 172 F.3d 1352, 50 USPQ2d 1447 (Fed. Cir. 1999).

[60]*In re Lowry*, 32 F.3d 1579, 32 USPQ2d 1031 (Fed. Cir. 1994).

[61]*In re Warmerdam*, 33 F.3d 1354, 31 USPQ2d 1754 (Fed. Cir. 1994).

[62]*In re Alappat*, 33 F.3d 1526, 31 USPQ2d 1545 (Fed. Cir. 1994). The court set forth the view that the Supreme Court in its algorithm cases was simply explaining a rather straightforward concept: that certain types of mathematical subject matter, standing alone, represent nothing more than abstract ideas until reduced to some type of practical application, and thus that

the fact that a claim would read on a general purpose computer programmed to carry out the claimed invention would not alone justify holding the claim unpatentable as directed to nonstatutory subject matter. Such programming, reasoned the court, creates a new machine, because a general purpose computer in effect becomes a special purpose computer once it is programmed to perform particular functions pursuant to instructions from software. In short, a computer is apparatus, not mathematics!

In late 1994, deciding *In re Trovato*,[63] the court touched the brakes a bit. The claims were seen to be drafted in illusory apparatus format as a guise. They were not drawn to a new kind of computer that the recited algorithm controlled, nor to a combination of the recited algorithm and a new memory for controlling a known computer. At most, the claims provided a systematic way in which to compute a number of interest. The court returned to its earlier decisions, indicating that even though a claimed process is not expressed in terms of a mathematical formula, application of the *Freeman-Walter-Abele* test is more refined than that. Words used in a claim operating on data to solve a problem can serve the same purpose as a formula. It recalled that ingenuity and utility have never been sufficient in themselves to garner patent protection. Thus, as the basic tools of scientific and technological work, mathematical calculations per se remain outside the sphere of patent protection.

The brakes did not remain on for long. In May of 1995, the court decided *In re Beauregard*,[64] which involved a Board rejection of computer program product claims on grounds of a printed matter objection. During the pendency of the appeal, the PTO Commissioner—to the surprise of many, including this author—had issued an order to the effect that "computer programs embodied in a tangible medium, such as floppy diskettes, are patentable subject matter." The court vacated and remanded to the Board. A few weeks later, the court, in banc, vacated sua sponte its earlier judgment in *Trovato* and remanded, indicating that the new PTO guidelines on the patentability of computer software are consistent with its decision in *Alappat*.[65]

---

subject matter is not, in and of itself, entitled to patent protection. The focus must be on the claim as a whole; it is not necessary to determine whether a claim contains, as merely a part of the whole, any mathematical subject matter which standing alone would not be entitled to patent protection. Here, the four claimed means elements functioned to transform one set of data to another through what may be viewed as a series of mathematical calculations. But that alone does not justify a holding that the claim as a whole is directed to nonstatutory subject matter. The claim is not so abstract and sweeping that it would wholly preempt the use of any apparatus employing the combination of mathematical calculations recited therein.

[63] *In re Travato*, 42 F.3d 1376, 33 USPQ2d 1194 (Fed. Cir. 1994).

[64] *In re Beauregard*, 53 F.3d 1583, 35 USPQ2d 1383 (Fed. Cir. 1995).

[65] *In re Trovato*, 60 F.3d 807, 35 USPQ2d 1570 (Fed. Cir. 1995). Two members of the in banc court dissented, arguing that the court should actually have reheard the matter, with briefing and argument, since neither the appellant nor the solicitor had requested a remand. Despite the possibility that some disagreement remains within the court, it seems safe to conclude that the Federal Circuit now considers computer programs embodied in a tangible medium as patentable subject matter.

(iii) Business Methods and Machine Functions

Methods that involve some variable reaction of a human partici-pant were typically not eligible. Early on, the CCPA felt that business systems and plans, even those that do not depend upon a judgmental human reaction, were probably ineligible[66] as methods, but that it might be possible to protect them in the context of machine claims.[67] The Federal Circuit has now laid to rest the business method excep-tion to statutory subject matter. Whether claims are directed to sub-ject matter within §101 should not turn on whether the claimed subject matter does "business" instead of something else. And whether a claim is too broad to be patentable is not to be judged under §101, but rather under §§102, 103, and 112.[68]

In a case presenting a claim to a method of competitively bidding on a plurality of items, the court held that where the only physical effect or result required by the claims is the entering of information into a record, such activity is insufficient to impart patentability to a claim involving the solving of a mathematical algorithm. Such a step is implicit in any application of an algorithm. Patentability of a process claim requires that there be some transformation or reduction of subject matter.[69]

There was some indication in early Supreme Court decisions that the inherent function of a machine could not properly be claimed as a process.[70] This lead was taken up by several lower courts, and the result was a good deal of confusion. In 1968, however, the CCPA abolished the rule to the extent that it prohibited a process claim on the ground that the sole disclosed apparatus would inherently carry out the recited process steps. Alternative means for carrying out the process are not required; the only restriction is that the inventor not be perceived as attempting merely to claim desirable results in the guise of a process.[71]

(iv) New Uses

The statute specifically provides that eligible processes include "a new use of a known process, machine, manufacture, composition

---

[66]*In re Patton,* 127 F.2d 324, 53 USPQ 376 (CCPA 1942).

[67]*In re Johnston,* 502 F.2d 765, 183 USPQ 172 (CCPA 1974).

[68]*State Street Bank & Trust Co. v. Signature Fin. Group Inc.,* 149 F.3d 1368, 47 USPQ2d 1596 (Fed. Cir. 1998). Near the end of 1999, 35 U.S.C. §273 was added to the patent statute. This enactment provides for a limited personal defense to an assertion of infringement of a business method patent where the defendant can establish that it reduced the invention to practice more than a year before the filing date of the patent and commercially used it prior to the filing date.

[69]*In re Schrader,* 22 F.3d 290, 30 USPQ2d 1455 (Fed. Cir. 1994). But see *AT&T Corp. v. Excel Comm Inc.,* 172 F.3d 1352, 50 USPQ2d 1447 (Fed. Cir. 1999).

[70]*Waxham v. Smith,* 294 U.S. 20, 24 USPQ 34 (1935); *Expanded Metal Co. v. Bradford,* 214 U.S. 366 (1909); *Westinghouse v. Boyden Power Brake Co.,* 170 U.S. 537 (1898); *Risdon Locomotive Works v. Medart,* 158 U.S. 68 (1895).

[71]*In re Tarczy-Hornoch,* 397 F.2d 856, 158 USPQ 141 (CCPA 1968).

of matter, or material."[72] Thus, even if a composition is old, a process using it in a new and unobvious way may be patentable.[73] In evaluating the patentability of new use claims, the question is whether the claimed method of use would have been obvious; it is not pertinent whether the compositions that are the subject of the use are themselves known or new or unobvious. The real question is whether the newly discovered utility would have been obvious. Obviousness requires some relationship between the use taught by the prior art and the use discovered by the patent applicant.[74] But merely setting out the scientific explanation of an inherent function of an old structure is not patentable.[75]

A new use of an old product or material must be claimed as a process though, and not as a product; an old product, being old, can never be patented as such.[76] However, if the product must be altered, even only slightly, to adapt it to the new use, then the invention may be patentable in a product context as well, provided of course that it can survive the obviousness inquiry.[77] It is also a general rule that merely discovering and claiming a new benefit of an old process cannot render the process again patentable.[78]

(c) Statutory Exclusions

Certain classes of inventions are, by statute, ineligible for patenting. For example, Congress has flatly prohibited patenting "any invention or discovery which is useful solely in the utilization of special nuclear material or atomic energy in an atomic weapon."[79] Similarly, no patent may be issued to a private applicant "for any invention which appears to the Commissioner of Patents to have significant utility in the conduct of aeronautical and space activities" in the absence of compliance with certain statutory requirements.[80] The CCPA has dealt with some questions arising under these statutes.[81]

---

[72]35 U.S.C. §100(b).

[73]*Loctite Corp. v. Ultraseal Ltd.,* 781 F.2d 861, 228 USPQ 90 (Fed. Cir. 1985). Predecessor courts have long recognized that the discovery of a new use is eligible for patenting as a method. E.g., *In re Shetty,* 566 F.2d 81, 195 USPQ 753 (CCPA 1977). See *Ansonia Brass & Copper Co. v. Electric Supply,* 144 U.S. 11 (1892).

[74]*In re Dillon,* 892 F.2d 1554, 13 USPQ2d 1337 (Fed. Cir. 1989).

[75]*In re King,* 801 F.2d 1324, 231 USPQ 136 (Fed. Cir. 1986).

[76]E.g., *In re Thuau,* 135 F.2d 344, 57 USPQ 324 (CCPA 1943). Indeed, it is beyond argument that no utility need be disclosed for a reference to be anticipatory of a claim to an old compound. Where an applicant discovered a new use for an old compound, and was given a method patent for that use, he was thereby rewarded fully for his contribution. Any more, in the form of a patent covering the old compound, would be a gratuity. *In re Schoenwald,* 964 F.2d 1122, 22 USPQ2d 1671 (Fed. Cir. 1992).

[77]E.g., *Hobbs v. Beach,* 180 U.S. 383 (1900); *Topliff v. Topliff,* 145 U.S. 156 (1892).

[78]*In re Woodruff,* 919 F.2d 1575, 16 USPQ2d 1934 (Fed. Cir. 1990).

[79]42 U.S.C. §2181(a).

[80]42 U.S.C. §2457(c).

[81]See Chisum, *Patents* §§1.06[4]&[5] (1985) where the cases are collected and analyzed.

A more important limitation is found in the patent statute itself,[82] concerning inventions whose publication or disclosure might be detrimental to the national security. The grant of a patent for such an invention can be withheld and the invention ordered kept secret.[83] Unauthorized disclosure of an invention that is the subject of a secrecy order can result in abandonment of the invention and forfeiture of rights.[84] A license for filing patent applications in foreign countries is required prior to six months after the filing of a U.S. patent application,[85] and a U.S. patent can be barred for filing abroad without a license.[86] Criminal penalties are provided.[87] At least one decision of a predecessor court foreshadows strict enforcement of these provisions by the Federal Circuit.[88]

(d) Semiconductor Chip Protection

The Semiconductor Chip Protection Act of 1984, which is codified at 17 U.S.C. §§901–914, arose from concerns that existing intellectual property laws did not provide adequate protection of proprietary rights in semiconductor chips that had been designed to perform a particular function. The Act adopted relevant aspects of existing intellectual property law, but for the most part created a new law, specifically adapted to the protection of design layouts of semiconductor chips. Inasmuch as cases arising under the Act are not within its exclusive jurisdictional mandate, the Federal Circuit will apply discernible regional circuit law to such issues.[89]

The court took a first look at the Act in *Brooktree v. Advanced Micro Devices.*[90] The patent system alone was deemed by Congress not to provide the desired scope of protection for mask works. Although electronic circuitry and electronic components are within the statutory subject matter of patentable invention, and some original circuitry may be patentable if it also meets the other requirements of the patent laws, Congress sought more expeditious protection against copying of original circuit layouts, whether or not they met the criteria of patentable invention. The Semiconductor Chip Protection Act of 1984 was an innovative solution to this problem. While some copyright principles underlie the law, as do some attributes of patent law, the

---

[82]35 U.S.C. §§181–188; the Invention Secrecy Act.

[83]35 U.S.C. §181.

[84]35 U.S.C. §182.

[85]35 U.S.C. §184.

[86]35 U.S.C. §185.

[87]35 U.S.C. §186.

[88]*In re Gaertner,* 604 F.2d 1348, 202 USPQ 714 (CCPA 1979).

[89]*Brooktree Corp. v. Advanced Micro Devices, Inc.,* 977 F.2d 1555, 24 USPQ2d 1401 (Fed. Cir. 1992).

[90]*Brooktree Corp. v. Advanced Micro Devices, Inc.,* 977 F.2d 1555, 24 USPQ2d 1401 (Fed. Cir. 1992).

Act was uniquely adapted to semiconductor mask works, in order to achieve appropriate protection for original designs while meeting the competitive needs of the industry and serving the public interest. It provides owners of registered mask works with the exclusive right to reproduce the mask work and to import or distribute a semiconductor chip in which the work is embodied. Mask works that are not original, or that consist of designs that are staple, commonplace, or familiar, or various modifications of such designs, are excluded from protection. Nor does protection extend to any "idea, procedure, process, system, method of operation, concept, principle, or discovery, regardless of the form in which it is described, explained, illustrated or embodied" in the mask work.

Under the Act, reverse engineering is a statutory defense. In performing reverse engineering one may disassemble, study, and analyze an existing chip in order to understand it. This knowledge may be used to create an original chip having a different design layout, but which performs the same or equivalent function as the existing chip, without penalty or prohibition. This practice leads to improved chips having form, fit, and function compatibility with the existing chip, thereby serving competition while advancing the state of technology.[91]

The Act provides that damages are to be measured as the actual damages suffered by the owner of the mask work plus the infringer's profits that are attributable to the infringement and not taken into account in computing the award of actual damages.[92]

(e) Statutory Invention Registration

A so-called statutory invention registration (SIR) is provided for in 35 U.S.C. §157. The inventor of the SIR has the same rights that

---

[91]This case provides an intensive study of evidentiary factors relating to proof of reverse engineering, with particular emphasis upon the significance of the "paper trail." In passing, the court rejected any notion that the sheer volume alone of documentation establishes the reverse engineering defense as a matter of law. The statute does not reflect an intent to excuse copying, as a matter of law, if the copier had first tried and failed to do the job without copying. The paper trail is evidence of independent effort, but it is not conclusive or incontrovertible proof of either originality or the absence of copying. The questions of originality and copying are heavily fact dependent, not absolutes of law. *Brooktree Corp. v. Advanced Micro Devices, Inc.,* 977 F.2d 1555, 24 USPQ2d 1401 (Fed. Cir. 1992).

[92]*Brooktree Corp. v. Advanced Micro Devices, Inc.,* 977 F.2d 1555, 24 USPQ2d 1401 (Fed. Cir. 1992). The court applied patent damages principles here, but expressly refrained from deciding whether all aspects of patent damages law will apply under the Act. On the other hand, the court applied copyright principles to some other questions. For example, it held that infringement under the Act does not require that all parts of the accused chip be copied. Also, costs and attorney fees were analyzed in copyright terms. Thus, fees may be denied in various situations, including (1) the presence of a complex or novel issue of law that the defendant litigates vigorously and in good faith; (2) the defendant's status as an innocent, rather than willful or knowing, infringer; (3) the plaintiff's prosecution of the case in bad faith; and (4) the defendant's good faith attempt to avoid infringement. Attorney fees decisions under the Act are to be reviewed under the abuse of discretion standard.

a patent provides to prevent others from patenting the invention. The inventor preserves the ability to protect the right to practice his or her own prior invention as against any later inventor, while forgoing the right to exclude others even if he or she is the prior inventor. Thus the SIR affords an inventor the possibility of securing the defensive aspects of a patent by obtaining the right to contest priority, while agreeing to publish the technology, thereby benefiting the public.[93]

§2.3 Utility

(a) General

For over 200 years, the concept of utility has occupied a central role in our patent system. The basic quid pro quo contemplated by the Constitution and Congress for granting a patent monopoly is the benefit derived by the public from an invention with substantial utility. Consequently, it is well established that a patent may not be granted to an inventor unless substantial or practical utility for the invention has been discovered and disclosed. Similarly, actual reduction to practice, which constitutes in law the final phase of invention, cannot be established absent a showing of practical utility.[94]

The utility requirement has its origin in Article I, section 8 of the Constitution, which indicates that the purpose of empowering Congress to authorize the granting of patents is "to promote progress of . . . useful arts."[95] The statute provides that only "useful" inventions and discoveries can be patented.[96] Although it might for a time have been supposed that the utility requirement was an anachronism that could safely be ignored, the Supreme Court in 1966 held unequivocally that a continuing condition for patentability is the demonstration of a specific and substantial utility. Mere interest for scientific investigation and research may not be substantial enough. Thus, the fact that a process works to produce the intended product, and the fact that the product belongs to a class of compounds that is the subject of serious scientific investigation, were not a sufficient demonstration of utility for the claimed process.[97]

Nonetheless, utility is a rarely litigated issue. A patent is presumed valid, and this includes a presumption of utility.[98] Utility is a

---

[93]*Hyatt v. Boone*, 146 F.3d 1128, 47 USPQ2d 1128 (Fed. Cir. 1998).

[94]*Fujikawa v. Wattanasin*, 93 F.3d 1559, 39 USPQ2d 1895 (Fed. Cir. 1996).

[95]*Stiftung v. Renishaw PLC*, 945 F.2d 1173, 20 USPQ2d 1094 (Fed. Cir. 1991).

[96]35 U.S.C. §101. *Stiftung v. Renishaw PLC*, 945 F.2d 1173, 20 USPQ2d 1094 (Fed. Cir. 1991).

[97]*Brenner v. Manson*, 383 U.S. 519, 148 USPQ 689 (1966).

[98]*Structural Rubber Prods. Co. v. Park Rubber Co.*, 749 F.2d 707, 223 USPQ 1264 (Fed. Cir. 1984); *Raytheon Co. v. Roper Corp.*, 724 F.2d 951, 220 USPQ 592 (Fed. Cir. 1983).

question of fact,[99] but in determining utility the claims must first be interpreted to define the invention that is to be tested for utility, and such interpretation is a legal matter.[100] Utility questions must be decided on their own unique factual circumstances.[101]

In certain cases, utility may be self-evident. Thus a correct finding of infringement of otherwise valid claims mandates as a matter of law a finding of utility.[102] Also, although utility does not require commercial marketability,[103] commercial success demonstrates utility.[104] The threshold of utility is not high. An invention is "useful" under §101 if it is capable of providing some identifiable benefit.[105]

The required substantial or practical utility must either be obvious, or discovered and disclosed.[106] If the written description fails to illuminate a credible utility, the PTO will make both a §112¶1 rejection for failure to teach how to use the invention and a §101 rejection for lack of utility. This dual rejection occurs because the how to use prong of §112 incorporates as a matter of law the requirement of §101 that the specification disclose as a matter of fact a practical utility for the invention. Thus, an applicant's failure to disclose how to use an invention may support a rejection under either §112¶1 for lack of enablement as a result of the specification's failure to disclose adequately to one ordinarily skilled in the art how to use the invention without undue experimentation, or §101 for lack of utility when there is a complete absence of data supporting the statements which set forth the desired results of the claimed invention. The PTO cannot make this type of rejection, however, unless it has reason to doubt the objective truth of the statements contained in the written description. The PTO may establish a reason to doubt an invention's asserted utility when the written description suggests an inherently unbelievable undertaking or involves implausible scientific principles.[107]

---

[99]*Process Control Corp. v. HydReclaim Corp.*, 190 F.3d 1350, 52 USPQ2d 1029 (Fed. Cir. 1999); *Stiftung v. Renishaw PLC*, 945 F.2d 1173, 20 USPQ2d 1094 (Fed. Cir. 1991); *Moleculon Res. Corp. v. CBS, Inc.*, 793 F.2d 1261, 229 USPQ 805 (Fed. Cir. 1986); *Cross v. Iizuka*, 753 F.2d 1040, 224 USPQ 739 (Fed. Cir. 1985). Issues of utility and enablement may involve consideration of complex scientific principles and disputed aspects of technology. Such issues are not treated as legal abstractions, but properly devolve on the trier of fact. Our system of justice does not require judge and jury to be independent experts in technology. In ascertaining the truth when the evidence is primarily scientific, as for other kinds of evidence, the trier of fact must make determinations of credibility, reliability, and weight. *Brooktree Corp. v. Advanced Micro Devices, Inc.*, 977 F.2d 1555, 24 USPQ2d 1401 (Fed. Cir. 1992).

[100]*Raytheon Co. v. Roper Corp.*, 724 F.2d 951, 220 USPQ 592 (Fed. Cir. 1983).

[101]*Cross v. Iizuka*, 753 F.2d 1040, 224 USPQ 739 (Fed. Cir. 1985).

[102]*United States Steel Corp. v. Phillips Petroleum Co.*, 865 F.2d 1247, 9 USPQ2d 1461 (Fed. Cir. 1989); *Raytheon Co. v. Roper Corp.*, 724 F.2d 951, 220 USPQ 592 (Fed. Cir. 1983).

[103]*Barmag Barmer Masch. AG v. Murata Mach., Ltd.*, 731 F.2d 831, 221 USPQ 561 (Fed. Cir. 1984). A finding that an invention is an improvement is not a prerequisite to patentability. It is possible for an invention to be less effective than existing devices but nevertheless meet the statutory criteria for patentability. *Custom Accessories, Inc. v. Jeffrey-Allan Indus., Inc.*, 807 F.2d 955, 1 USPQ2d 1196 (Fed. Cir. 1986).

[104]*Raytheon Co. v. Roper Corp.*, 724 F.2d 951, 220 USPQ 592 (Fed. Cir. 1983).

[105]*Juicy Whip Inc. v. Orange Bang Inc.*, 185 F.3d 1364, 51 USPQ2d 1700 (Fed. Cir. 1999).

[106]*Cross v. Iizuka*, 753 F.2d 1040, 224 USPQ 739 (Fed. Cir. 1985).

[107]*In re Cortright*, 165 F.3d 1353, 49 USPQ2d 1464 (Fed. Cir. 1999).

A claimed invention need not accomplish all of the objectives stated in the patent; when a properly claimed invention meets at least one stated objective, the utility requirement is satisfied.[108] Evidence of any practical utility is sufficient when the claim does not recite any particular utility.[109]

In a recent hard case, the court held that a disclosure that polypropylene granules could be pressed into a flexible film with a characteristic infrared spectrum was an insufficient disclosure of practical utility. The rationale was that the utility of a chemical compound may not reside in its potential role as an object of use-testing. To satisfy the utility requirement, the disclosure must assert a specific benefit in currently available form.[110]

The principle that inventions are invalid if they are principally designed to serve immoral or illegal purposes has not been applied broadly in recent years. For example, years ago courts invalidated patents on gambling devices on the ground that they were immoral, but that is no longer the law. The requirement of utility in patent law is not a directive to the PTO or the courts to serve as arbiters of deceptive trade practices. Other agencies, such as the Federal Trade Commission and the Food and Drug Administration, are assigned the task of protecting consumers from fraud and deception in the sale of food products. Of course, Congress is free to declare particular types of inventions unpatentable for a variety of reasons, including deceptiveness. Until such time as Congress does so, however, there is no basis in §101 to hold that inventions can be ruled unpatentable for lack of utility simply because they have the capacity to fool some members of the public.[111]

(b) Operability

As a general proposition, utility need not be proved unless a person skilled in the pertinent art would reasonably doubt the asserted utility. In such cases, it must appear that the patentee has supplied sufficient evidence to remove the doubt.

Utility requires a least a threshold showing of operability. The PTO bears the initial burden of showing prima facie that the claims

---

[108]*Stiftung v. Renishaw PLC,* 945 F.2d 1173, 20 USPQ2d 1094 (Fed. Cir. 1991); *Raytheon Co. v. Roper Corp.,* 724 F.2d 951, 220 USPQ 592 (Fed. Cir. 1983).

[109]*Cross v. Iizuka,* 753 F.2d 1040, 224 USPQ 739 (Fed. Cir. 1985).

[110]*In re Ziegler,* 992 F.2d 1197, 26 USPQ2d 1600 (Fed. Cir. 1993). One can speculate that this decision may have been influenced by the unsettling consequences of issuing a basic patent some 40 years after the invention was made. In the same case the court held that the appellant was collaterally estopped by a previous judgment in a multiparty interference from asserting that a disclosure that the polymer was "plastic-like" was a sufficient assertion of utility.

[111]*Juicy Whip Inc. v. Orange Bang Inc.,* 185 F.3d 1364, 51 USPQ2d 1700 (Fed. Cir. 1999). The patented beverage dispenser had a display bowl containing liquid that simulated a premix beverage, when in fact the beverage was mixed just prior to dispensing, in response to a customer order. The district court held the patent invalid for lack of utility, on the grounds that its purpose was to increase sales by deception (simulating a premix dispenser), and it

are unpatentable because of inoperativeness.[112] However, the very nature of the invention may raise a reasonable doubt sufficient to shift the burden to the inventor. In one interesting case, the invention was directed to improvement of the flavor of liquids by subjecting them to a magnetic field. The applicant conceded that the PTO had established a prima facie case of inoperativeness because of the unusual nature of the invention and undertook to rebut with evidence of taste tests. The taste tests were held unpersuasive because they were evidence of a type not convincing to the scientific community. Also, the tests covered only a few of the many liquids encompassed by the claims.[113]

The product or process sought to be patented must be "capable of being used to effect the object proposed."[114] Typically, operability is not questioned, unless the mode of operation alleged seems clearly to conflict with a recognized scientific principle.[115] However, the mere fact that something has not previously been done clearly is not, in itself, a sufficient basis for rejecting all applications purporting to disclose how to do it.[116]

There is a difficult borderline situation where the operability cannot be tested by any known scientific principles.[117] Clearly, each case must be approached individually, on its own unique facts. In a case involving a "perpetual motion" type of invention, the PTO was held justified in rejecting the claims under 35 U.S.C. §101, because the very nature of the claimed invention occasioned a reasonable skepticism as to its operability. And a reviewing district court was held not to have abused its discretion in requiring submission of a model of the device to the National Bureau of Standards for testing.[118]

---

improved the prior art only to the extent that it increased the sale of beverages. Naturally the Federal Circuit reversed.

[112]*Fregeau v. Mossinghoff*, 776 F.2d 1034, 227 USPQ 848 (Fed. Cir. 1985).

[113]*Fregeau v. Mossinghoff*, 776 F.2d 1034, 227 USPQ 848 (Fed. Cir. 1985). A rejection based upon failure to teach how to use the invention, pursuant to 35 U.S.C. §112, was also made. A specification that does not establish with certainty that the claimed invention will operate in the manner intended necessarily fails to satisfy the how to use requirement. See §5.2. However, the fact that dependent claims include species that might not meet the objects of the invention does not by itself prove that one skilled in the art cannot ascertain the scope of the asserted claims. That objection goes to possible inoperativeness under §101 or lack of enablement under §112. *North Am. Vaccine, Inc. v. American Cyanamid Co.*, 7 F.3d 1571, 28 USPQ2d 1333 (Fed. Cir. 1993).

[114]*Stiftung v. Renishaw PLC*, 945 F.2d 1173, 20 USPQ2d 1094, 1100 (Fed. Cir. 1991).

[115]*In re Chilowsky*, 229 F.2d 457, 108 USPQ 321 (CCPA 1956).

[116]*Gould v. Quigg*, 822 F.2d 1074, 3 USPQ2d 1302 (Fed. Cir. 1987).

[117]E.g., *In re Langer*, 503 F.2d 1380, 183 USPQ 288 (CCPA 1974); *In re Ferens*, 417 F.2d 1072, 163 USPQ 609 (CCPA 1969); *In re Perrigo*, 48 F.2d 965, 9 USPQ 152 (CCPA 1931).

[118]*In re Newman*, 782 F.2d 971, 228 USPQ 450 (Fed. Cir. 1986). It was held to be an abuse of discretion to permit NBS to destroy the model through tests, because it appeared that the PTO was attempting to determine not merely whether the device worked, but how. The PTO is not a guarantor of scientific theory, and it is not the province of the PTO to ascertain the scientific explanation underlying the operability of an invention. A portion of the district court's order barring the inventor or his representatives from certain phases of the NBS testing was also held an abuse of discretion. Evidence of ex parte tests is entitled to little or no weight and is given only negligible probative value. Moreover, "the objectivity of the tester is

Nonetheless, the court has been able to sidestep a square decision on whether an apparatus or method that appears to contradict the laws of thermodynamics can be patented.[119]

In some circumstances utility and enablement have a tendency to merge. If claimed subject matter is inoperable, the patent may indeed be invalid for failure to meet the utility requirement of §101 and the enablement requirement of §112.[120] However, the court has warned against confusing operability or enablement with the requirement for claim definiteness. The invention's operability may say nothing about a skilled artisan's understanding of the bounds of the claim.[121]

Certainly where a claim includes an incorrect or questionable theory or requires a means for accomplishing an unattainable result, it is invalid. The impossible cannot be enabled, and the invention would be inoperative as claimed, thus resulting in invalidity under both §101 and §112.[122] It is not a requirement of patentability that an inventor correctly set forth, or even know, how or why the invention works. Furthermore, statements that a physiological phenomenon was observed are not inherently suspect simply because the underlying basis for the observation cannot be predicted or explained.[123] But neither is the patent applicant relieved of the requirement of teaching how to achieve the claimed result, even if the theory of operation is not correctly explained or even understood.[124]

---

a fundamental rule not only of evidence but of conscience." Here an NBS spokesman had expressed skepticism to the press before any testing had begun. One wonders whether ex parte testing on the part of the applicant rather than the PTO will be rejected as quickly.

[119]*Newman v. Quigg*, 877 F.2d 1575, 11 USPQ2d 1340 (Fed. Cir. 1989). A special master found that Newman's perpetual motion machine was a contradiction of the laws of thermodynamics, but also found that the evidence before him established that the device produced more energy than it consumed. The district court rejected the master's recommendation of patentability solely on the basis that it contradicted physical laws and ordered NBS testing. The tests did not verify Newman's evidence. The Federal Circuit found no error in the submission to the NBS under the circumstances.

[120]*Brooktree Corp. v. Advanced Micro Devices, Inc.*, 977 F.2d 1555, 24 USPQ2d 1401 (Fed. Cir. 1992). Absence of utility can be the basis of a rejection under both 35 U.S.C. §§101 and 112. Obviously, if a claimed invention does not have utility, the specification cannot enable one to use it. *In re Brana*, 51 F.3d 1560, 34 USPQ2d 1437 (Fed. Cir. 1995). When an impossible limitation, such as a nonsensical method of operation, is clearly embodied within the claim, the claimed invention must be held invalid. While an otherwise valid patent covering a meritorious invention should not be struck down simply because of the patentee's misconceptions about scientific principles concerning the invention, when the claimed subject matter is inoperable, the patent may indeed be invalid for failure to meet the utility requirement of §101 and the enablement requirement of §112. *Process Control Corp. v. HydReclaim Corp.*, 190 F.3d 1350, 52 USPQ2d 1029 (Fed. Cir. 1999).

[121]*Miles Labs., Inc. v. Shandon, Inc.*, 997 F.2d 870, 27 USPQ2d 1123 (Fed. Cir. 1993).

[122]*Raytheon Co. v. Roper Corp.*, 724 F.2d 951, 220 USPQ 592 (Fed. Cir. 1983).

[123]*In re Cortright*, 165 F.3d 1353, 49 USPQ2d 1464 (Fed. Cir. 1999). The court held that the PTO had erred in suggesting that the applicant was required to prove the cause of resultant hair growth. However, where the claim itself purports to provide the cause (in this case, offsetting lower levels of a male hormone), and the specification shows only surmise and belief as opposed to observational proof, the claim does not satisfy the how to use requirement of §112. In this context, inherency may not be established by probabilities or possibilities. The mere fact that a certain thing may result from a given set of circumstances is not sufficient.

[124]*Newman v. Quigg*, 877 F.2d 1575, 11 USPQ2d 1340 (Fed. Cir. 1989).

Nevertheless, a defense of lack of utility cannot be sustained without proof of total incapacity.[125] A claim is not invalid for lack of operability simply because the invention does not work perfectly under all conditions.[126] The fact than an invention has only limited utility and is only operable in certain applications is not grounds for finding lack of utility. Only where there is complete absence of data supporting statements setting forth the desired results of the claimed invention will a §112 "how to use" defense be converted to a §101 utility defense.[127] Thus a claim read in a vacuum could lead one to the conclusion that the invention is inoperable. However, it is proper to ascertain the true meaning of the claim by interpreting it in light of the specification and the patent as a whole. This analysis may well lead to the conclusion that the invention is operable as claimed.[128] By the same token, a later dated publication can be relied upon as evidence of the level of skill in the art as of the application's filing date and as evidence that the device disclosed in the application would have been operative.[129]

It is possible that deliberately obtaining claims known to be directed to an inoperative embodiment of the invention may constitute inequitable conduct.[130]

Lack of utility due to inoperativeness is a question of fact.[131]

(c) Chemical Compounds and Human Utility

Properly or not, some special considerations have traditionally been thought to apply in the case of chemical compounds, particularly those with claimed therapeutic or pharmacological benefits. Thus it seems clear that a substance that is known to be useful only as an intermediate in the production of other compounds that have no

---

[125]*Brooktree Corp. v. Advanced Micro Devices, Inc.,* 977 F.2d 1555, 24 USPQ2d 1401 (Fed. Cir. 1992); *Envirotech Corp. v. Al George, Inc.,* 730 F.2d 753, 221 USPQ 473 (Fed. Cir. 1984).

[126]*National Recovery Tech. Inc. v. Magnetic Sep. Sys. Inc.,* 166 F.3d 1190, 49 USPQ2d 1671 (Fed. Cir. 1999).

[127]*Envirotech Corp. v. Al George, Inc.,* 730 F.2d 753, 221 USPQ 473 (Fed. Cir. 1984). See also *Tol-O-Matic, Inc. v. Proma Produckt-und Mktg. GmbH,* 945 F.2d 1546, 20 USPQ2d 1332 (Fed. Cir. 1991). See note 113 above.

[128]*Moleculon Res. Corp. v. CBS, Inc.,* 793 F.2d 1261, 229 USPQ 805 (Fed. Cir. 1986). The court seeks to interpret claims to preserve, rather than defeat, their validity, including the matter of operability. *Eastman Kodak Co. v. Goodyear Tire & Rubber Co.,* 114 F.3d 1547, 42 USPQ2d 1737 (Fed. Cir. 1997).

[129]*Gould v. Quigg,* 822 F.2d 1074, 3 USPQ2d 1302 (Fed. Cir. 1987). However, such a publication cannot supplement an insufficient disclosure in a prior dated application so as to render it enabling. *Id.*

[130]*Heidelberger Druckmaschinen AG v. Hantscho Comm. Prods., Inc.,* 21 F.3d 1068, 30 USPQ2d 1377 (Fed. Cir. 1994).

[131]*Brooktree Corp. v. Advanced Micro Devices, Inc.,* 977 F.2d 1555, 24 USPQ2d 1401 (Fed. Cir. 1992); *Fregeau v. Mossinghoff,* 776 F.2d 1034, 227 USPQ 848 (Fed. Cir. 1985). Although closely related to the legal question of enablement, operability under 35 U.S.C. §101 is a question of fact. *Newman v. Quigg,* 877 F.2d 1575, 11 USPQ2d 1340 (Fed. Cir. 1989).

established utility is not itself useful.[132] Proof that a compound will cause certain effects in laboratory animals may be sufficient utility; there is no requirement of therapeutic utility in humans.[133] Moreover, *in vitro* utility may be sufficient, particularly where *in vivo* activity is known in structurally similar compounds.[134]

On the other hand, a claimed method of administering such a compound to a patient to achieve a particular result will require *in vivo* testing.[135] And if a person of skill in the pertinent art would conclude, upon reading the specification, that the patentee intends that the invention be used for the treatment of humans, then the compound must be shown both safe[136] and effective for use on humans.[137] In the pharmaceutical arts, practical utility may be shown by adequate evidence of any pharmacological activity. It may be difficult to predict, however, whether a novel compound will exhibit pharmacological activity, even when the behavior of analogous compounds is known. Consequently, testing is often required to establish practical utility. But the test results need not absolutely prove that the compound is pharmacologically active. All that is required is that the tests be reasonably indicative of the desired pharmacological response. In other words, there must be a sufficient correlation between the tests and an asserted pharmacological activity so as to convince those skilled in the art, to a reasonable probability, that the novel compound will exhibit the asserted pharmacological behavior.[138] If more than a single utility is alleged, it is sufficient to establish only one.[139]

In its *Brana*[140] decision, the court took a hard look at what constitutes adequate disclosure and proof of human utility. The application indicated that the claimed compounds were useful for the "treatment of diseases" and were "antitumor substances." Had this been the only assertion of utility, the Board's rejection may have been sustainable. However, the specification also said that the compounds had "a better action and a better action spectrum as antitumor substances" than certain prior art compounds. Those compounds had been found to be highly effective against particular tumors. Thus the application was held to contain an allegation of a sufficiently specific use. Then the court turned to the question of whether the applicant had sufficiently

[132]*In re Kirk*, 376 F.2d 936, 153 USPQ 48 (CCPA 1967); *In re Joly*, 376 F.2d 906, 153 USPQ 45 (CCPA 1967).

[133]*Nelson v. Bowler*, 626 F.2d 853, 206 USPQ 881 (CCPA 1980).

[134]*Cross v. Iizuka*, 753 F.2d 1040, 224 USPQ 739 (Fed. Cir. 1985).

[135]*Fujikawa v. Wattanasin*, 93 F.3d 1559, 39 USPQ2d 1895 (Fed. Cir. 1996).

[136]*In re Hartop*, 311 F.2d 249, 135 USPQ 419 (CCPA 1962).

[137]*In re Langer*, 503 F.2d 1380, 183 USPQ 288 (CCPA 1974).

[138]*Fujikawa v. Wattanasin*, 93 F.3d 1559, 39 USPQ2d 1895 (Fed. Cir. 1996). The court was careful to point out that evidence of "any" pharmacological activity is sufficient only when the claim does not recite a particular utility. In contrast, when the claim recites a particular utility, it must be adequately shown.

[139]*In re Gottlieb*, 328 F.2d 1016, 140 USPQ 665 (CCPA 1964).

[140]*In re Brana*, 51 F.3d 1560, 34 USPQ2d 1437 (Fed. Cir. 1995).

proved the alleged utility. It confirmed that the PTO has the initial burden of challenging a presumptively correct assertion of utility in the disclosure. Only after the PTO provides evidence showing that one of ordinary skill in the art would reasonably doubt the asserted utility does the burden shift to the applicant to provide rebuttal evidence sufficient to convince such a person of the invention's asserted utility. The court held that the PTO had failed in that burden. There was no suggestion in the prior art that would lead one of skill in the art to question the asserted utility. Nor did the nature of the invention alone cause one of skill to reasonably doubt the asserted usefulness. The purpose of treating cancer with chemical compounds does not suggest an inherently unbelievable undertaking or involve implausible scientific principles.[141]

§2.4 Design Patents

The statute provides that a patent may be granted for a term of 14 years[142] for any "new, original and ornamental design for an article of manufacture."[143] A design patent protects the nonfunctional aspects of an ornamental design as shown in a patent.[144]

(a) Ornamentality Versus Functionality

Design and utility patents are based on different statutory provisions and involve different subject matter. The scope of protection afforded by each type of patent is different.[145] In general, a utility patent protects functional aspects and a design patent protects ornamental aspects of a product. If a patented design is primarily functional rather than ornamental, the patent is invalid.[146] It is unnecessary that a design be aesthetically pleasing. The "ornamental" requirement of the design statute means that the design must not

---

[141]The court went on to hold that, even had the PTO met its prima facie burden, the evidence submitted by the applicant was sufficient to prove the asserted utility. In passing, it noted that FDA approval is not a prerequisite for finding a compound useful within the meaning of the patent laws. Usefulness in patent law, and particularly in the context of pharmaceutical inventions, necessarily includes the expectation of further research and development. The state at which an invention in this field becomes useful is well before it is ready to be administered to humans.

[142]35 U.S.C. §173.

[143]35 U.S.C. §171. See *Hupp v. Siroflex of Am., Inc.,* 122 F.3d 1456, 43 USPQ2d 1887 (Fed. Cir. 1997).

[144]*Elmer v. ICC Fabricating, Inc.,* 67 F.3d 1571, 36 USPQ2d 1417 (Fed. Cir. 1995); *Keystone Ret. Wall Sys., Inc. v. Westrock, Inc.,* 997 F.2d 1444, 27 USPQ2d 1297 (Fed. Cir. 1993).

[145]*Carman Indus., Inc. v. Wahl,* 724 F.2d 932, 220 USPQ 481 (Fed. Cir. 1983).

[146]*Avia Group Int'l, Inc. v. L.A. Gear Calif., Inc.,* 853 F.2d 1557, 7 USPQ2d 1548 (Fed. Cir. 1988); *Power Controls Corp. v. Hybrinetics, Inc.,* 806 F.2d 234, 231 USPQ 774 (Fed. Cir. 1986). Indeed, the issuance of a design patent creates a presumption of nonfunctionality. *Power Controls Corp. v. Hybrinetics, Inc.,* 806 F.2d 234, 231 USPQ 774 (Fed. Cir. 1986).

be governed solely by function, i.e., that this is not the only possible form of the article that could perform its function. A design patent is for a useful article, but patentability is based on the design of the article, not the use. The design may contribute distinctiveness or consumer recognition, but an absence of artistic merit does not mean that the design is purely functional.[147]

Where there are several ways to achieve the function of an article of manufacture, the design of the article is more likely to serve a primarily ornamental purpose.[148] However, a failure to give dispositive effect to the existence of alternative designs in a validity analysis is not error. Consideration of alternative designs, if present, is a useful tool that may allow a court to conclude that a challenged design is not invalid for functionality. As such, alternative designs join the list of other appropriate considerations for assessing whether the patented design as a whole—its overall appearance—was dictated by functional considerations. These might include whether the protected design represents the best design; whether alternative designs would adversely affect the utility of the article; whether there are any concomitant utility patents; whether the advertising touts particular features of the design as having specific utility; and whether there are any elements in the design or an overall appearance clearly not dictated by function.[149]

When function dictates a design, protection would not promote the decorative arts, a purpose of the design patent statute. But a distinction exists between the functionality of an article or features thereof and the functionality of the particular design of such article or features thereof that perform a function. Were that not true, it would not be possible to obtain a design patent on a utilitarian article of manufacture, or to obtain both design and utility patents on the same article.[150] Thus, the utility of each of the various elements that

---

[147]*Seiko Epson Corp. v. Nu-Kote Int'l Inc.*, 190 F.3d 1360, 52 USPQ2d 1011 (Fed. Cir. 1999).

[148]*Berry Sterling Corp. v. Pescor Plastics, Inc.*, 122 F.3d 1452, 43 USPQ2d 1953 (Fed. Cir. 1997); *L.A. Gear, Inc. v. Thom McAn Shoe Co.*, 988 F.2d 1117, 25 USPQ2d 1913 (Fed. Cir. 1993). If a design is dictated solely by the function of the article, the patent is invalid because the design is not ornamental. A design is not dictated solely by its function when alternative designs for the article are available. Functionality is a determination that is reviewed for clear error in a bench trial. *Best Lock Corp. v. Ilco Unican Corp.*, 94 F.3d 1563, 40 USPQ2d 1048 (Fed. Cir. 1996). This case provides an interesting analysis of functionality. The patent was on a design for a blank key blade (not the entire finished key). Such a blank blade must be designed in order to perform its intended function, which is to fit into its corresponding lock's keyway. Thus, it is functional. The fact that the plaintiff also had a design patent on the corresponding keyway was not regarded as significant. The court seemed to hint that, had the patent in suit "claimed" the combination of a lock and key, the result might have been different. There was a vigorous dissent.

[149]*Berry Sterling Corp. v. Pescor Plastics, Inc.*, 122 F.3d 1452, 43 USPQ2d 1953 (Fed. Cir. 1997).

[150]*Avia Group Int'l, Inc. v. L.A. Gear Calif., Inc.*, 853 F.2d 1557, 7 USPQ2d 1548 (Fed. Cir. 1988). Thus a later filed design application can properly be a division of, and be entitled to the benefit of the filing date of, an earlier filed utility application. The support question under 35 U.S.C. §120 is simply a matter of whether the earlier application contains illustrations, whatever form they may take, depicting the design illustrated in the later application. *Racing*

comprise the design is not the relevant inquiry. In determining whether a design is primarily functional or primarily ornamental the claimed design is viewed in its entirety. The ultimate question is not the functional or decorative aspect of each separate feature, but the overall appearance of the article, in determining whether the claimed design is dictated by the utilitarian purpose of the article.[151]

The validity of a design patent does not require that the article be visible throughout its use.[152] It is a sound rule of thumb to presume the absence of ornamentality where the design cannot be perceived in its normal and intended use. But this is not a per se rule. In each case, the inquiry must extend to whether at some point in the life of the article an occasion arises where the appearance of the article becomes a matter of concern. The normal and intended use of an article is the period in the article's life beginning after completion of manufacture or assembly and ending with ultimate destruction, loss, or disappearance. Only the facts of specific cases will establish whether during that period the design can be observed in such a manner as to demonstrate ornamentality. For example, articles are designed for sale and display as well as for functional use, and the likelihood that articles would be observed during occasions of display or sale could have a substantial influence on the ornamentality of the article.[153]

Invalidity due to functionality is an affirmative defense to a claim of infringement of a design patent and must be proved by the party asserting the defense.[154]

(b) Infringement

It is not a design that is infringed, but the patent on it, which creates the right to exclude others for a limited time.[155] Infringement

---

Strollers, Inc. v. TRI Indus., Inc., 878 F.2d 1418, 11 USPQ2d 1300 (Fed. Cir. 1989). This decision seems to be in accord with *Kangaroos U.S.A., Inc. v. Caldor, Inc.*, 778 F.2d 1571, 228 USPQ 32 (Fed. Cir. 1985), which held without discussion that a utility application could be entitled to the filing date of an earlier filed design application. In *Racing Strollers*, the court expressly overruled *In re Campbell*, 212 F.2d 606, 101 USPQ 406 (CCPA 1954).

[151]*L.A. Gear, Inc. v. Thom McAn Shoe Co.*, 988 F.2d 1117, 25 USPQ2d 1913 (Fed. Cir. 1993). While analyzing elements of a design may be appropriate in some circumstances, the determination of whether the patented design is dictated by the function of the article of manufacture must ultimately rest on an analysis of its overall appearance. *Berry Sterling Corp. v. Pescor Plastics, Inc.*, 122 F.3d 1452, 43 USPQ2d 1953 (Fed. Cir. 1997).

[152]*Seiko Epson Corp. v. Nu-Kote Int'l Inc.*, 190 F.3d 1360, 52 USPQ2d 1011 (Fed. Cir. 1999).

[153]*In re Webb*, 916 F.2d 1553, 16 USPQ2d 1433 (Fed. Cir. 1990). Here the evidence showed that the applicant's design for a hip prosthesis was advertised and displayed at trade shows. In *Keystone Ret. Wall Sys., Inc. v. Westrock, Inc.*, 997 F.2d 1444, 27 USPQ2d 1297 (Fed. Cir. 1993), the court rejected the patentee's contention that the hidden portion of the design should be ignored for infringement purposes. An argument that hidden features of articles are not ornamental and cannot therefore be infringed confuses the test for design patentability with the standards for infringement.

[154]*L.A. Gear, Inc. v. Thom McAn Shoe Co.*, 988 F.2d 1117, 25 USPQ2d 1913 (Fed. Cir. 1993). Applying the presumption of validity, functionality must be established by clear and convincing evidence. *Id.*

[155]*Lee v. Dayton-Hudson Corp.*, 838 F.2d 1186, 5 USPQ2d 1625 (Fed. Cir. 1988).

of a design patent is defined by statute as the unauthorized manufacture or sale of the patented design or any colorable imitation thereof.[156] This is a question of fact, to be proved by a preponderance of the evidence.[157]

A design patent contains no written description; the drawings are the claims to the patented subject matter.[158] Though the court has remarked that a design patent claim has almost no scope,[159] it nonetheless insists that the infringement analysis demands proper claim construction to determine its meaning and scope.[160] The requirement that the court construe disputed claim language, as applied to design patents, must be adapted to the practice that a patented design is claimed as shown in its drawing. There is usually no description of the design in words.[161] The court has rejected an argument that the scope of a design patent is effectively determined by deciding infringement, rather than by construing the claim. Where a design contains both functional and nonfunctional elements, the scope of the claim must be construed in order to identify the nonfunctional aspects of the design as shown in the patent.[162] It is also incorrect to interpret the claim in view of the manufacturing specifications under which the patented design was developed. Rather, the court should address the article in the claimed design, which means, realistically, the article and its configuration as shown in the patent drawings.[163]

The test for infringement of a design patent is whether, in the eye of an ordinary observer, giving such attention as a purchaser usually gives, the patented and accused designs are substantially the same, and the resemblance is such as to deceive the observer, inducing him or her to purchase one supposing it to be the other.[164] This test

---

[156]*L.A. Gear, Inc. v. Thom McAn Shoe Co.*, 988 F.2d 1117, 25 USPQ2d 1913 (Fed. Cir. 1993). Patent infringement can be found for a design that is not identical to the patented design. *Braun Inc. v. Dynamics Corp.*, 975 F.2d 815, 24 USPQ2d 1121 (Fed. Cir. 1992).

[157]*Oddzon Prods., Inc. v. Just Toys, Inc.*, 122 F.3d 1396, 43 USPQ2d 1641 (Fed. Cir. 1997); *L.A. Gear, Inc. v. Thom McAn Shoe Co.*, 988 F.2d 1117, 25 USPQ2d 1913 (Fed. Cir. 1993).

[158]*Hupp v. Siroflex of Am., Inc.*, 122 F.3d 1456, 43 USPQ2d 1887 (Fed. Cir. 1997).

[159]*In re Mann*, 861 F.2d 1581, 8 USPQ2d 2030 (Fed. Cir. 1988).

[160]*Elmer v. ICC Fabricating, Inc.*, 67 F.3d 1571, 36 USPQ2d 1417 (Fed. Cir. 1995). The court provided a fascinating look at how it proposes to interpret claims in a design patent. The claim called for the "ornamental design as shown and described" in the patent. If features were functional and not ornamental, they could have been omitted from the drawings. Inasmuch as the features were included, the patentee effectively limited the scope of its patent claim by including those features in it.

[161]*Goodyear Tire & Rubber Co. v. Hercules Tire & Rubber Co.*, 48 USPQ2d 1767 (Fed. Cir. 1998). The claim was a design for a "tire tread." Both the patentee's embodiment and the accused device were truck tires. Although it would have been error to construe the claim as being limited to truck tires, it is not a matter of claim construction to determine the qualifications of the observer through whose eyes infringement is determined. Thus the district court properly selected a purchaser of truck tires as the ordinary observer.

[162]*Oddzon Prods., Inc. v. Just Toys, Inc.*, 122 F.3d 1396, 43 USPQ2d 1641 (Fed. Cir. 1997).

[163]*Berry Sterling Corp. v. Pescor Plastics, Inc.*, 122 F.3d 1452, 43 USPQ2d 1953 (Fed. Cir. 1997).

[164]*Avia Group Int'l, Inc. v. L.A. Gear Calif., Inc.*, 853 F.2d 1557, 7 USPQ2d 1548 (Fed. Cir. 1988); *Unette Corp. v. Unit Pack Co.*, 785 F.2d 1026, 228 USPQ 933 (Fed. Cir. 1986); *Shelcore, Inc. v. Durham Indus., Inc.*, 745 F.2d 621, 223 USPQ 584 (Fed. Cir. 1984); *Litton Sys., Inc. v. Whirlpool Corp.*, 728 F.2d 1423, 221 USPQ 97 (Fed. Cir. 1984). One instance of

is to be supplemented with the so-called point of novelty test: the requirement that the accused device must appropriate the novelty in the patented device that distinguishes it from the prior art.[165] The purpose of the point of novelty test is to focus on those aspects of a design that render it different from prior art designs.[166]

So, in determining whether a product design infringes a design patent, two distinct tests must be applied: the ordinary observer test and the point of novelty test. Under the first test, in determining the overall similarity of design, the ordinary observer must be deceived by the features common to the claimed and accused designs that are ornamental, not functional. The second test is distinct and requires in addition to the ordinary observer test that the accused device must appropriate the novelty in the patented device that distinguishes it from the prior art. Any merger of the point of novelty test and the ordinary observer test is legal error. It is error, for example, to look only to the point of novelty in applying the ordinary observer test.[167] Thus, the patentee of a design patent must prove both substantial similarity and appropriation of the point of novelty. The trial court cannot evade the point of novelty test by relying on the claimed overall design as the point of novelty.[168]

In conducting such analysis the patented design is viewed in its entirety, as it is claimed. As for other patented inventions, reference is made to the prior art and the prosecution history in order to give appropriate weight to the factors that contributed to patentability.[169] One cannot establish design patent infringement by showing similarity of only one part of a patented design if the designs as a whole are

---

actual confusion may not be sufficiently probative to create a genuine dispute of fact over design patent infringement, especially where the affidavit evidencing the confusion does not indicate whether it was caused by those aspects of the design that distinguish it from the prior art. *Winner Int'l Corp. v. Wolo Mfg. Corp.*, 905 F.2d 375, 15 USPQ2d 1076 (Fed. Cir. 1990). But it is not necessary in every case to introduce evidence of empirical sampling of ordinary observers as to deception in order to find design patent infringement. *Braun Inc. v. Dynamics Corp.*, 975 F.2d 815, 24 USPQ2d 1121 (Fed. Cir. 1992).

[165]*Lund Indus., Inc. v. GO Indus., Inc.*, 938 F.2d 1273, 19 USPQ2d 1383 (Fed. Cir. 1991); *Oakley, Inc. v. International Tropic-Cal, Inc.*, 923 F.2d 167, 17 USPQ2d 1401 (Fed. Cir. 1991); *Avia Group Int'l, Inc. v. L.A. Gear Calif., Inc.*, 853 F.2d 1557, 7 USPQ2d 1548 (Fed. Cir. 1988); *FMC Corp. v. Hennessy Indus., Inc.*, 836 F.2d 521, 5 USPQ2d 1272 (Fed. Cir. 1987); *Litton Sys., Inc. v. Whirlpool Corp.*, 728 F.2d 1423, 221 USPQ 97 (Fed. Cir. 1984). However, in *Lee v. Dayton-Hudson Corp.*, 838 F.2d 1186, 5 USPQ2d 1625 (Fed. Cir. 1988), the court seemed to retreat slightly from the "point of novelty" test, indicating that unless the "eye of the ordinary observer" test of essential deception is met, there is no need for detailed analysis in terms of the prior art.

[166]*Winner Int'l Corp. v. Wolo Mfg. Corp.*, 905 F.2d 375, 15 USPQ2d 1076 (Fed. Cir. 1990).

[167]*Unidynamics Corp. v. Automatic Prods. Int'l Ltd.*, 157 F.3d 1311, 48 USPQ2d 1099 (Fed. Cir. 1998). It is error to look only to the point of novelty in applying the ordinary observer test. *Unidynamics Corp. v. Automatic Prods. Int'l Ltd.*, 157 F.3d 1311, 48 USPQ2d 1099 (Fed. Cir. 1998). But see *L.A. Gear, Inc. v. Thom McAn Shoe Co.*, 988 F.2d 1117, 25 USPQ2d 1913 (Fed. Cir. 1993), in which the court emphasized that, while the accused design must appropriate the novelty that distinguished the patented design from the prior art, the ultimate question requires determining whether the effect of the whole design is substantially the same.

[168]*Sun Hill Indus., Inc. v. Easter Unlimited, Inc.*, 48 F.3d 1193, 33 USPQ2d 1925 (Fed. Cir. 1995). See also *Winner Int'l Corp. v. Wolo Mfg. Corp.*, 905 F.2d 375, 15 USPQ2d 1076 (Fed. Cir. 1990).

[169]*L.A. Gear, Inc. v. Thom McAn Shoe Co.*, 988 F.2d 1117, 25 USPQ2d 1913 (Fed. Cir. 1993).

substantially dissimilar. The test begins with an examination of the overall similarity of the patented and accused designs. A patented design is defined by the drawings in the patent, not just by one feature of the claimed design.[170] Courts should take into account similarities and differences in determining infringement of design patents.[171] The patented and accused designs do not have to be identical in order for design patent infringement to be found. It is the appearance of the design as a whole that is controlling.[172]

The doctrine of equivalents applies to design patents. But it applies only when the accused product includes features equivalent to the novel claimed design features. A patentee cannot invoke the doctrine to evade scrutiny of the point of novelty, because to do so would eviscerate the purpose of the point of novelty approach, which is to focus on those aspects of a design that render the design different from prior art designs.[173] Although some differences are acceptable, they must not be greater than those that distinguish over the art. Thus, in an art crowded with such designs, the range of equivalents is narrow.[174]

When the patented design and the design of the article sold by the patentee are substantially the same, it is not error to compare the patentee's and the accused articles directly. Indeed, such comparison may facilitate the analysis of whether an ordinary purchaser would be deceived into thinking that one were the other.[175] But the holder of a valid design patent need not have progressed to the manufacture and distribution of a purchasable product for its design patent to be infringed by another's product.[176] Thus, proper application of the test for design patent infringement usually requires that an accused design be compared to the claimed design, not to a commercial embodiment.[177] Indeed, comparing an accused product to the patentee's commercial embodiment of the claimed design risks relying on unclaimed and therefore irrelevant features as grounds for similarity or difference. It is legal error to base an infringement finding on features of the commercial embodiment that are not claimed.[178]

---

[170]*Keystone Ret. Wall Sys., Inc. v. Westrock, Inc.*, 997 F.2d 1444, 27 USPQ2d 1297 (Fed. Cir. 1993).

[171]*FMC Corp. v. Hennessy Indus., Inc.*, 836 F.2d 521, 5 USPQ2d 1272 (Fed. Cir. 1987).

[172]*Oddzon Prods., Inc. v. Just Toys, Inc.*, 122 F.3d 1396, 43 USPQ2d 1641 (Fed. Cir. 1997).

[173]*Sun Hill Indus., Inc. v. Easter Unlimited, Inc.*, 48 F.3d 1193, 33 USPQ2d 1925 (Fed. Cir. 1995). The designs must be equivalent in their ornamental, not functional, aspects. *Lee v. Dayton-Hudson Corp.*, 838 F.2d 1186, 5 USPQ2d 1625 (Fed. Cir. 1988).

[174]*Litton Sys., Inc. v. Whirlpool Corp.*, 728 F.2d 1423, 221 USPQ 97 (Fed. Cir. 1984).

[175]*L.A. Gear, Inc. v. Thom McAn Shoe Co.*, 988 F.2d 1117, 25 USPQ2d 1913 (Fed. Cir. 1993). See also *Lee v. Dayton-Hudson Corp.*, 838 F.2d 1186, 5 USPQ2d 1625 (Fed. Cir. 1988). The fact that color was involved does not make the comparison invalid. While color may be an improper consideration, there was no showing that the trial court was influenced by it.

[176]*Unette Corp. v. Unit Pack Co.*, 785 F.2d 1026, 228 USPQ 933 (Fed. Cir. 1986).

[177]*Payless Shoesource, Inc. v. Reebok Int'l Ltd.*, 998 F.2d 985, 27 USPQ2d 1516 (Fed. Cir. 1993).

[178]*Sun Hill Indus., Inc. v. Easter Unlimited, Inc.*, 48 F.3d 1193, 33 USPQ2d 1925 (Fed. Cir. 1995).

Design patent infringement does not concern itself with the broad issue of consumer behavior in the marketplace.[179] To find infringement, there need only be an appropriation of the patentee's protected design, not the patentee's market as well. The products need not be directly competitive; indeed, an infringer is liable even when the patent owner puts out no product. Clearly then, infringement is not avoided by selling to a different class of purchaser than that served by the patentee.[180]

Design patent infringement relates solely to the patented design and does not require proof of unfair competition in the marketplace or allow of avoidance of infringement by labeling.[181] Likelihood of confusion as to the source of the goods is therefore not a necessary or appropriate factor for determining infringement of a design patent. A determination that the shape of the alleged infringing design is not visible to the consumer at the time of sale, and therefore that the consumer is unlikely to be confused by the similarity in a competitor's product is inapposite. Concluding that a purchaser is unlikely to be confused only serves to blur the otherwise clear line that exists between the test for infringement of a design patent and the likelihood of confusion test for infringement of a trademark.[182]

By obtaining a design patent and not a utility patent, an inventor limits his or her patent protection to the ornamental design of the article. Design patents do not and cannot include claims to the structural or functional aspects of the article. Thus, it is the nonfunctional, design aspects that are pertinent to the determination of infringement. A device that copies the utilitarian or functional features of a patented design is not an infringement unless the ornamental aspects are also copied, so that the overall resemblance is such as to deceive.[183]

(c) Novelty and Loss of Right

In determining whether a design patent is invalid based on a description in a printed publication, the factual inquiry is the same as that which determines anticipation by prior publication of the subject matter of a utility patent. The publication must show the same subject matter as that of the patent, and must be identical in

---

[179]*Braun Inc. v. Dynamics Corp.*, 975 F.2d 815, 24 USPQ2d 1121 (Fed. Cir. 1992).

[180]*Avia Group Int'l, Inc. v. L.A. Gear Calif., Inc.*, 853 F.2d 1557, 7 USPQ2d 1548 (Fed. Cir. 1988).

[181]*L.A. Gear, Inc. v. Thom McAn Shoe Co.*, 988 F.2d 1117, 25 USPQ2d 1913 (Fed. Cir. 1993).

[182]*Unette Corp. v. Unit Pack Co.*, 785 F.2d 1026, 228 USPQ 933 (Fed. Cir. 1986). The court has observed that an argument that hidden features of articles are not ornamental and cannot therefore be infringed confuses the test for design patentability with the standards for infringement. *Keystone Ret. Wall Sys., Inc. v. Westrock, Inc.*, 997 F.2d 1444, 27 USPQ2d 1297 (Fed. Cir. 1993).

[183]*Read Corp. v. Portec, Inc.*, 970 F.2d 816, 23 USPQ2d 1426 (Fed. Cir. 1992); *Lee v. Dayton-Hudson Corp.*, 838 F.2d 1186, 5 USPQ2d 1625 (Fed. Cir. 1988). See also *Elmer v. ICC Fabricating, Inc.*, 67 F.3d 1571, 36 USPQ2d 1417 (Fed. Cir. 1995).

all material respects.[184] A claimed design is considered to be on sale, within the meaning of 35 U.S.C. §102(b), when an embodiment of the design was sold or offered for sale in this country more than one year before a filing date to which the claim is entitled (the critical date) and the sale or offer to sell was primarily for profit rather than for experimental purposes.[185]

Early on, the court indicated that the experimental use exception would not be available to avoid a public use bar.[186] Later, however, in *Tone v. Sysco*,[187] the court held that public use of a patented design could be negated by experimentation directed at optimizing the functional aspects of an article while not addressing the ornamental aspects of its design. More recently, in *Continental v. Owens-Brockway*,[188] the court refused to extend the *Tone* analysis to an on-sale situation.[189]

---

[184]*Hupp v. Siroflex of Am., Inc.,* 122 F.3d 1456, 43 USPQ2d 1887 (Fed. Cir. 1997).

[185]*Continental Plastic Containers Inc. v. Owens-Brockway Plastic Prods. Inc.,* 141 F.3d 1073, 46 USPQ2d 1277 (Fed. Cir. 1998). In this case, there was a contract to supply a customer with all of its requirements for the juice bottles that were the subject of the design patent. The contract was entered into prior to the critical date. Also prior to the critical date a wooden model and several three-dimensional drawings were complete and production molds were ordered and shipped. Although there were later changes in the design to overcome manufacturing difficulties, the court holds that the patented design was on sale.

[186]*In re Mann,* 861 F.2d 1581, 8 USPQ2d 2030 (Fed. Cir. 1988). "We see no way in which an ornamental design for an article of manufacture can be subject to the 'experimental use' exception applicable in the case of functioning machines, manufactures, or processes. Obtaining the reactions of people to a design—whether or not they like it—is not 'experimentation' in that sense. In the case of a design, if market testing shows that it has no appeal and the design is changed, the result is a new and different design; the original design remains just what it was. Design patents have almost no scope." The design in question was embodied in a wrought iron table that had been displayed at a trade show more than one year before the applicant's filing date. The court also rejected the applicant's argument that the design was not in public use because it was not used in its natural and intended way inasmuch as the table was "merely on display."

[187]*Tone Bros. Inc. v. Sysco Corp.,* 28 F.3d 1192, 31 USPQ2d 1321 (Fed. Cir. 1994).

[188]*Continental Plastic Containers Inc. v. Owens-Brockway Plastic Prods. Inc.,* 141 F.3d 1073, 46 USPQ2d 1277 (Fed. Cir. 1998).

[189]The majority justified its refusal to extend *Tone* to on-sale situations on two basic grounds. (1) The specific functions of an article of manufacture are not necessarily disclosed in a design patent. Thus, if *Tone* were to apply, not only would district courts likely be deluged with hindsight analysis as to what features were required to produce a functional article, but it would virtually require parties to seek judicial determinations in order to establish that which should be readily apparent from the face of the design patent. (2) Adopting the *Tone* approach would improperly imbue the patented design with additional limitations taken from a commercial embodiment. Actually, one wonders whether *Tone* itself is still good law. The *Owens-Brockway* majority goes on to observe that the policy behind experimental use negation is to give the inventor an opportunity to reduce the invention to practice. Thus, experimental use cannot occur after a reduction to practice. Since design inventions are reduced to practice as soon as an embodiment is constructed, experimental use negation is virtually inapplicable in the design patent context. Applying experimental use negation in the design patent context would allow entities to increase the life of their design patents merely by tarrying over the production of the article of manufacture. Judge Newman, in dissent, says that the majority has created a new rule specific to design patents in its holding that experimental use is "virtually inapplicable in the design patent context."

(d) Obviousness

Obviousness of a claimed design is a question of law based on underlying facts, and the standard of review is de novo.[190] There are naturally many similarities between design and utility patents. The tests for determining validity of a design patent are said to be identical with those for a utility patent.[191] Design patents must meet a nonobviousness requirement identical to that applicable to utility patents.[192] An expert's opinion on the legal conclusion of obviousness of a patented design is neither necessary nor controlling.[193]

The person of ordinary skill in the art is an ordinary designer of articles of the type at issue.[194] As with utility patents, obviousness is not determined as if the designer had hindsight knowledge of the patented design. When the patented design is a combination of selected elements in the prior art, a holding of obviousness requires that there be some teaching or suggestion whereby it would have been obvious to a designer of ordinary skill to make the particular selection and combination made by the patentee.[195] The scope of the prior art is not the universe of abstract design and artistic creativity, but designs of the same article of manufacture or of articles sufficiently similar that a person of ordinary skill would look to such articles for their designs.[196]

But it is improper to mix principles of obviousness for utility patents with those for ornamental design patents. Unlike an invention in a utility patent, a patented ornamental design has no use other than its visual appearance and its scope is limited to what is shown in the drawings. Therefore, in considering prior art references for purposes of determining patentability of designs, the focus must be on appearances and not uses. Accordingly, the focus must be on actual appearance rather than design concept. Viewing the principal prior art reference as a design concept produces a type of post-hoc rationalization of the claimed design that is improper.[197] Invalidating prior

---

[190]*In re Klein*, 987 F.2d 1569, 26 USPQ2d 1133 (Fed. Cir. 1993).

[191]*Litton Sys., Inc. v. Whirlpool Corp.*, 728 F.2d 1423, 221 USPQ 97 (Fed. Cir. 1984). See also *In re Borden*, 90 F.3d 1570, 39 USPQ2d 1524 (Fed. Cir. 1996).

[192]*Avia Group Int'l, Inc. v. L.A. Gear Calif., Inc.*, 853 F.2d 1557, 7 USPQ2d 1548 (Fed. Cir. 1988). Where a design claim covers plural alternative embodiments, a §103 rejection is proper if the prior art demonstrates the obviousness of any one of them. *In re Klein*, 987 F.2d 1569, 26 USPQ2d 1133 (Fed. Cir. 1993).

[193]*Avia Group Int'l, Inc. v. L.A. Gear Calif., Inc.*, 853 F.2d 1557, 7 USPQ2d 1548 (Fed. Cir. 1988).

[194]*In re Borden*, 90 F.3d 1570, 39 USPQ2d 1524 (Fed. Cir. 1996); *In re Carlson*, 983 F.2d 1032, 25 USPQ2d 1207 (Fed. Cir. 1993); *Avia Group Int'l, Inc. v. L.A. Gear Calif., Inc.*, 853 F.2d 1557, 7 USPQ2d 1548 (Fed. Cir. 1988); *Petersen Mfg. Co. v. Central Purchasing, Inc.*, 740 F.2d 1541, 222 USPQ 562 (Fed. Cir. 1984); *Litton Sys., Inc. v. Whirlpool Corp.*, 728 F.2d 1423, 221 USPQ 97 (Fed. Cir. 1984).

[195]*L.A. Gear, Inc. v. Thom McAn Shoe Co.*, 988 F.2d 1117, 25 USPQ2d 1913 (Fed. Cir. 1993).

[196]*Hupp v. Siroflex of Am., Inc.*, 122 F.3d 1456, 43 USPQ2d 1887 (Fed. Cir. 1997).

[197]*In re Harvey*, 12 F.3d 1061, 29 USPQ2d 1206 (Fed. Cir. 1993).

art must show or render obvious the ornamental features of a patented design rather than its functional features.[198]

The presumption of validity is the same for design and utility patents[199] and is a permissible basis for supporting a preliminary injunction in an appropriate design patent case.[200] Commercial success must be attributable to the ornamental features rather than the functional aspects of the design.[201] Copying is evidence of nonobviousness of a patented design.[202] Materiality in design patent prosecution is apparently the same as for utility prosecution.[203]

The court has hinted that there may be at least one significant difference in the validity context, however. Early on, the court explained that a design is a unitary thing and all portions are material in that they contribute to the appearance that constitutes a design.[204] It was therefore not surprising that the court initially indicated that the obviousness of a design, like any other invention, must be evaluated as a whole.[205] In a later case, however, the court seemed to indicate just the contrary, in a functionality setting.[206] A more recent decision does not entirely resolve the matter, although it does state that the teachings of combined references must be such as to have suggested the overall appearance of the claimed design.[207]

The Federal Circuit's *Harvey*[208] decision undertook to clarify the nature of the obviousness inquiry in view of a combination of references. It is improper to compare the visual impressions of selected, separate features of the prior art designs rather than the visual impression of the designs as a whole. A claimed design is not unpatentable for obviousness, even though all of its component features are found in the prior art, unless the prior art contains some suggestion to combine the components. And even if there is a suggestion to combine, if the prior art designs must be modified in more than one respect, then those modifications must be de minimis in nature and unrelated to the overall aesthetic appearance of the design. Thus, a

---

[198]*Oddzon Prods., Inc. v. Just Toys, Inc.*, 122 F.3d 1396, 43 USPQ2d 1641 (Fed. Cir. 1997).

[199]*Litton Sys., Inc. v. Whirlpool Corp.*, 728 F.2d 1423, 221 USPQ 97 (Fed. Cir. 1984).

[200]*Power Controls Corp. v. Hybrinetics, Inc.*, 806 F.2d 234, 231 USPQ 774 (Fed. Cir. 1986).

[201]*Avia Group Int'l, Inc. v. L.A. Gear Calif., Inc.*, 853 F.2d 1557, 7 USPQ2d 1548 (Fed. Cir. 1988); *Litton Sys., Inc. v. Whirlpool Corp.*, 728 F.2d 1423, 221 USPQ 97 (Fed. Cir. 1984).

[202]*Avia Group Int'l, Inc. v. L.A. Gear Calif., Inc.*, 853 F.2d 1557, 7 USPQ2d 1548 (Fed. Cir. 1988).

[203]*Pacific Furniture Mfg. Co. v. Preview Furniture Corp.*, 800 F.2d 1111, 231 USPQ 67 (Fed. Cir. 1986). In *Elk Corp. of Dallas v. GAF Build. Mat'ls Corp.*, 168 F.3d 28, 49 USPQ2d 1853 (Fed. Cir. 1999), the court found a design patent to be unenforceable because prior art designs that were not merely cumulative were not disclosed to the PTO.

[204]*In re Salmon*, 705 F.2d 1579, 217 USPQ 981 (Fed. Cir. 1984).

[205]*Petersen Mfg. Co. v. Central Purchasing, Inc.*, 740 F.2d 1541, 222 USPQ 562 (Fed. Cir. 1984).

[206]*Power Controls Corp. v. Hybrinetics, Inc.*, 806 F.2d 234, 231 USPQ 774 (Fed. Cir. 1986).

[207]*In re Sung Nam Cho*, 813 F.2d 378, 1 USPQ2d 1662 (Fed. Cir. 1987).

[208]*In re Harvey*, 12 F.3d 1061, 29 USPQ2d 1206 (Fed. Cir. 1993). See also *In re Borden*, 90 F.3d 1570, 39 USPQ2d 1524 (Fed. Cir. 1996).

proper obviousness rejection based on a combination of references requires that the visual ornamental features (design characteristics) of the claimed design appear in the prior art in a manner that suggests such features as used in the claimed design. If, however, the combined teachings suggest only components of a claimed design, but not its overall appearance, an obviousness rejection is inappropriate. A primary reference (basic design) must be cited having design characteristics that are basically the same as the claimed design. The designs of other references may then properly be relied upon for modification of such basic design when the references are so related that the appearance of certain ornamental features in one would have suggested application of those features to another.

The court now seems to have elevated the "primary reference" suggestion of *Harvey* to a standard rule of design obviousness analysis. Thus the first step in an obviousness analysis for a design patent requires a search of the prior art for a primary reference. This requires the trial court to (1) discern the correct visual impression created by the patented design as a whole and (2) determine whether there is a single reference that creates basically the same visual impression. In comparing the patented design to a prior art reference, the trial judge may determine almost instinctively whether the two designs create basically the same visual impression. Nonetheless, the judge must communicate the reasoning behind the decision. That explanation afford the parties a basis upon which to challenge, and also aids the appellate court in reviewing, the judge's ultimate decision. In the design patent context, however, the judge's explanation of the decision is more complicated because it involves an additional level of abstraction not required when comprehending the matter claimed in a utility patent. Unlike the readily available verbal description of the invention and of the prior art that exists in a utility patent case, a design patent case presents the judge only with visual descriptions. Given the lack of a visual language, the trial court must first translate these visual descriptions into words to evoke the visual image of the design. From this translation, the parties and appellate courts can discern the internal reasoning employed by the trial court to reach its decision as to whether or not a prior art design is basically the same as the claimed design.[209]

(e) Other Issues

The statutory provision governing the effective filing date of the subject matter of continuing applications, 35 U.S.C. §120, applies to

---

[209]*Durling v. Spectrum Furn. Co.*, 101 F.3d 100, 40 USPQ2d 1788 (Fed. Cir. 1996). There must be a reference with design characteristics that are basically the same as the claimed design in order to support a holding of obviousness. The correct application of this analytic approach is to ascertain whether, upon application of the *Graham v. Deere* factors to the invention viewed as a whole, this primary reference is known to have design characteristics

design patents as well as to utility patents. The common thread, and the criterion to be met, is whether the later claimed subject matter is described in the earlier application in compliance with §112¶1. Thus the earlier application must meet the written description requirement of §112. The test for sufficiency of the written description is the same, whether for a design or a utility patent. It is the drawings of the design patent that provide the description of the invention. Although linguists distinguish between a drawing and a writing, the drawings of the design patent are viewed in terms of the "written description" requirement of §112. Thus when an issue of priority arises under §120, one looks to the drawings of the earlier application for disclosure of the subject matter claimed in the later application. The inquiry is simply to determine whether the inventor had possession at the earlier date of what was claimed at the later date.[210] In the case of a design, the best mode requirement is not applicable, as a design has only one "mode" and it can be described only by illustrations showing what it looks like. As a practical matter, meeting the requirements of §112 in the case of a design is simply a question of whether the application contains illustrations, whatever form they may take, depicting the design invention.[211]

Under 35 U.S.C. §289 there is an alternative remedy for infringement of design patents: the entire profit of the infringer but not less than $250.[212] In the context of design patent infringement under §289, profits means pretax profits.[213] After a careful review of the parallel

---

of which the claimed design is an obvious variant. Obviousness is determined by ascertaining whether the applicable prior art contains any suggestion or motivation for making the modifications in the design of the primary reference in order to produce the claimed design. *Hupp v. Siroflex of Am., Inc.*, 122 F.3d 1456, 43 USPQ2d 1887 (Fed. Cir. 1997).

[210]*In re Daniels*, 144 F.3d 1452, 46 USPQ2d 1788 (Fed. Cir. 1998). In this case the court rejected the Board's theory that a design is a "unitary thing" and that any change in the drawing will therefore defeat a priority claim for a design application. The background of this case is interesting. It seems that an invention management company (later charged by the FTC with running a deceptive invention-promotion scheme) filed the original application. There was evidence that the company's clients were given a money-back guarantee that a patent would issue, and evidence that its draftsman would add decorative matter to the drawings to facilitate issuance as a design patent. Here the original application, a design for a leech trap, was filed with drawings showing the device decorated on each side with a pattern of leaves. The inventor later got new counsel, who filed a continuing application that simply omitted the leaf pattern. The court held that the leech trap as an article of manufacture was clearly visible in the earlier application, demonstrating to the artisan viewing that application that the inventor had possession at that time of the later claimed design of that article. The leaf ornamentation did not obscure the design of the trap, but was a mere indicium that did not override the underlying design.

[211]*Racing Strollers, Inc. v. TRI Indus., Inc.*, 878 F.2d 1418, 11 USPQ2d 1300 (Fed. Cir. 1989). Some added description in words may be useful to explain the illustration. *Id.*

[212]*Braun Inc. v. Dynamics Corp.*, 975 F.2d 815, 24 USPQ2d 1121 (Fed. Cir. 1992). Such a recovery cannot be increased under §284. *Id.* The act of infringement described in §289 is selling or exposing for sale any article to which the patented design has been applied. *Trans-World Mfg. Corp. v. Al Nyman & Sons*, 750 F.2d 1552, 224 USPQ 259 (Fed. Cir. 1984). The patented design was for a display rack for selling goods. The patentee was not entitled to the infringer's profits on the goods themselves. However, the racks may certainly have contributed to that profit, and the profit would therefore be relevant to a reasonable royalty under §284.

[213]*Nike Inc. v. Walmart Stores Inc.*, 138 F.3d 1437, 46 USPQ2d 1001 (Fed. Cir. 1998).

development of §§287(a) and 289, the court held that the patent marking provisions of §287(a) apply to the recovery of a design patent infringer's profit under §289. In order to reach this result, the court had to distinguish an earlier decision[214] holding that §284 does not authorize enhancement of §289 profits. That decision, it concluded, was not based upon drawing a rigorous distinction between damages and profits, but on the provision of §289 that bars the design patentee, upon recovering the infringer's profits, from twice recovering the profit made from the infringement.[215]

For discussion of issues arising in the context of design/utility double patenting, see §15.5(b).

§2.5 Plant Patents

Under 35 U.S.C. §161, a patent may be granted to anyone that invents or discovers, and asexually reproduces, any distinct and new variety of plant. Such a patent carries the right, pursuant to 35 U.S.C. §163, to exclude others from asexual reproduction of the plant, or from selling or using a plant so reproduced. In its *Imazio* decision,[216] the court provides a nice history of the Plant Patent Act and its incorporation in the Patent Act of 1952. In this fascinating opinion, the court interpreted the term "variety" in light of the asexual reproduction requirement and concluded that only a single plant, i.e., reproduction from one original specimen, is protected by a plant patent. Accordingly, "variety" cannot be read as affording patent protection to a range of plants. With this underpinning, the court then proceeded to construe the plant patent claim: the scope of the claim is the asexual progeny of the particular plant shown and described in the specification. Thus, it is not sufficient for infringement simply to prove that the alleged infringing plant has the same essential characteristics as the patent plant. It is a defense to plant patent infringement that the alleged infringing plant is not an asexual reproduction of the patented plant. Part of that proof could be that the defendant independently developed the allegedly infringing plant.[217]

A more recent enactment is the Plant Variety Protection Act (PVPA), which protects novel varieties of sexually reproduced seed,

---

[214]*Braun Inc. v. Dynamics Corp.,* 975 F.2d 815, 24 USPQ2d 1121 (Fed. Cir. 1992).

[215]*Nike Inc. v. Walmart Stores Inc.,* 138 F.3d 1437, 46 USPQ2d 1001 (Fed. Cir. 1998).

[216]*Imazio Nursery, Inc. v. Dania Greenhouses,* 69 F.3d 1560, 36 USPQ2d 1673 (Fed. Cir. 1995).

[217]Logic seems to indicate that infringement will require access of some kind, in order to perform the asexual reproduction. Will this mean that a finding of willful infringement, due to "copying," will inevitably follow a finding of infringement of a plant patent? It should also be noted that the *Imazio* decision recognized that its definition of variety is different than that used in the Plant Variety Protection Act. However, asexual reproduction is the cornerstone of plant patent protection, while sexual reproduction is the distinguishing feature of plant variety protection.

transplants, and plants. The PVPA extends protection to distinct, uniform, and stable new seed varieties. The developer of a novel variety obtains protection by acquiring a certificate of protection from the Plant Variety Protection Office. A PVPA certificate grants the breeder the right to exclude others from selling the variety, offering it for sale, reproducing, importing, or exporting it, or using it in producing a hybrid or different variety therefrom. PVPA protection lasts for 18 years, and the Act provides remedies for infringement of exclusive rights. Thus, the PVPA grants patent-like protection for sexually reproduced plants. The Federal Circuit has exclusive jurisdiction over appeals involving the PVPA.[218] The court applies its own substantive law to issues arising under the Plant Variety Protection Act.[219]

Among other activities, the unauthorized sale of seed harvested from crops grown with novel varieties is infringement of the right granted exclusively to a PVPA certificate holder. Under certain specified circumstances, however, farmers may save and sell seed harvested from crops grown from PVPA seed. Often farmers place harvested planting seed in plain brown bags for sale to other farmers. In a case of first impression, the Federal Circuit considered whether the sale of "brown bag" seed constituted an infringement of a PVPA certificate.[220] In a subsequent case, the court dealt with some other interesting infringement issues under the PVPA.[221]

The court has held that seeds and seed-grown plants are patentable subject matter under 35 U.S.C. §101. In so holding, it considered and rejected arguments that Congress, in passing the Plant Patent Act and the PVPA, intended to exclude plants from the purview of utility patent protection.[222]

---

[218]*Asgrow Seed Co. v. Winterboer*, 982 F.2d 486, 25 USPQ2d 1202 (Fed. Cir. 1992). The Act is found at 7 U.S.C. §§2321–2582.

[219]*Delta & Pine Land Co. v. Sinkers Corp.*, 177 F.3d 1343, 50 USPQ2d 1749 (Fed. Cir. 1999).

[220]*Asgrow Seed Co. v. Winterboer*, 982 F.2d 486, 25 USPQ2d 1202 (Fed. Cir. 1992). The defendants sold brown bag soybean seed harvested from crops planted with certified seed purchased from the plaintiff. The court held that the PVPA exempts such sales where the farmer's primary activity is growing a crop for consumption purposes; in other words, if more than half of the harvested crop is sold for consumption rather than seed, the seed sales are exempt. The court also held that the Act was not intended to limit such sales to a total amount of seed equal to that which the farmer would need to plant an ensuing crop. Several other detailed provisions of the PVPA are discussed in this opinion. The Supreme Court reversed, holding that a farmer may sell for reproductive purposes only such seed as the farmer has saved for the purpose of replanting his or her own acreage. *Asgrow Seed Co. v. Winterboer*, 513 U.S. 179, 33 USPQ2d 1430 (1995).

[221]*Delta & Pine Land Co. v. Sinkers Corp.*, 177 F.3d 1343, 50 USPQ2d 1749 (Fed. Cir. 1999).

[222]*Pioneer Hi-Bred Int'l Inc. v. J.E.M. Ag Supp. Inc.*, 200 F.3d 1374, 53 USPQ2d 1440 (Fed. Cir. 2000).

3

Novelty and Loss of Right

§3.1 Introduction

The fundamental qualitative condition for patentability is nonobviousness, as spelled out in 35 U.S.C. §103(a). That condition is the subject of Chapter 4. The topics of the current chapter are novelty and loss of right, which are dealt with in 35 U.S.C. §102. Section 102 also serves to define the prior art against which obviousness is measured under §103(a).

In order even to qualify for the nonobviousness inquiry, an invention or discovery must meet certain threshold criteria. Paramount among the patentability requirements is that which is sought to be patented must be new.[1] It has often been said that the person seeking a patent must be the "first and original" inventor. This is true to a certain extent. Certainly the invention must be original; under §102(f) one cannot knowingly patent the invention of another.

But must the inventor have been first? Not necessarily. In certain circumstances a person who independently makes an invention may be entitled to a patent even though another made the identical invention previously. Resolution of this question is often complex and difficult and may involve such factors as where the prior invention was made, whether it was accessible to the public and how, and the use that was made of it. Originality and priority are often collectively grouped under the term "novelty," which is not entirely inappropriate as a shorthand reference.

Novelty, however, is not the only prerequisite to the nonobviousness inquiry. Originality and priority may establish a right to a patent for a nonobvious invention, but it must also appear that the inventor has not, by some act or omission, lost that right to a patent. Loss of right has to do with so-called statutory bars, usually involving the running of a time period, and the issues here almost always require a determination of when the period began to run. For this reason, novelty and loss of right are questions that are often intimately related, and sometimes indistinguishable.

Thus, patents are available for useful inventions that were not obvious at the time the inventor did the work. But in order to qualify for a patent, it must appear that the person seeking the patent actually made the invention personally, and (with qualifications) made it before anyone else. More than that, the inventor must take steps to perfect his or her right to a patent in a timely way or lose the right. These, then, are the subjects of this chapter.

§3.2 Anticipation

Novelty and loss of right invoke a concept that has probably caused more difficulty than it is worth in the patent law. That concept

---

[1] *In re Schoenwald,* 964 F.2d 1122, 22 USPQ2d 1671 (Fed. Cir. 1992).

is identity, and it is usually expressed in the catchword "anticipation." At some risk of oversimplification, the rule may be stated as follows: lack of originality, or lack of priority, or a statutory bar, can be established only where the prior invention is identical to, or "anticipates," the invention sought to be patented. If there are differences between the prior work and the invention for which a patent is sought, §103(a) automatically comes into play, and the inquiry then becomes whether those differences are such that the invention would have been obvious.

All this sounds logical enough. But it does not take much exposure to patents and patent law until one realizes that instances of complete identity are comparatively rare. It almost never happens, for example, that a later inventor will, unknowingly at least, precisely duplicate the work of an earlier inventor. And even where there is a clear overlap of subject matter by two independent inventors (thus squarely raising a question of priority), those instances are more often than not resolved in the PTO by interference proceedings (see §15.2). If this be so, then it is reasonable to wonder why the patent law concerns itself with the concept of anticipation at all. Why not simply treat all questions of patentability in accordance with 35 U.S.C. §103(a), and let the obviousness inquiry resolve originality, priority, and loss of right as well? This question is neither idle nor easy to answer. But perhaps an attempt at some answers may provide a better understanding of the statutory scheme of patentability.

As will be seen in Chapter 4, the obviousness inquiry brings into play an entire panoply of indicators of patentability—objective evidence intended to persuade the decision maker that the invention was not obvious at the time it was made. Sometimes this evidence is exceedingly persuasive, to the point that it may be rightly said that the real purpose of it is to persuade the decision maker that the invention is entitled to patent protection *despite* its obviousness. Such evidence—commercial success, prior failure, long need, and the like—is generally held to be of no relevance to issues of originality, priority, and loss of right. In other words, objective evidence of patentability does not apply to novelty, only nonobviousness.

Perhaps this is reason enough to maintain the distinction between anticipation and obviousness: to prevent the decision maker from awarding protection to an invention identical to what had gone before. Indeed, one often encounters inventions that can by no stretch of the imagination be said to have been obvious—even after they are explained they still excite wonder at the elegance or power of the intellectual concepts involved. In such circumstances, the tendency of the decision maker might well be to find differences where none exist, simply to invoke the obviousness inquiry. This danger may well justify a careful preservation of the distinction between anticipation and obviousness.

Nevertheless, these answers are not entirely satisfactory. Perhaps the simplest and most satisfactory explanation is that the statutory sections dealing with novelty and loss of right after all serve another purpose—that of defining what the prior art is—and that is justification enough for their existence. In any event, the obviousness inquiry itself requires an isolation of the differences between the prior art and the subject matter sought to be patented, and once the prior art has been defined, the only way to find those differences is to know what is meant by identity, or as it is usually termed, anticipation.

(a) The General Test

Whether a reference is available as prior art, and whether it anticipates, are two quite separate questions.[2] The Federal Circuit has spoken clearly and at some length on the question of anticipation. At the outset, it warns us that anticipation as used in the case law prior to the Patent Act of 1952 may not have been used in the sense it is today.[3] Under modern decisions, anticipation requires that each and every element of the claimed invention be disclosed in a single prior art reference[4] or embodied in a single prior art device or practice.[5] The test is the same for a process. Anticipation requires identity of the claimed process and a process of the prior art; the claimed process, including each step thereof, must have been described or embodied, either expressly or inherently, in a single reference.[6] Those elements must either be inherent or disclosed expressly[7] and must be arranged as in the claim.[8] For anticipation, there must be no difference between the claimed invention and the reference disclosure, as viewed by a person of ordinary skill in the field of the invention.[9] It is the claims

---

[2]*Hodosh v. Block Drug Co.,* 786 F.2d 1136, 229 USPQ 182 (Fed. Cir. 1986).

[3]*Argus Chem. Corp. v. Fibre Glass-Evercoat Co.,* 759 F.2d 10, 225 USPQ 1100 (Fed. Cir. 1985).

[4]*In re Paulsen,* 30 F.3d 1475, 31 USPQ2d 1671 (Fed. Cir. 1994); *In re Spada,* 911 F.2d 705, 15 USPQ2d 1655 (Fed. Cir. 1990); *Richardson v. Suzuki Motor Co.,* 868 F.2d 1226, 9 USPQ2d 1913 (Fed. Cir. 1989); *Diversitech Corp. v. Century Steps, Inc.,* 850 F.2d 675, 7 USPQ2d 1315 (Fed. Cir. 1988); *Akzo N.V. v. United States ITC,* 808 F.2d 1471, 1 USPQ2d 1241 (Fed. Cir. 1986); *Orthokinetics, Inc. v. Safety Travel Chairs, Inc.,* 806 F.2d 1565, 1 USPQ2d 1081 (Fed. Cir. 1986); *Rolls-Royce Ltd. v. GTE Valeron Corp.,* 800 F.2d 1101, 231 USPQ 185 (Fed. Cir. 1986); *Kloster Speedsteel AB v. Crucible Inc.,* 793 F.2d 1565, 230 USPQ 81 (Fed. Cir. 1986); *Great Northern Corp. v. Davis Core & Pad Co.,* 782 F.2d 159, 228 USPQ 356 (Fed. Cir. 1986); *In re Donohue,* 766 F.2d 531, 226 USPQ 619 (Fed. Cir. 1985); *W.L. Gore & Assoc. v. Garlock, Inc.,* 721 F.2d 1540, 220 USPQ 303 (Fed. Cir. 1983); *SSIH Equip. S.A. v. United States ITC,* 713 F.2d 746, 218 USPQ 678 (Fed. Cir. 1983).

[5]*Minnesota Min. & Mfg. Co. v. Johnson & Johnson Orthopaedics, Inc.,* 976 F.2d 1559, 24 USPQ2d 1321 (Fed. Cir. 1992).

[6]*Glaverbel S.A. v. Northlake Mkt'g & Supp., Inc.,* 45 F.3d 1550, 33 USPQ2d 1496 (Fed. Cir. 1995).

[7]*Constant v. Advanced Micro-Devices, Inc.,* 848 F.2d 1560, 7 USPQ2d 1057 (Fed. Cir. 1988); *Verdegaal Bros., Inc. v. Union Oil Co.,* 814 F.2d 628, 2 USPQ2d 1051 (Fed. Cir. 1987); *Tyler Refrigeration v. Kysor Indus. Corp.,* 777 F.2d 687, 227 USPQ 845 (Fed. Cir. 1985); *RCA Corp. v. Applied Digital Data Sys., Inc.,* 730 F.2d 1440, 221 USPQ 385 (Fed. Cir. 1984); *Kalman v. Kimberly-Clark Corp.,* 713 F.2d 760, 218 USPQ 781 (Fed. Cir. 1983).

[8]*Richardson v. Suzuki Motor Co.,* 868 F.2d 1226, 9 USPQ2d 1913 (Fed. Cir. 1989); *Carella v. Starlight Archery & Pro Line Co.,* 804 F.2d 135, 231 USPQ 644 (Fed. Cir. 1986); *Lindemann Maschinenfabrik v. American Hoist & Derrick Co.,* 730 F.2d 1452, 221 USPQ 481 (Fed. Cir. 1984); *Connell v. Sears, Roebuck & Co.,* 722 F.2d 1542, 220 USPQ 193 (Fed. Cir. 1983).

[9]*Scripps Clinic & Res. Found. v. Genentech, Inc.,* 927 F.2d 1565, 18 USPQ2d 1001 (Fed. Cir. 1991).

that define the claimed invention. And it is claims, not specifications, that are anticipated.[10]

The corollary of the rule is that absence from the reference of any claimed element negates anticipation.[11] Almost is not enough. A prior art disclosure that almost meets the standard of anticipation may render the claim invalid under §103(a), but it does not anticipate.[12] Thus, anticipation of a patent claim requires a finding that the claim at issue "reads on" a prior art reference. In other words, if granting patent protection on the disputed claim would allow the patentee to exclude the public from practicing the prior art, then that claim is anticipated, regardless of whether it also covers subject matter not in the prior art.[13] Though a reference that lacks an element of the claims cannot anticipate them,[14] an unclaimed difference will not avoid anticipation.[15] Nor will the discovery of a previously unknown property permit the patenting of an old product.[16] If compositions are known, for any use or no use, they are not patentable as compositions, by force of §102. Only if they are new can they be patentable.[17]

It is beyond argument that no utility need be disclosed for a reference to be anticipatory of a claim to an old compound.[18] Recitation

---

[10]*Constant v. Advanced Micro-Devices, Inc.,* 848 F.2d 1560, 7 USPQ2d 1057, 1064 (Fed. Cir. 1988).

[11]*Kloster Speedsteel AB v. Crucible Inc.,* 793 F.2d 1565, 230 USPQ 81 (Fed. Cir. 1986).

[12]*Connell v. Sears, Roebuck & Co.,* 722 F.2d 1542, 220 USPQ 193 (Fed. Cir. 1983). Even though defenses under 35 U.S.C. §§102(a) and (g) may not be adequate, the evidence can be pertinent to the level of skill in the art for purposes of §103. *Orthopedic Equip. Co. v. United States,* 702 F.2d 1005, 217 USPQ 193 (Fed. Cir. 1983).

[13]*Atlas Powder Co. v. IRECO Inc.,* 190 F.3d 1342, 51 USPQ2d 1943 (Fed. Cir. 1999). Specifically, when a patent claims a chemical composition in terms of ranges of elements, any single prior art reference that falls within each of the ranges anticipates the claim. In chemical compounds, a single prior art species within the patent's claimed genus reads on the generic claim and anticipates. *Id.*

[14]*Carman Indus., Inc. v. Wahl,* 724 F.2d 932, 220 USPQ 481 (Fed. Cir. 1983). Whether a change is "material" for purposes of anticipation by public use is a factual question that cannot be resolved against the patentee on summary judgment. *Baker Oil Tools, Inc. v. Geo Vann, Inc.,* 828 F.2d 1588, 4 USPQ2d 1210 (Fed. Cir. 1987).

[15]*SSIH Equip. S.A. v. United States ITC,* 713 F.2d 746, 218 USPQ 678 (Fed. Cir. 1983). The term "consisting essentially of" in a claim does not negate anticipation by a reference that contains, as an essential ingredient, an element not listed in the claim. That term does, however, exclude ingredients that would materially affect the basic and novel characteristics of the claimed composition. *Atlas Powder Co. v. E.I. du Pont & Co.,* 750 F.2d 1569, 224 USPQ 409 (Fed. Cir. 1984).

[16]*Harris Corp. v. IXYS Corp.,* 114 F.3d 1149, 43 USPQ2d 1018 (Fed. Cir. 1997); *Titanium Metals Corp. v. Banner,* 778 F.2d 775, 227 USPQ 773 (Fed. Cir. 1985). That a claim may have the phrase "characterized by good corrosion resistance" does not change the fact that the claim is directed to an old alloy and is thus anticipated. When a claim covers several compositions, as by a recitation of ranges or otherwise, it is anticipated if one of them is in the prior art. *Id.* The discovery of a new property or use of a previously known composition, even when that property and use are unobvious from the prior art, cannot impart patentability to claims to the known composition. Thus the initial inquiry is to the novelty of the composition. Of course, the result may be different where the inventor is claiming the new use as a process. *In re Spada,* 911 F.2d 705, 15 USPQ2d 1655 (Fed. Cir. 1990).

[17]*In re Dillon,* 892 F.2d 1554, 13 USPQ2d 1337 (Fed. Cir. 1989). Products of identical chemical composition cannot have mutually exclusive properties. *In re Spada,* 911 F.2d 705, 15 USPQ2d 1655 (Fed. Cir. 1990).

[18]*In re Schoenwald,* 964 F.2d 1122, 22 USPQ2d 1671 (Fed. Cir. 1992).

of a new intended use for an old product does not make a claim to that old product patentable.[19] But where a reference makes no suggestion of any kind about its structural suitability for the claimed use, despite not explicitly describing anything inconsistent with that use, such a negative pregnant is not enough to show anticipation.[20]

Invalidity under §102 is an affirmative defense and the burden of proof is therefore on the patent challenger.[21] Thus a party asserting that a patent is anticipated under §102 must demonstrate, among other things, identity of invention.[22] There are many ways to express the concept of identity. Anticipation is sometimes said to require that all limitations of a claim be found in a reference, or "fully met" by it.[23] For a prior art reference to anticipate a claim, the reference must disclose each and every element of the claim with sufficient clarity to prove its existence in the prior art. Although this requirement presupposes the knowledge of one skilled in the art, that presumed knowledge does not grant a license to read into the prior art reference teachings that are not there. An expert's conclusory testimony, unsupported by the documentary evidence, cannot supplant the requirement of anticipatory disclosure in the prior art reference itself.[24]

Clearly, that which infringes if later anticipates if earlier.[25] However, that classic test should be modified to be "that which literally infringes," for infringement can occur under the doctrine of equivalents and, in such a situation, there would be no anticipation. Anticipation was, prior to the 1952 Act, used in a broader sense to encompass subject matter that, though different, was not "inventive." This latter concept was replaced with obviousness under §103, and anticipation thereafter became a restricted term of art in patent law, meaning that the claimed invention lacked novelty, or was unpatentable under 35 U.S.C. §102. All infringements of a claim do not "anticipate" in this sense. Some may be infringements under the doctrine of equivalents, which, if one wished to draw a parallel, is somewhat akin to obviousness.[26]

Basically, anticipation requires identity.[27] The identical invention must be shown in as complete detail as is contained in the patent

---

[19]*In re Schreiber,* 128 F.3d 1473, 44 USPQ2d 1429 (Fed. Cir. 1997).

[20]*Rowe v. Dror,* 112 F.3d 473, 42 USPQ2d 1550, 1555 (Fed. Cir. 1997).

[21]*Allied Colloids, Inc. v. American Cyanamid Co.,* 64 F.3d 1570, 35 USPQ2d 1840 (Fed. Cir. 1995).

[22]*Minnesota Min. & Mfg. Co. v. Johnson & Johnson Orthopaedics, Inc.,* 976 F.2d 1559, 24 USPQ2d 1321 (Fed. Cir. 1992).

[23]*Ralston Purina Co. v. Far-Mar-Co, Inc.,* 772 F.2d 1570, 227 USPQ 177 (Fed. Cir. 1985).

[24]*Motorola, Inc. v. Interdigital Tech. Corp.,* 121 F.3d 1461, 43 USPQ2d 1481 (Fed. Cir. 1997).

[25]*Polaroid Corp. v. Eastman Kodak Co.,* 789 F.2d 1556, 229 USPQ 561 (Fed. Cir. 1986). On the other hand, simply because an accused process infringes a prior art patent does not mean that the asserted claim is invalid for anticipation by that prior art patent. *W.L. Gore & Assoc. v. Garlock, Inc.,* 721 F.2d 1540, 220 USPQ 303 (Fed. Cir. 1983).

[26]*Lemar Marine, Inc. v. Barient, Inc.,* 827 F.2d 744, 3 USPQ2d 1766 (Fed. Cir. 1987).

[27]*Tyler Refrigeration v. Kysor Indus. Corp.,* 777 F.2d 687, 227 USPQ 845 (Fed. Cir. 1985); *Shatterproof Glass Corp. v. Libbey-Owens Ford Co.,* 758 F.2d 613, 225 USPQ 634 (Fed. Cir.

claim.[28] Concepts do not anticipate. Notions of concept, essence, or gist are no more useful in the context of §102 than elsewhere, because they divert the factfinder's attention from the subject matter of the invention as a whole.[29] But the law of anticipation does not require that the reference teach what the subject patent teaches.[30]

In deciding the issue of anticipation, the trier of fact must identify the elements of the claims, determine their meaning in light of the specification and prosecution history, and identify corresponding elements disclosed in the allegedly anticipating reference. It is therefore error to treat the claims as a mere catalog of separate parts, in disregard of the part-to-part relationships set forth in the claims that give those claims their meaning.[31] The focus must always be on the entirety of the claimed invention.[32] Despite the need for identity, anticipation is not a matter of ipsissimis verbis.[33]

The rule is that a court may not redraft a claim for purposes of avoiding a defense of anticipation; however, this rule applies where "extraneous" limitations from the specification are being read into the claim wholly apart from any need to interpret what the patentee meant by particular words or phrases in the claim. Thus, no litmus test can be given with respect to when the introductory words of a claim, the preamble, constitute a statement of purpose for a device or are, in themselves, structural limitations of a claim that can be relied upon to avoid anticipation. To say that a preamble statement is a limitation if it gives "meaning to the claim" may merely state the problem rather than lead one to an answer. The effect preamble language should be given can be resolved only on review of the entirety

---

1985); *Rosemount, Inc. v. Beckman Instruments, Inc.*, 727 F.2d 1540, 221 USPQ 1 (Fed. Cir. 1984); *Kalman v. Kimberly-Clark Corp.*, 713 F.2d 760, 218 USPQ 781 (Fed. Cir. 1983).

[28]*Richardson v. Suzuki Motor Co.*, 868 F.2d 1226, 9 USPQ2d 1913 (Fed. Cir. 1989). The claimed invention, as described in appropriately construed claims, must be the same as that of the reference, in order to anticipate. *Glaverbel S.A. v. Northlake Mkt'g & Supp., Inc.*, 45 F.3d 1550, 33 USPQ2d 1496 (Fed. Cir. 1995).

[29]*Panduit Corp. v. Dennison Mfg. Co.*, 774 F.2d 1082, 227 USPQ 337 (Fed. Cir. 1985).

[30]*Kalman v. Kimberly-Clark Corp.*, 713 F.2d 760, 218 USPQ 781, 789 (Fed. Cir. 1983). What a reference teaches is a question of fact. *In re Baird*, 16 F.3d 380, 29 USPQ2d 1550 (Fed. Cir. 1994).

[31]*Lindemann Maschinenfabrik v. American Hoist & Derrick Co.*, 730 F.2d 1452, 221 USPQ 481 (Fed. Cir. 1984). While experts may use the same words to describe both the claimed device and a prior art device, the prior art cannot anticipate the patent simply by possessing identically named parts, unless these parts also have the same structure or otherwise satisfy the claim limitations, and were understood to function in the same way by one skilled in the art. *Applied Med. Res. Corp. v. United States Surgical Corp.*, 147 F.3d 1374, 47 USPQ2d 1289 (Fed. Cir. 1998).

[32]*Structural Rubber Prods. Co. v. Park Rubber Co.*, 749 F.2d 707, 223 USPQ 1264 (Fed. Cir. 1984). See also *Panduit Corp. v. Dennison Mfg. Co.*, 774 F.2d 1082, 227 USPQ 337 (Fed. Cir. 1985).

[33]*Akzo N.V. v. United States ITC*, 808 F.2d 1471, 1 USPQ2d 1241 (Fed. Cir. 1986); *Structural Rubber Prods. Co. v. Park Rubber Co.*, 749 F.2d 707, 223 USPQ 1264 (Fed. Cir. 1984). An anticipatory reference need not duplicate word for word what is in the claims. *Standard Havens Prods., Inc. v. Gencor Indus., Inc.*, 953 F.2d 1360, 21 USPQ2d 1321 (Fed. Cir. 1992).

of the patent to gain an understanding of what the inventors actually invented and intended to encompass by the claim.[34]

Despite an early indication that equivalence may be sufficient for anticipation,[35] the court seems to have retreated somewhat when it found error in an instruction to that effect, terming it a legal theory pertinent to obviousness under §103 rather than anticipation under §102.[36] Nonetheless, equivalence may apply in a means-plus-function setting. Where an element is claimed as a means plus a function, the prior art must disclose structure capable of performing the functional limitation of the means in order to anticipate. The prior art element must at least be equivalent: it must function in substantially the same way to obtain substantially the same result.[37]

(b) Inherency

The prior art disclosure need not be express in order to anticipate.[38] Even if a prior art inventor does not recognize a function of his or her process, the process can anticipate if that function was inherent.[39] To establish inherency, the extrinsic evidence must make clear that the missing descriptive matter is necessarily present in the thing described in the reference, and that it would be so recognized by persons of ordinary skill.[40] Inherency is not necessarily coterminous with the knowledge of those of ordinary skill in the art. Artisans of ordinary skill may not recognize the inherent characteristics or functioning of the prior art. However, the discovery of a previously unappreciated property of a prior art composition, or of a scientific explanation for the prior art's functioning, does not render the old composition patentably new to the discoverer. Insufficient prior understanding of the inherent properties of a known composition does not defeat a finding of anticipation.[41]

---

[34]*Corning Glass Works v. Sumitomo Elec. U.S.A., Inc.,* 868 F.2d 1251, 9 USPQ2d 1962 (Fed. Cir. 1989).

[35]*Structural Rubber Prods. Co. v. Park Rubber Co.,* 749 F.2d 707, 223 USPQ 1264 (Fed. Cir. 1984).

[36]*Richardson v. Suzuki Motor Co.,* 868 F.2d 1226, 9 USPQ2d 1913 (Fed. Cir. 1989). See also text accompanying note 26 above.

[37]*RCA Corp. v. Applied Digital Data Sys., Inc.,* 730 F.2d 1440, 221 USPQ 385 (Fed. Cir. 1984). See also *In re Bond,* 910 F.2d 831, 15 USPQ2d 1566 (Fed. Cir. 1990).

[38]*Standard Havens Prods., Inc. v. Gencor Indus., Inc.,* 953 F.2d 1360, 21 USPQ2d 1321 (Fed. Cir. 1992); *Tyler Refrigeration v. Kysor Indus. Corp.,* 777 F.2d 687, 227 USPQ 845 (Fed. Cir. 1985); *RCA Corp. v. Applied Digital Data Sys., Inc.,* 730 F.2d 1440, 221 USPQ 385 (Fed. Cir. 1984); *Kalman v. Kimberly-Clark Corp.,* 713 F.2d 760, 218 USPQ 781 (Fed. Cir. 1983).

[39]*Verdegaal Bros., Inc. v. Union Oil Co.,* 814 F.2d 628, 2 USPQ2d 1051 (Fed. Cir. 1987). Where the result is a necessary consequence of what was deliberately intended, it is of no import that the authors of a reference did not appreciate the results. *Mehl/Biophile Int'l Corp. v. Milgraum,* 192 F.3d 1365, 52 USPQ2d 1303 (Fed. Cir. 1999). But an accidental or unwitting duplication of an invention cannot constitute an anticipation. *Scaltech Inc. v. Retec/Tetra L.L.C.,* 156 F.3d 1037, 48 USPQ2d 1037 (Fed. Cir. 1998).

[40]*In re Robertson,* 169 F.3d 743, 49 USPQ2d 1949 (Fed. Cir. 1999).

[41]*Atlas Powder Co. v. IRECO Inc.,* 190 F.3d 1342, 51 USPQ2d 1943 (Fed. Cir. 1999).

Inherency, however, may not be established by probabilities or possibilities. The mere fact that a certain thing may result from a given set of circumstances is not sufficient.[42] Occasional results are not inherent.[43] Under the principles of inherency, if a structure in the prior art necessarily functions in accordance with the limitations of a process or method claim, the claim is anticipated. This is not to say that the discovery of a new use for an old structure based on unknown properties of the structure might not be patentable to the discoverer as a process. However, merely setting out the scientific explanation of an inherent function is not patentable.[44] Congress has not seen fit to permit the patenting of an old product by one who has only discovered its inherent properties.[45]

The court seems inclined to draw a fine line between cases where property limitations need to be shown for anticipation and cases where such limitations need not be met. Structure alone may be inadequate to define the invention, making it appropriate to define the invention in part by property limitations.[46]

Of course, §102 prohibits the issuance of a patent if the reference discloses individual chemical species falling within the generic claims sought. In other words, species anticipate genera.[47] But the converse is not necessarily so.[48]

---

[42]*Scaltech Inc. v. Retec/Tetra L.L.C.*, 156 F.3d 1193, 51 USPQ2d 1055 (Fed. Cir. 1999); *In re Robertson*, 169 F.3d 743, 49 USPQ2d 1949 (Fed. Cir. 1999).

[43]*Mehl/Biophile Int'l Corp. v. Milgraum*, 192 F.3d 1365, 52 USPQ2d 1303, 1306 (Fed. Cir. 1999). It is possible that the court may be of the view that there is inherency only if a prior art example always yields the claimed invention. See *Glaxo, Inc. v. Novopharm Ltd.*, 52 F.3d 1043, 34 USPQ2d 1565 (Fed. Cir. 1995).

[44]*In re King*, 801 F.2d 1324, 231 USPQ 136 (Fed. Cir. 1986). If the natural result flowing from the operation of the process offered for sale would necessarily result in achievement of each of the claim limitations, then the claimed invention was offered for sale. *Scaltech Inc. v. Retec/Tetra L.L.C.*, 156 F.3d 1193, 51 USPQ2d 1055 (Fed. Cir. 1999). But the mere fact that a certain thing may result from a given set of circumstances is not sufficient to establish inherency. That which may be inherent is not necessarily known. *In re Rijckaert*, 9 F.3d 1531, 28 USPQ2d 1955 (Fed. Cir. 1993).

[45]*Titanium Metals Corp. v. Banner*, 778 F.2d 775, 227 USPQ 773 (Fed. Cir. 1985).

[46]*E.I. duPont & Co. v. Phillips Petroleum Co.*, 849 F.2d 1430, 7 USPQ2d 1129 (Fed. Cir. 1988). In the case of a polymer, structure alone was insufficient, and the patentee was entitled to define the invention in terms of properties as well. In such a situation, one attempting to invalidate the claim on grounds of anticipation must show that the prior art composition possessed the properties, although it need not be shown that the prior art inventor was aware of those properties. *Id.* Compare *Titanium Metals Corp. v. Banner*, 778 F.2d 775, 227 USPQ 773 (Fed. Cir. 1985), which dealt with an alloy. Once the alloy disclosed in the prior art reference was determined to possess the structural limitations of the claim, the burden shifted to the patentee to show that the alloy disclosed in the reference did not possess the claimed property.

[47]*In re Gosteli*, 872 F.2d 1008, 10 USPQ2d 1614 (Fed. Cir. 1989). The description of specific preferences in connection with a generic formula is determinative in any analysis of anticipation under §102. *Merck & Co. v. Biocraft Labs., Inc.*, 874 F.2d 804, 10 USPQ2d 1843 (Fed. Cir. 1989).

[48]In *Corning Glass Works v. Sumitomo Elec. U.S.A., Inc.*, 868 F.2d 1251, 9 USPQ2d 1962 (Fed. Cir. 1989), a prior art reference did not teach the specific constituent in question, but used a generic term and disclosed a list of several other specific examples. The challenger argued that the reference inherently taught the specific constituent, and thus anticipated, because it did not exclude the constituent. The court quickly rejected this argument, observing that if the theory were correct, a claim to a genus would inherently disclose all species within the genus.

Whether a claim limitation is inherent in a prior art reference for purposes of anticipation is a question of fact.[49] For a summary determination to be proper, there must be no genuine dispute whether the limitations of the claimed invention are disclosed, either explicitly or inherently, by an allegedly anticipating prior art reference.[50]

Although inherency is usually encountered in the §102 setting, it can also arise in the context of §103,[51] as will be seen in §4.4. If the inherency does not result in anticipation, then one must ask whether the inherency would have been obvious.[52]

(c) *Enablement*

In order to anticipate, a prior art reference must be enabling, thus placing the allegedly disclosed matter in the possession of the public.[53] The question of anticipation over a printed publication is whether the claims encompass and would enable the patentee to exclude others from making, using, or selling a product described in the publication.[54] The proper role of nonenabling references would be in the context of obviousness under 35 U.S.C. §103(a).[55]

---

[49]*Finnigan Corp. v. United States ITC*, 180 F.3d 1354, 51 USPQ2d 1001 (Fed. Cir. 1999). Whether a claim feature is inherent in a prior art reference is a factual issue on which extrinsic evidence may be submitted. *Hazani v. United States ITC*, 126 F.3d 1473, 44 USPQ2d 1358 (Fed. Cir. 1997).

[50]*Hazani v. United States ITC*, 126 F.3d 1473, 44 USPQ2d 1358 (Fed. Cir. 1997).

[51]*In re Napier*, 55 F.3d 610, 34 USPQ2d 1782 (Fed. Cir. 1995); *In re Grasselli*, 713 F.2d 731, 218 USPQ 769 (Fed. Cir. 1983).

[52]*Continental Can Co. v. Monsanto Co.*, 948 F.2d 1264, 20 USPQ2d 1746 (Fed. Cir. 1991); *Kloster Speedsteel AB v. Crucible Inc.*, 793 F.2d 1565, 230 USPQ 81 (Fed. Cir. 1986).

[53]*Akzo N.V. v. United States ITC*, 808 F.2d 1471, 1 USPQ2d 1241 (Fed. Cir. 1986); *Ashland Oil, Inc. v. Delta Resins & Refracs., Inc.*, 776 F.2d 281, 227 USPQ 657 (Fed. Cir. 1985); *Reading & Bates Constr. Co. v. Baker Energy Res. Corp.*, 748 F.2d 645, 223 USPQ 1168 (Fed. Cir. 1984). Apparently the fact that a system is experimental does not detract from its anticipatory value where it is described in an enabling document. *In re Baxter Travenol Labs.*, 952 F.2d 388, 21 USPQ2d 1281 (Fed. Cir. 1991).

[54]*Titanium Metals Corp. v. Banner*, 778 F.2d 775, 227 USPQ 773 (Fed. Cir. 1985). In *Helifix Ltd. v. Blok-Lok Ltd.*, 208 F.3d 1339, 54 USPQ2d 1299 (Fed. Cir. 2000), the reference publication did not expressly disclose a tool capable of practicing the method recited in the patent. The trial court nevertheless relied upon the fact that the PTO had issued a restriction requirement between the claimed method and the specific tool described in the patent specification. It interpreted the restriction requirement as reflecting the PTO's determination that other tools could be devised to practice the method. This was error. The restriction requirement between the method claimed and the specific tool described in the specification in no way bear on the enablement of a different tool.

[55]*Symbol Tech., Inc. v. Opticon, Inc.*, 935 F.2d 1569, 19 USPQ2d 1241 (Fed. Cir. 1991). In *Paperless Accounting, Inc. v. Bay Area Rapid Transit Sys.*, 804 F.2d 659, 231 USPQ 649 (Fed. Cir. 1986), the trial court had held that the claims in issue were not supported by a parent application, and that intervening foreign counterparts of the parent application anticipated the claims. In view of the fact that the foreign counterparts corresponded substantially to the disclosure of the parent, the Federal Circuit was troubled by that result. It reversed, reasoning that if the parent did not support the claims, it did not enable them; accordingly, neither did the foreign counterparts contain an enabling disclosure, and they could not therefore anticipate. In *Beckman Instr., Inc. v. LKB Produkter AB*, 892 F.2d 1547, 13 USPQ2d 1301 (Fed. Cir. 1989), the Federal Circuit approved a jury instruction to the effect that references relied upon to

Further, the reference must describe the applicant's claimed invention sufficiently to have placed a person of ordinary skill in the field of the invention in possession of it.[56] However, in the case of a genus claim that is anticipated by a prior art species, it may not be necessary to satisfy either of the principal requirements under 35 U.S.C. §112—written description and enablement—in order to render the genus unpatentable under §102.[57] It is possible for a specification to enable the practice of an invention as broadly as it is claimed and still not describe that invention. There is also a distinction between claim-anticipating disclosures and claim-supporting disclosures. A description of a single embodiment of broadly claimed subject matter constitutes a description of the invention for anticipation purposes, whereas the same information in a specification might not alone be enough to provide a description of that invention for purposes of adequate disclosure.[58]

(d) Combining References

The Federal Circuit regards it as hornbook law that anticipation must be found in a single reference, device, or process.[59] This does not mean, however, that references cannot be combined for purposes of anticipation.[60] Additional references may be used to interpret the allegedly anticipating reference and shed light on what it would have meant to those skilled in the art at the time.[61]

To serve as an anticipation when a reference is silent about an asserted inherent characteristic, the gap in the reference may be filled by recourse to extrinsic evidence. Such evidence must make clear that the missing descriptive matter is necessarily present in the thing

---

support a rejection for obviousness must provide an enabling disclosure. This holding must be reconciled with the statement, in the same case, that if a reference discloses an inoperative device, it is nonetheless prior art for all that it teaches.

[56]*In re Spada,* 911 F.2d 705, 15 USPQ2d 1655 (Fed. Cir. 1990). Express enablement is apparently unnecessary if the art is sufficiently advanced that one of ordinary skill would be capable of providing the necessary technical details. See *In re Paulsen,* 30 F.3d 1475, 31 USPQ2d 1671 (Fed. Cir. 1994).

[57]*Chester v. Miller,* 906 F.2d 1574, 15 USPQ2d 1333 (Fed. Cir. 1990). Here this reasoning led to a seemingly anomalous result. A party to an interference was attempting to rely upon an earlier filing date of a parent in a chain of applications that led to the CIP application under consideration. A patent had issued from one of the earlier applications, and the PTO rejected the party's CIP claims as anticipated. The party was barred from relying on the earlier filing date, because the parent did not satisfy the written description requirement for the subject matter of the CIP claims. Nonetheless, the issued patent anticipated. The court squarely held that even though a patent might satisfy a written description as to its own narrower claims, it might not satisfy the requirement as to broader claims that it nonetheless anticipates. In dictum, the court indicated that the same logic could apply in the enablement context.

[58]See *Vas-Cath Inc. v. Mahurkar,* 935 F.2d 1555, 19 USPQ2d 1111, 1115 (Fed. Cir. 1991).

[59]*Studiengesellschaft Kohle v. Dart Indus., Inc.,* 726 F.2d 724, 220 USPQ 841 (Fed. Cir. 1984).

[60]*In re Donohue,* 766 F.2d 531, 226 USPQ 619 (Fed. Cir. 1985).

[61]*Studiengesellschaft Kohle v. Dart Indus., Inc.,* 726 F.2d 724, 220 USPQ 841 (Fed. Cir. 1984).

described in the reference, and that it would be so recognized by persons of ordinary skill. Inherency, however, may not be established by probabilities or possibilities. The mere fact that a certain thing may result from a given set of circumstances is not sufficient. But if the disclosure is sufficient to show that the natural result flowing from the operation as taught would result in the performance of the questioned function, the disclosure should be regarded as sufficient. This modest flexibility in the rule that anticipation requires that every element of the claims appear in a single reference accommodates situations where the common knowledge of technologists is not recorded in the reference, that is, where technological facts are known to those in the field of the invention but not to judges.[62]

It is appropriate to look to a second reference to see whether the first gives possession of the invention to a person of ordinary skill in the art—in other words, to determine whether the first is enabling.[63] But it would be improper to rely upon a second reference for suggestion or motivation to combine teachings to meet the limitation—this is proper only under 35 U.S.C. §103.[64] Anticipation does not contemplate a random picking and choosing of prior art to find an element that will succeed.[65]

Incorporation by reference. Material not explicitly contained in the single, prior art document may still be considered for purposes of anticipation if that material is incorporated by reference into the

---

[62]*Continental Can Co. v. Monsanto Co.*, 948 F.2d 1264, 20 USPQ2d 1746 (Fed. Cir. 1991). For purposes of anticipation, extrinsic evidence may be considered when it is used to explain but not expand the meaning of a reference. *In re Baxter Travenol Labs.*, 952 F.2d 388, 21 USPQ2d 1281 (Fed. Cir. 1991).

[63]*In re Donohue*, 766 F.2d 531, 226 USPQ 619 (Fed. Cir. 1985).

[64]*In re Donohue*, 766 F.2d 531, 226 USPQ 619 (Fed. Cir. 1985); *Studiengesellschaft Kohle v. Dart Indus., Inc.*, 726 F.2d 724, 220 USPQ 841 (Fed. Cir. 1984). It is sometimes appropriate to consider extrinsic evidence to explain the disclosure of a reference. But such factual elaboration is necessarily of limited scope and probative value, for a finding of anticipation requires that all aspects of the claimed invention were already described in a single reference—a finding that is not supportable if it is necessary to prove facts beyond those disclosed in the reference in order to meet the claim limitations. The role of extrinsic evidence is to educate the decision maker to what the reference meant to persons of ordinary skill in the field of the invention, not to fill gaps in the reference. If it is necessary to reach beyond the boundaries of a single reference to provide missing disclosure of the claimed invention, the proper ground is not §102 anticipation, but §103 obviousness. *Scripps Clinic & Res. Found. v. Genentech, Inc.*, 927 F.2d 1565, 18 USPQ2d 1001 (Fed. Cir. 1991). The court seems willing to hold that a reference anticipates a claim if it discloses the claimed invention such that a skilled artisan could take its teachings in combination with his or her own knowledge of the particular art and thereby be in possession of the invention. *In re Graves*, 69 F.3d 1147, 36 USPQ2d 1697 (Fed. Cir. 1995). But is the court saying that in a situation where a secondary reference would normally be necessary, it can be dispensed with if the knowledge of a person of ordinary skill in the art can supply the missing teaching? If so, caution is suggested. This approach could further blur the boundary between §102 and §103.

[65]*Akzo N.V. v. United States ITC*, 808 F.2d 1471, 1 USPQ2d 1241 (Fed. Cir. 1986). The description of specific preferences in connection with a generic formula is determinative in an analysis of anticipation under §102. But in a §103(a) inquiry the fact that a specific embodiment is taught to be preferred is not controlling, since all disclosures of the prior art, including

document. Incorporation by reference provides a method for integrating material from various documents into a host document—a patent or printed publication in an anticipation determination—by citing such material in a manner that makes clear that the material is effectively part of the host document as if it were explicitly contained therein. To incorporate material by reference, the host document must identify with detailed particularity what specific material it incorporates and clearly indicate where that material is found in the various documents. Whether and to what extent material has been incorporated by reference into a host document is a question of law. The standard of one reasonably skilled in the art should be used to determine whether the host document describes the material to be incorporated by reference with sufficient particularity. No necessary contradiction exists given that incorporation by reference is a question of law while anticipation is a question of fact. Anticipation, put simply, requires that every element of the claimed invention be previously described in a single reference. Thus, if incorporation by reference comes into play in an anticipation determination, the court's role is to determine what material in addition to the host document constitutes the single reference. The factfinder's role, in turn, is to determine whether that single reference describes the claimed invention.[66]

(e) Relation to 35 U.S.C. §103(a)

It can be very important whether a PTO Board rejection is under 35 U.S.C. §102 or §103. In an obviousness setting, the art must contain a suggestion or motivation to modify it to function like the claimed invention. In an anticipation setting, where the only difference is in functional claim language, the applicant must show that the prior art does not have that function.[67] The court has, in the anticipation context, eschewed certain analytical techniques that it routinely uses in the obviousness setting. Thus, whether a reference is analogous art is irrelevant to whether that reference anticipates. A reference may be from an entirely different field of endeavor than that of the claimed invention or may be directed to an entirely different problem from the one addressed by the inventor, yet the reference will still anticipate if it explicitly or inherently discloses every limitation recited in the claims.[68] Also, a reference is no less anticipatory if, after disclosing the invention, the reference then disparages it. Thus, the

---

unpreferred embodiments, must be considered. *Merck & Co. v. Biocraft Labs., Inc.*, 874 F.2d 804, 10 USPQ2d 1843 (Fed. Cir. 1989).

[66]*Advanced Display Sys. Inc. v. Kent State Univ.*, 212 F.3d 1272, 54 USPQ2d 1673 (Fed. Cir. 2000). The doctrine of incorporation by reference has its roots in the law of wills and contracts. In those areas of jurisprudence, whether material is incorporated by reference presents a question of law. Logic therefore requires that incorporation by reference in the field of patent law is also a question of law. *Id.*

[67]*In re Mills*, 916 F.2d 680, 16 USPQ2d 1430 (Fed. Cir. 1990).

[68]*In re Schreiber*, 128 F.3d 1473, 44 USPQ2d 1429 (Fed. Cir. 1997).

question whether a reference "teaches away" from the invention is inapplicable to an anticipation analysis.[69]

Nonetheless, despite its best intentions and efforts, the Federal Circuit itself has been unable to achieve total purity in separating its analyses under §§102 and 103(a). Although it recognizes quite properly that a court is not "inescapably led" to a conclusion of obviousness just because the anticipation question was close,[70] the court has repeatedly remarked that anticipation is "the epitome of obviousness."[71]

With all respect, such statements are neither necessary nor harmless.[72] In one case a jury answered interrogatories about public use or sale in the affirmative but obviousness interrogatories in the negative. Apparently this jury did not feel that anticipation by public use or sale epitomized obviousness.[73] Moreover, such statements can lead to the view that a nonidentical device can be regarded as anticipating when the differences are not patentable distinctions.[74] This would be a very dangerous approach, for it would rob the inventor of the right to proffer objective evidence of nonobviousness.

Nonetheless, some shortcuts do make sense. Thus, where the district court held an independent claim to be nonobvious, it was reasonable to reverse, on a fortiori grounds, a holding that a dependent claim was anticipated (or obvious).[75]

(f) Prima Facie Anticipation

In an interference, if the PTO establishes a prima facie case of anticipation and enters an order to show cause why judgment should

---

[69]*Celeritas Tech. Ltd. v. Rockwell Int'l Corp.*, 150 F.3d 1354, 47 USPQ2d 1516 (Fed. Cir. 1998).

[70]*RCA Corp. v. Applied Digital Data Sys., Inc.*, 730 F.2d 1440, 221 USPQ 385 (Fed. Cir. 1984).

[71]*Jones v. Hardy*, 727 F.2d 1524, 220 USPQ 1021 (Fed. Cir. 1984). Although it is never necessary to so hold, a disclosure that anticipates also renders obvious, for anticipation is the epitome of obviousness, while the need to determine obviousness presumes anticipation is lacking. *Connell v. Sears, Roebuck & Co.*, 722 F.2d 1542, 220 USPQ 193 (Fed. Cir. 1983). Obviousness follows ipso facto from a conclusion of anticipation. *RCA Corp. v. Applied Digital Data Sys., Inc.*, 730 F.2d 1440, 221 USPQ 385 (Fed. Cir. 1984).

[72]We can all conceive of situations where anticipation may turn on a razor-thin point of inherency, yet the invention is completely unobvious. Consider a claim to a transuranic element that can be demonstrated by modern technology to have existed in an old atomic reactor, unbeknownst to anyone at the time. That element may well be anticipated, but all of the underlying factual inquiries would point to a conclusion of nonobviousness.

[73]*Allen Organ Co. v. Kimball Int'l, Inc.*, 839 F.2d 1556, 5 USPQ2d 1769 (Fed. Cir. 1988). The court had no difficulty in reconciling this inconsistency with the judgment of invalidity. The jury was instructed that public use and sale was a different subject than anticipation, and its findings on that question were perfectly consistent with the obviousness findings. The court felt it likely that the jury did not view the public use and sale transactions as part of the prior art for purposes of the obviousness inquiry.

[74]*Rosemount, Inc. v. Beckman Instruments, Inc.*, 727 F.2d 1540, 221 USPQ 1, 6 (Fed. Cir. 1984).

[75]*Hartness Int'l, Inc. v. Simplimatic Eng'g Co.*, 819 F.2d 1100, 2 USPQ2d 1826 (Fed. Cir. 1987). In *Ultradent Prods., Inc. v. Life-Like Cosmetics, Inc.*, 127 F.3d 1065, 44 USPQ2d 1336

not be entered against a party, the burden shifts to the party to overcome the prima facie case. Thus, if the PTO establishes a prima facie case that the prior art reference discloses every element of a claim, the burden would shift to the applicant to show that the reference does not enable or contain a written description of the anticipating subject matter.[76] A showing of virtual identity of compositions is sufficient to support a prima facie case of lack of novelty. In response, an applicant may argue that the inference of lack of novelty was not properly drawn, for example, if the PTO did not correctly apply or understand the subject matter of the reference, or if it drew unwarranted conclusions therefrom. However, when the PTO shows a sound basis for believing that the products of the applicant and the prior art are the same, the applicant has the burden of showing that they are not. A simple showing of newly discovered properties is insufficient, because such properties do not impart patentability to a known composition. Thus the applicant would have to overcome the apparent chemical identity of the claimed products and those of the prior art.[77]

The prima facie unpatentability analysis applies to inherent anticipation. A patent applicant is free to recite features of an apparatus either structurally or functionally. Yet choosing to define an element functionally, by what it does, carries with it a risk. Where the PTO has reason to believe that a functional limitation asserted to be critical for establishing novelty in the claimed subject matter may, in fact, be an inherent characteristic of the prior art, it possesses the authority to require the applicant to prove that the subject matter shown to be in the prior art does not possess the characteristic relied on. Thus, the PTO may find that a reference establishes a prima facie case of anticipation. The burden then shifts to the applicant to show that the prior art structure did not inherently possess the functionally defined limitations of the claimed apparatus.[78]

(g) *Review of Anticipation Findings*

Not unlike a determination of infringement, a determination of anticipation, as well as obviousness, involves two steps. First is construing the claim, a question of law for the court, followed by, in the case of anticipation or obviousness, a comparison of the construed

---

(Fed. Cir. 1997), the district court held a claim not invalid for anticipation on summary judgment, and the jury found the claim nonobvious. On appeal, the Federal Circuit reversed the summary judgment, finding anticipation. It brushed aside the argument that there is a conflict between a finding of anticipation and a jury verdict of nonobviousness, mainly on the ground that the error as to anticipation prejudiced the obviousness defense as well.

[76] *Chester v. Miller,* 906 F.2d 1574, 15 USPQ2d 1333 (Fed. Cir. 1990).

[77] *In re Spada,* 911 F.2d 705, 15 USPQ2d 1655 (Fed. Cir. 1990). The court seems to be saying that it is not enough to show different properties and then simply argue that because of that the compositions must be different. Rather, the court is requiring a positive showing of structural differences in the compositions themselves.

[78] *In re Schreiber,* 128 F.3d 1473, 44 USPQ2d 1429 (Fed. Cir. 1997).

claim to the prior art. This comparison process involves fact finding, and is for the factfinder in the first instance.[79] What a reference teaches is a question of fact.[80] Anticipation[81] and identity[82] are questions of fact. There is a separate presumption of novelty,[83] and the facts underlying a determination of anticipation must be proven by clear and convincing evidence.[84] The teaching cannot be vague.[85]

As a question of fact, anticipation is subject to review under the clearly erroneous standard.[86] Federal Circuit review of a finding of anticipation is conducted under the same standard whether it was made by a district court or by the PTO Board.[87] In the case of an ITC proceeding, the question is reviewed under the substantial evidence standard.[88]

From a jury's verdict of patent validity, it may be presumed that the jury found that no prior art reference completely embodied the method or apparatus of the claims in suit.[89] Thus, in the absence of special interrogatories, it is presumed from a general verdict of validity that the jury found differences between the claimed inventions and the prior art.[90] The appellate burden of the patent challenger in such a case is to establish that a reasonable juror could not have

---

[79]*Key Pharm. Inc. v. Hercon Labs. Corp.*, 161 F.3d 709, 48 USPQ2d 1911 (Fed. Cir. 1998).

[80]*In re Baird*, 16 F.3d 380, 29 USPQ2d 1550 (Fed. Cir. 1994).

[81]E.g., *Akzo N.V. v. United States ITC*, 808 F.2d 1471, 1 USPQ2d 1241 (Fed. Cir. 1986); *Carman Indus., Inc. v. Wahl*, 724 F.2d 932, 220 USPQ 481 (Fed. Cir. 1983).

[82]E.g., *Tyler Refrigeration v. Kysor Indus. Corp.*, 777 F.2d 687, 227 USPQ 845 (Fed. Cir. 1985); *Shatterproof Glass Corp. v. Libbey-Owens Ford Co.*, 758 F.2d 613, 225 USPQ 634 (Fed. Cir. 1985).

[83]*Structural Rubber Prods. Co. v. Park Rubber Co.*, 749 F.2d 707, 223 USPQ 1264 (Fed. Cir. 1984).

[84]*Diversitech Corp. v. Century Steps, Inc.*, 850 F.2d 675, 7 USPQ2d 1315 (Fed. Cir. 1988); *Carella v. Starlight Archery & Pro Line Co.*, 804 F.2d 135, 231 USPQ 644 (Fed. Cir. 1986).

[85]*W.L. Gore & Assoc. v. Garlock, Inc.*, 721 F.2d 1540, 220 USPQ 303 (Fed. Cir. 1983).

[86]*Glaxo, Inc. v. Novopharm Ltd.*, 52 F.3d 1043, 34 USPQ2d 1565 (Fed. Cir. 1995); *Glaverbel S.A. v. Northlake Mkt'g & Supp., Inc.*, 45 F.3d 1550, 33 USPQ2d 1496 (Fed. Cir. 1995); *In re Paulsen*, 30 F.3d 1475, 31 USPQ2d 1671 (Fed. Cir. 1994); *Minnesota Min. & Mfg. Co. v. Johnson & Johnson Orthopaedics, Inc.*, 976 F.2d 1559, 24 USPQ2d 1321 (Fed. Cir. 1992); *Diversitech Corp. v. Century Steps, Inc.*, 850 F.2d 675, 7 USPQ2d 1315 (Fed. Cir. 1988); *Allen Archery, Inc. v. Browning Mfg. Co.*, 819 F.2d 1087, 2 USPQ2d 1490 (Fed. Cir. 1987); *In re King*, 801 F.2d 1324, 231 USPQ 136 (Fed. Cir. 1986); *Tyler Refrigeration v. Kysor Indus. Corp.*, 777 F.2d 687, 227 USPQ 845 (Fed. Cir. 1985); *Lindemann Maschinenfabrik v. American Hoist & Derrick Co.*, 730 F.2d 1452, 221 USPQ 481 (Fed. Cir. 1984).

[87]*In re King*, 801 F.2d 1324, 231 USPQ 136 (Fed. Cir. 1986). Anticipation is a question of fact, and a Board decision on that question is reviewed for clear error. *In re Baxter Travenol Labs.*, 952 F.2d 388, 21 USPQ2d 1281 (Fed. Cir. 1991).

[88]*Texas Instr., Inc. v. United States ITC*, 988 F.2d 1165, 26 USPQ2d 1018 (Fed. Cir. 1993).

[89]*Shatterproof Glass Corp. v. Libbey-Owens Ford Co.*, 758 F.2d 613, 225 USPQ 634 (Fed. Cir. 1985).

[90]*Perkin-Elmer Corp. v. Computervision Corp.*, 732 F.2d 888, 221 USPQ 669 (Fed. Cir. 1984). But cf. *Allen Organ Co. v. Kimball Int'l, Inc.*, 839 F.2d 1556, 5 USPQ2d 1769 (Fed. Cir. 1988). A jury instruction that anticipation is established by a prior art disclosure that is "substantially the same," or that does not differ in "significant particulars," is erroneous. *Jamesbury Corp. v. Litton Indus. Prods., Inc.*, 756 F.2d 1556, 225 USPQ 253 (Fed. Cir. 1985).

found that the challenger had failed to overcome the presumption of novelty.[91]

Where a court of appeals had previously reversed a holding of anticipation, that holding is law of the case. The infringer therefore could not later advance the theory that the patent was invalid on the ground that it only represented the discovery of an inherent quality of the prior art.[92]

§3.3 Originality—Derivation

According to 35 U.S.C. §102(f), a person is not entitled to a patent if "he did not himself invent the subject matter sought to be patented." This simply states a fundamental principle of American patent law— what you patent must be your own invention: you cannot patent another's invention, nor can you patent an invention imported from abroad. As the Federal Circuit's predecessor court said, "being an inventor might be regarded as a preliminary legal requirement, for if he has not invented something, if he comes with something he knows was invented by someone else, he has no right even to approach the door" of the PTO.[93]

Thus, §102(f) requires that the patentee be the actual inventor of the subject matter patented. Derivation is reviewed as a question of fact. To show derivation, the party asserting invalidity must prove both prior conception of the invention by another and communication of that conception to the patentee.[94] It now seems clear that, for derivation, a communication of the complete claimed invention, in enabling detail, is required.[95]

---

[91]*Perkin-Elmer Corp. v. Computervision Corp.,* 732 F.2d 888, 221 USPQ 669 (Fed. Cir. 1984). Because anticipation is a factual determination, the critical question in the JNOV context is whether a reasonable juror could have found that the reference failed to anticipate; in the context of a motion for a new trial, it is whether the trial court abused its discretion in determining that a finding of no anticipation was not against the clear weight of the evidence. *Standard Havens Prods., Inc. v. Gencor Indus., Inc.,* 953 F.2d 1360, 21 USPQ2d 1321 (Fed. Cir. 1992).

[92]*Jones v. Hardy,* 727 F.2d 1524, 220 USPQ 1021, 1025 (Fed. Cir. 1984).

[93]*In re Bergy,* 596 F.2d 952, 201 USPQ 352 (CCPA 1979).

[94]*Gambro Lundia AB v. Baxter Healthcare Corp.,* 110 F.3d 1573, 42 USPQ2d 1378 (Fed. Cir. 1997).

[95]*Gambro Lundia AB v. Baxter Healthcare Corp.,* 110 F.3d 1573, 42 USPQ2d 1378 (Fed. Cir. 1997). In *Gambro,* the court indicated that §102(f) does not implicate the obviousness inquiry. This was contrary to its hint, in *New England Braiding Co. v. A.W. Chesterton Co.,* 970 F.2d 878, 23 USPQ2d 1622 (Fed. Cir. 1992), that there might be a §102(f)/§103 defense. The court subsequently expressly passed the question in *Lamb-Weston, Inc. v. McCain Foods, Ltd.,* 78 F.3d 540, 37 USPQ2d 1856 (Fed. Cir. 1996). Most recently, in *Oddzon Prods., Inc. v. Just Toys, Inc.,* 122 F.3d 1396, 43 USPQ2d 1641 (Fed. Cir. 1997), it squarely held, without even mentioning *Gambro,* that §102(f) does indeed define prior art that can be combined with other references under §103. Apparently the only way to rationalize these decisions is to conclude that, when the issue is invalidity under §102(f), the communication must have been a fully anticipatory concept; when the issue is obviousness, under §103, the communication of any relevant concept is to be treated as prior art, even though it does not anticipate the claimed

Prior conception, which must be proven by facts supported by clear and convincing evidence, is reviewed as a question of law based on underlying factual findings.[96] An inventor's testimony respecting the facts surrounding a claim of derivation cannot, standing alone, rise to the level of clear and convincing proof. Throughout the history of determination of patent rights, oral testimony by an alleged inventor asserting priority over a patentee's rights is regarded with skepticism, and as a result such testimony must be supported by some type of corroborating evidence.[97]

Although derivation and priority are akin in that both focus on inventorship, they are distinct concepts. A claim that a patentee derived an invention addresses originality—who invented the claimed subject matter. In a §102(f) attack on a patent or patent application, the proponent asserts that the patentee did not invent the claimed subject matter because the patentee derived the invention from another. The ultimate question of whether a patentee derived an invention from another is one of fact.[98] In an originality context the issue is not who is the first or prior inventor, but who made the invention. The inventorship issue to be decided is merely who conceived the invention for which patent protection is sought, and not who first conceived that invention.[99]

The Federal Circuit sometimes encounters questions relating to whether a particular person was or was not part of the "inventive entity" and thus should or should not be joined as an inventor.[100]

---

invention. One is left to wonder how the *Gambro* decision escaped the notice of the *Oddzon* panel and, if it did not, how that panel privately rationalized it.

[96]*Gambro Lundia AB v. Baxter Healthcare Corp.*, 110 F.3d 1573, 42 USPQ2d 1378 (Fed. Cir. 1997). While an inventor's statements made during the course of litigation might in some circumstances justify a court in concluding that the named inventor "did not himself invent the subject matter sought to be patented," it would require much stronger evidence that the named inventor was not the true inventor to justify a conclusion of clear and convincing evidence of invalidity. Despite some vagueness and inconsistency in the patentee's deposition testimony, she maintained throughout that she invented the claimed subject matter. As for the suggestion that her attorney might be the true inventor, an attorney's professional responsibility is to assist his or her client in defining the invention to obtain, if possible, a valid patent with maximum coverage. An attorney performing that role should not be a competitor of the client, asserting inventorship as a result of representing the client. Thus, to assert that proper performance of the attorney's role is a ground for invalidating the patent constitutes a failure to understand the proper role of a patent attorney. *Solomon v. Kimberly-Clark Corp.*, 216 F.3d 1372, 55 USPQ2d 1279 (Fed. Cir. 2000).

[97]*Price v. Symsek*, 988 F.2d 1187, 26 USPQ2d 1031 (Fed. Cir. 1993).

[98]*Price v. Symsek*, 988 F.2d 1187, 26 USPQ2d 1031 (Fed. Cir. 1993). To prove derivation in an interference proceeding, the person attacking the patent must establish prior conception of the claimed subject matter and communication of the conception to the adverse claimant. The determination of prior conception is a question of law based upon subsidiary factual findings. *Id.*

[99]*Sewall v. Walters*, 21 F.3d 411, 30 USPQ2d 1356 (Fed. Cir. 1994). In this case the court refused to recognize one worker as a joint inventor where he only designed circuits to carry out the other worker's idea and where that design effort was simply the exercise of the normal skill expected of an ordinary circuit designer.

[100]See §7.1(a). In *Richardson v. Suzuki Motor Co.*, 868 F.2d 1226, 9 USPQ2d 1913 (Fed. Cir. 1989), the jury found that the defendant had obtained a patent on an invention of the plaintiff. The court decreed assignment as a remedy, observing that courts are not powerless

Section 102(f) mandates that a patent accurately list the correct inventors of a claimed invention. Accordingly, if nonjoinder of an actual inventor is proved by clear and convincing evidence, a patent is rendered invalid. However, in cases of misjoinder and nonjoinder the operation of §102(f) is ameliorated by §256. This section is a savings provision. If a patentee demonstrates that inventorship can be corrected as provided for in §256, a district court must order correction of the patent, thus saving it from being rendered invalid. When a party asserts invalidity under §102(f) due to nonjoinder, a district court should first determine whether there exists clear and convincing proof that the alleged unnamed inventor was in fact a coinventor. Upon such a finding of incorrect inventorship, a patentee may invoke §256 to save the patent from invalidity. Accordingly, the patentee must then be given an opportunity to correct inventorship pursuant to that section. Nonjoinder may be corrected on notice and hearing of all parties concerned and upon a showing that the error occurred without any deceptive intent on the part of the unnamed inventor. But a patent with improper inventorship does not avoid invalidation simply because it might be corrected under §256. Rather, the patentee must claim entitlement to relief under the statute and the court must give the patentee an opportunity to correct the inventorship. If the inventorship is successfully corrected, §102(f) will not render the patent invalid. On the other hand, if the patentee does not claim relief under the statute and a party asserting invalidity proves incorrect inventorship, the court should hold the patent invalid for failure to comply with §102(f).[101]

Inurement involves a claim by an inventor that, as a matter of law, the acts of another person should accrue to the benefit of the inventor. Derivation involves the claim that the adverse party did not "invent" the subject matter of the count because that party derived the invention from another. To prove derivation in an interference proceeding, the party asserting derivation must establish prior conception of the claimed subject matter and communication of the conception to the adverse claimant. In order to establish inurement, an inventor must show, among other things, that the other person was working either explicitly or implicitly at the inventor's request. While derivation focuses on the communication of information between two parties, inurement focuses on the nature of the relationship between them. Communication of the conception by the inventor to the other party is not required to establish inurement.[102]

---

to redress wrongful appropriation of intellectual property by those subject to the court's jurisdiction. One wonders whether this patent would have been invalid under §102(f) had the defendant sued a third party for infringement. Would the invalidity have been "correctable" in a subsequent suit by the real inventor, or would collateral estoppel apply to the initial holding of invalidity?

[101]*Pannu v. Iolab Corp.*, 155 F.3d 1344, 47 USPQ2d 1657 (Fed. Cir. 1998).

[102]*Cooper v. Goldfarb*, 154 F.3d 1321, 47 USPQ2d 1896 (Fed. Cir. 1998).

§3.4 Prior Art

The real reason for denying patent rights is the basic principle that no patent should be granted that withdraws from the public domain technology already available to the public. Prior art is knowledge that is available, including what would be obvious from it, at a given time, to a person of ordinary skill in an art. Society, speaking through Congress, has said "thou shalt not take it away."[103] The statutory requirement that a patented invention be "new" is tested in accordance with 35 U.S.C. §102(a).[104] Any suggestion that a document is prior art because it appears before the filing date ignores the requirements of §102(a). That section explicitly refers to invention dates, not filing dates. Thus, under §102(a), a document is prior art only when published before the invention date. If the challenger establishes anticipation by a document published before the filing date, it then becomes the burden of the patentee to show that the claimed subject matter was invented prior to the date of publication. Section 102(g) governs this process.[105]

As we have seen, whether a reference is available as prior art, and whether it anticipates, are two quite separate questions.[106] The prior art status of a patent or publication, or a sale or use activity, is a legal question based on underlying fact issues.[107] The underlying facts need not be established beyond a reasonable doubt; the burden of proof to establish prior art is only by clear and convincing evidence.[108]

The knowledge of the prior art, of course, is presumed available to all, and it is irrelevant that the inventor may have been unaware

---

[103]*Kimberly-Clark Corp. v. Johnson & Johnson,* 745 F.2d 1437, 223 USPQ 603, 614 (Fed. Cir. 1984). The printed publication bar is grounded on the principle that once an invention is in the public domain, it is no longer patentable by anyone. *In re Hall,* 781 F.2d 897, 228 USPQ 453 (Fed. Cir. 1986).

[104]*Continental Can Co. v. Monsanto Co.,* 948 F.2d 1264, 20 USPQ2d 1746 (Fed. Cir. 1991).

[105]*Mahurkar v. C.R. Bard, Inc.,* 79 F.3d 1572, 38 USPQ2d 1288 (Fed. Cir. 1996).

[106]*Hodosh v. Block Drug Co.,* 786 F.2d 1136, 229 USPQ 182 (Fed. Cir. 1986).

[107]E.g., *Manville Sales Corp. v. Paramount Sys., Inc.,* 917 F.2d 544, 16 USPQ2d 1587 (Fed. Cir. 1990); *In re Cronyn,* 890 F.2d 1158, 13 USPQ2d 1070 (Fed. Cir. 1989); *Panduit Corp. v. Dennison Mfg. Co.,* 810 F.2d 1561, 1 USPQ2d 1593 (Fed. Cir. 1987); *J.A. LaPorte, Inc. v. Norfolk Dredging Co.,* 787 F.2d 1577, 229 USPQ 435 (Fed. Cir. 1986); *In re Hall,* 781 F.2d 897, 228 USPQ 453 (Fed. Cir. 1986); *Shatterproof Glass Corp. v. Libbey-Owens Ford Co.,* 758 F.2d 613, 225 USPQ 634 (Fed. Cir. 1985). In *Constant v. Advanced Micro-Devices, Inc.,* 848 F.2d 1560, 7 USPQ2d 1057 (Fed. Cir. 1988), a pro se patentee argued that it was unconstitutional for a court to invalidate his patent using prior art that was the result of government-funded research. His argument was that the Patent and Copyright Clause sets forth the only permissible means for the government to promote science. The court rejected this argument on the ground that the Constitution authorizes Congress to spend money to promote the "general welfare" and the definition of the general welfare and decisions on how to promote it are within the discretion of Congress. Government support for research and development is well within this discretionary power.

[108]*Trans-World Mfg. Corp. v. Al Nyman & Sons,* 750 F.2d 1552, 224 USPQ 259 (Fed. Cir. 1984). It is error to submit the question of whether a reference is prior art to the jury where there is no dispute about it. *Quaker City Gear Works, Inc. v. Skil Corp.,* 747 F.2d 1446, 223 USPQ 1161 (Fed. Cir. 1984).

of it.[109] But if material does not qualify as prior art on its own footing, the fact that the inventor knew about it does not matter—that will not raise it to the level of prior art.[110]

(a) Patenting

Under 35 U.S.C. §102(a), U.S. and foreign patents are prior art if they are prior to the applicant's invention date; and under §102(b), they are prior art (or statutory bars) if they are more than one year prior to the applicant's filing date, regardless when he or she made the invention. Although patents are the classical prior art, and probably the most frequently encountered obstacles to patentability, both in the PTO and in infringement litigation, there is not much controversy about their availability as references. Thus, patents are part of the literature of the art and are relevant for all they contain.[111]

35 U.S.C. §102(e). A patent application constitutes a constructive reduction to practice when filed and evidences a prior invention, which deprives a later invention of patentability.[112] Under §102(e), U.S. patents, at least those granted to a different inventive entity than the applicant,[113] are prior art as of their U.S. filing dates,[114] even though they may issue after the patent in question.[115] The court has held that although the inventions claimed in an application and in a patent were conceived by different inventive entities, the §102(e) exclusion for a patent granted to "another" is not necessarily satisfied

---

[109]*EWP Corp. v. Reliance Universal Inc.,* 755 F.2d 898, 225 USPQ 20 (Fed. Cir. 1985).

[110]*Kimberly-Clark Corp. v. Johnson & Johnson,* 745 F.2d 1437, 223 USPQ 603 (Fed. Cir. 1984). But see note 3:95 above.

[111]*In re Young,* 927 F.2d 588, 18 USPQ2d 1089 (Fed. Cir. 1991).

[112]*Rexam Indus. Corp. v. Eastman Kodak Co.,* 182 F.3d 1366, 51 USPQ2d 1457 (Fed. Cir. 1999).

[113]See *In re Costello,* 717 F.2d 1346, 219 USPQ 389 (Fed. Cir. 1983).

[114]*In re Bartfeld,* 925 F.2d 1450, 17 USPQ2d 1885 (Fed. Cir. 1991); *Hybritech Inc. v. Monoclonal Antibodies, Inc.,* 802 F.2d 1367, 231 USPQ 81 (Fed. Cir. 1986); *Martin v. Barber,* 755 F.2d 1564, 225 USPQ 233 (Fed. Cir. 1985). Although an applicant may rely upon a foreign filing date under 35 U.S.C. §119 to antedate a reference or win an interference, that filing date is not the effective date of his or her U.S. patent as a reference under §102(g) or §103(a). Nonetheless, the losing party in an interference with such a patent will be barred from obtaining claims that are patentably indistinguishable from the lost interference count. It is not that the count is prior art, but that the interference award is a judgment for purposes of preclusion by res judicata. The interference judgment conclusively determines that the winner is entitled to claim the patentable subject matter defined in the count. The judgment may therefore be used as a basis for rejection of claims to the same patentable invention. *In re Deckler,* 977 F.2d 1449, 24 USPQ2d 1448 (Fed. Cir. 1992).

[115]*Kloster Speedsteel AB v. Crucible Inc.,* 793 F.2d 1565, 230 USPQ 81 (Fed. Cir. 1986). Such a patent is sometimes referred to as "secret prior art" because, although it is effective as a reference as of its filing date under §102(e), its existence does not become known until it issues as a patent. *Sun Studs, Inc. v. ATA Equip. Leasing, Inc.,* 872 F.2d 978, 10 USPQ2d 1338 (Fed. Cir. 1989). Where patents are not in interference, the effective date of a U.S. patent as a reference is its filing date in the United States, not the date of conception or actual reduction to practice of the invention claimed or the subject matter disclosed. *Id.*

if the entities share one or more persons as joint inventors.[116] This holding arose in the context of anticipation; it is not clear whether the holding will eliminate any §102/§103 problem when there is a change of inventorship.[117]

Foreign patents typically enter the realm of prior art on the date that their contents become accessible to the public.[118] Actual knowledge of the contents is of course not required.[119] The question of whether a foreign patent document is a "patent" under §102(a) is one of law.[120]

The scope of a patent's claims determines what infringes the patent; it is no measure of what the patent discloses. Otherwise, Morse's telegraph patent claims, which were broad enough to cover a modern Telex, would also invalidate a patent on the Telex.[121] A failed experiment reported in the prosecution history of a patent renders it irrelevant as a prior art reference; another's experiment, imperfect and never perfected, will not serve either as an anticipation or as part of the prior art, for it has not served to enrich it.[122] On the

---

[116]*Applied Materials, Inc. v. Gemini Research Corp.*, 835 F.2d 279, 15 USPQ2d 1816 (Fed. Cir. 1987). The application that matured into patent AB and the application that matured into patent ABC grew from the same original application. The court simply held that the fact that inventor C was added to the later filed application does not necessarily make the former prior art. Is it crucial that both sprang from a common ancestor? Interesting situations can arise. In *In re Chu*, 66 F.3d 292, 36 USPQ2d 1089 (Fed. Cir. 1995), the PTO rejected the claims of a CIP application of inventors A and B over a §102(e) parent patent to inventor A. The court held that the 1984 amendment to §120 (which was effected by the addition of 35 U.S.C. §104(b)) means that complete identity of inventors is no longer required to obtain the filing date of a parent application. But here inventors A and B would only be entitled to the filing date of the parent A patent if it disclosed their claimed invention. Inasmuch as they were contesting that very question, and had argued on the merits that the patent to A did not disclose their joint invention, they were held to have conceded that it did not for priority purposes as well. Thus, the A patent was a proper reference that had to be distinguished on the merits.

[117]See also *In re Land*, 368 F.2d 866, 151 USPQ 621 (CCPA 1967). See 35 U.S.C. §103(c).

[118]See, e.g., *In re Ekenstam*, 256 F.2d 321, 118 USPQ 349 (CCPA 1958). Whether intervening foreign patent references are §102(b) bars depends on the content and dates of the foreign references and the priority dates to which the patent claims are entitled. *Paperless Accounting, Inc. v. Bay Area Rapid Transit Sys.*, 804 F.2d 659, 231 USPQ 649 (Fed. Cir. 1986). The court has held that a German Geschmacksmuster is a patent under §102(a). A Geschmacksmuster is a design registration obtained by an applicant from the German government after performing certain registration procedures. The applicant deposits an application, together with a drawing, photograph, or sample in a local city office. A list of such registrations is published in the German *Federal Gazette* and certified copies of the application materials are available from the city office. The Federal Circuit recognized that such materials, on display for public view in remote cities in a far-away land, may create a burden of discovery for one without the time, desire, or resources to journey there in person or by agent to observe what was registered and protected under German law. Such a burden, however, is by law imposed upon the hypothetical person of ordinary skill in the art who is charged with knowledge of all the contents of the relevant prior art. *In re Carlson*, 983 F.2d 1032, 25 USPQ2d 1207 (Fed. Cir. 1993). See also *In re Kathawala*, 9 F.3d 942, 28 USPQ2d 1785 (Fed. Cir. 1993), which holds that, at least for purposes of §102(d), a foreign patent need not be publicly available for the invention to be "patented." Patenting in a foreign country occurs when the patentee's rights under the patent become fixed.

[119]*In re Carlson*, 983 F.2d 1032, 25 USPQ2d 1207 (Fed. Cir. 1993).

[120]*In re Carlson*, 983 F.2d 1032, 25 USPQ2d 1207 (Fed. Cir. 1993).

[121]*In re Benno*, 768 F.2d 1340, 226 USPQ 683 (Fed. Cir. 1985). Of course, a claim is *part of* the disclosure of a patent. *Id.*

[122]*Fromson v. Advance Offset Plate, Inc.*, 755 F.2d 1549, 225 USPQ 26 (Fed. Cir. 1985).

other hand, obsolescence need not necessarily defeat a reference for what it discloses with respect to a claimed invention.[123]

Where an applicant's attorney characterizes a patent as "prior art," that explicit admission is sufficient to justify a district court holding that the patent is part of the prior art.[124] However, an admission by an attorney that a reference in a prior art brochure was to a patented process did not serve as a vehicle whereby the patent on the process, otherwise too late, also became prior art. The key factor is whether the brochure itself contains an enabling disclosure of the process.[125]

What of express or implied admissions arising out of the patentee's own actions or statements? The preamble of a so-called Jepson claim is impliedly admitted to be prior art.[126] But the court is firmly persuaded that prior art must have a statutory basis. Thus, if a Jepson preamble describes the inventor's own work, it is not prior art simply by virtue of the implied admission; it would have to stand on its own feet as a publication or other public disclosure prior to the critical date. On the other hand, if the preamble describes the work of a different inventive entity, it is prior art.[127] This reasoning also applies to the summary of prior art in the specification. It is common sense that an inventor, regardless of an admission, has knowledge of his or her own work; but this does not mean that one of ordinary skill in the art would have had knowledge of it.[128] Conversely, a statement in the specification that the properties of the claimed compound are about the same as the prior art properties is a statement of chemical fact that can be used against the applicant. It is not a part of his or her own teaching, which cannot be used against an applicant.[129] A patent applicant's statement of the purpose of his or her work is not prior art,[130] but a statement in a patent that something is in the prior art is binding on the applicant and patentee for determinations of anticipation and obviousness.[131]

Sole inventor A, and joint inventors A and B, are separate legal entities. Where the joint and sole inventions are related, inventor A

---

[123]*In re Etter,* 756 F.2d 852, 225 USPQ 1 (Fed. Cir. 1985).

[124]*Tyler Refrigeration v. Kysor Indus. Corp.,* 777 F.2d 687, 227 USPQ 845 (Fed. Cir. 1985).

[125]*Reading & Bates Constr. Co. v. Baker Energy Res. Corp.,* 748 F.2d 645, 223 USPQ 1168 (Fed. Cir. 1984). The court also went on, in a puzzling dictum, to express doubt whether the admission of an attorney as to what is prior art could have any binding effect on the court. *Id.* But see *Tyler Refrigeration v. Kysor Indus. Corp.,* 777 F.2d 687, 227 USPQ 845 (Fed. Cir. 1985).

[126]*Sjolund v. Musland,* 847 F.2d 1573, 6 USPQ2d 2020 (Fed. Cir. 1988); *Pentec, Inc. v. Graphic Controls Corp.,* 776 F.2d 309, 227 USPQ 766 (Fed. Cir. 1985). See also *Medtronic, Inc. v. Cardiac Pacemakers, Inc.,* 721 F.2d 1563, 220 USPQ 97 (Fed. Cir. 1983).

[127]*Reading & Bates Constr. Co. v. Baker Energy Res. Corp.,* 748 F.2d 645, 223 USPQ 1168 (Fed. Cir. 1984).

[128]*Reading & Bates Constr. Co. v. Baker Energy Res. Corp.,* 748 F.2d 645, 223 USPQ 1168 (Fed. Cir. 1984).

[129]*In re Thorpe,* 777 F.2d 695, 227 USPQ 964 (Fed. Cir. 1985).

[130]*In re Dow Chem. Co.,* 837 F.2d 469, 5 USPQ2d 1529 (Fed. Cir. 1988).

[131]*Constant v. Advanced Micro-Devices, Inc.,* 848 F.2d 1560, 7 USPQ2d 1057, 1063 (Fed. Cir. 1988).

may well have to disclose, under the best mode requirement of §112, the joint invention of A and B in the course of describing A's own sole invention. This does not amount to a disclosure of prior art with respect to the joint invention.[132]

It is error to treat original claims as prior art against reissue claims. This is so even where the reissue oath indicates that the inventor believes the original claims are unpatentable over a prior art reference. Such an oath does not constitute an admission that the reference anticipated those claims, and that the claims are therefore part of the prior art.[133]

(b) Publication

A printed publication in the United States or a foreign country is prior art under §102(a) if it was published prior to the applicant's date of invention and is a statutory bar under §102(b) if it was published more than a year before the filing date. The statutory phrase "printed publication" has been interpreted to give effect to ongoing advances in the technologies of data storage, retrieval, and dissemination. Because there are many ways in which a reference may be disseminated to the interested public, "public accessibility" has been called the touchstone in determining whether a reference constitutes a printed publication under §102. The publication bar must be approached on a case-by-case basis. The proponent of the publication bar must show that prior to the critical date the reference was sufficiently accessible, at least to those members of the public interested in the art, so that such a one by examining the reference could make the claimed invention without further research or experimentation.[134] Whether a document is a printed publication is a legal determination based on underlying fact issues.[135]

A document, to serve as a printed publication, must be generally available.[136] Thus, a paper presented orally to 50–500 persons, interested and of ordinary skill, and disseminated without restriction to at least six persons, more than a year prior to the filing date, constitutes prior art.[137] On the other hand, sending six copies of a brochure

---

[132]*In re Kaplan,* 789 F.2d 1574, 229 USPQ 678 (Fed. Cir. 1986).

[133]*Orthokinetics, Inc. v. Safety Travel Chairs, Inc.,* 806 F.2d 1565, 1 USPQ2d 1081 (Fed. Cir. 1986).

[134]*Constant v. Advanced Micro-Devices, Inc.,* 848 F.2d 1560, 7 USPQ2d 1057 (Fed. Cir. 1988); *In re Hall,* 781 F.2d 897, 228 USPQ 453 (Fed. Cir. 1986).

[135]*Northern Telecom, Inc. v. Datapoint Corp.,* 908 F.2d 931, 15 USPQ2d 1321 (Fed. Cir. 1990).

[136]*Northern Telecom, Inc. v. Datapoint Corp.,* 908 F.2d 931, 15 USPQ2d 1321 (Fed. Cir. 1990).

[137]*Massachusetts Inst. of Tech. v. AB Fortia,* 774 F.2d 1104, 227 USPQ 428 (Fed. Cir. 1985).

to a friend for the purpose of obtaining financial backing is not publication under §102.[138] In another case, the documents in question were reports that were distributed to about 50 persons or organizations involved in a complex military project. Although they were not under security classification, they bore the legend (or were of the type that should have) "reproduction or further dissemination is not authorized . . . not for public release." The court held that these materials were not printed publications because there was no clear and convincing evidence that anyone could have had access to the documents by the exercise of reasonable diligence.[139]

An inventor's own publication is of course prior art under 35 U.S.C. §103 if early enough. Thus, where an inventor publishes more than a year before filing, he or she is foreclosed from obtaining a patent on a method that would have been obvious from the publication, with or without the disclosure of other prior art.[140]

Evidence of routine business practice can be sufficient to prove that a reference was made accessible before a critical date. Accessibility goes to the issue of whether interested members of the relevant public could obtain the information if they wanted to. If accessibility is proved, there is no requirement to show that particular members of the public actually received the information.[141] It is not the law that accessibility can only be shown by evidence establishing a specific date of cataloging and shelving of a work before the critical date. While such evidence would be desirable in lending greater certainty to the accessibility determination, the realities of routine business practice counsel against requiring such evidence. The probative value of routine business practice to show the performance of a specific act has long been recognized. Competent evidence of general library practice may be relied upon to establish an approximate time when a document, such as a graduate thesis, became accessible.[142]

---

[138]*Preemption Devices, Inc. v. Minnesota Min. & Mfg. Co.,* 732 F.2d 903, 221 USPQ 841 (Fed. Cir. 1984). In one case a patent challenger sought to justify discovery against the American Physical Society on the ground that one of its anonymous prepublication referees might have disseminated a paper sufficiently to qualify it as prior art. The discovery was denied upon balancing the Society's need for confidentiality against the challenger's speculative interest. *Solarex Corp. v. Arco Solar, Inc.,* 870 F.2d 642, 10 USPQ2d 1247 (Fed. Cir. 1989).

[139]*Northern Telecom, Inc. v. Datapoint Corp.,* 908 F.2d 931, 15 USPQ2d 1321 (Fed. Cir. 1990).

[140]*In re O'Farrell,* 853 F.2d 894, 7 USPQ2d 1673 (Fed. Cir. 1988).

[141]*Constant v. Advanced Micro-Devices, Inc.,* 848 F.2d 1560, 7 USPQ2d 1057 (Fed. Cir. 1988).

[142]*In re Hall,* 781 F.2d 897, 228 USPQ 453 (Fed. Cir. 1986). In this case a single cataloged thesis in one university library was held to constitute sufficient accessibility where the evidence was that the thesis was received in November, and under routine practice would have been available for general use toward the end of December, given a critical date of February the next year. *In re Cronyn,* 890 F.2d 1158, 13 USPQ2d 1070 (Fed. Cir. 1989), held that a student thesis is not accessible to the public if it is neither cataloged nor indexed in a meaningful way. Undergraduate senior theses at Reed College were described on individual index cards, which were then filed alphabetically under the author's name. The three theses in question, which were held not to be printed publications, were among hundreds kept in a shoebox in the chemistry department library.

A publication must describe the claimed invention sufficiently to have placed the public in possession of it. Such possession is effected if one of ordinary skill in the art could have combined the publication's description of the invention with his or her own knowledge to make the claimed invention. Thus even if the claimed invention is disclosed in a printed publication, that disclosure will not suffice as an anticipation if it was not enabling. It is not necessary, however, that an invention disclosed in a publication shall have actually been made in order to satisfy the enablement requirement.[143]

(c) Use or Sale

The public use and on-sale bars are not limited to sales or uses by the inventor or one under the inventor's control, but may result from activities of a third party that anticipate the invention or render it obvious.[144] Under 35 U.S.C. §102(a), an applicant cannot have a patent if the subject matter claimed was "used by others in this country" before the applicant's invention of it. Under §102(b), he or she is barred if the invention was "in public use or on sale in this country, more than one year prior to" the application. Thus, §102(a) deals with the activities of a person other than the inventor, while the §102(b) bar may result from the activities of either the inventor or a third party.[145] Actions by the inventor occurring within the statutory one-year grace period under §102(b) are not prior art that will render the inventor's work anticipated or obvious.[146]

The policies that define the public use bar are: (1) discouraging the removal, from the public domain, of inventions that the public reasonably has come to believe are freely available, (2) favoring the prompt and widespread disclosure of inventions, (3) allowing the inventor a reasonable amount of time following sales activity to determine the potential economic value of a patent, and (4) prohibiting the inventor from commercially exploiting the invention for a period greater than the statutorily prescribed time.[147]

Prior art and the critical date. Both §102(a) and §102(b) also define prior art. For example, something that was in public use more

---

[143]*In re Donohue,* 766 F.2d 531, 226 USPQ 619, 621 (Fed. Cir. 1985). A printed publication must be enabling. *Solarex Corp. v. Arco Solar, Inc.,* 870 F.2d 642, 10 USPQ2d 1247 (Fed. Cir. 1989). In the case of a chemical compound an indication that a compound was successfully made is strong evidence of enablement; an indication of lack of success is strong evidence of lack of enablement; and an indication of no attempt does not evidence enablement one way or the other. *In re Donohue,* 766 F.2d 531, 226 USPQ 619 (Fed. Cir. 1985). This is a mixed question of fact and law. *In re Epstein,* 32 F.3d 1559, 31 USPQ2d 1817 (Fed. Cir. 1994).

[144]*In re Epstein,* 32 F.3d 1559, 31 USPQ2d 1817 (Fed. Cir. 1994).

[145]E.g., *J.A. LaPorte, Inc. v. Norfolk Dredging Co.,* 787 F.2d 1577, 229 USPQ 435 (Fed. Cir. 1986). The court has been able to pass the question of whether an offer for sale of the inventor's product by another, not expressly authorized by the inventor, would constitute a bar. *Seal-Flex, Inc. v. Athletic Track & Court Constr.,* 98 F.3d 1318, 40 USPQ2d 1450 (Fed. Cir. 1996).

[146]*Specialty Composites v. Cabot Corp.,* 845 F.2d 981, 6 USPQ2d 1601 (Fed. Cir. 1988).

[147]*Tone Bros., Inc. v. Sysco Corp.,* 28 F.3d 1192, 31 USPQ2d 1321 (Fed. Cir. 1994).

than a year prior to the inventor's filing date is prior art for obviousness purposes,[148] and such evidence can be combined with other prior
art references under 35 U.S.C. §103.[149] One year before the filing of
the application is referred to as the "critical date" for purposes of
measuring the "in public use or on sale" status of prior art.[150] If a
device was in public use or on sale before the critical date, then
that device becomes a reference under §103. Clearly, no reduction to
practice is required for a device to be prior art under §102(b), since
a §102(b)/§103 bar obviously concerns a device that is not a reduction
to practice of the claimed invention.[151]

    In order to qualify as prior art, a reference must have existed as
of the date of invention, which is normally presumed to be the filing
date of the application until an earlier date is proved.[152] But no reference, be it use or sale, publication or patent, that is prior art by virtue
of §102(b), as being more than one year prior to the inventor's filing
date, can be antedated by showing an earlier date of invention.[153]
Because this critical date—one year before the filing date—is determined retrospectively, those activities that will act as a bar must be
of such character that it is apparent at the time they are conducted
that patent filing must be completed within a year. Substantial property rights are at issue, and the trial court must determine with
precision when the bar came into being, for the bar must be proven
by clear and convincing evidence.[154]

---

[148]*Milliken Res. Corp. v. Dan River, Inc.,* 739 F.2d 587, 222 USPQ 571 (Fed. Cir. 1984).
If a device is in public use or on sale before the critical date, more than one year before the
application was filed, then that device becomes a reference under 35 U.S.C. §103. This is so
whether it was the inventor's use or sale, or that of a third person. *Baker Oil Tools, Inc. v.
Geo Vann, Inc.,* 828 F.2d 1588, 4 USPQ2d 1210 (Fed. Cir. 1987).

[149]*In re Kaslow,* 707 F.2d 1366, 217 USPQ 1089 (Fed. Cir. 1983). Section 102(b) may
create a bar to patentability either alone, if the device placed on sale is an anticipation of the
later claimed invention, or in conjunction with §103(a), if the claimed invention would have
been obvious from the device on sale in view of other prior art. *Keystone Ret. Wall Sys., Inc.
v. Westrock, Inc.,* 997 F.2d 1444, 27 USPQ2d 1297 (Fed. Cir. 1993). The filing of a design for
a building component with a municipal building department constituted public use so as to
qualify the design as prior art for purposes of an obviousness defense. *Concrete Unlimited Inc.
v. Cementcraft, Inc.,* 776 F.2d 1537, 227 USPQ 784 (Fed. Cir. 1985).

[150]*In re Epstein,* 32 F.3d 1559, 31 USPQ2d 1817 (Fed. Cir. 1994).

[151]*LaBounty Mfg., Inc. v. United States ITC,* 958 F.2d 1066, 22 USPQ2d 1025 (Fed. Cir.
1992). See also *Pfaff v. Wells Elec., Inc.,* 124 F.3d 1429, 43 USPQ2d 1928 (Fed. Cir. 1997),
aff'd, 525 U.S. 55, 48 USPQ2d 1641 (1998); *Keystone Ret. Wall Sys., Inc. v. Westrock, Inc.,* 997
F.2d 1444, 27 USPQ2d 1297 (Fed. Cir. 1993). Implicit in the operation of such a bar is the
absence of reduction to practice of the claimed invention as a requirement for the bar to operate.
The "invention," as claimed with all of its elements, is not the subject of the sale or use; if it
were, §103 would not be involved. *UMC Elec. Co. v. United States,* 816 F.2d 647, 2 USPQ2d
1465 (Fed. Cir. 1987).

[152]*Bausch & Lomb, Inc. v. Barnes-Hind, Inc.,* 796 F.2d 443, 230 USPQ 416 (Fed. Cir. 1986).

[153]*In re Foster,* 343 F.2d 980, 145 USPQ 166 (CCPA 1965). See *UMC Elec. Co. v. United
States,* 816 F.2d 647, 2 USPQ2d 1465 (Fed. Cir. 1987). A nonanticipating public use more than
one year before the claim's effective filing date may render the claim invalid for obviousness
under §103. *Elmer v. ICC Fabricating, Inc.,* 67 F.3d 1571, 36 USPQ2d 1417 (Fed. Cir. 1995).

[154]*Baker Oil Tools, Inc. v. Geo Vann, Inc.,* 828 F.2d 1588, 4 USPQ2d 1210 (Fed. Cir. 1987).
For example, the fact that a foreign patent attorney gave cautionary advice that a patent
application should be filed in the United States before a certain date—advice that was not
implemented—is not an admission of U.S. law or fact, and in particular does not compel a

Public use in general. Section 102(b) specifically provides for "public use," while §102(a) specifies only that the invention be "used by others." Nonetheless, use under §102(a) means use that is accessible to the public.[155] Public use is use by the inventor, or by a person who is not under any limitation, restriction, or obligation of secrecy to the inventor.[156] The nonsecret use of a claimed process in the usual course of producing articles for commercial purposes is a public use. If the use is consistent and reproducible, it is irrelevant that those using the invention may not have appreciated the results.[157] It is possible that, in order to qualify as prior art, the invention must be publicly used in its natural and intended way.[158]

Invalidity based on public use must be proved by clear and convincing evidence.[159] Once a prima facie case of public use before the critical date is made out, the inventor must come forward with clear and convincing evidence to counter that showing.[160] Whether or not an invention was in public use is a question of law based upon underlying

---

conclusion that the activity in question was a bar. *Allied Colloids, Inc. v. American Cyanamid Co.,* 64 F.3d 1570, 35 USPQ2d 1840 (Fed. Cir. 1995).

[155]*Carella v. Starlight Archery & Pro Line Co.,* 804 F.2d 135, 231 USPQ 644, 646 (Fed. Cir. 1986).

[156]*In re Smith,* 714 F.2d 1127, 218 USPQ 976 (Fed. Cir. 1983). In one interesting case, the inventor demonstrated models of his invention to colleagues and to his employer without any express agreement of confidentiality. The court held that there was no public use of the invention. The demonstration to colleagues was for the inventor's own private use and enjoyment. The invention was not given over for free and unrestricted use by another person. The employer's use was not commercial activity; a discussion between an employer and an employee does not by itself convert the employee's private pursuit into commercial enterprise with the employer. *Moleculon Res. Corp. v. CBS, Inc.,* 793 F.2d 1261, 229 USPQ 805 (Fed. Cir. 1986). In another case, the patients of a dentist were not asked to keep an orthodontic appliance secret, but it was beyond reasonable probability that the patients would show the device to others who would understand or want to duplicate it. In case of loss or breakage, the patient would expect that particular dentist to replace the appliance. Further, the dentist/patient relationship was said to establish the requisite control that an express vow of secrecy is designed to accomplish. *TP Labs., Inc. v. Professional Positioners, Inc.,* 724 F.2d 965, 220 USPQ 577 (Fed. Cir. 1984). In still another case, the device was shown to guests at a party in order to get feedback and generate discussion. The guests did not believe they were subject to secrecy or confidentiality restrictions. The inventor, who hosted the party, had an entry in her datebook that corroborated the date of the party. The court held that these facts established public use of the device. *Beachcombers v. Wildewood Creative Prods., Inc.,* 31 F.3d 1154, 31 USPQ2d 1653 (Fed. Cir. 1994).

[157]*W.L. Gore & Assoc. v. Garlock, Inc.,* 721 F.2d 1540, 220 USPQ 303 (Fed. Cir. 1983). One must take care to analyze just what the invention is that is said to be the subject of an invalidating use. In one case the claims covered a catalyst for polymerizing lower olefins, including propylene. The inventor had never used the catalyst to polymerize propylene but disclosed that possibility to another, who actually did it first. The defendant argued that if the claims were construed to cover the use of the catalyst in connection with propylene, they were invalid. The court disagreed and pointed out that because the claims were for a catalyst and not a process, it is immaterial who was the first to use the catalyst for propylene, so long as the inventor was the first to use the catalyst to polymerize lower olefins. *Studiengesellschaft Kohle v. Dart Indus., Inc.,* 726 F.2d 724, 220 USPQ 841 (Fed. Cir. 1984).

[158]*In re Mann,* 861 F.2d 1581, 8 USPQ2d 2030 (Fed. Cir. 1988).

[159]*Allied Colloids, Inc. v. American Cyanamid Co.,* 64 F.3d 1570, 35 USPQ2d 1840 (Fed. Cir. 1995).

[160]*Tone Bros., Inc. v. Sysco Corp.,* 28 F.3d 1192, 31 USPQ2d 1321 (Fed. Cir. 1994); *Hycor Corp. v. Schlueter Co.,* 740 F.2d 1529, 222 USPQ 553 (Fed. Cir. 1984). But see *Harrington Mfg. Co. v. Powell Mfg. Co.,* 815 F.2d 1478, 2 USPQ2d 1364 (Fed Cir. 1986).

issues of fact.[161] The facts underlying a conclusion of public use are subject to review under the clearly erroneous standard.[162]

Secret use. Secrecy alone does not necessarily negate public use.[163] As a general proposition, a commercial use by the inventor is a bar even if it is kept secret.[164] Thus, if the inventor's assignee produces a product by a patented method and offers it for sale before the critical date, the right to a method patent is lost, even though the method is not accessible to the public.[165] On the other hand, a patent on a process for making an article is not barred where a third party uses a machine secretly to practice the process and sells the product. The public could not learn the process by examining the product.[166]

On sale. To invoke the on-sale bar a defendant must prove that the complete claimed invention is embodied in or obvious in view of the thing sold or offered for sale before the critical date. The bar invalidates a patent for an invention offered for sale, even though not ready for satisfactory commercial marketing. If a patent owner seeks to avoid the bar on the basis that a sale or offer was experimental, a trial court must determine whether the patent owner sought the sale primarily for profit rather than as part of a testing program. To determine whether profit motivated a transaction, a court must examine the claimed features, the offeror's objective intent, and the totality of the circumstances.[167]

---

[161]*Tone Bros., Inc. v. Sysco Corp.*, 28 F.3d 1192, 31 USPQ2d 1321 (Fed. Cir. 1994).

[162]*Manville Sales Corp. v. Paramount Sys., Inc.*, 917 F.2d 544, 16 USPQ2d 1587 (Fed. Cir. 1990); *Harrington Mfg. Co. v. Powell Mfg. Co.*, 815 F.2d 1478, 2 USPQ2d 1364 (Fed Cir. 1986).

[163]*Kinzenbaw v. Deere & Co.*, 741 F.2d 383, 222 USPQ 929 (Fed. Cir. 1984).

[164]*Kinzenbaw v. Deere & Co.*, 741 F.2d 383, 222 USPQ 929 (Fed. Cir. 1984). The patentee had farmers use a device to test its warrantability, durability, and acceptability. The use was secret, but held to be commercial. And since the farmers were the agents of the patentee, it was a commercial use by the patentee. It should be noted that the patentee had conceded that it was not arguing the experimental use exception.

[165]*D.L. Auld Co. v. Chroma Graphics Corp.*, 714 F.2d 1144, 219 USPQ 13 (Fed. Cir. 1983). The result would be different if the actor had been one other than the inventor or someone with the inventor's authority. *Id.*

[166]*W.L. Gore & Assoc. v. Garlock, Inc.*, 721 F.2d 1540, 220 USPQ 303 (Fed. Cir. 1983). The third party apparently was honoring a purchase agreement clause to keep the machine secret; although outsiders could see the machine, there was no evidence that the process could be learned simply by viewing the machine.

[167]*Atlantic Thermoplastics Co. v. Faytex Corp.*, 970 F.2d 834, 23 USPQ2d 1481 (Fed. Cir. 1992). In a typical case where the patentee has placed some device on sale prior to the critical date, the accused infringer must demonstrate that this device actually embodied or rendered obvious the patented invention. But where the device that was allegedly on sale was the very device now accused to infringe, the allegation of infringement in and of itself satisfies that burden. *Vanmoor v. Wal-Mart Stores Inc.*, 201 F.3d 1363, 53 USPQ2d 1377 (Fed. Cir. 2000). The sale must be of the claimed invention, or something that would, by its addition to the prior art, render the invention obvious. *Ferag AG v. Quipp, Inc.*, 45 F.3d 1562, 33 USPQ2d 1512 (Fed. Cir. 1995); *UMC Elec. Co. v. United States,* 816 F.2d 647, 2 USPQ2d 1465 (Fed. Cir. 1987).

A single sale or offer to sell is enough to bar patentability.[168] The bar is not limited to sales by the inventor or one under his or her control but may result from activities of a third party,[169] acting either innocently or fraudulently.[170] The test of on sale requires (1) the complete invention claimed must have been embodied in or obvious in view of the thing offered for sale; (2) the invention must have been tested sufficiently to verify that it is operable and commercially marketable; and (3) the sale must have been primarily for profit rather than for experimental purposes.[171] The court has cautioned that a less stringent standard might be appropriate in some circumstances where the underlying statutory policies might otherwise be frustrated. These policies include (1) discouraging removal of inventions from the public domain that the public justifiably comes to believe are freely available, (2) favoring prompt and widespread disclosure of inventions, (3) giving the inventor a reasonable amount of time following the sales activity to determine the value of a patent, and (4) prohibiting an extension of the period for exploiting the invention.[172] The purpose of the on-sale bar is to disallow protection for an invention that was being commercialized more than one year prior to the filing of a patent application for that invention.[173] This question of law is not subject to a mechanical rule, but depends upon the totality of the circumstances. Commercialization is the central focus.[174]

An offer to sell is sufficient under the policies animating the statute, §102(b), which proscribes not a sale but a placing "on sale."[175]

---

[168]*Paragon Podiatry Lab., Inc. v. KLM Labs., Inc.*, 984 F.2d 1182, 25 USPQ2d 1561 (Fed. Cir. 1993); *Atlantic Thermoplastics Co. v. Faytex Corp.*, 970 F.2d 834, 23 USPQ2d 1481 (Fed. Cir. 1992); *Intel Corp. v. United States ITC*, 946 F.2d 821, 20 USPQ2d 1161 (Fed. Cir. 1991); *A.B. Chance Co. v. RTE Corp.*, 854 F.2d 1307, 7 USPQ2d 1881 (Fed. Cir. 1988); *In re Caveney*, 761 F.2d 671, 226 USPQ 1 (Fed. Cir. 1985).

[169]*J.A. LaPorte, Inc. v. Norfolk Dredging Co.*, 787 F.2d 1577, 229 USPQ 435 (Fed. Cir. 1986); *Pennwalt Corp. v. Akzona Inc.*, 740 F.2d 1573, 222 USPQ 833 (Fed. Cir. 1984).

[170]*Abbott Labs. v. Geneva Pharm. Inc.*, 182 F.3d 1315, 51 USPQ2d 1307, 1309 (Fed. Cir. 1999).

[171]*King Instrument Corp. v. Otari Corp.*, 767 F.2d 853, 226 USPQ 402 (Fed. Cir. 1985); *Barmag Barmer Masch. AG v. Murata Mach., Ltd.*, 731 F.2d 831, 221 USPQ 561 (Fed. Cir. 1984).

[172]*Envirotech Corp. v. Westech Eng'g, Inc.*, 904 F.2d 1571, 15 USPQ2d 1230 (Fed. Cir. 1990); *King Instrument Corp. v. Otari Corp.*, 767 F.2d 853, 226 USPQ 402 (Fed. Cir. 1985). See also *Ferag AG v. Quipp, Inc.*, 45 F.3d 1562, 33 USPQ2d 1512 (Fed. Cir. 1995).

[173]*RCA Corp. v. Data Gen. Corp.*, 887 F.2d 1056, 12 USPQ2d 1449 (Fed. Cir. 1989). One policy underlying the on-sale bar is to obtain widespread disclosure of new inventions to the public via patents as soon as possible; another is to prevent the inventor from commercially exploiting the exclusivity of the invention substantially beyond the statutorily authorized 17-year period. The bar cannot be determined by ascribing a label to certain activity so as to make it appear to be commercial, in lieu of considering whether the activity runs counter to the policies of the on-sale bar that are to be effectuated. *Id.* See also *U.S. Envtl. Prods., Inc. v. Westall*, 911 F.2d 713, 15 USPQ2d 1898 (Fed. Cir. 1990).

[174]*In re Mahurkar Hemodialysis Catheter*, 71 F.3d 1573, 37 USPQ2d 1138 (Fed. Cir. 1995). In this case there was a bona fide sale of a device that had been reduced to practice. Nonetheless, it was not made on ordinary commercial terms, and it did not place the invention in the public domain or lead the public to believe that it was freely available. The court affirmed a finding of no sale bar.

[175]*King Instrument Corp. v. Otari Corp.*, 767 F.2d 853, 226 USPQ 402 (Fed. Cir. 1985).

It is not necessary that a sale be consummated for the bar to operate. Even if no delivery is made prior to the critical date, the existence of a sales contract or the signing of a purchase agreement prior to that date has been held to demonstrate an on-sale status for the invention. No more than a firm offer to sell may be sufficient.[176] That an offer to sell is not accepted is immaterial.[177] But a bare offer to sell does not ipso facto satisfy the on-sale bar; the totality of the circumstances must always be considered in order to ascertain whether an offer of the new invention was in fact made.[178] A later offer to purchase does not mean that earlier activity did not constitute an offer to sell.[179] Sending a prototype to a customer to solicit a sale is sufficient to invoke the on-sale bar.[180] The fact that a buyer may have intended to order a different model has no bearing on whether the claimed invention was offered for sale. Thus, testimony that the buyer ordered a similar type of device would not alter the fact that the seller offered the actual invention.[181] But the inventor's attempted exploitation must be manifested as a definite sale or offer to sell the invention itself. Evidence that the patentee offered to sell one design, with the uncommunicated intent of attempting later to substitute its patented invention, therefore argues against a conclusion of on sale.[182]

Despite the phrase "in this country" found in §102(b), an offer to sell, made from England, nevertheless qualifies where it is made to a buyer at its place of business in the United States.[183]

A sale is a contract between parties to give and to pass rights of

---

[176]*Buildex, Inc. v. Kason Indus., Inc.,* 849 F.2d 1461, 7 USPQ2d 1325 (Fed. Cir. 1988). See also *STX LLC v. Brine Inc.,* 54 USPQ2d 1347 (Fed. Cir. 2000). The date of a purchase agreement is the effective date upon which an invention becomes part of the public domain. That delivery of the device embodying the invention came later is immaterial. *J.A. LaPorte, Inc. v. Norfolk Dredging Co.,* 787 F.2d 1577, 229 USPQ 435 (Fed. Cir. 1986).

[177]*RCA Corp. v. Data Gen. Corp.,* 887 F.2d 1056, 12 USPQ2d 1449 (Fed. Cir. 1989).

[178]*Envirotech Corp. v. Westech Eng'g, Inc.,* 904 F.2d 1571, 15 USPQ2d 1230 (Fed. Cir. 1990); *King Instrument Corp. v. Otari Corp.,* 767 F.2d 853, 226 USPQ 402 (Fed. Cir. 1985); *Shatterproof Glass Corp. v. Libbey-Owens Ford Co.,* 758 F.2d 613, 225 USPQ 634 (Fed. Cir. 1985).

[179]*Barmag Barmer Masch. AG v. Murata Mach., Ltd.,* 731 F.2d 831, 221 USPQ 561 (Fed. Cir. 1984).

[180]*Stearns v. Beckman Instruments, Inc.,* 737 F.2d 1565, 222 USPQ 457 (Fed. Cir. 1984). In *Intel Corp. v. United States ITC,* 946 F.2d 821, 20 USPQ2d 1161 (Fed. Cir. 1991), the patent owner distributed samples of the patented product to its salesmen three weeks prior to the critical date, with the expectation that they would be distributed to customers (the likelihood was that they were so distributed). The patent owner was clearly seeking a commercial advantage. Nonetheless, this did not amount to an on-sale bar because there was no clear and convincing evidence of an offer to sell, a sale, or a distribution to a customer prior to the critical date.

[181]*In re Caveney,* 761 F.2d 671, 226 USPQ 1 (Fed. Cir. 1985).

[182]*Envirotech Corp. v. Westech Eng'g, Inc.,* 904 F.2d 1571, 15 USPQ2d 1230 (Fed. Cir. 1990). The subjective, uncommunicated, and ultimate intention of the offeror, however clear, is not alone sufficient. *Id.*

[183]*In re Caveney,* 761 F.2d 671, 226 USPQ 1 (Fed. Cir. 1985).

property for consideration that the buyer pays or promises to pay the seller for the thing bought and sold. One cannot make such a contract with oneself. Accordingly, a sale or offer to sell under §102(b) must be between two separate entities.[184] But the court has refused to embrace unequivocally a "joint development" exception to the on-sale bar. Where the inventor sold to one who had provided the impetus for making the invention but was not a joint inventor, and where the sale was clearly motivated by profit, the court refused to accept the district court's characterization as one to which the on-sale bar was not intended to apply.[185]

Whether a promotion of a product to a customer is an offer accepted with an order, or a purchase order is an offer to buy accepted by delivery, either proposition results in a sale under UCC §2-206.[186] In one case the patentee had successfully bid on a contract proposal that called for experimental development of a system. The court held that the fact that the contract was for experimental development did not mean that the "offer to sell," i.e., to fulfill the contract, was not a "definite" offer. The requirement of a definite offer excludes merely indefinite or nebulous discussion about a possible sale. An offer to conduct experimental work may be as firm and definite, in the contract sense, as an offer to sell a product. Although such an offer may not constitute a bar because of policy considerations that allow an inventor to engage in experimentation to develop the invention, a definite offer is not made indefinite merely because it concerns experimental work. Nor is the on-sale bar negated by the fact that the contract calls for services, so long as the claimed invention results from those services.[187]

---

[184]*In re Caveney*, 761 F.2d 671, 226 USPQ 1 (Fed. Cir. 1985). The mere fact that a product is delivered to a distributor does not exempt the transaction, however, even where the distributor was owned 49% by the seller. *Id.* The question is whether the seller so controls the purchaser that the invention remains out of the public's hands. *Ferag AG v. Quipp, Inc.*, 45 F.3d 1562, 33 USPQ2d 1512 (Fed. Cir. 1995).

[185]*Buildex, Inc. v. Kason Indus., Inc.*, 849 F.2d 1461, 7 USPQ2d 1325 (Fed. Cir. 1988). The court rejected the trial court's reasoning that the policy against removing inventions from the public domain was not implicated because the invention was to be used exclusively by the person to whom the sale was made (an OEM manufacturer who had asked the inventor to try to develop the invention). The "public" is not limited to ultimate users of the product, but includes manufacturers as well. *Id.* But see *Continental Can Co. v. Monsanto Co.*, 948 F.2d 1264, 20 USPQ2d 1746 (Fed. Cir. 1991). In *Brasseler U.S.A. v. Stryker Sales Corp.*, 182 F.3d 888, 51 USPQ2d 1470 (Fed. Cir. 1999), a corporate manufacturer made 3,000 units and sold them to the corporate patent owner. Two of the inventors were employed by the patent owner, a third was the owner of the manufacturer, and the fourth was employed by the manufacturer. The patent owner had initiated development of the invention and had an agreement with the manufacturer that it would manufacturer the item only for the patent owner. The patent owner also performed additional manufacturing steps, but the units as supplied included all of the limitations of the claims. The court was unpersuaded by any of these factors. It distinguished this case from the situation in which an individual inventor takes a design to a fabricator and pays the fabricator for its services in fabricating a few sample products. It also indicated that even if the patent owner had been an "equitable" owner of the invention at the time of the transaction, the result would not have been different.

[186]*J.A. LaPorte, Inc. v. Norfolk Dredging Co.*, 787 F.2d 1577, 229 USPQ 435 (Fed. Cir. 1986).

[187]*RCA Corp. v. Data Gen. Corp.*, 887 F.2d 1056, 12 USPQ2d 1449 (Fed. Cir. 1989).

The policies underlying the on-sale bar concentrate on the inventor's attempt to exploit the invention rather than the potential purchaser's cognizance of it. Thus there is no requirement that the purchaser have actual knowledge of the invention.[188] It is not necessary that the sale documents themselves disclose the invention with respect to all claim elements. Merely offering to sell a product by way of an advertisement or invoice may be evidence of a definite offer for sale of a claimed invention even though no details are disclosed. That the offered product is in fact the claimed invention may be established by any relevant evidence, such as memoranda, drawings, correspondence, and testimony of witnesses.[189]

An assignment or sale of the *rights* to an invention, including potential patent rights, is not a sale of "the invention" within the meaning of §102(b).[190] Organizations that invite inventors to submit their ideas in order to obtain patent services and assistance in development and marketing are not ordinarily customers whereby contact with such an organization raises the on-sale bar. An inventor's quest for aid and advice in developing and patenting an invention is not an on-sale event as contemplated by §102(b).[191]

Evidence that the patentee claimed a date of first use for a trademark application that was prior to the critical date is not convincing of a barring sale, because the trademark application refers to the first use of the mark and not the invention.[192] On the other hand, the

---

[188]*Envirotech Corp. v. Westech Eng'g, Inc.*, 904 F.2d 1571, 15 USPQ2d 1230 (Fed. Cir. 1990). What the purchaser reasonably believes the inventor to be offering is relevant to whether, on balance, the offer objectively may be said to be of the patented invention. *Id.* The court found it significant that actual knowledge of the invention had only been communicated to a person other than the actual offeree. Compare *Ferag AG v. Quipp, Inc.*, 45 F.3d 1562, 33 USPQ2d 1512 (Fed. Cir. 1995), where the court indicated that while it is true, as in *Envirotech*, that failure to communicate an intent to sell the claimed invention is relevant, it is not controlling. The standard is more objective. Here the buyer had no reason to know that it was purchasing the patented invention, but it had no reason to expect to receive an old design either. The subjective intent of the seller was not clear at the time of the actual sales agreement, but it was made clear in a later order confirmation, prior to the critical date, that the intent was to supply the patented invention. Although the prior art would meet the agreed specifications, so would the patented invention. On these facts the court held that there was an offer to sell prior to the critical date.

[189]*RCA Corp. v. Data Gen. Corp.*, 887 F.2d 1056, 12 USPQ2d 1449 (Fed. Cir. 1989). In *Sonoscan, Inc. v. Sonotek, Inc.*, 936 F.2d 1261, 19 USPQ2d 1156 (Fed. Cir. 1991), the court, in finding that a quotation before the critical date constituted an offer to sell the patented invention, relied on: (1) testimony that, had the quotation been accepted, that which would have been delivered would have been the patented invention; and (2) a second quotation, made several days after the first and only a few days subsequent to the critical date, that unquestionably offered the patented invention. Thus, although the second quote was too late to qualify in and of itself as an offer to sell, it was used as evidence of what the first quote contemplated.

[190]*Moleculon Res. Corp. v. CBS, Inc.*, 793 F.2d 1261, 229 USPQ 805 (Fed. Cir. 1986). Accordingly, it is necessary to determine whether the purpose of negotiations was to obtain a contract for sale of the patented device, or to interest the other party in becoming a licensee. *Mas-Hamilton Group Inc. v. LaGard Inc.*, 156 F.3d 1206, 48 USPQ2d 1010 (Fed. Cir. 1998).

[191]*Hupp v. Siroflex of Am. Inc.*, 122 F.3d 1456, 43 USPQ2d 1887 (Fed. Cir. 1997).

[192]*Preemption Devices, Inc. v. Minnesota Min. & Mfg. Co.*, 732 F.2d 903, 221 USPQ 841 (Fed. Cir. 1984).

fact that a device was made from photographs of the inventor's own embodiment of the invention eliminates any question that the subject of the sale and the claimed subject matter of the patent were one and the same.[193]

The patent challenger has the burden of proving that there was a definite sale or offer to sell more than one year before the application for patent, and that the subject matter of the sale or offer to sell fully anticipated the claimed invention or would have rendered the claimed invention obvious by its addition to the art.[194] The trier of fact must determine whether the invention was completed and known to work for its intended purpose, or whether the inventor was continuing to develop and evaluate the invention; whether the inventor was merely exploring the market, or had made an unconditional offer to sell a completed invention.[195] The facts concerning an on-sale defense must be proved by clear and convincing evidence.[196] Likewise, the PTO has the initial burden to establish a prima facie case that the subject matter of the claims was on sale.[197] If these facts are established, the applicant or patent owner is called upon to come forward with an explanation of the circumstances surrounding what would otherwise appear to be commercialization outside the one-year grace period.[198] The ultimate question of patent validity is one of law, and whether an invention was on sale within the meaning of §102 is itself a subsidiary question of law,[199] based upon underlying factual considerations.[200]

---

[193]*J.A. LaPorte, Inc. v. Norfolk Dredging Co.*, 787 F.2d 1577, 229 USPQ 435 (Fed. Cir. 1986).

[194]*Envirotech Corp. v. Westech Eng'g, Inc.*, 904 F.2d 1571, 15 USPQ2d 1230 (Fed. Cir. 1990); *Buildex, Inc. v. Kason Indus., Inc.*, 849 F.2d 1461, 7 USPQ2d 1325 (Fed. Cir. 1988); *UMC Elec. Co. v. United States*, 816 F.2d 647, 2 USPQ2d 1465 (Fed. Cir. 1987).

[195]*Seal-Flex, Inc. v. Athletic Track & Court Constr.*, 98 F.3d 1318, 40 USPQ2d 1450 (Fed. Cir. 1996).

[196]*Seal-Flex, Inc. v. Athletic Track & Court Constr.*, 98 F.3d 1318, 40 USPQ2d 1450 (Fed. Cir. 1996); *Sonoscan, Inc. v. Sonotek, Inc.*, 936 F.2d 1261, 19 USPQ2d 1156 (Fed. Cir. 1991).

[197]*In re Brigance*, 792 F.2d 1103, 229 USPQ 988 (Fed. Cir. 1986). Note that the PTO need establish its prima facie case of sale only by a preponderance of the evidence, while a patent challenger in litigation must have clear and convincing evidence. *In re Caveney*, 761 F.2d 671, 226 USPQ 1 (Fed. Cir. 1985).

[198]*In re Hamilton*, 882 F.2d 1576, 11 USPQ2d 1890 (Fed. Cir. 1989); *UMC Elec. Co. v. United States*, 816 F.2d 647, 2 USPQ2d 1465 (Fed. Cir. 1987).

[199]*In re Mahurkar Hemodialysis Catheter*, 71 F.3d 1573, 37 USPQ2d 1138 (Fed. Cir. 1995); *Ferag AG v. Quipp, Inc.*, 45 F.3d 1562, 33 USPQ2d 1512 (Fed. Cir. 1995); *Paragon Podiatry Lab., Inc. v. KLM Labs., Inc.*, 984 F.2d 1182, 25 USPQ2d 1561 (Fed. Cir. 1993); *Atlantic Thermoplastics Co. v. Faytex Corp.*, 970 F.2d 834, 23 USPQ2d 1481 (Fed. Cir. 1992); *Manville Sales Corp. v. Paramount Sys., Inc.*, 917 F.2d 544, 16 USPQ2d 1587 (Fed. Cir. 1990); *Envirotech Corp. v. Westech Eng'g, Inc.*, 904 F.2d 1571, 15 USPQ2d 1230 (Fed. Cir. 1990); *UMC Elec. Co. v. United States*, 816 F.2d 647, 2 USPQ2d 1465 (Fed. Cir. 1987); *J.A. LaPorte, Inc. v. Norfolk Dredging Co.*, 787 F.2d 1577, 229 USPQ 435 (Fed. Cir. 1986); *Barmag Barmer Masch. AG v. Murata Mach., Ltd.*, 731 F.2d 831, 221 USPQ 561 (Fed. Cir. 1984).

[200]*Intel Corp. v. United States ITC*, 946 F.2d 821, 20 USPQ2d 1161 (Fed. Cir. 1991); *Sonoscan, Inc. v. Sonotek, Inc.*, 936 F.2d 1261, 19 USPQ2d 1156 (Fed. Cir. 1991); *Shatterproof Glass Corp. v. Libbey-Owens Ford Co.*, 758 F.2d 613, 225 USPQ 634 (Fed. Cir. 1985). The adequacy of testing, in the context of whether an invention can be said to have been on sale, is one of fact. *Biodex Corp. v. Loredan Biomedical, Inc.*, 946 F.2d 850, 20 USPQ2d 1252 (Fed. Cir. 1991). Resolution of the issue of experimental use is fact driven. *Paragon Podiatry Lab., Inc. v. KLM Labs., Inc.*, 984 F.2d 1182, 25 USPQ2d 1561 (Fed. Cir. 1993).

Ready for patenting—the Pfaff *rule.* The on-sale bar of §102(b) represents a balance of the policies of allowing the inventor a reasonable amount of time to ascertain the commercial value of an invention, while requiring prompt entry into the patent system after sales activity has begun. Thus the statute limits the period of commercial sale or offers of sale of an invention to one year, within which the patent application must be filed or forever barred.[201] The Federal Circuit early on adopted the view that the on-sale defense does not require that the goods actually be on hand at the time of the sale. However, it specifically passed the question whether a physical embodiment of some kind must have been in existence.[202] Though the court continued to skirt the question, it seemed to be signaling that a reduction to practice of some kind—sufficient at least to prove out the invention— would be required.[203]

When it finally did confront the issue squarely in *UMC v. United States*, the court held, in apparently unequivocal fashion, that the on-sale defense does not absolutely require a reduction to practice.[204] Upon closer analysis, however, the court's ruling seemed less than clear. It began by rejecting the invitation to adopt a "sufficiently reduced-to-practice" test, pointing out that there are no degrees of reduction to practice; either one has or has not occurred. Thus, it could only cause confusion in interference law, with its special technical considerations, and in operation of the on-sale bar, which is guided by entirely different policies, to adopt modifiers in connection with "reduction to practice," whatever the context.[205]

But the court went on to qualify its holding, indicating that it did not intend to sanction attacks on patents on the ground that the inventor or another offered for sale, before the critical date, the mere concept of the invention. Nor should inventors be forced to rush into the PTO prematurely. Nor did the court reject reduction to practice as an important analytical tool in an on-sale analysis. A holding that there has or has not been a reduction to practice of the claimed invention before the critical date might well determine whether the claimed invention was in fact the subject of the sale or offer to sell

---

[201]*Seal-Flex, Inc. v. Athletic Track & Court Constr.*, 98 F.3d 1318, 40 USPQ2d 1450, 1452–53 (Fed. Cir. 1996).

[202]*Barmag Barmer Masch. AG v. Murata Mach., Ltd.*, 731 F.2d 831, 221 USPQ 561 (Fed. Cir. 1984).

[203]See *Stearns v. Beckman Instruments, Inc.*, 737 F.2d 1565, 222 USPQ 457 (Fed. Cir. 1984); *King Instrument Corp. v. Otari Corp.*, 767 F.2d 853, 226 USPQ 402 (Fed. Cir. 1985); *Shatterproof Glass Corp. v. Libbey-Owens Ford Co.*, 758 F.2d 613, 225 USPQ 634 (Fed. Cir. 1985); *Great N. Corp. v. Davis Core & Pad Co.*, 782 F.2d 159, 228 USPQ 356 (Fed. Cir. 1986).

[204]*UMC Elec. Co. v. United States*, 816 F.2d 647, 2 USPQ2d 1465 (Fed. Cir. 1987). No reduction to practice is required for a device to be prior art under §102(b), since a §102(b)/§103 bar obviously concerns a device that is not a reduction to practice of the claimed invention. *LaBounty Mfg., Inc. v. United States ITC*, 958 F.2d 1066, 22 USPQ2d 1025 (Fed. Cir. 1992). See also *Keystone Ret. Wall Sys., Inc. v. Westrock, Inc.*, 997 F.2d 1444, 27 USPQ2d 1297 (Fed. Cir. 1993).

[205]*UMC Elec. Co. v. United States*, 816 F.2d 647, 2 USPQ2d 1465 (Fed. Cir. 1987).

or whether a sale was primarily for an experimental purpose. A holding that there is a reduction to practice of the claimed invention might, of course, lighten the burden of the party asserting the bar. All of the circumstances surrounding the sale or offer to sell, including the stage of development of the invention and the nature of the invention, would have to be considered and weighed against the policies underlying §102(b).[206] Under this "all-circumstances" test, then, the thrust of the inquiry seemed to be whether the inventor thought he or she had a product that could be and was offered to customers, not whether he or she could prevail under the technicalities of reduction to practice appropriate to determining priority of invention under interference law.[207]

It was against this background that the Supreme Court granted certiorari to review the decision of the Federal Circuit in *Pfaff v. Wells*.[208] In *Pfaff,* the Federal Circuit had looked to all the circumstances in holding that an invention that had not been reduced to practice as of the date it was on sale nevertheless barred a patent, because it had been sufficiently developed as of the on-sale date. The Supreme Court affirmed, but in so doing, swept away the all-circumstances test and replaced it with a simple inquiry: Was the claimed invention "ready for patenting" when it was placed on sale? If so, and if the on-sale event occurred more than a year before the application filing date, the right to a patent was lost. As the Court framed the new test:

> We conclude, therefore, that the on-sale bar applies when two conditions are satisfied before the critical date. First, the product must be the subject of a commercial offer for sale. An inventor can both understand and control the timing of the first commercial marketing of his invention.***

---

[206]*UMC Elec. Co. v. United States,* 816 F.2d 647, 2 USPQ2d 1465 (Fed. Cir. 1987). Actual reduction to practice of the subject invention means, among other things, that an actual embodiment that included all elements of the claim has been built. Thus a finding that an invention is reduced to practice prior to an offer to sell precludes any argument that the subject matter of the sale could not possibly be the invention as claimed because it was in only a preliminary stage of development. Also, experimental use, which means perfecting or completing an invention to the point of determining that it will work for its intended purpose, ends with an actual reduction to practice. *RCA Corp. v. Data Gen. Corp.,* 887 F.2d 1056, 12 USPQ2d 1449 (Fed. Cir. 1989). On the other hand, if the inventor had merely a conception or was working toward development of that conception, it can be said there was not yet any "invention" that could be placed on sale. *A.B. Chance Co. v. RTE Corp.,* 854 F.2d 1307, 7 USPQ2d 1881 (Fed. Cir. 1988); *UMC Elec. Co. v. United States,* 816 F.2d 647, 2 USPQ2d 1465 (Fed. Cir. 1987). The policy embodied in §102(b) does not require that the one-year period start to accrue on an invention that is not yet known to work satisfactorily for its intended purposes. Precedent illustrates a variety of factual situations wherein contacts with potential customers before an invention was completed did not start the accrual of the on-sale bar period. *Seal-Flex, Inc. v. Athletic Track & Court Constr.,* 98 F.3d 1318, 40 USPQ2d 1450 (Fed. Cir. 1996).

[207]*Paragon Podiatry Lab., Inc. v. KLM Labs., Inc.,* 984 F.2d 1182, 25 USPQ2d 1561 (Fed. Cir. 1993). See also *Robotic Vision Sys., Inc. v. View Eng'r, Inc.,* 112 F.3d 1163, 42 USPQ2d 1619 (Fed. Cir. 1997); *Micro Chem., Inc. v. Great Plains Chem. Co.,* 103 F.3d 1538, 41 USPQ2d 1238 (Fed. Cir. 1997).

[208]*Pfaff v. Wells Elec., Inc.,* 124 F.3d 1429, 43 USPQ2d 1928 (Fed. Cir. 1997).

Second, the invention must be ready for patenting. That condition may be satisfied in at least two ways: by proof of reduction to practice before the critical date; or by proof that prior to the critical date the inventor had prepared drawings or other descriptions of the invention that were sufficiently specific to enable a person skilled in the art to practice the invention.***[209]

One doubts that this new formulation will generate undue controversy; indeed, it is reasonable to expect that it will have a stabilizing effect.

In its first look at the issue following the Supreme Court decision, the Federal Circuit signaled its intention to follow the two-part test without balancing various policies according to the totality of the circumstances as may have been done in the past.[210] It has also made clear that the "invention" that has been offered for sale must, of course, be something within the scope of the claim. Hence, the first determination in the §102(b) analysis must be whether the subject of the barring activity met each of the limitations of the claim, and thus was an embodiment of the claimed invention. There is no requirement that the offer specifically identify these limitations. Nor is there a requirement that the patentee must have recognized the significance of these limitations at the time of offer. If the process that was offered for sale inherently possessed each of the claim limitations, then the process was on sale, whether or not the seller recognized that the process possessed the claimed characteristics.[211] As the court explained in another case, one of the primary purposes of the on-sale bar is to prohibit the withdrawal of inventions that have been placed into the public domain through commercialization. If the patentee's contrary argument were accepted, a person could buy or sell a compound whose exact nature had not been determined and then, years after those sales, file a patent application claiming the compound by reference to characteristics newly discovered.[212]

---

[209]*Pfaff v. Wells Elec., Inc.*, 525 U.S. 55, 48 USPQ2d 1641,1646–47 (1998).

[210]*Weatherchem Corp. v. J.L. Clark Inc.*, 163 F.3d 1326, 49 USPQ2d 1001 (Fed. Cir. 1998). See also *Brasseler U.S.A. v. Stryker Sales Corp.*, 182 F.3d 888, 51 USPQ2d 1470 (Fed. Cir. 1999). In *Weatherchem* the court concluded that there was a commercial offer for sale, which was sufficient even though delivery was not made, and no money changed hands, until after the critical date. It also concluded that the invention was ready for patenting. A drawing existed prior to the critical date that was admitted to disclose all of the elements of the claimed invention. The court found it significant that the buyer ordered large quantities before the critical date, thus demonstrating its confidence that the invention was complete and operative. Also, the manufacturer was able to produce the invention using the drawing in question.

[211]*Scaltech Inc. v. Retec/Tetra L.L.C.*, 156 F.3d 1193, 51 USPQ2d 1055 (Fed. Cir. 1999). *Pfaff* did not remove the requirement that the subject matter of the commercial offer for sale be something within the scope of the claim. *Tec Air Inc. v. Denso Mfg. Michigan Inc.*, 192 F.3d 1353, 52 USPQ2d 1294 (Fed. Cir. 1999). In *STX LLC v. Brine Inc.*, 54 USPQ2d 1347 (Fed. Cir. 2000), the claim called for a head for a lacrosse stick "which provides improved handling and playing characteristics" and then went on to describe the specific structure of the head. The court concluded that this preamble phrase was not a limitation of the claim. The fact that heads that were the subject of an offer to sell prior to the critical date might not have exhibited improved handling and playing characteristics was therefore irrelevant to either prong of the *Pfaff* on-sale test.

[212]*Abbott Labs. v. Geneva Pharm. Inc.*, 182 F.3d 1315, 51 USPQ2d 1307 (Fed. Cir. 1999).

The *Pfaff* "ready for patenting" test does not require presentation at trial of a single piece of evidence that would enable a patent attorney to draft the patent application. The test can be satisfied in at least two ways: by proof of reduction to practice before the critical date; or by proof that prior to the critical date the inventor had prepared drawings or other descriptions of the invention that were sufficiently specific to enable a person skilled in the art to practice the invention.[213] The court has also held that, under *Pfaff*, proof of conception is not necessary. A compound had been made abroad and sold in the United States, but nobody then knew that it constituted the particular crystalline form that was claimed. The court reasoned that it was nonetheless ready for patenting within the meaning of *Pfaff*, because it had been reduced to practice: the fact that it was sold under circumstances in which no question existed that it was useful proves that. The sale of the material obviates any need for inquiry into conception.[214]

Nonenabling sales. Sales or offers by one person of a claimed invention will bar another from obtaining a patent if the sale or offer to sell is made over a year before the latter's filing date. An exception to this general rule exists where a patented method is kept secret and remains secret after a sale of the unpatented product of the method. Such a sale prior to the critical date is a bar if made by the patentee or patent applicant, but not if made by another. However, if the sale or offer of sale by another results in an actual disclosure of the invention, it will be a bar.[215] Indeed, the Federal Circuit has indicated that a third-party sale need not always be informing; the question apparently is not whether a sale, even a third-party sale, "discloses" the invention at the time of sale, but whether the sale relates to a device that embodies the invention.[216]

---

[213]*Vanmoor v. Wal-Mart Stores Inc.*, 201 F.3d 1363, 53 USPQ2d 1377 (Fed. Cir. 2000).

[214]*Abbott Labs. v. Geneva Pharm. Inc.*, 182 F.3d 1315, 51 USPQ2d 1307 (Fed. Cir. 1999).

[215]*In re Caveney*, 761 F.2d 671, 226 USPQ 1 (Fed. Cir. 1985). But see *In re Mahurkar Hemodialysis Catheter*, 71 F.3d 1573, 37 USPQ2d 1138 (Fed. Cir. 1995), where the inventor's exclusive licensee sold two devices to a friendly customer in an effort to satisfy the requirements of the licensing agreement. The device had been reduced to practice and the sale was bona fide. Nonetheless, partly because the instructions packaged with the devices would have rendered them unusable for their intended purposes, the court affirmed a finding of no sale bar. In *Helifix Ltd. v. Blok-Lok Ltd.*, 208 F.3d 1339, 54 USPQ2d 1299 (Fed. Cir. 2000), after holding that a brochure did not appear to be enabling, because it did not disclose a tool for practicing the claimed method, the court went on to hold that the same infirmity existed with respect to an on-sale defense. The brochure itself did not establish that the invention was ready for patenting, so the defendant would have to establish that, at the pertinent time, the invention had been reduced to practice. Although the reduction to practice would not have to involve the specific tool disclosed in the patent, there would have to be a showing that some tool capable of being used to perform the claimed method had been developed.

[216]*J.A. LaPorte, Inc. v. Norfolk Dredging Co.*, 787 F.2d 1577, 229 USPQ 435 (Fed. Cir. 1986). Care should be taken, however, not to permit the PTO to "bootstrap" a hearsay statement that a product was on sale into an irrebuttable presumption that the product embodied the claimed invention. *In re Epstein*, 32 F.3d 1559, 31 USPQ2d 1817 (Fed. Cir. 1994), illustrates this potential concern. Published abstracts contained a description of a particular software product, identified the vendor, stated the date of first release or installation, and gave the number of current users. The date of publication of the abstracts did not antedate the critical

Experimental use or sale. The law of §102(b) is an implementation of the policy that if a patent is to be sought it must be applied for within a reasonable time after a completed invention has been placed in commerce. It is well recognized that an inventor's development of new technology may overlap with the ascertainment of market interest; indeed, market development often accompanies technical development, particularly in the latter phases of completion of an invention. Whether an incomplete invention reasonably requires evaluation under circumstances of actual conditions of use is a circumstance to be considered. But the policy of the on-sale bar does not tolerate a prolonged period of evaluation while the inventor is commercially exploiting the invention. In applying the standard of the totality of the circumstances it is necessary to consider the purpose of and the need for the testing and evaluation period.[217] In considering the matter of experimental use or sale, one must be mindful of the possible impact of the *Pfaff* "ready for patenting" rule discussed above.

Experimental use negates public use; when proved, it may show that particular acts, even if apparently public in a colloquial sense, do not constitute a public use within the meaning of §102.[218] Under long-standing judicial interpretation, a product embodying the patented invention, sold or offered for sale more than a year before the patent filing date, may escape the statutory bar where such sale was primarily for a bona fide experimental purpose, to perfect the invention, rather than for commercial exploitation. But any sales of the later patented product outside the grace period must be merely incidental to the primary purpose of experimentation.[219]

Secrecy is not determinative, either way. A secret commercial use by the inventor may be fatal, while an experimental use open to the public view may not constitute a bar.[220] An inventor may well need to have a customer test the invention to determine whether it

---

date, but the date of first release or installation did. In a remarkable decision, the Federal Circuit held that, despite the clear hearsay nature of the abstracts, they established without more that the products described were in public use or on sale more than a year before the critical date.

[217]*Seal-Flex, Inc. v. Athletic Track & Court Constr.*, 98 F.3d 1318, 40 USPQ2d 1450 (Fed. Cir. 1996). In this case the trial court refused summary judgment of public use, on grounds of experimental testing. Yet, when a track "like" the track being evaluated was offered for sale, it granted summary judgment of on sale. The Federal Circuit felt this was an inappropriate line of distinction, for an experimental track does not become a completed invention simply because of steps taken to interest potential customers.

[218]*Baxter Int'l, Inc. v. Cobe Labs., Inc.*, 88 F.3d 1054, 39 USPQ2d 1437 (Fed. Cir. 1996).

[219]*Paragon Podiatry Lab., Inc. v. KLM Labs., Inc.*, 984 F.2d 1182, 25 USPQ2d 1561 (Fed. Cir. 1993). A sale for experimental rather than commercial purposes may not constitute a statutory bar. *Armco, Inc. v. Cyclops Corp.*, 791 F.2d 147, 229 USPQ 721 (Fed. Cir. 1986).

[220]*TP Labs., Inc. v. Professional Positioners, Inc.*, 724 F.2d 965, 220 USPQ 577 (Fed. Cir. 1984). Although a written promise of confidentiality is a factor to be considered in appropriate circumstances, such as when persons other than the patentee conduct the experiments, the absence of such a promise does not make a use public as a matter of law, or outweigh the fact that no information of a confidential nature was communicated to others. *Allied Colloids, Inc. v. American Cyanamid Co.*, 64 F.3d 1570, 35 USPQ2d 1840 (Fed. Cir. 1995).

works as intended.[221] The §102(b) bar is avoided if the primary purpose of the work was experimental rather than mainly for the purpose of trade or profit. The law recognizes the inventor's need to test the invention, to ascertain whether the work is complete or further changes should be made, and to show that the invention will work for its intended purposes. The law further recognizes that such testing and development may encompass or even require disclosure to the public, without barring the inventor's access to the patent system.[222]

For an assertion of experimental use to have merit, it must be clear that the inventor kept control over his or her invention in the course of its testing. Although control is not the "lodestar" test in all cases involving experimental use, it is nonetheless an important factor. The experimental use doctrine operates in the inventor's favor to allow the inventor to refine the invention or to assess its value relative to the time and expense of prosecuting a patent application. If it is not the inventor or someone under his or her control or surveillance who does these things, there is no reason why he or she should be entitled to rely upon them to avoid the statute.[223]

The Federal Circuit has told us that experimental use is not an exception: the question, rather, is whether there is a public use; experimental use is simply not public use.[224] The court regards evidence of experimentation as part of the totality of the circumstances considered in a public use inquiry. The fact that there was experimentation occurring is relevant to the question of whether the activities of the inventor were at odds with any of the policies underlying the public use bar. In other words, the inquiry is not whether there was a public use and, if so, whether it was for a bona fide experimental purpose and thus excused. Rather, there is only one inquiry—was there a public use within the meaning of §102(b)?[225]

Where does the burden lie with respect to a showing of experimental purpose? Early on the court concluded that once a prima facie

---

[221]*U.S. Envtl. Prods., Inc. v. Westall,* 911 F.2d 713, 15 USPQ2d 1898 (Fed. Cir. 1990).

[222]*In re Mann,* 861 F.2d 1581, 8 USPQ2d 2030 (Fed. Cir. 1988). On the other hand, an invention can exist for purposes of the statutory bar even though it may be later refined or improved. *Id.* See also *Kolmes v. World Fibers Corp.,* 107 F.3d 1534, 41 USPQ2d 1829 (Fed. Cir. 1997).

[223]*In re Hamilton,* 882 F.2d 1576, 11 USPQ2d 1890 (Fed. Cir. 1989). Here an independent third party solicited and filled a "test order." The court adhered closely to standard agency principles and found that the third party was not the inventor's agent for purposes of this transaction. Thus the inventor could not have maintained sufficient control over any testing activity to qualify it as an experimental sale. See also *Lough v. Brunswick Corp.,* 86 F.3d 1113, 39 USPQ2d 1100 (Fed. Cir. 1996).

[224]*Harrington Mfg. Co. v. Powell Mfg. Co.,* 815 F.2d 1478, 2 USPQ2d 1364 (Fed Cir. 1986); *Hycor Corp. v. Schlueter Co.,* 740 F.2d 1529, 222 USPQ 553 (Fed. Cir. 1984). Experimental use is not an exception to public use, but "negates" it. *TP Labs., Inc. v. Professional Positioners, Inc.,* 724 F.2d 965, 220 USPQ 577 (Fed. Cir. 1984). But see *In re Brigance,* 792 F.2d 1103, 229 USPQ 988 (Fed. Cir. 1986). If a use is experimental, it is not, as a matter of law, a public use within the meaning of §102. *Lough v. Brunswick Corp.,* 86 F.3d 1113, 39 USPQ2d 1100 (Fed. Cir. 1996).

[225]*Tone Bros., Inc. v. Sysco Corp.,* 28 F.3d 1192, 31 USPQ2d 1321 (Fed. Cir. 1994).

case of use or sale is established, the burden of coming forward with countervailing evidence of experiment is on the patentee,[226] and it seems to have settled on this view.[227] A pair of decisions in the interim, however, injected a note of uncertainty as to whether the burden of showing lack of experimental purpose might not reside with the patent challenger in the first instance.[228]

Experiment must be the real purpose and not merely incidental to the use.[229] Objective evidence is preferred. The inventor's expression of his or her subjective intent to experiment is, without objective indicia, of little value, particularly if expressed after initiation of litigation.[230] An inventor's protestation of an intent to experiment, expressed for the first time during litigation, is of little evidentiary value. When sales are made in an ordinary commercial environment and the goods are placed outside the inventor's control, the inventor's secretly held subjective intent to experiment is unavailing without objective evidence to support the contention. A failure to communicate that intent to any of the purchasers or prospective purchasers is

---

[226]*D.L. Auld Co. v. Chroma Graphics Corp.*, 714 F.2d 1144, 219 USPQ 13 (Fed. Cir. 1983); *In re Smith*, 714 F.2d 1127, 218 USPQ 976 (Fed. Cir. 1983).

[227]*Tone Bros., Inc. v. Sysco Corp.*, 28 F.3d 1192, 31 USPQ2d 1321, 1323 n.4 (Fed. Cir. 1994); *U.S. Envtl. Prods., Inc. v. Westall*, 911 F.2d 713, 15 USPQ2d 1898 (Fed. Cir. 1990); *Harrington Mfg. Co. v. Powell Mfg. Co.*, 815 F.2d 1478, 2 USPQ2d 1364, 1367 & n.5 (Fed Cir. 1986); *Hycor Corp. v. Schlueter Co.*, 740 F.2d 1529, 222 USPQ 553 (Fed. Cir. 1984). Is the patentee's burden of proof one of clear and convincing evidence? These decisions are not entirely clear on that point. Compare *Tone* with *Harrington*. See also *In re Hamilton*, 882 F.2d 1576, 11 USPQ2d 1890 (Fed. Cir. 1989). On summary judgment, once an alleged infringer has presented facts sufficient to establish a prima facie case of public use, it falls to the patent owner to come forward with some evidence to the contrary sufficient to raise a genuine issue of material fact. Post hoc affidavit testimony alone, years after the events described and purporting to show an inventor's subjective experimental intent, will never satisfy the burden of establishing experimental use in a case where there is no contemporaneous evidence of experimental purpose and the objective evidence is to the contrary. *Sinskey v. Pharmacia Ophthalmics, Inc.*, 982 F.2d 494, 25 USPQ2d 1290 (Fed. Cir. 1992). The fact that an inventor had an intent to experiment in making a sale need not be overcome or disputed to invoke the statutory bar, and thus an averment to that effect does not in itself raise a genuine issue of material fact on summary judgment. *Paragon Podiatry Lab., Inc. v. KLM Labs., Inc.*, 984 F.2d 1182, 25 USPQ2d 1561 (Fed. Cir. 1993).

[228]Compare *TP Labs., Inc. v. Professional Positioners, Inc.*, 724 F.2d 965, 220 USPQ 577 (Fed. Cir. 1984), with *Barmag Barmer Masch. AG v. Murata Mach., Ltd.*, 731 F.2d 831, 221 USPQ 561 (Fed. Cir. 1984).

[229]*In re Smith*, 714 F.2d 1127, 218 USPQ 976 (Fed. Cir. 1983).

[230]*Harrington Mfg. Co. v. Powell Mfg. Co.*, 815 F.2d 1478, 2 USPQ2d 1364 (Fed Cir. 1986); *In re Brigance*, 792 F.2d 1103, 229 USPQ 988 (Fed. Cir. 1986); *TP Labs., Inc. v. Professional Positioners, Inc.*, 724 F.2d 965, 220 USPQ 577 (Fed. Cir. 1984); *In re Smith*, 714 F.2d 1127, 218 USPQ 976 (Fed. Cir. 1983). Where one co-inventor demonstrates the invention under circumstances amounting to a public disclosure, it is immaterial that the other co-inventor felt uncertain as to whether the invention would work. Any co-inventor is free to make, use, or sell an invention in the absence of an agreement to the contrary. *Harrington Mfg. Co. v. Powell Mfg. Co.*, 815 F.2d 1478, 2 USPQ2d 1364 (Fed Cir. 1986). In *Moxness Prods., Inc. v. Xomed, Inc.*, 891 F.2d 890, 13 USPQ2d 1169 (Fed. Cir. 1989), the court found error in the trial court's grant of JNOV based upon an expressed disregard of the inventor's oral testimony that conflicted with documentary evidence on the issue of whether a sale was for experimental purposes. The trial court apparently felt obliged to disregard the testimony in view of *In re Theis*, 610 F.2d 786, 284 USPQ 188 (CCPA 1979). The Federal Circuit did not overrule *Theis*, but distinguished it on the basis that it did not involve JNOV.

fatal.[231] Indeed, intent is merely a fact to be taken into account in resolving the ultimate legal question, and it is generally a factor of minimal value.[232]

The ultimate question of patent validity is one of law. Whether an invention was on sale within the meaning of §102(b) is itself a subsidiary question of law, but resolution of the issue of experimental use is fact driven.[233] A bare finding of prototype testing and development is inadequate to support a determination of experimental use.[234] Relevant factors include the nature of the activity that occurred in public; the public access to and knowledge of the use; whether there was any confidentiality obligation imposed on persons who observed the use; whether progress records or other indicia of experimental activity were kept; whether persons other than the inventor or those acting for the inventor conducted the experiments; how many tests were conducted; the scale of the tests compared with commercial conditions; the length of the test period in comparison with tests of similar products; and whether payment was made for the product of the test. There may be additional factors in a particular case; all circumstances must be considered.[235] Failure to make a profit is not conclusive; neither is the fact that the customer was advised and understood that the system was experimental. Such evidence may be outweighed by evidence that no testing schedule was adhered to and no records were maintained; that the inventor lacked control over the invention and its use; that the installation was used for promotional activities in an effort to make other sales; and that there was no secrecy.[236]

---

[231]*LaBounty Mfg., Inc. v. United States ITC,* 958 F.2d 1066, 22 USPQ2d 1025 (Fed. Cir. 1992). An assertion of experimental sales requires, at a minimum, that the customers be made aware of the experimentation. *Paragon Podiatry Lab., Inc. v. KLM Labs., Inc.,* 984 F.2d 1182, 25 USPQ2d 1561 (Fed. Cir. 1993).

[232]*Paragon Podiatry Lab., Inc. v. KLM Labs., Inc.,* 984 F.2d 1182, 25 USPQ2d 1561 (Fed. Cir. 1993).

[233]*Paragon Podiatry Lab., Inc. v. KLM Labs., Inc.,* 984 F.2d 1182, 25 USPQ2d 1561 (Fed. Cir. 1993).

[234]*Atlantic Thermoplastics Co. v. Faytex Corp.,* 5 F.3d 1477, 28 USPQ2d 1343 (Fed. Cir. 1993).

[235]*Allied Colloids, Inc. v. American Cyanamid Co.,* 64 F.3d 1570, 35 USPQ2d 1840 (Fed. Cir. 1995). See also *Sinskey v. Pharmacia Ophthalmics, Inc.,* 982 F.2d 494, 25 USPQ2d 1290 (Fed. Cir. 1992); *In re Brigance,* 792 F.2d 1103, 229 USPQ 988 (Fed. Cir. 1986); *Hycor Corp. v. Schlueter Co.,* 740 F.2d 1529, 222 USPQ 553 (Fed. Cir. 1984); *TP Labs., Inc. v. Professional Positioners, Inc.,* 724 F.2d 965, 220 USPQ 577 (Fed. Cir. 1984). Payment is a factor to be weighed but does not per se overcome an experimental purpose defense to an on-sale defense. *In re Hamilton,* 882 F.2d 1576, 11 USPQ2d 1890 (Fed. Cir. 1989). The absence of payment for tests supports an inference that the tests were for the benefit of the patentee and thus contravenes the inference of public use by or for the potential customer. *Allied Colloids, Inc. v. American Cyanamid Co.,* 64 F.3d 1570, 35 USPQ2d 1840 (Fed. Cir. 1995). Various factors are pertinent, e.g., whether there was a need for testing by other than the patentee, the amount of control exercised, the state of development of the invention, whether payments were made and the basis thereof, whether confidentiality was required, and whether technological changes were made. All must be considered in light of the public policy underlying §102(b). The on-sale bar is really measured by the time the public came into possession of the invention. *Continental Can Co. v. Monsanto Co.,* 948 F.2d 1264, 20 USPQ2d 1746 (Fed. Cir. 1991).

[236]*U.S. Envtl. Prods., Inc. v. Westall,* 911 F.2d 713, 15 USPQ2d 1898 (Fed. Cir. 1990).

The testing must somehow be related to the claimed features of the invention.[237] Certainly the fine-tuning of an invention by a stranger, after reduction to practice, for its own unique purposes, where the testing is independent of and not controlled by the patentee, is not experimental.[238] The fact that customers are given a money-back guarantee if they are dissatisfied does not establish an experimental relationship between the seller and buyer. Nor does the fact that some customers return devices for unsatisfactory performance. It is well settled that testing of a device to determine suitability for a customer's unclaimed need is not experimental use that will negate commercialization by the inventor.[239]

Where the evidence indicates that a market test was an experiment to see whether a consumer would buy the product, the experimental use exception does not apply.[240] Thus the court takes the view that the experimental use exception does not apply in the case of a design patent. Obtaining reactions of people to a design—that is, whether or not they like it—is not "experimentation." If market testing shows that the design has no appeal, and it is changed, the result is a new and different design; the original design remains just what it was.[241] But the court has held that experimentation directed to functional features of a product also containing an ornamental design may negate what otherwise would be considered a public use within the meaning of §102(b). Among the factors that should be considered

---

[237]*In re Brigance*, 792 F.2d 1103, 229 USPQ 988 (Fed. Cir. 1986); *Western Mar. Elec., Inc. v. Furuno Elec. Co.*, 764 F.2d 840, 226 USPQ 334 (Fed. Cir. 1985); *In re Smith*, 714 F.2d 1127, 218 USPQ 976 (Fed. Cir. 1983). Where a feature is in some claims but not others, experimentation as to that feature does not save the claims that do not include the feature. *In re Brigance*, 792 F.2d 1103, 229 USPQ 988 (Fed. Cir. 1986). But see *Grain Processing Corp. v. American Maize-Products Co.*, 840 F.2d 902, 5 USPQ2d 1788 (Fed. Cir. 1988), where it was shown to be industry custom to submit samples of proposed products to food manufacturers for determination of the product's utility. This testing was necessary because such products might interact adversely with other food ingredients in the manufacturer's products. The testing period was short, only very small quantities of samples were shipped, and they were free of charge. The court found nothing inconsistent with experimentation and thus concluded that there was no public use. In *Manville Sales Corp. v. Paramount Sys., Inc.*, 917 F.2d 544, 16 USPQ2d 1587 (Fed. Cir. 1990), the invention was designed to be used outdoors in adverse weather, so the court found no difficulty in concluding that testing in actual outdoor conditions was reasonable, and that experimentation was the principal purpose of the use and sale. But testing simply to determine whether a device is sufficiently durable is not testing to determine if the device as claimed would work for its intended purpose. *Paragon Podiatry Lab., Inc. v. KLM Labs., Inc.*, 984 F.2d 1182, 25 USPQ2d 1561 (Fed. Cir. 1993).

[238]*Baxter Int'l, Inc. v. Cobe Labs., Inc.*, 88 F.3d 1054, 39 USPQ2d 1437 (Fed. Cir. 1996). Standard security measures taken by the customer, rather than special requirements imposed by the seller, do not tend to reflect an experimental purpose. *Petrolite Corp. v. Baker Hughes Inc.*, 96 F.3d 1423, 40 USPQ2d 1201 (Fed. Cir. 1996).

[239]*LaBounty Mfg., Inc. v. United States ITC*, 958 F.2d 1066, 22 USPQ2d 1025 (Fed. Cir. 1992).

[240]*In re Smith*, 714 F.2d 1127, 218 USPQ 976 (Fed. Cir. 1983). But the fact that testing leads to and is followed by commercial success does not convert the test activity into an invalidating public use. The dispositive consideration is whether the inventor was in fact testing the invention. *Allied Colloids, Inc. v. American Cyanamid Co.*, 64 F.3d 1570, 35 USPQ2d 1840 (Fed. Cir. 1995).

[241]*In re Mann*, 861 F.2d 1581, 8 USPQ2d 2030 (Fed. Cir. 1988).

are (1) the length of the test period and the number of tests as compared with a similar type of test on a similar type of design, (2) whether a user made any payment for the device, (3) whether a user agreed to secrecy, (4) whether records were kept of the progress of the test, and (5) whether persons other than the designer conducted the asserted experiments.[242]

That testing was done on the commercial premises of another, and that the owner of the premises, the inventor, and even the public, benefit from the testing, do not alone negate a conclusion of experimental use.[243] Nor do advertisements for sale necessarily convert experimental use into barring commercial use.[244] Commercial purpose underlies virtually every contract between an inventor and a potential customer. When testing an invention entails customer contact, that does not convert an otherwise experimental purpose into a public use.[245]

On the other hand, the court is willing to hold that the fact a method worked on a noncommercial scale is sufficient to show that the use was not experimental, even though the products were marked "laboratory samples," and even though there were later experiments to achieve tooling for mass production.[246] Likewise, a patentee failed to show experimental use where the invention was provided to third parties without any confidentiality obligations, photographs of the invention were employed for marketing purposes, the invention was promoted in freely circulated sales literature, and the patentee was unable to point to any significant documentary evidence of testing.[247] The activity must represent a bona fide effort to perfect the invention or to ascertain whether it will answer its intended purpose. If commercial exploitation occurs, it must be merely incidental to the primary purpose of experimentation to perfect the invention.[248] In one case

---

[242]*Tone Bros., Inc. v. Sysco Corp.*, 28 F.3d 1192, 31 USPQ2d 1321 (Fed. Cir. 1994). The court undertook to distinguish *In re Mann* (note 241 above), on the basis that there, in view of the commercial nature of a trade show, an exploitative purpose seems to have been present. Here, the showing was for the purpose of testing functional features such as feel, hold, and handling. The court also suggests that some of the broad language of *Mann* may have been dicta. (One ventures to suggest that this comment is, in itself, the purest dictum, given the fact that *Mann* did not even address the issue of whether experimental use may be found in testing directed to functional aspects of a design.)

[243]*Hycor Corp. v. Schlueter Co.*, 740 F.2d 1529, 222 USPQ 553 (Fed. Cir. 1984).

[244]*Reactive Metals & Alloys Corp. v. ESM, Inc.*, 769 F.2d 1578, 226 USPQ 821 (Fed. Cir. 1985).

[245]*Allied Colloids, Inc. v. American Cyanamid Co.*, 64 F.3d 1570, 35 USPQ2d 1840 (Fed. Cir. 1995).

[246]*D.L. Auld Co. v. Chroma Graphics Corp.*, 714 F.2d 1144, 219 USPQ 13 (Fed. Cir. 1983).

[247]*Hycor Corp. v. Schlueter Co.*, 740 F.2d 1529, 222 USPQ 553 (Fed. Cir. 1984).

[248]*Pennwalt Corp. v. Akzona Inc.*, 740 F.2d 1573, 222 USPQ 833 (Fed. Cir. 1984). The fact that a sale or use occurs under a regulatory testing procedure does not make such uses or sales per se experimental. Here the sales were made under a temporary EPA permit, and the real goal of the activity under that permit was to obtain a commercial label. The purposes of the experimental activity under §102(b) and EPA regulations are quite different. In the former, the purpose is to prove the invention; in the latter, the purpose is to obtain the right to commercialize it. *Id.*

an inventor demonstrated a prototype to a journalist, who was not enjoined to secrecy, and who published an article prior to the critical date. Although the article was nonenabling, it reported that the invention worked flawlessly for its intended purposes, and even gave its approximate cost. This was a clear indication of commercial motive.[249]

Assertions of a reduction to practice in the context of an interference tend to refute assertions of experimentation and can be considered as evidence in determining whether a use was experimental.[250] Experimental use does not defeat the on-sale bar once the invention has been reduced to practice.[251] The court has rejected the argument that there can be no on-sale bar where the claimed invention, albeit reduced to practice, was part of a larger combination that was not yet reduced to practice and was still in the experimental stage. The experimental use exception is not applied to the subject matter of the offer as a whole, but only as to the claimed invention itself.[252]

(d) Prior Invention or Knowledge

If the claimed subject matter was known to others in this country prior to the applicant's invention of it, 35 U.S.C. §102(a) forbids a patent. If the invention was first made in this country by another who did not abandon, suppress, or conceal it, §102(g) forbids a patent. This author for a long time supposed that the two statutory provisions were mutually exclusive, and that §102(a) defined prior art while §102(g) was limited to interference practice and related priority contests. After all, it is quite clear that if an invention was known to another before the applicant made it, then the applicant was not the first inventor. That being the case, there was surely no need for §102(g), with its additional baggage of abandonment, suppression,

---

[249]*Harrington Mfg. Co. v. Powell Mfg. Co.*, 815 F.2d 1478, 2 USPQ2d 1364 (Fed Cir. 1986). There was no evidence that there was some public necessity requiring the demonstration, which was obviously for the purpose of gaining public recognition.

[250]*Baker Oil Tools, Inc. v. Geo Vann, Inc.*, 828 F.2d 1588, 4 USPQ2d 1210 (Fed. Cir. 1987). The court refused to give preclusive or estoppel effect to the assertions, however. In *Baxter Int'l, Inc. v. Cobe Labs., Inc.*, 88 F.3d 1054, 39 USPQ2d 1437 (Fed. Cir. 1996), the court more or less discounted the fact that an alleged prior user had filed his own patent application, with the usual declaration averring that the invention had not been in public use. The court felt that this was a statement of his own appraisal of the relevant facts, made in relation to his own application for patent, and should not bind a court later evaluating those facts, especially in relation to another's application for patent.

[251]*Atlantic Thermoplastics Co. v. Faytex Corp.*, 5 F.3d 1477, 28 USPQ2d 1343 (Fed. Cir. 1993). After actual reduction to practice, but more than a year before the application was filed, the government, employer of the inventor, contracted with a supplier to provide several thousand units for a test program. This was held to be an invalidating offer for sale. The fact that the sale was made in the context of a cost-plus research and development program does not suffice to avoid the bar. Nor does the fact that the products sold to the government were to be used for testing rather than deployment. Nor is it of consequence that the sale was made by a third party, not the inventor, or that the product was constructed and the sale made pursuant to the buyer's directions. *Zacharin v. United States*, 213 F.3d 1366, 55 USPQ2d 1047 (Fed. Cir. 2000).

[252]*RCA Corp. v. Data Gen. Corp.*, 887 F.2d 1056, 12 USPQ2d 1449 (Fed. Cir. 1989).

and concealment, unless it were intended to apply to an entirely different set of circumstances, like interferences.

This author was wrong. The Federal Circuit has held that §102(g) is a type of anticipation.[253] More than that, activity under §102(g) can be used as prior art for obviousness inquiries under 35 U.S.C. §103.[254] The court has scarcely begun to probe the interrelationships and intricacies of the two statutory provisions, and there is bound to be significant activity in this area.

Prior knowledge. Public policy does not favor the use of secret prior art.[255] Section 102(a) establishes that a person cannot patent what was already known to others. If the invention was known to or used by others in this country before the date of the patentee's invention, the later inventor has not contributed to the store of knowledge, and has no entitlement to a patent. Accordingly, in order to invalidate a patent based on prior knowledge or use, that knowledge or use must have been available to the public. Therefore, notwithstanding abandonment of the prior use—which may preclude a challenge under §102(g)—prior knowledge or use by others may invalidate a patent under §102(a) if the prior knowledge or use was accessible to the public. Section 102(b) establishes a one-year grace period based on publication or public use or sale, after which an inventor is barred from access to the patent system. Section 102(b), unlike §102(a), is primarily concerned with the policy that encourages an inventor to enter the patent system promptly, while recognizing a one-year period of public knowledge or use or commercial exploitation before the patent application must be filed. Thus an inventor's own prior commercial use, albeit kept secret, may constitute a public use or sale under §102(b), barring him or her from obtaining a patent. However, when an asserted prior use is not that of the applicant, §102(b) is not a bar when that prior use or knowledge is not available to the public.[256] Although in some circumstances unsupported oral testimony can be sufficient to prove prior knowledge or use, it must be regarded with suspicion and subjected to close scrutiny.[257]

---

[253]*New Idea Farm Equip. Corp. v. Sperry Corp.*, 916 F.2d 1561, 16 USPQ2d 1424 (Fed. Cir. 1990); *Hybritech Inc. v. Monoclonal Antibodies, Inc.*, 802 F.2d 1367, 231 USPQ 81 (Fed. Cir. 1986).

[254]*Hybritech Inc. v. Monoclonal Antibodies, Inc.*, 802 F.2d 1367, 231 USPQ 81 (Fed. Cir. 1986). Nonetheless, the court has said that the lost count of an interference is not prior art against a different invention, for "prior art" in the sense of §102(g) cannot be the basis of a §102(a) rejection, the invention not being publicly known or used. *In re Zletz*, 893 F.2d 319, 13 USPQ2d 1320 (Fed. Cir. 1989).

[255]*Kimberly-Clark Corp. v. Johnson & Johnson*, 745 F.2d 1437, 223 USPQ 603 (Fed. Cir. 1984). See *E.I. duPont & Co. v. Phillips Petroleum Co.*, 849 F.2d 1430, 7 USPQ2d 1129 (Fed. Cir. 1988).

[256]*Woodland Trust v. Flowertree Nursery Inc.*, 148 F.3d 1368, 47 USPQ2d 1363 (Fed. Cir. 1998). In order for knowledge to qualify as prior art under §102(a), it must have been accessible to the public. *Carella v. Starlight Archery & Pro Line Co.*, 804 F.2d 135, 231 USPQ 644 (Fed. Cir. 1986).

[257]*Carella v. Starlight Archery & Pro Line Co.*, 804 F.2d 135, 231 USPQ 644 (Fed. Cir. 1986). Oral testimony to establish the existence of allegedly anticipatory devices has long been viewed with skepticism. *Sjolund v. Musland*, 847 F.2d 1573, 6 USPQ2d 2020 (Fed. Cir. 1988).

Prior invention. United States patent law embraces the principle that the patent right is granted to the first inventor rather than the first to file a patent application.[258] Thus, a patent may be invalid as anticipated due to the prior conception and reduction to practice by another of the patentee's invention, pursuant to §102(g).[259]

Section 102(g) contains the basic rule for determining priority. It also provides basic protection for the inventive process, shielding in particular the creative steps of conception and reduction to practice. In the United States, the person who first reduces an invention to practice is prima facie the first and true inventor. However, the person who first conceives, and in a mental sense, first invents, may date the patentable invention back to the time of its conception, if the conception can be connected with the reduction to practice by reasonable diligence, so that they are substantially one continuous act.[260] A detailed analysis of the fundamental principles underlying §102(g) is set forth in §15.2, which deals with interference proceedings. Nonetheless, a brief discussion of a few of the cases that deal with §102(g) as a self-standing invalidity defense is appropriate here.

In order for prior invention to be prior art under §102(g), it must be reduced to practice.[261] A principal purpose of §102(g) is to ensure that a patent is awarded to a first inventor. However, it also encourages prompt public disclosure of an invention by penalizing the unexcused delay or failure of a first inventor to share the benefit of the knowledge of the invention with the public after the invention has been completed. One way a prior inventor may avoid the disqualifying effect of §102(g) is by promptly filing a patent application claiming the invention. In the usual context of an interference proceeding, each inventor involved in the proceeding will have filed a patent application, one of which may have matured into a patent. However, §102(g) is applicable in other contexts as well, such as when it is asserted a basis for invalidating a patent in defense to an infringement suit. In such a case the first inventor may seek to avoid a determination of abandonment by showing that he or she marketed or sold a commercial embodiment of the invention or described the invention in a publicly disseminated document. If the prior inventor's activities following completing of the invention do not evidence abandonment, suppression, or concealment, §102(g) will bar a later inventor from obtaining a patent.[262]

Under §102(g), a distinction must be drawn between deliberate suppression or concealment of an invention, which is probably not

---

[258]*Paulik v. Rizkalla,* 760 F.2d 1270, 226 USPQ 224 (Fed. Cir. 1985).

[259]*Texas Instr., Inc. v. United States ITC,* 988 F.2d 1165, 26 USPQ2d 1018 (Fed. Cir. 1993).

[260]*Mahurkar v. C.R. Bard, Inc.,* 79 F.3d 1572, 38 USPQ2d 1288 (Fed. Cir. 1996).

[261]*Kimberly-Clark Corp. v. Johnson & Johnson,* 745 F.2d 1437, 223 USPQ 603 (Fed. Cir. 1984). Reduction to practice in this context means that an invention be sufficiently tested to demonstrate that it will work for its intended purpose. If the usefulness of a compound for its intended purpose is not inherently apparent, it must be tested to demonstrate that it will perform with sufficient success. *Id.* See also *Checkpoint Sys., Inc. v. United States ITC,* 54 F.3d 756, 35 USPQ2d 1042 (Fed. Cir. 1995).

[262]*Checkpoint Sys., Inc. v. United States ITC,* 54 F.3d 756, 35 USPQ2d 1042 (Fed. Cir. 1995).

curable by resumption of work, and a legal inference of suppression or concealment based on "too long" a delay. The first probably results in an absolute forfeiture, while the second can be cured.[263] A mere delay in filing, even a long one, does not result in a "forfeiture" of patent rights, and §102(g) does not take cognizance of mere delay except in priority contests, where the equities of two applicants for the same invention are fully evaluated.[264] As between a prior inventor who benefits from a process by selling its product but suppresses, conceals, or otherwise keeps the process from the public, and a later inventor who promptly files a patent application from which the public will gain a disclosure of the process, the law favors the latter.[265] When determining whether an inventor has abandoned, suppressed, or concealed an invention, a period of delay between completion of the invention and subsequent public disclosure may or may not be of legal consequence. The delay may be inconsequential if, for example, it is reasonable in length or excused by the activities of the inventor. There is no particular length of delay that is per se unreasonable. Rather, a determination of abandonment, suppression, or concealment has consistently been based on equitable principles and public policy as applied to the facts of each case. A court must determine whether, under the facts before it, any delay was reasonable or excused as a matter of law.[266]

A two-judge panel of the Federal Circuit has expressly held that prior work under 35 U.S.C. §102(g) is prior art for purposes of §103 if it satisfies the requirements of §102(g), that is, if it was not abandoned, suppressed, or concealed.[267] The court specifically rejected as dictum the implication in a decision of a predecessor court[268] that there is a further requirement that the §102(g) work be known to the art or to the inventor before the invention was made. Despite lingering concerns about so-called secret prior art, the panel concluded that the requirement of no abandonment, suppression, or concealment should mollify such concerns somewhat.[269] The panel made it clear that because work was secret does not necessarily mean that it was "abandoned, suppressed, or concealed" within the meaning of §102(g), however. For example, the filing of a patent application maintains secrecy

---

[263]*Paulik v. Rizkalla,* 760 F.2d 1270, 226 USPQ 224 (Fed. Cir. 1985).

[264]*Panduit Corp. v. Dennison Mfg. Co.,* 774 F.2d 1082, 227 USPQ 337 (Fed. Cir. 1985).

[265]*W.L. Gore & Assoc. v. Garlock, Inc.,* 721 F.2d 1540, 220 USPQ 303 (Fed. Cir. 1983).

[266]*Checkpoint Sys., Inc. v. United States ITC,* 54 F.3d 756, 35 USPQ2d 1042 (Fed. Cir. 1995). Although the challenger bears the burden of establishing, by clear and convincing evidence, the facts that support the ultimate legal conclusion of invalidity under §102(g), the court has not expressly held that standard applicable to the facts relating to abandonment, suppression, or concealment. *Id.*

[267]*E.I. duPont & Co. v. Phillips Petroleum Co.,* 849 F.2d 1430, 7 USPQ2d 1129 (Fed. Cir. 1988).

[268]*In re Clemens,* 622 F.2d 1029, 206 USPQ 289 (CCPA 1980).

[269]*E.I. duPont & Co. v. Phillips Petroleum Co.,* 849 F.2d 1430, 7 USPQ2d 1129 (Fed. Cir. 1988). The panel also specifically recognized the impact of the 1984 amendments to §103 that alter the situation where the inventors are commonly employed. See notes 273–74 and accompanying text.

but cuts against abandonment, suppression, or concealment. The conclusion depends upon the facts of each case.[270]

The eventual development of this nuance promises to be interesting. In a later case the court attempted to harmonize §§102(e) and (g), on the apparent basis that under §102(e) an entire patent disclosure is a reference, but only as of its filing date, while under §102(g) only the specific matter that was the subject of the prior invention is prior art, but it becomes so as of the date of its conception or actual reduction to practice.[271] Thus a disclosure in a reference U.S. patent is not governed by §102(g) but by §102(e), and that disclosure can be antedated by a showing of prior invention without resort to an interference proceeding. On the other hand, where the subject matter sought to be antedated is *claimed* in the reference U.S. patent, an interference must be had to determine priority.[272]

The court had held that prior work by another in the same company could be, consistent with §102(g), applied as prior art under 35 U.S.C. §103.[273] Such holdings were obviated by a November 1984 amendment to §103, which effectively removed commonly owned prior invention activities from the ambit of §103 prior art.[274] However, if the first inventor does not have an obligation to assign to the common employer, the prior invention may be prior art. In an unusual case, one employee had conceived the invention and worked toward an eventual commercialization of it, but filed no patent application. Another employee invented it independently later and filed an application that matured into the patent in suit, which was assigned to the employer. Although the first inventor may have lost the right to obtain a patent, his work was not thereby disqualified as prior art. The court felt that if a valid patent were to be obtained, the first inventor, who is favored by U.S. law, could not be cavalierly tossed aside in favor of a second inventor with whom the employer had more advantageous contract rights.[275]

---

[270]*E.I. duPont & Co. v. Phillips Petroleum Co.,* 849 F.2d 1430, 7 USPQ2d 1129 (Fed. Cir. 1988). The court also appears to distinguish between abandonment, suppression, and concealment of the invention, and of data regarding the invention, such as data concerning whether a composition had certain properties. The panel seemed to hold that under no circumstances would such data be inadmissible simply because it, rather than the invention itself, had been concealed.

[271]*Sun Studs, Inc. v. ATA Equip. Leasing, Inc.,* 872 F.2d 978, 10 USPQ2d 1338 (Fed. Cir. 1989).

[272]*In re Zletz,* 893 F.2d 319, 13 USPQ2d 1320 (Fed. Cir. 1989). Thus, a losing party to an interference is entitled to claim subject matter other than that of the interference count, provided the requirements of patentability are met, and subject to those constraints that flow from the adverse decision in the interference. *Id.*

[273]*Kimberly-Clark Corp. v. Johnson & Johnson,* 745 F.2d 1437, 223 USPQ 603 (Fed. Cir. 1984).

[274]*In re Longi,* 759 F.2d 887, 225 USPQ 645, 650 & n.7 (Fed. Cir. 1985). See also *E.I. duPont & Co. v. Phillips Petroleum Co.,* 849 F.2d 1430, 7 USPQ2d 1129 (Fed. Cir. 1988).

[275]*Checkpoint Sys., Inc. v. United States ITC,* 54 F.3d 756, 35 USPQ2d 1042 (Fed. Cir. 1995). The court characterized the patent owner's arguments about abandonment, suppression, or concealment as "a new definition of 'chutzpah'."

Corroboration of prior invention. The matter of corroboration of prior invention has been addressed in a trio of recent cases. In *Woodland v. Flowertree,* the court explained that there is a very heavy burden to be met by one challenging validity when the only evidence is the oral testimony of interested persons and their friends, particularly as to long-past events. Corroboration of oral evidence of prior invention is the general rule in patent disputes. In assessing corroboration, the court endorses the following criteria: (1) the relationship between the corroborating witness and the alleged prior user, (2) the time period between the event and trial, (3) the interest of the corroborating witness in the subject matter in suit, (4) contradiction or impeachment of the witness's testimony, (5) the extent and details of the corroborating testimony, (6) the witness's familiarity with the subject matter of the patented invention and the prior use, (7) the probability that a prior use could occur considering the state of the art at the time, and (8) the impact of the invention on the industry and the commercial value of its practice. Such an analysis can be described as application of a "rule of reason" to the corroboration requirement. In this case the court was particularly concerned about the lack of any physical record of an alleged prior activity that was said to have begun 30 years prior, but only continued for a decade and was not reactivated until the defendant learned of the patentee's practices. It observed that early Supreme Court decisions reinforce the heavy burden when establishing prior public knowledge and use based on long-past events. The Supreme Court's view of human nature as well as human recollection, whether deemed cynical or realistic, retains its cogency. This view is reinforced, in modern times, by the ubiquitous paper trail of virtually all commercial activity. It is rare indeed that some physical record (e.g., a written document such as notes, letters, invoices, notebooks, or a sketch or drawing or photograph showing the device, a model, or some other contemporaneous record) does not exist. In this case, the court was impressed by the absence, despite the asserted many years of commercial and public use, of any physical record to support the oral evidence. The relationship of the witnesses and the fact that the asserted prior uses ended 20 years before the trial, and were abandoned until the defendant reportedly learned of the patentee's practices, underscored the failure of this oral evidence to provide clear and convincing evidence of prior knowledge and use.[276]

Six months later, in *Thomson v. Quixote,* the court appeared to retreat slightly from the *Woodland* approach. It held that, in a case involving a prior invention defense under §102(g), corroboration is required only when the testifying inventor is asserting a claim of

---

[276]*Woodland Trust v. Flowertree Nursery Inc.,* 148 F.3d 1368, 47 USPQ2d 1363 (Fed. Cir. 1998). The court was actually considering a defense of prior knowledge and use under 35 U.S.C. §102(a). In *Finnigan Corp. v. United States ITC,* 180 F.3d 1354, 51 USPQ2d 1001 (Fed. Cir. 1999), the court expressly concluded that a witness's uncorroborated testimony is equally suspect as clear and convincing evidence if it relates to use of the invention in public before

derivation or priority of his or her invention and is a named party, an employee of or assignor to a named party, or otherwise is in a position where he or she stands to gain, directly and substantially, by his or her invention being found to have priority over the patent claims at issue. The court observed that the cases that discuss skepticism of uncorroborated inventor testimony directed to establishing priority over an opponent's patent claim involve situations where the inventor is self-interested in the outcome of the trial and is thereby tempted to "remember" facts favorable to his or her case. The clear and convincing standard of proof required to establish priority, along with the numerous methods in the Federal Rules of Civil Procedure and Evidence by which a party may test, challenge, impeach, and rebut oral testimony, normally protect patentees from erroneous findings of invalidity. Thus, the corroboration rule is needed only to counterbalance the self-interest of a testifying inventor against the patentee.[277]

A few months after *Thomson v. Quixote,* the court had another look at the question. This time, the panel, which included the author of *Quixote,* concluded that *Quixote's* facts "did not present the question of the necessity of corroboration *vel non,* but rather the sufficiency of the corroborating evidence, a distinct inquiry involving an assessment of the totality of the circumstances, including consideration of 'the interest of the corroborating witness in the subject matter of the suit.' " Thus, the court appeared to overrule *Quixote* sub silento, holding that, while the level of interest of the testifying witness is an important consideration when such testimony is offered to corroborate another witness's testimony, corroboration is required of any witness whose testimony alone is asserted to invalidate a patent, regardless of his or her level of interest. In other words, the uncorroborated testimony cannot surmount the hurdle that the clear and convincing evidence standard imposes in proving patent invalidity.[278]

§3.5 Statutory Bars

There are several types of events that result in a loss of a right to a patent. Under 35 U.S.C. §102(c), the right to a patent for an

---

invention by the patentee (§102(a)), use of the invention in public one year before the patentee filed a patent application (§102(b)), or invention before the patentee (§102(g)).

[277]*Thomson S.A. v. Quixote Corp.,* 166 F.3d 1172, 49 USPQ2d 1530 (Fed. Cir. 1999). The court rejected an argument that the corroboration rule was required here inasmuch as the testifying witnesses were involved in businesses that supplied goods and services to the defendant; this was not seen to rise to the level of self-interest required to justify triggering application of the corroboration rule.

[278]*Finnigan Corp. v. United States ITC,* 180 F.3d 1354, 51 USPQ2d 1001, 1011 (Fed. Cir. 1999). In *Oney v. Ratliff,* 182 F.3d 893, 51 USPQ2d 1697 (Fed. Cir. 1999), the court remanded a summary judgment of invalidity for prior invention because the district court failed to apply the *Woodland* corroboration factors.

invention is lost if the inventor abandons the invention. The Federal Circuit has not yet dealt with this bar.

Section §102(d) forbids a U.S. patent if a foreign counterpart issues before the U.S. version on an application filed more than a year prior to the U.S. filing date. In its first look at a §102(d) situation, the court provided some guidelines as to what is meant by "patented" in a foreign country.[279] First, it held that a foreign patent need not be publicly available for the invention to be "patented" under §102(d). Patenting in a foreign country occurs when the patentee's rights under the patent become fixed. Second, it held that the fact that the foreign patent might be invalid under the law of the country that granted it was irrelevant. Where a foreign patent issues with claims directed to the same invention as the U.S. application, it is patented within the meaning of §102(d). Otherwise U.S. courts and the PTO would have to resolve esoteric legal questions that might arise under the patent laws of numerous foreign countries. The court also demonstrated a willingness to ascribe a fairly broad meaning to the term "invention" as used in that section of the statute. The U.S. application claimed a compound, while the foreign patent was directed to processes for making that compound. The court felt that the term "invention" must have a meaning consistent with the policy and purpose underlying §102(d), and thus held that a foreign patent application fully disclosing the invention and having the potential to claim it in a number of different ways satisfies §102(d), so that the bar should be applied.[280]

The remaining bar provision, §102(b), has been examined at length in the foregoing sections. Basically, it provides the inventor with a year of grace within which to file a patent application. Public policy favors prompt and widespread disclosure of inventions to the public, while giving the inventor a reasonable amount of time—one year by statute—to determine whether a patent is worthwhile, and at the same time precluding attempts by the inventor or his or her assignee from commercially exploiting the invention more than a year before the patent application is filed.[281] The public interest is thought to be served by permitting the inventor time to perfect his or her invention before filing an application.[282] The general purpose behind §102(b) bars is to require inventors to assert with due diligence their right to a patent through the prompt filing of a patent application.[283]

---

[279]*In re Kathawala*, 9 F.3d 942, 28 USPQ2d 1785 (Fed. Cir. 1993).

[280]This was so even though the foreign patent law in question may not have permitted claims to the composition itself.

[281]*Western Mar. Elec., Inc. v. Furuno Elec. Co.*, 764 F.2d 840, 226 USPQ 334 (Fed. Cir. 1985).

[282]*TP Labs., Inc. v. Professional Positioners, Inc.*, 724 F.2d 965, 220 USPQ 577 (Fed. Cir. 1984).

[283]*LaBounty Mfg., Inc. v. United States ITC*, 958 F.2d 1066, 22 USPQ2d 1025 (Fed. Cir. 1992).

The most commonly encountered §102(b) bar is that invoked by the invention being on sale. The purposes of the on-sale bar define its terms, but its sole purpose is not to preclude the award of a patent to one who is not the first inventor.[284] The policies underlying this bar concentrate on the attempt by the inventor to exploit the invention, not whether the potential purchaser was cognizant of the invention.[285] These policies (1) prevent removing inventions from the public domain that the public justifiably comes to believe are freely available due to commercialization, (2) favor prompt and widespread disclosure of inventions to the public, and (3) provide the inventor with evaluation time.[286] The on-sale bar encourages early disclosure and prevents extension of the statutory patent term.[287]

Those activities that will act as a bar must be of such character that it is apparent at the time they are conducted that a patent application must be on file within a year. Substantial property rights are at issue, and a court has to determine with precision when the bar came into existence, for the bar must be proven by clear and convincing evidence.[288]

The court has recently indicated that 35 U.S.C. §135(b), which forbids a claim that is the same or substantially the same as a claim of an issued patent unless presented prior to one year before the grant of the patent, is a type of statutory bar.[289]

---

[284]*J.A. LaPorte, Inc. v. Norfolk Dredging Co.*, 787 F.2d 1577, 229 USPQ 435 (Fed. Cir. 1986).

[285]*King Instrument Corp. v. Otari Corp.*, 767 F.2d 853, 226 USPQ 402 (Fed. Cir. 1985). Accordingly, the purchaser need not have actual knowledge of the invention for it to be on sale. *Id.*

[286]*In re Caveney*, 761 F.2d 671, 226 USPQ 1 (Fed. Cir. 1985). As an example, where a person photographs the inventor's device in Canada, without objection by the inventor; makes the device in the United States and sells it there, without objection by the inventor; and enters into an arrangement with the inventor to finance the inventor's U.S. patent, the inventor can hardly be heard to complain if his or her patent is thereby invalidated. He or she is not an innocent victim, for such conduct violates one of the principal policies of §102(b), which is to encourage early filing. *J.A. LaPorte, Inc. v. Norfolk Dredging Co.*, 787 F.2d 1577, 229 USPQ 435 (Fed. Cir. 1986).

[287]*Intel Corp. v. United States ITC*, 946 F.2d 821, 20 USPQ2d 1161 (Fed. Cir. 1991).

[288]*Baker Oil Tools, Inc. v. Geo Vann, Inc.*, 828 F.2d 1588, 4 USPQ2d 1210 (Fed. Cir. 1987).

[289]*In re McGrew*, 120 F.3d 1236, 43 USPQ2d 1633 (Fed. Cir. 1997).

4

Nonobviousness

§4.1 Introduction

Throughout the first 60 years of the U.S. patent system, the principal conditions for patentability were novelty and utility. Any eligible subject matter could be patented provided it were new and useful and not antagonistic to the public policy of the time.

In the middle of the 19th century a new condition for patentability was born. The birth was humble, arriving in the context of a case involving a patent on clay doorknobs. In *Hotchkiss v. Greenwood,*[1] the Supreme Court was confronted with a jury instruction to the effect that the patent was void if no other ingenuity or skill was necessary to construct the knob than that of an ordinary mechanic acquainted with the business. The high Court affirmed, holding that unless "more ingenuity and skill . . . were required . . . than were possessed by an ordinary mechanic acquainted with the business, there was an absence of that degree of skill and ingenuity which constitute essential elements of every invention. In other words, the improvement is the work of the skillful mechanic, not that of the inventor."[2] These simple words ushered in a century of confusion and conflicting precedent that any patent lawyer practicing near the end of the period would quickly—and even sometimes proudly—confirm to be unsurpassed by that generated in respect of any other issue in American law.

The test of "inventive novelty" or "invention" or even, in the approach of the more thoughtful courts, "nonobviousness," which emerged from this period, was amorphous and subjective, with as many faces as names. Objective indicia of patentability, such as commercial success, long-felt need, and prior failure, were wholeheartedly embraced by some courts and flatly rejected by others. During the final two decades of the period, however, the tide seemed to swing permanently against the patentee, particularly in the Supreme Court. A patent owner unlucky enough to get to that Court had about one chance in five of walking away with a valid patent.[3] The Court went so far as to suggest that only those inventions involving a "flash of creative genius" would be patentable.[4] Finally, in its last look at patentability prior to the Patent Act of 1952, the Court cautioned

---

[1] 52 U.S. 248 (1851).

[2] 52 U.S. at 266–67.

[3] 2 Chisum, *Patents* §5.02(3) (1985).

[4] *Cuno Eng'g Corp. v. Automatic Devices Corp.*, 314 U.S. 84, 51 USPQ 272 (1941).

that "Courts should scrutinize combination patent claims with a care proportioned to the difficulty and improbability of finding invention in an assembly of old elements."[5]

This was quite enough for the patent bar and, ultimately, Congress. The keystone provision of the sweeping revision to the patent laws embodied in the Patent Act of 1952 was 35 U.S.C. §103, which was directed toward "moderating the extreme degrees of strictness exhibited by a number of judicial opinions over the past dozen or more years," and intended to have a "stabilizing effect and minimize great departures which have appeared in some cases."[6]

Whether §103 has yet accomplished this admirable purpose is the primary focus of this chapter. The fascinating legal history of nonobviousness as a condition for patentability and the equally fascinating story of the struggles of the courts to apply §103 in the years following its January 1, 1953, effective date are, in any detail, beyond the scope of this work. Rather, this chapter deals with the efforts of the Federal Circuit to apply the law in a consistent and intelligent fashion and, in the process, to dispel the harmful effects of decades of confusion and misunderstanding.

§4.2   The Statutory Inquiry

(a)   Section 103 and Graham v. Deere

Section 103 was carefully and tightly written. Its title is "Conditions for patentability; non-obvious subject matter," and it goes on to say:

> A patent may not be obtained though the invention is not identically disclosed or described as set forth in section 102 of this title, if the differences between the subject matter sought to be patented and the prior art are such that the subject matter as a whole would have been obvious to a person having ordinary skill in the art to which said subject matter pertains. Patentability shall not be negatived by the manner in which the invention was made.[7]

In the first decade following passage of §103, the various courts of appeals developed sharply divergent views as to its intention and meaning. Judge Learned Hand, in an early case, made clear his feeling that the statute was intended to relax the stricter standard that had emerged from the last quarter-century of Supreme Court decisions

---

[5]*Great Atl. & Pac. Tea Co. v. Supermarket Equip. Corp.*, 340 U.S. 147, 87 USPQ 303 (1950).

[6]Federico, *Commentary on the New Patent Act*, 35 U.S.C.A. 1 (1954). Original §103, by virtue of amendments adding subsections (b) and (c), is now known as §103(a). These designations—§103 and §103(a)–are used interchangeably throughout this book.

[7]35 U.S.C. §103(a).

and to restore the original standard of *Hotchkiss v. Greenwood.*[8] Other courts took the view that §103 was a simple codification of the law existing as of its promulgation. The division was apparent enough so that a 1963 commentary undertook to classify the First, Fifth, Sixth, Eighth, and Ninth Circuits as believers in the codification theory and the Second, Third, Fourth, and D.C. Circuits as embracing the Hand/ *Hotchkiss* view.[9]

The Supreme Court, meanwhile, had put down its pen. More than a dozen years of judicial patina accumulated on §103 before the Court chose to speak. But when it did, it spoke with unusual clarity and force. In *Graham v. John Deere Co.*,[10] it announced a test that has since become the standard guideline for assessing patentability. Recognizing that the ultimate question of patent validity is one of law, the Court nevertheless defined several basic factual inquiries. Thus, under §103:

> the scope and content of the prior art are to be determined; differences between the prior art and the claims at issue are to be ascertained; and the level of ordinary skill in the pertinent art resolved. Against this background, the obviousness or nonobviousness of the subject matter is determined.[11]

Of equal significance was the next statement:

> Such secondary considerations as commercial success, long felt but unsolved needs, failure of others, etc., might be utilized to give light to the circumstances surrounding the origins of the subject matter sought to be patented. As indicia of obviousness or nonobviousness, these inquiries may have relevancy.[12]

The Court quite correctly pointed out that such considerations:

> focus attention on economic and motivational rather than technical issues and are, therefore, more susceptible of judicial treatment than are the highly technical facts often present in patent litigation. . . . Such inquiries may lend a helping hand to the judiciary which . . . is most ill-fitted to discharge the technological duties cast upon it by patent legislation. . . . They may also "guard against slipping into use of hindsight" . . . and to resist the temptation to read into the prior art the teachings of the invention in issue.[13]

In a companion case decided the same day, the Court went on to say that "known disadvantages in old devices which would naturally discourage the search for new inventions may be taken into account in determining obviousness."[14]

---

[8]*Lyon v. Bausch & Lomb Optical Co.*, 224 F.2d 530, 106 USPQ 1 (2d Cir. 1955).

[9]See Comment, "The Standard of Patentability," 63 *Colum. L. Rev.* 306 (1963).

[10]383 U.S. 1, 148 USPQ 459 (1966).

[11]383 U.S. at 17.

[12]383 U.S. at 17–18.

[13]383 U.S. at 35–36.

[14]*United States v. Adams*, 383 U.S. 39, 52, 148 USPQ 479 (1965).

At last, patentees and accused infringers, the patent bar, and the federal bench had been provided with the framework of an objective factual analysis that could be used as a guide to the prediction and resolution of the nonobviousness condition for patentability. This is not to say that the period between *Graham v. Deere* and the ascendance of the Federal Circuit has been free from difficulty—far from it. The Supreme Court itself has had unfortunate lapses, suggesting that §103 requires a synergistic result in a combination of old elements[15] and seemingly resurrecting the "special scrutiny" standard for combination inventions.[16] These lapses, unfortunately, have been at least partly responsible for a level of confusion and divergence of approach rivaling that prevailing prior to *Graham v. Deere*.

It can be left to the scholars of jurisprudence to say why. For our purposes, it matters only that this state of affairs was undoubtedly a primary motive underlying the very creation of the Court of Appeals for the Federal Circuit. The court has recognized that one of its main tasks is to bring about uniformity in the substantive patent law.[17] The court believes that the technological incentives fostered by the patent system depend on consistent interpretation of the law, and that faithful adherence to the patent statute and guiding precedent fosters uniformity in result.[18] Nowhere has it pursued consistency more relentlessly than in its treatment of §103. The remainder of this chapter will summarize the work of the Federal Circuit on this fundamental question of obviousness.

(b) The Federal Circuit Formulation

(i) The Basic Test

The Federal Circuit has, insofar as humanly possible, attempted to be faithful to the *Graham v. Deere* obviousness approach. Yet it has not sought to generalize. It has recognized that the job of deciding obviousness may be sometimes easy and sometimes hard, and not all those charged with the task may agree in a given case. But such is the way of the law.[19]

Obviousness is a question of law and like all legal conclusions it is reached after answers to a series of potential fact questions have been found—and it is reached in the light of those answers. In the ordinary patent case, the trier of fact must answer the *Graham* inquiries relating to (1) the scope and content of the prior art, (2) the differences between the art and the claims at issue, (3) the level of

---

[15]*Anderson's-Black Rock, Inc. v. Pavement Salvage Co.*, 396 U.S. 57, 163 USPQ 673 (1969).

[16]*Sakraida v. Ag Pro, Inc.*, 425 U.S. 273, 189 USPQ 449 (1976).

[17]*Panduit Corp. v. All States Plastic Mfg. Co.*, 744 F.2d 1564, 223 USPQ 465 (Fed. Cir. 1984).

[18]*Interconnect Planning Corp. v. Feil*, 774 F.2d 1132, 227 USPQ 543 (Fed. Cir. 1985).

[19]*In re Durden*, 763 F.2d 1406, 226 USPQ 359 (Fed. Cir. 1985).

ordinary skill in the art, and (4) whatever objective evidence may be present.[20] A reasoned resolution of the basis for upholding or invalidating patents is mandated by *Graham v. Deere*. Unlike a verdict on negligence to which the fact trier is expected to contribute the sense of the community, a decision on patent validity does not benefit from the fact trier's communal sense of patentability. A patentee, as well as an accused infringer for that matter, is entitled to have its position judged only by the standard that Congress has written into the statute.[21] Indeed, the test is an all-American one. The patent laws of the United States are the laws governing a determination of obviousness of a U.S. patent in a federal court.[22]

The obviousness determination, in short, is one of inquiry not quality.[23] Lawsuits arise out of the affairs of people, real people facing real problems, and nowhere is this more true than in the obviousness setting.[24] The Federal Circuit insists that what it terms the "real world story" of the invention not be obscured by lawyer's games played with the patent and the prior art. That human, real world story forms a major part of the landscape of the case and often reflects the inadequacy of the prior art and compels a conclusion of nonobviousness.[25] Thus, obviousness must be considered in light of the problem facing the inventor.[26]

Each obviousness case must of course be decided on its own particular facts.[27] For that reason, what the Federal Circuit or its predecessors have said in discussing different fact situations is not to be taken as having universal application. It would be easier to have some clear general rule by which all obviousness cases could be decided, and some judges might be tempted to formulate one. But the question arises in such an unpredictable variety of ways and in such different forms that it would be unwise to try. Today's rule would likely be regretted in tomorrow's case.[28] There are no all-purpose criteria for applying the law of obviousness to every factual situation. No one precedent or rationale can be controlling in all possible areas

---

[20]*Specialty Composites v. Cabot Corp.*, 845 F.2d 981, 6 USPQ2d 1601 (Fed. Cir. 1988); *Allen Archery, Inc. v. Browning Mfg. Co.*, 819 F.2d 1087, 2 USPQ2d 1490 (Fed. Cir. 1987); *Connell v. Sears, Roebuck & Co.*, 722 F.2d 1542, 220 USPQ 193 (Fed. Cir. 1983).

[21]*Structural Rubber Prods. Co. v. Park Rubber Co.*, 749 F.2d 707, 223 USPQ 1264 (Fed. Cir. 1984). The court has likened the obviousness inquiry to infringement under the doctrine of equivalents and anticipation to literal infringement. *Lemar Marine, Inc. v. Barient, Inc.*, 827 F.2d 744, 3 USPQ2d 1766 (Fed. Cir. 1987).

[22]*Medtronic, Inc. v. Daig Corp.*, 789 F.2d 903, 229 USPQ 664 (Fed. Cir. 1986). The argument that the court should adopt the conclusion of a German tribunal holding the German counterpart patent obvious was termed specious.

[23]*Schenck, A.G. v. Nortron Corp.*, 713 F.2d 782, 218 USPQ 698 (Fed. Cir. 1983).

[24]*Rosemount, Inc. v. Beckman Instruments, Inc.*, 727 F.2d 1540, 221 USPQ 1 (Fed. Cir. 1984).

[25]*Panduit Corp. v. Dennison Mfg. Co.*, 774 F.2d 1082, 227 USPQ 337 (Fed. Cir. 1985).

[26]E.g., *Northern Telecom, Inc. v. Datapoint Corp.*, 908 F.2d 931, 15 USPQ2d 1321 (Fed. Cir. 1990).

[27]*In re Durden*, 763 F.2d 1406, 226 USPQ 359 (Fed. Cir. 1985).

[28]*In re Durden*, 763 F.2d 1406, 226 USPQ 359, 362 (Fed. Cir. 1985).

of human creativity. The uniform application of the law of obviousness is essential to the commercial incentive that is the core of the patent system. The obligation of the decision maker is to apply the law consistently to the evidence for each new invention. All relevant facts must be considered, while recognizing that it is inappropriate to squeeze new factual situations into preestablished pigeonholes.[29]

(ii) The Timing of the Inquiry

Although events occurring several months after the invention may sometimes be considered contemporaneous and therefore some evidence relative to obviousness,[30] §103 demands that obviousness be tested as of "the time the invention was made."[31] The analytic focus is upon the state of knowledge at the time the invention was made.[32] Indeed, it has been said that facts determinable only after the invention was made may serve to evidence nonobviousness, but not obviousness. Thus the obviousness test cannot include a requirement that the invention demonstrate unusual or surprising results or have an effect greater than the prior art, since this would focus on facts determinable only after the invention was made.[33] Likewise, it is entirely improper to ask whether the invention "is" or "would be" obvious; the question is whether it "would have been obvious." The judge now knows all about the invention; he or she must determine whether it would have been obvious to those who knew only about the prior art.[34] He or she must view the prior art without reading into it the patent's teachings.[35]

To draw on hindsight knowledge of the patented invention, when the prior art does not contain or suggest that knowledge, is to use the invention as a template for its own reconstruction—an illogical and inappropriate process by which to determine patentability. The invention must be viewed not after the blueprint has been drawn by the inventor, but as it would have been perceived in the state of the art that existed at the time the invention was made.[36] And although

---

[29]*In re Eli Lilly & Co.*, 902 F.2d 943, 14 USPQ2d 1741 (Fed. Cir. 1990).

[30]*Ashland Oil, Inc. v. Delta Resins & Refracs., Inc.*, 776 F.2d 281, 227 USPQ 657 (Fed. Cir. 1985); *Stewart-Warner Corp. v. City of Pontiac*, 767 F.2d 1563, 226 USPQ 676 (Fed. Cir. 1985); *Lindemann Maschinenfabrik v. American Hoist & Derrick Co.*, 730 F.2d 1452, 221 USPQ 481 (Fed. Cir. 1984); *In re Farrenkopf*, 713 F.2d 714, 219 USPQ 1 (Fed. Cir. 1983).

[31]35 U.S.C. §103.

[32]*In re Raynes*, 7 F.3d 1037, 28 USPQ2d 1630 (Fed. Cir. 1993).

[33]*Kansas Jack, Inc. v. Kuhn*, 719 F.2d 1144, 219 USPQ 857 (Fed. Cir. 1983). A retrospective view of inherency is not a substitute for some teaching or suggestion that supports the selection and use of the various elements in the particular claimed combination. That which may be inherent is not necessarily known. Obviousness cannot be predicated on what is unknown. *In re Newell*, 891 F.2d 899, 13 USPQ2d 1248 (Fed. Cir. 1989).

[34]*Panduit Corp. v. Dennison Mfg. Co.*, 774 F.2d 1082, 227 USPQ 337 (Fed. Cir. 1985); *Rosemount, Inc. v. Beckman Instruments, Inc.*, 727 F.2d 1540, 221 USPQ 1 (Fed. Cir. 1984).

[35]*Vandenberg v. Dairy Equip. Co.*, 740 F.2d 1560, 224 USPQ 195 (Fed. Cir. 1984); *Kansas Jack, Inc. v. Kuhn*, 719 F.2d 1144, 219 USPQ 857 (Fed. Cir. 1983).

[36]*Sensonics, Inc. v. Aerosonic Corp.*, 81 F.3d 1566, 38 USPQ2d 1551 (Fed. Cir. 1996).

the person skilled in the art is presumed to know the art—indeed, he or she is pictured as working in a shop with the art hanging on the walls round about—the art in question is only that which he or she would have selected without the advantage of hindsight or knowledge of the invention.[37] Measuring a claimed invention against the standard established by §103 requires the oft-difficult but critical step of casting the mind back to the time of invention, to consider the thinking of one of ordinary skill in the art, guided only by the prior art references and the then-accepted wisdom in the field. Close adherence to this methodology is especially important in the case of less technologically complex inventions, where the very ease with which the invention can be understood may prompt one to fall victim to the insidious effect of a hindsight syndrome wherein that which only the inventor taught is used against its teacher. The best defense against the subtle powerful attraction of a hindsight-based obviousness analysis is rigorous application of the requirement for a showing of the teaching or motivation to combine prior art references.[38]

Thus, the Federal Circuit regards hindsight as an insidious and powerful phenomenon and insists upon use of the statutory phrase "would have been obvious," which tends to remind the decision maker of the need to cast the mind back to the time the invention was made.[39] Thus the obviousness standard, while easy to expound, is sometimes difficult to apply. It requires the decision maker to return to the time the invention was made.[40] This is not a facile statutory interpretation, for the quality of nonobviousness is not easy to measure, particularly when challenged years after the invention was made.[41] That which may be made clear and thus obvious to a court, with the invention fully diagrammed, may have been a breakthrough of substantial dimension when first unveiled.[42] Hindsight is a tempting but forbidden zone.[43]

(iii) The Whole of the Evidence

The court must view the totality of the evidence to avoid the hindsight syndrome wherein that which only the inventor taught is used against its teacher.[44] All evidence must be considered.[45] There is no legal authority for the view that the court, in an evaluation of

---

[37]*Union Carbide Corp. v. American Can Co.*, 724 F.2d 1567, 220 USPQ 584 (Fed. Cir. 1984).

[38]*In re Dembiczak*, 175 F.3d 994, 50 USPQ2d 1614 (Fed. Cir. 1999).

[39]*Panduit Corp. v. Dennison Mfg. Co.*, 774 F.2d 1082, 227 USPQ 337 (Fed. Cir. 1985).

[40]*Uniroyal, Inc. v. Rudkin-Wiley Corp.*, 837 F.2d 1044, 5 USPQ2d 1434 (Fed. Cir. 1988). See also *Litton Sys., Inc. v. Honeywell, Inc.*,87 F.3d 1559, 39 USPQ2d 1321 (Fed. Cir. 1996).

[41]*Interconnect Planning Corp. v. Feil*, 774 F.2d 1132, 227 USPQ 543 (Fed. Cir. 1985).

[42]*Interconnect Planning Corp. v. Feil*, 774 F.2d 1132, 227 USPQ 543 (Fed. Cir. 1985); *Panduit Corp. v. Dennison Mfg. Co.*, 774 F.2d 1082, 227 USPQ 337 (Fed. Cir. 1985).

[43]*Loctite Corp. v. Ultraseal Ltd.*, 781 F.2d 861, 228 USPQ 90, 98 (Fed. Cir. 1985).

[44]*In re Corkill*, 771 F.2d 1496, 226 USPQ 1005 (Fed. Cir. 1985).

[45]*Environmental Designs, Ltd. v. Union Oil Co.*, 713 F.2d 693, 218 USPQ 865 (Fed. Cir. 1983).

obviousness, must first determine that the prior art is more pertinent than the prior art considered by the PTO. Any relevant evidence, whether more or less pertinent, can be considered in an analysis of obviousness.[46] The obviousness inquiry rests on a foundation constructed of all relevant and probative facts found in light of all the evidence; if that foundation crumbles, the legal conclusion on which it rests must fall.[47] In particular, each prior art reference must be evaluated as an entirety, and all of the prior art must be evaluated as a whole.[48] The test for obviousness is what the combined teachings of the references would have suggested to one of ordinary skill in the art.[49]

(iv) The Legal Conclusion

Obviousness is, after all, a legal conclusion.[50] It is a question of law to be determined from the facts.[51] It is freely reviewable on appeal[52] for correctness or error as a matter of law and not under the clearly erroneous standard that is applicable to fact findings.[53]

The reasoning of the trial court cannot be ignored, since faulty reasoning is likely to lead to a wrong result. But an appellant must show not only faulty reasoning, but a wrong result. To reverse, the reviewing court must be convinced that the decision maker engaged in faulty analysis in applying the law to the facts, and that a correct application would bring a different result.[54] If on the essential facts, arrived at through proper application of the relevant law, it agrees with the trial court's conclusion, any error concerning nonessential facts ascribed to the trial court in reaching that conclusion is harmless and not a basis for reversal.[55] That the parties fervently dispute the

---

[46]*Constant v. Advanced Micro-Devices, Inc.*, 848 F.2d 1560, 7 USPQ2d 1057 (Fed. Cir. 1988).

[47]*Connell v. Sears, Roebuck & Co.*, 722 F.2d 1542, 220 USPQ 193 (Fed. Cir. 1983).

[48]*In re Evanega*, 829 F.2d 1110, 4 USPQ2d 1249 (Fed. Cir. 1987); *Panduit Corp. v. Dennison Mfg. Co.*, 774 F.2d 1082, 227 USPQ 337 (Fed. Cir. 1985); *EWP Corp. v. Reliance Universal Inc.*, 755 F.2d 898, 225 USPQ 20 (Fed. Cir. 1985).

[49]*In re Young*, 927 F.2d 588, 18 USPQ2d 1089 (Fed. Cir. 1991).

[50]E.g., *Aktiebolaget Karlstads v. United States ITC*, 705 F.2d 1565, 217 USPQ 865 (Fed. Cir. 1983).

[51]*In re Geiger*, 815 F.2d 686, 2 USPQ2d 1276 (Fed. Cir. 1987); *In re De Blauwe*, 736 F.2d 699, 222 USPQ 191 (Fed. Cir. 1984). Whether an invention would have been obvious in terms of §103 is ultimately a legal judgment, dependent upon the factual evidence adduced. *Burlington Indus. Inc. v. Quigg*, 822 F.2d 1581, 3 USPQ2d 1436 (Fed. Cir. 1987).

[52]*EWP Corp. v. Reliance Universal Inc.*, 755 F.2d 898, 225 USPQ 20 (Fed. Cir. 1985). But that does not mean that the reviewing court may proceed on a paper record as though no trial had taken place. To prevail the appellant must convince the court that the judgment cannot stand on the record created at trial. *Polaroid Corp. v. Eastman Kodak Co.*, 789 F.2d 1556, 229 USPQ 561 (Fed. Cir. 1986).

[53]E.g., *Panduit Corp. v. Dennison Mfg. Co.*, 810 F.2d 1561, 1 USPQ 1593 (Fed. Cir. 1987); *In re De Blauwe*, 736 F.2d 699, 222 USPQ 191 (Fed. Cir. 1984).

[54]*Cable Elec. Prods., Inc. v. Genmark, Inc.*, 770 F.2d 1015, 226 USPQ 881 (Fed. Cir. 1985); *Union Carbide Corp. v. American Can Co.*, 724 F.2d 1567, 220 USPQ 584 (Fed. Cir. 1984).

[55]*Gardner v. TEC Sys., Inc.*, 725 F.2d 1338, 220 USPQ 777 (Fed. Cir. 1984).

ultimate conclusion of obviousness is not enough to raise a factual question.[56]

The Federal Circuit has taken on a very full role in reviewing obviousness determinations. It regards as its task to consider the facts, either as properly found by the fact finder or as stipulated to or otherwise uncontested by the parties, and then to reach its own conclusion on obviousness. It will affirm if it agrees with the trial court's conclusion, reverse if it does not, and vacate and remand for new or additional findings if it feels the record lacks facts essential to formulating a conclusion.[57] With all respect, experience may demonstrate that this reach is overlong. The court seems to be saying that the trial court need not have been wrong, the reviewing court need only disagree.[58]

For a brief period, court watchers thought perhaps the Supreme Court might intervene. In 1986, the Court granted certiorari[59] in *Panduit v. Dennison,*[60] vacated, and remanded for further consideration "on the complex issue of the degree to which the obviousness is one of fact," governed on review by Federal Rule of Civil Procedure 52(a).[61] In its second *Panduit* opinion,[62] the Federal Circuit analyzed the question exhaustively and left no doubt about its view: although the four *Graham v. Deere* inquiries are basically factual and therefore invoke Rule 52(a), the ultimate question of obviousness is one of law,

---

[56]*Structural Rubber Prods. Co. v. Park Rubber Co.,* 749 F.2d 707, 223 USPQ 1264 (Fed. Cir. 1984).

[57]*Gardner v. TEC Sys., Inc.,* 725 F.2d 1338, 220 USPQ 777 (Fed. Cir. 1984).

[58]See *Panduit Corp. v. Dennison Mfg. Co.,* 810 F.2d 1561, 1 USPQ2d 1593 (Fed. Cir. 1987). In reaching its own conclusion regarding obviousness, the court need not give deference to a particular analytical construct utilized in a district court's opinion. *Gillette Co. v. S.C. Johnson & Son,* 919 F.2d 720, 16 USPQ2d 1923 (Fed. Cir. 1990). In an ITC case the underlying factual determinations are reviewed under the substantial evidence standard and the holding of obviousness is reviewed de novo. *Texas Instr., Inc. v. United States ITC,* 988 F.2d 1165, 26 USPQ2d 1018 (Fed. Cir. 1993); *Intel Corp. v. United States ITC,* 946 F.2d 821, 20 USPQ2d 1161 (Fed. Cir. 1991). Since obviousness is a question of law, the Federal Circuit is not bound by the ITC's ultimate determination on that matter. *Akzo N.V. v. United States ITC,* 808 F.2d 1471, 1 USPQ2d 1241 (Fed. Cir. 1986). The court reviews the PTO Board's ultimate determination of obviousness de novo, but the Board's underlying factual findings are reviewed on the substantial evidence standard. E.g., *In re Kotzab,* 217 F.3d 1365, 55 USPQ2d 1313, 1316 (Fed. Cir. 2000). The court has rejected out of hand a suggestion that a decision of the PTO Board of Appeals on obviousness be affirmed as a matter of law if it has a "rational basis." *In re McCarthy,* 763 F.2d 411, 226 USPQ 99 (Fed. Cir. 1985). Perhaps a "rational basis" test would be showing a bit too much deference to the lower body, and yet it seems unwise for an appellate court to preoccupy itself with matters of disagreement instead of error. The Federal Circuit reviews de novo a Board determination of whether a claimed invention would have been obvious. *In re Raynes,* 7 F.3d 1037, 28 USPQ2d 1630 (Fed. Cir. 1993). The ultimate determination of obviousness is a question of law that the court reviews without deference to the Board's judgment. It is the court's responsibility to make the final conclusion based upon its reading of the record before it, giving appropriate deference to the Board's underlying factual determinations, such as what a reference teaches. *In re Napier,* 55 F.3d 610, 34 USPQ2d 1782 (Fed. Cir. 1995).

[59]475 U.S. 809, 229 USPQ 478 (1986).

[60]*Panduit Corp. v. Dennison Mfg. Co.,* 774 F.2d 1082, 227 USPQ 337 (Fed. Cir. 1985).

[61]475 U.S. at 811, 229 USPQ at 479.

[62]*Panduit Corp. v. Dennison Mfg. Co.,* 810 F.2d 1561, 1 USPQ2d 1593 (Fed. Cir. 1987).

reviewable for correctness.[63] The degree to which the obviousness determination involves facts, and is thus subject to the clearly erroneous standard of Rule 52(a), is that degree required to erect a foundation of facts sufficient to support the legal conclusion.[64]

In a nonjury case, the general rule is that the district court must find the facts specially and state separately its legal conclusions. In patent cases, the need for express *Graham v. Deere* findings takes on special significance, as a guard against hindsight. The reviewing court must be convinced that the trial court actually applied *Graham* and must be presented with enough express and necessarily implied findings to know the basis of the trial court's opinion.[65] However, the fact that the trial court appears to adopt the arguments of a party does not necessarily mean that it shirked its responsibility to make such findings.[66] Nor is the rule so severe as to require the trial judge to articulate every imaginable permutation and combination of prior art teachings. While a complete discussion of the prior art would remove all doubt about whether the trial court properly reviewed the prior art for its total teachings, it may be presumed that the fact finder reviews all the evidence presented unless it explicitly expresses otherwise.[67]

Obviousness is not a term readily understood by a jury; it is overladen with layperson's meanings different from its legal connotation in the patent law.[68] Thus, although it is clearly not error to submit the question of obviousness to a jury, as long as the submission is accompanied by appropriate instructions on the law,[69] it is error for

---

[63]*Panduit Corp. v. Dennison Mfg. Co.,* 810 F.2d 1561, 1 USPQ2d 1593 (Fed. Cir. 1987). The Supreme Court denied certiorari the second time around. 481 U.S. 1052 (1987). Nonetheless, the court continues to recognize that the obviousness inquiry is highly fact specific by statutory design. E.g., *In re Brouwer,* 77 F.3d 1185, 37 USPQ2d 1663 (Fed. Cir. 1996); *In re Ochiai,* 71 F.3d 1565, 37 USPQ2d 1127 (Fed. Cir. 1995).

[64]*Ryco, Inc. v. Ag-Bag Corp.,* 857 F.2d 1418, 8 USPQ2d 1323 (Fed. Cir. 1988).

[65]*Loctite Corp. v. Ultraseal Ltd.,* 781 F.2d 861, 228 USPQ 90 (Fed. Cir. 1985). A district court's discussion of obviousness did not mention *Graham,* but it did make the specific factual findings required for a determination of obviousness. Thus, although it would have been preferable if the court had enumerated the *Graham* factors and systematically presented its analysis in terms of those factors, there is no reversible error if it is clear the required factual determinations were actually made and considered while applying the proper legal standard of obviousness. *Specialty Composites v. Cabot Corp.,* 845 F.2d 981, 6 USPQ2d 1601 (Fed. Cir. 1988).

[66]*Ashland Oil, Inc. v. Delta Resins & Refracs., Inc.,* 776 F.2d 281, 227 USPQ 657 (Fed. Cir. 1985).

[67]*Medtronic, Inc. v. Daig Corp.,* 789 F.2d 903, 229 USPQ 664 (Fed. Cir. 1986).

[68]*In re Hayes Microcomputer Patent Litig.,* 982 F.2d 1527, 25 USPQ2d 1241 (Fed. Cir. 1992); *Structural Rubber Prods. Co. v. Park Rubber Co.,* 749 F.2d 707, 223 USPQ 1264 (Fed. Cir. 1984). The court has likened the obviousness inquiry to that of the doctrine of equivalents. *Richardson v. Suzuki Motor Co.,* 868 F.2d 1226, 9 USPQ2d 1913 (Fed. Cir. 1989).

[69]*Railroad Dynamics, Inc. v. A. Stucki Co.,* 727 F.2d 1506, 220 USPQ 929 (Fed. Cir. 1984). When the legal conclusion of obviousness is submitted to the jury, it is technically improper to characterize that question as a special verdict under Rule 49(a), FRCP, because that rule only provides for the submission of fact questions to the jury. *Newell Cos. v. Kenney Mfg. Co.,* 864 F.2d 757, 9 USPQ2d 1417 (Fed. Cir. 1988); *Sjolund v. Musland,* 847 F.2d 1573, 6 USPQ2d 2020 (Fed. Cir. 1988).

the trial court to abdicate its responsibility to inform the jury of how §103 applies to the particular case.[70]

In its *Newell* decision,[71] the court took *Panduit v. Dennison*[72] to its next logical step in squarely holding that a trial court may direct a verdict on a disputed issue of obviousness where there are no disputed issues of material fact underlying that issue. Thus it would appear that, just as the Federal Circuit may disregard a pure legal conclusion of obviousness simply on grounds of disagreement with the trial judge, so may the trial judge reject the conclusion of the jury on that question if the material facts are established or undisputed. And it would seem that the trial court is not restricted by any quantum of proof or "lofty" standard when it applies the legal test for obviousness to a set of undisputed facts.[73]

The Federal Circuit does not sit as a fact finder. Only if those facts supported by substantial evidence will not in law support the jury's conclusion of obviousness can it be said that the jury committed an error of law. A de novo review of obviousness would amount to nothing different than "that the parties mail us the patent and the prior art and ask whether we think the claimed invention would have been obvious."[74]

(c) Obsolete Subtests and Forbidden Shortcuts

Federal district courts are well advised to apply the Federal Circuit's formulation of the obviousness test with close attention to substance and form. The court has rooted out backsliding from the literal language of the *Graham v. Deere* inquiry with an almost evangelical fervor. And yet such departures from orthodoxy do not always result in reversal,[75] particularly where it is clear that the *Graham* analysis played a meaningful part in the lower court's decision.[76] The Federal Circuit reminds us often that it reviews judgments not opinions, and therefore an error in philosophical approach on obviousness is not crucial unless it is apparent that the district court reached the wrong result.[77]

Nevertheless, language in a jury instruction to the effect that the jury must give careful scrutiny before endorsing the patent monopoly constitutes prejudicial error, in that it suggests that the jury must

---

[70]*Structural Rubber Prods. Co. v. Park Rubber Co.*, 749 F.2d 707, 223 USPQ 1264 (Fed. Cir. 1984).

[71]*Newell Cos. v. Kenney Mfg. Co.*, 864 F.2d 757, 9 USPQ2d 1417 (Fed. Cir. 1988).

[72]*Panduit Corp. v. Dennison Mfg. Co.*, 810 F.2d 1561, 1 USPQ2d 1593 (Fed. Cir. 1987).

[73]*Newell Cos. v. Kenney Mfg. Co.*, 864 F.2d 757, 9 USPQ2d 1417 (Fed. Cir. 1988).

[74]*Railroad Dynamics, Inc. v. A. Stucki Co.*, 727 F.2d 1506, 220 USPQ 929 (Fed. Cir. 1984).

[75]E.g., *Chore-Time Equip., Inc. v. Cumberland Corp.*, 713 F.2d 774, 218 USPQ 673 (Fed. Cir. 1983).

[76]*Jervis B. Webb Co. v. Southern Sys., Inc.*, 742 F.2d 1388, 222 USPQ 943 (Fed. Cir. 1984).

[77]*Milliken Res. Corp. v. Dan River, Inc.*, 739 F.2d 587, 222 USPQ 571 (Fed. Cir. 1984).

find the patent valid.[78] A court never declares a patent valid;[79] it is only necessary to hold that the challenger of validity failed to carry its burden.[80] A district court that believes it must decide whether it considers an invention patentable misconstrues its role, which is simply to determine whether the patent's challenger has carried its burden of proving by clear and convincing evidence the facts compelling a conclusion of invalidity.[81]

The court has cautioned against giving too much weight to the actions of foreign tribunals confronted with the same prior art. The theories and laws of patentability vary from country to country, as do the examination practices. International uniformity in theory and practice has not been achieved.[82]

The Federal Circuit has been quick to reject efforts to circumvent the more painstaking *Graham v. Deere* analysis. In case after case, we are told that lack of synergism is not an element of an obviousness determination,[83] even though a synergistic result may point toward nonobviousness.[84] The "flash of genius" test is no longer viable.[85] The question mandated by §103 is patentability, not "invention"; a district court is not required to conclude whether something was or was not "invented," nor whether it is subjectively "worthy" of patent protection.[86] The dispositive question is not whether the claimed device is an invention; rather, it is whether the invention satisfies the standards of patentability. To suggest that a new combination is not necessarily an invention or otherwise to require some concept of "inventiveness" or flash of genius for patentability would improperly misplace the focus of 35 U.S.C. §103.[87] And it is error to hold that mere "innovation"

---

[78]*Jamesbury Corp. v. Litton Indus. Prods., Inc.,* 756 F.2d 1556, 225 USPQ 253 (Fed. Cir. 1985).

[79]*Envirotech Corp. v. Al George, Inc.,* 730 F.2d 753, 221 USPQ 473 (Fed. Cir. 1984).

[80]*Environmental Designs, Ltd. v. Union Oil Co.,* 713 F.2d 693, 218 USPQ 865 (Fed. Cir. 1983).

[81]*Panduit Corp. v. Dennison Mfg. Co.,* 774 F.2d 1082, 227 USPQ 337 (Fed. Cir. 1985).

[82]*Heidelberger Druckmaschinen AG v. Hantscho Comm. Prods., Inc.,* 21 F.3d 1068, 30 USPQ2d 1377 (Fed. Cir. 1994).

[83]E.g., *Jervis B. Webb Co. v. Southern Sys., Inc.,* 742 F.2d 1388, 222 USPQ 943 (Fed. Cir. 1984); *Gardner v. TEC Sys., Inc.,* 725 F.2d 1338, 220 USPQ 777 (Fed. Cir. 1984); *Chore-Time Equip., Inc. v. Cumberland Corp.,* 713 F.2d 774, 218 USPQ 673 (Fed. Cir. 1983).

[84]*Custom Accessories, Inc. v. Jeffrey-Allan Indus., Inc.,* 807 F.2d 955, 1 USPQ2d 1196 (Fed. Cir. 1986); *Stratoflex, Inc. v. Aeroquip Corp.,* 713 F.2d 1530, 218 USPQ 871 (Fed. Cir. 1983). Synergism is probative only of nonobviousness; the obverse is not true. *Ryko Mfg. Co. v. Nu-Star, Inc.,* 950 F.2d 714, 21 USPQ2d 1053 (Fed. Cir. 1991). Synergism is not a requirement of nonobviousness, but when an inventor tries to distinguish the claims from the prior art by introducing evidence of unexpected synergistic properties, the evidence should at least demonstrate an effect greater than the sum of the several effects taken separately. *Merck & Co. v. Biocraft Labs., Inc.,* 874 F.2d 804, 10 USPQ2d 1843 (Fed. Cir. 1989).

[85]*Vandenberg v. Dairy Equip. Co.,* 740 F.2d 1560, 224 USPQ 195 (Fed. Cir. 1984).

[86]*Lindemann Maschinenfabrik v. American Hoist & Derrick Co.,* 730 F.2d 1452, 221 USPQ 481 (Fed. Cir. 1984).

[87]*Custom Accessories, Inc. v. Jeffrey-Allan Indus., Inc.,* 807 F.2d 955, 1 USPQ2d 1196 (Fed. Cir. 1986).

is not "invention"; innovation is always invention, perhaps just not always patentable invention.[88]

Despite constant prodding from the Federal Circuit, some district courts continue to stray from the path of righteousness. Thus the court has found it necessary to remind us that most technological advance is the fruit of methodical, persistent investigation.[89] Patents for such advances are consistent with the congressional mandate, somewhat inartfully expressed in §103, that "patentability shall not be negatived by the manner in which the invention was made."[90]

The fact that known principles are employed does not make an invention obvious; most patentable inventions employ known principles.[91] Nor does obviousness necessarily follow from a conclusion that the invention is but the product of the "natural evolution of the prior art."[92] The use of an "obvious to try" test ignores problem recognition as an element of the obviousness inquiry and is improper.[93] A general incentive does not make obvious a particular result, nor does the existence of techniques by which those efforts can be carried out.[94] The court has repeatedly emphasized that "obvious to try" is not the standard under §103. However, the meaning of the maxim is sometimes lost. Any invention that would in fact have been obvious would also have been, in a sense, obvious to try. The real question is: When is an invention that was obvious to try nevertheless nonobvious?[95] The court postulates three situations that seem to lead to the conclusion that it would have been obvious to try: (1) to vary all parameters or try each of numerous possible choices until one possibly arrived at a successful result, where the prior art gave either no indication of which parameters were critical or no direction as to which of many possible choices is likely to be successful; (2) to explore a new technology or general approach that seemed to be a promising

---

[88]*Richdel, Inc. v. Sunspool Corp.*, 714 F.2d 1573, 219 USPQ 8 (Fed. Cir. 1983).

[89]*In re Dow Chem. Co.*, 837 F.2d 469, 5 USPQ2d 1529 (Fed. Cir. 1988).

[90]35 U.S.C. §103(a). That an inventor has probed the strengths and weaknesses of the prior art and discovered an improvement that escaped those who came before is indicative of unobviousness, not obviousness. *Fromson v. Anitec Printing Plates Inc.*, 132 F.3d 1437, 45 USPQ2d 1269 (Fed. Cir. 1997).

[91]*Lindemann Maschinenfabrik v. American Hoist & Derrick Co.*, 730 F.2d 1452, 221 USPQ 481, 489 (Fed. Cir. 1984).

[92]*State Indus., Inc. v. Rheem Mfg. Co.*, 769 F.2d 762, 227 USPQ 375 (Fed. Cir. 1985).

[93]*Gillette Co. v. S.C. Johnson & Son*, 919 F.2d 720, 16 USPQ2d 1923 (Fed. Cir. 1990); *In re Fine*, 837 F.2d 1071, 5 USPQ2d 1596 (Fed. Cir. 1988); *In re Geiger*, 815 F.2d 686, 2 USPQ2d 1276 (Fed. Cir. 1987); *N.V. Akzo v. E.I. Dupont de Nemours*, 810 F.2d 1148, 1 USPQ2d 1704 (Fed. Cir. 1987); *Hybritech Inc. v. Monoclonal Antibodies, Inc.*, 802 F.2d 1367, 231 USPQ 81 (Fed. Cir. 1986); *In re Merck & Co.*, 800 F.2d 1091, 231 USPQ 375 (Fed. Cir. 1986); *Loctite Corp. v. Ultraseal Ltd.*, 781 F.2d 861, 228 USPQ 90 (Fed. Cir. 1985); *Jones v. Hardy*, 727 F.2d 1524, 220 USPQ 1021 (Fed. Cir. 1984).

[94]*In re Deuel*, 51 F.3d 1552, 34 USPQ2d 1210 (Fed. Cir. 1995).

[95]*In re O'Farrell*, 853 F.2d 894, 7 USPQ2d 1673 (Fed. Cir. 1988). The jurors could not reach a unanimous verdict on the question of whether a person of ordinary skill, presented with the problem and being familiar with all the prior art, but unaware of the patented invention, would be "led to do" what the inventor did. This was held to provide strong support for the unanimous verdict that the claim was valid; reasonable jurors could have concluded

field of experimentation, where the prior art gave only general guidance as to the particular form of the claimed invention or how to achieve it; and (3) where the reference contained detailed enabling methodology for practicing the claimed invention, a suggestion to modify the prior art to practice the claimed invention, and evidence suggesting that it would be successful. The first two situations result in nonobviousness, while the third does not.[96]

The court has also had to reject an "obvious to experiment" approach. Selective hindsight is no more applicable to the design of experiments than it is to the combination of prior art teachings. There must be a reason or suggestion in the art for selecting the procedure used, other than the knowledge learned from the applicant's disclosure.[97]

The test under §103 is not what "one might contemplate," but whether the references, taken as a whole, would suggest the invention to one of ordinary skill in the art.[98] Inherency and obviousness are distinct concepts. If the inherency does not result in anticipation, then one must ask whether the inherency would have been obvious.[99]

Finally, and perhaps most important, there is no special rule for combination patents.[100] It simply obfuscates the inquiry to posit a nonstatutory classification labeled combination patents.[101] The law must be the same for all patents and types of inventions. A level playing ground for the marketplace of ideas is as necessary for technological innovation as it is for politics and social policy.[102] Virtually all inventions are combinations and virtually all are combinations of old elements.[103] That all the elements of an invention may have been old, or some old and some new, or all new, is simply irrelevant to the

---

that the challenger had failed to meet the burden of proving invalidity by clear and convincing evidence. *Richardson v. Suzuki Motor Co.*, 868 F.2d 1226, 9 USPQ2d 1913 (Fed. Cir. 1989).

[96]*In re O'Farrell*, 853 F.2d 894, 7 USPQ2d 1673 (Fed. Cir. 1988). It should be noted that the reference was the inventors' own publication. In *Amgen, Inc. v. Chugai Pharma. Co.*, 927 F.2d 1200, 18 USPQ2d 1016 (Fed. Cir. 1991), the court rejected an "obvious to try" approach in evaluating the patentability of a gene. The proper analysis would have been whether, at the relevant time, one of ordinary skill in the art would have had a reasonable expectation of success in screening a DNA library with a prior art technique in order to obtain the claimed gene.

[97]*In re Dow Chem. Co.*, 837 F.2d 469, 5 USPQ2d 1529 (Fed. Cir. 1988). But see *In re Eli Lilly & Co.*, 902 F.2d 943, 14 USPQ2d 1741 (Fed. Cir. 1990).

[98]*Medtronic, Inc. v. Cardiac Pacemakers, Inc.*, 721 F.2d 1563, 220 USPQ 97 (Fed. Cir. 1983).

[99]*Kloster Speedsteel AB v. Crucible Inc.*, 793 F.2d 1565, 230 USPQ 81 (Fed. Cir. 1986).

[100]*Jervis B. Webb Co. v. Southern Sys., Inc.*, 742 F.2d 1388, 222 USPQ 943 (Fed. Cir. 1984). But see *Sakraida v. Ag Pro, Inc.*, 425 U.S. 273, 189 USPQ 489 (1976). The patentability of combinations of old elements is of ancient authority. *In re Wright*, 848 F.2d 1216, 6 USPQ2d 1959 (Fed. Cir. 1988).

[101]*Medtronic, Inc. v. Cardiac Pacemakers, Inc.*, 721 F.2d 1563, 220 USPQ 97 (Fed. Cir. 1983).

[102]*Panduit Corp. v. Dennison Mfg. Co.*, 810 F.2d 1561, 1 USPQ2d 1593 (Fed. Cir. 1987).

[103]*Panduit Corp. v. Dennison Mfg. Co.*, 810 F.2d 1561, 1 USPQ2d 1593 (Fed. Cir. 1987); *Richdel, Inc. v. Sunspool Corp.*, 714 F.2d 1573, 219 USPQ 8 (Fed. Cir. 1983); *Environmental Designs, Ltd. v. Union Oil Co.*, 713 F.2d 693, 218 USPQ 865 (Fed. Cir. 1983). Although a genus

obviousness inquiry.[104] Casting an invention as a combination of old elements leads improperly to an analysis of the claimed invention by the parts, not by the whole. A traditional problem with focusing on a patent as a combination of old elements is the attendant notion that patentability is undeserving without some synergistic or even different effect.[105]

The Federal Circuit demands that counsel set forth the law accurately. In particular, it is the duty of the lawyer to impart to the trial judge the proper test for obviousness. Submitting to the court language like "any differences would have been obvious" violates the axiom that the claimed invention as a whole must be evaluated. And arguing that "it would be obvious" shifts the focus to the wrong period of time.[106]

Despite its zeal, the court may itself have been guilty of uncritically embracing a shorthand test that could do mischief to §103. The court has on several occasions informed us that anticipation is the "epitome" or "ultimate" of obviousness.[107] Nothing could be further from the truth; one can imagine many old inventions that are anything but obvious. Epitomizing obviousness in this way is unnecessary and dangerous.[108]

§4.3 Level of Ordinary Skill in the Art

The person of ordinary skill in the art is a theoretical construct used in determining obviousness under §103, and is not descriptive

---

is anticipated by a species, the court has refused to adopt any per se rule that a subcombination is rendered obvious by a combination. *In re Emert,* 124 F.3d 1458, 44 USPQ2d 1149 (Fed. Cir. 1997).

[104]*Custom Accessories, Inc. v. Jeffrey-Allan Indus., Inc.,* 807 F.2d 955, 1 USPQ2d 1196 (Fed. Cir. 1986); *Environmental Designs, Ltd. v. Union Oil Co.,* 713 F.2d 693, 218 USPQ 865 (Fed. Cir. 1983).

[105]*Custom Accessories, Inc. v. Jeffrey-Allan Indus., Inc.,* 807 F.2d 955, 1 USPQ2d 1196 (Fed. Cir. 1986). Although it recognizes that it has used a "clear suggestion" test for obviousness in other cases, the court has declined to decide whether that is an overly rigorous test. Instead, it falls back on the standard "invention as a whole" test, which avoids improper focus on the obviousness of substitutions and differences. *Gillette Co. v. S.C. Johnson & Son,* 919 F.2d 720, 16 USPQ2d 1923 (Fed. Cir. 1990).

[106]*Hybritech Inc. v. Monoclonal Antibodies, Inc.,* 802 F.2d 1367, 231 USPQ 81 (Fed. Cir. 1986).

[107]*Jones v. Hardy,* 727 F.2d 1524, 220 USPQ 1021 (Fed. Cir. 1984); *Connell v. Sears, Roebuck & Co.,* 722 F.2d 1542, 220 USPQ 193 (Fed. Cir. 1983). Anticipation is the ultimate of obviousness. *In re Baxter Travenol Labs.,* 952 F.2d 388, 21 USPQ2d 1281 (Fed. Cir. 1991). In *Mendenhall v. Cedarapids, Inc.,* 5 F.3d 1556, 28 USPQ2d 1081 (Fed. Cir. 1993), the jury concluded that certain claims were anticipated but not obvious. The court held that this did not justify a new trial where the evidence supported the anticipation result, despite the legal homily that anticipation is the epitome of obviousness. *In re Robertson,* 169 F.3d 743, 49 USPQ2d 1949 (Fed. Cir. 1999), involved a Board rejection on obviousness that was premised on its finding of anticipation, coupled with the rubric that anticipation is the ultimate of obviousness. The Federal Circuit reversed the anticipation finding, and would not consider the PTO's attempt to augment the Board's obviousness ruling on appeal.

[108]See discussion at notes 3:70–74.

of some particular individual.[109] Here the decision maker confronts a "ghost," not unlike the "reasonable man" and other legal phantoms. To reach a proper conclusion under §103, the decision maker must step backward in time and into the shoes worn by that "person" when the invention was unknown and just before it was made. In light of all the evidence, the decision maker must then determine whether the patent challenger has convincingly established that the claimed invention as a whole would have been obvious at that time to that person. The answer to this question partakes more of the nature of law than of fact, for it is an ultimate conclusion based on a foundation formed of all the probative facts.[110] The primary value of the requirement that the level of skill be ascertained lies in its tendency to focus the mind of the decision maker away from what would presently be obvious to that decision maker and toward what would, when the invention was made, have been obvious to one of ordinary skill in the art.[111]

Three questions seem pertinent here: Who is this person? What is ordinary skill? What does this person of ordinary skill know? Somewhat surprisingly, the Federal Circuit has not demanded specific findings on the level of skill, particularly on summary judgment, where the subject matter of the patent and the prior art are easily understandable,[112] or where the prior art itself reflects an appropriate level and a need for testimony is not shown.[113] A failure to make a finding as to level of skill, or an incorrect finding, constitutes reversible error only if it influences the ultimate conclusion on obviousness.[114] There are instances where no error could be forthcoming, as in a finding that an invention would have been obvious to one of the lowest level of skill (a layperson), or that the invention would have been unobvious to those of extraordinary skill (i.e., other inventors in the art).[115] Any error in choosing too high a level of skill in determining that the invention would not have been obvious could not be prejudicial to the accused infringer and would not be grounds for reversal.[116] And in the context of a summary judgment motion, the trial judge is really resolving the question by reference to the skill of the layperson,

[109]*Endress + Hauser, Inc. v. Hawk Meas. Sys. Pty.*, 122 F.3d 1040, 43 USPQ2d 1849 (Fed. Cir. 1997).

[110]*Panduit Corp. v. Dennison Mfg. Co.*, 810 F.2d 1561, 1 USPQ2d 1593 (Fed. Cir. 1987).

[111]*Kloster Speedsteel AB v. Crucible Inc.*, 793 F.2d 1565, 230 USPQ 81 (Fed. Cir. 1986).

[112]*Chore-Time Equip., Inc. v. Cumberland Corp.*, 713 F.2d 774, 218 USPQ 673 (Fed. Cir. 1983).

[113]*Litton Indus. Prods., Inc. v. Solid State Sys. Corp.*, 755 F.2d 158, 225 USPQ 34 (Fed. Cir. 1985).

[114]*Custom Accessories, Inc. v. Jeffrey-Allan Indus., Inc.*, 807 F.2d 955, 1 USPQ2d 1196 (Fed. Cir. 1986); *Kloster Speedsteel AB v. Crucible Inc.*, 793 F.2d 1565, 230 USPQ 81 (Fed. Cir. 1986).

[115]*Kloster Speedsteel AB v. Crucible Inc.*, 793 F.2d 1565, 230 USPQ 81 (Fed. Cir. 1986). The court termed it a waste of time to complain about the district court having looked to other inventors in the field to establish the level of skill.

[116]*Specialty Composites v. Cabot Corp.*, 845 F.2d 981, 6 USPQ2d 1601 (Fed. Cir. 1988).

which is, except in rare circumstances, the most favorable view for the patentee.[117]

Nonetheless, that the question of obviousness is legal does not mean that "to a judge" may be substituted for the statutory phrase "to one of ordinary skill in the art." Thus the question is not answerable by a judge on the sole basis of what he or she thinks ought to be patentable under §103.[118] Under our economic and patent systems, valuation of the worth of an inventor's contribution is left to the public, not to the judiciary, in determining patentability. A judge is nowhere authorized to declare a patent invalid on his or her personal evaluation. Judges are not to decide whether they think a particular invention "ought" to be patented. Were it otherwise, a letter to the court would do, and trials, Title 35, and the PTO would be unnecessary.[119]

(a) The Person of Ordinary Skill

The hypothetical person skilled in the art is not the judge, nor a layperson, nor one skilled in remote arts, nor a genius in the art at hand,[120] nor the inventor—the invention is not to be evaluated through the eyes of the actual inventor.[121] Indeed, the court has said that the actual inventor's skill is irrelevant to the inquiry, and this for a very important reason. Inventors, as a class, according to the concepts underlying the Constitution and the statutes that have created the patent system, are thought to possess a special something that sets them apart from workers of ordinary skill. Thus obviousness should not be determined by inquiring into what patentees—that is, inventors—would have known or likely would have done faced with the revelations of the prior art. Similarly, a person of ordinary skill

---

[117]*Union Carbide Corp. v. American Can Co.,* 724 F.2d 1567, 220 USPQ 584 (Fed. Cir. 1984). It is improper, on motion for summary judgment of invalidity for obviousness, to draw inferences against a patentee on questions of the knowledge of one of ordinary skill in the art. *Rockwell Int'l Corp. v. United States,* 147 F.3d 1358, 47 USPQ2d 1027 (Fed. Cir. 1998).

[118]*Polaroid Corp. v. Eastman Kodak Co.,* 789 F.2d 1556, 229 USPQ 561 (Fed. Cir. 1986). It is clear that the decision maker—judge, jury, or examiner—need not be a person of skill in the art. The technical background and other professional qualifications of the particular examiners-in-chief making up a PTO Board panel are not legally relevant in an appeal to the Board under 35 U.S.C. §134, just as the technical qualifications of a judge are irrelevant in a §141 appeal to the Federal Circuit or a §145 review in the District Court for the District of Columbia. A Board member need not possess "ordinary skill" in a particular art area to be qualified to render a patentability determination on a claimed invention drawn to that art. *In re Nilssen,* 851 F.2d 1401, 7 USPQ2d 1500 (Fed. Cir. 1988).

[119]*Panduit Corp. v. Dennison Mfg. Co.,* 810 F.2d 1561, 1 USPQ2d 1593 (Fed. Cir. 1987). Nonetheless, it is not error for a judge, unskilled in the pertinent art, to decide the legal question of validity without the testimony of a qualified expert in that field. *Avia Group Int'l, Inc. v. L.A. Gear Calif., Inc.,* 853 F.2d 1557, 7 USPQ2d 1548 (Fed. Cir. 1988).

[120]*Environmental Designs, Ltd. v. Union Oil Co.,* 713 F.2d 693, 218 USPQ 865 (Fed. Cir. 1983).

[121]*Arkie Lures, Inc. v. Gene Larew Tackle, Inc.,* 119 F.3d 953, 43 USPQ2d 1294 (Fed. Cir. 1997); *Interconnect Planning Corp. v. Feil,* 774 F.2d 1132, 227 USPQ 543 (Fed. Cir. 1985); *Stewart-Warner Corp. v. City of Pontiac,* 767 F.2d 1563, 226 USPQ 676 (Fed. Cir. 1985).

in the art is also presumed to be one who thinks along the lines of conventional wisdom in the art and is not one who undertakes to innovate, whether by extraordinary insights or by patient and often expensive systematic research.[122] Thus, the testimony of an inventor that she devised an idea to try, and thought the idea would be successful, does not itself compel a conclusion of obviousness; the actual inventor may have possessed exceptional skill.[123]

In design cases, the hypothetical person is a designer of ordinary capability who designs articles of the type patented, rather than an ordinary observer or consumer.[124]

(b) The Level of Ordinary Skill

The level of skill in the art is a prism or lens through which a judge or jury views the prior art and the claimed invention. This reference point prevents these deciders from using their own insight or, worse yet, hindsight, to gauge obviousness.[125] The importance of resolving the level of ordinary skill lies in the necessity of maintaining objectivity in the obviousness inquiry. The court must ascertain what would have been objectively obvious to one of ordinary skill rather than what was subjectively obvious to the inventor. Probative factors are the educational level of the inventor and those who work in the industry and the sophistication of the technology involved.[126]

Other factors to be determined in ascertaining the level of ordinary skill are the various prior art approaches employed, the types of problems encountered in the art, the rapidity with which innovations are made, the sophistication of the technology involved, and the educational background and experience of those actively working in the field, including the inventor.[127] Not all such factors may be present

---

[122]*Standard Oil Co. v. American Cyanamid Co.,* 774 F.2d 448, 227 USPQ 293 (Fed. Cir. 1985).

[123]*Loctite Corp. v. Ultraseal Ltd.,* 781 F.2d 861, 228 USPQ 90 (Fed. Cir. 1985). A disgruntled former employee refused to execute patent application documents, stating that he had not invented anything in that connection while with his former employer. The trial court seemed impressed by this refusal to sign, but the Federal Circuit felt that led to error. A determination of obviousness should always be made in view of hypothetical persons skilled in the art and not the actual inventor. *Bausch & Lomb, Inc. v. Barnes-Hind, Inc.,* 796 F.2d 443, 230 USPQ 416 (Fed. Cir. 1986).

[124]*In re Carlson,* 983 F.2d 1032, 25 USPQ2d 1207 (Fed. Cir. 1993); *Pacific Furniture Mfg. Co. v. Preview Furniture Corp.,* 800 F.2d 1111, 231 USPQ 67 (Fed. Cir. 1986); *Petersen Mfg. Co. v. Central Purchasing, Inc.,* 740 F.2d 1541, 222 USPQ 562 (Fed. Cir. 1984); *Litton Sys., Inc. v. Whirlpool Corp.,* 728 F.2d 1423, 221 USPQ 97 (Fed. Cir. 1984).

[125]*Al-Site Corp. v. VSI Int'l Inc.,* 174 F.3d 1308, 50 USPQ2d 1161 (Fed. Cir. 1999).

[126]*Ryko Mfg. Co. v. Nu-Star, Inc.,* 950 F.2d 714, 21 USPQ2d 1053 (Fed. Cir. 1991). It is not always necessary for the trial court to articulate its resolution of the level of skill. *Id.* The trier of fact determines the level of skill to ensure proper objectivity at the outset of the obviousness inquiry. *Litton Sys., Inc. v. Honeywell, Inc.,* 87 F.3d 1559, 39 USPQ2d 1321 (Fed. Cir. 1996).

[127]*Custom Accessories, Inc. v. Jeffrey-Allan Indus., Inc.,* 807 F.2d 955, 1 USPQ2d 1196 (Fed. Cir. 1986); *Bausch & Lomb, Inc. v. Barnes-Hind, Inc.,* 796 F.2d 443, 230 USPQ 416 (Fed. Cir. 1986); *Vandenberg v. Dairy Equip. Co.,* 740 F.2d 1560, 224 USPQ 195 (Fed. Cir. 1984);

in every case, and one or more of them may predominate.[128] The education of the actual inventor, however, is by no means conclusive on the question of ordinary skill.[129] Even so, the inventor's admissions may be important. Where the patentee had argued during prosecution that certain substitutions could be made by a routineer without undue experimentation, that admission was relied upon to reject his argument that the level of skill in the art was high.[130]

Of course, it is as of the time the invention was made that the level of ordinary skill must be determined and analyzed.[131] Nevertheless, material that is not technically prior art can be used as evidence of the level of skill in the art as of about the pertinent date.[132]

It is probable that the Federal Circuit believes that an invention is more likely to have been obvious where the level of ordinary skill in the art was high.[133] In keeping with this attitude, the court will quickly reject any nonobviousness argument that presumes stupidity rather than skill.[134]

(c) The Knowledge of the Person of Skill

The hypothetical person of ordinary skill is presumed to have knowledge of all references that are sufficiently related to one another

---

Environmental Designs, Ltd. v. Union Oil Co., 713 F.2d 693, 218 USPQ 865 (Fed. Cir. 1983); *Orthopedic Equip. Co. v. All Orthopedic Appls., Inc.*, 707 F.2d 1376, 217 USPQ 1281 (Fed. Cir. 1983). A district court errs when it fails to consider these factors, and instead constructs a hypothetical person skilled in the art by assuming that such a person is someone who is familiar with the pertinent literature and is likely to attend trade shows. *Helifix Ltd. v. Blok-Lok Ltd.*, 208 F.3d 1339, 54 USPQ2d 1299 (Fed. Cir. 2000).

[128]*In re GPAC, Inc.*, 57 F.3d 1573, 35 USPQ2d 1116 (Fed. Cir. 1995); *Custom Accessories, Inc. v. Jeffrey-Allan Indus., Inc.*, 807 F.2d 955, 1 USPQ2d 1196 (Fed. Cir. 1986).

[129]*Custom Accessories, Inc. v. Jeffrey-Allan Indus., Inc.*, 807 F.2d 955, 1 USPQ2d 1196 (Fed. Cir. 1986); *Orthopedic Equip. Co. v. All Orthopedic Appls., Inc.*, 707 F.2d 1376, 217 USPQ 1281 (Fed. Cir. 1983).

[130]*Constant v. Advanced Micro-Devices, Inc.*, 848 F.2d 1560, 7 USPQ2d 1057 (Fed. Cir. 1988).

[131]*Stewart-Warner Corp. v. City of Pontiac*, 767 F.2d 1563, 226 USPQ 676 (Fed. Cir. 1985).

[132]*Gould v. Quigg*, 822 F.2d 1074, 3 USPQ2d 1302 (Fed. Cir. 1987); *In re Merck & Co.*, 800 F.2d 1091, 231 USPQ 375 (Fed. Cir. 1986); *Ashland Oil, Inc. v. Delta Resins & Refracs., Inc.*, 776 F.2d 281, 227 USPQ 657 (Fed. Cir. 1985); *Thomas & Betts Corp. v. Litton Sys., Inc.*, 720 F.2d 1572, 220 USPQ 1 (Fed. Cir. 1983); *Orthopedic Equip. Co. v. United States*, 702 F.2d 1005, 217 USPQ 193 (Fed. Cir. 1983).

[133]See *Vandenberg v. Dairy Equip. Co.*, 740 F.2d 1560, 224 USPQ 195 (Fed. Cir. 1984). Use of an extraordinary level of skill in arriving at a determination of nonobviousness is not reversible error because it does not harm the accused infringer. *Specialty Composites v. Cabot Corp.*, 845 F.2d 981, 6 USPQ2d 1601 (Fed. Cir. 1988). With all respect, could it not be argued that one of extraordinary skill in the art might know too much, and thus be amazed when the routineer successfully stumbles along an "obvious" course? In that case, the person of extraordinary skill would have found the invention unobvious, while the person of ordinary skill would have regarded it as obvious. The court seems to have rejected this argument, albeit without much discussion, in a closely analogous context. See *In re Dow Chem. Co.*, 837 F.2d 469, 5 USPQ2d 1529 (Fed. Cir. 1988).

[134]*In re Sovish*, 769 F.2d 738, 226 USPQ 771, 774 (Fed. Cir. 1985).

and to the pertinent art[135] and to have knowledge of all arts reasonably pertinent to the particular problem with which the inventor was involved.[136] The court has expressly rejected a challenge to its long-standing precedent that the hypothetical person of ordinary skill in the art is presumed to be aware of all prior art in the field of the inventor's endeavor and of prior art solutions for a common problem even if outside that field.[137] The question is whether what the inventor did would have been obvious to one of ordinary skill attempting to solve the problem upon which the inventor was working.[138]

The hypothetical person must be viewed as working in his or her shop with the prior art references—which the person is presumed to know—hanging on the walls around him or her.[139] However, that prior art is only that which the hypothetical person would have selected without the advantage of hindsight and may not be gathered with the claimed invention in mind.[140] In determining whether a suggestion can fairly be gleaned from the prior art, the full field of the invention must be considered, for the person of ordinary skill is charged with knowledge of the entire body of technological literature, including that which might lead away from the claimed invention.[141]

Most emphatically, the actual inventor is not presumed to have had actual knowledge of the prior art. The presumed knowledge of the art is of course available to all, and it is irrelevant that the actual inventor may have been unaware of it.[142] But great mischief could result from presuming that the inventor had actual knowledge of the art. Such a concept:

> is a witches' brew which could do untold damage to patentees if ingested into the body of patent law. Even the fumes of this brew, whoever originated it, are so stupefying that they have driven us to analyze anew this ancient presumption of knowledge of prior art on the part of

---

[135]*In re Sernaker,* 702 F.2d 989, 217 USPQ 1 (Fed. Cir. 1983).

[136]*Custom Accessories, Inc. v. Jeffrey-Allan Indus., Inc.,* 807 F.2d 955, 1 USPQ2d 1196 (Fed. Cir. 1986); *Pentec, Inc. v. Graphic Controls Corp.,* 776 F.2d 309, 227 USPQ 766 (Fed. Cir. 1985).

[137]*In re Nilssen,* 851 F.2d 1401, 7 USPQ2d 1500 (Fed. Cir. 1988).

[138]*In re Wright,* 848 F.2d 1216, 6 USPQ2d 1959 (Fed. Cir. 1988).

[139]*Union Carbide Corp. v. American Can Co.,* 724 F.2d 1567, 220 USPQ 584 (Fed. Cir. 1984).

[140]*Pentec, Inc. v. Graphic Controls Corp.,* 776 F.2d 309, 227 USPQ 766 (Fed. Cir. 1985); *Union Carbide Corp. v. American Can Co.,* 724 F.2d 1567, 220 USPQ 584 (Fed. Cir. 1984). That knowledge may have been within the province of the ordinary artisan does not in and of itself make it so, absent clear and convincing evidence of such knowledge. *Smiths Indus. Med. Sys. Inc. v. Vital Signs Inc.,* 183 F.3d 1347, 51 USPQ2d 1415 (Fed. Cir. 1999).

[141]*In re Dow Chem. Co.,* 837 F.2d 469, 5 USPQ2d 1529 (Fed. Cir. 1988).

[142]*EWP Corp. v. Reliance Universal Inc.,* 755 F.2d 898, 225 USPQ 20 (Fed. Cir. 1985). Indeed, the court has now hinted that it may be irrelevant that the person of ordinary skill could not, under the circumstances of a particular case, have been aware of certain prior art. *E.I. duPont & Co. v. Phillips Petroleum Co.,* 849 F.2d 1430, 7 USPQ2d 1129 (Fed. Cir. 1988). Similarly, evidence of secondary considerations is considered independently of what any real person knows about the prior art. To require that actual inventors in the field have the omni-science of the hypothetical person in the art is contrary to case law. *Hodosh v. Block Drug Co.,* 786 F.2d 1136, 229 USPQ 182 (Fed. Cir. 1986).

inventors. . . . Realistically, courts never have judged patentability by what the real inventor/applicant/patentee could or would do. Real inventors, as a class, vary in their capacities from ignorant geniuses to Nobel laureates; the courts have always applied a standard based on an imaginary worker of their own devising whom they have equated with the inventor.[143]

§4.4 Scope and Content of the Prior Art

An inventor's own publication is of course prior art under §103 if early enough. Thus, where an inventor publishes more than a year before filing, he or she forecloses obtaining a patent on an invention that would have been obvious from the publication, with or without the disclosure of other prior art.[144] A foreign patent application publication is prior art for what it teaches, even though no patent was obtained.[145]

The prior art is not limited to patents or publications, of course. Firsthand practical knowledge of unsolved needs in the art, by an expert, is evidence of the state of the art.[146] A statement in a patent that something is in the prior art is binding upon the patentee for determinations of anticipation and obviousness.[147] Evidence of public use or sale is relevant to the obviousness inquiry and can be combined with other prior art under §103.[148] Section 102(b) may create a bar to patentability either alone, if the device placed on sale is an anticipation of the later claimed invention, or in conjunction with §103, if the claimed invention would have been obvious from the on-sale device in view of the other prior art. If a device was in public use or on sale before the critical date, then that device becomes a reference under §103.[149] The court has recently held that §102(f), which deals with derivation, defines prior art that can be combined with other references under §103.[150] A two-judge panel of the court has held that prior

---

[143]*Kimberly-Clark Corp. v. Johnson & Johnson*, 745 F.2d 1437, 223 USPQ 603, 610 (Fed. Cir. 1984).

[144]*In re O'Farrell*, 853 F.2d 894, 7 USPQ2d 1673 (Fed. Cir. 1988).

[145]*Valmet Paper Mach., Inc. v. Beloit Corp.*, 105 F.3d 1409, 41 USPQ2d 1619 (Fed. Cir. 1997).

[146]*In re Piasecki*, 745 F.2d 1468, 223 USPQ 785 (Fed. Cir. 1984).

[147]*Constant v. Advanced Micro-Devices, Inc.*, 848 F.2d 1560, 7 USPQ2d 1057 (Fed. Cir. 1988).

[148]*Elmer v. ICC Fabricating, Inc.*, 67 F.3d 1571, 36 USPQ2d 1417 (Fed. Cir. 1995); *In re Kaslow*, 707 F.2d 1366, 217 USPQ 1089 (Fed. Cir. 1983). See also *Lockwood v. American Airlines, Inc.*, 107 F.3d 1565, 41 USPQ2d 1961 (Fed. Cir. 1997).

[149]*Keystone Ret. Wall Sys., Inc. v. Westrock, Inc.*, 997 F.2d 1444, 27 USPQ2d 1297 (Fed. Cir. 1993); *LaBounty Mfg., Inc. v. United States ITC*, 958 F.2d 1066, 22 USPQ2d 1025 (Fed. Cir. 1992).

[150]*Oddzon Prods., Inc. v. Just Toys, Inc.*, 122 F.3d 1396, 43 USPQ2d 1641 (Fed. Cir. 1997). In a case dealing with derivation, *Gambro Lundia AB v. Baxter Healthcare Corp.*, 110 F.3d 1573, 42 USPQ2d 1378 (Fed. Cir. 1997), the court had indicated that §102(f) does not implicate the obviousness inquiry. This was contrary to its earlier suggestion, in *New England Braiding Co. v. A.W. Chesterton Co.*, 970 F.2d 878, 23 USPQ2d 1622 (Fed. Cir. 1992), that there could

work under 35 U.S.C. §102(g) is prior art for purposes of §103 if it was not abandoned, suppressed, or concealed, despite lingering concerns about "secret prior art."[151] The combined teachings of the prior art as a whole must be considered.[152]

One must proceed with extreme caution here, however. There is a great tendency to elevate to prior art status subject matter that simply does not qualify. As an example, it is wholly improper, in a reissue or reexamination setting, to treat original invalid claims as prior art and to focus only on the differences between those claims and the new claims.[153] But the court appears willing to permit the PTO to employ hearsay evidence to establish the prior art status of certain documents.[154] The court will even rely upon judicial notice to fill out the prior art.[155]

Analogous art. As already indicated, the imaginary person of ordinary skill is presumed to have been aware of all arts reasonably pertinent to the particular problem confronting the actual inventor at the time.[156] Although §103 does not, by its terms, define the art to

---

be a §102(f)/§103 defense. The matter was subsequently expressly passed in *Lamb-Weston, Inc. v. McCain Foods, Ltd.*, 78 F.3d 540, 37 USPQ2d 1856 (Fed. Cir. 1996). The *Oddzon* panel did not offer to distinguish *Gambro*; indeed, the case was not even mentioned. The only way the author has been able to rationalize these decisions is to conclude that, when the issue is invalidity under §102(f), the communication must have been of a fully anticipatory concept; when the issue is obviousness under §103, the communication of any relevant concept is to be treated as prior art, even though it does not anticipate the claimed invention. If the *Oddzon* rule is applied broadly, it would seem that anything of pertinence that is taught to an inventor by another can constitute prior art.

[151]*E.I. duPont & Co. v. Phillips Petroleum Co.*, 849 F.2d 1430, 7 USPQ2d 1129 (Fed. Cir. 1988). The panel specifically rejected, as dictum, the implication in *In re Clemens*, 622 F.2d 1029, 206 USPQ 289 (CCPA 1980), that there is a further requirement that the §102(g) work be known to the art or to the patentee before he or she made the invention. It also recognized the impact of the amendment to §103 (2d paragraph, last sentence; now §103(c)), which alters the situation where the inventors are commonly employed. The 1984 amendment to §103 was in part intended to overturn a line of cases under which a prior invention that was not public could be treated as §102(g)/§103 prior art with respect to a later invention made by another employee of the same organization. The practical consequence of these decisions was that research organizations were given an incentive to discourage information sharing and collaboration among their researchers, thus impeding research, because one inventor's unpublished work might be prior art against another's. Congress amended §103 to eliminate this problem and thereby to encourage team research. *Kimberly-Clark Corp. v. Procter & Gamble Distrib. Co.*, 973 F.2d 911, 23 USPQ2d 1921 (Fed. Cir. 1992).

[152]*EWP Corp. v. Reliance Universal Inc.*, 755 F.2d 898, 225 USPQ 20 (Fed. Cir. 1985).

[153]*Interconnect Planning Corp. v. Feil*, 774 F.2d 1132, 227 USPQ 543 (Fed. Cir. 1985). In *Greenwood v. Hattori Seiko Co.*, 900 F.2d 238, 14 USPQ2d 1474 (Fed. Cir. 1990), the examiner in a reexamination proceeding rejected the claims and the patentee antedated the references, which resulted in the issuance of a reexamination certificate. On a motion for summary judgment, the trial court found that the showing of an earlier invention date by the patentee was defective, and thus purported to "restore" the examiner's rejection. The Federal Circuit, not surprisingly, vacated and remanded, holding that the trial court's action failed to comport with the required *Graham* analysis.

[154]See *In re Epstein*, 32 F.3d 1559, 31 USPQ2d 1817 (Fed. Cir. 1994). See also *Lockwood v. American Airlines, Inc.*, 107 F.3d 1565, 41 USPQ2d 1961 (Fed. Cir. 1997).

[155]*In re Raynes*, 7 F.3d 1037, 28 USPQ2d 1630 (Fed. Cir. 1993).

[156]*Pentec, Inc. v. Graphic Controls Corp.*, 776 F.2d 309, 227 USPQ 766 (Fed. Cir. 1985).

which the subject matter sought to be patented pertains, this determination is frequently couched in terms of whether the art is analogous or not, that is, whether the art is too remote to be treated as prior art. Whether a reference in the prior art is analogous is a fact question, reviewed under the clearly erroneous standard. Two criteria are used: (1) whether the art is from the same field of endeavor, regardless of the problem addressed; and (2) if the reference is not within the field of the inventor's endeavor, whether it still is reasonably pertinent to the particular problems with which the inventor is involved. If a reference disclosure has the same purpose as the claimed invention, the reference relates to the same problem, and that fact supports use of the reference to determine obviousness. If it is directed to a different purpose, the inventor would accordingly have had less motivation or occasion to consider it.[157] Accordingly, the trier of fact must look first to the nature of the problem with which the inventor was working. If the reference is not within the field of the inventor's endeavor, the fact finder then looks at whether the field of the reference is reasonably pertinent to that problem.[158] The hypothetical person of ordinary skill is presumed to have the ability to select and utilize knowledge from other arts that are reasonably pertinent. Thus, teachings of references from an analogous field properly may be combined with those from the specific field of endeavor in which the inventor was working.[159] Analogous art is simply that which is not too remote to be treated as prior art, and so labeling it merely connotes that it is relevant to a consideration of obviousness under §103.[160]

Of course, difficulties can arise in making the determination of what is pertinent or not. Hindsight selection of the pertinent art must be avoided at all cost.[161] Defining the problem in terms of its solution reveals improper hindsight in the selection of the prior art relevant to obviousness.[162] Patent examination is necessarily conducted by hindsight, with complete knowledge of the applicant's invention, and the courts have recognized the subjective aspects of determining whether an inventor would reasonably be motivated to go to the

---

[157]*In re Clay*, 966 F.2d 656, 23 USPQ2d 1058 (Fed. Cir. 1992). See also *Heidelberger Druckmaschinen AG v. Hantscho Comm. Prods., Inc.*, 21 F.3d 1068, 30 USPQ2d 1377 (Fed. Cir. 1994).

[158]*In re GPAC, Inc.*, 57 F.3d 1573, 35 USPQ2d 1116 (Fed. Cir. 1995); *In re Paulsen*, 30 F.3d 1475, 31 USPQ2d 1671 (Fed. Cir. 1994); *Wang Labs., Inc. v. Toshiba Corp.*, 993 F.2d 858, 26 USPQ2d 1767 (Fed. Cir. 1993); *Ryko Mfg. Co. v. Nu-Star, Inc.*, 950 F.2d 714, 21 USPQ2d 1053 (Fed. Cir. 1991); *In re Gorman*, 933 F.2d 982, 18 USPQ2d 1885 (Fed. Cir. 1991); *Finish Eng'g Co. v. Zerpa Indus., Inc.*, 806 F.2d 1041, 1 USPQ2d 1114 (Fed. Cir. 1986); *Bausch & Lomb, Inc. v. Barnes-Hind, Inc.*, 796 F.2d 443, 230 USPQ 416 (Fed. Cir. 1986); *In re Deminski*, 796 F.2d 436, 230 USPQ 313 (Fed. Cir. 1986); *Shatterproof Glass Corp. v. Libbey-Owens Ford Co.*, 758 F.2d 613, 225 USPQ 634 (Fed. Cir. 1985).

[159]*Cable Elec. Prods., Inc. v. Genmark, Inc.*, 770 F.2d 1015, 226 USPQ 881 (Fed. Cir. 1985).

[160]*In re Sovish*, 769 F.2d 738, 226 USPQ 771 (Fed. Cir. 1985).

[161]*Union Carbide Corp. v. American Can Co.*, 724 F.2d 1567, 220 USPQ 584 (Fed. Cir. 1984).

[162]*Monarch Knitting Mach. Corp. v. Sulzer Morat Gmbh*, 139 F.3d 877, 45 USPQ2d 1977 (Fed. Cir. 1998).

field in which the examiner found the reference in order to solve the problem facing the inventor. The combination of elements from nonanalogous sources, in a manner that reconstructs the applicant's invention only with the benefit of hindsight, is insufficient to present a prima facie case of obviousness.[163]

When the references are in the same field as the applicant's invention, knowledge thereof may be presumed,[164] but too broad a definition of the specific problem confronting the inventor can lead a court into error.[165] Pitfalls also await the unwary litigant. For example, it is extremely difficult to argue that a particular field is not the relevant art when one uses an expert in that field.[166] And certainly the pertinent art includes references referred to by the parties as part of the art.[167] It is self-evident that any reference that fully anticipates certain claims of a patent or that was the source of ideas used by the inventor when he or she conceived the invention is relevant and can be considered on the issue of obviousness.[168]

Teaching and teaching away. What the prior art taught or suggested, or what knowledge is available, is a factual determination.[169] A reference must be considered not only for what it expressly teaches, but also for what it fairly suggests.[170] A reference must be considered for everything it teaches by way of technology and is not limited to the particular invention it is describing or (in the case of a patent)

---

[163]*In re Oetiker,* 977 F.2d 1443, 24 USPQ2d 1443 (Fed. Cir. 1992). Technologies that are but "distant cousins" can justify a finding of nonanalogous art. *Litton Sys., Inc. v. Honeywell, Inc.,* 87 F.3d 1559, 39 USPQ2d 1321 (Fed. Cir. 1996).

[164]*In re Dance,* 160 F.3d 1339, 48 USPQ2d 1635 (Fed. Cir. 1998).

[165]*Lindemann Maschinenfabrik v. American Hoist & Derrick Co.,* 730 F.2d 1452, 221 USPQ 481 (Fed. Cir. 1984). This case is somewhat puzzling. The district court was held to have erred in defining the scope of the art to include certain prior art, and yet the Federal Circuit rejected the patentee's argument that such art was nonanalogous.

[166]*Orthopedic Equip. Co. v. United States,* 702 F.2d 1005, 217 USPQ 193 (Fed. Cir. 1983).

[167]*ACS Hosp. Sys., Inc. v. Montefiore Hosp.,* 732 F.2d 1572, 221 USPQ 929 (Fed. Cir. 1984). It may be possible to read this case as suggesting that references cited during PTO prosecution are ipso facto part of the pertinent art. However, a stipulation that certain matters were prior art is not a stipulation that such prior art is analogous. *Wang Labs., Inc. v. Toshiba Corp.,* 993 F.2d 858, 26 USPQ2d 1767 (Fed. Cir. 1993). The court has held that where the examiner states that particular art is nonanalogous, that is sufficient to raise a genuine issue of material fact and defeat summary judgment. *Finish Eng'g Co. v. Zerpa Indus., Inc.,* 806 F.2d 1041, 1 USPQ2d 1114 (Fed. Cir. 1986).

[168]*Constant v. Advanced Micro-Devices, Inc.,* 848 F.2d 1560, 7 USPQ2d 1057 (Fed. Cir. 1988). If an invention would have been obvious in light of certain prior art references, it is irrelevant that it would not have been obvious from other references. *Id.*

[169]*Ashland Oil, Inc. v. Delta Resins & Refracs., Inc.,* 776 F.2d 281, 227 USPQ 657 (Fed. Cir. 1985). What a reference teaches is a question of fact. *In re Beattie,* 974 F.2d 1309, 24 USPQ2d 1040 (Fed. Cir. 1992). Whether a patent or publication is in the prior art is a legal question. Whether something legally within the prior art is analogous is a fact question concerning the "content" of the art. *Panduit Corp. v. Dennison Mfg. Co.,* 810 F.2d 1561, 1 USPQ2d 1593 (Fed. Cir. 1987).

[170]*In re Baird,* 16 F.3d 380, 29 USPQ2d 1550 (Fed. Cir. 1994). What a reference teaches, and what it suggests, constitute two different inquiries. *In re Lueders,* 111 F.3d 1569, 42 USPQ2d 1481 (Fed. Cir. 1997).

attempting to protect.[171] For example, a relevant property of a compound cannot be ignored in the determination of obviousness.[172] Although inherency and obviousness are distinct legal concepts,[173] the inherent teaching of a prior art reference, a factual question, arises in the obviousness setting as well as under 35 U.S.C. §102.[174] However, a retrospective view of inherency is not a substitute for some teaching or suggestion that supports the selection and use of the various elements in the particular claimed combination. That which may be inherent is not necessarily known. Obviousness cannot be predicated on what is unknown.[175]

A reference must be considered for all that it taught, disclosures that diverge and teach away from the invention at hand as well as disclosures that point toward and teach the invention.[176] A reference may be said to teach away when a person of ordinary skill, upon reading it, would be discouraged from following the path set out in the reference, or would be led in a direction divergent from the path taken by the inventor.[177] The degree of teaching away will of course depend on the particular facts; in general, a reference will teach away if it suggests that the line of development flowing from the reference's disclosure is unlikely to be productive of the result sought by the inventor.[178] It is improper to take statements in the prior art wholly out of context and give them meanings they would not have had to one skilled in the art having no knowledge of the claimed invention, or to anyone else who can read the prior art with understanding.[179] It is impermissible within the framework of §103 to pick and choose

---

[171]*EWP Corp. v. Reliance Universal Inc.,* 755 F.2d 898, 225 USPQ 20 (Fed. Cir. 1985). The description of specific preferences in connection with a generic formula is determinative in an analysis of anticipation under §102. But in a §103 inquiry the fact that a specific embodiment is taught to be preferred is not controlling inasmuch as all disclosures of the prior art, including unpreferred embodiments, must be considered. *Merck & Co. v. Biocraft Labs., Inc.,* 874 F.2d 804, 10 USPQ2d 1843 (Fed. Cir. 1989). If a prior art structure performs the claimed function, it need not have been commercially viable. *In re Queener,* 796 F.2d 461, 230 USPQ 438 (Fed. Cir. 1986).

[172]*In re Chupp,* 816 F.2d 643, 2 USPQ2d 1437 (Fed. Cir. 1987); *In re Lalu,* 747 F.2d 703, 223 USPQ 1257 (Fed. Cir. 1984).

[173]*W.L. Gore & Assoc. v. Garlock, Inc.,* 721 F.2d 1540, 220 USPQ 303 (Fed. Cir. 1983).

[174]*In re Grasselli,* 713 F.2d 731, 218 USPQ 769 (Fed. Cir. 1983). The inherent teaching of a prior art reference, a question of fact, arises both in the context of anticipation and obviousness. *In re Napier,* 55 F.3d 610, 34 USPQ2d 1782 (Fed. Cir. 1995).

[175]*In re Rijckaert,* 9 F.3d 1531, 28 USPQ2d 1955 (Fed. Cir. 1993); *In re Newell,* 891 F.2d 899, 13 USPQ2d 1248 (Fed. Cir. 1989).

[176]*In re Dow Chem. Co.,* 837 F.2d 469, 5 USPQ2d 1529 (Fed. Cir. 1988); *Panduit Corp. v. Dennison Mfg. Co.,* 810 F.2d 1561, 1 USPQ2d 1593 (Fed. Cir. 1987); *Akzo N.V. v. United States ITC,* 808 F.2d 1471, 1 USPQ2d 1241 (Fed. Cir. 1986); *Ashland Oil, Inc. v. Delta Resins & Refracs., Inc.,* 776 F.2d 281, 227 USPQ 657 (Fed. Cir. 1985). Whether a reference teaches toward or away from the claimed invention is a question of fact. *Para-Ordnance Mfg. v. SGS Importers Int'l, Inc.,* 73 F.3d 1085, 37 USPQ2d 1237 (Fed. Cir. 1995).

[177]*Monarch Knitting Mach. Corp. v. Sulzer Morat Gmbh,* 139 F.3d 877, 45 USPQ2d 1977 (Fed. Cir. 1998); *Para-Ordnance Mfg. v. SGS Importers Int'l, Inc.,* 73 F.3d 1085, 37 USPQ2d 1237 (Fed. Cir. 1995); *In re Gurley,* 27 F.3d 551, 31 USPQ2d 1130 (Fed. Cir. 1994).

[178]*In re Gurley,* 27 F.3d 551, 31 USPQ2d 1130 (Fed. Cir. 1994).

[179]*In re Wright,* 866 F.2d 422, 9 USPQ2d 1649 (Fed. Cir. 1989).

from any one reference only so much of it as will support a given position, to the exclusion of other parts necessary to the full appreciation of what such reference fairly suggests to one of ordinary skill in the art.[180]

Where a reference warns against rather than teaches the invention, one cannot be expected to combine it with another teaching.[181] But the fact that a reference may be concerned with a different problem does not necessarily mean that it teaches away, if those skilled in the art would recognize its broader teaching.[182] Nor does the fact that the prior art suggested that the addition of an element could be costly and a source of possible error necessarily teach away, where the evidence shows that extra expense would not be a discouragement and that the potential for error would not be regarded as a significant drawback by one skilled in the art.[183] Simplicity of the prior art is rarely a characteristic that weighs against obviousness of a more complicated device with added function.[184] It is improper to downgrade a reference on the basis that it teaches away, unless it teaches away in the context of the combination of references.[185] When prior art contains apparently conflicting references, each must be weighed for its power to suggest solutions to an artisan of ordinary skill; the degree to which one reference might accurately discredit another must be considered.[186] Nevertheless, it is error not to give due regard for disclosures in references that teach away.[187]

Must prior art be enabling in order to provide a basis for an obviousness determination? One doubts it, yet the court has approved a jury instruction to that effect. However, in the same case the court indicated that even if a reference discloses an inoperative device it is prior art for all that it teaches.[188]

Determining whether there is a suggestion or motivation to modify a prior art reference is one aspect of determining the scope and

---

[180]*Bausch & Lomb, Inc. v. Barnes-Hind, Inc.*, 796 F.2d 443, 230 USPQ 416 (Fed. Cir. 1986); *In re Hedges*, 783 F.2d 1038, 228 USPQ 685 (Fed. Cir. 1986).

[181]*In re Fine*, 837 F.2d 1071, 5 USPQ2d 1596 (Fed. Cir. 1988).

[182]*In re Heck*, 699 F.2d 1331, 216 USPQ 1038 (Fed. Cir. 1983).

[183]*In re Farrenkopf*, 713 F.2d 714, 219 USPQ 1 (Fed. Cir. 1983). The message of this case seems to be that arguments about teaching away are perfectly susceptible to rebuttal evidence, like any others.

[184]*In re Dance*, 160 F.3d 1339, 48 USPQ2d 1635 (Fed. Cir. 1998).

[185]*In re Merck & Co.*, 800 F.2d 1091, 231 USPQ 375 (Fed. Cir. 1986).

[186]*In re Young*, 927 F.2d 588, 18 USPQ2d 1089 (Fed. Cir. 1991).

[187]*W.L. Gore & Assoc. v. Garlock, Inc.*, 721 F.2d 1540, 220 USPQ 303 (Fed. Cir. 1983).

[188]*Beckman Instr., Inc. v. LKB Produkter AB*, 892 F.2d 1547, 13 USPQ2d 1301, 1304 (Fed. Cir. 1989). See also *Paperless Accounting, Inc. v. Bay Area Rapid Transit Sys.*, 804 F.2d 659, 231 USPQ 649 (Fed. Cir. 1986). While a reference must enable practice of the invention in order to anticipate under §102, a nonenabling reference may qualify as prior art for purposes of determining obviousness under §103. *Symbol Tech., Inc. v. Opticon, Inc.*, 935 F.2d 1569, 19 USPQ2d 1241 (Fed. Cir. 1991). See *Lockwood v. American Airlines, Inc.*, 107 F.3d 1565, 41 USPQ2d 1961 (Fed. Cir. 1997), for a situation involving use of a system whose essential algorithms were secret. Public use of the high level aspects of the system was held sufficient to make the system prior art that could be combined with other prior art in an obviousness analysis.

content of the prior art, a fact question subsidiary to the ultimate conclusion of obviousness.[189]

§4.5 Differences Between Prior Art and Invention

The subject matter that must have been obvious, in order to deny patentability under §103, is the entirety of the claimed invention, a concept Congress nailed down with the statutory phrase "as a whole."[190] It is error to hold that the differences must be unobvious.[191] The focus is not merely on the differences between the claimed invention and the prior art, but on the claimed "subject matter as a whole."[192] Though the difference may be slight, it may also have been the key to success, and it is error to insist that the patentee show a "remarkable degree of difference."[193] Whether or not changes from the prior art are "minor," they must be evaluated in terms of the whole invention, including whether the prior art provides any teaching or suggestion to one of ordinary skill in the art to make the changes that would produce the patentee's method and device.[194] The court must evaluate the claim as a whole and not unduly focus on one facet of the claimed invention. However, the differences between the claimed invention and the prior art need to be identified to place the obviousness analysis into proper perspective. Where there is only a single difference, that facet will necessarily be significant in the analysis.[195]

It may even be that the existence of some difference does not automatically invoke the obviousness inquiry. In testing the limits of the boundary between §102 and §103, the court held that a reference anticipates a claim if it discloses the claimed invention such that a skilled artisan could take its teachings in combination with his or her own knowledge of the particular art and be in possession of the

---

[189]*Sibia Neurosciences Inc. v. Cadus Pharm. Corp.*, 225 F.3d 1349, 55 USPQ2d 1927 (Fed. Cir. 2000). Where a jury returns a verdict in favor of the patentee, it must be presumed that all factual disputes, such as the motivation to modify, were resolved in its favor. *Id.*

[190]*Panduit Corp. v. Dennison Mfg. Co.*, 810 F.2d 1561, 1 USPQ2d 1593, 1603 (Fed. Cir. 1987). See also *Stewart-Warner Corp. v. City of Pontiac*, 767 F.2d 1563, 226 USPQ 676 (Fed. Cir. 1985).

[191]*Richdel, Inc. v. Sunspool Corp.*, 714 F.2d 1573, 219 USPQ 8 (Fed. Cir. 1983); *Stratoflex, Inc. v. Aeroquip Corp.*, 713 F.2d 1530, 218 USPQ 871 (Fed. Cir. 1983).

[192]*Hybritech Inc. v. Monoclonal Antibodies, Inc.*, 802 F.2d 1367, 231 USPQ 81 (Fed. Cir. 1986); *In re Kaslow*, 707 F.2d 1366, 217 USPQ 1089 (Fed. Cir. 1983).

[193]*Jones v. Hardy*, 727 F.2d 1524, 220 USPQ 1021 (Fed. Cir. 1984).

[194]*Northern Telecom, Inc. v. Datapoint Corp.*, 908 F.2d 931, 15 USPQ2d 1321 (Fed. Cir. 1990).

[195]*Ryko Mfg. Co. v. Nu-Star, Inc.*, 950 F.2d 714, 21 USPQ2d 1053 (Fed. Cir. 1991). *In re Gal*, 980 F.2d 717, 25 USPQ2d 1076 (Fed. Cir. 1992), illustrates how the court will approach the problem of ascertaining the differences between the claimed invention and the prior art where the subject matter at hand is custom designed integrated circuit chips made up of many standard logic cells.

invention.[196] On the other hand, in appropriate circumstances, a single prior art reference can render a claim obvious.[197]

In order for apparatus claims to distinguish over the prior art, it is not necessary to show "operational differences." Apparatus claims cover what a device is, not what a device does. An invention need not operate differently than the prior art to be patentable, but need only be different—or, perhaps more accurately, unobviously different.[198]

In the case of a chemical compound, the claimed subject matter as a whole may include the unclaimed properties of the compound. A compound and all its properties are inseparable. Thus evidence of unobvious or unexpected advantageous properties may rebut a prima facie case of obviousness based on structural similarities.[199] Factors including unexpected results, new features, solution of a different problem, and novel properties are all considerations in the determination of obviousness. When such factors are described in the specification they are weighed in determining, in the first instance, whether the prior art presents a prima facie case of obviousness. When such factors are brought out in prosecution before the PTO, they are considered in determining whether a prima facie case, if made based on the prior art, has been rebutted. In either case, the requisite view of the whole invention mandates consideration of not only its structure but also its properties and the problem solved.[200]

Indeed, when a new and useful compound is invented or discovered, having a particular use, it is often the case that what is really a single invention may be viewed legally as having three or more different aspects permitting it to be claimed in different ways, for example: (1) the compound itself; (2) the method or process of making the compound; and (3) the method or process of using the compound

---

[196]*In re Graves,* 69 F.3d 1147, 36 USPQ2d 1697 (Fed. Cir. 1995). Caution is advised here. An overbroad application of this approach could be used to avoid some of the important aspects of the obviousness inquiry, such as the requirement for a suggestion or motivation to combine references.

[197]*Sibia Neurosciences Inc. v. Cadus Pharm. Corp.,* 225 F.3d 1349, 55 USPQ2d 1927 (Fed. Cir. 2000).

[198]*Hewlett-Packard Co. v. Bausch & Lomb, Inc.,* 909 F.2d 1464, 15 USPQ2d 1525 (Fed. Cir. 1990). The PTO must consider all claim limitations when determining patentability of an invention over the prior art, and may not disregard claim limitations comprised of, e.g., printed matter. *In re Lowry,* 32 F.3d 1579, 32 USPQ2d 1031 (Fed. Cir. 1994).

[199]*In re Chupp,* 816 F.2d 643, 2 USPQ2d 1437 (Fed. Cir. 1987). Such evidence may include data showing that a compound is unexpectedly superior in a property it shares with prior art compounds. In short, a compound can be patented on the basis of its properties. This raises important and interesting considerations. In this case the compound was expected to have herbicidal activity, but turned out to have unexpectedly superior activity for several uses. Its activity for other uses was inferior to the prior art. The PTO argued that a patent on the compound would prevent its use in those expected areas. The Federal Circuit indicated that this concern was misplaced and likened the argument to an "undue breadth" rejection, which was discredited long ago in *In re Ackermann,* 444 F.2d 1172, 170 USPQ 340 (CCPA 1971). Moreover (and this seems questionable), the court allowed that nobody would want to use the compound to produce inferior results, or fight lawsuits over such uses. This, with all respect, is needless speculation.

[200]*In re Wright,* 848 F.2d 1216, 6 USPQ2d 1959 (Fed. Cir. 1988).

for its intended purpose. One must be careful to distinguish a method of making a new and unobvious compound from a method of using it for its intended purpose. The method of making it may be old or obvious. But the method of use may be patentable because of the properties of the compound. It is error to treat the compound and its properties as prior art when evaluating the patentability of method of use claims. Requiring that the result of the method of use be unpredictable before unobviousness can be found does just that.[201]

The court in its in banc *Dillon* decision[202] expounded at length on the question of the inseparability of a compound and its characteristics. *Dillon* is discussed below in §4.7 in the treatment of prima facie obviousness. In a dictum the *Dillon* court also indicated that its previous *Durden*[203] decision did not hold that all methods involving old process steps are obvious. Thus, when any applicant properly presents and argues suitable method claims, they should be examined in light of all relevant factors, free from any presumed controlling effect of *Durden*. That case simply concluded that the particularly claimed process there was obvious; it refused to adopt an unvarying rule that the fact that nonobvious starting materials and nonobvious products are involved ipso facto renders the process nonobvious. Such an invariant rule always leading to the opposite conclusion is likewise not the law.[204] The court has since confirmed that dictum, observing that reliance upon such per se rules of obviousness, while administratively convenient for the PTO, is legally incorrect and must cease.[205]

Gist of the invention. Although consideration of an invention's "gist" is appropriate in some contexts (e.g., in determining infringement under the doctrine of equivalents; see §6.3(a)(ii)), when determining obviousness there is no legally recognizable or protected "essence," or "gist," or "heart" of the invention.[206] Distillation down to a gist or core is a superficial mode of analysis that disregards elements of the whole.[207] It is improper to regard the improvement or the advantage as the invention.[208] It is error to restrict the obviousness analysis to one step of a claimed multistep process[209] or to focus only on the

---

[201]*In re Pleuddmann,* 910 F.2d 823, 15 USPQ2d 1738 (Fed. Cir. 1990).

[202]*In re Dillon,* 919 F.2d 688, 16 USPQ2d 1897 (Fed. Cir. 1990).

[203]*In re Durden,* 763 F.2d 1406, 226 USPQ 359 (Fed. Cir. 1985).

[204]*In re Dillon,* 919 F.2d 688, 16 USPQ2d 1897 (Fed. Cir. 1990).

[205]*In re Ochiai,* 71 F.3d 1565, 37 USPQ2d 1127 (Fed. Cir. 1995). The court reversed the rejection of a process claim that employed a well-known reaction on a nonobvious starting material to make a nonobvious end product. See also *In re Brouwer,* 77 F.3d 1185, 37 USPQ2d 1663 (Fed. Cir. 1996).

[206]*Para-Ordnance Mfg. v. SGS Importers Int'l, Inc.,* 73 F.3d 1085, 37 USPQ2d 1237 (Fed. Cir. 1995); *Everpure, Inc. v. Cuno, Inc.,* 875 F.2d 300, 10 USPQ2d 1855 (Fed. Cir. 1989); *Loctite Corp. v. Ultraseal Ltd.,* 781 F.2d 861, 228 USPQ 90 (Fed. Cir. 1985); *Medtronic, Inc. v. Cardiac Pacemakers, Inc.,* 721 F.2d 1563, 220 USPQ 97 (Fed. Cir. 1983); *Stratoflex, Inc. v. Aeroquip Corp.,* 713 F.2d 1530, 218 USPQ 871 (Fed. Cir. 1983).

[207]*Bausch & Lomb, Inc. v. Barnes-Hind, Inc.,* 796 F.2d 443, 230 USPQ 416 (Fed. Cir. 1986).

[208]*Jones v. Hardy,* 727 F.2d 1524, 220 USPQ 1021 (Fed. Cir. 1984).

[209]*W.L. Gore & Assoc. v. Garlock, Inc.,* 721 F.2d 1540, 220 USPQ 303 (Fed. Cir. 1983).

point of novelty.[210] Reducing a claimed invention to an idea and then determining patentability of that idea is the wrong approach. Ideas are not patentable; claimed structures and methods are.[211] That "features," even distinguishing features, of the claimed invention are disclosed in the prior art is not alone sufficient to compel a conclusion of obviousness. It is common to find features somewhere in the prior art, but it is not features but the subject matter as a whole that must be evaluated under 35 U.S.C. §103.[212]

Claimed invention. Equally important is the admonition that patents are not obvious—claimed inventions are.[213] Claims, not embodiments, are the focus of the obviousness inquiry.[214] It is the claims that define the invention. It is therefore error to compare unclaimed features with the prior art to determine the patentability of the invention.[215] It is the subject matter of the claim that constitutes what is "sought to be patented" and that is, therefore, the sole object of the court's concern in determining obviousness.[216] Whether a preamble limitation of intended purpose or use constitutes a limitation is a matter to be determined on the facts of each case in view of the claimed invention as a whole.[217] A whereby clause that merely states the result of the limitations in the claim adds nothing to the patentability or substance of the claim.[218] Unclaimed functions of a claimed means cannot be used to distinguish over prior art.[219]

---

[210]*Litton Sys., Inc. v. Whirlpool Corp.,* 728 F.2d 1423, 221 USPQ 97 (Fed. Cir. 1984). It should be noted that this case does approve a point of novelty approach in determining infringement of a design patent.

[211]*Jones v. Hardy,* 727 F.2d 1524, 220 USPQ 1021 (Fed. Cir. 1984).

[212]*Connell v. Sears, Roebuck & Co.,* 722 F.2d 1542, 220 USPQ 193 (Fed. Cir. 1983). By the same token, a prior art patent must be considered in its entirety. The mere absence of an explicit requirement in one example of a specification cannot be taken as an affirmative statement that the requirement is not necessary, where other examples call for the requirement. *In re Evanega,* 829 F.2d 1110, 4 USPQ2d 1249 (Fed. Cir. 1987).

[213]*Richdel, Inc. v. Sunspool Corp.,* 714 F.2d 1573, 219 USPQ 8 (Fed. Cir. 1983).

[214]*Windsurfing Int'l, Inc. v. AMF, Inc.,* 782 F.2d 995, 228 USPQ 562 (Fed. Cir. 1986); *Jackson Jordon, Inc. v. Plasser Am. Corp.,* 747 F.2d 1567, 224 USPQ 1 (Fed. Cir. 1984).

[215]*Uniroyal, Inc. v. Rudkin-Wiley Corp.,* 837 F.2d 1044, 5 USPQ2d 1434 (Fed. Cir. 1988). But see notes 4:199–200 and accompanying text.

[216]*In re Sovish,* 769 F.2d 738, 226 USPQ 771 (Fed. Cir. 1985). In evaluating the patentability of new use claims, the question is whether the claimed method of use would have been obvious; it is not pertinent whether the compositions that are the subject of the use are themselves known or new or unobvious. The real question is whether the newly discovered utility would have been obvious. *In re Dillon,* 892 F.2d 1554, 13 USPQ2d 1337, *vacated,* 919 F.2d 688, 16 USPQ2d 1897 (Fed. Cir. 1990).

[217]*In re Stencel,* 828 F.2d 751, 4 USPQ2d 1071 (Fed. Cir. 1987). Here the claim was to a tool, a driver for a particular collar. The preamble recited limitations about the collar. The PTO found prior art drivers for other purposes that were very similar. The court held that those references would not have taught or suggested the structure of the claimed driver in the absence of prior knowledge about the inventor's collar system. To ignore the preamble statements in that connection would be like using the inventor's own collar system as prior art against him, which it was not. It should be noted that other limitations in the body of the claim referred back to the collar, so that a close connection could be made between the preamble and the body of the claim in that respect.

[218]*Texas Instr., Inc. v. United States ITC,* 988 F.2d 1165, 26 USPQ2d 1018 (Fed. Cir. 1993).

[219]*In re Schreiber,* 128 F.3d 1473, 44 USPQ2d 1429 (Fed. Cir. 1997).

Claims must be evaluated separately, rather than as a single unit of claims tied together.[220] Where one claim is not invalid, the presence of all its limitations in another claim preserves the latter's validity.[221] A merger of separate claim limitations into a single element is likewise improper, because limitations give meaning to the various elements of a claim.[222] The court must evaluate the patentability of a claim as it finds it.[223] The importance of the claim as a measure of the invention is underscored by the fact that where the Federal Circuit, in holding no infringement, reversed a claim construction upon which an obviousness argument was predicated, it could not reach the substantive obviousness question.[224]

It is the prior public knowledge—the "prior art"—by which patentability is tested. A patentee may set the metes and bounds of that which is sought to be patented, and it is not material whether the phenomena just outside these claim limits are qualitatively different from that which is claimed. The patentee is not required to show that some technological discontinuity exists between the claimed invention and the subject matter just outside the claims, but only that the claimed subject matter would have been nonobvious in view of the prior art.[225]

Combinations. Finally, any assertion that a combination of old elements can never rise to the level of patentable invention is incorrect because §103 requires the invention to be considered as a whole.[226] The conditions for patentability of combination inventions are the same as those for other inventions.[227] A combination may be patentable whether it be composed of elements all new, partly new, or all old.[228] Indeed,

---

[220]*Milliken Res. Corp. v. Dan River, Inc.,* 739 F.2d 587, 222 USPQ 571 (Fed. Cir. 1984). Here it was clear that the lower court had given the patentee the benefit of all possible limitations in a group of claims in holding them invalid, so no prejudice could be shown by a unitary treatment and the error was therefore harmless.

[221]*Panduit Corp. v. Dennison Mfg. Co.,* 810 F.2d 1561, 1 USPQ2d 1593 (Fed. Cir. 1987). Conversely, once a broad and representative claim has been declared invalid, there is no error in holding dependent claims invalid in the absence of any indication that they contain other limitations that might have rendered nonobvious the inventions set forth as wholes in those claims. *N.V. Akzo v. E.I. duPont & Co.,* 810 F.2d 1148, 1 USPQ2d 1704 (Fed. Cir. 1987). Dependent claims are nonobvious under §103 if the independent claims from which they depend are nonobvious. *In re Fine,* 837 F.2d 1071, 5 USPQ2d 1596 (Fed. Cir. 1988). The mere fact that a claim is a "picture claim" (i.e., one that recites in detail all of the features of an invention) is never, in itself, a justification for the allowance of such a claim. *In re Gorman,* 933 F.2d 982, 18 USPQ2d 1885 (Fed. Cir. 1991).

[222]*Panduit Corp. v. Dennison Mfg. Co.,* 774 F.2d 1082, 227 USPQ 337 (Fed. Cir. 1985).

[223]*In re Durden,* 763 F.2d 1406, 226 USPQ 359 (Fed. Cir. 1985).

[224]*E.I duPont & Co. v. Phillips Petroleum Co.,* 849 F.2d 1430, 7 USPQ2d 1129 (Fed. Cir. 1988); *McGill Inc. v. John Zink Co.,* 736 F.2d 666, 221 USPQ 944 (Fed. Cir. 1984).

[225]*Andrew Corp. v. Gabriel Elec., Inc.,* 847 F.2d 819, 6 USPQ2d 2010 (Fed. Cir. 1988).

[226]*Schenck, A.G. v. Nortron Corp.,* 713 F.2d 782, 218 USPQ 698 (Fed. Cir. 1983). See also *Richdel, Inc. v. Sunspool Corp.,* 714 F.2d 1573, 219 USPQ 8 (Fed. Cir. 1983).

[227]*Jervis B. Webb Co. v. Southern Sys., Inc.,* 742 F.2d 1388, 222 USPQ 943 (Fed. Cir. 1984).

[228]*Rosemount, Inc. v. Beckman Instruments, Inc.,* 727 F.2d 1540, 221 USPQ 1 (Fed. Cir. 1984).

that all elements of an invention may have been old (the normal situation), or some old and some new, or all new, is however, simply irrelevant. Virtually all inventions are combinations and virtually all are combinations of old elements. A court must consider what the prior art as a whole would have suggested to one skilled in the art.[229]

§4.6 Objective Evidence of Nonobviousness

Recall the words of the Supreme Court:

> Such secondary considerations as commercial success, long felt but unsolved needs, failure of others, etc., might be utilized to give light to the circumstances surrounding the origins of the subject matter sought to be patented. As indicia of obviousness or nonobviousness, these inquiries may have relevancy.[230]

We are able now safely to strike the "may" in the last sentence. The Federal Circuit has emphatically and repeatedly held that objective evidence of nonobviousness must be taken into account always and not just when the decision maker is in doubt.[231] Objective evidence is not merely icing on the cake.[232] Indeed, it is always error to exclude evidence of secondary indicators.[233]

The reason such evidence is relevant is because patent lawsuits "arise out of the affairs of people, real people facing real problems."[234]

---

[229]*Environmental Designs, Ltd. v. Union Oil Co.,* 713 F.2d 693, 218 USPQ 865, 870 (Fed. Cir. 1983). There is no such thing as a patented portion of a patented combination. It is the combination, not any portion or element thereof, that is patented. *Porter v. Farmers Supply Serv., Inc.,* 790 F.2d 882, 229 USPQ 814 (Fed. Cir. 1986).

[230]*Graham v. John Deere Co.,* 383 U.S. 1, 17–18, 148 USPQ 459 (1966).

[231]E.g., *Hybritech Inc. v. Monoclonal Antibodies, Inc.,* 802 F.2d 1367, 231 USPQ 81 (Fed. Cir. 1986); *Bausch & Lomb, Inc. v. Barnes-Hind, Inc.,* 796 F.2d 443, 230 USPQ 416 (Fed. Cir. 1986); *Cable Elec. Prods., Inc. v. Genmark, Inc.,* 770 F.2d 1015, 226 USPQ 881 (Fed. Cir. 1985); *Jones v. Hardy,* 727 F.2d 1524, 220 USPQ 1021 (Fed. Cir. 1984); *Medtronic, Inc. v. Cardiac Pacemakers, Inc.,* 721 F.2d 1563, 220 USPQ 97 (Fed. Cir. 1983). That evidence is secondary in time does not mean that it is secondary in importance. *Truswal Sys. Corp v. Hydro-Air Eng'g, Inc.,* 813 F.2d 1207, 2 USPQ2d 1034 (Fed. Cir. 1987). Evidence arising out of secondary considerations must always be considered. But the existence of such evidence does not control the obviousness determination. *Richardson-Vicks, Inc. v. Upjohn Co.,* 122 F.3d 1476, 44 USPQ2d 1181 (Fed. Cir. 1997).

[232]*Hybritech Inc. v. Monoclonal Antibodies, Inc.,* 802 F.2d 1367, 231 USPQ 81 (Fed. Cir. 1986).

[233]*Stratoflex, Inc. v. Aeroquip Corp.,* 713 F.2d 1530, 218 USPQ 871 (Fed. Cir. 1983). In this case the district court received the evidence and made findings, but did not consider them. This was harmless error inasmuch as the evidence was available for review by the Federal Circuit; a remand would have been wasteful.

[234]*Rosemount, Inc. v. Beckman Instruments, Inc.,* 727 F.2d 1540, 221 USPQ 1 (Fed. Cir. 1984). Despite this view of reality, the court has held it a non sequitur to refuse to consider secondary indicators in the absence of evidence that those working in the industry actually knew of the prior art. *Hodosh v. Block Drug Co.,* 786 F.2d 1136, 229 USPQ 182 (Fed. Cir. 1986). (Apparently the district court felt that had the workers in the field known of the art, there would have been no secondary considerations such as prior failure.) Evidence of secondary considerations is taken into account independently of what any real person knows about the prior art. Such considerations are objective criteria that help illuminate the subjective determination involved in the hypothesis used to draw the legal conclusion of obviousness based upon the

The significance of a new structure is often better measured in the marketplace than in the courtroom.[235] Such evidence can often serve "as insurance against the insidious attraction of the siren hindsight when confronted with a difficult task of evaluating the prior art"; it may tend to "reassure the decision maker."[236] Objective evidence of secondary considerations may in any given case be entitled to more or less weight, depending upon its nature and its relationship to the merits of the invention. It may be the most pertinent, probative, and revealing evidence available to the decision maker in reaching its conclusion. It is incumbent upon the decision maker to recognize that evidence of secondary considerations may be particularly strong and entitled to such weight that it may be decisive.[237] For example, despite a finding that the prior art was so close that it prima facie suggested the combination to one of skill in the art, the court was willing to reverse in view of a strong showing of commercial success and other secondary indicators.[238] Prior art cannot be evaluated in isolation, but must be considered in the light of the secondary considerations bearing on obviousness.[239] There is no question but that the Federal Circuit regards secondary considerations as a fourth factual inquiry under the *Graham v. Deere* obviousness analysis.[240] It is important to understand, however, that the absence of objective evidence does not preclude a holding of nonobviousness; such evidence is not a requirement for patentability. The absence of objective evidence is a neutral factor.[241]

The importance of secondary considerations to an inventor is likely to lead the Federal Circuit to be strict in its view that anticipation, under 35 U.S.C. §102, requires identity. Objective evidence of nonobviousness is probably not relevant to a novelty inquiry, and an overly broad view of anticipation could result in depriving a patentee or applicant of potent and persuasive arguments in favor of patentability.[242]

---

first three factual *Graham v. Deere* inquiries. Thus, to require that actual inventors in the field have the omniscience of the hypothetical person in the art is not only contrary to case law, but eliminates a useful tool for trial judges faced with a nonobviousness determination. *Id.* It is suggested, however, that a showing of prior failure would certainly be more persuasive if it occurred in the face of full actual knowledge of the pertinent prior art.

[235]*Continental Can Co. v. Monsanto Co.*, 948 F.2d 1264, 20 USPQ2d 1746 (Fed. Cir. 1991).

[236]*W.L. Gore & Assoc. v. Garlock, Inc.*, 721 F.2d 1540, 220 USPQ 303, 313 (Fed. Cir. 1983).

[237]*Ashland Oil, Inc. v. Delta Resins & Refracs., Inc.*, 776 F.2d 281, 227 USPQ 657 (Fed. Cir. 1985).

[238]*Simmons Fastener Corp. v. Illinois Tool Works, Inc.*, 739 F.2d 1573, 222 USPQ 744 (Fed. Cir. 1984).

[239]*Alco Standard Corp. v. Tennessee Valley Auth.*, 808 F.2d 1490, 1 USPQ2d 1337 (Fed. Cir. 1986).

[240]*Vandenberg v. Dairy Equip. Co.*, 740 F.2d 1560, 224 USPQ 195 (Fed. Cir. 1984).

[241]*Custom Accessories, Inc. v. Jeffrey-Allan Indus., Inc.*, 807 F.2d 955, 1 USPQ2d 1196 (Fed. Cir. 1986); *Medtronic Inc. v. Intermedics, Inc.*, 799 F.2d 734, 230 USPQ 641 (Fed. Cir. 1986).

[242]Cf. *Rosemount, Inc. v. Beckman Instruments, Inc.*, 727 F.2d 1540, 221 USPQ 1 (Fed. Cir. 1984). See discussion at notes 3:70–74.

(a) The Required Nexus

A nexus is required between the merits of the claimed invention and the evidence offered, if that evidence is to be given substantial weight en route to a conclusion on the obviousness issue.[243] The Federal Circuit has served notice that it will be strict in requiring that commercial success be shown to be the result of the patented invention and not also found in the prior art.[244] Commercial success is relevant only if it flows from the merits of the claimed invention. Where all the evidence is to the effect that the popularity of a product is due to an unclaimed feature, the fact finder is not entitled to draw the inference that the success of the product is due to the merits of the claimed invention.[245] While a finding that commercial success is well beyond the effect of promotional efforts will justify a nexus finding,[246] it may be difficult to attribute a nexus in a multipatent suit.[247] In each case the evidence will have to be carefully appraised in relation to the specific facts involved.[248]

The burden of proof as to nexus resides with the patentee. In meeting its burden, the patentee must come forward with evidence sufficient to constitute a prima facie case of the requisite nexus. A prima facie case is generally made out when the patentee shows both that there is commercial success and that the product or method that is successful is the invention disclosed and claimed in the patent. When the thing that is commercially successful is not coextensive with the patented invention—for example, if the patented invention is only a component of a commercially successful machine or process— the patentee must show prima facie a legally sufficient relationship between that which is patented and that which is sold. When the patentee has presented a prima facie case of nexus, the burden of coming forward with evidence in rebuttal shifts to the challenger, as in any civil litigation. It is thus the task of the challenger to adduce

---

[243]E.g., *Cable Elec. Prods., Inc. v. Genmark, Inc.,* 770 F.2d 1015, 226 USPQ 881 (Fed. Cir. 1985); *Vandenberg v. Dairy Equip. Co.,* 740 F.2d 1560, 224 USPQ 195 (Fed. Cir. 1984); *Simmons Fastener Corp. v. Illinois Tool Works, Inc.,* 739 F.2d 1573, 222 USPQ 744 (Fed. Cir. 1984); *Stratoflex, Inc. v. Aeroquip Corp.,* 713 F.2d 1530, 218 USPQ 871 (Fed. Cir. 1983).

[244]*Richdel, Inc. v. Sunspool Corp.,* 714 F.2d 1573, 219 USPQ 8 (Fed. Cir. 1983); *In re Sneed,* 710 F.2d 1544, 218 USPQ 385 (Fed. Cir. 1983).

[245]*Sjolund v. Musland,* 847 F.2d 1573, 6 USPQ2d 2020 (Fed. Cir. 1988).

[246]*Windsurfing Int'l, Inc. v. AMF, Inc.,* 782 F.2d 995, 228 USPQ 562 (Fed. Cir. 1986).

[247]*Aktiebolaget Karlstads v. United States ITC,* 705 F.2d 1565, 217 USPQ 865 (Fed. Cir. 1983).

[248]*Cable Elec. Prods., Inc. v. Genmark, Inc.,* 770 F.2d 1015, 226 USPQ 881 (Fed. Cir. 1985). An argument was made that the success of an energy-saving device was due to an oil crisis and not the merits of the device. However, the evidence showed an interest in such energy-saving techniques long before the oil crisis and a failure to achieve success. *Uniroyal, Inc. v. Rudkin-Wiley Corp.,* 837 F.2d 1044, 5 USPQ2d 1434 (Fed. Cir. 1988). Copying and use of the patented feature of a device, while other features were not copied, gives rise to an inference that there was a nexus between the patented feature and the commercial success of the device. If the feature was not critical to success, why was it copied? *Hughes Tool Co. v. Dresser Indus., Inc.,* 816 F.2d 1549, 2 USPQ2d 1396 (Fed. Cir. 1987).

evidence to show that the commercial success was due to extraneous factors other than the patented invention, such as advertising or superior workmanship. Argument and conjecture are insufficient. Once a prima facie case is made the court must consider the evidence on both sides of the question, with such weight as is warranted.[249]

Prima facie evidence of nexus is established if there was commercial success and if the invention claimed in the patent is that which was commercially successful.[250] A patentee is not required to prove as part of its prima facie case that the commercial success of the patented invention is not due to factors other than the patented invention. It is sufficient to show that the commercial success was of the patented invention itself. A requirement for proof of the negative of all imaginable contributing factors would be unfairly burdensome and contrary to the ordinary rules of evidence.[251] It is not necessary that the patented invention be solely responsible for the commercial success, in order for this factor to be given weight appropriate to the evidence, along with other pertinent factors.[252]

Objective evidence of patentability must be commensurate in scope with the claims that the evidence is offered to support.[253] Thus, in a design patent case, the commercial success must be attributable to the design, not an improved function.[254]

(b) Commercial Success

There is no doubt that a strong showing of commercial success, attributable to the merits of the claimed invention, is powerful and persuasive evidence of nonobviousness. And there is no doubt that the commercial success of the infringer's product is as relevant as that of the patentee. As the court has observed, an attack on commercial success evidence comes with poor grace from an infringer who achieved its own great commercial success and became one of the industry leaders by making and selling its own copy of the patented invention.[255] It is error to say that no amount of commercial success

---

[249]*Demaco Corp. v. F. Von Langsdorff Lic., Ltd.*, 851 F.2d 1387, 7 USPQ2d 1222 (Fed. Cir. 1988). See also *J.T. Eaton & Co. v. Atlantic Paste & Glue Co.*, 106 F.3d 1563, 41 USPQ2d 1641 (Fed. Cir. 1997).

[250]*Ryko Mfg. Co. v. Nu-Star, Inc.*, 950 F.2d 714, 21 USPQ2d 1053 (Fed. Cir. 1991). The court actually used the words "the invention disclosed in the patent." Surely it meant the invention *claimed* rather than the invention *disclosed*. A patentee need not show that all possible embodiments within the claims were successfully commercialized in order to rely on the success in the marketplace of the embodiment that was commercialized. *Applied Mtls. Inc. v. Advanced Semi. Mtls, Inc.*, 98 F.3d 1563, 40 USPQ2d 1481 (Fed. Cir. 1996).

[251]*Demaco Corp. v. F. Von Langsdorff Lic., Ltd.*, 851 F.2d 1387, 7 USPQ2d 1222 (Fed. Cir. 1988).

[252]*Continental Can Co. v. Monsanto Co.*, 948 F.2d 1264, 20 USPQ2d 1746 (Fed. Cir. 1991).

[253]*In re Grasselli*, 713 F.2d 731, 218 USPQ 769 (Fed. Cir. 1983).

[254]*Avia Group Int'l, Inc. v. L.A. Gear Calif., Inc.*, 853 F.2d 1557, 7 USPQ2d 1548 (Fed. Cir. 1988); *Litton Sys., Inc. v. Whirlpool Corp.*, 728 F.2d 1423, 221 USPQ 97 (Fed. Cir. 1984).

[255]*Panduit Corp. v. Dennison Mfg. Co.*, 774 F.2d 1082, 227 USPQ 337 (Fed. Cir. 1985). See also *Akzo N.V. v. United States ITC*, 808 F.2d 1471, 1 USPQ2d 1241 (Fed. Cir. 1986).

can save a particular invention, because this demonstrates that the court has made the legal conclusion of obviousness without first considering all evidence of nonobviousness.[256] Commercial success must be considered before a conclusion on obviousness is reached.[257] Conversely, lack of commercialization of an invention cannot alone support a holding of invalidity of a patent on that invention.[258] Proof of commercial success, however, is not simply a matter of producing sales figures. The patentee must be prepared with evidence of market share, growth in market share, and replacement of earlier sales by others.[259] Evidence of commercial success can be downgraded where there is no showing that the sales represent a substantial share of any definable market or that the profitability is anything out of the ordinary in the industry involved.[260] Sales figures cannot be given controlling weight in determining the effect of commercial success where the patent owner was the market leader well before the introduction of the patented invention. Sponsorship by a market leader may be largely responsible for the success of the invention.[261]

And of course the patentee must be prepared with a clear showing of the nexus between the sales and the merits of the invention.[262] The commercial success of an actual product may be due entirely to improvements or modifications made to the invention claimed in the patent. In such cases, the success is not pertinent to the nonobviousness of the invention. This is not to say, however, that inherent advantages in the invention are not to be taken into account in determining nonobviousness.[263] It is improper to put "sales pitch" features in patent claims, since their sole function is to point out distinctly the matter that is patented, not its advantages. But it is entirely proper for a court to take into account advantages flowing directly from the patented invention in determining nonobviousness, for such

---

[256]*W.L. Gore & Assoc. v. Garlock, Inc.,* 721 F.2d 1540, 220 USPQ 303 (Fed. Cir. 1983).

[257]*Demaco Corp. v. F. Von Langsdorff Lic., Ltd.,* 851 F.2d 1387, 7 USPQ2d 1222 (Fed. Cir. 1988); *Lindemann Maschinenfabrik v. American Hoist & Derrick Co.,* 730 F.2d 1452, 221 USPQ 481 (Fed. Cir. 1984).

[258]*Datascope Corp. v. SMEC, Inc.,* 776 F.2d 320, 227 USPQ 838 (Fed. Cir. 1985).

[259]*Kansas Jack, Inc. v. Kuhn,* 719 F.2d 1144, 219 USPQ 857 (Fed. Cir. 1983). In the ex parte process of examining a patent application, the PTO lacks the means or resources to gather evidence that supports or refutes the applicant's assertion that sales constitute commercial success. Consequently, the PTO must rely upon the applicant to provide hard evidence of commercial success. Evidence related solely to the number of units sold provides a very weak showing of commercial success, if any. Also, the personal opinion of the applicant as to nexus is insufficient; there must be some evidence showing that the customer bought the device because of features of the claimed invention. *In re Huang,* 100 F.3d 1568 (Fed. Cir. 1996).

[260]*Cable Elec. Prods., Inc. v. Genmark, Inc.,* 770 F.2d 1015, 226 USPQ 881 (Fed. Cir. 1985).

[261]*Pentec, Inc. v. Graphic Controls Corp.,* 776 F.2d 309, 227 USPQ 766 (Fed. Cir. 1985).

[262]E.g., *Kansas Jack, Inc. v. Kuhn,* 719 F.2d 1144, 219 USPQ 857 (Fed. Cir. 1983).

[263]*In re Vamco Mach., Inc.,* 752 F.2d 1564, 224 USPQ 617 (Fed. Cir. 1985). Mere passage of time may not be enough to discredit a nexus with commercial success. *Kloster Speedsteel AB v. Crucible Inc.,* 793 F.2d 1565, 230 USPQ 81 (Fed. Cir. 1986). In this case, the parties had stipulated commercial success, and then on appeal the infringer attacked the nexus. The Federal Circuit viewed this as an apparent and disquieting effort to renege on the stipulation but went on to consider the attack on the merits anyway.

advantages are the foundation of commercial success.[264] Evidence of commercial success occurring abroad is relevant (if attributable to the merits of the claimed invention), and it is improper for a court to reject it.[265]

The Federal Circuit has firmly rejected the argument that a patentee is not entitled to discover an alleged infringer's sales until the patentee has established a right to an accounting. Such information is relevant to patentability, on grounds of commercial success. Thus, even in the case of a nonparty, no useful purpose would be served in converting every hearing on a motion to quash a subpoena for sales information into a trial on infringement and bases of sales. The patentee may not, and is unlikely to in any event, demand sales information on products totally and clearly remote from the claimed invention.[266] Thus, no full-fledged trial on infringement and nexus need be conducted at the discovery stage in order to demonstrate the relevance of sales information. But where the district court does call for a nexus showing, an appellant claiming error must show that the absence of such a demand would have compelled a different result.[267]

(c) *Other Objective Indicators*

Objective evidence of nonobviousness is not limited to commercial success. Indeed, some of the most potent evidence supporting the patentability of an invention is found outside the marketplace.

Copying. The fact that an accused infringer did not copy any prior art device, but found it necessary to copy the claimed invention, is strong evidence of nonobviousness.[268] Copying is an indicium of nonobviousness and is to be given proper weight. It is not necessary for the patentee to prove that the customer of a copied device knew of and desired every attribute set out in the patent document.[269] It is a mistake, however, to expect the Federal Circuit to be uncritical in embracing such evidence. Thus, copying is not a persuasive argument where the accused infringer's effort to produce its own solution was

---

[264]*Preemption Devices, Inc. v. Minnesota Min. & Mfg. Co.,* 732 F.2d 903, 221 USPQ 841 (Fed. Cir. 1984).

[265]*Lindemann Maschinenfabrik v. American Hoist & Derrick Co.,* 730 F.2d 1452, 221 USPQ 481 (Fed. Cir. 1984).

[266]*Truswal Sys. Corp v. Hydro-Air Eng'g, Inc.,* 813 F.2d 1207, 2 USPQ2d 1034 (Fed. Cir. 1987). Here it was sufficient that the nonparty's products had been charged to infringe, though no suit had been brought.

[267]*American Standard, Inc. v. Pfizer, Inc.,* 828 F.2d 734, 3 USPQ 2d 1817, 1821–22 (Fed. Cir. 1987).

[268]*Specialty Composites v. Cabot Corp.,* 845 F.2d 981, 6 USPQ2d 1601 (Fed. Cir. 1988); *Panduit Corp. v. Dennison Mfg. Co.,* 774 F.2d 1082, 227 USPQ 337 (Fed. Cir. 1985). See also *Windsurfing Int'l, Inc. v. AMF, Inc.,* 782 F.2d 995, 228 USPQ 562 (Fed. Cir. 1986). Copying is evidence of nonobviousness of a patented design. *Avia Group Int'l, Inc. v. L.A. Gear Calif., Inc.,* 853 F.2d 1557, 7 USPQ2d 1548 (Fed. Cir. 1988).

[269]*Diversitech Corp. v. Century Steps, Inc.,* 850 F.2d 675, 7 USPQ2d 1315 (Fed. Cir. 1988).

not extensive, its product is not identical to the claimed invention, and it vigorously denies infringement.[270] In one particularly perceptive opinion, the Court was unmoved by alleged copying because the project was given a low priority by the infringer and thus there was no real pressure to develop its own independent product, because the infringer did not entirely fail in its own independent efforts and, most significantly, because the real copying seemed to be dimensional, rather than conceptual.[271]

In the end analysis, the court will require a nexus between the copying and the merits of the invention, just as in the case of commercial success. Access to and analysis of other products in the market are hardly rare, even in the design stages of competing devices. While access in combination with similarity can create a strong inference of copying, something more is needed to make that action significant to a determination of the obviousness issue. Copying may demonstrate a general lack of concern for patent property, or a contempt for the specific patent in question—which could be argued to show obviousness; or a contempt for the ability or willingness of the particular patentee to enforce that patent—which would require deeper inquiry. Even widespread copying in the industry could point to other conclusions, depending on the attitudes existing toward patent property and the accepted practices in the industry. Perhaps copying will turn out to be more relevant in the context of other evidence of nonobviousness.[272]

Prior failure. The litigation argument that an innovation is really quite ordinary carries diminished weight when offered by those who had tried and failed to solve the same problem, and then promptly adopted the solution that they are denigrating at trial.[273] Thus failure of others to provide a feasible solution to a long-standing problem is probative of nonobviousness.[274] The court regards a strong showing of prior failure by others, including the accused infringer, to be "virtually irrefutable" evidence that the claimed invention would not have been obvious.[275] One trial court viewed failure as an indication that a later invention, based upon a different principle, would have been obvious, because the inventor would know from the failure that he or she

---

[270]*Pentec, Inc. v. Graphic Controls Corp.*, 776 F.2d 309, 227 USPQ 766 (Fed. Cir. 1985).

[271]*Vandenberg v. Dairy Equip. Co.*, 740 F.2d 1560, 224 USPQ 195 (Fed. Cir. 1984). The latter ground is somewhat surprising, since one would have assumed that slavish copying, down to the last dimensional detail, would have been more impressive. But the decision is of course correct in assigning more importance to the copying of the concept than of the dimensions.

[272]*Cable Elec. Prods., Inc. v. Genmark, Inc.*, 770 F.2d 1015, 226 USPQ 881 (Fed. Cir. 1985). By the same token, the Federal Circuit will not abide any speculation by the district court that similarities are due to obviousness of design rather than deliberate mimicry, as this case makes clear.

[273]*Heidelberger Druckmaschinen AG v. Hantscho Comm. Prods., Inc.*, 21 F.3d 1068, 30 USPQ2d 1377 (Fed. Cir. 1994).

[274]*Intel Corp. v. United States ITC*, 946 F.2d 821, 20 USPQ2d 1161 (Fed. Cir. 1991).

[275]*Panduit Corp. v. Dennison Mfg. Co.*, 774 F.2d 1082, 227 USPQ 337 (Fed. Cir. 1985).

should try some other approach. The Federal Circuit was quick to point out that under this reasoning it would be progressively more difficult, after a succession of failures, to secure a patent on an invention that provided a solution to a long-felt need. That would be contrary to the well-established rule that failure of others to provide a feasible solution to a long-standing problem is probative of nonobviousness.[276] A failed experiment reported in the prosecution history of a patent renders it irrelevant as a prior art reference; another's experiment, imperfect and never perfected, will not serve either as an anticipation or as part of the prior art, for it has not served to enrich the art.[277]

However, prior failure is not persuasive where the person who failed did not have knowledge of the best art and, more important, was not motivated to try because of satisfaction with the way things were.[278] If a prior art structure performs the claimed function, it need not have been commercially viable.[279]

Licenses. While evidence of licenses under the patent may be persuasive of industry respect for the claimed invention, and thus persuasive of nonobviousness,[280] such evidence will not, like evidence of copying, be accepted uncritically. Thus, a long period of no infringement does not necessarily indicate respect for the strength of the patent; it may well result from a desire to avoid the costs of litigation.[281] Where the PTO issues a patent because the examiner did not consider close prior art, it is not unusual to see astute businessmen capitalize on it by erecting a temporarily successful licensing program thereon. Such programs are not infallible guides to patentability. They sometimes succeed because they are mutually beneficial to the licensed group or because of business judgments that it is cheaper to take licenses than to defend infringement suits, or for other reasons unrelated to the unobviousness of the licensed subject matter.[282]

Long-standing problem or need. The nature of the problem that persisted in the art, and the inventor's solution, are factors to be considered in determining whether the invention would have been obvious to a person of ordinary skill in that art.[283] Hypothetical combinations of the prior art are not likely to defeat a patent where the evidence shows that several long-standing problems were solved.[284]

---

[276]*Uniroyal, Inc. v. Rudkin-Wiley Corp.*, 837 F.2d 1044, 5 USPQ2d 1434 (Fed. Cir. 1988).

[277]*Fromson v. Advance Offset Plate, Inc.*, 755 F.2d 1549, 225 USPQ 26 (Fed. Cir. 1985).

[278]*In re Sneed*, 710 F.2d 1544, 218 USPQ 385 (Fed. Cir. 1983).

[279]*In re Queener*, 796 F.2d 461, 230 USPQ 438 (Fed. Cir. 1986).

[280]Cf. *In re Sernaker*, 702 F.2d 989, 217 USPQ 1, 7 (Fed. Cir. 1983).

[281]*Pentec, Inc. v. Graphic Controls Corp.*, 776 F.2d 309, 227 USPQ 766 (Fed. Cir. 1985).

[282]*EWP Corp. v. Reliance Universal Inc.*, 755 F.2d 898, 225 USPQ 20 (Fed. Cir. 1985).

[283]*Northern Telecom, Inc. v. Datapoint Corp.*, 908 F.2d 931, 15 USPQ2d 1321 (Fed. Cir. 1990).

[284]*Kalman v. Kimberly-Clark Corp.*, 713 F.2d 760, 218 USPQ 781 (Fed. Cir. 1983).

Long-felt need in the face of prior art later asserted to lead to a solution tends to negate the proposition that the combination of such prior art would have been obvious.[285] Long-felt need and prior failure are a useful guide in determining how a person of ordinary skill in the field would have viewed the patented invention at the time it was made.[286] Recognition of need and difficulties encountered by those skilled in the field are classical indicia of unobviousness. An argument that long-felt need is prima facie evidence of obviousness is contrary to logic as well as law. That there were other attempts and various combinations and procedures tried in the past does not render obvious the later successful one.[287]

On the other hand, a long-felt need is not essential as secondary evidence; it is but one type of evidence useful in the obviousness determination.[288] The person of skill in the art need not have been aware of the problem or seeking a solution, and the inventor is not required to have been the winner of a race to a common goal. The invention may create a new want and still be nonobvious.[289] To say that the missing step can be supplied by the very nature of the problem to be solved begs the question where there is no showing that the problem had been previously identified anywhere in the prior art.[290]

Unexpected results. Unexpected results may be strong support for unobviousness. Surprise and amazement by experts is important evidence. This is in accord with the approach that the obviousness inquiry should not focus solely on the product created, but also on the circumstances of the creation.[291] That which would have been surprising to a person of ordinary skill in a particular art would not have been obvious.[292] The fact that experts at the time perceived the invention as an exceptional technological achievement is good evidence of nonobviousness,[293] as is unpredictability.[294] An insight

---

[285]*Micro Chem., Inc. v. Great Plains Chem. Co.*, 103 F.3d 1538, 41 USPQ2d 1238 (Fed. Cir. 1997).

[286]*Heidelberger Druckmaschinen AG v. Hantscho Comm. Prods., Inc.*, 21 F.3d 1068, 30 USPQ2d 1377 (Fed. Cir. 1994).

[287]*In re Dow Chem. Co.*, 837 F.2d 469, 5 USPQ2d 1529 (Fed. Cir. 1988).

[288]*Windsurfing Int'l, Inc. v. AMF, Inc.*, 782 F.2d 995, 228 USPQ 562 (Fed. Cir. 1986).

[289]*Leinoff v. Louis Milona & Sons*, 726 F.2d 734, 220 USPQ 845 (Fed. Cir. 1984).

[290]*In re Zurko*, 111 F.3d 887, 42 USPQ2d 1476 (Fed. Cir. 1997).

[291]*Specialty Composites v. Cabot Corp.*, 845 F.2d 981, 6 USPQ2d 1601 (Fed. Cir. 1988); *Lindemann Maschinenfabrik v. American Hoist & Derrick Co.*, 730 F.2d 1452, 221 USPQ 481 (Fed. Cir. 1984).

[292]*In re Soni*, 54 F.3d 746, 34 USPQ2d 1684 (Fed. Cir. 1995). The principle applies most often to the less predictable fields, such as chemistry, where minor changes in a product or process may yield substantially different results. *Id.*

[293]*Interconnect Planning Corp. v. Feil*, 774 F.2d 1132, 227 USPQ 543 (Fed. Cir. 1985). In *Burlington Indus. Inc. v. Quigg*, 822 F.2d 1581, 3 USPQ2d 1436 (Fed. Cir. 1987), the court was impressed by the fact that noted experts expressed disbelief and one referred to the invention as a totally unexpected breakthrough.

[294]*W.L. Gore & Assoc. v. Garlock, Inc.*, 721 F.2d 1540, 220 USPQ 303 (Fed. Cir. 1983). However, obviousness does not require absolute predictability. A reasonable expectation that

that is contrary to the understanding and expectations of the art points to patentability.[295] Proceeding contrary to accepted wisdom of the art is strong evidence of nonobviousness.[296]

Nonetheless, unexpected results must be established by factual evidence, and mere argument or conclusory statements do not suffice; also, the unexpected results must be superior to results achieved by the prior art, and if comparative tests are made, the comparison must be made to the closest prior art.[297] Synergism is not a requirement of nonobviousness, but when an inventor tries to distinguish the claims from the prior art by introducing evidence of unexpected synergistic properties, the evidence should at least demonstrate an effect greater than the sum of the several effects taken separately.[298] Unexpected results over one of two equally close prior art references does not automatically establish nonobviousness.[299]

While an unexpected result may be evidence of nonobviousness, it is not a requirement.[300] It is therefore wholly erroneous to instruct a jury that the elements making up a claimed invention must perform a new and unexpected function in combination.[301] But it would likewise be error to hold that absolute predictability, rather than a reasonable expectation of success, is necessary to a conclusion of obviousness.[302] Obviousness does not require absolute predictability of success. Indeed, for many inventions that seem quite obvious, there is no absolute predictability of success until the invention is reduced to practice. There is always at least a possibility of unexpected results

---

the beneficial result will be achieved is sufficient. *In re Merck & Co.*, 800 F.2d 1091, 231 USPQ 375 (Fed. Cir. 1986).

[295]*Schenck, A.G. v. Nortron Corp.*, 713 F.2d 782, 218 USPQ 698 (Fed. Cir. 1983).

[296]*In re Hedges*, 783 F.2d 1038, 228 USPQ 685 (Fed. Cir. 1986); *W.L. Gore & Assoc. v. Garlock, Inc.*, 721 F.2d 1540, 220 USPQ 303 (Fed. Cir. 1983).

[297]*In re De Blauwe*, 736 F.2d 699, 222 USPQ 191 (Fed. Cir. 1984). See also *In re Baxter Travenol Labs.*, 952 F.2d 388, 21 USPQ2d 1281 (Fed. Cir. 1991). But see *In re Soni*, 54 F.3d 746, 34 USPQ2d 1684 (Fed. Cir. 1995), where the panel majority seemed to feel that an applicant's statement that the demonstrated better results were unexpected is sufficient. Indeed, it seemed simply to rely upon the applicant's duty of candor—the premise being that the applicant would not lie. The dissent, on the other hand, complains that the majority has eliminated altogether the requirement for objective proof that the observed improvement was indeed unexpected.

[298]*Merck & Co. v. Biocraft Labs., Inc.*, 874 F.2d 804, 10 USPQ2d 1843 (Fed. Cir. 1989).

[299]*In re Johnson*, 747 F.2d 1456, 223 USPQ 1260 (Fed. Cir. 1984).

[300]*Panduit Corp. v. Dennison Mfg. Co.*, 774 F.2d 1082, 227 USPQ 337 (Fed. Cir. 1985). But changes in dosages of pharmaceuticals normally do not lend patentability unless the results obtained at the designated concentrations are unexpectedly good. *Merck & Co. v. Biocraft Labs., Inc.*, 874 F.2d 804, 10 USPQ2d 1843 (Fed. Cir. 1989); *Smithkline Diagnostics, Inc. v. Helena Labs. Corp.*, 859 F.2d 878, 8 USPQ2d 1468 (Fed. Cir. 1988). Where the difference between the claimed invention and the prior art is some range or other variable within the claims, patentability requires a showing that the particular range is critical, generally by showing that the claimed range achieves unexpected results relative to the prior art range. *In re Woodruff*, 919 F.2d 1575, 16 USPQ2d 1934 (Fed. Cir. 1990).

[301]*American Hoist & Derrick Co. v. Sowa & Sons, Inc.*, 725 F.2d 1350, 220 USPQ 763 (Fed. Cir. 1984).

[302]*In re Longi*, 759 F.2d 887, 225 USPQ 645 (Fed. Cir. 1985).

that would then provide an objective basis for showing that the invention, although apparently obvious, was in law nonobvious. For obviousness, all that is required is a reasonable expectation of success.[303] But peer recognition of the benefits of the invention is not evidence of obviousness.[304]

Skepticism. General skepticism of those in the art—not amounting to teaching away—is also relevant and persuasive evidence of nonobviousness. In effect, teaching away is a more pointed and probative form of skepticism expressed in the prior art. In any case, the presence of either of these indicia gives insight into the question of obviousness.[305] Skepticism about the merits of the invention, or about whether it will solve the problem, is important evidence of nonobviousness. Indeed, the court has gone so far as to indicate that skepticism on the part of the infringer's own engineers must render an obviousness defense frivolous.[306] The skepticism of an expert, expressed before the inventor proved him wrong, is entitled to fair evidentiary weight, as are the several years of research that preceded the invention.[307] Doing what those skilled in the art suggested should not be done is a fact strongly probative of nonobviousness.[308] On the other hand, it is not a requirement for patentability that persons of ordinary skill in the art would expect the new idea to fail.[309]

Independent development. Of course, not all objective evidence is inherently favorable to the inventor. Although the court has noted the relevance of contemporaneous independent invention to the level of ordinary knowledge or skill in the art, it has also acknowledged the view that this evidence is relevant as a secondary consideration.[310] Thus, independent creation of the invention by others may be an indication of obviousness, but it must be shown to be contemporaneous

---

[303]*In re O'Farrell,* 853 F.2d 894, 7 USPQ2d 1673 (Fed. Cir. 1988).

[304]*In re Piasecki,* 745 F.2d 1468, 223 USPQ 785, 790 (Fed. Cir. 1984).

[305]*Monarch Knitting Mach. Corp. v. Sulzer Morat Gmbh,* 139 F.3d 877, 45 USPQ2d 1977 (Fed. Cir. 1998).

[306]*Amstar Corp. v. Envirotech Corp.,* 730 F.2d 1476, 221 USPQ 649 (Fed. Cir. 1984). See also *Gillette Co. v. S.C. Johnson & Son,* 919 F.2d 720, 16 USPQ2d 1923 (Fed. Cir. 1990).

[307]*In re O'Farrell,* 853 F.2d 894, 7 USPQ2d 1673 (Fed. Cir. 1988). In this case the Federal Circuit rejected an argument that the skepticism of one of greater than ordinary skill should not carry much weight. Because he knew more than those of ordinary skill, he would have expected failure, while the less learned and experienced persons of ordinary skill would have expected success. The court's answer to this argument—that persons of ordinary skill did not previously make the invention despite decades of experimentation and a recognition of need—is not entirely satisfactory. Does this mean that if there had not been long need and experimentation the skepticism of a person of exceptional skill could be disregarded?

[308]*Kloster Speedsteel AB v. Crucible Inc.,* 793 F.2d 1565, 230 USPQ 81 (Fed. Cir. 1986).

[309]*In re Dow Chem. Co.,* 837 F.2d 469, 5 USPQ2d 1529 (Fed. Cir. 1988).

[310]*Monarch Knitting Mach. Corp. v. Sulzer Morat Gmbh,* 139 F.3d 877, 45 USPQ2d 1977 (Fed. Cir. 1998).

with, not well after, the work of the patentee.[311] Five years later is too late.[312]

Prior litigation. The court has not yet really come to grips with the significance of prior litigation in determining nonobviousness. It has speculated that prior litigation may be evidence of secondary considerations such as commercial success or copying, but it is at the same time extremely sensitive to the risk of prejudice that such evidence carries.[313] It has cautioned against giving too much weight to the actions of foreign tribunals.[314]

§4.7 Resolution of the Legal Question

If the obviousness inquiry mandated by 35 U.S.C. §103 is faithfully adhered to, and if the *Graham v. Deere* findings are made, with appropriate attention to objective evidence, the legal conclusion of obviousness or nonobviousness falls into place with surprising ease. Congress was on the right track when it wrote the statute, and the Supreme Court kept the train on the rails with its *Graham v. Deere* decision. The main danger faced by the Federal Circuit may be sheer boredom. It is tempting, always, to think up new ways to say the same thing.[315] This is dangerous in legal method. A new term or phrase may take on meaning of its own, far beyond what was intended by the author. We have seen this happen far too often in the development of the law of obviousness. Let this be an earnest plea, then, to the Federal Circuit to avoid the temptation to turn a phrase when it comes to obviousness. Far better to affirm, or reverse, in an unpublished order than to permit careless wording to become a rule of decision.

It is impossible, of course, to avoid the promulgation of subtests, because of the wide variety of technical subject matter and factual circumstance that must be scrutinized under the obviousness inquiry. The remainder of this chapter is devoted to a brief look at some of these. Again, one hopes that they are viewed more as convenient tools of classification rather than mandatory logical routes to the legal conclusion of §103.

---

[311]*Stewart-Warner Corp. v. City of Pontiac,* 767 F.2d 1563, 226 USPQ 676 (Fed. Cir. 1985). Simultaneous development may or may not be indicative of obviousness. Indeed, the interference statute, 35 U.S.C. §135, specifically contemplates situations where a valid patent will issue to one of two inventors who made the invention nearly simultaneously. *Hybritech Inc. v. Monoclonal Antibodies, Inc.,* 802 F.2d 1367, 231 USPQ 81 (Fed. Cir. 1986).

[312]*Lindemann Maschinenfabrik v. American Hoist & Derrick Co.,* 730 F.2d 1452, 221 USPQ 481 (Fed. Cir. 1984).

[313]*Mendenhall v. Cedarapids, Inc.,* 5 F.3d 1556, 28 USPQ2d 1081 (Fed. Cir. 1993). See also notes 1:197–200 and accompanying text.

[314]See note 4:82 and accompanying text.

[315]The court has referred to this tendency as a "penchant for elegant variation." *Burlington Indus., Inc. v. Dayco Corp.,* 849 F.2d 1418, 7 USPQ2d 1158, 1160–61 (Fed. Cir. 1988).

(a) Combining References

When a patent describes a new mechanical device that can be viewed as a new combination or arrangement of mechanical components, the legal conclusion of obviousness requires that there be some suggestion, motivation, or teaching in the prior art whereby the person of ordinary skill would have selected the components that the inventor selected and used them to make the new device.[316] Likewise, the mere fact that it is possible to find two isolated disclosures that might be combined in such a way as to produce a new compound does not necessarily render such production obvious unless the art also contains something to suggest the desirability of the proposed combination.[317] Thus, the absence of a suggestion to combine is dispositive in an obviousness determination.[318] In appropriate circumstances, a single prior art reference can render a claim obvious. However, there must be a showing of a suggestion or motivation to modify the teachings of that reference to the claimed invention in order to support the obviousness conclusion. This suggestion or motivation may be derived from the prior art reference itself, from the knowledge of one of ordinary skill in the art, or from the nature of the problem to be solved.[319]

To properly combine references, there must have been some teaching, suggestion, or inference in the references, or knowledge generally available to one of ordinary skill in the art, that would have led one to combine the relevant teachings. What the references teach or suggest, or what knowledge is available, is a factual determination. But after making those determinations, the decision maker must subjectively analyze them to decide whether the teachings of the references could have been combined. This then is a legal conclusion.[320]

We have already considered at length the presumption of validity, and its function of burden allocation.[321] Nowhere does the presumption

---

[316]*C.R. Bard Inc. v. M3 Sys. Inc.,* 157 F.3d 1340, 48 USPQ2d 1225 (Fed. Cir. 1998). There must be something in the prior art as a whole to suggest the desirability, and thus the obviousness, of making the combination. *Heidelberger Druckmaschinen AG v. Hantscho Comm. Prods., Inc.,* 21 F.3d 1068, 30 USPQ2d 1377 (Fed. Cir. 1994); *In re Geiger,* 815 F.2d 686, 2 USPQ2d 1276 (Fed. Cir. 1987); *Alco Standard Corp. v. Tennessee Valley Auth.,* 808 F.2d 1490, 1 USPQ2d 1337 (Fed. Cir. 1986); *Custom Accessories, Inc. v. Jeffrey-Allan Indus., Inc.,* 807 F.2d 955, 1 USPQ2d 1196 (Fed. Cir. 1986); *Carella v. Starlight Archery & Pro Line Co.,* 804 F.2d 135, 231 USPQ 644 (Fed. Cir. 1986); *Lindemann Maschinenfabrik v. American Hoist & Derrick Co.,* 730 F.2d 1452, 221 USPQ 481 (Fed. Cir. 1984). See also *Vandenberg v. Dairy Equip. Co.,* 740 F.2d 1560, 224 USPQ 195 (Fed. Cir. 1984); *Kansas Jack, Inc. v. Kuhn,* 719 F.2d 1144, 219 USPQ 857 (Fed. Cir. 1983).

[317]*In re Grabiak,* 769 F.2d 729, 226 USPQ 870 (Fed. Cir. 1985).

[318]*Gambro Lundia AB v. Baxter Healthcare Corp.,* 110 F.3d 1573, 42 USPQ2d 1378 (Fed. Cir. 1997).

[319]*Sibia Neurosciences Inc. v. Cadus Pharm. Corp.,* 225 F.3d 1349, 55 USPQ2d 1927 (Fed. Cir. 2000).

[320]*Ashland Oil, Inc. v. Delta Resins & Refracs., Inc.,* 776 F.2d 281, 227 USPQ 657 (Fed. Cir. 1985). Whether a reference provides a motivation to combine its teachings with others is a factual determination. *Tec Air, Inc. v. Denso Mfg. Michigan, Inc.,* 192 F.3d 1353, 52 USPQ2d 1294, 1297-98 (Fed. Cir. 1999).

[321]See §1.5.

have more force than in the matter of combining prior art references. Thus, the law does not impose on the patentee the burden of establishing that the combined teachings of the individual prior art references would not have led one of skill in the art to the invention. Where the party asserting invalidity must rely upon a combination of prior art references to establish invalidity, that party bears the burden of showing some teaching or suggestion in these references that supports their use in combination. It is legal error to place this burden on the patentee.[322] An infringer cannot pick and choose among individual parts of assorted prior art references as a mosaic to recreate a facsimile of the claimed invention.[323] The questions to be resolved are whether a consideration of the teachings of all or any of the references would have suggested (expressly or by implication) the possibility of achieving further improvement by combining such teachings along the line of the claimed invention, and whether that invention achieved more than a combination that any or all of the references suggested.[324] The notion that combination claims can be declared invalid merely upon finding similar elements in separate prior patents would necessarily destroy virtually all patents and cannot be the law under the statute.[325]

It is improper to use the inventor's patent as an instruction book on how to reconstruct the prior art.[326] The consistent criterion for determination of obviousness is whether the prior art would have suggested to one of ordinary skill in the art that the process should be carried out and would have a reasonable likelihood of success, viewed in the light of the prior art. Both the suggestion and the expectation of success must be founded in the prior art, not in the applicant's disclosure.[327] The problem confronted by the inventor must

---

[322]*Ashland Oil, Inc. v. Delta Resins & Refracs., Inc.*, 776 F.2d 281, 227 USPQ 657 (Fed. Cir. 1985).

[323]*Akzo N.V. v. United States ITC*, 808 F.2d 1471, 1 USPQ2d 1241 (Fed. Cir. 1986). A determination of obviousness must involve more than indiscriminately combining prior art; a motivation or suggestion to combine must exist. *Micro Chem., Inc. v. Great Plains Chem. Co.*, 103 F.3d 1538, 41 USPQ2d 1238 (Fed. Cir. 1997).

[324]*Smithkline Diagnostics, Inc. v. Helena Labs. Corp.*, 859 F.2d 878, 8 USPQ2d 1468 (Fed. Cir. 1988); *In re Sernaker*, 702 F.2d 989, 217 USPQ 1 (Fed. Cir. 1983).

[325]*Panduit Corp. v. Dennison Mfg. Co.*, 810 F.2d 1561, 1 USPQ2d 1593 (Fed. Cir. 1987). A holding that combination claims are invalid based merely upon finding similar elements in separate prior art patents would be contrary to statute and would defeat the congressional purpose in enacting Title 35. *Smithkline Diagnostics, Inc. v. Helena Labs. Corp.*, 859 F.2d 878, 8 USPQ2d 1468 (Fed. Cir. 1988).

[326]*Panduit Corp. v. Dennison Mfg. Co.*, 810 F.2d 1561, 1 USPQ2d 1593 (Fed. Cir. 1987). See also *Sensonics, Inc. v. Aerosonic Corp.*, 81 F.3d 1566, 38 USPQ2d 1551 (Fed. Cir. 1996). When prior art references require selective combination by the court to render obvious a subsequent invention, there must be some reasons for the combination other than the hindsight gleaned from the invention itself. Something in the prior art as a whole must suggest the desirability, and thus the obviousness, of making the combination. *Uniroyal, Inc. v. Rudkin-Wiley Corp.*, 837 F.2d 1044, 5 USPQ2d 1434 (Fed. Cir. 1988).

[327]*In re O'Farrell*, 853 F.2d 894, 7 USPQ2d 1673 (Fed. Cir. 1988). See also *In re Vaeck*, 947 F.2d 488, 20 USPQ2d 1438 (Fed. Cir. 1991). A long period of research by the inventor tends to show that one skilled in the art would have had no reasonable expectation of success

be considered in determining whether it would have been obvious to combine references in order to solve that problem.[328]

During prosecution, an examiner may often find every element of a claimed invention in the prior art. If identification of each claimed element in the prior art were sufficient to negate patentability, very few patents would ever issue. Furthermore, rejecting patents solely by finding prior art corollaries for the claimed elements would permit an examiner to use the claimed invention itself as a blueprint for piecing together elements in the prior art to defeat the patentability of the claimed invention. Such an approach would be an illogical and inappropriate process by which to determine patentability. To prevent the use of hindsight based on the invention to defeat patentability of the invention, the law requires the examiner to show a motivation to combine the references that create the case of obviousness. In other words, the examiner must show reasons that the skilled artisan, confronted with the same problems as the inventor and with no knowledge of the claimed invention, would select the elements from the cited prior art references for combination in the manner claimed.[329] The court has identified three possible sources for a motivation to combine references: the nature of the problem to be solved, the teachings of the prior art, and the knowledge of persons of ordinary skill in the art.[330] The range of sources available, however, does not diminish the requirement for actual evidence. That is, the showing must be clear and particular. Broad conclusory statements regarding the teaching of multiple references, standing alone, are not evidence. In addition to demonstrating the propriety of an obviousness analysis, particular factual findings regarding the suggestion, teaching, or motivation to combine serve a number of important purposes, including: (1) clear explication of the position adopted by the examiner and the Board; (2) identification of the factual disputes, if any, between the applicant and the Board; and (3) facilitation of review on appeal.[331]

---

in combining the prior art. *Micro Chem., Inc. v. Great Plains Chem. Co.,* 103 F.3d 1538, 41 USPQ2d 1238 (Fed. Cir. 1997).

[328]*Northern Telecom, Inc. v. Datapoint Corp.,* 908 F.2d 931, 15 USPQ2d 1321 (Fed. Cir. 1990); *Diversitech Corp. v. Century Steps, Inc.,* 850 F.2d 675, 7 USPQ2d 1315 (Fed. Cir. 1988). Although the suggestion to combine references may flow from the nature of the problem, it more often comes from the teachings of the pertinent references, or from the ordinary knowledge of those skilled in the art that certain references are of special importance in a particular field. *In re Rouffet,* 149 F.3d 1350, 47 USPQ2d 1453 (Fed. Cir. 1998).

[329]*In re Rouffet,* 149 F.3d 1350, 47 USPQ2d 1453 (Fed. Cir. 1998).

[330]*In re Dembiczak,* 175 F.3d 994, 50 USPQ2d 1614 (Fed. Cir. 1999); *Al-Site Corp. v. VSI Int'l Inc.,* 174 F.3d 1308, 50 USPQ2d 1161 (Fed. Cir. 1999); *In re Rouffet,* 149 F.3d 1350, 47 USPQ2d 1453 (Fed. Cir. 1998).

[331]*In re Dembiczak,* 175 F.3d 994, 50 USPQ2d 1614 (Fed. Cir. 1999). The suggestion to modify a structure need not be found in the reference that discloses the structure, but there must be some logical reason apparent from positive, concrete evidence that justifies a combination of primary and secondary references. *In re Laskowski,* 871 F.2d 115, 10 USPQ2d 1397 (Fed. Cir. 1989). Where the required modification is to turn an element upside down, and it would be inoperable for its intended purpose when turned upside down, there is a teaching away rather than a suggestion to modify. *In re Gordon,* 733 F.2d 900 (Fed. Cir. 1984).

Thus, a suggestion to combine may come from the prior art, as filtered through the knowledge of one skilled in the art.[332] Motivation to make a combination can be found in the knowledge of one of ordinary skill in the art.[333] Rarely, however, will the skill in the art component operate to supply missing knowledge or prior art to reach an obviousness judgment. Skill in the art does not act as a bridge over gaps in substantive presentation of an obviousness case, but instead supplies the primary guarantee of objectivity in the process.[334] The same caution applies to patent prosecution. While the skill level is a component of the inquiry for a suggestion to combine, a lofty level of skill alone does not suffice to supply a motivation to combine. Otherwise a high level of ordinary skill in an art field would almost always preclude patentable inventions. As the court has often noted, invention itself is the process of combining prior art in a nonobvious manner. Therefore, even when the level of skill in the art is high, the Board must identify specifically the principle, known to one of ordinary skill, that suggests the claimed combination. In other words, the Board must explain the reasons one of ordinary skill in the art would have been motivated to select the references and to combine them to render the claimed invention obvious.[335]

However, a suggestion to modify the art to produce the claimed combination need not be expressly stated in one or all of the references.[336] The extent to which such suggestion must be explicit in, or may be fairly inferred from, the references is decided on the facts of each case, in light of the prior art and its relationship to the invention.

---

[332]*Motorola, Inc. v. Interdigital Tech. Corp.*, 121 F.3d 1461, 43 USPQ2d 1481 (Fed. Cir. 1997).

[333]*Pfaff v. Wells Elec., Inc.*, 124 F.3d 1429, 43 USPQ2d 1928 (Fed. Cir. 1997), *aff'd*, 525 U.S. 55, 48 USPQ2d 1641 (1998).

[334]*Al-Site Corp. v. VSI Int'l Inc.*, 174 F.3d 1308, 50 USPQ2d 1161, 1171 (Fed. Cir. 1999).

[335]*In re Rouffet*, 149 F.3d 1350, 47 USPQ2d 1453 (Fed. Cir. 1998). In this case, the Board simply invoked the high level of skill in the art to provide the necessary motivation to combine. It did not, however, explain what specific understanding or technological principle within the knowledge of one of ordinary skill in the art would have suggested the combination. If such a rote invocation could suffice to supply a motivation to combine, the more sophisticated scientific fields would rarely, if ever, experience a patentable technical advance. Instead, in complex scientific fields, the Board could routinely identify the prior art elements in an application, invoke the lofty level of skill, and rest its case for rejection. To counter this potential weakness in the obviousness construct, the suggestion to combine requirement stands as a critical safeguard against hindsight analysis and rote application of the legal test for obviousness. Because the Board did not explain the specific understanding or principle within the knowledge of a skilled artisan that would motivate one with no knowledge of the invention to make the combination, the court infers that the examiner selected these references with the assistance of hindsight. But the law forbids the use of hindsight in the selection of references that comprise the case of obviousness. Lacking a motivation to combine references, the Board therefore did not show a proper prima facie case of obviousness.

[336]*B.F. Goodrich Co. v. Aircraft Braking Sys. Corp.*, 72 F.3d 1577, 37 USPQ2d 1314 (Fed. Cir. 1996); *Cable Elec. Prods., Inc. v. Genmark, Inc.*, 770 F.2d 1015, 226 USPQ 881 (Fed. Cir. 1985). The court has rejected an argument that it adopt an approach whereby references may not be combined to formulate obviousness rejections absent an express suggestion in one prior art reference to look to another specific reference. *In re Nilssen*, 851 F.2d 1401, 7 USPQ2d 1500 (Fed. Cir. 1988).

As in all §103 determinations, the decision maker must bring judgment to bear.[337] Indeed, the court appears willing to infer a motivation to make a combination from the very nature of the subject matter involved, at least in appropriate cases. It begins with the self-evident proposition that mankind—in particular, inventors—strives to improve that which already exists. The nature of the problem to be solved may lead inventors to look to references relating to possible solutions to that problem.[338]

Nor is it necessary that the references be physically combinable.[339] A claim may have been obvious in view of a combination of references even if the features of one reference cannot be substituted physically into the structure of the other references.[340] This is particularly so where there is no mismatch between the technologies of the references, even though the combination does not make good economic sense.[341] But evidence that a combination was not viewed as technically feasible must be considered, for conventional wisdom that a combination should not be made is evidence of unobviousness.[342] Trade-offs often concern what is feasible, not what is, on balance, desirable. Motivation to combine requires the latter. The fact that the motivating benefit comes at the expense of another benefit, however, should not nullify its use as a basis to modify the disclosure of one reference with the teachings of another. Instead, the benefits, both lost and gained, should be weighed against one another.[343]

That a given combination would not be made by businesspersons for economic reasons does not mean that persons skilled in the art would not make the combination because of some technological incompatibility; only a direct showing as to the latter would be pertinent.[344] As long as some motivation or suggestion to combine the references is provided by the prior art taken as a whole, the law does not require that the references be combined for the reasons contemplated by the inventor.[345]

Nonobviousness cannot be established by attacking references individually where the rejection is based upon the teaching of a combination of references. Each reference must be read, not in isolation,

---

[337]*In re Gorman,* 933 F.2d 982, 18 USPQ2d 1885 (Fed. Cir. 1991).

[338]*Pro-Mold & Tool Co. v. Great Lakes Plastics, Inc.,* 75 F.3d 1568, 37 USPQ2d 1626 (Fed. Cir. 1996).

[339]*In re Sneed,* 710 F.2d 1544, 218 USPQ 385 (Fed. Cir. 1983).

[340]*In re Yamamoto,* 740 F.2d 1569, 222 USPQ 934 (Fed. Cir. 1984).

[341]*Orthopedic Equip. Co. v. United States,* 702 F.2d 1005, 217 USPQ 193 (Fed. Cir. 1983).

[342]*Arkie Lures, Inc. v. Gene Larew Tackle, Inc.,* 119 F.3d 953, 43 USPQ2d 1294 (Fed. Cir. 1997).

[343]*Winner Int'l Royalty Corp. v. Wang,* 202 F.3d 1340, 53 USPQ2d 1580 (Fed. Cir. 2000).

[344]*In re Farrenkopf,* 713 F.2d 714, 219 USPQ 1 (Fed. Cir. 1983).

[345]*In re Beattie,* 974 F.2d 1309, 24 USPQ2d 1040 (Fed. Cir. 1992). The court demonstrated a willingness to allow a fairly long reach in finding a motivation to combine in *Lamb-Weston, Inc. v. McCain Foods, Ltd.,* 78 F.3d 540, 37 USPQ2d 1856 (Fed. Cir. 1996), where the motivation to combine two references was said to reside in the nonconfidential product of devices that had been disclosed in confidence to the inventors.

but for what it fairly teaches in combination with the prior art as a whole. Thus it is improper to downgrade a reference on the basis that it teaches away, unless it teaches away in the context of the combination of references.[346]

Where the straightforward quality of the invention and the art make the required combination quite apparent, it is not error for the district court to fail to make a specific determination as to how the teachings of the references could be combined to produce the patented invention.[347] Also, inasmuch as the conclusion of obviousness is said to be strengthened where teachings are repeated in a number of references,[348] the Federal Circuit is willing to assume that the district court's citation of several references without delineating a single one of the group for combination was for the purpose of demonstrating the widespread knowledge in the art of each feature involved.[349]

A "trend" might very well constitute a suggestion or teaching to one of ordinary skill in the art to make "minor" changes from the prior art in accordance with that trend to produce the claimed invention. Whether the prior art discloses a "trend" is a question of fact. The existence of a trend depends on the content of the prior art, i.e., what the prior art would have taught one of ordinary skill in this art at the time of this invention. But before the trial court may examine the existence of a trend, it must resolve an antecedent question, namely, whether the prior art contains a suggestion or motivation to combine references to form a trend. Stated otherwise, what would have impelled one of ordinary skill to recognize a relationship between the problem and the solution? If those of ordinary skill would have recognized a relationship, then, and only then, does the trial court proceed to examine whether the prior art in fact contains a coherent teaching about that relationship. Thus, before proceeding to find a trend, the trial court must discern whether one of ordinary skill would have had a motivation to combine references to form a trend.[350]

(b) Prima Facie Obviousness

The Federal Circuit has embraced a theory of prima facie obviousness for use in ex parte prosecution in the PTO. The prima facie case

---

[346]*In re Merck & Co.*, 800 F.2d 1091, 231 USPQ 375 (Fed. Cir. 1986). The fact that it is necessary to combine the teachings of several references in order to support an obviousness rejection does not of itself weigh against a holding of obviousness. The criterion is not the number of references, but what they would have meant to a person of ordinary skill in the field of the invention. *In re Gorman*, 933 F.2d 982, 18 USPQ2d 1885 (Fed. Cir. 1991).

[347]*Cable Elec. Prods., Inc. v. Genmark, Inc.*, 770 F.2d 1015, 226 USPQ 881 (Fed. Cir. 1985). But even simple differences require some suggestion in the prior art to make the change. *In re Chu*, 66 F.3d 292, 36 USPQ2d 1089 (Fed. Cir. 1995).

[348]*Kansas Jack, Inc. v. Kuhn*, 719 F.2d 1144, 219 USPQ 857 (Fed. Cir. 1983).

[349]*Cable Elec. Prods., Inc. v. Genmark, Inc.*, 770 F.2d 1015, 226 USPQ 881 (Fed. Cir. 1985).

[350]*Monarch Knitting Mach. Corp. v. Sulzer Morat Gmbh*, 139 F.3d 877, 45 USPQ2d 1977, 1981-82 (Fed. Cir. 1998).

is a procedural tool that, as used in patent examination, means not only that the evidence of the prior art would reasonably allow the conclusion that the examiner seeks, but also that the prior art compels such a conclusion if the applicant produces no evidence or argument to rebut it.[351] The PTO has the initial burden of producing a factual basis for a rejection under §103. In other words, the PTO must establish a case of prima facie obviousness. Then the applicant is obliged to come forward with rebuttal, which is merely a showing of facts supporting the opposite conclusion. This approach is a procedural mechanism to allocate in an orderly way the burdens of going forward and persuasion as between the examiner and the applicant. It should be understood, however, that the applicant's rebuttal must not be evaluated only for its ability to knock down the prima facie case of obviousness; it also must be evaluated together with the facts on which that case was based. In short, the examiner must consider all of the evidence anew, and an earlier conclusion should not be regarded as set in concrete.[352] Prima facie obviousness refers only to the initial examination step. If examination at the initial stage does not produce a prima facie case of unpatentability, then without more the applicant is entitled to a grant of the patent.[353]

Some examples may illustrate the theory. In determining whether a case of prima facie obviousness exists, it is necessary to ascertain whether the prior art teachings would appear to be sufficient to one of ordinary skill in the art to suggest making the claimed substitution or other modification. The prior art must provide one of ordinary skill in the art the motivation to make the proposed molecular modifications needed to arrive at the claimed compound.[354] In

---

[351]*In re Spada,* 911 F.2d 705, 15 USPQ2d 1655 (Fed. Cir. 1990).

[352]*In re Piasecki,* 745 F.2d 1468, 223 USPQ 785 (Fed. Cir. 1984). See also *In re Oetiker,* 977 F.2d 1443, 24 USPQ2d 1443 (Fed. Cir. 1992); *In re Fritch,* 972 F.2d 1260, 23 USPQ2d 1780 (Fed. Cir. 1992). The PTO has the burden under §103 to establish a prima facie case of obviousness. It can satisfy this burden only by showing some objective teaching in the prior art or knowledge generally available to one of ordinary skill in the art that would lead that individual to combine the relevant teachings of the references. *In re Fine,* 837 F.2d 1071, 5 USPQ2d 1596 (Fed. Cir. 1988). A prima facie case of obviousness is established when the teachings from the prior art itself would appear to have suggested the claimed subject matter to a person of ordinary skill in the art. *In re Rijckaert,* 9 F.3d 1531, 28 USPQ2d 1955 (Fed. Cir. 1993). Apparently the PTO can rely upon hearsay evidence in making out its prima facie case. See *In re Epstein,* 32 F.3d 1559, 31 USPQ2d 1817 (Fed. Cir. 1994).

[353]*In re Oetiker,* 977 F.2d 1443, 24 USPQ2d 1443 (Fed. Cir. 1992).

[354]*In re Lalu,* 747 F.2d 703, 223 USPQ 1257 (Fed. Cir. 1984). The mere fact that the prior art may be modified in the manner suggested by an examiner does not make the modification obvious unless the prior art suggests the desirability of the modification. A modification that renders the prior art inoperable for its intended purpose is inappropriate. *In re Fritch,* 972 F.2d 1260, 23 USPQ2d 1780 (Fed. Cir. 1992). The claimed compound in *In re Jones,* 958 F.2d 347, 21 USPQ2d 1941 (Fed. Cir. 1992), fell within a genus of compounds disclosed in a prior art reference. The reference also disclosed that the genus had the same utility as that of the claimed species and was structurally similar. Nonetheless, no case of prima facie obviousness had been made out. For one thing, the reference genus may well have been infinite in scope; for another, there was no evidence, other than the PTO's speculation, that one of ordinary skill would have been motivated to make the modifications of the prior art necessary to arrive at the claimed compound. More recently, the court has made it clear that the fact that a claimed

deciding whether a prima facie case of obviousness has been made out, a new compound's utility must be considered.[355] But when chemical compounds have very close structural similarities and similar utilities, without more a prima facie case of obviousness may be made. When such close structural similarity to prior art compounds is shown, the burden of coming forward shifts to the applicant, and evidence affirmatively supporting unobviousness is required.[356] Where the difference between the claimed invention and the prior art is some range or other variable within the claims, patentability requires a showing that the particular range is critical, generally by showing that the claimed range achieves unexpected results relative to the prior art range.[357] Under this standard, it is not inventive to discover the optimum or workable ranges by routine experimentation. Only if the results of optimizing a variable are unexpectedly good can a patent be obtained for the claimed critical range.[358] Even though a modification results in great improvement and utility over the prior art, it may still not be patentable if the modification was within the capabilities of one skilled in the art, unless the claimed ranges "produce a new

---

compound may be encompassed by a disclosed generic formula does not by itself render that compound obvious. *In re Baird,* 16 F.2d 380, 29 USPQ2d 1550 (Fed. Cir. 1994). The prior art contained a generic disclosure that encompassed more than 100 million different diphenols, only one of which was the bisphenol A of the claimed compound. There was nothing in the reference suggesting that one should select the variables necessary to achieve bisphenol A, despite the fact that many of the diphenols specifically enumerated in the reference were derivatives of bisphenol A. Thus, the court reasoned, the reference did not suggest bisphenol A and therefore did not motivate the selection of that to arrive at the claimed compounds. It is interesting to note that the PTO has indicated that it does not intend to follow this decision; the examining corps has been directed to disregard *Baird* in assessing prima facie obviousness. See 1161 O.G. 314 (memorandum dated March 22, 1994).

[355]*In re Dillon,* 919 F.2d 688, 16 USPQ2d 1897 (Fed. Cir. 1990).

[356]*In re Nielson,* 816 F.2d 1562, 2 USPQ2d 1525 (Fed. Cir. 1987); *In re Grabiak,* 769 F.2d 729, 226 USPQ 870 (Fed. Cir. 1985). See also *In re Merck & Co.,* 800 F.2d 1091, 231 USPQ 375 (Fed. Cir. 1986). Prima facie obviousness can be rebutted by a showing of unexpected results. But obviousness does not require absolute predictability. Only a reasonable expectation that the beneficial result will be achieved is necessary. *Id.* One way for a patent applicant to rebut a prima facie case of obviousness based upon chemical similarity is to make a showing of unexpected results, i.e., to show that the claimed invention exhibits some superior property or advantage that a person of ordinary skill in the relevant art would have found surprising or unexpected. *In re Soni,* 54 F.3d 746, 34 USPQ2d 1684 (Fed. Cir. 1995). An examination for unexpected results is a factual, evidentiary inquiry, which is reviewed for clear error. *In re Geisler,* 116 F.3d 1465, 43 USPQ2d 1362 (Fed. Cir. 1997); *In re Mayne,* 104 F.3d 1339, 41 USPQ2d 1451 (Fed. Cir. 1997). Apparently an applicant can, through the use of a continuation application, introduce new evidence to overcome a finding of prima facie obviousness in the original application, even a finding that has been affirmed on appeal by a court. See *Applied Mtls, Inc. v. Advanced Semi. Mtls, Inc.,* 98 F.3d 1563, 40 USPQ2d 1481 (Fed. Cir. 1996); *Applied Mtls, Inc. v. Gemini Research Corp.,* 835 F.2d 279, 15 USPQ2d 1816 (Fed. Cir. 1987). Evidence and arguments relied upon by the applicant to rebut the prima facie case of obviousness need not be within the specification in order to be considered. There is no logical support for a contrary rule, given that obviousness is determined by the totality of the record including, in some instances most significantly, the evidence and arguments proffered during the give and take of ex parte prosecution. *In re Chu,* 66 F.3d 292, 36 USPQ2d 1089 (Fed. Cir. 1995).

[357]*In re Geisler,* 116 F.3d 1465, 43 USPQ2d 1362 (Fed. Cir. 1997); *In re Woodruff,* 919 F.2d 1575, 16 USPQ2d 1934 (Fed. Cir. 1990).

[358]*In re Geisler,* 116 F.3d 1465, 43 USPQ2d 1362 (Fed. Cir. 1997).

and unexpected result which is different in kind and not merely in degree from the results of the prior art."[359]

Thus, where the prior art recognizes the effectiveness of an element for a short period, the burden is upon the applicant to show that it would not have been obvious that the element would be effective for longer periods.[360] And the fact that performance of a compound is comparable to that of the prior art does not necessarily imply that the structures are identical, but it may justify a holding that the PTO has adduced a prima facie case of obviousness, thus shifting to the applicant the burden of proving that the prior art products do not necessarily or inherently possess the characteristics of the claimed product.[361] Generalization should be avoided insofar as specific chemical structures are alleged to be prima facie obvious one from the other. Nevertheless, the mere fact that biological activity is involved does not rule out prima facie obviousness.[362]

---

[359]*In re Huang,* 100 F.3d 1568 (Fed. Cir. 1996). Naked attorney argument is not the kind of factual evidence that is required to rebut a prima facie case of obviousness and is insufficient to establish unexpected results. *In re Geisler,* 116 F.3d 1465, 43 USPQ2d 1362 (Fed. Cir. 1997).

[360]*In re Farrenkopf,* 713 F.2d 714, 219 USPQ 1 (Fed. Cir. 1983).

[361]*In re Wright,* 848 F.2d 1216, 6 USPQ2d 1959 (Fed. Cir. 1988); *In re Thorpe,* 777 F.2d 695, 227 USPQ 964 (Fed. Cir. 1985). But it is not necessary in order to establish a prima facie case of obviousness that both a structural similarity between a claimed and prior art compound (or a key component of a composition) be shown and that there be a suggestion in or expectation from the prior art that the claimed compound or composition will have the same or a similar utility as the one newly discovered by the applicant. *In re Dillon,* 919 F.2d 688, 16 USPQ2d 1897 (Fed. Cir. 1990). To the extent *In re Wright, supra,* holds otherwise, it was overruled in *Dillon.* Properties must be considered in the overall evaluation of obviousness, and the lack of any disclosure of useful properties for a prior art compound may indicate a lack of motivation to make related compounds, thereby precluding a prima facie case. But it is not correct that similarity of structure and a suggestion of the activity of an applicant's compounds in the prior art are necessary before a prima facie case is established. *Id.*

[362]*In re Grabiak,* 769 F.2d 729, 226 USPQ 870 (Fed. Cir. 1985). The court has rejected the proposition that the established relationship in the genetic code between a nucleic acid and the protein it encodes also makes a gene prima facie obvious over its correspondent protein. It may be true that, knowing the structure of the protein, one can use the genetic code to hypothesize possible structures for the corresponding gene and that one thus has the potential for obtaining that gene. However, because of the degeneracy of the genetic code, there is a vast number of nucleotide sequences that might code for a specific protein. Therefore, given the failure of the prior art to suggest which of those possibilities is the claimed human sequence, the invention would not have been obvious. In so holding, the court refused to say that a gene is never rendered obvious when the amino acid sequence of its coded protein is known. Nor would it express an opinion concerning the reverse proposition, that knowledge of the structure of a DNA might make a coded protein obvious. *In re Bell,* 991 F.2d 781, 26 USPQ2d 1529 (Fed. Cir. 1993). The fact that one can conceive a general process in advance for preparing an undefined compound does not mean that a claimed specific compound was precisely envisioned and therefore obvious. A substance may indeed be defined by its process of preparation. That occurs, however, when it has already been prepared by that process and one therefore knows that the result of that process is the stated compound. Thus, the existence of a general method of isolating DNA molecules is essentially irrelevant to the question whether the specific molecules themselves would have been obvious, in the absence of other prior art that suggests the claimed DNAs. A prior art disclosure of a process reciting a particular compound or obvious variant thereof as a product of the process is, of course, another matter, raising issues of anticipation as well as obviousness. Moreover, where there is prior art that suggests a claimed compound, the existence, or lack thereof, of an enabling process for making that compound is surely a factor in any patentability determination. There must, however, still be prior art that suggests the claimed compound in order for a prima facie case of obviousness to be made out. Just as

The court has specifically adopted the doctrine of *In re Papesch,*[363] which holds that a compound and all its properties are inseparable. Evidence of unobvious or unexpected advantageous properties may rebut a prima facie case of obviousness based on structural similarities. Such evidence may include data showing that a compound is unexpectedly superior in a property it shares with prior art compounds. These properties need not produce superior results in every environment in which the compound may be used. To be patentable, a compound need not excel over prior art compounds in all common properties. Evidence that a compound is unexpectedly superior in one of a spectrum of common properties can be enough to rebut a prima facie case of obviousness.[364]

Indeed, the court had squarely decided, albeit through a divided panel in its initial *Dillon* decision, that a prima facie case of obviousness cannot be based upon structural similarity alone, without consideration of the properties and utility of the claimed new compound.[365] At the same time, the discovery of a new property or use of a previously known composition, even when that property and use are unobvious from the prior art, cannot impart patentability to claims for the known composition. Products of identical chemical composition cannot have mutually exclusive properties. Thus the initial inquiry is to the novelty of the composition.[366] In an in banc reconsideration of *Dillon*, the court expounded at length on the middle ground. Thus, structural similarity between claimed and prior art subject matter, proved by combining references or otherwise, where the prior art gives some reason or motivation to make the claimed compositions, creates a prima facie case of obviousness. The burden and opportunity then fall on an applicant to rebut the prima facie case. Such rebuttal can consist of a comparison of test data showing that the claimed compositions possess unexpectedly improved properties or properties that the prior art does not have, that the art is so deficient that there is no motivation to make what might otherwise appear to be obvious changes, or any other argument or presentation of evidence that is pertinent. There is no question that all evidence of the properties of the claimed compositions and the prior art must be considered in determining the ultimate question of patentability, but it is also clear

---

a broad genus does not necessarily render obvious each compound within its scope, so knowledge of a protein does not give one a conception of a particular DNA encoding it. *In re Deuel*, 51 F.3d 1552, 34 USPQ2d 1210 (Fed. Cir. 1995).

[363]315 F.2d 381, 137 USPQ 43 (CCPA 1963).

[364]*In re Chupp*, 816 F.2d 643, 2 USPQ2d 1437 (Fed. Cir. 1987). Changes in dosages of pharmaceuticals normally do not lend patentability unless the results obtained at the designated concentrations are unexpectedly good. *Merck & Co. v. Biocraft Labs., Inc.*, 874 F.2d 804, 10 USPQ2d 1843 (Fed. Cir. 1989).

[365]*In re Dillon*, 892 F.2d 1554, 13 USPQ2d 1337, *vacated*, 919 F.2d 688, 16 USPQ2d 1897 (Fed. Cir. 1990).

[366]*In re Spada*, 911 F.2d 705, 15 USPQ2d 1655 (Fed. Cir. 1990). Of course, the result may be different where the inventor is claiming the new use as a process. *Id.* See, e.g., *In re Pleuddmann*, 910 F.2d 823, 15 USPQ2d 1738 (Fed. Cir. 1990).

that the discovery that a claimed composition possesses a property not disclosed for the prior art subject matter does not by itself defeat a prima facie case.[367]

Normally a prima facie case is based upon structural similarity, i.e., an established structural relationship between a prior art compound and the claimed compound. Structural relationships may provide the requisite motivation or suggestion to modify known compounds to obtain new compounds. But in the case of a gene that is yet structurally undefined, it would have been highly unlikely for one of ordinary skill in the art to contemplate what was ultimately obtained. What cannot be contemplated or conceived cannot be obvious. A general motivation to search for some gene that exists does not necessarily make obvious a specifically defined gene that is subsequently obtained as a result of that search.[368]

In general, a reference that teaches away cannot serve to create a prima facie case of obviousness. However, this is not an abstract rule, for it may not be applicable in all circumstances. For example, the use of a known or obvious material does not become patentable simply because it has been described as inferior to some other product for the same use.[369]

It should be understood that prima facie obviousness applies to all technological classes of inventions, not just the chemical arts.[370]

(c) Miscellaneous Statements

The court has made several statements in ruling on obviousness that may point the way to future rulings for the astute practitioner.

Reliance upon general principles of engineering or physics, or upon the common experience of humankind, is inappropriate to the obviousness inquiry. First, the statute says nothing about such matters, but instead speaks of prior art. Second, such reliance raises a standard impossible for any patent to meet. Humans do not create from nothing; they must employ principles of physics and engineering and their own experience. It cannot be the law that the only inventions patentable are those that cannot be explained by any known principles of engineering or physics.[371] The mere fact that a device or process

---

[367]*In re Dillon,* 919 F.2d 688, 16 USPQ2d 1897 (Fed. Cir. 1990). It should be noted that the applicant did not separately appeal use claims, and thus she could not rely upon use limitations as distinctions. Judge Newman, joined by Judges Cowen and Mayer, filed a lengthy and perceptive dissenting opinion. This decision can be fully understood only by careful study and analysis of both opinions. See also *In re Baxter Travenol Labs.,* 952 F.2d 388, 21 USPQ2d 1281 (Fed. Cir. 1991).

[368]*In re Deuel,* 51 F.3d 1552, 34 USPQ2d 1210 (Fed. Cir. 1995).

[369]*In re Gurley,* 27 F.3d 551, 31 USPQ2d 1130 (Fed. Cir. 1994).

[370]*In re Oetiker,* 977 F.2d 1443, 24 USPQ2d 1443, 1444–45 (Fed. Cir. 1992).

[371]*Panduit Corp. v. Dennison Mfg. Co.,* 774 F.2d 1082, 227 USPQ 337 (Fed. Cir. 1985). Be assured, however, that a scientifically meaningless claim limitation will not be given weight

utilizes a known scientific principle does not make that device or process obvious.[372]

The law imposes no obligation on a patent applicant to determine what is going on in the technological gap between the claimed invention and the prior art, or to set the claim limits at the precise technological edge of the invention. Patentability is not measured against the closest point on the road to invention. Much technological change that meets the criterion of unobviousness, when viewed in light of the prior art, has a fuzzy boundary at its point of origin. Technological differences from prior art usually become more pronounced with distance from the boundary, but the changes may become manifest gradually. Indeed, the location of the boundary may well change with the available precision of measurement.[373]

The opinions or the contemporaneous beliefs of those skilled in the field, as to the nonobviousness of an invention, merit fair weight.[374] However, where the references and invention are easily understandable, there may be no need for expert explanatory testimony; certainly there is no rule that the trial court cannot, as a matter of law, make factual determinations on obviousness without expert analysis on behalf of the accused infringer.[375]

There is no presumptive correlation that two similar processes form substantially the same product where the processes differ by a materially limiting step.[376] Similarly, there is no rule that where an article patent is invalid, a method claim based entirely upon the use of the article is also unpatentable. However, in some cases, where the claimed apparatus and method are so interrelated that a separate *Graham v. Deere* analysis would be superfluous, there is no need to go further.[377] Where a product-by-process claim is rejected over a prior art product that appears to be identical, though produced by a different process, the burden is upon the applicant to come forward with evidence establishing an unobvious difference between the claimed product and the prior art product.[378]

The requirement of unobviousness in the case of chemical inventions is the same as for other types of inventions.[379] This is also

---

for purposes of determining nonobviousness. *N.V. Akzo v. E.I. Dupont de Nemours,* 810 F.2d 1148, 1 USPQ2d 1704 (Fed. Cir. 1987).

[372]*Uniroyal, Inc. v. Rudkin-Wiley Corp.,* 837 F.2d 1044, 5 USPQ2d 1434 (Fed. Cir. 1988).

[373]*Andrew Corp. v. Gabriel Elec., Inc.,* 847 F.2d 819, 6 USPQ2d 2010 (Fed. Cir. 1988).

[374]*In re Corkill,* 771 F.2d 1496, 226 USPQ 1005 (Fed. Cir. 1985).

[375]*Union Carbide Corp. v. American Can Co.,* 724 F.2d 1567, 220 USPQ 584 (Fed. Cir. 1984).

[376]*Ashland Oil, Inc. v. Delta Resins & Refracs., Inc.,* 776 F.2d 281, 227 USPQ 657 (Fed. Cir. 1985).

[377]*Union Carbide Corp. v. American Can Co.,* 724 F.2d 1567, 220 USPQ 584 (Fed. Cir. 1984). On the other hand, the grant of method claims directed to the use of a compound can be persuasive of the compound's nonobviousness. *In re Chupp,* 816 F.2d 643, 2 USPQ2d 1437 (Fed. Cir. 1987).

[378]*In re Marosi,* 710 F.2d 799, 218 USPQ 289 (Fed. Cir. 1983).

[379]*In re Johnson,* 747 F.2d 1456, 223 USPQ 1260 (Fed. Cir. 1984).

true for design inventions, although the evaluation of the prior art necessarily involves consideration of what are indicated to be the distinguishing characteristics of the claimed design. A combination of references may be the basis for obviousness of a design.[380]

Quite remarkably, a finding that an invention is an improvement is not a prerequisite to patentability. It is possible for an invention to be less effective than existing devices but nevertheless meet the statutory criteria for patentability.[381] The inquiry is not whether there was a "real discovery of merit" or whether the claimed invention offered a "new solution," but whether the claimed subject matter as a whole would have been obvious at the time the invention was made to a person having ordinary skill in the art.[382] Nor does the statute require complexity. Though technology has burgeoned, the patent system is not limited to sophisticated technologies and powerful corporations. Nowhere in the statute or the Constitution is the patent system opened only to those who make complex inventions difficult for judges to understand and foreclosed to those who make less mysterious inventions that a judge can understand after hearing the inventor's explanation of the invention and the engineering principles employed. The constitutional purpose is to encourage disclosure of patentable contributions to progress in the useful arts, all the useful arts, not just the esoteric.[383] Simplicity is not inimical to patentability.[384]

---

[380]*Petersen Mfg. Co. v. Central Purchasing, Inc.,* 740 F.2d 1541, 222 USPQ 562 (Fed. Cir. 1984). Design patents must meet a nonobviousness requirement identical to that applicable to utility patents. Obviousness is determined from the vantage of the designer of ordinary capability who designs articles of the type at issue. *Avia Group Int'l, Inc. v. L.A. Gear Calif., Inc.,* 853 F.2d 1557, 7 USPQ2d 1548 (Fed. Cir. 1988).

[381]*Demaco Corp. v. F. Von Langsdorff Lic., Ltd.,* 851 F.2d 1387, 7 USPQ2d 1222 (Fed. Cir. 1988); *Custom Accessories, Inc. v. Jeffrey-Allan Indus., Inc.,* 807 F.2d 955, 1 USPQ2d 1196 (Fed. Cir. 1986). Nothing in the patent statute requires that an invention be superior to the prior art to be patentable. *Ryco, Inc. v. Ag-Bag Corp.,* 857 F.2d 1418, 8 USPQ2d 1323 (Fed. Cir. 1988).

[382]*Monarch Knitting Mach. Corp. v. Sulzer Morat Gmbh,* 139 F.3d 877, 45 USPQ2d 1977 (Fed. Cir. 1998).

[383]*Panduit Corp. v. Dennison Mfg. Co.,* 810 F.2d 1561, 1 USPQ2d 1593 (Fed. Cir. 1987).

[384]*In re Oetiker,* 977 F.2d 1443, 24 USPQ2d 1443, 1446 (Fed. Cir. 1992). Simplicity may represent a significant and unobvious advance over the complexity of prior devices. *Sensonics, Inc. v. Aerosonic Corp.,* 81 F.3d 1566, 38 USPQ2d 1551 (Fed. Cir. 1996).

5

Specification and Claims

§5.1 Introduction

The specification and claims of a patent constitute one of the most difficult legal instruments to draw.[1] It is also fair to say that the specification and claims of a patent cause more trouble for judges and lawyers than most legal instruments.

The section of the patent statute that sets the standards for content of specification and structure of claims has taken on increased importance with the advent of the Federal Circuit. Section 112 provides, in part, that:

---

[1]*Slimfold Mfg. Co. v. Kinkead Indus., Inc.,* 810 F.2d 1113, 1 USPQ2d 1563 (Fed. Cir. 1987). In a mild criticism of an attorney's explanation that he used "shorthand," thus confusing the examiner and resulting in a summary judgment of inequitable conduct (which was vacated in this case), the court said: "Shorthand is a method of transcribing words by which the skilled stenographer can keep up with most persons' spoken words, but at a cost of having a script, readable only by himself, whereas the slower conventional method of arabic script is supposed to be readable by anyone not illiterate. In a patent, language readable only by the author is inappropriate. Besides arabic script, we all learn in school a penchant for 'elegant variation,' i.e., a reluctance to repeat even a single word more than once in a paragraph. If San Francisco is named once, on the next reference it becomes 'the Pacific Coast port above mentioned,' or even more elegantly, 'the City on the Golden Gate.' This is how we learn to write. . . . A patent, like any other legal document, is likely to have its intentions defeated by 'elegant variation,'

The specification shall contain a written description of the invention, and of the manner and process of making and using it, in such full, clear, concise, and exact terms as to enable any person skilled in the art to which it pertains, or with which it is most nearly connected, to make and use the same, and shall set forth the best mode contemplated by the inventor of carrying out his invention.

The specification shall conclude with one or more claims particularly pointing out and distinctly claiming the subject matter which the applicant regards as his invention. . . . [2]

In other words, the invention that is the subject of the patent must be described and claimed, in a rather formal way. The written description must teach a person of ordinary skill in the art how to make and use that claimed invention without undue experimentation. More than that, the inventor must make a reasonably full disclosure, showing how to practice the invention in the best way known to him or her at the time of filing the application. This chapter treats these basic subjects and also considers some problems, largely time bars, that can arise if the original written description is not adequate. Finally, it concludes with a discussion of the rules governing claim interpretation, as an appropriate introduction to the following chapter, which deals with infringement.

§5.2 Enabling Disclosure

The original 1790 Patent Act contained a requirement for an enabling disclosure,[3] and the present provision, §112, reflects a remarkably similar requirement. It was early held that a patent lacking in enablement was invalid and that a defective specification could be pleaded as a defense to a patent infringement suit.[4] Invalidity resulted not from any intent to deceive the public, but rather from a sort of failure of consideration—the public had given the patentee a privilege of exclusivity and in return was entitled, upon expiration of the privilege, to practice the invention.[5] It is good to keep in mind, in considering enablement, and in the discussions of best mode and claim adequacy that follow, that a party asserting invalidity based upon failure

---

which should be reserved for less mundane documents." *Burlington Indus., Inc. v. Dayco Corp.,* 849 F.2d 1418, 7 USPQ2d 1158, 1160–61 (Fed. Cir. 1988).

[2]35 U.S.C. §112. The third, fourth, and fifth paragraphs of §112 deal with dependent claims. The sixth paragraph is more substantive: it authorizes "means plus function" claims and indicates how they are to be construed. See §5.6(f). 35 U.S.C. §§113–115 have to do with drawings, models, and the applicant's oath, respectively. The court says that, under §112, it is clear that the specification of a patent consists of, and contains, both a written description of the invention and the claims. It also recognizes that, in present day usage, this statutory structure is not always adhered to. Thus, it is not uncommon for the claims and specification to be treated as distinct entities. *In re Dossel,* 115 F.3d 942, 42 USPQ2d 1881 (Fed. Cir. 1997).

[3]Act of April 10, 1790, ch. 7, §2, 1 Stat. 109.

[4]*Grant v. Raymond,* 31 U.S. 218 (1832).

[5]31 U.S. at 247.

to comply with §112 bears no less a burden and no fewer responsibilities than any other patent challenger; the standard is clear and convincing proof.[6]

Although not explicitly recited in §112, the specification of a patent must teach those skilled in the art how to make and use the full scope of the claimed invention without undue experimentation.[7] The elements of the modern enablement requirement may therefore be stated as follows: a patent application must, (1) when filed, (2) contain a written description of the invention, (3) sufficiently clear and complete to enable (4) one of ordinary skill in the art to which the invention pertains, to make and use the invention, (5) as claimed, (6) without undue experimentation. The Federal Circuit has had much to say about each of these elements.

(a) General

Enablement is a question of law,[8] subject to de novo review,[9] but it may well involve subsidiary questions of law or fact[10] and is amenable to resolution by a jury.[11] Issues of enablement may involve consideration of complex scientific principles and disputed aspects of technology. Such issues are not treated as legal abstractions, but properly

---

[6]*United States v. Telectronics, Inc.*, 857 F.2d 778, 8 USPQ2d 1217 (Fed. Cir. 1988); *Ralston Purina Co. v. Far-Mar-Co, Inc.*, 772 F.2d 1570, 227 USPQ 177 (Fed. Cir. 1985). See also *Northern Telecom, Inc. v. Datapoint Corp.*, 908 F.2d 931, 15 USPQ2d 1321 (Fed. Cir. 1990). An examiner may reject a claim if it is reasonable to conclude that one skilled in the art would be unable to carry out the claimed invention. It is reasonable for an examiner to have such doubt where the elements at issue are integral to the practice of the invention and neither the patent application nor the prior art described their structure. In such a case, the applicant then has the burden of overcoming the rejection. It is not sufficient to provide the structural and functional details of the elements in question only through an expert's affidavit unless that information is shown to have been known in the art. Moreover, an expert's opinion on the ultimate legal issue must be supported by something more than a conclusory statement. *In re Buchner,* 929 F.2d 660, 18 USPQ2d 1331 (Fed. Cir. 1991). See also *In re Wright*, 999 F.2d 155, 27 USPQ2d 1510 (Fed. Cir. 1993).

[7]*In re Wright*, 999 F.2d 155, 27 USPQ2d 1510 (Fed. Cir. 1993).

[8]*Amgen, Inc. v. Chugai Pharm. Co.*, 927 F.2d 1200, 18 USPQ2d 1016 (Fed. Cir. 1991); *Northern Telecom, Inc. v. Datapoint Corp.*, 908 F.2d 931, 15 USPQ2d 1321 (Fed. Cir. 1990); *Gould v. Quigg*, 822 F.2d 1074, 3 USPQ2d 1302 (Fed. Cir. 1987); *Hybritech Inc. v. Monoclonal Antibodies, Inc.*, 802 F.2d 1367, 231 USPQ 81 (Fed. Cir. 1986); *Moleculon Res. Corp. v. CBS, Inc.*, 793 F.2d 1261 (Fed. Cir. 1986); *DeGeorge v. Bernier*, 768 F.2d 1318, 226 USPQ 758 (Fed. Cir. 1985); *Cross v. Iizuka*, 753 F.2d 1040, 224 USPQ 739 (Fed. Cir. 1985); *Lindemann Maschinenfabrik v. American Hoist & Derrick Co.*, 730 F.2d 1452, 221 USPQ 481 (Fed. Cir. 1984); *Raytheon Co. v. Roper Corp.*, 724 F.2d 951, 220 USPQ 592 (Fed. Cir. 1983). Despite being a closely related question, operability under 35 U.S.C. §101 is a question of fact. *Newman v. Quigg*, 877 F.2d 1575, 11 USPQ2d 1340 (Fed. Cir. 1989).

[9]*Enzo Biochem Inc. v. Calgene Inc.*, 188 F.3d 1362, 52 USPQ2d 1129 (Fed. Cir. 1999); *Process Control Corp. v. HydReclaim Corp.*, 190 F.3d 1350, 52 USPQ2d 1029 (Fed. Cir. 1999).

[10]*Johns Hopkins Univ. v. Cellpro Inc.*, 152 F.3d 1342, 47 USPQ2d 1705 (Fed. Cir. 1998); *Utter v. Hiraga*, 845 F.2d 993, 6 USPQ2d 1709 (Fed. Cir. 1988); *Spectra-Physics, Inc. v. Coherent, Inc.*, 827 F.2d 1524, 3 USPQ2d 1737 (Fed. Cir. 1987); *Quaker City Gear Works, Inc. v. Skil Corp.*, 747 F.2d 1446, 223 USPQ 1161 (Fed. Cir. 1984). The underlying factual findings are reviewed for clear error. *Enzo Biochem Inc. v. Calgene Inc.*, 188 F.3d 1362, 52 USPQ2d 1129 (Fed. Cir. 1999); *In re Goodman*, 11 F.3d 1046 (Fed. Cir. 1993).

[11]*Allen Organ Co. v. Kimball Int'l, Inc.*, 839 F.2d 1556, 5 USPQ2d 1769 (Fed. Cir. 1988); *Spectra-Physics, Inc. v. Coherent, Inc.*, 827 F.2d 1524, 3 USPQ2d 1737 (Fed. Cir. 1987).

devolve on the trier of fact. Our system of justice does not require judge and jury to be independent experts in technology. In ascertaining the truth when the evidence is primarily scientific, as for other kinds of evidence, the trier of fact must make determinations of credibility, reliability, and weight.[12]

The relevant time frame for measuring enablement is the date of filing the application[13] not the time of trial.[14] Thus later occurring developments are of no significance regarding what one of skill in the art would believe as of the filing date.[15]

A specification disclosure that contains a teaching of the manner and process of making and using the invention in terms that correspond in scope to those used in describing and defining the subject matter sought to be patented must be taken as in compliance with the enablement requirement unless there is reason to doubt the objective truth of the statements that are relied on for enabling support. Thus, once an examiner accepts the sufficiency of a specification, an applicant has no further burden to prove by extrinsic evidence that the application was enabling. The burden would then shift to an opponent, for example, a rival in an interference, to come forward with contrary evidence.[16]

Potential infringers should be cautioned that the Federal Circuit may look with a jaundiced eye upon a nonenablement defense interposed by a copier.[17]

Best mode requirement. Compliance with the best mode requirement focuses on a different matter than does compliance with the enablement requirement. Enablement looks to placing the subject

---

[12]*Brooktree Corp. v. Advanced Micro Devices, Inc.*, 977 F.2d 1555, 24 USPQ2d 1401 (Fed. Cir. 1992).

[13]*Vas-Cath Inc. v. Mahurkar*, 935 F.2d 1555, 19 USPQ2d 1111 (Fed. Cir. 1991); *Gould v. Quigg*, 822 F.2d 1074, 3 USPQ2d 1302 (Fed. Cir. 1987); *Hybritech Inc. v. Monoclonal Antibodies, Inc.*, 802 F.2d 1367, 231 USPQ 81 (Fed. Cir. 1986); *White Consol. Indus., Inc. v. Vega Servo-Control, Inc.*, 713 F.2d 788, 218 USPQ 961 (Fed. Cir. 1983). Failure to meet a requirement of patentability, such as enablement, does not of itself establish the intent element of inequitable conduct. *Therma-Tru Corp. v. Peachtree Doors Inc.*, 44 F.3d 988, 33 USPQ2d 1274 (Fed. Cir. 1994). The date for evaluating a best mode disclosure in a continuation application is the date of the earlier application with respect to common subject matter. *Transco Prods., Inc. v. Performance Contr., Inc.*, 38 F.3d 551, 32 USPQ2d 1077 (Fed. Cir. 1994). The court has rejected the argument that it might constitute inequitable conduct to fail to disclose, prior to issue of a patent, a best mode or enabling detail discovered after the application was filed. The rationale is that disclosure is closed when the application is filed, and there is no opportunity for an inventor to include subsequent improvements or modifications in an application or patent after filing, because of the prohibition against new matter. Inasmuch as there can be no obligation to do so, there is no penalty for failure to do so. *Engel Indus., Inc. v. Lockformer Co.*, 946 F.2d 1528, 20 USPQ2d 1300 (Fed. Cir. 1991). It should be noted that this decision does not appear to address the question whether a best mode or enabling detail must be updated when a continuing application is filed.

[14]*Gould v. Quigg*, 822 F.2d 1074, 3 USPQ2d 1302 (Fed. Cir. 1987); *W.L. Gore & Assoc. v. Garlock, Inc.*, 721 F.2d 1540, 220 USPQ 303 (Fed. Cir. 1983).

[15]*In re Wright*, 999 F.2d 155, 27 USPQ2d 1510 (Fed. Cir. 1993).

[16]*Fiers v. Revel*, 984 F.2d 1164, 25 USPQ2d 1601 (Fed. Cir. 1993).

[17]*W.L. Gore & Assoc. v. Garlock, Inc.*, 721 F.2d 1540, 220 USPQ 303 (Fed. Cir. 1983).

matter of the claims generally in the possession of the public. Nonenablement is the failure to disclose any mode and does not depend on the applicant advocating a particular embodiment or method for making the invention.[18] The enablement requirement is met if the description enables any mode of making and using the claimed invention.[19]

Description requirement. The description requirement is different from enablement and requires that the invention be described in such a way that it is clear that the applicant invented what is claimed. A patent discloses only that which it describes, whether specifically or in general terms, so as to convey intelligence to one capable of understanding.[20] The purpose of the description requirement is to state what is needed to fulfill the enablement criteria. The written description must therefore communicate that which is necessary to enable the skilled artisan to make and use the claimed invention. A description that does not meet this requirement is legally insufficient.[21]

Consideration of the written description requirement often arises in the context of "new matter" problems (discussed in §5.5). Also, the requirements of the first paragraph of §112 apply to priority claims under §119[22] and §120.[23]

Living organisms. Where an invention depends on the use of living materials such as microorganisms or cultured cells, it may be impossible to enable the public to make the invention (i.e., to obtain these living materials) solely by means of a written disclosure. One means that has been developed for complying with the enablement requirement is to deposit the living materials in cell depositories, which will distribute samples to those who wish to practice the invention after the patent issues. Administrative guidelines and judicial decisions have clarified the conditions under which a deposit can satisfy the requirements of 35 U.S.C. §112.[24] Nonetheless, a deposit

---

[18]*Spectra-Physics, Inc. v. Coherent, Inc.,* 827 F.2d 1524, 3 USPQ 2d 1737 (Fed. Cir. 1987). In practical terms, however, where only an alternative embodiment is enabled, the disclosure of the best mode may be inadequate. But that is a question separate and distinct from the question whether the specification enabled one to make the invention at all. *Id.*

[19]*Engel Indus., Inc. v. Lockformer Co.,* 946 F.2d 1528, 20 USPQ2d 1300 (Fed. Cir. 1991).

[20]*In re Benno,* 768 F.2d 1340, 226 USPQ 683, 686 (Fed. Cir. 1985).

[21]*Kennecott Corp. v. Kyocera Int'l, Inc.,* 835 F.2d 1419, 5 USPQ2d 1194 (Fed. Cir. 1987).

[22]*Bigham v. Godtfredsen,* 857 F.2d 1415, 8 USPQ2d 1266 (Fed. Cir. 1988). The court apparently prefers to handle failure to disclose any mode as a written description defect rather than a best mode defect. *Id.*

[23]*Chester v. Miller,* 906 F.2d 1574, 15 USPQ2d 1333 (Fed. Cir. 1990).

[24]*In re Wands,* 858 F.2d 731, 8 USPQ2d 1400 (Fed. Cir. 1988). A deposit may also satisfy the best mode requirement of §112 and can be used to establish the filing date of the application as the prima facie date of invention. A deposit may also be used to satisfy the requirement under §114 that the PTO be guaranteed access to the invention during pendency of the application. *Id.* Although a public deposit of an organism can satisfy the enablement requirement of §112, a deposit of DNA inserts must be part of the record before it can provide evidence to support a

is not always necessary to satisfy the enablement requirement. No deposit is necessary if the biological organisms can be obtained from readily available sources or derived from readily available starting materials through routine screening that does not require undue experimentation. Whether the specification in an application involving living cells is enabled without a deposit must be decided on the facts of a particular case. Where the starting materials are available to the public and the screening and preparation methods are either known to the art or disclosed in the application, the sole issue is whether it would require undue experimentation to produce the claimed invention.[25]

(b) Claimed Invention

It is for the invention as claimed that enablement must exist, and not some other.[26] Thus, it is sufficient to disclose the details of the claimed circuitry without disclosing the details of all related, unclaimed circuitry with which the claimed circuitry might be interfaced.[27] Patents are not production documents, and nothing in the

---

particular claim construction. The party proffering evidence to the trial court must offer and explain that evidence in terms accessible to the court. A court has no scientific resources or expertise to derive a DNA sequence from a raw deposit and apply its legal reasoning to that result. *Schering Corp. v. Amgen Inc.,* 222 F.3d 1347, 55 USPQ2d 1650 (Fed. Cir. 2000).

[25]*In re Wands,* 858 F.2d 731, 8 USPQ2d 1400 (Fed. Cir. 1988). In *Amgen, Inc. v. Chugai Pharm. Co.,* 927 F.2d 1200, 18 USPQ2d 1016 (Fed. Cir. 1991), the best mode for a claim to a host cell transfected with a particular gene involved a special strain of hamster ovary cells. The inventor adequately disclosed how to obtain and isolate that strain. Thus, in view of the fact that one of skill in the art could, without undue experimentation, prepare the necessary biological samples from known materials based on the written description in the patent specification, it was not necessary to place a cell culture in a public depository. The court contrasted this with a situation where the biological samples could only be obtained from nature, as in the case of a unique soil sample. In another case, *In re Lundak,* 773 F.2d 1216, 227 USPQ 90 (Fed. Cir. 1985), the applicant did not make a required deposit of microorganisms until several days after the application was filed. The court held that the deposit added nothing to the written description. As long as the procedure followed ensures availability of the microorganism to the PTO during prosecution, and to the public after the patent issues, the enablement requirement is satisfied.

[26]*Christianson v. Colt Indus. Oper. Corp.,* 822 F.2d 1544, 3 USPQ2d 1241 (Fed. Cir. 1987), *vacated on jurisdictional grounds and remanded,* 486 U.S. 800, 7 USPQ2d 1109 (1988); *Raytheon Co. v. Roper Corp.,* 724 F.2d 951, 220 USPQ 592 (Fed. Cir. 1983). The question of adequacy of support must be resolved on the basis of what the claim sets forth rather than what it embraces. Adequacy is judged in relation to the scope of the claims, but the scope must be evaluated as it would have been as of the filing date, using the then-existing skill and state of the art. The fact that later discoveries result in a fuller understanding of what the claim covers is immaterial. *United States Steel Corp. v. Phillips Petroleum Co.,* 865 F.2d 1247, 9 USPQ2d 1461 (Fed. Cir. 1989). In *Enzo Biochem Inc. v. Calgene Inc.,* 188 F.3d 1362, 52 USPQ2d 1129 (Fed. Cir. 1999), the court refused to impute invalidity for nonenablement, which it found as to two patents, to a third simply on the ground that all three shared a common specification. While evidence of invalidity regarding the claims of one patent may certainly apply to those of another, a party may not avoid its burden of proof by making a blanket statement that its proofs with respect to one patent apply to another and not provide a formal analysis as to why that is true.

[27]*DeGeorge v. Bernier,* 768 F.2d 1318, 226 USPQ 758 (Fed. Cir. 1985). Patent specifications were never intended to be production specifications. *Id.*

patent law requires that a patentee must disclose data on how to mass-produce the invented product, in patents obtained either on individual parts of the product or on the entire product. Thus the law has never required that a patentee who elects to manufacture its claimed invention must disclose in its patent those dimensions, tolerances, drawings, and other parameters of mass production not necessary to enable one skilled in the art to practice (as distinguished from mass-produce) the invention. Nor is it an objective of the patent system to supply, free of charge, production data and production drawings to competing manufacturers. And that is good, for such a requirement would be irrational. Many inventions are never manufactured; the decision to manufacture may be taken well after the patent has issued; printing a thousand or more documents in the patent would often be required. For those and other reasons, the law requires that patents disclose inventions, not mass-production data, and that patents enable the practice of inventions, not the organization and operation of factories. The requirement for disclosure of sufficient information to enable one skilled in the art to practice the best mode of the claimed invention is and has been proven fully adequate for over 150 years.[28]

Scope of enablement. The court has recently observed that the enablement requirement ensures that the public knowledge is enriched by the patent specification to a degree at least commensurate with the scope of the claims. The scope of the claims therefore must be less than or equal to the scope of the enablement.[29] It had earlier indicated that the scope of the protection must bear a reasonable relationship to the scope of enablement.[30] But its decisions seem to foreshadow a painstaking, case-by-case development of this proposition.[31] This issue, although viewed here in the context of enablement,

---

[28]*Christianson v. Colt Indus. Oper. Corp.*, 822 F.2d 1544, 3 USPQ 2d 1241 (Fed. Cir. 1987). This case was vacated on jurisdictional grounds by the Supreme Court and remanded for retransfer to the Seventh Circuit. *Christianson v. Colt Indus. Oper. Corp.*, 486 U.S. 800, 7 USPQ2d 1109 (1988). For the similar views of the Seventh Circuit on the merits, see *Christianson v. Colt Indus. Oper. Corp.*, 870 F.2d 1292, 10 USPQ2d 1352 (7th Cir. 1989).

[29]*National Recovery Tech. Inc. v. Magnetic Sep. Sys. Inc.*, 166 F.3d 1190, 49 USPQ2d 1671 (Fed. Cir. 1999). Enabling a proxy for the claimed invention is not the same as enabling the claimed invention itself. In this case, while the written description enabled one of ordinary skill to approximate the claimed function of the invention, it did not enable the ideal solution to the problem, and it was the ideal solution that was claimed.

[30]*In re Wright*, 999 F.2d 155, 27 USPQ2d 1510 (Fed. Cir. 1993).

[31]In *United States v. Telectronics, Inc.*, 857 F.2d 778, 8 USPQ2d 1217 (Fed. Cir. 1988), the specification was enabling only for the use of stainless steel electrodes, while the claims were not limited in the types of materials that could be employed for electrodes. In finding a lack of enablement, the district court emphasized the time and cost of doing certain studies that would be necessary for materials other than stainless steel. In reversing, the Federal Circuit held that such factors may be taken into account but in this case they did not, standing alone, persuade the court that the necessary experimentation would be excessive. Is not this result explainable on the basis that stainless steel was adequately disclosed? Is it not sufficient that one embodiment is properly disclosed along with the general manner in which other embodiments could be tested out? Or is the court implying that unlimited claims require a

is closely related to the also recently emergent proposition that the written description may be fatally inadequate if it does not convey possession of the invention as broadly as it is claimed.[32]

In the PTO, a lack of enablement rejection under §112¶1 is appropriate where the written description fails to teach those in the art to make and use the invention as broadly as it is claimed without undue experimentation. This rejection takes several forms. The PTO will make a scope of enablement rejection where the written description enables something within the scope of the claims, but the claims are not limited to that scope. This type of rejection is marked by language stating that the specification does not enable one of ordinary skill to use the invention commensurate with the scope of the claims. On the other hand, if the written description does not enable any subject matter within the scope of the claims, the PTO will make a general enablement rejection, stating that the specification does not teach how to make or use the invention.[33] Although patent applicants are not required to disclose every species encompassed by their claims, even in an unpredictable art, there must be sufficient disclosure, either through illustrative examples or terminology, to teach those of ordinary skill how to make and use the invention as broadly as it is claimed.[34]

(c) Person of Ordinary Skill

A patent speaks to a person of ordinary skill in the art, not the general public.[35] The question is whether the disclosure is sufficient to enable one skilled in the art to practice the claimed invention.[36] When an invention, in its different aspects, involves distinct arts, the specification is adequate if it enables the adepts of each art, those

---

broader scope of enablement? In *Amgen, Inc. v. Chugai Pharm. Co.*, 927 F.2d 1200, 18 USPQ2d 1016 (Fed. Cir. 1991), the claim attempted to cover all analogs of a particular gene, but the specification taught how to make and use only a few of the thousands or perhaps millions of possibilities. The court held that the disclosure was not sufficiently enabling to support a generic claim. In another facet of this interesting case, the court held that in view of evidence that those skilled in the art would construe the claims to refer to in vivo activity, the preparation techniques described in the patent were not enabling, inasmuch as they were the result of in vitro testing.

[32]See the discussion of *Gentry Gallery Inc. v. Berkline Corp.*, 134 F.3d 1473, 45 USPQ2d 1498 (Fed. Cir. 1998), at notes 5:196–201.

[33]*In re Cortright*, 165 F.3d 1353, 49 USPQ2d 1464 (Fed. Cir. 1999).

[34]*In re Vaeck*, 947 F.2d 488, 20 USPQ2d 1438, 1445 (Fed. Cir. 1991). The fact that dependent claims include species that might not meet the objects of the invention may go to inoperativeness under §101 or lack of enablement under §112. *North Am. Vaccine, Inc. v. American Cyanamid Co.*, 7 F.3d 1571, 28 USPQ2d 1333 (Fed. Cir. 1993).

[35]*W.L. Gore & Assoc. v. Garlock, Inc.*, 721 F.2d 1540, 220 USPQ 303 (Fed. Cir. 1983).

[36]*Lindemann Maschinenfabrik v. American Hoist & Derrick Co.*, 730 F.2d 1452, 221 USPQ 481 (Fed. Cir. 1984). When the challenged subject matter is a computer program that implements a claimed device or method, enablement is determined from the viewpoint of a skilled programmer using the knowledge and skill with which such a person is charged. *Northern Telecom, Inc. v. Datapoint Corp.*, 908 F.2d 931, 15 USPQ2d 1321 (Fed. Cir. 1990).

who have the best chance of being enabled, to carry out the aspect proper to their specialty.[37]

Enablement presupposes availability. Incorporation by reference to a document does not satisfy the enablement requirement if it is unavailable to a person skilled in the art.[38] A later dated publication cannot supplement an insufficient disclosure in a prior dated application to render it enabling. It can, however, be relied upon as evidence of the level of skill in the art as of the application filing date, and as evidence that the device disclosed in the application would have been operative.[39]

By the same token, although it is not necessarily fatal to keep an element of an invention a trade secret and refer to it by name only, if there are equivalents known, and known to be equivalents, the equivalents must be available to a person of skill in the art.[40] It is not necessary to explain every detail, since the inventor is speaking to persons of ordinary skill.[41] Where there is uncontradicted evidence of what a term means to those skilled in the art, the fact that the specification lacks a formula (even though formulae were later developed) is not fatal.[42]

A patent applicant, of course, may be his or her own lexicographer,[43] because the dictionary cannot keep up with technology.[44] This permits patents even where the inventor is not schooled in the terminology of the technical art to which the invention pertains, or where there is a need to coin new expressions with which to communicate the invention. So long as the meaning of an expression is made reasonably clear and its use is consistent within the patent's disclosure, an inventor is permitted to define his or her own terms.[45] Nothing more than objective enablement is required, and therefore it is irrelevant whether this teaching is provided through broad terminology or illustrative examples.[46]

(d) No Undue Experimentation

A patent need not teach, and preferably omits, what is well known in the art.[47] Section 112¶1 permits resort to material outside of the

---

[37]*Enzo Biochem Inc. v. Calgene Inc.*, 188 F.3d 1362, 52 USPQ2d 1129 (Fed. Cir. 1999).

[38]*Quaker City Gear Works, Inc. v. Skil Corp.*, 747 F.2d 1446, 223 USPQ 1161 (Fed. Cir. 1984).

[39]*Gould v. Quigg*, 822 F.2d 1074, 3 USPQ2d 1302 (Fed. Cir. 1987).

[40]*White Consol. Indus., Inc. v. Vega Servo-Control, Inc.*, 713 F.2d 788, 218 USPQ 961 (Fed. Cir. 1983).

[41]*In re Wands*, 858 F.2d 731, 8 USPQ2d 1400 (Fed. Cir. 1988); *DeGeorge v. Bernier*, 768 F.2d 1318, 226 USPQ 758 (Fed. Cir. 1985).

[42]*W.L. Gore & Assoc. v. Garlock, Inc.*, 721 F.2d 1540, 220 USPQ 303 (Fed. Cir. 1983).

[43]*W.L. Gore & Assoc. v. Garlock, Inc.*, 721 F.2d 1540, 220 USPQ 303 (Fed. Cir. 1983).

[44]*Fromson v. Advance Offset Plate, Inc.*, 720 F.2d 1565, 219 USPQ 1137 (Fed. Cir. 1983).

[45]*Lear Siegler, Inc. v. Aeroquip Corp.*, 733 F.2d 881, 221 USPQ 1025 (Fed. Cir. 1984).

[46]*In re Wright*, 999 F.2d 155, 27 USPQ2d 1510 (Fed. Cir. 1993).

[47]*Spectra-Physics, Inc. v. Coherent, Inc.*, 827 F.2d 1524, 3 USPQ2d 1737 (Fed. Cir. 1987); *Hybritech Inc. v. Monoclonal Antibodies, Inc.*, 802 F.2d 1367, 231 USPQ 81 (Fed. Cir. 1986).

specification in order to satisfy the enablement portion of the statute because it makes no sense to encumber the specification of a patent with all the knowledge of the past concerning how to make and use the claimed invention. One skilled in the art knows how to make and use a bolt, a wheel, a gear, a transistor, or a known chemical starting material. The specification would be of enormous and unnecessary length if one had to literally reinvent and describe the wheel.[48] Nonetheless, practice of the invention must not require undue experimentation.[49] What is "undue" defies precise definition. That some experimentation is necessary does not preclude enablement,[50] but it is clear that any required experimentation must be reasonable.[51]

The key word is "undue" not "experimentation." The term "undue experimentation" does not appear in the statute. Whether undue experimentation is required is not a single, simple factual determination, but rather is a conclusion reached by weighing many factual considerations. Factors to be considered include (1) the quantity of experimentation necessary, (2) the amount of direction or guidance presented, (3) the presence or absence of working examples, (4) the nature of the invention, (5) the state of the prior art, (6) the relative skill of those in the art, (7) the predictability or unpredictability of the art, and (8) the breadth of the claims.[52] Some trial and error is permissible.[53]

Patent protection is granted in return for an enabling disclosure of an invention, not for vague intimations of general ideas that may or may not be workable. Tossing out the mere germ of an idea does not constitute enabling disclosure. While every aspect of a generic claim certainly need not have been carried out by an inventor, or exemplified in the specification, reasonable detail must be provided in order to enable members of the public to understand and carry out the invention. It is true that a specification need not disclose what is well known in the art. However, that general, oft-repeated

---

See also *Paperless Accounting, Inc. v. Bay Area Rapid Transit Sys.,* 804 F.2d 659, 231 USPQ 649 (Fed. Cir. 1986).

[48]*Atmel Corp. v. Information Storage Devices Inc.,* 198 F.3d 1374, 53 USPQ2d 1225, 1230 (Fed. Cir. 1999).

[49]*Lindemann Maschinenfabrik v. American Hoist & Derrick Co.,* 730 F.2d 1452, 221 USPQ 481 (Fed. Cir. 1984). See also *Hybritech Inc. v. Monoclonal Antibodies, Inc.,* 802 F.2d 1367, 231 USPQ 81 (Fed. Cir. 1986).

[50]*Amgen, Inc. v. Chugai Pharm. Co.,* 927 F.2d 1200, 18 USPQ2d 1016 (Fed. Cir. 1991); *DeGeorge v. Bernier,* 768 F.2d 1318, 226 USPQ 758 (Fed. Cir. 1985).

[51]*White Consol. Indus., Inc. v. Vega Servo-Control, Inc.,* 713 F.2d 788, 218 USPQ 961 (Fed. Cir. 1983).

[52]*In re Wands,* 858 F.2d 731, 8 USPQ2d 1400 (Fed. Cir. 1988). With respect to the last element, claim breadth, see discussion beginning at note 5:29. These *"Wands"* factors for evaluating the issue of undue experimentation are applicable in inter partes litigation as well as ex parte prosecution. In neither situation is any prediction required; in both, the enablement determination is made retrospectively, by looking back to the filing date and determining whether undue experimentation would have been required at that time. *Enzo Biochem Inc. v. Calgene Inc.,* 188 F.3d 1362, 52 USPQ2d 1129 (Fed. Cir. 1999).

[53]*W.L. Gore & Assoc. v. Garlock, Inc.,* 721 F.2d 1540, 220 USPQ 303 (Fed. Cir. 1983). For example, in *PPG Indus., Inc. v. Guardian Indus.,* 75 F.3d 1558, 37 USPQ2d 1618 (Fed. Cir. 1996), a test procedure described in the specification was flawed. Nonetheless, there was no

statement is merely a rule of supplementation, not a substitute for a basic enabling disclosure. It means that the omission of minor details does not cause a specification to fail to meet the enablement requirement. However, when there is no disclosure of any specific starting material or of any of the conditions under which a process can be carried out, undue experimentation is required; there is a failure to meet the enablement requirement that cannot be rectified by asserting that all the disclosure related to the process is within the skill of the art. It is the specification, not the knowledge of one skilled in the art, that must supply the novel aspects of an invention in order to constitute adequate enablement.[54]

When the challenged subject matter is a computer program that implements a claimed device or method, enablement is determined from the viewpoint of a skilled programmer using the knowledge and skill with which such a person is charged. The amount of disclosure that will enable practice of an invention that utilizes a computer program may vary according to the nature of the invention, the role of the program in carrying it out, and the complexity of the contemplated programming, all from the viewpoint of the skilled programmer. The question is whether a programmer of ordinary skill could write a satisfactory program with ordinary effort.[55] When disclosure of software is required, it is generally sufficient if the functions of the software are disclosed, it usually being the case that creation of the specific source code is within the skill of the art.[56]

The court has rejected an argument that, by criticizing prior art in the specification, the patentee directs persons of ordinary skill in the art away from utilizing portions of prior art structures and thus fails to enable his or her own invention.[57]

An inventor need not comprehend the scientific principles upon which the practical effectiveness of the invention rests. An expression of theory merely as a belief is appropriate and will not be used to limit the claims; indeed, §112 does not require a statement of theory or belief.[58] But while it is not a requirement of patentability that an

---

failure of enablement because the error in the test procedure could have easily been detected and remedied.

[54]*Genentech, Inc. v. Novo Nordisk, A/S,* 108 F.3d 1361, 42 USPQ2d 1001 (Fed. Cir. 1997). Indeed, it may be sufficient if enablement of use is obvious from the prior art. Thus where claims were directed to a compound with pharmacological activity (no specific therapeutic properties were claimed), a failure to specify dosages was not fatal in view of the disclosure of dosages in similar prior art compounds. *Cross v. Iizuka,* 753 F.2d 1040, 224 USPQ 739 (Fed. Cir. 1985).

[55]*Northern Telecom, Inc. v. Datapoint Corp.,* 908 F.2d 931, 15 USPQ2d 1321 (Fed. Cir. 1990). See also *White Consol. Indus., Inc. v. Vega Servo-Control, Inc.,* 713 F.2d 788, 218 USPQ 961 (Fed. Cir. 1983).

[56]*Robotic Vision Sys., Inc. v. View Eng'r, Inc.,* 112 F.3d 1163, 42 USPQ2d 1619 (Fed. Cir. 1997).

[57]*Utter v. Hiraga,* 845 F.2d 993, 6 USPQ2d 1709 (Fed. Cir. 1988). The basis seems to be that overcoming the applicant's criticism of the prior art would not have required undue experimentation.

[58]*Fromson v. Advance Offset Plate, Inc.,* 720 F.2d 1565, 219 USPQ 1137 (Fed. Cir. 1983). By the same token, however, it would be incongruous for an accused infringer to shoulder the

inventor correctly set forth, or even know, how or why the invention works, neither is the patent applicant relieved of the requirement of teaching how to achieve the claimed result, even if the theory of operation is not correctly explained or even understood.[59] The inventor is not entirely free to speculate. When a claim includes an incorrect or questionable theory or requires a means for accomplishing an unattainable result, it is invalid, probably on two grounds: (1) the impossible cannot be enabled, and (2) the invention would be inoperative, under either §112 or §101.[60]

Lack of enablement and absence of utility are closely related grounds of unpatentability.[61] Thus, if the written description fails to illuminate a credible utility, the PTO will make both a §112¶1 rejection for failure to teach how to use the invention and a §101 rejection for lack of utility. This dual rejection occurs because the how to use prong of §112 incorporates as a matter of law the requirement of §101 that the specification disclose as a matter of fact a practical utility for the invention. Thus, an applicant's failure to disclose how to use an invention may support a rejection under either §112¶1 for lack of enablement as a result of the specification's failure to disclose adequately to one ordinarily skilled in the art how to use the invention without undue experimentation, or §101 for lack of utility when there is a complete absence of data supporting the statements that set forth the desired results of the claimed invention. The PTO cannot make this type of rejection, however, unless it has reason to doubt the objective truth of the statements contained in the written description. The PTO may establish a reason to doubt an invention's asserted utility when the written description suggests an inherently unbelievable undertaking or involves implausible scientific principles.[62]

A claim is not invalid for lack of operability simply because the invention does not work perfectly under all conditions. But whether

---

burden of explaining why an invention did not work when the teachings of the specification have been followed, just as an inventor need not know how or why his or her invention does work in order to obtain a patent. *Enzo Biochem Inc. v. Calgene Inc.*, 188 F.3d 1362, 52 USPQ2d 1129 (Fed. Cir. 1999).

[59]*Newman v. Quigg*, 877 F.2d 1575, 11 USPQ2d 1340 (Fed. Cir. 1989). Furthermore, statements that a phenomenon was observed are not inherently suspect simply because the underlying basis for the observation cannot be predicted or explained. However, where the claim itself purports to provide the cause, and the specification shows only surmise and belief as opposed to observational proof, the claim does not satisfy the how to use requirement of §112. In this context, inherency may not be established by probabilities or possibilities. The mere fact that a certain thing may result from a given set of circumstances is not sufficient. *In re Cortright*, 165 F.3d 1353, 49 USPQ2d 1464 (Fed. Cir. 1999).

[60]*Raytheon Co. v. Roper Corp.*, 724 F.2d 951, 220 USPQ 592 (Fed. Cir. 1983). Absence of utility can be the basis of a rejection under both §101 and §112. Obviously, if a claimed invention does not have utility, the specification cannot enable one to use it. *In re Brana*, 51 F.3d 1560, 34 USPQ2d 1437 (Fed. Cir. 1995). If claimed subject matter is inoperable, the patent may indeed be invalid for failure to meet the utility requirement of §101 and the enablement requirement of §112. *Brooktree Corp. v. Advanced Micro Devices, Inc.*, 977 F.2d 1555, 24 USPQ2d 1401 (Fed. Cir. 1992). See the discussion in §2.3(b).

[61]*Process Control Corp. v. HydReclaim Corp.*, 190 F.3d 1350, 52 USPQ2d 1029 (Fed. Cir. 1999).

[62]*In re Cortright*, 165 F.3d 1353, 49 USPQ2d 1464 (Fed. Cir. 1999).

a patented device or process is operable is a different inquiry than whether a particular claim is enabled by the specification. With respect to enablement the relevant inquiry lies in the relationship between the specification, the claims, and the knowledge of one of ordinary skill in the art. If, by following the steps set forth in the specification, one of ordinary skill in the art is not able to replicate the claimed invention without undue experimentation, the claim has not been enabled as required by §112¶1.[63] Accordingly, a specification that does not establish with certainty that the claimed invention will operate in the manner intended necessarily fails to satisfy the how-to-use requirement.[64] If a patent claim fails to meet the utility requirement because it is not useful or operative, then it also fails to meet the how-to-use aspect of the enablement requirement.[65] Nevertheless, the fact that some claimed combinations are inoperative does not necessarily render them invalid. It is not a function of claims to specifically exclude all possible inoperative substances. But if the number of inoperative combinations becomes significant, forcing one of ordinary skill in the art to experiment unduly in order to practice the claimed invention, invalidity might result.[66]

A so-called single-means claim is improper because it covers every conceivable way of achieving the desired result, while the specification shows only a few at best. Invalidity results, not under some "undue breadth" formulation, but for lack of enabling disclosure, because the single-means claim "reads on subject matter as to which the specification is not enabling."[67] If an invention pertains to an art where the results are predictable (e.g., mechanical as opposed to chemical arts), a broad claim can be enabled by disclosure of a single embodiment, and it is not invalid for lack of enablement simply because it reads on another embodiment of the invention that is inadequately disclosed. This is also the logical implication of having a separate best mode requirement that contemplates that the specification can enable one to make and use the invention generally and still be defective for failure to disclose a single preferred embodiment.[68] On the other hand, the scope of the claims must bear a reasonable correlation to the scope of enablement provided by the specification. This means that the disclosure must adequately guide the worker to determine, without undue experimentation, which species among

---

[63]*National Recovery Tech. Inc. v. Magnetic Sep. Sys. Inc.*, 166 F.3d 1190, 49 USPQ2d 1671 (Fed. Cir. 1999).

[64]*Fregeau v. Mossinghoff,* 776 F.2d 1034, 227 USPQ 848 (Fed. Cir. 1985). Thus, where the invention was directed to improving the flavor of liquids by subjecting them to a magnetic field, taste-test results were rejected as inadequate because they were scientifically unconvincing and covered only a few of the many liquids encompassed by the claims. *Id.*

[65]*Process Control Corp. v. HydReclaim Corp.,* 190 F.3d 1350, 52 USPQ2d 1029 (Fed. Cir. 1999).

[66]*Atlas Powder Co. v. E.I. du Pont & Co.,* 750 F.2d 1569, 224 USPQ 409 (Fed. Cir. 1984).

[67]*In re Hyatt,* 708 F.2d 712, 218 USPQ 195 (Fed. Cir. 1983).

[68]*Spectra-Physics, Inc. v. Coherent, Inc.,* 827 F.2d 1524, 3 USPQ2d 1737 (Fed. Cir. 1987).

all those encompassed by a claimed genus possess the disclosed utility.[69]

The mere fact that examples are prophetic does not automatically result in a nonenabling disclosure; likewise, the fact that examples do not result in optimal performance does not mean that they are failures, so as to render the specification nonenabling.[70]

§5.3   Best Mode

Compliance with the best mode requirement focuses on a different matter than does compliance with the enablement requirement. Enablement looks to placing the subject matter of the claims generally in the possession of the public. If, however, the applicant develops specific instrumentalities or techniques that are recognized at the time of filing as the best way of carrying out the invention, then the best mode requirement imposes an obligation to disclose that information to the public as well.[71] The best mode requirement is intended to ensure that a patent applicant plays fair and square with the patent system. It is a requirement that the quid pro quo of the patent grant be satisfied. One must not receive the right to exclude others unless at the time of filing one has provided an adequate disclosure of the best mode known to him or her of carrying out the invention.[72]

The best mode requirement is a subjective test in that the statute requires a disclosure only of that which the inventor, not someone else, contemplates as the best mode of carrying out the invention.[73] Not surprisingly then, best mode is a question of fact,[74] and the district court's decision is reviewable for clear error,[75] or in a jury case,

---

[69]*In re Vaeck*, 947 F.2d 488, 20 USPQ2d 1438 (Fed. Cir. 1991).

[70]*Atlas Powder Co. v. E.I. du Pont & Co.*, 750 F.2d 1569, 224 USPQ 409, 414 (Fed. Cir. 1984).

[71]*Spectra-Physics, Inc. v. Coherent, Inc.*, 827 F.2d 1524, 3 USPQ2d 1737 (Fed. Cir. 1987).

[72]*Amgen, Inc. v. Chugai Pharm. Co.*, 927 F.2d 1200, 18 USPQ2d 1016 (Fed. Cir. 1991). The best mode requirement creates a statutory, bargained-for exchange by which a patentee obtains the right to exclude others from practicing the claimed invention for a certain time period, and the public receives knowledge of the preferred embodiments for practicing the claimed invention. *Eli Lilly & Co. v. Barr Labs. Inc.*, 222 F.3d 973, 55 USPQ2d 1609 (Fed. Cir. 2000).

[73]35 U.S.C. §112. There is no duty for an inventor to disclose details of which he or she was not aware. *Gargoyles, Inc. v. United States*, 113 F.3d 1572, 42 USPQ2d 1760 (Fed. Cir. 1997).

[74]*Christianson v. Colt Indus. Oper. Corp.*, 822 F.2d 1544, 3 USPQ2d 1241 (Fed. Cir. 1987), *vacated on jurisdictional grounds and remanded*, 486 U.S. 800, 7 USPQ2d 1109 (1988); *DeGeorge v. Bernier*, 768 F.2d 1318, 226 USPQ 758 (Fed. Cir. 1985); *McGill Inc. v. John Zink Co.*, 736 F.2d 666, 221 USPQ 944 (Fed. Cir. 1984). In order to grant a motion for JNOV as to lack of best mode, it is necessary for the court to decide as a matter of law that, upon the evidence presented at trial, reasonable minds could not have found that the best mode requirement was satisfied. *Dana Corp. v. IPC Ltd.*, 860 F.2d 415, 8 USPQ2d 1692 (Fed. Cir. 1988).

[75]*Minco, Inc. v. Combustion Eng'g, Inc.*, 95 F.3d 1109, 40 USPQ2d 1001 (Fed. Cir. 1996); *Engel Indus., Inc. v. Lockformer Co.*, 946 F.2d 1528, 20 USPQ2d 1300 (Fed. Cir. 1991); *Northern Telecom, Inc. v. Datapoint Corp.*, 908 F.2d 931, 15 USPQ2d 1321 (Fed. Cir. 1990); *Diversitech*

substantial evidence,[76] but this assumes a proper legal understanding of the best mode requirement.[77] Thus, invalidity for failure of compliance with the best mode requirement, as a question of fact, requires proof by clear and convincing evidence that the inventor knew of and concealed a better mode of carrying out the invention than was set forth in the specification.[78] Compliance depends upon the applicant's state of mind,[79] and the issue turns on the evaluation of the testimony of witnesses as well as the technological significance of the structure, both of which are within the province of the fact finder.[80]

A proper best mode analysis has two components. The first is whether, at the time the inventor filed the patent application, he or she knew of a mode of practicing the claimed invention that he or she considered to be better than any other. This part of the inquiry is wholly subjective, and resolves whether the inventor must disclose any facts in addition to those sufficient for enablement. If the inventor in fact contemplated such a preferred mode, the second part of the analysis compares what he or she knew with what was disclosed: Is the disclosure adequate to enable one skilled in the art to practice the best mode or, contrariwise, has the inventor "concealed" his or her preferred mode from the "public"? Assessing the adequacy of this disclosure, as opposed to its necessity, is largely an objective inquiry that depends upon the scope of the claimed invention and the level of skill in the art. Notwithstanding the mixed nature of the best mode inquiry, and perhaps because of its routine focus upon its subjective component, the courts treat the question as a whole as factual.[81]

Corp. v. Century Steps, Inc., 850 F.2d 675, 7 USPQ2d 1315 (Fed. Cir. 1988); *Spectra-Physics, Inc. v. Coherent, Inc.,* 827 F.2d 1524, 3 USPQ2d 1737 (Fed. Cir. 1987).

[76]*Great Northern Corp. v. Henry Molded Prods., Inc.,* 94 F.3d 1569, 39 USPQ2d 1997 (Fed. Cir. 1996).

[77]*Spectra-Physics, Inc. v. Coherent, Inc.,* 827 F.2d 1524, 3 USPQ2d 1737 (Fed. Cir. 1987).

[78]*Transco Prods., Inc. v. Performance Contr., Inc.,* 38 F.3d 551, 32 USPQ2d 1077 (Fed. Cir. 1994); *Scripps Clinic & Res. Found. v. Genentech, Inc.,* 927 F.2d 1565, 18 USPQ2d 1001 (Fed. Cir. 1991). Failure of compliance must be proved by clear and convincing evidence. *Engel Indus., Inc. v. Lockformer Co.,* 946 F.2d 1528, 20 USPQ2d 1300 (Fed. Cir. 1991).

[79]*Spectra-Physics, Inc. v. Coherent, Inc.,* 827 F.2d 1524, 3 USPQ2d 1737 (Fed. Cir. 1987). Compliance with the best mode requirement focuses on the state of mind of the inventor at the time the application is filed. The inventor's intent controls. *Minco, Inc. v. Combustion Eng'g, Inc.,* 95 F.3d 1109, 40 USPQ2d 1001 (Fed. Cir. 1996).

[80]*Diversitech Corp. v. Century Steps, Inc.,* 850 F.2d 675, 7 USPQ2d 1315 (Fed. Cir. 1988).

[81]*Chemcast Corp. v. Arco Indus. Corp.,* 913 F.2d 923, 16 USPQ2d 1033 (Fed. Cir. 1990). See also *United States Gypsum Co. v. National Gypsum Co.,* 74 F.3d 1209, 37 USPQ2d 1388 (Fed. Cir. 1996); *In re Hayes Microcomputer Patent Litig.,* 982 F.2d 1527, 25 USPQ2d 1241 (Fed. Cir. 1992); *Amgen, Inc. v. Chugai Pharm. Co.,* 927 F.2d 1200, 18 USPQ2d 1016 (Fed. Cir. 1991). Because the first component of the best mode requirement—whether at the time of filing the application the inventor knew of a mode that he or she considered to be better than any other—focuses on the applicant's state of mind, a question of fact, the court reviews this aspect of a jury's verdict for substantial evidence. *Applied Med. Res. Corp. v. United States Surgical Corp.,* 147 F.3d 1374, 47 USPQ2d 1289 (Fed. Cir. 1998).

It is the best mode of carrying out the claimed invention that must be disclosed.[82] Each claim must be considered for compliance.[83]

Nonenablement is the failure to disclose any mode and does not depend on the applicant advocating a particular embodiment or method for making the invention. In practical terms, where only an alternative embodiment is enabled, the disclosure of the best mode may be inadequate. But that is a question separate and distinct from the question whether the specification enabled one to make the invention at all. The logical implication of a separate best mode requirement is that the specification can enable one to make and use the invention and nonetheless be defective because it fails to disclose the inventor's preferred embodiment.[84] The court apparently prefers to analyze failures to disclose "any mode" under the written description requirement rather than in terms of best mode.[85]

Failure to comply with the best mode requirement amounts to concealing the preferred mode contemplated by the applicant at the time of filing the application. There is no objective standard; instead, only evidence of concealment—actual or intentional—is to be considered. In order to result in affirmance of a best mode rejection or to sustain a defense based on failure to satisfy the best mode requirement, the evidence must tend to show that the quality of the best mode disclosure is so poor as to effectively result in concealment.[86]

---

[82]*Randomex, Inc. v. Scopus Corp.*, 849 F.2d 585, 7 USPQ2d 1050 (Fed. Cir. 1988); *Christianson v. Colt Indus. Oper. Corp.*, 822 F.2d 1544, 3 USPQ2d 1241 (Fed. Cir. 1987), *vacated on jurisdictional grounds and remanded*, 486 U.S. 800, 7 USPQ2d 1109 (1988); *DeGeorge v. Bernier*, 768 F.2d 1318, 226 USPQ 758 (Fed. Cir. 1985). Compare *Northern Telecom, Inc. v. Datapoint Corp.*, 908 F.2d 931, 15 USPQ2d 1321 (Fed. Cir. 1990), where an objective of the invention was to capture data on ordinary audio tape. The patentee knew prior to filing that such tape was not the best and purchased different tape of its own design and specification. Such tape should have been disclosed in order to satisfy the best mode requirement. This can be contrasted with *Northern Telecom Ltd. v. Samsung Elec. Co.*, 215 F.3d 1281, 55 USPQ2d 1065 (Fed. Cir. 2000), where the claim was for a process of gaseous etching. The preferred use of the process was for fine line etching, but that was not a claim limitation. There was no disclosure of the best mode of achieving fine line etching, but the court held that was unnecessary, in view of the breadth of the claim.

[83]*Engel Indus., Inc. v. Lockformer Co.*, 946 F.2d 1528, 20 USPQ2d 1300 (Fed. Cir. 1991). Absent inequitable conduct, a best mode defense affects only those claims covering subject matter, the practice of which has not been disclosed in compliance with the best mode requirement. *Amgen, Inc. v. Chugai Pharm. Co.*, 927 F.2d 1200, 18 USPQ2d 1016 (Fed. Cir. 1991).

[84]*Spectra-Physics, Inc. v. Coherent, Inc.*, 827 F.2d 1524, 3 USPQ2d 1737 (Fed. Cir. 1987). A specification can be enabling and yet fail to disclose the best mode. Indeed, most of the cases in which the court has found the best mode requirement unfulfilled addressed situations where the inventor failed to disclose unclaimed elements that were nevertheless necessary to practice the best mode of carrying out the claimed invention. *Chemcast Corp. v. Arco Indus. Corp.*, 913 F.2d 923, 16 USPQ2d 1033 (Fed. Cir. 1990).

[85]*Bigham v. Godtfredsen*, 857 F.2d 1415, 8 USPQ2d 1266, 1269 (Fed. Cir. 1988).

[86]*Randomex, Inc. v. Scopus Corp.*, 849 F.2d 585, 7 USPQ2d 1050 (Fed. Cir. 1988); *Spectra-Physics, Inc. v. Coherent, Inc.*, 827 F.2d 1524, 3 USPQ2d 1737 (Fed. Cir. 1987); *DeGeorge v. Bernier*, 768 F.2d 1318, 226 USPQ 758 (Fed. Cir. 1985). It must be shown that the applicant knew of and concealed a better mode than he or she disclosed. *Hybritech Inc. v. Monoclonal Antibodies, Inc.*, 802 F.2d 1367, 231 USPQ 81 (Fed. Cir. 1986). But it is not required that specific intent to conceal be shown. Inasmuch as the inquiry as to adequacy of the disclosure of the best mode is objective, it is clear that a disclosure can be so objectively inadequate as

Intentional concealment of the best mode and disclosure of an inoperable mode instead constitutes inequitable conduct that renders the patent unenforceable.[87]

The purpose of the best mode requirement is to restrain inventors from applying for patents while at the same time concealing from the public preferred embodiments of their inventions. Accordingly, compliance exists when an inventor discloses his or her preferred embodiment.[88] The disclosure of that preferred embodiment need be no more extensive or complete than that required to satisfy the enabling requirement; otherwise, patent disclosures would turn into production specifications, which they were never intended to be.[89] As a general rule, where software constitutes part of a best mode of carrying out an invention, description of such a best mode is satisfied by a disclosure of the functions of the software. This is because, normally, writing code for such software is within the skill of the art, not requiring undue experimentation, once its functions have been disclosed.[90]

The best mode requirement assures that inventors do not conceal the best mode known to them when they file a patent application, but the "best mode" is that of practicing the claimed invention. It has nothing to do with mass production or with sales to customers having particular requirements.[91] The extent of information that an inventor must disclose depends on the scope of the claimed invention. Accordingly, an inventor need not disclose a mode for obtaining unclaimed

---

to effectively conceal the best mode, and that is sufficient. *United States Gypsum Co. v. National Gypsum Co.,* 74 F.3d 1209, 37 USPQ2d 1388 (Fed. Cir. 1996). If an inventor appreciates a best mode for carrying out the invention, invalidity may result from failure to disclose it, regardless of whether the inventor specifically intended to conceal it. *Minco, Inc. v. Combustion Eng'g, Inc.,* 95 F.3d 1109, 40 USPQ2d 1001 (Fed. Cir. 1996).

[87] *Consolidated Alum Corp. v. Foseco Int'l Ltd.,* 910 F.2d 804, 15 USPQ2d 1481 (Fed. Cir. 1990). Of course, a failure to disclose the best mode does not automatically equate with inequitable conduct; intent must be shown. *In re Hayes Microcomputer Patent Litig.,* 982 F.2d 1527, 25 USPQ2d 1241 (Fed. Cir. 1992). While in appropriate circumstances a failure to disclose the best mode may be so egregious as to constitute inequitable conduct, specific intent to deceive is not a required element of a best mode defense. *Graco, Inc. v. Binks Mfg. Co.,* 60 F.3d 785, 35 USPQ2d 1255 (Fed. Cir. 1995).

[88] *Dana Corp. v. IPC Ltd.,* 860 F.2d 415, 8 USPQ2d 1692 (Fed. Cir. 1988); *DeGeorge v. Bernier,* 768 F.2d 1318, 226 USPQ 758 (Fed. Cir. 1985). See also *Transco Prods., Inc. v. Performance Contr., Inc.,* 38 F.3d 551, 32 USPQ2d 1077 (Fed. Cir. 1994).

[89] *In re Gay,* 309 F.2d 769, 135 USPQ 311 (CCPA 1962). A patent disclosure is not a production specification, and technical details apparent to a person of ordinary skill need not be included in the specification. *Engel Indus., Inc. v. Lockformer Co.,* 946 F.2d 1528, 20 USPQ2d 1300 (Fed. Cir. 1991).

[90] *Fonar Corp. v. General Elec. Co.,* 107 F.3d 1543, 41 USPQ2d 1801 (Fed. Cir. 1997). This same reasoning would seem to apply to many semiconductor chips.

[91] *Christianson v. Colt Indus. Oper. Corp.,* 822 F.2d 1544, 3 USPQ2d 1241 (Fed. Cir. 1987). This case was vacated on jurisdictional grounds by the Supreme Court and remanded for retransfer to the Seventh Circuit. *Christianson v. Colt Indus. Oper. Corp.,* 486 U.S. 800, 7 USPQ2d 1109 (1988). For the similar views of the Seventh Circuit on the merits, see *Christianson v. Colt Indus. Oper. Corp.,* 870 F.2d 1292, 10 USPQ2d 1352 (7th Cir. 1989). Unclaimed subject matter is not subject to the disclosure requirements of §112. The reasons are pragmatic: the disclosure would be boundless and the pitfalls endless. *Engel Indus., Inc. v. Lockformer Co.,* 946 F.2d 1528, 20 USPQ2d 1300 (Fed. Cir. 1991).

subject matter unless the subject matter is novel and essential for carrying out the best mode of the invention. To be sure, if the best mode for carrying out a claimed invention involves novel subject matter, then an inventor must disclose a method for obtaining that subject matter even if it is unclaimed. But the best mode requirement does not extend to production details or routine details. Production details, which do not concern the quality or nature of the claimed invention, relate to commercial and manufacturing considerations such as equipment on hand, certain available materials, prior relationships with suppliers, expected volume of production, and costs. Routine details, on the other hand, implicate the quality and nature of invention, but their disclosure is unnecessary because they are readily apparent to one of ordinary skill in the art.[92]

So an inventor need not disclose manufacturing data or the requirements of a particular customer if that information is not part of the best mode of practicing the claimed invention. But the converse is also true. Whether characterizable as manufacturing data, customer requirements, or even trade secrets, information necessary to practice the best mode simply must be disclosed.[93] An applicant is obliged to disclose nonclaimed elements necessary to the operation or carrying out of the invention to which the patent is directed. However, where the invention relates only to a part of, or one aspect of, a device, an applicant is not required to disclose a nonclaimed element necessary to the operation of the overall device, but not necessary to the operation of the invention to which the patent is directed.[94]

A description of particular materials or sources or of a particular method or technique selected for manufacture may or may not be required as part of a best mode disclosure respecting a device. Thus, the particulars of making a prototype or even a commercial embodiment do not necessarily equate with the best mode of carrying out an invention. The inventor's manufacturing materials or sources or techniques used to make a device may vary from wholly irrelevant to critical. There is no mechanical rule that a best mode violation occurs because the inventor failed to disclose particular manufacturing procedures beyond the information sufficient for enablement. One

---

[92]*Eli Lilly & Co. v. Barr Labs. Inc.,* 222 F.3d 973, 55 USPQ2d 1609 (Fed. Cir. 2000). The court uses the term "production details" in two senses. First it is used to refer to commercial considerations such as the equipment on hand, or prior relationships with suppliers that were satisfactory. Such commercial considerations do not constitute a best mode of practicing the claimed invention because they do not relate to the quality or nature of the invention. The term is also used to refer to details that do relate to the quality or nature of the invention but need not be disclosed because they are routine—i.e., details of production about which those of ordinary skill in the art would already know. In this context, the omitted detail constitutes a best mode but the disclosure is deemed adequate because the detail is routine. *Young Dental Mfg. Co. v. Q3 Special Prods., Inc.,* 112 F.3d 1137, 42 USPQ2d 1589 (Fed. Cir. 1997); *Great Northern Corp. v. Henry Molded Prods., Inc.,* 94 F.3d 1569, 39 USPQ2d 1997 (Fed. Cir. 1996).

[93]*Chemcast Corp. v. Arco Indus. Corp.,* 913 F.2d 923, 16 USPQ2d 1033 (Fed. Cir. 1990).

[94]*Applied Med. Res. Corp. v. United States Surgical Corp.,* 147 F.3d 1374, 47 USPQ2d 1289 (Fed. Cir. 1998).

must look at the scope of the invention, the skill of the art, the evidence as to the inventor's belief, and all of the circumstances in order to evaluate whether the inventor's failure to disclose particulars of manufacture gives rise to an inference that he or she concealed information that one of ordinary skill in the art would not know.[95] An inventor's manufacturing materials or sources or techniques used to make a device may vary from wholly irrelevant to critical.[96] Sometimes a step or material or source or technique considered "best" in a manufacturing circumstance may have been selected for a reason that has nothing to do with the statutory "best mode," such as that the manufacturing equipment was on hand, certain materials were available, prior relations with the supplier were satisfactory, or other reasons having nothing to do with development of the invention.[97]

There is no objective standard by which to judge the adequacy of a best mode disclosure. Instead, only evidence of concealment, whether accidental or intentional, is considered. The specificity of disclosure required to comply with the best mode requirement must be determined by the knowledge of facts within the possession of the inventor at the time of filing the application.[98] However, statements

---

[95]*Wahl Instr., Inc. v. Acvious, Inc.,* 950 F.2d 1575, 21 USPQ2d 1123 (Fed. Cir. 1991). Disclosure concerning the best mode of practicing an invention must be distinguished for best mode purposes from disclosure for optimum commercial production. The former is required; the latter is not. *United States Gypsum Co. v. National Gypsum Co.,* 74 F.3d 1209, 37 USPQ2d 1388 (Fed. Cir. 1996). The failure to disclose the commercial mode does not ipso facto result in a §112 violation. The focus is not what a particular user decides to make and sell or even in what field the invention is most likely to find success. Rather, the parameters of a §112 inquiry are set by the claims. *Zygo Corp. v. Wyko Corp.,* 79 F.3d 1563, 38 USPQ2d 1281 (Fed. Cir. 1996). Even where there is a general reference to the best mode of practicing the claimed invention, the quality of the disclosure may be so poor as to effectively conceal it. However, the best mode requirement does not require an inventor to disclose production details so long as the means to carry out the invention are disclosed. Such details include supplier or trade name information where it is not needed or would be mere surplusage. Such information must be provided only when a skilled artisan could not practice the best mode of the claimed invention absent the information. *Transco Prods., Inc. v. Performance Contr., Inc.,* 38 F.3d 551, 32 USPQ2d 1077 (Fed. Cir. 1994).

[96]*Transco Prods., Inc. v. Performance Contr., Inc.,* 38 F.3d 551, 32 USPQ2d 1077 (Fed. Cir. 1994).

[97]*Wahl Instr., Inc. v. Acvious, Inc.,* 950 F.2d 1575, 21 USPQ2d 1123 (Fed. Cir. 1991). This case is a good example of just how fact-specific the best mode inquiry can be. The inventor had described in detail two alternative methods of making the claimed item, but not a third, which turned out to be the one he ultimately settled on for a commercial product. If the specification had simply indicated that "any suitable or desirable means of incorporating a layer of temperature indicating material within a plastic body" could be employed, that probably would have been sufficient for enablement and best mode as to the plastic body. But by going further, the specification became more vulnerable to a best mode attack. The court was, not surprisingly, troubled by this result and thus reversed a summary judgment of failure to disclose the best mode. One factor supporting the decision was that the inventor had filed his application after a commercial device had been made; had it been otherwise, there would have been no best mode defense. Also, although the person of skill in the art was one versed in temperature-indicating devices, the manufacturer would have been one versed in plastics fabrication. The "best" technique might not have been apparent to the former, but would certainly have been apparent to the latter. Perhaps the teaching of this case is that best mode may be satisfied if one of ordinary skill in the art who wishes to have a device made would achieve the best mode by taking it to an experienced fabricator of such devices.

[98]*Dana Corp. v. IPC Ltd.,* 860 F.2d 415, 8 USPQ2d 1692 (Fed. Cir. 1988); *Spectra-Physics, Inc. v. Coherent, Inc.,* 827 F.2d 1524, 3 USPQ2d 1737 (Fed. Cir. 1987). Compliance with the

about the lack of an objective standard should not be taken too literally. The best mode inquiry focuses on the inventor's state of mind as of the time the application was filed—a subjective, factual question.[99] But this focus is not exclusive. Both the level of skill in the art and the scope of the claimed invention are additional, objective metes and bounds of a best mode disclosure. Of necessity, the disclosure required by §112 is directed to those skilled in the art. Therefore one must consider the level of skill in the relevant art in determining whether a specification discloses the best mode. Whether a best mode disclosure is adequate, that is, whether the inventor concealed a better mode than was disclosed, is a function of not only what the inventor knew but also how one skilled in the art would have understood the disclosure. The other objective limitation on the extent of the disclosure necessary to comply with the best mode requirement is, of course, the scope of the claimed invention. It is concealment of the best mode of practicing the claimed invention that §112 is designed to prohibit.[100]

It is not up to the courts to decide how an inventor should disclose the best mode, but whether he or she has done so adequately.[101] What is required is an adequate disclosure of the best mode, not a guarantee that every aspect of the specification be precisely and universally reproducible.[102] The best mode requirement is directed to persons of ordinary skill in the art at the time the application is filed.[103] But the best mode requirement is not satisfied by reference to the level of skill in the art; rather, it entails a comparison of the disclosure in the specification with facts known to the inventor regarding the invention at the time the application was filed. Section 112 states explicitly that disclosure must be made of the best mode "contemplated by the

---

best mode requirement is governed by the inventor's state of mind with respect to the invention that is described and claimed in the patent application, at the time of filing. *Engel Indus., Inc. v. Lockformer Co.*, 946 F.2d 1528, 20 USPQ2d 1300 (Fed. Cir. 1991).

[99]*In re Hayes Microcomputer Patent Litig.*, 982 F.2d 1527, 25 USPQ2d 1241 (Fed. Cir. 1992), provides a good example. It appeared that the inventor believed that the best mode of his invention was to store a program as firmware, but not that he believed that the various details of the specific firmware listing actually used in his commercial product constituted the best mode. Thus, the fact that his patent only disclosed the general function of the firmware, without teaching mathematical formulas, flow charts, or a firmware program listing, did not violate the best mode requirement.

[100]*Chemcast Corp. v. Arco Indus. Corp.*, 913 F.2d 923, 16 USPQ2d 1033 (Fed. Cir. 1990).

[101]*Spectra-Physics, Inc. v. Coherent, Inc.*, 827 F.2d 1524, 3 USPQ 2d 1737 (Fed. Cir. 1987). But there is no per se requirement to provide names for sources of materials absent evidence that the name of the source would not be known or easily available. *Wahl Instr., Inc. v. Acvious, Inc.*, 950 F.2d 1575, 21 USPQ2d 1123 (Fed. Cir. 1991). A deposit of microorganisms may satisfy the best mode requirement. *In re Wands*, 858 F.2d 731, 8 USPQ2d 1400 (Fed. Cir. 1988).

[102]*Amgen, Inc. v. Chugai Pharm. Co.*, 927 F.2d 1200, 18 USPQ2d 1016 (Fed. Cir. 1991).

[103]*Randomex, Inc. v. Scopus Corp.*, 849 F.2d 585, 7 USPQ2d 1050 (Fed. Cir. 1988). Where the inventor discloses the best mode indiscriminately with other possible embodiments, the best mode requirement is nonetheless satisfied if one of ordinary skill in the art could readily determine which was best. *Id.* One wonders whether the result would be the same in the face of evidence that the best mode was buried in a jumble of other embodiments deliberately, for the purpose of obscuring the fact that it was preferred.

inventor." It is therefore incorrect to argue that the requirement may be met solely by reference to what was known in the prior art.[104] Certainly a patentee cannot cure its failure to disclose the best mode of practicing the invention at the time the application was filed by later selling a commercial product embodying the invention. Compliance with §112 cannot depend on whether a patentee later commercializes the invention. Moreover, those skilled in the art should not have to reverse engineer the commercial product; the specification of the patent should inform them of the best mode.[105]

In attempting to clarify the best mode requirement, the court in a dictum proposed this example: if one should invent an internal combustion engine, the best mode requirement would require him or her to divulge the fuel on which it would run best, but would not require him or her to disclose the formula for the fuel. Every requirement would be met if the patentee said that his or her engine ran smoothly and powerfully on Brand X fuel or equal. Making engines and making fuel are different arts.[106]

The best mode known to the inventor, and required to be disclosed, need not necessarily have been developed by the inventor himself or herself. It often happens that coworkers make improvements jointly with or independently of the inventor. Such improvements, if they are known to the inventor at the time of filing and otherwise constitute the best mode, must be disclosed.[107] A sharply divided panel of the court has held, unequivocally, that an assignee corporation's knowledge cannot be imputed to its employee, the inventor, for purposes of evaluating compliance with the best mode requirement.[108]

---

[104]*Dana Corp. v. IPC Ltd.*, 860 F.2d 415, 8 USPQ2d 1692 (Fed. Cir. 1988). The patent was for a valve stem seal. The inventor knew, before filing, that no seal design was acceptable using untreated rubber, that surface treatment was necessary to satisfactory performance of the seal, and that two designs were quite acceptable with fluoride surface treatment. Also, the seals first sold by the patentee were fluoride treated. No reference to fluoride treatment was made in the specification, although other surface treatments were set out as useful in some instances. Despite the fact that fluoride treatment of rubber was well known in the art, the court held that JNOV should have been granted on best mode grounds and reversed, holding the patent invalid.

[105]*United States Gypsum Co. v. National Gypsum Co.*, 74 F.3d 1209, 37 USPQ2d 1388 (Fed. Cir. 1996).

[106]*Randomex, Inc. v. Scopus Corp.*, 849 F.2d 585, 7 USPQ2d 1050 (Fed. Cir. 1988). This was a divided court.

[107]*Aktiebolaget Karlstads v. United States ITC*, 705 F.2d 1565, 217 USPQ 865 (Fed. Cir. 1983). However, such disclosures are not prior art against a later filed application claiming the improvement, unless the timing of the disclosure constitutes a one-year statutory bar against the second application under 35 U.S.C. §102(b). *In re Kaplan,* 789 F.2d 1574, 229 USPQ 678 (Fed. Cir. 1986). The best mode need not be developed by the patent applicant. It may be the commercial product of a third party, or even another's trade secret. The best mode can be, but does not need to be, claimed in the application; it merely needs to be disclosed. That the inventor, or a coinventor, may be entitled to a patent on the improvement does not negate the requirement of disclosure of the improvement, assuming an inventor contemplated the improvement as the best mode for his or her invention. *Graco, Inc. v. Binks Mfg. Co.,* 60 F.3d 785, 35 USPQ2d 1255 (Fed. Cir. 1995).

[108]*Glaxo, Inc. v. Novopharm Ltd.*, 52 F.3d 1043, 1053, 34 USPQ2d 1565 (Fed. Cir. 1995). Employees of the corporation working in other departments knew of a better mode, but did

The patentee is required to disclose what he or she knows. Thus, the fact that a formulation that is part of the best mode is a trade secret and is offered by the supplier on an exclusive basis only to the patentee does not excuse a failure to disclose at least the supplier's designation. Whatever the scope of the supplier's trade secret, to the extent it includes information known by the inventor that she or he considers part of her or his preferred mode, such information must be divulged. Moreover, whether and to whom the supplier chooses to sell its products cannot control the extent to which the inventor must disclose the best mode. Were it otherwise, inventors could readily circumvent the best mode requirement by concluding exclusive agreements with the suppliers of their preferred materials.[109]

The law does not require the impossible and hence does not require than an applicant describe in the specification every conceivable and possible future embodiment of the invention. The law requires that the inventor describe only the best mode known to him or her at the time of filing the application.[110] The court has now squarely held that the date for evaluating a best mode disclosure in a continuation application is the date of the earlier application as to common subject matter. In other words, there is no duty to update the disclosure of the continuation with respect to best mode information. This is said to be in keeping with district court holdings that the date for determining compliance with the best mode requirement for a reissue application is the filing date of the original and not that of the reissue and, for a U.S. application based upon a foreign application, the filing date of the foreign application.[111]

---

not disclose it to the inventor. Indeed, the in-house patent attorney knew of the better mode and expressed concern about the best mode disclosure. Nonetheless, a deliberate decision was made to keep the best mode a trade secret. The majority opinion goes so far as to state that no disclosure of that better mode was required even if it turned out that the corporation had deliberately screened the inventor from knowledge of it; the best mode requirement focuses solely upon what the inventor knows and nothing else. This reasoning provoked a sharp dissent from Judge Mayer, who accused the majority of blessing "corporate shell games resulting from organizational gerrymandering and willful ignorance by which one can secure the monopoly of a patent while hiding the best mode of practicing the invention the law expects to be made public in return for its protection." In attempting to dispel the force of the dissent, the majority held that a patent attorney does not enter into an agency relationship with the inventor for purposes of what is disclosed in the inventor's patent application, even though an agency relationship may exist where the attorney is prosecuting the application. No law was cited, only the ad hominem that an attorney's authority "does not include inventing." In the experience of this author, patent attorneys do a great deal of inventing. It would not be entirely surprising to see the court revisit this issue in the future.

[109]*Chemcast Corp. v. Arco Indus. Corp.*, 913 F.2d 923, 16 USPQ2d 1033 (Fed. Cir. 1990).

[110]*SRI Int'l v. Matsushita Elec. Corp.*, 775 F.2d 1107, 227 USPQ 577 (Fed. Cir. 1985). See also *Texas Instr., Inc. v. United States ITC*, 805 F.2d 1558, 231 USPQ 833 (Fed. Cir. 1986). See the discussion of later-discovered information at note 6:12.

[111]*Transco Prods., Inc. v. Performance Contr., Inc.*, 38 F.3d 551, 32 USPQ2d 1077 (Fed. Cir. 1994). In a concurring opinion in *Applied Mtls, Inc. v. Advanced Semi. Mtls, Inc.*, 98 F.3d 1563, 40 USPQ2d 1481, 1493 (Fed. Cir. 1996), the view was expressed that inventors must update the best mode disclosure when filing a CIP that added new matter pertinent to the best mode of practicing the invention claimed in the CIP.

In the case of a design, the best mode requirement is not applicable, as a design has only one "mode" and it can be described only by illustrations showing what it looks like.[112]

§5.4 Adequacy of Claims

It is elementary that the property right bestowed by a patent is measured, in the first instance, by the claims.[113] The term "claims" has been used in patent legislation since the Patent Act of 1836 to define the invention that an applicant believes is patentable. Since that time, the term has represented that portion of the specification that defines the patent owner's property rights in the invention.[114] The function of claims is twofold: to point out what the invention is in such a way as to distinguish it from the prior art; and to define the scope of protection afforded by the patent. In both of those aspects, claims are not technical descriptions of the disclosed inventions but are legal documents, like the descriptions of lands by metes and bounds in a deed, which define the area conveyed but do not describe the land.[115] A claim in a patent provides the metes and bounds of the right that the patent confers on the patentee to exclude others from making, using, or selling the protected invention. The language of a claim describes and points out the invention by a series of limiting words or phrases; these are the "limitations."[116] It is the claim, not the specification, that distinguishes what infringes from what does not.[117] That a claim may be broader than the specific embodiment disclosed in the specification is itself of no moment.[118]

It is axiomatic that the claims define the invention that an applicant believes is patentable.[119] In keeping with the importance of this role, the second paragraph of §112 requires the claims to particularly point out and distinctly claim the subject matter that the patent applicant regards as his or her invention. "Distinctly" means simply that the claim must have a clear and definite meaning when construed in the light of the complete patent document.[120] The requirement of distinctness in claiming guards against unreasonable advantages to

---

[112]*Racing Strollers, Inc. v. TRI Indus., Inc.*, 878 F.2d 1418, 11 USPQ2d 1300 (Fed. Cir. 1989).

[113]*A.B. Dick Co. v. Burroughs Corp.*, 713 F.2d 700, 218 USPQ 965 (Fed. Cir. 1983).

[114]*Hoechst-Roussel Pharm., Inc. v. Lehman*, 109 F.3d 756, 42 USPQ2d 1220 (Fed. Cir. 1997).

[115]*In re Vamco Mach., Inc.*, 752 F.2d 1564, 224 USPQ 617 (Fed. Cir. 1985).

[116]*Corning Glass Works v. Sumitomo Elec. U.S.A., Inc.*, 868 F.2d 1251, 9 USPQ2d 1962 (Fed. Cir. 1989).

[117]*W.L. Gore & Assoc. v. Garlock, Inc.*, 721 F.2d 1540, 220 USPQ 303 (Fed. Cir. 1983).

[118]*Ralston Purina Co. v. Far-Mar-Co, Inc.*, 772 F.2d 1570, 227 USPQ 177 (Fed. Cir. 1985).

[119]*In re Van Geuns*, 988 F.2d 1181, 26 USPQ2d 1057 (Fed. Cir. 1993).

[120]*Miles Labs., Inc. v. Shandon, Inc.*, 997 F.2d 870, 27 USPQ2d 1123 (Fed. Cir. 1993); *Standard Oil Co. v. American Cyanamid Co.*, 774 F.2d 448, 227 USPQ 293 (Fed. Cir. 1985).

the patentee and disadvantages to others arising from uncertainty as to their respective rights.[121] Whether a claim is invalid for indefiniteness depends on whether those skilled in the art would understand what is claimed,[122] or the scope[123] or bounds[124] of the claim, when it is read in light of the specification.

An essential purpose of patent examination is to fashion claims that are precise, clear, correct, and unambiguous. Only in this way can uncertainties of claim scope be removed, as much as possible, during the administrative process. Thus the inquiry during examination is patentability of the invention as the applicant regards it; and if the claims do not particularly point out and distinctly claim, in the words of §112, that which examination shows the applicant is entitled to claim as his or her invention, the appropriate PTO action is to reject the claims for that reason.[125] The second paragraph of §112 puts the burden of precise claim drafting squarely on the applicant.[126]

The matter of claim adequacy or "definiteness"—compliance with the second paragraph of §112—is generally said to be a question of law.[127] Nonetheless, the test for adequacy is whether one skilled in the art would understand all the language in the claims when they are read in light of the specification, as they must be.[128] Despite having said that ambiguity, undue breadth, vagueness, and triviality are

---

[121]*Athletic Alternatives, Inc. v. Prince Mfg., Inc.*, 73 F.3d 1573, 37 USPQ2d 1365 (Fed. Cir. 1996).

[122]*Morton Int'l, Inc. v. Cardinal Chem. Co.*, 5 F.3d 1464, 28 USPQ2d 1190 (Fed. Cir. 1993). The claimed compounds could not be identified by testing and thus a potential infringer could not determine whether it was infringing. The claims were therefore held indefinite.

[123]*In re Warmerdam*, 33 F.3d 1354, 31 USPQ2d 1754 (Fed. Cir. 1994); *North Am. Vaccine, Inc. v. American Cyanamid Co.*, 7 F.3d 1571, 28 USPQ2d 1333 (Fed. Cir. 1993).

[124]*Credle v. Bond*, 25 F.3d 1566, 30 USPQ2d 1911 (Fed. Cir. 1994). If the claims so read reasonably apprise such a person of the scope of the invention, §112 demands no more. *Miles Labs., Inc. v. Shandon, Inc.*, 997 F.2d 870, 27 USPQ2d 1123 (Fed. Cir. 1993).

[125]*In re Zletz*, 893 F.2d 319, 13 USPQ2d 1320 (Fed. Cir. 1989).

[126]*In re Morris*, 127 F.3d 1048, 44 USPQ2d 1023 (Fed. Cir. 1997).

[127]*Orthokinetics, Inc. v. Safety Travel Chairs, Inc.*, 806 F.2d 1565, 1 USPQ2d 1081 (Fed. Cir. 1986); *Shatterproof Glass Corp. v. Libbey-Owens Ford Co.*, 758 F.2d 613, 225 USPQ 634 (Fed. Cir. 1985). Compliance with the definiteness requirement is a question of law that is reviewed de novo. *Credle v. Bond*, 25 F.3d 1566, 30 USPQ2d 1911 (Fed. Cir. 1994); *North Am. Vaccine, Inc. v. American Cyanamid Co.*, 7 F.3d 1571, 28 USPQ2d 1333 (Fed. Cir. 1993). The ultimate conclusion of indefiniteness is one of law which the Federal Circuit is free to review anew on appeal. *In re Warmerdam*, 33 F.3d 1354, 31 USPQ2d 1754 (Fed. Cir. 1994). In a jury case, the questions are whether the jury's express or implied findings of fact are supported by substantial evidence, and whether those findings supported the conclusion of indefiniteness. *Beachcombers v. Wildewood Creative Prods., Inc.*, 31 F.3d 1154, 31 USPQ2d 1653 (Fed. Cir. 1994).

[128]*Orthokinetics, Inc. v. Safety Travel Chairs, Inc.*, 806 F.2d 1565, 1 USPQ2d 1081 (Fed. Cir. 1986); *Rosemount, Inc. v. Beckman Instruments, Inc.*, 727 F.2d 1540, 221 USPQ 1 (Fed. Cir. 1984). Reference to the testimony of witnesses who expressed difficulty in comprehending the claim language at issue has been held insufficient to sustain a contention of claim indefiniteness. *Allen Archery, Inc. v. Browning Mfg. Co.*, 819 F.2d 1087, 2 USPQ2d 1490 (Fed. Cir. 1987). Where an applicant expressly states, throughout the application and claims, that the invention includes a particular limitation, it would be contrary to the definiteness requirement to permit the applicant to avoid that limitation in a later infringement suit. *Unique Concepts, Inc. v. Brown*, 939 F.2d 1558, 19 USPQ2d 1500 (Fed. Cir. 1991).

matters that go to claim validity for failure to comply with the second paragraph of §112, not to interpretation or construction,[129] the Federal Circuit has now come to the view that resolution of claim definiteness issues is part of the court's performance of its duty as construer of patent claims. Accordingly, extrinsic evidence is irrelevant to the issue of indefiniteness where the meaning of the term in question is unambiguously set forth in the specification.[130]

For a claim to comply with §112¶2, it must satisfy two requirements: first, it must set forth what "the applicant regards as his invention," and second, it must do so with sufficient particularity and distinctness. During the prosecution of a patent application, a claim's compliance with both portions of §112¶2, may be analyzed by consideration of evidence beyond the patent specification, including an inventor's statements to the PTO. It is not inappropriate for the PTO or a reviewing tribunal to consider such evidence extrinsic to the patent application in light of the goals of the examination process and the fact that pending claims can be freely amended to comport with those goals. On the other hand, when a court analyzes whether issued claims comply with §112¶2, the evidence considered in that analysis should be more limited. As for the "definiteness" portion of §112¶2, it is well settled that a court will typically limit its inquiry to the way one of skill in the art would interpret the claims in view of the written description portion of the specification. There is no reason for a different standard to be applied to the question of whether a claim complies with the portion of the statute that requires the claim to set forth that which the inventor regards as his or her invention. A more limited range of evidence should be considered in evaluating validity as opposed to patentability under either portion of §112¶2, because the language of issued claims is generally fixed (subject to the limited possibilities of reissue and reexamination), the claims are no longer construed as broadly as is reasonably possible, and what the patentee subjectively intended the claims to mean is largely irrelevant to the claim's objective meaning and scope. The inquiry under §112¶2 focuses on whether the claims, as interpreted in view of the written description, adequately perform their function of notifying the public of the patentee's right to exclude. It is particularly inappropriate to consider inventor testimony obtained in the context of litigation in assessing validity under §112¶2 in view of the absence of probative value of such testimony. Although that "which the applicant regards as his invention" is subjective language, once the patent

---

[129]*Intervet Am., Inc. v. Kee-Vet Labs., Inc.,* 887 F.2d 1050, 12 USPQ2d 1474 (Fed. Cir. 1989). The requirements of §112 governing the written description and claim definiteness have as their purpose the avoidance of the kind of ambiguity that requires extrinsic evidence to resolve. If a patent's claims are sufficiently unambiguous for the PTO, there should exist no factual ambiguity when those claims are later construed by a court of law in an infringement action. *Markman v. Westview Instr., Inc.,* 52 F.3d 967, 34 USPQ2d 1321 (Fed. Cir. 1995).

[130]*Personalized Media Comm. LLC v. United States ITC,* 161 F.3d 696, 48 USPQ2d 1880, 1888 (Fed. Cir. 1998).

issues, the claims and written description must be viewed objectively, from the standpoint of a person of skill in the art.[131]

The amount of detail required to be included depends upon the particular invention and the prior art and is not to be viewed in the abstract but in conjunction with whether the specification is in compliance with the first paragraph of §112. If the claims, read with the specification, reasonably apprise those skilled in the art of both the utilization and the scope of the invention, and if the language is as precise as the subject matter permits, the courts can demand no more.[132] While a claim must be read in accordance with the precepts of English grammar,[133] the patentee is not limited by the dictionary and may be his or her own lexicographer.[134] Of course, the patentee's definition of a word or phrase, to the extent it differs from the conventional definition, must be clearly set forth in the specification.[135]

The law imposes no obligation on a patent applicant to determine what is going on in the technological gap between the claimed invention and the prior art, or to set the claim limits at the precise technological edge of the invention. A claim is not fatally indefinite for failing specifically to delineate the point at which the change in physical phenomenon occurs. A contrary rule would prevent a patentee from obtaining claims that do not coincide with, or claim less than, the exact point at which a change in the physical phenomenon occurs; it would require the patentee always to discover that point, no matter how prolonged or expensive the additional research; and it would bar patent protection when the change is by nature gradual or incremental at its transition, whether or not unobvious in view of the prior art.[136]

Experience and precedent have shown that questions of definiteness will be decided on a case-by-case basis, and that any effort to generalize a set of rules is futile. The Federal Circuit has just begun its work in this area, but it has a tremendous reservoir of CCPA precedent to draw upon.[137] It is important to keep separate the concepts of inadequate disclosure and indefiniteness of claims. A fatally vague claim does not by any means render the specification nonenabling.[138] Likewise, definiteness should not be confused with the operability requirement. The invention's operability may say nothing

---

[131]*Solomon v. Kimberly-Clark Corp.*, 216 F.3d 1372, 55 USPQ2d 1279 (Fed. Cir. 2000). The court did recognize that the determination of the perspective of one of skill in the art may involve reference to evidence extrinsic to the patent, such as prior art and witness testimony. 55 USPQ2d at 1282 n.4.

[132]*Miles Labs., Inc. v. Shandon, Inc.*, 997 F.2d 870, 27 USPQ2d 1123 (Fed. Cir. 1993); *Hybritech Inc. v. Monoclonal Antibodies, Inc.*, 802 F.2d 1367, 231 USPQ 81 (Fed. Cir. 1986); *Shatterproof Glass Corp. v. Libbey-Owens Ford Co.*, 758 F.2d 613, 225 USPQ 634 (Fed. Cir. 1985).

[133]*In re Hyatt*, 708 F.2d 712, 218 USPQ 195 (Fed. Cir. 1983).

[134]*Fromson v. Advance Offset Plate, Inc.*, 720 F.2d 1565, 219 USPQ 1137 (Fed. Cir. 1983).

[135]*Beachcombers v. Wildewood Creative Prods., Inc.*, 31 F.3d 1154, 31 USPQ2d 1653 (Fed. Cir. 1994).

[136]*Andrew Corp. v. Gabriel Elec., Inc.*, 847 F.2d 819, 6 USPQ2d 2010 (Fed. Cir. 1988).

[137]The cases are collected in Chisum, *Patents* §8.3 (1987).

[138]*Standard Oil Co. v. American Cyanamid Co.*, 774 F.2d 448, 227 USPQ 293 (Fed. Cir. 1985). See also *In re Dossel*, 115 F.3d 942, 42 USPQ2d 1881 (Fed. Cir. 1997).

about a skilled artisan's understanding of the bounds of the claim.[139] Remember, it is the specification that describes the invention, not the claims. The "full, clear, concise and exact" requirement of the first paragraph of §112 applies only to the specification, not the claims. It is inappropriate to speak of indefiniteness of the "patent"; only claims are subject to that criticism.[140]

It is also important to keep separate the concepts of obviousness and claim definiteness. Thus, an argument that the claims, properly construed, are broader than the scope of the evidence relating to obviousness will be considered by the court to raise an issue of adequacy, rather than an issue of claim construction pertinent to obviousness.[141] Nonetheless, indefiniteness has to do with validity, not infringement. A claim may be infringed, but the infringer would not be liable if the claim is invalid for indefiniteness under §112.[142]

One principle has been settled: words of degree do not in themselves render a claim indefinite.[143] Despite varying results even in Supreme Court decisions,[144] a phrase such as "substantially equal to" can be definite if it be shown that a person of skill in the art would understand the limitation. That some claim language may not be precise does not automatically render the claim invalid. When a word of degree is used the court must determine whether the specification provides some standard for measuring that degree.[145] Terms such as "close to," "substantially equal," "closely approximate," and "approach each other" are ubiquitous in patent claims. Such usages, when serving reasonably to describe the claimed subject matter to those of skill in the field of the invention, and to distinguish the claimed subject matter from the prior art, have been accepted in patent examination and upheld by the courts.[146]

---

[139]*Miles Labs., Inc. v. Shandon, Inc.*, 997 F.2d 870, 27 USPQ2d 1123 (Fed. Cir. 1993).

[140]*Orthokinetics, Inc. v. Safety Travel Chairs, Inc.*, 806 F.2d 1565, 1 USPQ2d 1081 (Fed. Cir. 1986).

[141]*Burlington Indus. Inc. v. Quigg*, 822 F.2d 1581, 3 USPQ2d 1436 (Fed. Cir. 1987).

[142]*Kingsdown Med. Cons, Ltd. v. Hollister, Inc.*, 863 F.2d 867, 9 USPQ2d 1384 (Fed. Cir. 1988). Ambiguous claims, whenever possible, should be construed to preserve their validity. This rule of construction, however, does not justify reading into a claim a limitation that it does not contain and that the patentee deleted from the claim during prosecution. It is therefore error to construe a claim narrowly to avoid a holding of new matter, thereby resulting in a determination of no infringement. *Texas Instr., Inc. v. United States ITC*, 871 F.2d 1054, 10 USPQ2d 1257 (Fed. Cir. 1989).

[143]*Seattle Box Co. v. Industrial Crat. & Pack., Inc.*, 731 F.2d 818, 221 USPQ 568 (Fed. Cir. 1984); *In re Marosi*, 710 F.2d 799, 218 USPQ 289 (Fed. Cir. 1983).

[144]Compare *Eibel Process Co. v. Minnesota & Ontario Paper Co.*, 261 U.S. 45 (1923) with *United Carbon Co. v. Binney & Smith Co.*, 317 U.S. 228, 55 USPQ 381 (1942).

[145]*Seattle Box Co. v. Industrial Crat. & Pack., Inc.*, 731 F.2d 818, 221 USPQ 568 (Fed. Cir. 1984).

[146]*Andrew Corp. v. Gabriel Elec., Inc.*, 847 F.2d 819, 6 USPQ2d 2010, 2012 (Fed. Cir. 1988). Likewise, the court will not approve "bootstrap" arguments regarding indefiniteness. In order to find infringement, the district court would have had to find that a thin coating was equivalent to no coating. It took the approach that such a finding was no different from writing the word "thin" into the patent claims, and if that were done, the claims would be indefinite, since there was no rational standard for determining what "thin" meant in this context. The

Technical terms are not per se indefinite when expressed in qualitative terms without numerical limits. Mathematical precision should not be imposed for its own sake; a patentee has the right to claim the invention in terms that would be understood by persons of skill in the field of the invention.[147] Open-ended claims (e.g., "highly purified") are not inherently improper. As for all claims their appropriateness depends on the particular facts of the invention, the disclosure, and the prior art. They may be supported if there is an inherent, albeit not precisely known, upper limit and if the specification enables one of skill in the art to approach that limit.[148] "Partially soluble" has been held to be too vague a term.[149]

It is improper to include "sales pitch" features in claims, inasmuch as the function of claims is to point out distinctly the matter that is patented, not its advantages.[150] A patentee may claim less than the entire invention.[151] A claim to a new product is not legally required to include critical limitations.[152] The court seems prepared to draw a very fine line between cases where property limitations need to be shown for purposes of anticipation and cases where such limitations need not be shown. The distinction, which involves considerations of claim adequacy, depends upon whether structure alone may be inadequate to define the invention, thus making it appropriate to

---

Federal Circuit disapproved this reasoning on the ground that it is improper for a court to redraft claims and then hold them invalid. *Diversitech Corp. v. Century Steps, Inc.*, 850 F.2d 675, 7 USPQ2d 1315 (Fed. Cir. 1988). This aspect of the case is probably dictum, because the court went on to hold that the patentee was estopped under the circumstances to claim equivalents.

[147]*Modine Mfg. Co. v. United States ITC*, 75 F.3d 1545, 37 USPQ2d 1609 (Fed. Cir. 1996).

[148]*Scripps Clinic & Res. Found. v. Genentech, Inc.*, 927 F.2d 1565, 18 USPQ2d 1001 (Fed. Cir. 1991).

[149]*Standard Oil Co. v. American Cyanamid Co.*, 774 F.2d 448, 227 USPQ 293 (Fed. Cir. 1985). In *Eiselstein v. Frank*, 52 F.3d 1035, 34 USPQ2d 1467 (Fed. Cir. 1995), the court, while recognizing that the word "about" can lead to indefiniteness, found that a disclosure of 45%–55% would support a claim limitation to "about 45% to about 55%" but not a claim to "about 50% to about 60%." It also held that the term "essentially" was vague. Claims calling for a genetic material having a specific activity of "about" so much were held indefinite in *Amgen, Inc. v. Chugai Pharm. Co.*, 927 F.2d 1200, 18 USPQ2d 1016 (Fed. Cir. 1991). When the meaning of claims is in doubt, especially where there is close prior art, they may be declared invalid. However, the court took pains to caution that this holding should not be understood as ruling out any and all uses of the term "about" in patent claims.

[150]*Preemption Devices, Inc. v. Minnesota Min. & Mfg. Co.*, 732 F.2d 903, 221 USPQ 841 (Fed. Cir. 1984).

[151]*Andrew Corp. v. Gabriel Elec., Inc.*, 847 F.2d 819, 6 USPQ2d 2010 (Fed. Cir. 1988).

[152]*W.L. Gore & Assoc. v. Garlock, Inc.*, 721 F.2d 1540, 220 USPQ 303 (Fed. Cir. 1983). The phrase "so dimensioned" was held definite where the claims were intended to cover the use of the invention with various types of automobiles. That a particular device on which the claims read may fit within some cars and not others is of no moment. The phrase "so dimensioned" is as accurate as the subject matter permits, automobiles being of various sizes. As long as those of ordinary skill in the art realized that the dimensions could be easily obtained, the second paragraph of §112 requires no more. The patent law does not require that all possible lengths corresponding to the spaces in hundreds of different automobiles be listed in the patent, let alone that they be listed in the claims. *Orthokinetics, Inc. v. Safety Travel Chairs, Inc.*, 806 F.2d 1565, 1 USPQ2d 1081 (Fed. Cir. 1986).

define the invention in part by property limitations.[153] Product-by-process claims, while permitted, are not specifically discussed in the patent statute. The practice and governing law have developed in response to the need to enable an applicant to claim an otherwise patentable product that resists definition by other than the process by which it is made.[154]

Claims that include a substantial number of inoperatives are properly rejectable under §112 because they do not correspond in scope to what the inventor regards as the invention.[155] Similarly, the discredited "old combination" defense (i.e., where the invention is merely an improvement of one element of the combination, a claim to the whole combination is invalid)[156] is really an indefiniteness defense under §112, on the theory that the claim does not point out that which the patentee regards as the invention.[157] But the fact that dependent claims include species that might not meet the objects of the invention does not by itself prove that one skilled in the art cannot ascertain the scope of the asserted claims. That objection goes to possible inoperativeness under §101 or lack of enablement under §112.[158]

It is entirely consistent with the claim definiteness requirement of the second paragraph of §112 to present subcombination claims drawn to only one aspect or combination of elements of an invention that has utility separate and apart from other aspects of the invention. It is not necessary that a claim recite each and every element needed for the practical utilization of the claimed subject matter. So long as the recited structure is capable of performing its claimed purpose, greater utility or more definite claiming is not required.[159]

The court adheres to its predecessor's rejection of "undue breadth" objections.[160] A patent applicant is entitled to claim the invention

---

[153]*E.I. duPont & Co. v. Phillips Petroleum Co.*, 849 F.2d 1430, 7 USPQ2d 1129 (Fed. Cir. 1988). The court contrasted *Titanium Metals Corp. v. Banner*, 778 F.2d 775, 227 USPQ 773 (Fed. Cir. 1985), which involved an alloy. Once the alloy disclosed in the prior art reference was determined to possess the structural limitations of the claim, the burden shifted to the patentee to show that the alloy disclosed in the reference did not possess the claimed property. But where, as in the polymer at issue in the *duPont* case, structure alone was insufficient, the patentee was entitled to define the invention in terms of properties as well. Thus the issue is not whether one can get a patent for discovering a new property of an old composition of matter, but whether the claimed composition, as defined in part by various property parameters, is new.

[154]*In re Thorpe*, 777 F.2d 695, 227 USPQ 964 (Fed. Cir. 1985). Product-by-process claims recite how a product is made, not how it is used. *Mentor Corp. v. Coloplast, Inc.*, 998 F.2d 992, 27 USPQ2d 1521 (Fed. Cir. 1993).

[155]*In re Corkill*, 771 F.2d 1496, 226 USPQ 1005 (Fed. Cir. 1985).

[156]See *Lincoln Eng'g Co. v. Stewart Warner Corp.*, 303 U.S. 545, 37 USPQ 1 (1938).

[157]*Radio Steel & Mfg. Co. v. MTD Prods., Inc.*, 731 F.2d 840, 221 USPQ 657 (Fed. Cir. 1984).

[158]*North Am. Vaccine, Inc. v. American Cyanamid Co.*, 7 F.3d 1571, 28 USPQ2d 1333 (Fed. Cir. 1993). The court went on to remark that if a species within a dependent claim does not meet the limitations of the independent claim, arguably it is not included within the scope of that dependent claim.

[159]*Stiftung v. Renishaw PLC*, 945 F.2d 1173, 20 USPQ2d 1094 (Fed. Cir. 1991).

[160]E.g., *In re Ackermann*, 444 F.2d 1172, 170 USPQ 340 (CCPA 1971). In one case a compound was expected to have herbicidal activity, but turned out to have unexpectedly superior activity for several uses. Its activity for other uses was expected, but was inferior to the prior

generically when it is described sufficiently to meet the requirements of §112.[161]

The Federal Circuit will be much more strict in its enforcement of the definiteness requirement while an application is in prosecution, because the applicant is still in a position to amend its claims to achieve compliance.[162] This attitude is likely to apply to all prosecution, including reexamination and reissue.[163]

Functional language in a claim is permitted by the last paragraph of §112, which provides:

> An element in a claim for a combination may be expressed as a means or step for performing a specified function without the recital of structure, material or acts in support thereof, and such claim shall be construed to cover the corresponding structure, material or acts described in the specification and equivalents thereof.[164]

It seems clear that this enactment was intended to overcome a Supreme Court decision[165] that had cast serious doubt upon the use of functional language in claims.[166] In the context of a means-plus-function clause, failure to describe adequately the necessary structure, material, or acts in the written description means that the drafter has failed to comply with the second paragraph of §112, which requires that all claims must particularly point out and distinctly claim the subject matter which the applicant regards as the invention. The first paragraph of §112, which provides the requirements for what must be contained in the written description regardless of whether claims are written in means-plus-function form, is not implicated in such a situation.[167]

---

art. The PTO argued that a patent on the compound would prevent its use in those expected areas. The court indicated this concern was misplaced, and likened the argument to the discredited "undue breadth" rejection. *In re Chupp,* 816 F.2d 643, 2 USPQ2d 1437 (Fed. Cir. 1987). The court also indicated that nobody would want to use the compound to produce inferior results or fight lawsuits over such uses. This seems questionable. What if the superior prior compound were itself the subject of an unexpired patent? In *United States Steel Corp. v. Phillips Petroleum Co.,* 865 F.2d 1247, 9 USPQ2d 1461 (Fed. Cir. 1989), the infringer was arguing that the question of support in an earlier application must be resolved on the basis of what the claim embraces rather than what it sets forth. Thus, if it embraces subject matter for which no adequate basis existed in the underlying disclosure, the claim is too broad. Again the court rejected the argument as sounding too much like an "overbreadth" defense.

[161]*Amgen, Inc. v. Chugai Pharm. Co.,* 927 F.2d 1200, 18 USPQ2d 1016 (Fed. Cir. 1991).

[162]*In re Corkill,* 771 F.2d 1496, 226 USPQ 1005 (Fed. Cir. 1985).

[163]Cf. *In re Etter,* 756 F.2d 852, 225 USPQ 1 (Fed. Cir. 1985); *In re Yamamoto,* 740 F.2d 1569, 222 USPQ 934 (Fed. Cir. 1984).

[164]35 U.S.C. §112¶6.

[165]*Halliburton Oil Well Cementing Co. v. Walker,* 329 U.S. 1, 71 USPQ 175 (1946).

[166]*In re Fuetterer,* 319 F.2d 259, 138 USPQ 217 (CCPA 1963). Absent the sixth paragraph of 35 U.S.C. §112, claim language that requires only a means for performing a function might be indefinite. *Laitram Corp. v. Rexnord, Inc.,* 939 F.2d 1533, 19 USPQ2d 1367 (Fed. Cir. 1991).

[167]*In re Dossel,* 115 F.3d 942, 42 USPQ2d 1881 (Fed. Cir. 1997). See also *Atmel Corp. v. Information Storage Devices Inc.,* 198 F.3d 1374, 53 USPQ2d 1225 (Fed. Cir. 1999). This topic is discussed in detail in §5.6(f).

Claim multiplicity does not itself reflect either claim confusion or contradiction.[168] Although the court has been critical of parties who submit the infringement issue on a "plethora of dependent claims," it does recognize that if validity were in issue, dependent claims might serve a useful role, for a necessarily narrower dependent claim may be valid when the claim from which it depends is not.[169]

§5.5 New Matter, Support, and the Description Requirement

Section 132 of the Patent Act provides that "no amendment shall introduce new matter into the disclosure of the invention." The fundamental inquiry is whether the material added by amendment was inherently contained in the original application.[170] A function or property that is inherent in a claimed product can be expressly described in an amendment and is not new matter.[171]

Support. The new matter prohibition is closely related to the requirement, said to be found in the first paragraph of §112, that the specification support the claims.[172] In determining whether a later application is entitled to the filing date of an earlier one under 35 U.S.C. §120, the question is whether the later claim would have been correctly rejected for support if it had been considered as of the time of the earlier filing date.[173] The specific basis for the support requirement is not entirely clear. It could be argued that the enablement requirement presupposes support; yet, it can be conceived that one of skill in the art could be enabled to make and use the claimed invention without an express disclosure of a particular claim element. And indeed, adding material that is already known to and available to the public, to the extent it is not new matter, does not deprive an applicant of its original filing date.[174]

Description requirement. Perhaps a better basis for the support rule is the description requirement, which insists that the specification "contain a written description of the invention."[175] While one does

---

[168]*Panduit Corp. v. Dennison Mfg. Co.*, 774 F.2d 1082, 227 USPQ 337 (Fed. Cir. 1985).

[169]*Wahpeton Canvas Co. v. Frontier, Inc.*, 870 F.2d 1546, 10 USPQ2d 1201 (Fed. Cir. 1989).

[170]*Schering Corp. v. Amgen Inc.*, 222 F.3d 1347, 55 USPQ2d 1650 (Fed. Cir. 2000). An amendment that conforms the written specification to the original drawing or claims, or that clarifies something inherent in the original disclosure, does not introduce new matter. See *Litton Sys., Inc. v. Whirlpool Corp.*, 728 F.2d 1423, 221 USPQ 97 (Fed. Cir. 1984).

[171]*Kennecott Corp. v. Kyocera Int'l, Inc.*, 835 F.2d 1419, 5 USPQ2d 1194 (Fed. Cir. 1987).

[172]*Pennwalt Corp. v. Akzona Inc.*, 740 F.2d 1573, 222 USPQ 833 (Fed. Cir. 1984); *In re Kaslow*, 707 F.2d 1366, 217 USPQ 1089 (Fed. Cir. 1983).

[173]*United States Steel Corp. v. Phillips Petroleum Co.*, 865 F.2d 1247, 9 USPQ2d 1461 (Fed. Cir. 1989).

[174]*Paperless Accounting, Inc. v. Bay Area Rapid Transit Sys.*, 804 F.2d 659, 231 USPQ 649 (Fed. Cir. 1986).

[175]E.g., *Kennecott Corp. v. Kyocera Int'l, Inc.*, 835 F.2d 1419, 5 USPQ2d 1194 (Fed. Cir. 1987); *In re Wilder*, 736 F.2d 1516, 222 USPQ 369 (Fed. Cir. 1984). Indeed, the court has said

not need to have carried out one's invention before filing a patent application, one does need to be able to describe that invention with particularity.[176] The description is of course judged from the viewpoint of one of ordinary skill in the art.[177] The fact finder must determine if one skilled in the art, reading the original specification, would immediately discern the limitation at issue in the parent application. In other words, does the disclosure of the application being relied upon reasonably convey to the artisan that the inventor had possession at that time of the later claimed subject matter? Before making any factual determination about the disclosure of any newly added material, the trial court must examine the circumstances surrounding the prosecution of the parent application.[178]

The description requirement most often comes into play where claims not presented in the application when filed are presented thereafter. But it also arises when applicants seek the benefit of the filing date of earlier foreign or domestic applications under 35 U.S.C. §§119 or 120. These situations all involve the question of adequate support for the claims at issue; the question is also sometimes analyzed in the context of new matter. Finally, the written description requirement similarly arises in the interference context, where the issue is whether a party can "make the count."[179] The written description requirement is the same for a claim copied for purposes of instituting an interference as for a claim presented during ex parte prosecution of a patent application.[180] The question of "intent to claim" in a reissue proceeding (i.e., is that which is claimed in the reissue something that could have been claimed on the basis of the original disclosure?) is analogous to the written description requirement under §112.[181]

When the scope of a claim has been changed by amendment in such a way as to justify an assertion that it is directed to a different invention than was the original claim, it is proper to inquire whether the newly claimed subject matter was described as the invention of

---

that compliance with §112 is negated if undue experimentation is required because of an inadequate or incomplete description. *In re Lundak,* 773 F.2d 1216, 227 USPQ 90 (Fed. Cir. 1985). A rejection for lack of support in the specification is a rejection under the written description requirement of the first paragraph of §112. *Pall Corp. v. Micron Separations, Inc.,* 66 F.3d 1211, 36 USPQ2d 1225 (Fed. Cir. 1995).

[176]*Fiers v. Revel,* 984 F.2d 1164, 25 USPQ2d 1601 (Fed. Cir. 1993).

[177]*Wang Labs., Inc. v. Toshiba Corp.,* 993 F.2d 858, 26 USPQ2d 1767 (Fed. Cir. 1993).

[178]*Waldemar Link v. Osteonics Corp.,* 32 F.3d 556, 31 USPQ2d 1855 (Fed. Cir. 1994).

[179]*Vas-Cath Inc. v. Mahurkar,* 935 F.2d 1555, 19 USPQ2d 1111 (Fed. Cir. 1991). This decision includes a comprehensive historical analysis of the written description requirement. The court also undertook to resolve any possible confusion between certain of its earlier decisions (see note 5:175), as follows: §112 requires a written description of the invention which is separate and distinct from the enablement requirement. The purpose of the written description is broader than merely to explain how to make and use the invention. The applicant must also convey with reasonable clarity to those skilled in the art that, as of the filing date sought, he or she was in possession of the invention. The invention is, for purposes of that inquiry, whatever is now being claimed.

[180]*In re Spina,* 975 F.2d 854, 24 USPQ2d 1142 (Fed. Cir. 1992).

[181]*In re Amos,* 953 F.2d 613, 21 USPQ2d 1271 (Fed. Cir. 1991).

the applicant in the patent application when filed. If the essence of the original disclosure supports the new claim limitation, the new limitation is not new matter.[182] Each claim of a patent must be separately analyzed for compliance with the written description requirement.[183] The specification must be sufficiently clear that persons of skill in the art will recognize that the inventor made the invention having those limitations.[184]

A specification may, within the meaning of 35 U.S.C. §112, contain a written description of a broadly claimed invention without describing all species that the claim encompasses.[185] On the other hand, even though a patent might contain a sufficient written description as to its own narrower claims, it might not satisfy the requirement as to broader claims that it nonetheless anticipates.[186] In order to satisfy the written description requirement for an invention that is claimed as a DNA, more is required than reference to a potential method for isolating it. The written description must set forth a precise definition, similar to that required for conception, such as a structure, formula, chemical name, or physical properties.[187]

The adequate written description requirement, which is distinct from the enablement and best mode requirements, serves to ensure that the inventor had possession, as of the filing date of the application relied on, of the specific subject matter later claimed; how the specification accomplishes this is not material. The applicant does not have to utilize any particular form of disclosure to describe the subject matter claimed.[188] The fact that a disclosure is very short is immaterial. Certainly no length requirement exists for a disclosure to adequately describe an invention. While some inventions require more

---

[182]*In re Wright*, 866 F.2d 422, 9 USPQ2d 1649 (Fed. Cir. 1989). The court also took issue with the PTO Board for discussing the examiner's new matter rejection in terms of the clarity of the meaning of the limitation; it felt this was an irrelevant inquiry because the limitation was composed of "common, garden variety words known to every English-speaking person."

[183]*Vas-Cath Inc. v. Mahurkar*, 935 F.2d 1555, 19 USPQ2d 1111 (Fed. Cir. 1991). For example, in *Eiselstein v. Frank*, 52 F.3d 1035, 34 USPQ2d 1467 (Fed. Cir. 1995), the court held that a disclosure of 45%–55% supported a claim limitation of "about 45% to about 55%" but not another claim that was limited to "about 50% to about 60%."

[184]*In re Spina*, 975 F.2d 854, 24 USPQ2d 1142 (Fed. Cir. 1992).

[185]*Utter v. Hiraga*, 845 F.2d 993, 6 USPQ2d 1709 (Fed. Cir. 1988).

[186]*Chester v. Miller*, 906 F.2d 1574, 15 USPQ2d 1333 (Fed. Cir. 1990). It is possible for a specification to enable the practice of an invention as broadly as it is claimed and still not describe that invention. There is also a distinction between claim-anticipating disclosures and claim-supporting disclosures. A description of a single embodiment of broadly claimed subject matter constitutes a description of the invention for anticipation purposes whereas the same information in a specification might not alone be enough to provide a description of that invention for purposes of adequate disclosure. *Vas-Cath Inc. v. Mahurkar*, 935 F.2d 1555, 19 USPQ2d 1111 (Fed. Cir. 1991).

[187]*Regents of Univ. of Calif. v. Eli Lilly & Co.*, 119 F.3d 1559, 43 USPQ2d 1398 (Fed. Cir. 1997); *Fiers v. Revel*, 984 F.2d 1164, 25 USPQ2d 1601 (Fed. Cir. 1993). This is analogous to the problem encountered with a so-called single means claim, which does not comply with the first paragraph of §112. Claiming all DNAs that achieve a result without defining what means will do so is not in compliance with the description requirement; it is an attempt to preempt the future before it has arrived.

[188]*In re Alton*, 76 F.3d 1168, 37 USPQ2d 1578 (Fed. Cir. 1996).

disclosure, the adequacy of the description of an invention depends on its content in relation to the particular invention, not its length.[189] Under proper circumstances, drawings alone may provide a written description of an invention sufficient to satisfy the requirement of §112.[190] An ipsis verbis disclosure is not necessary to satisfy the written description requirement of §112. In the case of chemical compounds, however, simply describing a large genus of compounds is not sufficient to satisfy the written description requirement as to particular species or subgenuses. There must be some "blazemarks" pointing the way to particular claimed compound.[191] A description that renders obvious a claimed invention is not sufficient to satisfy the written description requirement.[192]

The description requirement involves questions of fact, and the boundaries of the requirement are sure to be developed on a case-by-case basis.[193] Similarly, although the ultimate question of support under §112 is one of law, it is dependent upon underlying factual and

---

[189]*In re Hayes Microcomputer Patent Litig.*, 982 F.2d 1527, 25 USPQ2d 1241 (Fed. Cir. 1992).

[190]*Vas-Cath Inc. v. Mahurkar*, 935 F.2d 1555, 19 USPQ2d 1111 (Fed. Cir. 1991). Whether the drawings are those of a design or a utility application is not determinative, although in most cases the latter are much more detailed. In this case an earlier design application was relied upon, and the district court held that there was no support for a claimed range of variation because the design drawings did not necessarily exclude all values outside the claimed range. The Federal Circuit held this to be an improper legal standard. Consideration of what the drawings conveyed to persons of ordinary skill in the art is essential. The issue is whether one skilled in the art could derive the claimed ranges from the design drawings. *Id.* See also *Wang Labs., Inc. v. Toshiba Corp.*, 993 F.2d 858, 26 USPQ2d 1767 (Fed. Cir. 1993). A later application is entitled to the earlier filing date for all common subject matter that is contained in the earlier application, whether the subject matter appears in the body of the specification or in the claims or drawings. *Modine Mfg. Co. v. United States ITC*, 75 F.3d 1545, 37 USPQ2d 1609 (Fed. Cir. 1996).

[191]*Fujikawa v. Wattanasin*, 93 F.3d 1559, 39 USPQ2d 1895 (Fed. Cir. 1996). The written description requirement does not require identical descriptions of claimed compounds, but it requires enough disclosure in the patent to show one of skill in the art that the inventor invented what is claimed. Neither the Patent Act nor the case law requires a description of the exact chemical component of each combination that falls within the claimed ranges. *Union Oil Co. of Calif. v. Atlantic Richfield Co.*, 208 F.3d 989, 54 USPQ2d 1227 (Fed. Cir. 2000).

[192]*Regents of Univ. of Calif. v. Eli Lilly & Co.*, 119 F.3d 1559, 43 USPQ2d 1398 (Fed. Cir. 1997); *Tronzo v. Biomet Inc.*, 156 F.3d 1154, 47 USPQ2d 1829 (Fed. Cir. 1998); *Lockwood v. American Airlines, Inc.*, 107 F.3d 1565, 41 USPQ2d 1961 (Fed. Cir. 1997).

[193]*Ralston Purina Co. v. Far-Mar-Co, Inc.*, 772 F.2d 1570, 227 USPQ 177 (Fed. Cir. 1985). Compliance with the written description requirement is a question of fact. *In re Alton*, 76 F.3d 1168, 37 USPQ2d 1578 (Fed. Cir. 1996); *Wang Labs., Inc. v. Toshiba Corp.*, 993 F.2d 858, 26 USPQ2d 1767 (Fed. Cir. 1993); *In re Hayes Microcomputer Patent Litig.*, 982 F.2d 1527, 25 USPQ2d 1241 (Fed. Cir. 1992); *Utter v. Hiraga*, 845 F.2d 993, 6 USPQ2d 1709 (Fed. Cir. 1988). Compliance with the written description requirement is a question of fact, to be reviewed under the clearly erroneous standard. *Hyatt v. Boone*, 146 F.3d 1128, 47 USPQ2d 1128 (Fed. Cir. 1998); *Gentry Gallery, Inc. v. Berkline Corp.*, 134 F.3d 1473, 45 USPQ2d 1498 (Fed. Cir. 1998); *Kolmes v. World Fibers Corp.*, 107 F.3d 1534, 41 USPQ2d 1829 (Fed. Cir. 1997); *Fiers v. Revel*, 984 F.2d 1164, 25 USPQ2d 1601 (Fed. Cir. 1993); *In re Spina*, 975 F.2d 854, 24 USPQ2d 1142 (Fed. Cir. 1992); *Vas-Cath Inc. v. Mahurkar*, 935 F.2d 1555, 19 USPQ2d 1111 (Fed. Cir. 1991). But see *Kennecott Corp. v. Kyocera Int'l, Inc.*, 835 F.2d 1419, 5 USPQ2d 1194 (Fed. Cir. 1987), which seems to indicate that the written description requirement presents a legal question depending upon the particular facts of the case.

legal findings.[194] The court has indicated that, because of the fact-sensitive nature of the inquiry, caution in application of precedents in this area is required.[195]

The Gentry Gallery *doctrine.* The Federal Circuit appears to be in the early stages of development of a doctrine resting upon the principle that when the preferred embodiment is fairly described in the specification as the invention itself, the claims are not necessarily entitled to a scope broader than that embodiment.[196] Its decision in *Gentry Gallery*[197] is the latest clear exemplar of this doctrinal trend. As the court put the matter:

> It is a truism that a claim need not be limited to a preferred embodiment. However, in a given case, the scope of the right to exclude may be limited by a narrow disclosure. * * *
> In sum, the cases * * * do not stand for the proposition that an applicant can broaden his claims to the extent that they are effectively bounded only by the prior art. Rather, they make clear that claims may be no broader than the supporting disclosure, and therefore that a narrow disclosure will limit claim breadth.

At first glance, this language would seem to provide some support for the view that the claim should therefore be construed more narrowly, to comport with the scope of the written description. But it is important to observe precisely what it was that the court actually did about the perceived discrepancy between disclosure and claim in *Gentry.* Rather than treat the matter as a claim construction issue, or even an infringement issue, the court analyzed it as a question of compliance with the written description requirement of 35 U.S.C. §112¶1. Rather surprisingly, it held the claim invalid for want of an adequate written description.

In so doing, the court came at the written description issue in a somewhat unusual way. Rather than going through the usual analysis of whether a person skilled in the art would understand that the

---

[194]*Paperless Accounting, Inc. v. Bay Area Rapid Transit Sys.,* 804 F.2d 659, 231 USPQ 649 (Fed. Cir. 1986). If such findings have not been made below, it is inappropriate for the reviewing court to decide support ab initio. *Id.* Determination of whether a priority document contains sufficient disclosure under §112 is a question of law; but compliance with the written description aspect of that requirement is a question of fact. *Waldemar Link v. Osteonics Corp.,* 32 F.3d 556, 31 USPQ2d 1855 (Fed. Cir. 1994).

[195]*Union Oil Co. of Calif. v. Atlantic Richfield Co.,* 208 F.3d 989, 54 USPQ2d 1227 (Fed. Cir. 2000).

[196]See *Modine Mfg. Co. v. United States ITC,* 75 F.3d 1545, 37 USPQ2d 1609, 1612 (Fed. Cir. 1996).

[197]*Gentry Gallery, Inc. v. Berkline Corp.,* 134 F.3d 1473, 45 USPQ2d 1498 (Fed. Cir. 1998). See also *Fromson v. Anitec Printing Plates Inc.,* 132 F.3d 1437, 45 USPQ2d 1269 (Fed. Cir. 1997) (one cannot interpret a claim to be broader than what is contained in the specification and claims as filed); *Vehicular Tech. Corp. v. Titan Wheel Int'l, Inc.,* 141 F.3d 1084, 46 USPQ2d 1257 (Fed. Cir. 1998). In a more recent case, the court observed that *Gentry* considers the situation where the patent's disclosure makes crystal clear that a particular (i.e., narrow) understanding of a claim term is an essential element of the disclosed invention. *Johnson Worldwide Assoc. Inc. v. Zebco Corp.,* 175 F.3d 985, 50 USPQ2d 1607 (Fed. Cir. 1999).

inventors had possession of the claimed invention, it asked whether such a person would understand that an essential aspect of the invention had not been made a claim limitation. It is difficult to say at this point whether the court has created, or intends to create, a per se invalidity defense based upon the written description requirement. One fundamental problem will be how to know where to draw the line between permissible claim construction, to save the claim, and *Gentry* treatment, to invalidate it. What we may very well see as the matter develops is an increased focus, not on whether the patent claims must be construed as limited to the materials and techniques actually disclosed, but on whether the inventors of the patents provided a written description adequate to convey to a skilled artisan that they had possession of a broader or different invention than that.

At least one member of the court feels that *Gentry* is simply a reflection of the long-standing rule that claims in an application that are broader than the disclosure are not allowable.[198] But developing the true meaning of this rather simple statement is likely to prove extremely difficult. Even under this approach, a court would, in each case where the claims are broader than the particular embodiments disclosed, have to engage in a painstaking factual analysis of whether a person of ordinary skill in the art would regard the omitted limitation as critical to the disclosed invention.[199]

With all respect, there may be ways to approach this problem that do not require a new test for compliance with the written description requirement. Claim construction does not appear to be a viable option, because it would usually require the court to import a limitation from

---

[198]In its first clear chance to expound the meaning of *Gentry*, the court hedged. In *Reiffin v. Microsoft Corp.*, 214 F.3d 1342, 54 USPQ2d 1915 (Fed. Cir. 2000), the district court essentially followed *Gentry* and held the patents invalid for failure to provide an adequate written description of the invention. In a per curiam opinion, the appellate panel reversed, with a concurring opinion by Judge Newman. The panel majority held that the lower court erred in looking to the adequacy of the written description in the parent application rather than the CIP upon which the patents issued. There was no contention by Microsoft that those CIP applications did not support the claims; however, there was an underlying dispute as to whether Reiffin would need the filing date of the parent to avoid prior art. The majority was thus able to circumvent *Gentry* and remand. Judge Newman felt that the *Gentry* issue should be confronted, because it appeared that the lower court will ultimately have to evaluate entitlement to the parent filing date. She left no doubt that, in her view, *Gentry* is limited to a situation where the omitted limitation is the only possible embodiment, and where a variation would be outside the stated purpose of the invention. This, she says, is simply a reflection of the long-standing rule that claims in an application that are broader than the disclosure are not allowable.

[199]This process has already begun. In a very recent case, *Lampi Corp. v. American Power Prods. Inc.*, 228 F.3d 1365, 56 USPQ2d 1445 (Fed. Cir. 2000), the court was confronted with a claim limitation to a "housing having two separable half-shells." The specification disclosed identical half-shells, and indicated that this was to permit interchangeability in manufacture and assembly. The court seemed to feel that the written description was not so specific as to the need for identity as to fail to support the broader claim limitation. It distinguished *Tronzo v. Biomet Inc.*, 156 F.3d 1154, 47 USPQ2d 1829 (Fed. Cir. 1998). There the court had held that a claim limitation that read broadly on various shapes was not supported where there was nothing in the specification to suggest that shapes other than conical were necessarily a part of the disclosure. Indeed, the court there felt that the specification clearly suggested the contrary by asserting advantages of the conical shape over prior art shapes. With all respect, this distinction, if there is one, seems rather thin. For an example of how Judge Newman might

the specification into the claim—a technique that is strictly forbidden. However, the matter could reasonably be viewed as a failure to comply with the requirement of §112¶2 that an applicant claim the "subject matter which the applicant regards as his invention."[200] An even better approach might be to regard such a situation as a prime candidate for application of the reverse doctrine of equivalents. That defense is invoked when claims are written more broadly than the disclosure warrants. The purpose of restricting the scope of such claims is not only to avoid a holding of infringement when a court deems it appropriate but often is to preserve the validity of claims with respect to their original intended scope.[201]

New matter in general. Whatever the source of the new matter prohibition, the test for claim support under the first paragraph of §112 is whether the disclosure as originally filed reasonably conveys to the artisan that the inventor had possession at that time of the later claimed subject matter, rather than the presence or absence of literal support.[202] A phrase added to a claim by amendment cannot enlarge the scope of the claim beyond that supported in the specification and cannot change the disclosure in a way contrary to its substance as filed.[203] Whether particular technological information is new matter depends on the facts of the case: the nature of the disclosure, the state of the art, and the nature of the added matter. The presumption of validity is based in part on the expertise of patent examiners presumed to have done their job; indeed, it may be viewed as a presumption of administrative correctness. It follows that when the PTO allows an amendment without objection on grounds of new matter, the patent is entitled to an especially weighty presumption in that regard.[204]

The PTO bears the initial burden of presenting a prima facie case of unpatentability. Insofar as the written description requirement is

---

propose to apply such an analysis, see *Wang Labs. Inc. v. America Online Inc.,* 197 F.3d 1377, 53 USPQ2d 1161, 1165 (Fed. Cir. 1999).

[200]See, e.g., *Litton Sys. Inc. v. Honeywell Inc.,* 140 F.3d 1449, 46 USPQ2d 1321, 1329–30 (Fed. Cir. 1998). The PTO sometimes rejects claims under §112¶2 on the grounds that the applicants are not claiming what they regarded as their invention. Without evidence to the contrary, an examiner generally should presume that a claim recites what the applicant regards as the invention. Moreover, some material submitted by the applicant, other than the specification, must warrant this type of §112 rejection. Thus, an examiner generally makes a "regards as the invention" rejection only as an applicant's position becomes clear over the course of prosecution. In other words, this rejection almost always follows some other rejection of the inventive material set forth in the claim. *Id.*

[201]*Texas Instr., Inc. v. United States ITC,* 846 F.2d 1369, 6 USPQ2d 1886, 1889 (Fed. Cir. 1988).

[202]*Ralston Purina Co. v. Far-Mar-Co, Inc.,* 772 F.2d 1570, 227 USPQ 177 (Fed. Cir. 1985); *In re Kaslow,* 707 F.2d 1366, 217 USPQ 1089 (Fed. Cir. 1983).

[203]*Tandon Corp. v. United States ITC,* 831 F.2d 1017, 4 USPQ2d 1283 (Fed. Cir. 1987).

[204]*Brooktree Corp. v. Advanced Micro Devices, Inc.,* 977 F.2d 1555, 24 USPQ2d 1401 (Fed. Cir. 1992). Here the amendment to the claims was "for video display." This was held to be an "embellishment" and thus not new matter. As a consequence, arguments as to best mode, enablement, and written description were also rejected.

concerned, that burden is discharged by presenting evidence or reasons why persons skilled in the art would not recognize in the disclosure a description of the invention defined by the claims. Thus the burden placed on the examiner varies, depending upon what the applicant claims. If the applicant claims embodiments of the invention that are completely outside the scope of the specification, then the examiner need only establish this fact to make out a prima facie case. If, on the other hand, the specification contains a description of the claimed invention, albeit not in the identical words, then the examiner must provide reasons why one of ordinary skill in the art would not consider the description sufficient. Once the examiner carries the burden of making out a prima facie case of unpatentability, the burden of coming forward with evidence or argument shifts to the applicant. To overcome a prima facie case, an applicant must show that the invention as claimed is adequately described.[205]

During prosecution of an application, claims amended with limitations that are unsupported by the original disclosure are rejected under §112 as lacking support, while unsupported amendments to the abstract, drawing, or specification are objected to as new matter under §132.[206] During the prosecution of a patent application, the examiner acts as a fact finder. If an examiner determines that an amended claim recites elements without support in the parent disclosure, the proper basis of rejection is under the first paragraph of §112. If the examiner finally rejects a claim as lacking support in the disclosure, applicants generally have a choice. They may appeal the decision on the merits. Alternatively, they may elect to file a continuing application and reargue the point. Or else they can file a CIP application adding support for the rejected claims, thereby restricting claims containing any new matter to the later filing date of the CIP. A CIP thus does not explicitly memorialize the filing date accorded particular claims. Accordingly, when a priority date dispute arises, the trial court must examine closely the prosecution history to discover the proper date for each claim at issue.[207]

What if new matter does slip by in an amendment? Possibly the patent might be invalid under §112.[208] Typically, however, the issue arises in infringement suits in the context of a claim being supported only by new matter. Then the claim is vulnerable to a validity attack on grounds of defective oath, or statutory bar, or both.[209] It seems a

---

[205]*In re Alton,* 76 F.3d 1168, 37 USPQ2d 1578 (Fed. Cir. 1996).

[206]*Pennwalt Corp. v. Akzona Inc.,* 740 F.2d 1573, 222 USPQ 833 (Fed. Cir. 1984). Claims added by amendment and drawn to an invention not so described in the specification are drawn to new matter and prohibited by 35 U.S.C. §132. Claims to subject matter described in the specification are not new matter. *Kolmes v. World Fibers Corp.,* 107 F.3d 1534, 41 USPQ2d 1829 (Fed. Cir. 1997).

[207]*Waldemar Link v. Osteonics Corp.,* 32 F.3d 556, 31 USPQ2d 1855 (Fed. Cir. 1994).

[208]*Litton Sys., Inc. v. Whirlpool Corp.,* 728 F.2d 1423, 221 USPQ 97 (Fed. Cir. 1984).

[209]*Railroad Dynamics, Inc. v. A. Stucki Co.,* 727 F.2d 1506, 220 USPQ 929 (Fed. Cir. 1984); *Dresser Indus. v. United States,* 432 F.2d 787, 167 USPQ 473 (Ct. Cl. 1970). The theory,

safe prediction that the Federal Circuit will demand that a good deal of weight be given the PTO determination that new matter has not been introduced and will insist that the statutory presumption of validity apply here with full force and effect.[210] It is the burden of the patent challenger to come forward with proof of lack of support, even where the patentee must have support to rely upon an earlier filing date.[211]

A claim is part of the disclosure. Thus where a patent application as filed contains a claim that specifically discloses something not disclosed in the descriptive part of the specification, the applicant may amend the specification without being charged with adding new matter.[212] Also, the addition by amendment of information that adds nothing to the substance of the disclosure—as for example, the name and address of a microorganism depository—is not within the new matter prohibition.[213]

The only proper way to introduce new matter is by filing a CIP application. This is provided for in §120. The result is a sort of dual filing date being accorded different parts of the disclosure: the original date to the original material and any clarification thereof, and the later date to any new material not inherent in the original and any claim limitations not supported by the original.[214] Entitlement to priority under §120 is a matter of law, and receives plenary review on appeal. Any disputed factual questions are reviewed on the clearly erroneous standard.[215]

Effective filing date. In order to be entitled to the filing date of an earlier application, the invention must have been disclosed in the

---

of course, is that the oath is defective because it does not relate, as of its execution, to the claimed invention; similarly, statutory bars may intervene in the period between the original filing and the addition of the new matter.

[210]See *In re Smythe,* 480 F.2d 1376, 178 USPQ 279 (CCPA 1973).

[211]*Ralston Purina Co. v. Far-Mar-Co, Inc.,* 772 F.2d 1570, 227 USPQ 177 (Fed. Cir. 1985).

[212]*In re Benno,* 768 F.2d 1340, 226 USPQ 683 (Fed. Cir. 1985). Original claims as filed are part of the patent specification. *Northern Telecom, Inc. v. Datapoint Corp.,* 908 F.2d 931, 15 USPQ2d 1321 (Fed. Cir. 1990). See also *Hyatt v. Boone,* 146 F.3d 1128, 47 USPQ2d 1128 (Fed. Cir. 1998).

[213]*In re Lundak,* 773 F.2d 1216, 227 USPQ 90 (Fed. Cir. 1985).

[214]E.g., *Waldemar Link v. Osteonics Corp.,* 32 F.3d 556, 31 USPQ2d 1855 (Fed. Cir. 1994). See also *Augustine Med. Inc. v. Gaymar Indus. Inc.,* 181 F.3d 1291, 50 USPQ2d 1900 (Fed. Cir. 1999). This can be a very significant distinction. In one hard case the examiner objected to an amendment as containing new matter and the applicant filed a CIP oath. As to the newly added material, the applicant was estopped to deny that it was new matter because he had filed the new oath. He was limited to the date of the new oath (rather than the date of the amendment) as to the new material and was barred by his own prior sale as a result. *Litton Sys., Inc. v. Whirlpool Corp.,* 728 F.2d 1423, 221 USPQ 97 (Fed. Cir. 1984). Interestingly, an alleged oral compromise with the examiner, to the effect that the applicant would be entitled to the date of the amendment rather than the oath, was held ineffective by virtue of the rule that the substance of interviews with examiners must be reduced to writing.

[215]*In re Daniels,* 144 F.3d 1452, 46 USPQ2d 1788 (Fed. Cir. 1998). Review of factual determinations is now undoubtedly under the substantial evidence standard. See, e.g., *In re Gartside,* 203 F.3d 1305, 53 USPQ2d 1769 (Fed. Cir. 2000).

manner provided by the first paragraph of 35 U.S.C. §112.[216] Thus, for CIP claims to receive the benefit of a parent filing date under §120, the parent must satisfy the written description requirement of §112. This ensures that the inventor had possession of the later claimed invention on the filing date of the earlier application.[217] To be entitled to the filing date of an earlier application in a chain of applications, there must have been a continuing disclosure through the chain, without hiatus.[218] An invention may be described in different ways and still be the same invention. Thus a parent and a CIP need not use the identical words, if the earlier application shows the subject matter that is claimed in the later application, with adequate direction as to how to obtain it. Section 120 does not require that the invention be described in the same way or comply with §112 in the same way in both applications.[219]

But entitlement to a filing date does not extend to subject matter that is not disclosed but would be obvious over what is expressly disclosed. It extends only to that which is disclosed. While the meaning of terms, phrases, or diagrams in a disclosure is to be explained or interpreted from the vantage point of one skilled in the art, all the claim limitations must appear in the specification. The question is not whether a claimed invention is an obvious variant of that which is disclosed. Rather, a prior application itself must describe an invention, and do so in sufficient detail that one skilled in the art can clearly conclude that the inventor invented the claimed invention as of the filing date sought. In particular, it is not sufficient for purposes of the written description requirement that the disclosure, when combined with the knowledge in the art, would lead one to speculate as to modifications that the inventor might have envisioned but failed to disclose.[220] For an earlier filed application to serve as constructive reduction to practice of the subject matter of a claim, the applicant must describe the subject matter in terms that establish that he or

---

[216]*Racing Strollers, Inc. v. TRI Indus., Inc.*, 878 F.2d 1418, 11 USPQ2d 1300 (Fed. Cir. 1989).

[217]*Kennecott Corp. v. Kyocera Int'l, Inc.*, 835 F.2d 1419, 5 USPQ2d 1194 (Fed. Cir. 1987). See also *Tronzo v. Biomet Inc.*, 156 F.3d 1154, 47 USPQ2d 1829 (Fed. Cir. 1998); *Therma-Tru Corp. v. Peachtree Doors Inc.*, 44 F.3d 988, 33 USPQ2d 1274 (Fed. Cir. 1994). It is possible for a patent to contain sufficient disclosure to satisfy the written description requirement as to its own narrower claims, and yet fail to satisfy the requirement as to broader claims that it nonetheless anticipates. This seeming anomaly typically occurs where the patent discloses a species of a genus later sought to be claimed in a CIP of the application that matured into the patent. *Chester v. Miller*, 906 F.2d 1574, 15 USPQ2d 1333 (Fed. Cir. 1990).

[218]*Lockwood v. American Airlines, Inc.*, 107 F.3d 1565, 41 USPQ2d 1961 (Fed. Cir. 1997); *Eiselstein v. Frank*, 52 F.3d 1035, 34 USPQ2d 1467 (Fed. Cir. 1995).

[219]*Kennecott Corp. v. Kyocera Int'l, Inc.*, 835 F.2d 1419, 5 USPQ2d 1194 (Fed. Cir. 1987). See also *Eiselstein v. Frank*, 52 F.3d 1035, 34 USPQ2d 1467 (Fed. Cir. 1995).

[220]*Lockwood v. American Airlines, Inc.*, 107 F.3d 1565, 41 USPQ2d 1961 (Fed. Cir. 1997). A disclosure in a parent application that merely renders the later-claimed invention obvious is not sufficient to meet the written description requirement; the disclosure must describe the claimed invention with all its limitations. In order for a disclosure to be inherent, the missing descriptive matter must necessarily be present in the parent application's specification such that one skilled in the art would recognize such a disclosure. *Tronzo v. Biomet Inc.*, 156 F.3d

she was in possession of the later-claimed invention, including all of the elements and limitations presented in the claim at the time of the earlier filing. Although known details need not be included in a patent specification, when an explicit limitation in a claim is not present in the written description whose benefit is sought, it must be shown that a person of ordinary skill would have understood, at the time the patent application was filed, that the description requires that limitation. It is insufficient as written description, for purposes of establishing priority of invention, to provide a specification that does not unambiguously describe all limitations of the claim.[221]

In those cases where a CIP contains claims that depend upon an enlarged disclosure for support, that must of course be considered when it is required to establish dates of compliance with §112. But the mere filing of a CIP with additional matter or revised claims is not of itself an admission that the matter is new, or that the original application was legally insufficient to support the claims. Law and policy liberally authorize the filing of CIP applications for a number of reasons, whether to enlarge the disclosure to include new technological information, thereby providing the public with knowledge of recent developments or improvements; or to enable more extensive prosecution or improved draftsmanship of the specification or claims; or to provide a vehicle for prosecution of nonelected claims.[222] Absent a clear rejection based upon lack of an adequate written disclosure of the invention, estoppel does not follow merely from the filing of a CIP. Estoppel arises only when an unambiguous rejection gives rise to a choice of appealing or accepting the rejection, and the applicant accepts the rejection and expressly or impliedly concedes its correctness.[223]

A party who relies on an earlier filed foreign application under 35 U.S.C. §119, or a domestic application under §120, has the burden to show that the foreign or parent application supports later added

---

1154, 47 USPQ2d 1829 (Fed. Cir. 1998). See also *Regents of Univ. of Calif. v. Eli Lilly & Co.,* 119 F.3d 1559, 43 USPQ2d 1398 (Fed. Cir. 1997).

[221]*Hyatt v. Boone,* 146 F.3d 1128, 47 USPQ2d 1128 (Fed. Cir. 1998). The court found no fault with the standard applied by the Board ("the necessary and only reasonable construction") for written description compliance. In the end, the purpose of the description requirement is to ensure that the inventor had possession, as of the filing date of the application relied on, of the specific subject matter later claimed. Thus, the written description must include all of the limitations of the claim or interference count, or the applicant must show that any absent text is necessarily comprehended in the description provided and would have been so understood at the time the patent application was filed.

[222]*Paperless Accounting, Inc. v. Bay Area Rapid Transit Sys.,* 804 F.2d 659, 231 USPQ 649 (Fed. Cir. 1986).

[223]*Waldemar Link v. Osteonics Corp.,* 32 F.3d 556, 31 USPQ2d 1855 (Fed. Cir. 1994). The examiner had objected to the specification as lacking an adequate written description. The applicant canceled the original claims and submitted new ones. The examiner issued a final rejection based on §102 and §103 and did not repeat either §112 or §132 as a ground for objection or rejection. After filing a CIP, the parent was abandoned. In reversing the district court's holding that the applicant was estopped from asserting a priority date earlier than the CIP filing date, the court held that this case was more like *Paperless Accounting* (see text accompanying note 5:222) than *Litton* (see note 5:214).

claims under §112.[224] A function or property that is inherent in a claimed product can be expressly described in an amendment and is not new matter. By the same token, a CIP that claims an inherent property and adds a description of the property is entitled to the filing date of the parent under §120. The standard of inherency in interference practice, that an element is inherently disclosed if the necessary and only reasonable construction to be given the disclosure by one skilled in the art is one that lends clear support to the element, is consistent with this.[225] However, where an invention is claimed as unspecified structure for performing specific functions, there is no support for that invention in an earlier application that does not disclose those functions, even though it may disclose structure that would inherently perform those functions.[226]

There is no statutory prohibition against reliance upon an earlier design application in a later utility application, so long as the earlier application meets the §112 requirements as to the invention claimed in the later application.[227] Likewise, a later filed design application can properly be a division, and be entitled to the benefit of the filing date of an earlier filed utility application.[228]

Late claiming. A discussion of new matter would be incomplete without some mention of the so-called late claiming doctrine. For

---

[224]*Utter v. Hiraga*, 845 F.2d 993, 6 USPQ2d 1709 (Fed. Cir. 1988). In order to be entitled to the benefit of an earlier filed foreign application, the applicant must prove that the foreign application meets the requirements of the first paragraph of §112. The how-to-use prong of §112 incorporates as a matter of law the requirement of §101 that a specification disclose as a matter of fact a practical utility for the invention. Thus, in order to obtain the benefit of an earlier foreign filing date the applicant must show that the foreign application disclosed practical utility for the invention. *In re Ziegler*, 992 F.2d 1197, 26 USPQ2d 1600 (Fed. Cir. 1993). Perhaps more importantly, the earlier application must satisfy the written description requirement. *Fiers v. Revel*, 984 F.2d 1164, 25 USPQ2d 1601 (Fed. Cir. 1993). See also *In re Gosteli*, 872 F.2d 1008, 10 USPQ2d 1614 (Fed. Cir. 1989). There the claims at issue were to a genus and subgenus, while an intervening prior art reference disclosed species falling within those claims. The applicant's foreign priority application disclosed the species, but did not provide an adequate written description to support the genus and subgenus. The court held that the applicant could not rely upon the foreign priority date under 35 U.S.C. §119; only if the claims were directed to the species would the result be different. This holding seems clearly inconsistent with *In re Zeigler*, 347 F.2d 642, 146 USPQ 76 (CCPA 1965), which had been viewed as holding that a foreign application need show support for only so much of the claimed invention as is disclosed in the reference in order to achieve a priority date for the entirety of the claimed invention. The Federal Circuit declined to overrule *Zeigler* on the basis of its perception that any inconsistency had already been removed sub silento by later CCPA decisions.

[225]*Kennecott Corp. v. Kyocera Int'l, Inc.*, 835 F.2d 1419, 5 USPQ2d 1194 (Fed. Cir. 1987). Thus, where a CIP adds a written description and photomicrographs of a structure of a compound that was described and claimed in the parent application and also adds claim terms relating to the structure, and where the structure was admitted to be inherent in the compound, the CIP satisfied the description requirement of §112, and the new claims were entitled to the parent filing date. *Id.* A later explicit description of an inherent property in a CIP does not deprive the product of the benefit of the filing date of the earlier application. *Therma-Tru Corp. v. Peachtree Doors Inc.*, 44 F.3d 988, 33 USPQ2d 1274 (Fed. Cir. 1994).

[226]*Mendenhall v. Cedarapids, Inc.*, 5 F.3d 1556, 28 USPQ2d 1081 (Fed. Cir. 1993).

[227]*Kangaroos U.S.A., Inc. v. Caldor, Inc.*, 778 F.2d 1571, 228 USPQ 32 (Fed. Cir. 1985).

[228]*Racing Strollers, Inc. v. TRI Indus., Inc.*, 878 F.2d 1418, 11 USPQ2d 1300 (Fed. Cir. 1989). The court, sitting in banc, expressly overruled the contrary holding of *In re Campbell*, 212 F.2d 606, 101 USPQ 406 (CCPA 1954).

many years it was supposed by some that the Supreme Court had established a rule prohibiting the belated claiming of originally disclosed but unclaimed subject matter, at some time (measured by the statutory bar period) after a public use or sale by the applicant or a competitor.[229] The CCPA corrected this misapprehension, holding that the late claiming doctrine was really nothing more than an application of the rule against new matter: if a claim is unsupported except by new matter, it will be, for purposes of assessing statutory bars, limited to the date upon which it, or its new matter support, was first presented to the PTO.[230] This rejection of any independent doctrine of late claiming that would prohibit the claiming of originally disclosed matter was so unequivocal that the Federal Circuit now refers to late claiming as an inappropriate and long-ago discredited label.[231]

§5.6 Claim Construction

It is the claims that measure the invention.[232] In construing a claim, courts can neither broaden nor narrow them to give the patentee something different than what was set forth.[233] The construction of claims is simply a way of elaborating the normally terse language of the claims, in order to understand and explain, but not to change, the scope of the claims.[234] Proper claim construction necessarily precedes a determination of whether the claims read on the accused devices for infringement purposes.[235] Improper claim construction can therefore distort the entire infringement analysis.[236] Indeed, claim

---

[229]See *Muncie Gear Works v. Outboard, Marine & Mfg. Co.*, 315 U.S. 759, 53 USPQ 1 (1942).

[230]E.g., *Westphal v. Fawzi*, 666 F.2d 575, 212 USPQ 321 (CCPA 1981).

[231]*Railroad Dynamics, Inc. v. A. Stucki Co.*, 727 F.2d 1506, 220 USPQ 929, 940 (Fed. Cir. 1984).

[232]*Smithkline Diagnostics, Inc. v. Helena Labs. Corp.*, 859 F.2d 878, 8 USPQ2d 1468 (Fed. Cir. 1988); *Constant v. Advanced Micro-Devices, Inc.*, 848 F.2d 1560, 7 USPQ2d 1057 (Fed. Cir. 1988); *SRI Int'l v. Matsushita Elec. Corp.*, 775 F.2d 1107, 227 USPQ 577 (Fed. Cir. 1985).

[233]*Texas Instr., Inc. v. United States ITC*, 988 F.2d 1165, 26 USPQ2d 1018 (Fed. Cir. 1993).

[234]*Scripps Clinic & Res. Found. v. Genentech, Inc.*, 927 F.2d 1565, 18 USPQ2d 1001 (Fed. Cir. 1991).

[235]*Smithkline Diagnostics, Inc. v. Helena Labs. Corp.*, 859 F.2d 878, 8 USPQ2d 1468 (Fed. Cir. 1988); *Fonar Corp. v. Johnson & Johnson*, 821 F.2d 627, 3 USPQ2d 1109 (Fed. Cir. 1987); *Moeller v. Ionetics, Inc.*, 794 F.2d 653, 229 USPQ 992 (Fed. Cir. 1986); *Mannesmann Demag Corp. v. Engineered Metal Prods. Co.*, 793 F.2d 1279, 230 USPQ 45 (Fed. Cir. 1986); *Lemelson v. United States*, 752 F.2d 1538, 224 USPQ 526 (Fed. Cir. 1985); *Atlas Powder Co. v. E.I. du Pont & Co.*, 750 F.2d 1569, 224 USPQ 409 (Fed. Cir. 1984). The court makes no distinction between claim "interpretation" and claim "construction," but it has for consistency adopted the latter term when referring to the first step in an infringement analysis. *Markman v. Westview Instr., Inc.*, 52 F.3d 967, 34 USPQ2d 1321, 1326n.6 (Fed. Cir. 1995).

[236]*Key Mfg. Group, Inc. v. Microdot, Inc.*, 925 F.2d 1444, 17 USPQ2d 1806 (Fed. Cir. 1991); *Smithkline Diagnostics, Inc. v. Helena Labs. Corp.*, 859 F.2d 878, 8 USPQ2d 1468 (Fed. Cir. 1988); *ZMI Corp. v. Cardiac Resuscitator Corp.*, 844 F.2d 1576, 6 USPQ2d 1557 (Fed. Cir. 1988); *Bausch & Lomb, Inc. v. Barnes-Hind, Inc.*, 796 F.2d 443, 230 USPQ 416 (Fed. Cir. 1986); *Moeller v. Ionetics, Inc.*, 794 F.2d 653, 229 USPQ 992 (Fed. Cir. 1986).

construction will normally control the remainder of the decisional process.[237]

(a) The Markman Rule—Claim Construction as a Matter of Law

Issues of claim construction—what do the claims mean?—are for the court to decide and explicate on the record.[238] In its in banc *Markman*[239] decision, the Federal Circuit undertook to settle inconsistencies in its precedent regarding the nature of claim interpretation. It held that, in a case tried to a jury, the court has the power and obligation to construe as a matter of law the meaning of the language used in the patent claims. A patent covers the invention that the court, in construing its provisions, decides that it describes and claims. Because claim construction is a matter of law, the construction given the claims is reviewed de novo on appeal. Thus, it is not improper for a trial court to take the issue of claim construction away from the jury. This ordinarily can be accomplished by the court in framing its charge to the jury, but may also be done in the context of dispositive motions such as those seeking judgment as a matter of law.

---

[237]*Panduit Corp. v. Dennison Mfg. Co.*, 810 F.2d 1561, 1 USPQ2d 1593 (Fed. Cir. 1987). When the prior art is compared with erroneously interpreted claims, findings of differences between the prior art and the claims will necessarily be clearly erroneous. *Id.* If needed to impart clarity or avoid ambiguity, the prosecution history and the prior art may also be consulted in order to ascertain whether the patentee's invention is novel or was previously known to the art. *Glaverbel S.A. v. Northlake Mkt'g & Supp., Inc.*, 45 F.3d 1550, 33 USPQ2d 1496 (Fed. Cir. 1995). In *E.I. duPont & Co. v. Phillips Petroleum Co.*, 849 F.2d 1430, 7 USPQ2d 1129 (Fed. Cir. 1988), the court found it necessary to remand for a redetermination of obviousness because the district court had employed improper claim interpretation. Implicit in the court's review of a Board anticipation analysis is that the claim must first have been correctly construed to define the scope and meaning of each contested limitation. *Gechter v. Davidson*, 116 F.3d 1454, 43 USPQ2d 1030 (Fed. Cir. 1997).

[238]*Genentech, Inc. v. Wellcome Found. Ltd.*, 29 F.3d 1555, 31 USPQ2d 1161 (Fed. Cir. 1994).

[239]*Markman v. Westview Instr., Inc.*, 52 F.3d 967, 34 USPQ2d 1321 (Fed. Cir. 1995). For cases prior to *Markman*, see, e.g., *Morton Int'l, Inc. v. Cardinal Chem. Co.*, 959 F.2d 948, 22 USPQ2d 1231 (Fed. Cir. 1992); *Whittaker Corp. v. UNR Indus., Inc.*, 911 F.2d 709, 15 USPQ2d 1742 (Fed. Cir. 1990); *C.R. Bard, Inc. v. Advanced Card. Sys., Inc.*, 911 F.2d 670, 15 USPQ2d 1540 (Fed. Cir. 1990); *Hormone Res. Found., Inc. v. Genentech, Inc.*, 904 F.2d 1558, 15 USPQ2d 1039 (Fed. Cir. 1990); *Marsh-McBirney, Inc. v. Montedoro-Whitney Corp.*, 882 F.2d 498, 11 USPQ2d 1794 (Fed. Cir. 1989); *Snellman v. Ricoh Co.*, 862 F.2d 283, 8 USPQ2d 1996 (Fed. Cir. 1988); *Smithkline Diagnostics, Inc. v. Helena Labs. Corp.*, 859 F.2d 878, 8 USPQ2d 1468 (Fed. Cir. 1988); *ZMI Corp. v. Cardiac Resuscitator Corp.*, 844 F.2d 1576, 6 USPQ2d 1557 (Fed. Cir. 1988); *Grain Processing Corp. v. American Maize-Products Co.*, 840 F.2d 902, 5 USPQ2d 1788 (Fed. Cir. 1988); *Uniroyal, Inc. v. Rudkin-Wiley Corp.*, 837 F.2d 1044, 5 USPQ2d 1434 (Fed. Cir. 1988); *Perini Am., Inc. v. Paper Converting Mach. Co.*, 832 F.2d 581, 4 USPQ2d 1621 (Fed. Cir. 1987); *Vieau v. Japax, Inc.*, 823 F.2d 1510, 3 USPQ2d 1094 (Fed. Cir. 1987); *H.H. Robertson Co. v. United Steel Deck, Inc.*, 820 F.2d 384, 2 USPQ2d 1926 (Fed. Cir. 1987); *Slimfold Mfg. Co. v. Kinkead Indus., Inc.*, 810 F.2d 1113, 1 USPQ2d 1563 (Fed. Cir. 1987); *Moeller v. Ionetics, Inc.*, 794 F.2d 653, 229 USPQ 992 (Fed. Cir. 1986); *Mannesmann Demag Corp. v. Engineered Metal Prods. Co.*, 793 F.2d 1279, 230 USPQ 45 (Fed. Cir. 1986); *Moleculon Res. Corp. v. CBS, Inc.*, 793 F.2d 1261, 229 USPQ 805 (Fed. Cir. 1986); *Loctite Corp. v. Ultraseal Ltd.*, 781 F.2d 861, 228 USPQ 90 (Fed. Cir. 1985); *SRI Int'l v. Matsushita Elec. Corp.*, 775 F.2d 1107, 227 USPQ 577 (Fed. Cir. 1985); *Palumbo v. Don-Joy Co.*, 762 F.2d 969, 226 USPQ 5 (Fed. Cir. 1985); *McGill Inc. v. John Zink Co.*, 736 F.2d 666, 221 USPQ 944 (Fed. Cir. 1984).

In justifying its ruling, the *Markman* majority had many interesting things to say about the nature of patents, particularly in the course of rejecting a contract interpretation analogy as a guideline to claim interpretation. The constitutional ramifications of the decision also were fully addressed. These matters are discussed in other chapters of this book. It is sufficient here simply to note the court's adherence to the proposition that the focus in construing disputed terms in claim language is not the subjective intent of the inventor and examiner when they used a particular term. Rather, the focus is on the objective test of what one of ordinary skill in the art at the time of the invention would have understood the term to mean.

The *Markman* majority opinion is valuable for its systematic review of the types of evidence that can be considered in claim construction. Thus, for claim construction purposes, the written description of the patent may act as a sort of dictionary, which explains the invention and may define terms used in the claims. But the written description part of the specification itself does not delimit the right to exclude. That is the function and purpose of claims.

The judge should also consider the prosecution history, if it is in evidence. This undisputed public record of proceedings in the PTO is of primary significance in understanding the claims. The court has broad power to look as a matter of law to the prosecution history of the patent in order to ascertain the true meaning of language used in the patent claims. But it, like the written description, cannot be used to enlarge, diminish, or vary the limitations in the claims.

Finally, the *Markman* majority turned to the subject of extrinsic evidence, which it defined as all evidence external to the patent and prosecution history, including expert and inventor testimony, dictionaries, and learned treatises. At the outset, it noted that the requirements of 35 U.S.C. §112 governing the written description and claim definiteness have as their purpose the avoidance of the kind of ambiguity that allows introduction of extrinsic evidence in contract interpretation. Patent applications, unlike contracts, are reviewed by patent examiners, quasi-judicial officials trained in the law and presumed to have some expertise in interpreting the prior art and to be familiar from their work with the level of skill in the art. If the patent's claims are sufficiently unambiguous for the PTO, there should exist no factual ambiguity when those same claims are later construed by a court of law in an infringement action. Thus, extrinsic evidence is not for the purpose of clarifying ambiguity in claim interpretation.

Nonetheless, a judge is not usually a person conversant in the particular technical art involved and is not the hypothetical person skilled in the art to whom a patent is addressed. Extrinsic evidence, therefore, may be necessary to inform the court about the language in which the patent is written. It is not ambiguity in the document that creates the need for extrinsic evidence but rather unfamiliarity of the court with the terminology of the art to which the patent pertains. Such evidence may be helpful to explain scientific principles, the meaning of technical terms, and terms of art that appear in the patent and prosecution history. Extrinsic evidence may demonstrate the state of the art at the time of the invention. It is useful to show what was then old, to distinguish what was new, and to aid the court in the construction of the patent.

This use of extrinsic evidence as to the true meaning of the claim language is discretionary with the trial court.[240] It can accept evidence it finds helpful, and reject other evidence as unhelpful, and resolve disputes en route to pronouncing the meaning of the claim language as a matter of law based on the patent documents themselves. Thus, although construction may be enlightened by such extrinsic evidence as is helpful, it is still based upon the patent and its prosecution history.

The *Markman* majority went on to say more about the role of expert and inventor testimony as extrinsic evidence in claim construction. When such persons testify about how a claim should be construed, their testimony amounts to no more than legal opinion, being precisely the process of construction that the court must undertake. As to these types of opinions, the court has complete discretion to adopt the expert legal opinion as its own, to find guidance from it, or to ignore it entirely or even exclude it. Where legal experts offer their conflicting views of how the patent should be construed, or where the legal expert's view of how the patent should be construed conflicts with the patent document itself, such conflict does not create a question of fact nor can the expert opinion bind the court or relieve the court of its obligation to construe the claims according to the tenor of the patent. This opinion testimony also does not change or affect the de novo appellate review standard for ascertaining the meaning of the claim language.[241]

Although the *Markman* holding was largely unequivocal, serious questions immediately arose about its scope and even its longevity. The Federal Circuit itself hinted, in an obscure footnote,[242] that its ruling might not apply to questions of equivalence under §112.[243]

---

[240]The trial court is best situated to gauge the relevance and need for additional evidence to explicate claim terms. *Eastman Kodak Co. v. Goodyear Tire & Rubber Co.*, 114 F.3d 1547, 42 USPQ2d 1737 (Fed. Cir. 1997).

[241]*Markman v. Westview Instr., Inc.*, 52 F.3d 967, 34 USPQ2d 1321 (Fed. Cir. 1995). Evidence extrinsic to the patent and prosecution history, such as technical expert testimony, cannot be relied on to change the meaning of the claims when that meaning is made clear by those documents. Thus, such expert testimony cannot create a genuine issue of material fact precluding summary judgment because it is, under the circumstances, entitled to no weight. Any other rule would be unfair to competitors who must be able to rely on the patent documents themselves, without consideration of expert opinion that then does not even exist, in ascertaining the scope of a patentee's right to exclude. *Southwall Tech., Inc. v. Cardinal IG Co.*, 54 F.3d 1570, 34 USPQ2d 1673 (Fed. Cir. 1995).

[242]"As that issue is not before us today, we express no opinion on the issue of whether a determination of equivalents under Section 112, para. 6 is a question of law or fact." 52 F.3d at 977 n.8.

[243]The court seems finally to have settled on regarding the matter as a question of fact. See discussion accompanying notes 5:388–392.

In October of 1995 the Supreme Court granted certiorari,[244] creating much uncertainty. The anecdotal evidence is to the effect that many pending infringement cases were stayed or otherwise delayed pending Supreme Court review.[245] The Supreme Court's decision,[246] issued in April 1996, came as something of an anticlimax. A unanimous court, speaking through Mr. Justice Souter, affirmed, holding that the construction of a patent, including terms of art within its claim, is exclusively within the province of the court.[247] The decision is of interest mainly for its historical analysis of the issue. In the end, the Court provided only a couple of insights that may prove reliable in guiding the lower courts, including the Federal Circuit, as they continue to grapple with the *Markman* legacy. First, the Court did allow that credibility judgments have to be made about the experts who testify in patent cases, and in theory there could be a case in which a simple credibility judgment would suffice to choose between experts whose testimony was equally consistent with a patent's internal logic. But the Court doubted that trial courts would encounter many cases like that, expecting rather that any credibility determinations will be subsumed within the necessarily sophisticated analysis of the whole document, a much more likely job for the judge than for the jury. Second, the Court, in justifying its holding on grounds of uniformity in construction of a given patent, made it clear that such judgments will nonetheless not result in issue preclusion against new and independent infringement defendants even within a given jurisdiction, and the required uniformity will have to flow instead through the application of stare decisis.[248]

So far the court has followed *Markman* faithfully. Asserted claims must be interpreted by the trial court as a matter of law to determine their meaning and scope.[249] The court regards this as an obligation

---

[244]The grant was to consider the following question: "In patent infringement action for damages, is there right to jury trial under Seventh Amendment of genuine factual disputes about meaning of patent?" 34 USPQ2d 1321, 64 U.S.L.W. 3201 (U.S. Oct. 3, 1995).

[245]This author was personally involved in several such cases and knew of many more.

[246]517 U.S. 370, 38 USPQ2d 1461 (1996).

[247]One supposes that seemingly contrary prior statements by the Federal Circuit did not survive the Supreme Court's ruling. For example, in *Tol-O-Matic, Inc. v. Proma Produckt-und Mktg. GmbH,* 945 F.2d 1546, 20 USPQ2d 1332 (Fed. Cir. 1991), the court indicated that when the meaning of a term in a patent claim is unclear, subject to varying interpretations, or ambiguous, the jury may interpret the term en route to deciding the issue of infringement. In *Read Corp. v. Portec, Inc.,* 970 F.2d 816, 23 USPQ2d 1426 (Fed. Cir. 1992), it was said that where the trial court's interpretation is not set forth in its instructions to the jury, it must perform its role of deciding this issue in ruling on a JNOV motion. It seems likely that trial courts now must always instruct the jury as to the appropriate legal claim construction.

[248]This dictum by the Supreme Court seems directly contrary to *Del Mar Avionics, Inc. v. Quinton Instr. Co.,* 836 F.2d 1320, 5 USPQ2d 1255 (Fed. Cir. 1987), where the Federal Circuit indicated that, to the extent that the underlying facts are based on identical premises, the prior findings of another court and the claim construction based thereon are law of the case (or res judicata) and are not available for reinterpretation.

[249]*Southwall Tech., Inc. v. Cardinal IG Co.,* 54 F.3d 1570, 34 USPQ2d 1673 (Fed. Cir. 1995). Indeed, a jury's claim construction is, at best, an advisory determination. *Laitram Corp. v. NEC Corp.,* 62 F.3d 1388, 36 USPQ2d 1206 (Fed. Cir. 1995).

of the trial judge that is independent of the views asserted by the adversary parties. In other words, it is insufficient for the judge simply to choose between the asserted constructions of the parties without an independent analysis.[250]

The two major areas of uncertainty swirling in the wake of *Markman* are practical and extremely important ones. At what stage of the proceedings and in what context or format is the claim construction to be undertaken? And what evidence is to be considered? The answers to these questions are certain to occupy the Federal Circuit and the trial courts for years to come, but some beginnings have already been made.

Stage of the proceedings. As to the first major question—how and when should the determination be made—*Markman* itself had some tentative suggestions, such as resolving the matter in the framework of jury instructions or in the context of dispositive motions such as JMOL. Indeed, where the parties do not dispute any relevant facts regarding the accused product but disagree over which of two possible meanings of a claim is the proper one, the question of literal infringement collapses to one of claim construction and is thus amenable to summary judgment.[251]

The court has taken care to point out that *Markman* does not obligate the trial judge to undertake a conclusive interpretation of claims at an early stage in a case. A trial court may exercise its discretion to interpret the claims at a time when the parties have presented a full picture of the claimed invention and prior art.[252] A district court has broad powers of case management, including the power to limit discovery to relevant subject matter and to adjust discovery as appropriate to each phase of litigation. When a particular issue may be dispositive, the court may stay discovery concerning other issues until the critical issue is resolved. Thus the trial court's management of discovery at the claim construction stage may serve the salutary goals of speed and economy, and is appropriate in cases in which the dispute may be resolved at this stage without compromise of justice. Nonetheless, the Federal Circuit declines to adopt a uniform rule that claim construction should be done no earlier than the end of discovery. The stage at which the claims are construed may vary with the issues, their complexity, the potentially dispositive nature

---

[250]*Exxon Chem. Patents, Inc. v. Lubrizol Corp.,* 64 F.3d 1553, 35 USPQ2d 1801, 1803 (Fed. Cir. 1995). See also *Rodime PLC v. Seagate Tech. Inc.,* 174 F.3d 1294, 50 USPQ2d 1429 (Fed. Cir. 1999).

[251]*Athletic Alternatives, Inc. v. Prince Mfg., Inc.,* 73 F.3d 1573, 37 USPQ2d 1365 (Fed. Cir. 1996).

[252]*Sofamor Danek Group, Inc. v. DePuy-Motech, Inc.,* 74 F.3d 1216, 37 USPQ2d 1529 (Fed. Cir. 1996). For example, the trial court has no obligation to interpret claims conclusively and finally during a preliminary injunction proceeding. See also *Metaullics Sys. Co. v. Cooper,* 100 F.3d 938, 40 USPQ2d 1798 (Fed. Cir. 1996).

of the construction, and other considerations of the particular case.[253] Despite such assurances, however, anecdotal evidence surely foreshadows the ubiquitous rise of a procedure that, quite descriptively, is quickly becoming known as the *"Markman* hearing," where a trial court actually holds an evidentiary hearing, often prior to trial, for the purpose of arriving at a claim construction that can serve as a guide for further conduct of the litigation.[254]

It seems clear that *Markman* does not require that the trial judge repeat or restate every claim term in order to comply with the principle that claim construction is for the court. Claim construction is a matter of resolution of disputed meanings and technical scope, to clarify and when necessary to explain what the patentee covered by the claims, for use in the determination of infringement. It is not an obligatory exercise in redundancy.[255]

Intrinsic versus extrinsic evidence–the Vitronics *case.* No matter how and at what stage of the proceedings the job of claim construction is done, the more difficult set of problems has to do with the type of evidence that the court must, on the one hand, and may, on the other, consider in arriving at that decision. Again, the Federal Circuit made a start in *Markman* itself, in attempting to distinguish between and define intrinsic and extrinsic evidence. More recently, a panel of the court revisited that question in *Vitronics v. Conceptronic,*[256] with a somewhat surprisingly vigorous discouragement of trial court reliance on extrinsic evidence. *Vitronics* deserves attention if only in an effort to predict whether this attitude will prevail across the full court.

The *Vitronics* decision began unremarkably. Thus, in interpreting an asserted claim, the court should look first to the intrinsic evidence of record, i.e., the patent itself, including the claims, the specification, and, if in evidence, the prosecution history. Such intrinsic evidence is the most significant source of the legally operative meaning of disputed claim language. Although the words in a claim are generally given their ordinary and customary meaning, a patentee may choose to be his or her own lexicographer and use terms in a manner other than their ordinary meaning, as long as the special

---

[253]*Vivid Tech. Inc. v. American Sci. & Eng'g Inc.,* 200 F.3d 795, 53 USPQ2d 1289 (Fed. Cir. 1999).

[254]This author has already participated as an expert witness and as a special master in many such hearings, at various stages of the proceedings. In this day of common bifurcation between liability and damages, and even trifurcation of liability into infringement on the one hand and validity and enforceability on the other, another segmentation of the patent litigation corpus may seem a bit much unless clearly justified on grounds of economy, efficiency, and the interest of justice. As for the latter desideratum, it is obviously tempting to avoid much effort by adopting a claim construction that will necessarily result in summary judgment on the infringement issue. A cynical observer might view this as a handy transformation of a factual issue—infringement—into a legal issue—claim construction.

[255]*United States Surgical Corp. v. Ethicon, Inc.,* 103 F.3d 1554, 41 USPQ2d 1225 (Fed. Cir. 1997).

[256]*Vitronics Corp. v. Conceptronic, Inc.,* 90 F.3d 1576, 39 USPQ2d 1573 (Fed. Cir. 1996).

definition of the term is clearly stated in the patent specification or file history. Thus, it is always necessary to review the specification to determine whether the inventor has used any terms in a manner inconsistent with their ordinary meaning. The specification acts as a dictionary when it expressly defines terms used in the claims or when it defines terms by implication. Inasmuch as the specification must contain an enabling written description of the invention, it is always highly relevant and usually dispositive. It is the single best guide to the meaning of a disputed term. The prosecution history is also relevant. It contains the complete record of the PTO proceedings, including any express representations made by the applicant regarding the scope of the claims. As such, it is often of critical significance in determining the meaning of the claims.

The *Vitronics* court then went on to observe that, in most situations, an analysis of the intrinsic evidence alone will resolve any ambiguity in a disputed claim term. In such circumstances, it is improper to rely on extrinsic evidence. The claims, specification, and file history, rather than extrinsic evidence, constitute the public record of the patentee's claim, a record on which the public is entitled to rely. In other words, competitors are entitled to review the public record, apply the established rules of claim construction, ascertain the scope of the patentee's claimed invention and, thus, design around the claimed invention. Allowing the public record to be altered or changed by extrinsic evidence introduced at trial, such as expert testimony, would make this right meaningless. The same holds true whether it is the patentee or the alleged infringer who seeks to alter the scope of the claims.

Thus, only if there is still some genuine ambiguity in the claims, after consideration of all available intrinsic evidence, should the trial court resort to extrinsic evidence such as expert testimony. And even if the judge decides to hear all possible evidence before construing the claims, expert testimony inconsistent with the intrinsic evidence should be accorded no weight. Extrinsic evidence in general, and expert testimony in particular, may be used only to help the court come to the proper understanding of the claims; it may not be used to vary or contradict the claim language. Nor may it contradict the import of other parts of the specification. Nor may the inventor's subjective intent as to claim scope, when unexpressed in the patent documents, have any effect.

Strong language, indeed. The *Vitronics* panel did go on to suggest that reliance on expert testimony and other extrinsic evidence solely to help understand the underlying technology is not improper. But testimony on the technology is far different from other expert testimony, whether it be of an attorney, a technical expert, or the inventor, on the proper construction of a disputed claim term. The latter kind of testimony may be relied upon only if the patent documents are insufficient; such instances will rarely, if ever, occur. And even in those rare instances, prior art documents and dictionaries, although to a lesser extent, are more objective and reliable guides. Unlike expert testimony, these sources are accessible to the public in advance of litigation. They are to be preferred over opinion testimony, whether by an attorney or artisan in the field of technology to which the patent is directed. Indeed, opinion testimony on claim construction should be treated with the utmost caution, for it is no better than opinion testimony on the meaning of statutory terms.[257]

Whether the Federal Circuit as a whole will embrace the *Vitronics* decision's seeming discouragement of extrinsic evidence as a claim construction consideration is a question that make take years to answer.[258] The court rather quickly disavowed the notion that *Markman* stands for the proposition that extrinsic evidence including expert testimony amounts to no more than legal opinion and is entitled to no weight. *Markman* held that the trial court has wide latitude in the kinds of aids, including testimony of witnesses, employed to assist in the job of claim interpretation as a matter of law.[259] Trial courts generally can hear expert testimony for background and education on the technology implicated by the claim construction issues, and trial courts have broad discretion in this regard. Furthermore, a trial court is quite correct in hearing and relying on expert testimony on an ultimate claim construction question in cases in which the intrinsic evidence does not answer the question. What is disapproved of is an attempt to use extrinsic evidence to arrive at a claim construction that is clearly at odds with the claim construction mandated by the claims themselves, the written description, and the prosecution history, in other words, with the written record of the patent. Thus, if the meaning of a disputed claim term is clear from the intrinsic evidence—the written record—that meaning, and no other, must prevail; it cannot be altered or superseded by witness testimony or other external sources simply because one of the parties wishes it were otherwise. Competitors are entitled to rely on the public record of the

---

[257]*Vitronics Corp. v. Conceptronic, Inc.*, 90 F.3d 1576, 39 USPQ2d 1573, 1579 (Fed. Cir. 1996).

[258]Perhaps a middle ground can be found in decisions like *Hoechst Celanese Corp. v. BP Chem. Ltd.*, 78 F.3d 1575, 38 USPQ2d 1126 (Fed. Cir. 1996), which was decided in the interim between *Markman* and *Vitronics*. In *Hoechst* the court first reminds us that it need not look to extrinsic technical evidence. But then it confesses that such evidence is necessary for it in this case to make a decision, because its judges are not "personally qualified to know the scientific meanings" of the words at issue. It goes on to consider and weigh the conflicting expert testimony and general and technical dictionary definitions, and ultimately comes to a conclusion. Along the way, it looks at the inventor's testimony, reminds us again that *Markman* requires that no deference be given to inventor testimony about the meaning of the claims, but then concludes that the inventor's testimony enlarges its understanding of the technology and the usage of the disputed terms. If one thing is clear, it is that the court has taken upon itself an enormous task by insisting that claim interpretation is a question of law that is subject to plenary review. Cases like *Hoechst* and *Ethicon Endo-Surgery, Inc. v. United States Surgical Corp.*, 93 F.3d 1572, 40 USPQ2d 1019 (Fed. Cir. 1996) are illustrations of the massive effort that can go into just the review process. Roughly one-third of the precedential patent decisions of the Federal Circuit handed down in the interval between the fourth and fifth editions of this book involved substantive discussions of claim interpretation.

[259]*Endress + Hauser, Inc. v. Hawk Meas. Sys. Pty.*, 122 F.3d 1040, 43 USPQ2d 1849 (Fed. Cir. 1997).

patent, and if the meaning of the patent is plain, the public record is conclusive.[260]

Under *Vitronics*, it is entirely appropriate, perhaps even preferable, for a court to consult trustworthy extrinsic evidence to ensure that the claim construction it is tending to from the patent file is not inconsistent with clearly expressed, plainly apposite, and widely held understandings in the pertinent technical field. This is especially the case with respect to technical terms, as opposed to nontechnical terms in general usage or terms of art in the claim drafting art, such as "comprising." Indeed, a patent is both a technical and a legal document. While a judge is well equipped to interpret the legal aspects of the document, he or she must also interpret the technical aspects of the document, and its overall meaning, from the vantage point of one skilled in the art. Although the patent file may often be sufficient to permit the judge to interpret the technical aspects of the patent properly, consultation of extrinsic evidence is particularly appropriate to ensure that his or her understanding of the technical aspects of the patent is not entirely at variance with the understanding of one skilled in the art.[261] Thus the court believes that, although *Markman* presents a useful general rule, it is adaptable to the needs of the particular case. For example, extrinsic evidence may be particularly helpful to the court when a specific technical aspect that is potentially of dispositive weight was not discussed in the specification or explored during the patent prosecution.[262]

Nonetheless, the court continues to insist that, when an analysis of the intrinsic evidence alone will resolve any ambiguity in a disputed claim term, it is improper to rely on extrinsic evidence.[263] The intrinsic evidence should usually be sufficient to enable one to determine the meaning of a claim term.[264] Thus the court will likely continue to call for observation of these guidelines: to determine the proper meaning of claims a court first considers the so-called intrinsic evidence, i.e.,

---

[260]*Key Pharm. Inc. v. Hercon Labs. Corp.*, 161 F.3d 709, 48 USPQ2d 1911 (Fed. Cir. 1998). In *Mantech Envtl. Corp. v. Hudson Envtl. Serv. Inc.*, 152 F.3d 1368, 47 USPQ2d 1732 (Fed. Cir. 1998), the court held that the district court was legally correct both in admitting and accepting the testimony of the parties' expert witnesses for the purpose of background in the technical area at issue, and then basing its claim construction solely upon intrinsic evidence. Although such information always may be admitted by the trial court to educate itself about the patent and the relevant technology, the claims and the written description remain the primary and more authoritative sources of claim construction.

[261]*Pitney Bowes Inc. v. Hewlett-Packard Co.*, 182 F.3d 1298, 51 USPQ2d 1161 (Fed. Cir. 1999).

[262]*Fromson v. Anitec Printing Plates Inc.*, 132 F.3d 1437, 45 USPQ2d 1269 (Fed. Cir. 1997). When the specification explains and defines a term used in the claims, without ambiguity or incompleteness, there is no need to search further for the meaning of the term. However, when such definition is challenged it is often appropriate, despite facial clarity and sufficiency of the specification and the prosecution history, to receive evidence of the meaning and usage of terms of art from persons experienced in the field of the invention. *ATD Corp. v. Lydall Inc.*, 159 F.3d 534, 48 USPQ2d 1321 (Fed. Cir. 1998).

[263]*Kegel Co. v. AMF Bowling, Inc.*, 127 F.3d 1420, 44 USPQ2d 1123 (Fed. Cir. 1997).

[264]*Bell & Howell DMP Co. v. Altek Sys.*, 132 F.3d 701, 45 USPQ2d 1033 (Fed. Cir. 1997).

the claims, the written description, and, if in evidence, the prosecution history. Even within the intrinsic evidence, however, there is a hierarchy of analytical tools. The actual words of the claim are the controlling focus. The written description is considered, in particular to determine if the patentee acted as his or her own lexicographer, as the law permits, and ascribed a certain meaning to those claim terms. If not, the ordinary meaning, to one skilled in the art, of the claim language controls. The prosecution history is relevant because it may contain contemporaneous exchanges between the patent applicant and the PTO about what the claims mean. If upon examination of this intrinsic evidence the meaning of the claim language is sufficiently clear, resort to "extrinsic" evidence, such as treatises and technical references, as well as expert testimony when appropriate, should not be necessary. However, if after consideration of the intrinsic evidence there remains doubt as to the exact meaning of the claim terms, consideration of extrinsic evidence may be necessary to determine the proper construction.[265]

(b) Ordinary Meaning and Inventor Lexicography

Several broad principles govern claim interpretation. Claim construction begins, as it must, with the words of the claims.[266] We have already seen that a patentee may be his or her own lexicographer,[267] provided he or she defines the terms,[268] where there is a need to coin new expressions with which to communicate the invention, or where the inventor is not schooled in the terminology of the technical art to which the invention pertains.[269] Thus, the inventor's definition and explanation of the meaning of a word, as evidenced by the specification, controls the interpretation of that claim term, as opposed, for example, to dictionary definitions.[270]

---

[265]*Digital Biometrics Inc. v. Identix Inc.*, 149 F.3d 1335, 47 USPQ2d 1418, 1424 (Fed. Cir. 1998).

[266]*Vehicular Techs. Corp. v. Titan Wheel Int'l*, 141 F.3d 1084, 46 USPQ2d 1257 (Fed. Cir. 1998).

[267]*ZMI Corp. v. Cardiac Resuscitator Corp.*, 844 F.2d 1576, 6 USPQ2d 1557 (Fed. Cir. 1988); *Fonar Corp. v. Johnson & Johnson*, 821 F.2d 627, 3 USPQ2d 1109 (Fed. Cir. 1987); *Loctite Corp. v. Ultraseal Ltd.*, 781 F.2d 861, 228 USPQ 90 (Fed. Cir. 1985); *Fromson v. Advance Offset Plate, Inc.*, 720 F.2d 1565, 219 USPQ 1137 (Fed. Cir. 1983). Although a patentee may be his or her own lexicographer, the patent specification must support the asserted definition. *Constant v. Advanced Micro-Devices, Inc.*, 848 F.2d 1560, 7 USPQ2d 1057 (Fed. Cir. 1988). The patent law allows the inventor to be one's own lexicographer, but one may not compose one's own standards of patentability. *Merck & Co. v. Biocraft Labs., Inc.*, 874 F.2d 804, 10 USPQ2d 1843 (Fed. Cir. 1989). It is a well-established axiom in patent law that a patentee is free to be his or her own lexicographer and thus may use terms in a manner contrary to or inconsistent with one or more of their ordinary meanings. For this reason, an analysis of the specification and prosecution history is important to proper claim construction. *Hormone Res. Found., Inc. v. Genentech, Inc.*, 904 F.2d 1558, 15 USPQ2d 1039 (Fed. Cir. 1990).

[268]*Novo Nordisk of N.A., Inc. v. Genentech, Inc.*, 77 F.3d 1364, 37 USPQ2d 1773 (Fed. Cir. 1996). A patentee is entitled to provide his or her own definition for the terms used in a patent claim, including the transition phrase "consisting essentially of." *PPG Indus. Inc. v. Guardian Indus. Corp.*, 156 F.3d 1351, 48 USPQ2d 1351 (Fed. Cir. 1998).

[269]*Lear Siegler, Inc. v. Aeroquip Corp.*, 733 F.2d 881, 221 USPQ 1025 (Fed. Cir. 1984).

[270]*Serrano v. Telular Corp.*, 111 F.3d 1578, 42 USPQ2d 1538 (Fed. Cir. 1997).

By the same token, a claim must be read in accordance with the precepts of English grammar.[271] The ordinary and accustomed meaning of a disputed claim term is presumed to be the correct one, subject to the following provisions. First, a different meaning clearly and deliberately set forth in the intrinsic materials—the written description or the prosecution history—will control. Second, if the ordinary and accustomed meaning of a disputed term would deprive the claim of clarity, then further reference must be made to the intrinsic— or in some cases, extrinsic—evidence to ascertain the proper meaning. In either case, a party wishing to alter the meaning of a clear claim term must overcome the presumption that the ordinary and accustomed meaning is the proper one, demonstrating why such an alteration is required.[272]

The claim term's ordinary and accustomed meaning initially serves as a default meaning because the patentee may act as a lexicographer and ascribe a different, or modified, meaning to the term. The court, therefore, must examine a patent's specification and prosecution history to determine whether the patentee has given the term an unconventional meaning. If the patentee has not done so, the term's ordinary and accustomed meaning controls.[273] Where an inventor chooses to be his or her own lexicographer and to give terms uncommon meanings, he or she must set out this uncommon definition in some manner within the patent disclosure.[274]

Thus the claim language itself defines the scope of the claim. The construing court does not accord the specification, prosecution history, and other relevant evidence the same weight as the claims themselves, but consults these sources to give the necessary context to the claim language. Nonetheless, without manifest clarity in the claim language alone, the court will consult other sources about the intended meaning

---

[271]*In re Hyatt,* 708 F.2d 712, 218 USPQ 195, 197 (Fed. Cir. 1983). For example, modifiers of a term are usually in proximity to such term. *DeGeorge v. Bernier,* 768 F.2d 1318, 226 USPQ 758 (Fed. Cir. 1985).

[272]*K-2 Corp. v. Salomon S.A.,* 191 F.3d 1356, 52 USPQ2d 1001 (Fed. Cir. 1999).

[273]*Hockerson-Halberstadt Inc. v. Avia Group Int'l Inc.,* 222 F.3d 951, 55 USPQ2d 1487 (Fed. Cir. 2000). Words will be given their ordinary and accustomed meaning unless it appears that the inventor used them differently. *Gentex Corp. v. Donnelly Corp.,* 69 F.3d 527, 36 USPQ2d 1667 (Fed. Cir. 1995); *Nike Inc. v. Wolverine World Wide, Inc.,* 43 F.3d 644, 33 USPQ2d 1038 (Fed. Cir. 1994); *Carroll Touch, Inc. v. Electro Mechanical Sys., Inc.,* 3 F.3d 404, 27 USPQ2d 1836 (Fed. Cir. 1993); *Envirotech Corp. v. Al George, Inc.,* 730 F.2d 753, 221 USPQ 473 (Fed. Cir. 1984). Resort must be had to the specification and prosecution history to determine if the inventor used the disputed terms differently than their ordinary accustomed meaning. *Hoechst Celanese Corp. v. BP Chem. Ltd.,* 78 F.3d 1575, 38 USPQ2d 1126 (Fed. Cir. 1996); *ZMI Corp. v. Cardiac Resuscitator Corp.,* 844 F.2d 1576, 6 USPQ2d 1557 (Fed. Cir. 1988). When the specification does not use a term in a special or unique way, its ordinary meaning to one skilled in the art controls. *Ekchian v. Home Depot, Inc.,* 104 F.3d 1299, 41 USPQ2d 1364 (Fed. Cir. 1997). See *Hoganas AB v. Dresser Indus., Inc.,* 9 F.3d 948, 28 USPQ2d 1936 (Fed. Cir. 1993), for a fascinating exposition of the meaning of "straw-shaped, channel-forming elements."

[274]*Intellicall, Inc. v. Phonometrics, Inc.,* 952 F.2d 1384, 21 USPQ2d 1383 (Fed. Cir. 1992). See also *Beachcombers v. Wildewood Creative Prods., Inc.,* 31 F.3d 1154, 31 USPQ2d 1653 (Fed. Cir. 1994). The caveat is that any special definition given to a word must be clearly defined in the specification. *Markman v. Westview Instr., Inc.,* 52 F.3d 967, 34 USPQ2d 1321 (Fed. Cir. 1995).

of the claim language.[275] But where a specification contains neither a definition of a phrase nor a suggestion that the inventor sought to assign to the claim terms anything but their ordinary and accustomed meanings, those are the meanings that must be given them.[276] Without an express intent to impart a novel meaning to claim terms, an inventor's claim terms take on their ordinary meaning.[277] Some illustrations appear in the footnote.[278]

The law provides a patentee with the opportunity to define his or her own claim terms because the public may not be schooled in the terminology of the technical art or there may not be an extant term of singular meaning for the structure or concept that is being claimed. But absent a special and particular definition created by the patent applicant, terms in a claim are to be given their ordinary and accustomed meaning. Thus, when a claim term is expressed in general descriptive words, the court will not ordinarily limit the term to a numerical range that may appear in the written description or in other claims. Nor will it, in the broader situation, add a narrowing modifier before an otherwise general term that stands unmodified in a claim. For example, if an apparatus claim recites a general structure (e.g., a noun) without limiting that structure to a specific subset of structures (e.g., with an adjective), it will generally construe the claim to cover all known types of that structure that are supported by the patent disclosure. However, a common meaning, such as one expressed in a relevant dictionary, that flies in the face of the patent disclosure, is undeserving of fealty. Thus, where there are several common meanings for a claim term, the patent disclosure serves to point away from the improper meanings and toward the proper meaning. Ultimately, the interpretation to be given a term can only

---

[275]*Eastman Kodak Co. v. Goodyear Tire & Rubber Co.*, 114 F.3d 1547, 42 USPQ2d 1737 (Fed. Cir. 1997).

[276]*Athletic Alternatives, Inc. v. Prince Mfg., Inc.*, 73 F.3d 1573, 37 USPQ2d 1365 (Fed. Cir. 1996).

[277]*Kegel Co. v. AMF Bowling, Inc.*, 127 F.3d 1420, 44 USPQ2d 1123 (Fed. Cir. 1997).

[278]While use of the singular form of a word does not preclude a meaning that includes the plural, logic precludes reading a rule that permits singular usage to encompass the plural to require instead the plural meaning. *Embrex Inc. v. Service Eng'g Corp.*, 216 F.3d 1343, 55 USPQ2d 1161 (Fed. Cir. 2000). In *York Prods., Inc. v. Central Tractor Farm & Fam. Ctr.*, 99 F.3d 1568, 40 USPQ2d 1619 (Fed. Cir. 1996), the trial court, for no apparent good reason, found that "plurality" meant more than three. The Federal Circuit reversed on the basis that the ordinary meaning of plurality is more than one. In another case, in considering an argument about the meaning of the word "permanently," the court remarked that it would be hard pressed to describe anything as "permanent" if that term is understood to require an infinite duration. But claim construction is not philosophy; one need not wring one's hands when considering the implications of a metaphysical analysis of claim terms. Instead, one need only recognize that claim construction is firmly anchored in reality by the understanding of those of ordinary skill in the art. *K-2 Corp. v. Salomon S.A.*, 191 F.3d 1356, 52 USPQ2d 1001 (Fed. Cir. 1999). In *Mantech Envtl. Corp. v. Hudson Envtl. Serv. Inc.*, 152 F.3d 1368, 47 USPQ2d 1732 (Fed. Cir. 1998), the court relied upon the plain language of the claim to hold that the recited method steps must be performed sequentially, in the order given. In *Robot Vision Sys. Inc. v. View Eng'g Inc.*, 189 F.3d 1370, 51 USPQ2d 1949 (Fed. Cir. 1999), the court refused to interpret the term "providing" as requiring the separate manufacture of the component in question, rather than the selection and use of a preexisting component.

be determined and confirmed with a full understanding of what the inventors actually invented and intended to envelop with the claim. The construction that stays true to the claim language and most naturally aligns with the patent's description of the invention will be, in the end, the correct construction. A claim construction is persuasive, not because it follows a certain rule, but because it defines terms in the context of the whole patent.[279]

Special terms of art. There are special terms of art that are commonly understood. For example, the phrase "consisting of" is a term of art in patent law signifying restriction and exclusion, while, in contrast, the term "comprising" indicates an open-ended construction. In simple terms, a drafter uses the phrase "consisting of" to mean "I claim what follows and nothing else." A drafter uses the term "comprising" to mean "I claim at least what follows and potentially more."[280] The signal "comprising" is thus generally understood to signify that the claims do not exclude the presence in the accused apparatus or method of factors in addition to those explicitly recited. It implements the general rule that absent some special circumstance or estoppel that excludes the additional factor, infringement is not avoided by the presence of elements or steps in addition to those specifically recited in the claim.[281] The claim term "including" is synonymous with "comprising," thereby permitting the inclusion of unnamed components.[282] "Comprise" is a broader term than "consist."[283]

---

[279]*Renishaw plc v. Marposs Societa' per Azione,* 158 F.3d 1243, 48 USPQ2d 1117 (Fed. Cir. 1998).

[280]*Vehicular Tech. Corp. v. Titan Wheel Int'l Inc.,* 212 F.3d 1377, 54 USPQ2d 1841 (Fed. Cir. 2000).

[281]*Vivid Tech. Inc. v. American Sci. & Eng'g Inc.,* 200 F.3d 795, 53 USPQ2d 1289 (Fed. Cir. 1999). If a patent requires A, and the accused device or process uses A and B, infringement will be avoided only if the patent's definition of A excludes the possibility of B. Statements in the patent simply noting a distinction between A and B are thus unhelpful: what matters is not that the patent describes A and B as different, but whether, according to the patent, A and B must be mutually exclusive. *Northern Telecom Ltd. v. Samsung Elec. Co.,* 215 F.3d 1281, 55 USPQ2d 1065 (Fed. Cir. 2000). Use of the term "comprising" results in an "open" claim that will read on devices that add additional elements. *Stiftung v. Renishaw PLC,* 945 F.2d 1173, 20 USPQ2d 1094 (Fed. Cir. 1991). "Comprising" is a term of art used in claim language that means that the named elements are essential, but other elements may be added and still form a construct within the scope of the claim. *Rowe v. Dror,* 112 F.3d 473, 42 USPQ2d 1550 (Fed. Cir. 1997). A claim employing the transitional term "comprising" does not exclude additional, unrecited elements or method steps. *Moleculon Res. Corp. v. CBS, Inc.,* 793 F.2d 1261, 229 USPQ 805 (Fed. Cir. 1986). "Comprising" is not a weasel word with which to abrogate claim limitations. *Spectrum Int'l Inc. v. Sterilite Corp.,* 164 F.3d 1372, 49 USPQ2d 1065 (Fed. Cir. 1998). In *Phillips Pet. Co. v. Huntsman Polymers Corp.,* 157 F.3d 866, 48 USPQ2d 1161 (Fed. Cir. 1998), the court held that a claim to a "block copolymer comprising" excluded compositions that contain only an insignificant number of block copolymer molecules.

[282]*Hewlett-Packard Co. v. Repeat-O-Type Stencil,* 123 F.3d 1445, 43 USPQ2d 1650 (Fed. Cir. 1997). The claim word "including" is not construed in a lexicographic vacuum, but in the context of the specification and drawings. *Toro Co. v. White Consol. Indus. Inc.,* 199 F.3d 1295, 53 USPQ2d 1065 (Fed. Cir. 1999).

[283]*Georgia-Pacific Corp. v. United States Gypsum Co.,* 195 F.3d 1322, 52 USPQ2d 1590 (Fed. Cir. 1999).

"Consisting essentially of" is a transition phrase commonly used to signal a partially open claim in a patent. Typically, "consisting essentially of" precedes a list of ingredients in a composition claim or a series of steps in a process claim. By using the term "consisting essentially of," the drafter signals that the invention necessarily includes the listed ingredients and is open to unlisted ingredients that do not materially affect the basic and novel properties of the invention.[284] Thus, a "consisting essentially of" claim occupies a middle ground between closed claims that are written in a "consisting of" format and fully open claims that are drafted in a "comprising" format. Such a claim necessarily contains some inherent imprecision. The resolution of whether a given unlisted ingredient materially affects the basic and novel properties of the invention is a question of infringement for the trier of fact rather than one of claim construction for the court.[285]

The court has repeatedly emphasized that an indefinite article "a" or "an" in patent parlance carries the meaning of "one or more" in open-ended claims containing the transitional phrase "comprising." Unless the claim is specific as to the number of elements, the article "a" receives a singular interpretation only in rare circumstances when the patentee evinces a clear intent to so limit the article. Under this conventional rule, the claim limitation "a," without more, requires at least one. The written description supplies additional context for understanding whether the claim language limits the patent scope to a single unitary element or extends to encompass a device with multiple elements. Moreover, standing alone, a disclosure of a preferred or exemplary embodiment encompassing a singular element does not disclaim a plural embodiment. Thus, as the rule dictates, when the claim language or context calls for further inquiry, the court consults the written description for a clear intent to limit the invention to a singular embodiment. Prosecution history also may assist claim interpretation; an applicant may disclaim before the PTO a plural interpretation and thus lose the benefit of the customary meaning of indefinite articles in patent claims. Accordingly, when claim language or context suggests an ambiguity in application of the general meaning of an article, the court undertakes an examination of the written description and the prosecution history to ascertain whether to limit the meaning of "a" or "an."[286]

---

[284]*PPG Indus. Inc. v. Guardian Indus. Corp.*, 156 F.3d 1351, 48 USPQ2d 1351 (Fed. Cir. 1998). See also *Water Techs. Corp. v. Calco, Ltd.*, 850 F.2d 660, 7 USPQ2d 1097 (Fed. Cir. 1988); *Atlas Powder Co. v. E.I. du Pont & Co.*, 750 F.2d 1569, 224 USPQ 409 (Fed. Cir. 1984).

[285]*PPG Indus. Inc. v. Guardian Indus. Corp.*, 156 F.3d 1351, 48 USPQ2d 1351 (Fed. Cir. 1998). Where the phrase "consisting of" does not appear in the claim preamble and thus limits only the element set forth in the clause in which it appears, it does not exclude all other elements from the claim as a whole. *Mannesmann Demag Corp. v. Engineered Metal Prods. Co.*, 793 F.2d 1279, 230 USPQ 45 (Fed. Cir. 1986).

[286]*KCJ Corp. v. Kinetic Concepts Inc.*, 223 F.3d 1351, 55 USPQ2d 1835 (Fed. Cir. 2000). The article "a" suggests the singular. However, patent claim parlance also recognizes that an article can carry the meaning of "one or more," for example in a claim using the transitional

A "whereby" clause that merely states the result of the limitations in the claim adds nothing to the patentability or substance of the claim.[287] The term "integrally formed" has received some attention from the court.[288]

The use of the term "about" permits some leeway in the amount of a required constituent in a claim.[289] Such broadening usages as "about" must be given reasonable scope; they must be viewed by the decision maker as they would be understood by persons experienced in the field of the invention. Although it is rarely feasible to attach a precise limit to "about," the usage can usually be understood in light of the technology embodied in the invention. When the claims are applied to an accused device, it is a question of technologic fact whether the accused device meets a reasonable meaning of "about" in the particular circumstances.[290]

(c) Intrinsic Evidence

We know from *Markman* and *Vitronics* that intrinsic evidence refers to the so-called patent documents, including the claims themselves, the specification and drawings of the patent, and its prosecution history. The role of the specification and prosecution history are discussed in some detail in this subsection. Some standard general rules about how claims are to be viewed are discussed in subsection (g) below.

---

phrase "comprising." *Abtox, Inc. v. Exitron Corp.*, 122 F.3d 1019, 43 USPQ2d 1545, *amended opinion,* 46 USPQ2d 1735 (Fed. Cir. 1997). While the article "a" or "an" may suggest "one," those articles can mean "one" or "more than one," depending on the context in which the article is used. *Elkay Mfg. Co. v. Ebco Mfg. Co.*, 192 F.3d 970, 52 USPQ2d 1109 (Fed. Cir. 1999). In a somewhat murky 2–1 decision, the majority recognized that it is generally accepted in patent parlance that "a" or "an" can mean one or more. However, the court seemed to require an indication in the specification that the inventor intended the word to have other than its normal singular meaning. *North Am. Vaccine, Inc. v. American Cyanamid Co.*, 7 F.3d 1571, 28 USPQ2d 1333 (Fed. Cir. 1993).

[287]*Texas Instr., Inc. v. United States ITC*, 988 F.2d 1165, 26 USPQ2d 1018 (Fed. Cir. 1993).

[288]*In re Morris*, 127 F.3d 1048, 44 USPQ2d 1023 (Fed. Cir. 1997); *Hazani v. United States ITC*, 126 F.3d 1473, 44 USPQ2d 1358 (Fed. Cir. 1997).

[289]*Haynes Int'l, Inc. v. Jessop Steel Co.*, 8 F.3d 1573, 28 USPQ2d 1652 (Fed. Cir. 1993). See also *Eiselstein v. Frank*, 52 F.3d 1035, 34 USPQ2d 1467 (Fed. Cir. 1995); *Conopco, Inc. v. May Dep't Stores Co.*, 46 F.3d 1556, 32 USPQ2d 1225 (Fed. Cir. 1994). The meaning of the word "about" in a patent claim depends on the technological facts of the particular case; there is no universal meaning of the word in claim interpretation. *Pall Corp. v. Micron Separations, Inc.*, 66 F.3d 1211, 36 USPQ2d 1225 (Fed. Cir. 1995). In *Jeneric/Pentron Inc. v. Dillon Co.*, 205 F.3d 1377, 54 USPQ2d 1086 (Fed. Cir. 2000), the claim used the word "about" to qualify values with respect to ranges of certain properties. By contrast, when it came to constituents, the claim used precise numerical values. The court construed the claim as limited to those precise ranges for constituents, particularly in view of the fact that those ranges appeared to be necessary to distinguish the claims over the prior art. A patentee may not rely on the precise ranges of the claims to distinguish itself from prior art during prosecution and then later construe the ranges more broadly during an infringement action.

[290]*Modine Mfg. Co. v. United States ITC*, 75 F.3d 1545, 37 USPQ2d 1609 (Fed. Cir. 1996). In other words, the court seems to be saying that "about" is usually self-construing, and the real issue becomes the factual question of infringement.

Questions are sure to arise concerning whether the prior art in general is intrinsic or extrinsic evidence, but a reasonable approach seems to be that prior art that played a role in the prosecution is intrinsic while other prior art may be more reasonably viewed as extrinsic. Until the court speaks clearly on this matter, that will be the approach employed here.

It is the person of ordinary skill in the field of the invention through whose eyes the claims are construed. Such person is deemed to read the words used in the patent documents with an understanding of their meaning in the field, and to have knowledge of any special meaning and usage in the field. The inventor's words that are used to describe the invention—the inventor's lexicography—must be understood and interpreted by the court as they would be understood and interpreted by a person in that field of technology. Thus the court starts the decision-making process by reviewing the same resources as would that person, viz., the patent specification and the prosecution history. These documents have legal as well as technological content, for they show not only the framework of the invention as viewed by the inventor, but also the issues of patentability as viewed by the patent examiner.[291]

Claim as a whole. A claim must be read as a whole, rather than element by element.[292] Indeed, it may be preferable to analyze a claim in terms of its limitations, which give meaning to the various elements of the claim.[293] A court commits fundamental legal error when it analyzes each claim by a single word description of one part of the claimed invention. In patent law, a word means nothing outside the claim and the description in the specification. A disregard of claim limitations would render claim examination in the PTO meaningless. If a court may so rewrite claims, the entire statutory-regulatory structure that governs the drafting, submission, examination, allowance, and enforceability of claims would crumble.[294] There is no legally recognizable or protected gist or heart of the invention.[295] Reliance upon a finding that a "novel element" of a structural invention lies in the operation of a specification-described embodiment of the claimed structure would render meaningless the statutory requirement for claiming, the statutory requirement for treating claims individually,

---

[291]*Multiform Desiccants Inc. v. Medzam Ltd.*, 133 F.3d 1473, 45 USPQ2d 1429 (Fed. Cir. 1998).

[292]*Texas Instr., Inc. v. United States ITC*, 846 F.2d 1369, 6 USPQ2d 1886 (Fed. Cir. 1988); *Ball Corp. v. United States*, 729 F.2d 1429, 221 USPQ 289 (Fed. Cir. 1984); *In re Gulack*, 703 F.2d 1381, 217 USPQ 401 (Fed. Cir. 1983).

[293]*In re Warmerdam*, 33 F.3d 1354, 31 USPQ2d 1754 (Fed. Cir. 1994); *Panduit Corp. v. Dennison Mfg. Co.*, 774 F.2d 1082, 227 USPQ 337 (Fed. Cir. 1985).

[294]*Panduit Corp. v. Dennison Mfg. Co.*, 810 F.2d 1561, 1 USPQ2d 1593 (Fed. Cir. 1987).

[295]*Everpure, Inc. v. Cuno, Inc.*, 875 F.2d 300, 10 USPQ2d 1855 (Fed. Cir. 1989); *W.L. Gore & Assoc. v. Garlock, Inc.*, 721 F.2d 1540, 220 USPQ 303 (Fed. Cir. 1983). There is no such thing as a patented portion of a patented combination. *Porter v. Farmers Supply Serv., Inc.*, 790 F.2d 882, 229 USPQ 814 (Fed. Cir. 1986).

and the entire examination system centering on the allowance or rejection of claims.[296]

It cannot be said that a part of a claim is "claimed" subject matter. Claims, being definitions that must be read as a whole, do not "claim" or cover or protect all that their words may disclose. Even though a claim to an A-B-C combination of steps may contain a detailed description of step A, that does not give the patentee any patent right in step A alone and it is legally incorrect to say that step A is "patented."[297]

Specification. A technical term used in a patent document is interpreted as having the meaning that it would be given by persons experienced in the field of the invention, unless it is apparent from the patent and the prosecution history that the inventor used the term with a different meaning. Thus, it is always necessary to review the specification to determine whether the inventor has used any terms in a manner inconsistent with their ordinary meaning.[298] The specification that is relevant to claim construction is the specification of the patent in which the claims reside.[299]

The specification informs, but does not control, claim construction. Rather, the claim language itself governs the meaning of the claim.[300] Thus claims are always construed in light of the specification,[301] but that does not mean that the claims incorporate all disclosures of the specification.[302] Conversely, a patent claim should be construed to encompass at least one disclosed embodiment in the written description portion of the patent specification. This maxim flows from the statutory requirement that the specification shall contain a written description of the invention, which requires a patent applicant to disclose in the specification sufficient subject matter to support the breadth of the claims. A claim construction that does not

---

[296]*SRI Int'l v. Matsushita Elec. Corp.,* 775 F.2d 1107, 227 USPQ 577 (Fed. Cir. 1985).

[297]*General Foods Corp. v. Studiengesellschaft Kohle mbH,* 972 F.2d 1272, 23 USPQ2d 1839 (Fed. Cir. 1992). Claims must be read as a whole in analyzing a defense of double patenting. *Id.*

[298]*CVI/Beta Ventures, Inc. v. Tura LP,* 112 F.3d 1146, 42 USPQ2d 1577 (Fed. Cir. 1997).

[299]*Young Dental Mfg. Co. v. Q3 Special Prods., Inc.,* 112 F.3d 1137, 42 USPQ2d 1589 (Fed. Cir. 1997). See also, e.g., *Rowe v. Dror,* 112 F.3d 473, 42 USPQ2d 1550 (Fed. Cir. 1997). In determining whether a patented invention is anticipated, the claims are read in the context of the patent specification in which they arise and in which the invention is described. *Glaverbel S.A. v. Northlake Mkt'g & Supp., Inc.,* 45 F.3d 1550, 33 USPQ2d 1496 (Fed. Cir. 1995).

[300]*Envirco Corp. v. Clestra Cleanroom Inc.,* 209 F.3d 1360, 54 USPQ2d 1449 (Fed. Cir. 2000).

[301]E.g., *D.M.I., Inc. v. Deere & Co.,* 755 F.2d 1570, 225 USPQ 236 (Fed. Cir. 1985).

[302]*Constant v. Advanced Micro-Devices, Inc.,* 848 F.2d 1560, 7 USPQ2d 1057 (Fed. Cir. 1988); *Sjolund v. Musland,* 847 F.2d 1573, 6 USPQ2d 2020 (Fed. Cir. 1988); *Loctite Corp. v. Ultraseal Ltd.,* 781 F.2d 861, 228 USPQ 90 (Fed. Cir. 1985); *Lemelson v. United States,* 752 F.2d 1538, 224 USPQ 526 (Fed. Cir. 1985); *J.P. Stevens & Co. v. Lex Tex Ltd.,* 747 F.2d 1553, 223 USPQ 1089 (Fed. Cir. 1984); *Raytheon Co. v. Roper Corp.,* 724 F.2d 951, 220 USPQ 592 (Fed. Cir. 1983).

encompass a disclosed embodiment is thus rarely, if ever, correct and would require highly persuasive evidentiary support.[303]

There is sometimes a fine line between reading a claim in light of the specification, and reading a limitation into the claim from the specification.[304] While examples disclosed in the preferred embodiment may aid in the proper interpretation of a claim term, the scope of a claim is not necessarily limited by such examples.[305] Thus, what is patented is not restricted to the examples but is defined by the words in the claims if those claims are supported by the specification. Where a specification does not require a limitation, that limitation should not be read into the claims.[306] While it is entirely proper to use the specification to interpret what the patentee meant by a word or phrase in the claim, this is not to be confused with adding an extraneous limitation appearing in the specification, which is improper.[307] If everything in the specification were required to be read into the claims, or if structural claims were to be limited to devices operated precisely as a specification-described embodiment is operated, there would be no need for claims. Nor could an applicant, regardless of the prior art, claim more broadly than that embodiment. Nor would a basis remain for the statutory necessity that an applicant conclude the specification with claims particularly pointing out and distinctly claiming the subject matter that the applicant regards as his or her invention.[308] Just because a patent is narrow does not mean

---

[303]*Johns Hopkins Univ. v. Cellpro Inc.*, 152 F.3d 1342, 47 USPQ2d 1705 (Fed. Cir. 1998); *Vitronics Corp. v. Conceptronic, Inc.*, 90 F.3d 1576, 39 USPQ2d 1573 (Fed. Cir. 1996). A claim interpretation that excludes the preferred embodiment is rarely, if ever, correct. *Gentry Gallery, Inc. v. Berkline Corp.*, 134 F.3d 1473, 45 USPQ2d 1498 (Fed. Cir. 1998). It is unlikely that an inventor would define the invention in a way that excludes the preferred embodiment or that those skilled in the art would read it that way. *Hoechst Celanese Corp. v. BP Chem. Ltd.*, 78 F.3d 1575, 38 USPQ2d 1126 (Fed. Cir. 1996). A claim construction that would exclude the preferred embodiment described in the specification cannot be sustained. *Burke Inc. v. Bruno Indep. Living Aids Inc.*, 183 F.3d 1334, 51 USPQ2d 1295 (Fed. Cir. 1999). Despite these observations, the court in *Elekta Instr. S.A. v. O.U.R. Sci. Int'l Inc.*, 214 F.3d 1302, 54 USPQ2d 1910 (Fed. Cir. 2000), concluded that it was dealing with the rare case in which the only correct interpretation was one that excluded the only disclosed embodiment.

[304]*Comark Comm. Inc. v. Harris Corp.*, 156 F.3d 1182, 48 USPQ2d 1001 (Fed. Cir. 1998). But mere observation by the district court that the written description discloses only a particular structure does not constitute reading that structure into the claims as a limitation. It is entirely proper to use the specification as a starting point for construing disputed language. *Laitram Corp. v. Morehouse Indus. Inc.*, 143 F.3d 1456, 46 USPQ2d 1609 (Fed. Cir. 1998).

[305]*Ekchian v. Home Depot, Inc.*, 104 F.3d 1299, 41 USPQ2d 1364 (Fed. Cir. 1997). Claims, not the specification embodiments, define the scope of the protection. *American Permahedge, Inc. v. Barcana, Inc.*, 105 F.3d 1441, 41 USPQ2d 1614 (Fed. Cir. 1997).

[306]*Specialty Composites v. Cabot Corp.*, 845 F.2d 981, 6 USPQ2d 1601 (Fed. Cir. 1988). The fact that the examples showed only external plasticizers did not mean that the word "plasticizer" in the claims should be read to exclude internal plasticizers, where there was other evidence of record to support a broader interpretation. Also, some narrower dependent claims included external plasticizers as a limitation, so that limitation should not be read into the broader independent claims.

[307]*E.I. duPont & Co. v. Phillips Petroleum Co.*, 849 F.2d 1430, 7 USPQ2d 1129 (Fed. Cir. 1988). By "extraneous" is meant a limitation read into a claim from the specification wholly apart from any need to interpret what the patentee meant by particular words or phrases in the claim. *Id.*

[308]*SRI Int'l v. Matsushita Elec. Corp.*, 775 F.2d 1107, 227 USPQ 577 (Fed. Cir. 1985).

that the claims are to be limited to the specific embodiments disclosed in the specification.[309]

Nonetheless, it would run counter to the requirement that a claim particularly point out and distinctly claim the invention, were an inventor to expressly state, throughout the application and claims, that the invention includes a particular limitation, and then be allowed to avoid that limitation in a later infringement suit by reference to one paragraph in the specification that states an alternative lacking that limitation.[310] All rules of construction must be understood in terms of the factual situations that produced them, and applied in fidelity to their origins. Thus, it is true that the description of the preferred embodiment in the specification does not limit the claims to that embodiment. However, when the preferred embodiment is described in the specification as the invention itself, the claims are not necessarily entitled to a scope broader than that embodiment.[311] It is a truism that a claim need not be limited to a preferred embodiment. However, in a given case, the scope of the right to exclude may be limited by a narrow disclosure. In sum, the cases do not stand for the proposition that an applicant can broaden his or her claims to the extent that they are effectively bounded only by the prior art. Rather, they make clear that claims may be no broader than the supporting disclosure, and therefore that a narrow disclosure will limit claim breadth.[312]

Claim terms cannot be narrowed by reference to the written description or prosecution history unless the language of the claims invites reference to those sources. In other words, there must be a textual reference in the actual language of the claim with which to associate a proffered claim construction. The case law demonstrates two situations where a sufficient reason exists to require the entry of a definition of a claim term other than its ordinary and accustomed meaning. The first arises if the patentee has chosen to be his or her own lexicographer by clearly setting forth an explicit definition for a claim term. The second is where the term or terms chosen by the patentee so deprive the claim of clarity that there is no means by

---

[309]*Aktiebolaget Karlstads v. United States ITC*, 705 F.2d 1565, 217 USPQ 865 (Fed. Cir. 1983). References to a preferred embodiment, such as those often present in a specification, are not claim limitations. *Laitram Corp. v. Cambridge Wire Cloth Co.*, 863 F.2d 855, 9 USPQ2d 1289 (Fed. Cir. 1988). However, one cannot interpret a claim to be broader than what is contained in the specification and claims as filed. *Tandon Corp. v. United States ITC*, 831 F.2d 1017, 4 USPQ2d 1283 (Fed. Cir. 1987). Although the specification may well indicate that certain embodiments are preferred, particular embodiments appearing in the specification will not be read into the claims when the claim language is broader than such embodiments. *Electro Med. Sys. S.A. v. Cooper Life Sciences, Inc.*, 34 F.3d 1048, 32 USPQ2d 1017 (Fed. Cir. 1994).

[310]*Unique Concepts, Inc. v. Brown*, 939 F.2d 1558, 19 USPQ2d 1500 (Fed. Cir. 1991).

[311]*Modine Mfg. Co. v. United States ITC*, 75 F.3d 1545, 37 USPQ2d 1609 (Fed. Cir. 1996). Here the specification was amended to change an original range of .015–.070 to a smaller range of .015–.040 inch. Thus, the claimed limitation "relatively small" was held not to extend to .070 inch. However, this did not preclude an attempt to show literal infringement for dimensions over .040 or to establish equivalency.

[312]*Gentry Gallery, Inc. v. Berkline Corp.*, 134 F.3d 1473, 45 USPQ2d 1498 (Fed. Cir. 1998).

which the scope of the claim may be ascertained from the language used. In these two circumstances, a term or terms used in the claim invites—or indeed, requires—reference to intrinsic, or in some cases, extrinsic evidence to determine the scope of the claim language.[313] A party wishing to use statements in the written description to confine or otherwise affect a patent's scope must, at the very least, point to a term or terms in the claim with which to draw in those statements. Without any claim term that is susceptible of clarification by the written description, there is no legitimate way to narrow the property right. If one need not rely on a limitation to interpret what the patentee meant by a particular term or phrase in a claim, that limitation is "extraneous" and cannot constrain the claim.[314]

Courts cannot alter what the patentee has chosen to claim as the invention. No matter how great the temptations of fairness or policy making, courts do not rework claims. They only interpret them.[315] Nonetheless, the requirement of distinctness in claiming guards against unreasonable advantages to the patentee and disadvantages to others arising from uncertainty as to their respective rights. Thus, in a claim construction context, where there is an equal choice between a broader and a narrower meaning of a claim, and there is an enabling disclosure that indicates that the applicant is at least entitled to a claim having the narrower meaning, the notice function of the claim is best served by adopting the narrower meaning.[316]

It is well established that patent drawings do not define the precise proportions of the elements and may not be relied on to show particular sizes if the specification is completely silent on the issue.[317]

---

[313]*Johnson Worldwide Assoc. Inc. v. Zebco Corp.,* 175 F.3d 985, 50 USPQ2d 1607 (Fed. Cir. 1999).

[314]*Renishaw plc v. Marposs Societa' per Azione,* 158 F.3d 1243, 48 USPQ2d 1117 (Fed. Cir. 1998).

[315]*Intervet Am., Inc. v. Kee-Vet Labs., Inc.,* 887 F.2d 1050, 12 USPQ2d 1474 (Fed. Cir. 1989). It is incorrect to construe the claims contrary to the specification, and then to hold the claims invalid because they are contrary to the specification; the claims are construed in accordance with the rest of the specification of which they are a part, and not contrary to it. *C.R. Bard Inc. v. M3 Sys. Inc.,* 157 F.3d 1340, 48 USPQ2d 1225 (Fed. Cir. 1998). In *Becton Dickinson & Co. v. C.R. Bard, Inc.,* 922 F.2d 792, 17 USPQ2d 1097 (Fed. Cir. 1990), the district court reworked the claims to an extent that the Federal Circuit was moved to characterize as reflecting an "egregious misunderstanding of the law." On summary judgment, independent claim 1 was found not invalid but also not infringed, while independent claims 6 and 7 were found invalid for obviousness. The district court then proceeded to rewrite claims 6 and 7 as though they were dependent upon claim 1 and concluded that such hypothetical claims would be valid but not infringed, for the same reasons as claim 1.

[316]*Athletic Alternatives, Inc. v. Prince Mfg., Inc.,* 73 F.3d 1573, 37 USPQ2d 1365 (Fed. Cir. 1996). See also *Northern Telecom Ltd. v. Samsung Elec. Co.,* 215 F.3d 1281, 55 USPQ2d 1065 (Fed. Cir. 2000); *Digital Biometrics Inc. v. Identix Inc.,* 149 F.3d 1335, 47 USPQ2d 1418 (Fed. Cir. 1998).

[317]*Hockerson-Halberstadt Inc. v. Avia Group Int'l Inc.,* 222 F.3d 951, 55 USPQ2d 1487 (Fed. Cir. 2000). Thus, a reasonable competitor, being aware that figures in a patent are not drawn to scale unless otherwise indicated, would understand arguments in the prosecution history that clearly disclaim a particular construction even though those arguments might appear erroneous in light of the drawings. *Id.*

Title and abstract. The title of a patent appears to be nearly irrelevant to claim construction. Certainly, MPEP §606.01 provides that the examiner may require a change in the title if the proffered title is not descriptive of the invention claimed. However, it goes on to explain that "this may result in slightly longer titles, but the loss in brevity of the title will be more than offset by the gain in its informative value in indexing, classifying, searching, etc." Thus, as indicated by the MPEP itself, the purpose of the title is not to demarcate the precise boundaries of the claimed invention but rather to provide a useful reference tool for future classification purposes. In any event, if courts do not read limitations into the claims from the specification that are not found in the claims themselves, then they certainly will not read limitations into the claims from the patent title. Consequently, an amendment of the patent title during prosecution should not be regarded as having the same or similar effect as an amendment of the claims themselves by the applicant.[318] Despite the statement in PTO Rule 72(b) that the "abstract shall not be used for interpreting the scope of the claims," the court is willing to use the abstract as a source of intrinsic evidence as to the meaning of claims. It seems to feel that the rule is one that governs the conduct of patent examiners and does not address the process by which courts construe claims in infringement actions.[319]

Prosecution history. The prosecution history can be utilized as a claim construction tool apart from the pure estoppel context (see §6.3(b)).[320] Indeed, the Federal Circuit appears now to be of the view that the prosecution history is always relevant to a proper interpretation of a claim.[321] In that context, unless altering claim language to escape a rejection, an applicant only limits claims during prosecution by clearly disavowing claim coverage.[322] But a change made during

---

[318]*Pitney Bowes Inc. v. Hewlett-Packard Co.,* 182 F.3d 1298, 51 USPQ2d 1161 (Fed. Cir. 1999).

[319]*Hill-Rom Co. v. Kinetic Concepts Inc.,* 209 F.3d 1337, 54 USPQ2d 1437, 1440 n.1 (Fed. Cir. 2000).

[320]*Advance Transformer Co. v. Levinson,* 837 F.2d 1081, 5 USPQ2d 1600 (Fed. Cir. 1988); *Moleculon Res. Corp. v. CBS, Inc.,* 793 F.2d 1261, 229 USPQ 805 (Fed. Cir. 1986); *McGill Inc. v. John Zink Co.,* 736 F.2d 666, 221 USPQ 944 (Fed. Cir. 1984). In *Jurgens v. McKasy,* 927 F.2d 1552, 18 USPQ2d 1031 (Fed. Cir. 1991), the court placed heavy emphasis on the examiner's reasons for allowance and the prosecuting attorney's apparent agreement with the examiner's claim interpretation as expressed in those reasons.

[321]*Amhil Enters. Ltd. v. Wawa, Inc.,* 81 F.3d 1554, 38 USPQ2d 1471 (Fed. Cir. 1996). The prosecution history is relevant to claim coverage in a literal infringement analysis. *York Prods., Inc. v. Central Tractor Farm & Fam. Ctr.,* 99 F.3d 1568, 40 USPQ2d 1619 (Fed. Cir. 1996).

[322]*York Prods., Inc. v. Central Tractor Farm & Fam. Ctr.,* 99 F.3d 1568, 40 USPQ2d 1619 (Fed. Cir. 1996). See also *Jonsson v. Stanley Works,* 903 F.2d 812, 14 USPQ2d 1863 (Fed. Cir. 1990). The fact that an examiner placed no reliance on an applicant's statement distinguishing prior art does not mean that the statement is inconsequential for purposes of claim construction. *Laitram Corp. v. Morehouse Indus. Inc.,* 143 F.3d 1456, 46 USPQ2d 1609 (Fed. Cir. 1998). That prosecution shifts to a different focus does not blunt the impact of remarks made to overcome a prior rejection. The significance of such remarks is no different than in a case in which the claims are allowed in response to an amendment. *Desper Prods. Inc. v. QSound*

prosecution, even if not required by the prior art, may be relied upon by the public at least for claim interpretation purposes, if it was conspicuous and unambiguous.[323] Prosecution history is an important source of intrinsic evidence in interpreting claims because it is a contemporaneous exchange between the applicant and the examiner. The public has the right to rely on an applicant's remarks made in seeking allowance of claims.[324]

Thus the same statements in the prosecution history can be used both to interpret the claims and to determine whether there is prosecution history estoppel. But the two doctrines must be carefully distinguished. Claim interpretation in view of the prosecution history is a preliminary step in determining literal infringement, while prosecution history estoppel applies as a limitation to the DOE after the claims have been properly interpreted and no literal infringement is found. Estoppel does not involve a reinterpretation of the claims.[325]

Using the file history and arguments made during prosecution to ascertain the true meaning of what the inventor intended to convey in the claims is different from prosecution history estoppel, which is applied as a limitation upon the DOE after the claims have been properly interpreted. It is improper to consider prosecution history arguments only for the latter purpose. Nor need the PTO examiner have relied upon such arguments in order to make them relevant for claim interpretation purposes. They shed light on what the applicant meant by certain terms. On the other hand, merely because certain prosecution history is used to define the claims more narrowly does not preclude the possibility of an appropriate range of equivalents under the DOE. In other words, the two purposes must be kept separate.[326]

Labs. Inc., 157 F.3d 1325, 48 USPQ2d 1088 (Fed. Cir. 1998). In *EMI Group N.A. Inc. v. Intel Corp.,* 157 F.3d 887, 48 USPQ2d 1181 (Fed. Cir. 1998), the claim term "relatively thicker" was held to mean a ratio of at least 1.77 to 1. Although this ratio was not defined in the specification, it was invoked during prosecution to distinguish the claimed invention from the prior art.

[323]*Modine Mfg. Co. v. United States ITC,* 75 F.3d 1545, 37 USPQ2d 1609 (Fed. Cir. 1996). It is incorrect to construe a claim as encompassing the scope that was relinquished in order to obtain allowance of another claim, despite a difference in the words used. *Id.* In construing the claims in view of prosecution history or in deciding whether to estop a patentee from asserting a certain range of equivalents, a court may only explore the reason (right or wrong) for the objection and the manner in which the amendment addressed and avoided the objection. The correctness of the examiner's rejection is not at issue. *Regents of Univ. of Calif. v. Eli Lilly & Co.,* 119 F.3d 1559, 43 USPQ2d 1398 (Fed. Cir. 1997).

[324]*Desper Prods. Inc. v. QSound Labs. Inc.,* 157 F.3d 1325, 48 USPQ2d 1088 (Fed. Cir. 1998). The prosecution history constitutes a public record of the patentee's representations concerning the scope and meaning of the claims, and competitors are entitled to rely on those representations when ascertaining the degree of lawful conduct, such as designing around the claimed invention. *Hockerson-Halberstadt Inc. v. Avia Group Int'l Inc.,* 222 F.3d 951, 55 USPQ2d 1487 (Fed. Cir. 2000).

[325]*Loctite Corp. v. Ultraseal Ltd.,* 781 F.2d 861, 228 USPQ 90 (Fed. Cir. 1985).

[326]*Southwall Tech., Inc. v. Cardinal IG Co.,* 54 F.3d 1570, 34 USPQ2d 1673 (Fed. Cir. 1995); *E.I. duPont & Co. v. Phillips Petroleum Co.,* 849 F.2d 1430, 7 USPQ2d 1129 (Fed. Cir. 1988). In *Senmed, Inc. v. Richard-Allan Med. Indus., Inc.,* 888 F.2d 815, 12 USPQ2d 1508 (Fed. Cir. 1989), the court treated the same amendment and remarks both as a restriction

There is a clear line of distinction between using the contents of the prosecution history to reach an understanding about disputed claim language and the doctrine of prosecution history estoppel, which estops or limits later expansion of the protection accorded by the claim under the DOE when the claims have been purposefully amended or distinguished over relevant art to give up scope. Thus, it is technically correct to say that the doctrine of prosecution history estoppel is irrelevant to determination of literal claim scope. On the other hand, a particular interpretation of a claim term may have been disclaimed by the inventor during prosecution. Thus it is incorrect to ignore the prosecution history when interpreting claims.[327] Indeed, it is sometimes difficult to determine where construction leaves off and estoppel begins. The court sometimes gives great weight to the prosecution history even though there is no equivalence issue and thus no possibility of technical estoppel. Prosecution history is especially important when the invention involves a crowded art field, or when there is particular prior art that the applicant is trying to distinguish.[328]

The court has come to recognize that its previous characterization of claims as being "expanded" or "broadened" under the DOE was inaccurate. To say that the DOE extends or enlarges the claims is a contradiction in terms. The claims—i.e., the scope of patent protection as defined by the claims—remain the same, and application of the doctrine simply expands the exclusionary right to "equivalents" of what is claimed. The DOE, by definition, involves going beyond any permissible interpretation of the claim language.[329]

Of course, arguments made during prosecution regarding the meaning of a claim term are relevant to the interpretation of that term in every claim of the patent absent a clear indication to the contrary.[330] The prosecution history of a parent application in a chain

---

on claim construction, for purposes of literal infringement, and as an estoppel, for purposes of equivalence.

[327]*Biodex Corp. v. Loredan Biomedical, Inc.,* 946 F.2d 850, 20 USPQ2d 1252 (Fed. Cir. 1991). As a general matter, the claims of a patent are not limited by preferred embodiments. However, through statements made during prosecution or reexamination an applicant for a patent or a patent owner may commit to a particular meaning for a patent term, which meaning is then binding in litigation. *CVI/Beta Ventures, Inc. v. Tura LP,* 112 F.3d 1146, 42 USPQ2d 1577 (Fed. Cir. 1997).

[328]*Lemelson v. General Mills, Inc.,* 968 F.2d 1202, 23 USPQ2d 1284 (Fed. Cir. 1992). Here the original claim had five elements, but was amended to add two more elements in response to a rejection. The court held that the patentee was foreclosed from arguing that the additional elements were not necessary to avoid the art. That being the case, the jury must have found that the two additional clauses added something not found in the prior art but found in the accused device. But there was no evidence that the accused device contained those elements. Thus no reasonable jury could have read the claim both as valid over the art and as infringed by the accused device; in the context of the prosecution history, those were inherently inconsistent conclusions.

[329]*Wilson Sporting Goods Co. v. David Geoffrey & Assoc.,* 904 F.2d 677, 14 USPQ2d 1942 (Fed. Cir. 1990).

[330]*Digital Biometrics Inc. v. Identix Inc.,* 149 F.3d 1335, 47 USPQ2d 1418 (Fed. Cir. 1998); *Southwall Tech., Inc. v. Cardinal IG Co.,* 54 F.3d 1570, 34 USPQ2d 1673 (Fed. Cir. 1995).

may be relevant to claim interpretation. Also, it is improper to construe a term differently in one patent than another, where they have common ancestry.[331]

Statements made during reissue or reexamination proceedings are relevant as prosecution history when interpreting claims.[332] Also, statements made in an Information Disclosure Statement (IDS) can be the basis for a court to interpret the scope of the claims and can even create an estoppel that will preclude a finding of infringement by equivalents. An IDS is a part of the prosecution history upon which the examiner, the courts, and the public are entitled to rely.[333] But the court has cautioned on giving too much weight to a formal Citation of Prior Art. If filed after issuance and just before or during litigation, it may very well contain self-serving statements.[334] An unequivocal statement in a petition to make special may be used to limit the scope of a claim for literal infringement.[335] Because interference proceedings are part of the public record and shed light on the meaning of claims, it is proper to rely on the record of those proceedings in construing claims.[336]

Other admissions and estoppels. The court appears to recognize the possibility that admissions or other preclusive circumstances may impact claim interpretation. Thus, it found no error in the district court having relied upon remarks made during prosecution of one of the two patents in suit to interpret the claims of the other.[337] On the other hand, it quite correctly refused to consider arguments made by a different attorney, prosecuting later patent applications for a

---

[331]*Abtox, Inc. v. Exitron Corp.*, 122 F.3d 1019, 43 USPQ2d 1545, *amended opinion*, 46 USPQ2d 1735 (Fed. Cir. 1997). When multiple patents derive from the same initial application, the prosecution history regarding a claim limitation in any patent that has issued applies with equal force to subsequently issued patents that contain the same claim limitation. *Elkay Mfg. Co. v. Ebco Mfg. Co.*, 192 F.3d 970, 52 USPQ2d 1109 (Fed. Cir. 1999).

[332]*Spectrum Int'l Inc. v. Sterilite Corp.*, 164 F.3d 1372, 49 USPQ2d 1065 (Fed. Cir. 1998); *E.I. duPont & Co. v. Phillips Petroleum Co.*, 849 F.2d 1430, 7 USPQ2d 1129 (Fed. Cir. 1988). Where an identical claim is carried over on reissue, the prosecution history of the reissue is nevertheless relevant in construing the claim. *Howes v. Medical Components, Inc.*, 814 F.2d 638, 2 USPQ2d 1271 (Fed. Cir. 1987). But the fact that an accused infringer seeking reexamination may have admitted that the claims were broad enough to encompass a particular structure is irrelevant to construction of the claims. It is the applicant's representations during prosecution that potentially shed light on the construction of the claims, not the representations of a reexamination requester. *Laitram Corp. v. Morehouse Indus. Inc.*, 143 F.3d 1456, 46 USPQ2d 1609 (Fed. Cir. 1998).

[333]*Ekchian v. Home Depot, Inc.*, 104 F.3d 1299, 41 USPQ2d 1364 (Fed. Cir. 1997).

[334]*Moleculon Res. Corp. v. CBS, Inc.*, 793 F.2d 1261, 229 USPQ 805 (Fed. Cir. 1986).

[335]*Gentry Gallery, Inc. v. Berkline Corp.*, 134 F.3d 1473, 45 USPQ2d 1498 (Fed. Cir. 1998).

[336]*Phillips Pet. Co. v. Huntsman Polymers Corp.*, 157 F.3d 866, 48 USPQ2d 1161 (Fed. Cir. 1998).

[337]*Jonsson v. Stanley Works*, 903 F.2d 812, 14 USPQ2d 1863 (Fed. Cir. 1990). Nor was the court troubled by the contention that the district court was interpreting one claim in each of the patents as having exactly the same scope. This was explainable on the ground that one of the claims was a means-plus-function claim, and thus its scope was cut back to equivalents of the structure shown in the specification, which turned out to be the same scope as the other patent.

different inventor (albeit owned by the same assignee), as limiting the scope of the claims in suit.[338] It has also refused to use a statement in the letter of an executive of the corporate patent owner, to a licensee, that certain compounds were outside the claims as limiting the scope of the claims in a suit by the licensee against a third-party infringer.[339] When it comes to the question of which should control, an erroneous remark by an attorney in the course of prosecution of an application, or the claims of the patent as finally worded and issued by the PTO as an official grant, the law allows for no choice: the claims themselves control.[340]

The court does seem prepared to apply the doctrine of *Smith v. Hall*,[341] which is that a patentee, once having sought and obtained a broad construction of its claim in an action against one accused infringer, is barred, in a subsequent action against a different accused infringer, from arguing a narrow construction of the claim so as to avoid anticipation. However, the rule is not applicable where the patentee in the first case seeks a narrow construction that is not adopted by the first court.[342]

(d) Extrinsic Evidence

So what is extrinsic evidence and when is it to be consulted for purposes of claim construction? The *Vitronics*[343] decision provides at least some partial answers. Thus, extrinsic evidence is that which is external to the patent and file history, such as expert testimony, inventor testimony, dictionaries, and technical treatises and articles. It will usually be the accused infringer that is proffering extrinsic evidence, for the court regards a patent owner's contention that the

---

[338]*Water Techs. Corp. v. Calco, Ltd.*, 850 F.2d 660, 7 USPQ2d 1097 (Fed. Cir. 1988).

[339]*Water Techs. Corp. v. Calco, Ltd.*, 850 F.2d 660, 7 USPQ2d 1097 (Fed. Cir. 1988). The court explained that there was no estoppel or preclusion because there was no evidence that the third party had relied upon the statement to justify its activities. Perhaps so, but the decision seems to preclude any use of the statement, even as evidence.

[340]*Intervet Am., Inc. v. Kee-Vet Labs., Inc.*, 887 F.2d 1050, 12 USPQ2d 1474 (Fed. Cir. 1989). Here the attorney, in remarks accompanying an amendment, erroneously indicated that all claims contained a limitation, when in fact only one claim did. The court held it error to interpret the remaining claims as though they contained that limitation. The court did recognize, however, that such an attorney statement might be held against the patentee on a theory of estoppel if the patentee were attempting to expand the literal meaning of the claim and if the prosecution history showed that the expanded scope would be inclusive of subject matter that the attorney had, in order to get the claim allowed, represented to the PTO was not intended to be comprehended by the claim. It appeared in this case that the PTO examiner was not misled or deceived by the erroneous statement.

[341]301 U.S. 216 (1937).

[342]*Hybritech, Inc. v. Abbott Labs.*, 849 F.2d 1446, 7 USPQ2d 1191 (Fed. Cir. 1988). The court appears to regard the rule of *Smith v. Hall* as resting upon collateral estoppel, and well it might be in view of *Blonder-Tongue* (see §18.5(b)). The doctrine also appears to be consistent with the definition of preclusion by inconsistent positions (see §7.2(e)).

[343]*Vitronics Corp. v. Conceptronic, Inc.*, 90 F.3d 1576, 39 USPQ2d 1573 (Fed. Cir. 1996).

evidence intrinsic to its own patent is ambiguous and insufficient to construe the claims as somewhat ironic.[344]

Prior art, dictionaries, and treatises. As to treatises and articles, the court feels that they are worthy of special note. Judges are free to consult such resources at any time in order to better understand the underlying technology. They may also rely on dictionary definitions to the extent they do not contradict any definition found in or ascertained by a reading of the patent documents. In addition, a court in its discretion may admit and rely on prior art proffered by one of the parties, whether or not cited in the specification or the file history. This prior art can often help to demonstrate how a disputed term is used by those skilled in the art. Such art may make it unnecessary to rely on expert testimony and may save much trial time. As compared to expert testimony, which often only indicates what a particular expert believes a term means, prior art references may also be more indicative of what all those skilled in the art generally believe a certain term means. However, reliance on such evidence is unnecessary, and indeed improper, when the disputed terms can be understood from a careful reading of the public record.[345]

Courts must exercise caution lest dictionary definitions, usually the least controversial source of extrinsic evidence, be converted into technical terms of art having legal, not linguistic, significance. The best source for understanding a technical term is the specification from which it arose, informed, as needed, by the prosecution history. The evolution of restrictions in the claims, in the course of examination in the PTO, reveals how those closest to the patenting process— the inventor and the patent examiner—viewed the subject matter. When the specification explains and defines a term used in the claims, without ambiguity or incompleteness, there is no need to search further for the meaning of the term.[346]

---

[344]*Sextant Avionique S.A. v. Analog Devices Inc.*, 172 F.3d 813, 49 USPQ2d 1865, 1870 (Fed. Cir. 1999).

[345]*Vitronics Corp. v. Conceptronic, Inc.*, 90 F.3d 1576, 39 USPQ2d 1573 (Fed. Cir. 1996). Even when prior art is not cited in the written description or the prosecution history, it may assist in ascertaining the meaning of a term to a person skilled in the art. When prior art that sheds light on the meaning of a term is cited by the patentee, it can have particular value as a guide to the proper construction of the term, because it may indicate not only the meaning of the term to persons skilled in the art, but also that the patentee intended to adopt that meaning. *Arthur A. Collins Inc. v. Northern Telecom Ltd.*, 216 F.3d 1042, 55 USPQ2d 1143 (Fed. Cir. 2000). When the intrinsic record is clear the court does not give weight to an inconsistent dictionary definition. *Digital Biometrics Inc. v. Identix Inc.*, 149 F.3d 1335, 47 USPQ2d 1418 (Fed. Cir. 1998). In *United States Surgical Corp. v. Ethicon, Inc.*, 103 F.3d 1554, 41 USPQ2d 1225 (Fed. Cir. 1997), the court held that the provision of a dictionary to the jury, at its request and over the objections of both parties, was harmless error if error at all.

[346]*Multiform Desiccants Inc. v. Medzam Ltd.*, 133 F.3d 1473, 45 USPQ2d 1429 (Fed. Cir. 1998). The patentee had known of the accused device during prosecution, and had offered dictionary definitions in an attempt to provide a basis for broader coverage. The district court rejected those definitions offered during prosecution and the Federal Circuit agreed. In *Hill-Rom Co. v. Kinetic Concepts Inc.*, 209 F.3d 1337, 54 USPQ2d 1437 (Fed. Cir. 2000), the court looked to a dictionary to determine the ordinary meaning of the word "cushion." It then found that definition consistent with the usage in the patent.

In *Toro v. White*,[347] the court explained more fully its view of the propriety of consulting dictionaries. The dictionary definitions of common words are often less useful than the patent documents themselves in establishing the usage of ordinary words in connection with the claimed subject matter. This is not an issue of the richness of language, or variety or imprecision in the usage of words. Determining the limits of a patent claim requires understanding its terms in the context in which they were used by the inventor, considered by the examiner, and understood in the field of the invention. In judicial "claim construction" the court must achieve the same understanding of the patent, as a document whose meaning and scope have legal consequences, as would a person experienced in the technology of the invention. Such a person would not rely solely on a dictionary of general linguistic usage, but would understand the claims in light of the specification and the prior art, guided by the prosecution history and experience in the technologic field. Dictionaries are useful additional sources, as is the guidance of technical/scientific experts and other relevant evidence, in addition to the patent documents themselves, that may aid the judge in achieving the understanding and viewpoint of a person having experience in the field of the invention. However, dictionaries provide general definitions, rarely in sufficient detail to resolve close questions in particular contexts.

The pioneer status of the invention also requires consideration. A basic patent on a pioneering invention is entitled to be interpreted broadly.[348] The courts have recognized that patented inventions vary in their technological or industrial significance. There is not a discontinuous transition from "mere improvement" to "pioneer." The judicially "liberal" view of both claim interpretation and equivalency accorded a pioneer invention is not a manifestation of a different legal standard based on an abstract legal concept denominated "pioneer." Rather, the liberal view flows directly from the relative sparseness of prior art in nascent fields of technology. However, pioneer status does not change the way infringement is determined. The patentee's disclosure, the prosecution history, and the prior art still provide the background against which the scope of claims is determined.[349]

The court has held that it is not necessary to consider the prior art in determining equivalents under 35 U.S.C. §112¶6.[350]

Inventor testimony. The testimony of an inventor and his or her attorney concerning claim construction is entitled to little or no consideration. The testimony of an inventor often is a self-serving, after-the-fact attempt to state what should have been part of his or her patent application. The testimony of any attorney amounts to no more

---

[347]*Toro Co. v. White Consol. Indus. Inc.*, 199 F.3d 1295, 53 USPQ2d 1065 (Fed. Cir. 1999).

[348]*Texas Instr., Inc. v. United States ITC*, 805 F.2d 1558, 231 USPQ 833 (Fed. Cir. 1986).

[349]*Texas Instr., Inc. v. United States ITC*, 846 F.2d 1369, 6 USPQ2d 1886 (Fed. Cir. 1988).

[350]*Intel Corp. v. United States ITC*, 946 F.2d 821, 20 USPQ2d 1161 (Fed. Cir. 1991). See the discussion accompanying note 5:405.

than legal opinion—it is precisely the process of construction that the court must undertake.[351] By the same token, an inventor's subjective intent is of little or no probative weight in determining the scope of the claims, except as documented in the prosecution history.[352] But the problem the inventor was attempting to solve, as discerned from the specification and the prosecution history, is a relevant consideration.[353]

Although in *Markman* the Federal Circuit stated that the subjective intent of the inventor when he or she used a particular term is of little or no probative weight in determining the scope of a claim, this statement does not disqualify the inventor as a witness, or overrule the large body of precedent that recognizes the value of the inventor's testimony. The court did not hold that the inventor cannot explain the technology and what was invented and claimed; it held only that the inventor cannot by later testimony change the invention and the claims from their meaning at the time the patent was drafted and granted. Patents are written not for laymen, but for and by persons experienced in the field of the invention. An inventor is a competent witness to explain the invention and what was intended to be conveyed by the specification and covered by the claims. The testimony of the inventor may also provide background information, including explanation of the problems that existed at the time the invention was made and the inventor's solution to these problems. Although *Markman* and other precedent caution against creative reconstruction of an invention by interested persons, courts are not novices in receiving and weighing expertise on both sides of an issue.[354]

Expert testimony. Once a dispute over claim construction arises, experts should not be heard to inject a new meaning into terms that is inconsistent with what the inventor set forth in his or her patent and communicated, first to the patent examiner and ultimately to the public. Patents should be interpreted on the basis of their intrinsic record, not on the testimony of after-the-fact experts who played no

---

[351]*Bell & Howell DMP Co. v. Altek Sys.*, 132 F.3d 701, 45 USPQ2d 1033 (Fed. Cir. 1997). An inventor's after-the-fact testimony is of little weight compared to the clear import of the patent disclosure itself. *Roton Barrier, Inc. v. Stanley Works,* 79 F.3d 1112, 37 USPQ2d 1816 (Fed. Cir. 1996). Similarly, the court found error, albeit harmless, in a district court's reliance on an inventor's earlier published work to interpret the scope of his patent claims. It reasoned that a patent is to be interpreted by what it states rather than by what the inventor wrote in a scientific publication. There is no inconsistency between writing a paper (or giving a speech) on a particular embodiment of an invention and then claiming one's invention more broadly in a patent application. Patents often teach embodiments not carried out in the laboratory; scientific papers rarely do. *North Am. Vaccine, Inc. v. American Cyanamid Co.,* 7 F.3d 1571, 28 USPQ2d 1333 (Fed. Cir. 1993).

[352]*Engel Indus., Inc. v. Lockformer Co.,* 96 F.3d 1398, 40 USPQ2d 1161 (Fed. Cir. 1996).

[353]*CVI/Beta Ventures, Inc. v. Tura LP,* 112 F.3d 1146, 42 USPQ2d 1577 (Fed. Cir. 1997).

[354]*Voice Tech. Group Inc. v. VMC Sys. Inc.,* 164 F.3d 605, 49 USPQ2d 1333 (Fed. Cir. 1999). The Supreme Court in *Daubert v. Merrell Dow Pharms. Inc.,* 509 U.S. 579, 27 USPQ2d 1200 (1993), instructed trial judges to exclude scientifically unqualified witnesses, not those with superior qualifications. *Id.*

part in the creation and prosecution of the patent. Use of expert
testimony to explain an invention may be useful. But reliance on
extrinsic evidence to interpret claims is proper only when the claim
language remains genuinely ambiguous after consideration of the
intrinsic evidence, i.e., when the intrinsic evidence is insufficient to
enable the court to construe disputed claim terms. Accordingly, any
expert testimony that is inconsistent with unambiguous intrinsic evidence should be accorded no weight.[355] Expert testimony is often useful
to clarify the patented technology and to explain its meaning through
the eyes of experience, but it may not correct errors or erase limitations or otherwise diverge from the description of the invention as
contained in the patent documents.[356]

While *Markman* makes it clear that expert technical testimony
on claim construction is limited to aiding the court in understanding
the technology, the Federal Circuit itself finds such testimony of
valuable assistance in some cases.[357] It feels that, even under *Markman*, expert testimony about how those skilled in the art would interpret certain language in the claim may be considered when appropriate as an inherent part of the process of claim construction and
as an aid in arriving at the proper construction of the claim.[358] Patent
claims are normally construed as they would be by those of ordinary
skill in the art,[359] as of the application date,[360] and it is proper for the
trial judge to read the claims as would one of skill in the art.[361]

Expert testimony is of value as evidence of how those skilled in
the art would view the language.[362] The use of experts is generally a
matter of discretion with the trial judge, but that discretion is not
unlimited. In a patent case involving complex scientific principles, it
is particularly helpful to see how those skilled in the art would interpret the claims.[363]

---

[355]*Bell & Howell DMP Co. v. Altek Sys.*, 132 F.3d 701, 45 USPQ2d 1033 (Fed. Cir. 1997).
Trial testimony regarding the meaning of a claim cannot vary the meaning of a claim that is
established either by the claim itself or by the claim as correctly understood by reference to
the specification and the file history. *J.T. Eaton & Co. v. Atlantic Paste & Glue Co.*, 106 F.3d
1563, 41 USPQ2d 1641 (Fed. Cir. 1997).

[356]*Aqua-Aerobic Sys. Inc. v. Aerators Inc.*, 211 F.3d 1241, 54 USPQ2d 1566 (Fed. Cir. 2000).

[357]E.g., *National Presto Indus., Inc. v. West Bend Co.*, 76 F.3d 1185, 37 USPQ2d 1685
(Fed. Cir. 1996).

[358]*Tanabe Seiyaku Co. v. United States ITC*, 109 F.3d 726, 41 USPQ2d 1976 (Fed. Cir.
1997). See the discussion accompanying notes 5:258–262.

[359]*Electro Med. Sys. S.A. v. Cooper Life Sciences, Inc.*, 34 F.3d 1048, 32 USPQ2d 1017
(Fed. Cir. 1994); *Smithkline Diagnostics, Inc. v. Helena Labs. Corp.*, 859 F.2d 878, 8 USPQ2d
1468 (Fed. Cir. 1988); *Loctite Corp. v. Ultraseal Ltd.*, 781 F.2d 861, 228 USPQ 90 (Fed. Cir.
1985); *Palumbo v. Don-Joy Co.*, 762 F.2d 969, 226 USPQ 5 (Fed. Cir. 1985); *Fromson v. Advance
Offset Plate, Inc.*, 720 F.2d 1565, 219 USPQ 1137 (Fed. Cir. 1983).

[360]*Wiener v. NEC Elec., Inc.*, 102 F.3d 534, 41 USPQ2d 1023 (Fed. Cir. 1996).

[361]*Schenck, A.G. v. Nortron Corp.*, 713 F.2d 782, 218 USPQ 698 (Fed. Cir. 1983).

[362]*Fonar Corp. v. Johnson & Johnson*, 821 F.2d 627, 3 USPQ2d 1109 (Fed. Cir. 1987);
Moeller v. Ionetics, Inc., 794 F.2d 653, 229 USPQ 992 (Fed. Cir. 1986); *McGill Inc. v. John
Zink Co.*, 736 F.2d 666, 221 USPQ 944 (Fed. Cir. 1984).

[363]*Moeller v. Ionetics, Inc.*, 794 F.2d 653, 229 USPQ 992 (Fed. Cir. 1986). The testimony
of one skilled in the art about the meaning of claim terms at the time of the invention will

Thus, although claim interpretation is a question of law, expert testimony is admissible to explain the meaning of technical terms in the claims and to provide an opinion on the ultimate question of infringement.[364] Nonetheless, if the terms do not have a special meaning to those skilled in the art, the court can properly construe the claims as a matter of law.[365] A party is not required to proffer expert testimony on claim interpretation.[366]

(e) Factual Underpinnings and Appellate Review

Inasmuch as claim construction is a question of law,[367] a dispute on that issue normally does not preclude summary judgment[368] and the standard of appellate review is merely error, not clear error.[369]

---

almost always qualify as relevant evidence. *Eastman Kodak Co. v. Goodyear Tire & Rubber Co.*, 114 F.3d 1547, 42 USPQ2d 1737 (Fed. Cir. 1997). For example, industry practice can be a factor in claim interpretation. *Tillotson, Ltd. v. Walbro Corp.*, 831 F.2d 1033, 4 USPQ2d 1450 (Fed. Cir. 1987).

[364]*Snellman v. Ricoh Co.*, 862 F.2d 283, 8 USPQ2d 1996 (Fed. Cir. 1988).

[365]*Howes v. Medical Components, Inc.*, 814 F.2d 638, 2 USPQ2d 1271 (Fed. Cir. 1987). An affidavit consisting of opinions about the meaning and application of various phrases and provisions of a claim does not necessarily create factual disputes that preclude the grant of a summary judgment of infringement. *Townsend Eng'r Co. v. HiTec Co.*, 829 F.2d 1086, 4 USPQ2d 1136 (Fed. Cir. 1987). In an interesting dissent, Judge Nichols suggested that judges might have to resort to their "gut feeling of what the inventor really meant to say." His premise was that there is a "growing inability of speakers and writers, lawyers, technicians, and laymen, to say what they intend to say with accuracy and clarity." *ZMI Corp. v. Cardiac Resuscitator Corp.*, 844 F.2d 1576, 1583, 6 USPQ2d 1557 (Fed. Cir. 1988).

[366]*Moleculon Res. Corp. v. CBS, Inc.*, 793 F.2d 1261, 229 USPQ 805 (Fed. Cir. 1986). The court indicated that an argument to the contrary bordered on the frivolous.

[367]*Read Corp. v. Portec, Inc.*, 970 F.2d 816, 23 USPQ2d 1426 (Fed. Cir. 1992); *Lemelson v. General Mills, Inc.*, 968 F.2d 1202, 23 USPQ2d 1284 (Fed. Cir. 1992); *Tandon Corp. v. United States ITC*, 831 F.2d 1017, 4 USPQ2d 1283 (Fed. Cir. 1987); *Vieau v. Japax, Inc.*, 823 F.2d 1510, 3 USPQ2d 1094 (Fed. Cir. 1987); *Panduit Corp. v. Dennison Mfg. Co.*, 810 F.2d 1561, 1 USPQ2d 1593 (Fed. Cir. 1987); *Moleculon Res. Corp. v. CBS, Inc.*, 793 F.2d 1261 (Fed. Cir. 1986); *Windsurfing Int'l, Inc. v. AMF, Inc.*, 782 F.2d 995, 228 USPQ 562 (Fed. Cir. 1986); *Loctite Corp. v. Ultraseal Ltd.*, 781 F.2d 861, 228 USPQ 90 (Fed. Cir. 1985). The scope of a claim is a matter of law. *Water Techs. Corp. v. Calco, Ltd.*, 850 F.2d 660, 7 USPQ2d 1097 (Fed. Cir. 1988). Interpreting a term in a claim, as is interpretation of the claim as a whole, is a question of law. *Hormone Res. Found., Inc. v. Genentech, Inc.*, 904 F.2d 1558, 15 USPQ2d 1039 (Fed. Cir. 1990).

[368]*Wolverine World Wide, Inc. v. Nike, Inc.*, 38 F.3d 1192, 32 USPQ2d 1338 (Fed. Cir. 1994); *Becton Dickinson & Co. v. C.R. Bard, Inc.*, 922 F.2d 792, 17 USPQ2d 1097 (Fed. Cir. 1990); *George v. Honda Motor Co.*, 802 F.2d 432, 231 USPQ 382 (Fed. Cir. 1986); *Molinaro v. Fannon/Courier Corp.*, 745 F.2d 651, 223 USPQ 706 (Fed. Cir. 1984). However, if complex scientific principles are involved or expert testimony is needed to explain a disputed term, then an underlying factual question may arise that makes summary judgment improper. *Howes v. Medical Components, Inc.*, 814 F.2d 638, 2 USPQ2d 1271 (Fed. Cir. 1987). Claim interpretation may depend upon conflicting evidentiary material that can give rise to a genuine factual dispute. Resolution of any such factual dispute is required for proper claim interpretation. *C.R. Bard, Inc. v. Advanced Card. Sys., Inc.*, 911 F.2d 670, 15 USPQ2d 1540 (Fed. Cir. 1990).

[369]*Lemelson v. United States*, 752 F.2d 1538, 224 USPQ 526 (Fed. Cir. 1985). Claim interpretation is a question of law and is freely reviewable on appeal. *Whittaker Corp. v. UNR Indus., Inc.*, 911 F.2d 709, 15 USPQ2d 1742 (Fed. Cir. 1990); *Durango Assoc., Inc. v. Reflange, Inc.*, 843 F.2d 1349, 6 USPQ2d 1290 (Fed. Cir. 1988). Review of claim interpretation, as an issue of law, is plenary. *Intervet Am., Inc. v. Kee-Vet Labs., Inc.*, 887 F.2d 1050, 12 USPQ2d 1474 (Fed. Cir. 1989). Claim interpretation is subject to de novo review. *Carroll Touch, Inc. v.*

Where there is no assertion that the words on which the issue of infringement turns have anything other than their common, ordinary meanings, the interpretation of the claim is a question of law freely reviewable on appeal.[370] In reviewing the interpretation of the meaning of claims, the reviewing court need not defer to the district court either under a clearly erroneous standard or otherwise.[371] But when the interpretation of claims requires findings of underlying fact, those findings are reviewed in accordance with the appropriate evidentiary standard.[372]

In a pre-*Markman* decision, *Perini Am. v. Paper Converting*,[373] the court expounded the proposition that claim interpretation is a

---

Electro Mechanical Sys., Inc., Inc., 3 F.3d 404, 27 USPQ2d 1836 (Fed. Cir. 1993); *Texas Instr., Inc. v. United States ITC,* 988 F.2d 1165, 26 USPQ2d 1018 (Fed. Cir. 1993); *Intel Corp. v. United States ITC,* 946 F.2d 821, 20 USPQ2d 1161 (Fed. Cir. 1991). However, when the meaning of key terms of the claim is disputed and extrinsic evidence is necessary to explain the terms, then underlying factual questions may arise. Those factual findings are reviewed in accordance with the appropriate evidentiary standard, i.e., clear error in a bench trial. *Minnesota Min. & Mfg. Co. v. Johnson & Johnson Orthopaedics, Inc.,* 976 F.2d 1559, 24 USPQ2d 1321 (Fed. Cir. 1992). Interpretation of an interference count is a question of law that the court reviews de novo. *Davis v. Loesch,* 998 F.2d 963, 27 USPQ2d 1440 (Fed. Cir. 1993).

[370]*Key Mfg. Group, Inc. v. Microdot, Inc.,* 925 F.2d 1444, 17 USPQ2d 1806 (Fed. Cir. 1991).

[371]*Exxon Chem. Patents, Inc. v. Lubrizol Corp.,* 64 F.3d 1553, 35 USPQ2d 1801 (Fed. Cir. 1995); *Specialty Composites v. Cabot Corp.,* 845 F.2d 981, 6 USPQ2d 1601 (Fed. Cir. 1988). See also *Smithkline Diagnostics, Inc. v. Helena Labs. Corp.,* 859 F.2d 878, 8 USPQ2d 1468 (Fed. Cir. 1988). On claim interpretation, as in the case of other legal questions, the Federal Circuit is suggesting that a district court's judgment is entitled to no deference. Yet this legal question is admittedly based entirely upon purely factual inquiry concerning the claim, the specification, the prosecution history, and other claims in the patent, all construed as they would be by one of ordinary skill in the art. Inasmuch as it is the trial court, or jury, that conducts this factual inquiry, perhaps its ultimate conclusion on the question should be entitled to some deference. Indeed, perhaps the entire question should be regarded as factual rather than legal. The matter seems to be causing at least Judge Newman some difficulty. In *Advanced Card. Sys., Inc. v. Scimed Life Sys., Inc.,* 887 F.2d 1070, 12 USPQ2d 1539 (Fed. Cir. 1989), the district court granted summary judgment of no infringement based on its interpretation of the meaning of a term in the claim. A 2–1 majority of the appeal panel found that the meaning of the term was not clear, and vacated and remanded. In dissent, Judge Newman pointed out that (1) claim interpretation is a question of law and (2) the underlying facts that were being relied on by the parties (statements in specification, prosecution history, other claims, prior art) were not in dispute. Thus Judge Newman felt that the district court's judgment was procedurally proper and should have been reviewed on the merits. In *Senmed, Inc. v. Richard-Allan Med. Indus., Inc.,* 888 F.2d 815, 12 USPQ2d 1508 (Fed. Cir. 1989), the jury found infringement but the panel majority found that the jury verdict was based upon a claim interpretation that was wrong as a matter of law. In her dissent from the reversal, Judge Newman indicated that more deference should have been given the verdict. In *Key Pharm. Inc. v. Hercon Labs. Corp.,* 161 F.3d 709, 48 USPQ2d 1911 (Fed. Cir. 1998), the court observed that its standard of review of claim construction is now firmly established: it exercises independent review. However, it does not start from scratch; rather it begins with and carefully considers the trial court's work. It also recognizes that its decisions on claim construction have national stare decisis effect. *Id.* See *Burke Inc. v. Bruno Indep. Living Aids Inc.,* 183 F.3d 1334, 51 USPQ2d 1295 (Fed. Cir. 1999), for how this works in the case of a nonprecedential decision under Federal Circuit Rule 47.6(b).

[372]*Tandon Corp. v. United States ITC,* 831 F.2d 1017, 4 USPQ2d 1283 (Fed. Cir. 1987). In this case the appropriate standard of review was substantial evidence, because the court was reviewing an ITC order. In an infringement case the appropriate standard would be clear error. *Perini Am., Inc. v. Paper Converting Mach. Co.,* 832 F.2d 581, 4 USPQ2d 1621 (Fed. Cir. 1987).

[373]*Perini Am., Inc. v. Paper Converting Mach. Co.,* 832 F.2d 581, 4 USPQ2d 1621 (Fed. Cir. 1987).

conclusion of law. Like all legal conclusions, that conclusion rises out of and rests on a foundation built of established (undisputed or correctly found) facts. Interpretation of a claim, or of its scope, should not be assayed until that foundation is in place. If the meaning of terms in the claim, the specification, other claims, or the prosecution history is disputed, that dispute must be resolved as a question of fact before interpretation can begin. Confusion may be caused by the circumstances in which resolution of questions about the meaning of terms dictates the ultimate claim interpretation. But that is not unusual, legal conclusions being dictated by established facts and not the other way around, and it does not change the nature of the meaning-of-terms inquiry from one of fact to one of law. With the meaning of terms established, it may still be necessary to interpret the claim. It is that interpretation based on established facts that constitutes a legal conclusion reviewable as a matter of law.[374]

In a later case the court indicated that *Perini* is not to be read as holding that a disagreement over the meaning of a term in a claim ipso facto raises an issue of fact, thus precluding summary judgment. A disputed issue of fact may arise in connection with interpretation of a term in a claim if there is a genuine evidentiary conflict created by the underlying probative evidence pertinent to the claim's interpretation. However, in the absence of such an evidentiary conflict, claim interpretation may be resolved as an issue of law by the court on summary judgment, taking into account the specification, prosecution history, and other evidence. Conflicting opinions on the meaning of a term that are merely conclusory do not create such evidentiary conflict.[375]

More recently, in *Cybor v. FAS*, the court sat in banc to resolve a perceived conflict among its decisions. It held, unequivocally, that claim construction is a pure question of law and, that being the case, it will review de novo any allegedly fact-based questions relating to claim construction. In other words, the clearly erroneous rule does not apply to any findings or conclusions that the trial judge may have reached while construing the claims. Three members of the court sharply disagreed with this approach.[376] That the Federal Circuit may review a lower tribunal's claim construction de novo does not require

---

[374]*Perini Am., Inc. v. Paper Converting Mach. Co.*, 832 F.2d 581, 4 USPQ2d 1621 (Fed. Cir. 1987). But is not some deference due the fact finder here? See note 5:371. Where the parties do not dispute any relevant facts regarding the accused product, but disagree over possible claim interpretations, the question of literal infringement collapses into claim construction and is amenable to summary judgment. *General Mills, Inc. v. Hunt-Wesson, Inc.*, 103 F.3d 978, 41 USPQ2d 1440 (Fed. Cir. 1997).

[375]*Johnston v. IVAC Corp.*, 885 F.2d 1574, 12 USPQ2d 1382 (Fed. Cir. 1989). See also *Becton Dickinson & Co. v. C.R. Bard, Inc.*, 922 F.2d 792, 17 USPQ2d 1097 (Fed. Cir. 1990). Where a disputed term in a claim would be understood to have its ordinary meaning by one of skill in the art, extrinsic evidence that the inventor may have subjectively intended a different meaning does not preclude summary judgment. In such instance, there is no genuine dispute respecting a material fact. *Intellicall, Inc. v. Phonometrics, Inc.*, 952 F.2d 1384, 21 USPQ2d 1383 (Fed. Cir. 1992).

[376]*Cybor Corp. v. FAS Tech. Inc.*, 138 F.3d 1448, 46 USPQ2d 1169 (Fed. Cir. 1998).

it to consider claim construction arguments that were not raised below. A party's argument should not be a moving target. The argument at the trial and appellate level should be consistent, thereby ensuring a clear presentation of the issue to be resolved, an adequate opportunity for response and evidentiary development by the opposing party, and a record reviewable by the appellate court that is properly crystallized around and responsive to the asserted argument. The court's freedom to review claim construction de novo does not require it to effectively retry claim construction de novo by consideration of novel arguments not first presented to the tribunal whose decision is on review.[377]

In *Key v. Hercon,* the court addressed an unusual situation, where the appellant was urging that the district court erred in adopting the very claim construction that appellant advanced below. Although the function of an appellate court is to correct errors committed at trial, it looks with extreme disfavor on the party's assertion that the trial court committed error in adopting its proffered claim construction. Ordinarily, doctrines of estoppel, waiver, invited error, or the like would prohibit a party from asserting as error a position that it had advocated at the trial. Allowing parties in a patent suit to assert error in such situations would open the door to mischief and judicial inefficiency. For example, a party could advocate a certain claim construction at trial believing that that claim construction will result in favorable resolution of infringement or validity issues. If the trial court adopts that claim construction but resolves the infringement or validity issues unfavorably, the party could thereafter assert a new claim construction to get the proverbial second bite, possibly necessitating a retrial. The impropriety of asserting a position that the trial court adopts and then complaining about it on appeal should be obvious on its face, and litigants hardly need warning not to engage in such conduct.[378]

(f) Means-Plus-Function Elements

Section 112 itself directs that "means-plus-function" (MPF)[379] claims are to be construed to cover both the disclosed structure and equivalents thereof. Thus unless there is a clear basis for it in the

---

[377]*Finnigan Corp. v. United States ITC,* 180 F.3d 1354, 51 USPQ2d 1001 (Fed. Cir. 1999).

[378]*Key Pharm. Inc. v. Hercon Labs. Corp.,* 161 F.3d 709, 48 USPQ2d 1911 (Fed. Cir. 1998). The court went on to note, however, that in none of its prior opinions has it had occasion to publicly condemn this behavior. Moreover, the appellee did not object to the conduct or seek to invoke estoppel or other preclusive principles. Thus, in an abundance of fairness, and to preclude any argument by the appellant that it was not on notice, it chose instead to independently review the correctness of the trial court's claim construction. See also *Northern Telecom Ltd. v. Samsung Elec. Co.,* 215 F.3d 1281, 55 USPQ2d 1065 (Fed. Cir. 2000).

[379]The acronym MPF is occasionally used in this section for brevity. It is intended to encompass both means-plus-function and step-plus-function elements unless the context is to the contrary.

record, it is improper to limit a MPF claim to the particular means set forth in the specification. Patentees are required to disclose in the specification some enabling means for accomplishing the function, but there is and can be no requirement that applicants describe or predict every possible means of accomplishing that function. The statute was written precisely to avoid a holding that a MPF limitation must be read to cover only the disclosed means.[380]

Relation to the doctrine of equivalents. Equivalence under §112 is not precisely the same as the doctrine of equivalents (DOE) for infringement purposes (see §6.3(a)). For one thing a finding of §112 equivalence can lead to a finding of literal infringement.[381] Under the DOE, the question is whether the entirety of the accused device or process falls within a range of equivalence to which the claim is entitled, while under §112 the sole question is whether the single means in the accused device, which performs the stated function, is an equivalent of the corresponding means described in the specification as performing that function.[382] For another thing, equivalents under §112 is a pertinent consideration in the anticipation context.[383]

Thus, the sixth paragraph of §112 does not expand the scope of a claim. An element of a claim described as a means for performing a function, if read literally, would encompass any means for performing the function. Section 112 operates to cut back on the types of means that could literally satisfy the claim language—equivalents of disclosed structure. On the other hand, the statute has no effect on the function specified—it does not extend the element to equivalent functions. Properly understood, the provision operates more like the reverse doctrine of equivalents than the DOE because it restricts the scope of the literal claim language.[384]

---

[380]*Medtronic Inc. v. Intermedics, Inc.,* 799 F.2d 734, 230 USPQ 641 (Fed. Cir. 1986); *D.M.I., Inc. v. Deere & Co.,* 755 F.2d 1570, 225 USPQ 236 (Fed. Cir. 1985). This is true also when interpreting claims for purposes of the written description requirement (i.e., support). It is improper to limit means clauses to only the precise structure shown in the applications from which and to which a claim is copied for an interference proceeding. Equivalents of those structures are also pertinent. A claim is not interpreted one way in light of the specification in which it was originally granted and another way in light of the specification into which it is copied as a proposed interference count. *In re Spina,* 975 F.2d 854, 24 USPQ2d 1142 (Fed. Cir. 1992). See also *Rowe v. Dror,* 112 F.3d 473, 42 USPQ2d 1550 (Fed. Cir. 1997).

[381]*Palumbo v. Don-Joy Co.,* 762 F.2d 969, 226 USPQ 5 (Fed. Cir. 1985).

[382]*D.M.I., Inc. v. Deere & Co.,* 755 F.2d 1570, 225 USPQ 236 (Fed. Cir. 1985). In the context of a means-plus-function clause, failure to describe adequately the necessary structure, material, or acts in the written description means that the drafter has failed to comply with the second paragraph of §112, which requires that all claims must particularly point out and distinctly claim the subject matter which the applicant regards as the invention. *In re Dossel,* 115 F.3d 942, 42 USPQ2d 1881 (Fed. Cir. 1997).

[383]E.g., *In re Bond,* 910 F.2d 831, 15 USPQ2d 1566 (Fed. Cir. 1990).

[384]*Johnston v. IVAC Corp.,* 885 F.2d 1574, 12 USPQ2d 1382 (Fed. Cir. 1989). In *In re Iwahashi,* 888 F.2d 1370, 12 USPQ2d 1908 (Fed. Cir. 1989), the court reaffirmed the rule that a means-plus-function limitation is not interpreted to cover all means for accomplishing that function, but only the means described in the specification and any equivalents thereof. Any

In *Valmont v. Reinke,*[385] the Federal Circuit expanded upon the relationship of §112 equivalents to the traditional DOE. Section 112 permits MPF language in a combination claim, but with a string attached. The attaching string limits the applicant to the structure, material, or acts in the specification and their equivalents. The DOE has a different purpose and application. It prevents a copyist from evading patent claims with insubstantial changes. An equivalent under the DOE results from an insubstantial change that, from the perspective of one of ordinary skill in the art, adds nothing of significance to the claimed invention. But §112 and the DOE have something in common. The word "equivalent" in §112 invokes the familiar concept of an insubstantial change that adds nothing of significance. In the context of §112, however, an equivalent results from an insubstantial change that adds nothing of significance to the structure, material, or acts disclosed in the patent specification.

In *IMS v. Haas,*[386] the court attempted to illuminate the difference between equivalent structures and structural equivalency. In light of the similarity of the tests for equivalence under §112¶6 and the DOE, the context of the invention should be considered when performing a MPF equivalence analysis just as it is in a DOE determination. As a consequence, two structures that are equivalent in one environment may not be equivalent in another. More particularly, when in a claimed "means" limitation the disclosed physical structure is of little or no importance to the claimed invention, there may be a broader range of equivalent structures than if the physical characteristics of the structure are critical in performing the claimed function in the context of the claimed invention. Thus, a rigid comparison of physical structures in a vacuum may be inappropriate in a particular case. Indeed, the statute requires two structures to be equivalent, but it does not require them to be "structurally equivalent," i.e., it does not mandate an equivalency comparison that necessarily focuses heavily or exclusively on physical structure. In some cases, an analysis of insubstantial differences in the context of the invention results in a finding of equivalence under §112¶6, even though two structures arguably would not be considered equivalent structures in other contexts, e.g., if performing functions other than the claimed function. In other cases, in which the specific physical features of the structure corresponding to the "means" limitation may have more relevance to the claimed invention, a finding of noninfringement results.

MPF equivalency. For literal infringement of a §112¶6 limitation, the fact finder must determine whether the accused device performs an identical function to the one recited in the MPF clause. If the

---

statement to the contrary in *In re Sweet*, 393 F.2d 837, 157 USPQ 495 (CCPA 1968) was rejected as incorrect.

[385]*Valmont Indus., Inc. v. Reinke Mfg. Co.*, 983 F.2d 1039, 25 USPQ2d 1451 (Fed. Cir. 1993).

[386]*IMS Tech. Inc. v. Haas Automation Inc.*, 206 F.3d 1422, 54 USPQ2d 1129 (Fed. Cir. 2000).

identical function is performed, the fact finder must then determine whether the accused device utilizes the same structure or materials as described in the specification, or their equivalents.[387] Despite repeated statements that §112¶6 equivalence is a question of fact,[388] the court specifically left that question open in *Markman*.[389] In a series of decisions subsequent to *Markman*, the court took pains,[390] sometimes great pains,[391] to keep the question open. More recently, in a divided panel decision, the court finally held, unequivocally, that §112¶6 equivalency is a question of fact.[392] A decision on the matter can be reversed only if it is clearly erroneous. The sole question is whether the single means in the accused device that performs the function stated in the claim is the same as, or an equivalent of, the corresponding structure described in the patentee's specification as performing that function. The court must compare the accused structure with the disclosed structure and must find equivalent structure as well as identity of claimed function for that structure.[393] The matter of §112 equivalency is specifically addressed in §6.3(a)(iv), in association with the more general topic of the traditional DOE.

Construction of MPF elements. So if the Federal Circuit has finally concluded, albeit somewhat hesitantly, that §112 equivalency is a question of fact, what of the remaining issues posed by §112¶6? Whether the language of a claim is to be interpreted according to §112¶6, i.e., whether a claim limitation is in MPF format, is a matter

---

[387]*Mas-Hamilton Group Inc. v. LaGard Inc.*, 156 F.3d 1206, 48 USPQ2d 1010 (Fed. Cir. 1998).

[388]*Carroll Touch, Inc. v. Electro Mechanical Sys., Inc.*, 3 F.3d 404, 27 USPQ2d 1836 (Fed. Cir. 1993); *King Instr. Corp. v. Otari Corp.*, 767 F.2d 853, 226 USPQ 402 (Fed. Cir. 1985); *Palumbo v. Don-Joy Co.*, 762 F.2d 969, 226 USPQ 5 (Fed. Cir. 1985). The determination whether an accused device is a §112¶6 equivalent of the described embodiment is a question of fact and can be reversed only if it is clearly erroneous. *Durango Assoc., Inc. v. Reflange, Inc.*, 843 F.2d 1349, 6 USPQ2d 1290 (Fed. Cir. 1988). Section 112¶6 equivalence is a question of fact as is regular equivalence and reverse equivalence. *Hartness Int'l, Inc. v. Simplimatic Eng'g Co.*, 819 F.2d 1100, 2 USPQ2d 1826 (Fed. Cir. 1987).

[389]*Markman v. Westview Instr., Inc.*, 52 F.3d 967, 977 n.8, 34 USPQ2d 1321 (Fed. Cir. 1995).

[390]*Cybor Corp. v. FAS Tech. Inc.*, 138 F.3d 1448, 46 USPQ2d 1169 (Fed. Cir. 1998); *Kegel Co. v. AMF Bowling, Inc.*, 127 F.3d 1420, 44 USPQ2d 1123 (Fed. Cir. 1997). But see *Hebert v. Lisle Corp.*, 99 F.3d 1109, 40 USPQ2d 1611 (Fed. Cir. 1996), where the court said questions of the technologic equivalency of a claimed invention and an accused device are not questions of claim construction; they are questions of fact and require determination by the trier of fact, based on evidence.

[391]*Chiuminatta Concrete Concepts Inc. v. Cardinal Indus. Inc.*, 145 F.3d 1303, 46 USPQ2d 1752 (Fed. Cir. 1998).

[392]*Odetics Inc. v. Storage Tech. Corp.*, 185 F.3d 1259, 51 USPQ2d 1225 (Fed. Cir. 1999). See also *IMS Tech. Inc. v. Haas Automation Inc.*, 206 F.3d 1422, 54 USPQ2d 1129 (Fed. Cir. 2000). Cf. *Mas-Hamilton Group Inc. v. LaGard Inc.*, 156 F.3d 1206, 48 USPQ2d 1010 (Fed. Cir. 1998).

[393]*Durango Assoc., Inc. v. Reflange, Inc.*, 843 F.2d 1349, 6 USPQ2d 1290 (Fed. Cir. 1988). In *O.I. Corp. v. Tekmar Co.*, 115 F.3d 1576, 42 USPQ2d 1777 (Fed. Cir. 1997), the court held that the language "means for passing the analyte slug through a passage" is a MPF element, but "passage" is not part of the recited means. It is the place where the function occurs, not the structure that accomplishes it. The court then went on to construe the term "passage," in the ordinary way, by looking at the specification and prosecution history.

of claim construction and is thus a question of law, reviewed de novo. Once a court establishes that a MPF limitation is at issue, it must construe that limitation, thereby determining what the claimed function is and what structures disclosed in the written description correspond to the "means" for performing that function. These issues are likewise questions of law, reviewed de novo.[394]

One would expect that determination of the function should not be too controversial, inasmuch as the function must be spelled out in the claims.[395] Determination of corresponding structure, though, can present a very bothersome question: How much of the disclosed means does one include in order to assess §112¶6 equivalence?[396] Structural aspects that are unrelated to the recited function are not what the statute contemplates as structure corresponding to the recited function.[397] A structure disclosed in the specification is only deemed to be "corresponding structure" if the specification clearly links or associates that structure to the function recited in the claim. The duty to link or associate structure in the specification with the function is the quid pro quo for the convenience of employing §112¶6.[398]

---

[394]*Kemco Sales Inc. v. Control Papers Co.*, 208 F.3d 1352, 54 USPQ2d 1308 (Fed. Cir. 2000). See also *Overhead Door Corp. v. Chamberlain Group Inc.*, 194 F.3d 1261, 52 USPQ2d 1321 (Fed. Cir. 1999) (corresponding structure); *Unidynamics Corp. v. Automatic Prods. Int'l Ltd.*, 157 F.3d 1311, 48 USPQ2d 1099 (Fed. Cir. 1998) (associated function); *Mas-Hamilton Group Inc. v. LaGard Inc.*, 156 F.3d 1206, 48 USPQ2d 1010 (Fed. Cir. 1998) (corresponding structure); *Chiuminatta Concrete Concepts Inc. v. Cardinal Indus. Inc.*, 145 F.3d 1303, 46 USPQ2d 1752 (Fed. Cir. 1998) (associated function and corresponding structure).

[395]The statute does not permit limitation of a means-plus-function claim by adopting a function different from that explicitly recited in the claim. *Micro Chem. Inc. v. Great Plains Chem. Co.*, 194 F.3d 1258, 52 USPQ2d 1258 (Fed. Cir. 1999).

See *Smiths Indus. Med. Sys. Inc. v. Vital Signs Inc.*, 183 F.3d 1347, 51 USPQ2d 1415 (Fed. Cir. 1999), where the court found error in the trial court's construction of the functional portion of a MPF element.

[396]In *Dawn Equip. Corp. v. Kentucky Farms Inc.*, 140 F.3d 1009, 46 USPQ2d 1109 (Fed. Cir. 1998), the court was able to sidestep the question because it found that, even excluding the disputed portion, there was no infringement.

[397]*Chiuminatta Concrete Concepts Inc. v. Cardinal Indus. Inc.*, 145 F.3d 1303, 46 USPQ2d 1752 (Fed. Cir. 1998). Nor does the statute permit incorporation of structure from the written description beyond that necessary to perform the claimed function. After identifying the function of the MPF element, the court looks to the written description to identify the structure corresponding to that function. Identification of corresponding structure may embrace more than the preferred embodiment. A MPF claim encompasses all structure in the specification corresponding to that element and equivalent structures. *Micro Chem. Inc. v. Great Plains Chem. Co.*, 194 F.3d 1258, 52 USPQ2d 1258 (Fed. Cir. 1999). Also, the statute does not limit all terms in a MPF clause to what is disclosed in the written description and equivalents thereof; §112¶6 applies only to interpretation of the means or step that performs a recited function when a claim recites insufficient structure or acts for performing the function. *IMS Tech. Inc. v. Haas Automation Inc.*, 206 F.3d 1422, 54 USPQ2d 1129 (Fed. Cir. 2000).

[398]*Kahn v. General Motors Corp.*, 135 F.3d 1472, 45 USPQ2d 1608 (Fed. Cir. 1998). See also *York Prods., Inc. v. Central Tractor Farm & Fam. Ctr.*, 99 F.3d 1568, 40 USPQ2d 1619 (Fed. Cir. 1996). If the specification does not adequately disclose a particular structure as that which performs the recited function, then the claim does not particularly point out and distinctly claim that particular means. *B. Braun Med., Inc. v. Abbott Labs.*, 124 F.3d 1419, 43 USPQ2d 1896 (Fed. Cir. 1997). The court did indicate, however, that the unlinked structure could still be found a §112¶6 equivalent. *Id.*

Where a specification discloses two structurally very different embodiments of an element for performing a recited function, the court is not required to articulate a single claim interpretation consonant with all structures in the specification corresponding to the claimed function. Under §112¶6 the court need only identify the alternative structures that perform the recited function, and the claim will cover those and any equivalent structures.[399]

In a 2–1 panel decision, the court considered, in the context of the various paragraphs of 35 U.S.C. §112, the necessity for an express disclosure of some structure to support a MPF element. It reasoned that the question of claim definiteness under §112¶2 is based upon the understanding of one skilled in the art, and this extends to the question of whether sufficient structure has been disclosed to support a MPF limitation under §112¶6. In answering this question, it must be determined whether the corresponding structure of a MPF limitation is disclosed in the written description in such a manner that one skilled in the art will know and understand what structure corresponds to the means limitation. Otherwise, one does not know what the claim means. Fulfillment of the §112¶6 tradeoff cannot be satisfied when there is a total omission of structure. There must be structure in the specification. This conclusion is not inconsistent with the fact that the knowledge of one skilled in the particular art may be used to understand what structure the specification discloses, or that even a dictionary or other documentary source may be resorted to for such assistance, because such resources may only be employed in relation to structure that is disclosed in the specification. Paragraph 6 of §112 does not contemplate the kind of open-ended reference to extrinsic works that §112¶1, the enablement provision, does. Paragraph 1 permits resort to material outside of the specification in order to satisfy the enablement portion of the statute because it makes no sense to encumber the specification of a patent with all the knowledge of the past concerning how to make and use the claimed invention. Paragraph 6, however, does not have the expansive purpose of paragraph 1. It sets forth a simple requirement, a quid pro quo, in order to utilize a generic means expression. All one needs to do in order to obtain the benefit of that claiming device is to recite some structure corresponding to the means in the specification, as the statute states, so that one can readily ascertain what the claim means and comply with the particularity requirement of §112¶2. The requirement of specific structure in §112¶6 thus does not raise the specter of an unending disclosure of what everyone in the field knows that such a requirement in §112¶1 would entail. If this interpretation of the statute results in a slight amount of additional written description appearing in patent specifications, compared with total omission of

---

[399]*Ishida Co. v. Taylor,* 221 F.3d 1310, 55 USPQ2d 1449 (Fed. Cir. 2000).

structure, that is the trade-off necessitated by an applicant's use of the statute's permissive generic means term.[400]

Also, the court has warned that a virtual lack of disclosure of structure to support a MPF limitation does not indicate that the limitation reads on any and all means for performing the structure. For example, the structure of a microprocessor programmed to carry out an algorithm is limited by the disclosed algorithm. Thus, in a MPF claim in which the disclosed structure is a computer, or microprocessor, programmed to carry out an algorithm, the disclosed structure is not the general purpose computer, but rather the special purpose computer programmed to perform the disclosed algorithm.[401]

The statutorily required construction under §112¶6 must proceed on a limitation-by-limitation basis, not dissimilar to the analysis under the DOE.[402] In interpreting a MPF claim, several factors may be considered, including the language of the claim, other claims in the patent, the specification, the prosecution history, and expert testimony.[403] In dealing with a MPF limitation, a focus on the "plain meaning" of the terms, without resort to the limited features contained in the specification, the prosecution history, and a factual inquiry into equivalents, might create an erroneously broad scope.[404]

The role of prior art. But the court has held, squarely, that it is not necessary to consider the prior art in applying §112 equivalents. Even if the prior art discloses the same or an equivalent structure, the claim will not be limited in scope thereby. It is only necessary to determine what is an equivalent to the structure disclosed in the specification that is performing the function at issue. When prior art is considered in the context of the DOE, the purpose is to ensure that the patent holder does not obtain a broader right to exclude under that doctrine than could have been obtained from the PTO. But the

---

[400]*Atmel Corp. v. Information Storage Devices Inc.*, 198 F.3d 1374, 53 USPQ2d 1225 (Fed. Cir. 1999). The court seemed to hold that a nonpatent document incorporated by reference into the specification could not be relied upon to supply the necessary structure. Nonetheless, it was able to find sufficient disclosure of §112¶6 structure simply from the fact that the evidence indicated that a person of ordinary skill in the art would have been able to ascertain the structure from the very title of the incorporated document.

[401]*WMS Gaming Inc. v. International Game Tech.*, 184 F.3d 1339, 51 USPQ2d 1385 (Fed. Cir. 1999).

[402]*Endress + Hauser, Inc. v. Hawk Meas. Sys. Pty.*, 122 F.3d 1040, 43 USPQ2d 1849 (Fed. Cir. 1997).

[403]*Durango Assoc., Inc. v. Reflange, Inc.*, 843 F.2d 1349, 6 USPQ2d 1290 (Fed. Cir. 1988); *Rite-Hite Corp. v. Kelley Co.*, 819 F.2d 1120, 2 USPQ2d 1915 (Fed. Cir. 1987). In a dictum, the court indicated that the doctrine of claim differentiation may have to yield to §112¶(6). Thus, where a MPF element must be interpreted, due to §112¶(6), to require structure that is specified in another claim, that requirement cannot be avoided under the doctrine of claim differentiation. *Laitram Corp. v. Rexnord, Inc.*, 939 F.2d 1533, 19 USPQ2d 1367 (Fed. Cir. 1991). A MPF limitation is not made open-ended by the presence of another claim specifically claiming the disclosed structure that underlies the means clause or an equivalent of that structure. *C.R. Bard Inc. v. M3 Sys. Inc.*, 157 F.3d 1340, 48 USPQ2d 1225 (Fed. Cir. 1998).

[404]*Biodex Corp. v. Loredan Biomedical, Inc.*, 946 F.2d 850, 20 USPQ2d 1252, 1262 (Fed. Cir. 1991).

policies underlying that concept are not served by restricting claim limitations in the same manner. Thus, under §112¶6 the aids for determining a structural equivalent to the structure disclosed in the patent are the same as those used in interpreting any other type of claim language, namely, the specification, the prosecution history, other claims in the patent, and expert testimony.[405]

Identification of MPF elements. The court has worked hard to find a solid test for determining whether a particular claim element is a statutory means- or step-plus-function element and thus subject to the construction mandated by §112¶6. Its most recent efforts can be summarized like this: if the word "means" appears in a claim element in association with a function, the court presumes that §112¶6 applies. This presumption collapses, however, if the claim itself recites sufficient structure, material, or acts to perform the claimed function. Without the term "means," a claim element is presumed to fall outside MPF strictures. Once again, however, that presumption can collapse when an element lacking the term "means" nonetheless relies on functional terms rather than structure or mate-

---

[405]*Intel Corp. v. United States ITC*, 946 F.2d 821, 20 USPQ2d 1161 (Fed. Cir. 1991). Despite a clear suggestion in *In re Bond*, 910 F.2d 831, 15 USPQ2d 1566 (Fed. Cir. 1990), to the contrary, the PTO had applied a different standard during prosecution and gave notice that it intended to continue that practice. See "Applicability of the last paragraph of 35 U.S.C. §112 to patentability determinations before the Patent and Trademark Office," 1134 O.G. 631 (December 13, 1991). This apparent conflict was resolved in *In re Donaldson*, 16 F.3d 1189, 29 USPQ2d 1845 (Fed. Cir. 1994). There the court held that the PTO is obliged, by virtue of §112,¶6, to interpret MPF clauses to cover only the disclosed structure and equivalents. This does not conflict with the principle that claims in prosecution are to be given their broadest reasonable interpretation, for such an interpretation is the broadest permitted by law. *Alpex Computer Co. v. Nintendo Co.*, 102 F.3d 1214, 40 USPQ2d 1667 (Fed. Cir. 1997), should be read carefully in this context. There the court seemed to apply a "bar" against inconsistent positions (the next thing to a prosecution history estoppel?) by reason of distinctions over the prior art that had been made concerning the same MPF elements in other claims. In *Applied Med. Res. Corp. v. United States Surgical Corp.*, 147 F.3d 1374, 47 USPQ2d 1289 (Fed. Cir. 1998), the court reaffirmed that the prior art is not a consideration in determining MPF equivalency, this time in the context of the exclusion of expert testimony that sought to establish that nothing in the prior art is available as an equivalent for purposes of §112¶6. In *Clearstream Wastewater Sys. Inc. v. Hydro-Action Inc.*, 206 F.3d 1440, 54 USPQ2d 1185 (Fed. Cir. 2000), the court attempted to explain the notion that prior art may not be a consideration in construing MPF equivalents. Here the means in question was described in the patent as a flexible conduit system. The patent pointed out the disadvantages of the prior art rigid conduit system. The accused infringer used the prior art conduit system as its structure for performing the recited function. The court concluded that the MPF element could be interpreted to cover both the disclosed flexible system and the rigid prior art system as an equivalent. The court justified its holding on three grounds. First, although the specification taught away from the rigid system, it did not indicate that the rigid system could not perform the recited function, as was the case in *Signtech USA Ltd v. Vutek Inc.*, 174 F.3d 1352, 50 USPQ2d 1372 (Fed. Cir. 1999). Second, unlike the situation in *Sofamor Danek Group, Inc. v. DePuy-Motech, Inc.*, 74 F.3d 1216, 37 USPQ2d 1529 (Fed. Cir. 1996), the claim included another element that appeared to be the real point of novelty. Third, the fact that other claims were specific to the flexible system supported the broader interpretation for the claim in question, under the doctrine of claim differentiation. Combination claims can consist of new combinations of old elements or combinations of new and old elements. Because old elements are part of combination claims, claim limitations may, and often do, read on the prior art.

rial to describe performance of the claimed function.[406] Thus, in determining whether a claim element falls within §112¶6, the court presumes an applicant advisedly used the word "means" to invoke the statutory mandates for MPF clauses. Two specific rules, however, overcome this presumption. First, a claim element that uses the word "means" but recites no function corresponding to the means does not invoke §112¶6. Second, even if the claim element specifies a function, if it also recites sufficient structure or material for performing that function, §112¶6 does not apply. In making the first determination, the court relies primarily on the claim language itself, keeping in mind that a claim need not claim every function of a working device. Rather, a claim may specify improvements in one function without claiming the entire machine with its many functions. In making the second determination, it must also be kept in mind that a claim need not recite every last detail of structure disclosed in the specification for performing the claimed function. Instead, the claim need only recite "sufficient" structure to perform entirely the claimed function.[407]

Thus, if the word "means" appears in a claim element in combination with a function, it is presumed to be a MPF element to which §112¶6 applies. Nevertheless, according to its express terms, §112¶6 governs only claim elements that do not recite sufficient structural limitations. Therefore, the presumption that §112¶6 applies is overcome if the claim itself recites sufficient structure or material for performing the claimed function. Although use of the phrase "means for" (or "step for") is not the only way to invoke §112¶6, that terminology typically does so while other formulations generally do not. Therefore, when an element of a claim does not use the term "means," treatment as a MPF claim element is generally not appropriate. However, when it is apparent that the element invokes purely functional terms, without the additional recital of specific structure or material for performing that function, the claim element may be a MPF element despite the lack of express MPF language.[408] The use of the term

---

[406]*Micro Chem. Inc. v. Great Plains Chem. Co.*, 194 F.3d 1258, 52 USPQ2d 1258 (Fed. Cir. 1999).

[407]*Rodime PLC v. Seagate Tech. Inc.*, 174 F.3d 1294, 50 USPQ2d 1429 (Fed. Cir. 1999). See also *Sage Prods., Inc. v. Devon Indus., Inc.*, 126 F.3d 1420, 44 USPQ2d 1103 (Fed. Cir. 1997).

[408]*Al-Site Corp. v. VSI Int'l Inc.*, 174 F.3d 1308, 50 USPQ2d 1161 (Fed. Cir. 1999). See also *Personalized Media Comm. LLC v. United States ITC*, 161 F.3d 696, 48 USPQ2d 1880 (Fed. Cir. 1998); *Ethicon Inc. v. United States Surgical Corp.*, 135 F.3d 1456, 45 USPQ2d 1545 (Fed. Cir. 1998); *Cole v. Kimberly-Clark Corp.*, 102 F.3d 524, 41 USPQ2d 1001 (Fed. Cir. 1996); *York Prods., Inc. v. Central Tractor Farm & Fam. Ctr.*, 99 F.3d 1568, 40 USPQ2d 1619 (Fed. Cir. 1996); *Greenberg v. Ethicon Endo-Surgery, Inc.*, 91 F.3d 1580, 39 USPQ2d 1783 (Fed. Cir. 1996). When an apparatus claim does not recite definite structure in support of a defined function, it is subject to §112¶6. *Fonar Corp. v. General Elec. Co.*, 107 F.3d 1543, 41 USPQ2d 1801 (Fed. Cir. 1997). While traditional means language does not automatically make an element a MPF element, conversely, lack of such language does not prevent a limitation from being construed as a MPF limitation. If the recited element is not shown to have a generally understood structural meaning in the art, and if the language used is purely functional, the fact that the word "means" is not employed does not avoid the narrowing effect of §112¶6. *Mas-Hamilton Group Inc. v. LaGard Inc.*, 156 F.3d 1206, 48 USPQ2d 1010 (Fed. Cir. 1998). "Ink delivery means" is equivalent to "means for ink delivery" in the context of determining whether

"means" generally (but not always) shows that the patent applicant has chosen the option of MPF format invoking §112¶6 construction. The recitation of some structure in a MPF element does not preclude the applicability of §112¶6 when it merely serves to further specify the function of the means.[409]

A concession by a party regarding the applicability of §112¶6 does not relieve the court of its responsibility to interpret the claims as a matter of law. To interpret the claims, the court must decide the subsidiary question of whether the claim element disputed by the parties invokes §112¶6 in the first instance. Only by undertaking this inquiry can the court ensure consistency in statutory application. Moreover, its claim interpretation may affect entities beyond the parties to the case.[410]

Method claims. In *O.I. v. Tekmar*,[411] the court held, squarely and unequivocally, that §112¶6 applies to method claims. The analysis is interesting: structure and material go with means, and acts go with steps. Thus, §112¶6 is implicated when the claim recites step plus function without supporting acts. However, there must be a function associated with the particular step.[412] The court feels that if it were to construe every process claim containing steps described by an "ing" verb, such as passing, heating, reacting, etc., as a step-plus-function limitation, it would be limiting process claims in a manner never intended by Congress. Also, just because method claims "parallel" apparatus claims that contain MPF elements does not necessarily mean that the method claims must also be construed that way. Each claim must be independently reviewed in order to determine if it is subject to the requirements of §112¶6.[413]

(g) Some Standard Rules

Timing of the inquiry. Despite some earlier hints that other time frames might be appropriate,[414] the court has now clearly identified

---

it should qualify for means-function treatment under §112¶6. *Signtech USA Ltd v. Vutek Inc.*, 174 F.3d 1352, 50 USPQ2d 1372 (Fed. Cir. 1999). In *Envirco Corp. v. Clestra Cleanroom Inc.*, 209 F.3d 1360, 54 USPQ2d 1449 (Fed. Cir. 2000), the court held that "baffle means" was not a MPF element, because "baffle" is itself a structural term and the claims also further defined it as having "inner surfaces for directing airflow." In *Kemco Sales Inc. v. Control Papers Co.*, 208 F.3d 1352, 54 USPQ2d 1308 (Fed. Cir. 2000), the court held that "plastic envelope closing means" was a MPF limitation.

[409]*Unidynamics Corp. v. Automatic Prods. Int'l Ltd.*, 157 F.3d 1311, 48 USPQ2d 1099 (Fed. Cir. 1998).

[410]*Rodime PLC v. Seagate Tech. Inc.*, 174 F.3d 1294, 50 USPQ2d 1429 (Fed. Cir. 1999).

[411]*O.I. Corp. v. Tekmar Co.*, 115 F.3d 1576, 42 USPQ2d 1777 (Fed. Cir. 1997).

[412]The court rejected the argument that a preamble statement of purpose for the overall process constituted an associated function for the separate step clauses. A statement in a preamble of a result that necessarily follows from performing a series of steps does not convert each of those steps into step-plus-function clauses. See also *Serrano v. Telular Corp.*, 111 F.3d 1578, 42 USPQ2d 1538 (Fed. Cir. 1997).

[413]*O.I. Corp. v. Tekmar Co.*, 115 F.3d 1576, 42 USPQ2d 1777 (Fed. Cir. 1997).

[414]In *Markman* itself, the Federal Circuit said "the focus is on the objective test of what one of ordinary skill in the art at the time of the invention would have understood the term

the date of filing the application as the relevant time at which the claim construction inquiry must be evaluated.[415]

Consistency. Consistency in claim interpretation is important.[416] An inventor may not be heard to proffer an interpretation that would alter the undisputed public record (claim, specification, prosecution history) and treat the claim as a "nose of wax."[417] Words defined in the specification must be given the same meaning when used in a claim.[418] In some cases, a claim term can be given a different meaning in the various claims of the same patent, when a patent so provides. But in the absence of any evidence to the contrary, a court must presume that the use of different terms in the claims connotes different meanings.[419] An independent claim must not be interpreted in a way that is inconsistent with a claim that depends from it.[420]

That explicit arguments made during prosecution to overcome prior art can lead to narrow claim interpretations makes sense, because the public has a right to rely on such definitive statements made during prosecution. Indeed, by distinguishing the claimed invention over the prior art, an applicant is indicating what the claims do not cover. Therefore, a patentee, after relinquishing subject matter to distinguish a prior art reference asserted by the PTO during prosecution, cannot during subsequent litigation escape reliance by the defendant upon this unambiguous surrender of subject matter. Accordingly, claims may not be construed one way in order to obtain

---

to mean." 34 USPQ2d at 1335. In *Voice Tech. Group Inc. v. VMC Sys. Inc.,* 164 F.3d 605, 49 USPQ2d 1333, 1341 (Fed. Cir. 1999), the court remarked that an inventor cannot "by later testimony change the invention and the claims from their meaning at the time the patent was drafted and granted." In *Al-Site Corp. v. VSI Int'l Inc.,* 174 F.3d 1308, 50 USPQ2d 1161, 1168 (Fed. Cir. 1999), the court observed that "the literal meaning of a claim is fixed upon its issuance."

[415]*Schering Corp. v. Amgen Inc.,* 222 F.3d 1347, 55 USPQ2d 1650, 1654 (Fed. Cir. 2000). It refused to consider information that had been published several months after the filing date of the application. The court did, however, seem to leave room for the possibility that the date of invention, if it as a matter of record preceded the filing date, might be appropriate.

[416]*Schenck, A.G. v. Nortron Corp.,* 713 F.2d 782, 218 USPQ 698 (Fed. Cir. 1983).

[417]*Southwall Tech., Inc. v. Cardinal IG Co.,* 54 F.3d 1570, 34 USPQ2d 1673 (Fed. Cir. 1995); *Senmed, Inc. v. Richard-Allan Med. Indus., Inc.,* 888 F.2d 815, 12 USPQ2d 1508 (Fed. Cir. 1989).

[418]*Fonar Corp. v. Johnson & Johnson,* 821 F.2d 627, 3 USPQ2d 1109 (Fed. Cir. 1987); *McGill Inc. v. John Zink Co.,* 736 F.2d 666, 221 USPQ 944 (Fed. Cir. 1984). Construction of a claim in a manner inconsistent with the specification is error. *Howes v. Medical Components, Inc.,* 814 F.2d 638, 2 USPQ2d 1271 (Fed. Cir. 1987). Nevertheless, a patent's written description can set forth more than one definition of a claim term. Where the language of the written description is sufficient to put a reader on notice of the different uses of a term, and where those uses are further apparent from publicly available documents referenced in the patent file, it is appropriate to depart from the normal rule of construing seemingly identical terms in the same manner. This entirely accords with the public notice function of claims. *Pitney Bowes Inc. v. Hewlett-Packard Co.,* 182 F.3d 1298, 51 USPQ2d 1161 (Fed. Cir. 1999).

[419]*CAE Screenplates Inc. v. Heinrich Fiedler GmbH,* 224 F.3d 1308, 55 USPQ2d 1804 (Fed. Cir. 2000). Unless the patent otherwise provides, a claim term cannot be given a different meaning in the various claims of the same patent. Interpretation of a disputed claim term thus requires reference to the other claims. *Georgia-Pacific Corp. v. United States Gypsum Co.,* 195 F.3d 1322, 52 USPQ2d 1590 (Fed. Cir. 1999).

[420]*Wright Med. Tech., Inc. v. Osteonics Corp.,* 122 F.3d 1440, 43 USPQ2d 1837 (Fed. Cir. 1997).

their allowance and in a different way against accused infringers.[421] It is thus legally improper to treat structural claims one way when considering validity and another when considering infringement.[422] It is axiomatic that the claims must be construed in the same way for infringement that they were for determining validity,[423] including both literal infringement and infringement under the DOE.[424] In determining the patentability of product-by-process claims, the process limitations are not considered. But for infringement purposes, and presumably for purposes of validity as well, such claims are limited to a product prepared by the process set forth in the claims.[425] Consistency may transcend a particular proceeding, for claim interpretation is subject to the law of the case doctrine.[426]

Accused infringement. Determination of actual infringement is not in every case limited to literalism. Thus the court has recognized that if the accused infringer argues that the claim, as read in light of the aforementioned factors, does not actually read on its device, claim interpretation is required.[427] But is the accused device a permissible reference in claim interpretation? The court says no.[428] The claims should not be construed to "cover" or not to "cover" the accused device, for that procedure would make infringement a matter of judicial whim. It is only after the claims have been construed without reference to the accused device that those claims, so construed, are

---

[421]*Spectrum Int'l Inc. v. Sterilite Corp.,* 164 F.3d 1372, 49 USPQ2d 1065 (Fed. Cir. 1998).

[422]*Connell v. Sears, Roebuck & Co.,* 722 F.2d 1542, 220 USPQ 193 (Fed. Cir. 1983). Claims may not be construed one way in order to obtain their allowance and in a contrary way against infringers. *Lockwood v. American Airlines, Inc.,* 107 F.3d 1565, 41 USPQ2d 1961 (Fed. Cir. 1997); *Tandon Corp. v. United States ITC,* 831 F.2d 1017, 4 USPQ2d 1283 (Fed. Cir. 1987). To permit an inventor to expressly state, throughout the application and claims, that the invention includes a particular limitation, and then be allowed to avoid that limitation in a later infringement suit would run counter to the requirement that a claim particularly point out and distinctly claim the invention. *Unique Concepts, Inc. v. Brown,* 939 F.2d 1558, 19 USPQ2d 1500 (Fed. Cir. 1991).

[423]*Intervet Am., Inc. v. Kee-Vet Labs., Inc.,* 887 F.2d 1050, 12 USPQ2d 1474 (Fed. Cir. 1989); *Smithkline Diagnostics, Inc. v. Helena Labs. Corp.,* 859 F.2d 878, 8 USPQ2d 1468 (Fed. Cir. 1988); *W.L. Gore & Assoc., Inc. v. Garlock, Inc.,* 842 F.2d 1275, 6 USPQ2d 1277 (Fed. Cir. 1988). Claims mean the same for validity and infringement. *Atlantic Thermoplastics Co. v. Faytex Corp.,* 970 F.2d 834, 23 USPQ2d 1481 (Fed. Cir. 1992).

[424]*Senmed, Inc. v. Richard-Allan Med. Indus., Inc.,* 888 F.2d 815, 12 USPQ2d 1508 (Fed. Cir. 1989). See also *Uniroyal, Inc. v. Rudkin-Wiley Corp.,* 939 F.2d 1540, 19 USPQ2d 1432 (Fed. Cir. 1991).

[425]A contrary indication in *Scripps Clinic & Res. Found. v. Genentech, Inc.,* 927 F.2d 1565, 18 USPQ2d 1001 (Fed. Cir. 1991), was expressly disavowed in *Atlantic Thermoplastics Co. v. Faytex Corp.,* 970 F.2d 834, 23 USPQ2d 1481 (Fed. Cir. 1992), much to the consternation of several members of the court. See note 5:491.

[426]*W.L. Gore & Assoc., Inc. v. Garlock, Inc.,* 842 F.2d 1275, 6 USPQ2d 1277, 1281 (Fed. Cir. 1988); *Del Mar Avionics, Inc. v. Quinton Instr. Co.,* 836 F.2d 1320, 5 USPQ2d 1255 (Fed. Cir. 1987); *Stearns v. Beckman Instruments, Inc.,* 737 F.2d 1565, 222 USPQ 457 (Fed. Cir. 1984).

[427]*SRI Int'l v. Matsushita Elec. Corp.,* 775 F.2d 1107, 227 USPQ 577 (Fed. Cir. 1985).

[428]*Young Dental Mfg. Co. v. Q3 Special Prods., Inc.,* 112 F.3d 1137, 42 USPQ2d 1589 (Fed. Cir. 1997).

applied to the accused device to determine infringement.[429] But sometimes it may be impossible even to frame a claim interpretation issue without reference to the accused infringement.[430] It is correct that although the claims are construed objectively and without reference to the accused device, only those terms need be construed that are in controversy, and only to the extent necessary to resolve the controversy. It is therefore routine case management to require litigants to identify the aspects of their case that are material to the dispute.[431]

Claims are often drafted using terminology that is not as precise or specific as it might be. As long as the result complies with the statutory requirement to particularly point out and distinctly claim the subject matter that the applicant regards as the invention, that practice is permissible. That does not mean, however, that a court, under the rubric of claim construction, may give a claim whatever additional precision or specificity is necessary to facilitate a comparison between the claim and the accused product. Rather, after the court has defined the claim with whatever specificity and precision is warranted by the language of the claim and the evidence bearing on the proper construction, the task of determining whether the construed claim reads on the accused product is for the finder of fact.[432]

Claim differentiation. Each claim defines a separate invention.[433] The scope of each individual claim must be examined on its own merits, apart from other claims, even in the same patent.[434] Thus while evidence of the scope of a claim may be found from review of other claims,[435] narrow claim limitations cannot be read into broad

---

[429]*SRI Int'l v. Matsushita Elec. Corp.,* 775 F.2d 1107, 227 USPQ 577 (Fed. Cir. 1985). Of course, the particular accused product or process must be kept in mind, for it is efficient to focus on the construction of only the disputed elements or limitations of the claim. *Scripps Clinic & Res. Found. v. Genentech, Inc.,* 927 F.2d 1565, 18 USPQ2d 1001 (Fed. Cir. 1991).

[430]In *Hilgraeve Corp. v. McAfee Assoc. Inc.,* 224 F.3d 1349, 55 USPQ2d 1656 (Fed. Cir. 2000), the question was whether a claim requirement that incoming data be screened for a computer virus prior to storage could be interpreted to cover storage prior to screening, albeit with user perception that the screening occurred first. In *Conopco, Inc. v. May Dep't Stores Co.,* 46 F.3d 1556, 32 USPQ2d 1225 (Fed. Cir. 1994), the claim interpretation issue was whether the claimed ratio of "about 40:1" could be interpreted to cover an accused ratio of 163:1. In *Pall Corp. v. Micron Separations, Inc.,* 66 F.3d 1211, 36 USPQ2d 1225 (Fed. Cir. 1995), the question was whether "about 5:1 to about 7:1" could be interpreted to cover 4:1. It seems obvious that these "interpretation" issues cannot even be identified until one has examined the accused infringement and compared it to the claim. In other cases, it is difficult to avoid the conclusion that the claim construction exercise was conducted without any regard for the infringement issues. See, e.g., *Amhil Enters. Ltd. v. Wawa, Inc.,* 81 F.3d 1554, 38 USPQ2d 1471 (Fed. Cir. 1996); *PPG Indus., Inc. v. Guardian Indus.,* 75 F.3d 1558, 37 USPQ2d 1618 (Fed. Cir. 1996).

[431]*Vivid Tech. Inc. v. American Sci. & Eng'g Inc.,* 200 F.3d 795, 53 USPQ2d 1289 (Fed. Cir. 1999).

[432]*PPG Indus. Inc. v. Guardian Indus. Corp.,* 156 F.3d 1351, 48 USPQ2d 1351 (Fed. Cir. 1998).

[433]*Jones v. Hardy,* 727 F.2d 1524, 220 USPQ 1021 (Fed. Cir. 1984).

[434]*Lemelson v. TRW, Inc.,* 760 F.2d 1254, 225 USPQ 697 (Fed. Cir. 1985). But see *DeGeorge v. Bernier,* 768 F.2d 1318, 226 USPQ 758 (Fed. Cir. 1985).

[435]*Fromson v. Advance Offset Plate, Inc.,* 720 F.2d 1565, 219 USPQ 1137 (Fed. Cir. 1983). Interpretation of a disputed claim term requires reference not only to the specification and

claims either to avoid invalidity or to escape infringement.[436] To do so constitutes legal error.[437]

But claims are not born, and do not live, in isolation. Each is related to other claims, to the specification and drawing, to the prior art, to any attorney's remarks, to copending and continuing applications, and often to earlier or later versions of itself in light of amendments made to it.[438] A claim interpretation that would result in one claim having the same scope as another claim is presumptively unreasonable.[439] The doctrine of claim differentiation, which is ultimately based on the common sense notion that different words or phrases used in separate claims are presumed to indicate that the claims have different meanings and scope, normally means that limitations stated in dependent claims are not to be read into the independent claim from which they depend.[440] Thus, there is presumed to be a difference in meaning and scope when different words or phrases are used in separate claims. To the extent that the absence of such difference in meaning and scope would make a claim superfluous, the doctrine of claim differentiation states the presumption that the difference between claims is significant. At the same time, practice

---

prosecution history, but also to other claims. The fact that one must look to other claims using the same term when interpreting it in an asserted claim mandates that the term be interpreted consistently in all claims. Accordingly, arguments made during prosecution regarding the meaning of a claim term are relevant to the interpretation of that term in every claim of the patent absent a clear indication to the contrary. *Southwall Tech., Inc. v. Cardinal IG Co.*, 54 F.3d 1570, 34 USPQ2d 1673 (Fed. Cir. 1995).

[436]*Marsh-McBirney, Inc. v. Montedoro-Whitney Corp.*, 882 F.2d 498, 11 USPQ2d 1794 (Fed. Cir. 1989); *Uniroyal, Inc. v. Rudkin-Wiley Corp.*, 837 F.2d 1044, 5 USPQ2d 1434 (Fed. Cir. 1988); *Rite-Hite Corp. v. Kelley Co.*, 819 F.2d 1120, 2 USPQ2d 1915 (Fed. Cir. 1987); *SRI Int'l v. Matsushita Elec. Corp.*, 775 F.2d 1107, 227 USPQ 577 (Fed. Cir. 1985); *Jervis B. Webb Co. v. Southern Sys., Inc.*, 742 F.2d 1388, 222 USPQ 943 (Fed. Cir. 1984); *Amstar Corp. v. Envirotech Corp.*, 730 F.2d 1476, 221 USPQ 649 (Fed. Cir. 1984); *Raytheon Co. v. Roper Corp.*, 724 F.2d 951, 220 USPQ 592 (Fed. Cir. 1983); *Caterpillar Tractor Co. v. Berco, S.P.A.*, 714 F.2d 1110, 219 USPQ 185 (Fed. Cir. 1983).

[437]*Grain Processing Corp. v. American Maize-Products Co.*, 840 F.2d 902, 5 USPQ2d 1788 (Fed. Cir. 1988); *Palumbo v. Don-Joy Co.*, 762 F.2d 969, 226 USPQ 5 (Fed. Cir. 1985). The court obviously feels strongly about this rule. It has been called a fixed rule that enjoys an immutable and universally applicable status comparatively rare among rules of law. Without it, says the court, the entire statutory and regulatory structure governing the drafting, submission, examination, allowance, and enforceability of claims would crumble. *D.M.I., Inc. v. Deere & Co.*, 755 F.2d 1570, 225 USPQ 236 (Fed. Cir. 1985).

[438]*Kingsdown Med. Cons, Ltd. v. Hollister, Inc.*, 863 F.2d 867, 9 USPQ2d 1384 (Fed. Cir. 1988).

[439]*Beachcombers v. Wildewood Creative Prods., Inc.*, 31 F.3d 1154, 31 USPQ2d 1653 (Fed. Cir. 1994). Ordinarily a claim element that is claimed in general descriptive words, when a numerical range appears in the specification and in other claims, is not limited to the numbers in the specification or the other claims. It is usually incorrect to read numerical precision into a claim from which it is absent, particularly when other claims contain the numerical limitation. When a limitation is included in several claims but is stated in terms of apparently different scope, there is a presumption that a difference in scope is intended and is real. Such a presumption can be overcome, but the evidence must be clear and persuasive. *Modine Mfg. Co. v. United States ITC*, 75 F.3d 1545, 37 USPQ2d 1609 (Fed. Cir. 1996). But the doctrine of claim differentiation cannot restore to the claims a scope that has been shown to be unwarranted. *Fromson v. Anitec Printing Plates Inc.*, 132 F.3d 1437, 45 USPQ2d 1269 (Fed. Cir. 1997).

[440]*Karlin Tech. Inc. v. Surgical Dynamics Inc.*, 177 F.3d 968, 50 USPQ2d 1465 (Fed. Cir. 1999).

has long recognized that claims may be multiplied to define the metes and bounds of the invention in a variety of different ways. Thus two claims that read differently can cover the same subject matter.[441]

Claim differentiation only creates a presumption that each claim in a patent has a different scope; it is not a hard and fast rule of construction. That the patentee chose several words in drafting a particular limitation of one claim, but fewer (though similar) words in drafting the corresponding limitation in another, does not mandate different interpretations of the two limitations, since defining a state of affairs with multiple terms should help, rather than hinder, understanding. Moreover, that the claims are presumed to differ in scope does not mean that every limitation must be distinguished from its counterpart in another claim, but only that at least one limitation must differ.[442]

The doctrine of claim differentiation cannot broaden claims beyond the scope that is supported by the specification. The presumption that separate claims have different scope is a guide, not a rigid rule.[443] Claim differentiation therefore does not always control claim construction. If a claim will bear only one interpretation, similarity with another claim will have to be tolerated.[444]

The doctrine of claim differentiation cannot overshadow the express and contrary intentions of the patent draftsman. It is not unusual that separate claims may define the invention using different terminology, especially where independent claims are involved.[445] While it is true that dependent claims can aid in interpreting the scope of claims from which they depend, they are only an aid to interpretation and are not conclusive. The dependent claim tail cannot wag the independent claim dog.[446] Also, the doctrine of claim differentiation cannot override the sixth paragraph of 35 U.S.C. §112.[447]

---

[441]*Tandon Corp. v. United States ITC*, 831 F.2d 1017, 4 USPQ2d 1283 (Fed. Cir. 1987). The doctrine of claim differentiation cannot broaden claims beyond their correct scope, determined in light of the specification and the prosecution history and any relevant extrinsic evidence. Claims that are written in different words may ultimately cover substantially the same subject matter. *Multiform Desiccants Inc. v. Medzam Ltd.*, 133 F.3d 1473, 45 USPQ2d 1429 (Fed. Cir. 1998).

[442]*Kraft Foods Inc. v. International Trading Co.*, 203 F.3d 1362, 53 USPQ2d 1814 (Fed. Cir. 2000).

[443]*ATD Corp. v. Lydall Inc.*, 159 F.3d 534, 48 USPQ2d 1321 (Fed. Cir. 1998). See also *Tate Access Floors Inc. v. Maxcess Tech. Inc.*, 222 F.3d 958, 55 USPQ2d 1513 (Fed. Cir. 2000). While the doctrine of claim differentiation is not a hard and fast rule of construction, it does create a presumption that each claim in a patent has a different scope. *Comark Comm. Inc. v. Harris Corp.*, 156 F.3d 1182, 48 USPQ2d 1001 (Fed. Cir. 1998).

[444]*Laitram Corp. v. Morehouse Indus. Inc.*, 143 F.3d 1456, 46 USPQ2d 1609 (Fed. Cir. 1998).

[445]*Hormone Res. Found., Inc. v. Genentech, Inc.*, 904 F.2d 1558, 15 USPQ2d 1039 (Fed. Cir. 1990).

[446]*North Am. Vaccine, Inc. v. American Cyanamid Co.*, 7 F.3d 1571, 28 USPQ2d 1333, 1337 (Fed. Cir. 1993).

[447]*Laitram Corp. v. Rexnord, Inc.*, 939 F.2d 1533, 19 USPQ2d 1367 (Fed. Cir. 1991). See also *O.I. Corp. v. Tekmar Co.*, 115 F.3d 1576, 42 USPQ2d 1777 (Fed. Cir. 1997).

Claim type. The claims defining some inventions can by competent draftsmanship be directed to either a method or an apparatus. There is nothing improper in this state of affairs, and the exercise of the inventor's option on how to claim his or her invention is to be respected in interpreting the claims. But once they issue in a particular form, the protected invention is, as a matter of law, that form. Thus, a method claim protects a method and is not to be interpreted as directed to equipment, even equipment for performing the claimed method.[448] Apparatus distinctions are said to be irrelevant in determining infringement of process claims.[449] Yet a structural recitation in a method claim step can be construed as a limitation on the claim.[450] There is no requirement that a machine claim that incorporates process steps must conform to the conventional definition of a product-by-process claim.[451] Machine claims having means clauses may only be reasonably viewed as process claims if there is no supporting structure in the written description that corresponds to the claimed means elements.[452]

Claim limitations. The words of a claim describe and point out the invention by a series of limiting words or phrases—limitations.[453] It is said to be elementary patent law that all limitations are material.[454] References to "elements" can be misleading. The term is often used to refer to structural parts of the accused device or of a device embodying the invention. It is also used in the phrase, in 35 U.S.C. §112, "element of a claim." An element of an embodiment of an invention may be set forth in the claim. But it is the limitation of a claim that counts in determining both validity and infringement. Because claims are composed of a number of limitations, the limitations have on occasion been referred to as claim elements or elements of the claim, but clarity is advanced when sufficient wording is employed

---

[448]*Bandag, Inc. v. Al Bolser's Tire Stores, Inc.,* 750 F.2d 903, 223 USPQ 982 (Fed. Cir. 1984).

[449]*Polaroid Corp. v. Eastman Kodak Co.,* 789 F.2d 1556, 229 USPQ 561 (Fed. Cir. 1986); *Amstar Corp. v. Envirotech Corp.,* 730 F.2d 1476, 221 USPQ 649 (Fed. Cir. 1984).

[450]*Moleculon Res. Corp. v. CBS, Inc.,* 793 F.2d 1261, 229 USPQ 805 (Fed. Cir. 1986).

[451]*In re Warmerdam,* 33 F.3d 1354, 31 USPQ2d 1754 (Fed. Cir. 1994). The claim was to a machine having a memory containing data representing a hierarchy determined by the method of another claim. The court also expressed uncertainty as to whether the claim might not actually be a proper product-by-process claim, inasmuch as the storage of data in a memory physically alters the memory and thus in some sense gives rise to a new memory. In *Hazani v. United States ITC,* 126 F.3d 1473, 44 USPQ2d 1358 (Fed. Cir. 1997), the court held that a limitation in a product claim, calling for a "chemically engraved" surface, is more a description of structure rather than the process used to achieve it, and therefore does not convert the claim into a product-by-process claim.

[452]*State Street Bank & Trust Co. v. Signature Fin. Group Inc.,* 149 F.3d 1368, 47 USPQ2d 1596 (Fed. Cir. 1998).

[453]*Corning Glass Works v. Sumitomo Elec. U.S.A., Inc.,* 868 F.2d 1251, 9 USPQ2d 1962 (Fed. Cir. 1989).

[454]*Glaxo, Inc. v. Novopharm, Ltd.,* 110 F.3d 1562 (Fed. Cir. 1997). See also *Ashland Oil, Inc. v. Delta Resins & Refracs., Inc.,* 776 F.2d 281, 227 USPQ 657 (Fed. Cir. 1985). But cf. *Parks v. Fine,* 773 F.2d 1577, 227 USPQ 432 (Fed. Cir. 1985).

to indicate when "element" is intended to mean a component of an accused device or of an embodiment of an invention and when it is intended to mean a feature set forth in or as a limitation in a claim.[455] The court seems to have adopted the "All Elements" rule for infringement, but indicates that "element" means "limitation" in that context. "Element" may also be used to mean a series of limitations that, taken together, make up a component of the claimed invention.[456]

References to a preferred embodiment, such as those often present in a specification, are not claim limitations.[457] A dependent claim includes all of the limitations of the claims from which it depends and must be viewed as though it had originally been an independent claim.[458] Thus, where one claim is valid, the presence of all its limitations in another claim preserves the latter's validity.[459]

Preamble statements. Claim preambles, like all other claim language, are construed consistently with established claim construction principles. A preamble has the import that the claim as a whole suggests for it.[460] Generally the preamble does not limit the claims,[461] and thus preamble statements of intended use are not claim limitations.[462] However, statements appearing in the preamble may be necessary to give meaning to the claim and properly define the invention.[463] A preamble may serve a variety of purposes, depending on its content. It may limit the scope of the claim, for example when patentability depends on limitations stated in the preamble, or when the preamble contributes to the definition of the claimed invention.

---

[455]*Perkin-Elmer Corp. v. Westinghouse Elec. Corp.*, 822 F.2d 1529, 3 USPQ2d 1321 (Fed. Cir. 1987).

[456]*Corning Glass Works v. Sumitomo Elec. U.S.A., Inc.*, 868 F.2d 1251, 9 USPQ2d 1962 (Fed. Cir. 1989).

[457]*Laitram Corp. v. Cambridge Wire Cloth Co.*, 863 F.2d 855, 9 USPQ2d 1289 (Fed. Cir. 1988).

[458]*Kloster Speedsteel AB v. Crucible Inc.*, 793 F.2d 1565, 230 USPQ 81 (Fed. Cir. 1986).

[459]*Panduit Corp. v. Dennison Mfg. Co.*, 810 F.2d 1561, 1 USPQ2d 1593 (Fed. Cir. 1987). Each claim is separately presumed valid. *Kloster Speedsteel AB v. Crucible Inc.*, 793 F.2d 1565, 230 USPQ 81 (Fed. Cir. 1986). Dependent claims are nonobvious under 35 U.S.C. §103 if the independent claims from which they depend are nonobvious. *In re Fine*, 837 F.2d 1071, 5 USPQ2d 1596 (Fed. Cir. 1988). But a dependent claim whose patentability is not argued separately from that of its parent independent claim falls with the parent. *Environmental Instr., Inc. v. Sutron Corp.*, 877 F.2d 1561, 11 USPQ2d 1132 (Fed. Cir. 1989).

[460]*Bell Comm. Research v. Vitalink Comm. Corp.*, 55 F.3d 615, 34 USPQ2d 1816 (Fed. Cir. 1995).

[461]*DeGeorge v. Bernier*, 768 F.2d 1318, 226 USPQ 758 (Fed. Cir. 1985). A statement in a preamble of a result that necessarily follows from performing a series of steps does not convert each of those steps into step-plus-function clauses. *O.I. Corp. v. Tekmar Co.*, 115 F.3d 1576, 42 USPQ2d 1777 (Fed. Cir. 1997).

[462]*Loctite Corp. v. Ultraseal Ltd.*, 781 F.2d 861, 228 USPQ 90 (Fed. Cir. 1985).

[463]*Bell Comm. Research v. Vitalink Comm. Corp.*, 55 F.3d 615, 34 USPQ2d 1816 (Fed. Cir. 1995); *In re Paulsen*, 30 F.3d 1475, 31 USPQ2d 1671 (Fed. Cir. 1994); *Gerber Garment Tech., Inc. v. Lectra Sys., Inc.*, 916 F.2d 683, 16 USPQ2d 1436 (Fed. Cir. 1990); *Perkin-Elmer Corp. v. Computervision Corp.*, 732 F.2d 888, 221 USPQ 669 (Fed. Cir. 1984). See also *Phillips Pet. Co. v. Huntsman Polymers Corp.*, 157 F.3d 866, 48 USPQ2d 1161 (Fed. Cir. 1998); *Porter v. Farmers Supply Serv., Inc.*, 790 F.2d 882, 229 USPQ 814 (Fed. Cir. 1986).

Where, however, the preamble simply states the intended use or purpose of the invention, it usually does not limit the scope of the claim unless the preamble provides antecedents for ensuing claim terms and limits the claim accordingly.[464]

To say that a preamble phrase is a limitation if it gives "meaning to the claim" may merely state the problem rather than lead to the answer. No litmus test can be given with respect to when the introductory portions of a claim, the preamble, constitute a statement of purpose for a device or are, in themselves, additional structural limitations of a claim that can be relied upon to avoid anticipation.[465] Whether a preamble stating an intended purpose constitutes a limitation to the claim depends on whether the language is essential to particularly point out the invention.[466] The effect preamble language should be given can be resolved only on review of the entirety of the patent to gain an understanding of what the inventors actually invented and intended to encompass by the claim.[467] This is a matter to be determined on the facts of each case in view of the claimed invention as a whole.[468]

---

[464]*C.R. Bard Inc. v. M3 Sys. Inc.*, 157 F.3d 1340, 48 USPQ2d 1225 (Fed. Cir. 1998). In *Union Oil Co. of Calif. v. Atlantic Richfield Co.*, 208 F.3d 989, 54 USPQ2d 1227 (Fed. Cir. 2000), the claims called for "an unleaded gasoline suitable for combustion in an automotive engine." The court noted that the scope of such composition claims cannot embrace only certain uses of that composition. Otherwise they would mutate into method claims. The district court correctly applied this principle, refusing to narrow the scope of the claimed compositions to specific uses. However, the district court concluded that the claims cover "fuels that will regularly be used in autos, not that conceivably could be." It therefore limited the claims to standard automotive gasoline, thus excluding aviation fuels or racing fuels. Inasmuch as this interpretation had ample support in the specification, the Federal Circuit affirmed.

[465]*Corning Glass Works v. Sumitomo Elec. U.S.A., Inc.*, 868 F.2d 1251, 9 USPQ2d 1962 (Fed. Cir. 1989).

[466]*Diversitech Corp. v. Century Steps, Inc.*, 850 F.2d 675, 7 USPQ2d 1315 (Fed. Cir. 1988).

[467]*Corning Glass Works v. Sumitomo Elec. U.S.A., Inc.*, 868 F.2d 1251, 9 USPQ2d 1962 (Fed. Cir. 1989). Review of the patent in its entirety should be made to determine whether the inventors intended such recital to represent an additional structural limitation or merely introductory language. *In re Paulsen*, 30 F.3d 1475, 31 USPQ2d 1671 (Fed. Cir. 1994). The preamble called for a computer and the claim went on to describe the construction of a housing for the computer. The court found that the term "computer" was one that breathed life into the claim and was thus a necessary limitation. Nonetheless, the court interpreted the word to cover a calculator because there was no clear redefinition of the term computer in the specification that would exclude a calculator.

[468]*In re Stencel*, 828 F.2d 751, 4 USPQ2d 1071 (Fed. Cir. 1987). Here the claim was to a tool, a driver for a particular collar. The preamble recited limitations about the collar. The PTO found drivers for other purposes that were very similar. The court held that those references would not have taught or suggested the structure of the claimed driver in the absence of prior knowledge about the inventor's collar system. To ignore the preamble statements in that connection would be like using the inventor's own collar system as prior art against him, which it was not. The court accordingly reversed the PTO's obviousness rejection. It should be noted that other limitations in the body of the claim referred back to the collar, so that a close connection could be made between the preamble and the body of the claim in that respect. In *Intervet Am., Inc. v. Kee-Vet Labs., Inc.*, 887 F.2d 1050, 12 USPQ2d 1474 (Fed. Cir. 1989), the case was remanded so that the lower court could consider whether the fact that the attorney had called a preamble recitation a "limitation" in his remarks accompanying an amendment would impact the question. In *IMS Tech. Inc. v. Haas Automation Inc.*, 206 F.3d 1422, 54 USPQ2d 1129 (Fed. Cir. 2000), the court held that a preamble calling for a "control apparatus for controlling the relative motion between a tool and a workpiece" did not limit the scope of

Whether a preamble stating the purpose and context of the invention constitutes a limitation of the claimed process is determined on the facts of each case in light of the overall form of the claim, and the invention as described in the specification and illuminated in the prosecution history. It is thus appropriate to determine whether the term in the preamble serves to define the invention that is claimed, or is simply a description of the prior art.[469] Where a patentee uses the claim preamble to recite structural limitations of the claimed invention, the PTO and courts give effect to that usage. Conversely, where a patentee defines a structurally complete invention in the claim body and uses the preamble only to state a purpose or intended use for the invention, the preamble is not a claim limitation. The inquiry involves examination of the entire patent record to determine what invention the patentee intended to define and protect.[470]

The court has said that a term that breathes life into the claims is a necessary limitation even though it appears in the preamble.[471] But where the effect of words in the preamble is ambiguous at best, a compelling reason must exist before the language can be given weight.[472]

A so-called Jepson claim usually consists of a preamble and an improvement clause.[473] The Jepson form of claiming allows a patentee to use the preamble to recite elements or steps of the claimed invention that are conventional or known. When this form is employed, the claim preamble defines not only the context of the claimed invention, but also its scope. The use of the Jepson form evidences an intention to use the preamble to define, in part, the structural elements of the claimed invention.[474] Thus, in a Jepson claim the preamble is impliedly admitted to be prior art unless it reflects the inventor's own work,

---

the claim to a control apparatus separate from the machine tool itself. The claim would be infringed by any apparatus encompassing all of the limitations in the body of the claim. Such an infringing apparatus may be a machine tool apparatus that includes the claimed control features or a control apparatus that is separate from and communicates with a machine tool apparatus.

[469]*Rowe v. Dror*, 112 F.3d 473, 42 USPQ2d 1550 (Fed. Cir. 1997). Here the court held that a preamble recitation of "angioplasty" is a structural limitation of a catheter claim.

[470]*Applied Mtls, Inc. v. Advanced Semi. Mtls, Inc.*, 98 F.3d 1563, 40 USPQ2d 1481 (Fed. Cir. 1996). In *STX LLC v. Brine Inc.*, 54 USPQ2d 1347 (Fed. Cir. 2000), the court supported its conclusion that a preamble phrase was not a limitation of the claim by noting that the patent examiner's rejection of the claim for obviousness even after the preamble language was added suggests that the phrase was not essential in distinguishing it over the prior art and was not decisive in securing allowance of the claim during prosecution.

[471]*Loctite Corp. v. Ultraseal Ltd.*, 781 F.2d 861, 228 USPQ 90 (Fed. Cir. 1985).

[472]*DeGeorge v. Bernier*, 768 F.2d 1318, 226 USPQ 758 (Fed. Cir. 1985).

[473]E.g., *Pentec, Inc. v. Graphic Controls Corp.*, 776 F.2d 309, 227 USPQ 766 (Fed. Cir. 1985); *Reading & Bates Constr. Co. v. Baker Energy Res. Corp.*, 748 F.2d 645, 223 USPQ 1168 (Fed. Cir. 1984); *Medtronic, Inc. v. Cardiac Pacemakers, Inc.*, 721 F.2d 1563, 220 USPQ 97 (Fed. Cir. 1983). The court says that in a Jepson claim, the "inventive" portion must lie in the clause beginning "the improvement comprising." *Ethicon Endo-Surgery, Inc. v. United States Surgical Corp.*, 93 F.3d 1572, 40 USPQ2d 1019 (Fed. Cir. 1996).

[474]*Kegel Co. v. AMF Bowling, Inc.*, 127 F.3d 1420, 44 USPQ2d 1123 (Fed. Cir. 1997).

but the claimed invention consists of the preamble in combination with the improvement.[475]

Other reasons for interpretation. The two major reasons for interpreting claims are to determine their scope for infringement purposes and to test for obviousness under §103.[476] But there are other reasons. Indefiniteness under §112¶2 is not only a question of law, but part of the court's performance of its duty as the construer of patent claims. Accordingly, extrinsic evidence is irrelevant to the issue of indefiniteness where the meaning of the term in question is unambiguously set forth in the specification.[477] In determining utility, the claims must first be interpreted to define the invention to be tested for utility.[478] In deciding anticipation, the trier of fact must identify the elements of the claims, determine their meaning in light of the specification and prosecution history, and identify corresponding elements disclosed in the allegedly anticipating reference. It is therefore error to treat the claims as a mere catalog of separate parts, in disregard of the part-to-part relationships set forth in the claims that give the claims their meaning.[479]

It may be required to interpret claims in order to decide an issue of substantial identity of claims, in the context of a question involving consonance for double-patenting purposes.[480] Where interpretation is required of a claim that is copied for interference purposes, the copied claim is viewed in the context of the patent from which it was copied.[481] Interference counts are given the broadest reasonable interpretation possible, and resort to the specification is necessary only when there are ambiguities inherent in the claim language or obvious from arguments of counsel.[482]

Litigation versus prosecution. Not surprisingly, claims are construed quite differently depending upon whether they are in the PTO

---

[475]*Sjolund v. Musland,* 847 F.2d 1573, 6 USPQ2d 2020 (Fed. Cir. 1988); *Pentec, Inc. v. Graphic Controls Corp.,* 776 F.2d 309, 227 USPQ 766 (Fed. Cir. 1985). Cf. *Medtronic, Inc. v. Cardiac Pacemakers, Inc.,* 721 F.2d 1563, 220 USPQ 97 (Fed. Cir. 1983).

[476]There must be *some* reason, however. The fact that there may have been disputes as to claim interpretation issues will not prohibit a summary judgment of validity unless the issues are shown to be material to validity or unless there is an issue of conflicting claim interpretations with respect to validity and infringement. *National Presto Indus., Inc. v. West Bend Co.,* 76 F.3d 1185, 37 USPQ2d 1685 (Fed. Cir. 1996).

[477]*Personalized Media Comm. LLC v. United States ITC,* 161 F.3d 696, 48 USPQ2d 1880 (Fed. Cir. 1998).

[478]*Raytheon Co. v. Roper Corp.,* 724 F.2d 951, 220 USPQ 592 (Fed. Cir. 1983).

[479]*Lindemann Maschinenfabrik v. American Hoist & Derrick Co.,* 730 F.2d 1452, 221 USPQ 481 (Fed. Cir. 1984).

[480]*Symbol Tech., Inc. v. Opticon, Inc.,* 935 F.2d 1569, 19 USPQ2d 1241 (Fed. Cir. 1991).

[481]*In re Spina,* 975 F.2d 854, 24 USPQ2d 1142 (Fed. Cir. 1992). A claim is not interpreted one way in light of the specification in which it originally was granted and another way in light of the specification into which it is copied as a proposed interference count. *Id.* But see *Rowe v. Dror,* 112 F.3d 473, 42 USPQ2d 1550 (Fed. Cir. 1997).

[482]*Davis v. Loesch,* 998 F.2d 963, 27 USPQ2d 1440 (Fed. Cir. 1993).

or in court. Claims that are still in prosecution can be amended.[483] Thus, in proceedings before the PTO, claims are to be given their broadest reasonable interpretation consistent with the specification.[484] This rule applies to reissue and reexamination prosecution as well as original prosecution.[485] The rule reduces the possibility that allowed claims will be given a broader scope than is justified.[486]

Claims may be amended for the purpose of distinguishing cited references or in response to objections raised under 35 U.S.C. §112. Issues of judicial claim construction such as arise after patent issuance, for example, during infringement litigation, have no place in the prosecution of pending claims before the PTO, during which any ambiguity or excessive breadth may be corrected by merely changing the claim.[487] When the applicant states the meaning that the claim terms are intended to have, the claims are examined with that meaning, in order to achieve a complete exploration of the applicant's invention and its relation to the prior art. Thus the inquiry during examination is patentability of the invention as the applicant regards it.[488]

This approach does not apply in litigation, where there is no opportunity to amend the claims. There the claims should be construed, if possible, to uphold their validity.[489] Claims should be read

---

[483]*In re Yamamoto,* 740 F.2d 1569, 222 USPQ 934 (Fed. Cir. 1984).

[484]*In re Van Geuns,* 988 F.2d 1181, 26 USPQ2d 1057 (Fed. Cir. 1993); *Burlington Indus. Inc. v. Quigg,* 822 F.2d 1581, 3 USPQ2d 1436 (Fed. Cir. 1987); *In re Sneed,* 710 F.2d 1544, 218 USPQ 385 (Fed. Cir. 1983). *Markman* did not impact this rule. *In re Morris,* 127 F.3d 1048, 44 USPQ2d 1023 (Fed. Cir. 1997). However, this rule does not relieve the PTO of its essential task of examining the entire patent disclosure to discern the meaning of claim words and phrases. *Rowe v. Dror,* 112 F.3d 473, 42 USPQ2d 1550 (Fed. Cir. 1997). Although the PTO must give claims their broadest reasonable interpretation, this interpretation must be consistent with the one that those skilled in the art would reach. Prior art references may be indicative of what all those skilled in the art generally believe a certain term means and can often help to demonstrate how a disputed term is used by those skilled in the art. Accordingly, the PTO's interpretation of claim terms should not be so broad that it conflicts with the meaning given to identical terms in other patents from analogous art. *Voice Tech. Group Inc. v. VMC Sys. Inc.,* 164 F.3d 605, 49 USPQ2d 1333 (Fed. Cir. 1999). The broadest reasonable interpretation for a MPF clause is that it covers only the disclosed structure and equivalents. *In re Donaldson Co.,* 16 F.3d 1189, 29 USPQ2d 1845 (Fed. Cir. 1994). The PTO is not exempt from applying this analysis during prosecution. *In re Alappat,* 33 F.3d 1526, 31 USPQ2d 1545 (Fed. Cir. 1994).

[485]*DeGeorge v. Bernier,* 768 F.2d 1318, 226 USPQ 758 (Fed. Cir. 1985); *In re Etter,* 756 F.2d 852, 225 USPQ 1 (Fed. Cir. 1985). The fact that a patent is simultaneously being litigated and reexamined does not alter the rule that claims subject to amendment should be construed as broadly as possible. *In re Yamamoto,* 740 F.2d 1569, 222 USPQ 934 (Fed. Cir. 1984).

[486]*In re Yamamoto,* 740 F.2d 1569, 222 USPQ 934 (Fed. Cir. 1984). The broad interpretation rule for claims in prosecution is so pervasive that an applicant's good faith belief that the claims would be narrowly construed to avoid uncited prior art would have been unreasonable and might therefore not preclude a finding of gross negligence in failing to cite that art. *J.P. Stevens & Co. v. Lex Tex Ltd.,* 747 F.2d 1553, 223 USPQ 1089 (Fed. Cir. 1984).

[487]*Burlington Indus. Inc. v. Quigg,* 822 F.2d 1581, 3 USPQ2d 1436 (Fed. Cir. 1987).

[488]*In re Zletz,* 893 F.2d 319, 13 USPQ2d 1320 (Fed. Cir. 1989).

[489]*Whittaker Corp. v. UNR Indus., Inc.,* 911 F.2d 709, 15 USPQ2d 1742 (Fed. Cir. 1990); *Lemar Marine, Inc. v. Barient, Inc.,* 827 F.2d 744, 3 USPQ2d 1766 (Fed. Cir. 1987); *DeGeorge v. Bernier,* 768 F.2d 1318, 226 USPQ 758 (Fed. Cir. 1985); *ACS Hosp. Sys., Inc. v. Montefiore Hosp.,* 732 F.2d 1572, 221 USPQ 929 (Fed. Cir. 1984). A narrow claim construction is not prejudicial to the patentee on the issue of obviousness. The more narrowly a claim is construed

in a way that avoids ensnaring prior art if it is possible to do so.[490] The court has extended this reasoning to product-by-process claims as well. The court permits the PTO to give such claims their broadest reasonable meaning when determining patentability. During litigation determining validity or infringement, however, this approach is inapplicable. The PTO's treatment of a product-by-process claim as a product claim for patentability inquiries is consistent with its policy of giving claims their broadest reasonable interpretation. The same rule, however, will not apply in validity and infringement litigation.[491] There are limits on the litigation approach, though. The place to define the terms of the claims is in the specification, and the time to do it is during prosecution. Litigation-induced definitions by the inventor, coming near the end of the term of his or her patent, can have no effect on what the words of the document do in fact convey and have conveyed to the public during its term.[492]

One note of realism seems indicated. The court says, from time to time, that it is improper to attempt to avoid invalidity by importing claim limitations from narrower claims or even from the specification.[493] And yet it is difficult to read the decision in *United States v. Adams*[494] without concluding that the Supreme Court did precisely that in order to sustain the validity of what it regarded as a worthwhile invention. Many decisions of the regional circuits, the district courts,

---

the more likely the claim may be upheld in light of the prior art. *Newell Cos. v. Kenney Mfg. Co.*, 864 F.2d 757, 9 USPQ2d 1417 (Fed. Cir. 1988). The purpose of restricting the scope of claims through the reverse doctrine of equivalents often is to preserve the validity of claims with respect to their original intended scope. *Texas Instr., Inc. v. United States ITC*, 846 F.2d 1369, 6 USPQ2d 1886 (Fed. Cir. 1988). When claims are amenable to more than one construction, they should when reasonably possible be interpreted so as to preserve their validity. *Modine Mfg. Co. v. United States ITC*, 75 F.3d 1545, 37 USPQ2d 1609 (Fed. Cir. 1996). This applies to the question of operability. *Eastman Kodak Co. v. Goodyear Tire & Rubber Co.*, 114 F.3d 1547, 42 USPQ2d 1737 (Fed. Cir. 1997). Ambiguous claims, whenever possible, should be construed to preserve their validity. This rule of construction, however, does not justify reading into a claim a limitation that it does not contain and that the patentee deleted from the claim during prosecution. Narrow construction of a claim to avoid a holding of new matter is therefore error. Either there is new matter or there is not. *Texas Instr., Inc. v. United States ITC*, 871 F.2d 1054, 10 USPQ2d 1257 (Fed. Cir. 1989).

[490]*Harris Corp. v. IXYS Corp.*, 114 F.3d 1149, 43 USPQ2d 1018 (Fed. Cir. 1997).

[491]*Atlantic Thermoplastics Co. v. Faytex Corp.*, 970 F.2d 834, 23 USPQ2d 1481 (Fed. Cir. 1992). Thus, despite a contrary earlier holding in *Scripps Clinic & Res. Found. v. Genentech, Inc.*, 927 F.2d 1565, 18 USPQ2d 1001 (Fed. Cir. 1991), the court now holds that, for infringement purposes, product-by-process claims do not cover an identical product made by a different process. See also note 6:425. In a fascinating display of intramural disagreement, Judge Rich's dissent from a denial of rehearing in banc in *Atlantic Thermoplastics* termed the panel's rationale "insulting," "mutiny," "heresy," and, quite remarkably, "illegal." His dissenting opinion is reported at 974 F.2d 1279, 23 USPQ2d 1801. A separate concurring opinion by Judge Rader in support of the panel decision appears at 974 F.2d 1299, 24 USPQ2d 1138. More recently, in *Mentor Corp. v. Coloplast, Inc.*, 998 F.2d 992, 27 USPQ2d 1521 (Fed. Cir. 1993), the court was able to avoid the problem by deciding that the claims in question were not in fact product-by-process claims.

[492]*Lear Siegler, Inc. v. Aeroquip Corp.*, 733 F.2d 881, 221 USPQ 1025 (Fed. Cir. 1984).

[493]E.g., *Jervis B. Webb Co. v. Southern Sys., Inc.*, 742 F.2d 1388, 222 USPQ 943 (Fed. Cir. 1984).

[494]383 U.S. 39, 148 USPQ 479 (1965).

and perhaps even the Federal Circuit itself are, in the end analysis, explainable on no other basis.

Nonetheless, the Federal Circuit seems clearly unwilling to engage in this approach to claim construction. In one case[495] it offered to distinguish *Adams* on the ground that there the Supreme Court simply relied on the unclaimed limitation when considering rebuttal of the challenger's obviousness argument. With all respect, this distinction is rather finely drawn. Be that as it may, it seems safe to conclude that, *Adams* or no *Adams,* the Federal Circuit will not "save" claims by reading extraneous limitations into them.[496] Thus, the court has explained that it has consistently employed the caveat, "if possible," to its instruction that claims should be construed to sustain their validity. It has also admonished against judicial rewriting of claims to preserve validity. Therefore, if the only claim construction that is consistent with the claim's language and the written description renders the claim invalid, then the axiom does not apply and the claim is simply invalid.[497]

In a pair of recent cases, the court seems to be sending mixed signals about claim construction versus invalidity. In the first, the court adopted a claim construction that rendered the patent invalid. It held that the second occurrence of a phrase in the claim meant the same thing as the first occurrence. It brushed aside the district court's attempt to construe the claim in a way that would have it make sense, and found that the correct construction of the claim is one that is admittedly nonsensical. It concluded that, when an impossible limitation, such as a nonsensical method of operation, is clearly embodied within the claim, the claimed invention must be held invalid.[498] In the second, the question was whether a "frame of information" was limited to character-based systems, which was the embodiment described in the specification, or whether it could also cover bit-mapped systems. Despite the parties' agreement that the term "frame" can in general usage be applied to both, the court found that because a bit-mapped system was not described in the specification, the term had to be limited to character-based systems. It appeared that the court was taken by the fact that the specification did not enable a bit-mapped embodiment, and there was evidence that the inventors had been unable to implement one. The court acknowledged that enablement is a requirement for patentability, but responded that claims are not properly construed to have a meaning or scope that

---

[495]*E.I. duPont & Co. v. Phillips Petroleum Co.,* 849 F.2d 1430, 7 USPQ2d 1129 (Fed. Cir. 1988).

[496]*Corning Glass Works v. Sumitomo Elec. U.S.A., Inc.,* 868 F.2d 1251, 9 USPQ2d 1962 (Fed. Cir. 1989).

[497]*Rhine v. Casio Inc.,* 183 F.3d 1342, 51 USPQ2d 1377 (Fed. Cir. 1999). The court also warns, however, that a defendant cannot avoid a full-blown validity analysis by raising the specter of invalidity during the claim construction phase. *Id.*

[498]*Process Control Corp. v. HydReclaim Corp.,* 190 F.3d 1350, 52 USPQ2d 1029 (Fed. Cir. 1999).

would lead to their invalidity for failure to satisfy the requirements for patentability. Although a claim is not invalid simply because it embraces subject matter that is not specifically illustrated, in order to be covered by the claims that subject matter must be sufficiently described as the applicant's invention to meet the requirements of §112.[499]

---

[499]*Wang Labs. Inc. v. America Online Inc.,* 197 F.3d 1377, 53 USPQ2d 1161 (Fed. Cir. 1999). This statement has grave implications: taken literally, it could mean that a claim literally covers nothing that is not enabled in the specification. See the discussion of *Gentry Gallery* accompanying notes 5:196–201.

II
Infringement

6

Direct and Contributory Infringement

§6.1 Introduction

The statutory definition of direct infringement is deceptively simple. Section 271(a) provides that:

> Except as otherwise provided in this title, whoever without authority makes, uses, offers to sell or sells any patented invention, within the United States or imports into the United States any patented invention during the term of the patent therefor, infringes the patent.[1]

From time to time interesting questions can arise regarding the nature of the acts of making, using, or selling. The words "making" or "using," for example, can invoke the nearly unfathomable mysteries of repair versus reconstruction. Nice questions can be found in the phrases "within the United States" and "during the term." And an entire segment of the law of patent licenses is comprehended by the words "without authority." But far and away the most significant question of direct infringement centers around the innocuous words "patented invention." It is here that we grapple with the matter of claim interpretation and encounter the difficult concepts of equivalents and prosecution history estoppel. The basic question is straightforward enough: Did the accused infringer misappropriate the patented invention? But the answer requires us to know what the patented invention is, and this is the hardest inquiry in the patent law, as we have already seen in considering patentability and claim interpretation.

Once that difficult question is addressed and answered, however, the remainder of the direct infringement inquiry falls into place quite nicely. We then ask only whether the properly construed claim reads on the accused product or process.[2] Not surprisingly, this inquiry has

---

[1]35 U.S.C. §271(a).

[2]*Atlas Powder Co. v. E.I. du Pont & Co.,* 750 F.2d 1569, 224 USPQ 409 (Fed. Cir. 1984).

created very little law in the Federal Circuit. It is, after all, a matter of fact, and findings on the subject are not disturbed unless clearly erroneous.[3] In truth, the cases dealing with literal infringement amount to little more than a catalog of helpful hints and cautions. It is a different story entirely when there is no literal infringement, and the court must therefore confront the twin topics of the doctrine of equivalents (DOE) and prosecution history estoppel (PHE). Here the court has spoken in substance and depth, although not always with the clarity that marks its opinions on other subjects.

One initial problem must be dealt with by the writer—be it commentator or judge—who wishes to discuss equivalents and estoppel. The court early on taught us that infringement poses two quite distinct questions: What is the thing patented? and Has that thing been made by the accused infringer?[4] It is difficult to know whether to classify equivalents and estoppel with the first, or with the second. One important commentator seems to treat these questions in the context of claim interpretation,[5] and this makes a certain amount of sense. The problem is not purely academic, either, for as we have seen, claim interpretation is a question of law, while infringement is a question of fact.[6] The Federal Circuit seems minded to view equivalents as a question of fact[7] and PHE as a question of law.[8] This dichotomy does not assist us in attempting to group the issues in either category: claim readability or claim interpretation. Nonetheless, the approach taken here is to treat equivalents and estoppel as "infringement" issues rather than "interpretation" issues, simply because that appears to be a more traditional way of looking at those questions.

§6.2 Direct Infringement

(a) General

(i) Fundamental Concepts

Patent infringement is a tort,[9] but not an intentional tort. Intent is not an element of infringement. Therefore, independent development does not excuse infringement of the patent owner's right to exclude.[10]

---

[3]*Windsurfing Int'l, Inc. v. AMF, Inc.,* 782 F.2d 995, 228 USPQ 562 (Fed. Cir. 1986).

[4]*SSIH Equip. S.A. v. United States ITC,* 713 F.2d 746, 218 USPQ 678 (Fed. Cir. 1983).

[5]Chisum, *Patents,* Ch. 18 (1982).

[6]E.g., *SSIH Equip. S.A. v. United States ITC,* 713 F.2d 746, 218 USPQ 678 (Fed. Cir. 1983).

[7]*Sun Studs, Inc. v. ATA Equip. Leasing, Inc.,* 872 F.2d 978, 10 USPQ2d 1338 (Fed. Cir. 1989); *Radio Steel & Mfg. Co. v. MTD Prods., Inc.,* 731 F.2d 840, 221 USPQ 657 (Fed. Cir. 1984).

[8]*LaBounty Mfg., Inc. v. United States ITC,* 867 F.2d 1572, 9 USPQ2d 1995 (Fed. Cir. 1989).

[9]*Orthokinetics, Inc. v. Safety Travel Chairs, Inc.,* 806 F.2d 1565, 1 USPQ2d 1081 (Fed. Cir. 1986).

[10]*Hilton Davis Chem. Co. v. Warner-Jenkinson Co.,* 62 F.3d 1512, 35 USPQ2d 1641, 1646 (Fed. Cir. 1995), *rev'd on other grounds, Warner-Jenkinson Co. v. Hilton Davis Chem. Co.,* 520 U.S. 17, 41 USPQ2d 1865 (1997).

There is no intent element to direct infringement. If a device is capable of being operated in an infringing mode, it need not be shown that customers were told how to do it, or even that they were told it was possible.[11] Thus, unlike copyright infringement, copying is not a requisite to liability, and there is no requirement of knowledge or intent, at least for direct infringement.

On the other side of the coin, it is legitimate to deliberately design around a patent.[12] One of the benefits of the patent system is the incentive it provides for "designing around" patented inventions, thus creating innovations. Of course, determining when a patented device has been "designed around" enough to avoid infringement is a difficult determination to make. One cannot know for certain that changes are sufficient to avoid infringement until a judge or a jury has made that determination.[13]

The term "claims" has been used in patent legislation since the Patent Act of 1836 to define the invention that an applicant believes is patentable. Since that time, the term has represented that portion of the specification that defines the patent owner's property rights in the invention. This concept of a claim is related to, but distinct from, the concept of infringement. Direct infringement consists of making, using, offering to sell, or selling the invention defined by the claims of a patent, without the authority of the patent owner. With respect to direct infringement, then, the claims define the patent owner's property rights whereas infringement is the act of trespassing upon those rights. The relationship between infringement and the claims becomes even more tenuous under the DOE, where a product is deemed to infringe the patentee's right to exclude even though the product does not fall within the scope of the patent's claims. In sum, the concept of a claim is different from the concept of infringement, and, as a result, the plain meaning of claims is not the same as the plain meaning of infringement.[14]

The Federal Circuit has said repeatedly that direct infringement requires a two-step analysis. The patented invention as indicated by the claim language must first be defined—this is the legal question of claim interpretation. Then the trier of fact must judge whether the claims as properly interpreted cover the accused device or process.[15]

---

[11]*Intel Corp. v. United States ITC,* 946 F.2d 821, 20 USPQ2d 1161 (Fed. Cir. 1991). But see note 6:112.

[12]*Kimberly-Clark Corp. v. Johnson & Johnson,* 745 F.2d 1437, 223 USPQ 603 (Fed. Cir. 1984).

[13]*Read Corp. v. Portec, Inc.,* 970 F.2d 816, 23 USPQ2d 1426 (Fed. Cir. 1992).

[14]*Hoechst-Roussel Pharm., Inc. v. Lehman,* 109 F.3d 756, 42 USPQ2d 1220 (Fed. Cir. 1997).

[15]*Becton Dickinson & Co. v. C.R. Bard, Inc.,* 922 F.2d 792, 17 USPQ2d 1097 (Fed. Cir. 1990); *Hormone Res. Found., Inc. v. Genentech, Inc.,* 904 F.2d 1558, 15 USPQ2d 1039 (Fed. Cir. 1990); *Smithkline Diagnostics, Inc. v. Helena Labs. Corp.,* 859 F.2d 878, 8 USPQ2d 1468 (Fed. Cir. 1988); *ZMI Corp. v. Cardiac Resuscitator Corp.,* 844 F.2d 1576, 6 USPQ2d 1557 (Fed. Cir. 1988); *Grain Processing Corp. v. American Maize-Products Co.,* 840 F.2d 902, 5 USPQ2d 1788 (Fed. Cir. 1988); *Vieau v. Japax, Inc.,* 823 F.2d 1510, 3 USPQ2d 1094 (Fed. Cir. 1987); *Fonar Corp. v. Johnson & Johnson,* 821 F.2d 627, 3 USPQ2d 1109 (Fed. Cir. 1987); *Moleculon*

Thus the matter resolves itself into two questions: What is patented? and Has what is patented been made, used, or sold by another?[16] Because claim construction is the first step in determining infringement, improper claim construction can distort the entire infringement analysis.[17] The latter question, whether the properly construed claims read on the accused process or product,[18] is one of fact,[19] to be determined by the jury in a jury case.[20]

Where the fact finder is a jury, it is not improper under certain circumstances to leave the overall question of infringement to the jury.[21] In such cases, where the overall question of infringement is answered by the jury and a losing party's motion for JNOV is denied, appellate review is limited. In order to obtain reversal, the losing party must demonstrate that no reasonable juror could have interpreted the claim in a fashion that supports the conclusion on infringement. And if the jury does not make express findings on claim construction, the appellate court must presume the existence of facts necessary to support such a claim construction and look to see whether those

---

Res. Corp. v. CBS, Inc., 793 F.2d 1261, 229 USPQ 805 (Fed. Cir. 1986); *Mannesmann Demag Corp. v. Engineered Metal Prods. Co.*, 793 F.2d 1279, 230 USPQ 45 (Fed. Cir. 1986); *Standard Oil Co. v. American Cyanamid Co.*, 774 F.2d 448, 227 USPQ 293 (Fed. Cir. 1985); *Palumbo v. Don-Joy Co.*, 762 F.2d 969, 226 USPQ 5 (Fed. Cir. 1985); *Jamesbury Corp. v. Litton Indus. Prods., Inc.*, 756 F.2d 1556, 225 USPQ 253 (Fed. Cir. 1985); *Atlas Powder Co. v. E.I. du Pont & Co.*, 750 F.2d 1569, 224 USPQ 409 (Fed. Cir. 1984); *McGill Inc. v. John Zink Co.*, 736 F.2d 666, 221 USPQ 944 (Fed. Cir. 1984); *Envirotech Corp. v. Al George, Inc.*, 730 F.2d 753, 221 USPQ 473 (Fed. Cir. 1984); *Caterpillar Tractor Co. v. Berco, S.P.A.*, 714 F.2d 1110, 219 USPQ 185 (Fed. Cir. 1983). Although claim interpretation is a question of law, expert testimony is admissible to explain the meaning of technical terms in the claims and to give an opinion on the ultimate question of infringement. *Snellman v. Ricoh Co.*, 862 F.2d 283, 8 USPQ2d 1996 (Fed. Cir. 1988).

[16]*Fromson v. Advance Offset Plate, Inc.*, 720 F.2d 1565, 219 USPQ 1137 (Fed. Cir. 1983); *SSIH Equip. S.A. v. United States ITC*, 713 F.2d 746, 218 USPQ 678 (Fed. Cir. 1983).

[17]*ZMI Corp. v. Cardiac Resuscitator Corp.*, 844 F.2d 1576, 6 USPQ2d 1557 (Fed. Cir. 1988); *Bausch & Lomb, Inc. v. Barnes-Hind, Inc.*, 796 F.2d 443, 230 USPQ 416 (Fed. Cir. 1986); *Moeller v. Ionetics, Inc.*, 794 F.2d 653, 229 USPQ 992 (Fed. Cir. 1986).

[18]*Atlas Powder Co. v. E.I. du Pont & Co.*, 750 F.2d 1569, 224 USPQ 409 (Fed. Cir. 1984).

[19]E.g., *Intervet Am., Inc. v. Kee-Vet Labs., Inc.*, 887 F.2d 1050, 12 USPQ2d 1474 (Fed. Cir. 1989); *Under Sea Indus., Inc. v. Dacor Corp.*, 833 F.2d 1551, 4 USPQ2d 1772 (Fed. Cir. 1987); *Perini Am., Inc. v. Paper Converting Mach. Co.*, 832 F.2d 581, 4 USPQ2d 1621 (Fed. Cir. 1987); *Windsurfing Int'l, Inc. v. AMF, Inc.*, 782 F.2d 995, 228 USPQ 562 (Fed. Cir. 1986); *Shatterproof Glass Corp. v. Libbey-Owens Ford Co.*, 758 F.2d 613, 225 USPQ 634 (Fed. Cir. 1985); *Jamesbury Corp. v. Litton Indus. Prods., Inc.*, 756 F.2d 1556, 225 USPQ 253 (Fed. Cir. 1985); *Amstar Corp. v. Envirotech Corp.*, 730 F.2d 1476, 221 USPQ 649 (Fed. Cir. 1984). Though infringement is a factual question, it is of course of no consequence that the district court puts its finding on that question among the conclusions of law. *Fromson v. Western Litho Plate & Supp. Co.*, 853 F.2d 1568, 7 USPQ2d 1606 (Fed. Cir. 1988). Whether an imprecise claim limitation, such as the phrase "about 100% per second," is literally met is a question of fact for the trial court. And where the only evidence on the point consisted merely of the opinion testimony of the patentee's expert, without supporting tests or data, the district court was under no obligation to accept it. *W.L. Gore & Assoc. v. Garlock, Inc.*, 842 F.2d 1275, 6 USPQ2d 1277 (Fed. Cir. 1988). One wonders, however, precisely what the district court is using to reject the expert's opinion. Its own expertise? Gut feeling?

[20]*Witco Chem. Corp. v. Peachtree Doors, Inc.*, 787 F.2d 1545, 229 USPQ 188 (Fed. Cir. 1986).

[21]*McGill Inc. v. John Zink Co.*, 736 F.2d 666, 221 USPQ 944 (Fed. Cir. 1984). This case also indicates that the judge may determine in the first instance, as a matter of law, whether the claim language is disputed and would therefore require extrinsic evidence as to meaning.

facts were supported by substantial evidence.[22] A judge's findings on infringement are reviewed under the clearly erroneous standard.[23] Determination of literal infringement in an ITC proceeding is reviewed as a question of fact on a substantial evidence standard.[24]

Because of the factual nature of the infringement inquiry, the Federal Circuit has cautioned several times that a summary judgment motion on that issue must be approached with great care by the district court.[25] Nevertheless, summary judgment on the issue is appropriate where comparison of a properly interpreted claim with an uncontested description of the accused device reflects absence of a genuine issue of material fact.[26] A dispute as to the legal issue of claim interpretation does not necessarily preclude summary judgment. Where there is no dispute as to the facts underlying that legal issue, the function of applying claims to the accused device is the province of the district court.[27]

It is axiomatic that the patentee bears the burden of proving infringement.[28] The burden is on the patentee to show infringement, literal or by equivalents,[29] by a preponderance of the evidence.[30] Dur-

---

[22]*Sun Studs, Inc. v. ATA Equip. Leasing, Inc.*, 872 F.2d 978, 10 USPQ2d 1338 (Fed. Cir. 1989); *McGill Inc. v. John Zink Co.*, 736 F.2d 666, 221 USPQ 944 (Fed. Cir. 1984). A jury's finding of infringement must be upheld if it is supported by substantial evidence. *Braun Inc. v. Dynamics Corp.*, 975 F.2d 815, 24 USPQ2d 1121 (Fed. Cir. 1992).

[23]*Miles Labs., Inc. v. Shandon, Inc.*, 997 F.2d 870, 27 USPQ2d 1123 (Fed. Cir. 1993).

[24]*Texas Instr., Inc. v. United States ITC*, 988 F.2d 1165, 26 USPQ2d 1018 (Fed. Cir. 1993); *LaBounty Mfg., Inc. v. United States ITC*, 867 F.2d 1572, 9 USPQ2d 1995 (Fed. Cir. 1989).

[25]*SRI Int'l v. Matsushita Elec. Corp.*, 775 F.2d 1107, 227 USPQ 577 (Fed. Cir. 1985); *Palumbo v. Don-Joy Co.*, 762 F.2d 969, 226 USPQ 5 (Fed. Cir. 1985); *D.M.I., Inc. v. Deere & Co.*, 755 F.2d 1570, 225 USPQ 236 (Fed. Cir. 1985).

[26]*Chemical Eng'g Corp. v. Essef Indus., Inc.*, 795 F.2d 1565, 230 USPQ 385 (Fed. Cir. 1986); *Porter v. Farmers Supply Serv., Inc.*, 790 F.2d 882, 229 USPQ 814 (Fed. Cir. 1986); *Palumbo v. Don-Joy Co.*, 762 F.2d 969, 226 USPQ 5 (Fed. Cir. 1985).

[27]*Becton Dickinson & Co. v. C.R. Bard, Inc.*, 922 F.2d 792, 17 USPQ2d 1097 (Fed. Cir. 1990); *Martin v. Barber*, 755 F.2d 1564, 225 USPQ 233 (Fed. Cir. 1985). In a somewhat questionable ruling, the court used this reasoning to support an award of expenses for failure to admit. The patentee had refused to admit a request seeking an admission that the accused product did not contain a certain element. The patentee argued that the request sought an admission that would effectively concede the absence of literal infringement. The argument was rejected, and expenses awarded against the patentee, on the ground that it was for the court to decide whether the missing element was necessary for infringement. *Chemical Eng'g Corp. v. Essef Indus., Inc.*, 795 F.2d 1565, 230 USPQ 385 (Fed. Cir. 1986). An affidavit consisting of opinions about the meaning and application of various phrases and provisions of a claim does not necessarily create factual disputes that preclude the grant of a summary judgment of infringement. *Townsend Eng'r Co. v. HiTec Co.*, 829 F.2d 1086, 4 USPQ2d 1136 (Fed. Cir. 1987).

[28]*Ultra-Tex Surfaces Inc. v. Hill Bros. Chem. Co.*, 204 F.3d 1360, 53 USPQ2d 1892 (Fed. Cir. 2000).

[29]*Lemelson v. United States*, 752 F.2d 1538, 224 USPQ 526 (Fed. Cir. 1985).

[30]*Kegel Co. v. AMF Bowling, Inc.*, 127 F.3d 1420, 44 USPQ2d 1123 (Fed. Cir. 1997); *Braun Inc. v. Dynamics Corp.*, 975 F.2d 815, 24 USPQ2d 1121 (Fed. Cir. 1992); *Laitram Corp. v. Rexnord, Inc.*, 939 F.2d 1533, 19 USPQ2d 1367 (Fed. Cir. 1991); *Symbol Tech., Inc. v. Opticon, Inc.*, 935 F.2d 1569, 19 USPQ2d 1241 (Fed. Cir. 1991); *Smithkline Diagnostics, Inc. v. Helena Labs. Corp.*, 859 F.2d 878, 8 USPQ2d 1468 (Fed. Cir. 1988); *ZMI Corp. v. Cardiac Resuscitator Corp.*, 844 F.2d 1576, 6 USPQ2d 1557 (Fed. Cir. 1988); *Rite-Hite Corp. v. Kelley Co.*, 819 F.2d 1120, 2 USPQ2d 1915 (Fed. Cir. 1987); *Mannesmann Demag Corp. v. Engineered Metal Prods. Co.*, 793 F.2d 1279, 230 USPQ 45 (Fed. Cir. 1986); *Jamesbury Corp. v. Litton Indus. Prods., Inc.*, 756 F.2d 1556, 225 USPQ 253 (Fed. Cir. 1985); *Envirotech Corp. v. Al George, Inc.*, 730

ing an accounting, as during the liability trial, a patentee must prove infringement by a preponderance of the evidence.[31] In order to discharge this burden, the patentee must focus on the claims, for it is elementary that the property right bestowed by a patent is measured, in the first instance, by the claims.[32]

One is liable for patent infringement if a single claim be infringed.[33] It is axiomatic that dependent claims cannot be found infringed unless the claims from which they depend have been found to be infringed. One may infringe an independent claim and not infringe a claim dependent on that claim. The reverse is not true. One who does not infringe an independent claim cannot infringe a claim dependent on, and thus containing all the limitations of, that claim.[34]

The court appears to have adopted what it terms the "All Limitations Rule" for infringement.[35] Under that rule, to establish infringement of a patent every limitation set forth in a claim must be found in an accused product or process exactly or by a substantial equivalent.[36]

F.2d 753, 221 USPQ 473 (Fed. Cir. 1984). The patentee is well advised to be prepared with some positive evidence in response to a motion for summary judgment of noninfringement. The court has termed the filing of a complaint and the continuance of judicial proceedings in the absence of a specific charge of infringement to be "at best bizarre." *Chemical Eng'g Corp. v. Essef Indus., Inc.,* 795 F.2d 1565, 230 USPQ 385 (Fed. Cir. 1986). In *Under Sea Indus., Inc. v. Dacor Corp.,* 833 F.2d 1551, 4 USPQ2d 1772 (Fed. Cir. 1987), the lower court had erred in placing the burden of showing noninfringement on the defendant. Nonetheless, the court felt the error harmless where the lower court's finding of equivalence was not clearly erroneous. With all respect, this seems unfair to the accused infringer, who is wrongly saddled with the burden at trial and then has the clear burden on appeal to show that the resultant finding was clearly erroneous.

[31]*Amstar Corp. v. Envirotech Corp.,* 823 F.2d 1538, 3 USPQ2d 1412 (Fed. Cir. 1987).

[32]*A.B. Dick Co. v. Burroughs Corp.,* 713 F.2d 700, 218 USPQ 965 (Fed. Cir. 1983). And it is the claimed subject matter in its entirety that is the proper focus. The court deems frivolous any argument that suggests a holding of infringement might preclude use of a particular claim element outside the claimed combination. See *Panduit Corp. v. Dennison Mfg. Co.,* 774 F.2d 1082, 227 USPQ 337 (Fed. Cir. 1985).

[33]*Panduit Corp. v. Dennison Mfg. Co.,* 836 F.2d 1329, 5 USPQ2d 1266 (Fed. Cir. 1987). See also *Wahpeton Canvas Co. v. Frontier, Inc.,* 870 F.2d 1546, 10 USPQ2d 1201 (Fed. Cir. 1989).

[34]*Wahpeton Canvas Co. v. Frontier, Inc.,* 870 F.2d 1546, 10 USPQ2d 1201 (Fed. Cir. 1989). The jury found some dependent claims noninfringed, but did not answer an interrogatory as to independent claims from which they depended. The patentee's failure to seek resubmission to the jury of that interrogatory doomed its effort to overturn the noninfringement holding as to the dependent claims, on the theory that dependent claims cannot be found infringed unless the claims from which they depend have been found to be infringed. One wonders whether this would hold true in a situation where the patentee deliberately fails to place infringement of independent claims in issue, perhaps for fear of an invalidity holding. In another context, it appears that a finding of noninfringement of an independent claim will not automatically result in a finding of noninfringement of dependent claims. Using the "hypothetical claim" analysis for equivalents that was postulated in *Wilson Sporting Goods Co. v. David Geoffrey & Assoc.,* 904 F.2d 677, 14 USPQ2d 1942 (Fed. Cir. 1990), it is possible that the narrower dependent claims may escape the prior art and still be entitled to a range of equivalents that would cover the accused structure. See also *Wolverine World Wide, Inc. v. Nike, Inc.,* 38 F.3d 1192, 32 USPQ2d 1338 (Fed. Cir. 1994); *Carroll Touch, Inc. v. Electro Mechanical Sys., Inc.,* 3 F.3d 404, 27 USPQ2d 1836 (Fed. Cir. 1993); *Becton Dickinson & Co. v. C.R. Bard, Inc.,* 922 F.2d 792, 17 USPQ2d 1097 (Fed. Cir. 1990).

[35]*Corning Glass Works v. Sumitomo Elec. U.S.A., Inc.,* 868 F.2d 1251, 9 USPQ2d 1962 (Fed. Cir. 1989).

[36]*Laitram Corp. v. Rexnord, Inc.,* 939 F.2d 1533, 19 USPQ2d 1367 (Fed. Cir. 1991); *Key Mfg. Group, Inc. v. Microdot, Inc.,* 925 F.2d 1444, 17 USPQ2d 1806 (Fed. Cir. 1991); *Johnston v. IVAC Corp.,* 885 F.2d 1574, 12 USPQ2d 1382 (Fed. Cir. 1989).

It is elementary patent law that all limitations are material.[37] Because each element of a claim is material and essential, the patentee must show the presence of every element or its substantial equivalent in the accused device.[38] The court has specifically held that in determining both literalism and equivalence, the focus must be on the individual claim elements rather than the invention as a whole.[39] Literal infringement therefore requires that the accused device embody every element of the claim,[40] but this does not necessitate a slavish conformity to words of insignificance.[41]

That evidence of infringement may be circumstantial does not make it any less credible or persuasive, particularly where there is no countering evidence.[42] Proof of infringement does not require the plaintiff to produce an actual infringing device that the accused infringer sold. It is true that infringement must be established by comparison of the claims with devices sold before suit was filed, but the court has held that this could be done by showing (1) a stipulation that the defendant sells devices, and (2) proof that it advertises infringing devices.[43] Nor is a party required to proffer expert testimony on claim interpretation or on application of the claim language to the accused device. Indeed, the court has indicated that an argument to the contrary borders on the frivolous.[44]

In an interesting standoff, the district court believed both sides' experts and concluded that the evidence was in "equipoise." It therefore held that the patentee had not met its burden of proving infringe-

---

[37]*Glaxo, Inc. v. Novopharm, Ltd.*, 110 F.3d 1562 (Fed. Cir. 1997).

[38]*Charles Greiner & Co. v. Mari-Med Mfg., Inc.*, 962 F.2d 1031, 22 USPQ2d 1526 (Fed. Cir. 1992); *Unique Concepts, Inc. v. Brown*, 939 F.2d 1558, 19 USPQ2d 1500 (Fed. Cir. 1991); *Julien v. Zeringue*, 864 F.2d 1569, 9 USPQ2d 1552 (Fed. Cir. 1989); *Smithkline Diagnostics, Inc. v. Helena Labs. Corp.*, 859 F.2d 878, 8 USPQ2d 1468 (Fed. Cir. 1988); *Lemelson v. United States*, 752 F.2d 1538, 224 USPQ 526 (Fed. Cir. 1985).

[39]*Pennwalt Corp. v. Durand-Wayland, Inc.*, 833 F.2d 931, 4 USPQ2d 1737 (Fed. Cir. 1987).

[40]*ZMI Corp. v. Cardiac Resuscitator Corp.*, 844 F.2d 1576, 6 USPQ2d 1557 (Fed. Cir. 1988); *Hi-Life Prods., Inc. v. American Nat'l Water-Mattress Corp.*, 842 F.2d 323, 6 USPQ2d 1132 (Fed. Cir. 1988); *Mannesmann Demag Corp. v. Engineered Metal Prods. Co.*, 793 F.2d 1279, 230 USPQ 45 (Fed. Cir. 1986); *Stewart-Warner Corp. v. City of Pontiac*, 767 F.2d 1563, 226 USPQ 676 (Fed. Cir. 1985). Where a claim does not read on an accused device exactly, there can be no literal infringement. *Johnston v. IVAC Corp.*, 885 F.2d 1574, 12 USPQ2d 1382 (Fed. Cir. 1989).

[41]*Builders Concrete, Inc. v. Bremerton Concrete Prods. Co.*, 757 F.2d 255, 225 USPQ 240 (Fed. Cir. 1985).

[42]*Alco Standard Corp. v. Tennessee Valley Auth.*, 808 F.2d 1490, 1 USPQ2d 1337 (Fed. Cir. 1986). The evidence was a manual and a letter, indicating that an accused device performed certain functions. The court was willing to accept these as evidence that the device had the necessary claimed means to perform those functions. *Id.*

[43]*Allen Archery, Inc. v. Browning Mfg. Co.*, 819 F.2d 1087, 2 USPQ2d 1490 (Fed. Cir. 1987).

[44]*Moleculon Res. Corp. v. CBS, Inc.*, 793 F.2d 1261, 229 USPQ 805 (Fed. Cir. 1986). The district court did not abuse its discretion in refusing to grant a new trial where the expert witness had reviewed pertinent schematics but had not inspected the physical device and could not read the software source code. It was proper to have concluded that the expert's testimony as to infringement was competent in view of evidence that a physical inspection would have been useless, and that the source code was not the "best evidence" concerning the operation

ment by a preponderance. The Federal Circuit could not accept this logic.[45]

Reverse equivalents. The determination of whether the words of a claim literally read on the accused subject matter does not always end the infringement inquiry. A claim that is not literally infringed may in proper circumstances be held to cover equivalents; this topic is discussed in §6.3 below. Similarly, a determination that the claim words read literally on the accused matter is but an initial hurdle. If the patentee makes such a showing, the burden then shifts to the accused infringer to show, if it can, the fact of noninfringement under the so-called reverse doctrine of equivalents.[46] Under that doctrine there is no infringement, despite literal readability, if the accused product or process is so far changed in principle that it performs the function of the claimed invention in a substantially different way.[47] The reverse DOE is invoked when claims are written more broadly than the disclosure warrants. The purpose of restricting the scope of such claims is not only to avoid a holding of infringement when a court deems it appropriate, but often is to preserve the validity of claims with respect to their original intended scope.[48] The doctrine acknowledges that one may only appear to have appropriated the patented contribution.[49]

The reverse DOE might better be called a doctrine of nonequivalence. Its invocation requires both (1) that there must be apparent literal infringement of the words of the claims, and (2) that the accused device must be sufficiently different from that which is patented that despite the apparent literal infringement the claims are interpreted to negate infringement.[50] The court has specifically approved the use of a test that focuses upon whether the "principle" of the contribution made by the inventor is changed in an accused product.[51]

The reverse DOE becomes an issue only when the accused device falls within the literal words of the claim.[52] Because products on which

---

of the device. *Data Line Corp. v. Micro Techs., Inc.,* 813 F.2d 1196, 1 USPQ2d 2052 (Fed. Cir. 1987).

[45]*Andrew Corp. v. Gabriel Elec., Inc.,* 847 F.2d 819, 6 USPQ2d 2010 (Fed. Cir. 1988).

[46]*SRI Int'l v. Matsushita Elec. Corp.,* 775 F.2d 1107, 227 USPQ 577 (Fed. Cir. 1985).

[47]*Smithkline Diagnostics, Inc. v. Helena Labs. Corp.,* 859 F.2d 878, 8 USPQ2d 1468 (Fed. Cir. 1988); *Loctite Corp. v. Ultraseal Ltd.,* 781 F.2d 861, 228 USPQ 90 (Fed. Cir. 1985); *SRI Int'l v. Matsushita Elec. Corp.,* 775 F.2d 1107, 227 USPQ 577 (Fed. Cir. 1985).

[48]*Texas Instr., Inc. v. United States ITC,* 846 F.2d 1369, 6 USPQ2d 1886 (Fed. Cir. 1988). Just as the purpose of the doctrine of equivalents is to prevent pirating of the patentee's invention, so the purpose of the reverse doctrine of equivalents is to prevent unwarranted extension of the claims beyond a fair scope of the patentee's invention. The issues raised by new technologies require considered analysis. *Scripps Clinic & Res. Found. v. Genentech, Inc.,* 927 F.2d 1565, 18 USPQ2d 1001 (Fed. Cir. 1991).

[49]*SRI Int'l v. Matsushita Elec. Corp.,* 775 F.2d 1107, 227 USPQ 577 (Fed. Cir. 1985).

[50]*Texas Instr., Inc. v. United States ITC,* 846 F.2d 1369, 6 USPQ2d 1886 (Fed. Cir. 1988). But is the doctrine really one of claim interpretation?

[51]*United States Steel Corp. v. Phillips Petroleum Co.,* 865 F.2d 1247, 9 USPQ2d 1461 (Fed. Cir. 1989).

[52]*Martin v. Barber,* 755 F.2d 1564, 225 USPQ 233 (Fed. Cir. 1985).

patent claims are word-for-word readable often are in fact the same, perform the same function in the same way, and achieve the same result as the claimed invention, a defense based on the doctrine is rarely offered.[53] The fact that an infringer's product may be superior to the patentee's certainly does not call for application of the doctrine.[54] By the same token, one who takes a claimed structure and merely uses it in a way that differs from that in which a specification-described embodiment uses it, does not thereby escape infringement under the doctrine.[55]

Reverse equivalents was held to be a question of law in an early case,[56] but the court has since made it clear that the issue is factual. Infringement, whether literal or by equivalents, is a factual inquiry, and the DOE can be used to expand the claims or to restrict them as in the case of the reverse doctrine.[57]

Section 112 equivalents. The sixth paragraph of 35 U.S.C. §112 provides that a so-called means-plus-function claim shall be construed to cover the corresponding structure, material, or acts described in the specification and "equivalents thereof." Despite the word "equivalents," this inquiry under §112 is really one of literal infringement[58] and the court has warned against confusion with the traditional DOE.[59] However, in one of the court's early opinions on equivalents,[60] some very basic concepts were found to apply both to §112 equivalents and to the traditional DOE. Accordingly, the subject of §112 equivalents is treated in detail in §6.3.

Domination. The concept of domination is an important one in the study of infringement. It is a phenomenon growing out of the fact that patents have claims; one patent can have a broad or generic claim that reads on an invention defined by a narrower or more specific claim in another patent. The first dominates the second because the more narrowly claimed invention cannot be practiced without infringing the broader claim. The broader claim embraces or encompasses the subject matter defined by the narrower claim. One patent dominates another if a claim of the first reads on a device built or process

---

[53]*SRI Int'l v. Matsushita Elec. Corp.*, 775 F.2d 1107, 227 USPQ 577 (Fed. Cir. 1985). If one wishes to raise the defense, one must be explicit. The court has held one does not preserve a reverse doctrine of equivalents argument simply by mounting a defense to infringement, either literal or by equivalents. *Texas Instr., Inc. v. United States ITC*, 988 F.2d 1165, 26 USPQ2d 1018 (Fed. Cir. 1993).

[54]*Studiengesellschaft Kohle v. Dart Indus., Inc.*, 726 F.2d 724, 220 USPQ 841 (Fed. Cir. 1984).

[55]*SRI Int'l v. Matsushita Elec. Corp.*, 775 F.2d 1107, 227 USPQ 577 (Fed. Cir. 1985).

[56]*Kalman v. Kimberly-Clark Corp.*, 713 F.2d 760, 218 USPQ 781 (Fed. Cir. 1983).

[57]*SRI Int'l v. Matsushita Elec. Corp.*, 775 F.2d 1107, 227 USPQ 577 (Fed. Cir. 1985).

[58]*Palumbo v. Don-Joy Co.*, 762 F.2d 969, 226 USPQ 5 (Fed. Cir. 1985).

[59]*D.M.I., Inc. v. Deere & Co.*, 755 F.2d 1570, 225 USPQ 236 (Fed. Cir. 1985).

[60]*Texas Instr., Inc. v. United States ITC*, 805 F.2d 1558, 231 USPQ 833 (Fed. Cir. 1986).

practiced according to the second patent disclosure.[61] Thus a product may infringe more than one patent, and one may not be able to practice the invention protected by an improvement patent unless one has a license under the basic patent.[62] Devices that have been modified to such an extent that the modification may be separately patented may nonetheless infringe.[63]

Validity versus infringement. Although an invalid patent claim cannot give rise to liability for patent infringement, it is better practice always to decide both validity and infringement at the same time, since the issues may well overlap.[64] Infringement may be an important indicator of validity.[65] For example, if an accused infringer had no problem copying the patent, its §112 defenses may sound hollow.[66] By the same token, the validity findings may be helpful in the infringement inquiry; the pioneer nature of the invention may make it easier to find infringement.[67] On the other hand, that which infringes if later anticipates if earlier.[68] And arguments against infringement may be indistinguishably interwoven with the factual underpinnings of validity and enforceability determinations.[69]

The requirement for consistency in attacking both issues also calls for deciding both at the same time.[70] In determining the validity

---

[61]*In re Kaplan,* 789 F.2d 1574, 229 USPQ 678 (Fed. Cir. 1986).

[62]*Milliken Res. Corp. v. Dan River, Inc.,* 739 F.2d 587, 222 USPQ 571 (Fed. Cir. 1984). In holding that an infringer was not guilty of contempt, the court seemed impressed by the fact that after the injunction, the infringer had modified its process to include elements of another comparable patented process and had begun paying royalty thereon to the other patentee. Did the court overlook the concept of domination, or was the fact that the issue was contempt an overriding factor? *American Original Corp. v. Jenkins Food Corp.,* 774 F.2d 459, 227 USPQ 299 (Fed. Cir. 1985).

[63]*Texas Instr., Inc. v. United States ITC,* 805 F.2d 1558, 231 USPQ 833 (Fed. Cir. 1986).

[64]*Medtronic, Inc. v. Cardiac Pacemakers, Inc.,* 721 F.2d 1563, 220 USPQ 97 (Fed. Cir. 1983).

[65]*Stratoflex, Inc. v. Aeroquip Corp.,* 713 F.2d 1530, 218 USPQ 871 (Fed. Cir. 1983).

[66]*W.L. Gore & Assoc. v. Garlock, Inc.,* 721 F.2d 1540, 220 USPQ 303 (Fed. Cir. 1983).

[67]*Amstar Corp. v. Envirotech Corp.,* 730 F.2d 1476, 221 USPQ 649 (Fed. Cir. 1984). Conversely, a patent that issues in a crowded art cannot be considered pioneer for infringement purposes. *Chemical Eng'g Corp. v. Essef Indus., Inc.,* 795 F.2d 1565, 230 USPQ 385 (Fed. Cir. 1986).

[68]*Polaroid Corp. v. Eastman Kodak Co.,* 789 F.2d 1556, 229 USPQ 561 (Fed. Cir. 1986). Nonetheless, the court has rejected, perhaps for the first time, an argument that in order to establish literal infringement, the patentee must prove that the accused devices embody all the limitations in the asserted claims and, in addition, the accused devices must not be an adoption of the combined teachings of the prior art. Although such an analysis may be used under *Wilson Sporting Goods* (see the discussion beginning at note 6:296) to limit the permissible range of equivalents, it is inappropriate in a literal infringement inquiry. *Baxter Healthcare Corp. v. Spectramed, Inc.,* 49 F.3d 1575, 34 USPQ2d 1120 (Fed. Cir. 1995). Near the end of 1999, 35 U.S.C. §273 was added to the patent statute. This enactment provides for a limited personal defense to an assertion of infringement of a business method patent where the defendant can establish that it reduced the invention to practice more than a year before the filing date of the patent and commercially used it prior to the filing date.

[69]*Witco Chem. Corp. v. Peachtree Doors, Inc.,* 787 F.2d 1545, 229 USPQ 188 (Fed. Cir. 1986).

[70]It is legally improper to treat structural claims one way when considering validity and another when considering infringement. *Connell v. Sears, Roebuck & Co.,* 722 F.2d 1542, 220 USPQ 193 (Fed. Cir. 1983). In this case the court held it improper for the patentee to deprecate

of product-by-process claims in litigation, it appears that the product is construed as limited by the process stated in the claims. By the same token, a correct reading of product-by-process claims for infringement purposes is that they cover only a product prepared by the process set forth in the claims.[71]

Declaratory judgment plaintiffs who have been threatened with suit are at full liberty to deny infringement and often do. But they are also at liberty to admit infringement while asserting that the patent is invalid and that no liability for the infringement can therefore exist.[72] Where a district court has held a patent invalid, the defendant has a legal right to do the act claimed to be infringing, even though the district court decision is on appeal.[73]

(ii) Literal Infringement

A patent confers the right to exclude others from making, using, or selling the invention defined by the claims.[74] The acts of making, using, offering to sell, and selling are considered in the next section. In this section, we are concerned only with whether the accused matter is the invention defined by the claims. In this inquiry, as in the question of construction and interpretation of claim language, the cases are little more than a collection of helpful guides to decision. There are no broad rules, naturally enough, because of the intensely factual nature of the inquiry.

In considering infringement, as with all other issues in patent law, it is the claims that measure the property right bestowed by a patent.[75] The disclosure of a patent is in the public domain save as the claims forbid. The claims alone delimit the right to exclude; only they may be infringed.[76] Infringement, literal or by equivalents, is

---

art because it showed hair curlers, not unsnarlers, and then assert infringement on the part of a curler on the ground that it could be used as an unsnarler. This healthy consistency is much more difficult to achieve when issues are decided separately.

[71]*Atlantic Thermoplastics Co. v. Faytex Corp.,* 970 F.2d 834, 23 USPQ2d 1481 (Fed. Cir. 1992). The court had previously held in *Scripps Clinic & Res. Found. v. Genentech, Inc.,* 927 F.2d 1565, 18 USPQ2d 1001 (Fed. Cir. 1991), that product-by-process claims are not limited by the process for either purpose. In overruling *Scripps,* the court made an exhaustive analysis of Supreme Court and other precedent, and concluded that the *Scripps* rule would require the court to exclude claim limitations from its infringement analysis, which is forbidden under the All-Elements Rule. The court also recognized that PTO policy is to read the claim as not limited by the process in determining patentability.

[72]*International Med. Pros. v. Gore Ent. Holdings, Inc.,* 787 F.2d 572, 229 USPQ 278 (Fed. Cir. 1986).

[73]*Akzo N.V. v. United States ITC,* 808 F.2d 1471, 1 USPQ2d 1241 (Fed. Cir. 1986).

[74]*Standard Oil Co. v. American Cyanamid Co.,* 774 F.2d 448, 227 USPQ 293 (Fed. Cir. 1985).

[75]*Perini Am., Inc. v. Paper Converting Mach. Co.,* 832 F.2d 581, 4 USPQ2d 1621 (Fed. Cir. 1987); *A.B. Dick Co. v. Burroughs Corp.,* 713 F.2d 700, 218 USPQ 965 (Fed. Cir. 1983).

[76]*Environmental Instr., Inc. v. Sutron Corp.,* 877 F.2d 1561, 11 USPQ2d 1132 (Fed. Cir. 1989). Thus the court rejects the notion that literal infringement can be found where the accused device employs the principal teachings of the patent and is, with one exception, a virtual Chinese copy. *Id.* There is no legally recognizable or protected essential element, gist,

therefore determined by comparing an accused product or process, not with a preferred embodiment described in the patent or with a commercialized embodiment of the patent, but with the properly and previously construed claims in suit.[77] A patentee need produce no commercial device,[78] and it is error to compare the accused product to the patentee's commercial product.[79] Infringement is determined on the basis of the claims, not on the basis of a comparison with the patentee's commercial embodiment of the claimed invention.[80] Conversely, it is the accused commercial device that must be analyzed for infringement, not merely disclosures in the accused infringer's own patent.[81]

There is no abstract guide to determining when a modified device crosses the boundary with respect to the reasonable scope of the patent claims. Indeed, the determination of infringement is not made in the abstract but in the context of the claimed invention and the accused device.[82] A finding of literal infringement requires that the asserted claims, as properly construed, read on the accused product.[83] A claim covers or reads on an accused device if the device embodies every limitation of the claim, either literally or by a substantial equivalent.[84] Literal infringement is found where the accused device falls within the scope of the asserted claims as properly interpreted. For

---

or heart of an invention in a combination patent. *Everpure, Inc. v. Cuno, Inc.*, 875 F.2d 300, 10 USPQ2d 1855 (Fed. Cir. 1989). A patentee cannot prevail by proving infringement of claims originally filed but not in its patent. *Stein Assoc., Inc. v. Heat & Control, Inc.*, 748 F.2d 653, 223 USPQ 1277 (Fed. Cir. 1984).

[77]*SRI Int'l v. Matsushita Elec. Corp.*, 775 F.2d 1107, 227 USPQ 577 (Fed. Cir. 1985); *Martin v. Barber*, 755 F.2d 1564, 225 USPQ 233 (Fed. Cir. 1985); *Amstar Corp. v. Envirotech Corp.*, 730 F.2d 1476, 221 USPQ 649 (Fed. Cir. 1984). See also *Lund Indus., Inc. v. GO Indus., Inc.*, 938 F.2d 1273, 19 USPQ2d 1383 (Fed. Cir. 1991); *Datascope Corp. v. SMEC, Inc.*, 879 F.2d 820, 11 USPQ2d 1321 (Fed. Cir. 1989).

[78]*Perkin-Elmer Corp. v. Computervision Corp.*, 732 F.2d 888, 221 USPQ 669 (Fed. Cir. 1984).

[79]*Loctite Corp. v. Ultraseal Ltd.*, 781 F.2d 861, 228 USPQ 90 (Fed. Cir. 1985); *Yarway Corp. v. Eur-Control USA Inc.*, 775 F.2d 268, 227 USPQ 352 (Fed. Cir. 1985).

[80]*Spectrum Int'l Inc. v. Sterilite Corp.*, 164 F.3d 1372, 49 USPQ2d 1065 (Fed. Cir. 1998); *ACS Hosp. Sys., Inc. v. Montefiore Hosp.*, 732 F.2d 1572, 221 USPQ 929 (Fed. Cir. 1984). *Zenith Labs., Inc. v. Bristol-Myers Squibb Co.*, 19 F.3d 1418, 30 USPQ2d 1048, 32 USPQ2d 1017 (Fed. Cir. 1994), provides an interesting example of the importance of this rule. The issue was whether there was sufficient proof that the patented monohydrate form of the drug was actually found in the stomachs of patients who ingested the accused hemihydrate form. The claim contained a limitation that the compound exhibit certain x-ray diffraction properties. Instead of obtaining a sample from a patient's stomach, the patentee convinced the trial court that the accused drug actually did convert in the patient's stomach, and then submitted x-ray diffraction evidence with respect to the patented compound. This was improper. In determining whether a claim has been infringed, the scientific theories utilized must establish the presence of the limitations recited in the claim by reference to the accused substance not the patentee's commercial substance.

[81]*Chemical Eng'g Corp. v. Essef Indus., Inc.*, 795 F.2d 1565, 230 USPQ 385 (Fed. Cir. 1986).

[82]*Texas Instr., Inc. v. United States ITC*, 805 F.2d 1558, 231 USPQ 833 (Fed. Cir. 1986).

[83]*Morton Int'l, Inc. v. Cardinal Chem. Co.*, 5 F.3d 1464, 28 USPQ2d 1190 (Fed. Cir. 1993).

[84]*Carroll Touch, Inc. v. Electro Mechanical Sys., Inc.*, 3 F.3d 404, 27 USPQ2d 1836 (Fed. Cir. 1993).

literal infringement, each limitation of the claim must be met by the accused device exactly, any deviation from the claim precluding a finding of infringement.[85] If an express claim limitation is absent from an accused product, there can be no literal infringement as a matter of law.[86]

Even in the case of an injunction against patent infringement, a judgment of contempt for violation of the injunction requires a finding that the modified or new device falls within the admitted or adjudicated scope of the claims.[87] Some decisions have indicated that infringement may be determined by comparison with a device adjudicated as an infringement. In the sense that things equal to the same thing are equal to each other, this may be so in cases where the adjudicated device is a precise literal infringement of the claims. In such cases, comparison with the adjudicated device may serve as a handy method of reaching a determination. However, whether one is determining infringement at trial, in an accounting, or in a contempt proceeding, it must be remembered that it is a claim that is infringed and a claimed invention that is patented. Thus, comparison with an adjudicated device cannot serve to encompass within the patent's exclusionary scope a device that does not in fact constitute an infringement of the claim, either literally or under the DOE. In making a finding that the accused new device is an infringement, the court cannot avoid looking at the claims of the patent.[88]

The addition of a component,[89] or ingredient,[90] or step[91] to the claimed invention will not necessarily avoid infringement, even if the additional element provides an additional function,[92] unless added features produce a radically different system.[93] Indeed, the court has

---

[85]*Lantech, Inc. v. Keip Mach. Co.*, 32 F.3d 542, 31 USPQ2d 1666 (Fed. Cir. 1994).

[86]*Wolverine World Wide, Inc. v. Nike, Inc.*, 38 F.3d 1192, 32 USPQ2d 1338 (Fed. Cir. 1994).

[87]*KSM Fastening Sys., Inc. v. H.A. Jones Co.*, 776 F.2d 1522, 227 USPQ 676 (Fed. Cir. 1985).

[88]*Amstar Corp. v. Envirotech Corp.*, 823 F.2d 1538, 3 USPQ2d 1412 (Fed. Cir. 1987). There is really not much leeway here. In *Del Mar Avionics, Inc. v. Quinton Instr. Co.*, 836 F.2d 1320, 5 USPQ2d 1255 (Fed. Cir. 1987), another court had adjudicated that A infringed and C did not. *Both* parties were arguing that the adjudications should be res judicata as to B, which was similar but not identical to both A and C. The Federal Circuit quickly concluded that a device not previously before a court, and shown to differ from those structures previously litigated, requires determination on its own facts.

[89]*Loctite Corp. v. Ultraseal Ltd.*, 781 F.2d 861, 228 USPQ 90 (Fed. Cir. 1985).

[90]*Atlas Powder Co. v. E.I. du Pont & Co.*, 750 F.2d 1569, 224 USPQ 409 (Fed. Cir. 1984).

[91]*Standard Havens Prods., Inc. v. Gencor Indus., Inc.*, 953 F.2d 1360, 21 USPQ2d 1321 (Fed. Cir. 1992); *Bio-Rad Labs., Inc. v. Nicolet Instr. Corp.*, 739 F.2d 604, 222 USPQ 654 (Fed. Cir. 1984). It is fallacious to argue that infringement is avoided by adding a prior art step to a patented process. *Shamrock Techs. Inc. v. Medical Sterilization, Inc.*, 903 F.2d 789, 14 USPQ2d 1728 (Fed. Cir. 1990).

[92]*Northern Telecom, Inc. v. Datapoint Corp.*, 908 F.2d 931, 15 USPQ2d 1321 (Fed. Cir. 1990); *Radio Steel & Mfg. Co. v. MTD Prods., Inc.*, 731 F.2d 840, 221 USPQ 657 (Fed. Cir. 1984).

[93]*Data Line Corp. v. Micro Techs., Inc.*, 813 F.2d 1196, 1 USPQ2d 2052 (Fed. Cir. 1987). If a patent requires A, and the accused device or process uses A and B, infringement will be avoided only if the patent's definition of A excludes the possibility of B. Statements in the patent simply noting a distinction between A and B are thus unhelpful: what matters is not that the patent describes A and B as different, but whether, according to the patent, A and B

said that it has never required that a claim read on the entirety of an accused device in order to be infringed. If it reads merely on a part of an accused device, that is enough for infringement.[94] A device that embodies improvements on a claimed structure does not automatically avoid the reach of the claim.[95] The fact of separate patentability presents no legal or evidentiary presumption of noninfringement.[96] The court regards it as fundamental that one cannot avoid infringement merely by adding elements if each element recited in the claims is found in the accused device.[97] A contrary argument by counsel was termed a "reverse" statement of the law of infringement and was a principal factor in an award of double costs on appeal.[98]

The fact that claims are to a combination of elements does not in any way limit their scope in the infringement context.[99] There is no such thing as a patented portion of a patented combination. It is the combination, not any portion or element thereof, that is protected.[100] The court took the trouble to sit in banc to decide that, unlike the obviousness determination, the infringement inquiry requires attention to each claim element rather than the invention as a whole.[101] There is no legally recognizable or protected gist or heart of the invention, and it is error for the trial court to restrict a multistep

---

must be mutually exclusive. *Northern Telecom Ltd. v. Samsung Elec. Co.*, 215 F.3d 1281, 55 USPQ2d 1065 (Fed. Cir. 2000). While adding elements may, in certain instances, fail to prevent a finding of infringement, it will prevent a finding of literal infringement where the claim is specific as to the number of elements and adding elements eliminates an inherent feature of the claim. *Insituform Tech., Inc. v. CAT Contr., Inc.*, 99 F.3d 1098, 40 USPQ2d 1602 (Fed. Cir. 1996). In *Jeneric/Pentron Inc. v. Dillon Co.*, 205 F.3d 1377, 54 USPQ2d 1086 (Fed. Cir. 2000), one constituent of the accused product fell outside the claimed range. The patentee argued that the excess material in the accused product was for a purpose other than that described in the patent, and pointed to the open-ended "comprising" language of the claim. The court was quick to point out that it rejects any attempt to carve out a portion of a constituent according to functions not recited in the claim.

[94]*SunTiger Inc. v. Scientific Res. Fund Group*, 189 F.3d 1327, 51 USPQ2d 1811 (Fed. Cir. 1999).

[95]*Richardson v. Suzuki Motor Co.*, 868 F.2d 1226, 9 USPQ2d 1913 (Fed. Cir. 1989). Advances subsequent to the patent may still infringe. *Marsh-McBirney, Inc. v. Montedoro-Whitney Corp.*, 882 F.2d 498, 11 USPQ2d 1794 (Fed. Cir. 1989).

[96]*Hoechst Celanese Corp. v. BP Chem. Ltd.*, 78 F.3d 1575, 38 USPQ2d 1126 (Fed. Cir. 1996).

[97]*Stiftung v. Renishaw PLC*, 945 F.2d 1173, 20 USPQ2d 1094 (Fed. Cir. 1991); *Mannesmann Demag Corp. v. Engineered Metal Prods. Co.*, 793 F.2d 1279, 230 USPQ 45 (Fed. Cir. 1986); *A.B. Dick Co. v. Burroughs Corp.*, 713 F.2d 700, 218 USPQ 965 (Fed. Cir. 1983). Adding features to an accused device will not result in noninfringement if all the limitations in the claims, or equivalents thereof, are present in the accused device. *Uniroyal, Inc. v. Rudkin-Wiley Corp.*, 837 F.2d 1044, 5 USPQ2d 1434 (Fed. Cir. 1988). Where the claim language reads directly on the accused device, additional structure present in such device may, in appropriate circumstances, be disregarded in an infringement analysis. *Becton Dickinson & Co. v. C.R. Bard, Inc.*, 922 F.2d 792, 17 USPQ2d 1097 (Fed. Cir. 1990).

[98]*Amstar Corp. v. Envirotech Corp.*, 730 F.2d 1476, 221 USPQ 649 (Fed. Cir. 1984).

[99]*Amstar Corp. v. Envirotech Corp.*, 730 F.2d 1476, 221 USPQ 649 (Fed. Cir. 1984).

[100]*Porter v. Farmers Supply Serv., Inc.*, 790 F.2d 882, 229 USPQ 814 (Fed. Cir. 1986). There is no legally recognizable or protected essential element, gist, or heart of an invention in a combination patent. *Everpure, Inc. v. Cuno, Inc.*, 875 F.2d 300, 10 USPQ2d 1855 (Fed. Cir. 1989).

[101]*Pennwalt Corp. v. Durand-Wayland, Inc.*, 833 F.2d 931, 4 USPQ2d 1737 (Fed. Cir. 1987).

claim to one step, either to find infringement by one who uses only that step, or to find invalidity over art that discloses only that step.[102]

Apparatus distinctions not claimed are not controlling in determining infringement of process claims.[103] However, the court has held that a structural recitation in a method claim step can be construed as a limitation on the claim. Whether it does so limit the claim depends on the claim language, the specification, the prosecution history, and the other claims of the patent. Thus, where a claim called for a step of performing a particular act, and the accused structure was incapable of that act, it was error to find literal infringement.[104]

Where it is clear that the claims call for a device in its installed state, infringement must be determined by reference to what the accused device is like after installation.[105] A product claim is infringed by any product containing every claim limitation, regardless of how the product is made.[106] There need not be one-to-one correspondence between the components of an accused device and the claimed invention.[107]

Imperfect practice of an invention does not avoid infringement.[108] Inefficient infringement is infringement still.[109] Nor will a mere change in size due to improved miniaturization by technological advance in itself save an accused device from infringement.[110] Improvement upon a patented device does not necessarily avoid infringement.[111]

When an accused device may be easily altered to infringe, interesting questions arise. The court feels that a device does not infringe simply because it is possible to alter it in a way that would satisfy all the limitations of a patent claim. The question is not what it might have been made to do, but what it was intended to do and did do.

---

[102]*W.L. Gore & Assoc. v. Garlock, Inc.,* 721 F.2d 1540, 220 USPQ 303 (Fed. Cir. 1983). However, the court does seem willing to permit focus upon whether the "principle" of the contribution made by the inventor is changed in an accused product, at least for purposes of determining reverse equivalents. *United States Steel Corp. v. Phillips Petroleum Co.,* 865 F.2d 1247, 9 USPQ2d 1461 (Fed. Cir. 1989).

[103]*Polaroid Corp. v. Eastman Kodak Co.,* 789 F.2d 1556, 229 USPQ 561 (Fed. Cir. 1986). The converse is also true. Although apparatus claims give patent protection covering all uses for the claimed apparatus, a patent owner cannot use the patent laws to proscribe use of another noninfringing apparatus to perform a method that is not claimed. *Augustine Med. Inc. v. Gaymar Indus. Inc.,* 181 F.3d 1291, 50 USPQ2d 1900 (Fed. Cir. 1999).

[104]*Moleculon Res. Corp. v. CBS, Inc.,* 793 F.2d 1261, 229 USPQ 805 (Fed. Cir. 1986).

[105]*Rawlplug Co. v. Illinois Tool Works, Inc.,* 11 F.3d 1036, 28 USPQ2d 1908 (Fed. Cir. 1993). The claim was for a masonry anchor.

[106]*Exxon Chem. Patents, Inc. v. Lubrizol Corp.,* 64 F.3d 1553, 35 USPQ2d 1801 (Fed. Cir. 1995).

[107]*Festo Corp. v. Shoketsu KKK Co.,* 72 F.3d 857, 37 USPQ2d 1163 (Fed. Cir. 1995).

[108]*Paper Converting Mach. Co. v. Magna-Graphics Corp.,* 745 F.2d 11, 223 USPQ 591 (Fed. Cir. 1984).

[109]*Festo Corp. v. Shoketsu KKK Co.,* 72 F.3d 857, 37 USPQ2d 1163 (Fed. Cir. 1995); *Shamrock Techs., Inc. v. Medical Sterilization, Inc.,* 903 F.2d 789, 14 USPQ2d 1728 (Fed. Cir. 1990).

[110]*Texas Instr., Inc. v. United States ITC,* 805 F.2d 1558, 231 USPQ 833 (Fed. Cir. 1986).

[111]*Stiftung v. Renishaw PLC,* 945 F.2d 1173, 20 USPQ2d 1094 (Fed. Cir. 1991).

Of course, if a device is designed to be altered or assembled before operation, the manufacturer may be held liable for infringement if the device, as altered or assembled, infringes a valid patent.[112] A device does not infringe simply because it is possible to alter it in a way that would satisfy all the limitations of a patent claim.[113] An accused product that sometimes, but not always, embodies a claimed method nonetheless infringes.[114]

(iii) The Prohibited Acts

The statute broadly prohibits (1) making, using, selling, offering to sell, or importing, (2) within the United States, (3) during the term of the patent.[115] The phrase "offer to sell" was added to 35 U.S.C. §271(a) to conform U.S. law to the April 1994 Uruguay Round's Trade-Related Aspects of Intellectual Property Agreement. Additionally, a new subsection, §271(i), was added defining an "offer for sale" or an "offer to sell" as "that in which the sale will occur before the expiration of the term of the patent." The amendment to §271(a) represents a distinct change to the bases for patent infringement, because liability arose previously only as the result of an actual sale.[116]

Making, use, offer, and sale. Only one of the activities enumerated under §271(a) is required for infringement; thus, use alone is actionable, without either manufacture or sale.[117] The Federal Circuit promises to interpret these words broadly. In one case the defendant neither made nor sold, but simply furnished infringing display racks to its customers, free of charge, for their use. This was held to constitute use by the defendant and was therefore an infringement.[118] And

---

[112]*High Tech Med. Instr., Inc. v. New Image Indus., Inc.*, 49 F.3d 1551, 33 USPQ2d 2005 (Fed. Cir. 1995). The claim required that a camera be rotatably coupled to a body member. In the accused device, the original and intended operating configuration was a rigid coupling, but two set screws could be loosened so that it was capable of being rotated. The court found there was no reason to disregard the set screws in determining the character of the coupling for infringement purposes; it accordingly held no likelihood of success on the infringement issue. It distinguished *Intel Corp. v. United States ITC*, 946 F.2d 821, 20 USPQ 1161 (Fed. Cir. 1991) on the ground that there, the claimed invention was an integrated circuit programmable to operate in a certain manner. The accused device, although not specifically designed or sold to operate in that manner, could be programmed so to do.

[113]*Kegel Co. v. AMF Bowling, Inc.*, 127 F.3d 1420, 44 USPQ2d 1123 (Fed. Cir. 1997).

[114]*Bell Comm. Research v. Vitalink Comm. Corp.*, 55 F.3d 615, 34 USPQ2d 1816, 1822 (Fed. Cir. 1995).

[115]35 U.S.C. §271(a).

[116]*3D Sys. Inc. v. Aarotech Labs. Inc.*,160 F.3d 1373, 48 USPQ2d 1773 (Fed. Cir. 1998). The court has held that an offer to donate equipment to a school does not constitute an offer to sell within the meaning of §271(a). *HollyAnne Corp. v. TFT Inc.*, 199 F.3d 1304, 53 USPQ2d 1201 (Fed. Cir. 1999).

[117]*Roche Prods., Inc. v. Bolar Pharm. Co.*, 733 F.2d 858, 221 USPQ 937 (Fed. Cir. 1984).

[118]*Trans-World Mfg. Corp. v. Al Nyman & Sons*, 750 F.2d 1552, 224 USPQ 259 (Fed. Cir. 1984). The district court enjoined manufacture and sale but failed to enjoin use. This was held to be an abuse of discretion, inasmuch as an injunction against use was the only effective relief.

certainly, demonstration of an accused device in satisfaction of a prescribed bidding procedure constitutes infringement.[119] However, a threat of sale does not constitute an act of infringement.[120] Nor does the dissemination of information concerning the design and specifications of a patented invention.[121] The court has held, at least for jurisdictional purposes, that a letter containing a description of the allegedly infringing merchandise and the price at which it can be purchased constitutes an offer to sell, even where the letter contains a specific disclaimer to the contrary. In so holding, it seemed to signal that it will apply a fairly liberal construction to this new infringement provision. It also rejected the suggestion that decisional authority relating to on-sale issues under 35 U.S.C. §102(b) should control the analysis. The policies underlying §102(b) and §271(a) are very different.[122]

 Generally, infringement of an apparatus claim by a user can occur only when the claimed combination has been assembled and is used or is available for use. The court will not require a showing of actual use if it is clear that, as assembled, the accused device would infringe an apparatus claim; however, the mere fact that the device might be assembled in an infringing configuration is probably not alone sufficient.[123] To show infringement of method claims, a plaintiff

---

[119]*TVI Energy Corp. v. Blane,* 806 F.2d 1057, 1 USPQ2d 1071 (Fed. Cir. 1986). This case involved bids for a government contract, so that the sole remedy in any event would lie in the Claims Court.

[120]*Eli Lilly & Co. v. Medtronic, Inc.,* 915 F.2d 670 (Fed. Cir. 1990).

[121]*McElmurry v. Arkansas Power & Light Co.,* 995 F.2d 1576, 27 USPQ2d 1129 (Fed. Cir. 1993).

[122]*3D Sys. Inc. v. Aarotech Labs. Inc.,*160 F.3d 1373, 48 USPQ2d 1773 (Fed. Cir. 1998). In *Rotec Indus. Inc. v. Mitsubishi Corp.,* 215 F.3d 1246, 55 USPQ2d 1001 (Fed. Cir. 2000), the court addressed some important issues regarding the meaning of "offer to sell," but the 2–1 panel decision raises as many questions as it answers. Several domestic and foreign companies joined forces in response to a bid request to supply the patented system to a concern in China. The bid document and sales contract were executed outside the United States. No component of the system that was ultimately sold originated in the United States. There were meetings among the suppliers in the United States, but no admissible evidence that representatives of the Chinese concern were present. The patent owner contended that the activity in the United States amounted to an offer to sell under §271(a) and "supply" or "causing to supply" under §271(f)(2). As a preliminary matter, the panel majority decided that an "offer to sell" is to be interpreted according to its ordinary meaning in contract law, as revealed by traditional sources of authority. On the matter of whether the U.S. activity constituted an offer to sell under §271(a), the court found that the absence of a third party (such as the buyer) from the meetings was conclusive. There was simply no evidence upon which a jury could find that an offer to sell had occurred in this country. In reaching that conclusion, however, the panel majority, according to Judge Newman's concurring opinion, assumed that an offer made in the United States, to sell a system all of whose components would be made in foreign countries, for sale, installation, and use in a foreign country, would infringe the U.S. patent. Judge Newman disagrees with this proposition, and would have decided that there was no infringement under §271(a) on that basis. The panel majority disposed of the patent owner's §271(f)(2) claim on the ground that "offer to sell" in §271(a) should not be engrafted onto §271(f)(2). In other words, the phrase "supplies or causes to be supplied" does not comprehend offers to supply components of patented systems. See note 6:445 below.

[123]*Lemelson v. United States,* 752 F.2d 1538, 224 USPQ 526 (Fed. Cir. 1985).

must prove the modes in which the accused devices have been operated and the manner in which those modes infringe the patent claims. Simply proving delivery and use of a device capable of being used, in some mode, to infringe a method claim may not be enough.[124] The court has indicated that the law is unequivocal that the sale of equipment to perform a process is not a direct infringement of a patent claiming the process.[125]

There is a limited experimental use exception in infringement cases. Where the use is for amusement, or to satisfy idle curiosity, or for strictly philosophical inquiry, there may be no liability for infringement. But testing an invention just prior to expiration of a patent covering it does not fall within the exception, where the tests are in keeping with the legitimate business of the infringer who wishes to use the invention after expiration.[126] The court recognizes that it has construed the experimental use and de minimus exceptions to infringement liability very narrowly.[127]

Process patents. Historically, it was not an act of patent infringement to import into the United States a product made abroad by a process patented in the United States. Congress, concerned that foreign competitors were appropriating valuable American inventions, enacted the Process Patent Amendments Act of 1988 (PPAA).[128] Prior to the enactment of the 1988 statute, a patentee holding a process patent could sue for infringement if others used the process in this country, but had no cause of action if such persons used the patented process abroad to manufacture products, and then imported, used, or sold the products in this country. In that setting, the process patent owner's only legal recourse was to seek an exclusion order for such products from the ITC.[129] The PPAA made it an act of patent infringement, pursuant to 35 U.S.C. §271(g), to import, sell, or use in the

---

[124]*Lemelson v. United States,* 752 F.2d 1538, 224 USPQ 526 (Fed. Cir. 1985). But see 35 U.S.C. §271(g). See also *Zygo Corp. v. Wyko Corp.,* 79 F.3d 1563, 38 USPQ2d 1281 (Fed. Cir. 1996).

[125]*Joy Techs., Inc. v. Flakt, Inc.,* 6 F.3d 770, 28 USPQ2d 1378 (Fed. Cir. 1993). However, demonstration by a manufacturer, at open houses attended by customers, of equipment useful for practicing a claimed process, apparently can constitute direct infringement of process claims. *Mendenhall v. Cedarapids, Inc.,* 5 F.3d 1556, 28 USPQ2d 1081, 1100 (Fed. Cir. 1993).

[126]*Roche Prods., Inc. v. Bolar Pharm. Co.,* 733 F.2d 858, 221 USPQ 937 (Fed. Cir. 1984). This holding is now reflected in the statute. See 35 U.S.C. §271(e)(2) & (4) (added November 1984). A corollary provision maintains a limited exemption for development and submission activities required by the FDA. See 35 U.S.C. §271(e)(1) & (3).

[127]*Embrex Inc. v. Service Eng'g Corp.,* 216 F.3d 1343, 55 USPQ2d 1161 (Fed. Cir. 2000). In a concurring opinion Judge Rader urged the court to disavow any such excuses for infringement.

[128]*Novo Nordisk of N.A., Inc. v. Genentech, Inc.,* 77 F.3d 1364, 37 USPQ2d 1773 (Fed. Cir. 1996).

[129]*Eli Lilly & Co. v. American Cyanamid Co.,* 82 F.3d 1568, 38 USPQ2d 1705 (Fed. Cir. 1996).

United States, without authorization, a product made by a process patented in the United States. A provision concerning offers to sell was added to §271(g) by the Uruguay Round Agreements Act (URAA), effective January 1, 1996. Pursuant to 35 U.S.C. §295, the accused infringer's product is presumed to have been made by the patented process if the trial court finds that (1) a substantial likelihood exists that the product was made by the patented process, and (2) the patentee made a reasonable effort to determine the process actually used in the production of the product but was unable to so determine. If the trial court makes such findings, the burden of establishing that the product was not made by the patented process is on the accused infringer.[130]

Under the so-called "grandfather clause" exception to §271(g), there is no liability if the accused infringer can establish either (1) that the product was already in substantial and continuous sale or use on January 1, 1988, or (2) that it made substantial preparation for such sale or use before that date. Substantial preparation must consist of activities closely associated with the practice of the claimed invention.[131] Also, a concern raised during consideration of the process patent legislation was whether and to what extent the new legislation would affect products other than the direct and unaltered products of patented processes—that is, whether the new statute would apply when a product was produced abroad by a patented process but then modified or incorporated into other products before being imported into this country. Congress addressed that issue by providing that a product that is "made by" a patented process within the meaning of the statute will not be considered to be so made after (1) it is materially

---

[130]*Novo Nordisk of N.A., Inc. v. Genentech, Inc.,* 77 F.3d 1364, 37 USPQ2d 1773 (Fed. Cir. 1996). Section 295 on its face is a burden-shifting mechanism. As a general proposition, the law places the burden of proving infringement on the patentee who alleges it. When two conditions are met, the statute shifts that burden and requires the alleged infringer to disprove infringement. The two conditions are that a substantial likelihood exists that the product was made by the patented process, and that the plaintiff has made a reasonable effort to determine the process actually used in the production of the product and was unable so to determine. The statute also has a significant punitive element. It provides the trial court with a potent weapon to use against a noncooperative defendant. The statute thus works for the benefit of a patentee, but it also serves the needs of the court as a mechanism for enforcing its processes and orders. Whether each of the two prongs of §295 has been met is not determined subjectively by the plaintiff, but is determined objectively by the court. The specific point during a trial when the trial court should decide a §295 motion raised by the patentee will vary with the facts and circumstances of each case. It would be as arbitrary to identify a specific point at which the court must make its §295 decision as it would be to mandate a specific point in a proceeding when a court must enter summary judgment. The patentee has every right to urge the court to apply §295 when circumstances warrant it; likewise, the court has every right to exercise its discretion in determining at what point in the decisional process the statute will be brought into play. *Nutrinova Nutrition Spec. v. United States ITC,* 224 F.3d 1356, 55 USPQ2d 1951 (Fed. Cir. 2000).

[131]*Bio-Technology Gen. Corp. v. Genentech, Inc.,* 80 F.3d 1553, 38 USPQ2d 1321 (Fed. Cir. 1996). This interesting case involved the argument that a single use, abroad, of the patented method before the enactment of the statute amounted to infringement.

changed by subsequent processes, or (2) it becomes a trivial and nonessential component of another product.[132]

FDA approval. The Drug Price Competition and Patent Term Restoration Act of 1984 addressed two distinct problems created by the legal requirements for premarket FDA approval of drugs and medical devices. At the front end, a patent owner's effective patent term was shortened by the time spent obtaining approval. To avoid this unintended distortion of the purposes of the Patent Act, Congress provided for extending the term of patents relating to products that could not be marketed before undergoing a lengthy approval process. This distortion was remedied in 35 U.S.C. §156.[133]

At the other end of a patent term, the delay attendant on obtaining FDA approval for a competing product that utilized the patented invention had the effect in some situations of extending the patentee's exclusive rights beyond the patent term. Since a competing product could not be made or used while the patent was still in effect without infringing, the process for obtaining FDA approval could not be undertaken until the original patent expired.[134] At the urging of the generic drug manufacturers, Congress enacted 35 U.S.C. §271(e)(1), which exempts use of a "patented invention" solely in relation to development and submission of information under a federal law that "regulates the manufacture, use, or sale of drugs." The objective was for the drug manufacturers to be able to place generic substitutes for a patented drug on the market the day after the patent expired.[135]

While §271(e)(2) provides the federal courts with jurisdiction to hear infringement cases regarding claims directed to drugs or methods of using drugs, it does not provide jurisdiction to hear infringement cases regarding claims directed to methods for making drugs. In the context of an abbreviated new drug application (ANDA),[136] such a case would require resort to the Declaratory

---

[132]*Eli Lilly & Co. v. American Cyanamid Co.*, 82 F.3d 1568, 38 USPQ2d 1705 (Fed. Cir. 1996). Whether the product of a patented process is a "trivial and nonessential component" of another product is necessarily a question of degree. Even less well defined is the question whether the product of a patented process has been "materially changed" before its importation into this country. While applying that statutory language may be relatively easy in extreme cases, it is not at all easy in a closer case. Here the court made an exhaustive analysis of the legislative history and, on that basis, rejected the patent owner's theory that the language should be construed in light of its underlying purpose, which is to protect the economic value of U.S. process patents. In a highly fact-specific holding, the court seemed to signal a fairly expansive reading of the term "material change."

[133]*Telectronics Pacing Sys., Inc. v. Ventritex, Inc.*, 982 F.2d 1520, 25 USPQ2d 1196 (Fed. Cir. 1992). See also *Unimed, Inc. v. Quigg*, 888 F.2d 826, 12 USPQ2d 1644 (Fed. Cir. 1989); *Eli Lilly & Co. v. Medtronic, Inc.*, 872 F.2d 402, 10 USPQ2d 1304 (Fed. Cir. 1989), *aff'd*, 496 U.S. 661, 15 USPQ2d 1121 (1990).

[134]*Telectronics Pacing Sys., Inc. v. Ventritex, Inc.*, 982 F.2d 1520, 25 USPQ2d 1196 (Fed. Cir. 1992). This was a consequence of the Federal Circuit's *Roche* decision. See note 6:126.

[135]*Eli Lilly & Co. v. Medtronic, Inc.*, 872 F.2d 402, 10 USPQ2d 1304 (Fed. Cir. 1989), *aff'd*, 496 U.S. 661, 15 USPQ2d 1121 (1990).

[136]*Bayer AG v. Elan Pharm. Res. Corp.*, 212 F.3d 1241, 54 USPQ2d 1710 (Fed. Cir. 2000), contains a useful summary of ANDA procedure.

Judgment Act.[137] Both §156 and §271(e)(1) cover medical devices as well as drugs.[138]

Early on, the court indicated that the filing of an ANDA with the FDA is a technical act of infringement under §271(e)(2).[139] In a later case, however, it held that the patentee's burden of proving ultimate infringement is not met by the filing of the ANDA. The relevant inquiry is whether the patentee has proven by a preponderance of the evidence that the alleged infringer will likely market an infringing product. What is likely to be sold, or preferably, what will be sold, will ultimately determine whether infringement exists. This requires examination of all relevant evidence, not just the ANDA itself.[140]

The statute specifically provides an ANDA applicant immunity from allegations of infringement for acts that are necessary in preparing an ANDA. The production of a biobatch, and the submission of a certificate of quality and analysis regarding this biobatch, are required in the ANDA application process. Thus, even if the biobatch falls within the scope of the claims, the statute specifically indicates that such actions cannot constitute infringement. In addition, the focus of the infringement inquiry under §271(e)(2)(A) is on the product that will be sold after the FDA's approval of the ANDA, not on the biobatch that is produced to facilitate FDA approval. The filing of an ANDA is considered an act of infringement under §271(e)(2)(A), but this "act" is merely a vehicle to create case or controversy jurisdiction to enable a court to promptly resolve a dispute concerning an infringement that will happen in the future.[141] The court has sidestepped the

---

[137]*Glaxo, Inc. v. Novopharm, Ltd.,* 110 F.3d 1562 (Fed. Cir. 1997). Here, the defendant had sent a letter indicating that it intended to market the product after the expiration of the drug patent but before the expiration of the method of making patent, and had also submitted an ANDA accompanied by data sufficient to make FDA approval imminent. Thus the district court properly exercised its discretion to hear the DJ action. In *Hoechst-Roussel Pharm., Inc. v. Lehman,* 109 F.3d 756, 42 USPQ2d 1220 (Fed. Cir. 1997), the court confronted the question of whether a patent "claims" a product in the context of §156. It applied a conservative view of "claims," to mean what the claim in terms covers rather than what activity will infringe it. Thus, a product which would infringe only because, when administered, it would metabolize into the claimed product, was held to be outside the term extension provisions of §156.

[138]*Eli Lilly & Co. v. Medtronic, Inc.,* 872 F.2d 402, 10 USPQ2d 1304 (Fed. Cir. 1989), *aff'd,* 496 U.S. 661, 15 USPQ2d 1121 (1990). The noninfringement shield of §271(e)(1) applies to Class II medical devices as well as to the Class III devices considered in *Eli Lilly. Abtox, Inc. v. Exitron Corp.,* 122 F.3d 1019, 43 USPQ2d 1545, *amended opinion,* 46 USPQ2d 1735 (Fed. Cir. 1997). Demonstration of an accused device for the purpose of obtaining clinical investigators constitutes an exempt use reasonably related to FDA approval under §271(e)(1). *Telectronics Pacing Sys., Inc. v. Ventritex, Inc.,* 982 F.2d 1520, 25 USPQ2d 1196 (Fed. Cir. 1992).

[139]*Merck & Co. v. Biocraft Labs., Inc.,* 874 F.2d 804, 10 USPQ2d 1843 (Fed. Cir. 1989). However, under 21 U.S.C. §355 a generic manufacturer can file an ANDA if it certifies its belief that the patent is invalid or will not be infringed by its proposed manufacture, use, or sale of the drug, and notifies the patent owner of the reasons for its belief. If the patent owner brings an infringement suit, the FDA cannot approve the application unless the patent is declared invalid or not infringed. *Id.*

[140]*Glaxo, Inc. v. Novopharm, Ltd.,* 110 F.3d 1562 (Fed. Cir. 1997).

[141]*Bayer AG v. Elan Pharm. Res. Corp.,* 212 F.3d 1241, 54 USPQ2d 1710 (Fed. Cir. 2000). The court distinguished *Glaxo, Inc. v. Novopharm, Ltd.,* 110 F.3d 1562 (Fed. Cir. 1997), on the

interesting question of whether use of data obtained during infringement, for purposes other than FDA approval under §271(e)(1), constitutes infringement.[142]

Within the United States. The "United States" includes its territories and possessions, such as Puerto Rico and the U.S. Virgin Islands.[143] In analyzing the territorial reach of a U.S. patent, it is important to keep in mind the actionability of each of the separate acts of making, using, and selling. Thus, where the claimed invention is made in this country, it is irrelevant where it is sold.[144] By the same token, one who acquires infringing products in the United States and then resells them in a foreign country does not infringe.[145] In a controversial 1972 decision, the Supreme Court held that one who makes all the parts of a patented device in the United States and sells them for assembly in a foreign country is not a direct infringer, for one has not made, used, or sold the patented device in the United States.[146] Congress responded with the passage of 35 U.S.C. §271(f) in 1984, which makes such activity a direct infringement if it amounts to inducement to complete the assembly abroad.[147]

On the other hand, one who purchases a product abroad infringes a U.S. patent on that product if one uses or sells it in the United States.[148] The use of a patented invention in a foreign vessel, aircraft, or vehicle that is temporarily or accidentally in the United States does not, under certain circumstances, constitute infringement.[149] The

---

ground that the ANDA specification in that case did not define the compound in a manner that directly addressed the issue of infringement. Here, the ANDA specification described a well-defined compound so that the ultimate issue of infringement was straightforward.

[142]*Ortho Pharm Corp. v. Smith*, 959 F.2d 936, 22 USPQ2d 1119 (Fed. Cir. 1992). In *Telectronics Pacing Sys., Inc. v. Ventritex, Inc.*, 982 F.2d 1520, 25 USPQ2d 1196 (Fed. Cir. 1992), the court held that the use of derived test data for fund raising and other business purposes, being in itself a noninfringing act, does not destroy the §271(e)(1) exemption.

[143]35 U.S.C. §100(c).

[144]*Railroad Dynamics, Inc. v. A. Stucki Co.*, 727 F.2d 1506, 220 USPQ 929 (Fed. Cir. 1984).

[145]*Dowagiac Mfg. Co. v. Minnesota Moline Plow*, 235 U.S. 641 (1915). See 35 U.S.C. §271(g) for the converse situation. Neither export from the United States nor use in a foreign country of a product covered by a U.S. patent constitutes infringement. *Johns Hopkins Univ. v. Cellpro Inc.*, 152 F.3d 1342, 47 USPQ2d 1705 (Fed. Cir. 1998). In *Tieleman Food Equip., B.V. v. Stork Gamco, Inc.*, 56 F.3d 1373, 35 USPQ2d 1568 (Fed. Cir. 1995), an injunction prohibited making and selling without reference to geographic area. The infringing defendant made equipment abroad and sold it both abroad and in the United States. The injunction was vacated to the extent that it prohibited acts outside the country. There can be no infringement of a U.S. patent without some nexus to this country.

[146]*Deepsouth Packing Co. v. Laitram Corp.*, 406 U.S. 518, 173 USPQ 769 (1972).

[147]35 U.S.C. §271(f)(1). Section 271(f)(2) likewise condemns the sale of a specially adapted nonstaple component for use in a foreign country. It is not likely that §271(f) otherwise alters the basic principle that there can be no contributory infringement or inducement in the absence of a direct infringement. See *Deepsouth Packing Co. v. Laitram Corp.*, 406 U.S. 518, 173 USPQ 769 (1972).

[148]*Boesch v. Graff*, 133 U.S. 697 (1890). This is so even where the sale abroad is authorized by the laws of that country. However, purchase abroad from the U.S. patent owner would immunize use or resale in the United States.

[149]*Brown v. Dushesne*, 60 U.S. 183 (1857). The *Brown* holding was codified in 35 U.S.C. §272.

use or sale in the United States of products produced abroad by a process that is patented in the United States is treated above in the discussion of process patents.[150]

During the term of the patent. The Uruguay Round Agreements Act amended the patent law to provide that for patents in force on June 8, 1995, the patent term is the greater of 17 years from grant or 20 years from filing. The act also creates a limited safe harbor for persons who commenced acts or made substantial investment toward commission of acts, before June 8, 1995, that become infringing because of the extension of the patent period. Patentees may not assert their traditional patent remedies for infringing acts committed by such persons during the so-called Delta period (between original expiration and extended expiration). In exchange, qualifying persons must pay an equitable remuneration to the patentee.[151]

Issues can arise regarding each of the chronological boundaries of the term of the patent, beginning and end. A predecessor court indicated that use after issuance, of a device acquired or made prior to issuance of a patent covering it, constitutes infringement.[152] But mere possession of a product that becomes covered by a subsequently issued patent does not constitute an infringement of that patent until the product is used, sold, or offered for sale in the United States during the term of the patent.[153] A more compelling case can be made for devices made before, but not used until after, expiration of the patent. In one case the defendant had built all the parts and subassemblies for a machine, but had not tested it as a whole prior to expiration; the machine was shipped on the understanding that it would not be completely assembled and used until after expiration. The court held that infringement had occurred prior to expiration. The machine parts, unassembled, had no useful noninfringing purpose, and the patentee lost the profit on a sale it could have made during the life of the patent.[154]

---

[150]See discussion accompanying notes 6:128–132.

[151]*DuPont Merck Pharm. Co. v. Bristol-Meyers Squibb Co.,* 62 F.3d 1397, 35 USPQ2d 1718 (Fed. Cir. 1995). See 35 U.S.C. §154. The court here was confronted with an extremely complex situation involving the impact and relationship of the patent term extension on and to the ANDA procedure for FDA approval under §271(e)(1). See also *Bristol-Myers Squibb Co. v. Royce Labs., Inc.,* 69 F.3d 1130, 36 USPQ2d 1641 (Fed. Cir. 1995); *Merck & Co. v. Biocraft Labs., Inc.,* 874 F.2d 804, 10 USPQ2d 1843 (Fed. Cir. 1989).

[152]*Cohen v. United States,* 487 F.2d 525, 179 USPQ 859 (Ct. Cl. 1973); *Coakwell v. United States,* 372 F.2d 508, 153 USPQ 307 (Ct. Cl. 1967). A different result may obtain, however, where the device is acquired from, or made with the consent of, the prospective patentee.

[153]*Johns Hopkins Univ. v. Cellpro Inc.,* 152 F.3d 1342, 47 USPQ2d 1705 (Fed. Cir. 1998).

[154]*Paper Converting Mach. Co. v. Magna-Graphics Corp.,* 745 F.2d 11, 223 USPQ 591 (Fed. Cir. 1984). Compare *Deepsouth Packing Co. v. Laitram Corp.,* 406 U.S. 518, 173 USPQ 769 (1972). See also *Roche Prods., Inc. v. Bolar Pharm. Co.,* 733 F.2d 858, 221 USPQ 937 (Fed. Cir. 1984). In *Joy Technologies, Inc. v. Flakt, Inc.,* 6 F.3d 770, 28 USPQ2d 1378 (Fed. Cir. 1993), the defendant was enjoined from building or contracting to build plants that would be used to infringe the patented method after the patent expired. The Federal Circuit vacated the injunction and remanded to permit the district court to fashion an injunction that would prevent infringement during the term of the patent, e.g., completion of a plant that could and might be used during the term of the patent. The court seemed to be willing to permit such

(b) Repair versus Reconstruction

In its famous *Aro I* decision,[155] the Supreme Court reaffirmed the undoubted right of the lawful owner of a patented device to preserve its fitness for further use by repairing it. The high Court also gave lip service to its much earlier *Cotton-Tie* decision,[156] where it had held that reconstruction of a patented device, to the point of a second creation of the patented invention, was not legitimate repair, but unlawful direct infringement. The distinction is that the law entitles the purchaser of a patented apparatus to repair and replace worn or broken parts, but replacement that amounts to a second creation of the patented entity is not permissible.[157]

The decisions of the lower courts, and the Supreme Court, between *Aro I* and *Cotton-Tie* have shed little light on the supposed distinction between lawful repair and unlawful reconstruction. Decisions since *Aro I,* if anything, have clouded the view. A comprehensive analysis of the decisions is beyond the scope of this work.[158]

The Federal Circuit agrees that even an unconditional sale of a patented device is subject to the prohibition against reconstruction of the thing patented. A purchaser's right to use a patented device does not extend to reconstructing it, for reconstruction is deemed analogous to construction of a new device. However, repair is permissible.[159] The first case to reach the court that presented substantive repair/reconstruction issues was an easy one, and the court's opinion was quite properly circumscribed as a result.[160] The case involved frequent replacement of worn cutting disks in a patented tomato harvesting mechanism. The court clearly felt that the patentee was attempting to extend its patent rights in the harvester combination to cover the unpatented cutting disks and concluded that the accused activity was legitimate repair.

The teaching of this case is simply that the legal distinction between repair and reconstruction is not affected by whether the element of the combination that has been replaced is an essential or distinguishing part of the invention. As the court observed, a license to use a patented combination (which every purchaser gets) includes

---

an injunction if there were no way to disable the equipment so that direct infringement of the patented method could not occur prior to expiration. It distinguished *Paper Converting* on the ground that the present case involved a patented method, while in *Paper Converting* the defendant had made all parts, tested subassemblies, and then sold the patented apparatus disassembled, with an agreement that it would not be finally assembled until after the patent expired.

[155] *Aro Mfg. Co. v. Convertible Top Replacement Co.,* 365 U.S. 336, 128 USPQ 354 (1961).

[156] *American Cotton-Tie Co. v. Simmons,* 106 U.S. 89 (1882).

[157] *Lummus Indus., Inc. v. D.M. & E. Corp.,* 862 F.2d 267, 8 USPQ2d 1983 (Fed. Cir. 1988). The court approved a jury finding that replacing cutter reels in an apparatus for cutting fibers, in order to change the length of the fibers, is impermissible reconstruction.

[158] See Chisum, *Patents,* §16.03(3) for a review of the authorities.

[159] *Mallinckrodt, Inc. v. Medipart, Inc.,* 976 F.2d 700, 24 USPQ2d 1173 (Fed. Cir. 1992).

[160] *Porter v. Farmers Supply Serv., Inc.,* 790 F.2d 882, 229 USPQ 814 (Fed. Cir. 1986).

the right to preserve its fitness for use so far as it may be affected by wear or breakage. A licensed user therefore may replace any element no matter how essential it may be to the patented combination, as long as the replaced element is not itself separately claimed.[161] The Federal Circuit feels that the Supreme Court has taken an expansive view of conduct that constitutes permissible repair of a patented combination of unpatented elements. Thus the size or relative importance of the replacement part to the patented combination is not relevant when determining whether conduct constitutes repair or reconstruction. Nor is the doctrine of repair limited to temporary or minor repairs. It encompasses any repair that is necessary for the maintenance of the use of the whole of the patented combination through replacement of a spent, unpatented element.[162]

The court seems to have rejected economic spentness as an analytical tool. Objective economic decisions by the user, when it repairs or scraps a device, have no bearing on whether the device is "spent" under *Aro I*.[163] The use of a production-line method of rebuilding cannot convert permissible repair to impermissible reconstruction. Disassembly of the patented combination by a production rebuilder does not constitute voluntary destruction of the patented combination so that it becomes spent.[164]

The second repair/reconstruction case to reach the Federal Circuit illustrated this principle very well. Damages had already been paid in full by the defendant, and it had thus received an implied license, extending throughout the useful life of the infringing devices,

---

[161]*Porter v. Farmers Supply Serv., Inc.*, 790 F.2d 882, 229 USPQ 814 (Fed. Cir. 1986). See also *Everpure, Inc. v. Cuno, Inc.*, 875 F.2d 300, 10 USPQ2d 1855 (Fed. Cir. 1989).

[162]*Sage Prods., Inc. v. Devon Indus., Inc.*, 45 F.3d 1575, 33 USPQ2d 1765 (Fed. Cir. 1995). The device in question was a system for disposing of sharp medical instruments, including an outer enclosure and a removable inner container intended to be disposed of when full. The patentee did not argue that replacing a damaged inner container is reconstruction. Rather, it maintained that a genuine dispute existed about whether undamaged containers that were filled with medical waste were in fact spent, used up, or in need of repair at all as a result of being filled with medical waste. The court denied ever having said that an element is spent only when it is impossible to reuse it. Instead, it indicated that when it is neither practical nor feasible to continue using an element that is intended to be replaced, the element is effectively spent. The patentee also argued that, inasmuch as the claims did not require the inner container to be disposable, but only removable, it would be impermissible reconstruction to supply containers in a system used to deal with waste that is not hazardous. The court did not completely reject that position, but held that the facts did not bear it out. With all respect, this decision is not very instructive. In a later case, *Kendall Co. v. Progressive Med. Tech., Inc.*, 85 F.3d 1570, 38 USPQ2d 1917 (Fed. Cir. 1996), the result seemed to be a logical extension of *Sage*. The claim covered a medical device including a pair of pressure sleeves, a pump for supplying pressurized fluid to the sleeves, and connecting tubes. The patentee sold its system with the notice that the sleeves were for a single patient use only. The defendant provided replacement sleeves for use with the patentee's system. The court found no infringement even though the sleeves were not worn out when replaced. It observed that premature repair is the business of the purchaser of the product, who owns it, rather than the patentee, who sold it.

[163]*Dana Corp. v. American Precision Co.*, 827 F.2d 755, 3 USPQ2d 1852 (Fed. Cir. 1987). In a dictum, the court indicated that caution should be exercised in placing values, economic or otherwise, on the elements of a patented combination. *FMC Corp. v. Up-Right, Inc.*, 21 F.3d 1073, 30 USPQ2d 1361 (Fed. Cir. 1994).

[164]*Dana Corp. v. American Precision Co.*, 827 F.2d 755, 3 USPQ2d 1852 (Fed. Cir. 1987).

to sell its customers unpatented spare parts attributable to repair of those devices.[165] But the court distinguished between repair parts and "reconstruction" parts. Sale of spare parts for reconstruction, or possibly at the onset of the sale as mere extra parts, or spare parts connected with new, unlicensed machine sales, may be an infringement.[166] The doctrine of permissible repair allows one lawfully using a patented combination to preserve and maintain the combination by making repairs or replacing unpatented component parts necessary for continued use. Replacement of worn or spent parts in a patented combination constitutes repair not reconstruction.[167] The court also appears to have rejected an analysis of sequential replacement on the ground that it would be unworkable from a practical standpoint. The owner of a machine would have to reevaluate just how much of the machine is made up of nonoriginal parts each time the machine is repaired. Thus, sequential replacement of parts is permissible repair so long as no single instance of repair does not in and of itself constitute reconstruction.[168]

There are a number of factors that must be considered in determining whether a defendant has made a new article after the original has become spent, including the nature of the defendant's actions, the nature of the device and how it is designed (i.e., whether one of the components of the patented combination has a shorter useful life than the whole), whether a market has developed to manufacture or

---

[165]*King Instr. Corp. v. Otari Corp.,* 814 F.2d 1560, 2 USPQ2d 1201 (Fed. Cir. 1987). In *Carborundum Co. v. Molten Metal Equip. Innovations,* 72 F.3d 872, 37 USPQ2d 1169 (Fed. Cir. 1995), the district court enjoined the infringer from supplying repair parts for devices on which it had already paid damages. The infringer argued that it had an implied license to repair as a result of the payment of damages. The patentee argued that the injunction was necessary because it would otherwise be deprived of compensation for future repair parts sales. The court analyzed the question this way: once a patentee has been fully compensated by an infringer for the use of a device embodying the patented invention, a court may not grant an injunction preventing the infringer from using or repairing that device. But here the patentee had proved entitlement to lost profits for the sale of pumps and what the trial court referred to as convoyed sales of repair parts. The patentee did not attempt to obtain compensation for future repair parts because of the injunction. Thus, a modification of the injunction would allow the sale of future repair parts for which the patentee had received no compensation. Note that the court indicated that this result is not inconsistent with *King v. Otari,* above.

[166]*King Instr. Corp. v. Otari Corp.,* 814 F.2d 1560, 2 USPQ2d 1201 (Fed. Cir. 1987). See *Standard Havens Prods., Inc. v. Gencor Indus., Inc.,* 953 F.2d 1360, 21 USPQ2d 1321 (Fed. Cir. 1992).

[167]*Everpure, Inc. v. Cuno, Inc.,* 875 F.2d 300, 10 USPQ2d 1855 (Fed. Cir. 1989). The patent claimed a combination of a head and an attached filter cartridge. The neck of the cartridge was removably inserted into the head and had channels for directing fluid to and from a filter sealed within the cartridge. The patentee sold entire cartridges for periodic replacement during the much longer life of the head, while the accused infringer supplied, free of charge to its customers, an adaptor that enabled attachment of the accused cartridge to the patentee's head. The court held that this was repair not reconstruction, emphasizing the fact that it was the patentee who chose to design the system so that the entire cartridge, including its sealed neck and filter, is spent when the filter wears out.

[168]*FMC Corp. v. Up-Right, Inc.,* 21 F.3d 1073, 30 USPQ2d 1361 (Fed. Cir. 1994). The patented grape harvesters had a majority of their parts sequentially replaced over the years due to wear or breakage. The court passed the difficult issue of how much repair to a grape harvester made altogether at any single point in time would have risen to the level of reconstruction of a spent harvester.

service the part at issue, and objective evidence of the intent of the patentee.[169] But a noncontractual intention is simply the seller's hope or wish, rather than an enforceable restriction.[170]

The court has specifically passed the question whether it would be illegal as a misuse to license repair parts. A license called for royalty on "replacement parts sold by licensee for the reconstruction of" patented compound bows. The argument was that this amounted to misuse where royalty was paid on parts used for repair rather than reconstruction. The lower court held that acceptance of royalties on repair parts was the result of mistake and an inability to differentiate between repair and reconstruction parts in the context of the claimed bows, and not the result of an intent to extend the patent monopoly to unpatented articles. The Federal Circuit found this acceptable. [171]

The rule that there can be no contributory infringement in the absence of direct infringement applies in full force in the context of repair vs. reconstruction. Thus, for the sale of replacement parts to have constituted contributory infringement, the use of a device containing those replacement parts must have constituted direct infringement.[172] On the other side of the coin, even repair is infringement if the owner or user is not authorized; for example, the traditional rule is that repair of an unlicensed device constitutes infringement.[173] It is doubtful, however, whether this applies to the government. It would seem that the United States may repair whatever it has, even if possession is unauthorized.[174]

---

[169]*Aktiebolag v. E.J. Co.*, 121 F.3d 669, 43 USPQ2d 1620 (Fed. Cir. 1997). In this case, the patent claim covered a drill with a unique carbide tip geometry. The defendant resharpened the patented drills and the patentee did not charge that to be infringement. However, when the tip was chipped or cracked, or sufficiently worn down so that it could not be resharpened, the defendant sometimes replaced the carbide tip. The parties agreed that in such cases the drill had reached the end of its useful life unless it could be retipped. On these facts, the court held that the defendant was guilty of infringing reconstruction.

[170]*Hewlett-Packard Co. v. Repeat-O-Type Stencil*, 123 F.3d 1445, 43 USPQ2d 1650 (Fed. Cir. 1997). The court held it was not impermissible reconstruction, where the defendant bought new Hewlett-Packard ink jet cartridges, modified them so they could be refilled by the purchaser, and resold them. One important factor was that Hewlett-Packard engineered the structure so that all its components would last beyond the life of a single reservoir of ink. In other words, the components were not "spent" once the ink ran dry. The fact that it intended that the cartridges not be refillable does not create a limitation on the right of a purchaser to use, sell, or modify a patented product as long as a reconstruction of the patented combination is avoided.

[171]*Allen Archery, Inc. v. Browning Mfg. Co.*, 819 F.2d 1087, 2 USPQ2d 1490 (Fed. Cir. 1987). In *Tieleman Food Equip., B.V. v. Stork Gamco, Inc.*, 56 F.3d 1373, 35 USPQ2d 1568 (Fed. Cir. 1995), an injunction prohibited the infringer from selling "replacement parts." To the extent that the parts were separately patented, this was proper. But to the extent that it prohibited sales of unpatented replacement parts for repair of infringing devices for which the patentee had already been compensated by money damages, it required modification.

[172]*FMC Corp. v. Up-Right, Inc.*, 21 F.3d 1073, 30 USPQ2d 1361 (Fed. Cir. 1994).

[173]*Mallinckrodt, Inc. v. Medipart, Inc.*, 976 F.2d 700, 24 USPQ2d 1173 (Fed. Cir. 1992). In this case the patented devices were sold for one use only, under a label license. The defendant reconditioned the devices for a second use by the original purchaser. Thus, if the restriction to a single use is found valid (upon remand), then the reconditioning, whether or not reconstruction, would amount to infringement.

[174]See *Motorola, Inc. v. United States*, 729 F.2d 765, 221 USPQ 297 (Fed. Cir. 1984).

Whether an act is repair or reconstruction is a question of law that is reviewed de novo.[175]

(c) Implied License

A license is, of course, an affirmative defense to a claim of patent infringement. The traditional express license—a contractual device—is explored in Chapter 7. But it seems appropriate to consider here, in this chapter dealing with infringement, the impact of license rights implied by operation of law.

All or part of the right to exclude may be waived by granting a license, which may be express or implied. Although most licenses are express, a license may be implied and an implied license, like an express license, is a defense to patent infringement.[176] In patent law, an implied license merely signifies a patentee's waiver of the statutory right to exclude others. Such licenses arise by acquiescence, by conduct, by equitable estoppel, or by legal estoppel. These labels describe not different kinds of licenses, but rather different categories of conduct that lead to the same conclusion: an implied license. The label denotes the rationale for reaching the legal result.[177]

Generally, when a seller sells a product without restriction, it in effect promises the purchaser that it will not interfere with the purchaser's full enjoyment of the product purchased. The buyer has an implied license under any patents of the seller that dominate the product or any uses of the product to which the parties might reasonably contemplate the product will be put.[178] The notion that a license may be implied in the circumstances surrounding the sale of, or other authorization to use, a patented invention has its roots deep in fundamental patent law concepts. Perhaps the most important of these basic principles is that expressed in the Supreme Court's *Univis Lens*[179] decision: the first authorized sale of an article embodying a patented invention exhausts the patent rights in that article. In other words, the purchaser of a patented invention has the right to use it, and to preserve its fitness for its intended use, without interference

---

[175]*Aktiebolag v. E.J. Co.*, 121 F.3d 669, 43 USPQ2d 1620, 1622 (Fed. Cir. 1997).

[176]*Carborundum Co. v. Molten Metal Equip. Innovations,* 72 F.3d 872, 37 USPQ2d 1169 (Fed. Cir. 1995).

[177]*Wang Labs., Inc. v. Mitsubishi Elec. Am., Inc.,* 103 F.3d 1571, 41 USPQ2d 1263 (Fed. Cir. 1997).

[178]*Hewlett-Packard Co. v. Repeat-O-Type Stencil*, 123 F.3d 1445, 43 USPQ2d 1650 (Fed. Cir. 1997). The authority to use and sell a purchased device, however, does not include the right to make a new device or to reconstruct one that has been spent. *Id.* In this case, the defendant bought new Hewlett-Packard ink jet cartridges, modified them so they could be refilled by the purchaser, and resold them. This did not amount to infringement of a method patent directed to providing ink reservoirs with ink. The sale of the cartridge carried with it an implied license to use it in a manner that might infringe the method patent, despite the fact that Hewlett-Packard did not intend that the cartridges should be refilled with ink.

[179]*United States v. Univis Lens Co.*, 316 U.S. 241, 53 USPQ 404 (1942).

from the patentee.[180] The Federal Circuit seems to have embraced this idea without reservation.[181] To enforce the contracts of the patentee, the law may imply a license where a patent holder sells or authorizes the sale of a patent product. Thus an authorized sale of a patented product places that product beyond the reach of the patent. In return for this implied license, a patent holder receives a reward for inventive work in the first sale of the patented product. Patentees are entitled to but one royalty for the patented invention.[182] A purchaser of licensed products is free to use or resell the products. Such further use and sale is beyond the reach of the patent statutes under *Univis Lens*.[183] This long-standing principle applies similarly to a sale of a patented product manufactured by a licensee acting within the scope of its license.[184]

---

[180]*Porter v. Farmers Supply Serv., Inc.,* 790 F.2d 882, 229 USPQ 814 (Fed. Cir. 1986). Thus, sale of items especially adapted for use in a patented process is not contributory infringement or inducement, where the purchaser has an implied license to practice the patented process by virtue of authorized ownership of a special machine. There is no contributory infringement without direct infringement. *Met-Coil Sys. Corp. v. Korners Unlimited, Inc.,* 803 F.2d 684, 231 USPQ 474 (Fed. Cir. 1986).

[181]*Bandag, Inc. v. Al Bolser's Tire Stores, Inc.,* 750 F.2d 903, 223 USPQ 982 (Fed. Cir. 1984).

[182]*McCoy v. Mitsuboshi Cutlery, Inc.,* 67 F.3d 917, 36 USPQ2d 1289 (Fed. Cir. 1995). In some cases, the law implies a license where the patent holder does not authorize the sale of a patented product—an involuntary sale. Here the patentee contracted with the defendant to have the defendant produce 150,000 patented knives. When the defendant offered the knives, the patentee refused to accept or pay for them. The defendant repeatedly advised the patentee of its intent to sell the knives to mitigate damages, and attempted to negotiate, but the patentee remained silent. There was no suggestion that the knives were defective. Under the Texas version of the UCC, a seller is entitled to resell goods upon a buyer's wrongful refusal to pay. On these facts, the court held that an implied license properly enforces the patentee's promise to pay for the knives, reflects the defendant's commercial efforts to resolve the matter, and recognizes its rights to mitigate under Texas UCC law.

[183]*Intel Corp. v. ULSI Sys. Tech., Inc.,* 995 F.2d 1566, 27 USPQ2d 1136 (Fed. Cir. 1993); *Intel Corp. v. United States ITC,* 946 F.2d 821, 20 USPQ2d 1161 (Fed. Cir. 1991).

[184]*Intel Corp. v. ULSI Sys. Tech., Inc.,* 995 F.2d 1566, 27 USPQ2d 1136 (Fed. Cir. 1993). What is authorized is not always an easy question to answer. Here H-P had a license from Intel and was acting as a foundry for ULSI to produce chips. The court found that the foundry contract was not simply one in which H-P was to provide fabrication services, but actually involved the sale of chips from H-P to ULSI. The court rejected several arguments: (1) that the sale of chips by H-P constituted a de facto sublicense prohibited by the agreement; and (2) that the licensed seller of a patented product must own intellectual property rights to the product in order for there to be a sale (apparently the chip was based on a ULSI design not an H-P design). There was a vigorous dissent. In *Intel Corp. v. United States ITC,* 946 F.2d 821, 20 USPQ2d 1161 (Fed. Cir. 1991), Sanyo was permitted under its license from Intel to make, use, and sell "Sanyo" products. The defendant contracted with Sanyo to serve as a foundry to make products for the defendant to sell. The court held that the foundry activity was not authorized and therefore the defendant's resale was infringement. In *Cyrix Corp. v. SGS-Thompson Microelectronics, Inc.,* 77 F.3d 1381, 37 USPQ2d 1884 (Fed. Cir. 1996), two situations were presented. Under the first, a license from Intel to IBM granted the right to sell "IBM Licensed Products." IBM acted as a foundry for Cyrix, producing products that Cyrix designed. The court found no liability. In the second, another Intel licensee, ST, initially acted as a foundry for Cyrix-designed products, but then farmed the work out to an Italian affiliate and resold to Cyrix. There was a "have-made" clause in ST's agreement with Intel, and also a prohibition against sublicenses. The court also resolved this aspect against Intel. These foundry cases are certain to be highly fact dependent and almost always turn on the language of the express contract. In *Unidisco, Inc. v. Schattner,* 824 F.2d 965, 3 USPQ2d 1439 (Fed. Cir. 1987), which involved an exclusive license with no right to sublicense, the licensee appointed an exclusive distributor and sold the licensed product to the distributor for resale. The patentee

The doctrines of legal estoppel and equitable estoppel have been applied by courts to imply a license. Legal estoppel is merely shorthand for saying that a grantor of a property right or interest cannot derogate from the granted right by its own subsequent acts. The rationale for that is to estop the grantor from taking back that for which it received consideration.[185] A formal finding of equitable estoppel is not required as a prerequisite to a legal conclusion of implied license. That would remove all distinction between the doctrines. The primary difference between the estoppel analysis in implied license cases and the analysis in equitable estoppel cases is that implied license looks for an affirmative grant of consent or permission to make, use, or sell, i.e., a license. Equitable estoppel, on the other hand, focuses on misleading conduct suggesting that the patentee will not enforce patent rights.[186]

A license is implied by full compensation.[187] Thus, an infringer who has paid damages for its original infringement receives an implied license, extending throughout the useful life of the original machines, to supply customers with repair parts.[188] In the absence of a showing that a lost profits award would not fully compensate for infringement, a patentee is not entitled to enjoin further use of infringing devices.[189]

It is important, here as elsewhere, to focus upon just what is the invention that is claimed in the patent. Thus, where the patent claims a method, the sale of equipment for performing that method does not exhaust any rights in the patent.[190] There are two requirements for the grant of a license implied by the sale of nonpatented equipment used to practice a patented invention. First, the equipment involved must have no noninfringing uses. Second, the circumstances of the sale must plainly indicate that the grant of a license should be inferred. The inquiry does not end there, however. After it is determined that a license should be implied, the court must look further to the

---

sued the distributor for patent infringement, claiming that the arrangement amounted to a sublicense in violation of the agreement. The court disagreed. Thus, when the distributor acquired the licensed product from an authorized seller—the exclusive licensee—it also acquired the right to resell the product and its resales therefore were not infringing.

[185]*Spindelfabrik S., S. & G. GmbH v. Schubert & Salzer Mas. Ak.,* 829 F.2d 1075, 4 USPQ2d 1044 (Fed. Cir. 1987). The facts are interesting. The defendant infringer got a license under patent A. The patentee then sold patent A to plaintiff, who also owned patent B. Defendant argued that because it would have had an implied license under patent B if that patent had been owned by the original owner of patent A, the plaintiff was legally estopped to charge infringement of patent B. Not so, says court, clearly rejecting defendant's theory that plaintiff had "stepped into the shoes" of the original owner. See also *Wang Labs. Inc. v. Mitsubishi Elec. Am., Inc.,* 103 F.3d 1571, 41 USPQ2d 1263 (Fed. Cir. 1997).

[186]*Wang Labs. Inc. v. Mitsubishi Elec. Am., Inc.,* 103 F.3d 1571, 41 USPQ2d 1263 (Fed. Cir. 1997).

[187]*Stickle v. Heublein, Inc.,* 716 F.2d 1550, 219 USPQ 377 (Fed. Cir. 1983).

[188]*King Instr. Corp. v. Otari Corp.,* 814 F.2d 1560, 2 USPQ2d 1201 (Fed. Cir. 1987). That license does not extend to "reconstruction" parts. *Id.*

[189]*Amstar Corp. v. Envirotech Corp.,* 823 F.2d 1538, 3 USPQ2d 1412 (Fed. Cir. 1987).

[190]*Bandag, Inc. v. Al Bolser's Tire Stores, Inc.,* 750 F.2d 903, 223 USPQ 982 (Fed. Cir. 1984).

circumstances of the sale to determine the scope of the implied license. This determination must be based on what the parties reasonably intended as to the scope of the implied license based on the circumstances of the sale. One party's unilateral expectations as to the scope of the implied license are irrelevant.[191]

The cases are illustrative. A purchaser of toothpaste containing a desensitizing agent was held to receive an implied license to practice a claimed method of desensitizing teeth by applying that agent.[192] A contract that expressly granted the right to manufacture a product, but did not address any patents by which the product is made, was held to imply a license under a patent covering another product used to make the licensed product.[193] The law also implies a license to practice a claimed method to one who purchases a claimed apparatus for use in that method.[194] On the other hand, the fact that alternatives to infringement are unavailable or unreasonable might aid in establishing an implied license, but such a license does not result from the sale of equipment having uses that do not infringe, even if the use is only as replacement parts.[195] When a party argues that the sale of a device carries with it an implied license to use that device in practicing a patented invention, the party must show that the purchased device has no noninfringing uses.[196]

---

[191]*Carborundum Co. v. Molten Metal Equip. Innovations,* 72 F.3d 872, 37 USPQ2d 1169 (Fed. Cir. 1995). Here the patentee sold an unpatented pump, the only use for which was in its patented system. It is clear that a license was implied under the patent, and the pump purchasers were free to purchase the other elements of the patented system from any source. Otherwise the pump was worthless. However, the implied license did not extend for the life of the patent, but rather for the life of the pump. Had the patentee sold the entire system, that sale would have created an implied license for the useful life of the apparatus, and would have provided the right to repair it. In such case the patentee's customers would have had the right to purchase the pump from another source. But in choosing to sell only the pump, the patentee chose to forego revenue from sales of other elements of the system. A patentee is generally entitled to determine how it wishes to commercialize its invention in order to optimize its economic benefit from the patent grant. It should be noted that the court dismissed an argument that restrictions to an implied license must be express, on the ground that limiting an implied license created by the sale of a component to the life of that component is not a restriction. It is inherent in the nature of the product that is sold. A patentee is not required to express restrictions in conjunction with the sale of a device when the excluded activities are clearly beyond the scope of the implied license. It should also be noted that there was evidence of an upfront payment, but the court in a dictum treated this as more akin to a first-time engineering charge rather than a one-time royalty payment for an implied license to practice the invention for the life of the patent. See also *Met-Coil Sys. Corp. v. Korners Unlimited, Inc.,* 803 F.2d 684, 231 USPQ 474 (Fed. Cir. 1986).

[192]*Hodosh v. Block Drug. Co.,* 833 F.2d 1575, 4 USPQ2d 1935 (Fed. Cir. 1987).

[193]*Ortho Pharm. Corp. v. Genetics Inst., Inc.,* 52 F.3d 1026, 34 USPQ2d 1444 (Fed. Cir. 1995). The court applied California law.

[194]*Devices for Med., Inc. v. Boehl,* 822 F.2d 1062, 3 USPQ2d 1288 (Fed. Cir. 1987).

[195]*Bandag, Inc. v. Al Bolser's Tire Stores, Inc.,* 750 F.2d 903, 223 USPQ 982 (Fed. Cir. 1984). The court seems minded to insist that the purchaser be stuck with a virtual "white elephant" before a license will be implied.

[196]*Glass Equip. Dev. Inc. v. Besten Inc.,* 174 F.3d 1337, 50 USPQ2d 1300 (Fed. Cir. 1999). Here the district court improperly limited the analysis to the time of the summary judgment motion, effectively ignoring prior noninfringing uses. It also erred in requiring that a noninfringing use had to be the most profitable alternative.

The burden of proving that an implied license exists is on the party asserting implied license as a defense to infringement.[197] The existence of an implied license is a legal question,[198] and the court therefore has plenary review.[199] Whether express or implied, a license is a contract governed by ordinary principles of state contract law.[200]

An implied license can arise from the "entire course of conduct," but this requires something akin to equitable estoppel. Such a license cannot arise out of the unilateral expectations or even reasonable hopes of one party, unless the patentee gave the infringer some basis for such expectations at the time they were formed.[201] The necessary findings are that (1) a relationship existed between the patentee and the accused infringer, (2) within that relationship, the patentee had granted a right to use its inventions, (3) the patentee received valuable consideration for that grant of right, (4) the patentee denied that an implied license existed, and (5) the patentee's statements and conduct created the impression that it consented to the accused infringer making, using, or selling the patented inventions.[202]

In one case a patentee had contracted to provide machines to the defendant but failed in an attempt to supply them. The defendant covered the contract by purchasing improved machines from another source. The court held no implied license to obtain the improved machines, because those were not the machines the patentee contracted to provide.[203] In another case, the court held that postpurchase notices to customers, indicating that no implied license to practice the patented process was conferred by virtue of the machine purchase, was of no avail. Such notices were not part of the circumstances at the time of the sale, when the implied license would have arisen. After-the-fact notices are of no use in ascertaining the intent of the patentee and its customers at the time of the sale.[204]

---

[197]*Augustine Med. Inc. v. Progressive Dynamics Inc.*, 194 F.3d 1367, 52 USPQ2d 1515 (Fed. Cir. 1999); *Carborundum Co. v. Molten Metal Equip. Innovations*, 72 F.3d 872, 37 USPQ2d 1169 (Fed. Cir. 1995); *Met-Coil Sys. Corp. v. Korners Unlimited, Inc.*, 803 F.2d 684, 231 USPQ 474 (Fed. Cir. 1986); *Bandag, Inc. v. Al Bolser's Tire Stores, Inc.*, 750 F.2d 903, 223 USPQ 982 (Fed. Cir. 1984).

[198]*Met-Coil Sys. Corp. v. Korners Unlimited, Inc.*, 803 F.2d 684, 231 USPQ 474 (Fed. Cir. 1986).

[199]*Carborundum Co. v. Molten Metal Equip. Innovations*, 72 F.3d 872, 37 USPQ2d 1169 (Fed. Cir. 1995). The implied license defense is an issue of law that is reviewed de novo. *Augustine Med. Inc. v. Progressive Dynamics Inc.*, 194 F.3d 1367, 52 USPQ2d 1515 (Fed. Cir. 1999); *Glass Equip. Dev. Inc. v. Besten Inc.*, 174 F.3d 1337, 50 USPQ2d 1300 (Fed. Cir. 1999); *Wang Labs., Inc. v. Mitsubishi Elec. Am., Inc.*, 103 F.3d 1571, 41 USPQ2d 1263 (Fed. Cir. 1997).

[200]*McCoy v. Mitsuboshi Cutlery, Inc.*, 67 F.3d 917, 36 USPQ2d 1289 (Fed. Cir. 1995).

[201]*Bandag, Inc. v. Al Bolser's Tire Stores, Inc.*, 750 F.2d 903, 223 USPQ 982 (Fed. Cir. 1984); *Stickle v. Heublein, Inc.*, 716 F.2d 1550, 219 USPQ 377 (Fed. Cir. 1983). See also *McCoy v. Mitsuboshi Cutlery, Inc.*, 67 F.3d 917, 36 USPQ2d 1289 (Fed. Cir. 1995). The court has even suggested that failure to obtain a legal opinion on infringement might well negate any reliance that could form a basis for implied license. *Bandag, Inc. v. Al Bolser's Tire Stores, Inc.*, 750 F.2d 903, 223 USPQ 982 (Fed. Cir. 1984).

[202]*Wang Labs., Inc. v. Mitsubishi Elec. Am., Inc.*, 103 F.3d 1571, 41 USPQ2d 1263 (Fed. Cir. 1997).

[203]*Stickle v. Heublein, Inc.*, 716 F.2d 1550, 219 USPQ 377 (Fed. Cir. 1983).

[204]*Met-Coil Sys. Corp. v. Korners Unlimited, Inc.*, 803 F.2d 684, 231 USPQ 474 (Fed. Cir. 1986). The legality of such a notice even at the time of sale is open to question. It could be

A shopright has been described as a form of implied license, founded on estoppel or acquiescence.[205]

§6.3 The Doctrine of Equivalents

If accused matter falls clearly within the patent claim, infringement is made out and that is the end of it.[206] But what if the accused product or process does not employ every last literal detail of the claimed invention? Is there any protection for the patentee?

The doctrine of equivalents (DOE)[207] evolved as an affirmative response to this question. This section will examine the doctrine as it is applied by the Federal Circuit and will explore the principal limitations on the doctrine: changes in technology, the state of the prior art, and the prosecution history of the patent. The last—prosecution history estoppel—is the subject of a separate subsection, §6.3(b).

(a) Equivalents in General

Although the requirements of literal infringement are not met, infringement may still be found if the structures are equivalent. The classical test for equivalence was whether the accused device performs substantially the same function in substantially the same way to obtain substantially the same result.[208] So, too, in the case of a composition, where the accused substance avoids literal infringement by

---

argued that such a notice would have the effect of requiring the combined purchase of a staple (the machine) and a presumed nonstaple (the items used with the machine).

[205]*McElmurry v. Arkansas Power & Light Co.*, 995 F.2d 1576, 27 USPQ2d 1129 (Fed. Cir. 1993); *Lariscey v. United States*, 949 F.2d 1137, 20 USPQ2d 1845 (Fed. Cir. 1991). Shoprights are discussed in §7.1(b).

[206]*Graver Tank & Mfg. Co. v. Linde Air Prods. Co.*, 339 U.S. 605, 85 USPQ 328 (1950). This is the classical equivalents decision.

[207]The court appears to be willing to use the terms "equivalents" and "equivalence" interchangeably, as in "doctrine of equivalence." See *Nestier Corp. v. Menasha Corp.*, 739 F.2d 1576, 222 USPQ 747 (Fed. Cir. 1984). The convention adopted in this book is "doctrine of equivalents," more by habit and tradition than out of any notion of propriety. The court also occasionally employs "DOE" as a convenient, space-saving acronym. See, e.g., *Zodiac Pool Care Inc. v. Hoffinger Indus. Inc.*, 206 F.3d 1408, 54 USPQ2d 1141 (Fed. Cir. 2000). That acronym is often used in this chapter as well.

[208]E.g., *Read Corp. v. Portec, Inc.*, 970 F.2d 816, 23 USPQ2d 1426 (Fed. Cir. 1992); *Pennwalt Corp. v. Durand-Wayland, Inc.*, 833 F.2d 931, 4 USPQ2d 1737 (Fed. Cir. 1987); *Stewart-Warner Corp. v. City of Pontiac*, 767 F.2d 1563, 226 USPQ 676 (Fed. Cir. 1985). In *Sofamor Danek Group, Inc. v. DePuy-Motech, Inc.*, 74 F.3d 1216, 37 USPQ2d 1529 (Fed. Cir. 1996), a panel adopted the acronym FWR to describe the function-way-result test. Whether this will be picked up by others remains to be seen. The doctrine of equivalents is not a license to ignore claim limitations. Under the doctrine, the accused device and the claimed invention cannot work in substantially the same way if a limitation or its equivalent is missing. *Dolly, Inc. v. Spalding & Evenflo Co.*, 16 F.3d 394, 29 USPQ2d 1767 (Fed. Cir. 1994). Assessing equivalency involves a determination of whether the claimed invention and alleged infringing device, which are necessarily different (else there would be literal infringement), perform substantially the same function in substantially the same way to give the same or substantially the same result. *Perkin-Elmer Corp. v. Computervision Corp.*, 732 F.2d 888, 221 USPQ 669

changing one ingredient, it is appropriate for a court to consider in assessing equivalence whether the changed ingredient has the same purpose, quality, and function as the claimed ingredient. This is in full accord with the basic "function, way and result" test for equivalence.[209]

Analysis of patent infringement entails two inquiries: determination of the scope of the claims, as a matter of law; and the factual finding of whether the properly construed claims encompass the accused structure. This analytical framework applies whether claims are asserted to be infringed literally or by application of the DOE.[210] The court seems willing to pass direct infringement and decide equivalents as an alternative.[211] The implications of this need to be fully explored. For example, does this mean that the court is inclined to regard the two routes of analysis as parts of a single continuum, with direct infringement at one end and no equivalence at the other?[212]

Equivalence is a question of fact, reviewable under the clearly erroneous standard.[213] Faced with a finding of no literal infringement, the patentee's burden becomes one of establishing by a preponderance of the evidence that the accused device performs substantially the same function in substantially the same way to obtain substantially the same result as the claimed invention.[214] In a jury trial, the theory

---

(Fed. Cir. 1984). Equivalence of subsequently developed devices is not established by showing only accomplishment of the same result. *Zygo Corp. v. Wyko Corp.*, 79 F.3d 1563, 38 USPQ2d 1281 (Fed. Cir. 1996); *Texas Instr., Inc. v. United States ITC*, 805 F.2d 1558, 231 USPQ 833 (Fed. Cir. 1986).

[209]*Atlas Powder Co. v. E.I. du Pont & Co.*, 750 F.2d 1569, 224 USPQ 409 (Fed. Cir. 1984).

[210]*Texas Instr., Inc. v. United States ITC*, 805 F.2d 1558, 231 USPQ 833 (Fed. Cir. 1986). See also *Uniroyal, Inc. v. Rudkin-Wiley Corp.*, 939 F.2d 1540, 19 USPQ2d 1432 (Fed. Cir. 1991).

[211]*Under Sea Indus., Inc. v. Dacor Corp.*, 833 F.2d 1551, 4 USPQ2d 1772 (Fed. Cir. 1987).

[212]The transition may be gradual between literal infringement by substantially identical structures and infringement by equivalent structures. *Builders Concrete, Inc. v. Bremerton Concrete Prods. Co.*, 757 F.2d 255, 225 USPQ 240, 241 (Fed. Cir. 1985).

[213]*Insta-Foam Prods., Inc. v. Universal Foam Sys., Inc.*, 906 F.2d 698, 15 USPQ2d 1295 (Fed. Cir. 1990); *Jonsson v. Stanley Works*, 903 F.2d 812, 14 USPQ2d 1863 (Fed. Cir. 1990); *Sun Studs, Inc. v. ATA Equip. Leasing, Inc.*, 872 F.2d 978, 10 USPQ2d 1338 (Fed. Cir. 1989); *Ryco, Inc. v. Ag-Bag Corp.*, 857 F.2d 1418, 8 USPQ2d 1323 (Fed. Cir. 1988); *Uniroyal, Inc. v. Rudkin-Wiley Corp.*, 837 F.2d 1044, 5 USPQ2d 1434 (Fed. Cir. 1988); *Perkin-Elmer Corp. v. Westinghouse Elec. Corp.*, 822 F.2d 1529, 3 USPQ2d 1321 (Fed. Cir. 1987); *Hartness Int'l, Inc. v. Simplimatic Eng'g Co.*, 819 F.2d 1100, 2 USPQ2d 1826 (Fed. Cir. 1987); *Great Northern Corp. v. Davis Core & Pad Co.*, 782 F.2d 159, 228 USPQ 356 (Fed. Cir. 1986); *Shatterproof Glass Corp. v. Libbey-Owens Ford Co.*, 758 F.2d 613, 225 USPQ 634 (Fed. Cir. 1985); *Lemelson v. United States*, 752 F.2d 1538, 224 USPQ 526 (Fed. Cir. 1985); *American Hosp. Supply Corp. v. Travenol Labs., Inc.*, 745 F.2d 1, 223 USPQ 577 (Fed. Cir. 1984); *Radio Steel & Mfg. Co. v. MTD Prods., Inc.*, 731 F.2d 840, 221 USPQ 657 (Fed. Cir. 1984); *Envirotech Corp. v. Al George, Inc.*, 730 F.2d 753, 221 USPQ 473 (Fed. Cir. 1984); *Thomas & Betts Corp. v. Litton Sys., Inc.*, 720 F.2d 1572, 220 USPQ 1 (Fed. Cir. 1983). Questions of the technologic equivalency of a claimed invention and an accused device are not questions of claim construction. They are questions of fact, and require determination by the trier of fact, based on evidence. *Hebert v. Lisle Corp.*, 99 F.3d 1109, 40 USPQ2d 1611 (Fed. Cir. 1996). It is better practice for the trial court to make separate findings on equivalence. *Lemelson v. United States*, 752 F.2d 1538, 224 USPQ 526 (Fed. Cir. 1985). Review of an ITC factual finding on equivalents is under the substantial evidence standard. *Texas Instr., Inc. v. United States ITC*, 988 F.2d 1165, 26 USPQ2d 1018 (Fed. Cir. 1993).

[214]*Datascope Corp. v. SMEC, Inc.*, 776 F.2d 320, 227 USPQ 838 (Fed. Cir. 1985); *Lemelson v. United States*, 752 F.2d 1538, 224 USPQ 526 (Fed. Cir. 1985).

of equivalence is not necessarily included in or a part of literal infringement theory. A jury cannot be expected to make a determination of equivalence absent evidence and argument on the subject.[215] Thus, where a jury is given instructions as to literal infringement but not equivalence, a jury verdict of infringement cannot stand unless the accused device literally infringes the claim.[216]

The court has exhibited a good deal of concern about the way in which equivalents is presented to a jury. Thus, a jury must be separately directed to the proof of each element of the doctrine: function performed, means by which function is performed, and result achieved. The party asserting infringement must present evidence and argument concerning the doctrine and each of its elements. The elements must be presented in the form of particularized testimony and linking argument. Otherwise, a jury is more or less put to sea without guiding charts, and there is too much risk the jury will simply compare the two inventions as to overall similarity.[217] Mere generalized testimony as to equivalence is insufficient as a matter of law to support a jury verdict finding infringement under the DOE. The evidence and argument on the DOE cannot be merely subsumed in plaintiff's case of literal infringement. This is to ensure that a jury is provided with the proper evidentiary foundation from which it may permissibly conclude that a claim limitation has been met by an equivalent.[218]

---

[215]*Nestier Corp. v. Menasha Corp.*, 739 F.2d 1576, 222 USPQ 747 (Fed. Cir. 1984).

[216]*Data Line Corp. v. Micro Techs., Inc.*, 813 F.2d 1196, 1 USPQ2d 2052 (Fed. Cir. 1987).

[217]*Lear Siegler, Inc. v. Sealy Mattress Co.*, 873 F.2d 1422, 10 USPQ2d 1767 (Fed. Cir. 1989). In her remarkable dissent in *Malta v. Schulmerich Carillons, Inc.*, 952 F.2d 1320, 21 USPQ2d 1161 (Fed. Cir. 1991), Judge Newman accuses the majority of creating a new rule for determining equivalents, at least in a jury trial. According to her, the requirement of *Lear Siegler* that there be "particularized testimony and linking argument" has the effect, as employed by the majority, of creating a fourth prong to the function-way-result test: that of "why" a device is equivalent. The court seemed to back away from *Lear Siegler* and *Malta* in *National Presto Indus., Inc. v. West Bend Co.*, 76 F.3d 1185, 37 USPQ2d 1685 (Fed. Cir. 1996), when it indicated that those decisions do not require a particular formulaic exposition of evidence and argument about equivalency by witnesses and lawyers. Shortly thereafter, however, it disavowed any significant retreat from the rule that a patentee must still provide particularized testimony and linking argument as to the insubstantiality of the differences or with respect to the function-way-and result test. *Texas Instr., Inc. v. Cypress Semiconductor Corp.*, 90 F.3d 1558, 39 USPQ2d 1492 (Fed. Cir. 1996). But it is not necessary that expert witnesses opine in terms of the three-part test for equivalency, at least before a body having the expertise of the ITC. *Intel Corp. v. United States ITC*, 946 F.2d 821, 20 USPQ2d 1161 (Fed. Cir. 1991).

[218]*Comark Comm. Inc. v. Harris Corp.*, 156 F.3d 1182, 48 USPQ2d 1001 (Fed. Cir. 1998). In *General Elec. Co. v. Nintendo Co.*, 179 F.3d 1350, 50 USPQ2d 1910 (Fed. Cir. 1999), the court affirmed a summary judgment of noninfringement because the patentee did not present sufficient evidence for a reasonable jury to find infringement under the doctrine of equivalents. In *Dawn Equip. Corp. v. Kentucky Farms Inc.*, 140 F.3d 1009, 46 USPQ2d 1109 (Fed. Cir. 1998), it suggested that district courts might want to consider directing a verdict on equivalents when it appears that a reasonable jury could not find in favor of the patentee.

(i) Purpose of the Doctrine

The DOE was judicially devised to do equity.[219] It is an equitable doctrine intended, in situations where there is no literal infringement but liability is nevertheless appropriate, to prevent what is in essence a pirating of the patentee's invention.[220] To hold a patentee to the precise claim language in all cases could turn the patent grant into a hollow and useless thing.[221] The doctrine was established to make it impossible for the unscrupulous copyist to make unimportant and insubstantial changes and substitutions in the patent that, although adding nothing, would be enough to take the copied matter outside the claim and hence outside the reach of law.[222]

The court has expounded at some length on this theme and sounded an unmistakable note of caution, observing that equivalency is by its nature inimical to the basic precept of patent law that the claims are the measure of the grant. The doctrine, ubiquitous since its origin, exists solely for the equitable purpose of preventing an infringer from stealing the benefit of an invention. To achieve this purpose, equivalency is judicially determined by reviewing the content of the patent, the prior art, and the accused device, and essentially redefining the scope of the claims. This constitutes a deviation from the need of the public to know the precise legal limits of patent protection without recourse to judicial ruling.[223] On the one hand, claims must be particular and distinct so that the public has fair notice of what the patentee and the PTO have agreed constitute the metes and bounds of the claimed invention. Notice permits other parties to avoid actions that infringe the patent and to design around the patent. On the other hand, the patentee should not be deprived of the benefits of his or her patent by competitors who appropriate the sense of an invention while barely avoiding the literal language of the claims. Thus, although designing around patents to make new inventions is encouraged, piracy is not. The DOE emerged to deal with this problem.[224] The incentive to innovation that flows from

---

[219]*Hughes Aircraft Co. v. United States,* 717 F.2d 1351, 219 USPQ 473 (Fed. Cir. 1983).

[220]*Texas Instr., Inc. v. United States ITC,* 988 F.2d 1165, 26 USPQ2d 1018 (Fed. Cir. 1993); *Hormone Res. Found., Inc. v. Genentech, Inc.,* 904 F.2d 1558, 15 USPQ2d 1039 (Fed. Cir. 1990). See also *Miles Labs., Inc. v. Shandon, Inc.,* 997 F.2d 870, 27 USPQ2d 1123 (Fed. Cir. 1993).

[221]*Corning Glass Works v. Sumitomo Elec. U.S.A., Inc.,* 868 F.2d 1, 9 USPQ2d 1962 (Fed. Cir. 1989).

[222]*Yarway Corp. v. Eur-Control USA Inc.,* 775 F.2d 268, 227 USPQ 352 (Fed. Cir. 1985); *Martin v. Barber,* 755 F.2d 1564, 225 USPQ 233 (Fed. Cir. 1985); *Radio Steel & Mfg. Co. v. MTD Prods., Inc.,* 731 F.2d 840, 221 USPQ 657 (Fed. Cir. 1984). The doctrine is also said to be designed to protect inventors from unanticipated equivalents. *Kinzenbaw v. Deere & Co.,* 741 F.2d 383, 222 USPQ 929 (Fed. Cir. 1984).

[223]*Texas Instr., Inc. v. United States ITC,* 805 F.2d 1558, 231 USPQ 833 (Fed. Cir. 1986). The court had previously cautioned against expansion of the doctrine too far, to the point where patent counsel cannot rely at all on what the claims recite when advising a client as to infringement. *Great Northern Corp. v. Davis Core & Pad Co.,* 782 F.2d 159, 228 USPQ 356 (Fed. Cir. 1986).

[224]*London v. Carson Pirie Scott & Co.,* 946 F.2d 1534, 20 USPQ2d 1456 (Fed. Cir. 1991).

inventing around an adversely held patent must be preserved. To the extent that the DOE represents an exception to the requirement that the claims define the metes and bounds of the patent protection, it is only to serve the real purpose of the doctrine, which is to temper unsparing logic and serve the greater interest of justice.[225]

In dealing with the DOE, the court faces a difficult dichotomy. On one side rests the very important necessity of employing the clearest possible wording in preparing the specification and claims of a patent, one of the most difficult legal instruments to draw with accuracy. On the other lies the equally important necessity of determining infringement without the risk of injustice that may result from a blindered focus on words alone. The former, set out in 35 U.S.C. §112, recognizes a competitor's need for precise wording as an aid in avoiding infringement. The latter is called the DOE. Requiring a look at all the words while resisting their tyranny, and requiring, because the claims measure the invention, a look at all claim limitations, the doctrine in a proper case prevents an infringer from stealing the benefits of an invention. In that sense the doctrine recognizes a fact of the real business world: words are not misappropriated, claimed inventions are.[226] Each case in which infringement by equivalents is asserted turns on its facts and requires the trier of fact to balance the competing public policies of avoiding a "fraud on the patent" and the need for reasonable certainty by the public as to the scope of the patent grant.[227]

Though the DOE is designed to do equity and to relieve an inventor from a semantic straitjacket when equity requires, it is not designed to permit wholesale redrafting of a claim to cover nonequivalent devices, i.e., to permit a claim expansion that would encompass more than an insubstantial change.[228] Certainly the doctrine cannot be used to erase meaningful structural and functional limitations of the claim on which the public is entitled to rely in avoiding infringement. Thus where a broad term is employed in one claim, and a narrower term, used with respect to only one embodiment is employed in another claim, the implication is that infringement of the second claim can be avoided by not meeting that narrower term.[229] The concept of equivalency cannot embrace a structure that is specifically

---

[225]*Texas Instr., Inc. v. United States ITC,* 805 F.2d 1558, 231 USPQ 833 (Fed. Cir. 1986). This case can be read to foreshadow a less expansive application of the doctrine of equivalents in future cases. See also *Slimfold Mfg. Co. v. Kinkead Indus.,* 932 F.2d 1453, 18 USPQ2d 1842 (Fed. Cir. 1991).

[226]*Laitram Corp. v. Cambridge Wire Cloth Co.,* 863 F.2d 855, 9 USPQ2d 1289 (Fed. Cir. 1988).

[227]*Sun Studs, Inc. v. ATA Equip. Leasing, Inc.,* 872 F.2d 978, 10 USPQ2d 1338 (Fed. Cir. 1989).

[228]*Hormone Res. Found., Inc. v. Genentech, Inc.,* 904 F.2d 1558, 15 USPQ2d 1039 (Fed. Cir. 1990); *Perkin-Elmer Corp. v. Westinghouse Elec. Corp.,* 822 F.2d 1529, 3 USPQ2d 1321 (Fed. Cir. 1987).

[229]*Malta v. Schulmerich Carillons, Inc.,* 952 F.2d 1320, 21 USPQ2d 1161 (Fed. Cir. 1991). But see *Laitram Corp. v. Rexnord, Inc.,* 939 F.2d 1533, 19 USPQ2d 1367 (Fed. Cir. 1991).

excluded from the scope of the claims.[230] While the DOE extends the claims beyond their literal words, it does not prevent the manufacture, use, or sale by others of every device generally similar to the patented invention.[231]

But to the extent that courts, including the Federal Circuit itself, may have previously characterized claims as being "expanded" or "broadened" under the DOE, those characterizations are now said to be inaccurate. To say that the doctrine extends or enlarges claims is a contradiction in terms. The claims—i.e., the scope of patent protection as defined by the claims—remain the same. Application of the doctrine expands the right to exclude to "equivalents" of what is claimed. The doctrine, by definition, involves going beyond any permissible interpretation of the claim language; i.e., it involves determining whether the accused product is "equivalent" to what is described by the claim language.[232]

(ii) Application of the Doctrine

The Pennwalt *and* Warner-Jenkinson *decisions.* Infringement under the DOE cannot be established unless every limitation of a claim is satisfied either exactly or by a substantial equivalent.[233] This focus on individual claim elements when applying the DOE has prevailed, more or less, since the court decided *Pennwalt.*[234] Sitting in banc the court there held, by a 7–4 majority, that any infringement analysis under the DOE must deal with each claimed element, rather than a less focused consideration of the invention as a whole.[235] The principal dissenting opinion indicated the view that this approach is at odds with prior decisions[236] and fails to harmonize the policy of

---

[230]*Athletic Alternatives, Inc. v. Prince Mfg., Inc.,* 73 F.3d 1573, 37 USPQ2d 1365 (Fed. Cir. 1996).

[231]*Lear Siegler, Inc. v. Sealy Mattress Co.,* 873 F.2d 1422, 10 USPQ2d 1767 (Fed. Cir. 1989).

[232]*Wilson Sporting Goods Co. v. David Geoffrey & Assoc.,* 904 F.2d 677, 14 USPQ2d 1942 (Fed. Cir. 1990). The doctrine of equivalents cannot extend or enlarge the scope of the claims. The claims—i.e., the scope of patent protection as defined by the claims—remain the same and application of the doctrine expands the right to exclude to encompass equivalents of what is claimed. *Dolly, Inc. v. Spalding & Evenflo Co.,* 16 F.3d 394, 29 USPQ2d 1767 (Fed. Cir. 1994). But see *Environmental Instr., Inc. v. Sutron Corp.,* 877 F.2d 1561, 11 USPQ2d 1132 (Fed. Cir. 1989).

[233]E.g., *Carroll Touch, Inc. v. Electro Mechanical Sys. Inc.,* 3 F.3d 404, 27 USPQ2d 1836 (Fed. Cir. 1993).

[234]*Pennwalt Corp. v. Durand-Wayland, Inc.,* 833 F.2d 931, 4 USPQ2d 1737 (Fed. Cir. 1987).

[235]*Pennwalt Corp. v. Durand-Wayland, Inc.,* 833 F.2d 931, 4 USPQ2d 1737 (Fed. Cir. 1987). The device disclosed in the specification was hardwired circuitry, and the accused device used a microprocessor. It appears that the device did not perform some of the claimed functions, or equivalent functions, even though the microprocessor was capable of being programmed to perform those functions. It should be noted that the prosecution history revealed that certain of those specific functional limitations had been inserted to avoid prior art, and this may have led the court to a more restricted view of equivalence as to function—it felt that the accused device did not perform a function within the permissible range of equivalent functions permitted by the prosecution history.

[236]E.g., *Hughes Aircraft Co. v. United States,* 717 F.2d 1351, 219 USPQ 473 (Fed. Cir. 1983). In another look at *Hughes,* a majority concluded that *Pennwalt* had neither overruled

giving the public fair notice of what is patented with that of giving the inventor fair protection for what was invented. In a special dissent, Judge Newman provided an interesting historical review purporting to show that the DOE was historically applied to the invention as a whole. In a special concurring opinion, Judge Nies argued that the decision is not at odds with prior decisions—the "All Elements" rule was so pervasive that prior decisions applied it unconsciously.[237]

There followed a rather low-key tension between these rival points of view.[238] In *Dolly v. Spalding*,[239] the court undertook to expound a little more on the *Pennwalt* approach. *Pennwalt* requires an equivalent for every limitation of the claim, even though the equivalent may not be present in the corresponding component of the accused device. Thus, the doctrine does not require a one-to-one correspondence between components of the accused device and the claimed invention. An accused device may infringe under the DOE even though a combination of its components performs a function performed by a single element in the patented invention. Equivalency can also exist when separate claim limitations are combined into a single component of the accused device. But the court cannot convert a multilimitation claim into one of fewer limitations to support a

---

it or indicated that it was inconsistent. *Hughes Aircraft Co. v. United States,* 86 F.3d 1566, 39 USPQ2d 1065 (Fed. Cir. 1996).

[237]Judge Nies also gives great weight, almost in a due process context, to the idea that the public must be put on notice as to what is forbidden by a patent.

[238]For example, compare *Corning Glass Works v. Sumitomo Elec. U.S.A., Inc.,* 868 F.2d 1251, 9 USPQ2d 1962 (Fed. Cir. 1989) (nothing is taken from the public domain when the issue of equivalency is directed to a limitation only, in contrast to the entirety of the claimed invention), with *Richardson v. Suzuki Motor Co.,* 868 F.2d 1226, 9 USPQ2d 1913 (Fed. Cir. 1989) (verdict of no equivalents reversed where special verdict isolated a specific claim element so that it was removed from the perspective that is obtained only when the claimed invention is viewed in its entirety). But the court emphatically reaffirmed the vitality of *Pennwalt* in *Becton Dickinson & Co. v. C.R. Bard, Inc.,* 922 F.2d 792, 17 USPQ2d 1097 (Fed. Cir. 1990): whether necessary or not, after issuance of the patent all limitations in a claim are material and must be met exactly or equivalently in an accused device; only then can it be found that the two devices—claimed and accused—work in substantially the same way. See also *Intellicall, Inc. v. Phonometrics, Inc.,* 952 F.2d 1384, 21 USPQ2d 1383 (Fed. Cir. 1992). Indeed, the court feels so strongly about the *Pennwalt* All Limitations Rule that it has taken pains to indicate that, as a matter of terminology, it will speak only of "infringement" of a claim and of an "equivalent" to a limitation of a claim. Specifically, the court will avoid speaking of equivalency between the accused device and the patented invention. To speak of "equivalency" to the invention is technically inaccurate and creates confusion. The statutory requirement for liability is infringement of a patent, not equivalency between devices or methods. Equivalency to limitations of the claim must be the focus of the inquiry, particularly in jury trials. Otherwise, laypeople may be led to comparison of devices, rather than between the accused device and the claim, and to rely on generalities in the overall purpose of the devices. *Read Corp. v. Portec, Inc.,* 970 F.2d 816, 23 USPQ2d 1426 (Fed. Cir. 1992). However, the court has emphatically denied that *Pennwalt* set forth any determinative test for deciding the equivalence of a particular limitation. Thus, while the three-prong test of function-way-result may be an acceptable way of showing equivalency with respect to a limitation, it is not the only way. The test necessarily varies from case to case. *Malta v. Schulmerich Carillons, Inc.,* 952 F.2d 1320, 21 USPQ2d 1161 (Fed. Cir. 1991). On balance, it can be fairly said that the court, though not invariable in its adherence to *Pennwalt,* was at least giving it loud lip service.

[239]*Dolly, Inc. v. Spalding & Evenflo Co.,* 16 F.3d 394, 29 USPQ2d 1767 (Fed. Cir. 1994). But see *Ethicon Endo-Surgery Inc. v. United States Surgical Corp.,* 149 F.3d 1309, 47 USPQ2d 1272 (Fed. Cir. 1998).

finding of equivalency. In short, the concept of equivalency cannot embrace a structure that is specifically excluded from the claims. The accused device must contain every limitation or its equivalent.

This, then, was the setting against which, in its long-awaited in banc decision in *Hilton Davis v. Warner-Jenkinson*,[240] the court took another long, hard look at the DOE. When the smoke cleared, very little had changed. The court held that the application of the DOE rests on the substantiality of the differences between the claimed and accused products or processes, assessed according to an objective standard.[241] Thus, a finding of infringement under the doctrine requires proof of insubstantial differences between the claimed and accused products or processes. Often the function-way-result test will suffice to show the extent of the differences. In such cases, the parties will understandably focus on the evidence of function, way, and result, and the fact finder will apply the doctrine based on that evidence. Other factors, however, such as evidence of copying or designing around, may also inform the test for infringement under the DOE. No judge can anticipate whether such other factors will arise in a given case. Instead, the presence of such factors will depend on the way the parties frame their arguments.

Warner-Jenkinson also emphatically reaffirms that infringement under the DOE is an issue of fact to be submitted to the jury with proper instructions, or to be decided by the judge in a bench trial. In either event, the matter is not discretionary with the district judge. Nothing limits the type of evidence that either party may proffer in support of a factor it considers probative under the doctrine. The trial judge simply has a duty to decide whether the proffered evidence is relevant. This duty to assess relevance is no different in a DOE case than in any other type of case. Relevance will be self-evident to the judge in a case tried to the bench. In a jury trial, however, the judge must admit only relevant evidence, and instruct the jury to consider only the admitted evidence in reaching its decision.

The vantage point of one of ordinary skill in the relevant art provides the perspective for assessing the substantiality of the differences. The test is objective, with proof of the substantiality of the differences resting on objective evidence rather than unexplained subjective conclusions, whether offered by an expert witness or otherwise. The proper time frame for assessing substantiality is the time of infringement.

---

[240]*Hilton Davis Chem. Co. v. Warner-Jenkinson Co.*, 62 F.3d 1512, 35 USPQ2d 1641 (Fed. Cir. 1995).

[241]The court had signaled this direction in cases such as *Atlanta Motoring Access., Inc. v. Saratoga Tech., Inc.*, 33 F.3d 1362, 31 USPQ2d 1929 (Fed. Cir. 1994); *Valmont Indus., Inc. v. Reinke Mfg. Co.*, 983 F.2d 1039, 25 USPQ2d 1451 (Fed. Cir. 1993); *Hormone Res. Found., Inc. v. Genentech, Inc.*, 904 F.2d 1558, 15 USPQ2d 1039 (Fed. Cir. 1990); *Perkin-Elmer Corp. v. Westinghouse Elec. Corp.*, 822 F.2d 1529, 3 USPQ2d 1321 (Fed. Cir. 1987). In this sense, it becomes clear that equivalents is a legal theory that is more akin to obviousness than to anticipation. *Richardson v. Suzuki Motor Co.*, 868 F.2d 1226, 9 USPQ2d 1913 (Fed. Cir. 1989).

Thus, *Warner-Jenkinson* seems simply to have elevated substantiality of the differences to the focus of the equivalency inquiry, in place of the more familiar three-part test of similarity in function, way, and result. Although function-way-result remains a viable technique for assessing substantiality, it is not the exclusive test.[242] Other evidence is also relevant. Evidence of known interchangeability on the part of persons of ordinary skill in the art is potent evidence that such a person would have considered the change insubstantial.[243] Without such evidence, the patentee will need other objective technological evidence demonstrating that the substitute nevertheless represents a change that the ordinary artisan would have considered insubstantial at the time of the infringement. Evidence of copying is also relevant, not because the DOE rests on the subjective awareness or motivation of the accused infringer, but rather because copying suggests that the differences between the claimed and accused products or processes—measured objectively—are insubstantial. When an attempt to copy occurs, the fact finder may infer that the copyist, presumably one of some skill in the art, has made a fair copy, with only insubstantial changes. Such an inference should not dominate the analysis, however. Instead, where the inference arises, it must be weighed together with the other evidence relevant to the substantiality of the differences.[244]

Indeed, it is now clear that infringement under the DOE does not require bad faith or some other subjective component. Intent is not an element. An independently developed product or process that falls within the patent claims or includes only insubstantial differences nevertheless infringes. Those who make only insubstantial changes to a patented product or process are liable for infringement, regardless of their awareness of the patent and its disclosure. On the other hand, evidence of designing around is also relevant to infringement under the DOE. The ability of the public to design around—to use the patent disclosure to design a product or process that does not infringe, but like the claimed invention is an improvement over the prior art—is one of the important public benefits that justify awarding the patent owner exclusive rights to an invention. When a competitor becomes aware of a patent and attempts to design around its claims, the fact finder may infer that the competitor, presumably one of skill in the art, has designed substantial changes into the new product to

---

[242]If the parties, however, present primarily evidence of function, way, and result, such presentation may suffice to satisfy the doctrine of equivalents. *Sofamor Danek Group, Inc. v. DePuy-Motech, Inc.*, 74 F.3d 1216, 37 USPQ2d 1529 (Fed. Cir. 1996). But see *Roton Barrier, Inc. v. Stanley Works*, 79 F.3d 1112, 37 USPQ2d 1816 (Fed. Cir. 1996).

[243]E.g., *Multiform Desiccants Inc. v. Medzam Ltd.*, 133 F.3d 1473, 45 USPQ2d 1429 (Fed. Cir. 1998); *Sofamor Danek Group, Inc. v. DePuy-Motech, Inc.*, 74 F.3d 1216, 37 USPQ2d 1529 (Fed. Cir. 1996). But the fact of interchangeability is not always dispositive of equivalency, where the functions performed are not substantially the same. *Unidynamics Corp. v. Automatic Prods. Int'l Ltd.*, 157 F.3d 1311, 48 USPQ2d 1099 (Fed. Cir. 1998).

[244]This aspect of the Federal Circuit decision probably did not survive the Supreme Court's review. See text accompanying note 6:251.

avoid infringement.[245] The strength of this inference may vary from case to case. Evidence of designing around therefore weighs against finding infringement under the DOE.

Finally, evidence that the accused infringer developed its product or process through independent research is not directly relevant to the question of infringement under the DOE. Independent development means that the accused infringer had no knowledge of the patented invention when it developed its product or process. Without knowledge, the independent developer could not have set out to make its product or process either similar to or different from the claimed invention. Unlike copying or designing around, therefore, independent development itself produces no information about the substantiality of the differences. Such evidence is highly relevant, however, to refute a patent owner's contention that the DOE applies because the accused infringer copied, i.e., intentionally appropriated the substance of the claimed invention. When the patent owner asserts copying, evidence that the accused infringer developed its product or process without knowing of the patent becomes relevant in rebuttal.[246]

In 1996 the Supreme Court granted certiorari to review *Warner-Jenkinson* and in March 1997 reversed and remanded.[247] The decision of the Supreme Court is at once notable for what it did not decide. Despite widespread expectation among the members of the patent bar that the matter would finally be addressed, the Court found it unnecessary, given its resolution of the case, to decide whether application of the DOE is a task for the judge or for the jury. Thus the Federal Circuit's holding that equivalents is a question for the jury to decide currently stands as the law.[248]

As presented to the Court by the petitioner, the case afforded an opportunity to consider broad and basic attacks on the very foundation of the DOE itself. The Supreme Court responded with almost surgical precision, and quickly rejected all of those attacks. First, the Court held that the doctrine did survive the 1952 Patent Act revision, and declined to overrule *Graver Tank*.[249] Next the Court rejected a strong

---

[245]E.g., *Roton Barrier, Inc. v. Stanley Works,* 79 F.3d 1112, 37 USPQ2d 1816 (Fed. Cir. 1996). But see text accompanying note 6:251.

[246]*Hilton Davis Chem. Co. v. Warner-Jenkinson Co.,* 62 F.3d 1512, 35 USPQ2d 1641 (Fed. Cir. 1995).

[247]*Warner-Jenkinson Co. v. Hilton Davis Chem. Co.,* 520 U.S. 17, 41 USPQ2d 1865 (1997).

[248]One has good reason to believe it will remain the law. The Supreme Court indicated that there was ample support in its own prior cases for that holding and, indeed, offered some gratuitous guidance to the Federal Circuit as to how to "implement procedural improvements to promote certainty, consistency, and reviewability to this area of the law." 41 USPQ2d at 1875 n.8. But see *Tate Access Floors Inc. v. Maxcess Tech. Inc.,* 222 F.3d 958, 55 USPQ2d 1513, 1521 n.6 (Fed. Cir. 2000), where the Federal Circuit held, seemingly as a matter of law, that "a claim with a limitation as clear and decisive as 'black' can hardly be infringed under the doctrine of equivalents by a product that is brown."

[249]Most of petitioner's arguments had been considered and rejected by the Court in *Graver Tank & Mfg. Co. v. Linde Air Prods. Co.,* 339 U.S. 605, 85 USPQ 328 (1950), and it was not about to engage in an expansive reconsideration of those. The new argument was that Congress had negated the traditional doctrine of equivalents when it enacted 35 U.S.C. §112¶6. The

argument that any surrender of subject matter during prosecution establishes a bright line beyond which no equivalents may be claimed. This aspect of the decision is analyzed at length below in §6.3(b), dealing with prosecution history estoppel (PHE). The Court also rejected the petitioner's proposal that, in order to minimize conflict with the notice function of patent claims, the DOE should be limited to equivalents that are disclosed within the patent itself. In so embracing after arising equivalents, it necessarily reaffirmed the proposition that equivalency is to be determined as of the time of infringement.[250]

Finally, the Court addressed those matters that had been considered at length in the Federal Circuit opinion. It will be recalled that the Federal Circuit, despite its clear rejection of intent as an element of the doctrine, did suggest some rather convoluted considerations involving evidence of copying or designing around the patented invention as indicators of equivalence or lack of it. The Court remarked that this approach left much to be desired, and forcefully reaffirmed that intent plays no role and that copying or piracy are not prerequisites for application of the DOE. Instead, it suggested that evidence of independent experimentation may be relevant to the known interchangeability of substitutes, which is an important objective factor bearing on whether the accused device is substantially the same as the patented invention.[251] In the end, however, the Court did not purport to dictate a particular linguistic framework for analytical purposes. It left open to future development by the Federal Circuit what formulation—be it function-way-result, insubstantial difference, or some other incantation—may best suit a particular case.[252]

Most importantly, the Court expressed its concern that the decision of the Federal Circuit had not given sufficient attention to the need to preserve some meaning for each element in a claim.[253] This, together with the PHE issues, was the reason for the remand. The Court commended a focus on individual claim elements and a special vigilance against allowing the concept of equivalence to eliminate completely any such elements. As it put the matter:

> Each element contained in a patent claim is deemed material to defining the scope of the patented invention, and thus the doctrine of equivalents must be applied to individual elements of the claim, not to the invention as a whole. It is important to ensure that the application

---

Court disposed of this by pointing out that Congress could easily have responded to *Graver Tank* with similar targeted legislation, but did not. 41 USPQ2d at 1870–71.

[250]41 USPQ at 1871–72, 1874.

[251]41 USPQ at 1874.

[252]The Court was candid in observing that the function-way-result test, while sometimes suitable for analyzing mechanical devices, often provides a poor framework for analyzing other products or processes. At the same time, the insubstantial differences test offers little additional guidance as to what might render any given difference insubstantial. 41 USPQ2d 1875.

[253]It should be noted that the Federal Circuit had already expressed the view that its decision in *Hilton-Davis* did not eliminate the need to prove equivalency on a limitation-by-limitation basis. *Texas Instr., Inc. v. Cypress Semiconductor Corp.,* 90 F.3d 1558, 39 USPQ2d 1492 (Fed. Cir. 1996).

of the doctrine, even as to an individual element, is not allowed such broad play as to effectively eliminate that element in its entirety.[254]

This can only be regarded as a rather forceful reaffirmation of the majority rationale in *Pennwalt*.

The ramifications of the Supreme Court opinion in *Warner-Jenkinson* are sure to take years to develop.[255] In the meantime, one can be reasonably safe in predicting that the Federal Circuit will adhere faithfully at least to the letter of the rule that demands an equivalents analysis on an element-by-element basis.[256] Prior equivalents cases whose holdings or statement of the law may bear serious reexamination in light of *Warner-Jenkinson* are collected in the note.[257]

Pioneer status. A pioneer invention is definitely entitled to a broader range of equivalents,[258] while a narrow improvement in a crowded field enjoys a more circumscribed application of the doctrine.[259] The concept of "pioneer" arises from an ancient jurisprudence,

---

[254]41 USPQ2d at 1871.

[255]Certainly the court did not overreact when dealing with the case on remand from the Supreme Court. It simply gave a very brief review of the facts and reaffirmed its prior decision of equivalency. It then remanded to the trial court for a finding on the reason for the amendment, so that the PHE issue could be resolved. *Hilton Davis Chem. Co. v. Warner-Jenkinson Co.,* 114 F.3d 1161, 43 USPQ2d 1152 (Fed. Cir. 1997). In a case decided within days of the Supreme Court decision, it affirmed a finding of no equivalence and, in so doing, consulted various kinds of evidence on the question of whether the difference was substantial. The evidence included (1) the sharply restricted nature of the claims (a person of ordinary skill in the art would have understood that the inventor could have used more generic language), (2) preapplication experiments by the inventor also suggesting a lack of interchangeability, and (3) arguments made in foreign prosecution that were consistent with a conclusion of substantial difference. *Tanabe Seiyaku Co. v. United States ITC,* 109 F.3d 726, 41 USPQ2d 1976 (Fed. Cir. 1997).

[256]See, e.g., *Phonometrics Inc. v. Northern Telecom Inc.,* 133 F.3d 1459, 45 USPQ2d 1421 (Fed. Cir. 1998). In *Hughes Aircraft Co. v. United States,* 140 F.3d 1470, 46 USPQ2d 1285 (Fed. Cir. 1998), the court reconsidered its prior decision, reported at 717 F.2d 1351, 219 USPQ 473 (Fed. Cir. 1983), pursuant to a grant-vacate-remand order of the Supreme Court (in light of *Warner-Jenkinson*). It concluded that its analysis in the earlier *Hughes* opinion satisfied the All Elements Rule as stated in *Warner-Jenkinson,* which it believes is consistent with *Pennwalt.* In *Canton Bio-Medical Inc. v. Integrated Liner Tech. Inc.,* 216 F.3d 1367, 55 USPQ2d 1378 (Fed. Cir. 2000), the court made it clear that infringement of process inventions is subject to the "All Elements Rule," whereby each of the claimed steps of a patented process must be performed in an infringing process, literally or by an equivalent of that step, with due attention to the role of each step in the context of the patented invention.

[257]See the following for statements about equivalency to the claimed invention as a whole: *Intel Corp. v. United States ITC,* 946 F.2d 821, 20 USPQ2d 1161 (Fed. Cir. 1991); *Sun Studs, Inc. v. ATA Equip. Leasing, Inc.,* 872 F.2d 978, 10 USPQ2d 1338 (Fed. Cir. 1989); *Corning Glass Works v. Sumitomo Elec. U.S.A., Inc.,* 868 F.2d 1251, 9 USPQ2d 1962 (Fed. Cir. 1989). Hints, like that in *London v. Carson Pirie Scott & Co.,* 946 F.2d 1534, 20 USPQ2d 1456 (Fed. Cir. 1991), that the doctrine may be limited only to certain classes of case, probably can be safely disregarded.

[258]*Perkin-Elmer Corp. v. Westinghouse Elec. Corp.,* 822 F.2d 1529, 3 USPQ2d 1321 (Fed. Cir. 1987); *Kinzenbaw v. Deere & Co.,* 741 F.2d 383, 222 USPQ 929 (Fed. Cir. 1984); *Thomas & Betts Corp. v. Litton Sys., Inc.,* 720 F.2d 1572, 220 USPQ 1 (Fed. Cir. 1983).

[259]*Hughes Aircraft Co. v. United States,* 717 F.2d 1351, 219 USPQ 473 (Fed. Cir. 1983). A mechanical combination in a crowded field is entitled only to a narrow scope of equivalents. *Slimfold Mfg. Co. v. Kinkead Indus.,* 932 F.2d 1453, 18 USPQ2d 1842 (Fed. Cir. 1991).

reflecting judicial appreciation that a broad breakthrough invention merits a broader scope of equivalents than does a narrow improvement in a crowded technology. But the "pioneer" is not a separate class of invention, carrying a unique body of law. The wide range of technological advance between pioneering breakthrough and modest improvement accommodates gradations in scope of equivalency. The place of a particular invention in this spectrum depends on all the circumstances and is decided as a factual matter.[260]

That an invention is a combination of known elements is not relevant in determining either patentability or status as a pioneer invention. Virtually all inventions are combinations of old, known elements. Pioneer status has to do with the position occupied by the invention in the art to which it pertains, or which it creates, not with whether it is a combination of known elements.[261] For the occasional pioneering invention, devoid of significant prior art, whose boundaries probe the policy behind the law, there are no immutable rules.[262] The courts early recognized that patented inventions vary in their technological or industrial significance. Indeed, inventions vary as greatly as human imagination permits. There is not a discontinuous transition from "mere improvement" to "pioneer." History shows that the rules of law governing infringement determinations are amenable to consistent application despite the variety of contexts that arise. The judicially "liberal" view of both claim interpretation and equivalency accorded a pioneer invention is not a manifestation of a different legal standard based on an abstract legal concept denominated "pioneer." Rather, the liberal view flows directly from the relative sparseness of prior art in nascent fields of technology. However, pioneer status does not change the way infringement is determined. The patentee's disclosure, the prosecution history, and the prior art still provide the background against which the scope of claims is determined.[263] The range of permissible equivalents depends upon the extent and nature of the invention and may be more generously interpreted for a basic invention than for a less dramatic technological advance.[264]

No objective legal test separates pioneers from nonpioneers. Furthermore, it is impossible to predict the future of any given technology and thereby determine the likelihood that an invention will open vast new vistas of innovation. The peripheral claiming system itself,

---

[260]*Sun Studs, Inc. v. ATA Equip. Leasing, Inc.*, 872 F.2d 978, 10 USPQ2d 1338 (Fed. Cir. 1989).

[261]*Mac Corp. v. Williams Patent Crusher Co.*, 767 F.2d 882, 226 USPQ 515 (Fed. Cir. 1985).

[262]*Texas Instr., Inc. v. United States ITC*, 805 F.2d 1558, 231 USPQ 833 (Fed. Cir. 1986).

[263]*Texas Instr., Inc. v. United States ITC*, 846 F.2d 1369, 6 USPQ2d 1886 (Fed. Cir. 1988). Perhaps it is more accurate to say, therefore, that pioneer inventions *can*, because of the prior art, be afforded a broader range of equivalents, rather than that such inventions *must* be afforded a broader range.

[264]*Texas Instr., Inc. v. United States ITC*, 805 F.2d 1558, 231 USPQ 833 (Fed. Cir. 1986). The doctrine applies to patented designs as well. Where the art is crowded with designs, the range of equivalents is narrow. *Litton Sys., Inc. v. Whirlpool Corp.*, 728 F.2d 1423, 221 USPQ 97 (Fed. Cir. 1984).

however, makes the best distinction between pioneers and nonpioneers. Pioneers enjoy the benefits of their contribution to the art in the form of broader claims. Without extensive prior art to confine and cabin their claims, pioneers acquire broader claims than nonpioneers who must craft narrow claims to evade the strictures of a crowded art field. Thus, claim scope itself generally supplies broader exclusive entitlements to the pioneer. Moreover, a pioneer generally need not fear traditional limits on the application of the DOE such as prior art or PHE, because amendments or arguments to overcome the prior art are generally unnecessary in true pioneer applications.[265] But it is not necessary that an inventor be entitled to a broad claim covering all possible products in a line of products before a court may award an invention pioneer status, or a range of equivalents sufficient to encompass a particular accused product. It is commonplace for claims to inventions, pioneer and nonpioneer, to be amended during prosecution. Though the "area of equivalence" may vary, the DOE is applicable to both.[266]

Gist of claimed invention. Although the court has said that there is, for purposes of the obviousness inquiry, no legally recognizable or protected "gist" or "essence" or "heart" of the invention, such concepts may be useful in determining equivalence.[267] Thus, it has been said that consideration of the essence, gist, or heart of the invention may be helpful in determining infringement under the DOE. Such statements may not be read as implying that specific claim limitations can be ignored as insignificant or immaterial in determining infringement. They must be read as shorthand for the principle that the infringer should not appropriate the invention by making substitutions for those limitations, when the substitutions do not substantially change the function performed, or the way it is performed, by the invention.[268]

Similarly, it is the limitations and functions of the invention described in the claims, not the elements or functions of the accused device, that establish the reference point for the DOE. Thus, infringement under the DOE is not precluded merely because the accused device performs functions in addition to those performed by the claimed device. It is sufficient that the accused device performs substantially the same functions in substantially the same way to achieve

---

[265]*Augustine Med. Inc. v. Gaymar Indus. Inc.,* 181 F.3d 1291, 50 USPQ2d 1900 (Fed. Cir. 1999).

[266]*Laitram Corp. v. Cambridge Wire Cloth Co.,* 863 F.2d 855, 9 USPQ2d 1289 (Fed. Cir. 1988). But see the discussion of the *Festo* decision in §6.3(b)(v).

[267]*Loctite Corp. v. Ultraseal Ltd.,* 781 F.2d 861, 228 USPQ 90 (Fed. Cir. 1985); *Atlas Powder Co. v. E.I. du Pont & Co.,* 750 F.2d 1569, 224 USPQ 409 (Fed. Cir. 1984); *Medtronic, Inc. v. Cardiac Pacemakers, Inc.,* 721 F.2d 1563, 220 USPQ 97 (Fed. Cir. 1983). Cf. *United States Steel Corp. v. Phillips Petroleum Co.,* 865 F.2d 1247, 9 USPQ2d 1461 (Fed. Cir. 1989).

[268]*Perkin-Elmer Corp. v. Westinghouse Elec. Corp.,* 822 F.2d 1529, 3 USPQ2d 1321 (Fed. Cir. 1987).

substantially the same result as does the claimed invention.[269] The issue of whether the "way" or "result" prongs of the test are met may be highly dependent upon how broadly one defines the "function." The operative definition for purposes of equivalency analysis is the intended function as seen in the context of the patent, the prosecution history, and the prior art.[270]

Claims are normally construed as they would be by those of ordinary skill in the art. An important factor in the determination of equivalence is whether persons reasonably skilled in the art would have known of the interchangeability of an ingredient not contained in the patent with one that was.[271] But it is not required that those skilled in the art knew, at the time the patent application was filed, of the asserted equivalent means of performing the claimed function; that equivalence is determined as of the time infringement takes place.[272] Properties of a patented device that are discovered after the application has been filed may be pertinent to a function-way-result analysis when considering infringement under the DOE.[273] And of course, the patent specification need not disclose the equivalent element and the fact that it is a proper substitute in order for the doctrine to apply.[274]

Substantial equivalence. It is now well settled that each element of a claim is material and essential, and that in order for a court to find

---

[269]*Insta-Foam Prods., Inc. v. Universal Foam Sys., Inc.*, 906 F.2d 698, 15 USPQ2d 1295 (Fed. Cir. 1990). Infringement under the doctrine does not vanish merely because the accused device performs functions in addition to those performed by the claimed device. *Miles Labs., Inc. v. Shandon, Inc.*, 997 F.2d 870, 27 USPQ2d 1123 (Fed. Cir. 1993).

[270]*Genentech, Inc. v. Wellcome Found. Ltd.*, 29 F.3d 1555, 31 USPQ2d 1161 (Fed. Cir. 1994). For example, in *Zenith Labs., Inc. v. Bristol-Myers Squibb Co.*, 19 F.3d 1418, 30 USPQ2d 1048, 32 USPQ2d 1017 (Fed. Cir. 1994), the patentee was unable to satisfy the function prong of the test. It was clear from the prosecution history that the primary function of the claimed form of the drug was to facilitate preingestion manufacturing, and the accused drug did not even remotely perform that function.

[271]*Sofamor Danek Group, Inc. v. DePuy-Motech, Inc.*, 74 F.3d 1216, 37 USPQ2d 1529 (Fed. Cir. 1996); *Perkin-Elmer Corp. v. Westinghouse Elec. Corp.*, 822 F.2d 1529, 3 USPQ2d 1321 (Fed. Cir. 1987); *Palumbo v. Don-Joy Co.*, 762 F.2d 969, 226 USPQ 5 (Fed. Cir. 1985). Substitution of an ingredient known to be an equivalent to that required by the claim presents a classic example for a finding of infringement under the doctrine of equivalents. *Corning Glass Works v. Sumitomo Elec. U.S.A., Inc.*, 868 F.2d 1251, 9 USPQ2d 1962 (Fed. Cir. 1989). Interchangeability is a useful consideration when determining whether two specific structures are equivalents. *Rite-Hite Corp. v. Kelley Co.*, 819 F.2d 1120, 2 USPQ2d 1915 (Fed. Cir. 1987). The court has noted the interchangeability of hardware and software. Thus, the fact that a mechanical switch would necessarily require a human operator does not mean that a software switch can never be its equivalent. The "user operated" characteristic of a mechanical switch would not necessarily preclude a finding that software performs equivalently without human intervention. *Overhead Door Corp. v. Chamberlain Group Inc.*, 194 F.3d 1261, 52 USPQ2d 1321 (Fed. Cir. 1999). But an interchangeable device is not necessarily an equivalent device. *Key Mfg. Group, Inc. v. Microdot, Inc.*, 925 F.2d 1444, 17 USPQ2d 1806 (Fed. Cir. 1991).

[272]*Texas Instr., Inc. v. United States ITC*, 805 F.2d 1558, 231 USPQ 833 (Fed. Cir. 1986); *Atlas Powder Co. v. E.I. du Pont & Co.*, 750 F.2d 1569, 224 USPQ 409 (Fed. Cir. 1984); *American Hosp. Supply Corp. v. Travenol Labs., Inc.*, 745 F.2d 1, 223 USPQ 577 (Fed. Cir. 1984).

[273]*Engel Indus., Inc. v. Lockformer Co.*, 96 F.3d 1398, 40 USPQ2d 1161 (Fed. Cir. 1996).

[274]*Thomas & Betts Corp. v. Litton Sys., Inc.*, 720 F.2d 1572, 220 USPQ 1 (Fed. Cir. 1983).

infringement, the plaintiff must show the presence of every element or its substantial equivalent in the accused device. To be a "substantial equivalent" the element substituted in the accused device for the element set forth in the claim must not be such as would substantially change the way in which the function of the claimed invention is performed.[275] It is commonplace when devices are sold in competition that they perform substantially the same function and achieve substantially the same end result. But this does not make an accused device an infringement under the DOE if it performs the function and achieves the result in a substantially different way than the claimed invention.[276] Substantially the same way is shown if every limitation of a claim is satisfied either exactly or by a substantial equivalent in the accused device.[277] The fact that two devices achieve substantially the same result creates no presumption that they do so in substantially the same way. Such an argument turns the analysis of equivalence on its head. Much less does that fact create a presumption that the infringer must "destroy." The patentee has the burden of proof to show that the accused device infringes the patent claims, and to do so under the DOE requires a showing that all three components of the equivalency test are met.[278] Thus, a patentee must prove substantial identity as to each of the function, way, and result prongs of the DOE.[279]

Proof of equivalence can be made in any form: through testimony of experts or others versed in the technology; by documents, including texts and treatises; and, of course, by the disclosures of the prior art.[280] However, the court seems inclined to give little weight to conclusory

---

[275]*Wolverine World Wide, Inc. v. Nike, Inc.*, 38 F.3d 1192, 32 USPQ2d 1338 (Fed. Cir. 1994); *Pennwalt Corp. v. Durand-Wayland, Inc.*, 833 F.2d 931, 4 USPQ2d 1737 (Fed. Cir. 1987); *Perkin-Elmer Corp. v. Westinghouse Elec. Corp.*, 822 F.2d 1529, 3 USPQ2d 1321 (Fed. Cir. 1987). An "equivalent" of a claim limitation cannot substantially alter the manner of performing the claimed function. Where an accused device performs substantially the same function to achieve substantially the same result but in a substantially different manner, there is no infringement. *Dolly, Inc. v. Spalding & Evenflo Co.*, 16 F.3d 394, 29 USPQ2d 1767 (Fed. Cir. 1994). But equivalency is not defeated by using an additional step to achieve what the patentee does in one step. *EMI Group N.A. Inc. v. Intel Corp.*, 157 F.3d 887, 48 USPQ2d 1181 (Fed. Cir. 1998). Processes are equivalent, in terms of the law of patent infringement, when there is no substantial difference between the patented process and the accused process. *Canton Bio-Medical Inc. v. Integrated Liner Tech. Inc.*, 216 F.3d 1367, 55 USPQ2d 1378 (Fed. Cir. 2000).

[276]*Perkin-Elmer Corp. v. Westinghouse Elec. Corp.*, 822 F.2d 1529, 3 USPQ2d 1321 (Fed. Cir. 1987).

[277]*LaBounty Mfg., Inc. v. United States ITC*, 867 F.2d 1572, 9 USPQ2d 1995 (Fed. Cir. 1989). However, the substitute need not be in the exact same location specified by the claim. *Zygo Corp. v. Wyko Corp.*, 79 F.3d 1563, 38 USPQ2d 1281 (Fed. Cir. 1996).

[278]*Universal Gym Equip., Inc. v. ERWA Exercise Equip. Ltd.*, 827 F.2d 1542, 4 USPQ2d 1035 (Fed. Cir. 1987). See also *Moleculon Res. Corp. v. CBS, Inc.*, 872 F.2d 407, 10 USPQ2d 1390 (Fed. Cir. 1989). A finding of equivalency just because the same result is achieved is a flagrant abuse of the term "equivalent." *Zygo Corp. v. Wyko Corp.*, 79 F.3d 1563, 38 USPQ2d 1281 (Fed. Cir. 1996).

[279]*Genentech, Inc. v. Wellcome Found. Ltd.*, 29 F.3d 1555, 31 USPQ2d 1161 (Fed. Cir. 1994); *Malta v. Schulmerich Carillons, Inc.*, 952 F.2d 1320, 21 USPQ2d 1161 (Fed. Cir. 1991).

[280]*Martin v. Barber*, 755 F.2d 1564, 225 USPQ 233 (Fed. Cir. 1985). See also *Tanabe Seiyaku Co. v. United States ITC*, 109 F.3d 726, 41 USPQ2d 1976 (Fed. Cir. 1997).

statements on equivalence offered by expert witnesses; it will quite clearly be looking for factual evidence of equivalence.[281]

Things equal to each other may not be equal to the same thing, and it may not be properly assumed that merely because an accused device is, in a sense, equivalent to an admittedly infringing device it is necessarily equivalent to the claimed invention.[282] Likewise, the mere fact that an accused composition is itself patented does not mean it is not equivalent to a patented composition, although that could be so if the improvement patent were granted because of unexpected results. Where the defendant has appropriated the material features of the patent, infringement will be found even when those features have been supplemented and modified to such an extent that the defendant may be entitled to a patent for the improvement. The issuance of such a patent merely raises a presumption of validity, not a presumption of noninfringement.[283] But the fact of separate patentability is certainly relevant and entitled to due weight on the question of substantiality of the differences.[284]

Other rulings are illustrative. A patentee is not estopped to claim equivalence merely because he or she tried to use the accused equivalent and failed.[285] Equal performance is not required to establish equivalency.[286] The mere fact that a particular embodiment was not mentioned in instructions to foreign counsel does not establish that it is not an equivalent.[287] Evidence that an accused infringer intended to make a product that was compatible (nested) with the patentee's

---

[281]*Lemelson v. United States,* 752 F.2d 1538, 224 USPQ 526 (Fed. Cir. 1985). Expert testimony that any shape would be equivalent to an element described in the claim as having a particular shape does not compel a finding of equivalence. Such a result would effectively write the specific shape limitation out of the claim. *Tronzo v. Biomet Inc.,* 156 F.3d 1154, 47 USPQ2d 1829 (Fed. Cir. 1998). But *Tronzo* does not stand for the proposition that a claim limitation describing a specific shape of a claimed structure cannot be infringed under the DOE by a differently shaped structure. Instead, *Tronzo* merely applies conventional DOE law, including the "all elements" or "all limitations" rule. *Optical Disc Corp. v. Del Mar Avionics,* 208 F.3d 1324, 54 USPQ2d 1289 (Fed. Cir. 2000).

[282]*Datascope Corp. v. Kontron Inc.,* 786 F.2d 398, 229 USPQ 41 (Fed. Cir. 1986).

[283]*Atlas Powder Co. v. E.I. du Pont & Co.,* 750 F.2d 1569, 224 USPQ 409 (Fed. Cir. 1984). See also *Datascope Corp. v. Kontron Inc.,* 786 F.2d 398, 229 USPQ 41 (Fed. Cir. 1986). But see *Hoganas AB v. Dresser Indus., Inc.,* 9 F.3d 948, 28 USPQ2d 1936 (Fed. Cir. 1993). That the accused device is an improvement on the claimed subject matter does not avoid infringement even under the doctrine of equivalents. *Ryco, Inc. v. Ag-Bag Corp.,* 857 F.2d 1418, 8 USPQ2d 1323 (Fed. Cir. 1988). The fact that an accused process may be better or more efficient than the claimed process does not necessarily establish that the differences are substantial. *Insituform Tech. Inc. v. Cat Contr. Inc.,* 156 F.3d 1199, 48 USPQ2d 1610 (Fed. Cir. 1998).

[284]*Zygo Corp. v. Wyko Corp.,* 79 F.3d 1563, 38 USPQ2d 1281 (Fed. Cir. 1996); *National Presto Indus., Inc. v. West Bend Co.,* 76 F.3d 1185, 37 USPQ2d 1685 (Fed. Cir. 1996). But see *Fiskars Inc. v Hunt Mfg. Co.,* 221 F.3d 1318, 55 USPQ2d 1569 (Fed. Cir. 2000), where the court observed that since it is well established that separate patentability does not avoid equivalency as a matter of law, it will not intrude upon a trial court's evidentiary ruling, excluding such evidence. The admission or exclusion of evidence not material to the issue of infringement is consigned to the discretion of the trial judge.

[285]*Atlas Powder Co. v. E.I. du Pont & Co.,* 750 F.2d 1569, 224 USPQ 409 (Fed. Cir. 1984).

[286]*Modine Mfg. Co. v. United States ITC,* 75 F.3d 1545, 37 USPQ2d 1609 (Fed. Cir. 1996).

[287]*Caterpillar Tractor Co. v. Berco, S.P.A.,* 714 F.2d 1110, 219 USPQ 185 (Fed. Cir. 1983).

product does not necessarily result in equivalence; the test is still equivalence of function, means, and result.[288] It is improper for a court to redraft the claims in order to find equivalence and then hold them invalid.[289]

(iii) Limitations on the Doctrine

The DOE exists in some tension with other core tenets of the patent law, perhaps most notably the requirement that the patentee particularly point out and distinctly claim the subject matter that the applicant regards as the invention, pursuant to 35 U.S.C. §112¶2, and the function of patent claims to provide notice to competitors regarding the scope of the patent grant. The courts have responded to such concerns by developing an array of legal limitations, formulations, and tests regarding the application of the DOE. These efforts reflect two animating concepts. The first is that the DOE is limited. It cannot allow a patent claim to encompass subject matter that could not have been patented; nor can it be used to ignore the actual language of the patent. Thus, the DOE cannot allow a patent to encompass subject matter existing in the prior art. Nor may it allow coverage of obvious, or "trivial," variations of the prior art, for such subject matter could not have been lawfully patented in the first instance. It is also fundamental that the text of the claim must be closely followed: each element contained in a patent claim is deemed material to defining the scope of the patented invention, and thus the DOE must be applied to individual elements of the claim, not to the invention as a whole. Therefore, the DOE cannot be used to vitiate an element from the claim in its entirety. Similarly, where the patent document expressly identifies a role for a claim limitation, the DOE cannot be used to capture subject matter that does not substantially fulfill that role. These restrictions on the DOE pose questions of law. The second conceptual limitation on the DOE is the idea that the patentee may not use the doctrine to recover subject matter that has been surrendered. For example, PHE will exclude from the DOE any subject matter that was, by amendment or argument during prosecution, relinquished. In a similar vein, particular subject matter disclosed in the patent specification but not claimed is deemed to have been surrendered. Again, these are questions of law. Taken together, these concepts reflect an approach of maintaining a principled application of the DOE while hewing closely to the doctrine's original purpose: to prevent fraud on a patent. Where these limitations are inapplicable, the DOE operates to prevent an infringer from

---

[288]*Nestier Corp. v. Menasha Corp.*, 739 F.2d 1576, 222 USPQ 747 (Fed. Cir. 1984).

[289]*Diversitech Corp. v. Century Steps, Inc.*, 850 F.2d 675, 7 USPQ2d 1315 (Fed. Cir. 1988). In order to find infringement the trial court would have had to find that a thin coating was equivalent to no coating. It took the approach that such a finding would be no different from writing the word "thin" into the patent claims, and if that were done, the claims would be

stealing the benefit of an invention. To have this effect, however, the DOE must, as noted, remain within the boundaries established by the prior art, the scope of the patent claims themselves, and any surrendered subject matter.[290] Case law has established that the prior art and PHE provide independent "policy oriented" limitations on the DOE.[291] The most developed of these limitations from the theoretical legal standpoint—conduct during prosecution—is discussed in §6.3(b) under the topic of PHE. The others, including concepts that are just beginning to emerge, are discussed below.

Prior art and the hypothetical claim analysis. The limitation posed by the prior art is simply that the asserted range of equivalents may not encompass the prior art at the very point at which the claims distinguish from that art.[292] That issue—whether an asserted range of equivalents would cover what is already in the public domain—is one of law.[293] Because claims are to be construed, if possible, to sustain validity, if a construction sufficient to find infringement would result in invalidity, the proper legal conclusion is noninfringement, not invalidity.[294] Indeed, where validity is not in issue, application of the DOE should not amount to a backhanded attack on validity. Where

---

indefinite, since there was no rational standard for determining what thin meant in that context. The Federal Circuit disapproved this reasoning.

[290]*K-2 Corp. v. Salomon S.A.*, 191 F.3d 1356, 52 USPQ2d 1001 (Fed. Cir. 1999). Thus, if equivalence appears, infringement will be found unless (1) arguments or amendments made by the applicant during prosecution estop the patentee from asserting a range of equivalents broad enough to encompass the accused product or process; or (2) the equivalent device is within the public domain, i.e., found in the prior art. *Ryco, Inc. v. Ag-Bag Corp.*, 857 F.2d 1418, 8 USPQ2d 1323 (Fed. Cir. 1988); *Pennwalt Corp. v. Durand-Wayland, Inc.*, 833 F.2d 931, 4 USPQ2d 1737 (Fed. Cir. 1987); *Loctite Corp. v. Ultraseal Ltd.*, 781 F.2d 861, 228 USPQ 90 (Fed. Cir. 1985); *Perkin-Elmer Corp. v. Computervision Corp.*, 732 F.2d 888, 221 USPQ 669 (Fed. Cir. 1984); *Carman Indus., Inc. v. Wahl*, 724 F.2d 932, 220 USPQ 481 (Fed. Cir. 1983). Determination of either condition does not, however, require reassessment of validity or a reinterpretation of the claims as written. *Perkin-Elmer Corp. v. Computervision Corp.*, 732 F.2d 888, 221 USPQ 669 (Fed. Cir. 1984). In order to support a preliminary injunction the required finding of likelihood of success on infringement under the doctrine of equivalents should include findings not only as to the three-part test but findings on file wrapper estoppel and on whether the range of equivalents ensnares the prior art. *Conair Group v. Automatik App. GmbH*, 944 F.2d 862, 20 USPQ2d 1067 (Fed. Cir. 1991).

[291]*Sextant Avionique S.A. v. Analog Devices Inc.*, 172 F.3d 813, 49 USPQ2d 1865 (Fed. Cir. 1999).

[292]*Stewart-Warner Corp. v. City of Pontiac*, 767 F.2d 1563, 226 USPQ 676 (Fed. Cir. 1985). It is well established that limitations in a claim cannot be given a range of equivalents so wide as to cause the claim to encompass anything in the prior art. *Senmed, Inc. v. Richard-Allan Med. Indus., Inc.*, 888 F.2d 815, 12 USPQ2d 1508 (Fed. Cir. 1989). Claims may not be enlarged by equivalents to encompass the teachings of the prior art. *Tandon Corp. v. United States ITC*, 831 F.2d 1017, 4 USPQ2d 1283 (Fed. Cir. 1987). That an element of an accused device already existed in the prior art, however, does not bar equivalency as to that element. *Fiskars Inc. v Hunt Mfg. Co.*, 221 F.3d 1318, 55 USPQ2d 1569 (Fed. Cir. 2000). Prior art is not a consideration in analyzing equivalency under 35 U.S.C. §112. See note 6:336.

[293]*Wilson Sporting Goods Co. v. David Geoffrey & Assoc.*, 904 F.2d 677, 14 USPQ2d 1942 (Fed. Cir. 1990).

[294]*Carman Indus., Inc. v. Wahl*, 724 F.2d 932, 220 USPQ 481 (Fed. Cir. 1983).

validity is not challenged, the court is less free to limit the application of equivalents in light of the prior art.[295]

In its *Wilson Sporting Goods* decision,[296] the court expounded at some length on the impact of prior art upon the range of equivalents that a patent may enjoy. First the court posed and answered the question, why, if the doctrine does not involve expanding the claims, should the prior art be a limitation on the range of permissible equivalents? It is not because claims are construed narrowly if necessary to sustain their validity; the DOE is not a claim interpretation issue. Nor is it because to hold otherwise would allow the patentee to preempt a product that was in the public domain prior to the invention. The accused product in most infringement cases was never in the public domain—it was developed long after the invention and differs in several respects from the prior art. The answer is that a patentee should not be able to obtain, under the DOE, coverage that it could not lawfully have obtained from the PTO by literal claims. The doctrine exists to prevent a fraud on a patent, not to give a patentee something that it could not have got from the PTO had it tried. Thus, since prior art always limits that which an inventor could have claimed, it limits the range of permissible equivalents of a claim.[297]

The *Wilson* court went on to use that reasoning as the basis for a new test for assessing the impact of the prior art in applying the DOE. Under the *Wilson* test, a court is to visualize a hypothetical patent claim, sufficient in scope to literally cover the accused product. The pertinent question then becomes whether that hypothetical claim could have been allowed by the PTO over the prior art. If not, then it would be improper to permit the patentee to obtain that coverage in an infringement suit under the DOE. If the hypothetical claim could have been allowed, then prior art is not a bar to infringement under the doctrine. Viewing the issue in this manner allows use of traditional patentability rules and permits a more precise analysis than determining whether an accused product (which has no claim limitations on which to focus) would have been obvious in view of the prior art. It also reminds the analyst that the patentee is seeking patent coverage beyond the limits considered by the PTO examiner.[298]

It seems safe to expect that many questions about the hypothetical claim approach remain to be explored. The *Wilson* decision itself identified two interesting ramifications. First, a finding of noninfringement of an independent claim using this analysis does not,

---

[295]*Thomas & Betts Corp. v. Litton Sys., Inc.*, 720 F.2d 1572, 220 USPQ 1 (Fed. Cir. 1983). There may be an important lesson here for accused infringers.

[296]*Wilson Sporting Goods Co. v. David Geoffrey & Assoc.*, 904 F.2d 677, 14 USPQ2d 1942 (Fed. Cir. 1990).

[297]*Wilson Sporting Goods Co. v. David Geoffrey & Assoc.*, 904 F.2d 677, 14 USPQ2d 1942 (Fed. Cir. 1990). See also *Marquip Inc. v. Fosber Am. Inc.*, 198 F.3d 1363, 53 USPQ2d 1015 (Fed. Cir. 1999).

[298]*Wilson Sporting Goods Co. v. David Geoffrey & Assoc.*, 904 F.2d 677, 14 USPQ2d 1942 (Fed. Cir. 1990).

unlike the normal case, automatically result in a finding of noninfringement of dependent claims. The dependent claims are narrower and they may escape the prior art and still be entitled to a range of equivalents that would cover the accused structure.[299]

The second ramification was the court's observation that, as part of its normal burden of proving infringement, the patentee will bear the burden of showing that the range of equivalents it seeks does not ensnare the prior art. This does not undermine the presumption of validity of the actual patent claims, which will remain valid whether or not the patentee succeeds in persuading the court that it is entitled to the range of equivalents it seeks.[300] However, the court has since indicated that it is an affirmative defense of the accused infringer to allege and to show that it is practicing the prior art. When the patentee has presented a prima facie case of infringement, the burden shifts to the accused infringer to come forward with evidence to establish this defense. The patentee is not required to negate an affirmative defense that has not been pled and supported with evidence. Where the accused infringer does not allege that its device is in the prior art, or that a hypothetical claim covering its device would be unpatentable, there is nothing for the patentee to rebut.[301]

In the second edition of this book the author guessed that it was safe to believe that the hypothetical claim analysis would become the standard against which to assess the prior art limitations on the DOE. This guess was based on the fact that, very shortly after *Wilson*, the Federal Circuit used the technique in deciding another case.[302] But the court has since indicated that a *Wilson* analysis is not obligatory in every equivalents determination, though it helps define the limits imposed by prior art on the range of equivalents. It does not envision application of a full-blown patentability analysis to a hypothetical claim; it simply acknowledges that prior art limits the coverage available under the DOE.[303] Two questions immediately arise: (1) How

---

[299]*Wilson Sporting Goods Co. v. David Geoffrey & Assoc.,* 904 F.2d 677, 14 USPQ2d 1942 (Fed. Cir. 1990). This represents a narrow, counterintuitive exception to the general principle that, when one does not infringe a broader claim, one cannot infringe a dependent claim containing all of that broader claim's limitations plus more. It was based on the proposition that a broader claim might fail the *Wilson* test, while a narrower claim could pass it and thus be infringed. *Streamfeeder LLC v. Sure-Feed Inc.,* 175 F.3d 974, 50 USPQ2d 1515 (Fed. Cir. 1999).

[300]*Wilson Sporting Goods Co. v. David Geoffrey & Assoc.,* 904 F.2d 677, 14 USPQ2d 1942 (Fed. Cir. 1990).

[301]*Fiskars Inc. v Hunt Mfg. Co.,* 221 F.3d 1318, 55 USPQ2d 1569 (Fed. Cir. 2000). See also *National Presto Indus., Inc. v. West Bend Co.,* 76 F.3d 1185, 37 USPQ2d 1685 (Fed. Cir. 1996).

[302]*Insta-Foam Prods., Inc. v. Universal Foam Sys., Inc.,* 906 F.2d 698, 15 USPQ2d 1295 (Fed. Cir. 1990). See also *Jurgens v. McKasy,* 927 F.2d 1552, 18 USPQ2d 1031 (Fed. Cir. 1991). *Wilson* created an analytical framework, in the form of the hypothetical claim analysis, to determine the extent to which the prior art limits the application of the doctrine of equivalents. *Conroy v. Reebok Int'l,* 14 F.3d 1570, 29 USPQ2d 1373 (Fed. Cir. 1994). The determination of whether the scope of equivalents accorded to a particular claim would encompass the prior art is an issue of law that is reviewed de novo. *Streamfeeder LLC v. Sure-Feed Inc.,* 175 F.3d 974, 50 USPQ2d 1515 (Fed. Cir. 1999).

[303]*Key Mfg. Group, Inc. v. Microdot, Inc.,* 925 F.2d 1444, 17 USPQ2d 1806 (Fed. Cir. 1991). See also *National Presto Indus., Inc. v. West Bend Co.,* 76 F.3d 1185, 37 USPQ2d 1685

does one know when to apply the hypothetical claim analysis? and (2) How much less than full blown may the patentability analysis be? The court has at least partially answered the second question by indicating that if such an analysis is undertaken, it must include some sort of obviousness inquiry.[304] *Wilson* is an optional way of evaluating whether the prior art limits the application of the DOE. But if a trial court purports to employ a *Wilson* analysis, it must do so properly.[305]

Under the *Wilson* methodology, the patentee may propose a hypothetical claim that is broad enough in scope to literally read on the accused device. If the hypothetical claim could have been allowed by the PTO in view of the prior art, then the prior art does not preclude the application of the DOE and infringement may be found. On the other hand, as in the PTO's examination process, references may be combined to prove that the hypothetical claim would have been obvious to one of ordinary skill in the art and thus would not have been allowed. The burden of going forward with evidence to show that the accused device is in the prior art is upon the accused infringer, but the burden of persuasion that the hypothetical claim does not ensnare the prior art remains with the patentee. The hypothetical claim analysis cannot be used to redraft granted claims in litigation by narrowing and broadening a claim at the same time. A hypothetical claim analysis is not an opportunity to freely redraft granted claims. That opportunity existed in the PTO, where the submitted claims were examined for patentability. Other statutorily prescribed procedures exist for postgrant modification of claims in the PTO in appropriate circumstances. While use of a hypothetical claim may permit a minor extension of a claim to cover subject matter that is substantially equivalent to that literally claimed, one cannot, in the course of litigation and outside of the PTO, cut and trim, expanding here, and narrowing

---

(Fed. Cir. 1996). In *International Visual Corp. v. Crown Metal Mfg. Co.*, 991 F.2d 768, 26 USPQ2d 1588 (Fed. Cir. 1993), the court indicated that the hypothetical claim analysis is an "optional" way of evaluating whether prior art limits the application of the doctrine of equivalents. It is simply a way of expressing the well-established principle that a patentee should not be able to obtain, under the doctrine of equivalents, coverage that it could not lawfully have obtained from the PTO by literal claims.

[304]*We Care, Inc. v. Ultra-Mark Int'l Corp.*, 930 F.2d 1567, 18 USPQ2d 1562 (Fed. Cir. 1991). See also *General Am. Trans. Corp. v. Cryo-Trans, Inc.*, 93 F.3d 766, 39 USPQ2d 1801 (Fed. Cir. 1996). If the hypothetical claim analysis is utilized, a court is required to visualize a hypothetical claim that enlarges the scope of an issued claim so that it literally covers an accused device and to determine whether that hypothetical claim would have been patentable over the prior art. *International Visual Corp. v. Crown Metal Mfg. Co.*, 991 F.2d 768, 26 USPQ2d 1588 (Fed. Cir. 1993). Where a claim drawn literally to cover the accused device would not be patentable over the prior art on obviousness grounds, there is no infringement. *Key Mfg. Group, Inc. v. Microdot, Inc.*, 925 F.2d 1444, 17 USPQ2d 1806 (Fed. Cir. 1991). Must one do a complete *Graham v. Deere* analysis, including a consideration of objective indicia of nonobviousness?

[305]*Conroy v. Reebok Int'l*, 14 F.3d 1570, 29 USPQ2d 1373 (Fed. Cir. 1994). The trial court held, as a matter of law, that because the element in question was present in the prior art as well as the accused device, the patentee was precluded from urging that it was the equivalent of the corresponding claim element. This was of course error. The failure to apply an analysis of the claim consistent with the Federal Circuit's jurisprudence regarding anticipation and obviousness resulted in an overbroad restriction by the prior art on the application of the doctrine of equivalents.

there, to arrive at a claim that encompasses an accused device, but avoids the prior art. Slight broadening is permitted at that point, but not narrowing.[306]

Technological advances. The court has established a third, and potentially very significant, limitation on the DOE. It has always been thought that an embellishment made possible by technological advances may not permit an accused device to escape the web of infringement.[307] Indeed, that has been suggested as one of the purposes underlying the doctrine—to protect inventors from unanticipated equivalents.[308] It is therefore incorrect to suggest that the DOE can be invoked only for subject matter that is disclosed and enabled in the patent specification but not claimed. It is not controlling whether the inventor foresaw and described the potential equivalent at the time the patent application was filed.[309]

But in *Texas Instruments v. ITC*,[310] the court made it clear that while prior art and prosecution history are necessary considerations in applying the DOE, they do not of themselves control the breadth of equivalents available under the doctrine. A third factor—technological advances—also plays an important role. Thus, where extensive technological advances in all the claimed functions result in multiple departures from literal readability, the totality of change in the accused device may be too much to support a holding of infringement.

In *Texas Instruments* the court was confronted with a situation where rapidly developing semiconductor technology had resulted in an accused product that had several elements that employed means differing from the means disclosed in the patent. Although each means might, standing alone, have been an equivalent, the court was unable to find infringement, based upon the rule that the claimed invention as a whole must be considered in determining whether there is infringement by the accused devices, also considered as a whole. The court considered it inappropriate to view each change as if it were the only change from the disclosed embodiments of the invention. It is the entirety of the technology embodied in the accused devices that must be compared with the patent disclosure. Viewing all of the

---

[306]*Streamfeeder LLC v. Sure-Feed Inc.*, 175 F.3d 974, 50 USPQ2d 1515 (Fed. Cir. 1999). In *Ultra-Tex Surfaces Inc. v. Hill Bros. Chem. Co.*, 204 F.3d 1360, 53 USPQ2d 1892 (Fed. Cir. 2000), the court remarked that the hypothetical claim is only a device for limited, not substantial, inclusion of unclaimed subject matter and not for exclusion of unduly limiting subject matter. Curiously, the court went on to conclude that the hypothetical claim would nonetheless not have been patentable, even with the narrowed limitations, because it covered processes that were in public use more than a year prior to the filing date. But these processes apparently were the same as the accused process. One wonders whether and when the court will finally adopt the common sense rule of law that an accused infringement that was itself part of the prior art can never generate liability, under any theory.

[307]*Datascope Corp. v. SMEC, Inc.*, 776 F.2d 320, 227 USPQ 838 (Fed. Cir. 1985).

[308]See *Kinzenbaw v. Deere & Co.*, 741 F.2d 383, 222 USPQ 929 (Fed. Cir. 1984).

[309]*Pall Corp. v. Micron Separations, Inc.*, 66 F.3d 1211, 36 USPQ2d 1225 (Fed. Cir. 1995).

[310]*Texas Instr., Inc. v. United States ITC*, 805 F.2d 1558, 231 USPQ 833 (Fed. Cir. 1986).

modifications, they reflected more than mere substitution of an embellishment made possible by improved technology.[311] On a motion for reconsideration, the court adhered to its prior ruling in *Texas Instruments.*[312] The claimed functions were in the prior art, and the patentability of the combination depended on the totality of changes in the structures by which the functions were performed. Thus, for purposes of infringement the equivalency of each changed means is evaluated in the context of the accused device as a whole. Each function in a claim is part of a combination, not a separate invention. Where all functions are performed but multiple means are changed, the equivalency of each changed means is appropriately determined in light of the other structural changes in the combination. As in all cases involving assertions of equivalency, wherein the patentee seeks to apply its claims to structures not disclosed by the patentee, the court is required to exercise judgment. In cases of complex inventions, the judgment must take account of situations where the components of the claimed combination are of varying importance or are changed to varying degrees. This is done by viewing the components in combination.[313]

But if *Texas Instruments* demands that focus be upon the combination as a whole when all functions are performed, albeit by multiple changed means, the court just as clearly demands, in its *Pennwalt* decision,[314] as emphatically reconfirmed both by it and the Supreme Court in *Warner-Jenkinson,*[315] a focus on individual elements where some functions are missing. How does one harmonize *Pennwalt* and *Texas Instruments*? If the individual functions performed by the elements of a claimed combination are all present in the accused device, the court looks to the quantity and quality of the changes in the means for performing those functions, and this analysis, according to *Texas Instruments,* is made in the context of the claimed combination as a whole. If, on the other hand, certain functions of those individual elements are not performed, either literally or equivalently, then *Pennwalt* makes it clear that an equivalent functional result for the combination as a whole will nonetheless not result in infringement of the claim. What is the importance of these two decisions? For the moment, they would seem nothing more than appropriate guidelines

---

[311]*Texas Instr., Inc. v. United States ITC,* 805 F.2d 1558, 231 USPQ 833 (Fed. Cir. 1986). Although the bulk of the discussion took place in connection with the question of equivalency under §112, the court made it clear that the ruling applied to the traditional doctrine of equivalents as well. However, there are important differences between the two contexts, especially with reference to the need to consider the prior art, and the coverage of after-arising technology. See §6.3(a)(iv).

[312]*Texas Instr., Inc. v. United States ITC,* 805 F.2d 1558, 231 USPQ 833 (Fed. Cir. 1986), *on reconsideration,* 846 F.2d 1369, 6 USPQ2d 1886 (Fed. Cir. 1988).

[313]*Texas Instr., Inc. v. United States ITC,* 846 F.2d 1369, 6 USPQ2d 1886 (Fed. Cir. 1988). See also *Sun Studs, Inc. v. ATA Equip. Leasing, Inc.,* 872 F.2d 978, 10 USPQ2d 1338 (Fed. Cir. 1989).

[314]*Pennwalt Corp. v. Durand-Wayland, Inc.,* 833 F.2d 931, 4 USPQ2d 1737 (Fed. Cir. 1987).

[315]See discussion beginning at note 6:240.

to proper analytical technique, but this could well change as subsequent cases deal with more difficult situations.

The doctrine of Miller v. Bridgeport Brass. The court recently, and somewhat surprisingly, applied the rule of *Miller v. Bridgeport Brass Co.*,[316] in holding that subject matter disclosed but not claimed in a patent application is dedicated to the public. The upshot in the case at hand was that the rule prevents a finding of infringement under the DOE where the specification discloses the alleged equivalent structure but the claim does not literally cover it. The rationale is that a patentee may not narrowly claim an invention and then, in the course of an infringement suit, argue that the DOE should permit a finding of infringement because the specification discloses the equivalence. Such a result would merely encourage a patent applicant to present a broad disclosure in the specification of the application and file narrow claims, avoiding examination of broader claims that the applicant could have filed consistent with the specification.[317] In a later case, *Sage v. Devon*, the court expanded on this theme. Where a skilled patent drafter would have foreseen the limiting potential of the particular claim language used, the law restricts the application of the DOE without further fact finding. As between the patentee who had a clear opportunity to negotiate broader claims but did not do so, and the public at large, it is the patentee who must bear the consequences of failure to seek protection for a foreseeable alteration of the claimed structure.[318]

Thus, for a patentee who has claimed an invention narrowly, there may not be infringement under the DOE in many cases, even though the patentee might have been able to claim more broadly. If it were otherwise, then claims would be reduced to functional abstracts,

---

[316]104 U.S. 350 (1881).

[317]*Maxwell v. J. Baker, Inc.*, 86 F.3d 1098, 39 USPQ2d 1001 (Fed. Cir. 1996). The court also cited its own decision in *Unique Concepts, Inc. v. Brown*, 939 F.2d 1558, 19 USPQ2d 1500 (Fed. Cir. 1991). In *YBM Magnex Inc. v. United States ITC*, 145 F.3d 1317, 46 USPQ2d 1843 (Fed. Cir. 1998), the court noted that the ITC had read *Maxwell v. J. Baker* as establishing a broad new rule that the doctrine of equivalents is not applicable to subject matter that is disclosed but not claimed. The court took pains to limit *Maxwell* strictly to its facts: the specification disclosed two distinct alternative embodiments and the claims only covered one of them. The thought was that this enabled the applicant to avoid examination of the unclaimed alternative, and that would be a justification for denying the opportunity to enforce the unclaimed embodiment as an equivalent of the one that was claimed. In an order entered January 24, 2001 in appeal No. 99-1076, the court sua sponte decided to consider, in banc, whether and under what circumstances a patentee can rely upon the doctrine of equivalents with respect to unclaimed subject matter disclosed in the specification.

[318]*Sage Prods., Inc. v. Devon Indus., Inc.*, 126 F.3d 1420, 44 USPQ2d 1103 (Fed. Cir. 1997). The court recognized that this policy places a premium on forethought in claim drafting, but it nonetheless disclaimed any implication that the applicant in the case at hand was not adequately represented before the PTO. Rather, the court concluded that the record demonstrated a clear intention to claim the limited structure and no more. With all respect, this may have been so, but it is difficult to imagine many patent applicants who do not want the broadest protection their patent disclosure will support. This decision may foreshadow increased attention—in hindsight, of course—to the drafting skills of patent attorneys and agents, and clearly raises the possibility of a new class of malpractice complaints.

devoid of meaningful structural limitations on which the public could rely. So, in certain cases, the law restricts application of the DOE without further fact finding.[319] The *Sage v. Devon* decision recognizes that its reasoning places a premium on forethought in patent drafting. Indeed, that premium could lead to higher costs of patent prosecution. But the alternative rule—allowing broad play for the DOE to encompass foreseeable variations, not just of a claim element, but of a patent claim—also leads to higher costs. Society at large would bear these latter costs in the form of virtual foreclosure of competitive activity within the penumbra of each issued patent claim. Because the DOE blurs the line of demarcation between infringing and noninfringing activity, it creates a zone of uncertainty, into which competitors tread only at their peril. Given a choice of imposing the higher costs of careful prosecution on patentees, or imposing the costs of foreclosed business activity on the public at large, the court believes the costs are properly imposed on the group best positioned to determine whether or not a particular invention warrants investment at a higher level, that is to say, the patentees.[320]

The "All-Advantages Rule". Where a patent claim recites a specific function for an element of the claim and the written description reiterates the importance of that particular function, a patentee may not later argue, during the course of litigation, that an accused device lacking that functionality is equivalent.[321] This is elementary patent law. But a split panel may have taken this rule a step further in *Vehicular v. Titan,* suggesting that if a claim limitation must play a role in the context of the specific claim language, then an accused device that cannot play that role, or that plays a substantially different role, cannot infringe under the DOE. The question of whether an

---

[319]*Sage Prods., Inc. v. Devon Indus., Inc.,* 126 F.3d 1420, 44 USPQ2d 1103 (Fed. Cir. 1997). The court indicated that in the present case, a skilled patent drafter would have foreseen the limiting potential of the particular claim language used. No subtlety of language or complexity of the technology, nor any subsequent change in the state of the art, such as later-developed technology, obfuscated the significance of the limitation at the time of its incorporation into the claim. If the applicant had desired broad patent protection it could have sought claims with fewer structural encumbrances. Had it done so, the PTO could have fulfilled its statutory role in helping to ensure that exclusive rights issue only to those who have, in fact, contributed something new, useful, and unobvious. Instead, it left the PTO with manifestly limited claims that it later sought to expand through the doctrine of equivalents. But as between the patentee who had a clear opportunity to negotiate broader claims but did not do so, and the public at large, it is the patentee who must bear the cost of its failure to seek protection for this foreseeable alteration of its claimed structure.

[320]*Sage Prods., Inc. v. Devon Indus., Inc.,* 126 F.3d 1420, 44 USPQ2d 1103 (Fed. Cir. 1997). In *Zodiac Pool Care Inc. v. Hoffinger Indus. Inc.,* 206 F.3d 1408, 54 USPQ2d 1141 (Fed. Cir. 2000), the court relied heavily on *Sage* in finding no infringement under the DOE. But it did not appear to base its conclusion on the proposition that makes *Sage* so important, i.e., that the alterations were foreseeable. Instead, it simply said that the patent contained a clear structural limitation such that, given the proper construction of the limitation, a verdict of infringement under the DOE would reduce the claims to nothing more than functional abstracts, devoid of meaningful structural limitations on which the public could rely. Perhaps this foreshadows a simplistic new way to decide that no reasonable jury could find equivalents. All that is necessary is that the court find that the structural limitations are extremely clear.

[321]*Sage Prods., Inc. v. Devon Indus., Inc.,* 126 F.3d 1420, 44 USPQ2d 1103 (Fed. Cir. 1997).

explicit function has been identified with a claim limitation entails an examination of the claim and the explanation of it found in the written description of the patent. In some cases, the patent's prosecution history also may reveal the identification of a specific function relating to claimed structure. This may result from an amendment to claim language that was made to overcome, for example, a prior art rejection by the examiner. In such cases, the judicial analysis of whether structure and its associated function has been surrendered is conducted under the rubric of prosecution history estoppel. The available scope of protection of a patent under the DOE is not, however, limited solely by PHE. A separate body of case law confirms that a patentee may otherwise lose the right to assert coverage of allegedly equivalent structure or matter.[322] Thus, statements in the patent specification clearly inform a reader of the patent about the role played by the disputed claim element and the scope the patentee intended the patent to cover. They affect the interpretation of the patent given by the patent examiner in determining whether the claims are patentable over the prior art and by competitors attempting to avoid infringement; likewise, they must affect the range of equivalents allowed by the court.[323]

(iv) Section 112 Equivalence

The sixth paragraph of §112 provides that:

> An element in a claim for a combination may be expressed as a means or step for performing a specified function without the recital of structure, material, or acts in support thereof, and such claim shall be construed to cover the corresponding structure, material, or acts described in the specification and equivalents thereof.

Accordingly, if all other limitations in such a claim are literally met, and the accused device is shown to contain an equivalent of the structure that was identified in the means-plus-function (MPF)[324] limitation of the claim and disclosed in the specification, infringement is said to be "literal" as distinguished from infringement under the DOE.[325] In considering equivalents under 35 U.S.C. §112¶6, the function performed by the accused device must be identical with that

---

[322]*Vehicular Techs. Corp. v. Titan Wheel Int'l,* 141 F.3d 1084, 46 USPQ2d 1257 (Fed. Cir. 1998). The court indicated that the case law to which it referred establishes that, through statements made during prosecution of a patent application, it can become evident that an asserted equivalent is beyond coverage under the doctrine of equivalents.

[323]*Vehicular Techs. Corp. v. Titan Wheel Int'l,* 141 F.3d 1084, 46 USPQ2d 1257 (Fed. Cir. 1998). In her dissent, Judge Newman characterizes the majority opinion as imposing a new rule of law: there is now no liability for infringement by an equivalent device if the equivalent does not possess the unclaimed advantages or functions described in the specification. She dubs this the "All-Advantages Rule."

[324]The acronym MPF is occasionally used in this section for brevity. It is intended to encompass both means-plus-function and step-plus-function elements unless the context is to the contrary.

[325]*Data Line Corp. v. Micro Techs., Inc.,* 813 F.2d 1196, 1 USPQ2d 2052 (Fed. Cir. 1987).

found in the claim element, not just equivalent. The test is equivalent structure to perform identical function.[326]

Thus, literal infringement of a §112¶6 limitation requires that the relevant structure in the accused device perform the identical function recited in the claim and be identical or equivalent to the corresponding structure in the specification. Functional identity and either structural identity or equivalence are both necessary. Structural equivalence under §112¶6 is an application of the DOE in a restrictive role. As such, their tests for equivalence are closely related, involving similar analyses of insubstantiality of differences. In the DOE context, the following test is often used: if the "function, way, or result" of the assertedly substitute structure is substantially different from that described by the claim limitation, equivalence is not established. But this tripartite test developed for the doctrine of equivalents is not wholly transferable to the §112¶6 statutory equivalence context. Instead, the statutory equivalence analysis, while rooted in similar concepts of insubstantial differences as its DOE counterpart, is narrower. This is because, under §112¶6 equivalence, functional identity is required; thus the equivalence (indeed, identity) of the "function" of the assertedly substitute structure, material, or acts must be first established in order to reach the statutory equivalence analysis. The content of the test for insubstantial differences under §112¶6 thus reduces to "way" and "result." That is, the statutory equivalence analysis requires a determination of whether the "way" the assertedly substitute structure performs the claimed function, and the "result" of that performance, is substantially different from the "way" the claimed function is performed by the "corresponding structure, acts, or materials described in the specification," or its "result." Structural equivalence under §112¶6 is met only if the differences are insubstantial, that is, if the assertedly equivalent structure performs the claimed function in substantially the same way to achieve substantially the same result as the corresponding structure described in the specification.[327]

---

[326]*Pennwalt Corp. v. Durand-Wayland, Inc.*, 833 F.2d 931, 4 USPQ2d 1737 (Fed. Cir. 1987). The court also rejected a converse argument: that if the accused structure performs the identical function, it is per se structurally equivalent. *Id.* An example is found in *In re Hayes Microcomputer Patent Litig.*, 982 F.2d 1527, 25 USPQ2d 1241 (Fed. Cir. 1992), where the claimed means was a microprocessor for performing certain specified functions. The patentee's expert witness simply testified that the accused device included a microprocessor and was functionally equivalent to the claimed invention. That was held sufficient to support the jury's conclusion that the means were structurally equivalent.

[327]*Odetics Inc. v. Storage Tech. Corp.*, 185 F.3d 1259, 51 USPQ2d 1225 (Fed. Cir. 1999). See also *Kemco Sales Inc. v. Control Papers Co.*, 208 F.3d 1352, 54 USPQ2d 1308 (Fed. Cir. 2000); *Alpex Computer Co. v. Nintendo Co.*, 102 F.3d 1214, 40 USPQ2d 1667 (Fed. Cir. 1997); *Sun Studs, Inc. v. ATA Equip. Leasing, Inc.*, 872 F.2d 978, 10 USPQ2d 1338 (Fed. Cir. 1989); *Texas Instr., Inc. v. United States ITC*, 805 F.2d 1558, 231 USPQ 833 (Fed. Cir. 1986); *Palumbo v. Don-Joy Co.*, 762 F.2d 969, 226 USPQ 5 (Fed. Cir. 1985); *D.M.I., Inc. v. Deere & Co.*, 755 F.2d 1570, 225 USPQ 236 (Fed. Cir. 1985). A reduced version of the well-known tripartite test for the doctrine of equivalents has been applied in the §112¶6 context to determine if the differences are insubstantial, i.e., after determining that the accused device performs the identical function, as required by statute, whether it performs the function in substantially

So we see that although equivalence analyses under §112¶6 and the DOE are not coextensive and have different origins and purposes, their tests for equivalence are closely related. As the court pointed out in *Chiuminatta v. Cardinal,* both protect the substance of a patentee's right to exclude by preventing mere colorable differences or slight improvements from escaping infringement, the former, by incorporating equivalents of disclosed structures into the literal scope of a functional claim limitation, and the latter, by holding as infringements equivalents that are beyond the literal scope of the claim. They do so by applying similar analyses of insubstantiality of the differences. Thus, a finding of a lack of literal infringement for lack of equivalent structure under a MPF limitation may preclude a finding of equivalence under the DOE. There is an important difference, however. The DOE is necessary because one cannot predict the future. Due to technological advances, a variant of an invention may be developed after the patent is granted, and that variant may constitute so insubstantial a change from what is claimed in the patent that it should be held to be an infringement. Such a variant, based on after-developed technology, could not have been disclosed in the patent. Even if such an element is found not to be a §112¶6 equivalent because it is not equivalent to the structure disclosed in the patent, this analysis should not foreclose it from being an equivalent under the DOE. But where the equivalence issue does not involve later developed technologies, but rather involves technology that predates the invention itself, a finding of nonequivalence for §112¶6 purposes should preclude a contrary finding under the DOE. There is no policy-based reason why a patentee should get two bites at the apple. If he or she could have included in the patent what is now alleged to be equivalent, and did not, leading to a conclusion that an accused device lacks an equivalent to the disclosed structure, why should the issue of equivalence have to be litigated a second time (except in the case of variants of the invention based on after-developed technologies)? An element of a device cannot be "not equivalent" and equivalent to the same structure.[328]

---

the same way to achieve substantially the same result. *IMS Tech. Inc. v. Haas Automation Inc.,* 206 F.3d 1422, 54 USPQ2d 1129 (Fed. Cir. 2000).

[328]*Chiuminatta Concrete Concepts Inc. v. Cardinal Indus. Inc.,* 145 F.3d 1303, 46 USPQ2d 1752 (Fed. Cir. 1998). A finding of no literal infringement for lack of equivalent structure under a MPF limitation may preclude a finding of equivalence under the doctrine of equivalents. Both equivalence inquiries, after all, apply similar analyses of insubstantiality of the differences. This confluence occurs because infringement requires, either literally or under the doctrine of equivalents, that the accused product or process incorporate each limitation of the claimed invention. Therefore, if an accused product or process performs the identical function and yet avoids literal infringement for lack of a §112¶6 structural equivalent, it may well fail to infringe the same functional element under the doctrine of equivalents. This same reasoning may be applied in reverse in certain circumstances. *Al-Site Corp. v. VSI Int'l Inc.,* 174 F.3d 1308, 50 USPQ2d 1161 (Fed. Cir. 1999). Not long prior to *Chiuminatta* each member of a three-judge panel had engaged in interesting dicta on this very subject. See *Dawn Equip. Corp. v. Kentucky Farms Inc.,* 140 F.3d 1009, 46 USPQ2d 1109 (Fed. Cir. 1998). But *Chiuminatta's* preclusion of a finding of infringement under the doctrine of equivalents for preexisting technology after an adverse holding of no literal infringement for the same technology applies only to MPF

In a later case, the court carried *Chiuminatta* a bit further, and held that a structural equivalent under §112¶6 must have been available at the time of the issuance of the claim. An equivalent structure or act under §112¶6 cannot embrace technology developed after the issuance of the patent because the literal meaning of a claim is fixed upon its issuance. An "after-arising equivalent" infringes, if at all, under the traditional DOE. Thus, the temporal difference between patent issuance and infringement distinguishes an equivalent under §112¶6 from an equivalent under the DOE. In other words, an equivalent structure or act under §112¶6 for literal infringement must have been available at the time of patent issuance while an equivalent under the DOE may arise after patent issuance and before the time of infringement. An "after-arising" technology could thus infringe under the DOE without infringing literally as a §112¶6 equivalent. A proposed equivalent must have arisen at a definite period in time, i.e., either before or after patent issuance. If before, a §112¶6 structural equivalents analysis applies and any analysis for equivalent structure under the DOE collapses into the §112¶6 analysis. If after, a nontextual infringement analysis proceeds under the DOE. Patent policy supports application of the DOE to a claim element expressed in MPF form in the case of "after-arising" technology because a patent draftsman has no way to anticipate and account for later developed substitutes for a claim element. Therefore, the DOE appropriately allows marginally broader coverage than §112¶6.[329]

In another case, a divided panel held that *Chiuminatta* does not compel the conclusion that *Pennwalt* and *Warner-Jenkinson* command a component-by-component analysis of structural equivalence under §112¶6. It is of course axiomatic that each element contained in a patent claim is deemed material to determining the scope of the patented invention. Thus a claim limitation written in §112¶6 form, like all claim limitations, must be met, literally or equivalently, for infringement to lie. But such a limitation is literally met by structure, materials, or acts in the accused device that perform the claimed function in substantially the same way to achieve substantially the same result. The individual components, if any, of an overall structure that corresponds to the claimed function are not claim limitations. Rather, the claim limitation is the overall structure corresponding to

---

claim limitations. Where the patentee does not use the MPF format, the resolution of infringement under the doctrine of equivalents would not allow the patentee "two bites at the apple," since the resolution of the literal infringement question would not address the issue of equivalence in a claim drawn to structure rather than to MPF. Thus, for a claim limitation not drafted in MPF language, the mere fact that the asserted equivalent structure was preexisting technology does not foreclose a finding of infringement under the doctrine of equivalents. *Kraft Foods Inc. v. International Trading Co.,* 203 F.3d 1362, 53 USPQ2d 1814 (Fed. Cir. 2000). But see the discussion beginning at note 6:318.

[329]*Al-Site Corp. v. VSI Int'l Inc.,* 174 F.3d 1308, 50 USPQ2d 1161 (Fed. Cir. 1999). Strangely enough, six months earlier, the court had indicated that, for purposes of infringement under §112¶6, the accused equivalent structure need not have been known at the time the patented invention was made. *C.R. Bard Inc. v. M3 Sys. Inc.,* 157 F.3d 1340, 48 USPQ2d 1225 (Fed. Cir. 1998). It seems unlikely that the court is consciously distinguishing between the date of

the claimed function. This is why structures with different numbers of parts may still be equivalent under §112¶6, thereby meeting the claim limitation. The appropriate degree of specificity is provided by the statute itself; the relevant structure is that which "corresponds" to the claimed function. Further deconstruction or parsing is incorrect.[330]

So a structure in an accused device is equivalent to the disclosed structure corresponding to a MPF element if it is insubstantially different from the disclosed structure.[331] In *IMS v. Haas Automation,*[332] the court walked a fine line in attempting to illuminate the difference between equivalent structures and structural equivalency. In light of the similarity of the tests for equivalence under §112¶6 and the doctrine of equivalents, the context of the invention should be considered when performing a MPF equivalence analysis just as it is in a doctrine of equivalents determination. As a result, two structures that are equivalent in one environment may not be equivalent in another. More particularly, when in a claimed "means" limitation the disclosed physical structure is of little or no importance to the claimed invention, there may be a broader range of equivalent structures than if the physical characteristics of the structure are critical in performing the claimed function in the context of the claimed invention. Thus, a rigid comparison of physical structures in a vacuum may be inappropriate in a particular case. Indeed, the statute requires two structures to be equivalent, but it does not require them to be "structurally equivalent," i.e., it does not mandate an equivalency comparison that necessarily focuses heavily or exclusively on physical structure. In some cases, an analysis of insubstantial differences in the context of the invention results in a finding of equivalence under §112¶6 even though two structures arguably would not be considered equivalent structures in other contexts, e.g., if performing functions other than the claimed function. In other cases, in which the specific physical features of the structure corresponding to the "means" limitation may have more relevance to the claimed invention, a finding of noninfringement results.

The *Chuiminatta* court seemed to downplay interchangeability as an indicator of §112¶6 equivalency. Almost by definition, two structures that perform the same function may be substituted for one another. The question of known interchangeability is not whether both structures serve the same function, but whether it was known that one structure was an equivalent of another. Moreover, a finding of known interchangeability, while an important factor in determining

---

invention and the date of patenting in this context. See also *Ishida Co. v. Taylor,* 221 F.3d 1310, 55 USPQ2d 1449 (Fed. Cir. 2000).

[330]*Odetics Inc. v. Storage Tech. Corp.,* 185 F.3d 1259, 51 USPQ2d 1225 (Fed. Cir. 1999).

[331]*Cortland Line Co. v. Orvis Co.,* 203 F.3d 1353, 53 USPQ2d 1734 (Fed. Cir. 2000).

[332]*IMS Tech. Inc. v. Haas Automation Inc.,* 206 F.3d 1422, 54 USPQ2d 1129 (Fed. Cir. 2000).

equivalence, is certainly not dispositive.[333] Where the patent specification indicates that a structure like that in the accused device is incapable of achieving the goal of the invention, a conclusion that the structure was not a §112¶6 equivalent of the disclosed structure is justified.[334] The fact that two structures may perform unrelated and, more to the point, unclaimed functions differently or not at all is simply not pertinent to the measure of §112¶6 equivalents.[335]

The court has squarely held that it is not necessary to consider the prior art in applying §112 equivalents. Even if the prior art discloses the same or an equivalent structure, the claim will not be limited in scope thereby. It is only necessary to determine what is an equivalent to the structure disclosed in the specification that is performing the function at issue. When prior art is considered in the context of the DOE, the purpose is to ensure that the patent holder does not obtain a broader right to exclude under that doctrine than could have been obtained from the PTO. But the policies underlying that concept are not served by restricting claim limitations in the same manner. Thus, under §112, the aids for determining a structural equivalent to the structure disclosed in the patent are the same as those used in interpreting any other type of claim language, namely, the specification, the prosecution history, other claims in the patent, and expert testimony. Although *Texas Instruments* suggested that there might be some similarities between the equivalence analysis under §112 and under the traditional DOE, it did not suggest that prior art should be considered in determining literal satisfaction of a MPF claim limitation.[336]

The sixth paragraph of §112, while permitting equivalents, is nonetheless restrictive. It was adopted after the *Graver* decision[337] and thus the test that can be derived from *Graver*—that literal infringement is satisfied by any means that performs the function of a claim element—does not survive paragraph six. Paragraph six rules out the possibility that any and every means that perform the function specified in the claim literally satisfies that limitation. The function must be performed by an equivalent of the means disclosed in the patent.[338] Paragraph six does not expand the scope of a claim. An element of a claim described as a means for performing a function, if read literally, would encompass any means for performing the function. The sixth paragraph of §112 operates to cut back on the types

---

[333]*Chiuminatta Concrete Concepts Inc. v. Cardinal Indus. Inc.*, 145 F.3d 1303, 46 USPQ2d 1752 (Fed. Cir. 1998). But see *IMS Tech. Inc. v. Haas Automation Inc.*, 206 F.3d 1422, 54 USPQ2d 1129 (Fed. Cir. 2000), where the court recognized that evidence of known interchangeability between structure in the accused device and the disclosed structure has been considered an important factor.

[334]*Signtech USA Ltd v. Vutek Inc.*, 174 F.3d 1352, 50 USPQ2d 1372 (Fed. Cir. 1999).

[335]*Odetics Inc. v. Storage Tech. Corp.*, 185 F.3d 1259, 51 USPQ2d 1225 (Fed. Cir. 1999).

[336]*Intel Corp. v. United States ITC*, 946 F.2d 821, 20 USPQ2d 1161 (Fed. Cir. 1991).

[337]See note 6:206.

[338]*Pennwalt Corp. v. Durand-Wayland, Inc.*, 833 F.2d 931, 4 USPQ2d 1737 (Fed. Cir. 1987).

of means that could literally satisfy the claim language. On the other hand, the provision has no effect on the function specified—it does not extend the element to equivalent functions. Properly understood the provision operates more like the reverse DOE than the DOE because it restricts the scope of the literal claim language.[339]

The purpose of the sixth paragraph of §112 is to grant the inventor of a combination invention a fair scope that is not dependent on a catalogue of alternative embodiments in the specification. The claimed invention is not to be limited to preferred embodiments or specific examples in the specification. The details of performing each step need not be included in the claims unless required to distinguish the claimed invention from the prior art, or otherwise specifically point out and distinctly claim the invention. Nor must all possible methods of carrying out each step of the combination be described in the specification.[340]

While the scope of claims under paragraph six of §112 is a legal determination,[341] the scope of such equivalents is a question of fact, and once the accused device has been found to be an equivalent then literal infringement has properly been established.[342] It is the burden of the patentee to show, with respect to a claim limitation in MPF form, that the structure in the accused device that performs that function is the same as or an equivalent of the structure disclosed in the specification.[343] If infringement is found by a jury under such circumstances, the issue is whether a reasonable jury could have found the accused infringement to contain an equivalent of the means actually disclosed in the patent.[344] As aids in determining the breadth of §112 equivalence, the prosecution history, the other claims in the

---

[339]*Johnston v. IVAC Corp.*, 885 F.2d 1574, 12 USPQ2d 1382 (Fed. Cir. 1989). See also *Valmont Indus., Inc. v. Reinke Mfg. Co.*, 983 F.2d 1039, 25 USPQ2d 1451 (Fed. Cir. 1993). In an interesting situation, the result of a §112 equivalents analysis was that two claims, one from each of two separate patents, turned out to have exactly the same scope. *Jonsson v. Stanley Works*, 903 F.2d 812, 14 USPQ2d 1863 (Fed. Cir. 1990).

[340]*Texas Instr., Inc. v. United States ITC*, 805 F.2d 1558, 231 USPQ 833 (Fed. Cir. 1986).

[341]*Texas Instr., Inc. v. United States ITC*, 805 F.2d 1558, 231 USPQ 833 (Fed. Cir. 1986).

[342]*Odetics Inc. v. Storage Tech. Corp.*, 185 F.3d 1259, 51 USPQ2d 1225 (Fed. Cir. 1999); *Carroll Touch, Inc. v. Electro Mechanical Sys., Inc.*, 3 F.3d 404, 27 USPQ2d 1836 (Fed. Cir. 1993); *King Instr. Corp. v. Otari Corp.*, 767 F.2d 853, 226 USPQ 402 (Fed. Cir. 1985); *Palumbo v. Don-Joy Co.*, 762 F.2d 969, 226 USPQ 5 (Fed. Cir. 1985). See also *IMS Tech. Inc. v. Haas Automation Inc.*, 206 F.3d 1422, 54 USPQ2d 1129 (Fed. Cir. 2000). The determination whether an accused device is a §112 equivalent of the described embodiment is a question of fact and can be reversed only if it is clearly erroneous. *Durango Assoc., Inc. v. Reflange, Inc.*, 843 F.2d 1349, 6 USPQ2d 1290 (Fed. Cir. 1988). Section 112 equivalence is a question of fact as is regular equivalence and reverse equivalence. *Hartness Int'l, Inc. v. Simplimatic Eng'g Co.*, 819 F.2d 1100, 2 USPQ2d 1826 (Fed. Cir. 1987). See text accompanying notes 5:388–392.

[343]*Pennwalt Corp. v. Durand-Wayland, Inc.*, 833 F.2d 931, 4 USPQ2d 1737 (Fed. Cir. 1987). Nonetheless, under FRE 705 it is permissible for an expert witness to give an opinion on the ultimate question of infringement without providing the factual foundation for the opinion. Thus, an expert may give an opinion on literal infringement without testifying as to §112 equivalency. *Symbol Tech., Inc. v. Opticon, Inc.*, 935 F.2d 1569, 19 USPQ2d 1241 (Fed. Cir. 1991).

[344]*Data Line Corp. v. Micro Techs., Inc.*, 813 F.2d 1196, 1 USPQ2d 2052 (Fed. Cir. 1987).

patent, expert testimony, and the language of the asserted claims may be considered in addition to the specification.[345] Prosecution history is relevant to the construction of a claim written in MPF form. Indeed, just as PHE may act to estop an equivalence argument under the DOE, positions taken before the PTO may bar an inconsistent position on claim construction under §112¶6. Clear assertions made in support of patentability thus may affect the range of equivalents under §112¶6. The relevant inquiry is whether a competitor would reasonably believe that the applicant had surrendered the relevant subject matter.[346]

The pioneer status of the invention also requires consideration.[347] Indeed, the inquiry is not devoid of equitable considerations, particularly when determining the breadth of means claims in complex and rapidly evolving technologies. There is a limit on changed means of performing a claimed function. There must be outer boundaries to the scope of the sixth paragraph of §112 when the factual situation strains the rote application of the rule. There is no abstract guide to determining when a modified device crosses the boundary with respect to the reasonable scope of patent claims. Indeed, the determination of infringement is not made in the abstract but in the context of the claimed invention and the accused devices.[348]

(b) Prosecution History Estoppel

(i) In General

In applying the DOE, a court must avoid significant conflict with the fundamental principle that claims define the limits of patent protection. One important rule that prevents this clash is PHE.[349] The Supreme Court in *Warner-Jenkinson*[350] recently confirmed that *Graver Tank*[351] did not dispose of PHE as a legal limitation on the

---

[345]*Texas Instr., Inc. v. United States ITC,* 805 F.2d 1558, 231 USPQ 833 (Fed. Cir. 1986); *King Instr. Corp. v. Otari Corp.,* 767 F.2d 853, 226 USPQ 402 (Fed. Cir. 1985); *Palumbo v. Don-Joy Co.,* 762 F.2d 969, 226 USPQ 5 (Fed. Cir. 1985). Does PHE apply to §112 equivalency analyses? It is difficult to read *Alpex Computer Co. v. Nintendo Co.,* 102 F.3d 1214, 40 USPQ2d 1667 (Fed. Cir. 1997), any other way. See also *Cybor Corp. v. FAS Tech. Inc.,* 138 F.3d 1448, 46 USPQ2d 1169, 1175 (Fed. Cir. 1998). The fact that the asserted equivalent means is an improvement does not preclude a finding of infringement. *Texas Instr., Inc. v. United States ITC,* 805 F.2d 1558, 231 USPQ 833 (Fed. Cir. 1986).

[346]*Cybor Corp. v. FAS Tech. Inc.,* 138 F.3d 1448, 46 USPQ2d 1169, 1175 (Fed. Cir. 1998).

[347]*Texas Instr., Inc. v. United States ITC,* 805 F.2d 1558, 231 USPQ 833 (Fed. Cir. 1986).

[348]*Texas Instr., Inc. v. United States ITC,* 805 F.2d 1558, 231 USPQ 833 (Fed. Cir. 1986). As we have seen, multiple equivalents may avoid infringement under the doctrine of equivalents and, by the same token, avoid literal infringement even with reference to §112 equivalency. *Id.*

[349]*Charles Greiner & Co. v. Mari-Med Mfg., Inc.,* 962 F.2d 1031, 22 USPQ2d 1526 (Fed. Cir. 1992).

[350]*Warner-Jenkinson Co. v. Hilton Davis Chem. Co.,* 520 U.S. 17, 41 USPQ2d 1865 (1997).

[351]See note 6:249.

DOE and that it continues to be available as a defense to an infringement claim.

There are limitations to the DOE. The doctrine has been judicially devised to do equity in situations where there is no literal infringement but liability is nevertheless appropriate to prevent what is in essence a pirating of the patentee's invention. Concomitantly, two policy-oriented limitations, applied as questions of law, have developed. First, the doctrine will not extend to an infringing device within the public domain, i.e., found in the prior art at the time the patent issued. Second, PHE will not allow the patentee to recapture through equivalence certain coverage given up during prosecution.[352] Under the doctrine of PHE, claim amendments and arguments may preclude a patentee from recapturing what was foregone during prosecution of the patent application. Similarly, the range of equivalents to which a claimed invention is entitled may never be so great as to encompass a structure in the prior art. The doctrines of PHE and equivalents are equitable in nature, requiring courts to engage in a balancing analysis guided by the equitable and public policy principles underlying the doctrines involved and by the facts of the particular case.[353]

The doctrine of prosecution history (or "file wrapper") estoppel[354] is an equitable tool for determining the permissible scope of patent claims.[355] The essence of PHE is that a patentee should not be able to obtain, through litigation, coverage of subject matter relinquished during prosecution. The legal standard for determining what subject matter was relinquished is an objective one, measured from the vantage point of what a competitor was reasonably entitled to conclude, from the prosecution history, that the applicant gave up to procure issuance of the patent.[356] Material representations made to the PTO

[352]*Loctite Corp. v. Ultraseal Ltd.*, 781 F.2d 861, 228 USPQ 90 (Fed. Cir. 1985). Determination of either condition does not, however, require reassessment of validity or a reinterpretation of the claims as written. *Perkin-Elmer Corp. v. Computervision Corp.*, 732 F.2d 888, 221 USPQ 669 (Fed. Cir. 1984). See also *Loctite Corp. v. Ultraseal Ltd.*, 781 F.2d 861, 228 USPQ 90 (Fed. Cir. 1985). But see *Wilson Sporting Goods Co. v. David Geoffrey & Assoc.*, 904 F.2d 677, 14 USPQ2d 1942 (Fed. Cir. 1990).

[353]*Black & Decker, Inc. v. Hoover Serv. Ctr.*, 886 F.2d 1285, 12 USPQ2d 1250 (Fed. Cir. 1989). See also *Sofamor Danek Group, Inc. v. DePuy-Motech, Inc.*, 74 F.3d 1216, 37 USPQ2d 1529 (Fed. Cir. 1996).

[354]Although the doctrine has long and widely been referred to as "file wrapper estoppel," the Federal Circuit has indicated a preference for "prosecution history estoppel." *Amstar Corp. v. Envirotech Corp.*, 730 F.2d 1476, 221 USPQ 649 (Fed. Cir. 1984).

[355]*Mannesmann Demag Corp. v. Engineered Metal Prods. Co.*, 793 F.2d 1279, 230 USPQ 45 (Fed. Cir. 1986); *Builders Concrete, Inc. v. Bremerton Concrete Prods. Co.*, 757 F.2d 255, 225 USPQ 240 (Fed. Cir. 1985).

[356]*Mark I Mkt'g Corp. v. R.R. Donnelley & Sons*, 66 F.3d 285, 36 USPQ2d 1095 (Fed. Cir. 1995); *Haynes Int'l, Inc. v. Jessop Steel Co.*, 8 F.3d 1573, 28 USPQ2d 1652 (Fed. Cir. 1993). Of course the court recognizes that claims speak to one of ordinary skill in the art, while this test measures from the vantage point of a reasonable competitor. Under the circumstances, these formulations are not inconsistent. See also *Hoganas AB v. Dresser Indus., Inc.*, 9 F.3d 948, 28 USPQ2d 1936 (Fed. Cir. 1993). In examining the prosecution history in an estoppel analysis, the court does not look to the subjective intent of the applicant and what the applicant subjectively believed or intended that he or she was giving up to the public. Rather, the standard for determining what subject matter was surrendered is objective and depends on what a

in response to references cited by the PTO, with the result that the scope of the patent claims is changed in order to obtain the patent grant, are pertinent to the subsequent determination of the permissible scope of the patent claims.[357] The doctrine bars a patentee from construing its claims in a way that would resurrect subject matter previously surrendered during prosecution of the patent application.[358] It limits a patentee's reliance upon the DOE by preventing it from contending later that its claims should be interpreted as if limitations added by amendment were not present or that claims abandoned are still present. Further, when the patentee relies upon the DOE, it opens the door to rebuttal based upon prior representations made by it to the PTO that appear in the file history of its patent.[359]

The Federal Circuit has said that file wrapper estoppel is irrelevant where there is literal infringement.[360] Do not take this statement too broadly. The court occasionally lapses into a seeming application of the doctrine in a literal infringement setting.[361] The court explains the matter this way: there is a clear line of distinction between using the contents of the prosecution history to reach an understanding about disputed claim language and the doctrine of PHE, which estops or limits later expansion of the protection accorded by the claim

---

competitor, reading the prosecution history, would reasonably conclude was given up by the applicant. *Insituform Tech., Inc. v. CAT Contr., Inc.*, 99 F.3d 1098, 40 USPQ2d 1602 (Fed. Cir. 1996). A patentee is not free to retrade or renege on a deal struck with the PTO during patent prosecution. *Sage Prods., Inc. v. Devon Indus., Inc.*, 126 F.3d 1420, 44 USPQ2d 1103 (Fed. Cir. 1997).

[357]*Builders Concrete, Inc. v. Bremerton Concrete Prods. Co.*, 757 F.2d 255, 225 USPQ 240 (Fed. Cir. 1985). A straightforward example of the application of the doctrine is found in *Dixie USA, Inc. v. Infab Corp.*, 927 F.2d 584, 17 USPQ2d 1968 (Fed. Cir. 1991). In response to a rejection, the applicant amended the claim to require that openings be rectangular and round and argued that none of the prior art disclosed both rectangular and round openings. The accused structure had rectangular openings but no round ones and thus estoppel prevented a finding of infringement.

[358]*Mark I Mkt'g Corp. v. R.R. Donnelley & Sons*, 66 F.3d 285, 36 USPQ2d 1095 (Fed. Cir. 1995); *Texas Instr., Inc. v. United States ITC*, 988 F.2d 1165, 26 USPQ2d 1018 (Fed. Cir. 1993); *Jonsson v. Stanley Works*, 903 F.2d 812, 14 USPQ2d 1863 (Fed. Cir. 1990); *Mannesmann Demag Corp. v. Engineered Metal Prods. Co.*, 793 F.2d 1279, 230 USPQ 45 (Fed. Cir. 1986); *Thomas & Betts Corp. v. Litton Sys., Inc.*, 720 F.2d 1572, 220 USPQ 1 (Fed. Cir. 1983). For example, when an accused device is the same as a disclosed embodiment, and claims covering the disclosed embodiment are rejected and canceled, the yielded claim scope cannot be recovered in order to encompass the accused device through the doctrine of equivalents. *Diversitech Corp. v. Century Steps, Inc.*, 850 F.2d 675, 7 USPQ2d 1315 (Fed. Cir. 1988). The rejected claim was to a device with a coating on all sides; the final claims recited a coating on top and sides only. The specification said a coating could be put on the bottom as well. The defendant put a thin coating on the bottom and the patentee argued equivalency. Inasmuch as equivalence was demonstrated in the specification, the Federal Circuit's refusal to accept this argument is clearly grounded on estoppel. Although the claim was not amended, the broader claim from which it depended was canceled.

[359]*Thomas & Betts Corp. v. Litton Sys., Inc.*, 720 F.2d 1572, 220 USPQ 1 (Fed. Cir. 1983).

[360]*Fromson v. Advance Offset Plate, Inc.*, 720 F.2d 1565, 219 USPQ 1137 (Fed. Cir. 1983).

[361]See, e.g., *Key Mfg. Group, Inc. v. Microdot, Inc.*, 925 F.2d 1444, 17 USPQ2d 1806 (Fed. Cir. 1991). Certainly literal claim coverage would be limited by a clear disavowal of coverage during prosecution. *York Prods., Inc. v. Central Tractor Farm & Fam. Ctr.*, 99 F.3d 1568, 40 USPQ2d 1619 (Fed. Cir. 1996).

under the DOE when the claims have been purposefully amended or distinguished over relevant art to give up scope. Thus, it is technically correct to say that the doctrine of PHE is irrelevant to determination of literal claim scope. On the other hand, a particular interpretation of a claim term may have been disclaimed by the inventor during prosecution. Thus it is incorrect to ignore the prosecution history when interpreting claims.[362] The prosecution history is especially important when the invention involves a crowded art field, or when there is particular prior art that the applicant is trying to distinguish.[363]

Thus, the same statements in the prosecution history can be used both to interpret the claims and to determine whether there is PHE. The two doctrines must be distinguished. Interpreting claims in view of the prosecution history applies as a preliminary step in determining literal infringement. PHE applies as a limitation to the DOE after the claims have been properly interpreted and no literal infringement is found.[364] Using the file history and arguments made during prosecution to ascertain the true meaning of what the inventor intended to convey in the claims is different from PHE, which is applied as a limitation upon the DOE after the claims have been properly interpreted. It is improper to consider prosecution history arguments only for the latter purpose. Nor need the PTO examiner have relied upon such arguments in order to make them relevant for claim interpretation purposes. They shed light on what the applicant meant by certain terms. On the other hand, merely because certain prosecution history is used to define the claims more narrowly does not preclude the possibility of an appropriate range of equivalents under the DOE. In other words, the two purposes must be kept separate.[365]

Different standards of estoppel apply before and after a patent issues. It is much easier to ameliorate an act or omission before the patent issues. A patent attorney should not be able to choose one course of action within the PTO with the anticipation that, if later checked, he or she can always choose an alternate course of prosecution in a trial before a federal judge.[366] Nonetheless, it is clearly not

---

[362]*Biodex Corp. v. Loredan Biomedical, Inc.*, 946 F.2d 850, 20 USPQ2d 1252 (Fed. Cir. 1991).

[363]*Lemelson v. General Mills, Inc.*, 968 F.2d 1202, 23 USPQ2d 1284 (Fed. Cir. 1992).

[364]*Loctite Corp. v. Ultraseal Ltd.*, 781 F.2d 861, 228 USPQ 90 (Fed. Cir. 1985). See also *Moleculon Res. Corp. v. CBS, Inc.*, 793 F.2d 1261, 229 USPQ 805 (Fed. Cir. 1986); *McGill Inc. v. John Zink Co.*, 736 F.2d 666, 221 USPQ 944 (Fed. Cir. 1984). Apparently the court is willing to apply an estoppel to a question of §112¶6 equivalency. *Alpex Computer Co. v. Nintendo Co.*, 102 F.3d 1214, 40 USPQ2d 1667 (Fed. Cir. 1997).

[365]*E.I. duPont & Co. v. Phillips Petroleum Co.*, 849 F.2d 1430, 7 USPQ2d 1129 (Fed. Cir. 1988). But this is much more difficult than it sounds, for judges and for lawyers. See also *Southwall Tech., Inc. v. Cardinal IG Co.*, 54 F.3d 1570, 34 USPQ2d 1673 (Fed. Cir. 1995); *Senmed, Inc. v. Richard-Allan Med. Indus., Inc.*, 888 F.2d 815, 12 USPQ2d 1508 (Fed. Cir. 1989).

[366]*Litton Sys., Inc. v. Whirlpool Corp.*, 728 F.2d 1423, 221 USPQ 97 (Fed. Cir. 1984). In *In re Morris*, 127 F.3d 1048, 44 USPQ2d 1023 (Fed. Cir. 1997), the applicant added a limitation, but never argued that it distinguished over the prior art. On appeal, it advocated a narrow interpretation of the language in order to do just that. This, according to the court, looks like a veiled attempt to avoid the potential future effects of PHE. Such evasiveness cannot be

improper for an attorney to seek to distinguish, in a subsequent infringement action, arguments made to the PTO.[367] The court will not consider arguments made by a different attorney, prosecuting a later patent application, for a different inventor, as limiting the scope of the claims in a patent, even though both patent and application are owned by the same assignee.[368]

The doctrine of PHE is not an independent ground for relief.[369] It is an affirmative defense and must be pleaded.[370] The accused infringer must do more than create a "fog of false estoppel."[371]

The application of PHE is a question of law[372] and is reviewed for legal correctness.[373] Whether or not an amendment was made for reasons of patentability is a legal question.[374]

(ii) Amendments Versus Remarks

The Federal Circuit has said that remarks, as well as amendments, can create a PHE, at least where the reason for the remark is to avoid the prior art.[375] The court has recently come down with

---

condoned. This case may signal a policy directed to nipping evasiveness in the bud, before the patent issues.

[367]*Stratoflex, Inc. v. Aeroquip Corp.*, 713 F.2d 1530, 218 USPQ 871 (Fed. Cir. 1983). A contrary rule would automatically disqualify the prosecuting attorney from handling the litigation.

[368]*Water Techs. Corp. v. Calco, Ltd.*, 850 F.2d 660, 7 USPQ2d 1097 (Fed. Cir. 1988). See also *Laitram Corp. v. Cambridge Wire Cloth Co.*, 863 F.2d 855, 9 USPQ2d 1289 (Fed. Cir. 1988).

[369]*Ball Corp. v. United States*, 729 F.2d 1429, 221 USPQ 289 (Fed. Cir. 1984).

[370]*Carman Indus., Inc. v. Wahl*, 724 F.2d 932, 220 USPQ 481 (Fed. Cir. 1983).

[371]*Amstar Corp. v. Envirotech Corp.*, 730 F.2d 1476, 221 USPQ 649, 656 (Fed. Cir. 1984). A classical estoppel occurs where the accused infringer does more than make minor immaterial changes and instead adopts the very element that the inventor had eliminated from his or her claims for the stated purpose of avoiding the examiner's rejection. *Kinzenbaw v. Deere & Co.*, 741 F.2d 383, 222 USPQ 929 (Fed. Cir. 1984).

[372]*Mark I Mkt'g Corp. v. R.R. Donnelley & Sons*, 66 F.3d 285, 36 USPQ2d 1095 (Fed. Cir. 1995); *Wang Labs., Inc. v. Toshiba Corp.*, 993 F.2d 858, 26 USPQ2d 1767 (Fed. Cir. 1993). See also *Modine Mfg. Co. v. United States ITC*, 75 F.3d 1545, 37 USPQ2d 1609 (Fed. Cir. 1996). But see *Thomas & Betts Corp. v. Litton Sys., Inc.*, 720 F.2d 1572, 220 USPQ 1 (Fed. Cir. 1983).

[373]*LaBounty Mfg., Inc. v. United States ITC*, 867 F.2d 1572, 9 USPQ2d 1995 (Fed. Cir. 1989). PHE is subject to de novo review. *Loral Fairchild Corp. v. Sony Corp.*, 181 F.3d 1313, 50 USPQ2d 1865 (Fed. Cir. 1999). PHE is a policy-oriented limitation to the range of equivalents available to the patent, a limitation reviewed by the Federal Circuit as a matter of law. *Texas Instr., Inc. v. United States ITC*, 988 F.2d 1165, 26 USPQ2d 1018 (Fed. Cir. 1993). The court regards itself as free to undertake a complete and independent analysis of the issue. *Hoganas AB v. Dresser Indus., Inc.*, 9 F.3d 948, 28 USPQ2d 1936 (Fed. Cir. 1993).

[374]*K-2 Corp. v. Salomon S.A.*, 191 F.3d 1356, 52 USPQ2d 1001 (Fed. Cir. 1999).

[375]*Townsend Eng'r Co. v. HiTec Co.*, 829 F.2d 1086, 4 USPQ2d 1136 (Fed. Cir. 1987); *Hughes Aircraft Co. v. United States*, 717 F.2d 1351, 219 USPQ 473 (Fed. Cir. 1983). One case that apparently squarely so holds involved a claim to a process using ionic copper as a catalyst. The specification indicated that metallic copper used alone was ineffective, and the attorney also responded to the examiner's prior art rejection of the claim by distinguishing the art on the ground that it disclosed metallic copper, "which is outside the claims." It was held that the patentee, by this "disclaimer or concession" had surrendered any interpretation of its claim that would include metallic copper catalysts. *Standard Oil Co. v. American Cyanamid Co.*, 774 F.2d 448, 227 USPQ 293 (Fed. Cir. 1985).

some significant decisions in this area, but they will of course have to be reevaluated in light of the Supreme Court's *Warner-Jenkinson*[376] ruling, and the court's own *Festo*[377] decision, both discussed at length in the following section. In *Haynes v. Jessop,*[378] the court listed a broad range of activities that can give rise to PHE despite no amendment to a claim. These include (1) statements contained in a disclosure document placed in the PTO file as well as representations made during the prosecution of a parent application, (2) remarks made during prosecution of a claim not in suit as well as statements made after the examiner indicated the claims in suit were allowable, and (3) arguments submitted to obtain the patent.[379] In *Southwall v. Cardinal,*[380] the patentee was relying on *Read v. Portec*[381] for the proposition that unless the accused device contains all the features of the prior art used in distinguishing the asserted claims, estoppel cannot apply. The court disagreed. *Read* held that multiple arguments do not always create multiple estoppels, not that they never do. The correct view is that sometimes they do and sometimes they do not. The prosecution history as a whole must be examined in determining whether, based on a particular argument, a particular estoppel applies. For instance, any argument made regarding the need to distinguish the prior art does create a separate estoppel, regardless of other distinctions made. Thus, PHE is not limited only to the embodiments shown in the prior art. In other words, the limits imposed by PHE on the permissible range of equivalents can be broader than those imposed by the prior art.[382]

The *Southwall v. Cardinal* opinion went on to elaborate: estoppel extends beyond the basis of patentability. Clear assertions made during prosecution in support of patentability, whether or not actually required to secure allowance of the claim, may also create an estoppel. And once an argument is made regarding a claim term so as to create an estoppel, the estoppel will apply to that term in other claims. Competitors must be able to rely on the definition of a claim term given in the prosecution history, even when the term is later incorporated into different claims, in order to understand what constitutes infringement. Given the metamorphosis that claims often go through during prosecution, it is often impossible to trace the lineage of the

---

[376]*Warner-Jenkinson Co. v. Hilton Davis Chem. Co.*, 520 U.S. 17, 41 USPQ2d 1865 (1997).

[377]*Festo Corp. v. Shoketsu KKK Co.,* 234 F.3d 558, 56 USPQ2d 1865 (Fed. Cir. 2000).

[378]*Haynes Int'l, Inc. v. Jessop Steel Co.,* 8 F.3d 1573, 28 USPQ2d 1652 (Fed. Cir. 1993).

[379]Perhaps this discussion may have been unnecessary. The claim in question had never been amended in the classical sense. But because it was a dependent claim later rewritten in independent form, that action was the equivalent of amending the original independent claim. Viewed that way, there was an amendment.

[380]*Southwall Tech., Inc. v. Cardinal IG Co.*, 54 F.3d 1570, 34 USPQ2d 1673 (Fed. Cir. 1995).

[381]*Read Corp. v. Portec, Inc.,* 970 F.2d 816, 23 USPQ2d 1426 (Fed. Cir. 1992); see the discussion at note 6:387.

[382]See the discussion at note 6:385.

finally allowed claims to decide which arguments pertained to which claims.[383]

Thus an amendment to the claim being asserted is not absolutely necessary in order to create a PHE.[384] Positions taken in order to obtain allowance of an applicant's claims are pertinent to an understanding and interpretation of the claims that are granted by the PTO and may work an estoppel as against a subsequent different or broader interpretation.[385] However, remarks in prosecution that emphasize a structural distinction between a claim and the prior art cannot be read as limiting the claim to a particular method of operation. It is important to keep structure and operation separate in such an analysis.[386] Every statement made by a patentee during prosecution to distinguish a prior art reference does not create a separate estoppel. Arguments must be viewed in context. Thus, pointing out several differences that support patentability does not necessarily create an estoppel with respect to any particular one of those distinctions, and certainly does not create an estoppel respecting each.[387] Can failure to argue (or more to the point, prosecute to the bitter end) work an estoppel?[388]

---

[383]*Southwall Tech., Inc. v. Cardinal IG Co.*, 54 F.3d 1570, 34 USPQ2d 1673 (Fed. Cir. 1995).

[384]*Builders Concrete, Inc. v. Bremerton Concrete Prods. Co.*, 757 F.2d 255, 225 USPQ 240 (Fed. Cir. 1985). Where the same passage was added to another, unasserted claim, and the applicant argued patentability over the art based upon that passage, estoppel would apply. *Id.* It may be that an inference of reliance by the examiner upon a position taken during prosecution is required for an estoppel. In *Zenith Labs., Inc. v. Bristol-Myers Squibb Co.*, 19 F.3d 1418, 30 USPQ2d 1048, 32 USPQ2d 1017 (Fed. Cir. 1994), the patentee had emphasized the superior manufacturing-related benefits of the claimed monohydrate form of a drug, and the accused infringer argued that the patentee should therefore be estopped to assert that the accused hemihydrate form infringed even if it were converted to monohydrate after ingestion. The court disagreed. It was not clear that the statements as to superiority played a significant role in the examiner's decision to allow the claim. Although actual reliance by the examiner need not be shown, the circumstances must be such as to permit the inference that such reliance in fact occurred. A showing that the conduct in question played a material role in the issuance of the patent usually suffices. Although the prosecution history serves as a limit on the scope of claims by excluding any interpretation of the language that would permit the patentee to assert a meaning that was disclaimed or disavowed to obtain allowance, it is likewise improper to read a limitation into a claim wholly apart from any need to interpret what the patentee meant by particular words or phrases. Here the claim contained nothing that would limit it to the preingestion form of the drug. One wonders if this is a claim construction holding or an infringement holding.

[385]*Advance Transformer Co. v. Levinson,* 837 F.2d 1081, 5 USPQ2d 1600 (Fed. Cir. 1988). In *Intervet Am., Inc. v. Kee-Vet Labs., Inc.,* 887 F.2d 1050, 12 USPQ2d 1474 (Fed. Cir. 1989), the attorney in remarks accompanying an amendment erroneously indicated that all claims contained a limitation, when in fact only one claim did. The court held it error to interpret the remaining claims as though they contained that limitation. However, such an attorney statement might be held against the patentee on a theory of estoppel if the patentee is attempting to expand the literal meaning of the claim, and the prosecution history shows that the enlarged scope would include subject matter that the attorney had said was not included.

[386]*SRI Int'l v. Matsushita Elec. Corp.,* 775 F.2d 1107, 227 USPQ 577 (Fed. Cir. 1985).

[387]*Read Corp. v. Portec, Inc.,* 970 F.2d 816, 23 USPQ2d 1426 (Fed. Cir. 1992). Claims whose allowance was not due to a particular argument are not subject to estoppel deriving from that argument. *Fiskars Inc. v Hunt Mfg. Co.,* 221 F.3d 1318, 55 USPQ2d 1569 (Fed. Cir. 2000).

[388]In her concurring opinion in *Haynes Int'l, Inc. v. Jessop Steel Co.,* 8 F.3d 1573, 28 USPQ2d 1652 (Fed. Cir. 1993), Judge Newman worried that the majority opinion may be

In the end, the pertinent prosecution history for estoppel purposes is the entire record of proceedings in the PTO, including representations made to the examiner that the invention is patentable. Amendment of a claim in light of a prior art reference is not the sine qua non for estoppel. Unmistakable assertions made by the applicant in support of patentability, whether or not required to secure the allowance of the claim, also may operate to preclude the patentee from asserting equivalency between a limitation of the claim and a substituted structure or process step. Application of this test requires, in each case, examination of the prosecution history taken as a whole. Other players in the marketplace are entitled to rely on the record made in the PTO in determining the meaning and scope of the patent.[389]

The prosecution history must be examined as a whole in determining whether estoppel applies. This includes all applications in a chain of parentage.[390] Statements made in an IDS can be the basis for a court to interpret the scope of the claims of a granted patent. Also, arguments in an IDS can create an estoppel, and thus preclude a finding of infringement under the DOE. An IDS is a part of the prosecution history on which the examiner, the courts, and the public are entitled to rely. The party submitting it intends the statements to be relied on. It is reasonable to infer, absent an indication to the contrary, that an examiner will consider an IDS when determining whether to allow the claims; the courts and the public may rely on it as well.[391] Arguments made by an applicant in a petition to make

---

"misinterpreted as enlarging the scope of prosecution history estoppel." This worry may be valid, for the majority opinion can certainly be read to suggest that failure to continue prosecution beyond full examination may itself be a ground of estoppel. The court later granted rehearing for the limited purpose of changing certain language in the original opinion. Essentially, it removed references to reissue to make it clear that the prior holding referred to further prosecution by continuation application rather than by reissue. Again, Judge Newman voiced objection to any requirement that an applicant must continue to prosecute a claim in order to escape PHE and be entitled to rely upon the doctrine of equivalents. *Haynes Int'l, Inc. v. Jessop Steel Co.,* 15 F.3d 1076 (Fed. Cir. 1994).

[389]*Texas Instr., Inc. v. United States ITC,* 988 F.2d 1165, 26 USPQ2d 1018 (Fed. Cir. 1993).

[390]*Mark I Mkt'g Corp. v. R.R. Donnelley & Sons,* 66 F.3d 285, 36 USPQ2d 1095 (Fed. Cir. 1995). Here the patentee never narrowed the claims by amendment; instead, it chose to file a continuing application containing narrower claims. The court held this made no difference. Estoppel is not avoided by failing to respond to a rejection and instead meeting the substance of the rejection by filing a narrower continuing application. See also *Augustine Med. Inc. v. Gaymar Indus. Inc.,* 181 F.3d 1291, 50 USPQ2d 1900 (Fed. Cir. 1999); *Pall Corp. v. Micron Separations, Inc.,* 66 F.3d 1211, 36 USPQ2d 1225 (Fed. Cir. 1995).

[391]*Ekchian v. Home Depot, Inc.,* 104 F.3d 1299, 41 USPQ2d 1364 (Fed. Cir. 1997). See also *Serrano v. Telular Corp.,* 111 F.3d 1578, 42 USPQ2d 1538 (Fed. Cir. 1997). It is not necessary that a reference be specifically cited by the examiner as the reason for a rejection in order for it to give rise to an estoppel. Arguments made by an applicant in an IDS or otherwise during prosecution may form the basis of an estoppel without regard to whether the argument was made in response to a rejection or the prior art was cited by the examiner. *Litton Sys., Inc. v. Honeywell Inc.,* 140 F.3d 1449, 46 USPQ2d 1321 (Fed. Cir. 1998). For purposes of claim interpretation, and probably estoppel as well, a formal Citation of Prior Art pursuant to 35 U.S.C. §301 is part of the prosecution history. However, the court has cautioned on how much weight to give statements in such documents; if filed after issuance and just before or during

special can create an estoppel, and thus preclude a finding of infringement under the DOE.[392]

Arguments made during prosecution regarding the meaning of a claim term are relevant to the interpretation of that term in every claim of the patent absent a clear indication to the contrary.[393] However, arguments about an element do not create an estoppel as to claims that do not include the element.[394]

When a claim limitation is added in order to overcome a specific cited reference, estoppel as to that limitation is generated whether the limitation is added by amendment to pending claims, or by the submission of new claims containing the limitation.[395] Crucial amendments can conceivably be obscured by a complete rewriting of the claims.[396] Cancellation of a claim that is written broadly does not always generate an estoppel to narrower subject matter. The particular facts must be considered.[397]

Section 112 and new matter. The filing of a CIP application, in and of itself, is not an admission of the correctness of a rejection. Law and policy liberally authorize the filing of CIP applications for a number of reasons, whether to enlarge the disclosure to include new technological information, thereby providing the public with knowledge of recent developments or improvements; or to enable more extensive prosecution or improved draftsmanship of specification or claims; or to provide a vehicle for prosecution of nonelected claims.[398]

But if a patentee acquiesces in a rejection, such as new matter, lack of best mode, or insufficient disclosure, and files a CIP, he or she is estopped to argue that the rejection was erroneous.[399] The burden is on the infringer to establish a prima facie case of acquiescence, after which the patentee must come forward with countervailing evidence to rebut it. For example, the patentee could show that

---

litigation, the statements may well be self-serving. *Moleculon Res. Corp. v. CBS, Inc.*, 793 F.2d 1261, 229 USPQ 805 (Fed. Cir. 1986).

[392]*Gentry Gallery, Inc. v. Berkline Corp.*, 134 F.3d 1473, 45 USPQ2d 1498 (Fed. Cir. 1998). Here the distinction drawn over the prior art was so unequivocal that the court also used it to limit the scope of the claim for literal infringement.

[393]*Southwall Tech., Inc. v. Cardinal IG Co.*, 54 F.3d 1570, 34 USPQ2d 1673 (Fed. Cir. 1995). See also *American Permahedge, Inc. v. Barcana, Inc.*, 105 F.3d 1441, 41 USPQ2d 1614 (Fed. Cir. 1997).

[394]*Serrano v. Telular Corp.*, 111 F.3d 1578, 42 USPQ2d 1538 (Fed. Cir. 1997). In *Hebert v. Lisle Corp.*, 99 F.3d 1109, 40 USPQ2d 1611 (Fed. Cir. 1996), the court was able to pass an interesting question involving method claims that had originally been prosecuted as apparatus claims.

[395]*Pall Corp. v. Hemasure Inc.*, 181 F.3d 1305, 50 USPQ2d 1947 (Fed. Cir. 1999).

[396]*Great Northern Corp. v. Davis Core & Pad Co.*, 782 F.2d 159, 228 USPQ 356 (Fed. Cir. 1986) ("the applicant did not clearly surrender anything specific by rewriting his claims").

[397]*EMI Group N.A. Inc. v. Intel Corp.*, 157 F.3d 887, 48 USPQ2d 1181 (Fed. Cir. 1998).

[398]*Paperless Accounting, Inc. v. Bay Area Rapid Transit Sys.*, 804 F.2d 659, 231 USPQ 649 (Fed. Cir. 1986).

[399]*Pennwalt Corp. v. Akzona Inc.*, 740 F.2d 1573, 222 USPQ 833 (Fed. Cir. 1984); *Litton Sys., Inc. v. Whirlpool Corp.*, 728 F.2d 1423, 221 USPQ 97 (Fed. Cir. 1984).

he or she filed the CIP to disclose improvements developed after the filing date of the original. The infringer, on the other hand, can establish a prima facie case by showing that the CIP added material that seemed calculated to cure the rejection or objection.[400]

The court has held that the remarks made to overcome a rejection or objection under §112 do not create an estoppel.[401] This holding will of course need to be reevaluated in light of the recent *Festo*[402] decision, discussed below.

(iii) Reason for Amendment—The Festo *Decision*

Early on, the Federal Circuit insisted that it was error for a trial court to conclude that if the claims were once narrowed for whatever reason, the DOE cannot be invoked under any circumstances.[403] In its 1997 *Warner-Jenkinson*[404] decision, the Supreme Court emphatically reaffirmed that principle. Somewhat unexpectedly, it addressed certain matters that had long needed definitive attention. First, it made clear that where the reason for a change in a claim was not related to avoiding the prior art, or otherwise to address a specific concern that arguably would have rendered the claimed subject matter unpatentable, the change may introduce a new element, but it does not necessarily preclude infringement by equivalents of that element.[405] Next, *Warner-Jenkinson* disavowed any suggestion that, where a claim change is made to overcome a rejection based upon the prior art, a court is free to review the correctness of that rejection when deciding whether to apply PHE. Such concerns are properly addressed on direct appeal from the denial of a patent and will not be revisited in an infringement action.[406]

---

[400]*Pennwalt Corp. v. Akzona Inc.*, 740 F.2d 1573, 222 USPQ 833 (Fed. Cir. 1984).

[401]*Environmental Designs, Ltd. v. Union Oil Co.*, 713 F.2d 693, 218 USPQ 865 (Fed. Cir. 1983). See also *Caterpillar Tractor Co. v. Berco, S.P.A.*, 714 F.2d 1110, 219 USPQ 185 (Fed. Cir. 1983).

[402]*Festo Corp. v. Shoketsu KKK Co.*, 234 F.3d 558, 56 USPQ2d 1865 (Fed. Cir. 2000).

[403]*Bayer Aktiengesellschaft v. Duphar Int'l Research B.V.*, 738 F.2d 1237, 222 USPQ 649, 653 (Fed. Cir. 1984).

[404]*Warner-Jenkinson Co. v. Hilton Davis Chem. Co.*, 520 U.S. 17, 41 USPQ2d 1865 (1997).

[405]41 USPQ2d at 1872. In so holding, the Court recognized that there are a variety of other reasons why the PTO may request a change in claim language, often without the intent to limit equivalents or, indeed, with the expectation that the language it required would in many cases allow for a range of equivalents.

[406]In a case decided shortly after *Warner-Jenkinson,* the Federal Circuit observed that in construing the claims in view of prosecution history or in deciding whether to estop a patentee from asserting a certain range of equivalents, a court may only explore the reason (right or wrong) for the objection and the manner in which the amendment addressed and avoided the objection. The correctness of the examiner's rejection is not at issue. *Regents of Univ. of Calif. v. Eli Lilly & Co.*, 119 F.3d 1559, 43 USPQ2d 1398 (Fed. Cir. 1997). Thus, when an applicant disagrees with the examiner's prior art rejection and fails to prevail by argument, it has two choices: either to amend the claim or to appeal the rejection. It may not both make the amendment and then challenge its necessity in a subsequent infringement action on the allowed claim. A patentee does not have a second chance to relitigate the merits of a prior art rejection that caused an amendment to be made to gain allowance of the claims. *Bai v. L&L Wings Inc.*, 160 F.3d 1350, 48 USPQ2d 1674 (Fed. Cir. 1998). When arguments and amendments are made to distinguish a prior art reference, it is immaterial that the reference could have been

What is permissible for a court to explore, then, is the reason (right or wrong) for a rejection or objection and the manner in which the amendment addressed and avoided it. It was here that the *Warner-Jenkinson* Court set up a new rule to guide this exploration. The absence of a reason for an amendment, in the Court's view, should not avoid an estoppel. Accordingly, the patent owner must bear the burden of establishing the reason for an amendment required during prosecution.[407] The court will then decide whether that reason is sufficient to overcome PHE as a bar to application of the DOE to the element added by that amendment. Where no explanation is established, however, the court should presume that the PTO had a substantial reason related to patentability for including the limiting element added by amendment. In those circumstances, PHE will bar application of the DOE as to that element. This approach, in the view of the Supreme Court, gives proper deference to the role of claims in defining an invention and providing public notice, and to the primacy of the PTO in ensuring that the claims allowed cover only subject matter that is properly patentable. Applied in this fashion, PHE places reasonable limits on the DOE, and further insulates the doctrine from any feared conflict with the patent statute.[408]

Although not automatically erecting an estoppel, an amendment made for reasons other than patentability may still give rise to an estoppel. The court has acknowledged that even arguments made during prosecution without amendments to claim language, if sufficient to evince a clear and unmistakable surrender of subject matter, may estop an applicant from recapturing that surrendered matter under the DOE. Estoppel by clear and unmistakable surrender without claim amendments may arise even when the arguments to the examiner were not necessary to distinguish prior art. This principle presupposes that the applicant has made the surrender unmistakable enough that the public may reasonably rely on it. By logical extension, if an applicant makes an amendment unrelated to patentability that evinces an unmistakable surrender, that action will preclude recapture of the surrendered subject matter under the DOE.[409]

---

distinguished on other grounds. *Desper Prods. Inc. v. QSound Labs. Inc.*, 157 F.3d 1325, 48 USPQ2d 1088 (Fed. Cir. 1998).

[407]The Court used the words "the reason for an amendment *required* during patent prosecution" (emphasis supplied) and presumably employed the word "required" advisedly. 41 USPQ2d at 1873. In the fourth edition of this book the author predicted that much litigation could be expected over whether the new *Warner-Jenkinson* rules apply when the amendment was not "required" by the PTO. This prediction was very quickly squelched in *Festo Corp. v. Shoketsu KKK Co.*, 234 F.3d 558, 56 USPQ2d 1865 (Fed. Cir. 2000), where the court held that voluntary amendments made for reasons relating to patentability create estoppels. See discussion at note 6:419.

[408]On remand from the Supreme Court the Federal Circuit in turn remanded to the trial court for a finding on the reason for the amendment, so that the PHE issue could be resolved. *Hilton Davis Chem. Co. v. Warner-Jenkinson Co.*, 114 F.3d 1161, 43 USPQ2d 1152 (Fed. Cir. 1997).

[409]*Litton Sys., Inc. v. Honeywell Inc.*, 140 F.3d 1449, 46 USPQ2d 1321 (Fed. Cir. 1998). See also *Bayer AG v. Elan Pharm. Res. Corp.*, 212 F.3d 1241, 54 USPQ2d 1710 (Fed. Cir. 2000).

In the fourth edition of this book, the author remarked that a good deal of clarifying litigation was to be expected, but in the end *Warner-Jenkinson* did not seem to have done severe damage to earlier Federal Circuit decisions dealing with this aspect of PHE. Less than three years later, however, virtually all those earlier decisions were swept away by a breathtaking in banc ruling of the Federal Circuit. In its initial decision in *Festo v. Shoketsu*,[410] the panel affirmed a judgment of infringement under the DOE. A petition for certiori was filed and, in the interim, the Supreme Court decided *Warner-Jenkinson*. The Supreme Court also granted certiorari in *Festo*, and vacated and remanded for further consideration in light of *Warner-Jenkinson*. On remand, a Federal Circuit panel again affirmed the judgment of infringement under the DOE. Thereafter, however, the court granted a petition for rehearing in banc, setting up five specific questions that it intended to address.[411]

The first of those questions dealt squarely with the reason for an amendment. In its in banc *Festo* decision,[412] the court held, with only a single dissent, that a substantial reason related to patentability is not limited to overcoming prior art, but includes other reasons related to the statutory requirements for a patent. Therefore, an amendment that narrows the scope of a claim for any reason related to the statutory requirements for a patent will give rise to PHE with respect to the amended claim element. Among the possible reasons related to patentability that are not based on prior art, the court mentioned utility and patentable subject matter issues under 35 U.S.C. §101, the enablement, best mode, and written description requirements of §112¶1, and the claiming requirements of §112¶2.[413]

One now expects some fascinating litigation over what is, and what is not, a reason related to the statutory requirements for a patent. In the meantime, it seems safe to conclude that many of the previous statements on the reason for an amendment, set forth in the cases collected in the footnote, are obsolete.[414] Nonetheless, they

---

[410]*Festo Corp. v. Shoketsu KKK Co.*, 72 F.3d 857, 37 USPQ2d 1161 (Fed. Cir. 1995).

[411]*Festo Corp. v. Shoketsu KKK Co.*, 187 F.3d 1381, 51 USPQ2d 1959, 1959–60 (Fed. Cir. 1999).

[412]*Festo Corp. v. Shoketsu KKK Co.*, 234 F.3d 558, 56 USPQ2d 1865 (Fed. Cir. 2000).

[413]56 USPQ2d 1870–71.

[414]*Merck & Co. v. Mylan Pharm. Inc.*, 190 F.3d 1335, 51 USPQ2d 1954 (Fed. Cir. 1999); *Loral Fairchild Corp. v. Sony Corp.*, 181 F.3d 1313, 50 USPQ2d 1865 (Fed. Cir. 1999); *Sextant Avionique S.A. v. Analog Devices Inc.*, 172 F.3d 813, 49 USPQ2d 1865 (Fed. Cir. 1999); *Bai v. L&L Wings Inc.*, 160 F.3d 1350, 48 USPQ2d 1674 (Fed. Cir. 1998); *Litton Sys., Inc. v. Honeywell Inc.*, 140 F.3d 1449, 46 USPQ2d 1321 (Fed. Cir. 1998); *Vaupel Textilmaschinen KG v. Meccanical Euro Italia S.P.A.*, 944 F.2d 870, 20 USPQ2d 1045 (Fed. Cir. 1991); *Insta-Foam Prods., Inc. v. Universal Foam Sys., Inc.*, 906 F.2d 698, 15 USPQ2d 1295 (Fed. Cir. 1990); *Environmental Instr., Inc. v. Sutron Corp.*, 877 F.2d 1561, 11 USPQ2d 1132 (Fed. Cir. 1989); *Sun Studs, Inc. v. ATA Equip. Leasing, Inc.*, 872 F.2d 978, 10 USPQ2d 1338 (Fed. Cir. 1989); *Andrew Corp. v. Gabriel Elec., Inc.*, 847 F.2d 819, 6 USPQ2d 2010 (Fed. Cir. 1988); *Hi-Life Prods., Inc. v. American Nat'l Water-Mattress Corp.*, 842 F.2d 323, 6 USPQ2d 1132 (Fed. Cir. 1988); *Mannesmann Demag Corp. v. Engineered Metal Prods. Co.*, 793 F.2d 1279, 230 USPQ 45 (Fed. Cir.

may shed light on what, if anything, the Federal Circuit would regard as an amendment not related to patentability.[415]

The Warner-Jenkinson *presumption.* In ultimately deciding the merits of the DOE issues presented, the in banc *Festo* court addressed the matter of how a patent owner can discharge the burden of establishing the reason for an amendment. This was not one of the five questions that prompted the court to sit in banc, but it was necessary to the ultimate determination. The court squarely held that a patent owner seeking to establish the reason for an amendment must base its arguments "solely upon the public record of the patent's prosecution."[416] In other words, patent owners are not permitted to rely on evidence extrinsic to the prosecution history to demonstrate that an amendment made during prosecution has a purpose unrelated to patentability. This holding prompted a vigorous dissent from Judge Newman. Her concern is that the rule renders the *Warner-Jenkinson* presumption irrebutable. As she reasoned:

> Thus the majority holds that the rebuttable presumption concerning the reason for an amendment, which presumption arises when the prosecution record is silent as to the reason for the amendment, cannot be rebutted with evidence outside of the prosecution record. The rebuttable presumption thereby becomes irrebuttable, because the prosecution record is necessarily silent in order for the presumption to arise at all.[417]

With all respect to the majority, this logic has a certain appeal.[418]

(iv) Voluntary Amendments–The Festo Decision

The second question addressed by the in banc *Festo* decision had to do with the impact of claim amendments that were not required by the examiner or made in response to a rejection by an examiner for a stated reason. The court squarely held that voluntary claim amendments are treated the same as other amendments. Therefore, a voluntary amendment that narrows the scope of a claim for a reason related to the statutory requirements for a patent will give rise to

---

1986); *Loctite Corp. v. Ultraseal Ltd.,* 781 F.2d 861, 228 USPQ 90 (Fed. Cir. 1985); *Caterpillar Tractor Co. v. Berco, S.P.A.,* 714 F.2d 1110, 219 USPQ 185 (Fed. Cir. 1983).

[415]See, e.g., *Pall Corp. v. Micron Separations, Inc.,* 66 F.3d 1211, 36 USPQ2d 1225 (Fed. Cir. 1995), where the court observed that when claim changes or arguments are made in order to more particularly point out the invention, the purpose is to impart precision, not to overcome prior art. Such prosecution is not presumed to raise an estoppel, but is reviewed on its facts, with the guidance of precedent. For another example, limiting the claims because of a restriction requirement would not necessarily invoke file history estoppel. *Bayer Aktiengesellschaft v. Duphar Int'l Research B.V.,* 738 F.2d 1237, 222 USPQ 649 (Fed. Cir. 1984).

[416]56 USPQ2d at 1886.

[417]56 USPQ2d at 1924.

[418]It at least engendered sufficient concern among the majority to cause it to include a footnote "to make it clear that, in determining the reason for an amendment, a court can properly consider any attorney argument regarding the reason for the amendment that is supported by the prosecution history record." 56 USPQ2d 1886 n.6.

PHE as to the amended claim element. Both voluntary amendments and amendments required by the PTO signal to the public that subject matter has been surrendered. There is no reason why PHE should arise if the PTO rejects a claim because it believes the claim to be unpatentable, but not arise if the applicant amends a claim because he believes the claim to be unpatentable.[419]

Prior cases are collected in the footnote.[420]

(v) Scope of Estoppel–The Festo Decision

Prior to *Warner-Jenkinson*, the court seemed committed to the proposition that an amendment does not necessarily create a broad estoppel.[421] It held that the mere fact that a claim limitation was added to overcome a prior art rejection does not automatically preclude some range of equivalents with respect to that limitation. The prior art must always be analyzed, not to determine whether the claim would have been allowable without the amendment, but to determine whether the prior art permits the sought-for equivalence. There is no mechanical rule for determining PHE's effect on the range of equivalents.[422] Thus, an amendment may result in a limiting effect on the range of equivalents ranging from great to small to zero.[423]

---

[419]56 USPQ2d at 1871–72.

[420]In cases where a patentee's amendments were not required in response to an examiner's rejection or critical to the allowance of the claims, no estoppel has been found. *Mannesmann Demag Corp. v. Engineered Metal Prods. Co.,* 793 F.2d 1279, 230 USPQ 45 (Fed. Cir. 1986). But the Federal Circuit apparently disapproved of any speculative inquiries as to the necessity, from the standpoint of patentability, of an amendment clearly made to avoid a reference. See *Prodyne Enters., Inc. v. Julie Pomerantz, Inc.,* 743 F.2d 1581, 223 USPQ 477 (Fed. Cir. 1984). When a rejection based on prior art did not dictate the claim change that was made, it is necessary to look at the specific change and the reason, in ascertaining whether an estoppel has arisen by virtue of the change. A nonsubstantive change or a change that did not in fact determine patentability does not create an estoppel. *Pall Corp. v. Micron Separations, Inc.,* 66 F.3d 1211, 36 USPQ2d 1225 (Fed. Cir. 1995). In one case, a limitation specifying a tube of uniform outer diameter was added to distinguish art that showed protuberances along the length of the tube and thus did not estop the patentee from claiming coverage of a tapered tip on the tube. *Howes v. Medical Components, Inc.,* 814 F.2d 638, 2 USPQ2d 1271 (Fed. Cir. 1987). In *Hi-Life Prods., Inc. v. American Nat'l Water-Mattress Corp.,* 842 F.2d 323, 6 USPQ2d 1132 (Fed. Cir. 1988), the prior art showed the use of an element in another environment. In an interview with the PTO examiner, the applicant amended the claim to specify that particular element in his particular environment. The court refused to find an estoppel, reasoning that the limitation was shown in the art, and therefore the amendment was not necessary to avoid the art.

[421]*Hughes Aircraft Co. v. United States,* 717 F.2d 1351, 219 USPQ 473 (Fed. Cir. 1983). In *Haynes Int'l, Inc. v. Jessop Steel Co.,* 8 F.3d 1573, 28 USPQ2d 1652 (Fed. Cir. 1993), the trial court concluded that the patentee was estopped from asserting any range of equivalents for the claim. Although that holding was in error because the broad issue was not raised by the facts of the case, the Federal Circuit found it to be harmless error inasmuch as it concluded that the patentee was estopped from asserting coverage of the accused product.

[422]*LaBounty Mfg., Inc. v. United States ITC,* 867 F.2d 1572, 9 USPQ2d 1995 (Fed. Cir. 1989).

[423]*Hormone Res. Found., Inc. v. Genentech, Inc.,* 904 F.2d 1558, 15 USPQ2d 1039 (Fed. Cir. 1990); *Black & Decker, Inc. v. Hoover Serv. Ctr.,* 886 F.2d 1285, 12 USPQ2d 1250 (Fed. Cir. 1989).

Not long after *Warner-Jenkinson,* the court took another look at its earlier opinion[424] in *Hughes v. United States,* pursuant to a grant-vacate-remand order issued by the Supreme Court in light of *Warner-Jenkinson.* The government vigorously contended that, under *Warner-Jenkinson,* an estoppel acts as an absolute bar that precludes any equivalence to a claim limitation that was added to overcome a patentability rejection, regardless of what subject matter was surrendered. Under this rule, the patentee would be limited to the literal scope of the particular claim limitation. The court disagreed, reasoning that the key to PHE is the surrender or disclaimer of subject matter by the patentee, which the patentee is then unable to reclaim through the DOE. If the accused device does not fall within the range of subject matter surrendered, PHE does not preclude infringement under the DOE.[425] Shortly thereafter, in *Litton v. Honeywell,* the court took a deeper look at the doctrine of PHE in the wake of *Warner-Jenkinson.* It concluded that the Supreme Court adhered to the long-standing doctrine that an estoppel only bars recapture of that subject matter actually surrendered during prosecution. The common practice of amending a claim during prosecution, even amending to overcome prior art, does not necessarily surrender all subject matter beyond the literal scope of the amended claim limitation.[426]

All this hard work was largely consigned to the dust bin when the in banc *Festo* court addressed its third question: If a claim amendment creates PHE, what range of equivalents, if any, is available under the DOE for the claim element so amended? A deeply divided court held that when a claim amendment creates PHE with regard to a claim element, there is no range of equivalents available for the amended claim element. Application of the doctrine of equivalents to the claim element is completely barred.[427] The fourth question was related: When no explanation for a claim amendment is established, thus invoking the presumption of PHE under *Warner-Jenkinson,* what range of equivalents, if any, is available under the DOE for the claim element so amended? This one was easy and the answer was unanimous: when no explanation for a claim amendment is established, no range of equivalents is available for the claim element so

---

[424]*Hughes Aircraft Co. v. United States,* 717 F.2d 1351, 219 USPQ 473 (Fed. Cir. 1983).

[425]*Hughes Aircraft Co. v. United States,* 140 F.3d 1470, 46 USPQ2d 1285 (Fed. Cir. 1998).

[426]*Litton Sys., Inc. v. Honeywell Inc.,* 140 F.3d 1449, 46 USPQ2d 1321 (Fed. Cir. 1998). It is clear that the court is not unanimous on this point. Two dissenters from a denial of a petition for rehearing in banc in *Hughes v. United States* expressed the hope that the Solicitor General would petition for certiorari. *Hughes Aircraft Co. v. United States,* 148 F.3d 1384, 47 USPQ2d 1542 (Fed. Cir. 1998). And in *Litton v. Honeywell* itself there were several dissents and a concurring opinion on an order declining rehearing in banc. *Litton Sys., Inc. v. Honeywell Inc.,* 145 F.3d 1472, 47 USPQ2d 1106 (Fed. Cir. 1998). In *Merck & Co. v. Mylan Pharm. Inc.,* 190 F.3d 1335, 51 USPQ2d 1954 (Fed. Cir. 1999), a panel observed that estoppel is not automatic as to everything beyond the literal scope of the claim; its extent must be determined from what was relinquished, in light of the prior art.

[427]56 USPQ2d at 1872.

amended.[428] But on the third question, the court split 8–4, with a very vocal minority contending that some range of equivalents should be afforded in appropriate situations.[429] Indeed, one of the members of the majority wrote a special concurring opinion, remarking that the majority approach was "a second-best solution," and lamenting the loss of flexibility that would be available to judges if the matter were instead treated as a matter of "equitable law." Unlike the dissenters, however, this member of the majority forecasts an *increased* reliance on the DOE:

> Patent counsels may decide that past practice gives up too much under the new rules, and instead may start claiming narrowly with the hope of avoiding rejections and consequent amendments. Literal infringement will become harder to prove because claims will be drafted more narrowly and with greater specificity. That itself may be to the good, since much of current patent litigation involves claim construction issues resulting from the vague, sometimes almost incomprehensible, manner in which claims have been drafted.
>
> An unintended consequence, however, may be that patent litigation will lean ever more heavily on the doctrine of equivalents, especially in those cases in which the patent application, containing narrowly drawn claims, was approved without any amendment in the area that affects the accused product. The patentee may have little choice but to insist on enforcement under the doctrine of equivalents, if the patent is to be enforced at all. Since today's decision does not change the basic rule of analysis for infringement claims under the doctrine of equivalents, the outcome in those cases will continue to be tested under the pre-existing "insubstantial differences" and its surrogate "function-way-result," with all the game-playing those indeterminate phrases provide.
>
> In time then, the supposed benefits of the doctrinal improvements contained in today's decision may prove illusory.[430]

---

[428]56 USPQ2d at 1880. Indeed, the *Warner-Jenkinson* Court had so held, 520 U.S. at 33. And the Federal Circuit itself had previously concluded that where the *Warner-Jenkinson* presumption is applicable, no analysis of the scope of the estoppel is required; the estoppel is absolute. A patentee's failure to clarify the reason for the amendment and thereby rebut the presumption should not work to the detriment of the public by allowing an uncertain range of equivalency to remain as to the limitation at issue. *Sextant Avionique S.A. v. Analog Devices Inc.*, 172 F.3d 813, 49 USPQ2d 1865 (Fed. Cir. 1999).

[429]The detailed views of the dissenters should be read to be fully appreciated. For our purposes, it is sufficient to observe one consistent overriding theme. Thus, Judge Michel asserts that "the majority's holding effectively strips most patentees of their rights to assert infringement under the doctrine of equivalents." Judge Rader feels that, "by barring all application of the doctrine of equivalents for amended claims, this court does not account at all for the primary role of the doctrine." Judge Linn says that "the majority's new rule hands the unscrupulous copyist a free ride on potentially valuable patented technology, as long as the copyist merely follows the prosecution history road map and makes a change, no matter how trivial or insubstantial, to an element otherwise covered by such a narrowed claim limitation." Judge Newman puts it this way: "The result is to negate infringement by equivalents, as a matter of law, thereby providing a blueprint for ready imitation of patented products." Thus, all of the four dissenters believe that the majority rule will restrict access to the DOE. Judge Michel also made the important point that, by failing to provide that the new rule would have only prospective application, most of the 1,200,000 unexpired patents existing today would be in jeopardy, not having been prosecuted with the consequences of the new rule in mind.

[430]56 USPQ2d at 1891.

A full analysis of the reasoning of the majority and minority opinions in *Festo* is well beyond the scope of this work. Suffice to say that the majority articulated the following as a major justification for its adoption of the complete bar rule:

> Thus, under the complete bar approach, technological advances that would have lain in the unknown, undefined zone around the literal terms of a narrowed claim under the flexible bar approach will not go wasted and undeveloped due to fear of litigation. The public will be free to improve on the patented technology and design around it without being inhibited by the threat of a lawsuit because the changes could possibly fall within the scope of equivalents left after a claim element has been narrowed by amendment for a reason related to patentability. This certainty will stimulate investment in improvements and design-arounds because the risk of infringement will be easier to determine. In general, the difficulty in counseling the public and the patentee on the scope of protection provided by an amended element is greatly reduced under the complete bar approach due to the certainty and predictability such a bar produces.[431]

Thus, under *Festo*, the analysis of PHE relative to an amendment (whether by amending a pending claim, rewriting a claim, or substituting a new claim) of a particular claim element is conducted like this: the court first determines whether the amendment narrowed the literal scope of the claim.[432] If it did, estoppel will apply unless the patent owner establishes, by reference to the prosecution history, that the amendment was made for a purpose unrelated to patentability. If the patent owner fails in this, PHE completely bars application of the DOE to that claim element. The ramifications of this new approach are not clear at this point, nor is its potential impact upon both patent prosecution and infringement litigation. If nothing more, it certainly behooves the prosecuting patent attorney to take especial care to explain the purpose of an amendment that is believed not to relate to patentability. Further insight is likely to be gained only by a painful process of case-by-case development.

§6.4 Inducement and Contributory Infringement

Liability for patent infringement is not confined to those who commit the acts of direct infringement specified in 35 U.S.C. §271(a).[433] Section 271(b) provides that "whoever actively induces infringement

---

[431]56 USPQ2d at 1879.

[432]An interesting twist in *Festo* had to do with the fact that a claim in means-plus-function format was replaced with a claim that recited corresponding structure to perform the recited function. This had the effect of narrowing the claim with respect to that element, because the means-plus-function format would have covered equivalents of the corresponding structure as well. 56 USPQ2d at 1888.

[433]Except in the case of the government, which can be sued only for direct infringement, not inducement or contributory infringement. *Motorola, Inc. v. United States*, 729 F.2d 765, 221 USPQ 297 (Fed. Cir. 1984). The government has not waived sovereign immunity for

of a patent shall be liable as an infringer." And §271(c) defines contributory infringement as selling:

> a component of a patented machine, manufacture, combination or composition, or a material or apparatus for use in practicing a patented process, constituting a material part of the invention, knowing the same to be especially made or especially adapted for use in an infringement of such patent, and not a staple article or commodity of commerce suitable for substantial noninfringing use * * * .

The legislative history of §271 indicates that no substantive change in the scope of what constituted contributory infringement was intended by the enactment. However, the single concept of contributory infringement was divided between subsections (b) and (c) into "active inducement" (a type of direct infringement) and contributory infringement. Section 271(c) codified the prohibition against the common type of contributory infringement, where a seller would sell a component that was itself not technically covered by the claims of a product or process patent but that had no other use except with the claimed product or process. Section 271(c) makes it clear that only proof of a defendant's knowledge, not intent, that its activity caused infringement is necessary to establish liability. The case law further makes it clear that there must not only be knowledge that the component was especially made or adapted for a particular use, but also knowledge of the patent that proscribes that use. Although §271(b) is silent on the subject, it requires proof of actual intent to cause the acts that constitute the infringement. Such intent may be shown by circumstantial evidence.[434]

(a) The Direct Infringement Requirement

Perhaps the cardinal principle here is that there can be neither inducement of infringement[435] nor contributory infringement in the absence of a direct infringement.[436] Neither form of "dependent infringement"—contributory or inducement—can occur without an act

---

collateral acts like inducement and contributory infringement. *Gargoyles, Inc. v. United States,* 113 F.3d 1572, 42 USPQ2d 1760 (Fed. Cir. 1997).

[434]*Hewlett-Packard Co. v. Bausch & Lomb Inc.,* 909 F.2d 1464, 15 USPQ2d 1525 (Fed. Cir. 1990).

[435]*Micro Chem., Inc. v. Great Plains Chem. Co.,* 103 F.3d 1538, 41 USPQ2d 1238 (Fed. Cir. 1997); *Everpure, Inc. v. Cuno, Inc.,* 875 F.2d 300, 10 USPQ2d 1855 (Fed. Cir. 1989); *Water Techs. Corp. v. Calco, Ltd.,* 850 F.2d 660, 7 USPQ2d 1097 (Fed. Cir. 1988); *Met-Coil Sys. Corp. v. Korners Unlimited, Inc.,* 803 F.2d 684, 231 USPQ 474 (Fed. Cir. 1986).

[436]*FMC Corp. v. Up-Right, Inc.,* 21 F.3d 1073, 30 USPQ2d 1361 (Fed. Cir. 1994); *Everpure, Inc. v. Cuno, Inc.,* 875 F.2d 300, 10 USPQ2d 1855 (Fed. Cir. 1989); *Preemption Devices, Inc. v. Minnesota Min. & Mfg. Co.,* 803 F.2d 1170, 231 USPQ 297 (Fed. Cir. 1986); *Refac Int'l Ltd. v. IBM,* 798 F.2d 459, 230 USPQ 537 (Fed. Cir. 1986); *Porter v. Farmers Supply Serv., Inc.,* 790 F.2d 882, 229 USPQ 814 (Fed. Cir. 1986); *Molinaro v. Fannon/Courier Corp.,* 745 F.2d 651, 223 USPQ 706 (Fed. Cir. 1984). Defendant sold specially adapted items for use in a patented process, but the sales were to persons who had an implied license to practice the patented process by virtue of ownership of a special machine. Thus, there was no direct infringe-

of direct infringement.[437] This innocuous and perfectly logical rule gave rise to one of the truly outrageous decisions in the history of the patent law, *Deepsouth Packing Co. v. Laitram Corp.*[438] There the Supreme Court held that one who manufactured in the United States all of the parts of a patented machine and then shipped them in boxes to customers in foreign countries where they could be assembled into a complete machine in less than an hour was neither a direct infringer nor a contributory infringer. The alleged direct infringement, "making" the complete machine, was not actionable because it occurred abroad. And the defendant was not guilty of contributory infringement because no act of direct infringement had occurred in the United States.

In its first look at a *Deepsouth*-type situation, the Federal Circuit took pains to distinguish that decision. A patent was about to expire, and the defendant knew that the machine it had contracted to build and deliver would probably infringe. The machine was built but not tested as a whole; only subassemblies were completed and tested. The subassemblies were then shipped on the understanding that the machine was not to be completely assembled and used until after the patent had expired. This was held to be infringement. First, although *Deepsouth* manifested a horror of giving extraterritorial effect to a U.S. patent, there is no corresponding horror of a valid U.S. patent providing economic benefits not cut off entirely upon expiration of the patent.[439] Second, *Deepsouth* established a rule of "operable assembly"; if an operable assembly is tested, infringement occurs. Here the delivery was of a machine completed in the sense that it was ready for complete assembly and had no useful noninfringing purpose when delivered.[440]

Whatever the validity of these distinctions, the matter is now moot. In 1984 Congress responded to *Deepsouth* by adding 35 U.S.C. §271(f). Section 271(f)(1) converts a *Deepsouth* situation into inducement, and §271(f)(2) provides that the fact that what would otherwise be a direct infringement occurs abroad does not prevent liability for contributory infringement. The drafters of §271(c) explicitly recognized that without protection from contributory infringers, owners of method patents would have no effective protection. It would be impractical and undesirable to require the patentee to sue all ultimate

---

ment on the part of the machine owners, and consequently no contributory infringement or inducement on the part of defendant. *Met-Coil Sys. Corp. v. Korners Unlimited, Inc.,* 803 F.2d 684, 231 USPQ 474 (Fed. Cir. 1986).

[437]*Joy Techs., Inc. v. Flakt, Inc.,* 6 F.3d 770, 28 USPQ2d 1378 (Fed. Cir. 1993).

[438]406 U.S. 518, 173 USPQ 769 (1972).

[439]*Paper Converting Mach. Co. v. Magna-Graphics Corp.,* 745 F.2d 11, 223 USPQ 591 (Fed. Cir. 1984). This distinction must be taken with a grain of salt. One of the fundamentals of U.S. patent law is its abhorrence of postexpiration effect. See, e.g., *Brulotte v. Thys Co.,* 379 U.S. 29, 143 USPQ 264 (1964).

[440]*Paper Converting Mach. Co. v. Magna-Graphics Corp.,* 745 F.2d 11, 223 USPQ 591 (Fed. Cir. 1984).

consumers.[441] The provision overruling *Deepsouth,* 35 U.S.C. §271(f), was not retroactive.[442] The *Deepsouth* doctrine cannot be avoided simply by arguing that the decision is not applicable to a determination of the amount of damages where a U.S. infringer competed in the United States for sales against a U.S. patentee.[443] A loophole remains, for 35 U.S.C. §271(f) apparently does not cover the sale, in the United States, of unpatented apparatus for use in practicing a patented method abroad. Although the sale of the apparatus would amount to contributory infringement if it were used to practice the method in the United States, there is no infringement in the circumstance because the direct infringement—the practice of the method—takes place abroad. Nor did the foreign user ship products made by the patented process back to the United States, thus avoiding the reach of §271(g).[444] A 2–1 panel of the court has also held that "offer to sell" in §271(a) should not be engrafted onto §271(f)(2). In other words, the phrase "supplies or causes to be supplied" does not comprehend offers to supply components of patented systems.[445]

(b) Contributory Infringement

Despite the rule that there can be no contributory infringement in the absence of direct infringement, it is not necessary that direct infringers be joined as parties to a suit against a contributory infringer.[446] Discovery can elicit proof of direct infringement.[447] Direct evidence of direct infringement is not required; circumstantial evidence will suffice.[448] Indeed, direct infringement may be inferred from evidence that an accused component has no practical use other than in an infringing system.[449]

---

[441]*Hodosh v. Block Drug. Co.,* 833 F.2d 1575, 4 USPQ2d 1935 (Fed. Cir. 1987).

[442]*Amstar Corp. v. Envirotech Corp.,* 823 F.2d 1538, 3 USPQ2d 1412 (Fed. Cir. 1987).

[443]*Amstar Corp. v. Envirotech Corp.,* 823 F.2d 1538, 3 USPQ2d 1412 (Fed. Cir. 1987).

[444]*Standard Havens Prods., Inc. v. Gencor Indus., Inc.,* 953 F.2d 1360, 21 USPQ2d 1321 (Fed. Cir. 1992).

[445]*Rotec Indus. Inc. v. Mitsubishi Corp.,* 215 F.3d 1246, 55 USPQ2d 1001 (Fed. Cir. 2000). According to Judge Newman's concurring opinion, this conclusion is dictum. Her reasoning is that the majority assumed that *Deepsouth* is still valid, insofar as it requires that direct infringement of a combination patent requires an operable assembly of the whole and not just the manufacture of its parts. Thus the majority was effectively concluding that a §271(a) offer to sell would necessarily have to be an offer to sell the operable assembly. She accuses the majority of using *Deepsouth* to remove the benefit of the "offer to sell" amendment to §271(a) from the loophole-plugging effect of §271(f). She believes that the question of whether an offer to supply components of a patented system is actionable is too important and complex to dispose of in dictum.

[446]*Dana Corp. v. American Precision Co.,* 827 F.2d 755, 3 USPQ2d 1852 (Fed. Cir. 1987); *Refac Int'l Ltd. v. IBM,* 798 F.2d 459, 230 USPQ 537 (Fed. Cir. 1986); *Refac Int'l, Ltd. v. IBM,* 790 F.2d 79, 229 USPQ 712 (Fed. Cir. 1986).

[447]*Refac Int'l Ltd. v. IBM,* 798 F.2d 459, 230 USPQ 537 (Fed. Cir. 1986).

[448]*Moleculon Res. Corp. v. CBS, Inc.,* 793 F.2d 1261, 229 USPQ 805 (Fed. Cir. 1986).

[449]*Preemption Devices, Inc. v. Minnesota Min. & Mfg. Co.,* 803 F.2d 1170, 231 USPQ 297 (Fed. Cir. 1986).

The rule that there can be no contributory infringement without direct infringement apparently will not toll the running of the limitations period. Thus, where the sale of a catalyst took place more than six years prior to suit, but the use of the catalyst in a patented process occurred within the limitations period, there can nevertheless be no recovery for the catalyst sale on a contributory infringement theory.[450] Of course, once a patentee has collected, from a direct infringer, damages sufficient to put it in the position it would have occupied had there been no infringement, it cannot thereafter collect actual damages from a person liable only for contributing to that same infringement.[451]

The Federal Circuit holds that a patentee must show that an alleged contributory infringer knew that the combination for which its components were especially made was both patented and infringing. Such knowledge can be inferred from the fact that the alleged contributory infringer knew (1) that there were only two systems available at the time—the patented one and an infringing one, and (2) that the only market for its components was for use in the infringing system.[452] It is therefore error to award damages for contributory infringement that occurs prior to the infringer's knowledge of the patent.[453]

When a charge of contributory infringement is predicated entirely on the sale of an article of commerce that is used by the purchaser to infringe a patent, the public interest in access to that article of commerce is necessarily implicated.[454] The court has indicated that the fact that a component has no substantial noninfringing use makes it a nonstaple.[455]

The contributory infringement and misuse inquiries, though obviously intertwined, require analysis of the actions of different entities. In considering a plaintiff's claim of contributory infringement under §271(c), a court must review the defendant's acts. In considering a defense of patent misuse, a court must review the plaintiff's acts in light of 35 U.S.C. §271(d). The proper focus in a contributory infringement/misuse setting is on the product actually sold and not on an ingredient of that product.[456]

---

[450]*Standard Oil Co. v. Nippon Shokubai K. K. Co.*, 754 F.2d 345, 224 USPQ 863 (Fed. Cir. 1985).

[451]*King Instr. Corp. v. Otari Corp.*, 767 F.2d 853, 226 USPQ 402 (Fed. Cir. 1985).

[452]*Preemption Devices, Inc. v. Minnesota Min. & Mfg. Co.*, 803 F.2d 1170, 231 USPQ 297 (Fed. Cir. 1986).

[453]*Trell v. Marlee Elec. Corp.*, 912 F.2d 1443, 16 USPQ2d 1059 (Fed. Cir. 1990).

[454]*C.R. Bard, Inc. v. Advanced Card. Sys., Inc.*, 911 F.2d 670, 15 USPQ2d 1540 (Fed. Cir. 1990).

[455]*Preemption Devices, Inc. v. Minnesota Min. & Mfg. Co.*, 803 F.2d 1170, 231 USPQ 297 (Fed. Cir. 1986). This does not necessarily follow. Why did Congress use both phrases?

[456]*Hodosh v. Block Drug. Co.*, 833 F.2d 1575, 4 USPQ2d 1935 (Fed. Cir. 1987). The patent claimed a method of desensitizing teeth by applying potassium nitrate. The infringer sold toothpaste with potassium nitrate and argued that any attempt to prohibit such sales was tantamount to prohibiting the sale of potassium nitrate itself. The court held that the proper

(c) Active Inducement

The statutory liability for inducement of infringement derives from the common law, wherein acts that the actor knows will lead to the commission of a wrong by another place shared liability for the wrong on the actor.[457] The Federal Circuit reads §271(b) broadly to include liability of corporate officials who actively aid and abet their corporation's infringements.[458] The tort of inducement under §271(b) when applied to invoke personal liability, is premised on a concept of tortfeasance whereby persons in authority and control may in appropriate circumstances be deemed liable for wrongdoing, when inducing direct infringement by another.[459] A person infringes by actively and knowingly aiding and abetting another's direct infringement. Although §271(b) does not use the word "knowing," the case law and legislative history uniformly assert such a requirement.[460] Proof of intent to induce infringement is necessary, but direct evidence is not required; circumstantial evidence may suffice.[461] A crucial element of induced infringement is that the inducer must have actual or constructive knowledge of the patent.[462]

It is well settled that corporate officers who actively aid and abet their corporation's infringement may be personally liable for inducing infringement under §271(b), regardless of whether the corporation is

---

focus is on the composition as a whole, which may be far different from the individual ingredients. For example, it might be shown at trial that the toothpaste containing potassium nitrate was especially made and sold for infringing use and had a far narrower range of noninfringing uses, if any, than potassium nitrate or pure toothpaste alone. On the other hand, it might be shown that the accused composition has a "substantial" noninfringing use on teeth that do not need desensitizing.

[457]*National Presto Indus., Inc. v. West Bend Co.*, 76 F.3d 1185, 37 USPQ2d 1685 (Fed. Cir. 1996).

[458]*Power Lift, Inc. v. Lang Tools, Inc.*, 774 F.2d 478, 227 USPQ 435 (Fed. Cir. 1985).

[459]*Sensonics, Inc. v. Aerosonic Corp.*, 81 F.3d 1566, 38 USPQ2d 1551 (Fed. Cir. 1996). Here the individual was founder, owner, president, CEO, and chief engineer of the defendant infringer. He testified that he did not have authority to control or discontinue production of the accused device after he became aware of the patent or as the litigation progressed. The district court did not believe his testimony. The court affirmed a finding of personal liability.

[460]*Water Techs. Corp. v. Calco, Ltd.*, 850 F.2d 660, 7 USPQ2d 1097 (Fed. Cir. 1988). See also *C.R. Bard, Inc. v. Advanced Card. Sys., Inc.*, 911 F.2d 670, 15 USPQ2d 1540 (Fed. Cir. 1990).

[461]*Water Techs. Corp. v. Calco, Ltd.*, 850 F.2d 660, 7 USPQ2d 1097 (Fed. Cir. 1988). Here an individual licensed the infringer to make certain products and gave the infringer the formula for the material from which the products were made. That material was the subject of the plaintiff's patent. The individual had himself filed an application on a modified form of the material, and he argued that this fact, plus the fact that he subjectively believed that the material did not infringe, precluded any finding of specific, knowing intent to induce infringement by his licensee. The court disagreed on the ground that he had no opinion of counsel indicating that his modified material did not infringe and also on the ground that, under his license with the infringer, he had control over the design of the licensed product. These facts provided sufficient circumstantial evidence upon which to base a finding of inducement. In another interesting aspect, the fact that the individual's own direct infringement was de minimus did not excuse him from liability for all damages attributable to the direct infringement of his licensee.

[462]*Insituform Tech. Inc. v. Cat Contr. Inc.*, 156 F.3d 1199, 48 USPQ2d 1610 (Fed. Cir. 1998).

the alter ego of the corporate officer.[463] But if the corporation is not the alter ego of its officers or owners, they must be guilty of some deliberate, knowing misconduct. It must be established that they possessed specific intent to encourage the corporation's infringement and not merely that they had knowledge of the acts alleged to constitute infringement. In other words, the patentee has the burden to show that the individual's actions induced the infringing act and that he or she knew or should have known that his or her actions would induce actual infringement.[464]

Acts of a corporate officer that are within the scope of the officer's responsibility are not always sufficient grounds for penetrating the corporate protection and imposing personal liability. The policy considerations that underlie the corporate structure yield to personal liability for corporate acts only in limited circumstances. In general, a corporate officer is personally liable for his or her tortuous acts, just as any individual may be liable for a civil wrong. This general rule does not depend on the same grounds as piercing the corporate veil, such as inadequate capitalization, use of the corporate form for fraudulent purposes, or failure to comply with the formalities of corporate organization. When personal wrongdoing is not supported by legitimate corporate activity, the courts have assigned personal liability for wrongful actions even when taken on behalf of the corporation. However, this liability has been qualified, in extensive jurisprudence, by the distinction between commercial torts committed in the course of the officer's employment, and negligent and other culpable wrongful acts. Thus when a person in a control position causes the corporation to commit a civil wrong, imposition of personal liability requires consideration of the nature of the wrong, the culpability of the act, and whether the person acted in his or her personal interest or that of the corporation. The decisions have not always distinguished among the various legal premises, i.e.: (1) justification for piercing the corporate veil based on such criteria as absence of corporate assets or use of the corporate form for illegal purposes; (2) corporate commitment of a commercial tort (such as patent infringement or interference with contract or business advantage) caused by the officer acting as agent of the corporation; (3) similar actions that are exacerbated by culpable intent or bad faith on the part of the officer; or (4) personal commitment of a fraudulent or grossly negligent act.[465]

---

[463]*Orthokinetics, Inc. v. Safety Travel Chairs, Inc.*, 806 F.2d 1565, 1 USPQ2d 1081 (Fed. Cir. 1986). Corporate officers are presumably aware of what they are doing, and in that sense they can be said to have acted willfully. However, that does not mean that their acts must rise to the level recognized by the law as constituting willful infringement before they can be liable for infringement by their corporation. *Id.*

[464]*Micro Chem. Inc. v. Great Plains Chem. Co.*, 194 F.3d 1258, 52 USPQ2d 1258 (Fed. Cir. 1999); *Manville Sales Corp. v. Paramount Sys., Inc.*, 917 F.2d 544, 16 USPQ2d 1587 (Fed. Cir. 1990).

[465]*Hoover Group Inc. v. Custom Metalcraft, Inc.*, 84 F.3d 1408, 38 USPQ2d 1860 (Fed. Cir. 1996). In this case, it was not alleged that the corporate structure was a sham or existed merely to shield the individual from liability. Although he controlled the corporate entity, the

One related corporation can be liable for another's direct infringement only if the evidence reveals active inducement or circumstances justifying disregard of the status of the two as distinct, separate corporations.[466]

The principle of liability for aiding and abetting the wrongful acts of others is not imposed retrospectively, to make illegal an act that was not illegal when it was done. That is, if the thing that was abetted was not illegal at the time of abetment, but depended on some future event that might not occur (such as issuance of the patent), liability cannot be retroactively imposed. Thus, §271(b) does not reach persons who deliberately place later-infringing items into the chain of commerce before the patent issues.[467] Similarly, servicing and repair of a machine that was sold under circumstances that did not subject the seller to damages (prior to actual or constructive notice) cannot amount to inducement.[468]

In one interesting case, patent claims to a method of solving a puzzle could be directly infringed only by the puzzle user. Thus the puzzle manufacturer could be guilty only of inducing infringement.[469]

---

trial court did not pierce the corporate veil. The individual had made a straightforward commercial response to the assertions of patent infringement, including prompt consultations with counsel. Also, there was no finding that he actively and knowingly assisted the corporation's infringement, thus failing the requirement of culpable action. Certainly it is an insufficient basis for personal liability that he merely had knowledge of the acts alleged to constitute infringement.

[466]*A. Stucki Co. v. Worthington Indus., Inc.*, 849 F.2d 593, 7 USPQ2d 1066 (Fed. Cir. 1988). Mere ownership of stock is not enough to pierce the corporation veil. Here, the defendant indirectly owned 50% of the stock of an adjudged infringer, but there was no evidence that it had control over the infringer's actions and could have stopped the infringement. The "failure to stop" argument was also insufficient to support an inducement theory, even though the defendant was aware of the infringer's operations and knew that there was litigation, that infringement had been admitted, and that damages could be substantial if the validity of the patent was upheld. In *Hewlett-Packard Co. v. Bausch & Lomb Inc.*, 909 F.2d 1464, 15 USPQ2d 1525 (Fed. Cir. 1990), the court found lack of intent to induce infringement based upon the following facts: defendant sold a business that included an infringing line of products. The business was sold lock, stock, and barrel, without any retainer of interest or control, but there were several conditions associated with the sale: (1) the defendant gave the purchaser a license under a patent of defendant that happened to be the best prior art against the patent in suit; (2) the defendant indemnified, up to a cap limit, the purchaser against liability for infringement of the patent in suit; (3) there was an agreement to work jointly on a product that would not infringe the patent in suit; and (4) the purchaser agreed not to communicate with the plaintiff about the patent in suit.

[467]*National Presto Indus., Inc. v. West Bend Co.*, 76 F.3d 1185, 37 USPQ2d 1685 (Fed. Cir. 1996). Preissuance activities alone cannot establish inducement to infringe. *Micro Chem. Inc. v. Great Plains Chem. Co.*, 194 F.3d 1258, 52 USPQ2d 1258 (Fed. Cir. 1999).

[468]*Fonar Corp. v. General Elec. Co.*, 107 F.3d 1543, 41 USPQ2d 1801 (Fed. Cir. 1997).

[469]*Moleculon Res. Corp. v. CBS, Inc.*, 793 F.2d 1261, 229 USPQ 805 (Fed. Cir. 1986). The patentee offered no direct proof of puzzle use but offered circumstantial proof in the form of evidence of extensive sales of the puzzle, dissemination of an instruction sheet teaching the method, and the availability of a solution booklet. This evidence was sufficient to establish the requisite direct infringement. *Id.*

III

Ownership and Enforcement

7

Ownership of Patent Rights

This chapter, necessarily somewhat brief because of the Federal Circuit's limited subject matter jurisdiction, will examine how patent rights are acquired and owned.

There is a reasonably comprehensive statutory scheme governing inventorship and ownership.[1] Ownership springs from invention.[2] It is elementary that inventorship and ownership are separate issues. An application for a patent must be made by or on behalf of the actual inventor or inventors of the subject matter claimed therein. Thus inventorship is a question of who actually invented the subject matter claimed in a patent. Ownership, however, is a question of who owns legal title to the subject matter claimed in a patent, patents having the attributes of personal property. At the heart of any ownership analysis lies the question of who first invented the subject matter at issue, because the patent right initially vests in the inventor who may then, barring any restrictions to the contrary, transfer that right to another, and so forth. However, who ultimately possesses ownership rights in that subject matter has no bearing whatsoever on the question of who actually invented that subject matter.[3]

§7.1 Ownership by Grant

(a) Inventorship

In general. The patent statute provides that "whoever invents or discovers" any patentable subject matter "may obtain a patent therefor."[4] Only natural persons can be inventors.[5] The "inventor," in patent law, is the person or persons who conceived the patented invention.[6] Conception is the touchstone of inventorship.[7] Conception, and consequently inventorship, are questions of law that the Federal Circuit reviews de novo; any facts underlying a conclusion of inventorship are reviewed for clear error.[8] The so-called derivation defense,

---

[1]35 U.S.C. §§101, 116, 117, & 118 (inventorship); 35 U.S.C. §§100(d), 117, 118, 152, 261, & 262 (ownership).

[2]*Teets v. Chromalloy Gas Turbine Corp.,* 83 F.3d 403, 38 USPQ2d 1695 (Fed. Cir. 1996).

[3]*Beech Aircraft Corp. v. EDO Corp.,* 990 F.2d 1237 (Fed. Cir. 1993). Ownership and inventorship are separate issues. *Sewall v. Walters,* 21 F.3d 411, 30 USPQ2d 1356 (Fed. Cir. 1994).

[4]35 U.S.C. §101.

[5]*Beech Aircraft Corp. v. EDO Corp.,* 990 F.2d 1237 (Fed. Cir. 1993).

[6]*C.R. Bard Inc. v. M3 Sys. Inc.,* 157 F.3d 1340, 48 USPQ2d 1225 (Fed. Cir. 1998).

[7]*Ethicon Inc. v. United States Surgical Corp.,* 135 F.3d 1456, 45 USPQ2d 1545 (Fed. Cir. 1998); *Fina Oil & Chem. Co. v. Ewen,* 123 F.3d 1466, 43 USPQ2d 1935 (Fed. Cir. 1997); *Burroughs Wellcome Co. v. Barr Labs., Inc.,* 40 F.3d 1223, 32 USPQ2d 1915 (Fed. Cir. 1994). To be a joint inventor, one must contribute to the conception of an invention. *Pro-Mold & Tool Co. v. Great Lakes Plastics, Inc.,* 75 F.3d 1568, 37 USPQ2d 1626 (Fed. Cir. 1996). Determining inventorship is nothing more than determining who conceived the subject matter at issue, whether that subject matter is recited in a claim in an application or in a count in an interference. *Sewall v. Walters,* 21 F.3d 411, 30 USPQ2d 1356 (Fed. Cir. 1994). This case came to the court in the context of an originality contest as opposed to a priority context. In an originality case the issue is not who is the first or prior inventor, but who made the invention. The inventorship issue to be decided is merely who conceived the invention for which patent protection is sought, and not who first conceived that invention.

[8]*Ethicon Inc. v. United States Surgical Corp.,* 135 F.3d 1456, 45 USPQ2d 1545 (Fed. Cir. 1998); *Fina Oil & Chem. Co. v. Ewen,* 123 F.3d 1466, 43 USPQ2d 1935 (Fed. Cir. 1997); *Sewall v. Walters,* 21 F.3d 411, 30 USPQ2d 1356 (Fed. Cir. 1994).

under 35 U.S.C. §102(f), is also based on the requirement that the patentee be the actual inventor of the subject matter patented.[9]

In case of death or incapacity, the inventor's legal representatives may make and prosecute the patent application.[10] And one entitled to the patent by contract or operation of law may, under certain circumstances, apply for and obtain the patent if the inventor cannot or will not.[11]

Joint inventorship. The first paragraph of 35 U.S.C. §116 provides that:

> When an invention is made by two or more persons jointly, they shall apply for patent jointly. .... Inventors may apply for a patent jointly even though (1) they did not physically work together or at the same time, (2) each did not make the same type or amount of contribution, or (3) each did not make a contribution to the subject matter of every claim of the patent.

The issue of joint inventorship is governed by §116, which sets no explicit lower limit on the quantum or quality of inventive contribution required for a person to qualify as a joint inventor. Rather, a joint invention is simply the product of a collaboration between two or more persons working together to solve the problem addressed. The determination of whether a person is a joint inventor is fact specific, and no bright line standard will suffice in every case.[12] People may be joint inventors even though they do not physically work on the invention together or at the same time, and even though each does not make the same type or amount of contribution. The statute does not set forth the minimum quality or quantity of contribution required for joint inventorship.[13]

Thus, a patented invention may be the work of two or more joint inventors. Because conception is the touchstone of inventorship, each joint inventor must generally contribute to the conception of the invention. Conception is the formation in the mind of the inventor of a definite and permanent idea of the complete and operative invention, as it is thereafter to be applied in practice. An idea is sufficiently definite and permanent when only ordinary skill would be necessary to reduce the invention to practice, without extensive research or experimentation. The conceived invention must include every feature of the subject matter claimed in the patent. Nevertheless, for the conception of a joint invention, each of the joint inventors need not make the same type or amount of contribution to the invention. Rather, each needs to perform only a part of the task that produces

---

[9]See the discussion of this defense in §3.3.

[10]35 U.S.C. §117.

[11]35 U.S.C. §118.

[12]*Fina Oil & Chem. Co. v. Ewen*, 123 F.3d 1466, 43 USPQ2d 1935 (Fed. Cir. 1997).

[13]*Burroughs Wellcome Co. v. Barr Labs., Inc.*, 40 F.3d 1223, 32 USPQ2d 1915 (Fed. Cir. 1994).

the invention. On the other hand, one does not qualify as a joint inventor by merely assisting the actual inventor after conception of the claimed invention. One who simply provides the inventor with well-known principles or explains the state of the art without ever having a firm and definite idea of the claimed combination as a whole does not qualify as a joint inventor. Moreover, depending on the scope of a patent's claims, one of ordinary skill in the art who simply reduced the inventor's idea to practice is not necessarily a joint inventor, even if the specification discloses that embodiment to satisfy the best mode requirement. Furthermore, a coinventor need not make a contribution to every claim of a patent. A contribution to one claim is enough. Thus, the critical question for joint conception is who conceived, as that term is used in the patent law, the subject matter of the claims at issue.[14] All that is required of a joint inventor is that he or she (1) contribute in some significant manner to the conception or reduction to practice of the invention, (2) make a contribution to the claimed invention that is not insignificant in quality, when that contribution is measured against the dimension of the full invention, and (3) do more than merely explain to the real inventors well-known concepts or the current state of the art.[15]

It is accordingly clear that if a person supplies the required quantum of inventive contribution, that person does not lose his or her status as a joint inventor just because he or she used the services, ideas, and aid of others in the process of perfecting the invention.[16] However, those others may also in appropriate circumstances become joint inventors by their contributions.[17] A person is not precluded from being a joint inventor simply because his or her contribution to a collaborative effort is experimental. Instead, the qualitative contribution of each collaborator is the key—each inventor must contribute to the joint arrival at a definite and permanent idea of the invention as it will be used in practice.[18] On the other hand, requesting someone

---

[14]*Ethicon Inc. v. United States Surgical Corp.*, 135 F.3d 1456, 45 USPQ2d 1545 (Fed. Cir. 1998).

[15]*Pannu v. Iolab Corp.*, 155 F.3d 1344, 47 USPQ2d 1657 (Fed. Cir. 1998).

[16]*Fina Oil & Chem. Co. v. Ewen*, 123 F.3d 1466, 43 USPQ2d 1935 (Fed. Cir. 1997). An inventor may use the services, ideas, and aid of others in the process of perfecting his or her invention without losing his or her right to a patent. *Hess v. Advanced Cardiovascular Sys., Inc.*, 106 F.3d 976, 41 USPQ2d 1782 (Fed. Cir. 1997); *Shatterproof Glass Corp. v. Libbey-Owens Ford Co.*, 758 F.2d 613, 225 USPQ 634 (Fed. Cir. 1985). Others may provide services in perfecting the invention conceived by another without becoming an "inventor" by operation of law. *C.R. Bard Inc. v. M3 Sys. Inc.*, 157 F.3d 1340, 48 USPQ2d 1225 (Fed. Cir. 1998). The contributor of any disclosed means of a means-plus-function claim element is a joint inventor as to that claim, unless one asserting sole inventorship can show that the contribution of that means was simply a reduction to practice of the sole inventor's broader concept. *Ethicon Inc. v. United States Surgical Corp.*, 135 F.3d 1456, 45 USPQ2d 1545 (Fed. Cir. 1998). In *Sewall v. Walters*, 21 F.3d 411, 30 USPQ2d 1356 (Fed. Cir. 1994), the court refused to recognize one worker as a joint inventor where he only designed circuits to carry out the other worker's idea and where that design effort was simply the exercise of the normal skill expected of an ordinary circuit designer.

[17]*Fina Oil & Chem. Co. v. Ewen*, 123 F.3d 1466, 43 USPQ2d 1935 (Fed. Cir. 1997).

[18]*Burroughs Wellcome Co. v. Barr Labs., Inc.*, 40 F.3d 1223, 32 USPQ2d 1915 (Fed. Cir. 1994). The doctrine of simultaneous conception and reduction to practice states that, in some

to produce something without saying just what it is to be or how to do it is not what the patent law recognizes as invention.[19]

Any joint inventor is free to make, use, or sell the invention in the absence of an agreement to the contrary.[20] A sole inventor (A) and joint inventors (A and B) are separate legal entities, a legal proposition from which certain legal consequences flow, such as who must apply for a patent.[21]

Correction of inventorship. The third paragraph of §116 provides for correction of inventorship error in a pending application, where the error arises without any deceptive intention.[22] The 1984 amendments to 35 U.S.C. §116 made it clear that each joint inventor need not have made a contribution to the subject matter of every claim of a patent.[23] But the 1984 amendments to §116 did not eliminate collaboration as a requirement for joint invention. Thus, a patent issued to a later inventor cannot be corrected to include the name of an earlier inventor (and thereby to obtain the benefit of the earlier invention date), even one within the same organization, where the

---

instances, an inventor may only be able to establish a conception by pointing to a reduction to practice through a successful experiment. But it applies to the entire invention and is used to resolve priority disputes. It cannot be used, in a dispute concerning joint inventorship, to show that because the first person did not conceive or reduce to practice the entire claimed invention, that person did not at least contribute in some significant way to the ultimate conception. *Fina Oil & Chem. Co. v. Ewen,* 123 F.3d 1466, 43 USPQ2d 1935 (Fed. Cir. 1997).

[19]*Morgan v. Hirsch,* 728 F.2d 1449, 221 USPQ 193 (Fed. Cir. 1984).

[20]*Harrington Mfg. Co. v. Powell Mfg. Co.,* 815 F.2d 1478, 2 USPQ2d 1364 (Fed Cir. 1986). A joint inventor as to even one claim enjoys a presumption of ownership in the entire patent. This rule presents the prospect that a coinventor of only one claim might gain entitlement to ownership of a patent with dozens of claims. Where inventors choose to cooperate in the inventive process, their joint inventions may become joint property without some express agreement to the contrary. *Ethicon Inc. v. United States Surgical Corp.,* 135 F.3d 1456, 45 USPQ2d 1545 (Fed. Cir. 1998).

[21]*In re Kaplan,* 789 F.2d 1574, 229 USPQ 678 (Fed. Cir. 1986).

[22]*Stark v. Advanced Magnetics, Inc.,* 119 F.3d 1551, 43 USPQ2d 1321 (Fed. Cir. 1997). A jury instruction that indicates that the patent must be found invalid if the inventor was not the actual and only inventor is an oversimplification, in that it does not recognize the possibility of curing improper inventorship. *Shatterproof Glass Corp. v. Libbey-Owens Ford Co.,* 758 F.2d 613, 225 USPQ 634 (Fed. Cir. 1985). This case also indicated that it was not incumbent upon the patentee to disclaim, during the course of litigation, claims that were subject to a controverted inventorship challenge. See 35 U.S.C. §253. The interpretation of 35 U.S.C. §116 is a question of law freely reviewable on appeal. *Kimberly-Clark Corp. v. Procter & Gamble Distrib. Co.,* 973 F.2d 911, 23 USPQ2d 1921 (Fed. Cir. 1992). A petition to correct inventorship may be filed during reissue proceedings. *C.R. Bard Inc. v. M3 Sys. Inc.,* 157 F.3d 1340, 48 USPQ2d 1225 (Fed. Cir. 1998).

[23]*Smithkline Diagnostics, Inc. v. Helena Labs. Corp.,* 859 F.2d 878, 8 USPQ2d 1468 (Fed. Cir. 1988). The amendments are not (by the enacting statute) retroactively applicable in litigation pending the date of enactment. Nonetheless, in an interesting bit of jurisprudence, the court effectively applied them retroactively on the following basis: there was a split among the circuits prior to the 1984 amendments—the "all claims" rule was not uniformly accepted as the substantive law at that time. Inasmuch as it is doubtful that Congress intended the nonretroactivity provision of the enabling act to give a litigant a right to invoke the law of a particular circuit where there are conflicts on an issue, the nonretroactivity provision of the enacting statute does not negate the applicability of amended §116 in cases pending on the 1984 enactment date.

work of the earlier inventor was unknown to the later inventor at the time of the later invention.[24]

Closely related to §116 is 35 U.S.C. §256. The difficulty of determining legal inventorship has been recognized, and, to avoid inadvertent invalidity, §256 permits correction of the designated inventorship of a patent.[25] Before the enactment of §256, patentees and their assignees committed inventorship errors at their peril; misjoinder or nonjoinder of an inventor rendered the patent invalid. Section 256 affords the opportunity to correct the patent. If the patentees and their assignees agree, correction can be had on application to the PTO Commissioner. In the event agreement is not attained, however, the second paragraph of §256 permits redress in federal court.[26]

In the case of nonjoinder, there is another potential ground for invalidity independent of §§116 and 256. Section 102(f) mandates that a patent accurately list the correct inventors of a claimed invention. Accordingly, if nonjoinder of an actual inventor is proved by clear and convincing evidence, a patent is rendered invalid. However, in cases of nonjoinder the operation of §102(f) is ameliorated by §256. This section is a savings provision. If a patentee demonstrates that inventorship can be corrected as provided for in §256, a district court must order correction of the patent, thus saving it from being rendered invalid. When a party asserts invalidity under §102(f) due to nonjoinder, a district court should first determine whether there exists clear and convincing proof that the alleged unnamed inventor was in fact a coinventor. Upon such a finding of incorrect inventorship, a patentee may invoke §256 to save the patent from invalidity. Accordingly, the patentee must then be given an opportunity to correct inventorship pursuant to that section. Nonjoinder may be corrected on notice and hearing of all parties concerned and upon a showing that the error occurred without any deceptive intent on the part of the unnamed inventor. But a patent with improper inventorship does not avoid invalidation simply because it might be corrected under §256. Rather, the patentee must claim entitlement to relief under the statute and the court must give the patentee an opportunity to correct the inventorship. If the inventorship is successfully corrected, §102(f) will not render the patent invalid. On the other hand, if the patentee does not claim relief under the statute and a party asserting invalidity proves incorrect inventorship, the court should hold the patent invalid for failure to comply with §102(f).[27]

---

[24]*Kimberly-Clark Corp. v. Procter & Gamble Distrib. Co.*, 973 F.2d 911, 23 USPQ2d 1921 (Fed. Cir. 1992). See *Checkpoint Sys., Inc. v. United States ITC*, 54 F.3d 756, 35 USPQ2d 1042 (Fed. Cir. 1995), for a situation involving a possible joint invention that became part of the prior art under §102(g), thus precluding correction of a later-issued patent to one of the inventors.

[25]*C.R. Bard Inc. v. M3 Sys. Inc.*, 157 F.3d 1340, 48 USPQ2d 1225 (Fed. Cir. 1998).

[26]*MCV, Inc. v. King-Seeley Thermos Co.*, 870 F.2d 1568, 10 USPQ2d 1287 (Fed. Cir. 1989). The standards of the first paragraph of §256 relating to misjoinder and nonjoinder apply to both the PTO Commissioner and the courts. *Stark v. Advanced Magnetics, Inc.*, 119 F.3d 1551, 43 USPQ2d 1321 (Fed. Cir. 1997).

[27]*Pannu v. Iolab Corp.*, 155 F.3d 1344, 47 USPQ2d 1657 (Fed. Cir. 1998).

It is said that the purpose of §256 is to provide a remedy for a bona fide mistake in inventorship.[28] However, §256 allows deletion of a misjoined inventor whether the error occurred by deception or by innocent mistake. The statute also allows addition of an unnamed actual inventor, but the error of nonjoinder cannot betray any deceptive intent by that inventor. In other words, correction is available in all misjoinder cases where there is an error and in those nonjoinder cases where the unnamed inventor is free of deceptive intent.[29]

The principles of jurisdiction applicable to declaratory judgment suits are not implicated in inventorship disputes; the cause of action is itself created by 35 U.S.C. §256, which explicitly authorizes judicial resolution of coinventorship contests over issued patents. Thus, a suit for determination of coinventorship and consequent correction of a patent arises under the patent law.[30] However, declaratory judgment jurisdiction is evaluated by applying the well-pleaded complaint rule, considering the hypothetical complaint that the declaratory defendant would have brought. In the case of an action for a declaration that the inventors on a patent were properly named, this would be a complaint for correction of inventorship under §256, which provides a cause of action to interested parties to have the inventorship of a patent changed to reflect the true inventors of the subject matter claimed in the patent. A patentee or its assignee may state a claim under this section even where there is not a consensus on the correct inventorship as long as all parties are given notice and an opportunity to be heard. Thus, a declaratory plaintiff may establish an actual controversy in this context by averring that (1) it holds a recognized interest in a patent that could be adversely affected by an action brought under §256, and (2) another party with a right to bring an

---

[28]*Stark v. Advanced Magnetics, Inc.*, 29 F.3d 1570, 31 USPQ2d 1290 (Fed. Cir. 1994).

[29]*Stark v. Advanced Magnetics, Inc.*, 119 F.3d 1551, 43 USPQ2d 1321 (Fed. Cir. 1997). Here the nonjoined inventor was alleging that his collaborators deliberately and fraudulently omitted him as an inventor. Thus the court rejected the collaborators' argument that their own deceptive intention would prevent correction of inventorship. Only if the nonjoined inventor had deceptive intention would this be so. The majority of this 2–1 panel worried about the consequences of its permitting correction of inventorship where the named inventors may have had fraudulent intention in leaving off the nonjoined inventor. It concluded, as in *Burroughs Wellcome Co. v. Barr Labs., Inc.*, 40 F.3d 1223, 32 USPQ2d 1915 (Fed. Cir. 1994), that the patent may well be unenforceable for inequitable conduct when any coinventors are omitted with deceptive intention. It also supposed that the patent would be unenforceable even by the innocent nonjoined inventor, despite the fact that this issue was neither ripe nor presented. As it said, one bad apple spoils the entire barrel. Thus, although the nonjoined inventor might have a state law fraud claim against the listed inventors, the patent would not be enforceable by anybody. See also *University of Colorado Found. v. American Cyanamid Co.*, 196 F.3d 1366, 52 USPQ2d 1801 (Fed. Cir. 1999).

[30]*MCV, Inc. v. King-Seeley Thermos Co.*, 870 F.2d 1568, 10 USPQ2d 1287 (Fed. Cir. 1989). The court has said that a federal court has no independent jurisdiction over an action seeking a declaratory judgment of inventorship. Any controversy between the parties, if one exists, can only be contractual, and the fact that a contract action may involve a determination of the true inventor does not convert that action into one arising under the patent laws. *Consolidated World Housewares, Inc. v. Finkle*, 829 F.2d 261, 4 USPQ2d 1565 (Fed. Cir. 1987). Though proper inventorship may be the subject of future prosecution, it is not ancillary to priority in

action under §256 has created in the declaratory plaintiff a reasonable apprehension that it will do so.[31]

Section 256 does not limit the time during which inventorship can be corrected. It thus serves the public policy of preserving property rights from avoidable forfeiture. On the other hand, equity disfavors undue and prejudicial delay by a person who may have an interest in the property of another. Synthesizing these equitable interests, the defenses of laches and estoppel have been applied in §256 actions.[32] Nonetheless, diligence is not an absolute legal requisite for an action to correct inventorship under §256.[33] Whether diligent action is required in a particular case must be determined on the facts of that case. Lack of diligence may be an appropriate basis for barring legal action when there is an affirmative obligation on the claimant to act promptly and without significant pause in establishing a legal right. The common law has recognized that varying degrees of diligence may be required, depending on the circumstances. For example, a higher degree of diligence is appropriate when the claimant is chargeable with injury or disadvantage to another due to the claimant's failure to act expeditiously. Thus, there are circumstances where diligence is an appropriate requisite to pursuit of a particular legal right, whether or not the defenses of laches or estoppel may be invoked against the claimant.[34] Where there are several patents at issue in litigation, each is a separate chose in action. It is thus incorrect as a matter of law to hold that correction of several subsequently issued patents would be barred upon a finding of lack of diligence as to the first. This is by analogy to the law of laches, where the general rule is that the laches period does not accrue until each patent issues, even if the patents are interrelated.[35]

Even where correction of inventorship is not properly in issue, the courts have power to decree a remedy of assignment to redress

---

an interference. *DeGeorge v. Bernier*, 768 F.2d 1318, 226 USPQ 758 (Fed. Cir. 1985); *Case v. CPC Int'l*, 730 F.2d 745, 221 USPQ 196 (Fed. Cir. 1984).

[31]*Fina Oil & Chem. Co. v. Ewen*, 123 F.3d 1466, 43 USPQ2d 1935 (Fed. Cir. 1997).

[32]*Stark v. Advanced Magnetics, Inc.*, 29 F.3d 1570, 31 USPQ2d 1290 (Fed. Cir. 1994). Equitable estoppel will apply to inventorship contests; the putative coinventor must be diligent in acting to preserve his or her rights. *MCV, Inc. v. King-Seeley Thermos Co.*, 870 F.2d 1568, 10 USPQ2d 1287 (Fed. Cir. 1989). See also *Advanced Cardiovascular Sys., Inc. v. Scimed Life Sys., Inc.*, 988 F.2d 1157, 26 USPQ2d 1038 (Fed. Cir. 1993). The fact that one joint inventor allowed his part of the invention to become prior art more than a year before the filing date apparently does not disqualify him as a joint inventor. *Pannu v. Iolab Corp.*, 155 F.3d 1344, 47 USPQ2d 1657 (Fed. Cir. 1998).

[33]*Stark v. Advanced Magnetics, Inc.*, 29 F.3d 1570, 31 USPQ2d 1290 (Fed. Cir. 1994). In so holding, the court pointed out that although 37 C.F.R. §1.48 requires diligence, that rule relates to correction of inventorship under 35 U.S.C. §116 while an application is pending. Rule 324 (37 C.F.R. §1.324), which implements §256, has no express requirement for diligence.

[34]*Stark v. Advanced Magnetics, Inc.*, 29 F.3d 1570, 31 USPQ2d 1290 (Fed. Cir. 1994). The court held that a period from patent issuance to filing suit to correct inventorship, ranging from five months to under four years for six individual patents, did not bar the §256 action.

[35]*Stark v. Advanced Magnetics, Inc.*, 29 F.3d 1570, 31 USPQ2d 1290 (Fed. Cir. 1994).

wrongful appropriation of intellectual property by those subject to the court's jurisdiction.[36]

Presumption of correct inventorship; burden of proof. The burden of showing misjoinder or nonjoinder of inventors is a heavy one and must be proved by clear and convincing evidence, both as to patent applications under §116 and issued patents under §256. This rule rests on important policy considerations. The inventors as named in an issued patent are presumed to be correct. The temptation for persons who consulted with the inventor and provided materials and advice, to reconstruct, so as to further their own position, the extent of their contribution to the conception of the invention is simply too great to permit a lower standard than clear and convincing evidence.[37]

It has long been the rule that one who asserts "inventor" status must provide clear and convincing evidence of supporting facts, including corroborating evidence.[38] An inventor's testimony respecting the facts surrounding a claim of derivation or priority of invention cannot, standing alone, rise to the level of clear and convincing proof. The rule is the same for an alleged coinventor's testimony. Thus, an alleged coinventor must supply evidence to corroborate his or her testimony. Whether the inventor's testimony has been sufficiently corroborated is evaluated under a "rule of reason" analysis. Under this analysis, an evaluation of all pertinent evidence must be made so that a sound determination of the credibility of the alleged inventor's story may be reached. Corroborating evidence may take many forms. Often contemporaneous documents prepared by a putative inventor serve to corroborate an inventor's testimony. Circumstantial evidence about the inventive process may also corroborate. Additionally, oral testimony of someone other than the alleged inventor may corroborate. Taken together, the alleged coinventor's testimony and the corroborating evidence must show inventorship by clear and convincing evidence. This requirement is not to be taken lightly. Under the rule of reason standard for corroborating evidence, the trial court must consider corroborating evidence in context, make necessary credibility determinations, and assign appropriate probative weight to the evidence to determine whether clear and convincing evidence

---

[36]*Richardson v. Suzuki Motor Co.,* 868 F.2d 1226, 9 USPQ2d 1913 (Fed. Cir. 1989). This appears to have been a case of derivation under 35 U.S.C. §102(f), where the defendant had wrongfully obtained a patent on the plaintiff's invention, which had been disclosed to the defendant in confidence.

[37]*Hess v. Advanced Cardiovascular Sys., Inc.,* 106 F.3d 976, 41 USPQ2d 1782 (Fed. Cir. 1997). See also *Fina Oil & Chem. Co. v. Ewen,* 123 F.3d 1466, 43 USPQ2d 1935 (Fed. Cir. 1997). Patent issuance creates a presumption that the named inventors are the true and only inventors. *Ethicon Inc. v. United States Surgical Corp.,* 135 F.3d 1456, 45 USPQ2d 1545 (Fed. Cir. 1998). The inventors as named in an issued patent are presumed to be correct, and the simple fact that a large number of individuals are listed does not destroy that presumption. *Canon Computer Sys. Inc v. NuKote Int'l Inc.,* 134 F.3d 1085, 45 USPQ2d 1355 (Fed. Cir. 1998).

[38]*C.R. Bard Inc. v. M3 Sys. Inc.,* 157 F.3d 1340, 48 USPQ2d 1225 (Fed. Cir. 1998).

supports a claim of coinventorship. Accordingly, there need not be corroboration for every factual issue contested by the parties.[39]

(b) Employee/Employer Relationships: Shoprights

The Federal Circuit has begun to confront some of the issues that can arise in the case of the employed inventor, such as shoprights or refusals to assign.[40] The act of invention itself vests an inventor with a common law or "natural" right to make, use, and sell the invention absent conflicting patent rights in others and, in certain circumstances, may similarly vest such rights in an employer of the inventor.[41] An invention presumptively belongs to its creator. This simple proposition becomes more complex when one creates while employed by another person. Consistent with the presumption that the inventor owns his or her invention, an individual owns the patent rights even though the invention was conceived and/or reduced to practice during the course of employment. At the same time, however, the law recognizes that employers may have an interest in the creative products of their employees. For example, an employer may obtain a shopright in employee inventions where it has contributed to the development of the invention. A shopright permits the employer to use the employee's invention without liability for infringement. In addition, contract law allows individuals to freely structure their transactions and employee relationships. An employee may thus freely consent by contract to assign all rights in inventive ideas to the employer.[42]

The general rule is that, absent contractual arrangements to the contrary, an independent discovery belongs to the employee unless it is within the scope and purpose of the employment. The shopright is an exception to that general rule. A common law doctrine founded on equitable principles, the shopright allows an employer to use, without payment to the employee, an employee's invention that was made using the employer's time, materials, facilities, or equipment.

---

[39]*Ethicon Inc. v. United States Surgical Corp.*, 135 F.3d 1456, 45 USPQ2d 1545 (Fed. Cir. 1998). Every putative inventor must provide corroborating evidence of any asserted contributions to the conception of the invention. Like conception of the entire invention, a contribution to conception is a mental act that cannot be accurately verified without corroboration. *Fina Oil & Chem. Co. v. Ewen*, 123 F.3d 1466, 43 USPQ2d 1935 (Fed. Cir. 1997).

[40]In *Bausch & Lomb, Inc. v. Barnes-Hind, Inc.*, 796 F.2d 443, 230 USPQ 416 (Fed. Cir. 1986), a coinventor had left his original employer to work for a competitor. He at first refused when asked to execute patent documents, indicating that he had not invented anything in that connection while with his original employer. The district court seemed impressed by the refusal to sign, but the Federal Circuit gave the refusal little weight in the obviousness determination in view of the inventor's self-interest as an employee of a competitor.

[41]*Arachnid, Inc. v. Merit Indus., Inc.*, 939 F.2d 1574, 19 USPQ2d 1513 (Fed. Cir. 1991). Employment, salary, and bonuses are all valid forms of consideration for an assignment of an invention from an employee to an employer. *Carroll Touch, Inc. v. Electro Mechanical Sys., Inc.*, 3 F.3d 404, 27 USPQ2d 1836 (Fed. Cir. 1993).

[42]*Teets v. Chromalloy Gas Turbine Corp.*, 83 F.3d 403, 38 USPQ2d 1695 (Fed. Cir. 1996).

The shopright has been described as a form of implied license, founded on estoppel or acquiescence. It has been applied to tangible and intangible property, including trade secrets.[43] A shopright entitles its possessor to duplicate the invention or to procure it from outside vendors or contractors.[44]

Thus a shopright is generally accepted as being a right that is created at common law, when the circumstances demand it, under principles of equity and fairness, entitling an employer to use without charge an invention patented by one or more of its employees without liability for infringement. Many courts have characterized a shopright as being a type of implied license; others as a form of equitable estoppel. The Federal Circuit feels that the proper methodology is to look to the totality of the circumstances on a case-by-case basis and determine whether the facts of a particular case demand, under principles of equity and fairness, a finding that a shopright exists. In such an analysis one should look to such factors as the circumstances surrounding the development of the patented invention and the inventor's activities respecting that invention, once developed, to determine whether equity and fairness demand that the employer be allowed to use that invention in its business. A factually driven analysis such as this ensures that the principles of equity and fairness underlying the shopright rule are considered.[45]

Even without an express contract to assign, employers may still claim an employee's inventive work where the employer specifically hires or directs the employee to exercise invention faculties. When the purpose for employment thus focuses on invention, the employee has received full compensation for his or her inventive work. But an employer cannot claim ownership of an employee's invention unless the contract of employment by express terms or unequivocal inference shows that the employee was hired for the express purpose of producing the thing patented. Thus, when an employer hires a person for general service and the employee invents on the side, the invention belongs to the employee. However, the employer may claim ownership of the invention if the employer hires a person for the specific purpose of making the invention. Even if hired for a general purpose, an employee with the specific task of developing a device or process may cede ownership of the invention from that task to the employer. To apply this contract principle, a court must examine the employment relationship at the time of the inventive work to determine if the parties entered an implied-in-fact contract to assign patent rights. Such a contract is an agreement founded upon a meeting of the minds,

---

[43]*Lariscey v. United States*, 949 F.2d 1137, 20 USPQ2d 1845 (Fed. Cir. 1991). In this interesting case the court found that the Federal Prison Industries did not acquire a shopright in an inmate's invention.

[44]*McElmurry v. Arkansas Power & Light Co.*, 995 F.2d 1576, 27 USPQ2d 1129 (Fed. Cir. 1993).

[45]*McElmurry v. Arkansas Power & Light Co.*, 995 F.2d 1576, 27 USPQ2d 1129 (Fed. Cir. 1993).

which, although not embodied in an express contract, is inferred as a fact from conduct of the parties showing, in light of the surrounding circumstances, their tacit understanding. By comparison, an implied-in-law contract is a fiction of law where a promise is imputed to perform a legal duty, as to repay money obtained by fraud or duress.[46]

§7.2 Ownership by Acquisition

(a) Assignments

Patents and trademarks, like other personal property, may be conveyed from the inventor or registrant, although a trademark cannot be validly assigned unless accompanied by its goodwill garnered in the marketplace. Both governing statutes (35 U.S.C. §261 for patents and 15 U.S.C. §1060 for trademarks) require the assignments to be in writing; but recording is necessary only to protect the assignee from subsequent bona fide purchasers without notice.[47]

Property rights in an invention are by definition personal property. An application for patent as well as the patent itself may be assigned. Indeed, rights in an invention may be assigned and legal title to an ensuing patent will pass to the assignee upon grant of the patent. If an assignment of rights in an invention is made prior to the existence of the invention, this may be viewed as an assignment of an expectant interest. Although such assignments are valid, the assignee holds at most an equitable title. Once an invention is made and a patent application filed, however, legal title to the rights accruing thereunder would be in the assignee, and the assignor-inventor would have nothing remaining to assign.[48] The owner or licensee of a patent cannot convey that which it does not possess.[49]

Where a contract expressly grants rights in any future invention, no further act would ordinarily be required once an invention came into being; the transfer of title would occur by operation of law.[50] On

---

[46]*Teets v. Chromalloy Gas Turbine Corp.,* 83 F.3d 403, 38 USPQ2d 1695 (Fed. Cir. 1996). As a matter of common law, state contract principles provide the rules for identifying and enforcing implied-in-fact contracts. Most states, however, follow Supreme Court decisions involving ownership of inventive rights. The existence of an implied-in-fact contract to assign inventive rights is a question of fact that is reviewed for clear error. *Id.*

[47]*GAIA Tech., Inc. v. Reconversion Tech., Inc.,* 93 F.3d 774, 39 USPQ2d 1826 (Fed. Cir. 1996).

[48]*Filmtec Corp. v. Allied-Signal Inc.,* 939 F.2d 1568, 19 USPQ2d 1508 (Fed. Cir. 1991).

[49]*Prima Tek II L.L.C. v. A-Roo Co.,* 222 F.3d 1372, 55 USPQ2d 1742 (Fed. Cir. 2000).

[50]*Filmtec Corp. v. Allied-Signal Inc.,* 939 F.2d 1568, 19 USPQ2d 1508 (Fed. Cir. 1991). In *Filmtec Corp. v. Hydranautics,* 982 F.2d 1546, 25 USPQ2d 1283 (Fed. Cir. 1992), the federal legislation underlying government-funded research required the contracting employer to include in its employment agreements a provision that the government would retain title to inventions made by the employee. Thus, the fact that the inventor was not bound by the contract is of no moment. Nor does it make any difference that the formalities of the statute, including issuance of the patent to the United States, were not complied with. When the invention was conceived by the employee working on the contract research, title to that invention immediately

the other hand, an agreement to assign is not an assignment. A provision that all rights to inventions developed during a consulting period "will be assigned" does not rise to the level of a present assignment of an existing invention, effective to transfer all legal and equitable rights therein to the proposed assignee and to extinguish any rights of the proposed assignor. Nor does it amount to a present assignment of an expectant interest. Although an agreement to assign in the future inventions not yet developed may vest the promisee with equitable rights in those inventions once made, such an agreement does not by itself vest legal title to patents on the inventions.[51]

An assignment of a patent may be either absolute, or by way of a mortgage and liable to be defeated by nonperformance of a condition subsequent.[52]

Patents are specifically given the attributes of personal property by virtue of 35 U.S.C. §261. Section 261 goes on to provide that patents, patent applications, "or any interest therein, shall be assignable in law by an instrument in writing."[53] Section 261 also provides that such a conveyance is void as against a subsequent purchaser for value without notice unless it is recorded in the PTO within three months, or prior to the subsequent transaction.

Merely recording an assignment does not evidence its validity as a title conveyance, nor does it create subject matter jurisdiction under 28 U.S.C. §1338.[54] By the same token, recording under §261 is not necessary in order to give validity to an exclusive license.[55] It is well established that when a legal titleholder of a patent transfers his or her title to a third party purchaser for value without notice of an outstanding equitable claim or title, the purchaser takes the entire ownership of the patent, free of any prior equitable encumbrance. The patent statute takes this a step further and adopts, in §261, the principle of the real property recording acts. Thus, a bona fide purchaser for value cuts off the rights of a prior assignee who has failed to record the prior assignment in the PTO. The statute is intended to cut off legal interests, while the common law rule affected only equitable interests.[56]

Under §261 a subsequent purchaser must be in fact a purchaser for a valuable consideration. This requirement is different from the

---

vested in the government by operation of law. The employee had no right to assign it to the employer, then or later.

[51]*Arachnid, Inc. v. Merit Indus., Inc.,* 939 F.2d 1574, 19 USPQ2d 1513 (Fed. Cir. 1991). Compare *Speedplay Inc. v. Bebop Inc.,* 211 F.3d 1245, 53 USPQ2d 1984 (Fed. Cir. 2000).

[52]*Vaupel Textilmaschinen KG v. Meccanical Euro Italia S.P.A.,* 944 F.2d 870, 20 USPQ2d 1045 (Fed. Cir. 1991).

[53]*Enzo APA & Son v. Geapag A.G.,* 134 F.3d 1090, 45 USPQ2d 1368 (Fed. Cir. 1998).

[54]*Beghin-Say Int'l, Inc. v. Ole-Bendt Rasmussen,* 733 F.2d 1568, 221 USPQ 1121 (Fed. Cir. 1984).

[55]*Weinar v. Rollform Inc.,* 744 F.2d 797, 223 USPQ 369 (Fed. Cir. 1984).

[56]*Filmtec Corp. v. Allied-Signal Inc.,* 939 F.2d 1568, 19 USPQ2d 1508 (Fed. Cir. 1991). See also *Heidelberg Harris Inc. v. Loebach,* 145 F.3d 1454, 46 USPQ2d 1948 (Fed. Cir. 1998).

classic notion of a purchaser under a deed of grant, where the requirement of consideration was a formality. Under §261, the subsequent purchaser, in order to cut off the rights of the prior purchaser, must be more than a donee or other gratuitous transferee. There must be in fact valuable consideration paid so that the subsequent purchaser can, as a matter of law, claim record reliance as a premise upon which the purchase was made.[57] As a general proposition, in order to defeat a bona fide purchaser defense on the basis of notice, the purchaser must have received the notice before it has paid the consideration or performed its purchase obligations.[58] The court has indicated that employment, salary, and bonuses are all valid forms of consideration for an employee's assignment to his or her employer.[59]

The courts are not powerless to decree assignment of a patent to the true inventor in cases of derivation.[60] In the absence of a showing that a putative owner had parted with ownership prior to death, there is a presumption that he or she was the owner at death.[61]

The court has resurrected the doctrine of assignor estoppel. That subject is discussed in §7.2(e).

(b) Assignments versus Licenses: Standing to Sue

This section should be read in conjunction with §8.1(a)(iv). Section 281 provides that a "patentee" shall have remedy by civil action for infringement of a patent. The term patentee, under §100(d), includes not only the patentee to whom the patent was issued but also the successors in title to the patentee. Courts look to the substance of an agreement to determine whether it has the effect of an assignment and thus satisfies the statutory requirement that the patentee must sue. Where a patentee makes an assignment of all significant rights under the patent, such assignee may be deemed the effective patentee under the statute and has standing to bring a suit in its own name for infringement.[62] A conveyance of legal title by the patentee can be

---

[57]*Filmtec Corp. v. Allied-Signal Inc.*, 939 F.2d 1568, 19 USPQ2d 1508 (Fed. Cir. 1991). The court seems willing to apply standard notions of privity to the notice requirement. It indicated in this same case that if one of the founders of a company is on notice of the assignment provisions of his or her own prior employment contract with a former employer, the new company is likewise on notice.

[58]*Heidelberg Harris Inc. v. Loebach*, 145 F.3d 1454, 46 USPQ2d 1948 (Fed. Cir. 1998). The court declined an invitation to adopt the proposition that a bona fide purchaser for value forfeits its right to rely on the rule unless it takes legal action against the party from whom it made the purchase.

[59]*Carroll Touch, Inc. v. Electro Mechanical Sys., Inc.*, 3 F.3d 404, 27 USPQ2d 1836, 1842 (Fed. Cir. 1993).

[60]*Richardson v. Suzuki Motor Co.*, 868 F.2d 1226, 9 USPQ2d 1913 (Fed. Cir. 1989).

[61]*Stickle v. Heublein, Inc.*, 716 F.2d 1550, 219 USPQ 377 (Fed. Cir. 1983). Passing of title by will is governed by state law. *Id.*

[62]*Enzo APA & Son v. Geapag A.G.*, 134 F.3d 1090, 45 USPQ2d 1368 (Fed. Cir. 1998); *Ortho Pharm. Corp. v. Genetics Inst., Inc.*, 52 F.3d 1026, 34 USPQ2d 1444 (Fed. Cir. 1995). See *Ethicon Inc. v. United States Surgical Corp.*, 135 F.3d 1456, 45 USPQ2d 1545 (Fed. Cir.

made only of (1) the entire patent, (2) an undivided part or share of the entire patent, or (3) all rights under the patent in a specified geographical region of the United States. A transfer of any of these is an assignment and vests the assignee with title in the patent, and a right to sue infringers (either alone, in cases (1) and (3), or, in case (2), jointly with the assignor). A transfer of less than one of these three interests is a license, not an assignment of legal title, and it gives the licensee no right to sue for infringement at law in the licensor's own name. Under certain circumstances, a licensee may possess sufficient interest in the patent to have standing to sue as a coplaintiff with the patentee. Such a licensee is usually an exclusive licensee.[63] Thus, although a patentee has standing to sue in its own name, an exclusive licensee that does not have all substantial rights has standing to sue third parties only as a coplaintiff with the patentee. At least one exception to that rule exists, however: an exclusive licensee that does not have all substantial rights does have standing to sue in its own name when necessary to prevent an absolute failure of justice, as where the patentee is the infringer, and cannot sue itself. On the other hand, a bare licensee has no standing at all.[64]

A licensing arrangement conferring standing must, logically, resemble an assignment in both form and substance.[65] To determine whether a provision in an agreement constitutes an assignment or a license, one must ascertain the intention of the parties and examine the substance of what was granted. An assignment of an interest in an invention secured by patent is a contract and, like all other contracts, is to be construed so as to carry out the intent of the parties. Whether a transfer constitutes a sale or a license is determined by the substance of the transaction. A transfer will suffice as a sale if it appears from the agreement and the surrounding circumstances that the parties intended that the patentee surrender all substantial rights to the invention. Whether a transfer of a particular right or interest under a patent is an assignment or a license does not depend upon the name by which it calls itself, but upon the legal effect of its provisions. The term "assignment" has a particular meaning in patent law, implying formal transfer of title. A formal assignment may not be required in order to transfer all substantial rights.[66]

1998), for a discussion of standing in the context of co-ownership. The congressional policy expressed in §262 is that co-owners are at the mercy of one another.

[63]*Rite-Hite Corp. v. Kelley Co.*, 56 F.3d 1538, 35 USPQ2d 1065 (Fed. Cir. 1995). See also *Enzo APA & Son v. Geapag A.G.*, 134 F.3d 1090, 45 USPQ2d 1368 (Fed. Cir. 1998); *Arnold Corp. v. Hydrotech Sys., Inc.*, 109 F.3d 1567, 42 USPQ2d 1129 (Fed. Cir. 1997); *Minco, Inc. v. Combustion Eng'g, Inc.*, 95 F.3d 1109, 40 USPQ2d 1001 (Fed. Cir. 1996).

[64]*Textile Prods. Inc. v. Mead Corp.*, 134 F.3d 1481, 45 USPQ2d 1633 (Fed. Cir. 1998).

[65]*Enzo APA & Son v. Geapag A.G.*, 134 F.3d 1090, 45 USPQ2d 1368 (Fed. Cir. 1998). If the courts were to expand the virtual assignment exception to include verbal licenses, the exception would swallow the rule. Parties would be free to engage in revisionist history, circumventing the certainty provided by the writing requirement of §261 by claiming to be patentee by virtue of a verbal licensing arrangement. *Id.*

[66]*Vaupel Textilmaschinen KG v. Meccanical Euro Italia S.P.A.*, 944 F.2d 870, 20 USPQ2d 1045 (Fed. Cir. 1991). In determining whether a grant of all substantial rights was intended,

The use of the word "exclusive" is not controlling; what matters is the substance of the arrangement. Because patent rights are rights to exclude others, a licensee is an exclusive licensee only if the patentee has promised, expressly or impliedly, that others shall be excluded from practicing the invention within the field covered by the license. Put another way, an exclusive license is a license to practice the invention, accompanied by the patent owner's promise that others shall be excluded from practicing it within the field of use wherein the licensee is given leave. Thus, if a patentee-licensor is free to grant licenses to others, licensees under that patent are not exclusive licensees.[67]

Generally, one seeking money damages for patent infringement must have held legal title to the patent at the time of the infringement.[68] An assignee may bring an action to redress any violations of the exclusive rights conferred by the patent. Infringement, however, harms only the owner of the patent at the time of the infringing acts. Thus the conveyance of the patent does not normally include the right to recover for injury occurring to a prior owner. The right to sue for past infringement is not transferred unless the assignment agreement manifests an intent to transfer this right. Neither statute nor common

---

it is helpful to look at what rights have been retained by the grantor, not only what was granted. In this case, the grantor retained (1) a veto right on sublicensing, (2) the right to obtain foreign patents on the invention, (3) a reversionary right to the patent in the event of bankruptcy or termination of production by the grantee, and (4) a right to receive infringement damages. On the other hand, the grantor transferred the right to sue for infringement, subject only to an obligation to inform the grantor. On balance, the court concluded that this transaction transferred all substantial rights. In *Prima Tek II L.L.C. v. A-Roo Co.*, 222 F.3d 1372, 55 USPQ2d 1742 (Fed. Cir. 2000), the court observed that a licensee's right to sublicense is an important consideration in evaluating whether a license agreement transfers all substantial rights. A mere "sublicensing veto," which requires the licensee to obtain written consent of the patent owner for all sublicenses (as in *Vaupel*, supra), may be only a minor derogation from the grant of rights and thus not deprive the licensee of standing to sue in its own name. However, the agreement in this case went far beyond a mere sublicensing veto. Instead of simply allowing the patent owner to approve or disapprove sublicenses, it required that the licensee execute a sublicense to a particular party and to no one else. Because the licensee's rights under the agreement were significantly diminished by the sublicense requirement, it could not be said that the requirement was merely a "minor derogation" from the grant of rights.

[67]*Textile Prods. Inc. v. Mead Corp.*, 134 F.3d 1481, 45 USPQ2d 1633 (Fed. Cir. 1998). A contract to produce for the patent owner its total requirements for a patented product does not automatically convert the exclusive supplier into an exclusive licensee of the patent. The contractual manufacturing rights of a party do not alone confer a right to exclude all others from making an invention. To qualify as an exclusive license, an agreement must clearly manifest the patentee's promise to refrain from granting to anyone else a license in the area of exclusivity. In this case, which involved a complex contract, the court held that the supplier did not have standing to assert patent infringement against the patent owner and its secondary supplier.

[68]*Rite-Hite Corp. v. Kelley Co.*, 56 F.3d 1538, 35 USPQ2d 1065 (Fed. Cir. 1995). Nunc pro tunc assignments are not sufficient to confer retroactive standing because, as a general matter, parties should possess rights before seeking to have them vindicated in court. *Enzo APA & Son v. Geapag A.G.*, 134 F.3d 1090, 45 USPQ2d 1368 (Fed. Cir. 1998). In *Mas-Hamilton Group Inc. v. LaGard Inc.*, 156 F.3d 1206, 48 USPQ2d 1010 (Fed. Cir. 1998), the patent owner, a declaratory judgment defendant, assigned the patent during the pendency of the appeal. The assignment did not expressly transfer right to sue for past infringement, but this was cured by a later supplemental assignment. The court held that both the original owner and the assignee have standing to prosecute the appeal. While it is true that nunc pro tunc assignments

law precedent, however, requires a particular formula or set prescription of words to express that conveyance.[69]

Thus ownership of a patent is normally a requisite to sue for infringement,[70] and standing to recover damages for past infringement requires an express assignment of that right.[71] On the other hand, the court appears to have approved the holding of its predecessor[72] that, in patent litigation between private parties, equitable rights of ownership of strangers to the suit cannot be raised as defenses against the legal titleholder of a patent.[73]

(c) Licenses

A patent confers on its holder the right to exclude others from making, using, or selling what is described in its claims. Implicit in

---

are not sufficient to confer retroactive standing, here standing was not deficient at the time the declaratory suit was filed, nor at the time the appeal was filed.

[69]*Minco, Inc. v. Combustion Eng'g, Inc.,* 95 F.3d 1109, 40 USPQ2d 1001 (Fed. Cir. 1996). Determining whether the right to sue for prior infringement has been transferred turns on the proper construction of the assignment agreements, which is a matter of state contract law. Here the assignment documents specifically invoked Tennessee law.

[70]*Speedco, Inc. v. Estes,* 853 F.2d 909, 7 USPQ2d 1637 (Fed. Cir. 1988). There, a patent was sold for cash and a note. After making one payment the assignee quit paying on the ground that the patent had been procured by fraud. The assignee then brought a declaratory judgment action seeking an evaluation by the district court as to the validity and enforceability of the patent and reformation of the terms of the assignment in accordance with the district court's determination of the real value of what was conveyed. The Federal Circuit held that this was not a case arising under the patent laws, inasmuch as the only claim the declaratory defendant could have brought, in the absence of a complete renouncement of the assignment by the assignee, was a state law contract action to enforce the terms of the contract and recover the overdue payments owed on the note. He would not be required, as an element of such a claim, to show that the patent is valid, for patents are presumed valid. Invalidity would only be a defense to the state contract action. On the other hand, since ownership of a patent is normally a requisite to sue for infringement, the defendant would somehow have to regain title. The situation was distinguished from that in *C.R. Bard, Inc. v. Schwartz,* 716 F.2d 874, 219 USPQ 197 (Fed. Cir. 1983), where the declaratory plaintiff was a licensee, not an assignee. There the declaratory defendant retained title and could have terminated the license and sued for infringement. It should also be noted that, in view of the disposition of the case on jurisdictional grounds, the court did not decide whether an assignee has standing to challenge the validity of a patent in a suit against the assignor. But see *Diamond Scientific Co. v. Ambico, Inc.,* 848 F.2d 1220, 6 USPQ2d 2028 (Fed. Cir. 1988).

[71]*Arachnid, Inc. v. Merit Indus., Inc.,* 939 F.2d 1574, 19 USPQ2d 1513 (Fed. Cir. 1991). The extremely complex title situation that was addressed by the court in this case illustrates the need for special care in drafting and analyzing assignments and assignment agreements. See also *Heidelberg Harris Inc. v. Loebach,* 145 F.3d 1454, 46 USPQ2d 1948 (Fed. Cir. 1998). In *GAIA Tech., Inc. v. Reconversion Tech., Inc.,* 93 F.3d 774, 39 USPQ2d 1826 (Fed. Cir. 1996), the court held that an assignment of patent and trademark rights executed after the litigation was commenced but made effective prior to filing of suit did not confer standing on the assignee retroactively.

[72]*Dorr-Oliver, Inc. v. United States,* 432 F.2d 447, 165 USPQ 517 (Ct. Cl. 1970). Despite the rule, the government was permitted to raise a title defense because of the anti-assignment statute (31 U.S.C. §203), which prohibited the assignment of any claim for patent infringement against the United States that arose prior to the time a plaintiff acquired title to the patent.

[73]*Filmtec Corp. v. Hydranautics,* 982 F.2d 1546, 25 USPQ2d 1283 (Fed. Cir. 1992). Here, the defendant was permitted to raise the defense that title was actually in the government rather than the plaintiff; but here, as in *Dorr-Oliver* (see note 7:72), there was a federal statute

the right to exclude is the ability to waive that right, i.e., to license activities that would otherwise be excluded.[74] This right, like any other property right, is subject to the contractual obligations of its owner and the applicable law. Thus a patent owner may contract to confer a license on another party. In most instances under contract law, a patent owner intentionally creates an express license. A licensee, of course, has an affirmative defense to a claim of patent infringement.[75] A license agreement is a contract governed by ordinary principles of state contract law.[76] Construction of a license agreement is a question of state contract law that the court reviews de novo.[77]

A patent license agreement is in essence nothing more than a promise by the licensor not to sue the licensee.[78] Even if it is couched in terms of "licensee is given the right to make, use, or sell X," the agreement cannot convey that absolute right because not even the patentee of X is given that right. His or her right is merely one to exclude others from making, using, or selling X. Indeed, the patentee of X and his or her licensee, when making, using, or selling X, can be subject to suit under other patents. In any event, patent license agreements can be written to convey different scopes of promises not to sue, e.g., a promise not to sue under a specific patent or, more broadly, a promise not to sue under any patent the licensor now has or may acquire in the future.[79] The proprietary rights granted by any

involved, which provided that title to any invention made or conceived under a FNERDA contract "shall vest" in the United States. It should be noted that, as an alternative ground for its decision, the court also found that the defendant was a third-party beneficiary of a contract between the plaintiff and the government.

[74]*Prima Tek II L.L.C. v. A-Roo Co.*, 222 F.3d 1372, 55 USPQ2d 1742 (Fed. Cir. 2000).

[75]*McCoy v. Mitsuboshi Cutlery, Inc.*, 67 F.3d 917, 36 USPQ2d 1289 (Fed. Cir. 1995). In the case of a license agreement having a rescission clause, a patentee in a suit for infringement can properly assert that it owned the patent at the time of infringement and that the defendant is infringing the patent. In such cases, the plaintiff does not seek any specific equitable relief as a prerequisite to bringing the infringement claim. Thus, the district court can treat the defendant's claim of a license as a defense to the assertion that he is infringing, and the court can decide that issue first as a matter of efficient management of the trial. However, when the infringement suit involves an assignment, unless the assignment may be declared null and void by operation of law—either through a forfeiture provision present in the agreement or under a provision of applicable state law—an assignor suing for infringement must first affirmatively seek equitable relief from a court to rescind or cancel the assignment. Until ownership is restored in the assignor, there can be no act of infringement by the assignee. *Jim Arnold Corp. v. Hydrotech Sys., Inc.*, 109 F.3d 1567, 42 USPQ2d 1119 (Fed. Cir. 1997).

[76]*Interspiro USA, Inc. v. Figgie Int'l, Inc.*, 18 F.3d 927, 30 USPQ2d 1070 (Fed. Cir. 1994); *Power Lift, Inc. v. Weatherford Nipple-Up Sys., Inc.*, 871 F.2d 1082, 10 USPQ2d 1464 (Fed. Cir. 1989).

[77]*Heidelberg Harris Inc. v. Loebach*, 145 F.3d 1454, 46 USPQ2d 1948 (Fed. Cir. 1998); *Studiengesellschaft Kohle, M.B.H. v. Hercules, Inc.*, 105 F.3d 629, 41 USPQ2d 1518 (Fed. Cir. 1997). The issue whether a license or sublicense exists based on a given set of facts is one of law. *Adelberg Labs., Inc. v. Miles, Inc.*, 921 F.2d 1267, 17 USPQ2d 1111 (Fed. Cir. 1990).

[78]*Jim Arnold Corp. v. Hydrotech Sys., Inc.*, 109 F.3d 1567, 42 USPQ2d 1119, 1127 (Fed. Cir. 1997); *Fromson v. Western Litho Plate & Supp. Co.*, 853 F.2d 1568, 7 USPQ2d 1606 (Fed. Cir. 1988); *Spindelfabrik S.S.&G. GmbH v. Schubert & Salzer Mas. Ak.*, 829 F.2d 1075, 4 USPQ2d 1044 (Fed. Cir. 1987).

[79]*Spindelfabrik S.S.&G. GmbH v. Schubert & Salzer Mas. Ak.*, 829 F.2d 1075, 4 USPQ2d 1044 (Fed. Cir. 1987).

patent are the rights to exclude others from making, using, or selling the invention in the United States. A patent license may have the effect between the parties to the license of transferring some of those proprietary rights from the patentee to its licensee. Such license then does more than provide a covenant not to sue, i.e., a bare license. In addition, the license makes the licensee the beneficial owner of some identifiable part of the patentee's bundle of rights to exclude others. Thus, a licensee with proprietary rights in the patent is generally called an exclusive licensee.[80] Determining whether a licensee is an exclusive licensee or a bare licensee is a question of ascertaining the intent of the parties to the license as manifested by the terms of their agreement and examining the substance of the grant. The use of the word "exclusive" is not controlling; what matters is the substance of the arrangement. Because patent rights are rights to exclude others, a licensee is an exclusive licensee only if the patentee has promised, expressly or impliedly, that others shall be excluded from practicing the invention within the field covered by the license. Put another way, an exclusive license is a license to practice the invention, accompanied by the patent owner's promise that others shall be excluded from practicing it within the field of use wherein the licensee is given leave. Thus, if a patentee-licensor is free to grant licenses to others, licensees under that patent are not exclusive licensees.[81]

There are significant differences between exclusive and nonexclusive licenses. An exclusive licensee can be awarded damages if properly joined as a plaintiff, while a bare licensee may not be entitled to recovery.[82] Indeed, a true exclusive licensee can sue the patent owner for patent infringement,[83] while a nonexclusive licensee has no standing to sue for infringement.[84]

Each co-owner of a U.S. patent is ordinarily free to make, use, offer to sell, and sell the patented invention without regard to the wishes of any other co-owner. The ownership rights of each carry the

---

[80]*Ortho Pharm. Corp. v. Genetics Inst., Inc.*, 52 F.3d 1026, 34 USPQ2d 1444 (Fed. Cir. 1995).

[81]*Textile Prods. Inc. v. Mead Corp.,* 134 F.3d 1481, 45 USPQ2d 1633 (Fed. Cir. 1998).

[82]*Weinar v. Rollform Inc.,* 744 F.2d 797, 223 USPQ 369 (Fed. Cir. 1984). The licensee here was actually an exclusive distributor who had the exclusive right to sell by contract. The court dismissed as disingenuous the argument that his right was not exclusive because the patentee was also selling—to him.

[83]*Yarway Corp. v. Eur-Control USA Inc.,* 775 F.2d 268, 227 USPQ 352 (Fed. Cir. 1985). Note that such a suit is one arising under the patent laws for purposes of Federal Circuit jurisdiction. The mere fact that a patent dispute arises between contracting parties does not necessarily lead to the conclusion that the cause of action is one under contract rather than one under the patent laws. *Id.* However, a claim of failure to pay royalties due under a patent license agreement is one arising out of state contract law, not "arising under" the patent law. *Schwarzkopf Dev. Corp. v. Ti-Coating, Inc.,* 800 F.2d 240, 231 USPQ 47 (Fed. Cir. 1986).

[84]*Kalman v. Berlyn Corp.,* 914 F.2d 1473, 16 USPQ2d 1093 (Fed. Cir. 1990). However, when the sole licensee has been shown to be directly damaged by an infringer in a two-supplier market, and when the nexus between the sole licensee and the patentee is close and clearly defined, the sole licensee must be recognized as the real party in interest. *Id.* See *Ortho Pharm. Corp. v. Genetics Inst., Inc.,* 52 F.3d 1026, 34 USPQ2d 1444 (Fed. Cir. 1995) and *Rite-Hite Corp. v. Kelley Co.,* 56 F.3d 1538, 35 USPQ2d 1065 (Fed. Cir. 1995), for a full discussion of this issue. These topics are discussed in more detail in §7.2(b) and §8.1(a)(iv).

right to license others, a right that also does not require the consent of any other co-owner. Thus, unless the co-owner has given up these rights through an agreement to the contrary, it may not be prohibited from exploiting its rights in the patent, including the right to grant licenses to third parties on whatever conditions it chooses. However, the grant of a license by one co-owner cannot deprive the other co-owner of the right to sue for accrued damages for past infringement. That would require a release, not a license, and the rights of a patent co-owner, absent agreement to the contrary, do not extend to granting a release that would defeat an action by other co-owners to recover damages for past infringement. Thus, the power to grant a license does not render the unilateral right to sue valueless. The grant of a license simply limits the relief that other co-owners can obtain by exercising their unilateral right to sue.[85] By virtue of the unilateral right to sue, the second co-owner can still force the first co-owner to join an infringement action against the licensee to recover the second co-owner's accrued damages for past infringement. Thus, a prospective license is not per se incompatible with a unilateral right to sue.[86]

Breaches of patent license agreements other than simple failure to pay royalties can and do come before the court. For example, the court has indicated that damages may be available to a licensor against a licensee who fails to affix a patent marking in accordance with a specific provision of the license.[87]

Where termination of a license agreement would cause loss of market share and possible litigation against the licensee and its customers, those factors could result in irreparable harm, thus justifying

---

[85]*Schering Corp. v. Roussel-UCLAF SA,* 104 F.3d 341, 41 USPQ2d 1359 (Fed. Cir. 1997). Here there was an agreement that contained a provision governing the rights and obligations of the co-owners in the event of infringement by a third party. One sued the third party for infringement and, two weeks later, the other granted the third party a license. The Federal Circuit held that the agreement did not restrict the right to grant a license to the third party and therefore affirmed a summary judgment of no infringement by the third party. In so holding, the court reasoned that the co-owner's grant of a license was not inconsistent with its agreement obligation to provide reasonable assistance in connection with the litigation. See also *Ethicon Inc. v. United States Surgical Corp.,* 135 F.3d 1456, 45 USPQ2d 1545 (Fed. Cir. 1998).

[86]*Ethicon Inc. v. United States Surgical Corp.,* 135 F.3d 1456, 45 USPQ2d 1545 (Fed. Cir. 1998). Here a coinventor granted a "retroactive license" to the infringer. It was clear that this was intended to operative as a prospective license and a release for past infringement. The court held that the coinventor could not release the infringer from liability to the other owner of the patent. However, the coinventor refused to consent to an infringement suit and would not join as a plaintiff. Thus the suit had to be dismissed for want of a necessary party. The result is essentially the same as a release.

[87]*Yarway Corp. v. Eur-Control USA Inc.,* 775 F.2d 268, 227 USPQ 352 (Fed. Cir. 1985). In *Lisle Corp. v. Edwards,* 777 F.2d 693, 227 USPQ 894 (Fed. Cir. 1985), the licensee failed to mark as required by the license. After the failure was called to his attention, he began to mark within the contractual period for curing breaches. The court held this was sufficient; it would have been unduly burdensome if not impossible to recall all products and mark them. Thus the licensor was not entitled to terminate, and the lower court should decree specific performance of the license agreement and enjoin the licensor from suing for infringement.

a preliminary injunction against termination.[88] State contract law may prevent termination under certain circumstances.[89]

Where a license prohibits sublicensing, it is no breach for the licensee to make products for a third party to sell under the third party's trademark.[90] A license between the plaintiff patentee and Sanyo permitted the latter to make, use, and sell "Sanyo" products. The defendant contracted with Sanyo to produce products for the defendant to sell. The court found that to be unlicensed activity and thus an infringement.[91] An exclusive licensee with no right to sublicense may nonetheless sell the licensed product to an exclusive distributor for resale.[92] Where a license agreement has a choice of forum clause that controls the venue of any suit for breach of the agreement, suit will be dismissed if brought elsewhere.[93] Where a license is not contingent upon any future event other than the passage of time, the license vests as of the date of the agreement, although its rights and obligations may not be effective until the period of time has passed.[94]

In its important *Lear* decision,[95] the Supreme Court held that a patent licensee is not estopped from contesting the validity of the licensed patent. The Federal Circuit views *Lear* as a patent policy statement that encourages prompt adjudication of patent validity by permitting a licensee to cease payments due under a license contract while challenging the validity of the patent. It does not, however, permit a licensee to avoid facing the consequences that such an action would bring; it only prevents the affirmative enforcement by the

---

[88]*Cordis Corp. v. Medtronic, Inc.*, 835 F.2d 859, 5 USPQ2d 1118 (Fed. Cir. 1987). The plaintiff began to produce product A and product B at about the same time. It concluded it might have a problem with A and took a license from the patentee/defendant. It paid royalties on A, but about four years after the license the patentee indicated that B was an infringement and advised that it would terminate the license unless plaintiff paid a substantial sum for a paid-up license on B. Plaintiff brought an action for declaratory judgment of noninfringement and obtained a preliminary injunction against termination. In affirming, the Federal Circuit observed that this was not a situation where the plaintiff was attempting to avoid the natural consequences of failure to pay royalties. It is still paying on A and never has paid on B.

[89]An Oklahoma statute provided relief from forfeiture under equitable circumstances in the absence of fraud or gross negligence. Where the licensee had tendered full compensation, and the court below had added attorney fees, the Federal Circuit had no difficulty in holding that the licensee's payment of royalties on a quarterly basis rather than monthly, as required by the contract, did not justify termination. The licensor's argument that this is a form of compulsory licensing was rejected on the ground that the licensor had agreed to accept money as full compensation for its voluntary loss of the right to exclude, and it was simply being denied the chance to recapture that right. *Power Lift, Inc. v. Weatherford Nipple-Up Sys., Inc.* 871 F.2d 1082, 10 USPQ2d 1464 (Fed. Cir. 1989).

[90]*Lisle Corp. v. Edwards*, 777 F.2d 693, 227 USPQ 894 (Fed. Cir. 1985). The court characterized this argument as specious.

[91]*Intel Corp. v. United States ITC*, 946 F.2d 821, 20 USPQ2d 1161 (Fed. Cir. 1991). For similar cases, see note 6:148 above.

[92]*Unidisco, Inc. v. Schattner*, 824 F.2d 965, 3 USPQ2d 1439 (Fed. Cir. 1987).

[93]*Warner & Swasey Co. v. Salvagnini Transferica S.P.A.*, 806 F.2d 1045, 231 USPQ 972 (Fed. Cir. 1986). Even though the suit was one for infringement, the clause controls, because the suit is ultimately based on a breach of the license.

[94]*Heidelberg Harris Inc. v. Loebach*, 145 F.3d 1454, 46 USPQ2d 1948 (Fed. Cir. 1998).

[95]*Lear, Inc. v. Adkins*, 395 U.S. 653, 162 USPQ 1 (1969).

licensor of the royalty payment provisions of the license agreement while the patent's validity is being challenged by the licensee.[96] The question of entitlement to royalties paid or due prior to an adjudication of invalidity will probably depend upon who mounts the validity challenge and what the basis for invalidity is. Congress has not seen fit to create an implied warranty of validity in license agreements, so that absent fraud or misconduct a patentee should not be held responsible for the issuance of an invalid patent. The likely result is that a licensee can recoup royalties it pays during its own challenge to validity, but cannot recover royalties paid during a challenge by a third party, absent fraud in the procurement.[97]

Where a state court specifically based its decision on state law governing breach of contract, a patent licensee who breached the agreement in bad faith was properly precluded by the state court's judgment from using the licensed inventions, whatever might eventually be the fate of the licensed patents in a copending federal court action.[98]

The court does not appear to be too picky about the integration rule. An infringer signed a license agreement, but a few days later the patentee sent a letter acknowledging oral modifications of the written agreement. The infringer was bound by the written agreement. In view of the fact that the modifications merely noted that the patentee would not enforce certain provisions of the license and might afford the infringer a more favorable royalty in the future, the infringer's obligations under the written agreement were not abrogated.[99]

(d) Contract Law in General

In connection with its rather broad jurisdiction over matters arising from various government boards of contract appeals,[100] the Federal Circuit occasionally deals with principles of contract law that have application to patent agreements. In general, the court will apply the law of the regional circuit, including its choice of law rules,

---

[96]*Cordis Corp. v. Medtronic, Inc.,* 780 F.2d 991, 228 USPQ 189 (Fed. Cir. 1985).

[97]*Cordis Corp. v. Medtronic, Inc.,* 780 F.2d 991, 228 USPQ 189 (Fed. Cir. 1985). If a licensee fails to pay during a third-party challenge, it runs the risk of being terminated and sued for infringement. The court has not held unequivocally that escrow payments will not solve this problem, but surely one cannot count on that as a solution. *Id.*

[98]*In re Oximetrix, Inc.,* 748 F.2d 637, 223 USPQ 1068 (Fed. Cir. 1984). On a similar question, the court has also passed the question whether a state court judgment that royalties were owing would preclude the licensee from recouping royalties in the event the licensee were later successful with its invalidity defense in a copending action in federal court. In view of the unsettled nature of the recoupment question in general, it was proper to refuse to enjoin the state court action on this basis. *Intermedics Infusaid, Inc. v. Regents of Univ. of Minn.,* 804 F.2d 129, 231 USPQ 653 (Fed. Cir. 1986).

[99]*Allen Archery, Inc. v. Browning Mfg. Co.,* 819 F.2d 1087, 2 USPQ2d 1490 (Fed. Cir. 1987).

[100]See, e.g., 28 U.S.C. §1295(a)(10), (b), & (c).

to determine what substantive law, usually that of a state, governs a particular contract dispute. Thus, the enforceability of a settlement agreement, although arising in the context of a patent infringement case, is governed by the law of the appropriate state, including its statute of frauds.[101]

The Seventh Amendment preserves a right to a jury trial on issues of fact in damages suits for breach of contract between private party litigants.[102]

Interpretation. One familiar principle is that a contract must be interpreted in accordance with the parties' understanding as shown by their conduct before the controversy.[103] One may not ignore the interpretation and performance of a contract, whether termed "mistake" or not, that occurred before a dispute arose.[104]

An interpretation that gives reasonable meaning to all parts of a contract will be preferred to one that leaves portions of the contract meaningless.[105] In resolving a disputed interpretation of a contract, words and other conduct are interpreted in the light of all the circumstances, and if the principal purpose of the parties is ascertainable, it is given great weight. The avowed goal and primary function of the court is the ascertainment of the intention of the parties. The parties' intent must be gathered from the instrument as a whole, from the perspective of a reasonably intelligent person acquainted with the contemporary circumstances.[106] In contract interpretation,

---

[101]*Sun Studs, Inc. v. Applied Theory Assocs.*, 772 F.2d 1557, 227 USPQ 81 (Fed. Cir. 1985). See also *Gjerlov v. Schuyler Labs., Inc.*, 131 F.3d 1016, 44 USPQ2d 1881 (Fed. Cir. 1997); *S & T Mfg. Co. v. County of Hillsborough, Fla.*, 815 F.2d 676, 2 USPQ2d 1280 (Fed. Cir. 1987). In ascertaining whether a subsequent change in state law may be accommodated by a contract, the original intention of the parties must be considered. *Alvin, Ltd. v. United States Postal Serv.*, 816 F.2d 1562 (Fed. Cir. 1987). An insurance policy is a contract, and the court therefore applies the relevant state contract law in construing the terms of the policy. *U.S. Test Inc. v. NDE Envtl. Corp.*, 196 F.3d 1376, 52 USPQ2d 1845 (Fed. Cir. 1999). The court applied Louisiana law, and held that an insurance policy requiring defense of suits for "advertising injury," where advertising injury was defined as "infringement of copyright, title, or slogan," did not obligate the insurer to defend against a patent infringement claim.

[102]*Seaboard Lumber Co. v. United States*, 903 F.2d 1560 (Fed. Cir. 1990). The acceptance of contract provisions providing for dispute resolution in a forum where there is no entitlement to a jury trial may satisfy the voluntary and knowing standard for waiver of right to jury trial. *Id.* In its important decision in *Markman v. Westview Instr., Inc.*, 52 F.3d 967, 34 USPQ2d 1321 (Fed. Cir. 1995), the court considered at length and ultimately rejected an argument that claim interpretation should be regarded as analogous to contract interpretation for purposes of evaluating the right to a jury trial. The in banc opinion is of interest here for what it has to say about contracts.

[103]*Julius Goldman's Egg City v. United States*, 697 F.2d 1051 (Fed. Cir. 1983); *Blinderman Constr. Co. v. United States*, 695 F.2d 552 (Fed. Cir. 1982).

[104]*Alvin, Ltd. v. United States Postal Serv.*, 816 F.2d 1562 (Fed. Cir. 1987).

[105]*Fortec Constructors v. United States*, 760 F.2d 1288 (Fed. Cir. 1985). A court must view a single provision of a contract in the way that gives meaning to, and provides internal harmony among, all parts of the contract. The term "including" can be read as one of addition rather than limitation. *Ethicon Inc. v. United States Surgical Corp.*, 135 F.3d 1456, 45 USPQ2d 1545 (Fed. Cir. 1998).

[106]*Alvin, Ltd. v. United States Postal Serv.*, 816 F.2d 1562 (Fed. Cir. 1987). When a contract indicates a clear intention by both parties to be bound, but leaves the price indefinite, the court

the plain and unambiguous meaning of a written agreement controls. Evidence of trade practice does not trump unambiguous contract language.[107] No contract provision should be construed as being in conflict with another unless no other reasonable interpretation is possible.[108] Where specific and general terms in a contract are in conflict, those which relate to a particular matter control over the more general language.[109]

Wherever possible, words of a contract should be given their ordinary and common meaning.[110] One who contests a reasonable construction must show that both parties understood the language to mean something else, or at least that the contester had no reason to know of the reasonable construction at the time.[111]

If a contract is reasonably susceptible of more than one interpretation, it is ambiguous. Where such a latent ambiguity exists, the court will construe the ambiguous term against the drafter of the contract when the nondrafter's interpretation is reasonable. This promotes care and completeness by the drafter.[112] If the language at issue was patently ambiguous at the time of drafting, then the nondrafting party was under a duty to inquire as to its meaning.[113] When determining whether contract language is patently ambiguous, the language must be placed at a point along the spectrum of ambiguity. There is a gray area between the point along this spectrum at which a document requires more exacting language and that at which additional detail will add nothing but worthless surplusage.[114] A contract will be construed against its drafter.[115]

State law controls in matters of interpretation of contracts,[116] including patent license agreements.[117] Contract interpretation is a

---

can enforce the contract by determining a reasonable price. *Aviation Contractor Employees, Inc. v. United States*, 945 F.2d 1568 (Fed. Cir. 1991). Obviously, where two parties disagree on the meaning of a contract term, an interpretation that fails to meet one party's purpose will very likely meet the other party's purpose. *Novamedix Ltd. v. NDM Acquisition Corp.*, 166 F.3d 1177, 49 USPQ2d 1613 (Fed. Cir. 1999).

[107]*Craft Mach. Works, Inc. v. United States*, 926 F.2d 1110 (Fed. Cir. 1991).

[108]*United States v. Johnson Controls, Inc.*, 713 F.2d 1541 (Fed. Cir. 1983). Different contractual provisions may use the same term in a different context to encompass a different meaning. *Craft Mach. Works, Inc. v. United States*, 926 F.2d 1110 (Fed. Cir. 1991).

[109]*Hills Materials Co. v. Rice*, 982 F.2d 514 (Fed. Cir. 1992).

[110]*Hills Materials Co. v. Rice*, 982 F.2d 514 (Fed. Cir. 1992).

[111]*L.S.S. Leasing Corp. v. United States*, 695 F.2d 1359 (Fed. Cir. 1982).

[112]*Hills Materials Co. v. Rice*, 982 F.2d 514 (Fed. Cir. 1992). See also *Studiengesellschaft Kohle, mBH v. Hercules, Inc.*, 105 F.3d 629, 41 USPQ2d 1518 (Fed. Cir. 1997).

[113]*Fort Vancouver Plywood Co. v. United States*, 860 F.2d 409 (Fed. Cir. 1988).

[114]*Fort Vancouver Plywood Co. v. United States*, 860 F.2d 409 (Fed. Cir. 1988).

[115]*L.S.S. Leasing Corp. v. United States*, 695 F.2d 1359 (Fed. Cir. 1982). Under the rule of contra proferentum, a contract is construed against its drafter if the interpretation advanced by the nondrafter is reasonable. *Fort Vancouver Plywood Co. v. United States*, 860 F.2d 409 (Fed. Cir. 1988).

[116]*American Med. Sys., Inc. v. Medical Eng'g Corp.*, 6 F.3d 1523, 28 USPQ2d 1321 (Fed. Cir. 1993).

[117]*Interspiro USA, Inc. v. Figgie Int'l, Inc.*, 18 F.3d 927, 30 USPQ2d 1070 (Fed. Cir. 1994).

matter of law and thus is amenable to decision on summary judgment.[118] Interpretation of an unambiguous contract provision is a question of law that is subject to de novo review.[119] Because contract interpretation is a matter of law, the Federal Circuit reviews de novo the interpretation of the ITC and the Claims Court.[120] The proper interpretation of a pretrial stipulation, like any contract, presents a legal question that is addressed on appeal de novo. The inquiry begins with the language of the stipulation memorializing the intent of the parties.[121]

Implied contracts. An implied-in-fact contract is one founded upon a meeting of minds which, although not embodied in an express contract, is inferred as a fact from conduct of the parties showing, in light of the surrounding circumstances, their tacit understanding. The existence of an express contract precludes the existence of an implied contract dealing with the same subject, unless the implied contract is entirely unrelated to the express contract.[122]

Rescission, reformation, and duress. Where there has been a mutual mistake of material fact, resulting in a contract that does not faithfully embody the parties' actual intent, reformation, rescission, and restitution may be available to the adversely affected party.[123] Although the courts well recognize the public as well as private interest in the finality of settlements, as for all contracts a settlement will not be enforced if it is tainted by fraud or another condition that warrants its rescission.[124] A party who rescinds a contract must place the other party in status quo by restoring the consideration or whatever was received under the contract.[125]

In the absence of fraud, mistake, accident, or illegality, a court cannot change the terms of a contract.[126] In general, reformation is an appropriate remedy when the terms of a contract do not accurately

---

[118]*Government Sys. Advisors, Inc. v. United States,* 847 F.2d 811 (Fed. Cir. 1988).

[119]*American Med. Sys., Inc. v. Medical Eng'g Corp.,* 6 F.3d 1523, 28 USPQ2d 1321 (Fed. Cir. 1993).

[120]*Texas Instr., Inc. v. United States ITC,* 988 F.2d 1165, 26 USPQ2d 1018 (Fed. Cir. 1993); *Craft Mach. Works, Inc. v. United States,* 926 F.2d 1110 (Fed. Cir. 1991).

[121]*Kearns v. Chrysler Corp.,* 32 F.3d 1541, 31 USPQ2d 1746 (Fed. Cir. 1994).

[122]*Atlas Corp. v. United States,* 895 F.2d 745 (Fed. Cir. 1990).

[123]*Roseburg Lumber Co. v. Madigan,* 978 F.2d 660 (Fed. Cir. 1992).

[124]*Bradley v. Chiron Corp.,* 136 F.3d 1370, 45 USPQ2d 1819 (Fed. Cir. 1998). In *RCA Corp. v. Data Gen. Corp.,* 887 F.2d 1056, 12 USPQ2d 1449 (Fed. Cir. 1989), the plaintiff claimed that the defendant had entered into a license agreement with a secret intent never to pay royalties; thus, plaintiff argued that it would never have entered the agreement but for the deception. The trial court denied plaintiff's claim for rescission and breach damages, but the record was not clear as to the basis for the judgment. On appeal, the plaintiff appeared to urge that the district court had erred in failing to permit it to collect "royalties." The Federal Circuit was able to skirt some difficult issues by ruling that plaintiff had not sued for enforcement of the license; thus, in appealing a denial of "royalties" it was appealing the wrong question.

[125]*Dahl v. United States,* 695 F.2d 1373 (Fed. Cir. 1982).

[126]*Atlas Corp. v. United States,* 895 F.2d 745 (Fed. Cir. 1990).

reflect the intention of the parties at the time of drafting.[127] Reformation serves to bring the parties' written contract in accord with their agreement.[128] Reformation is also available as an equitable remedy when the parties to a contract have made a mutual mistake of fact.[129] The purpose of reforming a contract on the basis of mutual mistake is to make a defective writing conform to the agreement of the parties upon which there was a meeting of the minds. A mutual mistake as to a fact or factor, even a material one, will not support relief if the contract itself puts the risk of such a mistake on the party seeking reformation.[130] But reformation is not available for a unilateral mistake, such as bad business judgment, in the absence of fraud or misrepresentation.[131]

Thus a party seeking to state a claim for reformation of a contract under the doctrine of mutual mistake must allege four elements: (1) the parties to the contract were mistaken in their belief regarding a fact; (2) that mistaken belief constituted a basic assumption underlying the contract; (3) the mistake had a material effect on the bargain; and (4) the contract did not put the risk of the mistake on the party seeking reformation. A "mistake" that can support reformation is a belief that is not in accord with the facts. To satisfy this element of a reformation claim, a plaintiff must allege that it held an erroneous belief as to an existing fact. If the existence of a fact is not known to the contracting parties, they cannot have a belief concerning that fact; therefore, there can be no "mistake."[132]

In ascertaining the actual contractual intent when one of the parties asserts that the mutual intent was different from that shown in the written word, the Federal Circuit applies the classic principle: if the parties have made a memorial of their bargain, their actual intent is ineffective unless it is expressed in some way in the writing, or unless it can be made the basis for reformation of the writing. The subjective intent of one of the parties, if contrary to the unambiguous and reasonable text of the written contract, is not a basis for reforming the contract. A party contesting the reasonable construction of contract language must show either that both parties had a contrary intent, or that the party seeking relief had no reason to know of that reasonable construction at the time of making the agreement.[133]

The three requirements to establish duress are exacting: (1) that one side involuntarily accepted the terms of another; (2) that circum-

---

[127]*American Employers Ins. Co. v. United States*, 812 F.2d 700 (Fed. Cir. 1987). See also *Bowen-McLaughlin-York Co. v. United States*, 813 F.2d 1221 (Fed. Cir. 1987).

[128]*Atlas Corp. v. United States*, 895 F.2d 745 (Fed. Cir. 1990).

[129]*American Employers Ins. Co. v. United States*, 812 F.2d 700 (Fed. Cir. 1987).

[130]*Emerald Maintenance, Inc. v. United States*, 925 F.2d 1425 (Fed. Cir. 1991).

[131]*Bowen-McLaughlin-York Co. v. United States*, 813 F.2d 1221 (Fed. Cir. 1987): *American Employers Ins. Co. v. United States*, 812 F.2d 700 (Fed. Cir. 1987).

[132]*Atlas Corp. v. United States*, 895 F.2d 745 (Fed. Cir. 1990). See also *Dairyland Power Coop. v. United States*, 16 F.3d 1197 (Fed. Cir. 1994); *Roseburg Lumber Co. v. Madigan*, 978 F.2d 660 (Fed. Cir. 1992).

[133]*City of Oxnard v. United States*, 851 F.2d 344 (Fed. Cir. 1988).

stances permitted no alternative; and (3) that those circumstances were the result of coercive acts of the other side.[134]

Agreement to agree. The requirement for certainty in contracts serves two purposes. One is the need to determine whether the parties in fact intended to contract at all, and the other relates to the ability of a court to determine when a breach has occurred and to formulate an appropriate remedy. Once it is determined that the parties did indeed intend to create a contract, courts should be slow to deny enforcement on the basis of indefiniteness in the contract. While some courts have invalidated so-called agreements to agree, the emerging view is that an agreement that specifies that certain terms will be agreed on by future negotiation is sufficiently definite, because it impliedly places an obligation on the parties to negotiate in good faith. Such an obligation gives the contract certainty by allowing the courts to determine when a breach has occurred by determining whether the parties have negotiated in good faith.[135]

Authority. A purported agreement with the United States is not binding unless the party can show that the official with whom the agreement was made had authority to bind the government.[136] Parties are presumed to have entered into a valid and binding contract.[137] The government enters into contracts as does a private person, and its contracts are governed by the common law.[138] The meaning of a contract cannot change simply because the government changes its interpretation of the law.[139] Administrative actions taken in violation of statutory authorization or requirement are of no effect, and courts are bound to strike down illegal contracts. A contractor therefore assumes the risk that a government agency has actual authority to enter into a contract, and if it does not, damages cannot be recovered. No damages can be awarded for breach of a nullity.[140] If the theory of recovery is express contract, then the absence of a signature of someone authorized to contract is fatal, absent estoppel or apparent authority. And the same general proposition holds if the theory is implied contract: the person whose acts might bind the party must have authority, actual or apparent.[141] Agency is a consensual relationship in which the agent agrees to act upon the instructions of the principal.[142]

---

[134]*Employers Ins. of Wausau v. United States,* 764 F.2d 1572 (Fed. Cir. 1985).

[135]*Aviation Contractor Employees, Inc. v. United States,* 945 F.2d 1568 (Fed. Cir. 1991).

[136]*S.E.R., Jobs for Prog., Inc. v. United States,* 759 F.2d 1 (Fed. Cir. 1985).

[137]*Alvin, Ltd. v. United States Postal Serv.,* 816 F.2d 1562 (Fed. Cir. 1987).

[138]*Alvin, Ltd. v. United States Postal Serv.,* 816 F.2d 1562 (Fed. Cir. 1987).

[139]*Craft Mach. Works, Inc. v. United States,* 926 F.2d 1110 (Fed. Cir. 1991).

[140]*United States v. Amdahl Corp.,* 786 F.2d 387 (Fed. Cir. 1986).

[141]*City of Alexandria v. United States,* 737 F.2d 1022 (Fed. Cir. 1984).

[142]*In re Hamilton,* 882 F.2d 1576, 11 USPQ2d 1890 (Fed. Cir. 1989).

Sales and the UCC. Plainly, the common, or usual meaning of the term "sale" includes those situations in which a contract has been made between two parties who agree to transfer title and possession of specific property for a price. The Uniform Commercial Code has been recognized as the general law governing the sale of goods and is another useful, though not authoritative, source in determining the ordinary commercial meaning of the term "sale." Section 2-106, which defines the various terms used throughout the UCC, states that a contract for sale includes both a present sale of goods and a contract to sell goods at a future time. Section 2-106 further states that a present sale means a sale that is accomplished by the making of the contract. Therefore, the UCC is in accordance with other sources in defining the term "sale" as having been accomplished when a contract for the transfer of goods has been completed.[143] A sale is a contract between parties to give and to pass rights of property for consideration which the buyer pays or promises to pay the seller for the thing bought and sold. One cannot make a contract with oneself. Thus, for a legitimate sale to occur, the buyer and seller must be two separate entities.[144]

The world of commercial transactions is not limited to a binary world in which an agreement that passes title to goods must be either a contract for sale of goods or a contract for sale of services. Many commercial transactions are not governed by Article 2 of the UCC: sale of land or securities, assignment of a contract right, or granting a license under a patent or copyright, to name just a few. Thus, a settlement agreement under which the patentee was given title to the infringer's inventory of infringing goods was not a "contract for sale of goods" and therefore did not invoke the implied warranties of merchantability and fitness of the UCC.[145] Whether a promotion of a product to a customer is an offer to sell accepted with an order, or a purchase order is an offer to buy accepted by delivery, either proposition results in a sale under §2-206 of the Uniform Commercial Code.[146]

Contract damages. Contract law has long been held to preclude recovery for speculative damages. This principle applies to the threshold issue of whether damages have actually been sustained, however,

---

[143]*Enercon GmbH v. United States ITC,* 151 F.3d 1376, 47 USPQ2d 1725 (Fed. Cir. 1998). This case dealt with the meaning of the term "sale" in 19 U.S.C. §1337.

[144]*In re Caveney,* 761 F.2d 671, 226 USPQ 1 (Fed. Cir. 1985).

[145]*Novamedix Ltd. v. NDM Acquisition Corp.,* 166 F.3d 1177, 49 USPQ2d 1613 (Fed. Cir. 1999). The agreement is no more a contract for the sale of goods than it is a licensing agreement for patents. In fact, it is neither exclusively; it is a mixed contract, similar to a mixed contract for the provision of both goods and services. It should therefore be analyzed as a mixed contract. This invokes (under N.Y. law), the predominant purpose test. Here the essential nature of the agreement was to settle a patent infringement lawsuit, not the sale of goods.

[146]*J.A. LaPorte, Inc. v. Norfolk Dredging Co.,* 787 F.2d 1577, 229 USPQ 435 (Fed. Cir. 1986). Under the UCC, a merchant warrants freedom from liability for infringement but a buyer who furnishes specifications must hold the seller harmless. *Cover v. Hydramatic Packing Co.,* 83 F.3d 1390, 38 USPQ2d 1783 (Fed. Cir. 1996). The UCC requires notice of breach of

and does not bar the award of damages for a proven injury of uncertain measure.[147] The court applies the law of the applicable state in evaluating damages for breach of contract.[148]

(e) Licensee and Assignor Estoppel

The Federal Circuit had previously recognized that the Supreme Court's *Lear* decision[149] explicitly abolished licensee estoppel.[150] Nonetheless, in *Diamond v. Ambico*[151] the court resurrected the doctrine of assignor estoppel, which is an equitable doctrine that prevents one who has assigned the rights to a patent or patent application from later contending that what was assigned is a nullity. The estoppel also operates to bar other parties in privity with the assignor, such as a corporation founded by the assignor. The estoppel historically has applied to invalidity challenges based on novelty, utility, and obviousness. It is frequently justified (1) to prevent unfairness and injustice, (2) to prevent one from benefiting from one's own wrong, (3) by analogy to estoppel by deed in real estate, and (4) by analogy to a landlord-tenant relationship. In resurrecting the doctrine, the court fully recognized the doubt cast upon assignor estoppel by *Lear* and other decisions.[152] It also recognized that four district court decisions and one court of appeals decision had indicated that the doctrine no longer prevails, while two district courts had acknowledged the doctrine but refused to apply it on the facts. Nonetheless, in the face of this mass of contrary authority, the Federal Circuit in *Ambico* held that the doctrine does retain vitality and may be applied on a case-by-case equitable evaluation to estop an assignor from raising challenges based upon 35 U.S.C. §§102, 103, and 112.[153]

---

warranty. Where a vendor is informed of problems and agrees to modify the product, the notice provision is satisfied. *Stickle v. Heublein, Inc.*, 716 F.2d 1550, 219 USPQ 377 (Fed. Cir. 1983). Under the Texas version of the UCC, a seller is entitled to resell goods upon a buyer's wrongful refusal to pay. *McCoy v. Mitsuboshi Cutlery, Inc.*, 67 F.3d 917, 36 USPQ2d 1289 (Fed. Cir. 1995).

[147]*Roseburg Lumber Co. v. Madigan*, 978 F.2d 660 (Fed. Cir. 1992).

[148]*U.S. Valves Inc. v. Dray*, 212 F.3d 1368, 54 USPQ2d 1834, 1838 (Fed. Cir. 2000).

[149]*Lear, Inc. v. Adkins*, 395 U.S. 653, 162 USPQ 1 (1969).

[150]*Cordis Corp. v. Medtronic, Inc.*, 780 F.2d 991, 228 USPQ 189 (Fed. Cir. 1985). See text accompanying notes 7:96–97.

[151]*Diamond Scientific Co. v. Ambico, Inc.*, 848 F.2d 1220, 6 USPQ2d 2028 (Fed. Cir. 1988).

[152]In *Westinghouse Elec. & Mfg. Co. v. Formica Insulation Co.*, 266 U.S. 342 (1924), the Supreme Court endorsed the rule that an assignor and those in privity with the assignor can be estopped from challenging the validity of the assigned patent. However, the assignor was permitted to present evidence of the state of the art for the purpose of construing and narrowing the claims of the patent. This accommodation permitted the assignor to defend against the infringement suit by attempting to show that the accused device fell outside the proper scope of the claims of the patent, yet prevented the assignor from attacking the patent's validity. Later, in *Scott Paper v. Marcalus Mfg. Co.*, 326 U.S. 249 (1945), the Court carved out another exception, holding that the doctrine was not available to the assignee to foreclose the assignor from asserting the right to make use of the prior art invention of an expired patent that anticipates that of the assigned patent.

[153]*Diamond Scientific Co. v. Ambico, Inc.*, 848 F.2d 1220, 6 USPQ2d 2028 (Fed. Cir. 1988). In so holding, the court appeared to concentrate on the unfairness and injustice rationale for

The court began by distinguishing between licensee estoppel and assignor estoppel. The public policy that favors allowing a licensee to contest the validity of the patent is not present in the assignment situation. Unlike the licensee who might be forced to continue to pay for a potentially invalid patent, the assignor who would challenge the patent has already been fully paid for the patent rights. The court also distinguished assignee and assignor estoppel. If an assignee of a patent were allowed to challenge the patent, it could be placed in the legally awkward position of simultaneously attacking and defending the validity of the same patent. In the case of an assignor, an estoppel prevents it from later contending that what was assigned was a nullity, or from benefiting from its own wrong. Finally, the court recognized that, despite the public policy that encourages challenges to potentially invalid patents, there are still circumstances in which the equities of the contractual relationship between the parties should deprive one party (or others in privity with it) of the right to bring that challenge.[154]

In the case at hand, the court felt that it was significant that the assignor actively participated in the preparation and prosecution of the application. On the other hand, it regarded as irrelevant the fact that the assignment was of a pending application, thus opening the possibility that the assignee could later have amended the claims. The assignment was of the rights to the invention, irrespective of the particular language in the claims describing the invention when the patent was ultimately granted. Moreover, to the extent the assignee might have broadened the claims beyond what could be validly claimed in light of the prior art, the assignor could submit evidence to narrow the scope of the claims—estopping an assignor does not necessarily prevent it from successfully defending against an infringement claim.[155]

The *Ambico* court held that the doctrine of assignor estoppel is an issue directly related to patent law and is therefore not governed by the law of the regional circuit.[156] Thus the court is largely unrestrained by the views of other courts in answering the many questions[157] that are sure to arise as it redevelops the doctrine. Since

---

estoppel. It is the implicit representation by the assignor that the patent rights that it is assigning, presumably for value, are not worthless, that sets the assignor apart from the rest of the world and can deprive it of the ability later to challenge the validity of the patent. To allow the assignor to make that representation at the time of the assignment (to its advantage) and later to repudiate it (again to its advantage) could work an injustice against the assignee. In a concurring opinion, one judge argues for premising the doctrine of assignor estoppel on the laws of contract and property transfers rather than an equitable case-by-case evaluation. She suggests that the public policy expressed in *Lear* weakens the rule of law and disserves the national interest, and she feels that patents should never be singled out as the only property right that is treated by law as exempt from the normal precepts of commercial bargain and sale.

[154]*Diamond Scientific Co. v. Ambico, Inc.,* 848 F.2d 1220, 6 USPQ2d 2028 (Fed. Cir. 1988).

[155]See note 7:152. An estopped party may argue for a narrow claim construction, or that the accused devices are within the prior art and therefore cannot infringe. *Mentor Graphics Corp. v. Quickturn Des. Sys. Inc.,* 150 F.3d 1374, 47 USPQ2d 1683 (Fed. Cir. 1998).

[156]*Diamond Scientific, Co. v. Ambico, Inc.,* 848 F.2d 1220, 6 USPQ2d 2028 (Fed. Cir. 1988).

[157]For example, how will the doctrine be squared with the concept of a request for reexamination on behalf of an undisclosed principal? Could not the assignor get an attorney to prosecute

Ambico the court has squarely held that assignor estoppel applies to unenforceability defenses based upon inequitable conduct as well as ordinary invalidity defenses.[158] The court has also held that assignor estoppel can be considered and applied in a proceeding under 19 U.S.C. §1337 in the ITC.[159] It has held that assignor estoppel does not preclude the estopped party from arguing that the patentee is itself collaterally estopped from asserting a patent found invalid in a prior proceeding.[160]

The court has more recently begun to treat the matter as governed by a presumption. Due to the intrinsic unfairness in allowing an assignor to challenge the validity of the patent it assigned, the implicit representation of validity contained in an assignment of a patent for value raises the presumption that an estoppel will apply. Without exceptional circumstances (such as an express reservation by the assignor of the right to challenge the validity of the patent or an express waiver by the assignee of the right to assert assignor estoppel), one who assigns a patent surrenders with that assignment the right to later challenge the validity of the assigned patent.[161]

The scope of the estoppel has also received attention. Where a party assigns a patent, and the equities demand application of estoppel, the analysis is straightforward. The assignor implicitly attests to the value of the assigned patent. The assignor's representations cover no more or less than the assigned rights. Thus a defendant may submit evidence to help properly construe or narrow the claims of the assigned patent, though estopped to challenge their validity. Where, however, a party assigns an invention or patent application, and the equities advise application of estoppel, the analysis is more elaborate. The range of relevant and competent evidence in fixing the limits of the estoppel should be more liberal than in the case of an assignment of a granted patent. This does not require a liberal definition of the invention in favor of the assignee. Rather, it permits admission of more evidence to determine carefully the limits of the estoppel. Because the bounds of the invention are less certain, ample evidence must be considered to define the assignor's representations.[162]

---

a reexamination request on the same grounds and thus achieve the same result? But cf. *Shamrock Techs. Inc. v. Medical Sterilization, Inc.*, 903 F.2d 789, 14 USPQ2d 1728 (Fed. Cir. 1990).

[158]*Shamrock Techs. Inc. v. Medical Sterilization, Inc.*, 903 F.2d 789, 14 USPQ2d 1728 (Fed. Cir. 1990). The court does indicate, however, that in a proper case general principles of equity may preclude use of assignor estoppel to bar a viable equitable defense arising from postassignment events. *Id.*

[159]*Intel Corp. v. United States ITC*, 946 F.2d 821, 20 USPQ2d 1161 (Fed. Cir. 1991).

[160]*Mentor Graphics Corp. v. Quickturn Des. Sys. Inc.*, 150 F.3d 1374, 47 USPQ2d 1683 (Fed. Cir. 1998).

[161]*Mentor Graphics Corp. v. Quickturn Des. Sys. Inc.*, 150 F.3d 1374, 47 USPQ2d 1683 (Fed. Cir. 1998). In this case the sales agreement that transferred ownership of the patent contained a disclaimer of any warranty that the patent was valid. This was held not to overcome the presumption of assignor estoppel.

[162]*Q.G. Prods., Inc. v. Shorty, Inc.*, 992 F.2d 1211, 26 USPQ2d 1778 (Fed. Cir. 1993). Here the accused infringer had assigned a pending application. The assignee later filed a CIP application and the patent in suit resulted. The accused infringer argued, not without some

So long as the right to challenge validity is not directly curtailed, it appears that *Ambico* will be unhesitatingly applied. A consulting agreement contained a clause providing that the consultant would assist in protecting, defending, and enforcing any patent resulting from the contract work. The consultant later infringed and challenged validity. This was held to be a breach of the agreement, thus justifying a refusal to share royalties as provided by the agreement. The Federal Circuit rejected the argument that the protection clause was void and unenforceable under *Lear*. The promise to protect and defend was a legitimate concern of the contracting parties in view of the fact that development of technology and invention was the core purpose of the contract. Here the consultant was not prevented from contesting validity, but when he did, he became liable for the consequences of his breach.[163] Similarly, although there was an indication in *Ambico* that an assignor might still raise "usual defenses" to a contract of assignment, the court will take care to distinguish such defenses from those that really relate to the validity of the patent itself. Thus, an assignor's argument that he was misled as to inventorship and patentability when he signed the declaration was held to relate to viability of the patent application and therefore to patent validity rather than validity of the assignment contract.[164] The court has rejected an attempt to avoid estoppel by a coinventor whose excuse was that he did not realize at the time he executed the assignment that he was assigning his rights to the claimed invention.[165]

The court has also rejected an argument that *Lear* mandates breach of contract damages where a licensee fails to pay royalties. *Lear* simply does not address that issue. *Lear* abrogated the doctrine of licensee estoppel principles that had developed under state law. *Lear* does not discuss a licensor's right to royalties where a license agreement is entered into after a patent issues. Nor does it deal with a licensor's right to terminate or rescind a license agreement, or

---

logic, that the differences between the two applications precluded assignor estoppel. The Federal Circuit disagreed, based upon a close and complex factual analysis, finding that the differences added by the CIP application were not what persuaded the PTO of the ultimate validity of the claims. The court also emphasized two equitable factors: the fact that the accused infringer had received value for its assignment, and the fact that it knew of one of its principal invalidity contentions as of the time of the assignment. One wonders whether the reasoning of this case would apply to a broadened reissue, for example, if it were the original patent that had been assigned rather than an invention or pending application.

[163]*Sun Studs, Inc. v. ATA Equip. Leasing, Inc.*, 872 F.2d 978, 10 USPQ2d 1338 (Fed. Cir. 1989).

[164]*Shamrock Techs. Inc. v. Medical Sterilization, Inc.*, 903 F.2d 789, 14 USPQ2d 1728 (Fed. Cir. 1990).

[165]*Carroll Touch, Inc. v. Electro Mechanical Sys., Inc.*, 3 F.3d 404, 27 USPQ2d 1836 (Fed. Cir. 1993). The court felt that if the coinventor was indeed mistaken, it was a mistake attributable solely to his own imprudence. The court also underscored the importance of the oath, observing that it could hardly permit a party to avoid the effects of an equitable doctrine by claiming that he violated an oath; equity cannot aid the violator of an oath. The court brushed aside the argument that the coinventor received no compensation for the patent application or the assignment of the invention by pointing out that employment, salary, and bonuses are all valid forms of consideration for such an assignment.

dictate what must be held a breach of contract, or what damages must be awarded for a breach, or under what circumstances, if any, a licensee can recover royalties paid. Those questions continue to be matters dependent upon particular fact situations, contract provisions, and state contract law, albeit they must be resolved in harmony with general principles discernible from *Lear*.[166] The fact that an assignor takes back a license and becomes a licensee as well does not prevent application of assignor estoppel. Apparently an assignor-licensee is in a different situation from an ordinary licensee.[167]

A determination whether assignor estoppel applies in a particular case requires a balancing of the equities between the parties. That determination is a matter committed to the sound discretion of the trial court and is therefore reviewed for abuse of discretion.[168] Assignor estoppel is an equitable doctrine that is mainly concerned with the balance of the equities between the parties. Those in privity with the assignor partake of that balance; hence, extension of the estoppel to those in privity is justified. What constitutes privity varies, depending upon the purpose for which privity is asserted. Privity, like the doctrine of assignor estoppel itself, is determined upon a balance of the equities. For example, if an inventor assigns an invention to his or her employer and leaves to join another company, whether the latter is in privity and thus bound by the doctrine will depend on the equities dictated by the relationship between the inventor and his or her new employer in light of the infringing acts. The closer that relationship, the more the equities will favor binding the new employer.[169] A rule setting aside estoppel after a corporate transaction would chart a clear course for assignors to profit from a scheme of slovenly prosecution, marketing of flawed patents, and infringement.[170] It is not necessary

---

[166]*RCA Corp. v. Data Gen. Corp.*, 887 F.2d 1056, 12 USPQ2d 1449 (Fed. Cir. 1989).

[167]*Acoustical Design, Inc. v. Control Elec. Co.*, 932 F.2d 939, 18 USPQ2d 939 (Fed. Cir. 1991). Indeed, even the ordinary licensee is not immune from at least an occasional raised judicial eyebrow. In *General Foods Corp. v. Studiengesellschaft Kohle mbH*, 972 F.2d 1272, 23 USPQ2d 1839 (Fed. Cir. 1992), the court observed that it seemed "odd" that a licensee would enjoy the fruits of a license for 10 years and then come up with the contention that the patent is invalid for double patenting. One wonders whether such commentary reflects the decision-making process.

[168]*Carroll Touch, Inc. v. Electro Mechanical Sys., Inc.*, 3 F.3d 404, 27 USPQ2d 1836 (Fed. Cir. 1993).

[169]*Shamrock Techs. Inc. v. Medical Sterilization, Inc.*, 903 F.2d 789, 14 USPQ2d 1728 (Fed. Cir. 1990). Here the inventor/assignor left the plaintiff company to join the defendant infringer as vice president of operations; he had 50,000 shares of stock; as soon as he was hired, defendant built a facility for the infringing process; he oversaw the design and construction of the facility and was in charge of the operation; and he participated in the decision to go ahead with the project. On these facts, he was found to be far more than a mere employee, and defendant was held to be in privity with him and therefore estopped. In *Intel Corp. v. United States ITC*, 946 F.2d 821, 20 USPQ2d 1161 (Fed. Cir. 1991), the court held not only that the inventor's own company was in privity, but that another company involved with them in a joint development program was also estopped. See also *Mentor Graphics Corp. v. Quickturn Des. Sys. Inc.*, 150 F.3d 1374, 47 USPQ2d 1683 (Fed. Cir. 1998).

[170]*Mentor Graphics Corp. v. Quickturn Des. Sys. Inc.*, 150 F.3d 1374, 47 USPQ2d 1683 (Fed. Cir. 1998).

to conclude that there was an illicit purpose in order to find privity. It is only necessary to determine whether the infringer availed itself of the inventor's knowledge and assistance to conduct the infringement.[171]

(f) Equitable, Legal, and Judicial Estoppel and the Doctrine of Preclusion by Inconsistent Positions

Some of these matters are related to the topics of res judicata and preclusion by judgment, which are discussed at length in §13.5. Nonetheless, some are difficult to classify under those headings and are therefore grouped here for convenience. Other related topics are implied license (§6.2(c)), interference estoppel (§15.2(e)), marking estoppel (§9.4(d)), and estoppel associated with laches (§9.3).

The doctrines of legal estoppel and equitable estoppel have been applied by courts to imply a license. Legal estoppel is merely shorthand for saying that a grantor of a property right or interest cannot derogate from the right granted by his or her own subsequent acts. The rationale for that is to estop the grantor from taking back that for which it received consideration.[172]

In resurrecting the doctrine of assignor estoppel (see §7.2(e) above) the court has rejected any analysis based upon traditional principles of equitable estoppel. Assignor estoppel is the functional equivalent of estoppel by deed, which is a form of legal, not equitable, estoppel.[173]

The court examined the familiar principles of equitable estoppel in a case involving the government. The plaintiff contended that the government was equitably estopped to deny that an invention had been reduced to practice prior to a contract because, it said, the government had agreed, during the negotiation of the contract, that there had been a reduction to practice. The court observed that four elements are necessary for equitable estoppel: (1) the government believed that it had expressed such agreement, (2) the government intended the contractor to enter into the contract in reliance on that agreement, (3) the contractor did not know the true facts (i.e., that the government did not really agree that the invention had been reduced to practice), and (4) the contractor must have relied upon the government's conduct to its detriment.[174] The court has refused

---

[171]*Intel Corp. v. United States ITC*, 946 F.2d 821, 20 USPQ2d 1161, 1176 (Fed. Cir. 1991).

[172]*Spindelfabrik S., S. & G. GmbH v. Schubert & Salzer Mas. Ak.*, 829 F.2d 1075, 4 USPQ2d 1044 (Fed. Cir. 1987). See §7.2(e).

[173]*Diamond Scientific Co. v. Ambico, Inc.*, 848 F.2d 1220, 6 USPQ2d 2028 (Fed. Cir. 1988). But this need not confine the court's application of the doctrine—the analysis must be concerned mainly with the balance of equities between the parties. *Id.*

[174]*Hazeltine Corp. v. United States*, 820 F.2d 1190, 2 USPQ2d 1744 (Fed. Cir. 1987). There was held to be no estoppel because plaintiff could not show that the government believed it had expressed agreement that there had been a reduction to practice. In *Zacharin v. United States*, 213 F.3d 1366, 55 USPQ2d 1047 (Fed. Cir. 2000), the patentee made his invention

to use a statement in a letter from an executive of a corporate patent owner to a licensee, to the effect that certain compounds were outside the patent claims, as limiting the scope of the claims in a suit by the licensee against a third party infringer. There was no estoppel because there was no evidence that the third party relied on the statement to justify its activities.[175] In a design patent case, the defendant supplier had indemnified a large retailer. The plaintiff patent owner did not join the retailer because of assurances from defendant that it could provide any and all relief. After losing, the defendant argued that it should be permitted to deduct, from the "total profit" permitted by the design patent statute (35 U.S.C. §289), the profits of the retailer. The Federal Circuit disagreed. Actions induced by attorney representations cannot be disclaimed by their instigator. Reliance by the plaintiff was sought and obtained, and it was not unreasonable. Having induced that reliance, the defendant cannot now renounce the consequences.[176]

The doctrine of judicial estoppel is the general proposition that where a party assumes a certain position in a legal proceeding, and succeeds in maintaining that position, it may not thereafter, simply because its interests have changed, assume a contrary position. A court employs this doctrine where it appears that a litigant is playing fast and loose with the courts and when intentional self-contradiction is being used as a means of obtaining unfair advantage in a forum provided for suitors seeking justice. In order to be subject to judicial estoppel, a party, having obtained a litigation benefit, must have attempted to invoke the authority of one tribunal to override a bargain made with another.[177] The issue of judicial estoppel is considered to

---

while employed by the government, and government attorneys filed the patent application. The patentee was later declared to have all rights in the invention. At the time the application was filed, both the patentee and the government attorneys were aware of a possible statutory bar. In its suit against the government for infringement, the patentee urged that the government should be estopped to raise the statutory bar as a defense. The court held that in order for equitable estoppel to be successfully asserted against the government, some form of affirmative misconduct must be shown in addition to the traditional requirements of estoppel. There was no evidence that the government attorneys had given the patentee incorrect legal advice or engaged in any other affirmative misconduct.

[175]*Water Techs. Corp. v. Calco, Ltd.,* 850 F.2d 660, 7 USPQ2d 1097 (Fed. Cir. 1988).

[176]*L.A. Gear, Inc. v. Thom McAn Shoe Co.,* 988 F.2d 1117, 25 USPQ2d 1913 (Fed. Cir. 1993).

[177]*Wang Labs., Inc. v. Applied Computer Sci., Inc.,* 958 F.2d 355, 22 USPQ2d 1055 (Fed. Cir. 1992). Just before trial the parties met and then informed the court by phone that they had agreed to settle. The court dismissed the case without prejudice to reopening by a certain date if settlement was not consummated. The parties never signed their draft agreement, and they continued to squabble while the court's set date went by. The plaintiff then moved to vacate the dismissal order and enforce the unexecuted settlement agreement. The district court judicially estopped the defendant from contending that a settlement had not been reached pursuant to the phone call and draft agreement. On appeal the Federal Circuit held that there was no estoppel because the defendant had not obtained a litigation benefit. Both parties had benefited from the phone call, and defendant's attempt to avoid the settlement was not an effort to invoke the authority of one tribunal to override a bargain made with another. In *Super Sack Mfg. Corp. v. Chase Packaging Corp.,* 57 F.3d 1054, 35 USPQ2d 1139 (Fed. Cir. 1995), the court held that a statement made in motion papers and briefs, to the effect that plaintiff would not assert its patents against any product that defendant was making as of the commencement of the litigation, will work a permanent estoppel. In *U.S. Philips Corp. v. Sears, Roebuck*

be procedural and is thus decided under the law of the regional circuit.[178] The decision whether to invoke judicial estoppel lies within the court's discretion and a refusal to apply the doctrine is reviewed under the abuse of discretion standard.[179] The doctrine of judicial estoppel is not followed by a majority of jurisdictions.[180]

The court had previously touched upon the doctrine of preclusion by inconsistent positions in an early case.[181] In *Hybritech v. Abbott*,[182] it expressly adopted the doctrine in the face of an argument that its prior discussion was dictum only. Under the doctrine, a patent holder is not precluded from taking a position in a subsequent action inconsistent with a position taken in a prior action unless the opposing party can demonstrate either (1) personal reliance on the decision granted in the prior suit, (2) prejudice to its litigation of the issues in the present suit by reason of the decision in the prior suit, or (3) the patent holder's apparent misuse of the court.[183] The court has also adopted the doctrine of *Smith v. Hall*,[184] which holds that a patentee, once having sought and obtained a broad construction of its claim in an action against one accused infringer, is barred, in a subsequent action against a different accused infringer, from arguing a narrow construction of its claim so as to avoid anticipation.[185]

Quasi-estoppel is an equitable doctrine preventing one from repudiating an act or assertion if it would harm another who reasonably relied on the act or assertion. This appears to be in contradistinction

---

& Co., 55 F.3d 592, 34 USPQ2d 1699 (Fed. Cir. 1995), the court appeared to apply a judicial estoppel where a party had argued in one district court that certain issues should be tried there, and later argued in another district court that it had the absolute right to relitigate the same issues. The court indicated that it had the firm impression that the party was attempting to play fast and loose with the judicial system. See also *Data Gen. Corp. v. Johnson*, 78 F.3d 1556 (Fed. Cir. 1996). In *Northern Telecom Ltd. v. Samsung Elec. Co.*, 215 F.3d 1281, 55 USPQ2d 1065 (Fed. Cir. 2000), a party on appeal alleged error in the claim construction that it had successfully advocated below. The court was able to pass the question of judicial estoppel because it found little merit in the party's challenge to the construction.

[178]*Wang Labs., Inc. v. Applied Computer Sci., Inc.*, 958 F.2d 355, 22 USPQ2d 1055 (Fed. Cir. 1992); *Water Techs. Corp. v. Calco, Ltd.*, 850 F.2d 660, 7 USPQ2d 1097 (Fed. Cir. 1988). One wonders whether the doctrine of judicial estoppel is not the same as the doctrine of preclusion by inconsistent positions, which the court has itself applied, probably using its own law. See notes 7:181–185 and accompanying text. Apparently administrative boards have authority to apply judicial estoppel as well as courts. *Data Gen. Corp. v. Johnson*, 78 F.3d 1556 (Fed. Cir. 1996).

[179]*Data Gen. Corp. v. Johnson*, 78 F.3d 1556 (Fed. Cir. 1996).

[180]*Water Techs. Corp. v. Calco, Ltd.*, 850 F.2d 660, 7 USPQ2d 1097 (Fed. Cir. 1988). The court found that the Seventh Circuit has considered and applied the doctrine. It was inapplicable here, however, because there had been no judicial acceptance of the asserted previous inconsistent position, and thus no risk of inconsistent results, no effect on the integrity of the judicial process, and no perception that the court had been misled.

[181]*Jackson Jordon, Inc. v. Plasser Am. Corp.*, 747 F.2d 1567, 224 USPQ 1 (Fed. Cir. 1984).

[182]*Hybritech, Inc. v. Abbott Labs.*, 849 F.2d 1446, 7 USPQ2d 1191 (Fed. Cir. 1988).

[183]*Hybritech, Inc. v. Abbott Labs.*, 849 F.2d 1446, 7 USPQ2d 1191 (Fed. Cir. 1988).

[184]301 U.S. 216 (1937).

[185]*Hybritech, Inc. v. Abbott Labs.*, 849 F.2d 1446, 7 USPQ2d 1191 (Fed. Cir. 1988). The Federal Circuit calls this collateral estoppel and well it might be in view of *Blonder-Tongue*. (See §18.5(b).) But the holding seems to fit the doctrine of preclusion by inconsistent positions (or judicial estoppel, for that matter) quite well. In any event, the court refused to apply the

to judicial estoppel, which is that where a party successfully urges a particular position in a legal proceeding, it is estopped from taking a contrary position in a subsequent proceeding where its interests have changed.[186]

§7.3 Government Ownership

There is a very comprehensive statutory scheme regulating the interest of the federal government in patents on inventions made with federal assistance.[187] In addition, other federal legislation often touches on the subject. For example, under the Saline Water Conversion Act, all patents resulting from research developed by government expenditure are available to the "general public." Inasmuch as the defendant was a member of the general public, it was entitled to practice any patented invention made under a contract for such research. The only question was whether the patented invention was made or conceived during the term of the contract.[188]

The court dealt with the constitutionality of Executive Order 10096, which establishes an administrative procedure for determining ownership of inventions made by government employees. It held that the Order did not result in a taking of property without due process and was therefore valid under the Fifth Amendment. The procedural safeguards in the Order and its accompanying regulations are sufficient.[189]

---

rule here, where the patentee sought a narrow construction in the first case but the court did not adopt that construction.

[186]*In re Baker Hughes Inc.*, 215 F.3d 1297, 55 USPQ2d 1149 (Fed. Cir. 2000). The appellant had, while the patent was owned by another, requested reexamination, asserting that the claims were unpatentable over a particular reference. When it acquired the patent, the appellant became the patent's defender in the reexamination proceeding. The PTO Director argued that the appellant should be quasi-estopped to deny unpatentability over that reference. The court disagreed. Quasi-estoppel is a seldom-utilized doctrine that appears predominately in tax cases. It is also known as the "duty of consistency." The court recognized that the appellant's change of position with regard to patentability put it in an unusual, and perhaps suspect, position. However, there was no showing that it made any specific factual misstatements in its request for reexamination or that the PTO relied on any such misstatements. Moreover, the PTO is charged with making an independent determination concerning the patentability of inventions. The fact that appellant once opposed the maintenance of the patent and now defends it does not change the PTO's duty to conduct the reexamination. Finally, there was no showing that the PTO or the public has suffered any harm from the change of position.

[187]E.g., 35 U.S.C. §§200–212.

[188]*Filmtec Corp. v. Hydranautics*, 982 F.2d 1546, 25 USPQ2d 1283 (Fed. Cir. 1992). The fact that the inventor was not bound by the contract is of no moment, inasmuch as the underlying legislation required the contracting employer to include in its employment contracts a provision that the government would retain title to inventions made by the employee. Nor does the fact that the formalities of the statute, including issuance to the United States, were not complied with, make any difference. When the invention was conceived by the employee working under the contract, title to that invention immediately vested in the United States by operation of law. The employee had no right to assign it to his employer, then or later.

[189]*Heinemann v. United States*, 796 F.2d 451, 230 USPQ 430 (Fed. Cir. 1986). Determinations under Order 10096 (including appeals thereof to the PTO Commissioner) are final agency actions reviewable under the Administrative Procedure Act. *Id.*

Not only does the United States own patents, but it can and does sue for infringement.[190] Under 35 U.S.C. §207(a)(2), federal agencies are empowered to grant licenses under federally owned patents, including the right of enforcement.[191] It would appear that the government may obtain shoprights to inventions of federal prison inmates under appropriate circumstances.[192] Interesting jurisdictional questions can arise in the context of government ownership determinations pursuant to 42 U.S.C. §5908.[193]

---

[190]See *United States v. Telectronics, Inc.,* 857 F.2d 778, 8 USPQ2d 1217 (Fed. Cir. 1988), in which the government sued on a patent, lost below, appealed, and ultimately won.

[191]*Nutrition 21 v. United States,* 930 F.2d 862, 18 USPQ2d 1351 (Fed. Cir. 1991). Although *Wireless Tel. Co. v. Radio Corp.,* 269 U.S. 459 (1926), holds that both the owner and the exclusive licensee are generally necessary parties, the court here reversed an involuntary joinder of the United States as a plaintiff to an infringement suit brought by its exclusive licensee. Public policy dictates that the government should not be required to make its limited litigation resources available each time one of its licensees seeks to sue for infringement.

[192]See *Lariscey v. United States,* 949 F.2d 1137, 20 USPQ2d 1845 (Fed. Cir. 1991).

[193]See *Cedars-Sinai Med. Ctr. v. Watkins,* 11 F.3d 1573, 29 USPQ2d 1188 (Fed. Cir. 1993).

8

Infringement Litigation— Jurisdiction and Procedure

One's patent is being infringed. What does one do? The simple solution is to ignore it. The more complex solutions keep a thousand patent lawyers busy virtually the whole of their time. One threatens, one cajoles, one negotiates, and ultimately—and probably far too often—one goes to the law and litigates. It is this latter—and very Anglo-American—alternative that is the subject of the next three chapters. And it is a subject dear to the heart of the author, for it is how he has made his living these past 35 years.

§8.1 Jurisdiction and Venue

(a) Subject Matter Jurisdiction

(i) General

Under 28 U.S.C. §1338(a) federal district courts have original and exclusive jurisdiction of any civil action arising under any act of Congress relating to patents. Under the Patent Act of 1952, "a patentee shall have remedy by civil action for infringement of his patent."[1] There is no doubt, therefore, that federal district courts have jurisdiction, exclusive of the state courts, over patent infringement actions.[2]

---

[1]35 U.S.C. §281.

[2]No doubt, that is, unless the determination of whether there has been patent infringement depends upon the construction of the provisions of a contract, in which case there may be plenty of doubt. Compare *Air Prods. & Chems., Inc. v. Reichhold Chems., Inc.,* 755 F.2d 1559, 225 USPQ 121 (Fed. Cir. 1985), with *Yarway Corp. v. Eur-Control USA Inc.,* 775 F.2d 268, 227 USPQ 352 (Fed. Cir. 1985).

Doubt only arises where it is not clear that the civil action is one for patent infringement.

Historically, a cause of action seeking equitable relief in aid of a request for relief at law could not be sought in the same action. The two forms of relief had to be pursued separately, one in a court of equity and the other in a court of law. But since the adoption of the Federal Rules of Civil Procedure in 1938, parties may join claims to relief regardless of whether they are legal or equitable. Accordingly, to the extent that prior decisions on federal patent jurisdiction were based on the separation of law and equity, such decisions fail to provide guidance applicable to modern cases.[3]

General principles. Where a court has no jurisdiction, it has no power to do anything but strike the case from its docket.[4] A court without jurisdiction must simply announce its lack of jurisdiction and dismiss the proceeding.[5] Federal courts therefore have the power, and the duty, to examine their own jurisdiction,[6] and an appellate court is obliged to notice want of jurisdiction in the lower court.[7] The Federal Circuit reviews decisions about subject matter jurisdiction de novo.[8]

All federal courts are courts of limited jurisdiction,[9] and that jurisdiction cannot be conferred by waiver, acquiescence, or mutual consent.[10] Parties by agreement or otherwise are incapable of either adding to or detracting from a court's jurisdiction.[11] Mere recitation of a basis for jurisdiction, by either a party or a court, cannot control

---

[3]*Kunkel v. Topmaster Int'l, Inc.,* 906 F.2d 693, 15 USPQ2d 1367 (Fed. Cir. 1990).

[4]*Johns-Manville Corp. v. United States,* 893 F.2d 324 (Fed. Cir. 1989).

[5]*National Presto Indus. v. Dazey Corp.,* 107 F.3d 1576, 42 USPQ2d 1070 (Fed. Cir. 1997).

[6]*Williams v. Secretary of Navy,* 787 F.2d 552 (Fed. Cir. 1986); *Aleut Tribe v. United States,* 702 F.2d 1015 (Fed. Cir. 1983).

[7]*Minnesota Chippewa Tribe v. United States,* 768 F.2d 338 (Fed. Cir. 1985); *Coastal Corp. v. United States,* 713 F.2d 728 (Fed. Cir. 1983). Thus where a statute of limitations is jurisdictional, the limitations issue can be considered on appeal even though not raised below—or by the parties on appeal. *Minnesota Chippewa Tribe v. United States,* 768 F.2d 338 (Fed. Cir. 1985). Compliance with the statute of limitations of the Claims Court (generally six years under 28 U.S.C. §2501) is a jurisdictional matter. *Hart v. United States,* 910 F.2d 814 (Fed. Cir. 1990); *Jones v. United States,* 801 F.2d 1334 (Fed. Cir. 1986). Jurisdiction of a lower court, including the Claims Court, is a matter for its own decision in the first instance. *Lindahl v. Office of Personnel Management,* 718 F.2d 391 (Fed. Cir. 1983). While the Federal Circuit does not generally condone or entertain arguments raised for the first time on appeal, it may sua sponte consider all bases for the district court's jurisdiction. *Broughton Lumber Co. v. Yeutter,* 939 F.2d 1547 (Fed. Cir. 1991).

[8]*Manville Sales Corp. v. Paramount Sys., Inc.,* 917 F.2d 544, 16 USPQ2d 1587 (Fed. Cir. 1990); *Kunkel v. Topmaster Int'l, Inc.,* 906 F.2d 693, 15 USPQ2d 1367 (Fed. Cir. 1990).

[9]*Mars, Inc. v. Kabushiki-Kaisha Nippon Conlux,* 24 F.3d 1368, 30 USPQ2d 1621 (Fed. Cir. 1994); *Williams v. Secretary of Navy,* 787 F.2d 552 (Fed. Cir. 1986); *Lindahl v. Office of Personnel Management,* 718 F.2d 391 (Fed. Cir. 1983).

[10]*Gould v. Control Laser Corp.,* 866 F.2d 1391, 9 USPQ2d 1718 (Fed. Cir. 1989); *Coastal Corp. v. United States,* 713 F.2d 728 (Fed. Cir. 1983). Indeed, a party is not prevented from subsequently challenging a court's jurisdiction that the party itself had previously invoked. *Glasstech, Inc. v. AB Kyro OY,* 769 F.2d 1574, 226 USPQ 949 (Fed. Cir. 1985).

[11]*Utter v. Hiraga,* 845 F.2d 993, 6 USPQ2d 1709 (Fed. Cir. 1988).

and cannot alter the scope of the court's statutory mandate.[12] Conjecture alone cannot serve as a grant of jurisdiction.[13]

A federal court's jurisdiction is limited to that conferred by Congress.[14] It is a fundamental principle, embedded in the Constitution, that all federal courts, except the Supreme Court, are established by Congress and possess only the jurisdiction granted to them by the Congress.[15] The limits upon federal jurisdiction, whether imposed by Congress or the Constitution, must be neither disregarded nor evaded.[16]

Although federal question jurisdiction is initially determined on the allegations in the complaint,[17] substance not form is controlling.[18] Characterizing issues as primary and secondary is of no aid to the court in the determination of subject matter jurisdiction.[19] In determining subject matter jurisdiction, the court must consider as a whole the substance of the claim in addition to the language of the complaint and may also consider jurisdictional facts outside the pleadings. The party who brings suit is master to decide what law it will rely upon, and jurisdiction generally depends upon the case made and the relief demanded by the plaintiff. A court must review and analyze the plaintiff's pleadings, with special attention directed to the relief requested by the plaintiff.[20]

Two well-established principles of subject matter jurisdiction are that federal question jurisdiction is created by a nonfrivolous assertion of a federal claim in a well-pleaded complaint and that such jurisdiction, once established, is not ordinarily defeated by a subsequent change in circumstances.[21] All of these qualifications are important: frivolous claims do not create jurisdiction.[22] Jurisdiction is determined at the time the suit is filed and, after vesting, cannot be ousted by subsequent events, including action by the parties.[23] Similarly,

---

[12]*Williams v. Secretary of Navy*, 787 F.2d 552 (Fed. Cir. 1986).

[13]*Lindahl v. Office of Personnel Management*, 718 F.2d 391 (Fed. Cir. 1983).

[14]*Allied Corp. v. United States ITC*, 850 F.2d 1573, 7 USPQ2d 1303 (Fed. Cir. 1988).

[15]*In re United States*, 877 F.2d 1568 (Fed. Cir. 1989).

[16]*Mars, Inc. v. Kabushiki-Kaisha Nippon Conlux*, 24 F.3d 1368, 30 USPQ2d 1621 (Fed. Cir. 1994).

[17]*Atari, Inc. v. JS & A Group, Inc.*, 747 F.2d 1422, 223 USPQ 1074 (Fed. Cir. 1984).

[18]*Williams v. Secretary of Navy*, 787 F.2d 552 (Fed. Cir. 1986).

[19]*Air Prods. & Chems., Inc. v. Reichhold Chems., Inc.*, 755 F.2d 1559, 225 USPQ 121, 124 (Fed. Cir. 1985).

[20]*Air Prods. & Chems., Inc. v. Reichhold Chems., Inc.*, 755 F.2d 1559, 225 USPQ 121 (Fed. Cir. 1985). However, although leniency with respect to more formal matters should be extended to a pro se party, a court may not similarly take a liberal view of jurisdictional requirements and set a different rule for pro se litigants only. *Kelley v. Department of Labor*, 812 F.2d 1378 (Fed. Cir. 1987). In personam and subject matter jurisdictional facts must be pled. *Spectronics Corp. v. H.B. Fuller Co.*, 940 F.2d 631, 19 USPQ2d 1545 (Fed. Cir. 1991).

[21]*Albert v. Kevex Corp.*, 729 F.2d 757, 221 USPQ 202 (Fed. Cir. 1984).

[22]*Atari, Inc. v. JS & A Group, Inc.*, 747 F.2d 1422, 223 USPQ 1074 (Fed. Cir. 1984).

[23]*F. Alderete Gen. Contractors v. United States*, 714 F.2d 1476 (Fed. Cir. 1983). See also *ATL, Inc. v. United States*, 736 F.2d 677 (Fed. Cir. 1984); *Beghin-Say Int'l, Inc. v. Ole-Bendt Rasmussen*, 733 F.2d 1568, 221 USPQ 1121 (Fed. Cir. 1984). But cf. *Imagineering, Inc. v. Van*

later events may not create jurisdiction where none existed at the time of filing the complaint.[24]

In addition, Article III of the Constitution limits the role of federal courts to adjudication of actual "cases" and "controversies."[25] The existence of jurisdiction does not confirm a court's ability to supply relief. The issue must also be justiciable; it depends on whether the duty asserted can be judicially identified and its breach judicially determined, and whether protection for the right asserted can be judicially molded.[26] Justiciability and the controversy requirement are discussed below in connection with topics such as declaratory judgment jurisdiction, standing, and mootness.

Subject matter jurisdictional facts must be pled and proved when challenged.[27] On reviewing a motion to dismiss for lack of subject matter jurisdiction, the court must take as true the factual allegations set forth in the complaint.[28] If a motion to dismiss challenges the truth of the jurisdictional facts alleged in the complaint, the district court may consider relevant evidence in order to resolve the factual dispute. In such case the plaintiff bears the burden of establishing subject matter jurisdiction by a preponderance of the evidence. However, the plaintiff must be given an opportunity to be heard before dismissal is ordered.[29] Briefs, exhibits, and affidavits can be considered in connection with a motion under Rule 12(b)(1), FRCP, to dismiss for lack of subject matter jurisdiction.[30] Normally a motion for summary judgment seeks a judgment on the merits, while a motion to dismiss for lack of subject matter jurisdiction seeks a judgment in abatement in that it does not bar future claims. Thus, such a motion to dismiss on jurisdictional grounds should properly be brought under Rule 12(b)(1).[31] The commentators indicate that summary judgment

---

Klassens, Inc., 53 F.3d 1260, 34 USPQ2d 1526 (Fed. Cir. 1995), where the case as filed included a design patent infringement claim and Lanham Act claims. Before trial the design patent claim was dropped and the trial court dismissed a declaratory judgment counterclaim directed to the design patent. The only remaining patent-related issue was the defendant's claim for attorney fees under 35 U.S.C. §285 incurred in the defense of the design patent claim. This was held to be a claim arising under the patent law so that the Federal Circuit accordingly had jurisdiction over the Lanham Act claims as well.

[24]*Spectronics Corp. v. H.B. Fuller Co.*, 940 F.2d 631, 19 USPQ2d 1545 (Fed. Cir. 1991).

[25]*Boeing Co. v. Commissioner of Patents*, 853 F.2d 878, 7 USPQ2d 1487 (Fed. Cir. 1988). For example, the assertion of a single patent claim at trial does not create a case of actual controversy respecting other claims of the patent, and a judgment invalidating the other claims will accordingly be vacated. *Carroll Touch, Inc. v. Electro Mechanical Sys., Inc.*, 3 F.3d 404, 27 USPQ2d 1836 (Fed. Cir. 1993). That an agency may choose to render advisory opinions cannot create for one displeased with its advice a cause of action cognizable in an Article III court. *Allied Corp. v. United States ITC*, 850 F.2d 1573, 7 USPQ2d 1303 (Fed. Cir. 1988).

[26]*Murphy v. United States*, 993 F.2d 871 (Fed. Cir. 1993).

[27]*Spectronics Corp. v. H.B. Fuller Co.*, 940 F.2d 631, 19 USPQ2d 1545 (Fed. Cir. 1991).

[28]*Reynolds v. Army & Air Force Exch. Serv.*, 846 F.2d 746 (Fed. Cir. 1988); *Air Prods. & Chems., Inc. v. Reichhold Chems., Inc.*, 755 F.2d 1559, 225 USPQ 121 (Fed. Cir. 1985).

[29]*Reynolds v. Army & Air Force Exch. Serv.*, 846 F.2d 746 (Fed. Cir. 1988).

[30]*Vink v. Schijf*, 839 F.2d 676, 5 USPQ2d 1728 (Fed. Cir. 1988).

[31]*Indium Corp. v. Semi-Alloys, Inc.*, 781 F.2d 879, 228 USPQ 845 (Fed. Cir. 1985). In deciding Rule 12(b) motions, a court can consider evidentiary matters outside the pleadings;

is an inappropriate vehicle for jurisdictional inquiries.[32] Despite an apparent lapse on the question[33] the Federal Circuit now seems to have adopted that view.[34]

The burden of establishing jurisdiction in the district court lies with the party seeking to invoke the court's jurisdiction.[35] If a Rule 12(b)(1) motion simply challenges the court's subject matter jurisdiction based on the sufficiency of the pleading's allegations—i.e., where the movant presents a "facial" attack on the pleading—then those allegations are taken as true and construed in a light most favorable to the complainant. If the Rule 12(b)(1) motion denies or controverts the pleader's allegations of jurisdiction, however, the movant is deemed to be challenging the factual basis for the court's subject matter jurisdiction. In such a case, the allegations in the complaint are not controlling and only uncontroverted factual allegations are accepted as true for purposes of the motion. All other facts underlying the controverted jurisdictional allegations are in dispute and are subject to factfinding by the district court. In establishing the predicate jurisdictional facts, a court is not restricted to the face of the pleadings, but may review evidence extrinsic to the pleadings, including affidavits and deposition testimony.[36] If the facts reveal any reasonable basis upon which the nonmovant might prevail, the motion will be denied.[37]

It is often the case, where a tribunal's subject matter jurisdiction is based on the same statute that gives rise to the federal right, that the jurisdictional requirements mesh with the factual requirements necessary to prevail on the merits. In such a situation the tribunal should assume jurisdiction and treat (and dismiss on, if necessary) the merits of the case.[38] The presence of a valid defense does not oust

---

thus, it would not be improper for a district court to treat a summary judgment motion as a suggestion of lack of subject matter jurisdiction.

[32] 5 Wright & Miller, *Federal Practice and Procedure* 547 (1969); 2A *Moore's Federal Practice* §12.07(2.-1)(1986).

[33] See *Goodyear Tire & Rubber Co. v. Releasomers, Inc.*, 824 F.2d 953, 3 USPQ2d 1310 (Fed. Cir. 1987).

[34] See *Vink v. Schijf*, 839 F.2d 676, 5 USPQ2d 1728 (Fed. Cir. 1988).

[35] *National Presto Indus. v. Dazey Corp.*, 107 F.3d 1576, 42 USPQ2d 1070 (Fed. Cir. 1997); *Mars, Inc. v. Kabushiki-Kaisha Nippon Conlux*, 24 F.3d 1368, 30 USPQ2d 1621 (Fed. Cir. 1994); *Cedars-Sinai Med. Ctr. v. Watkins*, 11 F.3d 1573, 29 USPQ2d 1188 (Fed. Cir. 1993).

[36] *Cedars-Sinai Med. Ctr. v. Watkins*, 11 F.3d 1573, 29 USPQ2d 1188 (Fed. Cir. 1993). By contrast, a motion to dismiss for failure to state a claim upon which relief can be granted under Rule 12(b)(6) always takes the allegations of the complaint as true and favorable to the nonmoving party. *Id.* Compare *Ephraim v. Brown*, 82 F.3d 399 (Fed. Cir. 1996).

[37] *Mars, Inc. v. Kabushiki-Kaisha Nippon Conlux*, 24 F.3d 1368, 30 USPQ2d 1621 (Fed. Cir. 1994).

[38] *Amgen, Inc. v. United States ITC*, 902 F.2d 1532, 14 USPQ2d 1734 (Fed. Cir. 1990). *Exxon Chem. Patents, Inc. v. Lubrizol Corp.*, 935 F.2d 1263, 19 USPQ2d 1061 (Fed. Cir. 1991), presents an interesting example. A proper listing for the issuing patent appeared in the proper issue of the *Official Gazette* and the owner brought suit that day. However, the patent was not printed until later and the Commissioner did not sign the patent until several weeks later. The defendant moved to dismiss the suit for lack of jurisdiction, on the ground that there was no patent when the suit was brought. The court held that jurisdiction depends upon whether

a tribunal of jurisdiction unless, of course, the defense is jurisdictional. If it did, the only cases decided on the merits would hold for victorious plaintiffs, and no successful defense would generate a res judicata bar. Where the defendant has a valid defense and there are no material disputed facts, it may move for summary judgment or dismissal for failure to state a claim upon which relief can be granted, depending upon the proofs needed. The distinction between lack of jurisdiction and failure to state a claim upon which relief can be granted is an important one. A dismissal on the merits carries res judicata effect and dismissal for want of jurisdiction does not.[39] However, a dismissal for lack of jurisdiction may be given res judicata effect as to the jurisdictional issue.[40]

Arising under the patent laws. The appellate jurisdiction of the Federal Circuit includes (and is exclusive with respect to) final decisions of district courts where the subject matter jurisdiction of those courts is based, "in whole or in part," on 28 U.S.C. §1338.[41] The fundamental question of whether a civil action arises under a federal law relating to patents is accordingly treated in detail in that context. See §16.1(b). A few special problems deserve consideration here, however.

The fundamental test ought to be whether the claimant asserts before the district court some right or privilege that would be defeated by one or sustained by an opposite construction of the patent laws.[42] But what is an act of Congress relating to patents? It is sufficient here to summarize the general guidelines set out by the Supreme Court in *Christianson v. Colt.*[43]

In order to demonstrate that a case is one arising under federal patent law, the plaintiff must set up some right, title, or interest under the patent laws, or at least make it appear that some right or privilege will be defeated by one construction or sustained by the opposite construction of those laws. Jurisdiction under §1338 extends

---

the plaintiff actually pleaded the elements required by the patent laws for a patent infringement claim. When a challenge to jurisdiction is in fact directed only to the merits of a question of patent law, it is proper for the district court to accept jurisdiction. The question of whether a valid patent existed when suit was brought remains to be tried as a question of patent law. Compare *GAF Building Mat. Corp. v. Elk Corp. of Dallas,* 90 F.3d 479, 39 USPQ2d 1463 (Fed. Cir. 1996). But see *Laitram Corp. v. Cambridge Wire Cloth Co.,* 919 F.2d 1579, 16 USPQ2d 1929 (Fed. Cir. 1990). Neither intent nor preparation constitutes infringement under 35 U.S.C. §271. Thus, in the absence of evidence that an accused construction had actually been made, used, or sold as of the commencement of the action, the court should dismiss for want of jurisdiction.

[39]*Do-Well Mach. Shop, Inc. v. United States,* 870 F.2d 637 (Fed. Cir. 1989). If the predicate facts are not proved after the court assumes jurisdiction, the decision is deemed to be on the merits, resolving the substantive claim. *Ephraim v. Brown,* 82 F.3d 399 (Fed. Cir. 1996).

[40]*Amgen, Inc. v. United States ITC,* 902 F.2d 1532, 14 USPQ2d 1734 (Fed. Cir. 1990).

[41]28 U.S.C. §1295(a).

[42]*Dubost v. United States PTO,* 777 F.2d 1561, 227 USPQ 977 (Fed. Cir. 1985); *Beghin-Say Int'l, Inc. v. Ole-Bendt Rasmussen,* 733 F.2d 1568, 221 USPQ 1121 (Fed. Cir. 1984).

[43]*Christianson v. Colt Indus. Oper. Corp.,* 486 U.S. 800, 7 USPQ2d 1109 (1988).

only to those cases in which a well-pleaded complaint establishes either that federal patent law creates the cause of action or that the plaintiff's right to relief necessarily depends on resolution of a substantial question of federal patent law, in that patent law is a necessary element of one of the well-pleaded claims. Under the well-pleaded complaint rule, whether a claim arises under patent law must be determined from what necessarily appears in the plaintiff's statement of its own claim, unaided by anything alleged in anticipation or avoidance of defenses, even if the defense is anticipated in the plaintiff's complaint and even if both parties admit that the defense is the only question truly at issue in the case.[44] A plaintiff may not defeat §1338 jurisdiction by omitting to plead necessary federal patent law questions.[45]

However, merely because the involved statute relates to patents does not mean that the claim arises under the patent laws. In general, a claim arises under the particular statute that creates the cause of action.[46] Thus, even though jurisdiction may lie over a declaratory judgment action based upon threatened infringement, threatened infringement does not itself create a claim for infringement under 35 U.S.C. §271(a), and there is therefore no "arising under" jurisdiction over a claim for an injunction against threatened infringement.[47] Interfering subject matter is a jurisdictional requirement for a claim of interfering patents under 35 U.S.C. §291, and lack of interference renders the district court powerless to adjudge a patent invalid.[48]

---

[44]*Christianson v. Colt Indus. Oper. Corp.*, 486 U.S. 800, 7 USPQ2d 1109 (1988). The Federal Circuit has extended the well-pleaded complaint rule to include well-pleaded compulsory counterclaims. Thus, an in banc court held that it has jurisdiction over an appeal in a case in which the complaint was based on diversity (seeking a declaratory judgment of no misappropriation of trade secrets) but a compulsory counterclaim for patent infringement was present. The court did not decide what the result would be in the event the counterclaim were permissive only. *AeroJet-General Corp. v. Machine Tool Works*, 895 F.2d 736, 13 USPQ2d 1670 (Fed. Cir. 1990). The court feels that, under *Christianson,* a claim supported by alternative theories in the complaint may not form the basis for §1338 jurisdiction unless patent law is essential to each of those theories. *American Tel. & Tel. Co. v. Integrated Network Corp.,* 972 F.2d 1321, 23 USPQ2d 1918 (Fed. Cir. 1992). The matter can sometimes turn on state law. Thus, under Texas law, a business disparagement claim based upon a false accusation of patent infringement requires the plaintiff to demonstrate that its accused product does not infringe. Under Massachusetts law, the defendant patentee has the burden to show the truth of its statements about infringement. A federal court therefore has jurisdiction of the Texas claim but not the Massachusetts claim. *Additive Cont'l & Meas. Sys., Inc. v. Flowdata, Inc.,* 986 F.2d 476, 25 USPQ2d 1798 (Fed. Cir. 1993). A claim supported by alternative theories may not form the basis for §1338(a) jurisdiction unless patent law is essential to each of those theories; similarly, an alternative legal defense raising a question of patent law is insufficient to confer jurisdiction. *Cedars-Sinai Med. Ctr. v. Watkins,* 11 F.3d 1573, 29 USPQ2d 1188 (Fed. Cir. 1993).

[45]*Christianson v. Colt Indus. Oper. Corp.,* 486 U.S. 800, 7 USPQ2d 1109 (1988).

[46]*Atari, Inc. v. JS & A Group, Inc.,* 747 F.2d 1422, 223 USPQ 1074 (Fed. Cir. 1984).

[47]*Lang v. Pacific Marine & Supply Co.,* 895 F.2d 761, 13 USPQ2d 1820 (Fed. Cir. 1990).

[48]*Albert v. Kevex Corp.,* 729 F.2d 757, 221 USPQ 202 (Fed. Cir. 1984). This despite the fact that there was interfering subject matter prior to a disclaimer that cured it. See also *Albert v. Kevex Corp.,* 741 F.2d 396, 223 USPQ 1 (Fed. Cir. 1984). The proper vehicle would have been a declaratory judgment action. Section 291 gives patent owners a separate and distinct basis of jurisdiction if two patents interfere. Were it not so, §291 would be redundant with §271, since a party could always assert prior invention as a defense under §102(g). *Kimberly-Clark Corp. v. Procter & Gamble Distrib. Co.,* 973 F.2d 911, 23 USPQ2d 1921 (Fed. Cir. 1992).

There can be no jurisdiction over a claim for false marking under 35 U.S.C. §292 until the article allegedly mismarked actually exists. The article must be completed before §292 will allow a claim.[49]

On the other hand, judicial resolution of coinventorship contests over issued patents is explicitly authorized by 35 U.S.C. §256. Thus, a suit for determination of coinventorship and correction of a patent under §256 arises under the patent law. Relief depends on resolution of a substantial question of patent law: the definition of the invention and the issue of inventorship. If coinventorship is found, then the court would have to consider the question of whether nonjoinder was without deceptive intention. One answer would permit correction of the patent; the other could invalidate it.[50] A federal district court has jurisdiction, apparently pursuant to the general mandamus statute, 28 U.S.C. §1651, to review a decision of the PTO Commissioner on a petition to revive a patent application. Whatever may be the scope of the Commissioner's discretion, the existence of that discretion does not bar judicial review of the Commissioner's decision. Also, the action in the district court is one arising under the patent laws, in that it depends on resolution of a substantial question of federal patent law.[51]

An action requesting a district court to remove a cloud on title to a patent application and to declare it the plaintiff's property is not an action arising under the patent laws, and a federal district court has no jurisdiction. The fact that a contract of assignment is recorded in the PTO does not create jurisdiction, and there is nothing in 35 U.S.C. §261 (which governs assignments) that creates a right of action in federal courts to seek contract interpretation.[52] The court recognizes that it generally lacks jurisdiction over a simple contractual dispute involving construction of patent terms familiar to the patent law. But where the contract involves a federal statute, the situation must be closely examined to determine whether the action arises under the statute and whether the statute relates to patents. Thus, an action seeking a declaration that a Department of Energy ownership determination under 42 U.S.C. §5908 is invalid is one arising under an act of Congress relating to patents. This is so principally because §5908 in essence instructs the Commissioner to issue a patent to the United States, rather than the named inventor, once the statutory requirements are satisfied.[53] Under 16 U.S.C. §831r, the Tennessee

---

Thus validity, priority, and related issues have a source of jurisdiction under §291 distinct from an infringement action, and the fact that the parties are not accusing one another of infringement does not eliminate their right to relief under §291. *Id.*

[49]*Lang v. Pacific Marine & Supply Co.,* 895 F.2d 761, 13 USPQ2d 1820 (Fed. Cir. 1990).

[50]*MCV, Inc. v. King-Seeley Thermos Co.,* 870 F.2d 1568, 10 USPQ2d 1287 (Fed. Cir. 1989). This is a clear holding that §256 creates a cause of action to determine and correct inventorship.

[51]*Morganroth v. Quigg,* 885 F.2d 843, 12 USPQ2d 1125 (Fed. Cir. 1989).

[52]*Beghin-Say Int'l, Inc. v. Ole-Bendt Rasmussen,* 733 F.2d 1568, 221 USPQ 1121 (Fed. Cir. 1984).

[53]*Cedars-Sinai Med. Ctr. v. Watkins,* 11 F.3d 1573, 29 USPQ2d 1188 (Fed. Cir. 1993). In a dictum, the court questioned whether a direct challenge to the ownership determination under the Administrative Procedure Act would form the basis for §1338(a) jurisdiction.

Valley Authority has the right, when necessary, to infringe patents, and the owner has the right to recover reasonable compensation in a district court. Such a case is one arising under an act of Congress relating to patents.[54] It seems clear enough that an action to enforce a foreign patent would not arise under the federal patent laws.[55]

Interesting jurisdictional questions can arise in the context of patent license agreements. It has been said that a claim of failure to pay royalties due under a patent license agreement is one arising out of state contract law, not arising under the patent law. Likewise, a case cannot arise under federal law where the patent claim is merely a defense to a state court action.[56] Thus state courts may decide patent questions.[57] But neither is a federal district court precluded in patent suits from resolving nonpatent questions, and the fact that a question of contract law must be decided prior to reaching the patent infringement question does not defeat federal subject matter jurisdiction. That the resolution of a question of state law may render federal questions moot does not deprive a federal court of subject matter jurisdiction where the plaintiff bases its claim upon, and seeks remedies under, the patent laws.[58]

That a nonfederal issue (e.g., ownership of a patent) must be resolved before the federal issue (e.g., infringement of the patent) is immaterial in determining whether there is federal jurisdiction.[59] However, to invoke the jurisdiction of a federal court under §1338, it is necessary that a plaintiff allege facts that demonstrate that it, and not the defendant, owns the patent rights upon which the infringement suit is premised. Furthermore, this allegation of ownership must have a plausible foundation. Federal jurisdiction cannot lie based on allegations that are frivolous or insubstantial. Thus, if a plaintiff cannot in good faith allege such facts because, absent judicial intervention to change the situation, under the terms of a contract or deed of assignment the rights at issue are held by the defendant, federal court is not the place to seek that initial judicial intervention. It may seem strange at first blush that the question of whether a patent is valid and infringed ordinarily is one for federal courts, while the question of who owns the patent rights and on what

---

[54]*Alco Standard Corp. v. Tennessee Valley Auth.*, 808 F.2d 1490, 1 USPQ2d 1337 (Fed. Cir. 1986).

[55]Cf. *Stein Assoc., Inc. v. Heat & Control, Inc.*, 748 F.2d 653, 223 USPQ 1277 (Fed. Cir. 1984). But see the discussion of *Mars, Inc. v. Kabushiki-Kaisha Nippon Conlux*, 24 F.3d 1368, 30 USPQ2d 1621 (Fed. Cir. 1994), accompanying notes 8:77–80.

[56]*Schwarzkopf Dev. Corp. v. Ti-Coating, Inc.*, 800 F.2d 240, 231 USPQ 47 (Fed. Cir. 1986).

[57]*Christianson v. Colt Indus. Oper. Corp.*, 822 F.2d 1544, 3 USPQ2d 1241 (Fed. Cir. 1987), *vacated on jurisdictional grounds and remanded*, 486 U.S. 800, 7 USPQ2d 1109 (1988).

[58]*Kunkel v. Topmaster Int'l, Inc.*, 906 F.2d 693, 15 USPQ2d 1367 (Fed. Cir. 1990); *Air Prods. & Chems., Inc. v. Reichhold Chems., Inc.*, 755 F.2d 1559, 225 USPQ 121 (Fed. Cir. 1985). It is possible that the result might be different if the contract itself required a court ruling to establish a right to terminate the license. In *U.S. Valves Inc. v. Dray*, 212 F.3d 1368, 54 USPQ2d 1834 (Fed. Cir. 2000), the court held that a federal court has jurisdiction over action for breach of a license agreement where one of the issues is whether the product is covered by the licensed patent.

[59]*Vink v. Schijf*, 839 F.2d 676, 5 USPQ2d 1728 (Fed. Cir. 1988).

terms typically is a question exclusively for state courts. Yet that long has been the law. It is well settled that if the patentee pleads a cause of action based on rights created by a contract, or on the common law of torts, the case is not one arising under the patent laws. Licenses are considered as nothing more than a promise by the licensor not to sue the licensee, and title to the patent does not change hands under a license agreement. However, assignments pass title to the patentee's rights, with all the accompanying rights of ownership, from the patentee to the assignee. Therefore, in the case of a license agreement having a rescission clause, a patentee in a suit for infringement can properly assert that it owned the patent at the time of infringement and that the defendant is infringing the patent. In such cases, the plaintiff does not seek any specific equitable relief as a prerequisite to bringing the infringement claim. However, when the infringement suit involves an assignment, unless the assignment may be declared null and void by operation of law—either through a forfeiture provision present in the agreement or under a provision of applicable state law—an assignor suing for infringement must first affirmatively seek equitable relief from a court to rescind or cancel the assignment. Until ownership is restored in the assignor, there can be no act of infringement by the assignee. Federal question jurisdiction must exist at the time the complaint is filed for a federal court to exercise authority over the case, and without first receiving equitable relief that restores to the assignor title to the patent, any claim of ownership by the assignor will be unfounded. Further, because an action to rescind or cancel an assignment is a state law based claim, absent diversity jurisdiction it is to a state court that plaintiff must look in seeking a forfeiture.[60]

A suit by an exclusive licensee against the licensor for infringement of the licensed patents seeks the relief afforded by the patent laws and in substance arises under the patent laws. The mere fact that a patent dispute arises between contracting parties does not necessarily lead to the conclusion that the cause of action is one under contract rather than patent rights.[61] On the other hand, where the determination of whether there has been an infringement of a patent depends upon the construction of the provisions of a contract and not upon the construction of an act of Congress relating to patents, the controversy is not one arising under the patent laws.[62] Individual contract provisions can be significant.[63]

---

[60]*Jim Arnold Corp. v. Hydrotech Sys., Inc.,* 109 F.3d 1567, 42 USPQ2d 1119 (Fed. Cir. 1997).

[61]*Yarway Corp. v. Eur-Control USA Inc.,* 775 F.2d 268, 227 USPQ 352 (Fed. Cir. 1985). See also *Kunkel v. Topmaster Int'l, Inc.,* 906 F.2d 693, 15 USPQ2d 1367 (Fed. Cir. 1990).

[62]*Air Prods. & Chems., Inc. v. Reichhold Chems., Inc.,* 755 F.2d 1559, 225 USPQ 121 (Fed. Cir. 1985). Even the transient appearance of a counterclaim for declaratory judgment of invalidity and noninfringement (dismissed during the pleading stages) will not confer jurisdiction in such a case. *Schwarzkopf Dev. Corp. v. Ti-Coating, Inc.,* 800 F.2d 240, 231 USPQ 47 (Fed. Cir. 1986).

[63]A choice of forum clause (Italy) in a license agreement was enforced, and the case dismissed, even though the suit was for patent infringement. *Warner & Swasey Co. v. Salvagnini*

A federal district court may not interpret and enforce a settlement agreement that terminated prior litigation unless it has some federal jurisdictional basis for enforcing a contract between the parties. Neither the Federal Rules nor any statute give federal courts the inherent power to interpret and enforce settlement agreements, even those that pertain to litigation originally pending in federal courts, absent some independent basis of jurisdiction. One such basis is ancillary jurisdiction, which may be exercised over a settlement agreement (1) to permit disposition by a single court of claims that are, in varying respects and degrees, factually interdependent, and (2) to enable a court to function successfully, i.e., to manage its proceedings, vindicate its authority, and effectuate its decrees. But under the first circumstance (single court disposition of factually interdependent claims) entry of judgment, such as a consent judgment, terminates both the federal case and any basis for ancillary federal jurisdiction over the contractual agreement that occasioned the termination. Thus, for federal courts to enforce the settlement agreement, the dispute must involve some ongoing source of federal jurisdiction to which the nonfederal matter may be considered ancillary.[64] Under the second source of ancillary jurisdiction (successful functioning of the court), an order or judgment of the court must incorporate the settlement agreement such that a breach of the agreement also violates the court's decree.[65]

Diversity and amount in controversy. The purpose behind the diversity jurisdiction statute, 28 U.S.C. §1332, is to ensure an impartial tribunal for citizens of different states.[66] Because the jurisdiction of the Federal Circuit is limited to review of cases arising under federal laws, the court is not likely to have to deal with diversity of citizenship and amount in controversy on any substantial basis.[67]

Transferica S.P.A., 806 F.2d 1045, 231 USPQ 972 (Fed. Cir. 1986). A reference in the complaint to the license as a means of assessing reasonable damages did not make the action one arising under state contract law rather than the patent laws. *Air Prods. & Chems., Inc. v. Reichhold Chems., Inc.*, 755 F.2d 1559, 225 USPQ 121 (Fed. Cir. 1985). In *American Tel. & Tel. Co. v. Integrated Network Corp.*, 972 F.2d 1321, 23 USPQ2d 1918 (Fed. Cir. 1992), the court assumed without deciding that construction of a term in a contract could sustain §1338 jurisdiction. However, it was quick to point out that it did not find that proposition intuitively obvious and that it could find no cases that so hold.

[64]*National Presto Indus. v. Dazey Corp.*, 107 F.3d 1576, 42 USPQ2d 1070 (Fed. Cir. 1997). The court was able to pass the question of whether a district court's inherent but limited contempt power is sufficiently robust to support ancillary jurisdiction, for it found that the contempt power of the district court was not invoked by the proceedings below. See also *Interspiro USA, Inc. v. Figgie Int'l, Inc.*, 18 F.3d 927, 30 USPQ2d 1070 (Fed. Cir. 1994).

[65]*National Presto Indus. v. Dazey Corp.*, 107 F.3d 1576, 42 USPQ2d 1070 (Fed. Cir. 1997).

[66]*UNR Indus., Inc. v. United States*, 911 F.2d 654 (Fed. Cir. 1990).

[67]District court jurisdiction of federal questions is not dependent upon the amount in controversy. See Revision Notes to 28 U.S.C. §1331. Aggregation of claims by individual plaintiffs for jurisdictional purposes is permitted only when there is a single title or right in which they have a common and undivided interest. Similar rules apply to class actions. Where the members of the class are not suing with respect to a common interest, there will be no aggregation of claims. The claim of each member of the class must be examined separately to determine

Nonetheless, the court has had occasion to point out that diversity is tested as of the filing date of a complaint and cannot be changed by the action of a party thereafter,[68] and that the amount in controversy for jurisdictional purposes must be ascertained by the requests in the pleadings, without consideration of success on the merits.[69] Also, the mere fact that diversity is alleged in the complaint as the basis for jurisdiction does not necessarily mean that the case is not one cognizable under 28 U.S.C. §1338(a). Where the complaint asks for an injunction against patent infringement, it is a patent case.[70]

Pendent and supplemental jurisdiction. Pursuant to 35 U.S.C. §1338(b), district courts have original jurisdiction of civil actions asserting a claim of unfair competition when joined with a "substantial and related claim" under the patent laws. The doctrine of pendent jurisdiction is one of discretion, and the standard of review is abuse of discretion.[71] Whether or not an act constitutes the tort of unfair competition under §1338(b) is a question of law that the Federal Circuit reviews de novo.[72]

Section 1338(b) was enacted to authorize a federal court to assume jurisdiction over a nonfederal unfair competition claim joined in the same case with a federal cause of action arising from U.S. patent, copyright, plant variety protection, or trademark laws, in an effort to avoid piecemeal litigation.[73] Where state issues substantially predominate, whether in terms of proof or the scope of the issues raised or the remedy sought, a court may decline to exercise jurisdiction. Section 1338(b) does not curtail such discretion.[74] Thus a state or federal claim of unfair competition may be appended to a related claim of patent infringement under 28 U.S.C. §1338(b). However, this is a jurisdictional statute that does not create the substantive right

---

whether it meets the jurisdictional requirement. *Chula Vista Sch. Dist. v. Bennett,* 824 F.2d 1573 (Fed. Cir. 1987).

[68]*Beghin-Say Int'l, Inc. v. Ole-Bendt Rasmussen,* 733 F.2d 1568, 221 USPQ 1121 (Fed. Cir. 1984).

[69]*Zumerling v. Devine,* 769 F.2d 745 (Fed. Cir. 1985).

[70]*Chemical Eng'g Corp. v. Marlo, Inc.,* 754 F.2d 331, 222 USPQ 738 (Fed. Cir. 1984).

[71]*Verdegaal Bros., Inc. v. Union Oil Co.,* 750 F.2d 947, 224 USPQ 249 (Fed. Cir. 1984). The Federal Circuit will apply regional circuit law, where discernible, in evaluating the district court's exercise of discretion on matters of pendent jurisdiction. *Id.* It is also within the discretion of the court to allow amendment of a complaint to add an alternative claim for breach of contract over which the court could also exercise pendent jurisdiction if it chose to do so. *Kunkel v. Topmaster Int'l, Inc.,* 906 F.2d 693, 15 USPQ2d 1367 (Fed. Cir. 1990).

[72]*Mars, Inc. v. Kabushiki-Kaisha Nippon Conlux,* 24 F.3d 1368, 30 USPQ2d 1621 (Fed. Cir. 1994).

[73]*Mars, Inc. v. Kabushiki-Kaisha Nippon Conlux,* 24 F.3d 1368, 30 USPQ2d 1621 (Fed. Cir. 1994).

[74]*Conopco, Inc. v. May Dep't Stores Co.,* 46 F.3d 1556, 32 USPQ2d 1225 (Fed. Cir. 1994). The court was able to pass the question of supplemental jurisdiction under 28 U.S.C. §1367, because that statute applies only to civil actions commenced on or after December 1, 1990, ruling out the present case.

underlying the claim. A litigant must find its substantive rights else-where.[75] The court indicates that pendent jurisdiction requires that the two claims in question "derive from a common nucleus of opera-tive fact."[76]

In its *Mars* decision,[77] the court undertook to flesh out the mean-ing of "unfair competition" as used in §1338(b). It started with the observation that when Congress borrows a common law term in a statute, absent a contrary instruction it is presumed to adopt the term's widely accepted common law meaning. The common law con-cept of unfair competition had not been confined to any rigid definition and encompasses a variety of types of commercial or business conduct considered "contrary to good conscience," including acts of trademark and trade dress infringement, false advertising, dilution, and trade secret theft. However, infringement of patent rights, domestic or for-eign, is not generally recognized as coming within the rubric of unfair competition. Unfair competition law and patent law have long existed as distinct and independent bodies of law, each with different origins and each protecting different rights. The law of unfair competition generally protects consumers and competitors from deceptive or un-ethical conduct in commerce. Patent law, on the other hand, protects a patent owner from the unauthorized use by others of the patented invention, irrespective of whether deception or unfairness exists. The distinction is also evident in the general statutory framework enacted by Congress. Whereas patent law is completely preempted by federal law, the law of unfair competition, despite some federal encroachment, remains largely free from federal exclusivity. The provisions of the federal patent law are not in pari materia with the state and federal provisions governing unfair competition. Moreover, §1338(b) itself expressly sets a claim of unfair competition apart from a claim arising under U.S. patent law. Although it does not make a comparable distinction regarding a claim arising under foreign patent law, that alone does not allow equation of these dissimilar causes of action.[78]

After deciding that a claim for infringement of a foreign patent is not a claim for unfair competition within the meaning of 28 U.S.C.

---

[75]*Mars, Inc. v. Kabushiki-Kaisha Nippon Conlux*, 24 F.3d 1368, 30 USPQ2d 1621 (Fed. Cir. 1994). There is no federal common law of unfair competition. *Water Techs. Corp. v. Calco, Ltd.*, 850 F.2d 660, 7 USPQ2d 1097 (Fed. Cir. 1988).

[76]*Windsurfing Int'l Inc. v. AMF Inc.*, 828 F.2d 755, 4 USPQ2d 1053 (Fed. Cir. 1987). The party was arguing that the district court had pendent jurisdiction to consider a challenge to another's trademarks, because it had alleged patent misuse with respect to trademark provis-ions of the other's patent licenses. The Federal Circuit denied jurisdiction on the ground that there was no identity of the trademarks and the patented inventions.

[77]*Mars, Inc. v. Kabushiki-Kaisha Nippon Conlux*, 24 F.3d 1368, 30 USPQ2d 1621 (Fed. Cir. 1994). The context of this decision was whether the district court had pendent or supplemental jurisdiction over a claim for infringement of a Japanese patent.

[78]Thus, in the absence of clear evidence that a claim of infringement of a foreign patent was intended by Congress to qualify as a claim of unfair competition under §1338(b), the court holds squarely, as a matter of law, that it does not. *Mars, Inc. v. Kabushiki-Kaisha Nippon Conlux*, 24 F.3d 1368, 30 USPQ2d 1621 (Fed. Cir. 1994).

§1338(b), the *Mars* court turned to the matter of supplemental jurisdiction under 28 U.S.C. §1367.[79] Under that doctrine, a federal court possesses the power to entertain a nonfederal claim if it is joined with a related federal claim such that the entire action before the court comprises but one constitutional "case." The requisite relatedness exists for jurisdictional purposes when the claims derive from a "common nucleus of operative fact" and, as such, would ordinarily be expected to be tried in one proceeding. Finally, when this power to hear a nonfederal claim is found to exist, the exercise of jurisdiction over it is nonetheless discretionary with the trial court.[80] A court may decline to exercise supplemental jurisdiction under certain circumstances spelled out in §1367(c), including where there has been a dismissal of all claims over which the court had original jurisdiction.[81]

A federal bankruptcy court can decide patent infringement claims.[82]

Sovereign immunity. The constitutional aspects of sovereign immunity and the matter of state immunity from patent infringement suits are treated in detail in §18.4. The terms of the government's consent to be sued in any particular court define that court's jurisdiction to entertain the suit.[83] Statutes waiving sovereign immunity are

---

[79]Section 1367 codified the basic principles articulated by the Supreme Court in *United Mine Workers v. Gibbs*, 383 U.S. 715 (1966).

[80]*Mars, Inc. v. Kabushiki-Kaisha Nippon Conlux*, 24 F.3d 1368, 30 USPQ2d 1621 (Fed. Cir. 1994). Applying these general principles, the Federal Circuit concluded that the district court lacked power under §1367(a) to hear a Japanese patent infringement claim because there were differences between the U.S. and Japanese patents, the accused devices and acts, and, of course, the governing laws. It seems clear that the court left some room for the exercise of federal jurisdiction over a foreign patent claim in an appropriate case. One can certainly foresee the possibility that a Canadian counterpart patent, for example, having identical or similar claims, could be asserted together with its U.S. sibling patent against the same device in a federal district court.

[81]*GAIA Tech., Inc. v. Reconversion Tech., Inc.*, 93 F.3d 774, 39 USPQ2d 1826 (Fed. Cir. 1996). Here, having dismissed the related patent and trademark claims, the court vacated the judgment as to the state law claims and remanded for a determination by the district court of whether it wishes to continue to entertain the state claims, a matter within its discretion. Note that the court entered subsequent orders at 104 F.3d 1296, 1298, which suggest that it may give further consideration to this issue. In *Textile Prods. Inc. v. Mead Corp.*, 134 F.3d 1481, 45 USPQ2d 1633 (Fed. Cir. 1998), a patent infringement claim was dismissed for lack of standing, and the trial court also dismissed a contract claim with prejudice. A simple dismissal for lack of jurisdiction would have been proper. There was no diversity, so the only basis for jurisdiction over the contract claim was supplemental jurisdiction. Once the patent infringement claim was dismissed, there was no longer any supplemental jurisdiction to consider the contract claim. Inasmuch as a lack of subject matter jurisdiction usually justifies only a dismissal, not a dismissal with prejudice, it was error to dismiss it with prejudice.

[82]*Institut Pasteur v. Cambridge Biotech Corp.*, 186 F.3d 1356, 51 USPQ2d 1321 (Fed. Cir. 1999). A patent infringement claim in bankruptcy court is, like other tort claims, an assertion of a right to payment and therefore constitutes a bankruptcy "claim." It is therefore a "core proceeding" within the meaning of 28 U.S.C. §157(b)(2)(B). *Id.*

[83]*NEC Corp. v. United States*, 806 F.2d 247 (Fed. Cir. 1986). However, in the context of a suit against a private party in a district court, 28 U.S.C. §1498(a) is not jurisdictional, but simply provides an affirmative defense that can be waived. *Manville Sales Corp. v. Paramount Sys., Inc.*, 917 F.2d 544, 16 USPQ2d 1587 (Fed. Cir. 1990).

strictly construed.[84] Also, the conditions upon which the government consents to be sued must be strictly observed and are not subject to implied limitations.[85] The Federal Circuit has held that the Tort Claims Act, 28 U.S.C. §1346(b), did not waive immunity with respect to suit against the PTO Commissioner on the ground that he erred in instituting an interference proceeding.[86]

Effect of appeal or other action. Typically, the filing of a notice of appeal removes jurisdiction from the district court. In general, a valid appeal ousts the district court of jurisdiction to proceed with any matters involved in the appeal. Sometimes a fine line is drawn. Thus in one case the district court ordered a preliminary injunction but did not issue supporting findings and conclusions until after the notice of appeal had been filed. The belated findings were viewed as "illegitimate" and the case was remanded.[87] But in another case, the district court made oral findings and conclusions and entered a judgment, then later submitted more polished, formal, written findings. The losing party appealed first from the judgment and then from the entry of the written findings. The Federal Circuit decided that the written findings were effective and that the appeal should be decided with reference to them.[88]

The court has held that the trial court had jurisdiction to consider a motion brought under Rule 37, FRCP, for expenses for failure to admit pursuant to Rule 36, after appeal from a grant of summary judgment.[89] On the other hand, a district court is without jurisdiction subsequent to an order of the Multidistrict Litigation Panel transferring the action to another district court.[90]

The regional circuits are split on whether a district court, after final judgment, retains jurisdiction from the original action (under §1338) or must have independent jurisdiction (e.g., diversity) to enforce a settlement agreement that was not incorporated into the final

---

[84]*Beachboard v. United States,* 727 F.2d 1092 (Fed. Cir. 1984). Note that the Claims Court can dismiss a case on grounds of laches even though it lacks jurisdiction over equitable claims. *Foster v. United States,* 733 F.2d 88 (Fed. Cir. 1984).

[85]*NEC Corp. v. United States,* 806 F.2d 247 (Fed. Cir. 1986).

[86]*Case v. CPC Int'l,* 730 F.2d 745, 221 USPQ 196 (Fed. Cir. 1984).

[87]*Chemlawn Serv. Corp. v. GNC Pumps, Inc.,* 823 F.2d 515, 3 USPQ2d 1313 (Fed. Cir. 1987) (Fifth Circuit law). This was not one of those unusual cases where effective review on the merits would be possible without the aid of findings and conclusions, and to rely on the belated findings and conclusions would have been improper since it might encourage other district courts to circumvent the requirements of Rule 52(a), FRCP.

[88]*Under Sea Indus., Inc. v. Dacor Corp.,* 833 F.2d 1551, 4 USPQ2d 1772 (Fed. Cir. 1987). The second appeal was ineffective, inasmuch as appeals are taken from judgments not findings and conclusions. Nonetheless, there is nothing to prevent a district judge from entering written findings subsequent to judgment where he had indicated to the parties that he intended to do that. The court here seems to be viewing the written set as simply a formalized version of the oral set.

[89]*Chemical Eng'g Corp. v. Essef Indus., Inc.,* 795 F.2d 1565, 230 USPQ 385 (Fed. Cir. 1986). The Rule 37 motion was filed long before the appeal briefs were due.

[90]*Glasstech, Inc. v. AB Kyro OY,* 769 F.2d 1574, 226 USPQ 949 (Fed. Cir. 1985).

judgment. The Federal Circuit has resolved the matter in favor of retention of jurisdiction.[91] Clearly, a court may retain jurisdiction to enforce an agreement settling a case over which it once presided by incorporating the agreement into an order of dismissal. The order need not use the word "incorporate" or any other magic form of words; rather, the court need only manifest an inferable intent to retain jurisdiction.[92] Settlement moots an action, although jurisdiction remains with the district court to enter a consent judgment.[93]

A trial court has discretion to dismiss a complaint that simply duplicates another pending related action.[94]

(ii) Declaratory Judgments in General

In a case of actual controversy within its jurisdiction, a federal district court may declare the rights and other legal relations of the parties.[95] The key words are "a case of actual controversy." Federal courts do not issue advisory opinions.[96] Indeed, under the "case or controversy" requirement of Article III of the Constitution, a federal court is without power to give advisory opinions, because such opinions cannot affect the rights of the litigants in the cases before it.[97] A declaratory judgment action may be brought in order to resolve an actual controversy between interested parties. The purpose of the Declaratory Judgment Act is to enable a person who is reasonably at legal risk because of an unresolved dispute to obtain judicial resolution of that dispute without having to await the commencement of legal action by the other side. It accommodates the situation wherein the interests of one side to the dispute may be served by delay in

---

[91]*Joy Mfg. Co. v. National Mine Serv. Co.*, 810 F.2d 1127, 1 USPQ2d 1627 (Fed. Cir. 1987). However, a divided panel indicated, in a dictum, that there would be no contempt jurisdiction for violation of the agreement. *Id.*

[92]*Interspiro USA, Inc. v. Figgie Int'l, Inc.*, 18 F.3d 927, 30 USPQ2d 1070 (Fed. Cir. 1994). The court applied Third Circuit law in reaching this decision. Was this really necessary, in view of the court's prior willingness (see note 8:91 and accompanying text) to resolve a split among the regional circuits as to whether there need be any incorporation at all? Certainly *Figgie* implies that an action to enforce an agreement settling a patent infringement case is one arising under the patent laws.

[93]*Gould v. Control Laser Corp.*, 866 F.2d 1391, 9 USPQ2d 1718 (Fed. Cir. 1989). The settlement licensed the defendant under claims found valid, and an explicit reservation in the settlement agreement of the issue regarding invalid claims could not serve to maintain the controversy between the parties.

[94]*Finch v. Hughes Aircraft Co.*, 926 F.2d 1574, 17 USPQ2d 1914 (Fed. Cir. 1991).

[95]28 U.S.C. §2201.

[96]*Goodyear Tire & Rubber Co. v. Releasomers, Inc.*, 824 F.2d 953, 3 USPQ2d 1310 (Fed. Cir. 1987); *International Med. Pros. v. Gore Ent. Holdings, Inc.*, 787 F.2d 572, 229 USPQ 278 (Fed. Cir. 1986).

[97]*United States v. Cook*, 795 F.2d 987 (Fed. Cir. 1986). The Declaratory Judgment Act, 28 U.S.C. §2201(a), parallels Article III of the Constitution, requiring an actual controversy between the parties before a federal court may exercise jurisdiction. This requires the presence of a substantial controversy, between parties having adverse legal interests, of sufficient immediacy and reality to warrant the issuance of a declaratory judgment. *EMC Corp. v. Norand Corp.*, 89 F.3d 807, 39 USPQ2d 1451 (Fed. Cir. 1996).

taking legal action. However, the controversy must be actual, not hypothetical or of uncertain prospective occurrence. The requirement of actual controversy encompasses concepts such as ripeness, standing, and the prohibition against advisory judicial rulings.[98]

The competing considerations in declaratory judgment jurisdiction are of constitutional dimension: (1) there must be an actual controversy over which a federal court may exercise jurisdiction; and (2) to proceed in the absence of a case or controversy would involve the court in rendering a forbidden advisory opinion. In deciding between these competing considerations there is no specific, all-purpose test.[99] The statutory authorization is the same as the constitutional requirement: declaratory judgment jurisdiction is predicated upon the existence of a case or controversy between the parties.[100]

What counts, then, is whether an actual controversy exists.[101] A justiciable case or controversy requires a real and substantial dispute affecting the legal rights and obligations of parties having adverse interests.[102] The sole requirement for jurisdiction under the Declaratory Judgment Act is that the conflict be real and immediate, i.e., that there be a true, actual "controversy" as required by the Act.[103] Declaratory judgment jurisdiction exists when an examination of the totality of the circumstances indicates that an actual controversy exists between the parties involved.[104] The burden is on the plaintiff to establish the existence of the controversy, both at the time of the complaint and continuing thereafter.[105] The jurisdictional facts must

---

[98]*BP Chems. Ltd. v. Union Carbide Corp.*, 4 F.3d 975, 28 USPQ2d 1124 (Fed. Cir. 1993).

[99]*Arrowhead Indus. Water, Inc. v. Ecolochem, Inc.*, 846 F.2d 731, 6 USPQ2d 1685 (Fed. Cir. 1988).

[100]*Goodyear Tire & Rubber Co. v. Releasomers, Inc.*, 824 F.2d 953, 3 USPQ2d 1310 (Fed. Cir. 1987); *Jervis B. Webb Co. v. Southern Sys., Inc.*, 742 F.2d 1388, 222 USPQ 943 (Fed. Cir. 1984).

[101]*International Med. Pros. v. Gore Ent. Holdings, Inc.*, 787 F.2d 572, 229 USPQ 278 (Fed. Cir. 1986).

[102]*C.R. Bard, Inc. v. Schwartz*, 716 F.2d 874, 219 USPQ 197 (Fed. Cir. 1983).

[103]*Arrowhead Indus. Water, Inc. v. Ecolochem, Inc.*, 846 F.2d 731, 6 USPQ2d 1685 (Fed. Cir. 1988).

[104]*Shell Oil Co. v. Amoco Corp.*, 970 F.2d 885, 23 USPQ2d 1627 (Fed. Cir. 1992); *Indium Corp. v. Semi-Alloys, Inc.*, 781 F.2d 879, 228 USPQ 845 (Fed. Cir. 1985). In *Arrowhead Indus. Water, Inc. v. Ecolochem, Inc.*, 846 F.2d 731, 6 USPQ2d 1685 (Fed. Cir. 1988), the plaintiff filed a declaratory judgment complaint that was dismissed for want of an actual controversy. A new complaint was filed, alleging an additional jurisdictional fact. The court rejected as totally insupportable the defendant's argument that jurisdiction should turn on whether the additional jurisdictional fact alone can establish the controversy.

[105]*International Med. Pros. v. Gore Ent. Holdings, Inc.*, 787 F.2d 572, 229 USPQ 278 (Fed. Cir. 1986); *Indium Corp. v. Semi- Alloys, Inc.*, 781 F.2d 879, 228 USPQ 845 (Fed. Cir. 1985). The controversy must exist as of the filing of the complaint seeking the declaratory judgment and may well have to continue until conclusion of the action. See *Jervis B. Webb Co. v. Southern Sys., Inc.*, 742 F.2d 1388, 222 USPQ 943 (Fed. Cir. 1984). The reasonable apprehension test is an objective one, to be applied to the facts at the time the complaint is filed. Thus, an actual suit filed by the defendant against the plaintiff months after the declaratory judgment action was filed cannot be considered in assessing the reasonable apprehension of suit. *West Interactive Corp. v. First Data Resources, Inc.*, 972 F.2d 1295, 23 USPQ2d 1927 (Fed. Cir. 1992).

be alleged in the complaint,[106] and if the defendant denies the factual allegations that allegedly support the existence of a case or controversy, the party seeking the declaratory judgment must prove the underlying facts.[107]

If the jurisdictional facts are undisputed, the question of declaratory judgment jurisdiction is one of law, and the clearly erroneous standard is not involved.[108] There is no absolute right to a declaratory judgment. The statute says a court "may" grant one. Hence, when there is a clear controversy and thus jurisdiction, a district court's decision on whether to exercise that jurisdiction is discretionary.[109] The Declaratory Judgment Act places a remedial arrow in the district court's quiver and creates an opportunity, rather than a duty, to grant a new form of relief to qualifying litigants.[110]

The Federal Circuit recognizes that the Supreme Court regards the district court's discretion in this respect as uniquely broad and insists that the appellate courts use a deferential abuse of discretion standard for review.[111] But the district court's discretion on declaratory judgment jurisdiction is not unfettered. It cannot, for example, decline jurisdiction as a matter of whim or personal disinclination. But there is no requirement that special circumstances must be present. Considerations of practicality and wise judicial administration are sufficient.[112]

Certainly a dismissal must provide some insight as to the exercise of such discretion.[113] The reason for giving this limited discretion to the district court is to enable it to make a reasoned judgment whether the investment of judicial time and resources in a declaratory action

---

[106]*International Med. Pros. v. Gore Ent. Holdings, Inc.,* 787 F.2d 572, 229 USPQ 278 (Fed. Cir. 1986).

[107]*Jervis B. Webb Co. v. Southern Sys., Inc.,* 742 F.2d 1388, 222 USPQ 943 (Fed. Cir. 1984).

[108]*Arrowhead Indus. Water, Inc. v. Ecolochem, Inc.,* 846 F.2d 731, 6 USPQ2d 1685 (Fed. Cir. 1988). Whether an actual controversy exists upon particular facts is a question of law and is subject to plenary appellate review. The district court's factual findings pertinent thereto are reviewed for clear error under Rule 52(a), FRCP. *BP Chems. Ltd. v. Union Carbide Corp.,* 4 F.3d 975, 28 USPQ2d 1124 (Fed. Cir. 1993). The district court's view of the fact pattern before it is not to be lightly disregarded. *Super Sack Mfg. Corp. v. Chase Packaging Corp.,* 57 F.3d 1054, 35 USPQ2d 1139 (Fed. Cir. 1995).

[109]*Arrowhead Indus. Water, Inc. v. Ecolochem, Inc.,* 846 F.2d 731, 6 USPQ2d 1685 (Fed. Cir. 1988). Dismissal for lack of declaratory judgment jurisdiction is reviewed as a matter of law, keeping in mind that the district court's view of the legal effect of the fact pattern before it is not to be easily disregarded. *Spectronics Corp. v. H.B. Fuller Co.,* 940 F.2d 631, 19 USPQ2d 1545 (Fed. Cir. 1991).

[110]*EMC Corp. v. Norand Corp.,* 89 F.3d 807, 39 USPQ2d 1451, 1454 (Fed. Cir. 1996).

[111]*EMC Corp. v. Norand Corp.,* 89 F.3d 807, 39 USPQ2d 1451 (Fed. Cir. 1996). Compare, e.g., *Genentech, Inc. v. Eli Lilly & Co.,* 998 F.2d 931, 27 USPQ2d 1241 (Fed. Cir. 1993).

[112]*EMC Corp. v. Norand Corp.,* 89 F.3d 807, 39 USPQ2d 1451 (Fed. Cir. 1996). Nor can it dismiss a declaratory judgment action merely because a parallel infringement suit was subsequently filed in another district; to take such action without any other reasons would be contrary to the general rule favoring the forum of the first filed action. *Id.* The court must make a reasoned judgment whether the investment of time and resources will be worthwhile. *Serco Servs. Co. v. Kelley Co.,* 51 F.3d 1037, 34 USPQ2d 1217 (Fed. Cir. 1995).

[113]*Goodyear Tire & Rubber Co. v. Releasomers, Inc.,* 824 F.2d 953, 3 USPQ2d 1310 (Fed. Cir. 1987).

will prove worthwhile in resolving a justiciable dispute. Situations justifying exercise of discretion to accept jurisdiction include (1) when the judgment will serve a useful purpose in clarifying and settling the legal relations in issue, and (2) when it will terminate and afford relief from the uncertainty, insecurity, and controversy giving rise to the proceeding.[114]

When a court enters an order that a party does not like, the party's recourse is to seek relief on appeal; it is not appropriate for the party to contest the court's order by filing a new action seeking a declaratory judgment challenging the court's ruling in the first case. This is not a case in which the party seeking declaratory relief argues that it cannot obtain a just adjudication of its rights in the first action and that declaratory relief is necessary to preserve important rights that otherwise would be unjustifiably lost. If permitted, such a strategy would undermine three strong and related policies of federal procedure: (1) that litigation relating to a single matter should take place in a single action, (2) that a district court's order in one action should be reviewed by the statutory method of appeal, not by a collateral proceeding for a declaratory judgment, and (3) that, with limited exceptions, review of a district court's ruling should take place only after a final judgment is entered in the case.[115]

Where Federal Circuit jurisdiction over a trademark issue arises only because the district court's jurisdiction was based in part on 28 U.S.C. §1338(a), the court will look to the law of the regional circuit to determine the existence of a case or controversy on that issue.[116] But where the issue clearly implicates the jurisprudential responsibilities of the court in a field within its exclusive jurisdiction, such as a patent case, the court does not regard itself as bound by decisions of the regional circuits on declaratory judgment jurisdiction.[117]

In promulgating the Declaratory Judgment Act, Congress intended to prevent avoidable damages from being incurred by a person

---

[114]*Minnesota Min. & Mfg. Co. v. Norton Co.*, 929 F.2d 670, 18 USPQ2d 1302 (Fed. Cir. 1991). However, the statement that such a decision lies within the discretion of the trial court does not rigidly fix the decision's reviewability. In this case the court clearly signals a broader standard of review by indicating that it must determine whether the district court properly balanced the needs of the plaintiff and the consequences of exercising jurisdiction. That determination does not depend on particular observations of witnesses by the trial court and thus the trial court's decision is not accorded the narrow review reserved for such discretionary decisions.

[115]*Glitsch Inc. v. Koch Eng'g Co.*, 216 F.3d 1382, 55 USPQ2d 1374 (Fed. Cir. 2000). In an infringement case, the defendant had sought to amend its answer to assert a misuse defense. The district court denied the motion as untimely. The party then brought a separate declaratory judgment action asserting misuse. The district court granted summary judgment on the ground that the party had waived its right to litigate the defense. The Federal Circuit affirmed, not on the basis of waiver, but on the ground that the party was not entitled to use a declaratory judgment action to collaterally attack the district court's order in the first action denying its motion to amend its answer.

[116]*Windsurfing Int'l, Inc. v. AMF Inc.*, 828 F.2d 755, 4 USPQ2d 1053 (Fed. Cir. 1987).

[117]*Goodyear Tire & Rubber Co. v. Releasomers, Inc.*, 824 F.2d 953, 3 USPQ2d 1310 (Fed. Cir. 1987). The decision to assume declaratory judgment jurisdiction in a case where the patent in question is involved in an interference is of importance to the development of patent law. Accordingly, the court regards it as a matter that falls within its exclusive subject matter

uncertain of his or her rights and threatened with damage by delayed adjudication. Where a party and its customers have been threatened with the prospect of infringement, and it continues to sell products it believes do not infringe, its potential liability grows.[118] Patent suits, like any others, must reflect an actual controversy and be within the original jurisdiction of the trial court. For a federal court to have jurisdiction of a declaratory judgment action in a patent case where diversity is not present, it must first find that the case arises under the patent laws.[119] Where there is no diversity between the parties, the federal Declaratory Judgment Act, 28 U.S.C. §2201, does not create an independent source of federal court jurisdiction.[120]

Thus, a declaratory action neither confers nor constrains jurisdiction or immunity. The Declaratory Judgment Act does not provide a substantive right; it provides a procedure whereby an aggrieved person may obtain a declaration of legal rights and relations. It is the Patent Act that states the law; the declaratory judgment procedure may be invoked when there is a controversy concerning an assertion of substantive rights under the Patent Act. To determine jurisdiction or immunity as to a particular cause of action it is necessary to look to the substantive violation and other relevant criteria, not to the procedure for obtaining relief. An action seeking a declaration of patent invalidity arises under the patent law, as do actions seeking a declaration of infringement or noninfringement.[121]

Declaratory judgment jurisdiction is evaluated by applying the well-pleaded complaint rule, considering the hypothetical complaint that the declaratory defendant would have brought.[122] If, but for the availability of the declaratory judgment procedure, the federal claim would arise only as a defense to a state-created cause of action, jurisdiction is lacking in the federal court.[123] The court has made it clear

---

jurisdiction and will not defer to the law of the regional circuit. *Minnesota Min. & Mfg. Co. v. Norton Co.,* 929 F.2d 670, 18 USPQ2d 1302 (Fed. Cir. 1991).

[118]*Minnesota Min. & Mfg. Co. v. Norton Co.,* 929 F.2d 670, 18 USPQ2d 1302 (Fed. Cir. 1991). In this case the declaratory plaintiff had instituted an interference with the patent in suit and an award of priority in its favor would moot the infringement question. Nonetheless, the Federal Circuit reversed the lower court's discretionary dismissal of the action.

[119]*C.R. Bard, Inc. v. Schwartz,* 716 F.2d 874, 219 USPQ 197 (Fed. Cir. 1983). The declaratory judgment statute, 28 U.S.C. §2201, creates an additional remedy where the court has original jurisdiction. *Id.*

[120]*Speedco, Inc. v. Estes,* 853 F.2d 909, 7 USPQ2d 1637 (Fed. Cir. 1988). See *MCV, Inc. v. King-Seeley Thermos Co.,* 870 F.2d 1568, 10 USPQ2d 1287 (Fed. Cir. 1989).

[121]*Genentech, Inc. v. Eli Lilly & Co.,* 998 F.2d 931, 27 USPQ2d 1241 (Fed. Cir. 1993). In *Merck & Co. v. Kessler,* 80 F.3d 1543, 38 USPQ2d 1347 (Fed. Cir. 1996), several plaintiffs with drug patents whose terms had been extended persuaded the court that an actual controversy was present in their declaratory judgment action against the FDA and the PTO seeking a review of a final determination of the PTO regarding the interplay of the Hatch-Waxman Act and the URAA.

[122]*Fina Oil & Chem. Co. v. Ewen,* 123 F.3d 1466, 43 USPQ2d 1935 (Fed. Cir. 1997).

[123]*Speedco, Inc. v. Estes,* 853 F.2d 909, 7 USPQ2d 1637 (Fed. Cir. 1988). Here the inventor had sold the patent for cash and a promissory note. The assignee made one payment on the note and then quit paying on the ground that the inventor had obtained the patent fraudulently. The assignee also brought a federal declaratory judgment action, seeking a determination by

that, at least in patent matters, the fact that an issue arises in the context of a declaratory judgment action does not affect the underlying right to a jury trial.[124]

Declaratory judgment actions involving trademarks are analogous to those involving patents.[125] The test for determining whether an actual case or controversy exists in a declaratory judgment action involving trademarks is likewise two pronged. First, the declaratory plaintiff must have a real and reasonable apprehension of litigation. Second, the declaratory plaintiff must have engaged in a course of conduct that brought it into adversarial conflict with the declaratory defendant.[126]

Despite the broad language in 28 U.S.C. §2201, the Claims Court lacks declaratory judgment jurisdiction. The enabling statute, 28 U.S.C. §1491, does not purport to confer such jurisdiction; that would require a statute specifically waiving sovereign immunity and authorizing declaratory judgments.[127]

(iii) Declaratory Judgments in Patent Cases

Inasmuch as a declaratory judgment respecting patent validity would otherwise be merely advisory, an actual controversy is required.[128] In patent cases this means there must be a reasonable threat that the patentee will bring an infringement suit against the alleged infringer.[129] A declaratory judgment plaintiff has the burden of establishing that it reasonably believed the patentee had intent to initiate a patent infringement suit.[130] On appeal, the Federal Circuit

---

the court as to the validity and enforceability of the patent, and reformation of the terms of the assignment in accordance with the court's evaluation of the real value of the patent. The Federal Circuit held this was not a case arising under the patent laws. The only claim the declaratory defendant could have brought, in the absence of a complete renouncement of the assignment by the assignee, was a state law contract action to enforce the terms of the contract and recover the overdue payments owed on the note. The inventor would not be required, as an element of such a claim, to show that the patent is valid, for patents are presumed valid. Invalidity would only be a defense to the state contract action. On the other hand, since ownership of a patent is normally a requisite to sue for infringement, the defendant would somehow have to regain title. This makes the case distinguishable from *C.R. Bard, Inc. v. Schwartz*, 716 F.2d 874, 219 USPQ 197 (Fed. Cir. 1983), where the declaratory plaintiff was a licensee, not an assignee. There the declaratory defendant retained title and could have terminated the license and sued for infringement.

[124]*In re Lockwood*, 50 F.3d 966, 33 USPQ2d 1406 (Fed. Cir. 1995). The Supreme Court granted certiorari to review this case, but the issue was mooted by agreement of the parties.

[125]*Windsurfing Int'l Inc. v. AMF Inc.*, 828 F.2d 755, 4 USPQ2d 1053 (Fed. Cir. 1987).

[126]*Windsurfing Int'l Inc. v. AMF Inc.*, 828 F.2d 755, 4 USPQ2d 1053 (Fed. Cir. 1987). Here the plaintiff merely had a desire to use the mark, but did not choose to go ahead and use it and fight it out in court. A mere commercial interest is not sufficient. A justiciable controversy is one that touches the legal relations of parties having adverse legal interests. *Id.*

[127]*Beachboard v. United States*, 727 F.2d 1092 (Fed. Cir. 1984).

[128]*International Med. Pros. v. Gore Ent. Holdings, Inc.*, 787 F.2d 572, 229 USPQ 278 (Fed. Cir. 1986).

[129]*C.R. Bard, Inc. v. Schwartz*, 716 F.2d 874, 219 USPQ 197 (Fed. Cir. 1983).

[130]*West Interactive Corp. v. First Data Resources, Inc.*, 972 F.2d 1295, 23 USPQ2d 1927 (Fed. Cir. 1992); *Shell Oil Co. v. Amoco Corp.*, 970 F.2d 885, 23 USPQ2d 1627 (Fed. Cir. 1992).

must determine whether the trial court erred in finding that the plaintiff failed to meet that burden. The legal effect of the parties' conduct, and in particular whether it was sufficient to create an actual controversy, is a question of law that is reviewed de novo. The Federal Circuit applies its own law.[131] The actual controversy requirement is satisfied when a defendant patentee's conduct has created on the part of the declaratory judgment plaintiff a reasonable apprehension that it will face an infringement suit if it commences or continues the activity in question and when it has actually produced the accused device or has prepared to produce such a device.[132] The same reasoning applies in a case of threatened infringement: if the controversy requirement is met by a sufficient allegation of immediacy and reality, there is no reason why a patentee should be unable to seek a declaration of infringement against a future infringer.[133]

In *Arrowhead v. Ecolochem,*[134] the court expounded at some length on what it terms a two-pronged test for determining declaratory judgment jurisdiction in patent cases. First, the defendant's conduct must have created on the part of the plaintiff a reasonable apprehension that the defendant will initiate suit if the plaintiff continues the allegedly infringing activity. Second, the plaintiff must actually have either produced the device or prepared to produce the device. The test is objective and is applied to the facts existing when the complaint is filed. Its first prong looks to defendant's conduct; its second to that of plaintiff. Basically, the test requires two core elements: (1) acts of defendant indicating an intent to enforce its patent; and (2) acts of plaintiff that might subject it or its customers to suit for patent infringement.[135]

Plaintiff's conduct must be such as to establish that it has a true interest to be protected by the declaratory judgment. A plaintiff may

---

[131]*Shell Oil Co. v. Amoco Corp.,* 970 F.2d 885, 23 USPQ2d 1627 (Fed. Cir. 1992).

[132]*Cordis Corp. v. Medtronic, Inc.,* 835 F.2d 859, 5 USPQ2d 1118 (Fed. Cir. 1987); *Goodyear Tire & Rubber Co. v. Releasomers, Inc.,* 824 F.2d 953, 3 USPQ2d 1310 (Fed. Cir. 1987); *International Med. Pros. v. Gore Ent. Holdings, Inc.,* 787 F.2d 572, 229 USPQ 278 (Fed. Cir. 1986); *Indium Corp. v. Semi-Alloys, Inc.,* 781 F.2d 879, 228 USPQ 845 (Fed. Cir. 1985); *Jervis B. Webb Co. v. Southern Sys., Inc.,* 742 F.2d 1388, 222 USPQ 943 (Fed. Cir. 1984).

[133]*Lang v. Pacific Marine & Supply Co.,* 895 F.2d 761, 13 USPQ2d 1820 (Fed. Cir. 1990). The accused infringing ship's hull was under construction, but would not be finished until at least nine months after the complaint was filed. This was not of sufficient immediacy to meet the actual controversy requirement, and the court affirmed the dismissal of the declaratory judgment claim for lack of jurisdiction. In *Telectronics Pacing Sys., Inc. v. Ventritex, Inc.,* 982 F.2d 1520, 25 USPQ2d 1196 (Fed. Cir. 1992), the defendant was engaged in the process of obtaining FDA approval for a medical device and was thus not an infringer by virtue of 35 U.S.C. §271(e)(1). At the commencement of suit, the device had only recently begun clinical trials and was years away from potential FDA approval. There was no certainty that the device when approved would be the same device that began clinical trials, inasmuch as product changes during testing are contemplated by statute. On these facts the declaratory judgment claim was dismissed for want of jurisdiction.

[134]*Arrowhead Indus. Water, Inc. v. Ecolochem, Inc.,* 846 F.2d 731, 6 USPQ2d 1685 (Fed. Cir. 1988).

[135]*Arrowhead Indus. Water, Inc. v. Ecolochem, Inc.,* 846 F.2d 731, 6 USPQ2d 1685 (Fed. Cir. 1988). See also, e.g., *EMC Corp. v. Norand Corp.,* 89 F.3d 807, 39 USPQ2d 1451 (Fed. Cir.

not, for example, obtain a declaratory judgment merely because it would like an advisory opinion on whether it would be liable for patent infringement if it were to initiate some merely contemplated activity. The plaintiff must be engaged in an actual making, selling, or using activity subject to an infringement charge, or must have made meaningful preparation for such activity. The former admits of rather straightforward proofs; the latter can be more problematic. Whether a declaratory plaintiff's ability and definite intention to undertake a potentially infringing activity constitutes sufficient "preparation" is a question of degree to be resolved on a case-by-case basis.[136]

Reasonable apprehension of suit. The injury of which a declaratory judgment plaintiff complains is a wrongful restraint on the free exploitation of noninfringing goods. One of those restraints may be the threat of an infringement suit, as communicated in a cease-and-desist letter. In the event a patentee casts its net of cease-and-desist letters too widely and entangles some noninfringing products, a plaintiff may have little recourse other than a declaratory judgment action to disentangle its noninfringing business. In those instances, the cease-and-desist letters are the cause of the entanglement and at least partially give rise to the plaintiff's action.[137] The defendant's conduct must be such as to indicate its intent to enforce its patent. If it has expressly charged a current activity of the plaintiff as an infringement, there is clearly an actual controversy, certainty has rendered apprehension irrelevant, and one need say no more.[138] In light of the subtleties of lawyer language, however, the courts have not required an express infringement charge.[139] When the defendant's conduct, including its statements, falls short of an express charge, one must consider the totality of the circumstances. If the circumstances warrant, a reasonable apprehension may be found in the absence of any communication from defendant to plaintiff. If, on the other hand, the defendant has done nothing but obtain a patent, there can be no

---

1996); *BP Chems. Ltd. v. Union Carbide Corp.*, 4 F.3d 975, 28 USPQ2d 1124 (Fed. Cir. 1993); *Genentech, Inc. v. Eli Lilly & Co.*, 998 F.2d 931, 27 USPQ2d 1241 (Fed. Cir. 1993).

[136]*Arrowhead Indus. Water, Inc. v. Ecolochem, Inc.*, 846 F.2d 731, 6 USPQ2d 1685 (Fed. Cir. 1988). On the question of infringing activity, an interest in practicing the invention of another does not satisfy the infringement prong of the two-part test. That a superior process is patented to another, and unavailable for use without a license, does not of itself create a justiciable controversy. *BP Chems. Ltd. v. Union Carbide Corp.*, 4 F.3d 975, 28 USPQ2d 1124 (Fed. Cir. 1993).

[137]*Red Wing Shoe Co. v. Hockerson-Halberstadt Inc.*, 148 F.3d 1355, 47 USPQ2d 1192 (Fed. Cir. 1998).

[138]*Arrowhead Indus. Water, Inc. v. Ecolochem, Inc.*, 846 F.2d 731, 6 USPQ2d 1685 (Fed. Cir. 1988). What if the patent owner, for purpose of forestalling a laches defense, provides written notice of its intent to enforce its patent? See, e.g., *Vaupel Textilmaschinen KG v. Meccanical Euro Italia S.P.A.*, 944 F.2d 870, 20 USPQ2d 1045 (Fed. Cir. 1991). Would this satisfy the immediacy requirement for declaratory judgment jurisdiction?

[139]*EMC Corp. v. Norand Corp.*, 89 F.3d 807, 39 USPQ2d 1451 (Fed. Cir. 1996); *Shell Oil Co. v. Amoco Corp.*, 970 F.2d 885, 23 USPQ2d 1627 (Fed. Cir. 1992); *Arrowhead Indus. Water, Inc. v. Ecolochem, Inc.*, 846 F.2d 731, 6 USPQ2d 1685 (Fed. Cir. 1988); *Goodyear Tire & Rubber Co. v. Releasomers, Inc.*, 824 F.2d 953, 3 USPQ2d 1310 (Fed. Cir. 1987).

basis for the required apprehension, a rule that protects quiescent patent owners against unwarranted litigation.[140] In what this author regards as something of an understatement, the court was quite candid about the reasonable apprehension inquiry:

> There is not always an easy demarcation between a reasonable apprehension on the part of a would-be infringer, and the situation whereby a patent, by its existence, inhibits unauthorized practice of its subject matter. The relationships are rarely as simple as they appear in judicial opinions.[141]

Of course, a patent must exist. A threat is not sufficient to create a case of actual controversy unless it is made with respect to a patent that has issued before the declaratory complaint is filed. Where suit was brought a month before the patent issued, the subsequent issuance did not cure the lack of a controversy.[142]

The court appears to be trending toward a narrow view of what constitutes a reasonable apprehension of suit, at least in the context of licensing negotiations. In one case, a statement that certain activities "fall within" patent claims was regarded as merely constituting a statement of the patentee's position in negotiations relative to the declaratory plaintiff's position. Also, the fact that the patentee answered "yes" when asked whether it intended to enforce its patent was seen to be merely reflexive and obligatory in license negotiations.[143] Although access to declaratory procedures in patent cases does not

---

[140]*Arrowhead Indus. Water, Inc. v. Ecolochem, Inc.,* 846 F.2d 731, 6 USPQ2d 1685 (Fed. Cir. 1988). Here the patentee wrote a customer, saying that plaintiff was not licensed and that any use of the patented process would be a direct infringement. It also wrote plaintiff and said that it had reason to believe that plaintiff had initiated or contemplated practice of the patented process, demanded immediate cessation, and indicated that it had not hesitated to protect its patent rights whenever appropriate. It later sued another infringer and asked the court in that case for a finding indicating that both the defendant there and the plaintiff here were practicing a process that infringes its patent. On this set of facts, the Federal Circuit found it difficult, if not impossible, to imagine how a prudent executive confronted with the totality of this conduct could resist the onset of a most reasonable apprehension that his or her company was next in line to be sued. Indeed, considering the realities of business life, such an executive could incur the wrath of stockholders if he or she either continued to offer the process without seeking a resolution of the obvious conflict, or supinely and unjustifiably abandoned the process. That the plaintiff's letter skillfully skirted an express charge of infringement was in this case meaningless.

[141]*BP Chems. Ltd. v. Union Carbide Corp.,* 4 F.3d 975, 28 USPQ2d 1124, 1128 (Fed. Cir. 1993).

[142]*GAF Building Mat. Corp. v. Elk Corp. of Dallas,* 90 F.3d 479, 39 USPQ2d 1463 (Fed. Cir. 1996).

[143]*Shell Oil Co. v. Amoco Corp.,* 970 F.2d 885, 23 USPQ2d 1627 (Fed. Cir. 1992). Any time parties are in negotiation over patent rights, the possibility of a lawsuit looms in the background. No patent owner with any sense would open negotiations by assuring the opposite party that it does not intend to enforce the patent under any circumstances. The threat of enforcement is the entire source of the patentee's bargaining power. Thus, it is unrealistic to suggest that some negotiating patentees intend to enforce their patents while some do not, and that the first group is subject to declaratory judgment actions while the second is not. *EMC Corp. v. Norand Corp.,* 89 F.3d 807, 39 USPQ2d 1451 (Fed. Cir. 1996). Although a patent owner's refusal to give assurances that it will not enforce its patent is relevant to the determination of reasonable apprehension of suit, it is not dispositive. *BP Chems. Ltd. v. Union Carbide Corp.,* 4 F.3d 975, 28 USPQ2d 1124 (Fed. Cir. 1993).

necessarily require an explicit threat of suit, there must be more than ongoing license negotiations. The reasonable apprehension of suit test requires more than the nervous state of mind of a possible infringer; it requires that the objective circumstances support such an apprehension.[144] Such "jawboning" is apparently not to be taken too seriously by potential infringers.[145] The test for finding a controversy for jurisdictional purposes is a pragmatic one and cannot turn on whether the parties use polite terms in dealing with one another or engage in more bellicose saber rattling. The need to look to substance rather than form is especially important in this area, because in many instances the parties are sensitive to the prospect of a declaratory judgment action and couch their exchanges in terms designed either to create or defeat declaratory judgment jurisdiction. The inquiry does not turn on whether the parties have used particular magic words in communicating with one another.[146]

Conduct of the defendant with respect to other litigation plays a strong role in determining the reasonableness of the declaratory plaintiff's apprehension. In one case the defendant had already sued the plaintiff for a large sum in state court, alleging misappropriation of trade secrets that involved the same technology as the patents at issue in the declaratory judgment complaint. The defendant had informed plaintiff of the patents and had made some innuendoes that could reasonably have led plaintiff to believe that a suit would be filed. Thus the fact that the defendant's president attested that he had never expressly authorized a suit for patent infringement was insufficient to avoid declaratory judgment jurisdiction. Intentions may change over time. The state court action amounted to a course of conduct that showed a willingness to protect the technology and that was sufficient to create a reasonable apprehension of suit.[147]

---

[144]*Phillips Plastics Corp. v. Kato Hatsujou K.K.*, 57 F.3d 1051, 35 USPQ2d 1222 (Fed. Cir. 1995). The patentee had written the declaratory plaintiff, stating that its products were covered by a patent and inviting plaintiff to take a license. Plaintiff responded that the patent was invalid. The patentee then filed for reissue and the plaintiff participated as a protester. After reissue, the patentee again wrote plaintiff, enclosing a copy of the reissued patent and offering a license. After some negotiation, plaintiff filed suit. The court agreed with plaintiff's argument that one who may become liable for infringement should not be subject to manipulation by a patentee who uses careful phrases in order to avoid explicit threats, thus denying recourse to the courts while damages accrue. Nonetheless, it held that negotiations had not really broken down and that the objective circumstances did not support a reasonable apprehension of litigation.

[145]In *West Interactive Corp. v. First Data Resources, Inc.*, 972 F.2d 1295, 23 USPQ2d 1927 (Fed. Cir. 1992), the fact that the inventor, an employee of a subsidiary of the patent owner, told the plaintiff that infringement of the patents would lead to legal problems was not sufficient, even in light of the patent owner's litigious history.

[146]*EMC Corp. v. Norand Corp.*, 89 F.3d 807, 39 USPQ2d 1451 (Fed. Cir. 1996).

[147]*Goodyear Tire & Rubber Co. v. Releasomers, Inc.*, 824 F.2d 953, 3 USPQ2d 1310 (Fed. Cir. 1987). Related litigation may be evidence of a reasonable apprehension. *Shell Oil Co. v. Amoco Corp.*, 970 F.2d 885, 23 USPQ2d 1627 (Fed. Cir. 1992). But see *West Interactive Corp. v. First Data Resources, Inc.*, 972 F.2d 1295, 23 USPQ2d 1927 (Fed. Cir. 1992), where the fact that defendant had already sued three other infringers was dismissed as pertinent but not conclusive, in that it did not show that defendant "invariably pursues litigation against alleged infringers."

What is going on in the industry, particularly other litigation, is relevant to the question of reasonable apprehension. A patentee can hardly be surprised if a company follows the prudent business course of monitoring a suit involving the same patent that the patentee is writing to the company and its customer about. Nothing in the law requires a competitor to blind itself to anything going on in its field of business. The law does not require enterprises to keep their heads in the sand while a patentee picks them off one by one at its leisure.[148]

The test is an objective one; a purely subjective apprehension of an infringement suit is insufficient to satisfy the actual controversy requirement.[149] In assessing reasonable apprehension of suit it is the objective words and actions of the patent owner that are controlling. Although such words and actions are not viewed in isolation of their intended effect on the listener, a subjective apprehension is insufficient without objective substance.[150]

There is of course no rule that a party seeking a declaratory judgment of patent invalidity must show an actual controversy by admitting infringement. Declaratory judgment plaintiffs who have been threatened with suit are at full liberty to deny infringement and often do. They are also at liberty to admit infringement while asserting that the patent is invalid and that no liability for the infringement can therefore exist. Admission of infringement is to be encouraged as a means of limiting the issues to be tried. But such an admission can have legal consequences beyond those that might result from an admission that one is making a product or practicing a process that is accused or that might at trial be found to be an infringement.[151] It would be incongruous to require that one seeking a declaration of noninfringement prove its process or product is the "same as" or "identical" to the patented process or product. The requirement is simply that the declaratory judgment plaintiff show use or preparation for use of a process that might at trial be found to be an infringement.[152] A nonparty to a pending infringement suit is of course under no obligation to seek intervention or to bring a declaratory judgment action.[153]

---

[148]*Arrowhead Indus. Water, Inc. v. Ecolochem, Inc.*, 846 F.2d 731, 6 USPQ2d 1685 (Fed. Cir. 1988). Certainly the fact that a competitor is suing a third party and asking the court there to find that one's company is a coinfringer can hardly contribute to euphoria. *Id.*

[149]*Indium Corp. v. Semi-Alloys, Inc.*, 781 F.2d 879, 228 USPQ 845 (Fed. Cir. 1985). This case may reflect a less than expansive reach on the part of the Federal Circuit with regard to declaratory judgment jurisdiction. The patentee had written the plaintiff and offered an opportunity to discuss a nonexclusive license, had sued other companies on the patents in question, and had sued the plaintiff for unfair competition in state court.

[150]*BP Chems. Ltd. v. Union Carbide Corp.*, 4 F.3d 975, 28 USPQ2d 1124 (Fed. Cir. 1993).

[151]*International Med. Pros. v. Gore Ent. Holdings, Inc.*, 787 F.2d 572, 229 USPQ 278 (Fed. Cir. 1986). It is difficult to conceive, however, of a justiciable controversy where neither party says there is any possibility of infringement. *Id.*

[152]*Arrowhead Indus. Water, Inc. v. Ecolochem, Inc.*, 846 F.2d 731, 6 USPQ2d 1685 (Fed. Cir. 1988).

[153]*Truswal Sys. Corp v. Hydro-Air Eng'g, Inc.*, 813 F.2d 1207, 2 USPQ2d 1034 (Fed. Cir. 1987). Of course, if the nonparty chooses not to do so, it cannot complain about the outcome. *Id.*

The Federal Circuit has said that the existence of a case or controversy is evaluated on a claim-by-claim basis in patent infringement litigation. Thus, where a complaint charges infringement of only some claims, a declaratory judgment counterclaim that raises the rest must be independently evaluated for reasonable apprehension of suit and preparations to infringe. [154] However, it is possible that this rule will be honored as much in the breach as in the observance, simply by oversight. [155]

In the first edition of this book the proposition was stated that a patentee cannot unilaterally remove the validity issue if the accused infringer has challenged the validity of the patent claim in a declaratory judgment counterclaim. [156] Later decisions cast substantial doubt on that proposition, [157] but the Supreme Court appears now to have confirmed it. [158]

An actual controversy must be extant at all stages of review, not merely at the time the complaint is filed. Subsequent events can

---

[154] *Jervis B. Webb Co. v. Southern Sys., Inc.*, 742 F.2d 1388, 222 USPQ 943 (Fed. Cir. 1984). Certainly this does not preclude a counterclaim on all claims where the complaint is on all claims, or a complaint for declaratory judgment on all claims in response to general accusations of infringement. Nor does it preclude a judgment declaring that all claims are invalid when the proofs at trial establish a generalized basis such as fraud or derivation. *Id.* On the other hand, where a complaint is amended prior to trial to drop several claims of the patent, it is error to hold the entire patent invalid in the absence of a declaratory judgment counterclaim. *Stearns v. Beckman Instr., Inc.*, 737 F.2d 1565, 222 USPQ 457 (Fed. Cir. 1984). In *Tol-O-Matic, Inc. v. Proma Produckt-und Mktg. GmbH*, 945 F.2d 1546, 20 USPQ2d 1332 (Fed. Cir. 1991), the accused infringer brought an action seeking a declaration that it did not infringe any claim of the defendant's patent. Only claim 25 was tried, on a stipulation that it was representative of claims 25–31. No evidence was introduced at trial on claims 1–24 or 32. The plaintiff was successful and on appeal argued that the judgment should cover all claims, not just claims 25–31, on the ground that the patentee had the burden of proof as to infringement and offered no evidence on the remaining claims. In rejecting this argument, the Federal Circuit said that pleadings do not suffice to support a judgment when the subject matter was not litigated or fairly placed in issue during the trial. There must be sufficient and explicit notice of the claims at risk. When the pleadings are not in complete harmony with the issues that were litigated and adjudicated, it is the pleadings that may be conformed to the judgment, not vice versa. But in *Westvaco Corp. v. International Paper Co.*, 991 F.2d 735, 26 USPQ2d 1353 (Fed. Cir. 1993), the plaintiff brought a declaratory judgment action to invalidate all of the claims and the defendant patent owner counterclaimed for infringement of fewer than all. The district court found all claims to be not invalid. On appeal, plaintiff argued that the lower court lacked jurisdiction as to the claims not asserted by the patent owner. The Federal Circuit refused to vacate the judgment as to those claims. The basis for the declaratory judgment jurisdiction was a general accusation of infringement that had never been withdrawn. Also, the plaintiff introduced evidence on invalidity of the unasserted claims at trial.

[155] See *Connell v. Sears, Roebuck & Co.*, 722 F.2d 1542, 220 USPQ 193 (Fed. Cir. 1983).

[156] See note 8:63 in the first edition, citing *Shelcore, Inc. v. Durham Indus., Inc.*, 745 F.2d 621, 223 USPQ 584 (Fed. Cir. 1984).

[157] E.g., *Perini Am., Inc. v. Paper Converting Mach. Co.*, 832 F.2d 581, 4 USPQ2d 1621 (Fed. Cir. 1987); *Vieau v. Japax, Inc.*, 823 F.2d 1510, 3 USPQ2d 1094 (Fed. Cir. 1987); *Fonar Corp. v. Johnson & Johnson*, 821 F.2d 627, 3 USPQ2d 1109 (Fed. Cir. 1987). The question is discussed in a more generalized context in §16.3(h).

[158] *Cardinal Chem. Co. v. Morton Int'l, Inc.*, 508 U.S. 83, 26 USPQ2d 1721 (1993). See *Morton Int'l, Inc. v. Cardinal Chem. Co.*, 5 F.3d 1464, 28 USPQ2d 1190 (Fed. Cir. 1993). In a recent case, the Federal Circuit interpreted *Cardinal* as being a relatively narrow decision, because it noted factors that in an unusual case might justify a refusal to reach the merits of a validity determination. Thus, the Federal Circuit interprets *Cardinal* this way: an affirmed finding of noninfringement does not, without more, justify a reviewing court's refusal to reach

change the picture.[159] And yet the Federal Circuit fully recognizes that the Declaratory Judgment Act serves the policies underlying the patent laws by enabling a test of the validity and infringement of patents that are possibly being used only as what Learned Hand called "scarecrows."[160] Indeed, one panel of the court said:

> This appeal presents a type of the sad and saddening scenario that led to enactment of the Declaratory Judgment Act. . . . In the patent version of that scenario, a patent owner engages in a danse macabre, brandishing a Democlean threat with a sheathed sword.
>
> . . . Guerrilla-like, the patent owner attempts extrajudicial patent enforcement with scare-the-customer-and-run tactics that infect the competitive environment of the business community with uncertainty and insecurity. . . . Before the Act, competitors victimized by that tactic were rendered helpless and immobile so long as the patent owner refused to grasp the nettle and sue. After the Act, those competitors were no longer restricted to an *in terrorem* choice between the incurrence of a growing potential liability for patent infringement and abandonment of their

---

the trial court's conclusion as to validity. *Super Sack Mfg. Corp. v. Chase Packaging Corp.*, 57 F.3d 1054, 35 USPQ2d 1139 (Fed. Cir. 1995).

[159]Where the patentee charged infringement of certain claims in the complaint, but abandoned the charge prior to trial and steadfastly refused thereafter to assert infringement of those claims, it was not error to refuse to decide the defendant's declaratory judgment counterclaim as to those claims. *Grain Processing Corp. v. American Maize-Products Co.*, 840 F.2d 902, 5 USPQ2d 1788 (Fed. Cir. 1988). But see *Environmental Instr., Inc. v. Sutron Corp.*, 877 F.2d 1561, 11 USPQ2d 1132 (Fed. Cir. 1989). In *Spectronics Corp. v. H.B. Fuller Co.*, 940 F.2d 631, 19 USPQ2d 1545 (Fed. Cir. 1991), there had been a sufficient controversy when the case was commenced, but the defendant patentee filed a reissue application and agreed not to sue the plaintiff on any of the original claims of the patent. Under these circumstances, the actual controversy did not survive and the district court was correct in dismissing the declaratory judgment action. Inasmuch as there was no guarantee that a reissue patent would eventually issue, and no way to tell what its claims might be, the plaintiff could not demonstrate that its present activity was a potential infringement of any existing patent claims. In *Amana Ref. Inc. v. Quadlux Inc.*, 172 F.3d 852, 50 USPQ2d 1304 (Fed. Cir. 1999), a covenant not to sue for infringement of a patent with respect to any product previously or currently advertised, manufactured, marketed, or sold, removed any reasonable apprehension of an infringement suit based on activities preceding the covenant, and thus divested the court of jurisdiction over a declaratory judgment action. The fact that plaintiff had new products in the pipeline did not alter this result, for an actual controversy cannot be based on a fear of litigation over future products. In *Super Sack Mfg. Corp. v. Chase Packaging Corp.*, 57 F.3d 1054, 35 USPQ2d 1139 (Fed. Cir. 1995), plaintiff sued for infringement and defendant counterclaimed for a declaratory judgment of invalidity and noninfringement. Plaintiff later decided to drop its claim, and unconditionally agreed that it would never assert the patents against any product that defendant was making as of the commencement of the litigation. The court held that this circumstance caused defendant's declaratory counterclaim to fail the second prong of the test for justiciability: the putative infringer's present activity must place it at risk of infringement liability. The mere possibility of a future infringement suit based upon future acts was simply too speculative a basis for jurisdiction. In *Fina Research S.A. v. Baroid Ltd.*, 141 F.3d 1479, 46 USPQ2d 1461 (Fed. Cir. 1998), the court indicated that a covenant not to sue is not the only way to dispel the pall of an already existing reasonable apprehension. The threat may dissipate because of, for example, changed circumstances. Such an exception to the requirements of *Super Sack* and *Spectronics* must necessarily be a narrow one, however. A later disavowal of threats to sue does not necessarily remove the reasonable apprehension of suit that the threats engender. Otherwise, a patentholder could attempt extrajudicial patent enforcement with scare-and-run tactics.

[160]*Bresnick v. United States Vitamin Corp.*, 139 F.2d 239, 242, 59 USPQ 345, 348 (2d Cir. 1943).

enterprises; they could clear the air by suing for a judgment that would settle the conflict of interests.[161]

Standing of licensees. Prior to the formation of the Federal Circuit, the regional circuits were split on whether a licensee could bring a declaratory judgment action to have the licensed patent declared invalid while the license is in effect. The Third Circuit had answered in the negative, on the ground that no infringement suit is possible while the license is effective.[162] The Second Circuit was in the affirmative, reasoning that nonpayment of royalties can subject a licensee to federal claims.[163] The Federal Circuit rejected the Third Circuit's flat prohibition and applied its standard "totality of the circumstances" test to determine whether there was a reasonable apprehension of an infringement suit.[164]

In another license case, the plaintiff was paying royalty on device A. The patentee indicated that device B also infringed and demanded a large payment for a paid-up future license on device B while making it clear that such payment would not relieve the plaintiff from past liability on device B. The court held that plaintiff had a reasonable apprehension of being sued for patent infringement on device B. This is different from a typical situation where the licensee raises noninfringement merely as a defense to a state contract action; here the plaintiff was asserting noninfringement and estoppel, both as bars to an infringement action.[165] In an interesting variation, the declaratory judgment plaintiff was a nonmanufacturing licensor. It made the argument that the two-part test for declaratory jurisdiction does not accommodate the situation where its licensing business is being undermined by threats directed to its actual or potential licensees. It asserted two legal interests: (1) its competitive interest in licensing technology, and (2) its liability for indemnification should its licensees be sued for infringement. The Federal Circuit rejected both interests because both required an actual controversy involving the indemnitee

---

[161]*Arrowhead Indus. Water, Inc. v. Ecolochem, Inc.*, 846 F.2d 731, 6 USPQ2d 1685, 1688 (Fed. Cir. 1988). But a reasonable apprehension of suit does not arise when a patentee does nothing more than exercise its lawful commercial prerogatives and, in so doing, puts a competitor in the position of having to choose between abandoning a particular business venture or bringing matters to a head by engaging in arguably infringing activity. *Cygnus Therapeutics Sys. v. Alza Corp.*, 92 F.3d 1153, 39 USPQ2d 1666 (Fed. Cir. 1996).

[162]*Thiokol Chem. Corp. v. Burlington Indus., Inc.*, 448 F.2d 1328, 171 USPQ 193 (3d Cir. 1971).

[163]*Warner-Jenkinson Co. v. Allied Chem. Corp.*, 567 F.2d 184, 193 USPQ 753 (2d Cir. 1977).

[164]*C.R. Bard, Inc. v. Schwartz*, 716 F.2d 874, 219 USPQ 197 (Fed. Cir. 1983). The licensee had quit paying royalties and the patentee had sued in state court to recover royalties. But the patentee had the right under the license to cancel the agreement and sue for infringement. In an affidavit in support of a motion to dismiss the licensee's federal declaratory judgment action, it was indicated that the patentee had no intention of canceling, but his attorney would not flatly state that no suit for infringement would be brought. Held: intentions may change over time. The plaintiff licensee had a reasonable apprehension that it would be sued for infringement.

[165]*Cordis Corp. v. Medtronic, Inc.*, 835 F.2d 859, 5 USPQ2d 1118 (Fed. Cir. 1987).

and there was none. In particular, the agreement to defend or indemnify a third person does not provide the actual controversy whereby the defender or indemnitor may bring a declaratory action on its own behalf when there is no actual controversy involving the indemnitee. The indemnitor's standing in such case is derivative, not original and independent.[166]

Future products and threatened infringement. An actual controversy cannot be based on a fear of litigation over future products.[167] But the court has squarely held that there may be jurisdiction for a declaration of rights in the face of threatened infringement. To meet the controversy requirement, two elements must be present: (1) the defendant must be engaged in an activity directed toward making, selling, or using subject to an infringement charge, or be making meaningful preparation for such activity; and (2) acts of the defendant must indicate a refusal to change the course of its actions in the face of acts by the patentee sufficient to create a reasonable apprehension that a suit will be forthcoming. The latter element ensures that the controversy is definite and concrete between parties having adverse legal interests.[168] Determining whether concrete steps have been taken with the intent to conduct activity that could constitute infringement is generally a more demanding task when the activity constitutes inducement of infringement instead of direct infringement, because the former involves the activities of at least two parties and the latter usually only those of one. Nonetheless, the court has declined to

---

[166]*BP Chems. Ltd. v. Union Carbide Corp.*, 4 F.3d 975, 28 USPQ2d 1124 (Fed. Cir. 1993). In a dictum, the court also pointed out that the decision to exercise declaratory judgment jurisdiction is discretionary. The fact that the indemnified licensees were missing from the case was grounds for a concern that the exercise of jurisdiction would not afford complete relief from the uncertainty, insecurity, and controversy giving rise to the proceeding.

[167]*Amana Ref. Inc. v. Quadlux Inc.*, 172 F.3d 852, 50 USPQ2d 1304 (Fed. Cir. 1999).

[168]*Lang v. Pacific Marine & Supply Co.*, 895 F.2d 761, 13 USPQ2d 1820 (Fed. Cir. 1990). A threat of sale does not constitute an act of infringement under 35 U.S.C. §271. *Eli Lilly & Co. v. Medtronic, Inc.*, 915 F.2d 670 (Fed. Cir. 1990). But see the discussion of offers to sell in §6.2(iii). While 35 U.S.C. §271(e)(2) provides the federal courts with jurisdiction to hear infringement cases regarding claims directed to drugs or methods of using drugs, it does not provide jurisdiction to hear infringement cases regarding claims directed to methods for making drugs. In the context of an ANDA, such a case would require resort to the Declaratory Judgment Act. A patentee may seek a declaration that a person will infringe a patent in the future, provided there is a sufficient allegation of immediacy and reality. Here, the defendant had sent a letter indicating that it intended to market the product after the expiration of the drug patent but before the expiration of the method of making patent, and had also submitted an ANDA accompanied by data sufficient to make FDA approval imminent. Thus the district court properly exercised its discretion to hear the DJ action. *Glaxo, Inc. v. Novopharm, Ltd.*, 110 F.3d 1562 (Fed. Cir. 1997). In *Laitram Corp. v. Cambridge Wire Cloth Co.*, 919 F.2d 1579, 16 USPQ2d 1929 (Fed. Cir. 1990), the parties had apparently concocted some possible constructions for purposes of a summary judgment motion, but none had actually been made. The Federal Circuit vacated the summary judgment of noninfringement and indicated that the case should have been dismissed for want of jurisdiction, on the ground that neither intent nor preparation constitutes infringement under 35 U.S.C. §271. The court did hint once again that there might have been jurisdiction over an action for a declaration of infringement.

create a per se rule that an actual controversy predicated on inducement may exist only if direct infringement has already occurred.[169]

Priority of litigation. The question of whether a properly brought
declaratory action to determine patent rights should yield to a later
filed suit for patent infringement raises the issue of national uniformity in patent cases and invokes the special obligation of the Federal
Circuit to avoid creating opportunities for dispositive differences
among the regional circuits. Thus the court has refused to apply to
patent cases the rule that an action for declaration of noninfringement
of a trademark should give way to a later filed suit for trademark
infringement. Such a rule would automatically grant the patentee
the choice of forum, whether the patentee had sought—or sought to
avoid—judicial resolution of the controversy. Instead, the court has
decided to apply the general rule whereby the forum of the first filed
case is favored, unless considerations of judicial and litigant economy,
and the just and effective disposition of disputes, require otherwise.
Such exceptions are not rare and are made when justice or expediency
requires, as in any issue of choice of forum. Considerations include
convenience and availability of witnesses, absence of jurisdiction over
all necessary or desirable parties, possibility of consolidation with
related litigation, and identity of the real party in interest. Of importance are conservation of judicial resources and comprehensive disposition of litigation. These considerations, which affect transfer to or
dismissal in favor of another forum, do not change simply because
the first filed action is for a declaratory judgment.[170]

Other relief. Along the same lines, can an action lie for a declaratory judgment of patent validity? Possibly so, where there is a strong
showing of an actual threat of infringement.[171] In the case of an action
for a declaration that the inventors on a patent were properly named,
the hypothetical complaint that the declaratory defendant would have
brought would be one for correction of inventorship under 35 U.S.C.
§256, which provides a cause of action to interested parties to have

---

[169]*Fina Research S.A. v. Baroid Ltd.,* 141 F.3d 1479, 46 USPQ2d 1461 (Fed. Cir. 1998).

[170]*Genentech, Inc. v. Eli Lilly & Co.,* 998 F.2d 931, 27 USPQ2d 1241 (Fed. Cir. 1993). In
so saying, the court did recognize that first filed suits have sometimes been dismissed in favor
of later filed actions when forum shopping was the only motive for the filing of the first suit.
See also *EMC Corp. v. Norand Corp.,* 89 F.3d 807, 39 USPQ2d 1451 (Fed. Cir. 1996). In *Serco
Servs. Co. v. Kelley Co.,* 51 F.3d 1037, 34 USPQ2d 1217 (Fed. Cir. 1995), the court distinguished
Genentech on the facts and found that the trial court had not abused its discretion in dismissing
a declaratory judgment action that had been filed three days before an infringement suit. The
trial court had considered the convenience of the parties and witnesses, and also the fact that
the accused infringer had been warned that the patentee was going to file its infringement
suit on a particular day and therefore filed its declaratory suit as an anticipatory preemption.
Despite its recognition that the impact of forum shopping has been tempered by the Federal
Circuit's own creation, thus making the stakes of a race to the courthouse less severe, it had
no difficulty in approving the district court's dismissal of the declaratory judgment action
as anticipatory.

[171]See *Chemical Eng'g Corp. v. Marlo, Inc.,* 754 F.2d 331, 222 USPQ 738 (Fed. Cir. 1984).

the inventorship of a patent changed to reflect the true inventors of the subject matter claimed in the patent. Thus, a declaratory plaintiff may establish an actual controversy in this context by averring: (1) that it holds a recognized interest in a patent that could be adversely affected by an action brought under §256, and (2) another party with a right to bring an action under §256 has created in the declaratory plaintiff a reasonable apprehension that it will do so.[172]

Federal district courts do not have original jurisdiction to conduct an interference. Thus a party who had acquired by separate contracts the interests of separate inventive entities in the same invention was not entitled to a declaratory judgment as to which was the true inventor.[173]

(iv) Standing to Litigate

The question of a party's standing to bring a case is a jurisdictional one that is reviewed de novo.[174] Standing is closely related to the case or controversy requirement. Standing, in the constitutional dimension, is one of the doctrines that cluster about Article III (e.g., mootness, ripeness, political question) to define further the case or controversy requirement that limits the federal judicial power in our system of government. Those who do not possess Article III standing may not litigate in the courts of the United States.[175] Under the Constitution the judicial power of Article III courts extends only to cases of actual controversy. One aspect of a case or controversy is that the litigant is entitled to have the court decide the merits of the dispute or of particular issues. Whether a party has a sufficient stake in an otherwise justiciable controversy to obtain judicial resolution of that controversy is what has traditionally been referred to as the question of standing to sue.[176]

In cases where a plaintiff asserts a procedural entitlement, such as judicial review, from a federal statute or its implementing regulations, the standing and reviewability inquiries tend to merge. The question of jurisdiction requires a focus on the legal rights or interests

---

[172]*Fina Oil & Chem. Co. v. Ewen*, 123 F.3d 1466, 43 USPQ2d 1935 (Fed. Cir. 1997). The mere fact that the court looked to a state court action between the parties to find evidence of a reasonable apprehension in this case does not mean that the hypothetical declaratory judgment claim may be based only on the actual claim brought in state court. If a federal claim is made in state court, removal is the appropriate route; where there is no federal claim, a declaratory plaintiff is not limited to the actual state claims made.

[173]*Consolidated World Housewares, Inc. v. Finkle*, 829 F.2d 261, 4 USPQ2d 1565 (Fed. Cir. 1987). The plaintiff had entered into a contract with one of the putative inventors that looked suspiciously like it called for collusive litigation to get the matter in a federal court and before the Federal Circuit. The court, which said this conduct "paints a picture appalling," felt that the plaintiff ought to have made his own decision as to inventorship and accepted the consequences, rather than try to get a court to decide it for him.

[174]*GAIA Tech., Inc. v. Reconversion Tech., Inc.*, 93 F.3d 774, 39 USPQ2d 1826 (Fed. Cir. 1996).

[175]*McKinney v. Department of Treasury*, 799 F.2d 1544 (Fed. Cir. 1986).

[176]*Animal Legal Defense Fund v. Quigg*, 932 F.2d 920, 18 USPQ2d 920 (Fed. Cir. 1991).

that devolve from the relevant statute. Congress may provide for judicial review of some issues at the behest of particular parties, but not others.[177]

The question of standing involves the determination of whether a particular litigant is entitled to invoke the jurisdiction of a federal court to decide the merits of a dispute or of particular issues.[178] The focus is on the qualifications and status of the party seeking to bring its complaint before the court and not on the issues it wishes to have resolved.[179] It is elemental that there must be parties before there is a case or controversy. The fact that seemingly adverse parties appear on two sides of an action is not controlling. If one party is actually and formally in control of the other party, adjudication must be refused. Actual control is not even necessary; the ability to control suffices. If one party has the ability to control the other, the case is moot for lack of adversariness.[180]

The rules of standing are threshold determinants of the propriety of judicial intervention, and it is the responsibility of the plaintiff to demonstrate that it is a proper party to invoke judicial resolution of the dispute and exercise of the court's remedial powers.[181] When standing is placed in issue, there is a two-step analysis that involves both the constitutional limitations and the prudential limitations that circumscribe standing. As an initial matter, the court must ensure that the litigant satisfies the requirements of Article III of the Constitution. Once the court determines that the litigant satisfies the constitutional aspects, it must consider whether any prudential limitations restrain the court from exercising its judicial power.[182]

The principal limitation imposed by Article III is that a litigant seeking to invoke the court's authority must show that it personally has suffered some actual or threatened injury as a result of the putatively illegal conduct of the defendant. In addition, Article III requires the litigant to establish that there is a causal connection between the litigant's injury and the putatively illegal conduct of the defendant and that this injury is likely to be redressed should the court grant the relief requested. The injury may be either economic or noneconomic in nature, but it must be judicially cognizable, or personal, or distinct and palpable, or concrete, or a specific present objective harm. It may not be abstract, conjectural, or hypothetical.[183]

---

[177]*Syntex (U.S.A.) Inc. v. United States PTO,* 882 F.2d 1570, 11 USPQ2d 1866 (Fed. Cir. 1989).

[178]*McKinney v. Department of Treasury,* 799 F.2d 1544 (Fed. Cir. 1986).

[179]*McKinney v. Department of Treasury,* 799 F.2d 1544 (Fed. Cir. 1986); *Reid v. Department of Commerce,* 793 F.2d 277 (Fed. Cir. 1986).

[180]*Gould v. Control Laser Corp.,* 866 F.2d 1391, 9 USPQ2d 1718 (Fed. Cir. 1989).

[181]*Reid v. Department of Commerce,* 793 F.2d 277 (Fed. Cir. 1986).

[182]*Boeing Co. v. Commissioner of Patents,* 853 F.2d 878, 7 USPQ2d 1487 (Fed. Cir. 1988); *McKinney v. Department of Treasury,* 799 F.2d 1544 (Fed. Cir. 1986).

[183]*Boeing Co. v. Commissioner of Patents,* 853 F.2d 878, 7 USPQ2d 1487 (Fed. Cir. 1988); *McKinney v. Department of Treasury,* 799 F.2d 1544 (Fed. Cir. 1986). See also *Animal Legal*

Where the actual or threatened injury required by Article III exists solely by virtue of statutes creating legal rights that have been invaded, the standing question depends upon whether the statutory provision on which the claim rests properly can be understood as granting persons in the litigant's position a right to judicial relief.[184] A patent is a creature of statute, as is the right of a patentee to have a remedy for infringement of his or her patent. Suit must be brought on the patent, as ownership only of the invention gives no right to exclude, which is obtained only from the patent grant. In order to exercise that right, a plaintiff must necessarily have standing as comprehended by the patent statute.[185] For example, the public interest in airing charges of fraudulent procurement of a patent does not outweigh the public policy that dictates dismissal of litigation where there is neither standing (because of lack of antitrust injury) nor jurisdiction (because of absence of an actual controversy).[186]

The mere assertion of a right to have the government act in accordance with the law is not sufficient, in and of itself. Nor is an interest in a problem, no matter how long-standing the interest or how qualified the litigant in matters relating to the problem.[187] In an interesting case, the Federal Circuit has held that a patentee may or may not have standing to sue to challenge the lawfulness of regulations relating to reexamination procedure, depending upon actual prejudice.[188]

In *Animal Legal Defense Fund v. Quigg*,[189] the court considered a proposed challenge, under the Administrative Procedures Act, to a PTO Notice that stated that the PTO "now considers non-naturally occurring, non-human multicellular organisms, including animals, to be patentable subject matter." Its decision provides an interesting look at several standing questions. For one thing, there is no right

---

Defense Fund v. Quigg, 932 F.2d 920, 18 USPQ2d 920 (Fed. Cir. 1991); *Reid v. Department of Commerce*, 793 F.2d 277 (Fed. Cir. 1986). An exclusive licensee can be awarded damages if properly joined as a plaintiff. *Weinar v. Rollform, Inc.*, 744 F.2d 797, 223 USPQ 369 (Fed. Cir. 1984). See also *Kalman v. Berlyn Corp.*, 914 F.2d 1473, 16 USPQ2d 1093 (Fed. Cir. 1990).

[184]*Reid v. Department of Commerce*, 793 F.2d 277 (Fed. Cir. 1986).

[185]*Arachnid, Inc. v. Merit Indus., Inc.*, 939 F.2d 1574, 19 USPQ2d 1513 (Fed. Cir. 1991).

[186]*Indium Corp. v. Semi-Alloys, Inc.*, 781 F.2d 879, 228 USPQ 845 (Fed. Cir. 1985).

[187]*McKinney v. Department of Treasury*, 799 F.2d 1544 (Fed. Cir. 1986). Nor is the continued existence of a patent sufficient to create standing, without conduct creating a reasonable apprehension of a suit for infringement. Without such an apprehension, the alleged injury is indistinguishable from any injury that the issuance of a patent might cause the general public. *Boeing Co. v. Commissioner of Patents*, 853 F.2d 878, 7 USPQ2d 1487 (Fed. Cir. 1988).

[188]*Patlex Corp. v. Mossinghoff*, 758 F.2d 594, 225 USPQ 243 (Fed. Cir. 1985). The patentee had conceded that the requester had indeed raised a substantial new question of patentability, thus justifying the PTO examiner's order for reexamination. Inasmuch as the challenged regulations related to the rights of patentees prior to entry of an order for reexamination, this patentee was not prejudiced by them. In a later decision in the same case, the court found that the patentee had standing to challenge the lawfulness and constitutionality of certain reexamination regulations where he had made no concession as to the existence of a substantial new question of patentability. *Patlex Corp. v. Mossinghoff*, 771 F.2d 480, 226 USPQ 985 (Fed. Cir. 1985).

[189]*Animal Legal Defense Fund v. Quigg*, 932 F.2d 920, 18 USPQ2d 920 (Fed. Cir. 1991).

in nonapplicants to object to the way in which patent applications of others are prosecuted. A third party has no right to intervene in the prosecution of a particular patent application to prevent issuance of an allegedly invalid patent. For another, interests that are merely value preferences (e.g., anticruelty) can be shared by any citizen with the same bona fide special interest. Thus there is a requirement of injury-in-fact. This requires a careful showing of causation.

The fact that a party may have standing to bring a cancellation proceeding in the PTO does not automatically create a case or controversy sufficient to establish jurisdiction in a district court.[190] A nonpatentee requester for reexamination is neither an applicant entitled to appeal under 35 U.S.C. §145 nor a patent owner entitled to appeal under §306. Thus, such a requester, even one who has intervened in a §145 action, has no independent statutory right to bring a §145 action.[191] Every perceived injury caused by improper agency action does not carry a right to immediate judicial redress. A right to immediate judicial review must be granted or reasonably inferred from a particular statute. For example, a potential infringer may not sue the PTO seeking retraction of a patent issued to another by reason of its improper allowance by the PTO. A remedy must await confrontation with the patent owner. The same is true with respect to a reissued patent. And although a third-party reexamination requester has some rights vis-a-vis the PTO, such a requester has no right to challenge the validity of the reexamination certificate by suit against the PTO.[192]

In addition to federal judicial power, the standing doctrine also embraces several judicially self-imposed limits on the exercise of federal jurisdiction. These prudential restrictions include a general prohibition precluding a litigant from raising another person's legal rights, a rule barring adjudication of generalized grievances more appropriately addressed in the representative branch, and a requirement that a plaintiff's complaint fall within the zone of interests protected by the law involved.[193] A federal court should normally refrain from exercise of its judicial power unless the litigant asserts an injury peculiar to itself or to a distinct group of which it is a part, rather than an interest shared in substantially equal measure by all or a large class of citizens. In addition, the litigant must show that its complaint falls within the zone of interests to be protected or regulated by the statute or constitutional guarantee in question.[194]

---

[190]*Windsurfing Int'l Inc. v. AMF Inc.,* 828 F.2d 755, 4 USPQ2d 1053 (Fed. Cir. 1987).

[191]*Boeing Co. v. Commissioner of Patents,* 853 F.2d 878, 7 USPQ2d 1487 (Fed. Cir. 1988).

[192]*Syntex (U.S.A.) Inc. v. United States PTO,* 882 F.2d 1570, 11 USPQ2d 1866 (Fed. Cir. 1989).

[193]*McKinney v. Department of Treasury,* 799 F.2d 1544 (Fed. Cir. 1986); *Reid v. Department of Commerce,* 793 F.2d 277 (Fed. Cir. 1986).

[194]*Boeing Co. v. Commissioner of Patents,* 853 F.2d 878, 7 USPQ2d 1487 (Fed. Cir. 1988). The Administrative Procedure Act gives standing to any person adversely affected or aggrieved by an agency action within the meaning of a relevant statute. But it is the patent statute, not the APA itself, that is the relevant statute in PTO matters. Thus, if a party is to be deemed

Nonetheless, Congress, through the exercise of its legislative power, can resolve the question of prudential limitations on standing one way or the other. It may, by statute, grant a right of action, either expressly or by clear implication, to persons seeking relief on the basis of the legal rights or interests of third persons. Logically, Congress can also deny such a right of action.[195]

In general, a litigant must assert an injury peculiar to itself or to a distinct group of which it is a part, rather than an interest shared in substantially equal measure by all or a large part of the populace.[196] With respect to the Article III injury requirement, it is recognized that an association may have standing to assert the claims of its members, even where the association itself has not suffered injury from the challenged action; but the organization derives its own standing in part by showing that its members have incurred actual or threatened injury. Associational or organizational standing requires that the organization show that (1) its members would otherwise have standing to sue in their own right; (2) the interests it seeks to protect are germane to the organization's purpose; and (3) neither the claims asserted nor the relief requested requires the participation of the individual members in the lawsuit.[197]

Standing to sue for infringement.[198] The patent law provides, in 35 U.S.C. §281, that a "patentee" shall have remedy by civil action for infringement of a patent. The term patentee, under §100(d), includes not only the patentee to whom the patent was issued but also the successors in title to the patentee.[199] This has been interpreted to require that a suit for infringement must ordinarily be brought by a party holding legal title to the patent.[200] But where a patentee makes an assignment of all significant rights under the patent, the assignee

---

within the zone of interests for standing purposes, it must fall within the zone of interests protected by the patent laws. Simply because patents are issued for the public good does not satisfy this test. Otherwise, any members of the public who perceived that they would be harmed by an issued patent they believed to be invalid would be able to bring a collateral attack on the validity of issued patents. *Animal Legal Defense Fund v. Quigg,* 932 F.2d 920, 18 USPQ2d 920 (Fed. Cir. 1991).

[195]*Reid v. Department of Commerce,* 793 F.2d 277 (Fed. Cir. 1986).

[196]*McKinney v. Department of Treasury,* 799 F.2d 1544 (Fed. Cir. 1986).

[197]*McKinney v. Department of Treasury,* 799 F.2d 1544 (Fed. Cir. 1986); *Reid v. Department of Commerce,* 793 F.2d 277 (Fed. Cir. 1986).

[198]This section should be read in conjunction with the discussion of assignments and exclusive licenses in §7.2(b).

[199]*Enzo APA & Son v. Geapag A.G.,* 134 F.3d 1090, 45 USPQ2d 1368 (Fed. Cir. 1998); *Rite-Hite Corp. v. Kelley Co.,* 56 F.3d 1538, 35 USPQ2d 1065 (Fed. Cir. 1995); *Ortho Pharm. Corp. v. Genetics Inst., Inc.,* 52 F.3d 1026, 34 USPQ2d 1444 (Fed. Cir. 1995). The right to sue for infringement is ordinarily an incident of legal title to the patent. *Abbott Labs. v. Diamedix Corp.,* 47 F.3d 1128, 33 USPQ2d 1771 (Fed. Cir. 1995).

[200]*Enzo APA & Son v. Geapag A.G.,* 134 F.3d 1090, 45 USPQ2d 1368 (Fed. Cir. 1998). Only a patentee may bring an action for patent infringement. *Textile Prods. Inc. v. Mead Corp.,* 134 F.3d 1481, 45 USPQ2d 1633 (Fed. Cir. 1998).

may be deemed the effective patentee under the statute and has standing to bring a suit in its own name for infringement.[201]

A conveyance of legal title by the patentee can be made only of (1) the entire patent, (2) an undivided part or share of the entire patent, or (3) all rights under the patent in a specified geographical region of the United States. A transfer of any of these is an assignment and vests the assignee with title in the patent and a right to sue infringers (either alone, as in cases (1) and (3), or, in case (2), jointly with the assignor). A transfer of less than one of these three interests is a license, not an assignment of legal title, and it gives the licensee no right to sue for infringement at law in the licensor's own name.[202]

An exclusive license is equivalent to an assignment and may therefore confer standing upon the licensee to sue for patent infringement. Conversely, a "bare licensee"—one who enjoys only a nonexclusive license—has no standing to sue for infringement. The court adheres to the principle that a patentee should be joined, either voluntarily or involuntarily, in any infringement suit brought by an exclusive licensee. However, this general rule—which is prudential rather than constitutional in nature—is subject to an exception. The exception is that, where the patentee makes an assignment of all substantial rights under the patent, the assignee may be deemed the effective "patentee" under §281 and thus may have standing to maintain an infringement suit in its own name.[203] Unless there is a transfer of all substantial rights under the patent, the conveyance is a license rather than an assignment, and the patent owner is a necessary party to an infringement action brought by the licensee.[204] Also, saying that a licensee must sue with or in the name of the patentee does not mean that every licensee under a patent has a rightful place

---

[201]*Enzo APA & Son v. Geapag A.G.*, 134 F.3d 1090, 45 USPQ2d 1368 (Fed. Cir. 1998); *Ortho Pharm. Corp. v. Genetics Inst., Inc.*, 52 F.3d 1026, 34 USPQ2d 1444 (Fed. Cir. 1995).

[202]*Rite-Hite Corp. v. Kelley Co.*, 56 F.3d 1538, 35 USPQ2d 1065 (Fed. Cir. 1995). See also *Enzo APA & Son v. Geapag A.G.*, 134 F.3d 1090, 45 USPQ2d 1368 (Fed. Cir. 1998). Nunc pro tunc assignments are not sufficient to confer retroactive standing because, as a general matter, parties should possess rights before seeking to have them vindicated in court. *Id.* An assignment of patent rights executed after the litigation commenced but made effective prior to the filing of suit does not confer standing on the assignee retroactively. *GAIA Tech., Inc. v. Reconversion Tech., Inc.*, 93 F.3d 774, 39 USPQ2d 1826 (Fed. Cir. 1996). In *Mas-Hamilton Group Inc. v. LaGard Inc.*, 156 F.3d 1206, 48 USPQ2d 1010 (Fed. Cir. 1998), the patent owner, defendant in a declaratory judgment action, assigned the patent during the pendency of the appeal. The assignment did not expressly transfer the right to sue for past infringement, but this was cured by a later supplementary assignment. The court held that both the original owner and the assignee have standing to prosecute the appeal. While it is true that nunc pro tunc assignments are not sufficient to confer retroactive standing, here standing was not deficient at the time the declaratory suit was filed, nor at the time the appeal was filed.

[203]*Prima Tek II L.L.C. v. A-Roo Co.*, 222 F.3d 1372, 55 USPQ2d 1742 (Fed. Cir. 2000).

[204]*Abbott Labs. v. Diamedix Corp.*, 47 F.3d 1128, 33 USPQ2d 1771 (Fed. Cir. 1995). See also *Minco, Inc. v. Combustion Eng'g, Inc.*, 95 F.3d 1109, 40 USPQ2d 1001 (Fed. Cir. 1996). Compare *Speedplay Inc. v. Bebop Inc.*, 211 F.3d 1245, 53 USPQ2d 1984 (Fed. Cir. 2000). However, an exclusive licensee that does not have all substantial rights does have standing to sue in its own name when necessary to prevent an absolute failure of justice, as where the patentee is the infringer, and cannot sue itself. *Textile Prods. Inc. v. Mead Corp.*, 134 F.3d 1481, 45 USPQ2d 1633 (Fed. Cir. 1998).

in an infringement suit. A licensee must have standing under the patent statute. A license may amount to no more than a covenant not to sue the licensee, with the patentee reserving the right to grant others the same right. A holder of such a nonexclusive license suffers no legal injury from infringement and thus has no standing to bring suit or even join in a suit with the patentee.[205]

Thus in certain limited circumstances, standing has been accorded, where all substantial rights under the patent have been transferred in the form of an exclusive license, rendering the licensee the virtual assignee. A licensing arrangement conferring standing must, logically, resemble an assignment in both form and substance.[206] To be an exclusive licensee for standing purposes, a party must have received not only the right to practice the invention within a given territory, but also the patentee's express or implied promise that others shall be excluded from practicing the invention within that territory as well. If the party has not received an express or implied promise of exclusivity under the patent, it has a bare license and has received only the patentee's promise that the party will not be sued for infringement.[207] To determine whether a license agreement has conveyed all substantial rights in a patent, and is thus tantamount to an assignment, the court must ascertain the intention of the parties and examine the substance of what was granted. In so doing, it is helpful to look at what rights were retained by the grantor.[208] The use of the word "exclusive" is not controlling; what matters is the substance of the arrangement. Because patent rights are rights to exclude others, a licensee is an exclusive licensee only if the patentee has promised, expressly or impliedly, that others shall be excluded from practicing the invention within the field covered by the license. Put another way, an exclusive license is a license to practice the invention, accompanied by the patent owner's promise that others shall be excluded from practicing it within the field of use wherein the licensee is given leave. Thus, if a patentee-licensor is free to grant

---

[205]*Ortho Pharm. Corp. v. Genetics Inst., Inc.*, 52 F.3d 1026, 34 USPQ2d 1444 (Fed. Cir. 1995). A bare licensee, who has no right to exclude others, has no legally recognized interest that entitles it to bring or join an infringement action. *Abbott Labs. v. Diamedix Corp.*, 47 F.3d 1128, 33 USPQ2d 1771 (Fed. Cir. 1995).

[206]*Enzo APA & Son v. Geapag A.G.*, 134 F.3d 1090, 45 USPQ2d 1368 (Fed. Cir. 1998). Under §261, "[a]pplications for patent, patents, or any interest therein, shall be assignable in law by an instrument in writing." If the courts were to expand the virtual assignment exception to include oral licenses, the exception would swallow the rule. Parties would be free to engage in revisionist history, circumventing the certainty provided by the writing requirement of §261 by claiming to be patentee by virtue of a verbal licensing arrangement. *Id.*

[207]*Rite-Hite Corp. v. Kelley Co.*, 56 F.3d 1538, 35 USPQ2d 1065 (Fed. Cir. 1995). The court held that independent sales organizations who resold the patented product lacked standing to recover damages. They argued that they should be allowed to join as coplaintiffs because each had a virtually exclusive license to sell products made by the patentee to particular customers in an exclusive sales territory. The court regarded the exclusivity as applying only to sales territories, not to patent rights.

[208]*Prima Tek II L.L.C. v. A-Roo Co.*, 222 F.3d 1372, 55 USPQ2d 1742 (Fed. Cir. 2000). The fact that title may revert back to the licensor under the terms of the agreement does not necessarily make the licensor an indispensable party. *Id.*

licenses to others, licensees under that patent are not exclusive licensees.[209]

Economic injury alone therefore does not provide standing to sue under the patent statute. To have coplaintiff standing in an infringement suit, a licensee must hold some of the proprietary sticks from the bundle of patent rights, albeit a lesser share of rights in the patent than for an assignment and standing to sue alone. But a right to sue clause in an agreement has no effect on standing, one way or the other. A licensee with sufficient proprietary interest in a patent has standing regardless of whether the licensing agreement so provides. By the same token, a right to sue clause cannot negate the requirement that, for coplaintiff standing, a licensee must have beneficial ownership of some of the patentee's proprietary rights.[210]

The consequence of recognizing coplaintiff standing is that the licensee has a right to bring suit on the patent, albeit in the name of the licensor, whether or not the license so provides and regardless of the patentee's cooperation. Further, the patentee/licensor suffers the legal consequences of litigation brought in its name. The requirement that a licensee sue in the name of the patentee is not merely a formality. The patentee is brought into the suit for substantive reasons, namely, to protect its own interest in connection with the charged acts of infringement and to enable the alleged infringer to respond in one action to all claims of infringement for those acts.[211]

One of the underlying policies of the rule requiring joinder of the patent owner is to prevent duplicative litigation against a single accused infringer. This does not mean, however, that a patent owner's agreement to be bound by all judgments against a licensee necessarily resolves the issue of standing. Standing to sue for infringement depends entirely on the putative plaintiff's proprietary interest in the

---

[209]*Textile Prods. Inc. v. Mead Corp.,* 134 F.3d 1481, 45 USPQ2d 1633 (Fed. Cir. 1998). A contract to produce for the patent owner its total requirements for a patented product does not automatically convert the exclusive supplier into an exclusive licensee of the patent. The contractual manufacturing rights of a party do not alone confer a right to exclude all others from making an invention. To qualify as an exclusive license, an agreement must clearly manifest the patentee's promise to refrain from granting to anyone else a license in the area of exclusivity. In this case, which involved a complex contract, the court held that the supplier did not have standing to assert patent infringement against the patent owner and its secondary supplier.

[210]*Ortho Pharm. Corp. v. Genetics Inst., Inc.,* 52 F.3d 1026, 34 USPQ2d 1444 (Fed. Cir. 1995). In this case an agreement expressly granted the right to make a product but did not address any patents by which the product was made. Under California law, such a provision implied a license under a patent that covered a product used to make the ultimate licensed product. The agreement also granted the exclusive right to sell the ultimate product abroad. On these facts the Federal Circuit held that the licensee had no standing to bring or join a suit for infringement of the patent. The patent provided no rights respecting the ultimate product per se. Moreover, inasmuch as a U.S. patent grants the right to exclude others only in this country, the right to sell the ultimate product abroad was not a proprietary right arising from the patent. Thus, with respect to rights under the patent, the licensee had only a nonexclusive right to make the patented product in the United States.

[211]*Ortho Pharm. Corp. v. Genetics Inst., Inc.,* 52 F.3d 1026, 34 USPQ2d 1444 (Fed. Cir. 1995).

patent, not on any contractual arrangements among the parties regarding who may sue and who will be bound by judgments. Just as a "right to sue" clause cannot confer standing on a bare licensee, neither can a patent owner's agreement to be bound by judgments against a licensee circumvent the rule that the patent owner must ordinarily join, in any infringement action, an exclusive licensee who possesses less than all substantial rights in the patent. To hold otherwise would be to allow a patent owner to effectively grant a "hunting license," solely for the purpose of litigation, in the form of a pro forma exclusive license, e.g., covering only a minuscule territory.[212]

The merits of injury allegations have no bearing on the question of standing. However, one aspect of standing is that the requested relief would rectify the plaintiff's alleged injuries.[213] One seeking to recover money damages for infringement of a U.S. patent (an action at law) must have held the legal title to the patent during the time of the infringement. The principal exception is where the assignment of a patent is coupled with an assignment of a right of action for past infringements. The latter must be express and cannot be inferred from an assignment of the patent itself. Other recognized exceptions confer standing upon nonowners to join infringement suits as coplaintiffs with the patent, such as licensees and exclusive vendors of the patented product. But one who owns only the equitable title can seek only equitable relief—an injunction but not damages.[214] Thus, a nonexclusive licensee of a patent has no standing to sue for infringement. But when the sole licensee has been shown to be directly damaged by an infringer in a two-supplier market, and when the nexus between the sole licensee and the patentee is close and clearly defined, the licensee must be recognized as the real party in interest. This gives effect to the congressional mandate in 35 U.S.C. §284 that the damages shall be adequate to compensate for the infringement.[215]

An action for infringement must join as plaintiffs all co-owners. Further, as a matter of substantive patent law, all co-owners must ordinarily consent to join as plaintiffs in an infringement suit. Two established exceptions exist. First, when any patent owner has granted an exclusive license, it stands in a relationship of trust to its licensee and must permit the licensee to sue in the patent owner's name. Second, the obligation may arise by contract among co-owners. If, by agreement, a co-owner waives its right to refuse to join suit, its

---

[212]*Prima Tek II L.L.C. v. A-Roo Co.,* 222 F.3d 1372, 55 USPQ2d 1742 (Fed. Cir. 2000).

[213]*Syntex (U.S.A.) Inc. v. United States PTO,* 882 F.2d 1570, 11 USPQ2d 1866 (Fed. Cir. 1989). The plaintiff was simply urging that a reexamination was improperly conducted. But it is pure speculation that a "properly" conducted reexamination would have resulted in cancellation of all patent claims, thus alleviating plaintiff's injury.

[214]*Arachnid, Inc. v. Merit Indus., Inc.,* 939 F.2d 1574, 19 USPQ2d 1513 (Fed. Cir. 1991). See also *Heidelberg Harris Inc. v. Loebach,* 145 F.3d 1454, 46 USPQ2d 1948 (Fed. Cir. 1998). But neither statute nor common law precedent requires a particular formula or set prescription of words to express the conveyance of a right of action for past infringements. *Minco, Inc. v. Combustion Eng'g, Inc.,* 95 F.3d 1109, 40 USPQ2d 1001 (Fed. Cir. 1996).

[215]*Kalman v. Berlyn Corp.,* 914 F.2d 1473, 16 USPQ2d 1093 (Fed. Cir. 1990).

co-owners may subsequently force it to join in a suit against infringers. Consequently, one co-owner has the right to impede the other co-owner's ability to sue infringers by refusing to voluntarily join in such a suit. This rule finds support in 35 U.S.C. §262, which provides that, in the absence of any agreement to the contrary, each of the joint owners of a patent may make, use, offer to sell, or sell the patented invention within the United States, or import the patented invention into the United States, without the consent of and without accounting to the other owners. This freedom to exploit the patent without a duty to account to other co-owners also allows co-owners to freely license others to exploit the patent without the consent of other co-owners. Thus, the congressional policy expressed by §262 is that patent co-owners are at the mercy of one another.[216]

Mootness and ripeness. Questions of mootness and ripeness, like standing, are closely related to the case or controversy inquiry. Mootness of an action relates to the basic dispute between the parties, not merely the relief requested. Thus, although subsequent acts may moot a request for particular relief, or a count, the constitutional requirement of a case or controversy may be supplied by the availability of other relief.[217] Mootness is discussed in detail in §16.3(h), largely in the context of a claim or issue becoming moot prior to appellate review.[218] On issues of mootness and ripeness that do not pertain to patent law questions, the Federal Circuit will apply the law of the regional circuit.[219]

Of course, so long as an issue remains moot, a district court need not decide a motion raising it, but rather may defer it, or deny or dismiss it as moot. But once the issue is no longer moot, the motion must be decided. It is critical to the orderly administration of justice that, when a non-moot motion is properly presented, it must be considered.[220]

---

[216]*Ethicon Inc. v. United States Surgical Corp.,* 135 F.3d 1456, 45 USPQ2d 1545, 1554 (Fed. Cir. 1998).

[217]*Intrepid v. Pollock,* 907 F.2d 1125 (Fed. Cir. 1990). A party in an ITC proceeding argued that its unilateral decision to stop manufacturing an earlier design mooted the infringement issue (inasmuch as only injunctive-type relief is available in the ITC). The Federal Circuit rejected this argument on the ground that mere voluntary cessation of allegedly illegal conduct does not moot a case; if it did, the courts would be compelled to leave the party free to return to its old ways. *Intel Corp. v. United States ITC,* 946 F.2d 821, 20 USPQ2d 1161 (Fed. Cir. 1991). A reissue, coupled with a covenant not to sue on any original claims of the patent, mooted an actual controversy regarding infringement of the original patent. *Spectronics Corp. v. H.B. Fuller Co.,* 940 F.2d 631, 19 USPQ2d 1545 (Fed. Cir. 1991).

[218]See, e.g., *Amstar Corp. v. Envirotech Corp.,* 823 F.2d 1538, 3 USPQ2d 1412 (Fed. Cir. 1987); *Fonar Corp. v. Johnson & Johnson,* 821 F.2d 627, 3 USPQ2d 1109 (Fed. Cir. 1987).

[219]*Molins PLC v. Quigg,* 837 F.2d 1064, 5 USPQ2d 1526 (Fed. Cir. 1988). When reviewing a district court's conclusion that the causes of action in a case are not ripe for adjudication, and are therefore beyond the Article III jurisdiction of the federal courts, the Federal Circuit applies regional circuit law. Under Ninth Circuit law, a dismissal under Rule 12(b)(1) for lack of subject matter jurisdiction is reviewed de novo. In the context of a ripeness determination, the underlying factual findings must be accepted unless clearly erroneous. *Cedars-Sinai Med. Ctr. v. Watkins,* 11 F.3d 1573, 29 USPQ2d 1188 (Fed. Cir. 1993).

[220]*Laitram Corp. v. NEC Corp.,* 115 F.3d 947, 42 USPQ2d 1897 (Fed. Cir. 1997).

The court has laid down some general guidelines for analyzing ripeness issues. A case or controversy may be constitutionally ripe for review but that does not automatically invoke review. Prudential considerations must also be satisfied.[221] In determining whether a challenge to an administrative action is ripe for review, a two-fold inquiry must be made: first to determine whether the issues tendered are appropriate for judicial resolution, and second to assess the hardship to the parties if judicial relief to the parties is denied at that stage. This in essence requires the court to balance its interest in deciding the issue in a more concrete setting against the hardship to the parties caused by delaying review. Thus if the hardship is slight, only a minimum showing of countervailing judicial or administrative interest is needed to tip the balance against judicial review. In resolving the fitness prong of the ripeness issue, the court must determine if the challenged action raises purely legal questions. If so, it is presumptively fit for judicial review unless the courts or agency would benefit from postponement of review until the agency's policy has crystallized or the question arises in a more concrete setting.[222]

Using this analysis, the court decided that a facial challenge to the PTO's "first action final rejection" policy was not ripe for review. Although the question is presumptively fit for judicial challenge, an appraisal of the policy would benefit from review in a more concrete setting in view of long-standing agency practice. Thus review should be delayed absent a countervailing hardship to the requesting party.[223] An action seeking a declaratory judgment invalidating a government ownership determination under 42 U.S.C. §5908 was also dismissed for want of jurisdiction on ripeness grounds.[224]

A district court's decision not to exercise jurisdiction under the mandamus statute for federal officers (28 U.S.C. §1361) is a discretionary one. Section 1361 is intended to provide a remedy only if the plaintiff has exhausted all other avenues of relief and only if the defendant owes the plaintiff a clear nondiscretionary duty. Where judicial review is available in another court, mandamus is unavailable

---

[221]*Molins PLC v. Quigg,* 837 F.2d 1064, 5 USPQ2d 1526 (Fed. Cir. 1988).

[222]*Molins PLC v. Quigg,* 837 F.2d 1064, 5 USPQ2d 1526 (Fed. Cir. 1988). See also *Cedars-Sinai Med. Ctr. v. Watkins,* 11 F.3d 1573, 29 USPQ2d 1188 (Fed. Cir. 1993).

[223]*Molins PLC v. Quigg,* 837 F.2d 1064, 5 USPQ2d 1526 (Fed. Cir. 1988). The party argued that it frequently files U.S. applications and that the policy would therefore have a continuing impact on the manner in which it conducts its affairs. This is not the type of hardship that warrants immediate consideration of an issue presented in abstract form, however. The only burden on the party would be that it would have to file another petition to challenge the policy when and if it is applied against it in another application.

[224]*Cedars-Sinai Med. Ctr. v. Watkins,* 11 F.3d 1573, 29 USPQ2d 1188 (Fed. Cir. 1993). The U.S. patent application in issue was involved in an interference, thus making that matter not yet fit for adjudication. As to foreign patent rights based on the U.S. application, it was clear that the §5908 determination could have an adverse effect on the plaintiff's ability to license those rights; thus, the fitness prong was satisfied. However, the case failed the hardship prong of the ripeness test because there was no evidence to demonstrate that the determination was in fact directly and substantially interfering with any foreign licensing efforts.

under this statute.[225] Indeed, mandamus is ordinarily unavailable where a statutory method of appeal has been prescribed.[226]

(v) Removal of Actions

Any civil action of which federal district courts have original jurisdiction may, if brought in a state court, be removed by the defendant to the federal district court embracing the location of the state court.[227] The procedure governing removal of actions is laid out in 28 U.S.C. §§1441–1452. In general, removal itself is an ex parte matter, accomplished by filing a petition in the appropriate federal district court.[228] A defendant may properly remove an action if the district court to which it seeks removal has subject matter jurisdiction at the time of removal.[229] Once a case is removed, the state court may take no further action, and any further state proceedings will be vacated.[230] A plaintiff may challenge the propriety of the removal by moving to remand to the state court.[231] Remands are not reviewable by appeal, mandamus, or otherwise.[232]

State courts may determine issues of patent law in appropriate cases, and a suit for business damage caused by threats to sue on a patent is not itself a suit under the patent laws. However, where the plaintiff also alleges patent infringement, and it appears that such an allegation is more than merely incidental to its other claims, the case belongs in federal court.[233] A case is not removable unless the complaint in state court shows on its face that resolution of the case depends on a federal question. That a defense raises a federal question is immaterial.[234] But a plaintiff may not defeat removal by omitting

---

[225]*Franchi v. Manbeck,* 972 F.2d 1283, 23 USPQ2d 1847 (Fed. Cir. 1992).

[226]*Franchi v. Manbeck,* 972 F.2d 1283, 23 USPQ2d 1847 (Fed. Cir. 1992). Thus, the exclusive forum for review of a PTO decision refusing to register an attorney to practice is that prescribed by 35 U.S.C. §32, not by mandamus in any district court. *Id.*

[227]28 U.S.C. §1441.

[228]28 U.S.C. §1446.

[229]*Additive Cont'l & Meas. Sys., Inc. v. Flowdata, Inc.,* 986 F.2d 476, 25 USPQ2d 1798 (Fed. Cir. 1993).

[230]*Syntex Ophthalmics, Inc. v. Novicky,* 745 F.2d 1423, 223 USPQ 695 (Fed. Cir. 1984).

[231]28 U.S.C. §1447.

[232]*In re Oximetrix, Inc.,* 748 F.2d 637, 223 USPQ 1068 (Fed. Cir. 1984).

[233]*In re Snap-On Tools Corp.,* 720 F.2d 654, 220 USPQ 8 (Fed. Cir. 1983).

[234]*In re Oximetrix, Inc.,* 748 F.2d 637, 223 USPQ 1068 (Fed. Cir. 1984). In *Additive Cont'l & Meas. Sys., Inc. v. Flowdata, Inc.,* 986 F.2d 476, 25 USPQ2d 1798 (Fed. Cir. 1993), the plaintiff had alleged in Texas state court that the defendant had committed business disparagement by accusing it of patent infringement. Under Texas law, such a claim requires the plaintiff to prove as part of its prima face case the falsity of the statement. Thus, the plaintiff would have to show that its product did not infringe the defendant's patent. Inasmuch as this would require resolution of a substantial question of federal patent law, the federal district court would have jurisdiction. In affirming the district court's denial of remand to the Texas state court, the Federal Circuit distinguished *American Well Works Co. v. Layne & Bowler Co.,* 241 U.S. 257 (1916). There the claim arose under Massachusetts law which, unlike Texas law, required the defendant patent owner to prove the truth of its statements of infringement as a defense to a plaintiff's disparagement action. In another case the court has expressly passed the question

to plead necessary federal questions in a complaint.[235] If after a removal it appears that for some reason the federal court cannot act, the case should be dismissed rather than remanded to a state court that lacks jurisdiction.[236]

The timing of the federal-state actions is crucial. Counts in a state case at the time of appeal to the state appellate court cannot be removed, inasmuch as the federal court's jurisdiction derives only from the state trial court. A count added after the state appeal, on the other hand, is removable. Moreover, after a final judgment in federal court, it is too late to move to remand a claim to state court.[237]

(b) Venue

Venue, of course, relates to the locale in which a suit may be properly instituted and not to the power of the court to hear the case or reach the parties.[238] The power to hear has been discussed above as a matter of subject matter jurisdiction, and the power to reach will be discussed in the next section as a matter of personal jurisdiction.

Venue, which connotes locality, serves the purpose of protecting a defendant from the inconvenience of having to defend an action in a trial court that is either remote from the defendant's residence or from the place where the acts underlying the controversy occurred. The venue statutes achieve this by limiting a plaintiff's choice of forum to only certain courts from among all those that might otherwise acquire personal jurisdiction over the defendant.[239]

The basic patent venue statute, 28 U.S.C. §1400(b), provides that patent infringement suits may be brought in the district where the defendant resides, or where it has committed acts of infringement and has a regular and established place of business.[240] It was previously clear that §1400(b) was the sole and exclusive provision controlling corporate venue in patent infringement actions and was not to be supplemented by the general corporate venue statute, 28 U.S.C.

---

whether the filing in a state court of a counterclaim for patent infringement is sufficient alone to support removal to federal court. *AeroJet-General Corp. v. Machine Tool Works,* 895 F.2d 736, 13 USPQ2d 1670 (Fed. Cir. 1990). The court has also passed the question whether construction of a term in a contract can sustain jurisdiction under 35 U.S.C. §1338(a) and thus defeat remand. *American Tel. & Tel. Co. v. Integrated Network Corp.,* 972 F.2d 1321, 23 USPQ2d 1918 (Fed. Cir. 1992).

[235]*Christianson v. Colt Indus. Oper. Corp.,* 486 U.S. 800, 7 USPQ2d 1109 (1988).

[236]*In re Snap-On Tools Corp.,* 720 F.2d 654, 220 USPQ 8 (Fed. Cir. 1983).

[237]*Syntex Ophthalmics, Inc. v. Novicky,* 745 F.2d 1423, 223 USPQ 695, 700 (Fed. Cir. 1984).

[238]*Minnesota Min. & Mfg. Co. v. Eco Chem, Inc.,* 757 F.2d 1256, 225 USPQ 350 (Fed. Cir. 1985). Indeed, 28 U.S.C. §1406(b) provides that nothing shall impair district court jurisdiction where a party does not interpose timely and sufficient objection to venue. *Eastman Kodak Co. v. Goodyear Tire & Rubber Co.,* 114 F.3d 1547, 42 USPQ2d 1737 (Fed. Cir. 1997).

[239]*VE Holding Corp. v. Johnson Gas Appliance Co.,* 917 F.2d 1574, 16 USPQ2d 1614 (Fed. Cir. 1990). Venue requirements exist for the benefit of defendants. *Hoover Group Inc. v. Custom Metalcraft, Inc.,* 84 F.3d 1408, 38 USPQ2d 1860 (Fed. Cir. 1996).

[240]*In re Cordis Corp.,* 769 F.2d 733, 226 USPQ 784 (Fed. Cir. 1985).

§1391(c).[241] Thus, for purposes of §1400(b), a corporation was a resident only of the state in which it is incorporated.[242] In 1988, however, §1391(c) was amended to provide that a corporate defendant resides in any district where there would be personal jurisdiction over it at the time the action is commenced. The court has expressly held that this new definition of corporate residence applies to §1400(b).[243] Thus, the remaining criteria in §1400(b), "acts of infringement" and "regular and established place of business," are likely to come into play only where an individual or other noncorporate entity is being sued for infringement.

Section 1400(b) is not to be liberally construed.[244] Nonetheless, the issue of infringement on the merits is not reached in considering whether a defendant "has committed acts of infringement," but only whether accused acts took place in the forum district.[245] Similarly, in determining whether a defendant has a "regular and established place of business" in the judicial district, the appropriate inquiry is whether the defendant does its business in that district through a permanent and continuous presence there and not whether it has a fixed physical presence in the sense of a formal office or store.[246] Venue is based on the facts alleged in the well-pleaded complaint.[247]

A declaratory judgment action alleging that a patent is invalid and not infringed—the mirror image of a suit for patent infringement—is governed by the general venue statutes, not §1400(b).[248]

Piercing the corporate veil may be appropriate in order to establish patent venue. Thus, venue is proper as to individuals who are alter egos of a corporation, by virtue of proper venue as to the corporation.[249] Also, venue for personal liability of a corporation's officer or

---

[241]*In re Cordis Corp.*, 769 F.2d 733, 226 USPQ 784 (Fed. Cir. 1985). Surely the court did not mean to suggest that the venue of infringement suits against aliens is not governed by 28 U.S.C. §1391(d), which provides that an alien may be sued in any district. *Brunette Mach. Works v. Kochum Indus., Inc.*, 406 U.S. 706, 174 USPQ 1 (1972). It should also be noted that suits against patentees that are not residents of the United States (e.g., declaratory judgment actions) may be brought in the U.S. District Court for the District of Columbia. 35 U.S.C. §293.

[242]*In re Cordis Corp.*, 769 F.2d 733, 226 USPQ 784 (Fed. Cir. 1985).

[243]*VE Holding Corp. v. Johnson Gas Appliance Co.*, 917 F.2d 1574, 16 USPQ2d 1614 (Fed. Cir. 1990). This definition is narrower than allowing venue wherever a corporation could be served with process, but is somewhat broader than that encompassed by the previous standard of place of incorporation. *Id.*

[244]*In re Cordis Corp.*, 769 F.2d 733, 226 USPQ 784 (Fed. Cir. 1985).

[245]*In re Cordis Corp.*, 769 F.2d 733, 226 USPQ 784 (Fed. Cir. 1985).

[246]*In re Cordis Corp.*, 769 F.2d 733, 226 USPQ 784 (Fed. Cir. 1985). The court refused to disturb a denial of a motion to dismiss for improper venue, where the accused corporation maintained two full-time sales representatives within the district. Such determinations are highly fact intensive.

[247]*Hoover Group Inc. v. Custom Metalcraft, Inc.*, 84 F.3d 1408, 38 USPQ2d 1860 (Fed. Cir. 1996).

[248]*VE Holding Corp. v. Johnson Gas Appliance Co.*, 917 F.2d 1574, 16 USPQ2d 1614 (Fed. Cir. 1990).

[249]*Minnesota Min. & Mfg. Co. v. Eco Chem, Inc.*, 757 F.2d 1256, 225 USPQ 350 (Fed. Cir. 1985). The court also indicated, in dicta, that venue would be (1) proper as to a corporation by virtue of the acts of alter egos, (2) proper as to a parent by virtue of the acts of a wholly owned

owner for acts of infringement by the corporation, whether or not the facts support piercing the corporate veil, may reasonably be based on the venue provisions for the corporation.[250] However, venue as to corporate employees charged with personal liability for acts taken as individuals, not as the alter ego of the corporation, does not flow automatically to forums in which venue is proper as to the corporation.[251]

Transfers and multidistrict litigation. Parties may seek transfers to a more convenient forum under 28 U.S.C. §1404(a), or to a proper forum under §1406(a). A transfer order is interlocutory, not final and appealable. Transfers to a more convenient forum are reviewable only by mandamus.[252] Where a court dismisses for want of personal jurisdiction, it cannot order a transfer under 28 U.S.C. 1404(a).[253] A motion to transfer under §1404(a) is governed by the law of the regional circuit.[254]

The judicial panel on multidistrict litigation is authorized, pursuant to 28 U.S.C. §1407, to transfer to any district court, for coordinated or consolidated pretrial proceedings, civil actions pending in more than one district and involving one or more common questions of fact. The panel must determine that coordinated pretrial proceedings will be for the convenience of parties and witnesses and will promote the just and efficient conduct of such actions. The purpose of the statute is the avoidance of conflicting and duplicative pretrial demands on parties and witnesses in related cases. Among the factors pertinent to the choice of forum for transfer and consolidation by the panel are: (1) one or more cases already in that court, (2) that court has already developed familiarity with the issues, (3) that court is a central location for witnesses and counsel, (4) relevant documents and witnesses are located in that forum, and (5) a common party is located there.[255]

(c) Personal Jurisdiction

Amenability to service and the exercise of personal jurisdiction are linked together in the federal courts. Under Rule 4(e), a federal

---

subsidiary, and (3) proper as to one corporation by virtue of the acts of another intimately connected corporation. Also, joinder of a successor corporation under Rule 25(c), FRCP, does not disturb venue. *Id.*

[250]*Hoover Group Inc. v. Custom Metalcraft, Inc.,* 84 F.3d 1408, 38 USPQ2d 1860 (Fed. Cir. 1996).

[251]*Hoover Group Inc. v. Custom Metalcraft, Inc.,* 84 F.3d 1408, 38 USPQ2d 1860 (Fed. Cir. 1996).

[252]*Wood v. United States,* 961 F.2d 195 (Fed. Cir. 1992). The Federal Circuit may consider venue transfer questions raised under the All Writs Statute, 28 U.S.C. §1651. *In re Regents of the Univ. of Calif.,* 964 F.2d 1128 (Fed. Cir. 1992). The denial of a motion to transfer under §1404(a) does not bar coordination of pretrial procedures under 28 U.S.C. §1407. *Id.*

[253]*HollyAnne Corp. v. TFT Inc.,* 199 F.3d 1304, 53 USPQ2d 1201 (Fed. Cir. 1999).

[254]*Winner Int'l Royalty Corp. v. Wang,* 202 F.3d 1340, 53 USPQ2d 1580 (Fed. Cir. 2000).

[255]*In re Regents of the Univ. of Calif.,* 964 F.2d 1128 (Fed. Cir. 1992). The Federal Circuit may consider by extraordinary writ transfer and consolidation orders of the multidistrict panel.

court normally looks either to a federal statute or to the long-arm statute of the state in which it sits to determine whether a defendant is amenable to service.[256] But the Federal Circuit decides in personam jurisdiction questions in patent infringement cases purely as a matter of federal law. The tort of patent infringement exists solely by virtue of federal statute, and defining its contours inevitably entails the construction of that statute—not a state long-arm statute. The latter simply creates a general, procedural rule that torts committed in the state give rise to jurisdiction over potential defendants. It is not the source of the substantive right and does not purport to affect its scope or nature. So while the federal choice of law rule concerning personal jurisdiction requires the court to look to state law in the first instance, the character of the particular tort alleged requires a look back to federal law on the conceptualization of the tort and its situs.[257]

Where subject matter jurisdiction over an action exists by virtue of a federal question rather than diversity, the due process consideration is that of the Fifth Amendment. The Federal Circuit recognizes that the Supreme Court's jurisprudence has thus far included only state and diversity cases, and thus explicates only the demands of the Fourteenth Amendment. Nonetheless, the court applies that jurisprudence, including the minimum contacts standard, to personal jurisdiction in federal question cases, such as those arising under the patent laws. The most recent summarization of minimum contacts theory looks to whether the defendant has purposefully directed its activities at residents of the forum and whether the litigation results from alleged injuries that arise out of or relate to those activities. Where the defendant deliberately has engaged in significant activities within a state, or has created continuing obligations between itself and residents of the forum, it has availed itself of the privilege of conducting business there. Because its activities are shielded by the benefits and protections of the forum's laws it is presumptively not unreasonable to require it to submit to the burdens of litigation in that forum as well.[258]

For a long time, the Federal Circuit had no opportunity to confront the constitutional limits on exercise of in personam jurisdiction by the federal courts whose judgments it reviews.[259] The nearest the court came to grappling with the constitutional "minimum contacts" concept was its holding that a court that has jurisdiction over a

---

Id. In *Regents of Univ. of Calif. v. Eli Lilly & Co.*, 119 F.3d 1559, 43 USPQ2d 1398 (Fed. Cir. 1997), the court was able to pass the question of whether a case transferred under 28 U.S.C. §1407(a) for consolidated pretrial proceedings must be returned for trial on the merits to the court from which it was transferred.

[256]*Akro Corp. v. Luker*, 45 F.3d 1541, 33 USPQ2d 1505 (Fed. Cir. 1995).

[257]*North Am. Philips Corp. v. American Vending Sales, Inc.*, 35 F.3d 1576, 32 USPQ2d 1203 (Fed. Cir. 1994).

[258]*Akro Corp. v. Luker*, 45 F.3d 1541, 33 USPQ2d 1505 (Fed. Cir. 1995).

[259]The court itself suggested that questions of personal jurisdiction might begin to be encountered more frequently in patent infringement cases due to the 1988 amendments to the venue statutes. Venue, at least in the corporate setting, used to be a much stricter requirement.

corporation has jurisdiction over its alter egos.[260] In the same case, it held that where the district court had in personam jurisdiction over the original corporate party and a successor corporation was properly served and joined, the district court has in personam jurisdiction over the successor corporation without regard to its contacts with the forum. The theory is that the successor is not joined because its substantive rights are in question, but rather because it has come to own the property in issue.[261]

In *Beverly Hills Fan*,[262] the court finally had an opportunity to consider a serious question of personal jurisdiction in a patent infringement case. One defendant was a Chinese corporation that manufactured the accused fans in Taiwan and the second corporate defendant was a New Jersey importer. Neither had assets or employees in the forum state, Virginia. Neither was licensed to do business nor had an agent for service of process in Virginia, and both denied direct shipments of the fans into Virginia. The evidence showed that one of the fans had been purchased by the plaintiff from a retail outlet in Virginia, and that a manual accompanying the fan identified the importer as the source and warrantor of the product. Also, three months after the complaint was filed, there were at least 50 of the fans for sale at six retail outlets in Virginia.[263] On these facts, the Federal Circuit held that both due process and the Virginia long-arm statute were satisfied.

As an initial matter, the court decided that it should apply its own law rather than regional circuit law to such questions. Although in one sense the due process issue is procedural, it is a critical determinant of whether and in what forum a patentee can seek redress for infringement of its rights. The regional circuits have not reached a uniform approach to the stream of commerce theory that governs the underlying jurisdictional issue. Application of regional circuit law would not therefore promote the Federal Circuit's mandate of achieving national uniformity in the field of patent law. Conversely, the

---

Now it is coextensive with personal jurisdiction. *VE Holding Corp. v. Johnson Gas Appliance Co.*, 917 F.2d 1574, 16 USPQ2d 1614 (Fed. Cir. 1990).

[260]*Minnesota Min. & Mfg. Co. v. Eco Chem, Inc.*, 757 F.2d 1256, 225 USPQ 350 (Fed. Cir. 1985).

[261]*Minnesota Min. & Mfg. Co. v. Eco Chem, Inc.*, 757 F.2d 1256, 225 USPQ 350 (Fed. Cir. 1985).

[262]*Beverly Hills Fan Co. v. Royal Sovereign Corp.*, 21 F.3d 1558, 30 USPQ2d 1001 (Fed. Cir. 1994).

[263]This item of evidence is noteworthy for two reasons. First, it was based on an affidavit reporting on telephone conversations with unnamed employees of the retail outlets. Despite the obvious hearsay nature of this evidence, the court seemed impressed by the fact that the defendants could have independently verified the accuracy of the affidavit statements. More significantly, the evidence had to do with contacts with the forum state occurring after the filing of the complaint. The Federal Circuit distinguished a case involving a single tortious act that inflicted discrete injury upon the victim. Here, by contrast, the causes of action, direct infringement and inducement, both involve continuous infliction of injury upon the victim. In a case involving a continuous tort, such as patent infringement, it would be arbitrary to identify a single moment after which the defendants' contacts with the forum necessarily become

creation and application of a uniform body of Federal Circuit law in this area would clearly promote judicial efficiency, would not create undue conflict and confusion at the district court level, and would be consistent with that mandate. Moreover, it would further the elimination of forum shopping.[264] Thus, with regard to the federal constitutional due process analysis of a defendant's contacts with the forum state in patent cases, the court does not defer to the interpretations of other federal and state courts. However, in interpreting the meaning of state long-arm statutes, it elects to defer to the interpretations of the relevant state and federal courts, including their determinations regarding whether or not such statutes are intended to reach to the limit of federal due process.[265]

The *Beverly Hills Fan* court then turned to the merits of the minimum contacts theory of jurisdictional due process. The requirement for purposeful minimum contacts helps ensure that nonresidents have fair warning that a particular activity may subject them to litigation within the forum. Fair warning is desirable, for nonresidents are thus able to organize their affairs, alleviate the risk of burdensome litigation by procuring insurance and the like, and otherwise plan for the possibility that litigation in the forum might ensue. Moreover, notwithstanding the existence of purposeful minimum contacts, a due process determination requires one further step. Even if the requisite minimum contacts have been found through an application of the stream of commerce theory or otherwise, if it would be unreasonable[266] for the forum to assert jurisdiction under all the facts

---

irrelevant to the issue of personal jurisdiction. *Beverly Hills Fan Co. v. Royal Sovereign Corp.*, 21 F.3d 1558, 30 USPQ2d 1001 (Fed. Cir. 1994).

[264]*Beverly Hills Fan Co. v. Royal Sovereign Corp.*, 21 F.3d 1558, 30 USPQ2d 1001 (Fed. Cir. 1994). See also *Dainippon Screen Mfg. Co. v. CFMT Inc.*, 142 F.3d 1266, 46 USPQ2d 1616 (Fed. Cir. 1998). The jurisdictional issues presented by an out-of-state patentee defending a declaratory judgment action are no less intimately involved with the substance of the patent laws than that of an out-of-state accused infringer. Accordingly, the court applies its own law. *Akro Corp. v. Luker*, 45 F.3d 1541, 33 USPQ2d 1505 (Fed. Cir. 1995). See also *Red Wing Shoe Co. v. Hockerson-Halberstadt Inc.*, 148 F.3d 1355, 47 USPQ2d 1192 (Fed. Cir. 1998). Indeed, where there is a patent infringement claim joined with state law claims, the district court is obligated to apply Federal Circuit law, rather than regional circuit law, to personal jurisdiction questions on both sets of claims. *3D Sys. Inc. v. Aarotech Labs. Inc.*,160 F.3d 1373, 48 USPQ2d 1773 (Fed. Cir. 1998). However, where a claim for declaratory judgment of noninfringement is dismissed for lack of subject matter jurisdiction, leaving only state law trade libel and defamation claims, regional circuit law may be applied. *Amana Ref. Inc. v. Quadlux Inc.*, 172 F.3d 852, 50 USPQ2d 1304 (Fed. Cir. 1999).

[265]*Graphic Controls Corp. v. Utah Med. Prods. Inc.*, 149 F.3d 1382, 47 USPQ2d 1622 (Fed. Cir. 1998). In *3D Sys. Inc. v. Aarotech Labs. Inc.*,160 F.3d 1373, 48 USPQ2d 1773 (Fed. Cir. 1998), the court noted that it has rejected previous attempts to shape its personal jurisdiction law through state common law definitions of federal statutory terms. While it may be appropriate to speak loosely of patent infringement as a tort, more accurately the cause of action for patent infringement is created and defined by statute. Defining the contours of the tort of infringement, which exists solely by virtue of federal statute, entails the construction of the federal statute and not a state's common or statutory law. The tort of patent infringement due to an "offer to sell" is a federal statutory creation and is not limited by state contract law. The statutory character of the "offer to sell" requires a look back to federal law on the conceptualization of the "offer to sell" itself.

[266]The court concluded that there was an intentional distribution channel formed by the defendants and the retailer, and that the defendants knew, or reasonably could have foreseen,

and circumstances, then due process requires that jurisdiction be denied.[267] In general, such cases are limited to the rare situation in which the plaintiff's interest[268] and the state's interest are so attenuated that they are clearly outweighed by the burden of subjecting the defendant to litigation within the forum. A state has an interest in discouraging injuries that occur within the state, including patent infringement. It also has an interest in cooperating with other states to provide a forum for litigating the plaintiff's cause of action. In a patent infringement case, the plaintiff will be able to seek redress for sales in other states as well, and those states will thus be spared the burden of providing a forum. And the defendants will be protected from harassment resulting from multiple suits.[269]

Finally, the court focused on Virginia's long-arm statute. Although it appeared that the Virginia legislature intended the statute to extend its jurisdiction as far as due process would allow, it also appeared that the intention was that the particulars of the statute be satisfied even though it might be argued that a lesser standard

---

that a termination point of the channel was Virginia. Their conduct and connections with Virginia were therefore such that they should reasonably have anticipated being brought into court there. *Beverly Hills Fan Co. v. Royal Sovereign Corp.*, 21 F.3d 1558, 30 USPQ2d 1001 (Fed. Cir. 1994).

[267]In a later case, *Akro Corp. v. Luker*, 45 F.3d 1541, 33 USPQ2d 1505 (Fed. Cir. 1995), the court further explained the additional fairness inquiry. Satisfaction of the two fundamental inquiries, whether the defendant purposefully directed its activities at residents of the state and, if so, whether the litigation results from alleged injuries that arise from or relate to those activities, while necessary, is not always sufficient to justify personal jurisdiction over the defendant. If the assertion of jurisdiction fails to comport with notions of fair play and substantial justice, the court must be satisfied that the defendant has not presented a compelling case that jurisdiction would be constitutionally unreasonable. But the burden of proof as to this final prong is on the defendant. It should be noted that the court also seemed to suggest that the considerations of fairness must be matters that could not be addressed by filing a motion for change of venue under 28 U.S.C. §1404(a). In *Dainippon Screen Mfg. Co. v. CFMT Inc.*, 142 F.3d 1266, 46 USPQ2d 1616 (Fed. Cir. 1998), the defendant patent holding company exclusively licensed its parent corporation, which competed with the declaratory plaintiff in the forum state. The defendant itself issued threats of infringement suit to plaintiff there. The notion that a parent company can incorporate a holding company in another state, transfer its patents to the holding company, arrange to have those patents licensed back to itself by virtue of its complete control over the holding company, and threaten its competitors with infringement without fear of being a declaratory judgment defendant, save perhaps in the state of incorporation of the holding company, qualified for one of the Federal Circuit's "chutzpah" awards. While a patent holding subsidiary is a legitimate creature and may provide certain business advantages, it cannot fairly be used to insulate patent owners from defending declaratory judgment actions in those forums where its parent company operates under the patent and engages in activities sufficient to create personal jurisdiction and declaratory judgment jurisdiction.

[268]The court recognized that, although a plaintiff's residence in the forum may, because of the defendant's relationship with the plaintiff, enhance defendant's contacts with the forum, plaintiff's residence there is not a separate requirement. Lack of residence will not defeat jurisdiction established on the basis of the defendant's contacts. *Beverly Hills Fan Co. v. Royal Sovereign Corp.*, 21 F.3d 1558, 30 USPQ2d 1001 (Fed. Cir. 1994).

[269]In considering prejudice to the defendants, the court even addressed the Eastern District of Virginia's celebrated "rocket docket" (five months average from joining issue to trial in civil cases). It observed that merely because it may be to the plaintiff's advantage to litigate a patent infringement case there does not militate against its right to have access to that court where there is a question of personal jurisdiction. *Beverly Hills Fan Co. v. Royal Sovereign Corp.*, 21 F.3d 1558, 30 USPQ2d 1001 (Fed. Cir. 1994).

would meet due process. Thus, a separate analysis was required.[270] First, the court concluded that the situs of the injury in the context of patent infringement is the location at which the infringing activity directly impacts on the interests of the patentee, such as the situs of the infringing sales, rather than the residence of the patentee. Among the most important rights in the bundle of rights owned by a patent holder is the right to exclude others. This right is not limited to a particular situs, but exists anywhere the patent is recognized. A patent is a federally created property right, valid throughout the United States. Its legal situs would seem to be anywhere it is called into play. As an example, the right to exclude is violated at the situs where a sale occurs. Similarly, economic loss occurs to the patent holder at the place where the infringing sale is made because the patent owner loses business there. This loss is immediate when the patent holder is marketing a competing product. And even if it is not, the loss may be no less real since the sale represents a loss in potential revenue through licensing or other arrangements. Additionally, a focus on the place where the infringing sales are made is consistent with other areas of intellectual property law such as trademark and copyright.[271]

In a subsequent case,[272] the court reaffirmed the *Beverly Hills* holding that patent infringement occurs where the infringing sales are made. It rejected mechanical tests such as where title passes, and flatly held that to sell an infringing article to a buyer in a state is to commit a tort[273] there (though not necessarily only there). That conclusion is not arrived at without difficulty, however. The selling of an infringing article, unlike the making and the using of it, which as purely physical occurrences are relatively straightforward to place, has both a physical and a conceptual dimension to it. That is to say, it is possible to define the situs of the tort of infringement-by-sale either in real terms as including the location of the seller and the buyer and perhaps the points along the shipment route in between, or in formal terms as the single point at which some legally operative

---

[270]In Ohio, the statute provides that a court may exercise personal jurisdiction over a person as to a cause of action arising from the person's transacting any business in the state. This has been held to extend to the greatest permissible reach consistent with due process. *Akro Corp. v. Luker*, 45 F.3d 1541, 33 USPQ2d 1505 (Fed. Cir. 1995).

[271]Virginia's statute also requires that substantial revenue be derived from goods used or consumed or services rendered within the state; such revenue need not be related to the tortious injury in question. The court held that an admitted 3% of the defendant's revenues owing to an unrelated product, coupled with an inference of substantial absolute revenues derived from infringing sales within the state, satisfied this requirement. *Beverly Hills Fan Co. v. Royal Sovereign Corp.*, 21 F.3d 1558, 30 USPQ2d 1001 (Fed. Cir. 1994).

[272]*North Am. Philips Corp. v. American Vending Sales, Inc.*, 35 F.3d 1576, 32 USPQ2d 1203 (Fed. Cir. 1994).

[273]The court noted that while it may be appropriate to speak loosely of patent infringement as a tort, more accurately the cause of action for patent infringement is created and defined by statute. 35 U.S.C. §271 does not speak generally of the tort of patent infringement, but specifically of a liability that arises upon the making, using, or selling of an infringing article. Thus the statute on its face clearly suggests the conception that the "tort" of patent infringement occurs where the offending act is committed and not where the injury is felt. *North Am. Philips Corp. v. American Vending Sales, Inc.*, 35 F.3d 1576, 32 USPQ2d 1203 (Fed. Cir. 1994).

act took place (such as the place where the sales transaction would be deemed to have occurred as a matter of commercial law).[274] Thus, determining whether jurisdiction exists over an out-of-state defendant involves two inquiries: whether a forum state's long-arm statute permits the assertion of jurisdiction and whether assertion of personal jurisdiction violates federal due process.[275] However, where the forum state's long-arm statute is coextensive with the limits of due process, the two inquiries collapse into one: whether jurisdiction comports with due process.[276] In those states where the long-arm statute is coextensive with the limits of due process, the focus of the inquiry involves consideration of three factors: whether the defendant purposefully directed its activities at residents of the forum, whether the claim arises out of or relates to the defendant's activities with the forum, and whether assertion of personal jurisdiction is reasonable and fair.[277] The minimum contacts test examines the number and nature of a defendant's contacts with the forum. In general, when the cause of action at issue arises out of or relates to those contacts, a court may properly assert personal jurisdiction, even if those contacts are isolated and sporadic. Jurisdiction in this situation has the name "specific" jurisdiction. In fact, even a single act can support jurisdiction, so long as it creates a substantial connection with the forum, as opposed to an attenuated affiliation. In contrast, a defendant whose contacts with a forum are continuous and systematic may be subject to jurisdiction even when the cause of action has no relation to those contacts. Jurisdiction in this situation has the name general jurisdiction. In both situations, contacts only add to the quantum for personal jurisdiction when purposefully directed at the forum or its residents. Random, fortuitous, or attenuated contacts do not count in the minimum contacts calculus. Similarly, contacts resulting from the unilateral activity of others do not count.[278]

---

[274]The goods were delivered f.o.b. Texas and California, not Illinois, where they were ultimately shipped to the distributor. The court held that these circumstances satisfied due process. Illinois has an interest in prohibiting the importation of infringing articles into its territory and regulating the conduct of distributors with respect to subsequent resales. Surely the reasonable market participant in the modern commercial world has to expect to be haled into the courts of a state, however distant, to answer for any liability based at least in part on importation. *North Am. Philips Corp. v. American Vending Sales, Inc.*, 35 F.3d 1576, 32 USPQ2d 1203 (Fed. Cir. 1994).

[275]*Graphic Controls Corp. v. Utah Med. Prods. Inc.*, 149 F.3d 1382, 47 USPQ2d 1622 (Fed. Cir. 1998); *Dainippon Screen Mfg. Co. v. CFMT Inc.*, 142 F.3d 1266, 46 USPQ2d 1616 (Fed. Cir. 1998); *Genetic Implant Sys., Inc. v. Core-Vent Corp.*, 123 F.3d 1455, 43 USPQ2d 1786 (Fed. Cir. 1997).

[276]*Dainippon Screen Mfg. Co. v. CFMT Inc.*, 142 F.3d 1266, 46 USPQ2d 1616 (Fed. Cir. 1998).

[277]*Genetic Implant Sys., Inc. v. Core-Vent Corp.*, 123 F.3d 1455, 43 USPQ2d 1786 (Fed. Cir. 1997).

[278]*Red Wing Shoe Co. v. Hockerson-Halberstadt Inc.*, 148 F.3d 1355, 47 USPQ2d 1192 (Fed. Cir. 1998). In *3D Sys. Inc. v. Aarotech Labs. Inc.*, 160 F.3d 1373, 48 USPQ2d 1773 (Fed. Cir. 1998), the court reaffirmed and applied the three-pronged test for specific jurisdiction. On the second prong—whether the cause of action arises out of or directly relates to those activities—it finds that an offer to sell is sufficient. It rejected the suggestion that state law should control that determination, and turned instead to the "offer to sell" provision of 35 U.S.C. §271(a).

The court has also considered personal jurisdiction over declaratory judgment defendants. In one case the defendant patentee sent warning letters to the Ohio plaintiff's patent counsel (albeit the counsel was located in North Carolina). The patentee also entered into an exclusive license agreement with an Ohio company. Thus the activity was purposefully directed at Ohio residents. And the plaintiff's cause of action arose out of or related to those activities, satisfying the second prong of the minimum contacts analysis. Finally, as to fairness and constitutional reasonableness, it is clear that Ohio had a manifest interest in providing its residents with a convenient forum for redressing injuries inflicted by out-of-state actors. The injury complained of—restraint of plaintiff's production of goods by means of a noninfringed, invalid, or unenforceable patent—falls well within the boundaries of the sorts of injuries that Ohio has an interest in discouraging.[279] In a later case, the threatened infringer sued an Italian patentee, and its Iowa exclusive licensee, in California. The court found that the Italian patentee had purposefully directed its activities at the forum state, and its exclusive licensee purposefully initiated the interaction with the plaintiff that resulted in the declaratory judgment action. All the reasons for adopting and applying the stream of commerce theory to the question of personal jurisdiction over an out-of-state alleged infringer as defendant are equally applicable to the same question regarding an out-of-state patentee as defendant. Under the circumstances the California court certainly had the power to decide the issues brought before it, and its exercise of jurisdiction would not be contrary to concepts of fair play and substantial justice.[280]

The sending of infringement notices, without more activity in a forum state, is not sufficient to satisfy the requirements of due process.[281] Even though cease-and-desist letters alone are often substantially related to the cause of action, thus providing minimum contacts, principles of fair play and substantial justice afford a patentee sufficient latitude to inform others of its patent rights without subjecting

---

[279]*Akro Corp. v. Luker*, 45 F.3d 1541, 33 USPQ2d 1505 (Fed. Cir. 1995). An offer to donate equipment to a school does not constitute an offer to sell within the meaning of 35 U.S.C. §271(a), and thus such activity does not give rise to the cause of action for purposes of the second prong of the *Akro* test for specific jurisdiction.

[280]*Viam Corp. v. Iowa Export-Import Trading Co.*, 84 F.3d 424, 38 USPQ2d 1833 (Fed. Cir. 1996).

[281]*Genetic Implant Sys., Inc. v. Core-Vent Corp.*, 123 F.3d 1455, 43 USPQ2d 1786 (Fed. Cir. 1997). Here, however, there was much more, including a program to develop a market within the state and the appointment of a distributor who sold into the state (a situation analogous to the grant of a patent license). The fact that some of these activities may have occurred prior to issuance of the patent is irrelevant. It is jurisdiction that is at issue, not liability for patent infringement. In *Graphic Controls Corp. v. Utah Med. Prods. Inc.*, 149 F.3d 1382, 47 USPQ2d 1622 (Fed. Cir. 1998), the court found that, under New York law, the state long-arm statute does not extend to the limits of due process. It then found that the plaintiff's cause of action must arise out of the business activities in the state, and that those activities must be such that the defendant projects itself into the state to purposefully avail itself of the benefits and protections of the state's laws. It concluded that defendant's cease-and-desist letters, which gave rise to the declaratory judgment cause of action, were of insufficient quality and degree to be considered transaction of business under New York law.

itself to jurisdiction in a foreign forum. A patentee should not subject itself to personal jurisdiction in a forum solely by informing a party who happens to be located there of suspected infringement. Grounding personal jurisdiction on such contacts alone would not comport with principles of fairness. Moreover, an offer for a license within a cease-and-desist letter does not somehow convert that letter into something more than it was already. An offer to license is more closely akin to an offer for settlement of a disputed claim rather than an arm's-length negotiation in anticipation of a long-term continuing business relationship. Treating such hybrid cease-and-desist letters differently would also be contrary to fair play and substantial justice by providing disincentives for the initiation of settlement negotiations.[282]

A divided panel of the court has held that filing an ANDA with the FDA office in Maryland does not support personal jurisdiction for a patent infringement action there.[283] Letters sent by the patentee to distributors in states other than the forum state were held insufficient to support in personam jurisdiction in a trade libel action.[284]

Failure to object to service of process as insufficient, in a motion to dismiss a cross-claim, constitutes a waiver of the objection.[285]

A district court determination that it lacks personal jurisdiction of a party—a question of law—is reviewed without deference,[286] while disputed facts underlying this legal determination are reviewed for clear error.[287]

---

[282]*Red Wing Shoe Co. v. Hockerson-Halberstadt Inc.*, 148 F.3d 1355, 47 USPQ2d 1192 (Fed. Cir. 1998). In this case, the patent owner defendant sold no product in the forum state, but had many licensees who did. The court rejected several of the declaratory plaintiff's arguments that this additional factor should suffice to submit the defendant to personal jurisdiction there. Thus, doing business with a company that does business in the forum state is not the same as doing business there. Contacts resulting from the unilateral activity of another party or third person are not attributable to a defendant. Also, receipt of royalty income from licensees for sales made in the forum state is irrelevant. And it would be improper to describe the licensees, none of whom were residents of the forum state, as a distribution channel in order to invoke a "stream of commerce" theory. The defendant's product is a covenant not to sue, not a device incorporating the patented technology.

[283]*Zeneca Ltd. v. Mylan Pharm. Inc.*, 173 F.3d 829, 50 USPQ2d 1294 (Fed. Cir. 1999). One judge dissented without opinion. One judge applied the so-called government contacts exception, holding that entry into Maryland by a nonresident for the purpose of contacting a federal government agency does not provide a basis for the assertion of in personam jurisdiction. The third judge opined that such an activity is not a contact with the state at all; the defendant did not purposefully avail itself of the benefits of the laws of Maryland or direct its activities at Maryland residents. Thus, according to the third judge, the court need not adopt the government contacts exception.

[284]*Amana Ref. Inc. v. Quadlux Inc.*, 172 F.3d 852, 50 USPQ2d 1304 (Fed. Cir. 1999).

[285]*United States v. Rush*, 804 F.2d 645 (Fed. Cir. 1986).

[286]*Viam Corp. v. Iowa Export-Import Trading Co.*, 84 F.3d 424, 38 USPQ2d 1833 (Fed. Cir. 1996). A district court's ultimate conclusion as to whether it has in personam jurisdiction, and any subsidiary conclusions regarding the legal effect of particular jurisdictional facts, present questions of law subject to review de novo. *North Am. Philips Corp. v. American Vending Sales, Inc.*, 35 F.3d 1576, 32 USPQ2d 1203 (Fed. Cir. 1994). See also *Graphic Controls Corp. v. Utah Med. Prods. Inc.*, 149 F.3d 1382, 47 USPQ2d 1622 (Fed. Cir. 1998); *Genetic Implant Sys., Inc. v. Core-Vent Corp.*, 123 F.3d 1455, 43 USPQ2d 1786 (Fed. Cir. 1997); *Akro Corp. v. Luker*, 45 F.3d 1541, 33 USPQ2d 1505 (Fed. Cir. 1995).

[287]*Dainippon Screen Mfg. Co. v. CFMT Inc.*, 142 F.3d 1266, 46 USPQ2d 1616, 1619 (Fed. Cir. 1998).

§8.2 Federal Procedure

The Federal Rules of Civil and Appellate Procedure and the Federal Rules of Evidence are and should be applied in patent cases no differently from their application in any other type of case.[288] The Federal Rules of Civil Procedure are more than guidelines for orderly litigation; they ensure that the proceedings are conducted fairly, with the objective of uncovering the truth and in accordance with the fundamental principles of due process.[289] It is well established that a court's procedural rules promulgated pursuant to statutory authorization are deemed to have the force and effect of law.[290]

(a) Pleading and Joinder

The principal function of procedural rules should be to serve as useful guides to help, not hinder, persons who have a legal right to bring their problems before the courts. The Federal Rules of Civil Procedure reject the notion that pleading is a game of skill in which one misstep by counsel may be decisive as to the outcome and instead accept the principle that the purpose of pleading is to facilitate a proper decision on the merits.[291]

Rule 12 motions. Rule 12(b), FRCP, permits certain defenses to be raised, at the option of the pleader, by motion. Motions under Rule 12(b)(1), directed at jurisdictional issues, are discussed elsewhere.[292] The presence of a valid defense does not oust a tribunal of jurisdiction unless, of course, the defense is jurisdictional. Where the defendant has a valid defense and there are no material disputed facts, it may move for summary judgment or dismissal for failure to state a claim upon which relief can be granted, depending upon the proofs needed.[293] Rule 12(b)(2) provides for motions to dismiss for lack of personal jurisdiction. Where the plaintiff's factual allegations are not directly

---

[288]*SRI Int'l v. Matsushita Elec. Corp.,* 775 F.2d 1107, 227 USPQ 577 (Fed. Cir. 1985).

[289]*In re Newman,* 782 F.2d 971, 228 USPQ 450 (Fed. Cir. 1986). Strict compliance with local procedural rules is, of course, always desirable. *D.L. Auld Co. v. Chroma Graphics Corp.,* 714 F.2d 1144, 219 USPQ 13 (Fed. Cir. 1983). It is possible that the Federal Circuit may have misapprehended the source of the Federal Rules of Civil Procedure in *Eaton Corp. v. Appliance Valves Corp.,* 790 F.2d 874, 229 USPQ 668 (Fed. Cir. 1986), where the comment was made that Rule 26, FRCP, reflects the clear intent of Congress that courts be permissive in the introduction of relevant evidence. With all respect, the Federal Rules are promulgated by the U.S. Supreme Court, and the only involvement of Congress is a requirement that the Court report them to Congress 90 days prior to the effective date so that Congress can change any laws that may conflict with the rules. See 28 U.S.C. §2072.

[290]*M.A. Mortenson Co. v. United States,* 996 F.2d 1177 (Fed. Cir. 1993).

[291]*Cornwall v. U.S. Constr. Mfg., Inc.,* 800 F.2d 250, 231 USPQ 64 (Fed. Cir. 1986). Leniency with respect to formal matters should normally be extended to a pro se party. *Kelley v. Department of Labor,* 812 F.2d 1378 (Fed. Cir. 1987).

[292]See text accompanying 8:27–37.

[293]*Do-Well Mach. Shop, Inc. v. United States,* 870 F.2d 637 (Fed. Cir. 1989).

controverted by such a motion, they are taken as true for purposes of determining jurisdiction.[294]

Rule 12(b)(6) authorizes a defendant to move, before filing a responsive pleading, for dismissal of the complaint. Such a motion challenges the legal theory of the complaint, not the sufficiency of any evidence that might be adduced. The purpose of the rule is to allow the court to eliminate actions that are fatally flawed in their legal premises and destined to failure, and thus to spare litigants the burdens of unnecessary pretrial and trial activity.[295] Such a motion, which cuts off a claimant at the threshold, must be denied unless it appears beyond doubt that the plaintiff can prove no set of facts in support of its claim that would entitle it to relief.[296] The question of whether a Rule 12(b)(6) motion was properly granted is a purely procedural question not pertaining to patent law, to which the court applies the rule of the regional circuit.[297]

The Rule 12(b)(6) pleading requirements for a complaint of patent infringement cannot be extended to require a plaintiff to specifically include each element of the claims of the asserted patent. Such requirements do not demand that a patentee amend its pleading to include specific allegations about each limitation once a court has construed the claims of the patent. To impose such requirements would contravene the notice pleading standard, and would add needless steps to the already complex process of patent litigation. Instead, a patentee need only plead facts sufficient to place the alleged infringer on notice. This requirement ensures that an accused infringer has sufficient knowledge of the facts alleged to enable it to answer the complaint and defend itself.[298]

---

[294]*Akro Corp. v. Luker*, 45 F.3d 1541, 33 USPQ2d 1505 (Fed. Cir. 1995). Hearsay evidence that bears circumstantial indicia of reliability may be admitted for purposes of determining whether personal jurisdiction obtains. *Id.*

[295]*Advanced Cardiovascular Sys., Inc. v. Scimed Life Sys., Inc.*, 988 F.2d 1157, 26 USPQ2d 1038 (Fed. Cir. 1993). But a complaint need not specify the correct legal theory, or point to the right statute, to survive a motion to dismiss. Thus, the fact that the plaintiff may have selected the law of the wrong state in support of its trade secret claim does not justify dismissal. *C&F Packing Co. v. IBP Inc.*, 224 F.3d 1296, 55 USPQ2d 1865 (Fed. Cir. 2000).

[296]*Highland Falls-Fort Dist. v. United States*, 48 F.3d 1166 (Fed. Cir. 1995); *Advanced Cardiovascular Sys., Inc. v. Scimed Life Sys., Inc.*, 988 F.2d 1157, 26 USPQ2d 1038 (Fed. Cir. 1993); *Constant v. Advanced Micro-Devices, Inc.*, 848 F.2d 1560, 7 USPQ2d 1057 (Fed. Cir. 1988). A dismissal, even sua sponte, for failure to state a claim on which relief could be granted does not violate due process. In such a case, the court is simply stating that, as a matter of law, the party's case is untenable, and no additional proceedings could have enabled the party to prove any set of facts entitling it to prevail. *Constant v. United States*, 929 F.2d 654, 18 USPQ2d 1298 (Fed. Cir. 1991). Under the simplified notice pleading of the Federal Rules, the allegations of a complaint or petition should be construed liberally and the complaint should not be dismissed for failure to state a claim unless it appears beyond doubt that the plaintiff can prove no set of facts in support of its claim that would entitle it to relief. *Scotch Whisky Ass'n v. U.S. Distilled Prods. Co.*, 952 F.2d 1317, 21 USPQ2d 1145 (Fed. Cir. 1991).

[297]*C&F Packing Co. v. IBP Inc.*, 224 F.3d 1865, 55 USPQ2d 1865 (Fed. Cir. 2000).

[298]*Phonometrics Inc. v. Hospitality Franchise Sys. Inc.*, 203 F.3d 790, 53 USPQ2d 1762 (Fed. Cir. 2000). In this case, the complaint alleged ownership of the asserted patent, named each individual defendant, cited the patent that was allegedly infringed, described the means by which the defendants allegedly infringed, and pointed to the specific sections of the patent

In keeping with the rules governing dismissal under Rule 12(b)(6) the factual statements in the complaint are accepted as true. The dismissal of a claim under Rule 12(b)(6) is proper only when, on the complainant's version of the facts, the premises of a cognizable claim have not been stated. The appellate court, like the district court, tests the sufficiency of the complaint as a matter of law, accepting as true all well-pleaded allegations of fact, construed in the light most favorable to the plaintiff. Conclusory allegations of law and unwarranted inferences of fact do not suffice to support a claim.[299] In order to be sustained, a Rule 12(b)(6) dismissal must be correct as a matter of law when the allegations of the complaint are taken as true.[300] Disputed issues are construed favorably to the complainant and all reasonable inferences are drawn in its favor.[301] To the extent that factual questions are raised and are material to the result, dismissal is improper unless there is no reasonable view of the facts that could support the claim.[302]

A motion to dismiss under Rule 12(b)(6) may rest on plaintiff's lack of standing.[303] However, the strictures of Rule 12(b)(6) are not readily applicable to a determination of laches. Although a Rule 12(b)(6) motion may be grounded on an affirmative defense, the defense of laches usually requires factual development beyond the content of the complaint.[304]

Rule 12(b)(6) provides that if matters outside the complainant's pleading are presented to the court the motion shall be treated as one for summary judgment under Rule 56. But there is a significant difference. A movant's challenge to the sufficiency of the complaint as a matter of law, brought under Rule 12(b)(6), is not sufficient notice that the nonmovant must respond as if to a motion for summary

---

law invoked. It thus contained enough detail to allow the defendants to answer, and Rule 12(b)(6) requires no more.

[299]*Bradley v. Chiron Corp.,* 136 F.3d 1370, 45 USPQ2d 1819 (Fed. Cir. 1998). See also *Highland Falls-Fort Dist. v. United States,* 48 F.3d 1166 (Fed. Cir. 1995); *Abbott Labs. v. Brennan,* 952 F.2d 1346, 21 USPQ2d 1192 (Fed. Cir. 1992). In an antitrust action the complaint need only allege sufficient facts from which the court can discern the elements of an injury resulting from an act forbidden by the antitrust laws. But allegations of legal conclusions are insufficient to withstand a motion to dismiss. *Id.* Whether a complaint is properly dismissed for failure to state a claim upon which relief can be granted is a question of law that is reviewed de novo. *Dehne v. United States,* 970 F.2d 890 (Fed. Cir. 1992). No deference is owed to the holding of the trial court. *Advanced Cardiovascular Sys., Inc. v. Scimed Life Sys., Inc.,* 988 F.2d 1157, 26 USPQ2d 1038 (Fed. Cir. 1993).

[300]*Bristol-Myers Squibb Co. v. Royce Labs., Inc.,* 69 F.3d 1130, 36 USPQ2d 1641 (Fed. Cir. 1995); *Advanced Cardiovascular Sys., Inc. v. Scimed Life Sys., Inc.,* 988 F.2d 1157, 26 USPQ2d 1038 (Fed. Cir. 1993).

[301]*Cedars-Sinai Med. Ctr. v. Watkins,* 11 F.3d 1573, 29 USPQ2d 1188 (Fed. Cir. 1993); *Advanced Cardiovascular Sys., Inc. v. Scimed Life Sys., Inc.,* 988 F.2d 1157, 26 USPQ2d 1038 (Fed. Cir. 1993); *Atlas Corp. v. United States,* 895 F.2d 745 (Fed. Cir. 1990).

[302]*Advanced Cardiovascular Sys., Inc. v. Scimed Life Sys., Inc.,* 988 F.2d 1157, 26 USPQ2d 1038 (Fed. Cir. 1993).

[303]*Animal Legal Defense Fund v. Quigg,* 932 F.2d 920, 18 USPQ2d 920 (Fed. Cir. 1991). See the discussion of standing in §8.1(a)(iv).

[304]*Advanced Cardiovascular Sys., Inc. v. Scimed Life Sys., Inc.,* 988 F.2d 1157, 26 USPQ2d 1038 (Fed. Cir. 1993).

judgment, by placing material facts in dispute. Rule 56 imposes a substantial burden upon the nonmovant to place in dispute the material facts of the case. In contrast, on motion to dismiss on the complainant's pleading it is improper for the court to decide the case on facts not pleaded by the complainant, unless the complainant had notice thereof and the opportunity to proceed in accordance with the rules of summary judgment.[305] It may also make a significant difference whether a claim is dismissed on jurisdictional grounds, under Rule 12(b)(1), or for failure to state a claim under Rule 12(b)(6). For example, if the pleading of a federal claim survives jurisdictional scrutiny, it may support supplemental jurisdiction over state law claims under 28 U.S.C. §1367.[306]

Rule 12(e) authorizes a motion for a more definite statement. The court has branded as bordering the frivolous a contention that the strong public policy of a Supreme Court decision relieved it from the requirement to specify its cause of action in its pleadings.[307] Although nothing in the language of Rule 12(f) explicitly prohibits a court from examining materials beyond the pleadings on a motion to strike, some courts have noted that the general rule is otherwise. The Federal Circuit says that ordinarily a court should be able to determine the legal sufficiency of a defense from the pleadings. However, when a plaintiff raises an equitable challenge to a defense, such as assignor estoppel, a court ought to have a bit more latitude to consider materials beyond the pleadings, particularly if they present uncontested factual matters.[308]

Affirmative defenses and counterclaims. Rule 8(c), FRCP, provides that affirmative defenses must be pleaded and sets forth a sizable list. In addition, 35 U.S.C. §282 denominates the following as defenses and requires that they be pleaded: noninfringement, absence of liability for infringement, unenforceability, invalidity for failure to

---

[305]*Advanced Cardiovascular Sys., Inc. v. Scimed Life Sys., Inc.,* 988 F.2d 1157, 26 USPQ2d 1038 (Fed. Cir. 1993).

[306]*Hunter Douglas Inc. v. Harmonic Design Inc.,* 153 F.3d 1318, 47 USPQ2d 1769 (Fed. Cir. 1998). The court dismissed, on jurisdictional grounds, a claim purporting to state a cause of action to enforce an alleged federal right to copy and use that which is in the public domain.

[307]*Ballard Med. Prods. v. Wright,* 823 F.2d 527, 3 USPQ2d 1337, 1339 (Fed. Cir. 1987). A RICO plaintiff must, under 18 U.S.C. §1964(c), allege an injury to its business or property by reason of a violation of 18 U.S.C. §1962(b). The allegations of RICO violations must be pled with sufficient specificity so as to place the party being sued on notice of the issues involved in the suit. *Formax, Inc. v. Hostert,* 841 F.2d 388, 5 USPQ2d 1939 (Fed. Cir. 1988) (Seventh Circuit law). An allegation that the defendant mailed misappropriated trade secret information to a series of customers on specific dates satisfies the requirement that the content of the communications and the scheme to defraud be listed in the complaint. *Id.* The rules of pleading require that the circumstances constituting fraud or mistake shall be stated with particularity. *Bradley v. Chiron Corp.,* 136 F.3d 1370, 45 USPQ2d 1819 (Fed. Cir. 1998). This case contains a nice discussion of the elements required, under California law, for rescission of a settlement agreement on grounds of mistake or fraud, and also how those elements must be pleaded in a federal complaint.

[308]*Diamond Scientific Co. v. Ambico, Inc.,* 848 F.2d 1220, 6 USPQ2d 2028 (Fed. Cir. 1988). Here the court felt that, because of the equitable nature of the estoppel doctrine, it was not

meet the conditions for patentability or for failure to comply with §§112 or 251, and "any other fact or act made a defense by this title."

Under 35 U.S.C. §282 federal courts are permitted to adjudicate the validity of patents when invalidity is raised as an affirmative defense in infringement suits. Congress was fully within its constitutional power when it delegated this authority to the courts.[309] The validity of a patent is always subject to plenary challenge on its merits. A court may invalidate a patent on any substantive ground, whether or not that ground was considered by the patent examiner.[310]

The Federal Circuit has instructed that any matter that does not controvert the opposing party's prima facie case is to be affirmatively pleaded. Thus, invalidity is an affirmative defense that must be pleaded. Simply denying an allegation that the patent was duly and legally issued is not sufficient.[311] Other affirmative defenses that must be pleaded are prosecution history estoppel,[312] implied license,[313] practicing the prior art,[314] misuse,[315] intervening rights,[316] and double patenting.[317] Inequitable conduct is a separate defense to patent infringement.[318] Res judicata and collateral estoppel are affirmative defenses that must be pleaded. [319] The fact that infringing use was solely for the government is not jurisdictional, but provides simply an affirmative defense that is waived if not pleaded.[320]

---

improper for the district court to have considered some matters outside the strict confines of the pleadings in deciding whether to apply assignor estoppel.

[309]*Constant v. Advanced Micro-Devices, Inc.,* 848 F.2d 1560, 7 USPQ2d 1057 (Fed. Cir. 1988).

[310]*Magnivision, Inc. v. Bonneau Co.,* 115 F.3d 956, 42 USPQ2d 1925 (Fed. Cir. 1997).

[311]*Cornwall v. U.S. Constr. Mfg., Inc.,* 800 F.2d 250, 231 USPQ 64 (Fed. Cir. 1986). Invalidity due to functionality is an affirmative defense to a claim of infringement of a design patent and must be proved by the party asserting the defense. *L.A. Gear, Inc. v. Thom McAn Shoe Co.,* 988 F.2d 1117, 25 USPQ2d 1913 (Fed. Cir.1993).

[312]*Carman Indus., Inc. v. Wahl,* 724 F.2d 932, 220 USPQ 481 (Fed. Cir. 1983).

[313]*Carborundum Co. v. Molten Metal Equip. Innovations,* 72 F.3d 872, 37 USPQ2d 1169 (Fed. Cir. 1995).

[314]*Fiskars Inc. v Hunt Mfg. Co.,* 221 F.3d 1318, 55 USPQ2d 1569 (Fed. Cir. 2000).

[315]*Senza-Gel Corp. v. Seiffhart,* 803 F.2d 661, 231 USPQ 363 (Fed. Cir. 1986); *Windsurfing Int'l, Inc. v. AMF, Inc.,* 782 F.2d 995, 228 USPQ 562 (Fed. Cir. 1986); *Bio-Rad Labs., Inc. v. Nicolet Instr. Corp.,* 739 F.2d 604, 222 USPQ 654 (Fed. Cir. 1984). A counterclaimant on a *Walker Process* antitrust theory was confronted with the running of the statute of limitations. It argued that Rule 11, FRCP, had prohibited it from earlier pleading a *Walker Process* claim without more information. The Federal Circuit observed that such an argument came in bad grace because the counterclaimant had filed a boilerplate answer with many "information and belief" allegations that never saw the light of day at trial. Probably the court felt that the counterclaimant was simply using this as a hindsight argument to excuse a failure to plead the counterclaim earlier. *Korody-Colyer Corp. v. General Motors Corp.,* 828 F.2d 1572, 4 USPQ2d 1203 (Fed. Cir. 1987). It does seem, however, that there could eventually be real tension in this area if Rule 11 enforcement becomes any more vigorous.

[316]*Underwater Devices, Inc. v. Morrison-Knudsen Co.,* 717 F.2d 1380, 219 USPQ 569 (Fed. Cir. 1983). See *Windsurfing Int'l, Inc. v. AMF, Inc.,* 782 F.2d 995, 228 USPQ 562 (Fed. Cir. 1986). The court views absolute intervening rights as a damages issue. *Bic Leisure Prods., Inc. v. Windsurfing Int'l, Inc.,* 1 F.3d 1214, 27 USPQ2d 1671 (Fed. Cir. 1993).

[317]*Symbol Tech., Inc. v. Opticon, Inc.,* 935 F.2d 1569, 19 USPQ2d 1241 (Fed. Cir. 1991).

[318]*A.B. Chance Co. v. RTE Corp.,* 854 F.2d 1307, 7 USPQ2d 1881 (Fed. Cir. 1988).

[319]*Dana Corp. v. NOK, Inc.,* 882 F.2d 505, 11 USPQ2d 1883 (Fed. Cir. 1989).

[320]*Manville Sales Corp. v. Paramount Sys., Inc.,* 917 F.2d 544, 16 USPQ2d 1587 (Fed. Cir. 1990).

A compulsory counterclaim is one arising out of the transaction or occurrence that is the subject matter of the opposing party's claim, and a permissive counterclaim is any other.[321] The right to file a counterclaim for patent infringement in response to an action seeking a declaratory judgment of patent noninfringement is unique to patent law and warrants a uniform national rule.[322] In order to be classed as a compulsory counterclaim, Rule 13(a), FRCP, requires that the claim (1) exist at the time of pleading, (2) arise out of the same transaction or occurrence as the opposing party's claim, and (3) not require for adjudication parties over whom the court may not acquire jurisdiction. The scope of "transaction or occurrence" is liberally interpreted, as the court determines whether there is a logical relationship between the claim in suit and the counterclaim.[323] A compulsory counterclaim need not have an independent jurisdictional basis. It must be filed, at the pleading stage or later by leave of court, or be abandoned.[324]

Thus, a patent owner must, in response to a claim for a declaratory judgment of invalidity and noninfringement, counterclaim for patent infringement or be forever barred.[325] Rule 13(a) recognizes that when disputed issues arise from the same operative facts, fairness as well as efficiency require that the issues be raised for resolution in the same action. There are four tests, satisfaction of any one of which can render a counterclaim compulsory: (1) whether the legal and factual issues raised by the claim and counterclaim are largely the same; (2) whether, absent the compulsory counterclaim rule, res judicata would bar a subsequent suit on the counterclaim; (3) whether substantially the same evidence supports or refutes both the claim and counterclaim; or (4) whether there is a logical relation between the claim and counterclaim. A counterclaim for patent infringement, in an action for declaration of noninfringement of the same patent, readily meets all four of these criteria. Thus, when the same patent is at issue in an action for declaration of noninfringement, a counterclaim for patent infringement is compulsory and if not made is deemed waived. Such a counterclaim ordinarily should not be refused entry.

---

[321]*Employers Ins. of Wausau v. United States,* 764 F.2d 1572 (Fed. Cir. 1985). The institution of a plaintiff's suit suspends the running of limitations on a compulsory counterclaim while the suit is pending, but a permissive counterclaim does not generate a like tolling.

[322]*Vivid Tech. Inc. v. American Sci. & Eng'g Inc.,* 200 F.3d 795, 53 USPQ2d 1289 (Fed. Cir. 1999).

[323]*Genentech Inc. v. University of Califonia,* 143 F.3d 1446, 46 USPQ2d 1586 (Fed. Cir. 1998) (applying Seventh Circuit law). Despite noting a lack of unanimity among the circuits as to whether antitrust counterclaims in patent infringement suits are compulsory, the court found that the district court did not exceed its discretionary authority in enjoining a party before it from filing separate antitrust claims in other forums.

[324]*AeroJet-General Corp. v. Machine Tool Works,* 895 F.2d 736, 13 USPQ2d 1670 (Fed. Cir. 1990). Regional circuit law governs questions of res judicata that arise as a consequence of the compulsory counterclaim provisions of Rule 13(a), FRCP. *Beech Aircraft Corp. v. EDO Corp.,* 990 F.2d 1237 (Fed. Cir. 1993).

[325]*Genentech, Inc. v. Eli Lilly & Co.,* 998 F.2d 931, 27 USPQ2d 1241, 1252-53 (Fed. Cir. 1993). A counterclaim must be compulsory in order to be raised as of right in an area of law

An otherwise proper counterclaim that would not succeed on its substantive merits should ordinarily be disposed of on its merits and not by refusal to accept its filing.[326]

Amendments to pleadings. Where a supplemental pleading with respect to events occurring after the initial pleading relates to the same cause of action originally pleaded, it may be an abuse of discretion to deny the amendment. Similarly, a complaint may be amended where a new form of relief is being sought.[327] Several factors govern the consideration of a motion to amend pleadings: (1) undue delay; (2) bad faith; (3) prejudice to the nonmovant; and (4) futility of the amendment. The single most important factor is whether prejudice would result, but the nonmovant bears the burden of showing why the amendment should not be permitted.[328] Delay is also important, and delay and prejudice reinforce one another: the longer the delay, the less prejudice the nonmovant need show. At some point delay becomes fatal.[329] Although delay itself is an insufficient ground to deny amendment to a pleading, if the delay is "undue" the district court may refuse to permit amendment.[330]

After a responsive pleading has been served, the standards for adding parties are the same whether the motion is made under Rule 15 or Rule 21. In the absence of facts such as undue delay, bad faith,

---

in which a state is otherwise immune from suit. Also, it must be in recoupment of the state claim. *Id.*

[326]*Vivid Tech. Inc. v. American Sci. & Eng'g Inc.,* 200 F.3d 795, 53 USPQ2d 1289 (Fed. Cir. 1999).

[327]*Intrepid v. Pollock,* 907 F.2d 1125 (Fed. Cir. 1990).

[328]*Senza-Gel Corp. v. Seiffhart,* 803 F.2d 661, 231 USPQ 363 (Fed. Cir. 1986).

[329]*Tenneco Resins, Inc. v. Reeves Bros., Inc.,* 752 F.2d 630, 224 USPQ 536 (Fed. Cir. 1985). Where a party had delayed five years before moving to amend its pleading to assert patent invalidity, and where the patent owner had conducted discovery on the assumption that validity was not in issue, it was not an abuse of discretion to refuse the amendment, even in view of the policy of ridding the public of invalid patents. In *Glaverbel S.A. v. Northlake Mktg. & Supp., Inc.,* 45 F.3d 1550, 33 USPQ2d 1496 (Fed. Cir. 1995), the court affirmed a trial judge's refusal to permit evidence on inoperability, where the challenger had requested leave to amend its counterclaim to assert that defense one week before trial. It should be noted that the challenger had pleaded noncompliance with 35 U.S.C. §101, but gave no details.

[330]*Datascope Corp. v. SMEC, Inc.,* 962 F.2d 1043, 22 USPQ2d 1573 (Fed. Cir. 1992). The motion was filed almost nine years after commencement of suit. There had been a liability trial, a damages trial, two appeals, and a further damages hearing. At the last damages hearing there was a total award of over $4 million, whereupon the defendant filed for reorganization under Chapter 11 of the Bankruptcy Act. At this point the plaintiff sought to amend the complaint to add the defendant's president and principal stockholder as a party. The Federal Circuit found no abuse of discretion in denial of the motion. See also *Charles Greiner & Co. v. Mari-Med Mfg., Inc.,* 962 F.2d 1031, 22 USPQ2d 1526 (Fed. Cir. 1992). In *Korody-Colyer Corp. v. General Motors Corp.,* 828 F.2d 1572, 4 USPQ2d 1203 (Fed. Cir. 1987), the defendant had pleaded an antitrust counterclaim (based on tying) that was stayed pending trial of patent issues. The patent trial resulted in a holding of fraud in the procurement, and the defendant then attempted to amend its pleading to add a *Walker Process* counterclaim (see *Walker Process Equip., Inc. v. Food Mach. & Chem. Corp.,* 382 U.S. 172, 147 USPQ 404 (1965)). The court held that the counterclaim was barred by the statute of limitations. There was no "relation back" between the tying counterclaim, which involved nonpatented parts, and the *Walker Process* counterclaim, which involved patented parts, because the original pleading did not give "adequate notice" of the *Walker Process* claim under Rule 15(c), FRCP. The mere fact that

or prejudice to the opposing party, leave to amend to add a party should be freely given.[331] Whether an amendment to add a party pursuant to Rule 15(c) relates back to the date of the original pleading depends upon four factors, all of which must be satisfied: (1) the basic claim must have arisen out of the conduct set forth in the original pleading; (2) the party to be brought in must have received such notice that it will not be prejudiced in maintaining its defense; (3) that party must or should have known that, but for a mistake concerning identity, the action would have been brought against it; and (4) the second and third requirements must have been fulfilled within the prescribed limitations period. [332]

In reviewing an order denying a motion to amend a complaint to add a party, the Federal Circuit looks to the law of the regional circuit.[333] Whether or not to permit an amendment to the pleadings rests with the sound discretion of the trial judge, whose decision may be overturned only if the court abuses that discretion.[334] Apparently a party may obtain immediate review of a denial of a motion to amend by voluntarily dismissing its complaint.[335] It is within the discretion of the court to allow amendment of a complaint to add an alternative

---

the tying pleading used the phrase "among other things" could not possibly have provided fair notice of a *Walker Process* claim.

[331]*Kalman v. Berlyn Corp.,* 914 F.2d 1473, 16 USPQ2d 1093 (Fed. Cir. 1990).

[332]*Fromson v. Citiplate, Inc.,* 886 F.2d 1300, 12 USPQ2d 1299 (Fed. Cir. 1989). Here the additional individual parties were 50% owners of the defendant infringer and were found to have participated in and approved of the infringement of the patent. A motion was made to amend the pleadings to add them as parties before trial, and they successfully resisted on the ground that their defendant company was solvent. After trial and an adverse judgment their company declared bankruptcy and the plaintiff moved to amend to add them as parties. The Federal Circuit held that the district court committed no error in permitting the amendment to relate back. The individuals could not have been surprised, and they themselves created the mistake in identity of the proper party to be sued through their false assurances of solvency of the company. The cases are legion holding corporate officers and directors personally liable for participating in, inducing, and approving acts of patent infringement by a corporation.

[333]*Datascope Corp. v. SMEC, Inc.,* 962 F.2d 1043, 22 USPQ2d 1573 (Fed. Cir. 1992); *Kalman v. Berlyn Corp.,* 914 F.2d 1473, 16 USPQ2d 1093 (Fed. Cir. 1990).

[334]*Datascope Corp. v. SMEC, Inc.,* 962 F.2d 1043, 22 USPQ2d 1573 (Fed. Cir. 1992); *Charles Greiner & Co. v. Mari-Med Mfg., Inc.,* 962 F.2d 1031, 22 USPQ2d 1526 (Fed. Cir. 1992); *Tenneco Resins, Inc. v. Reeves Bros., Inc.,* 752 F.2d 630, 224 USPQ 536 (Fed. Cir. 1985); *Trans-World Mfg. Corp. v. Al Nyman & Sons,* 750 F.2d 1552, 224 USPQ 259 (Fed. Cir. 1984); *Jervis B. Webb Co. v. Southern Sys., Inc.,* 742 F.2d 1388, 222 USPQ 943 (Fed. Cir. 1984). An appeal from the denial of a motion to file an amended or supplemental pleading invokes an abuse of discretion standard of review. A misinterpretation of Rule 15, FRCP, would itself constitute an abuse of discretion. *Intrepid v. Pollock,* 907 F.2d 1125 (Fed. Cir. 1990). Outright denial of a motion to amend without any justifying reason is not an exercise of discretion; it is merely abuse of that discretion and inconsistent with the spirit of the Federal Rules. *Kalman v. Berlyn Corp.,* 914 F.2d 1473, 16 USPQ2d 1093 (Fed. Cir. 1990). In *Cornwall v. U.S. Constr. Mfg., Inc.,* 800 F.2d 250, 231 USPQ 64 (Fed. Cir. 1986), the court, applying Eleventh Circuit law, found abuse of discretion in a denial of a motion to amend to assert invalidity, where the defendant had denied that the patent was duly and legally issued and had indicated in the pretrial stipulation that it contended the patent was invalid.

[335]*St. Paul F. & M. Ins. Co. v. United States,* 959 F.2d 960 (Fed. Cir. 1992). The court distinguished this from a "voluntary" dismissal in the usual sense of a consent judgment; the general rule is that a party cannot appeal a voluntary judgment.

claim for breach of contract over which the court could exercise pendent jurisdiction if it chose to do so.[336] A judgment can be entered regarding claims that were actually litigated without objection, even though they were not asserted in the pleadings.[337] Amendment of pleadings after trial requires a showing that the issue was actually tried by the implied or express consent of the opposing party. The inquiry would include a determination of whether the opposing party would be prejudiced by the implied amendment, whether it had a fair opportunity to defend, and whether it could offer any additional evidence if the case were to be retried on the different theory.[338]

In *Christianson v. Colt,*[339] the Supreme Court passed the question whether a court could furnish itself a jurisdictional basis unsupported by the pleadings by deeming the complaint amended in light of the parties' "express or implied consent" to litigate a claim under Rule 15(b), FRCP. There was, in the Court's view, no evidence of any consent among the parties to litigate a patent law claim.

In one interesting case, the patentee found out about a new model shortly after the complaint was filed and long before trial, but did not charge infringement for three years and moved for contempt only after an injunctive order was entered on the original accused devices. The patentee had never asked leave to supplement the complaint, which would have been the proper procedure in view of the rule that only acts committed before the complaint is filed may be considered at trial. The court held that the district court acted properly in finding contempt and enjoining the new model, but in refusing damages.[340]

Rule 41(a)(1), FRCP, unambiguously gives a plaintiff the right to dismiss an action before the defendant serves an answer or a motion for summary judgment. Such voluntary dismissal is a matter of right running to the plaintiff that may not be extinguished or circumscribed by adversary or court.[341] The Federal Circuit has adopted the view that when a plaintiff seeks voluntary dismissal of fewer than all claims, Rule 41(a) does not apply, since it expressly deals with dismissal of an "action." Thus, such a "dismissal" is really a Rule 15 amendment to the complaint.[342]

Joinder of parties and claims. Often a party asking a court to disregard corporate existence will attempt to show that the corporation was merely the alter ego of its officers. More generally, a court

---

[336]*Kunkel v. Topmaster Int'l, Inc.,* 906 F.2d 693, 15 USPQ2d 1367 (Fed. Cir. 1990).

[337]*Jervis B. Webb Co. v. Southern Sys., Inc.,* 742 F.2d 1388, 222 USPQ 943 (Fed. Cir. 1984).

[338]*Trans-World Mfg. Corp. v. Al Nyman & Sons,* 750 F.2d 1552, 224 USPQ 259 (Fed. Cir. 1984).

[339]*Christianson v. Colt Indus. Oper. Corp.,* 486 U.S. 800, 7 USPQ2d 1109 (1988).

[340]*Rosemount, Inc. v. Beckman Instr., Inc.,* 727 F.2d 1540, 221 USPQ 1 (Fed. Cir. 1984). This decision seems to be based upon a laches theory. However, the court made it clear that it was not establishing a per se laches rule that all postcomplaint activity must be accused immediately. Three years was simply too long.

[341]*Eastalco Alum. Co. v. United States,* 995 F.2d 201 (Fed. Cir. 1993).

[342]*Gronholz v. Sears, Roebuck & Co.,* 836 F.2d 515, 5 USPQ2d 1269 (Fed. Cir. 1987).

may exert its equitable powers and disregard the corporate entity if it decides that piercing the veil will prevent fraud, illegality, injustice, a contravention of public policy, or prevent the corporation from shielding someone from criminal liability. The court must start, however, from the general rule that the corporate entity should be recognized and upheld, unless specific, unusual circumstances call for an exception. Moreover, unless there is at least specific intent to escape liability for a particular tort, the cause of justice does not require disregarding the corporate entity.[343]

Thus, acts of a corporate officer that are within the scope of the officer's responsibility are not always sufficient grounds for penetrating the corporate protection and imposing personal liability. The policy considerations that underlie the corporate structure yield to personal liability for corporate acts only in limited circumstances. In general, a corporate officer is personally liable for his or her tortious acts, just as any individual may be liable for a civil wrong. This general rule does not depend on the same grounds as piercing the corporate veil, such as inadequate capitalization, use of the corporate form for fraudulent purposes, or failure to comply with the formalities of corporate organization. When personal wrongdoing is not supported by legitimate corporate activity, the courts have assigned personal liability for wrongful actions even when taken on behalf of the corporation. However, this liability has been qualified, in extensive jurisprudence, by the distinction between commercial torts committed in the course of the officer's employment, and negligent and other culpable wrongful acts. Thus when a person in a control position causes the corporation to commit a civil wrong, imposition of personal liability requires consideration of the nature of the wrong, the culpability of the act, and whether the person acted in his or her personal interest or that of the corporation. The decisions have not always distinguished among the various legal premises, i.e. (1) justification for piercing the corporate veil based on such criteria as absence of corporate assets or use of the corporate form for illegal purposes; (2) corporate commitment of a commercial tort (such as interference with contract or business advantage, or patent infringement) caused by the officer acting as agent of the corporation; (3) similar actions that are exacerbated by culpable intent or bad faith on the part of the officer; or (4) personal commission of a fraudulent or grossly negligent act. In this case, it was not alleged that the corporate structure was a sham or

---

[343]*Manville Sales Corp. v. Paramount Sys., Inc.,* 917 F.2d 544, 16 USPQ2d 1587 (Fed. Cir. 1990). The corporate form is not to be lightly cast aside. A court must start from the general rule that the corporate entity should be recognized and upheld, unless specific, unusual circumstances call for an exception or unless there is at least specific intent to escape liability for a particular tort. *3D Sys. Inc. v. Aarotech Labs. Inc.,*160 F.3d 1373, 48 USPQ2d 1773 (Fed. Cir. 1998). Personal liability under 35 U.S.C. §271(a) requires sufficient evidence to justify piercing the corporate veil. The corporate entity deserves respect and legal recognition unless specific, unusual circumstances justify disregarding the corporate structure. The most common reason for disregarding the corporate structure is that the corporation was merely the alter ego of its officers. *Al-Site Corp. v. VSI Int'l Inc.,* 174 F.3d 1308, 50 USPQ2d 1161 (Fed. Cir. 1999).

existed merely to shield the individual from liability. Although he controlled the corporate entity, the trial court did not pierce the corporate veil.[344]

But regardless whether the circumstances are such that a court should disregard the corporate entity and pierce the corporate veil, corporate officers who actively assist their corporation's infringement may be personally liable for inducement.[345] It is well settled that corporate officers who actively aid and abet their corporation's infringement may be personally liable for inducing infringement under 35 U.S.C. §271(b) regardless of whether the corporation is the alter ego of the corporate officer.[346] Section 271(b) is to be read broadly, and such a reading clearly can include liability for corporate officials who actively aid and abet their corporation's infringements.[347] Infringement is a tort, and officers of a corporation are personally liable

---

[344]*Hoover Group Inc. v. Custom Metalcraft, Inc.*, 84 F.3d 1408, 38 USPQ2d 1860 (Fed. Cir. 1996). Here the individual made a straightforward commercial response to the assertions of patent infringement, including prompt consultations with counsel. Also, there was no finding that he actively and knowingly assisted the corporation's infringement. Certainly it is an insufficient basis for personal liability that he merely had knowledge of the acts alleged to constitute infringement. In *Genetic Implant Sys., Inc. v. Core-Vent Corp.*, 123 F.3d 1455, 43 USPQ2d 1786 (Fed. Cir. 1997), the court refused to ignore the corporate form and subject an individual to jurisdiction in a declaratory judgment action against him and his company. He was president, CEO, and sole owner, but there was no showing that he actually disregarded the corporate entity or personally participated in illegal conduct. In *Ohio Cellular Prods. Corp. v. Nelson*, 175 F.3d 1343, 50 USPQ2d 1481 (Fed. Cir. 1999), a patent owned by a corporation was found unenforceable for inequitable conduct. The trial court held the corporation liable for attorney fees. The inventor, who was also president and sole shareholder of the corporation, and who had prosecuted the application and committed the inequitable conduct, had his lawyer write the successful defendant, suggesting if it tried to collect the fees award, he would liquidate the company. The defendant moved to join the inventor, and the trial court added him as a party and immediately entered judgment against him as well. The Federal Circuit, over a vigorous dissent by Judge Newman, affirmed. Its decision was not based on piercing the corporate veil, but rather on the fact that the individual had adequate notice and would not be substantially prejudiced. His clear control over and participation in the litigation, and his central role in the wrongdoing, were the critical factors. The Supreme Court granted certiorari and, not surprisingly, reversed and remanded. *Nelson v. Adams USA Inc.*, ___ U.S. ___, 54 USPQ2d 1513 (2000). The rationale was a failure of due process. The individual was never afforded a proper opportunity to respond to the claim, but was adjudged liable the very first moment his personal liability was legally at issue. The high Court recognized that the Federal Circuit's essential position was that there was sufficient identity between the individual and his corporation to bind him without further ado. The Federal Circuit did not conclude that these factors would have justified imposition of liability on a veil-piercing theory; rather, it felt that no basis had been advanced to believe anything different or additional would have been done in defense had the individual been a party from the outset. The Supreme Court firmly rejected this as speculation, and observed that judicial predictions about the outcome of hypothesized litigation cannot substitute for the actual opportunity to defend that due process affords every party against whom a claim is stated.

[345]*Manville Sales Corp. v. Paramount Sys., Inc.*, 917 F.2d 544, 16 USPQ2d 1587 (Fed. Cir. 1990). Nonetheless, unless the corporate structure is a sham, personal liability for inducement to infringe is not automatic, but must be supported by personal culpability. *Hoover Group Inc. v. Custom Metalcraft, Inc.*, 84 F.3d 1408, 38 USPQ2d 1860 (Fed. Cir. 1996).

[346]*Sensonics, Inc. v. Aerosonic Corp.*, 81 F.3d 1566, 38 USPQ2d 1551 (Fed. Cir. 1996); *Orthokinetics, Inc. v. Safety Travel Chairs, Inc.*, 806 F.2d 1565, 1 USPQ2d 1081 (Fed. Cir. 1986). See *Shamrock Techs. Inc. v. Medical Sterilization, Inc.*, 903 F.2d 789, 14 USPQ2d 1728 (Fed. Cir. 1990), for an interesting analysis of privity between inventor and employer in the context of assignor estoppel.

[347]*Power Lift, Inc. v. Lang Tools, Inc.*, 774 F.2d 478, 227 USPQ 435 (Fed. Cir. 1985).

for the tortious conduct of the corporation if they personally took part in the commission of the tort or specifically directed other officers, agents, or employees of the corporation to commit the tortious act. Courts in many cases have recognized and imposed personal liability on corporate officers for participating in, inducing, and approving acts of patent infringement.[348] However, corporate officers must be shown to have knowingly induced infringement. It must be established that they possessed specific intent to encourage the corporation's infringement and not merely that they had knowledge of the acts alleged to constitute infringement. The patentee has the burden to show that the alleged infringer's actions induced the infringing acts and that it knew or should have known that its actions would induce actual infringement.[349] Pre-issuance activities alone cannot establish inducement to infringe on the part of a corporate officer.[350]

One related corporation can be liable for another's direct infringement only if the evidence reveals circumstances justifying disregard of the status of the two as distinct, separate corporations. Mere ownership of stock is not enough to justify piercing the corporate veil.[351]

Proving direct infringement is essential to proving contributory infringement under §271(c), but it is not necessary to join the direct infringers as parties, inasmuch as discovery can elicit proof of direct infringement.[352]

A patentee that does not voluntarily join an action prosecuted by its exclusive licensee can be joined as a defendant or, in a proper case, made an involuntary plaintiff if it is not subject to service of process.[353] The policy underlying the requirement to join the owner when an exclusive licensee brings suit is to prevent the possibility of two suits on the same patent against a single infringer. Under Rule

---

[348]*Orthokinetics, Inc. v. Safety Travel Chairs, Inc.*, 806 F.2d 1565, 1 USPQ2d 1081 (Fed. Cir. 1986). Here the court reversed a finding of no personal liability where the individuals owned all the stock, held all the directorships, were directly responsible for the design and production of the infringing product, and were the only ones who stood to benefit from the infringing sales. See also *Fromson v. Citiplate, Inc.*, 886 F.2d 1300, 12 USPQ2d 1299 (Fed. Cir. 1989).

[349]*Manville Sales Corp. v. Paramount Sys., Inc.*, 917 F.2d 544, 16 USPQ2d 1587 (Fed. Cir. 1990). Here the lower court found that the corporate officers were not the alter ego of the corporation, but found them personally liable on the ground that they took actions that caused the copying of the patented invention. The Federal Circuit reversed as an abuse of discretion. There was no evidence that they knew of the patent and their acts were within the scope of their employment. It appears that if the corporation is not the alter ego of the officers, they must be guilty of some deliberate, knowing misconduct.

[350]*Micro Chem. Inc. v. Great Plains Chem. Co.*, 194 F.3d 1258, 52 USPQ2d 1258 (Fed. Cir. 1999).

[351]*A. Stucki Co. v. Worthington Indus., Inc.*, 849 F.2d 593, 7 USPQ2d 1066 (Fed. Cir. 1988). Here the defendant indirectly owned 50% of the stock of an adjudged infringer, but there was no evidence that it had control over the infringer's actions and could have stopped the infringement. For the extremely complex sequel to this case see *A. Stucki Co. v. Buckeye Steel Castings Co.*, 963 F.2d 360, 22 USPQ2d 1581 (Fed. Cir. 1992).

[352]*Refac Int'l, Ltd. v. IBM*, 798 F.2d 459, 230 USPQ 537 (Fed. Cir. 1986); *Refac Int'l, Ltd. v. IBM*, 790 F.2d 79, 229 USPQ 712 (Fed. Cir. 1986).

[353]*Abbott Labs. v. Diamedix Corp.*, 47 F.3d 1128, 33 USPQ2d 1771 (Fed. Cir. 1995).

19, FRCP, a court must undertake a two-step analysis to determine whether a person should be joined. A person is necessary if complete relief cannot be accorded among those already parties, or if the disposition of an action may leave persons already parties subject to a substantial risk of incurring double, multiple, or otherwise inconsistent obligations.[354] Even if a patent owner is a necessary party under Rule 19(a) because it would be prejudiced by a holding of invalidity of its patent, this prejudice does not automatically make it indispensable under Rule 19(b).[355] The authority of an appellate court, under Rule 27, FRAP, to join a patent owner as an indispensable party in order to correct standing and thus preserve jurisdiction should be exercised sparingly.[356] Related issues are discussed in §8.1(a)(iv) in the context of standing to litigate.

---

[354]*Vaupel Textilmaschinen KG v. Meccanical Euro Italia S.P.A.*, 944 F.2d 870, 20 USPQ2d 1045 (Fed. Cir. 1991). In *Nutrition 21 v. United States,* 930 F.2d 862, 18 USPQ2d 1351 (Fed. Cir. 1991), the government owned a patent and gave plaintiff an exclusive license for certain products, a nonexclusive license for other products, and reserved a nonexclusive license for itself on all products. It also empowered plaintiff to bring suit in its own name, to collect damages, and to settle, provided the government had a continuing right to intervene. The plaintiff sued an infringer and joined the government under Rule 19(a). The Federal Circuit held that the government was not a necessary party and reversed its joinder as an involuntary plaintiff. Under 35 U.S.C. §207(a)(2), federal agencies may license patents owned by the United States, including the right to enforce those patents. Public policy indicates that the government should not be required to make its limited litigation resources available each time one of its licensees seeks to bring an infringement suit. Although *Independent Wireless Tel. Co. v. Radio Corp.*, 269 U.S. 459 (1926), may hold that both the owner and exclusive licensee of a patent are generally necessary parties, that case did not involve a patent owned by the United States, nor was the license predicated on §207.

[355]*Dainippon Screen Mfg. Co. v. CFMT Inc.,* 142 F.3d 1266, 46 USPQ2d 1616 (Fed. Cir. 1998). Here, the absent patent owner was the wholly-owned subsidiary of the declaratory defendant, which had an exclusive license under the patents. The first factor of Rule 19(b) is party prejudice. The court found that the exclusive licensee and the patent owner shared the common goal of defending the patent. Moreover, to the extent that it would be prejudiced if the suit were to proceed in its absence, the patent owner could intervene. The second factor, the court's ability to shape relief to avoid prejudice, is of little relevance in the context of a patent declaratory judgment suit because the relief sought in such a suit does not depend upon the patentee's presence in court. The third factor, adequacy of the judgment, favors maintenance of the suit in the patent owner's absence because a declaration of invalidity or noninfringement would fully serve the declaratory plaintiff's interest in ensuring that it is free from claims of patent infringement. In this regard, it is relevant that a declaratory judgment suit is not one in which the plaintiff seeks relief that will require an affirmative act by the absentee, therefore making the case essentially hollow if it were to proceed in the patent owner's absence. The fourth factor, whether the plaintiff will have an adequate remedy if the case is dismissed, favors dismissal if there exists another forum in which all parties could be joined in the suit. However, the fact that an alternative forum exists does not automatically warrant dismissal of the case given the mandate of Rule 19(b) to consider all of the relevant factors and the equities of the situation. Here the court considered it highly relevant that the patent owner was merely its parent's holding company for the patent in suit. It should be noted that all of this ruling was probably dicta, inasmuch as the court had already held that personal jurisdiction over the holding company was proper. In *Dow Chem. Co. v. Exxon Corp.,* 139 F.3d 1470, 46 USPQ2d 1120 (Fed. Cir. 1998), the court held that the patent owner, a subsidiary of the defendant, was not an indispensable party in a suit for interference with contract relations based upon inequitable conduct. The defendant had the right to sue for infringement, the right to defend the subsidiary in litigation concerning the patent, and the right to sublicense it. Accordingly, the court found that the defendant would adequately protect the absent patent owner's interests.

[356]*Prima Tek II L.L.C. v. A-Roo Co.,* 222 F.3d 1372, 55 USPQ2d 1742 (Fed. Cir. 2000).

In an interesting intervention case under Rule 24, FRCP, the plaintiff had filed an action in the district court to reinstate his lapsed patent pursuant to 5 U.S.C. §§701–706. Summary judgment was granted in his favor and he immediately added the reinstated patent to an already-pending infringement suit involving another patent. The defendant there moved to intervene in the reinstatement suit. The motion was denied and the proposed intervener appealed both the denial of intervention and the grant of summary judgment of reinstatement. The Federal Circuit held that intervention as of right was properly denied on the ground that the accused infringer's ability to protect its interest in the infringement suit would not be impaired by the reinstatement of the patent. The reinstatement decision would not bind the court handling the infringement case, and the accused infringer could appeal in that case if it is precluded from raising a lapsed-patent defense.[357] In an unusual case, the court affirmed a refusal to permit an accused patent infringer from intervening in an ADR proceeding between the patentee and another accused infringer.[358]

Rule 25, FRCP, which deals with transfers of interest, applies only to pending litigation. Thus a successor in interest cannot be added to a settled action.[359]

Joinder of parties is an issue not unique to patent law; hence the Federal Circuit will apply the discernible law of the regional circuit.[360] In reviewing a denial of a motion for permissive intervention the court applies regional circuit law.[361] Whether a party is indispensable under Rule 19(b), FRCP, is a matter of regional circuit law.[362]

(b) Discovery

Discovery is regulated by Rules 26–37 and 45, FRCP. The scope and conduct of discovery are committed to the discretion of the trial

---

[357]*Chapman v. Manbeck*, 931 F.2d 46, 18 USPQ2d 1565 (Fed. Cir. 1991). The court also refused to disturb the district court's discretionary refusal to allow permissive intervention.

[358]*Haworth, Inc. v. Steelcase, Inc.*, 12 F.3d 1090, 29 USPQ2d 1368 (Fed. Cir. 1993).

[359]*Horphag Res. Ltd. v. Consac Indus., Inc.*, 116 F.3d 1450, 42 USPQ2d 1567 (Fed. Cir. 1997).

[360]*Katz v. Lear Siegler, Inc.*, 909 F.2d 1459, 15 USPQ2d 1554 (Fed. Cir. 1990). Here the court selected a de novo standard of review and then decided that the district court was correct in ordering joinder of a licensee as a counterdefendant to a declaratory judgment counterclaim. The joinder would not defeat jurisdiction and would facilitate a determination of the plaintiff's capacity to sue for patent infringement. An argument could be made that this question raises patent law issues, and therefore the Federal Circuit might wish to develop its own law on the subject.

[361]*Haworth, Inc. v. Steelcase, Inc.*, 12 F.3d 1090, 29 USPQ2d 1368 (Fed. Cir. 1993). Under Sixth Circuit law, the standard of review of such an order is abuse of discretion. An abuse of discretion exists where the court's decision relies on clearly erroneous findings of fact, improperly applies the law or uses an erroneous legal standard, or is simply arbitrary and unjustifiable under the circumstances.

[362]*Dainippon Screen Mfg. Co. v. CFMT Inc.*, 142 F.3d 1266, 46 USPQ2d 1616, 1619 (Fed. Cir. 1998).

court.[363] In a discovery dispute, a determination that a district court has the power to order discovery does not end the inquiry; it must also be determined whether an abuse of discretion occurred in exercising that power.[364] A district judge who has presided over the action for several years is in the best position to assess whether the party seeking discovery has shown some reasonable relationship between the claimed invention and the information sought.[365]

Discovery orders made by a court in which a case is pending are not appealable as of right, being merely interlocutory, until the entry of final judgment in a suit. When a party pursues discovery outside the jurisdiction in which the suit is pending, however, the jurisdiction of the local district court may be invoked to rule on discovery issues in an ancillary proceeding. An order terminating that type of proceeding is final and thus gives a right of appeal.[366] However, an order in such a proceeding denying a motion to quash a subpoena is not final and thus not appealable.[367] Where the order denies the motion to quash in part, and the party against whom the discovery is sought cross-appeals, the Federal Circuit may exercise pendent jurisdiction even though the cross-appeal is not independently reviewable.[368]

(i) Discovery in General

It is a premise of modern litigation that the Federal Rules contemplate liberal discovery, in the interest of just and complete resolution of disputes. Relevancy for the purposes of Rule 26, FRCP, is broadly construed. However, the potential for discovery abuse is ever present, and courts are authorized to limit discovery to that which is proper and warranted in the circumstances of the case.[369]

An objective of Rule 26 is to guard against redundant or disproportionate discovery by giving the court authority to reduce the amount

---

[363]*Florsheim Shoe Co. v. United States,* 744 F.2d 787 (Fed. Cir. 1984).

[364]*United States v. Cook,* 795 F.2d 987 (Fed. Cir. 1986); *Heat & Control, Inc. v. Hester Indus. Inc.,* 785 F.2d 1017, 228 USPQ 926 (Fed. Cir. 1986) (applying Fourth Circuit law); *Florsheim Shoe Co. v. United States,* 744 F.2d 787 (Fed. Cir. 1984). The standard of review is abuse of discretion. *Dorf & Stanton Comm., Inc. v. Molson Breweries,* 100 F.3d 919, 40 USPQ2d 1761 (Fed. Cir. 1996); *Katz v. Batavia Mar. & Sporting Supp., Inc.,* 984 F.2d 422, 25 USPQ2d 1547 (Fed. Cir. 1993).

[365]*American Standard, Inc. v. Pfizer, Inc.,* 828 F.2d 734, 3 USPQ2d 1817 (Fed. Cir. 1987).

[366]*Katz v. Batavia Mar. & Sporting Supp., Inc.,* 984 F.2d 422, 25 USPQ2d 1547 (Fed. Cir. 1993); *Micro Motion, Inc. v. Kane Steel Co.,* 894 F.2d 1318, 13 USPQ2d 1696 (Fed. Cir. 1990); *Solarex Corp. v. Arco Solar, Inc.,* 870 F.2d 642, 10 USPQ2d 1247 (Fed. Cir. 1989). See also *Haworth, Inc. v. Herman Miller, Inc.,* 998 F.2d 975, 27 USPQ2d 1469 (Fed. Cir. 1993).

[367]*Micro Motion, Inc. v. Kane Steel Co.,* 894 F.2d 1318, 13 USPQ2d 1696 (Fed. Cir. 1990). In *Micro Motion, Inc. v. Exac Corp.,* 876 F.2d 1574, 11 USPQ2d 1070 (Fed. Cir. 1989), the court noted that it was mindful of the harshness inherent in requiring a witness to place himself in contempt to create a final appealable decision. Nonetheless, the court does not wish to make itself a second-stage motion court to review pretrial applications of all nonparty witnesses alleging some damage because of the litigation.

[368]*Micro Motion, Inc. v. Kane Steel Co.,* 894 F.2d 1318, 13 USPQ2d 1696 (Fed. Cir. 1990).

[369]*Katz v. Batavia Mar. & Sporting Supp., Inc.,* 984 F.2d 422, 25 USPQ2d 1547 (Fed. Cir. 1993).

of discovery that may be directed to matters that are otherwise proper subjects of inquiry. The factors to be balanced by the trial court in determining the propriety of discovery are the relevance of the discovery sought, the requesting party's need, and the potential hardship to the opposing party.[370] Where proof of either relevance or need is not established, discovery is properly denied. Need is enhanced when information is uniquely available from the party from whom it is sought. Need is diminished when the information is available elsewhere.[371] Rule 26(g) specifically requires that the party or its attorney seeking discovery must certify that it has made reasonable inquiry and that the request is warranted.[372] Rule 26(b)(1), FRCP, allows discovery of any nonprivileged matter that is relevant to the subject matter involved in the pending action. The rule has boundaries, however. Discovery of matter not reasonably calculated to lead to the discovery of admissible evidence is outside its scope.[373] Relevance under Rule 26(b)(1) is construed more broadly for discovery than for trial.[374] Nonetheless, while the requirement that discovery be relevant to the subject matter involved is broadly construed, the divergent situations to which it must apply makes it impossible to provide a rigid definition of this phrase. Clearly discovery is allowed to flesh out a pattern of facts already known to a party relating to an issue necessarily in the case. At the other extreme, requested information is not relevant to the subject matter involved in the pending action if the inquiry is based on the party's mere suspicion or speculation. The area in between raises the difficult discovery questions where discretionary decisions must be made.[375]

Thus, while the expression "fishing expedition" has been generally denigrated as a reason for objecting to discovery, in some situations it remains apt. If suit is brought on a mere suspicion of infringement, discovery would not be allowed based on an allegation alone. A bare allegation of wrongdoing is not a fair reason for requiring a defendant to undertake financial burdens and risks to further a plaintiff's case. The discovery rules are designed to assist a party to prove a claim it reasonably believes to be viable without discovery,

---

[370]*Heat & Control, Inc. v. Hester Indus. Inc.*, 785 F.2d 1017, 228 USPQ 926 (Fed. Cir. 1986).

[371]*American Standard, Inc. v. Pfizer, Inc.*, 828 F.2d 734, 3 USPQ2d 1817 (Fed. Cir. 1987). The court found no abuse of discretion here in refusing discovery of sales data, while it did find an abuse on similar facts in *Truswal Sys. Corp v. Hydro-Air Eng'g, Inc.*, 813 F.2d 1207, 2 USPQ2d 1034 (Fed. Cir. 1987). For the government to make requests that would require plaintiffs in turn to seek information from the government itself clearly exceeds the bounds for which discovery is provided to litigants. *Hendler v. United States,* 952 F.2d 1364 (Fed. Cir. 1991). In *Haworth, Inc. v. Herman Miller, Inc.*, 998 F.2d 975, 27 USPQ2d 1469 (Fed. Cir. 1993), the court found no abuse of discretion in denying third party discovery in an ancillary forum without first having moved to compel the discovery from a party in the forum court.

[372]*Micro Motion, Inc. v. Kane Steel Co.*, 894 F.2d 1318, 13 USPQ2d 1696 (Fed. Cir. 1990). The reasonable inquiry is also required by Rule 11, FRCP. *Id.*

[373]*American Standard, Inc. v. Pfizer, Inc.*, 828 F.2d 734, 3 USPQ2d 1817 (Fed. Cir. 1987).

[374]*Truswal Sys. Corp. v. Hydro-Air Eng'g, Inc.*, 813 F.2d 1207, 2 USPQ2d 1034 (Fed. Cir. 1987).

[375]*Micro Motion, Inc. v. Kane Steel Co.*, 894 F.2d 1318, 13 USPQ2d 1696 (Fed. Cir. 1990).

not to find out if it has any basis for a claim. That the discovery might uncover evidence showing that a plaintiff has a legitimate claim does not justify the discovery request.[376]

Discovery of persons not party to the litigation is contemplated by the rules. Although Rule 26(b) applies equally to discovery of nonparties, the fact of nonparty status may be considered by the court in weighing the burdens imposed in the circumstances.[377]

One seeking discovery of confidential sales information must show some relationship between the claimed invention and the information sought, and that the information is reasonably necessary for a fair opportunity to develop and prepare the case for trial.[378] It is reasonable to provide a nonparty from whom discovery is sought, at a minimum, with the same protection for discovery of information regarding infringement that it would have received had it been sued for infringement. Rule 26(g) requires a party to make a "reasonable inquiry" before seeking discovery, and parallels the thrust of Rule 11 with respect to making allegations in a complaint.[379] But no full-fledged trial on infringement and nexus need be conducted at the discovery stage in order to demonstrate the relevance of sales information.[380] Delay can create prejudice: possible witnesses may disperse, memories fade, documents become lost or destroyed.[381] A court whose jurisdiction is limited to ancillary or discovery matters should be cautious in determining what is relevant to the main action, because of its unfamiliarity with the main action. Where there is doubt over relevance, the court should be permissive.[382] But this is not an immutable rule. It may be that there are serious relevancy questions that have not been, or could not be, given meaningful consideration in the main action. For example, both patentee and accused infringer might well be interested in information from a nonparty competitor, and it might not be in the interest of either of them to raise relevancy

---

[376]*Micro Motion, Inc. v. Kane Steel Co.,* 894 F.2d 1318, 13 USPQ2d 1696 (Fed. Cir. 1990).

[377]*Katz v. Batavia Mar. & Sporting Supp., Inc.,* 984 F.2d 422, 25 USPQ2d 1547 (Fed. Cir. 1993). See also *Haworth, Inc. v. Herman Miller, Inc.,* 998 F.2d 975, 27 USPQ2d 1469 (Fed. Cir. 1993).

[378]*American Standard, Inc. v. Pfizer, Inc.,* 828 F.2d 734, 3 USPQ2d 1817 (Fed. Cir. 1987).

[379]*Micro Motion, Inc. v. Kane Steel Co.,* 894 F.2d 1318, 13 USPQ2d 1696 (Fed. Cir. 1990). The patentee was seeking discovery as to a nonparty competitor's devices, so that he could show they were infringing and thus no impediment to lost profits. The court felt the patentee should have been able to make some threshold showing that these devices infringe, without subjecting the competitor to discovery. An unfounded suspicion regarding infringement does not support discovery into that subject matter. *Id.*

[380]*American Standard, Inc. v. Pfizer, Inc.,* 828 F.2d 734, 3 USPQ2d 1817 (Fed. Cir. 1987). But where the district court does call for a nexus showing, the appellant must demonstrate that the absence of such a demand would have compelled a different result. *Id.*

[381]*Tenneco Resins, Inc. v. Reeves Bros., Inc.,* 752 F.2d 630, 224 USPQ 536 (Fed. Cir. 1985).

[382]*Truswal Sys. Corp. v. Hydro-Air Eng'g, Inc.,* 813 F.2d 1207, 2 USPQ2d 1034 (Fed. Cir. 1987); *Heat & Control, Inc. v. Hester Indus. Inc.,* 785 F.2d 1017, 228 USPQ 926 (Fed. Cir. 1986).

objections.[383] In general, the need for discovery in an ancillary proceeding is diminished when the information is available elsewhere.[384]

The applicable law on discovery matters is that of the regional circuit, supplemented if necessary by that of other regional circuits, and the Federal Rules of Civil Procedure.[385] If the regional circuit has not spoken, the court must predict how that circuit would decide the issue in light of such criteria as the decisions of that circuit's district courts, other circuits' decisions, and public policy.[386] In a patent infringement action, a determination of relevance for discovery purposes implicates substantive patent law, and the court therefore applies its own law rather than that of the regional circuit.[387]

(ii) Subpoenas

Under Rule 45, FRCP, a district court may quash or modify a subpoena if it finds that to grant the discovery would be unreasonable and oppressive. Rule 45 must be read in light of Rule 26, which defines the scope of discovery.[388] The burden of proving that a subpoena is oppressive is on the party moving to quash and is a heavy one. The burden is greater still when the relief is requested before the discovery has commenced. When a court is confronted with a motion to quash, its duty is not to deny discovery altogether but to reduce the demand to a reasonable level, considering the parties' concerns.[389] The district court must balance the relevance of the discovery sought, the requesting party's need, and the potential hardship to the party subject to the subpoena. In assessing the burden of complying with the subpoena, the court may consider as one factor that the deponent is not a party. The administration of justice would not be aided, however,

---

[383]*Micro Motion, Inc. v. Kane Steel Co.*, 894 F.2d 1318, 13 USPQ2d 1696 (Fed. Cir. 1990). This is important in deciding whether to permit discovery of relevant and necessary information pursuant to a protective order, or to preclude the discovery entirely. In cases where the company from whom discovery is sought has an affinity with a party to the main litigation, a protective order may be effective protection to a nonparty. But where the nonparty is a competitor of both parties to the main litigation, it would be unrealistic to believe that either party would serve as an effective champion to maintain confidentiality and limit public disclosure during trial. The nonparty would, in fact, lose all control of the situation since disclosure of its information depends on the action by a court before which it has no standing. *Id.*

[384]*Haworth, Inc. v. Herman Miller, Inc.*, 998 F.2d 975, 27 USPQ2d 1469 (Fed. Cir. 1993).

[385]*Truswal Sys. Corp. v. Hydro-Air Eng'g, Inc.*, 813 F.2d 1207, 2 USPQ2d 1034 (Fed. Cir. 1987). Under the Seventh Circuit's abuse of discretion standard, the relevant inquiry is not how the reviewing judges would have ruled if they had been considering the case in the first place, but rather whether any reasonable person could agree with the district court. *American Standard, Inc. v. Pfizer, Inc.*, 828 F.2d 734, 3 USPQ2d 1817 (Fed. Cir. 1987). Whether a response to a document request under Rule 30(b)(5) merited sanctions presents a procedural issue not unique to patent law and regional circuit law controls. *Badalamenti v. Dunham's, Inc.*, 896 F.2d 1359, 13 USPQ2d 1967 (Fed. Cir. 1990).

[386]*Badalamenti v. Dunham's, Inc.*, 896 F.2d 1359, 13 USPQ2d 1967 (Fed. Cir. 1990).

[387]*Micro Motion, Inc. v. Kane Steel Co.*, 894 F.2d 1318, 13 USPQ2d 1696, 1702 n.8 (Fed. Cir. 1990).

[388]*Heat & Control, Inc. v. Hester Indus. Inc.*, 785 F.2d 1017, 228 USPQ 926 (Fed. Cir. 1986).

[389]*Heat & Control, Inc. v. Hester Indus. Inc.*, 785 F.2d 1017, 228 USPQ 926 (Fed. Cir. 1986).

by a rule relieving all persons from giving particular evidence on the sole ground that they are not parties to the suit.[390]

The quashing of a subpoena ad testificatum is rarely granted. Until the subpoenaed person is asked specific questions during the deposition, the deponent has, in virtually all cases, no basis to invoke the protective principles of Rule 26(c) in advance of the appearance, except as to the convenience of the time or place for the deposition. Thus the general rule is that a properly served person must appear in accordance with a deposition notice or subpoena.[391]

A subpoena for records in a civil case must of course meet certain standards. The court must make sure that the subpoena has been served pursuant to lawful authority, is for a lawful purpose, is relevant to the lawful purpose, and is not unreasonable.[392]

(iii) Protective Orders

While the Federal Rules unquestionably allow broad discovery, a right to discovery is not unlimited. As a matter of procedure, to secure protection from discovery, a nonparty may invoke the inherent power of the court, or Rule 45(b) if appropriate, to quash a subpoena. Under Rule 45(d), a nonparty subpoenaed for testimony and production of documents may move for a protective order under Rule 26(c), including an order that discovery not be had. Confidential commercial information warrants special protection under Rule 26(c)(7). A nonparty also may merely object to production of documents and things. By merely objecting, such discovery is foreclosed except pursuant to an order of the court. While the burdens may vary somewhat depending on which rule or procedure is invoked, the substantive considerations for denying a party discovery are generally the same and may be gleaned from Rule 26(b), (c), and (g). Discovery may not be had regarding a matter that is not relevant. Even if relevant, discovery is not permitted where no need is shown, or compliance would be unduly burdensome, or where harm to the person from whom discovery is sought outweighs the need of the person seeking the information.[393]

Under Rule 26(c), protective orders are available for a variety of purposes. A protective order does not eliminate the requirements of relevance and need for the information; it is the burden of the party seeking discovery to establish a need for the breadth of the information sought in response to the responding party's prima facie showing that

---

[390]*Truswal Sys. Corp. v. Hydro-Air Eng'g, Inc.,* 813 F.2d 1207, 2 USPQ2d 1034 (Fed. Cir. 1987).

[391]*Micro Motion, Inc. v. Kane Steel Co.,* 894 F.2d 1318, 13 USPQ2d 1696 (Fed. Cir. 1990). However, under Rule 30(b)(6), which allows the subpoena of an unnamed deponent who must be able to testify as to particular matters concerning his or her company, the substantive matters into which inquiry will be made at the deposition may well be revealed in advance. *Id.*

[392]*McDonnell Douglas Corp. v. United States,* 754 F.2d 364 (Fed. Cir. 1985).

[393]*Micro Motion, Inc. v. Kane Steel Co.,* 894 F.2d 1318, 13 USPQ2d 1696 (Fed. Cir. 1990).

the discovery would be burdensome.[394] Where a motion to dismiss raised only legal issues for which factual discovery was not necessary or appropriate, it was no abuse of discretion to suspend discovery pending disposition of the motion.[395] In one case the moving party argued that the information sought need not be produced because it was secret and proprietary and also because it was available from other sources. The Federal Circuit noted this apparent paradox, but went on to hold that selective disclosure of protectable trade secrets is not per se unreasonable and oppressive when appropriate protective measures are imposed.[396]

A trade secret or other confidential research, development, or commercial information may be the subject of a protective order under Rule 26(c)(7), FRCP. One seeking a protective order under that rule must first establish that the information sought is confidential, and then demonstrate that disclosure might be harmful. Courts have presumed that disclosure to a competitor is more harmful than disclosure to a noncompetitor. Once confidentiality and potential harm are shown, the burden shifts to the party seeking discovery to establish that disclosure of trade secrets and confidential information is relevant and necessary to its case.[397] In an interesting case, the court balanced the competing interests and found that the interest of the American Physical Society in protecting the confidentiality of its anonymous, prepublication referees outweighed the defendant's merely speculative interest in establishing a paper as prior art.[398]

Confidential information is a common subject for a protective order. In-house counsel cannot be excluded from access to confidential information simply on the ground that they are in-house rather than retained. Exclusion of counsel must be done on a rational factual basis.[399] On the other hand, a protective order by the ITC, limiting access to confidential information to outside counsel only and denying access to house counsel, was upheld against very vigorous attack. The reasoning was that the ITC is heavily dependent upon voluntary submission of information, and disclosure of sensitive materials to any adversary would have a chilling effect on the parties' willingness to provide the confidential information essential to the Commission's fact-finding processes.[400]

---

[394]*Katz v. Batavia Mar. & Sporting Supp., Inc.,* 984 F.2d 422, 25 USPQ2d 1547 (Fed. Cir. 1993).

[395]*Florsheim Shoe Co. v. United States,* 744 F.2d 787 (Fed. Cir. 1984).

[396]*Heat & Control, Inc. v. Hester Indus. Inc.,* 785 F.2d 1017, 228 USPQ 926 (Fed. Cir. 1986).

[397]*American Standard, Inc. v. Pfizer, Inc.,* 828 F.2d 734, 3 USPQ2d 1817 (Fed. Cir. 1987). See *In re Jenoptik AG,* 109 F.3d 721, 41 USPQ2d 1950 (Fed. Cir. 1997), for an interesting situation involving the possible use in Germany of U.S. depositions, which might circumvent the usual confidentiality safeguards available in a German court.

[398]*Solarex Corp. v. Arco Solar, Inc.,* 870 F.2d 642, 10 USPQ2d 1247 (Fed. Cir. 1989). Both the lower court and the Federal Circuit passed the proposition, advanced by the APS, that there should be a qualified privilege to protect a scholarly journal's peer review process.

[399]*U.S. Steel Corp. v. United States,* 730 F.2d 1465 (Fed. Cir. 1984).

[400]*Akzo N.V. v. United States ITC,* 808 F.2d 1471, 1 USPQ2d 1241 (Fed. Cir. 1986).

The Federal Circuit has held that the mental process of an agency head is not subject to inquiry in a judicial or administrative proceeding.[401] This is consistent with a disposition on the part of the court to forbid inquiry, by deposition testimony, into the thought processes of a PTO examiner engaged in deciding whether or not to allow patent claims.[402]

The court has firmly rejected any notion that a patentee is not entitled to discover an alleged infringer's sales until the patentee has established a right to an accounting. Such information is relevant to patentability, as tending to show commercial success.[403] Similarly, the court has indicated that sales information of a nonparty is relevant, at least for discovery purposes, so long as the products are not totally and clearly remote from the claimed invention. No useful purpose is served in converting every hearing on a motion to quash a subpoena for sales information into a full-fledged trial on infringement.[404] Rule 26(d), which pertains to controlling the sequence and timing of discovery, may be invoked as a mechanism for accommodating the competing interests of those involved in the discovery process, for example, by delaying discovery on damages until liability is established.[405] A district court has broad powers of case management, including the power to limit discovery to relevant subject matter and to adjust discovery as appropriate to each phase of litigation. When a particular issue may be dispositive, the court may stay discovery concerning other issues until the critical issue is resolved.[406]

In reviewing questions concerning violation of protective orders, the Federal Circuit applies regional circuit law. In the Fourth Circuit, violation of a protective order, which is a form of civil contempt, must be proved by clear and convincing evidence. A district court's finding that a protective order has not been violated will be reversed only if clearly erroneous.[407]

---

[401]*Bacon v. Department of HUD,* 757 F.2d 265 (Fed. Cir. 1985).

[402]See §10.4(b).

[403]*American Standard, Inc. v. Pfizer, Inc.,* 828 F.2d 734, 3 USPQ2d 1817 (Fed. Cir. 1987); *Truswal Sys. Corp. v. Hydro-Air Eng'g, Inc.,* 813 F.2d 1207, 2 USPQ2d 1034 (Fed. Cir. 1987).

[404]*Truswal Sys. Corp. v. Hydro-Air Eng'g, Inc.,* 813 F.2d 1207, 2 USPQ2d 1034 (Fed. Cir. 1987). In *Micro Motion, Inc. v. Kane Steel Co.,* 894 F.2d 1318, 13 USPQ2d 1696 (Fed. Cir. 1990), the patentee was seeking discovery against nonparty competitors. Its purpose was to show that it would have made the infringer's sales but for the infringement, in that the devices of the competitors were either infringements themselves or unacceptable noninfringing alternatives. The court denied the discovery on the ground that the patentee had made no threshold showing that the devices were infringing. Along the way, however, it seemed to indicate that a patentee has no absolute right to pursue any and every alternative theory of damages, no matter how complicated or tenuous. It justified this view on the ground that a court has discretion to deny a plaintiff's proposed method of proof that imposes too great a burden on court proceedings.

[405]*Micro Motion, Inc. v. Kane Steel Co.,* 894 F.2d 1318, 13 USPQ2d 1696 (Fed. Cir. 1990).

[406]*Vivid Tech. Inc. v. American Sci. & Eng'g Inc.,* 200 F.3d 795, 53 USPQ2d 1289, 1295 (Fed. Cir. 1999). Thus the court's management of discovery at the claim construction stage may serve the salutary goals of speed and economy, and is appropriate in cases in which the dispute may be resolved at this stage without compromise of justice. *Id.*

[407]*Glaxo, Inc. v. Novopharm, Ltd.,* 110 F.3d 1562 (Fed. Cir. 1997). Here the finding was that all of the alleged trade secrets were to be found in documents submitted as exhibits not under seal. Dissemination or use of such information did not violate the protective order.

(iv) Sanctions

The Federal Circuit applies the law of the pertinent regional circuit when the precise issue to be addressed involves an interpretation of the FRCP, such as a discovery sanction.[408] Rule 37, FRCP, provides for a variety of sanctions for failure to cooperate in the discovery process. The standard of review of orders granting or denying discovery sanctions is also abuse of discretion.[409] A plaintiff with a proven meritorious claim may have that claim taken away if the plaintiff's conduct—or that of its lawyer—is so offensive to the court and so violative of established norms as to justify punishment this severe. As a general rule, trial courts are given wide discretion to manage the course of a trial and to direct the conduct of counsel. But this discretion is not without limits and is reviewed for abuse.[410]

An abuse of discretion on a discovery sanction may be found when (1) the court's decision is clearly unreasonable, arbitrary, or fanciful; (2) the decision is based on an erroneous conclusion of law; (3) the court's findings are clearly erroneous; or (4) the record contains no evidence upon which the district court rationally could have based its decision.[411] An order imposing sanctions on a party for violating an order compelling discovery is neither a final order appealable under 28 U.S.C. §1295(a)(3) nor an appealable interlocutory order of §1292(c). The order is appealable, if at all, under the collateral order doctrine.[412] But a trial court's discretion to impose sanctions is not unfettered, especially when the de facto result of the sanction is dismissal. There are constitutional limitations upon the power of courts, even in aid of their own valid processes, to dismiss an action without affording a party the opportunity for a hearing on the merits of its cause. The harsh remedy of de facto dismissal is appropriate

---

[408]*Seal-Flex Inc. v. Athletic Track & Court Constr.*, 172 F.3d 836, 50 USPQ2d 1225 (Fed. Cir. 1999); *Wexell v. Komar Indus., Inc.*, 18 F.3d 916, 29 USPQ2d 2017 (Fed. Cir. 1994).

[409]*Wexell v. Komar Indus., Inc.*, 18 F.3d 916, 29 USPQ2d 2017 (Fed. Cir. 1994); *Refac Int'l, Ltd. v. Hitachi, Ltd.*, 921 F.2d 1247, 16 USPQ2d 1347 (Fed. Cir. 1990); *Ingalls Shipbuilding, Inc. v. United States*, 857 F.2d 1448 (Fed. Cir. 1988); *Minnesota Min. & Mfg. Co. v. Eco Chem, Inc.*, 757 F.2d 1256, 225 USPQ 350 (Fed. Cir. 1985); *Stock Pot Restaurant, Inc. v. Stockpot, Inc.*, 737 F.2d 1576, 222 USPQ 665 (Fed. Cir. 1984). The sanction will not be disturbed unless upon a weighing of the relevant factors the reviewing court is left with a definite and firm conviction that the court below committed a clear error of judgment. The question is not whether the reviewing court as an original matter would have granted the sanction. *Adkins v. United States*, 816 F.2d 1562 (Fed. Cir. 1987). The district court's determination that a party disobeyed a discovery order is entitled to considerable weight because the district court judge is best equipped to assess the circumstances of the noncompliance. *Nike, Inc. v. Wolverine World Wide, Inc.*, 43 F.3d 644, 33 USPQ2d 1038 (Fed. Cir. 1994).

[410]*Hendler v. United States*, 952 F.2d 1364 (Fed. Cir. 1991).

[411]*Badalamenti v. Dunham's, Inc.*, 896 F.2d 1359, 13 USPQ2d 1967 (Fed. Cir. 1990). See also *Western Elec. Co. v. Piezo Tech., Inc.*, 860 F.2d 428, 8 USPQ2d 1853 (Fed. Cir. 1988). A district court's determination of the law and the application thereof to the facts is not a matter within its discretion. *Id.*

[412]*M.A. Mortenson Co. v. United States*, 877 F.2d 50 (Fed. Cir. 1989). Here the court held unappealable, under the collateral order doctrine, an order awarding attorney fees as part of the sanctions against the United States for failure to comply with discovery orders!

where the failure to comply with a pretrial discovery order is due to willfulness, bad faith, or fault on the part of a litigant.[413]

The available sanctions can be of fatal significance, such as default judgment[414] or dismissal.[415] Severe sanctions such as taking allegations as established and awarding judgment on that basis, dismissal, and default judgment are authorized only in extreme circumstances. To warrant imposition of these severe sanctions, the violations must be due to willfulness, bad faith, or fault. The district court must take into account: (1) the public's interest in expeditious resolution of litigation; (2) the court's need to manage its docket; (3) the risk of prejudice to the defendants; (4) the public policy favoring disposition of cases on their merits; and (5) the availability of less drastic sanctions.[416]

The court follows the Supreme Court's guidelines in *National Hockey*.[417] A discovery sanction should meet the judicial goal of punishing the errant party in order to deter others who would otherwise be inclined to pursue similar behavior. Also, it must be just and related to the particular claim at issue.[418] The sanction of dismissal is intended to be both a punishment for the offender and a deterrent to others. Ordinarily, it is applied in those cases where a party is explicitly ordered by the court to provide discovery and thereafter fails to respond in a proper or timely manner. Rule 37, FRCP, should not be construed to authorize dismissal when the failure to comply was due to inability and not to willfulness, bad faith, or any fault of the party. Absent that showing, an exercise of the power in proper circumstances is necessary to prevent undue delays in the disposition of pending cases and to avoid congestion in the calendars of district courts.[419]

---

[413]*Ingalls Shipbuilding, Inc. v. United States*, 857 F.2d 1448 (Fed. Cir. 1988). See also *Tennant Co. v. Hako Minuteman, Inc.*, 878 F.2d 1413, 11 USPQ2d 1303 (Fed. Cir. 1989).

[414]*Minnesota Min. & Mfg. Co. v. Eco Chem, Inc.*, 757 F.2d 1256, 225 USPQ 350 (Fed. Cir. 1985). There was no abuse of discretion in granting default judgment where a party failed completely to answer interrogatories, obtained seven extensions of time to answer the complaint, failed to appear at scheduled hearings and to schedule hearings for its own motions, and disbanded a corporate entity without informing the court.

[415]*Stock Pot Restaurant, Inc. v. Stockpot, Inc.*, 737 F.2d 1576, 222 USPQ 665 (Fed. Cir. 1984). No abuse of discretion in denial of a motion to dismiss for failure to appear for deposition, where the motion to dismiss was not filed for many months thereafter.

[416]*Refac Int'l, Ltd. v. Hitachi, Ltd.*, 921 F.2d 1247, 16 USPQ2d 1347 (Fed. Cir. 1990). Here the court affirmed the district court's dismissal of the patentee's complaint, and an award of attorney fees, based upon plaintiff's failure to comply with an order requiring it to specify its charge of infringement. The appeal by plaintiff was also held to be frivolous and plaintiff was ordered to pay the attorney fees of the defendants and double their costs on appeal.

[417]*National Hockey League v. Metropolitan Hockey Club, Inc.*, 427 U.S. 639 (1976).

[418]*Cochran Consulting, Inc. v. Uwatec USA, Inc.*, 102 F.3d 1224, 41 USPQ2d 1161 (Fed. Cir. 1996). Due process requires that a claim dismissed for failure to comply with a discovery order must be specifically related to the particular claim that was at issue in the order. *Seal-Flex Inc. v. Athletic Track & Court Constr.*, 172 F.3d 836, 50 USPQ2d 1225 (Fed. Cir. 1999).

[419]*Adkins v. United States*, 816 F.2d 1562 (Fed. Cir. 1987). See also *Wexell v. Komar Indus., Inc.*, 18 F.3d 916, 29 USPQ2d 2017 (Fed. Cir. 1994) (Sixth Circuit law). In *Hendler v. United States*, 952 F.2d 1364 (Fed. Cir. 1991), the court reversed a Rule 37 dismissal as an abuse of discretion where the plaintiff had failed to produce information that the plaintiff would have had to obtain from the government itself. To use discovery as an alternative to its own

But because dismissal is universally recognized as a sanction of last resort, courts are required, before imposing that sanction, to consider fully all the surrounding circumstances, such as the degree of culpability, the amount of prejudice, and the availability of less drastic sanctions.[420]

Examples of application of the *National Hockey* guidelines provide contrast. In one case the court found no abuse of discretion in a dismissal of the complaint for failure to answer interrogatories after three extensions of time, a motion, a court-ordered deadline, and a warning to counsel.[421] In another, it was an abuse to preclude the government from introducing evidence on a crucial issue (in practical effect a dismissal) for inadequate interrogatory answers. Under the circumstances the court felt that the government should have been given a predicate "warning order" setting out the deficiencies and giving the government a chance to comply.[422] In another case, the trial court at a pretrial conference orally ordered the parties to provide full disclosure, indicating that anything responsive that was not disclosed would not be usable at trial. Defendant sought information regarding plaintiff's theory of infringement. Plaintiff indicated in a letter that it had not made any contention regarding infringement by equivalents, but reserved the right to do so after an investigation by its technical expert. Discovery closed without further disclosure as to the doctrine of equivalents. The district court, in response to a Rule 37 motion, precluded plaintiff from urging equivalents at trial. The Federal Circuit affirmed, noting that an oral order can provide the basis for a Rule 37 sanction.[423]

In a case involving an "abuse of the judicial process in startling dimensions," the Federal Circuit was even willing to affirm a summary judgment of dismissal that was clearly intended as a discovery sanction.[424] But discovery sanctions are intended to deter intentional abuse of the discovery process, not as a means to resolve the merits of a case. Where the problem is a perceived inadequacy of proof, not the failure to provide it, dismissal as a sanction under Rule 37 is not warranted.[425]

Rule 37(b)(2) permits a court to order a party to pay the reasonable expenses, including attorney fees, caused by that party's failure

---

preparation of a defense or to harass the plaintiff comes close to governmental abuse of the judicial process.

[420]*Genentech, Inc. v. United States ITC,* 122 F.3d 1409, 43 USPQ2d 1722 (Fed. Cir. 1997).

[421]*Adkins v. United States,* 816 F.2d 1562 (Fed. Cir. 1987).

[422]*Ingalls Shipbuilding, Inc. v. United States,* 857 F.2d 1448 (Fed. Cir. 1988).

[423]*Nike, Inc. v. Wolverine World Wide, Inc.,* 43 F.3d 644, 33 USPQ2d 1038 (Fed. Cir. 1994).

[424]*Wright v. United States,* 728 F.2d 1459 (Fed. Cir. 1984). The court sua sponte awarded double costs and $500 in view of the egregious nature of the plaintiff's persistent bad faith course of conduct.

[425]*Ingalls Shipbuilding, Inc. v. United States,* 857 F.2d 1448 (Fed. Cir. 1988). No Rule 37 sanction is appropriate when a litigant's failure is not the result of bad faith or misconduct. Failure to set forth in discovery facts sufficient to establish a cause of action is not proof of bad faith. *Hendler v. United States,* 952 F.2d 1364 (Fed. Cir. 1991).

to comply with a discovery order.[426] Even though a party meets the time constraints of 35 U.S.C. §282 for identifying prior art, a trial court may exclude prior art if it was not identified during the discovery process.[427] The court has indicated that the available sanctions do not include limitation of prejudgment interest.[428]

In an interesting case, the district court sanctioned an attorney for misconduct in responding to discovery, based upon a magistrate's finding. The district court held a hearing at which the magistrate testified. The Federal Circuit held that such a hearing fully met the constitutional due process requirements of notice and an opportunity to respond.[429] In another case, the court reversed the trial judge's denial of a motion for a new trial largely on the basis of discovery misconduct.[430]

In what may turn out to be an extremely significant decision, the court approved an award of expenses under Rule 37(c) for failure to admit pursuant to Rule 36. The accused infringer had asked for an admission that its product lacked a certain element, and the patentee refused. After obtaining a judgment of noninfringement, the accused infringer moved for expenses. The court rejected the argument that the request sought an admission that would effectively concede the absence of literal infringement. The reasoning was that infringement is a legal issue, and it is for the court to decide whether the element is necessary for infringement.[431] If this ruling is applied broadly, it can have far-reaching consequences. It does not take a particularly clever lawyer to construct a Rule 36 request for admissions that will have the practical effect of requiring his or her opponent to admit or deny infringement, and turn about is certainly fair play. Thus, this

---

[426]*DH Tech. Inc. v. Synergystex Int'l Inc.*, 154 F.3d 1333, 47 USPQ2d 1865 (Fed. Cir. 1998).

[427]*ATD Corp. v. Lydall Inc.*, 159 F.3d 534, 48 USPQ2d 1321, 1333–34 (Fed. Cir. 1998).

[428]*Bio-Rad Labs., Inc. v. Nicolet Instr. Corp.*, 807 F.2d 964, 1 USPQ2d 1191 (Fed. Cir. 1986). Discovery-related conduct may evoke sanctions under other rules as well. In *Katz v. Batavia Mar. & Sporting Supp., Inc.*, 984 F.2d 422, 25 USPQ2d 1547 (Fed. Cir. 1993), the district court's order quashing discovery was affirmed. Nonetheless, the Federal Circuit awarded costs under Rule 39, FRAP, to the party seeking discovery, because the notice of motion to quash had not been given in a manner calculated to avoid the expense of traveling to the deposition site.

[429]*Fromson v. Citiplate, Inc.*, 886 F.2d 1300, 12 USPQ2d 1299 (Fed. Cir. 1989).

[430]*Advanced Display Sys. Inc. v. Kent State Univ.*, 212 F.3d 1272, 54 USPQ2d 1673 (Fed. Cir. 2000). The court had some strong words to describe counsel's conduct: "Indeed, to say that counsel's conduct during discovery raises the collective eyebrow of this court would be to understate the severity of their transgressions. Counsel tactics during discovery evinced a brazen disregard for the legal process. Throughout discovery, counsel's strategy consisted of efforts to obfuscate, cover-up, and subvert evidence that was properly discoverable and response to Kent's requests.*** In a case such as this, in which counsel deliberately and repeatedly flouts discovery requests and disregards the Federal Rules of Civil Procedure, the sanction of a new trial fits the transgression. Indeed, the acts of ADS's counsel strike at the heart of the discovery process, and they deprived Kent of its full measure of a right to a fair trial based upon all the relevant evidence." 54 USPQ2d at 1684. In remanding, the court strongly encouraged the lower court to follow through by reviewing counsel's conduct and considering, within its discretion, disciplinary actions and additional sanctions beyond the granting of a new trial.

[431]*Chemical Eng'g Corp. v. Essef Indus., Inc.*, 795 F.2d 1565, 230 USPQ 385 (Fed. Cir. 1986).

decision could result in all parties being at risk of having to pay a successful opponent's expenses on the infringement issue.[432]

A party served with a document request under Rule 34 or 30(b)(5) is required to respond. It may either agree to produce documents as requested, respond by objecting, or move for a protective order. If it chooses to ignore the request, it is subject to sanctions under Rule 37(d), but sanctions under Rule 37(b) are unavailable unless a violation of an order for discovery is involved. If it responds to the request by objecting, it need not seek a protective order, but some courts award sanctions where the response is so evasive or misleading as to be tantamount to no response at all.[433] The discovery rules require that a party have ownership, custody, or control of a demanded document before a sanction may properly be imposed for failure to produce the document. Rule 37 is not a legal requirement to do the impossible, and the courts have declined to assess a penalty for a failure to do that which it may not have been in the power of the party to do.[434]

(c) Pretrial Practice

(i) Pretrial Conferences and Orders

Rule 16, FRCP, deals with pretrial conferences and orders in quite comprehensive detail. The Federal Circuit is in accord with the goals underlying the rule. It has recognized that trials conducted in keeping with the statutorily assigned burdens would not result in assured victory, or more victories, for either side and has therefore indicated that trial courts should consider pretrial orders designed to facilitate such trials.[435] Similarly, in jury cases courts should consider pretrial orders that specify precisely what the jury will be asked to do after it has been given instructions prepared in light of the evidence

---

[432]Inasmuch as the standard of review on discovery sanctions is abuse of discretion, it will be that much more difficult for the Federal Circuit to control overenthusiastic trial judges on Rule 37(c) sanctions. But see *Badalamenti v. Dunham's, Inc.,* 896 F.2d 1359, 13 USPQ2d 1967 (Fed. Cir. 1990).

[433]*Badalamenti v. Dunham's, Inc.,* 896 F.2d 1359, 13 USPQ2d 1967 (Fed. Cir. 1990). Here the court passed the question whether the Sixth Circuit would adopt this view, because it found that the response was not so evasive as to constitute a failure to respond. The Federal Circuit also refused to find that the conduct was such that it would fall within the district court's inherent authority to sanction for discovery violations. Apparently some of the documents that fell within the request were invalidating prior art that the defendant later obtained from another source. The lower court apparently considered them crucial, for it awarded $100,000 against the plaintiff and its lawyer. The moral seems to be that the party seeking the discovery must be persistent and follow up on its requests, no matter how crucial the withheld information turns out to be.

[434]*Cochran Consulting, Inc. v. Uwatec USA, Inc.,* 102 F.3d 1224, 41 USPQ2d 1161 (Fed. Cir. 1996). This interesting case involved an attempt to discover ROM code used in an infringing device. The complicating factor was that the code belonged to a Swiss company that was not a party. The Federal Circuit analysis of Supreme Court precedent governing such situations is instructive.

[435]*Orthokinetics, Inc. v. Safety Travel Chairs, Inc.,* 806 F.2d 1565, 1 USPQ2d 1081 (Fed. Cir. 1986).

and at the end of its deliberations.[436] The court promises to take pretrial orders seriously.[437] Due regard will also be given to pretrial stipulations.[438]

Care must be taken with stipulations, both giving and receiving. A defendant stipulated validity and infringement and took the case to trial on lack of notice under 35 U.S.C. §287. The jury found no notice and no damages, and the trial court entered a judgment of dismissal. The Federal Circuit affirmed a denial of the plaintiff's motion for a judgment of validity and infringement on the ground that the stipulation was clearly not intended to permit such a judgment. But a denial of the plaintiff's request for an injunction was also affirmed on the same basis. This is an entirely different matter, for it would seem that a trial of validity and infringement could not have been avoided if the plaintiff had wished to press for injunctive relief below, stipulation or no stipulation.[439] In another case, the parties had stipulated in the trial court that four claims would be "representative." On a first appeal that resulted in a reversal of the district court's holding of invalidity, the Federal Circuit made a statement that only the representative claims were considered on appeal. The defendant interpreted this to mean that the fate of the other, nonrepresentative claims was unresolved and objected to the district court's judgment that all of the claims were valid. The defendant's appeal from that judgment was dismissed as frivolous.[440]

Where the parties agreed in a joint pretrial statement that a factual issue existed, it was error for the trial court to grant summary judgment sua sponte on grounds involving that issue.[441] But while a pretrial stipulation may direct the evidence to be offered, it does not

---

[436]*Orthokinetics, Inc. v. Safety Travel Chairs, Inc.*, 806 F.2d 1565, 1 USPQ2d 1081 (Fed. Cir. 1986). Indeed, a Rule 16 conference may well be the last opportunity to preserve some very important rights. See *American Med. Sys., Inc. v. Medical Eng'g Corp.*, 6 F.3d 1523, 28 USPQ2d 1321 (Fed. Cir. 1993).

[437]In affirming an exclusion of certain exhibits, the court observed that "it is well settled that documents not marked and identified before trial may be excluded." *Devices for Med., Inc. v. Boehl*, 822 F.2d 1062, 3 USPQ2d 1288 (Fed. Cir. 1987). Surely the court did not mean to suggest that such a rule is universally followed by district courts; it seems quite clearly to be a matter of local practice, or even the preference of individual judges. In *Claude E. Atkins Enter., Inc. v. United States*, 899 F.2d 1180 (Fed. Cir. 1990), there had been a history of failure to comply with court orders regarding status reports and pretrial submissions. Finally the trial court ordered the parties to submit pretrial statements on the evidence to be introduced at trial. Plaintiff failed to do so and the court dismissed, sua sponte, for failure to prosecute.

[438]See *Kloster Speedsteel AB v. Crucible Inc.*, 793 F.2d 1565, 230 USPQ 81 (Fed. Cir. 1986). The parties had stipulated commercial success, but on appeal the infringer attacked this secondary indicium on the basis of lack of nexus. The court viewed this as an apparent and disquieting attempt to renege on the stipulation but went on to consider the nexus argument on the merits nonetheless.

[439]*Devices for Med., Inc. v. Boehl*, 822 F.2d 1062, 3 USPQ2d 1288 (Fed. Cir. 1987).

[440]*Panduit Corp. v. Dennison Mfg. Co.*, 836 F.2d 1329, 5 USPQ2d 1266 (Fed. Cir. 1987). Apparently the court of appeals felt that defendant's new counsel was attempting to renege on a stipulation that predecessor counsel had made. It should be noted that the author's law firm was defendant's new counsel in this case; the author hopes and believes that such relationship has not affected the discussion of this case.

[441]*Skaw v. United States*, 740 F.2d 932 (Fed. Cir. 1984).

empower the trial court to decide an issue not properly before it.[442] Nothing in Rule 16(e) indicates that a pretrial order from a first trial controls the range of evidence to be considered in a second trial. Indeed, such a cramped interpretation would greatly hobble the parties in meaningfully relitigating an issue that the court has decided requires retrial.[443]

The court has held that it is not bound by stipulations of law. Parties may stipulate any facts they wish. But the attempted stipulation as to a legal conclusion might result in the court rendering an advisory opinion.[444]

(ii) Pretrial Motions

There are ways other than summary judgment to avoid or postpone a trial on some or all of the issues presented. Normally a motion for summary judgment seeks a judgment on the merits, while a motion to dismiss for lack of subject matter jurisdiction seeks a judgment in abatement in that it does not bar future claims. Thus the motion to dismiss should properly be brought under Rule 12(b)(1), FRCP. However, in deciding such motions a court can consider evidentiary matters outside the pleadings, and summary judgment motions can in appropriate cases be treated as Rule 12(b) motions.[445] Motions under Rule 12 are discussed in §8.2(a).[446] Rule 7, FRCP, requires that motions state with particularity the grounds therefor. The purpose is to provide notice to both the court and the opposing party, so that the court knows how to process the motion correctly and the opposing party has a meaningful opportunity to respond.[447] The substance of a motion, rather than its linguistic form alone, determines its nature and thus its legal effect.[448]

Rule 41(a)(1), FRCP, unambiguously gives a plaintiff the right to dismiss an action before the defendant serves an answer or motion for summary judgment. Such voluntary dismissal is a matter of right running to the plaintiff that may not be extinguished by adversary or court.[449]

---

[442]*Stearns v. Beckman Instr., Inc.*, 737 F.2d 1565, 222 USPQ 457 (Fed. Cir. 1984). Where the complaint was amended prior to trial to remove certain claims, it was improper to adjudicate the validity of all claims.

[443]*Johns Hopkins Univ. v. Cellpro Inc.*, 152 F.3d 1342, 47 USPQ2d 1705 (Fed. Cir. 1998). The court held that a party had not waived its right to rely on a reference that it did not assert during a first trial, where the district court, in a posttrial ruling, made a particular claim construction and ordered a new trial.

[444]*Technicon Instr., Corp. v. Alpkem Corp.*, 866 F.2d 417, 9 USPQ2d 1540 (Fed. Cir. 1989).

[445]*Indium Corp. v. Semi-Alloys, Inc.*, 781 F.2d 879, 228 USPQ 845 (Fed. Cir. 1985).

[446]See also text accompanying notes 8:27–37.

[447]*Registration Control Sys., Inc. v. Compusystems, Inc.*, 922 F.2d 805, 17 USPQ2d 1212 (Fed. Cir. 1990). Apparently the court will follow regional circuit precedent in determining sufficient particularity under Rule 7.

[448]*Super Sack Mfg. Corp. v. Chase Packaging Corp.*, 57 F.3d 1054, 35 USPQ2d 1139 (Fed. Cir. 1995).

[449]*Eastalco Alum. Co. v. United States*, 995 F.2d 201 (Fed. Cir. 1993).

The specific point at which the trial court should decide a motion under 35 U.S.C. §295 (for benefit of the patented process presumption) will vary with the facts and circumstances of each case. It would be as arbitrary to identify a specific point at which the court must make its §295 decision as it would be to mandate a specific point in a proceeding when a court must enter summary judgment.[450]

(iii) Separation and Severance

Severance of a claim is obtained under Rule 21, FRCP; separation under Rule 42(b). Separation for trial under Rule 42(b) does not result in "severance."[451] The purpose of ordering separate trials under Rule 42(b) is to promote convenience, expedition, and economy, to avoid delay and prejudice, and to preserve the right to a jury trial.[452] A district court has broad discretion in separating issues and claims for trial as part of its discretion in trial management. It may, therefore, order a trial on unenforceability separate from an infringement trial that may involve an invalidity defense. But the discretion in ordering an equitable claim to be tried first is narrowly limited and must wherever possible be exercised to preserve jury trial.[453] In patent cases involving antitrust claims, it is standard practice for trial courts to separate the patent issues for earlier trial as that is the most likely way to result in a just final disposition of the litigation.[454] In discussing the need to reveal an attorney's opinion, the court has suggested that it may be useful to have separate trials on liability and on willfulness and damages. That way, the accused infringer need only disclose its attorney's opinion if it is found liable.[455]

---

[450]*Nutrinova Nutrition Spec. v. United States ITC*, 224 F.3d 1356, 55 USPQ2d 1951 (Fed. Cir. 2000).

[451]*In re Innotron Diagnostics*, 800 F.2d 1077, 231 USPQ 178 (Fed. Cir. 1986); *Atari, Inc. v. JS&A Group, Inc.*, 747 F.2d 1422, 223 USPQ 1074 (Fed. Cir. 1984).

[452]*Atari, Inc. v. JS&A Group, Inc.*, 747 F.2d 1422, 223 USPQ 1074 (Fed. Cir. 1984). Action on a motion for separation is procedural, not substantive. *Id.* The standard of review is abuse of discretion. *In re Innotron Diagnostics*, 800 F.2d 1077, 231 USPQ 178 (Fed. Cir. 1986). In *Cabinet Vision v. Cabnetware*, 129 F.3d 595, 44 USPQ2d 1683 (Fed. Cir. 1997), the district court erred in a matter of separation of issues for jury trial, but it indicated that any error was invited by one of the parties. The Federal Circuit observed that such an error cannot be excused, even if the party failed to advise the court on how to separate and manage those issues that were for the court and those that were for the jury. Interpretation of the law is the responsibility of the court.

[453]*Gardco Mfg., Inc. v. Herst Lighting Co.*, 820 F.2d 1209, 2 USPQ2d 2015 (Fed. Cir. 1987). The court held here that (1) the defense of inequitable conduct is equitable in nature and does not give rise to the right of trial by jury, and (2) that an inequitable conduct issue may be tried first, without a jury, if the factual issues resolved thereby are not so common with those relating to the jury issues of validity and infringement that a jury trial of those issues would be precluded by the earlier bench trial.

[454]*In re Innotron Diagnostics*, 800 F.2d 1077, 231 USPQ 178 (Fed. Cir. 1986).

[455]*Fromson v. Western Litho Plate & Supp. Co.*, 853 F.2d 1568, 7 USPQ2d 1606 (Fed. Cir. 1988).

Inasmuch as such questions clearly implicate the jurisprudential responsibilities of the Federal Circuit with respect to patent law, the court is not bound by regional circuit precedent.[456]

(iv) Stays and Dismissals

Courts have inherent power to manage their dockets and stay proceedings, including the authority to order a stay pending conclusion of a PTO reexamination.[457] A federal district court may also stay its own proceedings in favor of a state case, where the outcome of the state case might moot, or have preclusive effect on, the federal case, and where the state case would not resolve matters of federal law.[458] To promote efficient judicial management and conservation of judicial resources, a court may enjoin parties under its jurisdiction from proceeding with a concurrent action involving the same or related issues. In deciding whether to enjoin concurrent litigation, the court must determine whether resolution of the case disposes of the other litigation.[459]

The Federal Circuit clearly recognizes a "customer suit" doctrine, whereby litigation against or brought by the manufacturer of infringing goods takes precedence over a suit by the patent owner against customers of the manufacturer.[460] The doctrine is based on the manufacturer's presumed greater interest in defending its actions against charges of patent infringement, and to guard against possibility of abuse. In cases in which the doctrine is applied, the second suit would resolve all charges against the customers in the stayed suit.[461]

The public policy favoring expeditious resolution of disputes is of particular weight when dealing with wasting assets such as patents.[462] The premise behind a decision to enjoin[463] or stay concurrent proceedings is that they involve the same issues and parties. But where the

---

[456]*Gardco Mfg., Inc. v. Herst Lighting Co.*, 820 F.2d 1209, 2 USPQ2d 2015, 2018 (Fed. Cir. 1987).

[457]*Ethicon v. Quigg*, 849 F.2d 1422, 7 USPQ2d 1152 (Fed. Cir. 1988). In *Slip Track Sys. Inc. v. Metal Lite Inc.*, 159 F.3d 1337, 48 USPQ2d 1055 (Fed. Cir. 1998), the court held that a stay of an interfering patents suit pending the outcome of reexamination was improper. The principal point of contention is which party was the first to invent the subject matter claimed in the two patents. The issue of priority cannot be determined by reexamination. Accordingly, if carried to completion on the limited statutory scope that is available in reexamination, the reexamination proceeding would result in cancellation of the claims of the second filed patent in light of the first filed, without any exploration of which party was the first to invent the claimed subject matter. The question of whether a district court case should be stayed pending the outcome of PTO proceedings is governed by Federal Circuit law.

[458]*Intermedics Infusaid, Inc. v. Regents of Univ. of Minn.*, 804 F.2d 129, 231 USPQ 653 (Fed. Cir. 1986). A stay order is generally not a final appealable order, unless it would effectively put a party out of court. On appeal, the standard of review is abuse of discretion. *Id.*

[459]*In re Van Geuns*, 946 F.2d 845, 20 USPQ2d 1291 (Fed. Cir. 1991).

[460]*Katz v. Lear Siegler, Inc.*, 909 F.2d 1459, 15 USPQ2d 1554, 1558 (Fed. Cir. 1990).

[461]*Kahn v. General Motors Corp.*, 889 F.2d 1078, 12 USPQ2d 1997 (Fed. Cir. 1989).

[462]*Katz v. Lear Siegler, Inc.*, 909 F.2d 1459, 15 USPQ2d 1554 (Fed. Cir. 1990).

[463]*Kahn v. General Motors Corp.*, 889 F.2d 1078, 12 USPQ2d 1997 (Fed. Cir. 1989).

stayed or enjoined proceeding clearly involves many issues, such as the provenance, performance, and disposition of a contract, that are not at issue in the other case, there is insufficient reason to delay resolution of either.[464] The general rule is that the first suit should have priority. Restraint of the first filed suit is made only to prevent wrong or injustice. There are two exceptions: (1) where forum shopping alone motivated the choice of situs for the first suit, and (2) the "customer suit" doctrine.[465] A district court has the inherent power to control the disposition of the cases on its docket with economy of time and effort for itself, for counsel, and for litigants. Incident to this power is the court's ability to dismiss a lawsuit. Dismissal without prejudice may operate as an alternative to a stay of proceedings.[466]

The purpose of 28 U.S.C. §1292(c)(2), which allows interlocutory appeals in patent cases, was to permit a stay of a damages trial, not compel one. There is thus no conflict between that statute and Rule 62(a), FRCP, which grants discretion to stay or proceed with the damages trial during an appeal.[467]

§8.3 Attorneys and Their Conduct

The authority of a U.S. court of appeals over matters concerning the administration of its bar is well recognized. Membership in a state bar or admission to practice before the highest court of a state is a prerequisite to admission to the bar of a federal court. Absence or loss of state bar status may absolutely destroy the condition of fair private and professional character, without the possession of which there could be no possible right to continue to be a member of a federal bar.[468]

Where a party voluntarily chooses an attorney, it cannot be heard to complain about the attorney's incompetence, at least in a civil case.[469] Having made the choice, the client "cannot now avoid the consequences of the acts or omissions of this freely selected agent."[470]

---

[464]*Katz v. Lear Siegler, Inc.*, 909 F.2d 1459, 15 USPQ2d 1554 (Fed. Cir. 1990).

[465]*Kahn v. General Motors Corp.*, 889 F.2d 1078, 12 USPQ2d 1997 (Fed. Cir. 1989).

[466]*L.E.A. Dynatech, Inc. v. Allina*, 49 F.3d 1527, 33 USPQ2d 1839 (Fed. Cir. 1995). The patent in suit had been taken back to the PTO for reissue during the pendency of the litigation. The application was pending for 17 months and the examiner finally rejected all of the claims. The duration of an appeal of the final rejection was indefinite. Under these circumstances the Federal Circuit approved the district court's dismissal without prejudice as an alternative to a stay.

[467]*In re Calmar, Inc.*, 854 F.2d 461, 7 USPQ2d 1730 (Fed. Cir. 1988). The Federal Circuit typically denies motions to stay damages trials during appeals in patent cases. *Id.*

[468]*In re Martin*, 120 F.3d 256 (Fed. Cir. 1997).

[469]*Johnson v. Department of Treasury*, 721 F.2d 361 (Fed. Cir. 1983).

[470]*Link v. Wabash Railroad Co.*, 370 U.S. 626 (1962). Thus, attorney negligence is not a valid excuse for a party's failure to submit all available evidence when attempting to provoke an interference. Parties are deemed bound by the acts of their freely selected lawyer-agents and are considered to have notice of all facts, notice of which can be charged upon the attorney.

It thus behooves the patent litigant to choose its lawyer wisely and well, if the comments and criticism emanating from the Federal Circuit bench are any indicator of the quality of its bar. This author ventures to state—without any statistical support save a strong gut feeling—that no court of the United States has leveled more vocal criticism of its bar in so short a time than the Federal Circuit has in its first few years of existence. Whether it is deserved or not, the legal scholar will have to judge. But make no mistake about it, the Federal Circuit can be a perilous place to practice law.[471]

The court put the handwriting on the wall in highly visible scarlet letters when it criticized the plaintiff's inexperienced counsel, and awarded double costs and a fine, for the plaintiff's having appealed the trial court's grant of a motion for JNOV.[472] In other words, plaintiff got a jury verdict of validity and infringement, the trial judge set it aside, and the plaintiff's consequent appeal was seen to be frivolous! There is no mistaking the message in that result.

(a) *Rule 11 Violations and Other Attorney Misconduct*

The court has said that the limit lines of lawyering are not always clear.[473] That is unfortunate, for they should be. Let us see whether the reported decisions of the Federal Circuit are any help.

Rule 11 violations. Rule 11, FRCP, requires attorneys and pro se litigants to conduct a reasonable inquiry into the law and facts before signing pleadings, written motions, and other documents, and prescribes sanctions for violation of these obligations. The court's confrontations with Rule 11 have been sparse but reasonably instructive.[474] Rule 11 imposes a duty on attorneys to certify by their signature that (1) they have read the pleadings or the motions they file and (2) the pleading or motion is well grounded in fact, has a colorable basis in law, and is not filed for an improper purpose. Rule 11 imposes a duty on attorneys to certify that they have conducted a reasonable

---

Huston v. Ladner, 973 F.2d 1564, 23 USPQ2d 1910 (Fed. Cir. 1992). Notice to counsel is notice to the client unless the applicable notice provision expressly requires otherwise. *Belton Indus., Inc. v. United States,* 6 F.3d 756 (Fed. Cir. 1993). Any other notion would be wholly inconsistent with our system of representative litigation, in which each party is deemed bound by the acts of its lawyer-agent and is considered to have notice of all facts, notice of which can be charged upon the attorney. *Super Sack Mfg. Corp. v. Chase Packaging Corp.*, 57 F.3d 1054, 35 USPQ2d 1139 (Fed. Cir. 1995).

[471]See, e.g., *Pac-Tec, Inc. v. Amerace Corp.,* 903 F.2d 796, 14 USPQ2d 1871 (Fed. Cir. 1990).

[472]*Connell v. Sears, Roebuck &* Co., 722 F.2d 1542, 220 USPQ 193 (Fed. Cir. 1983).

[473]*Railroad Dynamics, Inc. v. A. Stucki Co.,* 727 F.2d 1506, 220 USPQ 929 (Fed. Cir. 1984).

[474]Rule 11 took its modern form in 1983 and then was substantially amended in 1993. It is important in assessing a decision to know which version governed the case. For example, in *Judin v. United States,* 110 F.3d 780, 42 USPQ2d 1300 (Fed. Cir. 1997), the court was dealing with Rule 11 of the Court of Federal Claims, which is patterned after the 1983 version of Rule 11, FRCP. The court specifically passed the question whether it would reach the same decision under the 1993 version of Rule 11.

inquiry and have determined that any papers filed with the court are factually and legally tenable. The central purpose of Rule 11 is to deter baseless filings.[475]

Thus, Rule 11 calls for sanctions to be imposed on a party for making arguments or filing claims that are frivolous, legally unreasonable, without factual foundation, or asserted for an improper purpose. A frivolous argument or claim is one that is both baseless and made without a reasonable and competent inquiry.[476] Although a Rule 11 determination includes both factual and legal issues, all aspects of the determination are reviewed for an abuse of discretion, because the district court is better situated than the court of appeals to marshal the pertinent facts and apply the fact-dependent legal standard.[477] The abuse of discretion standard also applies to the choice of appropriate sanctions, although once a violation has been found imposition of sanctions is mandatory.[478] In many cases it is not necessary for a district court to elaborate on its denial of a request for Rule 11 sanctions. Sanctions are often sought in cases in which they are manifestly unwarranted, and it would impose an undue burden on district courts to require a detailed explanation for the denial of sanctions in every case. When the requesting party makes a strong showing that Rule 11 violations may have occurred, however, the district court should provide some explanation for disregarding the proffered showing.[479]

The court's first square confrontation with Rule 11 was in the context of an alleged failure on the part of the attorney who signed the complaint to make reasonable inquiry concerning infringement. The district court had dismissed the complaint and awarded attorney fees as sanctions under Rule 37, FRCP, and apparently felt that it was unnecessary to resolve the defendant's additional request for Rule 11 sanctions. The Federal Circuit remanded for a determination of whether Rule 11 was violated when the complaint was signed and, if so, an imposition of an appropriate sanction on the attorney, his client, or both. The court stressed that the question of whether a litigant's position is well grounded and legally tenable for Rule 11 purposes is fact specific and requires some assessment of the signer's credibility.[480]

---

[475]*View Eng'g Inc. v. Robotic Vision Sys. Inc.*, 208 F.3d 981, 54 USPQ2d 1179 (Fed. Cir. 2000).

[476]*S. Bravo Sys., Inc. v. Containment Tech. Corp.*, 96 F.3d 1372, 40 USPQ2d 1140 (Fed. Cir. 1996).

[477]*S. Bravo Sys., Inc. v. Containment Tech. Corp.*, 96 F.3d 1372, 40 USPQ2d 1140 (Fed. Cir. 1996). Rule 11 sanctions are reviewed for the error underlying them under the abuse of discretion standard. The abuse of discretion standard applies to both the decision to sanction, and the amount of the sanction. *View Eng'g Inc. v. Robotic Vision Sys. Inc.*, 208 F.3d 981, 54 USPQ2d 1179 (Fed. Cir. 2000).

[478]*Refac Int'l, Ltd. v. Hitachi, Ltd.*, 921 F.2d 1247, 16 USPQ2d 1347 (Fed. Cir. 1990).

[479]*S. Bravo Sys., Inc. v. Containment Tech. Corp.*, 96 F.3d 1372, 40 USPQ2d 1140 (Fed. Cir. 1996).

[480]*Refac Int'l, Ltd. v. Hitachi, Ltd.*, 921 F.2d 1247, 16 USPQ2d 1347 (Fed. Cir. 1990). The court has since had occasion to consider several substantive Rule 11 matters in the patent law context. *Hoffmann-La-Roche Inc. v. Invamed Inc.*, 213 F.3d 1359, 54 USPQ2d 1846 (Fed. Cir. 2000), provides a good of example of adequate prefiling investigation for purposes of Rule 11.

In a more recent case, the court affirmed a Rule 11 sanction where the patentee's attorney filed a counterclaim for infringement of eight patents in response to a declaratory judgment action alleging invalidity and noninfringement of one of those patents. In an intensely factual analysis, it concluded that the attorney had not made sufficient inquiry. It held that Rule 11 requires the attorney, at a bare minimum, to apply the claims of each and every patent that is being brought into the lawsuit to an accused device and conclude that there is a reasonable basis for a finding of infringement of at least one claim of each patent so asserted. The presence of an infringement analysis plays the key role in determining the reasonableness of the prefiling inquiry made in a patent infringement case under Rule 11. A patent suit can be an expensive proposition. Defending against baseless claims of infringement subjects the alleged infringer to undue costs, which is precisely the scenario Rule 11 contemplates. Performing a prefiling assessment of the basis of each infringement claim is, therefore, extremely important. In bringing a claim of infringement, the patent holder, if challenged, must be prepared to demonstrate to both the court and the alleged infringer exactly why it believed before filing the claim that it had a reasonable chance of proving infringement. Failure to do so should ordinarily result in the district court expressing its broad discretion in favor of Rule 11 sanctions, at least in the absence of a sound excuse or considerable mitigating circumstances.[481]

The court has suggested that it may not be possible to postulate a case in which it would be an abuse of discretion for a court to

---

The patentee could not tell whether the defendant's product was made by the patented process. Reverse engineering was not possible. Upon reasonable inquiry, the defendant refused to disclose its manufacturing process. Accordingly, the patentee filed an infringement suit on information and belief. The court held that this set of circumstances did not violate Rule 11 and did not compel a finding that the case was exceptional under 35 U.S.C. §285. See also *Cambridge Prods., Ltd. v. Penn Nutrients, Inc.,* 962 F.2d 1048, 22 USPQ2d 1577 (Fed. Cir. 1992). In *In re Hayes Microcomputer Patent Litig.,* 982 F.2d 1527, 25 USPQ2d 1241 (Fed. Cir. 1992), the court found no abuse of discretion in the district court's refusal to award Rule 11 sanctions against the defendant for what might have been regarded as an ill-advised pursuit of an inequitable conduct defense. In *S. Bravo Sys., Inc. v. Containment Tech. Corp.,* 96 F.3d 1372, 40 USPQ2d 1140 (Fed. Cir. 1996), it appeared that the patentee's attorneys relied upon their client's lay opinion that the accused device infringed. This was sufficient to require a remand of the district court's denial of Rule 11 sanctions. If on remand it is found that the attorneys conducted no investigation of the factual and legal merits of the client's claims other than to rely on his lay opinion, it would be difficult to avoid the conclusion that sanctions are appropriate. In *Judin v. United States,* 110 F.3d 780, 42 USPQ2d 1300 (Fed. Cir. 1997), the court directed Rule 11 sanctions where the patentee and his attorney made no reasonable effort to ascertain whether the accused device satisfied two key claim limitations. They failed to obtain, or even attempt to obtain, a sample of the device and thus never compared the accused device with the patent claims prior to filing the complaint. The fact that an expert hired after the complaint was filed was able to come up with colorable doctrine of equivalents arguments (that were ultimately rejected by the district court) did not cure the failure to conduct a proper Rule 11 prefiling investigation.

[481]*View Eng'g Inc. v. Robotic Vision Sys. Inc.,* 208 F.3d 981, 54 USPQ2d 1179 (Fed. Cir. 2000). The court rejected, as an excuse, the argument that the plaintiff had been uncooperative in permitting prelitigation investigation. This case is also noteworthy for its discussion of how a monetary sanction under Rule 11 should be assessed, using a so-called lodestar approach. Among other things, the court rejected a plea by the sanctioned law firm that an award of $98,000 would be ruinous to it.

deny Rule 11 sanctions even though the legal position said to be sanctionable was accepted by that court.[482] In imposing Rule 11 sanctions, a court may allocate sanctions between an attorney and client according to their relative fault. Attorneys are usually held solely responsible when the filing violating Rule 11 is unwarranted by law. However, an attorney and client may be held jointly and severally liable for filings that are not well grounded in fact.[483]

Rule 11 sanctions are available only in federal trial court proceedings, not on appeal.[484] But the court has indicated that it will adhere to the spirit of Rule 11 in its dealings with the lawyers who appear before it. Indeed, it has pointed out that while it may be justifiable to refuse to hold lawyers personally liable under Rule 11 on the ground that they may have been misled by their clients, the appellate setting is different; counsel usually knows when there is no basis for an appeal and thus should be held personally liable.[485]

A district court decision imposing Rule 11 sanctions is not final, and hence not appealable, until the amount of the sanction has been decided.[486] Regional circuit law governs Rule 11 determinations.[487]

Other misconduct. The court has held that the imposition of sanctions against a party's attorneys, under 28 U.S.C. §1927, for multiplying the proceedings unreasonably and vexatiously, requires an opportunity for a hearing on the record. Although the court suggested that a motion under Rule 59(e), FRCP, for reconsideration of the sanction order is to be favored as a way of eliminating an appeal or a remand, it did recognize that reconsideration after a decision is rendered is no substitute for a predecision hearing.[488] Liability under §1927 does not require that the actions were taken in bad faith.[489]

---

[482]*Additive Con. & Meas. Sys., Inc. v. Flowdata, Inc.,* 96 F.3d 1390, 40 USPQ2d 1106 (Fed. Cir. 1996).

[483]*Judin v. United States,* 110 F.3d 780, 42 USPQ2d 1300 (Fed. Cir. 1997). Under Rule 11, reliance on forwarding cocounsel may in certain circumstances satisfy an attorney's duty of reasonable inquiry, although an attorney who signs a pleading cannot simply delegate to forwarding cocounsel his or her duty of reasonable inquiry. Also, Under Rule 11, for a party represented by an attorney, the "person who signed" the pleading refers to the individual attorney who signed the pleading, not the attorney's firm. *Id.*

[484]*A. Hirsh, Inc. v. United States,* 948 F.2d 1240 (Fed. Cir. 1991).

[485]*Chemical Eng'g Corp. v. Marlo, Inc.,* 754 F.2d 331, 222 USPQ 738 (Fed. Cir. 1984). Thus, the Federal Circuit is willing to exercise its own disciplinary authority under Rule 46(c), FRAP. In *In re Solerwitz,* 848 F.2d 1573 (Fed. Cir. 1988), the court suspended an attorney for one year for reasons centering around the filing of numerous frivolous appeals.

[486]*View Eng'g, Inc. v. Robotic Vision Sys., Inc.,* 115 F.3d 962, 42 USPQ2d 1956 (Fed. Cir. 1997).

[487]*Abbott Labs. v. Brennan,* 952 F.2d 1346, 21 USPQ2d 1192 (Fed. Cir. 1992).

[488]*Beatrice Foods Co. v. New England Printing & Lith. Co.,* 899 F.2d 1171, 14 USPQ2d 1020 (Fed. Cir. 1990). The court reviews all aspects of a sanctions award under §1927 for abuse of discretion. Although a finding of bad faith is required to impose sanctions under §1927, knowing or reckless conduct meets this standard, and the lack of an explicit finding of bad faith by the trial judge will not preclude sanctions when the record supports such a finding. *Baldwin Hardware Corp. v. Franksu Enter. Corp.,* 78 F.3d 550, 37 USPQ2d 1829 (Fed. Cir. 1996).

[489]*Fiskars Inc. v Hunt Mfg. Co.,* 221 F.3d 1318, 55 USPQ2d 1569 (Fed. Cir. 2000). But see *Baldwin Hardware* at note 8:488.

An abuse of the judicial process resides as much in the presentation of a knowingly frivolous defense as in the filing of a knowingly frivolous complaint or appeal.[490] Counsel's role as an officer of the court should not be subservient to his or her role as an advocate. An attorney should not file a motion simply on the ground that it will save the client money, if it appears that it will inconvenience the court![491] The assertion that a judge improperly participated in a case from which he or she should have recused constitutes a charge most grave. Counsel should not make such an assertion precipitously or recklessly, nor on unsupported rumor, conjecture, and speculation. To do so is to trifle with the court and the administration of justice.[492] Attacking a trial judge as lacking in skill, understanding, or legal competence is improper argument and wholly ineffective, if not counterproductive. It has no tendency to prove anything.[493]

The role of counsel includes that of explaining, when necessary, the esoterics of patent law to the district court. If counsel fails in that role, that failure cannot be cured by arguments made on appeal.[494] It is crucial that counsel set forth the law accurately. More particularly, it is the duty of counsel to impart to the judge that the obviousness question requires a structured approach.[495] Presentation of the infringement issue on an overgrown claims jungle is an unprofessional exercise not in clarification but in obfuscation.[496]

Distortion of the record, by deleting critical language in a quotation, reflects a lack of candor in violation of Rule 3.3 of the Model

---

[490]*Amstar Corp. v. Envirotech Corp.*, 730 F.2d 1476, 221 USPQ 649 (Fed. Cir. 1984) (asserting invalidity with no basis for it, or in the face of strong countervailing evidence, may well be frivolous); *Railroad Dynamics, Inc. v. A. Stucki Co.*, 727 F.2d 1506, 220 USPQ 929 (Fed. Cir. 1984). See also *Chemical Eng'g Corp. v. Essef Indus., Inc.*, 795 F.2d 1565, 230 USPQ 385 (Fed. Cir. 1986) (filing of a complaint and continuance of judicial proceedings without specifying charge of infringement termed "at best bizarre"). In *Imagineering, Inc. v. Van Klassens, Inc.*, 53 F.3d 1260, 34 USPQ2d 1526 (Fed. Cir. 1995), the trial court sanctioned defendant and its attorney for failure to withdraw voluntarily a declaratory judgment counterclaim after plaintiff had admitted the patent was invalid and had dismissed its patent infringement claim. This was held to be an abuse of discretion, largely because the plaintiff had refused to stipulate to invalidity. Thus, withdrawal of the counterclaim might have resulted in a waiver of objection to errors that the district court may have committed, including a denial of attorney fees. Other sanctions found to be an abuse of discretion were for filing motions to compel a deposition and to dismiss for lack of jurisdiction and venue.

[491]*Crostic v. Veterans Admin.*, 730 F.2d 1464 (Fed. Cir. 1984).

[492]*Maier v. Orr*, 758 F.2d 1578 (Fed. Cir. 1985).

[493]*Preemption Devices, Inc. v. Minnesota Min. & Mfg. Co.*, 732 F.2d 903, 221 USPQ 841 (Fed. Cir. 1984). See also *Interspiro USA, Inc. v. Figgie Int'l, Inc.*, 18 F.3d 927, 30 USPQ2d 1070 (Fed. Cir. 1994).

[494]*Senza-Gel Corp. v. Seiffhart*, 803 F.2d 661, 231 USPQ 363 (Fed. Cir. 1986).

[495]*Hybritech Inc. v. Monoclonal Antibodies, Inc.*, 802 F.2d 1367, 231 USPQ 81 (Fed. Cir. 1986). Modifications by addition of elements do not avoid infringement. A contrary argument by counsel was termed a "reverse statement" of the law of infringement and was a principal factor in an award of double costs on appeal. *Amstar Corp. v. Envirotech Corp.*, 730 F.2d 1476, 221 USPQ 649 (Fed. Cir. 1984). A deliberate mischaracterization of a decision goes beyond legitimate advocacy. *Octocom Sys., Inc. v. Houston Computer Serv., Inc.*, 918 F.2d 937, 16 USPQ2d 1783 (Fed. Cir. 1990).

[496]*Wahpeton Canvas Co. v. Frontier, Inc.*, 870 F.2d 1546, 10 USPQ2d 1201, 1206 n.6 (Fed. Cir. 1989).

Rules of Professional Conduct, wastes the time of the court and opposing counsel, and imposes unnecessary costs on the parties and on the public.[497] The notion that counsel may strenuously and repeatedly emphasize a fact contrary to the record, may consider that conduct mere error, and may still consider his or her preparation diligent, is anathema to the proper, fair, and expeditious administration of appellate justice. That conduct constitutes a dereliction of duty owed the court.[498] Counsel's obligation to the client, as well as to the court, is to know the record and present it accurately. Clients have a fundamental interest in the fair and truthful administration of justice that far exceeds their monetary interest in a particular case.[499] The law is not a sport where winning is everything, and neither a trial nor an appeal should be only an exercise in gamesmanship. Counsel should not trade charges and countercharges. Pointing to misstatements is appropriate, but motivational analysis is not. Judges have much and many better things to do than to referee irrelevant cat-fights of counsel.[500]

Frivolous procedural gambits can result in awards of fees and costs against the attorney personally.[501] A trial court has wide discretion in designing an appropriate remedial sanction for attorney misconduct.[502] In matters of attorney discipline, marked deference is owed to the discretionary rulings of the judge conducting the trial.[503] In

---

[497]*Amstar Corp. v. Envirotech Corp.*, 730 F.2d 1476, 221 USPQ 649 (Fed. Cir. 1984). See also *Paulik v. Rizkalla*, 796 F.2d 456, 230 USPQ 434 (Fed. Cir. 1986).

[498]*Glaros v. H.H. Robertson Co.*, 797 F.2d 1564, 230 USPQ 393 (Fed. Cir. 1986). Here the counsel stated an untruth, but one that could have easily been checked. In an interesting twist, the court refused sanctions to the other party on the ground that he should at least have called the offending party to advise him of the error. Misrepresentation of the import and content of the record on appeal was found to justify an award of attorney fees against counsel personally in *Cambridge Prods., Ltd. v. Penn Nutrients, Inc.*, 962 F.2d 1048, 22 USPQ2d 1577 (Fed. Cir. 1992).

[499]*Pac-Tec, Inc. v. Amerace Corp.*, 903 F.2d 796, 14 USPQ2d 1871 (Fed. Cir. 1990).

[500]*Glaros v. H.H. Robertson Co.*, 797 F.2d 1564, 230 USPQ 393 (Fed. Cir. 1986). In *Nordberg, Inc. v. Telsmith, Inc.*, 82 F.3d 394, 38 USPQ2d 1593 (Fed. Cir. 1996), the court had some strong things to say about intemperate remarks directed at opposing counsel during oral argument.

[501]*In re Oximetrix, Inc.*, 748 F.2d 637, 223 USPQ 1068 (Fed. Cir. 1984); *Colt Indus. Oper. Corp. v. Index-Werke K.G.*, 739 F.2d 622 (Fed. Cir. 1984).

[502]*In re Mark Indus.*, 751 F.2d 1219, 224 USPQ 521 (Fed. Cir. 1984). An award of attorney fees under Rules 11 or 37 is subject to review under an abuse of discretion standard. *New Idea Farm Equip. Corp. v. Sperry Corp.*, 916 F.2d 1561, 16 USPQ2d 1424 (Fed. Cir. 1990). The abuse of discretion standard governs review of decisions about sanctions and attorney fees under Rule 11 and 35 U.S.C. §285. *Cambridge Prods., Ltd. v. Penn Nutrients, Inc.*, 962 F.2d 1048, 22 USPQ2d 1577 (Fed. Cir. 1992). In the matter of sanctions particular deference is owed the trial court's discretion, for the trial judge has viewed the matter at first hand, has considered all the circumstances, and made assessments of credibility and other intangibles that escape the written record. *Abbott Labs. v. Brennan*, 952 F.2d 1346, 21 USPQ2d 1192 (Fed. Cir. 1992). The terms of a disciplinary order entered under the trial court's inherent authority to sanction attorneys for unprofessional conduct are reviewed for abuse of discretion. *Baldwin Hardware Corp. v. Franksu Enter. Corp.*, 78 F.3d 550, 37 USPQ2d 1829 (Fed. Cir. 1996).

[503]*Fiskars Inc. v Hunt Mfg. Co.*, 221 F.3d 1318, 55 USPQ2d 1569 (Fed. Cir. 2000). See also *Thermocycle Int'l, Inc. v. A.F. Hinrichsen Sales Corp.*, 851 F.2d 339, 7 USPQ2d 1407 (Fed. Cir. 1988).

one case the plaintiff's attorney on the first day of trial moved for an order in limine to prevent defendant from introducing a line of evidence that would require plaintiff's counsel to give testimony contrary to plaintiff's interest. The district court denied the motion, denied counsel's request to withdraw, disqualified counsel, and granted default judgment against plaintiff. The Federal Circuit, applying regional circuit law, concluded that the penalty was highly disproportionate and constituted an abuse of discretion. It emphasized that uncertainties in application of the canons of professional conduct to a situation weigh in mitigation of an extreme sanction of default judgment, as does a plaintiff's right to judicial resolution of its dispute in the absence of any evidence of deliberate wrongdoing.[504]

(b) Conduct Before the PTO

The patent law vests the PTO Director, not the courts, with the responsibility to protect PTO proceedings from unqualified practitioners. A court may disturb the Director's decisions regarding a potential practitioner's qualifications only if it finds that the Director abused his or her discretion in denying a petitioner's application. Under 35 U.S.C. §31, the Director has the discretionary authority to regulate the practice of patent agents before the PTO.[505]

The provision of the Patent Act that deals with suspension or exclusion from practice of agents and attorneys before the PTO (35 U.S.C. §32) is an act of Congress relating to patents within the meaning of 28 U.S.C. §1338(a). And a petition filed in a federal district court seeking to overturn the action of the PTO in failing to award the petitioner a passing grade on the examination for registration as a patent agent is a civil action under §32. Thus, the Federal Circuit has jurisdiction of an appeal from a denial of the petition.[506]

In *Jaskiewicz v. Mossinghoff,*[507] the court provided some valuable insights regarding the role of the PTO in attorney discipline. The statute itself, 35 U.S.C. §32, authorizes suspension or exclusion of any attorney from practice before the PTO for incompetence or disrepute, for failure to comply with regulations, or for gross misconduct. The PTO is under severe limitations as to time and staffing, and it is incumbent upon attorneys and agents who prosecute patent applications to follow the procedural rules of the PTO.[508] Similarly, 37 C.F.R. §1.344 directs practitioners before the PTO to conform to

---

[504]*Thermocycle Int'l, Inc. v. A.F. Hinrichsen Sales Corp.,* 851 F.2d 339, 7 USPQ2d 1407 (Fed. Cir. 1988).

[505]*Premysler v. Lehman,* 71 F.3d 387, 37 USPQ2d 1057 (Fed. Cir. 1995).

[506]*Wyden v. Commissioner of Patents,* 807 F.2d 934, 231 USPQ 918 (Fed. Cir. 1986).

[507]*Jaskiewicz v. Mossinghoff,* 822 F.2d 1053, 3 USPQ2d 1294 (Fed. Cir. 1987).

[508]*Jaskiewicz v. Mossinghoff,* 822 F.2d 1053, 3 USPQ2d 1294 (Fed. Cir. 1987).

the standards of ethical and professional conduct set forth in the Code of Professional Responsibility of the American Bar Association.[509]

Finally, the court made it clear that the sanctions available under PTO Rule 56 (37 C.F.R. §1.56) are not limited to holding a patent unenforceable. In instances where a person entitled to practice before the PTO has breached the duty of candor and good faith in prosecuting a patent application, it may well be appropriate or necessary to issue sanctions directly against that attorney or agent—at least in circumstances where there has been an intent to deceive, defraud, or make misrepresentations to the PTO. Rule 56 is applied in disciplinary proceedings, not as a case of failure to comply with regulations, but because an intentional violation of Rule 56 amounts to gross misconduct or conduct violative of the ABA Disciplinary Rules.[510] Thus the court found that the PTO had properly based its disciplinary proceeding both on Rule 56 and the ABA Disciplinary Rules. Applying the principle that findings of misconduct must be supported by clear and convincing evidence, which is the standard normally applicable to proof of fraud, the court reversed on two counts and affirmed on another.[511] The court also remanded for the PTO to reconsider its sanction of two years' suspension and five years' probation.[512]

In matters involving attorney disciplinary proceedings, the PTO must prove its charges by clear and convincing evidence. In reviewing such a PTO determination under 35 U.S.C. §32, a district court must consider whether there was substantial evidence to support the action of the PTO. In other words, both the district court and the Federal Circuit must decide whether a reasonable mind could have found the evidence of attorney misconduct clear and convincing.[513]

A patent attorney is often faced with choices during a patent prosecution. If he or she makes a mistake, the PTO permits the patentee to institute reissue or reexamination proceedings in certain instances. But the attorney should not be able to choose one course

---

[509]*Jaskiewicz v. Mossinghoff,* 822 F.2d 1053, 3 USPQ2d 1294 (Fed. Cir. 1987). The court impliedly approved this regulation, but noted that disciplinary action under the ABA Model Rules is properly pursued under the Disciplinary Rules but not under the more general Canons of Ethics.

[510]*Jaskiewicz v. Mossinghoff,* 822 F.2d 1053, 3 USPQ2d 1294 (Fed. Cir. 1987).

[511]*Jaskiewicz v. Mossinghoff,* 822 F.2d 1053, 3 USPQ2d 1294 (Fed. Cir. 1987). Because of the nature of disciplinary proceedings, it is incumbent upon the Commissioner to prove that the attorney or agent is not fit to practice before the PTO. It is therefore error to require the attorney to corroborate his or her testimony; the burden of proof remains with the Commissioner to prove that the attorney is no longer worthy of office. *Id.*

[512]The court felt this penalty was excessive under the circumstances. The attorney was 63 years old and had been a solo practitioner for many years with a theretofore blameless record. No patentee or applicant had lost any rights as a consequence of his actions. The suspension would likely preclude him from ever practicing again, because he would lose his practice in the interim. The consequences of effective disbarment are especially serious because the attorney is not only deprived of professional honor but also stripped permanently of his chosen means to a livelihood. *Jaskiewicz v. Mossinghoff,* 822 F.2d 1053, 3 USPQ2d 1294 (Fed. Cir. 1987).

[513]*Klein v. Peterson,* 866 F.2d 412, 9 USPQ2d 1558, 1559 (Fed. Cir. 1989).

of action within the PTO with the anticipation that he or she can always choose an alternate course of action in a trial before a federal judge.[514] Nonetheless, it is clearly not improper for an attorney to seek, in a subsequent infringement action, to distinguish arguments made to the PTO.[515]

The duty of candor owed the PTO during ex parte prosecution is a very different thing from that in a court proceeding where the adversary system of justice prevails. Counsel's obligation to be candid does not go so far as to require him or her to volunteer uncertainties such as whatever might be in his or her mind about the contents of a reference.[516] In considering the duty of disclosure, the applicant includes both the patentee and the attorney who prosecuted the application, because the knowledge and actions of the attorney are chargeable to the applicant.[517]

It is not within the bounds of propriety for a law firm to assist a client in obtaining a patent that was equitably owned by another and then lead the attack against the patent's validity once it is transferred to its rightful owner. Such a situation is not comparable to advancing a legal theory for one client and taking a contrary position for another in unrelated proceedings.[518]

In a case involving a suggestion that the patent attorney might be the true inventor, thus resulting in invalidity under 35 U.S.C. §102(f), the court observed that an attorney's professional responsibility is to assist his or her client in defining the invention to obtain, if possible, a valid patent with maximum coverage. An attorney performing that role should not be a competitor of the client, asserting inventorship as a result of representing the client. Thus, to assert that proper performance of the attorney's role is a ground for invalidating the patent constitutes a failure to understand the proper role of a patent attorney.[519]

---

[514]*Litton Sys., Inc. v. Whirlpool Corp.*, 728 F.2d 1423, 221 USPQ 97 (Fed. Cir. 1984).

[515]*Sun Studs, Inc. v. Applied Theory Assocs.*, 772 F.2d 1557, 227 USPQ 81 (Fed. Cir. 1985). Any other result would automatically disqualify the attorney who handled the prosecution from trying the infringement suit.

[516]*Atlas Powder Co. v. Ireco Chems.*, 773 F.2d 1230, 227 USPQ 289 (Fed. Cir. 1985). There is serious question whether a nonparty to previous litigation in which a lapse of candor may have occurred could take advantage of it in another case. *Id.*

[517]*FMC Corp. v. Manitowoc Co.*, 835 F.2d 1411, 5 USPQ2d 1112 (Fed. Cir. 1987).

[518]*Sun Studs, Inc. v. Applied Theory Assocs.*, 772 F.2d 1557, 227 USPQ 81 (Fed. Cir. 1985). In *Molins PLC v. Textron, Inc.*, 48 F.3d 1172, 33 USPQ2d 1823 (Fed. Cir. 1995), the same attorney was prosecuting applications for two separate clients, containing potentially overlapping or conflicting claims. The Federal Circuit recognized that the position of the attorney was fraught with possible conflict of interest, because his representation of two clients seeking patents in closely related technologies created a risk of sacrificing the interest of one client for that of the other and of failing to discharge his duty of candor to the PTO with respect to each. But the conflict of interest question was not before the court. Instead, in the context of inequitable conduct, it held that the claims of one of the applications were cumulative to art already of record and thus were not material to the prosecution of the other application.

[519]*Solomon v. Kimberly-Clark Corp.*, 216 F.3d 1372, 55 USPQ2d 1279 (Fed. Cir. 2000).

(c) Attorney Disqualification

Attorney disqualification is part of a court's duty to safeguard the sacrosanct privacy of the attorney-client relationship that is necessary to maintain public confidence in the legal profession and to protect the integrity of the judicial process. The principal concern is that an attorney shall maintain the confidentiality of the information that he or she obtains from a client.[520] An important policy is the preservation of secrets and confidences communicated to the lawyer by the former client. The client has the right to expect that confidences disclosed to his or her lawyer will not be shared with others and will not be used against him or her by the former lawyer or by lawyers associated with his or her former lawyers. The presumption that a lawyer switching sides shares confidences with associates is essential to protecting these confidences.[521] Also important is the integrity of the trial process.[522] Indeed, a court may move on its own where it believes that the public interest is implicated in an attorney disqualification matter.[523]

A disqualification order discredits the bar generally and the individual attorney particularly, and judges must therefore exercise caution not to paint with a broad brush unless a specifically identifiable impropriety has actually occurred.[524] But a disqualification order will not be disturbed if the record reveals any sound basis for the court's action. It will be reversed only where it is not based on articulable principles, or where the court either misperceives the relevant rule of law or abuses its discretion.[525] The applicable law is that of the regional circuit,[526] or in the absence of clear authority there, the rule

---

[520]*Panduit Corp. v. All States Plastic Mfg. Co.*, 744 F.2d 1564, 223 USPQ 465 (Fed. Cir. 1984).

[521]*Atasi Corp. v. Seagate Tech.*, 847 F.2d 826, 6 USPQ2d 1955 (Fed. Cir. 1988) (9th Circuit law).

[522]*Telectronics Prop., Ltd. v. Medtronic, Inc.*, 836 F.2d 1332, 5 USPQ2d 1424 (Fed. Cir. 1988) (Second Circuit law).

[523]*Sun Studs, Inc. v. Applied Theory Assocs.*, 772 F.2d 1557, 227 USPQ 81 (Fed. Cir. 1985).

[524]*Panduit Corp. v. All States Plastic Mfg. Co.*, 744 F.2d 1564, 223 USPQ 465 (Fed. Cir. 1984).

[525]*Telectronics Prop., Ltd. v. Medtronic, Inc.*, 836 F.2d 1332, 5 USPQ2d 1424 (Fed. Cir. 1988); *Sun Studs, Inc. v. Applied Theory Assocs.*, 772 F.2d 1557, 227 USPQ 81 (Fed. Cir. 1985). A district court has primary responsibility for controlling the conduct of the lawyers practicing before it. An order of the trial court exercising its discretion in fulfilling that responsibility will not be disturbed if the record reveals any sound basis for the disqualification. A disqualification order will be reversed only where the district court misperceives the relevant rule of law or abuses its discretion. *Atasi Corp. v. Seagate Tech.*, 847 F.2d 826, 6 USPQ2d 1955 (Fed. Cir. 1988).

[526]E.g., *Picker Int'l, Inc. v. Varian Assoc., Inc.*, 869 F.2d 578, 10 USPQ2d 1122 (Fed. Cir. 1989); *Atasi Corp. v. Seagate Tech.*, 847 F.2d 826, 6 USPQ2d 1955 (Fed. Cir. 1988); *Telectronics Prop., Ltd. v. Medtronic, Inc.*, 836 F.2d 1332, 5 USPQ2d 1424 (Fed. Cir. 1988); *Panduit Corp. v. All States Plastic Mfg. Co.*, 744 F.2d 1564, 223 USPQ 465 (Fed. Cir. 1984). The court feels that it is improper to predict how a regional circuit would rule unless such a prediction is essential to disposition of the appeal. *Atasi Corp. v. Seagate Tech.*, 847 F.2d 826, 6 USPQ2d 1955 (Fed. Cir. 1988). Here the court found that the presumption of shared confidences had

gleaned from the general weight of authority.[527] The test for disqualification is whether the former representation by the attorney changing sides is substantially related to the current representation. However, the test does not depend on whether actual confidences were received or on the length of the former representation.[528] Once one of a law firm's members is found to have been counsel for an adverse party in a substantially related matter the entire firm must be disqualified, whether or not the other lawyers of the firm were actually exposed to the confidential information possessed by the attorney switching firms. A presumption exists that the other members of the firm shared in the confidential information. This presumption applies to an "of counsel" attorney as well as partners and associates, especially if he or she is more than a de minimus "of counsel."[529]

The presumption of shared confidences among attorneys is rebuttable. In order to rebut it, objective and verifiable evidence is called for. A court can properly refuse to accept subjective affidavits of attorneys, because lawyers are not always aware of their receipt or use of confidential information. An example of objective evidence would be the construction of a so-called Chinese Wall or screen between an attorney and other members of his or her firm.[530] In a dictum, the Federal Circuit observed that the Chinese Wall (actual physical screening) is a more effective technique for avoiding shared confidences than the "cone of silence" (self-imposed silence by the attorney in question).[531]

The fiduciary relationship existing between lawyer and client extends to preliminary consultation by a prospective client with a view to retention of the lawyer, even though actual employment does not result.[532] A power of attorney does not ipso facto create an attorney-client relationship. In a situation where the inventor is employed by a corporation, he or she would normally give a power of attorney to the corporation's regular patent counsel. Should that inventor later be an accused infringer, this would not mean that the corporation's regular patent counsel should be automatically disqualified from handling the matter for the corporation. Facts to be considered are what the parties expected, and equities such as the length of time of representation in total, and timeliness of the motion to disqualify.[533]

---

not been overcome and therefore found it unnecessary to predict whether the Ninth Circuit, which has not spoken on the subject, would hold that the presumption is rebuttable in any event.

[527] *EZ Paintr Corp. v. Padco, Inc.*, 746 F.2d 1459, 223 USPQ 1065 (Fed. Cir. 1984).

[528] *Atasi Corp. v. Seagate Tech.*, 847 F.2d 826, 6 USPQ2d 1955 (Fed. Cir. 1988). Under Ninth Circuit law, the possible harshness of the rule is mitigated by the "peripheral representation" standard, under which the attorney may avoid disqualification by showing that he or she had no personal involvement in the matter. Here, however, the attorney's signature appeared on pleadings, and he had helped prepare a brief and visited the client's facilities on two occasions. *Id.*

[529] *Atasi Corp. v. Seagate Tech.*, 847 F.2d 826, 6 USPQ2d 1955 (Fed. Cir. 1988).

[530] *EZ Paintr Corp. v. Padco, Inc.*, 746 F.2d 1459, 223 USPQ 1065 (Fed. Cir. 1984).

[531] *Atasi Corp. v. Seagate Tech.*, 847 F.2d 826, 6 USPQ2d 1955 (Fed. Cir. 1988). One wonders whether the distinctions between the two techniques are very clear.

[532] *Kearns v. Fred Lavery Porsche Audi Co.*, 745 F.2d 600, 223 USPQ 881 (Fed. Cir. 1984).

[533] *Sun Studs, Inc. v. Applied Theory Assocs.*, 772 F.2d 1557, 227 USPQ 81 (Fed. Cir. 1985).

The ABA Code of Professional Responsibility may provide appropriate guidance in disqualification proceedings, but the court will review the canons very carefully. In one unusual situation, the former inside and outside counsel of the corporation that originally obtained the patent were now similarly representing the accused licensee/infringer. The inside counsel had participated in the prosecution; the outside counsel had not, but did work with the same inventor and prosecuted other cases. The present patent owner, also the present employer of the inventor, moved to disqualify both. The court's analysis is instructive.[534]

Although the sanction of disqualification does not follow automatically from a violation of DR 5-105, the duty of undivided loyalty owed existing clients is a large factor. Conflicts of interest may increase as mergers between law firms become more common, but to allow the merged firm to pick and choose which clients will survive the merger would violate the duty of undivided loyalty.[535]

Mere delay is not normally a defense to a motion for disqualification. The court typically looks for something more, e.g., an affirmative statement by the moving party that there was no problem or an indication that the motion was brought for tactical reasons.[536] A former client may waive its right to object to counsel of an opposing party on the ground of conflict of interest where it knowingly refrains from asserting the right promptly. The doctrine of waiver exists as a means to balance the competing policies relevant to imputed disqualification. The policy of preserving the former client's confidences is opposed by the policy of giving the opposing party the freedom of choice of legal counsel. The doctrine of waiver protects the opposing party's freedom of choice of legal counsel.[537] The court will, however, look carefully at a claim of waiver by permission, to see whether there is an element of duress.[538]

In one case the issue of disqualification was raised informally more than a year after the action was begun, and the motion to disqualify was not brought for nearly 18 months. But the motion was not tardy, even so, in view of correspondence between counsel seeking an explanation of whether confidences had been exchanged and a long period of settlement negotiations.[539] Where attorneys have already withdrawn, any question of whether they should have been disqualified is moot.[540]

---

[534]*Telectronics Prop., Ltd. v. Medtronic, Inc.*, 836 F.2d 1332, 5 USPQ2d 1424 (Fed. Cir. 1988) (Second Circuit law).

[535]*Picker Int'l, Inc. v. Varian Assoc., Inc.*, 869 F.2d 578, 10 USPQ2d 1122 (Fed. Cir. 1989).

[536]*EZ Paintr Corp. v. Padco, Inc.*, 746 F.2d 1459, 223 USPQ 1065 (Fed. Cir. 1984).

[537]*Atasi Corp. v. Seagate Tech.*, 847 F.2d 826, 6 USPQ2d 1955 (Fed. Cir. 1988) (Ninth Circuit law). Here there was only a six-month delay and no evidence that the motion to disqualify was used in an abusive manner as a part of litigation tactics, so the disqualification order was affirmed.

[538]*Picker Int'l, Inc. v. Varian Assoc., Inc.*, 869 F.2d 578, 10 USPQ2d 1122 (Fed. Cir. 1989).

[539]*Kearns v. Fred Lavery Porsche Audi Co.*, 745 F.2d 600, 223 USPQ 881 (Fed. Cir. 1984).

[540]*Thermocycle Int'l, Inc. v. A.F. Hinrichsen Sales Corp.*, 851 F.2d 339, 7 USPQ2d 1407 (Fed. Cir. 1988).

(d) Miscellaneous

A corporation without counsel cannot be party to an appeal, and its president cannot appear pro se for himself or herself and also for the corporation.[541] House counsel are officers of the court, just like outside counsel, and are bound by the same ethical considerations and subject to the same sanctions.[542]

An inmate of a federal prison made an invention working in the prison shop and filed a pro se suit in the Claims Court asking that a patent attorney be assigned to prosecute a patent application for him. The Federal Circuit affirmed a denial of the request. In civil proceedings the right to counsel is highly circumscribed. A strong presumption that there is a right to appointed counsel exists only when the indigent may lose his or her personal freedom. Beyond that narrow framework, the Supreme Court has not recognized a constitutional right to appointed counsel in civil matters. Congress has provided by statute for mandatory or discretionary appointment of counsel in specified situations, but these do not apply here.[543]

---

[541]*Jones v. Hardy,* 727 F.2d 1524, 220 USPQ 1021 (Fed. Cir. 1984).

[542]*U.S. Steel Corp. v. United States,* 730 F.2d 1465 (Fed. Cir. 1984).

[543]*Lariscey v. United States,* 861 F.2d 1267, 8 USPQ2d 2007 (Fed. Cir. 1988). The court passed the question whether the Claims Court has power under any circumstances to appoint counsel.

9

Infringement Litigation—Defenses

§9.1 General

The Patent Act of 1952 itself provides that the following "shall be defenses in any action involving the validity or infringement of a patent and shall be pleaded":

(1) Noninfringement, absence of liability for infringement, or unenforceability,

(2) Invalidity of the patent or any claim in suit on any ground specified in part II of this title as a condition for patentability,

(3) Invalidity of the patent or any claim in suit for failure to comply with any requirement of sections 112 or 251 of this title,

(4) Any other fact or act made a defense by this title.[1]

Most of the defenses that are enumerated in the patent statute, and some that are not, are discussed at length elsewhere in this book. Thus invalidity for ineligible subject matter, and for lack of utility or operability, is discussed in Chapter 2. Invalidity due to statutory bars or anticipation or derivation is the subject of Chapter 3. Obviousness, the principal invalidity defense, is dealt with in Chapter 4. And the various §112 defenses, such as absence of best mode and enabling disclosure, claim indefiniteness, and inadequacy of written description, are the concerns of Chapter 5. Double patenting and failure to satisfy the requirements of the reissue statute are discussed in Chapter 15.

Standing and the various jurisdictional, venue, and other objections that can be asserted by way of a Rule 12(b) motion are treated in Chapter 8. The noninfringement defense is the focus of Chapter 6. Absence of liability for infringement is also discussed in Chapter 6 in the context of implied license, and in Chapter 15 in the context of intervening rights.

Finally, there are several defenses that fall in the category of unenforceability, or absence of liability, that are treated specially here. Inequitable conduct and misuse both result in unenforceability. Laches, it may be supposed, results in absence of liability, while estoppel may render the patent unenforceable. By the same token, statutory limitations on damages and failure to mark or otherwise

---

[1]35 U.S.C. §282. Although §282 does not specifically mention 35 U.S.C. §305 as an invalidity defense to a patent infringement suit, the Federal Circuit has held that impermissible enlargement of claim scope in violation of §305 does indeed result in invalidity. *Quantum Corp. v. Rodime, PLC,* 65 F.3d 1577, 36 USPQ2d 1162 (Fed. Cir. 1995). Imperfection in patent examination, whether by the examiner or the applicant, does not create a new defense called "prosecution irregularities" and does not displace the experience-based criteria of the inequitable conduct cases. Procedural lapses during examination, should they occur, do not provide grounds of invalidity. Absent proof of inequitable conduct, the examiner's or the applicant's absolute compliance with the internal rules of patent examination becomes irrelevant after the patent has issued. *Magnivision, Inc. v. Bonneau Co.,* 115 F.3d 956, 42 USPQ2d 1925 (Fed. Cir. 1997).

give notice all limit liability for infringement. These are explored below. First, however, it is necessary to examine a special requirement that the statute imposes for certain defenses.

§9.2 Section 282 Notice

The invalidity defenses that depend upon prior art, such as anticipation and obviousness, can be asserted only upon special notice to the patentee. The statute requires notice in the pleadings or otherwise, in writing at least 30 days before trial, of:

> the country, number, date, and name of the patentee of any patent, the title, date, and page numbers of any publication to be relied upon as anticipation of the patent in suit or . . . as showing the state of the art, and the name and address of any person who may be relied upon as the prior inventor or as having prior knowledge of or as having previously used or offered for sale the invention of the patent in suit. In the absence of such notice proof of the said matters may not be made at the trial except on such terms as the court requires.[2]

The objective of the statute is to prevent unfair and prejudicial surprise by the production of unexpected and unprepared-for prior art references at trial. Notice of prior art must be such as effectively to allow an opportunity for the patent owner to prepare to address it at trial. Witnesses may have to review the document, and rebuttal evidence may have to be sought out and examined. The document noticed may shape the course of the trial. What counts is notice of intent to rely. Therefore, merely mentioning the reference in a pretrial paper, and neglecting to indicate that it will be used at trial, normally does not constitute adequate notice. But the statutory requirement of notice does not dictate an arbitrary or absolute rule barring introduction of relevant, material evidence on the purely formalistic fact that notice of reliance was lacking. The statute also permits the trial court to determine whether, in its sound discretion, a party has been deprived of an adequate opportunity to present its case, even though statutory notice is lacking. The boundaries of the district court's discretion under §282 are defined by unfair, prejudicial harm.[3]

Section 282 does not trump the Federal Rules of Civil Procedure. Thus, even though a party meets the time constraints of §282 for identifying prior art, a trial court may exclude prior art if it was not identified during the discovery process. When the court has set and the parties have agreed to a discovery period, that procedure necessarily governs that trial. Although §282 sets a minimum period for the identification of prior art to be introduced as evidence of anticipation, a specific judicial directive for the timing of discovery establishes the

---

[2]35 U.S.C. §282.

[3]*Eaton Corp. v. Appliance Valves Corp.*, 790 F.2d 874, 229 USPQ 668 (Fed. Cir. 1986).

procedures to which the parties are bound. The purpose of §282, like that of the Federal Rules, is to prevent unfair and prejudicial surprise, not to facilitate last-minute production of evidence.[4]

§9.3 Laches and Estoppel

In its landmark 1992 in banc decision in *A.C. Aukerman Co. v. R.L. Chaides Construction Co.,*[5] the court undertook to clarify and, in certain respects, rewrite the law of laches and estoppel in the context of patent infringement litigation. An earlier panel decision[6] had, apparently sua sponte, discarded the six-year presumption of unreasonable delay and prejudice that had been almost universally accepted in prior cases. The panel decision was soon vacated[7] and, after almost a year of uncertainty among patent litigants and judges in many cases, the court finally announced its in banc decision.[8]

To say that the *Aukerman* court took a fresh look at laches and estoppel is something of an understatement. Indeed, its review was penetrating and exhaustive, as demonstrated by the fact that it went so far as to actually reaffirm that both laches and estoppel are cognizable under 35 U.S.C. §282 as equitable defenses to a claim for patent infringement.[9] Concentrating first on laches, the court essentially reconfirmed the following basic tenets:

(1) Where the defense of laches is established, the patentee's claim for damages prior to suit may be barred.

(2) Two elements underlie the defense: (a) the patentee's delay in bringing suit was unreasonable and inexcusable, and (b) the alleged

---

[4]*ATD Corp. v. Lydall Inc.,* 159 F.3d 534, 48 USPQ2d 1321 (Fed. Cir. 1998).

[5]*A.C. Aukerman Co. v. R.L. Chaides Constr. Co.,* 960 F.2d 1020, 22 USPQ2d 1321 (Fed. Cir. 1992).

[6]*A.C. Aukerman Co. v. R.L. Chaides Constr. Co.,* 18 USPQ2d 1618 (1991). The original panel decision relied heavily upon a military pay case, *Cornetta v. United States,* 851 F.2d 1372 (Fed. Cir. 1988).

[7]*A.C. Aukerman Co. v. R.L. Chaides Constr. Co.,* 935 F.2d 1262, 18 USPQ2d 2056 (1991).

[8]The decision was unanimous except for a partial dissent by the author of the original panel decision.

[9]In so doing it had to reject at least three separate arguments against applying laches in a patent infringement case. (1) Laches should not be applied within the period prescribed by the statute of limitations. The court reasoned that in 35 U.S.C. §286 Congress imposed an arbitrary limitation on the period for which damages may be awarded on any claim for patent infringement. Laches, on the other hand, invokes the discretionary power of the court to limit the defendant's liability by reason of the equities between the particular parties. Recognition of laches as a defense thus does not affect the general enforceability of the patent against others or the presumption of its validity under §282. (2) Laches, by reason of being an equitable defense, may be applied only to monetary awards resulting from an equitable accounting, not to legal claims for damages. (3) It is improper to utilize laches as a defense to completely bar recovery of prefiling damages flowing from a continuing tort, such as patent infringement. *A.C. Aukerman Co. v. R.L. Chaides Constr. Co.,* 960 F.2d 1020, 22 USPQ2d 1321 (Fed. Cir. 1992). *Aukerman* applies in trademark opposition and cancellation proceedings as well. *Lincoln Logs Ltd. v. Lincoln Pre-cut Log Homes, Inc.,* 971 F.2d 732, 23 USPQ2d 1701 (Fed. Cir. 1992).

infringer suffered material prejudice attributable to the delay.[10] A district court should consider these facts and all of the evidence and other circumstances to determine whether equity should intercede to bar prefiling damages.

(3) A presumption of laches arises where the patentee delays bringing suit for more than six years after the date the patentee knew or should have known of the alleged infringing activity.

(4) The presumption has the effect of shifting the burden of going forward with evidence, not the burden of persuasion.

Thus, a six-year delay in filing suit after actual or constructive knowledge of the alleged infringement creates a prima facie defense of laches. Without the benefit of the presumption, the defendant must prove unreasonable and inexcusable delay that caused prejudice or injury.[11] So far, this is pretty standard stuff. But in expounding the nature and effect of the six-year presumption, the *Aukerman* court began to break some new ground. First the court explained that, without the presumption, the two elements of unreasonable delay and prejudice might reasonably be inferred from the length of the delay, but not necessarily. With the presumption, though, those facts must be inferred absent rebuttal evidence.

The court then generalized the presumption of laches in terms of Rule 301, FRE, which makes it clear that a presumption imposes on the party against whom it is directed the burden of going forward with evidence, but not the burden of proof in the sense of the risk of nonpersuasion. Rule 301 embodies what is known as the "bursting bubble" theory of presumptions, under which a presumption is not merely rebuttable but completely vanishes upon the introduction of evidence sufficient to support a finding of the nonexistence of the presumed fact. That is, the evidence must be sufficient to put the existence of a presumed fact into genuine dispute. Nonetheless, the defendant at all times bears the ultimate burden of persuasion on the affirmative defense of laches.[12]

Thus, laches works like this: as an initial response to a defendant's evidence of at least a six-year delay, a patentee may offer proof that the delay has not in fact been six years, that the time it first learned or should have known of the infringement after the patent

---

[10]In addition to *Aukerman,* see also *Eastman Kodak Co. v. Goodyear Tire & Rubber Co.,* 114 F.3d 1547, 42 USPQ2d 1737 (Fed. Cir. 1997); *Gasser Chair Co. v. Infanti Chair Mfg. Corp.,* 60 F.3d 770, 34 USPQ2d 1822 (Fed. Cir. 1995); *Meyers v. Brooks Shoe Inc.,* 912 F.2d 1459, 16 USPQ2d 1055 (Fed. Cir. 1990); *Jamesbury Corp. v. Litton Indus. Prods., Inc.,* 839 F.2d 1544, 5 USPQ2d 1779 (Fed. Cir. 1988); *Bott v. Four Star Corp.,* 807 F.2d 1567, 1 USPQ2d 1210 (Fed. Cir. 1986); *Mainland Indus., Inc. v. Standal's Patents Ltd.,* 799 F.2d 746, 230 USPQ 772 (Fed. Cir. 1986); *S.E.R., Jobs for Prog., Inc. v. United States,* 759 F.2d 1 (Fed. Cir. 1985); *Leinoff v. Louis Milona & Sons,* 726 F.2d 734, 220 USPQ 845 (Fed. Cir. 1984).

[11]*Eastman Kodak Co. v. Goodyear Tire & Rubber Co.,* 114 F.3d 1547, 42 USPQ2d 1737 (Fed. Cir. 1997).

[12]At this point the court expressly overruled any of its previous decisions that may have indicated that the ultimate burden of persuasion shifts. *A.C. Aukerman Co. v. R.L. Chaides Constr. Co.,* 960 F.2d 1020, 22 USPQ2d 1321 (Fed. Cir. 1992).

issued was within six years before filing suit. If a patentee is successful on this factual issue, no presumption arises. In the event a presumption does arise, the patentee may offer proof directed to rebutting the laches factors. Such proof may be directed to showing either that the delay was reasonable or that the defendant suffered no prejudice or both. By raising a genuine issue respecting either factual element, the presumption as to both is overcome (a "double bursting bubble"), and this is so even if the patentee's evidence may ultimately be rejected as not persuasive. Elimination of the presumption does not mean that the patentee has precluded the possibility of a laches defense; it does mean, however, that the presumption of laches plays no role in the ultimate decision. The facts of unreasonable delay and prejudice then must be proved and judged on the totality of the evidence presented.[13]

So how may the defendant prevail without a presumption of laches? Where the *Auckerman* presumption does not apply, the accused infringer bears the burden on such questions as (1) whether it lacked notice of the patentee's intent to sue after the close of other litigation, and (2) economic or evidentiary prejudice.[14] Material prejudice resulting from delay may be either economic or evidentiary. Evidentiary or "defense" prejudice may arise by reason of a defendant's inability to present a full and fair defense on the merits due to the loss of records, the death of a witness, or the unreliability of memories of long past events, thereby undermining the court's ability to judge the facts.[15] Economic prejudice may arise where a defendant and possibly others will suffer the loss of monetary investments or incur damages that likely would have been prevented by earlier suit. Such damages or monetary losses are not merely those attributable to a finding of liability for infringement, for economic prejudice would then arise in every suit. The courts must look for a change in the economic position of the alleged infringer during the period of delay.[16] Where a defendant is indifferent to whether the patentee will sue because of a belief that the patent is invalid, it may be difficult to show prejudice resulting from delay. Even a considerable investment during a delay period is not a result of the delay if it was a deliberate business decision to ignore a warning and to proceed as if nothing had occurred. The infringer must prove that the change in economic

---

[13]*A.C. Aukerman Co. v. R.L. Chaides Constr. Co.*, 960 F.2d 1020, 22 USPQ2d 1321 (Fed. Cir. 1992).

[14]*Hall v. Aqua Queen Mfg., Inc.*, 93 F.3d 1548, 39 USPQ2d 1925 (Fed. Cir. 1996).

[15]*A.C. Aukerman Co. v. R.L. Chaides Constr. Co.*, 960 F.2d 1020, 22 USPQ2d 1321 (Fed. Cir. 1992). Testimonial evidence is frequently critical to invalidity defenses and almost always so respecting unenforceability. *Id.*

[16]It is not enough that the alleged infringer changed its position by investing in production of the allegedly infringing device. The change must be because of and as a result of the delay, not simply a business decision to capitalize on a market opportunity. *Hemstreet v. Computer Entry Sys. Corp.*, 972 F.2d 1290, 23 USPQ2d 1860 (Fed. Cir. 1992).

position would not have occurred had the patentee sued earlier.[17] On the other hand, this does not mean that a patentee may intentionally lie silently in wait watching damages escalate, particularly where an infringer, had it had notice, could have switched to a noninfringing product. Indeed, economic prejudice is not a simple concept but rather is likely to be a slippery issue to resolve.

The *Aukerman* court then turned to the relationship of laches and equitable estoppel. In the simplest form of laches, there need be no direct contact between patentee and infringer prior to suit. In other instances, the patentee may make an objection and then do nothing more for years. Where there has been contact or a relationship between the parties during the delay period that may give rise to an inference that the plaintiff has abandoned its claim against the defendant, the facts may lend themselves to analysis under principles of equitable estoppel as well as laches. But the two defenses are not the same. Laches focuses on the reasonableness of the plaintiff's delay, while estoppel focuses on what the defendant has been led reasonably to believe from the plaintiff's conduct. Thus, for laches, the length of delay, the seriousness of prejudice, the reasonableness of excuses, and the defendant's conduct or culpability must be weighed to determine whether the patentee dealt unfairly with the alleged infringer by not promptly bringing suit.

The remedies, of course, are also different. Laches bars only retrospective relief, while estoppel entirely bars assertion of the patent claim.[18] In other words, laches bars the right to recover damages for the period prior to filing a complaint for patent infringement.[19] After noting that an equitable estoppel defense may wholly bar the patentee's claim,[20] the court outlined the three elements of estoppel in the context of patent infringement litigation:

(1) The patentee, through misleading conduct, leads the alleged infringer reasonably to infer that the patentee does not intend to enforce its patent against that infringer. "Conduct" may include specific statements, action, inaction, or silence where there was an obligation to speak.[21] This element, unlike laches, requires that the infringer

---

[17]*Gasser Chair Co. v. Infanti Chair Mfg. Corp.*, 60 F.3d 770, 34 USPQ2d 1822 (Fed. Cir. 1995).

[18]*A.C. Aukerman Co. v. R.L. Chaides Constr. Co.*, 960 F.2d 1020, 22 USPQ2d 1321 (Fed. Cir. 1992); *Adelberg Labs., Inc. v. Miles, Inc.*, 921 F.2d 1267, 17 USPQ2d 1111 (Fed. Cir. 1990); *Hottel Corp. v. Seaman Corp.*, 833 F.2d 1570, 4 USPQ2d 1939 (Fed. Cir. 1987).

[19]See cases cited in note 9:10.

[20]*Meyers v. Brooks Shoe Inc.*, 912 F.2d 1459, 16 USPQ2d 1055 (Fed. Cir. 1990); *Mainland Indus., Inc. v. Standal's Patents Ltd.*, 799 F.2d 746, 230 USPQ 772 (Fed. Cir. 1986); *Young Eng'rs, Inc. v. United States ITC*, 721 F.2d 1305, 219 USPQ 1142 (Fed. Cir. 1983).

[21]Although equitable estoppel may in some instances be based upon a misleading silence, mere silence must be accompanied by some other factor that indicates the silence was sufficiently misleading as to amount to bad faith. *Hemstreet v. Computer Entry Sys. Corp.*, 972 F.2d 1290, 23 USPQ2d 1860 (Fed. Cir. 1992). The patentee must communicate to the accused infringer (by words, conduct, or silence) that the patentee will not pursue an infringement claim. *B. Braun Med., Inc. v. Abbott Labs.*, 124 F.3d 1419, 43 USPQ2d 1896 (Fed. Cir. 1997). "Conduct"

be aware of the patent and be able to infer that the patentee knows of its activities.

(2) The alleged infringer relies on the patentee's misleading conduct.

(3) Due to its reliance, the alleged infringer will be materially prejudiced if the patentee is allowed to proceed with its claim. The second and third elements are not the same, although they are frequently confused. An infringer can build a plant entirely unaware of the patent and then be enjoined from using it; although harmed, the infringer could not show reliance on the patentee's conduct.

Thus the *Aukerman* court substantially redefined the elements of equitable estoppel. As a result, it felt the need to overrule expressly its previous statement[22] of the estoppel test because it confusingly intertwined the elements of laches and estoppel. More than that, the court squarely held that the six-year presumption does not apply with respect to estoppel.[23] This is only logical, inasmuch as the presumed laches factors of delay and prejudice are no longer elements of estoppel.

Laches is an equitable defense and its existence must be determined in each case under its particular facts. It is a question primarily addressed to the discretion of the trial court.[24] As the court made clear in *Aukerman,* laches is not established by undue delay and prejudice. Those factors merely lay the foundation for the trial court's exercise of discretion.[25] The district court's exercise of discretion is reviewed to determine whether the decision was clearly unreasonable, arbitrary, or fanciful, based on clearly erroneous findings of fact or an erroneous conclusion of law, or supported by no rational basis in the record.[26]

---

may include specific statements, action, inaction, or silence where there was an obligation to speak. *Scholle Corp. v. Blackhawk Molding Co.,* 133 F.3d 1469, 45 USPQ2d 1468 (Fed. Cir. 1998).

[22]Thus *Jamesbury Corp. v. Litton Indus. Prods., Inc.,* 756 F.2d 1556, 225 USPQ 253 (Fed. Cir. 1985), and similar cases stand overruled in that respect.

[23]In a dictum in *Jamesbury Corp. v. Litton Indus. Prods., Inc.,* 839 F.2d 1544, 5 USPQ2d 1779 (Fed. Cir. 1988), the court had cast some doubt on whether a six-year delay raises presumptions of unreasonable and inexcusable inaction and prejudice to the accused infringer in the context of estoppel. In *Adelberg Labs., Inc. v. Miles, Inc.,* 921 F.2d 1267, 17 USPQ2d 1111 (Fed. Cir. 1990), the court indicated, without actually deciding, that the laches presumptions do not apply in the estoppel context.

[24]*Gasser Chair Co. v. Infanti Chair Mfg. Corp.,* 60 F.3d 770, 34 USPQ2d 1822 (Fed. Cir. 1995); *A.C. Aukerman Co. v. R.L. Chaides Constr. Co.,* 960 F.2d 1020, 22 USPQ2d 1321 (Fed. Cir. 1992); *Vaupel Textilmaschinen KG v. Meccanical Euro Italia S.P.A.,* 944 F.2d 870, 20 USPQ2d 1045 (Fed. Cir. 1991); *Adelberg Labs., Inc. v. Miles, Inc.,* 921 F.2d 1267, 17 USPQ2d 1111 (Fed. Cir. 1990); *Bott v. Four Star Corp.,* 807 F.2d 1567, 1 USPQ2d 1210 (Fed. Cir. 1986). Laches is an affirmative defense rather than an equitable claim for relief. *Foster v. United States,* 733 F.2d 88 (Fed. Cir. 1984). Laches and estoppel both depend on the facts of the particular case and are matters within the trial court's discretion that will not be set aside absent a showing of abuse of discretion. *Jamesbury Corp. v. Litton Indus. Prods., Inc.,* 839 F.2d 1544, 5 USPQ2d 1779 (Fed. Cir. 1988).

[25]*A.C. Aukerman Co. v. R.L. Chaides Constr. Co.,* 960 F.2d 1020, 22 USPQ2d 1321 (Fed. Cir. 1992). Laches and estoppel are equitable defenses, committed to the sound discretion of the trial court. Both ultimately turn on underlying factual determinations. *Hemstreet v. Computer Entry Sys. Corp.,* 972 F.2d 1290, 23 USPQ2d 1860 (Fed. Cir. 1992).

[26]*Vaupel Textilmaschinen KG v. Meccanical Euro Italia S.P.A.,* 944 F.2d 870, 20 USPQ2d 1045 (Fed. Cir. 1991). Application of the laches bar is reviewed under the abuse of discretion

The *Aukerman* presumption places a burden of production of evidence on the patentee. This burden relates to both the excusability of the delay and the lack of prejudice resulting from the delay. A defendant can remain utterly mute on the issue of prejudice and nonetheless prevail.[27] In *Aukerman* the court expressly adopted the preponderance of evidence standard for laches and estoppel, at least in the absence of special circumstances, such as fraud or intentional misconduct. Nonetheless, a determination of laches is not made upon the application of mechanical rules. The defense, being personal to the particular party and equitable in nature, must have flexibility in its application. A court must look at all of the particular facts and circumstances of each case and weigh the equities of the parties. Likewise, when exercising its discretion as to equitable estoppel, the court must take into consideration all evidence regarding the equities, even where all three elements of estoppel are established.[28]

In determining laches, the court must consider when the patent owner knew or should have known of the defendant's alleged infringement.[29] The court has held, unequivocally, that patentees have an affirmative duty to police their rights. For example, sales, marketing, publication, or public use of a product similar to or embodying technology similar to the patented invention, or published descriptions of the defendant's potentially infringing activities, give rise to a duty to investigate whether there is infringement. Furthermore, constructive knowledge of the infringement may be imputed to the patentee even where it has no actual knowledge of the sales, marketing, publication, public use, or other conspicuous activities of potential infringement if these activities are sufficiently prevalent in the inventor's field of endeavor. The patentee who is negligently or willfully oblivious to these types of activities cannot later claim lack of knowledge as justification for escaping the application of laches. Allocating the burden to patentees to seek out infringers is proper, furthermore, because compared to potential infringers, they are in the best position to know the scope of their patent protection and, therefore, also to know likely places to find infringement. This superior knowledge generally allows them to incur comparatively lower costs in investigating potentially infringing activities than competitors would incur conducting patent

---

standard. *Hall v. Aqua Queen Mfg., Inc.*, 93 F.3d 1548, 39 USPQ2d 1925 (Fed. Cir. 1996). A district court's finding of equitable estoppel is reviewed under an abuse of discretion standard. *Scholle Corp. v. Blackhawk Molding Co.*, 133 F.3d 1469, 45 USPQ2d 1468 (Fed. Cir. 1998). The Federal Circuit may reverse a discretionary decision if it rests on an erroneous interpretation of law or clearly erroneous factual underpinnings. Without such error, however, a laches determination stands unless it evinces unreasonable judgment in weighing relevant factors. *Eastman Kodak Co. v. Goodyear Tire & Rubber Co.*, 114 F.3d 1547, 42 USPQ2d 1737 (Fed. Cir. 1997).

[27]*Hall v. Aqua Queen Mfg., Inc.*, 93 F.3d 1548, 39 USPQ2d 1925 (Fed. Cir. 1996).

[28]*A.C. Aukerman Co. v. R.L. Chaides Constr. Co.*, 960 F.2d 1020, 22 USPQ2d 1321 (Fed. Cir. 1992).

[29]*Eastman Kodak Co. v. Goodyear Tire & Rubber Co.*, 114 F.3d 1547, 42 USPQ2d 1737 (Fed. Cir. 1997); *Adelberg Labs., Inc. v. Miles, Inc.*, 921 F.2d 1267, 17 USPQ2d 1111 (Fed. Cir. 1990); *Meyers v. Brooks Shoe Inc.*, 912 F.2d 1459, 16 USPQ2d 1055 (Fed. Cir. 1990).

searches on every aspect of their products and notifying the patentee of their results.[30]

The court has specifically rejected constructive notice as a basis for laches. Absent actual notice, the facts must support a duty of inquiry.[31] Like infringement, the period of delay does not begin until the patent issues, at the earliest.[32] However, it may begin with the first contact on the subject between patentee and infringer, even though infringement has not yet begun.[33]

In deciding laches, a court must also consider and weigh any justification offered by the plaintiff for its delay. Excuses that have been recognized include other litigation, negotiations with the accused, poverty and illness, war, the extent of the infringement, and disputes over title to the patent.[34] Poverty, by itself, is never an excuse for laches purposes, although it may be considered as a factor where there is some legally cognizable excuse for an unreasonable delay. A patentee's inability to find willing counsel is also widely rejected as a legally cognizable reason to excuse an unreasonable delay in filing suit.[35]

---

[30]*Wanlass v. General Elec. Co.*, 148 F.3d 1334, 46 USPQ2d 1915 (Fed. Cir. 1998). In *Wanlass v. Fedders Corp.*, 145 F.3d 1461, 47 USPQ2d 1097 (Fed. Cir. 1998), a 2–1 panel may have injected a note of uncertainty. One judge felt the district court had imposed, at least on summary judgment, an unreasonable burden of inquiry in holding that Wanlass had constructive knowledge of the infringement. Another judge concurred in the result, but worried that the result cannot be reconciled with the sweeping language of *Wanlass v. General Electric*, supra. The dissent is based on the view that under the circumstances, as established by undisputed facts, Wanlass had an obligation to test.

[31]*Advanced Cardiovascular Sys., Inc. v. Scimed Life Sys., Inc.*, 988 F.2d 1157, 26 USPQ2d 1038 (Fed. Cir. 1993). The "knew or should have known" criterion is appropriate to actions to correct inventorship as well as actions for infringement. Thus, it is error to measure the laches delay period for a putative inventor's action to correct inventorship from the date of patent issuance, in the absence of proof that the putative inventor knew or should have known that the patent issued and omitted him or her as a joint inventor. *Id.*

[32]*A.C. Aukerman Co. v. R.L. Chaides Constr. Co.*, 960 F.2d 1020, 22 USPQ2d 1321 (Fed. Cir. 1992); *Meyers v. Brooks Shoe Inc.*, 912 F.2d 1459, 16 USPQ2d 1055 (Fed. Cir. 1990); *Bott v. Four Star Corp.*, 807 F.2d 1567, 1 USPQ2d 1210 (Fed. Cir. 1986). Where there are several patents at issue, the general rule is that the laches period does not accrue until each patent issues, even if they are interrelated. *Stark v. Advanced Magnetics, Inc.*, 29 F.3d 1570, 31 USPQ2d 1290 (Fed. Cir. 1994).

[33]*Leinoff v. Louis Milona & Sons*, 726 F.2d 734, 220 USPQ 845 (Fed. Cir. 1984).

[34]*A.C. Aukerman Co. v. R.L. Chaides Constr. Co.*, 960 F.2d 1020, 22 USPQ2d 1321 (Fed. Cir. 1992). In *Bio-Technology Gen. Corp. v. Genentech, Inc.*, 80 F.3d 1553, 38 USPQ2d 1321 (Fed. Cir. 1996), the court held that the fact that importation of a product made abroad by a process patented in the United States was not an infringement prior to the enactment of 35 U.S.C. §271(g) would vitiate any conclusion of unreasonable delay that included that preenactment period. In *Hemstreet v. Computer Entry Sys. Corp.*, 972 F.2d 1290, 23 USPQ2d 1860 (Fed. Cir. 1992), the plaintiff introduced evidence that the delay was attributable to other litigation and a reexamination. This was more than sufficient to raise a genuine dispute as to whether the display was excusable. The bubble was burst and defendant was put to its proof on both factors: unreasonable and inexcusable delay and prejudice resulting from that delay. In *Gasser Chair Co. v. Infanti Chair Mfg. Corp.*, 60 F.3d 770, 34 USPQ2d 1822 (Fed. Cir. 1995), the court indicated that a delay might be justified where the parties had early on entered into an agreement whereby the defendant promised to refrain from making the infringing device; at a later encounter, the plaintiff may have been justified in believing that the defendant would honor the earlier agreement and thus in refraining from immediate suit.

[35]*Hall v. Aqua Queen Mfg., Inc.*, 93 F.3d 1548, 39 USPQ2d 1925 (Fed. Cir. 1996).

The equities may or may not require that the plaintiff communicate its reasons for delay to the defendant.[36] A prejudice argument is severely undercut where the defendant has explicit notice of the other litigation and an implicit awareness that it may soon face litigation if it refuses to license. If the plaintiff has an established sequential license-or-litigate pattern, the defendant's position is worsened.[37]

The court recognizes that delay may be excused by the fact that the patentee had no means of learning of the infringement, or that the infringer deliberately sought to conceal its activities.[38] Thus, in determining the length of delay for laches, a court must look at the time the patentee knew, or in the exercise of reasonable diligence should have known, of the alleged infringing activity.[39] Intervening corporate entities may not serve as insulators with respect to imputed knowledge. Thus, a patentee is responsible for knowledge of infringement by the defendant's corporate predecessor; the defendant is responsible for knowledge of a notice of infringement given that predecessor by the patentee; and the defendant is entitled to rely upon lack of communication (misleading silence) with that predecessor as well as with itself.[40]

Reliance is not required for laches but is essential to equitable estoppel,[41] although it may not be required to prove actual reliance where the only possible inference from the record is that the patentee would leave the accused infringer unmolested.[42] To show reliance, the infringer must have had a relationship or communication with the plaintiff that lulls the infringer into a sense of security in going ahead with its investments.[43]

---

[36]*Hemstreet v. Computer Entry Sys. Corp.*, 972 F.2d 1290, 23 USPQ2d 1860 (Fed. Cir. 1992); *A.C. Aukerman Co. v. R.L. Chaides Constr. Co.*, 960 F.2d 1020, 22 USPQ2d 1321 (Fed. Cir. 1992).

[37]*Hemstreet v. Computer Entry Sys. Corp.*, 972 F.2d 1290, 23 USPQ2d 1860 (Fed. Cir. 1992).

[38]*Fromson v. Western Litho Plate & Supp. Co.*, 853 F.2d 1568, 7 USPQ2d 1606 (Fed. Cir. 1988). The defendant's policy of secrecy and denial of infringement upon inquiry can be relevant here. *Eastman Kodak Co. v. Goodyear Tire & Rubber Co.*, 114 F.3d 1547, 42 USPQ2d 1737 (Fed. Cir. 1997).

[39]*Jamesbury Corp. v. Litton Indus. Prods., Inc.*, 839 F.2d 1544, 5 USPQ2d 1779 (Fed. Cir. 1988). Here the court was willing to start the period at the time that the patentee had, in an action against the government in the Claims Court, identified the defendant's products as among those it was complaining about. The patentee's argument that this was not knowledge of the actual infringing activity, because the defendant did not make nongovernment sales until later, was rejected.

[40]*Jamesbury Corp. v. Litton Indus. Prods., Inc.*, 839 F.2d 1544, 5 USPQ2d 1779 (Fed. Cir. 1988). Query: Will this reasoning apply to questions of marking and notice under 35 U.S.C. §287 as well?

[41]*Gasser Chair Co. v. Infanti Chair Mfg. Corp.*, 60 F.3d 770, 34 USPQ2d 1822 (Fed. Cir. 1995).

[42]*ABB Robotics, Inc. v. GMFanuc Robotics Corp.*, 52 F.3d 1062, 34 USPQ2d 1597 (Fed. Cir. 1995). In order to prove reliance for purposes of equitable estoppel, an accused infringer must produce contemporaneous evidence demonstrating such reliance, not just post hoc conclusory statements. *Hall v. Aqua Queen Mfg., Inc.*, 93 F.3d 1548, 39 USPQ2d 1925 (Fed. Cir. 1996).

[43]*Gasser Chair Co. v. Infanti Chair Mfg. Corp.*, 60 F.3d 770, 34 USPQ2d 1822 (Fed. Cir. 1995).

Detrimental reliance may be established by investments made in the manufacture of the accused devices.[44] Indeed, increasing sales alone may be enough to show economic prejudice. Capital investments by the accused infringer are not necessarily a prerequisite to a finding of material economic prejudice.[45] Material prejudice may be established by testimony from a corporate president that he would have sold the company, rather than make continued capital investments, had he known of the allegation of infringement.[46] Although the principles of equity ignore no form of prejudice, the prejudice element of laches is not established solely because the raising of the claim would delay other litigation. Justice requires that an issue in legitimate dispute not be held forfeited merely because it would complicate other pending litigation.[47]

However, the court has clearly held that the existence of other litigation may be acceptable as an excuse for delay, especially if the infringer is aware of it;[48] perhaps even foreign litigation may serve to excuse delay.[49] For other litigation to excuse a delay in bringing suit there must be adequate notice of the proceeding. The notice must inform the alleged infringer of the other proceeding and of the patentee's intention to enforce its patent upon completion of that proceeding.[50] The notice of intent to enforce must be specific; a mere statement that the subject is under consideration by the patentee's lawyers is insufficient.[51]

To successfully invoke the "other litigation" excuse for delay, it is not necessary that both the notice of other litigation and of a patentee's intent to sue after that other litigation is terminated be

---

[44]*Jamesbury Corp. v. Litton Indus. Prods., Inc.,* 839 F.2d 1544, 5 USPQ2d 1779 (Fed. Cir. 1988). The court was not required to decide whether reliance upon an opinion of noninfringement tends to negate an argument that the defendant was relying on the patentee's inaction. In *A.C. Aukerman Co. v. R.L. Chaides Constr. Co.,* 960 F.2d 1020, 22 USPQ2d 1321 (Fed. Cir. 1992), the court indicated a preference for treating detrimental reliance as two separate elements of estoppel: reliance and detriment. This, said the court, "adds some clarity in this confusing area of the law."

[45]*ABB Robotics, Inc. v. GMFanuc Robotics Corp.,* 52 F.3d 1062, 34 USPQ2d 1597, 1600 (Fed. Cir. 1995).

[46]*Jamesbury Corp. v. Litton Indus. Prods., Inc.,* 839 F.2d 1544, 5 USPQ2d 1779 (Fed. Cir. 1988).

[47]*Advanced Cardiovascular Sys., Inc. v. Scimed Life Sys., Inc.,* 988 F.2d 1157, 26 USPQ2d 1038 (Fed. Cir. 1993).

[48]*Leinoff v. Louis Milona & Sons,* 726 F.2d 734, 220 USPQ 845 (Fed. Cir. 1984).

[49]*Mainland Indus., Inc. v. Standal's Patents Ltd.,* 799 F.2d 746, 230 USPQ 772 (Fed. Cir. 1986).

[50]*Vaupel Textilmaschinen KG v. Meccanical Euro Italia S.P.A.,* 944 F.2d 870, 20 USPQ2d 1045 (Fed. Cir. 1991); *Meyers v. Brooks Shoe Inc.,* 912 F.2d 1459, 16 USPQ2d 1055 (Fed. Cir. 1990); *Hottel Corp. v. Seaman Corp.,* 833 F.2d 1570, 4 USPQ2d 1939 (Fed. Cir. 1987). But there is no rigid requirement that notice of the other litigation actually be given. If a defendant is, for example, aware of the litigation from other sources, it would place form over substance to require a specific notice. *A.C. Aukerman Co. v. R.L. Chaides Constr. Co.,* 960 F.2d 1020, 22 USPQ2d 1321 (Fed. Cir. 1992).

[51]*Jamesbury Corp. v. Litton Indus. Prods., Inc.,* 839 F.2d 1544, 5 USPQ2d 1779 (Fed. Cir. 1988). There is no rigid requirement that a patentee notify an infringer that it will be sued after the conclusion of other pending litigation on the patent. However, where there is

expressly stated in writing. The important question is whether the infringer had reason to know of the other litigation and reason to believe that it was likely to be sued. But notice is important for several reasons. It informs the accused infringer so that it can alter its activities to avoid liability, or bring a declaratory judgment action if the delay in waiting for a judicial determination would be a burden upon its proposed activities. To establish whether adequate notice was given, the court must look not only at the actions of the patentee but also at evidence showing whether the alleged infringer was in fact on notice of an existing lawsuit.[52] In an estoppel context, the patentee must generally notify an accused infringer about other litigation. This is only logical, inasmuch as the fact of other litigation cannot have had a bearing on the reasonableness of the infringer's inference that it would be left unmolested unless the infringer somehow knew about it.[53]

The court has specifically passed the questions whether a reexamination proceeding qualifies as "other litigation" that can be relied upon to excuse a delay, and whether other litigation with respect to one of several related patents can excuse delay with respect to all.[54] But the court has squarely held that reissue proceedings can qualify as "other litigation"[55] and has hinted that reexamination may as well.[56] A dictum suggests that the Federal Circuit will not accept a "pattern of litigation" argument as a counter to the "other litigation" excuse.[57]

Delay attributable to the PTO rather than the patentee may also be excusable, especially where there is no detrimental reliance.[58] Unclean hands or egregious conduct on the part of the infringer may also result in the denial of a laches or estoppel defense.[59] Willful infringement may, under certain circumstances, excuse delay in bringing suit.[60] Thus, plagiarizing or copying a patented invention

---

prior contact between the patentee and that infringer, the overall equities may require appropriate notice. *Hall v. Aqua Queen Mfg., Inc.,* 93 F.3d 1548, 39 USPQ2d 1925 (Fed. Cir. 1996).

[52]*Vaupel Textilmaschinen KG v. Meccanical Euro Italia S.P.A.,* 944 F.2d 870, 20 USPQ2d 1045 (Fed. Cir. 1991).

[53]*A.C. Aukerman Co. v. R.L. Chaides Constr. Co.,* 960 F.2d 1020, 22 USPQ2d 1321 (Fed. Cir. 1992).

[54]*Hottel Corp. v. Seaman Corp.,* 833 F.2d 1570, 4 USPQ2d 1939 (Fed. Cir. 1987).

[55]*Vaupel Textilmaschinen KG v. Meccanical Euro Italia S.P.A.,* 944 F.2d 870, 20 USPQ2d 1045 (Fed. Cir. 1991).

[56]*Hemstreet v. Computer Entry Sys. Corp.,* 972 F.2d 1290, 23 USPQ2d 1860 (Fed. Cir. 1992).

[57]*Jamesbury Corp. v. Litton Indus. Prods., Inc.,* 839 F.2d 1544, 5 USPQ2d 1779 (Fed. Cir. 1988). The defendant argued that the patentee had established a pattern of prompt litigation against other infringers, and since defendant was not sued it could reasonably conclude that the patentee did not intend to sue it. The court rejected this argument on the basis that it would defeat the rationale for the "other litigation" excuse, which is that the high cost of patent litigation and, in some cases, the comparatively small amounts recoverable from each infringer, justify not requiring the patentee to sue everybody at the same time.

[58]*Studiengesellschaft Kohle v. Northern Petrochem. Co.,* 784 F.2d 351, 228 USPQ 837 (Fed. Cir. 1986).

[59]See *Leinoff v. Louis Milona & Sons,* 726 F.2d 734, 220 USPQ 845 (Fed. Cir. 1984). Copying can be egregious conduct that will shift the equities in the plaintiff's favor in a laches situation. *Gasser Chair Co. v. Infanti Chair Mfg. Corp.,* 60 F.3d 770, 34 USPQ2d 1822 (Fed.

constitutes egregious conduct of the type that changes the equities in favor of a patentee and defeats a defense of laches.[61] In one case the patentee attempted to justify a delay of over 10 years in bringing suit on the grounds that it had a subjective belief that the defendant was sublicensed by the patentee's exclusive licensee. Thus, reasoned the patentee, it would have been a violation of Rule 11, FRCP, to have sued earlier. The court rejected this excuse on the basis that, on the facts, the patentee's subjective belief was unreasonable.[62]

The fact-intensive nature of the laches and estoppel inquiry makes results difficult to predict. Patentees do not have a general duty either to grant patent infringement clearance or else sue any rival who so asks. But when the course of dealings between a patentee and an alleged infringer is such that the alleged infringer reasonably infers from the patentee's misleading conduct or inaction that the patentee has waived its patent rights, then the first element of equitable estoppel has been established absent a statement to the contrary by the patentee.[63] In one case, five years of silence after a refusal to license did not create estoppel.[64] In another, the patentee found out

---

Cir. 1995). As with laches, egregious conduct must be considered as part of the equitable estoppel determination. *Id.*

[60]*Hall v. Aqua Queen Mfg., Inc.,* 93 F.3d 1548, 39 USPQ2d 1925 (Fed. Cir. 1996). Here the court rejected the excuse based upon the fact that the defendant relied on an opinion letter of invalidity that was rendered to other members of the industry.

[61]*Bott v. Four Star Corp.,* 807 F.2d 1567, 1 USPQ2d 1210 (Fed. Cir. 1986). Here the Federal Circuit was so enthusiastic about the countereffect of the copying that it did not even bother to remand, despite a lack of a specific finding below that the infringer was guilty of egregious conduct. In *A.C. Aukerman Co. v. R.L. Chaides Constr. Co.,* 960 F.2d 1020, 22 USPQ2d 1321 (Fed. Cir. 1992), the plaintiff had countered the estoppel defense with some evidence, including an admission, that the defendant had copied the patented structure. This was rejected by the district court on the ground that plaintiff should have proved infringement. The Federal Circuit found error in this. The summary judgment motion was not one for infringement but for estoppel, and the defendant therefore had the burden of proof that the device it called a "copy" did not infringe. One supposes the result might have been different had there not been an admission of "copying."

[62]*Adelberg Labs., Inc. v. Miles, Inc.,* 921 F.2d 1267, 17 USPQ2d 1111 (Fed. Cir. 1990). Plaintiff also argued that it was only seeking damages for the period after the alleged sublicense became ineffective and, therefore, laches should not apply to postsublicense infringement. The court refused to bifurcate the damages/laches period in that fashion.

[63]*Scholle Corp. v. Blackhawk Molding Co.,* 133 F.3d 1469, 45 USPQ2d 1468 (Fed. Cir. 1998). In this case defendant came out with a device and plaintiff sent a cease-and-desist letter. A few months later plaintiff sued another competitor. Meanwhile, defendant began designing around and came out with a new device. Two months later defendant sent the new device to plaintiff and indicated a belief that it did not infringe; it said it would consider the device noninfringing unless plaintiff advised otherwise. Plaintiff did not respond, and finally sued three years later. During the interim, there were meetings between defendant and plaintiff on a variety of subjects, including the patent, the litigation against the competitor, possible merger, etc. At no time did plaintiff suggest the new product might be infringing. The court found equitable estoppel.

[64]*Studiengesellschaft Kohle v. Dart Indus., Inc.,* 726 F.2d 724, 220 USPQ 841 (Fed. Cir. 1984). The court also held that it was not error for the district court to have required the infringer to show that it would not have expanded its facilities if the patentee had asserted the patent. Does this mean the burden is on the infringer to show reliance? Where the patentee and its exclusive licensee both charged the defendant with infringement and then did nothing for 10 years, this was sufficient to induce a reasonable belief that the patentee had abandoned its claim. *Adelberg Labs., Inc. v. Miles, Inc.,* 921 F.2d 1267, 17 USPQ2d 1111 (Fed. Cir. 1990).

about a new model shortly after filing a patent infringement complaint and long before trial, but did not charge infringement for three years, never asked to supplement the complaint, and moved for contempt only after an injunctive order was entered on the model that was the subject of the original complaint. Under these circumstances, it was proper to find contempt and enjoin the new model, but refuse damages.[65] The court has made it clear that in multipatent suits, laches must be evaluated separately for each patent.[66] It is possible that a change in the infringing activities may disrupt the laches period, especially if the change is unknown to the patentee.[67]

Bankruptcy may play a role. The patentee had charged defendant's predecessor with infringement several years prior to an order of reorganization, but did not bring an action until after the reorganization. The Federal Circuit vacated a summary judgment in favor of the defendant, on grounds, among others, that it was not established by undisputed evidence that the plaintiff had abandoned its claim or acquiesced in the predecessor's denial of infringement, and that there was no evidence that the patentee had intentionally misled the predecessor by its silence.[68] A patentee cannot avoid the consequences of laches by transferring the patent. Its actions are imputed to the assignee.[69]

Silence alone is not sufficient affirmative conduct to give rise to estoppel. Some evidence must exist to show that the silence was sufficiently misleading to amount to bad faith. It must be sufficiently misleading to induce the alleged infringer reasonably to infer that the patentee has abandoned its claims.[70] The fact that a defendant

---

In *MCV, Inc. v. King-Seeley Thermos Co.*, 870 F.2d 1568, 10 USPQ2d 1287 (Fed. Cir. 1989), the court found prejudice in the face of less than a six-year delay.

[65]*Rosemount, Inc. v. Beckman Instr., Inc.*, 727 F.2d 1540, 221 USPQ 1 (Fed. Cir. 1984). The court made it clear that it was not establishing a per se laches rule that all postcomplaint products must be accused immediately, however.

[66]*Meyers v. Brooks Shoe Inc.*, 912 F.2d 1459, 16 USPQ2d 1055 (Fed. Cir. 1990). The court found error in basing a laches decision on a single period for three patents that had issued over a span of several years. In particular, the court felt that it was reasonable for the patentee to await the issuance of the second patent, which was a division of the first; both were alleged to be infringed by the same products. Awaiting issuance of the second to sue on both at once conserved the resources of the parties and the courts. The court indicated that there may be times when a patentee must bring suit before the expected issuance of the second of two patents, but this was not one of them.

[67]*A.C. Aukerman Co. v. R.L. Chaides Constr. Co.*, 960 F.2d 1020, 22 USPQ2d 1321 (Fed. Cir. 1992).

[68]*Broomall Indus. v. Data Design Logic Sys., Inc.*, 786 F.2d 401, 229 USPQ 38 (Fed. Cir. 1986).

[69]*Eastman Kodak Co. v. Goodyear Tire & Rubber Co.*, 114 F.3d 1547, 42 USPQ2d 1737 (Fed. Cir. 1997).

[70]*Adelberg Labs., Inc. v. Miles, Inc.*, 921 F.2d 1267, 17 USPQ2d 1111 (Fed. Cir. 1990); *Jamesbury Corp. v. Litton Indus. Prods., Inc.*, 839 F.2d 1544, 5 USPQ2d 1779 (Fed. Cir. 1988); *Hottel Corp. v. Seaman Corp.*, 833 F.2d 1570, 4 USPQ2d 1939 (Fed. Cir. 1987). Silence alone will not create an estoppel unless there was a clear duty to speak, or somehow the patentee's continued silence reinforces the defendant's inference from the plaintiff's known acquiescence that the defendant will be unmolested. *A.C. Aukerman Co. v. R.L. Chaides Constr. Co.*, 960 F.2d 1020, 22 USPQ2d 1321 (Fed. Cir. 1992).

does not actually have a belief that the patentee has abandoned its claim does not destroy the estoppel defense if such a belief would have been reasonable. An accused infringer does not lose its right reasonably to rely upon misleading conduct and silence simply by taking sensible measures to protect itself, such as the preparation of certain documents in anticipation of litigation.[71] The silence must be intentionally misleading, e.g., a communication indicating that the patentee would take immediate action, which if not followed up might indicate that it had dropped the matter.[72] In *Aukerman,* the court expressly held that fraud or wrongful intent is not necessary to create an estoppel, and it is therefore not necessary that a patentee's silence be intentionally misleading. On the other hand, such considerations may affect the overall equities, and bad faith silence may encompass cases where there is a duty to speak.[73] Misleading action may be silence, if it is accompanied by some other factor indicating that the silence was sufficiently misleading to amount to bad faith. Nor is it essential that the period of silence be preceded by a threat of immediate and vigorous enforcement. This is the most common scenario, but it is not the only set of facts that can support a finding of misleading silence.[74]

Quite logically, estoppel applies in ITC proceedings, where there are exclusion orders but no damages available as relief,[75] while laches applies in Claims Court proceedings, where damages in the form of compensation may be had, but no injunctive relief is available.[76] In district court infringement litigation, questions may arise regarding the scope of laches. In one case the patentee acknowledged that it was not entitled to damages for sales of devices made during the period of laches, but argued that it was entitled to a permanent injunction against use and repair of those devices subsequent to the laches period. This was on the theory that the continued use of the

---

[71]*Adelberg Labs., Inc. v. Miles, Inc.,* 921 F.2d 1267, 17 USPQ2d 1111 (Fed. Cir. 1990).

[72]*Hottel Corp. v. Seaman Corp.,* 833 F.2d 1570, 4 USPQ2d 1939 (Fed. Cir. 1987). In this case the court found conflicting evidence on whether the patentee's periods of silence could reasonably be interpreted by the infringer as an indication that the patentee had abandoned his claims, and thus reversed a summary judgment of estoppel. In another case the court found misleading silence in the fact that the last letter prior to suit, some eight years later, indicated that the patentee was considering the infringer's denial of infringement. *Jamesbury Corp. v. Litton Indus. Prods., Inc.,* 839 F.2d 1544, 5 USPQ2d 1779 (Fed. Cir. 1988). In *Meyers v. Brooks Shoe Inc.,* 912 F.2d 1459, 16 USPQ2d 1055 (Fed. Cir. 1990), the court indicated that a suggestion of infringement coupled with an offer to license followed by silence does not suffice to establish estoppel, unless the silence is sufficiently misleading to induce the alleged infringer reasonably to infer that the patentee has abandoned its claim. The court held that no estoppel resulted from a telephone call suggesting that there was infringement, but unaccompanied by a threat of immediate suit, or even a hint that litigation was being contemplated.

[73]*A.C. Aukerman Co. v. R.L. Chaides Constr. Co.,* 960 F.2d 1020, 22 USPQ2d 1321 (Fed. Cir. 1992).

[74]*ABB Robotics, Inc. v. GMFanuc Robotics Corp.,* 52 F.3d 1062, 34 USPQ2d 1597 (Fed. Cir. 1995). Here there was a charge of infringement followed by inaction and an extensive and complex prior relationship that were sufficient, taken as a whole, to mislead.

[75]*Young Eng'rs, Inc. v. United States ITC,* 721 F.2d 1305, 219 USPQ 1142 (Fed. Cir. 1983).

[76]*Foster v. United States,* 733 F.2d 88 (Fed. Cir. 1984).

precomplaint devices is a current (and indeed future) violation of 35 U.S.C. §271(a). The court held that this construes the scope of laches too narrowly. By inexcusably failing to exercise timely its right to exclude, the patentee, in effect, authorized the public to infringe—to "make, use, offer to sell, or sell" a patented invention—during the laches period. And it is well settled that an authorized sale of a patented product places that product beyond the reach of the patent. Likewise, the sale of an infringing product during the laches period is beyond the reach of the patent: the patentee cannot later enjoin the use of a product sold during that time.[77]

Estoppel also applies to suits to correct inventorship under 35 U.S.C. §256.[78] There may be differences in application of the principles of laches and estoppel to a trade dress situation as opposed to a patent situation. Unlike patent rights, which arise at issuance of the patent, rights in trade dress arise when the overall appearance attains recognition and association among the relevant consumer group. Thus the precise time at which trade dress rights accrue is uncertain. Trade dress rights are separate and distinct from patent rights in other ways as well. For example, the public interest element of trade dress law, which seeks to prevent consumer confusion over products with similar appearance, may lead a court to grant injunctive relief despite the plaintiff's delay in bringing suit.[79]

The court has indicated that the strictures of Rule 12(b)(6) are not readily applicable to a determination of laches. Although a Rule 12(b)(6) motion may be grounded upon an affirmative defense, the defense of laches usually requires factual development beyond the content of the complaint. The facts evidencing unreasonableness of the delay, lack of excuse, or material prejudice to the defendant are seldom set forth in the complaint and at the pleading stage of the

---

[77]*Odetics Inc. v. Storage Tech. Corp.*, 185 F.3d 1259, 51 USPQ2d 1225 (Fed. Cir. 1999). Moreover, allowing a patentee who commits laches to enjoin the further use of a precomplaint product would, in many cases, allow the patentee to recover royalties that laches specifically prevents. Using the leverage of an injunction, patentees could, in theory, extract at minimum a reasonable royalty from current users of the precomplaint infringing products. Indeed, one expects such a user would pay as much as it would cost to shift to a noninfringing product, an amount, given investment in infringing systems, perhaps far more than a reasonable royalty. These incentives would encourage patentees to adopt a strategy of ambush rather than providing fair notice. *Id.*

[78]Laches and estoppel have been applied in actions under §256. *Stark v. Advanced Magnetics, Inc.*, 29 F.3d 1570, 31 USPQ2d 1290 (Fed. Cir. 1994). A delay of more than six years after the omitted inventor knew or should have known of the issuance of the patent will produce a rebuttable presumption of laches in an action to correct inventorship. *Advanced Cardiovascular Sys., Inc. v. Scimed Life Sys., Inc.*, 988 F.2d 1157, 26 USPQ2d 1038 (Fed. Cir. 1993). In *MCV, Inc. v. King-Seeley Thermos Co.*, 870 F.2d 1568, 10 USPQ2d 1287 (Fed. Cir. 1989), the court analyzed all factors, including prejudice, and found estoppel based on a four-year delay. The court dismissed the plaintiff's argument that detrimental reliance would never be justified in a §256 case, because 35 U.S.C. §116 requires the applicant to identify all known inventors. Estoppel is an equitable concept; it is not defeated by an inequitable attempt to invoke a statutory requirement.

[79]*Gasser Chair Co. v. Infanti Chair Mfg. Corp.*, 60 F.3d 770, 34 USPQ2d 1822 (Fed. Cir. 1995).

proceedings cannot be decided against the complainant based solely on presumptions.[80]

Diligence. The court has indicated that there are circumstances wherein diligence is an appropriate requisite to pursuit of a particular legal right, whether or not the defenses of laches or estoppel may be invoked against the claimant. Lack of diligence may be a basis for barring legal action when there is an affirmative obligation on the claimant to act promptly and without significant pause in establishing a legal right. The common law has recognized that varying degrees of diligence may be required, depending on the circumstances. For example, a higher degree of diligence is appropriate when the claimant is chargeable with injury or disadvantage to another due to the claimant's failure to act expeditiously.[81]

§9.4 Limitations, Marking, and Notice

(a) Limitations

The patent statute of limitations, 35 U.S.C. §286, provides that no recovery shall be had for any infringement committed more than six years prior to the filing of the complaint or counterclaim for infringement in the action. This is not a statute of limitations in the sense that it limits the bringing of an action; it only limits the period during which recovery may be had.[82] Violations of patent rights are continuing events.[83]

The institution of a plaintiff's suit suspends the running of limitations on a compulsory counterclaim while the suit is pending.[84] But the court has made it clear that there is no tolling of the statute of limitations by equitable considerations, unlike laches and estoppel.[85]

The court has dealt with one unusual situation in the limitations context. A sale of a catalyst took place more than six years prior to suit, but the catalyst was first used in the infringing process within

---

[80]*Advanced Cardiovascular Sys., Inc. v. Scimed Life Sys., Inc.*, 988 F.2d 1157, 26 USPQ2d 1038 (Fed. Cir. 1993).

[81]*Stark v. Advanced Magnetics, Inc.*, 29 F.3d 1570, 31 USPQ2d 1290 (Fed. Cir. 1994). Here the court held that diligence is not an absolute legal requisite for an action under 35 U.S.C. §256 to correct inventorship. Whether diligent action is required in a particular case must be determined on the facts of that case.

[82]*Standard Oil Co. v. Nippon Shokubai K.K. Co.*, 754 F.2d 345, 224 USPQ 863 (Fed. Cir. 1985).

[83]*Genentech, Inc. v. Eli Lilly & Co.*, 998 F.2d 931, 27 USPQ2d 1241 (Fed. Cir. 1993).

[84]*Employers Ins. of Wausau v. United States*, 764 F.2d 1572 (Fed. Cir. 1985). A permissive counterclaim does not generate a like tolling. A compulsory counterclaim is one arising out of the transaction or occurrence that is the subject of the opposing party's claim, and a permissive counterclaim is any other. *Id.*

[85]*A. Stucki Co. v. Buckeye Steel Castings Co.*, 963 F.2d 360, 22 USPQ2d 1581 (Fed. Cir. 1992).

the six-year period. The court held that the rule that there can be no contributory infringement in the absence of a direct infringement does not control here; the act that later became contributory infringement took place outside the limitations period, so there can be no recovery for the contributory infringement.[86]

The court encounters an occasional limitations issue outside the context of patent infringement. The court has passed the question of when a civil RICO cause of action accrues, noting that the regional circuits are divided on the question.[87] Compliance with the Claims Court statute of limitations is jurisdictional.[88] The six-year statute of limitations (28 U.S.C. §2501) on actions against the United States is a jurisdictional requirement attached by Congress as a condition of the government's waiver of sovereign immunity and, as such, must be strictly construed. Exceptions to the limitations and conditions upon which the government consents to be sued are not to be implied. Inasmuch as the six-year period serves as a jurisdictional limitation rather than simply as an affirmative defense, it is not capable of waiver or subject to an estoppel, whether pled or not.[89]

A claim first accrues and the six-year statute begins to run when all the events have occurred that fix the liability of the government and entitle the claimant to institute an action. The statute of limitations is a meritorious defense, in itself serving a public interest. It protects the government from having to defend suits long after the events sued upon have occurred. And it puts an end to the possibility of litigation after a reasonable time. As a statute of repose, it is intended both to limit the opportunity to file suits and to limit the obligation to defend against them. The government is not required to keep its courts open indefinitely for one who neglects or refuses to apply for redress until it may fairly be presumed that the means by which the other party might disprove a claim are lost in the lapse of time.[90]

However, a statute of limitations can be tolled in proper circumstances, even in suits against the government. Thus the statute can be tolled where the government fraudulently or deliberately conceals material facts relevant to a plaintiff's claim so that the plaintiff was unaware of their existence and could not have discovered the basis

---

[86]*Standard Oil Co. v. Nippon Shokubai K. K. Co.,* 754 F.2d 345, 224 USPQ 863 (Fed. Cir. 1985). Section 286 is applicable against inducers or contributory infringers as well as direct infringers. Where a patentee complains of no acts of contributory infringement within the six-year period prior to commencement of the action, no recovery can be had, regardless of whether there was direct infringement within that period. *A. Stucki Co. v. Buckeye Steel Castings Co.,* 963 F.2d 360, 22 USPQ2d 1581 (Fed. Cir. 1992).

[87]*A. Stucki Co. v. Buckeye Steel Castings Co.,* 963 F.2d 360, 22 USPQ2d 1581 (Fed. Cir. 1992).

[88]*Jones v. United States,* 801 F.2d 1334 (Fed. Cir. 1986). The general statute (28 U.S.C. §2501) is six years. An action for breach of a fiduciary duty accrues when the trust beneficiary knew or should have known of the breach. *Id.*

[89]*Hart v. United States,* 910 F.2d 814 (Fed. Cir. 1990); *Hopland Band of Pomo Indians v. United States,* 855 F.2d 1573 (Fed. Cir. 1988).

[90]*Hart v. United States,* 910 F.2d 814 (Fed. Cir. 1990).

of its claim. But it is not necessary that the plaintiff obtain a complete understanding of all the facts before the tolling ceases and the statute begins to run.[91] Whether equitable tolling is permitted under a statute of limitations raises a pure question of federal law involving statutory interpretation; such matters are reviewed de novo by the Federal Circuit.[92]

A statute of limitation sets out the maximum period of time during which an action can be brought or a right enforced. The statute begins to run on the date of accrual, which is the date the plaintiff discovers (or should discover) the injury. This date is often the same as—but sometimes later than—the date on which the wrong that injures the plaintiff occurs. The doctrine of equitable tolling stops the running of the statute of limitation if, despite all due diligence, plaintiffs are unable to obtain essential information concerning the existence of their claim. But the doctrine of equitable tolling does not apply to statutes of repose. A statute of repose cuts off a cause of action at a certain time irrespective of the time of accrual of the cause of action. Thus, equitable tolling is generally available unless the statute indicates a contrary intent, e.g., by establishing an outer date for bringing an action.[93]

Although it is not always clearly stated or recognized in the case law, the distinction that must be drawn is that between tolling the commencement of the running of the statute (a tolling of the accrual) and tolling the running of the statute once commenced (a tolling of the statute). In suits against the government the distinction can be critical, because tolling of accrual is routinely allowed, while tolling of running seldom is, due to the jurisdictional nature of the statute.[94]

It is possible that fraud in the procurement of a patent could amount to fraudulent concealment that would toll the running of the limitations statute on both a federal antitrust claim and a state tort claim based on the fraudulent procurement.[95] The statute of limitations for a false marking action under 35 U.S.C. §292 is that set forth in 28 U.S.C. §2462, which imposes a five-year limit on any action for the enforcement of any civil fine.[96]

(b) Marking and Notice

The patent statute, 35 U.S.C. §287, provides for notice to the public by marking the patented article. In the event of a failure so to mark,

---

[91]*Hopland Band of Pomo Indians v. United States,* 855 F.2d 1573 (Fed. Cir. 1988).

[92]*Weddel v. Secretary, Health & Hum. Serv.,* 100 F.3d 929 (Fed. Cir. 1996).

[93]*Weddel v. Secretary, Health & Hum. Serv.,* 100 F.3d 929 (Fed. Cir. 1996).

[94]*Hopland Band of Pomo Indians v. United States,* 855 F.2d 1573 (Fed. Cir. 1988).

[95]*Albert v. Kevex Corp.,* 729 F.2d 757, 221 USPQ 202 (Fed. Cir. 1984).

[96]*Arcadia Mach. & Tool Inc. v. Sturm, Ruger & Co.,* 786 F.2d 1124, 229 USPQ 124 (Fed. Cir. 1986).

no damages shall be recovered by the patentee in any action for infringement, except on proof that the infringer was notified of the infringement and continued to infringe thereafter, in which event damages may be recovered only for infringement occurring after such notice. Filing of an action for infringement shall constitute such notice.

Thus the statute requires either actual or constructive notice that the article is patented, or no damages can be recovered by the patentee. The purpose behind the marking statute is to give notice to the public of the patent.[97] The patent owner has the burden of pleading and proving at trial that it complied with the statutory requirements for marking or notice. Compliance with §287(a) is a question of fact.[98]

Absent notice, actual or constructive, knowledge of a patent is irrelevant. Section 287 requires "notice of the infringement."[99] Actual notice of infringement requires the affirmative communication of a specific charge of infringement against a specific accused product or device. It is irrelevant whether the defendant knows of the patent or of its own infringement. The correct approach under §287 must focus on the action of the patentee, not the knowledge or understanding of the infringer.[100]

There are several important limitations on this requirement. First, neither marking nor actual notice is required if the patented invention is not made or sold by the patentee or someone acting under its authority.[101] A licensee who makes or sells a patented article does so "for or under" the patentee within the meaning of 35 U.S.C. §287, thereby limiting the patentee's damage recovery when the patented article is not marked.[102] In the cases of third parties that are unrelated

---

[97]*American Med. Sys., Inc. v. Medical Eng'g Corp.*, 6 F.3d 1523, 28 USPQ2d 1321 (Fed. Cir. 1993). In *Cover v. Hydramatic Packing Co.*, 83 F.3d 1390, 38 USPQ2d 1783 (Fed. Cir. 1996), the court considered whether §287 might preempt state commercial law such as the UCC.

[98]*Maxwell v. J. Baker, Inc.*, 86 F.3d 1098, 39 USPQ2d 1001 (Fed. Cir. 1996). In *Wiener v. NEC Elec., Inc.*, 102 F.3d 534, 41 USPQ2d 1023 (Fed. Cir. 1996), the evidence showed that certain devices were marked by hand with pen and ink. The court concluded that a reasonable fact finder could conclude that the devices were properly marked.

[99]*Devices for Med., Inc. v. Boehl*, 822 F.2d 1062, 3 USPQ2d 1288 (Fed. Cir. 1987). The defendant had stipulated to infringement and tried only the notice issue. The Federal Circuit regarded plaintiff's argument that the stipulation of infringement made notice unnecessary as "simply irrational."

[100]*Amsted Indus. v. Buckeye Steel Castings Co.*, 24 F.3d 178, 30 USPQ2d 1462 (Fed. Cir. 1994). Thus, a broadside letter to the industry, informing it of the patent and warning against infringement, is not notice of the infringement within the meaning of §287. The court passed the question whether it would be sufficient if the infringer acknowledges a specific communication to be a notice of infringement.

[101]*Wine Ry. Appliance Co. v. Enterprise Ry. Equip. Co.*, 297 U.S. 387 (1936).

[102]*Amsted Indus. v. Buckeye Steel Castings Co.*, 24 F.3d 178, 30 USPQ2d 1462 (Fed. Cir. 1994). In this case the court held squarely that this applies as well to a situation where the patentee makes an element of the patented invention and sells it to a customer, who then completes the claimed structure. Such a sale impliedly authorizes the customer to make, use, and sell the patented invention and marking is therefore required. The court rejected the patentee's argument that it would have been guilty of false marking under §292 had it placed the marking on the element that it did sell. See also *Maxwell v. J. Baker, Inc.*, 86 F.3d 1098, 39 USPQ2d 1001 (Fed. Cir. 1996).

to the patentee, however, it is often more difficult for the patentee to ensure compliance. Thus a rule of reason approach is justified and substantial compliance may be found to satisfy the marking statute. The court may consider whether the patentee made reasonable efforts to ensure compliance.[103]

Second, §287 applies only to patented articles, and neither actual nor constructive notice is required where the patent claims only a process.[104] Where a patent contains both article and method claims, and both are charged to infringe, marking is necessary, whether the method be one for using the article[105] or one for making it.[106]

In one case the court undertook an exhaustive review of the case law of when and to what extent a patented device must be marked. It held, in light of the permissive wording of §287 and the policy of encouraging notice by marking, that the statute precludes recovery of damages only for infringement for any time prior to compliance with the marking or actual notice requirements of the statute. Therefore, a delay between issuance of the patent and compliance with the marking provisions of §287 will not prevent recovery of damages after the date that marking has begun.[107] The court cautioned, however, that once marking has begun, it must be substantially consistent and continuous in order for the party to avail itself of the constructive notice provisions of the statute.[108]

Based upon a careful review of the parallel development of §287(a) and 35 U.S.C. §289, the court has held that the patent marking

---

[103]*Maxwell v. J. Baker, Inc.*, 86 F.3d 1098, 39 USPQ2d 1001 (Fed. Cir. 1996). Here it appeared that 95% of the products sold by the licensee of the patentee were marked. The patentee even went so far as to notify the licensee's suppliers of the need to mark. This was held to support a jury determination of compliance with the marking statute.

[104]*American Med. Sys., Inc. v. Medical Eng'g Corp.*, 6 F.3d 1523, 28 USPQ2d 1321 (Fed. Cir. 1993); *Bandag, Inc. v. Gerrard Tire Co.*, 704 F.2d 1578, 217 USPQ 977 (Fed. Cir. 1983).

[105]*Devices for Med., Inc. v. Boehl*, 822 F.2d 1062, 3 USPQ2d 1288 (Fed. Cir. 1987). The patentee did not require its licensee to mark the product, and there was no evidence that a patent marking had ever appeared on the product. The court reasoned that, having sold the product unmarked (or having permitted its licensee to do so), the patentee can hardly maintain entitlement to damages for use of the product by a purchaser uninformed that use would violate the method claims. This holding appears to answer the question left open in *Hanson v. Alpine Valley Ski Area, Inc.*, 718 F.2d 1075, 219 USPQ 679 (Fed. Cir. 1983), although it may be possible to draw distinctions in specific factual settings.

[106]*American Med. Sys., Inc. v. Medical Eng'g Corp.*, 6 F.3d 1523, 28 USPQ2d 1321 (Fed. Cir. 1993).

[107]*American Med. Sys., Inc. v. Medical Eng'g Corp.*, 6 F.3d 1523, 28 USPQ2d 1321 (Fed. Cir. 1993). The patentee shipped several thousand unmarked devices before the patent issued, and about 2,000 after it issued, and did not begin shipping marked devices until over three months after issue.

[108]*American Med. Sys., Inc. v. Medical Eng'g Corp.*, 6 F.3d 1523, 28 USPQ2d 1321 (Fed. Cir. 1993). The court held that marking alone without distribution provides no notice to the public where unmarked products are continuing to be shipped. The world cannot be put on notice if the patentee marks certain products but continues to ship unmarked products. Therefore, the patentee was not in full compliance with §287 while it continued to ship its unmarked products, which continued to mislead the public into thinking that the product was freely available. Full compliance was not achieved until it consistently marked substantially all of its patent products and was no longer distributing unmarked products.

provisions of §287(a) apply to the recovery of a design patent infringer's profit under §289.[109]

The criteria for actual notice under §287(a) are not coextensive with the criteria for filing a declaratory judgment action. Thus, actual notice may be achieved without creating a case of actual controversy in terms of 28 U.S.C. §2201. It is not controlling whether the patentee threatens suit, demands cessation of infringement, or offers a license under the patent. Although there are numerous possible variations in form and content, the purpose of the actual notice requirement is met when the recipient is notified, with sufficient specificity, that the patent holder believes that the recipient of the notice may be an infringer. Thus, the actual notice requirement is satisfied when the recipient is informed of the identity of the patent and the activity that is believed to be an infringement, accompanied by a proposal to abate the infringement, whether by license or otherwise.[110] In the case of actual notice, the notice of the infringement must come from the patentee not the infringer. Thus, where an infringer's attorney advises it that it is infringing, that is not the notice contemplated by §287.[111]

Failure of a licensee to mark in accordance with a specific contractual requirement may be actionable.[112] Failure to raise at trial an issue of limitation of damages by failure to mark precludes raising the issue on appeal.[113] Notice, actual or constructive by marking, is not a prerequisite to recovery against the government under 28 U.S.C. §1498.[114]

Courts have enjoined infringement notices when the patent owner acted in bad faith, for example by making threats without intending to file suit, or sending notices indiscriminately to all members of the trade, or when it has no good faith belief in the validity of its patent. But a patentee that has a good faith belief that its patents are being infringed violates no protected right when it so

---

[109]*Nike, Inc. v. Walmart Stores Inc.*, 138 F.3d 1437, 46 USPQ2d 1001 (Fed. Cir. 1998). In order to reach this result, the court had to distinguish *Braun Inc. v. Dynamics Corp.*, 975 F.2d 815, 24 USPQ2d 1121 (Fed. Cir. 1992). There, it had held that §284 does not authorize enhancement of §289 profits. This decision, it concluded, was not based upon drawing a rigorous distinction between damages and profits, but on the provision of §289 that bars the design patentee, upon recovering the infringer's profits, from "twice recover[ing] the profit made from the infringement."

[110]*SRI Int'l, Inc. v. Advanced Tech. Labs., Inc.*, 127 F.3d 1462, 44 USPQ2d 1422 (Fed. Cir. 1997). Here it was found sufficient to have said, in writing, that the patentee believed that certain specified products may infringe the patent (which was enclosed) and that a license was available. In *Ralston Purina Co. v. Far-Mar-Co, Inc.*, 772 F.2d 1570, 227 USPQ 177, 181 (Fed. Cir. 1985), the court indicated that an offer of a license is actual notice of another's patent rights, at least in the context of creating a duty of due care not to infringe.

[111]*American Med. Sys., Inc. v. Medical Eng'g Corp.*, 6 F.3d 1523, 28 USPQ2d 1321 (Fed. Cir. 1993).

[112]See *Lisle Corp. v. Edwards*, 777 F.2d 693, 227 USPQ 894 (Fed. Cir. 1985); *Yarway Corp. v. Eur-Control USA Inc.*, 775 F.2d 268, 227 USPQ 352 (Fed. Cir. 1985). Could the damages for breach of contract include loss of damages to the patentee due to the lack of marking?

[113]*Weinar v. Rollform Inc.*, 744 F.2d 797, 223 USPQ 369 (Fed. Cir. 1984).

[114]*Motorola, Inc. v. United States*, 729 F.2d 765, 221 USPQ 297 (Fed. Cir. 1984).

notifies infringers. And an accused infringer should not be insulated from knowledge and fair warning of potential liability or deprived of the opportunity to respond to threatened litigation.[115] Thus, communication to possible infringers concerning patent rights is not improper if the patent holder has a good faith belief in the accuracy of the communication. Although "bad faith" may encompass subjective as well as objective considerations, and the patent holder's notice is not irrelevant to a determination of bad faith, a competitive commercial purpose is not of itself improper, and bad faith is not supported when the information is objectively accurate. In general, a threshold showing of incorrectness or falsity, or disregard for either, is required in order to find bad faith in the communication of information about the existence or pendency of patent rights. Indeed, a patentee, acting in good faith on its belief as to the nature and scope of its rights, is fully permitted to press those rights even though it may misconceive what those rights are. It has long been recognized that patents would be of little value if infringers of them could not be notified of the consequences of infringement or proceeded against in the courts. Such action considered by itself cannot be said to be illegal. Thus it is not improper for a patent owner to advise possible infringers of its belief that a particular product may infringe the patent. A patentee has the right to inform a potential infringer of the existence of the patent, whereby the recipient of the information may adjust its activities, perhaps seek a license, or otherwise act to protect itself. The statute contemplates such notice. Federal law has uniformly upheld a patentee's right to publicize the issuance of patents and to so inform potential infringers. Indeed, judicially mandated silence would preserve the ignorance of potential infringers whose liability could build.[116]

(c) False Marking

Section 292 of Title 35 provides for civil penalties against those who falsely mark products with an indication that they are patented, or that a patent has been applied for. There can be no violation of §292 unless it be shown that the false marking was intentional, and for the purpose of deceiving the public.[117] There is no jurisdiction over a claim for false marking until the article allegedly mismarked actually exists. The article must be completed before §292 will allow a claim.[118] Marking "patent pending" simply means that the product

---

[115]*Mallinckrodt, Inc. v. Medipart, Inc.,* 976 F.2d 700, 24 USPQ2d 1173 (Fed. Cir. 1992). Having reversed a summary judgment of patent misuse, the court also vacated an injunction prohibiting the patent owner from sending out infringement notices.

[116]*Mikohn Gaming Corp. v. Acres Gaming Inc.,* 165 F.3d 891, 49 USPQ2d 1308 (Fed. Cir. 1998).

[117]*Arcadia Mach. & Tool Inc. v. Sturm, Ruger & Co.,* 786 F.2d 1124, 229 USPQ 124 (Fed. Cir. 1986).

[118]*Lang. v. Pacific Marine & Supply Co.,* 895 F.2d 761, 13 USPQ2d 1820 (Fed. Cir. 1990). But cf. *Amsted Indus. v. Buckeye Steel Castings Co.,* 24 F.3d 178, 30 USPQ2d 1462 (Fed. Cir. 1994).

is made in accordance with a pending patent application; patents are never "pending," but this is no violation of §292.[119] The phrase "may be manufactured under" certain patents is not deceptive; nor is the omission of applicable patents from a label; nor are inadvertent errors that are the result of oversight or caused by patent expirations.[120]

(d) Marking Estoppel

The court has not yet squarely passed on the validity of the so-called marking estoppel doctrine under which a party, usually a licensee, who marks its product with the patent number is estopped to deny that the product is covered by the patent.[121] However, the court has held that an admittedly noninfringing product cannot be converted by estoppel to an infringing product. The defendant had first marketed a product containing hemoglobin, which infringed, and then substituted lead acetate, which admittedly did not infringe. Nonetheless, it failed to alter a package insert stating that the product contained hemoglobin. On the theory that customers would not have purchased the defendant's product if they had known it contained lead acetate rather than hemoglobin, plaintiff argued that defendant should be estopped to deny infringement. The court distinguished the marking estoppel cases on the ground that since defendant never took a license, liability for royalty payments was not at issue, and defendant had not erroneously placed a patent number on its product, but erroneously identified a component.[122]

§9.5 Fraudulent Procurement and Inequitable Conduct

(a) Introduction

Inequitable conduct is an offense against the PTO and the public. The offense is committed most commonly by intentional failures to submit material references to an examiner, or by making knowing false or misleading statements to the examiner, such that it can confidently be said that by deceitful intent the patent prosecution

---

[119]*Arcadia Mach. & Tool Inc. v. Sturm, Ruger & Co.*, 786 F.2d 1124, 229 USPQ 124 (Fed. Cir. 1986).

[120]*Arcadia Mach. & Tool Inc. v. Sturm, Ruger & Co.*, 786 F.2d 1124, 229 USPQ 124 (Fed. Cir. 1986). Failure to remove patent markings for some time after expiration is not justification for refusing prejudgment interest. *Radio Steel & Mfg. Co. v. MTD Prods., Inc.*, 788 F.2d 1554, 229 USPQ 431 (Fed. Cir. 1986).

[121]See, e.g., *Crane Co. v. Aeroquip Corp.*, 364 F. Supp. 547, 179 USPQ 596, *aff'd in part & rev'd in part on other grounds*, 504 F.2d 1086, 183 USPQ 577 (7th Cir. 1974).

[122]*Smithkline Diagnostics, Inc. v. Helena Labs. Corp.*, 859 F.2d 878, 8 USPQ2d 1468 (Fed. Cir. 1988). One wonders whether the result would be the same if there were evidence that the component was deliberately misidentified.

process has been subverted. Although the conduct giving rise to judgments of unenforceability thus occurs before the examiner, the offense deserves its penalty because the processes of the PTO have been transgressed.[123]

Applicants for patents are required to prosecute patent applications in the PTO with candor, good faith, and honesty. This duty extends also to the applicants' representatives. A breach of the duty constitutes inequitable conduct. Inequitable conduct includes affirmative misrepresentations of a material fact, failure to disclose material information, or submission of false material information, coupled with an intent to deceive. One who alleges inequitable conduct arising from a failure to disclose prior art must offer clear and convincing proof of the materiality of the prior art, knowledge chargeable to the applicant of that prior art and of its materiality, the applicant's failure to disclose the prior art, and intent to mislead the PTO. The withholding of information must meet thresholds of both materiality and intent. Once threshold findings of materiality and intent are established, the court must weigh them to determine whether the equities warrant a conclusion that inequitable conduct occurred. In light of all the circumstances, an inequitable conduct judgment must be made concerning whether the applicant's conduct is so culpable that the patent should not be enforced. The ultimate determination of inequitable conduct is committed to the trial judge's discretion and is reviewed under an abuse of discretion standard. Findings of materiality and intent are subject to the clearly erroneous standard.[124]

The Federal Circuit has been very active in the area of fraud or, as it prefers to call it, "inequitable conduct,"[125] that is alleged to have occurred during the prosecution of a patent application before the PTO. A careful review of this activity leaves one with the distinct impression that the court will scrutinize charges of fraud very closely and will be disinclined to uphold an inequitable conduct defense in the absence of truly egregious conduct, such as falsification of data, or a clear showing of intent to deceive.[126] For example, there is nothing improper, illegal, or inequitable in filing a patent application for the purpose of obtaining a right to exclude a known competitor's product from the market; nor is it in any manner improper to amend or insert claims intended to cover a competitor's product which the applicant's attorney has learned about during prosecution of a patent application. Any such amendment or insertion must comply with all statutes and regulations, of course, but if it does, its genesis in the marketplace

---

[123]*Akron Polymer Cont. Corp. v. Exxel Cont. Inc.*, 148 F.3d 1380, 47 USPQ2d 1533 (Fed. Cir. 1998).

[124]*Molins PLC v. Textron, Inc.*, 48 F.3d 1172, 33 USPQ2d 1823 (Fed. Cir. 1995).

[125]E.g., *J.P. Stevens & Co. v. Lex Tex Ltd.*, 747 F.2d 1553, 223 USPQ 1089 (Fed. Cir. 1984).

[126]See, e.g., *Hycor Corp. v. Schlueter Co.*, 740 F.2d 1529, 222 USPQ 553 (Fed. Cir. 1984); *Kansas Jack, Inc. v. Kuhn*, 719 F.2d 1144, 219 USPQ 857 (Fed. Cir. 1983).

is simply irrelevant and cannot of itself evidence deceitful intent.[127] Imperfection in patent examination, whether by the examiner or the applicant, does not create a new defense called "prosecution irregularities" and does not displace the experience-based criteria of the inequitable conduct cases. Absent proof of inequitable conduct, the examiner's or the applicant's absolute compliance with the internal rules of patent examination becomes irrelevant after the patent has issued.[128]

To be sure, the court recognizes that there is an important public interest in protecting the integrity of the patent issuing process and in preventing the enforcement of patents procured by fraud.[129] Despite this strong public interest, the PTO has decided to withdraw from any policing activity. In a Notice dated September 8, 1988,[130] the PTO Commissioner indicated that it would no longer investigate and reject original or reissue applications under 37 C.F.R. §1.56.[131] The expressed reason for this new "hands-off" policy was that the PTO is not an appropriate forum for determining intent to mislead.[132] Thus we may expect, if anything, that the frequency and intensity of inequitable conduct litigation in the courts will increase.

The violation of the duty of disclosure that renders a patent unenforceable has its basis in the inventor's duty of candor to the PTO during prosecution, which is an ex parte proceeding.[133] On the other hand, the court has gone out of its way to remark that fraud in the PTO has been overplayed, is appearing in nearly every patent suit, and is "cluttering up" the patent system.[134] Fraud, says the

---

[127]*Kingsdown Med. Cons, Ltd. v. Hollister, Inc.,* 863 F.2d 867, 9 USPQ2d 1384 (Fed. Cir. 1988).

[128]*Magnivision, Inc. v. Bonneau Co.,* 115 F.3d 956, 42 USPQ2d 1925 (Fed. Cir. 1997). But in *Critikon, Inc. v. Becton Dickinson Vascular Access, Inc.,* 120 F.3d 1253, 43 USPQ2d 1666 (Fed. Cir. 1997), the court reversed a finding of no inequitable conduct, relying heavily on the fact that the applicant's attorney did not disclose, during a reissue proceeding, the fact that the original patent was in litigation. In *DH Tech. Inc. v. Synergystex Int'l Inc.,* 154 F.3d 1333, 47 USPQ2d 1865 (Fed. Cir. 1998), the court observed that honest mistakes can be corrected, but not attempts to fraudulently pay the small entity issue fee while maintaining an enforceable patent.

[129]*Smith Int'l, Inc. v. Hughes Tool Co.,* 759 F.2d 1572, 225 USPQ 889 (Fed. Cir. 1985).

[130]*Patent and Trademark Office Implementation of 37 C.F.R. 1.56,* 1095 O.G. 16 (Oct. 11, 1988).

[131]This new policy may have been foreshadowed in *Lutzker v. Plet,* 843 F.2d 1364, 6 USPQ2d 1370 (Fed. Cir. 1988), where the court reviewed a PTO Board award of interference priority based on two grounds: (1) abandonment, suppression, and concealment; and (2) fraud. The court affirmed on the first ground and found it unnecessary to consider the failure to comply with 37 C.F.R. §1.56(a).

[132]The PTO reads Federal Circuit decisions such as *In re Harita,* 847 F.2d 801, 6 USPQ2d 1930 (Fed. Cir. 1988) and *FMC Corp. v. Manitowoc Co.,* 835 F.2d 1411, 5 USPQ2d 1112 (Fed. Cir. 1987), as requiring "a high level of proof of intent to mislead." 1095 O.G. 16.

[133]*Atlas Powder Co. v. Ireco Chems.,* 773 F.2d 1230, 227 USPQ 289 (Fed. Cir. 1985). The court carefully distinguishes between ex parte patent prosecution and adversary patent litigation. In the latter, counsel's obligation to be candid does not go as far as to require him or her to volunteer uncertainties such as whatever might be in his or her mind about the contents of a reference. Moreover, even if counsel were guilty of a lapse in candor, there is serious doubt whether a nonparty to that litigation could take advantage of it in another case. *Id.*

[134]*Kimberly-Clark Corp. v. Johnson & Johnson,* 745 F.2d 1437, 223 USPQ 603 (Fed. Cir. 1984). The court even instructed that it is better to say fraud "in" the PTO rather than fraud

Federal Circuit, is a "much-abused and too often last-resort allegation."[135] Inequitable conduct is not, and should not be, a magic incantation to be asserted against every patentee.[136] As one panel put it:

> The habit of charging inequitable conduct in almost every major patent case has become an absolute plague. Reputable lawyers seem to feel compelled to make the charge against other reputable lawyers on the slenderest grounds, to represent their client's interests adequately, perhaps. They get anywhere with the accusation in but a small percentage of the cases, but such charges are not inconsequential on that account. They destroy the respect for one another's integrity, for being fellow members of an honorable profession, that used to make the bar a valuable help to the courts in making a sound disposition of their cases, and to sustain the good name of the bar itself. A patent litigant should be made to feel, therefore, that an unsupported charge of "inequitable conduct in the Patent Office" is a negative contribution to the rightful administration of justice. The charge was formerly known as "fraud on the Patent Office," a more pejorative term, but the change of name does not make the thing itself smell any sweeter. Even after complete testimony the court should find inequitable conduct only if shown by clear and convincing evidence. A *summary judgment* that a reputable attorney has been guilty of inequitable conduct, over his denials, ought to be, and can properly be, rare indeed.[137]

Thus we find this "important public interest" yielding to discretionary doctrines such as law of the case[138] and standing.[139] And we find the court describing a summary judgment of fraud or inequitable conduct as a draconian result.[140] Indeed, there is some indication that the court may even be willing to consider an in pari delicto argument in evaluating fraud defenses.[141] In the end analysis, unjustified accusations of inequitable conduct are offensive and unprofessional. Separating one from the other is a difficult task assigned to trial courts,

---

"on" the PTO. It is the American public that is represented by the PTO; the agency itself is in no way defrauded and has nothing to lose. *Id.*

[135]*E.I. duPont & Co. v. Phillips Petroleum Co.*, 849 F.2d 1430, 7 USPQ2d 1129 (Fed. Cir. 1988); *Preemption Devices, Inc. v. Minnesota Min. & Mfg. Co.*, 732 F.2d 903, 221 USPQ 841 (Fed. Cir. 1984).

[136]*FMC Corp. v. Manitowoc Co.*, 835 F.2d 1411, 5 USPQ2d 1112 (Fed. Cir. 1987).

[137]*Burlington Indus., Inc. v. Dayco Corp.*, 849 F.2d 1418, 7 USPQ2d 1158, 1161 (Fed. Cir. 1988). Yes, but what of the disreputable client of a reputable attorney? Once again, the court's statement tends to discourage the reasonable advocacy demanded by our adversary system of justice.

[138]*Smith Int'l, Inc. v. Hughes Tool Co.*, 759 F.2d 1572, 225 USPQ 889 (Fed. Cir. 1985). The general policy against review of conceded or unappealed issues will not, however, prevail against the policy against fraud. *Thompson-Hayward Chem. Co. v. Rohm & Haas Co.*, 745 F.2d 27, 223 USPQ 690 (Fed. Cir. 1984).

[139]*Indium Corp. v. Semi-Alloys, Inc.*, 781 F.2d 879, 228 USPQ 845 (Fed. Cir. 1985).

[140]*Kangaroos U.S.A., Inc. v. Caldor, Inc.*, 778 F.2d 1571, 228 USPQ 32 (Fed. Cir. 1985). No doubt cases in this category vary immensely in their factual situations and must be decided on a case-by-case basis. *Kimberly-Clark Corp. v. Johnson & Johnson*, 745 F.2d 1437, 223 USPQ 603 (Fed. Cir. 1984). But this is no more true here than for many other fact-intensive issues that are perfectly appropriate for summary judgment if there is no genuine issue of material fact to be decided. See *Paragon Podiatry Lab., Inc. v. KLM Labs., Inc.*, 984 F.2d 1182, 25 USPQ2d 1561 (Fed. Cir. 1993).

[141]In a dictum, the court indicated that it would not look with favor on a defense of fraudulent procurement where the defendant had originally acquired some of the patents in

which have the opportunity to find facts, hear witnesses, and judge credibility. Things can "fall through the floorboards" and not arise from an intent to deceive. But those who are not "up front" with the PTO run the risk that, years later, a fact finder might conclude that they intended to deceive.[142]

(b) Relation to Common Law Fraud

Fraud in the procurement of a patent requires proof of the elements of fraud as developed in the common law: (1) that a false representation of a material fact was made, (2) with the intent to deceive, (3) which induced the deceived party to act in justifiable reliance on the misrepresentation, and (4) which caused injury that would not otherwise have occurred. The tort of fraud requires that there was a successful deception, and action taken by the person deceived that would not have otherwise been taken. Applied to patent prosecution, fraud requires (1) a false representation or deliberate omission of a fact material to patentability, (2) made with the intent to deceive the patent examiner, (3) on which the examiner justifiably relied in granting the patent, and (4) but for which misrepresentation or deliberate omission the patent would not have been granted. A finding of fraud can of itself render the patent unenforceable, and when accompanied by the elements of violation of the Sherman Act, can incur additional consequences. To establish fraud for purposes of antitrust violation the defendant "must make a greater showing of scienter and materiality" than when seeking unenforceability based on conduct before the Patent Office. Knowing and willful fraud must be shown, and is predicate to potential antitrust violation. The requirements of common law fraud are in contrast with the broader sweep of "inequitable conduct," an equitable defense that may be satisfied when material information is withheld with the intent to deceive the examiner, whether or not the examiner is shown to have relied thereon.[143] Also, the subjective good faith of the patentee or his

---

question, and had actually filed the application for one of them, before assigning them to the plaintiff. *Minnesota Min. & Mfg. Co. v. Eco Chem, Inc.,* 757 F.2d 1256, 225 USPQ 350 (Fed. Cir. 1985).

[142]*Molins PLC v. Textron, Inc.*, 48 F.3d 1172, 33 USPQ2d 1823 (Fed. Cir. 1995).

[143]*C.R. Bard Inc. v. M3 Sys. Inc.,* 157 F.3d 1340, 48 USPQ2d 1225 (Fed. Cir. 1998). Common law fraud requires (1) misrepresentation of a material fact, (2) intent to deceive or a state of mind so reckless respecting the consequences as to be the equivalent of intent, (3) justifiable reliance on the misrepresentation by the party deceived, inducing him or her to act thereon, and (4) injury to the party deceived resulting from reliance on the misrepresentation. *American Hoist & Derrick Co. v. Sowa & Sons, Inc.,* 725 F.2d 1350, 220 USPQ 763 (Fed. Cir. 1984). Intent to deceive is a necessary component of common law fraud and is also a material factor in the determination of inequitable conduct before the PTO, as the doctrine has evolved to enforce the high standards of conduct required of patent practitioners. *Kangaroos U.S.A., Inc. v. Caldor, Inc.,* 778 F.2d 1571, 228 USPQ 32 (Fed. Cir. 1985). Conduct before the PTO that may render a patent unenforceable is broader than common law fraud and includes affirmative acts of commission as well as acts of omission. *J.P. Stevens & Co. v. Lex Tex Ltd.,* 747 F.2d 1553, 223 USPQ 1089 (Fed. Cir. 1984).

or her attorney, though it might afford a complete defense to the common law tort of fraud or deceit, does not negate inequitable conduct. Rather, the question is whether a reasonable person in the position of the patentee or his or her attorney, knew or should have known that the information was material.[144]

(c) *Summary Judgment and Right to Jury Trial*

In a case of first impression, the Federal Circuit held that (1) the defense of inequitable conduct is equitable in nature and does not give rise to the right of trial by jury, and (2) an inequitable conduct issue may be tried first, without a jury, if the factual issues resolved thereby are not so common with those relating to the jury issues of validity and infringement that a jury trial of those issues would be precluded by the earlier bench trial.[145] Thus, there are several ways in which a trial court may handle the issue of inequitable conduct during a jury trial. It can reserve the entire issue unto itself, it can submit special interrogatories to the jury on the facts of materiality and intent, or it can instruct the jury to find and weigh the facts of materiality and intent and decide the ultimate question of inequitable conduct. Absent a clear showing of prejudice or failure to achieve a fair trial, the trial court's choice of procedure will not be disturbed.[146]

The inquiry involved in ruling on a motion for summary judgment necessarily implicates the substantive evidentiary standard of proof that would apply at the trial on the merits. Thus a summary judgment of inequitable conduct would require an undisputed showing of materiality and intent by clear and convincing evidence.[147] The court has been less than enthusiastic about summary judgments of unenforceability based upon inequitable conduct.[148]

---

[144]*Argus Chem. Corp. v. Fibre Glass-Evercoat Co.,* 759 F.2d 10, 225 USPQ 1100 (Fed. Cir. 1985).

[145]*Gardco Mfg., Inc. v. Herst Lighting Co.,* 820 F.2d 1209, 2 USPQ2d 2015 (Fed. Cir. 1987). Here the court held the patent unenforceable due to failure to disclose the patentee's own prior art devices. That this evidence might also be used to establish invalidity did not mean that the issue of invalidity was precluded. A patent may be valid and yet be rendered unenforceable for misuse or inequitable conduct. Similarly, a valid patent may be infringed, but there will be no liability to the patentee when the patent is unenforceable. Thus the issue of conduct of the applicant in the PTO, raised in the nonjury portion of the trial, and the separated validity and infringement issues are distinct and without commonality either as claims or in relation to the underlying fact issues. See also *Paragon Podiatry Lab., Inc. v. KLM Labs., Inc.,* 984 F.2d 1182, 25 USPQ2d 1561 (Fed. Cir. 1993).

[146]*Hebert v. Lisle Corp.,* 99 F.3d 1109, 40 USPQ2d 1611 (Fed. Cir. 1996). See also note 9:156.

[147]*Baker Oil Tools, Inc. v. Geo Vann, Inc.,* 828 F.2d 1588, 4 USPQ2d 1210 (Fed. Cir. 1987).

[148]See *Burlington Indus., Inc. v. Dayco Corp.,* 849 F.2d 1418, 7 USPQ2d 1158 (Fed. Cir. 1988). See also note 9:137. But see *Paragon Podiatry Lab., Inc. v. KLM Labs., Inc.,* 984 F.2d 1182, 25 USPQ2d 1561 (Fed. Cir. 1993). If a bare declaration of lack of intent to mislead where a false material affidavit is submitted to the PTO were to raise a genuine issue, summary judgment would be precluded in all cases except where no response at all is made. However, such a declaration amounts to no more than would a conclusory denial in a pleading, which

(d) Burden of Proof

Although inequitable conduct requires less stringent proofs as to both materiality and intent than common law fraud, mere evidence of simple negligence, oversight, or an erroneous judgment made in good faith is not sufficient to render a patent unenforceable.[149] Establishing that a patent was procured by fraud or with such egregious conduct as to render it unenforceable requires clear, unequivocal, and convincing evidence of an intentional misrepresentation or withholding of a material fact from the PTO.[150] The drawing of inferences, particularly in respect of an intent-implicating question, is peculiarly within the province of the fact finder that observed the witnesses. Since the fact finder has personally heard the testimony and observed the demeanor of the witnesses, the appellate court accords deference to its assessment of a witness's credibility and character. However, given the ease with which a relatively routine act of patent prosecution can be portrayed as intended to mislead or deceive, clear and convincing evidence of conduct sufficient to support an inference of culpable intent is required.[151]

Although a patentee's actions may raise a suspicion of misrepresentation, a holding of fraud cannot be based on suspicion.[152] A party asserting the defense of fraud has a heavy burden,[153] and that burden is more difficult where the PTO has reaffirmed the patentability of the claims over undisclosed prior art, as in a reissue.[154] To be guilty of inequitable conduct, one must have intended to act inequitably. Consequently, one who alleges a "failure to disclose" type of inequitable conduct must offer clear and convincing proof of: (1) prior art or information that is material; (2) knowledge chargeable to the applicant of that prior art or information and of its materiality; and

---

under Rule 56, FRCP, is insufficient to create a genuine issue. The declaration must at least state facts supporting a plausible justification or excuse for the misrepresentation. *Id.*

[149]*Orthopedic Equip. Co. v. All Orthopedic Appls., Inc.,* 707 F.2d 1376, 217 USPQ 1281 (Fed. Cir. 1983).

[150]*Modine Mfg. Co. v. Allen Group, Inc.,* 917 F.2d 538, 16 USPQ2d 1622 (Fed. Cir. 1990); *Specialty Composites v. Cabot Corp.,* 845 F.2d 981, 6 USPQ2d 1601 (Fed. Cir. 1988); *Driscoll v. Cebalo,* 731 F.2d 878, 221 USPQ 745 (Fed. Cir. 1984); *Orthopedic Equip. Co. v. All Orthopedic Appls., Inc.,* 707 F.2d 1376, 217 USPQ 1281 (Fed. Cir. 1983). See also *Akzo N.V. v. United States ITC,* 808 F.2d 1471, 1 USPQ2d 1241 (Fed. Cir. 1986); *In re Jerabek,* 789 F.2d 886, 229 USPQ 530 (Fed. Cir. 1986); *J.P. Stevens & Co. v. Lex Tex Ltd.,* 747 F.2d 1553, 223 USPQ 1089 (Fed. Cir. 1984). This same rule applies even where the patent has not been issued but is still pending before the PTO, as in an interference. *Driscoll v. Cebalo,* 731 F.2d 878, 221 USPQ 745 (Fed. Cir. 1984). It is thoroughly established that inequitable conduct of the "violation of duty of disclosure" variety must be established by clear and convincing evidence. What must be so established is (1) the materiality of the undisclosed, suppressed, or misrepresented prior art or statutory bar and (2) the intent of the person not disclosing to thereby deceive or mislead the PTO. *In re Harita,* 847 F.2d 801, 6 USPQ2d 1930 (Fed. Cir. 1988).

[151]*Molins PLC v. Textron, Inc.,* 48 F.3d 1172, 33 USPQ2d 1823 (Fed. Cir. 1995).

[152]*Vandenberg v. Dairy Equip. Co.,* 740 F.2d 1560, 224 USPQ 195 (Fed. Cir. 1984).

[153]*Kansas Jack, Inc. v. Kuhn,* 719 F.2d 1144, 219 USPQ 857 (Fed. Cir. 1983); *Environmental Designs, Ltd. v. Union Oil Co.,* 713 F.2d 693, 218 USPQ 865 (Fed. Cir. 1983).

[154]*American Hoist & Derrick Co. v. Sowa & Sons, Inc.,* 725 F.2d 1350, 220 USPQ 763 (Fed. Cir. 1984).

(3) failure of the applicant to disclose the art or information resulting from an intent to mislead the PTO. That proof may be rebutted by: (a) a showing that the prior art or information was not material (because it is less pertinent than or merely cumulative with prior art or information cited to or by the PTO); (b) if the prior art or information was material, a showing that applicant did not know of that art or information; (c) if applicant did know of that art or information, a showing that applicant did not know of its materiality; or (d) a showing that applicant's failure to disclose the art or information did not result from an intent to mislead the PTO. Thus a balancing of overlapping considerations is involved in determining, in view of all the circumstances, the presence or absence of inequitable conduct.[155]

(e) The Balancing Test

In an early decision, the court recognized that in patent cases breach of the disclosure duty does not itself render the patent invalid or unenforceable, and fraud may be determined only by careful balancing of intent in light of materiality. Inasmuch as this balancing is not a fact, nor a mere application of law to facts, it requires discretion.[156] Thus materiality and intent are intertwined. A greater showing of materiality may create an inference that failure to disclose was wrongful, while a specific showing of wrongful intent can lower the standard of materiality.[157] This reasoning has led to a fairly workable test: once the thresholds of materiality and intent are established, the court conducts a balancing test to determine, as a matter of law, whether the scales tilt to a conclusion that inequitable conduct

---

[155]*FMC Corp. v. Manitowoc Co.*, 835 F.2d 1411, 5 USPQ2d 1112 (Fed. Cir. 1987). See also *Fox Indus., Inc. v. Structural Preservation Sys., Inc.*, 922 F.2d 801, 17 USPQ2d 1579 (Fed. Cir. 1991).

[156]*American Hoist & Derrick Co. v. Sowa & Sons, Inc.*, 725 F.2d 1350, 220 USPQ 763 (Fed. Cir. 1984). The court in this case had much to say about the role of the jury in a fraud determination. The terms "fraudulently withhold" and "fraudulent representation" should not be used in instructions, since they cause only confusion and do not direct the jury to relevant factual inquiries. Because the jury must determine how convincing has been the proof of intent, it should be instructed that it may find a showing on this element to be lacking entirely or that it may find intent to have been shown by any relevant degree of proof from inference to direct evidence. On materiality, the jury should be instructed to determine the pertinency of withheld information, a factual matter, and then resolve materiality in light thereof, using one of the several tests for materiality. Finally, it would be error to instruct the jury that withheld information must have had a material influence on the PTO examiner, in the absence of any testimony from the examiner. *Id.*

[157]*Under Sea Indus., Inc. v. Dacor Corp.*, 833 F.2d 1551, 4 USPQ2d 1772 (Fed. Cir. 1987); *Kimberly-Clark Corp. v. Johnson & Johnson*, 745 F.2d 1437, 223 USPQ 603 (Fed. Cir. 1984). In one case the court dismissed a contention that the district court had applied an improper standard of materiality in referring to a particular reference as not being "highly material," observing that the district court's opinion as a whole indicated that there was no imposition of an improperly high standard. *Specialty Composites v. Cabot Corp.*, 845 F.2d 981, 6 USPQ2d 1601 (Fed. Cir. 1988). This seems fair enough, but the court also indicated that there was a "presumption" that the district court applied the standard of *J.P. Stevens Co. v. Lex Tex Ltd.*, 747 F.2d 1553, 223 USPQ 1089 (Fed. Cir. 1984), simply because the case was cited! Such a presumption seems dangerous and unnecessary.

occurred.[158] The more material the omission or misrepresentation, the lower the level of intent required.[159] Indeed, gross negligence can be the standard when the misrepresentation has a high degree of materiality. Simple negligence, however, or an error in judgment is never sufficient for a holding of inequitable conduct.[160] Also, subjective good faith can fend off a charge of inequitable conduct, depending upon the balance. For example, if it is the patentee's own prior sale that is withheld, good faith may not save the patent. On the other hand, where the attorney who prosecutes the application testifies that he or she did not regard a reference as pertinent, good faith may prevail.[161]

(f) Materiality

Early on, the Federal Circuit recognized that there are at least four workable tests for materiality. The PTO works with the standard set forth in 37 C.F.R. §1.56, which is that information is material if there is a substantial likelihood that a reasonable examiner would have considered it important in deciding whether to allow the application to issue as a patent. This is the broadest test and aligns with how one ought to conduct business with the PTO.[162] Under this standard, a prior art reference that is merely cumulative is not material.[163] Attorneys have to make judgments on many matters, and to avoid a charge

---

[158]*Halliburton Co. v. Schlumberger Tech. Corp.*, 925 F.2d 1435, 17 USPQ2d 1834 (Fed. Cir. 1991); *Specialty Composites v. Cabot Corp.*, 845 F.2d 981, 6 USPQ2d 1601 (Fed. Cir. 1988); *In re Jerabek*, 789 F.2d 886, 229 USPQ 530 (Fed. Cir. 1986). Both materiality and intent to withhold must be shown before these elements can be balanced in determining whether the applicant was guilty of inequitable conduct in patent prosecution. *Andrew Corp. v. Gabriel Elec., Inc.*, 847 F.2d 819, 6 USPQ2d 2010 (Fed. Cir. 1988).

[159]*Akzo N.V. v. United States ITC*, 808 F.2d 1471, 1 USPQ2d 1241 (Fed. Cir. 1986). The quantum of intent evidence necessary for inequitable conduct depends, in part, on the materiality of the information. Overstatements and exaggerations do not rise to the level of gross falsification. *Gambro Lundia AB v. Baxter Healthcare Corp.*, 110 F.3d 1573, 42 USPQ2d 1378 (Fed. Cir. 1997).

[160]*N.V. Akzo v. E.I. duPont de Nemours*, 810 F.2d 1148, 1 USPQ2d 1704 (Fed. Cir. 1987).

[161]*Allen Archery, Inc. v. Browning Mfg. Co.*, 819 F.2d 1087, 2 USPQ2d 1490, 1495–96 (Fed. Cir. 1987); *Laitram Corp. v. Cambridge Wire Cloth Co.*, 785 F.2d 292, 228 USPQ 935 (Fed. Cir. 1986).

[162]*American Hoist & Derrick Co. v. Sowa & Sons, Inc.*, 725 F.2d 1350, 220 USPQ 763 (Fed. Cir. 1984). Rule 56 was extensively revised in 1990. See the discussion at note 9:175.

[163]*Engel Indus., Inc. v. Lockformer Co.*, 946 F.2d 1528, 20 USPQ2d 1300 (Fed. Cir. 1991); *Scripps Clinic & Res. Found. v. Genentech, Inc.*, 927 F.2d 1565, 18 USPQ2d 1001 (Fed. Cir. 1991); *Specialty Composites v. Cabot Corp.*, 845 F.2d 981, 6 USPQ2d 1601 (Fed. Cir. 1988); *J.P. Stevens & Co. v. Lex Tex Ltd.*, 747 F.2d 1553, 223 USPQ 1089 (Fed. Cir. 1984). References that are less material than those considered by the PTO, although material themselves, need not be disclosed. *Halliburton Co. v. Schlumberger Tech. Corp.*, 925 F.2d 1435, 17 USPQ2d 1834 (Fed. Cir. 1991). Nothing in law or logic requires an applicant to submit merely cumulative references for PTO review. *Rolls-Royce Ltd. v. GTE Valeron Corp.*, 800 F.2d 1101, 231 USPQ 185 (Fed. Cir. 1986). However, a withheld reference may be highly material when it discloses a more complete combination of relevant features, even if those features are before the patent examiner in other references. *Semiconductor Energy Lab. Co. v. Samsung Elec. Co.*, 204 F.3d 1368, 54 USPQ2d 1001 (Fed. Cir. 2000).

of inequitable conduct, they do not have to raise and explain to the PTO all problems they have considered.[164]

Other recognized tests are "objective but for," "subjective but for," and "but it may have."[165] The latter means that the information might reasonably have affected the examiner's decision as to patentability and poses a legal question. Subjective "but for" is a purely factual test, and objective "but for" is closely intertwined with intent.[166] For some time it was difficult to know which of these tests the court favored, but the choice seemed to boil down to the PTO's own Rule 56 standard, and the objective but for test. Most recently, the court termed the PTO Rule 56 "reasonable examiner" rule as the major standard for materiality.[167] Nondisclosed or false information is material if there is a substantial likelihood that a reasonable examiner would have considered the omitted reference or false information important in deciding whether to allow the application to issue as a patent.[168] The standard to be applied is not whether a particular examiner would consider the information to be important, or actually be misled by the alleged misrepresentations. Rather, it is that of a reasonable examiner.[169]

On the other hand, the balancing approach described above in §9.5(e) seems to invoke an objective but for analysis. Thus, if under the objective but for test it is found that information was crucial to

---

[164]*Reactive Metals & Alloys Corp. v. ESM, Inc.*, 769 F.2d 1578, 226 USPQ 821 (Fed. Cir. 1985). An applicant need not disclose to the PTO all use or sale activities that occurred prior to the application date. Such activities may or may not be material. For example, there is no point in bringing to the PTO's attention sales activities that did not take place before the one-year grace period, or sales that are accompanied by a showing that they were for experimental purposes. On the other hand, commercial sales known to have occurred more than one year prior to filing are prior art and fall within the disclosure duty. *Id.* In *Paragon Podiatry Lab., Inc. v. KLM Labs., Inc.*, 984 F.2d 1182, 25 USPQ2d 1561 (Fed. Cir. 1993), the court took pains to indicate that its holding in *Reactive Metals*, above, does not excuse an attorney from disclosing, based solely upon the inventor's representations, precritical date sales in the face of objective evidence that the sales were commercial in nature. The decision whether or not to disclose sales made before the critical date should, where the case is close, be resolved by disclosure, not by the applicant's unilateral decision. In a jury case it is error to instruct that an applicant must "fully disclose all pertinent facts which may affect the decision" of the PTO. *American Hoist & Derrick Co. v. Sowa & Sons, Inc.*, 725 F.2d 1350, 220 USPQ 763 (Fed. Cir. 1984).

[165]*J.P. Stevens & Co. v. Lex Tex Ltd.*, 747 F.2d 1553, 223 USPQ 1089 (Fed. Cir. 1984).

[166]*American Hoist & Derrick Co. v. Sowa & Sons, Inc.*, 725 F.2d 1350, 220 USPQ 763 (Fed. Cir. 1984).

[167]*Akzo N.V. v. United States ITC*, 808 F.2d 1471, 1 USPQ2d 1241 (Fed. Cir. 1986). See also *Halliburton Co. v. Schlumberger Tech. Corp.*, 925 F.2d 1435, 17 USPQ2d 1834 (Fed. Cir. 1991); *Pacific Furniture Mfg. Co. v. Preview Furniture Corp.*, 800 F.2d 1111, 231 USPQ 67 (Fed. Cir. 1986). In *Merck & Co. v. Danbury Pharmical, Inc.*, 873 F.2d 1418, 10 USPQ2d 1682 (Fed. Cir. 1989), the court made it clear that materiality is not to be judged under a "but for" test. Instead, materiality may be established by a showing that a reasonable examiner would consider withheld prior art important in deciding whether to issue the patent. Here the withheld prior art did not render the invention obvious, but the court nonetheless found that it was material.

[168]*Specialty Composites v. Cabot Corp.*, 845 F.2d 981, 6 USPQ2d 1601 (Fed. Cir. 1988).

[169]*Western Elec. Co. v. Piezo Tech., Inc.*, 860 F.2d 428, 8 USPQ2d 1853 (Fed. Cir. 1988). Thus inquiry into the importance that a particular examiner may have placed on the representations, by testing his or her knowledge of the prior art, is wholly irrelevant. *Id.*

a reasonable examiner, then gross negligence may be sufficient; on the other hand, if information was important but not crucial, then something more than gross negligence or recklessness may be required, and good faith judgment or honest mistake may be a defense.[170]

The level of materiality may be high or low.[171] Moreover, it is plain that the disclosure duty has changed over the years.[172] Nonetheless, the court has come to the view that the 1977 amendments to 37 C.F.R. §1.56 merely codified the existing PTO policy on inequitable conduct and were consistent with the standards of conduct prevailing in the early 1970s,[173] even though the law may not have been as clear then as it is today.[174] Under the 1990 revisions to Rule 56, information is material to patentability when it is not cumulative to information already of record or being made of record in the application and (1) it establishes, by itself or in combination with other information, a prima facie case of unpatentability of a claim, or (2) it refutes, or is inconsistent with, a position the applicant takes in (i) opposing an argument of unpatentability relied on by the PTO, or (ii) asserting an argument of patentability. The court has held that this new rule is not retroactive and applies only to activities after March 16, 1992.[175] It has not yet squarely addressed the impact, if any, of the new rule on existing formulations of the materiality standard, although in a recent case it appeared to apply, without comment, the standard of materiality set forth in new Rule 56.[176]

There was for some time another large unanswered question regarding materiality. Clearly, where claims are later rejected over withheld references, as in a reissue proceeding, that alone establishes

---

[170]*American Hoist & Derrick Co. v. Sowa & Sons, Inc.,* 725 F.2d 1350, 220 USPQ 763 (Fed. Cir. 1984).

[171]*FMC Corp. v. Manitowoc Co.,* 835 F.2d 1411, 5 USPQ2d 1112 (Fed. Cir. 1987). In *Lummus Indus., Inc. v. D.M. & E. Corp.,* 862 F.2d 267, 8 USPQ2d 1983 (Fed. Cir. 1988), the court rejected the concept of a rule of per se high materiality (as in the case of anticipation) that would remove from judge and jury the authority to find facts respecting both anticipation and materiality, based solely on an examiner's rejection for anticipation.

[172]*In re Harita,* 847 F.2d 801, 6 USPQ2d 1930 (Fed. Cir. 1988). It is a mischaracterization, says the court, to call 37 C.F.R. §1.56 a "codification," for it has inaugurated a whole new way of life in the prosecution of patent applications. It has effectively made applicants, their associates, and their attorneys partners with the PTO examining corps in producing for PTO consideration the prior art that is needed to operate a reasonably effective examination system. *Id.*

[173]*Fox Indus., Inc. v. Structural Preservation Sys., Inc.,* 922 F.2d 801, 17 USPQ2d 1579 (Fed. Cir. 1991). This is so despite the seemingly contrary prior view of the court that it was a mischaracterization to call 37 C.F.R. §1.56 a codification. *In re Harita,* 847 F.2d 801, 6 USPQ2d 1930 (Fed. Cir. 1988).

[174]*Manville Sales Corp. v. Paramount Sys., Inc.,* 917 F.2d 544, 16 USPQ2d 1587 (Fed. Cir. 1990). The basic tenets of inequitable conduct as summarized in *J.P. Stevens & Co. v. Lex Tex Ltd.,* 747 F.2d 1553, 223 USPQ 1089 (Fed. Cir. 1984), were the law by 1977. *Id.* The *J.P. Stevens* standard of proper conduct in the PTO was applicable as early as 1973–74. *Molins PLC v. Textron, Inc.,* 48 F.3d 1172, 33 USPQ2d 1823 (Fed. Cir. 1995).

[175]*Molins PLC v. Textron, Inc.,* 48 F.3d 1172, 33 USPQ2d 1823 (Fed. Cir. 1995).

[176]*Semiconductor Energy Lab. Co. v. Samsung Elec. Co.,* 204 F.3d 1368, 54 USPQ2d 1001, 1005 (Fed. Cir. 2000).

materiality.[177] A finding that a withheld reference anticipates a claim satisfies the most stringent standard of materiality.[178] But must a reference be invalidating in order to be fatally material? The court was for awhile sending conflicting signals on this question.[179] But it now seems clear that inequitable conduct may be found absent unpatentability.[180] A difference in a single element, however important to the patented invention, is not automatically dispositive of the issue of materiality. In other words, materiality is not analyzed in a vacuum. It is not dependent on a single element viewed in isolation. Rather, it is judged based upon the overall degree of similarity between the omitted reference and the claimed invention in light of the other prior art before the examiner.[181] A misrepresentation need not be relied upon by the examiner in deciding to allow a patent. The matter misrepresented need only be within a reasonable examiner's realm of consideration.[182]

Despite these questions, some things are quite clear concerning materiality. Even where an applicant fails to disclose an otherwise material prior art reference, that failure will not support a finding of inequitable conduct if the reference is simply cumulative to other references, i.e., if the reference teaches no more than what a reasonable examiner would consider to be taught by the prior art already before the PTO.[183] Information that is not technically prior art is not material.[184] But if a patentee's expert witness admits that art "would

---

[177]*In re Jerabek,* 789 F.2d 886, 229 USPQ 530 (Fed. Cir. 1986); *J.P. Stevens & Co. v. Lex Tex Ltd.,* 747 F.2d 1553, 223 USPQ 1089 (Fed. Cir. 1984).

[178]*Fox Indus., Inc. v. Structural Preservation Sys., Inc.,* 922 F.2d 801, 17 USPQ2d 1579 (Fed. Cir. 1991).

[179]Compare *Laitram Corp. v. Cambridge Wire Cloth Co.,* 785 F.2d 292, 228 USPQ 935 (Fed. Cir. 1986), with *A.B. Dick Co. v. Burroughs Corp.,* 798 F.2d 1392, 230 USPQ 849 (Fed. Cir. 1986). See also *Kimberly-Clark Corp. v. Johnson & Johnson,* 745 F.2d 1437, 223 USPQ 603 (Fed. Cir. 1984); *Driscoll v. Cebalo,* 731 F.2d 878, 221 USPQ 745 (Fed. Cir. 1984).

[180]*Gardco Mfg., Inc. v. Herst Lighting Co.,* 820 F.2d 1209, 2 USPQ2d 2015 (Fed. Cir. 1987). In determining the inequitable conduct issue, a district court need not make explicit findings on whether undisclosed art anticipates the claimed invention or whether it would have rendered the claimed invention obvious under 35 U.S.C. §103. *Id.* A reference is not immaterial simply because the claims are eventually deemed by an examiner to be patentable thereover. *Molins PLC v. Textron, Inc.,* 48 F.3d 1172, 33 USPQ2d 1823 (Fed. Cir. 1995).

[181]*Baxter Int'l Inc. v. McGaw Inc.,* 149 F.3d 1321, 47 USPQ2d 1225 (Fed. Cir. 1998).

[182]*Merck & Co. v. Danbury Pharmical, Inc.,* 873 F.2d 1418, 10 USPQ2d 1682 (Fed. Cir. 1989).

[183]*Regents of Univ. of Calif. v. Eli Lilly & Co.,* 119 F.3d 1559, 43 USPQ2d 1398 (Fed. Cir. 1997).

[184]*Northern Telecom, Inc. v. Datapoint Corp.,* 908 F.2d 931, 15 USPQ2d 1321 (Fed. Cir. 1990); *Environmental Designs, Ltd. v. Union Oil Co.,* 713 F.2d 693, 218 USPQ 865 (Fed. Cir. 1983). Actions by the inventor himself occurring within the statutory one-year grace period under 35 U.S.C. §102 are not prior art that will render the inventor's work anticipated or obvious, and it is not inequitable conduct to fail to disclose such art to the PTO during prosecution. *Specialty Composites v. Cabot Corp.,* 845 F.2d 981, 6 USPQ2d 1601 (Fed. Cir. 1988). An asserted public use bar that is not supportable on the evidence at trial cannot be deemed material and culpable without a full trial. *Allied Colloids, Inc. v. American Cyanamid Co.,* 64 F.3d 1570, 35 USPQ2d 1840 (Fed. Cir. 1995).

be pertinent for consideration," it is material for purposes of an inequitable conduct inquiry.[185] Concealment of sales information can be particularly egregious because, unlike an applicant's failure to disclose, for example, a material patent reference, the PTO has no way of securing sales information on its own.[186] In contrast to cases where allegations of fraud are based on the withholding of prior art, there is no room to argue that submission of false affidavits is not material.[187] Similarly, intentional concealment of the best mode and disclosure of an inoperable mode instead amounts to inequitable conduct.[188] However, the court is apparently willing to permit misrepresentations in the body of a patent application so long as they are not material.[189]

It is not inequitable conduct to fail to disclose, prior to issue of the patent, a best mode or enabling detail discovered after the application was filed. The rationale is that disclosure is closed when the application is filed, and there is no opportunity for an inventor

---

[185]*Argus Chem. Corp. v. Fibre Glass-Evercoat Co.*, 759 F.2d 10, 225 USPQ 1100 (Fed. Cir. 1985). Admissions can cut both ways. In *Sensonics, Inc. v. Aerosonic Corp.*, 81 F.3d 1566, 38 USPQ2d 1551 (Fed. Cir. 1996), the court observed that the failure of the accused infringer to include a reference in its own request for reexamination of the patent in suit weighed heavily against its argument that the reference was material.

[186]*Paragon Podiatry Lab., Inc. v. KLM Labs., Inc.*, 984 F.2d 1182, 25 USPQ2d 1561 (Fed. Cir. 1993).

[187]*Rohm & Haas Co. v. Crystal Chem. Co.*, 722 F.2d 1556, 220 USPQ 289 (Fed. Cir. 1983). A patent may be held unenforceable by reason of a patentee's submission of material false information with an intent to deceive. *General Electro Music Corp. v. Samick Music Corp.*, 19 F.3d 1405, 30 USPQ2d 1149 (Fed. Cir. 1994). An honest mistake in an affidavit does not constitute inequitable conduct. *Allen Archery, Inc. v. Browning Mfg. Co.*, 819 F.2d 1087, 2 USPQ2d 1490 (Fed. Cir. 1987). However, that statements in an affidavit are true does not alone negate a finding of inequitable conduct, because truthful statements can be crafted in a misleading manner through intentional omission of particular relevant facts. *B.F. Goodrich Co. v. Aircraft Braking Sys. Corp.*, 72 F.3d 1577, 37 USPQ2d 1314 (Fed. Cir. 1996). An inventor cannot submit a misleading affidavit among a plurality of affidavits and later argue that it was the nonmisleading affidavit that resulted in allowance, thus effectively curing the defective affidavit; each ipso facto has a certain level of materiality. *Refac Int'l, Ltd. v. Lotus Dev. Corp.*, 81 F.3d 1576 (Fed. Cir. 1996). The court also rejected an argument that the misleading submission had no probative value because it consisted only of opinion, not facts. The court indicated that this argument qualifies only for a Chutzpah award, not a reversal. *Id.*

[188]*Consolidated Alum Corp. v. Foseco Int'l Ltd.*, 910 F.2d 804, 15 USPQ2d 1481 (Fed. Cir. 1990). However, a failure to disclose the best mode does not automatically equate with inequitable conduct because of the intent requirement. *In re Hayes Microcomputer Patent Litig.*, 982 F.2d 1527, 25 USPQ2d 1241 (Fed. Cir. 1992). While in appropriate circumstances a failure to disclose the best mode may be so egregious as to constitute inequitable conduct, specific intent to deceive is not a required element of a best mode defense. *Graco, Inc. v. Binks Mfg. Co.*, 60 F.3d 785, 35 USPQ2d 1255 (Fed. Cir. 1995). Failure to meet a requirement of patentability, such as enablement, does not of itself establish the intent element of inequitable conduct. *Therma-Tru Corp. v. Peachtree Doors Inc.*, 44 F.3d 988, 33 USPQ2d 1274 (Fed. Cir. 1994).

[189]*Regents of Univ. of Calif. v. Eli Lilly & Co.*, 119 F.3d 1559, 43 USPQ2d 1398 (Fed. Cir. 1997). The applicants knowingly used a particular uncertified plasmid (apparently the NIH certifies such plasmids for use) to hasten their determination of DNA sequences. In the examples of their patent application, they indicated that they had used a certified plasmid. The court concluded that the district court abused its discretion in holding the patent to be unenforceable for inequitable conduct. The reasoning seems to be lack of materiality: the result would not have been different if the uncertified plasmid had actually been identified in the examples, because both worked equally well. Also, a reasonable examiner would not have considered noncompliance with the NIH guidelines to be material to patentability. The court rejected

to include subsequent improvements or modifications in an application or patent after filing, because of the prohibition against new matter. Inasmuch as there can be no obligation to do so, there is no penalty for failure to do so.[190]

Although knowledge by a patentee of a nondisclosed reference goes to intent and not materiality, the fact that the reference was the starting point in the patentee's design process is evidence of materiality.[191] Courts may certainly look outside the involved claim in determining, in the first place, whether inequitable conduct did in fact occur. Claims are not born, and do not live, in isolation. Each is related to other claims, to the specification and drawings, to the prior art, to any attorney's remarks, to copending and continuing applications, and often to earlier or later versions of itself in light of amendments made to it.[192] A breach of the duty of candor early in the prosecution may render unenforceable all claims that eventually issue from the same or a related application. Thus, where an attorney knows that prior art is material to the patentability of claims he or she has drafted, he or she has an obligation to disclose it to the PTO notwithstanding the fact that none of the claims ultimately issued in the form in which they were drafted. A fortuitous rejection does not cure a breach of the duty of candor.[193]

(g) *Knowledge*

For inequitable conduct, applicants must be chargeable with knowledge of the existence of the prior art or information, for it is

---

defendant's argument that, had the applicant complied with the NIH guidelines, the application might have been delayed and the applicant might not have been the first to file.

[190]*Engel Indus., Inc. v. Lockformer Co.*, 946 F.2d 1528, 20 USPQ2d 1300 (Fed. Cir. 1991). This case does not appear to touch the question of whether a best mode disclosure must be updated when a continuing application is filed.

[191]*Pacific Furniture Mfg. Co. v. Preview Furniture Corp.*, 800 F.2d 1111, 231 USPQ 67 (Fed. Cir. 1986). However, in its first look at the issue, the court refused to hold that the failure of the applicant to disclose that certain information had been derived from another, and was therefore prior art under 35 U.S.C. §102(f)/§103, amounted to inequitable conduct. The court felt that prior law on the subject was so unclear that the requisite deceptive intention could not have been present. *Oddzon Prods., Inc. v. Just Toys, Inc.*, 122 F.3d 1396, 43 USPQ2d 1641 (Fed. Cir. 1997).

[192]*Kingsdown Med. Cons, Ltd. v. Hollister, Inc.*, 863 F.2d 867, 9 USPQ2d 1384 (Fed. Cir. 1988).

[193]*Fox Indus., Inc. v. Structural Preservation Sys., Inc.*, 922 F.2d 801, 17 USPQ2d 1579, 1581 (Fed. Cir. 1991). This was a particularly egregious situation, inasmuch as the attorney had used the patentee's brochure, published more than a year before filing, as source material in drafting the application. Compare *Scripps Clinic & Res. Found. v. Genentech, Inc.*, 927 F.2d 1565, 18 USPQ2d 1001 (Fed. Cir. 1991), where the court said that a reference that is material only to withdrawn claims cannot be the basis of a holding of inequitable conduct. The court justified this on the reasoning that an applicant has a right to decline to do work (collecting comparative data to distinguish a reference) suggested by the PTO and to withdraw the claims, without incurring liability for inequitable conduct. In *Glaverbel S.A. v. Northlake Mkt'g & Supp., Inc.*, 45 F.3d 1550, 33 USPQ2d 1496 (Fed. Cir. 1995), the patentee knew of a reference during the original prosecution, but it came to light only during reexamination. It was used by the PTO in a rejection during reexamination, but that rejection was later withdrawn. In a seemingly unrelated passage of its opinion, the Federal Circuit indicated that reduction in

impossible to disclose the unknown. Similarly, an applicant must be chargeable with knowledge of the materiality of the art or information. Yet an applicant who knew of the art or information cannot intentionally avoid learning of its materiality through gross negligence—it may be found that the applicant should have known of that materiality.[194] As a general rule, there is no duty to conduct a prior art search, and thus there is no duty to disclose art of which an applicant "could" have been aware.[195] However, one should not be able to cultivate ignorance, or to disregard numerous warnings that material information or prior art may exist, merely to avoid actual knowledge of that information or prior art. When one does that, the "should have known" factor becomes operative.[196] Under the rules of the PTO, the duty of disclosure rests on the inventor, each attorney or agent who prepares or prosecutes an application, and on every other individual who is substantively involved in the preparation or prosecution of the application and who is associated with the inventor, with the assignee, or with anyone to whom there is an obligation to assign the application.[197]

Actual or imputed knowledge of withheld information is pertinent to intent if on the part of the applicant and is pertinent to materiality if on the part of the PTO. In one case the court seemed to excuse a nondisclosure because the attorney was not aware of the reference, and there was no evidence that the inventor was trained to evaluate what is and is not prior art.[198] In considering the disclosure duty, the applicant includes both the patentee and the attorney who prosecuted the application, because the knowledge and actions of the attorney are chargeable to the applicant.[199] In another case, the lower court

---

claim scope during reexamination is not of itself probative of material withholding with intent to deceive and supports no such inference.

[194]*FMC Corp. v. Manitowoc Co.*, 835 F.2d 1411, 5 USPQ2d 1112 (Fed. Cir. 1987).

[195]*Nordberg, Inc. v. Telsmith, Inc.*, 82 F.3d 394, 38 USPQ2d 1593 (Fed. Cir. 1996); *FMC Corp. v. Hennessy Indus., Inc.*, 836 F.2d 521, 5 USPQ2d 1272 (Fed. Cir. 1987). An applicant is not obligated to disclose search results where the search fails to turn up prior art as close as that cited by the examiner. *Hebert v. Lisle Corp.*, 99 F.3d 1109, 40 USPQ2d 1611 (Fed. Cir. 1996).

[196]*FMC Corp. v. Hennessy Indus., Inc.*, 836 F.2d 521, 5 USPQ2d 1272 (Fed. Cir. 1987). The Federal Circuit will not hold unenforceable a patent once granted in the absence of an intent to mislead, although the nondisclosure of facts of which the applicant should have known the materiality may justify an inference of intent to mislead in appropriate cases. *Burlington Indus., Inc. v. Dayco Corp.*, 849 F.2d 1418, 7 USPQ2d 1158 (Fed. Cir. 1988).

[197]*Molins PLC v. Textron, Inc.*, 48 F.3d 1172, 33 USPQ2d 1823 (Fed. Cir. 1995).

[198]*Kansas Jack, Inc. v. Kuhn*, 719 F.2d 1144, 219 USPQ 857 (Fed. Cir. 1983). Where the inventor is uncertain whether particular activities are actually prior art, and they turn out not to be, there is no obligation to disclose them. *Hebert v. Lisle Corp.*, 99 F.3d 1109, 40 USPQ2d 1611 (Fed. Cir. 1996). An inventor indicated that he had "heard of" a particular use, but had never seen one, did not know the manufacturer, and did not consider it pertinent even if true. It was not inequitable conduct to fail to disclose this anecdotal use to the PTO. *Hartness Int'l, Inc. v. Simplimatic Eng'g Co.*, 819 F.2d 1100, 2 USPQ2d 1826 (Fed. Cir. 1987). A prior art reference was received in the inventor's office a month before his patent issued, but there was no evidence that he saw it or had personal knowledge of it. The court found no inequitable conduct. *Kolmes v. World Fibers Corp.*, 107 F.3d 1534, 41 USPQ2d 1829 (Fed. Cir. 1997).

[199]*FMC Corp. v. Manitowoc Co.*, 835 F.2d 1411, 5 USPQ2d 1112 (Fed. Cir. 1987). The duty of candor rests on the inventor as well as the attorney. *Fox Indus., Inc. v. Structural Preservation Sys., Inc.*, 922 F.2d 801, 17 USPQ2d 1579 (Fed. Cir. 1991).

had found fraud on the basis that the inventor was presumed to know the prior art. Naturally the Federal Circuit rejected this concept as leading to an "absurd result."[200]

Inequitable conduct cannot be based on an applicant's failure to disclose a prior art reference if the examiner independently discovers that reference.[201] Thus the fact that the examiner actually knew about the withheld prior art may well preclude a finding of materiality. But a mere possibility that he or she could have known is not enough. Where inequitable conduct is at issue, mere possibilities are not enough.[202] It cannot be presumed, at least where fraud or other egregious conduct is concerned, that the PTO considered prior art if it was not cited during prosecution. Any presumption that an examiner is aware of all prior art in the classifications he or she searched does not apply in the fraud context.[203]

A lapse on the part of the examiner will not excuse fraud or gross negligence on the part of an applicant.[204] But although an oversight on the part of the examiner does not exculpate an applicant whose acts are intentionally deceptive, any doubt as to whether the examiner lapsed in his or her duty should not increase the burden on the applicant. The applicant's obligation of candor does not replace the examiner's duty to examine the claims.[205] Thus, the court has said

---

[200]*Kimberly-Clark Corp. v. Johnson & Johnson,* 745 F.2d 1437, 223 USPQ 603, 610 (Fed. Cir. 1984).

[201]*Litton Sys., Inc. v. Honeywell, Inc.,*87 F.3d 1559, 39 USPQ2d 1321 (Fed. Cir. 1996).

[202]*J.P. Stevens & Co. v. Lex Tex Ltd.,* 747 F.2d 1553, 223 USPQ 1089 (Fed. Cir. 1984). When a reference was before the PTO, whether through the examiner's search or the applicant's disclosure, it cannot be deemed to have been withheld from the examiner. *Scripps Clinic & Res. Found. v. Genentech, Inc.,* 927 F.2d 1565, 18 USPQ2d 1001 (Fed. Cir. 1991). It is of course conceivable that the manner of citing a reference, e.g., "burying" it in a multitude of other references, could in itself amount to inequitable conduct. However, in *Molins PLC v. Textron, Inc.,* 48 F.3d 1172, 33 USPQ2d 1823 (Fed. Cir. 1995), the court reversed a finding of intent to mislead on that basis as clearly erroneous.

[203]*Driscoll v. Cebalo,* 731 F.2d 878, 221 USPQ 745 (Fed. Cir. 1984). In one case the court assumed, without deciding, the correctness of the proposition that when an examiner represents that he has reviewed specific prior art, the duty of candor does not require the applicant to advocate that the examiner should have cited that art as material when he fails to do so. Nonetheless, the case was distinguishable in that the only representation by the examiner was that he had searched the class and subclass in which the omitted art was contained—not that he had reviewed the specific omitted art. An indication of a generalized search does not of itself relieve the applicant from the duty of candor. *FMC Corp. v. Hennessy Indus., Inc.,* 836 F.2d 521, 5 USPQ2d 1272 (Fed. Cir. 1987).

[204]*Kangaroos U.S.A., Inc. v. Caldor, Inc.,* 778 F.2d 1571, 228 USPQ 32 (Fed. Cir. 1985). This case involved an alleged fraudulent claim of priority. The examiner did not demand verification of priority entitlement in the face of an intervening reference. Nonetheless, summary judgment was inappropriate because the attorney's intent in making the priority claim was important.

[205]*Northern Telecom, Inc. v. Datapoint Corp.,* 908 F.2d 931, 15 USPQ2d 1321 (Fed. Cir. 1990). In this case the court appears to hold that the fact that a party's underlying conduct may be acceptable may well exculpate the party from an inequitable conduct holding even where the party misrepresents the nature of the underlying conduct to the PTO. Here the applicant submitted a Rule 312 amendment, making five changes to the specification that arguably enlarged the scope of the claims. He prefaced the amendment with the statement that the changes were to correct "typographical errors and other such discrepancies." The court found that the claims as originally filed were already of that scope, and therefore accepted the applicant's argument that the amendment simply conformed the descriptive text of the

that where two copending applications owned by the same company are before an examiner, he or she has a duty to know of them both to be sure they claim distinct inventions.[206] But the fact that an examiner cites a specific reference in his or her examination of another, unrelated patent that issued earlier than the patent in suit does not mean that he or she was aware of the reference so as to relieve the applicant from citing it. The duty of candor requires more than an assumption that the examiner will recall something from a previous application.[207]

Where a patentee's own prior device is described in the body of the patent as prior art, there is no fraud even though it is not identified as the inventor's own work.[208] A patentee cannot justify nondisclosure by arguing that the material was disclosed in a copending application that was mentioned in his or her patent. A copending application is not prior art, and a reference to it does not thereby advise the PTO as to what was actually in the prior art.[209] However, under §609 of the MPEP, a reference is not required to be resubmitted in prosecuting a divisional application. In view of §609 it cannot be inequitable conduct for an applicant not to resubmit, in the divisional application, the information that was cited or submitted in the parent application.[210]

(h) Intent

Inequitable conduct carries the consequence of permanent unenforceability of the patent claims. Forfeiture is not favored as a remedy for actions not shown to be culpable.[211] Inequitable conduct therefore requires an intent to act inequitably.[212]

---

specification to the claims. That, plus the fact that the nature of the amendments was clear on their face, and all the pertinent information was squarely before the examiner in a single document, led the court to conclude that the lower court's finding of intent was clearly erroneous. In *Fiskars Inc. v Hunt Mfg. Co.,* 221 F.3d 1318, 55 USPQ2d 1569 (Fed. Cir. 2000), the applicant submitted several references listed on a PTO Form 1449 and the examiner drew a line through one, indicating (in accordance with MPEP §609) that it was not considered. The accused infringer argued that the applicant should have stressed the relevance of the reference. The court disagreed, pointing out that the requirement that an applicant explain the relevance of the reference listed on a Form 1449 was removed in 1992. An applicant cannot be guilty of inequitable conduct if the reference was cited to the examiner, whether or not it was a ground of rejection by the examiner. Although the examiner's reason for lining out the reference was unknown, the applicant's citation of it as prior art defeats the charge that it was withheld with deceptive intent. An applicant is not required to tell the PTO twice about the same prior art, on pain of loss of the patent for inequitable conduct.

[206]*Kimberly-Clark Corp. v. Johnson & Johnson,* 745 F.2d 1437, 223 USPQ 603 (Fed. Cir. 1984). This seems to suggest the applicant of one is under no duty to alert the examiner to the other.

[207]*FMC Corp. v. Hennessy Indus., Inc.,* 836 F.2d 521, 5 USPQ2d 1272 (Fed. Cir. 1987).

[208]*Vandenberg v. Dairy Equip. Co.,* 740 F.2d 1560, 224 USPQ 195 (Fed. Cir. 1984).

[209]*Gardco Mfg., Inc. v. Herst Lighting Co.,* 820 F.2d 1209, 2 USPQ2d 2015 (Fed. Cir. 1987).

[210]*ATD Corp. v. Lydall Inc.,* 159 F.3d 534, 48 USPQ2d 1321 (Fed. Cir. 1998).

[211]*Tol-O-Matic, Inc. v. Proma Produckt-und Mktg. GmbH,* 945 F.2d 1546, 20 USPQ2d 1332 (Fed. Cir. 1991).

[212]*Halliburton Co. v. Schlumberger Tech. Corp.,* 925 F.2d 1435, 17 USPQ2d 1834 (Fed. Cir. 1991).

Fraud or inequitable conduct requires proof of a threshold intent. Intent to deceive should be determined in light of the realities of patent practice, and not as a matter of strict liability whatever the nature of the action before the PTO. Given the ease with which a relatively routine act of patent prosecution can be portrayed as intended to mislead or deceive, clear and convincing evidence of conduct sufficient to support an inference of culpable intent is required.[213]

The facts in inequitable conduct cases rarely, if ever, include direct evidence of admitted deceitful conduct. The intent element of the offense is in the main proven by inferences drawn from facts, with the collection of inferences permitting a confident judgment that deceit has occurred.[214] Thus intent may be proven by showing acts the natural consequences of which are presumably intended by the actor.[215] Some evidence on the issue of intent must exist, although it need not be direct and may be inferred from the patentee's conduct,[216] such as reckless disregard or gross negligence as to the truth.[217] Proof of deliberate scheming is not needed; gross negligence may be sufficient in light of the total circumstances. Gross negligence is present when the applicant or his or her attorney, judged as a reasonable person in that position, knew or should have known of the materiality of a withheld reference.[218] But the required finding of intent to deceive cannot be inferred solely from a finding of gross negligence,[219] and not every district court finding of gross negligence necessarily compels a finding of intentional nondisclosure; subjective good faith is a factor

---

[213]*Northern Telecom, Inc. v. Datapoint Corp.*, 908 F.2d 931, 15 USPQ2d 1321 (Fed. Cir. 1990).

[214]*Akron Polymer Cont. Corp. v. Exxel Cont. Inc.*, 148 F.3d 1380, 47 USPQ2d 1533 (Fed. Cir. 1998). In this case, the same lawyers prosecuted copending applications (V and K) for the same assignee, before different examiners. There was sufficient overlap in the two to raise double patenting concerns. The attorneys did not disclose the pendency of application V to the examiner in the prosecution of application K, which became the patent in suit, until after a notice of allowance in the K prosecution. However, they did disclose the existence of application K to the examiner handling application V. This was seen to point away from an intent to deceive and the court found that a threshold level of deceitful intent had not been shown.

[215]*Molins PLC v. Textron, Inc.*, 48 F.3d 1172, 33 USPQ2d 1823 (Fed. Cir. 1995); *J.P. Stevens & Co. v. Lex Tex Ltd.*, 747 F.2d 1553, 223 USPQ 1089 (Fed. Cir. 1984); *Kansas Jack, Inc. v. Kuhn*, 719 F.2d 1144, 219 USPQ 857 (Fed. Cir. 1983); *Merck & Co. v. Danbury Pharmical, Inc.*, 873 F.2d 1418, 10 USPQ2d 1682 (Fed. Cir. 1989). A finding of intent to deceive is necessary to sustain a charge of inequitable conduct. However, such a finding does not necessarily require direct proof of subjective wrongful intent. *RCA Corp. v. Data Gen. Corp.*, 887 F.2d 1056, 12 USPQ2d 1449 (Fed. Cir. 1989).

[216]*Smithkline Diagnostics, Inc. v. Helena Labs. Corp.*, 859 F.2d 878, 8 USPQ2d 1468 (Fed. Cir. 1988).

[217]*W.L. Gore & Assoc. v. Garlock, Inc.*, 721 F.2d 1540, 220 USPQ 303 (Fed. Cir. 1983); *Kansas Jack, Inc. v. Kuhn*, 719 F.2d 1144, 219 USPQ 857 (Fed. Cir. 1983).

[218]*Specialty Composites v. Cabot Corp.*, 845 F.2d 981, 6 USPQ2d 1601 (Fed. Cir. 1988); *J.P. Stevens & Co. v. Lex Tex Ltd.*, 747 F.2d 1553, 223 USPQ 1089 (Fed. Cir. 1984). See also *In re Jerabek*, 789 F.2d 886, 229 USPQ 530 (Fed. Cir. 1986); *Reactive Metals & Alloys Corp. v. ESM, Inc.*, 769 F.2d 1578, 226 USPQ 821 (Fed. Cir. 1985).

[219]*Hoffman-La Roche Inc. v. Lemmon Co.*, 906 F.2d 684, 15 USPQ2d 1363 (Fed. Cir. 1990).

to be considered.[220] And certainly simple negligence, oversight, or an erroneous judgment made in good faith are insufficient.[221]

In its *Kingsdown* ruling the court, sitting in banc, proposed to clarify the relationship of gross negligence and intent. It held that a finding that particular conduct amounts to gross negligence does not of itself justify an inference of intent to deceive; the involved conduct, viewed in light of all the evidence indicative of good faith, must indicate sufficient culpability to require a finding of intent to deceive.[222] Certainly it is clear that gross negligence alone will not *compel* an inference of intent to deceive. But it is not clear whether the court was saying that gross negligence alone can never *support* an inference of intent, even if there is no evidence indicative of good faith, or simply that evidence of good faith, if present, must always be considered.

In a subsequent case, the court explained further: a finding of gross negligence alone is insufficient to support a holding of inequitable conduct. Inequitable conduct requires a finding of intent to mislead or deceive the PTO. Such intent usually can only be found as a matter of inference from circumstantial evidence. Although the proof of gross negligence may be circumstantial evidence that gives rise to an inference of intent to mislead in some instances, the label "gross negligence" covers too wide a range of culpable conduct to create such an inference in all cases. Thus grossly negligent conduct may or may not compel an inference of an intent to mislead. Such an inference depends upon the totality of the circumstances, including the nature and level of culpability of the conduct and the absence or presence of affirmative evidence of good faith. An actual finding of intent to mislead is necessary.[223] Thus, under *Kingsdown* the court must view the involved conduct in light of all the evidence and must then determine whether that conduct in its totality manifests a sufficiently culpable state of mind to warrant a determination that it was inequitable.[224] The alleged conduct must not amount merely to the improper performance of, or omission of, an act one ought to have performed. Rather, clear and convincing evidence must prove that an applicant

---

[220]*FMC Corp. v. Hennessy Indus., Inc.,* 836 F.2d 521, 5 USPQ2d 1272 (Fed. Cir. 1987).

[221]*Specialty Composites v. Cabot Corp.,* 845 F.2d 981, 6 USPQ2d 1601 (Fed. Cir. 1988); *J.P. Stevens & Co. v. Lex Tex Ltd.,* 747 F.2d 1553, 223 USPQ 1089 (Fed. Cir. 1984). See also *Reactive Metals & Alloys Corp. v. ESM, Inc.,* 769 F.2d 1578, 226 USPQ 821 (Fed. Cir. 1985).

[222]*Kingsdown Med. Cons, Ltd. v. Hollister, Inc.,* 863 F.2d 867, 9 USPQ2d 1384 (Fed. Cir. 1988).

[223]*Hewlett-Packard Co. v. Bausch & Lomb, Inc.,* 882 F.2d 1556, 11 USPQ2d 1750 (Fed. Cir. 1989). Here the district court found that false affidavits during reissue were made with "studied ignorance" of the facts and "reckless indifference" for the truth. But it did not actually make a finding of intent, so a remand was in order. Grossly negligent conduct may or may not compel an inference of an intent to mislead. *Manville Sales Corp. v. Paramount Sys., Inc.,* 917 F.2d 544, 16 USPQ2d 1587 (Fed. Cir. 1990).

[224]*Halliburton Co. v. Schlumberger Tech. Corp.,* 925 F.2d 1435, 17 USPQ2d 1834 (Fed. Cir. 1991); *Consolidated Alum Corp. v. Foseco Int'l Ltd.,* 910 F.2d 804, 15 USPQ2d 1481 (Fed. Cir. 1990).

had the specific intent to accomplish an act that the applicant ought not to have performed, such as misleading or deceiving the PTO.[225]

No single factor or combination of factors can be said always to require an inference of intent to mislead; yet a patentee facing a high level of materiality and clear proof that it knew or should have known of that materiality can expect to find it difficult to establish subjective good faith sufficient to prevent the drawing of an inference of intent to mislead. A mere denial of intent to mislead will not suffice in such circumstances.[226] Considerations touching materiality and the applicant's knowledge thereof overlap those touching the applicant's intent because of inferences of intent that may be drawn from the former. Yet intent is a question of fact, and an applicant who knew or should have known of the art or information, and of its materiality, is not automatically precluded thereby from an effort to convince the fact finder that the failure to disclose was nonetheless not due to an intent to mislead the PTO—that, in light of all the circumstances of the case, an inference of intent to mislead is not warranted.[227]

The court suggests that a refusal to infer intent to mislead does not mean that a court is insisting upon a "smoking gun" or an outright confession.[228] Yet the decisions sometimes fail to infer intent to withhold very highly material art. In one case a failure to disclose an anticipatory reference was excused on the ground that both the inventor and his attorney believed, in complete good faith, that the reference neither anticipated nor rendered obvious the claims.[229] In another, a failure to disclose an anticipatory reference was excused because of a separate finding that the attorney did not intend to withhold the information.[230] And in another, failure to disclose an anticipatory reference was excused on the ground that the Japanese attorney who became aware of it was ignorant of the disclosure duty.[231]

---

[225]*Molins PLC v. Textron, Inc.*, 48 F.3d 1172, 33 USPQ2d 1823 (Fed. Cir. 1995).

[226]*FMC Corp. v. Manitowoc Co.*, 835 F.2d 1411, 5 USPQ2d 1112 (Fed. Cir. 1987). Proof of high materiality and that the applicant knew or should have known of that materiality makes it difficult to show good faith to overcome an inference of intent to mislead. *Semiconductor Energy Lab. Co. v. Samsung Elec. Co.*, 204 F.3d 1368, 54 USPQ2d 1001 (Fed. Cir. 2000).

[227]*FMC Corp. v. Manitowoc Co.*, 835 F.2d 1411, 5 USPQ2d 1112 (Fed. Cir. 1987). An intent to mislead cannot be inferred solely from a failure to present material prior art of which an applicant is aware. *Braun Inc. v. Dynamics Corp.*, 975 F.2d 815, 24 USPQ2d 1121 (Fed. Cir. 1992).

[228]*Paragon Podiatry Lab., Inc. v. KLM Labs., Inc.*, 984 F.2d 1182, 25 USPQ2d 1561, 1567 (Fed. Cir. 1993); *FMC Corp. v. Manitowoc Co.*, 835 F.2d 1411, 5 USPQ2d 1112 (Fed. Cir. 1987).

[229]*Allen Archery, Inc. v. Browning Mfg. Co.*, 819 F.2d 1087, 2 USPQ2d 1490 (Fed. Cir. 1987).

[230]*Allen Organ Co. v. Kimball Int'l, Inc.*, 839 F.2d 1556, 5 USPQ2d 1769 (Fed. Cir. 1988). This was a jury case, and the proper inquiry was said to be whether a reasonable jury could have found an absence of intent in the face of such a high degree of materiality.

[231]*In re Harita*, 847 F.2d 801, 6 USPQ2d 1930 (Fed. Cir. 1988). The court emphasized that there was no evidence of deliberate scheming, no misstatement, only silence, and prompt filing of a reissue application to cure the problem. See also *Demaco Corp. v. F. Von Langsdorff Lic., Ltd.*, 851 F.2d 1387, 7 USPQ2d 1222 (Fed. Cir. 1988), where the district court had found the requisite intent to conceal a reference, but the Federal Circuit reversed the finding as clearly erroneous. The American attorney had asked the German attorney for all references cited against the German counterpart. The German sent a list that included the missing

Intent is a factual matter that is rarely free from dispute.[232] Accordingly, cases should be evaluated on their individual facts. Certainly where none of the cited references showed a key element of a claimed process, and the withheld references teach that element, the applicant should have known that the withheld references would be important to the PTO, and intent is established.[233] The fact that an applicant is licensed under a withheld patent is an important factor in establishing intent.[234]

Gross negligence is supported by the fact that counsel used a withheld reference as art in a Japanese opposition and had also instructed a British associate to amend British counterpart claims to avoid the reference.[235] The fact that a withheld reference was the basis for rejection of foreign counterpart claims is important in establishing intent. Differences in foreign patent laws may be important in other contexts, but not in determining intent in an inequitable conduct case.[236] The court is mindful of the complexities of conducting a worldwide patent prosecution in a crowded art, attempting to represent one's client or company properly, and yet fulfill one's duty to various patent offices. But failure to cite to the PTO a material reference cited elsewhere in the world justifies a strong inference that the withholding was intentional.[237] However, the details of foreign prosecution are not an additional category of material information. Although international search reports may contain information material to patentability if they identify closer prior art than that which was before the U.S. examiner, it is the reference itself, not the information generated in prosecuting foreign counterparts, that is material to prosecution in the United States.[238]

The need for case-by-case evaluation of the intent factor continues. In one case the inventor failed to disclose his own prior device that was found to have been on sale. Although it was not an anticipation, it

---

reference but not a copy of it. The American attorney asked for a copy and the German said it was not necessary. Perhaps the result is explainable by the fact that the reference was listed in a German priority document that was filed with the PTO. Also, a concurring member of the panel felt that the reference was not, as the district court had found, material and that the majority should therefore not have reached the intent issue.

[232]*Albert v. Kevex Corp.*, 729 F.2d 757, 221 USPQ 202 (Fed. Cir. 1984).

[233]*J.P. Stevens & Co. v. Lex Tex Ltd.*, 747 F.2d 1553, 223 USPQ 1089 (Fed. Cir. 1984). Even where the withheld art is not material the patentee must use due care. A mistaken reissue declaration as to how and when the patentee became aware of such art was found to be grossly negligent, although insufficient to support a conclusion of inequitable conduct. *State Indus., Inc. v. Rheem Mfg. Co.*, 769 F.2d 762, 227 USPQ 375 (Fed. Cir. 1985).

[234]*J.P. Stevens & Co. v. Lex Tex Ltd.*, 747 F.2d 1553, 223 USPQ 1089 (Fed. Cir. 1984).

[235]*In re Jerabek*, 789 F.2d 886, 229 USPQ 530 (Fed. Cir. 1986).

[236]*J.P. Stevens & Co. v. Lex Tex Ltd.*, 747 F.2d 1553, 223 USPQ 1089 (Fed. Cir. 1984).

[237]*Molins PLC v. Textron, Inc.*, 48 F.3d 1172, 33 USPQ2d 1823 (Fed. Cir. 1995). Here the British patent agent focused on a reference several times during foreign counterpart prosecution and characterized it as the closest known art. Yet he did not cite it during the U.S. prosecution. The reference was found to disclose relevant features beyond those shown in the other prior art and was the basis of amendment and distinction in the foreign counterpart prosecution. The Federal Circuit affirmed a finding of intent to mislead under these circumstances.

[238]*ATD Corp. v. Lydall Inc.*, 159 F.3d 534, 48 USPQ2d 1321 (Fed. Cir. 1998).

taught features that were the focus of much PTO argument about distinctions over other prior art. The Federal Circuit confirmed an inference of culpable intent, largely on the basis that, by withholding his own prior art device, the inventor was able to make an argument that he could not otherwise have made. The fact that there was a close question of experimentation associated with the sale was unpersuasive; close cases should be resolved by disclosure, not unilaterally by the applicant.[239] In another case, a competitor's interfering patent issued after payment of the final fee. The company patent attorney, despite knowledge of the interfering patent, let his company's patent issue, and disclosed the interfering patent to the PTO in connection with a sibling application claiming related subject matter. The attorney's testimony was that he lacked sufficient time prior to issuance to make a determination as to "what the heck to do about it." Although the court felt that prudence might have dictated telling the PTO about the interfering patent immediately, there was no evidence of an intent to deceive by letting the patent issue.[240] An applicant's German agent learned, during European prosecution, that the alternative embodiment of one drawing figure, to which some U.S. claims were directed, was inoperative. At that time, the U.S. application had been allowed but not issued. The accused infringer argued that it was inequitable conduct to have permitted those claims to issue. The agent testified that it never occurred to him to inform the PTO prior to issue. The Federal Circuit affirmed the district court's finding of no intent.[241]

A failure to disclose a reference that was known to be material to a broader claim that had been canceled is gross negligence where a narrower claim is at least prima facie obvious over the withheld reference.[242] But the court has rejected the proposition that a failure to disclaim or reissue, and a continuation of the litigation after an

---

[239]*LaBounty Mfg., Inc. v. United States ITC,* 958 F.2d 1066, 22 USPQ2d 1025 (Fed. Cir. 1992). The decision whether or not to disclose sales made before the critical date should, where the case is close, be resolved by disclosure, not by the applicant's unilateral decision. Absent explanation, evidence of a knowing failure to disclose sales that bear all of the earmarks of commercialization reasonably supports an inference that the inventor's attorney intended to mislead the PTO. *Paragon Podiatry Lab., Inc. v. KLM Labs., Inc.,* 984 F.2d 1182, 25 USPQ2d 1561 (Fed. Cir. 1993).

[240]*Kimberly-Clark Corp. v. Procter & Gamble Distrib. Co.,* 973 F.2d 911, 23 USPQ2d 1921 (Fed. Cir. 1992).

[241]*Heidelberger Druckmaschinen AG v. Hantscho Comm. Prods., Inc.,* 21 F.3d 1068, 30 USPQ2d 1377 (Fed. Cir. 1994). It should be noted that the claims in question were disclaimed early in the litigation by the patent owner.

[242]*Driscoll v. Cebalo,* 731 F.2d 878, 221 USPQ 745 (Fed. Cir. 1984). The fact that the application was still in prosecution had no effect. An applicant who is guilty of gross negligence should not be exculpated simply because the PTO fortuitously has not yet reached the point of allowing the application. *Id.* A breach of duty early in the prosecution may render unenforceable all claims that eventually issue from the same or a related application. Where an attorney knows that prior art is material to the patentability of claims he or she has drafted, there is an obligation to disclose the art to the PTO notwithstanding the fact that none of the claims ultimately issued in the form in which he or she drafted them. A fortuitous rejection does not cure a breach of the duty of candor. *Fox Indus., Inc. v. Structural Preservation Sys., Inc.,* 922 F.2d 801, 17 USPQ2d 1579 (Fed. Cir. 1991). But see *Scripps Clinic & Res. Found. v. Genentech, Inc.,* 927 F.2d 1565, 18 USPQ2d 1001 (Fed. Cir. 1991).

error is brought to the patentee's intention, is proof that the error was intentional. A suggestion that patentees should abandon their suits, or disclaim or reissue, in response to every charge of inequitable conduct was viewed as nothing short of ridiculous. The right of patentees to resist such charges must not be chilled to extinction by fear that a failure to disclaim or reissue will be used against them as evidence that their original intent was deceitful. A requirement for disclaimer or reissue to avoid adverse inferences would merely encourage the proliferation of inequitable conduct charges.[243]

There is no doubt that subjective good faith can be a defense to a charge of inequitable conduct.[244] It is not inequitable conduct to omit telling the patent examiner information that the applicant in good faith believes is not material to patentability.[245] But a good faith belief that claims should be narrowly construed to avoid uncited prior art will not necessarily preclude a finding of recklessness or gross negligence in failing to cite that art. The references may be important in assessing patentability, whatever may be the applicant's view. Moreover, the applicant should have known that, during prosecution, claims are given their broadest reasonable interpretation; hence the applicant's narrow claim interpretation would have been unreasonable.[246]

Where the conduct is affirmative falsification rather than withholding information, intent is more easily established. The affirmative act of submitting an affidavit must be construed as having been intended to be relied upon.[247] And the state of mind of an affiant is not important where the natural consequences of his or her false affidavit are to mislead.[248] But an honest mistake in an affidavit does not constitute inequitable conduct.[249]

---

[243]*Kingsdown Med. Cons, Ltd. v. Hollister, Inc.,* 863 F.2d 867, 9 USPQ2d 1384, 1391 (Fed. Cir. 1988).

[244]*Allen Archery, Inc. v. Browning Mfg. Co.,* 819 F.2d 1087, 2 USPQ2d 1490 (Fed. Cir. 1987).

[245]*Allied Colloids, Inc. v. American Cyanamid Co.,* 64 F.3d 1570, 35 USPQ2d 1840 (Fed. Cir. 1995).

[246]*J.P. Stevens & Co. v. Lex Tex Ltd.,* 747 F.2d 1553, 223 USPQ 1089 (Fed. Cir. 1984).

[247]*Refac Int'l, Ltd. v. Lotus Dev. Corp.,* 81 F.3d 1576 (Fed. Cir. 1996).

[248]*Rohm & Haas Co. v. Crystal Chem. Co.,* 722 F.2d 1556, 220 USPQ 289 (Fed. Cir. 1983). That statements in an affidavit are true does not alone negate a finding of inequitable conduct, because truthful statements can be crafted in a misleading manner through intentional omission of particular relevant facts. *B.F. Goodrich Co. v. Aircraft Braking Sys. Corp.,* 72 F.3d 1577, 37 USPQ2d 1314 (Fed. Cir. 1996). In *Paragon Podiatry Lab., Inc. v. KLM Labs., Inc.,* 984 F.2d 1182, 25 USPQ2d 1561 (Fed. Cir. 1993), the applicant submitted Rule 132 affidavits and characterized the affiants as disinterested third parties. It turned out that each had owned stock in the applicant's company and that one or more had been paid consultants for the company. The court held this to be sufficient evidence of intent to mislead and affirmed a summary judgment of inequitable conduct. See also *Refac Int'l, Ltd. v. Lotus Dev. Corp.,* 81 F.3d 1576 (Fed. Cir. 1996), where an omission concerning the employment background of a Rule 132 declarant was likewise held to be improper. In *Litton Sys., Inc. v. Honeywell, Inc.,* 87 F.3d 1559, 39 USPQ2d 1321 (Fed. Cir. 1996), the court rejected as a basis for an inequitable conduct defense an argument that the applicant was not sufficiently forthcoming about an expert declarant's lack of qualifications and expertise with respect to some aspects of his declaration.

[249]*Allen Archery, Inc. v. Browning Mfg. Co.,* 819 F.2d 1087, 2 USPQ2d 1490 (Fed. Cir. 1987). So long as a patentee complies with PTO rules by describing prophetic examples in the present tense, there is no inequitable conduct. *Atlas Powder Co. v. E.I. du Pont & Co.,* 750

Ministerial acts are more vulnerable to errors that by definition result from inattention and not from the scienter involved in the more egregious acts of omission and commission that have been seen as reflecting the deceitful intent element of inequitable conduct. It is not possible to counter the "I didn't know" excuse with a "should have known" accountability approach when faced with a pure error, which by definition is done unintentionally.[250]

A holding of unenforceability based on the filing of a false oath requires that the oath be false, and made with knowledge of the falsity.[251] A patent may well be unenforceable for inequitable conduct when any coinventors are omitted with deceptive intention.[252] A petition to make an application special must contain a declaration that a prior art search was conducted, or that the applicant has a good knowledge of the pertinent prior art. A jury found that a prior art search meant a formal search by an attorney or paid searcher in the PTO files, or an equivalent computer search. The applicant had not made such a search, nor did it state that it had good personal knowledge of the prior art. The court held as a matter of law that this statement was material because it was made to secure expedited examination of the application.[253]

In a recent case involving an untranslated foreign language reference, the court postulated a new doctrine of "constructive withholding." By submitting an entire untranslated reference to the PTO along with a one-page, partial translation focusing on less material portions and a concise statement directed to those less material portions, the applicant left the examiner with the impression that the examiner did not need to conduct any further translation or investigation. Thus,

---

F.2d 1569, 224 USPQ 409 (Fed. Cir. 1984). In *Glaxo, Inc. v. Novopharm Ltd.*, 52 F.3d 1043, 34 USPQ2d 1565 (Fed. Cir. 1995), the trial court found that an affidavit submitted during prosecution was misleading and that the misstatement it contained was material. Nonetheless it concluded that an inference of intent to mislead was not warranted. Apparently the affiant implied that test data had been obtained in a particular way when it had not. But the affiant believed, and correctly as it turned out, that test data so obtained would support his conclusion. The Federal Circuit affirmed.

[250]*Kingsdown Med. Cons, Ltd. v. Hollister, Inc.*, 863 F.2d 867, 9 USPQ2d 1384 (Fed. Cir. 1988). This rationale seems more directed to lack of knowledge rather than lack of intent, however. The "ministerial" act in question involved incorrect identification of a claim as one that had been allowed in a parent application when in fact it had been rejected for indefiniteness.

[251]*Hebert v. Lisle Corp.*, 99 F.3d 1109, 40 USPQ2d 1611 (Fed. Cir. 1996). Here the court held that it was not a violation to file an oath without indicating that the invention had been used more than a year before the filing date, when the jury verdict was that such use did not invalidate the patent. In *Seiko Epson Corp. v. Nu-Kote Int'l Inc.*, 190 F.3d 1360, 52 USPQ2d 1011 (Fed. Cir. 1999), the district court held that a failure to submit native language declarations concerning the prior art rendered the patent per se unenforceable for inequitable conduct. The Federal Circuit rejected that view, explaining that technical violations of PTO procedures, absent fraud or intentional deception, are not inequitable conduct that would invalidate the patent. The courts have consistently rejected the notion of per se forfeiture based on nonfraudulent failure to comply with a rule of practice before the PTO.

[252]*Stark v. Advanced Magnetics, Inc.*, 119 F.3d 1551, 43 USPQ2d 1321 (Fed. Cir. 1997).

[253]*General Electro Music Corp. v. Samick Music Corp.*, 19 F.3d 1405, 30 USPQ2d 1149 (Fed. Cir. 1994). The jury rejected the applicant's attorney's denials of intent to mislead; the Federal Circuit held that the jury's assessment in this respect was entitled to great deference.

the applicant deliberately deceived the examiner into thinking that the reference was less relevant than it really was, and constructively withheld the reference from the PTO. Though the examiner is indeed presumed to have done his or her job correctly, there is no support in the law for a presumption that the examiner will understand foreign languages such as Japanese or will request a costly complete translation of every submitted foreign language document, particularly in the absence of any reason to do so. Consequently, while the examiner's initials require that it be presumed that he or she considered the reference, this presumption extends only to the examiner's consideration of the brief translated portion and the concise statement. Any contention that the PTO should not require applicants to translate all foreign references into English misses the critical point. The duty at issue in this case was the duty of candor, not a duty of translation. The duty of candor does not require that the applicant translate every foreign reference, but only that the applicant refrain from submitting partial translations and concise explanations that it knows will misdirect the examiner's attention from the reference's relevant teaching. Here, the desirability of the examiner securing a full translation was masked by the affirmatively misleading concise statement and one-page translation.[254]

It is standard practice for an applicant in an interference to obscure dates on documents and simply aver that the documents antedate the filing date of the adverse patent. The mere fact that this is done carries no weight as evidence of culpable intent.[255]

In a situation where the best mode was concealed and an inoperable mode disclosed instead, the court expressly equated a finding of intentional concealment under the mask of the fictitious mode with a finding of intent to deceive.[256]

---

[254]*Semiconductor Energy Lab. Co. v. Samsung Elec. Co.,* 204 F.3d 1368, 54 USPQ2d 1001 (Fed. Cir. 2000). The court found the untranslated portions noncumulative and material. As evidence of its good faith, the applicant urged that it had complied with PTO Rule 98 and MPEP §609A(3). In dismissing these arguments, the court commented that an applicant cannot overcome a finding of deceitful intent merely by showing that it did certain things properly. Though Rule 98 requires that the applicant provide any existing translation of a foreign reference, Rule 98 provides neither a safe harbor nor a shield against allegations of inequitable conduct. It merely provides a floor for required submissions of translations of foreign applications, not a ceiling; it is by no means an excuse or license for concealing material portions of a prior art reference. Similarly, though MPEP §609A(3) allows the applicant some discretion in the manner in which it phrases its concise explanation, it nowhere authorizes the applicant to intentionally omit altogether key teachings of the reference. If the concise statement requirement allowed applicants to selectively disclose what they know as long as what they selected for disclosure was accurate, applicants could easily mislead the examiner by explaining all but one of the relevant elements, thereby leaving the examiner with the impression that the reference did not anticipate, render obvious, or otherwise make unpatentable the claimed invention.

[255]*Baker Oil Tools, Inc. v. Geo Vann, Inc.,* 828 F.2d 1588, 4 USPQ2d 1210 (Fed. Cir. 1987).

[256]*Consolidated Alum Corp. v. Foseco Int'l Ltd.,* 910 F.2d 804, 15 USPQ2d 1481 (Fed. Cir. 1990). While in appropriate circumstances a failure to disclose the best mode may be so egregious as to constitute inequitable conduct, specific intent to deceive is not a required element of a best mode defense. *Graco, Inc. v. Binks Mfg. Co.,* 60 F.3d 785, 35 USPQ2d 1255 (Fed. Cir. 1995). Failure to meet a requirement of patentability, such as enablement, does not of itself

(i) Appellate Review

In *Kingsdown* the court held that inequitable conduct is an equitable issue and, as such, its resolution is committed to the sound discretion of the trial court and is reviewed under an abuse of discretion standard. Accordingly, the court will not simply substitute its judgment for that of the trial court in relation to inequitable conduct.[257] Presumably the clearly erroneous standard will continue to apply to the underlying factual questions of materiality, intent, and the like.[258]

The ultimate question of whether inequitable conduct occurred is equitable in nature, committed to the discretion of the trial court, and will not be overturned unless it is clear that the determination is based upon a jury's findings of fact that are unsupported by substantial evidence, or a misapplication or misinterpretation of applicable law, or that the ruling evidences a clear error of judgment on the part of the district court.[259]

The ultimate question of fraud is one of law, but the underlying elements are largely factual determinations.[260] Good faith, intent to deceive, scienter, and honest mistake are all questions of fact.[261] Intent is a factual determination particularly within the province of the trier of fact. A jury finding of absence of intent is subject to review on the same basis as other jury factual findings.[262]

Thus, materiality and intent are subject to the clearly erroneous standard of review, and the court must affirm findings on those questions unless it is left with a definite and firm conviction that error has occurred. But if the threshold of materiality and intent is crossed, the court must determine as a matter of law whether inequitable

---

establish the intent element of inequitable conduct. *Therma-Tru Corp. v. Peachtree Doors Inc.*, 44 F.3d 988, 33 USPQ2d 1274 (Fed. Cir. 1994).

[257]*Kingsdown Med. Cons, Ltd. v. Hollister, Inc.*, 863 F.2d 867, 9 USPQ2d 1384 (Fed. Cir. 1988). See also *Minnesota Min. & Mfg. Co. v. Johnson & Johnson Orthopaedics, Inc.*, 976 F.2d 1559, 24 USPQ2d 1321 (Fed. Cir. 1992); *Fox Indus., Inc. v. Structural Preservation Sys., Inc.*, 922 F.2d 801, 17 USPQ2d 1579 (Fed. Cir. 1991); *Hoffman-La Roche Inc. v. Lemmon Co.*, 906 F.2d 684, 15 USPQ2d 1363 (Fed. Cir. 1990).

[258]*Amgen, Inc. v. Chugai Pharm. Co.*, 927 F.2d 1200, 18 USPQ2d 1016 (Fed. Cir. 1991); *Halliburton Co. v. Schlumberger Tech. Corp.*, 925 F.2d 1435, 17 USPQ2d 1834 (Fed. Cir. 1991). See text accompanying notes 9:260–263.

[259]*Modine Mfg. Co. v. Allen Group, Inc.*, 917 F.2d 538, 16 USPQ2d 1622 (Fed. Cir. 1990). See also *General Electro Music Corp. v. Samick Music Corp.*, 19 F.3d 1405, 30 USPQ2d 1149 (Fed. Cir. 1994).

[260]*American Hoist & Derrick Co. v. Sowa & Sons, Inc.*, 725 F.2d 1350, 220 USPQ 763 (Fed. Cir. 1984).

[261]*Kangaroos U.S.A., Inc. v. Caldor, Inc.*, 778 F.2d 1571, 228 USPQ 32 (Fed. Cir. 1985).

[262]*Modine Mfg. Co. v. Allen Group, Inc.*, 917 F.2d 538, 16 USPQ2d 1622 (Fed. Cir. 1990); *Allen Organ Co. v. Kimball Int'l, Inc.*, 839 F.2d 1556, 5 USPQ2d 1769 (Fed. Cir. 1988). A trial judge has broad discretion in trial management, and therefore may permit the jury to decide intent while reserving to itself the ultimate question of inequitable conduct. In that case its ruling would be reviewed on the abuse of discretion standard. *Tol-O-Matic, Inc. v. Proma Produckt-und Mktg. GmbH*, 945 F.2d 1546, 20 USPQ2d 1332 (Fed. Cir. 1991).

conduct has occurred.[263] When the pertinent facts related to inequitable conduct are undisputed, the court of appeals need not remand for the trial court to make findings and conclusions but may resolve the issue.[264] The court has served notice that one's legal duty of candor to the PTO will not be judged by the least common denominator.[265]

(j) Effect of Fraud or Inequitable Conduct

Issues of inequitable conduct are most difficult both for trial courts and reviewing appellate courts. One who has engaged in inequitable conduct has inflicted damage on the patent examining system, obtaining a statutory period of exclusivity by improper means, and on the public, which must face an unlawfully granted patent. Loss of one's patent and damage to reputation are justified penalties for such conduct.[266] Fraud or inequitable conduct does not render a patent invalid; rather, the patent becomes unenforceable. Although the practical effect may be the same, the legal concepts are quite different.[267] On the other hand, a decision holding the patent invalid does not moot an inequitable conduct issue where the accused infringer is seeking attorney fees as a consequence of the inequitable conduct.[268] Inequitable conduct with respect to less than all the claims renders the entire patent unenforceable.[269] And although some conduct that renders a patent unenforceable can be purged so that the patent later

---

[263]*Specialty Composites v. Cabot Corp.*, 845 F.2d 981, 6 USPQ2d 1601 (Fed. Cir. 1988); *J.P. Stevens & Co. v. Lex Tex Ltd.*, 747 F.2d 1553, 223 USPQ 1089 (Fed. Cir. 1984). See also *Carella v. Starlight Archery & Pro Line Co.*, 804 F.2d 135, 231 USPQ 644 (Fed. Cir. 1986); *In re Jerabek*, 789 F.2d 886, 229 USPQ 530 (Fed. Cir. 1986). Thus the court can uphold a finding of gross negligence, but reverse a legal conclusion of inequitable conduct. *State Indus., Inc. v. Rheem Mfg. Co.*, 769 F.2d 762, 227 USPQ 375 (Fed. Cir. 1985). Where the district court remarked that it was not "implying improper motives," this statement was taken as an indication that it had not made a finding of intent, and its summary judgment of unenforceability for inequitable conduct therefore had to be reversed. *Scripps Clinic & Res. Found. v. Genentech, Inc.*, 927 F.2d 1565, 18 USPQ2d 1001 (Fed. Cir. 1991).

[264]*Smithkline Diagnostics, Inc. v. Helena Labs. Corp.*, 859 F.2d 878, 8 USPQ2d 1468 (Fed. Cir. 1988).

[265]*Argus Chem. Corp. v. Fibre Glass-Evercoat Co.*, 759 F.2d 10, 225 USPQ 1100 (Fed. Cir. 1985). Thus, an attorney's testimony on the practice followed by other attorneys is irrelevant. *Id.*

[266]*Molins PLC v. Textron, Inc.*, 48 F.3d 1172, 33 USPQ2d 1823 (Fed. Cir. 1995).

[267]*Minnesota Min. & Mfg. Co. v. Johnson & Johnson Orthopaedics, Inc.*, 976 F.2d 1559, 24 USPQ2d 1321 (Fed. Cir. 1992). See also *Korody-Colyer Corp. v. General Motors Corp.*, 760 F.2d 1293, 225 USPQ 1099 (Fed. Cir. 1985). Where two of three patents in suit are expired, with one of those invalid and the other not infringed, and the unexpired patent is also not infringed, the question of unenforceability of any of them is moot, even though inequitable conduct itself may be relevant to a nonmoot attorney fees question, and "fraud" might be relevant to further proceedings on an antitrust count. *FMC Corp. v. Hennessy Indus., Inc.*, 836 F.2d 521, 5 USPQ2d 1272 (Fed. Cir. 1987).

[268]*Paragon Podiatry Lab., Inc. v. KLM Labs., Inc.*, 984 F.2d 1182, 25 USPQ2d 1561 (Fed. Cir. 1993).

[269]*Kingsdown Med. Cons, Ltd. v. Hollister, Inc.*, 863 F.2d 867, 9 USPQ2d 1384 (Fed. Cir. 1988); *Lummus Indus., Inc. v. D.M.& E. Corp.*, 862 F.2d 267, 8 USPQ2d 1983 (Fed. Cir. 1988); *J.P. Stevens & Co. v. Lex Tex Ltd.*, 747 F.2d 1553, 223 USPQ 1089 (Fed. Cir. 1984). Failure to disclose prior art designs that were not merely cumulative will render a design patent

becomes enforceable, fraud is incurable and results in permanent unenforceability.[270]

With respect to inequitable conduct, it is appropriate to give the same extent of unenforceability to a reissue patent as to an original patent. The same level of misconduct is required in both instances. Thus, as in the case of an original patent, if inequitable conduct is found during the prosecution of a reissue application, all the claims of the reissue patent are rendered unenforceable, even those carried over without change from the original patent.[271] Reissue is not available to obtain new claims and thereby rehabilitate a patent obtained by inequitable conduct.[272]

Inequitable conduct may render a patent unenforceable, but this differs from the "fraud" required to support a *"Walker Process"* type antitrust claim.[273]

Fraud in the procurement of one patent does not necessarily render a related patent unenforceable; typically the fraud in order to have that effect must be committed upon the court itself.[274] However, under the *Keystone Driller* doctrine,[275] unenforceability of one patent may, under certain circumstances, impact the enforceability of other patents owned by the wrongdoer. The Federal Circuit successfully avoided grappling directly with this problem in one case by vacating a moot judgment of unenforceability.[276] More recently, however, it has specifically rejected the suggestion that *Keystone Driller* should be limited to fraud on the court, and has held that inequitable conduct with respect to one patent may so permeate the others that all are unenforceable.[277]

A finding of inequitable conduct in the prosecution of a patent in a chain of applications does not necessarily render another patent in

---

unenforceable. *Elk Corp. of Dallas v. GAF Bldg. Mat'ls Corp.*, 168 F.3d 28, 49 USPQ2d 1853 (Fed. Cir. 1999).

[270]*Rohm & Haas Co. v. Crystal Chem. Co.*, 722 F.2d 1556, 220 USPQ 289 (Fed. Cir. 1983). Fraud can be cured during prosecution. The applicant must expressly advise the PTO of the fraud and the actual facts and must establish patentability based on the actual facts. The cure must be demonstrated, like the defense of fraud itself, by clear, unequivocal, and convincing evidence. *Id.*

[271]*Hewlett-Packard Co. v. Bausch & Lomb, Inc.*, 882 F.2d 1556, 11 USPQ2d 1750 (Fed. Cir. 1989).

[272]*Hewlett-Packard Co. v. Bausch & Lomb, Inc.*, 882 F.2d 1556, 11 USPQ2d 1750 (Fed. Cir. 1989).

[273]*Hewlett-Packard Co. v. Bausch & Lomb, Inc.*, 882 F.2d 1556, 11 USPQ2d 1750 (Fed. Cir. 1989); *FMC Corp. v. Hennessy Indus., Inc.*, 836 F.2d 521, 5 USPQ2d 1272 (Fed. Cir. 1987). See §11.3 below.

[274]*SSIH Equip. S.A. v. United States ITC*, 713 F.2d 746, 218 USPQ 678 (Fed. Cir. 1983). Inequitable conduct with respect to a patent that was not asserted is not relevant to inequitable conduct respecting patents that were asserted. *FMC Corp. v. Hennessy Indus., Inc.*, 836 F.2d 521, 5 USPQ2d 1272 (Fed. Cir. 1987). The defense of unclean hands applies only with respect to the right in suit. *Bio-Technology Gen'l Corp. v. Genentech, Inc.*, 80 F.3d 1553, 38 USPQ2d 1321 (Fed. Cir. 1996).

[275]*Keystone Driller Co. v. General Excavator Co.*, 290 U.S. 240 (1933).

[276]*Texas Instr., Inc. v. United States ITC*, 851 F.2d 342, 7 USPQ2d 1509 (Fed. Cir. 1988).

[277]*Consolidated Alum Corp. v. Foseco Int'l Ltd.*, 910 F.2d 804, 15 USPQ2d 1481 (Fed. Cir. 1990).

the chain unenforceable. The court recognizes that its earlier decisions clearly stand for the proposition that cancellation or amendment of a claim tainted by inequitable conduct will not excuse the patentee's intentional failure to disclose material references, and that inequitable conduct with respect to one claim renders the entire patent unenforceable. However, where the claims are subsequently separated from those tainted by inequitable conduct through a divisional application, and where the issued claims have no relation to the omitted prior art, the patent issued from the divisional application will not also be unenforceable due to inequitable conduct committed in the parent application.[278]

The court has held that a state tort action for abuse of process cannot be invoked as a remedy for inequitable or other unsavory conduct of parties to proceedings in the PTO. The patent grant is within the exclusive purview of federal law. Although certain traditional state law concerns may properly be raised when patent rights are litigated, the conduct of litigants in administrative proceedings before the PTO is not remediable by state action in tort, at least unless it be shown that the entire federal agency action is a "sham" within the meaning of the *Noerr/Pennington* doctrine. A contrary result would in effect create another forum for litigating issues arising from the administrative process, or a new system of judicial overview of actions before the PTO. This would not harmonize with the traditional judicial disfavor of collateral attack, under the common law, on proceedings before the PTO. Thus, the federal administrative process of examining and issuing patents, including proceedings before the PTO's boards, is not subject to collateral review in terms of the common law tort of abuse of process. The PTO procedures themselves provide a remedy for any malfeasance on the part of litigants, and an additional state action would be an inappropriate collateral intrusion on the regulatory procedures of the PTO under the guise of a complaint sounding in tort and would be contrary to Congress's preemptive regulation in the area of patent law.[279]

Obtaining a patent through inequitable conduct does not violate §43(a) of the Lanham Act. The established remedy for inequitable conduct is unenforceability of the patent. If a trial court considers that the case is an exceptional one, which is often found when the patent has been improperly procured, attorney fees can be awarded. Moreover, enforcement of a patent procured by fraud on the PTO may be violative of §2 of the Sherman Act provided the other elements necessary to a §2 case are present. Thus there are adequate remedies

---

[278]*Baxter Int'l Inc. v. McGaw Inc.*, 149 F.3d 1321, 47 USPQ2d 1225 (Fed. Cir. 1998).

[279]*Abbott Labs. v. Brennan*, 952 F.2d 1346, 21 USPQ2d 1192 (Fed. Cir. 1992). But see *Dow Chem. Co. v. Exxon Corp.*, 139 F.3d 1470, 46 USPQ2d 1120 (Fed. Cir. 1998), where the court held that state courts, or federal courts adjudicating state law claims, may hear a state law tort claim for intentional interference with actual and prospective contractual relations that implicates the patent law issue of inequitable conduct.

to deal with inequitable conduct when it is found. Resort to federal unfair competition law is not one of them.[280]

Antitrust claims based upon fraud in the procurement of a patent are discussed in §11.3(d).

§9.6 Summary Judgment

Patent litigation frequently is complex, long, and difficult. Parties have available in patent cases, however, discovery procedures, evidentiary rules, and partial or complete summary judgment, to narrow the issues for trial. A party must either use these procedures or meet its burden of proof at trial.[281] Summary judgment is governed by Rule 56, FRCP. Under Rule 56(c), summary judgment is proper "if the pleadings, depositions, answers to interrogatories, and admissions on file, together with the affidavits, if any, show that there is no genuine issue as to any material fact and that the moving party is entitled to a judgment as a matter of law." If there is a real dispute about a material fact or factual inference, summary judgment is inappropriate; the factual dispute should be reserved for trial.[282] Rule 56(d) provides that if the court is unable to grant all the relief requested and determines that a trial is necessary, it shall if practicable specify the facts that appear without substantial controversy.

(a) General Principles

The primary principles governing summary judgment are very well settled. A summary judgment is not proper when material issues of fact requiring trial to resolve are present. Evidence and inferences must be viewed and drawn in a light most favorable to the nonmoving party. The moving party bears the burden of showing absence of a material fact issue, and doubt will be resolved against that party.[283] A factual question is material if a reasonable jury could return a

---

[280]*Pro-Mold & Tool Co. v. Great Lakes Plastics, Inc.,* 75 F.3d 1568, 37 USPQ2d 1626 (Fed. Cir. 1996).

[281]*Rohm & Haas Co. v. Brotech Corp.,* 127 F.3d 1089, 44 USPQ2d 1459 (Fed. Cir. 1997).

[282]*Meyers v. Brooks Shoe Inc.,* 912 F.2d 1459, 16 USPQ2d 1055 (Fed. Cir. 1990).

[283]*A.B. Chance Co. v. RTE Corp.,* 854 F.2d 1307, 7 USPQ2d 1881 (Fed. Cir. 1988); *Hi-Life Prods., Inc. v. American Nat'l Water-Mattress Corp.,* 842 F.2d 323, 6 USPQ2d 1132 (Fed. Cir. 1988); *Armco, Inc. v. Cyclops Corp.,* 791 F.2d 147, 229 USPQ 721 (Fed. Cir. 1986); *Hodosh v. Block Drug Co.,* 786 F.2d 1136, 229 USPQ 182 (Fed. Cir. 1986); *SRI Int'l v. Matsushita Elec. Corp.,* 775 F.2d 1107, 227 USPQ 577 (Fed. Cir. 1985); *Palumbo v. Don-Joy Co.,* 762 F.2d 969, 226 USPQ 5 (Fed. Cir. 1985); *Lemelson v. TRW, Inc.,* 760 F.2d 1254, 225 USPQ 697 (Fed. Cir. 1985); *Martin v. Barber,* 755 F.2d 1564, 225 USPQ 233 (Fed. Cir. 1985). To sustain a motion for summary judgment the court must determine that there is no triable issue of material fact, because on the version most favorable to the party opposing the motion, that party still cannot prevail. *Burlington Indus., Inc. v. Dayco Corp.,* 849 F.2d 1418, 7 USPQ2d 1158 (Fed. Cir. 1988).

verdict for the nonmoving party based at least in part on its determination of the factual question.[284] A material fact is one that may affect the decision, whereby the finding of that fact is relevant and necessary to the proceedings. A genuine dispute is shown to exist if sufficient evidence is presented such that a reasonable fact finder could decide the question in favor of the nonmoving party. The evidence submitted by the nonmovant in opposition to the motion is to be believed, and all justifiable inferences are to be drawn in its favor. While the nonmoving party is not required to present its entire case in response to a motion for summary judgment, to defeat the motion the nonmovant must present sufficient evidence to show an evidentiary conflict as to the material fact in dispute, with due consideration to the evidentiary burdens.[285] And where the moving party has the burden of proof on a claim or defense raised in a summary judgment motion, it must show that the undisputed facts establish every element of the claim or defense.[286] Thus the inquiry involved in a ruling on a motion for summary judgment necessarily implicates the substantive evidentiary standard of proof that would apply at the trial on the merits.[287]

When the moving party does not have the burden of proof on the issue that is the subject of the summary judgment motion, the movant nonetheless bears the initial burden of coming forward with sufficient evidence to demonstrate that there is no material issue of fact that would preclude summary judgment, and that it is entitled to judgment as a matter of law. If the movant meets its initial burden, the burden of coming forward shifts to the party opposing the motion. The opposing party does not, at this stage, have the burden of establishing that it is entitled to judgment in its favor; it need only show either that the movant did not establish that it is entitled to judgment on undisputed facts or on the opposer's version of the facts, or that there are material issues of fact that require resolution at trial. On an issue for which the moving party does not have the burden of proof at trial, the moving party may meet its initial burden on the motion either by providing evidence that negates an essential element of the opposing party's case, or by showing that the evidence on file (such as pleadings, depositions, and admissions) establishes no material issue of fact and that the opposer will not be able to prove an essential element of its case.[288]

---

[284]*Scripps Clinic & Res. Found. v. Genentech, Inc.*, 927 F.2d 1565, 18 USPQ2d 1001 (Fed. Cir. 1991).

[285]*Opryland USA Inc. v. Great Am. Music Show, Inc.*, 970 F.2d 847, 23 USPQ2d 1471 (Fed. Cir. 1992). See also *Tone Bros., Inc. v. Sysco Corp.*, 28 F.3d 1192, 31 USPQ2d 1321 (Fed. Cir. 1994); *Keystone Ret. Wall Sys., Inc. v. Westrock, Inc.*, 997 F.2d 1444, 27 USPQ2d 1297 (Fed. Cir. 1993). A material fact is one whose finding is necessary to the proceedings. *Festo Corp. v. Shoketsu KKK Co.*, 72 F.3d 857, 37 USPQ2d 1163 (Fed. Cir. 1995).

[286]*Meyers v. Brooks Shoe Inc.*, 912 F.2d 1459, 16 USPQ2d 1055 (Fed. Cir. 1990).

[287]*Baker Oil Tools, Inc. v. Geo Vann, Inc.*, 828 F.2d 1588, 4 USPQ2d 1210 (Fed. Cir. 1987).

[288]*Vivid Tech. Inc. v. American Sci. & Eng'g Inc.*, 200 F.3d 795, 53 USPQ2d 1289 (Fed. Cir. 1999).

Where both parties file dispositive motions, and neither challenges nor denies the material facts relied upon by the other, the trial court may properly enter judgment on the issue of law, based upon the material facts contained in the motions.[289] But the fact that both parties move for summary judgment does not mean that the court must grant judgment as a matter of law for one side or the other; summary judgment in favor of either party is not proper if disputes remain as to material facts.[290] Summary judgment is authorized where it is quite clear what the truth is.[291]

Countering the motion. The party opposing the motion is required merely to point to an evidentiary conflict created on the record.[292] Nonetheless, it must show an evidentiary conflict; mere denials or conclusory statements are of course insufficient.[293] If the evidence is merely colorable, or is not significantly probative, summary judgment may be granted.[294] Where the movant has supported its summary judgment motion with affidavits or other evidence that, unopposed, would establish its right to judgment, the nonmovant may not rest upon general denials in its pleadings or otherwise but must proffer countering evidence sufficient to create a genuine factual dispute. A dispute is genuine only if, on the entirety of the record, a reasonable jury could resolve a factual matter in favor of the nonmovant.[295] There can be no genuine issue as to any material fact where the nonmoving party's proof is deficient in meeting an essential part of the applicable legal standard, since such failure renders all other facts immaterial.[296] An affirmative defense must be raised in response to a summary judgment motion, or it is waived.[297]

[289]*Heinemann v. United States,* 796 F.2d 451, 230 USPQ 430 (Fed. Cir. 1986).

[290]*Scripps Clinic & Res. Found. v. Genentech, Inc.,* 927 F.2d 1565, 18 USPQ2d 1001 (Fed. Cir. 1991); *Prineville Sawmill Co. v. United States,* 859 F.2d 905 (Fed. Cir. 1988); *Mingus Constructors, Inc. v. United States,* 812 F.2d 1387 (Fed. Cir. 1987). Separate motions for summary judgment from each party are not necessarily an admission that no material facts remain at issue. *Massey v. Del Labs., Inc.,* 118 F.3d 1568, 43 USPQ2d 1367 (Fed. Cir. 1997).

[291]*Hodosh v. Block Drug Co.,* 786 F.2d 1136, 229 USPQ 182 (Fed. Cir. 1986); *Interpart Corp. v. Italia,* 777 F.2d 678, 228 USPQ 124 (Fed. Cir. 1985).

[292]*Armco, Inc. v. Cyclops Corp.,* 791 F.2d 147, 229 USPQ 721 (Fed. Cir. 1986). Such issues of material fact should not be resolved conclusively in the nonmovant's favor, however.

[293]*Armco, Inc. v. Cyclops Corp.,* 791 F.2d 147, 229 USPQ 721 (Fed. Cir. 1986); *Hodosh v. Block Drug Co.,* 786 F.2d 1136, 229 USPQ 182 (Fed. Cir. 1986); *Interpart Corp. v. Italia,* 777 F.2d 678, 228 USPQ 124 (Fed. Cir. 1985); *SRI Int'l v. Matsushita Elec. Corp.,* 775 F.2d 1107, 227 USPQ 577 (Fed. Cir. 1985). There must be a showing of sufficient information to require a judge or jury to resolve the conflicting different versions of the truth through trial. *Harrington Mfg. Co. v. Powell Mfg. Co.,* 815 F.2d 1478, 2 USPQ2d 1364 (Fed Cir. 1986).

[294]*Scripps Clinic & Res. Found. v. Genentech, Inc.,* 927 F.2d 1565, 18 USPQ2d 1001 (Fed. Cir. 1991).

[295]*Sweats Fashions, Inc. v. Pannill Knitting Co.,* 833 F.2d 1560, 4 USPQ2d 1793 (Fed. Cir. 1987). Summary judgment may be granted when no reasonable jury could return a verdict for the nonmoving party. *Oddzon Prods., Inc. v. Just Toys, Inc.,* 122 F.3d 1396, 43 USPQ2d 1641 (Fed. Cir. 1997).

[296]*London v. Carson Pirie Scott & Co.,* 946 F.2d 1534, 20 USPQ2d 1456 (Fed. Cir. 1991). See also *Dairyland Power Coop. v. United States,* 16 F.3d 1197 (Fed. Cir. 1994).

[297]*Diversey Lever Inc. v. Ecolab Inc.,* 191 F.3d 1350, 52 USPQ2d 1062 (Fed. Cir. 1999).

A motion for summary judgment may be opposed by any of the kinds of evidentiary materials listed in Rule 56(c), except the mere pleadings themselves.[298] The nonmovant may not rest on its conclusory pleadings but must set out, usually in an affidavit by one with knowledge of specific facts, what specific evidence could be offered at trial. A nonmovant runs the risk of a grant of summary judgment by failing to disclose the evidentiary basis for its claim. Summary judgment need not be denied merely to satisfy a litigant's speculative hope of finding some evidence that might tend to support a complaint.[299] The truth of a disputed material fact cannot be established on attorney statement alone.[300] Where objective evidence is required to establish a claim, summary judgment will not be defeated by evidence of subjective motivation.[301]

Mere conclusory statements and denials do not take on dignity by placing them in affidavit form to counter a motion for summary judgment.[302] Thus, an expert's unsupported conclusion on the ultimate issue of infringement is insufficient to raise a genuine issue of material fact. Although such testimony of an expert witness may be proper during trial when the opposing party can challenge the factual basis of the expert's opinion during cross-examination, the affidavit of an expert submitted in opposition to a motion for summary judgment must do more by setting forth specific facts showing that there is a genuine issue for trial. Thus, the expert must set forth the factual foundation for the opinion—such as a statement regarding the structure found in the accused product—in sufficient detail for the court to determine whether that factual foundation would support a finding of infringement under the claim construction adopted by the court, with all reasonable inferences drawn in favor of the nonmovant.[303] Under Rule 56(e), evidence presented in an affidavit must be evidence that would be admissible if presented at trial through the testimony of the affiant as a sworn witness.[304]

A party cannot create an issue of fact by supplying an affidavit contradicting its prior deposition testimony, without explaining the contradiction or attempting to resolve the disparity. Where a party has been examined extensively at deposition and then seeks to create an issue of fact through a later, inconsistent declaration, it has the

---

[298]*Finish Eng'g Co. v. Zerpa Indus., Inc.*, 806 F.2d 1041, 1 USPQ2d 1114 (Fed. Cir. 1986).

[299]*Pure Gold, Inc. v. Syntex (U.S.A.), Inc.*, 739 F.2d 624, 222 USPQ 741 (Fed. Cir. 1984).

[300]*Vivid Tech. Inc. v. American Sci. & Eng'g Inc.*, 200 F.3d 795, 53 USPQ2d 1289 (Fed. Cir. 1999).

[301]*Carroll Touch, Inc. v. Electro Mechanical Sys., Inc.*, 3 F.3d 404, 27 USPQ2d 1836 (Fed. Cir. 1993).

[302]*Sweats Fashions, Inc. v. Pannill Knitting Co.*, 833 F.2d 1560, 4 USPQ2d 1793 (Fed. Cir. 1987).

[303]*Arthur A. Collins Inc. v. Northern Telecom Ltd.*, 216 F.3d 1042, 55 USPQ2d 1143 (Fed. Cir. 2000).

[304]*Scosche Indus., Inc. v. Visor Gear, Inc.*, 121 F.3d 675, 43 USPQ2d 1659 (Fed. Cir. 1997). An affidavit asserted that the affiant was told by person A that person B had made a statement to A. The affidavit assertion was for the purpose of proving that the statement had been made

duty to provide a satisfactory explanation for the discrepancy at the time the declaration is filed. To allow the party to preclude summary judgment simply by contradicting its own prior statements would seriously impair the utility of Rule 56. Thus, a trial court may properly disregard such a declaration in assessing the existence of a genuine issue of fact.[305]

At the same time, where a party does not respond to the movant's list of "undisputed facts" with affidavits or other evidence, it cannot upon appeal attack a summary judgment on that basis.[306] The party opposing summary judgment need not, however, prove the contrary but only must come forward with evidence showing that such proof is possible.[307]

On the other hand, if the evidentiary matter in support of a motion for summary judgment does not establish the absence of a genuine issue, summary judgment must be denied even if no opposing evidentiary matter is presented.[308] The burden of the movant is not to produce evidence showing the absence of a genuine issue of material fact, but simply to "show"—that is, point out to the district court— that there is an absence of evidence to support the nonmoving party's case.[309] On the other hand, the nonmovant must present sufficient evidence for a jury to return a verdict in its favor on an issue it asserts is disputed.[310]

Rule 56(f) considerations. Rule 56(e) states that a party opposing summary judgment must set forth specific facts showing that there is a genuine issue for trial. However, this requirement in turn is qualified by Rule 56(f), which provides that summary judgment may be refused where the nonmoving party has not had the opportunity to discover information that is essential to its opposition. The safeguard to which Rule 56(f) is directed is that a nonmovant cannot be deprived of the discovery needed to place at issue material factual questions in opposition to the motion. Rule 56(f) requires the nonmoving party to state, by affidavit, reasons why discovery is needed to support its opposition.[311] Summary judgment is inappropriate unless

---

by B to A. This would be hearsay even if the affiant were testifying at trial and is thus inappropriate evidence in a summary judgment proceeding. *Id.*

[305]*Sinskey v. Pharmacia Ophthalmics, Inc.,* 982 F.2d 494, 25 USPQ2d 1290 (Fed. Cir. 1992).

[306]*Jamesbury Corp. v. Litton Indus. Prods., Inc.,* 839 F.2d 1544, 5 USPQ2d 1779 (Fed. Cir. 1988). See also *Petrolite Corp. v. Baker Hughes Inc.,* 96 F.3d 1423, 40 USPQ2d 1201 (Fed. Cir. 1996).

[307]*D.L. Auld Co. v. Chroma Graphics Corp.,* 714 F.2d 1144, 219 USPQ 13 (Fed. Cir. 1983). It is difficult to establish the existence of a fact issue by attempting to contradict admissions, however. *Id.*

[308]*Broomall Indus. v. Data Design Logic Sys., Inc.,* 786 F.2d 401, 229 USPQ 38 (Fed. Cir. 1986).

[309]*Dairyland Power Coop. v. United States,* 16 F.3d 1197 (Fed. Cir. 1994); *Conroy v. Reebok Int'l,* 14 F.3d 1570, 29 USPQ2d 1373 (Fed. Cir. 1994); *Sweats Fashions, Inc. v. Pannill Knitting Co.,* 833 F.2d 1560, 4 USPQ2d 1793 (Fed. Cir. 1987).

[310]*A.B. Chance Co. v. RTE Corp.,* 854 F.2d 1307, 7 USPQ2d 1881 (Fed. Cir. 1988). When there is substantial evidence to support a factual conclusion, summary judgment to the contrary

a tribunal permits the parties adequate time for discovery. If a party submits a proper Rule 56(f) affidavit indicating that it has had no opportunity to gather evidence through discovery on a pertinent subject, a grant of summary judgment will be vacated and remanded.[312]

For example, the grant of summary judgment of noninfringement, with respect to accused devices whose components or methods are not readily observable and are in dispute, requires sufficient discovery to assure that the issue has been fully and fairly resolved. Rule 56(f) serves the dual purpose of safeguarding against too hasty a grant of summary judgment, while requiring that parties who seek time for additional discovery have not been dilatory. Such parties must make an authoritative and timely proffer, show good cause for the failure to have discovered these essential facts sooner, present a plausible basis for the belief that there are discoverable facts sufficient to raise a genuine and material issue, and show that the facts are discoverable within a reasonable amount of time. When a movant satisfies these requirements a strong presumption arises in favor of relief.[313] However, a party may not simply assert in its brief that discovery was necessary and thereby overturn summary judgment when it failed to comply with the requirement of Rule 56(f) to set out reasons for the need for discovery in an affidavit.[314] Moreover, a party cannot forestall summary judgment by arguing that it has not had an opportunity to complete its discovery when it has not pursued its discovery rights with vigor.[315] A trial court's denial of a motion for further discovery under Rule 56(f) will not be deemed an abuse of discretion if there is no reason to believe that it will lead to the denial of a pending motion for summary judgment. The moving party must demonstrate specifically how postponement of a ruling on the motion would enable

---

is improper. *Lifescan, Inc. v. Home Diagnostics, Inc.,* 76 F.3d 358, 37 USPQ2d 1595 (Fed. Cir. 1996).

[311]*Opryland USA Inc. v. Great Am. Music Show, Inc.,* 970 F.2d 847, 23 USPQ2d 1471 (Fed. Cir. 1992). A litigant's right to discovery is fully protected by Rule 56(f), FRCP, which allows a court to refuse summary judgment if a litigant shows by affidavit that additional discovery is necessary to uncover facts essential to justify its position. *Avia Group Int'l, Inc. v. L.A. Gear Calif., Inc.,* 853 F.2d 1557, 7 USPQ2d 1548 (Fed. Cir. 1988).

[312]*Dunkin' Donuts of Am., Inc. v. Metallurgical Exoproducts Corp.,* 840 F.2d 917, 6 USPQ2d 1026 (Fed. Cir. 1988).

[313]*Vivid Tech. Inc. v. American Sci. & Eng'g Inc.,* 200 F.3d 795, 53 USPQ2d 1289 (Fed. Cir. 1999). When a party who opposes a Rule 56(f) motion has control of the requested information, this factor weighs heavily in favor of relief under Rule 56(f). *Id.*

[314]*Sweats Fashions, Inc. v. Pannill Knitting Co.,* 833 F.2d 1560, 4 USPQ2d 1793 (Fed. Cir. 1987). A litigant's complaint that it needed discovery will not be heard on appeal when discovery was precluded by its own failure to seek Rule 56(f) protection. *Avia Group Int'l, Inc. v. L.A. Gear Calif., Inc.,* 853 F.2d 1557, 7 USPQ2d 1548 (Fed. Cir. 1988). The rule was specifically intended to deal with the problem of premature motions for summary judgment. *Spectra Corp. v. Lutz,* 839 F.2d 1579, 5 USPQ2d 1867 (Fed. Cir. 1988). It was therefore no abuse of discretion to refuse to delay ruling on a motion for summary judgment where the opposing party had already conducted 11 months of discovery and had filed no Rule 56(f) affidavit. Summary judgment need not be denied merely to satisfy a litigant's speculative hope of finding some evidence through discovery that might tend to support a complaint. *Id.*

[315]*Scosche Indus., Inc. v. Visor Gear, Inc.,* 121 F.3d 675, 43 USPQ2d 1659 (Fed. Cir. 1997).

it, by discovery or other means, to rebut the movant's showing of the absence of a genuine issue of fact. It may not simply rely on vague assertions that additional discovery will produced needed, but unspecified, facts. The rule does not require clairvoyance on the part of the moving party, but the movant is required to state with some precision the materials it hopes to obtain with further discovery, and exactly how it expects those materials would help it in opposing summary judgment.[316] Entitlement to discovery under Rule 56(f), FRCP, is decided according to the law of the regional circuit.[317]

Purpose and cautions. The purpose of summary judgment is not to deprive a litigant of a trial, but to avoid an unnecessary trial when only one outcome can ensue.[318] Summary judgment is thus an important means of conserving judicial and other resources, but it must be carefully employed, for an improvident grant may deny a party a chance to prove a worthy case, and an improvident denial may force on a party and the court an unnecessary trial.[319]

There is no right to a jury trial where there are no issues of fact to be tried by a jury, and a proper summary judgment therefore does not violate the Seventh Amendment.[320] Ample due process safeguards are available in the summary judgment procedures of Rule 56. A litigant is not "deprived" of a trial upon grant of summary judgment where the evidence of record at the time of the motion supports its

---

[316]*Simmons Oil Corp. v. Tesoro Pet. Corp.*, 86 F.3d 1138 (Fed. Cir. 1996). Rule 56(e) requires an affiant to set forth admissible evidence establishing a genuine issue of material fact requiring trial. Rule 56(f) requires an affiant to state reasons why he or she cannot present by affidavit facts essential to justify the opposition to the motion for summary judgment. This requires more than a simple assertion that discovery is necessary. If all one had to do to obtain a grant of a Rule 56(f) motion were to allege possession by the movant of "certain information" and "other evidence," every summary judgment decision would have to be delayed while the nonmovant fishes in the movant's files. The request for discovery must be focused. It must show what facts are sought and how they are reasonably expected to create a genuine issue. *Keebler Co. v. Murray Bakery Prods.*, 866 F.2d 1386, 9 USPQ2d 1736 (Fed. Cir. 1989).

[317]*Vivid Tech. Inc. v. American Sci. & Eng'g Inc.*, 200 F.3d 795, 53 USPQ2d 1289, 1297 (Fed. Cir. 1999).

[318]*Vivid Tech. Inc. v. American Sci. & Eng'g Inc.*, 200 F.3d 795, 53 USPQ2d 1289 (Fed. Cir. 1999). In any type of lawsuit the purpose of summary judgment is to avoid an unnecessary trial. *Continental Can Co. v. Monsanto Co.*, 948 F.2d 1264, 20 USPQ2d 1746 (Fed. Cir. 1991); *Lemelson v. TRW, Inc.*, 760 F.2d 1254, 225 USPQ 697 (Fed. Cir. 1985). Rule 56 is a vehicle of convenience to parties and courts, for use when the circumstances warrant. *Glaverbel S.A. v. Northlake Mkt'g & Supp., Inc.*, 45 F.3d 1550, 33 USPQ2d 1496 (Fed. Cir. 1995).

[319]*Lemelson v. TRW, Inc.*, 760 F.2d 1254, 225 USPQ 697 (Fed. Cir. 1985); *D.L. Auld Co. v. Chroma Graphics Corp.*, 714 F.2d 1144, 219 USPQ 13 (Fed. Cir. 1983).

[320]*Constant v. Advanced Micro-Devices, Inc.*, 848 F.2d 1560, 7 USPQ2d 1057 (Fed. Cir. 1988). Cf. *Paragon Podiatry Lab., Inc. v. KLM Labs., Inc.*, 984 F.2d 1182, 25 USPQ2d 1561 (Fed. Cir. 1993). However, a motion for summary judgment before trial is not a substitute for a motion for judgment as a matter of law at the close of all evidence. Thus, a failure to raise an issue by motion for judgment as a matter of law means that the sufficiency of the evidence underlying a district court's denial of JNOV on that issue is unreviewable on appeal, even where the issue was the subject of a motion for summary judgment. *Wang Labs., Inc. v. Toshiba Corp.*, 993 F.2d 858, 26 USPQ2d 1767 (Fed. Cir. 1993).

opponent on all key issues and the nonmovant fails to put in sufficient evidence to create a triable issue of any material fact.[321]

The fact-intensive nature of certain cases argues against the precipitous grant of summary judgment. Because the remedy can be harsh in its finality, its application must be accompanied by careful concern for the entire record and the relevant law.[322] Though speedy and inexpensive, summary judgment is nonetheless a lethal weapon, and courts must be mindful of its aims and targets and beware of overkill in its use.[323] Summary judgment may deny the nonmovant its day (i.e., a trial) in court, and experience has shown that a trial often establishes facts and inferences not gleanable from papers submitted pretrial.[324] Summary proceedings on a documentary record do not always result in a full and fair adjudication.[325] In short, summary judgment is a drastic remedy.[326]

The Federal Circuit interprets *Anderson v. Liberty Lobby, Inc.*[327] as having expanded the group of situations in which summary judgment is appropriate. Specifically, a nonmovant must do more than merely raise some doubt as to the existence of a fact; evidence must be forthcoming from the nonmovant that would be sufficient to require submission to the jury of the dispute over the fact.[328] Summary judgment procedure is properly regarded not as a disfavored procedural shortcut, but rather as an integral part of the Federal Rules as a whole, which are designed to secure the just, speedy, and inexpensive determination of every action.[329]

The Federal Rules do not contemplate that a court may dispose of a cause by summary judgment when the basis for the judgment

---

[321]*Avia Group Int'l, Inc. v. L.A. Gear Calif., Inc.*, 853 F.2d 1557, 7 USPQ2d 1548 (Fed. Cir. 1988).

[322]*Yuba Goldfields, Inc. v. United States*, 723 F.2d 884 (Fed. Cir. 1983).

[323]*Kangaroos U.S.A., Inc. v. Caldor, Inc.*, 778 F.2d 1571, 228 USPQ 32 (Fed. Cir. 1985); *SRI Int'l v. Matsushita Elec. Corp.*, 775 F.2d 1107, 227 USPQ 577 (Fed. Cir. 1985).

[324]*SRI Int'l v. Matsushita Elec. Corp.*, 775 F.2d 1107, 227 USPQ 577 (Fed. Cir. 1985).

[325]*Interconnect Planning Corp. v. Feil*, 774 F.2d 1132, 227 USPQ 543 (Fed. Cir. 1985). To the extent that apparent inconsistencies among several affidavits submitted in support of a motion for summary judgment raised questions of credibility and weight, whether of witness or of interpretation of scientific data, those questions were improperly resolved on summary judgment. Trial by document is an inadequate substitute for trial with witnesses, who are subject to examination and cross-examination in the presence of the decisionmaker. *Scripps Clinic & Res. Found. v. Genentech, Inc.*, 927 F.2d 1565, 18 USPQ2d 1001 (Fed. Cir. 1991). In a summary judgment proceeding, a court may consider exhibits that were made a part of a deposition record. *Glaverbel S.A. v. Northlake Mkt'g & Supp., Inc.*, 45 F.3d 1550, 33 USPQ2d 1496 (Fed. Cir. 1995).

[326]*Selva & Sons v. Nina Footwear, Inc.*, 705 F.2d 1316, 217 USPQ 641 (Fed. Cir. 1983).

[327]477 U.S. 242 (1986).

[328]*Scripps Clinic & Res. Found. v. Genentech, Inc.*, 927 F.2d 1565, 18 USPQ2d 1001 (Fed. Cir. 1991); *Avia Group Int'l, Inc. v. L.A. Gear Calif., Inc.*, 853 F.2d 1557, 7 USPQ2d 1548 (Fed. Cir. 1988). Summary judgment may be granted when no reasonable jury could return a verdict for the nonmoving party. *Nike, Inc. v. Wolverine World Wide, Inc.*, 43 F.3d 644, 33 USPQ2d 1038 (Fed. Cir. 1994).

[329]*Avia Group Int'l, Inc. v. L.A. Gear Calif., Inc.*, 853 F.2d 1557, 7 USPQ2d 1548 (Fed. Cir. 1988); *Sweats Fashions, Inc. v. Pannill Knitting Co.*, 833 F.2d 1560, 4 USPQ2d 1793 (Fed. Cir. 1987).

was not raised by the movant with sufficient precision for the nonmovant to respond.[330] Also, a party has a right to know what procedural theory is being employed, and should not be taken by surprise. Where the nonmovant expects only threshold matters to be decided, it is error to then decide the merits without opportunity for discovery and other preparation.[331] But must a responding party bring a cross-motion for summary judgment in order to have the matter decided on the merits? Not necessarily. A district court has the power to enter summary judgment sua sponte, so long as the losing party is on notice that it must come forward with all its evidence.[332] There is nothing inherently improper about the district court entering summary judgment for a nonmovant. In many cases, where the factual record has been well developed before the summary judgment stage, the grant of summary judgment to the nonmovant may well be the most efficient manner to decide a case.[333]

(b) Specific Issues

Patentability. Summary judgment is as appropriate in a patent case as any other where there is no genuine issue of material fact and the movant is entitled to judgment as a matter of law.[334] But while it may facilitate the disposition of legally meritless suits, when

---

[330]*Kangaroos U.S.A., Inc. v. Caldor, Inc.,* 778 F.2d 1571, 228 USPQ 32 (Fed. Cir. 1985); *Cooper v. Ford Motor Co.,* 748 F.2d 677, 223 USPQ 1286 (Fed. Cir. 1984). Summary judgment cannot be used to determine causes that are not before the court by pleading or otherwise. *Flowdata, Inc. v. Cotton,* 57 F.3d 1046 (Fed. Cir. 1995).

[331]*Selva & Sons v. Nina Footwear, Inc.,* 705 F.2d 1316, 217 USPQ 641 (Fed. Cir. 1983). If a lower tribunal is to convert a motion under Rule 12(b)(6), FRCP, to one for summary judgment, it must do so in a way to permit the opposer to respond. See also *Advanced Cardiovascular Sys., Inc. v. Scimed Life Sys., Inc.,* 988 F.2d 1157, 26 USPQ2d 1038 (Fed. Cir. 1993).

[332]*International Visual Corp. v. Crown Metal Mfg. Co.,* 991 F.2d 768, 26 USPQ2d 1588 (Fed. Cir. 1993).

[333]*Massey v. Del Labs., Inc.,* 118 F.3d 1568, 43 USPQ2d 1367 (Fed. Cir. 1997). Defendant moved for summary judgment of invalidity based on anticipation but did not move on obviousness. The district court found no anticipation but went ahead and held the patent invalid for obviousness. The Federal Circuit concluded that the patentee had not had a full and fair opportunity to ventilate the issues. *Id.* Where the patentee moved for summary judgment of infringement and the defendant moved for summary judgment of invalidity but not noninfringement, the Federal Circuit saw nothing improper in the district court's entry of summary judgment of noninfringement. *International Visual Corp. v. Crown Metal Mfg. Co.,* 991 F.2d 768, 26 USPQ2d 1588 (Fed. Cir. 1993). In *National Presto Indus., Inc. v. West Bend Co.,* 76 F.3d 1185, 37 USPQ2d 1685 (Fed. Cir. 1996), the accused infringer moved for summary judgment of invalidity but the patentee did not cross-move. Nonetheless, the Federal Circuit approved a sua sponte grant of partial summary judgment that the patent was not invalid.

[334]*C.R. Bard, Inc. v. Advanced Card. Sys., Inc.,* 911 F.2d 670, 15 USPQ2d 1540 (Fed. Cir. 1990); *Howes v. Medical Components, Inc.,* 814 F.2d 638, 2 USPQ2d 1271 (Fed. Cir. 1987); *Moeller v. Ionetics, Inc.,* 794 F.2d 653, 229 USPQ 992 (Fed. Cir. 1986); *Hodosh v. Block Drug Co.,* 786 F.2d 1136, 229 USPQ 182 (Fed. Cir. 1986); *SRI Int'l v. Matsushita Elec. Corp.,* 775 F.2d 1107, 227 USPQ 577 (Fed. Cir. 1985); *Brenner v. United States,* 773 F.2d 306, 227 USPQ 159 (Fed. Cir. 1985); *Cooper v. Ford Motor Co.,* 748 F.2d 677, 223 USPQ 1286 (Fed. Cir. 1984); *Barmag Barmer Masch. AG v. Murata Mach., Ltd.,* 731 F.2d 831, 221 USPQ 561 (Fed. Cir. 1984). It is no longer debatable that the issues in a patent case are subject to summary judgment. *Avia Group Int'l, Inc. v. L.A. Gear Calif., Inc.,* 853 F.2d 1557, 7 USPQ2d 1548 (Fed. Cir. 1988).

summary judgment is improvidently granted the effect is to prolong litigation and increase its burdens. This is of particular concern in patent disputes, where the patent property is a wasting asset and justice is ill served by delay in final resolution.[335]

Materiality is viewed in light of the legal standard to be applied.[336] If the issue is obviousness, the first question is whether there exists any genuine issue as to any fact material to the *Graham v. Deere* inquiries.[337] A patentee who moves for summary judgment that the patent is not invalid need not introduce any evidence due to the presumption of validity.[338] If the accused infringer is able, in its motion for summary judgment, to establish a prima facie case for overcoming the presumption of validity, then the burden shifts and the nonmovant patentee has the duty of submitting evidence setting forth specific facts raising a genuine issue for trial.[339] But it is improper, on motion for summary judgment of invalidity for obviousness, to draw inferences against the patentee on questions of the knowledge of one of ordinary skill in the art or secondary considerations.[340] All that is required is a showing of a question of material fact sufficient to raise a genuine issue. Thus where one skilled in the art makes such statements that are not merely conclusory, but are facts set forth in sufficient detail by a knowledgeable declarant, summary judgment is improper.[341] But it is incumbent on the trial judge to look beyond mere denials or arguments with respect to scope and content of the art, differences, level of skill, and so forth. Certainly summary judgment can be granted in the face of an expert affidavit that expresses no

---

[335]*Continental Can Co. v. Monsanto Co.*, 948 F.2d 1264, 20 USPQ2d 1746 (Fed. Cir. 1991).

[336]*Barmag Barmer Masch. AG v. Murata Mach., Ltd.*, 731 F.2d 831, 221 USPQ 561 (Fed. Cir. 1984). The substantive law will identify which facts are material. *Becton Dickinson & Co. v. C.R. Bard, Inc.*, 922 F.2d 792, 17 USPQ2d 1097 (Fed. Cir. 1990).

[337]*Cable Elec. Prods., Inc. v. Genmark, Inc.*, 770 F.2d 1015, 226 USPQ 881 (Fed. Cir. 1985); *Cooper v. Ford Motor Co.*, 748 F.2d 677, 223 USPQ 1286 (Fed. Cir. 1984). In *Greenwood v. Hattori Seiko Co.*, 900 F.2d 238, 14 USPQ2d 1474 (Fed. Cir. 1990), the patentee sued for infringement and a reexamination request was filed. The examiner rejected the claims but the patentee antedated the references and the examiner issued a reexamination certificate. On summary judgment, the trial court held the patentee's showing of prior invention was defective, and purported to "restore" the reexamination examiner's rejection. The Federal Circuit, naturally enough, vacated and remanded on the ground that adoption of the examiner's initial position disregards the presumption of validity and fails to comport with the required *Graham v. Deere* analysis.

[338]*Massey v. Del Labs., Inc.*, 118 F.3d 1568, 43 USPQ2d 1367 (Fed. Cir. 1997).

[339]*Cable Elec. Prods., Inc. v. Genmark, Inc.*, 770 F.2d 1015, 226 USPQ 881 (Fed. Cir. 1985).

[340]*Rockwell Int'l Corp. v. United States*, 147 F.3d 1358, 47 USPQ2d 1027 (Fed. Cir. 1998).

[341]*Palumbo v. Don-Joy Co.*, 762 F.2d 969, 226 USPQ 5 (Fed. Cir. 1985). The determination whether prior art is analogous involves some factual issues concerning whether the reference is within the field of the inventor's endeavor or reasonably pertinent to the problem with which the invention was involved. Where the PTO examiner states that a particular piece of prior art is nonanalogous, that is sufficient to raise a genuine issue of material fact and defeat summary judgment. *Finish Eng'g Co. v. Zerpa Indus., Inc.*, 806 F.2d 1041, 1 USPQ2d 1114 (Fed. Cir. 1986). See also *Hodosh v. Block Drug Co.*, 786 F.2d 1136, 229 USPQ 182 (Fed. Cir. 1986) (summary judgment inappropriate where questions of material fact remain with respect to the meaning of various terms in ancient Ming Dynasty Chinese writings).

more than a conclusory opinion that ignores rather than conflicts with the evidence of record.[342]

Even conflicting opinions of experts on the obviousness issue do not necessarily raise a genuine issue of material fact sufficient to defeat a motion for summary judgment.[343] Moreover, where the references and invention in issue are easily understandable, there is no need for expert explanatory testimony.[344] Indeed, the Federal Circuit found no error in a holding by the trial court, on summary judgment, that the subject matter of the patent and the prior art were so easily understandable that no factual determination of the level of ordinary skill in the art was necessary.[345]

Whether a change is "material" for purposes of anticipation by public use is a factual question that cannot be resolved against the patentee on summary judgment.[346] For a summary determination to be proper, there must be no genuine dispute whether the limitations of a claimed invention are disclosed, either explicitly or inherently, by an allegedly anticipating prior art reference.[347] The patentee may have a special obligation to come forward with evidence in response to a prima facie showing of use or sale.[348]

---

[342]*Union Carbide Corp. v. American Can Co.*, 724 F.2d 1567, 220 USPQ 584 (Fed. Cir. 1984).

[343]*Avia Group Int'l, Inc. v. L.A. Gear Calif., Inc.*, 853 F.2d 1557, 7 USPQ2d 1548 (Fed. Cir. 1988); *Cable Elec. Prods., Inc. v. Genmark, Inc.*, 770 F.2d 1015, 226 USPQ 881 (Fed. Cir. 1985); *Petersen Mfg. Co. v. Central Purchasing, Inc.*, 740 F.2d 1541, 222 USPQ 562 (Fed. Cir. 1984) (design patent). In one very interesting case the defendant had relied upon the testimony of the plaintiff's expert witness in connection with the defendant's successful motion for partial summary judgment. Upon later trial of the remaining issues, the defendant attacked the qualifications of the plaintiff's expert, the plaintiff agreed, and the expert was disqualified. On appeal, the plaintiff sought to overcome the partial summary judgment by arguing that there was a genuine issue as to the qualifications of the expert. The court held that the defendant's attack did not amount to an admission under Rule 56(c) and characterized the plaintiff's strategy as grotesque and in poor grace. *Glaros v. H.H. Robertson Co.*, 797 F.2d 1564, 230 USPQ 393 (Fed. Cir. 1986).

[344]*Union Carbide Corp. v. American Can Co.*, 724 F.2d 1567, 220 USPQ 584 (Fed. Cir. 1984). The court observed that a trial would produce more argument but no more enlightenment. This may be so, but we respectfully caution against any rule that encourages trial courts to make factual determinations simply on the basis that the invention is easily understandable. Cf. *Petersen Mfg. Co. v. Central Purchasing, Inc.*, 740 F.2d 1541, 222 USPQ 562 (Fed. Cir. 1984).

[345]*Chore-Time Equip., Inc. v. Cumberland Corp.*, 713 F.2d 774, 218 USPQ 673 (Fed. Cir. 1983). Again, such holdings could be dangerous. The very conclusion that the patent and prior art are easily understandable might well be a hotly disputed factual issue.

[346]*Baker Oil Tools, Inc. v. Geo Vann, Inc.*, 828 F.2d 1588, 4 USPQ2d 1210 (Fed. Cir. 1987).

[347]*Hazani v. United States ITC*, 126 F.3d 1473, 44 USPQ2d 1358 (Fed. Cir. 1997).

[348]Once an alleged infringer has presented facts sufficient to establish a prima facie case of public use, it falls to the patent owner to come forward with some evidence to the contrary sufficient to raise a genuine issue of material fact. *Sinskey v. Pharmacia Ophthalmics, Inc.*, 982 F.2d 494, 25 USPQ2d 1290 (Fed. Cir. 1992). An inventor's subjective intent as to whether a public use was commercially motivated is immaterial when objective evidence points otherwise; thus the matter can be resolved on summary judgment. *Harrington Mfg. Co. v. Powell Mfg. Co.*, 815 F.2d 1478, 2 USPQ2d 1364 (Fed Cir. 1986). An averment that an inventor had an intent to experiment in making a sale does not in itself raise a genuine issue of material fact. *Paragon Podiatry Lab., Inc. v. KLM Labs., Inc.*, 984 F.2d 1182, 25 USPQ2d 1561 (Fed. Cir. 1993).

Infringement. The Federal Circuit has indicated that a motion for summary judgment on the issue of infringement must be approached with great care by the district court.[349] Indeed, because infringement itself is a fact issue, a district court must approach a motion for summary judgment of infringement or noninfringement with a care proportioned to the likelihood of its being inappropriate.[350] Nonetheless, the court has also recognized that it is at least conceivable that comparison of a properly interpreted claim with a stipulated or uncontested description of an accused device or process would reflect such an absence of material fact issues as to warrant summary judgment of infringement or noninfringement.[351]

Noninfringement under the doctrine of equivalents is also a matter that can be resolved by summary judgment.[352] Whether a claim is infringed under the doctrine of equivalents may be decided on summary judgment if no reasonable jury could determine that the limitation and the element at issue are equivalent.[353] This standard sets a high hurdle that the Federal Circuit does not lightly attempt to surmount.[354]

---

[349]*Cole v. Kimberly-Clark Corp.*, 102 F.3d 524, 41 USPQ2d 1001 (Fed. Cir. 1996); *Palumbo v. Don-Joy Co.*, 762 F.2d 969, 226 USPQ 5 (Fed. Cir. 1985). Summary judgment may, however, properly be decided as a matter of law when no genuine issue of material fact exists and no expert testimony is required to explain the nature of the patented invention or the accused product or to assist in their comparison. *Amhil Enters. Ltd. v. Wawa, Inc.*, 81 F.3d 1554, 38 USPQ2d 1471 (Fed. Cir. 1996).

[350]*Chemical Eng'g Corp. v. Essef Indus., Inc.*, 795 F.2d 1565, 230 USPQ 385 (Fed. Cir. 1986); *SRI Int'l v. Matsushita Elec. Corp.*, 775 F.2d 1107, 227 USPQ 577 (Fed. Cir. 1985); *D.M.I., Inc. v. Deere & Co.*, 755 F.2d 1570, 225 USPQ 236 (Fed. Cir. 1985).

[351]*D.M.I., Inc. v. Deere & Co.*, 755 F.2d 1570, 225 USPQ 236 (Fed. Cir. 1985). See also *Chemical Eng'g Corp. v. Essef Indus., Inc.*, 795 F.2d 1565, 230 USPQ 385 (Fed. Cir. 1986); *Porter v. Farmers Supply Serv., Inc.*, 790 F.2d 882, 229 USPQ 814 (Fed. Cir. 1986); *Palumbo v. Don-Joy Co.*, 762 F.2d 969, 226 USPQ 5 (Fed. Cir. 1985).

[352]*Brenner v. United States*, 773 F.2d 306, 227 USPQ 159 (Fed. Cir. 1985). A summary judgment of noninfringement will be upheld where the claims do not read on the accused structure to establish literal infringement and a prosecution history estoppel makes clear that no actual infringement under the doctrine of equivalents can be found. *Townsend Eng'r Co. v. HiTec Co.*, 829 F.2d 1086, 4 USPQ2d 1136 (Fed. Cir. 1987). It is incorrect to suppose that a nonmovant has no duty to submit evidence with respect to infringement under the doctrine of equivalents in a summary judgment situation. A movant may prevail by pointing out the absence of evidence to support the nonmoving party's case. *Intellicall, Inc. v. Phonometrics, Inc.*, 952 F.2d 1384, 21 USPQ2d 1383 (Fed. Cir. 1992). In *General Elec. Co. v. Nintendo Co.*, 179 F.3d 1350, 50 USPQ2d 1910 (Fed. Cir. 1999), the court affirmed a summary judgment of noninfringement because the patentee did not present sufficient evidence for a reasonable jury to find infringement under the doctrine of equivalents. In *Wiener v. NEC Elec., Inc.*, 102 F.3d 534, 41 USPQ2d 1023 (Fed. Cir. 1996), the court rejected an expert declaration submitted in connection with a summary judgment motion because its statements about equivalency were too conclusory to constitute substantial evidence.

[353]*Zelinski v. Brunswick Corp.*, 185 F.3d 1311, 51 USPQ2d 1590 (Fed. Cir. 1999). In this case, the only evidence submitted by the patent owner was the conclusory statement by a patent attorney expert to the effect that "because there is literal infringement, there is infringement under the doctrine of equivalents." The court found this failed to provide the necessary evidentiary basis to support a claim that there was a genuine issue of material fact on equivalence. The court also rejected the argument that the trial judge's characterization of the statement as "conclusory" constituted impermissible fact finding. The trial judge was simply trying to determine whether the expert's statement raised a genuine issue for trial.

[354]*Vehicular Tech. Corp. v. Titan Wheel Int'l Inc.*, 212 F.3d 1377, 54 USPQ2d 1841 (Fed. Cir. 2000).

Because prosecution history estoppel is a purely legal issue, an affidavit testifying as to what a reasonable competitor would conclude from the prosecution history cannot create a genuine issue of material fact so as to bar summary judgment.[355]

One instance of actual confusion may not be sufficiently probative to create a genuine dispute of fact over design patent infringement, especially where the affidavit evidencing the confusion does not indicate whether it was caused by those aspects of the design that distinguish it from the prior art.[356]

Claim interpretation. A dispute as to the legal issue of claim interpretation does not preclude summary judgment. Where the facts underlying the issue of infringement are undisputed, the function of applying claims to the accused device is the province of the district court.[357] Indeed, it is quite clear that the determination of the scope of patent claims is a question of law, and a dispute respecting that legal issue does not preclude summary judgment.[358] However, underlying factual disputes may arise that preclude summary judgment. If complex scientific principles are involved or expert testimony is needed to explain a disputed term, for example, then an underlying factual question may arise that makes summary judgment improper. On the other hand, if the terms do not have a special meaning to those skilled in the art, the court can properly construe the claims as a matter of law without resort to expert evidence.[359] Where the parties do not dispute any relevant facts regarding the accused product, but disagree over possible claim interpretations, the question of literal infringement collapses into claim construction and is amenable to summary judgment.[360]

An affidavit consisting of opinions about the meaning and application of various phrases and provisions of a claim does not necessarily create factual disputes that preclude the grant of a summary judgment of infringement.[361] The court has specifically rejected the contention that a disagreement over the meaning of a term in a claim ipso facto raises an issue of fact that would preclude summary judgment. A disputed issue of fact may arise in connection with interpretation of a term in a claim if there is a genuine evidentiary conflict created by

---

[355]*Bayer AG v. . Elan Pharm. Res. Corp.*, 212 F.3d 1241, 54 USPQ2d 1710 (Fed. Cir. 2000).

[356]*Winner Int'l Corp. v. Wolo Mfg. Corp.*, 905 F.2d 375, 15 USPQ2d 1076 (Fed. Cir. 1990).

[357]*Martin v. Barber*, 755 F.2d 1564, 225 USPQ 233 (Fed. Cir. 1985).

[358]*Becton Dickinson & Co. v. C.R. Bard, Inc.*, 922 F.2d 792, 17 USPQ2d 1097 (Fed. Cir. 1990); *George v. Honda Motor Co.*, 802 F.2d 432, 231 USPQ 382 (Fed. Cir. 1986); *Molinaro v. Fannon/Courier Corp.*, 745 F.2d 651, 223 USPQ 706 (Fed. Cir. 1984).

[359]*Howes v. Medical Components, Inc.*, 814 F.2d 638, 2 USPQ2d 1271 (Fed. Cir. 1987).

[360]*General Mills, Inc. v. Hunt-Wesson, Inc.*, 103 F.3d 978, 41 USPQ2d 1440 (Fed. Cir. 1997); *Athletic Alternatives, Inc. v. Prince Mfg., Inc.*, 73 F.3d 1573, 37 USPQ2d 1365 (Fed. Cir. 1996).

[361]*Townsend Eng'r Co. v. HiTec Co.*, 829 F.2d 1086, 4 USPQ2d 1136 (Fed. Cir. 1987).

the underlying probative evidence pertinent to the claim's interpretation. However, without such an evidentiary conflict, claim interpretation may be resolved as an issue of law by the court on summary judgment.[362] Evidence extrinsic to the patent and prosecution history, such as expert testimony, cannot be relied on to change the meaning of the claims when that meaning is made clear by those documents. Thus, such evidence cannot create a genuine issue of material fact precluding summary judgment because it is, under the circumstances, entitled to no weight.[363]

The question of substantial identity between claims, being a matter of claim interpretation, is a question of law and can be resolved by summary judgment.[364] But a summary judgment based upon a conclusion that reissue claims were broader than the originals may implicate underlying factual issues of claim construction that require a trial.[365] The legal adequacy of a patentee's reason for requesting reissue is a question of law. If the facts material to that question are not in dispute, the matter can be resolved by summary judgment.[366]

Other issues. The court has said that antitrust relevant market definition is both highly factual and important and is therefore not a suitable subject for determination on summary judgment.[367] Likewise, summary procedures should be used sparingly where motive and intent play leading roles. A summary judgment of fraud or inequitable conduct, reached while denying the person so accused the opportunity to be heard on the issue, is a draconian result.[368] A summary judgment of inequitable conduct would therefore require an undisputed showing of materiality and intent by clear and convincing evidence.[369] Nonetheless, the court appears willing to affirm a summary judgment of inequitable conduct in an appropriate case, particularly where the

---

[362]*Johnston v. IVAC Corp.*, 885 F.2d 1574, 12 USPQ2d 1382 (Fed. Cir. 1989). See also *Wolverine World Wide, Inc. v. Nike, Inc.*, 38 F.3d 1192, 32 USPQ2d 1338 (Fed. Cir. 1994). Where a disputed term in a claim would be understood to have its ordinary meaning by one of ordinary skill in the art, extrinsic evidence that the inventor may have subjectively intended a different meaning does not preclude summary judgment. *Intellicall, Inc. v. Phonometrics, Inc.*, 952 F.2d 1384, 21 USPQ2d 1383 (Fed. Cir. 1992).

[363]*Southwall Tech., Inc. v. Cardinal IG Co.*, 54 F.3d 1570, 34 USPQ2d 1673 (Fed. Cir. 1995).

[364]*Interconnect Planning Corp. v. Feil*, 774 F.2d 1132, 227 USPQ 543 (Fed. Cir. 1985).

[365]*Tillotson, Ltd. v. Walbro Corp.*, 831 F.2d 1033, 4 USPQ2d 1450 (Fed. Cir. 1987).

[366]*Scripps Clinic & Res. Found. v. Genentech, Inc.*, 927 F.2d 1565, 18 USPQ2d 1001 (Fed. Cir. 1991).

[367]*Albert v. Kevex Corp.*, 741 F.2d 396, 223 USPQ 1 (Fed. Cir. 1984). With all respect, it is difficult to see why the importance of an issue should have any bearing on the appropriateness of summary judgment.

[368]*Kangaroos U.S.A., Inc. v. Caldor, Inc.*, 778 F.2d 1571, 228 USPQ 32 (Fed. Cir. 1985). Again, it is difficult to see how a summary judgment proceeding constitutes denial of an opportunity to be heard.

[369]*Baker Oil Tools, Inc. v. Geo Vann, Inc.*, 828 F.2d 1588, 4 USPQ2d 1210 (Fed. Cir. 1987). In vacating a summary judgment of unenforceability based upon inequitable conduct, the court said "rather than anyone being a crook, it is surely a permissible inference that both the applicant's attorney and the examiner were alike confused, not being possessed of the analytical vision of hindsight. This may be a mistaken inference, but on summary judgment it cannot be

sole issue is the correctness of the district court's conclusion that there was no genuine issue respecting intent to deceive.[370]

Disputes as to foreign language terms may preclude summary judgment.[371] Contract interpretation is a matter of law and thus is amenable to decision on summary judgment.[372] The court has also in effect allowed summary judgment on the issue of declaratory judgment jurisdiction, but perhaps improperly so.[373]

(c) Form and Review of Summary Judgment

It is not required that a district judge render findings of fact and conclusions of law when a complete summary judgment is entered, and the judgment cannot be reversed on that ground alone.[374] In granting summary judgment the district court need not function as an arbiter among differing versions of every factual reality for which evidentiary support has been presented.[375] Factfinding is an inappropriate exercise on summary judgment, at either the trial level or the appellate level.[376] Indeed, it might per se imply the impropriety of a grant of summary judgment.[377] But while there is no requirement that a trial judge make findings of fact in granting a motion for summary judgment, findings are often extremely helpful to a reviewing court. It is certainly helpful to have a statement of the undisputed facts.[378] If the trial court's underlying holdings would otherwise be

---

rejected out of hand in favor of a less plausible sinister interpretation." *Burlington Indus., Inc. v. Dayco Corp.*, 849 F.2d 1418, 7 USPQ2d 1158 (Fed. Cir. 1988).

[370]*Paragon Podiatry Lab., Inc. v. KLM Labs., Inc.*, 984 F.2d 1182, 25 USPQ2d 1561 (Fed. Cir. 1993). If a bare declaration of lack of intent to mislead (where a false, material affidavit is submitted to the PTO) were to raise a genuine issue, summary judgment would be precluded in all cases except where the patent owner makes no response at all. However, such a declaration amounts to no more than would a conclusory denial in a pleading, which, under Rule 56, is insufficient to create a genuine issue. The declaration must at least state facts supporting a plausible justification or excuse for the misrepresentation. *Id.*

[371]*Hodosh v. Block Drug Co.*, 786 F.2d 1136, 229 USPQ 182 (Fed. Cir. 1986).

[372]*Government Sys. Advisors, Inc. v. United States*, 847 F.2d 811 (Fed. Cir. 1988).

[373]*Goodyear Tire & Rubber Co. v. Releasomers, Inc.*, 824 F.2d 953, 3 USPQ2d 1310 (Fed. Cir. 1987). See text accompanying notes 8:32–34.

[374]*Petersen Mfg. Co. v. Central Purchasing, Inc.*, 740 F.2d 1541, 222 USPQ 562 (Fed. Cir. 1984). It manifests incorrect expectations to fault a district court for failure to find particular facts in granting summary judgment. *Cable Elec. Prods., Inc. v. Genmark, Inc.*, 770 F.2d 1015, 226 USPQ 881 (Fed. Cir. 1985).

[375]*Cable Elec. Prods., Inc. v. Genmark, Inc.*, 770 F.2d 1015, 226 USPQ 881 (Fed. Cir. 1985).

[376]*Lemelson v. TRW, Inc.*, 760 F.2d 1254, 225 USPQ 697 (Fed. Cir. 1985).

[377]*Cable Elec. Prods., Inc. v. Genmark, Inc.*, 770 F.2d 1015, 226 USPQ 881 (Fed. Cir. 1985).

[378]*Tillotson, Ltd. v. Walbro Corp.*, 831 F.2d 1033, 4 USPQ2d 1450 (Fed. Cir. 1987). The mere fact that a judge in deciding a motion for summary judgment speaks of "findings of fact" supporting a judgment does not mean that he or she must have weighed evidence and resolved a genuine issue of fact. A statement of the undisputed facts on summary judgment is of great assistance to the reviewing court, and the district court commits no error where it "finds" only that there is no bona fide dispute of fact. *Avia Group Int'l, Inc. v. L.A. Gear Calif., Inc.*, 853 F.2d 1557, 7 USPQ2d 1548 (Fed. Cir. 1988).

ambiguous or unascertainable, the reasons for entering summary judgment must be stated somewhere in the record.[379]

The issue of material fact required to be present in order to entitle a party to proceed to trial in the face of an adverse motion for summary judgment need not be resolved conclusively in favor of the party asserting its existence. All that is required is a showing of sufficient evidence supportive of the existence of the claimed factual dispute to require a judge or jury to resolve the differing versions of the truth through a trial.[380] A full statement of the basis for the judgment facilitates appellate review, and there does exist in complicated cases the risk of an unnecessary reversal if the logic that resulted in a grant of summary judgment cannot be discerned.[381] But the requirement is pragmatic, with an eye toward judicial economy and communication with the litigants.[382]

To succeed on appeal, a party must show that it submitted evidence of the existence of a genuine issue of material fact prior to the grant of summary judgment.[383] On appeal from a grant of summary judgment the record will be viewed in the light most favorable to the party against whom summary judgment was granted.[384] The appellate court will not retry the motion; its review is based on the record—evidence actually presented—not on assorted evidentiary might-have-beens.[385]

In general, when a district court grants summary judgment, an appellate court reviews without deference to the trial court whether there are disputed material facts, and independently whether the prevailing party is entitled to judgment as a matter of law. By contrast, when a district court denies summary judgment, that decision is reviewed with considerable deference to the trial court.[386] Thus, the reviewing court determines for itself whether the standards for summary judgment have been met and is not bound in any respect by the trial court's ruling that there was no material factual dispute present.[387] Even if a district court properly finds that no genuine issue

---

[379]*Telectronics Pacing Sys., Inc. v. Ventritex, Inc.,* 982 F.2d 1520, 25 USPQ2d 1196 (Fed. Cir. 1992).

[380]*Lemelson v. TRW, Inc.,* 760 F.2d 1254, 225 USPQ 697 (Fed. Cir. 1985).

[381]*Cable Elec. Prods., Inc. v. Genmark, Inc.,* 770 F.2d 1015, 226 USPQ 881 (Fed. Cir. 1985); *Petersen Mfg. Co. v. Central Purchasing, Inc.,* 740 F.2d 1541, 222 USPQ 562 (Fed. Cir. 1984).

[382]*Cable Elec. Prods., Inc. v. Genmark, Inc.,* 770 F.2d 1015, 226 USPQ 881 (Fed. Cir. 1985).

[383]*Glaros v. H.H. Robertson Co.,* 797 F.2d 1564, 230 USPQ 393 (Fed. Cir. 1986).

[384]*Confederated Tribes v. United States,* 964 F.2d 1102 (Fed. Cir. 1992).

[385]*Chemical Eng'g Corp. v. Essef Indus., Inc.,* 795 F.2d 1565, 230 USPQ 385 (Fed. Cir. 1986).

[386]*SunTiger Inc. v. Scientific Res. Fund Group,* 189 F.3d 1327, 51 USPQ2d 1811 (Fed. Cir. 1999).

[387]*Intellicall, Inc. v. Phonometrics, Inc.,* 952 F.2d 1384, 21 USPQ2d 1383 (Fed. Cir. 1992); *Vas-Cath Inc. v. Mahurkar,* 935 F.2d 1555, 19 USPQ2d 1111 (Fed. Cir. 1991); *C.R. Bard, Inc. v. Advanced Card. Sys., Inc.,* 911 F.2d 670, 15 USPQ2d 1540 (Fed. Cir. 1990); *Prineville Sawmill Co. v. United States,* 859 F.2d 905 (Fed. Cir. 1988); *Armco, Inc. v. Cyclops Corp.,* 791 F.2d 147, 229 USPQ 721 (Fed. Cir. 1986). However, where the parties concede that there are no genuine issues of material fact, the appellate court need only decide the same question of law decided

of material fact is raised, reversal is still required if the court engaged in a faulty legal analysis in applying the law to the facts, and if a correct application of the law to those facts might bring a different result.[388] The party against which summary judgment is granted is not estopped by the filing of its own motion for summary judgment from asserting on review that there are genuine issues of material fact that prevent entry of judgment as a matter of law against it. But a cross-motion for summary judgment on the identical issues makes suspect an assertion on appeal that there were disputed factual questions.[389]

A reversal of summary judgment on appeal is not dispositive, but merely remits the case for trial.[390] However, in reversing a summary judgment an appellate court will often rule on legal errors where those issues will be raised at trial.[391] Indeed, it may be proper in some cases for an appellate court that disagrees with a district court's decision granting summary judgment in favor of the moving party, to reverse and remand with instructions to award summary judgment in favor of the nonmoving party.[392] Where the parties concede that there are no genuine issues of material fact, the appellate court need only decide the same question of law decided by the district court on summary judgment.[393]

In the appeal of a grant of summary judgment, such factual inferences as are material to the grant are not reviewed under the clearly erroneous standard, as if they were findings of fact made following a trial of issues. As a district court has no genuine discretion in determining whether to grant summary judgment, a reviewing court must determine de novo that the strict standard to be applied by the district court has been met. To affirm a grant of summary judgment, an appellate court must accordingly determine that the

---

by the district court on summary judgment. *Glaxo Oper. UK Ltd. v. Quigg,* 894 F.2d 392, 13 USPQ2d 1628 (Fed. Cir. 1990). The court reviews the propriety of a summary judgment decision de novo. *Conroy v. Reebok Int'l,* 14 F.3d 1570, 29 USPQ2d 1373 (Fed. Cir. 1994); *Dehne v. United States,* 970 F.2d 890 (Fed. Cir. 1992). The question of the propriety of summary judgment itself is subject to complete and independent review by the Federal Circuit. *Cohen v. United States,* 995 F.2d 205 (Fed. Cir. 1993). Such a standard provides the court with substantial latitude. *Confederated Tribes v. United States,* 964 F.2d 1102 (Fed. Cir. 1992).

[388]*Palumbo v. Don-Joy Co.,* 762 F.2d 969, 226 USPQ 5 (Fed. Cir. 1985).

[389]*Mingus Constructors, Inc. v. United States,* 812 F.2d 1387 (Fed. Cir. 1987).

[390]*SRI Int'l v. Matsushita Elec. Corp.,* 775 F.2d 1107, 227 USPQ 577 (Fed. Cir. 1985).

[391]*Palumbo v. Don-Joy Co.,* 762 F.2d 969, 226 USPQ 5 (Fed. Cir. 1985).

[392]*Litton Indus. Prods., Inc. v. Solid State Sys. Corp.,* 755 F.2d 158, 225 USPQ 34 (Fed. Cir. 1985). A district court also has the power to enter summary judgment sua sponte, so long as the losing party is on notice that it must come forward with all of its evidence. *International Visual Corp. v. Crown Metal Mfg. Co.,* 991 F.2d 768, 26 USPQ2d 1588 (Fed. Cir. 1993). In *Pall Corp. v. Hemasure Inc.,* 181 F.3d 1305, 50 USPQ2d 1947 (Fed. Cir. 1999), the trial court decided that the claim was literally infringed on summary judgment, and therefore did not decide infringement by equivalents. The Federal Circuit reversed the literal infringement judgment, and also reached out and decided that there was no infringement under the doctrine of equivalents as well.

[393]*Glaxo Oper. UK Ltd. v. Quigg,* 894 F.2d 392, 13 USPQ2d 1628 (Fed. Cir. 1990).

record demonstrates an absence of any actual dispute as to factual inferences that would have a material impact on the entitlement of the summary judgment movant to judgment as a matter of law.[394] In a takings case, the court indicated that there may be some discretionary leeway with respect to summary judgment. It observed that, in order to handle a litigation in an orderly and expeditious manner, a district court has discretion to deny summary judgment on issues in which it might otherwise be appropriate, particularly in fact-intensive matters.[395]

An order granting a judgment on certain issues is a judgment on those issues. It forecloses further dispute on those issues at the trial stage. An order denying a motion for summary judgment, on the other hand, is merely a judge's determination that genuine issues of material fact exist. It is not a judgment and does not foreclose trial on the issues on which summary judgment was sought. It does not settle or even tentatively decide anything about the merits of the claim. Denial of summary judgment is strictly a pretrial order that decides only one thing—that the case should go to trial. An order denying a motion for summary judgment is interlocutory, nonfinal, and nonappealable. Nor is it usually properly reviewable on an appeal from the final judgment entered after trial.[396] However, a denial of a motion for summary judgment may be appealed, even after a final judgment at trial, if the motion involved a purely legal question and the factual disputes resolved at trial do not affect the resolution of that legal question. A party may preserve the matter for appeal by

---

[394]*A.B. Chance Co. v. RTE Corp.*, 854 F.2d 1307, 7 USPQ2d 1881 (Fed. Cir. 1988); *Lemelson v. TRW, Inc.*, 760 F.2d 1254, 225 USPQ 697 (Fed. Cir. 1985). In reviewing a trial court's grant of summary judgment, an appellate court is not bound by the clearly erroneous rule because proper summary judgment is not based on debatable findings of fact. *Burlington Indus., Inc. v. Dayco Corp.*, 849 F.2d 1418, 7 USPQ2d 1158 (Fed. Cir. 1988). The question is not the weight of the evidence but the presence of a genuine issue of material fact, and an appellant need only show that one or more of the facts on which the district court relied was genuinely in dispute. *Avia Group Int'l, Inc. v. L.A. Gear Calif., Inc.*, 853 F.2d 1557, 7 USPQ2d 1548 (Fed. Cir. 1988).

[395]*Confederated Tribes v. United States*, 964 F.2d 1102 (Fed. Cir. 1992).

[396]*Glaros v. H.H. Robertson Co.*, 797 F.2d 1564, 230 USPQ 393 (Fed. Cir. 1986). See also *Lermer Germany GMBH v. Lermer Corp.*, 94 F.3d 1575, 39 USPQ2d 2014 (Fed. Cir. 1996); *Senza-Gel Corp. v. Seiffhart*, 803 F.2d 661, 231 USPQ 363 (Fed. Cir. 1986). When a matter comes before an appellate court following a summary judgment, the appellate court is free to adopt a ground advanced by the appellee in seeking summary judgment but not adopted by the trial court. Such an approach does not convert an argument advanced by one of the parties into an impermissible interlocutory appeal of a denial of summary judgment. *Glaxo Inc. v. TorPharm Inc.*, 153 F.3d 1366, 47 USPQ2d 1836 (Fed. Cir. 1998). In *Tone Bros., Inc. v. Sysco Corp.*, 28 F.3d 1192, 31 USPQ2d 1321 (Fed. Cir. 1994), the district court granted a motion for summary judgment of invalidity of a design patent and denied it as to noninfringement. Upon the patentee's appeal from the invalidity judgment, the defendant argued as an alternate ground for affirmance that the district court had erred in denying the motion as to noninfringement. The Federal Circuit refused to consider this alternate ground, reasoning that it was not suited to address the merits of such a fact-intensive issue prior to the district court having done so.

renewing the issue at trial or by including it in a memoranda of law or proposed conclusions of law.[397]

A Rule 56(d) order granting a partial summary judgment from which no immediate appeal lies is merged into the final judgment and reviewable on appeal from that final judgment.[398]

---

[397]*United Tech. Corp. v. Chromalloy Gas Turbine Corp.*, 189 F.3d 1338, 51 USPQ2d 1838 (Fed. Cir. 1999).

[398]*Glaros v. H.H. Robertson Co.*, 797 F.2d 1564, 230 USPQ 393 (Fed. Cir. 1986). If a Rule 56(d) order contains findings fundamental to further conduct of the case or intertwined with a judgment that is properly appealable, those findings may be reviewed. *Palumbo v. Don-Joy Co.*, 762 F.2d 969, 226 USPQ 5 (Fed. Cir. 1985).

10

Infringement Litigation—
Trial and Judgment

§10.1 Trial Conduct

Trial courts have the right and duty to manage proceedings before them to ensure both expedition and fairness and must be granted a wide discretion in carrying out that duty.[1] Indeed, the Federal Rules recognize the need for the exercise of discretion by the trial court in carrying out its duty of managing the judicial process, the business of the court, and the administration of justice. The proper exercise of that discretion should not be impeded by second guessing at the appellate level.[2] Thus a court of appeals will intervene in a district court's management of a case only to satisfy an overwhelming legal requirement or to prevent manifest injustice.[3] Trials must be fair not perfect.[4]

Trials establish facts.[5] If summary judgment is inappropriate, fact issues must be resolved by trial in which the conflicting views of the experts will be subject to the refining fire of cross-examination, a more effective means of arriving at legal conclusions than perusal of ex parte affidavits and declarations of partisan experts lobbed at each other from opposing trenches.[6]

The issues resolved by a court are defined by the facts in the case and the law applied; they are not necessarily limited to those briefed by the parties.[7] On the other hand, a trial judge is under no obligation to consider a defense abandoned at trial.[8]

---

[1]*Glaros v. H.H. Robertson Co.*, 797 F.2d 1564, 230 USPQ 393 (Fed. Cir. 1986); *Railroad Dynamics, Inc. v. A. Stucki Co.*, 727 F.2d 1506, 220 USPQ 929 (Fed. Cir. 1984). A trial judge has broad discretion in trial management. *Tol-O-Matic, Inc. v. Proma Produckt-und Mktg. GmbH*, 945 F.2d 1546, 20 USPQ2d 1332 (Fed. Cir. 1991). See also *Motorola, Inc. v. Interdigital Tech. Corp.*, 121 F.3d 1461, 43 USPQ2d 1481 (Fed. Cir. 1997). As a general rule, trial courts are given wide discretion to manage the course of a trial and to direct the conduct of counsel. But this discretion is not without limits and is reviewed for abuse. *Hendler v. United States*, 952 F.2d 1364 (Fed. Cir. 1991). A good example of the breadth of that discretion is illustrated in *Abbott Labs. v. Diamedix Corp.*, 47 F.3d 1128, 33 USPQ2d 1771 (Fed. Cir. 1995), where, upon remand, the Federal Circuit expressly left open the task of "refereeing disputes" as to how a litigation "control" clause in a license agreement was to be implemented at trial.

[2]*Rosemount, Inc. v. Beckman Instr., Inc.*, 727 F.2d 1540, 221 USPQ 1 (Fed. Cir. 1984). A trial on a motion for preliminary injunction and for contempt of a previous injunction took only six hours. The appellant argued on appeal that only minutes were allowed for consideration of the infringement issues on two of the three patents involved. The court disregarded the argument because the objection had not been made to the court below. *Laitram Corp. v. Cambridge Wire Cloth Co.*, 863 F.2d 855, 9 USPQ2d 1289 (Fed. Cir. 1988).

[3]*In re International Med. P.R. Assoc.*, 739 F.2d 618 (Fed. Cir. 1984). The trial court is in a much better position than the appellate court to determine whether maintenance of a schedule will work an injustice. *Id.*

[4]*Newell Cos. v. Kenney Mfg. Co.*, 864 F.2d 757, 9 USPQ2d 1417 (Fed. Cir. 1988); *Devices for Med., Inc. v. Boehl*, 822 F.2d 1062, 3 USPQ2d 1288 (Fed. Cir. 1987).

[5]*Atari, Inc. v. JS & A Group, Inc.*, 747 F.2d 1422, 223 USPQ 1074 (Fed. Cir. 1984).

[6]*Hodosh v. Block Drug Co.*, 786 F.2d 1136, 229 USPQ 182 (Fed. Cir. 1986).

[7]*Zenith Radio Corp. v. United States*, 783 F.2d 184 (Fed. Cir. 1986).

[8]*Windsurfing Int'l, Inc. v. AMF, Inc.*, 782 F.2d 995, 228 USPQ 562 (Fed. Cir. 1986). Intervening rights is an affirmative defense that must be raised at trial; submitting affidavits at a posttrial hearing was not sufficient. *Id.* A party's deliberate refusal to appear at trial and prosecute its counterclaim authorizes the judge to dismiss the counterclaim for failure to prosecute. *Syntex Ophthalmics, Inc. v. Novicky*, 795 F.2d 983, 230 USPQ 427 (Fed. Cir. 1986).

§10.2 Magistrates, Masters, and Judges

The Magistrate's Act, which provides for consensual reference to a magistrate for trial,[9] is constitutional.[10] Such a reference to conduct "any and all further proceedings" certainly authorizes a magistrate to enter summary judgment.[11]

The role of a federal district court vis-à-vis a master is governed by Rule 53, FRCP.[12] The federal courts have the inherent power to appoint persons unconnected with the court to aid judges in the performance of specific duties.[13] This includes the power to appoint masters without the consent of the parties. Reference of issues to a master, even compulsory reference, does not violate the Seventh Amendment right to a trial by a jury, inasmuch as the master's findings can be read to the jury under Rule 53(e)(3).[14] The findings and report of a special master may be presented along with other evidence for consideration by the jury. The report will, unless rejected by the court, be admitted at the jury trial as evidence of facts and findings embodied therein; but it will be treated, at most, as prima facie evidence thereof. The parties remain free to call, examine, and cross-examine witnesses as if the report had not been made. No incident of the jury trial is modified or taken away either by the preliminary, tentative hearing before the master or by the use to which the report may be put. The master's report is evidence, and as such may be referred to in arguments of counsel.[15]

Masters can properly aid the court in evaluating issues of patent validity and infringement in the context of motions for summary judgment and have often done so.[16] A master need not have the same expertise in the technology as the inventor. Where complicated issues of patent law are involved, the appointment of an experienced patent

---

[9]28 U.S.C. §636(c).

[10]*D.L. Auld Co. v. Chroma Graphics Corp.,* 753 F.2d 1029, 224 USPQ 737 (Fed. Cir. 1985).

[11]*D.L. Auld Co. v. Chroma Graphics Corp.,* 753 F.2d 1029, 224 USPQ 737 (Fed. Cir. 1985). A contrary contention was termed frivolous. See also *D.L. Auld Co. v. Chroma Graphics Corp.,* 714 F.2d 1144, 219 USPQ 13 (Fed. Cir. 1983).

[12]*Milliken Res. Corp. v. Dan River, Inc.,* 739 F.2d 587, 222 USPQ 571 (Fed. Cir. 1984).

[13]*Festo Corp. v. Shoketsu KKK Co.,* 72 F.3d 857, 37 USPQ2d 1163 (Fed. Cir. 1995); *Constant v. Advanced Micro-Devices, Inc.,* 848 F.2d 1560, 7 USPQ2d 1057 (Fed. Cir. 1988).

[14]*Constant v. Advanced Micro-Devices, Inc.,* 848 F.2d 1560, 7 USPQ2d 1057 (Fed. Cir. 1988).

[15]*Festo Corp. v. Shoketsu KKK Co.,* 72 F.3d 857, 37 USPQ2d 1163 (Fed. Cir. 1995). Here the court found no harmful error in the fact that the district court allowed the jury to have copies of the master's report rather than simply having it read to them.

[16]*Constant v. Advanced Micro-Devices, Inc.,* 848 F.2d 1560, 7 USPQ2d 1057 (Fed. Cir. 1988). See also *Festo Corp. v. Shoketsu KKK Co.,* 72 F.3d 857, 37 USPQ2d 1163 (Fed. Cir. 1995). In *Riverwood Int'l Corp. v. Mead Corp.,* 212 F.3d 1365, 54 USPQ2d 1763 (Fed. Cir. 2000), a special master heard the evidence, made findings of fact, and concluded that the claims would have been obvious. The district court accepted the findings in whole and without modification, but concluded that the claims would not have been obvious. The Federal Circuit reversed, concluding that the findings would support only the legal conclusion of obviousness.

attorney is quite appropriate.[17] In a nonjury trial, complexity alone does not warrant reference to a master. However, the strict "exceptional condition" standard of Rule 53(b) relates only to actions tried without a jury.[18]

One must object to a reference to a master at the time the reference is made.[19] A party cannot wait to see whether it likes a master's findings before challenging the use of a master. Failure to object in a timely fashion constitutes a waiver.[20] A judge reviewing a master's determination is not obligated to accept an erroneous legal theory of the case, even if both parties pursued that theory before the master.[21]

It is not error for a judge, unskilled in the pertinent art, to decide the legal question of validity without the testimony of a qualified expert in that field.[22] Patent issues may involve consideration of complex scientific principles and disputed aspects of technology. Such issues are not treated as legal abstractions, but properly devolve on the trier of fact. Our system of justice does not require judge and jury to be independent experts in technology. In ascertaining the truth when the evidence is primarily scientific, as for other kinds of evidence, the trier of fact must make determinations of credibility, reliability, and weight.[23] Courts of law are not the optimal fora for trying questions of scientific truth; even less are appellate courts equipped to choose among conflicting scientific theories. Judges are dependent on the quality and strength of the scientific evidence brought before them. The trial judge who hears the witnesses and does the initial assessment of the evidence deserves considerable latitude in eventually choosing sides based on what is ultimately an educated guess. That is what judging is about.[24]

The technical qualifications of a judge are irrelevant in appeals to the Federal Circuit under 35 U.S.C. §141 or to the District Court for the District of Columbia under §145.[25] Questioning the competency of the district judge is not recommended. The Federal Circuit has

---

[17]*Constant v. Advanced Micro-Devices, Inc.*, 848 F.2d 1560, 7 USPQ2d 1057 (Fed. Cir. 1988).

[18]*Festo Corp. v. Shoketsu KKK Co.*, 72 F.3d 857, 37 USPQ2d 1163 (Fed. Cir. 1995).

[19]*Phonometrics Inc. v. Northern Telecom Inc.*, 133 F.3d 1459, 45 USPQ2d 1421 (Fed. Cir. 1998).

[20]*Constant v. Advanced Micro-Devices, Inc.*, 848 F.2d 1560, 7 USPQ2d 1057 (Fed. Cir. 1988).

[21]*Studiengesellschaft Kohle v. Dart Indus., Inc.*, 862 F.2d 1564, 9 USPQ2d 1273 (Fed. Cir. 1988).

[22]*Avia Group Int'l, Inc. v. L.A. Gear Calif., Inc.*, 853 F.2d 1557, 7 USPQ2d 1548 (Fed. Cir. 1988).

[23]*Brooktree Corp. v. Advanced Micro Devices, Inc.*, 977 F.2d 1555, 24 USPQ2d 1401 (Fed. Cir. 1992).

[24]*Zenith Labs., Inc. v. Bristol-Myers Squibb Co.*, 19 F.3d 1418, 30 USPQ2d 1048, 32 USPQ2d 1017 (Fed. Cir. 1994).

[25]*In re Nilssen*, 851 F.2d 1401, 7 USPQ2d 1500 (Fed. Cir. 1988).

termed such tactics "reprehensible."[26] All courts are legally competent to decide the issues that properly come before them.[27]

Recusal. The Due Process Clause may sometimes bar trial by judges who have no actual bias and who would do their very best to weigh the scales of justice equally between contending parties. To perform its high function in the best way, justice must satisfy the appearance of justice. The standard to be applied is what a reasonable person would believe about the judge's impartiality in view of all the facts. In deciding on recusal, it is important for a federal judge to reach his or her own determination, without calling upon counsel to express their views as to the desirability of the judge remaining in the case.[28] Opinions formed by the judge on the basis of facts introduced or events occurring in the court of the current proceedings, or of prior proceedings, do not constitute a basis for a bias or partiality motion unless they display a deep-seated favoritism or antagonism that would make fair judgment impossible. Thus, judicial remarks during the course of a trial that are critical or disapproving of, or even hostile to, counsel, the parties, or their cases, ordinarily do not support a bias or partiality challenge. Not establishing bias or partiality are expressions of impatience, dissatisfaction, annoyance, and even anger, that are within the bounds of what imperfect men and women, even after having been confirmed as federal judges, sometimes display. A judge's ordinary efforts at courtroom administration—even a stern and short-tempered judge's ordinary efforts at courtroom administration—remain immune. To warrant recusal, bias or prejudice must be directed against a party, and bias exhibited against an attorney will only merit recusal when it results in material and identifiable harm to that party's case.[29]

Actions to disqualify a judge for bias or prejudice upon affidavit of a party are provided for in 28 U.S.C. §144. Section 455 of the same title provides for recusal under certain specified conditions. Section 455(b) may be viewed as presuming bias or prejudice when any of its listed circumstances are present. Although there is a specific timeliness requirement for actions under §144, there is none under §455. The passage of time is merely one factor and the concept of timeliness merges into and is subsumed in the concepts of equity, fairness, and

---

[26]*Interspiro USA, Inc. v. Figgie Int'l, Inc.*, 18 F.3d 927, 30 USPQ2d 1070 (Fed. Cir. 1994).

[27]*Polymer Tech., Inc. v. Bridwell H.A.*, 103 F.3d 970, 41 USPQ2d 1185, 1191–92 (Fed. Cir. 1996). Here the argument was that because the district court had limited patent law experience, it should be presumed that there was error in ruling on a motion for a preliminary injunction. The Federal Circuit found the argument "wholly inappropriate and, indeed, offensive."

[28]*Hewlett-Packard Co. v. Bausch & Lomb, Inc.*, 882 F.2d 1556, 11 USPQ2d 1750 (Fed. Cir. 1989).

[29]*Baldwin Hardware Corp. v. Franksu Enter. Corp.*, 78 F.3d 550, 37 USPQ2d 1829 (Fed. Cir. 1996). See also *Pac-Tec, Inc. v. Amerace Corp.*, 903 F.2d 796, 14 USPQ2d 1871 (Fed. Cir. 1990).

justice.[30] Sources such as prior unrelated proceedings, and local bar assessments of general competence, are not relevant to the issue of judicial bias or prejudice warranting recusal in a particular case.[31]

A violation of 28 U.S.C. §455 does not in itself automatically deprive the judge of jurisdiction. The remedies for disqualification are left to the judiciary. In determining whether a judgment should be vacated for violation of §455, it is appropriate to consider the risk of injustice to the parties in this and other cases, and the risk of undermining the public's confidence in the judicial process. There is a distinction in the fairness quotient of prospective and retrospective remedies.[32]

A motion to vacate a judgment based on an assertion that the trial judge should have disqualified himself or herself is a matter unrelated to patent law and is decided by reference to the law of the regional circuit.[33] The standard of review on appeal from a denial of a motion to vacate a recused judge's prior orders is abuse of discretion.[34]

§10.3 Jury Practice

The procedural aspects of jury trials are governed largely by Rules 47–51, FRCP. In its decision in *Structural Rubber v. Park*,[35] the Federal Circuit provided a fairly comprehensive review and summary of its views on jury practice. A good overview of the subject can be had from the court's opinion there, taken in light of Rules 47–51. By amendment to the Federal Rules of Civil Procedure effective December 1, 1991, motions for JNOV and for directed verdict are now

---

[30]*Polaroid Corp. v. Eastman Kodak Co.*, 866 F.2d 1415, 9 USPQ2d 1877 (Fed. Cir. 1989).

[31]*Baldwin Hardware Corp. v. Franksu Enter. Corp.*, 78 F.3d 550, 37 USPQ2d 1829 (Fed. Cir. 1996). In this case the Federal Circuit refused to order a complete trial transcript, at government expense, to help appellant prove judicial bias or prejudice.

[32]*Polaroid Corp. v. Eastman Kodak Co.*, 866 F.2d 1415, 9 USPQ2d 1877 (Fed. Cir. 1989). Here the judge disqualified herself sua sponte after she became a shareholder in Kodak by virtue of an inheritance. She had advised the parties of the decedent's ownership over six years previously, before trial started. She denied a rather belated motion to vacate all her previous orders and the Federal Circuit affirmed. The risk of injustice to the parties seemed to weigh heavily on the Polaroid side, and the public's confidence in the judicial process would be less likely injured by adherence to the result than if the law were to countenance a sundering of the result more than six years later on grounds other than the merits. In *Baldwin Hardware Corp. v. Franksu Enter. Corp.*, 78 F.3d 550, 37 USPQ2d 1829 (Fed. Cir. 1996), the judge's mother owned shares of parent company of plaintiff. The shares were kept in a trust that had as one of its beneficiaries the judge. The trust sold the shares two months after the suit was filed and one month before the judge entered his first substantive order in the case. The judge knew nothing of this until after trial had begun, 18 months later. The court held a recusal motion under these circumstances bordered on the frivolous.

[33]*Hewlett-Packard Co. v. Bausch & Lomb, Inc.*, 882 F.2d 1556, 11 USPQ2d 1750 (Fed. Cir. 1989); *Polaroid Corp. v. Eastman Kodak Co.*, 866 F.2d 1415, 9 USPQ2d 1877 (Fed. Cir. 1989). See also *Baldwin Hardware Corp. v. Franksu Enter. Corp.*, 78 F.3d 550, 37 USPQ2d 1829 (Fed. Cir. 1996).

[34]*Polaroid Corp. v. Eastman Kodak Co.*, 866 F.2d 1415, 9 USPQ2d 1877 (Fed. Cir. 1989).

[35]*Structural Rubber Prods. Co. v. Park Rubber Co.*, 749 F.2d 707, 223 USPQ 1264 (Fed. Cir. 1984).

denominated motions for judgment as a matter of law (JMOL). The change in name was made in order to emphasize the correlation in standards for grant of these motions as well as motions for summary judgment under Rule 56 and was not intended to change the existing standard of review.[36]

(a) *Right to Jury Trial*

A right to a jury trial in federal court must arise out of the Seventh Amendment or be granted by a federal statute. The Seventh Amendment preserves the right to a jury trial in those actions in which the right existed at common law when the amendment was adopted in 1791.[37] The views expressed on the meaning of this right have ranged from endorsing the absolute sanctity of a right to have a jury decide the law as well as the facts, to no right to a jury trial at all where the issues are complex.[38] It appears that the Federal Circuit will be taking a middle view. Despite some early criticism of the use of juries in general to resolve patent disputes,[39] there is little doubt that the right to a jury trial on patent issues that may arise in a suit for patent infringement is fully protected by the Seventh Amendment,[40] despite concerns about technological complexity. The court has observed that the Seventh Amendment does not permit rationing of the right. Scholarly disputes over the use of jury trials in complex cases have to do with the right itself, centering on whether lay juries are capable of making correct factual determinations in such cases. Patent issues are not necessarily more complicated than issues in cases such as antitrust, medical injury, and product liability.[41]

---

[36]*Brooktree Corp. v. Advanced Micro Devices, Inc.,* 977 F.2d 1555, 24 USPQ2d 1401 (Fed. Cir. 1992). See also *Wang Labs., Inc. v. Toshiba Corp.,* 993 F.2d 858, 26 USPQ2d 1767 (Fed. Cir. 1993).

[37]*Washington Int'l Ins. Co. v. United States,* 863 F.2d 877 (Fed. Cir. 1988). An action against the government, however, is not a suit at common law within the purview of the Seventh Amendment. It has long been settled that the Seventh Amendment right to trial by jury does not apply in actions against the federal government. *Id.* The Seventh Amendment preserves a right to a jury trial on issues of fact in suits for breach of contract damages between private party litigants. *Seaboard Lumber Co. v. United States,* 903 F.2d 1560 (Fed. Cir. 1990). A party in an action against the United States has a right to trial by jury only where Congress has affirmatively and unambiguously granted that right by statute; the right must be one of the terms of the government's consent to be sued. *Washington Int'l Ins. Co. v. United States,* 863 F.2d 877 (Fed. Cir. 1988). Under 28 U.S.C. §1876 a party is not granted a right to a jury trial in the Court of International Trade. That is an enabling statute that simply sets forth the procedures to be followed when such an action is tried before a jury. *Id.*

[38]*Structural Rubber Prods. Co. v. Park Rubber Co.,* 749 F.2d 707, 223 USPQ 1264 (Fed. Cir. 1984).

[39]See *American Hoist & Derrick Co. v. Sowa & Sons, Inc.,* 725 F.2d 1350, 220 USPQ 763 (Fed. Cir. 1984).

[40]*Patlex Corp. v. Mossinghoff,* 758 F.2d 594, 225 USPQ 243 (Fed. Cir. 1985).

[41]*Connell v. Sears, Roebuck & Co.,* 722 F.2d 1542, 220 USPQ 193 (Fed. Cir. 1983). Issues of utility and enablement may involve consideration of complex scientific principles and disputed aspects of technology. Such issues are not treated as legal abstractions, but properly devolve

In its *In re Lockwood*[42] decision, the court emphatically reaffirmed that there is an absolute Seventh Amendment right to a jury trial on questions of patent validity, whether they arise in the context of an infringement action or an action seeking a declaratory judgment of invalidity. Indeed, the right to trial by jury in such a case is sufficiently important that mandamus will lie to protect it. The opinion is a virtual textbook on the history both of declaratory judgment actions and of the right to jury trial on the factual issues underlying the validity defense. In its *Markman*[43] decision, the court held that claim construction is a question of law that a trial court can take from the jury. It found, however, that this holding does not deprive parties of part of their right to a jury trial in patent infringement cases. The patentee's right to a jury trial on the application of the properly construed claim to the accused device is preserved.[44]

Thus, the Seventh Amendment preserves the right to jury trial, including the common law practice of permitting the jury to draw legal conclusions based upon its fact findings, in light of legal instructions. Although the court is ultimately responsible for upholding the law applicable to the facts found, it cannot substitute its view for that of the jury since that would be an effective denial of the right to jury trial.[45]

The reexamination statute is not invalid as a deprivation of the right to a jury trial.[46] Nor does separation of patent issues from antitrust issues violate the right to jury trial.[47] Once a party invokes the core jurisdiction of the bankruptcy court by filing a proof of claim, even a claim for patent infringement, that party has no Seventh Amendment right to a jury trial.[48]

The question of separation of inequitable conduct issues for nonjury trial is two-fold: (1) whether a separate nonjury trial may be ordered at all, and (2) if it can, whether a separate nonjury trial may

---

on the trier of fact. Our system of justice does not require judge and jury to be independent experts in technology. In ascertaining the truth when the evidence is primarily scientific, as for other kinds of evidence, the trier of fact must make determinations of credibility. *Brooktree Corp. v. Advanced Micro Devices, Inc.,* 977 F.2d 1555, 24 USPQ2d 1401 (Fed. Cir. 1992).

[42]*In re Lockwood,* 50 F.3d 966, 33 USPQ2d 1406 (Fed. Cir. 1995).

[43]*Markman v. Westview Instr., Inc.,* 52 F.3d 967, 34 USPQ2d 1321 (Fed. Cir. 1995).

[44]The court rationalized this view partly on the basis that claim interpretation is more akin to statutory interpretation than interpretation of a contract. Both patents and statutes are public documents and both may create liability in third persons who were not part of the process that created them. Contract interpretation often seeks to determine the intent of the parties, whereas statutory interpretation only deals with the collective intent of the legislative body. *Markman v. Westview Instr., Inc.,* 52 F.3d 967, 34 USPQ2d 1321 (Fed. Cir. 1995). In affirming, the Supreme Court found that evidence of common law practice at the time of the framing does not entail application of the Seventh Amendment's jury guarantee to the construction of patent claims. 517 U.S. 370, 38 USPQ2d 1461 (1996).

[45]*Connell v. Sears, Roebuck & Co.,* 722 F.2d 1542, 220 USPQ 193 (Fed. Cir. 1983).

[46]*Patlex Corp. v. Mossinghoff,* 758 F.2d 594, 225 USPQ 243 (Fed. Cir. 1985). See also *Joy Tech., Inc. v. Manbeck,* 959 F.2d 226, 22 USPQ2d 1153 (Fed. Cir. 1992).

[47]*In re Innotron Diagnostics,* 800 F.2d 1077, 231 USPQ 178 (Fed. Cir. 1986).

[48]*Institut Pasteur v. Cambridge Biotech Corp.,* 186 F.3d 1356, 51 USPQ2d 1321 (Fed. Cir. 1999).

precede the jury trial to which the patentee would be entitled on the legal issues of validity and infringement.[49] Under Rule 42(b), FRCP, a district court has broad discretion in separating issues and claims for trial as part of its discretion in the management of trials. It may, therefore, order a trial on unenforceability separate from an infringement trial that may involve an invalidity defense. But the discretion in ordering an equitable claim to be tried first is narrowly limited and must wherever possible be exercised to preserve jury trial.[50] Nonetheless, in a case of first impression the court decided (1) that the defense of inequitable conduct is equitable in nature and does not give rise to the right of trial by jury, and (2) that an inequitable conduct issue may be tried first, without a jury, if the factual issues resolved thereby are not so common with those relating to the jury issues of validity and infringement that a jury trial of those issues would be precluded by the earlier bench trial.[51] Thus, there are several ways in which a trial court may handle the issue of inequitable conduct during a jury trial. It can reserve the entire issue unto itself; it can submit special interrogatories to the jury on the facts of materiality and intent; or it can instruct the jury to find and weigh the facts of materiality and intent and decide the ultimate question of inequitable conduct. Absent a clear showing of prejudice or failure to achieve a fair trial, the trial court's choice of procedure will not be disturbed.[52]

---

[49]*Gardco Mfg., Inc. v. Herst Lighting Co.,* 820 F.2d 1209, 2 USPQ2d 2015 (Fed. Cir. 1987). The question clearly implicates the jurisprudential responsibilities of the Federal Circuit with respect to patent law, and it is thus not bound by regional circuit precedent. *Id.*

[50]*Gardco Mfg., Inc. v. Herst Lighting Co.,* 820 F.2d 1209, 2 USPQ2d 2015 (Fed. Cir. 1987). See also *Cabinet Vision v. Cabnetware,* 129 F.3d 595, 44 USPQ2d 1683 (Fed. Cir. 1997). The fact that error in a matter of separation of issues for jury trial was invited by one of the parties cannot be excused, even if the party failed to advise the court on how to separate and manage those issues that were for the court and those that were for the jury. Interpretation of the law is the responsibility of the court. *Id.*

[51]*Gardco Mfg., Inc. v. Herst Lighting Co.,* 820 F.2d 1209, 2 USPQ2d 2015 (Fed. Cir. 1987). Here the court held the patent unenforceable due to failure to disclose the patentee's own prior art devices. That this evidence might also be used to establish invalidity did not mean that the issue of invalidity was precluded. A patent may be valid and yet be rendered unenforceable for misuse or inequitable conduct. Similarly, a valid patent may be infringed, i.e., the accused device may fall within the scope of the claim, but there will be no liability to the patentee when the patent is unenforceable. Thus the issue of conduct of the applicant in the PTO, raised in the nonjury trial, and the separated validity and infringement issues are distinct and without commonality either as claims or in relation to the underlying fact issues. See also *Paragon Podiatry Lab., Inc. v. KLM Labs., Inc.,* 984 F.2d 1182, 25 USPQ2d 1561 (Fed. Cir. 1993). In *Cabinet Vision v. Cabnetware,* 129 F.3d 595, 44 USPQ2d 1683 (Fed. Cir. 1997), there was an inequitable conduct defense and a *Walker Process* antitrust counterclaim. Because of the antitrust counterclaim, the district court let the jury decide the underlying facts. It found no inequitable conduct and thus did not reach the counterclaim. The district court then treated the jury verdict in this respect as advisory only as to inequitable conduct and not binding as to the antitrust counterclaim. This was error. The facts underlying the defense and the counterclaim had such substantial commonality that the jury's resolution of them could not be merely advisory under the circumstances, and was binding as to the antitrust counterclaim. Note that the real problem here stemmed from the order in which the questions were presented to the jury.

[52]*Hebert v. Lisle Corp.,* 99 F.3d 1109, 40 USPQ2d 1611 (Fed. Cir. 1996). However, the court has pointed out that disputed issues of fact underlying the issue of inequitable conduct

There is no right to a jury trial where there are no issues of fact to be tried by the jury, and a proper summary judgment therefore does not violate the Seventh Amendment.[53] Reference of issues to a master, even compulsory reference, does not violate the right to jury trial.[54] The court has observed[55] that a party in an action at law has a right to a jury trial, not a jury verdict. Thus it is permissible for a trial court to direct a verdict on obviousness if there are no disputes as to underlying factual questions.[56]

A private litigant may waive its right to a jury in civil cases. Waiver can be either express or implied. Waiver requires only that the party waiving such right do so voluntarily and knowingly based on the facts of the case.[57] Because waiver of a jury trial is a procedural matter not unique to patent law, and is accomplished pursuant to local rules, the court looks to the law of the regional circuit.[58]

---

are not jury questions, the issue being entirely equitable in nature. Thus, the facts are ordinarily for the court to resolve, accompanied by findings of fact under Rule 52(a). Correction of error is more difficult when the fact issues respecting inequitable conduct are decided by a jury by means of special verdicts. Review in that instance is under the stringent substantial evidence standard. *General Electro Music Corp. v. Samick Music Corp.*, 19 F.3d 1405, 30 USPQ2d 1149 (Fed. Cir. 1994). Serious problems can arise if the judge and jury attack related issues simultaneously. In *Therma-Tru Corp. v. Peachtree Doors Inc.*, 44 F.3d 988, 33 USPQ2d 1274 (Fed. Cir. 1994), the jury retired to decide validity and infringement and the judge simultaneously decided inequitable conduct. The invalidity defenses included nonenablement and the jury found the patent valid. Meanwhile, the judge found inequitable conduct on the ground that the withheld information had to do with enablement. The Federal Circuit, in a 2–1 decision, found this to be improper jurisprudence. When a party has a right to a jury trial on an issue involved in a legal claim, the judge is bound by the jury's determination of that issue as it affects his or her disposition of an accompanying equitable claim. The fact that the determinations by the jury and the judge are simultaneous does not authorize judicial findings independent of and contrary to the facts found by the jury in reaching its verdict.

[53]*Constant v. Advanced Micro-Devices, Inc.*, 848 F.2d 1560, 7 USPQ2d 1057 (Fed. Cir. 1988). That a grant of summary judgment takes a case from the jury is in no sense a denial of a right to a trial by jury. Summary judgment can lie only where no dispute with respect to a material fact is "genuine." A dispute is genuine if the evidence is such that a reasonable jury could return a verdict for the nonmoving party. *Johnston v. IVAC Corp.*, 885 F.2d 1574, 12 USPQ2d 1382 (Fed. Cir. 1989).

[54]*Constant v. Advanced Micro-Devices, Inc.*, 848 F.2d 1560, 7 USPQ2d 1057 (Fed. Cir. 1988).

[55]*Newell Cos. v. Kenney Mfg. Co.*, 864 F.2d 757, 9 USPQ2d 1417 (Fed. Cir. 1988).

[56]See text accompanying notes 10:156–158.

[57]*Seaboard Lumber Co. v. United States*, 903 F.2d 1560 (Fed. Cir. 1990). The acceptance of contract provisions providing for dispute resolution in a forum where there is no entitlement to a jury trial may satisfy the "voluntary" and "knowing" standard. *Id.* Where a trial court omits, and the parties fail to demand, submission of certain issues of fact to the jury, a jury trial on those issues is waived. *Baxter Healthcare Corp. v. Spectramed, Inc.*, 49 F.3d 1575, 34 USPQ2d 1120 (Fed. Cir. 1995). In *American Med. Sys., Inc. v. Medical Eng'g Corp.*, 6 F.3d 1523, 28 USPQ2d 1321 (Fed. Cir. 1993), the original complaint demanding a jury trial was filed but never served. Later pleadings did not demand a jury, nor did the defendant raise the matter at the Rule 16 pretrial conference. On these facts the court held that the trial judge was correct in finding that defendant had waived its right to a jury. In *Transmatic, Inc. v. Gulton Indus., Inc.*, 53 F.3d 1270, 35 USPQ2d 1035 (Fed. Cir. 1995), the trial court ordered a bench trial with an advisory jury and the parties did not object. Later, the plaintiff objected to the lack of a binding jury trial on certain issues. The trial court held that there had been a waiver and the Federal Circuit agreed, applying Sixth Circuit law.

[58]*Cabinet Vision v. Cabnetware*, 129 F.3d 595, 44 USPQ2d 1683 (Fed. Cir. 1997).

(b) Legal Questions

Litigants have the right to have a case tried in a manner that ensures factual questions are determined by the jury and the decisions on legal issues are made by the court. Various techniques to accomplish this are available under the Federal Rules and under the inherent powers of a judge to control the course of a jury trial. But it is incumbent upon the parties to present proper motions or requests to the court and also to be certain that the court has a working familiarity of the law applicable to the case before the trial begins.[59] So long as instructions on the law and general verdicts remain permissible elements of a jury trial, it is idle to speak of the jury solely as a fact-finding body.[60]

Thus there is neither error nor danger inherent in submitting questions of law to a jury so long as it is adequately instructed,[61] but the instructions must identify in some clear manner what underlying factual issues the jury is expected to resolve.[62] Unless the instructions are adequate, the trial court must reach an independent conclusion on legal questions.[63] In some situations, where the process is neither a determination of fact nor a mere application of law to facts but requires balancing and judicial discretion, the court must do it.[64] That a jury has answered a legal question may not in itself require reversal. Of a certainty, however, that circumstance cannot serve to relieve the trial judge or the appellate court of the judicial duty to ensure that the law is correctly applied.[65] Where no objection is made to the submission of a legal issue to the jury, the court treats the jury's verdict on the legal issue as a resolution of all genuinely disputed underlying factual issues in favor of the verdict winner.[66]

The merger of law and equity dissolved the distinction once governing issues submissible to a jury. Thus equitable issues such as unclean hands can be decided by a jury.[67] Nonetheless, even while

---

[59]*Structural Rubber Prods. Co. v. Park Rubber Co.*, 749 F.2d 707, 223 USPQ 1264 (Fed. Cir. 1984).

[60]*Railroad Dynamics, Inc. v. A. Stucki Co.*, 727 F.2d 1506, 220 USPQ 929 (Fed. Cir. 1984).

[61]*Bio-Rad Labs., Inc. v. Nicolet Instr. Corp.*, 739 F.2d 604, 222 USPQ 654 (Fed. Cir. 1984); *Railroad Dynamics, Inc. v. A. Stucki Co.*, 727 F.2d 1506, 220 USPQ 929 (Fed. Cir. 1984); *White v. Jeffrey Min. Mach. Co.*, 723 F.2d 1553, 220 USPQ 703 (Fed. Cir. 1983).

[62]*Quaker City Gear Works, Inc. v. Skil Corp.*, 747 F.2d 1446, 223 USPQ 1161 (Fed. Cir. 1984). Indeed, courts should consider pretrial orders in jury trials that specify precisely what the jury will be asked to do after it has been given instructions prepared in light of the evidence and at the end of its deliberations. *Orthokinetics, Inc. v. Safety Travel Chairs, Inc.*, 806 F.2d 1565, 1 USPQ2d 1081 (Fed. Cir. 1986).

[63]*White v. Jeffrey Min. Mach. Co.*, 723 F.2d 1553, 220 USPQ 703 (Fed. Cir. 1983).

[64]*American Hoist & Derrick Co. v. Sowa & Sons, Inc.*, 725 F.2d 1350, 220 USPQ 763 (Fed. Cir. 1984) (balancing intent in light of materiality for fraud).

[65]*Senmed, Inc. v. Richard-Allan Med. Indus., Inc.*, 888 F.2d 815, 12 USPQ2d 1508 (Fed. Cir. 1989).

[66]*Mendenhall v. Cedarapids, Inc.*, 5 F.3d 1556, 28 USPQ2d 1081 (Fed. Cir. 1993).

[67]*Connell v. Sears, Roebuck & Co.*, 722 F.2d 1542, 220 USPQ 193 (Fed. Cir. 1983). See also *Bio-Rad Labs., Inc. v. Nicolet Instr. Corp.*, 739 F.2d 604, 222 USPQ 654 (Fed. Cir. 1984) (patent misuse).

recognizing that a jury's fact findings common to a legal claim and an equitable defense are to be accepted by the court in ruling on the defense, the court has questioned resolution by the jury of equitable issues.[68]

(c) Jury Instructions

Jury instructions should be tailored to the dispute in the case[69] and must be confined to the issues as presented by the pleadings and evidence.[70] The particular findings the jury must make before it can reach a verdict are controlled by the court's instructions to the jury.[71] However valid a proffered instruction may be as an abstract proposition, it cannot be given after a trial involving no evidence relating to it.[72]

Jury instructions should be read in their entirety.[73] An instruction that is defective because of a misstatement of law is not cured simply by a correct statement appearing elsewhere. More is required of jury instructions than to state the law correctly somewhere in the instructions. The question, once a misstatement has been made, is whether the error was so egregious, considering the instructions as a whole, as to require the verdict to be set aside.[74] Jury instructions must be both legally correct and sufficiently comprehensive to address factual issues for which there is disputed evidence of record. But a party has no vested right in its own carefully couched form of words in an instruction. In order to prevail on appeal the party must demonstrate that the instructions read in their entirety were incorrect or incomplete as given and then show that the suggested instruction could

---

[68]*Quaker City Gear Works, Inc. v. Skil Corp.,* 747 F.2d 1446, 223 USPQ 1161 (Fed. Cir. 1984). In *B. Braun Med., Inc. v. Abbott Labs.,* 124 F.3d 1419, 43 USPQ2d 1896 (Fed. Cir. 1997), the court was able to pass the question whether, over objection, a trial court may ever submit an equitable issue, such as misuse, to a jury, either under Rule 39(b), FRCP, or under other authority.

[69]*Jamesbury Corp. v. Litton Indus. Prods., Inc.,* 756 F.2d 1556, 225 USPQ 253 (Fed. Cir. 1985).

[70]*American Hoist & Derrick Co. v. Sowa & Sons, Inc.,* 725 F.2d 1350, 220 USPQ 763 (Fed. Cir. 1984).

[71]*DMI, Inc. v. Deere & Co.,* 802 F.2d 421, 231 USPQ 276 (Fed. Cir. 1986); *Bio-Rad Labs., Inc. v. Nicolet Instr. Corp.,* 739 F.2d 604, 222 USPQ 654 (Fed. Cir. 1984); *Perkin-Elmer Corp. v. Computervision Corp.,* 732 F.2d 888, 221 USPQ 669 (Fed. Cir. 1984).

[72]*DMI, Inc. v. Deere & Co.,* 802 F.2d 421, 231 USPQ 276 (Fed. Cir. 1986). Conjecture and speculation are not competent evidence in this respect.

[73]*Jurgens v. McKasy,* 927 F.2d 1552, 18 USPQ2d 1031 (Fed. Cir. 1991); *Fonar Corp. v. Johnson & Johnson,* 821 F.2d 627, 3 USPQ2d 1109 (Fed. Cir. 1987); *Orthokinetics, Inc. v. Safety Travel Chairs, Inc.,* 806 F.2d 1565, 1 USPQ2d 1081 (Fed. Cir. 1986). Although interrogatories to a jury should be directed to factual matters, it is not error to call an instruction coupled with a request for verdict an "interrogatory." *Railroad Dynamics, Inc. v. A. Stucki Co.,* 727 F.2d 1506, 220 USPQ 929 (Fed. Cir. 1984). A new trial on the ground of erroneous instructions is permissible only when it is clear that an error in instructions as a whole was such as to have misled the jury. *New Idea Farm Equip. Corp. v. Sperry Corp.,* 916 F.2d 1561, 16 USPQ2d 1424 (Fed. Cir. 1990).

[74]*Jamesbury Corp. v. Litton Indus. Prods., Inc.,* 756 F.2d 1556, 225 USPQ 253 (Fed. Cir. 1985).

have cured the error.[75] A new trial is ordered only when errors in the instructions as a whole clearly misled the jury.[76] The standard of review of jury instructions is prejudicial legal error.[77]

A failure to object to an instruction before the jury retires precludes raising the propriety of the instruction later.[78] Thus, failure to proffer timely, specific objections to jury instructions precludes consideration of any such objection on appeal unless great injustice would result.[79] There is an affirmative obligation to timely raise objections to instructions or interrogatories on the basis of potential confusion of the jury in resolving questions. Failure to object prior to the verdict may well result in waiver of any postverdict challenge.[80] This rule was designed to avoid the "heads-or-tails" ploy by which counsel stands mute when an erroneous instruction is given, hoping for a favorable verdict and planning to use the erroneous instruction on appeal if the verdict be unfavorable.[81] Nonetheless, the court will sometimes reverse despite a failure to object to an instruction, if that is the only way to correct plain error.[82] It should be noted that the law presumes that the jury followed the trial court's instructions.[83]

---

[75]*Biodex Corp. v. Loredan Biomedical, Inc.*, 946 F.2d 850, 20 USPQ2d 1252 (Fed. Cir. 1991). See also *Goodwall Constr. Co. v. Beers Constr. Co.*, 991 F.2d 751, 26 USPQ2d 1420 (Fed. Cir. 1993); *Delta-X Corp. v. Baker Hughes Prod. Tools, Inc.*, 984 F.2d 410, 25 USPQ2d 1447 (Fed. Cir. 1993).

[76]*Delta-X Corp. v. Baker Hughes Prod. Tools, Inc.*, 984 F.2d 410, 25 USPQ2d 1447 (Fed. Cir. 1993).

[77]*Mendenhall v. Cedarapids, Inc.*, 5 F.3d 1556, 28 USPQ2d 1081 (Fed. Cir. 1993); *Jamesbury Corp. v. Litton Indus. Prods., Inc.*, 756 F.2d 1556, 225 USPQ 253 (Fed. Cir. 1985).

[78]*Modine Mfg. Co. v. Allen Group, Inc.*, 917 F.2d 538, 16 USPQ2d 1622 (Fed. Cir. 1990); *Weinar v. Rollform Inc.*, 744 F.2d 797, 223 USPQ 369 (Fed. Cir. 1984). For example, failure to object to an instruction that indicates a reference is prior art precludes the losing party from raising on appeal the issue of whether the reference is prior art as a matter of law. *Verdegaal Bros., Inc. v. Union Oil Co.*, 814 F.2d 628, 2 USPQ2d 1051 (Fed. Cir. 1987). Nor can a party complain that a trial court failed to give an instruction that it was not requested to give. *Data Line Corp. v. Micro Techs., Inc.*, 813 F.2d 1196, 1 USPQ2d 2052 (Fed. Cir. 1987). Unchallenged jury instructions state the law to be applied on review of the jury verdict. *Brooktree Corp. v. Advanced Micro Devices, Inc.*, 977 F.2d 1555, 24 USPQ2d 1401 (Fed. Cir. 1992). In *Hupp v. Siroflex of Am., Inc.*, 122 F.3d 1456, 43 USPQ2d 1887 (Fed. Cir. 1997), the court expressed some rather serious misgivings about a jury instruction on infringement that also required the jury to find the patent valid. The argument was that since the jury had found the patent invalid, it might have thought that it had to find the patent not infringed. But the court refused to order a new trial because the complaining party did not object when the instruction was given and did not seek clarification of the verdict before the jury was dismissed.

[79]*Lummus Indus., Inc. v. D.M. & E. Corp.*, 862 F.2d 267, 8 USPQ2d 1983 (Fed. Cir. 1988); *Orthokinetics, Inc. v. Safety Travel Chairs, Inc.*, 806 F.2d 1565, 1 USPQ2d 1081 (Fed. Cir. 1986); *Medtronic Inc. v. Intermedics, Inc.*, 799 F.2d 734, 230 USPQ 641 (Fed. Cir. 1986); *Bio-Rad Labs., Inc. v. Nicolet Instr. Corp.*, 739 F.2d 604, 222 USPQ 654 (Fed. Cir. 1984). See also *Goodwall Constr. Co. v. Beers Constr. Co.*, 991 F.2d 751, 26 USPQ2d 1420 (Fed. Cir. 1993).

[80]*Allen Organ Co. v. Kimball Int'l, Inc.*, 839 F.2d 1556, 5 USPQ2d 1769 (Fed. Cir. 1988). The court, in an apparent dictum, also indicated that an instruction to which no timely objection is made becomes law of the case. Would not waiver suffice?

[81]*Glaros v. H.H. Robertson Co.*, 797 F.2d 1564, 230 USPQ 393 (Fed. Cir. 1986).

[82]*American Hoist & Derrick Co. v. Sowa & Sons, Inc.*, 725 F.2d 1350, 220 USPQ 763 (Fed. Cir. 1984). But see *Brooktree Corp. v. Advanced Micro Devices, Inc.*, 977 F.2d 1555, 24 USPQ2d 1401 (Fed. Cir. 1992).

[83]*Weinar v. Rollform Inc.*, 744 F.2d 797, 223 USPQ 369, 377 (Fed. Cir. 1984).

(d) Patent Issues

There are no special rules for patent jury cases; the law and rules of procedure generally applicable to civil jury cases apply without exception in patent jury cases.[84] The role of a trial court in a patent jury trial should not be significantly different from its role in a patent bench trial with respect to legal issues.[85]

It is no error to submit the question of obviousness to a jury.[86] It is established that the jury may decide the questions of anticipation and obviousness, either as separate special verdicts or en route to a verdict on the question of validity.[87] When the legal question of obviousness is submitted to the jury, it is technically improper to characterize the question as a special verdict under Rule 49(a), FRCP, because that rule only provides for the submission of fact questions to the jury.[88]

Legal questions are routinely submitted to the jury in other types of cases. The obviousness inquiry is somewhat like negligence; one skilled in the art is like the hypothetical reasonable person.[89] But unlike a verdict on negligence to which the jury is expected to contribute the sense of the community, a decision on patent validity does not benefit from the jury's communal sense of patentability. A patentee, as well as an infringer, is entitled to have its position judged only by the standard that Congress has written into the statute. Thus, a party has a right, upon proper requests, to have the trial court delineate in its instructions what facts in the particular case must be found to reach a conclusion of obviousness and what facts require a contrary answer.[90] The duty of the trial court, therefore, is to give instructions that are meaningful, not in terms of some abstract case, but which can be understood and given effect by the jury once it resolves the issues of fact that are in dispute. To repeat statutory language is not sufficient unless its meaning and application to the facts are clear without explanation. Obviousness is not a term readily understood by a jury; it is overladen with laypersons' meanings different from its legal connotations in the patent law. It is thus error for the trial court to abdicate its responsibility to inform the jury of how the

---

[84]*Railroad Dynamics, Inc. v. A. Stucki Co.*, 727 F.2d 1506, 220 USPQ 929 (Fed. Cir. 1984); *Connell v. Sears, Roebuck & Co.*, 722 F.2d 1542, 220 USPQ 193 (Fed. Cir. 1983).

[85]*Structural Rubber Prods. Co. v. Park Rubber Co.*, 749 F.2d 707, 223 USPQ 1264 (Fed. Cir. 1984).

[86]*Railroad Dynamics, Inc. v. A. Stucki Co.*, 727 F.2d 1506, 220 USPQ 929 (Fed. Cir. 1984); *Connell v. Sears, Roebuck &* Co., 722 F.2d 1542, 220 USPQ 193 (Fed. Cir. 1983). Obviousness is a legal determination that may be submitted to a jury with proper instruction. *In re Hayes Microcomputer Patent Litig.*, 982 F.2d 1527, 25 USPQ2d 1241 (Fed. Cir. 1992).

[87]*Richardson v. Suzuki Motor Co.*, 868 F.2d 1226, 9 USPQ2d 1913 (Fed. Cir. 1989).

[88]*Newell Cos. v. Kenney Mfg. Co.*, 864 F.2d 757, 9 USPQ2d 1417 (Fed. Cir. 1988); *Sjolund v. Musland*, 847 F.2d 1573, 6 USPQ2d 2020 (Fed. Cir. 1988).

[89]*Connell v. Sears, Roebuck & Co.*, 722 F.2d 1542, 220 USPQ 193 (Fed. Cir. 1983).

[90]*Structural Rubber Prods. Co. v. Park Rubber Co.*, 749 F.2d 707, 223 USPQ 1264 (Fed. Cir. 1984).

obviousness statute applies to the particular case.[91] Instructions on obviousness should track §103 and make clear, at a minimum, that the jury must consider the invention as a whole and must walk in the shoes of one skilled in the art at the time the invention was made.[92]

Rulings on instructions as to various patent issues demonstrate the court's concern that the jury is adequately and accurately instructed on the patent law. Certainly outdated or obsolete statements of the law will be quickly rejected. For example, it was held wholly erroneous to instruct the jury that the elements making up the claimed invention must perform a new and unexpected function in the combination.[93] Likewise, language in an instruction to the effect that the jury must give careful scrutiny before endorsing the patent monopoly constituted prejudicial legal error.[94] It was also error to instruct that the presumption of validity can be overcome merely by a preponderance of the evidence if the patent examiner was misled as to the meaning of certain prior art.[95]

An instruction that anticipation is established by a prior art disclosure that is "substantially the same" or that does not differ in "significant particulars" is erroneous.[96] It is also error to give an instruction that suggests the jury should decide whether a person of ordinary skill in the art would actually know about the prior art references.[97] Although enablement is ultimately a question of law, there may be underlying factual issues involved, and it is amenable to resolution by the jury.[98]

---

[91]*Structural Rubber Prods. Co. v. Park Rubber Co.*, 749 F.2d 707, 223 USPQ 1264 (Fed. Cir. 1984).

[92]*Connell v. Sears, Roebuck & Co.*, 722 F.2d 1542, 220 USPQ 193 (Fed. Cir. 1983). *United States Surgical Corp. v. Ethicon, Inc.*, 103 F.3d 1554, 41 USPQ2d 1225 (Fed. Cir. 1997), is instructive with respect to the propriety of various instructions, and suggested instructions, dealing with the obviousness inquiry.

[93]*American Hoist & Derrick Co. v. Sowa & Sons, Inc.*, 725 F.2d 1350, 220 USPQ 763 (Fed. Cir. 1984).

[94]*Jamesbury Corp. v. Litton Indus. Prods., Inc.*, 756 F.2d 1556, 225 USPQ 253 (Fed. Cir. 1985).

[95]*Jamesbury Corp. v. Litton Indus. Prods., Inc.*, 756 F.2d 1556, 225 USPQ 253 (Fed. Cir. 1985). On the other hand, a jury should be instructed that the PTO has found the claims patentable on reissue over additional prior art, and the defendant's burden has therefore become more difficult, both as to patentability and fraud. *American Hoist & Derrick Co. v. Sowa & Sons, Inc.*, 725 F.2d 1350, 220 USPQ 763 (Fed. Cir. 1984).

[96]*Jamesbury Corp. v. Litton Indus. Prods., Inc.*, 756 F.2d 1556, 225 USPQ 253 (Fed. Cir. 1985). Indeed, where it was admitted that no single prior art reference taught the claimed invention, it was error to submit the question of lack of novelty to the jury, and when they returned a verdict, it was reversible error not to correct it by JMOL. The trial court does not sit to approve miscarriages of justice. *Structural Rubber Prods. Co. v. Park Rubber Co.*, 749 F.2d 707, 223 USPQ 1264 (Fed. Cir. 1984). Likewise, it is error to submit the question of whether a reference is prior art to the jury where there is no dispute about it. *Quaker City Gear Works, Inc. v. Skil Corp.*, 747 F.2d 1446, 223 USPQ 1161 (Fed. Cir. 1984). A jury finding that there "was no prior art" cannot possibly stand in the face of numerous clearly relevant prior art patents in the trial record. *Connell v. Sears, Roebuck & Co.*, 722 F.2d 1542, 220 USPQ 193 (Fed. Cir. 1983).

[97]*Quaker City Gear Works, Inc. v. Skil Corp.*, 747 F.2d 1446, 223 USPQ 1161 (Fed. Cir. 1984).

[98]*Allen Organ Co. v. Kimball Int'l, Inc.*, 839 F.2d 1556, 5 USPQ2d 1769 (Fed. Cir. 1988); *Spectra-Physics, Inc. v. Coherent, Inc.*, 827 F.2d 1524, 3 USPQ2d 1737 (Fed. Cir. 1987).

A jury instruction that indicates the patent must be found invalid if the inventor was not the actual and only inventor is an oversimplification, in that it does not recognize the possibility of curing improper inventorship.[99] And it is error to fail to instruct the jury on reasonable or established royalty or lost profits and speak instead only in terms of "monetary loss."[100]

The court has now held squarely that claim interpretation is for the judge not the jury, and that this rule does not deprive parties of their right to a jury trial in patent infringement cases. The patentee's right to a jury trial on the application of the properly construed claim to the accused device is preserved.[101] When the question of infringement is given to a jury, there is a special burden placed on the trial judge—as well as the parties—to ensure that the second step in the infringement analysis, that of comparing the claims to the accused product or process, does not cause the first step, interpreting the claims properly, to get short shrift.[102]

In *Hilton-Davis*,[103] the court held that infringement under the doctrine of equivalents is an issue of fact to be submitted to the jury with proper instructions. In a jury trial, the theory of equivalence is not necessarily included in or a part of literal infringement theory. This may be so in a bench trial, but a jury cannot be expected to make a determination of equivalence absent evidence and argument on the subject. Thus, there is no error in refusing to instruct the jury on equivalence where no competent evidence on the subject, other than evidence of literal infringement, was offered at trial.[104] On the other hand, where a jury is given instructions as to literal infringement but not equivalents, a jury verdict of infringement cannot stand unless the accused device literally infringes the claim.[105] A jury must be separately directed to the proof of each element of the doctrine of equivalents: function performed, means by which the function is performed, and result achieved. The party asserting infringement

---

[99]*Shatterproof Glass Corp. v. Libbey-Owens Ford Co.*, 758 F.2d 613, 225 USPQ 634 (Fed. Cir. 1985).

[100]*American Hoist & Derrick Co. v. Sowa & Sons, Inc.*, 725 F.2d 1350, 220 USPQ 763, 775 (Fed. Cir. 1984).

[101]*Markman v. Westview Instr., Inc.*, 52 F.3d 967, 34 USPQ2d 1321 (Fed. Cir. 1995). In view of *Markman*, the court will apparently treat jury determinations of claim construction issues as advisory only. See *Laitram Corp. v. NEC Corp.*, 62 F.3d 1388, 36 USPQ2d 1206 (Fed. Cir. 1995). But see *Tol-O-Matic, Inc. v. Proma Produckt-und Mktg. GmbH*, 945 F.2d 1546, 20 USPQ2d 1332 (Fed. Cir. 1991).

[102]*Lemelson v. General Mills, Inc.*, 968 F.2d 1202, 23 USPQ2d 1284 (Fed. Cir. 1992). Claim interpretation is a question of law for the court. Where the court's interpretation is not set forth in its instructions to the jury, the court must perform its role of deciding this issue in ruling on the JMOL motion. *Read Corp. v. Portec, Inc.*, 970 F.2d 816, 23 USPQ2d 1426 (Fed. Cir. 1992).

[103]*Hilton Davis Chem. Co. v. Warner-Jenkinson Co.*, 62 F.3d 1512, 35 USPQ2d 1641 (Fed. Cir. 1995). The Supreme Court, in its review of the case, found it unnecessary to decide this matter. See text accompanying note 6:248.

[104]*Nestier Corp. v. Menasha Corp.*, 739 F.2d 1576, 222 USPQ 747 (Fed. Cir. 1984).

[105]*Data Line Corp. v. Micro Techs., Inc.*, 813 F.2d 1196, 1 USPQ2d 2052 (Fed. Cir. 1987).

must present evidence and argument concerning the doctrine and each of its elements. The evidence and argument cannot merely be subsumed in the plaintiff's case of literal infringement. The elements must be presented in the form of particularized testimony and linking argument. Otherwise, a jury is more or less put to sea without guiding charts, and there is too much risk the jury will simply compare the invention and the accused infringement as to overall similarity.[106]

Absent sufficient basis for directing a verdict, a party has a right of jury determination of the question of willful infringement. Willfulness of behavior is a classical jury question of intent.[107]

A trial court can permit the jury to decide intent, but reserve to itself the ultimate question of inequitable conduct.[108] The Federal Circuit is particularly careful about instructions regarding fraud and inequitable conduct. An instruction should not employ the terms "fraudulent representation" and "fraudulently withhold," because they cause only confusion and do not direct the jury to relevant factual inquiries. Since the jury must determine how convincing has been the proof of intent, it should be instructed that it may find a showing on this element to be lacking entirely or that it may find intent to have been shown by any relevant degree of proof, from inference (gross negligence or recklessness) to direct evidence (a deliberate scheme). Where there is no testimony from the examiner, it is error to instruct the jury that withheld information must have a "material influence upon the examiner" or that the applicant must "fully disclose all pertinent facts which may affect the decision" of the PTO. The jury should be instructed to determine the pertinency of the withheld information (a question of fact) and then resolve materiality in light thereof, using one of the several tests for materiality.[109]

(e) Form of Verdict

A trial judge has broad discretion in trial management, including choice of general or special jury verdicts or interrogatories.[110] A jury

---

[106]*Lear Siegler, Inc. v. Sealy Mattress Co.*, 873 F.2d 1422, 10 USPQ2d 1767 (Fed. Cir. 1989). See also *Richardson v. Suzuki Motor Co.*, 868 F.2d 1226, 9 USPQ2d 1913 (Fed. Cir. 1989) (too narrow a definition of "equivalent" results in reversal of verdict of no equivalents). It is important to focus on equivalency to limitations of the claim, rather than equivalency to the invention, particularly in jury trials. Otherwise laypersons may be led to comparison of devices, rather than between the accused device and the claim, and to rely on generalities in the overall purpose of the devices. *Read Corp. v. Portec, Inc.*, 970 F.2d 816, 23 USPQ2d 1426 (Fed. Cir. 1992).

[107]*Richardson v. Suzuki Motor Co.*, 868 F.2d 1226, 9 USPQ2d 1913 (Fed. Cir. 1989).

[108]*Tol-O-Matic, Inc. v. Proma Produckt-und Mktg. GmbH*, 945 F.2d 1546, 20 USPQ2d 1332 (Fed. Cir. 1991).

[109]*American Hoist & Derrick Co. v. Sowa & Sons, Inc.*, 725 F.2d 1350, 220 USPQ 763 (Fed. Cir. 1984).

[110]*Tol-O-Matic, Inc. v. Proma Produckt-und Mktg. GmbH*, 945 F.2d 1546, 20 USPQ2d 1332 (Fed. Cir. 1991). The specificity of a verdict is within the discretion of the trial judge. *Hoechst Celanese Corp. v. BP Chem. Ltd.*, 78 F.3d 1575, 38 USPQ2d 1126 (Fed. Cir. 1996).

in a civil case can return a naked general verdict. Such a verdict involves a presumption that the jury found the facts and reached the legal conclusion undergirding its verdict. But it leaves a wide area of uncertainty on review, and appellate judges have expressed grave concern about the use of a general verdict in civil cases. There are several ways to alleviate the uncertainty: (1) a special verdict under Rule 49(a) in which the jury answers specific fact questions; (2) a general verdict with interrogatories under Rule 49(b); and (3) legal instructions under Rule 51. In addition, Rule 50(a) provides for a directed verdict, and Rule 50(b) for JMOL. Rule 59(a) provides for new trial on many grounds, including a determination that the jury reached its verdict as a result of passion and prejudice. Finally, Rule 52 makes it clear that, when using an advisory jury, the court must make its own findings of fact and conclusions of law. These rules safeguard against unruly or "rogue elephant" juries and ensure reliability of jury verdicts.[111] A party by its proposal of or acquiescence in a verdict form waives objection, except under egregious circumstances.[112]

Under Rule 49(a), FRCP, the jury makes written findings on each factual issue, and the court applies the law to the jury's findings. Rule 49(b) is a middle course between the simple general verdict and the special verdict procedure of Rule 49(a) in that it focuses the jury's attention on the controlling points at issue, and the interrogatory answers provide a check on the propriety of the general verdict.[113] The distinction between special verdicts and special interrogatories is unclear. Rule 49(a) applies to special verdicts, while Rule 49(b) applies to general verdicts, which may be accompanied by special interrogatories.[114] Judgment may be entered when a jury functioning under Rule 49(a) has returned answers to some but not all interrogatories if the answers returned are dispositive of the case.[115]

---

[111]*Connell v. Sears, Roebuck & Co.*, 722 F.2d 1542, 220 USPQ 193 (Fed. Cir. 1983).

[112]*Hoechst Celanese Corp. v. BP Chem. Ltd.*, 78 F.3d 1575, 38 USPQ2d 1126 (Fed. Cir. 1996).

[113]*Allen Organ Co. v. Kimball Int'l, Inc.*, 839 F.2d 1556, 5 USPQ2d 1769 (Fed. Cir. 1988). The label "verdict" in Rule 49(a) is an unfortunate choice. Special verdicts are just jury answers to factual interrogatories. "Verdict" was apparently employed because returning verdicts is what juries do. Doubtless the drafters expected courts and counsel to distinguish between a general verdict, naked or accompanied by answers to interrogatories under Rule 49(b) (in returning either of which a jury finds the facts, applies the law as instructed, and designates the winning side), and a special verdict (in returning which a jury supplies only written answers to fact questions). *Wahpeton Canvas Co. v. Frontier, Inc.*, 870 F.2d 1546, 10 USPQ2d 1201 (Fed. Cir. 1989).

[114]*Arachnid, Inc. v. Medalist Mktg. Corp.*, 972 F.2d 1300, 23 USPQ2d 1946 (Fed. Cir. 1992).

[115]*Wahpeton Canvas Co. v. Frontier, Inc.*, 870 F.2d 1546, 10 USPQ2d 1201 (Fed. Cir. 1989). Here, a finding that a device does not infringe an independent claim on which the jury answered could not be said to compel a finding that the device does not infringe a different independent claim on which the jury did not answer. In *Goodwall Constr. Co. v. Beers Constr. Co.*, 991 F.2d 751, 26 USPQ2d 1420 (Fed. Cir. 1993), the verdict form provided blanks to answer yes or no to both literal infringement and infringement by equivalents. The trial judge had instructed that if the jury found literal infringement and answered "yes" in that blank, it should not consider equivalents and should put a "no" in that blank, which is precisely what happened.

A compilation of written findings on each issue of fact is a special verdict. The practice contemplates that the judge will submit only factual questions to the jury and will then apply the law, supplementing if necessary any factual determinations not submitted to the jury. If the verdict does not answer all the questions, it may, unless wholly defective, be accepted for those issues that are resolved. A party may request reconsideration by the jury of unresolved factual issues or may be entitled to a retrial of those issues. But if the party agrees to an instruction that the jury need not answer all the questions, the right to trial by jury of those questions may be waived, and the court would be empowered to complete the findings, apply the law, and direct entry of judgment. Where the court determines that the answers given are reconcilable (not hopelessly in conflict), the special verdict should be recorded as such and after the law is applied, the court should direct entry of judgment. If the answers in a special verdict do not support a party's contention, it should move for JMOL, since it wishes to challenge the sufficiency of the evidence supporting those answers. Finally, the court is not free to make a specific finding that overrules an implicit and inherent finding of the jury within a broader question; rather, the court must accept the jury's determination unless it is not supported by substantial evidence.[116] The Federal Circuit has given a strong indication that it favors the use of special verdicts under Rule 49(a) as a means of simplifying the jury instruction writing process.[117] Where a special verdict form asks the jury to answer only an ultimate question, the jury instructions serve as the most direct guide as to what facts the jury found.[118]

A court is bound to find special verdicts consistent if it can do so under a fair reading of them.[119] The issue of inconsistent jury findings is a procedural matter not unique to patent law and the Federal Circuit accordingly applies the discernable law of the forum.[120] Under

---

The judge then quite properly concluded that the jury had not decided anything about equivalents and went on to consider the matter himself. He concluded that a reasonable jury would have found infringement under the doctrine of equivalents and entered judgment to that effect. Although he approached the matter under Rule 50(b) rather than Rule 49(a), which would have been the proper avenue, no error resulted. It should be noted that because neither party had objected to the judge's instruction on the matter, both were deemed to have waived the right to a jury trial on equivalents if the jury found literal infringement.

[116]*Quaker City Gear Works, Inc. v. Skil Corp.*, 747 F.2d 1446, 223 USPQ 1161 (Fed. Cir. 1984).

[117]*Richardson-Vicks, Inc. v. Upjohn Co.*, 122 F.3d 1476, 44 USPQ2d 1181 (Fed. Cir. 1997); *Structural Rubber Prods. Co. v. Park Rubber Co.*, 749 F.2d 707, 223 USPQ 1264 (Fed. Cir. 1984).

[118]*Wang Labs., Inc. v. Mitsubishi Elec. Am., Inc.*, 103 F.3d 1571, 41 USPQ2d 1263 (Fed. Cir. 1997).

[119]*Richardson v. Suzuki Motor Co.*, 868 F.2d 1226, 9 USPQ2d 1913 (Fed. Cir. 1989). In *Beckman Instr., Inc. v. LKB Produkter AB*, 892 F.2d 1547, 13 USPQ2d 1301 (Fed. Cir. 1989), the court found no problem reconciling a jury finding of validity and infringement as to method claims with a finding of invalidity and noninfringement as to apparatus claims of the same patent.

[120]*Arachnid, Inc. v. Medalist Mktg. Corp.*, 972 F.2d 1300, 23 USPQ2d 1946 (Fed. Cir. 1992). Under Ninth Circuit law, a party may challenge the consistency of a jury verdict for the first time in a posttrial motion, and need not raise it before the jury is discharged. However,

Seventh Circuit law, when interrogatory answers are inconsistent with each other, and the general verdict is consistent with less than all of the interrogatory answers, there is an obligation under Rule 49(b) to seek return of the jury. It is not clear whether a similar waiver would result under Rule 49(a). In any event, when it is possible to reconcile the jury's answers, such reconciliation is always preferable to the grant of a new trial.[121]

When a jury returns a general verdict unaccompanied by special interrogatories, the law presumes the existence of fact findings implied from the jury's having reached that verdict.[122] The general verdict thus includes the jury's legal conclusion and a set of implied fact findings necessary to support the legal conclusion encompassed in the verdict.[123] Under the general verdict/multiple defenses rule, even if most of the possible grounds for an invalidity or unenforceability verdict are supported by substantial evidence, a new trial must be ordered if any one of the possible grounds is unsupported by substantial evidence.[124] When liability is argued to the jury on alternate legal theories, one of which is not legally correct or is not a permissible

---

such a challenge must be made at the district court level, and cannot be raised for the first time on appeal. *Id.*

[121]*Allen Organ Co. v. Kimball Int'l, Inc.,* 839 F.2d 1556, 5 USPQ2d 1769 (Fed. Cir. 1988). Here the jury answered interrogatories about public use and sale in the affirmative, but answered obviousness interrogatories in the negative. The court had no difficulty in reconciling this inconsistency with the judgment of invalidity. It is likely that the jury did not view the public use and sale circumstances as part of the prior art for purposes of the obviousness inquiry. See also *Mendenhall v. Cedarapids, Inc.,* 5 F.3d 1556, 28 USPQ2d 1081 (Fed. Cir. 1993) (certain claims held invalid for public use but not obvious). In *Baxter Healthcare Corp. v. Spectramed, Inc.,* 49 F.3d 1575, 34 USPQ2d 1120 (Fed. Cir. 1995), the jury had deadlocked on a special interrogatory as to validity and the patentee argued that the district court should have entered judgment in its favor, on the ground that the defendant had failed to meet its burden of proving invalidity on those issues by clear and convincing evidence. The issue was very real, inasmuch as a JMOL of noninfringement was reversed. The Federal Circuit, without explanation, simply said "We disagree," and remanded for the district court to decide the validity issue. In *Richardson v. Suzuki Motor Co.,* 868 F.2d 1226, 9 USPQ2d 1913 (Fed. Cir. 1989), the jury could not reach a unanimous verdict on the question of whether a person of ordinary skill, presented with the problem and being familiar with all the prior art, would be "led to do" what the inventor did. However, the jury did reach a unanimous verdict that the claim was valid. The court was able to resolve this apparent inconsistency on the following reasoning: the question for the jury was whether the challenger met its burden of proving invalidity by clear and convincing evidence; and the question on review is whether reasonable jurors could have concluded that the challenger failed to meet that burden. The jury's lack of unanimity on the special verdict could reasonably be taken to mean that invalidity had not been proved by clear and convincing evidence.

[122]*DMI, Inc. v. Deere & Co.,* 802 F.2d 421, 231 USPQ 276 (Fed. Cir. 1986); *Bio-Rad Labs., Inc. v. Nicolet Instr. Corp.,* 739 F.2d 604, 222 USPQ 654 (Fed. Cir. 1984); *Perkin-Elmer Corp. v. Computervision Corp.,* 732 F.2d 888, 221 USPQ 669 (Fed. Cir. 1984); *Railroad Dynamics, Inc. v. A. Stucki Co.,* 727 F.2d 1506, 220 USPQ 929 (Fed. Cir. 1984). It is well settled that a jury is presumed to have resolved disputed factual issues in favor of the verdict winner. However, it may not be presumed that the jury found facts on which there is no evidence. Nor is the jury free to discard probative admissions and undisputed facts. *Newell Cos. v. Kenney Mfg. Co.,* 864 F.2d 757, 9 USPQ2d 1417 (Fed. Cir. 1988).

[123]*Railroad Dynamics, Inc. v. A. Stucki Co.,* 727 F.2d 1506, 220 USPQ 929 (Fed. Cir. 1984). It is not an abuse of discretion to fashion multiple general verdict questions to conform to the multiple claims and devices at issue in a patent infringement case.

[124]*Arachnid, Inc. v. Medalist Mktg. Corp.,* 972 F.2d 1300, 23 USPQ2d 1946 (Fed. Cir. 1992).

jury question, a general verdict of liability cannot stand lest it have been based on the incorrect or impermissible theory. This principle has been applied to multiple claims as well as to multiple theories, when one of the claims or theories should not have been submitted to the jury.[125] Obviously, then, the presence of special interrogatories greatly facilitates the role of the trial judge on motion for JMOL and new trial and eases the job of the appellate court.[126] One advantage of the use of separate verdicts is that some may be accepted for those issues that are resolved according to the evidence and the law and others need not be relied upon or may even be rejected outright. Thus, a new trial may be avoided entirely or be necessary on only certain issues. The trial judge reserves a large measure of control over the judgment to be entered.[127]

The Federal Circuit has indicated a very strong preference for the use of interrogatories on the controlling facts in patent disputes. Failure to use interrogatories invokes a heavy burden of convincing the reviewing court that the trial judge did not abuse his or her discretion. Their use facilitates appellate review by freeing the court from having to survey every possible basis for the jury's decision. It also accords with the inherent divisional lines between the roles of judge and jury and may help avoid lengthy retrials by permitting application of the harmless error standard of review.[128] Nonetheless, the court has taken pains to explain that it is not insisting that interrogatories must be submitted to the jury on the question of obviousness—only that it is advantageous. A judgment based on a verdict cannot be vacated solely for failure to do so; whether to do so is in the discretion of the trial court and reviewable only upon a showing of abuse.[129] Findings duplicating a jury's interrogatory answers are unnecessary and may even cause problems, for those that recast the jury's actual language, although not inconsistent, may

---

[125]*Mitsubishi Elec. Corp. v. Ampex Corp.*, 190 F.3d 1300, 51 USPQ2d 1910 (Fed. Cir. 1999). Here the general question of invalidity was submitted to the jury, but defendant was asserting three separate grounds. The court held that plaintiff had not objected sufficiently to this procedure to preserve the matter for appeal. It went on, however, to hold that the instructions relating to each individual ground for invalidity were proper.

[126]*Vieau v. Japax, Inc.*, 823 F.2d 1510, 3 USPQ2d 1094 (Fed. Cir. 1987); *Bio-Rad Labs., Inc. v. Nicolet Instr. Corp.*, 739 F.2d 604, 222 USPQ 654 (Fed. Cir. 1984); *Perkin-Elmer Corp. v. Computervision Corp.*, 732 F.2d 888, 221 USPQ 669 (Fed. Cir. 1984); *Railroad Dynamics, Inc. v. A. Stucki Co.*, 727 F.2d 1506, 220 USPQ 929 (Fed. Cir. 1984).

[127]*Mendenhall v. Cedarapids, Inc.*, 5 F.3d 1556, 28 USPQ2d 1081 (Fed. Cir. 1993).

[128]*American Hoist & Derrick Co. v. Sowa & Sons, Inc.*, 725 F.2d 1350, 220 USPQ 763 (Fed. Cir. 1984). See also *White v. Jeffrey Min. Mach. Co.*, 723 F.2d 1553, 220 USPQ 703 (Fed. Cir. 1983); *Yuba Goldfields, Inc. v. United States*, 723 F.2d 884 (Fed. Cir. 1983). Certainly a trial court may not solicit only a legal conclusion from the jury and then act as a fact finder preliminary to expressing agreement with the jury's legal determination. *American Hoist & Derrick Co. v. Sowa & Sons, Inc.*, 725 F.2d 1350, 220 USPQ 763 (Fed. Cir. 1984).

[129]*Allen Organ Co. v. Kimball Int'l, Inc.*, 839 F.2d 1556, 5 USPQ2d 1769 (Fed. Cir. 1988); *Weinar v. Rollform Inc.*, 744 F.2d 797, 223 USPQ 369 (Fed. Cir. 1984). The form of a jury verdict is within the discretion of the trial judge. *Lummus Indus., Inc. v. D.M. & E. Corp.*, 862 F.2d 267, 8 USPQ2d 1983 (Fed. Cir. 1988).

enable the appellant to focus its attack on the findings rather than the jury's verdict.[130]

All fact findings of a jury are nonadvisory unless made in an area expressly removed from the jury verdict. Thus it is neither appropriate nor necessary for a trial court to label as "advisory" a jury finding as to willful infringement and to make its own finding, in order to exercise its statutory discretion to award increased damages.[131] The court regards advisory verdicts as a "discredited procedure."[132]

(f) Posttrial Practice in Jury Cases

It should be kept in mind that, in accordance with the amendment to the Federal Rules effective December 1, 1991, motions for JNOV and for directed verdict are now denominated motions for judgment as a matter of law (JMOL).[133] The court now refers to "judgment as a matter of law" by using the acronym JMOL in place of JNOV.[134] Under Rule 50(b), when a motion for JMOL is made after a verdict is returned, the court may allow the judgment to stand, order a new trial, or direct entry of judgment as a matter of law.[135]

If prejudicial error occurred, or if the verdict is against the clear weight of the evidence, a new trial may be granted as an alternative to JMOL.[136] Rule 59 allows a trial court to grant a new trial on all or part of the issues tried to a jury for any of the reasons for which new trials have been granted in actions at law in federal courts. These include cases where the verdict is against the great weight of the

---

[130]*Glaros v. H.H. Robertson Co.*, 797 F.2d 1564, 230 USPQ 393 (Fed. Cir. 1986).

[131]*Shiley, Inc. v. Bentley Labs., Inc.*, 794 F.2d 1561, 230 USPQ 112 (Fed. Cir. 1986). Increased damages are assigned to the court, whether the facts of willful conduct justifying an increase are found by a jury or by the court. If the jury finds willful infringement and it is not overturned on motion for JMOL, then the court has discretion to award increased damages. If the finding of the jury is no willful infringement and its verdict is not overturned on JMOL, no basis for assessing increased damages exists. *Id.*

[132]*Richardson v. Suzuki Motor Co.*, 868 F.2d 1226, 9 USPQ2d 1913 (Fed. Cir. 1989). In *Transmatic, Inc. v. Gulton Indus., Inc.*, 53 F.3d 1270, 35 USPQ2d 1035 (Fed. Cir. 1995), the trial court used an advisory jury and simply accepted its damages award without making sufficiently comprehensive and detailed findings of fact of its own. This was error. The use of an advisory jury does not free the trial court from its obligation under Rule 52(a).

[133]*Brooktree Corp. v. Advanced Micro Devices, Inc.*, 977 F.2d 1555, 24 USPQ2d 1401 (Fed. Cir. 1992).

[134]*Amsted Indus. v. Buckeye Steel Castings Co.*, 24 F.3d 178, 30 USPQ2d 1462 (Fed. Cir. 1994).

[135]*Laitram Corp. v. NEC Corp.*, 115 F.3d 947, 42 USPQ2d 1897 (Fed. Cir. 1997).

[136]*New Idea Farm Equip. Corp. v. Sperry Corp.*, 916 F.2d 1561, 16 USPQ2d 1424 (Fed. Cir. 1990); *Shatterproof Glass Corp. v. Libbey-Owens Ford Co.*, 758 F.2d 613, 225 USPQ 634 (Fed. Cir. 1985). Rule 59(a) provides for a new trial where the jury reaches its verdict as a result of passion and prejudice. *Connell v. Sears, Roebuck & Co.*, 722 F.2d 1542, 220 USPQ 193 (Fed. Cir. 1983). The difference between JMOL and new trial motions can be understood by considering a factual patent question like anticipation. The critical question in the JMOL context is whether a reasonable juror could have found that the reference failed to anticipate; in the context of a motion for a new trial, it is whether the trial court abused its discretion in determining that a finding of no anticipation was not against the clear weight of the evidence. *Standard Havens Prods., Inc. v. Gencor Indus., Inc.*, 953 F.2d 1360, 21 USPQ2d 1321 (Fed. Cir. 1992).

evidence. The court may thus grant a new trial even where substantial evidence supports the verdict, if the verdict is against the clear weight of evidence. This discretionary authority is aided in part by the ability of the trial judge to weigh the evidence and assess the credibility of witnesses. Unlike a JMOL, the trial judge need not view the evidence from the perspective most favorable to the prevailing party.[137] Improper coercion of a jury can amount to an unfair trial. A trial court should be wary not to actually or seemingly influence a jury to forego their conscientious convictions in order to reach a verdict when at an impasse.[138]

An appeal from a denial of a mistrial motion or a motion for a new trial should generally be taken from the final judgment.[139] The Federal Circuit reviews the grant or denial of a motion for a new trial under the abuse of discretion standard.[140] That question turns on whether an error occurred in the conduct of the trial that was so grievous as to have rendered the trial unfair.[141] In reviewing the trial court's denial of a new trial, the court of appeals reviews the jury instructions as a whole to determine whether clear error occurred, such that the jury was misled.[142] It may be inappropriate to order a partial new trial. A partial retrial may not be resorted to unless it clearly appears that the issue to be retried is so distinct and separable from the others that a new trial of it alone may be had without injustice.[143]

---

[137]*Litton Sys., Inc. v. Honeywell, Inc.*, 87 F.3d 1559, 39 USPQ2d 1321 (Fed. Cir. 1996). Note that in this case the court affirmed the trial judge's grant of a new trial on the $1.2 billion dollar damage award. It felt the trial judge was in the best position to evaluate the plaintiff's damage theory as propounded by its expert—it agreed that the model was too speculative.

[138]*Witco Chem. Corp. v. Peachtree Doors, Inc.*, 787 F.2d 1545, 229 USPQ 188 (Fed. Cir. 1986). After a long trial and long deliberations, the jury remained at an impasse on infringement. The trial judge, recognizing their weariness, decided to excuse them indefinitely subject to recall. Then the jury was recalled and issued additional instructions, after which they rendered a prompt verdict. That sequence of events, in the view of the Federal Circuit, seemingly coerced the jury into reaching a verdict, any verdict, for the sake of reaching an agreement, any agreement, in order to end the trial.

[139]*Witco Chem. Corp. v. Peachtree Doors, Inc.*, 787 F.2d 1545, 229 USPQ 188 (Fed. Cir. 1986).

[140]*Orthokinetics, Inc. v. Safety Travel Chairs, Inc.*, 806 F.2d 1565, 1 USPQ2d 1081 (Fed. Cir. 1986); *Witco Chem. Corp. v. Peachtree Doors, Inc.*, 787 F.2d 1545, 229 USPQ 188 (Fed. Cir. 1986); *Shatterproof Glass Corp. v. Libbey-Owens Ford Co.*, 758 F.2d 613, 225 USPQ 634 (Fed. Cir. 1985); *Bio-Rad Labs., Inc. v. Nicolet Instr. Corp.*, 739 F.2d 604, 222 USPQ 654 (Fed. Cir. 1984). Where the basis for the motion is abuse of the discovery process, that question is particularly within the province of the trial judge. *Bio-Rad Labs., Inc. v. Nicolet Instr. Corp.*, 739 F.2d 604, 222 USPQ 654 (Fed. Cir. 1984).

[141]*Orthokinetics, Inc. v. Safety Travel Chairs, Inc.*, 806 F.2d 1565, 1 USPQ2d 1081 (Fed. Cir. 1986). The moving party failed to show sufficient prejudice despite (1) having had to deliver final arguments prior to having a substantially completed version of special verdict interrogatories, (2) failure to obtain instructions regarding alternative mandatory verdicts, and (3) possible confusion as to whether the verdict on obviousness was advisory rather than binding. *Id.*

[142]*Shatterproof Glass Corp. v. Libbey-Owens Ford Co.*, 758 F.2d 613, 225 USPQ 634 (Fed. Cir. 1985).

[143]*Witco Chem. Corp. v. Peachtree Doors, Inc.*, 787 F.2d 1545, 229 USPQ 188 (Fed. Cir. 1986). Infringement issues were so indistinguishably woven with the factual underpinnings of

Where a district court grants a new trial conditioned on the appellate court's reversal of JMOL, the case ordinarily will go back for new trial unless the appellate court directs otherwise. In considering a motion for new trial, the district court has wide discretion and may consider the credibility of witnesses and weigh evidence.[144]

The case law has developed a set of guidelines governing consideration of motions for JMOL, consistent with the Seventh Amendment guarantee. A court must (1) consider all the evidence, (2) in a light most favorable to the nonmovant, (3) drawing reasonable inferences favorable to the nonmovant, (4) without determining credibility of witnesses, and (5) without substituting its choice for that of the jury between conflicting elements of evidence. If, having done all this properly, it concludes that reasonable persons could not have reached a verdict for the nonmovant, it must grant the motion.[145] This ultimate conclusion is really a two-step determination: (1) What facts are supported by substantial evidence? and (2) Do those facts support the legal conclusion necessarily drawn by the jury en route to its verdict?[146] In the first step the judge avoids invasion of the jury's right to select reasonably from probative evidence and evaluate credibility. In the second the judge avoids miscarriage of justice by reaching a different legal conclusion when necessary.[147]

The court usually takes a hands-off attitude on jury determinations of credibility. Thus, a jury's assessment of the character of a

---

validity, enforceability, and contract issues that it would have been inappropriate to have more than one jury decide those questions.

[144]*Moxness Prods., Inc. v. Xomed, Inc.*, 891 F.2d 890, 13 USPQ2d 1169 (Fed. Cir. 1989).

[145]*Allied Colloids, Inc. v. American Cyanamid Co.*, 64 F.3d 1570, 35 USPQ2d 1840 (Fed. Cir. 1995); *New Idea Farm Equip. Corp. v. Sperry Corp.*, 916 F.2d 1561, 16 USPQ2d 1424 (Fed. Cir. 1990); *Sun Studs, Inc. v. ATA Equip. Leasing, Inc.*, 872 F.2d 978, 10 USPQ2d 1338 (Fed. Cir. 1989); *Wahpeton Canvas Co. v. Frontier, Inc.*, 870 F.2d 1546, 10 USPQ2d 1201 (Fed. Cir. 1989); *Dana Corp. v. IPC Ltd.*, 860 F.2d 415, 8 USPQ2d 1692 (Fed. Cir. 1988); *Connell v. Sears, Roebuck & Co.*, 722 F.2d 1542, 220 USPQ 193 (Fed. Cir. 1983). See also *Verdegaal Bros., Inc. v. Union Oil Co.*, 814 F.2d 628, 2 USPQ2d 1051 (Fed. Cir. 1987); *Orthokinetics, Inc. v. Safety Travel Chairs, Inc.*, 806 F.2d 1565, 1 USPQ2d 1081 (Fed. Cir. 1986); *DMI, Inc. v. Deere & Co.*, 802 F.2d 421, 231 USPQ 276 (Fed. Cir. 1986); *Mainland Indus., Inc. v. Standal's Patents Ltd.*, 799 F.2d 746, 230 USPQ 772 (Fed. Cir. 1986). There is no question that a court may take an issue from a jury on a directed verdict or JMOL motion at least in the same circumstances where it could have granted summary judgment. *Newell Cos. v. Kenney Mfg. Co.*, 864 F.2d 757, 9 USPQ2d 1417 (Fed. Cir. 1988).

[146]*Read Corp. v. Portec, Inc.*, 970 F.2d 816, 23 USPQ2d 1426 (Fed. Cir. 1992); *Dana Corp. v. IPC Ltd.*, 860 F.2d 415, 8 USPQ2d 1692 (Fed. Cir. 1988); *Perkin-Elmer Corp. v. Computervision Corp.*, 732 F.2d 888, 221 USPQ 669 (Fed. Cir. 1984); *Railroad Dynamics, Inc. v. A. Stucki Co.*, 727 F.2d 1506, 220 USPQ 929 (Fed. Cir. 1984).

[147]*Dana Corp. v. IPC Ltd.*, 860 F.2d 415, 8 USPQ2d 1692 (Fed. Cir. 1988); *Railroad Dynamics, Inc. v. A. Stucki Co.*, 727 F.2d 1506, 220 USPQ 929 (Fed. Cir. 1984). The trial court cannot let its own view of which side has the better case or what it would have done as a juror influence it. *Connell v. Sears, Roebuck & Co.*, 722 F.2d 1542, 220 USPQ 193 (Fed. Cir. 1983). The trial court cannot consider the credibility of witnesses or weigh the evidence. *Moxness Prods., Inc. v. Xomed, Inc.*, 891 F.2d 890, 13 USPQ2d 1169 (Fed. Cir. 1989). But it is not role reversal for the judge to say he or she would have made the same findings as those made by the jury, nor to determine whether there is sufficient evidence of record to support the jury's implied findings. *Railroad Dynamics, Inc. v. A. Stucki Co.*, 727 F.2d 1506, 220 USPQ 929 (Fed. Cir. 1984).

witness is entitled to great deference.[148] It is within the province of the jury to determine the credibility of a witness and the weight to be given the testimony; indeed, the jury is not required to accept testimony as true, even if it is uncontradicted.[149] In reviewing the record on motion for JMOL, the trial judge may not account for witness credibility, weigh evidence, or vary from the jury's verdict, unless— viewing the evidence in the light most favorable to the nonmoving party—substantial evidence does not support that verdict. The jury alone weighs conflicting evidence and the credibility of witnesses.[150] In connection with a motion for JMOL, the jury's resolution of the factual disputes is reviewed for substantial evidence and the review of any conclusion respecting an issue of law based upon facts supported by substantial evidence is de novo.[151]

Substantial evidence, in the context of the first step, is such relevant evidence from the record taken as a whole as might be accepted by a reasonable mind as adequate to support the finding under review.[152] A district court is not required to evaluate the evidence to determine whether the jury could have found otherwise. The district court is also not required to assume that the jury believed all or indeed any of the evidence in evaluating whether there was sufficient evidence to support the jury's finding. Simply because evidence is offered at trial does not mean that the court must assume the jury believed the evidence or gave it the same weight as does the profferor of such evidence.[153]

Where the instructions and special interrogatories are adequate to delineate the basis for the court's decision, no written analysis on the motion is necessary.[154] But where the judgment of a trial court is so terse that it lacks any rationale for its decisions on the parties' various posttrial motions, one option for the reviewing court, not to be discarded lightly, is to vacate the judgment and remand the matter for a full explication of the reasons for the court's rejection of the jury's findings. Another option is to examine the record to determine whether the facts support the judgment. This avoids the inefficiencies of having the appellate court review and decide the issue twice.[155]

---

[148]*General Electro Music Corp. v. Samick Music Corp.*, 19 F.3d 1405, 30 USPQ2d 1149 (Fed. Cir. 1994). As the finder of fact, the jury receives deference for its function of weighing witness demeanor, credibility, and meaning. *Al-Site Corp. v. VSI Int'l Inc.*, 174 F.3d 1308, 50 USPQ2d 1161 (Fed. Cir. 1999).

[149]*Amsted Indus. v. Buckeye Steel Castings Co.*, 24 F.3d 178, 30 USPQ2d 1462 (Fed. Cir. 1994).

[150]*Litton Sys., Inc. v. Honeywell, Inc.*, 87 F.3d 1559, 39 USPQ2d 1321 (Fed. Cir. 1996).

[151]*Mendenhall v. Cedarapids, Inc.*, 5 F.3d 1556, 28 USPQ2d 1081 (Fed. Cir. 1993).

[152]*Dana Corp. v. IPC Ltd.*, 860 F.2d 415, 8 USPQ2d 1692 (Fed. Cir. 1988); *Perkin-Elmer Corp. v. Computervision Corp.*, 732 F.2d 888, 221 USPQ 669 (Fed. Cir. 1984). Substantial evidence is more than a mere scintilla. *Genentech, Inc. v. Wellcome Found. Ltd.*, 29 F.3d 1555, 31 USPQ2d 1161 (Fed. Cir. 1994).

[153]*Comark Comm. Inc. v. Harris Corp.*, 156 F.3d 1182, 48 USPQ2d 1001, 1010 (Fed. Cir. 1998).

[154]*Medtronic Inc. v. Intermedics, Inc.*, 799 F.2d 734, 230 USPQ 641 (Fed. Cir. 1986).

[155]*Baxter Healthcare Corp. v. Spectramed, Inc.*, 49 F.3d 1575, 34 USPQ2d 1120 (Fed. Cir. 1995). The trial judge in this case actually indicated, in the presence of the jury and prior to

In *Newell v. Kenney,*[156] a decision that seems likely to create some controversy, a divided panel of the court held that it is not improper to direct a verdict on a disputed issue of obviousness where there are no disputed issues of material fact underlying that issue. The majority felt that none of the court's previous decisions prohibits the trial judge from substituting his or her judgment for that of the jury on the legal question of obviousness where there are no factual matters in dispute. It justified the holding as consistent with a grant of summary judgment on the obviousness issue where there are no disputed factual issues, and with *Panduit v. Dennison,*[157] which holds that the application of the statutory standard of obviousness to a set of established facts is a question of law subject to full and independent review on appeal. In a vigorous dissent Judge Newman termed the majority holding a "change in the right to jury trial of the question of unobviousness." Her fundamental concern is that obviousness is not a "pure" question of law, separable from its factual components. Whatever may be the proper approach to appellate review of bench trials on obviousness, which was the focus of *Panduit v. Dennison,* Judge Newman urges that it should not deprive a litigant of the right to have the obviousness of its invention determined by a jury.[158] Judge Newman's dissent, which is interesting and instructive, leaves one with the distinct impression that this subject could receive further airing.

A motion on unanswered interrogatories is not one for JMOL. A special verdict is a compilation of answers returned and a motion for JMOL seeks a judgment notwithstanding that verdict. Thus a motion as to unreturned interrogatories is simply one for judgment, under Rule 50(b).[159] Courts have held that in some circumstances judgment may be entered under Rule 50(b) when the jury cannot arrive at a general verdict. However, the Federal Circuit has passed the question whether Rule 50(b) can be applied to unanswered questions when a special verdict is formed of answers to only some questions.[160]

When a jury, charged with returning special interrogatories pursuant to Rule 49(a), fails to agree unanimously on some of the answers, a trial judge has available several different procedural actions prior to dismissing the jury. First the judge could simply resubmit the issue to the jury for further deliberations in hope of obtaining a unanimous

---

dismissing it, a feeling that it would be necessary to declare a mistrial. Later, the judge decided the case based upon answers to some interrogatories and in light of the posttrial motions. The Federal Circuit simply regarded the judge's earlier statement as an intent that was not acted upon.

[156]*Newell Cos. v. Kenney Mfg. Co.,* 864 F.2d 757, 9 USPQ2d 1417 (Fed. Cir. 1988).

[157]*Panduit Corp. v. Dennison Mfg. Co.,* 810 F.2d 1561, 1 USPQ2d 1593 (Fed. Cir. 1987). See discussion at §4.2(b)(iv).

[158]*Newell Cos. v. Kenney Mfg. Co.,* 864 F.2d 757, 9 USPQ2d 1417 (Fed. Cir. 1988).

[159]*Wahpeton Canvas Co. v. Frontier, Inc.,* 870 F.2d 1546, 10 USPQ2d 1201 (Fed. Cir. 1989).

[160]*Wahpeton Canvas Co. v. Frontier, Inc.,* 870 F.2d 1546, 10 USPQ2d 1201 (Fed. Cir. 1989). Here the district court took it upon itself to supply its own answer to the unanswered inquiries. Thus it did not direct the entry of judgment as if the requested verdict had been directed, but instead entered its own judgment on its own findings.

verdict. Second, the judge could ask the parties if they would be willing to forego the requirement of unanimity and accept a majority verdict. Third, the judge could enter judgment on the basis of the unanimous verdicts if they are dispositive of the case. Fourth, the judge could declare the entire case a mistrial and order it reheard in its entirety with a different jury. Finally, it could, in certain situations, order a partial retrial only as to those issues that were not unanimously agreed upon by the jury.[161]

These guidelines are fully applicable to patent cases.[162] Thus the rule for JMOL in a patent infringement suit is inquiry, under the proper legal standard of patentability, as to whether the evidence (and the inferences reasonably drawn therefrom), when viewed in the light most favorable to the nonmovant and without weighing credibility, is or is not substantial.[163] The requirement that the court draw "inferences" favorable to the nonmovant relates only to factual inferences, not to legal conclusions based on an established set of facts, even though those facts do not all favor that conclusion.[164] Care must be taken so as not to create a burden where there is none. A patent owner is never in law required to prove facts establishing validity, though it may be well advised to prove such facts in rebuttal of a patent challenger's case. The result is that when a verdict of validity is tested by motion for JMOL, the question is whether the challenger's evidence withstood the patentee's rebuttal evidence to the extent that reasonable jurors could not have concluded that the patent was valid. When the verdict connotes invalidity, a properly instructed jury has necessarily determined that the challenger's evidence met the burden imposed under 35 U.S.C. §282.[165]

An issue must be raised in a motion for a directed verdict at the close of the evidence in order to challenge the trial court's denial of a motion for JMOL. If it is not, the appealing party loses the benefit

---

[161]*Baxter Healthcare Corp. v. Spectramed, Inc.*, 49 F.3d 1575, 34 USPQ2d 1120 (Fed. Cir. 1995).

[162]*Connell v. Sears, Roebuck & Co.*, 722 F.2d 1542, 220 USPQ 193 (Fed. Cir. 1983). See also *Shatterproof Glass Corp. v. Libbey-Owens Ford Co.*, 758 F.2d 613, 225 USPQ 634 (Fed. Cir. 1985); *Weinar v. Rollform Inc.*, 744 F.2d 797, 223 USPQ 369 (Fed. Cir. 1984).

[163]*Connell v. Sears, Roebuck & Co.*, 722 F.2d 1542, 220 USPQ 193 (Fed. Cir. 1983). The court may grant the motion for JMOL if the facts found on substantial evidence are insufficient to support, or contrary to, the jury's legal conclusion, or if the facts found, though they would be capable of supporting the legal conclusion, were based upon evidence less than substantial. *Id.*

[164]*Newell Cos. v. Kenney Mfg. Co.*, 864 F.2d 757, 9 USPQ2d 1417 (Fed. Cir. 1988).

[165]*Railroad Dynamics, Inc. v. A. Stucki Co.*, 727 F.2d 1506, 220 USPQ 929 (Fed. Cir. 1984). Normally, evidence presented by a patentee-plaintiff will not support a grant of a JMOL invalidating a patent. That is because the burden is on an accused infringer to show by clear and convincing evidence facts supporting the conclusion that the patent is invalid. Accordingly, grant of JMOL in favor of a party bearing the burden of proof may be granted only where (1) the movant has established its case by evidence that the jury would not be at liberty to disbelieve and (2) the only reasonable conclusion is in the movant's favor. However, in unusual cases, an admission made by a plaintiff's witness can be sufficient to support entry of a JMOL in favor of a defendant after the close of the plaintiff's case in chief, even where the defendant bears the burden of proof on the decided issue. Thus, where the patentee, during its case in chief, introduced inventor testimony that established failure to disclose the best mode, entry of JMOL

of the substantial evidence rule on the issue.[166] A failure to bring a timely motion for directed verdict dramatically changes the standard of review with respect to fact issues decided by the jury. It results in a waiver of the right to challenge presumed jury findings as unsupported by substantial evidence. The appellant may then only challenge the judgment on the ground that the judge committed an error of law or an abuse of discretion.[167] Rule 50(a) requires that a motion for directed verdict shall state the specific grounds therefor. Thus if a party fails to specify an issue, it may not subsequently challenge the jury's verdict on that issue. Even a specific reference to the issue in a motion for JMOL does not cure the prior failure to include the issue in the motion for a directed verdict.[168] Even the timing is significant. Failure to renew, after the close of all evidence, an unsuccessful motion made at the close of the defendant's case will waive the issues that were the subject of the original motion.[169] However, the failure

---

at the close of plaintiff's case was appropriate. *Nobelpharma AB v. Implant Innovations Inc.,* 141 F.3d 1059, 46 USPQ2d 1097 (Fed. Cir. 1998).

[166]*Power Lift, Inc. v. Lang Tools, Inc.,* 774 F.2d 478, 227 USPQ 435 (Fed. Cir. 1985). The party failed to raise the issues of lost profits and claim validity. Those issues could have been reviewed, under the abuse of discretion standard, on appeal of a denial of a motion for new trial. In this case, however, the denial of the motion for a new trial was not a reviewable final judgment, and the only reviewable order was the trial court's judgment entered on the jury verdict. *Id.* Only judgments can be appealed. Where no judgment was entered on a laches defense, the moving party could not have cross-appealed the denial of its motion for a directed verdict on that issue. Moreover, only a party adversely affected by a judgment can appeal and the moving party was not adversely affected by a judgment of invalidity. Thus, since that party could not have cross-appealed, its failure to do so has no effect on the law of the case. Its laches defense is not precluded by law of the case because the defense was not conclusively determined by the denial of its motion for directed verdict. *Jamesbury Corp. v. Litton Indus. Prods., Inc.,* 839 F.2d 1544, 5 USPQ2d 1779 (Fed. Cir. 1988).

[167]*Jurgens v. McKasy,* 927 F.2d 1552, 18 USPQ2d 1031 (Fed. Cir. 1991). Providing the opportunity to the nonmovant to repair gaps in its proofs is the reason Rule 50(b) is rigorously applied. *Hoechst Celanese Corp. v. BP Chem. Ltd.,* 78 F.3d 1575, 38 USPQ2d 1126 (Fed. Cir. 1996).

[168]*Orthokinetics, Inc. v. Safety Travel Chairs, Inc.,* 806 F.2d 1565, 1 USPQ2d 1081 (Fed. Cir. 1986) (motion for directed verdict on infringement will not cure failure to have moved for directed verdict on willful infringement; infringement and willful infringement are not the same thing); *Kinzenbaw v. Deere & Co.,* 741 F.2d 383, 222 USPQ 929 (Fed. Cir. 1984) (failure to specify public use as issue). The simple statement "I would move for a directed verdict at the close of all the evidence at this time on both the issue of noninfringement and invalidity" is not sufficiently specific to satisfy the purpose of Rule 50(a), i.e., to notify the adversary of holes in its evidence so that they might be filled, if possible, before the case goes to the jury. *Wilson Sporting Goods Co. v. David Geoffrey & Assoc.,* 904 F.2d 677, 14 USPQ2d 1942 (Fed. Cir. 1990). Under Rule 50(b), FRCP, JMOL can be granted only in accordance with a party's motion for a directed verdict. At the close of plaintiff's case the accused infringer moved for a directed verdict on the issue of noninfringement on the ground that the "evidence is insufficient." The trial court later granted JMOL on the ground that there had been no testimony and linking argument as to function/way/result for equivalency. The Federal Circuit felt that the directed verdict motion was adequate to support that JMOL. *Malta v. Schulmerich Carillons, Inc.,* 952 F.2d 1320, 21 USPQ2d 1161 (Fed. Cir. 1991).

[169]*Nestier Corp. v. Menasha Corp.,* 739 F.2d 1576, 222 USPQ 747 (Fed. Cir. 1984). The patentee's motion was for a directed verdict on validity and willful infringement. When this was denied, the patentee put on his rebuttal evidence and did not renew the motion or move for a new trial or JMOL after the verdict. In *Wilson Sporting Goods Co. v. David Geoffrey & Assoc.,* 904 F.2d 677, 14 USPQ2d 1942 (Fed. Cir. 1990), the court held that a motion for JMOL need not be filed within 10 days after entry of judgment; service within that time is sufficient.

of the opposing party to object to an issue when included in a motion for JMOL may cure a failure to include it in a motion for directed verdict.[170]

The Federal Circuit has adopted the rule that a motion for a directed verdict is not the same as a motion for judgment under Rule 41(b) in a nonjury case. The former raises questions of law only.[171] Nor is a motion for summary judgment before trial a substitute for a motion for directed verdict (or judgment as a matter of law) at the close of all evidence.[172] Whether the evidence is sufficient to create an issue of fact for the jury is a legal question.[173]

(g) Appellate Review

The Federal Circuit follows regional circuit law on questions of jury procedure.[174] Unchallenged jury instructions state the law to be applied on review of the jury verdict.[175] Jury instructions are reviewed for correctness, with due attention to their clarity, objectivity, and adequacy, taken as a whole.[176]

In *Zodiac Pool Care Inc. v. Hoffinger Indus. Inc.*, 206 F.3d 1408, 54 USPQ2d 1141 (Fed. Cir. 2000), the district judge remarked that he understood the motion to have been renewed by oral statements of counsel, so there was no abuse of discretion in granting JMOL.

[170]*Orthokinetics, Inc. v. Safety Travel Chairs, Inc.*, 806 F.2d 1565, 1 USPQ2d 1081 (Fed. Cir. 1986). But see *Delta-X Corp. v. Baker Hughes Prod. Tools, Inc.*, 984 F.2d 410, 25 USPQ2d 1447 (Fed. Cir. 1993).

[171]*Stearns v. Beckman Instr., Inc.*, 737 F.2d 1565, 222 USPQ 457 (Fed. Cir. 1984).

[172]*Wang Labs., Inc. v. Toshiba Corp.*, 993 F.2d 858, 26 USPQ2d 1767 (Fed. Cir. 1993). However, a defense previously raised in a motion for summary judgment is not waived by failing to raise it in a JMOL motion. *Streamfeeder LLC v. Sure-Feed Inc.*, 175 F.3d 974, 50 USPQ2d 1515 (Fed. Cir. 1999).

[173]*Jamesbury Corp. v. Litton Indus. Prods., Inc.*, 756 F.2d 1556, 225 USPQ 253 (Fed. Cir. 1985).

[174]*Wilson Sporting Goods Co. v. David Geoffrey & Assoc.*, 904 F.2d 677, 14 USPQ2d 1942 (Fed. Cir. 1990) (timeliness of motion for JMOL); *Arachnid, Inc. v. Medalist Mktg. Corp.*, 972 F.2d 1300, 23 USPQ2d 1946 (Fed. Cir. 1992); *Beckman Instr., Inc. v. LKB Produkter AB*, 892 F.2d 1547, 13 USPQ2d 1301 (Fed. Cir. 1989); *Moxness Prods., Inc. v. Xomed, Inc.*, 891 F.2d 890, 13 USPQ2d 1169 (Fed. Cir. 1989); *Wahpeton Canvas Co. v. Frontier, Inc.*, 870 F.2d 1546, 10 USPQ2d 1201 (Fed. Cir. 1989) (motion for JMOL); *Newell Cos. v. Kenney Mfg. Co.*, 864 F.2d 757, 9 USPQ2d 1417 (Fed. Cir. 1988) (reserving ruling on motion for directed verdict until after verdict); *Lummus Indus., Inc. v. D.M.& E. Corp.*, 862 F.2d 267, 8 USPQ2d 1983 (Fed. Cir. 1988) (jury instructions); *Sjolund v. Musland*, 847 F.2d 1573, 6 USPQ2d 2020 (Fed. Cir. 1988) (denial of motion for JMOL); *Allen Organ Co. v. Kimball Int'l, Inc.*, 839 F.2d 1556, 5 USPQ2d 1769 (Fed. Cir. 1988) (inconsistent jury findings or verdicts). Apparently the court will not always apply regional circuit law to questions of jury procedure. In *Biodex Corp. v. Loredan Biomedical, Inc.*, 946 F.2d 850, 20 USPQ2d 1252 (Fed. Cir. 1991), it decided that it would apply its own law governing the reviewability of fact findings made by a jury in a patent trial absent any postverdict motions. It passed the question whether regional circuit law applies to review of postverdict motions but did indicate that the law appeared uniform in any event.

[175]*Brooktree Corp. v. Advanced Micro Devices, Inc.*, 977 F.2d 1555, 24 USPQ2d 1401 (Fed. Cir. 1992). But the Federal Circuit follows the general rule that in reviewing the law on a properly laid and renewed motion for JMOL, it is not bound by the instructions given the jury, even if they were not objected to below. *Markman v. Westview Instr., Inc.*, 52 F.3d 967, 34 USPQ2d 1321 (Fed. Cir. 1995).

[176]*United States Surgical Corp. v. Ethicon, Inc.*, 103 F.3d 1554, 41 USPQ2d 1225 (Fed. Cir. 1997).

District courts have broad authority and discretion in controlling the conduct of a trial, including the form by which a jury returns its verdict, and will not be interfered with unless an abuse of discretion is shown.[177] Jury verdicts themselves must be treated with great deference, but not so great as to require acceptance of findings where they are clearly and unquestionably not supported by substantial evidence. To so hold would render the trial and submission of evidence a farce.[178] Nonetheless, the standard of appellate review differs from a bench trial: findings of fact by the jury are more difficult to set aside, being reviewed only for reasonableness under the substantial evidence test; those of a trial judge are reviewed under the clearly erroneous rule.[179] The high standard for reviewing verdicts involving fact questions makes any such appeal a very chancy proposition.[180] An appellate tribunal is abjured to determine whether a jury verdict can be sustained, on any reasonable theory.[181] The Federal Circuit is not at liberty to substitute its selection of credible evidence for the selection made by the jury.[182] The jury's verdict must stand unless the evidence is of such quality and weight that reasonable persons in the exercise of impartial judgment could not have returned that verdict.[183]

In a jury trial there are two decision makers, judge and jury. In general the judge decides issues of law and issues committed to his or her discretion and the jury decides issues of fact that are material to the case and in genuine dispute. The appellate court reviews decisions made by the judge for prejudicial legal error (e.g., jury instructions) or abuse of discretion (e.g., increasing damages), the standard depending upon the particular issue. In contrast, the evidence underlying a jury verdict on an issue of fact is reviewed to determine whether the jury's decision was supported by substantial evidence. Between these simple extremes are issues of law submitted to the jury upon disputed facts. The standard of review for such issues (e.g., a jury special verdict on obviousness where the underlying facts were disputed) has two parts. The appellate court first presumes that the jury resolved the underlying factual disputes in favor of the verdict winner and leaves those presumed findings undisturbed if they are supported by substantial evidence. It then examines the legal conclusion de novo to see whether it is correct in light of those presumed jury fact findings.[184]

---

[177]*Railroad Dynamics, Inc. v. A. Stucki Co.*, 727 F.2d 1506, 220 USPQ 929 (Fed. Cir. 1984).

[178]*Connell v. Sears, Roebuck & Co.*, 722 F.2d 1542, 220 USPQ 193 (Fed. Cir. 1983).

[179]*Richardson v. Suzuki Motor Co.*, 868 F.2d 1226, 9 USPQ2d 1913 (Fed. Cir. 1989); *Railroad Dynamics, Inc. v. A. Stucki Co.*, 727 F.2d 1506, 220 USPQ 929 (Fed. Cir. 1984).

[180]*Munoz v. Strahm Farms, Inc.*, 69 F.3d 501, 36 USPQ2d 1499 (Fed. Cir. 1995).

[181]*Richardson v. Suzuki Motor Co.*, 868 F.2d 1226, 9 USPQ2d 1913 (Fed. Cir. 1989).

[182]*Wahpeton Canvas Co. v. Frontier, Inc.*, 870 F.2d 1546, 10 USPQ2d 1201, 1207 (Fed. Cir. 1989).

[183]*Tol-O-Matic, Inc. v. Proma Produckt-und Mktg. GmbH,* 945 F.2d 1546, 20 USPQ2d 1332 (Fed. Cir. 1991).

[184]*Jurgens v. McKasy*, 927 F.2d 1552, 18 USPQ2d 1031 (Fed. Cir. 1991).

Where no motions for JMOL or new trial are filed, and appeal is directly from the judgment entered on the jury verdict, review for sufficiency of evidence is extremely limited or nonexistent; prejudicial legal error must be shown to have occurred in the conduct of the trial, and the action of an appellate court is limited to affirmance or remand for new trial.[185] The court has held, squarely and unequivocally, that it cannot review the sufficiency of the evidence after a jury verdict absent some postverdict disposition, either by a deferred ruling or upon a postverdict motion.[186] Reversal is not available to an appellant who merely establishes error in instructions or other procedures employed at trial. If error could have prejudicially affected the verdict, the appellate court may only order that the judgment be vacated and a new trial granted, because the appellate court cannot say what verdict the jury would reach when properly instructed or when proper procedure is followed. Where the error was harmless—that is, where the evidence is such that the same verdict necessarily would have been reached—affirmance is required since a new trial would be a waste of time.[187]

It thus behooves counsel to file nonfrivolous motions for JMOL and for new trial. Otherwise the appellate court cannot reverse or order judgment for the appellant.[188] If prejudicial error occurred, or if the verdict is against the clear weight of the evidence, a new trial may be granted, in the discretion of the district judge, as an alternative to JNOV. On review, the court of appeals must determine whether that discretion has been abused.[189] That question turns on whether

---

[185]*Structural Rubber Prods. Co. v. Park Rubber Co.*, 749 F.2d 707, 223 USPQ 1264 (Fed. Cir. 1984). See also *Biodex Corp. v. Loredan Biomedical, Inc.*, 946 F.2d 850, 20 USPQ2d 1252 (Fed. Cir. 1991). Where a party fails to make a motion for JMOL at the close of the evidence, the sufficiency of the evidence underlying presumed jury findings cannot be challenged through a renewed motion for JMOL or on appeal. Nonetheless, the party may challenge the judgment on the ground that the judge committed an error of law or abused his or her discretion, i.e., it may challenge the judge's legal conclusion on obviousness, the judge's jury instructions, and any other issue that was the province of the court rather than the jury and to which it timely objected at trial. *Young Dental Mfg. Co. v. Q3 Special Prods., Inc.*, 112 F.3d 1137, 42 USPQ2d 1589 (Fed. Cir. 1997).

[186]*Biodex Corp. v. Loredan Biomedical, Inc.*, 946 F.2d 850, 20 USPQ2d 1252 (Fed. Cir. 1991). In this case an oral motion at the close of testimony for a directed verdict, never ruled on by the judge, did not suffice to preserve the right of review on the sufficiency of the evidence. In *Wang Labs., Inc. v. Toshiba Corp.*, 993 F.2d 858, 26 USPQ2d 1767 (Fed. Cir. 1993), the court held that a failure to raise an issue by motion for judgment as a matter of law means that the sufficiency of the evidence underlying a district court's denial of JMOL on that issue is unreviewable on appeal, even where the issue was the subject of a pretrial motion for summary judgment.

[187]*Weinar v. Rollform Inc.*, 744 F.2d 797, 223 USPQ 369 (Fed. Cir. 1984). As a result, it is difficult to conceive of a procedural error so grave that reversal would be warranted. A party may obtain a new trial only by showing that error affected its substantial rights. One is entitled to a fair, not a perfect, trial. *Fonar Corp. v. Johnson & Johnson*, 821 F.2d 627, 3 USPQ2d 1109 (Fed. Cir. 1987). The adequacy of jury instructions is reviewed for prejudicial legal error. *Mendenhall v. Cedarapids, Inc.*, 5 F.3d 1556, 28 USPQ2d 1081 (Fed. Cir. 1993).

[188]*Devices for Med., Inc. v. Boehl*, 822 F.2d 1062, 3 USPQ2d 1288 (Fed. Cir. 1987); *Railroad Dynamics, Inc. v. A. Stucki Co.*, 727 F.2d 1506, 220 USPQ 929 (Fed. Cir. 1984). An appeal may not be treated as a substitute for a motion for JMOL. *Id.*

[189]*Shatterproof Glass Corp. v. Libbey-Owens Ford Co.*, 758 F.2d 613, 225 USPQ 634 (Fed. Cir. 1985).

an error occurred in the conduct of the trial that was so grievous as to have rendered the trial unfair.[190] In reviewing the trial court's denial of a new trial, the court of appeals reviews the jury instructions as a whole to determine whether clear error took place, such that the jury was misled.[191]

The propriety of denial of a JMOL motion is a question of law subject to de novo review.[192] On appeal after denial of a motion for JMOL the appellant must show either (1) that the presumed or express findings are not supported by substantial evidence or (2) if so supported, the legal conclusions implied from the verdict cannot be supported by those findings. In sum, the appellant must show either that reasonable jurors could not have made the presumed findings or that the conclusions necessary to the general verdict were not supported.[193] Since each of these determinations is a question of law, the reviewing court is governed by the same standard on review. Thus, a party seeking reversal of a grant or denial of a motion JNOV must convince the appellate court that the trial court erroneously applied one or both steps.[194] In reviewing a decision denying a motion for JMOL, the Federal Circuit does not approach the issues as if there had been no trial. It reviews the evidence as a whole and ascertains whether the verdict is in accordance with the law and whether there was substantial evidence in support of the jury's verdict. Where the testimony and argument are in conflict on virtually all fact questions, due deference must be given to the opportunity of the jury and the

---

[190]*DMI, Inc. v. Deere & Co.*, 802 F.2d 421, 231 USPQ 276 (Fed. Cir. 1986).

[191]*DMI, Inc. v. Deere & Co.*, 802 F.2d 421, 231 USPQ 276 (Fed. Cir. 1986). To be successful on an appeal from a judgment entered on a denial of a motion for a new trial, the appellant must show abuse of discretion. *Shearing v. Iolab Corp.*, 975 F.2d 1541, 24 USPQ2d 1133 (Fed. Cir. 1992); *Railroad Dynamics, Inc. v. A. Stucki Co.*, 727 F.2d 1506, 220 USPQ 929 (Fed. Cir. 1984).

[192]*Braun Inc. v. Dynamics Corp.*, 975 F.2d 815, 24 USPQ2d 1121 (Fed. Cir. 1992).

[193]*New Idea Farm Equip. Corp. v. Sperry Corp.*, 916 F.2d 1561, 16 USPQ2d 1424 (Fed. Cir. 1990); *Bio-Rad Labs., Inc. v. Nicolet Instr. Corp.*, 739 F.2d 604, 222 USPQ 654 (Fed. Cir. 1984). See also *Shearing v. Iolab Corp.*, 975 F.2d 1541, 24 USPQ2d 1133 (Fed. Cir. 1992); *Modine Mfg. Co. v. Allen Group, Inc.*, 917 F.2d 538, 16 USPQ2d 1622 (Fed. Cir. 1990); *New Idea Farm Equip. Corp. v. Sperry Corp.*, 916 F.2d 1561, 16 USPQ2d 1424 (Fed. Cir. 1990). This standard applies in general to judgments entered on a verdict after denial of a Rule 50(b) judgment as a matter of law. *Mentor Corp. v. Coloplast, Inc.*, 998 F.2d 992, 27 USPQ2d 1521 (Fed. Cir. 1993). In *Dana Corp. v. IPC Ltd.*, 860 F.2d 415, 8 USPQ2d 1692 (Fed. Cir. 1988), the court held that reasonable minds could not have found that the best mode requirement was satisfied. In *Sjolund v. Musland*, 847 F.2d 1573, 6 USPQ2d 2020 (Fed. Cir. 1988), the court held that a reasonable jury could only have found the invention obvious. See also *Verdegaal Bros., Inc. v. Union Oil Co.*, 814 F.2d 628, 2 USPQ2d 1051 (Fed. Cir. 1987); *Data Line Corp. v. Micro Techs., Inc.*, 813 F.2d 1196, 1 USPQ2d 2052 (Fed. Cir. 1987); *Mainland Indus., Inc. v. Standal's Patents Ltd.*, 799 F.2d 746, 230 USPQ 772 (Fed. Cir. 1986); *Medtronic Inc. v. Intermedics, Inc.*, 799 F.2d 734, 230 USPQ 641 (Fed. Cir. 1986); *Glaros v. H.H. Robertson Co.*, 797 F.2d 1564, 230 USPQ 393 (Fed. Cir. 1986); *Perkin-Elmer Corp. v. Computervision Corp.*, 732 F.2d 888, 221 USPQ 669 (Fed. Cir. 1984); *Railroad Dynamics, Inc. v. A. Stucki Co.*, 727 F.2d 1506, 220 USPQ 929 (Fed. Cir. 1984). Where there are multiple defenses presented, this is a heavy burden. The winner only has to show substantial evidence on one defense. *Weinar v. Rollform Inc.*, 744 F.2d 797, 223 USPQ 369 (Fed. Cir. 1984).

[194]*Dana Corp. v. IPC Ltd.*, 860 F.2d 415, 8 USPQ2d 1692 (Fed. Cir. 1988). See also *Litton Sys., Inc. v. Honeywell, Inc.*, 87 F.3d 1559, 39 USPQ2d 1321 (Fed. Cir. 1996). A grant of JMOL

trial judge to have observed the witnesses and viewed the exhibits over a lengthy trial.[195] On appeal to determine the correctness of the district court's ruling on JMOL, the court of appeals applies the JMOL standard anew.[196] On a review of a motion for JMOL, the court retains the power and duty to say what the correct law is, and then to examine the factual issues submitted to the jury and determine whether findings thereon are supported by substantial evidence and in turn support the verdict under the law. The Federal Circuit follows the general rule that in reviewing the law on a properly laid and renewed motion for JMOL, it is not bound by the instructions given the jury, even if they were not objected to below.[197]

The burden on one who appeals the grant of a motion for JMOL is to show that the jury's factual findings were supported by at least substantial evidence and the legal conclusions made by the jury can be supported by those findings.[198] A grant of JMOL under Rule 50(a) is subject to de novo review. The reviewing court applies the same standard as the district court, examining the record in the light most favorable to the nonmovant and drawing inferences in its favor. The JMOL may be affirmed only if there is no legally sufficient evidentiary basis for a reasonable jury to find otherwise, and, thus, the judgment entered is the only one possible under the controlling law.[199] The appellate court must affirm a grant of a directed verdict unless the appellant shows that a jury could reasonably have returned a verdict in its favor on the presentation it had made when all justifiable inferences are drawn in its favor. The mere existence of a scintilla of evidence in support of the appellant's position will be insufficient; there must be evidence on which the jury could reasonably find for appellant.[200] Substantial evidence is such relevant evidence from the

---

is given plenary review on appeal. *York Prods., Inc. v. Central Tractor Farm & Fam. Ctr.*, 99 F.3d 1568, 40 USPQ2d 1619 (Fed. Cir. 1996).

[195]*Shatterproof Glass Corp. v. Libbey-Owens Ford Co.*, 758 F.2d 613, 225 USPQ 634 (Fed. Cir. 1985). It should be kept in mind that it is the judge who was present at trial who is best positioned to review the evidence and events at trial. *Railroad Dynamics, Inc. v. A. Stucki Co.*, 727 F.2d 1506, 220 USPQ 929 (Fed. Cir. 1984). Issues of credibility of witnesses are for the jury and are not amenable to appellate review. *Brooktree Corp. v. Advanced Micro Devices, Inc.*, 977 F.2d 1555, 24 USPQ2d 1401 (Fed. Cir. 1992).

[196]*Read Corp. v. Portec, Inc.*, 970 F.2d 816, 23 USPQ2d 1426 (Fed. Cir. 1992). In applying the JMOL standard anew, the Federal Circuit is bound by those same constraints in testing the sufficiency of the evidence in support of the jury's verdict. *Litton Sys., Inc. v. Honeywell, Inc.*, 87 F.3d 1559, 39 USPQ2d 1321 (Fed. Cir. 1996).

[197]*Markman v. Westview Instr., Inc.*, 52 F.3d 967, 34 USPQ2d 1321 (Fed. Cir. 1995).

[198]*Vieau v. Japax, Inc.*, 823 F.2d 1510, 3 USPQ2d 1094 (Fed. Cir. 1987); *Fonar Corp. v. Johnson & Johnson*, 821 F.2d 627, 3 USPQ2d 1109 (Fed. Cir. 1987). A trial judge properly grants JMOL when the evidence permits only one reasonable conclusion as to the verdict. *Litton Sys., Inc. v. Honeywell, Inc.*, 87 F.3d 1559, 39 USPQ2d 1321 (Fed. Cir. 1996). A grant of JMOL is given plenary review on appeal. *York Prods, Inc. v. Central Tractor Farm & Fam. Ctr.*, 99 F.3d 1568, 40 USPQ2d 1619 (Fed. Cir. 1996).

[199]*Eastman Kodak Co. v. Goodyear Tire & Rubber Co.*, 114 F.3d 1547, 42 USPQ2d 1737 (Fed. Cir. 1997).

[200]*A. Stucki Co. v. Worthington Indus., Inc.*, 849 F.2d 593, 7 USPQ2d 1066 (Fed. Cir. 1988). Substantial evidence is more than a mere scintilla. *Genentech, Inc. v. Wellcome Found. Ltd.*, 29 F.3d 1555, 31 USPQ2d 1161 (Fed. Cir. 1994).

record taken as a whole that might be accepted by a reasonable mind as adequate to support the finding under review. If the jury's factual findings, on the evidence presented, could have been made by a reasonable jury, the appellant may prevail only by showing that those findings cannot support the jury's legal conclusion.[201]

There is a judicial preference in favor of granting a JMOL over a directed verdict. The rationale behind the preference is the effect of an appellate court's reversal of a judgment in each situation. With a directed verdict, the entire case must be retried if the judgment is overturned, while with a JMOL the jury verdict can be entered as the judgment should the appellate court reverse. Thus, it is in the interest of efficient judicial administration for a court to withhold ruling on a motion for directed verdict in favor of deciding a motion for JMOL.[202] Review of a district court's grant of a directed verdict is plenary. The district court was correct only if under the governing law there can be but one reasonable conclusion as to the verdict.[203] But in reviewing the propriety of a directed verdict the appellate court does not weigh the evidence, consider the credibility of witnesses, or decide disputed facts.[204] Where a district court grants a new trial conditioned on reversal of JMOL, the case will ordinarily be retried unless the appellate court directs otherwise.[205]

The court has given some instructive comment on its review of jury verdicts on several patent issues. Thus, where the verdict is one of validity, the true question on appeal is whether the defendant, who bears the burden, submitted such evidence as would preclude a reasonable jury from reaching a verdict of validity. The fact basis for the verdict need not be spelled out by the jury; it is sufficient if there be a basis for the verdict in the evidence.[206] From a jury's verdict of patent validity, it may be presumed that the jury found that no prior art reference completely embodied the method or apparatus of the claims in suit.[207] The standard of review on the conclusion of obviousness is the same whether rendered by judge or jury—it is a question

---

[201]*Tol-O-Matic, Inc. v. Proma Produckt-und Mktg. GmbH*, 945 F.2d 1546, 20 USPQ2d 1332 (Fed. Cir. 1991); *Vieau v. Japax, Inc.*, 823 F.2d 1510, 3 USPQ2d 1094 (Fed. Cir. 1987); *Fonar Corp. v. Johnson & Johnson*, 821 F.2d 627, 3 USPQ2d 1109 (Fed. Cir. 1987); *DMI, Inc. v. Deere & Co.*, 802 F.2d 421, 231 USPQ 276 (Fed. Cir. 1986).

[202]*Jamesbury Corp. v. Litton Indus. Prods., Inc.*, 839 F.2d 1544, 5 USPQ2d 1779 (Fed. Cir. 1988). See also *Allied Colloids, Inc. v. American Cyanamid Co.*, 64 F.3d 1570, 35 USPQ2d 1840 (Fed. Cir. 1995).

[203]*Arachnid, Inc. v. Merit Indus., Inc.*, 939 F.2d 1574, 19 USPQ2d 1513 (Fed. Cir. 1991).

[204]*Allied Colloids, Inc. v. American Cyanamid Co.*, 64 F.3d 1570, 35 USPQ2d 1840 (Fed. Cir. 1995).

[205]*Moxness Prods., Inc. v. Xomed, Inc.*, 891 F.2d 890, 13 USPQ2d 1169 (Fed. Cir. 1989).

[206]*Weinar v. Rollform Inc.*, 744 F.2d 797, 223 USPQ 369 (Fed. Cir. 1984). See also *Perkin-Elmer Corp. v. Computervision Corp.*, 732 F.2d 888, 221 USPQ 669 (Fed. Cir. 1984).

[207]*Shatterproof Glass Corp. v. Libbey-Owens Ford Co.*, 758 F.2d 613, 225 USPQ 634 (Fed. Cir. 1985); *Perkin-Elmer Corp. v. Computervision Corp.*, 732 F.2d 888, 221 USPQ 669 (Fed. Cir. 1984). See also *Shearing v. Iolab Corp.*, 975 F.2d 1541, 24 USPQ2d 1133 (Fed. Cir. 1992). In *Motorola, Inc. v. Interdigital Tech. Corp.*, 121 F.3d 1461, 43 USPQ2d 1481 (Fed. Cir. 1997), the jury was given a special verdict form that asked it to decide whether any of the many

of law.[208] In reviewing a grant of JMOL on obviousness, the appellate court must recreate the facts as they may have been found by the jury, and assess the record evidence in the light most favorable to the verdict winner. But in so doing, it must not abdicate its role as the ultimate decision maker on the legal question of obviousness.[209]

Where a jury is asked to decide a question of law that depends on underlying factual determinations, the jury's legal conclusion is subject to independent review by the court on appeal.[210] Whether the statutory requirement of "error" has been met is an issue of law that is reviewed de novo. The legal conclusion is based on underlying factual inquiries that are reviewed, in a jury case, for substantial evidence.[211]

When reviewing a jury finding on an equitable issue normally reserved for the court such as patent misuse, the court first presumes that the jury resolved the underlying factual disputes in favor of the verdict winner and leaves those presumed findings undisturbed if they are supported by substantial evidence. Then, in a manner analogous to its review of legal conclusions, it examines the conclusion de novo to see whether it is correct in light of the jury fact findings.[212]

Best mode is a question of fact. Thus where the jury finds that the defendant failed to prove that the best mode was not disclosed, the jury determination stands unless not supported by substantial evidence.[213] Where the jury finds a claim indefinite, the standard of review is whether the jury's express or implied findings of fact were supported by substantial evidence, and whether those findings supported the conclusion of indefiniteness.[214]

---

claims in issue had been proven obvious. The form went on to require that, if the answer was yes, the jury was to list the specific prior art that it felt rendered each such claim obvious. The jury listed prior art that the accused infringer conceded did not render some claims obvious. The trial judge entered JMOL as to those claims and the Federal Circuit affirmed. Legal formalities govern special verdicts. Here the jury delivered only one verdict and it is that verdict that must be reviewed. To look behind the special verdict and hypothesize some general verdict of obviousness would open a Pandora's box. A reviewing court simply has no tools to distinguish a jury's inadvertent oversight from a jury's mistaken, though genuinely held, view. Thus the court declined to infer a permissible jury verdict based on appropriate prior art.

[208]*Structural Rubber Prods. Co. v. Park Rubber Co.,* 749 F.2d 707, 223 USPQ 1264 (Fed. Cir. 1984).

[209]*Richardson-Vicks, Inc. v. Upjohn Co.,* 122 F.3d 1476, 44 USPQ2d 1181 (Fed. Cir. 1997).

[210]*Sjolund v. Musland,* 847 F.2d 1573, 6 USPQ2d 2020 (Fed. Cir. 1988).

[211]*Mentor Corp. v. Coloplast, Inc.,* 998 F.2d 992, 27 USPQ2d 1521 (Fed. Cir. 1993).

[212]*Virginia Panel Corp. v. MAC Panel Co.,* 133 F.3d 860, 45 USPQ2d 1225 (Fed. Cir. 1997).

[213]*McGill Inc. v. John Zink Co.,* 736 F.2d 666, 221 USPQ 944 (Fed. Cir. 1984). The court found in *Dana Corp. v. IPC Ltd.,* 860 F.2d 415, 8 USPQ2d 1692 (Fed. Cir. 1988), that the district court had applied the wrong legal standard on best mode. Rather than remand, however, it went on to decide the case because it felt there were sufficient established facts of record to enable it to exercise its discretion to determine the merits of the trial court's denial of a JMOL motion. In reversing, the court had to conclude that reasonable minds could not have found that the best mode requirement was satisfied.

[214]*Beachcombers v. Wildewood Creative Prods., Inc.,* 31 F.3d 1154, 31 USPQ2d 1653 (Fed. Cir. 1994).

The court has approved a responsible procedure whereby a patentee, who objects to the trial court's jury instructions on claim interpretation, consents to entry of JMOL to expedite its appeal and conserve resources.[215]

The issue of patent infringement is one of fact to be proven by a preponderance of the evidence, and a jury's finding of infringement must be upheld if it is supported by substantial evidence.[216] A jury's determination of willfulness is reviewed by the same standard.[217]

Jury damage awards, unless the product of passion and prejudice, are not easily overturned or modified on appeal.[218] A jury award of damages is reviewed on the reasonable jury/substantial evidence standard.[219]

Where the overall question of infringement is answered by the jury and the losing party's motion for JMOL is denied, appellate court review is limited. In order to obtain reversal, the losing party must demonstrate that no reasonable juror could have interpreted the claim in a fashion that supports the conclusion on infringement.[220] Of course, a verdict for a plaintiff, for example, infringement of a design patent, cannot stand where the plaintiff fails wholly to offer proof with respect to an element of its cause of action, for example, ornamental similarity and likelihood of confusion therein.[221]

---

[215]*York Prods., Inc. v. Central Tractor Farm & Fam. Ctr.,* 99 F.3d 1568, 40 USPQ2d 1619 (Fed. Cir. 1996).

[216]*Braun Inc. v. Dynamics Corp.,* 975 F.2d 815, 24 USPQ2d 1121 (Fed. Cir. 1992). In *Comark Comm. Inc. v. Harris Corp.,* 156 F.3d 1182, 48 USPQ2d 1001 (Fed. Cir. 1998), the claim element in question was but one of many disputed elements and the jury may have found that element literally present, rather than by equivalents, and yet still have found the claim to be infringed under the doctrine of equivalents. In order to arrive at its verdict of infringement under the doctrine of equivalents, the jury must have found that one or more claim elements were met by equivalents, and could have found the remainder of the claim elements were met literally. The jury may well have found that all elements were met by equivalents rather than literally. Because no special verdict interrogatory was used to determine which elements were met literally and which were met equivalently, the court could not presume to ascertain which elements the jury found to be met only by equivalents. Thus, the jury verdict must be upheld if there is sufficient evidence of equivalents and linking testimony such that a reasonable jury could have found that at least one element was met by equivalents.

[217]*Braun Inc. v. Dynamics Corp.,* 975 F.2d 815, 24 USPQ2d 1121 (Fed. Cir. 1992). In finding willful infringement, a jury is required to find by clear and convincing evidence in view of the totality of the circumstances that the infringer acted in disregard of the patent and lacked a reasonable basis for believing it had a right to do what it did. On appeal the issue is whether that finding was supported by substantial evidence. The appellate court reviews the evidence in the light most favorable to the prevailing party, drawing all reasonable inferences in its favor, to determine whether reasonable persons could have reached the jury's verdict. *Amsted Indus. v. Buckeye Steel Castings Co.,* 24 F.3d 178, 30 USPQ2d 1462 (Fed. Cir. 1994).

[218]*Weinar v. Rollform Inc.,* 744 F.2d 797, 223 USPQ 369 (Fed. Cir. 1984).

[219]*Richardson v. Suzuki Motor Co.,* 868 F.2d 1226, 9 USPQ2d 1913 (Fed. Cir. 1989).

[220]*Tol-O-Matic, Inc. v. Proma Produckt-und Mktg. GmbH,* 945 F.2d 1546, 20 USPQ2d 1332 (Fed. Cir. 1991). In *McGill Inc. v. John Zink Co.,* 736 F.2d 666, 221 USPQ 944 (Fed. Cir. 1984), the jury did not make express findings on claim construction, so that the court had to presume the existence of facts necessary to support such a claim construction and then see whether such facts were supported by substantial evidence. For equivalents under §112, the issue is whether a reasonable jury could have found the accused infringement to contain an equivalent of the means actually disclosed in the patent. *Data Line Corp. v. Micro Techs., Inc.,* 813 F.2d 1196, 1 USPQ2d 2052 (Fed. Cir. 1987).

[221]*Read Corp. v. Portec, Inc.,* 970 F.2d 816, 23 USPQ2d 1426 (Fed. Cir. 1992).

§10.4 Evidence and Witnesses

Like most federal courts of appeals, the Federal Circuit is not swamped with evidentiary issues. This is because error may not be predicated on an evidentiary ruling unless a substantial right of a party is involved.[222] Not all errors warrant annulment of the trial process. A trial need not be perfect; it must, however, be fair. Thus the Federal Rules of Evidence require that the issues presented at trial be relevant to the matter in dispute, and be supported by admissible evidence that is free of unfair prejudice. Although a trial court has substantial discretion in determining the evidence to be admitted, the ultimate fact must be of consequence to the determination of the evidence, under FRE 401. As provided in FRE 401–403, admissible evidence must be relevant in that it must tend to make a consequential fact more or less probable. The purposes of the FRE include assuring that irrelevant evidence does not unfairly prejudice the trial. Unfair prejudice is an undue tendency to suggest decision on an improper basis, commonly, though not necessarily, an emotional one. The obligation of the trial judge to act as "gatekeeper" is founded on the potential for prejudice.[223]

When balancing probative value against possible prejudice, the trial court has broad discretion. A trial court's admission or exclusion of evidence on grounds of relevance is reviewed for abuse of discretion.[224] Excluded evidence is viewed in the light most favorable to its proponent, giving the evidence its maximum reasonable probative force and its minimum reasonable prejudicial value. The reviewing court, in order to reverse such a decision made at trial, must be firmly convinced that a prejudicial mistake was made.[225] There is no

---

[222]*DMI, Inc. v. Deere & Co.*, 802 F.2d 421, 231 USPQ 276 (Fed. Cir. 1986); *Mainland Indus., Inc. v. Standal's Patents Ltd.*, 799 F.2d 746, 230 USPQ 772 (Fed. Cir. 1986).

[223]*Magnivision, Inc. v. Bonneau Co.*, 115 F.3d 956, 42 USPQ2d 1925, 1929 (Fed. Cir. 1997).

[224]*Kolmes v. World Fibers Corp.*, 107 F.3d 1534, 41 USPQ2d 1829 (Fed. Cir. 1997); *Roton Barrier, Inc. v. Stanley Works*, 79 F.3d 1112, 37 USPQ2d 1816 (Fed. Cir. 1996); *Munoz v. Strahm Farms, Inc.*, 69 F.3d 501, 36 USPQ2d 1499 (Fed. Cir. 1995); *Abbott Labs. v. Brennan*, 952 F.2d 1346, 21 USPQ2d 1192 (Fed. Cir. 1992). The court reviews evidentiary rulings with extreme deference. *National Presto Indus., Inc. v. West Bend Co.*, 76 F.3d 1185, 37 USPQ2d 1685 (Fed. Cir. 1996). The admission or exclusion of evidence not material to the issue of infringement is consigned to the discretion of the trial judge. *Fiskars Inc. v Hunt Mfg. Co.*, 221 F.3d 1318, 55 USPQ2d 1569 (Fed. Cir. 2000).

[225]*Abbott Labs. v. Brennan*, 952 F.2d 1346, 21 USPQ2d 1192 (Fed. Cir. 1992). It must be shown that admission or exclusion of the challenged evidence prejudiced substantial rights and was thus not harmless error. *Kolmes v. World Fibers Corp.*, 107 F.3d 1534, 41 USPQ2d 1829 (Fed. Cir. 1997); *Munoz v. Strahm Farms, Inc.*, 69 F.3d 501, 36 USPQ2d 1499 (Fed. Cir. 1995). In matters of trial management the district court has a limited right to be wrong without incurring appellate intrusion. Appellate review of evidentiary rulings is extremely restricted; it must be shown that there was manifest error, such as a reasonable likelihood that the improper exclusion of evidence prejudiced the outcome. *National Presto Indus., Inc. v. West Bend Co.*, 76 F.3d 1185, 37 USPQ2d 1685 (Fed. Cir. 1996). If evidence of marginal probative worth necessitates lengthy rebuttal, it imparts disproportionate weight to an irrelevant issue. And a jury instruction that implicitly endorses the issue can add weight to its prejudicial impact. *Magnivision, Inc. v. Bonneau Co.*, 115 F.3d 956, 42 USPQ2d 1925 (Fed. Cir. 1997).

reversible error unless the admission or exclusion of evidence appears to be inconsistent with substantial justice.[226]

The court has rejected the notion that error in admitting evidence is harmless merely because there exists substantial evidence to support the finding even without the tainted evidence. Instead, the question is whether the admission of the evidence affected the substantial rights of the party opposing it. A number of factors have guided the courts in their determinations of whether error is harmless, including (1) whether erroneously admitted evidence was the primary evidence relied upon, (2) whether the aggrieved party was nonetheless able to present the substance of its claim, (3) the existence and usefulness of curative jury instructions, (4) the extent of jury argument based on tainted evidence, (5) whether erroneously admitted evidence was merely cumulative, and (6) whether other evidence was overwhelming.[227]

When the court does review evidentiary matters not unique to patent issues, it applies the law of the regional circuit.[228] The Federal Rules of Evidence are and should be applied in patent cases no differently from their application in any other type of case.[229]

(a) Witnesses in General

The function of witnesses, expert and otherwise, is to assist the court in determining and comprehending facts.[230] Testimonial evidence is frequently critical to invalidity defenses and almost always so respecting unenforceability.[231] The credibility of a witness and the weight to be given his or her testimony are matters for the trier of

---

[226]*Abbott Labs. v. Brennan*, 952 F.2d 1346, 21 USPQ2d 1192 (Fed. Cir. 1992). In this case the court applied Sixth Circuit law. It found no abuse of discretion in permitting a party to call witnesses that it identified only the day before trial, on the ground that it was surprised that the other party's witnesses would be testifying on a particular subject.

[227]*ATD Corp. v. Lydall Inc.*, 159 F.3d 534, 48 USPQ2d 1321 (Fed. Cir. 1998).

[228]*Rodime PLC v. Seagate Tech. Inc.*, 174 F.3d 1294, 50 USPQ2d 1429 (Fed. Cir. 1999); *Ethicon Inc. v. United States Surgical Corp.*, 135 F.3d 1456, 45 USPQ2d 1545 (Fed. Cir. 1998); *Dorf & Stanton Comm., Inc. v. Molson Breweries*, 100 F.3d 919, 40 USPQ2d 1761 (Fed. Cir. 1996); *Abbott Labs. v. Brennan*, 952 F.2d 1346, 21 USPQ2d 1192 (Fed. Cir. 1992); *Mainland Indus., Inc. v. Standal's Patents Ltd.*, 799 F.2d 746, 230 USPQ 772 (Fed. Cir. 1986). The abuse of discretion standard is applied generally to review of evidentiary rulings in the federal system. *ATD Corp. v. Lydall Inc.*, 159 F.3d 534, 48 USPQ2d 1321 (Fed. Cir. 1998). In *In re Spalding Sports Worldwide Inc.*, 203 F.3d 800, 53 USPQ2d 1747 (Fed. Cir. 2000), the Federal Circuit applied its own law to the issue of whether the attorney-client privilege applies to an invention record prepared and submitted to house counsel. It distinguished *In re Regents of Univ. of Calif.*, 101 F.3d 1386, 40 USPQ2d 1784 (Fed. Cir. 1996), on the ground that the issue there (whether a licensor and a licensee are joint clients for purposes of privilege under the community of interest doctrine) was not unique to patent law.

[229]*SRI Int'l v. Matsushita Elec. Corp.*, 775 F.2d 1107, 227 USPQ 577 (Fed. Cir. 1985). See also *Symbol Tech., Inc. v. Opticon, Inc.*, 935 F.2d 1569, 19 USPQ2d 1241 (Fed. Cir. 1991).

[230]*EWP Corp. v. Reliance Universal Inc.*, 755 F.2d 898, 225 USPQ 20 (Fed. Cir. 1985).

[231]*A.C. Aukerman Co. v. R.L. Chaides Constr. Co.*, 960 F.2d 1020, 22 USPQ2d 1321 (Fed. Cir. 1992).

fact.[232] The drawing of inferences, particularly in respect of an intent-implicating question, is peculiarly within the province of the fact finder that observed the witnesses. Since the fact finder has personally heard the testimony and observed the demeanor of the witnesses, the appellate court accords deference to the fact finder's assessment of a witness's credibility and character.[233]

That some parts of a witness's testimony may be attacked is a common phenomenon. It supplies no basis, however, for holding that the fact finder is not entitled to credit other parts of that witness's testimony.[234] The mere fact that a long time has passed between a person's testimony at trial and the date that his or her testimony is directed to is not in itself sufficient to discredit that testimony.[235] The fact that a witness has no demonstrated financial interest in the outcome of the suit supports the trustworthiness of his or her testimony.[236] But a witness's pecuniary interest in the outcome of a case goes to the probative weight of testimony, not its admissibility.[237] In the end, however, trial courts have and must continue to have the right to reject the testimony of a witness, a right that can be defeated only when clear error is shown. That a trial court's opinion does not contain language expressly discrediting a witness's testimony does not license an appellate court to reweigh that testimony and to make its own credibility determinations.[238]

When a party knows of witnesses on a material issue and chooses not to call them despite the fact they are within its control to produce, the fact finder may draw the inference that the testimony would have been unfavorable. Generally the opposing party must establish that the missing witness was peculiarly within the adversary's power to produce by showing that the witness was unavailable to be called, for an unfavorable inference is not drawn from the lack of testimony by one who is equally available to be called by either party.[239]

---

[232]*Gyromat Corp. v. Champion Spark Plug Co.*, 735 F.2d 549, 222 USPQ 4 (Fed. Cir. 1984).

[233]*Molins PLC v. Textron, Inc.*, 48 F.3d 1172, 33 USPQ2d 1823 (Fed. Cir. 1995).

[234]*DeSarno v. Department of Commerce*, 761 F.2d 657 (Fed. Cir. 1985).

[235]*Gould v. Quigg*, 822 F.2d 1074, 3 USPQ2d 1302 (Fed. Cir. 1987).

[236]*Sjolund v. Musland*, 847 F.2d 1573, 6 USPQ2d 2020 (Fed. Cir. 1988).

[237]*Ethicon Inc. v. United States Surgical Corp.*, 135 F.3d 1456, 45 USPQ2d 1545 (Fed. Cir. 1998). In this case the accused infringer found a person who claimed to be coinventor. He was given an immediate payment of $300,000, and future payments of up to $100,000 per year for 10 years were contingent upon the infringer prevailing in the infringement litigation. In return, the person granted the infringer an exclusive license and agreed to testify in the proceeding to correct inventorship. The court held his testimony was admissible. The license agreement terms did not constitute payment for his testimony as a fact witness. A patent license agreement that binds the inventor to participate in subsequent litigation is very common. This sort of agreement simply assures the licensee that it will be able to defend the property in which it has purchased an interest.

[238]*Polaroid Corp. v. Eastman Kodak Co.*, 789 F.2d 1556, 229 USPQ 561 (Fed. Cir. 1986). Where a presiding official expressly finds a witness credible, the reviewing court cannot substitute a contrary credibility determination based on a cold paper record. *DeSarno v. Department of Commerce*, 761 F.2d 657 (Fed. Cir. 1985).

[239]*A.B. Dick Co. v. Burroughs Corp.*, 798 F.2d 1392, 230 USPQ 849 (Fed. Cir. 1986) (dictum). This generalization is not applicable where the likelihood of bias of the potential

(b) Patent Examiners and Other Officials

United States v. Morgan[240] permits an official exercising a quasiju-dicial function to testify as to relevant matters of fact so long as the factual inquiries do not probe into the mental processes employed by the official in formulating the decision in question. In *Western Electric v. Piezo,*[241] the Federal Circuit explored the boundaries of the *Morgan* doctrine as it applies to the testimony of patent examiners. Patent examiners are quasijudicial officials. The general rule has been that a patent examiner cannot be compelled to testify regarding his or her "mental processes" in reaching a decision on a patent application. The courts have held, however, that patent examiners may be deposed if the questions are limited to factual matters and if the questioning does not delve into hypothetical or speculative areas or the examiner's bases, reasons, mental processes, analyses, or conclusions.[242]

The *Piezo* decision holds that, in general, a patent examiner may not be compelled to answer questions that probe his or her technical knowledge of the subject matter of the patent. Although such ques-tions may be factual in form, they are typically not asked to obtain technical information or facts relating to the conduct of the proceed-ing; rather, they seek only to determine the extent of the examiner's knowledge in the particular art. Questions directed at "scoping out" the bounds of the examiner's technical knowledge may indicate, either separately or as a group, the considerations or factors that he or she took into account during the examination process. The examiner's knowledge of the relevant prior art is, to a large part, the product of his or her consideration of the references. Later recollection of what he or she knew at the time of the proceeding may be indicative of technical areas or prior art he or she deemed important, while unim-portant matters may be forgotten. The state of his or her knowledge is, therefore, inextricably intertwined with his or her reasoning and action in examining the patent. Disclosure of the details of his or her technical knowledge inherently provides at least some, and more likely substantial, insight into his or her mental processes in evaluat-ing the application and pertinent references.[243]

---

witness is great, and in such a case the witness is not considered equally available to both parties (e.g., employees or inventors with contractual obligation to testify). *Id.* Where a party does put an employee on the stand, impeachment on cross-examination is certainly available to the opposing party. See *Shiley, Inc. v. Bentley Labs., Inc.,* 794 F.2d 1561, 230 USPQ 112 (Fed. Cir. 1986).

[240]313 U.S. 409 (1941).

[241]*Western Elec. Co. v. Piezo Tech., Inc.,* 860 F.2d 428, 8 USPQ2d 1853 (Fed. Cir. 1988).

[242]*Green v. Rich Iron Co.,* 944 F.2d 852, 20 USPQ2d 1075 (Fed. Cir. 1991); *Western Elec. Co. v. Piezo Tech., Inc.,* 860 F.2d 428, 8 USPQ2d 1853 (Fed. Cir. 1988). See also *Magnivision, Inc. v. Bonneau Co.,* 115 F.3d 956, 42 USPQ2d 1925 (Fed. Cir. 1997).

[243]*Western Elec. Co. v. Piezo Tech., Inc.,* 860 F.2d 428, 8 USPQ2d 1853 (Fed. Cir. 1988).

The *Piezo* panel went further, however, and justified its decision as supportive of the integrity of the quasijudicial administrative process. The court felt that questions about an examiner's technical knowledge of the particular art tend to be disruptive of the decision-making process and thereby interfere with the PTO's administrative functions. By asking those questions in anticipation that the examiner does not know the answers or is not fully conversant with the technical area, a party could attempt to discredit the examiner and ease its burden of persuasion. It is no more appropriate to question a patent examiner's technical expertise than it is to question the quality of a judge's law school education or judicial experience. Furthermore, questions that might discredit an examiner are irrelevant because it is not the particular examiner's expertise that gives the decisions presumptive correctness but the authority duly vested in him or her by his or her appointment as a patent examiner.[244]

(c) Expert Witnesses

A trial judge has sole discretion to decide whether or not he or she needs, or even just desires, an expert's assistance to understand a patent, and the Federal Circuit has said that it will not disturb that discretion except in the clearest case.[245] Certainly where the references and invention are easily understandable, there may be no need for expert explanatory testimony.[246] Moreover, the Federal Circuit is not disposed to ignore what it can observe with its own eyes and determine with its own hands, simply for want of some expert to testify about it or some affiant to put the obvious down on paper over his or her notarized signature. A sample is a potent witness.[247] Nonetheless, it is well recognized that the persuasiveness

---

[244]*Western Elec. Co. v. Piezo Tech., Inc.,* 860 F.2d 428, 8 USPQ2d 1853 (Fed. Cir. 1988). In another interesting sidelight, the court in this case likened the "reasonable examiner" for inequitable conduct purposes to the hypothetical man of skill in the art. The patentee had argued that the examiner was an independent and impartial expert who could be relied upon to recognize and reject misleading statements about the prior art. In rejecting the accused infringer's counterargument that it needed testimony from the examiner to test this thesis, the court observed that the standard to be applied is not whether a particular examiner would be misled by alleged misrepresentations, but whether a "reasonable" examiner would be. Thus the knowledge of this particular examiner is irrelevant.

[245]*General Electro Music Corp. v. Samick Music Corp.,* 19 F.3d 1405, 30 USPQ2d 1149 (Fed. Cir. 1994); *Abbott Labs. v. Brennan,* 952 F.2d 1346, 21 USPQ2d 1192 (Fed. Cir. 1992); *Acoustical Design, Inc. v. Control Elec. Co.,* 932 F.2d 939, 18 USPQ2d 939 (Fed. Cir. 1991); *Seattle Box Co. v. Industrial Crat. & Pack., Inc.,* 731 F.2d 818, 221 USPQ 568 (Fed. Cir. 1984). Admissibility of expert testimony in the Claims Court is within the trial judge's discretion. *Milmark Serv., Inc. v. United States,* 731 F.2d 855 (Fed. Cir. 1984).

[246]*Union Carbide Corp. v. American Can Co.,* 724 F.2d 1567, 220 USPQ 584 (Fed. Cir. 1984). It is not error for a judge, unskilled in the pertinent art, to decide the legal question of validity without the testimony of a qualified expert in that field. *Avia Group Int'l, Inc. v. L.A. Gear Calif., Inc.,* 853 F.2d 1557, 7 USPQ2d 1548 (Fed. Cir. 1988).

[247]*In re Benno,* 768 F.2d 1340, 226 USPQ 683 (Fed. Cir. 1985).

of the presentation of complex technology-based issues to laypersons depends heavily on the relative skill of the experts.[248]

The role of expert testimony as extrinsic evidence in claim construction has begun to receive closer attention. When such persons testify about how a claim should be construed, their testimony amounts to no more than a legal opinion, being precisely the process of construction that the court must undertake. As to these types of opinions, the court has complete discretion to adopt the expert legal opinion as its own, to find guidance from it, or to ignore it entirely or even exclude it. When legal experts offer their conflicting views of how the patent should be construed, or when the legal expert's view of how the patent should be construed conflicts with the patent document itself, such conflict does not create a question of fact, nor can the expert opinion bind the court or relieve the court of its obligation to construe the claims according to the tenor of the patent.[249]

Experience has shown that opposite opinions of persons professing to be experts may be obtained to any amount.[250] If an appellant could establish clear error in a district court's findings by merely citing a contrary view advocated at trial by the appellant's expert, the fact-finding role of the district court would be rendered meaningless.[251] Courts of law are not the optimal fora for trying questions of scientific truth. Even less are appellate courts equipped to choose among conflicting scientific theories. Judges are dependent on the quality and strength of the scientific evidence brought before them. The trial judge who hears the witnesses and does the initial assessment of the evidence deserves considerable latitude in eventually choosing sides based on what is ultimately an educated guess—that is what judging is about.[252] Where the evidence consists solely of competing expert opinions, the court of appeals has no basis for overturning the district court's credibility determinations.[253] Likewise, a conflict in the legal

---

[248]*Mitsubishi Elec. Corp. v. Ampex Corp.*, 190 F.3d 1300, 51 USPQ2d 1910, 1920 (Fed. Cir. 1999).

[249]*Markman v. Westview Instr., Inc.*, 52 F.3d 967, 34 USPQ2d 1321 (Fed. Cir. 1995). Pre-*Markman* statements to the contrary must be read with caution. Thus, in *Moeller v. Ionetics, Inc.*, 794 F.2d 653, 229 USPQ 992 (Fed. Cir. 1986), it was said that the trial court's discretion in the use of experts is not unlimited. In a patent case involving complex scientific principles, it is particularly helpful to see how those skilled in the art would interpret the claim. Indeed, the test of claim interpretation is directed to one skilled in the art, and it makes sense therefore to elicit testimony from such individuals. See also *McGill Inc. v. John Zink Co.*, 736 F.2d 666, 221 USPQ 944 (Fed. Cir. 1984). Independent expert testimony may be used for the purpose of establishing facts such as the meaning of various terms to those skilled in the art. *Martin v. Mayer*, 823 F.2d 500, 3 USPQ2d 1333 (Fed. Cir. 1987). Although claim interpretation is a question of law, expert testimony is admissible to explain the meaning of technical terms in the claims and to give an opinion on the ultimate question of infringement. *Snellman v. Ricoh Co.*, 862 F.2d 283, 8 USPQ2d 1996 (Fed. Cir. 1988).

[250]*Hodosh v. Block Drug Co.*, 786 F.2d 1136, 229 USPQ 182 (Fed. Cir. 1986).

[251]*Rolls-Royce Ltd. v. GTE Valeron Corp.*, 800 F.2d 1101, 231 USPQ 185 (Fed. Cir. 1986).

[252]*Zenith Labs., Inc. v. Bristol-Myers Squibb Co.*, 19 F.3d 1418, 30 USPQ2d 1048, 32 USPQ2d 1017 (Fed. Cir. 1994).

[253]*Amstar Corp. v. Envirotech Corp.*, 823 F.2d 1538, 3 USPQ2d 1412 (Fed. Cir. 1987).

opinions of experts creates no dispute of fact that would defeat summary judgment.[254]

In an interesting standoff, the district court seemed to believe both sides' experts, concluded that the evidence was in "equipoise," and therefore held that the patentee had not met its burden of proving infringement by a preponderance. The Federal Circuit would not permit the district court to escape so easily its responsibility of choosing between reasonable-sounding experts. A true equipoise of evidence may indeed defeat the party with the burden of proof, but there is no authority for holding evidence to be in equipoise for the sole reason that a court cannot decide between conflicting experts. Given the complexity of modern technology, it may well happen that qualified experts will appear on both sides, that their testimony will conflict, and that the testimony or the technology or both will be difficult to understand. However, to decline to decide the issue when conflicting evidence appears to be counterbalancing, solely because the subject matter is technically complex, will defeat the party with the burden of proof without a fair hearing. Such treatment would remove complex technological issues from the purview of justice; this cannot reflect the correct judicial response to a world increasingly bound to technology.[255]

While objective factual evidence going toward a determination under 35 U.S.C. §103 is preferable to statements of opinion on the issue, the nature of the matter sought to be established, as well as the strength of the opposing evidence, must be taken into consideration in assessing the probative value of expert opinion. Opinion testimony rendered by experts must be given consideration, and while not controlling, generally is entitled to some weight. Lack of factual support for expert opinion going to factual determinations, however, may render the testimony of little probative value in a validity inquiry.[256]

A district court is not obliged to adopt a conclusion stated by an expert witness. The court's obligation is to weigh expert and other testimony; but it is the court's, not the expert's, responsibility to

---

[254]*Avia Group Int'l, Inc. v. L.A. Gear Calif., Inc.*, 853 F.2d 1557, 7 USPQ2d 1548 (Fed. Cir. 1988).

[255]*Andrew Corp. v. Gabriel Elec., Inc.*, 847 F.2d 819, 6 USPQ2d 2010 (Fed. Cir. 1988).

[256]*Ashland Oil, Inc. v. Delta Resins & Refracs., Inc.*, 776 F.2d 281, 227 USPQ 657 (Fed. Cir. 1985). But see *Data Line Corp. v. Micro Techs., Inc.*, 813 F.2d 1196, 1 USPQ2d 2052 (Fed. Cir. 1987). Expert affidavits submitted to the PTO by the applicant are entitled to little or no weight if they are mere opinions unsupported by facts. *In re Etter*, 756 F.2d 852, 225 USPQ 1 (Fed. Cir. 1985). The Federal Rules of Civil Procedure encourage discovery of information held by expert witnesses in order to narrow issues and eliminate surprise at trial. *DMI, Inc. v. Deere & Co.*, 802 F.2d 421, 231 USPQ 276 (Fed. Cir. 1986). Refusal to provide such discovery can result in exclusion of evidence. See *Rosemount, Inc. v. Beckman Instr., Inc.*, 727 F.2d 1540, 221 USPQ 1 (Fed. Cir. 1984). Evidence on obviousness may be presented through the testimony of experts. *Burlington Indus. Inc. v. Quigg*, 822 F.2d 1581, 3 USPQ2d 1436 (Fed. Cir. 1987). The person of ordinary skill in the art is a theoretical construct used in determining obviousness under §103, and is not descriptive of some particular individual. To suggest that the construct applies to particular individuals could mean that a person of exceptional skill in the art would be disqualified from testifying as an expert because not ordinary enough. *Endress + Hauser, Inc. v. Hawk Meas. Sys. Pty.*, 122 F.3d 1040, 43 USPQ2d 1849 (Fed. Cir. 1997).

decide the case.[257] A judge or jury is not required to accept expert testimony even if it is uncontradicted. There may be such inherent improbability in the statements of a witness as to induce the court or jury to disregard his or her evidence, even in the absence of any direct conflicting testimony.[258] Thus, where the evidence of infringement consists merely of one expert's opinion, without supporting tests or data, the district court is under no obligation to accept it.[259]

Rule 705, FRE, functions to abbreviate trials by permitting opinion testimony without factual foundation. Patent cases, so often typified by lengthy testimony on complex technical issues, are particularly served by this purpose.[260] But the fact that under Rule 705, FRE, an expert is not always required to disclose the facts and data underlying his or her opinion does not mean that the court is required to credit the testimony when the opposing party fails to probe those underlying facts by cross-examination, especially if that testimony is inherently unbelievable.[261] An expert's opinion on the legal conclusion of obviousness of a patented design is neither necessary nor controlling.[262] An expert's opinion on the ultimate legal conclusion is neither required

---

[257]*Del Mar Avionics, Inc. v. Quinton Instr. Co.,* 836 F.2d 1320, 5 USPQ2d 1255 (Fed. Cir. 1987). In *Applied Med. Res. Corp. v. United States Surgical Corp.,* 147 F.3d 1374, 47 USPQ2d 1289 (Fed. Cir. 1998), the court found no error in the exclusion of evidence of a ruling of an ALJ in an interference, whose reasoning was similar to that being propounded by an expert witness on the question of substantiality of differences. The witness's credibility as an expert and the probative quality of his testimony come from his experience, presentation, and reasoning, and not those of the administrative patent judge. This narrow exclusion merely prevented the party from augmenting the credibility of its expert's testimony by aligning it with the ALJ's factual finding. Such alignment could conflate factual inquiries—the ALJ's finding and a finding on the substantiality of differences—in a way that might prejudice or overshadow the later, more directly relevant finding.

[258]*U.S. Philips Corp. v. Windmere Corp.,* 861 F.2d 695, 8 USPQ2d 1885 (Fed. Cir. 1988). The court has embraced the views of the Supreme Court on unproven science in *Daubert v. Merrell Dow Pharm., Inc.,* 509 U.S. 579 (1993). See *Hebert v. Lisle Corp.,* 99 F.3d 1109, 40 USPQ2d 1611 (Fed. Cir. 1996). See also *Kumho Tire Co. v. Carmichael,* 526 U.S. 137, 50 USPQ2d 1177 (1999). Courts are not novices in receiving and weighing expertise on both sides of an issue. The Supreme Court in *Daubert* instructed trial judges to exclude scientifically unqualified witnesses, not those with superior qualifications. *Voice Tech. Group Inc. v. VMC Sys. Inc.,* 164 F.3d 605, 49 USPQ2d 1333 (Fed. Cir. 1999).

[259]*W.L. Gore & Assoc., Inc. v. Garlock, Inc.,* 842 F.2d 1275, 6 USPQ2d 1277 (Fed. Cir. 1988). Caution is indicated here, however. Surely a district court must have some evidence to support a contrary finding other than its own gut feeling that the expert is wrong.

[260]*Symbol Tech., Inc. v. Opticon, Inc.,* 935 F.2d 1569, 19 USPQ2d 1241 (Fed. Cir. 1991). Although an expert's unsupported conclusion may be proper during trial when the opposing party can challenge the factual basis of the expert's opinion through cross-examination, the affidavit of an expert submitted in opposition to a motion for summary judgment must do more. It must set forth specific facts showing that there is a genuine issue for trial. *Arthur A. Collins Inc. v. Northern Telecom Ltd.,* 216 F.3d 1042, 55 USPQ2d 1143 (Fed. Cir. 2000). An expert's affidavit on the purely legal issue of prosecution history estoppel cannot create a genuine issue of material fact that would bar summary judgment. *Bayer AG v. Elan Pharm. Res. Corp.,* 212 F.3d 1241, 54 USPQ2d 1710 (Fed. Cir. 2000).

[261]*Studiengesellschaft Kohle v. Dart Indus., Inc.,* 862 F.2d 1564, 9 USPQ2d 1273 (Fed. Cir. 1988). See also *Rohm & Haas Co. v. Brotech Corp.,* 127 F.3d 1089, 44 USPQ2d 1459 (Fed. Cir. 1997).

[262]*Avia Group Int'l, Inc. v. L.A. Gear Calif., Inc.,* 853 F.2d 1557, 7 USPQ2d 1548 (Fed. Cir. 1988).

nor indeed evidence at all.[263] It is not necessary that expert witnesses opine in terms of the three-part test for the doctrine of equivalents, at least before a body having the expertise of the ITC.[264]

While the opinion testimony of a party having a direct interest in the pending litigation is less persuasive than opinion testimony by a disinterested party, it cannot be disregarded for that reason alone and may be relied upon when sufficiently convincing.[265] What about a lawyer associated with a party? Certainly the court has roundly criticized actual and even indirect testimony from a lawyer.[266] On the other hand, it has been quite willing to accept the testimony of a patent lawyer on issues such as file history estoppel and claim differentiation, indicating with apparent approval that "in the manner not unusual in patent cases, he testified about questions of patent law as if it were foreign law."[267] However, it will be as quick to reject incorrect legal propositions announced by a patent law expert as it is to disregard unproven science. Incorrect statements of law are no more admissible through experts than are falsifiable legal theories.[268]

---

[263]*Mendenhall v. Cedarapids, Inc.*, 5 F.3d 1556, 28 USPQ2d 1081 (Fed. Cir. 1993). The court went on to say that the spectacle of experts arguing over the legal conclusion of obviousness before a jury, even if not error, should be avoided inasmuch as such opinions are not substantive evidence. The practice of using such experts developed in bench trials where they informed the judge, like a brief, on the intricacies of patent law. With all respect, this author believes that making a jury understand the preferred route to decision is difficult enough, without discouraging the use of one of the most useful tools in the trial lawyer's kit.

[264]*Intel Corp. v. United States ITC*, 946 F.2d 821, 20 USPQ2d 1161 (Fed. Cir. 1991). It is permissible for an expert to give an opinion on the ultimate question of infringement without providing the factual foundation for the opinion. *Symbol Tech., Inc. v. Opticon, Inc.*, 935 F.2d 1569, 19 USPQ2d 1241 (Fed. Cir. 1991). Here the plaintiff's expert gave an opinion without testifying as to §112 equivalents and the defendant failed to cross-examine on the subject. The plaintiff took a profound risk that defendant would, on cross, demonstrate noninfringement; but the defendant chose not to expose any defects in the opinion. The defendant cannot therefore recoup for its failed litigation strategy by arguing, on appeal, that the plaintiff failed to make a prima facie showing of infringement because it did not address §112 equivalents.

[265]*Ashland Oil, Inc. v. Delta Resins & Refracs., Inc.*, 776 F.2d 281, 227 USPQ 657 (Fed. Cir. 1985). Evidence of ex parte testing is entitled to little or no weight and is given only negligible probative value. The objectivity of the tester is a fundamental rule not only of evidence but of conscience. *In re Newman*, 782 F.2d 971, 228 USPQ 450 (Fed. Cir. 1986). Disregarding the testimony of an expert, for bias, as to what a prior art reference teaches does not eliminate the reference itself as evidence. *Verdegaal Bros., Inc. v. Union Oil Co.*, 814 F.2d 628, 2 USPQ2d 1051 (Fed. Cir. 1987).

[266]*Panduit Corp. v. Dennison Mfg. Co.*, 774 F.2d 1082, 227 USPQ 337 (Fed. Cir. 1985); *Connell v. Sears, Roebuck & Co.*, 722 F.2d 1542, 220 USPQ 193 (Fed. Cir. 1983). Attorney's argument is no substitute for evidence. *Johnston v. IVAC Corp.*, 885 F.2d 1574, 12 USPQ2d 1382 (Fed. Cir. 1989).

[267]*Yarway Corp. v. Eur-Control USA Inc.*, 775 F.2d 268, 227 USPQ 352 (Fed. Cir. 1985). In federal courts foreign law is a question of law to be determined by expert evidence or any other relevant source. *Merck & Co. v. United States ITC*, 774 F.2d 483, 227 USPQ 779 (Fed. Cir. 1985). In another case, the refusal to permit a patent law professor to testify on obviousness was held no abuse of discretion, where he did not possess technical expertise in the art. *Medtronic Inc. v. Intermedics, Inc.*, 799 F.2d 734, 230 USPQ 641 (Fed. Cir. 1986). In *Endress + Hauser, Inc. v. Hawk Meas. Sys. Pty.*, 122 F.3d 1040, 43 USPQ2d 1849 (Fed. Cir. 1997), the court noted the impropriety of patent lawyers testifying as expert witnesses and giving their opinion regarding the proper interpretation of a claim as a matter of law, the ultimate issue for the court to decide.

[268]*Hebert v. Lisle Corp.*, 99 F.3d 1109, 40 USPQ2d 1611 (Fed. Cir. 1996).

It is now clear that expert witness fees are not recoverable under 35 U.S.C. §285.[269]

(d) Admissions and Hearsay

Counsel's arguments are not evidence.[270] But certainly statements by an attorney can bind the client.[271] However, where a litigant is pro se, only his or her simple statements of fact, and not his or her legal conclusions, will be binding.[272]

Although a pleading may constitute an admission, a party is entitled to plead inconsistently in alternative defenses. Nor should judicial estoppel be invoked to preclude a position inconsistent with an earlier pleading unless the party received a benefit from the previously taken position in the form of judicial success. Where there is no judicial acceptance of the earlier position, there is no risk of inconsistent results, no effect on the integrity of the judicial process, and no perception that the court has been misled.[273] Issues such as admission by pleadings and judicial estoppel are considered to be procedural and thus decided under the law of the regional circuit.[274]

A report prepared by one government agency is an admission of the government generally, if it was part of the agency's duties to make the report.[275]

Because of the general trustworthiness of regularly kept records and the need for such evidence in many cases, the business records

---

[269]*Amsted Indus. v. Buckeye Steel Castings Co.*, 23 F.3d 374, 30 USPQ2d 1470 (Fed. Cir. 1994). This case overruled the court's previous holding in *Mathis v. Spears*, 857 F.2d 749, 8 USPQ2d 1029 (Fed. Cir. 1988), in light of *West Virginia Univ. Hosps., Inc. v. Casey*, 499 U.S. 83 (1991), where it was held that attorney fees did not encompass expert witness fees; explicit statutory reference to expert witness fees is required in order to supersede 28 U.S.C. §1821(b). See also *Crawford Fitting Co. v. J.T. Gibbons, Inc.*, 482 U.S. 437 (1987), where the Court held that when a prevailing party seeks reimbursement for fees paid to its own expert witnesses, a federal court is, absent contract or explicit statutory authority to the contrary, bound by 28 U.S.C. §1821(b), which limits expert witness fee awards under §1920 to $40 a day for each day's attendance and for the time necessarily occupied in travel to and from the place of attendance.

[270]*C.R. Bard, Inc. v. Advanced Card. Sys., Inc.*, 911 F.2d 670, 15 USPQ2d 1540 (Fed. Cir. 1990); *Johnston v. IVAC Corp.*, 885 F.2d 1574, 12 USPQ2d 1382 (Fed. Cir. 1989); *Senza-Gel Corp. v. Seiffhart*, 803 F.2d 661, 231 USPQ 363 (Fed. Cir. 1986). But see *Perkin-Elmer Corp. v. Computervision Corp.*, 732 F.2d 888, 221 USPQ 669 (Fed. Cir. 1984).

[271]*Tyler Refrigeration v. Kysor Indus. Corp.*, 777 F.2d 687, 227 USPQ 845 (Fed. Cir. 1985).

[272]*Syntex Ophthalmics, Inc. v. Novicky*, 745 F.2d 1423, 223 USPQ 695 (Fed. Cir. 1984).

[273]*Water Techs. Corp. v. Calco, Ltd.*, 850 F.2d 660, 7 USPQ2d 1097 (Fed. Cir. 1988). The plaintiff, an exclusive licensee, had at an earlier stage in the case pleaded as a defense to the licensor's (joined as an involuntary plaintiff) claim for royalties that the patents were invalid. That portion of the controversy was settled, and the defendant infringer was urging that the pleading constituted an admission of invalidity.

[274]*Water Techs. Corp. v. Calco, Ltd.*, 850 F.2d 660, 7 USPQ2d 1097 (Fed. Cir. 1988).

[275]*Skaw v. United States*, 740 F.2d 932 (Fed. Cir. 1984). Also, there is a general rule that public reports issued by agencies of the government are admissible regardless of duty. *Id.* In *Standard Havens Prods., Inc. v. Gencor Indus., Inc.*, 953 F.2d 1360, 21 USPQ2d 1321 (Fed. Cir. 1992), the court rejected an argument that it was error to have admitted a PTO certificate of correction in evidence as a public record exception to the hearsay rule, where the PTO later withdrew the certificate, thus casting doubt on its trustworthiness.

exception to the hearsay rule expressed in Rule 803(6) has been construed generously in favor of admissibility. District courts, moreover, are accorded broad discretion in determining whether a proper foundation has been laid for admitting business records.[276] The custodian or other qualified witness who must authenticate business records under Rule 803(6) need not be the person who prepared or maintained the records, or even an employee of the record-keeping entity, as long as the witness understands the system used to prepare the records. Moreover, the sufficiency of the foundation evidence must be assessed in light of the nature of the documents at issue; documents that are standard records of the type regularly maintained by firms in a particular industry may require less by way of foundation testimony than less conventional documents proffered for admission as business records.[277] Reliability is the basis for admitting evidence under the business records exception.[278]

Hearsay may be used in administrative proceedings and may be treated as substantial evidence, even without corroboration, if to a reasonable mind the circumstances are such as to lend it credence.[279] The court has made it clear that where documents appear on their face to be accurate and reliable, and where the applicant proffers no evidence to support arguments to the contrary, the PTO may assume the truthfulness of the statements contained therein. The inapplicability of hearsay evidence rules in ex parte PTO examination is appropriate in light of the purpose and reason for the hearsay rule, which is the theory that many possible sources of inaccuracy and untrustworthiness that may lie underneath the untested assertion of a witness can best be brought to light and exposed, if they exist, by the test of cross-examination. During ex parte examination applicants are free to investigate hearsay assertions relied upon by an examiner during the three-to-six month period available to respond to an office action. They also have the right to introduce rebuttal evidence under 37 C.F.R. §1.132. If they wish to cross-examine the authors of written hearsay assertions they may bring a civil action under 35 U.S.C.

---

[276]*Conoco Inc. v. Department of Energy,* 99 F.3d 387 (Fed. Cir. 1996).

[277]*Conoco Inc. v. Department of Energy,* 99 F.3d 387 (Fed. Cir. 1996). Doubtless there must be some reliable testimony, however. In *Kolmes v. World Fibers Corp.,* 107 F.3d 1534, 41 USPQ2d 1829 (Fed. Cir. 1997), documents were excluded as hearsay because they were not properly authenticated under the business records exception of FRE 802 and 803(6). An attempt to authenticate them by affidavit was rejected as insufficient, and the only live witness was not shown to be a custodian or other qualified witness under the business records exception, nor did he testify concerning the record-keeping process relating to the documents.

[278]*Munoz v. Strahm Farms, Inc.,* 69 F.3d 501, 36 USPQ2d 1499 (Fed. Cir. 1995). Here the question was foundation for photos that had been sent to Kodak for processing.

[279]*Hayes v. Department of Navy,* 727 F.2d 1535 (Fed. Cir. 1984). The general rule is that administrative agencies like the PTO are not bound by the rules of evidence that govern judicial proceedings. Agencies may provide for the application of evidence rules, as the PTO has done in patent interference and public use proceedings, both of which are inter partes in nature. However, the PTO has not made any special provision for evidence rules during ex parte examination. *In re Epstein,* 32 F.3d 1559, 31 USPQ2d 1817 (Fed. Cir. 1994).

§145.[280] Indeed, affidavit and deposition statements developed in inter partes cases may be used in PTO proceedings; such evidence may be more reliable and complete than ex parte evidence due to the adversary nature of the proceedings. However, the credibility of such statements must be established by clear and convincing evidence, which may require corroboration.[281]

Under Rule 56(e), FRCP, evidence presented in an affidavit must be evidence that would be admissible if presented at trial through the testimony of the affiant as a sworn witness. Thus, in an affidavit asserting that the affiant was told by person A that person B had made a statement to A, the assertion was for the purpose of proving that the statement had been made by B to A. This would be hearsay even if the affiant were testifying at trial and is thus inappropriate evidence in a summary judgment proceeding.[282]

The court occasionally is confronted with issues concerning exceptions to the rule against hearsay.[283] The two residual hearsay exceptions in the Federal Rules, FRE 803(24) and 804(b)(5), were meant to be reserved for exceptional cases. They were not intended to confer a broad license on trial judges to admit hearsay statements that do not fall within one of the other exceptions contained in Rules 803 and 804(b). Rule 803(24) provides that the evidence proffered must possess circumstantial guarantees of trustworthiness equivalent to those possessed by evidence admissible under the other Rule 803 exceptions. In addition, the court must determine that the evidence proffered is more probative on the point for which it is offered than any other evidence the proponent can procure through reasonable efforts, and that the general purposes of the rules and the interests of justice will best be served by admission.[284]

The court appears willing to accept hearsay evidence as part of a response to a motion to dismiss for lack of personal jurisdiction.[285] In one unusual case the court found no error in permitting the jury to view a videotape of a deposition of the inventor that had been

---

[280]*In re Epstein*, 32 F.3d 1559, 31 USPQ2d 1817 (Fed. Cir. 1994).

[281]*In re Sneed*, 710 F.2d 1544, 218 USPQ 385 (Fed. Cir. 1983).

[282]*Scosche Indus., Inc. v. Visor Gear, Inc.*, 121 F.3d 675, 43 USPQ2d 1659, 1664 (Fed. Cir. 1997).

[283]In *Rotec Indus. Inc. v. Mitsubishi Corp.*, 215 F.3d 1246, 55 USPQ2d 1001 (Fed. Cir. 2000), a witness indicated that he was told by a declarant that a certain meeting had taken place. The court rejected the argument that the statement was admissible to prove the fact of the meeting on the ground that it was made in furtherance of a conspiracy. At best, the statement revealed purportedly truthful information (the fact of the meeting) to the alleged victim of the conspiracy (the witness or his company). The court also rejected the argument that the statement was an admission of a party agent. There was no evidence that the witness could affect the legal relationships of the parties.

[284]*Conoco Inc. v. Department of Energy,* 99 F.3d 387 (Fed. Cir. 1996).

[285]*Beverly Hills Fan Co. v. Royal Sovereign Corp.*, 21 F.3d 1558, 30 USPQ2d 1001 (Fed. Cir. 1994). The court seemed impressed by the fact that the moving party could have independently verified the accuracy of the facts established in an affidavit that reported on telephone conversations with unnamed employees of a retail outlet. See also *Akro Corp. v. Luker*, 45 F.3d 1541, 33 USPQ2d 1505 (Fed. Cir. 1995).

taken in litigation in Canada. It was clear that the opposing party in the Canadian case possessed the requisite interest, opportunity, and motive to develop the issues fully on cross-examination; that compliance with Canadian law was not contested; that the issues in both cases were similar; and that the trial judge regarded the tape as sufficiently trustworthy to be used to ascertain the truth.[286]

(e) Burdens and Presumptions

The statutory presumption of patent validity established by 35 U.S.C. §282, and the burden it places upon the patent challenger, have been discussed at length in §1.5. In general, presumptions of fact are created to assist in certain circumstances where direct proof of a matter is for one reason or another rendered difficult. They arise out of considerations of fairness, public policy, and probability, and are useful devices for allocating the burden of production of evidence between the parties. However, derived as they are from considerations of fairness and policy, they must not be given mechanical application.[287]

The presumptions relating to laches and estoppel are treated in §9.3. Such presumptions are controlled by Rule 301, FRE, which embodies what is known as the bursting bubble theory of presumptions. In this theory, a presumption is not merely rebuttable but completely vanishes upon the introduction of evidence sufficient to support a finding of the nonexistence of the presumed fact. That is, the evidence must be sufficient to put the existence of a presumed fact into genuine dispute.[288]

Identifying the appropriate burden of proof is important, because adoption of an incorrect and more difficult burden cannot ordinarily be classified as harmless error.[289] In American law, preponderance of the evidence is the rock bottom burden at the fact-finding level in civil litigation.[290] Preponderance of the evidence, in civil or administrative actions, means the greater weight of evidence: evidence that is more convincing than the evidence that is offered in opposition to it.[291] The preponderance standard requires only that the fact finder believe that the existence of a fact is more probable than its nonexistence

---

[286]*Mainland Indus., Inc. v. Standal's Patents Ltd.,* 799 F.2d 746, 230 USPQ 772 (Fed. Cir. 1986). The inventor had died prior to the U.S. trial. It was also clear that the judge found no indication that the jury was unduly influenced by sympathy for the inventor.

[287]*Panduit Corp. v. All States Plastic Mfg. Co.,* 744 F.2d 1564, 223 USPQ 465 (Fed. Cir. 1984).

[288]*A.C. Aukerman Co. v. R.L. Chaides Constr. Co.,* 960 F.2d 1020, 22 USPQ2d 1321 (Fed. Cir. 1992).

[289]*Price v. Symsek,* 988 F.2d 1187, 26 USPQ2d 1031 (Fed. Cir. 1993).

[290]*SSIH Equip. S.A. v. United States ITC,* 718 F.2d 365 (Fed. Cir. 1983).

[291]*St. Paul F. & M. Ins. Co. v. United States,* 6 F.3d 763 (Fed. Cir. 1993); *Hale v. Department of Transp.,* 772 F.2d 882 (Fed. Cir. 1985).

before it may find in favor of the party that has the burden to persuade the fact finder of the fact's existence.[292]

Moving up the scale, the clear and convincing standard is different from, and lesser than, the beyond a reasonable doubt standard.[293] The clear and convincing standard of proof is an intermediate standard that lies somewhere between proof beyond a reasonable doubt and a preponderance of the evidence. Although not susceptible to precise definition, clear and convincing evidence has been described as evidence that produces in the mind of the trier of fact an abiding conviction that the truth of the factual contention is highly probable.[294] But even under the clear and convincing standard, proof need not be airtight. The law requires persuasion not perfection.[295]

Once the standard of proof for a particular issue has been determined, it applies without regard to the circumstances of a particular case. Litigants can always assert, and sometimes effectively, that their cases involve special circumstances.[296]

Drawing an inference on an inference is not the role of the fact finder. But impermissibly using an inference to establish a fact should not be confused with permissibly drawing an inference from an already established fact. From proof of a certain fact or facts it may be logical to conclude that another fact does or does not exist. The conclusion is reached by inference, which involves only reason and experience.[297] Proof of a prima facie case compels the conclusion sought to be proved unless evidence sufficient to rebut the conclusion is produced.[298]

(f) Offers of Compromise

An unaccepted offer of settlement ordinarily is not admissible evidence to show either the existence or amount of liability. The rule reflects the reality that permitting consideration of settlement offers as indicative of an admission of liability in the amount of the offer would seriously discourage parties from discussing settlement or making offers. The law favors settlement of litigation, which reduces the burden on courts and counsel and mitigates the antagonism and hostility that protracted litigation leading to judgment may cause.[299]

---

[292]*Bosies v. Benedict*, 27 F.3d 539, 30 USPQ2d 1862 (Fed. Cir. 1994).

[293]*DeGeorge v. Bernier*, 768 F.2d 1318, 226 USPQ 758 (Fed. Cir. 1985).

[294]*Buildex, Inc. v. Kason Indus., Inc.*, 849 F.2d 1461, 7 USPQ2d 1325 (Fed. Cir. 1988).

[295]*Buildex, Inc. v. Kason Indus., Inc.*, 849 F.2d 1461, 7 USPQ2d 1325 (Fed. Cir. 1988).

[296]*Hess v. Advanced Cardiovascular Sys., Inc.*, 106 F.3d 976, 41 USPQ2d 1782 (Fed. Cir. 1997).

[297]*FMC Corp. v. Manitowoc Co.*, 835 F.2d 1411, 5 USPQ2d 1112, 1116 (Fed. Cir. 1987).

[298]*Hale v. Department of Transp.*, 772 F.2d 882 (Fed. Cir. 1985).

[299]*Cheyenne River Sioux Tribe v. United States*, 806 F.2d 1046 (Fed. Cir. 1986). See also *Medtronic Inc. v. Intermedics, Inc.*, 799 F.2d 734, 230 USPQ 641 (Fed. Cir. 1986).

Thus, an offer to license at a given rate if made as an offer of compromise in contemplation of litigation is inadmissible under Rule 408, FRE.[300] However, an offer to license is not inadmissible under Rule 408 if there was no actual dispute in progress at the time of the offer.[301] Rule 407, FRE, bars evidence of subsequent remedial action in proving culpability for a prior act or event. The policy implemented by Rule 407 is to avoid inhibiting postaccident repair, lest additional injury occur. The court has hinted that Rule 407 applies to willfulness determinations in the patent infringement context.[302]

(g) Privilege and Work Product

The attorney-client privilege protects the confidentiality of communications between attorney and client made for the purpose of obtaining legal advice. The work product privilege protects the attorney's thought processes and legal recommendations.[303] In what may turn out to be a fairly significant decision the Federal Circuit provided some guidance on matters of attorney-client privilege. In *American Standard v. Pfizer,*[304] the court reminded us that the purpose[305] of the attorney-client privilege is to encourage full and frank communication between attorneys and their clients by assuring clients that their disclosures will be held in confidence. It protects communications made in confidence by clients to their lawyers for the purpose of obtaining legal advice. In keeping with this policy, it expressly repudiated any notion that in-house and outside patent counsel's validity opinions are never protected by the attorney-client privilege.[306] The controversial portion of the *American Standard* decision has to do with whether the privilege protects the legal advice given or other

---

[300]*Hanson v. Alpine Valley Ski Area, Inc.,* 718 F.2d 1075, 219 USPQ 679 (Fed. Cir. 1983).

[301]*Deere & Co. v. International Harvester Co.,* 710 F.2d 1551, 218 USPQ 481 (Fed. Cir. 1983).

[302]*Pall Corp. v. Micron Separations, Inc.,* 66 F.3d 1211, 36 USPQ2d 1225 (Fed. Cir. 1995).

[303]*Genentech, Inc. v. United States ITC,* 122 F.3d 1409, 43 USPQ2d 1722 (Fed. Cir. 1997). There is no legal principle that even remotely supports the notion that an otherwise discoverable document alchemically metamorphosizes into privileged work product simply because an attorney photocopies it. *Advanced Display Sys. Inc. v. Kent State Univ.,* 212 F.3d 1272, 54 USPQ2d 1673 (Fed. Cir. 2000).

[304]*American Standard, Inc. v. Pfizer, Inc.,* 828 F.2d 734, 3 USPQ2d 1817 (Fed. Cir. 1987).

[305]The attorney-client privilege encourages full and frank communication between attorneys and their clients and thereby promotes broader public interests in the observance of law and administration of justice. Thus the privilege protects a client's confidential communications to an attorney necessary to obtain legal counseling. *Shearing v. Iolab Corp.,* 975 F.2d 1541, 24 USPQ2d 1133 (Fed. Cir. 1992). The court held there was no privilege because the lawyer was testifying about a conversation had with the client at a time when the lawyer was not acting as attorney for the client.

[306]*American Standard, Inc. v. Pfizer, Inc.,* 828 F.2d 734, 3 USPQ2d 1817 (Fed. Cir. 1987). The court also repudiated any view that a validity opinion based on publicly available information, as most such opinions are, is for that reason alone outside the privilege. Further, it repudiated the view that what the attorney told the client in an opinion letter is always irrelevant.

communications from the attorney to the client. In a split decision, the court held that where it is clear than an opinion letter relies on nonconfidential information, regardless of its source, and does not reveal any confidential communications of the client, it is not privileged. This holding may be interpreted as meaning that the attorney's advice in and of itself is not privileged.[307]

The work product immunity belongs to both the attorney and the client while the attorney-client privilege belongs to the client alone. The attorney-client privilege evaporates upon any voluntary disclosure of confidential information to a third party; the purpose of the work product immunity is not in all cases frustrated by a similar disclosure. That purpose is to prevent the disclosure of an attorney's mental impressions and thought processes either to an opponent in the litigation for which the attorney generated and recorded those impressions, or to a third party with interests not common to those of the party asserting the privilege.[308] Once the attorney-client privilege has been waived, it is generally lost for all purposes and in all forums. Although the Federal Circuit is aware that a small number of courts have recognized a limited waiver doctrine, it has never recognized limited waivers.[309]

To invoke the crime-fraud exception, a party challenging the attorney-client privilege must make a prima facie showing that the communication was made in furtherance of a crime or fraud. In the context of inequitable conduct, the party challenging the privilege on that basis must make a prima facie showing that the communication (here an invention record) was made in furtherance of common law fraud of the *Walker Process* type. Although the party seeking to overcome the attorney-client privilege need not conclusively prove fraud,

---

[307]The court did recognize that in some circumstances the disclosure of the bare fact that counsel was consulted might chill the willingness of citizens to approach a lawyer's office. More importantly, the disclosure of the lawyer's communication could in itself disclose, directly or indirectly, what the client told the lawyer. The majority of the panel seemed quite willing to accommodate these concerns on a case-by-case basis. But the holding provoked a sharp dissent from Judge Newman, who expressed the view that classical legal opinions that communicate legal advice from attorney to client have been and should continue to be regarded as subject to the privilege. One may reasonably suppose that this debate is not over. The court has applied *American Standard* in holding that a memo from an Assistant Attorney General to the Solicitor General only constituted work product and was not privileged where it did not betray any communications between the client (the IRS) and the attorney (the Justice Department). *Carter v. Gibbs,* 909 F.2d 1450 (Fed. Cir. 1990).

[308]*Carter v. Gibbs,* 909 F.2d 1450 (Fed. Cir. 1990). The rule seems to be that voluntary, albeit inadvertent, disclosure of work product to an adversary in the litigation for which the attorney produced that information constitutes a waiver. Here the court held that a waiver of the work product immunity resulted when the government inadvertently attached a copy of a Justice Department memorandum to the opposing party's copy of a motion for an extension of time. But see *Genentech, Inc. v. United States ITC,* 122 F.3d 1409, 43 USPQ2d 1722 (Fed. Cir. 1997), where the court recognized that some courts find an exception to the waiver when the disclosure is inadvertent. For instance, if the party has used reasonable effort to protect a confidence, courts may find a subsequent disclosure inadvertent and thus not a waiver of privilege.

[309]*Genentech, Inc. v. United States ITC,* 122 F.3d 1409, 43 USPQ2d 1722 (Fed. Cir. 1997). The court did seem to leave the door open for a limited waiver if the protective order governing the litigation expressly so provides.

or necessarily submit direct evidence to make a prima facie showing of fraud, a mere allegation of failure to cite a reference to the PTO will not suffice. In actuality, a citation of prior art in an invention record in the absence of evidence of a purpose to conceal that art would seem to be the opposite of furthering fraud; it informs the patent attorney or agent of the closest prior art. What the attorney then does with that information is another matter, but inclusion of the closest prior art in an invention record does not alone provide evidence of furthering a fraud.[310]

When the same attorney represents the interest of two or more entities on the same matter, those represented are viewed as joint clients for purposes of privilege. The protection of communications among clients and attorneys allied in a common legal cause has long been recognized. The issue is not who employed the attorney but whether the attorney was acting in a professional relationship to the person asserting the privilege. This relationship hinges upon the client's belief that it is consulting a lawyer in that capacity and its manifested intention to seek professional legal advice.[311]

It is well established that the attorney-client privilege is not limited to actions taken and advice obtained in anticipation of litigation. Persons seek legal advice and assistance in order to meet legal requirements and to plan their conduct; such steps serve the public interest in achieving compliance with law and facilitating the administration of justice, and indeed may aver litigation.[312] Consultation with counsel during patent prosecution meets the criteria of compliance with law and meeting legal requirements, thereby reducing or avoiding litigation, and is within the scope of subject matter that is subject to the attorney-client privilege.[313]

In its *Spalding*[314] decision, the court held, as a matter of first impression, that an invention record submitted to a corporate legal department is protected by the attorney-client privilege. The court refused to dissect the document to evaluate separately each of its components. It was enough that the overall tenor of the document indicated that it was a request for legal advice or services. Moreover, it is not necessary expressly to request confidential legal assistance when that request is implied. Finally, to the extent that the invention record may contain technical information, or refer to prior art, the inclusion of such information does not render the document discoverable, because requests for legal advice on patentability or for legal services in preparing a patent application necessarily require the

---

[310]*In re Spalding Sports Worldwide Inc.*, 203 F.3d 800, 53 USPQ2d 1747 (Fed. Cir. 2000).

[311]*In re Regents of Univ. of Calif.*, 101 F.3d 1386, 40 USPQ2d 1784 (Fed. Cir. 1996). When prelitigation advice and assistance serve a shared legal interest, the parties to that interest do not lose the privilege when litigation arises. *Id.*

[312]*In re Regents of Univ. of Calif.*, 101 F.3d 1386, 40 USPQ2d 1784 (Fed. Cir. 1996).

[313]*In re Regents of Univ. of Calif.*, 101 F.3d 1386, 40 USPQ2d 1784 (Fed. Cir. 1996).

[314]*In re Spalding Sports Worldwide Inc.*, 203 F.3d 800, 53 USPQ2d 1747 (Fed. Cir. 2000).

evaluation of technical information such as prior art. In any event, an attorney cannot evaluate patentability or prepare a competent patent application without knowing the prior art and obtaining relevant technical information from the inventors. Accordingly, since the invention record was prepared and submitted primarily for the purpose of obtaining legal advice on patentability and legal services in preparing a patent application, it is privileged in its entirety.

The executive privilege, which has been analogized to the work product privilege, protects agency officials' deliberations, advisory opinions, and recommendations in order to promote frank discussion of legal or policy matters in the decision-making process.[315] There is also a state secrets privilege, which is absolute.[316]

The attorney-client privilege promotes confidential relations that may well deal with the very suit in question. The work product immunity protects the attorney's thought processes and legal recommendations, which also may bear directly on the suit in question. A party does not automatically waive these privileges, which protect the formulation of legal opinions and litigation strategy, simply by bringing suit. There are three approaches in ruling on whether by instituting litigation a plaintiff waives attorney-client, work product, or executive privilege: (1) automatic waiver; (2) balancing need for discovery against need for protecting secrecy; and (3) the so-called *Hearns* test. Under *Hearns* there is waiver if assertion of the privilege was a result of some affirmative act, such as filing suit, by the asserting party; through this affirmative act, the asserting party put the protected information at issue by making it relevant to the case; and application of the privilege would have denied the opposing party access to information vital to its defense. The Federal Circuit has rejected the automatic waiver approach on the ground that such privileges involve questions too subtle and sensitive to be breached without a more penetrating analysis. However, it has not yet decided between the balancing and *Hearns* tests.[317]

In an important statement on the question of when and whether to reveal an attorney's opinion, the court suggested that it may be useful to have separate trials on liability and on willfulness and damages. That way the accused infringer need only disclose an attorney's opinion if it is found liable.[318] Of course, the assertion of privilege with respect to infringement and validity opinions of counsel may support the drawing of adverse inferences.[319] But assertion of the privilege does not raise an irrebuttable presumption of willfulness.

---

[315]*Zenith Radio Corp. v. United States*, 764 F.2d 1577 (Fed. Cir. 1985).

[316]*Langenegger v. United States*, 756 F.2d 1565 (Fed. Cir. 1985).

[317]*Zenith Radio Corp. v. United States*, 764 F.2d 1577 (Fed. Cir. 1985). In this case, the showing of need was insufficient. Mere relevance does not make information vital, and need is difficult to show where the information is available from another source.

[318]*Fromson v. Western Litho Plate & Supp. Co.*, 853 F.2d 1568, 7 USPQ2d 1606 (Fed. Cir. 1988). See also *Quantum Corp. v. Tandon Corp.*, 940 F.2d 642, 19 USPQ2d 1799 (Fed. Cir. 1991).

[319]*L.A. Gear, Inc. v. Thom McAn Shoe Co.*, 988 F.2d 1117, 25 USPQ2d 1913 (Fed. Cir. 1993).

Such a rule would not accommodate consideration of other facts, nor would it respect the right of a party to assert the privilege.[320]

Although discovery orders are not routinely appealable, a writ of mandamus may be sought to prevent the wrongful exposure of privileged communications.[321] A district court's finding that a party has waived the attorney-client privilege is reviewed under the abuse of discretion standard.[322]

Application of the attorney-client privilege is a question of fact.[323]

(h) Miscellaneous Matters

The trial judge has the duty of assuring the relevance of the proposed evidence to the issue requiring decision.[324] Rule 403, FRE, provides an exception to the admissibility of relevant evidence, where its probative value is substantially outweighed by the danger of unfair prejudice. Rule 403 exclusions are reviewed under an abuse of discretion standard.[325] Many matters under Rule 403 are not easily resolved in the patent law context. The court has struggled with the Rule 403 admissibility of evidence of prior litigation involving the same patent.[326]

Demonstrative evidence may be excluded if its probative value is substantially outweighed by the danger of unfair prejudice, confusion of the issues, or misleading the jury, or by considerations of undue delay, waste of time, or needless presentation of cumulative evidence. Such a determination is within the trial court's considerable discretion.[327]

Circumstantial evidence, says the court, is sufficient to prove direct infringement and may indeed be more certain, satisfying, and

---

[320]*Electro Med. Sys. S.A. v. Cooper Life Sciences, Inc.*, 34 F.3d 1048, 32 USPQ2d 1017 (Fed. Cir. 1994).

[321]*In re Regents of Univ. of Calif.*, 101 F.3d 1386, 40 USPQ2d 1784 (Fed. Cir. 1996). Mandamus review may be granted of discovery orders that turn on claims of privilege when (1) there is raised an important issue of first impression, (2) the privilege would be lost if review were denied until final judgment, and (3) immediate resolution would avoid the development of doctrine that would undermine the privilege. *Id.*

[322]*Dorf & Stanton Comm., Inc. v. Molson Breweries*, 100 F.3d 919, 40 USPQ2d 1761 (Fed. Cir. 1996).

[323]*American Standard, Inc. v. Pfizer, Inc.*, 828 F.2d 734, 3 USPQ2d 1817, 1824 (Fed. Cir. 1987).

[324]*National Presto Indus., Inc. v. West Bend Co.*, 76 F.3d 1185, 37 USPQ2d 1685 (Fed. Cir. 1996).

[325]*Mendenhall v. Cedarapids, Inc.*, 5 F.3d 1556, 28 USPQ2d 1081 (Fed. Cir. 1993). The decision to admit or exclude evidence is within the sound discretion of the trial court and will be reversed on appeal only for a clear abuse of that discretion. *Kearns v. Chrysler Corp.*, 32 F.3d 1541, 31 USPQ2d 1746 (Fed. Cir. 1994).

[326]*Mendenhall v. Cedarapids, Inc.*, 5 F.3d 1556, 28 USPQ2d 1081 (Fed. Cir. 1993).

[327]*Young Dental Mfg. Co. v. Q3 Special Prods., Inc.*, 112 F.3d 1137, 42 USPQ2d 1589 (Fed. Cir. 1997).

persuasive than direct evidence.[328] Oral testimony to establish the existence of allegedly anticipatory devices has long been viewed with skepticism.[329] In administrative cases circumstantial evidence can be used to prove the elements of a charge, including the element of intent,[330] and can also provide corroboration.[331]

The general rule on supplementing a record with new evidence is that appellate courts can act on no evidence that was not before the trial court, nor receive any paper that was not used at the hearing. However, there is an exception, at least in cases dealing with the construction of treaties. The public acts and proclamations of governments, and those of their publicly recognized agents, in carrying into effect treaties, are historical and notorious facts of which the court can take regular judicial notice.[332] The court will take judicial notice of the content of court records, such as a protective order entered in another case.[333] It will take notice of papers in an interference record.[334] The court is apparently willing to take judicial notice of a patent that, although not part of the appeal record, was referred to at argument and is publicly accessible.[335]

Courts may take judicial notice of facts of universal notoriety, which need not be proved, and of whatever is generally known within their jurisdictions. To that end, dictionaries and encyclopedias may be consulted.[336] Judicial notice may be taken of common everyday mechanical concepts in appropriate circumstances.[337] The court has taken notice of the ubiquitous use of video to display programming and other information.[338] But in response to an argument, in a RICO

---

[328]*Moleculon Res. Corp. v. CBS, Inc.,* 793 F.2d 1261, 229 USPQ 805 (Fed. Cir. 1986). Claims to a method of solving a puzzle could be infringed only by the puzzle user. There was no direct evidence of use, but plenty of evidence of sales, with instructions. This evidence was held sufficient to establish a direct infringement predicate for inducement of infringement.

[329]*Sjolund v. Musland,* 847 F.2d 1573, 6 USPQ2d 2020 (Fed. Cir. 1988).

[330]*DeWitt v. Department of Navy,* 747 F.2d 1442 (Fed. Cir. 1984).

[331]*In re Sneed,* 710 F.2d 1544, 218 USPQ 385 (Fed. Cir. 1983).

[332]*Coplin v. United States,* 761 F.2d 688 (Fed. Cir. 1985). The court warned that this holding should not lightly be extended to a broader application of the doctrine.

[333]*Genentech, Inc. v. United States ITC,* 122 F.3d 1409, 43 USPQ2d 1722 (Fed. Cir. 1997).

[334]*Genentech, Inc. v. Chiron Corp.,* 112 F.3d 495, 42 USPQ2d 1608 (Fed. Cir. 1997).

[335]*Hoganas AB v. Dresser Indus., Inc.,* 9 F.3d 948, 28 USPQ2d 1936 (Fed. Cir. 1993).

[336]*B.V.D. Licensing Corp. v. Body Action Design, Inc.,* 846 F.2d 727, 6 USPQ2d 1719 (Fed. Cir. 1988). With his typical thoughtful jurisprudence, Judge Nichols in a concurring opinion made a plea for wide but careful use of the doctrine, saying that "Judicial notice fills the gaps. It is just as well for a judicial author to say so when he is doing this, and every now and then to take a side glance at Fed. R. of Evid. 201 to be sure he is using judicial notice correctly." 846 F.2d at 729. Despite this caveat, the court in a subsequent case was willing to take judicial notice of the widespread use of carbonless paper in manifold business forms. *In re Wright,* 866 F.2d 422, 9 USPQ2d 1649 (Fed. Cir. 1989). The court has also taken judicial notice of the "adjudicative fact" that a first office action in a reexamination rejected the claims of the patent before it. *Standard Havens Prods., Inc. v. Gencor Indus., Inc.,* 897 F.2d 511, 13 USPQ2d 2029 (Fed. Cir. 1990).

[337]*In re Oetiker,* 977 F.2d 1443, 24 USPQ2d 1443 (Fed. Cir. 1992).

[338]*In re Raynes,* 7 F.3d 1037, 28 USPQ2d 1630 (Fed. Cir. 1993).

case, that common sense suggested certain facts as a possibility, the court observed that common sense is not evidence.[339]

If a court finds that evidence has been destroyed, and that the destruction was carried out in bad faith, it may then infer that the evidence would have been unfavorable to the destroying party if introduced in court.[340]

§10.5 Findings of Fact

In a nonjury trial, Rule 52(a), FRCP, requires that the court shall find the facts specially and state separately its conclusions of law thereon. Where the court fails to make findings, the judgment will normally be vacated and the action remanded for appropriate findings to be made. The rule does not place a severe burden upon the trial judge, for he or she need only make brief, definite, and pertinent findings and conclusions upon the contested matters. Moreover, where a full understanding may be had without the aid of separate findings, there is a narrow exception to the general rule.[341] When granting an injunction, Rule 52(a), FRCP, requires that a court set forth the findings of fact and conclusions of law that are the basis of its decision. The district court need not make binding findings of fact, but at the very least must find probabilities that the necessary facts can be proved.[342]

A district court need follow no prescribed grammatical formulation in expressing its findings and conclusions, but the reviewing court must attempt to discern from the district court's opinion or action the bases, albeit unexpressed, for its findings and conclusions.[343] It is common practice for a district court, after a full trial, to include in its required findings the facts in a case that are not disputed as well as those it resolved on the basis of conflicting evidence. A court's findings after trial must be viewed simply as a statement of the facts, some of which were disputed and some not, that support its ultimate conclusions.[344]

---

[339]*A. Stucki Co. v. Worthington Indus., Inc.,* 849 F.2d 593, 7 USPQ2d 1066 (Fed. Cir. 1988).

[340]*Eaton Corp. v. Appliance Valves Corp.,* 790 F.2d 874, 229 USPQ 668 (Fed. Cir. 1986). In *Cablestrand Corp. v. Wallshein,* 989 F.2d 472, 26 USPQ2d 1079 (Fed. Cir. 1993), the district court after a bench trial entered judgment but made no findings of fact or conclusions of law. The Federal Circuit held that it had no basis on which to review the appealed judgment and remanded for entry of findings and conclusions.

[341]*Loctite Corp. v. Ultraseal Ltd.,* 781 F.2d 861, 228 USPQ 90 (Fed. Cir. 1985).

[342]*Atari Games Corp. v. Nintendo of Am., Inc.,* 897 F.2d 1572, 14 USPQ2d 1034 (Fed. Cir. 1990).

[343]*Fromson v. Western Litho Plate & Supp. Co.,* 853 F.2d 1568, 7 USPQ2d 1606 (Fed. Cir. 1988). The naked phrase "not appropriate" in connection with a request for attorney fees is insufficient, requiring a remand for an ultimate finding on exceptionality, accompanied by subsidiary findings reflecting the reasons underlying the district court's exercise of discretion in awarding or denying attorney fees in light of its findings. *Id.*

[344]*Avia Group Int'l, Inc. v. L.A. Gear Calif., Inc.,* 853 F.2d 1557, 7 USPQ2d 1548 (Fed. Cir. 1988).

The ultimate test of the adequacy of findings is whether they are sufficiently comprehensive and pertinent to the issue to form a basis for the decision. How many and specific the findings need be are questions to be resolved on a case-by-case basis.[345] A district court is not obligated to list, and reject, factors that might have supported a contrary conclusion.[346] Oral findings and conclusions by a district court may be sufficient to indicate the basis of the trial judge's decision and provide an adequate foundation for appellate review.[347] Where a trial judge is identified with the practice of delivering orally from the bench opinions and fact findings in complex cases, thus saving time and conserving judicial energy, a transcript of that oral presentation should have the same dignity as written findings and conclusions.[348]

One cannot meet the burden of showing that findings are clearly erroneous merely by showing that the trial court adopted the winning party's submissions.[349] Thus, it is acceptable for a trial court to adopt many or most of the parties' proposed findings of fact and conclusions of law, particularly if they are skillfully and wisely drafted. Such adoption, even if wholesale, does not alter the standard of review.[350] Findings are no less those of the court because they were proposed by counsel.[351] But an apparent absence of personal attention by the trial court need not be disregarded; particularly where the adopted findings are those proposed by a party before trial, there is a greater chance that they may be clearly erroneous.[352] A complete failure to make findings has been characterized as a dereliction of duty.[353]

---

[345]*Loctite Corp. v. Ultraseal Ltd.*, 781 F.2d 861, 228 USPQ 90 (Fed. Cir. 1985). The mere fact that the district court does not include findings and conclusions on all the evidence does not mean that it was not considered. *N.V. Akzo v. E.I. duPont de Nemours*, 810 F.2d 1148, 1 USPQ2d 1704 (Fed. Cir. 1987). Simply because a judge fails to mention evidence does not mean that it was not considered. *Winner Int'l Corp. v. Wolo Mfg. Corp.*, 905 F.2d 375, 15 USPQ2d 1076 (Fed. Cir. 1990).

[346]*J.P. Stevens Co. v. Lex Tex Ltd.*, 822 F.2d 1047, 3 USPQ2d 1235 (Fed. Cir. 1987). In denying a motion for a preliminary injunction, the district court did not err in not making detailed findings on peripheral issues for which adequate foundation was not provided by the moving party. *Xeta, Inc. v. Atex, Inc.*, 852 F.2d 1280, 7 USPQ2d 1471 (Fed. Cir. 1988).

[347]*Albert v. Kevex Corp.*, 729 F.2d 757, 221 USPQ 202 (Fed. Cir. 1984).

[348]*Florida Rock Indus., Inc. v. United States*, 791 F.2d 893 (Fed. Cir. 1986). But written findings, once adopted, become the findings and conclusions of the court regardless of their source. *Under Sea Indus., Inc. v. Dacor Corp.*, 833 F.2d 1551, 4 USPQ2d 1772 (Fed. Cir. 1987). A losing party criticized the trial court's opinion, which was issued before the trial testimony was transcribed, because it contained language similar to that in the winning party's brief. However, the testimony, when transcribed, was found to support the judge's findings. *Durango Assoc., Inc. v. Reflange, Inc.*, 843 F.2d 1349, 6 USPQ2d 1290 (Fed. Cir. 1988).

[349]*FMC Corp. v. Manitowoc Co.*, 835 F.2d 1411, 5 USPQ2d 1112 (Fed. Cir. 1987); *Rosemount, Inc. v. Beckman Instr., Inc.*, 727 F.2d 1540, 221 USPQ 1 (Fed. Cir. 1984).

[350]*Roton Barrier, Inc. v. Stanley Works*, 79 F.3d 1112, 37 USPQ2d 1816 (Fed. Cir. 1996).

[351]*Litton Sys., Inc. v. Sundstrand Corp.*, 750 F.2d 952, 224 USPQ 252 (Fed. Cir. 1984).

[352]*Lindemann Maschinenfabrik v. American Hoist & Derrick Co.*, 730 F.2d 1452, 221 USPQ 481 (Fed. Cir. 1984). The fact that the district court adopts findings and conclusions prepared after trial by the prevailing party is no reason to invalidate them. *Under Sea Indus., Inc. v. Dacor Corp.*, 833 F.2d 1551, 4 USPQ2d 1772 (Fed. Cir. 1987). The court distinguished *Lindemann*, supra, on the ground that the findings there were prepared before trial and no supporting evidence for some of them was forthcoming at trial.

[353]*Loctite Corp. v. Ultraseal Ltd.*, 781 F.2d 861, 228 USPQ 90 (Fed. Cir. 1985); *Seattle Box Co. v. Industrial Crat. & Pack., Inc.*, 756 F.2d 1574, 225 USPQ 357 (Fed. Cir. 1985). It

§10.6 Judgments

Appeals are to be taken from judgments, not findings and conclusions.[354] Whether a written set of findings submitted after entry of judgment on an oral set is effective depends upon regional circuit law.[355] But the preferred practice is clearly to hold up entry of judgment pursuant to Rule 58, FRCP.[356]

Where fewer than all claims of a patent are charged to be infringed, it is error to frame the judgment to apply to all.[357] It would be inappropriate for a district court to state in its judgment form that four patents were valid if only one claim of each were asserted and tried. In the absence of any indication that the four claims tried were stipulated to be representative, the district court should consider whether its judgment should be recast to limit it to the claims in suit.[358]

Pleadings do not suffice to support a judgment when the subject matter was not litigated or fairly placed in issue during the trial. There must be sufficient and explicit notice of the patent claims at risk. When the pleadings are not in complete harmony with the issues that were litigated and adjudicated, it is the pleadings that may be conformed to the judgment, not vice versa.[359]

(a) Posttrial Practice

In nonjury cases, a new trial may be granted pursuant to Rule 59, FRCP, or relief from a judgment may be obtained in appropriate situations under Rule 60. Rule 59(b) requires that a motion for new trial be made not later than 10 days after entry of judgment, while Rule 60(b) simply specifies a reasonable time (or, under some circumstances, one year).

A denial or grant of a motion for a new trial is reviewed under an abuse of discretion standard.[360] That question turns on whether

---

was not error to fail to specify in the opinion which claims were held to be infringed where the judgment itself specified the infringed claims. *Atlas Powder Co. v. E.I. du Pont & Co.,* 750 F.2d 1569, 224 USPQ 409 (Fed. Cir. 1984). There is a greater need for express findings on certain issues, such as obviousness. *Loctite Corp. v. Ultraseal Ltd.,* 781 F.2d 861, 228 USPQ 90 (Fed. Cir. 1985). A district court need not make findings of fact and conclusions of law in denying a motion to reopen evidence. A summary denial of such a motion without opinion in no way implies that the court did not consider the newly submitted evidence. *Enzo Biochem Inc. v. Calgene Inc.,* 188 F.3d 1362, 52 USPQ2d 1129 (Fed. Cir. 1999).

[354]*Under Sea Indus., Inc. v. Dacor Corp.,* 833 F.2d 1551, 4 USPQ2d 1772, 1775 (Fed. Cir. 1987).

[355]*Hybritech, Inc. v. Abbott Labs.,* 849 F.2d 1446, 7 USPQ2d 1191 (Fed. Cir. 1988); *Under Sea Indus., Inc. v. Dacor Corp.,* 833 F.2d 1551, 4 USPQ2d 1772 (Fed. Cir. 1987).

[356]*Hybritech, Inc. v. Abbott Labs.,* 849 F.2d 1446, 7 USPQ2d 1191 (Fed. Cir. 1988).

[357]*Diversitech Corp. v. Century Steps, Inc.,* 850 F.2d 675, 7 USPQ2d 1315 (Fed. Cir. 1988).

[358]*Dow Chem. Co. v. American Cyanamid Co.,* 816 F.2d 617, 2 USPQ2d 1350 (Fed. Cir. 1987).

[359]*Tol-O-Matic, Inc. v. Proma Produckt-und Mktg. GmbH,* 945 F.2d 1546, 20 USPQ2d 1332 (Fed. Cir. 1991).

[360]*Orthokinetics, Inc. v. Safety Travel Chairs, Inc.,* 806 F.2d 1565, 1 USPQ2d 1081 (Fed. Cir. 1986); *Underwater Devices, Inc. v. Morrison-Knudsen Co.,* 717 F.2d 1380, 219 USPQ 569

an error occurred in the conduct of the trial that was so grievous as to have rendered the trial unfair.[361] A party may obtain a new trial only by showing that error affected its substantial rights. One is entitled to a fair, not a perfect, trial.[362] A new trial for newly discovered prior art would require a showing that the movant was diligent, that the new art is not merely cumulative, and that it is material and, if considered, would probably produce a different result.[363] Motions under Rules 59 and 60 cannot be used as a backdoor device to secure review. Where the losing party raised a best mode defense for the first time in a Rule 59 motion for a new trial, it was improper to assert that the district court's denial of the motion constituted a decision on the merits of the best mode issue that could be reviewed on appeal.[364] And the issue of inventorship, raised for the first time in an unsuccessful Rule 60(b) motion after trial, will not be entertained on appeal.[365]

The Federal Circuit has rejected an argument (apparently based on Rule 54(b), FRCP) that a timely new trial motion enables the district court to retain jurisdiction to grant relief not requested by the motion.[366]

Rule 60(a) provides for relief from clerical errors. For example, it is an appropriate procedure to resolve doubt as to whether the district court intended to double damages or to treble them.[367]

Rule 60(b) provides for relief from judgment under several explicitly defined circumstances. In considering the issue of excusable neglect for purposes of Rule 60(b)(1), a court should pay attention to three factors: (1) whether the nondefaulting party will be prejudiced; (2) whether the defaulting party has a meritorious defense; and

---

(Fed. Cir. 1983). Motions for new trial are committed to the discretion of the district court. Requiring a party to play by the Rules of Civil Procedure cannot be equated with the substantial injustice that may under other circumstances warrant remand for a new trial. Indeed, a remand subjecting a party to another trial at the behest of an adversary who failed to comply with the rules may itself be an injustice to the former. Though the rules should be liberally construed, they were established to take the guesswork out of trials, not to add to it. *Snellman v. Ricoh Co.*, 836 F.2d 528, 5 USPQ2d 1341 (Fed. Cir. 1987).

[361]*Orthokinetics, Inc. v. Safety Travel Chairs, Inc.*, 806 F.2d 1565, 1 USPQ2d 1081 (Fed. Cir. 1986).

[362]*Fonar Corp. v. Johnson & Johnson*, 821 F.2d 627, 3 USPQ2d 1109 (Fed. Cir. 1987).

[363]*Underwater Devices, Inc. v. Morrison-Knudsen Co.*, 717 F.2d 1380, 219 USPQ 569 (Fed. Cir. 1983). In *WMS Gaming Inc. v. International Game Tech.*, 184 F.3d 1339, 51 USPQ2d 1385 (Fed. Cir. 1999), the district court did not abuse its discretion in finding that the due diligence standard extends to both the party and its attorneys.

[364]*CPG Prods. Corp. v. Pegasus Luggage, Inc.*, 776 F.2d 1007, 227 USPQ 497 (Fed. Cir. 1985). Rule 60 is not a substitute for appeal. *Amstar Corp. v. Envirotech Corp.*, 823 F.2d 1538, 3 USPQ2d 1412 (Fed. Cir. 1987).

[365]*CPG Prods. Corp. v. Pegasus Luggage, Inc.*, 776 F.2d 1007, 227 USPQ 497 (Fed. Cir. 1985).

[366]*Snellman v. Ricoh Co.*, 836 F.2d 528, 5 USPQ2d 1341 (Fed. Cir. 1987). The action involved patent infringement and breach of contract claims and a counterclaim for breach of contract. The defendant moved for a new trial on "all issues," but only specifically referred to the infringement and breach claims and not the breach counterclaim. This was insufficient under Rule 7(b)(1). Accordingly, the motion did not constitute a Rule 59 motion as to the counterclaim.

[367]*Bott v. Four Star Corp.*, 807 F.2d 1567, 1 USPQ2d 1210 (Fed. Cir. 1986).

(3) whether culpable conduct of the defaulting party led to the default. These factors are not to be applied in the disjunctive, such that a finding that any one of them is unfavorable to the defaulting party requires denial of the motion for relief. Rather, the three factors are to be balanced and weighed. In addition, there is no requirement that the moving party show extraordinary circumstances. Finally, it must appear that the moving party acted willfully in violating the trial court's rules and procedures. As a consequence, default judgment is inappropriate if a party merely has notice of the claim against it and fails to file an answer.[368]

Rule 60(b)(2) deals with newly discovered evidence which by due diligence could not have been discovered in time to move for a new trial under Rule 59(b). The due diligence limitation of Rule 60(b)(2) serves the salutary purpose of providing finality to judicial decisions and orders by preventing belated attempts to reopen judgment on the basis of facts that the moving party could have discovered at the time of trial.[369] Determining whether newly discovered evidence warrants a new trial entails the following three-prong analysis: (1) the probability that the evidence would have changed the outcome of the trial; (2) whether the evidence could have been discovered earlier through the moving party's due diligence; and (3) whether the evidence is merely cumulative or impeaching.[370]

The savings clause of Rule 60(b) retains the power of a court to set aside a judgment for "fraud upon the court." The Federal Circuit has decided that inequitable conduct in the prosecution of a patent

---

[368]*Information Sys. & Net. Corp. v. United States,* 994 F.2d 792 (Fed. Cir. 1993).

[369]*Smith Int'l, Inc. v. Hughes Tool Co.,* 759 F.2d 1572, 225 USPQ 889 (Fed. Cir. 1985). In *Standard Havens Prods., Inc. v. Gencor Indus., Inc.,* 953 F.2d 1360, 21 USPQ2d 1321 (Fed. Cir. 1992), the PTO issued a certificate of correction on the day trial started but later withdrew it and sua sponte instituted a reexamination. The Federal Circuit rejected defendant's argument that a new trial should have been granted when the PTO withdrew the certificate, but it did not foreclose the question of whether a Rule 60(b)(2) motion should be granted after a final ruling in the reexamination. In *Amstar Corp. v. Envirotech Corp.,* 823 F.2d 1538, 3 USPQ2d 1412 (Fed. Cir. 1987), a Rule 60(b) motion based on newly discovered prior art was filed more than a year after the judgment on validity but within a year of an appellate decision dealing with the infringement portion of the judgment. The motion was held untimely under Rule 60(b)(2) or (3). However, the infringer argued that the one-year time limit does not apply where there has been fraud on the court and suggested that failure to disclose prior art to the court amounts to fraud on the court. The Federal Circuit held that fraud on the court, other than fraud as to jurisdiction, is fraud directed to the judicial machinery itself and not fraud between the parties or false statements or perjury.

[370]*Advanced Display Sys. Inc. v. Kent State Univ.,* 212 F.3d 1272, 54 USPQ2d 1673 (Fed. Cir. 2000). Here the newly discovered evidence was a previously suppressed deposition in which testimony was given concerning prior failure and copying. In remanding for a new trial on obviousness, the court concluded that the patentee had been diligent in its effort to discover the evidence, and that the testimony constituted highly probative evidence of nonobviousness given that after initial deliberations the jury was in equipoise on the issue of obviousness, and this newly discovered evidence could have been the tipping factor for finding the patent to be not invalid. The court also felt that a new trial was appropriate on infringement as well. It should be understood that case involved what the court clearly felt was a particularly egregious instance of misconduct during discovery. It should be noted, however, that allegations of nondisclosure in pretrial discovery will not support an action for fraud on the court. *Amstar Corp. v. Envirotech Corp.,* 823 F.2d 1538, 3 USPQ2d 1412 (Fed. Cir. 1987).

application does not constitute fraud upon a court that enters a consent judgment based upon the unenforceable patent. The fact that Rule 60(b) contains two distinct fraud provisions (see Rule 60(b)(3)) means that not all fraud is "fraud upon the court." The savings clause must be construed very narrowly because the otherwise nebulous concept of fraud upon the court could easily overwhelm the specific fraud provision of subparagraph (3), with its one-year time limitation. Fraud upon the court should embrace only that species of fraud that attempts to subvert the integrity of the court itself, or that is a fraud perpetrated by officers of the court, so that the judicial machinery cannot perform in the usual manner its impartial task of adjudicating cases that come to it. Fraud upon the court is thus typically confined to the most egregious cases, such as bribery of a judge or juror, or improper influence exerted on the court by an attorney, wherein the integrity of the court and its ability to function impartially is directly impinged.[371]

Under Rule 60(b)(5) ("no longer equitable that the judgment should have prospective application"), the party seeking relief has the burden to demonstrate that continued operation of the judgment will result in inequity.[372] Under Rule 60(b)(6) ("any other reason justifying relief from the operation of the judgment"), the party must show that circumstances surrounding the judgment created a substantial danger of an unjust result. A change in law after entry of judgment does not alone justify such relief, even if coupled with a possible or

---

[371]*Broyhill Furn. Indus. v. Craftmaster Furn. Corp.*, 12 F.3d 1080, 29 USPQ2d 1283 (Fed. Cir. 1993). The Federal Circuit distinguished *Hazel-Atlas Glass Co. v. Hartford-Empire Co.*, 322 U.S. 238 (1944), on the ground that there the falsified evidence was presented to the court as well as to the PTO. A party had moved to set aside a consent judgment enjoining infringement, on the ground that the patent had been found in another case to have been procured by fraud. The motion was filed more than a year after the entry of the consent judgment and thus could not qualify under Rule 60(b)(3). The Federal Circuit also concluded that the motion did not stand up under Rule 60(b)(4), which provides for relief from judgments that are "void" and does not have the one-year time limit. A judgment is not void merely because it is or may be erroneous, or because the precedent upon which it was based is later altered or even overruled. Rather, it is well established that a judgment is void for purposes of Rule 60(b)(4) only when the court that rendered the judgment lacked jurisdiction or failed to act in accordance with due process of law. In *Fraige v. American-National Watermattress Corp.*, 996 F.2d 295, 27 USPQ2d 1149 (Fed. Cir. 1993), the president of the accused infringer fraudulently altered a prior art advertisement so that it became a bar to patentability under 35 U.S.C. §102(b). The jury found the patent invalid on three separate grounds: §102, §103, and §112. The patent owner proved the fraud and moved for relief from judgment under Rule 60(b)(3). The district court denied the motion on the basis that the alternative grounds could support the invalidity judgment. The Federal Circuit found this to be an abuse of discretion, in that the district court should not have attempted to evaluate the effect of the fraud on the jury. The Federal Circuit placed heavy emphasis on *Hazel-Atlas*, supra, which holds that a court cannot accurately assess the effects of fraudulent conduct and, therefore, should presume that the defrauding party would commit the fraud only when confident of its effectiveness. The fraud was a wrong against the judicial system as well as the patent owner, and it impacted the validity of an issued patent, which is a matter of public concern.

[372]*Ashland Oil, Inc. v. Delta Oil Prods. Corp.*, 806 F.2d 1031, 1 USPQ2d 1073 (Fed. Cir. 1986) (Seventh Circuit law).

actual loss of money.[373] Unless exceptional or extraordinary circumstances are shown, a Rule 60(b)(6) motion is generally not granted.[374]

A motion to amend or alter a judgment under Rule 59(e), FRCP, while not required, is often desirable in that it can make issues reviewable and avoid the imposition of a return visit to a busy district court.[375] The question whether a district court retains jurisdiction to alter or amend its judgment under Rule 59 is a procedural issue not unique to patent law and is therefore decided under regional circuit law.[376] Under Eleventh Circuit law, the 10-day time limit imposed by Rule 59(e) is jurisdictional, and a district court has no inherent authority and cannot, sua sponte, modify its judgment outside of the 10-day limit.[377] Care must be taken in the timing of appeals in relation to motions under Rule 59(e), because a notice of appeal filed before the disposition of such a motion is ineffective.[378] Also, one must distinguish between a motion under Rule 59(e) and one under Rule 60(b)(2). There is no requirement under Rule 59(e) for a showing that the evidence could not by due diligence have been discovered earlier.[379]

A decision under Rule 60(b) is final and appealable.[380] The grant or denial of a motion for relief from judgment under Rule 60(b) is discretionary, and the standard of review is abuse of discretion.[381]

---

[373]*Ashland Oil, Inc. v. Delta Oil Prods. Corp.*, 806 F.2d 1031, 1 USPQ2d 1073 (Fed. Cir. 1986). The argument was that the Seventh Circuit had failed to consider commercial success because the case was not "close," and that the Federal Circuit had repudiated such a view of the law. In *W.L. Gore & Assoc. v. C.R. Bard, Inc.*, 977 F.2d 558, 24 USPQ2d 1451 (Fed. Cir. 1992), the court indicated that when the parties have chosen to submit to a consent decree instead of seeking a more favorable judgment, their burden under Rule 60(b) is perhaps even more formidable than had they litigated and lost. See text accompanying note 10:407.

[374]*CTS Corp. v. Piher Int'l Corp.*, 727 F.2d 1550, 221 USPQ 11 (Fed. Cir. 1984). See *Case v. BSAF Wyandotte*, 737 F.2d 1034, 222 USPQ 737 (Fed. Cir. 1984), for an example of strict application of Rule 60(b) (pro se plaintiff missed date for filing notice of appeal).

[375]*Nickson Indus., Inc. v. Rol Mfg. Co.*, 847 F.2d 795, 6 USPQ2d 1878 (Fed. Cir. 1988). The district court had apparently ignored the winning patentee's request for an injunction and the Federal Circuit refused to rule on the request, thus requiring a remand.

[376]*Sun-Tek Indus., Inc. v. Kennedy Sky Lites, Inc.*, 848 F.2d 179, 6 USPQ2d 2017 (Fed. Cir. 1988).

[377]*Sun-Tek Indus., Inc. v. Kennedy Sky Lites, Inc.*, 848 F.2d 179, 6 USPQ2d 2017 (Fed. Cir. 1988). The district court had entered a judgment that included a specific finding that the case was not exceptional. Later, outside the 10-day limit, it entered an amended judgment finding the case was exceptional. No Rule 59 motion was ever filed, but the court had specially retained jurisdiction on attorney fees. The Federal Circuit vacated the amended judgment on the ground that the district court was not acting within the jurisdiction that it had retained. It did not merely award attorney fees consistent with its judgment—it reversed the part of its judgment relating to exceptionality. To permit the district court to reverse the unchallenged and unreserved part of its judgment would undermine the finality of judgments.

[378]*Tylo Sauna, S.A. v. Amerec Corp.*, 826 F.2d 7, 3 USPQ2d 1792 (Fed. Cir. 1987).

[379]*Beverly Hills Fan Co. v. Royal Sovereign Corp.*, 21 F.3d 1558, 30 USPQ2d 1001 (Fed. Cir. 1994).

[380]*Ashland Oil, Inc. v. Delta Oil Prods. Corp.*, 806 F.2d 1031, 1 USPQ2d 1073 (Fed. Cir. 1986).

[381]*Broyhill Furn. Indus. v. Craftmaster Furn. Corp.*, 12 F.3d 1080, 29 USPQ2d 1283 (Fed. Cir. 1993); *Fraige v. American-National Watermattress Corp.*, 996 F.2d 295, 27 USPQ2d 1149 (Fed. Cir. 1993); *Ashland Oil, Inc. v. Delta Oil Prods. Corp.*, 806 F.2d 1031, 1 USPQ2d 1073 (Fed. Cir. 1986); *United States v. Atkinson*, 748 F.2d 659 (Fed. Cir. 1984); *Case v. BSAF Wyandotte*, 737 F.2d 1034, 222 USPQ 737 (Fed. Cir. 1984); *CTS Corp. v. Piher Int'l Corp.*, 727

However, the underlying fact findings by the trial court in support of a denial of a Rule 60(b) motion must be upheld unless they are clearly erroneous.[382] In reviewing rulings under Rule 60(b), the Federal Circuit generally defers to the law of the regional circuit because such rulings commonly involve procedural matters that are not unique to patent law. However, where the district court's Rule 60(b) determination turns on substantive matters unique to patent law, the Federal Circuit applies its own law.[383] The filing of a Rule 60(b) motion for relief from judgment does not substitute for, or toll the time prescribed for, filing a notice of appeal.[384]

After an appeal, the district court is absolutely bound by the Federal Circuit's decision, and ultimately must enter a judgment on the portion affected by the decision.[385] An inferior court has no power or authority to deviate from the mandate issued by an appellate court.[386]

(b) Rule 41(b) Motions

Rule 41(b), FRCP, provides that in a nonjury case, the defendant may, after the plaintiff has presented its case, move for a dismissal on the ground that upon the facts and the law the plaintiff has shown no right to relief. A Rule 41(b) motion is not the same as a motion for a directed verdict in a jury case. The latter motion raises a question of law only, and factual conflicts cannot be resolved.[387] Under Rule 41(b), the trial judge evaluates and resolves conflicts of evidence and

---

F.2d 1550, 221 USPQ 11 (Fed. Cir. 1984). The balance of all factors arising in a Rule 60(b) motion is committed to the sound discretion of the court. Although an abuse of discretion may be shown when the trial court committed a clear error of judgment, it is not sufficient that the reviewing court could have reached a different result. *W.L. Gore & Assoc. v. C.R. Bard, Inc.,* 977 F.2d 558, 24 USPQ2d 1451 (Fed. Cir. 1992). A trial on the merits is favored over default judgment, and close cases should be resolved in favor of the party seeking to set aside a default. Thus, when a court has denied a party's motion to be relieved from default judgment, a glaring abuse of discretion is not required for reversal and even a slight abuse may justify relieving the party from the harsh sanction of default. Rule 60(b) is applied most liberally to judgments in default. *Information Sys. & Net. Corp. v. United States,* 994 F.2d 792 (Fed. Cir. 1993).

[382]*CTS Corp. v. Piher Int'l Corp.,* 727 F.2d 1550, 221 USPQ 11 (Fed. Cir. 1984).

[383]*Broyhill Furn. Indus. v. Craftmaster Furn. Corp.,* 12 F.3d 1080, 29 USPQ2d 1283 (Fed. Cir. 1993). Unless the ruling raises some question unique to patent law, the applicable law is that of the regional circuit. *Amstar Corp. v. Envirotech Corp.,* 823 F.2d 1538, 3 USPQ2d 1412 (Fed. Cir. 1987); *Ashland Oil, Inc. v. Delta Oil Prods. Corp.,* 806 F.2d 1031, 1 USPQ2d 1073 (Fed. Cir. 1986). The general question of relief from judgment under Rule 60(b) is not exclusive to the Federal Circuit. *W.L. Gore & Assoc. v. C.R. Bard, Inc.,* 977 F.2d 558, 24 USPQ2d 1451 (Fed. Cir. 1992). Rule 60(b) motions are governed by the law of the regional circuit. *Marquip Inc. v. Fosber Am. Inc.,* 198 F.3d 1363, 53 USPQ2d 1015 (Fed. Cir. 1999).

[384]*United States v. Atkinson,* 748 F.2d 659 (Fed. Cir. 1984).

[385]*King Instrument Corp. v. Otari Corp.,* 814 F.2d 1560, 2 USPQ2d 1201 (Fed. Cir. 1987). It was not an abuse of discretion for the district court to enter that judgment immediately, rather than waiting until it decided the remanded portions of its original judgment. *Id.*

[386]*In re Wella A.G.,* 858 F.2d 725, 8 USPQ2d 1365 (Fed. Cir. 1988). The rule is equally applicable to the duty of an administrative agency, such as the PTO Board, to comply with the mandate issued by a reviewing court. *Id.* See also *In re Roberts,* 846 F.2d 1360, 6 USPQ2d 1772 (Fed. Cir. 1988).

[387]*Stearns v. Beckman Instr., Inc.,* 737 F.2d 1565, 222 USPQ 457 (Fed. Cir. 1984).

credibility, and findings entered as a result of such a motion are reviewed under the same clearly erroneous standard as are findings entered at the close of all the evidence.[388] Indeed, the court may sustain the defendant's Rule 41(b) motion even though plaintiff's evidence establishes a prima facie case on the merits, if there is evidence contrary to plaintiff's position on the record.[389] A dismissal pursuant to Rule 41(b) is deemed to be on the merits unless the dismissing court specifies otherwise.[390]

(c) Consent Decrees and Settlements

The law favors settlement of litigation, which reduces the burden on courts and counsel and mitigates the antagonism and hostility that protracted litigation leading to judgment may cause.[391] Settlement moots an action, although jurisdiction remains with the district court to enter a consent judgment.[392] There is a compelling public interest in upholding and enforcing settlement agreements voluntarily entered into.[393] Thus, a consent order embodying a settlement agreement is a final judgment; it is accompanied by finality as stark as an adjudication after full trial.[394]

The Federal Circuit has indicated[395] that it will follow the views of the *Restatement*[396] on claim and issue preclusion. Thus a prior consent decree in a case involving a different claim for relief would have no preclusive effect because no issues were litigated.[397] It is generally correct that a judgment entered pursuant to a stipulation will give rise only to claim preclusion, not issue preclusion. However, where rulings on specific issues are made after a full and fair opportunity to litigate, and those rulings are firm and consistent with a subsequent settlement agreement and the judgment actually entered in the case, issue preclusion can be applied to the judgment. The

---

[388]*Lemelson v. United States,* 752 F.2d 1538, 224 USPQ 526 (Fed. Cir. 1985).

[389]*Stearns v. Beckman Instr., Inc.,* 737 F.2d 1565, 222 USPQ 457 (Fed. Cir. 1984).

[390]*Kearns v. General Motors Corp.,* 94 F.3d 1553, 39 USPQ2d 1949 (Fed. Cir. 1996). But Rule 41(b) does not reasonably impose res judicata upon causes of action that were not pled in the dismissed action. *Id.*

[391]*S & T Mfg. Co. v. County of Hillsborough, Fla.,* 815 F.2d 676, 2 USPQ2d 1280 (Fed. Cir. 1987); *Cheyenne River Sioux Tribe v. United States,* 806 F.2d 1046 (Fed. Cir. 1986); *Bergh v. Department of Transp.,* 794 F.2d 1575 (Fed. Cir. 1986).

[392]*Gould v. Control Laser Corp.,* 866 F.2d 1391, 9 USPQ2d 1718 (Fed. Cir. 1989). The general rule is that when settlement moots an action, vacatur of the judgment is appropriate, although there may be circumstances when this is not so. *U.S. Philips Corp. v. Windmere Corp.,* 971 F.2d 728, 23 USPQ2d 1709 (Fed. Cir. 1992).

[393]*Hemstreet v. Spiegel, Inc.,* 851 F.2d 348, 7 USPQ2d 1502 (Fed. Cir. 1988).

[394]*W.L. Gore & Assoc. v. C.R. Bard, Inc.,* 977 F.2d 558, 24 USPQ2d 1451 (Fed. Cir. 1992).

[395]*Foster v. Hallco Mfg. Co.,* 947 F.2d 469, 20 USPQ2d 1241 (Fed. Cir. 1991); *Chromalloy Am. Corp. v. Kenneth Gordon, Ltd.,* 736 F.2d 694, 222 USPQ 187 (Fed. Cir. 1984).

[396]*Restatement (Second) of Judgments* 131 (1982).

[397]*Chromalloy Am. Corp. v. Kenneth Gordon, Ltd.,* 736 F.2d 694, 222 USPQ 187 (Fed. Cir. 1984).

stipulated judgment must, like a contract, be construed to determine its effect in light of all of the circumstances, including the intent of the parties.[398] No issue preclusion attaches to lost issues that cannot be appealed, e.g., where a party wins on its claim but loses on an issue. But a voluntary relinquishment of one's right to appeal, as by a stipulated judgment of dismissal, where one stands as an overall loser, does not fall within that rationale.[399]

The court is willing to view a consent decree as a contract, separate and apart from any technical question of res judicata. Thus, even where no preclusion is found, the court must also inquire whether interpretation of a consent decree as a contract would bar a claim or defense.[400] A consent decree will therefore be construed as a contract for enforcement purposes, and aids to construction, such as circumstances surrounding formation of the decree and the technical meanings words may have had to the parties, may be considered.[401] Indeed, due process requires that a consent decree be construed in accordance with the circumstances under which it was entered.[402] Nonetheless, the scope of a consent decree must be discerned within its four corners and not by reference to what might satisfy the purposes of one of the parties to it or by what might have been written had the plaintiff established its factual claims and legal theories in litigation.[403]

In *Foster v. Hallco*,[404] the court expanded further on its view of a consent decree as a contract. Where a judgment is entered by consent

---

[398]*Hartley v. Mentor Corp.*, 869 F.2d 1469, 10 USPQ2d 1138 (Fed. Cir. 1989). The patentee dismissed his claim with prejudice after the trial court had held the patent invalid on the merits. Inasmuch as that holding provided one possible ground to support the stipulated dismissal, the judgment operates as an adjudication on the merits of the claim. As part of the settlement the defendant had likewise dismissed its declaratory judgment counterclaim, and the plaintiff argued that this dismissal was inconsistent with the invalidity ruling and thus should negate any issue preclusion resulting from the dismissal of the claim. The Federal Circuit rejected this argument on the ground that a stipulated dismissal with prejudice of a declaratory judgment action does not resolve the merits of the underlying claim. With all respect, the author of this book has on at least one occasion obtained a summary judgment of validity and infringement based upon the preclusive effect of a stipulated dismissal of a prior declaratory judgment counterclaim.

[399]*Hartley v. Mentor Corp.*, 869 F.2d 1469, 10 USPQ2d 1138 (Fed. Cir. 1989).

[400]*Chromalloy Am. Corp. v. Kenneth Gordon, Ltd.*, 736 F.2d 694, 222 USPQ 187 (Fed. Cir. 1984).

[401]*H.F. Allen Orchards v. United States*, 749 F.2d 1571 (Fed. Cir. 1984). See also *S & T Mfg. Co. v. County of Hillsborough, Fla.*, 815 F.2d 676, 2 USPQ2d 1280 (Fed. Cir. 1987); *Joy Mfg. Co. v. National Mine Serv. Co.*, 810 F.2d 1127, 1 USPQ2d 1627 (Fed. Cir. 1987).

[402]*KSM Fastening Sys., Inc. v. H.A. Jones Co.*, 776 F.2d 1522, 227 USPQ 676 (Fed. Cir. 1985). This applies to injunctions entered by consent as well. An adjudged device conceivably could have been found not to fall within the scope of the claims upon a full trial. Nevertheless, under a consent decree the device is an admitted infringement, and the claims of the patent may be construed in light of that admission when the court undertakes to determine whether a modified device is also an infringement in contempt proceedings.

[403]*H.F. Allen Orchards v. United States*, 749 F.2d 1571 (Fed. Cir. 1984). While issues of patent infringement do give rise to individual causes of action, those individual causes of action cannot override the unambiguous language of a settlement agreement that releases all possible future claims related to the matters settled by the agreement. *Augustine Med. Inc. v. Progressive Dynamics Inc.*, 194 F.3d 1367, 52 USPQ2d 1515 (Fed. Cir. 1999).

[404]*Foster v. Hallco Mfg. Co.*, 947 F.2d 469, 20 USPQ2d 1241 (Fed. Cir. 1991).

prior to trial on any issue, no issue may be said to have been fully, fairly, or actually litigated, and issue preclusion does not arise. There is, however, a form of issue preclusion that is not dependent upon actual litigation. Thus, if a consent judgment, by its terms, indicates that the parties intend to preclude any challenge to the validity of a particular patent, even in subsequent litigation involving a new cause of action, then that issue can be precluded. But such an intention should not readily be inferred. The teaching of this case seems to be that if the patentee wishes a consent decree to preclude future challenges to validity by the particular accused infringer that is party to the decree, that intention should be expressly recited.

A party may expressly reserve in a consent judgment the right to relitigate some or all issues that would have otherwise been barred between the same parties. Any such reservation must be discerned within the four corners of the consent decree, and cannot be expanded beyond the decree's express terms.[405] However, one must be extremely careful with consent judgments, so as not to foreclose, unwittingly, the right to review on certain underlying rulings of the court. When a case between the parties has been settled, there is no actual matter in controversy essential to the decision of the particular matter before the court. Inasmuch as an agreement of the parties cannot confer jurisdiction on a court, a settlement that purports to dispose of everything except that portion of the court's ruling that holds some claims invalid cannot create jurisdiction for an appeal of that question.[406]

The court's contract theory of consent orders certainly impacts the question of relief from a consent judgment under Rule 60(b), FRCP. When parties have chosen to submit to a consent decree instead of seeking a more favorable result, the burden under Rule 60(b) is

---

[405]*Epic Metals Corp. v. H.H. Robertson Co.,* 870 F.2d 1574, 10 USPQ2d 1296 (Fed. Cir. 1989). Here the consent judgment provided that the patent was valid over the art before the PTO and the art considered in another litigation. It expressly did not decide whether a proposed structure was an infringement, and reserved the right to contest infringement on the basis that the structure was following the prior art or was an obvious modification of it. Two panel members held that this express language nonetheless does not reserve the right to challenge validity on new prior art; the only express reservation is on infringement. The third panel member (concurring on other grounds) felt that the plain intent of the consent judgment was to permit a challenge to validity on new prior art.

[406]*Gould v. Control Laser Corp.,* 866 F.2d 1391, 9 USPQ2d 1718 (Fed. Cir. 1989). The district court found the claims infringed, but some valid and some invalid. The parties settled, and defendant took a license under the valid claims. The plaintiff then attempted to appeal the judgment of invalidity. Two members of the panel felt that the explicit reservation in the settlement agreement of the issue regarding the invalid claims cannot serve to maintain the controversy between the parties, and voted to dismiss the appeal for lack of jurisdiction. In a partial dissent, the third panel member urged that the holding of invalidity should be vacated. The majority justified its refusal to vacate on the ground that the case did not become moot during the appeal process—rather, a consent decree was entered pursuant to agreement of the parties, and that mooted any possibility of the plaintiff taking an appeal. The majority reasoned that vacating the invalidity judgment would preclude a collateral estoppel defense in a later case—in effect, deciding the *Blonder- Tongue* issue before it even arises. In *St. Paul F. & M. Ins. Co. v. United States,* 959 F.2d 960 (Fed. Cir. 1992), the district court refused to permit amendment of the complaint, and the plaintiff voluntarily dismissed so that it could appeal

perhaps more formidable than had they litigated to judgment. Although modification of a consent order is not precluded in appropriately exceptional circumstances, it must be shown that absent such relief an extreme and unexpected hardship will result. The equities presented by the facts of the particular case must be examined. For a judgment entered on consent, the asserted reasons for the requested modification must be evaluated in the context of the negotiated bargain between the parties at the time of the settlement, for this bargain adds weight to the policies of res judicata. But a decree may not be changed in the interests of a defendant if the purposes of the litigation as incorporated in the decree have not been fully achieved. That a contract voluntarily made turns out to be less or more favorable to one of the parties is insufficient ground for judicial intervention.[407] A court should not construe a consent judgment beyond its express terms simply because the decree as written does not serve the asserted purpose of one of the parties to the settlement. By the same token, it is not required that any interpretation of a consent decree that is in accord with one or the other party's purposes must be discarded for that reason alone. Obviously, where two parties disagree on the meaning of a contract term, an interpretation that fails to meet one party's purpose will very likely meet the other party's purpose.[408]

Although the courts well recognize the public as well as private interest in the finality of settlements, as for all contracts a settlement will not be enforced if it is tainted by fraud or another condition that warrants its rescission.[409]

There is no principle that precludes the government from settling, upon whatever terms it deems suitable, cases in which it determines

---

the denial. This was not a voluntary dismissal in the usual sense of a consent judgment and thus did not affect the right to appeal.

[407]*W.L. Gore & Assoc. v. C.R. Bard, Inc.,* 977 F.2d 558, 24 USPQ2d 1451 (Fed. Cir. 1992). Here the defendant moved for relief from the consent judgment on grounds of a change in law, citing the new infringement statute, 35 U.S.C. §271(e). The Federal Circuit held that the defendant was not entitled to relief and, in so doing, distinguished the line of so-called institutional reform cases on the basis that the decrees involved there reach beyond the parties and impact on the public's right to the sound and efficient operation of its institutions. By contrast, in commercial litigation such as patent infringement suits, the decrees affect only the parties to the particular case. They are commercial litigants who have negotiated a voluntary contract that has simply been accepted by the court in termination of litigation. Although the public purpose of an intervening change in law is a factor to be weighed, here it did not outweigh the public policy of an overriding interest in the finality and repose of judgments on consent. It should be noted that the court was careful to avoid expressing any opinion on what might be the outcome if the defendant simply went ahead with uses that would fall within the scope of §271(e); thus, the court effectively passed the question whether the consent decree would survive a direct challenge under the statute.

[408]*Novamedix Ltd. v. NDM Acquisition Corp.,* 166 F.3d 1177, 49 USPQ2d 1613 (Fed. Cir. 1999).

[409]*Bradley v. Chiron Corp.,* 136 F.3d 1370, 45 USPQ2d 1819 (Fed. Cir. 1998). In *Broyhill Furn. Indus. v. Craftmaster Furn. Corp.,* 12 F.3d 1080, 29 USPQ2d 1283 (Fed. Cir. 1993), the court was able to pass the question of whether a later judgment of inequitable conduct in a case against another defendant would justify relief from a consent judgment under Rule 60(b)(3), which deals with fraud. The court did hold, however, that the inequitable conduct did not result in a void judgment under Rule 60(b)(4) or "fraud upon the court" under the savings clause of Rule 60(b).

that the likelihood of success is so low as to make continued litigation inappropriate. The decision whether to settle a particular case and upon what terms is a matter particularly within the discretion of the agency conducting the litigation.[410] Where a party does settle with the government, or anyone else for that matter, it may be equitably estopped to attack the settlement. Those who employ the judicial appellate process to attack a settlement through which controversy has been set to rest bear a properly heavy burden; they must show that the contract is tainted with invalidity, either by fraud or mutual mistake.[411] An ITC consent order, like a cease-and-desist order or an exclusion order, is enforceable by civil penalty imposed by the Commission and recoverable in the district court in the event of nonpayment.[412]

One aspect of consent decrees in patent cases that is sure to be controversial concerns the applicable law. Generally, interpretation of a settlement agreement is not an issue unique to patent law, even if arising in the context of a patent infringement suit.[413] The Federal Circuit has decided that the enforceability of a settlement agreement, albeit arising in the context of a patent infringement case, is not a patent issue. Accordingly, it will look to regional circuit law, including regional circuit precedent on choice of law.[414] If regional circuit law (and perhaps by reference to choice of law rules, state law) is held to control the enforceability of consent decrees that purport to adjudicate patent validity, minor chaos could result.

---

[410]*Bergh v. Department of Transp.,* 794 F.2d 1575 (Fed. Cir. 1986).

[411]*Asberry v. United States Postal Serv.,* 692 F.2d 1378 (Fed. Cir. 1982). In *S & T Mfg. Co. v. County of Hillsborough, Fla.,* 815 F.2d 676, 2 USPQ2d 1280 (Fed. Cir. 1987), the court awarded damages for frivolous appeal where the party attempted to attack a settlement agreement on appeal. The parties had participated in a court settlement conference and signed a partial transcript that purported to reflect their agreement. The following day, one party prepared a sketch illustrating what would be regarded as noninfringing, and the other party made changes and initialed it. When it came time to sign the formal settlement papers, the initialing party balked. The district court found as a fact that there had been a meeting of the minds, and the Federal Circuit, applying Eleventh Circuit law, which regards the question of whether parties have entered into a contract as one of fact, found no clear error and affirmed.

[412]*San Huan New Mt'ls High Tech Inc. v. United States ITC,*161 F.3d 1347, 48 USPQ2d 1865 (Fed. Cir. 1998). Here the court held that a respondent was precluded, by a consent order of the ITC entered in its original investigation, from contesting certain issues, such as the impact of prior art on the scope of equivalents, in an enforcement proceeding.

[413]*Novamedix Ltd. v. NDM Acquisition Corp.,* 166 F.3d 1177, 49 USPQ2d 1613 (Fed. Cir. 1999).

[414]*Sun Studs, Inc. v. Applied Theory Assocs.,* 772 F.2d 1557, 227 USPQ 81 (Fed. Cir. 1985). Here the regional circuit law indicated that a settlement agreement is to be resolved under state rather than federal law; the Federal Circuit accordingly applied substantive state law to hold a settlement agreement in a patent infringement case unenforceable for failure to comply with the statute of frauds. See also *Augustine Med. Inc. v. Progressive Dynamics Inc.,* 194 F.3d 1367, 52 USPQ2d 1515 (Fed. Cir. 1999); *Gjerlov v. Schuyler Labs., Inc.,* 131 F.3d 1016, 44 USPQ2d 1881 (Fed. Cir. 1997); *S & T Mfg. Co. v. County of Hillsborough, Fla.,* 815 F.2d 676, 2 USPQ2d 1280 (Fed. Cir. 1987). The court looks to regional circuit law to determine the res judicata effect of consent judgments. Under Third Circuit law, consent judgments have the same force and effect as judgments entered after a trial on the merits, *Epic Metals Corp. v. H.H. Robertson Co.,* 870 F.2d 1574, 10 USPQ2d 1296 (Fed. Cir. 1989), and a court may retain jurisdiction to enforce an agreement settling a case over which it once presided by incorporating

In *Lear, Inc. v. Adkins*,[415] the Supreme Court overruled the doctrine of licensee estoppel, which barred a patent licensee from contesting the validity of the licensed patent.[416] Although *Lear* did not deal specifically with consent judgments of validity, the regional circuits have applied its public policy utterances in varying fashion.[417] The Federal Circuit has now made it clear that it will apply its own law to the question of whether the public policies expressed in *Lear* override the general principles of res judicata that would otherwise apply to consent judgments. But on the application of those general principles of res judicata to consent judgments, regional circuit law is applied.[418] It remains to be seen how the Federal Circuit will deal with this question when it is squarely presented. The court has held that a party cannot avoid a settlement commitment, voluntarily made, to continue payments even in the event of a later holding of unenforceability. The policy of *Lear* must yield, in the case of settlement untainted by any fraud, to the policy of encouraging settlement.[419]

In *Foster v. Hallco*,[420] the court held unequivocally that *Lear* does not permit challenges to validity where, under normal principles of res judicata applicable to a consent judgment, such challenges would be precluded. *Lear* did not involve a judgment but only a license. No court has ever suggested that *Lear* intended to abrogate the application of res judicata to judgments imposed by a court after full litigation. Nor should it prohibit the application of res judicata in the consent judgment setting. A binding consent judgment encourages patent owners to agree to settlement and to remove its force would

---

the agreement into an order of dismissal. *Interspiro USA, Inc. v. Figgie Int'l, Inc.*, 18 F.3d 927, 30 USPQ2d 1070 (Fed. Cir. 1994).

[415]395 U.S. 653, 162 USPQ 1 (1969).

[416]*C.R. Bard, Inc. v. Schwartz*, 716 F.2d 874, 219 USPQ 197 (Fed. Cir. 1983).

[417]See, e.g., *Am. Equip. Corp. v. Wikomi Mfg. Co.*, 630 F.2d 544, 208 USPQ 465 (7th Cir. 1980), which holds that a consent judgment of validity will not be enforced absent an express or implied adjudication of infringement.

[418]*Foster v. Hallco Mfg. Co.*, 947 F.2d 469, 20 USPQ2d 1241 (Fed. Cir. 1991). The court applied its own law in deciding whether a consent judgment enjoining infringement of a patent should be set aside following a judicial determination that the patent was procured by inequitable conduct. *Broyhill Furn. Indus. v. Craftmaster Furn. Corp.*, 12 F.3d 1080, 29 USPQ2d 1283 (Fed. Cir. 1993).

[419]*Hemstreet v. Spiegel, Inc.*, 851 F.2d 348, 7 USPQ2d 1502 (Fed. Cir. 1988). The defendant infringer settled after one week of trial by taking a license, which provided that payments would be made even if the patent were later held invalid or unenforceable. The action was dismissed. The patent was later held unenforceable for inequitable conduct. The defendant sought an order relieving it from making payments under the license. The Federal Circuit found it unnecessary to decide whether, under Seventh Circuit law, the settlement order constituted an adjudication of validity and infringement and thus became res judicata on the enforceability issue. In *Broyhill Furn. Indus. v. Craftmaster Furn. Corp.*, 12 F.3d 1080, 29 USPQ2d 1283 (Fed. Cir. 1993), the parties had entered into a consent judgment enjoining infringement. The patent was later held unenforceable because of inequitable conduct during its prosecution. The accused infringer moved pursuant to Rule 60(b), FRCP, to set aside the consent judgment. Inasmuch as the motion was outside the one-year limitation of subsection (3) of Rule 60(b), which deals with fraud, it had to be grounded on the savings clause of the rule, dealing with fraud on the court. Applying its own law, the Federal Circuit found that inequitable conduct does not constitute fraud on the court.

[420]*Foster v. Hallco Mfg. Co.*, 947 F.2d 469, 20 USPQ2d 1241 (Fed. Cir. 1991).

have an adverse effect on settlement negotiations.[421] Thus, under the court's contract theory of consent decrees, future challenges to validity may be precluded, but such an intention should not readily be inferred. A narrow construction strikes a reasonable balance between the policy considerations of *Lear* and those favoring voluntary settlement of patent litigation.[422]

A federal district court may not interpret and enforce a settlement agreement that terminated prior litigation unless it has some federal jurisdictional basis for enforcing a contract between the parties. Neither the Federal Rules nor any statute gives federal courts the inherent power to interpret and enforce settlement agreements, even those that pertain to litigation originally pending in federal courts, absent some independent basis of jurisdiction. One such basis is ancillary jurisdiction, which may be exercised over a settlement agreement (1) to permit disposition, by a single court, of claims that are, in varying respects and degrees, factually interdependent, and (2) to enable a court to function successfully, i.e., to manage its proceedings, vindicate its authority, and effectuate its decrees. But under the first circumstance (single court disposition of factually interdependent claims) entry of judgment, such as a consent judgment, terminates both the federal case and any basis for ancillary federal jurisdiction over the contractual agreement that occasioned the termination. Thus, for federal courts to enforce the settlement agreement, the dispute must involve some ongoing source of federal jurisdiction to which the nonfederal matter may be considered ancillary.[423] Under the second source of ancillary jurisdiction (successful functioning of the court), an order or judgment of the court must incorporate the settlement agreement such that a breach of the agreement also violates the court's decree.[424] A motion to enforce an agreement settling

---

[421]Res judicata embodies the public policy of putting an end to litigation. In its simplest construct, it precludes the relitigation of a claim, or cause of action, or any possible defense to the cause of action that is ended by a judgment of the court. This aspect of res judicata, known as claim preclusion, applies whether the judgment is rendered after trial and imposed by the court or entered upon the consent of the parties. *Foster v. Hallco Mfg. Co.,* 947 F.2d 469, 20 USPQ2d 1241 (Fed. Cir. 1991).

[422]*Foster v. Hallco Mfg. Co.,* 947 F.2d 469, 20 USPQ2d 1241 (Fed. Cir. 1991). A consent judgment of patent validity may preclude a party from asserting invalidity in subsequent litigation involving new accused products, so long as the agreement manifests an intent to be bound. However, any surrender of the right to challenge validity of a patent is construed narrowly. In *Foster v. Hallco,* the court refused to hold that a consent judgment had surrendered the invalidity defense as to future accused products, even though the agreement stated that the patents were "valid and enforceable in all respects." *Foster* requires more for a waiver of the invalidity defense as to future accused products. *Diversey Lever Inc. v. Ecolab Inc.,* 191 F.3d 1350, 52 USPQ2d 1062 (Fed. Cir. 1999). Here, the settlement agreement provided that the defendant would not "directly or indirectly aid, assist or participate in any action contesting the validity" of the patents. By that language, the defendant surrendered its right to challenge the validity of the patents in any context.

[423]*National Presto Indus. v. Dazey Corp.,* 107 F.3d 1576, 42 USPQ2d 1070 (Fed. Cir. 1997). In this case, the court was able to pass the question of whether a district court's inherent but limited contempt power is sufficiently robust to support ancillary jurisdiction, for it found that the contempt power of the district court was not invoked by the proceedings below. See also *Joy Mfg. Co. v. National Mine Serv. Co.,* 810 F.2d 1127, 1 USPQ2d 1627 (Fed. Cir. 1987).

[424]*National Presto Indus. v. Dazey Corp.,* 107 F.3d 1576, 42 USPQ2d 1070 (Fed. Cir. 1997). In *Interspiro USA, Inc. v. Figgie Int'l, Inc.,* 18 F.3d 927, 30 USPQ2d 1070 (Fed. Cir.

a patent infringement action arises under the patent laws if the district court retains jurisdiction to enforce the agreement. However, where breach of the agreement does not itself establish infringement of the patent, it is error to determine damages based upon 35 U.S.C. §284. Rather, the trial court should look to state contract law regarding damages for breach of contract. So too with an award of attorney fees under §285.[425] The court has rejected an attempt to use judicial estoppel to enforce an unexecuted settlement agreement.[426]

In an interesting situation, the defendant agreed in a pretrial stipulation to be bound by a judgment in another case against another party charged with infringing the plaintiff's patent. The stipulation covered validity and enforceability, but excluded any consent judgment. The other party vigorously contested validity and enforceability at trial, lost, and exhausted all available posttrial remedies. It then reached a settlement on the issue of damages that mooted its posttrial motions and forced it to forfeit its appellate rights. The Federal Circuit held that this was not a consent judgment within the meaning of the stipulation. It made short work of the defendant's argument that public policy should rescue it from a decision that it later finds to have been imprudently made. On the contrary, the court felt that public policy favors preventing the defendant from reneging on an agreement into which it freely entered and upon which both the plaintiff and the trial court relied.[427]

1994), the court noted that under Third Circuit law, a court may retain jurisdiction to enforce an agreement settling a case over which it once presided by incorporating the agreement into an order of dismissal. The order need not use the word "incorporate" or any other magic form of words; rather, the court need only manifest an inferable intent to retain jurisdiction. The court unequivocally held that attorney fees under 35 U.S.C. §285 may be awarded in an action to enforce such an agreement. Its reasoning also implies that such a case is one arising under the patent laws.

[425]*Gjerlov v. Schuyler Labs., Inc.*, 131 F.3d 1016, 44 USPQ2d 1881 (Fed. Cir. 1997).

[426]*Wang Labs., Inc. v. Applied Computer Sci., Inc.*, 958 F.2d 355, 22 USPQ2d 1055 (Fed. Cir. 1992). The parties met just before trial and informed the court by telephone that they had agreed to settle. The case was dismissed without prejudice to reopening by a certain date if the settlement was not consummated. The parties came up with a draft agreement, but it was never signed and the squabbling continued. After the date set by the court had passed, the plaintiff moved to enforce the unexecuted settlement agreement. The district court granted the motion, judicially estopping defendant from contending that settlement had not been reached pursuant to the phone call and the draft agreement. The Federal Circuit disagreed, pointing out that a court does not have power to impose a settlement agreement when there was never a meeting of the minds. But in *Core-Vent Corp. v. Implant Innovations, Inc.*, 53 F.3d 1252, 34 USPQ2d 1581 (Fed. Cir. 1995), it appears that a meeting of the minds was reached. After trial had commenced, the parties informed the judge that they had reached a settlement. The judge had plaintiff's attorney state the terms of the settlement for the record. The statement was quite comprehensive and detailed; among other things it contemplated a royalty bearing, license, past damages, and a consent judgment of validity and infringement. The judge polled the parties and their counsel and all expressed satisfaction with the statement, whereupon the judge dismissed the jury. Inevitably, a dispute ensued over both the language of the judgment itself and the terms of a formal license agreement. The plaintiff submitted a proposed judgment that tracked the open court statement quite closely, and the judge entered it. The Federal Circuit affirmed. The teaching of this case seems to be that if a litigant requires special provisions, they had better be expressed at the time a statement is made in court, rather than hoping to rely upon later arguments concerning standard practice and usage in licensing.

[427]*Kearns v. Chrysler Corp.*, 32 F.3d 1541, 31 USPQ2d 1746 (Fed. Cir. 1994).

Offers of judgment are governed by Rule 68, FRCP. Because a Rule 68 judgment is the product of an agreement between the parties, the parties define the scope of the judgment. Like consent decrees, Rule 68 judgments are interpreted according to general principles of contract law.[428]

---

[428]*Scosche Indus., Inc. v. Visor Gear, Inc.*, 121 F.3d 675, 43 USPQ2d 1659 (Fed. Cir. 1997). Here the plaintiff brought a declaratory action for invalidity and defendant counterclaimed for infringement. Plaintiff offered judgment on the counterclaim and defendant accepted. The holding was that the lower court erroneously granted summary judgment dismissing the invalidity claim (which plaintiff wanted to remain alive because it also had some unfair competition claims involving the patent).

11

Other Litigation

The Federal Circuit reviews decisions involving patents, or subject matter closely related to patents, in several settings other than traditional patent infringement actions. Some, like patent suits against the government in the Court of Federal Claims and patent proceedings before the United States International Trade Commission (ITC), are direct analogs of patent infringement cases. Others arise in the context of administrative review, such as decisions from PTO tribunals (discussed at length in Chapter 15) and decisions of district courts reviewing those tribunals' actions under 35 U.S.C. §§145 and 146, discussed below in §11.4(a). Finally, the court sees a variety of patent-related matters, usually in the context of defenses or companion claims in patent infringement cases. These consist largely of antitrust, inequitable conduct, and trade secret issues. This chapter will examine the Federal Circuit's treatment of these ancillary and incidental questions.

§11.1 Court of Federal Claims (Formerly Claims Court)

(a) General powers

There are three exceptions to the constitutional command that the judicial power of the United States be vested in Article III courts: cases in territorial courts, courts-martial cases, and cases involving "public rights." The Court of Federal Claims, an Article I court, can exercise the judicial power of the United States under certain circumstances.[1] Those circumstances are spelled out in a comprehensive statutory framework.[2]

In general, the power of the Court of Federal Claims to grant equitable relief is limited to those claims that are themselves within the power of the court.[3] It does not have declaratory judgment jurisdic-

---

[1] *United States v. Rush,* 804 F.2d 645 (Fed. Cir. 1986).

[2] 28 U.S.C. §§1491–1509. It is a fundamental principle, embedded in the Constitution, that all federal courts, except the Supreme Court, are established by Congress and possess only the jurisdiction granted to them by Congress. The powers of an Article I court, such as the Court of Federal Claims, are limited by what has been given it by specific act of Congress and by its own rules adopted pursuant to congressional authority. *In re United States,* 877 F.2d 1568 (Fed. Cir. 1989).

[3] *ATL, Inc. v. United States,* 736 F.2d 677 (Fed. Cir. 1984). In an interesting case an inmate of a federal prison made an invention working in the prison shop. He filed a pro se suit in the Court of Federal Claims, asking that a patent attorney be assigned to prosecute a patent application for him and that the government be enjoined from using his inventions. The Federal Circuit agreed with the Court of Federal Claims that it had no jurisdiction. *Lariscey v. United States,* 861 F.2d 1267, 8 USPQ2d 2007 (Fed. Cir. 1988). The Court of Federal Claims allowed him to amend his complaint to assert claims for violation of the Fifth Amendment "taking"

tion.[4] But where the prime effort of a plaintiff is to obtain money from the government, the exclusive jurisdiction of the Court of Federal Claims cannot be avoided by drafting a complaint that appears to seek only injunctive, mandatory, or declaratory relief against the government.[5]

The Court of Federal Claims can constitutionally decide cross-claims by the government against third parties in "public rights" cases, i.e., matters arising between the government and persons subject to its authority in connection with the performance of the constitutional functions of the executive and legislative branches that historically could have been determined exclusively by those branches.[6] The Court of Federal Claims is without jurisdiction to adjudicate the government's claims against third parties unless (1) the government's claim is for the recovery of money that it has already paid out in respect of the transaction or matter that constitutes the subject matter of the suit, or (2) the third party appears and asserts a claim or an interest in a claim against the United States. Moreover, situation (1) applies only where the government is sued for money that was incorrectly disbursed to a third party under a mistake of fact or law. Thus, the Court of Federal Claims has no jurisdiction to determine a third-party defendant's contractual obligations to indemnify the government. Although a third-party defendant may assist the government in the defense of the case, and may offer additional evidence on its own behalf and advance such legal contentions as it deems appropriate in the protection of its interest, such status does not affect the jurisdiction of the Court of Federal Claims.[7] Likewise, it has no jurisdiction over a contract implied in law.[8]

A "taking" of personal property, for Fifth Amendment purposes, is defined as a direct interference with or disturbance of property rights by the deliberate exercise of government power. The Fifth Amendment is designed not to limit that interference but to secure compensation in the event of otherwise proper interference amounting to a taking. In accordance with these principles, the court has held that a federal prison inmate may, under appropriate circumstances, seek redress in the Court of Federal Claims against the government for a taking of trade secret rights developed while the prisoner was incarcerated.[9]

clause and for breach of implied contract. His request for appointment of a lawyer was refused, and that was the question being appealed. The Federal Circuit affirmed the refusal to provide counsel without deciding whether the Court of Federal Claims had power in any event to appoint counsel.

[4]*Beachboard v. United States*, 727 F.2d 1092 (Fed. Cir. 1984).

[5]*Chula Vista Sch. Dist. v. Bennett*, 824 F.2d 1573 (Fed. Cir. 1987).

[6]*United States v. Rush*, 804 F.2d 645 (Fed. Cir. 1986).

[7]*Penda Corp. v. United States*, 44 F.3d 967, 33 USPQ2d 1200 (Fed. Cir. 1994). See also *United States v. Rush*, 804 F.2d 645 (Fed. Cir. 1986).

[8]*Atlas Corp. v. United States*, 895 F.2d 745 (Fed. Cir. 1990).

[9]*Lariscey v. United States*, 949 F.2d 1137, 20 USPQ2d 1845 (Fed. Cir. 1991).

Compliance with the Court of Federal Claims statute of limitations (six years generally under 28 U.S.C. §2501) is jurisdictional in nature.[10] On review of final agency actions in the Court of Federal Claims the standard is "arbitrary, capricious, abuse of discretion, or otherwise not in accordance with law."[11] The Federal Circuit applies the clearly erroneous standard to factual findings of the Court of Federal Claims.[12]

The Federal Circuit has held that 28 U.S.C. §2505, which provides that any judge of the Court of Federal Claims may sit at any place within the United States, does not authorize the Court of Federal Claims to conduct proceedings abroad.[13]

(b) Sovereign Immunity

The terms of the government's consent to be sued in any particular court define that court's jurisdiction to entertain the suit. Conditions upon which the government consents to be sued must be strictly observed and are not subject to implied limitations.[14] Thus, waivers of sovereign immunity are to be strictly construed.[15] The six-year statute of limitations, 28 U.S.C. §2501, on actions against the United States is a jurisdictional requirement attached by Congress as a condition of the government's waiver of sovereign immunity and, as such, must be strictly construed. Exceptions to the limitations and conditions upon which the government consents to be sued are not to be implied.[16] Thus, the United States cannot be held liable for costs without its consent.[17] And it is well settled that attorney fees cannot

---

[10]*Hart v. United States,* 910 F.2d 814 (Fed. Cir. 1990); *Hopland Band of Pomo Indians v. United States,* 855 F.2d 1573 (Fed. Cir. 1988); *Jones v. United States,* 801 F.2d 1334 (Fed. Cir. 1986). The court has discussed at some length the difference between tolling the statute and tolling the accrual of the limitations period; the difference was said to be significant in suits against the government due to the jurisdictional nature of the statute. See §9.4(a). Inasmuch as the limitations period serves as a jurisdictional limitation rather than simply as an affirmative defense, it is not capable of waiver or subject to an estoppel, whether pled or not. *Hopland Band of Pomo Indians v. United States,* 855 F.2d 1573 (Fed. Cir. 1988).

[11]*Heinemann v. United States,* 796 F.2d 451, 230 USPQ 430 (Fed. Cir. 1986).

[12]*Hankins Constr. Co. v. United States,* 838 F.2d 1194 (Fed. Cir. 1988); *Alger v. United States,* 741 F.2d 391 (Fed. Cir. 1984).

[13]*In re United States,* 877 F.2d 1568 (Fed. Cir. 1989). The Court of Federal Claims had ordered that the trial of a government contract appeal action brought by a West German company would be held in a suitable U.S. consulate in West Germany.

[14]*NEC Corp. v. United States,* 806 F.2d 247 (Fed. Cir. 1986). See also *Hart v. United States,* 910 F.2d 814 (Fed. Cir. 1990).

[15]*United States v. Johnson Controls, Inc.,* 713 F.2d 1541 (Fed. Cir. 1983). 28 U.S.C. §1491 does not purport to give the Court of Federal Claims declaratory judgment jurisdiction. That would require a statute specifically waiving sovereign immunity and authorizing declaratory judgments. *Beachboard v. United States,* 727 F.2d 1092 (Fed. Cir. 1984).

[16]*Hart v. United States,* 910 F.2d 814 (Fed. Cir. 1990); *Hopland Band of Pomo Indians v. United States,* 855 F.2d 1573 (Fed. Cir. 1988).

[17]*Johns-Manville Corp. v. United States,* 893 F.2d 324 (Fed. Cir. 1989).

be awarded against the federal government unless specifically authorized by a statutory waiver of sovereign immunity. Such statutory authorization must be express and specific; it cannot be extended beyond the statute's literal terms and it cannot be implied.[18] The government has, however, waived immunity with respect to monetary sanctions for discovery abuses in cases over which the Court of Federal Claims has jurisdiction.[19]

A right to a jury trial in a federal court must arise out of the Seventh Amendment or be granted by a federal statute. The Seventh Amendment preserves the right to a jury trial in those actions in which the right existed at common law when the amendment was adopted in 1791. An action against the government, however, is not a suit at common law; it has long been settled that the Seventh Amendment right to trial by jury does not apply in actions against the government. Thus, a party in an action against the United States has a right to trial by jury only where Congress has affirmatively and unambiguously granted that right by statute, as one of the terms of the government's consent to be sued.[20]

(c) Section 1498 Actions

The patent jurisdiction of the Court of Federal Claims is spelled out in 28 U.S.C. §1498:

> (a) Whenever an invention described in and covered by a patent of the United States is used or manufactured by or for the United States without license of the owner thereof or lawful right to use or manufacture the same, the owner's remedy shall be by action against the United States in the United States Court of Federal Claims for the recovery of his reasonable and entire compensation for such use and manufacture. . . .

The statute goes on to provide that use or manufacture by anyone with the "authorization or consent" of the government is use or manufacture by the government. Section 1498 requires that suits against manufacturers who produce goods for the government be filed against the government in the Court of Federal Claims. When a manufacturer sells a product to both the government and a third party, the normal course of events is parallel patent infringement proceedings in a district court for the nongovernment sales.[21]

---

[18]*Saldana v. Merit Sys. Prot. Bd.,* 766 F.2d 514 (Fed. Cir. 1985). Congress, in waiving sovereign immunity, may prescribe the forum and conditions under which it can be sued, and such waivers cannot be implied but must be unequivocally expressed. *In re United States,* 877 F.2d 1568 (Fed. Cir. 1989).

[19]*M.A. Mortenson Co. v. United States,* 996 F.2d 1177 (Fed. Cir. 1993).

[20]*Washington Int'l Ins. Co. v. United States,* 863 F.2d 877 (Fed. Cir. 1988). The court held that 28 U.S.C. §1876 does not grant a party a right to a jury trial in the Court of International Trade.

[21]*Nasatka v. Delta Scientific Corp.,* 58 F.3d 1578, 35 USPQ2d 1374 (Fed. Cir. 1995).

The government's unlicensed use of a patented invention is properly viewed as a taking of property under the Fifth Amendment through the government's exercise of its power of eminent domain, and the patent holder's remedy for such use is reasonable and entire compensation under 28 U.S.C. §1498(a). Because recovery is based on eminent domain, the proper measure is what the owner has lost, not what the taker has gained. Generally, the preferred manner of reasonably and entirely compensating the patent owner is to require the government to pay a reasonable royalty for its license as well as damages for its delay in paying the royalty.[22] Lost profits are available against the government as well, although consequential damages are not.[23]

Inasmuch as the theoretical basis for a §1498 action is eminent domain, the government in this context is not in the position of an ordinary infringer, but rather a compulsory, nonexclusive licensee.[24] Thus, injunctive relief is not available against the government in the Court of Claims,[25] and it is likely that a district court cannot even enjoin a threatened sale to the United States.[26] A patent owner may not use its patent to cut the government off from sources of supply, either at the bid stage or during performance of a government contract. It is therefore impermissible to enjoin a private party from bidding on government contracts to supply articles that have been held to infringe a patent.[27]

---

[22]*Hughes Aircraft Co. v. United States,* 86 F.3d 1566, 39 USPQ2d 1065 (Fed. Cir. 1996).

[23]*Gargoyles, Inc. v. United States,* 113 F.3d 1572, 42 USPQ2d 1760 (Fed. Cir. 1997).

[24]*Motorola, Inc. v. United States,* 729 F.2d 765, 221 USPQ 297 (Fed. Cir. 1984). It is lawful for a licensee to repair, while an unlicensed infringer cannot lawfully repair, the infringing device. Apparently the government is always treated like a licensee in this respect; in other words, the government can repair whatever it has, even if its possession is not authorized. *Id.* In dealing with a laches defense, the court was willing to start the delay period at the point in time that the patentee had, in an action against the government in the Court of Federal Claims, identified the defendant's products as among those it was complaining about. *Jamesbury Corp. v. Litton Indus. Prods., Inc.,* 839 F.2d 1544, 5 USPQ2d 1779 (Fed. Cir. 1988). The court rejected the patentee's argument that, since the defendant did not make nongovernment sales until later, this was not really knowledge of infringing activity.

[25]*Motorola, Inc. v. United States,* 729 F.2d 765, 221 USPQ 297 (Fed. Cir. 1984).

[26]*TVI Energy Corp. v. Blane,* 806 F.2d 1057, 1 USPQ2d 1071 (Fed. Cir. 1986). A presale demonstration was use for the United States, and the sole remedy was in the Court of Federal Claims. *Id.* In *Manville Sales Corp. v. Paramount Sys., Inc.,* 917 F.2d 544, 16 USPQ2d 1587 (Fed. Cir. 1990), the court reviewed *Sperry Gyroscope Co. v. Arma Eng'g Co.,* 271 U.S. 232 (1926), and concluded that it stands for the proposition that §1498(a) is not jurisdictional, but simply provides an affirmative defense in patent infringement cases in district courts. Thus, failure to raise the defense that sales were to the government amounts to a waiver. The court distinguished *TVI,* supra, on the ground that it did not mean there that the trial court actually lacked jurisdiction, but only that the outcome of the case was the same as though it had.

[27]*Trojan, Inc. v. Shat-R-Shield, Inc.,* 885 F.2d 854, 12 USPQ2d 1132 (Fed. Cir. 1989). In one case the defendant argued that an injunction was too broad because it would, if read literally, prevent defendant from supplying to the government. The court refused to modify the injunction, on the basis of the following reasoning: a patent is a grant of the right to exclude others from making, using, or selling the invention claimed. Taken at face value, this would seem to be a right to prevent a manufacturer from selling its product to the United States. But it is not, because 28 U.S.C. §1498 says it is not. The patentee takes its patent from the government subject to the government's eminent domain right to obtain what it needs from

The policy behind the authorization or consent provision of §1498 was to relieve private government contractors from expensive litigation with patentees, possible injunctions, payment of royalties, and punitive damages.[28] Authorization or consent by the government can be expressed in a form other than a formal letter. In proper circumstances, authorization can be implied.[29]

The Federal Circuit has cautioned that the concepts, phrases, and words commonly used in the patent field do not always connote the same meaning in a §1498 case.[30] The government can be sued only for direct infringement, not inducement or contributory infringement.[31] In a suit against the government, "use" is the prohibited activity. Although a showing of actual use may not be required if it is clear that, as assembled, an accused device would infringe, the mere fact that a device might possibly be assembled in an infringing configuration is probably not enough.[32] Notice, actual or constructive (as by marking under 35 U.S.C. §287), is not a prerequisite to recovery against the United States under §1498.[33]

Money judgments of the Court of Federal Claims bear compound interest under 28 U.S.C. §1961, but the statute is silent as to prejudgment interest. The Federal Circuit has indicated that, despite the fact that simple interest may have been "traditional" in Fifth Amendment cases, compound interest may more nearly fit with the policy to accomplish justice as between a patentee and the United States.[34] Increased

---

manufacturers, and to use what it obtains. The government has graciously consented, in that same statute, to be sued in the Court of Federal Claims for reasonable and entire compensation, for what would be infringement if committed by a private person. The same principles apply to injunctions, which are nothing more than the giving of the aid of the courts to the enforcement of the patentee's right to exclude. Though injunctions may seem to say that making for and selling to the government is forbidden, injunctions based upon patent rights cannot in reality do that because of §1498. *W.L. Gore & Assoc., Inc. v. Garlock, Inc.,* 842 F.2d 1275, 6 USPQ2d 1277 (Fed. Cir. 1988).

[28]*TVI Energy Corp. v. Blane,* 806 F.2d 1057, 1 USPQ2d 1071 (Fed. Cir. 1986). This 1918 amendment to the statute was at the behest of the Secretary of the Navy, who cited difficulties in procuring goods from private manufacturers necessary to meet military requirements in World War I. *Id.*

[29]*TVI Energy Corp. v. Blane,* 806 F.2d 1057, 1 USPQ2d 1071 (Fed. Cir. 1986). Where government bidding procedure guidelines require a demonstration, authorization can be implied.

[30]*Motorola, Inc. v. United States,* 729 F.2d 765, 221 USPQ 297 (Fed. Cir. 1984).

[31]*Motorola, Inc. v. United States,* 729 F.2d 765, 221 USPQ 297 (Fed. Cir. 1984). The government has not waived sovereign immunity for collateral acts like inducement and contributory infringement. *Gargoyles, Inc. v. United States,* 113 F.3d 1572, 42 USPQ2d 1760 (Fed. Cir. 1997).

[32]*Lemelson v. United States,* 752 F.2d 1538, 224 USPQ 526 (Fed. Cir. 1985). Generally, infringement of an apparatus claim can occur only when the claimed combination has been assembled and is used or is available for use. *Id.*

[33]*Motorola, Inc. v. United States,* 729 F.2d 765, 221 USPQ 297 (Fed. Cir. 1984).

[34]*Dynamics Corp. v. United States,* 766 F.2d 518, 226 USPQ 622 (Fed. Cir. 1985). The court remanded for consideration of whether "reasonable and entire compensation" may include compounded prejudgment interest. The court also remarked that delay damages are an attempt to repay a patentee for the loss of money to which it had a right. Delay damages should therefore be adequate to compensate the patentee for the lost use of its money during the relevant accounting period.

damages and attorney fees are not available against the government in a §1498 case.[35] An award of costs to the prevailing party in suits involving the government is provided for in 28 U.S.C. §2412(a). It does not, however, authorize the Court of Federal Claims to award costs in a case that is dismissed for want of jurisdiction.[36]

Decisions of the Court of Federal Claims are reviewed by the Federal Circuit for errors of law and clear errors of fact.[37] It reviews in plenary fashion whether the Court of Federal Claims properly grants summary judgment or properly dismisses for failure to state a claim upon which relief can be granted, as both are questions of law.[38] Valuation determinations for purposes of eminent domain are reviewed for clear error as are determinations of what constitutes a reasonable royalty.[39]

§11.2 International Trade Commission

(a) In General

Unfair methods of competition and unfair acts in the importation of articles into the United States are unlawful, pursuant to 19 U.S.C. §1337, if they meet certain conditions or have certain effects or tendencies. Under Part II of the Tariff Act of 1930[40] the United States International Trade Commission (ITC) is invested with the authority, among other things, to deal with such unlawful acts and to order exclusion of such articles from entry into the country.

Patent infringement, as by importing and selling a product that, although made abroad, is covered by a U.S. patent, is clearly an unfair act or method of competition under §1337.[41] By statute,[42] the importation and sale of an unpatented product produced abroad by a process covered by a U.S. patent is likewise a prohibited act.[43] But

---

[35]*Motorola, Inc. v. United States,* 729 F.2d 765, 221 USPQ 297 (Fed. Cir. 1984).

[36]*Johns-Manville Corp. v. United States,* 893 F.2d 324 (Fed. Cir. 1989). The American common law rules regarding the award of costs are modified by 28 U.S.C. §1919, which provides for costs whenever an action in a district court or the Court of International Trade is dismissed for lack of jurisdiction. It does not, however, apply to the Court of Federal Claims. *Id.*

[37]*Atlas Corp. v. United States,* 895 F.2d 745 (Fed. Cir. 1990). Because contract interpretation is a matter of law, the Federal Circuit reviews the interpretation of the Court of Federal Claims de novo. *Craft Mach. Works, Inc. v. United States,* 926 F.2d 1110 (Fed. Cir. 1991).

[38]*Dairyland Power Coop. v. United States,* 16 F.3d 1197 (Fed. Cir. 1994). Legal conclusions of the Court of Federal Claims, such as a grant of summary judgment, are reviewed de novo. Such a standard provides the Federal Circuit with substantial latitude. *Confederated Tribes v. United States,* 964 F.2d 1102 (Fed. Cir. 1992).

[39]*Hughes Aircraft Co. v. United States,* 86 F.3d 1566, 39 USPQ2d 1065 (Fed. Cir. 1996).

[40]19 U.S.C. §§1330–1340.

[41]*Massachusetts Inst. of Tech. v. AB Fortia,* 774 F.2d 1104, 227 USPQ 428, 431 (Fed. Cir. 1985). A sale for importation includes the situation in which a contract for goods has been formed in accordance with the UCC. *Enercon GmbH v. United States ITC,* 151 F.3d 1376, 47 USPQ2d 1725 (Fed. Cir. 1998).

[42]19 U.S.C. §1337(a)(1)(B)(ii).

[43]*Akzo N.V. v. United States ITC,* 808 F.2d 1471, 1 USPQ2d 1241 (Fed. Cir. 1986); *Massachusetts Inst. of Tech. v. AB Fortia,* 774 F.2d 1104, 227 USPQ 428 (Fed. Cir. 1985). So,

§1337 is not merely the international extension of the U.S. patent, trademark, and copyright laws.[44] To prove a violation, a complainant must show both an unfair act and a resulting detrimental effect or tendency.[45] More is required than simply proof of continuing infringement of a valid patent; a §1337 proceeding is not designed solely to protect a patentee from loss.[46]

Defenses to a charge of unfair competition under §1337 include both noninfringement and invalidity, as well as proof that the acts involved do not relate to a domestic industry.[47] However, there is no warrant for the ITC to ignore the presumption that the PTO properly did its job in granting a patent. The concern of the ITC for the public health and welfare, and for a competitive economy, is not inimical to the public policy that undergirds 35 U.S.C. §282. Inasmuch as patent invalidity is a statutory defense, not a regulatory duty, the ITC has no authority to redetermine patent validity when no defense of validity has been raised.[48]

It is often the case, where a tribunal's subject matter jurisdiction is based on the same statute that gives rise to the federal right, that the jurisdictional requirements mesh with the factual requirements necessary to prevail on the merits. In such a situation the tribunal should assume jurisdiction and treat (and dismiss on, if necessary) the merits of the case. Thus, the ITC should not dismiss a complaint for lack of jurisdiction simply because it does not believe that the complainant will be able to sustain its allegations of infringement.[49]

Section 1337 permits termination of an investigation only in the event of a settlement. The court applied this with strict literalism in rejecting a termination that had been based upon an arbitration clause in an underlying license agreement between the parties. Despite the ITC's obligation to consider all defenses, and notwithstanding the broad federal policy favoring arbitration of international transactions, an equitable defense cannot be raised to abort an inquiry before the public interest can be considered.[50]

---

too, with importation of a product produced abroad by trade secret misappropriation. *Viscofan, S.A. v. United States ITC,* 787 F.2d 544, 229 USPQ 118 (Fed. Cir. 1986). In *Amgen, Inc. v. United States ITC,* 902 F.2d 1532, 14 USPQ2d 1734 (Fed. Cir. 1990), the issue was whether the statute was intended to prohibit the importation of articles made abroad by a process in which a product claimed in a U.S. patent is employed. The court decided the question in the negative. Congress used the term "covered by the claims" in the normal parlance of patent lawyers, to whom a patent "covering" a process is a patent containing at least one claim defining a process.

[44]*Corning Glass Works v. United States ITC,* 799 F.2d 1559, 230 USPQ 822 (Fed. Cir. 1986); *Warner Bros., Inc. v. United States ITC,* 787 F.2d 562, 229 USPQ 126 (Fed. Cir. 1986); *Textron, Inc. v. United States ITC,* 753 F.2d 1019, 224 USPQ 625 (Fed. Cir. 1985).

[45]E.g., *New England Butt Co. v. United States ITC,* 756 F.2d 874, 225 USPQ 260 (Fed. Cir. 1985).

[46]*Corning Glass Works v. United States ITC,* 799 F.2d 1559, 230 USPQ 822 (Fed. Cir. 1986).

[47]*Massachusetts Inst. of Tech. v. AB Fortia,* 774 F.2d 1104, 227 USPQ 428 (Fed. Cir. 1985).

[48]*Lannom Mfg. Co. v. United States ITC,* 799 F.2d 1572, 231 USPQ 32 (Fed. Cir. 1986).

[49]*Amgen, Inc. v. United States ITC,* 902 F.2d 1532, 14 USPQ2d 1734 (Fed. Cir. 1990).

[50]*Farrel Corp. v. United States ITC,* 949 F.2d 1147, 20 USPQ2d 1912 (Fed. Cir. 1991). Once it begins a §1337 investigation, the ITC is authorized to terminate the investigation only

Equitable estoppel applies in ITC proceedings as well as infringement litigation.[51] Assignor estoppel can be considered and applied in §1337 cases before the ITC.[52] However, inequitable conduct involving a different patent will not bar a complainant from relief.[53] The ITC will apply res judicata principles in its own proceedings, both issue preclusion[54] and claim preclusion.[55] However, ITC decisions regarding patent issues have no preclusive effect in court proceedings.[56]

The ITC has authority to grant temporary injunctive relief, and its practice should be to exercise that authority in a parallel fashion to district courts. It applies the four standard factors for preliminary injunctions, and the court of appeals reviews on the basis of abuse of discretion.[57]

The Federal Circuit apparently approves the six-factor test that the ITC uses in assessing civil penalties for violating its orders. This analysis balances (1) the good or bad faith of the respondent, (2) the injury to the public, (3) the respondent's ability to pay, (4) the extent to which the respondent has benefited from its violations, (5) the need to vindicate the authority of the Commission, and (6) the public interest.[58] An ITC consent order, like a cease-and-desist order or an exclusion order, is enforceable by civil penalty imposed by the Commission and recoverable in the district court in the event of nonpayment.[59]

---

in limited and specific circumstances: after its entry of a consent order or approval of a settlement agreement. The court here declined to decide whether the ITC also has authority to terminate an investigation where the complaint is withdrawn without objection, or where the issue becomes moot (e.g., due to expiration of the patent).

[51]*Young Eng'rs, Inc. v. United States ITC,* 721 F.2d 1305, 219 USPQ 1142 (Fed. Cir. 1983).

[52]*Intel Corp. v. United States ITC,* 946 F.2d 821, 20 USPQ2d 1161 (Fed. Cir. 1991).

[53]*Akzo N.V. v. United States ITC,* 808 F.2d 1471, 1 USPQ2d 1241 (Fed. Cir. 1986). The argument was that the complainant was infringing a patent of the alleged §1337 violator. It should be noted that this argument was very weak in any event, because that patent had been held invalid in a district court judgment that was also on appeal.

[54]*SSIH Equip. S.A. v. United States ITC,* 713 F.2d 746, 218 USPQ 678 (Fed. Cir. 1983) (applying the *Blonder-Tongue* doctrine). In *San Huan New Mt'ls High Tech Inc. v. United States ITC,* 161 F.3d 1347, 48 USPQ2d 1865 (Fed. Cir. 1998), the court held that a respondent was precluded, by a consent order of the ITC entered in its original investigation, from contesting certain issues, such as the impact of prior art on the scope of equivalents, in an enforcement proceeding.

[55]*Young Eng'rs, Inc. v. United States ITC,* 721 F.2d 1305, 219 USPQ 1142 (Fed. Cir. 1983).

[56]*Bio-Technology Gen'l Corp. v. Genentech, Inc.,* 80 F.3d 1553, 38 USPQ2d 1321 (Fed. Cir. 1996). Thus, it would seem inappropriate to stay a district court suit pending an ITC action, particularly where the ITC matter can be resolved without deciding patent issues (e.g., lack of injury to domestic industry). *Corning Glass Works v. United States ITC,* 799 F.2d 1559, 230 USPQ 822 (Fed. Cir. 1986). Certainly where an order terminating an ITC investigation is not appealable, it will have no collateral estoppel or res judicata effect. *Block v. United States ITC,* 777 F.2d 1568, 228 USPQ 37 (Fed. Cir. 1985).

[57]*Rosemount, Inc. v. United States ITC,* 910 F.2d 819, 15 USPQ2d 1569 (Fed. Cir. 1990).

[58]*San Huan New Mt'ls High Tech Inc. v. United States ITC,*161 F.3d 1347, 48 USPQ2d 1865 (Fed. Cir. 1998). The court found in this case that the ITC's assessment of a civil penalty violated neither the Excessive Fines Clause of the Eighth Amendment nor the Due Process Clause.

[59]*San Huan New Mt'ls High Tech Inc. v. United States ITC,* 161 F.3d 1347, 48 USPQ2d 1865 (Fed. Cir. 1998). Section 1337(f)(2), which authorizes the Commission when necessary to

(b) Procedure

Under 19 U.S.C. §1337, the ITC has exclusive authority to investigate, either on the basis of a complaint or on its own initiative, allegations that foreign importers are engaging in unfair methods of competition or infringing a U.S. patent. The statute also establishes procedures the ITC must follow in its investigations and sets a strict timetable for their completion. Through its staff, it conducts the investigations independently of the wishes of the parties, and in reaching its final determination on an alleged violation it must consider factors that may or may not interest the parties: the public health and welfare, competitive conditions in the U.S. economy, the production of like or directly competitive articles in the United States, and U.S. consumers.[60]

An ITC investigation must be completed, and a determination made, within one year.[61] The Federal Circuit has held that this time limit applies to the initial determination of the ITC rather than an order modified after partial presidential disapproval.[62] The President may disapprove ITC determinations on policy grounds.[63] Where the President disapproves a portion of a remedy, there is no need for new ITC proceedings; the determination simply remains in effect to the extent not disapproved, and the ITC can issue a new remedy order based upon the valid portion of the prior determination.[64]

The ITC is heavily dependent upon voluntary submission of information, and disclosure of sensitive materials to any adversary would have a chilling effect on the parties' willingness to provide the confidential information essential to the ITC's fact-finding processes. Accordingly, the Federal Circuit will be favorably inclined toward strict discovery protective orders.[65]

Proceedings before the ITC under §1337 have been challenged as inherently judicial and involving essentially private rights, and therefore requiring adjudication by a constitutional Article III court. The Federal Circuit has responded that §1337 is a valid delegation of the broad congressional power for the public purpose of providing an adequate remedy for domestic industries against unfair practices beginning abroad and culminating in importation. Although it is true that private rights may be affected, the thrust of the statute is directed

---

collect the penalty by action in the district court, does not contemplate a de novo trial. It is simply a collection proceeding, and the statute and rules do not permit retrial, in such a proceeding, of the issues of fact and law relating to liability and amount of penalty. *Id.*

[60]*Farrel Corp. v. United States ITC,* 949 F.2d 1147, 20 USPQ2d 1912 (Fed. Cir. 1991).

[61]Or 18 months in more complicated cases. 19 U.S.C. §1337(b)(1).

[62]*Young Eng'rs, Inc. v. United States ITC,* 721 F.2d 1305, 219 USPQ 1142 (Fed. Cir. 1983).

[63]19 U.S.C. §1337(g)(2).

[64]*Young Eng'rs, Inc. v. United States ITC,* 721 F.2d 1305, 219 USPQ 1142 (Fed. Cir. 1983). If the President suggests a narrower order, the ITC can likewise rely upon the record of its initial proceeding. *Aktiebolaget Karlstads v. United States ITC,* 705 F.2d 1565, 217 USPQ 865 (Fed. Cir. 1983).

[65]*Akzo N.V. v. United States ITC,* 808 F.2d 1471, 1 USPQ2d 1241 (Fed. Cir. 1986).

toward the protection of the public interest from unfair trade practices in international commerce.[66] Likewise, ITC procedures do not violate U.S. treaty obligations by discriminating on the basis of nationality. There is nothing in any applicable treaty that guarantees an alien the rights that would have been afforded a domestic corporation if sued in a district court; the only guarantee is that the alien will be afforded the same rights as a domestic corporation in a §1337 proceeding before the ITC.[67]

(c) Domestic Industry

Effective August 23, 1988, 19 U.S.C. §1337 was amended extensively.[68] Among the more important changes was the elimination of the substantial injury requirement in cases where the unfair practice involves infringement of a U.S. patent. Although the requirement that a related industry in this country exist or be in the process of establishment remains, the discussion in earlier editions of this book dealing with the substantial injury requirement has been rendered moot by those changes. The cases are collected in the footnote.[69] Apparently the elimination of the injury requirement was retroactive and controlled pending investigations.[70]

Products manufactured abroad under the authority of the complainant, and then imported to the United States for sale, are not part of the domestic industry.[71] The patentee does nothing in such instances to contribute to opportunities for employment of domestic industrial workers.[72] The court has held that members of the domestic industry are not immune to remedial orders under §1337. The domestic industry requirement is a jurisdictional prerequisite to ITC action under §1337, not a congressional pardon for unlawful conduct.[73]

---

[66]*Akzo N.V. v. United States ITC,* 808 F.2d 1471, 1 USPQ2d 1241 (Fed. Cir. 1986).

[67]*Akzo N.V. v. United States ITC,* 808 F.2d 1471, 1 USPQ2d 1241 (Fed. Cir. 1986).

[68]Pub. L. No. 100-418.

[69]*Fischer & Porter Co. v. United States ITC,* 831 F.2d 1574, 4 USPQ2d 1700 (Fed. Cir. 1987); *Akzo N.V. v. United States ITC,* 808 F.2d 1471, 1 USPQ2d 1241 (Fed. Cir. 1986); *Corning Glass Works v. United States ITC,* 799 F.2d 1559, 230 USPQ 822 (Fed. Cir. 1986); *Warner Bros., Inc. v. United States ITC,* 787 F.2d 562, 229 USPQ 126 (Fed. Cir. 1986); *Textron, Inc. v. United States ITC,* 753 F.2d 1019, 224 USPQ 625 (Fed. Cir. 1985).

[70]*Hyundai Elec. Indus. Co. v. United States ITC,* 899 F.2d 1204, 14 USPQ2d 1396 (Fed. Cir. 1990).

[71]*Schaper Mfg. Co. v. United States ITC,* 717 F.2d 1368, 219 USPQ 665 (Fed. Cir. 1983). See also *Corning Glass Works v. United States ITC,* 799 F.2d 1559, 230 USPQ 822 (Fed. Cir. 1986).

[72]*Corning Glass Works v. United States ITC,* 799 F.2d 1559, 230 USPQ 822 (Fed. Cir. 1986).

[73]*Texas Instr., Inc. v. United States ITC,* 988 F.2d 1165, 26 USPQ2d 1018 (Fed. Cir. 1993). The court had previously held that domestic competitors who infringe the patent cannot be taken into account in assessing the domestic industry. The ITC is not in a position to try a multiplicity of infringement actions against domestic infringers as part of an investigation.

(d) Federal Circuit Review

An ITC proceeding is not a civil action.[74] Pursuant to §1337(c), the standard of review for ITC determinations is established by 5 U.S.C. §706, which provides that the reviewing court shall decide all relevant questions of law. Thus the Federal Circuit is not bound by the ITC's interpretation of statutory provisions. However, even though an issue may be denominated one of law, the court is not free simply to substitute its view for that of the ITC. The court must decide whether the ITC definitions or standards are reasonable in light of the language, policies, and legislative history of the statute.[75] What this boils down to, however, is that ITC legal conclusions are reviewed for correctness.[76] The legal conclusion of obviousness, in particular, is freely reviewable,[77] and the court does not consider itself bound by the ITC's ultimate determination on that matter.[78] Thus a holding of obviousness is reviewed de novo but the underlying factual determinations are reviewed under the substantial evidence standard.[79] The court reviews de novo the ITC's legal determinations, including those relating to claim interpretation and patent validity.[80] It is the primary responsibility of the ITC to administer the trade laws and not the patent laws.[81]

On issues of fact, the court's scope of review of ITC findings is narrowly limited.[82] If the ITC uses the correct legal standard, the Federal Circuit is bound to accept its findings of fact if they are supported by substantial evidence.[83] The substantial evidence standard therefore applies to factual determinations such as anticipation,

---

[74]*SSIH Equip. S.A. v. United States ITC,* 713 F.2d 746, 218 USPQ 678 (Fed. Cir. 1983).

[75]*Corning Glass Works v. United States ITC,* 799 F.2d 1559, 230 USPQ 822 (Fed. Cir. 1986). The court reviews final determinations of the ITC in accordance with Chapter 7 of the Administrative Procedure Act, 5 U.S.C. §§701–706. *Genentech, Inc. v. United States ITC,* 122 F.3d 1409, 43 USPQ2d 1722 (Fed. Cir. 1997).

[76]*Texas Instr., Inc. v. United States ITC,* 805 F.2d 1558, 231 USPQ 833 (Fed. Cir. 1986); *American Hosp. Supply Corp. v. Travenol Labs., Inc.,* 745 F.2d 1, 223 USPQ 577 (Fed. Cir. 1984); *SSIH Equip. S.A. v. United States ITC,* 713 F.2d 746, 218 USPQ 678 (Fed. Cir. 1983). The meaning or interpretation of precedent is a question of law, and an ITC determination thereof is given de novo review by the Federal Circuit. *YBM Magnex Inc. v. United States ITC,* 145 F.3d 1317, 46 USPQ2d 1843 (Fed. Cir. 1998).

[77]*Surface Tech. v. United States ITC,* 801 F.2d 1336, 231 USPQ 192 (Fed. Cir. 1986).

[78]*Akzo N.V. v. United States ITC,* 808 F.2d 1471, 1 USPQ2d 1241 (Fed. Cir. 1986); *Aktiebolaget Karlstads v. United States ITC,* 705 F.2d 1565, 217 USPQ 865 (Fed. Cir. 1983).

[79]*Texas Instr., Inc. v. United States ITC,* 988 F.2d 1165, 26 USPQ2d 1018 (Fed. Cir. 1993); *Intel Corp. v. United States ITC,* 946 F.2d 821, 20 USPQ2d 1161 (Fed. Cir. 1991).

[80]*Checkpoint Sys., Inc. v. United States ITC,* 54 F.3d 756, 35 USPQ2d 1042 (Fed. Cir. 1995).

[81]*Tandon Corp. v. United States ITC,* 831 F.2d 1017, 4 USPQ2d 1283 (Fed. Cir. 1987).

[82]*Corning Glass Works v. United States ITC,* 799 F.2d 1559, 230 USPQ 822 (Fed. Cir. 1986).

[83]*Tanabe Seiyaku Co. v. United States ITC,* 109 F.3d 726, 41 USPQ2d 1976 (Fed. Cir. 1997); *Akzo N.V. v. United States ITC,* 808 F.2d 1471, 1 USPQ2d 1241 (Fed. Cir. 1986); *Texas Instr., Inc. v. United States ITC,* 805 F.2d 1558, 231 USPQ 833 (Fed. Cir. 1986); *New England Butt Co. v. United States ITC,* 756 F.2d 874, 225 USPQ 260 (Fed. Cir. 1985). This is different from the clearly erroneous standard of review applied to civil actions. *American Hosp. Supply Corp. v. Travenol Labs., Inc.,* 745 F.2d 1, 223 USPQ 577 (Fed. Cir. 1984); *SSIH Equip. S.A. v.*

prior invention, and infringement, both literal and by equivalents.[84] There is a significant difference between this standard and the clearly erroneous standard, and in a close case the difference can be controlling. It was the intent of Congress that greater weight and finality be accorded to the ITC's findings than those of a trial court.[85]

The ITC can issue an order only if it is "in accordance with substantial evidence." This requires weighing the evidence with respect to reliability, materiality, relevance, probativeness, and quantity. On the other hand, the Federal Circuit reviews the ITC determination to see whether it is unsupported by substantial evidence, a far different standard that requires no weighing.[86] This is the same as the stringent standard applicable to a trial court in taking a case from a jury or in review of a jury verdict on a motion for JNOV.[87] The substantial evidence standard does not allow a court to conduct a de novo investigation of the evidence on the record before it and reach an independent conclusion; rather, the court's review is limited to deciding whether there is sufficient evidence in the record considered as a whole to support the agency's findings. The mere fact that a reasonable person might reach some other conclusion is insufficient for a reviewing court to overturn the ITC's conclusion.[88] Summary determinations, however, are reviewed as a matter of law. Because the ALJ has not made any factual determinations at that stage in the proceedings, the substantial evidence standard of review is not applicable.[89]

The Federal Circuit reviews the final determination of the ITC, not the ALJ's initial decision or the Commission's "reversal" of it. The standard is whether the determination is arbitrary, capricious, an abuse of discretion, or otherwise not in accordance with law or unsupported by substantial evidence. The fact that a contrary determination of the ALJ and the dissenting members of the Commission would be sustained if it were the decision under review does not mean that

---

United States ITC, 713 F.2d 746, 218 USPQ 678 (Fed. Cir. 1983). Under the substantial evidence standard, the court will not disturb the ITC's findings if they are supported by such relevant evidence as a reasonable mind might accept as adequate to support a conclusion. *Checkpoint Sys., Inc. v. United States ITC*, 54 F.3d 756, 35 USPQ2d 1042 (Fed. Cir. 1995).

[84]*Texas Instr., Inc. v. United States ITC*, 988 F.2d 1165, 26 USPQ2d 1018 (Fed. Cir. 1993). The standard of review of an ITC obviousness determination is whether there is substantial evidence to support the fact findings underlying the legal conclusion of obviousness. *Surface Tech. v. United States ITC*, 801 F.2d 1336, 231 USPQ 192 (Fed. Cir. 1986). Determination of literal infringement is a factual inquiry and, in an ITC proceeding, is reviewed on a substantial evidence standard. *LaBounty Mfg., Inc. v. United States ITC*, 867 F.2d 1572, 9 USPQ2d 1995 (Fed. Cir. 1989).

[85]*Tandon Corp. v. United States ITC*, 831 F.2d 1017, 4 USPQ2d 1283 (Fed. Cir. 1987). The court seems inclined to accord a measure of deference to the evidentiary and procedural rulings of the ITC. See *Hazani v. United States ITC*, 126 F.3d 1473, 44 USPQ2d 1358 (Fed. Cir. 1997).

[86]*Fischer & Porter Co. v. United States ITC*, 831 F.2d 1574, 4 USPQ2d 1700 (Fed. Cir. 1987).

[87]*Corning Glass Works v. United States ITC*, 799 F.2d 1559, 230 USPQ 822 (Fed. Cir. 1986); *SSIH Equip. S.A. v. United States ITC*, 713 F.2d 746, 218 USPQ 678 (Fed. Cir. 1983).

[88]*Akzo N.V. v. United States ITC*, 808 F.2d 1471, 1 USPQ2d 1241 (Fed. Cir. 1986).

[89]*Hazani v. United States ITC*, 126 F.3d 1473, 44 USPQ2d 1358, 1360 (Fed. Cir. 1997).

the majority's determination must be overturned. Both decisions may be reasonable, based on the entirety of the record. The Federal Circuit may not substitute its judgment for the Commission's final determination merely on the ground that it believes the ALJ's view is "more reasonable" than that of the Commission.[90]

Deference must be given to an interpretation of a statute by the agency charged with its administration. With respect to the meaning of the statutory requirements that an unfair method of competition must have a particular effect or tendency, it is particularly within the province and expertise of the ITC to define those phrases.[91] Review of an injury determination is therefore limited to deciding whether the Commission's decision is supported by substantial evidence and whether the determination is, on the record, arbitrary, capricious, or an abuse of discretion.[92] It is not necessary that expert witnesses opine in terms of the three-part test for the doctrine of equivalents before a body having the expertise of the ITC.[93]

The ITC likewise has broad discretion in selecting the form, scope, and extent of the remedy, and judicial review of its choice of remedy is necessarily limited. The court will not interfere except where the remedy selected has no reasonable relation to the unlawful practices found to exist.[94] Inasmuch as an ITC matter is one involving the public interest, there may be justification for broader remedies than in private infringement litigation.[95]

---

[90]*Fischer & Porter Co. v. United States ITC*, 831 F.2d 1574, 4 USPQ2d 1700 (Fed. Cir. 1987).

[91]*Fischer & Porter Co. v. United States ITC*, 831 F.2d 1574, 4 USPQ2d 1700 (Fed. Cir. 1987); *Corning Glass Works v. United States ITC*, 799 F.2d 1559, 230 USPQ 822 (Fed. Cir. 1986). In contrast, the ITC is not charged with administration of the patent statute, and the Federal Circuit does not therefore defer to its interpretation of patent law. *Corning Glass Works v. United States ITC*, 799 F.2d 1559, 230 USPQ 822 (Fed. Cir. 1986).

[92]*Akzo N.V. v. United States ITC*, 808 F.2d 1471, 1 USPQ2d 1241 (Fed. Cir. 1986).

[93]*Intel Corp. v. United States ITC*, 946 F.2d 821, 20 USPQ2d 1161 (Fed. Cir. 1991).

[94]*Viscofan, S.A. v. United States ITC*, 787 F.2d 544, 229 USPQ 118 (Fed. Cir. 1986). Here there was no abuse found in setting the period of exclusion as the time it would have taken a wrongdoer to develop, by lawful means, the process whose secrets it had misappropriated. It was also proper to set the starting date for that period as of the order itself, rather than the date of theft of the trade secrets.

[95]*Viscofan, S.A. v. United States ITC*, 787 F.2d 544, 229 USPQ 118 (Fed. Cir. 1986). The fact that the process may use nonproprietary technology does not necessarily render the order too broad; where the trade secret aspects of the process are not independent of the public aspects, the process itself may be precluded. The wrongdoer can always petition the ITC for modification of the order if it can demonstrate an ability to make the product without any of the secret technology. *Id. Hyundai Elec. Indus. Co. v. United States ITC*, 899 F.2d 1204, 14 USPQ2d 1396 (Fed. Cir. 1990), is interesting from the standpoint of how an exclusion remedy should be fashioned. The ITC's discretion with respect to remedies is not unlimited, however. In *Biocraft Labs., Inc. v. United States ITC*, 947 F.2d 483, 20 USPQ2d 1446 (Fed. Cir. 1991), it issued a temporary cease-and-desist order against the respondent. The respondent posted a bond that permitted it to dispose of infringing product already imported, and also provided that there would be no forfeiture with respect to conduct that was otherwise authorized. Later there was a settlement and the respondent petitioned, with the consent of the complainant, for release of the bond. The ITC refused on the ground that the conduct was not authorized when the bond was posted, but only after the event through the settlement agreement. Its justifications were that the bond is the price that respondents must pay for the right to continue acts that may constitute §1337 violations, that there is a strong public interest in temporary

In sum, the substantial evidence standard of review applies only to ITC determinations of substantive violation. Determinations on the public interest, the nature of the domestic market, bonding, and remedy are subject to a less stringent standard of judicial review. Thus, ITC remedy determinations are reviewed under the arbitrary and capricious, abuse of discretion standard: if the ITC has considered the relevant factors and not made a clear error of judgment, the court affirms its choice of remedy.[96] A sanction imposed by the ITC under its rules is also reviewed for abuse of discretion.[97]

The Federal Circuit will not review what the ITC has not decided. Thus, where the ITC reaches a "no violation" determination on the basis of a single dispositive issue, the court will not review other matters.[98] The court has labeled this single-issue approach as risky, however. Although the ITC should not be precluded from taking that risk where the conclusion reached on one dispositive issue appears to it inevitable and unassailable,[99] a failure to decide other issues can inhibit expeditious resolution of matters before the ITC.[100] Where the Federal Circuit affirms a finding of no injury, it will vacate ITC findings on patent issues as moot.[101]

The ITC can issue orders barring only future conduct. Neither exclusion nor cease-and-desist orders are applicable once a patent expires. Thus, when a patent expires on its way through the appeal process, the proper practice is to vacate the determination and remand

---

relief, and that the money goes to the U.S. Treasury, not the complainant. The Federal Circuit found the ITC's refusal to release the bond to be an abuse of discretion, inasmuch as the purpose of the bond is to protect the complainant as well as the public interest.

[96]*Hyundai Elec. Indus. Co. v. United States ITC,* 899 F.2d 1204, 14 USPQ2d 1396 (Fed. Cir. 1990). The court seemed to feel this result was foreshadowed in *Viscofan, S.A. v. United States ITC,* 787 F.2d 544, 229 USPQ 118 (Fed. Cir. 1986). In reviewing an ITC order dealing with temporary injunctive relief, the Federal Circuit employs the abuse of discretion standard. The decision may thus be set aside if it rests on a foundation of an erroneous understanding of the law or on clearly erroneous findings of fact; otherwise, it may be set aside only if, based on the facts, it is patently unreasonable, arbitrary, or fanciful. *Rosemount, Inc. v. United States ITC,* 910 F.2d 819, 15 USPQ2d 1569 (Fed. Cir. 1990).

[97]*Genentech, Inc. v. United States ITC,* 122 F.3d 1409, 43 USPQ2d 1722 (Fed. Cir. 1997). An abuse occurs if the sanction decision (1) is clearly unreasonable, arbitrary, or fanciful, (2) is based on an erroneous conclusion of law, (3) rests on clearly erroneous fact findings, or (4) follows from a record that contains no evidence on which the decision-making body could rationally base its decision. *Id.*

[98]*Beloit Corp. v. Valmet OY,* 742 F.2d 1421 (Fed. Cir. 1984). On the other hand, where the ITC affirms an administrative law judge's conclusion that there was a violation, without rejecting or refusing to take a position on any part of the ALJ's initial determination, all conclusions of the ALJ necessary for a finding of a violation are reviewable by the court. *Akzo N.V. v. United States ITC,* 808 F.2d 1471, 1 USPQ2d 1241 (Fed. Cir. 1986).

[99]*Beloit Corp. v. Valmet OY,* 742 F.2d 1421 (Fed. Cir. 1984).

[100]*Lannom Mfg. Co. v. United States ITC,* 799 F.2d 1572, 231 USPQ 32 (Fed. Cir. 1986). The ITC expressly neither affirmed nor reversed the ALJ on infringement. Thus the court was unable to review on the merits the question of injury. Although there may be circumstances wherein no injury will be shown even if all doubt as to infringement is resolved in favor the complainant, here the determination of which goods were covered by the patent claims was essential to the ensuing determination of injury, and a remand was necessary.

[101]*Fischer & Porter Co. v. United States ITC,* 831 F.2d 1574, 4 USPQ2d 1700 (Fed. Cir. 1987); *Corning Glass Works v. United States ITC,* 799 F.2d 1559, 230 USPQ 822 (Fed. Cir. 1986).

to the ITC with instructions to dismiss as moot the portion of the complaint relating to that patent.[102] And where a determination of injury is based upon two valid patents, and one is held invalid on appeal, it is appropriate to remand for another determination of injury based upon only the valid patent.[103]

When a petitioner loses an ITC complaint and appeals, the winning respondents cannot appeal, and their cross-appeals must be dismissed for lack of standing. However, they can participate in the petitioner's appeal, but only to the extent that they may raise matters in support of the ITC's determination of no violation; they may not be heard on matters as to which the ITC has taken no position.[104] Where it is clear that an ITC exclusion order would cover the components of a nonparty when incorporated into the excluded infringing products of the respondent, the nonparty may appeal as "any person adversely affected by a final determination of the Commission" under 19 U.S.C. §1337(c).[105]

If a party fails to raise, in a petition for review by the full Commission, an issue decided by the ALJ, it waives review of that issue by the Federal Circuit.[106]

The Federal Circuit can review only final determinations of the ITC. A final determination is a final administrative decision on the merits, excluding or refusing to exclude articles from entry. A determination is not final if there are issues remaining regarding remedy, or if there are ongoing enforcement proceedings.[107] The Federal Circuit has jurisdiction to review final determination decisions of the ITC on the merits, that is, those that exclude or refuse to exclude articles from entry.[108] Thus, the court has no statutory authority to review ITC advisory opinions. Under 28 U.S.C. §1295(a)(6) it may review only "final determinations" of the ITC, and advisory opinions are not final determinations. What counts is not the nature or thoroughness of the agency proceeding, but the effect of the determination. An

---

[102]*Texas Instr., Inc. v. United States ITC,* 851 F.2d 342, 7 USPQ2d 1509 (Fed. Cir. 1988).

[103]*Aktiebolaget Karlstads v. United States ITC,* 705 F.2d 1565, 217 USPQ 865 (Fed. Cir. 1983). Where two patents expire on the same day, only one need be considered on appeal. Thus where the ITC entered an order barring import of any devices infringing either patent, and the court upheld the validity and infringement determinations as to one, it was able to vacate the ITC's validity, enforceability, and infringement determinations as to the other. *Texas Instr., Inc. v. United States ITC,* 871 F.2d 1054, 10 USPQ2d 1257 (Fed. Cir. 1989). One wonders whether it will always be clear which of the two patents to deal with.

[104]*Surface Tech. v. United States ITC,* 780 F.2d 29 (Fed. Cir. 1985).

[105]*LSI Computer Sys., Inc. v. United States ITC,* 832 F.2d 588, 4 USPQ2d 1705 (Fed. Cir. 1987). The plain meaning of "any person" controls in the absence of legislative history to the contrary; the legislative history showed no intention to limit appeals to "parties" only. The requirement that the person be "adversely affected" will prevent judicial chaos. *Id.* It should be noted that the nonparty appellant had not sought to intervene and did not participate in the proceeding except by providing deposition testimony in response to subpoenas.

[106]*Allied Corp. v. United States ITC,* 850 F.2d 1573, 7 USPQ2d 1303 (Fed. Cir. 1988) (claim construction).

[107]*Crucible Mt'ls Corp. v. United States ITC,* 127 F.3d 1057 (Fed. Cir. 1997).

[108]*Amgen, Inc. v. United States ITC,* 902 F.2d 1532, 14 USPQ2d 1734 (Fed. Cir. 1990).

agency may not issue what it calls advisory opinions and attempt to make some appealable and some not on the basis of its selection among types of proceedings, or on the basis of how those opinions are treated by other agencies. If the ITC wishes one of its pronouncements to have effect as a final determination, it knows how to accomplish that objective. The lack of finality inherent in the word "advisory" dooms review.[109]

Similarly, the Federal Circuit lacks jurisdiction of an appeal from an ITC order terminating an investigation as "abated."[110] The court also lacks jurisdiction to review an ITC order refusing to declassify certain confidential business information.[111] On the other hand, an ITC decision dismissing a complaint for lack of subject matter jurisdiction is intrinsically a final determination not to exclude articles from entry and is thus reviewable.[112]

The Federal Circuit has jurisdiction to review a modified exclusion order despite the fact that the statute, 19 U.S.C. §1337(c), limits review to determination under subsections (d), (e), and (f), and authority for exclusion order modification is found only in subsection (h). There is a general rule that judicial review will not be precluded on the sole ground that specific procedures for judicial review of a particular agency action are not spelled out in a statute. An order modifying an original order inherently relates to the propriety of the original and affects its validity.[113]

§11.3 Patent-Antitrust

Many patent infringement suits involve antitrust issues. These can arise either in the context of patent misuse defenses or direct claims and counterclaims for violation of federal antitrust laws. In general, the Federal Circuit will approach a federal antitrust claim as would the regional court of appeals for the circuit that includes the district court whose judgment is being reviewed.[114] However, in

---

[109]*Allied Corp. v. United States ITC,* 850 F.2d 1573, 7 USPQ2d 1303 (Fed. Cir. 1988).

[110]*Block v. United States ITC,* 777 F.2d 1568, 228 USPQ 37 (Fed. Cir. 1985).

[111]*Viscofan, S.A. v. United States ITC,* 787 F.2d 544, 229 USPQ 118 (Fed. Cir. 1986). The requester wanted the material for use in another proceeding, not to aid in the ITC proceeding. Thus the order was not ancillary to review of the exclusion order.

[112]*Amgen, Inc. v. United States ITC,* 902 F.2d 1532, 14 USPQ2d 1734 (Fed. Cir. 1990).

[113]*Allied Corp. v. United States ITC,* 850 F.2d 1573, 7 USPQ2d 1303 (Fed. Cir. 1988). A party may appeal a final determination modifying a remedial order issued by the ITC where the modification is adverse to the party. *Crucible Mt'ls Corp. v. United States ITC,* 127 F.3d 1057 (Fed. Cir. 1997).

[114]*Korody-Colyer Corp. v. General Motors Corp.,* 828 F.2d 1572, 4 USPQ2d 1203 (Fed. Cir. 1987); *Argus Chem. Corp. v. Fibre Glass-Evercoat Co.,* 812 F.2d 1381, 1 USPQ2d 1971 (Fed. Cir. 1987); *Loctite Corp. v. Ultraseal Ltd.,* 781 F.2d 861, 228 USPQ 90 (Fed. Cir. 1985).

deciding whether conduct in procuring or enforcing a patent is sufficient to strip a patentee of its immunity from the antitrust laws,
Federal Circuit law applies.[115]

At the outset, the court recognizes that the federal antitrust laws
do not create a federal law of unfair competition or purport to afford
remedies for all torts committed by or against persons engaged in
interstate commerce. Nor do the antitrust laws negate the patentee's
right to exclude others from patent property. The patent and antitrust
laws are complementary, the patent system serving to encourage
invention and the bringing of new products to market by adjusting
investment risk, and the antitrust laws serving to foster industrial
competition. The patent and antitrust laws serve the public in different ways, both of importance to the nation.[116]

(a) Standing and Immunity

The Department of Justice, the Federal Trade Commission, state
attorneys general, and private parties may enforce the federal antitrust laws. Private parties may bring suit for violation of the Sherman
and Clayton Acts under §4 and §16 of the Clayton Act. A private
party, however, must meet certain standards to qualify for standing
to sue under these provisions. One such requirement is that a private
party must allege an antitrust injury, which is an injury of the type
the antitrust laws were intended to prevent and flows from that which
makes the defendant's acts unlawful. The purpose of the antitrust
injury requirement is to ensure that the harm for which the plaintiff
seeks compensation corresponds to the rationale for finding a violation
of the antitrust laws in the first place. It further ensures that plaintiffs
only recover if the loss is the result of a competition-reducing aspect
or effect of the defendant's behavior rather than a competition-
increasing or neutral aspect of that behavior.[117]

Standing to bring a private antitrust damage action is limited
to those injured in their business or property by reason of anything
forbidden in the antitrust laws. Criteria for ascertaining whether a
claim of injury is sufficient to establish antitrust standing include:
(1) whether there is a causal connection between an antitrust violation
and harm to the plaintiff, and whether the defendants intended to
cause that harm; (2) whether the nature of plaintiff's alleged injury

---

[115]*Nobelpharma AB v. Implant Innovations Inc.*, 141 F.3d 1059, 46 USPQ2d 1097 (Fed.
Cir. 1998). This conclusion applies equally to all antitrust claims premised on the bringing of
a patent infringement suit. *Id.* The court applies its own law in deciding whether a refusal to
license or sell patented parts constitutes a violation of the antitrust laws; however, when
evaluating that conduct with respect to copyrighted diagnostic software, it applies regional
circuit law. *In re Independent Serv. Org. Antitrust Litig.*, 203 F.3d 1322, 53 USPQ2d 1852 (Fed.
Cir. 2000).

[116]*Intergraph Corp. v. Intel Corp.*, 195 F.3d 1346, 52 USPQ2d 1641, 1652 (Fed. Cir. 1999).

[117]*Eastman Kodak Co. v. Goodyear Tire & Rubber Co.*, 114 F.3d 1547, 42 USPQ2d 1737
(Fed. Cir. 1997).

was of the type the antitrust laws were intended to forestall; (3) the directness or indirectness of the asserted injury; (4) whether the claim rests on some abstract or speculative measure of harm; and (5) the strong interest in keeping the scope of complex antitrust trials within judicially manageable limits, avoiding both duplicative recoveries and the complex apportionment of damages.[118] The interest sought to be protected by the antitrust laws is the welfare of the consumer.[119]

The state action doctrine, although grounded on general principles of federalism, relates specifically to state sovereignty in state legislatively authorized activity. The doctrine provides immunity, or "exemption" as it is sometimes called, from federal competition laws when the state is performing official actions, whether or not such actions are anticompetitive in effect. To warrant such immunity, the anticompetitive acts must be taken in the state's "sovereign capacity" and not as a market participant in competition with commercial enterprise. If the allegedly immune anticompetitive acts are not explicitly ordered by a legislative arm of state government, they must be conducted pursuant to legislative authorization that contemplates such acts.[120]

The *Noerr/Pennington* doctrine immunizes good faith access to the courts. The Federal Circuit believes that the "sham" litigation exception to *Noerr/Pennington* incorporates an objective as well as a subjective prong. Thus, if there is no objective evidence that a patent infringement action is so baseless that no reasonable litigant could realistically expect to secure favorable relief, the court need not consider the patentee's subjective motivations in bringing the suit.[121]

(b) Monopolization

Section 2 of the Sherman Act deals with monopolization, and attempts and conspiracies to monopolize. In contrast, §7 of the Clayton Act deals with monopolistic tendencies in their incipiency and well before they have attained such effects as would justify a Sherman Act proceeding. Thus, §7 may prohibit an acquisition, such as the acquisition of some patent licenses, if the effect of such acquisition

---

[118]*Indium Corp. v. Semi-Alloys, Inc.*, 781 F.2d 879, 228 USPQ 845 (Fed. Cir. 1985).

[119]*FMC Corp. v. Manitowoc Co.*, 835 F.2d 1411, 5 USPQ2d 1112 (Fed. Cir. 1987).

[120]*Genentech, Inc. v. Eli Lilly & Co.*, 998 F.2d 931, 27 USPQ2d 1241 (Fed. Cir. 1993). The court was able to pass the question of whether a state university's licensing activities establish a market participant exception to state action immunity by finding that the activities were not in restraint of trade and therefore not in violation of antitrust principles.

[121]*Carroll Touch, Inc. v. Electro Mechanical Sys., Inc.*, 3 F.3d 404, 27 USPQ2d 1836 (Fed. Cir. 1993). In such a case, the matter can be disposed of by summary judgment. *Id.* In *U.S. Philips Corp. v. Sears, Roebuck & Co.*, 55 F.3d 592, 34 USPQ2d 1699 (Fed. Cir. 1995), the court quite properly held that a winning lawsuit is by definition a reasonable effort at petitioning for redress and therefore not a sham. However, the majority opinion went on to volunteer that the "place to challenge litigation as sham is in the asserted sham litigation." One can easily postulate situations where this is impossible, e.g., a sham state court action that gives rise to a federal antitrust claim.

may be substantially to lessen competition, or to tend to create a monopoly.[122]

On one hand, a patent owner must be allowed to protect the property right given to it under the patent laws. On the other hand, it may not use the property right granted by a patent to extend its power in the marketplace improperly, i.e., beyond the limits of what Congress intended the patent laws to give. The fact that a patent is obtained does not wholly insulate the patent owner from the antitrust laws. When a patent owner uses its patent rights not only as a shield to protect the invention but as a sword to eviscerate competition unfairly, that owner may be found to have abused the grant and may become liable for antitrust violations when sufficient power in the relevant market is present. Therefore, patent owners may incur antitrust liability for enforcement of a patent known to be obtained through fraud, or known to be invalid, where a license of a patent compels the purchase of unpatented goods, or where there is an overall scheme to use the patent to violate the antitrust laws.[123]

When the patented product is merely one of many products that actively compete on the market, few problems arise between the property rights of a patent owner and the antitrust laws. However, when the patented product is so successful that it creates its own economic market or consumes a large segment of an existing market, the aims and objectives of the patent and antitrust laws may seem, at first glance, wholly at odds. However, the two bodies of law are actually complementary, as both are aimed at encouraging innovation, industry, and competition.[124] Mere procurement of a patent, whatever the conduct of the applicant in the procurement, cannot without more affect the welfare of the consumer and cannot in itself violate the antitrust laws. Thus there is no relationship between the antitrust laws and a patent that is valid, properly procured, and enforced.[125]

---

[122]*Eastman Kodak Co. v. Goodyear Tire & Rubber Co.*, 114 F.3d 1547, 42 USPQ2d 1737 (Fed. Cir. 1997).

[123]*Atari Games Corp. v. Nintendo of Am., Inc.*, 897 F.2d 1572, 14 USPQ2d 1034 (Fed. Cir. 1990). Intellectual property rights do not confer a privilege to violate the antitrust laws. *In re Independent Serv. Org. Antitrust Litig.*, 203 F.3d 1322, 53 USPQ2d 1852 (Fed. Cir. 2000).

[124]*Atari Games Corp. v. Nintendo of Am., Inc.*, 897 F.2d 1572, 14 USPQ2d 1034 (Fed. Cir. 1990). Nondisclosure of trade secrets in patent applications is not inconsistent with the objectives of the patent system, and the patentee is not thereby extending its exclusionary rights in the patented inventions. *Christianson v. Colt Indus. Oper. Corp.*, 822 F.2d 1544, 3 USPQ2d 1241 (Fed. Cir. 1987), *vacated on jurisdictional grounds & remanded*, 486 U.S. 800, 7 USPQ2d 1109 (1988).

[125]*FMC Corp. v. Manitowoc Co.*, 835 F.2d 1411, 5 USPQ2d 1112 (Fed. Cir. 1987). In *Atari Games Corp. v. Nintendo of Am., Inc.*, 897 F.2d 1572, 14 USPQ2d 1034 (Fed. Cir. 1990), the court reversed a preliminary injunction forbidding the patentee from filing suits for infringement against the accused infringer's customers. The court remarked that Congress has specifically granted patent owners the right to commence a civil suit in order to protect their inventions. Thus a preliminary injunction takes on special significance when the injunction involves patent rights and antitrust allegations. The court also observed that, because patents are cloaked in a presumption of validity, a patent infringement suit is presumed to be brought in good faith. Surely the court did not intend this observation to apply without condition to the infringement issue, where the patentee bears the burden of proof. One could conceive of a suit commenced

The bringing of a lawsuit to enforce legal rights does not of itself constitute violation of the antitrust laws or patent misuse. There must be bad faith and improper purpose in bringing the suit, in implementation of an illegal restraint of trade. A purpose is improper if its goal is not to win a favorable judgment, but to harass a competitor and deter others from competition by engaging the litigation process itself, regardless of the outcome.[126]

The offense of monopoly under §2 of the Sherman Act has two elements: (1) the possession of monopoly power in the relevant market and (2) the willful acquisition or maintenance of that power as distinguished from growth or development as a consequence of a superior product, business acumen, or historic accident.[127] To establish an illegal attempt to monopolize, a plaintiff must prove (1) a specific intent to monopolize, and (2) a dangerous probability that the attempt would be successful in achieving a monopoly in the relevant market.[128]

Relevant market definition is both highly factual and important and is therefore not a suitable subject for determination on summary judgment.[129] It is not presumed that the patent-based right to exclude necessarily establishes market power in antitrust terms. The virtually

---

with the knowledge that there was no infringement; this could well result in conflict with the antitrust laws.

[126]*Glaverbel S.A. v. Northlake Mkt'g & Supp., Inc.*, 45 F.3d 1550, 33 USPQ2d 1496 (Fed. Cir. 1995). The defendant was arguing that it was being sued abroad by the patent owner on foreign patents covering the same technology and that the cost of the litigation was crippling. The court made short work of this: parties who engage in international business may indeed encounter litigation in foreign courts; such actions, and their cost and consequences, do not of themselves constitute violation of the Sherman Act. In *Eastman Kodak Co. v. Goodyear Tire & Rubber Co.*, 114 F.3d 1547, 42 USPQ2d 1737 (Fed. Cir. 1997), the court reasoned that the simple acquisition and enforcement of patent rights did not create an antitrust injury because the accused infringer would have suffered the same consequences had the rights been acquired and enforced by another party or, indeed, retained and enforced by the original owner.

[127]*U.S. Philips Corp. v. Windmere Corp.*, 861 F.2d 695, 8 USPQ2d 1885 (Fed. Cir. 1988). Evidence that a firm holding 90% percent of a market that has substantial entry barriers drastically slashes its prices in response to the competition of a new entrant, for the purpose and with the effect of eliminating that entrant, is sufficient to show monopolization. *Id.* In *C.R. Bard Inc. v. M3 Sys. Inc.*, 157 F.3d 1340, 48 USPQ2d 1225 (Fed. Cir. 1998), the patent owner had a patent on a reusable biopsy gun and a separate patent on the needle. The court upheld a jury verdict of intent to monopolize based upon the fact that the patent owner made modification so that competitive nonpatented needles would not fit without an adaptor. In order to prevail on such an antitrust claim, it had to be shown that the patent owner made the change for predatory reasons, i.e., for the purpose of injuring competitors in the replacement needle market, rather than for improving the operation of the gun. There was substantial evidence that the real reasons for modifying the gun were to raise the cost of entry to potential makers of replacement needles, to make doctors apprehensive about using nonpatented needles, and to preclude the use of "copycat" needles. There were findings of a relevant product market for replacement needles for such guns and that the patent owner had monopoly power in that market.

[128]*Loctite Corp. v. Ultraseal Ltd.*, 781 F.2d 861, 228 USPQ 90 (Fed. Cir. 1985). In an antitrust action the complaint need only allege sufficient facts from which the court can discern the elements of an injury resulting from an act forbidden by the antitrust laws. The elements of a claim for attempted monopolization are (1) specific intent to monopolize, (2) anticompetitive conduct, and (3) dangerous probability of success. *Abbott Labs. v. Brennan*, 952 F.2d 1346, 21 USPQ2d 1192 (Fed. Cir. 1992).

[129]*Albert v. Kevex Corp.*, 741 F.2d 396, 223 USPQ 1 (Fed. Cir. 1984).

unlimited variety and scope of patented inventions and market situations militate against per se rules in these complex areas. Unless the patent has been obtained by fraud such that the market position had been gained illegally, the patent right to exclude does not constitute monopoly power prohibited by the Sherman Act.[130] The trier of fact need not engage in the meaningless exercise of market definition where no wrongful conduct has been shown.[131]

Price competition is not itself an antitrust violation. The law that prohibits predatory pricing practices does not routinely bar a seller from lowering its prices to compete with a competitor's lower prices. Predatory intent is a requisite.[132] The Sherman Act does not convert all harsh commercial actions into antitrust violations. Unilateral conduct that may adversely affect another's business situation, but is not intended to monopolize that business, does not violate the Sherman Act.[133]

Patenting and licensing the results of research is not a violation of antitrust principles, and the grant of an exclusive license is a lawful incident of the right to exclude provided by the patent laws. A patent owner's right to select its licensees, its decision to grant exclusive or nonexclusive licenses or to sue for infringement, and its pursuit of optimum royalty income are not in themselves restraints of trade.[134]

---

[130]*C.R. Bard Inc. v. M3 Sys. Inc.*, 157 F.3d 1340, 48 USPQ2d 1225 (Fed. Cir. 1998). A patent alone does not demonstrate market power. *In re Independent Serv. Org. Antitrust Litig.*, 203 F.3d 1322, 53 USPQ2d 1852 (Fed. Cir. 2000).

[131]*Akzo N.V. v. United States ITC*, 808 F.2d 1471, 1 USPQ2d 1241 (Fed. Cir. 1986). In an unusual case, the parties stipulated that if the patent were invalid for lack of enablement, then the plaintiff would be guilty of violation of §2 of the Sherman Act. The district court found the patent invalid and entered judgment of antitrust violation, and plaintiff appealed the invalidity ruling. The Federal Circuit refused to decide the issue on the ground that it might amount to an advisory opinion. The case was remanded for findings on antitrust elements such as whether the suit had been prosecuted by plaintiff with knowledge of the invalidity. *Technicon Instr. Corp. v. Alpkem Corp.*, 866 F.2d 417, 9 USPQ2d 1540 (Fed. Cir. 1989). The court indicated that a full trial would not be necessary—that the parties could stipulate any facts they wished. But the stipulation could not be treated as an agreement concerning the legal effect of admitted facts, inasmuch as the court cannot be controlled by agreement of counsel on a question of law. It seems that the practical effect may be that the parties cannot get review of the enablement ruling, because it might be difficult for the plaintiff to bring itself to stipulate to bad faith, which would appear to be the one factual matter that must be decided, either by trial or agreement.

[132]*Xeta, Inc. v. Atex, Inc.*, 852 F.2d 1280, 7 USPQ2d 1471 (Fed. Cir. 1988). Violation of the Robinson-Patman Act requires, inter alia, that the same commodity be sold to separate customers at different prices during the same time period. *Id.*

[133]*Intergraph Corp. v. Intel Corp.*, 195 F.3d 1346, 52 USPQ2d 1641 (Fed. Cir. 1999). Intergraph sued Intel for patent infringement and, in response, Intel withdrew or reduced technical assistance and special benefits, particularly prerelease access to Intel's new products. The district court granted a preliminary injunction against Intel, finding a likelihood that its actions violated the antitrust laws. The Federal Circuit reversed. The opinion provides a nice review of the law in this area, and deals with such issues as the "essential facility" theory, refusals to deal, leveraging of monopoly power, coercive reciprocity and tying, and conspiracy. The court found that none of these theories, taken individually, reflected a violation of the Sherman Act, and rejected the notion that if there is a fraction of validity to each theory, the sum of those fractions may be used to prove a violation.

[134]*Genentech, Inc. v. Eli Lilly & Co.*, 998 F.2d 931, 27 USPQ2d 1241 (Fed. Cir. 1993). In this case the patent owner was a state university. In *In re Independent Serv. Org. Antitrust Litig.*, 203 F.3d 1322, 53 USPQ2d 1852 (Fed. Cir. 2000), a copier maker refused to license

And certainly a patentee that has a good faith belief that its patents are being infringed violates no protected right when it so notifies infringers. Nor should an accused infringer be insulated from knowledge and fair warning of potential liability, or deprived of the opportunity to respond to threatened litigation.[135]

(c) Per Se Illegality

The court has not yet had an opportunity to give much consideration to cases under §1 of the Sherman Act, particularly those falling within the per se category. It has held that there was no per se anticompetitive effect resulting from a "value-in-use" pricing program, where the patentee sold a product made by a patented process at prices appropriate to the ultimate end use. The customers could use the product for other end uses but had to agree that if they did, or if they resold the product, they would pay a differential.[136]

To show an illegal tie, three elements must be demonstrated: (1) the purchase of one product (the tying product) must be conditioned on the purchase of another product (the tied product); (2) the defendant must have sufficient economic power with respect to the tying product to appreciably restrain free competition in the market for the tied product; and (3) the amount of commerce affected must be not insubstantial.[137] In dicta, the court has indicated that certain license restrictions are not per se antitrust violations, such as restricting the sale of game cartridges outside the United States or limiting the number of cartridges that can be distributed.[138]

One troublesome area that the court has begun to explore is the potential tension between postsale restrictions, on the one hand, and the *Univis Lens*[139] doctrine, on the other. Under *Univis Lens,* the first

---

or sell its patented copier parts and copyrighted diagnostic software to independent service organizations. The court held that this was not, as a matter of law, a violation of §2 of the Sherman Act. There is no more reason to inquire into the subjective motivation of the maker in refusing to sell or license its patented works than there is in evaluating the subjective motivation of a patentee in bringing suit to enforce that same right. In the absence of any indication of illegal tying, fraud in the PTO, or sham litigation, the patent holder may enforce the statutory right to exclude others from making, using, or selling the claimed invention free from liability under the antitrust laws. The court will not inquire into subjective motivation for exerting statutory rights, even though a refusal to sell or license a patented invention may have an anticompetitive effect, so long as that anticompetitive effect is not illegally extended beyond the statutory patent grant. It is the infringement defendant and not the patentee that bears the burden to show that one of these exceptional situations exists.

[135]*Mallinckrodt, Inc. v. Medipart, Inc.,* 976 F.2d 700, 24 USPQ2d 1173 (Fed. Cir. 1992).

[136]*Akzo N.V. v. United States ITC,* 808 F.2d 1471, 1 USPQ2d 1241 (Fed. Cir. 1986).

[137]*Xeta, Inc. v. Atex, Inc.,* 852 F.2d 1280, 7 USPQ2d 1471 (Fed. Cir. 1988). The court affirmed a denial of a preliminary injunction where the allegation was that the defendant had conditioned the sale of its proprietary software on the customer's purchase of its hardware, and enforced the tie with an announced disclaimer of warranty and technical service obligations when components are used in foreign systems.

[138]*Atari Games Corp. v. Nintendo of Am., Inc.,* 897 F.2d 1572, 14 USPQ2d 1034 (Fed. Cir. 1990).

[139]*United States v. Univis Lens Co.,* 316 U.S. 241, 53 USPQ 404 (1942).

authorized sale of an article embodying a patented invention exhausts the patent rights in that article. Nonetheless, the court has refused the invitation to condemn all postsale restrictions as patent misuse. A sale may be conditioned, so long as the condition does not violate some other law or policy. The question is whether the restriction is reasonably within the patent grant, or whether the patentee has ventured beyond it and into behavior having an anticompetitive effect not justifiable under the rule of reason.[140] A patentee is generally entitled to determine how it wishes to commercialize its invention in order to optimize its economic benefit from the patent grant.[141]

(d) *Fraudulent Procurement and Sham Litigation*

A patent owner who brings a lawsuit to enforce the statutory right to exclude others from making, using, or selling the claimed invention is exempt from the antitrust laws, even though such a suit may have an anticompetitive effect, unless the infringement defendant proves that the asserted patent was obtained through knowing and willful fraud, or that the infringement suit was a mere sham to cover what is actually no more than an attempt to interfere directly with the business relationships of a competitor.[142]

The Federal Circuit recognizes that a fraudulently procured patent may give rise to a violation of §2 of the Sherman Act or §5 of the FTC Act.[143] The court uses the term *"Walker Process* claim" to mean liability, if all prerequisites of §2 of the Sherman Act are shown, for (1) enforcement of a patent known to have been procured by fraud, or (2) bad faith enforcement of a patent known to be invalid.[144] After passing the question in previous cases, the court has also held that *Walker Process* and the Supreme Court's decision in *Professional Real Estate Investors (PRE)*[145] provide alternative legal grounds on which a patentee may be stripped of its immunity from the antitrust laws.

---

[140]*Mallinckrodt, Inc. v. Medipart, Inc.,* 976 F.2d 700, 24 USPQ2d 1173 (Fed. Cir. 1992). At issue was the validity of a "label license" that specified that the sale of the patented medical treatment device was for a single use (i.e., disposable) only. The court refused to accept the district judge's view that all postsale restrictions are invalid as patent misuse. The court also made it clear that, in judging the validity of a postsale restriction, it is unimportant whether the purchaser acquires the patented device directly from the patentee or from a licensee.

[141]*Carborundum Co. v. Molten Metal Equip. Innovations,* 72 F.3d 872, 37 USPQ2d 1169 (Fed. Cir. 1995).

[142]*Glass Equip. Dev. Inc. v. Besten Inc.,* 174 F.3d 1337, 50 USPQ2d 1300 (Fed. Cir. 1999).

[143]*Litton Indus. Prods., Inc. v. Solid State Sys. Corp.,* 755 F.2d 158, 225 USPQ 34 (Fed. Cir. 1985); *American Hoist & Derrick Co. v. Sowa & Sons, Inc.,* 725 F.2d 1350, 220 USPQ 763 (Fed. Cir. 1984). It does not, however, constitute unfair competition under §43(a) of the Lanham Act. *Pro-Mold & Tool Co. v. Great Lakes Plastics, Inc.,* 75 F.3d 1568, 37 USPQ2d 1626, 1631 (Fed. Cir. 1996).

[144]*Korody-Colyer Corp. v. General Motors Corp.,* 828 F.2d 1572, 4 USPQ2d 1203 (Fed. Cir. 1987). See *Walker Process Equip., Inc. v. Food Mach. & Chem. Corp.,* 382 U.S. 172, 147 USPQ 404 (1965).

[145]*Professional Real Estate Investors, Inc. v. Columbia Pictures Indus., Inc.,* 508 U.S. 49 (1993).

Both legal theories may be applied to the same conduct; each provides its own basis for depriving a patent owner of immunity from the antitrust laws; either or both may be applicable to a particular party's conduct in obtaining and enforcing a patent. Consequently, if the elements of *Walker Process* fraud, as well as the other criteria for antitrust liability, are met, such liability can be imposed without the additional sham inquiry required under *PRE*. That is because *Walker Process* antitrust liability is based on the knowing assertion of a patent procured by fraud on the PTO, very specific conduct that is clearly reprehensible. On the other hand, irrespective of the patent applicant's conduct before the PTO, an antitrust claim can also be based on a *PRE* allegation that a suit is baseless; in order to prove that a suit was within the "sham" exception to immunity, an antitrust plaintiff must prove that the suit was both objectively baseless and subjectively motivated by a desire to impose collateral, anticompetitive injury rather than to obtain a justifiable legal remedy. Thus, under *PRE*, a sham suit must be both subjectively brought in bad faith and based on a theory of either infringement or validity that is objectively baseless. Accordingly, if a suit is not objectively baseless, an antitrust defendant's subjective motivation is immaterial. In contrast with a *Walker Process* claim, a patentee's activities in procuring the patent are not necessarily at issue. It is the bringing of a lawsuit that is subjectively and objectively baseless that must be proved.[146]

To support a conclusion of sham litigation, the lawsuit must be objectively meritless such that no reasonable litigant could expect success on the merits, and it must be found that the baseless lawsuit conceals an attempt to interfere directly with the business relationships of a competitor. Thus although sham litigation as a tactic to destroy competition can lead to antitrust violation, sham litigation requires more than a failed legal theory. Neither the bringing of an unsuccessful suit to enforce patent rights, nor the effort to enforce a patent that ultimately falls to invalidity, subjects the suitor to antitrust liability. Since a principal purpose of the patent system is to provide innovators with a property right upon which investment and other commercial commitments can be made, the patentee must have the right of enforcement of a duly granted patent, unencumbered by punitive consequences should the patent's validity or infringement not survive litigation. The law recognizes a presumption that the assertion of a duly granted patent is made in good faith, and this presumption is overcome only by affirmative evidence of bad faith.[147]

In *Walker Process*, the Supreme Court held that in order to strip a patentee of its exemption from the antitrust laws because of its attempting to enforce its patent monopoly, an antitrust plaintiff is first required to prove that the patentee obtained the patent by knowingly and willfully misrepresenting facts to the PTO. The plaintiff in

---

[146]*Nobelpharma AB v. Implant Innovations Inc.,* 141 F.3d 1059, 46 USPQ2d 1097 (Fed. Cir. 1998).

[147]*C.R. Bard Inc. v. M3 Sys. Inc.,* 157 F.3d 1340, 48 USPQ2d 1225 (Fed. Cir. 1998).

the patent infringement suit must also have been aware of the fraud when bringing suit.[148] Under *Walker Process* the maintenance and enforcement of a patent procured by knowing and willful fraud may meet the intent and conduct elements of violation of the Sherman Act, provided that the ability to lessen or destroy competition, including market power in the relevant market, can also be shown. A patent does not of itself establish a presumption of market power in the antitrust sense. The commercial advantage gained by new technology and its protection by patent do not convert the possessor thereof into a prohibited monopolist. The patent right must be coupled with violation of §2 of the Sherman Act, and the elements of a §2 violation must be met. Determination of whether the patentee meets the Sherman Act elements of monopolization or an attempt to monopolize is governed by the rules of application of the antitrust laws to market participants, with due consideration to the exclusivity that inheres in the patent grant. Analysis under the rule of reason takes into consideration the policy underlying the patent grant and the national interest served, for the public purpose of the patent grant as an incentive to invention, investment, and disclosure is achieved solely by the statutory right to exclude.[149]

Fraudulent procurement is not a per se violation. A patent is not a monopoly, and therefore the theory that a fraudulently procured patent was an illegal monopoly all along fails.[150] Without some effort at enforcement, a patent cannot serve as the foundation for a *Walker Process* type monopolization case.[151] Nonetheless, treble damages may be recovered where a patentee maintains and enforces a patent that it knows to have been procured by inequitable conduct.[152] The relevant market must be pleaded and proved.[153] A bare allegation that a patentee obtained a patent through inequitable conduct does not establish a violation of the Sherman Act.[154]

Mere "technical fraud" is not enough; an honest mistake will not support a §2 claim.[155] A finding of *Walker Process* fraud requires higher threshold showings of both intent and materiality than does a finding

---

[148]*Nobelpharma AB v. Implant Innovations Inc.*, 141 F.3d 1059, 46 USPQ2d 1097 (Fed. Cir. 1998).

[149]*Abbott Labs. v. Brennan*, 952 F.2d 1346, 21 USPQ2d 1192 (Fed. Cir. 1992).

[150]*American Hoist & Derrick Co. v. Sowa & Sons, Inc.*, 725 F.2d 1350, 220 USPQ 763 (Fed. Cir. 1984). The burden of demonstrating procompetitive effects shifts only where the evidence shows that the challenged practice has the hallmarks of anticompetitive behavior; namely, that it has operated to raise prices and reduce output. *Akzo N.V. v. United States ITC*, 808 F.2d 1471, 1 USPQ2d 1241 (Fed. Cir. 1986).

[151]*Cygnus Therapeutics Sys. v. Alza Corp.*, 92 F.3d 1153, 39 USPQ2d 1666 (Fed. Cir. 1996).

[152]*Argus Chem. Corp. v. Fibre Glass-Evercoat Co.*, 812 F.2d 1381, 1 USPQ2d 1971 (Fed. Cir. 1987); *Litton Indus. Prods., Inc. v. Solid State Sys. Corp.*, 755 F.2d 158, 225 USPQ 34 (Fed. Cir. 1985).

[153]*American Hoist & Derrick Co. v. Sowa & Sons, Inc.*, 725 F.2d 1350, 220 USPQ 763 (Fed. Cir. 1984).

[154]*Allen Archery, Inc. v. Browning Mfg. Co.*, 819 F.2d 1087, 2 USPQ2d 1490 (Fed. Cir. 1987).

[155]*American Hoist & Derrick Co. v. Sowa & Sons, Inc.*, 725 F.2d 1350, 220 USPQ 763 (Fed. Cir. 1984).

of inequitable conduct. Moreover, unlike a finding of inequitable conduct, a finding of *Walker Process* fraud may not be based upon an equitable balancing of lesser degrees of materiality and intent. Rather, it must be based on independent and clear evidence of deceptive intent together with a clear showing of reliance, i.e., that the patent would not have issued but for the misrepresentation or omission.[156] The distinction between inequitable conduct that can lead to a declaration of patent unenforceability and fraud that can lead to antitrust damages is similar to raising a shield as distinguished from unsheathing a sword. Thus, a party that fails to establish inequitable conduct can hardly expect to prevail on a *Walker Process* claim.[157] In short, *Walker Process* fraud is a more serious offense than inequitable conduct.[158]

An assertion of a patent through trial and appeal does not constitute a "continuing violation," in the context of a *Walker Process* antitrust claim, for purposes of the antitrust statute of limitations. The initiation of the lawsuit or other enforcement proceeding is the final, immutable act in the violation, and the statute begins to run at that point.[159]

---

[156]*Nobelpharma AB v. Implant Innovations Inc.*, 141 F.3d 1059, 46 USPQ2d 1097 (Fed. Cir. 1998). See also *C.R. Bard Inc. v. M3 Sys. Inc.*, 157 F.3d 1340, 48 USPQ2d 1225 (Fed. Cir. 1998); *Argus Chem. Corp. v. Fibre Glass-Evercoat Co.*, 812 F.2d 1381, 1 USPQ2d 1971 (Fed. Cir. 1987); *Litton Indus. Prods., Inc. v. Solid State Sys. Corp.*, 755 F.2d 158, 225 USPQ 34 (Fed. Cir. 1985); *American Hoist & Derrick Co. v. Sowa & Sons, Inc.*, 725 F.2d 1350, 220 USPQ 763 (Fed. Cir. 1984).

[157]*FMC Corp. v. Manitowoc Co.*, 835 F.2d 1411, 5 USPQ2d 1112 (Fed. Cir. 1987). An extremely high level of misconduct, actual fraud, is necessary to sustain a *Walker Process* antitrust claim. When a party seeks to collect monetary damages from a patentee because of alleged violations of the antitrust laws, it is appropriate to require a higher degree of misconduct for that damage award than when a party asserts only a defense against an infringement claim. *Hewlett-Packard Co. v. Bausch & Lomb, Inc.*, 882 F.2d 1556, 11 USPQ2d 1750 (Fed. Cir. 1989). Inequitable conduct may render a patent unenforceable, but it differs from the "fraud" required to support a *Walker Process* type antitrust claim. *FMC Corp. v. Hennessy Indus., Inc.*, 836 F.2d 521, 5 USPQ2d 1272 (Fed. Cir. 1987).

[158]*Nobelpharma AB v. Implant Innovations Inc.*, 141 F.3d 1059, 46 USPQ2d 1097 (Fed. Cir. 1998). Inequitable conduct is a broader, more inclusive concept than the common law fraud needed to support a *Walker Process* claim. Inequitable conduct is a lesser offense than common law fraud, and includes types of conduct less serious than knowing and willful fraud. Inequitable conduct is thus an equitable defense in a patent infringement action and serves as a shield, while a more serious finding of fraud potentially exposes a patentee to antitrust liability and thus serves as a sword. Antitrust liability can include treble damages. In contrast, the remedies for inequitable conduct, while serious enough, only include unenforceability of the affected patent or patents and possible attorney fees. *Id.*

[159]*Korody-Colyer Corp. v. General Motors Corp.*, 828 F.2d 1572, 4 USPQ2d 1203 (Fed. Cir. 1987). This case contains some interesting sidelights. The antitrust claimant argued that Rule 11, FRCP, prohibited it from having pled the *Walker Process* claim earlier, without more information. The argument was rejected, but it could have validity under certain circumstances. The claimant also argued that there was "relation back" of the *Walker Process* claim to an earlier pleaded tying claim. This argument was rejected on the ground that the original tying pleading did not give adequate notice of the *Walker Process* claim under Rule 15(c), FRCP. Ninth Circuit law was applied.

(e) Patent Misuse

The enforceability of restrictions on the use of patented goods derives from the patent grant, which is in classical terms of property, the right to exclude. This right to exclude may be waived in whole or in part. The conditions of such waiver are subject to patent, contract, antitrust, and any other applicable law, as well as equitable considerations such as are reflected in the law of patent misuse. As in other areas of commerce, private parties may contract as they choose, provided that no law is violated thereby. The concept of patent misuse arose to restrain practices that did not in themselves violate any law, but that drew anticompetitive strength from the patent right, and thus were deemed to be contrary to public policy. The policy purpose was to prevent a patentee from using the patent to obtain market benefit beyond that which inheres in the statutory patent right.[160] The defense of patent misuse arises from the equitable doctrine of unclean hands, and relates generally to the use of patent rights to obtain or to coerce an unfair commercial advantage. Patent misuse relates primarily to a patentee's actions that affect competition in unpatented goods or that otherwise extend the economic effect beyond the scope of the patent grant. Patent misuse is viewed as a broader wrong than antitrust violation because of the economic power that may be derived from the patentee's right to exclude. Thus misuse may arise when the conditions of antitrust violation are not met. The key inquiry is whether, by imposing conditions that derive their force from the patent, the patentee has impermissibly broadened the scope of the patent grant with anticompetitive effect. Although the defense of patent misuse indeed evolved to protect against "wrongful" use of patents, the catalog of practices labeled "patent misuse" does not include a general notion of "wrongful" use. In application, the doctrine has largely been confined to a handful of specific practices. Although the law should not condone wrongful commercial activity, the body of misuse law and precedent need not be enlarged into an open-ended pitfall for patent-supported commerce.[161]

Thus, patent misuse is an affirmative defense to an accusation of patent infringement, the successful assertion of which requires that the alleged infringer show that the patentee has impermissibly broadened the physical or temporal scope of the patent grant with anticompetitive effect. The courts have identified certain specific practices as constituting per se patent misuse, including so-called tying arrangements in which a patentee conditions a license under the patent on the purchase of a separable, staple good, and arrangements in which a patentee effectively extends the term of its patent by requiring postexpiration royalties. Congress, however, has established that other specific practices may not support a finding of patent

---

[160] *Mallinckrodt, Inc. v. Medipart, Inc.,* 976 F.2d 700, 24 USPQ2d 1173 (Fed. Cir. 1992).

[161] *C.R. Bard Inc. v. M3 Sys. Inc.,* 157 F.3d 1340, 48 USPQ2d 1225 (Fed. Cir. 1998). The patent misuse doctrine, born from the equitable doctrine of unclean hands, is a method of

misuse. A 1988 amendment to 35 U.S.C. §271(d) provides that, in the absence of market power, even a tying arrangement does not constitute patent misuse. When a practice alleged to constitute patent misuse is neither per se patent misuse nor specifically excluded from a misuse analysis by §271(d), a court must determine if that practice is reasonably within the patent grant, i.e., that it relates to subject matter within the scope of the patent claims. If so, the practice does not have the effect of broadening the scope of the patent claims and thus cannot constitute patent misuse. If, on the other hand, the practice has the effect of extending the patentee's statutory rights and does so with an anticompetitive effect, that practice must then be analyzed in accordance with the rule of reason. Under the rule of reason, the finder of fact must decide whether the questioned practice imposes an unreasonable restraint on competition, taking into account a variety of factors, including specific information about the relevant business, its condition before and after the restraint was imposed, and the restraint's history, nature, and effect.[162]

As a general matter, an unconditional sale of a patented device exhausts the patentee's right to control the purchaser's use of the device thereafter. The theory behind this rule is that in such a transaction, the patentee has bargained for, and received, an amount equal to the full value of the goods. This exhaustion doctrine, however, does not apply to an expressly conditional sale or license. In such a transaction, it is more reasonable to infer that the parties negotiated a price that reflects only the value of the "use" rights conferred by the patentee. As a result, express conditions accompanying the sale or license of a patented product are generally upheld. Such conditions,

---

limiting abuse of patent rights separate from the antitrust laws. *B. Braun Med., Inc. v. Abbott Labs.*, 124 F.3d 1419, 43 USPQ2d 1896 (Fed. Cir. 1997).

[162]*Virginia Panel Corp. v. MAC Panel Co.*, 133 F.3d 860, 45 USPQ2d 1225 (Fed. Cir. 1997). Threats to void or limit warranties do not constitute use of a patent to control unpatented products. Voiding a warranty is not use of a patent at all. In addition, voiding a warranty on a product already sold, while possibly a breach of warranty, cannot be a tying arrangement because the purchaser is not deciding whether to buy a product. As for future sales, the threat is not to refuse to license, but only to limit a warranty, which is a matter of contract law between buyer and seller having no misuse implications. Moreover, threats to limit or void warranties presumably reflect a patentee's unwillingness to extend free repair or replacement services to usage of its product that it cannot control. Also, truncated negotiations that might have resulted in a license agreement requiring the licensee to purchase unpatented, staple goods, do not constitute patent misuse. *Id.* The contributory infringement and misuse inquiries, although intertwined, require analysis of the actions of different entities. In considering a plaintiff's claim of contributory infringement under §271(c), a court must review the defendant's acts. In considering a defense of patent misuse, a court must review the plaintiff's actions in light of §271(d). Here the patent claimed a method of desensitizing teeth by applying potassium nitrate. The accused infringer sold toothpaste containing potassium nitrate and argued that an attempt to prohibit sale of the toothpaste was tantamount to prohibiting the sale of potassium nitrate. The court held that the proper focus is on the composition as a whole, which may be far different from individual ingredients. For example, it might be shown at trial that the toothpaste containing potassium nitrate was especially made and sold for an infringing use and had a far narrower range of noninfringing uses, if any, than potassium nitrate or pure toothpaste alone. On the other hand, it might be shown that the accused composition has a "substantial" noninfringing use on teeth that do not need desensitizing. *Hodosh v. Block Drug Co.*, 833 F.2d 1575, 4 USPQ2d 1935 (Fed. Cir. 1987).

however, are contractual in nature and are subject to antitrust, patent, contract, and any other applicable law, as well as equitable considerations such as misuse. Accordingly, conditions that violate some law or equitable consideration are unenforceable. On the other hand, violation of valid conditions entitles the patentee to a remedy for either patent infringement or breach of contract. The key inquiry is whether, by imposing the condition, the patentee has impermissibly broadened the physical or temporal scope of the patent grant with anticompetitive effect. Two common examples of such impermissible broadening are using a patent that enjoys market power (in this connection, see 35 U.S.C. §271(d)(5), which permits such restrictions where the patent does not confer market power) in the relevant market to restrain competition in an unpatented product, and employing the patent beyond its statutory term. In contrast, field of use restrictions are generally upheld, and any anticompetitive effects they may cause are reviewed in accordance with the rule of reason.[163]

That a patent owner sends infringement notices to various government contractors, even notices that threaten suit and injunctions, does not indicate that it is attempting to broaden its patent monopoly. A patentee must be allowed to make its rights known to a potential infringer so that the latter can determine whether to cease its allegedly infringing activities, negotiate a license if one is offered, or decide to run the risk of liability and the imposition of an injunction.[164]

---

[163]*B. Braun Med., Inc. v. Abbott Labs.*, 124 F.3d 1419, 43 USPQ2d 1896 (Fed. Cir. 1997). In *Mallinckrodt, Inc. v. Medipart, Inc.*, 976 F.2d 700, 24 USPQ2d 1173 (Fed. Cir. 1992), the patented invention was a medical treatment device that the patentee sold under a "label license" that specified a single use (i.e., disposable) only. The district court felt that any postsale restriction was invalid as a misuse and, accordingly, granted summary judgment of noninfringement in favor of the defendant, who reconditioned the devices for a second use by the original purchaser. The Federal Circuit remanded for a determination of whether the postsale restriction was reasonably within the patent grant, or whether the patentee had ventured beyond it into behavior having an anticompetitive effect not justifiable under the rule of reason. The Federal Circuit reasoned that, if the restriction to a single use were found permissible, then the reconditioning, whether or not reconstruction, would amount to infringement, on the basis of the traditional rule that even repair of an unlicensed device constitutes infringement. On the other hand, even an unconditioned sale of a patented device is subject to the prohibition against reconstruction of the thing patented. The court also observed that, in judging the validity of a postsale restriction, it is unimportant whether the purchaser acquires the patented device directly from the patentee, or from a licensee.

[164]*Virginia Panel Corp. v. MAC Panel Co.*, 133 F.3d 860, 45 USPQ2d 1225 (Fed. Cir. 1997). This applies even to warning a company that, at least in its role as a supplier to the United States, could not be subject to liability or enjoined from practicing the claimed invention. While 28 U.S.C. §1498 clearly restricts a patentee's remedies against government contractors' infringing acts, it does not make those acts noninfringing and it certainly does not prohibit the sending of infringement notices to government contractors. The statute only provides an affirmative defense for applicable government contractors by establishing that, as to goods "used or manufactured by or for the United States," the contractor will not be liable for its infringing acts. Moreover, the Federal Acquisition Regulations (FAR) explicitly contemplate that patentees will send infringement notices directly to contractors. The FAR provisions, which impose contractual obligations on government contractors, instruct contractors to notify their respective contracting officers promptly and in reasonable detail of each notice or claim of patent infringement based on the performance of the contract. Furthermore, even if a jury should conclude that the patent owner attempted to extend the remedial scope of its patents by sending infringement notices where no injunction could be obtained, such conduct did not

Royalties may be based on unpatented components if that provides a convenient means for measuring the value of the license.[165] The court has passed the question of whether it would be illegal as a misuse to license "repair" parts.[166]

The court has held clearly that a finding of patent misuse does not create entitlement to damages in favor of the accused infringer. Nor can the defense of misuse be converted to an affirmative claim for damages simply by pleading it as a declaratory judgment counterclaim.[167] A party that did not raise the issue of patent misuse in one action may raise that issue in another action based on a separate assertion of infringement, whether as a defense against the claim of infringement or in a request for declaratory relief.[168]

§11.4 Miscellaneous Litigation

(a) *District Court Review of the PTO*

(i) *Ex Parte Proceedings*

An applicant dissatisfied with a decision of the PTO Board has a choice, under 35 U.S.C. §145, of appealing to the Federal Circuit or bringing a civil action against the Commissioner in the District Court for the District of Columbia.[169] Such an action is one to set

---

violate the rule of reason. The patent owner could not have been certain that the allegedly infringing devices were only to be used by the government. *Id.*

[165]*Engel Indus., Inc. v. Lockformer Co.*, 96 F.3d 1398, 40 USPQ2d 1161 (Fed. Cir. 1996). The court does suggest, however, that such a provision must be voluntary.

[166]*Allen Archery, Inc. v. Browning Mfg. Co.*, 819 F.2d 1087, 2 USPQ2d 1490 (Fed. Cir. 1987). The license agreement indicated that no royalty was to be paid on repair parts, and the lower court found that acceptance of royalty on such parts was the result of mistake and an inability to differentiate between repair and reconstruction parts in the context of the patented combination.

[167]*B. Braun Med., Inc. v. Abbott Labs.*, 124 F.3d 1419, 43 USPQ2d 1896 (Fed. Cir. 1997). However, the court did hint that a district court, in its discretion, might use the "other and further relief" provision of 28 U.S.C. §2202 to permit an accused infringer to assert an affirmative claim for damages based upon the same operative facts that would underlie a misuse defense, e.g., as an antitrust claim or a breach of contract theory. *Id.* Violation of the antitrust laws, in this case §2 of the Sherman Act, requires more exacting proof than suffices to demonstrate patent misuse. For example, violation of the antitrust laws always requires an intent to monopolize, market power in a defined relevant market (which may be broader than that defined by the patent), and damages attributable to the conduct asserted to be in violation of the antitrust laws. Certainly conduct that is insufficient to support a misuse defense cannot support an otherwise flawed antitrust judgment. Where the conduct underlying the allegations of misuse does not amount to patent misuse, the same conduct cannot support a judgment that it violated the Sherman Act. *Virginia Panel Corp. v. MAC Panel Co.*, 133 F.3d 860, 45 USPQ2d 1225 (Fed. Cir. 1997).

[168]*Glitsch Inc. v. Koch Eng'g Co.*, 216 F.3d 1382, 55 USPQ2d 1374, 1377 (Fed. Cir. 2000).

[169]*Abbott Labs. v. Brennan*, 952 F.2d 1346, 21 USPQ2d 1192 (Fed. Cir. 1992). If the appeal is by a party to an interference, it can be brought in any district court having venue and personal jurisdiction. 35 U.S.C. §146. The Federal Circuit has exclusive jurisdiction over appeals in these actions by virtue of 28 U.S.C. §1295(a)(4)(C). See §16.1(e). When judgment is taken against both parties, and each pursues a different route of review, interesting jurisdictional

aside or overturn the Board's decision. The district court should apply the clearly erroneous standard utilized by appellate courts. However, the standard must be adapted to permit introduction of additional evidence. The result is that even in the absence of additional evidence affecting a particular finding of the Board, it may be set aside by the district court if clearly erroneous. On the other hand, where new evidence is presented to the district court on a disputed fact question, a de novo finding will be necessary to take such evidence into account together with the evidence that was originally before the Board.[170]

An action under 35 U.S.C. §145 is in essence an action to set aside a decision of the Board and to resolve questions of patentability to the extent issues are raised at trial. But the district court lacks authority to direct the PTO to issue a patent. It matters not that additional evidence is permitted and that the district court may make de novo findings. It is presumed that the PTO will follow a proper order issued by that court and perform the duties imposed by statute. The district court may only authorize the PTO to issue a patent upon compliance with the requirements of law.[171]

While the evidentiary record before the Board serves as the evidentiary nucleus of the district court proceeding in a §145 action, the parties are entitled to submit additional evidence.[172] The district court in a §145 appeal has a powerful advantage over the Board and the examiner, because it hears and sees witnesses.[173] When additional evidence is adduced beyond that before the PTO the factual weight must be determined afresh. However, it is fruitless to suggest that the district court cannot reach a different conclusion on the same evidence that was before the PTO. The right to a fresh look by a court of general jurisdiction, upon refusal by the PTO to grant a patent, has long been established. The legislative purpose of §145 is de novo review.[174]

---

problems can arise. See *In re Van Geuns,* 946 F.2d 845, 20 USPQ2d 1291 (Fed. Cir. 1991). Note that the Commissioner may appeal an adverse decision of the District of Columbia District Court to the Federal Circuit. See *Unimed, Inc. v. Quigg,* 888 F.2d 826, 12 USPQ2d 1644 (Fed. Cir. 1989).

[170]*Fregeau v. Mossinghoff,* 776 F.2d 1034, 227 USPQ 848 (Fed. Cir. 1985). In an action under 35 U.S.C. §145, the district court can set aside the Board's fact findings only if they are clearly erroneous, but if new evidence is presented on a disputed question of fact, a de novo fact finding is made by the district court. Thus, although enablement is a question of law, where extensive additional evidence directed to the factual underpinnings of that question was presented to the district court, the Federal Circuit's review would be as for any bench trial: clear error in fact findings and error in law. *Gould v. Quigg,* 822 F.2d 1074, 3 USPQ2d 1302 (Fed. Cir. 1987). To the extent that these cases suggest use of the clearly erroneous standard, they should be carefully reevaluated in light of the Supreme Court decision in *Dickinson v. Zurko,* 527 U.S. 150, 50 USPQ2d 1930 (1999), *reversing In re Zurko,* 142 F.3d 1447, 46 USPQ2d 1691 (Fed. Cir. 1998). See §17.1(b).

[171]*Gould v. Quigg,* 822 F.2d 1074, 3 USPQ2d 1302 (Fed. Cir. 1987). See also *In re Wella A.G.,* 858 F.2d 725, 8 USPQ2d 1365 (Fed. Cir. 1988).

[172]*Gould v. Quigg,* 822 F.2d 1074, 3 USPQ2d 1302 (Fed. Cir. 1987).

[173]*Burlington Indus. Inc. v. Quigg,* 822 F.2d 1581, 3 USPQ2d 1436 (Fed. Cir. 1987).

[174]*Burlington Indus. Inc. v. Quigg,* 822 F.2d 1581, 3 USPQ2d 1436 (Fed. Cir. 1987).

Unless a party is prejudiced thereby or due process is denied, expeditious justice is better served by avoiding artificial restrictions on the district court's authority to resolve all issues reasonably raised in a §145 proceeding. Thus, while the Board will normally have decided every issue that is raised before the district court, the court is not required to obtain, or suspend all proceedings while the applicant obtains, a full administrative Board decision for every fresh aspect that arises during the course of the judicial proceeding.[175]

One who requests reexamination, other than the patentee, is not an applicant entitled to appeal under 35 U.S.C. §145. Thus, such a requester, even one who has intervened in a §145 action, has no independent statutory right to bring a §145 action.[176] When Congress added the reexamination mechanism in 1981, it did not amend the language of 35 U.S.C. §145 that provides that expenses of civil actions to review PTO proceedings "shall be paid by the applicant." Thus a §145 proceeding to review a reexamination carries a risk of an assessment of costs against the patent owner.[177]

(ii) Interference Proceedings

A party to an interference proceeding in the PTO may likewise appeal a Board decision directly to the Federal Circuit or, alternatively, may proceed to a district court under 35 U.S.C. §146 for a hybrid appeal/trial de novo in which the PTO record is admitted on motion of either party.[178] An appeal to the Federal Circuit must be

---

[175]*Newman v. Quigg,* 877 F.2d 1575, 11 USPQ2d 1340 (Fed. Cir. 1989).

[176]*Boeing Co. v. Commissioner of Patents,* 853 F.2d 878, 7 USPQ2d 1487 (Fed. Cir. 1988). The patentee and the PTO had jointly requested the district court to remand to the PTO, and the intervener/reexamination-requester was unhappy with this approach and attempted to appeal to the Federal Circuit. The appeal was dismissed for lack of standing.

[177]*Joy Tech., Inc. v. Manbeck,* 959 F.2d 226, 22 USPQ2d 1153 (Fed. Cir. 1992).

[178]*General Instr. Corp. v. Scientific-Atlanta, Inc.,* 995 F.2d 209 (Fed. Cir. 1993). See also *Case v. CPC Int'l,* 730 F.2d 745, 221 USPQ 196 (Fed. Cir. 1984). Parties to an interference dissatisfied with the PTO Board decision have a choice of appealing to the Federal Circuit under §141 or commencing a civil action in an appropriate district court under §146. In a direct appeal, the appellee is the PTO, while in a §146 action the other party to the interference is usually the defendant. *In re Van Geuns,* 946 F.2d 845, 20 USPQ2d 1291 (Fed. Cir. 1991). This case provides a good historical account of interference practice particularly in the context of review; it also gives some of the legislative history of the 1984 amendments that streamlined interference procedures. In *Rexam Indus. Corp. v. Eastman Kodak Co.,* 182 F.3d 1366, 51 USPQ2d 1457 (Fed. Cir. 1999), the court allowed a patent applicant that prevailed in an interference before the Board of Patent Appeals and Interferences based only on the constructive reduction to practice represented by its patent application, to continue to contest priority in a succeeding civil action under §146, notwithstanding the patent applicant's acquiescence, during pendency of that action, to entry of final judgment against it on priority grounds in another interference involving the same inventions but a different adversary. Priority issues that have been fully developed and presented to the Board for decision in interference proceedings should be decided by the Board even if a count is deemed unpatentable to one party. The fact that the issue comes before a district court in a §146 proceeding is of no moment, since such an action is derivative of the interference conducted in the PTO. Priority was at issue at the Board level; it can also be at the district court level. Issues properly raised at the Board are fair ground for litigation in the district court. The public interest in ensuring that only those patents that claim patentable subject matter are issued and maintained is best served when a district

dismissed if any adverse party to the interference files a timely notice of election to have all further proceedings conducted in a district court under §146. In that event, the appellant must then file a §146 action in order to obtain judicial review.[179]

A §146 action is derivative of the interference conducted in the PTO.[180] Under §146, the administrative record developed at the PTO may be admitted without prejudice to the right of the parties to take further testimony. But the right to offer new evidence is not unlimited. While the expression "de novo" is often used to describe a §146 action, the statute does not use that language or state that new issues can be freely raised. Rather, the district court is authorized on review to accept new testimony, but normally only as to issues raised by the parties during the proceedings below or by the Board's decision. In order for an issue to have been raised adequately so that it qualifies for consideration in a §146 proceeding, it should have been raised as specified in the PTO's interference rules. Failing that, the district court may exercise its discretion, but there must be some justification for admitting new evidence. Factors to be considered are due diligence or countervailing suppression, bad faith, or gross negligence on the part of the offering party, intervening changes in law, the insertion of a new issue or new evidence deserving of a response or further elaboration, etc. In short, the right to raise new issues in a §146 action is really limited to compelling circumstances.[181]

In an early decision,[182] the Federal Circuit left open three questions: (1) whether under some circumstances a district court may properly restrict the admission of testimony on an issue raised before the Board; (2) how one demonstrates that an issue has been raised before the Board in a manner sufficient to qualify it for testimonial admission in a §146 proceeding; and (3) whether a district court may admit testimony in a §146 proceeding on an issue concededly not raised in any fashion before the Board. More recently, the court has answered the second and third questions. Thus, as to the second, more is required than passing reference to the subject matter during

---

court considering review of a decision of the Board resolves all issues of priority and patentability that have been raised and fully developed.

[179]*Wu v. Wang*, 129 F.3d 1237, 44 USPQ2d 1641 (Fed. Cir. 1997). In this case the adverse party filed an election and then went ahead and filed its own §146 action in California. The appellant countered with a §146 action in the District of Columbia and moved the Federal Circuit to enjoin the adverse party from prosecuting the California action. The motion was granted, because it is the appellant that gets to choose the appropriate forum under §146. The court did indicate, however, that an appropriate transfer motion could be entertained by the District of Columbia court.

[180]*Rexam Indus. Corp. v. Eastman Kodak Co.*, 182 F.3d 1366, 51 USPQ2d 1457 (Fed. Cir. 1999).

[181]*Conservolite, Inc. v. Widmayer*, 21 F.3d 1098, 30 USPQ2d 1626 (Fed. Cir. 1994). Here the district court made a ruling in a §146 case that was tantamount to a holding that the parties were not claiming the same patentable invention. Inasmuch as this issue is at the very heart of an interference, it should have been raised in the PTO and could not be considered by the district court for the first time in a §146 appeal.

[182]*Case v. CPC Int'l*, 730 F.2d 745, 221 USPQ 196 (Fed. Cir. 1984).

the course of the interference proceeding. For the most part, parties should raise issues in the manner clearly specified in the PTO's interference regulations. Short of such compliance, issues may only be deemed raised for §146 purposes if the record clearly demonstrates that the issue was undeniably placed before the examiner-in-chief, and one or more parties insisted that the issue be resolved in the process of deciding which of the parties was entitled to priority. As to the third, the court simply noted that district court review of an interference under §146 was an equitable remedy of long standing. As such, the district court may, in appropriate circumstances, exercise its discretion and admit testimony on issues even though they were not raised before the Board.[183]

In any event, the court has held squarely that the admission of live testimony on all matters before the Board in a §146 action makes a fact finder of the district court and requires a de novo trial. Thus, although the live testimony before the district court might be the same as or similar to testimony before the Board in the form of affidavits and deposition transcripts, a district court should still make de novo factual findings, while treating the record before the Board when offered by a party as if it were originally taken and produced in the district court.[184]

(b) Interfering Patents

The rights to which one is entitled by ownership of a patent are principally the right to exclude others from making, using, and selling patented subject matter. The fact that the PTO issues patents to two parties on the same invention is a serious impediment to the enjoyment of this essential right to exclude. Neither patent owner knows if its patent is valid in light of the other's patent, the presumption of validity having been eroded by the grant of an interfering

---

[183]*General Instr. Corp. v. Scientific-Atlanta, Inc.*, 995 F.2d 209 (Fed. Cir. 1993). In order for an issue to have been raised adequately so that it qualifies for consideration in a §146 proceeding, it should have been raised as specified in the PTO's interference rules. Failing that, the district court may exercise its discretion, but there must be justification for admitting new evidence. In short, the right to raise new issues in a §146 action is limited to compelling circumstances. *Conservolite, Inc. v. Widmayer*, 21 F.3d 1098, 30 USPQ2d 1626 (Fed. Cir. 1994). The court listed factors to be considered: due diligence or countervailing suppressing, bad faith or gross negligence on the part of the offering party; intervening changes in law; the insertion of a new issue or new evidence deserving of a response or further elaboration; and other considerations. The issue in question was whether both parties were claiming the same patentable invention. The court held that inasmuch as this issue is at the very heart of an interference, it should have been raised in the PTO and could not be considered by the district court for the first time in a §146 appeal.

[184]*Winner Int'l Royalty Corp. v. Wang*, 202 F.3d 1340, 53 USPQ2d 1580 (Fed. Cir. 2000). It should be noted that the court qualified its holding by passing the question of whether the de novo standard would apply to issues that were not the subject of live testimony in the district court. It should also be noted that this decision does not squarely confront the impact that *Dickinson v. Zurko*, 527 U.S. 150, 50 USPQ2d 1930 (1999), may have as to issues that are not subject to de novo review. See also *In re Kotzab*, 217 F.3d 1365, 55 USPQ2d 1313 (Fed. Cir. 2000).

patent. One owner has a patent that it will lose if asserted against third parties, thereby incurring for itself, the accused infringer, and the public unneeded expense. The other has to assert or defend its patent before its presumption of validity, at least regarding priority of invention, is meaningful. Section 291 provides a means for resolving the contested issue of priority of invention solely between two patent owners, without involving third parties.[185]

Occasionally, despite the best efforts of the PTO, two patents with interfering claims are issued. Under 35 U.S.C. §291, the owner of such a patent may have relief against the owner of another by civil action. Interference is a jurisdictional requirement for a §291 action, and if a party cures the interference by filing a disclaimer of the interfering claims, the district court lacks power to proceed further.[186] Section 291 gives patent owners a separate and distinct basis of jurisdiction if two patents interfere. In such situations, validity, priority, and related issues have a source of jurisdiction under §291 distinct from that of an infringement action under 35 U.S.C. §271.[187]

Interfering patents are not patents that are or may be infringed by the same device; they are patents that claim the same subject matter. It is thus correct, and necessary, to compare claims, not disclosures, when comparing issued patents under 35 U.S.C. §291. It is not the district court's responsibility to determine, from the respective specifications, whether interfering claims could have been granted in each patent. The threshold issue under §291 is whether the patents contain claims to the same subject matter.[188]

In an interesting case, interfering patents issued on the same day, and the owner of the first filed instigated reexamination of the second filed. The PTO rejected the second as anticipated by the first, and refused to permit the owner of the second to swear behind the first, citing MPEP §706.02(b)(4). The owner of the second brought an interfering patents suit under §291. The owner of the first filed moved to stay pending the outcome of reexamination, and the trial court granted the stay. The stay was reversed by the Federal Circuit. The stay was improper because a foreseeable consequence of staying the interfering patents suit in favor of the reexamination proceedings

---

[185]*Kimberly-Clark Corp. v. Procter & Gamble Distrib. Co.,* 973 F.2d 911, 23 USPQ2d 1921 (Fed. Cir. 1992).

[186]*Albert v. Kevex Corp.,* 729 F.2d 757, 221 USPQ 202 (Fed. Cir. 1984).

[187]*Kimberly-Clark Corp. v. Procter & Gamble Distrib. Co.,* 973 F.2d 911, 23 USPQ2d 1921 (Fed. Cir. 1992). Were it not so, §291 would be redundant with §271, inasmuch as a party could always assert prior invention as a defense under 35 U.S.C. §102(g). *Id.*

[188]*Advance Transformer Co. v. Levinson,* 837 F.2d 1081, 5 USPQ2d 1600 (Fed. Cir. 1988). As a guide to determining whether the claimed subject matter is the same, the district court did not err in looking at whether the claims cross-read on the disclosure of the other's patent and thus whether each patentee could have made, based on his or her own disclosure, the claims that were granted to the other. Also, although it cannot be a controlling factor, the fact that the party seeking a declaration of interfering patents made no attempt to provoke an interference during the pendency of his or her application, and the fact that the PTO declared no interference, are factors to be considered as evidence of an absence of identity of the claimed inventions. *Id.*

was that the second filed owner would be unable to raise the issue of priority of invention in any forum. The principal point of contention was which party was the first to invent the subject matter claimed in the two patents. The issue of priority could not be determined by reexamination, which is an ex parte procedure with the limited focus of utilizing the expertise of the PTO to consider the effect of uncited prior art on the validity of a granted patent. Accordingly, if carried to completion, the reexamination proceeding would result in cancellation of the claims of the second filed patent in light of the first filed, without any exploration of which party was the first to invent the claimed subject matter. Because an interference in the PTO was unavailable, the second filed owner's only option was to institute an interfering patents suit under §291. An interfering patents suit allows the priority of invention issue to be litigated between two issued patents that claim identical subject matter. That purpose would be defeated if the party holding the patent with an earlier filing date could avoid a priority contest by requesting a reexamination of the patent with a later filing date and obtaining a stay of the interfering patents suit pending the outcome of the reexamination. For that reason, the district court should move forward with the interfering patents suit rather than staying the suit in favor of the PTO proceeding.[189]

In an inequitable conduct context, the court affirmed a finding of no intent to deceive where an attorney had apparently knowingly permitted an interfering patent to issue without advising the PTO.[190]

(c) Trade Secrets and Unfair Competition

(i) In General

The common law concept of unfair competition has not been codified to any rigid definition and encompasses a variety of types of commercial or business conduct considered "contrary to good conscience," including acts of trademark and trade dress infringement, false advertising, dilution, and trade secret theft. However, infringement of patent rights, domestic or foreign, is not generally recognized as coming within the rubric of unfair competition. Unfair competition law and patent law have long existed as distinct and independent bodies of law, each with different origins and each protecting different rights. The law of unfair competition generally protects consumers and competitors from deceptive or unethical conduct in commerce. Patent law, on the other hand, protects a patent owner from the

---

[189]*Slip Track Sys. Inc. v. Metal Lite Inc.,* 159 F.3d 1337, 48 USPQ2d 1055 (Fed. Cir. 1998).

[190]*Kimberly-Clark Corp. v. Procter & Gamble Distrib. Co.,* 973 F.2d 911, 23 USPQ2d 1921 (Fed. Cir. 1992).

unauthorized use by others of the patented invention, irrespective of whether deception or unfairness exists.[191]

A federal court is authorized under 28 U.S.C. §1338(b) to assume jurisdiction over a nonfederal unfair competition claim joined in the same case with a federal cause of action arising from U.S. patent, copyright, plant variety protection, or trademark laws; this is an effort by Congress to avoid piecemeal litigation. However, §1338(b) creates no substantive basis for a claim of unfair competition. Thus, an asserted claim of unfair competition that a plaintiff seeks to join with a related federal claim must find a substantive basis in some other, independent source of law.[192]

The Federal Circuit thus sometimes encounters state trade secret and unfair competition issues and even claims for relief as part of its work. It applies regional circuit law on unfair competition.[193] This will include the familiar concept that a federal district court must apply the choice of law rules of the state in which it sits.[194] There is no federal law of unfair competition.[195] Unfair competition and trademark infringement, like patent infringement, involve questions of fact reviewed under the clearly erroneous[196] or substantial evidence[197] standards. However, the determination of likelihood of confusion is the ultimate conclusion of law to be decided by the court and, as a result, a de novo standard of review is applicable.[198]

(ii) Federal/State and Federal/Federal Tensions

The distinction between the law of unfair competition and patent law is evident in the general statutory framework enacted by Congress. Whereas patent law is completely preempted by federal law,

---

[191]*Mars, Inc. v. Kabushiki-Kaisha Nippon Conlux*, 24 F.3d 1368, 30 USPQ2d 1621 (Fed. Cir. 1994).

[192]*Mars, Inc. v. Kabushiki-Kaisha Nippon Conlux*, 24 F.3d 1368, 30 USPQ2d 1621 (Fed. Cir. 1994). Whether or not an act constitutes the tort of unfair competition under §1338(b) is a question of law that the Federal Circuit reviews de novo. *Id.*

[193]*Jurgens v. McKasy*, 927 F.2d 1552, 18 USPQ2d 1031 (Fed. Cir. 1991); *Cicena Ltd. v. Columbia Tel. Group*, 900 F.2d 1546, 14 USPQ2d 1401 (Fed. Cir. 1990); *Power Controls Corp. v. Hybrinetics, Inc.*, 806 F.2d 234, 231 USPQ 774 (Fed. Cir. 1986). In deciding questions of false designation of origin under §43(a) of the Lanham Act, the court applies regional circuit law. *Al-Site Corp. v. VSI Int'l Inc.*, 174 F.3d 1308, 50 USPQ2d 1161 (Fed. Cir. 1999); *Keystone Ret. Wall Sys., Inc. v. Westrock, Inc.*, 997 F.2d 1444, 27 USPQ2d 1297 (Fed. Cir. 1993); *L.A. Gear, Inc. v. Thom McAn Shoe Co.*, 988 F.2d 1117, 25 USPQ2d 1913 (Fed. Cir. 1993); *Oakley, Inc. v. International Tropic-Cal, Inc.*, 923 F.2d 167, 17 USPQ2d 1401 (Fed. Cir. 1991).

[194]*Syntex Ophthalmics, Inc. v. Novicky*, 745 F.2d 1423, 223 USPQ 695 (Fed. Cir. 1984). Thus the Federal Circuit will discover and apply, as would the Seventh Circuit and a federal district court in Illinois, the Illinois rule that an action based upon misappropriation of proprietary information or trade secrets is governed by the law of the place where the alleged wrong was committed or the wrongful benefit obtained. *Id.*

[195]*Water Techs. Corp. v. Calco, Ltd.*, 850 F.2d 660, 7 USPQ2d 1097 (Fed. Cir. 1988).

[196]*Charles Greiner & Co. v. Mari-Med Mfg., Inc.*, 962 F.2d 1031, 22 USPQ2d 1526 (Fed. Cir. 1992).

[197]*Braun Inc. v. Dynamics Corp.*, 975 F.2d 815, 24 USPQ2d 1121 (Fed. Cir. 1992).

[198]*Braun Inc. v. Dynamics Corp.*, 975 F.2d 815, 24 USPQ2d 1121 (Fed. Cir. 1992).

the law of unfair competition, despite some federal encroachment, remains largely free from federal exclusivity.[199] The topic of federal preemption of state law is discussed in detail in §1.4(c).

Federal statutes provide very narrow grounds for relief from unfair competition. For example, §43(a) of the Lanham Act, 15 U.S.C. §1125(a), is effective generally in the area of protection of trade identity and false advertising. In the area of international trade, under 19 U.S.C. §1337(a), U.S. companies are protected from "unfair methods of competition" in the importation of goods.[200]

Patent infringement is not the unfair competition envisaged in §43(a) of the Lanham Act.[201] But a distinct cause of action for unfair competition may arise in a factual context that also gives rise to a patent infringement claim.[202] The fact that certain conduct is actionable under one federal law, and, in conjunction with other additional conduct, is also actionable under another federal law, does not, without more, create an impermissible conflict between the federal acts. To the contrary, the overriding principle for resolving apparent conflicts among federal laws is to give appropriate effect to each.[203] In determining whether patent law conflicts with rights created by other federal laws, the Federal Circuit applies its own law rather than that of the regional circuit.[204]

For example, the privileged right of a patentee to notify the public of its patent rights is statutorily rooted in the patent laws at 35 U.S.C. §287, which authorizes patentholders to "give notice to the public" of a patent by marking its patented articles and makes marking or specific notice to the accused infringer a prerequisite to the recovery of damages. Principles for resolving conflict among federal acts require recognition of this precept of patent law. Accordingly, before a patentee may be held liable under §43(a) of the Lanham Act for marketplace activity in support of its patent, and thus be deprived of the right to make statements about potential infringement of its patent, the marketplace activity must have been undertaken in bad faith. This prerequisite is a function of the interaction between the Lanham Act and patent law, and is in addition to the elements required by §43(a) itself, as §43(a) alone does not require bad faith. Adding a bad faith requirement to a §43(a) claim in this context gives effect both to the

---

[199]*Mars, Inc. v. Kabushiki-Kaisha Nippon Conlux*, 24 F.3d 1368, 30 USPQ2d 1621 (Fed. Cir. 1994).

[200]*Water Techs. Corp. v. Calco, Ltd.*, 850 F.2d 660, 7 USPQ2d 1097 (Fed. Cir. 1988).

[201]See *CPG Prods. Corp. v. Pegasus Luggage, Inc.*, 776 F.2d 1007, 227 USPQ 497 (Fed. Cir. 1985). Patent infringement per se does not give rise to an action for unfair competition. *S. Bravo Sys., Inc. v. Containment Tech. Corp.*, 96 F.3d 1372, 40 USPQ2d 1140 (Fed. Cir. 1996).

[202]*Water Techs. Corp. v. Calco, Ltd.*, 850 F.2d 660, 7 USPQ2d 1097, 1105 (Fed. Cir. 1988).

[203]*Zenith Elec. Corp. v. Exzec Inc.*, 182 F.3d 1340, 51 USPQ2d 1337 (Fed. Cir. 1999). For example, the gravamen of a Lanham Act §43(a) claim is marketplace misconduct, whereas that of an antitrust claim based upon a bad faith infringement suit or a *Walker Process* theory is abuse of the administrative and judicial process. *Id.*

[204]*Midwest Indus. Inc. v. Karavan Trailers Inc.*, 175 F.3d 1356, 50 USPQ2d 1672 (Fed. Cir. 1999).

rights of patentees as protected by the patent laws under ordinary circumstances, and to the salutary purposes of the Lanham Act to promote fair competition in the marketplace. As thus understood, there is no conflict between the demands of the Lanham Act and the patent law, and a patentee is easily able to comply with both. Furthermore, patent law is not frustrated because bad faith marketplace statements concerning patents do not further the purposes of the patent law, namely, providing an incentive to invent, promoting the full disclosure of inventions, and ensuring that ideas in the public domain remain there. On the other hand, with respect to the Lanham Act, recognizing a §43(a) claim in this context will further its statutory purpose of preventing deception and unfair competition in the marketplace, and requiring bad faith will not unduly thwart that purpose. In sum, imposing §43(a) liability on a patentee for marketplace statements regarding infringement and scope of its patent, assuming such statements otherwise satisfy the elements of §43(a), does not impermissibly conflict with the patent laws as long as the statements are proven to have been made in bad faith.[205]

In the absence of special circumstances, it is not unfair competition to enforce a patent that is later held invalid.[206] Nor does obtaining a patent through inequitable conduct violate §43(a) of the Lanham Act. The established remedy for inequitable conduct is unenforceability of the patent. If a trial court considers that the case is an exceptional one, which is often found when the patent has been improperly procured, attorney fees can be awarded. Moreover, enforcement of a patent procured by fraud on the PTO may be violative of §2 of the Sherman Act provided the other elements necessary to a §2 case are present. Thus there are adequate remedies to deal with inequitable conduct when it is found. Resort to federal unfair competition law is not one of them.[207] The courts have the power to redress wrongful appropriation of intellectual property by decreeing a remedy of assignment.[208] A wrongfully obtained injunction is not a basis for an unfair competition claim, where the complainant let the injunction be entered by default.[209]

(iii) *Trade Secret Fundamentals*

The creator and builder of a machine that is not patented or otherwise divulged to the public has certain common law rights that

---

[205]*Zenith Elec. Corp. v. Exzec Inc.*, 182 F.3d 1340, 51 USPQ2d 1337 (Fed. Cir. 1999).

[206]*Concrete Unlimited Inc. v. Cementcraft, Inc.*, 776 F.2d 1537, 227 USPQ 784 (Fed. Cir. 1985).

[207]*Pro-Mold & Tool Co. v. Great Lakes Plastics, Inc.*, 75 F.3d 1568, 37 USPQ2d 1626 (Fed. Cir. 1996). The Federal Circuit does not defer to regional circuit law on this question. *Id.*

[208]*Richardson v. Suzuki Motor Co.*, 868 F.2d 1226, 9 USPQ2d 1913 (Fed. Cir. 1989). This is so even where the defendant has obtained a patent on an invention of the plaintiff, thus raising patent law questions of proper inventorship and perhaps even derivation under 35 U.S.C. §102(f).

[209]*Shelcore, Inc. v. Durham Indus., Inc.*, 745 F.2d 621, 223 USPQ 584 (Fed. Cir. 1984).

accompany ownership of tangible personal property. These include the right to possession of the idea and its physical embodiments, the right to limit disclosure to others, and the right to contract for the terms of use by others. The laws governing ownership and use of unpatented property and unpublished information thus derive from theories of property, adapted to achieve fairness in commercial relationships, and are rooted in the common law. The law governing protection of trade secrets has developed in this common law context. There has evolved a complex of equitable and legal criteria designed to balance the protection of proprietary information against the public interest in the free flow of ideas.[210]

In accordance with common law rights, and where no statute abrogates those rights, the creator of a device has the right to make, use, and sell it. The common law does not provide the right to exclude others, and absent the right to exclude that is granted by the patent statute, an inventor's recourse to the common law requires that the invention meet the criteria of secrecy as appropriate to the circumstances. The foundation of trade secret law is explained in the *Restatement* as intended to protect commercial information from competitors who do not know or use it.[211] Where an inventor creates, builds, and uses a device in a particular state, the trade secrets laws of that state apply.[212]

The first step in any trade secret analysis is a determination of whether any trade secrets exist. It is not enough to point to broad areas of technology and assert that something there must have been secret and misappropriated. Once it is determined that specific trade secrets were maintained in confidence, the next step is to determine whether any of them were misappropriated.[213] The court has rejected an argument, based upon the analogous context of patent priority contests, that a trade secret holder must corroborate the existence of a trade secret with evidence beyond the testimony of interested parties. Patent interference law is concerned with priority of invention and does not set the standard for detecting the existence of a trade secret. In a patent priority contest it is the timing of inventive activities and the diligence of a putative inventor that is in issue, not the existence of the invention itself. Rather than apply inapposite patent law requirements, the court looks to the trade secret law of the relevant state in misappropriation cases.[214]

Under Illinois law, the necessary factors for a valid trade secret claim are (1) legally cognizable trade secrets; (2) misappropriation of the secrets from within a confidential relationship; (3) disclosure in

---

[210]*Lariscey v. United States,* 949 F.2d 1137, 20 USPQ2d 1845 (Fed. Cir. 1991).

[211]*Lariscey v. United States,* 949 F.2d 1137, 20 USPQ2d 1845 (Fed. Cir. 1991).

[212]*Lariscey v. United States,* 949 F.2d 1137, 20 USPQ2d 1845 (Fed. Cir. 1991).

[213]*Roton Barrier, Inc. v. Stanley Works,* 79 F.3d 1112, 37 USPQ2d 1816 (Fed. Cir. 1996).

[214]*C&F Packing Co. v. IBP Inc.,* 224 F.3d 1296, 55 USPQ2d 1865 (Fed. Cir. 2000). This case provides a good summary of Illinois trade secret law.

breach of the relationship; and (4) profit from the disclosure. A trade secret is a secret plan or process, tool, mechanism, or compound known only to its owner and those employees to whom it is necessary to confide it.[215] To be a trade secret under Indiana law, information must be kept secret, and economic benefit must be derived from that secrecy.[216] Under California law, the burden of proof is on the plaintiff to prove that its information meets the legal requirements of a protectable trade secret. Knowhow, improvements, data, and information are, when subject to a confidential relationship, intellectual property in the eyes of the law and are protected in accordance with law. This in turn requires either a contractual covenant or a confidential relationship as a premise of relief. The fact that a defendant might have developed on its own the information it received from the plaintiff does not mean that the information cannot be protected as a trade secret. Slavish copying is not necessary for misappropriation of trade secrets, nor does improvement or modification necessarily avoid liability.[217]

Matters of broad public knowledge or of general knowledge in an industry cannot constitute confidential information or trade secrets.[218] Information disclosed in patents prior to any alleged acts of misappropriation cannot possibly be a trade secret.[219] A disclosure at a meeting attended by industry representatives constitutes public disclosure even though there was a proprietary notice on a brochure distributed at the meeting. The important factor is that there was no secrecy agreement. Such an agreement does not follow from the unilateral acts of one person. In the absence of warnings to keep the information secret, the nonexistence of a secrecy agreement can be implied.[220] On the other hand, a disclosure of secret information to a government agency that has a regulation indicating that such information will not be disclosed to others except for evaluation creates an implied contract not to disclose.[221]

In an interesting case involving an invention by a federal prison inmate, the court developed at some length the recognition that proprietary information may be divulged to others within a defined group, in an environment protected from competitors, under circumstances that recognize its proprietary status. The pertinent inquiry is whether the recipient of the information is fairly apprised that it is deemed proprietary. The creator of a prototype device does not forfeit the possibility of compensation simply by demonstration to or testing by

---

[215]*Syntex Ophthalmics, Inc. v. Novicky,* 745 F.2d 1423, 223 USPQ 695 (Fed. Cir. 1984).

[216]*American Standard, Inc. v. Pfizer, Inc.,* 828 F.2d 734, 3 USPQ2d 1817 (Fed. Cir. 1987).

[217]*Richardson v. Suzuki Motor Co.,* 868 F.2d 1226, 9 USPQ2d 1913 (Fed. Cir. 1989).

[218]*Litton Sys., Inc. v. Sundstrand Corp.,* 750 F.2d 952, 224 USPQ 252 (Fed. Cir. 1984).

[219]*Water Techs. Corp. v. Calco, Ltd.,* 850 F.2d 660, 7 USPQ2d 1097 (Fed. Cir. 1988).

[220]*Correge v. Murphy,* 705 F.2d 1326, 217 USPQ 753 (Fed. Cir. 1983).

[221]*Airborne Data, Inc. v. United States,* 702 F.2d 1350, 217 USPQ 297 (Fed. Cir. 1983).

the intended user. When property rights are at issue, the common law weighs heavily against forfeiture by implication.[222]

A misappropriator of trade secrets has no authorization to continue to reap the benefits of its wrongful acts. Thus, a successful plaintiff is entitled to an injunction against continuing use of trade secrets.[223] The burden on a movant for preliminary injunction in a trade secret case includes a showing of imminent irreparable injury that is real and concrete. This is a difficult burden if the movant cannot first show that there is a reasonable likelihood of success, i.e., that it has secrets that have been misappropriated.[224] In one case a divided court found no abuse of discretion in a denial of a preliminary injunction in a trade secret case. The majority, relying on broad discretion in the trial judge, cited (1) uncertainty as to sufficient secrecy measures, (2) delay in invoking legal proceedings, (3) no showing of irreparable harm, and (4) an insufficient showing of likelihood of success. It appeared there were many suppliers and customers familiar with the information.[225]

Under Illinois trade secret law, punitive damages are penal in nature and their purpose is to deter the defendant and others from committing the same offense in the future. Such damages should be allowed with caution and confined within narrow limits. Illinois courts have distinguished between motivation by malice and motivation by competition and have awarded punitive damages in the former situation but not in the latter. The same analysis holds for attorney fees under the Illinois Trade Secrets Act.[226] Also in Illinois, an injunction in a trade secret case must be limited to the approximate length of time necessary for the defendant to duplicate the trade secret by lawful means.[227] However, in an ITC proceeding, it may be proper to set the period as the length of time necessary to develop both the secret and nonsecret aspects of a process.[228]

A trade secret or other confidential research, development, or commercial information may be the subject of a protective order under Rule 26(c)(7), FRCP. One seeking a protective order under that rule must establish that the information sought is confidential.[229]

---

[222]*Lariscey v. United States,* 949 F.2d 1137, 20 USPQ2d 1845 (Fed. Cir. 1991).

[223]*Richardson v. Suzuki Motor Co.,* 868 F.2d 1226, 9 USPQ2d 1913 (Fed. Cir. 1989).

[224]*Litton Sys., Inc. v. Sundstrand Corp.,* 750 F.2d 952, 224 USPQ 252 (Fed. Cir. 1984).

[225]*Formax, Inc. v. Hostert,* 841 F.2d 388, 5 USPQ2d 1939 (Fed. Cir. 1988). The dissenter pointed to the narrowness of the remedy sought (injunction against use, not reverse engineering).

[226]*Roton Barrier, Inc. v. Stanley Works,* 79 F.3d 1112, 37 USPQ2d 1816 (Fed. Cir. 1996).

[227]*Syntex Ophthalmics, Inc. v. Novicky,* 745 F.2d 1423, 223 USPQ 695 (Fed. Cir. 1984). In *Roton Barrier, Inc. v. Stanley Works,* 79 F.3d 1112, 37 USPQ2d 1816 (Fed. Cir. 1996), the court vacated an injunction that was broad enough to prohibit lawful activity, such as buying and reselling products from third parties who had not been privy to the plaintiff's trade secrets. It also vacated another injunction that simply prohibited the dissemination or use of the plaintiff's trade secrets, without specifying what they were.

[228]*Viscofan, S.A. v. United States ITC,* 787 F.2d 544, 229 USPQ 118 (Fed. Cir. 1986).

[229]*American Standard, Inc. v. Pfizer, Inc.,* 828 F.2d 734, 3 USPQ2d 1817 (Fed. Cir. 1987).

It is clear that confidential business information is property and that defrauding one out of such property by theft of a business secret falls within the definition of fraud under the mail and wire fraud statutes. Thus, sending illegally obtained confidential information by mail or wires can fulfill certain elements of a RICO violation.[230]

An agreement whereunder an inventor agrees to facilitate a manufacturer's testing and evaluation of an invention is a routine commercial arrangement. It does not convert the inventor's work in adapting his or her invention to the manufacturer's product into the work of a hired technician whose work product is automatically owned by the manufacturer, unless the agreement so provides.[231]

(iv) Trade Dress Fundamentals

Section 43(a) of the Lanham Act creates a federal cause of action for trade dress infringement.[232] Nonetheless, because trade dress issues are not unique to the exclusive jurisdiction of the Federal Circuit, it defers to the law of the regional circuits.[233]

The protection of trade dress is of common law origin. It is based upon recognition that the packaging of goods can serve as an indicator of source, and that similar packaging may confuse, mislead, or deceive the consumer. Trade dress protection is not limited to the exterior packaging of a product, for the design of a product itself may function as its packaging, serving to distinguish it from other products, and hence be protectable trade dress under §43(a). Trade dress of a product involves the total image of a product and may include features such as size, shape, color or color combinations, texture, or graphics. Trade dress is viewed as the overall combination and arrangement of design elements into the total image by which the product is perceived by the consuming public. The protection of trade dress has been liberally construed, for trade dress associated with a product that has accumulated goodwill is almost always an important ingredient in the salability of the product.[234] Unlike patent rights, which arise at issuance of the patent, rights in trade dress arise when the overall appearance attains recognition and association among the relevant consumer group. Thus, the precise time at which trade dress rights accrue is uncertain. Trade dress rights are separate and distinct from patent

---

[230]*Formax, Inc. v. Hostert,* 841 F.2d 388, 5 USPQ2d 1939 (Fed. Cir. 1988). The court relied upon *Carpenter v. United States,* 484 U.S. 19 (1987), in which the Supreme Court held that an employee defrauded his employer, a financial newspaper, by stealing the content of his as yet unpublished comments on stock values and selling that information to parties not entitled to have it, using the mails or wires.

[231]*Richardson v. Suzuki Motor Co.,* 868 F.2d 1226, 9 USPQ2d 1913 (Fed. Cir. 1989). A finding of fraudulent inducement to reveal trade secrets can result in punitive damages. *Id.*

[232]*Elmer v. ICC Fabricating, Inc.,* 67 F.3d 1571, 36 USPQ2d 1417 (Fed. Cir. 1995); *Tone Bros., Inc. v. Sysco Corp.,* 28 F.3d 1192, 31 USPQ2d 1321 (Fed. Cir. 1994).

[233]*Elmer v. ICC Fabricating, Inc.,* 67 F.3d 1571, 36 USPQ2d 1417 (Fed. Cir. 1995).

[234]*L.A. Gear, Inc. v. Thom McAn Shoe Co.,* 988 F.2d 1117, 25 USPQ2d 1913 (Fed. Cir. 1993). See also *Elmer v. ICC Fabricating, Inc.,* 67 F.3d 1571, 36 USPQ2d 1417 (Fed. Cir. 1995).

rights in other ways as well. For example, the public interest element of trade dress law, which seeks to prevent consumer confusion over products with similar appearance, may lead a court to grant injunctive relief despite a plaintiff's delay in bringing suit.[235]

The court holds, in accordance with the Supreme Court's *Two Pesos* decision,[236] that if the trade dress at issue is inherently distinctive, the plaintiff need only show that purchasers are likely to confuse it with the allegedly imitating goods. It is not necessary to prove secondary meaning. As the Federal Circuit explains the matter, trademarks may be (1) generic, (2) descriptive, (3) suggestive, (4) arbitrary, or (5) fanciful. Under *Two Pesos,* the latter three categories of marks are deemed inherently distinctive. Consequently, a trade dress is inherently distinctive if it is suggestive, arbitrary, or fanciful; in other words, if it is brand identifying—capable of identifying products or services as coming from a specific source.[237]

To succeed on a claim of trade dress infringement a party must prove that its trade dress was inherently distinctive or has acquired secondary meaning, that the trade dress of its products and those of the alleged infringer were confusingly similar, and that the appropriated features of the trade dress were not primarily functional.[238] Thus, trade dress for which protection is sought under §43(a) of the Lanham Act must serve as an indication of origin or source, either by virtue of inherent distinctiveness or by secondary meaning acquired through use.[239]

Only nonfunctional product features may receive trade dress protection. Trademark or trade dress law may not be used to secure patent-like protection for useful product features. A product feature is functional, and cannot serve as a trademark, if it is essential to the use or purpose of the article or if it affects the cost or quality of the article, that is, if exclusive use of the feature would put competitors at a significant nonreputation-related disadvantage. Patent law, not

---

[235]*Gasser Chair Co. v. Infanti Chair Mfg. Corp.,* 60 F.3d 770, 34 USPQ2d 1822 (Fed. Cir. 1995). This discussion was in the context of laches and estoppel.

[236]*Two Pesos, Inc. v. Taco Cabana,* 112 S.Ct. 2753, 23 USPQ2d 1081 (1992).

[237]*Braun Inc. v. Dynamics Corp.,* 975 F.2d 815, 24 USPQ2d 1121 (Fed. Cir. 1992). See also *Tone Bros., Inc. v. Sysco Corp.*, 28 F.3d 1192, 31 USPQ2d 1321 (Fed. Cir. 1994); *Keystone Ret. Wall Sys., Inc. v. Westrock, Inc.*, 997 F.2d 1444, 27 USPQ2d 1297 (Fed. Cir. 1993); *L.A. Gear, Inc. v. Thom McAn Shoe Co.*, 988 F.2d 1117, 25 USPQ2d 1913 (Fed. Cir. 1993).

[238]*Elmer v. ICC Fabricating, Inc.,* 67 F.3d 1571, 36 USPQ2d 1417 (Fed. Cir. 1995); *General Electro Music Corp. v. Samick Music Corp.*, 19 F.3d 1405, 30 USPQ2d 1149 (Fed. Cir. 1994).

[239]*Keystone Ret. Wall Sys., Inc. v. Westrock, Inc.,* 997 F.2d 1444, 27 USPQ2d 1297 (Fed. Cir. 1993); *L.A. Gear, Inc. v. Thom McAn Shoe Co.*, 988 F.2d 1117, 25 USPQ2d 1913 (Fed. Cir. 1993). In the latter case, the court recognized that similarity in appearance alone cannot establish source confusion as a matter of law. The right to copy unpatented and uncopyrighted designs of articles has been reaffirmed by the Supreme Court (see §1.4(c); see also *Elmer v. ICC Fabricating, Inc.,* 67 F.3d 1571, 36 USPQ2d 1417 (Fed. Cir. 1995)). Thus, even distinctive product designs cannot be absolutely shielded from copying; under §43(a), likelihood of confusion must be shown. Nonetheless, under Second Circuit law, intentional copying of trade dress creates a presumption of confusing similarity. Thus the burden of avoiding confusion, and the burden of proving that confusion has been avoided, are on the copier. Here the court found clear error in the finding of likelihood of confusion because of the sophistication of the product

trade dress law, is the principal means for providing exclusive rights in useful product features. Extending trademark and trade dress law to protect functional features might create perpetual, patent-like rights in unpatented or unpatentable items.[240] If products having the same utility cannot be made without duplicating the design, the product design is deemed essential to the function and is not protectable as a matter of trade dress.[241] But trade dress protection, under the Lanham Act or state law, does not depend on whether a patent has been obtained for the product or feature in question. To be sure, statements in a patent may provide evidence that the asserted trade dress is functional, and thus not entitled to legal protection. But the fact that a patent has been acquired does not convert what otherwise would have been protected trade dress into nonprotected matter.[242] The regional circuits differ on where the burden lies with respect to functionality.[243]

The party attempting to prove secondary meaning has the burden by a preponderance. Secondary meaning is a term of art that denotes that there is an association formed in the minds of the consumers between the mark and source or origin of the product. Such an association is provided by a variety of direct and circumstantial evidence. Secondary meaning must be shown to have existed prior to the date on which the accused infringer commenced using a confusingly similar trade dress. Secondary meaning can be called "acquired distinctiveness" as opposed to inherent distinctiveness.[244]

Cases applying regional circuit law to various trade dress issues are collected in the note.[245]

---

purchasers, and the conspicuous and permanent placement of the parties' respective trademarks on the product.

[240]*Elmer v. ICC Fabricating, Inc.,* 67 F.3d 1571, 36 USPQ2d 1417 (Fed. Cir. 1995).

[241]*L.A. Gear, Inc. v. Thom McAn Shoe Co.,* 988 F.2d 1117, 25 USPQ2d 1913 (Fed. Cir. 1993). The court accepted the Second Circuit's disapproval of the doctrine of "aesthetic functionality," under which an ornamental design may be excluded from the protection of §43(a) when the design is an important ingredient in the commercial success of the product.

[242]*Midwest Indus. Inc. v. Karavan Trailers Inc.,* 175 F.3d 1356, 50 USPQ2d 1672 (Fed. Cir. 1999).

[243]*Elmer v. ICC Fabricating, Inc.,* 67 F.3d 1571, 36 USPQ2d 1417 (Fed. Cir. 1995) (burden of proving nonfunctionality on plaintiff under Eleventh Circuit law); *Keystone Ret. Wall Sys., Inc. v. Westrock, Inc.,* 997 F.2d 1444, 27 USPQ2d 1297 (Fed. Cir. 1993) (burden of proving nonfunctionality on plaintiff under Ninth Circuit law); *L.A. Gear, Inc. v. Thom McAn Shoe Co.,* 988 F.2d 1117, 25 USPQ2d 1913 (Fed. Cir. 1993) (functionality burden on party asserting defense under Second Circuit law).

[244]*Tone Bros., Inc. v. Sysco Corp.,* 28 F.3d 1192, 31 USPQ2d 1321 (Fed. Cir. 1994). The anonymous source rule states that a consumer need not know the identity of the single source, and that all that is necessary to establish secondary meaning is that the consumer associate the trade dress with a single, albeit anonymous, source. The rule is directed to the situation where a typical buyer would not know the corporate identity of the source. *Id.*

[245]*Midwest Indus. Inc. v. Karavan Trailers Inc.,* 175 F.3d 1356, 50 USPQ2d 1672 (Fed. Cir. 1999); *Al-Site Corp. v. VSI Int'l Inc.,* 174 F.3d 1308, 50 USPQ2d 1161 (Fed. Cir. 1999); *Continental Plastic Containers Inc. v. Owens-Brockway Plastic Prods. Inc.,* 141 F.3d 1073, 46 USPQ2d 1277 (Fed. Cir. 1998); *Imagineering, Inc. v. Van Klassens, Inc.,* 53 F.3d 1260, 34 USPQ2d 1526 (Fed. Cir. 1995); *Conopco, Inc. v. May Dep't Stores Co.,* 46 F.3d 1556, 32 USPQ2d

(d) Other Torts

RICO litigation. A RICO plaintiff must (under 18 U.S.C. §1964(c)) allege an injury to its business or property by reason of a violation of 18 U.S.C. §1962(b). The allegations of RICO violations must be pled with sufficient specificity so as to place the party being sued on notice of the issues involved in the suit.[246] A RICO plaintiff must demonstrate a "pattern of racketeering activity" consisting of at least two instances of racketeering activity. Mail and wire fraud both qualify as predicate acts under the federal RICO statute. Applying its own law, the Federal Circuit has held that inequitable conduct before the PTO cannot qualify as an act of mail fraud or wire fraud for purposes of the predicate act requirement. In the context of the mail fraud statutes, the words "to defraud" commonly refer to wronging one in property rights by dishonest methods or schemes and usually signify the deprivation of something of value by trick, deceit, chicane, or overreaching. Although a patent is property, protected against appropriation both by individuals and by government, an application that has not yet matured into a patent cannot properly be deemed government property.[247]

The courts of appeals are divided as to when a civil RICO cause of action accrues. The majority rule is that the statute begins to run when the plaintiff discovers, or reasonably should have discovered, the basis for its civil RICO claim. The minority rule is that the claim accrues as of the last predicate act. The Federal Circuit passed the question in one case by deciding that the plaintiff's claim was barred under either rule.[248]

Tortious interference. The premise of a state action for tortious interference with contractual relations is that the wrongdoer intentionally induced or otherwise caused a third party not to enter into or continue a business relation with the plaintiff. Customers are wont to negotiate for the most favorable terms, and a potential customer is

---

1225 (Fed. Cir. 1994); *Jurgens v. McKasy,* 927 F.2d 1552, 18 USPQ2d 1031 (Fed. Cir. 1991); *Oakley, Inc. v. International Tropic-Cal, Inc.,* 923 F.2d 167, 17 USPQ2d 1401 (Fed. Cir. 1991).

[246]*Formax, Inc. v. Hostert,* 841 F.2d 388, 5 USPQ2d 1939 (Fed. Cir. 1988) (Seventh Circuit law). An allegation that the defendant mailed misappropriated trade secret information to a series of customers on specific dates satisfies the requirement that the content of the communications and the scheme to defraud be listed in the complaint. *Id.* See note 11:230 and accompanying text.

[247]*Semiconductor Energy Lab. Co. v. Samsung Elec. Co.,* 204 F.3d 1368, 54 USPQ2d 1001 (Fed. Cir. 2000). In another RICO case a patentee claimed that the defendant was liable for the fact that a bankrupt subsidiary could not satisfy infringement damages. The court refused to overturn a directed verdict, holding that the patentee was required to prove by at least a preponderance of the evidence that the defendant had, through a pattern of racketeering activity, caused the infringer's inability to pay damages. *A. Stucki Co. v. Worthington Indus., Inc.,* 849 F.2d 593, 7 USPQ2d 1066 (Fed. Cir. 1988).

[248]*A. Stucki Co. v. Buckeye Steel Castings Co.,* 963 F.2d 360, 22 USPQ2d 1581 (Fed. Cir. 1992). The claim was grounded on an alleged "bankruptcy plot" to avoid payment of damages.

certainly not barred from negotiating with more than one supplier.[249] Under California law, the elements of intentional interference with contractual relations are: (1) a valid contract between the plaintiff and a third party; (2) the defendant's knowledge of this contract; (3) the defendant's intentional acts to induce a breach or disruption of the contractual relationship; and (4) resulting damage. The elements of intentional interference with prospective economic advantage are: (1) an economic relationship between the plaintiff and a third party with probability of ripening into a future economic benefit for the plaintiff; (2) knowledge of the defendant about this relationship; (3) intentional acts by the defendant to disrupt the relationship; (4) actual disruption of the relationship; and (5) damages proximately caused by the defendant's acts. These elements presuppose a colorable economic relationship between the plaintiff and a third party with the potential to develop into a full contractual relationship. Evidence of the prospective relationship need not take the form of an offer, but must specifically show the possibility of future economic association. The privilege of free competition may be an affirmative defense. But to invoke this privilege, a competitor may not use wrongful means.[250]

In one case a patentee had granted an exclusive license with no right to sublicense, and the licensee thereafter appointed an exclusive distributor and sold the licensed product to the distributor for resale. The patentee sued the distributor for tortious interference with contract, claiming that the arrangement amounted to a sublicense in violation of the agreement. The court held that the arrangement was not a sublicense and that therefore there could not have been any tortious interference with the agreement, because the agreement was not breached.[251] A supplier that resells patented and trademarked items that the patentee refused to accept and pay for was held not to have committed unfair competition or tortious interference with prospective business relations.[252]

Abuse of process. In *Abbott v. Brennan,*[253] the court held that a state tort action for abuse of process cannot be invoked as a remedy for inequitable or other unsavory conduct of parties to proceedings in the PTO. The patent grant is within the exclusive purview of federal law. Although certain traditional state law concerns may properly be raised when patent rights are litigated, the conduct of litigants in administrative proceedings before the PTO is not remediable by state

---

[249]*Xeta, Inc. v. Atex, Inc.,* 852 F.2d 1280, 7 USPQ2d 1471 (Fed. Cir. 1988) (New Hampshire law).

[250]*Litton Sys., Inc. v. Honeywell, Inc.,* 87 F.3d 1559, 39 USPQ2d 1321 (Fed. Cir. 1996). In *Additive Cont'l & Meas. Sys., Inc. v. Flowdata, Inc.,* 986 F.2d 476, 25 USPQ2d 1798 (Fed. Cir. 1993), the court considered the elements of a claim of business disparagement based upon accusations of patent infringement.

[251]*Unidisco, Inc. v. Schattner,* 824 F.2d 965, 3 USPQ2d 1439 (Fed. Cir. 1987).

[252]*McCoy v. Mitsuboshi Cutlery, Inc.,* 67 F.3d 917, 36 USPQ2d 1289 (Fed. Cir. 1995).

[253]*Abbott Labs. v. Brennan,* 952 F.2d 1346, 21 USPQ2d 1192 (Fed. Cir. 1992).

action in tort, unless it be shown that the entire federal agency action is a "sham." A contrary result would in effect create another forum for litigating issues arising from the administrative process, or a new system of judicial overview of actions before the PTO. This would not harmonize with the traditional judicial disfavor of collateral attack, under the common law, on proceedings before the PTO. Thus, the federal administrative process of examining and issuing patents, including proceedings before the PTO's boards, is not subject to collateral review in terms of the common law tort of abuse of process. The PTO procedures themselves provide a remedy for any malfeasance on the part of litigants, and an additional state action would be an inappropriate collateral intrusion on the regulatory procedures of the PTO under the guise of a complaint sounding in tort and contrary to the preemptive regulation in the area of patent law.[254]

Assertions of infringement. There is nothing improper about a patentee's attempting to enforce its rights under the patent by advising potential infringers of its good faith belief that a particular product infringes.[255] Communication to possible infringers concerning patent rights is not improper if the patent holder has a good faith belief in the accuracy of the communication. Although "bad faith" may encompass subjective as well as objective considerations, and the patent holder's notice is not irrelevant to a determination of bad faith, a competitive commercial purpose is not of itself improper, and bad faith is not supported when the information is objectively accurate. In general, a threshold showing of incorrectness or falsity, or disregard for either, is required in order to find bad faith in the communication of information about the existence or pendency of patent rights. Indeed, a patentee, acting in good faith on its belief as to the nature and scope of its rights, is fully permitted to press those rights even though it may misconceive what those rights are. It has long been recognized that patents would be of little value if infringers of them could not be notified of the consequences of infringement or proceeded against in the courts. Such action considered by itself cannot be said to be illegal. Thus federal authority makes clear that it is not improper for a

---

[254]The court has also held that a claim under the New Jersey RICO statute predicated upon inequitable conduct is preempted by the federal patent law. *Semiconductor Energy Lab. Co. v. Samsung Elec. Co.*, 204 F.3d 1368, 54 USPQ2d 1001 (Fed. Cir. 2000). In *University of Colorado Found. v. American Cyanamid Co.*, 196 F.3d 1366, 52 USPQ2d 1801 (Fed. Cir. 1999), the court held that a claim for fraudulent nondisclosure of a patent application was not preempted by federal law. In interesting dicta on the matter of potential damages, the court reasoned as follows: because the plaintiffs did not themselves try to patent the invention, there could be no damages due to loss of prestige in having the patent. Moreover, inasmuch as the plaintiffs intended to permit the defendant to make and use the invention, the only financial opportunity that was lost was the payment that the defendant would have needed to make to plaintiffs to get them to cooperate in obtaining the patent. As joint owners, the plaintiffs and the defendant would not have needed to account to one another. By the same token, this means that the plaintiffs could have licensed others. Thus, the proper measure of damage is what the defendant would have paid to the plaintiffs for an exclusive license or assignment.

[255]*Scosche Indus., Inc. v. Visor Gear, Inc.*, 121 F.3d 675, 43 USPQ2d 1659 (Fed. Cir. 1997).

patent owner to advise possible infringers of its belief that a particular product may infringe the patent. A patentee has the right to inform a potential infringer of the existence of the patent, whereby the recipient of the information may adjust its activities, perhaps seek a license, or otherwise act to protect itself. The statute contemplates such notice. Federal law has uniformly upheld a patentee's right to publicize the issuance of patents and to so inform potential infringers. Indeed, judicially mandated silence would preserve the ignorance of potential infringers whose liability could build.[256]

In *Zenith v. Exzec,* the defendant brought Lanham Act §43(a) and state unfair competition counterclaims alleging that the plaintiff patentee made false representations of patent infringement and of defendant's inability to design around the patents. Under §43(a)(1)(B), the defendant would have to allege and ultimately prove that: (1) the plaintiff made a false or misleading statement of fact in commercial advertising or promotion about the defendant's goods or services, (2) the statement actually deceived or was likely to deceive a substantial segment of the intended audience, (3) the deception was material in that it was likely to influence purchasing decisions, (4) the plaintiff caused the statement to enter interstate commerce, and (5) the statement resulted in actual or probable injury to the defendant. The court examined a line of decisions that had distinguished between false representations of infringement and false representations of inability to avoid infringement, and that had held only the latter circumstances would support a §43(a) claim. The court declined to draw that distinction, holding instead that both types of representations, if made in bad faith, can be reached by §43(a).[257]

(e) Copyright and Semiconductor Chip Protection

Copyrights are discussed in Chapter 1 in the context of legal concepts that are closely associated with patents. See §1.4(a). The Semiconductor Chip Protection Act is treated in Chapter 2 in contrast with related but patentable subject matter. See §2.2(d).

§11.5 Alternative Dispute Resolution

In view of a 1982 amendment to the patent statute, the court may see more issues arising in the context of arbitration. Under 35

---

[256]*Mikohn Gaming Corp. v. Acres Gaming Inc.,* 165 F.3d 891, 49 USPQ2d 1308 (Fed. Cir. 1998).

[257]*Zenith Elec. Corp. v. Exzec Inc.,* 182 F.3d 1340, 51 USPQ2d 1337 (Fed. Cir. 1999). Exactly what constitutes bad faith remains to be determined on a case-by-case basis. Obviously, if the patentee knows that the patent is invalid, unenforceable, or not infringed, yet represents to the marketplace that a competitor is infringing the patent, a clear case of bad faith representations is made out. Furthermore, statements to the effect that a competitor is incapable of

U.S.C. §294, a voluntary arbitration clause in a patent license or other patent agreement is valid, irrevocable, and enforceable. Such procedures are to be governed by Title 9 of the United States Code.

It is clear that §294, which authorizes enforcement of agreements to arbitrate, cannot be relied upon to support the contention that a contract suit involving arbitration, during which issues of validity and infringement might be encountered, is one "arising under" the patent laws within the meaning of 28 U.S.C. §1338. That patent validity issues may have been injected during the course of an arbitration proceeding in a contract suit forms no basis for asserting that the district court's jurisdiction was based on §1338.[258]

In determining whether an issue is subject to arbitration, the court must determine whether the contracting parties agreed to arbitrate that dispute. The parties' intentions control, but those intentions are generously construed as to issues of arbitrability.[259] A total unilateral withholding of royalty might result in a waiver of the right to arbitrate under a patent license agreement; merely waiting until after the licensor files a complaint before requesting arbitration does not effect a waiver.[260] Despite a strong federal policy favoring arbitration of international transactions, an arbitration clause cannot justify termination of an ITC investigation before the public interest can be considered.[261]

There are cases in which application of collateral estoppel to an arbitrator's decision is justified. Though some courts have cited fairness as a criterion in deciding whether to apply collateral estoppel,

---

designing around the patent are inherently suspect. They are suspect not only because with sufficient effort it is likely that most patents can be designed around, but also because such a statement appears nearly impossible to confirm a priori. For these reasons, the bad faith element may be much easier to satisfy for statements of this type. *Id.*

[258]*Ballard Med. Prods. v. Wright*, 823 F.2d 527, 3 USPQ2d 1337 (Fed. Cir. 1987).

[259]*Rhone-Poulenc Spec. Ch. v. SCM Corp.*, 769 F.2d 1569, 226 USPQ 873 (Fed. Cir. 1985). Where a patent license clause said that any controversy arising out of the contract shall be settled by arbitration, it was clear error to hold that the parties did not intend patent infringement to be arbitrated. Determination of the scope and infringement of the patent is the quintessence of the agreement. *Id.* This case does not decide whether patent validity is arbitrable under such a provision, because the party moved only to arbitrate scope and infringement. In a later dictum, the Federal Circuit appears to have approved the concept that arbitrators in patent contract disputes have no roving commission to pass upon the validity of patents. It is likely that the parties to a contract must specifically place the issue of validity into arbitration. *Ballard Med. Prods. v. Wright*, 823 F.2d 527, 3 USPQ2d 1337, 1340 (Fed. Cir. 1987).

[260]*Rhone-Poulenc Spec. Ch. v. SCM Corp.*, 769 F.2d 1569, 226 USPQ 873 (Fed. Cir. 1985). The result could be different if the licensee first answers the complaint and then moves to stay pending arbitration. *Id.* In *Utter v. Hiraga*, 845 F.2d 993, 6 USPQ2d 1709 (Fed. Cir. 1988), an agreement provided that interference issues would be submitted to an arbitrator, whose decision would bind the parties "with no further right of appeal." The arbitrator was to decide disputed issues "unless the parties mutually agree otherwise in writing." Following the arbitrator's decision, the parties filed a stipulation with the PTO accepting the arbitrator's decision to refer certain issues to the PTO Board to enable the Board to make priority awards. A motion to dismiss an appeal from the ensuing Board decision was denied. There was no clear intent to waive the right to appeal from the Board's decision, and this was an appeal from the Board not the arbitrator. The stipulation constituted a written agreement that the arbitrator would not decide certain issues.

[261]*Farrel Corp. v. United States ITC*, 949 F.2d 1147, 20 USPQ2d 1912 (Fed. Cir. 1991).

it is not enough merely to label the application of collateral estoppel "unfair" because it follows procedures that may be different from those used before another adjudicating body. Unfairness sufficient to bar application of collateral estoppel requires a specific showing that the precise dispute was not fairly litigated and resolved before the arbitrator.[262] But the preclusive effect of prior arbitration awards is for individual resolution, absent a provision in the governing contract that requires earlier awards to bind subsequent arbitrators. In order for collateral estoppel to apply, it must be shown that the issue previously arbitrated is identical to the one now under arbitration. Courts should be careful not to judicialize the arbitration process. Arbitration normally envisions that each case be decided on its own under the controlling contract without undue reliance on other arbitration awards, even if the facts and circumstances are close. It is one thing to bind the parties by estoppel when the same facts have already been resolved by an earlier forum of competent authority. It is quite another to bind them when there is no precise correspondence of facts, circumstances, and timing.[263] In the absence of a specific contractual or statutory requirement, an arbitrator is under no duty to set out specific findings of fact to support an award.[264]

In an unusual case, the court affirmed the lower court's refusal to permit an accused patent infringer to intervene in an ADR proceeding between the patentee and another accused infringer.[265]

---

[262]*Kroeger v. United States Postal Serv.*, 865 F.2d 235 (Fed. Cir. 1988).

[263]*Gonce v. Veterans Admin.*, 872 F.2d 995 (Fed. Cir. 1989).

[264]*Gonce v. Veterans Admin.*, 872 F.2d 995 (Fed. Cir. 1989).

[265]*Haworth, Inc. v. Steelcase, Inc.*, 12 F.3d 1090, 29 USPQ2d 1368 (Fed. Cir. 1993).

IV

Remedies

12

Damages, Interest, and Costs

    A patentee has succeeded in persuading a judge or jury that its patent is valid and infringed and that it can enforce it against the infringer. What may it expect in the way of relief?

    Only a few years prior to the creation of the Federal Circuit, the answer would have been "Not much!" An injunction against further infringement could be expected, almost certainly, unless the patent had expired. But the damages assessed against the infringer were all too often insufficient to cover the patentee's attorney fees and other litigation expenses. Awards of treble damages and attorney fees, at least those that would survive appellate review, were rare.

Shortly after the Federal Circuit began to function, the Supreme Court decided *General Motors Corp. v. Devex Corp.*,[1] holding that prejudgment interest on patent infringement damages should be awarded absent some justification for denying such relief. The *Devex* holding was said to be consistent with the overriding purpose of Congress, reflected in 35 U.S.C. §284, of affording patent owners complete compensation. The statutory scheme was to ensure that the patent owner is placed in as good a position as it would have been in had the infringer entered into a reasonable royalty agreement.[2]

The Federal Circuit has fully embraced this positive approach toward complete compensation, and the pendulum is swinging at high speed in favor of the patent owner. Indeed, there may be cause for concern that patentees, insofar as reflected in the decisions of the Federal Circuit, are being overcompensated, at least in the area of increased damages and attorney fees. It is now conventional wisdom in the patent bar that a defendant in a patent infringement case, even one who is clearly not guilty of copying, had better have a thoughtful opinion of patent invalidity or noninfringement in its hip pocket. Patent infringement these days is a very risky business indeed, as will be seen in Chapter 14.

§12.1 Compensatory Damages

(a) General

The general rule regarding damages is that when a wrong has been done, and the law gives a remedy, the compensation shall be equal to the injury. The latter is the standard by which the former is to be measured. The injured party is to be placed, as near as may be, in the situation it would have occupied had the wrong not been committed. The rule applies to patent cases. Congress has sought to ensure that the patent owner would in fact receive full compensation for any damages it suffered as a result of the infringement.[3]

The statute provides that:

> Upon finding for the claimant the court shall award the claimant damages adequate to compensate for the infringement but in no event less than a reasonable royalty for the use made of the invention by the infringer ***.[4]

---

[1]461 U.S. 648 (1983).

[2]461 U.S. at 655.

[3]*Fromson v. Western Litho Plate & Supp. Co.*, 853 F.2d 1568, 7 USPQ2d 1606 (Fed. Cir. 1988). In patent cases, as in other commercial torts, damages are measured by inquiring, had the tortfeasor not committed the wrong, what would have been the financial position of the person wronged? *Brooktree Corp. v. Advanced Micro Devices, Inc.*, 977 F.2d 1555, 24 USPQ2d 1401 (Fed. Cir. 1992).

[4]35 U.S.C. §284. A motion to enforce an agreement settling a patent infringement action arises under the patent laws if the district court retains jurisdiction to enforce the agreement. However, where breach of the agreement does not itself establish infringement of the patent, it is error to determine damages based upon §284. Rather, the trial court should determine

Section 284 imposes no limitation on the types of harm resulting from infringement that the statute will redress. Its broad language awards damages for an injury as long as it resulted from the infringement. Recoverable damages are those that are the direct and foreseeable result of the infringement.[5]

The government's unlicensed use of a patented invention is properly viewed as a taking of property under the Fifth Amendment through the government's exercise of its power of eminent domain, and the patent holder's remedy for such use is reasonable and entire compensation under 28 U.S.C. §1498(a). Because recovery is based on eminent domain, the proper measure is what the owner has lost, not what the taker has gained. Generally, the preferred manner of reasonably and entirely compensating the patent owner is to require the government to pay a reasonable royalty for its license as well as damages for its delay in paying the royalty.[6]

The fact of infringement establishes the fact of damage because the patentee's right to exclude has been violated.[7] Thus, a patentee can bring an action for infringement without any evidence of damage or lost sales.[8] Indeed, a patentee qualifies for damages adequate to compensate for infringement even though it does not exploit its patent.[9] Not only is the patent owner afforded a statutory opportunity for injunctive relief,[10] but if there have been acts of infringement, it is entitled, without a showing of actual damage, to a statutory minimum of a reasonable royalty for that infringement.[11] Where a patentee fails to show causation and can point to no evidence that warrants a lost profits award, the court will require a determination of a reasonable royalty.[12] On the other hand, where a district court correctly

---

damages under state contract law regarding damages for breach of contract. So too with an award of attorney fees under 35 U.S.C. §285. *Gjerlov v. Schuyler Labs., Inc.,* 131 F.3d 1016, 44 USPQ2d 1881 (Fed. Cir. 1997).

[5]*King Instr. Corp. v. Perego,* 65 F.3d 941, 36 USPQ2d 1129 (Fed. Cir. 1995). Of course, notwithstanding the broad language of §284, judicial relief cannot redress every conceivable harm that can be traced to an alleged wrongdoing. For example, remote consequences, such as a heart attack of the inventor or loss in value of stock of a patentee corporation, caused indirectly by infringement, are not compensable. *Rite-Hite Corp. v. Kelley Co.,* 56 F.3d 1538, 35 USPQ2d 1065 (Fed. Cir. 1995).

[6]*Hughes Aircraft Co. v. United States,* 86 F.3d 1566, 39 USPQ2d 1065 (Fed. Cir. 1996). Valuation determinations for purposes of eminent domain are reviewed for clear error as are determinations of what constitutes a reasonable royalty. *Id.* The court has passed the question of whether lost profits against the government must be proved by clear and convincing evidence. It has held, however, that consequential damages are not recoverable under §1498. *Gargoyles, Inc. v. United States,* 113 F.3d 1572, 42 USPQ2d 1760 (Fed. Cir. 1997).

[7]*Lindemann Maschinenfabrik v. American Hoist & Derrick Co.,* 895 F.2d 1403, 13 USPQ2d 1871 (Fed. Cir. 1990).

[8]*Roche Prods., Inc. v. Bolar Pharm. Co.,* 733 F.2d 858, 221 USPQ 937 (Fed. Cir. 1984).

[9]*King Instr. Corp. v. Perego,* 65 F.3d 941, 36 USPQ2d 1129 (Fed. Cir. 1995).

[10]35 U.S.C. §283.

[11]E.g., *Stickle v. Heublein, Inc.,* 716 F.2d 1550, 219 USPQ 377 (Fed. Cir. 1983). Injunctions and damages must be tailored to the circumstances and be correlatively determined. *Id.*

[12]*Water Techs. Corp. v. Calco, Ltd.,* 850 F.2d 660, 7 USPQ2d 1097 (Fed. Cir. 1988). See also *Smithkline Diagnostics, Inc. v. Helena Labs. Corp.,* 926 F.2d 1161, 17 USPQ2d 1922 (Fed. Cir. 1991).

finds that lost profits is the proper measure of damages, it need not receive evidence pertinent to a reasonable royalty.[13]

An infringer's failure to profit from the infringement is immaterial. Damages are compensation for pecuniary loss suffered from infringement without regard to whether the defendant has gained or lost by its unlawful acts. The measure, when calculation is possible, is an amount needed to return the patent owner to the position it would have occupied had there been no infringement.[14] But damages cannot always be measured by looking at the pecuniary condition of the patentee before and after the infringement. This would prevent an award of damages where, for example, the patentee is not in the business. Thus, a reasonable royalty is the floor below which damages shall not fall.[15] The patent owner bears the burden of proof on damages. When the evidence is inadequate to establish actual or nearly actual damages, a court may employ a reasonable royalty as the floor below which a damage award may not fall. As used in 35 U.S.C. §284, "reasonable royalty" is handy shorthand for "damages." As the statute provides, the royalty is "for the use made of the invention by the infringer." Thus the calculation is not a mere academic exercise in setting some percentage figure as a "royalty." The determination remains one of damages to the injured party.[16]

The statute does not instruct a court on how to compute damages; the only congressional intent expressed ensures that a claimant receive adequate damages, not less than a reasonable royalty.[17] Damages adequate to compensate for the infringement are usually measured, depending upon the circumstances and the proof, as the patent owner's lost profits or as a reasonable royalty.[18] The measurement of actual damages is a question of fact.[19]

---

[13]*Beatrice Foods Co. v. New England Printing & Lith. Co.,* 899 F.2d 1171, 14 USPQ2d 1020 (Fed. Cir. 1990).

[14]*Weinar v. Rollform Inc.,* 744 F.2d 797, 223 USPQ 369 (Fed. Cir. 1984). Damages is the amount of loss to a patentee. *Smithkline Diagnostics, Inc. v. Helena Labs. Corp.,* 926 F.2d 1161, 17 USPQ2d 1922 (Fed. Cir. 1991).

[15]*State Indus., Inc. v. Mor-Flo Indus., Inc.,* 883 F.2d 1573, 12 USPQ2d 1026 (Fed. Cir. 1989); *Stickle v. Heublein, Inc.,* 716 F.2d 1550, 219 USPQ 377 (Fed. Cir. 1983). Although the statute states that the damage award shall not be less than a reasonable royalty, the purpose of this alternative is not to provide a simple accounting method, but to set a floor below which the courts are not authorized to go. *Del Mar Avionics, Inc. v. Quinton Instr. Co.,* 836 F.2d 1320, 5 USPQ2d 1255 (Fed. Cir. 1987).

[16]*Fromson v. Western Litho Plate & Supp. Co.,* 853 F.2d 1568, 7 USPQ2d 1606 (Fed. Cir. 1988).

[17]*Paper Converting Mach. Co. v. Magna-Graphics Corp.,* 745 F.2d 11, 223 USPQ 591 (Fed. Cir. 1984).

[18]*Beatrice Foods Co. v. New England Printing & Lith. Co.,* 899 F.2d 1171, 14 USPQ2d 1020 (Fed. Cir. 1990). Because the sale of devices that may be used to practice a patented method cannot infringe without proof of direct infringement, offers to sell such devices cannot supply adequate evidentiary support for a compensatory damage award. Thus, the patent owner is relegated to a reasonable royalty. *Embrex Inc. v. Service Eng'g Corp.,* 216 F.3d 1343, 55 USPQ2d 1161 (Fed. Cir. 2000).

[19]*Brooktree Corp. v. Advanced Micro Devices, Inc.,* 977 F.2d 1555, 24 USPQ2d 1401 (Fed. Cir. 1992).

Thus, the amount of a prevailing party's damages is a finding of fact on which the plaintiff bears the burden of proof by a preponderance of the evidence. Where the amount is fixed by the court, review is in accordance with the clearly erroneous standard of Rule 52(a), FRCP. Where the review is of a denial of a motion for JNOV, the more restrictive substantial evidence standard is employed. On the other hand, certain subsidiary decisions underlying a damage theory are discretionary with the court, such as the choice of an accounting method for determining profit margin or the methodology for arriving at a reasonable royalty. Such decisions are reviewed under the abuse of discretion standard. Finally, the principle that a judge has discretion to select methodology does not mean that he or she may choose between basing an award on lost profits or a reasonable royalty. If a winning patentee seeks and proves lost profits, it is entitled to an award reflecting that amount. A judge may, however, choose between reasonable alternative accounting methods for determining the amount of lost profits, or may, in his or her discretion, adopt a reasonable way to determine the number of infringing units.[20]

The district court has discretion in choosing the methodology for assessing and computing damages, and the only limitation on that discretion is that the award be adequate compensation and not less than a reasonable royalty.[21] Indeed, a patentee has no absolute right to pursue any and every alternative theory of damages, no matter how complicated or tenuous. A court has discretion to deny a proposed method of proof of damages that imposes too great a burden on court proceedings.[22] Simply because different accounting methods lead to different results does not make an award at the higher end of the spectrum more than adequate.[23]

Jury damage awards, unless the product of passion and prejudice, are not easily overturned or modified on appeal.[24] A jury's finding

---

[20]*Smithkline Diagnostics, Inc. v. Helena Labs. Corp.,* 926 F.2d 1161, 17 USPQ2d 1922 (Fed. Cir. 1991). See also *Stryker Corp. v. Intermedics Orthopedics, Inc.,* 96 F.3d 1409, 40 USPQ2d 1065 (Fed. Cir. 1996); *Unisplay S.A. v. American Elec. Sign Co.,* 69 F.3d 512, 36 USPQ2d 1540 (Fed. Cir. 1995); *Minnesota Min. & Mfg. Co. v. Johnson & Johnson Orthopaedics, Inc.,* 976 F.2d 1559, 24 USPQ2d 1321 (Fed. Cir. 1992).

[21]*King Instr. Corp. v. Otari Corp.,* 767 F.2d 853, 226 USPQ 402 (Fed. Cir. 1985); *Seattle Box Co. v. Industrial Crat. & Pack., Inc.,* 756 F.2d 1574, 225 USPQ 357 (Fed. Cir. 1985).

[22]*Micro Motion, Inc. v. Kane Steel Co.,* 894 F.2d 1318, 13 USPQ2d 1696 (Fed. Cir. 1990). This was a discovery situation. With all respect, it would seem that a party should have the right to make its proofs, no matter how complicated they are. It should be noted that one aspect that may have tipped the scales is the fact that the plaintiff had, at one point in the case, been willing to go to trial on damages without the evidence in question. Thus the court may have felt that the discovery was not absolutely necessary.

[23]*Seattle Box Co. v. Industrial Crat. & Pack., Inc.,* 756 F.2d 1574, 225 USPQ 357 (Fed. Cir. 1985); *Paper Converting Mach. Co. v. Magna-Graphics Corp.,* 745 F.2d 11, 223 USPQ 591 (Fed. Cir. 1984).

[24]*Weinar v. Rollform Inc.,* 744 F.2d 797, 223 USPQ 369 (Fed. Cir. 1984). However, it is error to fail to instruct a jury properly on reasonable or established royalty or lost profits. Instructions phrased in terms of "monetary loss" are inadequate. *Id.* A jury award of damages is reviewed on the reasonable jury/substantial evidence standard. *Richardson v. Suzuki Motor Co.,* 868 F.2d 1226, 9 USPQ2d 1913 (Fed. Cir. 1989).

must be upheld unless the amount is grossly excessive or monstrous, or based only on speculation or guesswork.[25] On the matter of remittitur, the court has adopted the maximum recovery rule, which requires it to remit the damage award to the highest amount the jury could properly have awarded based on the relevant evidence.[26] Grants of remittitur or new trial because of excessive damages awards are reviewed for abuse of discretion.[27]

The statute provides that "when the damages are not found by a jury, the court shall assess them."[28] Inasmuch as the trial court's assessment is discretionary, it will not be disturbed absent an abuse of that discretion.[29] An abuse of discretion may be established by showing that the district court made an error of law, or a clear error of judgment, or made findings that were clearly erroneous.[30] On appeal the reviewing court may not exercise de novo review over a finding on damages. This is so whether the basis for the finding is testimony, or physical or documentary evidence.[31]

It is the infringer's burden to show that the amount or method of assessing damages constituted an abuse of discretion.[32] On appeal an infringer cannot successfully argue that the district court abused its discretion and awarded too high a figure simply by substituting its own recomputation to arrive at a lower figure. Such an argument does not show error, but merely indicates the damages an infringer-appellant would prefer to pay. That the district court might have viewed the infringer's evidence more favorably is not a basis for reversal. Pointing to facts that might have supported a lower royalty rate does not sustain the burden of showing an abuse of discretion.[33]

Of course, no multiple recoveries can be had.[34] After a patentee has collected from a direct infringer damages sufficient to put it in

---

[25]*Brooktree Corp. v. Advanced Micro Devices, Inc.*, 977 F.2d 1555, 24 USPQ2d 1401 (Fed. Cir. 1992).

[26]*Oiness v. Walgreen Co.*, 88 F.3d 1025, 39 USPQ2d 1304 (Fed. Cir. 1996). The plaintiff then has a choice between accepting the reduction or facing a new trial on damages. *Unisplay S.A. v. American Elec. Sign Co.*, 69 F.3d 512, 36 USPQ2d 1540 (Fed. Cir. 1995).

[27]*Oiness v. Walgreen Co.*, 88 F.3d 1025, 39 USPQ2d 1304 (Fed. Cir. 1996).

[28]25 U.S.C. §284.

[29]*Manville Sales Corp. v. Paramount Sys., Inc.*, 917 F.2d 544, 16 USPQ2d 1587 (Fed. Cir. 1990); *State Indus., Inc. v. Mor-Flo Indus., Inc.*, 883 F.2d 1573, 12 USPQ2d 1026 (Fed. Cir. 1989); *CPG Prods. Corp. v. Pegasus Luggage, Inc.*, 776 F.2d 1007, 227 USPQ 497 (Fed. Cir. 1985); *Yarway Corp. v. Eur-Control USA Inc.*, 775 F.2d 268, 227 USPQ 352 (Fed. Cir. 1985).

[30]*Trell v. Marlee Elec. Corp.*, 912 F.2d 1443, 16 USPQ2d 1059 (Fed. Cir. 1990); *State Indus., Inc. v. Mor-Flo Indus., Inc.*, 883 F.2d 1573, 12 USPQ2d 1026 (Fed. Cir. 1989); *Fromson v. Western Litho Plate & Supp. Co.*, 853 F.2d 1568, 7 USPQ2d 1606 (Fed. Cir. 1988); *TWM Mfg. Co. v. Dura Corp.*, 789 F.2d 895, 229 USPQ 525 (Fed. Cir. 1986).

[31]*TWM Mfg. Co. v. Dura Corp.*, 789 F.2d 895, 229 USPQ 525 (Fed. Cir. 1986).

[32]*King Instr. Corp. v. Otari Corp.*, 767 F.2d 853, 226 USPQ 402 (Fed. Cir. 1985).

[33]*TWM Mfg. Co. v. Dura Corp.*, 789 F.2d 895, 229 USPQ 525 (Fed. Cir. 1986).

[34]*Weinar v. Rollform Inc.*, 744 F.2d 797, 223 USPQ 369 (Fed. Cir. 1984). Where the patentee recovers a reasonable royalty, an award of some portion of the difference between the infringer's actual sales price of its business to a third party and an expert's evaluation of the value of that business without the infringing equipment might well constitute double

the position it would have occupied had there been no infringement, it cannot thereafter collect actual damages from a person liable only for contributing to that same infringement.[35] Similarly, it has been held that only one recovery may be had where the same act (selling an accused device) constitutes both patent infringement and unfair competition.[36] It would seem that the quantum of damage is not affected by the number of claims infringed.[37] The court has hinted that it will always attempt to award more than mere nominal damages.[38]

The purpose of 28 U.S.C. §1292(c)(2), which allows interlocutory appeals in patent cases, was to permit a stay of a damages trial, not compel one. There is thus no conflict between that statute and Rule 62(a), FRCP, which grants discretion to stay or proceed with the damages trial during the appeal. Indeed, the Federal Circuit typically denies motions to stay damages trials during appeals in patent cases.[39]

(b) Actual Damages: Lost Profits

The general rule for determining the actual damages to a patentee that is itself producing the patented item is to determine the sales and profits lost to the patentee because of the infringement.[40]

---

recovery. *Minco, Inc. v. Combustion Eng'g, Inc.,* 95 F.3d 1109, 40 USPQ2d 1001 (Fed. Cir. 1996).

[35]*King Instr. Corp. v. Otari Corp.,* 767 F.2d 853, 226 USPQ 402 (Fed. Cir. 1985). Here the alleged contributory infringement was the sale of spare parts; it would seem that the patentee could recover an additional amount for the spare parts only if he could reasonably have anticipated the sale of spare parts himself in the absence of the direct infringement. *Id.* Even though an inducer's own direct infringement is de minimis, it is nonetheless liable for all damages attributable to the direct infringement that it actively induced. *Water Techs. Corp. v. Calco, Ltd.,* 850 F.2d 660, 7 USPQ2d 1097 (Fed. Cir. 1988).

[36]*CPG Prods. Corp. v. Pegasus Luggage, Inc.,* 776 F.2d 1007, 227 USPQ 497 (Fed. Cir. 1985). Here the Federal Circuit was applying Eleventh Circuit law.

[37]Cf. *Hartness Int'l, Inc. v. Simplimatic Eng'g Co.,* 819 F.2d 1100, 2 USPQ2d 1826 (Fed. Cir. 1987). Despite holding the independent claim nonobvious, the district court went on to hold a dependent claim anticipated. Naturally, the Federal Circuit reversed on a fortiori grounds. However, the court found it unnecessary to remand for a finding as to infringement of the dependent claim, because it was felt that damages would be unaffected by such a finding. In another case, the court criticized the patentee for submitting the infringement issue on appeal on a "plethora of dependent claims," observing that infringement of an independent claim would result in the same damage award as would infringement of all claims dependent thereon. *Wahpeton Canvas Co. v. Frontier, Inc.,* 870 F.2d 1546, 10 USPQ2d 1201 (Fed. Cir. 1989). Care might be suggested here. One could certainly conceive of situations where it would be logical to argue that the more claims of a patent that are infringed, the higher the "reasonable" royalty.

[38]*Roche Prods., Inc. v. Bolar Pharm. Co.,* 733 F.2d 858, 221 USPQ 937, 943 (Fed. Cir. 1984). "If the patent law precludes substantial damages, there exists a strange gap in the panoply (in its proper meaning, a suit of armor) of protection the patent statutes place around an aggrieved and injured patentee." The infringer had begun testing for FDA approval during the last six months before the patent expired. The court suggested that it might be appropriate to award damages sufficient to compensate for actual injury caused to the patentee by the infringer's unlawful head start.

[39]*In re Calmar, Inc.,* 854 F.2d 461, 7 USPQ2d 1730 (Fed. Cir. 1988).

[40]*Del Mar Avionics, Inc. v. Quinton Instr. Co.,* 836 F.2d 1320, 5 USPQ2d 1255 (Fed. Cir. 1987).

It is important at the outset to keep in mind the cardinal limitation of §284: a reasonable royalty is the absolute minimum to which a wronged patentee is entitled. Thus it is proper to award lost profits only to the extent that they exceed a reasonable royalty.[41] An award may be split between lost profits as actual damages to the extent they are proven and a reasonable royalty for the remainder.[42] It is also important to observe carefully the distinction between the profits lost to the patentee, and those that the infringer made. The patentee is clearly not entitled to the infringer's profits, although they can be used as a yardstick to measure the lost profits of the patentee in a proper case.[43] To the extent a patentee complains that infringement has damaged its ability to service foreign markets, it must rely on foreign patent protection.[44]

The "but for" test. Although it would be incorrect to bar a patentee who is not yet manufacturing the product from proving that its actual damages were larger than a reasonable royalty, the burden on a patentee who has not begun to manufacture the patented product is commensurately heavy.[45] To recover lost profits as opposed to royalties, a patent owner must prove a causal relation between the infringement and its loss of profits. The patent owner must show that "but for" the infringement, it would have made the infringer's sales.[46] The

---

[41]*TWM Mfg. Co. v. Dura Corp.*, 789 F.2d 895, 229 USPQ 525 (Fed. Cir. 1986). Perhaps this is not strictly so. In *Hartness Int'l, Inc. v. Simplimatic Eng'g Co.*, 819 F.2d 1100, 2 USPQ2d 1826 (Fed. Cir. 1987), the patentee proved lost profits of $158,000 but had previously taken the position that it should have a 70% royalty, which resulted in damages of only $81,000. The district court awarded the lower figure on the ground that the patentee was bound by its earlier position. The patentee did not appeal, but the infringer claimed that a 70% royalty was too high. In affirming on lack of abuse of discretion, the Federal Circuit observed that this was not really a reasonable royalty determination but simply a downward adjustment of actual lost profits.

[42]*State Indus., Inc. v. Mor-Flo Indus., Inc.*, 883 F.2d 1573, 12 USPQ2d 1026 (Fed. Cir. 1989).

[43]*Kori Corp. v. Wilco Marsh Buggies, Inc.*, 761 F.2d 649, 225 USPQ 985 (Fed. Cir. 1985). See also *Stickle v. Heublein, Inc.*, 716 F.2d 1550, 219 USPQ 377 (Fed. Cir. 1983). Infringer's profits are often considered in determining a reasonable royalty. *TWM Mfg. Co. v. Dura Corp.*, 789 F.2d 895, 229 USPQ 525 (Fed. Cir. 1986); *Trans-World Mfg. Corp. v. Al Nyman & Sons*, 750 F.2d 1552, 224 USPQ 259 (Fed. Cir. 1984). But see *Radio Steel & Mfg. Co. v. MTD Prods., Inc.*, 788 F.2d 1554, 229 USPQ 431 (Fed. Cir. 1986). The patent law long provided that a patentee could recover both its own damages and the infringer's profits. The law changed in 1946 to preclude recovery of the infringer's profits and allow recovery of damages only. *King Instr. Corp. v. Perego*, 65 F.3d 941, 36 USPQ2d 1129 (Fed. Cir. 1995). Thus, patent infringement carries no remedy of an accounting for an infringer's profits. Such profits can, however, be used to determine the reasonableness of the patentee's profit margins. *Water Techs. Corp. v. Calco, Ltd.*, 850 F.2d 660, 7 USPQ2d 1097 (Fed. Cir. 1988). Under the Semiconductor Chip Protection Act, damages are to be measured as the actual damages suffered by the owner of the mask work plus the infringer's profits that are attributable to the infringement and that are not taken into account in computing the award of actual damages. *Brooktree Corp. v. Advanced Micro Devices, Inc.*, 977 F.2d 1555, 24 USPQ2d 1401 (Fed. Cir. 1992).

[44]*Johns Hopkins Univ. v. Cellpro Inc.*, 152 F.3d 1342, 47 USPQ2d 1705 (Fed. Cir. 1998).

[45]*Hebert v. Lisle Corp.*, 99 F.3d 1109, 40 USPQ2d 1611 (Fed. Cir. 1996).

[46]*Bic Leisure Prods., Inc. v. Windsurfing Int'l, Inc.*, 1 F.3d 1214, 27 USPQ2d 1671 (Fed. Cir. 1993).

Federal Circuit seems to have embraced the Sixth Circuit's *Panduit*[47] "but for" test for lost profits.[48]

Thus the patentee must show causation, and a factual basis for causation is "but for."[49] In order to be entitled to lost profits, the patent owner must show: (1) a demand for the product during the period in question; (2) an absence, during that period, of acceptable noninfringing substitutes; (3) its own manufacturing and marketing capability to meet or exploit that demand; and (4) a detailed computation of the amount of the profit it would have made.[50] In short, it is the patentee's burden to prove, by a preponderance of the evidence,[51] that but for the infringement it would have made the sales.[52]

The requirement of causation implicates the patentee's manufacturing capacity and marketing capability, the desires of customers for the claimed invention, the relationship of the claimed invention to the product sold, and other factors pertinent to the particular market or parties. Causation is most easily found where only two companies, the patentee and the infringer, are in the market. Where there is evidence of a third-party competitor, the lost profits theory would appear to be nonviable inasmuch as the third party could have made the sale rather than the patentee. Under such circumstances, there appears to be no possible causation. But patentees have successfully urged modifications to the basic damage theory so as to cover situations other than the simple two-supplier market. There is precedent for finding causation despite an alternative source of supply if that source is an infringer or puts out a noninfringing product that is an unacceptable alternative, or if the source accounts for only insignificant sales. There is also precedent for lost profits damages calculated on a portion of an infringer's sales based on the patentee's

---

[47]*Panduit Corp. v. Stahlin Bros. Fibre Works,* 575 F.2d 1152, 197 USPQ 726 (6th Cir. 1978).

[48]E.g., *Gyromat Corp. v. Champion Spark Plug Co.,* 735 F.2d 549, 222 USPQ 4 (Fed. Cir. 1984). Nonetheless, the court has made it clear that the four-part *Panduit* test is not the exclusive standard for determining entitlement to lost profits. *Carella v. Starlight Archery & Pro Line Co.,* 804 F.2d 135, 231 USPQ 644 (Fed. Cir. 1986). *Panduit* is the court's "nonexclusive" standard. *State Indus., Inc. v. Mor-Flo Indus., Inc.,* 883 F.2d 1573, 12 USPQ2d 1026 (Fed. Cir. 1989). Where a patent owner maintains that it lost sales equal in quantity to the infringing sales, the four-part *Panduit* test applies. *Water Techs. Corp. v. Calco, Ltd.,* 850 F.2d 660, 7 USPQ2d 1097 (Fed. Cir. 1988).

[49]*Lam, Inc. v. Johns-Manville Corp.,* 718 F.2d 1056, 219 USPQ 670 (Fed. Cir. 1983).

[50]*Ryco, Inc. v. Ag-Bag Corp.,* 857 F.2d 1418, 8 USPQ2d 1323 (Fed. Cir. 1988); *Radio Steel & Mfg. Co. v. MTD Prods., Inc.,* 788 F.2d 1554, 229 USPQ 431 (Fed. Cir. 1986); *Yarway Corp. v. Eur-Control USA Inc.,* 775 F.2d 268, 227 USPQ 352 (Fed. Cir. 1985); *Seattle Box Co. v. Industrial Crat. & Pack., Inc.,* 756 F.2d 1574, 225 USPQ 357 (Fed. Cir. 1985); *Paper Converting Mach. Co. v. Magna-Graphics Corp.,* 745 F.2d 11, 223 USPQ 591 (Fed. Cir. 1984); *Gyromat Corp. v. Champion Spark Plug Co.,* 735 F.2d 549, 222 USPQ 4 (Fed. Cir. 1984).

[51]*Yarway Corp. v. Eur-Control USA Inc.,* 775 F.2d 268, 227 USPQ 352 (Fed. Cir. 1985).

[52]*King Instr. Corp. v. Otari Corp.,* 767 F.2d 853, 226 USPQ 402 (Fed. Cir. 1985); *Kori Corp. v. Wilco Marsh Buggies, Inc.,* 761 F.2d 649, 225 USPQ 985 (Fed. Cir. 1985); *Paper Converting Mach. Co. v. Magna-Graphics Corp.,* 745 F.2d 11, 223 USPQ 591 (Fed. Cir. 1984); *Bio-Rad Labs., Inc. v. Nicolet Inst. Corp.,* 739 F.2d 604, 222 USPQ 654 (Fed. Cir. 1984). An award of damages may be remanded in the absence of a finding that the patentee would have made the sales but for the infringement. *Bott v. Four Star Corp.,* 807 F.2d 1567, 1 USPQ2d 1210 (Fed. Cir. 1986).

market share.[53] A purchaser unable to obtain the infringing device is presumed to seek an acceptable substitute.[54]

Reconstructing the market, by definition a hypothetical enterprise, requires the patentee to project economic results that did not occur. To prevent the hypothetical from lapsing into pure speculation, the court requires sound economic proof of the nature of the market and likely outcomes with infringement factored out of the economic picture. Within this framework, trial courts consistently permit patentees to present market reconstruction theories showing all of the ways in which they would have been better off in the "but for world," and accordingly to recover lost profits in a wide variety of forms. But by the same token, a fair and accurate reconstruction of the "but for" market also must take into account, where relevant, alternative actions the infringer foreseeably would have undertaken had it not infringed. Without the infringing product, a rational would-be infringer is likely to offer an acceptable noninfringing alternative, if available, to compete with the patent owner rather than leave the market altogether. The competitor in the "but for" marketplace is hardly likely to surrender its complete market share when faced with a patent, if it can compete in some other lawful manner. Moreover, only by comparing the patented invention to its next-best available alternative—regardless of whether the alternative was actually produced and sold during the infringement—can the court discern the market value of the patent owner's exclusive right, and therefore its expected profit or reward, had the infringer's activities not prevented it from taking full economic advantage of this right. Thus, an accurate reconstruction of the hypothetical "but for" market takes into account any alternatives available to the infringer.[55]

All in all, the critical inquiry is whether the patentee has shown a reasonable probability that it would have made the infringing sales.[56] The but for test does not demand absolute proof.[57] It is not possible and is unnecessary to negate every possibility that a purchaser might have bought another product.[58] The patentee need not

---

[53]*Micro Motion, Inc. v. Kane Steel Co.*, 894 F.2d 1318, 13 USPQ2d 1696 (Fed. Cir. 1990).

[54]*Uniroyal, Inc. v. Rudkin-Wiley Corp.*, 939 F.2d 1540, 19 USPQ2d 1432 (Fed. Cir. 1991).

[55]*Grain Processing Corp. v. American Maize-Prods. Co.*, 185 F.3d 1341, 51 USPQ2d 1556 (Fed. Cir. 1999).

[56]*Bic Leisure Prods., Inc. v. Windsurfing Int'l, Inc.*, 1 F.3d 1214, 27 USPQ2d 1671 (Fed. Cir. 1993); *Water Techs. Corp. v. Calco, Ltd.*, 850 F.2d 660, 7 USPQ2d 1097 (Fed. Cir. 1988); *Del Mar Avionics, Inc. v. Quinton Instr. Co.*, 836 F.2d 1320, 5 USPQ2d 1255 (Fed. Cir. 1987); *Gyromat Corp. v. Champion Spark Plug Co.*, 735 F.2d 549, 222 USPQ 4 (Fed. Cir. 1984). When the patentee establishes the reasonableness of the inference that it would have made the infringing sales, it has sustained the burden of proving entitlement to lost profits for those sales. The onus is then placed on the infringer to show that it is unreasonable to infer that some or all of the infringing sales probably caused the patentee to suffer the loss of profits. *Kaufman Co. v. Lantech, Inc.*, 926 F.2d 1136, 17 USPQ2d 1828 (Fed. Cir. 1991).

[57]*American Hoist & Derrick Co. v. Sowa & Sons, Inc.*, 725 F.2d 1350, 220 USPQ 763 (Fed. Cir. 1984).

[58]*State Indus., Inc. v. Mor-Flo Indus., Inc.*, 883 F.2d 1573, 12 USPQ2d 1026 (Fed. Cir. 1989); *Marsh-McBirney, Inc. v. Montedoro-Whitney Corp.*, 882 F.2d 498, 11 USPQ2d 1794 (Fed.

prove causation as a certainty, but only as a reasonable probability.[59] The patent owner's burden of proof is not an absolute one, although liability does not extend to speculative profits.[60]

Nor is it absolutely necessary that the trial court make a specific finding of causation, where it is clear that it understood the requirement of causation and that such a finding naturally flowed from an ultimate finding of lost profits.[61] Where the plaintiff's sales decrease after the defendant begins to sell devices incorporating the designs and features of plaintiff's devices, causation can be inferred in the absence of any evidence by the defendant that there was some other convincing explanation for the plaintiff's loss of sales.[62]

The infringer's ability to customize and its reputation for competitive pricing do not tend to show that the patentee would not have made the sales but for the infringement.[63] Moreover, the fact that the patentee might not have competed for every infringing sale does not indicate that the inference the patentee would probably have made the sale absent the infringement is unreasonable.[64] In response to an argument that many sales were due to customer loyalty, the court held that it is illogical to consider the preference of customers for the infringer as a source of supply, because that presumes a legitimate choice between two manufacturers. The real question is whether a showing of loyalty of some customers overcomes the reasonable inference, when the patentee and infringers are the only suppliers of the

---

Cir. 1989); *Del Mar Avionics, Inc. v. Quinton Instr. Co.*, 836 F.2d 1320, 5 USPQ2d 1255 (Fed. Cir. 1987); *Carella v. Starlight Archery & Pro Line Co.*, 804 F.2d 135, 231 USPQ 644 (Fed. Cir. 1986); *Paper Converting Mach. Co. v. Magna-Graphics Corp.*, 745 F.2d 11, 223 USPQ 591 (Fed. Cir. 1984); *Gyromat Corp. v. Champion Spark Plug Co.*, 735 F.2d 549, 222 USPQ 4 (Fed. Cir. 1984).

[59]*Marsh-McBirney, Inc. v. Montedoro-Whitney Corp.*, 882 F.2d 498, 11 USPQ2d 1794 (Fed. Cir. 1989); *King Instr. Corp. v. Otari Corp.*, 767 F.2d 853, 226 USPQ 402 (Fed. Cir. 1985); *Bio-Rad Labs., Inc. v. Nicolet Inst. Corp.*, 739 F.2d 604, 222 USPQ 654 (Fed. Cir. 1984). Of course, the proof may not be speculative. *Yarway Corp. v. Eur-Control USA Inc.*, 775 F.2d 268, 227 USPQ 352 (Fed. Cir. 1985). In *Ryco, Inc. v. Ag-Bag Corp.*, 857 F.2d 1418, 8 USPQ2d 1323 (Fed. Cir. 1988), the court rejected a contention that a decline in the patentee's sales was due to a slump in the agricultural economy. That same slump must have affected the infringer's sales as well, and it is those sales that are relevant to lost profits.

[60]*State Indus., Inc. v. Mor-Flo Indus., Inc.*, 883 F.2d 1573, 12 USPQ2d 1026 (Fed. Cir. 1989).

[61]*Del Mar Avionics, Inc. v. Quinton Instr. Co.*, 836 F.2d 1320, 5 USPQ2d 1255 (Fed. Cir. 1987); *Amstar Corp. v. Envirotech Corp.*, 823 F.2d 1538, 3 USPQ2d 1412 (Fed. Cir. 1987); *King Instr. Corp. v. Otari Corp.*, 767 F.2d 853, 226 USPQ 402 (Fed. Cir. 1985). It may be possible to infer causation in a two-supplier market. *Lam, Inc. v. Johns-Manville Corp.*, 718 F.2d 1056, 219 USPQ 670 (Fed. Cir. 1983).

[62]*Universal Gym Equip., Inc. v. ERWA Exercise Equip. Ltd.*, 827 F.2d 1542, 4 USPQ2d 1035, 1043 (Fed. Cir. 1987).

[63]*Kaufman Co. v. Lantech, Inc.*, 926 F.2d 1136, 17 USPQ2d 1828 (Fed. Cir. 1991).

[64]*Kaufman Co. v. Lantech, Inc.*, 926 F.2d 1136, 17 USPQ2d 1828 (Fed. Cir. 1991). Here the patentee conceded that it would not have attempted to make sales to the infringer's distributors, but did establish that the infringing devices were typically resold by the distributors to customers within a year. In the case of lost profits determinations involving large installations, it is not of controlling significance that the patent owner did not bid on every infringing sale, even in a market having more than two suppliers. *Standard Havens Prods., Inc. v. Gencor Indus., Inc.*, 953 F.2d 1360, 21 USPQ2d 1321 (Fed. Cir. 1992).

patented product, that the patent owner would have made the sales made by the infringers.[65]

In *Bic v. Windsurfing,* the court again[66] indicated that the *Panduit* test is an acceptable but not exclusive test for determining "but for" causation. *Panduit* assumes that the patent owner and the infringer sell products sufficiently similar to compete in the same market segment. Both the "demand" and the "noninfringing alternative" *Panduit* factors rely on such an assumption. Similarly, the market share approach endorsed by the court in *State Industries*[67] assumes competition in the same market. But where the market is elastic, the patent owner and the infringer sell to different segments of the market, and the patent owner had valued its patent in terms of licensing royalties, by licensing nearly every competitor, a patent owner may not be entitled to lost profits. But it is entitled to royalties, including lost royalties that its own licensees would have paid it but for the infringement.[68]

Demand. A substantial number of sales by the infringer is said to be compelling evidence of demand for the patented product.[69]

Acceptable noninfringing substitutes. The court requires reliable economic proof of the market that establishes an accurate context to project the likely results "but for" the infringement. The availability of substitutes invariably will influence the market forces defining this "but for" marketplace.[70] It is axiomatic that if a device is not available for purchase, an infringer cannot argue that the device is an acceptable noninfringing alternative for the purpose of avoiding a lost profits award. A lost profits award reflects the realities of sales actually lost, not the possibilities of a hypothetical market that the infringer might have created.[71] But a substitute need not be openly on sale to be "available." Thus, with proper economic proof of availability, an acceptable substitute not on the market during the infringement may nonetheless become part of the lost profits calculus and therefore limit or preclude those damages.[72]

---

[65]*Datascope Corp. v. SMEC, Inc.,* 879 F.2d 820, 11 USPQ2d 1321 (Fed. Cir. 1989).

[66]See note 12:48.

[67]See note 12:104.

[68]*Bic Leisure Prods., Inc. v. Windsurfing Int'l, Inc.,* 1 F.3d 1214, 27 USPQ2d 1671, 1674 (Fed. Cir. 1993).

[69]*Gyromat Corp. v. Champion Spark Plug Co.,* 735 F.2d 549, 222 USPQ 4 (Fed. Cir. 1984).

[70]*Grain Processing Corp. v. American Maize-Prods. Co.,* 185 F.3d 1341, 51 USPQ2d 1556 (Fed. Cir. 1999).

[71]*Zygo Corp. v. Wyko Corp.,* 79 F.3d 1563, 38 USPQ2d 1281 (Fed. Cir. 1996).

[72]*Grain Processing Corp. v. American Maize-Prods. Co.,* 185 F.3d 1341, 51 USPQ2d 1556 (Fed. Cir. 1999). Accordingly, an available technology not on the market during the infringement period can constitute a noninfringing alternative. The critical time period for determining availability of an alternative is the period of infringement for which the patent owner claims damages, i.e., the "accounting period." Switching to a noninfringing substitute after the accounting period does not alone show availability of the noninfringing substitute during this critical

The word "acceptable" is also an important qualification on noninfringing substitutes.[73] Mere existence of a competing device does not make it an acceptable substitute. A product lacking the advantages of that patented can hardly be termed a substitute acceptable to the customer who wants those advantages.[74] The fact that some alternatives were available that incorporate some but not all of the patent claim elements does not establish that a finding of no acceptable noninfringing substitutes was erroneous. A contrary result would ignore the fact that the patent claim is a total combination of elements, viewed as a whole.[75] The fact that there are other infringing substitutes is obviously not significant.[76]

In deciding whether there are acceptable noninfringing alternatives for purposes of assessing damages, it appears the court will insist upon a rigorous infringement analysis.[77] Factors that point toward an absence of noninfringing alternatives include (1) failure of the infringer to design its own device, (2) an election to infringe despite having expended only minimal sums on design when notified of infringement, (3) willful infringement, (4) failure to successfully

---

time. When an alleged alternative is not on the market during the accounting period, a trial court may reasonably infer that it was not available as a noninfringing substitute at that time. The accused infringer then has the burden to overcome this inference by showing that the substitute was available during the accounting period. Mere speculation or conclusory assertions will not suffice to overcome the inference. After all, the infringer chose to produce the infringing, rather than noninfringing, product. Thus, the trial court must proceed with caution in assessing proof of the availability of substitutes not actually sold during the period of infringement. Acceptable substitutes that the infringer proves were available during the accounting period can preclude or limit lost profits; substitutes only theoretically possible will not. *Id.*

[73]*Yarway Corp. v. Eur-Control USA Inc.,* 775 F.2d 268, 227 USPQ 352 (Fed. Cir. 1985).

[74]*TWM Mfg. Co. v. Dura Corp.,* 789 F.2d 895, 229 USPQ 525 (Fed. Cir. 1986). The trial court found that none of the alleged substitutes possessed all the advantages of the patented device. The Federal Circuit, without deciding whether such a finding is absolutely required, simply indicated that the finding supported a determination of no acceptable substitutes. See also *Smithkline Diagnostics, Inc. v. Helena Labs. Corp.,* 926 F.2d 1161, 17 USPQ2d 1922 (Fed. Cir. 1991); *Kalman v. Berlyn Corp.,* 914 F.2d 1473, 16 USPQ2d 1093 (Fed. Cir. 1990). To be deemed acceptable, the alleged noninfringing substitute must not have a disparately higher price than or possess characteristics significantly different from the patented product. *Kaufman Co. v. Lantech, Inc.,* 926 F.2d 1136, 17 USPQ2d 1828 (Fed. Cir. 1991). To prove that there are no acceptable noninfringing substitutes, the patent owner must show either that the purchasers in the marketplace generally were willing to buy the patented product for its advantages, or that the specific purchasers of the infringing product purchased on that basis. *Standard Havens Prods., Inc. v. Gencor Indus., Inc.,* 953 F.2d 1360, 21 USPQ2d 1321 (Fed. Cir. 1992).

[75]*Radio Steel & Mfg. Co. v. MTD Prods., Inc.,* 788 F.2d 1554, 229 USPQ 431 (Fed. Cir. 1986).

[76]*Gyromat Corp. v. Champion Spark Plug Co.,* 735 F.2d 549, 222 USPQ 4 (Fed. Cir. 1984).

[77]*Datascope Corp. v. SMEC, Inc.,* 879 F.2d 820, 11 USPQ2d 1321 (Fed. Cir. 1989). The court found clear error in a finding that an alternative was noninfringing on the basis that the analysis was made with reference to the patentee's commercial embodiment rather than the patent claims. In *Comair Rotron, Inc. v. Nippon Densan Corp.,* 49 F.3d 1535, 33 USPQ2d 1929 (Fed. Cir. 1995), the defendant's accused device had been found, along with several other devices, to be an acceptable noninfringing substitute in a prior case on the same patent against a different defendant. Naturally the present defendant attempted to use that judgment as collateral estoppel on the infringement question. The lower court granted a summary judgment in its favor but the Federal Circuit reversed on the ground that the prior finding was not necessary to the judgment. Its reasoning seemed to be that economic complexities such as multiple competitors, some of whom infringe and some of whom don't, have not led to a bright line rule on this aspect of lost profits.

market other allegedly acceptable designs, (5) violation of an injunction against infringement, and (6) withdrawal from the business after enforcement of such an injunction.[78] Where the infringer ignores the supposed substitutes, its argument is of limited influence.[79] On the other hand, the fact that neither the patentee's nor the infringer's market share changed significantly after introduction of the accused device is very probative of the availability of noninfringing substitutes.[80] Consumer demand defines the relevant market and relative substitutability among products therein. Important factors shaping demand may include consumers' intended use for the patentee's product, similarity of physical and functional attributes of the patentee's product to alleged competing products, and price. Where the alleged substitute differs from the patentee's product in one or more of these respects, the patentee often must adduce economic data supporting its theory of the relevant market in order to show "but for" causation.[81]

In *Pall v. Micron*,[82] the court held squarely that (1) a product licensed to a third party as a result of litigation is a noninfringing substitute, but (2) such a product is not a noninfringing substitute during the period prior to the license, and (3) voluntary settlement of the litigation by licensing does not retrospectively transform an accused infringing product into a noninfringing substitute. It also held that, after such a license, lost profits are limited to the share of the defendant's sales that the patent owner would reasonably have made, with the remaining sales assessed according to a reasonable royalty. In this latter connection it rejected the patent owner's argument that such a result provides a windfall to the infringer, which was premised on the logic that when there are multiple infringers the infringement will be profitable to the remaining infringers once the patentee settles with any one of them. The court reasoned that the purpose of compensatory damages is not to punish the infringer, but to make the patentee whole. The correct point at which to solve this problem, apparently, is in the setting of the royalty rate and the discretionary multiplication of damages.[83]

The existence of noninfringing substitutes is a question of fact, reviewable under the clearly erroneous standard.[84]

---

[78]*TWM Mfg. Co. v. Dura Corp.*, 789 F.2d 895, 229 USPQ 525 (Fed. Cir. 1986). The fact that the patentee sells several lines of products, some patented and some not, does not of itself justify an inference that the lines are acceptable substitutes. *Kaufman Co. v. Lantech, Inc.*, 926 F.2d 1136, 17 USPQ2d 1828 (Fed. Cir. 1991).

[79]*TWM Mfg. Co. v. Dura Corp.*, 789 F.2d 895, 229 USPQ 525 (Fed. Cir. 1986).

[80]*Slimfold Mfg. Co. v. Kinkead Indus.*, 932 F.2d 1453, 18 USPQ2d 1842 (Fed. Cir. 1991).

[81]*Grain Processing Corp. v. American Maize-Prods. Co.*, 185 F.3d 1341, 51 USPQ2d 1556 (Fed. Cir. 1999).

[82]*Pall Corp. v. Micron Separations, Inc.*, 66 F.3d 1211, 36 USPQ2d 1225 (Fed. Cir. 1995).

[83]*Pall Corp. v. Micron Separations, Inc.*, 66 F.3d 1211, 36 USPQ2d 1225 (Fed. Cir. 1995). Apparently the noninfringing alternative must be available other than only through the patentee, however. See *Rite-Hite Corp. v. Kelley Co.*, 56 F.3d 1538, 35 USPQ2d 1065 (Fed. Cir. 1995).

[84]*Zygo Corp. v. Wyko Corp.*, 79 F.3d 1563, 38 USPQ2d 1281 (Fed. Cir. 1996); *Minnesota Min. & Mfg. Co. v. Johnson & Johnson Orthopaedics, Inc.*, 976 F.2d 1559, 24 USPQ2d 1321

Ability to meet demand. Aggressive development of the market by the patentee is good evidence of ability to meet the market demand.[85] Lost profits are a particularly appropriate measure of damages where the patentee and the infringer are the only suppliers in the market.[86] Lost profits for all sales are easier to obtain where there are only two suppliers in the market, the patent owner and the infringer.[87] However, lost profits may be too speculative where the patentee is not in the business of making the same machine as the infringer.[88] An exclusive licensee may be able to recover lost profits in an infringement suit, on the theory that it is entitled to be compensated on the basis of its ability to exploit the patent.[89]

Calculation of lost profits. The amount of lost profits cannot be speculative but need not be proved with unerring precision either.[90] The infringer bears the risk of any uncertainty as to computation,[91] especially where it is due to its failure to keep accurate or complete records.[92] The amount of detailed testimony and documentation regarding computations of the patentee's lost profits will vary with the

---

(Fed. Cir. 1992); *Radio Steel & Mfg. Co. v. MTD Prods., Inc.,* 788 F.2d 1554, 229 USPQ 431 (Fed. Cir. 1986).

[85]*Yarway Corp. v. Eur-Control USA Inc.,* 775 F.2d 268, 227 USPQ 352 (Fed. Cir. 1985).

[86]*Kori Corp. v. Wilco Marsh Buggies, Inc.,* 761 F.2d 649, 225 USPQ 985 (Fed. Cir. 1985); *Lam, Inc. v. Johns-Manville Corp.,* 718 F.2d 1056, 219 USPQ 670 (Fed. Cir. 1983).

[87]*Micro Motion, Inc. v. Kane Steel Co.,* 894 F.2d 1318, 13 USPQ2d 1696 (Fed. Cir. 1990); *Water Techs. Corp. v. Calco, Ltd.,* 850 F.2d 660, 7 USPQ2d 1097 (Fed. Cir. 1988). When the contesting parties are the only suppliers of the product, it is not inappropriate to infer that the patentee would have had the sales made by the infringer. *Marsh-McBirney, Inc. v. Montedoro-Whitney Corp.,* 882 F.2d 498, 11 USPQ2d 1794 (Fed. Cir. 1989).

[88]*Stickle v. Heublein, Inc.,* 716 F.2d 1550, 219 USPQ 377 (Fed. Cir. 1983). But see *Hebert v. Lisle Corp.,* 99 F.3d 1109, 40 USPQ2d 1611 (Fed. Cir. 1996). Expert testimony to the effect that, if the infringer had not been in the market, and if the patentee had been able to make all the sales that the infringer made, the patentee's sales would have increased 68% was held not to support a conclusion that the patentee would have made 68% of the infringer's sales but for the infringement. *Railroad Dynamics, Inc. v. A. Stucki Co.,* 727 F.2d 1506, 220 USPQ 929 (Fed. Cir. 1984). But see *King Instr. Corp. v. Perego,* 65 F.3d 941, 36 USPQ2d 1129 (Fed. Cir. 1995); *Rite-Hite Corp. v. Kelley Co.,* 56 F.3d 1538, 35 USPQ2d 1065 (Fed. Cir. 1995).

[89]*Kori Corp. v. Wilco Marsh Buggies, Inc.,* 761 F.2d 649, 225 USPQ 985 (Fed. Cir. 1985). A nonexclusive licensee may be limited to a reasonable royalty.

[90]*Bio-Rad Labs., Inc. v. Nicolet Inst. Corp.,* 739 F.2d 604, 222 USPQ 654 (Fed. Cir. 1984).

[91]*Yarway Corp. v. Eur-Control USA Inc.,* 775 F.2d 268, 227 USPQ 352 (Fed. Cir. 1985); *King Instr. Corp. v. Otari Corp.,* 767 F.2d 853, 226 USPQ 402 (Fed. Cir. 1985). When the amount of damages is not ascertainable with precision, reasonable doubt is appropriately resolved against the infringer. *Del Mar Avionics, Inc. v. Quinton Instr. Co.,* 836 F.2d 1320, 5 USPQ2d 1255 (Fed. Cir. 1987).

[92]*Hartness Int'l, Inc. v. Simplimatic Eng'g Co.,* 819 F.2d 1100, 2 USPQ2d 1826 (Fed. Cir. 1987); *Lam, Inc. v. Johns-Manville Corp.,* 718 F.2d 1056, 219 USPQ 670 (Fed. Cir. 1983). But see *Beatrice Foods Co. v. New England Printing & Lith. Co.,* 899 F.2d 1171, 14 USPQ2d 1020 (Fed. Cir. 1990), where the defendant destroyed many of its records, which made it impossible for the plaintiff to reconstruct all of the infringing sales. The district court awarded lost profits equal to the total sales that could be proved. The Federal Circuit held that the district court had no equitable discretion to equate gross provable sales with lost profits, and remanded. It did, however, indicate that if the records destruction seemed to warrant it, the district court on remand could exercise its discretion to increase damages, and thus end up with an award even greater than the defendant's gross sales.

size and complexity of the patentee's company and with the extent to which that information is challenged or contradicted by the infringer.[93]

Lost profits may be in the form of diverted sales, eroded prices, or increased expenses.[94] For example, if the patentee can show that it had to sell at a lower price in order to keep the infringer from making the sale, it can recover the difference.[95] Where the infringer's sales cause an artificial depression of the patentee's sales and thus depress the patentee's profit margin, the infringer should not be the beneficiary. It is therefore appropriate to use the patent owner's profit margin, unaffected by the infringing sales, to estimate what the patent owner's profits would have been in the absence of the infringement.[96]

In general, an infringer's sales at a lower price do not defeat the patentee's recovery of its losses at the patentee's price, for the principle of patent damages is to return the patentee to the pecuniary position it would have been in but for the infringement.[97] Thus, where the infringer's pricing practices forced the patentee to give discounts, the patentee would be entitled to recover those discounts in computing its lost profits.[98] Similarly, where the evidence showed that the infringement caused the patentee to reduce its price an average of $100 per unit, it was proper to award the patentee, in addition to its actual lost profits, $100 for each of its own sales and $100 for each of the infringer's sales.[99] Price erosion as a damages element can become extremely significant.[100] To prove price erosion damages, a patentee

---

[93]*Carella v. Starlight Archery & Pro Line Co.*, 804 F.2d 135, 231 USPQ 644 (Fed. Cir. 1986).

[94]*Amstar Corp. v. Envirotech Corp.*, 823 F.2d 1538, 3 USPQ2d 1412 (Fed. Cir. 1987); *Lam, Inc. v. Johns-Manville Corp.*, 718 F.2d 1056, 219 USPQ 670 (Fed. Cir. 1983).

[95]*Lam, Inc. v. Johns-Manville Corp.*, 718 F.2d 1056, 219 USPQ 670 (Fed. Cir. 1983). See also *Kalman v. Berlyn Corp.*, 914 F.2d 1473, 16 USPQ2d 1093 (Fed. Cir. 1990).

[96]*King Instr. Corp. v. Otari Corp.*, 767 F.2d 853, 226 USPQ 402 (Fed. Cir. 1985).

[97]*Ball Corp. v. Micron Separations, Inc.*, 66 F.3d 1211, 36 USPQ2d 1225 (Fed. Cir. 1995). It should be noted, however, that the court affirmed a lost profits rate that was less than the patentee's actual rate.

[98]*TWM Mfg. Co. v. Dura Corp.*, 789 F.2d 895, 229 USPQ 525 (Fed. Cir. 1986). A failure to consider the fact that the infringer sold at a lower price than the patent owner is not error from the standpoint of the infringer. The patent owner's disregard of that fact could only reduce the profit that it might have proved. *Ryco, Inc. v. Ag-Bag Corp.*, 857 F.2d 1418, 8 USPQ2d 1323 (Fed. Cir. 1988).

[99]*TWM Mfg. Co. v. Dura Corp.*, 789 F.2d 895, 229 USPQ 525 (Fed. Cir. 1986). Interestingly, there was a period during which reasonable royalty was found to be the appropriate measure of damage. During this period, the extra $100 was not awarded because it presumably would have been factored into the reasonable royalty calculation. In a combined patent and mask work infringement case, the court affirmed a lost profits award that included as an element losses due to the patent owner lowering prices as a result of the infringer's preinfringing announcement of the new product. In so doing, it noted that for products of high technology, the innovator's opportunity to recover the investment made in research and development is often concentrated in the few years immediately following introduction of a new product. *Brooktree Corp. v. Advanced Micro Devices, Inc.*, 977 F.2d 1555, 24 USPQ2d 1401 (Fed. Cir. 1992).

[100]In *Minnesota Min. & Mfg. Co. v. Johnson & Johnson Orthopaedics, Inc.*, 976 F.2d 1559, 24 USPQ2d 1321 (Fed. Cir. 1992), this factor apparently accounted for $29 million of the award.

must show that, but for the infringement, it would have been able to charge higher prices.[101] Whether competitive price reductions are properly included as lost profits is a question of fact.[102]

In lost profits determinations involving large installations, noninfringing installations cannot form the basis for a lost profits recovery, even if the sales of those noninfringing installations result from "bait-and-switch" tactics on the part of the infringer.[103]

Lost profits can be based on market shares.[104] If a patentee can show that its growth rate during the period of infringement was less than the rate projected from the preinfringement period, it can recover expected profits for the differential (less, of course, any actual lost profits on sales made by the infringer during the period). The court indicated that such a measure of damages was not unduly speculative or conjectural and seemed to justify it on such considerations as injury to goodwill and drain of resources and personnel caused by the litigation.[105] But projections of lost profits must not be speculative. The burden of proving future injury is commensurately greater than that for damages already incurred, for the future always harbors unknowns. While estimates of lost future profits may necessarily contain some speculative elements, the fact finder must have before it such facts and circumstances to enable it to make an estimate of damage based upon judgment not guesswork.[106]

In ITC cases, the court has recognized that it may be appropriate to employ a more lenient standard with respect to the actual quantum of lost sales, on the theory that an emerging domestic industry may need additional protection. However, the standard of proof remains the same: a but for analysis must be employed and that requires

---

[101]*Minco, Inc. v. Combustion Eng'g, Inc.,* 95 F.3d 1109, 40 USPQ2d 1001 (Fed. Cir. 1996).

[102]*Brooktree Corp. v. Advanced Micro Devices, Inc.,* 977 F.2d 1555, 24 USPQ2d 1401 (Fed. Cir. 1992).

[103]*Standard Havens Prods., Inc. v. Gencor Indus., Inc.,* 953 F.2d 1360, 21 USPQ2d 1321 (Fed. Cir. 1992).

[104]*State Indus., Inc. v. Mor-Flo Indus., Inc.,* 883 F.2d 1573, 12 USPQ2d 1026 (Fed. Cir. 1989). The patentee had 40% of a total market that consisted of infringements and a less preferable but noninfringing substitute. The district court effectively neutralized the noninfringing alternative by crediting each competitor in the market with its share of the total market. Thus, it held that the patentee was entitled to lost profits on 40% of the infringer's sales, and a reasonable royalty on the remaining 60%. See also *Micro Motion, Inc. v. Kane Steel Co.,* 894 F.2d 1318, 13 USPQ2d 1696 (Fed. Cir. 1990). In *Slimfold Mfg. Co. v. Kinkead Indus.,* 932 F.2d 1453, 18 USPQ2d 1842 (Fed. Cir. 1991), the court distinguished *State v. Mor-Flo* on the ground it held only that the grant of lost profits based on market share was not an abuse of discretion. That does not mean that a failure to award lost profits based on market share would necessarily constitute an abuse of discretion.

[105]*Lam, Inc. v. Johns-Manville Corp.,* 718 F.2d 1056, 219 USPQ 670 (Fed. Cir. 1983). The court was not required to deal with the possibility that the postinfringement growth rate might remain at the reduced level; here it picked up again to the preinfringement level. It should also be considered whether this decision might be limited to a market with only two suppliers.

[106]*Oiness v. Walgreen Co.,*88 F.3d 1025, 39 USPQ2d 1304 (Fed. Cir. 1996). Speculative or contingent profits, as opposed to those a plaintiff would certainly earn but for the default, are recoverable only when the record permits estimation of probable profits with reasonable certainty. *U.S. Valves Inc. v. Dray,* 212 F.3d 1368, 54 USPQ2d 1834 (Fed. Cir. 2000).

a showing that a sale by the infringer represented a lost sale to the industry.[107]

The court has indicated that it is willing to employ an "incremental profits" approach to calculating loss. This approach recognizes that it does not cost as much to produce unit *n+1* if the first *n* or fewer units have already paid the fixed costs.[108] The court also has vigorously embraced the "entire market rule" for lost profits calculations as well as reasonable royalty determinations.[109]

In *Rite-Hite v. Kelley*,[110] the patentee made two types of devices: a low priced unit that was covered by its patent, and a high priced unit that was not. The defendant's infringing device was intended to compete with the plaintiff's unpatented high priced unit. In an in banc decision, the court held that the patentee was entitled to recover profits that it lost on the diverted sales of the unpatented device. The court adopted a test of reasonable foreseeability, not unlike the concept of "proximate cause" traditionally encountered in tort law. Thus, lost sales of the unpatented device that directly competed with the infringing device were reasonably foreseeable and therefore compensable.[111]

---

[107]*Corning Glass Works v. United States ITC,* 799 F.2d 1559, 230 USPQ 822 (Fed. Cir. 1986).

[108]*Paper Converting Mach. Co. v. Magna-Graphics Corp.,* 745 F.2d 11, 223 USPQ 591 (Fed. Cir. 1984). Fixed costs are those that do not vary with increases in production, such as management salaries, property taxes, insurance, etc. *Id.* An award of incremental profits is well established and appropriate for determining damages for patent infringement where any increase in fixed costs per unit is found to be minimal. *State Indus., Inc. v. Mor-Flo Indus., Inc.,* 883 F.2d 1573, 12 USPQ2d 1026 (Fed. Cir. 1989).

[109]*State Indus., Inc. v. Mor-Flo Indus., Inc.,* 883 F.2d 1573, 12 USPQ2d 1026 (Fed. Cir. 1989); *Paper Converting Mach. Co. v. Magna-Graphics Corp.,* 745 F.2d 11, 223 USPQ 591 (Fed. Cir. 1984) (lost profits case). The *Panduit* test applies here as well. Thus, there must be a reasonable probability that the patentee would have made the sale of an unpatented accessory had the defendant not made the infringing sale. *Kaufman Co. v. Lantech, Inc.,* 926 F.2d 1136, 17 USPQ2d 1828 (Fed. Cir. 1991). See §12.1(d) for a general discussion of the entire market rule.

[110]*Rite-Hite Corp. v. Kelley Co.,* 56 F.3d 1538, 35 USPQ2d 1065 (Fed. Cir. 1995).

[111]The court rejected various policy arguments, such as that inventors should be encouraged by the law to practice their patented inventions, and that a patent cannot be used to restrict competition in the sale of products not covered by the patent. It also distinguished the noninfringing alternative prong of the lost profits test on the grounds that here, the noninfringing alternative was available only through the patentee. In a vigorous dissent, Judge Nies pointed out that the plaintiff could not mark the unpatented products with the patent number for notice purposes, and yet could recover for profits lost as a result of the diverted sales of those products. This, according to her, puts the patentee who does not practice the patented invention at an advantage versus one who does. The majority brushed this argument aside, implying that the lost sales had occurred after actual notice of the infringement. In *King Instr. Corp. v. Perego,* 65 F.3d 941, 36 USPQ2d 1129 (Fed. Cir. 1995), a 2–1 majority reaffirmed the *Rite-Hite* holding that lost profits are available to the patent owner despite its failure to produce the patented product. The dissent accused the majority of extending *Rite-Hite* to cover a situation where the patentee is not even putting out a competitive product; rather, it was one that did not offer the advantage of the patented device. At one point, the majority decision sets up a hypothetical situation that would lead to the result that "infringement may actually be profitable." With all respect, one might venture to inquire what is wrong with that? Is there something morally reprehensible about infringement if everyone profits? As the majority points out, Congress decided 50 years ago that a defendant infringer should no longer be made to disgorge its own profits; actual damages or a reasonable royalty are sufficient as long as they are adequate to compensate for the infringement.

(c) *Reasonable Royalty*

The two methods by which damages are usually calculated under 35 U.S.C. §284 are assessment of actual damages (the profits the patentee lost due to the infringement) or, if actual damages cannot be ascertained, determination of a reasonable royalty.[112]

The statute mandates a reasonable royalty as the floor below which damages shall not fall.[113] A reasonable royalty is the amount a person, desiring to manufacture, use, or sell a patented article as a business proposition, would be willing to pay as a royalty and yet be able to make a reasonable profit.[114]

Can damages be assessed at greater than a reasonable royalty without a lost profits analysis? Apparently so.[115] Yet care must be taken to avoid confusing the two modes of analysis.[116]

The hypothetical negotiation. In *Fromson v. Western,*[117] the court had some interesting things to say about the very concept of a reasonable royalty. Determining a fair and reasonable royalty is often a difficult judicial chore, seeming often to involve more the talents of a conjurer than those of a judge. Lacking adequate evidence of an

---

[112]*Trell v. Marlee Elec. Corp.,* 912 F.2d 1443, 16 USPQ2d 1059 (Fed. Cir. 1990). Where the plaintiff does not sell its invention in the United States, it must present evidence of a reasonable royalty. *Id.*

[113]35 U.S.C. §284. See *Stickle v. Heublein, Inc.,* 716 F.2d 1550, 219 USPQ 377 (Fed. Cir. 1983). A statement by the trial court that it was awarding "nominal" damages is not necessarily in conflict with the reasonable royalty standard as the statutory floor, where it appeared that the court was using that term to indicate that it was giving the plaintiff far less than it had demanded. *Lindemann Maschinenfabrik v. American Hoist & Derrick Co.,* 895 F.2d 1403, 13 USPQ2d 1871 (Fed. Cir. 1990).

[114]*Trans-World Mfg. Corp. v. Al Nyman & Sons,* 750 F.2d 1552, 224 USPQ 259 (Fed. Cir. 1984).

[115]In *Maxwell v. J. Baker, Inc.,* 86 F.3d 1098, 39 USPQ2d 1001 (Fed. Cir. 1996), the court found no abuse of discretion in a jury interrogatory that asked "What is the reasonable royalty? Was the plaintiff damaged in excess of the reasonable royalty and, if so, by how much?" This approach was justified in part by the absurdity of a hypothetical negotiation where the parties had previously been unable to reach agreement. This case stands for the proposition that the fact finder may consider additional factors to assist in the determination of adequate compensation for the infringement. See also note 12:125.

[116]In *Mahurkar v. C.R. Bard, Inc.,* 79 F.3d 1572, 38 USPQ2d 1288 (Fed. Cir. 1996), the trial court properly found a reasonable royalty rate but then assessed an additional 9% that it called a *"Panduit* kicker." The Federal Circuit viewed this as an enhancement of the damages award and reversed. *Panduit* had to do with lost profits, not reasonable royalty, and nowhere does that decision authorize additional damages or a "kicker" on top of a reasonable royalty. In *Rodime PLC v. Seagate Tech. Inc.,* 174 F.3d 1294, 50 USPQ2d 1429 (Fed. Cir. 1999), the plaintiff elected to forego lost profits as a measure of damages in favor of reasonable royalty. But it still sought "consequential business damages" resulting from the defendant's refusal to take a license (theoretically depriving plaintiff of an income stream sufficient to have enabled it to avoid bankruptcy). The Federal Circuit hinted that this might be acceptable methodology if the impending bankruptcy were factored into the hypothetical negotiations. But here the plaintiff sought such damages above and beyond the reasonable royalty. As such, these damages were merely a species of lost profits, which plaintiff had elected to forego.

[117]*Fromson v. Western Litho Plate & Supp. Co.,* 853 F.2d 1568, 7 USPQ2d 1606 (Fed. Cir. 1988).

established royalty, the court is left with the judge-created methodology described as "hypothetical negotiations between willing licensor and willing licensee." The reasonable royalty methodology encompasses fantasy and flexibility: fantasy because it requires a court to imagine what warring parties would have agreed to as willing negotiators; flexibility because it speaks of negotiations as of the time infringement began, yet permits and often requires a court to look to events and facts that occurred thereafter and that could not have been known to or predicted by the hypothesized negotiators. When one is forced to erect a hypothetical situation, it is easy to forget a basic reality—a license is fundamentally an agreement by the patent owner not to sue the licensee. In a normal negotiation, the potential licensee has three basic choices: (1) forego all use of the invention; (2) pay an agreed royalty; or (3) infringe the patent and risk litigation. The reasonable royalty methodology presumes that the licensee has made the second choice, when in fact it selected the third. Whatever royalty may result from employment of the methodology, the law is not without means for recognizing that an infringer is unlike a true "willing licensee"; nor is the law without means for placing the injured patentee in the situation it would have occupied if the wrong had not been committed. Increased damages under 35 U.S.C. §284 is one such means. Attorney fees in "exceptional" cases under §285 is another. Prejudgment interest is a third.

Like all methodologies based upon a hypothetical situation, there will be an element of uncertainty in determining a reasonable royalty. But a court is not at liberty, in pursuing the methodology, to abandon entirely the statutory standard of damages "adequate to compensate" for the infringement. The royalty arrived at must be reasonable under all the circumstances; that is, it must be at least a close approximation of what would be "adequate to compensate" for the "use made of the invention by the infringer" as required by §284.[118]

It is a hypothetical royalty resulting from arm's-length negotiations between a willing licensor and a willing licensee.[119] The willing licensor/licensee approach must be flexibly applied as a device in the aid of justice.[120] In using the test, it is important to understand that there is no actual willingness on either side.[121]

Section 284 does not mandate how the district court must compute a reasonable royalty, but only that it compensate for the infringement.[122] The court has held squarely that a district court is not limited

---

[118]*Fromson v. Western Litho Plate & Supp. Co.*, 853 F.2d 1568, 7 USPQ2d 1606 (Fed. Cir. 1988). See also *Trell v. Marlee Elec. Corp.*, 912 F.2d 1443, 16 USPQ2d 1059 (Fed. Cir. 1990).

[119]*State Indus., Inc. v. Mor-Flo Indus., Inc.*, 883 F.2d 1573, 12 USPQ2d 1026 (Fed. Cir. 1989); *TWM Mfg. Co. v. Dura Corp.*, 789 F.2d 895, 229 USPQ 525 (Fed. Cir. 1986).

[120]*TWM Mfg. Co. v. Dura Corp.*, 789 F.2d 895, 229 USPQ 525 (Fed. Cir. 1986). Relevant economic facts may inform this judicially-sanctioned speculation. *Mahurkar v. C.R. Bard, Inc.*, 79 F.3d 1572, 38 USPQ2d 1288 (Fed. Cir. 1996).

[121]*Hanson v. Alpine Valley Ski Area, Inc.*, 718 F.2d 1075, 219 USPQ 679 (Fed. Cir. 1983).

[122]*TWM Mfg. Co. v. Dura Corp.*, 789 F.2d 895, 229 USPQ 525 (Fed. Cir. 1986).

to selecting one or the other of the specific royalty figures urged by opposing parties as reasonable,[123] nor is a jury, although the award must be within the range encompassed by the record as a whole.[124] Also, damages can be increased above a reasonable royalty so that the award is adequate to compensate for the infringement. Such an increase can be justified either on the basis that reasonable means "reasonable for an infringer," or simply under the statute.[125]

That the patentee might have agreed to a lesser royalty is of little relevance, for to look only at that question would be to pretend that the infringement never happened. It would also make an election to infringe a handy means for competitors to impose a compulsory license policy upon every patent owner.[126] In determining the true measure of a reasonable royalty, a court should not select a diminished royalty rate that a patentee may have been forced to accept by the disrepute of its patent and the open defiance of its rights.[127] Nonetheless, it is important to leave the hypothetical licensee a profit margin.[128] On the other hand, it is not unreasonable to base the award on the expected profits of the patentee rather than the infringer, even though this turns out to be many times the infringer's net profit.[129] In contrast to a lost profits inquiry, the fact that an infringer could have continued to market a noninfringing alternative is a factor relevant to the determination of a proper royalty during hypothetical negotiations.[130]

The *Fromson* court also commented thoughtfully on the status of the individual inventor in the reasonable royalty compensation scheme. Historically, the methodology for determining a reasonable royalty has been problematic as a mechanism for doing justice to individual, nonmanufacturing patentees. Because courts routinely denied injunctions to such patentees, infringers could perceive nothing to fear but the possibility of a compulsory license at a reasonable

---

[123]*Smithkline Diagnostics, Inc. v. Helena Labs. Corp.*, 926 F.2d 1161, 17 USPQ2d 1922 (Fed. Cir. 1991).

[124]*Unisplay S.A. v. American Elec. Sign Co.*, 69 F.3d 512, 36 USPQ2d 1540 (Fed. Cir. 1995).

[125]*Stickle v. Heublein, Inc.*, 716 F.2d 1550, 219 USPQ 377 (Fed. Cir. 1983). See also *Maxwell v. J. Baker, Inc.*, 86 F.3d 1098, 39 USPQ2d 1001 (Fed. Cir. 1996). In *Slimfold Mfg. Co. v. Kinkead Indus.*, 932 F.2d 1453, 18 USPQ2d 1842 (Fed. Cir. 1991), the court approved an award of a reasonable royalty and an additional amount for cost savings in manufacture attributable to the patented invention. But see *Mahurkar v. C.R. Bard, Inc.*, 79 F.3d 1572, 38 USPQ2d 1288 (Fed. Cir. 1996).

[126]*TWM Mfg. Co. v. Dura Corp.*, 789 F.2d 895, 229 USPQ 525 (Fed. Cir. 1986). Courts have recognized the need to distinguish between royalties payable by infringers and noninfringers. *Fromson v. Western Litho Plate & Supp. Co.*, 853 F.2d 1568, 7 USPQ2d 1606 (Fed. Cir. 1988).

[127]*Fromson v. Western Litho Plate & Supp. Co.*, 853 F.2d 1568, 7 USPQ2d 1606 (Fed. Cir. 1988).

[128]*Hughes Tool Co. v. Dresser Indus., Inc.*, 816 F.2d 1549, 2 USPQ2d 1396 (Fed. Cir. 1987); *Hanson v. Alpine Valley Ski Area, Inc.*, 718 F.2d 1075, 219 USPQ 679 (Fed. Cir. 1983). Of course, it is proper to resolve difficulty in determining a reasonable royalty against an infringer that has lost its financial records. *TWM Mfg. Co. v. Dura Corp.*, 789 F.2d 895, 229 USPQ 525 (Fed. Cir. 1986).

[129]*Rite-Hite Corp. v. Kelley Co.*, 56 F.3d 1538, 35 USPQ2d 1065 (Fed. Cir. 1995).

[130]*Zygo Corp. v. Wyko Corp.*, 79 F.3d 1563, 38 USPQ2d 1281 (Fed. Cir. 1996).

royalty, resulting in some quarters in a lowered respect for the rights of such patentees and a failure to recognize the innovation-encouraging social purpose of the patent system. Thus a cold "bottom-line" logic would dictate to some a total disregard of the individual inventor's patent because if the case be lost, a license could be compelled, probably at the same royalty that would have been paid if the patentee's rights had been respected at the outset. Though the methodology must on occasion be used for want of a better one, it must be carefully applied to achieve a truly reasonable royalty, for the methodology risks creation of the perception that blatant, blind appropriation of inventions patented by individual, nonmanufacturing inventors is the profitable, "can't-lose" course.[131]

Compensation for infringement can take cognizance of the actual commercial consequences of the infringement, and the hypothetical negotiators for a reasonable royalty need not act as if there had been no infringement, no litigation, and no erosion of market position or patent value.[132] In applying the "reasonable royalty" methodology, emphasis on an individual inventor's lack of money and manufacturing capacity can tend to distinguish the respect due the patent rights of impecunious individual inventors from that due the patent rights of well-funded, well-lawyered, large manufacturing corporations. Any such distinction should be rejected as the disservice it is to the public interest in technological advancement.[133]

Infringer's anticipated profit. Among the factors to be considered in applying the willing licensor/licensee approach is the infringer's anticipated profit from the use of the patented invention, including the effect of using the patented item in promoting sales of other products of the licensee.[134] Evidence of the infringer's actual profits is generally admissible as probative of its anticipated profits.[135] Although the court has allowed that it is not illogical to hypothesize a negotiation as of the time of notice of infringement, it continues to insist that the hypothetical exercise be set at the time infringement

---

[131]*Fromson v. Western Litho Plate & Supp. Co.,* 853 F.2d 1568, 7 USPQ2d 1606 (Fed. Cir. 1988).

[132]*Sun Studs, Inc. v. ATA Equip. Leasing, Inc.,* 872 F.2d 978, 10 USPQ2d 1338 (Fed. Cir. 1989). The court refused to concern itself with whether the date of the hypothetical negotiations should be as of the date of contributory infringement, or of direct infringement, terming it "too fine" a line to draw.

[133]*Fromson v. Western Litho Plate & Supp. Co.,* 853 F.2d 1568, 7 USPQ2d 1606 (Fed. Cir. 1988).

[134]*Trans-World Mfg. Corp. v. Al Nyman & Sons,* 750 F.2d 1552, 224 USPQ 259 (Fed. Cir. 1984). See also *Trell v. Marlee Elec. Corp.,* 912 F.2d 1443, 16 USPQ2d 1059 (Fed. Cir. 1990). Collateral sales certainly may be taken into account in determining what a willing licensor would have charged a willing licensee. *Deere & Co. v. International Harvester Co.,* 710 F.2d 1551, 218 USPQ 481 (Fed. Cir. 1983).

[135]*TWM Mfg. Co. v. Dura Corp.,* 789 F.2d 895, 229 USPQ 525 (Fed. Cir. 1986); *Trans-World Mfg. Corp. v. Al Nyman & Sons,* 750 F.2d 1552, 224 USPQ 259 (Fed. Cir. 1984).

began.[136] A vast disparity between actual and hypothetically negotiated profits will rarely be sustainable when the invention was recognized by both parties as highly valuable at the time infringement began and a negotiation is hypothesized. Yet each case must be judged on its own merits in light of the evidentiary record created and introduced by counsel.[137] The infringer's actual profit, however, does not act as a cap on the amount of a reasonable royalty.[138] Nor does an industry standard profit. The court seems willing to employ an analytical approach in its weighting of anticipated profits.[139]

An award of a 25 percent royalty was based upon a finding that the infringer would have made a profit of 60 percent. The Federal Circuit, in analyzing the evidence, determined that the 60 percent expectation was profit on incremental investment rather than cost. The 60 percent finding was therefore seen to be clearly erroneous, and the 25 percent royalty was rejected as arbitrary.[140] On the other hand, the court found no abuse of discretion in applying a royalty rate to the selling price alone rather than to the selling price plus the royalty amount.[141]

---

[136]*Wang Labs., Inc. v. Toshiba Corp.*, 993 F.2d 858, 26 USPQ2d 1767 (Fed. Cir. 1993). The focus should be on the date infringement began rather than events subsequent to the initial infringement. *TWM Mfg. Co. v. Dura Corp.*, 789 F.2d 895, 229 USPQ 525 (Fed. Cir. 1986). See also *Unisplay S.A. v. American Elec. Sign Co.*, 69 F.3d 512, 36 USPQ2d 1540 (Fed. Cir. 1995).

[137]*Datascope Corp. v. SMEC, Inc.*, 879 F.2d 820, 11 USPQ2d 1321 (Fed. Cir. 1989).

[138]*State Indus., Inc. v. Mor-Flo Indus., Inc.*, 883 F.2d 1573, 12 USPQ2d 1026 (Fed. Cir. 1989); *Fromson v. Western Litho Plate & Supp. Co.*, 853 F.2d 1568, 7 USPQ2d 1606 (Fed. Cir. 1988). See also *Mahurkar v. C.R. Bard, Inc.*, 79 F.3d 1572, 38 USPQ2d 1288 (Fed. Cir. 1996). It is not unreasonable to base the award on the expected profits of the patentee rather than the infringer, even though this turns out to be many times the infringer's net profit. *Rite-Hite Corp. v. Kelley Co.*, 56 F.3d 1538, 35 USPQ2d 1065 (Fed. Cir. 1995). In *Snellman v. Ricoh Co.*, 862 F.2d 283, 8 USPQ2d 1996 (Fed. Cir. 1988), the jury awarded $12 million, which was more than four times the defendant's total sales. The justification was a reasonable royalty based upon a high, albeit disputed, projection of expected sales at the time infringement began. The district court felt this was a miscarriage of justice and granted a new trial on damages, with a resultant award of less than $1 million. The Federal Circuit vacated and remanded, either to reinstate the jury verdict or for a new trial based on its statements about what evidence is admissible on the issue. In *Radio Steel & Mfg. Co. v. MTD Prods., Inc.*, 788 F.2d 1554, 229 USPQ 431 (Fed. Cir. 1986), the court rejected an argument that a 10% royalty was unreasonable because it exceeded the infringer's profit. It should be noted that there was evidence that the profit figure was low because the infringing product was at the time used as a loss leader. In *Lindemann Maschinenfabrik v. American Hoist & Derrick Co.*, 895 F.2d 1403, 13 USPQ2d 1871 (Fed. Cir. 1990), the court termed an expert's statement that the infringer would, in hypothetical negotiations, agree to pay a royalty in excess of what it expected to make in profits "absurd" in light of the evidence in the case.

[139]*TWM Mfg. Co. v. Dura Corp.*, 789 F.2d 895, 229 USPQ 525 (Fed. Cir. 1986). The court affirmed a 30% royalty as reasonable, where the infringer projected an anticipated net profit of 37–42% and the industry standard net profit was 7–12%. Despite the infringer's anguished cry that this rate was grossly inflated and exorbitant, the court seemed to be persuaded by facts such as commercial success, long-felt need, copying, and the absence of competing products.

[140]*Hughes Tool Co. v. Dresser Indus., Inc.*, 816 F.2d 1549, 2 USPQ2d 1396 (Fed. Cir. 1987). There is no rule that a royalty be no higher than the infringer's net profit margin. Nor is it inappropriate for a district court to consider gross profits. *State Indus., Inc. v. Mor-Flo Indus., Inc.*, 883 F.2d 1573, 12 USPQ2d 1026 (Fed. Cir. 1989).

[141]*Nickson Indus., Inc. v. Rol Mfg. Co.*, 847 F.2d 795, 6 USPQ2d 1878 (Fed. Cir. 1988). This is an interesting theory—the patentee seems to be saying that the infringer would have

One interesting case dealt with the infringer's profits in the context of a patented design for a display rack for selling goods. Inasmuch as the infringing racks may well have contributed to the infringer's sales of, and therefore profits on, the goods themselves, those profits would be relevant to a reasonable royalty under §284.[142]

Established royalty. A very logical measure of a hypothetical reasonable royalty is an actual, established royalty. And even if there is no existing royalty rate, it is appropriate to consider royalties paid by others in the industry for use of a comparable patent.[143] The task is simplified when the record shows an established royalty for the patent in question or for related patents or products.[144] However, evidence of royalties for products entirely distinct from the patented product are insufficient to establish an industry standard.[145] Also, evidence of actual licenses that were negotiated some years after the date of first infringement may not be probative.[146] Conversely, established rates do not necessarily fix a ceiling for the royalty that may be assessed after an infringement trial.[147]

The reasonableness of a rate in a single license is sometimes questioned because there is no general acquiescence,[148] or because it involves only a minor competitor.[149] Thus, a single licensing agreement, without more, is insufficient proof of an established royalty. For a royalty to be established, it must be paid by such a number of persons as to indicate a general acquiescence in its reasonableness

---

upped its price to cover the royalty. Thus, if R is the nominal rate, the effective rate would be $R/(1 - R)$.

[142]*Trans-World Mfg. Corp. v. Al Nyman & Sons,* 750 F.2d 1552, 224 USPQ 259 (Fed. Cir. 1984). It should be noted that 35 U.S.C. §289 provides an additional remedy for infringement of design patents, over and above that available under 35 U.S.C. §284: the patentee is entitled to the total profit of the infringer (not less than $250). Here the total profit on the racks to which the patented design had been applied was small compared to the profit from the sale of the displayed goods. The patentee was not entitled to the profits from the sale of the goods under §289, but those profits were a consideration under §284. In *L.A. Gear, Inc. v. Thom McAn Shoe Co.,* 988 F.2d 1117, 25 USPQ2d 1913 (Fed. Cir. 1993), the defendant supplier had indemnified its large retail customer and plaintiff did not join the customer because of assurances from the defendant that it could provide any and all relief. Later, the defendant argued that it should be permitted to deduct, from the "total profit" under §289, the profits of the customer. The Federal Circuit rejected this argument on the grounds that actions induced by attorney representations cannot be disclaimed by their instigator. Reliance by the plaintiff was sought and obtained, and it was not unreasonable. Having induced that reliance, the defendant could not renounce the consequences.

[143]*American Original Corp. v. Jenkins Food Corp.,* 774 F.2d 459, 227 USPQ 299 (Fed. Cir. 1985).

[144]*Mahurkar v. C.R. Bard, Inc.,* 79 F.3d 1572, 38 USPQ2d 1288 (Fed. Cir. 1996).

[145]*Railroad Dynamics, Inc. v. A. Stucki Co.,* 727 F.2d 1506, 220 USPQ 929 (Fed. Cir. 1984).

[146]*Odetics Inc. v. Storage Tech. Corp.,* 185 F.3d 1259, 51 USPQ2d 1225 (Fed. Cir. 1999).

[147]*Bio-Rad Labs., Inc. v. Nicolet Inst. Corp.,* 739 F.2d 604, 222 USPQ 654 (Fed. Cir. 1984). A rate of one-third the selling price was held reasonable against evidence of industry rates of 3–10%. Cf. *Hanson v. Alpine Valley Ski Area, Inc.,* 718 F.2d 1075, 219 USPQ 679 (Fed. Cir. 1983).

[148]*Hanson v. Alpine Valley Ski Area, Inc.,* 718 F.2d 1075, 219 USPQ 679 (Fed. Cir. 1983).

[149]*Deere & Co. v. International Harvester Co.,* 710 F.2d 1551, 218 USPQ 481 (Fed. Cir. 1983).

by those who have occasion to use the invention. Where no established royalty exists, the court must use a hypothetical willing buyer/willing seller analysis.[150]

Where an established royalty exists, it will usually be the best measure of what is a reasonable royalty. Nonetheless, a reasonable royalty may be greater than an established royalty. For example, a higher figure may be awarded when the evidence clearly shows that widespread infringement made the established royalty artificially low. But the patentee must come forward with evidence that an established royalty rate makes the award inadequate.[151]

The general principle is that for an established royalty to be regarded as reasonable, it must relate to the value of the invention. In other words, the defendant's infringing acts must be commensurate in quality and extent with those that were contemplated under the actual license.[152] In calculating a reasonable royalty by reference to an established royalty, the court is perfectly willing to employ the detailed terms of the actual license.[153]

The requirement to determine actual damages is not diminished by the difficulty of the determination. The use of a royalty as a measure of damages is suited to those circumstances where there is an established royalty or licensing program, or where the patentee is not itself in the business, or where the profits are too speculative to estimate. But where a percentage figure is not an established royalty and is not found to be an approximation of the damages actually sustained, its imposition on a patent owner who would not have licensed its invention for that figure is a form of compulsory license, against the will and interest of the person wronged, in favor of the wrongdoer.[154] When lost profits are the measure, the amount is normally provable

---

[150]*Trell v. Marlee Elec. Corp.*, 912 F.2d 1443, 16 USPQ2d 1059 (Fed. Cir. 1990). In this case the district court settled upon a rate in a single agreement, and the defendant did not introduce any evidence to show that rate was unreasonable. Nonetheless, the Federal Circuit indicated that the defendant was not required to rebut proof of a royalty paid by another for an exclusive license that involved additional inventions. The burden was upon the plaintiff to show that the agreement rate was reasonable.

[151]*Nickson Indus., Inc. v. Rol Mfg. Co.*, 847 F.2d 795, 6 USPQ2d 1878 (Fed. Cir. 1988).

[152]*Bandag, Inc. v. Gerrard Tire Co.*, 704 F.2d 1578, 217 USPQ 977 (Fed. Cir. 1983). The existing license agreements also conferred trademark and other rights, and it was held error to fail to apportion between the patent and nonpatent elements of the established royalty.

[153]*Allen Archery, Inc. v. Browning Mfg. Co.*, 898 F.2d 787, 14 USPQ2d 1156 (Fed. Cir. 1990). Plaintiff's industry-wide license agreement provided for calculating the royalty as a percentage of the net selling price established in normal, bona fide, arm's-length transactions. The Federal Circuit found error in calculating a royalty based upon the infringer's sales to its subsidiary rather than the subsidiary's sales to customers.

[154]*Del Mar Avionics, Inc. v. Quinton Instr. Co.*, 836 F.2d 1320, 5 USPQ2d 1255 (Fed. Cir. 1987). Indeed, the principle underlying damage measurement is unchanged even when there is an established royalty, for it is reasonable to assume that such a royalty is a fair measure of the actual damage to a patentee who has authorized others to practice the patented invention. *Id.* The patentee's usual licensing approach should be considered in assessing a reasonable royalty. *Studiengesellschaft Kohle v. Dart Indus., Inc.*, 862 F.2d 1564, 9 USPQ2d 1273 (Fed. Cir. 1988). In *Sun Studs, Inc. v. ATA Equip. Leasing, Inc.*, 872 F.2d 978, 10 USPQ2d 1338 (Fed. Cir. 1989), the patentee was complaining that it should have received damages measured by the much higher value of the invention to the ultimate user rather than to the manufacturer

by the facts in evidence or as a factual inference from the evidence. When a reasonable royalty is the measure, the amount may again be considered a factual inference from the evidence, yet there is room for exercise of a common sense estimation of what the evidence shows would be a "reasonable" award. One challenging only the court's finding as to amount of damages awarded as a reasonable royalty must therefore show that the award is, in view of all the evidence, either so outrageously high or so outrageously low as to be unsupportable as an estimation of a reasonable royalty.[155]

Licensing offers. The court has refused to adopt any hard and fast rule that offers to license others at a particular rate establishes that rate as a ceiling for a reasonable royalty. The entirety of the circumstances, including the consequence of widespread infringement, must be considered.[156] A defendant may often seek to minimize the award of damages by presenting evidence of licensing offers at favorable rates. But offers to license present special problems. A royalty at which a patentee offers to license its invention, particularly when coupled with a claim of infringement, is not necessarily the same rate as that upon which a hypothetical willing licensee and willing licensor would agree.[157] Moreover, offers to license in settlement of actual or contemplated litigation may well be inadmissible under Rule 408, FRE.[158] However, evidence of a license agreement resulting from other litigation may be admissible where the agreement is not just an effort to resolve the dispute or avoid litigation. The avoidance of the risk and expense of litigation is always a potential motive for settlement.[159] Also, the terms of a settlement are admissible as to a reasonable royalty where litigation has established liability and the settling defendant was facing an accounting and an injunction. The patentee's argument that the settlement represents an erosion, because of the threat of the litigation causing the patentee to compromise, is not applicable in

---

or supplier of the invention. But its only established royalty was that to a supplier, and it made no effort to show at trial that it would have adopted a user royalty structure.

[155]*Lindemann Maschinenfabrik v. American Hoist & Derrick Co.,* 895 F.2d 1403, 13 USPQ2d 1871 (Fed. Cir. 1990). Although the reasonable royalty standard of 35 U.S.C. §284 obviates the need to show the fact of damage when infringement is admitted or proven, that does not mean that a patentee who puts on little or no satisfactory evidence of a reasonable royalty can successfully appeal on the ground that the amount awarded was not reasonable. *Id.*

[156]*Hughes Aircraft Co. v. United States,* 86 F.3d 1566, 39 USPQ2d 1065 (Fed. Cir. 1996).

[157]*American Original Corp. v. Jenkins Food Corp.,* 774 F.2d 459, 227 USPQ 299 (Fed. Cir. 1985).

[158]*Hanson v. Alpine Valley Ski Area, Inc.,* 718 F.2d 1075, 219 USPQ 679 (Fed. Cir. 1983). Such an offer is admissible in the absence of an actual contemporaneous dispute. *Deere & Co. v. International Harvester Co.,* 710 F.2d 1551, 218 USPQ 481 (Fed. Cir. 1983). See also *Studiengesellschaft Kohle v. Dart Indus., Inc.,* 862 F.2d 1564, 9 USPQ2d 1273 (Fed. Cir. 1988); *Snellman v. Ricoh Co.,* 862 F.2d 283, 8 USPQ2d 1996 (Fed. Cir. 1988).

[159]*Snellman v. Ricoh Co.,* 862 F.2d 283, 8 USPQ2d 1996 (Fed. Cir. 1988). The court distinguished *Deere & Co. v. International Harvester Co.,* 710 F.2d 1551, 218 USPQ 481 (Fed. Cir. 1983), on the ground that the license agreement being relied on here was to take effect only if the licensee's liability were upheld on appeal.

such a situation. Both parties know that the next step is the exact type of accounting exercise that is being undertaken in the present case.[160] Unaccepted offers to the industry,[161] or to major competitors that approach on their own initiative,[162] may lack probative value.

(d) Calculation

In proving damages, the patent owner's burden of proof is not absolute, but rather one of reasonable probability. The district court is thus free to use its discretion in choosing a method for calculating damages, as long as the measure of damages is just and reasonable.[163] The methodology of assessing and computing damages under 35 U.S.C. §284 is within the sound discretion of the district court, and the appellant therefore has the burden of establishing an abuse of discretion by showing an error of law, or a clear error of judgment, or findings that were clearly erroneous.[164]

Contract law has long been held to preclude recovery for speculative damages. This principle applies to the threshold issue of whether damages have actually been sustained, however, and does not bar the award of damages for a proven injury of uncertain measure.[165] This approach appears to govern patent infringement damages as well. Thus, estimates or compromises are not improper per se.[166] The

---

[160]*Studiengesellschaft Kohle v. Dart Indus., Inc.*, 862 F.2d 1564, 9 USPQ2d 1273 (Fed. Cir. 1988).

[161]*American Original Corp. v. Jenkins Food Corp.*, 774 F.2d 459, 227 USPQ 299 (Fed. Cir. 1985).

[162]*Deere & Co. v. International Harvester Co.*, 710 F.2d 1551, 218 USPQ 481, 486 (Fed. Cir. 1983).

[163]*Kori Corp. v. Wilco Marsh Buggies, Inc.*, 761 F.2d 649, 225 USPQ 985 (Fed. Cir. 1985).

[164]*Stryker Corp. v. Intermedics Orthopedics, Inc.*, 96 F.3d 1409, 40 USPQ2d 1065 (Fed. Cir. 1996); *Unisplay S.A. v. American Elec. Sign Co.*, 69 F.3d 512, 36 USPQ2d 1540 (Fed. Cir. 1995); *State Indus., Inc. v. Mor-Flo Indus., Inc.*, 883 F.2d 1573, 12 USPQ2d 1026 (Fed. Cir. 1989); *Hartness Int'l, Inc. v. Simplimatic Eng'g Co.*, 819 F.2d 1100, 2 USPQ2d 1826 (Fed. Cir. 1987). The methodology of assessing and computing damages under 35 U.S.C. §284 is within the sound discretion of the district court. To prevail on appeal, the appellant must convince the court of appeals that the district court abused its discretion by basing its award on clearly erroneous factual findings, legal error, or a manifest error of judgment. *Nickson Indus., Inc. v. Rol Mfg. Co.*, 847 F.2d 795, 6 USPQ2d 1878 (Fed. Cir. 1988).

[165]*Roseburg Lumber Co. v. Madigan*, 978 F.2d 660 (Fed. Cir. 1992). In *Brooktree Corp. v. Advanced Micro Devices, Inc.*, 977 F.2d 1555, 24 USPQ2d 1401 (Fed. Cir. 1992), the court approved a failure to permit the jury to consider whether projected future losses due to price erosion could be included in a damage award. That question was simply too speculative. Although projected future losses may be recovered when sufficiently supported, the burden of proving future injury is commensurately greater than that for damages already incurred.

[166]Testimony that a royalty of about 4%, coupled with a substantial down payment, would be reasonable does not mean that an award of 5% is speculative. *Shatterproof Glass Corp. v. Libbey-Owens Ford Co.*, 758 F.2d 613, 225 USPQ 634 (Fed. Cir. 1985). Testimony that an infringing process is used "maybe one-half or three-quarters" of the time does not render a two-thirds figure erroneous. *Bandag, Inc. v. Gerrard Tire Co.*, 704 F.2d 1578, 217 USPQ 977 (Fed. Cir. 1983). Acceptance of 2% as an annual price erosion figure is not erroneous in view of defendant's argument that there would have been no price inflation in the absence of the

determination of a damage award is not an exact science and the amount need not be proven with unerring precision. The trial court is required to approximate, if necessary, the amount to which the patent owner is entitled. In such a case, while the damages may not be determined by mere speculation or guess, it will be enough if the evidence shows the extent of the damages as a matter of just and reasonable inference, although the result be only approximate.[167] There is no absolute requirement for documentary corroboration where a court's determination of damages is based upon credible testimony only. It is not always necessary to produce books or records to support a damage award.[168] Fundamental principles of justice require the court to throw any risk of uncertainty upon the wrongdoer rather than upon the injured party,[169] and any doubts regarding the precise amount of damages must therefore be resolved against the infringer.[170] When manufacturing records are destroyed after the litigation commenced, strong inferences adverse to the infringer may be drawn.[171] Where it is impossible to make a mathematical or approximate apportionment between infringing and noninfringing items, the infringer must bear the burden and the entire risk.[172]

The traditional approach is to calculate damages based upon the use of a patented process or the sale of a patented product. However, alternatives are often appropriate. It is error to suppose that damages

---

infringement while plaintiff introduced evidence to show that it would have raised prices 4% per annum. *Minnesota Min. & Mfg. Co. v. Johnson & Johnson Orthopaedics, Inc.,* 976 F.2d 1559, 24 USPQ2d 1321 (Fed. Cir. 1992). Use of disjunctive "or" in license agreement supports failure to apportion between two licensed patents where only one infringed. *Underwater Devices, Inc. v. Morrison-Knudsen Co.,* 717 F.2d 1380, 219 USPQ 569 (Fed. Cir. 1983). No error in finding that patentee would have required uniformity among licensees. *Hanson v. Alpine Valley Ski Area, Inc.,* 718 F.2d 1075, 219 USPQ 679 (Fed. Cir. 1983). No merit to argument that a 10% royalty is too high because the invention is only a combination of old elements. *Radio Steel & Mfg. Co. v. MTD Prods., Inc.,* 788 F.2d 1554, 229 USPQ 431 (Fed. Cir. 1986).

[167]*Del Mar Avionics, Inc. v. Quinton Instr. Co.,* 836 F.2d 1320, 5 USPQ2d 1255 (Fed. Cir. 1987). Contempt damages, like other damages, need not be calculated with mathematical precision. All that is necessary is credible evidence sufficient to establish the amount of damages. Courts are allowed to act upon probable and inferential as well as direct and positive proof. *Graves v. Kemscop Group, Inc.,* 864 F.2d 754, 9 USPQ2d 1404 (Fed. Cir. 1988). The amount of damages is a question of fact and a jury award that is within the range of high and low values established by the evidence is not easily overturned on appeal. *Standard Havens Prods., Inc. v. Gencor Indus., Inc.,* 953 F.2d 1360, 21 USPQ2d 1321 (Fed. Cir. 1992).

[168]*Graves v. Kemscop Group, Inc.,* 864 F.2d 754, 9 USPQ2d 1404 (Fed. Cir. 1988).

[169]*Kori Corp. v. Wilco Marsh Buggies, Inc.,* 761 F.2d 649, 225 USPQ 985 (Fed. Cir. 1985). The principle that the infringer must bear the risk of uncertainty cannot alone justify increasing the actual damages, however. *Beatrice Foods Co. v. New England Printing & Lith. Co.,* 923 F.2d 1567, 17 USPQ2d 1553 (Fed. Cir. 1991).

[170]*Kaufman Co. v. Lantech, Inc.,* 926 F.2d 1136, 17 USPQ2d 1828 (Fed. Cir. 1991); *Gyromat Corp. v. Champion Spark Plug Co.,* 735 F.2d 549, 222 USPQ 4 (Fed. Cir. 1984).

[171]*Sensonics, Inc. v. Aerosonic Corp.,* 81 F.3d 1566, 38 USPQ2d 1551 (Fed. Cir. 1996).

[172]*Nickson Indus., Inc. v. Rol Mfg. Co.,* 847 F.2d 795, 6 USPQ2d 1878 (Fed. Cir. 1988). In this case, however, the infringer had prepared a document from which estimates could be made, and the patentee had introduced the document in evidence, albeit for a different purpose (to show discrepancies in the infringer's sales figures). The patentee argued that the document was too flaw-riddled to be credible and that it would be unfair to permit it to be relied upon for an unanticipated purpose. However, the court found a colloquy that indicated some forewarning that the document might be used to distinguish infringing and noninfringing sales and held that the patentee had failed to identify sufficient flaws to preclude such reliance. See also

can only be assessed based upon the number of units sold before
expiration of the patent. Manufacture is an act of infringement also,
so the correct measure is the number manufactured, regardless when
they were sold.[173] The court found no error in selecting as the royalty
base the amount of materials consumed in an infringing process,
where the patentee had other agreements that so provided.[174] Similarly, it is proper to measure damages for infringement of a patented
process by reference to sales of the product produced by the process.[175]
On the other hand, the court has approved an award based upon a
portion of the estimated savings produced by the patented invention,
rather than a royalty based upon actual use.[176] In other cases a flat
fee may be appropriate.[177] The patent owner may be entitled to lost
royalties that its own licensees would have paid it but for the infringement.[178]

Where the claimed invention is made in this country, it is of
course irrelevant for damages purposes where it is sold. It is therefore
proper to include foreign sales in damages calculations if the product
is made in this country.[179] The court has applied the reasoning of
Hanover Shoe[180] to patent infringement cases, in holding that British
corporate taxes should not be deducted from the computation of a
corporation's lost profits.[181]

It is error to award damages for contributory infringement that
occurs prior to the infringer's knowledge of the patent.[182]

The court has indicated that it views absolute intervening rights
as a damages issue—the identification of those sales that properly
serve as a measure of damages. Thus, it does not become ripe for
decision until the patent owner secures a liability judgment.[183]

The entire market rule. In the case of a patented product, it is
sometimes difficult to know to what, precisely, the royalty should be
applied. Where the claim is in so-called Jepson form, and the parties

---

Oiness v. Walgreen Co., 88 F.3d 1025, 39 USPQ2d 1304 (Fed. Cir. 1996), where the court rejected
a rather convoluted technique for estimating sales.

[173]*Sensonics, Inc. v. Aerosonic Corp.,* 81 F.3d 1566, 38 USPQ2d 1551 (Fed. Cir. 1996).

[174]*Bandag, Inc. v. Gerrard Tire Co.,* 704 F.2d 1578, 217 USPQ 977 (Fed. Cir. 1983).

[175]*Central Soya Co. v. Geo. A. Hormel & Co.,* 723 F.2d 1573, 220 USPQ 490 (Fed. Cir.
1983). The court rejected an argument, akin to file wrapper estoppel, that it would be wrong
to calculate damages by reference to the product, because all product claims had been voluntarily
surrendered during the prosecution of the patent.

[176]*Hanson v. Alpine Valley Ski Area, Inc.,* 718 F.2d 1075, 219 USPQ 679 (Fed. Cir. 1983).

[177]*Trans-World Mfg. Corp. v. Al Nyman & Sons,* 750 F.2d 1552, 224 USPQ 259 (Fed. Cir.
1984); *Stickle v. Heublein, Inc.,* 716 F.2d 1550, 219 USPQ 377 (Fed. Cir. 1983).

[178]*Bic Leisure Prods., Inc. v. Windsurfing Int'l, Inc.,* 1 F.3d 1214, 27 USPQ2d 1671 (Fed.
Cir. 1993).

[179]*Railroad Dynamics, Inc. v. A. Stucki Co.,* 727 F.2d 1506, 220 USPQ 929 (Fed. Cir.
1984). But cf. *Amstar Corp. v. Envirotech Corp.,* 823 F.2d 1538, 3 USPQ2d 1412 (Fed. Cir. 1987).

[180]*Hanover Shoe, Inc. v. United Shoe Mach. Corp.,* 392 U.S. 481 (1968).

[181]*Kalman v. Berlyn Corp.,* 914 F.2d 1473, 16 USPQ2d 1093 (Fed. Cir. 1990).

[182]*Trell v. Marlee Elec. Corp.,* 912 F.2d 1443, 16 USPQ2d 1059 (Fed. Cir. 1990).

[183]*Bic Leisure Prods., Inc. v. Windsurfing Int'l, Inc.,* 1 F.3d 1214, 27 USPQ2d 1671, 1677
(Fed. Cir. 1993).

sell and the customers buy the entire assembly rather than just the improved element, it is proper to apply royalty to the entire assembly.[184] And where a hypothetical licensee would have anticipated an increase in sales of collateral unpatented items because of the patented device, the patentee should be compensated accordingly.[185]

Thus the Federal Circuit has most definitely embraced the "entire market" rule of damages. The entire market value rule allows recovery based on the value of an entire apparatus containing several features, even though only one feature is patented. It is the financial and marketing dependence on the patented item under standard marketing procedures that determines whether the unpatented features of a machine should be included in calculating compensation for infringement. The ultimate determining factor is whether the patentee or its licensee can normally anticipate the sale of the unpatented components together with the patented components. Where there is no evidence that the unpatented components have been or could be used independently of the patented structure, then the patentee would normally have anticipated the sale of the entire machine, and damages based upon the entire market value are appropriate.[186] The question, then, is simply whether the patentee would have made the sale of the unpatented elements but for the infringement.[187]

---

[184]*Railroad Dynamics, Inc. v. A. Stucki Co.*, 727 F.2d 1506, 220 USPQ 929 (Fed. Cir. 1984).

[185]*TWM Mfg. Co. v. Dura Corp.*, 789 F.2d 895, 229 USPQ 525 (Fed. Cir. 1986). The infringer failed to show how many, if any, of the patented devices were sold alone, without the collateral unpatented items. Thus no apportionment could be made, and it was proper to include the unpatented items generally in the royalty base. *Id.* The value of collateral sales can be factored into the determination of a reasonable royalty rate. For example, the patented invention can be used to promote a whole line of products, some of which may not use the invention. *State Indus., Inc. v. Mor-Flo Indus., Inc.*, 883 F.2d 1573, 12 USPQ2d 1026 (Fed. Cir. 1989). The court has also approved the concept of lost profits for future parts sales. However, if the future parts sales are for installations upon which damages have been paid, the question will be whether those parts are for repair or reconstruction. If for repair, then there would be no damages. Thus the court may refuse to permit lost profits on future parts sales on the grounds that the matter is too speculative. For one thing, it is not yet known whether the defendant will pay the damage award for the past infringement, thus "authorizing" the installations and their future repair. *Standard Havens Prods., Inc. v. Gencor Indus., Inc.*, 953 F.2d 1360, 21 USPQ2d 1321 (Fed. Cir. 1992). Compare *Carborundum Co. v. Molten Metal Equip. Innovations*, 72 F.3d 872, 37 USPQ2d 1169 (Fed. Cir. 1995), which deals with this question in an injunctive setting.

[186]*Festo Corp. v. Shoketsu KKK Co.*, 72 F.3d 857, 37 USPQ2d 1163 (Fed. Cir. 1995); *TWM Mfg. Co. v. Dura Corp.*, 789 F.2d 895, 229 USPQ 525 (Fed. Cir. 1986); *King Instr. Corp. v. Otari Corp.*, 767 F.2d 853, 226 USPQ 402 (Fed. Cir. 1985); *Kori Corp. v. Wilco Marsh Buggies, Inc.*, 761 F.2d 649, 225 USPQ 985 (Fed. Cir. 1985); *Paper Converting Mach. Co. v. Magna-Graphics Corp.*, 745 F.2d 11, 223 USPQ 591 (Fed. Cir. 1984). Where the patent-related feature of a product is the basis for customer demand, it is appropriate to award lost profits based upon the profit margin on the product as a whole, under the entire market value rule. *State Indus., Inc. v. Mor-Flo Indus., Inc.*, 883 F.2d 1573, 12 USPQ2d 1026 (Fed. Cir. 1989). The entire market value rule allows a patentee to recover damages based on the value of an entire apparatus containing several features, when the feature patented constitutes the basis for customer demand. *Fonar Corp. v. General Elec. Co.*, 107 F.3d 1543, 41 USPQ2d 1801 (Fed. Cir. 1997); *Slimfold Mfg. Co. v. Kinkead Indus.*, 932 F.2d 1453, 18 USPQ2d 1842 (Fed. Cir. 1991).

[187]*Kaufman Co. v. Lantech, Inc.*, 926 F.2d 1136, 17 USPQ2d 1828 (Fed. Cir. 1991); *King Instr. Corp. v. Otari Corp.*, 767 F.2d 853, 226 USPQ 402 (Fed. Cir. 1985). Even where the infringer does not make the unpatented items, but simply purchases them and includes them

In its in banc decision in *Rite-Hite v. Kelley,*[188] the court restated the entire market value rule as it applies to unpatented components. In order to recover for sales of unpatented components sold with patented components, either by way of reasonable royalty or lost profits, it must be shown that the unpatented components function together with the patented component in some manner so as to produce a desired end product or result. All the components together must be analogous to components of a single assembly, or be parts of a complete machine, or they must constitute a functional unit. There can be no recovery for items that have essentially no functional relationship to the patented invention and that may have been sold with an infringing device only as a matter of convenience or business advantage. The court distinguished its holding that certain unpatented devices were compensable on the ground that they were directly competitive with the patented devices, while the unpatented components were sold with the patented devices only for convenience and business advantage. It is a clear purpose of the patent law to redress competitive damages resulting from infringement of the patent, but there is no basis for extending that recovery to include damages for items that are neither competitive with nor function with the patented invention.[189]

The court has expressed a preference that the expression "convoyed sales" be limited to sales made simultaneously with a basic item; repair parts should be called "derivative sales."[190]

§12.2 Interest and Costs

(a) Interest

The matter of interest on money judgments, attributable to the period after the judgment is entered, has been uncontroversial. By statute, 28 U.S.C. §1961, compound interest at Treasury bill rates is mandatory on money judgments of federal district courts[191] and the

---

for the convenience of the customer, they may be included in the entire market value. *TWM Mfg. Co. v. Dura Corp.,* 789 F.2d 895, 229 USPQ 525 (Fed. Cir. 1986).

[188]*Rite-Hite Corp. v. Kelley Co.,* 56 F.3d 1538, 35 USPQ2d 1065 (Fed. Cir. 1995).

[189]But see note 12:106. In *Stryker Corp. v. Intermedics Orthopedics, Inc.,* 96 F.3d 1409, 40 USPQ2d 1065 (Fed. Cir. 1996), the claim covered a hip implant with a sleeve. The accused implants were always offered with a sleeve option, although a sleeve was actually used only about one-fourth of the time. The evidence showed that surgeons needed the entire system in the operating room because in most circumstances the final decision on whether or not to install the implant with the sleeve was made in surgery. On these facts, the court held it was no error to award damages based on the total number of implants sold instead of the much smaller total number of sleeves sold. The basis seemed to be that it did not matter if the surgeon installed the implant without the sleeve, because the compensable injury had already occurred when the accused device was supplied to the surgeon rather than the patented device.

[190]*Carborundum Co. v. Molten Metal Equip. Innovations,* 72 F.3d 872, 37 USPQ2d 1169 (Fed. Cir. 1995).

[191]*Gyromat Corp. v. Champion Spark Plug Co.,* 735 F.2d 549, 222 USPQ 4 (Fed. Cir. 1984). The statement of the court in *Allen Archery, Inc. v. Browning Mfg. Co.,* 898 F.2d 787,

Court of Federal Claims.[192] Interest is allowed on "any money judgment" under 28 U.S.C. §1961. Any judgment in §1961 includes a judgment awarding attorney fees under 35 U.S.C. §285. Such interest is to be calculated from the date of entry of the judgment. The provision for calculating interest from entry of judgment deters use of the appellate process by the judgment debtor solely as a means of prolonging its free use of money owed the judgment creditor. Interest on an attorney fee award thus runs from the date of the judgment establishing the right to the award, not the date of the judgment establishing its quantum.[193] Where no statute specifically authorizes an award of prejudgment interest, such an award lies within the discretion of the court as part of its equitable powers.[194]

Only the question of prejudgment interest or, as it is sometimes called, "delay damages,"[195] has received any substantial attention in the Federal Circuit. As indicated at the beginning of this chapter, the Supreme Court's *Devex*[196] decision held that prejudgment interest on patent infringement damages was to be awarded absent some justification for denying such relief. The Federal Circuit has certainly been faithful to *Devex*.[197] The law is not without means for placing the injured patentee in the situation it would have occupied had the wrong not been committed. Prejudgment interest is such a means.[198] Although the trial court has discretion in the matter, prejudgment interest is compensatory and must be awarded absent justification for withholding it. Thus, where the trial court denies prejudgment interest without giving reasons, there is an abuse of discretion and the case must be remanded.[199] *Devex* arose in the context of damages based upon a reasonable royalty, but the court has made it clear that in the absence of special circumstances prejudgment interest should be granted on a lost profits award as well.[200] Prejudgment interest is the rule on both patent infringement and trade secret misappropriation damage awards.[201]

It is clear that *Devex* did not disturb the prior holding of the Supreme Court in *Duplate Corp. v. Triplex Safety Glass Co.*,[202] that a court has authority to award prejudgment interest on unliquidated

---

14 USPQ2d 1156 (Fed. Cir. 1990), to the effect that the district court had not abused its discretion in compounding postjudgment interest was therefore somewhat misleading.

[192]*Dynamics Corp. v. United States*, 766 F.2d 518, 226 USPQ 622 (Fed. Cir. 1985).

[193]*Mathis v. Spears*, 857 F.2d 749, 8 USPQ2d 1029 (Fed. Cir. 1988).

[194]*United States v. Imperial Food Imports*, 834 F.2d 1013 (Fed. Cir. 1987).

[195]See *Hughes Aircraft Co. v. United States*, 86 F.3d 1566, 39 USPQ2d 1065 (Fed. Cir. 1996).

[196]*General Motors Corp. v. Devex Corp.*, 461 U.S. 648, 217 USPQ 1185 (1983).

[197]E.g., *Stickle v. Heublein, Inc.*, 716 F.2d 1550, 219 USPQ 377 (Fed. Cir. 1983).

[198]*Fromson v. Western Litho Plate & Supp. Co.*, 853 F.2d 1568, 7 USPQ2d 1606 (Fed. Cir. 1988).

[199]*Laitram Corp. v. Cambridge Wire Cloth Co.*, 785 F.2d 292, 228 USPQ 935 (Fed. Cir. 1986); *Bio-Rad Labs., Inc. v. Nicolet Inst. Corp.*, 739 F.2d 604, 222 USPQ 654 (Fed. Cir. 1984).

[200]*Lummus Indus., Inc. v. D.M. & E. Corp.*, 862 F.2d 267, 8 USPQ2d 1983 (Fed. Cir. 1988); *Gyromat Corp. v. Champion Spark Plug Co.*, 735 F.2d 549, 222 USPQ 4 (Fed. Cir. 1984).

[201]*Richardson v. Suzuki Motor Co.*, 868 F.2d 1226, 9 USPQ2d 1913 (Fed. Cir. 1989).

[202]298 U.S. 448, 29 USPQ 306 (1936).

damages where there was bad faith or other exceptional circumstances. The Federal Circuit has now extended *Duplate* to cover attorney fee awards under 35 U.S.C. §285. Thus, a district court has discretion to award prejudgment interest on such awards, but need not do so in every case or, indeed, in every exceptional case.[203]

Inasmuch as prejudgment interest is not punitive but compensatory,[204] it cannot be applied to the punitive portion of an award.[205] There can be no prejudgment interest on the increased portion of treble damages,[206] nor can prejudgment interest itself be trebled.[207] Nonetheless, the district court has discretion and can select an award above the statutory rate, including prime interest or above.[208] The rate at which prejudgment interest is to be assessed is within the discretion of the trier of fact. There is no rule that it must be at the prime rate, nor is there a rule that it must be at some lesser, reasonable commercial rate for an investor, not a lender.[209] By the same token, the mere assertion that a particular rate is too low does not establish abuse of that discretion.[210]

The justification for refusing prejudgment interest should bear some relationship to the award of prejudgment interest, such as delay in the prosecution of the patent.[211] Difficulty in calculation is no justification for denying prejudgment interest.[212] Dilatory action during

---

[203]*Mathis v. Spears,* 857 F.2d 749, 8 USPQ2d 1029 (Fed. Cir. 1988). The court postulates a situation where litigation initiated in good faith may acquire an exceptional cast as it progresses. Presumably, it might be an abuse of discretion to award prejudgment interest on attorney fees in such a case, but not in a case where the litigation was conducted in bad faith from the beginning.

[204]*Lam, Inc. v. Johns-Manville Corp.,* 718 F.2d 1056, 219 USPQ 670 (Fed. Cir. 1983). Prejudgment interest is designed to compensate for the delay a patentee experiences in obtaining money it would have received sooner if no infringement occurred, while damages are enhanced as punishment. *Beatrice Foods Co. v. New England Printing & Lith. Co.,* 923 F.2d 1567, 17 USPQ2d 1553 (Fed. Cir. 1991).

[205]*Beatrice Foods Co. v. New England Printing & Lith. Co.,* 923 F.2d 1567, 17 USPQ2d 1553 (Fed. Cir. 1991); *Leinoff v. Louis Milona & Sons,* 726 F.2d 734, 220 USPQ 845 (Fed. Cir. 1984). Liquidated damages are not punitive if they are reasonable and the exact amount of actual damages would be difficult to prove. Thus prejudgment interest may be assessed, in appropriate circumstances, on liquidated damages. *United States v. Imperial Food Imports,* 834 F.2d 1013 (Fed. Cir. 1987).

[206]*Underwater Devices, Inc. v. Morrison-Knudsen Co.,* 717 F.2d 1380, 219 USPQ 569 (Fed. Cir. 1983). The purpose is to make plaintiff whole, not to punish.

[207]*Lam, Inc. v. Johns-Manville Corp.,* 718 F.2d 1056, 219 USPQ 670 (Fed. Cir. 1983).

[208]*Lam, Inc. v. Johns-Manville Corp.,* 718 F.2d 1056, 219 USPQ 670 (Fed. Cir. 1983).

[209]*Studiengesellschaft Kohle v. Dart Indus., Inc.,* 862 F.2d 1564, 9 USPQ2d 1273 (Fed. Cir. 1988). A patentee need not demonstrate that it borrowed at the prime rate or above in order to be entitled to prejudgment interest at that rate. *Uniroyal, Inc. v. Rudkin-Wiley Corp.,* 939 F.2d 1540, 19 USPQ2d 1432 (Fed. Cir. 1991). In *Hughes Aircraft Co. v. United States,* 86 F.3d 1566, 39 USPQ2d 1065 (Fed. Cir. 1996), the court rejected an interesting theory that, inasmuch as a loan to the government carries no risk, the rate should be that paid on Treasury bills.

[210]*Railroad Dynamics, Inc. v. A. Stucki Co.,* 727 F.2d 1506, 220 USPQ 929 (Fed. Cir. 1984).

[211]*Radio Steel & Mfg. Co. v. MTD Prods., Inc.,* 788 F.2d 1554, 229 USPQ 431 (Fed. Cir. 1986). The infringer argued that the patentee's failure to omit patent markings for some time after expiration should bar prejudgment interest as an equitable matter. The court held that postexpiration circumstances were irrelevant to the matter of prejudgment interest, which was for the period prior to expiration.

[212]*Sensonics, Inc. v. Aerosonic Corp.,* 81 F.3d 1566, 38 USPQ2d 1551 (Fed. Cir. 1996).

discovery, without resultant delay in the trial, does not justify limiting the period of prejudgment interest; a district court has available other sanctions to remedy abuses of the discovery process.[213] Generally, prejudgment interest should be awarded from the date of infringement to the date of judgment. District courts have discretion to limit prejudgment interest where, for example, the patent owner has caused undue delay in the lawsuit, but there must be justification bearing a relationship to the award.[214] Prejudgment interest on projected lost profits has been denied on the ground that it would amount to an award of interest for the use of money that had not yet been used.[215]

Inasmuch as the purpose of prejudgment interest is to compensate the patentee for its foregone use of the money between the time of the infringement and the date of the judgment, the merits of the infringer's challenges are immaterial in determining the amount of prejudgment interest.[216] It is also immaterial what use the plaintiff might have made of the money it should have received.[217]

An award of prejudgment interest to a patent owner for the period during which its patent was subject to a judgment of invalidity is appropriate if, after exercising its discretion, the district court decides that such an award is necessary to put the patent owner in as good a position as it would have enjoyed had the infringer entered into a reasonable royalty agreement when the infringement began.[218] Similarly, the court found an abuse of discretion in refusing to award prejudgment interest for the period during which a patent infringement case was stayed pending the outcome of another case on the

---

[213]*Bio-Rad Labs., Inc. v. Nicolet Instr. Corp.*, 807 F.2d 964, 1 USPQ2d 1191 (Fed. Cir. 1986). Where a complaint was filed one year after delivery of the first infringing device and eight months after termination of efforts to resolve the dispute, and trial began within a year of the first status conference, it was clearly erroneous to find that the trial had been unduly delayed. *Id.*

[214]*Nickson Indus., Inc. v. Rol Mfg. Co.*, 847 F.2d 795, 6 USPQ2d 1878 (Fed. Cir. 1988). Here the district court found no basis for withholding prejudgment interest but limited the award to the filing of the suit. The Federal Circuit vacated and remanded for an award running to judgment or a statement of reasons for limiting the term. See also *Lummus Indus., Inc. v. D.M. & E. Corp.*, 862 F.2d 267, 8 USPQ2d 1983 (Fed. Cir. 1988). Determining the dividing line between pre- and postjudgment interest is a question that is not unique to patent law. It invokes 28 U.S.C. §1961 and the court therefore looks to the law of the regional circuit. In the Sixth Circuit, that is the date damages were meaningfully ascertained. *Transmatic Inc. v. Gulton Indus. Inc.*, 180 F.3d 1343, 50 USPQ2d 1591 (Fed. Cir. 1999). In *Uniroyal, Inc. v. Rudkin-Wiley Corp.*, 939 F.2d 1540, 19 USPQ2d 1432 (Fed. Cir. 1991), the court found no error in refusing prejudgment interest during a period when the court proceedings were stayed at the joint request of both parties.

[215]*Oiness v. Walgreen Co.*, 88 F.3d 1025, 39 USPQ2d 1304 (Fed. Cir. 1996).

[216]*Bio-Rad Labs., Inc. v. Nicolet Instr. Corp.*, 807 F.2d 964, 1 USPQ2d 1191 (Fed. Cir. 1986). The merits may be relevant to avoidance of an increase in damages for willful infringement.

[217]*Allen Archery, Inc. v. Browning Mfg. Co.*, 898 F.2d 787, 14 USPQ2d 1156 (Fed. Cir. 1990). In *Hughes Aircraft Co. v. United States*, 86 F.3d 1566, 39 USPQ2d 1065 (Fed. Cir. 1996), the court extended to delay damages (prejudgment interest) the rule that a damage award need not be reduced by the amount of taxes that would had to have been paid.

[218]*Hughes Tool Co. v. Dresser Indus., Inc.*, 816 F.2d 1549, 2 USPQ2d 1396 (Fed. Cir. 1987). It appeared that the district court had concluded that prejudgment interest can never be awarded under such circumstances; this was legal error and required remand.

same patent, where the stay seemed reasonable and both parties apparently favored it.[219] In another case, a delay of nearly six years in bringing suit was held not to justify a denial of prejudgment interest where the patentee was in litigation during much of that period with the defendant's customer.[220]

In affirming an award of prejudgment interest calculated as simple interest at a state statutory rate, the court concluded that Congress did not intend to make the postjudgment rates and compounding of 28 U.S.C. §1961 mandatory with respect to prejudgment interest.[221] In dealing with the same question as applied to judgments of the Claims Court, the Federal Circuit was moved to note that, in particular cases, compound interest may more nearly fit with the policy to accomplish justice as between the plaintiff and the government. Thus the case was remanded to consider whether "reasonable and entire compensation" contemplates compounded prejudgment interest.[222]

In the end, the rate of prejudgment interest and whether it should be compounded or uncompounded are matters left largely to the discretion of the trial court. In exercising that discretion, however, the court must be guided by the purpose of prejudgment interest, which is to ensure that the patent owner is placed in as good a position as it would have been in had the infringer entered into a reasonable royalty agreement.[223] The grant or denial of prejudgment interest is reviewed to determine whether the district court abused the available range of discretion in so doing.[224]

(b) Costs

At early common law, no costs were awarded to either party. At least as early as 1278, English legislation changed that rule in actions at law. The English practice was adopted by American courts at an early time, and the ability to award costs has become more a part of the inherent authority of the courts than a matter of statutory authorization. Nonetheless, the American common law recognized

---

[219]*Allen Archery, Inc. v. Browning Mfg. Co.*, 898 F.2d 787, 14 USPQ2d 1156 (Fed. Cir. 1990).

[220]*Kalman v. Berlyn Corp.*, 914 F.2d 1473, 16 USPQ2d 1093 (Fed. Cir. 1990).

[221]*Gyromat Corp. v. Champion Spark Plug Co.*, 735 F.2d 549, 222 USPQ 4 (Fed. Cir. 1984).

[222]*Dynamics Corp. v. United States*, 766 F.2d 518, 226 USPQ 622 (Fed. Cir. 1985). It would seem that "delay damages" are appropriate under 28 U.S.C. §1498.

[223]*Bio-Rad Labs., Inc. v. Nicolet Instr. Corp.*, 807 F.2d 964, 1 USPQ2d 1191 (Fed. Cir. 1986). See also *Rite-Hite Corp. v. Kelley Co.*, 56 F.3d 1538, 35 USPQ2d 1065 (Fed. Cir. 1995). Where no evidence of record relating to the appropriate rate suggested the use of either the prime rate or the rate that the patentee paid on its corporate borrowings, it was an abuse of discretion to employ a 7% rate, uncompounded, as provided by state law. *Id.* The district court has discretion to award either simple or compound interest. *Hughes Aircraft Co. v. United States*, 86 F.3d 1566, 39 USPQ2d 1065 (Fed. Cir. 1996); *Nickson Indus., Inc. v. Rol Mfg. Co.*, 847 F.2d 795, 6 USPQ2d 1878 (Fed. Cir. 1988). The ascertainment of the prejudgment interest rate is within the sound discretion of the district court. *Kaufman Co. v. Lantech, Inc.*, 926 F.2d 1136, 17 USPQ2d 1828 (Fed. Cir. 1991).

[224]*Lummus Indus., Inc. v. D.M. & E. Corp.*, 862 F.2d 267, 8 USPQ2d 1983 (Fed. Cir. 1988).

limitations on the ability of a court to award costs. First, under the doctrine of sovereign immunity, the United States cannot be held liable for costs without its consent. Also, under the common law, a court that lacks jurisdiction over the subject matter does not have the power to award costs. These common law rules have been changed in both respects by statute. The prevailing party in suits involving the government is now entitled to costs by virtue of 28 U.S.C. §2412(a), and 28 U.S.C. §1919 provides for costs to be awarded whenever an action in a district court is dismissed for want of jurisdiction.[225] Rule 54(d)(1), FRCP, allows costs other than attorney fees to the prevailing party as of course.[226]

In deciding how to define "prevailing party" for purposes of Rule 54(d)(1), the court follows Supreme Court precedent. Thus, a plaintiff "prevails" when actual relief on the merits of its claim materially alters the legal relationship between the parties by modifying the defendant's behavior in a way that directly benefits the plaintiff. It should be understood, however, that whether a party is the prevailing party is only a threshold inquiry. A trial court may lawfully award minimal costs or no costs after considering the amount and nature of the party's success. This question of how much is decided according to regional circuit law and reviewed under an abuse of discretion standard.[227]

Inasmuch as costs at the district court level are largely a matter of statute[228] and are clearly within the discretion of the trial judge,[229] we may expect little attention to this subject by the Federal Circuit. Nevertheless, there have been a few decisions.

The expenses that a federal court may award as costs under its Rule 54(d)(1) discretionary authority are enumerated in 28 U.S.C. §1920.[230] In a dictum, the court has remarked that cost awards to winners are regarded as a fair price that losers pay for using the judicial system, and that a trial court should deny costs to winners

---

[225]*Johns-Manville Corp. v. United States,* 893 F.2d 324 (Fed. Cir. 1989). The specific holding was that §1919 does not apply to the Claims Court; nor does §2412(a) authorize the Claims Court to award costs in a case that is dismissed for want of jurisdiction, not even where lack of jurisdiction is not immediately apparent on the face of the pleadings. Where the Claims Court has no jurisdiction, it has no power to do anything but strike the case from its docket.

[226]*Manildra Milling Corp. v. Ogilvie Mills, Inc.,* 76 F.3d 1178, 37 USPQ2d 1707 (Fed. Cir. 1996).

[227]*Manildra Milling Corp. v. Ogilvie Mills, Inc.,* 76 F.3d 1178, 37 USPQ2d 1707 (Fed. Cir. 1996). A plaintiff who succeeds in having a competitor's patent declared invalid "prevails." *Id.*

[228]28 U.S.C. §1920.

[229]*Syntex Ophthalmics, Inc. v. Novicky,* 795 F.2d 983, 230 USPQ 427 (Fed. Cir. 1986).

[230]*Manildra Milling Corp. v. Ogilvie Mills, Inc.,* 76 F.3d 1178, 37 USPQ2d 1707 (Fed. Cir. 1996). Included are fees of the court reporter for all or any part of the stenographic transcript necessarily obtained for use in the case. This covers both trial and deposition testimony. As a general rule, daily trial transcript costs should not be awarded absent court approval prior to the trial; but a court may overlook lack of prior approval if the case is complex and the transcripts invaluable both to court and counsel. As for depositions, although use at trial is direct evidence of necessity, an item may still be reasonably necessary for use in the case even if unused at trial. The underlying inquiry is whether the depositions reasonably seemed necessary at the time they were taken. *Id.*

only when the award would be unjust. It may therefore turn out to be an abuse of discretion to disregard the presumption of costs to the prevailing party in the absence of a finding of special circumstances.[231]

In *Mathis v. Spears,*[232] the court held that necessary and reasonable expert witness fees may be included in awards of attorney fees under 35 U.S.C. §285. Costs are governed by Rule 54(d), FRCP, and 28 U.S.C. §§1821 and 1920, and the rule does not grant federal courts discretion to award witness fees beyond the limitations of the statute. But the rule and statues relate to good faith proceedings, i.e., to court resolutions of controversies about which reasonable persons may disagree. In such cases, the American Rule is that each party bears its own attorney fees and expenses, and Rule 54(d) and the statutes modify the American Rule only slightly, to provide for reimbursement to the winner for its relatively low "costs." However, nothing in the rule or statutes impedes or precludes a district court from exercising its inherent equitable power to make whole a party injured by an egregious abuse of the judicial process. Though courts have exercised that inherent power in the absence of express statutory authorization, Congress has not been unaware of the distinction between good faith litigation to which the American Rule applies and bad faith litigation to which it does not. Congress enacted §285 to codify in patent cases the "bad faith" equitable exception to the American Rule. It would be inconsistent with the intent of §285, which is to discourage conduct that falls within the scope of exceptional, to limit the prevailing party to something less than the fees and expenses to which it was subjected by "very exceptional" conduct. This includes necessary and reasonable expert witness fees.[233]

The lower court has the power to tax and award costs after a notice of appeal has been filed.[234] Indeed, a district court may award costs even when a case is settled, where the settlement agreement and stipulated order of dismissal do not address the matter.[235]

The court has affirmed awards of costs for translations and transcripts of oral arguments[236] and for depositions, even where they were not referred to in the lower court's opinion[237] or actually read into the record at trial.[238] In one unusual case, the court held that if one uses

---

[231]*Connell v. Sears, Roebuck & Co.,* 722 F.2d 1542, 220 USPQ 193 (Fed. Cir. 1983).

[232]*Mathis v. Spears,* 857 F.2d 749, 8 USPQ2d 1029 (Fed. Cir. 1988).

[233]*Mathis v. Spears,* 857 F.2d 749, 8 USPQ2d 1029 (Fed. Cir. 1988).

[234]*Chore-Time Equip., Inc. v. Cumberland Corp.,* 713 F.2d 774, 218 USPQ 673 (Fed. Cir. 1983).

[235]*Reactive Metals & Alloys Corp. v. ESM, Inc.,* 769 F.2d 1578, 226 USPQ 821 (Fed. Cir. 1985). The defendant had come up with some good prior art shortly before trial and the plaintiff voluntarily dismissed; thus the award of costs to the "prevailing" defendant was not an abuse of discretion. However, an accompanying award of attorney fees was reversed as clearly erroneous.

[236]*Chore-Time Equip., Inc. v. Cumberland Corp.,* 713 F.2d 774, 218 USPQ 673 (Fed. Cir. 1983).

[237]*Chore-Time Equip., Inc. v. Cumberland Corp.,* 713 F.2d 774, 218 USPQ 673 (Fed. Cir. 1983).

[238]*Syntex Ophthalmics, Inc. v. Novicky,* 795 F.2d 983, 230 USPQ 427 (Fed. Cir. 1986).

a word processor to produce multiple copies, as by printing several ribbon copies from an original stored in the machine, the costs would be reimbursable; but not so where the use of the word processor was simply as a fancy typewriter to produce a single ribbon copy from which multiple copies were made by another method.[239] Attorney fees do not typically include taxable costs.[240]

---

[239]*CTS Corp. v. Piher Int'l Corp.*, 754 F.2d 972, 221 USPQ 954 (Fed. Cir. 1984). Note that this case dealt with costs of appeal not trial. One would guess that technology has obsoleted this decision.

[240]*Bennett v. Department of Navy*, 699 F.2d 1140 (Fed. Cir. 1983).

13

Injunctive Relief

§13.1 Injunctions in General

Pursuant to 35 U.S.C. §283, the courts that have jurisdiction of patent cases "may grant injunctions in accordance with the principles of equity to prevent the violation of any right secured by patent, on such terms as the court deems reasonable."[1] This is clearly an important element of relief. Without injunctive power the patent owner would lack much of the leverage afforded by the right to exclude. Without the right to obtain an injunction, the right to exclude granted to the patentee would have only a fraction of the value it was intended to have and would no longer be as great an incentive to engage in the toils of scientific and technological research.[2]

(a) Injunctions Against Infringement

Because the principal value of a patent is its statutory right to exclude, the nature of the patent grant weighs against holding that monetary damages will always suffice to make the patentee whole. The patent statute provides injunctive relief to preserve the legal interests of the parties against future infringement that may have market effects never fully compensable in money.[3] Harm to reputation resulting from confusion between an inferior accused product and a patentee's superior product is a type of harm that is often not fully compensable by money because the damages caused are speculative and difficult to measure.[4] In matters involving patent rights, irreparable harm has been presumed when a clear showing has been made of patent validity and infringement. This presumption derives in part from the finite term of the patent grant, for patent expiration is not suspended during litigation, and the passage of time can work irremediable harm.[5]

It may come somewhat as a surprise, then, that injunctive relief under §283 is discretionary, not mandatory, and must be governed by historic equitable principles.[6] And it is the standards of the public interest, not the requirements of private litigation, that measure the need for injunctive relief.[7] The historic injunctive process was

---

[1]*High Tech Med. Instr., Inc. v. New Image Indus., Inc.*, 49 F.3d 1551, 33 USPQ2d 2005 (Fed. Cir. 1995).

[2]*Smith Int'l, Inc. v. Hughes Tool Co.*, 718 F.2d 1573, 219 USPQ 686 (Fed. Cir. 1983).

[3]*Reebok Int'l Ltd. v. J. Baker, Inc.*, 32 F.3d 1552, 31 USPQ2d 1781 (Fed. Cir. 1994); *Hybritech, Inc. v. Abbott Labs.*, 849 F.2d 1446, 7 USPQ2d 1191 (Fed. Cir. 1988).

[4]*Reebok Int'l Ltd. v. J. Baker, Inc.*, 32 F.3d 1552, 31 USPQ2d 1781 (Fed. Cir. 1994). However, such confusion is unlikely to occur or may be de minimis once the patentee stops making and advertising its patented product. *Id.*

[5]*Richardson v. Suzuki Motor Co.*, 868 F.2d 1226, 9 USPQ2d 1913 (Fed. Cir. 1989).

[6]*Roche Prods., Inc. v. Bolar Pharm. Co.*, 733 F.2d 858, 221 USPQ 937 (Fed. Cir. 1984). "If Congress wants the federal courts to issue injunctions without regard to historic equity principles, it is going to have to say so in explicit and even shameless language rarely if ever to be expected from a body itself made up very largely of American lawyers, having, probably, as much respect for traditional equity principles as do the courts."

[7]*Roche Prods., Inc. v. Bolar Pharm. Co.*, 733 F.2d 858, 221 USPQ 937 (Fed. Cir. 1984).

designed to deter, not to punish.[8] The purpose behind the injunction must be to prevent the violation of some right secured by the patent. It may not be punitive.[9]

Does this mean that the Federal Circuit, as favorably disposed as it seems to be toward patent enforcement, is likely to come down in favor of compulsory licensing, in effect if not in name? One doubts it.[10] While the grant of injunctive authority in patent cases is clearly in discretionary terms, injunctive relief against an infringer is the norm.[11] Once infringement is established, it is contrary to the laws of property, of which the patent law partakes, to deny the patentee's right to exclude others from use of its property. It is therefore the general rule that an injunction will issue when infringement has been adjudged, absent a sound reason for denying it.[12] The fact that the defendant has stopped infringing is generally not a reason for denying an injunction against future infringement unless the evidence is very persuasive that further infringement will not take place.[13]

Indeed, a patentee can bring an action for infringement without any evidence of damage or lost sales.[14] But an injunction under §283

---

[8]*Amstar Corp. v. Envirotech Corp.,* 823 F.2d 1538, 3 USPQ2d 1412 (Fed. Cir. 1987).

[9]*Joy Techs., Inc. v. Flakt, Inc.,* 6 F.3d 770, 28 USPQ2d 1378 (Fed. Cir. 1993). Punishment is not the proper purpose of injunctive relief under §283. *Johns Hopkins Univ. v. Cellpro Inc.,* 152 F.3d 1342, 47 USPQ2d 1705 (Fed. Cir. 1998).

[10]Certainly the court has inveighed against the concept of compulsory licensing in the context of preliminary injunctions. See *Atlas Powder Co. v. Ireco Chems.,* 773 F.2d 1230, 227 USPQ 289 (Fed. Cir. 1985), and text accompanying note 13:120. Yet there may be conflicting signals. In *Shatterproof Glass Corp. v. Libbey-Owens Ford Co.,* 758 F.2d 613, 225 USPQ 634 (Fed. Cir. 1985), the district court had denied the patentee's request for an injunction and granted a compulsory license to the infringer. Apparently the patentee did not appeal that relief, and the infringer was complaining only about the royalty charged for the license. But see *Windsurfing Int'l, Inc. v. AMF, Inc.,* 782 F.2d 995, 228 USPQ 562 (Fed. Cir. 1986). In other cases, the court has indicated that a damage award based upon a reasonable royalty that is a lump sum or flat fee will obviate the need for injunctive relief. Although the court views this merely as a license implied by full compensation, and not compulsory licensing, the effect may be the same. *Amstar Corp. v. Envirotech Corp.,* 823 F.2d 1538, 3 USPQ 2d 1412 (Fed. Cir. 1987); *Stickle v. Heublein, Inc.,* 716 F.2d 1550, 219 USPQ 377 (Fed. Cir. 1983). See also *Power Lift, Inc. v. Weatherford Nipple-Up Sys., Inc.,* 871 F.2d 1082, 10 USPQ2d 1464 (Fed. Cir. 1989); *Trans-World Mfg. Corp. v. Al Nyman & Sons,* 750 F.2d 1552, 224 USPQ 259 (Fed. Cir. 1984). Cf. *E.I. duPont de Nemours & Co. v. Phillips Petroleum Co.,* 835 F.2d 277, 5 USPQ2d 1109 (Fed. Cir. 1987).

[11]*KSM Fastening Sys., Inc. v. H.A. Jones Co.,* 776 F.2d 1522, 227 USPQ 676 (Fed. Cir. 1985).

[12]*Richardson v. Suzuki Motor Co.,* 868 F.2d 1226, 9 USPQ2d 1913 (Fed. Cir. 1989). Although the general rule is that an injunction should follow an infringement verdict, district courts, appropriate to questions of equity, enjoy considerable discretion in determining whether the facts of a situation require issuance of an injunction. *Odetics Inc. v. Storage Tech. Corp.,* 185 F.3d 1259, 51 USPQ2d 1225 (Fed. Cir. 1999).

[13]*W.L. Gore & Assoc., Inc. v. Garlock, Inc.,* 842 F.2d 1275, 6 USPQ2d 1277 (Fed. Cir. 1988).

[14]*Roche Prods., Inc. v. Bolar Pharm. Co.,* 733 F.2d 858, 221 USPQ 937 (Fed. Cir. 1984). There is, however, no independent federal jurisdiction over a claim for an injunction against threatened infringement. *Lang. v. Pacific Marine & Supply Co.,* 895 F.2d 761, 13 USPQ2d 1820 (Fed. Cir. 1990). Historically, courts routinely denied injunctions to individual, nonmanufacturing patentees. Under such circumstances infringers could perceive nothing to fear but the possibility of a compulsory license at a reasonable royalty, resulting in some quarters in a lowered respect for the rights of such patentees and a failure to recognize the innovation-encouraging social purpose of the patent system. *Fromson v. Western Litho Plate & Supp. Co.,* 853 F.2d 1568, 7 USPQ2d 1606 (Fed. Cir. 1988).

is only proper to the extent it is to prevent the violation of any right secured by patent. A determination that such right has been violated is, thus, a necessary predicate.[15] An injunction that prohibits making and selling without reference to geographic area is improper. There can be no infringement of a U.S. patent without some nexus to this country.[16] An injunction under §283 can reach extraterritorial activities, even if these activities do not themselves constitute infringement. It is necessary, however, that the injunction prevent infringement of a U.S. patent. For example, consider the preissuance manufacture of two machines, one of which is used after the patent is issued and the other of which is exported. An injunction requiring return of the exported machine, which was never made, used, or sold during the term of the patent in the United States, is beyond the scope of §283 and hence an abuse of discretion.[17]

An injunction that would prohibit sales of unpatented replacement parts for repair of infringing devices for which damages had already been obtained required modification.[18] A patentee is not entitled to a permanent injunction against use and repair, subsequent to a period of laches, of devices made during the laches period.[19]

---

[15]*Eli Lilly & Co. v. Medtronic, Inc.*, 915 F.2d 670 (Fed. Cir. 1990). In *Ortho Pharm Corp. v. Smith*, 959 F.2d 936, 22 USPQ2d 1119 (Fed. Cir. 1992), the court very neatly sidestepped the interesting question of the extent to which a permanent injunction could forbid the use of data obtained during infringement (other than for FDA approval purposes, which is dealt with under 35 U.S.C. §271(e)(1)). The court reasoned that, if it be assumed that such conduct is infringement, then it was prohibited under the existing injunction, which simply forbade further infringement. But if it be assumed that it is not infringement, then it would have to decide whether the district court had discretionary power under §283 to enjoin such conduct. Assuming further that the district court had such power, the patentee would have to demonstrate that it had abused its discretion in failing to exercise that power. But the patentee had only argued the question of whether the conduct was infringement, and that, said the Federal Circuit, is properly addressable in the context of contempt proceedings. The court also carefully avoided any resolution of whether an injunction against use of data can extend beyond the life of the infringed patent.

[16]*Tieleman Food Equip., B.V. v. Stork Gamco, Inc.*, 56 F.3d 1373, 35 USPQ2d 1568 (Fed. Cir. 1995).

[17]*Johns Hopkins Univ. v. Cellpro Inc.*, 152 F.3d 1342, 47 USPQ2d 1705 (Fed. Cir. 1998). In this case the district court abused its discretion in ordering repatriation of six vials of cellular material that had been made prior to issuance of the patent, exported to Canada after issuance, and used in Canada to supply markets outside the United States. The Federal Circuit reasoned like this: the repatriation aspect of the order does not enjoin activities that either have infringed the patent or are likely to do so and thus does not prevent infringement—the proper purpose of an injunction under §283. Mere possession of a product that becomes covered by a subsequently issued patent does not constitute an infringement of that patent until the product is used, sold, or offered for sale in the United States during the term of the patent. Likewise, neither export from the United States nor use in a foreign country of a product covered by a U.S. patent constitutes infringement.

[18]*Tieleman Food Equip., B.V. v. Stork Gamco, Inc.*, 56 F.3d 1373, 35 USPQ2d 1568 (Fed. Cir. 1995).

[19]*Odetics Inc. v. Storage Tech. Corp.*, 185 F.3d 1259, 51 USPQ2d 1225 (Fed. Cir. 1999).

Of course, the patentee must affirmatively seek an injunction.[20] When it does, the district court must determine whether an injunction is warranted.[21]

Where both damages and injunctive relief are appropriate, they must be tailored to the circumstances and correlatively determined.[22] The court seems quite willing to do its best to see that the patentee is protected. In one unusual case, the defendant had started testing for FDA approval during the last six months before the patent expired. In a dictum, the court indicated that an order requiring destruction of test results and records (to dissipate the head start resulting from the infringer's wrongful conduct) seemed harsh and contrary to public welfare. But the court also hinted strongly that more than nominal damages might be appropriate; perhaps enough to make up for the actual injury caused by jumping the gun.[23] The need for injunctive relief does not necessarily become more imperative as the end of the patent term approaches. Indeed, an injunction against infringement may be absolutely essential at the beginning of the term of the patent, for example, to enable a patent owner to establish a new business.[24]

What about injunctive orders that could have significant post-expiration effect? In *Kearns v. Chrysler*,[25] the patent owner was seeking a postexpiration injunction on the ground that money damages were inadequate compensation. The court of course denied this relief,

---

[20]In one unusual case, the defendant had stipulated validity and infringement below, and the case was tried on the question of notice of the infringement pursuant to 35 U.S.C. §287. The jury found no notice, and thus no damage, and the district court entered a judgment of dismissal. Although the patentee unsuccessfully demanded a judgment of validity and infringement based on the stipulation, there was apparently no similar request below for an injunction. The Federal Circuit brushed away the patentee's argument that the trial court should have entered an injunction based on the stipulation. *Devices for Med., Inc. v. Boehl*, 822 F.2d 1062, 3 USPQ2d 1288 (Fed. Cir. 1987). The end result is a patent admitted to be valid and infringed, but with no injunction against future infringement. Perhaps the defendant would not have stipulated validity and infringement in the face of a request for an injunction, and perhaps the appellate court was correct in refusing to permit the question to be raised belatedly on appeal. And yet it seems likely that had the plaintiff requested an injunction, the trial court would have had no choice but to permit a trial on the right to an injunction.

[21]*Nickson Indus., Inc. v. Rol Mfg. Co.*, 847 F.2d 795, 6 USPQ2d 1878 (Fed. Cir. 1988). Where the winning patentee had requested an injunction in its complaint and posttrial brief, but the district court did not mention injunctive relief in its judgment, the case had to be remanded so that the district court could either enjoin future infringement or state a sufficient reason for not doing so. The Federal Circuit declined the invitation to rule on the request for an injunction, on the ground that it is for the district court in the first instance to determine whether an injunction is warranted. The court did indicate, however, that a motion to amend or alter the judgment under Rule 59(e), FRCP, while not required, would have made the remanded issues reviewable and avoided the imposition of a return visit to a busy district court.

[22]*Stickle v. Heublein, Inc.*, 716 F.2d 1550, 219 USPQ 377, 387 (Fed. Cir. 1983).

[23]*Roche Prods., Inc. v. Bolar Pharm. Co.*, 733 F.2d 858, 221 USPQ 937 (Fed. Cir. 1984).

[24]*Woodard v. Sage Prods., Inc.*, 818 F.2d 841, 2 USPQ2d 1649 (Fed. Cir. 1987).

[25]*Kearns v. Chrysler Corp.*, 32 F.3d 1541, 31 USPQ2d 1746 (Fed. Cir. 1994). In *Additive Cont'l & Meas. Sys., Inc. v. Flowdata, Inc.*, 986 F.2d 476, 25 USPQ2d 1798 (Fed. Cir. 1993), the court found that a permanent injunction declaring that "plaintiff is forever barred from infringing [defendant's] patent" was too broad to satisfy Rule 65(d), FRCP. It should be noted that additional language in the injunctive order implied that the order might have been entered with the consent of both parties. Even if this consent was simply as to form, would not that prevent the enjoined party from contesting the scope of the injunction on appeal?

largely on the basis that §283 provides for injunctions only to "prevent the violations of any right secured by patent." Thus, when the rights secured by a patent are no longer protectable by virtue of expiration or unenforceability, entitlement to injunctive relief becomes moot. In *Joy v. Flakt*,[26] the court faced a more complicated situation. The defendant was enjoined from building or contracting to build plants that would be used to practice the patented method after expiration of the patent. The court vacated the injunction and remanded to permit the district court to fashion an injunction that would prevent infringement only during the term of the patent, e.g., completion of a plant that could and might be used before the patent expired. It appeared that the court would approve such an injunction if there were no way to disable the equipment so that direct infringement of the patented method could not occur prior to expiration.

(b) Framing Injunctive Relief

The Federal Circuit has, quite properly, declined the invitation to tell district courts how to frame injunctions in patent cases. Despite fears of district-level forum shopping, the court will allow trial judges wide latitude on the theory that it is uniformity of decision on contempt, rather than on framing injunctions, that should be the primary goal.[27] Nevertheless, although a trial court is given broad discretionary powers in shaping equitable decrees, injunctive relief should be narrowly tailored to fit the specific legal violations at hand.[28] By requiring specificity in injunctions, Rule 65(d), FRCP, relieves parties from the burden of adjudicating unwarranted contempt proceedings.[29]

This need for specificity is often difficult to meet in patent cases. Although in most cases a broad injunction against violation of a statute does not satisfy the specificity requirement, patent injunctions are frequently drafted broadly to prohibit "further infringement." This is reasonable because contempt proceedings, civil or criminal, are available only with respect to devices previously admitted or adjudged to infringe and to other devices that are no more than colorably

---

[26]*Joy Techs. Inc. v. Flakt, Inc.*, 6 F.3d 770, 28 USPQ2d 1378 (Fed. Cir. 1993). The court distinguished its decision in *Paper Converting* (see note 6:154 and accompanying text).

[27]*KSM Fastening Sys., Inc. v. H.A. Jones Co.*, 776 F.2d 1522, 227 USPQ 676 (Fed. Cir. 1985).

[28]*Gemveto Jewelry Co. v. Jeff Cooper Inc.*, 800 F.2d 256, 230 USPQ 876 (Fed. Cir. 1986). An injunction that imposes unnecessary restraints on the enjoined party's lawful activity will be vacated. *Id.*

[29]*Additive Cont'l & Meas. Sys., Inc. v. Flowdata, Inc.*, 986 F.2d 476, 25 USPQ2d 1798 (Fed. Cir. 1993). See also *Signtech USA Ltd v. Vutek Inc.*, 174 F.3d 1352, 50 USPQ2d 1372 (Fed. Cir. 1999). Rule 65(d) prohibits reference in an injunctive order to another document. In *Joy Techs. Inc. v. Flakt, Inc.*, 6 F.3d 770, 28 USPQ2d 1378 (Fed. Cir. 1993), the order granting the injunction and the specific acts enjoined against were set forth in separate documents. Although the court observed that this defect alone would require vacating and remanding the injunctive order for compliance as to form and specificity, the court nonetheless went ahead and decided the underlying issues that were the main focus of the appeal. This seems to have been appropriate under the circumstances.

different therefrom and that clearly are infringements of the patent.[30] A permanent injunction should prohibit infringement by any product of the infringer, not just those involved in the suit. The burden is on the infringer to avoid contempt.[31]

(c) Appellate Review

Section 283 grants the district courts broad discretion in determining whether the facts of a case warrant an injunction and in determining the scope of the injunctive relief. The grant, denial, or modification of an injunction under §283 is reviewable under an abuse of discretion standard.[32] However, although the standard of review for the issuance and scope of an injunction is abuse of discretion, whether the terms of the injunction fulfill the specificity mandates of Rule 65(d), FRCP, is a question of law that is reviewed de novo.[33] On appeal, review of denial of an injunction is narrow.[34] The appellant must meet the heavy burden of showing that the district court abused its discretion, committed an error of law, or seriously misjudged the evidence.[35]

But the trial court's discretion is not absolute,[36] and the Federal Circuit has not hesitated to intervene in appropriate cases. Thus, where the defendant neither made nor sold, but simply furnished

---

[30]*KSM Fastening Sys., Inc. v. H.A. Jones Co.*, 776 F.2d 1522, 227 USPQ 676 (Fed. Cir. 1985). See also *Signtech USA Ltd v. Vutek Inc.*, 174 F.3d 1352, 50 USPQ2d 1372 (Fed. Cir. 1999). Based upon a past history of egregious conduct on the part of the infringer, the district court fashioned an injunction requiring it to submit modified designs to the court for approval prior to attempting sales. The Federal Circuit approved this as a reflection of the old adage that those caught violating the law must expect some fencing in. *Spindelfabrik GmbH v. Schubert & Salzer*, 903 F.2d 1568, 14 USPQ2d 1913 (Fed. Cir. 1990). See also *Additive Cont. & Meas. Sys. Inc. v. Flowdata Inc.*, 154 F.3d 1345, 47 USPQ2d 1906 (Fed. Cir. 1998), where the court approved an injunction forbidding the party from undertaking any activities relative to the general subject matter of the patent without first obtaining leave of court. In *U.S. Valves Inc. v. Dray*, 212 F.3d 1368, 54 USPQ2d 1834 (Fed. Cir. 2000), the district court permanently enjoined the defendant from selling the device "covered under the license agreement." The Federal Circuit approved this language on the basis that, upon expiration of the patents, the device would no longer be "covered under the license agreement." The life of the injunction thus spans only the life of the license terms or until expiration of the patents. It is neither indefinite nor effective in perpetuity.

[31]*Smith Int'l, Inc. v. Hughes Tool Co.*, 718 F.2d 1573, 219 USPQ 686 (Fed. Cir. 1983).

[32]*Ortho Pharm Corp. v. Smith*, 959 F.2d 936, 22 USPQ2d 1119 (Fed. Cir. 1992). District courts are given broad discretion under §283 to determine whether the facts of a case warrant the grant of an injunction and to determine the scope of the injunction. *Joy Techs., Inc. v. Flakt, Inc.*, 6 F.3d 770, 28 USPQ2d 1378 (Fed. Cir. 1993). The grant of an injunction against infringement, and its scope, are reviewed for abuse of discretion. *Tieleman Food Equip., B.V. v. Stork Gamco, Inc.*, 56 F.3d 1373, 35 USPQ2d 1568 (Fed. Cir. 1995).

[33]*Signtech USA Ltd v. Vutek Inc.*, 174 F.3d 1352, 50 USPQ2d 1372 (Fed. Cir. 1999).

[34]*Smith Int'l, Inc. v. Hughes Tool Co.*, 718 F.2d 1573, 219 USPQ 686 (Fed. Cir. 1983). Denial is reviewed for abuse of discretion. *Odetics Inc. v. Storage Tech. Corp.*, 185 F.3d 1259, 51 USPQ2d 1225 (Fed. Cir. 1999).

[35]*Datascope Corp. v. Kontron Inc.*, 786 F.2d 398, 229 USPQ 41 (Fed. Cir. 1986); *Smith Int'l, Inc. v. Hughes Tool Co.*, 718 F.2d 1573, 219 USPQ 686 (Fed. Cir. 1983).

[36]*Smith Int'l, Inc. v. Hughes Tool Co.*, 718 F.2d 1573, 219 USPQ 686 (Fed. Cir. 1983).

infringing display racks to its customers, free, for their use, the district court abused its discretion by enjoining manufacture and sale, but failing, without explanation, to enjoin use.[37] In a trade secret case, state law required that injunctive relief be limited in duration to the approximate time necessary for the defendant to duplicate the secret by lawful means. A 20-year injunction based on evidence that the secret process took 20 man-years to develop was held an abuse of discretion, because it took no account of team efforts.[38] In another case, the court vacated an injunction that was broad enough to prohibit lawful activity, such as buying and reselling products from third parties who had not been privy to the plaintiff's trade secrets; it also vacated an injunction that simply prohibited the dissemination or use of the plaintiff's trade secrets without specifying what they were.[39] A refusal of an injunction grounded on the small size of the infringer, and the fact that the infringing product was its principal business, was held an abuse. The court remarked that "one who elects to build a business on a product found to infringe cannot be heard to complain if an injunction against continuing infringement destroys the business so elected."[40]

The reviewing court is not restricted in review of a grant of an injunction to the merits. A departure from the basic procedural requirements for issuance of an injunction may also require that the injunction be vacated. In determining the procedural requirements for the grant of an injunction, the Federal Circuit looks to regional circuit law. However, where that particular court has not spoken and it is unclear what view would prevail there, the Federal Circuit may look to other circuits for guidance.[41]

(d) *Injunctions Against Other Activity*

Injunctions, of course, are not limited to the purposes specified in §283. To promote efficient judicial management and conservation of judicial resources, a court for example may enjoin parties under its jurisdiction from proceeding with a concurrent action involving the same or related issues. In deciding whether to enjoin concurrent

---

[37]*Trans-World Mfg. Corp. v. Al Nyman & Sons,* 750 F.2d 1552, 224 USPQ 259 (Fed. Cir. 1984). The furnishing of the racks for use by the customers constituted use by the defendant and was an infringement. Under the circumstances, the only effective relief would be to enjoin use.

[38]*Syntex Ophthalmics, Inc. v. Novicky,* 745 F.2d 1423, 223 USPQ 695 (Fed. Cir. 1984).

[39]*Roton Barrier, Inc. v. Stanley Works,* 79 F.3d 1112, 37 USPQ2d 1816 (Fed. Cir. 1996).

[40]*Windsurfing Int'l, Inc. v. AMF, Inc.,* 782 F.2d 995, 228 USPQ 562, 568 n.12 (Fed. Cir. 1986).

[41]*Digital Equip. Corp. v. Emulex Corp.,* 805 F.2d 380, 231 USPQ 779 (Fed. Cir. 1986). An injunction staying concurrent litigation is, pursuant to First Circuit law, reviewed on the standard of abuse of discretion. Such review includes consideration of whether the district court applied incorrect law, or misapplied the law to the facts. *Katz v. Lear Siegler, Inc.,* 909 F.2d 1459, 15 USPQ2d 1554 (Fed. Cir. 1990).

litigation, the court must determine whether resolution of the case disposes of the other litigation.[42]

The Federal Circuit clearly recognizes a "customer suit" doctrine, whereby litigation against or brought by the manufacturer of infringing goods takes precedence over a suit by the patent owner against customers of the manufacturer. An injunction against proceeding with concurrent litigation does not require an analysis under the normal four-part standard for preliminary injunctions, particularly the question of likelihood of success on the merits. Rather, a primary question is whether the issues and parties are such that the disposition of one case would be dispositive of the other.[43] Thus, a district court has the discretionary power to enjoin a party from pursuing litigation before a foreign tribunal, but can exercise that power only if the parties and issues are the same and resolution of the domestic action will dispose of the foreign action.[44]

A misappropriator of trade secrets has no authorization of right to continue to reap the benefits of its wrongful acts. A successful plaintiff is therefore entitled to an injunction against continuing use of trade secrets.[45] In general, a court has the power to issue a mandatory injunction to restore the situation to the status quo when a party, with notice of impending injunction proceedings, completes or performs the action sought to be enjoined.[46] An injunction to prevent a party—at least one other than the patent owner—from continuing a reexamination proceeding is not available relief, because there is no review of the PTO's decision to reexamine, and the requester has no further role to play in any event once reexamination is ordered.[47] A threatened infringement of a patent does not create a claim for infringement under 35 U.S.C. §271, and there is therefore no federal question jurisdiction over a claim for an injunction against threatened infringement, even though an action for declaratory judgment may well lie.[48]

Infringement notices have been enjoined when the patentee acted in bad faith, for example, by making threats without intending to file suit, or sending notices indiscriminately to all members of the trade,

---

[42]*In re Van Geuns,* 946 F.2d 845, 20 USPQ2d 1291 (Fed. Cir. 1991). Apparently the Federal Circuit considers itself to have this power. Here it was being asked to enjoin prosecution of a district court action for review under 35 U.S.C. §146 pending outcome of the appeal; it refused on the ground that the parties and issues in the district court were different.

[43]*Katz v. Lear Siegler, Inc.,* 909 F.2d 1459, 15 USPQ2d 1554 (Fed. Cir. 1990). The fact that the customers had not agreed to be bound by the outcome of the manufacturer suit did not dissuade the court from affirming the injunction against the customer suit.

[44]*Stein Assoc., Inc. v. Heat & Control, Inc.,* 748 F.2d 653, 223 USPQ 1277 (Fed. Cir. 1984). In another case, the court refused to overturn the district court's refusal to enjoin a state court action, on the ground that the potential preclusive effect of a state court judgment in the matter was an open question. *Intermedics Infusaid, Inc. v. Regents of Univ. of Minn.,* 804 F.2d 129, 231 USPQ 653 (Fed. Cir. 1986).

[45]*Richardson v. Suzuki Motor Co.,* 868 F.2d 1226, 9 USPQ2d 1913 (Fed. Cir. 1989).

[46]*F. Alderete Gen. Contractors v. United States,* 714 F.2d 1476 (Fed. Cir. 1983).

[47]*Joy Mfg. Co. v. National Mine Serv. Co.,* 810 F.2d 1127, 1 USPQ2d 1627 (Fed. Cir. 1987).

[48]*Lang. v. Pacific Marine & Supply Co.,* 895 F.2d 761, 13 USPQ2d 1820 (Fed. Cir. 1990).

or when it has no good faith belief in the validity of the patent. But a patentee may not be enjoined to silence even as it publicly litigates issues of direct concern to the objects of the intended notice.[49]

(e) Binding Effect of Injunctions on Nonparties

Courts do not write legislation for members of the public at large; they frame decrees and judgments that bind the parties before them. For that reason, courts of equity have long observed the general rule that a court may not enter an injunction against a person who has not been made a party to the case before it. However, that does not mean that nonparties may not be held in contempt of court for violating injunctions directed at others. Courts have carefully distinguished between entering an injunction against a nonparty, which is forbidden, and holding a nonparty in contempt for aiding and abetting in the violation of an injunction that has been entered against a party, which is permitted. Rule 65(d), FRCP, codifies these principles. Thus, those who act in concert with an enjoined party may be held in contempt, but only for assisting the enjoined party in violating the injunction.[50]

As a general matter, a court may not enjoin a nonparty that has not appeared before it to have its rights legally adjudicated. Nonparties may be held in contempt, however, if they either abet the defendant, or are legally identified with it. That common law principle is reflected in the text of Rule 65(d), FRCP, which states that an injunction is binding on parties and "their officers, agents, servants, employees, and attorneys, and upon those persons in active concert and participation with them who receive actual notice of the order

---

[49]*Mallinckrodt, Inc. v. Medipart, Inc.,* 976 F.2d 700, 24 USPQ2d 1173 (Fed. Cir. 1992). The district court had granted a summary judgment of patent misuse and enjoined the patentee from sending out infringement notices. Upon reversing and remanding the misuse judgment, the Federal Circuit also vacated the judgment. A patentee that has a good faith belief that its patents are being infringed violates no protected right when it so notifies infringers. Nor should an accused infringer be insulated from knowledge and fair warning of potential liability or deprived of the opportunity to respond to threatened litigation.

[50]*Additive Con. & Meas. Sys., Inc. v. Flowdata, Inc.,* 96 F.3d 1390, 40 USPQ2d 1106 (Fed. Cir. 1996). In *Kloster Speedsteel AB v. Crucible Inc.,* 793 F.2d 1565, 230 USPQ 81 (Fed. Cir. 1986), after trial but before judgment a third party purchased the facility of the infringer. Rather than deciding a motion to join the third party, the district court entered an injunction that purported to bind the infringer and "successors in interest or assigns." Although such language may not enlarge the permissible scope of Rule 65, its effect seems to have been intended to bind those in privity with the infringer. Inasmuch as a nonparty who acquires assets of a defendant-infringer after a suit begins is in privity, this third party was held to be bound by the injunction, even though it had not had an opportunity to litigate on the merits before being enjoined. The court commented that any private agreement between the third party and the defendant-infringer as to liability is irrelevant as to the binding effect of the injunction. The court was critical of the entire transaction as an effort to avoid an injunction rather than simply refrain from infringement, indicating that the scheme did not reflect the highest ethical standards of the business community or bar. Another interesting aspect of the decision was the court's ruling that the third party had standing to appeal a refusal to modify the injunction, inasmuch as it was bound by that injunction.

by personal service or otherwise." The effect of an injunction on non-parties depends on an appraisal of their relations and behavior with the enjoined party and not upon mere construction of terms of the order. Thus, a person not legally identified with a party can be held in contempt only if there was active concert and participation. The general rule in civil contempt is that a party need not intend to violate an injunction to be found in contempt. Nonparties are differently situated. Nonparties are subject to contempt sanctions if they act with an enjoined party to bring about a result forbidden by the injunction, but only if they are aware of the injunction and know that their acts violate the injunction. And because actual notice is a requirement for contempt based on active concert and participation with an enjoined party, only those acts that take place after notice can serve as a basis for contempt.[51]

Rule 65(d) derives from the common law doctrine that a decree of injunction not only binds parties defendant but also those identified with them in interest, in privity with them, represented by them, or subject to their control. The rule does not specify successors and assigns as among those an injunction binds, and the appearance of those words in an enforcement order cannot enlarge its scope beyond that permitted by the rule. Successors and assigns may, however, be instrumentalities through which a defendant seeks to evade an order, or they may fall within the definition of persons in active concert or participation in the violation of an injunction. If they are, then by that fact they are brought within the scope of contempt proceedings under the Federal Rules of Civil Procedure. Thus, whether one brings oneself in contempt as a successor or assign depends on an appraisal of one's relations and behavior and not upon mere construction of the terms of the order itself.[52] An injunction would be of little value if its proscriptions could be evaded by the expedient of forming another entity to carry on the enjoined activity. For that reason, courts have consistently held that "successors" are within the scope of an injunction entered against a corporation and may be held in contempt for its violation. The question of the extent to which a federal injunction applies to nonparties is governed by Rule 65(d), not by state law. Successorship liability turns on whether there is a substantial continuity of interest between the two organizations. Thus, an injunction may survive the dissolution of the corporation at which it is directed and continue to bind any successor in interest to the original defendant. Such a rule is necessary to prevent an enjoined defendant from nullifying a decree by carrying out prohibited acts through aiders and abettors, although they were not parties to the original proceeding.[53]

---

[51]*Additive Cont. & Meas. Sys. Inc. v. Flowdata Inc.,* 154 F.3d 1345, 47 USPQ2d 1906 (Fed. Cir. 1998).

[52]*Eli Lilly & Co. v. Premo Pharm. Labs., Inc.,* 843 F.2d 1378, 6 USPQ2d 1367 (Fed. Cir. 1988).

[53]*Additive Cont. & Meas. Sys. Inc. v. Flowdata Inc.,* 154 F.3d 1345, 47 USPQ2d 1906 (Fed. Cir. 1998).

Applying this analytical technique, the court found that a successor corporation was not an instrumentality through which the original defendants were seeking to evade an order, or a person in active concert or participation with those defendants, where it was (1) not formed by the original individual or corporate defendants or any officer, director, agent, servant, employee, or attorney of any of them, (2) unaware of the injunction at the time it acquired its interest in the subject matter of the prior decree, and (3) not a mere continuation of the original defendant because it did not assume any significant liabilities and did not acquire certain assets.[54]

An employee of an enjoined corporation is usually not bound by an injunction after severing relations with the corporation. However, this is not so where a corporate officer is "legally identified" with a corporation. In general, an officer is legally identified with a corporation if the officer is so identified in interest with those named in the decree that it would be reasonable to conclude that his or her rights and interests have been represented and adjudicated in the original injunction proceeding. Factors that may be pertinent to the inquiry are the officer's position and responsibilities in the enjoined corporation, participation in the litigation that preceded the entry of the injunction, and the degree of similarity between his or her activities in the old and new businesses.[55]

A court may modify an injunction when it is satisfied that it has been turned into an instrument of wrong. The policies of res judicata are not totally inviolate when the judgment includes an injunction of prospective effect. The preclusive effect of a judgment must be balanced against the need, in sound judicial discretion, to modify a continuing injunction when circumstances have sufficiently changed. Lest the finality of judgment and the policy of ending litigation be unduly impeached, however, such modification requires not only that circumstances have changed, but that unexpected hardship and inequity have resulted.[56]

---

[54]*Eli Lilly & Co. v. Premo Pharm. Labs., Inc.,* 843 F.2d 1378, 6 USPQ2d 1367 (Fed. Cir. 1988). The successor corporation had acquired a New Drug Application indirectly from a party forbidden by injunction to produce the drug to which the NDA related. The district court felt that this amounted to acquisition of an interest in the subject matter of the prior decree, but the Federal Circuit disagreed. An NDA simply signifies that a drug has met federal safety and efficacy requirements; it is not equivalent to the product it addresses and it does not authorize anyone to make, use, or sell the drug, certainly not in derogation of another's patent rights. The Federal Circuit distinguished *Brunswick Corp. v. Chrysler Corp.,* 408 F.2d 335, 161 USPQ 65 (7th Cir. 1969). There the acquiring party was aware of a consent decree and purchased the entire business devoted to the production of the infringing products, including personnel and manufacturing facilities.

[55]*Additive Cont. & Meas. Sys. Inc. v. Flowdata Inc.,* 154 F.3d 1345, 47 USPQ2d 1906 (Fed. Cir. 1998). Here the officer was the incorporator and sole shareholder of the infringer corporation when it was formed. At all times he owned at least 90% of its stock, served as its president throughout the litigation, and represented its interests in that litigation. It had operated out of his home for some period of time, the same location from which he started and operated a successor corporation to market the redesigned device. His work on that device began while he was still serving as the original corporation's president. On these facts, he was properly held in contempt.

[56]*W.L. Gore & Assoc. v. C.R. Bard, Inc.,* 977 F.2d 558, 24 USPQ2d 1451 (Fed. Cir. 1992).

The All Writs Act (28 U.S.C. §1651) authorizes courts in certain circumstances to issue directives to persons who are not parties to an underlying lawsuit. Thus, a federal court may issue such commands as may be necessary or appropriate to effectuate and prevent the frustration of orders it has previously issued in the exercise of jurisdiction otherwise obtained. But the extraordinary remedy of enjoining nonparties must be reserved for extraordinary cases, in which the activities of third parties threaten to undermine the court's ability to render a binding judgment in the case before it. The All Writs Act cannot be employed as a general license for district courts to grant relief against nonparties whenever such measures seem useful or efficient. Thus, although an injunctive order prohibiting nonparties from doing certain acts may be more efficient than a separate lawsuit against those parties, the All Writs Act does not authorize that kind of adjudicative shortcut.[57]

(f) Government Involvement

Injunctive relief against future infringement is, of course, not available against the government in actions under 28 U.S.C. §1498.[58] In one case the defendant argued that an injunction was too broad because it would, read literally, prevent the defendant from supplying the government. The Federal Circuit refused to modify the injunction, on the following complex but undoubtedly correct reasoning: a patent is a grant of the right to exclude others from making, using, or selling the invention claimed. Taken at face value, this would seem to include the right to prevent a manufacturer from supplying an invention to the government. But it does not because 28 U.S.C. §1498 says it does not. The patentee takes his or her patent from the government subject to the government's eminent domain right to obtain what it needs from manufacturers and to use what it obtains. The government has graciously consented, in the same statute, to be sued in the Claims Court for reasonable and entire compensation for what would be infringement if done by a private person. These same principles apply to injunctions, which are nothing more than the giving of the aid of the courts to the enforcement of the patentee's right to exclude. Though injunctions may seem to say that making for and selling to the government is forbidden, injunctions based upon patent rights cannot in reality do that because of 28 U.S.C. §1498.[59] Similarly, 19 U.S.C.

---

[57]*Additive Con. & Meas. Sys., Inc. v. Flowdata, Inc.,* 96 F.3d 1390, 40 USPQ2d 1106 (Fed. Cir. 1996).

[58]*Motorola, Inc. v. United States,* 729 F.2d 765, 221 USPQ 297 (Fed. Cir. 1984). Indeed, it is likely that preliminary injunctive relief against a supplier's threatened sale to the government is not available. *TVI Energy Corp. v. Blane,* 806 F.2d 1057, 1 USPQ2d 1071 (Fed. Cir. 1986).

[59]*W.L. Gore & Assoc., Inc. v. Garlock, Inc.,* 842 F.2d 1275, 6 USPQ2d 1277 (Fed. Cir. 1988). The Federal Circuit did not discuss the district court's reason for refusing to modify the injunction, which was that the trial had taken place and the injunction was entered before the

§1337 does not function merely as an international extension of private rights under the patent statute, and therefore the statements of the Federal Circuit on the showing of injury required for the grant of an injunction in a patent infringement suit cannot be taken out of context and applied to the issuance of an exclusion order in a §1337 proceeding. More is required there than simply proof of continuing infringement of a valid enforceable patent.[60]

(g) Staying or Vacating Injunctions

Where an injunction has expired, and there are no current or future consequences that could keep alive any controversy over its terms or duration, the entire question is moot and should not be further considered. There is no need to vacate an expired injunction.[61] There are four factors that always guide the Federal Circuit's discretion to issue a stay pending appeal: (1) whether the stay applicant has made a strong showing that it is likely to succeed on the merits; (2) whether the applicant will be irreparably injured absent a stay; (3) whether issuance of the stay will substantially injure the other party's interest in the proceeding; and (4) where the public interest lies. Each factor need not be given equal weight, and the likelihood of success in the appeal is not a rigid concept. The four factors can effectively merge to a sliding scale of likelihood of success versus balance of harm.[62] Thus a stay of an injunction may be appropriate to preserve the status quo pending an appeal. However, a stay is not a judicial license to continue and greatly increase infringing activities.[63]

The court granted a stay of an injunction pending appeal in *duPont v. Phillips.*[64] During the pendency of the litigation, the patentee filed a reissue application as it was obligated to do under its license with third parties. The defendant refused to take a license, claiming that the patent was invalid. The PTO examiner entered a final rejection of the reissue application, and the patentee appealed in the PTO. While the PTO appeal was pending the patentee sued defendant for infringement, and the appeal was stayed in favor of

---

defendant even became involved in any government bidding. See also *Trojan, Inc. v. Shat-R-Shield, Inc.,* 885 F.2d 854, 12 USPQ2d 1132 (Fed. Cir. 1989).

[60]*Corning Glass Works v. United States ITC,* 799 F.2d 1559, 230 USPQ 822 (Fed. Cir. 1986).

[61]*Syntex Ophthalmics, Inc. v. Novicky,* 795 F.2d 983, 230 USPQ 427 (Fed. Cir. 1986).

[62]*Standard Havens Prods., Inc. v. Gencor Indus., Inc.,* 897 F.2d 511, 13 USPQ2d 2029 (Fed. Cir. 1990).

[63]*Bott v. Four Star Corp.,* 807 F.2d 1567, 1 USPQ2d 1210 (Fed. Cir. 1986). Where there was an enormous increase in infringing activity during the period of stay, it was appropriate to include that activity in the willful activity that was said to justify increased damages. *Id.* Anecdotal data suggest that the Federal Circuit is not easily persuaded to grant a stay pending appeal.

[64]*E.I. duPont de Nemours & Co. v. Phillips Petroleum Co.,* 835 F.2d 277, 5 USPQ2d 1109 (Fed. Cir. 1987).

the infringement litigation. The district court found the patent infringed and not invalid, and entered a permanent injunction, which it refused to stay. The Federal Circuit granted defendant's motion for a stay pending the appeal of the infringement judgment, citing several grounds: (1) the conflict between the PTO and the district court showed the existence of substantial legal issues of claim interpretation on appeal; (2) the defendant would have to retool, fundamentally transform that portion of its business, and stop making products that accounted for $200 million in annual sales; (3) there was a likelihood of a resultant shortage of the product in the market so that users might be unable to find supplies; and (4) the patentee's willingness to license all willing competitors, and its announced intention to divest itself of this aspect of its own business, put it in a different position than a patentee who is practicing its invention and fully excluding others.

Similarly, in *Standard Havens v. Gencor*,[65] a stay of execution pending appeal was granted. The success factor favored the infringer, on the ground that the PTO had granted a request for reexamination. The infringer also showed that it would suffer layoffs, insolvency, and perhaps extinction if the injunction were allowed to continue and the money judgment were executed. On the other hand, the patentee would not be greatly harmed, because it appeared that there was serious doubt whether it would be able to collect the full money judgment in the event the infringer were thrown into bankruptcy. The public interest did not appear to favor either side.

§13.2 Preliminary Injunctions and TROs

(a) In General

The authority provided by 35 U.S.C. §283 to grant injunctions in infringement actions extends to preliminary injunctions pending trial as well as permanent injunctions after a full determination on the merits. The standards applied to the grant of preliminary injunctions are the same in patent cases as in other areas of the law.[66] The purpose of a preliminary, or interlocutory, injunction is to preserve the status quo and to protect the respective rights of the parties pending a determination on the merits.[67] The need for findings and reasons to explain any injunctive relief that goes beyond maintaining

---

[65]*Standard Havens Prods., Inc. v. Gencor Indus., Inc.*, 897 F.2d 511, 13 USPQ2d 2029 (Fed. Cir. 1990).

[66]*High Tech Med. Instr., Inc. v. New Image Indus., Inc.*, 49 F.3d 1551, 33 USPQ2d 2005 (Fed. Cir. 1995).

[67]*Cordis Corp. v. Medtronic, Inc.*, 835 F.2d 859, 5 USPQ2d 1118 (Fed. Cir. 1987); *Cordis Corp. v. Medtronic, Inc.*, 780 F.2d 991, 228 USPQ 189 (Fed. Cir. 1985).

the status quo is especially critical at a preliminary stage in the proceedings.[68]

The status quo to be preserved is that state of affairs existing immediately before the filing of the litigation—the last uncontested status that preceded the pending controversy.[69] But the Federal Circuit has quite unceremoniously rejected any argument that preservation of the status quo is inconsistent with a preliminary injunction against patent infringement. The concept of status quo was not intended to allow an infringer to continue the alleged infringements at the rate they were occurring when the suit was filed. A preliminary injunction preserves the status quo if it prevents future trespasses but does not undertake to assess the pecuniary or other consequences of past trespasses.[70]

Whether or not to grant a preliminary injunction against patent infringement involves substantive matters unique to patent law and is therefore governed by the law of the Federal Circuit. However, as to purely procedural aspects of such injunctions, such as whether there has been compliance with Rules 52(a) and 65, FRCP, regional circuit law controls.[71] The court also applies the law of the regional circuit as to denial of a preliminary injunction against trademark infringement.[72] In an antitrust and unfair competition suit, a preliminary injunction prohibiting the defendant from filing lawsuits for contributory infringement against the plaintiff's customers is governed by the law of the regional circuit.[73]

Typically four factors must be considered: (1) the relative rights and hardships of the parties; (2) the likelihood of ultimate success

---

[68]*Digital Equip. Corp. v. Emulex Corp.*, 805 F.2d 380, 231 USPQ 779 (Fed. Cir. 1986).

[69]*Litton Sys., Inc. v. Sundstrand Corp.*, 750 F.2d 952, 224 USPQ 252 (Fed. Cir. 1984).

[70]*H.H. Robertson Co. v. United Steel Deck, Inc.*, 820 F.2d 384, 2 USPQ2d 1926 (Fed. Cir. 1987). If the infringer has allowed itself to become excessively dependent upon infringing sales, the "status quo" catchword does not necessarily allow it to continue such dependency. *Atlas Powder Co. v. Ireco Chems.*, 773 F.2d 1230, 227 USPQ 289 (Fed. Cir. 1985).

[71]*Hybritech, Inc. v. Abbott Labs.*, 849 F.2d 1446, 7 USPQ2d 1191 (Fed. Cir. 1988). See *Reebok Int'l Ltd. v. J. Baker, Inc.*, 32 F.3d 1552, 31 USPQ2d 1781 (Fed. Cir. 1994) (an appeal from a denial of a preliminary injunction based on patent infringement involves substantive issues unique to patent law and is governed by the law of the Federal Circuit); *Xeta, Inc. v. Atex, Inc.*, 852 F.2d 1280, 7 USPQ2d 1471 (Fed. Cir. 1988) (regional circuit law applies to standards for preliminary injunctive relief). Questions regarding an injunction bond are decided according to the law of the regional circuit. In the Fifth Circuit, a district court is within its discretion in declining to award the amount of the injunction bond (when a preliminary injunction is dissolved as a result of a contrary jury verdict), unless the plaintiff acted in bad faith in obtaining the injunction. *Hupp v. Siroflex of Am., Inc.*, 122 F.3d 1456, 43 USPQ2d 1887 (Fed. Cir. 1997).

[72]*Black & Decker, Inc. v. Hoover Serv. Ctr.*, 886 F.2d 1285, 12 USPQ2d 1250 (Fed. Cir. 1989).

[73]*Atari Games Corp. v. Nintendo of Am., Inc.*, 897 F.2d 1572, 14 USPQ2d 1034 (Fed. Cir. 1990). One wonders whether this rule should apply in a patent-antitrust setting. The questions presented may have as much to do with patent law as antitrust. Under Ninth Circuit law, a party may satisfy the four factors by demonstrating either (1) a combination of probable success on the merits and the possibility of irreparable injury, or (2) that serious questions of law are raised and the balance of hardships tips sharply in its favor. A serious question is one where the movant has a fair chance of success on the merits. *Id.*

on the merits; (3) the possibility of irreparable harm; and (4) the public interest.[74] The burden on an applicant for a preliminary injunction against patent infringement is to show a reasonable probability of eventual success in the litigation and a likelihood of irreparable injury pendente lite if the relief is not granted. In addition, the district court should take into account, when relevant, the possibility of harm to other interested persons from the grant or denial of an injunction and the public interest.[75]

Equity requires that no one element be dispositive, that each be weighed and measured against the others and against the relief requested.[76] If a preliminary injunction is granted by the trial court, the weakness of the showing regarding one factor may be overborne by the strength of others. If the injunction is denied, the absence of an adequate showing with regard to any one factor may be sufficient, given the weight or lack of it assigned the other factors, to justify the denial.[77] The matter of preliminary injunctive relief is committed to the sound discretion of the trial court, and a reversal requires a showing that the trial judge abused his or her discretion, committed an error of law, or seriously misjudged the evidence.[78]

---

[74]*Reebok Int'l Ltd. v. J. Baker, Inc.*, 32 F.3d 1552, 31 USPQ2d 1781 (Fed. Cir. 1994); *Intel Corp. v. ULSI Sys. Tech., Inc.*, 995 F.2d 1566, 27 USPQ2d 1136 (Fed. Cir. 1993); *Oakley, Inc. v. International Tropic-Cal, Inc.*, 923 F.2d 167, 17 USPQ2d 1401 (Fed. Cir. 1991); *Hybritech, Inc. v. Abbott Labs.*, 849 F.2d 1446, 7 USPQ2d 1191 (Fed. Cir. 1988); *T.J. Smith & Nephew Ltd. v. Consolidated Med. Equip., Inc.*, 821 F.2d 646, 3 USPQ2d 1316 (Fed. Cir. 1987); *Datascope Corp. v. Kontron Inc.*, 786 F.2d 398, 229 USPQ 41 (Fed. Cir. 1986); *Cordis Corp. v. Medtronic, Inc.*, 780 F.2d 991, 228 USPQ 189 (Fed. Cir. 1985).

[75]*H.H. Robertson Co. v. United Steel Deck, Inc.*, 820 F.2d 384, 2 USPQ2d 1926 (Fed. Cir. 1987).

[76]*Hybritech, Inc. v. Abbott Labs.*, 849 F.2d 1446, 7 USPQ2d 1191 (Fed. Cir. 1988); *H.H. Robertson Co. v. United Steel Deck, Inc.*, 820 F.2d 384, 2 USPQ2d 1926 (Fed. Cir. 1987); *Roper Corp. v. Litton Sys., Inc.*, 757 F.2d 1266, 225 USPQ 345 (Fed. Cir. 1985); *Smith Int'l, Inc. v. Hughes Tool Co.*, 718 F.2d 1573, 219 USPQ 686 (Fed. Cir. 1983).

[77]*Chrysler Motors Corp. v. Auto Body Panels of Ohio, Inc.*, 908 F.2d 951, 15 USPQ2d 1469 (Fed. Cir. 1990).

[78]*Oakley, Inc. v. International Tropic-Cal, Inc.*, 923 F.2d 167, 17 USPQ2d 1401 (Fed. Cir. 1991); *Chrysler Motors Corp. v. Auto Body Panels of Ohio, Inc.*, 908 F.2d 951, 15 USPQ2d 1469 (Fed. Cir. 1990); *Atari Games Corp. v. Nintendo of Am., Inc.*, 897 F.2d 1572, 14 USPQ2d 1034 (Fed. Cir. 1990); *Xeta, Inc. v. Atex, Inc.*, 852 F.2d 1280, 7 USPQ2d 1471 (Fed. Cir. 1988); *Cordis Corp. v. Medtronic, Inc.*, 835 F.2d 859, 5 USPQ2d 1118 (Fed. Cir. 1987); *T.J. Smith & Nephew Ltd. v. Consolidated Med. Equip., Inc.*, 821 F.2d 646, 3 USPQ2d 1316 (Fed. Cir. 1987); *H.H. Robertson Co. v. United Steel Deck, Inc.*, 820 F.2d 384, 2 USPQ2d 1926 (Fed. Cir. 1987); *Datascope Corp. v. Kontron Inc.*, 786 F.2d 398, 229 USPQ 41 (Fed. Cir. 1986); *Cordis Corp. v. Medtronic, Inc.*, 780 F.2d 991, 228 USPQ 189 (Fed. Cir. 1985); *Litton Sys., Inc. v. Sundstrand Corp.*, 750 F.2d 952, 224 USPQ 252 (Fed. Cir. 1984); *Stein Assoc., Inc. v. Heat & Control, Inc.*, 748 F.2d 653, 223 USPQ 1277 (Fed. Cir. 1984). The procedural requirements for, and scope of, preliminary injunctive relief are subject to review as well as the merits. *Digital Equip. Corp. v. Emulex Corp.*, 805 F.2d 380, 231 USPQ 779 (Fed. Cir. 1986). Although the issuance of an injunction is clearly within the discretion of the district court, the district court's discretion is not absolute and must be measured against the standards governing the issuance of an injunction. *Intel Corp. v. ULSI Sys. Tech., Inc.*, 995 F.2d 1566, 27 USPQ2d 1136 (Fed. Cir. 1993); *Hybritech, Inc. v. Abbott Labs.*, 849 F.2d 1446, 7 USPQ2d 1191 (Fed. Cir. 1988). The issuance of a preliminary injunction is within the discretion of the trial court, but that discretion is not absolute. *Lund Indus., Inc. v. GO Indus., Inc.*, 938 F.2d 1273, 19 USPQ2d 1383 (Fed. Cir. 1991). The grant or denial of a preliminary injunction is reviewed under an abuse of discretion standard. Findings of fact are subject to the clearly erroneous standard of Rule 52(a), FRCP,

When a preliminary injunction is granted, to obtain reversal on appeal an alleged infringer need only convince the appellate court that one of the factual premises is clearly erroneous. In contrast, when a preliminary injunction is denied, the movant carries a heavier burden to obtain a reversal. The movant must show not only that one or more of the factors relied on by the district court was clearly erroneous, but also that a denial of the preliminary relief sought would amount to an abuse of the court's discretion upon reversal of an erroneous finding.[79]

Preliminary injunctive relief has been rightly described as an extraordinary remedy not to be routinely granted.[80] In its first encounter with the issue of preliminary injunctive relief in a patent case, the Federal Circuit gave fair warning that such relief would not be easy to come by. It observed that unusually stringent standards had been developed in patent cases and attributed the reluctance to grant preliminary injunctions to distrust and unfamiliarity with patents and a belief that the PTO was inherently unreliable in its patentability determinations.[81] But the court has since made it clear that the standards applied to the grant of a preliminary injunction are no more or less stringent in patent cases than in other areas of the law. The existing standards for relief pendente lite, fairly applied, can accommodate any special circumstances that may arise.[82]

(b) Likelihood of Success on the Merits

The burden upon one who moves for preliminary relief in a patent case is no different than for other kinds of intellectual property, where only a clear showing is required. There need not have been a trial or a final adjudication of validity, nor is proof beyond question required,

---

and conclusions of law are reviewed de novo. *Black & Decker, Inc. v. Hoover Serv. Ctr.*, 886 F.2d 1285, 12 USPQ2d 1250 (Fed. Cir. 1989). An ITC order dealing with temporary injunctive relief may be set aside if it rests on a foundation of an erroneous understanding of the law or on clearly erroneous findings of fact; otherwise, it may be set aside only if, based on the facts, it is patently unreasonable, arbitrary, or fanciful. *Rosemount, Inc. v. United States ITC*, 910 F.2d 819, 15 USPQ2d 1569 (Fed. Cir. 1990).

[79]*New England Braiding Co. v. A.W. Chesterton Co.*, 970 F.2d 878, 23 USPQ2d 1622 (Fed. Cir. 1992). See also *Reebok Int'l Ltd. v. J. Baker, Inc.*, 32 F.3d 1552, 31 USPQ2d 1781 (Fed. Cir. 1994). An appellant has a heavy burden to overcome the denial of a motion for a preliminary injunction. *Payless Shoesource, Inc. v. Reebok Int'l Ltd.*, 998 F.2d 985, 27 USPQ2d 1516 (Fed. Cir. 1993).

[80]*Intel Corp. v. ULSI Sys. Tech., Inc.*, 995 F.2d 1566, 27 USPQ2d 1136 (Fed. Cir. 1993); *Black & Decker, Inc. v. Hoover Serv. Ctr.*, 886 F.2d 1285, 12 USPQ2d 1250 (Fed. Cir. 1989). See also *High Tech Med. Instr., Inc. v. New Image Indus., Inc.*, 49 F.3d 1551, 33 USPQ2d 2005 (Fed. Cir. 1995).

[81]*Smith Int'l, Inc. v. Hughes Tool Co.*, 718 F.2d 1573, 219 USPQ 686 (Fed. Cir. 1983).

[82]*H.H. Robertson Co. v. United Steel Deck, Inc.*, 820 F.2d 384, 2 USPQ2d 1926 (Fed. Cir. 1987). Statements that a preliminary injunction is a drastic and extraordinary remedy do not imply that it must be rare or practically unattainable, only that it is not granted as a matter of right; it must be thoroughly justified. *Polymer Tech., Inc. v. Bridwell H.A.*, 103 F.3d 970, 41 USPQ2d 1185 (Fed. Cir. 1996).

else nothing additional would be required to establish the liability of the accused infringer. When a patentee clearly shows that its patent is valid and infringed, a court may upon balance of all the competing equities preliminarily enjoin infringement.[83] Of course, if a title defense is raised, the patentee must show a reasonable likelihood of success on the merits as to ownership as well.[84] The burden is always on the movant to demonstrate entitlement to preliminary relief. But such entitlement is determined in the context of the presumptions and burdens that would inhere at trial on the merits. Thus, the patent challenger retains the burden of establishing invalidity, and the applicant for preliminary injunctive relief retains the burden of showing a reasonable likelihood that the attack on the validity of the patent would fail.[85]

It is understood, however, that the substantive issues of validity and infringement are not raised for final resolution by motions for preliminary injunctions.[86] A district court cannot be held to have erred in deciding that the patentee failed to make a sufficient showing of likelihood of success to support a preliminary injunction where the evidence presented in support of invalidity raises a substantial question, although the defense may not be entirely fleshed out. Given the time constraints within which an accused infringer must usually respond with evidence to a motion for preliminary injunction, a fully comprehensive presentation of its defenses cannot be reasonably required. Because severe time constraints are usual, it is recognized that a motion for a preliminary injunction must customarily be decided on the basis of procedures that are less formal and evidence that is less complete than in a trial on the merits. Indeed, such a record does not usually allow for a reliable resolution of the merits. While it is not the patentee's burden to prove validity, the patentee must show that the alleged infringer's defense lacks substantial merit.[87]

---

[83]*Atlas Powder Co. v. Ireco Chems.*, 773 F.2d 1230, 227 USPQ 289 (Fed. Cir. 1985). The court had earlier hinted at adoption of a test that would require proof beyond question of validity and infringement. *Smith Int'l, Inc. v. Hughes Tool Co.*, 718 F.2d 1573, 219 USPQ 686 (Fed. Cir. 1983).

[84]*Filmtec Corp. v. Allied-Signal Inc.*, 939 F.2d 1568, 19 USPQ2d 1508 (Fed. Cir. 1991).

[85]*H.H. Robertson Co. v. United Steel Deck, Inc.*, 820 F.2d 384, 2 USPQ2d 1926 (Fed. Cir. 1987).

[86]*Roper Corp. v. Litton Sys., Inc.*, 757 F.2d 1266, 225 USPQ 345 (Fed. Cir. 1985). Sometimes the court reaches out and decides or prejudges them, however. See, e.g., *Jeneric/Pentron Inc. v. Dillon Co.*, 205 F.3d 1377, 54 USPQ2d 1086 (Fed. Cir. 2000) (noninfringement); *Vehicular Techs. Corp. v. Titan Wheel Int'l*, 141 F.3d 1084, 46 USPQ2d 1257 (Fed. Cir. 1998) (nonequivalency); *Genentech, Inc. v. Novo Nordisk, A/S*, 108 F.3d 1361, 42 USPQ2d 1001 (Fed. Cir. 1997) (invalidity); *Novo Nordisk of N.A., Inc. v. Genentech, Inc.*, 77 F.3d 1364, 37 USPQ2d 1773 (Fed. Cir. 1996) (noninfringement).

[87]*New England Braiding Co. v. A.W. Chesterton Co.*, 970 F.2d 878, 23 USPQ2d 1622 (Fed. Cir. 1992). However, even a strong showing of misjoinder of inventors will not necessarily preclude the imposition of a preliminary injunction. Incorrect inventorship is a technical defect in a patent that may be easily curable. Even assuming misjoinder, an inventor's persuasive explanation of how any such error occurred will usually suffice to show a likelihood of success on the issue of validity. *Canon Computer Sys. Inc v. NuKote Int'l Inc.*, 134 F.3d 1085, 45 USPQ2d 1355 (Fed. Cir. 1998).

In establishing likelihood of success for a patentee, the required clear showing of validity demands prior adjudication, public acquiescence, or conclusive direct technical evidence.[88] However, a prior adjudication of validity need not have been between the same parties in order to support the grant of a preliminary injunction, nor need it have been a final adjudication. The question is not one of res judicata or collateral estoppel, but merely evidence tending to show likelihood of success.[89] Substantial weight may be given to a patent's litigation history in connection with a motion for relief pendente lite. A prior adjudication upholding patent validity, after a fully litigated trial involving similar issues of fact and law, contributes strong support to the grant of a preliminary injunction.[90] The district court is not bound, as a matter of law, by the prior adjudication of validity against a different defendant but it may, as an exercise of its discretion, give considerable weight to it.[91] Thus, where a patent had been held valid in earlier litigation against another, and the presently accused infringer made no effort to show invalidity, likelihood of success was taken as established. The accused infringer had an opportunity to make some showing in response to a motion for preliminary injunction, but failed to grasp it.[92] Moreover, a binding prior adjudication of infringement as between the same parties, coupled with an admission of infringement, may well obviate the necessity of a showing of irreparable harm.[93]

Can the presumption of validity alone support a preliminary injunction? The court seemed to suggest that it could, at least in a design patent case. However, the defendant came forward with strong evidence of functionality, and the patentee did not respond with countervailing evidence tending to establish validity. The result was a reversal of a preliminary injunction.[94] The court has since held that

---

[88]*Smith Int'l, Inc. v. Hughes Tool Co.*, 718 F.2d 1573, 219 USPQ 686 (Fed. Cir. 1983). A variety of formulations have been used to describe the quantum or sufficiency of the showing required for likelihood of success. These range from restrictive statements such as "reasonable certainty," "strong probability," and "substantial likelihood," to merely a "reasonable possibility" or a "probable chance." There have been suggestions that the standard interacts with the degree of harm that each party will suffer: the greater the harm, the less certainty required for likelihood of success. *New England Braiding Co. v. A.W. Chesterton Co.*, 970 F.2d 878, 23 USPQ2d 1622 (Fed. Cir. 1992).

[89]*Atlas Powder Co. v. Ireco Chems.*, 773 F.2d 1230, 227 USPQ 289 (Fed. Cir. 1985).

[90]*H.H. Robertson Co. v. United Steel Deck, Inc.*, 820 F.2d 384, 2 USPQ2d 1926 (Fed. Cir. 1987).

[91]*Hybritech, Inc. v. Abbott Labs.*, 849 F.2d 1446, 7 USPQ2d 1191 (Fed. Cir. 1988). Here the patent had previously been held valid by the Federal Circuit itself. However, it subsequently became involved in an interference in which its inventor was relegated to junior party status. Despite evidence that only 25% of junior parties prevail, the court found no error in the district court's conclusion that the plaintiff had established a likelihood of success with respect to validity.

[92]*Roper Corp. v. Litton Sys., Inc.*, 757 F.2d 1266, 225 USPQ 345 (Fed. Cir. 1985). It should be noted that the trial court's denial of a preliminary injunction was affirmed on other grounds.

[93]*Smith Int'l, Inc. v. Hughes Tool Co.*, 718 F.2d 1573, 219 USPQ 686 (Fed. Cir. 1983).

[94]*Power Controls Corp. v. Hybrinetics, Inc.*, 806 F.2d 234, 231 USPQ 774 (Fed. Cir. 1986). See also *Chrysler Motors Corp. v. Auto Body Panels of Ohio, Inc.*, 908 F.2d 951, 15 USPQ2d 1469 (Fed. Cir. 1990). The accused infringer does not have the same burden of clear and

the presumption of validity, being procedural not substantive, does not alone create a presumption of irreparable harm.[95] The presumption of validity is not evidence that can be weighed in determining likelihood of success. It simply acts as a procedural device that places the burden of going forward with evidence and the ultimate burden of persuasion of invalidity at trial on the alleged infringer. It does not relieve a patentee who moves for a preliminary injunction from carrying the normal burden of demonstrating that it will likely succeed on all disputed liability issues at trial, even when the issue concerns the patent's validity. At this preliminary stage the trial court does not resolve the validity question but rather must make an assessment of the persuasiveness of the challenger's evidence, recognizing that it is doing so without all evidence that may come out at trial.[96] A cautionary corollary is that a preliminary injunction improvidently granted may impart undeserved value to an unworthy patent.[97]

Likelihood of success also requires a clear showing of infringement. Certainly no authority supports the notion that a preliminary injunction against infringement may issue in response to rumors of a threat of infringement. Quite the contrary; a high burden of factual proof must be carried by a patentee seeking preliminary relief.[98] Nonetheless, the grant of a preliminary injunction does not require that infringement be proved beyond all question, or that there be no evidence supporting the viewpoint of the accused infringer. The grant turns on the likelihood that the patentee will meet its burden at trial of proving infringement.[99] The corollary proposition is that a denial of a preliminary injunction does not require that noninfringement be clear beyond all question.[100] An admission that an accused device is

---

convincing proof that he or she will have at trial. *Nutrition 21 v. United States,* 930 F.2d 867, 18 USPQ2d 1347 (Fed. Cir. 1991).

[95]*T.J. Smith & Nephew Ltd. v. Consolidated Med. Equip., Inc.,* 821 F.2d 646, 3 USPQ2d 1316 (Fed. Cir. 1987). It may be possible to read this case as signaling a retreat, albeit slight, from the court's earlier position that a prior adjudication of validity is not necessary for preliminary injunctive relief. See, e.g., *Roper Corp. v. Litton Sys., Inc.,* 757 F.2d 1266, 225 USPQ 345 (Fed. Cir. 1985); *Smith Int'l, Inc. v. Hughes Tool Co.,* 718 F.2d 1573, 219 USPQ 686 (Fed. Cir. 1983). But the court rather vehemently disclaims any such retreat in a footnote. 821 F.2d at 647 n.2. Where the accused infringer comes forward with some evidence of invalidity or unenforceability, a patentee cannot establish a likelihood of success on the merits simply by reliance upon the presumption of validity. *Nutrition 21 v. United States,* 930 F.2d 867, 18 USPQ2d 1347 (Fed. Cir. 1991).

[96]*New England Braiding Co. v. A.W. Chesterton Co.,* 970 F.2d 878, 23 USPQ2d 1622 (Fed. Cir. 1992).

[97]*H.H. Robertson Co. v. United Steel Deck, Inc.,* 820 F.2d 384, 2 USPQ2d 1926 (Fed. Cir. 1987).

[98]*Chemical Eng'g Corp. v. Marlo, Inc.,* 754 F.2d 331, 222 USPQ 738 (Fed. Cir. 1984).

[99]*H.H. Robertson Co. v. United Steel Deck, Inc.,* 820 F.2d 384, 2 USPQ2d 1926 (Fed. Cir. 1987).

[100]*Illinois Tool Works, Inc. v. Grip-Pak, Inc.,* 906 F.2d 679, 15 USPQ2d 1307 (Fed. Cir. 1990).

equivalent to a previously adjudicated device may constitute a clear showing of infringement.[101] The converse is also true.[102]

A reasonable likelihood of success as to infringement cannot be established by comparing a new accused device with one that previously had been admitted, as part of a settlement of an earlier lawsuit, to be an infringement. A proper infringement analysis requires comparison of the accused design to the patent claims not to another design.[103] When the required showing of infringement implicates the doctrine of equivalents, the court may insist upon a complete *Wilson Sporting Goods* analysis.[104]

(c) Public Interest

The public interest and the possibility of harm to other interested persons may be relevant.[105] Typically, in a patent infringement case, although there exists a public interest in protecting rights secured by valid patents, the focus of the district court's public interest analysis should be whether there is some critical public interest that would be injured by the grant of preliminary relief.[106] In one case, evidence that some doctors preferred to use the accused product was a factor in denying preliminary relief.[107] Another holding implies that preliminary injunctive relief to prevent a threatened sale of an infringing device to the government is not available under any circumstances.[108] However, the court has remarked, in the context of the public interest, that selling a lower priced product does not justify infringing a patent.[109]

---

[101]*Datascope Corp. v. Kontron Inc.*, 786 F.2d 398, 229 USPQ 41 (Fed. Cir. 1986). The patentee attempted to go a step further and demonstrate that a different accused device was equivalent to the first and therefore equivalent to the claimed invention. The court refused to regard this concatenation of equivalents as a clear showing of infringement.

[102]In *Jeneric/Pentron Inc. v. Dillon Co.*, 205 F.3d 1377, 54 USPQ2d 1086 (Fed. Cir. 2000), the district court, in deciding that there was no likelihood of success on the infringement issue, relied solely on the evidence submitted by the expert for one party. This was harmless error, if error at all, for strangely enough the expert relied upon was the patentee's expert; it seems that the patentee's expert opined that the accused product fell outside of the claimed range for one element, while the infringer's expert had the opposite opinion.

[103]*Lund Indus., Inc. v. GO Indus., Inc.*, 938 F.2d 1273, 19 USPQ2d 1383 (Fed. Cir. 1991). The court distinguished its earlier decision in *KSM Fastening Sys., Inc. v. H.A. Jones Co.*, 776 F.2d 1522, 227 USPQ 676 (Fed. Cir. 1985), on the basis that it involved a determination of the propriety of contempt proceedings rather than likelihood of success on infringement.

[104]*We Care, Inc. v. Ultra-Mark Int'l Corp.*, 930 F.2d 1567, 18 USPQ2d 1562 (Fed. Cir. 1991). See §6.3(a)(iii) for a discussion of *Wilson*.

[105]*Smith Int'l, Inc. v. Hughes Tool Co.*, 718 F.2d 1573, 219 USPQ 686 (Fed. Cir. 1983).

[106]*Hybritech, Inc. v. Abbott Labs.*, 849 F.2d 1446, 7 USPQ2d 1191 (Fed. Cir. 1988). Here the court affirmed a grant of preliminary injunctive relief as to all of the defendant's medical test kits except those used to detect cancer and hepatitis.

[107]*Datascope Corp. v. Kontron Inc.*, 786 F.2d 398, 229 USPQ 41 (Fed. Cir. 1986).

[108]*TVI Energy Corp. v. Blane*, 806 F.2d 1057, 1 USPQ2d 1071 (Fed. Cir. 1986).

[109]*Payless Shoesource, Inc. v. Reebok Int'l Ltd.*, 998 F.2d 985, 27 USPQ2d 1516 (Fed. Cir. 1993).

(d) Relative Hardships

Similarly, consideration must be given to relative hardships. An injunction should not be granted if its impact on the enjoined party would be more severe than the injury the moving party would suffer if it were not granted.[110] A preliminary injunction is a drastic remedy. The hardship on a preliminarily enjoined manufacturer who must withdraw its product from the market before trial can be devastating. On the other hand, the hardship on a patentee denied an injunction after showing a strong likelihood of success on validity and infringement consists in a frequently and equally serious delay in the exercise of its limited-in-time property right. Neither hardship can be controlling in all cases.[111] It would be error for a court to rely exclusively on the relative size of the parties in determining the equities between them. The impact of grant or denial of a preliminary injunction on each is a proper factor to be considered. However, the fact that one party is small and could be put out of business by a preliminary injunction does not insulate it if the other three factors are sufficient to tip the scale in the patentee's favor. Small parties have no special right to infringe patents simply because they are small.[112] The court has affirmed a preliminary injunction against infringement of a patent with only a year to run, even in the face of evidence that the injunction affected two-thirds of the defendant's sales and would result in the layoff of 200 employees.[113]

(e) Irreparable Harm

Likelihood of success is an important factor,[114] but it is not alone determinative. The court has hinted that irreparable harm may be equally important.[115] As a general rule, a showing of immediate irreparable harm is required, and a preliminary injunction will be refused

---

[110]*Litton Sys., Inc. v. Sundstrand Corp.*, 750 F.2d 952, 224 USPQ 252 (Fed. Cir. 1984).

[111]*Illinois Tool Works, Inc. v. Grip-Pak, Inc.*, 906 F.2d 679, 15 USPQ2d 1307 (Fed. Cir. 1990). Apparently the destructive effect of an injunction on a business is less troublesome to the court after trial and judgment than it is on a motion for preliminary injunctive relief, as well it might be.

[112]*Bell & Howell DMP Co. v. Altek Sys.*, 132 F.3d 701, 45 USPQ2d 1033 (Fed. Cir. 1997).

[113]*Atlas Powder Co. v. Ireco Chems.*, 773 F.2d 1230, 227 USPQ 289 (Fed. Cir. 1985). The court was unimpressed with the fact that the patent was near expiration, pointing out that "patent rights do not peter out as the end of the patent term, usually 17 years, is approached."

[114]In *Payless Shoesource, Inc. v. Reebok Int'l Ltd.*, 998 F.2d 985, 27 USPQ2d 1516 (Fed. Cir. 1993), the court found that the trial court had abused its discretion in determining that the movant was not likely to succeed on the merits of its design patent, trademark, and trade dress infringement claims. Recognizing that likelihood of success on the merits is but one prerequisite to the issue of a preliminary injunction, it went on to conclude that the trial court's erroneous determination as to likelihood of success may have tainted its resolution of other preliminary injunction factors, thus justifying a remand.

[115]*Illinois Tool Works, Inc. v. Grip-Pak, Inc.*, 906 F.2d 679, 15 USPQ2d 1307 (Fed. Cir. 1990).

where the infringer is solvent and money will adequately compensate.[116] There is no presumption that money damages will be inadequate.[117] Only a viable threat of serious harm that cannot be undone authorizes exercise of a court's equitable power to enjoin before the merits are fully determined. A preliminary injunction will not issue simply to prevent a mere possibility of injury, even where the prospective injury is great.[118] Nonetheless, a defendant's ability to compensate a plaintiff in money damages does not necessarily preclude issuance of a preliminary injunction.[119] An infringer's argument that infringement and related damages are fully compensable in money downplays the nature of the statutory right to exclude others from making, using, or selling the patented invention. While monetary relief is often the sole remedy for past infringement, it does not follow that a monetary award is also the sole remedy against future infringement. The patent statute further provides injunctive relief to preserve the legal interests of the parties against future infringement that may have market effects never fully compensable in money. If monetary relief were the sole relief afforded by the patent statute, then injunctions would be unnecessary and infringers could become compulsory licensees for as long as the litigation lasts.[120]

Moreover, it is clear that a threat of irreparable harm will be presumed in the face of a strong showing of likelihood of success on both validity and infringement, although a strong showing on a single

---

[116]*Smith Int'l, Inc. v. Hughes Tool Co.*, 718 F.2d 1573, 219 USPQ 686 (Fed. Cir. 1983).

[117]*Nutrition 21 v. United States*, 930 F.2d 867, 18 USPQ2d 1347 (Fed. Cir. 1991).

[118]*Cordis Corp. v. Medtronic, Inc.*, 780 F.2d 991, 228 USPQ 189 (Fed. Cir. 1985). If the right to exclude during the litigation period alone established irreparable harm, the presumption of irreparable harm stemming from a finding of likely success could never be rebutted, for every patentee whose motion for a preliminary injunction is denied loses the right to exclude an accused infringer from the marketplace pending the trial. *Reebok Int'l Ltd. v. J. Baker, Inc.*, 32 F.3d 1552, 31 USPQ2d 1781 (Fed. Cir. 1994).

[119]*Roper Corp. v. Litton Sys., Inc.*, 757 F.2d 1266, 225 USPQ 345 (Fed. Cir. 1985). It was held improper to focus solely upon defendant's statement that she would be able to meet any damages due the patentee. Irreparable harm does not depend solely upon the ability to satisfy a money judgment because money awards are not the sole remedy for future infringement. *Pretty Punch Shoppettes, Inc. v. Hauk*, 844 F.2d 782, 6 USPQ2d 1563 (Fed. Cir. 1988). On the other side of the coin, where termination of a license agreement would cause loss of market share and possible litigation against the licensee and its customers, those factors could result in irreparable harm, justifying a preliminary injunction forbidding termination. *Cordis Corp. v. Medtronic, Inc.*, 835 F.2d 859, 5 USPQ2d 1118 (Fed. Cir. 1987). A mere difficulty in calculating losses of market share, or speculation that such losses might occur, is not sufficient to show a threat of irreparable injury for purposes of a preliminary injunction. A reliance upon possible market share loss would apply in every patent case where the patentee practices the invention. *Nutrition 21 v. United States*, 930 F.2d 867, 18 USPQ2d 1347 (Fed. Cir. 1991).

[120]*H.H. Robertson Co. v. United Steel Deck, Inc.*, 820 F.2d 384, 2 USPQ2d 1926 (Fed. Cir. 1987); *Atlas Powder Co. v. Ireco Chems.*, 773 F.2d 1230, 227 USPQ 289 (Fed. Cir. 1985). Past applications of the concept that no patentee could ever be irreparably harmed when an alleged infringer is capable of responding in damages frequently disserved patentees and the patent system. But that disservice would not be cured by a rash of patentee motions for preliminary injunctions filed without full basis in equity. Application of a concept that every patentee is always irreparably harmed by an alleged infringer's pretrial sales would equally disserve the patent system. *Illinois Tool Works, Inc. v. Grip-Pak, Inc.*, 906 F.2d 679, 15 USPQ2d 1307 (Fed. Cir. 1990).

one of these issues may be insufficient to raise a presumption.[121] In matters involving patent rights, irreparable harm has been presumed when a clear showing has been made of patent validity and infringement. This presumption derives in part from the finite term of the patent grant, for patent expiration is not suspended during litigation and the passage of time can work irremediable harm. The opportunity to practice an invention during the notoriously lengthy course of patent litigation may itself tempt infringers. The nature of the patent grant thus weighs against holding that monetary damages will always suffice to make the patentee whole, for the principal value of a patent is its statutory right to exclude. The presumption of irreparable harm in patent cases is analogous to that in other forms of intellectual property.[122]

(f) Rebutting the Presumption of Irreparable Harm

The presumption of irreparable harm resulting from a strong preliminary showing of patent validity and continued infringement has been termed a "legal" presumption. This means only that it is judge made and in that sense legal. The presumption itself relates to the fact of injury. Like any other presumption of fact, it does not override the evidence of record. Thus, it may be rebutted by evidence of what the actual injury is likely to be.[123] The presumption of irreparable harm does not necessarily or automatically override the evidence of record. Like many other factual presumptions, it simply acts as a procedural device that shifts the ultimate burden of production on the question of irreparable harm onto the alleged infringer.[124] For

---

[121]*Chrysler Motors Corp. v. Auto Body Panels of Ohio, Inc.*, 908 F.2d 951, 15 USPQ2d 1469 (Fed. Cir. 1990); *Roper Corp. v. Litton Sys., Inc.*, 757 F.2d 1266, 225 USPQ 345 (Fed. Cir. 1985). See also *Bell & Howell DMP Co. v. Altek Sys.*, 132 F.3d 701, 45 USPQ2d 1033 (Fed. Cir. 1997); *Atlas Powder Co. v. Ireco Chems.*, 773 F.2d 1230, 227 USPQ 289 (Fed. Cir. 1985); *Smith Int'l, Inc. v. Hughes Tool Co.*, 718 F.2d 1573, 219 USPQ 686 (Fed. Cir. 1983). A presumption of irreparable harm can flow from a strong showing of likelihood of success. *Polymer Tech., Inc. v. Bridwell H.A.*, 103 F.3d 970, 41 USPQ2d 1185 (Fed. Cir. 1996); *Hybritech, Inc. v. Abbott Labs.*, 849 F.2d 1446, 7 USPQ2d 1191 (Fed. Cir. 1988). Where a trial court accords a presumption of irreparable harm based upon a strong showing of infringement and validity, and the Federal Circuit perceives clear error in the infringement finding, the finding of irreparable harm will of course be vacated as well. *Novo Nordisk of N.A., Inc. v. Genentech, Inc.*, 77 F.3d 1364, 37 USPQ2d 1773 (Fed. Cir. 1996).

[122]*H.H. Robertson Co. v. United Steel Deck, Inc.*, 820 F.2d 384, 2 USPQ2d 1926 (Fed. Cir. 1987). See also *Nutrition 21 v. United States*, 930 F.2d 867, 18 USPQ2d 1347 (Fed. Cir. 1991).

[123]*Rosemount, Inc. v. United States ITC*, 910 F.2d 819, 15 USPQ2d 1569 (Fed. Cir. 1990). The court expressly rejected an argument that the presumption can be overcome only by evidence of cessation of infringement (in this case, cessation of importation). See also *T.J. Smith & Nephew Ltd. v. Consolidated Med. Equip., Inc.*, 821 F.2d 646, 3 USPQ2d 1316 (Fed. Cir. 1987); *H.H. Robertson Co. v. United Steel Deck, Inc.*, 820 F.2d 384, 2 USPQ2d 1926 (Fed. Cir. 1987). The court has cast some doubt upon even the existence of the presumption in cases where the showing of likelihood of success is not strong, contrasting cases where there were previous holdings of validity. *Illinois Tool Works, Inc. v. Grip-Pak, Inc.*, 906 F.2d 679, 15 USPQ2d 1307 (Fed. Cir. 1990).

[124]*Reebok Int'l Ltd. v. J. Baker, Inc.*, 32 F.3d 1552, 31 USPQ2d 1781 (Fed. Cir. 1994).

example, despite a strong showing of past infringement, there was no evidence that the defendant was presently infringing or had definite plans to do so in the future. The patentee was not practicing the invention and had not shown that anything the defendant was doing would preclude the patentee's ability to license or enter the market. Under this totality of circumstances, the presumption of irreparable injury was rebutted; the status quo could be maintained without an injunction pendente lite.[125] Although a patentee's failure to practice an invention does not necessarily defeat the patentee's claim of irreparable harm, the lack of commercial activity by the patentee is a significant factor in the calculus.[126] The presumption may also be rebutted by a long delay in seeking a preliminary injunction and the granting of licenses, both of which are acts incompatible with the emphasis on the right to exclude that is the basis for the presumption in a proper case.[127]

The presumption of irreparable harm can be rebutted by evidence that (1) the nonmovant has or will soon cease the allegedly infringing activities, thus making an injunction unnecessary; (2) movants have engaged in a pattern of granting licenses under the patent, such that it may be reasonable to expect that invasion of the patent right can be recompensed with a royalty rather than with an injunction; or (3) movants unduly delayed in bringing suit, thereby negating the idea of irreparability.[128] A patentee does not have to sue all infringers at once. Picking off one infringer at a time is not inconsistent with being irreparably harmed. The failure to bring suit against other potential infringers may be relevant to an analysis of irreparable harm, but only when it indicates unreasonable delay in bringing suit, willingness to accept royalty-type damages in lieu of market exclusivity, or indifference in enforcing one's patent.[129]

Simply asserting that it will have sufficient funds to answer for future losses does not sustain a defendant's burden to rebut the presumption of irreparable harm. Competitors change the marketplace. Years after infringement has begun, it may be impossible to

---

[125]*Roper Corp. v. Litton Sys., Inc.*, 757 F.2d 1266, 225 USPQ 345 (Fed. Cir. 1985). The argument that the defendant's reentry into the market could preclude the patentee's entrance was regarded as simply too conjectural.

[126]*High Tech Med. Instr., Inc. v. New Image Indus., Inc.*, 49 F.3d 1551, 33 USPQ2d 2005 (Fed. Cir. 1995).

[127]*T.J. Smith & Nephew Ltd. v. Consolidated Med. Equip., Inc.*, 821 F.2d 646, 3 USPQ2d 1316 (Fed. Cir. 1987). The granting of a license to a third party evidences an absence of irreparable harm. *Illinois Tool Works, Inc. v. Grip-Pak, Inc.*, 906 F.2d 679, 15 USPQ2d 1307 (Fed. Cir. 1990). Although a showing of delay may be so significant as to preclude a determination of irreparable harm, such a showing does not preclude it as a matter of law. A period of delay is but one circumstance that the district court must consider in the context of the totality of the circumstances. *Hybritech, Inc. v. Abbott Labs.*, 849 F.2d 1446, 7 USPQ2d 1191 (Fed. Cir. 1988). Absent a good explanation, 17 months is a substantial period of delay that militates against the issuance of a preliminary injunction by demonstrating that there is no apparent urgency to the request for injunctive relief. *High Tech Med. Instr., Inc. v. New Image Indus., Inc.*, 49 F.3d 1551, 33 USPQ2d 2005 (Fed. Cir. 1995).

[128]*Polymer Tech., Inc. v. Bridwell H.A.*, 103 F.3d 970, 41 USPQ2d 1185 (Fed. Cir. 1996).

[129]*Polymer Tech., Inc. v. Bridwell H.A.*, 103 F.3d 970, 41 USPQ2d 1185 (Fed. Cir. 1996).

restore a patentee's exclusive position by an award of damages and a permanent injunction. Customers may have established relationships with infringers. The market is rarely the same when a market of multiple sellers is suddenly converted to one with a single seller by legal fiat. Requiring purchasers to pay higher prices after years of paying lower prices to infringers is not a reliable business option.[130] Evidence tending to show that the market for the patented product is limited does not rebut the presumption of irreparable harm. The right to exclude others from a specific market, no matter how large or small that market, is an essential element of the patent right. Inventors with small markets are as entitled to exclusivity under the patent statute as are those with large markets.[131] When the market for a patented product is in decline, the passage of time is particularly likely to irreparably harm the patentee. By the time the litigation is over, there may well be no market over which the patentee can exercise its patent right. A patentee is entitled to exclude others from the practice of its invention, even if noninfringing competition is taking away its market. While a patentee is not protected against noninfringing competition, it is protected against infringers even if its business is declining.[132]

And even when irreparable injury is presumed it is still necessary to consider the balance of hardships. The magnitude of the threatened injury to the patent owner is weighed, in the light of the strength of the showing of likelihood of success on the merits, against the injury to the accused infringer if the preliminary decision is in error. Results of other litigation involving the same patent may be taken into account, and the public interest is considered.[133] Although balance of hardships is one of the four factors to be considered in deciding whether to grant a preliminary injunction, there is no requirement that the district court expressly find that the balance tips in favor of the patentee in order to grant an injunction.[134]

(g) *Activity Other than Patent Infringement*

The Federal Circuit has considered preliminary injunctive relief against activity other than patent infringement. In one case the plaintiff sought a preliminary injunction against defendant filing a suit

---

[130]*Polymer Tech., Inc. v. Bridwell H.A.*, 103 F.3d 970, 41 USPQ2d 1185 (Fed. Cir. 1996).

[131]*Polymer Tech., Inc. v. Bridwell H.A.*, 103 F.3d 970, 41 USPQ2d 1185 (Fed. Cir. 1996). The court went on to hold that evidence of other possible causes for the plaintiff's loss of business, such as its principal's death, his wife's inexperience, and other competition, was insufficient to rebut the presumption. Being inexperienced in business also does not negate irreparable harm. Even a poor businessperson is entitled to the exclusionary rights of a patent.

[132]*Bell & Howell DMP Co. v. Altek Sys.*, 132 F.3d 701, 45 USPQ2d 1033 (Fed. Cir. 1997).

[133]*H.H. Robertson Co. v. United Steel Deck, Inc.*, 820 F.2d 384, 2 USPQ2d 1926 (Fed. Cir. 1987).

[134]*Hybritech, Inc. v. Abbott Labs.*, 849 F.2d 1446, 7 USPQ2d 1191 (Fed. Cir. 1988).

for patent infringement, on the ground that the patent was invalid for prior public use.[135] In a trademark case the court applied regional circuit law with respect to a denial of a preliminary injunction against infringement.[136] A preliminary injunction can be supported by a reasonable likelihood of success on either infringement of a presumptively valid design patent or a violation of §43(a) of the Lanham Act.[137] A preliminary injunction takes on special significance when the injunction involves patent rights and antitrust allegations.[138]

Preliminary injunctive relief may be available to prevent termination of a license agreement. In one interesting case, the plaintiff began to produce products A and B at about the same time. It concluded it might have an infringement problem with product A and took a license from the patentee defendant about three years later. It paid royalties on product A, but also brought a declaratory judgment action seeking to have the patents declared invalid. That action was dismissed after a holding of validity by another court. Four years after the inception of the license on product A, the defendant patentee indicated its belief that product B infringed and advised that it would terminate the license unless plaintiff would pay $1 million for a paid-up future license covering product B (apparently that payment would not dispose of past liability). Plaintiff brought a declaratory judgment action asserting the defenses of noninfringement, laches, and estoppel. The trial court granted plaintiff's motion for a preliminary injunction against termination of the license, and the Federal Circuit affirmed. It was clear that this was not a typical situation where the licensee was attempting to avoid the natural consequences of failure to pay royalties. Plaintiff was still paying with respect to product A and had never paid on product B. Among the factors considered were irreparable harm resulting from loss of market share and further litigation, and the public interest (the product was an electrical lead for a heart pacemaker).[139]

The burden on the movant for preliminary relief in a trade secret case includes a showing of imminent irreparable injury that is real and concrete. This is difficult to do if movant cannot first show that there is a reasonable likelihood of success, i.e., that it has secrets

---

[135]*Cordis Corp. v. Medtronic, Inc.*, 780 F.2d 991, 228 USPQ 189 (Fed. Cir. 1985). The court indicated that although it is possible that such evidence might be used to show likelihood of success on the merits in some situations, the presumption of validity militates against any such conclusion.

[136]*Black & Decker, Inc. v. Hoover Serv. Ctr.*, 886 F.2d 1285, 12 USPQ2d 1250 (Fed. Cir. 1989).

[137]*Oakley, Inc. v. International Tropic-Cal, Inc.*, 923 F.2d 167, 17 USPQ2d 1401 (Fed. Cir. 1991).

[138]*Atari Games Corp. v. Nintendo of Am., Inc.*, 897 F.2d 1572, 14 USPQ2d 1034 (Fed. Cir. 1990). The court reversed a preliminary injunction forbidding the patentee from filing suits for infringement against the accused infringer's customers.

[139]*Cordis Corp. v. Medtronic, Inc.*, 835 F.2d 859, 5 USPQ2d 1118 (Fed. Cir. 1987). It also appeared that plaintiff had made a showing of likelihood of success on noninfringement, laches and estoppel, and lack of coverage under the definition of licensed products.

that have been misappropriated. Unless this be shown, there is no threatened harm that would result from disclosure of the alleged secrets.[140] In a trade secret case a divided court found no abuse of discretion in a denial of a preliminary injunction. The majority, relying on broad discretion, cited (1) uncertainty as to the sufficiency of secrecy measures, (2) delay in invoking legal proceedings, (3) failure to show irreparable harm, and (4) an insufficient showing of likelihood of success.[141] Under First Circuit law, an antitrust plaintiff seeking a preliminary injunction must show that there is no adequate remedy at law, that the plaintiff will suffer irreparable injury absent the requested injunction, that such injury outweighs the harm an injunction would inflict on the defendant, that the plaintiff has shown a likelihood of success on the merits, and that the public interest will not be adversely affected by the grant of the requested injunction.[142]

(h) Findings and Conclusions

The procedural requirements for the grant of a preliminary injunction include notice, a statement of the reasons for an injunctive order, and the posting of security, all in accordance with Rule 65, FRCP. Further, Rule 52(a) requires that a preliminary injunction be supported by findings of fact. Otherwise the reviewing court has nothing before it to which appropriate appellate standards of review can be applied with respect to the merits of the injunction.[143]

Rule 52(a) does not place a severe burden upon the trial judge, for he or she need only make brief, definite, pertinent findings and conclusions upon the contested matters. However, the findings must be sufficient to permit meaningful review.[144] If a preliminary injunction is denied, the absence of an adequate showing with regard to any one of the four factors may be sufficient, given the weight or lack of it assigned the other factors by the trial court, to justify the denial.

---

[140]*Litton Sys., Inc. v. Sundstrand Corp.*, 750 F.2d 952, 224 USPQ 252 (Fed. Cir. 1984). No abuse of discretion was found in denial of the motion for preliminary injunction. The merits were a "toss-up" and granting the injunction would completely alter the status quo and cause greater hardship to the defendant.

[141]*Formax, Inc. v. Hostert*, 841 F.2d 388, 5 USPQ2d 1939 (Fed. Cir. 1988). It appeared that there were many suppliers and customers familiar with the information. The dissenter pointed to the narrowness of the remedy sought, which was merely a preliminary injunction against use, not against reverse engineering.

[142]*Xeta, Inc. v. Atex, Inc.*, 852 F.2d 1280, 7 USPQ2d 1471 (Fed. Cir. 1988). In the First Circuit, the probability-of-success component looms large. *Id.*

[143]*Digital Equip. Corp. v. Emulex Corp.*, 805 F.2d 380, 231 USPQ 779 (Fed. Cir. 1986).

[144]*Nutrition 21 v. United States*, 930 F.2d 867, 18 USPQ2d 1347 (Fed. Cir. 1991); *Pretty Punch Shoppettes, Inc. v. Hauk*, 844 F.2d 782, 6 USPQ2d 1563 (Fed. Cir. 1988). See also *Atari Games Corp. v. Nintendo of Am., Inc.*, 897 F.2d 1572, 14 USPQ2d 1034 (Fed. Cir. 1990). The test of adequacy of findings is whether they are sufficiently comprehensive and pertinent to the issue to form a basis for the decision. *Conair Group v. Automatik App. GmbH*, 944 F.2d 862, 20 USPQ2d 1067 (Fed. Cir. 1991); *Oakley, Inc. v. International Tropic-Cal, Inc.*, 923 F.2d 167, 17 USPQ2d 1401 (Fed. Cir. 1991).

Thus a trial court need not necessarily make findings as to each of the four factors in denying a preliminary injunction, especially where the denial is based upon one of the two critical facts: likelihood of success and irreparable harm. This is so even though a movant who clearly establishes likelihood of success receives the benefit of a presumption as to irreparable harm. The presumption can be rebutted. However, where the trial court denies the motion on the basis of no showing of irreparable harm, without having made findings on likelihood of success, it commits error, for it thereby deprives the movant of the presumption.[145]

Thus, a failure to issue any supporting findings and conclusions until after the notice of appeal had been filed demanded reversal and remand.[146] Similarly, a simple statement by the trial court that it was unconvinced as to the probability of the patentee prevailing on the merits of the issue of infringement, because there were too many issues of fact yet to be determined, was insufficient. The Federal Circuit felt that it had no basis for evaluating what facts entered into the trial court's infringement analysis or if that analysis comported with legal standards articulated by the Federal Circuit.[147] These cases seem to foreshadow a good deal of impatience with trial judges who grant or deny injunctions without giving adequate reasons.

Findings and conclusions made in connection with a motion for preliminary injunction are not binding at trial. There is always the possibility of new evidence changing the court's impression of the facts.[148] For example, the trial court has no obligation to interpret claims conclusively and finally during a preliminary injunction hearing. A trial court may exercise its discretion to interpret the claims

---

[145]*Reebok Int'l Ltd. v. J. Baker, Inc.*, 32 F.3d 1552, 31 USPQ2d 1781 (Fed. Cir. 1994). In this case the error was harmless because the nonmoving party had presented evidence sufficient to rebut the presumption.

[146]*Chemlawn Serv. Corp. v. GNC Pumps, Inc.*, 823 F.2d 515, 3 USPQ2d 1313 (Fed. Cir. 1987). The case was not one of those unusual ones where effective review on the merits of a preliminary injunction was possible without the aid of findings and conclusions. Inasmuch as the filing of the notice of appeal ousted the district court of jurisdiction to proceed with any matters involved in the appeal, the belated findings and conclusions were viewed as "illegitimate." It would have been improper to accept and rely upon them, since it might encourage other district courts to circumvent the requirements of Rule 52(a). It should be noted that the Federal Circuit was applying Fifth Circuit law in this case. In *Xeta, Inc. v. Atex, Inc.*, 852 F.2d 1280, 7 USPQ2d 1471 (Fed. Cir. 1988), however, the court held that the district court, in denying a motion for preliminary injunction, did not err in not making detailed findings on peripheral issues for which adequate foundation was not provided by the moving party.

[147]*Pretty Punch Shoppettes, Inc. v. Hauk*, 844 F.2d 782, 6 USPQ2d 1563 (Fed. Cir. 1988). Failure to provide adequate findings is an error of law. For example, findings on likelihood of success as to infringement under the doctrine of equivalents should include findings as to function, way, and result; whether the range of equivalents ensnares the prior art; and file wrapper estoppel. *Conair Group v. Automatik App. GmbH*, 944 F.2d 862, 20 USPQ2d 1067 (Fed. Cir. 1991). In *Oakley, Inc. v. International Tropic-Cal, Inc.*, 923 F.2d 167, 17 USPQ2d 1401 (Fed. Cir. 1991), the district court simply concluded that the patentee owned the design patent in suit and that there was substantial likelihood that it would prevail on the merits. This was held insufficient to support an injunction.

[148]*Illinois Tool Works, Inc. v. Grip-Pak, Inc.*, 906 F.2d 679, 15 USPQ2d 1307 (Fed. Cir. 1990). However, the court has hinted that it might treat its own determinations on a motion

at a time when the parties have presented a full picture of the claimed invention and prior art.[149] But although the court need not make binding findings, it must, at the very least, find probabilities that the necessary facts can be proved at trial.[150]

(i) Miscellaneous

The right to a hearing on a preliminary injunction is implicit in the notice requirement of Rule 65(a). The need for a hearing is especially pressing in a situation where relevant facts are in sharp dispute.[151] As a general rule, a preliminary injunction should not issue on the basis of affidavits alone. Moreover, a district court should be wary of issuing an injunction based solely upon allegations and conclusory affidavits submitted by the plaintiff.[152]

Once a preliminary injunction has been entered in compliance with an earlier mandate of an appellate court, it is doubtful that the trial court would have authority to dissolve it.[153]

The ITC has authority to grant temporary injunctive relief, and its practice should be to exercise that authority in a parallel fashion to district courts. It applies the four standard factors, and the court of appeals reviews on the basis of abuse of discretion.[154]

§13.3 Contempt Proceedings

Persons subject to an injunctive order issued by a court with jurisdiction are expected to obey that decree until it is modified or reversed, even if they have proper grounds to object to the order.[155] A civil contempt proceeding for violation of an injunction issued after patent litigation, while primarily for the benefit of the patent owner, nevertheless involves also the concept of an affront to the court for failure to obey its order.[156] The distinction between civil and criminal

---

for preliminary injunction as law of the case. *Black & Decker, Inc. v. Hoover Serv. Ctr.*, 886 F.2d 1285, 12 USPQ2d 1250 (Fed. Cir. 1989).

[149]*Sofamor Danek Group, Inc. v. DePuy-Motech, Inc.*, 74 F.3d 1216, 37 USPQ2d 1529 (Fed. Cir. 1996). See also *International Comm. Mt'ls., Inc. v. Ricoh Co.*, 108 F.3d 316, 41 USPQ2d 1957 (Fed. Cir. 1997).

[150]*Atari Games Corp. v. Nintendo of Am., Inc.*, 897 F.2d 1572, 14 USPQ2d 1034 (Fed. Cir. 1990).

[151]*Digital Equip. Corp. v. Emulex Corp.*, 805 F.2d 380, 231 USPQ 779 (Fed. Cir. 1986).

[152]*Atari Games Corp. v. Nintendo of Am., Inc.*, 897 F.2d 1572, 14 USPQ2d 1034 (Fed. Cir. 1990).

[153]*Smith Int'l, Inc. v. Hughes Tool Co.*, 759 F.2d 1572, 225 USPQ 889 (Fed. Cir. 1985).

[154]*Rosemount, Inc. v. United States ITC*, 910 F.2d 819, 15 USPQ2d 1569 (Fed. Cir. 1990).

[155]*Carborundum Co. v. Molten Metal Equip. Innovations*, 72 F.3d 872, 37 USPQ2d 1169, 1176 (Fed. Cir. 1995).

[156]*KSM Fastening Sys., Inc. v. H.A. Jones Co.*, 776 F.2d 1522, 227 USPQ 676 (Fed. Cir. 1985).

contempt lies in what the court primarily seeks to accomplish by imposing sentence in the proceedings. A civil contempt sanction is remedial, and for the benefit of the complainant, while a criminal contempt sentence is punitive, to vindicate the authority of the court. A contempt sanction is civil if the penalty is intended to coerce compliance with an order of the court or to compensate for losses or damages caused by noncompliance. Although a fine payable to the court normally is punitive, it is also remedial when the defendant can avoid paying the fine simply by performing the affirmative act required by the court's order. A judgment for civil contempt is conditional in nature. On the other hand, because criminal contempt is intended to vindicate the authority of the court, it cannot be purged by any act of the contemnor.[157]

A contempt order is final and appealable when the opportunity to purge the contempt has passed and the position of the parties has been affected by the contempt order. Courts have also viewed a contempt order as appealable when the effect of that order is to modify an injunction. However, when no sanction has been imposed for the contempt and there is no effect on continuing proceedings, interlocutory appeal is unnecessary and therefore unwarranted.[158] The abuse of discretion standard applies to review of a refusal to grant a motion for judgment of contempt. Review is narrowly circumscribed, and reversal is limited to denials based on an incorrect application of law or application of a proper legal standard to clearly erroneous findings.[159] Thus, the clearly erroneous standard applies to findings of civil contempt where the correct legal standards for a contempt proceeding are employed.[160]

Before entering a finding of contempt of an injunction in a patent infringement case, a district court must address two separate questions. The first is whether a contempt hearing is an appropriate forum in which to determine whether a redesigned device infringes, or whether the issue of infringement should be resolved in a separate infringement action. That decision turns on a comparison between

---

[157]*Spindelfabrik S., S. & G. GmbH v. Schubert & Salzer Mas. Ak.*, 903 F.2d 1568, 14 USPQ2d 1913 (Fed. Cir. 1990). The district court assessed a $2 million fine in a patent infringement contempt proceeding. Although the fine was to be paid to the patentee, it was not assessed as compensation. Nor was it coercive or conditional. Rather, it was designed to deter the infringer from future violations. Thus, despite the trial court's characterization of the fine as civil, the Federal Circuit held that it was a fine for criminal contempt. Inasmuch as the trial court did not follow the requisite procedures for criminal contempt, it had to be reversed. The reversal, however, was without prejudice to assessment of a new civil penalty that would be compensatory or have a conditional but coercive impact. *Id.*

[158]*Seiko Epson Corp. v. Nu-Kote Int'l Inc.*, 190 F.3d 1360, 52 USPQ2d 1011 (Fed. Cir. 1999).

[159]*Mac Corp. v. Williams Patent Crusher Co.*, 767 F.2d 882, 226 USPQ 515 (Fed. Cir. 1985). Where the court reverses a finding of noninfringement, it must nevertheless remand to enable the district court to exercise its discretion as to whether contempt has occurred. *Laitram Corp. v. Cambridge Wire Cloth Co.*, 863 F.2d 855, 9 USPQ2d 1289 (Fed. Cir. 1988).

[160]*Preemption Devices, Inc. v. Minnesota Min. & Mfg. Co.*, 803 F.2d 1170, 231 USPQ 297 (Fed. Cir. 1986).

the original infringing product and the redesigned device. If the differences are such that "substantial open issues" of infringement are raised by the new device, then contempt proceedings are inappropriate. If contempt proceedings are appropriate, the second question the district court must resolve is whether the new accused device infringes the claims of the patent. Within those general constraints, the district court has broad discretion to determine how best to enforce its injunctive decrees.[161]

Civil contempt is a severe remedy and should not be resorted to where there is a fair ground of doubt as to the wrongfulness of the defendant's conduct.[162] In answering the first question—appropriateness of contempt as a remedy—it must be kept in mind that an enjoined party is entitled to design around the claims of a patent without the threat of contempt proceedings with respect to every modified device.[163] In such a proceeding, the movant has the heavy burden of proving violation of the district court's order by clear and convincing evidence,[164] and the courts uniformly exercise restraint in affording the patent owner the benefit of contempt proceedings where the motion is brought to enforce an injunction against a manufacture that was not the subject of the original injunction.[165]

Once the patentee has obtained an injunction against infringement, it is not likely to institute a separate suit to enjoin a modified device. Rather, it is likely to proceed on a motion to punish for contempt. The advantages of this course are substantial. The adjudged infringer is already under the jurisdiction of the court and may be summoned to appear to respond on the merits, the contempt motion being merely part of the original action. Contempt proceedings are generally summary in nature and may be decided by the court on affidavits and exhibits without the formalities of a full trial, although the movant bears the heavy burden of proving violation by clear and convincing evidence. If a violation is found, the contemnor may be punished by a fine payable to the patent owner and imprisonment,

---

[161]*Additive Cont. & Meas. Sys. Inc. v. Flowdata Inc.*, 154 F.3d 1345, 47 USPQ2d 1906 (Fed. Cir. 1998). See also *KSM Fastening Sys., Inc. v. H.A. Jones Co.*, 776 F.2d 1522, 227 USPQ 676 (Fed. Cir. 1985).

[162]*Preemption Devices, Inc. v. Minnesota Min. & Mfg. Co.*, 803 F.2d 1170, 231 USPQ 297 (Fed. Cir. 1986); *KSM Fastening Sys., Inc. v. H.A. Jones Co.*, 776 F.2d 1522, 227 USPQ 676 (Fed. Cir. 1985); *Mac Corp. v. Williams Patent Crusher Co.*, 767 F.2d 882, 226 USPQ 515 (Fed. Cir. 1985).

[163]*KSM Fastening Sys., Inc. v. H.A. Jones Co.*, 776 F.2d 1522, 227 USPQ 676 (Fed. Cir. 1985). Nonetheless, the enjoined party bears the risk that the enjoining court may find the changes to be too insubstantial to avoid contempt.

[164]*Amstar Corp. v. Envirotech Corp.*, 823 F.2d 1538, 3 USPQ2d 1412 (Fed. Cir. 1987); *Preemption Devices, Inc. v. Minnesota Min. & Mfg. Co.*, 803 F.2d 1170, 231 USPQ 297 (Fed. Cir. 1986). The standard of proof for infringement is a preponderance of the evidence, while that for contempt is clear and convincing evidence. *Laitram Corp. v. Cambridge Wire Cloth Co.*, 863 F.2d 855, 9 USPQ2d 1289 (Fed. Cir. 1988).

[165]*KSM Fastening Sys., Inc. v. H.A. Jones Co.*, 776 F.2d 1522, 227 USPQ 676 (Fed. Cir. 1985).

even in civil contempt.[166] Whether or not to proceed by way of contempt rather than supplemental complaint is within the discretion of the district court and will not be disturbed if the district court follows the general rule for determining whether contempt is appropriate.[167]

Despite having passed the question the first time it was presented,[168] the Federal Circuit early on made it clear that contempt proceedings respecting a modified device are inappropriate if there is more than a colorable difference between the adjudged device and the modified one.[169] In *Arbek v. Moazzam*,[170] the court elaborated on this rule. Thus, to show contempt, the patent owner must prove by clear and convincing evidence that the modified device falls within the admitted or adjudicated scope of the claims and is, therefore, an infringement. A trial court may decide contempt motions on affidavits and exhibits without the formalities of a full trial. Additionally, in summary proceedings, an accused infringer may face fines, damages, or even imprisonment. For that reason, the court cautions that contempt is not a sword for wounding a former infringer who had made a good faith effort to modify a previous adjudged or admitted infringing device so as to remain in the market. Rather, the modifying party generally deserves the opportunity to litigate the infringement question at a new trial, particularly if expert and other testimony subject to cross-examination would be helpful or necessary. Thus, if there are substantial open issues with respect to infringement to be tried, contempt proceedings are inappropriate. The presence of such disputed issues creates a fair ground for doubt that the decree has been violated. This safeguards due process concerns. Accordingly, before reaching the ultimate question of whether an injunction against infringement has been violated, the trial court must consider a threshold question: whether substantial open infringement issues must be litigated.

---

[166]*KSM Fastening Sys., Inc. v. H.A. Jones Co.*, 776 F.2d 1522, 227 USPQ 676 (Fed. Cir. 1985). It is well established that formal service is not required in a contempt proceeding. However, parties to a contempt proceeding are entitled to adequate notice and an opportunity to be heard. *Additive Cont. & Meas. Sys. Inc. v. Flowdata Inc.*, 154 F.3d 1345, 47 USPQ2d 1906 (Fed. Cir. 1998).

[167]*KSM Fastening Sys., Inc. v. H.A. Jones Co.*, 776 F.2d 1522, 227 USPQ 676 (Fed. Cir. 1985).

[168]*Mac Corp. v. Williams Patent Crusher Co.*, 767 F.2d 882, 226 USPQ 515 (Fed. Cir. 1985).

[169]*KSM Fastening Sys., Inc. v. H.A. Jones Co.*, 776 F.2d 1522, 227 USPQ 676 (Fed. Cir. 1985).

[170]*Arbek Mfg., Inc. v. Moazzam*, 55 F.3d 1567, 34 USPQ2d 1670 (Fed. Cir. 1995). The trial court found, in the context of a contempt proceeding, that a modified device did not infringe. The Federal Circuit equated the finding with a "fair ground for doubt" that the injunctive order had been violated, and thus concluded that the trial court had detected "substantial open infringement issues" within the meaning of the *KSM* test. It then looked at the infringement question on the merits and concluded that there was substantial evidence to support the trial court's finding of no infringement. It therefore affirmed the denial of a preliminary injunction but vacated the noninfringement finding as premature. On remand, the patentee may well get a trial on the substantive infringement question in any event. This logic is interesting and probably correct.

The court has rejected any substantive test for colorability, such as the doctrine of equivalents,[171] and has instead adopted a procedural test. Under that test, the question is simply whether there are substantial new issues to be litigated. If so, a new or supplemental complaint must be filed.[172] A standard of appropriateness based on procedural considerations is more likely to meet due process requirements, considering the usual summary nature of contempt proceedings. The presence of disputed issues creates a fair ground for doubt that the decree has been violated and thus rules out contempt.[173]

Under the "substantial new issue" test the court will be able to utilize principles of claim and issue preclusion to determine what issues were settled by the original suit and what would have to be tried. Such a determination may vary depending upon whether the original suit was settled by consent or fully litigated. In a litigated case, the injunction must be interpreted in light of the rulings of the court on the scope of the claims. The patent owner may not, in contempt proceedings, seek to broaden the scope of the claims that were adjudicated and thereby "catch" the modified device. On the other hand, with a consent decree an adjudged device conceivably could have been found not to fall within the scope of the claims upon a full trial; nevertheless, such a device is an admitted infringement. Thus the claims of the patent may be construed in light of that admission when the court undertakes to determine whether a modified device is also an infringement in contempt proceedings.[174]

Other factors may influence the determination of appropriateness, such as timing of the motion for contempt[175] and the pendency of other actions.[176] In some instances a showing that a redesign has resulted in the issuance of a patent would be sufficient to require a separate lawsuit to litigate any potential infringement by the redesigned device.[177] The court seems to be of the view that there is no

---

[171]*KSM Fastening Sys., Inc. v. H.A. Jones Co.,* 776 F.2d 1522, 227 USPQ 676 (Fed. Cir. 1985). See also *Preemption Devices, Inc. v. Minnesota Min. & Mfg. Co.,* 803 F.2d 1170, 231 USPQ 297 (Fed. Cir. 1986).

[172]*KSM Fastening Sys., Inc. v. H.A. Jones Co.,* 776 F.2d 1522, 227 USPQ 676 (Fed. Cir. 1985).

[173]*KSM Fastening Sys., Inc. v. H.A. Jones Co.,* 776 F.2d 1522, 227 USPQ 676 (Fed. Cir. 1985). The court suggested one possible guideline: if expert or other testimony subject to cross-examination would be helpful or necessary in resolving the issues, contempt is likely to be inappropriate.

[174]*KSM Fastening Sys., Inc. v. H.A. Jones Co.,* 776 F.2d 1522, 227 USPQ 676 (Fed. Cir. 1985).

[175]*Rosemount, Inc. v. Beckman Instr., Inc.,* 727 F.2d 1540, 221 USPQ 1 (Fed. Cir. 1984). The patentee found out about a new model long before the original trial, but did not charge infringement, and moved for contempt only after an injunctive order was entered against the models that were charged in the original trial. The court upheld a finding of contempt, but refused damages, apparently on a laches theory.

[176]*Mac Corp. v. Williams Patent Crusher Co.,* 767 F.2d 882, 226 USPQ 515 (Fed. Cir. 1985). The court passed the question of whether the pendency of a declaratory judgment action seeking a declaration of noninfringement on the part of a new device would in all cases preclude a contempt proceeding for that device.

[177]*Additive Cont. & Meas. Sys. Inc. v. Flowdata Inc.,* 154 F.3d 1345, 47 USPQ2d 1906 (Fed. Cir. 1998). But where the file history of the patent shows that neither the original

contempt jurisdiction for violation of a settlement agreement that is not part of the trial court's actual judgment.[178] Whether a particular act, such as use of data obtained during infringement, is itself infringement and violative of an injunction against infringement may be an issue that is appropriately resolved in the contempt context.[179]

Once the appropriateness of contempt is determined, the question of violation is fairly straightforward. A judgment of contempt for violation of an injunction against patent infringement, by making, using, or selling a modified device, may not be upheld in the absence of a finding that the modified device falls within the admitted or adjudicated scope of the claims and is, therefore, an infringement.[180] Infringement is the sine qua non of a violation of an injunction against infringement.[181] Although the issue is violation vel non of the injunction, not patent infringement, devices that could not be enjoined as infringements on a separate complaint cannot possibly be deemed enjoined as infringements under an existing injunction in a contempt proceeding.[182] In making such a determination, the court cannot avoid looking at the patent claims.[183]

During an accounting, as during the liability trial, a patentee must prove infringement by a preponderance of the evidence. Some decisions have indicated that infringement may be determined by comparison with a device adjudicated as an infringement. In the sense that things equal to the same thing are equal to each other, this may be so in cases where the adjudicated device is a precise literal infringement of the claims. In such cases, comparison with the adjudicated device may serve as a handy method of reaching a determination. However, whether one is determining infringement at trial, in an accounting, or in a contempt proceeding, it must be remembered that it is a claim that is infringed and a claimed invention that is patented. Thus comparison with an adjudicated device cannot serve to encompass within the patent's exclusionary scope a device that does not in fact constitute an infringement of the claim, either literally or under the doctrine of equivalents. In a civil contempt proceeding,

---

infringing device nor the infringed patent was submitted to the patent examiner, the fact that the new design was patented does not demonstrate that it was more than colorably different from the infringing original. *Id.*

[178]*Joy Mfg. Co. v. National Mine Serv. Co.*, 810 F.2d 1127, 1 USPQ2d 1627 (Fed. Cir. 1987).

[179]*Ortho Pharm Corp. v. Smith*, 959 F.2d 936, 22 USPQ2d 1119 (Fed. Cir. 1992).

[180]*Joy Mfg. Co. v. National Mine Serv. Co.*, 810 F.2d 1127, 1 USPQ2d 1627 (Fed. Cir. 1987).

[181]*Preemption Devices, Inc. v. Minnesota Min. & Mfg. Co.*, 803 F.2d 1170, 231 USPQ 297 (Fed. Cir. 1986); *KSM Fastening Sys., Inc. v. H.A. Jones Co.*, 776 F.2d 1522, 227 USPQ 676 (Fed. Cir. 1985). Absent infringement, there cannot be contempt for violating an injunction against infringement. *Laitram Corp. v. Cambridge Wire Cloth Co.*, 863 F.2d 855, 9 USPQ2d 1289 (Fed. Cir. 1988).

[182]*KSM Fastening Sys., Inc. v. H.A. Jones Co.*, 776 F.2d 1522, 227 USPQ 676 (Fed. Cir. 1985).

[183]*Amstar Corp. v. Envirotech Corp.*, 823 F.2d 1538, 3 USPQ2d 1412 (Fed. Cir. 1987); *Preemption Devices, Inc. v. Minnesota Min. & Mfg. Co.*, 803 F.2d 1170, 231 USPQ 297 (Fed. Cir. 1986); *KSM Fastening Sys., Inc. v. H.A. Jones Co.*, 776 F.2d 1522, 227 USPQ 676 (Fed. Cir. 1985).

the movant must prove a violation by clear and convincing evidence. This therefore requires a showing that a redesign falls within the adjudicated scope of the claims. It is not enough to show simply that the redesign is the equivalent of the previously adjudicated devices.[184]

A permanent injunction should prohibit infringement by any product of the infringer, not just those involved in the suit. The burden is on the infringer to avoid a finding of contempt.[185] A nonparty, even one with notice, cannot be held in contempt of an injunction until shown to be in concert or participation with a party.[186] Those who act in concert with an enjoined party may be held in contempt, but only for assisting the enjoined party in violating the injunction.[187]

For an enjoined party the general rule is to keep a safe distance from the margin line. Where the party's attorney warns it to be careful, and the party obeys only the letter of the attorney's advice, it runs the risk of willful infringement.[188] Where an injunction is written narrowly against a particular infringing device, contempt may, nevertheless, be found on the basis of a modified infringing device. An enjoined party under a narrow decree will not be permitted to escape on a purely "in rem" theory that only a particular device is prohibited, where it is evident that the modifications do not avoid infringement and were made for the purpose of evasion of the court's order. The standard is whether the differences between the two devices are merely colorable.[189] The question of whether the differences are more than colorable can evoke a wide range of evidentiary factors. In one case the court seemed impressed by the fact that after the injunction, the infringer modified its process to include elements of another comparable patented process and began paying royalties thereon.[190]

The Federal Circuit declines the opportunity to tell district courts how to frame injunctions in patent cases, and allows wide latitude. As was noted earlier, it is uniformity in decisions on contempt, rather than on framing injunctions, that is the primary goal.[191] Although in most cases a broad injunction against violation of a statute does not satisfy the specificity requirement, patent injunctions are frequently

---

[184]*Amstar Corp. v. Envirotech Corp.*, 823 F.2d 1538, 3 USPQ2d 1412 (Fed. Cir. 1987).

[185]*Smith Int'l, Inc. v. Hughes Tool Co.*, 718 F.2d 1573, 219 USPQ 686 (Fed. Cir. 1983).

[186]*Spindelfabrik GmbH v. Schubert & Salzer Mas. Ak.*, 903 F.2d 1568, 14 USPQ2d 1913 (Fed. Cir. 1990).

[187]*Additive Con. & Meas. Sys., Inc. v. Flowdata, Inc.*, 96 F.3d 1390, 40 USPQ2d 1106 (Fed. Cir. 1996).

[188]*Paper Converting Mach. Co. v. Magna-Graphics Corp.*, 785 F.2d 1013, 228 USPQ 938 (Fed. Cir. 1986).

[189]*KSM Fastening Sys., Inc. v. H.A. Jones Co.*, 776 F.2d 1522, 227 USPQ 676 (Fed. Cir. 1985).

[190]*American Original Corp. v. Jenkins Food Corp.*, 774 F.2d 459, 227 USPQ 299 (Fed. Cir. 1985). Tests showed that the comparable patented process was not as effective as the process of the patent in suit.

[191]*KSM Fastening Sys., Inc. v. H.A. Jones Co.*, 776 F.2d 1522, 227 USPQ 676 (Fed. Cir. 1985).

drafted broadly to prohibit "further infringement." This is reasonable because contempt proceedings, civil or criminal, are available only with respect to devices previously admitted or adjudged to infringe and to other devices that are no more than colorably different therefrom and that clearly are infringements of the patent.[192] It seems likely that the court will hold that willful infringement is contumacious per se.[193]

Contempt damages in a patent infringement case do not raise issues unique to patent law and thus the Federal Circuit will apply the law of the regional circuit.[194] Regional circuit law also governs the definitions of civil and criminal contempt.[195]

Of course, one may not in a contempt proceeding challenge infringement on the ground that the patent is invalid. Validity of the patent is law of the case in such proceedings.[196]

---

[192]*KSM Fastening Sys., Inc. v. H.A. Jones Co.*, 776 F.2d 1522, 227 USPQ 676 (Fed. Cir. 1985).

[193]See *Paper Converting Mach. Co. v. Magna-Graphics Corp.*, 745 F.2d 11, 223 USPQ 591 (Fed. Cir. 1984).

[194]*Graves v. Kemscop Group, Inc.*, 864 F.2d 754, 9 USPQ2d 1404 (Fed. Cir. 1988). Under Seventh Circuit law, damages in a civil contempt action need not be proved by clear and convincing evidence; it is only the violation of the injunction itself that must be proved by clear and convincing evidence. Damages for civil contempt are within the discretion of the district court. *Id.*

[195]*Spindelfabrik S., S. & G. GmbH v. Schubert & Salzer Mas. Ak.*, 903 F.2d 1568, 14 USPQ2d 1913 (Fed. Cir. 1990).

[196]*KSM Fastening Sys., Inc. v. H.A. Jones Co.*, 776 F.2d 1522, 227 USPQ 676 (Fed. Cir. 1985).

14

Increased Damages and Attorney Fees

§14.1 General

The authority for punitive relief in patent cases is statutory. Whether damages are found by the jury or assessed by the judge, "in either event the court may increase the damages up to three times the amount found or assessed"[1] and "in exceptional cases may award reasonable attorney fees to the prevailing party."[2] Attorney fees may

---

[1]35 U.S.C. §284. Liquidated damages are not punitive if they are reasonable and the exact amount of actual damage would be difficult to prove. *United States v. Imperial Food Imports,* 834 F.2d 1013 (Fed. Cir. 1987).

[2]35 U.S.C. §285.

also be awarded for conduct in violation of Rule 11, FRCP, as a discovery sanction under Rule 37, FRCP, and for frivolous or vexatious conduct under Rule 38, FRAP, or 28 U.S.C. §1927. All of these concepts appear to be interrelated.[3] In addition, of course, state law may provide for an award of punitive damages in certain cases, such as fraudulent inducement to reveal trade secrets.[4]

One purpose of an increased damage award is to deter willful patent infringement by punishing the willful infringer.[5] The typical justification for increased damages, therefore, is a finding of willful infringement. However, there is no requirement for a showing of bad faith in order to award increased damages for willful infringement.[6] The measure of damages provides an opportunity for the trial court to balance equitable concerns as it determines whether and how to recompense the successful litigant.[7] The consequences of patent infringement include the assessment provided by statute of multiplied damages or attorney fees. Whether or not willfulness is found, the court has the authority to consider the degree of culpability of the tortfeasor.[8] Increased damages and attorney fees are simply means for placing the injured patentee in the situation it would have occupied if the wrong had not been committed.[9] Thus, there is no necessary inconsistency between awarding treble damages on account of willful infringement and denying attorney fees whether or not the case is deemed exceptional.[10]

On the other hand, one of the benefits of a patent system is its so-called negative incentive to design around a competitor's products, even when they are patented, thus bringing a steady flow of innovations to the market place. It should not be discouraged by punitive damage awards except in cases where conduct is so obnoxious as clearly to call for them. The world of competition is full of fair fights.[11] Provisions for increased damages under 35 U.S.C. §284 and attorney fees under §285 are available as deterrents to blatant, blind, willful infringement of valid patents.[12] Attorney fees are not to be routinely assessed against a losing party in litigation. They are awarded to

---

[3]*Western Mar. Elec., Inc. v. Furuno Elec. Co.,* 764 F.2d 840, 226 USPQ 334 (Fed. Cir. 1985).

[4]*Richardson v. Suzuki Motor Co.,* 868 F.2d 1226, 9 USPQ2d 1913 (Fed. Cir. 1989). See, e.g., *Roton Barrier, Inc. v. Stanley Works,* 79 F.3d 1112, 37 USPQ2d 1816 (Fed. Cir. 1996), for a case involving punitive damages under the Illinois Trade Secrets Act.

[5]*Avia Group Int'l, Inc. v. L.A. Gear Calif., Inc.,* 853 F.2d 1557, 7 USPQ2d 1548 (Fed. Cir. 1988).

[6]*TWM Mfg. Co. v. Dura Corp.,* 789 F.2d 895, 229 USPQ 525 (Fed. Cir. 1986); *S.C. Johnson & Son v. Carter-Wallace, Inc.,* 781 F.2d 198, 228 USPQ 367 (Fed. Cir. 1986).

[7]*S.C. Johnson & Son v. Carter-Wallace, Inc.,* 781 F.2d 198, 228 USPQ 367 (Fed. Cir. 1986).

[8]*Rite-Hite Corp. v. Kelley Co.,* 819 F.2d 1120, 2 USPQ2d 1915 (Fed. Cir. 1987).

[9]*Fromson v. Western Litho Plate & Supp. Co.,* 853 F.2d 1568, 7 USPQ2d 1606 (Fed. Cir. 1988).

[10]*Paper Converting Mach. Co. v. Magna-Graphics Corp.,* 785 F.2d 1013, 228 USPQ 938 (Fed. Cir. 1986).

[11]*State Indus., Inc. v. A.O. Smith Corp.,* 751 F.2d 1226, 224 USPQ 418 (Fed. Cir. 1985).

[12]*Mathis v. Spears,* 857 F.2d 749, 8 USPQ2d 1029 (Fed. Cir. 1988).

avoid a gross injustice and not to penalize a party for merely defending or prosecuting a lawsuit.[13]

From early on, federal courts refused to adopt the English rule requiring assessment of attorney fees against a losing party. Under the American Rule, the prevailing litigant is ordinarily not entitled to any attorney fees absent statutory authority. A rationale for this rule is that one should not be penalized for litigating.[14] Allowance of fees only in exceptional cases is based on the premise that courts should attempt to strike a balance between the interest of the patentee in protecting its statutory rights and the interest of the public in confining such rights to their legal limits.[15]

Is willful infringement exceptional conduct? Willful infringement may be seen as producing an unnecessary and outcome-certain lawsuit and thus may make a case so exceptional as to warrant attorney fees.[16] A finding of willful infringement is legally sufficient to meet the criterion of an "exceptional case," and under such circumstances it is within the trial court's discretionary authority to award attorney fees,[17] although an award of fees, because discretionary, does not automatically follow from the willfulness of an infringement.[18]

A finding of willful infringement does not mandate that damages be enhanced, much less mandate treble damages. The paramount determination in deciding to grant enhancement and the amount thereof is the egregiousness of the defendant's conduct based on all the facts and circumstances. The court must consider factors that render the infringer's conduct more culpable, as well as factors that are mitigating or ameliorating. These include (1) whether there was deliberate copying, (2) whether there was good faith belief that the patent was invalid or not infringed, (3) the infringer's behavior in

---

[13]*Revlon, Inc. v. Carson Prods. Co.,* 803 F.2d 676, 231 USPQ 472 (Fed. Cir. 1986).

[14]*Machinery Corp. v. Gullfiber AB,* 774 F.2d 467, 227 USPQ 368 (Fed. Cir. 1985).

[15]*S.C. Johnson & Son v. Carter-Wallace, Inc.,* 781 F.2d 198, 228 USPQ 367 (Fed. Cir. 1986); *Machinery Corp. v. Gullfiber AB,* 774 F.2d 467, 227 USPQ 368 (Fed. Cir. 1985). Not all successful defendants are entitled to attorney fees or to attorney fees and expenses. The requirement in §285 of establishing an exceptional case remains a formidable and adequate barrier to unwarranted awards. Similarly, the §285 requirement that the fees awarded be "reasonable" is a safeguard against excessive reimbursement. *Mathis v. Spears,* 857 F.2d 749, 8 USPQ2d 1029 (Fed. Cir. 1988). In *Yarway Corp. v. Eur-Control USA Inc.,* 775 F.2d 268, 227 USPQ 352, 359 (Fed. Cir. 1985), the trial court found bad faith, despite a nonfrivolous effort to design around the patent, apparently on the ground that the infringer was the patent owner who had exclusively licensed the plaintiff. In reversing, the court observed that where the parties are working under a contract, it would be logical to expect them to provide remedies for any breach in the contract itself, and recourse to the more punitive aspects of tort damages is therefore unnecessary. Attempting to avoid infringement and invent around a patent is not sufficient to justify the enhancement of damages or attorney fees. See also *Spindelfabrik S., S. & G. GmbH v. Schubert & Salzer Mas. Ak.,* 829 F.2d 1075, 4 USPQ2d 1044 (Fed. Cir. 1987).

[16]*Kloster Speedsteel AB v. Crucible Inc.,* 793 F.2d 1565, 230 USPQ 81 (Fed. Cir. 1986).

[17]*Del Mar Avionics, Inc. v. Quinton Instr. Co.,* 836 F.2d 1320, 5 USPQ2d 1255 (Fed. Cir. 1987).

[18]*Modine Mfg. Co. v. Allen Group, Inc.,* 917 F.2d 538, 16 USPQ2d 1622 (Fed. Cir. 1990); *Avia Group Int'l, Inc. v. L.A. Gear Calif., Inc.,* 853 F.2d 1557, 7 USPQ2d 1548 (Fed. Cir. 1988). See also *Brooktree Corp. v. Advanced Micro Devices, Inc.,* 977 F.2d 1555, 24 USPQ2d 1401 (Fed. Cir. 1992).

the litigation, (4) the infringer's size and financial condition, (5) closeness of the case, (6) duration of the infringer's misconduct, (7) remedial action by the infringer, (8) the infringer's motivation for harm, and (9) whether the infringer attempted to conceal its misconduct. These factors seem to be in accord with punitive damage considerations in other tort contexts.[19] The increase of damages based on willfulness of the infringement is within the discretionary authority of the trial court, informed by the court's familiarity with the matter in litigation and the interest of justice. In exercising its discretion the trial court may consider the weight of the evidence of willfulness. It thus considers the culpability of the infringer with due attention to any circumstances in mitigation, the closeness of the question, and any other facts pertinent to the award of exemplary damages.[20] Indeed, not only is it incumbent upon a trial court to articulate the basis for a finding of exceptional circumstances, but it is equally necessary to explain why the case was not exceptional in the face of a finding of willful infringement.[21]

Increased damages and attorney fees must be premised on willful infringement or bad faith.[22] In the initial determination of culpability, and thus liability for increased damages, "bad faith" properly refers to an infringer's failure to meet its affirmative duty to use due care in avoiding infringement of another's patent rights. If an infringer adequately performs that duty by determining, for example, that an asserted patent is invalid, that there is no infringement, or that its conduct is authorized by a license, it will not be held liable for increased damages. On the other hand, where it continues its infringing activity, and fails to investigate and determine, in good faith, that it possesses reasonable defenses to an accusation of patent infringement, the infringement is in bad faith. Such conduct occurs when an infringer merely copies a patented invention, or where it obtains incompetent, conclusory opinions of counsel only to use as a shield

---

[19]*Read Corp. v. Portec, Inc.,* 970 F.2d 816, 23 USPQ2d 1426 (Fed. Cir. 1992). Slavish copying is not required in order for copying to be a factor pointing toward willfulness. *Stryker Corp. v. Intermedics Orthopedics, Inc.,* 96 F.3d 1409, 40 USPQ2d 1065 (Fed. Cir. 1996).

[20]*Brooktree Corp. v. Advanced Micro Devices, Inc.,* 977 F.2d 1555, 24 USPQ2d 1401 (Fed. Cir. 1992). For example, enhanced damages may be regarded as inappropriate, despite a verdict finding of willfulness, because of the closeness of the issues. *Laitram Corp. v. NEC Corp.,* 115 F.3d 947, 42 USPQ2d 1897 (Fed. Cir. 1997).

[21]*Jurgens v. CBK, Ltd.,* 80 F.3d 1566, 38 USPQ2d 1397 (Fed. Cir. 1996); *Modine Mfg. Co. v. Allen Group, Inc.,* 917 F.2d 538, 16 USPQ2d 1622 (Fed. Cir. 1990); *Fromson v. Western Litho Plate & Supp. Co.,* 853 F.2d 1568, 7 USPQ2d 1606 (Fed. Cir. 1988); *S.C. Johnson & Son v. Carter-Wallace, Inc.,* 781 F.2d 198, 228 USPQ 367 (Fed. Cir. 1986).

[22]*Yarway Corp. v. Eur-Control USA Inc.,* 775 F.2d 268, 227 USPQ 352 (Fed. Cir. 1985). Enhanced damages may be awarded only as a penalty for an infringer's increased culpability, namely, willful infringement or bad faith. *Beatrice Foods Co. v. New England Printing & Lith. Co.,* 923 F.2d 1567, 17 USPQ2d 1553 (Fed. Cir. 1991). Here the district court had previously found that the infringement was not willful and that the infringer had not prolonged the litigation in bad faith, and therefore concluded that the case was not exceptional. Nonetheless, the district court was outraged at the infringer's intentional destruction of records, and therefore trebled the actual damages "to adequately compensate" the patentee. The Federal Circuit vacated the award on the ground that damages cannot be enhanced to award the patentee

against a later charge of willful infringement, rather than in a good faith attempt to avoid infringing another's patent. Thus, "bad faith" is more correctly called "bad faith infringement," and it is merely a type of willful infringement.[23]

In the end analysis, awards of increased damages and attorney fees should not be allowed to thwart efforts to challenge the validity of patents believed in good faith to be invalid. A party who has obtained advice of competent counsel, or otherwise acquired a basis for a bona fide belief that a patent is invalid, can be said to serve the patent system in challenging that patent in a lawsuit conducted fairly, honestly, and in good faith. Such a party should not have increased damages or attorney fees imposed solely because a court subsequently holds that belief unfounded, particularly when the issues may be fairly described as close.[24]

It is well settled that attorney fees cannot be awarded against the federal government unless specifically authorized by a statutory waiver of sovereign immunity. Such statutory authorization must be express and specific; it cannot be extended beyond the statute's literal terms and it cannot be implied.[25] Thus increased damages and attorney fees are not available against the government in a case under 28 U.S.C. §1498.[26]

The court has also squarely held that the alternative remedy for design patent infringement provided by 35 U.S.C. §289—recovery of an infringer's total profit—cannot be increased under §284, which provides only for "damages."[27]

§14.2 Willful Infringement

The primary consideration in determining willful infringement is whether the infringer, acting in good faith and upon due inquiry, had sound reason to believe that it had the right to act in the manner that was found to be infringing. The law does not search for minimally tolerable behavior, but requires prudent and ethical legal and commercial actions. The precedent displays the consistent theme of whether a prudent person would have had sound reason to believe that the patent was not infringed or was invalid or unenforceable and would be so held if litigated. A factor to be considered is whether the adjudged infringer relied on legal advice. When this defense is raised the court may consider the nature of the advice, the thoroughness and competence of the legal opinion presented, and its objectivity.

---

additional compensation to rectify what the trial court views as an inadequacy in the actual damages found.

[23]*Jurgens v. CBK, Ltd.,* 80 F.3d 1566, 38 USPQ2d 1397 (Fed. Cir. 1996).

[24]*Kloster Speedsteel AB v. Crucible Inc.,* 793 F.2d 1565, 230 USPQ 81 (Fed. Cir. 1986).

[25]*Saldana v. Merit Sys. Prot. Bd.,* 766 F.2d 514 (Fed. Cir. 1985).

[26]*Motorola, Inc. v. United States,* 729 F.2d 765, 221 USPQ 297 (Fed. Cir. 1984).

[27]*Braun Inc. v. Dynamics Corp.,* 975 F.2d 815, 24 USPQ2d 1121 (Fed. Cir. 1992).

The court will determine whether the advice of noninfringement or invalidity or unenforceability could have reasonably been relied on, and whether, on the totality of the circumstances, exculpatory factors avert a finding of willful infringement. The totality of the circumstances may include not only such aspects as the closeness or complexity of the legal and factual questions presented, but also commercial factors that may have affected the infringer's actions. Aspects in mitigation, such as whether there was independent invention or attempts to design around and avoid the patent or any other factors tending to show good faith, should be taken into account and given appropriate weight. Willful infringement is a question of fact, and must be established by clear and convincing evidence, for the boundary between unintentional and culpable acts is not always bright. Since the issue of willfulness not only raises issues of reasonableness and prudence, but is often accompanied by questions of intent, belief, and credibility, appellate review requires appropriate deference to the special role of the trial court in making such determinations. Thus a finding of willful infringement will be sustained unless the reviewing court has a definite and firm conviction that the trier of fact erred.[28]

The issue of willful infringement accordingly measures the infringing behavior, in the circumstances in which the infringer acted, against an objective standard of reasonable commercial behavior in the same circumstances. Willful infringement is thus a measure of reasonable commercial behavior in the context of the tort of patent infringement. The extent to which the infringer disregarded the property rights of the patentee, the deliberateness of the tortious acts, or other manifestations of unethical or injurious commercial conduct, may provide grounds for a finding of willful infringement and the enhancement of damages.[29] The boundary between unintentional and culpable acts is not always bright, for the facts often include subjective as well as objective elements. Thus willful infringement must be established by clear and convincing evidence, for it is a punitive finding and can have the consequence of multiplication of damages.[30] In finding willful infringement, a jury is required to find by clear and convincing evidence in view of the totality of the circumstances that the infringer acted in disregard of the patent and lacked a reasonable basis for believing that it had a right to do what it did. On appeal the issue is whether that finding was supported by substantial evidence.[31]

For a finding of willful infringement, it must appear that the infringer had no reasonable basis for believing it had a right to do

---

[28]*SRI Int'l, Inc. v. Advanced Tech. Labs., Inc.,* 127 F.3d 1462, 44 USPQ2d 1422 (Fed. Cir. 1997).

[29]*Hoechst Celanese Corp. v. BP Chem. Ltd.,* 78 F.3d 1575, 38 USPQ2d 1126 (Fed. Cir. 1996).

[30]*Pall Corp. v. Micron Separations, Inc.,* 66 F.3d 1211, 36 USPQ2d 1225 (Fed. Cir. 1995).

[31]*Amsted Indus. v. Buckeye Steel Castings Co.,* 24 F.3d 178, 30 USPQ2d 1462 (Fed. Cir. 1994).

the acts in question.[32] The test is whether, under all the circumstances, a reasonable person would prudently conduct himself or herself with any confidence that a court might hold the patent invalid or not infringed.[33] There must be an honest doubt of infringement or validity.[34] In determining whether an infringer acted in bad faith so as to merit an increase in damages awarded against it, the court will consider the totality of the circumstances, including (1) whether the infringer deliberately copied the ideas or design of another; (2) whether the infringer, when it knew of the other's patent protection, investigated its scope and formed a good faith belief that it was invalid or not infringed; and (3) the infringer's behavior as a party to the litigation.[35] Although the act of stipulating infringement may be considered a factor in a willfulness determination in appropriate circumstances, it cannot be the sole basis for enhancement of damages.[36]

Willfulness in infringement, as in life, is not an all-or-nothing trait, but one of degree. It recognizes that infringement may range from unknowing, or accidental, to deliberate, or reckless, disregard of a patentee's legal rights. The role of a finding of willfulness in the law of infringement is partly as a deterrent—an economic deterrent to the tort of infringement—and partly as a basis for making economically whole one who has been wronged, for example, by assessment of attorney fees. The term "willfulness" thus reflects a threshold of culpability in the act of infringement that, alone or with other considerations of the particular case, contributes to the court's assessment of the consequences of patent infringement.[37]

Willfulness is a determination as to a state of mind,[38] that must be made by examining the totality of the circumstances.[39] Proof must be by clear and convincing evidence.[40]

(a) The Opinion Requirement

Is there a duty to obtain an opinion of counsel? Certainly ongoing consultation with a patent lawyer is highly probative evidence of good faith.[41] On the other hand, an aggressive strategy, involving a decision

---

[32]*Rosemount, Inc. v. Beckman Instr., Inc.,* 727 F.2d 1540, 221 USPQ 1 (Fed. Cir. 1984); *Stickle v. Heublein, Inc.,* 716 F.2d 1550, 219 USPQ 377 (Fed. Cir. 1983).

[33]*Central Soya Co. v. Geo. A. Hormel & Co.,* 723 F.2d 1573, 220 USPQ 490 (Fed. Cir. 1983).

[34]*Rosemount, Inc. v. Beckman Instr., Inc.,* 727 F.2d 1540, 221 USPQ 1 (Fed. Cir. 1984).

[35]*Bott v. Four Star Corp.,* 807 F.2d 1567, 1 USPQ2d 1210 (Fed. Cir. 1986).

[36]*Graco, Inc. v. Binks Mfg. Co.,* 60 F.3d 785, 35 USPQ2d 1255 (Fed. Cir. 1995).

[37]*Rite-Hite Corp. v. Kelley Co.,* 819 F.2d 1120, 2 USPQ2d 1915 (Fed. Cir. 1987).

[38]*Read Corp. v. Portec, Inc.,* 970 F.2d 816, 23 USPQ2d 1426 (Fed. Cir. 1992).

[39]E.g., *Minnesota Min. & Mfg. Co. v. Johnson & Johnson Orthopaedics, Inc.,* 976 F.2d 1559, 24 USPQ2d 1321 (Fed. Cir. 1992); *Braun Inc. v. Dynamics Corp.,* 975 F.2d 815, 24 USPQ2d 1121 (Fed. Cir. 1992).

[40]E.g., *Braun Inc. v. Dynamics Corp.,* 975 F.2d 815, 24 USPQ2d 1121, 1127 (Fed. Cir. 1992).

[41]*Braun Inc. v. Dynamics Corp.,* 975 F.2d 815, 24 USPQ2d 1121 (Fed. Cir. 1992).

to forego advice of counsel and to bring a declaratory judgment action seeking to have the patent declared invalid, can well be a factor in a decision to award increased damages. An alleged infringer who intentionally blinds himself or herself to the facts and law, continues to infringe, and employs the judicial process with no solidly based expectation of success can hardly be surprised when its infringement is found to be willful.[42] Thus where a potential infringer has actual notice of another's patent rights, it has an affirmative duty of due care, and that affirmative duty will normally entail the obtaining of competent legal advice of counsel before infringing or continuing to infringe.[43]

The court has held that a copyist's reliance on counsel's Rule 11 obligations to support its assertion that it had a good faith belief in the invalidity or unenforceability of the patent was insufficient to overcome a finding of willful infringement. A defensive pleading of invalidity or unenforceability may pass muster under Rule 11, yet not provide adequate defense to a charge of willfulness.[44]

There is no rule excluding reliance upon house counsel opinions.[45] But house counsel's opinion may be insufficient, especially if he or she is not a patent attorney and does not examine the prosecution history of the patent[46] or if he or she was aware of other wrongdoing relating to the matter. In such circumstances, due care may require the opinion of outside counsel.[47]

---

[42]*Kloster Speedsteel AB v. Crucible Inc.*, 793 F.2d 1565, 230 USPQ 81 (Fed. Cir. 1986). Indeed, the mere fact that an accused infringer brought a declaratory judgment action is no evidence that there was a reasonable basis for believing it had a right to continue allegedly infringing activity. *Kaufman Co. v. Lantech*, 807 F.2d 970, 1 USPQ2d 1202 (Fed. Cir. 1986).

[43]*Critikon, Inc. v. Becton Dickinson Vascular Access, Inc.*, 120 F.3d 1253, 43 USPQ2d 1666 (Fed. Cir. 1997); *Minnesota Min. & Mfg. Co. v. Johnson & Johnson Orthopaedics, Inc.*, 976 F.2d 1559, 24 USPQ2d 1321 (Fed. Cir. 1992); *Read Corp. v. Portec, Inc.*, 970 F.2d 816, 23 USPQ2d 1426 (Fed. Cir. 1992); *Ortho Pharm Corp. v. Smith*, 959 F.2d 936, 22 USPQ2d 1119 (Fed. Cir. 1992); *Ryco, Inc. v. Ag-Bag Corp.*, 857 F.2d 1418, 8 USPQ2d 1323 (Fed. Cir. 1988); *Avia Group Int'l, Inc. v. L.A. Gear Calif., Inc.*, 853 F.2d 1557, 7 USPQ2d 1548 (Fed. Cir. 1988); *Spindelfabrik S., S. & G. GmbH v. Schubert & Salzer Mas. Ak.*, 829 F.2d 1075, 4 USPQ2d 1044 (Fed. Cir. 1987); *Bott v. Four Star Corp.*, 807 F.2d 1567, 1 USPQ2d 1210 (Fed. Cir. 1986); *Rolls-Royce Ltd. v. GTE Valeron Corp.*, 800 F.2d 1101, 231 USPQ 185 (Fed. Cir. 1986); *Great Northern Corp. v. Davis Core & Pad Co.*, 782 F.2d 159, 228 USPQ 356 (Fed. Cir. 1986); *Ralston Purina Co. v. Far-Mar-Co, Inc.*, 772 F.2d 1570, 227 USPQ 177 (Fed. Cir. 1985); *Bandag, Inc. v. Al Bolser's Tire Stores, Inc.*, 750 F.2d 903, 223 USPQ 982 (Fed. Cir. 1984); *Rosemount, Inc. v. Beckman Instr., Inc.*, 727 F.2d 1540, 221 USPQ 1 (Fed. Cir. 1984); *Central Soya Co. v. Geo. A. Hormel & Co.*, 723 F.2d 1573, 220 USPQ 490 (Fed. Cir. 1983); *Underwater Devices, Inc. v. Morrison-Knudsen Co.*, 717 F.2d 1380, 219 USPQ 569 (Fed. Cir. 1983). But see *King Instr. Corp. v. Otari Corp.*, 767 F.2d 853, 226 USPQ 402 (Fed. Cir. 1985).

[44]*L.A. Gear, Inc. v. Thom McAn Shoe Co.*, 988 F.2d 1117, 25 USPQ2d 1913 (Fed. Cir. 1993).

[45]*SRI Int'l, Inc. v. Advanced Tech. Labs., Inc.*, 127 F.3d 1462, 44 USPQ2d 1422 (Fed. Cir. 1997).

[46]*Underwater Devices, Inc. v. Morrison-Knudsen Co.*, 717 F.2d 1380, 219 USPQ 569 (Fed. Cir. 1983). Ordering the prosecution file is a normal and necessary step. *Id.* On the other hand, in *Studiengesellschaft Kohle v. Dart Indus., Inc.*, 862 F.2d 1564, 9 USPQ2d 1273 (Fed. Cir. 1988), a 2–1 panel found no clear error in a holding that the defendant had acted reasonably in electing to rely upon the opinion of inside counsel, a qualified patent attorney who had been monitoring the relevant field for three years.

[47]*Minnesota Min. & Mfg. Co. v. Johnson & Johnson Orthopaedics, Inc.*, 976 F.2d 1559, 24 USPQ2d 1321 (Fed. Cir. 1992).

But not every failure to seek an opinion of competent counsel will mandate an ultimate finding of willfulness. Conversely, that an opinion was obtained does not always and alone dictate a finding that the infringement was not willful.[48] Possession of a favorable opinion of counsel is not essential to avoid a willfulness determination; it is only one factor to be considered, albeit an important one.[49] The court has passed the question whether willful infringement can ever be purged by subsequent legal advice.[50]

Thus, consultation with counsel is indeed relevant evidence, as is the product of that consultation, its thoroughness, its objectivity, and its substance. To serve as exculpatory legal advice the opinion of counsel is viewed objectively, to determine whether it was obtained in a timely manner, whether counsel analyzed the relevant facts and explained the conclusions in light of the applicable law, and whether the opinion warranted a reasonable degree of certainty that the infringer had the legal right to conduct the infringing activity.[51] What matters is the nature of the opinion and what effect it had on an infringer's actions.[52] Those cases where willful infringement is found despite the presence of an opinion of counsel generally involve situations where the opinion of counsel was either ignored or found to be incompetent.[53] The emphasis must be on competency.[54] Objective evidence must be considered to determine whether a defendant was justified in relying on patent counsel's advice, i.e., whether the opinion was competent. Opinion letters should be reviewed to determine whether they evidence an adequate foundation based on a review of all necessary facts or whether they are conclusory on their face. Counsel's opinion must be thorough enough, as combined with other facts, to instill a belief in the infringer that a court might reasonably hold the patent is invalid, not infringed, or unenforceable. The letter should be reviewed for its overall tone, its discussion of case law,

---

[48]*Kloster Speedsteel AB v. Crucible Inc.*, 793 F.2d 1565, 230 USPQ 81 (Fed. Cir. 1986). Here, a finding of no willfulness was reversed as clearly erroneous because no opinion was sought despite a warning not to infringe more than a year before infringement began. See also *Ryco, Inc. v. Ag-Bag Corp.*, 857 F.2d 1418, 8 USPQ2d 1323 (Fed. Cir. 1988); *Avia Group Int'l, Inc. v. L.A. Gear Calif., Inc.*, 853 F.2d 1557, 7 USPQ2d 1548 (Fed. Cir. 1988); *Spindelfabrik S., S. & G. GmbH v. Schubert & Salzer Mas. Ak.*, 829 F.2d 1075, 4 USPQ2d 1044 (Fed. Cir. 1987). Absence of an opinion of counsel does not in every case require a finding of bad faith. *Studiengesellschaft Kohle v. Dart Indus., Inc.*, 862 F.2d 1564, 9 USPQ2d 1273 (Fed. Cir. 1988); *Nickson Indus., Inc. v. Rol Mfg. Co.*, 847 F.2d 795, 6 USPQ2d 1878 (Fed. Cir. 1988).

[49]*Electro Med. Sys. S.A. v. Cooper Life Sciences, Inc.*, 34 F.3d 1048, 32 USPQ2d 1017 (Fed. Cir. 1994).

[50]*SRI Int'l, Inc. v. Advanced Tech. Labs., Inc.*, 127 F.3d 1462, 44 USPQ2d 1422 (Fed. Cir. 1997).

[51]*SRI Int'l, Inc. v. Advanced Tech. Labs., Inc.*, 127 F.3d 1462, 44 USPQ2d 1422 (Fed. Cir. 1997).

[52]*Amsted Indus. v. Buckeye Steel Castings Co.*, 24 F.3d 178, 30 USPQ2d 1462 (Fed. Cir. 1994).

[53]*Read Corp. v. Portec, Inc.*, 970 F.2d 816, 23 USPQ2d 1426 (Fed. Cir. 1992).

[54]*Minnesota Min. & Mfg. Co. v. Johnson & Johnson Orthopaedics, Inc.*, 976 F.2d 1559, 24 USPQ2d 1321 (Fed. Cir. 1992).

its analysis of the particular facts, and its reference to inequitable conduct.[55] In order to provide a defense against willful infringement, counsel's opinion must be premised upon the best information known to the defendant. Otherwise, the opinion is likely to be inaccurate and will be ineffective to indicate the defendant's good faith intent. Whenever material information is intentionally withheld, or the best information is intentionally not made available to counsel during the preparation of the opinion, the opinion can no longer serve its prophylactic purpose of negating a finding of willful infringement.[56]

There is no per se rule. While an opinion or lack of an opinion is evidence going to an infringer's state of mind, its existence, or lack thereof, is not conclusive.[57] The weight that may fairly be placed on the presence or absence of an exculpatory opinion of counsel varies with the circumstances of each case and has not been amenable to development of a rigorous rule.[58] In ascertaining an alleged infringer's state of mind, a district court must look at the totality of circumstances in determining willfulness.[59]

Whether infringement is willful is by definition a question of the infringer's intent. While an opinion of counsel is an important factor in determining willfulness, its importance does not depend upon its legal correctness. Indeed, the question arises only where counsel turns out to have been wrong. Rather, the lawyer's opinion must be thorough enough, as combined with other factors, to instill a belief in the infringer that a court might reasonably hold the patent invalid, not

---

[55]*Westvaco Corp. v. International Paper Co.,* 991 F.2d 735, 26 USPQ2d 1353 (Fed. Cir. 1993). For example, in *Johns Hopkins Univ. v. Cellpro Inc.,* 152 F.3d 1342, 47 USPQ2d 1705 (Fed. Cir. 1998), the court held that an opinion of outside counsel could not have instilled in the defendant, through its knowledgeable patent advisor, a reasonable confidence that its activities did not infringe valid patents. The court cited the following defects: the opinion did not attempt to link the disclosures of the prior art references relied upon to establish anticipation or obviousness with the limitations of the claims of the patents. The opinion letter concluded that defendant did not infringe some claims but conspicuously omitted any reference to claims asserted in the action. Further, the opinion was merely conclusory as to its allegations concerning inequitable conduct, and made no mention that intent to deceive is a necessary component of this defense, a fact that is often difficult to establish.

[56]*Comark Comm. Inc. v. Harris Corp.,* 156 F.3d 1182, 48 USPQ2d 1001 (Fed. Cir. 1998). An infringer's uncontradicted testimony that he or she had a good faith belief that the patent was invalid need not be accepted by a jury as true where there is also evidence that the belief was based on an opinion that was in part predicated on faulty or incomplete information. *Amsted Indus. v. Buckeye Steel Castings Co.,* 24 F.3d 178, 30 USPQ2d 1462 (Fed. Cir. 1994). The evidence was that the client knew that the attorney did not fully understand the invention and was not aware of objective evidence of nonobviousness.

[57]*Rite-Hite Corp. v. Kelley Co.,* 819 F.2d 1120, 2 USPQ2d 1915 (Fed. Cir. 1987); *Rolls-Royce Ltd. v. GTE Valeron Corp.,* 800 F.2d 1101, 231 USPQ 185 (Fed. Cir. 1986); *Machinery Corp. v. Gullfiber AB,* 774 F.2d 467, 227 USPQ 368 (Fed. Cir. 1985). Simply because the infringer obtained an opinion on another patent does not mean that its failure to do so on the one in suit amounts to conscious disregard of it. *American Original Corp. v. Jenkins Food Corp.,* 774 F.2d 459, 227 USPQ 299 (Fed. Cir. 1985). Where the defendant did not consult an attorney for five months after the first notice letter, did not search for prior art until after suit, and continued to make and sell after suit, double damages were justified. *Del Mar Avionics, Inc. v. Quinton Instr. Co.,* 836 F.2d 1320, 5 USPQ2d 1255 (Fed. Cir. 1987).

[58]*Del Mar Avionics, Inc. v. Quinton Instr. Co.,* 836 F.2d 1320, 5 USPQ2d 1255 (Fed. Cir. 1987); *Rite-Hite Corp. v. Kelley Co.,* 819 F.2d 1120, 2 USPQ2d 1915 (Fed. Cir. 1987).

[59]*Machinery Corp. v. Gullfiber AB,* 774 F.2d 467, 227 USPQ 368 (Fed. Cir. 1985).

infringed, or unenforceable. Thus, the infringer's intent and reasonable beliefs are the primary focus of a willful infringement inquiry.[60] An important consideration in assessing willfulness is that there is nothing in the opinion itself that would alert a client to regard the opinion as a bad one.[61]

Certainly an opinion must be rendered in good faith and must not be disregarded.[62] For example, a conclusory account of defense counsel's aspirations for winning an infringement suit without any supporting reasons does not amount to an authoritative opinion upon which a good faith reliance on invalidity may be founded.[63] Reliance upon factual assumptions for the opinion must be reasonable.[64]

The client need not itself be able to evaluate the legal competence of its attorney's advice to avoid a finding of willfulness. The client would not need the attorney's advice at all in that event. That an opinion is "incompetent" must be shown by objective evidence. For example, an attorney may not have looked into the necessary facts and thus there would be no foundation for his or her opinion. A written opinion may be incompetent on its face by reason of its containing

---

[60]*Ortho Pharm Corp. v. Smith,* 959 F.2d 936, 22 USPQ2d 1119 (Fed. Cir. 1992). Here the court held that a failure to make a doctrine of equivalents analysis was not per se unreasonable. A critical factor in evaluating the effect of an opinion of counsel on willfulness is the reasonableness of a party's reliance on it. There is no requirement that an opinion must address validity to negate a finding of willful infringement, if it concludes that there is no infringement. Whether or not an opinion is legally correct is not the proper focus. *Graco, Inc. v. Binks Mfg. Co.,* 60 F.3d 785, 35 USPQ2d 1255 (Fed. Cir. 1995).

[61]*Read Corp. v. Portec, Inc.,* 970 F.2d 816, 23 USPQ2d 1426 (Fed. Cir. 1992). See note 14:56.

[62]*Machinery Corp. v. Gullfiber AB,* 774 F.2d 467, 227 USPQ 368 (Fed. Cir. 1985). Where an attorney advises the client to avoid a particular range of a constituent, but the client does not even measure the range for a long time after beginning production, and then only after adding another ingredient that might make a difference, any inference of good faith is negated and the client is in the same position as one who did not obtain an opinion of counsel. *Central Soya Co. v. Geo. A. Hormel & Co.,* 723 F.2d 1573, 220 USPQ 490 (Fed. Cir. 1983). In another case, the attorney advised the client, who was under an injunction, to avoid certain things. The client complied, but modified its activities, without informing the attorney, to include things that the attorney had not specifically advised against. In affirming a finding of willfulness, the court observed that the attorney had done what he could, and likened the client to a child who complains that its mother never warned it not to eat the daisies. *Paper Converting Mach. Co. v. Magna-Graphics Corp.,* 785 F.2d 1013, 228 USPQ 938 (Fed. Cir. 1986). The court indicated that there was a duty, because of the injunction, to be ultra careful. In *Graco, Inc. v. Binks Mfg. Co.,* 60 F.3d 785, 35 USPQ2d 1255 (Fed. Cir. 1995), a few devices were made without approval of counsel. The Federal Circuit viewed this as due to carelessness or inadvertency by technical personnel, not disregard of patent rights by management.

[63]*Bott v. Four Star Corp.,* 807 F.2d 1567, 1 USPQ2d 1210 (Fed. Cir. 1986); *Kori Corp. v. Wilco Marsh Buggies, Inc.,* 761 F.2d 649, 225 USPQ 985 (Fed. Cir. 1985). It may not satisfy the duty to seek and obtain competent legal advice where the party merely obtains an assurance from the manufacturer that it has obtained an opinion of invalidity and noninfringement, without actually seeing the opinion or investigating further. *Jurgens v. McKasy,* 927 F.2d 1552, 18 USPQ2d 1031 (Fed. Cir. 1991). In *Datascope Corp. v. SMEC, Inc.,* 879 F.2d 820, 11 USPQ2d 1321 (Fed. Cir. 1989), an opinion said nothing about validity, and considered only literal infringement, not equivalents (indeed, the Federal Circuit concluded that the opinion could not have dealt with equivalents because defendant's attorneys neither obtained nor consulted the prosecution history of the patent). The district court's conclusion of nonwillfulness, based largely on the opinion, was held clearly erroneous.

[64]*Minnesota Min. & Mfg. Co. v. Johnson & Johnson Orthopaedics, Inc.,* 976 F.2d 1559, 24 USPQ2d 1321, 1340 (Fed. Cir. 1992).

merely conclusory statements without discussion of facts or obviously presenting only a superficial or off-the-cuff analysis. But an opinion need not unequivocally state that the client will not be held liable for infringement. An honest opinion is more likely to speak of probabilities than certainties. A good test that the advice given is genuine and not merely self-serving is whether the asserted defenses are backed up with viable proof during a trial that raises substantial questions.[65]

Oral opinions are not favored because they have to be proved perhaps years after the event, based only on testimony that may be affected by faded memories and the forces of contemporaneous litigation.[66]

An accused infringer has the right to assert the attorney-client privilege. And when it refuses to produce an exculpatory opinion of counsel in response to a charge of willful infringement, an inference may be drawn that either no opinion was obtained or, if one was obtained, it was unfavorable. But assertion of the privilege does not raise an irrebuttable presumption of willfulness. Such a rule would not accommodate consideration of other facts, nor would it respect the right of a party to assert the privilege. Accordingly, an inference that an opinion was unfavorable does not foreclose consideration of other relevant factors. There are no hard and fast rules in respect of willfulness.[67]

In an important statement on the question of whether and when to reveal an attorney's opinion, the court has suggested that it may be useful to have separate trials on liability and on willfulness and damages. That way, the accused infringer need only disclose an attorney's opinion if it is found liable.[68] An accused infringer should not, without the trial court's careful consideration, be forced to choose between waiving the privilege in order to protect itself from a willfulness finding (in which case it may risk prejudicing itself on the question of liability) and maintaining the privilege (in which case it may

---

[65]*Read Corp. v. Portec, Inc.,* 970 F.2d 816, 23 USPQ2d 1426 (Fed. Cir. 1992). A failure of a lawyer to perform specific legal research prior to rendering an opinion does not per se render that opinion incompetent, particularly where the attorney has many years of experience in the patent specialty. *Id.* The fact that a letter speaks in terms of probabilities, and therefore can be said to be equivocal, does not require a finding of willfulness. *Westvaco Corp. v. International Paper Co.,* 991 F.2d 735, 26 USPQ2d 1353 (Fed. Cir. 1993).

[66]*Minnesota Min. & Mfg. Co. v. Johnson & Johnson Orthopaedics, Inc.,* 976 F.2d 1559, 24 USPQ2d 1321 (Fed. Cir. 1992).

[67]*Electro Med. Sys. S.A. v. Cooper Life Sciences, Inc.,* 34 F.3d 1048, 32 USPQ2d 1017 (Fed. Cir. 1994). Despite refusal to produce an opinion, the Federal Circuit reversed the determination of willfulness on the basis of other evidence: the infringement was de minimis and was accomplished only to avoid dismissal of a declaratory judgment suit and ensure prompt adjudication. The infringer's conduct throughout was to seek resolution of the controversy in court. Moreover, the merits questions were close.

[68]*Fromson v. Western Litho Plate & Supp. Co.,* 853 F.2d 1568, 7 USPQ2d 1606 (Fed. Cir. 1988). Here, however, willfulness and damages were tried with liability, and since the infringer failed to introduce an exculpatory opinion of counsel at trial, the court was free to infer that either no opinion was obtained or, if an opinion were obtained, it was contrary to the infringer's desire to initiate or continue its use of the patentee's invention.

risk being held to be a willful infringer if liability is found). Trial courts thus should give serious consideration to a separate trial on willfulness whenever the particular attorney-client communications, once inspected by the court in camera, reveal that the defendant is indeed confronted with this dilemma.[69]

(b) Notice of the Patent

Although a party may have a duty to seek and obtain competent legal advice before the initiation of any possible infringing activity, this is so only where the party has knowledge of the patent.[70]

What constitutes notice? Or, more to the point, when does the duty of care begin? It is obvious that a party cannot be held liable for infringement, and thus not for willful infringement, of a nonexistent patent.[71] Moreover, in our patent system patent applications are secret, and patentees are authorized to sue "innocent" manufacturers immediately after their patents issue and without warning. To hold such patentees entitled to increased damages or attorney fees on the ground of willful infringement, however, would be to reward use of the patent system as a form of ambush.[72] Nonetheless, as a general proposition, the fact that the accused party may have started its infringement before the patent issued, or before becoming aware of the patent, does not always bar an award of increased damages or attorney fees.[73] Although willfulness is generally based on conduct that occurred after a patent issued, prepatent conduct may also be used to support a finding of willfulness.[74]

In *Gustafson v. Intersystems,*[75] the court traced its evolving jurisprudence concerning circumstances where a product found to infringe at trial had been manufactured before the patent issued. In two early cases, the court had concluded nonwillfulness where there was no prior notice of the patent and suit followed within days after the patent

---

[69]*Quantum Corp. v. Tandon Corp.,* 940 F.2d 642, 19 USPQ2d 1799 (Fed. Cir. 1991). Indeed, the assertion of privilege with respect to infringement and validity opinions of counsel may support the drawing of adverse inferences. *L.A. Gear, Inc. v. Thom McAn Shoe Co.,* 988 F.2d 1117, 25 USPQ2d 1913 (Fed. Cir. 1993).

[70]*Jurgens v. McKasy,* 927 F.2d 1552, 18 USPQ2d 1031 (Fed. Cir. 1991).

[71]*Gustafson, Inc. v. Intersystems Indus. Prods., Inc.,* 897 F.2d 508, 13 USPQ2d 1972 (Fed. Cir. 1990).

[72]*Gustafson, Inc. v. Intersystems Indus. Prods., Inc.,* 897 F.2d 508, 13 USPQ2d 1972 (Fed. Cir. 1990).

[73]*Pacific Furniture Mfg. Co. v. Preview Furniture Corp.,* 800 F.2d 1111, 231 USPQ 67 (Fed. Cir. 1986).

[74]*Minnesota Min. & Mfg. Co. v. Johnson & Johnson Orthopaedics, Inc.,* 976 F.2d 1559, 24 USPQ2d 1321 (Fed. Cir. 1992).

[75]*Gustafson, Inc. v. Intersystems Indus. Prods., Inc.,* 897 F.2d 508, 13 USPQ2d 1972 (Fed. Cir. 1990).

issued.[76] In its next decision,[77] willfulness was sustained because a prior warning had been given and the infringer knew of the patent the day it issued. Thereafter, the court distinguished its earlier cases,[78] indicating that it had not laid down a per se rule that willful infringement could never be found when manufacture began before issue, and adopting a "totality of the circumstances" approach to analyzing willfulness.[79] Using that test, it later sustained willfulness findings for manufacture before issue where warnings had been given.[80]

In the *Gustafson* case itself, the court reversed a willfulness finding where the infringer's first knowledge of the patent came when it got sued. It would appear, therefore, that no knowledge at all will be important in defeating a willfulness finding, while a warning, even prior to infringement, will support a willfulness finding. As the court explained, whether an act is willful is by definition a question of the actor's intent, the answer to which must be inferred from all the circumstances. Hence, a party cannot be found to have willfully infringed a patent of which the party had no knowledge. Nor is there a universal rule that to avoid willfulness one must cease manufacture of a product immediately upon learning of a patent, or upon receipt of a patentee's charge of infringement, or upon the filing of suit. Exercising due care, a party may continue to manufacture and may present what in good faith it believes to be a legitimate defense without risk of being found on that basis alone a willful infringer. That such a defense proves unsuccessful does not establish that infringement was willful. However, presentation in bad faith of a totally unsupportable, frivolous defense may in itself provide a basis for attorney fees under §285 and may, in light of all the circumstances, also constitute some evidence that continued infringement was willful.[81]

The matter will certainly be developed on a case-by-case basis. For example, the court has refused to consider the conduct of an

[76]*American Original Corp. v. Jenkins Food Corp.,* 774 F.2d 459, 227 USPQ 299 (Fed. Cir. 1985); *State Indus., Inc. v. A.O. Smith Corp.,* 751 F.2d 1226, 224 USPQ 418 (Fed. Cir. 1985). In *American Original,* the infringing machine was altered, upon the advice of a contractor who did have legal counsel, in the hope of avoiding infringement.

[77]*Power Lift, Inc. v. Lang Tools, Inc.,* 774 F.2d 478, 227 USPQ 435 (Fed. Cir. 1985).

[78]See note 14:76.

[79]*Shiley, Inc. v. Bentley Labs., Inc.,* 794 F.2d 1561, 230 USPQ 112 (Fed. Cir. 1986). The fact that an infringer may have started its infringement before the patent issued or before it was aware of the patent does not bar an award of increased damages or attorney fees. *Avia Group Int'l, Inc. v. L.A. Gear Calif., Inc.,* 853 F.2d 1557, 7 USPQ2d 1548 (Fed. Cir. 1988).

[80]*Kaufman Co. v. Lantech,* 807 F.2d 970, 1 USPQ2d 1202 (Fed. Cir. 1986); *Pacific Furniture Mfg. Co. v. Preview Furniture Corp.,* 800 F.2d 1111, 231 USPQ 67 (Fed. Cir. 1986). In *National Presto Indus., Inc. v. West Bend Co.,* 76 F.3d 1185, 37 USPQ2d 1685 (Fed. Cir. 1996), the court rejected, as an exculpatory argument, the circumstance that the plaintiff filed suit on the day the patent issued. It appeared that the defendant knew of its issuance on that day and indeed had several months' advance warning. The district court increased the damages by one-half; this was affirmed.

[81]*Gustafson, Inc. v. Intersystems Indus. Prods., Inc.,* 897 F.2d 508, 13 USPQ2d 1972 (Fed. Cir. 1990).

infringer prior to its contact with an attorney, where the devices made during that period were prototypes only and not the real focus of the litigation.[82] In another case, the infringer had received some orders by the time it received an opinion on the patent, but no installations had been made. Before installation, modifications were made, although they turned out to be insufficient to avoid infringement. The Federal Circuit was unable to conclude in the face of such evidence that a finding of nonwillfulness was clearly erroneous.[83]

Does a patent-pending marking constitute notice for purposes of the willfulness inquiry? The court has said that to willfully infringe a patent, the patent must exist and one must have knowledge of it. A patent-pending notice gives one no knowledge whatsoever. It is not even a guarantee that an application has been filed. Filing an application is no guarantee any patent will issue, and a very substantial percentage of applications never result in patents. What the scope of claims in patents that do issue will be is something that is totally unforeseeable.[84]

(c) Particular Cases

The rejection of a license offer without even consulting house counsel is a factor that tends toward a finding of willfulness. The fact that the license offer was quickly withdrawn and suit filed within 60 days of the issuance of the patent does not overcome this; there is no rule that an infringer must be allowed a certain amount of time to "develop" willfulness.[85] Actually, a request for a license can cut both ways. It can be evidence of willfulness or evidence of an infringer's good faith if the infringer can show that it wanted a license as an alternative to unaffordable or expensive litigation costs.[86] But an unsuccessful attempt to obtain a license under the patent in suit

---

[82]*Radio Steel & Mfg. Co. v. MTD Prods., Inc.*, 788 F.2d 1554, 229 USPQ 431 (Fed. Cir. 1986). In *State Indus., Inc. v. Mor-Flo Indus., Inc.*, 883 F.2d 1573, 12 USPQ2d 1026 (Fed. Cir. 1989), the district court found that the infringement was not willful, based upon reliance on erroneous advice of counsel that there was no infringement. This finding, however, seemed inconsistent with the district court's other findings that the defendant purposely patterned its method upon that of the plaintiff, and that the defendant should have known it was infringing. Thus the Federal Circuit remanded to resolve the conflicting evidence. With all respect, it appeared that the district court had done its best to resolve the conflicting evidence and had come out on the side of nonwillfulness.

[83]*Amstar Corp. v. Envirotech Corp.*, 823 F.2d 1538, 3 USPQ2d 1412 (Fed. Cir. 1987).

[84]*State Indus., Inc. v. A.O. Smith Corp.*, 751 F.2d 1226, 224 USPQ 418 (Fed. Cir. 1985). Here the infringer did not copy the plaintiff's device but was spurred into activity by it. The court hints, however, that a finding of willful infringement might be supported by actual copying of a product bearing patent-applied-for markings.

[85]*Ralston Purina Co. v. Far-Mar-Co, Inc.*, 772 F.2d 1570, 227 USPQ 177 (Fed. Cir. 1985). The court also referred to the infringer's knowledge that the patentee had won an interference as support for the finding of willfulness.

[86]*King Instr. Corp. v. Otari Corp.*, 767 F.2d 853, 226 USPQ 402 (Fed. Cir. 1985).

demands a high degree of caution to avoid the possibility of infringement of that patent.[87] Again, willfulness must be evaluated on the totality of the surrounding circumstances.[88]

In the end analysis, willfulness determinations are unpredictable. Certainly, where a defendant is informed of the specific allegation of infringement and given a copy of the patent, where it takes no affirmative steps through consultation with counsel or otherwise to ascertain whether the patent is infringed, and where it deliberately continues its infringement, a finding of willfulness—even a reversal of the district court—is hardly surprising.[89] Nor is there error in a finding of willful infringement where the patentee offered a license and was ignored, and six years later advised of a validity holding and was still ignored.[90] An enormous increase in infringing activity during the period of a stay of an injunction pending appeal can appropriately be considered as part of the willful activity that justified increased damages.[91] An attempt to design a noninfringing alternative does not necessarily negate continuing sales of infringing devices during the redesign period.[92] Infringement after the Federal Circuit has affirmed a judgment on liability is particularly egregious.[93] Naturally enough, a statement by the president of the infringer to the effect that it would copy any machine that his customers requested, regardless of whether a patent was issued, will not sit well with the Federal Circuit when it is reviewing a finding of willful infringement.[94]

But the circumstances are not always so clear. The court has left undisturbed a finding of no willfulness where the evidence showed that the infringer had previously obtained an opinion on an earlier device and had abandoned the device when advised it would infringe, and yet had obtained no opinion on the device in suit.[95] An oral opinion that was based on the patent and an accused device, but not the prosecution history or prior art, was sufficient to support a finding

---

[87]*Spindelfabrik GmbH v. Schubert & Salzer*, 829 F.2d 1075, 4 USPQ2d 1044 (Fed. Cir. 1987). Here that factor overcame reliance upon the advice of German in-house counsel and resulted in a finding of willfulness and an award of increased damages and attorney fees.

[88]*King Instr. Corp. v. Otari Corp.*, 767 F.2d 853, 226 USPQ 402 (Fed. Cir. 1985).

[89]*CPG Prods. Corp. v. Pegasus Luggage, Inc.*, 776 F.2d 1007, 227 USPQ 497 (Fed. Cir. 1985). See also *Orthokinetics, Inc. v. Safety Travel Chairs, Inc.*, 806 F.2d 1565, 1 USPQ2d 1081 (Fed. Cir. 1986).

[90]*Leinoff v. Louis Milona & Sons*, 726 F.2d 734, 220 USPQ 845 (Fed. Cir. 1984).

[91]*Bott v. Four Star Corp.*, 807 F.2d 1567, 1 USPQ2d 1210 (Fed. Cir. 1986). A stay is not a judicial license to continue and greatly increase infringing activities. *Id.*

[92]*American Med. Sys., Inc. v. Medical Eng'g Corp.*, 6 F.3d 1523, 28 USPQ2d 1321 (Fed. Cir. 1993).

[93]*Bott v. Four Star Corp.*, 807 F.2d 1567, 1 USPQ2d 1210 (Fed. Cir. 1986).

[94]*Kaufman Co. v. Lantech*, 807 F.2d 970, 1 USPQ2d 1202 (Fed. Cir. 1986). He also remained at the patentee's trade show booth, observing operation of the device, despite being asked to leave.

[95]*Rolls-Royce Ltd. v. GTE Valeron Corp.*, 800 F.2d 1101, 231 USPQ 185 (Fed. Cir. 1986). Significant design changes, in most instances, would require a new opinion of counsel. *Critikon, Inc. v. Becton Dickinson Vascular Access, Inc.*, 120 F.3d 1253, 43 USPQ2d 1666 (Fed. Cir. 1997).

of no willfulness.[96] In another case, the infringer had known about the patent prior to commencing the infringing activity but was not aware of the patentee's charge of infringement until shortly prior to suit. No opinion of counsel was obtained; indeed, counsel was not consulted until after suit was filed. However, an officer of the infringer testified that he thought a lot of the features were covered by prior art, and the district court found that this amounted to a good faith belief that the patent was invalid. The Federal Circuit affirmed a finding of no willfulness.[97] On the other hand, an invalidity opinion based solely on file wrapper references does not, by itself, raise an inference of good faith substantial enough to overturn a trial court's finding of willfulness.[98] The lack of a separate doctrine of equivalents analysis in an opinion letter is not necessarily critical or dispositive where the opinion letter contains enough other indicia of competence.[99]

In one case the district court excluded evidence of a prior jury trial in which defendant's position was vindicated (the verdict was later overturned on motion) from a subsequent trial on willfulness and damages. The Federal Circuit found no abuse of discretion. The jury verdict came four years after defendant received notice of the patent and thus had no bearing upon the willfulness of defendant's conduct at that earlier time. Moreover, it had significant potential to confuse the second jury.[100] In another case a "green-light" opinion letter had been obtained by an industry defense group. The patentee's expert witness had criticized the letter on various grounds, including a failure to make a proper and full analysis under 35 U.S.C. §103. There was evidence that the accused device was designed to be compatible with the patented device. The defendant, as the founder of the industry group, was aware that its declaratory judgment litigation against the patent owner would be more effective if other members of the group did not take a license. All of these factors supported an

---

[96]*Radio Steel & Mfg. Co. v. MTD Prods., Inc.,* 788 F.2d 1554, 229 USPQ 431 (Fed. Cir. 1986). The court pointed out that this was not a case where the attorney was reluctantly pressured into an opinion by its client, or one in which the client had previously received a carefully prepared written opinion but had instead acted on the basis of an oral, off-the-cuff opinion. In those situations an oral opinion might not suffice to establish nonwillfulness.

[97]*Nickson Indus., Inc. v. Rol Mfg. Co.,* 847 F.2d 795, 6 USPQ2d 1878 (Fed. Cir. 1988).

[98]*Central Soya Co. v. Geo. A. Hormel & Co.,* 723 F.2d 1573, 220 USPQ 490 (Fed. Cir. 1983). A counsel's opinion is to be weighed on the question of good faith.

[99]*Westvaco Corp. v. International Paper Co.,* 991 F.2d 735, 26 USPQ2d 1353 (Fed. Cir. 1993). In *Hoechst Celanese Corp. v. BP Chem. Ltd.,* 78 F.3d 1575, 38 USPQ2d 1126 (Fed. Cir. 1996), the court declined an invitation to adopt a per se rule that infringement only under the doctrine of equivalents cannot be regarded as willful conduct. In *WMS Gaming Inc. v. International Game Tech.,* 184 F.3d 1339, 51 USPQ2d 1385 (Fed. Cir. 1999), the court reversed a finding of literal infringement but affirmed on infringement by equivalence. Under these circumstances, it vacated and remanded the finding of willful infringement for reconsideration in light of the conclusion of no literal infringement. It admonished the district court to bear in mind that the patent law encourages competitors to design or invent around existing patents.

[100]*Johns Hopkins Univ. v. Cellpro Inc.,* 152 F.3d 1342, 47 USPQ2d 1705 (Fed. Cir. 1998). See also *Odetics Inc. v. Storage Tech. Corp.,* 185 F.3d 1259, 51 USPQ2d 1225 (Fed. Cir. 1999).

inference by the jury that the defendant made its decision to infringe without a good faith belief in the invalidity of the patent and that it used the opinion letter as a basis for forming a patent defense group rather than as a genuine basis for decision making.[101] The court has held that a grant by the PTO of reexamination is not probative of unpatentability and thus the grant of reexamination does not automatically preclude a finding of willfulness. The grant of reexamination, although surely evidence that the criterion for reexamination has been met, does not establish a likelihood of patent invalidity.[102]

That someone has a patent right to exclude others from making the invention claimed in his or her patent does not mean that the invention cannot infringe claims of another's patent that are broad enough to encompass, i.e., to "dominate," the invention. Thus, an infringer probably cannot rely upon the fact that it has itself obtained a patent on the accused product as establishing a reasonable belief that it did not infringe.[103]

Absent sufficient basis for directing a verdict, a party has a right of jury determination of the question of willful infringement. Willfulness of behavior is a classical jury question of intent.[104]

In *Pall v. Micron,*[105] the court hinted that Rule 407, FRE, will apply to willfulness determinations. Rule 407 bars evidence of subsequent remedial action in proving culpability for a prior act or event; the policy implemented by the rule is to avoid inhibiting postaccident repair, lest additional injury occur. In *Pall*, the defendant switched largely to a new version after six years' production of the old version and after three years of litigation. It continued, however, to produce some quantities of the original version. The trial court found no willfulness as to the first six years of the original version, but did find willfulness as to the continued production of the old version after the switch. The Federal Circuit reversed. It recognized that patent infringement is a continuing tort, and an action even if innocent when begun does not automatically retain its purity as circumstances change; the filing of a lawsuit does not stop the clock insofar as culpability may arise from continuing disregard of the legal rights of the patentee. It also disavowed any rule that because an original infringement was found not to be willful, there is a greater burden on the patentee to prove willfulness as circumstances change. Nonetheless, it held that partial conversion to the new version was not probative of willfulness for the continuing product of the old version.

---

[101]*In re Hayes Microcomputer Patent Litig.,* 982 F.2d 1527, 25 USPQ2d 1241 (Fed. Cir. 1992).

[102]*Hoechst Celanese Corp. v. BP Chem. Ltd.,* 78 F.3d 1575, 38 USPQ2d 1126, 1133 (Fed. Cir. 1996).

[103]*Rolls-Royce Ltd. v. GTE Valeron Corp.,* 800 F.2d 1101, 231 USPQ 185 (Fed. Cir. 1986).

[104]*Richardson v. Suzuki Motor Co.,* 868 F.2d 1226, 9 USPQ2d 1913 (Fed. Cir. 1989).

[105]*Pall Corp. v. Micron Separations, Inc.,* 66 F.3d 1211, 36 USPQ2d 1225 (Fed. Cir. 1995).

§14.3 Other Exceptional Conduct

The court apparently has come to the view that infringement damages cannot be enhanced in the absence of a finding of willful infringement. The court characterized its previous suggestions that damages might be enhanced solely due to misconduct during litigation as dicta, and pointed out that other sanctions are generally available for litigation misconduct. Bad faith behavior of a party to the litigation is just a factor to be weighed in assessing the level of a defendant's culpability where an infringement is found to be willful. However, litigation misconduct may in itself make a case "exceptional," thus justifying an award of attorney fees.[106]

The increased damages portion of §284 requires a two-step inquiry. First, the fact finder must determine whether an infringer is guilty of conduct upon which increased damages may be based. If so, the court then determines, exercising its sound discretion, whether, and to what extent, to increase the damages award given the totality of the circumstances. Because increased damages are punitive, the requisite conduct for imposing them must include some degree of culpability. An act of willful infringement satisfies this culpability requirement and is, without doubt, sufficient to meet the first criterion for increasing a compensatory damages award. Increased damages also may be awarded because of bad faith on the other side. The correlation between bad faith, willful infringement, and increased damages, however, is sometimes misunderstood because the term "bad faith" has numerous patent law applications. Only some of these are relevant in determining the predicate culpability for an increased damages award. Bad faith is used, for example, in referring to misconduct in the prosecution or litigation over a patent. Such conduct includes inequitable conduct during patent prosecution, bringing vexatious or unjustified suits, attorney or client misconduct during litigation, or unnecessarily prolonging litigation. These acts by themselves, however, are not sufficient for an increased damages award under §284 because they are not related to the underlying act of infringement and say nothing about the culpability of the infringer. Only a culpable infringer can be held liable for increased damages, not an innocent one. The listed acts might be evaluated to determine if the infringer acted willfully in light of the totality of the surrounding circumstances. The ultimate fact to be proven, that is, the basis for increased damages, however, would be that the infringement was willful, not that litigation activities were improper. Thus, although an infringer's inequitable conduct in prosecuting its own patents, or its egregious conduct in infringement litigation may be sufficient for other sanctions or fee awards, or may be used as a factor in determining whether

---

[106]*Read Corp. v. Portec, Inc.,* 970 F.2d 816, 23 USPQ2d 1426 (Fed. Cir. 1992). See *Westvaco Corp. v. International Paper Co.,* 991 F.2d 735, 26 USPQ2d 1353 (Fed. Cir. 1993). But see *Delta-X Corp. v. Baker Hughes Prod. Tools, Inc.,* 984 F.2d 410, 25 USPQ2d 1447 (Fed. Cir.

or how much to increase a damages award once sufficient culpability is found, these actions are not sufficient independent bases to justify increased damages under §284.[107]

Enhanced damages are punitive not compensatory. Therefore, an infringer may generally avoid enhanced damages with a meritorious good faith defense and a substantial challenge to infringement.[108] Activities reflective of bad faith and thus suggesting exceptional circumstances include inequitable conduct during patent prosecution, misconduct during litigation, vexatious or unjustified litigation, or a frivolous suit.[109] District courts possess inherent power to assess attorney fees as a sanction when a party acts in bad faith, vexatiously, wantonly, or for oppressive reasons.[110] Courts have tools to punish egregious misconduct. These include attorney fees under §285, Rule 11, appellate Rule 38, or 28 U.S.C. 1927.[111]

(a) Inequitable Conduct

Inequitable conduct is a separate defense to patent infringement and, either alone or in conjunction with trial conduct, may constitute the basis for an award of attorney fees under 35 U.S.C. §285.[112] But not every case of proven inequitable conduct must result in an automatic attorney fee award or an evaluation of the case as "exceptional."[113] Thus the court has refused the invitation to establish as a rule that one who succeeds in invalidating a fraudulently procured patent should be awarded attorney fees unless the patentee can show compelling

---

1993), where the court continues to use language that suggests an award of enhanced damages might be supported by bad faith.

[107]*Jurgens v. CBK, Ltd.*, 80 F.3d 1566, 38 USPQ2d 1397 (Fed. Cir. 1996).

[108]*Delta-X Corp. v. Baker Hughes Prod. Tools, Inc.*, 984 F.2d 410, 25 USPQ2d 1447 (Fed. Cir. 1993).

[109]*Beckman Instr., Inc. v. LKB Produkter AB*, 892 F.2d 1547, 13 USPQ2d 1301 (Fed. Cir. 1989); *Standard Oil Co. v. American Cyanamid Co.*, 774 F.2d 448, 227 USPQ 293 (Fed. Cir. 1985); *Bayer Aktiengesellschaft v. Duphar Int'l Research B.V.*, 738 F.2d 1237, 222 USPQ 649 (Fed. Cir. 1984); *Stevenson v. Sears, Roebuck & Co.*, 713 F.2d 705, 218 USPQ 969 (Fed. Cir. 1983).

[110]*L.E.A. Dynatech, Inc. v. Allina*, 49 F.3d 1527, 33 USPQ2d 1839 (Fed. Cir. 1995).

[111]*Jurgens v. CBK, Ltd.*, 80 F.3d 1566, 38 USPQ2d 1397 (Fed. Cir. 1996).

[112]*A.B. Chance Co. v. RTE Corp.*, 854 F.2d 1307, 7 USPQ2d 1881 (Fed. Cir. 1988). Thus it was error for the district court to refuse an award of attorney fees without making a determination of whether the patentee had engaged in inequitable conduct as alleged, and a remand was required. *Id.* See also *Enzo Biochem Inc. v. Calgene Inc.*, 188 F.3d 1362, 52 USPQ2d 1129 (Fed. Cir. 1999). Inequitable conduct must, as a matter of law, be taken into account in deciding a request for attorney fees. *Pharmacia & Upjohn Co. v. Mylan Pharm. Inc.*, 182 F.3d 1356, 51 USPQ2d 1466 (Fed. Cir. 1999).

[113]*Consolidated Alum Corp. v. Foseco Int'l Ltd.*, 910 F.2d 804, 15 USPQ2d 1481 (Fed. Cir. 1990); *Hewlett-Packard Co. v. Bausch & Lomb, Inc.*, 882 F.2d 1556, 11 USPQ2d 1750 (Fed. Cir. 1989). See also *Gardco Mfg., Inc. v. Herst Lighting Co.*, 820 F.2d 1209, 2 USPQ2d 2015 (Fed. Cir. 1987). Here there was no showing that the district court was clearly erroneous in finding an absence of exceptional circumstances, and thus no showing of an abuse of discretion in failure to award attorney fees, despite the fact that the Federal Circuit indicated that the patentee's appeal of the finding of inequitable conduct would have been deemed frivolous if not for the presence of a jury trial issue of first impression.

countervailing circumstances.[114] Section 285 does not contemplate that a prevailing alleged infringer should be treated as a private attorney general for invalidating a fraudulently obtained patent. Rather its purpose is to provide discretion where it would be grossly unjust that the winner be left to bear the burden of its own counsel fees, which prevailing litigants normally bear.[115]

(b) Invalidity

A classical case of bad faith would exist where the patentee brings an infringement suit knowing the patent to be invalid or not infringed. It has been suggested that the presumption of validity might protect the patentee in cases where validity is an issue.[116] Where a patentee is sued for a declaratory judgment of invalidity and noninfringement, it can probably rely upon the presumption of validity alone to establish the nonexceptional nature of the case, provided there is no fraud or inequitable conduct, or unless it appears that the initial accusations that established the case or controversy were made in bad faith or that the litigation was conducted in an unreasonable manner.[117]

Nonetheless, bringing suit on a patent despite knowledge of earlier sales that would invalidate it justifies a holding of exceptionality.[118] By the same token, continuing with litigation after learning of invalidating sales can justify attorney fees.[119] On the other hand, a patentee should not automatically be penalized for pursuing an infringement action after a determination of invalidity in another suit.[120]

The court has said that the only deterrent to the improper bringing of clearly unwarranted suits on obviously invalid or unenforceable patents is §285.[121] No award under §285 can fully compensate a defendant subjected to bad faith litigation, e.g., for loss of executives' time and missed business opportunities. Thus that defendant cannot be

---

[114]*J.P. Stevens Co. v. Lex Tex Ltd.,* 822 F.2d 1047, 3 USPQ2d 1235 (Fed. Cir. 1987). The argument was that the court's prior decision in *Rohm & Haas Co. v. Crystal Chem. Co.,* 736 F.2d 688, 222 USPQ 97 (Fed. Cir. 1984), compels such a result, but the court rejected the argument on the basis that such a result would improperly shift the burden of proof.

[115]*J.P. Stevens Co. v. Lex Tex Ltd.,* 822 F.2d 1047, 3 USPQ2d 1235 (Fed. Cir. 1987). Both invalidating a fraudulently procured patent and sustaining a valid one are public services. *Id.*

[116]*Advance Transformer Co. v. Levinson,* 837 F.2d 1081, 5 USPQ2d 1600 (Fed. Cir. 1988); *Machinery Corp. v. Gullfiber AB,* 774 F.2d 467, 227 USPQ 368 (Fed. Cir. 1985).

[117]*Advance Transformer Co. v. Levinson,* 837 F.2d 1081, 5 USPQ2d 1600 (Fed. Cir. 1988).

[118]*Interpart Corp. v. Italia,* 777 F.2d 678, 228 USPQ 124 (Fed. Cir. 1985).

[119]*Hughes v. Novi Am., Inc.,* 724 F.2d 122, 220 USPQ 707 (Fed. Cir. 1984).

[120]*Stevenson v. Sears, Roebuck & Co.,* 713 F.2d 705, 218 USPQ 969 (Fed. Cir. 1983). It should be noted that here there had been a Court of Customs and Patent Appeals decision affirming a prior holding of validity by the USITC, so that the award of fees by the district court would seem to have been particularly inappropriate. See also *Morton Int'l, Inc. v. Cardinal Chem. Co.,* 5 F.3d 1464, 28 USPQ2d 1190 (Fed. Cir. 1993).

[121]*Mathis v. Spears,* 857 F.2d 749, 8 USPQ2d 1029 (Fed. Cir. 1988). This may be an overstatement. Certainly the antitrust laws provide a powerful deterrent in appropriate cases.

fully returned to the situation it would have occupied if the wrong had not been committed. In determining the compensatory quantum of an award under §285 in such an egregious case, therefore, the courts should not be, and have not been, limited to ordinary reimbursement of only those amounts paid by the injured party for purely legal services or precluded from ordinary reimbursement of legitimate expenses defendant was unfairly forced to pay.[122] When confronted with litigation brought in bad faith, a court's exercise of its inherent power to rectify, at least in part, the injustice done the defendant serves additionally to defend the court and the judicial process against abuse.[123]

(c) Noninfringement

A frivolous infringement suit is one that the patentee knew or, on reasonable investigation, should have known was baseless. A frivolous suit can be exceptional for purposes of 35 U.S.C. §285.[124] The court has held that there is no difference in the standards applicable to patentees and those applicable to infringers who engage in bad faith litigation. The different interests of the patentee and alleged infringer are adequately taken into account in the required evaluation of the totality of the circumstances. Thus the court rejected an argument by the patentee that the district court had based a finding of exceptionality upon an improper application of a "simple negligence" standard. The patentee filed a baseless infringement case through studied ignorance, which is substantially more than simple negligence.[125]

Ascertaining a patentee's state of mind in sending infringement notice letters to the trade also requires the court to take into account the totality of the circumstances. Failure to obtain advice of counsel does not conclusively establish a patentee's bad faith or in itself make the case exceptional. There must be proof of actual wrongful intent or gross negligence. The gross negligence standard requires willful, wanton, or reckless misconduct, or evidence of utter lack of all care.[126] The court has found no abuse of discretion in refusing attorney fees for voluntary dismissal of an infringement count where the patent was added to the suit by stipulation and dismissed with the consent

---

Also, one is prompted to wonder when the defects in a patent reach the point that it can be said to be "obviously" invalid.

[122]*Mathis v. Spears,* 857 F.2d 749, 8 USPQ2d 1029 (Fed. Cir. 1988).

[123]*Mathis v. Spears,* 857 F.2d 749, 8 USPQ2d 1029 (Fed. Cir. 1988).

[124]*Haynes Int'l, Inc. v. Jessop Steel Co.,* 8 F.3d 1573, 28 USPQ2d 1652 (Fed. Cir. 1993). The Federal Circuit found that the patentee's claim of infringement was not baseless because it had a reasonable chance of proving literal infringement. Thus the lower court's award of attorney fees was an abuse of discretion and had to be reversed.

[125]*Eltech Sys. Corp. v. PPG Indus, Inc.,* 903 F.2d 805, 14 USPQ2d 1965 (Fed. Cir. 1990).

[126]*Machinery Corp. v. Gullfiber AB,* 774 F.2d 467, 227 USPQ 368 (Fed. Cir. 1985).

of the accused party.[127] In another case, the accused infringer sought attorney fees for failure of the patentee to investigate infringement before sending a warning letter. The accused infringer brought a declaratory judgment action seeking to have the patent declared not infringed, but the patentee promptly admitted no infringement and sought a settlement. These factors, in addition to the possibility that the accused infringer may have had alternatives to bringing the declaratory judgment action, seemed to carry the day for the patentee.[128]

The court has held that obtaining a sample of the defendant's composition and analyzing it prior to filing suit met the standards for prefiling inquiry under Rule 11, despite defendant's argument that the plaintiff did not make any effort to determine whether the composition was made by the patented method.[129]

It is neither illegal nor bad faith for an applicant to amend claims in view of a competitor's product.[130]

(d) Frivolous Defenses

An abuse of the judicial process resides as much in the presentation of a knowingly frivolous defense as in the filing of a knowingly frivolous complaint or appeal.[131] However, merely losing on the defenses of invalidity or noninfringement is not enough to make a case exceptional.[132] The Federal Circuit does not approve "boilerplate" answers and defenses, but something more in the way of vexatious tactics is necessary to establish that defenses are asserted in bad faith.[133] The court has indicated that an assertion of invalidity with no basis for it, or in the face of strong countervailing evidence (i.e., skepticism of the infringer's own engineers), might well be frivolous.[134]

---

[127]*Shatterproof Glass Corp. v. Libbey-Owens Ford Co.,* 758 F.2d 613, 225 USPQ 634 (Fed. Cir. 1985).

[128]*Machinery Corp. v. Gullfiber AB,* 774 F.2d 467, 227 USPQ 368 (Fed. Cir. 1985).

[129]*Cambridge Prods., Ltd. v. Penn Nutrients, Inc.,* 962 F.2d 1048, 22 USPQ2d 1577 (Fed. Cir. 1992). In a fascinating turnabout, the court went on to sanction the defendant's attorney personally for misrepresenting the import and content of the record on appeal. *Hoffmann-La-Roche Inc. v. Invamed Inc.,* 213 F.3d 1359, 54 USPQ2d 1846 (Fed. Cir. 2000), provides a good illustration of what the court regards as adequate prefiling investigation for purposes both of Rule 11 and §285.

[130]*Multiform Desiccants Inc. v. Medzam Ltd.,* 133 F.3d 1473, 45 USPQ2d 1429 (Fed. Cir. 1998).

[131]*Amstar Corp. v. Envirotech Corp.,* 730 F.2d 1476, 221 USPQ 649 (Fed. Cir. 1984).

[132]*State Indus., Inc. v. A.O. Smith Corp.,* 751 F.2d 1226, 224 USPQ 418 (Fed. Cir. 1985).

[133]*Stickle v. Heublein, Inc.,* 716 F.2d 1550, 219 USPQ 377 (Fed. Cir. 1983). See also *Beckman Instr., Inc. v. LKB Produkter AB,* 892 F.2d 1547, 13 USPQ2d 1301 (Fed. Cir. 1989).

[134]*Amstar Corp. v. Envirotech Corp.,* 730 F.2d 1476, 221 USPQ 649 (Fed. Cir. 1984). In *Serrano v. Telular Corp.,* 111 F.3d 1578, 42 USPQ2d 1538 (Fed. Cir. 1997), the court found no abuse in awarding attorney fees where the conduct of the party required relitigation of certain issues already decided in another case, and where the accused devices were only slightly different from the previously enjoined devices.

(e) Conduct of Litigation

Despite the availability of monetary sanctions, including attorney fees, under Rule 37, FRCP, it would not appear that Rule 37 and 35 U.S.C. §285 are mutually exclusive. Thus, abuses of the discovery process may well amount to bad faith conduct.[135] Other examples of arguably exceptional circumstances arising from the conduct of litigation have included the wrongful obtaining of an injunction,[136] the unfounded removal of a case from state to federal court,[137] and failure of the patentee's counsel to advise defense counsel that the patent in suit was in the process of reissue.[138] The court has held that, as a matter of law, vexatious litigation tactics must be taken into consideration in deciding whether to award attorney fees under §285. However, it observed that an improvident allegation of willfulness or resistance to the imposition of collateral estoppel does not automatically warrant such an award.[139]

In one case a patentee had initially opposed a stay of proceedings, urging a swift trial, when it was confident of the validity of the patent claims. But after a reissue proceeding resulted in a final rejection, it did an about-face and urged a stay. This was sufficient to justify an award of attorney fees.[140] Selective destruction of patent prosecution records that takes place after the patent owner begins contemplating litigation may support an exceptionality finding.[141]

Judgments of a district court concerning good and bad faith conduct of litigation are not easily overturned.[142] The district court judge is in the best position to monitor the parties' litigation conduct and is also the most injured by misconduct at the pretrial and trial stages.[143]

(f) Attorney Conduct

What is the role of the lawyer in exceptionality determinations? It is an understatement to suggest that counsel is very deeply and

---

[135]*Reactive Metals & Alloys Corp. v. ESM, Inc.*, 769 F.2d 1578, 226 USPQ 821 (Fed. Cir. 1985); *Western Mar. Elec., Inc. v. Furuno Elec. Co.*, 764 F.2d 840, 226 USPQ 334 (Fed. Cir. 1985).

[136]*Shelcore, Inc. v. Durham Indus., Inc.*, 745 F.2d 621, 223 USPQ 584 (Fed. Cir. 1984).

[137]*In re Oximetrix, Inc.*, 748 F.2d 637, 223 USPQ 1068 (Fed. Cir. 1984). Fees were awarded here under Rule 11, FRCP, and 28 U.S.C. §1927.

[138]*In re Mark Indus.*, 751 F.2d 1219, 224 USPQ 521 (Fed. Cir. 1984). See also *Beckman Instr., Inc. v. LKB Produkter AB*, 892 F.2d 1547, 13 USPQ2d 1301 (Fed. Cir. 1989).

[139]*Pharmacia & Upjohn Co. v. Mylan Pharm. Inc.*, 182 F.3d 1356, 51 USPQ2d 1466 (Fed. Cir. 1999).

[140]*L.E.A. Dynatech, Inc. v. Allina*, 49 F.3d 1527, 33 USPQ2d 1839 (Fed. Cir. 1995).

[141]*Molins PLC v. Textron, Inc.*, 48 F.3d 1172, 33 USPQ2d 1823 (Fed. Cir. 1995). The district court also had relied, in part, on clearly erroneous findings of inequitable conduct, so a remand was necessary. The court did recognize that companies are entitled to maintain file destruction programs without being found to have improperly destroyed evidence. But the district court can best determine whether any destruction was part of an established and legitimate records disposal program.

[142]*Spectra-Physics, Inc. v. Coherent, Inc.*, 827 F.2d 1524, 3 USPQ2d 1737 (Fed. Cir. 1987).

[143]*Molins PLC v. Textron, Inc.*, 48 F.3d 1172, 33 USPQ2d 1823, 1833 (Fed. Cir. 1995).

personally involved, especially in the Federal Circuit. Although the court has passed the question of whether a party is responsible for the knowledge and acts of its counsel,[144] it is well understood that bad faith displayed in pretrial or trial stages of a case, by counsel or a party, may render the case exceptional.[145] More than that, the lawyer may be personally liable. Counsel have been held jointly and severally liable, with their clients, for frivolous mandamus petitions[146] and appeals.[147]

The court has also indicated that attorney fees may be awarded against an agent of a corporate party, if the agent's own conduct supports an exceptional case finding. There must be clear and convincing evidence that its actions were in fact tortious or were undertaken in a personal capacity and not as an agent.[148]

(g) Appellate Activity

An appeal that is clearly hopeless and unquestionably without any possible basis in fact or law wastes the time of the court and of opposing counsel and imposes unnecessary costs on the parties and on fellow citizens whose taxes support the court and its staff.[149] This has been the guiding philosophy of the Federal Circuit as it has grappled with the concepts of frivolousness and exceptionality at the appellate level.

Quite early on the court squarely held that attorney fees could be awarded for appellate activity under 35 U.S.C. §285 in cases in which the appeal itself is exceptional.[150] Thus it would appear that fees can be awarded under both the frivolous appeal standard of Rule 38, FRAP, and under the exceptional case standard of 35 U.S.C. §285.[151] Appellate attorney fees are apparently the sole province of

---

[144]*Hughes v. Novi Am., Inc.*, 724 F.2d 122, 220 USPQ 707 (Fed. Cir. 1984). Here it was clear that the party's employees had independent knowledge.

[145]*Kloster Speedsteel AB v. Crucible Inc.*, 793 F.2d 1565, 230 USPQ 81 (Fed. Cir. 1986). It does not necessarily reflect bad faith for counsel to take inconsistent positions in two litigations. *Orthopedic Equip. Co. v. All Orthopedic Appls., Inc.*, 707 F.2d 1376, 217 USPQ 1281 (Fed. Cir. 1983).

[146]*In re Oximetrix, Inc.*, 748 F.2d 637, 223 USPQ 1068 (Fed. Cir. 1984).

[147]*Colt Indus. Oper. Corp. v. Index-Werke K.G.*, 739 F.2d 622 (Fed. Cir. 1984).

[148]*Machinery Corp. v. Gullfiber AB*, 774 F.2d 467, 227 USPQ 368 (Fed. Cir. 1985). Here the individual had undertaken to make an infringement investigation for the corporate patent owner, and the accused infringer was seeking fees on the ground that the infringement allegation had been made in bad faith.

[149]*Porter v. Farmers Supply Serv., Inc.*, 790 F.2d 882, 229 USPQ 814 (Fed. Cir. 1986).

[150]*Rohm & Haas Co. v. Crystal Chem. Co.*, 736 F.2d 688, 222 USPQ 97 (Fed. Cir. 1984). See also *Paper Converting Mach. Co. v. Magna-Graphics Corp.*, 788 F.2d 1536, 229 USPQ 480 (Fed. Cir. 1986).

[151]*Porter v. Farmers Supply Serv., Inc.*, 790 F.2d 882, 229 USPQ 814 (Fed. Cir. 1986). But see *Shelcore, Inc. v. Durham Indus., Inc.*, 745 F.2d 621, 223 USPQ 584 (Fed. Cir. 1984). Under Rule 38, FRAP, counsel against whom fees and costs for a frivolous appeal are assessed is not entitled to notice or a hearing. *Sun-Tek Indus., Inc. v. Kennedy Sky-Lites, Inc.*, 865 F.2d 1254, 9 USPQ2d 1574 (Fed. Cir. 1989).

the Federal Circuit,[152] and affirmance of the trial court's denial of fees does not preclude the court from awarding fees resulting from opposing a frivolous appeal.[153]

An award of the attorney fees and costs incurred in defending a frivolous appeal, made pursuant to Rule 38, FRAP, is unlike an award of attorney fees under various fee-shifting statutes that call for "reasonable" attorney fees. It is intended to deter frivolous appeals and thus preserve the appellate calendar for cases worthy of consideration. Thus, in the absence of exceptional circumstances, the Federal Circuit will not stop to inquire whether the fees were reasonable, but merely whether they were actually expended.[154]

The fact that a dissenting opinion was filed in an appeal tends to refute the idea that the appeal was so unreasonable as to render it exceptional conduct.[155] Similarly, a partially successful appeal is not frivolous.[156]

An appeal to the Federal Circuit, seeking clarification of an order of the Court of Appeals for the District of Columbia, was characterized as a form of procedural and semantic gamesmanship abusive of the judicial process and wasteful of resources of the parties and the court.[157] The filing of a mandamus petition, where its lack of basis was so clear in fact and law that competent counsel could not possibly have failed to recognize it, was likewise found to be frivolous.[158]

14.4 Attorney Fees

Under the American Rule each party bears its own attorney fees and expenses. As an exception to that rule, courts have exercised their inherent equitable power to make whole a party injured by an egregious abuse of the judicial process. But in patent cases, that power is apparently limited to "exceptional cases."[159] A federal court has inherent power to impose sanctions, and this includes shifting litigation costs where a party has acted in bad faith, vexatiously, wantonly, or for oppressive reasons. Statutes governing sanctions do not displace this inherent power. When statutes or rules provide an adequate sanction for bad faith, a trial court should ordinarily rely on those express authorities for sanctions. But if in the informed

---

[152]*Rohm & Haas Co. v. Crystal Chem. Co.*, 736 F.2d 688, 222 USPQ 97 (Fed. Cir. 1984).

[153]*Porter v. Farmers Supply Serv., Inc.*, 790 F.2d 882, 229 USPQ 814 (Fed. Cir. 1986).

[154]*Sun-Tek Indus., Inc. v. Kennedy Sky-Lites, Inc.*, 865 F.2d 1254, 9 USPQ2d 1574 (Fed. Cir. 1989).

[155]*Paper Converting Mach. Co. v. Magna-Graphics Corp.*, 788 F.2d 1536, 229 USPQ 480 (Fed. Cir. 1986).

[156]*Vandenberg v. Dairy Equip. Co.*, 740 F.2d 1560, 224 USPQ 195 (Fed. Cir. 1984).

[157]*Colt Indus. Oper. Corp. v. Index-Werke K.G.*, 739 F.2d 622 (Fed. Cir. 1984).

[158]*In re Oximetrix, Inc.*, 748 F.2d 637, 223 USPQ 1068 (Fed. Cir. 1984).

[159]*SunTek Indus., Inc. v. Kennedy Sky Lites, Inc.*, 929 F.2d 676, 18 USPQ2d 1332 (Fed. Cir. 1991).

discretion of the court, neither the statute nor the rules are up to the task, the court may safely rely on its inherent power. There must be a finding of fraud or abuse of the judicial process. The reviewing court must distinguish between inappropriate conduct redressable under 35 U.S.C. §284 or §285 and egregious conduct that justifies resort to the inherent power to sanction. The court should resort to its inherent power only where the rules or statutes do not reach the acts that degrade the legal system.[160]

The patent statute provides for an award of attorney fees to the "prevailing party" in exceptional cases.[161] Attorney fees under §285 may be awarded for time incurred in the litigation of legitimate patent claims. Attorney fees are awarded to a "prevailing party" and are not restricted to patent owners.[162] Under 35 U.S.C. §285, for a party to obtain an award of attorney fees, (1) the case must be exceptional; (2) the trial court may exercise discretion; (3) the fees must be reasonable; and (4) they may be awarded only to the prevailing party.[163] In order to "prevail" within the meaning of §285, a plaintiff must have achieved some of the benefits sought in bringing suit, i.e., damages or an injunction.[164] Nor are all successful defendants entitled to attorney fees. The requirement in §285 of establishing an exceptional case remains a formidable and adequate barrier to unwarranted awards.

---

[160]*Amsted Indus. v. Buckeye Steel Castings Co.*, 23 F.3d 374, 30 USPQ2d 1470 (Fed. Cir. 1994). In this case the trial court found that the defendant copied the patent, lacked a good faith belief that it was invalid, denied infringement in the face of evidence to the contrary, and burdened the court with numerous motions. However, there was no fraudulent conduct, no false pleadings, and no tactics of oppression and harassment. There was no discovery abuse, no misleading evidence presented at trial, and in general no conduct amounting to abuse of the judicial process. Thus, although this state of the record was held to support an award of increased damages and attorney fees under §§284 and 285, the Federal Circuit felt it did not support an exercise of discretion to award an addition sanction, under the trial court's equitable powers, of the expert witness fees expended by the plaintiff.

[161]E.g., *Beckman Instr., Inc. v. LKB Produkter AB*, 892 F.2d 1547, 13 USPQ2d 1301 (Fed. Cir. 1989).

[162]*Interspiro USA, Inc. v. Figgie Int'l, Inc.*, 18 F.3d 927, 30 USPQ2d 1070 (Fed. Cir. 1994). In *Automated Bus. Mach. Inc. v. NEC Am. Inc.*, 202 F.3d 1353, 53 USPQ2d 1601 (Fed. Cir. 2000), the court affirmed an award of attorney fees that included fees paid by the defendant's grandparent corporation. Apparently, neither control of the litigation nor degree of participation is a critical factor.

[163]*Machinery Corp. v. Gullfiber AB*, 774 F.2d 467, 227 USPQ 368 (Fed. Cir. 1985). In *SunTek Indus., Inc. v. Kennedy Sky Lites, Inc.*, 929 F.2d 676, 18 USPQ2d 1332 (Fed. Cir. 1991), the district court found that the case was not exceptional. Subsequently, at a stage in the proceedings where it lacked jurisdiction, it amended the judgment to award attorney fees. The award was vacated on appeal on jurisdictional grounds, but in the meantime the amended judgment had been executed. On remand, the district court erroneously refused to order restitution of the attorney fees. Inasmuch as the district court could not properly award fees in a case that was not found to be exceptional, it could not achieve that same result under the guise of exercising equitable powers to deny restitution.

[164]*Gentry Gallery, Inc. v. Berkline Corp.*, 134 F.3d 1473, 45 USPQ2d 1498 (Fed. Cir. 1998). A plaintiff that successfully withstands an equitable conduct defense but loses on validity is not a prevailing party. When a plaintiff succeeds only in overcoming a defense raised to the claim it asserted in bringing suit, it is not "the prevailing party." *Id.* Where a summary judgment is vacated and the case remanded, there is no "prevailing party" and thus no basis for an award of attorney fees under §285. *DH Tech. Inc. v. Synergystex Int'l Inc.*, 154 F.3d 1333, 47 USPQ2d 1865 (Fed. Cir. 1998).

Similarly, the §285 requirement that the fees awarded be "reasonable" is a safeguard against excessive reimbursement.[165] Federal Circuit precedent governs the substantive interpretation of §285, which is unique to patent law.[166]

The purpose of §285 is to provide discretion where it would be grossly unjust that the winner be left to bear the burden of its own counsel fees, which prevailing litigants normally bear.[167] It is intended to reimburse a party that is injured when forced to undergo an exceptional case, not the party's attorneys.[168] The purpose of §285 when applied to accused infringers is generally said to be two-fold: one, it discourages infringement by penalizing the infringer; and two, it prevents gross injustice when the accused infringer has litigated in bad faith. Where there is no willful infringement, the purpose of discouraging infringement is not relevant. But an attorney fee award can in such a case be justified by the need to prevent gross injustice. This can be based on such matters as bad faith or litigation misconduct.[169] Thus, a decision holding a patent invalid does not moot an inequitable conduct issue where the accused infringer seeks attorney fees as a result.[170]

It is not entirely clear whether the party must prevail totally or just on the appealed issues.[171] However, the court has indicated that it may be an abuse of discretion to award fees for an entire case in a situation where some claims are held valid and infringed and others held invalid or not infringed.[172] Similarly, it would seem that fees may have to be apportioned carefully with regard to whether they resulted from a vexatious litigation strategy.[173]

Attorney fees do not typically include taxable costs,[174] but they do cover expenses.[175] In *Mathis v. Spears*,[176] the court spoke at length on the subject of expenses under §285. In nonexceptional cases, the American Rule is that each party bears its own attorney fees and expenses. But courts have exercised their inherent equitable power

---

[165]*Mathis v. Spears,* 857 F.2d 749, 8 USPQ2d 1029 (Fed. Cir. 1988).

[166]*Pharmacia & Upjohn Co. v. Mylan Pharm. Inc.,* 182 F.3d 1356, 51 USPQ2d 1466 (Fed. Cir. 1999).

[167]*Badalamenti v. Dunham's, Inc.,* 896 F.2d 1359, 13 USPQ2d 1967 (Fed. Cir. 1990).

[168]*Mathis v. Spears,* 857 F.2d 749, 8 USPQ2d 1029 (Fed. Cir. 1988).

[169]*Beckman Instr., Inc. v. LKB Produkter AB,* 892 F.2d 1547, 13 USPQ2d 1301 (Fed. Cir. 1989). Where fees are awarded solely on the basis of litigation misconduct, the award must bear some relation to the extent of the misconduct. *Read Corp. v. Portec, Inc.,* 970 F.2d 816, 23 USPQ2d 1426 (Fed. Cir. 1992).

[170]*Paragon Podiatry Lab., Inc. v. KLM Labs., Inc.,* 984 F.2d 1182, 25 USPQ2d 1561 (Fed. Cir. 1993).

[171]*Radio Steel & Mfg. Co. v. MTD Prods., Inc.,* 731 F.2d 840, 221 USPQ 657 (Fed. Cir. 1984).

[172]*Beckman Instr., Inc. v. LKB Produkter AB,* 892 F.2d 1547, 13 USPQ2d 1301 (Fed. Cir. 1989).

[173]*Beckman Instr., Inc. v. LKB Produkter AB,* 892 F.2d 1547, 13 USPQ2d 1301 (Fed. Cir. 1989).

[174]*Bennett v. Department of Navy,* 699 F.2d 1140 (Fed. Cir. 1983).

[175]*Central Soya Co. v. Geo. A. Hormel & Co.,* 723 F.2d 1573, 220 USPQ 490 (Fed. Cir. 1983).

[176]*Mathis v. Spears,* 857 F.2d 749, 8 USPQ2d 1029 (Fed. Cir. 1988).

to make whole a party injured by an egregious abuse of the judicial process. Congress enacted §285 to codify in patent cases the "bad faith" equitable exception to the American Rule. The intent was to discourage conduct that falls within the scope of exceptionality, by reimbursing the prevailing party for the fees and expenses to which it was subjected by the exceptional conduct.

The *Mathis* court did not hold that all awards under §285 may or must include expenses, or expenses of any particular type or amount. The district court's inherent equitable power and informed discretion remain available in determining the level of exceptionality rising out of the offender's particular conduct and in then determining, in light of that conduct, the compensatory quantum of the award, including the amount of attorney fees, what if any expenses shall be included, and the rate of prejudgment interest, if any, on the award.[177]

Those include the reasonable and necessary out-of-pocket expenses of providing a lawyer's services that are not covered by the hourly rate because they cannot always be anticipated with any certainty in a given case, that are routinely paid by counsel and billed to the client, that are not taxable costs or prohibited by statute, and that are not expenses incurred for the mere convenience of counsel.[178] The *Mathis* decision makes it clear that an attorney fee award can include necessary and reasonable lodging expenses of multiple attorneys for multiple defendants, and expenses for secretarial and paralegal services that were incurred when the volume of work relating to the litigation exceeded the normal secretarial workday, resulting in an out-of-pocket cost above and beyond normal office salaries.[179] Although *Mathis* also held that expert witness fees are recoverable under 35 U.S.C. §285, that portion of the decision has since been effectively vitiated by Supreme Court precedent.[180] Thus, expert witness fees are not recoverable under 35 U.S.C. §285.[181]

Apparently there is no doubt that fees may be awarded for in-house counsel work, at least during the period when in-house counsel is lead trial counsel.[182]

---

[177]*Mathis v. Spears,* 857 F.2d 749, 8 USPQ2d 1029 (Fed. Cir. 1988).

[178]*Bennett v. Department of Navy,* 699 F.2d 1140 (Fed. Cir. 1983).

[179]*Mathis v. Spears,* 857 F.2d 749, 8 USPQ2d 1029 (Fed. Cir. 1988). Fees and expenses of experts and consultants are awardable under §285. *Beckman Instr., Inc. v. LKB Produkter AB,* 892 F.2d 1547, 13 USPQ2d 1301 (Fed. Cir. 1989).

[180]In *Crawford Fitting Co. v. J.T. Gibbons, Inc.,* 482 U.S. 437 (1987), the Court held that when a prevailing party seeks reimbursement for fees paid to its own expert witnesses, a federal court is, absent contract or explicit statutory authority to the contrary, bound by 28 U.S.C. §1821(b), which limits expert witness fee awards under §1920 to $40 a day for each day's attendance and for the time necessarily occupied in travel to and from the place of attendance. And in *West Virginia Univ. Hosps., Inc. v. Casey,* 499 U.S. 83 (1991), the Court held that attorney fees did not encompass expert witness fees; explicit statutory reference to expert witness fees is required in order to supersede 28 U.S.C. §1821(b).

[181]*Amsted Indus. v. Buckeye Steel Castings Co.,* 23 F.3d 374, 30 USPQ2d 1470 (Fed. Cir. 1994).

[182]*PPG Indus., Inc. v. Celanese Polymer Spec. Co.,* 840 F.2d 1565, 6 USPQ2d 1010 (Fed. Cir. 1988).

Proof of fees should include an accounting of hours, billing rates, and some evidence to show the reasonableness of the rates in the community. The records should be organized so that the court can review the reasonableness of the time expended.[183] There is no judicial requirement for contemporaneous time records to qualify for a fee award. While such records are the most desirable way of proving time spent, they are not the only means. Attorney fees are allowable if they are based on records that are substantially reconstructed and reasonably accurate.[184] A client's bill may, if sufficiently detailed, substitute for lost billing records. But there must be some evidence to support the reasonableness of the billing rate charged and the number of hours expended. Although the issue of fees should be settled in the most expeditious manner possible, there must be some findings, certainly more than an "equitable instinct," supporting the fee award in order to provide a base for appellate review.[185] Customary fees are factors in determining a reasonable attorney fee.[186]

Reasonable rates for in-house counsel are to be calculated based on cost plus overhead. To allow a private firm market standard for in-house work would be to allow a nonlegal business corporation to use the services of in-house counsel and reap a profit therefrom.[187]

Where a prevailing party has obtained excellent results, its attorney should recover a fully compensatory fee. Normally this will encompass all hours reasonably expended on the litigation.[188] Reasonableness is also comprehended by the requirement that the fees be for work actually done on issues covered by the statutory provision for the fees.[189] Fees can be awarded for defenses not tried. Litigants in good faith may raise alternative legal grounds for a desired outcome, and the court's rejection of or failure to reach certain grounds is not a sufficient reason for reducing a fee.[190]

---

[183]*Lam, Inc. v. Johns-Manville Corp.*, 718 F.2d 1056, 219 USPQ 670 (Fed. Cir. 1983).

[184]*PPG Indus., Inc. v. Celanese Polymer Spec. Co.*, 840 F.2d 1565, 6 USPQ2d 1010 (Fed. Cir. 1988). It was an abuse of discretion to refuse any fees for in-house counsel work where the underlying documentation for time spent was affidavits corroborated by business records, all prepared within two years of the end of the time period in question. The court did note, however, that insufficient documentation may warrant a reduction in fees. The amount was therefore left to the discretion of the district court on remand. *Id.* Insufficient documentation may warrant a reduction in fees, but it does not relieve the district court of its obligation to award a reasonable fee. *Slimfold Mfg. Co. v. Kinkead Indus.*, 932 F.2d 1453, 18 USPQ2d 1842 (Fed. Cir. 1991).

[185]*Water Techs. Corp. v. Calco, Ltd.*, 850 F.2d 660, 7 USPQ2d 1097 (Fed. Cir. 1988).

[186]*Mathis v. Spears*, 857 F.2d 749, 8 USPQ2d 1029 (Fed. Cir. 1988). It was not improper for the trial court to consider the results of American Intellectual Property Law Association surveys of rates.

[187]*PPG Indus., Inc. v. Celanese Polymer Spec. Co.*, 840 F.2d 1565, 6 USPQ2d 1010 (Fed. Cir. 1988).

[188]*Mathis v. Spears*, 857 F.2d 749, 8 USPQ2d 1029 (Fed. Cir. 1988).

[189]*Hughes v. Novi Am., Inc.*, 724 F.2d 122, 220 USPQ 707 (Fed. Cir. 1984).

[190]*Mathis v. Spears*, 857 F.2d 749, 8 USPQ2d 1029 (Fed. Cir. 1988).

Under §285, fees cannot be awarded for work on nonpatent issues.[191] The court has held that attorney fees under §285 may be awarded in an action to enforce an agreement settling a patent infringement case.[192] But care must be taken to assure that a fee award does not cover work done in connection with a claim that does not warrant attorney fees.[193] Only if the nonpatent issues are so intertwined with the patent issues that the evidence would in large measure be material to both can fees be awarded for the entire case.[194]

It seems clear that fee awards may cover work other than strictly that done at the trial court level. Thus, the power to award attorney fees for appellate work is not the exclusive domain of an appellate court, and the trial court may award fees for prior appeals where such appeals are an integral part of the ongoing litigation.[195]

What about administrative proceedings? In *Webb v. Dyer County Board*,[196] the Supreme Court held that attorney fees should not be awarded in nonmandatory, nonjudicial proceedings where the party has the option of proceeding directly to court, unless the party can demonstrate that the work product was both useful and of a type ordinarily necessary. In deciding that fees should be awarded for protester participation in a protested reissue proceeding, the Federal Circuit seemingly distinguished *Webb* on the ground that the protester's participation was mandatory, or nearly so. Thus the district court on remand was instructed not to evaluate whether the protester's work was useful and necessary: it was presumed to be so because it was the same work that would have been performed if the case had proceeded to trial.[197] It seems reasonable to expect that this ruling will be applied to reexamination proceedings as well. Work done in a reexamination by an opposing party would seem to be no less necessary and useful than the work of a protester in a reissue proceeding.

Certainly an award under §285 is not limited to fees paid for counsel's work at trial. Fees incurred in discovery that was necessary to the outcome of the case are properly included in an award.[198]

One decision can be read as suggesting that increased damages are typically intended to cover attorney fees in whole or in major

---

[191]*Petersen Mfg. Co. v. Central Purchasing, Inc.,* 740 F.2d 1541, 222 USPQ 562 (Fed. Cir. 1984).

[192]*Interspiro USA, Inc. v. Figgie Int'l, Inc.,* 18 F.3d 927, 30 USPQ2d 1070 (Fed. Cir. 1994). The reasoning implies that such a claim is one arising under the patent laws.

[193]*Water Techs. Corp. v. Calco, Ltd.,* 850 F.2d 660, 7 USPQ2d 1097 (Fed. Cir. 1988).

[194]*Stickle v. Heublein, Inc.,* 716 F.2d 1550, 219 USPQ 377 (Fed. Cir. 1983).

[195]*PPG Indus., Inc. v. Celanese Polymer Spec. Co.,* 840 F.2d 1565, 6 USPQ2d 1010 (Fed. Cir. 1988).

[196]471 U.S. 234 (1985).

[197]*PPG Indus., Inc. v. Celanese Polymer Spec. Co.,* 840 F.2d 1565, 6 USPQ2d 1010 (Fed. Cir. 1988). The court also held that it was an abuse of discretion to deny attorney fees incurred by the protester as an intervener in the applicant's previous appeal to the Federal Circuit from the PTO Board decision rejecting the reissue application.

[198]*Mathis v. Spears,* 857 F.2d 749, 8 USPQ2d 1029 (Fed. Cir. 1988).

part.[199] A district court has discretion to award prejudgment interest on attorney fee awards under §285, but need not do so in every case, indeed, not even in every exceptional case.[200]

The liability of nonparties for fee awards is discussed in §8.2(a).[201]

14.5 Standard of Proof and Review

A finding of willfulness requires the fact finder to find that clear and convincing evidence shows that the infringer acted in disregard of the patent and had no reasonable basis for believing that it had a right to do the acts. This is a factual determination to be made after consideration of the totality of the circumstances. In making a determination of willfulness, the court is also required to consider mitigating or ameliorating factors. The determination is reviewed under a clearly erroneous standard.[202] Rule 52(a), FRCP, applies.[203] Because willfulness raises issues of reasonableness and prudence, and is often accompanied by questions of intent, belief, and credibility, appellate review requires appropriate deference to the special role of the trial court in making such determinations. Thus, a finding that infringement was not willful will be sustained unless the reviewing court has a definite and firm conviction that the trier of fact erred.[204]

Indeed, the broader determination of exceptionality is factual and is reviewed for clear error.[205] The prevailing party has the burden

---

[199]*Paper Converting Mach. Co. v. Magna-Graphics Corp.*, 788 F.2d 1536, 229 USPQ 480 (Fed. Cir. 1986).

[200]*Mathis v. Spears*, 857 F.2d 749, 8 USPQ2d 1029 (Fed. Cir. 1988).

[201]See, e.g., note 8:344.

[202]*American Med. Sys., Inc. v. Medical Eng'g Corp.*, 6 F.3d 1523, 28 USPQ2d 1321 (Fed. Cir. 1993). Willful infringement is a question of fact, reviewable under the clearly erroneous standard. *Bic Leisure Prods., Inc. v. Windsurfing Int'l, Inc.*, 1 F.3d 1214, 27 USPQ2d 1671 (Fed. Cir. 1993); *Westvaco Corp. v. International Paper Co.*, 991 F.2d 735, 26 USPQ2d 1353 (Fed. Cir. 1993); *L.A. Gear, Inc. v. Thom McAn Shoe Co.*, 988 F.2d 1117, 25 USPQ2d 1913 (Fed. Cir. 1993); *State Indus., Inc. v. Mor-Flo Indus., Inc.*, 883 F.2d 1573, 12 USPQ2d 1026 (Fed. Cir. 1989); *Avia Group Int'l, Inc. v. L.A. Gear Calif., Inc.*, 853 F.2d 1557, 7 USPQ2d 1548 (Fed. Cir. 1988); *Bott v. Four Star Corp.*, 807 F.2d 1567, 1 USPQ2d 1210 (Fed. Cir. 1986); *Kaufman Co. v. Lantech*, 807 F.2d 970, 1 USPQ2d 1202 (Fed. Cir. 1986); *CPG Prods. Corp. v. Pegasus Luggage, Inc.*, 776 F.2d 1007, 227 USPQ 497 (Fed. Cir. 1985); *Ralston Purina Co. v. Far-Mar-Co, Inc.*, 772 F.2d 1570, 227 USPQ 177 (Fed. Cir. 1985); *Kori Corp. v. Wilco Marsh Buggies, Inc.*, 761 F.2d 649, 225 USPQ 985 (Fed. Cir. 1985); *Leinoff v. Louis Milona & Sons*, 726 F.2d 734, 220 USPQ 845 (Fed. Cir. 1984); *Underwater Devices, Inc. v. Morrison-Knudsen Co.*, 717 F.2d 1380, 219 USPQ 569 (Fed. Cir. 1983).

[203]*Gustafson, Inc. v. Intersystems Indus. Prods., Inc.*, 897 F.2d 508, 13 USPQ2d 1972 (Fed. Cir. 1990); *Paper Converting Mach. Co. v. Magna-Graphics Corp.*, 785 F.2d 1013, 228 USPQ 938 (Fed. Cir. 1986).

[204]*Georgia-Pacific Corp. v. United States Gypsum Co.*, 195 F.3d 1322, 52 USPQ2d 1590 (Fed. Cir. 1999). The factual question of willful infringement is reviewed under the clearly erroneous standard. To overturn such a finding, the appellate court must have a firm conviction that a mistake was committed by the district court. *Rite-Hite Corp. v. Kelley Co.*, 819 F.2d 1120, 2 USPQ2d 1915 (Fed. Cir. 1987).

[205]*Fromson v. Western Litho Plate & Supp. Co.*, 853 F.2d 1568, 7 USPQ2d 1606 (Fed. Cir. 1988); *Spectra-Physics, Inc. v. Coherent, Inc.*, 827 F.2d 1524, 3 USPQ2d 1737 (Fed. Cir. 1987);

of proving by clear and convincing evidence that the case is exceptional.[206] Thus the standard of proof for willful infringement[207] and other types of exceptional conduct[208] is clear and convincing evidence. A finding of willful infringement is based upon a totality of the circumstances.[209] To establish willful infringement, a plaintiff must prove by clear and convincing evidence that the defendant acted with no reasonable basis for believing it had the right to do so. There are no hard and fast per se rules.[210]

Whether the infringer had a reasonable belief that the accused activity did not violate the law is a question of fact, as are other questions relevant to the issue of willfulness. Although fairness as between patentee and infringer is a consideration in the determination of whether illegal behavior warrants an enhanced penalty, the question does not thereby become "equitable." The issue of willful infringement remains with the trier of fact.[211] Absent sufficient basis for directing a verdict, a party has a right to jury determination of the question of willful infringement. Willfulness of behavior is a classical jury question of intent.[212] Thus, in a jury case, if there is any set of facts supported by substantial evidence and capable of supporting a jury determination of willfulness, it will be upheld.[213] Where a district court decides the attorney fees award on its merits, and enters a "final and appealable order," the order is a final decision over which the Federal Circuit may exercise appellate review.[214]

Kloster Speedsteel AB v. Crucible Inc., 793 F.2d 1565, 230 USPQ 81 (Fed. Cir. 1986). That the appellate court, sitting at trial, might have differently appraised the suit, is not a basis for holding that the district court's appraisal was erroneous. *Porter v. Farmers Supply Serv., Inc.,* 790 F.2d 882, 229 USPQ 814 (Fed. Cir. 1986).

[206]*Badalamenti v. Dunham's, Inc.,* 896 F.2d 1359, 13 USPQ2d 1967 (Fed. Cir. 1990).

[207]*Braun Inc. v. Dynamics Corp.,* 975 F.2d 815, 24 USPQ2d 1121 (Fed. Cir. 1992); *State Indus., Inc. v. Mor-Flo Indus., Inc.,* 883 F.2d 1573, 12 USPQ2d 1026 (Fed. Cir. 1989); *E.I. duPont & Co. v. Phillips Petroleum Co.,* 849 F.2d 1430, 7 USPQ2d 1129 (Fed. Cir. 1988).

[208]*Beckman Instr., Inc. v. LKB Produkter AB,* 892 F.2d 1547, 13 USPQ2d 1301 (Fed. Cir. 1989).

[209]*Minnesota Min. & Mfg. Co. v. Johnson & Johnson Orthopaedics, Inc.,* 976 F.2d 1559, 24 USPQ2d 1321 (Fed. Cir. 1992); *Braun Inc. v. Dynamics Corp.,* 975 F.2d 815, 24 USPQ2d 1121 (Fed. Cir. 1992); *Bott v. Four Star Corp.,* 807 F.2d 1567, 1 USPQ2d 1210 (Fed. Cir. 1986); *Kaufman Co. v. Lantech,* 807 F.2d 970, 1 USPQ2d 1202 (Fed. Cir. 1986); *Orthokinetics, Inc. v. Safety Travel Chairs, Inc.,* 806 F.2d 1565, 1 USPQ2d 1081 (Fed. Cir. 1986).

[210]*State Indus., Inc. v. Mor-Flo Indus., Inc.,* 883 F.2d 1573, 12 USPQ2d 1026 (Fed. Cir. 1989); *Studiengesellschaft Kohle v. Dart Indus., Inc.,* 862 F.2d 1564, 9 USPQ2d 1273 (Fed. Cir. 1988).

[211]*National Presto Indus., Inc. v. West Bend Co.,* 76 F.3d 1185, 37 USPQ2d 1685 (Fed. Cir. 1996).

[212]*Richardson v. Suzuki Motor Co.,* 868 F.2d 1226, 9 USPQ2d 1913 (Fed. Cir. 1989).

[213]*Orthokinetics, Inc. v. Safety Travel Chairs, Inc.,* 806 F.2d 1565, 1 USPQ2d 1081 (Fed. Cir. 1986). Infringement and willful infringement are not the same thing, and a motion for directed verdict on infringement will not cure a failure to move for directed verdict on willful infringement. *Id.* A jury's determination as to willfulness is reviewable under the substantial evidence standard. *Braun Inc. v. Dynamics Corp.,* 975 F.2d 815, 24 USPQ2d 1121 (Fed. Cir. 1992). See also *Hoechst Celanese Corp. v. BP Chem. Ltd.,* 78 F.3d 1575, 38 USPQ2d 1126 (Fed. Cir. 1996).

[214]*PPG Indus., Inc. v. Celanese Polymer Spec. Co.,* 840 F.2d 1565, 6 USPQ2d 1010 (Fed. Cir. 1988).

Once there is a finding of willfulness or bad faith, the decision whether to award attorney fees, and if so, in what amount, is within the discretion of the trial judge.[215] For fee-shifting issues particular deference is due to the trial judge, who had the opportunity to observe those intangibles missing from the appellate record.[216] In reviewing an award of attorney fees, the Federal Circuit first considers whether the district court's fact finding of an exceptional case was clearly erroneous, and whether the district court invoked the proper legal standards in making that decision. It then considers whether there was an abuse of discretion as to the award. The principles that guide review of discretion are whether the district court's decision was based on an erroneous conclusion of law or clearly erroneous factual findings, or whether the district court committed a clear error of judgment.[217]

Increased damages are also discretionary with the district court.[218] The mere fact that a district court declines to award the increased damages that may accompany a finding of willful infringement does not mean that the court found the infringement not willful.[219] Where an appellant cannot show the district court's finding of nonwillfulness to be clearly erroneous, there is no need to reach the question of whether the district court abused its discretion in declining to award increased damages or costs.[220]

Although a finding that a case is not exceptional has been said to be clearly within the discretion of the trial court,[221] the Federal Circuit has since taken pains to explain that the discretion of the

---

[215]*Badalamenti v. Dunham's, Inc.*, 896 F.2d 1359, 13 USPQ2d 1967 (Fed. Cir. 1990); *Gardco Mfg., Inc. v. Herst Lighting Co.*, 820 F.2d 1209, 2 USPQ2d 2015 (Fed. Cir. 1987); *Bott v. Four Star Corp.*, 807 F.2d 1567, 1 USPQ2d 1210 (Fed. Cir. 1986); *Kloster Speedsteel AB v. Crucible Inc.*, 793 F.2d 1565, 230 USPQ 81 (Fed. Cir. 1986); *S.C. Johnson & Son v. Carter-Wallace, Inc.*, 781 F.2d 198, 228 USPQ 367 (Fed. Cir. 1986); *Korody-Colyer Corp. v. General Motors Corp.*, 760 F.2d 1293, 225 USPQ 1099 (Fed. Cir. 1985); *Bayer Aktiengesellschaft v. Duphar Int'l Research B.V.*, 738 F.2d 1237, 222 USPQ 649 (Fed. Cir. 1984); *Hughes v. Novi Am., Inc.*, 724 F.2d 122, 220 USPQ 707 (Fed. Cir. 1984); *White Consol. Indus., Inc. v. Vega Servo-Control, Inc.*, 713 F.2d 788, 218 USPQ 961 (Fed. Cir. 1983).

[216]*Brooktree Corp. v. Advanced Micro-Devices, Inc.*, 977 F.2d 1555, 24 USPQ2d 1401 (Fed. Cir. 1992).

[217]*PPG Indus., Inc. v. Celanese Polymer Spec. Co.*, 840 F.2d 1565, 6 USPQ2d 1010 (Fed. Cir. 1988). See also *Cybor Corp. v. FAS Tech. Inc.*, 138 F.3d 1448, 46 USPQ2d 1169 (Fed. Cir. 1998); *Amsted Indus. v. Buckeye Steel Castings Co.*, 24 F.3d 178, 30 USPQ2d 1462 (Fed. Cir. 1994); *Beckman Instr., Inc. v. LKB Produkter AB*, 892 F.2d 1547, 13 USPQ2d 1301 (Fed. Cir. 1989). An award of attorney fees without basis in the record is an abuse of discretion. *Gustafson, Inc. v. Intersystems Indus. Prods., Inc.*, 897 F.2d 508, 13 USPQ2d 1972 (Fed. Cir. 1990). An award of attorney fees under Rules 11 or 37, FRCP, is likewise subject to review under an abuse of discretion standard. *New Idea Farm Equip. Corp. v. Sperry Corp.*, 916 F.2d 1561, 16 USPQ2d 1424 (Fed. Cir. 1990). The abuse of discretion standard governs review of decisions about sanctions and attorney fees under Rule 11 and 35 U.S.C. §285. *Cambridge Prods., Ltd. v. Penn Nutrients, Inc.*, 962 F.2d 1048, 22 USPQ2d 1577 (Fed. Cir. 1992).

[218]*State Indus., Inc. v. Mor-Flo Indus. Inc.*, 948 F.2d 1573, 20 USPQ2d 1738 (Fed. Cir. 1991); *Rosemount, Inc. v. Beckman Instr., Inc.*, 727 F.2d 1540, 221 USPQ 1 (Fed. Cir. 1984).

[219]*Kloster Speedsteel AB v. Crucible Inc.*, 793 F.2d 1565, 230 USPQ 81 (Fed. Cir. 1986).

[220]*Amstar Corp. v. Envirotech Corp.*, 823 F.2d 1538, 3 USPQ2d 1412 (Fed. Cir. 1987).

[221]*Orthopedic Equip. Co. v. All Orthopedic Appls., Inc.*, 707 F.2d 1376, 217 USPQ 1281 (Fed. Cir. 1983).

district court comes into play only after there has been a conclusion of exceptionality, reached without clear error in factual finding and with application of correct legal standards. Once the case is found to be exceptional, the district court may, but need not, award fees. Thus it is incorrect to say, ever, that exceptionality is a matter within the discretion of the lower court,[222] or of the jury in a jury case.[223] The proper approach to a motion for attorney fees under 35 U.S.C. §285 requires a two-step analysis. The district court must determine whether the case is exceptional; if it is, then it is within the court's discretion to award attorney fees to the prevailing party. It is only after a specific finding of exceptional circumstances has been made that the discretion to award attorney fees can be exercised. A decision concerning the award of attorney fees is reviewable only to determine whether the court has abused its discretion. An abuse of discretion may be established by showing that the district court either made an error of law, or a clear error of judgment, or exercised its discretion on findings that were clearly erroneous.[224]

Thus a finding of exceptional circumstances does not mandate an award of attorney fees,[225] nor does a finding of willful infringement demand an increase in damages.[226] Many factors can influence the decision, and the trial judge is in the best position to weigh considerations such as the closeness of the case, the tactics of counsel, the conduct of the parties, and any other factors that may contribute to a fair allocation of the burdens of litigation as between winner and

---

[222]*Reactive Metals & Alloys Corp. v. ESM, Inc.*, 769 F.2d 1578, 226 USPQ 821 (Fed. Cir. 1985). See also *Kloster Speedsteel AB v. Crucible Inc.*, 793 F.2d 1565, 230 USPQ 81 (Fed. Cir. 1986); *Hycor Corp. v. Schlueter Co.*, 740 F.2d 1529, 222 USPQ 553 (Fed. Cir. 1984).

[223]*Shiley, Inc. v. Bentley Labs., Inc.*, 794 F.2d 1561, 230 USPQ 112 (Fed. Cir. 1986). Increased damages are assigned to the court, whether the facts of willful infringement justifying an increase are found by a jury or by the court. If the jury finds willful infringement, and if that finding is not overturned on motion for JNOV, then the court has discretion to award increased damages. If the finding of the jury is no willful infringement, and that is not overturned on motion, no basis for assessing increased damages exists.

[224]*J.P. Stevens Co. v. Lex Tex Ltd.*, 822 F.2d 1047, 3 USPQ2d 1235 (Fed. Cir. 1987).

[225]*Odetics Inc. v. Storage Tech. Corp.*, 185 F.3d 1259, 51 USPQ2d 1225 (Fed. Cir. 1999); *Avia Group Int'l, Inc. v. L.A. Gear Calif., Inc.*, 853 F.2d 1557, 7 USPQ2d 1548 (Fed. Cir. 1988); *Reactive Metals & Alloys Corp. v. ESM, Inc.*, 769 F.2d 1578, 226 USPQ 821 (Fed. Cir. 1985). In *J.P. Stevens Co. v. Lex Tex Ltd.*, 822 F.2d 1047, 3 USPQ2d 1235 (Fed. Cir. 1987), a prior Federal Circuit holding of inequitable conduct was used by the trial court to support its conclusion that the case was exceptional. Somewhat surprisingly, the Federal Circuit nonetheless found no abuse of discretion in the lower court's denial of attorney fees. See also *Gardco Mfg., Inc. v. Herst Lighting Co.*, 820 F.2d 1209, 2 USPQ2d 2015 (Fed. Cir. 1987).

[226]Cf. *Brooktree Corp. v. Advanced Micro Devices, Inc.*, 977 F.2d 1555, 24 USPQ2d 1401 (Fed. Cir. 1992); *Kloster Speedsteel AB v. Crucible Inc.*, 793 F.2d 1565, 230 USPQ 81 (Fed. Cir. 1986). The patent statute's provision for increased damages is permissive not mandatory: a court "may" increase the damages up to three times the amount found or assessed. *State Indus., Inc. v. Mor-Flo Indus. Inc.*, 948 F.2d 1573, 20 USPQ2d 1738 (Fed. Cir. 1991). See also *Odetics Inc. v. Storage Tech. Corp.*, 185 F.3d 1259, 51 USPQ2d 1225 (Fed. Cir. 1999). There is no merit to an argument that a finding of willfulness but a denial of enhanced damages is necessarily an abuse of discretion. *Cybor Corp. v. FAS Tech. Inc.*, 138 F.3d 1448, 46 USPQ2d 1169 (Fed. Cir. 1998).

loser.[227] The trial judge is better able to assess the conduct of parties appearing before it than is the appellate court. Questions of misconduct often involve the tone and tenor of advocacy, rather than the literal words of the advocate. In such instances, a cold printed record cannot fully convey the aspects of conduct that a trial court might find egregious. Thus the Federal Circuit is careful to avoid substituting its assessment of facts for those of the judge who experienced them firsthand.[228] A trial court's exercise of discretion as to increased damages is informed by its familiarity with the matter in litigation and the interest of justice.[229]

To enable appellate review, a district court is obligated to explain the basis for an award of enhanced damages, particularly where the maximum amount is imposed. In order to impose the maximum trebling, the court's assessment of the level of culpability must be high.[230] The discretionary authority of the trial court in these matters will not be lightly disturbed.[231] The standard of review is abuse of discretion,[232] and awards of attorney fees cannot be overturned unless the trial court abuses its discretion or makes its determination with an erroneous conception of the law.[233]

But the exercise of discretion, though broad, is not unrestrained. The court's choice of discretionary ruling should be in furtherance of

---

[227]*National Presto Indus., Inc. v. West Bend Co.,* 76 F.3d 1185, 37 USPQ2d 1685 (Fed. Cir. 1996); *J.P. Stevens Co. v. Lex Tex Ltd.,* 822 F.2d 1047, 3 USPQ2d 1235 (Fed. Cir. 1987); *S.C. Johnson & Son v. Carter-Wallace, Inc.,* 781 F.2d 198, 228 USPQ 367 (Fed. Cir. 1986). See also *In re Mark Indus.,* 751 F.2d 1219, 224 USPQ 521 (Fed. Cir. 1984). Insufficient documentation may warrant a reduction in fees in the discretion of the district court. *PPG Indus., Inc. v. Celanese Polymer Spec. Co.,* 840 F.2d 1565, 6 USPQ2d 1010 (Fed. Cir. 1988). In *Virginia Panel Corp. v. MAC Panel Co.,* 133 F.3d 860, 45 USPQ2d 1225 (Fed. Cir. 1997), the jury found willful infringement, but the judge only awarded 10% enhancement of damages and denied attorney fees. This was not an abuse of discretion, based on the following findings: (1) the copying was only recklessly indifferent as opposed to deliberate, (2) the infringer conducted a marginally sufficient investigation of the asserted patents, albeit upon incomplete information, (3) its behavior as a party to the litigation was not unacceptable, (4) many of the issues were close questions, and (5) a large enhancement could drive the infringer out of business.

[228]*Motorola, Inc. v. Interdigital Tech. Corp.,* 121 F.3d 1461, 43 USPQ2d 1481 (Fed. Cir. 1997).

[229]*Del Mar Avionics, Inc. v. Quinton Instr. Co.,* 836 F.2d 1320, 5 USPQ2d 1255 (Fed. Cir. 1987). An award of double damages was affirmed in the face of contentions by the patentee that the award should have been trebled and by the infringer that there should have been no increase. In *In re Hayes Microcomputer Patent Litig.,* 982 F.2d 1527, 25 USPQ2d 1241 (Fed. Cir. 1992), the district court doubled the prejudgment damages and granted a permanent injunction, but then stayed the injunction pending appeal and required the infringer to pay a royalty into escrow during the pendency of the appeal. The patent owner argued that the court should have enhanced the interim escrowed royalty as well, but the Federal Circuit found no abuse of discretion in failing to do so.

[230]*Read Corp. v. Portec, Inc.,* 970 F.2d 816, 23 USPQ2d 1426 (Fed. Cir. 1992).

[231]*J.P. Stevens Co. v. Lex Tex Ltd.,* 822 F.2d 1047, 3 USPQ2d 1235 (Fed. Cir. 1987); *S.C. Johnson & Son v. Carter-Wallace, Inc.,* 781 F.2d 198, 228 USPQ 367 (Fed. Cir. 1986).

[232]*Korody-Colyer Corp. v. General Motors Corp.,* 760 F.2d 1293, 225 USPQ 1099 (Fed. Cir. 1985); *Hughes v. Novi Am., Inc.,* 724 F.2d 122, 220 USPQ 707 (Fed. Cir. 1984). The Federal Circuit reviews an award of attorney fees under the highly deferential abuse of discretion standard. *L.E.A. Dynatech, Inc. v. Allina,* 49 F.3d 1527, 33 USPQ2d 1839 (Fed. Cir. 1995).

[233]*Bayer Aktiengesellschaft v. Duphar Int'l Research B.V.,* 738 F.2d 1237, 222 USPQ 649 (Fed. Cir. 1984).

the policies of the laws that are being enforced, as informed by the court's familiarity with the matter in litigation and the interest of justice.[234] Findings adequate to permit meaningful review of the trial court's exercise of discretion are essential.[235] A finding of exceptionality is one of fact. A district court need follow no prescribed grammatical formulation in expressing its findings and conclusions, but the reviewing court must attempt to discern from the district court's opinion or action the bases, albeit unexpressed, for its findings and conclusions. Such discernment cannot be made from the naked phrase "not appropriate" in connection with attorney fees.[236] Not only is it incumbent upon a trial court to articulate the basis for a finding of exceptional circumstances, but it is equally necessary to explain why the case was not exceptional in the face of a finding of willful infringement.[237]

---

[234]*S.C. Johnson & Son v. Carter-Wallace, Inc.*, 781 F.2d 198, 228 USPQ 367 (Fed. Cir. 1986). Compare *J.P. Stevens Co. v. Lex Tex Ltd.*, 822 F.2d 1047, 3 USPQ2d 1235 (Fed. Cir. 1987).

[235]*S.C. Johnson & Son v. Carter-Wallace, Inc.*, 781 F.2d 198, 228 USPQ 367 (Fed. Cir. 1986); *Reactive Metals & Alloys Corp. v. ESM, Inc.*, 769 F.2d 1578, 226 USPQ 821 (Fed. Cir. 1985); *Paper Converting Mach. Co. v. Magna-Graphics Corp.*, 745 F.2d 11, 223 USPQ 591 (Fed. Cir. 1984); *Petersen Mfg. Co. v. Central Purchasing, Inc.*, 740 F.2d 1541, 222 USPQ 562 (Fed. Cir. 1984); *Hughes v. Novi Am., Inc.*, 724 F.2d 122, 220 USPQ 707 (Fed Cir. 1984). Findings in support of an award or denial of increased damages and attorney fees for willfulness must be made in the first instance by the trial court. *Fromson v. Western Litho Plate & Supp. Co.*, 853 F.2d 1568, 7 USPQ2d 1606 (Fed. Cir. 1988). While a finding of willful infringement does not mandate that damages be increased or that attorney fees be awarded, after an express finding of willful infringement a trial court should provide reasons for not increasing a damages award or for not finding a case exceptional for the purpose of awarding attorneys fees. Failure so to do can result in a remand. *Tate Access Floors Inc. v. Maxcess Tech. Inc.*, 222 F.3d 958, 55 USPQ2d 1513 (Fed. Cir. 2000). Remands for findings on exceptionality and attorney fees are unfortunate, and the parties should provide the district court an opportunity to explain or clarify its decision if possible. *Badalamenti v. Dunham's, Inc.*, 896 F.2d 1359, 13 USPQ2d 1967 (Fed. Cir. 1990). Where the record provides a sufficient basis upon which to review the trial court's exercise of discretion in denying attorney fees, no useful purpose would be served by a remand to enable the district court to tell the Federal Circuit in express terms what it already knows from the record. *Carroll Touch, Inc. v. Electro Mechanical Sys., Inc.*, 3 F.3d 404, 27 USPQ2d 1836 (Fed. Cir. 1993). Though findings on exceptionality and reasons underlying discretionary action on attorney fees are helpful to an appellate court, remand should not be a matter of rote in every case in which findings and reasons are not expressly set forth. An appellate court need not close its eyes to the record where there is a way clearly open to affirm the district court's action. *Consolidated Alum Corp. v. Foseco Int'l Ltd.*, 910 F.2d 804, 15 USPQ2d 1481 (Fed. Cir. 1990). However, where there was clear error in a finding of willfulness, requiring reversal of an increased damages award, the court also remanded the award of attorney fees that might nonetheless have been supportable on the record. The court seemed to feel that the erroneous willfulness finding might well have tainted the attorney fees award. *Westvaco Corp. v. International Paper Co.*, 991 F.2d 735, 26 USPQ2d 1353 (Fed. Cir. 1993). See also *Sensonics, Inc. v. Aerosonic Corp.*, 81 F.3d 1566, 38 USPQ2d 1551 (Fed. Cir. 1996).

[236]*Fromson v. Western Litho Plate & Supp. Co.*, 853 F.2d 1568, 7 USPQ2d 1606 (Fed. Cir. 1988). Accordingly, the case was remanded for an ultimate finding on exceptionality, accompanied by subsidiary findings reflecting the reasons underlying the district court's exercise of its discretion in awarding or denying attorney fees in light of its findings. Apparently §285 does not require that the district court actually use the word "exceptional" when awarding attorney fees, however. To vacate such an award on that basis would be to exalt form over substance, especially where the record supports such an award. *Goodwall Constr. Co. v. Beers Constr. Co.*, 991 F.2d 751, 26 USPQ2d 1420 (Fed. Cir. 1993).

[237]*Fromson v. Western Litho Plate & Supp. Co.*, 853 F.2d 1568, 7 USPQ2d 1606 (Fed. Cir. 1988); *S.C. Johnson & Son v. Carter-Wallace, Inc.*, 781 F.2d 198, 228 USPQ 367 (Fed. Cir. 1986). In *Jurgens v. CBK, Ltd.*, 80 F.3d 1566, 38 USPQ2d 1397 (Fed. Cir. 1996), the jury found bad faith infringement and the trial court held there was substantial evidence to support that

It seems clear that an exercise of discretion in denying attorney fees should focus on the unjustness of the denial as well as the conduct of the wrongful party.[238]

The party who seeks an award of attorney fees has the burden of proof of facts to establish the exceptional character of the case[239] by clear and convincing evidence.[240] A party does not waive a specifically pleaded claim for attorney fees under §285 by failing to include it in a motion for summary judgment of invalidity that is granted.[241]

The methodology of assessing a reasonable award of attorney fees under §285 is within the discretion of the district court. To show that the district court abused that discretion, the appellant must convince the reviewing court that the district court based its award on clearly erroneous factual findings, legal error, or a manifest error of judgment.[242] Federal appellate courts may review jury awards of punitive damages based on state law claims. The reviewing court must keep a verdict for punitive damages within reasonable bounds, considering the purpose to be achieved as well as the culpability of the defendant in the particular case. A punitive damage award must bear a reasonable relationship to plaintiff's injury and defendant's malicious intent, and must not become in part a windfall to the individual litigant.[243]

---

finding. Nonetheless, it refused to increase damages or award attorney fees on the grounds that the plaintiff did not clearly mark its own devices and that the defendant had obtained an opinion of counsel. This was found to be an abuse of discretion. In order to find bad faith, the jury necessarily had to reject reliance on the opinion of counsel. As for marking, the jury necessarily had determined that the defendant had notice of the patent.

[238]*J.P. Stevens Co. v. Lex Tex Ltd.*, 822 F.2d 1047, 3 USPQ2d 1235 (Fed. Cir. 1987). In *L.E.A. Dynatech, Inc. v. Allina*, 49 F.3d 1527, 33 USPQ2d 1839 (Fed. Cir. 1995), the court was able to pass the interesting question of whether the district court might not have abused its discretion in awarding fees, where the award would likely bankrupt the party.

[239]*Reactive Metals & Alloys Corp. v. ESM, Inc.*, 769 F.2d 1578, 226 USPQ 821 (Fed. Cir. 1985). It would improperly shift the burden to establish a rule that one who succeeds in invalidating a fraudulently procured patent should be awarded attorney fees unless the patentee can show compelling countervailing circumstances. *J.P. Stevens Co. v. Lex Tex Ltd.*, 822 F.2d 1047, 3 USPQ2d 1235 (Fed. Cir. 1987).

[240]*Carroll Touch, Inc. v. Electro Mechanical Sys., Inc.*, 3 F.3d 404, 27 USPQ2d 1836 (Fed. Cir. 1993). The standard of proof required to prove bad faith conduct is clear and convincing evidence. *Loctite Corp. v. Ultraseal Ltd.*, 781 F.2d 861, 228 USPQ 90 (Fed. Cir. 1985); *Reactive Metals & Alloys Corp. v. ESM, Inc.*, 769 F.2d 1578, 226 USPQ 821 (Fed. Cir. 1985).

[241]*Brasseler U.S.A. v. Stryker Sales Corp.*, 182 F.3d 888, 51 USPQ2d 1470 (Fed. Cir. 1999).

[242]*Mathis v. Spears*, 857 F.2d 749, 8 USPQ2d 1029 (Fed. Cir. 1988).

[243]*Imagineering, Inc. v. Van Klassens, Inc.*, 53 F.3d 1260, 34 USPQ2d 1526 (Fed. Cir. 1995). Here the punitive damages for a state law unfair competition claim were nearly five times the compensatory damages. The Federal Circuit regarded this a windfall recovery and remanded for a remittitur.

V
The Patent Office

15

Patent Prosecution

§15.1 Ex Parte Prosecution

Because of its jurisdiction of appeals from decisions of the PTO Board,[1] the Federal Circuit has ample opportunity to review both the procedural and substantive aspects of patent prosecution before the PTO. The great bulk of the issues confronted by the court have to do with matters of patentability, such as obviousness, anticipation, and compliance with 35 U.S.C. §112, and have been considered elsewhere in this book. The other major aspect of PTO practice that frequently reaches the court is the question of fraud and inequitable conduct, which is the subject of §9.5. The present section deals with PTO issues that are less often encountered by the Federal Circuit.

PTO regulations. Under 35 U.S.C. §6(a) the PTO Director may establish regulations, not inconsistent with law, for the conduct of proceedings in the PTO. The validity of such a regulation will be sustained so long as it is reasonably related to the purposes of the enabling legislation.[2] For example, the Director is primarily responsible for the application and enforcement of the narrow technical and specialized statutory and regulatory provisions governing abandonment and revival of patent applications. His or her interpretation of those provisions is entitled to considerable deference.[3] However, the

---

[1]35 U.S.C. §§141–144.

[2]*Ethicon v. Quigg,* 849 F.2d 1422, 7 USPQ2d 1152 (Fed. Cir. 1988). Interpretive rules, such as the General Requirements bulletin promulgated by the Director to interpret the regulations dealing with the practice of patent agents before the PTO, are not subject to the notice and comment requirements of 5 U.S.C. §552. Interpretive rules enable agencies to explain ambiguous terms in legislative enactments without having to undertake cumbersome proceedings. *Premysler v. Lehman,* 71 F.3d 387, 37 USPQ2d 1057 (Fed. Cir. 1995).

[3]*Morganroth v. Quigg,* 885 F.2d 843, 12 USPQ2d 1125 (Fed. Cir. 1989). A federal district court has jurisdiction, apparently under the general mandamus statute, 28 U.S.C. §1651, to review a decision of the Director on a petition to revive a patent application. Whatever may be the scope of the Director's discretion, the existence of that discretion does not bar judicial

rule-making powers of the Director are limited to the conduct of proceedings in the PTO; there is no general substantive rule-making power.[4] The Director, unlike the courts, has no inherent authority, only that which Congress gives.[5]

The PTO operates under a very comprehensive set of regulations.[6] The patent system as a whole benefits from clear, unambiguous rules.[7] The PTO is under severe limitations as to time and staffing, and it is incumbent upon attorneys and agents who prosecute patent applications to follow the procedural rules of the PTO.[8] The *Manual of Patent Examining Procedure* (MPEP) is an operating manual that describes procedures on which the public can rely.[9] The MPEP has no binding force on courts, but it is entitled to notice so far as it is an official interpretation of statutes or regulations with which it is not in conflict.[10] It is essentially a looseleaf training and instruction manual for examiners that is continually revised in piecemeal fashion, and it is not surprising to find inconsistencies in it. It does not have the force of law or the force of the Patent Rules of Practice.[11] Director's Notices are merely procedural memoranda setting forth guidelines for the PTO.[12] The court will disapprove MPEP provisions or Notice guidelines that it feels are erroneous.[13]

---

review. Also, inasmuch as the action for review is one arising under the patent laws, the Federal Circuit has jurisdiction of an appeal from the district court. *Id.* When a decision pursuant to a permissive statute concerns only PTO practice, the Federal Circuit reviews the decision for abuse of discretion. This likewise applies to decisions taken pursuant to a permissive regulation that is a proper exercise of authority granted under 35 U.S.C. §6(a). *Gerritsen v. Shirai,* 979 F.2d 1524, 24 USPQ2d 1912 (Fed. Cir. 1992). The Director may not exercise discretion in a way that contradicts the purposes of the patent statute or is completely contrary to reason. *Ray v. Lehman,* 55 F.3d 606, 34 USPQ2d 1786 (Fed. Cir. 1995).

[4]*Merck & Co. v. Kessler,* 80 F.3d 1543, 38 USPQ2d 1347 (Fed. Cir. 1996). The court in this case rejected the argument, advanced by both sides, that a PTO determination was entitled to "controlling weight." That degree of deference is reserved for review of statutory interpretations by agencies with substantive rule-making powers. PTO determinations are entitled only to the deference that is due based upon the thoroughness of its consideration and the validity of its reasoning.

[5]*Ethicon v. Quigg,* 849 F.2d 1422, 7 USPQ2d 1152 (Fed. Cir. 1988). Effective March 29, 2000, the Commissioner became known as the Director of the PTO. *Helfgott & Karas P.C. v. Dickinson,* 209 F.3d 1328, 54 USPQ2d 1425 (Fed. Cir. 2000).

[6]See Title 37, Code of Federal Regulations.

[7]*Waldemar Link v. Osteonics Corp.,* 32 F.3d 556, 31 USPQ2d 1855 Fed. Cir. 1994).

[8]*Jaskiewicz v. Mossinghoff,* 822 F.2d 1053, 3 USPQ2d 1294 (Fed. Cir. 1987).

[9]*Ethicon v. Quigg,* 849 F.2d 1422, 7 USPQ2d 1152 (Fed. Cir. 1988); *Paperless Accounting, Inc. v. Bay Area Rapid Transit Sys.,* 804 F.2d 659, 231 USPQ 649 (Fed. Cir. 1986). Patent attorneys and examiners commonly rely on the MPEP as a guide in procedural matters. *Syntex (U.S.A.) Inc. v. United States PTO,* 882 F.2d 1570, 11 USPQ2d 1866 (Fed. Cir. 1989).

[10]*Refac Int'l, Ltd. v. Lotus Dev. Corp.,* 81 F.3d 1576 (Fed. Cir. 1996); *Molins PLC v. Textron, Inc.,* 48 F.3d 1172, 33 USPQ2d 1823 (Fed. Cir. 1995); *Syntex (U.S.A.) Inc. v. United States PTO,* 882 F.2d 1570, 11 USPQ2d 1866 (Fed. Cir. 1989); *Molins PLC v. Quigg,* 837 F.2d 1064, 5 USPQ2d 1526 (Fed. Cir. 1988); *Litton Sys., Inc. v. Whirlpool Corp.,* 728 F.2d 1423, 221 USPQ 97 (Fed. Cir. 1984). The MPEP does not have the force of law, but it is well known to those registered to practice before the PTO and reflects the presumptions under which the PTO operates. *Critikon, Inc. v. Becton Dickinson Vascular Access, Inc.,* 120 F.3d 1253, 43 USPQ2d 1666 (Fed. Cir. 1997).

[11]*Racing Strollers, Inc. v. TRI Indus., Inc.,* 878 F.2d 1418, 11 USPQ2d 1300 (Fed. Cir. 1989).

[12]*In re Longi,* 759 F.2d 887, 225 USPQ 645 (Fed. Cir. 1985). Certainly where Notices are not even applied, they can have no bearing on the outcome of an appeal. *Id.*

[13]*In re Longi,* 759 F.2d 887, 225 USPQ 645 (Fed. Cir. 1985).

It is presumed that public officials do their assigned jobs.[14] There is accordingly a presumption that the PTO complies with its own rules, including those relating to review of the content of amendments filed by an applicant. A district court should not require more of an applicant than is required by the PTO.[15] A district court lacks authority to direct the PTO to issue a patent under 35 U.S.C. §145, but it is presumed that the PTO will follow a proper order issued by a court and perform the duties imposed by statute. The district court may only authorize the PTO to issue a patent upon compliance with requirements of law.[16]

There is no right in nonapplicants to object to the way in which patent applications of others are prosecuted. A third party has no right to intervene in the prosecution of a particular patent application to prevent issuance of an allegedly invalid patent.[17]

The patent law vests the PTO Director, not the courts, with the responsibility to protect PTO proceedings from unqualified practitioners. A court may disturb the Director's decisions regarding a potential practitioner's qualifications only if it finds that the Director abused his or her discretion in denying a petitioner's application. Under 35 U.S.C. §31, the Director has the discretionary authority to regulate the practice of patent agents before the PTO.[18]

Application and prosecution formalities. A patent application must include a specification and claims, a drawing, an oath or declaration, and a filing fee. Omission of any one makes the application incomplete and thus not entitled to a filing date.[19] Nonetheless, the Director does have discretion, and can waive minor defects.[20]

Indeed, 35 U.S.C. §26 specifically authorizes provisional acceptance of defectively executed documents. In enacting this provision,

---

[14]*Northern Telecom, Inc. v. Datapoint Corp.,* 908 F.2d 931, 15 USPQ2d 1321 (Fed. Cir. 1990).

[15]*Rite-Hite Corp. v. Kelley Co.,* 819 F.2d 1120, 2 USPQ2d 1915 (Fed. Cir. 1987). Nonetheless, while the PTO is presumed to have complied with all applicable rules, that presumption cannot overcome a clear statutory violation. *Baxter Int'l Inc. v. McGaw Inc.,* 149 F.3d 1321, 47 USPQ2d 1225 (Fed. Cir. 1998).

[16]*Gould v. Quigg,* 822 F.2d 1074, 3 USPQ2d 1302 (Fed. Cir. 1987). The concurring opinion of Judge Newman in *Exxon Chem. Patents, Inc. v. Lubrizol Corp.,* 935 F.2d 1263, 19 USPQ2d 1061 (Fed. Cir. 1991), provides a nice review of internal PTO procedures governing the actual issuance of patents.

[17]*Animal Legal Defense Fund v. Quigg,* 932 F.2d 920, 18 USPQ2d 1677 (Fed. Cir. 1991). Animal rights groups were attempting to challenge a PTO Notice that indicated that the PTO "now considers non-naturally occurring, non-human multicellular organisms, including animals, to be patentable subject matter."

[18]*Premysler v. Lehman,* 71 F.3d 387, 37 USPQ2d 1057 (Fed. Cir. 1995).

[19]*Litton Sys., Inc. v. Whirlpool Corp.,* 728 F.2d 1423, 221 USPQ 97 (Fed. Cir. 1984).

[20]*Dubost v. United States PTO,* 777 F.2d 1561, 227 USPQ 977 (Fed. Cir. 1985). The Federal Circuit reversed a determination that the PTO Director had no discretion to award a filing date where the applicant's check was unsigned and remanded for the Director to exercise his discretion. In an interesting side issue, the court held that it had jurisdiction over this case because the plaintiff asserted some right or privilege that would be defeated by one construction, or sustained by an opposite construction, of the patent laws.

Congress had in mind the dangers that overly rigid bureaucratic practices could and did pose for patent applicants. Before §26 was enacted, an irregularity in a patent application could bring the application process to a halt and jeopardize the date of priority, resulting in serious repercussions, including the loss of patent rights.[21]

Procedural lapses during examination, should they occur, do not provide grounds for invalidity. Absent proof of inequitable conduct, the examiner's or the applicant's absolute compliance with the internal rules of patent examination becomes irrelevant after the patent has issued. Imperfection in patent examination, whether by the examiner or the applicant, does not create a new defense called "prosecution irregularities" and does not displace the experience-based criteria of the inequitable conduct cases.[22] The court has demonstrated some empathy for those who engage in the complex yet crucial administrative process known as patent prosecution before the PTO. Mistakes are inevitable, much as all those involved try to minimize their possibility. Even if total elimination of mistakes is an illusory goal, their reasonable mitigation should not be. Sound judgment, flexibility, and the careful following of considered processes are critical to ensuring that small mistakes do not become large ones, and that mistakes of form do not overwhelm the correctness of substance.[23]

The PTO Director has no authority to revive an application that becomes abandoned by reason of the failure of the applicant to appeal to the Federal Circuit from a district court decision affirming a PTO Board decision rejecting the application.[24]

---

[21]*In re Bennett,* 766 F.2d 524, 226 USPQ 413 (Fed. Cir. 1985). The principle behind remedial provisions such as 35 U.S.C. §26 is to allow correction of those statutory rigors for which the penalty may be excessive under the circumstances. These relief provisions attempt to strike a balance between the need for consistency in administration of a complex statute, even if consistency occasionally results in forfeiture of substantive rights, and the need for fairness, which may place on the administering body the occasional burden of exercising discretion to avoid an unjust result. The balance chosen requires continual evaluation in light of the purposes served by the statute. It is not in the public interest to bar all possibility of legal or equitable relief, when such is sought to correct a harmless error. *Id.*

[22]*Magnivision, Inc. v. Bonneau Co.,* 115 F.3d 956, 42 USPQ2d 1925 (Fed. Cir. 1997). The court discussed at some length the requirement that the substance of an interview be recorded in writing. Much ado about this had been made at trial, as well as references to the remarkable persistence in wearing down the examiner. In view of the fact that the district court had already granted a summary judgment of no inequitable conduct, the Federal Circuit was unimpressed by these contentions as providing a free-standing defense, or indeed, as having any relevance to patent validity. See also *Seiko Epson Corp. v. Nu-Kote Int'l Inc.,* 190 F.3d 1360, 52 USPQ2d 1011 (Fed. Cir. 1999), which deals with native-language declarations under PTO Rule 69.

[23]*Helfgott & Karas P.C. v. Dickinson,* 209 F.3d 1328, 54 USPQ2d 1425 (Fed. Cir. 2000). This case involved an extremely complex series of mistakes, on both sides, in the handling of a Demand for International Preliminary Examination on an international patent application filed in the PTO under the PCT. The court ultimately held that the Director should have permitted correction.

[24]*Morganroth v. Quigg,* 885 F.2d 843, 12 USPQ2d 1125 (Fed. Cir. 1989). In its first look at a maintenance fee question, the Federal Circuit applied the same analysis that it uses in considering whether to revive abandoned applications under 35 U.S.C. §133: whether the party responsible for the payment exercised the due care of a reasonably prudent person. Inasmuch as 35 U.S.C. §41(c) has now been amended to allow reinstatement if the delay is merely

Examination and amendment. Patent applications are reviewed by patent examiners, quasijudicial officials, trained in the law and presumed to have some expertise in interpreting the references and to be familiar from their work with the level of skill in the art.[25] During the prosecution of a patent application, the examiner acts as a fact finder.[26]

An applicant has discretion to submit amendments after a final rejection. The examiner only permits such amendments upon a showing of good and sufficient reasons why they are necessary and were not earlier presented. A refusal to permit such an amendment is not a rejection on the merits and leaves the application in the same status it was in after the final rejection.[27]

Continuing and divisional applications. In general, a continuation application is one filed during the pendency of another application that contains at least part of the disclosure of the other application and names at least one inventor in common with that application. Continuation and divisional applications are alike in that they are both continuing applications based on the same disclosure as an earlier application. They differ, however, in what they claim. A continuation application claims the same invention claimed in an earlier application, although there may be some variation in the scope of the subject matter claimed. A divisional application, on the other hand, is one carved out of an earlier application that disclosed and claimed more than one independent invention. Thus, the divisional application claims only one or more, but not all, of the independent inventions of the earlier application. A CIP application is a continuing application containing a portion or all of the disclosure of an earlier application together with added matter not present in that earlier application. The term parent is often used to refer to the immediately preceding application upon which a continuation application claims priority; the term original is used to refer to the first application in a chain of continuing applications. The upshot is that, no matter what term is used to describe a continuation application, that application is entitled to the benefit of a filing date of an earlier application only as to common subject matter.[28] To be entitled to the filing date of an

---

unintentional, rather than unavoidable, it appears that due care is not even required. *Ray v. Lehman*, 55 F.3d 606, 34 USPQ2d 1786 (Fed. Cir. 1995).

[25]*Markman v. Westview Instr., Inc.*, 52 F.3d 967, 34 USPQ2d 1321 (Fed. Cir. 1995).

[26]*Waldemar Link v. Osteonics Corp.*, 32 F.3d 556, 31 USPQ2d 1855 (Fed. Cir. 1994).

[27]*Waldemar Link v. Osteonics Corp.*, 32 F.3d 556, 31 USPQ2d 1855 (Fed. Cir. 1994).

[28]*Transco Prods., Inc. v. Performance Contr., Inc.*, 38 F.3d 551, 32 USPQ2d 1077 (Fed. Cir. 1994). Continuation and divisional applications may be filed under any one of 37 C.F.R. §§1.53, 1.60, and 1.62, which provide different procedural benefits. CIP applications may be filed only pursuant to Rules 53 and 62. Continuation applications filed under Rules 53 and 60 must be filed prior to the patenting or abandonment of or termination of proceedings on the earlier application on which they are based. A continuation application filed under Rule 62 must be filed prior to the payment of the issue fee for, abandonment of, or termination of proceedings on, the earlier application.

earlier application in a chain of applications, there must have been a continuing disclosure through the chain, without hiatus.[29]

Priority and filing dates. Rule 131 (37 C.F.R. §1.131) provides an ex parte mechanism whereby a patent applicant may antedate subject matter in a reference even if the reference describes the same invention that is claimed by the applicant, provided that when the reference is a U.S. patent, the same invention is not claimed therein. A disclosure in a reference U.S. patent does not fall under 35 U.S.C. §102(g) but under §102(e), and thus can be antedated in accordance with Rule 131. But when the subject matter sought to be antedated is claimed in the reference U.S. patent, Rule 131 is not available and an interference must be had to determine priority.[30]

The purpose of filing a Rule 131 declaration is to demonstrate that the applicant's date of invention is prior to the effective date of the reference cited in support of a rejection. The rule allows the applicant to overcome the reference by showing that the invention in question was reduced to practice prior to the filing date of the reference.[31] A failed attempt to antedate a prior art reference does not constitute an admission that the prior art truly renders the subject matter of the application unpatentable. An affidavit or declaration under Rule 131 may be employed during prosecution in immediate response to a prior art rejection to overcome the rejection and therefore to obviate any unnecessary patentability argument. The PTO does not impose the burden of overcoming with argument prior art that is to be antedated under Rule 131. Otherwise, an applicant would rely on such an affidavit only as a last resort, out of fear that an early failure to antedate the allegedly invalidating reference would preclude a later attempt to overcome the reference by argument.[32]

Under certain circumstances, an applicant may be entitled to the filing date of an earlier filed application, domestic or foreign, with respect to some or all of the subject matter of a later filed application. For example, §120 provides that an application is entitled to the filing date of an earlier U.S. application if the invention was disclosed in the earlier in compliance with §112, if the two are copending, and if the later application contains or is amended to contain a reference to the first.[33] For a claim in a later filed application to be entitled to the filing date of an earlier application under §120, the earlier

---

[29]*Eiselstein v. Frank*, 52 F.3d 1035, 34 USPQ2d 1467 (Fed. Cir. 1995).

[30]*In re Zletz*, 893 F.2d 319, 13 USPQ2d 1320 (Fed. Cir. 1989). Where the reference is a patent that actually claims the invention, an interference proceeding may be necessary in order to determine priority. *In re Asahi/Am. Inc.*, 48 F.3d 1204, 37 USPQ2d 1204 (Fed. Cir. 1995).

[31]*In re Asahi/Am. Inc.*, 48 F.3d 1204, 37 USPQ2d 1204 (Fed. Cir. 1995). This case well illustrates the notion that some devices are so simple that a mere construction of them is all that is necessary to constitute reduction to practice. The Rule 131 declaration here simply showed that the claimed device was manufactured by an outside vendor and described in two trade publications prior to the reference date.

[32]*Credle v. Bond,* 25 F.3d 1566, 30 USPQ2d 1911 (Fed. Cir. 1994).

[33]*In re Costello,* 717 F.2d 1346, 219 USPQ 389 (Fed. Cir. 1983).

application must comply with the written description requirement of §112¶1.[34] If the second application contains new matter, it is a CIP and is entitled to the original filing date only as to the material originally disclosed and any part of the new disclosure that was inherent in the original.[35] There is no statutory prohibition against reliance on a design application for §120 priority, either for a later design application,[36] or a later utility application if the original design disclosure meets the §112 requirements as to the application claimed in the utility application.[37] However, §120 does require that the earlier application be for the same invention.[38] Also, the focus must be on the right application.[39] In order for a patent to be entitled to the filing date of an earlier application in a chain of applications of which it is a part, it must be shown that as to the invention claimed there has been continuing disclosure through the chain of applications, without hiatus.[40] Entitlement to priority under §120 is a matter of law, and receives plenary review on appeal. Any disputed factual questions are reviewed on the clearly erroneous standard.[41]

Under 35 U.S.C. §119, a U.S. applicant may also be entitled to the date of filing of a foreign counterpart application if he or she files

---

[34]*Tronzo v. Biomet Inc.,* 156 F.3d 1154, 47 USPQ2d 1829 (Fed. Cir. 1998).

[35]*Litton Sys., Inc. v. Whirlpool Corp.,* 728 F.2d 1423, 221 USPQ 97 (Fed. Cir. 1984). New matter cannot be added by amendment, but only by a continuing application in accordance with 35 U.S.C. §120. *Id.* Thus, claims amended with limitations unsupported by the original disclosure are rejected under §112 as lacking support, while unsupported amendments to the abstract, specification, and drawings are objected to as new matter. *Pennwalt Corp. v. Akzona Inc.,* 740 F.2d 1573, 222 USPQ 833 (Fed. Cir. 1984).

[36]*In re Salmon,* 705 F.2d 1579, 217 USPQ 981 (Fed. Cir. 1984). The court expressly overruled *In re Campbell,* 212 F.2d 606, 101 USPQ 406 (CCPA 1954), in holding that a later filed design application can properly be a division and be entitled to the filing date of an earlier filed utility application. *Racing Strollers, Inc. v. TRI Indus., Inc.,* 878 F.2d 1418, 11 USPQ2d 1300 (Fed. Cir. 1989). Meeting the requirements of 35 U.S.C. §112 in the case of a design is simply a question of whether the earlier application contains illustrations, whatever form they may take, depicting the design illustrated in the later application. The best mode requirement is not applicable, as a design has only one "mode" and it can be described only by illustrations showing what it looks like. *Id.*

[37]*Kangaroos U.S.A., Inc. v. Caldor, Inc.,* 778 F.2d 1571, 228 USPQ 32 (Fed. Cir. 1985).

[38]*In re Salmon,* 705 F.2d 1579, 217 USPQ 981 (Fed. Cir. 1984). Thus a design application showing a stool with a square seat will not support a design for a stool with a round seat. *Id.* Entitlement to a filing date does not extend to subject matter that is not disclosed but would be obvious over what is expressly disclosed. *Lockwood v. American Airlines, Inc.,* 107 F.3d 1565, 41 USPQ2d 1961 (Fed. Cir. 1997). *In re Chu,* 66 F.3d 292, 36 USPQ2d 1089 (Fed. Cir. 1995), presented in interesting issue involving different inventive entities. The PTO rejected claims in a CIP application of inventors A and B over a §102(e) parent patent to inventor A. The court held that the 1984 amendment to §120 that was effected by §104(b) means that complete identity of inventors is no longer required to obtain a parent filing date. But it went on to point out that A and B are entitled to the parent filing date of A only if the A patent discloses the invention claimed by A and B. Inasmuch as A and B were fighting that very question, and had argued that their claimed invention was not disclosed in A, they were held to have conceded that it was not for priority purposes as well. Thus, the A patent would be a proper reference that would have to be distinguished.

[39]*Kangaroos U.S.A., Inc. v. Caldor, Inc.,* 778 F.2d 1571, 228 USPQ 32 (Fed. Cir. 1985). It is error to require support in an earlier application if there is no intervening prior art. *Id.*

[40]*Lemelson v. TRW, Inc.,* 760 F.2d 1254, 225 USPQ 697 (Fed. Cir. 1985). See also *Lockwood v. American Airlines, Inc.,* 107 F.3d 1565, 41 USPQ2d 1961 (Fed. Cir. 1997).

[41]*In re Daniels,* 144 F.3d 1452, 46 USPQ2d 1788, 1790 (Fed. Cir. 1998).

in the United States within a year of the foreign filing.[42] An applicant may antedate prior art by relying on the benefit of a previously filed foreign application to establish an effective date earlier than that of the reference. But under §119, the claims set forth in a U.S. application are entitled to the earlier foreign priority date only if the corresponding foreign application supports the claims in the manner required by the first paragraph of §112.[43] A CIP application can be entitled to different priority dates for different claims. Claims containing any matter introduced in the CIP are accorded the filing date of the CIP application. However, matter disclosed in the parent application is entitled to the benefit of the filing date of the parent application. When a priority date dispute arises, the trial court must examine closely the prosecution history to discover the proper date for each claim at issue.[44]

Under 35 U.S.C. §156, there is a comprehensive scheme under which the PTO Director may entertain and approve applications for patent term extension. District court review of such decisions is governed by the Administrative Procedure Act, 5 U.S.C. §706(2)(A).[45]

Burdens and presumptions. A statute setting rules of procedure and assigning burdens to litigants in a court trial does not automatically become applicable to proceedings before the PTO.[46] Although patents are entitled to a presumption of validity under 35 U.S.C. §282, and a party asserting patent invalidity must support the assertion by facts constituting clear and convincing evidence, patent applications are not entitled to the procedural advantages of §282. The standard of proof required to properly reject the claims of a patent application is necessarily lower than that required to invalidate patent claims. The three standards of proof generally recognized are proof by a preponderance of the evidence, proof by clear and convincing evidence, and proof beyond a reasonable doubt. Because it is the only standard

---

[42]*In re Mulder,* 716 F.2d 1542, 219 USPQ 189 (Fed. Cir. 1983).

[43]*In re Gosteli,* 872 F.2d 1008, 10 USPQ2d 1614 (Fed. Cir. 1989). In order to get the foreign priority date, the foreign application must support what is being claimed by the applicant, not just what is shown by the reference. *Id.* The how-to-use prong of §112 incorporates as a matter of law the requirement of §101 that a specification disclose as a matter of fact a practical utility for the invention. Thus, in order to obtain the benefit of an earlier foreign filing date the applicant must show that the foreign application disclosed practical utility for the invention. *In re Ziegler,* 992 F.2d 1197, 26 USPQ2d 1600 (Fed. Cir. 1993). Perhaps more importantly, the earlier application must satisfy the written description requirement. *Fiers v. Revel,* 984 F.2d 1164, 25 USPQ2d 1601 (Fed. Cir. 1993).

[44]*Waldemar Link v. Osteonics Corp.,* 32 F.3d 556, 31 USPQ2d 1855 (Fed. Cir. 1994). See also *Augustine Med. Inc. v. Gaymar Indus. Inc.,* 181 F.3d 1291, 50 USPQ2d 1900 (Fed. Cir. 1999).

[45]*Glaxo Oper. UK Ltd. v. Quigg,* 894 F.2d 392, 13 USPQ2d 1628 (Fed. Cir. 1990). Because the patent term extension is determined by the PTO Director from a formula based upon the regulatory review period, any action contesting the Director's determination lies against the Secretary of Health and Human Services (or the FDA as the Secretary's delegate), who has the statutory authority to determine the review period. The Director has no authority to review and set aside a final determination of a regulatory review period made by the Secretary. *Astra v. Lehman,* 71 F.3d 1578, 37 USPQ2d 1212 (Fed. Cir. 1995).

[46]*In re Etter,* 756 F.2d 852, 225 USPQ 1 (Fed. Cir. 1985).

of proof lower than clear and convincing, preponderance of the evidence is the standard that must be met by the PTO in making rejections.[47]

Under 35 U.S.C. §132 the PTO must state the reasons for rejection. This requires that the applicant at least be informed of the broad statutory basis for the rejection so that he or she may determine what the issues are on which he or she can or should produce evidence. The statute is violated when a rejection is so uninformative that it prevents the applicant from recognizing and seeking to counter the grounds for rejection. But it does not require the PTO to explicitly preempt every possible response to a rejection.[48]

In ex parte prosecution, the PTO has the initial burden of producing a factual basis for a rejection. In other words, the PTO must establish a case of prima facie obviousness. Then the applicant is obliged to come forward with rebuttal, which is merely a showing of facts supporting the opposite conclusion. This approach is a procedural mechanism to allocate in an orderly way the burdens of going forward and persuasion as between the examiner and the applicant.[49] Similarly, once the PTO establishes a prima facie case of anticipation based on inherency, the burden shifts to the applicant to prove that the subject matter shown to be in the prior art does not possess the characteristic relied on by the PTO. It will not suffice merely to make an assertion that the inherent characteristic does not exist and challenge the PTO to prove the contrary by experiment or otherwise; the PTO is not equipped to perform such tasks.[50] Likewise, the PTO is entitled to reject an application for insufficient proof when the invention by its very nature occasions reasonable skepticism as to its operability.[51]

Thus, the process of patent prosecution is an interactive one. Once the PTO has made an initial determination that specified claims are not patentable (the prima facie case concept), the burden of production falls to the applicant to establish entitlement to a patent. This promotes the development of the written record before the PTO that provides the requisite written notice to the public as to what the applicant claims as the invention. Public notice is an important objective of patent prosecution before the PTO.[52]

---

[47]*In re Caveney,* 761 F.2d 671, 226 USPQ 1 (Fed. Cir. 1985). Except for fraud rejections, which require clear and convincing evidence. *Id.* Preponderance of the evidence is the standard that must be met by the PTO in making rejections. *In re Epstein,* 32 F.3d 1559, 31 USPQ2d 1817 (Fed. Cir. 1994).

[48]*Chester v. Miller,* 906 F.2d 1574, 15 USPQ2d 1333 (Fed. Cir. 1990). For example, §132 does not require the PTO to state specifically that a prior art reference describes and enables claims rejected as anticipated. *Id.*

[49]*In re Piasecki,* 745 F.2d 1468, 223 USPQ 785 (Fed. Cir. 1984).

[50]*In re King,* 801 F.2d 1324, 231 USPQ 136 (Fed. Cir. 1986).

[51]*In re Newman,* 782 F.2d 971, 228 USPQ 450 (Fed. Cir. 1986).

[52]*In re Morris,* 127 F.3d 1048, 44 USPQ2d 1023 (Fed. Cir. 1997).

Evidence. The general rule is that administrative agencies like the PTO are not bound by the rules of evidence that govern judicial proceedings. Agencies may provide for the application of evidence rules, as the PTO has done in patent interference and public use proceedings, both of which are inter partes in nature. However, the PTO has not made any special provision for evidence rules during ex parte examination. The inapplicability of hearsay evidence rules in ex parte PTO examination is appropriate in light of the purpose and reason for the hearsay rule, which is the theory that many possible sources of inaccuracy and untrustworthiness that may lie underneath the bare untested assertion of a witness can best be brought to light and exposed, if they exist, by the test of cross-examination. During ex parte examination applicants are free to investigate hearsay assertions relied upon by an examiner during the three- to six-month period available to respond to an office action. They also have the right to introduce rebuttal evidence under Rule 132. If they wish to cross-examine the authors of written hearsay assertions they may bring a civil action under 35 U.S.C. §145.[53] Thus, where documents appear on their face to be accurate and reliable, and where the applicant proffers no evidence to support arguments to the contrary, the PTO may assume the truthfulness of the statements contained therein to support a rejection. It then falls to the applicant to come forward with evidence to the contrary.[54]

How does an applicant rebut a prima facie showing by the PTO? Certainly affidavit evidence may be employed, although expert affidavits submitted to the PTO are entitled to little or no weight if they are mere opinions unsupported by facts.[55] Affidavits submitted to the PTO must contain more than mere unsupported conclusory statements as to the ultimate legal question at issue.[56] Affidavit and deposition statements developed in inter partes cases may be used in PTO proceedings. Indeed, such statements may be more reliable and complete than ex parte evidence due to the adversary nature of the proceedings. However, the credibility of such statements must be established by clear and convincing evidence, which may require

---

[53]*In re Epstein*, 32 F.3d 1559, 31 USPQ2d 1817 (Fed. Cir. 1994).

[54]*In re Epstein*, 32 F.3d 1559, 31 USPQ2d 1817 (Fed. Cir. 1994). Here published abstracts contained a description of a particular software product, identified the vendor, stated the date of first release or installation, and gave the number of current users. The date of publication of the abstracts did not antedate the critical date, but the date of first release or installation did. The court held that, despite the clear hearsay nature of the abstracts, they established without more that the products described were in public use or on sale more than a year before the critical date. Two of the panel members appear to analyze this problem on a prima facie case basis: although the PTO must show why the applicant is not entitled to a patent, it satisfies this burden initially with the abstracts.

[55]*In re Etter*, 756 F.2d 852, 225 USPQ 1 (Fed. Cir. 1985). The court has indicated that it is aware of no reason why opinion evidence relating to fact issues may not be considered by an examiner. *In re Alton*, 76 F.3d 1168, 37 USPQ2d 1578 (Fed. Cir. 1996).

[56]*In re Wright*, 999 F.2d 155, 27 USPQ2d 1510 (Fed. Cir. 1993).

corroboration.[57] So-called Rule 131 affidavits, used to overcome prior art references by establishing an earlier filing date, have their own special requirements.[58]

Appeals to the Board. The public responsibility of the PTO requires attentive performance of all aspects of the patent examination function. The PTO is charged with the duty of examining the claims contained in the patent application, and this includes review by the Board when an appeal is taken under 35 U.S.C. §134. It is not only unfair to the applicant, it is also inefficient to decline to review claims that are properly appealed and reasonably argued before the Board.[59] Nonetheless, claims stand or fall together unless they are separately argued.[60] Also, a party cannot wait until after the Board has rendered an adverse decision and then present new arguments in a request for reconsideration.[61]

The technical background and other professional qualifications of the particular examiners-in-chief making up a PTO Board panel are not legally relevant in an appeal to the Board under 35 U.S.C. §134, just as the technical qualifications of a judge are irrelevant in a §141 appeal to the Federal Circuit or an appeal under §145 to the District Court for the District of Columbia. A board member need not possess "ordinary skill" in a particular art area to be qualified to render a patentability determination on a claimed invention drawn to the art. The correctness of a board's decision depends on whether the decision is supported by the record, not on the technical background of the examiners-in-chief who decided the appeal.[62]

The PTO Board of Patent Appeals and Interferences is not bound by the FRCP, which by their terms apply only to district courts. Nor has it voluntarily bound itself to them. Nonetheless, the Federal Circuit feels that the Board must meet an equivalent standard, at least as to findings and conclusions. Thus, the Board is required to

---

[57]*In re Sneed,* 710 F.2d 1544, 218 USPQ 385 (Fed. Cir. 1983). Circumstantial evidence can provide the necessary corroboration. *Id.*

[58]See 37 C.F.R. §1.131. Rule 131 means what it says, even though it is to be liberally construed. *In re Mulder,* 716 F.2d 1542, 219 USPQ 189 (Fed. Cir. 1983). See also *In re Asahi / Am. Inc.,* 48 F.3d 1204, 37 USPQ2d 1204 (Fed. Cir. 1995); *In re Costello,* 717 F.2d 1346, 219 USPQ 389 (Fed. Cir. 1983).

[59]*In re Beaver,* 893 F.2d 329, 13 USPQ2d 1409 (Fed. Cir. 1989). The Board held that the applicant had not preserved the independent appeal of certain claims, on the ground that claims not separately argued stand or fall with those that are. The court reviewed the record and concluded that the Board was wrong—that the arguments for the claims in question, though concise, were sufficiently made to preserve the right of appeal.

[60]*In re Brouwer,* 77 F.3d 1185, 37 USPQ2d 1663 (Fed. Cir. 1996). Where an applicant on appeal does not separately argue the merits of dependent claims, they stand or fall with the independent claim. *In re Kemps,* 97 F.3d 1427, 40 USPQ2d 1309 (Fed. Cir. 1996).

[61]*Cooper v. Goldfarb,* 154 F.3d 1321, 47 USPQ2d 1896 (Fed. Cir. 1998). The question of whether a party properly raised an issue is a question of law based on subsidiary factual findings. Where there is no factual dispute as to what statements were contained in a final hearing brief, but only the legal significance to be accorded the statements, the court reviews de novo the Board's conclusion that the statements did not adequately raise the issue. *Id.*

[62]*In re Nilssen,* 851 F.2d 1401, 7 USPQ2d 1500 (Fed. Cir. 1988).

set forth in its opinions specific findings of fact and conclusions of law adequate to form a basis for review. For example, an anticipation analysis must be conducted on a limitation-by-limitation basis, with specific fact findings for each contested limitation and satisfactory explanations for such findings. Claim construction must also be explicit, at least as to any construction disputed by a party. A similar standard will apply to obviousness determinations.[63] In addition to demonstrating the propriety of an obviousness analysis, particular factual findings regarding the suggestion, teaching, or motivation to combine serve a number of important purposes, including (1) clear explication of the position adopted by the examiner and the Board, (2) identification of the factual disputes, if any, between the applicant and the Board, and (3) facilitation of review on appeal.[64]

Review of Board decisions. An applicant dissatisfied with a decision of the PTO Board has a choice, under 35 U.S.C. §145, of appealing to the Federal Circuit or bringing a civil action against the Director in the District Court for the District of Columbia.[65] District court review of Board decisions is discussed in §11.4(a).

PTO Board findings of fact may be set aside only if arbitrary, capricious, an abuse of discretion, or unsupported by substantial evidence.[66]

There is a general rule that courts should not overturn administrative decisions unless the administrative body not only has erred but has erred against objection made at the time appropriate under its practice. But practice before such agencies is controlled by each agency's own regulations, and where the rights of individuals are affected, it is incumbent upon agencies, including the PTO, to follow their own procedures. Weight should be given to the normal practices of the agency, as understood by practitioners before it.[67] Affirmance by the PTO Board of a rejection of a claim on any ground constitutes

---

[63]*In re Dembiczak,* 175 F.3d 994, 50 USPQ2d 1614 (Fed. Cir. 1999).

[64]*Gechter v. Davidson,* 116 F.3d 1454, 43 USPQ2d 1030 (Fed. Cir. 1997). Compare *In re Hyatt,* 211 F.3d 1367, 54 USPQ2d 1664 (Fed. Cir. 2000).

[65]*Abbott Labs. v. Brennan,* 952 F.2d 1346, 21 USPQ2d 1192 (Fed. Cir. 1992). The Director has no right to appeal a decision of the Board to the Federal Circuit. *In re Alappat,* 33 F.3d 1526, 31 USPQ2d 1545 (Fed. Cir. 1994). The repeated reenactment of 35 U.S.C. §141 reflects the belief of Congress that the Director does not need such right in view of his or her rule-making authority and degree of control over the Board. *Id.*

[66]*Dickinson v. Zurko,* 527 U.S. 150, 50 USPQ2d 1930 (1999), reversing *In re Zurko,* 142 F.3d 1447, 46 USPQ2d 1691 (Fed. Cir. 1998). In deciding a question not conclusively dealt with in *Dickinson v. Zurko,* the court has concluded that it will reviewing fact finding by the Board for substantial evidence rather than on the more deferential "arbitrary or capricious" standard. *In re Gartside,* 203 F.3d 1305, 53 USPQ2d 1769 (Fed. Cir. 2000). See also *In re Hyatt,* 211 F.3d 1367, 54 USPQ2d 1664 (Fed. Cir. 2000).

[67]*In re Nielson,* 816 F.2d 1562, 2 USPQ2d 1525 (Fed. Cir. 1987). The Board erroneously stated that the appellant did not argue certain claims. The PTO Solicitor urged that the appellant's subsequent failure to request the Board to reconsider this error resulted in a waiver of the right to argue those claims on appeal to the Federal Circuit. The Solicitor conceded that this was a new theory of an appellant's burdens before the PTO, and it was not PTO practice to require such requests. Naturally, the court rejected the Solicitor's position.

a general affirmance of the examiner's decision; but in order for an issue to be reviewed by the Federal Circuit, it must be clearly specified in the examiner's decision as a ground for rejection.[68] The court has also distinguished precedent holding that an agency tribunal must have an opportunity to consider procedural deficiencies prior to an appeal to a court; thus, a new ground of rejection entered by the Board is a final determination raising substantive issues and may be appealed without seeking reconsideration and presenting arguments to the Board.[69] The Board has no jurisdiction to review the merits of a restriction requirement, inasmuch as that is a matter within the discretion of the examiner and does not amount to a rejection of claims.[70]

It is untimely to submit evidence of unobviousness after an adverse Board decision without a showing of good and sufficient reasons why it was not earlier presented.[71]

An inferior court has no power or authority to deviate from the mandate issued by an appellate court. This rule is equally applicable to the duty of an administrative agency, such as the PTO Board, to comply with the mandate issued by a reviewing court.[72]

The Director is not bound by a Board decision that an applicant is entitled to a patent. Only a court can order the Director to act, not the Board. The ultimate authority regarding the granting of patents lies with the Director. For example, if the Board rejects an application, the Director can control the PTO's position in any appeal through the Solicitor of the PTO; the Board cannot demand that the Solicitor attempt to sustain the Board's decision. Conversely, if the Board approves an application, the Director has the option of refusing to sign a patent, an action that would be subject to a mandamus suit by the applicant. The Director has an obligation to refuse to grant a patent if he or she believes that doing so would be contrary to law. The Board is merely the highest level of the examining corps and operates subject to the Director's overall ultimate authority and responsibility.[73]

---

[68]*In re Webb*, 916 F.2d 1553, 16 USPQ2d 1433 (Fed. Cir. 1990).

[69]*In re Evanega*, 829 F.2d 1110, 4 USPQ2d 1249 (Fed. Cir. 1987). See also *Newman v. Quigg*, 877 F.2d 1575, 11 USPQ2d 1340 (Fed. Cir. 1989).

[70]*In re Watkinson*, 900 F.2d 230, 14 USPQ2d 1407 (Fed. Cir. 1990).

[71]*In re Nielson*, 816 F.2d 1562, 2 USPQ2d 1525 (Fed. Cir. 1987). The court has also approved the Board's practice under PTO Rule 197(b) in refusing to consider a second request for rehearing. Thus, the appellant was precluded from relying on the argument, raised for the first time in a second request, as a basis for overturning the Board's decision.

[72]*In re Wella A.G.*, 858 F.2d 725, 8 USPQ2d 1365 (Fed. Cir. 1988).

[73]*In re Alappat*, 33 F.3d 1526, 31 USPQ2d 1545 (Fed. Cir. 1994). In this case an original three-member Board rendered a decision and the examiner requested reconsideration. Commissioner Manbeck designated an expanded eight-member panel, including himself, to reconsider the case. The result was a 5–3 decision, with the original three panel members dissenting. The court held that this was within the Commissioner's authority under 35 U.S.C. §7(a). It also held that the action of the expanded Board in reconsidering the original decision was a "rehearing" within the meaning of §7; reconsideration and rehearing are interchangeable in this context. The holding is consistent with the broad supervisory authority given the Commis-

§15.2　Interference Proceedings

United States patent law embraces the principle that the patent right is granted to the first inventor rather than the first to file a patent application.[74] As a consequence this country has, almost unique in the world, a procedure for resolving patent "interferences." This procedure is conducted, in the first instance, in the PTO; federal district courts do not have original jurisdiction to conduct an interference.[75] Determination of priority of invention invokes a complex body of procedural and substantive law, applied in the first instance in administrative proceedings in accordance with 35 U.S.C. §135(a). The interference proceeding implements the principle of U.S. law that the right to a patent derives from priority of invention, not priority of patent application filing. The general rule is that the first person to conceive the invention is the first inventor, provided that when the first to conceive the invention is the last to reduce it to practice, the person who was first to conceive must have exercised reasonable diligence to an actual or constructive reduction to practice, from a time prior to conception by the other. Thus, during an interference proceeding evidence may be presented of conception, reduction to practice, and diligence, as appropriate to the positions of the parties, or a party may rely on the patent document to establish the facts of priority of invention.[76]

The Federal Circuit, not without justification, has branded the "tortuous interference practice" as a culprit for delay in the patenting process.[77] Interference proceedings are not only tortuous, they are virtually incomprehensible to the uninitiated. They are arcane and highly specialized.[78] Fortunately, the court provided a nice review of interference procedure in *General Instrument v. Scientific-Atlanta*,[79] which can serve as a brief introduction to the topic. Thus, a common two-party interference before the PTO is an administrative proceeding expected to be concluded in 24 months. Once the PTO sends a notice of declaration of interference to each party, it also sets a period for

---

sioner by 35 U.S.C. §6(a). The court distinguished its prior decision in *Animal Legal Defense Fund v. Quigg*, 932 F.2d 920, 18 USPQ2d 1677 (Fed. Cir. 1991), which had held that the Board was not the alter ego or agent of the Commissioner. It is clear that Congress did not intend the Board to be independent of any and all oversight by the Commissioner.

[74]*Paulik v. Rizkalla*, 760 F.2d 1270, 226 USPQ 224 (Fed. Cir. 1985). The unique premise of the U.S. patent system is that it rewards the first to invent, not the first to file. *Bruning v. Hirose*, 161 F.3d 681, 48 USPQ2d 1934 (Fed. Cir. 1998).

[75]*Consolidated World Housewares, Inc. v. Finkle*, 829 F.2d 261, 4 USPQ2d 1565 (Fed. Cir. 1987).

[76]*Hyatt v. Boone*, 146 F.3d 1128, 47 USPQ2d 1128 (Fed. Cir. 1998).

[77]*Studiengesellschaft Kohle v. Northern Petrochem. Co.*, 784 F.2d 351, 228 USPQ 837 (Fed. Cir. 1986).

[78]*Conservolite, Inc. v. Widmayer*, 21 F.3d 1098, 30 USPQ2d 1626 (Fed. Cir. 1994).

[79]*General Instr. Corp. v. Scientific-Atlanta, Inc.*, 995 F.2d 209 (Fed. Cir. 1993). *In re Van Geuns*, 946 F.2d 845, 20 USPQ2d 1291 (Fed. Cir. 1991), provides a good historical account of interference practice, particularly in the context of review; it also gives some of the legislative history of the 1984 amendments that streamlined interference procedures.

filing preliminary statements and preliminary motions, a period that usually is three months. A preliminary statement is a formal document that serves several purposes. Initially, it permits the issuance of show cause orders by an examiner-in-chief of the Board when it would be futile to take testimony. It also limits a party's proof on date of invention and provides notice of the opposing party's case at the close of the motions period in most situations. A preliminary statement may be filed at any time during the period for filing motions. It is filed in a sealed envelope and is usually unavailable to the opposing party until the examiner-in-chief in charge of the interference rules on the preliminary motions and directs that it be opened.

The preliminary motions are usually a critical part of an interference. Although the Board may consider any issue in order to prevent manifest injustice, a party may not raise any issue at the final hearing that properly could have been raised by a preliminary motion, a motion to correct inventorship, or in an opposition to these motions if the motions were successful, unless the party shows good cause for the failure to raise the issue in time. The Board may consider any properly raised issue which, in addition to issues raised in preliminary motions, may include issues of unpatentability presented by the examiner-in-chief. The parties aid in identifying such issues pursuant to their duty to disclose information material to patentability. Such information is submitted to the examiner-in-chief in information disclosure statements. If the rulings on the preliminary motions do not terminate the interference, the preliminary statements are served on the opposing party and opened.

Periods are then set for discovery and taking testimony. After a final hearing, the Board issues a decision. A party dissatisfied with the decision may seek reconsideration, or it may appeal directly to the Federal Circuit based on the Board record. Alternatively, a party may proceed to a district court for a hybrid appeal/trial de novo proceeding in which the PTO record is admitted on motion of either party, but may be supplemented by further testimony.

Under 37 C.F.R. §1.616, the examiner-in-chief and the Board have discretionary authority to sanction an interference party who fails to comply with an interference regulation. This represents a permissible exercise of the authority delegated to the PTO Director by Congress under 35 U.S.C. §6(a) and comports with the Administrative Procedure Act.[80] Either may impose an appropriate sanction, including granting judgment in an interference, against a party who fails

---

[80]*Gerritsen v. Shirai*, 979 F.2d 1524, 24 USPQ2d 1912 (Fed. Cir. 1992). Both a decision to sanction an interference party and the choice of sanction are reviewed for abuse of discretion. *Id.* The court concluded that it was appropriate for the Board to sanction a party for failure to file a belated preliminary motion and a showing of good cause. However, the court felt the Board abused its discretion in selecting the sanction, which was to preclude the party from raising certain issues. See also *Abrutyn v. Giovanniello*, 15 F.3d 1048, 29 USPQ2d 1615 (Fed. Cir. 1994).

to comply with the rules governing interferences, including filing deadlines.[81]

(a) Priority in General

The patent statute, 35 U.S.C. §102(g), provides that a person shall be entitled to a patent unless:

> before the applicant's invention thereof the invention was made in this country by another who had not abandoned, suppressed, or concealed it. In determining priority of invention there shall be considered not only the respective dates of conception and reduction to practice of the invention, but also the reasonable diligence of one who was first to conceive and last to reduce to practice, from a time prior to conception by the other.

Section 102(g) contains the basic rule for determining priority. It also provides basic protection for the inventive process, shielding in particular the creative steps of conception and reduction to practice. In the United States, the person who first reduces an invention to practice is prima facie the first and true inventor. However, the person who first conceives, and in a mental sense, first invents, may date the patentable invention back to the time of its conception, if the conception can be connected with the reduction to practice by reasonable diligence, so that they are substantially one continuous act.[82]

Interferences may be declared between pending applications or, pursuant to 35 U.S.C. §135(b), between an application and an issued patent.[83] An interference proceeding is principally declared to permit a determination of priority, to decide who among multiple patent applicants (or applicants and patentees) was the first to invent claimed subject matter. Issues of patentability can be considered, but infringement will not.[84] If the inventions at issue are either unpatentable to the parties or are not the same invention, no contest of priority as contemplated by §135 exists.[85]

---

[81]*Abrutyn v. Giovanniello*, 15 F.3d 1048, 29 USPQ2d 1615 (Fed. Cir. 1994). Due to a series of omissions involving failures to make and record assignments, the junior party in this case missed the deadline for filing a preliminary statement. The Board awarded default judgment to the senior party and the Federal Circuit affirmed. In an interesting twist, the PTO Director asked the court to remand instead, on the ground that the Board's penalty was too harsh. The Federal Circuit refused, largely on the ground that the PTO is not a party. Thus, although the PTO may regard the penalty as excessive, it is the opponent in the interference that is the party, and it vehemently disagrees with the PTO's change of heart.

[82]*Mahurkar v. C.R. Bard, Inc.*, 79 F.3d 1572, 38 USPQ2d 1288 (Fed. Cir. 1996). In a priority contest the party first to conceive and first to reduce to practice prevails. *New Idea Farm Equip. Corp. v. Sperry Corp.*, 916 F.2d 1561, 16 USPQ2d 1424 (Fed. Cir. 1990).

[83]The PTO lacks jurisdiction to adjudicate priority between issued patents. *Slip Track Sys. Inc. v. Metal Lite Inc.*, 159 F.3d 1337, 48 USPQ2d 1055 (Fed. Cir. 1998). Section 135(b) requires that a claim copied from an issued patent for purposes of interference must be made within a year of the issue of the patent. *Parks v. Fine*, 773 F.2d 1577, 227 USPQ 432 (Fed. Cir. 1985). For an interesting application of §135(b) in an ex parte context, see *In re McGrew*, 120 F.3d 1236, 43 USPQ2d 1633 (Fed. Cir. 1997).

[84]*Minnesota Min. & Mfg. Co. v. Norton Co.*, 929 F.2d 670, 18 USPQ2d 1302 (Fed. Cir. 1991).

[85]*Conservolite, Inc. v. Widmayer*, 21 F.3d 1098, 30 USPQ2d 1626 (Fed. Cir. 1994).

In order to establish priority in an interference, the party who files later is required to establish reduction to practice before the filing date of the party who filed first, or conception before that date coupled with reasonable diligence from just before that date to the filing date of the later filing party. However, in order to establish the prima facie case necessary to entitle a junior party to proceed with the interference, the later filing party is required only to prove at least so much of its case as would entitle it to an award of priority if the senior party were to rely only on its filing date and were not to rebut any of the junior party's case.[86] Where an interference is between pending applications, the junior party has the burden of proving its case for priority by a preponderance of the evidence.[87] The PTO must examine, analyze, and evaluate reasonably all pertinent evidence when weighing the credibility of an inventor's story. This is a rule of reason standard.[88] All evidence as to priority must be considered as a whole.[89]

The burden of proof, in connection with a motion attacking the benefit of a filing date accorded an opponent in an interference proceeding, is to establish the proposition at issue by a preponderance of the evidence. Under the new rules of the PTO, this burden lies upon the movant. Thus, while the burden initially may be on a party seeking to provoke an interference, or seeking to obtain entitlement to a priority date, once an interference has been declared and a party seeks to change the status of the parties by motion, the burden is then on the movant.[90] For a party involved in an interference to be accorded the benefit of the filing date of an earlier U.S. patent application, the earlier application either must be referred to in the declaration of the interference or must be made the subject of a motion "for benefit." When a party moves for benefit of an earlier filing date, the motion must show that the earlier application constitutes a constructive reduction to practice of the subject matter of the count.

---

[86]*Hahn v. Wong,* 892 F.2d 1028, 13 USPQ2d 1313 (Fed. Cir. 1989). See also *Schendel v. Curtis,* 83 F.3d 1399, 38 USPQ2d 1743 (Fed. Cir. 1996).

[87]*Morgan v. Hirsch,* 728 F.2d 1449, 221 USPQ 193 (Fed. Cir. 1984). See *Coleman v. Dines,* 754 F.2d 353, 224 USPQ 857 (Fed. Cir. 1985), for an unusual situation involving a substitution of applications and a consequent change from senior party to junior party. It is possible that a party can win an interference without testimony, simply on the basis of facts already of record in the PTO file. But if a party wants evidence considered, it must follow the procedural rules of the PTO Board. *Case v. CPC Int'l,* 730 F.2d 745, 221 USPQ 196 (Fed. Cir. 1984).

[88]*Holmwood v. Sugavanam,* 948 F.2d 1236, 20 USPQ2d 1712 (Fed. Cir. 1991). Under the rule of reason, the PTO cannot ignore the realities of technical operations in modern day research laboratories. *Id.*

[89]*Price v. Symsek,* 988 F.2d 1187, 26 USPQ2d 1031 (Fed. Cir. 1993).

[90]*Kubota v. Shibuya,,* 999 F.2d 517, 27 USPQ2d 1418 (Fed. Cir. 1993). It should be noted that the Director filed an amicus brief urging this result. The Director also took the position that this reapportionment of the burden of proof constituted a significant change in the law that created some confusion within the PTO and the practicing bar. Thus the Director urged, and the Federal Circuit agreed, that the case be remanded to permit a limited testimony period in which the movant could seek to satisfy its burden.

Thus, that party bears the burden of establishing support for the count in the earlier application.[91]

Both the patent statute and the regulations of the PTO authorize an interference between an application for a patent and an issued patent. Under the new interference rules adopted in 1984, if the effective filing date of the application is more than three months after the effective filing date of the patent, the applicant is required to file evidence demonstrating that the applicant is prima facie entitled to a judgment relative to the patent, and an explanation stating with particularity how that prima facie case is established. A primary examiner then determines whether a prima facie basis is alleged. If so, then the application goes to an examiner-in-chief for review. If the examiner-in-chief agrees, the interference proceeds. If not, an interference is declared but an order is entered stating the reasons for disagreement and directing the applicant to show cause why summary judgment should not be entered. A PTO Board panel then determines whether to enter summary judgment or permit the interference to proceed.[92] The standard of proof to establish priority of invention in an interference with an issued patent is clear and convincing evidence rather than proof beyond a reasonable doubt.[93] A junior party has the burden of proving prior conception and diligence. Where the interference is between an application and a patent that issued on a copending application, the applicable standard of proof is preponderance of the evidence. This standard differs from the clear and convincing standard that is applicable both to proof of derivation and proof of priority in an interference between an issued patent and an application that was filed for purposes of provoking an interference with the patent.[94]

Although derivation under 35 U.S.C. §102(f) and priority of invention are akin in that both focus on inventorship and both may be resolved by the Board in an interference action, they are distinct concepts. A claim that a patentee derived an invention addresses originality—who invented the subject matter of the count? Under this attack on a patent or patent application, the proponent asserts that the patentee or applicant did not invent the subject matter of the count because he or she derived the invention from another. To prove derivation in an interference proceeding, the proponent must

---

[91]*Credle v. Bond*, 25 F.3d 1566, 30 USPQ2d 1911 (Fed. Cir. 1994).

[92]*Hahn v. Wong*, 892 F.2d 1028, 13 USPQ2d 1313 (Fed. Cir. 1989). Whether a party seeking to initiate an interference has shown "good cause" for its failure to present, at the time of its original submission, evidence that it later wishes to submit, is a matter within the discretion of the Board. The 1984 rules revision imposes stricter standards for newly presented evidence. The "good cause" standard was intended to tighten the prior practice. Ignorance of counsel as to the provisions of the rules or the substantive requirements of the law is not good cause. *Id.* See also *Huston v. Ladner*, 973 F.2d 1564, 23 USPQ2d 1910 (Fed. Cir. 1992).

[93]*Price v. Symsek*, 988 F.2d 1187, 26 USPQ2d 1031 (Fed. Cir. 1993).

[94]*Bosies v. Benedict*, 27 F.3d 539, 30 USPQ2d 1862 (Fed. Cir. 1994). See also *Bruning v. Hirose*, 161 F.3d 681, 48 USPQ2d 1934 (Fed. Cir. 1998).

establish prior conception of the claimed subject matter and communication of the conception to the adverse claimant. While the ultimate question of whether a purported inventor derived the invention from another is one of fact, the determination of whether there was a prior conception is a question of law based upon subsidiary factual findings. Contrasted with derivation, a claim to priority of invention does not question whether the patentee invented the subject matter of the count, but instead focuses on which party *first* invented it. Priority goes to the first party to reduce an invention to practice unless the other party can show that it was the first to conceive the invention and that it exercised reasonable diligence in later reducing that invention to practice.[95]

Prior to the 1984 amendments to the patent statute the Board of Patent Interferences decided questions of priority, but not of patentability. Issues of patentability over the prior art were decided only by the Board of Appeals. Under the old statute and its implementing regulations, if issues of patentability were raised during an interference, the interference would be stayed, examination would proceed ex parte to resolve the patentability issue, and thereafter the interference proceeding would resume. If other issues of patentability were still pending at the conclusion of the interference, as was often the case, the application was once again returned to ex parte examination for resolution of those issues. Often, prosecution of the application included a decision of the Board of Appeals once examination by the examiner was finished. Thus, both boards and the examiner could be called upon in the prosecution of a single application involved in an interference. Congress became dissatisfied with the inefficiency of this "start-and-stop" process in which a case could "ping-pong" back and forth between interference and examination proceedings. Therefore, in 1984, Congress combined the Board of Patent Interferences with the Board of Patent Appeals to create the current Board of Patent Appeals and Interferences, and also amended 35 U.S.C. §135(a) to include the following provision: "The Board of Patent Appeals and Interferences shall determine questions of priority of the inventions and may determine questions of patentability." Consolidation of the two boards into one, with authority to consider questions both of patentability and of priority in a unified proceeding, was intended to streamline such proceedings before the PTO.[96] Thus, the PTO may,

---

[95]*Price v. Symsek,* 988 F.2d 1187, 26 USPQ2d 1031 (Fed. Cir. 1993).

[96]*Schulze v. Green,* 136 F.3d 786, 45 USPQ2d 1770 (Fed. Cir. 1998). The PTO Board at one time had jurisdiction only over priority and issues ancillary thereto. With the 1984 consolidation of the PTO Interferences Board and the Patent Appeals Board, it is no longer necessary to determine whether an issue is ancillary to priority, because the new Board will resolve both priority and patentability issues when both are fully presented. The public interest in the benefits of a patent system is best met by procedures that resolve administratively questions affecting patent validity that arise in the PTO. To do otherwise is contrary to the PTO's mission to grant presumptively valid patents. *Perkins v. Kwon,* 886 F.2d 325, 12 USPQ2d 1308 (Fed. Cir. 1989). Whether the Board possesses jurisdiction to continue an interference in order to decide patentability issues is a question of law that is reviewed de novo. But a decision

during the course of an interference, determine the patentability of any claim involved in the interference. In such cases, the PTO is passing on the patentability of claims, not counts.[97] Prior decisions respecting whether certain issues were ancillary to priority are collected in the note.[98]

(b) Right to Make the Counts

Under the old interference rules, a party copying claims for the purpose of provoking an interference bore the burden of proving by clear and convincing evidence that it had the right to make the claim. This right to make the claim turned on whether an applicant's disclosure supported the full scope of the claim under 35 U.S.C. §112.

---

to resolve issues of patentability that are not placed in issue by the parties to an interference is reviewed for abuse of discretion. *In re Gartside,* 203 F.3d 1305, 53 USPQ2d 1769 (Fed. Cir. 2000). In this case the court held that where the junior party patentee concedes that certain of its claims are unpatentable and authorizes cancellation of them, the Board nonetheless has jurisdiction to decide the patentability of those claims to the senior party applicant, and its decision to make that determination was appropriate.

[97]*Rowe v. Dror,* 112 F.3d 473, 42 USPQ2d 1550 (Fed. Cir. 1997). Thus, the PTO must separately determine the patentability of each claim in the interference, just as it would in an ex parte prosecution. However, where the party urging patentability does not separately address the patentability of each claim corresponding to a count, all such claims stand or fall together. *Id.* A patentability question, such as inventorship, if fairly raised and capable of being fully presented, must be resolved during the inter partes interference proceeding rather than during ex parte prosecution. The opposing party may well have a continuing interest in seeing that the patent does not issue to its opponent, even if it cannot win on the underlying priority question. *Schulze v. Green,* 136 F.3d 786, 45 USPQ2d 1770 (Fed. Cir. 1998). In this case there was a question of improper inventorship on the part of the applicant party. It filed a motion to correct inventorship but the motion was dismissed for failure to comply with certain technical requirements. When the preliminary statements were opened it became apparent that the patentee party could not prevail on priority. But inasmuch as the applicant party had never refiled its motion for correction of inventorship, the patentee party moved for judgment under §102(f). The Board entered judgment against the patentee party on priority and against the applicant party under §102(f). The Federal Circuit indicated that the applicant party should have refiled its motion, because the inventorship issue should have been decided inter partes. However, it vacated on the somewhat dubious ground that the applicant party was never put on "notice" by the PTO that its failure to refile its inventorship motion might be fatal.

[98]*DeGeorge v. Bernier,* 768 F.2d 1318, 226 USPQ 758 (Fed. Cir. 1985); *Case v. CPC Int'l,* 730 F.2d 745, 221 USPQ 196 (Fed. Cir. 1984) (joinder of inventors not ancillary); *Correge v. Murphy,* 705 F.2d 1326, 217 USPQ 753 (Fed. Cir. 1983) (patentability not ancillary). In one case the PTO Board found that neither party to the interference was the true inventor, but felt that it could not award against both parties. It therefore awarded priority to the senior party and simultaneously recommended to the Director that claims corresponding to the counts be rejected in both applications under 35 U.S.C. §102(f). The Federal Circuit affirmed but indicated that a more appropriate procedure would have been for the Board to suspend the interference so that its recommendation under §102(f) could be acted upon. *Morgan v. Hirsch,* 728 F.2d 1449, 221 USPQ 193 (Fed. Cir. 1984). See also *Coleman v. Dines,* 754 F.2d 353, 224 USPQ 857 (Fed. Cir. 1985) (prior invention not ancillary); *Case v. CPC Int'l,* 730 F.2d 745, 221 USPQ 196 (Fed. Cir. 1984) (breadth attack under §112 not ancillary); *Magdo v. Kooi,* 699 F.2d 1325, 216 USPQ 1033 (Fed. Cir. 1983) (adequacy under §112 and operability not ancillary; the court has not yet decided whether a challenge to best mode can be made in an interference); *Cross v. Iizuka,* 753 F.2d 1040, 224 USPQ 739 (Fed. Cir. 1985) (utility and enablement ancillary in §119 situations); *Woods v. Tsuchiya,* 754 F.2d 1571, 225 USPQ 11 (Fed. Cir. 1985) (some discovery questions not ancillary); *Parks v. Fine,* 783 F.2d 1036, 228 USPQ 677 (Fed. Cir. 1986) (dissolution not ancillary).

However, the right-to-make analysis is largely inapposite in the context of the new rules. As a prerequisite to the declaration of an interference between an application and an issued patent, the PTO must determine that the subject matter of the application claims, whether or not the language of the claim is identical to that of the patent claim, is patentable, and that the claims are drawn to the same invention. The declaration of an interference thus prima facie establishes those conditions. While the burden of establishing prima facie priority rests initially on a party seeking to provoke an interference, once an interference has been declared the burden is on a party who seeks to change the nature of the interference to take action by means of a suitable motion. Indeed, a party may not raise for consideration at final hearing a matter that properly could have been raised by a motion or opposition, unless the party shows good cause why the issue was not timely raised and except to prevent manifest injustice.[99]

It is axiomatic that the claims define the invention that an applicant believes is patentable. Although claims of one or more parties may be identical to a count of an interference, the count is not a claim to an invention; it is merely the vehicle for contesting the priority of invention and determining what evidence is relevant to the issue of priority. When the PTO considers patentability in an interference proceeding it rules on the patentability of a claim, not a count.[100]

The written description requirement is the same for a claim copied for purposes of interference as for a claim presented during ex parte prosecution of a patent application.[101] When an applicant selects language that is somewhat broad in scope, he or she takes the risk that others with specifically different structures may be able to meet the language selected.[102]

Prior cases dealing with right to make are collected in the footnote.[103]

(c) Conception and Reduction to Practice

In determining priority of invention, consideration of the gist or essence of the invention may be appropriate.[104] Conception requires

---

[99]*Conservolite, Inc. v. Widmayer,* 21 F.3d 1098, 30 USPQ2d 1626 (Fed. Cir. 1994).

[100]*In re Van Geuns,* 988 F.2d 1181, 26 USPQ2d 1057 (Fed. Cir. 1993).

[101]*In re Spina,* 975 F.2d 854, 24 USPQ2d 1142 (Fed. Cir. 1992).

[102]*Davis v. Loesch,* 998 F.2d 963, 27 USPQ2d 1440 (Fed. Cir. 1993).

[103]*Utter v. Hiraga,* 845 F.2d 993, 6 USPQ2d 1709 (Fed. Cir. 1988); *Kennecott Corp. v. Kyocera Int'l, Inc.,* 835 F.2d 1419, 5 USPQ2d 1194 (Fed. Cir. 1987); *Martin v. Mayer,* 823 F.2d 500, 3 USPQ2d 1333 (Fed. Cir. 1987); *Parks v. Fine,* 773 F.2d 1577, 227 USPQ 432 (Fed. Cir. 1985); *Ralston Purina Co. v. Far-Mar-Co, Inc.,* 772 F.2d 1570, 227 USPQ 177 (Fed. Cir. 1985); *DeGeorge v. Bernier,* 768 F.2d 1318, 226 USPQ 758 (Fed. Cir. 1985); *Woods v. Tsuchiya,* 754 F.2d 1571, 225 USPQ 11 (Fed. Cir. 1985); *Burson v. Carmichael,* 731 F.2d 849, 221 USPQ 664 (Fed. Cir. 1984); *Case v. CPC Int'l,* 730 F.2d 745, 221 USPQ 196 (Fed. Cir. 1984).

[104]*Perkin-Elmer Corp. v. Westinghouse Elec. Corp.,* 822 F.2d 1529, 3 USPQ2d 1321 (Fed. Cir. 1987).

more than a bare idea.[105] Conception is the formation in the mind of the inventor of a definite and permanent idea of the complete and operative invention, as it is to be thereafter applied in practice.[106] Actual reduction to practice requires that the claimed invention work for its intended purpose, and, as has long been the law, constructive reduction to practice occurs when a patent application on the claimed invention is filed.[107] The matter of joint conception and reduction to practice is discussed in detail in §7.1(a) under the topic of inventorship.

Conception. In *Burroughs Wellcome v. Barr*,[108] the court expounded its definition of conception. Thus, conception is the touchstone of inventorship, the completion of the mental part of invention. It is the formation in the mind of the inventor of a definite and permanent idea of the complete and operative invention, as it is thereafter to be applied in practice. Conception is complete only when the idea is so clearly defined in the inventor's mind that only ordinary skill would be necessary to reduce the invention to practice, without extensive research or experimentation. Because it is a mental act, courts require corroborating evidence of a contemporaneous disclosure that would enable one skilled in the art to make the invention. Thus, the test for conception is whether the inventor had an idea that was definite and permanent enough that one skilled in the art could understand the invention; the inventor must prove the conception by corroborating evidence, preferably by showing a contemporaneous disclosure. An idea is definite and permanent when the inventor has a specific, settled idea, a particular solution to the problem at hand, not just a general goal or research plan he or she hopes to pursue. The conception analysis necessarily turns on the inventor's ability to describe the invention with particularity. Until this can be done, he or she cannot prove possession of the complete mental picture of the invention. These rules ensure that patent rights attach only when an idea is so far developed that the inventor can point to a definite, particular invention.[109]

---

[105]*Burroughs Wellcome Co. v. Barr Labs., Inc.*, 40 F.3d 1223, 32 USPQ2d 1915 (Fed. Cir. 1994).

[106]E.g., *Cooper v. Goldfarb*, 154 F.3d 1321, 47 USPQ2d 1896 (Fed. Cir. 1998); *Kridl v. McCormick*, 105 F.3d 1446, 41 USPQ2d 1686 (Fed. Cir. 1997); *Filmtec Corp. v. Hydranautics*, 982 F.2d 1546, 25 USPQ2d 1283 (Fed. Cir. 1992). Since commercial success is not required for a reduction to practice, it certainly is not required for a conception. *Filmtec v. Hydranautics*, supra.

[107]*Hybritech Inc. v. Monoclonal Antibodies, Inc.*, 802 F.2d 1367, 231 USPQ 81 (Fed. Cir. 1986).

[108]*Burroughs Wellcome Co. v. Barr Labs., Inc.*, 40 F.3d 1223, 32 USPQ2d 1915 (Fed. Cir. 1994).

[109]The court's clear indication that the contemporaneous disclosure must be enabling is in accord with its earlier statement in *Sewall v. Walters*, 21 F.3d 411, 30 USPQ2d 1356 (Fed. Cir. 1994), to the effect that conception is complete when one of ordinary skill in the art could construct the apparatus without unduly extensive research or experimentation. At the same time, however, the court insists in *Burroughs Wellcome* that enablement and conception are distinct issues, and one need not necessarily meet the enablement standard of 35 U.S.C. §112

In some instances, an inventor is unable to establish a conception until he or she has reduced the invention to practice through a successful experiment. This situation results in a simultaneous conception and reduction to practice.[110] The *Burroughs Wellcome* decision also rejects the proposition that an inventor can never conceive an invention in an unpredictable or experimental field until reduction to practice is complete. It is undoubtedly true that in some circumstances, an inventor is unable to establish a conception until the invention has been reduced to practice through a successful experiment. But in such cases, it is not merely because the field is unpredictable; the alleged conception fails because it is incomplete. Under these circumstances, the reduction to practice can be the most definitive corroboration of conception, for where the idea is in constant flux, it is not definite and permanent. A conception is not complete if the subsequent course of experimentation, especially experimental failures, reveals uncertainty that so undermines the specificity of the inventor's idea that it is not yet a definite and permanent reflection of the complete invention as it will be used in practice. It is this factual uncertainty, not the general uncertainty surrounding experimental sciences, that bears on the problem of conception.[111]

It is conceivable that an inventor could prove prior conception by clear and convincing evidence despite the fact that no one piece of evidence in and of itself establishes the prior conception. It is sufficient if the picture painted by all of the evidence taken collectively

---

to prove conception. One wonders where the line is drawn. Of course, the court observed in *Sewall* that the existence of research or experimentation does not necessarily indicate, by itself, that complete conception did not exist. One must look for a nexus between the research or experimentation and the subject for which patent protection is sought.

[110]*Amgen, Inc. v. Chugai Pharm. Co.*, 927 F.2d 1200, 18 USPQ2d 1016 (Fed. Cir. 1991). In this case the court wrestled with the idea of conception of a gene. A gene is a chemical compound, albeit a complex one, and it is well established that conception of a chemical compound requires that the inventor be able to define it so as to distinguish it from other materials, and to describe how to obtain it. Conception does not occur unless one has a mental picture of the structure of the chemical, or is able to define it by its method of preparation, its physical or chemical properties, or whatever characteristics sufficiently distinguish it. It is not sufficient to define it solely by its principal biological property, because an alleged conception having no more specificity than that is simply a wish to know the identity of any material with that biological property. Thus, when an inventor is unable to envision the detailed constitution of a gene so as to distinguish it from other materials, as well as a method for obtaining it, conception has not been achieved until reduction to practice has occurred, i.e., until the gene has been isolated. In *Fiers v. Revel*, 984 F.2d 1164, 25 USPQ2d 1601 (Fed. Cir. 1993), the court undertook to clarify the *Amgen* holding. Thus, conception of a DNA, like conception of any chemical substance, requires a definition of that substance other than by its functional utility. In general, a DNA coding for a protein cannot be conceived until one knows the nucleotide sequence of the DNA. To the extent that conception may occur when one is able to define a chemical by its method of preparation, that would be valid only where the DNA is actually claimed in terms of its method of preparation. Before reduction to practice, conception only of a process for making a substance, with a conception of a structural or equivalent definition of that substance, can at most constitute a conception of the substance claimed as a process. Conception of a substance claimed per se without reference to a process requires conception of its structure, name, formula, or definitive chemical or physical properties.

[111]*Burroughs Wellcome Co. v. Barr Labs., Inc.*, 40 F.3d 1223, 32 USPQ2d 1915 (Fed. Cir. 1994). The doctrine of simultaneous conception and reduction to practice states that, in some instances, an inventor may only be able to establish a conception by pointing to a reduction

gives the fact finder an abiding conviction that the assertion of prior conception is highly probable.[112] A document is not itself a conception, for conception occurs in the inventor's mind, not on paper. The document simply corroborates a claim that the inventor had formulated a definite and permanent idea of the invention by the time the document was prepared.[113]

Conception of a chemical compound requires (1) the idea of the structure of the compound and (2) possession of an operative method of making it.[114] The difficulty that would arise in holding that a conception occurs when one has only the idea of a compound, defining it by its hoped-for function, is that would-be inventors would file patent applications before they had made their inventions and before they could describe them. That is not consistent with the statute or the policy behind the statute, which is to promote disclosure of inventions, not of research plans. While one does not need to have carried out one's invention before filing a patent application, one does need to be able to describe that invention with particularity.[115] When, as is often the case, a method of making a compound with conventional techniques is a matter of routine knowledge among those skilled in the art, a compound has been deemed to have been conceived when it is described, and the question of whether the conceiver was in possession of a method of making it is simply not raised.[116] Conception of a species within a genus may constitute conception of the genus.[117]

Corroboration of conception. An inventor's testimony, standing alone, is insufficient to prove conception. It requires corroboration.[118] Thus, an inventor's testimony respecting the facts surrounding a claim of derivation or priority of invention cannot, standing alone, rise to the level of clear and convincing proof. Throughout the history of the determination of patent rights, oral testimony by an alleged inventor asserting priority over a patentee's rights is regarded with skepticism, and as a result, such testimony must be supported by some type of corroborating evidence. Without some type of corroborating

---

to practice through a successful experiment. *Fina Oil & Chem. Co. v. Ewen*, 123 F.3d 1466, 43 USPQ2d 1935 (Fed. Cir. 1997).

[112]*Price v. Symsek*, 988 F.2d 1187, 26 USPQ2d 1031 (Fed. Cir. 1993).

[113]*Burroughs Wellcome Co. v. Barr Labs., Inc.*, 40 F.3d 1223, 32 USPQ2d 1915 (Fed. Cir. 1994).

[114]*Oka v. Youssefyeh*, 849 F.2d 581, 7 USPQ2d 1169 (Fed. Cir. 1988). Conception of a chemical compound requires that the inventor be able to define it so as to distinguish it from other materials, and to describe how to obtain it. *Bosies v. Benedict*, 27 F.3d 539, 30 USPQ2d 1862 (Fed. Cir. 1994). Conception of a chemical substance requires knowledge of both the specific chemical structure of the compound and an operative method of making it. *Fina Oil & Chem. Co. v. Ewen*, 123 F.3d 1466, 43 USPQ2d 1935 (Fed. Cir. 1997).

[115]*Fiers v. Revel*, 984 F.2d 1164, 25 USPQ2d 1601 (Fed. Cir. 1993).

[116]*Oka v. Youssefyeh*, 849 F.2d 581, 7 USPQ2d 1169 (Fed. Cir. 1988).

[117]*Oka v. Youssefyeh*, 849 F.2d 581, 7 USPQ2d 1169 (Fed. Cir. 1988).

[118]*Gambro Lundia AB v. Baxter Healthcare Corp.*, 110 F.3d 1573, 42 USPQ2d 1378 (Fed. Cir. 1997).

evidence, an alleged inventor's testimony cannot satisfy the clear and convincing standard.[119] The corroboration requirement arose out of a concern that inventors testifying in patent infringement cases would be tempted to remember facts favorable to their case by the lure of protecting their patent or defeating another's patent. While perhaps prophylactic in application given the unique abilities of trial court judges and juries to assess credibility, the rule provides a bright line for both district courts and the PTO to follow in addressing the difficult issues related to invention dates. In assessing corroboration of oral testimony, courts apply a rule of reason analysis.[120]

Thus, proof of conception requires a showing that each feature of the count was known to the inventor and communicated to the corroborating witness in sufficient fullness to enable one of skill in the art to make the invention. A rule of reason approach applies to conception, but some independent corroboration is necessary.[121] An evaluation of all pertinent evidence must be made so that a sound determination of the credibility of the inventor's story may be reached. Relevant factors include: (1) delay between the event and the trial; (2) interest of corroborating witnesses; (3) contradiction or impeachment; (4) corroboration; (5) the corroborating witnesses' familiarity with details of alleged prior work; (6) improbability of prior use considering the state of the art; (7) impact of the invention on the industry;

---

[119]*Price v. Symsek,* 988 F.2d 1187, 26 USPQ2d 1031 (Fed. Cir. 1993). The court disavows any per se rule that what a drawing discloses invariably must be supported by corroborating evidence. This is unlike a situation where an inventor is proffering oral testimony attempting to remember specifically what was conceived and when it was conceived, a situation where, over time, honest witnesses can convince themselves that they conceived the invention of a valuable patent. Thus, only an inventor's testimony requires corroboration before it can be considered. *Id.*

[120]*Mahurkar v. C.R. Bard, Inc.,* 79 F.3d 1572, 38 USPQ2d 1288 (Fed. Cir. 1996). There is no particular formula that an inventor must follow in providing corroboration of his or her testimony of conception. Rather, whether a putative inventor's testimony has been sufficiently corroborated is determined by a rule of reason analysis, in which an evaluation of all pertinent evidence must be made so that a sound determination of the credibility of the inventor's story may be reached. *Singh v. Brake,* 222 F.3d 1362, 55 USPQ2d 1673 (Fed. Cir. 2000).

[121]*Coleman v. Dines,* 754 F.2d 353, 224 USPQ 857 (Fed. Cir. 1985). See also *Kridl v. McCormick,* 105 F.3d 1446, 41 USPQ2d 1686 (Fed. Cir. 1997). The mere fact that the inventor coauthored a paper will not provide evidence of conception of a sole invention without more. *Coleman v. Dines,* supra. But corroboration is not required where a party seeks to prove conception through the use of physical exhibits. The trier of fact can conclude for itself what documents show, aided by testimony as to what they would mean to one skilled in the art. *Mahurkar v. C.R. Bard, Inc.,* 79 F.3d 1572, 38 USPQ2d 1288 (Fed. Cir. 1996). Under a rule of reason analysis, the fact that a notebook entry has not been promptly witnessed does not necessarily disqualify it in serving as corroboration of conception. Indeed, in some cases conception may be proved solely on the basis of laboratory notebook entries witnessed subsequent to their entry. *Singh v. Brake,* 222 F.3d 1362, 55 USPQ2d 1673 (Fed. Cir. 2000). See also *Hybritech Inc. v. Monoclonal Antibodies, Inc.,* 802 F.2d 1367, 231 USPQ 81 (Fed. Cir. 1986). In *Bosies v. Benedict,* 27 F.3d 539, 30 USPQ2d 1862 (Fed. Cir. 1994), the inventor had a notebook entry showing the structure of the claimed compound, except that a variable "n" was undefined. To meet the count, n would have to be in the range of 2 to 8. A corroborating witness testified that he understood n to mean 1 or 2. The court rejected this as sufficient corroboration of the conception. The conception test is whether every limitation of the count was then known to the inventor.

and (8) relationship between witness and alleged prior user.[122] A tribunal must make a reasonable analysis of all of the pertinent evidence to determine whether the inventor's testimony is credible. The tribunal must also bear in mind the purpose of corroboration, which is to prevent fraud by providing independent confirmation of the inventor's testimony.[123] An inventor need not know that the invention will work for conception to be complete. It need only be shown that he or she had the idea; the discovery that an invention actually works is part of its reduction to practice. A belief that the invention will work and the reasons for choosing a particular approach are irrelevant to conception.[124] Evidence need not always expressly show possession of the invention to corroborate conception. But just showing enough to have made the invention obvious may not be sufficient.[125]

The matter of corroboration is also discussed in §3.4(d), in the context of the defense of prior invention.

Reduction to practice. The filing of a patent application serves as conception and constructive reduction to practice of the subject matter described in the application. There is no need for proof or corroboration of the subject matter that is included in the application unless a date earlier than the filing date is sought to be established. Thus the inventor need not provide evidence of either conception or actual reduction to practice when relying on the content of the patent application. However, the patent application must comply with the legal requirements for support of the interference count. When a party to an interference seeks the benefit of an earlier filed U.S. patent application, the earlier application must meet the requirements of 35 U.S.C. §120 and §112¶1 for the subject matter of the count. The earlier application must contain a written description of the subject matter of the interference count, and must meet the enablement requirement.[126] An abandoned application cannot, if no subsequent

---

[122]*Price v. Symsek,* 988 F.2d 1187, 26 USPQ2d 1031 (Fed. Cir. 1993). See also *Schendel v. Curtis,* 83 F.3d 1399, 38 USPQ2d 1743 (Fed. Cir. 1996).

[123]*Kridl v. McCormick,* 105 F.3d 1446, 41 USPQ2d 1686 (Fed. Cir. 1997). The court explicitly held that an inventor's uncorroborated testimony that he conceived a utility for his invention may be accepted if there exists other corroborated evidence to indicate that the inventor's testimony is credible. Circumstances may make utility implicit. The court seems here to be saying that the question is whether a person of ordinary skill in the art would have accepted the inventor's uncorroborated testimony of intended use of his invention at the time of his conception.

[124]*Burroughs Wellcome Co. v. Barr Labs., Inc.,* 40 F.3d 1223, 32 USPQ2d 1915 (Fed. Cir. 1994).

[125]*Burroughs Wellcome Co. v. Barr Labs., Inc.,* 40 F.3d 1223, 32 USPQ2d 1915 (Fed. Cir. 1994).

[126]*Hyatt v. Boone,* 146 F.3d 1128, 47 USPQ2d 1128 (Fed. Cir. 1998). The filing of a patent application is a constructive reduction to practice. *Hazeltine Corp. v. United States,* 820 F.2d 1190, 2 USPQ2d 1744 (Fed. Cir. 1987).

application was copending with it, be considered a constructive reduction to practice; it is inoperative for any purpose save possibly as evidence of conception.[127]

Actual reduction to practice usually requires at least a testing of the invention. The invention must have been sufficiently tested to demonstrate that it will work for its intended purposes.[128] When testing is necessary to show actual reduction to practice, the embodiment relied upon as evidence of priority must actually work for its intended purpose. The testing required depends on the particular facts of each case, with the court guided by a common sense approach in weighing the sufficiency of the testing. Reduction to practice does not require that the invention, when tested, be in a commercially satisfactory stage of development. Similarly, testing need not show utility beyond a possibility of failure, but only a probability. Complex inventions and problems may require laboratory tests that accurately duplicate actual working conditions in practical use. Less complex inventions and problems do not demand such stringent testing. But the cases all share a common theme: the question is whether the testing in fact demonstrated a solution to the problem intended to be solved by the inventor. There is no requirement of commercial perfection nor absolute replication of the circumstances of the invention's ultimate use. But when the problem includes many uncertainties, more scrupulous testing is required.[129]

Proof of an actual reduction to practice requires a showing that the embodiment relied upon as evidence of priority actually worked for its intended purpose. This is so even if the intended purpose is not explicitly set forth in the counts of the interference. On the other hand, tests performed outside the intended environment can be sufficient to show reduction to practice if the testing conditions are sufficiently similar to those of the intended environment.[130] In the context of a patent rights clause in a government contract, reduction to practice occurs when it is established that the invention will perform its intended function beyond a possibility of failure, so that whatever minor adjustments are thereafter required may be considered mere

---

[127]*In re Costello,* 717 F.2d 1346, 219 USPQ 389 (Fed. Cir. 1983).

[128]*Holmwood v. Sugavanam,* 948 F.2d 1236, 20 USPQ2d 1712 (Fed. Cir. 1991); *Great Northern Corp. v. Davis Core & Pad Co.,* 782 F.2d 159, 228 USPQ 356 (Fed. Cir. 1986); *King Instr. Corp. v. Otari Corp.,* 767 F.2d 853, 226 USPQ 402 (Fed. Cir. 1985); *Kimberly-Clark Corp. v. Johnson & Johnson,* 745 F.2d 1437, 223 USPQ 603 (Fed. Cir. 1984).

[129]*Scott v. Finney,* 34 F.3d 1058, 32 USPQ2d 1115 (Fed. Cir. 1995). The invention was an inflatable penile implant. The court rejected a suggestion that actual human use testing was necessary to establish successful operation under actual human use conditions for a reasonable length of time. It would appear that the court felt that the PTO was requiring a showing of safety and effectiveness that is more properly left to the FDA.

[130]*DSL Dynamic Sciences Ltd. v. Union Switch & Signal, Inc.,* 928 F.2d 1122, 18 USPQ2d 1152 (Fed. Cir. 1991). Here the work involved testing and use of a coupler mount assembly with a caboose. In order to prove an actual reduction to practice, the party needed to show either that use of a coupler mount with a caboose is an intended purpose of the invention or that the tests performed on a caboose coupler sufficiently simulated the conditions present on a freight car coupler.

perfecting modifications. An invention that has been so reduced to practice is immediately ready to be adapted for practical use.[131] But there is no requirement that the invention be tested in a commercially satisfactory stage of development.[132]

Reduction to practice follows conception. To show actual reduction to practice, an inventor must demonstrate that the invention is suitable for its intended purpose. Depending on the character of the invention and the problem it solves, this showing may require test results. Less complicated inventions and problems do not demand stringent testing.[133] Indeed, some devices are so simple and their purpose and efficacy so obvious that their complete construction is sufficient to demonstrate workability.[134] But when testing is necessary to establish utility, there must be some recognition of successful testing prior to the critical date. It is not enough that the testing be completed before the critical date and ultimately prove successful, regardless of when that success is appreciated or recognized.[135]

To establish reduction to practice of a chemical composition, it is sufficient to prove that the inventor actually prepared the composition and knew it would work.[136] On the other hand, if the usefulness of a compound for its intended purpose is not inherently apparent, it must be tested to demonstrate that it will perform with sufficient success.[137] Actual reduction to practice, which constitutes in law the final phase of invention, cannot be established absent a showing of practical utility.[138] But if the claim is to a process for making a compound, reduction to practice does not require that the compound itself be tested for utility.[139]

---

[131]*Hazeltine Corp. v. United States,* 820 F.2d 1190, 2 USPQ2d 1744 (Fed. Cir. 1987). A contractor with such an invention therefore would reasonably seek a contract with the government for the production of a working prototype, or at the very least would file a patent application. Negotiation of a two-phase contract, the first phase of which was a research and development obligation viewed as a "study and design" phase, and performance of that first phase are inconsistent with the argument that a reduction to practice had occurred prior to the execution of the contract. *Id.*

[132]*Mahurkar v. C.R. Bard, Inc.,* 79 F.3d 1572, 38 USPQ2d 1288 (Fed. Cir. 1996); *King Instr. Corp. v. Otari Corp.,* 767 F.2d 853, 226 USPQ 402 (Fed. Cir. 1985); *Barmag Barmer Masch. AG v. Murata Mach., Ltd.,* 731 F.2d 831, 221 USPQ 561 (Fed. Cir. 1984). Thus, although events occurring after an alleged actual reduction to practice can cast doubt on whether reduction to practice has in fact taken place, a failure of several commercial devices made long after the asserted reduction does not necessarily mean that the device was inadequately tested. *DSL Dynamic Sciences Ltd. v. Union Switch & Signal, Inc.,* 928 F.2d 1122, 18 USPQ2d 1152 (Fed. Cir. 1991).

[133]*Mahurkar v. C.R. Bard, Inc.,* 79 F.3d 1572, 38 USPQ2d 1288 (Fed. Cir. 1996).

[134]*King Instr. Corp. v. Otari Corp.,* 767 F.2d 853, 226 USPQ 402 (Fed. Cir. 1985). However, the mere existence of assembly drawings does not by itself establish a reduction to practice. *Id.* See also *In re Asahi/Am. Inc.,* 48 F.3d 1204, 37 USPQ2d 1204 (Fed. Cir. 1995).

[135]*Estee Lauder Inc. v. L'Oreal S.A.,* 129 F.3d 588, 44 USPQ2d 1610 (Fed. Cir. 1997).

[136]*Hahn v. Wong,* 892 F.2d 1028, 13 USPQ2d 1313 (Fed. Cir. 1989).

[137]*Kimberly-Clark Corp. v. Johnson & Johnson,* 745 F.2d 1437, 223 USPQ 603 (Fed. Cir. 1984).

[138]*Fujikawa v. Wattanasin,* 93 F.3d 1559, 39 USPQ2d 1895 (Fed. Cir. 1996).

[139]*Shurie v. Richmond,* 699 F.2d 1156, 216 USPQ 1042 (Fed. Cir. 1983).

The physical embodiment relied upon as an actual reduction to practice must include every essential limitation of the count.[140] The two-pronged test for actual reduction to practice requires construction of an embodiment that meets every element of the claim, and testing to see that the embodiment works for its intended purpose. These are two distinct requirements that must be met. Thus, successful testing of an embodiment that lacks an element, even though it may contain an equivalent of that element, does not eliminate, or act as a surrogate for, the requirement that the embodiment contain every element. The doctrine of equivalents does not pertain to interference law.[141]

The rule that conception and reduction to practice cannot be established nunc pro tunc simply requires that in order for an experiment to constitute an actual reduction to practice, there must have been contemporaneous appreciation of the invention at issue by the inventor. Subsequent testing or later recognition may not be used to show that a party had contemporaneous appreciation of the invention. However, evidence of subsequent testing may be admitted for the purpose of showing that an embodiment was produced and that it met the limitations of the count.[142] There are no degrees of reduction to practice; either one has or has not occurred.[143]

Corroboration of reduction to practice. In order to establish an actual reduction to practice, an inventor's testimony must be corroborated by independent evidence. However, a "rule of reason" analysis is applied to determine whether an inventor's testimony regarding reduction to practice has been sufficiently corroborated. The rule requires an evaluation of all pertinent evidence when determining the credibility of an inventor's testimony. In order to corroborate a reduction to practice, it is not necessary to produce an actual over-the-shoulder observer. Rather, sufficient circumstantial evidence of an independent nature can satisfy the corroboration requirement. Furthermore, an actual reduction to practice does not require corroboration for every factual issue contested by the parties. But adoption

---

[140]*Correge v. Murphy,* 705 F.2d 1326, 217 USPQ 753 (Fed. Cir. 1983). A party cannot rely upon tests performed on a composition that fails to meet the limitations of the interference count to demonstrate that the composition works for its intended purpose. *Cooper v. Goldfarb,* 154 F.3d 1321, 47 USPQ2d 1896 (Fed. Cir. 1998). Where the count called for an airplane having a passenger cabin, a luggage compartment, and intervening floor with openings and ventilation devices, it is not enough to test merely the ventilation device; the test must be performed in an airplane mockup. *Id.* See also *UMC Elec. Co. v. United States,* 816 F.2d 647, 2 USPQ2d 1465 (Fed. Cir. 1987). Every limitation of the interference count must exist in the embodiment and be shown to have performed as intended. *Newkirk v. Lulejian,* 825 F.2d 1581, 3 USPQ2d 1793 (Fed. Cir. 1987). Thus, where the count called for a means for performing a step, the party had to show that the embodiment included the means and that he actually performed the step. *Id.*

[141]*Eaton v. Evans,* 204 F.3d 1094, 53 USPQ2d 1696, 1698 (Fed. Cir. 2000).

[142]*Cooper v. Goldfarb,* 154 F.3d 1321, 47 USPQ2d 1896 (Fed. Cir. 1998).

[143]*UMC Elec. Co. v. United States,* 816 F.2d 647, 2 USPQ2d 1465 (Fed. Cir. 1987). It can only cause confusion in interference law, with its special technical considerations, and in

of the rule of reason approach has not altered the requirement that evidence of corroboration must not depend solely on the inventor.[144]

The purpose of the rule requiring corroboration is to prevent fraud. Thus the inventor must provide independent corroborating evidence in addition to his or her own statements and documents. Such evidence may consist of testimony of a witness, other than an inventor, to the actual reduction to practice, or it may consist of evidence of surrounding facts and circumstances independent of information received from the inventor. Statements by a witness that he had read and understood a notebook entry as of a certain date do not corroborate a reduction to practice; they establish only that those pages existed as of that date. This may be part of a cohesive web of corroborating evidence that could establish reduction to practice, but it is insufficient standing alone.[145] In one case the inventor testified that he had practiced the claimed method as of a certain date and offered a page from his notebook that confirmed it. His proofs were held sufficiently corroborated by (1) testimony of a coworker that the inventor had obtained the supplies necessary to practice the method; (2) testimony of another coworker that he had seen a product produced by the method; and (3) general evidence that the company had an organized research program designed to create a record sufficient to corroborate inventions.[146] Only an inventor's testimony need be corroborated, not the testimony of a corroborating witness.[147]

To establish a date of invention, a party may not rely upon knowledge, use, or activity that took place in a foreign country, except as provided by 35 U.S.C. §104.[148] The activity relied upon for priority must have occurred in the United States. Thus, where the claim is to a process for making a compound, testing in the United States of the utility of the compound is insufficient if the compound is made by practicing the process in a foreign country.[149] Where testimony merely places acts within a stated time period, the inventor has not

---

operation of the on-sale bar, which is guided by entirely different policies, to adopt modifiers in connection with "reduction to practice," whatever the context. *Id.*

[144]*Cooper v. Goldfarb,* 154 F.3d 1321, 47 USPQ2d 1896 (Fed. Cir. 1998).

[145]*Hahn v. Wong,* 892 F.2d 1028, 13 USPQ2d 1313 (Fed. Cir. 1989). The court recognizes that the standard of proof required to corroborate a reduction to practice may be more stringent than that required to corroborate a conception. Thus, a notebook page may well show that the inventor conceived what was written on the page, whereas it may not show that the experiments were actually performed, as required for a reduction to practice. *Singh v. Brake,* 222 F.3d 1362, 55 USPQ2d 1673 (Fed. Cir. 2000). As with the conception element of priority, corroboration is required to support testimony regarding communication and reasonable diligence in reduction to practice. *Price v. Symsek,* 988 F.2d 1187, 26 USPQ2d 1031 (Fed. Cir. 1993).

[146]*Lacotte v. Thomas,* 758 F.2d 611, 225 USPQ 633 (Fed. Cir. 1985). When a putative inventor has obtained specific reagents with no substantial use other than to make the claimed chemical compound, that evidence is of significant corroborative value, both as to reduction to practice and conception. *Singh v. Brake,* 222 F.3d 1362, 55 USPQ2d 1673 (Fed. Cir. 2000).

[147]*Holmwood v. Sugavanam,* 948 F.2d 1236, 20 USPQ2d 1712 (Fed. Cir. 1991).

[148]*Holmwood v. Sugavanam,* 948 F.2d 1236, 20 USPQ2d 1712 (Fed. Cir. 1991).

[149]*Shurie v. Richmond,* 699 F.2d 1156, 216 USPQ 1042 (Fed. Cir. 1983).

established a date for his or her activities earlier than the last day of the period.[150]

(d) Diligence, Abandonment, and Suppression

The law does not inquire as to the fits and starts by which an invention is made, and a mere lapse of time will not prevent the inventor from receiving a patent. The sole exception to this principle resides in 35 U.S.C. §102(g) and the exigencies of the priority contest.[151] Generally, the party who establishes that it is the first to conceive and the first to reduce an invention to practice is entitled to a patent. However, the second party to conceive and reduce to practice the same invention will be awarded priority of invention if it can show that the first party to reduce to practice abandoned, suppressed, or concealed the invention.[152]

Under §102(g), a distinction must be drawn between deliberate suppression or concealment of an invention, which is probably not curable by resumption of work, and a legal inference of suppression or concealment based on "too long" a delay. The first probably results in an absolute forfeiture, while the second can be cured.[153] Intentional suppression refers to situations in which an inventor, designedly, and with the view of applying it indefinitely and exclusively for his or her own profit, withholds the invention from the public.[154] Abandonment can also be fatal to a party in interference.[155]

Where there is an unreasonable delay between the actual reduction to practice and the filing of a patent application, there is a basis for inferring abandonment, suppression, or concealment. However, the inventor's activities during the delay period may excuse the delay. For example, he or she may have worked during that period to improve

---

[150]*Oka v. Youssefyeh,* 849 F.2d 581, 7 USPQ2d 1169 (Fed. Cir. 1988). Thus, a Board finding that an invention was made during the last week of October fails to establish that the invention was made prior to October 31. Since the senior party's filing date was October 31, this results in a tie that the senior party wins. *Id.*

[151]*Paulik v. Rizkalla,* 760 F.2d 1270, 226 USPQ 224 (Fed. Cir. 1985).

[152]*Lutzker v. Plet,* 843 F.2d 1364, 6 USPQ2d 1370 (Fed. Cir. 1988).

[153]*Paulik v. Rizkalla,* 760 F.2d 1270, 226 USPQ 224 (Fed. Cir. 1985). Renewed activity can negate suppression or concealment. A decision maker with limited funds must decide whether additional research funds should be committed to a project that has been neglected for some time. In making this decision, it would certainly take into account the likelihood that the additional research might yield valuable patent rights. Furthermore, in evaluating the probability of securing those patent rights, an important consideration would be the earliest priority date to which the research would be entitled, especially in situations where the decision maker knows that it and its competitors are racing toward a common goal. Thus, the right to rely on renewed activity for purposes of priority would encourage the decision maker to fund the additional research. *Fujikawa v. Wattanasin,* 93 F.3d 1559, 39 USPQ2d 1895 (Fed. Cir. 1996).

[154]*Fujikawa v. Wattanasin,* 93 F.3d 1559, 39 USPQ2d 1895 (Fed. Cir. 1996).

[155]*Correge v. Murphy,* 705 F.2d 1326, 217 USPQ 753 (Fed. Cir. 1983). There was no presumption of intent to abandon where an actual reduction to practice was followed in seven months by a public disclosure, which was in turn followed in eight months by filing of an application. Diligence was not at issue.

or perfect the invention disclosed in the patent application. The law does not punish an inventor for attempting to perfect his or her process before he or she gives it to the public. Thus, an inference of suppression or concealment may be overcome with evidence that the reason for the delay was to perfect the invention. But where the delay is caused by working on refinements and improvements that are not reflected in the final patent application, or that go to commercialization of the invention, the delay will not be excused.[156]

Where a party has an actual reduction to practice followed by a long period of inactivity, it may not be able to use the earlier reduction for priority, but it can use it to show conception and attempt to show diligence from just before the other's entry into the field until its own application filing date.[157] Even where there is an inference of suppression or concealment, the applicant can show that it renewed activity on the invention and proceeded diligently until filing the application, beginning prior to the other party's entry into the field.[158]

Although spurring into resumption of work by the entry of the other into the field is not necessary to a finding of suppression or concealment, it is an important equitable factor.[159] Evidence that a first inventor was spurred to disclose by the activities of a second inventor has always been an important factor in priority determinations because it creates an inference that, but for the efforts of the second inventor, the public would never have gained knowledge of the invention.[160]

The junior party in an interference is required to establish reduction to practice before the senior party's filing date, or conception before that date coupled with reasonable diligence from just before that date to the junior party's own filing date.[161] One who is first to conceive but last to reduce to practice has the burden of establishing a prima facie case of reasonable diligence from a time immediately before the other's filing date until his or her own reduction to practice.

---

[156]*Lutzker v. Plet*, 843 F.2d 1364, 6 USPQ2d 1370 (Fed. Cir. 1988). The court approved a Board conclusion that a 51-month delay between actual reduction to practice and first public disclosure gave rise to an inference of an intent to abandon, suppress, or conceal the invention. The applicant's efforts to justify the delay were rejected as being primarily directed to commercialization (preparing production molds, a recipe book, and blister packaging). Moreover, there was evidence of a deliberate policy not to disclose to the public until the invention was ready for commercial production. See also *Fujikawa v. Wattanasin*, 93 F.3d 1559, 39 USPQ2d 1895 (Fed. Cir. 1996).

[157]*Paulik v. Rizkalla*, 796 F.2d 456, 230 USPQ 434 (Fed. Cir. 1986).

[158]*Lutzker v. Plet*, 843 F.2d 1364, 6 USPQ2d 1370 (Fed. Cir. 1988). Here the suppressing party showed a commercially viable version of the invention, which had been actually reduced to practice 51 months earlier, on the same day that the other party filed its patent application. This "same-day" renewal of activity was not "prior" to the other's entry into the field and thus could not overcome the inference of suppression.

[159]*Paulik v. Rizkalla*, 760 F.2d 1270, 226 USPQ 224 (Fed. Cir. 1985).

[160]*Fujikawa v. Wattanasin*, 93 F.3d 1559, 39 USPQ2d 1895 (Fed. Cir. 1996). In this case the court expressly passed the question of whether spurring as a result of activity by a third party (i.e., one not a party to the interference) qualifies to create that inference.

[161]*Oka v. Youssefyeh*, 849 F.2d 581, 7 USPQ2d 1169 (Fed. Cir. 1988). See also *Mahurkar v. C.R. Bard, Inc.*, 79 F.3d 1572, 38 USPQ2d 1288 (Fed. Cir. 1996).

The reasonable diligence standard balances the interest in rewarding and encouraging invention with the public's interest in the earliest possible disclosure of innovation.[162]

Diligence is subject to the rule of reason as determined in the particular circumstances of each case. Reasonable diligence can be shown if it is established that the attorney worked reasonably hard on the particular application in question during the critical period. It may not be possible for a patent attorney to begin working on an application at the moment the inventor makes the disclosure, because the attorney may already have a backlog of other cases demanding his or her attention. Generally, the patent attorney must show that unrelated cases are taken up in chronological order, and thus he or she has the burden of keeping good records of the dates when cases are docketed as well as the dates when specific work is done on the applications.[163] Setting aside a project to work on others, as a matter of choice, militates against reasonable diligence.[164] In determining the reasonableness of delay, the courts may consider the everyday problems and limitations encountered by an inventor, but delays caused by an inventor's efforts to refine an invention to the most marketable and profitable form are not acceptable as excuses.[165]

(e) Miscellaneous Interference Issues

Evidence. More evidentiary opportunities are available to parties in an interference than to an applicant in an ex parte examination and appeal to the Board. In an interference, unlike an ex parte proceeding, the Federal Rules of Evidence apply. In addition, both sides can submit testimony, initially in the form of affidavits, unless the

---

[162]*Griffith v. Kanamaru,* 816 F.2d 624, 2 USPQ2d 1361 (Fed. Cir. 1987).

[163]*Bey v. Kollonitsch,* 806 F.2d 1024, 231 USPQ 967 (Fed. Cir. 1986). In this case it was held that an inventor should not be penalized because his attorney reasonably prepared closely related applications together, thereby expediting the filing of the applications and the prompt disclosure to the public of the closely related inventions contained therein. Work on a related case is to be credited toward reasonable diligence if the work on the related case contributes substantially to the ultimate preparation of the involved application. The sheer number of related cases alone is not determinative as to whether they are sufficiently related. It is error to hold that the cases must be so related that they "had" to be worked on as a group. Here the attorney worked on 22 related applications over the critical period of 41 days, fully justifying a holding of attorney diligence.

[164]*Griffith v. Kanamaru,* 816 F.2d 624, 2 USPQ2d 1361 (Fed. Cir. 1987).

[165]*Griffith v. Kanamaru,* 816 F.2d 624, 2 USPQ2d 1361 (Fed. Cir. 1987). A college professor advanced some rather novel excuses for delay, all of which were rejected by the court. For one thing, he said he was waiting for the matriculation of a graduate student, to whom he had promised the work, and who needed the project for her degree. But there was no showing that she was the only person capable of doing the work, or even that she was uniquely qualified. Thus, the convenience of the timing of a semester schedule did not justify a three-month delay in beginning work toward reduction to practice. Similarly, the college had a policy of requiring outside funding for research, and the professor waited for commercial interest. Although this policy may have beneficial aspects, the patent laws should not be skewed or slanted to enable the college to have its cake and eat it too—to act in a noncommercial manner and yet preserve the pecuniary rewards of commercial exploitation for itself. *Id.*

testimony must be compelled. A party may "cross-examine" an affiant through oral deposition. Discovery, at least against the party opponent, is also available. However, although the parties will be given an opportunity to appear before the Board to present oral argument at a final hearing, at no point in the interference proceeding is a party allowed to present live testimony before the Board. The Board reviews testimony only in the form of affidavits and transcripts of depositions, and other facts in the form of responses to interrogatories and requests for admissions. Thus, although the proceeding before the Board in an interference differs from that following an ex parte examination, the two proceedings are the same in at least one important respect— in no case is live testimony given before the Board, which would allow the Board to observe demeanor, to hear the witnesses rebut one another's testimony in response to questioning from the parties and the judges, and thus to determine credibility.[166]

There is no rigorous rule excluding expert testimony in an interference. Independent expert testimony may be used for the purpose of establishing facts such as the meaning of various terms to those skilled in the art.[167]

It is standard practice for an applicant in an interference to obscure dates on documents and simply aver that the documents antedate the filing date of the adverse patent.[168]

Interpretation of counts. Interference counts should be given their broadest possible interpretation, and resort to the specification is necessary only where there are ambiguities inherent in the claim language or obvious from arguments of counsel.[169] The mere fact that the parties argue among themselves as to the meaning of the counts does not create ambiguity where none exists.[170] If there is such ambiguity, resort must be had to the specification of the patent from which the copied count came.[171] Limitations not clearly included in a count should not be read into it.[172] A count's proper construction must be discerned by examining the language of the count as a whole. In determining the true meaning of the language, the grammatical structure and syntax may be instructive.[173]

---

[166]*Winner Int'l Royalty Corp. v. Wang,* 202 F.3d 1340, 53 USPQ2d 1580, 1585 (Fed. Cir. 2000).

[167]*Martin v. Mayer,* 823 F.2d 500, 3 USPQ2d 1333 (Fed. Cir. 1987).

[168]*Baker Oil Tools, Inc. v. Geo Vann, Inc.,* 828 F.2d 1588, 4 USPQ2d 1210 (Fed. Cir. 1987).

[169]*Davis v. Loesch,* 998 F.2d 963, 27 USPQ2d 1440 (Fed. Cir. 1993); *DeGeorge v. Bernier,* 768 F.2d 1318, 226 USPQ 758 (Fed. Cir. 1985); *Woods v. Tsuchiya,* 754 F.2d 1571, 225 USPQ 11 (Fed. Cir. 1985).

[170]*Woods v. Tsuchiya,* 754 F.2d 1571, 225 USPQ 11 (Fed. Cir. 1985).

[171]*DeGeorge v. Bernier,* 768 F.2d 1318, 226 USPQ 758 (Fed. Cir. 1985). Where interpretation is required of a claim that is copied for interference purposes, the copied claim is viewed in the context of the patent from which it was copied. *In re Spina,* 975 F.2d 854, 24 USPQ2d 1142 (Fed. Cir. 1992).

[172]*Newkirk v. Lulejian,* 825 F.2d 1581, 3 USPQ2d 1793 (Fed. Cir. 1987).

[173]*Credle v. Bond,* 25 F.3d 1566, 30 USPQ2d 1911 (Fed. Cir. 1994).

In interpreting claims for purposes of the written description requirement (i.e., support), it is improper to limit means clauses to only the precise structures shown in the applications from which and to which a claim is copied. Equivalents of those structures are also pertinent. A claim is not interpreted one way in light of the specification in which it originally was granted, and another way in light of the specification into which it is copied as a proposed interference count.[174]

Other issues. Inurement involves a claim by an inventor that, as a matter of law, the acts of another person should accrue to the benefit of the inventor. Derivation involves the claim that the adverse party did not "invent" the subject matter of the count because that party derived the invention from another. To prove derivation in an interference proceeding, the party asserting derivation must establish prior conception of the claimed subject matter and communication of the conception to the adverse claimant. In order to establish inurement, an inventor must show, among other things, that the other person was working either explicitly or implicitly at the inventor's request. While derivation focuses on the communication of information between two parties, inurement focuses on the nature of the relationship between them. Communication of the conception by the inventor to the other party is not required to establish inurement.[175] At least three requirements must be met before a noninventor's recognition of the utility of an invention can inure to the benefit of the inventor. First, the inventor must have conceived of the invention. Second, the inventor must have had an expectation that the embodiment tested would work for the intended purpose of the invention. Third, the inventor must have submitted the embodiment for testing for the intended purpose of the invention.[176]

Sometimes inventorship issues are resolved by way of interference. In an originality case the issue is not who is the first or prior inventor, but who made the invention. The inventorship issue to be decided is thus merely who conceived the invention for which patent protection is sought, not who first conceived that invention.[177] An allegation that two persons were joint inventors of a count requires some degree of collaboration. A person who first conceived and first reduced an invention to practice cannot be a joint inventor with a person who allegedly did not even conceive until after the former's

---

[174]*In re Spina*, 975 F.2d 854, 24 USPQ2d 1142 (Fed. Cir. 1992).

[175]*Cooper v. Goldfarb*, 154 F.3d 1321, 47 USPQ2d 1896 (Fed. Cir. 1998).

[176]*Genentech, Inc. v. Chiron Corp.*, 220 F.3d 1345, 55 USPQ2d 1636 (Fed. Cir. 2000).

[177]*Sewall v. Walters*, 21 F.3d 411, 30 USPQ2d 1356 (Fed. Cir. 1994). In this case a corporation filed a joint application naming an employee and a consultant as joint inventors. The consultant later filed the identical application as a sole inventor. An interference was declared, but inasmuch as the consultant was also entitled to the filing date of the joint application, neither party was senior or junior with respect to priority. The issue was really one of joint or sole inventorship, and on that issue the consultant had the burden of proof because he was the second to file in his sole capacity.

reduction to practice; collaboration under such circumstances is simply not possible.[178]

In one case the court held that the Board abused its discretion in requiring the owner of two of the applications in a three-way interference to elect between them at a stage in the proceedings where it was not yet clear what the content of the final count would be or what proofs on dates of conception and reduction to practice the third party would seek to establish. Thus, the owner was unable to make a reasoned determination as to which of its applications would be the best upon which to proceed.[179]

Review. Parties to an interference dissatisfied with the PTO Board decision have a choice of appealing to the Federal Circuit under 35 U.S.C. §141 or commencing a civil action in an appropriate district court under §146.[180] An appeal to the Federal Circuit must be dismissed if any adverse party to the interference files a timely notice of election to have all further proceedings conducted in a district court under §146. In that event, the appellant must then file a §146 action in order to obtain judicial review.[181] District court review of interference proceedings is discussed in §11.4(a)(ii).

An issue not addressed at a final hearing before the PTO Board will not be considered on appeal to the Federal Circuit.[182] The issues of count construction,[183] priority,[184] conception,[185] reduction to practice,[186]

---

[178]*Credle v. Bond*, 25 F.3d 1566, 30 USPQ2d 1911 (Fed. Cir. 1994).

[179]*Barton v. Adang*, 162 F.3d 1140, 49 USPQ2d 1128 (Fed. Cir. 1998).

[180]*In re Van Geuns*, 946 F.2d 845, 20 USPQ2d 1291 (Fed. Cir. 1991).

[181]*Wu v. Wang*, 129 F.3d 1237, 44 USPQ2d 1641 (Fed. Cir. 1997). In this case the adverse party filed an election and then went ahead and filed its own §146 action in California. The appellant countered with a §146 action in the District of Columbia and moved the Federal Circuit to enjoin the adverse party from prosecuting the California action. The motion was granted, because it is the appellant that gets to choose the appropriate forum under §146. The court did indicate, however, that an appropriate transfer motion could be entertained by the D.C. district court. There was also a complex question as to whether the appellee was truly an "adverse party" entitled to file such an election.

[182]*Credle v. Bond*, 25 F.3d 1566, 30 USPQ2d 1911 (Fed. Cir. 1994).

[183]*Credle v. Bond*, 25 F.3d 1566, 30 USPQ2d 1911 (Fed. Cir. 1994); *Davis v. Loesch*, 998 F.2d 963, 27 USPQ2d 1440 (Fed. Cir. 1993); *DeGeorge v. Bernier*, 768 F.2d 1318, 226 USPQ 758 (Fed. Cir. 1985).

[184]*Kridl v. McCormick*, 105 F.3d 1446, 41 USPQ2d 1686 (Fed. Cir. 1997). Priority is a question of law that is to be determined based upon underlying factual determinations. *Conservolite, Inc. v. Widmayer*, 21 F.3d 1098, 30 USPQ2d 1626 (Fed. Cir. 1994); *Price v. Symsek*, 988 F.2d 1187, 26 USPQ2d 1031 (Fed. Cir. 1993).

[185]*Singh v. Brake*, 222 F.3d 1362, 55 USPQ2d 1673 (Fed. Cir. 2000); *Kridl v. McCormick*, 105 F.3d 1446, 41 USPQ2d 1686 (Fed. Cir. 1997); *Bosies v. Benedict*, 27 F.3d 539, 30 USPQ2d 1862 (Fed. Cir. 1994); *Sewall v. Walters*, 21 F.3d 411, 30 USPQ2d 1356 (Fed. Cir. 1994); *Filmtec Corp. v. Hydranautics*, 982 F.2d 1546, 25 USPQ2d 1283 (Fed. Cir. 1992).

[186]*Fujikawa v. Wattanasin*, 93 F.3d 1559, 39 USPQ2d 1895 (Fed. Cir. 1996); *Schendel v. Curtis*, 83 F.3d 1399, 38 USPQ2d 1743 (Fed. Cir. 1996); *In re Asahi/Am. Inc.*, 48 F.3d 1204, 37 USPQ2d 1204 (Fed. Cir. 1995); *Scott v. Finney*, 34 F.3d 1058, 32 USPQ2d 1115 (Fed. Cir. 1995); *Holmwood v. Sugavanam*, 948 F.2d 1236, 20 USPQ2d 1712 (Fed. Cir. 1991); *DSL Dynamic Sciences Ltd. v. Union Switch & Signal, Inc.*, 928 F.2d 1122, 18 USPQ2d 1152 (Fed. Cir. 1991).

and suppression or concealment[187] are questions of law that the court reviews de novo. Facts found by the PTO Board in interferences are reviewed under the substantial evidence standard.[188] What is disclosed in an application involved in an interference, and whether an application supports the subject matter of a count, are questions of fact.[189]

Where a party thinks it can prevail solely on the basis of its filing date and therefore does not introduce evidence of priority despite opportunity to do so, remand is not appropriate. There is no support in law for repeated bites at the apple.[190] The determination whether a party seeking to initiate an interference has shown good cause for its failure to present additional evidence at the time of its initial submission is a matter within the discretion of the Board.[191]

Estoppel. There are four types of interference estoppel. (1) Estoppel by dissolution prevents a junior party who had access to the senior party's application from obtaining claims to common patentable subject matter after an interference is dissolved. (2) Estoppel by judgment prevents a losing party in a previous interference between the same parties from making any claim (a) not patentably distinct from the counts in issue in that interference or (b) that reads on the disclosure of the winning party to which the losing party had access. (3) Equitable estoppel prevents the winning party in a previous interference terminated by judgment (or the senior party in an interference that ends in dissolution) from claiming patentably distinct subject matter to which the other party did not have access. (4) Estoppel for failure to file a motion to amend prevents a party who fails to file a timely interlocutory motion to amend from later claiming subject matter that could have been added by such a motion.[192] But the lost count of an interference is not prior art against a different invention, for

---

[187]*Fujikawa v. Wattanasin,* 93 F.3d 1559, 39 USPQ2d 1895 (Fed. Cir. 1996).

[188]*Singh v. Brake,* 222 F.3d 1362, 55 USPQ2d 1673 (Fed. Cir. 2000). Apparently, when the court concludes that the PTO did not have substantial evidence to support its determinations, the proper course is to remand. *Id.* See note 15:66, dealing with the impact of *Dickinson v. Zurko,* 527 U.S. 150, 50 USPQ2d 1930 (1999). For cases employing the old clearly erroneous standard, see *Kridl v. McCormick,* 105 F.3d 1446, 41 USPQ2d 1686 (Fed. Cir. 1997); *Fujikawa v. Wattanasin,* 93 F.3d 1559, 39 USPQ2d 1895 (Fed. Cir. 1996); *Schendel v. Curtis,* 83 F.3d 1399, 38 USPQ2d 1743 (Fed. Cir. 1996); *Holmwood v. Sugavanam,* 948 F.2d 1236, 20 USPQ2d 1712 (Fed. Cir. 1991); *Coleman v. Dines,* 754 F.2d 353, 224 USPQ 857 (Fed. Cir. 1985).

[189]*Credle v. Bond,* 25 F.3d 1566, 30 USPQ2d 1911 (Fed. Cir. 1994). Under the old interference practice, failure to appeal a decision on the right to make certain counts does not amount to an admission that a party has a right to make an appealed count. An unappealed adjudication of priority as to some counts does not give those counts a new status, as prior art or as evidence, with respect to support for other counts. *Martin v. Mayer,* 823 F.2d 500, 3 USPQ2d 1333 (Fed. Cir. 1987). A party whose right to make the count is not decided adversely to it cannot argue on appeal that the interference should not have been declared because it was not able to make the counts. *Newkirk v. Lulejian,* 825 F.2d 1581, 3 USPQ2d 1793 (Fed. Cir. 1987).

[190]*Burson v. Carmichael,* 731 F.2d 849, 221 USPQ 664 (Fed. Cir. 1984). Remand might be appropriate if the party introduces the evidence but the Board fails to consider it. *Id.*

[191]*Huston v. Ladner,* 973 F.2d 1564, 23 USPQ2d 1910 (Fed. Cir. 1992).

[192]*Woods v. Tsuchiya,* 754 F.2d 1571, 225 USPQ 11 (Fed. Cir. 1985).

"prior art" in the sense of 35 U.S.C. §102(g) cannot be the basis of a §102(a) rejection, the invention not being publicly known or used. Thus a losing party to an interference is entitled to claim subject matter other than that of the interference count, provided the requirements of patentability are met, and subject to those constraints that flow from the adverse decision in the interference.[193]

The losing party in an interference declared on a phantom count corresponding to interfering species claims of the parties is estopped in postinterference ex parte proceedings from obtaining a generic claim that would dominate the species claims of the winning party corresponding to the phantom count.[194] Where priority is awarded to a junior party by reason of the senior party's failure to comply with a discovery order, and where the ordered discovery was pertinent to the priority issue, the dismissal of the interference was held to have established facts sufficient to justify an estoppel by judgment against the senior party in a second interference between the two.[195]

The PTO rules permit a party to contest the designation of particular claims as corresponding to a count. If a party does not timely contest that designation, there is in effect a concession that all of the designated claims would be anticipated or made obvious if the count were actually prior art. This does not mean, however, that the party has conceded that claims corresponding to a count are anticipated or made obvious by the prior art when the subject matter of the count itself is determined to be unpatentable for obviousness. A party to an interference proceeding should be permitted to argue separately the patentability of claims designated as corresponding substantially

---

[193]*In re Zletz,* 893 F.2d 319, 13 USPQ2d 1320 (Fed. Cir. 1989). The court examined the possible tension between *In re Frilette,* 436 F.2d 496, 168 USPQ 368 (CCPA 1971), which held that a losing party to an interference, on showing that the invention now claimed is not "substantially the same" as that of the lost interference count, may employ the procedures of Rule 131 in order to antedate the filing date of the interfering application, and *In re Taub,* 348 F.2d 556, 146 USPQ 384 (CCPA 1965), which held that priority as to a genus may be shown by prior invention of a single species. In *In re Deckler,* 977 F.2d 1449, 24 USPQ2d 1448 (Fed. Cir. 1992), the court partially addressed the *"Hilmer"* cases, which appear to hold that the foreign filing date of a winning party in interference is nonetheless not the effective date of its U.S. patent as a reference under §102(g) or §103. Here the losing party was held to be barred, by collateral estoppel, from obtaining claims that were admittedly patentably indistinguishable from the lost interference count. The count is not prior art, but it is a judgment for res judicata purposes. Interference estoppel bars the assertion of claims for inventions that are patentably indistinct from those in an interference that the applicant had lost. The interference judgment conclusively determined that the winner was entitled to claim the patentable subject matter defined in the count. Thus, the judgment may be used as a basis for rejection of claims to the same patentable invention. If it were not given that preclusive effect, there could be a second interference.

[194]*In re Kroekel,* 803 F.2d 705, 231 USPQ 640 (Fed. Cir. 1986). Since the losing party might have raised the issue of the winning party's right to make the broad claims but failed to do so, it is now estopped from arguing that the winning party abandoned, suppressed, or concealed the subject matter of the generic claim, and that it is therefore entitled to a patent including such a claim. Of course, if the generic claim were somehow patentably distinct from the lost count, it could not be denied to the losing party on the sole ground of interference estoppel. Also, if the losing party had attempted to broaden the count, albeit unsuccessfully, he would not later be estopped from attempting to claim the broader subject matter.

[195]*Woods v. Tsuchiya,* 754 F.2d 1571, 225 USPQ 11 (Fed. Cir. 1985).

to a count, just as a party would be permitted to do in an ex parte prosecution and appeal.[196] In an interference, a claim is patentably distinct from the interference count if the apparatus claimed by the count does not render what is being claimed by the claim at issue obvious.[197]

A disclaimer in one interference, with different counts, does not effect a disclaimer in another.[198] Canceling narrow claims copied from another's application creates no estoppel.[199]

A party seeking to precipitate an interference filed a Rule 205 amendment and a Rule 204(c) statement averring reduction to practice of the invention of the counts prior to a particular date, and an interference was declared. The party later abandoned the interference. A defendant in an infringement suit argued that the party thereby admitted reduction to practice (and thus public use) of a device that meets the claims that ultimately issued in the party's patent. The Federal Circuit held that the statement and amendment were more than a pleading but not an adjudication—they were sworn statements of fact. As such, they could of course be considered as evidence in determining whether the uses were experimental or not (reduction to practice tends to refute assertions of experimentation). But they should not be given estoppel effect with respect to whether a completed invention existed at that time.[200] In another case a party obtained bifurcation of a count on the theory that the bromo and iodo forms of a compound were patentably distinct from the chloro form. It was held that the party could not thereafter urge a contrary theory by arguing that his earlier application, which described halogen in general with chloro as a specific example, provides an adequate written description of the bromo and iodo forms of the invention so as to obtain priority based upon his earlier application.[201]

Settlement. Pursuant to 35 U.S.C. §135(c), any agreement or understanding made in connection with or in contemplation of the termination of an interference must be filed with the PTO. This is to prevent anticompetitive settlements.[202]

---

[196]*In re Van Geuns,* 988 F.2d 1181, 26 USPQ2d 1057 (Fed. Cir. 1993). Of course, if a party chooses not to argue the claims separately, they would stand or fall together. *Id.*

[197]*Davis v. Loesch,* 998 F.2d 963, 27 USPQ2d 1440 (Fed. Cir. 1993).

[198]*Magdo v. Kooi,* 699 F.2d 1325, 216 USPQ 1033 (Fed. Cir. 1983). See *Guinn v. Kopf,* 96 F.3d 1419, 40 USPQ2d 1157 (Fed. Cir. 1996), where the court held that disclaiming all claims relating to an interference does not divest the PTO Board of jurisdiction.

[199]*Case v. CPC Int'l,* 730 F.2d 745, 221 USPQ 196 (Fed. Cir. 1984).

[200]*Baker Oil Tools, Inc. v. Geo Vann, Inc.,* 828 F.2d 1558, 4 USPQ2d 1210 (Fed. Cir. 1987). The result might well have been different had there been an inter partes, litigated adjudication by the PTO on the subject.

[201]*Bigham v. Godtfredsen,* 857 F.2d 1415, 8 USPQ2d 1266 (Fed. Cir. 1988).

[202]*CTS Corp. v. Piher Int'l Corp.,* 727 F.2d 1550, 221 USPQ 11 (Fed. Cir. 1984). Here the parties were engaged in related patent litigation that was settled by agreement, but the settlement was not filed with the PTO. Under the circumstances, the court held the settlement to

§15.3 Reissue

(a) General

A patent attorney is often faced with choices during a patent prosecution. If an attorney or patentee makes a mistake, the PTO permits the patentee to institute reissue or reexamination proceedings in certain instances.[203] The reissue statute balances the purpose of providing the patentee with an opportunity to correct errors of inadequate claim scope against the public interest in finality and certainty of patent rights.[204] Reissue is essentially a reprosecution of all claims. Thus original claims that a patentee wants to maintain unchanged may nonetheless be rejected on any statutory ground.[205] Reissue is an extraordinary procedure and not a substitute for PTO appeal procedures.[206]

The statute provides that:

> Whenever any patent is, through error without any deceptive intention, deemed wholly or partly inoperative or invalid, by reason of a defective specification or drawing, or by reason of the patentee claiming more or less than he had a right to claim in the patent, the Director shall, on the surrender of such patent and the payment of the fee required by law, reissue the patent for the invention disclosed in the original patent, and in accordance with a new and amended application, for the unexpired part of the term of the original patent. No new matter shall be introduced into the application. . . .
>
> No reissued patent shall be granted enlarging the scope of the claims of the original patent unless applied for within two years from the grant of the original patent.[207]

In enacting the reissue statute, Congress provided a statutory basis for correction of error. The statute is remedial in nature, based on fundamental principles of equity and fairness, and should be construed liberally. Nonetheless, not every event or circumstance that might be labeled error is correctable by reissue.[208] The whole purpose

---

be insufficiently connected with the termination of the interference and refused to permit a reopening of the settlement to declare the patent unenforceable under §135(c).

[203]*Litton Sys., Inc. v. Whirlpool Corp.,* 728 F.2d 1423, 221 USPQ 97 (Fed. Cir. 1984).

[204]*In re Graff,* 111 F.3d 874, 42 USPQ2d 1471 (Fed. Cir. 1997).

[205]*Hewlett-Packard Co. v. Bausch & Lomb, Inc.,* 882 F.2d 1556, 11 USPQ2d 1750 (Fed. Cir. 1989).

[206]*Ball Corp. v. United States,* 729 F.2d 1429, 221 USPQ 289 (Fed. Cir. 1984).

[207]35 U.S.C. §251.

[208]*In re Weiler,* 790 F.2d 1576, 229 USPQ 673 (Fed. Cir. 1986). The purpose of the reissue statute is to remedy errors, and all of the provisions of a unified statute must be read in harmony. Thus an error in actual compliance with the reissue statute does not insulate that error from the remedial reach and intent of provisions like §26. *In re Bennett,* 766 F.2d 524, 226 USPQ 413 (Fed. Cir. 1985). The reissue statute is remedial in nature, based on principles of equity and fairness, and should be liberally construed. In any given case, the statute should be so applied to the facts that justice will be done both to the patentee and the public. *In re Harita,* 847 F.2d 801, 6 USPQ2d 1930 (Fed. Cir. 1988). Reissue error is generally liberally construed. *Mentor Corp. v. Coloplast, Inc.,* 998 F.2d 992, 27 USPQ2d 1521 (Fed. Cir. 1993).

of reissue, as far as claims are concerned, is to permit limitations to be added to claims that are too broad or to be taken from claims that are too narrow.[209] A reissue oath or declaration must satisfy two requirements: it must show error in the patent and error in conduct. Typically the patentee wants broader claims if the prior art allows (the patentee claimed less than he or she had a right to claim), or narrower claims if the broad claims are invalid over prior art (the patentee claimed more than he or she had a right to).[210]

A patentee must base an application for reissue upon one of four specified grounds identified in §251: (1) an error in the specification, (2) a defective drawing, or original claims that are (3) too broad or (4) too narrow. The basis for a narrowing reissue has generally been the belated discovery of partially invalidating prior art. In contrast, a broadened reissue has generally been founded upon postissuance discovery of attorney error in understanding the scope of the invention. The oath for reissue must state that the patent is defective or partly inoperative or invalid because of one or more of these defects. It must also allege that the defect arose through error without deceptive intent. Finally, the PTO can reissue the patent only for the invention disclosed in the original patent, and no new matter can be introduced.[211] And an expired patent cannot be reissued; the statute is unequivocal in permitting reissue only "for the unexpired part of the term of the original patent."[212]

Error without deceptive intent. The reissue statute was not enacted as a panacea for all patent prosecution problems, nor as a grant to the patentee of a second opportunity to prosecute de novo its original application. Though the term "error" is to be interpreted liberally, it still requires inadvertence, accident, and mistake. Deliberate acts are excluded.[213] Thus, the reissue procedure does not give the patentee

---

[209]*In re Weiler,* 790 F.2d 1576, 229 USPQ 673 (Fed. Cir. 1986).

[210]*Hewlett-Packard Co. v. Bausch & Lomb, Inc.,* 882 F.2d 1556, 11 USPQ2d 1750 (Fed. Cir. 1989). Here the patentee maintained that his broad claims were valid; he simply wanted narrower claims in the event the broader claims should happen to be held invalid. In a sense, the patentee claimed neither too little nor too much in scope; rather, he included too few claims. The court recognized that the CCPA had tacitly approved, at least in dicta, the practice of allowing reissue for the purpose of including narrower claims as a hedge against possible invalidation of broad claims. It was able to avoid the question here because the reissue applicant was unable to show that the narrower claims were omitted by error. Thus, although there was error in the patent, there was no error in conduct.

[211]*In re Amos,* 953 F.2d 613, 21 USPQ2d 1271 (Fed. Cir. 1991).

[212]*In re Morgan,* 990 F.2d 1230, 26 USPQ2d 1392 (Fed. Cir. 1993). Here the reissue application was filed before expiration of the original patent, which expired while the appeal from a decision of the PTO Board was pending before the Federal Circuit. The court was apparently unimpressed by arguments based on the six-year postexpiration enforceability period, the fact that reexamination is possible after expiration, or the fact that the reissue application had been filed before expiration. The appeal was dismissed as moot.

[213]*In re Weiler,* 790 F.2d 1576, 229 USPQ 673 (Fed. Cir. 1986). See also *Hester Indus. v. Stein Inc.,* 142 F.3d 1472, 46 USPQ2d 1641 (Fed. Cir. 1998). Reissue is not available to obtain new claims and thereby rehabilitate a patent obtained by inequitable conduct. *Hewlett-Packard Co. v. Bausch & Lomb, Inc.,* 882 F.2d 1556, 11 USPQ2d 1750 (Fed. Cir. 1989).

a second opportunity to prosecute de novo the original application. Error under the reissue statute does not include a deliberate decision to surrender specific subject matter in order to overcome prior art, a decision that in light of subsequent developments in the marketplace might be regretted. The reissue statute cannot be construed in such a way that competitors, properly relying on the original prosecution history, become patent infringers when they do.[214]

An attorney's failure to appreciate the full scope of the invention is one of the most common sources of defects in patents.[215] This form of error has generally been accepted as sufficient to satisfy the "error" requirement of §251.[216] The fact that the error could have been discovered at the time of prosecution with a more thorough patentability search, or with improved communication between the inventors and the attorney, does not by itself preclude a patent owner from correcting defects through reissue.[217] Nonetheless, the court has rejected allegations of an inventor's ignorance of drafting and claiming technique, and his or her counsel's ignorance of the invention, as a basis for error. Such allegations could frequently be made and, if accepted as establishing error, would require the grant of reissues on anything and everything mentioned in a disclosure. There must be an indication of how the ignorance caused error in failure to claim an invention. Insight resulting from hindsight on the part of new counsel does not, in every case, establish error.[218] No doubt if two patent attorneys are given the task of drafting patent claims for the same invention, the

---

[214]*Mentor Corp. v. Coloplast, Inc.*, 998 F.2d 992, 27 USPQ2d 1521 (Fed. Cir. 1993). In order to make a prima facie showing of error in conduct, it is not enough for a reissue applicant to submit an oath or declaration that merely parrots the statutory language. *Hewlett-Packard Co. v. Bausch & Lomb, Inc.*, 882 F.2d 1556, 11 USPQ2d 1750 (Fed. Cir. 1989). Here the applicant simply declared that he had failed to include narrower claims, and did not explain how the failure came about. He argued that whenever it appears that narrower claims could have been obtained, error warranting reissue exists. The court rejected this theory on the ground that if it were correct it would be difficult to conceive of any extant patent for which a right of reissue would not exist. Thus the court is refusing to create a rule whereby error in conduct may be presumed absent evidence that the error in the patent was intentional.

[215]*Hester Indus. v. Stein Inc.*, 142 F.3d 1472, 46 USPQ2d 1641 (Fed. Cir. 1998); *Mentor Corp. v. Coloplast, Inc.*, 998 F.2d 992, 27 USPQ2d 1521 (Fed. Cir. 1993); *In re Wilder*, 736 F.2d 1516, 222 USPQ 369 (Fed. Cir. 1984).

[216]*Hester Indus. v. Stein Inc.*, 142 F.3d 1472, 46 USPQ2d 1641 (Fed. Cir. 1998). An inventor's failure to appreciate the scope of an invention at the time of the original patent grant, and thus an initial intent not to claim the omitted subject matter, is a remediable error. *C.R. Bard Inc. v. M3 Sys. Inc.*, 157 F.3d 1340, 48 USPQ2d 1225 (Fed. Cir. 1998). An attorney's failure to appreciate the full scope of the invention qualifies as an error under §251 and is correctable by reissue. *In re Clement*, 131 F.3d 1464, 45 USPQ2d 1161 (Fed. Cir. 1997).

[217]*In re Wilder*, 736 F.2d 1516, 222 USPQ 369 (Fed. Cir. 1984). This was an application for a broadened reissue. The attorney claimed error on the ground that he had assumed the prior art contained features that it in fact did not, thus leading him to claim less than the inventor was entitled to. The error was discovered later, when the full commercial success of the invention had become apparent, but it could have been discovered during prosecution.

[218]*In re Weiler*, 790 F.2d 1576, 229 USPQ 673 (Fed. Cir. 1986) (no error in claiming a method but failing to claim the product at all, or in acquiescing in a restriction requirement and failing to file a divisional application on nonelected claims). Deliberate cancellation of a claim can constitute correctable error if it occurs without deceptive intent and does not amount to an admission that the claim is unpatentable; inferences about intent can be drawn from

two attorneys will in all likelihood arrive at somewhat different claims of somewhat different scope. And such differences are even more likely when the second attorney drafts the new claims years later and with the distinct advantage of having knowledge of the product offered by an accused infringer. This reality does not justify recapturing surrendered subject matter under the mantra of "failure to appreciate the scope of the invention."[219]

An error of law is not excluded from the class of error subject to correction in accordance with the reissue statute. Although attorney error is not an open invitation to reissue in every case in which it may appear, the purpose of the reissue statute is to avoid forfeiture of substantive rights due to error made without intent to deceive. The law does not require that no competent attorney or alert inventor could have avoided the error sought to be corrected by the reissue. Failure of the attorney to claim the invention sufficiently broadly is one of the most common sources of defects. Subjective intent is not determinative of whether the applicant erred in claiming less than he or she had a right to claim.[220]

Courts sometimes speak of an "intent to claim" the subject matter of the reissue claim sought. The phrase does not appear in the statute and is but a judicial shorthand, signifying a means of measuring whether the statutorily required error is present. A showing that an applicant had an intent to claim subject matter he or she did not claim can go a long way to support a finding that error occurred; conversely, a showing that an applicant never had any such intent makes a finding of error extremely difficult if not impossible.[221] Section 251 does not include a separate requirement of an objective intent to claim. Rather, the essential inquiry under the "original patent" clause of §251 is whether one skilled in the art, reading the specification, would identify the subject matter of the new claims as invented and disclosed by the patentees. This inquiry is analogous to the written description requirement of 35 U.S.C. §112¶1.[222] Lack of compliance with §112 will foreclose a finding of intent to claim, but absence of §112 support dooms the application in any event. The converse is not true: compliance with §112 does not alone establish intent to claim and does not alone establish error in a failure to claim.[223]

---

changes in claim scope when other reliable evidence is not available. *Ball Corp. v. United States,* 729 F.2d 1429, 221 USPQ 289 (Fed. Cir. 1984).

[219]*Hester Indus. v. Stein Inc.,* 142 F.3d 1472, 46 USPQ2d 1641 (Fed. Cir. 1998).

[220]*Scripps Clinic & Res. Found. v. Genentech, Inc.,* 927 F.2d 1565, 18 USPQ2d 1001 (Fed. Cir. 1991).

[221]*In re Weiler,* 790 F.2d 1576, 229 USPQ 673 (Fed. Cir. 1986). Perhaps this is too strong a statement in view of an earlier caution by the court that lack of intent to claim is not an independent basis for denying a reissue application under §251. *In re Hounsfield,* 699 F.2d 1320, 216 USPQ 1045 (Fed. Cir. 1983). See also *Scripps Clinic & Res. Found. v. Genentech, Inc.,* 927 F.2d 1565, 18 USPQ2d 1001 (Fed. Cir. 1991).

[222]*Hester Indus. v. Stein Inc.,* 142 F.3d 1472, 46 USPQ2d 1641, 1651 (Fed. Cir. 1998).

[223]*In re Weiler,* 790 F.2d 1576, 229 USPQ 673 (Fed. Cir. 1986).

A mistaken acquiescence in a restriction requirement is not an error that can be corrected by reissue.[224]

Same invention. Section 251 authorizes reissue for "the" invention disclosed in the original patent, not for just "any" and "every" invention for which one may find some support in the disclosure of the original patent.[225] It is not necessary, however, that the claimed subject matter be described identically; it is sufficient if the disclosure originally filed conveys to those skilled in the art that the reissue applicant invented the subject matter later claimed.[226] Intent to claim can shed light on whether the claims of a reissue application are directed to the same invention as the original patent.[227] Intent to claim inquires whether that which is claimed in the reissue is something that could have been claimed on the basis of the original disclosure, given that the requisite inadvertent error has been demonstrated. This is analogous to the written description requirement under §112.[228]

Broadened claims. Section 251 puts a two-year time limit on applying for broader claims. If a broadening reissue application is on file within two years, the claims may be further broadened outside the two-year period. However, if a nonbroadened application is filed within two years, the first broadening may not be accomplished outside the two-year period.[229] A claim is broadened if it is broader in

[224]*In re Watkinson,* 900 F.2d 230, 14 USPQ2d 1407 (Fed. Cir. 1990). The examiner had required restriction between method and composition claims, and the applicant's patent agent thought the method claims to be unpatentable and so elected the composition claims without traverse. No divisional was ever filed. The court rejected, in dicta, the argument that the real "error" was the agent's belief that the method claims were unpatentable.

[225]*In re Weiler,* 790 F.2d 1576, 229 USPQ 673 (Fed. Cir. 1986). It is difficult to find error in the failure to claim inventions on the sole basis that they were disclosed. To so hold would render meaningless the statutory requirement that an applicant point out and distinctly claim subject matter that he or she regards as his or her invention. *Id.*

[226]*In re Wilder,* 736 F.2d 1516, 222 USPQ 369 (Fed. Cir. 1984). Where synchronous scanning was the only embodiment disclosed in the original patent, and the reissue claims were generic to synchronous and nonsynchronous scanning, a rejection of the reissue claims as drawn to subject matter not disclosed in the original was held proper. *Id.*

[227]*In re Hounsfield,* 699 F.2d 1320, 216 USPQ 1045 (Fed. Cir. 1983). To the extent the construct of an objective intent to claim is useful, it is only one factor that sheds light on whether the "original patent" clause of §251 is satisfied. *Hester Indus. v. Stein Inc.,* 142 F.3d 1472, 46 USPQ2d 1641 (Fed. Cir. 1998).

[228]*In re Amos,* 953 F.2d 613, 21 USPQ2d 1271 (Fed. Cir. 1991). The court rejected an objective "intent to claim" test that would have established that the new claims are not drawn to the same invention as the original merely by finding that the subject matter was not originally claimed. The court also declined to decide whether the "same invention" test under §251 is in every case coextensive with the written description requirement of §112.

[229]*In re Fotland,* 779 F.2d 31, 228 USPQ 193 (Fed. Cir. 1985). In *In re Graff,* 111 F.3d 874, 42 USPQ2d 1471 (Fed. Cir. 1997), the patentee filed a reissue application within two years with only the original claims (the reissue was filed to correct drawing error). More than two years after original issue, the patentee introduced broader claims by amendment. The examiner rejected them as too late, and the patentee filed a continuation application with the broader claims and let the original claims issue in a reissue patent. The Board held (1) continuations are not permitted in reissue practice, and (2) the broadened claims were filed

any respect than the original claim, even though it may be narrowed in other respects. It is immaterial that the broadening takes place with respect to an element that is of no patentable significance.[230] A claim of a reissue application is broader in scope than the original claims if it contains within its scope any conceivable apparatus or process that would not have infringed the original patent. A reissue claim that is broader in any respect is considered to be broader than the original claims even though it may be narrower in other respects.[231]

It is proper to permit a broadened reissue to cover an embodiment that was not disclosed in the patent and only discovered later. The issue is whether the original specification supports the broadened claims.[232] When a reissue applicant seeks to obtain a broadened version of a claim, one must look to see whether the disclosure reasonably conveys to one skilled in the art that the inventor had possession of the broad invention at the time the original application was filed. This speaks to the reason why the inventor failed to claim more broadly an invention he or she had claimed in the original, and not to a situation where he or she failed to claim that invention at all the first time around.[233]

The PTO has interpreted Rule 175 (37 C.F.R. §1.175) as requiring the reissue applicant to specify every difference between the original and reissue claims in its new oath or declaration. The court has approved this application of the rule, while at the same time indicating that the decision should not be interpreted as implying that the MPEP is binding upon the court.[234] In a later case, the court held a reissue patent invalid for failure of the declaration to explain claim differences that had been created during the reissue prosecution. Thus, when amendments correcting an overclaiming are made during reissue prosecution in response to a rejection, a patentee is obligated to file a supplemental declaration explaining the source of the overclaiming

---

too late. The Federal Circuit held that continuations of reissue applications are permissible, but affirmed the Board's second ground. *In re Doll*, 419 F.2d 925, 164 USPQ 218 (CCPA 1970), was distinguished on the ground that there the reissue application was filed with broadened claims within two years and further broadening was permitted outside the two-year period. Apparently the key is whether the public was put on notice, within two years, that any broadening would be sought. If not, the two-year period rules. In *Vectra Fitness Inc. v. TNWK Corp.*, 162 F.3d 1379, 49 USPQ2d 1144 (Fed. Cir. 1998), claims were obtained by reissue that were narrower than the broadest claims that issued in the original patent, but broader than the original claims that remained after the patentee filed a disclaimer. The reissue application was filed more than two years after the patent issued, but less than two years after the disclaimer. The court held, unequivocally, that §253, which provides that a disclaimer becomes part of the original patent, applies to reissue applications. Thus, the reissue claims were invalid under §251.

[230]*In re Bennett*, 766 F.2d 524, 226 USPQ 413 (Fed. Cir. 1985).

[231]*Tillotson, Ltd. v. Walbro Corp.*, 831 F.2d 1033, 4 USPQ2d 1450 (Fed. Cir. 1987). See also *Westvaco Corp. v. International Paper Co.*, 991 F.2d 735, 26 USPQ2d 1353 (Fed. Cir. 1993).

[232]*In re Peters*, 723 F.2d 891, 221 USPQ 952 (Fed. Cir. 1983). It is error to confine the patentee to the specific embodiment disclosed in the original patent. *Id.*

[233]*In re Weiler*, 790 F.2d 1576, 229 USPQ 673 (Fed. Cir. 1986).

[234]*In re Constant*, 827 F.2d 728, 3 USPQ2d 1479 (Fed. Cir. 1987). See MPEP §1444.

error, that it was nondeceptive and otherwise excusable, and how the amendment corrects the overclaiming.[235]

Recapture. Recapture bars a patentee from acquiring, through reissue, claims that are of the same or broader scope than those claims that were canceled from the original application.[236] Thus, if a patentee tries to recapture what he or she previously surrendered in order to obtain allowance of original patent claims, that deliberate withdrawal or amendment cannot be said to involve the inadvertence or mistake contemplated by §251. It is not an error of the kind that will justify the grant of a reissue patent that includes the matter withdrawn. It is precisely because the patentee amended the claims to overcome prior art that a member of the public is entitled to occupy the space abandoned by the patent applicant.[237]

The recapture rule, therefore, prevents a patentee from regaining through reissue the subject matter that was surrendered in an effort to obtain allowance of the original claims. Under this rule, claims that are broader than the original patent claims in a manner directly pertinent to the subject matter surrendered during prosecution are impermissible. The first step in applying the recapture rule is to determine whether and in what aspect the reissue claims are broader than the patent claims. For example, a reissue claim that deletes a limitation or element from the patent claims is broader in that limitation's aspect. Although the scope of the claims is the proper inquiry, claim language, including limitations, defines claim scope. Courts must determine in which aspects the reissue claim is broader, which includes broadening as a result of an omitted limitation. The second step is to determine whether the broader aspects of the reissue claims relate to surrendered subject matter. To determine whether an applicant surrendered particular subject matter, one looks to the prosecution history for arguments and changes to the claims made in an effort to overcome a prior art rejection. Although the recapture rule does not apply in the absence of evidence that the applicant's amendment was an admission that the scope of that claim was not in fact patentable, the court may draw inferences from changes in claim scope when other reliable evidence of the patentee's intent is not available. Deliberately canceling or amending a claim in an effort to overcome a reference strongly suggests that the applicant admits that the scope of the claim before the cancellation or amendment is

---

[235]*Nupla Corp. v. IXL Mft. Co.*, 114 F.3d 191, 42 USPQ2d 1711 (Fed. Cir. 1997). The moral here is, always check to see whether a supplemental declaration is required. Note that the court passed the question whether this rule would apply if the changes were only small language changes that did not affect the scope of the claims, or if the amendments had been specifically dictated by the examiner as necessary for allowance (in that event, the examiner would arguably already know what a supplemental declaration would point out).

[236]*Mentor Corp. v. Coloplast, Inc.*, 998 F.2d 992, 27 USPQ2d 1521 (Fed. Cir. 1993); *Ball Corp. v. United States*, 729 F.2d 1429, 221 USPQ 289 (Fed. Cir. 1984). Estoppel principles are subsumed in the recapture doctrine. *Id.*

[237]*Mentor Corp. v. Coloplast, Inc.*, 998 F.2d 992, 27 USPQ2d 1521 (Fed. Cir. 1993).

unpatentable, but it is not dispositive because other evidence in the prosecution history may indicate the contrary. Amending a claim by the inclusion of an additional limitation has exactly the same effect as if the claim as originally presented had been canceled and replaced by a new claim including that limitation.[238]

Once it is determined that an applicant has surrendered the subject matter of the canceled or amended claim, it must then be determined whether the surrendered subject matter has crept into the reissue claim. Comparing the reissue claim with the canceled claim is one way to do this. If the scope of the reissue claim is the same as or broader than that of the canceled claim, then the patentee is clearly attempting to recapture surrendered subject matter and the reissue claim is, therefore, unallowable. In contrast, a reissue claim narrower in scope escapes the recapture rule entirely. Some reissue claims, however, are broader than the canceled claim in some aspects, but narrower in others. The court analyzes such situations in this manner: (1) if the reissue claim is as broad as or broader than the canceled or amended claim in all aspects, the recapture rule bars the claim; (2) if it is narrower in all aspects, the recapture rule does not apply, but other rejections are possible; (3) if the reissue claim is broader in some aspects, but narrower in others, then: (a) if the reissue claim is as broad as or broader in an aspect germane to a prior art rejection, but narrower in another aspect completely unrelated to the rejection, the recapture rule bars the claim; (b) if the reissue claim is narrower in an aspect germane to prior art rejection, and broader in an aspect unrelated to the rejection, the recapture rule does not bar the claim, but other rejections are possible.[239]

---

[238]*In re Clement,* 131 F.3d 1464, 45 USPQ2d 1161 (Fed. Cir. 1997). See also *Hester Indus. v. Stein Inc.,* 142 F.3d 1472, 46 USPQ2d 1641 (Fed. Cir. 1998).

[239]*In re Clement,* 131 F.3d 1464, 45 USPQ2d 1161 (Fed. Cir. 1997). In the case at hand, the court found that the reissue claim was both broader and narrower in areas relevant to the prior art rejections. It concluded that on balance the claim was broader than it was narrower in a manner directly pertinent to the subject matter surrendered during prosecution, and therefore recapture applied. The court also recognized that in *Ball Corp. v. United States,* 729 F.2d 1429, 221 USPQ 289 (Fed. Cir. 1984), it had indicated that the recapture rule does not apply when the reissue claim is broader than the canceled claim in a manner unrelated to the alleged error supporting reissue, but did not address whether the recapture rule would apply if the broadening did relate to the alleged error. It described a scenario in which the patentee intentionally fails to enumerate an error so that it may eliminate a limitation that it argued distinguished the claim from a reference or that it added in an effort to overcome a reference, and then seeks protection under *Ball.* It therefore limited *Ball* to its facts: the recapture rule does not apply when the broadening not only relates to an aspect of the claim that was never narrowed to overcome prior art, or argued as distinguishing the claim from the prior art, but also is not materially related to the alleged error. In *Hester Indus. v. Stein Inc.,* 142 F.3d 1472, 46 USPQ2d 1641 (Fed. Cir. 1998), the court recognized that, while *Clement* suggested that a surrender can occur by way of arguments or claim changes made during prosecution of the original patent application, to date the cases in which it has found an impermissible recapture have involved claim amendments or cancellations. Indeed, it had expressly left open, in *Ball,* the question of whether argument without amendment can effect a surrender. In holding that it can, the court reasons that, in determining whether there is a surrender, the prosecution history of the original patent should be examined for evidence of an admission by the patent applicant regarding patentability. In this regard, claim amendments are relevant because an amendment to overcome a prior art rejection evidences an admission that the claim was not

Thus, a patentee is free to acquire, through reissue, claims that are narrower in scope than canceled original claims of the application that resulted in the original patent. In such a case, the recapture doctrine does not apply.[240] Obtaining broadened reissue claims with a scope equivalent to that in preamended claims of the original application does not amount to recapture in the absence of evidence that the amendment was somehow an admission that the original claims were not patentable.[241] Reissue claims that are broader in certain respects and narrower in others may avoid the effect of the recapture rule. If a reissue claim is broader in a way that does not attempt to reclaim what was surrendered earlier, the recapture rule may not apply.[242]

Review. Where the statutory requirements are met, reissue of a patent is not discretionary with the Director, but mandatory.[243] The Federal Circuit has declined to decide whether a district court has power to order the PTO to reopen and complete prosecution of a reissue application.[244] A reissue application without change to the specification or claims[245] is merely a request for an advisory opinion, and the Federal Circuit would lack jurisdiction of an appeal from a Board decision affirming the examiner's rejection of the application.[246] A district court may not compel a patentee to seek reissue when he or she insists there is no error in the patent.[247]

---

patentable. But amendment of a claim is not the only permissible predicate for establishing a surrender. Arguments made to overcome prior art can equally evidence an admission sufficient to give rise to a finding of surrender. There is no unfairness in binding the patentee to deliberate assertions made in order to obtain allowance of the original patent claims over the prior art. Indeed, fairness to the public must also be considered. In this respect, the recapture rule is quite similar to prosecution history estoppel, which prevents the application of the doctrine of equivalents in a manner contrary to the patent's prosecution history. Like the recapture rule, prosecution history estoppel prevents a patentee from regaining subject matter surrendered during prosecution in support of patentability. The same reasoning that led the court to conclude that arguments alone can give rise to prosecution history estoppel lends support to the proposition that arguments alone can give rise to a surrender for purposes of the recapture rule.

[240]*Whittaker Corp. v. UNR Indus., Inc.*, 911 F.2d 709, 15 USPQ2d 1742 (Fed. Cir. 1990).

[241]*Seattle Box Co. v. Industrial Crat. & Pack., Inc.*, 731 F.2d 818, 221 USPQ 568 (Fed. Cir. 1984). See also *Mentor Corp. v. Coloplast, Inc.*, 998 F.2d 992, 27 USPQ2d 1521 (Fed. Cir. 1993).

[242]*Mentor Corp. v. Coloplast, Inc.*, 998 F.2d 992, 27 USPQ2d 1521 (Fed. Cir. 1993).

[243]*Scripps Clinic & Res. Found. v. Genentech, Inc.*, 927 F.2d 1565, 18 USPQ2d 1001, 1009 (Fed. Cir. 1991).

[244]*Baker Perkins, Inc. v. Werner & Pfleiderer Corp.*, 710 F.2d 1561, 218 USPQ 577 (Fed. Cir. 1983). This interesting question would probably arise only upon appeal from a contempt citation against the PTO.

[245]As under the so-called Dann amendments, which were repealed July 1, 1982. Those provisions, which permitted inter partes protester participation in reissue proceedings, as well as "no-fault" reissues, were intended to economize time and expense for both the court and the litigants. In practice, the desired results were not achieved. After enactment of the reexamination legislation the Dann amendments were repealed. *PPG Indus., Inc. v. Celanese Polymer Spec. Co.*, 840 F.2d 1565, 6 USPQ2d 1010 (Fed. Cir. 1988).

[246]*In re Keil*, 808 F.2d 830, 1 USPQ2d 1427 (Fed. Cir. 1987).

[247]*Green v. Rich Iron Co.*, 944 F.2d 852, 20 USPQ2d 1075 (Fed. Cir. 1991). This was once common practice under the old "no-fault" reissue practice. *Id.* See note 15:245.

Whether the statutory requirement of "error" has been met is an issue of law that is reviewed de novo. The legal conclusion is based on underlying factual inquiries that are reviewed, in a jury case, for substantial evidence.[248] The legal adequacy of a patentee's reason for requesting reissue is a question of law. If the facts material to that question are not in dispute, the matter can be resolved by summary judgment.[249]

Presumption of validity. Claims in a reissue application of course enjoy no presumption of validity.[250] Even so, it is error to treat the original claims as prior art against reissue claims, despite an oath that the claims are believed to be unpatentable in view of a prior art reference. Such an oath does not constitute a binding admission that the reference anticipated those claims and that the claims are therefore part of the prior art.[251] As in the case of an original patent, if inequitable conduct is found during the prosecution of the reissue application, all the claims of the reissue patent are rendered unenforceable, even those carried over without change from the original patent.[252]

The burden of proving invalidity is made heavier by reissue, wherein art that invalidated the original patent receives close scrutiny by the PTO. Although a decision by the PTO on an original or reissue application is never binding or controlling, and the district court has an obligation to reach an independent conclusion, the examination procedure and its result must be given appropriate consideration and weight.[253] Statements made during reissue proceedings are relevant prosecution history when interpreting claims.[254] After reissue, the challenger's burden of proof, as an evidentiary matter, is usually more difficult to sustain.[255] Thus, a jury should be instructed that the PTO has found claims patentable on reissue over additional prior art, and that the defendant's burden has therefore become more difficult, both as to invalidity and fraud.[256]

---

[248]*Mentor Corp. v. Coloplast, Inc.,* 998 F.2d 992, 27 USPQ2d 1521 (Fed. Cir. 1993). See also *In re Clement,* 131 F.3d 1464, 45 USPQ2d 1161 (Fed. Cir. 1997).

[249]*Scripps Clinic & Res. Found. v. Genentech, Inc.,* 927 F.2d 1565, 18 USPQ2d 1001 (Fed. Cir. 1991).

[250]*In re Etter,* 756 F.2d 852, 225 USPQ 1 (Fed. Cir. 1985).

[251]*Orthokinetics, Inc. v. Safety Travel Chairs, Inc.,* 806 F.2d 1565, 1 USPQ2d 1081 (Fed. Cir. 1986).

[252]*Hewlett-Packard Co. v. Bausch & Lomb, Inc.,* 882 F.2d 1556, 11 USPQ2d 1750 (Fed. Cir. 1989). Normally, invalidation of a new claim added during reissue does not invalidate other claims carried over from the original patent. Here the invalidity of new claims was the result of a defective reissue oath. Nonetheless, the court held that the carryover claims were unaffected, even though the original patent had technically been surrendered.

[253]*Interconnect Planning Corp. v. Feil,* 774 F.2d 1132, 227 USPQ 543 (Fed. Cir. 1985). See also *Windsurfing Int'l, Inc. v. AMF, Inc.,* 782 F.2d 995, 228 USPQ 562 (Fed. Cir. 1986).

[254]*E.I. duPont & Co. v. Phillips Petroleum Co.,* 849 F.2d 1430, 7 USPQ2d 1129 (Fed. Cir. 1988).

[255]*Kaufman Co. v. Lantech,* 807 F.2d 970, 1 USPQ2d 1202 (Fed. Cir. 1986).

[256]*American Hoist & Derrick Co. v. Sowa & Sons, Inc.,* 725 F.2d 1350, 220 USPQ 763 (Fed. Cir. 1984).

(b) Intervening Rights

The first paragraph of 35 U.S.C. §252 makes it clear that surrender of the original patent upon reissue does not affect any pending action or abate any cause of action to the extent that the claims of the original and reissue patents are identical.[257] To the extent they are not identical, then the patentee has no rights prior to the reissue date, because the original patent has been surrendered and is extinguished.[258] In other words, §252 provides no liability for acts prior to the reissue date unless an identical claim is carried over.[259] This relatively straightforward concept is not strictly what is meant by "intervening rights," which is the subject of the second paragraph of §252.[260]

The court has now begun to characterize the defenses provided for in the second paragraph of §252 as "absolute" intervening rights and "equitable" intervening rights. Thus, an accused infringer has an absolute right to use or sell a product that was made, used, or purchased prior to the grant of the reissue patent as long as this activity does not infringe a claim of the reissue patent that was in the original patent. This absolute right covers only products already in existence at the time of the reissue. Equitable intervening rights is not absolute. It permits a court to provide for the continued manufacture, use, or sale to the extent and under such terms as the court deems equitable.[261]

Under the doctrine of intervening rights, as spelled out in the second paragraph of §252, an infringer may, because of prereissue activity, enjoy a personal intervening right to continue what would otherwise be infringing activity after the reissue. The underlying rationale for intervening rights is that the public has the right to use what is not specifically claimed in the original patent. Recapture through a reissue patent of what is dedicated to the public by omission in the original patent is permissible under specific conditions, but not at the expense of innocent parties. Therefore, one may be able to continue to infringe a reissue patent if the court decides that equity

---

[257]*Howes v. Medical Components, Inc.,* 814 F.2d 638, 2 USPQ2d 1271 (Fed. Cir. 1987).

[258]*Kaufman Co. v. Lantech,* 807 F.2d 970, 1 USPQ2d 1202 (Fed. Cir. 1986).

[259]*Seattle Box Co. v. Industrial Crat. & Pack., Inc.,* 731 F.2d 818, 221 USPQ 568 (Fed. Cir. 1984).

[260]*Fortel Corp. v. Phone-Mate, Inc.,* 825 F.2d 1577, 3 USPQ2d 1771 (Fed. Cir. 1987); *Kaufman Co. v. Lantech,* 807 F.2d 970, 1 USPQ2d 1202 (Fed. Cir. 1986).

[261]*Bic Leisure Prods., Inc. v. Windsurfing Int'l, Inc.,* 1 F.3d 1214, 27 USPQ2d 1671 (Fed. Cir. 1993). Despite the fact that §252 is clearly couched in language suggestive of a liability defense, the court in this case treated absolute intervening rights as a damages issue—the identification of those sales that properly serve as a measure of damages. Thus, it does not become an issue until the patent owner secures a liability judgment. It should be noted that these observations were made in the course of holding that the infringer's waiver of its equitable intervening rights defense and its failure to raise absolute intervening rights during the liability trial did not result in a consequential waiver of absolute intervening rights in connection with the damages trial.

dictates such a result.[262] Substantial preparation alone does not automatically vest an accused infringer with intervening rights under the second paragraph of §252. The trial court still retains discretion to grant intervening rights to the extent and under such terms as it deems equitable.[263]

"Identical," for purposes of §252, means "without substantive change."[264] This is so for both the first and the second paragraphs of §252.[265] The determination of whether reissue claims are "identical" to original claims is a question of law, reviewed de novo.[266]

Under the reissue statute, "identical" has consistently been interpreted to permit minor word changes. In essence, courts have held that it is the scope of the claim that must be identical, not that the identical words must be used. The standard applied is that of whether a particular change to the claims is substantive, such that the scope of the claims is no longer substantially identical. It is a reasonable standard, for it implements the purpose of the statute while enabling application to the facts in any given cases so that justice will be done.[267] Simply because an amendment during reexamination follows a rejection based on prior art does not mean per se that the claim was changed substantively. A rejection on prior art during the course of reexamination is not a PTO decision of unpatentability; rather, it is part of the prosecution history, and its significance depends on the particular facts and circumstances. To determine whether a claim change is substantive it is necessary to perform the same type of analysis that is used in the context of prosecution history estoppel, to determine the reason for the change.[268] A claim of a reissue application is broader in scope than the original claims if it contains within

---

[262]*Seattle Box Co. v. Industrial Crat. & Pack., Inc.*, 756 F.2d 1574, 225 USPQ 357 (Fed. Cir. 1985). Here the court permitted continued infringing use of items in inventory on the date the patent reissued, in view of the fact that the items had been designed with advice of counsel to avoid the original patent, and the infringer had orders prior to reissue. Another important factor is whether the items can be converted to noninfringements and at what cost and effort.

[263]*Westvaco Corp. v. International Paper Co.*, 991 F.2d 735, 26 USPQ2d 1353 (Fed. Cir. 1993). Thus a denial of intervening rights is reviewed under the abuse of discretion standard. *Id.*

[264]*Westvaco Corp. v. International Paper Co.*, 991 F.2d 735, 26 USPQ2d 1353 (Fed. Cir. 1993); *Laitram Corp. v. NEC Corp.*, 952 F.2d 1357, 21 USPQ2d 1276 (Fed. Cir. 1992). A new claim with a limitation "greater than or substantially equal to" is not identical to "greater than" because there was substantive change. *Seattle Box Co. v. Industrial Crat. & Pack., Inc.*, 731 F.2d 818, 221 USPQ 568 (Fed. Cir. 1984). In response to an indefiniteness rejection under §112, the reissue applicant changed "said collar" to "a collar on said sleeve," to give "said collar" an antecedent basis. This was held not to be a substantive change and thus not to destroy the "identical" nature of the claim for purposes of the reissue statute. The mere fact that the change was made in response to a §112 rejection does not make it substantive, nor did it broaden the claim. *Slimfold Mfg. Co. v. Kinkead Indus., Inc.*, 810 F.2d 1113, 1 USPQ2d 1563 (Fed. Cir. 1987).

[265]*Kaufman Co. v. Lantech*, 807 F.2d 970, 1 USPQ2d 1202 (Fed. Cir. 1986).

[266]*Westvaco Corp. v. International Paper Co.*, 991 F.2d 735, 26 USPQ2d 1353 (Fed. Cir. 1993).

[267]*Slimfold Mfg. Co. v. Kinkead Indus., Inc.*, 810 F.2d 1113, 1 USPQ2d 1563 (Fed. Cir. 1987). It is the scope of the claims that must be identical, not that the identical words must be used. *Westvaco Corp. v. International Paper Co.*, 991 F.2d 735, 26 USPQ2d 1353 (Fed. Cir. 1993).

[268]*Laitram Corp. v. NEC Corp.*, 952 F.2d 1357, 21 USPQ2d 1276 (Fed. Cir. 1992).

its scope any conceivable apparatus or process that would not have infringed the original patent.[269]

Intervening rights is an affirmative defense that must be raised at trial. Failure to plead it is a waiver. It cannot be raised for the first time on appeal.[270]

§15.4 Reexamination

The reexamination procedure was added to the patent law at the end of 1980.[271] It provides a means whereby a patentee, or any member of the public, may ascertain whether a substantial new question of patentability can be raised against an issued patent on the basis of documentary prior art—patents and printed publications.

Reexamination establishes a mechanism for enabling the PTO to review and correct an initial examination. Thus reexamination is conducted afresh, without the burdens and presumptions that accompany litigation of an issued patent.[272] Nonetheless, in enacting the reexamination statute, Congress did not authorize the PTO to evaluate patentability anew whenever there existed doubt as to a patent's validity. Rather, the PTO was authorized to reexamine an issued patent only within strictly defined limits. Reexamination was only intended for those instances in which the examiner did not have all of the relevant prior art at his or her disposal when the patentability of the invention was originally considered.[273] Reexamination will be limited to documentary art—patents and printed publications—except where the patentee admits that certain activities such as use or sale are part of the prior art.[274]

Purpose. The proponents of reexamination anticipated three principal benefits. First, reexamination based on references that were not previously included in the patentability examination could resolve validity disputes more quickly and less expensively than litigation. Second, courts would benefit from the expertise of the PTO on prior

---

[269]*Westvaco Corp. v. International Paper Co.*, 991 F.2d 735, 26 USPQ2d 1353 (Fed. Cir. 1993). In finding that the reissue claim was broader, the court found it significant that the patent owner had not sued the alleged infringer for infringement of the original; this was said to create an inference that even the patent owner believed the scope of the claims had changed.

[270]*Windsurfing Int'l, Inc. v. AMF, Inc.*, 782 F.2d 995, 228 USPQ 562 (Fed. Cir. 1986); *Underwater Devices, Inc. v. Morrison-Knudsen Co.*, 717 F.2d 1380, 219 USPQ 569 (Fed. Cir. 1983).

[271]35 U.S.C. §§301–307.

[272]*Laitram Corp. v. NEC Corp.*, 952 F.2d 1357, 21 USPQ2d 1276 (Fed. Cir. 1992).

[273]*In re Portola Packaging, Inc.*, 110 F.3d 786, 42 USPQ2d 1295 (Fed. Cir. 1997).

[274]*Quad Envtl. Tech. Corp. v. Union Sanitary Dist.*, 946 F.2d 870, 20 USPQ2d 1392 (Fed. Cir. 1991). Prior to the revision of MPEP §2217 in July 1989, the PTO would not consider prior uses or sales in a reexamination, even if they were admitted to be prior art. *Id.* In *In re Lonardo*, 119 F.3d 960, 43 USPQ2d 1262 (Fed. Cir. 1997), a split panel held that the PTO is authorized to consider obviousness-type double patenting on reexamination.

art that was not previously of record. Third, reexamination would strengthen confidence in patents whose validity was clouded because pertinent prior art had not previously been considered by the PTO. However, Congress recognized that the broad purpose must be balanced against the potential for abuse, whereby unwarranted reexaminations can harass the patentee and waste the patent life. The legislative record and the record of the interested public reflect a serious concern that reexamination not create new opportunities for abusive tactics and burdensome procedures. Thus, reexamination as enacted was carefully limited to new prior art, that is, new information about preexisting technology that may have escaped review at the time of the initial examination of the patent application.[275] The innate function of the reexamination process is to increase the reliability of the PTO's action in issuing a patent by reexamination of patents thought "doubtful." When the patent is concurrently involved in litigation, an auxiliary function is to free the court from any need to consider prior art without the benefit of the PTO's initial consideration. In a very real sense, the intent underlying reexamination is to "start over" in the PTO with respect to the limited examination areas involved—to reexamine the claims and to examine new or amended claims, as they would have been considered if they had been originally examined in light of all of the prior art of record in the reexamination proceeding.[276] When a substantial question exists with respect to the correctness of the original patent grant, it does not conflict but coincides with the nature of the patentee's right when the government reexamines the propriety of the grant it has made and thereafter reaffirms the grant, substitutes a new grant (amended or new claims), or withdraws the grant in whole or in part.[277]

The court understands that the PTO's goal is to perform thoroughly and conscientiously its function of allowing applications claiming only patentable subject matter, and that in order to do so it wishes to take advantage of a second opportunity to examine claims it once issued when reexamination gives it that chance. However, Congress did not grant the PTO such a broad mandate. Even when the door to the reexamination gate is opened, the PTO is not freed from the limitations Congress placed on the reexamination process. Whatever the basis on which reexamination is granted, it was intended to deal only with substantial new questions of patentability, essentially those based on prior art that was not before the examiner during an earlier

---

[275]*In re Recreative Techs. Corp.*, 83 F.3d 1394, 38 USPQ2d 1776 (Fed. Cir. 1996).

[276]*Ethicon v. Quigg*, 849 F.2d 1422, 7 USPQ2d 1152 (Fed. Cir. 1988); *In re Etter*, 756 F.2d 852, 225 USPQ 1 (Fed. Cir. 1985). Reexamination is a good way to find out how the examiner feels about new art. *Lindemann Maschinenfabrik v. American Hoist & Derrick Co.*, 730 F.2d 1452, 221 USPQ 481 (Fed. Cir. 1984).

[277]*In re Etter*, 756 F.2d 852, 225 USPQ 1 (Fed. Cir. 1985). The grant by the PTO of reexamination is not probative of unpatentability and thus does not automatically preclude a finding of willfulness. The grant of reexamination, although surely evidence that the criterion for reexamination has been met, does not establish a likelihood of patent invalidity. *Hoechst Celanese Corp. v. BP Chem. Ltd.*, 78 F.3d 1575, 38 USPQ2d 1126 (Fed. Cir. 1996).

examination.[278] Thus, the court has strictly circumscribed the definition of "new prior art." In one case, the examiner on reexamination rejected the claims as obvious over a single reference. The same obviousness rejection had been made during the original prosecution and was successfully overcome. The Board reversed the obviousness rejection but sua sponte rejected the claims as anticipated by that reference. The Federal Circuit held, unequivocally, that the PTO exceeded its authority under the reexamination statute. Inasmuch as no new issue of patentability was presented, the reexamination should have been terminated. The fact that the Board changed the ground sua sponte has no effect. It cannot have been the statutory intent that a patentee would not know whether there was a new ground of rejection, as required for reexamination, until the reexamination was completed on the old ground, was appealed to the Board, and was decided by the Board not on the old ground but on a possible new ground that was not previously part of the reexamination.[279]

In another case, reexamination was sought on the basis of new prior art. A rejection was made on that art and the applicant amended the claims to avoid the rejection. The examiner then rejected the amended claims based upon a combination of two pieces of art that had been cited during the original prosecution. The court disapproved this approach as well. A rejection made during reexamination does not raise a substantial new question of patentability if it is supported only by prior art previously considered by the PTO in relation to the same or broader claims. Claim amendments made during reexamination, which necessarily cannot broaden the scope of the claims, do not give the PTO authority to revisit previously considered questions of patentability. Since the original bases for concluding that a substantial new question of patentability existed to justify reexamination were withdrawn by the PTO during reexamination, leaving only arguments based on references previously considered by the PTO, the reexamination should have been terminated.[280] In a later case, reexamination was ordered on the basis of art that had been cited but not applied during original prosecution, but the ultimate rejection was based upon that art and some new art. The court reasoned that it does not review the decision of the PTO to institute a reexamination, but rather it reviews the Board's ultimate decision. Inasmuch as the Board's ultimate rejection satisfied the conditions for reexamination, it was proper.[281]

Effect. Inasmuch as the determination of whether a substantial new question of patentability exists is discretionary with the Director,

---

[278]*In re Portola Packaging, Inc.,* 110 F.3d 786, 42 USPQ2d 1295 (Fed. Cir. 1997).

[279]*In re Recreative Techs. Corp.,* 83 F.3d 1394, 38 USPQ2d 1776 (Fed. Cir. 1996). To the extent that §2258 of the MPEP, which defines the scope of reexamination to include reexamination of the patent in view of any pertinent patents or publications, including issues previously addressed by the PTO, is inconsistent with this holding, it is invalid. *Id.*

[280]*In re Portola Packaging, Inc.,* 110 F.3d 786, 42 USPQ2d 1295 (Fed. Cir. 1997).

[281]*In re Hiniker,* 150 F.3d 1362, 47 USPQ2d 1523 (Fed. Cir. 1998).

and not appealable, a denial of a request for reexamination does not deprive the requesting party of the right to contest validity in subsequent court proceedings.[282] There is nothing untoward about the PTO upholding the validity of a reexamined patent that the district court later finds invalid. This is essentially what occurs when a court finds a patent invalid after the PTO has granted it. It is important to understand that the district court and the PTO can consider different evidence. Accordingly, different results between the two forums may be entirely reasonable. And, if the district court determines a patent is not invalid, the PTO should consider its reexamination because, of course, the two forums have different standards of proof. A court's decision upholding a patent's validity is not ordinarily binding on another challenger of the patent's validity, and certainly collateral estoppel does not prevent the PTO from completing a reexamination in this situation.[283] To the extent the MPEP states[284] that the PTO is bound by a court's decision upholding a patent's validity, it is incorrect. On the other hand, if a court finds a patent invalid, the PTO may discontinue its reexamination. This is consistent with *Blonder-Tongue*.[285] Of course, in the end it is up to a court, not the PTO, to decide if the patentee had a full and fair chance to litigate the validity of the patent, but it is certainly permissible for the PTO to act on a standing judgment of invalidity unless and until a court has said it does not have res judicata effect.[286]

An examiner's decision on reexamination is evidence the court must consider in determining whether the party asserting invalidity has met its statutory burden by clear and convincing evidence.[287] After reexamination, the challenger's burden of proof is more difficult to sustain.[288] Statements made during reexamination proceedings are relevant prosecution history when interpreting claims.[289] The courts have inherent power to manage their dockets and stay proceedings, including the authority to order a stay pending conclusion of a PTO reexamination. On the other hand, the Director does not have authority to stay reexamination proceedings pending the outcome of district court infringement litigation.[290]

---

[282]*In re Etter*, 756 F.2d 852, 225 USPQ 1 (Fed. Cir. 1985).

[283]*Ethicon v. Quigg*, 849 F.2d 1422, 7 USPQ2d 1152 (Fed. Cir. 1988).

[284]MPEP §2286.

[285]See §18.5(b).

[286]*Ethicon v. Quigg*, 849 F.2d 1422, 7 USPQ2d 1152 (Fed. Cir. 1988).

[287]*Custom Accessories, Inc. v. Jeffrey-Allan Indus., Inc.*, 807 F.2d 955, 1 USPQ2d 1196 (Fed. Cir. 1986).

[288]*Kaufman Co. v. Lantech*, 807 F.2d 970, 1 USPQ2d 1202 (Fed. Cir. 1986); *Custom Accessories, Inc. v. Jeffrey-Allan Indus., Inc.*, 807 F.2d 955, 1 USPQ2d 1196 (Fed. Cir. 1986).

[289]*E.I. duPont & Co. v. Phillips Petroleum Co.*, 849 F.2d 1430, 7 USPQ2d 1129 (Fed. Cir. 1988). In the context of a charge of inequitable conduct, the court has remarked that no adverse inference flows from a patentee's actions in adjusting its claims on reexamination, whether or not the patentee itself initiated the reexamination. Thus, reduction in claim scope during reexamination is not of itself probative of material withholding with intent to deceive, and supports no such inference. *Glaverbel S.A. v. Northlake Mkt'g & Supp., Inc.*, 45 F.3d 1550, 33 USPQ2d 1496 (Fed. Cir. 1995).

[290]*Ethicon v. Quigg*, 849 F.2d 1422, 7 USPQ2d 1152 (Fed. Cir. 1988).

Intervening rights. The purpose of the reexamination procedure is to permit a patentee or other interested person to obtain review and if necessary correction of the claims resulting from the initial examination of the patent. Reexamination may entail changes in the claims, except that the claims cannot be enlarged. The effect of a reexamined patent during the period before issuance of the reexamination certificate is governed by 35 U.S.C. §307(b), which provides that the rules established in §252 for reissued patents shall apply to reexamined patents. Sections 307 and 252 shield those who deem an adversely held patent to be invalid; if the patentee later cures the infirmity by reissue or reexamination, the making of substantive changes in the claims is treated as an irrebuttable presumption that the original claims were materially flawed. Thus the statute relieves those who may have infringed the original claims from liability during the period before the claims are validated. Applying §252, when the reexamined or reissued claims are identical to those of the original patent, they shall "have effect continuously from the date of the original patent." Unless a claim granted or confirmed upon reexamination is identical to an original claim, the patent cannot be enforced against infringing activity that occurred before issuance of the reexamination certificate. "Identical" does not mean verbatim, but means at most without substantive change. Thus whether amendments made to overcome rejections based on prior art are substantive depends on the nature and scope of the amendments. There is no absolute rule for determining whether an amended claim is legally identical to an original claim. An amendment that clarifies the text of the claim or makes it more definite without affecting its scope is generally viewed as identical for the purpose of §252. Determination of whether a claim change during reexamination is substantive requires analysis of the scope of the original and reexamined claims in light of the specification, with attention to the references that occasioned the reexamination, as well as the prosecution history and any other relevant information.[291]

In determining whether the scope of a claim has been enlarged, the reexamination practice has shared the body of precedent developed for reissue determinations. Thus the court has held that a change of words does not always mean change of scope, and that the question of whether the claims have been materially or substantially enlarged must be determined upon the claim as a whole. However, if the patentee is seeking to recover subject matter that had been surrendered during the initial prosecution, this flexibility of analysis is eliminated,

---

[291]*Bloom Eng'g Co. v. North Am. Mfg. Co.,* 129 F.3d 1247, 44 USPQ2d 1859 (Fed. Cir. 1997). See §15.3(b) above. Claims amended during reexamination are entitled to the date of the original patent if they are without substantive change or are legally "identical" to the claims of the original patent. "Identical" does not mean verbatim, but rather means without substantive change. *Laitram Corp. v. NEC Corp.,* 952 F.2d 1357, 21 USPQ2d 1276 (Fed. Cir. 1992); *Tennant Co. v. Hako Minuteman, Inc.,* 878 F.2d 1413, 11 USPQ2d 1303 (Fed. Cir. 1989). Claims, though amended during reexamination, retain their original effective date unless changed in scope from the original patent. *Minco, Inc. v. Combustion Eng'g, Inc.,* 95 F.3d 1109, 40 USPQ2d 1001 (Fed. Cir. 1996). Restating dependent claims in independent form does not

for the prosecution history establishes the substantiality of the change and estops its recapture. Thus although the circumstances of presentation in the specification may temper the general rule that broadening of any term of a claim is fatal, even when other terms are narrowed, it is appropriate to consider other factors including whether the applicant intended to have originally covered the challenged subject matter.[292] The court refuses to hold that the doctrine of equivalents should be taken into account when evaluating an original claim to determine whether its scope has been impermissibly enlarged by amendment during reexamination. To do so, it says, would allow a patentee to transform a district court case based on infringement under the doctrine of equivalents into a case based on literal infringement simply by broadening claims during reexamination.[293]

The Federal Circuit has firmly rejected the argument that any amendment made during reexamination is substantive simply because of the fact that reexamination is granted only in the presence of a substantial new question of patentability. The legislative history in no way supports such a restrictive view. The substantial new question standard was incorporated to prevent abuse and harassment of patentees, not to manifest a congressional intent that any amendment in the reexamination proceeding must be deemed substantial and therefore trigger an intervening right.[294]

Reexamined claims, like reissued claims, that are not substantively identical with the originals cannot be enforced for the period prior to the issuance of the reexamination certificate. This is not, of course, the doctrine of intervening rights, which applies only to the period after the issuance of the certificate.[295]

Presumption of validity. The presumption of validity does not apply in reexamination proceedings.[296] It does not meet the statutory purpose of the presumption of administrative correctness to apply it

---

constitute a substantive change in claim scope. *Bloom Eng'g Co. v. North Am. Mfg. Co.*, 129 F.3d 1247, 44 USPQ2d 1859 (Fed. Cir. 1997).

[292]*Anderson v. International Eng'g & Mfg. Inc.*, 160 F.3d 1345, 48 USPQ2d 1631 (Fed. Cir. 1998).

[293]*Thermalloy, Inc. v. Aavid Eng'r, Inc.*, 121 F.3d 691, 43 USPQ2d 1846, 1849 (Fed. Cir. 1997).

[294]*Kaufman Co. v. Lantech*, 807 F.2d 970, 1 USPQ2d 1202 (Fed. Cir. 1986). Although it recognizes that it is difficult to conceive of many situations in which the scope of a rejected claim that became allowable when amended is not substantively changed by the amendment, the court continues to reject any per se rule, and to analyze the question of substantive change in light of an overall examination of the written description, the prosecution history, and the language of the respective claims. *Laitram Corp. v. NEC Corp.*, 163 F.3d 1342, 49 USPQ2d 1199 (Fed. Cir. 1998).

[295]*Fortel Corp. v. Phone-Mate, Inc.*, 825 F.2d 1577, 3 USPQ2d 1771 (Fed. Cir. 1987). The court now refers to the defense for the period prior to issuance as "absolute" intervening rights and for the period subsequent as "equitable" intervening rights. *Bic Leisure Prods., Inc. v. Windsurfing Int'l, Inc.*, 1 F.3d 1214, 27 USPQ2d 1671 (Fed. Cir. 1993).

[296]*Laitram Corp. v. NEC Corp.*, 952 F.2d 1357, 21 USPQ2d 1276 (Fed. Cir. 1992); *Ethicon v. Quigg*, 849 F.2d 1422, 7 USPQ2d 1152 (Fed. Cir. 1988); *In re Etter*, 756 F.2d 852, 225 USPQ 1 (Fed. Cir. 1985).

to a procedure whose purpose is the remedy of administrative error.[297] The presumption of validity is a rule of procedure placing the burden of persuasion on one who attacks a patent's validity. There is no such attacker in a reexamination, and hence no one on whom that burden may be placed. The examiner is not attacking the validity of a patent but is conducting a subjective examination of claims in the light of prior art. Even where a third party requests reexamination, it may be heard only on whether there is a substantial new question of patentability. In litigation, where a patentee cannot amend claims, or add new claims, the presumption, and the rule of claim construction that claims shall be construed to save them if possible, have important roles to play. In reexamination, where claims can be amended and new claims added, and where no litigating adversary is present, those roles and their rationale simply vanish.[298]

Procedure. No amendment or new claim enlarging the scope of a claim of the patent will be permitted in a reexamination proceeding. Whether amendments enlarge the scope of a claim is a matter of claim construction. A claim is enlarged if it includes within its scope any subject matter that would not have infringed the original patent. The test is the same as that used in applying the two-year limitation for broadened reissue claims. Such a claim is broader in scope than the original if it contains within its scope any conceivable apparatus or method that would not have infringed the original. A claim that is broader in any respect is considered to be broader than the original even though it may be narrower in other respects.[299] Whether claims have been enlarged is a matter of claim construction, a question of law subject to complete and independent review on appeal.[300] The prohibition of enlarged scope has serious consequences. The Federal Circuit has squarely held that, although 35 U.S.C. §282 does not specifically mention §305 as an invalidity defense, claims whose scope is enlarged by reexamination are invalid.[301]

---

[297]*Patlex Corp. v. Mossinghoff,* 758 F.2d 594, 225 USPQ 243 (Fed. Cir. 1985).

[298]*In re Etter,* 756 F.2d 852, 225 USPQ 1 (Fed. Cir. 1985).

[299]*Quantum Corp. v. Rodime, PLC,* 65 F.3d 1577, 36 USPQ2d 1162 (Fed. Cir. 1995); *In re Freeman,* 30 F.3d 1459, 31 USPQ2d 1444 (Fed. Cir. 1994). A reexamined claim has been broadened if it includes within its scope any subject matter that would not have infringed the original patent. *Hockerson-Halberstadt Inc. v. Converse Inc.,* 183 F.3d 1369, 51 USPQ2d 1518 (Fed. Cir. 1999); *Thermalloy, Inc. v. Aavid Eng'r, Inc.,* 121 F.3d 691, 43 USPQ2d 1846 (Fed. Cir. 1997). In an interesting twist, the Federal Circuit in *Freeman* applied collateral estoppel, based upon statements in its own prior ruling regarding claim construction in an infringement context, to the question of whether the reexamination claims were broader in scope than the original claims.

[300]*Quantum Corp. v. Rodime, PLC,* 65 F.3d 1577, 36 USPQ2d 1162 (Fed. Cir. 1995). The court held that changing a limitation of "at least 600" tracks per inch in a computer disk claim to "at least approximately 600" tracks per inch enlarged the scope of the claim. See also *Hockerson-Halberstadt Inc. v. Converse Inc.,* 183 F.3d 1369, 51 USPQ2d 1518 (Fed. Cir. 1999); *Anderson v. International Eng'g & Mfg. Inc.,* 160 F.3d 1345, 48 USPQ2d 1631 (Fed. Cir. 1998).

[301]*Quantum Corp. v. Rodime, PLC,* 65 F.3d 1577, 36 USPQ2d 1162 (Fed. Cir. 1995). The court rejected a suggestion that it should restrict the scope of the claim to its original language,

In prosecution, the PTO construes claims as broadly as possible to reduce the possibility that allowed claims will be given a broader scope than is justified.[302] Thus claims subject to reexamination will be given their broadest reasonable interpretation consistent with the specification, and limitations appearing in the specification are not to be read into the claims.[303] In reexamination, as in reissue and other prosecution, the applicant will have an opportunity to amend the claims, and the fact that the patent may also be involved in litigation should not make any difference. Claims in reexamination are to be construed as broadly as possible even though the patent is simultaneously in litigation.[304]

The Director has no authority to stay reexamination proceedings pending infringement litigation. The reexamination statute, 35 U.S.C. §305, requires that such proceedings be conducted with "special dispatch." Whatever else this phrase means, it does not admit of an indefinite suspension of reexamination proceedings pending conclusion of litigation.[305]

In reexamination proceedings, there is no review of the Director's decision to reexamine, and the requester (if other than the patentee) has no further role to play once reexamination is ordered.[306] Patent owners have the right to review of the examiner's final reexamination decision, but not directly by a court. The decision appealed to a court is that of the PTO Board, which may review an examiner's decision unfavorable to the patent owner. The government has no right to review of an examiner or Board decision favorable to the patent owner, and no one, not even the patent owner, may appeal a PTO decision denying a request for reexamination.[307] The same standard of review applies to reexamination as to other cases reaching the Federal Circuit: correctness of legal analysis and clear error as to factual analysis.[308]

---

thus avoiding a holding of infringement against any devices that would not have been covered by any of the original claims as they existed prior to reexamination. Although claims are to be construed, if possible, to sustain their validity, it is well settled that no matter how great the temptations of fairness or policy making, courts do not redraft claims.

[302]*In re Yamamoto,* 740 F.2d 1569, 222 USPQ 934 (Fed. Cir. 1984).

[303]*In re Etter,* 756 F.2d 852, 225 USPQ 1 (Fed. Cir. 1985).

[304]*In re Yamamoto,* 740 F.2d 1569, 222 USPQ 934 (Fed. Cir. 1984).

[305]*Ethicon v. Quigg,* 849 F.2d 1422, 7 USPQ2d 1152 (Fed. Cir. 1988). The court declined to decide the hypothetical question of whether the Director has the power to stay one reexamination if there are multiple concurrent proceedings pending in the PTO, but it did say that there is nothing to prevent the Director from conducting orderly proceedings within his office so long as he does not violate the statute. Special dispatch in the posited circumstances may call for coordinated activity to resolve issues seriatim, which would not necessarily violate congressional instructions so long as the reexamination was handled with special priority and progressed as quickly as possible.

[306]*Joy Mfg. Co. v. National Mine Serv. Co.,* 810 F.2d 1127, 1 USPQ2d 1627 (Fed. Cir. 1987). But see note 15:310 and accompanying text.

[307]*Syntex (U.S.A.) Inc. v. United States PTO,* 882 F.2d 1570, 11 USPQ2d 1866 (Fed. Cir. 1989).

[308]*In re Andersen,* 743 F.2d 1578, 223 USPQ 378 (Fed. Cir. 1984).

The patent statute specifies that any person has the right to request reexamination. The category of third-party requesters is, thus, open ended and includes, for example, attorneys representing a principal whose identity is not disclosed to the PTO or patentee. The requester must cite references and explain their pertinency. If reexamination is granted, a third-party requester has the right to reply to any statement submitted by the patent owner in response to the PTO's order granting reexamination. The statute gives third-party requesters no further, specific right to participate in the reexamination proceeding; indeed, it specifically prohibits further participation by third-party requesters during reexamination. Thus, a reexamination is conducted ex parte after it is instituted.[309] Near the end of 1999, 35 U.S.C. §§311–318 were added to the patent statute. This enactment provides for an optional inter partes reexamination procedure that may have significant ramifications.[310]

The Federal Circuit has held that a district court lacks power to order any party, whether patent owner or accused infringer, to seek reexamination. It distinguishes the undoubted power of a district court to order mediation or appoint a special master on the ground that both are provided for by the FRCP. The cases that concern the inherent power of a trial court to manage its docket do not support a broad inherent power that includes the authority to require a party to participate in a permissive, and potentially expensive, agency proceeding that the party within its rights chooses not to pursue.[311]

A nonpatentee requester for reexamination is not an applicant entitled to appeal under 35 U.S.C. §145 or a patent owner entitled to appeal under §306. Thus, such a requester, even one who has intervened in a §145 action, has no independent statutory right to bring a §145 action. Nor is any injury caused such a requester within the zone of interests protected by §§145 and 306 so as to give it standing to appeal in its role as an intervener.[312] It was expected that third persons would have an interest in the outcome of reexamination, but the existence of such interest does not change the congressional

---

[309]*Syntex (U.S.A.) Inc. v. United States PTO,* 882 F.2d 1570, 11 USPQ2d 1866 (Fed. Cir. 1989). The legislative intent was to provide specified limits to the participation of third parties, thus adding weight to the purpose of facilitating and expediting the reexamination proceeding, as against the possible advantages of a full inter partes contest. *In re Opprecht,* 868 F.2d 1264 (Fed. Cir. 1989). Nonetheless, in *In re Hiniker,* 150 F.3d 1362, 47 USPQ2d 1523 (Fed. Cir. 1998), the patent owner's failure to serve its request for oral argument before the Board on the requester resulted in a loss of the right to oral argument.

[310]The new procedure is detailed in Goldman & Choi, "The New Optional *Inter Partes* Reexamination Procedure and Its Strategic Use," 28 AIPLA Q.J. 307 (Fall 2000).

[311]*In re Continental Gen. Tire, Inc.,* 81 F.3d 1089, 38 USPQ2d 1365 (Fed. Cir. 1996). One wonders whether the district court would have the power to file for reexamination on its own. The court has also held that a district court lacks power to order a patentee to submit, in a reexamination, papers prepared by the alleged infringer. *Emerson Elec. Co. v. Davoil, Inc.,* 88 F.3d 1051, 39 USPQ2d 1474 (Fed. Cir. 1996).

[312]*In re Opprecht,* 868 F.2d 1264 (Fed. Cir. 1989); *Boeing Co. v. Commissioner of Patents,* 853 F.2d 878, 7 USPQ2d 1487 (Fed. Cir. 1988).

intent that the proceeding be limited in its inter partes attributes.[313]
A third-party requester cannot therefore obtain review of the PTO's
decision to issue a reexamination certificate by suing the PTO in
federal district court. Congress did not intend to confer such a right,
even where the challenge is based upon alleged procedural improprie-
ties in the reexamination process.[314] Not every perceived injury caused
by improper agency action carries a right to immediate judicial redress. A right to immediate judicial review must be granted or reasonably inferred from a particular statute. For example, a potential infringer may not sue the PTO seeking retraction of a patent issued to
another by reason of its improper allowance by the PTO. A remedy
must await confrontation with the patent owner. The same is true
with respect to a reissued patent. And although a third-party reexamination requester has some rights vis-a-vis the PTO, such a requester
has no right to challenge the validity of the reexamination certificate
by suit against the PTO.[315]

In an interesting situation, the appellant had, while the patent
was owned by another, requested reexamination, asserting that the
claims were unpatentable over a particular reference. When it acquired the patent, the appellant became the patent's defender in the
reexamination proceeding. The Director argued that the appellant
should be estopped to deny unpatentability over that reference. The
court recognized that the appellant's change of position with regard
to patentability put it in an unusual, and perhaps suspect, position.
However, there was no showing that it made any specific factual
misstatements in its request for reexamination or that the PTO relied
on any such misstatements. Moreover, the PTO is charged with making an independent determination concerning the patentability of
inventions. The fact that appellant once opposed the maintenance of
the patent and now defends it does not change the PTO's duty to
conduct the reexamination. Lastly, there was no showing that the
PTO or the public has suffered any harm from the change of position.
Appellant informed the PTO of a reference that had not been considered by the examiner in the patent's original examination, argued
that that reference raised a substantial new question of patentability,
and requested a reexamination. The PTO agreed that a substantial
new question of patentability was raised by the reference and granted

---

[313]*In re Opprecht*, 868 F.2d 1264 (Fed. Cir. 1989). Thus the court denied a request by a
party to stayed district court litigation involving the patent to intervene or appear amicus in
the patentee's appeal from the PTO Board. One suspects the court will not permit intervention
unless the outcome would be res judicata with respect to the proposed intervener.

[314]*Syntex (U.S.A.) Inc. v. United States PTO*, 882 F.2d 1570, 11 USPQ2d 1866 (Fed. Cir.
1989). The court distinguished *Ethicon v. Quigg*, 849 F.2d 1422, 7 USPQ2d 1152 (Fed. Cir.
1988), where it upheld the right of a third party to have the reexamination conducted with
dispatch. Nothing in the reexamination statute addressed that issue, while here it was clear
that Congress did not intend to grant a right to have a reexamination certificate set aside. The
creation of a right or remedy in a third party to challenge a result favorable to a patent owner
after ex parte prosecution would be unprecedented and cannot be inferred.

[315]*Syntex (U.S.A.) Inc. v. United States PTO*, 882 F.2d 1570, 11 USPQ2d 1866 (Fed.
Cir. 1989).

the request. The PTO had the same obligation and ability to reexamine the patent in light of the reference whether appellant was an opposer or a defender. The public interest lies in having valid patents upheld and invalid patents rendered invalid, and hence patents should be reexamined when a substantial question of patentability is raised. The proper result occurs irrespective of the owner's role in the process.[316]

Validity. Standing requires that a petitioner allege and show that it has been personally injured. Where no concession is made by the patentee as to the existence of a substantial new question of patentability, he or she has standing to challenge the lawfulness and constitutionality of certain regulations governing reexamination.[317] However, if he or she makes such a concession, and the challenged regulations relate to his or her rights prior to an order for reexamination, there is no justiciable controversy, and no standing.[318]

A PTO regulation that provided for doubt to be resolved in favor of ordering reexamination was held void as contrary to the statutory mandate underlying the reexamination process, which included a purpose to protect patentees from doubtful reexaminations.[319] Otherwise, it has been held that retrospective application of the reexamination statute does not violate Fifth Amendment due process, and that the statute is not invalid as a deprivation of the right to jury trial or of the right to have validity determined by an Article III court.[320] Congress was within its constitutional power when it created a reexamination procedure as an additional mechanism for the review of patents. The creation of reexamination did not divest the courts of any power to review patent validity.[321] The initial three-month period of silence following a request for reexamination does not offend due process, and the refund of part of the reexamination filing fee in the event reexamination is not ordered does not unduly weight the scales in favor of PTO grants of reexamination.[322]

§15.5 Double Patenting and Disclaimer

(a) Double Patenting in General

The doctrine that forbids so-called double patenting precludes one person from obtaining more than one valid patent for either

---

[316]*In re Baker Hughes Inc.*, 215 F.3d 1297, 55 USPQ2d 1149 (Fed. Cir. 2000).
[317]*Patlex Corp. v. Mossinghoff*, 771 F.2d 480, 226 USPQ 985 (Fed. Cir. 1985).
[318]*Patlex Corp. v. Mossinghoff*, 758 F.2d 594, 225 USPQ 243 (Fed. Cir. 1985).
[319]*Patlex Corp. v. Mossinghoff*, 771 F.2d 480, 226 USPQ 985 (Fed. Cir. 1985).
[320]*Joy Tech., Inc. v. Manbeck*, 959 F.2d 226, 22 USPQ2d 1153 (Fed. Cir. 1992); *Patlex Corp. v. Mossinghoff*, 758 F.2d 594, 225 USPQ 243 (Fed. Cir. 1985).
[321]*Constant v. Advanced Micro-Devices, Inc.*, 848 F.2d 1560, 7 USPQ2d 1057 (Fed. Cir. 1988).
[322]*Patlex Corp. v. Mossinghoff*, 771 F.2d 480, 226 USPQ 985 (Fed. Cir. 1985).

(1) the same invention, or (2) an obvious modification of the same invention.[323] The double patenting determination involves two inquiries. First, is the same invention claimed twice? This inquiry hinges upon the scope of the claims in question. If the claimed inventions are identical in scope, the proper rejection is under 35 U.S.C. §101 because an inventor is entitled to but a single patent for an invention. If one claimed invention has a broader scope than the other, the court must proceed to a second inquiry: whether one claim defines merely an obvious variation of the other patent claim. Without a patentable distinction—because the pending claim defines merely an obvious variation of the patented claim—the patentee may overcome the double patent rejection by filing a terminal disclaimer.[324] The basic concept of double patenting is that the same invention cannot be patented more than once, for that would result in a second patent that would expire some time after the first and extend the protection timewise. But double patenting law has always been more inclusive. Double patenting law principles extend to merely obvious variants of what has been patented as well.[325] The court has passed the question of whether there might be a third type of double patenting—"nonobvious" double patenting—which would forbid claims whose subject matter was fully disclosed in an earlier patent unless the applicant could show why the claims were not presented in the earlier patent.[326]

It is the claims that are compared when assessing double patenting.[327] The prohibition of "same invention" double patenting finds its support in 35 U.S.C. §101, which permits "a" patent. The term "same invention" in this context means an invention drawn to identical subject matter.[328] The test is whether the claims of the two patents cover the same thing: i.e., do they cross-read?[329] The Federal Circuit is of the view that, at least in the case of two utility patents, the mere fact that the claims are drawn to different statutory categories of inventions means that they are not drawn to the same invention.[330] Nor does the fact that the claims of one patent dominate the claims of another necessarily mean that they claim the same invention.[331]

---

[323]*In re Longi,* 759 F.2d 887, 225 USPQ 645 (Fed. Cir. 1985); *Carman Indus., Inc. v. Wahl,* 724 F.2d 932, 220 USPQ 481 (Fed. Cir. 1983).

[324]*In re Goodman,* 11 F.3d 1046 (Fed. Cir. 1993).

[325]*General Foods Corp. v. Studiengesellschaft Kohle mbH,* 972 F.2d 1272, 23 USPQ2d 1839 (Fed. Cir. 1992).

[326]*In re Lonardo,* 119 F.3d 960, 43 USPQ2d 1262 (Fed. Cir. 1997). See MPEP §804(B)(2).

[327]*Ortho Pharm Corp. v. Smith,* 959 F.2d 936, 22 USPQ2d 1119 (Fed. Cir. 1992). Claims are the determinants, and the claims must be read as a whole. *General Foods Corp. v. Studiengesellschaft Kohle mbH,* 972 F.2d 1272, 23 USPQ2d 1839 (Fed. Cir. 1992).

[328]*In re Longi,* 759 F.2d 887, 225 USPQ 645 (Fed. Cir. 1985). See also *Ortho Pharm Corp. v. Smith,* 959 F.2d 936, 22 USPQ2d 1119 (Fed. Cir. 1992).

[329]*Carman Indus., Inc. v. Wahl,* 724 F.2d 932, 220 USPQ 481 (Fed. Cir. 1983).

[330]*Studiengesellschaft Kohle v. Northern Petrochem. Co.,* 784 F.2d 351, 228 USPQ 837 (Fed. Cir. 1986) (no "same invention" double patenting where first patent covers catalyst, and second covers process of using it).

[331]*In re Kaplan,* 789 F.2d 1574, 229 USPQ 678 (Fed. Cir. 1986) (no "same invention" double patenting where first patent claims process, and second patent, dominated by first, claims that process using a specific solvent mixture).

Obviousness-type double patenting is a judicially created doctrine grounded in public policy (as reflected in the patent statute). The purpose is to prevent the extension of the term of a patent, even where an express statutory basis for a rejection or defense is missing, by prohibiting the issuance of claims in a second patent that are not patentably distinct from those in a first patent.[332] Another way to put it is that the doctrine prohibits claims in the second patent that define "merely an obvious variation" of an invention claimed in the first patent.[333] This is so the public can, upon expiration of the first patent, be free to practice obvious variations of the invention claimed. The inquiry is whether the claimed invention in the second patent or application would have been obvious from the subject matter of the claims of the first, in light of the prior art.[334] Such situations may arise when developments and improvements are made as the inventor or persons associated with the inventor continue to work in the field of an invention.[335] The doctrine was adopted out of necessity where the courts were faced with a situation in which claims in two applications were so very much alike as to effectively extend the life of the patent that issued first.[336]

An obviousness-type double patenting rejection is analogous to a rejection for obviousness under §103, except that the patent principally underlying the rejection is not considered prior art.[337] Therefore, the Federal Circuit will review under the same guidelines as employed in a true §103 situation: the clearly erroneous standard applies to underlying factual findings and the ultimate conclusion of obviousness is reviewed for correctness or error as a matter of law.[338] There

---

[332]*In re Longi*, 759 F.2d 887, 225 USPQ 645 (Fed. Cir. 1985). See also *In re Berg*, 140 F.3d 1428, 46 USPQ2d 1226 (Fed. Cir. 1998). The proper inquiry for obviousness-type double patenting is to compare the claims of the two patents to see whether they are patentably distinct. *Panduit Corp. v. Dennison Mfg. Co.*, 774 F.2d 1082, 227 USPQ 337 (Fed. Cir. 1985). Double patenting can also occur where a first patent's claims would have been obvious from the claims of a second patent. *In re Longi*, 759 F.2d 887, 225 USPQ 645 (Fed. Cir. 1985). See also *In re Goodman*, 11 F.3d 1046 (Fed. Cir. 1993).

[333]*In re Braat*, 937 F.2d 589, 19 USPQ2d 1289 (Fed. Cir. 1991).

[334]*Ortho Pharm Corp. v. Smith*, 959 F.2d 936, 22 USPQ2d 1119 (Fed. Cir. 1992). The argument that the claimed inventions do not overlap may have some significance in "same invention" type double patenting, but it is irrelevant in the obviousness context. Rejections on obviousness-type double patenting can be applied to clearly distinct inventions, each of which is considered patentable over the art absent the first. *In re Longi*, 759 F.2d 887, 225 USPQ 645 (Fed. Cir. 1985). The point of novelty approach is rejected in the double patenting context. *Litton Sys., Inc. v. Whirlpool Corp.*, 728 F.2d 1423, 221 USPQ 97 (Fed. Cir. 1984).

[335]*Quad Envtl. Tech. Corp. v. Union Sanitary Dist.*, 946 F.2d 870, 20 USPQ2d 1392 (Fed. Cir. 1991).

[336]*Gerber Garment Tech., Inc. v. Lectra Sys., Inc.*, 916 F.2d 683, 16 USPQ2d 1436 (Fed. Cir. 1990).

[337]*Quad Envtl. Tech. Corp. v. Union Sanitary Dist.*, 946 F.2d 870, 20 USPQ2d 1392 (Fed. Cir. 1991); *In re Longi*, 759 F.2d 887, 225 USPQ 645 (Fed. Cir. 1985). An applicant's disclosure cannot, of course, be used as prior art against him or her, even in an obviousness-type double patenting context. *In re Kaplan*, 789 F.2d 1574, 229 USPQ 678 (Fed. Cir. 1986). Patent claims may be invalidated on the basis of obviousness-type double patenting over a copending patent application where a terminal disclaimer has not been filed. This prevents extension of the patent term. *Hartness Int'l, Inc. v. Simplimatic Eng'g Co.*, 819 F.2d 1100, 2 USPQ2d 1826 (Fed. Cir. 1987).

[338]*In re Longi*, 759 F.2d 887, 225 USPQ 645 (Fed. Cir. 1985).

is a basic difference between obviousness-type double patenting rejections and standard obviousness rejections: double patenting depends entirely on what is claimed in an issued patent. Obviousness relates to what is disclosed (whether or not claimed) in a prior art reference (whether or not a patent). A prior art reference that renders claimed subject matter obvious under 35 U.S.C. §103 does not necessarily create an obviousness-type double patenting situation.[339] There is also a difficulty that arises in all obviousness-type double patenting cases—determining when a claim is or is not an obvious variation of another claim. A claim often does not describe any particular thing but instead defines the boundary of patent protection, and it is difficult to try to determine what is a mere obvious variation of a legal boundary. In making the determination, it is useful to compare the one claim with a tangible embodiment that is disclosed and falls within the scope of the other claim. But the patent disclosure must not be used as prior art.[340]

The Federal Circuit disfavors the use of the term "extension of monopoly" in general, and specifically in the double patenting context. Perhaps "patent rights" should be used instead of "monopoly." The difficulty with monopoly is that it is used in different senses in patent and antitrust law. Because of its antitrust connotations and association with illegality in connection therewith, it often evokes negative reactions inappropriate to a dispassionate analysis of patent law problems. In the double patenting context extension of monopoly cannot be used as a type designation of the two types of double patenting (obviousness and same invention), because the basis for both is a timewise extension of the patent rights, and both rest on the fact that a patent has been issued and later issuance of a second patent will continue protection for that same invention (or an obvious variation) beyond expiration of the first.[341]

Indeed, not all extensions of the patent right are foreclosed. Sometimes it happens that a later filed improvement patent issues before an earlier filed application on the basic invention. In such a situation, the court must apply a "two-way" patentability determination to the claims. In other words, in order to find obviousness-type double patenting, it must be found not only that the claims of the basic application are merely obvious variations of the claims of the improvement patent, but also that the patent claims are obvious variations of the application claims. Although such an analysis may result in a chronological extension of the patent right, it is not an improper extension. Any other holding would make the patentee's rights to the generic

---

[339]*In re Bartfeld,* 925 F.2d 1450, 17 USPQ2d 1885 (Fed. Cir. 1991).

[340]*In re Braat,* 937 F.2d 589, 19 USPQ2d 1289 (Fed. Cir. 1991). The disclosure of a patent cited in support of a double patenting rejection cannot be used as though it were prior art, even where the disclosure is found in the claims. *General Foods Corp. v. Studiengesellschaft Kohle mbH,* 972 F.2d 1272, 23 USPQ2d 1839 (Fed. Cir. 1992).

[341]*In re Kaplan,* 789 F.2d 1574, 229 USPQ 678 (Fed. Cir. 1986).

protection subject to the vagaries of the rates of progress of separate patent applications through the PTO.[342]

Thus, under the one-way test, the examiner asks whether the application claims are obvious over the patent claims. Under the two-way test, the examiner also asks whether the patent claims are obvious over the application claims. If not, the application claims later may be allowed. Thus, when the two-way test applies, some claims may be allowed that would have been rejected under the one-way test. The essential concern is to prevent rejections for obviousness-type double patenting when the applicants file first for a basic invention and later for an improvement, but, through no fault of the applicants, the PTO decides the applications in reverse order of filing, rejecting the basic application although it would have been allowed if the applications had been decided in the order of their filing. Under the two-way test, the court examines the application claim and the patent claim to determine whether each was obvious in view of the other, rather than considering only whether the application claim was patentably distinct from the patent claim. The two-way test, however, is a narrow exception to the general rule of the one-way test. Nevertheless, the notion survives that in certain unusual circumstances, the applicant should receive the benefit of the two-way test.[343]

---

[342]*In re Braat,* 937 F.2d 589, 19 USPQ2d 1289 (Fed. Cir. 1991). Actually, this was not strictly an "improvement" situation. Both the application and the patent disclosed and claimed separate subcombination inventions; the later filed but earlier issued application combined both subcombinations to form a third invention. Thus, although the claims to one of the subcombinations were an obvious variation over the combination claims, the claims to the combination were not obvious in view of the subcombination claims. The court distinguished *Braat* in *In re Goodman,* 11 F.3d 1046 (Fed. Cir. 1993), on the ground that *Braat* involved independent applications. In *Goodman,* the applicant chose to file a continuation to obtain early issuance of a narrow species claim. The earlier filed parent was still pending with generic claims. In a sense, those generic claims are "anticipated" by the species claim in the issued patent. In such a situation, no two-way analysis is required. The only way the applicant can get the generic claim is to file a terminal disclaimer. Otherwise, by adopting the easy course of filing a continuation or divisional application to gain a narrow claim, a patentee could gain an extension of the term on the species when the broad genus later issued. This practice would extend the exclusionary right past the term mandated by Congress. As the court later explained in *In re Emert,* 124 F.3d 1458, 44 USPQ2d 1149 (Fed. Cir. 1997), where a later filed application with narrower claims issues first, through no fault of the applicant, the court applies a two-way patentability test, as in *Braat.* But where the applicant has control, for example, by seeking early issuance of a narrow species claim while filing a continuation to pursue a broader claim, as in *Goodman,* the court will apply a one-way test. See also *Eli Lilly & Co. v. Barr Labs. Inc.,* 222 F.3d 973, 55 USPQ2d 1609 (Fed. Cir. 2000).

[343]*In re Berg,* 140 F.3d 1428, 46 USPQ2d 1226 (Fed. Cir. 1998). In this case the inventor filed two applications on the same day; one claimed the genus and the other a species. The disclosures were practically identical. All claims could have been filed in a single application. The species application issued, and the genus claims were rejected on grounds of obviousness-type double patenting. The court refused to apply the two-way test under the circumstances. It held that if an applicant can file all of its claims in one application, but elects not to, it is not entitled to the two-way treatment. The applicant takes a calculated risk that, by simultaneously filing two separate applications, it might gain the advantage of a quickly issued, narrow patent and also the advantage of a broader application, which took longer to issue as a patent but consequently had a later expiration date. Effectively extending the patent term, however, is precisely the result that the doctrine of obviousness-type double patenting was created to prevent. The two-way exception can only apply when the applicant could not avoid separate filings, and even then, only if the PTO controlled the rates of prosecution to cause the later

The question of whether the one-way test or the two-way test applies is one of law and therefore reviewed without deference.[344]

There is a heavy burden of proof on one seeking to show double patenting.[345] Double patenting is an affirmative defense that must be proved by clear and convincing evidence.[346] It is a question of law that is reviewed de novo.[347] De novo review of double patenting questions is appropriate because double patenting is a matter of what is claimed, and therefore is treated like claim construction upon appellate review.[348]

The double patenting challenge must be evaluated, like any other ground of invalidity, against individual claims. Thus, the fact that a nonasserted claim is invalid for double patenting does not necessarily mean that the entire patent is invalid.[349]

(b) Design/Utility Double Patenting

Double patenting is rare in the context of design vs. utility patents. Indeed, there is an argument that double patenting never applies in that setting. However, the Federal Circuit has effectively passed this question.[350] Double patenting in the design/utility context is a judicially created doctrine based purely on the public policy of preventing the extension of the term of a patent, even where an express statutory basis for the doctrine is lacking. In this context, as in utility/utility, or design/design, there are two kinds of double patenting: same invention and obviousness. If a device embodying the patentable design must infringe the utility claim, and a device embodying the patentable utility claim must infringe the design patent, the two cross-read and claim the same invention. In the second

---

filed species claims to issue before the claims for a genus in an earlier application. In the present case, the two applications could have been filed as one, so it was irrelevant who actually controlled the respective rates of prosecution.

[344]*In re Berg*, 140 F.3d 1428, 46 USPQ2d 1226 (Fed. Cir. 1998); *In re Emert*, 124 F.3d 1458, 44 USPQ2d 1149 (Fed. Cir. 1997).

[345]*Carman Indus., Inc. v. Wahl*, 724 F.2d 932, 220 USPQ 481 (Fed. Cir. 1983).

[346]*Symbol Tech., Inc. v. Opticon, Inc.*, 935 F.2d 1569, 19 USPQ2d 1241 (Fed. Cir. 1991).

[347]*In re Berg*, 140 F.3d 1428, 46 USPQ2d 1226 (Fed. Cir. 1998); *In re Lonardo*, 119 F.3d 960, 43 USPQ2d 1262 (Fed. Cir. 1997); *Texas Instr., Inc. v. United States ITC*, 988 F.2d 1165, 26 USPQ2d 1018 (Fed. Cir. 1993). A rejection under the doctrine of obviousness-type double patenting is a legal conclusion that is freely reviewable. *In re Goodman*, 11 F.3d 1046 (Fed. Cir. 1993).

[348]*Georgia-Pacific Corp. v. United States Gypsum Co.*, 195 F.3d 1322, 52 USPQ2d 1590 (Fed. Cir. 1999).

[349]*Ortho Pharm Corp. v. Smith*, 959 F.2d 936, 22 USPQ2d 1119 (Fed. Cir. 1992).

[350]*Carman Indus., Inc. v. Wahl*, 724 F.2d 932, 220 USPQ 481 (Fed. Cir. 1983). The argument is that if double patenting exists, one of the two patents must necessarily claim inappropriate subject matter. For example, if double patenting is found, "utility" subject matter will necessarily be common to both patents, and the design patent should be declared invalid for failure to satisfy the ornamentality requirements of 35 U.S.C. §171. The court here passed the question of whether double patenting can ever apply where one patent is invalid, thus effectively passing this argument as well.

type, the question is whether the claimed subject matter of the patent under attack would have been obvious from the claims, not the disclosure, of the other patent, and vice versa.[351]

(c) Restriction and Disclaimer

Two independent and distinct inventions cannot be claimed in the same patent. By statutory and common law, each patent establishes an independent and distinct property right.[352] Pursuant to 35 U.S.C. §121, the PTO may require an application to be restricted to one of two or more independent and distinct inventions. The PTO can issue a restriction requirement if it finds that two or more inventions claimed in a patent application are "independent and distinct." A process and apparatus for its practice can be restricted if either the process as claimed can be practiced by another materially different apparatus or by hand or the apparatus as claimed can be used to practice another and materially different process. In response to a restriction requirement, an applicant must elect one invention for examination. Claims to the nonelected invention are withdrawn from consideration and must be canceled before the application is allowed to issue as a patent.[353]

If restriction is required, the patentee is insulated from an obviousness-type double patenting attack. When Congress wrote §121, it considered whether to truncate the term of patents issued following requirements for restriction and decided not to.[354] Thus, if a potential applicant is unsure whether it has more than one patentably distinct set of claims, the PTO advises that it file all of the claims as one application. Then, as examination proceeds, if the PTO determines that more than one distinct invention was claimed in a single application, §121 authorizes the Director to restrict the claims in the application to a single invention. If the claims are so restricted, one or more divisional applications can then be filed containing the claims that were the subject of restriction. When such a divisional application is filed, the PTO is prohibited from using the claims of the patent issuing on the application that prompted the restriction requirement as a reference against the claims of any divisional application. Hence, by filing all of its related claims in one application, such an applicant is protected from an obviousness-type double patenting rejection if

---

[351]*Carman Indus., Inc. v. Wahl*, 724 F.2d 932, 220 USPQ 481 (Fed. Cir. 1983). The disclosure can be looked to, as always, to define terms in the claim. *Id.* Applying the two-way test of *Carman*, the court in *In re Dembiczak*, 175 F.3d 994, 50 USPQ2d 1614 (Fed. Cir. 1999), concluded that there was no design/utility double patenting in respect of the ubiquitous orange plastic trash bags that resemble Halloween-style pumpkins.

[352]*Kearns v. General Motors Corp.*, 94 F.3d 1553, 39 USPQ2d 1949 (Fed. Cir. 1996).

[353]*Helifix Ltd. v. Blok-Lok Ltd.*, 208 F.3d 1339, 54 USPQ2d 1299, 1305 (Fed. Cir. 2000).

[354]*Studiengesellschaft Kohle v. Northern Petrochem. Co.*, 784 F.2d 351, 228 USPQ 837 (Fed. Cir. 1986). The court did not decide whether 35 U.S.C. §121 automatically protects against a "same invention" type double patenting attack, but that result seems likely.

the PTO later determines the applicant has submitted claims to more than one patentable invention.[355]

In a restriction situation, the elected claims in the parent application can never be used as a traditional "reference" on which to reject the claims in a divisional application. That is not to say, however, that the elected claims may not be looked to in assessing compliance with the prohibition against claiming the same invention in two patents.[356] The court applies the doctrine of "consonance" to make that assessment. Plain common sense dictates that a divisional application filed as a result of a restriction requirement cannot contain claims drawn to the invention set forth in the claims elected and prosecuted to patent in the parent application. The divisional must have claims drawn only to the other invention. Thus, the claims in the divisional must be and remain "consonant"; that is, the line of demarcation between independent and distinct inventions that prompted the restriction requirement must be maintained. The divisional claims may not be so amended as to bring them back over the line. If the line is crossed, §121 provides no protection against double patenting.[357]

The protection against double patenting applies only to divisional applications that are filed as a result of a restriction requirement.[358] However, voluntary limitation of the term of a later issued patent is a convenient response to an obviousness-type double patenting rejection, when the statutory requirement of common ownership is met. Any possible enlargement of the term of exclusivity is eliminated, while enabling some limited protection to a patentee's later developments.[359]

Under 35 U.S.C. §253, a patentee or applicant may disclaim or dedicate to the public the entire term, or any terminal part of the term, of the patent. By the use of this so-called terminal disclaimer device, an applicant can overcome an obviousness-type double patenting rejection by providing that the second patent will expire with the first, thus freeing the public to use obvious modifications of the first after its expiration.[360] Where obviousness-type double patenting is

[355]*In re Berg,* 140 F.3d 1428, 46 USPQ2d 1226 (Fed. Cir. 1998).

[356]*Gerber Garment Tech., Inc. v. Lectra Sys., Inc.,* 916 F.2d 683, 16 USPQ2d 1436 (Fed. Cir. 1990).

[357]*Gerber Garment Tech., Inc. v. Lectra Sys., Inc.,* 916 F.2d 683, 16 USPQ2d 1436 (Fed. Cir. 1990). But see *Applied Mtls, Inc. v. Advanced Semi. Mtls, Inc.,* 98 F.3d 1563, 40 USPQ2d 1481 (Fed. Cir. 1996). The court has rejected any formalistic approach to consonance that places determinative significance on method versus apparatus claims. *Symbol Tech., Inc. v. Opticon, Inc.,* 935 F.2d 1569, 19 USPQ2d 1241 (Fed. Cir. 1991).

[358]*Gerber Garment Tech., Inc. v. Lectra Sys., Inc.,* 916 F.2d 683, 16 USPQ2d 1436 (Fed. Cir. 1990).

[359]*Quad Envtl. Tech. Corp. v. Union Sanitary Dist.,* 946 F.2d 870, 20 USPQ2d 1392 (Fed. Cir. 1991).

[360]*In re Longi,* 759 F.2d 887, 225 USPQ 645 (Fed. Cir. 1985). This is so even in the case of commonly owned applications with different inventive entities. Despite a contrary Commissioner's Notice, obviousness-type double patenting is applicable in such situations; and despite an apparently contrary MPEP guideline, a terminal disclaimer is available to overcome the double patenting problem. The *"In re Bass"* amendments to 35 U.S.C. §103 were not intended

recognized before issuance of a patent, the price extracted for obtaining the second patent is disclaimer of part of the term of protection for all claims in the patent—even those that standing alone would not run afoul of the rule against double patenting.[361] But a reference patent that is not of common ownership, or a publication or public use or sale more than one year before the filing date of the later filed application, cannot be removed as prior art by the filing of a terminal disclaimer.[362] Thus, terminal disclaimers are neither appropriate nor available means for overcoming §102(e)/§103 rejections. The purpose of a terminal disclaimer is to limit the term of a patent, not to remove a reference as prior art.[363]

Normally, a court should not look behind a terminal disclaimer to see whether it was really necessary.[364] A terminal disclaimer is not an admission of obviousness of the later filed claimed invention in light of the earlier filed disclosure, for that is not the basis of the disclaimer. It raises neither presumption nor estoppel as to the merits of the rejection.[365]

Section 253 also provides that "whenever, without any deceptive intention, a claim of a patent is invalid the remaining claims shall not thereby be rendered invalid," and goes on to provide for disclaimer of any complete claim of a patent. Similarly, 35 U.S.C. §288 provides that "whenever, without deceptive intention, a claim of a patent is invalid, an action may be maintained for the infringement of a claim of the patent which may be valid. The patentee shall recover no costs unless a disclaimer of the invalid claim has been entered at the Patent and Trademark Office before the commencement of the suit." A statutory disclaimer under §253 has the effect of canceling the

---

to have any impact on obviousness-type double patenting. *Id.* See also *Ortho Pharm Corp. v. Smith,* 959 F.2d 936, 22 USPQ2d 1119 (Fed. Cir. 1992).

[361]*Ortho Pharm Corp. v. Smith,* 959 F.2d 936, 22 USPQ2d 1119 (Fed. Cir. 1992). This unitary treatment of the claims with respect to their term of protection does not carry over into an obviousness-type double patenting attack on the claims after the patent is issued. *Id.*

[362]*Quad Envtl. Tech. Corp. v. Union Sanitary Dist.,* 946 F.2d 870, 20 USPQ2d 1392 (Fed. Cir. 1991).

[363]*In re Bartfeld,* 925 F.2d 1450, 17 USPQ2d 1885 (Fed. Cir. 1991).

[364]*Merck & Co. v. United States ITC,* 774 F.2d 483, 227 USPQ 779 (Fed. Cir. 1985). Here a terminal disclaimer on five patents included a standard clause to the effect that each patent would expire immediately if it ceased to be commonly owned with the others. The owner was permitted to attempt to establish that its later acquisition of four of the patents was merely for the purpose of effectuating and implementing an intent to have acquired all five in an earlier assignment.

[365]*Quad Envtl. Tech. Corp. v. Union Sanitary District,* 946 F.2d 870, 20 USPQ2d 1392 (Fed. Cir. 1991). The patentee had overcome an obviousness-type double patenting rejection over his own earlier patent by filing a terminal disclaimer. As it turned out, the invention of the earlier patent had been in public use more than a year before the filing date of the later patent. The court held that the disclaimer did not estop the patentee from contesting the merits of the obviousness of the invention claimed in the later patent in view of the public use of the earlier patented invention. In *Ortho Pharm. Corp. v. Smith,* 959 F.2d 936, 22 USPQ2d 1119 (Fed. Cir. 1992), a generic parent patent was invalid for double patenting over a species patent, and another species patent—the one in suit—had been terminally disclaimed with respect to the parent. The accused infringer argued that the species patent was also invalid for double

claims from the patent and the patent is viewed as though the disclaimed claims had never existed in the patent.[366] The Federal Circuit has held that it was not incumbent upon a patentee to disclaim, during the course of litigation, claims subject to a controverted inventorship challenge.[367]

The court has rejected the proposition that a failure to disclaim or reissue after an error is brought to the patentee's attention is proof that the error was intentional. A suggestion that patentees should abandon their suits, or disclaim or reissue, in response to every charge of inequitable conduct raised by an alleged infringer is, in the eyes of the court, nothing short of ridiculous. The right of patentees to resist such charges must not be chilled to extinction by fear that a failure to disclaim or reissue will be used against them as evidence that their original intent was deceitful. A requirement for disclaimer or reissue to avoid adverse inferences would merely encourage the proliferation of inequitable conduct charges.[368]

Failure of a patentee to disclaim an invalid patent claim does not prevent the patentee from enforcing any remaining claims in the same patent that are otherwise valid. The contrary rule of *Maytag Co. v. Hurley Mach. Co.*[369] did not survive the Patent Act of 1952, particularly 35 U.S.C. §§253 and 288.[370]

---

patenting as a result. The Federal Circuit rejected this as an "indirect" obviousness-type double patenting defense.

[366]*Guinn v. Kopf,* 96 F.3d 1419, 40 USPQ2d 1157 (Fed. Cir. 1996). In *Vectra Fitness Inc. v. TNWK Corp.,* 162 F.3d 1379, 49 USPQ2d 1144 (Fed. Cir. 1998), the PTO mishandled a disclaimer by failing to publish it in the OG, although it was placed in the application file. The court rejected an argument that this error somehow nullified the disclaimer.

[367]*Shatterproof Glass Corp. v. Libbey-Owens Ford Co.,* 758 F.2d 613, 225 USPQ 634 (Fed. Cir. 1985).

[368]*Kingsdown Med. Cons, Ltd. v. Hollister, Inc.,* 863 F.2d 867, 9 USPQ2d 1384 (Fed. Cir. 1988).

[369]307 U.S. 243 (1939).

[370]*Allen Archery, Inc. v. Browning Mfg. Co.,* 819 F.2d 1087, 2 USPQ2d 1490 (Fed. Cir. 1987).

VI
The Federal Circuit

16

Federal Circuit Jurisdiction and Appealability

The Federal Circuit was created, in part, for the purpose of achieving uniformity in the exposition and application of substantive patent law.[1] In creating the Federal Circuit, congressional emphasis was on the need for greater uniformity in patent law and for freeing the judicial process from the forum shopping caused by conflicting patent decisions of the regional circuits.[2] The burden of this chapter and the next is to show how patent law questions reach the court, and how they are handled once they are there.

Many nonpatent questions also reach the court, of course. Some of these arrive as part of patent cases, and some as a result of the court's other subject matter jurisdiction. Among other things, the Federal Courts Improvement Act grants the Federal Circuit exclusive appellate jurisdiction over a variety of cases involving the federal government.[3] In dealing with them, the court necessarily develops legal principles of more general application. Chapter 18 examines those broader principles to the extent that they are likely to have application to patent issues as well.

Jurisdiction, in the appellate context, can have several subtly different meanings. In the broadest sense, it connotes the power of the appellate court to act. Inasmuch as the Federal Circuit, like other federal appellate courts, is a legislative creation, its power derives solely from its statutory mandate; its jurisdiction is limited, and the statutory mandate cannot be altered.[4]

The narrower meanings of jurisdiction, for our purposes, have to do with what types of claims are subject to review, and in what lower tribunals those claims arise. These are the concern of §16.1 on subject matter jurisdiction. A third meaning focuses on the nature of the judgment or order that raises the question sought to be reviewed.

---

[1]E.g., *Atari, Inc. v. JS & A Group, Inc.,* 747 F.2d 1422, 223 USPQ 1074 (Fed. Cir. 1984); *Panduit Corp. v. All States Plastic Mfg. Co.,* 744 F.2d 1564, 223 USPQ 465 (Fed. Cir. 1984).

[2]*Christianson v. Colt Indus. Oper. Corp.,* 822 F.2d 1544, 3 USPQ2d 1241 (Fed. Cir. 1987), *vacated on jurisdictional grounds & remanded,* 486 U.S. 800, 7 USPQ2d 1109 (1988).

[3]*United States v. Hohri,* 482 U.S. 64 (1987).

[4]*Christianson v. Colt Indus. Oper. Corp.,* 822 F.2d 1544, 3 USPQ 2d 1241 (Fed. Cir. 1987), *vacated on jurisdictional grounds & remanded,* 486 U.S. 800, 7 USPQ2d 1109 (1988); *Williams v. Secretary of Navy,* 787 F.2d 552 (Fed. Cir. 1986).

This is the subject of §16.2, which deals with appealability. Nonjurisdictional reasons for refusing review of questions or claims are discussed in §16.3 under scope of review. The standards of review applicable to the various types of questions that come before the court are the subject of the next chapter, §17.1. The remainder of that chapter is devoted to the rules and significant practice idiosyncrasies of the court.

§16.1 Subject Matter Jurisdiction

(a) General Principles of Appellate Jurisdiction

Federal courts have the duty to examine and determine their own jurisdiction.[5] Despite the interests of judicial economy and the benefits to the parties in advancing litigation, no interest is served by an appellate decision under a jurisdictional cloud.[6] Thus it is the duty of the appellate court to raise, sua sponte, the question of its jurisdiction to hear an appeal.[7]

It is axiomatic that the initial inquiry in any appeal is whether the court to which appeal is taken has jurisdiction to hear the appeal. While in some matters of procedural or substantive law the Federal Circuit will follow the law as interpreted by the circuit in which the district court is located, such deference is inappropriate on issues of the Federal Circuit's own jurisdiction. The court has the duty to satisfy itself that an appeal is properly before it. It may, of course, look for guidance in the decisions of the regional circuit to which appeals from that district court would normally lie, as well as those of other courts. However, its decision to follow another circuit's interpretation of a common jurisdictional statute results from the persuasiveness of the analysis, not any binding effect.[8]

---

[5]*Williams v. Secretary of Navy,* 787 F.2d 552 (Fed. Cir. 1986); *Aleut Tribe v. United States,* 702 F.2d 1015 (Fed. Cir. 1983).

[6]*Glasstech, Inc. v. AB Kyro OY,* 769 F.2d 1574, 226 USPQ 949 (Fed. Cir. 1985).

[7]*In re Alappat,* 33 F.3d 1526, 31 USPQ2d 1545 (Fed. Cir. 1994); *Wang Labs., Inc. v. Applied Computer Sci., Inc.,* 958 F.2d 355, 22 USPQ2d 1055 (Fed. Cir. 1992); *Johannsen v. Pay Less Drug Stores, Inc.,* 917 F.2d 160, 16 USPQ2d 1697 (Fed. Cir. 1990); *Wyden v. Commissioner of Patents,* 807 F.2d 934, 231 USPQ 918 (Fed. Cir. 1986); *Shiley, Inc. v. Bentley Labs., Inc.,* 782 F.2d 992, 228 USPQ 543 (Fed. Cir. 1986); *Minnesota Chippewa Tribe v. United States,* 768 F.2d 338 (Fed. Cir. 1985); *Parker Bros. v. Tuxedo Monopoly, Inc.,* 757 F.2d 254, 226 USPQ 11 (Fed. Cir. 1985). In *Ballard Med. Prods. v. Wright,* 823 F.2d 527, 3 USPQ2d 1337 (Fed. Cir. 1987), counsel for a party who had moved to dismiss the appeal attempted to withdraw the motion at oral argument. The court indicated that counsel's statement was not alone effective to withdraw the motion; the court would be obliged to consider the jurisdictional question sua sponte in any event.

[8]*Woodard v. Sage Prods., Inc.,* 818 F.2d 841, 2 USPQ2d 1649 (Fed. Cir. 1987). All this, of course, is tempered by the Supreme Court's admonition in *Christianson v. Colt Indus. Operating Corp.,* 486 U.S. 800, 7 USPQ2d 1109 (1988), that law of the case principles be strictly observed in resolving jurisdictional conflicts. See §16.1(f). See also *Sanders Assoc., Inc. v. Summagraphics Corp.,* 2 F.3d 394, 27 USPQ2d 1853 (Fed. Cir. 1993); *Wang Labs., Inc. v. Applied Computer Sci., Inc.,* 958 F.2d 355, 22 USPQ2d 1055 (Fed. Cir. 1992).

Moreover, inasmuch as an appellate court has no jurisdiction to decide the merits of the case if the court from which the appeal was taken was without jurisdiction,[9] the Federal Circuit, like all courts,[10] has inherent jurisdiction to determine its own jurisdiction and that of the tribunal from which the appeal was taken.[11] Courts created by statute can have no jurisdiction but such as the statute confers. The statute confers on the Federal Circuit authority to make a single decision upon concluding that it lacks jurisdiction—whether to dismiss the case or, in the interest of justice, to transfer it to a court of appeals that does have jurisdiction. A court may not in any case, even in the interest of justice, extend its jurisdiction where none exists.[12] Lack of appellate subject matter jurisdiction is a defect in the court's authority to act at all, requiring dismissal or transfer of the appeal.[13]

The result of lack of jurisdiction in the lower tribunal is not reversal or affirmance, but dismissal of the appeal or vacation of the judgment. Thus, where the district court properly dismissed for lack of jurisdiction, the Federal Circuit would dismiss the appeal.[14] And where the district court entered an order after the case had been transferred to another court, the order would be vacated.[15]

The Federal Circuit strictly construes its jurisdiction in harmony with its congressional mandate.[16] Substance not form controls the determination.[17] Implicit in the mandate is the authority to recharacterize pleadings that would improperly evade the intent of Congress.[18]

---

[9]*Glasstech, Inc. v. AB Kyro OY*, 769 F.2d 1574, 226 USPQ 949 (Fed. Cir. 1985). For example, the Federal Circuit has no jurisdiction over an appeal from an advisory opinion. *In re Keil*, 808 F.2d 830, 1 USPQ2d 1427 (Fed. Cir. 1987).

[10]*Chemical Eng'g Corp. v. Marlo, Inc.*, 754 F.2d 331, 222 USPQ 738 (Fed. Cir. 1984).

[11]*Beghin-Say Int'l, Inc. v. Ole-Bendt Rasmussen*, 733 F.2d 1568, 221 USPQ 1121 (Fed. Cir. 1984); *C.R. Bard, Inc. v. Schwartz*, 716 F.2d 874, 219 USPQ 197 (Fed. Cir. 1983). The Federal Circuit has inherent jurisdiction to determine whether a lower tribunal had jurisdiction, and it reviews such an issue de novo. *Interspiro USA, Inc. v. Figgie Int'l, Inc.*, 18 F.3d 927, 30 USPQ2d 1070 (Fed. Cir. 1994).

[12]*Christianson v. Colt Indus. Operating Corp.*, 486 U.S. 800, 7 USPQ2d 1109 (1988).

[13]*AeroJet-General Corp. v. Machine Tool Works*, 895 F.2d 736, 13 USPQ2d 1670 (Fed. Cir. 1990). Thus lack of appellate subject matter jurisdiction precludes even a decision as to whether the appealed order is final or not. However, the appellate court may, for example, dismiss as untimely any appeal clearly brought beyond the statutory 30-day time limit. Such an appeal would be untimely in all courts and hence its transfer would be wasteful and its dismissal would not involve a decision on internal appealability questions such as finality or mootness. *Id.*

[14]*Beghin-Say Int'l, Inc. v. Ole-Bendt Rasmussen*, 733 F.2d 1568, 221 USPQ 1121 (Fed. Cir. 1984). The fact that the district court may have had diversity jurisdiction or some other federal question jurisdiction is not cognizable by the Federal Circuit, where jurisdiction was lacking under 28 U.S.C. §1338(a). See §16.1(b).

[15]*Glasstech, Inc. v. AB Kyro OY*, 769 F.2d 1574, 226 USPQ 949 (Fed. Cir. 1985).

[16]*Chemical Eng'g Corp. v. Marlo, Inc.*, 754 F.2d 331, 222 USPQ 738 (Fed. Cir. 1984). Congress is the source of jurisdiction granted federal courts other than the Supreme Court. *Christianson v. Colt Indus. Oper. Corp.*, 822 F.2d 1544, 3 USPQ 2d 1241 (Fed. Cir. 1987), vacated on jurisdictional grounds & remanded, 486 U.S. 800, 7 USPQ2d 1109 (1988).

[17]*Williams v. Secretary of Navy*, 787 F.2d 552 (Fed. Cir. 1986); *Chemical Eng'g Corp. v. Marlo, Inc.*, 754 F.2d 331, 222 USPQ 738 (Fed. Cir. 1984).

[18]*Chemical Eng'g Corp. v. Marlo, Inc.*, 754 F.2d 331, 222 USPQ 738 (Fed. Cir. 1984).

Jurisdiction cannot be conferred by waiver or acquiescence,[19] and mere recitation of a basis for jurisdiction, by either a party or a court, cannot be controlling.[20] Parties by agreement or otherwise are incapable of either adding to or detracting from a court's jurisdiction.[21] An agreement of the parties cannot confer jurisdiction on the court.[22]

The strictness of the jurisdictional inquiry is reflected in the view that the time within which a notice of appeal must be filed is "mandatory and jurisdictional," and dismissal of the appeal for untimeliness results under all but "unique circumstances."[23] All appellate jurisdiction is prospective only, in the sense that a notice of appeal may or may not be filed.[24] A motion under Rule 60(b), FRCP, for relief from judgment does not substitute for or toll the time prescribed for filing a notice of appeal,[25] even in the case of a pro se litigant who contended that he had been unable to find a docket entry showing judgment.[26] On the other hand, where it appeared that the district court intended a later judgment to be appealable, a failure to appeal from earlier orders was not fatal.[27]

Jurisdiction of the Federal Circuit is determined on a case basis, not an issue basis. It is the collection of proceedings below that must be viewed as of the time of appeal.[28] The court will look to the true nature of the action in the district court.[29]

---

[19]*In re Alappat*, 33 F.3d 1526, 31 USPQ2d 1545 (Fed. Cir. 1994); *Registration Control Sys., Inc. v. Compusystems, Inc.*, 922 F.2d 805, 17 USPQ2d 1212 (Fed. Cir. 1990); *Coastal Corp. v. United States*, 713 F.2d 728 (Fed. Cir. 1983).

[20]*Williams v. Secretary of Navy*, 787 F.2d 552 (Fed. Cir. 1986).

[21]*Utter v. Hiraga*, 845 F.2d 993, 6 USPQ2d 1709 (Fed. Cir. 1988). Here the parties had agreed to submit interference issues to an arbitrator, whose decision would bind the parties "with no further right of appeal." The arbitrator was to decide disputed issues "unless the parties mutually agree otherwise in writing." Following the arbitrator's decision, the parties filed a stipulation with the PTO accepting the arbitrator's decision to refer certain issues to the PTO Board to enable the Board to make priority awards. The Federal Circuit held that there was no clear intent to waive the right to appeal from the Board's decision. This appeal was from the Board not the arbitrator. Moreover, there was a written agreement (the stipulation) that the arbitrator would not decide certain issues. Thus the parties contemplated that there could be an appeal from the Board's decision. A motion to dismiss the appeal was accordingly denied.

[22]*Gould v. Control Laser Corp.*, 866 F.2d 1391, 9 USPQ2d 1718 (Fed. Cir. 1989).

[23]*Armstrong Rubber Co. v. United States*, 781 F.2d 889 (Fed. Cir. 1986). Unique circumstances include a situation where the district court grants an untimely motion for extension of time to appeal, believing the motion to have been timely. *Sofarelli Assoc., Inc. v. United States*, 716 F.2d 1395 (Fed. Cir. 1983). See §17.2(f).

[24]*Atari, Inc. v. JS & A Group, Inc.*, 747 F.2d 1422, 223 USPQ 1074 (Fed. Cir. 1984).

[25]*United States v. Atkinson*, 748 F.2d 659 (Fed. Cir. 1984).

[26]*Case v. BSAF Wyandotte*, 737 F.2d 1034, 222 USPQ 737 (Fed. Cir. 1984). One suspects that the district court disbelieved the story of the pro se litigant; there was contrary evidence.

[27]*Bandag, Inc. v. Al Bolser Tire Stores, Inc.*, 719 F.2d 392, 219 USPQ 1049 (Fed. Cir. 1983).

[28]*Christianson v. Colt Indus. Oper. Corp.*, 822 F.2d 1544, 3 USPQ 2d 1241 (Fed. Cir. 1987), *vacated on jurisdictional grounds & remanded*, 486 U.S. 800, 7 USPQ2d 1109 (1988); *Parker Bros. v. Tuxedo Monopoly, Inc.*, 757 F.2d 254, 226 USPQ 11 (Fed. Cir. 1985); *Atari, Inc. v. JS & A Group, Inc.*, 747 F.2d 1422, 223 USPQ 1074 (Fed. Cir. 1984).

[29]*Williams v. Secretary of Navy*, 787 F.2d 552 (Fed. Cir. 1986).

Unlike other courts of appeals, the Federal Circuit has no general supervisory authority over district courts.[30] Thus, the court will intervene in the district court's management of a case only to satisfy an overwhelming legal requirement or to prevent manifest injustice. The district court is in a much better position than the appellate court to determine, for example, whether trial scheduling will work an injustice.[31] Despite allegations of bias, the court lacks authority to reassign a case to another district judge.[32]

(b) *Patent Infringement Cases in District Courts*

A primary objective of Congress in creating the Federal Circuit was to bring about uniformity in the area of patent law.[33] The broad theme of the Federal Courts Improvement Act—increasing nationwide uniformity in certain fields of national law—is epitomized in the field of patent law. The availability of a clear, stable, uniform basis for evaluating matters of patentability and infringement renders more predictable the outcome of contemplated litigation, facilitates effective business planning, and adds confidence to investment in innovative new products and technology. Congress clearly wanted the Federal Circuit to get its hands on well-pleaded, nonfrivolous claims arising under the patent laws and thus to maximize the court's chances of achieving the congressional objectives underlying the Act.[34] Yet the court's first several years of jurisdictional inquiry have shown a somewhat surprising reluctance on its part to get its hands on every patent issue that arises in the federal court system.[35] By contrast, the court seems quite willing to decide nonpatent issues, even outside the patent context.[36]

---

[30]*Mississippi Chem. Corp. v. Swift Agric. Chem. Corp.*, 717 F.2d 1374, 219 USPQ 577 (Fed. Cir. 1983).

[31]*In re International Med. P.R. Assoc.*, 739 F.2d 618 (Fed. Cir. 1984).

[32]*Petersen Mfg. Co. v. Central Purchasing, Inc.*, 740 F.2d 1541, 222 USPQ 562 (Fed. Cir. 1984). The court felt obliged in this case to point out that "we do not sit to judge the character of district court judges." Of course not, but one hopes that this observation will not have an unduly chilling effect upon the rare but necessary motion for recusal. District courts should not be beyond reproach, even in the eyes of an appellate court of limited jurisdiction.

[33]*Panduit Corp. v. All States Plastic Mfg. Co.*, 744 F.2d 1564, 223 USPQ 465 (Fed. Cir. 1984). One of Congress's objectives in creating a Federal Circuit with exclusive jurisdiction over certain patent cases was to reduce the widespread lack of uniformity and uncertainty of legal doctrine that existed in the administration of patent law. *Christianson v. Colt Indus. Oper. Corp.*, 486 U.S. 800, 7 USPQ2d 1109 (1988).

[34]*AeroJet-General Corp. v. Machine Tool Works*, 895 F.2d 736, 13 USPQ2d 1670 (Fed. Cir. 1990).

[35]*Atari, Inc. v. JS & A Group, Inc.*, 747 F.2d 1422, 223 USPQ 1074 (Fed. Cir. 1984). The view that the Federal Circuit should take jurisdiction whenever that would facilitate patent law uniformity disregards the jurisdiction-granting role of the Congress. *Christianson v. Colt Indus. Oper. Corp.*, 822 F.2d 1544, 3 USPQ2d 1241 (Fed. Cir. 1987), *vacated on jurisdictional grounds & remanded*, 486 U.S. 800, 7 USPQ2d 1109 (1988).

[36]*Atari, Inc. v. JS & A Group, Inc.*, 747 F.2d 1422, 223 USPQ 1074 (Fed. Cir. 1984).

The principal jurisdictional statute, 28 U.S.C. §1295(a), provides that the Federal Circuit shall have exclusive jurisdiction of appeals from final decisions of district courts where the jurisdiction of those courts was based, "in whole or in part, on section 1338 of this title." Excepted are cases involving copyright or trademark claims but no patent claims.[37] Thus, Federal Circuit jurisdiction depends upon whether the jurisdiction of the district court was based, in whole or in part, on 28 U.S.C. §1338. The question is whether the jurisdiction of the district court could have been so based, and the fact that there may have been alternative jurisdictional bases has no bearing. Nor does the district court's view of its jurisdiction. The Federal Circuit is arbiter of its own jurisdiction and has the power to decide the threshold question independently of the conclusion reached by the district court. To say otherwise would produce absurd results, for its jurisdiction would then turn on statements of the district court.[38]

The reference statute, 28 U.S.C. §1338(a), provides that district courts have original and exclusive jurisdiction "of any civil action arising under any Act of Congress relating to patents."[39] Thus the jurisdictional mandate is simple and straightforward: the Federal Circuit has exclusive power to review final decisions in cases where the jurisdiction was based at least in part on a claim arising under the patent laws. In application, this mandate has not been quite that simple.

For example, the court has proposed the following jurisdictional test: whether the claimant asserts before the district court some right or privilege that would be defeated by one or sustained by an opposite construction of the patent laws.[40] But would this not, in some situations, lead to a different result than the rule that the jurisdiction of the Federal Circuit is determined on a case basis and not an issue

---

[37]Section 1338(a) confers jurisdiction over civil actions arising under patent, plant variety protection, copyright, and trademark laws. Thus the case in the district court must include a patent or plant variety claim in order for the Federal Circuit to have jurisdiction over the appeal. A case involving only a trademark or copyright claim, or both, albeit within the exclusive jurisdiction of the district court under §1338, is not reviewable by the Federal Circuit.

[38]*Christianson v. Colt Indus. Oper. Corp.*, 822 F.2d 1544, 3 USPQ2d 1241 (Fed. Cir. 1987), *vacated on jurisdictional grounds & remanded,* 486 U.S. 800, 7 USPQ2d 1109 (1988). The Federal Circuit's judgment was vacated by the Supreme Court on the ground that, without jurisdiction, the Federal Circuit lacked power to do anything except dismiss or transfer. On the merits of the jurisdictional inquiry, however, the Supreme Court did not seem to disagree with the Federal Circuit's analysis. Accordingly, although vacation by the Supreme Court may render the decision of the Federal Circuit technically unavailable as precedent for stare decisis purposes, that decision clearly reflects the thinking and probable direction of the Federal Circuit in future decisions. Thus it is treated here and elsewhere throughout this work (e.g., §§5.2 and 5.3) as though it were unaffected by the Supreme Court's order. Of course, a district court's determination of whether the claims before it arise under the patent laws is not determinative of the appellate jurisdiction of the Federal Circuit. *Franchi v. Manbeck,* 972 F.2d 1283, 23 USPQ2d 1847 (Fed. Cir. 1992).

[39]28 U.S.C. §1338(b) gives the district courts original jurisdiction over civil actions asserting unfair competition claims, such as misappropriation of trade secrets, "when joined with a substantial and related" patent, trademark, or copyright claim.

[40]*Dubost v. United States PTO,* 777 F.2d 1561, 227 USPQ 977 (Fed. Cir. 1985).

basis?[41] A mere allegation that the patent law is involved will not confer jurisdiction when that of the district court did not rest at least in part on a continuing claim arising under the patent laws.[42]

Also, we find the court instructing that its jurisdiction is normally determined when the district court complaint is filed. To impart certainty throughout the entire process of filing, pretrial, trial, and post-trial motions, appellate jurisdiction should normally be known and remain unaffected.[43] And yet the court tells us, indeed in the same opinion, that the term "case" at the time of an actual determination of appellate jurisdiction refers collectively to the proceedings that transpired at the district court level when viewed pragmatically at the time of appeal.[44]

Results in this area are therefore not entirely predictable. Where a case included both patent and copyright counts, and the district court separated the patent count for trial and granted a preliminary injunction on the copyright count, the Federal Circuit decided it had jurisdiction despite the separation of the patent count. What the result might be were the patent count dismissed or otherwise irrevocably discontinued, or severed under Rule 21, FRCP, is unclear.[45] The path of appeal is determined by the basis of jurisdiction in the district court and is not controlled by its decision or by the substance of the issues that are appealed. The reasons are pragmatic: to avoid creating fresh opportunities for forum shopping; to avoid bifurcation of issues and cases at trial and on appeal; to remove uncertainty and the abuses of procedural maneuvering; and, ultimately, to facilitate resolution of disputes. Thus the direction of appeal to the Federal Circuit does not change during or after trial, even when the only issues remaining

---

[41]*Bandag, Inc. v. Al Bolser's Tire Stores, Inc.,* 750 F.2d 903, 223 USPQ 982 (Fed. Cir. 1984). Congress granted the Federal Circuit patent case jurisdiction not patent issue jurisdiction. *Christianson v. Colt Indus. Oper. Corp.,* 822 F.2d 1544, 3 USPQ2d 1241 (Fed. Cir. 1987), *vacated on jurisdictional grounds & remanded,* 486 U.S. 800, 7 USPQ2d 1109 (1988).

[42]*Atari, Inc. v. JS & A Group, Inc.,* 747 F.2d 1422, 223 USPQ 1074 (Fed. Cir. 1984). The mere presence of a patent issue cannot of itself create a cause of action arising under the patent laws. *Consolidated World Housewares, Inc. v. Finkle,* 829 F.2d 261, 4 USPQ2d 1565 (Fed. Cir. 1987). But a federal bankruptcy court can decide patent infringement claims, and the Federal Circuit has jurisdiction over an appeal from a district court review of such a decision. *Institut Pasteur v. Cambridge Biotech Corp.,* 186 F.3d 1356, 51 USPQ2d 1321 (Fed. Cir. 1999).

[43]*Atari, Inc. v. JS & A Group, Inc.,* 747 F.2d 1422, 223 USPQ 1074 (Fed. Cir. 1984). Certainly pleadings filed after appeal cannot alter the jurisdictional basis for the appeal. *Schwarzkopf Dev. Corp. v. Ti-Coating, Inc.,* 800 F.2d 240, 231 USPQ 47 (Fed. Cir. 1986). The presence or absence of jurisdiction must be determined on the facts existing at the time the complaint under consideration was filed. *Arrowhead Indus. Water, Inc. v. Ecolochem, Inc.,* 846 F.2d 731, 6 USPQ2d 1685 (Fed. Cir. 1988). Appellate jurisdiction depends upon the nature of the case in the district court and not upon the issues presented for review. *U.S. Philips Corp. v. Windmere Corp.,* 861 F.2d 695, 8 USPQ2d 1885 (Fed. Cir. 1988). That patent validity issues may have been injected during the course of an arbitration proceeding in a contract suit forms no basis for asserting that the district court's jurisdiction was based on 28 U.S.C. §1338, and hence forms no basis for asserting jurisdiction in the Federal Circuit. *Ballard Med. Prods. v. Wright,* 823 F.2d 527, 3 USPQ2d 1337 (Fed. Cir. 1987).

[44]*Atari, Inc. v. JS & A Group, Inc.,* 747 F.2d 1422, 223 USPQ 1074 (Fed. Cir. 1984). See also *Bandag, Inc. v. Al Bolser's Tire Stores, Inc.,* 750 F.2d 903, 223 USPQ 982 (Fed. Cir. 1984).

[45]*Atari, Inc. v. JS & A Group, Inc.,* 747 F.2d 1422, 223 USPQ 1074 (Fed. Cir. 1984).

are not within its exclusive assignment.[46] Similarly, where patent and trademark claims are separately appealed, the court has jurisdiction over the trademark appeal. But it is unclear what result would obtain were the patent claim not appealed at all.[47] Where a district court has "arising under" patent jurisdiction originally, and retains jurisdiction to enforce a settlement agreement, the Federal Circuit has jurisdiction over an appeal from the enforcement proceedings.[48]

On the other hand, where the patent claims in a case had long been finally adjudicated with no possibility of reopening, and all that remained were antitrust issues, the Federal Circuit was willing to transfer the appeal to the Seventh Circuit, which had previous familiarity with the case.[49] But in another case where the Federal Circuit had already passed on the patent issues, it would decide the antitrust issues as well, applying regional circuit law where discernible.[50] Indeed, the court has since made it clear that its jurisdiction should not depend upon the happenstance that a district court decides the patent issues in a case before deciding the antitrust issues.[51]

Where a counterclaim for declaratory judgment of invalidity and noninfringement is dismissed without opposition by the counterclaimant in the pleading stage, leaving only a state court claim, there is no appellate jurisdiction. The transient appearance of the counterclaim did not give it irrevocable control of the jurisdictional basis of the case. As a result, the state court claim on appeal, reaching the Federal Circuit solely on the basis of diversity, did not acquire a basis for jurisdiction arising in whole or part under the patent laws.[52]

---

[46]*Abbott Labs. v. Brennan*, 952 F.2d 1346, 21 USPQ2d 1192 (Fed. Cir. 1992). See also *Zenith Elec. Corp. v. Exzec Inc.*, 182 F.3d 1340, 51 USPQ2d 1337 (Fed. Cir. 1999).

[47]*Bandag, Inc. v. Al Bolser's Tire Stores, Inc.*, 750 F.2d 903, 223 USPQ 982 (Fed. Cir. 1984).

[48]*Wang Labs., Inc. v. Applied Computer Sci., Inc.*, 958 F.2d 355, 22 USPQ2d 1055 (Fed. Cir. 1992). It should be noted that this holding was mandated by law of the case considerations, although there is no apparent reason to doubt its future applicability.

[49]*USM Corp. v. SPS Tech., Inc.*, 770 F.2d 1035, 226 USPQ 1038 (Fed. Cir. 1985).

[50]*Korody-Colyer Corp. v. General Motors Corp.*, 828 F.2d 1572, 4 USPQ2d 1203 (Fed. Cir. 1987). It would appear that *USM Corp. v. SPS Tech., Inc.*, 770 F.2d 1035, 226 USPQ 1038 (Fed. Cir. 1985), discussed at note 16:49, is strictly limited to its unusual procedural circumstances.

[51]*Technicon Instr., Corp. v. Alpkem Corp.*, 866 F.2d 417, 9 USPQ2d 1540 (Fed. Cir. 1989). The plaintiff had sued for patent infringement and the defendant counterclaimed for antitrust violation. The district court found no infringement and dismissed the complaint, and the Federal Circuit affirmed on appeal. The district court then entered judgment on the antitrust counterclaim and the plaintiff appealed. The court found that it had jurisdiction over the appeal, just as it did in *U.S. Philips Corp. v. Windmere Corp.*, 861 F.2d 695, 8 USPQ2d 1885 (Fed. Cir. 1988), where the appeal was from a directed verdict against the defendant on an antitrust counterclaim, rendered prior to any decision on the plaintiff's patent infringement claim.

[52]*Schwarzkopf Dev. Corp. v. Ti-Coating, Inc.*, 800 F.2d 240, 231 USPQ 47 (Fed. Cir. 1986). Some jurisdictional questions become extremely complex. In *Gronholz v. Sears, Roebuck & Co.*, 836 F.2d 515, 5 USPQ2d 1269 (Fed. Cir. 1987), the original complaint had counts for patent infringement and trade secret misappropriation. The defendant moved for summary judgment on the trade secret count, and the plaintiff moved for voluntary dismissal, under Rule 41(a), FRCP, of both counts. The trial court granted the unopposed motion to dismiss the patent count, but denied the motion for voluntary dismissal on the trade secret count and granted summary judgment instead. The plaintiff appealed the summary judgment to the Federal Circuit. The defendant's motion to transfer to the regional circuit was granted. The Federal

The well-pleaded complaint rule. In *Christianson v. Colt,*[53] the Federal Circuit signaled its intention to employ the traditional "well-pleaded complaint" rule as a tool for jurisdictional analysis. This case, which represents the first full-blown review of a Federal Circuit decision by the Supreme Court, had an interesting background. According to the Federal Circuit, the plaintiff brought an antitrust action alleging a concerted refusal to deal. The defense was that any boycott was justified by trade secrets. In opposition to that defense, and in anticipation of it, plaintiff pleaded that the trade secrets were unenforceable because the secrets should have been disclosed in certain of defendant's patents in order to comply with the best mode and enablement requirements of 35 U.S.C. §112. The district court granted summary judgment for plaintiff, and defendant appealed to the Federal Circuit. That court agreed with plaintiff that it lacked jurisdiction because the case did not arise under the patent laws, and in an unpublished order transferred the appeal to the Seventh Circuit pursuant to 28 U.S.C. §1631.

The case was briefed and argued to the Seventh Circuit on its merits, but that court sua sponte reexamined the jurisdictional question. After finding that law of the case principles did not compel adherence to the Federal Circuit's view of the jurisdictional issue, the Seventh Circuit found that it lacked jurisdiction because the case was one of those over which the Federal Circuit had exclusive jurisdiction. The Seventh Circuit accordingly ordered a retransfer to the Federal Circuit.[54]

This left the Federal Circuit in a quandary. It felt that the Seventh Circuit retransfer order was not binding upon it, because it was "clearly wrong." Yet it appreciated fully the unseemliness of a perpetual game of jurisdictional ping pong. Its solution, rather than to dismiss or retransfer the appeal, was to decide it on the merits, in the interest of justice. The net result, then, was that the Federal Circuit found itself in the unusual position of deciding a case over which it felt it lacked jurisdiction.

The Supreme Court granted certiorari and, after reaching the same conclusion as the Federal Circuit on the fundamental jurisdictional question, vacated the judgment with directions to remand to

---

Circuit adopted the view that Rule 41(a) does not apply to a voluntary dismissal of fewer than all claims, since the rule deals with dismissal of an "action." Thus, such a dismissal is in reality a Rule 15 amendment to the complaint. Application of the well-pleaded complaint rule to such an amended complaint leads to the conclusion that the case does not arise under the patent laws. But does this not mean that the district court itself lacked jurisdiction over the pendent trade secret claim (in the absence of diversity) and should have dismissed? The overwhelming weight of authority seems to say so. See 13B Wright, Miller & Cooper, *Federal Practice & Procedure* §3567.1 (1984). However, where there has already been a substantial commitment of federal judicial resources (as here on the motion for summary judgment), perhaps the federal courts are justified in keeping the case. See *Graf v. Elgin, J&E Ry. Co.,* 790 F.2d 1341 (7th Cir. 1986). Compare *Zenith Elec. Corp. v. Exzec Inc.,* 182 F.3d 1340, 51 USPQ2d 1337 (Fed. Cir. 1999).

[53]*Christianson v. Colt Indus. Oper. Corp.,* 822 F.2d 1544, 3 USPQ2d 1241 (Fed. Cir. 1987), *vacated on jurisdictional grounds & remanded,* 486 U.S. 800, 7 USPQ2d 1109 (1988).

[54]*Christianson v. Colt Indus. Oper. Corp.,* 798 F.2d 1051, 230 USPQ 840 (7th Cir. 1986).

the Seventh Circuit. Its reasoning was that courts created by statute can have no jurisdiction but such as the statute confers. The Federal Circuit was, by the transfer statute (28 U.S.C. §1631), limited to a choice between two simple alternatives once it found it lacked jurisdiction: dismiss or, in the interest of justice, transfer to a court of appeals that has jurisdiction. A court may not in any case, even in the interest of justice, extend its jurisdiction where none exists.[55]

The reasoning of the Supreme Court and that of the Federal Circuit on the underlying jurisdictional question seem mutually consistent, and rely in large measure on the well-pleaded complaint rule. In the Federal Circuit's view of the rule, whether an action arises under federal law must be determined from what necessarily appears in the plaintiff's statement of its own claim in the complaint, unaided by anything alleged in anticipation or avoidance of defenses that it is thought the defendant may interpose. A defense that raises a federal question is thus inadequate to confer federal jurisdiction, even if the defense is anticipated in the plaintiff's complaint, and even if both parties admit that the defense is the only question truly at issue in the case.[56]

The Supreme Court in *Christianson v. Colt* elaborated somewhat: in order to demonstrate that a case is one arising under federal patent law the plaintiff must set up some right, title, or interest under the patent laws, or at least make it appear that some right or privilege will be defeated by one construction or sustained by the opposite construction of those laws. Jurisdiction under 28 U.S.C. §1338 extends only to those cases in which a well-pleaded complaint establishes either that federal patent law creates the cause of action or that the plaintiff's right to relief necessarily depends on resolution of a substantial question of federal patent law, in that patent law is a necessary element of one of the well-pleaded claims.[57] The Court also indicated that, just as a plaintiff may not defeat removal by omitting to plead necessary federal questions in a complaint, so a plaintiff may not defeat §1338 jurisdiction by omitting to plead necessary federal patent law questions. Finally, the Supreme Court passed the question whether a court of appeals could furnish itself a jurisdictional basis unsupported by the pleadings by deeming the complaint amended in light of the parties' express or implied consent to litigate a claim under Rule 15(b), FRCP.[58]

The Federal Circuit has been faithful to the holdings of *Christianson v. Colt*. Within weeks of the Supreme Court decision it accepted a transfer from the First Circuit without substantive review of the

---

[55]*Christianson v. Colt Indus. Oper. Corp.*, 486 U.S. 800, 7 USPQ2d 1109 (1988).

[56]*Vink v. Schijf*, 839 F.2d 676, 5 USPQ2d 1728 (Fed. Cir. 1988); *Gronholz v. Sears, Roebuck & Co.*, 836 F.2d 515, 5 USPQ2d 1269 (Fed. Cir. 1987); *Christianson v. Colt Indus. Oper. Corp.*, 822 F.2d 1544, 3 USPQ2d 1241 (Fed. Cir. 1987), *vacated on jurisdictional grounds & remanded*, 486 U.S. 800, 7 USPQ2d 1109 (1988).

[57]*Christianson v. Colt Indus. Oper. Corp.*, 486 U.S. 800, 7 USPQ2d 1109 (1988).

[58]*Christianson v. Colt Indus. Oper. Corp.*, 486 U.S. 800, 7 USPQ2d 1109 (1988). The Court found no evidence of any consent among the parties to litigate a patent law claim, because the

correctness of the regional circuit's jurisdictional determination.[59] The court later remarked that it, like every other circuit court, must apply law of the case principles to transfer decisions of coordinate courts, notwithstanding that such a decision may implicate Federal Circuit jurisdiction.[60] It has also observed that a court may not in any case, even in the interest of justice, extend its jurisdiction where none exists.[61] In an in banc decision the court expanded the well-pleaded complaint rule to include well-pleaded compulsory counterclaims for patent infringement.[62] The court feels that, under *Christianson v. Colt,* a claim supported by alternative theories in the complaint may not form the basis for §1338 jurisdiction unless patent law is essential to each of those theories.[63]

It seems clear that different results may obtain if there is evidence of efforts to manipulate proceedings in the district court so as to invoke or avoid jurisdiction of the Federal Circuit.[64] The Federal Circuit has remarked that what appeared to be an agreement calling for collusive litigation to get the matter into a federal court (and ultimately before the Federal Circuit) "paints a picture appalling."[65] In another case, there had previously been a hearing and an appeal on some state court issues, and then a patent issued and the pleadings were amended to include a claim for patent infringement. The Federal Circuit held that it had jurisdiction over the whole of the case, including dependent nonpatent issues. There was no suggestion that the infringement claim was baseless or frivolous, or that its addition to the complaint was a tactical procedural maneuver. The court pointed out that the situation was identical to that which would have prevailed had the patent suit been filed separately and consolidated with the suit involving state court issues.[66]

State versus federal considerations. It has been argued that failure to find jurisdiction would subject a party to the unappealing prospect of having its patent rights determined in state court. The court took the opportunity to point out that the statutory limits on its own jurisdiction and that of the district courts can and do result

---

complaint was found to have alternate theories. Compare *Gronholz v. Sears, Roebuck & Co.,* 836 F.2d 515, 5 USPQ2d 1269 (Fed. Cir. 1987).

[59]*Xeta, Inc. v. Atex, Inc.,* 852 F.2d 1280, 7 USPQ2d 1471 (Fed. Cir. 1988).

[60]*Smith v. Orr,* 855 F.2d 1544 (Fed. Cir. 1988).

[61]*Johns-Manville Corp. v. United States,* 855 F.2d 1556 (Fed. Cir. 1988).

[62]*AeroJet-General Corp. v. Machine Tool Works,* 895 F.2d 736, 13 USPQ2d 1670 (Fed. Cir. 1990). The complaint was based upon diversity of citizenship, seeking a declaratory judgment of no misappropriation of trade secrets, and the counterclaim for patent infringement was found to be compulsory. In *DSC Comm. Corp. v. Pulse Comm.,* 170 F.3d 1354, 50 USPQ2d 1001 (Fed. Cir. 1999), the rule was extended to cover permissive counterclaims as well.

[63]*American Tel. & Tel. Co. v. Integrated Network Corp.,* 972 F.2d 1321, 23 USPQ2d 1918 (Fed. Cir. 1992).

[64]*USM Corp. v. SPS Tech., Inc.,* 770 F.2d 1035, 226 USPQ 1038 (Fed. Cir. 1985).

[65]*Consolidated World Housewares, Inc. v. Finkle,* 829 F.2d 261, 4 USPQ2d 1565 (Fed. Cir. 1987).

[66]*Eaton Corp. v. Appliance Valves Corp.,* 790 F.2d 874, 229 USPQ 668 (Fed. Cir. 1986).

in state courts resolving patent issues. The Federal Circuit was not intended by Congress to be the exclusive tribunal to hear appeals relating to patents or to be the only federal circuit court to hear appeals of patent law issues. The creation of the Federal Circuit did not alter the traditional allocation of patent issues between federal and state courts resulting from application of 28 U.S.C. §1338. State and federal courts often are required to interpret and apply laws from outside their respective jurisdictions in order to decide specific issues in cases properly before them. Presumably state courts and regional federal courts of appeals will look to the decisions of the Federal Circuit for guidance when those issues relate to patents.[67]

Despite the difficulty in formulating appropriate general tests, certain basic principles have clearly emerged. On the one hand, the Federal Circuit does not have exclusive jurisdiction over patent matters that may arise in a state court action. Rather, its jurisdiction is limited to appeals of cases in which the jurisdiction of the district court was based at least in part on §1338.[68] Thus a claim of failure to pay royalties due under a patent license agreement is one arising out of state contract law and not one arising under the patent law.[69] Likewise, a case cannot arise under federal law where the patent claim is merely a defense to a state court action.[70]

To determine whether a state law cause of action necessarily depends on resolution of a substantial question of federal patent law, in that patent law is a necessary element of one of the well-pleaded claims, *Christianson v. Colt* teaches that a court must look to the elements of the claims appearing on the face of the complaint. Such scrutiny of the claims pleaded is thorough, for the court must ascertain whether all the theories by which a plaintiff could prevail on a claim rely solely on resolving a substantial question of federal patent law. Using this approach, the court found §1338 jurisdiction over a state claim of injurious falsehood, based upon an assertion by the patentee that it held exclusive rights to make or sell devices covered by the patent. The only allegation of falsity was that the patent is invalid or unenforceable. Thus, the action satisfied the well-pleaded complaint rule, for a required element of the state law cause of action—a falsity— necessarily depends on a question of federal patent law. Moreover, all theories upon which the plaintiff could prevail depend upon resolving a question of federal patent law, because no other basis for falsity was pleaded by the plaintiff. And validity and enforceability are certainly substantial enough to convey §1338 jurisdiction.[71]

---

[67]*Speedco, Inc. v. Estes,* 853 F.2d 909, 7 USPQ2d 1637 (Fed. Cir. 1988).

[68]*In re Oximetrix, Inc.,* 748 F.2d 637, 223 USPQ 1068 (Fed. Cir. 1984). State courts may decide patent questions. *Christianson v. Colt Indus. Oper. Corp.,* 822 F.2d 1544, 3 USPQ2d 1241 (Fed. Cir. 1987), *vacated on jurisdictional grounds & remanded,* 486 U.S. 800, 7 USPQ2d 1109 (1988).

[69]*Schwarzkopf Dev. Corp. v. Ti-Coating, Inc.,* 800 F.2d 240, 231 USPQ 47 (Fed. Cir. 1986).

[70]*Schwarzkopf Dev. Corp. v. Ti-Coating, Inc.,* 800 F.2d 240, 231 USPQ 47 (Fed. Cir. 1986).

[71]*Hunter Douglas Inc. v. Harmonic Design Inc.,* 153 F.3d 1318, 47 USPQ2d 1769 (Fed. Cir. 1998).

It is clear that 35 U.S.C. §294, which authorizes enforcement of agreements to arbitrate, cannot be relied upon to support the contention that a contract suit involving arbitration, in the course of which issues of validity and infringement might be encountered, is one arising under the patent laws within the meaning of 28 U.S.C. §1338.[72] The scope of a licensed patent may control the scope of a license agreement, but that rule of contract law cannot possibly convert a suit for breach of contract into one arising under the patent laws as required to render the jurisdiction of the district court based on §1338.[73] That a contract action may involve a determination of the true inventor does not convert that action into one arising under the patent laws. The federal court therefore lacks jurisdiction over an action seeking a declaration of the true inventor, brought by one who had acquired by separate contracts the interest of separate inventive entities in the same invention. Federal district courts do not have original jurisdiction to conduct an interference, and any controversy between the parties is therefore contractual.[74]

On the other hand, the Federal Circuit has jurisdiction over pendent matters that are attached to a patent claim, including both traditional state questions and federal matters such as copyright or trademark or antitrust claims. Indeed, it has exclusive jurisdiction to review such matters, as long as the case involves a bona fide patent claim.[75] The court's exclusive jurisdiction over matters arising in whole or in part under the patent laws is not defeated by the fact that the patent claims have been dismissed with prejudice. The path of appeal is determined by the basis of jurisdiction in the district court, and is not controlled by the district court's decision or the substance of issues that are appealed. Because the complaint contained patent infringement claims, the district court's jurisdiction arose under 28 U.S.C. §1338(a). This established the path of appeal, giving the Federal Circuit exclusive jurisdiction.[76] The jurisdiction of

---

[72]*Ballard Med. Prods. v. Wright,* 823 F.2d 527, 3 USPQ2d 1337 (Fed. Cir. 1987).

[73]*Ballard Med. Prods. v. Wright,* 823 F.2d 527, 3 USPQ2d 1337 (Fed. Cir. 1987). The court has assumed without deciding that construction of a term in a contract could sustain jurisdiction under §1338(a) if it implicated patent law principles; however, it took pains to point out that it did not find that proposition intuitively obvious, and could find no cases that so hold. *American Tel. & Tel. Co. v. Integrated Network Corp.,* 972 F.2d 1321, 23 USPQ2d 1918 (Fed. Cir. 1992). The counts of the complaint were breach of contract, breach of fiduciary duty, misappropriation of proprietary information, and inducing breach of contract and misappropriation. The only possible patent question was the purport of language in the employment contract, which required assignment of all inventions conceived during employment. There was, in the court's view, no reason to assume this referred only to patentable inventions. In addition, the court offered that when an invention is conceived may be more a question of common sense than one of patent law. The phrase might have both patent and general law meanings, and the state court would be free to look for guidance to Federal Circuit decisions on conception.

[74]*Consolidated World Housewares, Inc. v. Finkle,* 829 F.2d 261, 4 USPQ2d 1565 (Fed. Cir. 1987).

[75]*Panduit Corp. v. All States Plastic Mfg. Co.,* 744 F.2d 1564, 223 USPQ 465 (Fed. Cir. 1984). See also *Cygnus Therapeutics Sys. v. Alza Corp.,* 92 F.3d 1153, 39 USPQ2d 1666 (Fed. Cir. 1996); *Micro Motion, Inc. v. Kane Steel Co.,* 894 F.2d 1318, 13 USPQ2d 1696 (Fed. Cir. 1990).

[76]*Zenith Elec. Corp. v. Exzec Inc.,* 182 F.3d 1340, 51 USPQ2d 1337 (Fed. Cir. 1999). But where a patent infringement claim that was joined with a pendent trade secret claim is volunta-

the Federal Circuit is over a final decision of a district court, not the patent portion of a final decision.[77] The court will assume jurisdiction over an appeal from an order quashing a subpoena in an ancillary proceeding where the principal action is a patent infringement case and the discovery sought relates to the patent infringement claim.[78]

The mere labeling and sequencing of pleadings in the trial tribunal cannot be allowed to control every exercise of the Federal Circuit's appellate jurisdiction. Nor can the mere presence in a case of issues other than those within the court's exclusive appellate jurisdiction serve to oust it of the jurisdiction it must and would otherwise exercise in carrying out its mission.[79]

Thus, the court will review a Lanham Act count, applying the law of the regional circuit, even though it would have not had jurisdiction over the Lanham Act count if it had not been joined with a patent infringement count.[80] So too with such questions as attorney disqualification,[81] unfair competition,[82] and other matters.[83] In such cases, the court will decide the nonpatent counts in light of the problems faced by the district court, including the law there applicable, and counsel are admonished that it is their duty and role to brief and argue the nonpatent counts just as if they were appearing before the regional circuit from which the case originated.[84]

That a nonfederal issue, such as ownership of a patent, must be resolved before a federal issue, such as infringement of the patent, is immaterial in determining whether there is federal jurisdiction.[85]

---

rily dismissed, the Federal Circuit lacks jurisdiction over an appeal from a summary judgment on the trade secret count. *Gronholz v. Sears, Roebuck & Co.*, 836 F.2d 515, 5 USPQ2d 1269 (Fed. Cir. 1987). The *Zenith* decision distinguished *Gronholz* on the ground that there the dismissal of the patent claim was without prejudice, thus operating as an amendment of the complaint. In *Nilssen v. Motorola Inc.*, 203 F.3d 782, 53 USPQ2d 1765 (Fed. Cir. 2), the court confirmed that the determinative factor is not whether the dismissal was voluntary or involuntary, but rather whether it was without prejudice to reasserting the patent claims. If so, the parties are left in the same legal position with respect to the patent claims as if they had never been filed, and the Federal Circuit lacks jurisdiction.

[77]*Atari, Inc. v. JS & A Group, Inc.*, 747 F.2d 1422, 223 USPQ 1074 (Fed. Cir. 1984). See also *United States v. Hohri*, 482 U.S. 64 (1987); *Schwarzkopf Dev. Corp. v. Ti-Coating, Inc.*, 800 F.2d 240, 231 USPQ 47 (Fed. Cir. 1986).

[78]*Micro Motion, Inc. v. Kane Steel Co.*, 894 F.2d 1318, 13 USPQ2d 1696 (Fed. Cir. 1990).

[79]*In re Innotron Diagnostics*, 800 F.2d 1077, 231 USPQ 178 (Fed. Cir. 1986).

[80]*Petersen Mfg. Co. v. Central Purchasing, Inc.*, 740 F.2d 1541, 222 USPQ 562 (Fed. Cir. 1984). The Lanham Act is codified in 15 U.S.C. §§1051–1127.

[81]*Panduit Corp. v. All States Plastic Mfg. Co.*, 744 F.2d 1564, 223 USPQ 465 (Fed. Cir. 1984).

[82]*Interpart Corp. v. Italia*, 777 F.2d 678, 228 USPQ 124 (Fed. Cir. 1985).

[83]*Cable Elec. Prods., Inc. v. Genmark, Inc.*, 770 F.2d 1015, 226 USPQ 881 (Fed. Cir. 1985).

[84]*Cable Elec. Prods., Inc. v. Genmark, Inc.*, 770 F.2d 1015, 226 USPQ 881 (Fed. Cir. 1985).

[85]*Vink v. Schijf*, 839 F.2d 676, 5 USPQ2d 1728 (Fed. Cir. 1988). The original complaint sought a declaratory judgment as to title to a patent, and an injunction against infringement. The complaint was amended to allege title in the plaintiff and patent infringement. Thus on its face the amended complaint set forth a patent law question sufficient to confer federal jurisdiction. The defendant argued that under *Luckett v. Delpark, Inc.*, 270 U.S. 496 (1926), a suit seeking a declaration of ownership of a patent does not arise under the patent laws, nor is subject matter jurisdiction conferred by the complainant requesting an injunction against future infringement after ownership is determined. The Federal Circuit pointed out, however, that the *Luckett* Court had indicated that if the complaint had been for patent infringement,

Miscellaneous patent questions. The true nature of the case controls. Thus the fact that diversity is alleged as the basis for jurisdiction does not necessarily mean that the case is not one cognizable under §1338. Where the diversity complaint requests an injunction against patent infringement, it is a patent case.[86] By the same token, a suit by an exclusive licensee against the licensor for infringement of the licensed patent seeks the relief afforded by the patent laws and in substance arises under the patent laws. The mere fact that a patent dispute arises between contracting parties does not necessarily lead to the conclusion that the cause of action is one under contract rather than patent.[87] The patent laws create no affirmative right supporting a cause of action against a competitor to assert a right to make or copy what is in the public domain and excluded from patent protection. Therefore, no basis under the federal patent laws exists to support a right to file a declaratory judgment counterclaim seeking a declaration that the defendant has a "right to copy" a design that it asserts is in the public domain. To argue that trade dress protection cannot be afforded to the plaintiff because the design is in the public domain is merely a defense to the plaintiff's claim for trade dress infringement. As an affirmative defense raised in response to a trade dress infringement claim, which admittedly does not "arise under" the patent laws, this defense does not give rise to jurisdiction under *Christianson*.[88]

A nonpatent antitrust action was consolidated with a patent infringement action. Later, certain issues were separated for trial and one of the parties sought mandamus. The Federal Circuit held that it had exclusive jurisdiction over any appeal under such circumstances. The consolidation in no way ousted the district court of jurisdiction over the patent case, and at the time the challenged separation order was issued, its jurisdiction over the entire consolidated case was based in part on §1338. This is no different than it would have been had the defendant in the antitrust case filed the patent claim as a counterclaim. There is but one lawsuit and its outcome will be substantially governed by considerations unique to the field of patent law.[89] Consolidation for trial does not produce the same jurisdictional effect as the filing of a patent action in the form of a counterclaim, particularly where the parties are different in the consolidated cases.[90]

A suit against the PTO to compel it to award the plaintiff an application filing date is one that the Federal Circuit may review on

---

the fact of an anticipated defense of lack of title would not have defeated federal jurisdiction. One would have to suppose that *Luckett* retains its vitality and that the unamended complaint in the principal case would have been dismissed for want of jurisdiction.

[86]*Chemical Eng'g Corp. v. Marlo, Inc.*, 754 F.2d 331, 222 USPQ 738 (Fed. Cir. 1984).

[87]*Yarway Corp. v. Eur-Control USA Inc.*, 775 F.2d 268, 227 USPQ 352 (Fed. Cir. 1985).

[88]*Leatherman Tool Group Inc. v. Cooper Indus. Inc.*, 131 F.3d 1011, 44 USPQ2d 1837 (Fed. Cir. 1997).

[89]*In re Innotron Diagnostics*, 800 F.2d 1077, 231 USPQ 178 (Fed. Cir. 1986).

[90]*Christianson v. Colt Indus. Oper. Corp.*, 822 F.2d 1544, 3 USPQ2d 1241 (Fed. Cir. 1987), *vacated on jurisdictional grounds & remanded*, 486 U.S. 800, 7 USPQ2d 1109 (1988). *Interpart Corp. v. Italia*, 777 F.2d 678, 228 USPQ 124 (Fed. Cir. 1985), is distinguishable on that basis.

appeal, for the plaintiff's right to priority would be sustained or defeated by a construction of the patent laws.[91] Similarly, a petition filed in the district court seeking to overturn the action of the PTO in failing to award the petitioner a passing grade on the examination for registration as a patent agent is a civil action under 35 U.S.C. §32, and §32 is an act of Congress relating to patents. Thus, the Federal Circuit has jurisdiction of an appeal from a denial of the petition.[92] Judicial resolution of coinventorship contests over issued patents is explicitly authorized by 35 U.S.C. §256. Thus a suit for determination of coinventorship and correction of a patent under §256 arises under the patent law.[93] An action brought in federal district court to review a decision of the PTO Commissioner on a petition to revive an abandoned patent application is one arising under the patent laws, in that it depends on resolution of a substantial question of federal patent law. The Federal Circuit accordingly has jurisdiction of an appeal from the district court's order.[94]

The Tennessee Valley Authority has the right, under 16 U.S.C. §831r, to infringe patents, and the owner has the right to recover reasonable compensation in a district court. Such a case is one arising under an act of Congress relating to patents, and the Federal Circuit accordingly has exclusive jurisdiction over the appeal.[95] The Federal Circuit also has exclusive jurisdiction over appeals involving the Plant Variety Protection Act.[96]

(c) Patent Compensation in the Court of Federal Claims

The Federal Circuit has exclusive jurisdiction of an appeal from a final decision of the United States Court of Federal Claims.[97] The Court of Federal Claims has jurisdiction over a variety of suits against the United States, as set forth in 28 U.S.C. §§1491–1509. The claims that concern us here are those arising under §1498, entitled "Patent and copyright cases." Section 1498 is a lengthy provision, establishing as it does the basic framework for patent infringement claims against the government. In capsule form, the statute provides that whenever a patented invention is used or manufactured by or for the United States, the patent owner's remedy "shall be by action against the

---

[91]*Dubost v. United States PTO,* 777 F.2d 1561, 227 USPQ 977 (Fed. Cir. 1985).

[92]*Wyden v. Commissioner of Patents,* 807 F.2d 934, 231 USPQ 918 (Fed. Cir. 1986). See also *Franchi v. Manbeck,* 972 F.2d 1283, 23 USPQ2d 1847 (Fed. Cir. 1992).

[93]*MCV, Inc. v. King-Seeley Thermos Co.,* 870 F.2d 1568, 10 USPQ2d 1287 (Fed. Cir. 1989). This appears to be a clear holding that §256 creates a cause of action to determine and correct inventorship.

[94]*Morganroth v. Quigg,* 885 F.2d 843, 12 USPQ2d 1125 (Fed. Cir. 1989).

[95]*Alco Standard Corp. v. Tennessee Valley Auth.,* 808 F.2d 1490, 1 USPQ2d 1337 (Fed. Cir. 1986).

[96]*Asgrow Seed Co. v. Winterboer,* 982 F.2d 486, 25 USPQ2d 1202 (Fed. Cir. 1992).

[97]28 U.S.C. §1295(a)(3).

United States in the United States Court of Federal Claims for the recovery of its reasonable and entire compensation for such use and manufacture." Special problems encountered in patent infringement suits against the government are discussed in §11.1.

This clear-cut jurisdictional grant has presented no problems. The court has made it clear that on substantive patent matters, federal trial courts are bound by Federal Circuit law, but on procedural matters they are to apply the law of the regional circuit. However, where the Federal Circuit hears all appeals from the trial court, as in the case of the Court of Federal Claims, Federal Circuit law governs on procedural matters as well.[98]

(d) Patent Determinations of the ITC

The Federal Circuit has exclusive jurisdiction to review the final determinations of the United States International Trade Commission relating to unfair trade practices in import trade, by virtue of 28 U.S.C. §1295(a)(6). The ITC has the statutory power to deal with unfair methods of competition and unfair acts in the importation of articles into the United States; these methods and acts include patent infringement.[99] The substantive and procedural patent law unique to the ITC is discussed in §11.2.

The Federal Circuit has no statutory authority to review advisory opinions of the ITC. Section 1295(a)(6) permits review of "final determinations" of the ITC, and advisory opinions are not final determinations. What counts is not the nature or thoroughness of the agency proceeding, but the effect of the determination. An agency may not issue what it calls advisory opinions and attempt to make some appealable and some not appealable on the basis of its selection among types of proceedings, or on the basis of how those opinions are treated by other agencies. If the ITC wishes one of its pronouncements to have effect as a final determination, it has the ability to accomplish that objective.[100]

The Federal Circuit has jurisdiction to review final determination decisions of the ITC on the merits, i.e., those that exclude or refuse to exclude articles from entry. An ITC decision dismissing a complaint for lack of subject matter jurisdiction is intrinsically a final determination not to exclude articles from entry and is thus reviewable.[101] On the other hand, the court has held that it lacks jurisdiction to review an order of the ITC refusing to declassify certain confidential business

---

[98]*Panduit Corp. v. All States Plastic Mfg. Co.*, 744 F.2d 1564, 223 USPQ 465 (Fed. Cir. 1984).

[99]19 U.S.C. §1337. The statute defines patent infringement as the importation of any product or article covered by the claims of any unexpired valid U.S. patent and, in addition, the importation of a product made by a process so covered.

[100]*Allied Corp. v. United States ITC*, 850 F.2d 1573, 7 USPQ2d 1303 (Fed. Cir. 1988).

[101]*Amgen, Inc. v. United States ITC*, 902 F.2d 1532, 14 USPQ2d 1734 (Fed. Cir. 1990).

information. The requester sought the information for use in another proceeding, not as an aid to challenge of an ITC exclusion order under review. The Federal Circuit's jurisdiction is limited to review of exclusion orders, and the refusal to declassify was not ancillary to such review.[102]

The Federal Circuit has jurisdiction to review a modified exclusion order despite the fact that the enabling statute, 19 U.S.C. §1337(c), limits review to determinations under subsections (d), (e), and (f) and authority for modification is found only in subsection (h). There is a general rule that judicial review will not be precluded on the sole ground that specific procedures for judicial review of a particular agency action are not spelled out in a statute. An order modifying an original order inherently relates to the propriety of the original and affects its validity.[103] The court will permit a nonparty to appeal as "any person adversely affected by a final determination of the" ITC under §1337(c).[104]

(e) Patent Determinations of the PTO

As provided in 28 U.S.C. §1295(a)(4)(A), the court has exclusive jurisdiction of appeals from decisions of the PTO Board of Patent Appeals and Interferences relating to patent applications and interferences. A corollary provision, §1295(a)(4)(C), confers exclusive jurisdiction over decisions of district courts on such matters, where the dissatisfied party has elected to seek review, in the first instance, by civil action pursuant to 35 U.S.C. §145 (patent applications; limited to the District Court for the District of Columbia) or 35 U.S.C. §146 (patent interferences; may be brought in other district courts). The two routes of appeal—one direct from the PTO Board and one with an intermediate proceeding by civil action in a district court—are mutually exclusive, but the Federal Circuit ends up as the court of last resort in either case, barring Supreme Court review. Actions under §§145 and 146 are discussed in §11.4(a).

Jurisdiction with respect to the PTO is limited to review of decisions of the PTO Board. Thus, the Federal Circuit does not have jurisdiction to review decisions of the Commissioner of Patents and Trademarks.[105] Nonetheless, the court has jurisdiction over an appeal from a district court order that purports to review a decision of the PTO Commissioner under the general mandamus statute, 28 U.S.C.

---

[102]*Viscofan, S.A. v. United States ITC,* 787 F.2d 544, 229 USPQ 118 (Fed. Cir. 1986).

[103]*Allied Corp. v. United States ITC,* 850 F.2d 1573, 7 USPQ2d 1303 (Fed. Cir. 1988).

[104]*LSI Computer Sys., Inc. v. United States ITC,* 832 F.2d 588, 4 USPQ2d 1705 (Fed. Cir. 1987).

[105]*In re Makari,* 708 F.2d 709, 218 USPQ 193 (Fed. Cir. 1983). Neither the PTO Board nor the Federal Circuit has jurisdiction to review the merits of a requirement for restriction, inasmuch as that is a matter within the discretion of the examiner and does not amount to a rejection of claims. *In re Watkinson,* 900 F.2d 230, 14 USPQ2d 1407 (Fed. Cir. 1990).

§1651.[106] The court also has jurisdiction of a suit brought under the Administrative Procedures Act, 5 U.S.C. §§702-06, asserting that the Director acted arbitrarily and capriciously in denying a petition. Although the APA is clearly not a patent law, the right to relief necessarily depends upon resolution of a substantial question of patent law—whether the Director violated the APA in applying its rules and regulations.[107]

Inasmuch as the PTO Interference Board itself has jurisdiction only to decide issues of priority and ancillary matters, the Federal Circuit's jurisdiction is similarly limited. Dissolution of an interference is not a matter ancillary to priority; only the Director or an examiner, and not the Board, have authority to dissolve an interference. Consequently, the Federal Circuit has no jurisdiction to review a Board decision refusing to dissolve an interference.[108]

(f) Transfers and the Regional Courts of Appeals

The Federal Circuit is a coequal member of a system of 13 appellate courts arranged in a single tier. It is not a superior member possessed of jurisdiction to review and reverse the judgments of the other 12. It has not been granted jurisdiction to engage in appellate review or rehearing of a final decision, or to recall or countermand a mandate, of a coordinate court of appeals.[109] The manner in which the Federal Circuit deals with regional circuit precedent and the circumstances under which it considers itself bound to follow that precedent are the subject of §17.2(b).

The judicial code provides, in 28 U.S.C. §1631, for transfers of appeals between the Federal Circuit and the regional circuits as an alternative to dismissal for lack of jurisdiction where such action appears to be in the interest of justice. The Supreme Court has instructed the Federal Circuit and its sister regional courts how to approach this question to avoid a perpetual game of jurisdictional table tennis: adhere strictly to law of the case principles.[110] Thus, the jurisdictional decision of the first court of appeals to entertain the question will normally prevail. The Supreme Court has also made it clear that when the Federal Circuit finds that it lacks jurisdiction it

---

[106]*Morganroth v. Quigg*, 885 F.2d 843, 12 USPQ2d 1125 (Fed. Cir. 1989).

[107]*Helfgott & Karas P.C. v. Dickinson*, 209 F.3d 1328, 54 USPQ2d 1425 (Fed. Cir. 2).

[108]*Parks v. Fine*, 783 F.2d 1036, 228 USPQ 677 (Fed. Cir. 1986). Interestingly, the Commissioner, as an amicus, successfully urged the court here to change a prior holding reversing the Board's decision refusing to dissolve. This case indicates that the court will not hesitate to refrain from exercising questionable jurisdiction even where it is convinced that the decision under review is wrong.

[109]*In re Roberts*, 846 F.2d 1360, 6 USPQ2d 1772 (Fed. Cir. 1988). The jurisdiction of the Federal Circuit is limited to review of judgments in relation to which a notice of appeal is filed after October 1, 1982. The court has no jurisdiction to reach back and redo anything done by a coordinate court of appeals on a notice of appeal filed prior to that date. *Id.*

[110]*Christianson v. Colt Indus. Oper. Corp.*, 486 U.S. 800, 7 USPQ2d 1109 (1988).

has authority to make but a single decision—dismiss the appeal or, in the interest of justice, transfer it to a regional court of appeals that does have jurisdiction.[111]

§16.2 Appealability

(a) *Final Decisions*

The Federal Circuit follows the "final judgment" rule.[112] Indeed, it is obliged so to do by 28 U.S.C. §1295, which specifies jurisdiction over "final" decisions or determinations.[113] Before exploring the concept of finality, it is well to consider briefly the closely related concept of standing, in the context of what is meant by a decision or determination.

Effect of decision. A decision is an order in which a right has been adjudicated.[114] And there must be an aggrieved party.[115] Only a party adversely affected by a judgment can appeal.[116] Thus a party is equitably estopped to attack a settlement on appeal unless the

---

[111]*Christianson v. Colt Indus. Oper. Corp.*, 486 U.S. 800, 7 USPQ2d 1109 (1988).

[112]E.g., *Cabot Corp. v. United States,* 788 F.2d 1539 (Fed. Cir. 1986).

[113]The statute specifies final decisions in district court patent cases under §1295(a)(1) and Court of Federal Claims cases under (a)(3), and final determinations of the ITC under (a)(6). Decisions of the PTO Board and of the district courts pursuant to 35 U.S.C. §§145 or 146 apparently need not be "final" under 28 U.S.C. §1295(a)(4)(A) and (C). See *Wagner Shokai, Inc. v. Kabushiki Kaisha Wako*, 699 F.2d 1390, 217 USPQ 98 (Fed. Cir. 1983).

[114]*Wagner Shokai, Inc. v. Kabushiki Kaisha Wako,* 699 F.2d 1390, 217 USPQ 98 (Fed. Cir. 1983). In *Sun-Tek Indus., Inc. v. Kennedy Sky Lites, Inc,* 856 F.2d 173, 8 USPQ2d 1154 (Fed. Cir. 1988), appellant sought review of an order increasing a supersedeas bond. But the bond had not been posted and judgment had already been executed. It was clear that appellant's counsel was simply seeking to overturn a finding, entered by the trial court during the supersedeas skirmishing below, to the effect that counsel had failed to honor the terms of the trial court's order regarding supersedeas. The Federal Circuit regarded this as an improper challenge to the finding itself, independent of the order, and dismissed for lack of jurisdiction on the ground that the challenged finding was not an appealable order. In *Fromson v. Citiplate, Inc.,* 886 F.2d 1300, 12 USPQ2d 1299 (Fed. Cir. 1989), the court, following regional circuit law, permitted an attorney to appeal from an opinion of a district court in which he was chastised by the judge. The Federal Circuit had misgivings, reasoning that efforts to expunge a district court's comments would appear to be more appropriately the subject of a mandamus petition. It distinguished *Sun-Tek* on the ground that there the party sought only to appeal a finding regarding the conduct of its counsel who was not a named appellant; in *Fromson,* the challenge was to a sanction (the adverse comments) and was asserted by counsel himself, a named appellant.

[115]*Aleut Tribe v. United States,* 702 F.2d 1015 (Fed. Cir. 1983). Apparently there need not be an opponent, however. In *Gerritsen v. Shirai,* 979 F.2d 1524, 24 USPQ2d 1912 (Fed. Cir. 1992), the PTO Board had imposed sanctions on one party to an interference. That party appealed, and the Commissioner filed an amicus brief, but the other party did not file a brief. The court refused to hold that the failure of the other party to respond or take a position regarding the appeal meant that it could not decide the appeal on the merits; it therefore denied the appellant's motion for judgment on the record.

[116]*Jamesbury Corp. v. Litton Indus. Prods., Inc.,* 839 F.2d 1544, 5 USPQ2d 1779 (Fed. Cir. 1988).

contract is tainted with invalidity, as by fraud or mutual mistake.[117] A party who makes a concession cannot challenge on appeal a finding on that point.[118] Normally a party cannot appeal a voluntary dismissal or consent judgment.[119]

A winning respondent in an ITC proceeding cannot appeal and can participate in the petitioner's appeal only to the extent of raising matters in support of the ITC's determination.[120] But even the possibility of prejudice to a petitioner does not necessarily make a determination appealable. Where the ITC terminates a self-initiated investigation (commenced at the request of a government agency) as "abated," there is no jurisdiction over the agency's appeal. Even though the agency might be prejudiced because the termination would not have collateral estoppel or res judicata effect, the decision to terminate is not a final determination.[121] By similar reasoning, while an order granting JNOV is appealable because it results in judgment in favor of the movant, orders denying JNOV or denying a motion for a new trial do not generally result in judgments and are not appealable. Denials of motions for JNOV, new trial, or mistrial are appealable only from a final judgment entered on the verdict.[122]

Rule 54(a), FRCP, describes a judgment as a decree or any order from which an appeal lies. A judgment is not appealable within the meaning of FRAP 4(a)(6) unless it is entered in compliance with Rules 58 and 79(a), FRCP. Rule 58 requires that every judgment shall be set forth on a separate document. Absent waiver, there is no judgment without a separate document. The purpose of this rule is to save

---

[117]*Asberry v. United States Postal Serv.*, 692 F.2d 1378 (Fed. Cir. 1982).

[118]*In re Caveney*, 761 F.2d 671, 226 USPQ 1 (Fed. Cir. 1985).

[119]*St. Paul F. & M. Ins. Co. v. United States*, 959 F.2d 960 (Fed. Cir. 1992). In this case, however, the lower court had refused to permit an amendment to the complaint, and the plaintiff asked for dismissal of its original complaint (which it admitted was, based upon newly discovered evidence, no longer factually supported) so it could appeal and obtain immediate review of the merits of its motion to amend. This was therefore not a voluntary dismissal in the usual sense of a consent judgment.

[120]*Surface Tech., Inc. v. United States ITC*, 780 F.2d 29 (Fed. Cir. 1985). By statute, any person adversely affected by a final determination of the ITC may appeal, whether or not a party. *LSI Computer Sys., Inc. v. United States ITC*, 832 F.2d 588, 4 USPQ2d 1705 (Fed. Cir. 1987). See 19 U.S.C. §1337(c). A party may appeal a final determination modifying a remedial order issued by the ITC where the modification is adverse to the party. *Crucible Materials Corp. v. United States ITC*, 127 F.3d 1057 (Fed. Cir. 1997).

[121]*Block v. United States ITC*, 777 F.2d 1568, 228 USPQ 37 (Fed. Cir. 1985). An advisory opinion of the ITC is not a final determination and is thus not reviewable by the Federal Circuit. *Allied Corp. v. United States ITC*, 850 F.2d 1573, 7 USPQ2d 1303 (Fed. Cir. 1988). That an agency may choose to render advisory opinions cannot create for one displeased with its advice a cause of action cognizable in an Article III court. A federal court's jurisdiction is limited to that conferred by Congress. Here the Federal Circuit found that it had no jurisdiction on the basis of lack of finality and did not reach the Article III case or controversy issue.

[122]*Witco Chem. Corp. v. Peachtree Doors, Inc.*, 787 F.2d 1545, 229 USPQ 188 (Fed. Cir. 1986); *Railroad Dynamics, Inc. v. A. Stucki Co.*, 727 F.2d 1506, 220 USPQ 929 (Fed. Cir. 1984). Only judgments can be appealed. Where no judgment was entered on a defense, the moving party could not have cross-appealed the denial of its motion for directed verdict on that issue. *Jamesbury Corp. v. Litton Indus. Prods., Inc*, 839 F.2d 1544, 5 USPQ2d 1779 (Fed. Cir. 1988). Appeals are to be taken from judgments, not findings and conclusions. *Under Sea Indus., Inc. v. Dacor Corp.*, 833 F.2d 1551, 4 USPQ2d 1772 (Fed. Cir. 1987).

litigants from losing the opportunity to appeal because they failed to recognize which docket entry constituted the entry of a final judgment. Rule 79(a) requires that judgments shall be entered in the civil docket. The docket entry must dispose of the issues and state a final declaration of the result.[123]

Finality of decision. Thus there must be a decision or determination adjudicating some right, and there must be a party aggrieved by that adjudication.[124] But more than that, the adjudication must be "final." The requirement of finality is an historic characteristic of federal appellate procedure. The rule demands that a party must ordinarily raise all claims of error in a single appeal following final judgment on the merits.[125] The rule reflects a strong congressional policy against piecemeal reviews and against obstructing or impeding an ongoing judicial proceeding by interlocutory appeals.[126] Bifurcation of appeals serves neither justice nor judicial efficiency.[127] The court applies regional circuit law to the question of finality.[128]

The court quite properly sat in banc to take a hard look at the finality requirements of its basic jurisdictional statute, 28 U.S.C. §1295(a). It found that under subsections 1, 2, 3, 5, 6, 9, and 10 there is an express requirement of finality, while under subsections 4 (appeals from district courts under 35 U.S.C. §145 and §146, and from PTO Boards), 7 (Secretary of Commerce findings), and 8 (Plant Variety Protection Act appeals) there is no express finality requirement. Nonetheless, based upon earlier CCPA decisions, it interpreted

---

[123]*Marsh-McBirney, Inc. v. Montedoro-Whitney Corp.,* 882 F.2d 498, 11 USPQ2d 1794 (Fed. Cir. 1989).

[124]In addition, the court has even been guided by a sense of "appropriateness" in deciding whether to take an appeal. In one unusual case the Court of Appeals for the District of Columbia had sent the matter back to the district court for further proceedings. On the second appeal, the losing party took the case to the Federal Circuit, but argued that the district court had misinterpreted the previous order of the D.C. Circuit. The Federal Circuit held that it would be inappropriate for it to review, interpret, or otherwise act with respect to an order of a sister court. It characterized the appeal as a "form of procedural and semantic gamesmanship abusive of the judicial process and wasteful of resources of the parties and the court," and awarded attorney fees against the appellant and its counsel. *Colt Indus. Operating Corp. v. Index-Werke K.G.,* 739 F.2d 622 (Fed. Cir. 1984).

[125]*Cabot Corp. v. United States,* 788 F.2d 1539 (Fed. Cir. 1986).

[126]*Heat & Control, Inc. v. Hester Indus. Inc.,* 785 F.2d 1017, 228 USPQ 926 (Fed. Cir. 1986). Appellate courts have historically disfavored piecemeal litigation and permitted appeals from complete and final judgments only. *W.L. Gore & Assoc. v. International Med. Pros. Res. Assoc.,* 975 F.2d 858, 24 USPQ2d 1195 (Fed. Cir. 1992).

[127]*Eaton Corp. v. Appliance Valves Corp.,* 790 F.2d 874, 229 USPQ 668 (Fed. Cir. 1986). Accordingly, an order remanding a matter to an administrative agency for further proceedings is not final even though it finally resolves an important legal issue. Such a result avoids unnecessary piecemeal appellate review without precluding later review of a legal issue or any other determination made on a complete administrative record. *Cabot Corp. v. United States,* 788 F.2d 1539 (Fed. Cir. 1986). See also *Jeannette Sheet Glass Corp. v. United States,* 803 F.2d 1576 (Fed. Cir. 1986).

[128]*Phonometrics Inc. v. Hospitality Franchise Sys. Inc.,* 203 F.3d 790, 53 USPQ2d 1762, 1764 (Fed. Cir. 2).

subsection 4 as though it incorporated an express finality requirement.[129]

Lack of finality is a defect in an order, having no effect on or relation to appellate subject matter jurisdiction, but simply precluding the exercise of such jurisdiction in deciding the merits of the order.[130] The term "final decision" can mean different things in different situations. Specifically a court decision can be "final" in the sense that a court is done with the action and has entered final judgment. Alternatively, a court decision can be final in the sense that the court has conclusively decided the controversy and the decision can no longer be attacked, either collaterally or by appeal. A better term for the latter type of final decision might be "conclusive" decision.[131] The court that enters the judgment is best qualified to assert whether it intended that judgment as final.[132]

In general, an order is final only when it ends the litigation on the merits and leaves nothing for the court to do but execute judgment.[133] One must be cautious with such a deceptively simple formulation, however. In a Claims Court judgment the claimant was given the most significant relief sought, but questions of attorney fees and costs remained. In other words, more remained than mere execution

---

[129]*Copelands' Enters., Inc. v. CNV, Inc.*, 887 F.2d 1065, 12 USPQ2d 1562 (Fed. Cir. 1989). Under §1295(a)(6) the Federal Circuit can review only final determinations of the ITC. A final determination is a final administrative decision on the merits, excluding or refusing to exclude articles from entry. The determination is not final if there are issues remaining regarding remedy, or if there are ongoing enforcement proceedings. *Crucible Materials Corp. v. United States ITC*, 127 F.3d 1057 (Fed. Cir. 1997).

[130]*AeroJet-General Corp. v. Machine Tool Works*, 895 F.2d 736, 13 USPQ2d 1670 (Fed. Cir. 1990).

[131]*Micro Motion, Inc. v. Kane Steel Co.*, 894 F.2d 1318, 13 USPQ2d 1696 (Fed. Cir. 1990).

[132]*PPG Indus., Inc. v. Celanese Polymer Spec. Co.*, 840 F.2d 1565, 6 USPQ2d 1010 (Fed. Cir. 1988). But the finality of a district court decision is not determined by the way the court characterizes the decision. Rather, the question to be answered is whether any issues remain to be decided by the court. *View Eng'g, Inc. v. Robotic Vision Sys., Inc.*, 115 F.3d 962, 42 USPQ2d 1956 (Fed. Cir. 1997).

[133]*Mendenhall v. Barber-Greene Co.*, 26 F.3d 1573, 31 USPQ2d 1001 (Fed. Cir. 1994); *PPG Indus., Inc. v. Celanese Polymer Spec. Co.*, 840 F.2d 1565, 6 USPQ2d 1010 (Fed. Cir. 1988); *Cabot Corp. v. United States*, 788 F.2d 1539 (Fed. Cir. 1986); *United States v. W.H. Moseley Co.*, 730 F.2d 1472 (Fed. Cir. 1984). The court espouses a liberal view of finality. Thus, if part of an order directs the defendant to pay a sum of money, and if the plaintiff is entitled to immediate execution, the order is final and appealable. *King Instr. Corp. v. Otari Corp.*, 814 F.2d 1560, 2 USPQ2d 1201 (Fed. Cir. 1987). Where a district court dismisses a claim with leave to amend, and the appeal is taken prior to the end of the period allowed for amendment, the court of appeals nonetheless has jurisdiction, even though the district court does not enter a final judgment until after the period for amendment has run. There is no prejudice to the appellee because of the premature notice of appeal, and a denial of jurisdiction would spin judicial wheels for no practical purpose. *Phonometrics Inc. v. Hospitality Franchise Sys. Inc.*, 203 F.3d 790, 53 USPQ2d 1762 (Fed. Cir. 2). In *Enzo Biochem Inc. v. Calgene Inc.*, 188 F.3d 1362, 52 USPQ2d 1129 (Fed. Cir. 1999), the district court granted judgment of invalidity as to two patents but refused to rule on a third, and dismissed the defendant's declaratory judgment counterclaim. The decision refusing to rule was inadvertently not cited in the final judgment order, as it should have been under FRCP 58. The court nonetheless concluded that it should exercise jurisdiction over the defendant's cross-appeal, on the ground that nothing further remained to be done.

of a judgment. Nevertheless, the court considered the judgment final and appealable.[134]

A judgment on a separately tried claim is normally not final and appealable until all claims are adjudicated.[135] Thus an order denying summary judgment on a trade secret claim but granting summary judgment on a patent claim is not appealable because it lacks finality.[136] In general, orders denying summary judgment motions and motions to dismiss are unappealable.[137] Indeed, a denial of a summary judgment is not only not a final judgment and not appealable, it is not a judgment at all. It is quite simply and solely a determination that one or more issues require a trial.[138] Such an order does not settle or even tentatively decide anything about the merits of the claim; it is interlocutory, nonfinal, and nonappealable.[139] An order granting partial summary judgment is not a final appealable order because it does not dispose of all claims raised. Thus, if a party wishes to appeal a partial summary judgment, it must ordinarily obtain a certification from the district court under Rule 54(b). At the same time, courts have generally understood the practical realities of litigation under these circumstances, and have permitted an appeal without a Rule 54(b) order when events subsequent to the partial judgment satisfy the purposes of the final judgment rule.[140]

---

[134]*Electro-Methods, Inc. v. United States,* 728 F.2d 1471 (Fed. Cir. 1984). The Federal Circuit views *Budinich v. Becton Dickinson & Co.,* 486 U.S. 196 (1988), as holding that a decision on the merits is a final decision for purposes of immediate appeal even though the recoverability or amount of attorney fees for the litigation remain to be determined. *Newell Cos. v. Kenney Mfg. Co.,* 864 F.2d 757, 9 USPQ2d 1417 (Fed. Cir. 1988). Where a district court decides an attorney fee award on its merits, and enters a "final and appealable order," the order is a final decision over which the Federal Circuit may exercise appellate review. *PPG Indus., Inc. v. Celanese Polymer Spec. Co.,* 840 F.2d 1565, 6 USPQ2d 1010 (Fed. Cir. 1988).

[135]*Atari, Inc. v. JS & A Group, Inc.,* 747 F.2d 1422, 223 USPQ 1074 (Fed. Cir. 1984).

[136]*Veach v. Vinyl Improvement Prods. Co.,* 700 F.2d 1390, 217 USPQ 97 (Fed. Cir. 1983). In an unusual situation, the trial court denied the plaintiff's motion for preliminary injunction as to one of several patents in suit and granted the defendant's motion for summary judgment of invalidity as to that patent. Plaintiff appealed the denial of the injunction, but inasmuch as the trial court had given no reasons for the denial, the order would have been incapable of review. Nonetheless, the Federal Circuit was willing to review the merits of the summary judgment because it was closely interrelated factually to the preliminary injunction question and because the parties had focused on invalidity on the quite reasonable assumption that it was the basis for the denial of the injunction. *Gerber Garment Tech., Inc. v. Lectra Sys., Inc.,* 916 F.2d 683, 16 USPQ2d 1436 (Fed. Cir. 1990). See also *Helifix Ltd. v. Blok-Lok Ltd.,* 208 F.3d 1339, 54 USPQ2d 1299 (Fed. Cir. 2).

[137]*Smith Int'l, Inc. v. Hughes Tool Co.,* 759 F.2d 1572, 225 USPQ 889 (Fed. Cir. 1985); *Parker Bros. v. Tuxedo Monopoly, Inc.,* 757 F.2d 254, 226 USPQ 11 (Fed. Cir. 1985); *Aleut Tribe v. United States,* 702 F.2d 1015 (Fed. Cir. 1983).

[138]*Senza-Gel Corp. v. Seiffhart,* 803 F.2d 661, 231 USPQ 363 (Fed. Cir. 1986); *Glaros v. H.H. Robertson Co.,* 797 F.2d 1564, 230 USPQ 393 (Fed. Cir. 1986). This barrier to appellate review holds even when the party that has sought summary judgment has requested a permanent injunction in its prayer for relief, so that the denial of the motion for summary judgment has the effect of denying, for the time being, a request for an injunction. *Lermer Germany GMBH v. Lermer Corp.,* 94 F.3d 1575, 39 USPQ2d 2014 (Fed. Cir. 1996).

[139]*Glaros v. H.H. Robertson Co.,* 797 F.2d 1564, 230 USPQ 393 (Fed. Cir. 1986).

[140]*CAE Screenplates Inc. v. Heinrich Fiedler GmbH,* 224 F.3d 1308, 55 USPQ2d 1804 (Fed. Cir. 2). In this case, the parties did not obtain a Rule 54(b) certification, but did appear to concede below that the partial summary judgment ruling would dispose of all issues in the

While an order granting a partial summary judgment (from which no immediate appeal lies) is merged into the final judgment and reviewable on appeal from that final judgment, an order denying summary judgment is not.[141] However, a denial of a motion for summary judgment may be appealed, even after a final judgment at trial, if the motion involved a purely legal question and the factual disputes resolved at trial do not affect the resolution of that legal question. A party may preserve the matter for appeal by renewing the issue at trial or by including it in a memoranda of law or proposed conclusions of law.[142] A ruling under Rule 60(b), FRCP, is final and appealable.[143]

As a general proposition, when a trial court disposes finally of a case, any interlocutory rulings merge with the final judgment. Thus both the order finally disposing of the case and the interlocutory orders are reviewable on appeal from the final judgment. However,

---

case. Their concession, however, was not sufficiently explicit. The court said it is loath to sanction this type of appellate practice. The demands placed on the dockets of both the appellate court and those of the federal district courts are severe enough without the added burden created by uncertain concessions made by parties eager for appellate review. Nevertheless, there is some flexibility in the finality rule in order that justice and the economic termination of litigation may not suffer from an overly strict adherence to formalism. It must be remembered that practical, not technical, considerations are to govern the application of principles of finality. At oral argument, counsel conceded under questioning that the district court's claim construction resolved the issue of noninfringement. This concession, although more appropriate had it been made before the district court, appears to satisfy the general purpose of the finality requirement. Accordingly, the court exercised jurisdiction over the merits of the appeal.

[141]*Glaros v. H.H. Robertson Co.*, 797 F.2d 1564, 230 USPQ 393 (Fed. Cir. 1986). The court termed appellant's effort to seek review of a denial of summary judgment improper and productive only of a waste of the court's time and the party's resources. In *Syntex Pharm. Int'l, Inc. v. K-Line Pharm., Ltd.*, 905 F.2d 1525, 15 USPQ2d 1239 (Fed. Cir. 1990), the trial court granted the patentee's motion for summary judgment of infringement and denied the infringer's motion for summary judgment of invalidity, and also set a trial for damages. Nonetheless, although its memorandum opinion indicated the patent was "valid as a matter of law," its order did not expressly hold the patent valid. The Federal Circuit dismissed the appeal on the ground that neither the grant of the motion on infringement nor the denial of the motion on invalidity was appealable. If the parties felt the order appealed from was ambiguous, and not in keeping with what appeared to be the trial court's clear intention, they should have sought to resolve the ambiguity below by requesting clarification or moving for certification under Rule 54(b). See also *Trilogy Comm., Inc. v. Times Fiber Comm., Inc.*, 109 F.3d 739, 42 USPQ2d 1129 (Fed. Cir. 1997). Despite its criticism of the appellant in *Glaros*, the court has recognized that in other circuits a denial of a summary judgment motion is appealable after entry of final judgment. *Scripps Clinic & Res. Found. v. Genentech, Inc.*, 927 F.2d 1565, 18 USPQ2d 1001 (Fed. Cir. 1991). In *DSC Comm. Corp. v. Pulse Comm.*, 170 F.3d 1354, 50 USPQ2d 1001 (Fed. Cir. 1999), the district court denied a motion for summary judgment of copyright misuse. At trial the copyright claims were dismissed on other grounds, so that the misuse defense was not considered. In remanding the judgment of dismissal, the court remarked that the misuse issue was not ripe for review. In *Pitney Bowes Inc. v. Hewlett-Packard Co.*, 182 F.3d 1298, 51 USPQ2d 1161 (Fed. Cir. 1999), the trial court granted a motion for summary judgment of noninfringement, and denied a motion for summary judgment of invalidity. On appeal, the noninfringement ruling was reversed. This rendered the invalidity ruling nonfinal. Consequently, the Federal Circuit dismissed the cross-appeal of that ruling.

[142]*United Tech. Corp. v. Chromalloy Gas Turbine Corp.*, 189 F.3d 1338, 51 USPQ2d 1838 (Fed. Cir. 1999).

[143]*Ashland Oil, Inc. v. Delta Oil Prods. Corp.*, 806 F.2d 1031, 1 USPQ2d 1073 (Fed. Cir. 1986). A decision on a Rule 60(b) motion, when the motion does not toll the time for filing an appeal from the final judgment, is a separate final action by the district court and, as such, must be appealed separately from the underlying action. *Phonometrics Inc. v. Northern Telecom Inc.*, 133 F.3d 1459, 45 USPQ2d 1421 (Fed. Cir. 1998).

some courts have carved out an exception: if the final order is a dismissal resulting from bad faith or dilatory conduct, then the interlocutory orders do not merge and do not become reviewable. To hold otherwise would open up a back door route to review of interlocutory orders and reward bad conduct.[144] The timing and sequence of order entry can be important. In one case the district court had ordered a new trial on damages, but later entered a judgment holding the patent invalid. On appeal from the judgment, the invalidity holding was reversed. Under the circumstances, the Federal Circuit would have no jurisdiction over the older order granting a new trial because it was interlocutory and unconditional.[145]

Not surprisingly, the court has indicated that orders closing discovery,[146] barring introduction of evidence,[147] imposing Rule 11 sanctions,[148] and quashing a subpoena (by the forum judge)[149] will be regarded as unappealable. Orders refusing to permit amendments to pleadings are not reviewable until final judgment.[150] Orders granting or denying stays and motions on attorney disqualification present special problems and are discussed below in connection with certifications and the collateral order doctrine.

It is important to understand that finality for purposes of collateral estoppel is not necessarily the same as for purposes of appealability. The first requires that the prior adjudication be sufficiently firm to be accorded conclusive effect; the party against whom the estoppel

---

[144]*Hendler v. United States,* 952 F.2d 1364 (Fed. Cir. 1991).

[145]*Randomex, Inc. v. Scopus Corp.,* 849 F.2d 585, 7 USPQ2d 1050 (Fed. Cir. 1988). Ordinarily an order for de novo consideration or for a new trial is not appealable. *Snellman v. Ricoh Co.,* 862 F.2d 283, 8 USPQ2d 1996 (Fed. Cir. 1988).

[146]*Veach v. Vinyl Improvement Prods. Co.,* 700 F.2d 1390, 217 USPQ 97 (Fed. Cir. 1983).

[147]*Smith Int'l, Inc. v. Hughes Tool Co.,* 759 F.2d 1572, 225 USPQ 889 (Fed. Cir. 1985). One appeals or cross-appeals from a judgment not from an evidentiary ruling. *Wahpeton Canvas Co. v. Frontier, Inc.,* 870 F.2d 1546, 10 USPQ2d 1201 (Fed. Cir. 1989).

[148]*View Eng'g, Inc. v. Robotic Vision Sys., Inc.,* 115 F.3d 962, 42 USPQ2d 1956 (Fed. Cir. 1997).

[149]*Heat & Control, Inc. v. Hester Indus. Inc.,* 785 F.2d 1017, 228 USPQ 926 (Fed. Cir. 1986). However, an order quashing a subpoena to a third party, entered in a supplementary proceeding brought in one district to obtain evidence for use in a case pending in another, is final and appealable, because the appellant would effectively be denied appellate review otherwise. *Katz v. Batavia Mar. & Sporting Supp., Inc.,* 984 F.2d 422, 25 USPQ2d 1547 (Fed. Cir. 1993); *Truswal Sys. Corp v. Hydro-Air Eng'g, Inc.,* 813 F.2d 1207, 2 USPQ2d 1034 (Fed. Cir. 1987). Discovery orders made by a court in which a case is pending are not appealable as of right, being merely interlocutory, until the entry of final judgment in the suit. When a party pursues discovery outside the jurisdiction in which the case is pending, however, the jurisdiction of the local district court may be invoked to rule on discovery issues in an ancillary proceeding. An order terminating that type of proceeding is final and thus gives a right of appeal. *Haworth, Inc. v. Herman Miller, Inc.,* 998 F.2d 975, 27 USPQ2d 1469 (Fed. Cir. 1993); *Solarex Corp. v. Arco Solar, Inc.,* 870 F.2d 642, 10 USPQ2d 1247 (Fed. Cir. 989). However, an order of a district court other than the forum that denies a motion to quash a subpoena is not final and cannot be appealed, in keeping with the general rule that orders allowing discovery are not appealable. *Micro Motion Inc. v. Exac Corp.,* 876 F.2d 1574, 11 USPQ2d 1070 (Fed. Cir. 1989). An order imposing sanctions on a party for violating an order compelling discovery is neither a final order appealable under 28 U.S.C. §1295(a)(3) nor an appealable interlocutory order under §1292(c). *M.A. Mortenson Co. v. United States,* 877 F.2d 50 (Fed. Cir. 1989).

[150]*St. Paul F. & M. Ins. Co. v. United States,* 959 F.2d 960 (Fed. Cir. 1992).

is asserted must have had the right, even if not exercised, to challenge on appeal the correctness of the earlier decision.[151]

The finality concept of district court litigation, requiring both liability and damages to be resolved before an appeal, is not necessarily applicable to agency board proceedings. The agency's characterization of a decision is not determinative of the finality issue, and the relevant statutes outlining the required administrative procedures must be examined. Where an appeal would not disrupt the administrative process, in that there is nothing more for the agency board to do, the reviewing court has jurisdiction.[152]

The court has considered whether a judgment that disposes of fewer than all actions consolidated by the district court into one case may be separately appealed. The district court consolidated two separate declaratory judgment actions, on two separate patents, into a single case. The fundamental question is whether such a consolidation is to be viewed as merging the actions or whether the actions retain their separate identities for purposes of appellate review. If the actions merge into one for jurisdictional purposes, appeal will be proper, absent certification under Rule 54(b), only after disposition of all of the claims in the consolidated case.[153]

Not every decision that is reviewed by the Federal Circuit is final, by any means. By statute, rule, and decision, various types of orders are made appealable despite lack of finality. These are the subjects of the next several sections.

(b) Appealable Interlocutory Decisions

(i) Judgments Final Except for Accounting

Pursuant to 28 U.S.C. §1292(c)(2), the Federal Circuit is given exclusive jurisdiction over judgments in civil actions for patent infringement that are final except for an accounting and that would otherwise be appealable. The regional circuits long enjoyed this exception to the finality rule. It accommodated the typical circumstance in patent cases where the trial of liability was severed from damages. This will be one of the common routes for patent cases to reach the court.

In determining whether a judgment is final except for an accounting, and therefore appealable under §1292(c)(2), the key is the binding effect in disposing of the patent infringement question. Section

---

[151]*Interconnect Planning Corp. v. Feil,* 774 F.2d 1132, 227 USPQ 543 (Fed. Cir. 1985).

[152]*Dewey Elec. Corp. v. United States,* 803 F.2d 650 (Fed. Cir. 1986).

[153]*Spraytex, Inc. v. DJS&T,* 96 F.3d 1377, 40 USPQ2d 1145 (Fed. Cir. 1996). Because this is an issue concerning its own jurisdiction, it applies its own law and not that of the regional circuit. In its own decisions, it found that it has treated consolidated cases as one merged unit for jurisdictional purposes. Consequently, absent Rule 54(b) certification, there may be no appeal of a judgment disposing of fewer than all aspects of a consolidated case.

1292(c)(2) still requires a judgment, not just the announcement of findings of fact and conclusions of law. It is unreasonable to suppose that a party is free to appeal every utterance of the trial court under the guise of §1292(c)(2), which is, after all, a limited exception to the normal rule that appeals must await final judgment on the whole case.[154] The purpose of §1292(c)(2) is to permit a stay of a damages trial, not compel one. There is thus no conflict between that statute and Rule 62(a), FRCP, which grants discretion to stay or proceed with the damages trial during the appeal. Indeed, the Federal Circuit typically denies motions to stay damages trials during appeals in patent cases.[155]

The phrase "final except for an accounting" means an accounting for patent infringement damages, not unfair competition damages. Thus, where the trial court found against the plaintiff on its patent infringement claim, but for it on its unfair competition claim, the pendency of the unfair competition accounting removed Federal Circuit jurisdiction under 28 U.S.C. §1292(c)(2).[156]

The Federal Circuit has held that where a district court found the defendant in contempt of a consent decree and deferred the question of damages, the contempt order was appealable under §1292(c)(2).[157] In another case, the trial court found the patent valid and determined the amount of damages and also indicated that it was awarding attorney fees and costs in an amount to be determined later. The Federal Circuit denied a motion to dismiss the appeal, pointing out that the exception to the finality rule for patent cases was enacted in response to the expense frequently involved in accounting proceedings and the losses incurred when recoveries are ultimately denied by reversal of decrees on the merits. Allowing an appeal where all that remains to be determined is the amount of attorney fees will prevent possible loss of time and expense and the need to explore what sometimes may be sensitive attorney records, and is in full harmony with the purposes of §1292(c)(2).[158]

(ii) Injunctive Orders

Section 1292(c)(1) gives the Federal Circuit jurisdiction of certain interlocutory orders in cases over which it would have jurisdiction of

---

[154]*Marsh-McBirney, Inc. v. Montedoro-Whitney Corp.*, 882 F.2d 498, 11 USPQ2d 1794 (Fed. Cir. 1989).

[155]*In re Calmar, Inc.*, 854 F.2d 461, 7 USPQ2d 1730 (Fed. Cir. 1988). The purpose of §1292(c)(2) is to permit district courts to stay and possibly avoid a burdensome determination of damages. *Mendenhall v. Barber-Greene Co.*, 26 F.3d 1573, 31 USPQ2d 1001 (Fed. Cir. 1994).

[156]*Johannsen v. Pay Less Drug Stores, Inc.*, 917 F.2d 160, 16 USPQ2d 1697 (Fed. Cir. 1990).

[157]*H.A. Jones Co. v. KSM Fastening Sys., Inc.*, 745 F.2d 630, 223 USPQ 689 (Fed. Cir. 1984).

[158]*Majorette Toys Inc. v. Darda, Inc.*, 798 F.2d 1390, 230 USPQ 541 (Fed. Cir. 1986). Thus a district court need not enter a partial final judgment under Rule 54(b) in a patent case that is final except for an accounting. *Shamrock Tech., Inc. v. Medical Sterilization, Inc.*, 903 F.2d 789, 14 USPQ2d 1728 (Fed. Cir. 1990). In *Johannsen v. Pay Less Drug Stores, Inc.*, 917 F.2d 160, 16 USPQ2d 1697 (Fed. Cir. 1990), the court indicated that recent Supreme Court decisions

an appeal from a final decision under §1295. These types of orders are enumerated in §1292(a) and include injunctive orders, orders dealing with receiverships, and orders in admiralty cases. For our purposes, the only significant category is set forth in §1292(a)(1), i.e., orders "granting, continuing, modifying, refusing or dissolving injunctions, or refusing to dissolve or modify injunctions."[159] This is a potent provision and if interpreted broadly can cover interlocutory orders dealing with matters quite far afield from traditional injunctions.

Nevertheless, the court has been quite restrictive in its view of §1292 injunction orders. In one case, the parties cross-moved for summary judgment to determine who was superior in license rights. The grant of the motion in favor of one party clearly meant that, so long as the interlocutory order granting the motion stands, the other party could not get injunctive relief. The court held that the order was not one refusing an injunction under §1292(a)(1) and was therefore not appealable under §1292(c)(1).[160] Similarly, a denial of a motion for a stay of a posttrial injunction pending appeal is neither a final decision nor an appealable interlocutory order,[161] and a matter that could be handled below routinely by a protective order is not an appealable injunction.[162] Nonetheless, an order directing reinstatement of an employee with various entitlements has been held sufficiently injunctive to justify appealability under §1292(a)(1).[163] Likewise, denial of a stay to permit arbitration was held to be an interlocutory order refusing an injunction and thus appealable.[164]

In determining whether a particular order is injunctive in nature, a court of appeals is not limited to the terminology used. Rather, it is necessary to look to the substantive effect of the order.[165] With

---

have held that the pending quantification of attorney fees and costs does not destroy finality for purposes of appeal. Thus the court's discussion of §1292(c)(2) in *Majorette Toys* was unnecessary.

[159]For example, an order continuing an injunction is immediately appealable. *King Instr. Corp. v. Otari Corp.*, 814 F.2d 1560, 2 USPQ2d 1201 (Fed. Cir. 1987). An order refusing to modify an injunction is immediately appealable and ordinarily receives separate and priority treatment. *Trojan, Inc. v. Shat-R-Shield, Inc.*, 885 F.2d 854, 12 USPQ2d 1132 (Fed. Cir. 1989). Where a contempt order also puts into place injunctive relief supplementary to the injunction found to have been violated, it is immediately appealable under 28 U.S.C. §1292(a)(1). *Eli Lilly & Co. v. Medtronic, Inc.*, 915 F.2d 670 (Fed. Cir. 1990). An interlocutory appeal from a permanent injunction, to the extent it considers questions of validity and infringement, is identical in substance to an appeal brought under §1292(c)(2). *Mendenhall v. Barber-Greene Co.*, 26 F.3d 1573, 31 USPQ2d 1001 (Fed. Cir. 1994).

[160]*Holmes v. Bendix Corp.*, 713 F.2d 792, 219 USPQ 6 (Fed. Cir. 1983). Note that the court distinguished an unpublished opinion in which it had dismissed a similar appeal, on the ground that there had been a voluntary dismissal which would preclude any appeal on the merits.

[161]*Shiley, Inc. v. Bentley Labs., Inc.*, 782 F.2d 992, 228 USPQ 543 (Fed. Cir. 1986).

[162]*Rigaku Corp. v. Ferrofluidics Corp.*, 800 F.2d 1115, 231 USPQ 139 (Fed. Cir. 1986).

[163]*Maier v. Orr*, 754 F.2d 973 (Fed. Cir. 1985).

[164]*Rhone-Poulenc Spec. Ch. v. SCM Corp.*, 769 F.2d 1569, 226 USPQ 873 (Fed. Cir. 1985).

[165]*Electronic Data Sys. Corp. v. General Servs. Admin.*, 792 F.2d 1569 (Fed. Cir. 1986). See also *Rigaku Corp. v. Ferrofluidics Corp.*, 800 F.2d 1115, 231 USPQ 139 (Fed. Cir. 1986); *Chaparral Comm., Inc. v. Boman Indus., Inc.*, 798 F.2d 456, 230 USPQ 535 (Fed. Cir. 1986).

the exception of orders that enjoin[166] or stay[167] commencement or prosecution of other actions, it can be broadly stated that an order incidental to a pending action that does not grant part or all of the ultimate injunctive relief sought is not an injunction, however mandatory or prohibitory its terms, and, indeed, notwithstanding the fact that it purports to enjoin.[168] If the order is injunctive, it must further be shown that it will have serious, perhaps irreparable, consequences[169] that can be effectually challenged only by immediate appeal.[170]

In *Woodward v. Sage*,[171] the Federal Circuit expressly adopted the so-called *Carson*[172] test for determining whether a ruling on an interlocutory matter effectively denies injunctive relief. Under that test, only those orders that have a serious, perhaps irreparable, consequence and cannot be effectually challenged except by immediate appeal are subject to interlocutory appeal under §1292(a)(1). As with specific denial of preliminary injunctive relief, the harm caused by an order that is deemed to deny a preliminary injunction cannot effectually be reviewed after the trial. By that time the question of relief or of maintaining the status quo during trial will have become moot. But the denial of a permanent injunction does not necessarily have this element of harm, that is, effectual unreviewability after trial. Thus, not every order that entirely disposes of a claim for a permanent injunction is immediately appealable as of right under §1292(a)(1)—not even those that effectively deny permanent injunctive relief based on the substantive merits of the claim. Section 1292 is construed narrowly.[173]

In *Sage*, the patent was likely to expire before a final appealable judgment would be entered. The patentee, who had lost a summary

---

Interlocutory appeals are not restricted to orders that specifically address the propriety of the denial of an injunction. An order may be appealable under 28 U.S.C. §1292(a)(1) if it has that substantive effect. *Woodard v. Sage Prods., Inc.*, 818 F.2d 841, 2 USPQ2d 1649 (Fed. Cir. 1987).

[166]An order granting an injunction against continuing suit in another forum is appealable as of right. *Katz v. Lear Siegler, Inc.*, 909 F.2d 1459, 15 USPQ2d 1554 (Fed. Cir. 1990).

[167]There is no functional distinction between a stay of a first filed suit and an injunction against prosecution of the first filed suit. Under the *Carson* test, an order staying a first filed customer suit for patent infringement in favor of a later filed declaratory judgment suit by the manufacturer will receive interlocutory review. *Kahn v. General Motors Corp.*, 889 F.2d 1078, 12 USPQ2d 1997 (Fed. Cir. 1989).

[168]*Rigaku Corp. v. Ferrofluidics Corp.*, 800 F.2d 1115, 231 USPQ 139 (Fed. Cir. 1986). An order of a federal district court denying a motion to enjoin a state court action is an order denying an injunction and is thus an appealable interlocutory order. *Intermedics Infusaid, Inc. v. Regents of Univ. of Minn.*, 804 F.2d 129, 231 USPQ 653 (Fed. Cir. 1986).

[169]*Intermedics Infusaid, Inc. v. Regents of Univ. of Minn.*, 804 F.2d 129, 231 USPQ 653 (Fed. Cir. 1986).

[170]*Chaparral Comm., Inc. v. Boman Indus., Inc.*, 798 F.2d 456, 230 USPQ 535 (Fed. Cir. 1986).

[171]*Woodard v. Sage Prods., Inc.*, 818 F.2d 841, 2 USPQ2d 1649 (Fed. Cir. 1987). The reader should be aware that the author's firm represented one of the parties in this case; it is hoped and believed that this involvement has in no way colored the author's analysis of this decision.

[172]*Carson v. American Brands, Inc.*, 450 U.S. 79 (1981).

[173]*Woodard v. Sage Prods., Inc.*, 818 F.2d 841, 2 USPQ2d 1649 (Fed. Cir. 1987).

judgment of infringement against one of the defendants, argued that an interlocutory appeal should be permitted because it needed injunctive relief against future infringements that may have market effects never fully compensable in money. The Federal Circuit rejected this argument on two basic grounds: (1) The *Carson* requirements must be apparent from the record; here there was no finding below that the infringer might capture a share of the market that could never be recovered by the patentee. The proper procedure would have been to move for entry of a judgment under Rule 54(b), FRCP, in order to develop a factual record if that motion were denied. (2) The patentee failed to move for a preliminary injunction, and that failure was a good indication that the status quo could continue until the ultimate conclusion of the litigation without the need for interlocutory appellate review.[174]

This holding involved dismissal of a patent infringement complaint against one of several defendants. The court has since extended the holding to a situation involving a complaint with multiple counts and a single defendant, i.e., dismissal of a patent infringement count with surviving counts for breach of contract and unfair competition. Again, there was no right to an immediate interlocutory appeal, despite a request for permanent injunctive relief, in the absence of a showing that the *Carson* criteria were satisfied.[175]

In formulating its version of the *Carson* test the court also reviewed its own prior holdings and concluded that they needed no modification other than the clarification that a litigant need not specifically alert a district court that its ruling on an interlocutory matter in effect denies an injunction, if the pleadings make that self-evident.[176]

A contempt order is final and appealable when the opportunity to purge the contempt has passed and the position of the parties has been affected by the contempt order. Courts have also viewed a contempt order as appealable when the effect of that order is to modify an injunction. However, when no sanction has been imposed for the contempt and there is no effect on continuing proceedings, interlocutory appeal is unnecessary and therefore unwarranted.[177]

The jurisdiction of the Federal Circuit to hear appeals from interlocutory injunctive orders is not limited to orders of district courts. It includes such orders from all tribunals within its exclusive appellate jurisdiction, including the Claims Court, the Court of International Trade, and the General Services Board of Contract Appeals.[178]

---

[174]*Woodard v. Sage Prods., Inc.,* 818 F.2d 841, 2 USPQ2d 1649 (Fed. Cir. 1987).

[175]*Norco Prods., Inc. v. Mecca Dev., Inc.,* 821 F.2d 644, 3 USPQ2d 1319 (Fed. Cir. 1987). See also *Enercon Indus. Corp. v. Pillar Corp.,* 105 F.3d 1437, 41 USPQ2d 1630 (Fed. Cir. 1997).

[176]*Woodard v. Sage Prods., Inc.,* 818 F.2d 841, 2 USPQ2d 1649 (Fed. Cir. 1987). See *Chaparral Comm., Inc. v. Boman Indus., Inc.,* 798 F.2d 456, 230 USPQ 535 (Fed. Cir. 1986).

[177]*Seiko Epson Corp. v. Nu-Kote Int'l Inc.,* 190 F.3d 1360, 52 USPQ2d 1011 (Fed. Cir. 1999).

[178]*Electronic Data Sys. Corp. v. General Servs. Admin.,* 792 F.2d 1569 (Fed. Cir. 1986).

(c) Certified Questions

Both rule and statute give the trial court an opportunity to participate in case management by indicating those otherwise interlocutory questions it feels are important or timely enough to warrant an immediate appeal.

Section 1292(b) certification. Under 28 U.S.C. §1292(b), regional circuits have discretionary jurisdiction over appeals from orders that the district court certifies as involving a controlling question of law as to which there is substantial ground for difference of opinion, and as to which an immediate appeal may materially advance the ultimate termination of the litigation. In an early case, the Federal Circuit held that under the statute as then written, it lacked jurisdiction to hear appeals on questions certified under §1292(b).[179] Congress later rectified the oversight by providing in §1292(c)(1) that the court has jurisdiction over interlocutory orders of the type described in §1292(b).

Despite this express grant, the court promises to be extremely sparing in the exercise of discretion[180] to accept questions certified under §1292(b). It has, however, permitted an appeal on an attorney disqualification order that was certified by the lower court[181] and on ordinary patent[182] and patent misuse questions.[183] In such appeals, it has jurisdiction to consider all questions material to the trial court's order, in addition to the certified questions.[184] Indeed, the court is perfectly willing to rewrite a question that has been certified for appeal under 28 U.S.C. §1292(b) before answering it, if it appears that the intention of the district court can be discerned and thereby served.[185]

The court has similar discretion under §1292(d)(2) to accept appeals from orders of the Court of Federal Claims certified as containing controlling questions. Review under §1292(d)(2) is likewise not limited to the certified question, and the appellate court can consider all questions material to the correctness of the interlocutory order, such as jurisdiction in the lower court.[186]

---

[179]*Harrington Mfg. Co. v. Powell Mfg. Co.,* 709 F.2d 710 (Fed. Cir. 1983).

[180]The granting of a petition for permission to appeal under 28 U.S.C. §1292(b) is discretionary with the court of appeals. *In re Convertible Rowing Exerciser Patent Litig.,* 903 F.2d 822 (Fed. Cir. 1990).

[181]*Picker Int'l, Inc. v. Varian Assoc., Inc.,* 869 F.2d 578, 10 USPQ2d 1122 (Fed. Cir. 1989); *Sun Studs, Inc. v. Applied Theory Assocs.,* 772 F.2d 1557, 227 USPQ 81 (Fed. Cir. 1985).

[182]*Moeller v. Ionetics, Inc.,* 794 F.2d 653, 229 USPQ 992 (Fed. Cir. 1986).

[183]*Hodosh v. Block Drug. Co.,* 833 F.2d 1575, 4 USPQ2d 1935 (Fed. Cir. 1987); *Senza-Gel Corp. v. Seiffhart,* 803 F.2d 661, 231 USPQ 363 (Fed. Cir. 1986).

[184]*Moeller v. Ionetics, Inc.,* 794 F.2d 653, 229 USPQ 992 (Fed. Cir. 1986).

[185]*Racing Strollers, Inc. v. TRI Indus., Inc.,* 878 F.2d 1418, 11 USPQ2d 1300 (Fed. Cir. 1989).

[186]*Minnesota Chippewa Tribe v. United States,* 768 F.2d 338 (Fed. Cir. 1985); *United States v. Connolly,* 716 F.2d 882 (Fed. Cir. 1983).

Rule 54(b) certification. A second certification technique is set forth in Rule 54(b), FRCP. Prior to the promulgation of the Federal Rules of Civil Procedure, generally there was no authority for treating anything less than the whole case as a judicial unit for purposes of appeal. However, the Federal Rules created increased opportunities for the liberal joinder of claims in multiple claim actions. As a result, litigation became more complex and multiple claim actions because more common. In the interests of sound judicial administration, Congress enacted Rule 54(b) to relax the restrictions upon what should be treated as a judicial unit for the purposes of appellate jurisdiction. The rule allows a district court to sever an individual claim that has been finally resolved. It acknowledges the policy that, in multiple claims actions, some final decisions on less than all of the claims should be appealable without waiting for a final decision on all of the claims.[187]

In cases involving multiple claims or parties, the district court may direct the entry of a final judgment as to one or more but fewer than all of the claims or parties, but only upon an express determination that there is no just reason for delay and upon an express direction for the entry of judgment. Technically, this technique results in a final and therefore appealable judgment, so that the appellate court has no discretion to reject the appeal. The Federal Circuit has held that a Rule 54(b) certification requires both an express direction for entry of judgment and an express determination that there is no just reason for delay. Where the latter was missing, the appeal was dismissed with leave to request correction by the court below.[188] It is not necessary, however, for a district court to make findings or give reasons for certifying an appeal under Rule 54(b), where the posture of the case and the factors justifying entry of judgment are readily apparent from the briefs and record.[189]

In order for Rule 54(b) to apply, the judgment must be final with respect to one or more claims. A judgment is not final unless it is an ultimate disposition of an individual claim entered in the court of a multiple claims action. Rule 54(b) does not come into play when mere defenses are left unadjudicated, but only when additional claims, counterclaims, or third-party claims remain unadjudicated.[190]

---

[187]*W.L. Gore & Assoc. v. International Med. Pros. Res. Assoc.,* 975 F.2d 858, 24 USPQ2d 1195 (Fed. Cir. 1992).

[188]*Aleut Tribe v. United States,* 702 F.2d 1015 (Fed. Cir. 1983). Under Rule 54(b) a district court must make an express statement of finality and indicate the lack of a just reason for delay. *Spraytex, Inc. v. DJS&T,* 96 F.3d 1377, 40 USPQ2d 1145 (Fed. Cir. 1996).

[189]*W.L. Gore & Assoc. v. International Med. Pros. Res. Assoc.,* 975 F.2d 858, 24 USPQ2d 1195 (Fed. Cir. 1992).

[190]*W.L. Gore & Assoc. v. International Med. Pros. Res. Assoc.,* 975 F.2d 858, 24 USPQ2d 1195 (Fed. Cir. 1992). Here the patent was held invalid and not infringed, and the fact that the court had not disposed of defendant's patent misuse defense did not destroy the finality of the judgment for purposes of Rule 54(b). Once the district court decided that the patent was invalid or not infringed, it no longer needed to address other defense. A defendant need only sustain one decisive defense, not all of them. The fact that the district court had bifurcated

Courts analyzing whether Rule 54(b) applies must focus on both the finality of the judgment and the separateness of the claims for relief.[191] Under Rule 54(b), the trial judge is a "dispatcher" who decides whether to release a decision for appellate consideration by making an express determination that there is no just reason for delay. The trial judge is permitted to determine, in the first instance, the appropriate time when each final decision upon one or more but less than all of the claims in a multiple claims action is ready for appeal. The knowledge bred of the district court's proximity to the case can be brought to bear on the question of the propriety of immediate review. Certification is therefore within the discretion of the trial judge who should carefully consider the competing equities.[192] But the requirement of finality is a statutory mandate and not a matter of discretion. The Supreme Court has rejected the view that the mere twin recitations of finality and no just reason for delay by the district court automatically renders a judgment appealable as a final decision. Instead, when an appeal is certified pursuant to Rule 54(b), an appellate court should review the finality of the judgment de novo in order to assure itself that it has jurisdiction. While the district court's determination that there is no just reason for delay is reviewed under an abuse of discretion standard, a district court cannot, in the exercise of its discretion, treat as final that which is not final. The separateness of the claims for relief, on the other hand, is a matter to be taken into account in reviewing the trial court's exercise of discretion in determining that there is no just reason to delay the appeal.[193]

An order imposing monetary sanctions on a party for violating a discovery order is not appealable under Rule 54(b) even when reduced to partial judgment. Rule 54(b) contemplates claims in the sense of the substantive right being asserted—the cause of action—rather than requests that are incidental to the procedure for obtaining a judicial award and enforcing it.[194] A district court need not, in a patent case that is final except for an accounting, enter a partial final judgment under Rule 54(b), inasmuch as such cases are appealable as of right under 28 U.S.C. §1292(c)(2).[195]

---

the misuse defense did not impact the finality of its judgment. The Federal Circuit also indicated that the asserted factual overlap of a related antitrust counterclaim did not demonstrate that the district court had abused its discretion in certifying the patent infringement claim for appeal under Rule 54(b).

[191]*W.L. Gore & Assoc. v. International Med. Pros. Res. Assoc.*, 975 F.2d 858, 24 USPQ2d 1195 (Fed. Cir. 1992).

[192]*Jeannette Sheet Glass Corp. v. United States*, 803 F.2d 1576 (Fed. Cir. 1986).

[193]*W.L. Gore & Assoc. v. International Med. Pros. Res. Assoc.*, 975 F.2d 858, 24 USPQ2d 1195 (Fed. Cir. 1992). The court reviews de novo the determination whether a judgment is final with respect to one or more claims, while the determination that there was no just reason for delay is reviewed under an abuse of discretion standard. The need for immediate appeal and the policy against piecemeal review are weighed. *Spraytex, Inc. v. DJS&T*, 96 F.3d 1377, 40 USPQ2d 1145 (Fed. Cir. 1996).

[194]*M.A. Mortenson Co. v. United States*, 877 F.2d 50 (Fed. Cir. 1989).

[195]*Shamrock Techs. Inc. v. Medical Sterilization, Inc.*, 903 F.2d 789, 14 USPQ2d 1728 (Fed. Cir. 1990).

A party should not be prejudiced by a failure to seek certification under Rule 54(b).[196] Denial of Rule 54(b) certification has been said to be proper where the case had been pending for 30 months and the factual issues underlying all counts were sufficiently intertwined that a separate appeal would complicate trial of the remaining counts.[197]

(d) Collateral Orders

Departures from the final judgment rule are permitted only when observance of it would practically defeat the right to any review at all.[198] Some orders that do not terminate the litigation are appealable under the collateral order exception to the finality requirement, because they are final in effect. To determine appealability of an order, an appellate court must balance the inconvenience and costs of piecemeal review against the danger of denying justice by delay.[199] Such orders finally determine claims of right separable from, and collateral to, rights asserted in the action.[200] In order to qualify, the order must at a minimum (1) conclusively determine the disputed question, (2) resolve an important issue completely separate from the merits of the action, and (3) be effectively unreviewable on appeal from a final judgment.[201] Some courts appear to add a fourth requirement, that the order present a serious and unsettled question, but the Federal Circuit formulation subsumes this under the second test of importance.[202] The final order rule reflects a strong congressional policy against piecemeal reviews and against obstructing or impeding an ongoing judicial proceeding by interlocutory appeals. The collateral order exception is a narrow one whose reach is limited to trial court orders affecting rights that will be irretrievably lost in the absence of an immediate appeal.[203]

A good example of such an order is one granting a motion to quash a subpoena, by a court other than the one before whom the underlying litigation is pending. Such an order entered by the forum court would normally not be appealable because it would be reviewable after final judgment on the merits. But where the forum court has no jurisdiction over the party subpoenaed, no such review would be possible, and if the matter is of sufficient importance, an appeal should be permitted.[204] Most discovery orders issued within the context of a primary proceeding fail to satisfy the requirement that they

---

[196]*Interconnect Planning Corp. v. Feil,* 774 F.2d 1132, 227 USPQ 543 (Fed. Cir. 1985).

[197]*Chaparral Comm., Inc. v. Boman Indus., Inc.,* 798 F.2d 456, 230 USPQ 535 (Fed. Cir. 1986).

[198]*Cabot Corp. v. United States,* 788 F.2d 1539 (Fed. Cir. 1986).

[199]*Heat & Control, Inc. v. Hester Indus. Inc.,* 785 F.2d 1017, 228 USPQ 926 (Fed. Cir. 1986).

[200]*United States v. W.H. Moseley Co.,* 730 F.2d 1472 (Fed. Cir. 1984).

[201]*Jeannette Sheet Glass Corp. v. United States,* 803 F.2d 1576 (Fed. Cir. 1986); *Cabot Corp. v. United States,* 788 F.2d 1539 (Fed. Cir. 1986).

[202]*Heat & Control, Inc. v. Hester Indus. Inc.,* 785 F.2d 1017, 228 USPQ 926 (Fed. Cir. 1986).

[203]*Jeannette Sheet Glass Corp. v. United States,* 803 F.2d 1576 (Fed. Cir. 1986).

[204]*Heat & Control, Inc. v. Hester Indus. Inc.,* 785 F.2d 1017, 228 USPQ 926 (Fed. Cir. 1986). The court saw no inconsistency in the fact that it would be the appellate body in each

be effectively unreviewable on appeal from a final judgment. Moreover, they are not truly collateral in that they are not completely separate from the merits.[205] By the same token, an order imposing sanctions on a party for violating an order compelling discovery is appealable, if at all, under the collateral order doctrine.[206]

Faced with an 8–3 split in the regional circuits, the Federal Circuit has sided with the minority in holding that an order denying a request for court-appointed counsel in a civil action is immediately appealable under the collateral order doctrine. An unconditional denial below conclusively determines the disputed question; that question does not enmesh the court in the factual and legal issues comprising the merits; and the denial makes the decision effectively unreviewable, for the appellate court may never know whether a different or better case could have been presented by counsel.[207]

A stay order is normally not a final, appealable order unless the stay effectively puts a party out of court[208] or is for an indefinite or very protracted period. Thus, the court will not permit an appeal from an order staying an infringement case pending reexamination by the

---

case. See also *Micro Motion Inc. v. Exac Corp.*, 876 F.2d 1574, 11 USPQ2d 1070 (Fed. Cir. 1989); *Solarex Corp. v. Arco Solar, Inc.*, 870 F.2d 642, 10 USPQ2d 1247 (Fed. Cir. 1989); *Truswal Sys. Corp v. Hydro-Air Eng'g, Inc.*, 813 F.2d 1207, 2 USPQ2d 1034 (Fed. Cir. 1987). An order quashing a subpoena in an ancillary proceeding not only terminates the proceeding but also is unreviewable on appeal of the final judgment in the principal action. Thus such an order is immediately appealable as of right. Where the order denies the motion to quash in part, and the party against whom the discovery was sought cross-appeals, the reviewing court may exercise pendent jurisdiction even though the cross-appeal is not independently reviewable. The issues are sufficiently intertwined factually and legally in both appeals. *Micro Motion Inc. v. Kane Steel Co.*, 894 F.2d 1318, 13 USPQ2d 1696 (Fed. Cir. 1990). It should be noted that the Federal Circuit held that it had jurisdiction over the main appeal because the discovery sought in the ancillary action related to a patent infringement claim in the principal action.

[205]*Quantum Corp. v. Tandon Corp.*, 940 F.2d 642, 19 USPQ2d 1799 (Fed. Cir. 1991). Nonparties may secure review of a discovery order by refusing to comply with it and appealing a consequent contempt order, which is considered final. That route is an "adequate alternative" that provides an "effective review" of the order. Thus, there is no justification for permitting interlocutory review either under the collateral order doctrine or by writ of mandamus, even where the government is the nonparty at risk. *Connaught Labs. Inc. v. SmithKline Beecham P.L.C.*, 165 F.3d 1368, 49 USPQ2d 1540 (Fed. Cir. 1999).

[206]*M.A. Mortenson Co. v. United States*, 877 F.2d 50 (Fed. Cir. 1989). An order awarding attorney fees as part of the sanctions against the government for failure to comply with discovery orders was held unappealable because the government failed to show that it would become effectively unreviewable on appeal from a final judgment. The government could not demonstrate that the other party would be unable to repay the sanction if the order were ultimately reversed, nor had it shown that it would be harmed by parting with the money until a final judgment could be obtained and appealed. In *Sanders Assoc., Inc. v. Summagraphics Corp.*, 2 F.3d 394, 27 USPQ2d 1853 (Fed. Cir. 1993), the court considered whether an order individually sanctioning a client and its attorney is immediately appealable. After an exhaustive review of regional circuit precedent, it held that making payments to a potential witness conditional on the outcome of the case is not necessarily separable from the underlying lawsuit and thus does not satisfy the second prong of the collateral order doctrine. In addition, the third prong is not satisfied because both the client and the attorney can obtain review of the sanction after final judgment is entered, even if there is no appeal on the merits by any party.

[207]*Lariscey v. United States*, 861 F.2d 1267, 8 USPQ2d 2007 (Fed. Cir. 1988). Note that on this question the court itself divided 2–1.

[208]*Intermedics Infusaid, Inc. v. Regents of Univ. of Minn.*, 804 F.2d 129, 231 USPQ 653 (Fed. Cir. 1986). The court specifically passed the "difficult" issue of whether an earlier filed state court action, for which the federal case was stayed, would be determinative. *Id.*

PTO; the Federal Circuit will have jurisdiction over any appeal from the reexamination, and the PTO must treat such matters with dispatch.[209] But the court has permitted an appeal from an order staying an interfering patents suit under 35 U.S.C. §291 pending reexamination of one of the patents in suit.[210] An order directing the PTO to reopen and complete prosecution of a reissue application is not appealable under the collateral order doctrine.[211] However, an order directing a patent owner to submit certain documents during a reexamination, though not final, is an appealable collateral order.[212] An order separating and staying trial as to customers, while proceeding as to manufacturers, is not appealable because it resolves no claim.[213] An order refusing bifurcation of issues is a routine, discretionary trial management matter; were such orders appealable before trial, a flood of piecemeal appeals would surely ensue.[214]

An order denying a motion to disqualify counsel is not appealable.[215] The grant of such a motion, however, seemed to be of sufficient importance and finality that the court was at first willing to permit appeals thereon under the collateral order doctrine.[216] A square holding to the contrary by the Supreme Court resulted in a corresponding change in view by the Federal Circuit, so that today attorney disqualification orders that are interlocutory can be reviewed only under 28

---

[209]*Gould v. Control Laser Corp.*, 705 F.2d 1340, 217 USPQ 985 (Fed. Cir. 1983).

[210]*Slip Track Sys. Inc. v. Metal Lite Inc.*, 159 F.3d 1337, 48 USPQ2d 1055 (Fed. Cir. 1998). The final judgment rule is subject to exceptions that allow litigants to challenge interlocutory orders of serious, perhaps irreparable, consequence. An order staying a case is generally not subject to appeal. That general rule does not prevent review of a stay, however, when it is clear that no further action is contemplated by the district court following the stay. Thus, federal courts have often found jurisdiction to review stays in favor of state court suits when the state court judgment would have a fully preclusive effect on the federal action or moot the federal action entirely. Stays in favor of administrative proceedings are similarly reviewed on an "effectively out of court" standard. The stay entered in this case was an appealable order because it effectively disposes of the district court action. The owner of the second filed patent cannot litigate priority issues in the PTO reexamination, nor can it swear behind the anticipatory first filed patent. Under those circumstances, the reexamination, if carried to completion, is likely to result in the cancellation of all of the claims of the second filed patent. That in turn would require a dismissal of the interfering patents suit, since a necessary condition for such an action is the existence of two valid and interfering patents. As a result, the district court would have no occasion to consider the issue of priority of invention following the resolution of the PTO proceeding. That consequence provides sufficient finality to make the stay order a "final decision" for appealability purposes. *Id.*

[211]*Baker Perkins, Inc. v. Werner & Pfleiderer Corp.*, 710 F.2d 1561, 218 USPQ 577 (Fed. Cir. 1983). The court seemed to suggest that the matter must first be presented to the PTO for compliance.

[212]*Emerson Elec. Co. v. Davoil, Inc.*,88 F.3d 1051, 39 USPQ2d 1474 (Fed. Cir. 1996).

[213]*Refac Int'l, Ltd. v. IBM*, 790 F.2d 79, 229 USPQ 712 (Fed. Cir. 1986). The appeal was held frivolous, largely because the appellant had not advised the court that the customers had agreed to be bound by any injunction entered against the manufacturers. The court later changed its mind as to its award of attorney fees, saying that the appellant's arguments "can on reconsideration be said to fall just within the ragged edge of the penumbra surrounding legitimate advocacy." *Refac Int'l, Ltd. v. IBM*, 798 F.2d 459, 230 USPQ 537 (Fed. Cir. 1986).

[214]*Quantum Corp. v. Tandon Corp.*, 940 F.2d 642, 19 USPQ2d 1799 (Fed. Cir. 1991).

[215]*C.P.C. v. Nosco Plastics, Inc.*, 719 F.2d 400 (Fed. Cir. 1983).

[216]*Panduit Corp. v. All States Plastic Mfg. Co.*, 744 F.2d 1564, 223 USPQ 465 (Fed. Cir. 1984); *In re International Med. P.R. Assoc.*, 739 F.2d 618 (Fed. Cir. 1984).

U.S.C. §1292(c)(1) if certified by the district court pursuant to §1292(b).[217]

The court recognizes a second limited exception to the final decision rule, in addition to the collateral order doctrine.[218] Under the so-called *Gillespie* rule, courts of appeals have power in cases of marginal finality to decide questions fundamental to the further conduct of the case.[219] In an early look at the *Gillespie* rule, the court may have engendered some confusion. In dealing with an order refusing to permit an amendment of reply pleadings to assert invalidity and unenforceability of a patent asserted by counterclaim, the court proposed a two-part rule for appealability of orders relating to pleadings: (1) Do the stricken allegations raise issues separate and distinct from those raised by the remaining allegations? and (2) Will the goal of judicial economy be served? The court seemed first to find that the stricken defenses were separate and distinct and then to find that they were so intertwined with other issues that judicial economy required a single trial.[220] Beyond question, however, the court reached the right result, both in holding that the order was not appealable under the collateral order doctrine because there would be an effective review on appeal from the final judgment and in holding that the question was fundamental to further conduct of the case and thus fit the *Gillespie* criterion. Perhaps "separate and distinct" may be taken to mean only that a judgment on the remaining questions would not moot the question that is the subject of the interlocutory order. In another case, the court correctly pointed out that a partial summary judgment relating to facts deemed established for trial is not a final judgment, but if the findings are fundamental to the further conduct of the case, or are intertwined with the summary judgment that is properly before the appellate court, they may be reviewed.[221]

Sitting in banc, the court has concluded that the Supreme Court itself has severely limited its *Gillespie* decision by confining it to its own unique facts. In the case before it, an attempted appeal from an interlocutory order of the PTO Trademark Trial and Appeal Board, the court concluded that inasmuch as facts similar to *Gillespie* could not possibly arise in such a setting, *Gillespie* no longer provides a viable basis for appeal of such orders.[222]

---

[217]*Sun Studs, Inc. v. Applied Theory Assocs.*, 772 F.2d 1557, 227 USPQ 81 (Fed. Cir. 1985). See *Richardson-Merrell, Inc. v. Koller*, 472 U.S. 424 (1985).

[218]*Tenneco Resins, Inc. v. Reeves Bros., Inc.*, 736 F.2d 1508, 222 USPQ 276 (Fed. Cir. 1984).

[219]*Gillespie v. United States Steel Corp.*, 379 U.S. 148 (1964).

[220]*Tenneco Resins, Inc. v. Reeves Bros., Inc.*, 736 F.2d 1508, 222 USPQ 276 (Fed. Cir. 1984).

[221]*Palumbo v. Don-Joy Co.*, 762 F.2d 969, 226 USPQ 5 (Fed. Cir. 1985). *Helifix Ltd. v. Blok-Lok Ltd.*, 208 F.3d 1339, 54 USPQ2d 1299 (Fed. Cir. 2), provides a good example of invocation of pendent appellate jurisdiction on the basis of "inextricably intertwined" issues. The district court denied a motion for a preliminary injunction and held the patent invalid on summary judgment. There were other claims in the case so both judgments were interlocutory, but the denial of the injunction was of course appealable. The court naturally exercised pendent jurisdiction over the appeal from the summary judgment. See also *Gerber Garment Tech., Inc. v. Lectra Sys., Inc.*, 916 F.2d 683, 16 USPQ2d 1436 (Fed. Cir. 1990).

[222]*Copelands' Enters. Inc. v. CNV, Inc.*, 887 F.2d 1065, 12 USPQ2d 1562 (Fed. Cir. 1989).

There is also some discretion to review related questions. Thus, an interlocutory order that ordinarily would not be appealable may be given discretionary appellate review when it is ancillary to other matters that are appealable. Consideration is given to the extent to which the appealable order involves factors pertinent to the otherwise nonappealable order, such that judicial efficiency and the interest of justice are served by review of the ancillary question.[223]

(e) *Extraordinary Writs*

Under the All Writs Act, 28 U.S.C. §1651(a), federal courts are empowered to "issue all writs necessary or appropriate in aid of their respective jurisdictions and agreeable to the usages and principles of law." This authority applies to the Federal Circuit.[224] Courts of appeals have traditionally construed their mandamus authority to extend to cases within their actual or potential appellate jurisdiction. Thus the mandamus authority of the Federal Circuit attaches when the jurisdiction of the district court is based, in whole or in part, on §§1338 or 1346.[225]

The mandamus statute is not a grant of jurisdiction. There must be some other basis for jurisdiction before an appellate court may issue the particular writ sought by a petition for mandamus.[226] The requirements for issuing a writ of mandamus are: (1) a clear duty on the part of the defendant to perform the action in question; (2) a clear right on the part of the plaintiff to demand the relief sought; and (3) an absence of an adequate alternative remedy.[227]

The Federal Circuit has no administrative authority over district courts.[228] Thus, although the court has mandamus power, it cannot be used for general supervision.[229] The mandamus statute is not an

[223]*Katz v. Lear Siegler, Inc.,* 909 F.2d 1459, 15 USPQ2d 1554 (Fed. Cir. 1990). Here there was an appealable order granting an injunction, and a nonappealable order joining a party. The two issues were sufficiently intertwined that the court exercised its discretion in favor of review of the joinder question.

[224]*In re Cordis Corp.,* 769 F.2d 733, 226 USPQ 784 (Fed. Cir. 1985); *In re Makari,* 708 F.2d 709, 218 USPQ 193 (Fed. Cir. 1983).

[225]*In re Innotron Diagnostics,* 800 F.2d 1077, 231 USPQ 178 (Fed. Cir. 1986). In a case within the Federal Circuit's appellate jurisdiction, it has jurisdiction to decide questions raised by extraordinary writ. Issues that are properly before it on appeal (such as venue) are no less within its jurisdiction when raised by extraordinary writ. *In re Regents of the Univ. of Calif.,* 964 F.2d 1128 (Fed. Cir. 1992).

[226]*In re Roberts,* 846 F.2d 1360, 6 USPQ2d 1772 (Fed. Cir. 1988).

[227]*Timken Co. v. United States,* 893 F.2d 337 (Fed. Cir. 1990); *Maier v. Orr,* 754 F.2d 973 (Fed. Cir. 1985).

[228]*In re Mark Indus.,* 751 F.2d 1219, 224 USPQ 521 (Fed. Cir. 1984); *In re Oximetrix, Inc.,* 748 F.2d 637, 223 USPQ 1068 (Fed. Cir. 1984); *In re International Med. P.R. Assoc.,* 739 F.2d 618 (Fed. Cir. 1984); *In re Precision Screen Mach., Inc.,* 729 F.2d 1428, 221 USPQ 1034 (Fed. Cir. 1984); *Mississippi Chem. Corp. v. Swift Agric. Chem. Corp.,* 717 F.2d 1374, 219 USPQ 577 (Fed. Cir. 1983).

[229]*Mississippi Chem. Corp. v. Swift Agric. Chem. Corp.,* 717 F.2d 1374, 219 USPQ 577 (Fed. Cir. 1983).

independent statutory grant of jurisdiction. Mandamus was traditionally employed to confine an inferior court to a lawful exercise of its
prescribed jurisdiction or to compel it to exercise its authority when
it is its duty to do so. Use of mandamus in exercising supervisory
authority has been approved, but only for the regional circuits not
the Federal Circuit. Administration, supervision, management, and
overseeing of courts within a regional circuit are the sole province of
that circuit court.[230]

Nevertheless, the authority of the All Writs Act is not limited to
instances in which failure to issue the writ would preclude an ultimate
appeal; it can be used to correct a clear abuse of discretion or usurpation of judicial discretion by the lower tribunal.[231]

The lines are not easy to draw. The court can always consider
petitions for mandamus in situations where the order would prevent
an appeal or otherwise frustrate the court's proper exercise of jurisdiction. But there are troublesome cases: (1) those implicating supervisory responsibilities of the regional circuit courts (e.g., judge assignments, calendar control, transfers, reference to master); (2) those that
arise in all types of cases but do not directly implicate the patent
doctrinal jurisprudence of the Federal Circuit (e.g., disqualification
of counsel); and (3) those that do directly implicate its patent doctrinal
jurisprudential responsibilities (e.g., separate trial of patent issues,
court-ordered tests for utility, refusal to apply 35 U.S.C. §82). In these
troublesome cases the court will limit the exercise of its power to
entertain petitions for mandamus to cases involving only "proper
circumstances." It is likely that proper circumstances will be found
only in category (3) situations.[232] For example, sanctions imposed on
counsel stemming from a controversy about the timing of the damages
portion of a patent trial and the appealability of an interlocutory
order under 28 U.S.C. §1292(c) are bound up with and controlled by
the doctrinal responsibilities of the court, and it thus has mandamus
jurisdiction to review such sanctions.[233]

Mandamus is no substitute for appeal.[234] The remedy of mandamus is a drastic one, to be invoked only in extraordinary situations.[235]
It is strong medicine to be reserved for the most serious and critical
ills, and if a rational and substantial legal argument can be made in

---

[230]*In re Innotron Diagnostics,* 800 F.2d 1077, 231 USPQ 178 (Fed. Cir. 1986).

[231]*In re Regents of Univ. of Calif.,* 101 F.3d 1386, 40 USPQ2d 1784 (Fed. Cir. 1996); *In re Continental Gen. Tire, Inc.,* 81 F.3d 1089, 38 USPQ2d 1365 (Fed. Cir. 1996); *In re Regents of the Univ. of Calif.,* 964 F.2d 1128 (Fed. Cir. 1992); *In re Calmar, Inc.,* 854 F.2d 461, 7 USPQ2d 1730 (Fed. Cir. 1988); *In re Newman,* 763 F.2d 407, 226 USPQ 997 (Fed. Cir. 1985); *In re Mark Indus.,* 751 F.2d 1219, 224 USPQ 521 (Fed. Cir. 1984); *In re International Med. P.R. Assoc.,* 739 F.2d 618 (Fed. Cir. 1984); *Mississippi Chem. Corp. v. Swift Agric. Chem. Corp.,* 717 F.2d 1374, 219 USPQ 577 (Fed. Cir. 1983). Mandamus can also be used by federal courts to compel administrative action. *Maier v. Orr,* 754 F.2d 973 (Fed. Cir. 1985).

[232]*In re Innotron Diagnostics,* 800 F.2d 1077, 231 USPQ 178 (Fed. Cir. 1986).

[233]*In re Calmar, Inc.,* 854 F.2d 461, 7 USPQ2d 1730 (Fed. Cir. 1988).

[234]*Case v. BSAF Wyandotte,* 737 F.2d 1034, 222 USPQ 737 (Fed. Cir. 1984).

[235]*In re Continental Gen. Tire, Inc.,* 81 F.3d 1089, 38 USPQ2d 1365 (Fed. Cir. 1996).

support of an order, the case is not appropriate for mandamus, even though on a normal appeal a court might find reversible error.[236] The burden is on the petitioner to show exceptional circumstances justifying the writ and to establish that its right to the writ is clear and indisputable.[237]

Specific holdings are illustrative. In the absence of a clear demonstration of abuse of discretion, an order refusing joinder of a party is not reviewable by mandamus, because there is no potential to frustrate appellate jurisdiction.[238] So too with orders granting or denying motions to disqualify counsel.[239] There may be exceptional cases where an appellate court is justified in issuing a writ directing the district court to execute a certificate under Rule 54(b), FRCP, but as a general proposition such a refusal will not be interfered with.[240] Similarly, mandamus is unavailable to review an order continuing or vacating a stay of proceedings[241] or denying a motion to dismiss for lack of venue.[242] A transfer order is interlocutory, not final and appealable. Transfers to a more convenient forum are therefore reviewable only by mandamus.[243] Thus, in a case within the Federal Circuit's appellate jurisdiction, it may consider venue transfer questions raised under the All Writs Statute, 28 U.S.C. §1651. More than that, it may consider by extraordinary writ transfer and consolidation orders of the Judicial Panel on Multidistrict Litigation.[244]

The right to trial by jury is sufficiently important that mandamus will lie to protect it. Thus, rather than await an appeal after trial on the merits, the Federal Circuit will grant a writ to preserve the right prior to trial.[245] Although discovery orders are not routinely appealable,[246] a writ of mandamus may be sought to prevent the wrongful exposure of privileged communications. Mandamus review may be granted of discovery orders that turn on claims of privilege when (1) there is raised an important issue of first impression, (2) the privilege would be lost if review were denied until final judgment, and (3) immediate resolution would avoid the development of doctrine that would undermine the privilege.[247]

---

[236]*In re Cordis Corp.*, 769 F.2d 733, 226 USPQ 784 (Fed. Cir. 1985).

[237]*In re Jenoptik AG*, 109 F.3d 721, 41 USPQ2d 1950 (Fed. Cir. 1997); *In re Continental Gen. Tire, Inc.*, 81 F.3d 1089, 38 USPQ2d 1365 (Fed. Cir. 1996); *In re Regents of the Univ. of Calif.*, 964 F.2d 1128 (Fed. Cir. 1992); *In re Innotron Diagnostics*, 800 F.2d 1077, 231 USPQ 178 (Fed. Cir. 1986).

[238]*In re Precision Screen Mach., Inc.*, 729 F.2d 1428, 221 USPQ 1034 (Fed. Cir. 1984).

[239]*In re International Med. P.R. Assoc.*, 739 F.2d 618 (Fed. Cir. 1984); *C.P.C. v. Nosco Plastics, Inc.*, 719 F.2d 400 (Fed. Cir. 1983).

[240]*Jeannette Sheet Glass Corp. v. United States*, 803 F.2d 1576 (Fed. Cir. 1986).

[241]*In re Oximetrix, Inc.*, 748 F.2d 637, 223 USPQ 1068 (Fed. Cir. 1984).

[242]*In re Cordis Corp.*, 769 F.2d 733, 226 USPQ 784 (Fed. Cir. 1985).

[243]*Wood v. United States*, 961 F.2d 195 (Fed. Cir. 1992).

[244]*In re Regents of the Univ. of Calif.*, 964 F.2d 1128 (Fed. Cir. 1992).

[245]*In re Lockwood*, 50 F.3d 966, 33 USPQ2d 1406 (Fed. Cir. 1995).

[246]E.g., *Connaught Labs. Inc. v. SmithKline Beecham P.L.C.*, 165 F.3d 1368, 49 USPQ2d 1540 (Fed. Cir. 1999).

[247]*In re Regents of Univ. of Calif.*, 101 F.3d 1386, 40 USPQ2d 1784 (Fed. Cir. 1996). In *In re Spalding Sports Worldwide Inc.*, 203 F.3d 800, 53 USPQ2d 1747 (Fed. Cir. 2), the court

A refusal to grant summary judgment based on collateral estoppel may justify a writ, inasmuch as review after trial would not be meaningful—the unnecessary trial would already have taken place.[248] A district court order directing that a patent applicant submit a working model of his invention to the National Bureau of Standards for possible destructive testing was also held to be reviewable by mandamus. A prima facie case of irreparable injury was shown in that no subsequent appeal would necessarily redress the damage caused by the destruction.[249]

The court will entertain a petition for a writ of mandamus directed at overturning an order relating to the separate trial of patent issues, because the writ could be in aid of its jurisdiction. This is particularly so where the separated issue is a potentially moot antitrust claim. If such petitions were directed to the regional circuits, there would be a risk of differing resolutions and consequent forum shopping.[250]

In one hard case, a writ was refused to review the denial of a motion to vacate and reenter judgment to facilitate appeal, where the movant had failed to file a timely notice of appeal.[251] The refusal of the writ appeared to be based upon no finding of abuse of discretion. It would seem, however, that a strong argument could be made that the order would frustrate the jurisdiction of the Federal Circuit unless some other route of review were available. Here the appellate court appeared to conduct a substantive review by direct appeal on the basis that the order was from a denial of a motion under Rule 60(b), FRCP.

Perhaps the court should be cautious about flat utterances to the effect that mandamus is not available for certain purposes. A pair of removal/remand decisions illustrate the need for caution. In the first case, the court reviewed by mandamus a remand by a federal district court back to state court after removal, on the perfectly correct ground that such review was in aid of its appellate jurisdiction.[252] If the remand stood without review, the Federal Circuit would never get the case. In a later decision, the court held, flatly, that remands of removed cases are not reviewable by appeal, mandamus, or otherwise.[253] This holding was limited to remands pursuant to 28 U.S.C. §1447(c), which deals with cases removed "improvidently and without jurisdiction," and the court was quick to point out that in the earlier case the remand was not stated to have been based on §1447(c). Even so, it is respectfully suggested that a flat holding that mandamus is

---

granted review by mandamus of the question whether the attorney-client privilege applies to an invention record submitted for patent evaluation. See *In re Jenoptik AG,* 109 F.3d 721, 41 USPQ2d 1950 (Fed. Cir. 1997), for a discussion of mandamus review of rulings affecting use of depositions in a foreign proceeding.

[248]*Mississippi Chem. Corp. v. Swift Agric. Chem. Corp.,* 717 F.2d 1374, 219 USPQ 577 (Fed. Cir. 1983).

[249]*In re Newman,* 782 F.2d 971, 228 USPQ 450 (Fed. Cir. 1986).

[250]*In re Innotron Diagnostics,* 800 F.2d 1077, 231 USPQ 178 (Fed. Cir. 1986).

[251]*Case v. BSAF Wyandotte,* 737 F.2d 1034, 222 USPQ 737 (Fed. Cir. 1984).

[252]*In re Snap-On Tools Corp.,* 720 F.2d 654, 220 USPQ 8 (Fed. Cir. 1983).

[253]*In re Oximetrix, Inc.,* 748 F.2d 637, 223 USPQ 1068 (Fed. Cir. 1984).

unavailable for §1447(c) remands goes too far. One can certainly envision circumstances under which the very finding of the district court as to improvident removal was itself an abuse of discretion or an usurpation of judicial power, thus justifying mandamus as an extraordinary remedy.[254]

The Federal Circuit's jurisdiction over all appeals from the PTO makes mandamus in that context somewhat unlikely. For example, the failure of the PTO to accord an applicant the benefit of a filing date does not justify a writ, because the court will ultimately hear any appeal from a final, unfavorable outcome.[255] Similarly, where the district court in an action under 35 U.S.C. §145 remanded to the PTO with directions that the applicant submit working models, mandamus would not issue in the absence of abuse of discretion or usurpation of judicial power. The district court would ultimately have to enter a final judgment, and if it were adverse to the applicant, the Federal Circuit would get the appeal.[256]

§16.3 Scope of Review

(a) General

Affirmance does not require that the reviewing court and the trial court reach a conclusion in precisely the same fashion.[257] A court of appeals may affirm the judgment of a district court on any ground, including grounds not relied upon by the district court.[258] The trial judge's reasoning cannot be ignored, since faulty reasoning is likely to lead to a wrong result. But an appellant must show not only faulty reasoning but also a wrong result.[259] Thus the Federal Circuit reminds

---

[254]Perhaps the court was reacting to petitioner's arguments in general, which it found "are totally without merit, are based on mutually exclusive concepts, and are drawn in disregard of the record." The court held the petition to be frivolous. *In re Oximetrix, Inc.,* 748 F.2d 637, 641, 223 USPQ 1068 (Fed. Cir. 1984).

[255]*In re Makari,* 708 F.2d 709, 218 USPQ 193 (Fed. Cir. 1983).

[256]*In re Newman,* 763 F.2d 407, 226 USPQ 997 (Fed. Cir. 1985). But see *In re Newman,* 782 F.2d 971, 228 USPQ 450 (Fed. Cir. 1986), and text accompanying note 16:249.

[257]*Gardner v. TEC Sys., Inc.,* 725 F.2d 1338, 220 USPQ 777 (Fed. Cir. 1984).

[258]*Bio-Rad Labs., Inc. v. Nicolet Instr. Corp.,* 807 F.2d 964, 1 USPQ2d 1191 (Fed. Cir. 1986). But application of this principle in certain cases is dubious. Particularly where the determination lies in the discretion of the district judge, the review should be directed to the stated basis for the exercise of discretion, and not other grounds upon which the district judge may have grounded his or her decision. *Id.* A party may defend a judgment on any ground properly raised below, so long as such affirmance would neither expand nor contract the rights established for either party by the judgment appealed from. *Consolidated Alum Corp. v. Foseco Int'l Ltd.,* 910 F.2d 804, 15 USPQ2d 1481 (Fed. Cir. 1990).

[259]*Union Carbide Corp. v. American Can Co.,* 724 F.2d 1567, 220 USPQ 584 (Fed. Cir. 1984).

us again and again that it is decisions that are appealed, not opin-ions,[260] or passing comments,[261] or mere language.[262] It is the validity of the judgment, not the quality of any opinion supporting it, that has legal significance, and the court's failure to cite any cases has no relevance to whether the court reached the correct legal result.[263] But where the language of the opinion indicates an erroneous basis for the decision, it will be reversed.[264] The court insists that it reviews judgments, not phrases in an opinion,[265] or expressions of the district court,[266] or language used in justification of the judgment appealed from,[267] or rhetoric.[268] The court reviews judgments, not opinions, and an error in philosophical approach is not crucial unless it be shown that the district court reached the wrong result.[269] Yet the analysis reflected in an opinion filed with the judgment appealed from may on occasion be so flawed as to obfuscate the true basis for the judgment or to establish that the judgment was erroneously based.[270] The court reviews judgments, not passing statements[271] or words.[272] Yet opinion language may indicate that a judgment is erroneously based,[273] and the district court's expression of the basis for its ruling may reflect

---

[260]*In re Hyatt,* 708 F.2d 712, 218 USPQ 195 (Fed. Cir. 1983). Judgments, orders, and mandates may be "vacated." Opinions may be revised, modified, withdrawn, and replaced. *In re Perry,* 918 F.2d 931 (Fed. Cir. 1990).

[261]*Structural Rubber Prods. Co. v. Park Rubber Co.,* 749 F.2d 707, 223 USPQ 1264 (Fed. Cir. 1984).

[262]*In re Weiler,* 790 F.2d 1576, 229 USPQ 673 (Fed. Cir. 1986).

[263]*Constant v. United States,* 929 F.2d 654, 18 USPQ2d 1298 (Fed. Cir. 1991).

[264]*In re Weiler,* 790 F.2d 1576, 229 USPQ 673 (Fed. Cir. 1986).

[265]*Howes v. Medical Components, Inc.,* 814 F.2d 638, 2 USPQ2d 1271 (Fed. Cir. 1987); *Kloster Speedsteel AB v. Crucible Inc.,* 793 F.2d 1565, 230 USPQ 81 (Fed. Cir. 1986); *Porter v. Farmers Supply Serv., Inc.,* 790 F.2d 882, 229 USPQ 814 (Fed. Cir. 1986).

[266]*International Medical Pros. v. Gore Ent. Holdings, Inc.,* 787 F.2d 572, 229 USPQ 278 (Fed. Cir. 1986).

[267]*Pentec, Inc. v. Graphic Controls Corp.,* 776 F.2d 309, 227 USPQ 766 (Fed. Cir. 1985).

[268]*Lindemann Maschinenfabrik v. American Hoist & Derrick Co.,* 730 F.2d 1452, 221 USPQ 481 (Fed. Cir. 1984). See note 114 above.

[269]*Milliken Res. Corp. v. Dan River, Inc.,* 739 F.2d 587, 222 USPQ 571 (Fed. Cir. 1984). See, e.g., *General Mills, Inc. v. Hunt-Wesson, Inc.,* 103 F.3d 978, 41 USPQ2d 1440 (Fed. Cir. 1997);. *Vandenberg v. Dairy Equip. Co.,* 740 F.2d 1560, 224 USPQ 195 (Fed. Cir. 1984).

[270]*Fromson v. Advance Offset Plate, Inc.,* 755 F.2d 1549, 225 USPQ 26 (Fed. Cir. 1985); *Stratoflex, Inc. v. Aeroquip Corp.,* 713 F.2d 1530, 218 USPQ 871 (Fed. Cir. 1983).

[271]*Perkin-Elmer Corp. v. Computervision Corp.,* 732 F.2d 888, 221 USPQ 669 (Fed. Cir. 1984); *Medtronic, Inc. v. Cardiac Pacemakers, Inc.,* 721 F.2d 1563, 220 USPQ 97 (Fed. Cir. 1983). One passing statement, taken out of context, may well not provide a basis for reversal. *American Med. Sys., Inc. v. Medical Eng'g Corp.,* 6 F.3d 1523, 28 USPQ2d 1321 (Fed. Cir. 1993).

[272]*Lindemann Maschinenfabrik v. American Hoist & Derrick Co.,* 895 F.2d 1403, 13 USPQ2d 1871 (Fed. Cir. 1990). Thus the fact that the trial court said it was awarding "nominal" damages was not necessarily in conflict with the reasonable royalty standard as the statutory floor for damages. The court felt the trial judge was simply indicating that he was giving the plaintiff less than it was demanding.

[273]*FMC Corp. v. Hennessy Indus., Inc.,* 836 F.2d 521, 5 USPQ2d 1272 (Fed. Cir. 1987); *Porter v. Farmers Supply Serv., Inc.,* 790 F.2d 882, 229 USPQ 814 (Fed. Cir. 1986).

an error of fact or law that requires reversal of the judgment if there is no support in the record for that basis.[274]

In the end analysis, a litigant is entitled to a fair hearing, not a perfect one. The district court's opinion may not have been perfect—few human products are. But surface blemishes do not compel reversal.[275]

(b) Findings and Conclusions

So the Federal Circuit reviews judgments and decisions, but will consider what the trial court said in reaching its decision. Must the trial court say anything at all? Rule 52(a), FRCP, requires that the trial court in a nonjury case "find the facts specially and state separately its conclusions of law thereon."[276] A district court may not merely state its findings in conclusory terms, but must provide sufficient detail to elucidate the reasoning by which the court reached its ultimate finding on an issue of fact or conclusion on an issue of law; otherwise, the appellate court is unable to carry out its appellate review function. Indeed, the trial court must also find subsidiary facts specially, not just the ultimate fact. If it fails to do so, its decision will ordinarily be vacated.[277]

Certainly oral findings and conclusions are sufficient to indicate the basis of the district court's decision and provide an adequate basis for appellate review.[278] But an appellate court lacks power to make findings of fact, and where the trial court fails to make findings, the judgment will normally be vacated and the case remanded for appropriate findings.[279] Where the judgment of the trial court lacks any rationale for its decisions on the postverdict motions of the parties, one option, not to be discarded lightly, is to vacate the judgment and remand the matter for a full explication of the reasons for the court's rejection of the jury's findings. Another option is to examine the record

---

[274]*International Medical Pros. v. Gore Ent. Holdings, Inc.,* 787 F.2d 572, 229 USPQ 278 (Fed. Cir. 1986).

[275]*Chemical Eng'g Corp. v. Essef Indus., Inc.,* 795 F.2d 1565, 230 USPQ 385, 390 (Fed. Cir. 1986). Trials must be fair not perfect. *Newell Cos. v. Kenney Mfg. Co.,* 864 F.2d 757, 9 USPQ2d 1417 (Fed. Cir. 1988).

[276]*Loctite Corp. v. Ultraseal Ltd.,* 781 F.2d 861, 228 USPQ 90 (Fed. Cir. 1985).

[277]*Gechter v. Davidson,* 116 F.3d 1454, 43 USPQ2d 1030 (Fed. Cir. 1997). Compare *In re Hyatt,* 211 F.3d 1367, 54 USPQ2d 1664 (Fed. Cir. 2).

[278]*Albert v. Kevex Corp.,* 729 F.2d 757, 221 USPQ 202 (Fed. Cir. 1984).

[279]*Loctite Corp. v. Ultraseal Ltd.,* 781 F.2d 861, 228 USPQ 90 (Fed. Cir. 1985); *Seattle Box Co. v. Industrial Crat. & Pack., Inc.,* 756 F.2d 1574, 225 USPQ 357 (Fed. Cir. 1985); *ACS Hosp. Sys., Inc. v. Montefiore Hosp.,* 732 F.2d 1572, 221 USPQ 929 (Fed. Cir. 1984). See *Cablestrand Corp. v. Wallshein,* 989 F.2d 472, 26 USPQ2d 1079 (Fed. Cir. 1993). In *Graco, Inc. v. Binks Mfg. Co.,* 60 F.3d 785, 35 USPQ2d 1255 (Fed. Cir. 1995), best mode was a seriously contested issue, and the defendant devoted several paragraphs of proposed findings to the matter. The plaintiff's proposed findings and the trial court's actual findings did not deal with the question; there was simply a holding that the patent was not invalid. This was insufficient to permit meaningful review of the best mode defense, so that a remand was necessary.

to determine whether the facts support the judgment. This avoids the inefficiencies of having the appellate court review and decide the issue twice.[280] But it is not the function of the appellate court to search the record and analyze the evidence in order to supply findings that the trial court failed to make.[281] The court has said that it may make a finding of fact on evidence that is undisputed. It may also make such a finding even when the evidence is disputed if, as a matter of law, the court could only make one finding of fact or decide the fact in only one way. Otherwise, protracted litigation and unnecessary delay and expense would occur.[282] But a failure to make specific findings may be an abuse of discretion.[283] Indeed, a district court may be forced to draw reasoned legal conclusions as well.[284]

When the opinion under review does not adequately set forth the reasons for its conclusion, the reviewing court cannot determine whether the lower court's decision is correct. The reviewing court must know what a decision means before the duty arises to say whether it is right or wrong,[285] and a failure to make findings has been characterized as a dereliction of duty.[286] Nevertheless, where full understanding may be had without the aid of separate findings, the Federal Circuit does recognize a narrow exception to Rule 52(a).[287] If the trial court has not misapplied the controlling legal standards in its evaluation of the evidence, its ultimate finding may be reviewed in order to conclude the controversy without unnecessary further expenditure of

---

[280]*Baxter Healthcare Corp. v. Spectramed, Inc.*, 49 F.3d 1575, 34 USPQ2d 1120 (Fed. Cir. 1995).

[281]*Atlantic Thermoplastics Co. v. Faytex Corp.*, 5 F.3d 1477, 28 USPQ2d 1343 (Fed. Cir. 1993).

[282]*Smithkline Diagnostics, Inc. v. Helena Labs. Corp.*, 859 F.2d 878, 8 USPQ2d 1468 (Fed. Cir. 1988). But is this not directly contrary to its earlier indication that an appellate court lacks *power* to make findings? See, e.g., cases cited in note 16:279.

[283]*Medtronic, Inc. v. Daig Corp.*, 789 F.2d 903, 229 USPQ 664 (Fed. Cir. 1986).

[284]*Truswal Sys. Corp v. Hydro-Air Eng'g, Inc.*, 813 F.2d 1207, 2 USPQ2d 1034 (Fed. Cir. 1987). Neither party cited case authority on the question at bar, and the district court based its decision on the sole ground that no case was cited. The Federal Circuit remanded with the observation that because a case is one of first impression is not itself a ground for decision.

[285]*McKeague v. United States*, 788 F.2d 755 (Fed. Cir. 1986). For example, the need for findings and reasons to explain any injunctive relief that goes beyond maintaining the status quo is especially critical at a preliminary stage of the proceedings. The procedural requirements include a statement of the reasons for a preliminary injunction under Rule 65, FRCP. Further, Rule 52(a) requires that a preliminary injunction be supported by findings of fact. Otherwise, the reviewing court has nothing before it to which appropriate appellate standards of review can be applied with respect to the merits of the injunction. *Digital Equip. Corp. v. Emulex Corp.*, 805 F.2d 380, 231 USPQ 779 (Fed. Cir. 1986).

[286]*Loctite Corp. v. Ultraseal Ltd.*, 781 F.2d 861, 228 USPQ 90 (Fed. Cir. 1985). In one such situation, even after a first remand the district court limited its statement to a mere ultimate conclusion, without any explanation whatever of the particular factors and facts it considered. It made no findings, failed to evaluate those facts that were previously established, and did not indicate the grounds for its exercise of discretion. The appellate court is at an obvious disadvantage in reviewing such a bald conclusion and would have to remand a second time unless the record left no question as to the decision that must result from a remand. *Seattle Box Co. v. Industrial Crat. & Pack., Inc.*, 756 F.2d 1574, 225 USPQ 357 (Fed. Cir. 1985).

[287]*Loctite Corp. v. Ultraseal Ltd.*, 781 F.2d 861, 228 USPQ 90 (Fed. Cir. 1985).

judicial resources, if possible.[288] Where there is a sufficient record, the relevant facts are not in dispute, no credibility determinations are needed, and it appears that there can be only one acceptable resolution of the problem, a remand is not required.[289] Remand should not be a matter of rote in every case in which findings and reasons are not expressly set forth. An appellate court need not close its eyes to the record where there is a way clearly open to affirm the district court's action.[290]

Rule 52(a) does not place a severe burden upon the trial judge, for he or she need only make brief, definite, pertinent findings and conclusions upon the contested matters. The ultimate test of the adequacy of findings is whether they are sufficiently comprehensive and pertinent to the issue to form a basis for the decision. How many and how specific the findings need be are questions to be resolved on a case-by-case basis.[291] A district court need follow no prescribed grammatical formulation in expressing its findings and conclusions.[292] The fact that evidence was not discussed below does not mean that it was not considered.[293] Failure to mention does not mean failure to consider when the evidence supplies support for the district court's determination.[294] A district court is not obligated to list, and reject,

---

[288]*ACS Hosp. Sys., Inc. v. Montefiore Hosp.*, 732 F.2d 1572, 221 USPQ 929 (Fed. Cir. 1984).

[289]*Seattle Box Co. v. Industrial Crat. & Pack., Inc.*, 756 F.2d 1574, 225 USPQ 357 (Fed. Cir. 1985).

[290]*Consolidated Alum Corp. v. Foseco Int'l Ltd.*, 910 F.2d 804, 15 USPQ2d 1481 (Fed. Cir. 1990).

[291]*Pretty Punch Shoppettes, Inc. v. Hauk*, 844 F.2d 782, 6 USPQ2d 1563 (Fed. Cir. 1988); *Loctite Corp. v. Ultraseal Ltd.*, 781 F.2d 861, 228 USPQ 90 (Fed. Cir. 1985). In one case the trial court simply indicated that it found no fraud. In some cases this might be insufficient to permit meaningful review, but here it was clear from its opinion that it was correct. Moreover, there was no evidence at trial bearing directly on the subject, and fraud was raised only in posttrial briefs. *Studiengesellschaft Kohle v. Dart Indus., Inc.*, 726 F.2d 724, 220 USPQ 841 (Fed. Cir. 1984). Although it seems clear that an exercise of discretion in denying attorney fees should focus on the unjustness of the denial as well as the conduct of the wrongful party, it was sufficient for the district court simply to say that in light of all the facts it would not be just to award fees. *J.P. Stevens Co. v. Lex Tex Ltd.*, 822 F.2d 1047, 3 USPQ2d 1235 (Fed. Cir. 1987). Although the issue of fees should be settled in the most expeditious manner possible, there must be some findings, certainly more than an "equitable instinct," supporting the fee award in order to provide a basis for appellate review. *Water Techs. Corp. v. Calco, Ltd.*, 850 F.2d 660, 7 USPQ2d 1097 (Fed. Cir. 1988). To enable appellate review, a district court is obligated to explain the basis for an award of enhanced damages, particularly where the maximum amount is imposed. *Read Co v. Portec, Inc.*, 970 F.2d 816, 23 USPQ2d 1426 (Fed. Cir. 1992). It would seem that a party who believes that the findings are inadequate should complain at the earliest opportunity. See *Glaverbel S.A. v. Northlake Mkt'g & Supp., Inc.*, 45 F.3d 1550, 33 USPQ2d 1496 (Fed. Cir. 1995). Not surprisingly, individual judges of the Federal Circuit sometimes find themselves in sharp disagreement as to whether or not findings are adequate to permit meaningful review. In *Atlantic Thermoplastics Co. v. Faytex Corp.*, 5 F.3d 1477, 28 USPQ2d 1343 (Fed. Cir. 1993), the majority of the panel found it necessary to remand for a second time because of what it regarded as inadequate findings. The dissenting judge, however, took the remarkable step of actually writing a hypothetical opinion that would support the judgment below.

[292]*Fromson v. Western Litho Plate & Supp. Co.*, 853 F.2d 1568, 7 USPQ2d 1606 (Fed. Cir. 1988).

[293]*Kansas Jack, Inc. v. Kuhn*, 719 F.2d 1144, 219 USPQ 857 (Fed. Cir. 1983).

[294]*FMC Corp. v. Hennessy Indus., Inc.*, 836 F.2d 521, 5 USPQ2d 1272 (Fed. Cir. 1987).

factors that might have supported a contrary conclusion.[295] It may be presumed that the fact finder reviews all the evidence presented unless it explicitly indicates otherwise.[296]

While certainly preferable from the viewpoint of a reviewing court, the trial court does not have to set forth explicitly findings and conclusions to support its decision on summary judgment. But if its underlying holdings would otherwise be ambiguous or unascertainable, the reasons for entering summary judgment must be stated somewhere in the record.[297]

Injunctions may impose special obligations on the district court.[298] Rule 52(a), FRCP, requires that the grant or denial of a preliminary injunction be supported by findings of fact. Those findings must be sufficient to permit meaningful review. It is insufficient simply for the district court to say that it is not convinced as to the probability of the patentee prevailing on the merits when it comes to the issue of infringement.[299]

Like a district court opinion, a Board opinion must contain sufficient findings and reasoning to permit meaningful appellate scrutiny. For example, an anticipation analysis must be conducted on a limitation-by-limitation basis, with specific fact findings for each contested limitation and satisfactory explanations for such findings. Claim construction must also be explicit, at least as to any construction disputed by a party. A similar standard will apply to obviousness determinations.[300] Federal Circuit review of PTO decisions is on the record before the PTO. When the Board affirms an examiner's rejection generally, without reviewing a particular ground the examiner relied on, that ground is assumed to be affirmed. Thus, in the absence of express

---

[295]*J.P. Stevens Co. v. Lex Tex Ltd.,* 822 F.2d 1047, 3 USPQ2d 1235 (Fed. Cir. 1987).

[296]*Medtronic, Inc. v. Daig Corp.,* 789 F.2d 903, 229 USPQ 664 (Fed. Cir. 1986). In an obviousness case the rule is not so severe as to require the trial judge to articulate every imaginable combination of prior art teachings. Such would, however, remove all doubt as to whether the trial court properly reviewed the prior art.

[297]*Telectronics Pacing Sys., Inc. v. Ventritex, Inc.,* 982 F.2d 1520, 25 USPQ2d 1196 (Fed. Cir. 1992).

[298]See *Chemlawn Serv. Corp. v. GNC Pumps, Inc.,* 823 F.2d 515, 3 USPQ2d 1313 (Fed. Cir. 1987).

[299]*Pretty Punch Shoppettes, Inc. v. Hauk,* 844 F.2d 782, 6 USPQ2d 1563 (Fed. Cir. 1988). The district court felt that too many issues of fact remained to be determined. But the patentee's expert had testified on infringement and both parties had briefed the issue. The Federal Circuit indicated that it had no basis for evaluating what facts entered into the trial court's infringement analysis, or whether that analysis comported with standards articulated by the Federal Circuit. Thus the denial of a preliminary injunction was vacated and remanded. This case foreshadows a deal of impatience with trial judges who deny injunctions without giving adequate reasons. Since *Pretty Punch,* several preliminary injunctions have been vacated due to inadequate findings of fact. *Conair Group v. Automatik App. GmbH,* 944 F.2d 862, 20 USPQ2d 1067 (Fed. Cir. 1991) (inadequate findings as to doctrine of equivalents); *Nutrition 21 v. United States,* 930 F.2d 867, 18 USPQ2d 1347 (Fed. Cir. 1991) (no findings on inequitable conduct); *Oakley, Inc. v. International Tropic-Cal, Inc.,* 923 F.2d 167, 17 USPQ2d 1401 (Fed. Cir. 1991). See also *Gerber Garment Tech., Inc. v. Lectra Sys., Inc.,* 916 F.2d 683, 16 USPQ2d 1436 (Fed. Cir. 1990).

[300]*Gechter v. Davidson,* 116 F.3d 1454, 43 USPQ2d 1030 (Fed. Cir. 1997).

reversal by the Board, it is appropriate for the reviewing court to consider such a ground.[301]

In a jury case, the presence of special interrogatories or a written opinion by the trial court makes it easier for the court of appeals, but the absence of these aids does not alter the standard of review.[302] Nor is the standard rendered inapplicable by the fact that the trial court adopts a party's proposed findings verbatim, although awareness of that circumstance may increase wariness on review.[303] It is clear that the use of an advisory jury does not free the trial court from its obligation under Rule 52(a).[304]

(c) Remands

A remand, with its accompanying expenditure of additional judicial resources, in a case thought to be completed, is a step not lightly taken. It is a step that should be limited to cases in which further action must be taken by the district court or in which the appellate court has no way open to it to affirm or reverse the district court's action under review.[305] For example, adoption of an incorrect and more difficult burden of proof cannot ordinarily be classified as harmless error.[306]

Normal practice, where a trial judge errs, is to remand to permit reconsideration under the proper legal standard. But where the record is clear and leaves no question as to what the result would be on remand, the appellate court can correct the error.[307] Thus, in an appropriate case a court of appeals may direct that judgment be granted

---

[301]*In re Nielson*, 816 F.2d 1562, 2 USPQ2d 1525 (Fed. Cir. 1987). In the reexamination setting, the court does not review the decision of the PTO to institute a reexamination, but rather it reviews the Board's ultimate decision. *In re Hiniker*, 150 F.3d 1362, 47 USPQ2d 1523 (Fed. Cir. 1998).

[302]*Bio-Rad Labs., Inc. v. Nicolet Inst. Corp.*, 739 F.2d 604, 222 USPQ 654 (Fed. Cir. 1984).

[303]*Hybritech Inc. v. Monoclonal Antibodies, Inc.*, 802 F.2d 1367, 231 USPQ 81 (Fed. Cir. 1986); *Pentec, Inc. v. Graphic Controls Corp.*, 776 F.2d 309, 227 USPQ 766 (Fed. Cir. 1985). The trial court's opinion came out before the trial testimony was transcribed, and the losing party criticized the opinion because it contained language similar to that in the winning party's brief. However, the Federal Circuit indicated that the testimony, when transcribed, supported the judge's findings. *Durango Assoc., Inc. v. Reflange, Inc.*, 843 F.2d 1349, 6 USPQ2d 1290 (Fed. Cir. 1988).

[304]*Transmatic, Inc. v. Gulton Indus., Inc.*, 53 F.3d 1270, 35 USPQ2d 1035 (Fed. Cir. 1995).

[305]*Consolidated Alum Corp. v. Foseco Int'l Ltd.*, 910 F.2d 804, 15 USPQ2d 1481 (Fed. Cir. 1990).

[306]*Price v. Symsek*, 988 F.2d 1187, 26 USPQ2d 1031 (Fed. Cir. 1993).

[307]*Baginsky v. United States*, 697 F.2d 1070 (Fed. Cir. 1983). Where it was clear that the infringer had plagiarized the patented invention, it was unnecessary to remand for a finding of egregious conduct sufficient to defeat a laches defense. *Bott v. Four Star Corp.*, 807 F.2d 1567, 1 USPQ2d 1210 (Fed. Cir. 1986). However, where there was doubt as to whether the district court intended to double or treble damages, a remand was the proper procedure. *Id.* Although it is always error to exclude evidence of secondary indicators of nonobviousness, it was harmless error for the district court, once having admitted the evidence and made findings, to fail to consider the impact of the indicators; the Federal Circuit was able to do that and avoid a wasteful remand. *Stratoflex, Inc. v. Aeroquip Corp.*, 713 F.2d 1530, 218 USPQ 871 (Fed.

against an appellee without permitting the appellee to seek a new trial from the district court. But the fact that the appellate court has the power to foreclose further proceedings in the district court does not imply that its judgments have that effect even when the court does not so direct. Only where the court is able to make an informed judgment based on the record before it would a decision by the court of appeals directing the entry of final judgment serve the purpose of Rule 50 to speed litigation and to avoid unnecessary retrials. And only where the burden on the appellee to raise its new trial issues before the appellate court is small will that be required. An appellee cannot be expected to preserve all issues that might conceivably give rise to a motion for a new trial, including those issues unrelated to the subject of the appeal. In a case that turns on claim construction, for example, a contrary rule would require an appellee to anticipate every possible claim construction that the appellate court might adopt and put forth grounds for a new trial under each possible claim construction.[308]

On the other hand, where relief such as prejudgment interest must be awarded absent some justification for withholding it, and the trial judge refuses the award but makes no determination as to justification, the case must be remanded.[309] A reviewing court must attempt to discern from the district court's opinion or action the bases, albeit unexpressed, for its findings and conclusions. Such discernment cannot be made from the naked phrase "not appropriate" in connection with attorney fees. Accordingly, a remand was required for an ultimate finding on exceptionality, accompanied by subsidiary findings reflecting the reasons underlying the district court's exercise of its discretion in awarding or denying attorney fees in light of its findings.[310] In like manner, a factual determination resting in part upon

---

Cir. 1983). Similarly, where the PTO Board correctly rejected a claim under 35 U.S.C. §112 but relied upon the wrong subparagraph of that section, it would be wasteful to remand inasmuch as the same result would obtain. *In re Hyatt*, 708 F.2d 712, 218 USPQ 195 (Fed. Cir. 1983).

[308]*Exxon Chem. Patents Inc. v. Lubrizol Corp.*, 137 F.3d 1475, 45 USPQ2d 1865, 1871 (Fed. Cir. 1998).

[309]*Bio-Rad Labs., Inc. v. Nicolet Inst. Corp.*, 739 F.2d 604, 222 USPQ 654 (Fed. Cir. 1984).

[310]*Fromson v. Western Litho Plate & Supp. Co.*, 853 F.2d 1568, 7 USPQ2d 1606 (Fed. Cir. 1988). See also *U.S. Envtl. Prods., Inc. v. Westall*, 911 F.2d 713, 15 USPQ2d 1898 (Fed. Cir. 1990); *Badalamenti v. Dunham's, Inc.*, 896 F.2d 1359, 13 USPQ2d 1967 (Fed. Cir. 1990); *A.B. Chance Co. v. RTE Corp.*, 854 F.2d 1307, 7 USPQ2d 1881 (Fed. Cir. 1988). But see *Consolidated Alum Corp. v. Foseco Int'l Ltd.*, 910 F.2d 804, 15 USPQ2d 1481 (Fed. Cir. 1990), where the court indicated that though findings on exceptionality and reasons underlying discretionary action on attorney fees are helpful to the appellate court, remand should not be a matter of rote in every case in which findings and reason are not expressly set forth. An appellate court need not close its eyes to the record where there is a way clearly open to affirm the district court's action. In *Westvaco Corp. v. International Paper Co.*, 991 F.2d 735, 26 USPQ2d 1353 (Fed. Cir. 1993), the Federal Circuit found that the district court had clearly erred in finding that the infringement was willful and thus its award of increased damages had to be reversed. Although its companion award of attorney fees might nonetheless have been supportable on the record even without willfulness, that award was vacated and remanded. The court seemed to feel that the erroneous willfulness finding might well have tainted the fees award. In *Carroll Touch, Inc. v. Electro Mechanical Sys., Inc.*, 3 F.3d 404, 27 USPQ2d 1836 (Fed. Cir. 1993), the

a misstatement of law is not reversed but simply remanded for further consideration and elaboration in light of the correct law.[311] The court feels that a trial judge is in the best position to determine whether a motion for a new trial meets the requirement of Rule 7, FRCP, that it identify with sufficient particularity the grounds therefor, so as to provide adequate notice. Accordingly, the Federal Circuit will decline to perform that discretionary inquiry in the first instance.[312]

An attempt to stipulate the legal effect of admitted facts will result in a remand. In one case the parties stipulated that if the patent were invalid for lack of enablement, the plaintiff was guilty of violation of §2 of the Sherman Act. The district court found the patent invalid and entered an antitrust judgment, and the plaintiff appealed the invalidity ruling. The court refused to decide the question and remanded for findings on elements of the antitrust violation. Although the parties are free to stipulate any facts they wish, any attempted stipulation as to the legal conclusion of antitrust violation might result in the court rendering an advisory opinion on the underlying enablement question.[313]

Obviousness cases. In obviousness cases, the need for express *Graham v. Deere* findings[314] takes on an especially significant role because of an occasional tendency of district courts to depart from the *Graham* test. The reviewing court must be convinced from the opinion that the trial court actually applied *Graham* and must be presented with enough express and necessarily implied findings to know the basis of the trial court's opinion.[315] Where a faulty analysis is used below, the case can be remanded for the district court to

---

victorious accused infringer argued that a remand was required because the district court had made no factual findings on exceptionality. The Federal Circuit disagreed, distinguishing its decisions in *Fromson* and *Badalamenti* on the ground that the record in the present case provided a sufficient basis upon which to review the trial court's exercise of discretion in denying attorney fees.

[311]*Bayer Aktiengesellschaft v. Duphar Int'l Research B.V.*, 738 F.2d 1237, 222 USPQ 649 (Fed. Cir. 1984). The magistrate made a determination that the suit was frivolous, but in so doing made an erroneous statement concerning the law of prosecution history estoppel. On remand, the magistrate could reconfirm his determination if it could be supported with other nonerroneous reasons.

[312]*Registration Control Sys., Inc. v. Compusystems, Inc.*, 922 F.2d 805, 17 USPQ2d 1212 (Fed. Cir. 1990).

[313]*Technicon Instr. Corp. v. Alpkem Corp.*, 866 F.2d 417, 9 USPQ2d 1540 (Fed. Cir. 1989).

[314]See §4.2.

[315]*Loctite Corp. v. Ultraseal Ltd.*, 781 F.2d 861, 228 USPQ 90 (Fed. Cir. 1985). See also *Custom Accessories, Inc. v. Jeffrey-Allan Indus., Inc.*, 807 F.2d 955, 1 USPQ2d 1196 (Fed. Cir. 1986). Failure to base an examination of obviousness on the factual findings required by *Graham v. Deere* (see §4.2 above) can require that the case be remanded for those findings to be made. *Specialty Composites v. Cabot Corp.*, 845 F.2d 981, 6 USPQ2d 1601 (Fed. Cir. 1988). Here the district court's discussion of obviousness did not mention *Graham,* but it did make the specific factual findings required for a determination of obviousness. Thus, although it would have been preferable if the court had enumerated the *Graham* factors and systematically presented its analysis in terms of those factors, there was no reversible error. It was clear that the required factual findings were actually made and considered while applying the proper legal standard of obviousness.

determine whether a new trial is necessary; if the parties stipulate to the facts, the district court can decide the legal issues relating to validity.[316] If a district court does not make findings necessary to resolution of the obviousness question and legal error is present, the appellate court would vacate in view of that legal error and remand for the district court to make the missing findings. If unassailable findings were made, but they could not support the judgment under a proper application of law, the appellate court may vacate or reverse but not make its own findings.[317]

The use of an obsolete subtest, such as synergism, does not absolutely require remand, since, as we know, the court reviews judgments not opinions.[318] In one interesting case, the district court held that there was anticipation by one reference, but no obviousness over a combination of other references. The Federal Circuit reversed on anticipation but refused to remand for a determination of obviousness involving the allegedly anticipatory reference.[319] It is clear that the court will not remand to decide unnecessary issues. Thus, where the district court held an independent claim nonobvious, the Federal Circuit naturally reversed, on a fortiori grounds, a holding that a dependent claim was anticipated or obvious. Nonetheless, although the district court had made no determination of infringement as to the dependent claim, no remand was necessary because the Federal Circuit felt that the outcome would have no impact on damages.[320] In many cases, a reversal on claim construction would necessitate a remand to the PTO, but sometimes the court will go ahead and decide the question of patentability based upon the correct claim construction.[321]

Other legal issues. The Federal Circuit will sometimes decide a legal question rather than remand, in the interest of avoiding delay.[322]

---

[316]*Envirotech Corp. v. Al George, Inc.*, 730 F.2d 753, 221 USPQ 473 (Fed. Cir. 1984).

[317]*Panduit Corp. v. Dennison Mfg. Co.*, 810 F.2d 1561, 1 USPQ2d 1593 (Fed. Cir. 1987). But the district court's failure to set forth an explicit explanation as to how a person of ordinary skill in the pertinent art would have combined the prior art in order to arrive at the claimed invention does not require reversal. The Federal Circuit is willing to look for and accept implicit findings of fact in the opinion of the trial court. *Para-Ordnance Mfg. v. SGS Importers Int'l, Inc.*, 73 F.3d 1085, 37 USPQ2d 1237 (Fed. Cir. 1995).

[318]*Chore-Time Equip., Inc. v. Cumberland Corp.*, 713 F.2d 774, 218 USPQ 673 (Fed. Cir. 1983).

[319]*RCA Corp. v. Applied Digital Data Sys., Inc.*, 730 F.2d 1440, 221 USPQ 385 (Fed. Cir. 1984). Perhaps this decision can be explained on grounds of waiver. See §16.3(d).

[320]*Hartness Int'l, Inc. v. Simplimatic Eng'g Co.*, 819 F.2d 1100, 2 USPQ2d 1826 (Fed. Cir. 1987).

[321]*In re Baker Hughes Inc.*, 215 F.3d 1297, 55 USPQ2d 1149 (Fed. Cir. 2).

[322]*DeGeorge v. Bernier*, 768 F.2d 1318, 226 USPQ 758 (Fed. Cir. 1985). For example, in *DuPont Merck Pharm. Co. v. Bristol-Meyers Squibb Co.*, 62 F.3d 1397, 35 USPQ2d 1718 (Fed. Cir. 1995), the court was confronted with the impact and relationship of the patent term extension provision of the Uruguay Round Agreements Act on and to the ANDA procedure for FDA approval under 35 U.S.C. §217(e)(1). After deciding that there was subject matter jurisdiction over a declaratory judgment action seeking to resolve those questions (and reversing the district court's dismissal on jurisdictional grounds), the court went on to decide the ultimate

Although the court may decide a legal issue not resolved below where the pertinent facts are undisputed, such a procedure is an aberration and limited to issues upon which the answer is clear. For the court to decide the parties' unadjudicated and unpresented issues would be unfair to the district court, the judicial process, and the parties themselves. An appellate court can hardly hold, for example, that the district court did or did not err in resolving issues it did not resolve and those it had no opportunity to resolve.[323] Where litigation has been protracted, it will sometimes pretermit the question of the district court's authority to take particular action and review the merits of the action or refusal to act, in order to expedite a final resolution of the case.[324] The court does not hesitate to provide guidance where appropriate. Thus, in reversing summary judgment it will often rule on legal errors where those issues will be raised at trial.[325]

The court is not disposed to ignore what it can observe with its own eyes and determine with its own hands, simply for want of some expert to testify about it or some affiant to put the obvious down on paper over his or her notarized signature. A sample is a potent witness. Although the court does not decide fact issues de novo, there is no issue where the matter can be plainly seen by inspection. In such situations, the interests of judicial economy and avoidance of undue burden on the parties militate against a remand, and the court will find the necessary fact.[326]

It is allowable to reason back from a judgment to the basis on which it stands, upon the principle that where a conclusion is indisputable and could have been drawn only from certain premises, the premises are equally indisputable with the conclusion. Thus, a request for a remand on the ground that the court below never decided whether an infringement charge was frivolous (and therefore a basis for an unfair competition claim) was denied where the court below did refuse a request for attorney fees that was based upon the identical assertion that the infringement charge was frivolous.[327] When the pertinent facts related to inequitable conduct are undisputed, the court of appeals need not remand for the trial court to make findings and conclusions but may resolve the issue.[328] In one case a plaintiff simply took the incorrect position that preclusion issues could not be

---

issues, which were fully briefed to the district court. It is no doubt significant that the appeal had been expedited.

[323]*Black & Decker, Inc. v. Hoover Serv. Ctr.*, 886 F.2d 1285, 12 USPQ2d 1250 (Fed. Cir. 1989).

[324]*Smith Int'l, Inc. v. Hughes Tool Co.*, 759 F.2d 1572, 225 USPQ 889 (Fed. Cir. 1985).

[325]*Palumbo v. Don-Joy Co.*, 762 F.2d 969, 226 USPQ 5 (Fed. Cir. 1985).

[326]*In re Benno*, 768 F.2d 1340, 226 USPQ 683 (Fed. Cir. 1985).

[327]*FMC Corp. v. Manitowoc Co.*, 835 F.2d 1411, 5 USPQ2d 1112 (Fed. Cir. 1987).

[328]*Smithkline Diagnostics, Inc. v. Helena Labs. Corp.*, 859 F.2d 878, 8 USPQ2d 1468 (Fed. Cir. 1988). In *Kimberly-Clark Corp. v. Procter & Gamble Distrib. Co.*, 973 F.2d 911, 23 USPQ2d 1921 (Fed. Cir. 1992), the court was willing to review inequitable conduct issues because they were so closely intertwined with the priority and validity issues that were being reviewed under the interfering patents statute, 35 U.S.C. §291.

applied in the appellate setting, and did not seek to supplement the record with evidence showing why res judicata or collateral estoppel should not be imposed. Thus, although those are affirmative defenses and must be pleaded, a remand for that purpose was not necessary.[329]

Effect on later proceedings. Absent contrary instructions, a remand for reconsideration leaves the precise manner of reconsideration—whether on the existing record or with additional testimony or other evidence—to the discretion of the trial court.[330] If in dealing with an issue the Federal Circuit makes rulings or observations that might affect other issues, a remand may well be in order.[331]

In a jury case, the patents were found invalid and the jury did not reach damages, but the trial court had excluded certain damages evidence. The Federal Circuit considered it appropriate to set forth its legal views on the propriety of the exclusion so as to avoid yet a third trial.[332] A reversal of a holding of not invalid as to some claims and a vacation of that holding as to other claims necessitated a vacation of the judgment of infringement as well. However, in the interest of judicial economy the court went on to consider some infringement issues.[333]

A judgment on less than all dispositive issues can be inefficient, requiring another long proceeding. For this reason, a district court should decide validity and infringement and enter a judgment on both issues when both are raised. Where a district judge indicates there is infringement, but makes no finding and enters no judgment on that issue, the case must be remanded for him or her to decide whether the record supports such a finding, or whether further trial is necessary.[334] In general, it is not open to a reviewing court to find de novo the facts necessary to support a judgment on grounds other than the one found to be erroneous, however clear those facts may appear and however attractive those grounds may be. A remand is

---

[329]*Dana Corp. v. NOK, Inc.,* 882 F.2d 505, 11 USPQ2d 1883 (Fed. Cir. 1989).

[330]*State Indus., Inc. v. Mor-Flo Indus. Inc.,* 948 F.2d 1573, 20 USPQ2d 1738 (Fed. Cir. 1991). Findings that are vacated or otherwise not left undisturbed are not law of the case in later proceedings. *Id.*

[331]Improper claim interpretation requires a remand for redetermination of obviousness. *E.I. duPont & Co. v. Phillips Petroleum Co.,* 849 F.2d 1430, 7 USPQ2d 1129 (Fed. Cir. 1988). In *Burlington Indus., Inc. v. Dayco Corp.,* 849 F.2d 1418, 7 USPQ2d 1158 (Fed. Cir. 1988), the district court granted summary judgment of unenforceability but denied summary judgment of obviousness and noninfringement. The patentee appealed, but the moving defendant did not. The Federal Circuit vacated the unenforceability judgment and remanded, remarking that the district court might, by what was said on the inequitable conduct issue, change its opinions as to what the patent means, which might, in turn, bear on the obviousness and noninfringement issues. The trial court was therefore free to reconsider its conclusions on all the issues it had previously passed upon.

[332]*Trans-World Mfg. Corp. v. Al Nyman & Sons,* 750 F.2d 1552, 224 USPQ 259 (Fed. Cir. 1984).

[333]*E.I. duPont & Co. v. Phillips Petroleum Co.,* 849 F.2d 1430, 7 USPQ2d 1129 (Fed. Cir. 1988).

[334]*Lindemann Maschinenfabrik v. American Hoist & Derrick Co.,* 730 F.2d 1452, 221 USPQ 481 (Fed. Cir. 1984).

necessary.[335] But the court expects the parties to do what they can to avoid remands. The court refused to rule on a winning patentee's request for an injunction (which the district court had apparently ignored), on the ground that it was for the district court in the first instance to determine whether an injunction was warranted. However, the court did comment that a motion to amend or alter the judgment under Rule 59(e), FRCP, while not required, would have made the remanded issues reviewable and avoided the imposition of a return visit to a busy district court.[336] Also, Rule 52(b) provides for postjudgment motions for findings not made. Counsel should not simply ignore that rule and head off to the appellate court to seek a remand for the making of those same findings.[337]

The court has refused to consider new prior art[338] or to decide infringement[339] in the first instance. The court is sending mixed signals concerning the length of its reach to decide infringement issues in the first instance. In *Exxon v. Lubrizol*,[340] after deciding that the trial judge had used an improper claim interpretation in instructing the jury, the court went on to inquire whether, under the proper claim interpretation, the evidence was such that a reasonable jury could have found literal infringement. In other cases, the court has continued to employ the more traditional approach of remanding undecided infringement questions.[341]

---

[335]*International Medical Pros. v. Gore Ent. Holdings, Inc.,* 787 F.2d 572, 229 USPQ 278 (Fed. Cir. 1986).

[336]*Nickson Indus., Inc. v. Rol Mfg. Co.,* 847 F.2d 795, 6 USPQ2d 1878 (Fed. Cir. 1988). Requiring a party to play by the rules cannot be equated with the substantial injustice that may under other circumstances warrant remand for a new trial. Indeed, a remand subjecting a party to another trial at the behest of an adversary who failed to comply with the rules may itself be an injustice to the former. *Snellman v. Ricoh Co.,* 836 F.2d 528, 5 USPQ2d 1341 (Fed. Cir. 1987).

[337]*Consolidated Alum Corp. v. Foseco Int'l Ltd.,* 910 F.2d 804, 15 USPQ2d 1481 (Fed. Cir. 1990).

[338]*Underwater Devices, Inc. v. Morrison-Knudsen Co.,* 717 F.2d 1380, 219 USPQ 569 (Fed. Cir. 1983). But see *Mehl/Biophile Int'l Corp. v. Milgraum,* 192 F.3d 1365, 52 USPQ2d 1303 (Fed. Cir. 1999), where the district court found anticipation by one reference and did not consider another in its anticipation analysis. The Federal Circuit disagreed as to the first reference but went on to find that the second reference did anticipate.

[339]*W.L. Gore & Assoc. v. Garlock, Inc.,* 721 F.2d 1540, 220 USPQ 303 (Fed. Cir. 1983).

[340]*Exxon Chem. Patents, Inc. v. Lubrizol Corp.,* 64 F.3d 1553, 35 USPQ2d 1801 (Fed. Cir. 1995). See also *CVI/Beta Ventures, Inc. v. Tura LP,* 112 F.3d 1146, 42 USPQ2d 1577 (Fed. Cir. 1997).

[341]See *Lantech, Inc. v. Keip Mach. Co.,* 32 F.3d 542, 31 USPQ2d 1666 (Fed. Cir. 1994) (where the district court decides only literal infringement and the Federal Circuit reverses, it will not go on to decide infringement under the doctrine of equivalents); *Tone Bros., Inc. v. Sysco Corp.,* 28 F.3d 1192, 31 USPQ2d 1321 (Fed. Cir. 1994) (where the district court denies a motion for summary judgment of noninfringement of a design patent because of presence of disputed issues of material fact, the Federal Circuit will not consider this alternative ground in support of the judgment). But see *Pall Corp. v. Hemasure Inc.,* 181 F.3d 1305, 50 USPQ2d 1947 (Fed. Cir. 1999) (where district court found literal infringement and did not decide equivalents, and the literal infringement judgment was reversed on appeal, the court went on to find no infringement under the doctrine of equivalents as well). In *Graco, Inc. v. Binks Mfg. Co.,* 60 F.3d 785, 35 USPQ2d 1255 (Fed. Cir. 1995), the district court opinion was devoid of any discussion of claim construction and simply stated a conclusory finding of no infringement.

Where the patentee fails to show causation and can point to no evidence that warrants a remand for reconsideration of a lost profits award, the court will remand for a determination of a reasonable royalty.[342] In a contempt proceeding, where the court reverses a finding of noninfringement, it nonetheless must remand to enable the district court to exercise its discretion as to whether contempt has occurred.[343] And where the defendant argued alternative grounds for dismissal, but the trial court based the dismissal on one ground only, it would be improper to argue on appeal the other ground; affirmance on such an alternative ground is appropriate only when affirmance does not require fact finding.[344]

In some cases the court truly has no choice. For example, a remand may be required in view of an intervening Supreme Court decision.[345] Where an order granting an injunction and a recital of the specific prohibitions enjoined against were set forth in separate documents, in violation of Rule 65(d), FRCP, this defect alone would require vacating and remanding the injunctive order for compliance as to form and specificity.[346] Where a district court denied a motion for a preliminary injunction two days after the Multidistrict Litigation Panel had transferred the case to another district, the Federal Circuit

---

The Federal Circuit held meaningful review was impossible and remanded. Thus, in most cases, upon detecting an error in claim interpretation, the court will remand for a finding on infringement. However, where the parties do not dispute the technical functioning of the accused device and application of the interpreted claims to the accused device does not create further disputes, it may proceed to analyze infringement. *Wiener v. NEC Elec., Inc.*, 102 F.3d 534, 41 USPQ2d 1023 (Fed. Cir. 1996). In *Arbek Mfg., Inc. v. Moazzam*, 55 F.3d 1567, 34 USPQ2d 1670 (Fed. Cir. 1995), the trial court made a finding that a modified device did not infringe in the context of a contempt proceeding. The Federal Circuit equated this finding with a "fair ground for doubt" and concluded that the trial court had detected "substantial open infringement issues." It then looked at the infringement issue on the merits and concluded that there was substantial evidence to support the finding of no infringement, which necessitated affirmance of the trial court's denial of the contempt motion. Nonetheless, it vacated and remanded the noninfringement finding as premature. The logic of this case, though complex, seems correct.

[342]*Water Techs. Corp. v. Calco, Ltd.*, 850 F.2d 660, 7 USPQ2d 1097 (Fed. Cir. 1988). In *Zygo Corp. v. Wyko Corp.*, 79 F.3d 1563, 38 USPQ2d 1281 (Fed. Cir. 1996), the court felt that the district court had failed to make adequate findings on the issue of acceptable noninfringing alternatives; it therefore remanded.

[343]*Laitram Corp. v. Cambridge Wire Cloth Co.*, 863 F.2d 855, 9 USPQ2d 1289 (Fed. Cir. 1988).

[344]*International Medical Pros. v. Gore Ent. Holdings, Inc.*, 787 F.2d 572, 229 USPQ 278 (Fed. Cir. 1986). In *Chemlawn Serv. Corp. v. GNC Pumps, Inc.*, 823 F.2d 515, 3 USPQ2d 1313 (Fed. Cir. 1987), the court apparently felt that Fifth Circuit law demanded a remand even where the failure to make appropriate findings was technical. The district court had ordered a preliminary injunction but did not issue supporting findings and conclusions until after the notice of appeal had been filed. The Federal Circuit concluded that (1) this was not one of those unusual cases where effective review on the merits was possible without the aid of findings and conclusions, and (2) the filing of the notice of appeal ousted the district court of jurisdiction to proceed with any matters involved in the appeal. Thus the belated findings and conclusions were "illegitimate," and it would be improper to accept and rely upon them since it might encourage other district courts to circumvent the requirements of Rule 52(a), FRCP.

[345]*Braun Inc. v. Dynamics Corp.*, 975 F.2d 815, 24 USPQ2d 1121 (Fed. Cir. 1992).

[346]*Joy Techs., Inc. v. Flakt, Inc.*, 6 F.3d 770, 28 USPQ2d 1378 (Fed. Cir. 1993). Nonetheless, the court went ahead and decided the underlying issues that were the main focus of the appeal.

could not decide the appeal on the merits, but was obliged to vacate and remand.[347] Where a case becomes moot while on appeal, the proper disposition is to vacate the judgment and remand with instructions to dismiss the complaint; it is not proper simply to dismiss the appeal.[348] For example, where there is no claim for damages and the patent expires during the pendency of the appeal, the plaintiff is no longer entitled to an injunction and a judgment dealing with the patent's validity is moot; the judgment is therefore vacated and the case remanded for dismissal of the infringement claim.[349]

An issue such as inequitable conduct may be relevant to more than one aspect of a case, thus requiring a remand for decision below.[350] In one case the district court found that the infringement was not willful, based upon advice of counsel. The Federal Circuit remanded to resolve what it perceived as an inconsistency between this finding and a finding of near copying.[351]

In some cases, the court may be without power to remand. For example, its lack of supervisory authority over district courts precludes a remand for reassignment to another judge on grounds of bias.[352]

In unusual cases the court will sometimes reach out to decide matters that ordinarily might be thought to be more suitable for initial decision by the lower courts.[353]

---

[347]*Glasstech, Inc. v. AB Kyro OY,* 769 F.2d 1574, 226 USPQ 949 (Fed. Cir. 1985). See also *Power Controls Corp. v. Hybrinetics, Inc.,* 806 F.2d 234, 231 USPQ 774 (Fed. Cir. 1986). In view of the fact that, under Ninth Circuit law, the district court lacked jurisdiction to modify its findings of fact and conclusions of law after a notice of appeal had been filed, the Federal Circuit could not review the modifications. However, it would have been a waste to remand without deciding anything, so the court did review the unmodified provisions of judgment as it stood at the time the appeal was filed. *Id.*

[348]*Gibralter Indus., Inc. v. United States,* 726 F.2d 747 (Fed. Cir. 1984). The subject of mootness is treated in §16.3(h).

[349]*Texas Instr., Inc. v. United States ITC,* 851 F.2d 342, 7 USPQ2d 1509 (Fed. Cir. 1988); *Kinzenbaw v. Deere & Co.,* 741 F.2d 383, 222 USPQ 929 (Fed. Cir. 1984).

[350]*Dana Corp. v. NOK, Inc.,* 882 F.2d 505, 11 USPQ2d 1883 (Fed. Cir. 1989). The court found the patent invalid on appeal and thus did not need to decide unenforceability. However, the same alleged inequitable conduct was relevant to a demand for attorney fees and a remand was necessary.

[351]*State Indus., Inc. v. Mor-Flo Indus. Inc.,* 883 F.2d 1573, 12 USPQ2d 1026 (Fed. Cir. 1989). With all respect, it appeared that the district court had done all it could to resolve the conflict and had come out on the side of nonwillfulness. On remand the district court again found no willfulness and the patentee appealed. This time around the Federal Circuit made it clear that its vacation of the previous findings had left the district court perfectly free to exercise its discretion; indeed, it found the patentee's appeal to be frivolous "given the difficulty of showing reversible error in discretionary rulings." *State Indus., Inc. v. Mor-Flo Indus. Inc.,* 948 F.2d 1573, 20 USPQ2d 1738 (Fed. Cir. 1991).

[352]*Petersen Mfg. Co. v. Central Purchasing, Inc.,* 740 F.2d 1541, 222 USPQ 562 (Fed. Cir. 1984).

[353]In *Mars, Inc. v. Kabushiki-Kaisha Nippon Conlux,* 24 F.3d 1368, 30 USPQ2d 1621 (Fed. Cir. 1994), the plaintiff had indicated that, if the Federal Circuit affirmed dismissal of its federal question claim (for infringement of a Japanese patent) on jurisdictional grounds, it would amend its complaint to plead diversity and assert the claim in that way. The defendant responded that it would, in that event, assert forum non conveniens as a ground for dismissal. The Federal Circuit, after dismissing the claim on jurisdictional grounds, went on to address

Tribunal or proceeding. The special nature of the proceedings below may affect the decision to remand. In appeals from decisions of the PTO Board, the PTO cannot raise a new ground of rejection or apply a new rationale to support a rejection. But the court cannot simply ignore the substance of the PTO's argument. The proper procedure would be to remand to afford the applicant an opportunity to produce evidence to counter the new argument. It would be unfair not to give the applicant this chance, for had the Board or examiner objected below, the applicant would have had the opportunity for compliance. If the PTO wishes to complain about lack of evidence, the complaint should be made while the applicant has a chance to do something about it, or there will be a remand.[354] Similarly, where the PTO Board improperly fails to consider certain evidence, a remand is in order.[355]

The Federal Circuit encourages remand motions where the parties agree that remand is desirable, or intervening law may warrant a remand, or the Board may wish to accede to some of the appellant's demands, or other circumstances are present that indicate a remand is appropriate. But remands to the PTO Board are not automatically granted absent such circumstances. Where the appellant had already expended the time, money, and effort to file its brief, a PTO motion to remand so that the Board could reevaluate the bases of its decision was denied.[356] The court has also rejected the proposition that the Board must be given an opportunity to reconsider a new ground of rejection prior to appeal.[357]

In a jury case, reversal is not available to the appellant who merely establishes error in instructions or other procedures employed at trial. If the error could have prejudicially affected the verdict, the appellate court may only vacate the judgment and remand for a new trial, because it cannot be said what the verdict would have been with proper instructions or procedure. And where the error was harmless—where the evidence was such that the same verdict necessarily would have been reached—affirmance is required since a remand for a new trial would be a waste. As a result, it is difficult to conceive of a procedural error so grave that reversal of a judgment on a jury verdict would be warranted.[358] In a best mode case, the court found that the

---

forum non conveniens "in the interest of judicial economy," concluding that "any attempt to replead jurisdiction based on diversity of citizenship at this point would seem ill-founded."

[354]*In re De Blauwe,* 736 F.2d 699, 222 USPQ 191 (Fed. Cir. 1984).

[355]*In re Margolis,* 785 F.2d 1029, 228 USPQ 940 (Fed. Cir. 1986).

[356]*In re Hester,* 838 F.2d 1193, 5 USPQ2d 1832 (Fed. Cir. 1988).

[357]*In re Evanega,* 829 F.2d 1110, 4 USPQ2d 1249 (Fed. Cir. 1987). The court distinguished a line of Supreme Court cases holding that an agency tribunal must have an opportunity to consider procedural deficiencies prior to an appeal to a court. Here the issue in question was substantive and had been raised by the PTO Board sua sponte.

[358]*Weinar v. Rollform Inc.,* 744 F.2d 797, 223 USPQ 369 (Fed. Cir. 1984). There is a judicial preference in favor of granting JNOV over a directed verdict. The rationale behind the preference is the effect of an appellate court's reversal of a judgment in each situation. With a directed verdict, the entire case must be retried if the judgment is overturned, while with a

district judge had applied the wrong legal standard. Rather than remand, however, it went on to decide the issue, because it felt that there were sufficient established facts of record to enable it to exercise its discretion to determine the merits of the JNOV motion that the trial court had denied on that incorrect legal standard.[359]

In an ITC case, the Commission expressly neither affirmed nor reversed the administrative law judge on infringement. Thus, the Federal Circuit was unable to review on the merits the question of injury. Although there may be circumstances wherein no injury will be shown even if all doubt as to infringement is resolved in favor of the complainant, here the determination of which goods were covered by the patent claims was essential to the ensuing determination of injury. The matter had to be remanded. The court took the opportunity to comment that the Commission's failure to resolve the infringement issue inhibited expeditious resolution of the matters before the ITC.[360] Where a determination of injury was based upon two valid patents, and the Federal Circuit held one invalid on appeal, a remand was appropriate for another determination of injury based only on the single valid patent.[361]

On the other hand, where the Federal Circuit affirms an ITC finding of no injury, it will vacate findings on patent issues as moot.[362] Inasmuch as the ITC can issue orders barring only future conduct, the expiration of a patent pending appeal of an ITC finding of unenforceability of the patent moots the appeal.[363] It has been said that the Federal Circuit does not sit to review that which the ITC has not decided. But where the ITC affirms the administrative law judge's conclusion that there has been a violation, and neither rejects any part of it nor indicates that it is taking no position on any part of it, all findings of the ALJ necessary for a conclusion of a violation are reviewable.[364]

The mandate rule. Upon return of the mandate, the district court cannot give relief beyond the scope of that mandate, but it may act on matters left open by the mandate. The mandate must be strictly

---

JNOV, the jury verdict can be entered as the judgment should the appellate court reverse. Thus, it is in the interest of efficient judicial administration for a court to withhold ruling on a motion for directed verdict in favor of deciding a motion for JNOV. *Jamesbury Corp. v. Litton Indus. Prods., Inc.* 839 F.2d 1544, 5 USPQ2d 1779 (Fed. Cir. 1988).

[359]*Dana Corp. v. IPC Ltd.,* 860 F.2d 415, 8 USPQ2d 1692 (Fed. Cir. 1988). In the context of this case, this required that the court determine as a matter of law that, upon the evidence presented at trial, reasonable minds could not have found that the best mode requirement was satisfied.

[360]*Lannom Mfg. Co. v. United States ITC,* 799 F.2d 1572, 231 USPQ 32 (Fed. Cir. 1986).

[361]*Aktiebolaget Karlstads v. United States ITC,* 705 F.2d 1565, 217 USPQ 865 (Fed. Cir. 1983).

[362]*Fischer & Porter Co. v. United States ITC,* 831 F.2d 1574, 4 USPQ2d 1700 (Fed. Cir. 1987); *Corning Glass Works v. United States ITC,* 799 F.2d 1559, 230 USPQ 822 (Fed. Cir. 1986).

[363]*Texas Instr., Inc. v. United States ITC,* 851 F.2d 342, 7 USPQ2d 1509 (Fed. Cir. 1988). See §16.3(h).

[364]*Akzo N.V. v. United States ITC,* 808 F.2d 1471, 1 USPQ2d 1241 (Fed. Cir. 1986).

obeyed and the district court's actions on remand should not be inconsistent with either the letter or the spirit of the mandate. Indeed, issues decided implicitly by the court of appeals may not be reexamined by the district court, although this rule applies only to those issues decided by necessary implication.[365] Nonetheless, while a mandate is controlling as to matters within its compass, on remand a lower court is free as to other issues.[366]

Interpretation of an appellate mandate[367] entails more than examining the language of the court's judgment in a vacuum. As an initial matter, every appellate court judgment vests jurisdiction in the district court to carry out some further proceedings. In some cases, those further proceedings may be purely ministerial, as when a judgment for the plaintiff is reversed and the only matters that remain for the district court are to dismiss the complaint and enter the judgment in the docket. Frequently, however, the disposition of a case in the court of appeals will require the district court to undertake more significant proceedings. In either case, the nature of the district court's remaining tasks is discerned not simply from the language of the judgment, but from the judgment in combination with the accompanying opinion. Thus, the single word "reversed" does not forbid the district court to take any action that is consistent with the appellate mandate, as informed by both the formal judgment issued by the court and the court's written opinion.[368] Where the court does

---

[365]*Laitram Corp. v. NEC Corp.,* 115 F.3d 947, 42 USPQ2d 1897 (Fed. Cir. 1997). Under the mandate rule, a district court is without choice in obeying the mandate of an appellate court. The rule is compulsory. The fact that a different court of appeals (here the Federal Circuit) from that issuing the mandate (here the Seventh Circuit) may ultimately get the next appeal does not change the mandate rule. *In re Roberts,* 846 F.2d 1360, 6 USPQ2d 1772 (Fed. Cir. 1988). An inferior court is without power or authority to deviate from the mandate issued by an appellate court. The rule is equally applicable to the duty of an administrative agency, such as the PTO Board, to comply with the mandate issued by a reviewing court. *In re Wella A.G.,* 858 F.2d 725, 8 USPQ2d 1365 (Fed. Cir. 1988). It is doubtful whether a district court would have authority to dissolve a preliminary injunction that it had entered, not in the exercise of its own discretion, but in compliance with an earlier appellate court mandate. *Smith Int'l, Inc. v. Hughes Tool Co.,* 759 F.2d 1572, 225 USPQ 889 (Fed. Cir. 1985).

[366]*Exxon Corp. v. United States,* 931 F.2d 874 (Fed. Cir. 1991). In *Laitram Corp. v. NEC Corp.,* 115 F.3d 947, 42 USPQ2d 1897 (Fed. Cir. 1997), the district court had granted JMOL of noninfringement and denied other JMOL motions as moot. On appeal the noninfringement JMOL was reversed and the case remanded with instructions to reinstate the jury verdict. The court ultimately held that its mandate did not preclude consideration and decision on the other motions.

[367]The court reviews the interpretation of its own mandate de novo. *Odetics Inc. v. Storage Tech. Corp.,* 185 F.3d 1259, 51 USPQ2d 1225 (Fed. Cir. 1999); *Engel Indus. Inc. v. Lockformer Co.,* 166 F.3d 1379, 49 USPQ2d 1618 (Fed. Cir. 1999).

[368]*Exxon Chem. Patents Inc. v. Lubrizol Corp.,* 137 F.3d 1475, 45 USPQ2d 1865 (Fed. Cir. 1998). In the trial court the patentee obtained a favorable claim construction and withdrew its proposed jury instructions on infringement by equivalents. On appeal, the Federal Circuit reversed that claim construction. On remand, the trial court denied the patentee's motion for a new trial on infringement by equivalents. The Federal Circuit held that the patentee did not abandon its doctrine of equivalents theory of liability by not submitting it to the jury or raising it on the previous appeal. Once the district judge construed the claim language in the patentee's favor, the doctrine of equivalents issue in the case became moot. It could not realistically be expected to request alternative jury instructions asking for an advisory verdict on whether the patent would be infringed under the doctrine of equivalents using the defendant's proposed

not order a remand on any of the issues presented on appeal, the scope of the mandate, and thus the scope of the matters removed from the district court's jurisdiction, is coterminous with the scope of the issues deemed presented to the court on appeal. The scope of the issues presented to the court on appeal must be measured by the scope of the judgment appealed from, not by the arguments advanced by the appellant. To hold otherwise would allow appellants to present appeals in a piecemeal and repeated fashion, and would lead to the untenable result that a party who has chosen not to argue a point on a first appeal should stand better as regards the law of the case than one who had argued and lost. The responsibility to review the judgments appealed to the court can be properly discharged only if the court assumes that the appellant has fully set forth its attack on the judgment below; only then will the court be able to address with confidence the range of issues determined by the appealed judgment. In other words, the court is entitled to assume that an appellant has raised all issues it deems important against a judgment appealed from. An issue that falls within the scope of the judgment appealed from but is not raised by the appellant in its opening brief on appeal is necessarily waived. Unless remanded by the court, all issues within the scope of the appealed judgment are deemed incorporated within the mandate and thus are precluded from further adjudication. Of course, the court must remain mindful that the interpretation of the scope of a court's mandate may be uncertain; both the letter and the spirit of the mandate must be considered. A judgment that does not specifically provide for a remand speaks only to the issues incorporated in the mandate; it is not necessarily incompatible with further proceedings to be undertaken in the district court. Only the issues actually decided—those within the scope of the judgment appealed from, minus those explicitly reserved or remanded by the court—are foreclosed from further consideration.[369]

(d) Waivers

The issues resolved by a trial court are defined by the facts in the case and the law applied; they are not necessarily limited to those briefed by the parties on appeal.[370] In general, an appellate court will only review a lower court's decision in light of the grounds and theories advanced below and will not consider a new argument raised for the first time on appeal.[371] A party cannot change horses; it would simply

---

claim construction. Nor could it, as appellee, have been expected to defend the judgment in its favor on the basis of a theory of liability that was never given to the jury. *Id.*

[369]*Engel Indus. Inc. v. Lockformer Co.,* 166 F.3d 1379, 49 USPQ2d 1618 (Fed. Cir. 1999).
[370]*Zenith Radio Corp. v. United States,* 783 F.2d 184 (Fed. Cir. 1986).
[371]*Bayer Aktiengesellschaft v. Duphar Int'l Research B.V.,* 738 F.2d 1237, 222 USPQ 649 (Fed. Cir. 1984).

be unfair to rerun the race.[372] An appellate court will consider an issue not presented below only if: (1) the issue involves a pure question of law and refusal to consider it would result in a miscarriage of justice; (2) the proper resolution is beyond any doubt; (3) the appellant had no opportunity to raise the objection at the district court level; (4) the issue presents significant questions of general impact or of great public concern; or (5) the interest of substantial justice is at stake.[373] However, as a general proposition, an appellate court may affirm a judgment of a district court on any ground the law and the record will support so long as that ground would not expand the relief granted. If the grounds urged in support of the judgment have not been presented to and passed upon by the trial court, an appellate court may prefer not to address them in the first instance. If, however, the ground urged is one of law, and that issue has been fully vetted by the parties on appeal, an appellate court may choose to decide the issue even if not passed on by the trial court.[374]

Nonetheless, the court will not normally consider issues that were not presented in the district court.[375] The failure of the record on appeal to make reference to an issue strongly suggests that it was not raised below and therefore could not be argued on appeal.[376] Indeed, the failure to designate a specific portion of a judgment in a notice of appeal precludes the court from considering issues relating thereto.[377] Normally an issue not raised by an appellant in its opening brief is waived, although that practice may as a matter of discretion not be adhered to where circumstances indicate that it would be basically unfair.[378]

---

[372]*Kloster Speedsteel AB v. Crucible Inc.,* 793 F.2d 1565, 230 USPQ 81 (Fed. Cir. 1986).

[373]*L.E.A. Dynatech, Inc. v. Allina,* 49 F.3d 1527, 33 USPQ2d 1839 (Fed. Cir. 1995).

[374]*Glaxo Inc. v. TorPharm Inc.,* 153 F.3d 1366, 47 USPQ2d 1836 (Fed. Cir. 1998). When a matter comes before an appellate court following a summary judgment, the appellate court is free to adopt a ground advanced by the appellee in seeking summary judgment but not adopted by the trial court. Such an approach does not convert an argument advanced by one of the parties into an impermissible interlocutory appeal of the denial of a summary judgment. *Id.*

[375]*Braun Inc. v. Dynamics Corp.,* 975 F.2d 815, 24 USPQ2d 1121 (Fed. Cir. 1992).

[376]*Atlas Powder Co. v. E.I. du Pont & Co.,* 750 F.2d 1569, 224 USPQ 409 (Fed. Cir. 1984).

[377]*Weinar v. Rollform Inc.,* 744 F.2d 797, 223 USPQ 369 (Fed. Cir. 1984).

[378]*Becton Dickinson & Co. v. C.R. Bard, Inc.,* 922 F.2d 792, 17 USPQ2d 1097 (Fed. Cir. 1990). Where an appellant gave an infringement issue only cursory and ambiguous treatment in its opening brief, mentioning it only in a footnote and omitting it from the statement of issues section of the brief, the issue was waived. *Conopco, Inc. v. May Dep't Stores Co.,* 46 F.3d 1556, 32 USPQ2d 1225 (Fed. Cir. 1994). See also *Amhil Enters. Ltd. v. Wawa, Inc.,* 81 F.3d 1554, 38 USPQ2d 1471 (Fed. Cir. 1996), where the appellant waived its right to appeal on the doctrine of equivalents by omitting it in the opening brief and mentioning it only once in the reply brief. In *Wang Labs., Inc. v. Toshiba Corp.,* 993 F.2d 858, 26 USPQ2d 1767 (Fed. Cir. 1993), one appellant raised prosecution history estoppel in its initial brief while the other did not. The court ultimately found estoppel and gave both appellants the benefit of that finding. In *Enercon GmbH v. United States ITC,* 151 F.3d 1376, 47 USPQ2d 1725 (Fed. Cir. 1998), the losing party did not challenge an ITC finding of infringement as an issue on appeal until the very end of its reply brief; this constituted a waiver. See also *Regents of Univ. of Calif. v. Eli Lilly & Co.,* 119 F.3d 1559, 43 USPQ2d 1398 (Fed. Cir. 1997).

Certainly a party who concedes[379] or abandons[380] a point cannot expect to be heard on that question. Invited error cannot be appealed.[381] And by any standard, an argument that is not raised in the district court, or in the appellate briefs, and is mentioned for the first

---

[379]*In re Caveney*, 761 F.2d 671, 226 USPQ 1 (Fed. Cir. 1985). Concessions must be made with care. The patentee conceded in its appeal brief that there was no literal infringement because the devices "lack the required low current and low current density." The patentee went on to argue that although the holding of literal infringement would therefore have to be reversed, the case should be remanded for findings on equivalents. However, the Federal Circuit viewed the concession as broad enough to mean that the accused devices did not perform substantially the same function in substantially the same way. Thus no remand was necessary. *ZMI Corp. v. Cardiac Resuscitator Corp.*, 844 F.2d 1576, 6 USPQ2d 1557 (Fed. Cir. 1988). So too with stipulations. The parties had stipulated in the trial court that four claims would be "representative." On the first appeal, the court made the statement that only the representative claims were considered on appeal. The district court's holding of invalidity was reversed. The defendant interpreted this to mean that the fate of the other, nonrepresentative claims was unresolved, and objected to the district court's judgment, upon remand, that all of the claims were valid. Defendant appealed from that judgment and the Federal Circuit dismissed the appeal as frivolous. Apparently the Federal Circuit felt that defendant's new counsel was attempting to renege on a stipulation that predecessor counsel had made. *Panduit Corp. v. Dennison Mfg. Co.*, 836 F.2d 1329, 5 USPQ2d 1266 (Fed. Cir. 1987). Merely acknowledging that a statement appears in a decision does not bind the party to the legal standard set forth in that statement. *Argus Chem. Corp. v. Fibre Glass-Evercoat Co.*, 759 F.2d 10, 225 USPQ 1100 (Fed. Cir. 1985). In *Snellman v. Ricoh Co.*, 862 F.2d 283, 8 USPQ2d 1996 (Fed. Cir. 1988), the district court granted a motion for a new trial on damages and limited plaintiff's evidence to the point where it was possible only to prove a smaller figure. Rather than go through a pointless trial, the plaintiff agreed to a judgment for the smaller amount. The Federal Circuit held that this was not a waiver, and the entire damages question could be appealed. In *Mendenhall v. Cedarapids, Inc.*, 5 F.3d 1556, 28 USPQ2d 1081 (Fed. Cir. 1993), a party conceded that some claims were invalid and argued that there was no basis for treating other claims differently. It was accordingly precluded from arguing that the other claims were not invalid. See also *Hoover Group, Inc. v. Custom Metalcraft, Inc.*, 66 F.3d 299, 36 USPQ2d 1101 (Fed. Cir. 1995) (waiver of obviousness defense).

[380]*Preemption Devices, Inc. v. Minnesota Min. & Mfg. Co.*, 732 F.2d 903, 221 USPQ 841 (Fed. Cir. 1984). Cf. *Kloster Speedsteel AB v. Crucible Inc.*, 793 F.2d 1565, 230 USPQ 81 (Fed. Cir. 1986). Where dependent claims are not argued separately from independent claims held to be invalid, the dependent claims are invalid as well. *Richardson-Vicks, Inc. v. Upjohn Co.*, 122 F.3d 1476, 44 USPQ2d 1181 (Fed. Cir. 1997). *Environmental Instr., Inc. v. Sutron Corp.*, 877 F.2d 1561, 11 USPQ2d 1132 (Fed. Cir. 1989); *Ryco, Inc. v. Ag-Bag Corp.*, 857 F.2d 1418, 8 USPQ2d 1323 (Fed. Cir. 1988). See also *In re Kemps*, 97 F.3d 1427, 40 USPQ2d 1309 (Fed. Cir. 1996); *In re Grams*, 888 F.2d 835, 12 USPQ2d 1824 (Fed. Cir. 1989).

[381]*Chemical Eng'g Corp. v. Essef Indus., Inc.*, 795 F.2d 1565, 230 USPQ 385 (Fed. Cir. 1986); *Weinar v. Rollform Inc.*, 744 F.2d 797, 223 USPQ 369 (Fed. Cir. 1984). In *Key Pharm. Inc. v. Hercon Labs. Corp.*, 161 F.3d 709, 48 USPQ2d 1911 (Fed. Cir. 1998), the court dealt with an unusual situation, where the appellant was urging that the district court erred in adopting the very claim construction that appellant advanced below. Although the function of an appellate court is to correct errors committed at trial, it viewed with extreme disfavor the appellant's assertion. Ordinarily, doctrines of estoppel, waiver, invited error, or the like would prohibit a party from asserting as error a position that it had advocated at the trial. Allowing parties in a patent suit to assert error in such situations would open the door to mischief and judicial inefficiency. For example, a party could advocate a certain claim construction at trial believing that that claim construction will result in favorable resolution of infringement or validity issues. If the trial court adopts that claim construction but resolves the infringement or validity issues unfavorably, the party could thereafter assert a new claim construction to get the proverbial second bite, possibly necessitating a retrial. The impropriety of asserting a position that the trial court adopts and then complaining about it on appeal should be obvious on its face, and litigants hardly need warning not to engage in such conduct. The court went on to note, however, that in none of its prior opinions had it had occasion to publicly condemn this behavior. Moreover, the appellee did not object to the conduct or seek to invoke estoppel or other preclusive principles. Thus, in an abundance of fairness, and to preclude any argument

time at oral argument, cannot be considered.[382] Under Rule 28(a)(6), FRAP, arguments may not be properly raised by incorporating them by reference from the appendix rather than discussing them in the brief.[383] Rehearing petitions are normally not a suitable vehicle for making new arguments to the appellate court.[384] Likewise, affirmative defenses such as intervening rights[385] or file wrapper estoppel, which should be pleaded, cannot be considered for the first time on appeal.[386]

Simply failing to deal with an issue below can be fatal on appeal. The court does not "review" that which was not presented to the district court.[387] It has refused to consider such questions as fraud,[388] best mode,[389] damages,[390] limitations,[391] motion for directed verdict or JNOV,[392]

---

by the appellant that it was not on notice, it chose instead to independently review the correctness of the trial court's claim construction. In *Becton Dickinson & Co. v. C.R. Bard, Inc.*, 922 F.2d 792, 17 USPQ2d 1097 (Fed. Cir. 1990), the district court found that independent claims 6 and 7, as written, were invalid under 35 U.S.C. §103. It then proceeded, quite improperly, to rewrite them to be dependent on claim 1 and found that, so rewritten, they were valid but not infringed. Both parties agreed this was wrong. On appeal the patentee argued only the issue of noninfringement of claims 1–5, and neither party made any argument concerning infringement or validity of the hypothetical rewritten claims 6 and 7. The Federal Circuit held that the patentee had waived its right to argue the validity of claims 6 and 7. The patentee had, in a motion below, treated the judgment as though it had passed on the validity of those claims. The court felt that this was a "knowing tactical decision" designed to set up for attack the "easy target of a meaningless ruling of noninfringement of hypothetical claims."

[382]*Fromson v. Advance Offset Plate, Inc.*, 720 F.2d 1565, 219 USPQ 1137 (Fed. Cir. 1983).

[383]*Graphic Controls Corp. v. Utah Med. Prods. Inc.*, 149 F.3d 1382, 47 USPQ2d 1622 (Fed. Cir. 1998).

[384]*Exxon Chem. Patents Inc. v. Lubrizol Corp.*, 137 F.3d 1475, 45 USPQ2d 1865 (Fed. Cir. 1998).

[385]*Underwater Devices, Inc. v. Morrison-Knudsen Co.*, 717 F.2d 1380, 219 USPQ 569 (Fed. Cir. 1983).

[386]*Carman Indus., Inc. v. Wahl*, 724 F.2d 932, 220 USPQ 481 (Fed. Cir. 1983).

[387]*Sage Prods., Inc. v. Devon Indus., Inc.*, 126 F.3d 1420, 44 USPQ2d 1103 (Fed. Cir. 1997).

[388]*Laitram Corp. v. Cambridge Wire Cloth Co.*, 785 F.2d 292, 228 USPQ 935 (Fed. Cir. 1986).

[389]*Great Northern Corp. v. Henry Molded Prods., Inc.*, 94 F.3d 1569, 39 USPQ2d 1997 (Fed. Cir. 1996); *CPG Prods. Corp. v. Pegasus Luggage, Inc.*, 776 F.2d 1007, 227 USPQ 497 (Fed. Cir. 1985).

[390]*CPG Prods. Corp. v. Pegasus Luggage, Inc.*, 776 F.2d 1007, 227 USPQ 497 (Fed. Cir. 1985). In *Bic Leisure Prods., Inc. v. Windsurfing Int'l, Inc.*, 1 F.3d 1214, 27 USPQ2d 1671 (Fed. Cir. 1993), the court decided that absolute intervening rights is a damages issue. Thus, the infringer's waiver of an equitable intervening rights defense, and its failure to raise absolute intervening rights during the liability trial, did not result in a consequential waiver of absolute intervening rights, which could be raised during the damages phase of the case.

[391]*Weinar v. Rollform Inc.*, 744 F.2d 797, 223 USPQ 369 (Fed. Cir. 1984).

[392]*Nestier Corp. v. Menasha Corp.*, 739 F.2d 1576, 222 USPQ 747 (Fed. Cir. 1984). But see *Orthokinetics, Inc. v. Safety Travel Chairs, Inc.*, 806 F.2d 1565, 1 USPQ2d 1081 (Fed. Cir. 1986). Such questions can be complicated by the need, in certain instances, to apply regional circuit law. In *Delta-X Corp. v. Baker Hughes Prod. Tools, Inc.*, 984 F.2d 410, 25 USPQ2d 1447 (Fed. Cir. 1993), the defendant had moved for JNOV without first having moved for a directed verdict, in apparent violation of Rule 50, FRCP. The plaintiff did not oppose the JNOV motion until after it was granted, and defendant argued that plaintiff should not be able to raise the Rule 50 challenge for the first time on appeal. The Federal Circuit concluded that, under Fifth Circuit law, it may address an issue for the first time on appeal if the issue concerns a pure question of law or if proper resolution of the issue is beyond doubt. Under that standard, the court found that the grant of JNOV was improper. In *York Prods., Inc. v. Central Tractor Farm & Fam. Ctr.*, 99 F.3d 1568, 40 USPQ2d 1619 (Fed. Cir. 1996), the patentee objected to the trial

claim interpretation,[393] obviousness,[394] new prior art,[395] nonanalogous art,[396] reverse doctrine of equivalents,[397] and other matters[398] that were not raised below. Indeed, merely raising the issue of infringement below does not justify assertion of an argument on appeal that was not specifically asserted below.[399]

The grant of a motion for summary judgment may present special considerations. A party does not waive a specifically pleaded claim for attorney fees under 35 U.S.C. §285 by failing to include it in a motion for summary judgment of invalidity that is granted.[400] Where a party does not respond to a moving party's list of "undisputed facts" with affidavits or other evidence, it cannot upon appeal attack a summary judgment on that basis.[401] Similarly, a litigant's complaint that it needed discovery to respond to a motion for summary judgment will not be heard on appeal when discovery was precluded by its own

---

court's jury instructions with respect to claim interpretation. After reserving its objections and clearly presenting the issues to the trial court, it consented to entry of JMOL to expedite its appeal and conserve resources. The Federal Circuit seemed pleased with this responsible procedure, and held there was no waiver of the right to appeal.

[393]*Sage Prods., Inc. v. Devon Indus., Inc.*, 126 F.3d 1420, 44 USPQ2d 1103 (Fed. Cir. 1997). The court's freedom to review claim construction de novo does not require it to effectively retry claim construction de novo by consideration of novel arguments not first presented to the tribunal whose decision is on review. *Finnigan Corp. v. United States ITC*, 180 F.3d 1354, 51 USPQ2d 1001 (Fed. Cir. 1999).

[394]*RCA Corp. v. Applied Digital Data Sys., Inc.*, 730 F.2d 1440, 221 USPQ 385 (Fed. Cir. 1984). In *Hoover Group, Inc. v. Custom Metalcraft, Inc.*, 66 F.3d 299, 36 USPQ2d 1101 (Fed. Cir. 1995), the defendant stipulated before trial that its patent expert would not testify on obviousness. The principal defense at trial was anticipation, and the district court indicated that the defendant failed to present any testimony supporting obviousness. Despite defendant's arguments that all of the necessary evidence was introduced at trial in the context of anticipation, the Federal Circuit held that the obviousness defense, although pleaded, had been waived and could not be raised on appeal.

[395]*Thomas & Betts Corp. v. Litton Sys., Inc.*, 720 F.2d 1572, 220 USPQ 1 (Fed. Cir. 1983). A party that argues a particular date for an on-sale bar cannot argue an earlier one on appeal. *Sewall v. Walters*, 21 F.3d 411, 30 USPQ2d 1356 (Fed. Cir. 1994).

[396]*In re Schreiber*, 128 F.3d 1473, 44 USPQ2d 1429 (Fed. Cir. 1997).

[397]*Texas Instr., Inc. v. United States ITC*, 988 F.2d 1165, 26 USPQ2d 1018, 1027 (Fed. Cir. 1993).

[398]*Allied Corp. v. United States ITC*, 850 F.2d 1573, 7 USPQ2d 1303 (Fed. Cir. 1988); *Hodosh v. Block Drug. Co.*, 833 F.2d 1575, 4 USPQ2d 1935 (Fed. Cir. 1987); *Brewer v. American Battle Mons. Comm'n*, 779 F.2d 663 (Fed. Cir. 1985); *D.L. Auld Co. v. Chroma Graphics Corp.*, 753 F.2d 1029, 224 USPQ 737 (Fed. Cir. 1985); *Bio-Rad Labs., Inc. v. Nicolet Inst. Corp.*, 739 F.2d 604, 222 USPQ 654 (Fed. Cir. 1984). Questions regarding compliance with due process and with provisions of the Administrative Procedure Act cannot be raised by an amicus where the appellant did not raise them. *In re Alappat*, 33 F.3d 1526, 31 USPQ2d 1545 (Fed. Cir. 1994). In *Pac-Tec, Inc. v. Amerace Corp.*, 903 F.2d 796, 14 USPQ2d 1871 (Fed. Cir. 1990), the court in dictum seemed to indicate that a party may not raise on appeal the argument that an injunction encompasses unadjudicated claims, unless that argument was first presented to the district court. But see *Trell v. Marlee Elec. Corp.*, 912 F.2d 1443, 16 USPQ2d 1059 (Fed. Cir. 1990), where the court indicated that a failure to raise below the issue of knowledge of the patent (in the context of contributory infringement occurring prior to knowledge) does not bar consideration of it for the first time on appeal.

[399]*Personalized Media Comm. LLC v. United States ITC*, 161 F.3d 696, 48 USPQ2d 1880 (Fed. Cir. 1998).

[400]*Brasseler U.S.A. v. Stryker Sales Corp.*, 182 F.3d 888, 51 USPQ2d 1470 (Fed. Cir. 1999).

[401]*Jamesbury Corp. v. Litton Indus. Prods., Inc.*, 839 F.2d 1544, 5 USPQ2d 1779 (Fed. Cir. 1988).

failure to seek protection under Rule 56(f), FRCP.[402] As the court points out, it is not among the purposes of the appellate process to rewrite the scenario produced by an appellant at trial. Nor is it among the roles of the court to entertain such efforts at rewriting.[403] An appeal is not a means for counsel to cure mistakes and omissions made at trial; judgments rendered after trial are based on what transpired at trial.[404] As the court put it in characteristic pithy language:

> this is another bizarre appeal in which this court is asked to undo the tangles, twists, and turns created by appellant's counsel in the proceedings before the trial court. When a witch's brew has been stirred in the crucible of litigation, it is not the role of this court to strain the concoction for chestnuts left to burn through vincible ignorance of the law. Nor is it our role to conduct a review de novo of rulings on motions or to order entry of judgments on issues never presented to the jury or to the trial court.[405]

On appeal, litigants cannot expect to be heard for the first time on objections that could and should have been raised in the trial court as to the conduct of the trial.[406] The propriety of record evidence to which a party did not timely object is effectively beyond appellate review.[407] Where an appellant failed to oppose the appellee's motion to dismiss in the trial court, it waived its right to contest the dismissal on any ground it could have raised below.[408] Where a party fails to object to instructions before the jury retires, it is precluded from assigning them as error on appeal. This rule was designed to avoid the heads-or-tails ploy by which counsel stands mute when an erroneous instruction is given, hoping for a favorable verdict and planning to complain of the erroneous instruction on appeal if the verdict be unfavorable.[409] Absent plain error, lawyers who give the trial judge no opportunity to consider the propriety of an event at trial simply

---

[402]*Avia Group Int'l, Inc. v. L.A. Gear Calif., Inc.*, 853 F.2d 1557, 7 USPQ2d 1548 (Fed. Cir. 1988).

[403]*CPG Prods. Corp. v. Pegasus Luggage, Inc.*, 776 F.2d 1007, 227 USPQ 497 (Fed. Cir. 1985).

[404]*Rolls-Royce Ltd. v. GTE Valeron Corp.*, 800 F.2d 1101, 231 USPQ 185 (Fed. Cir. 1986). It is not the purpose of the appellate process or the role of the Federal Circuit to rectify mistakes made by counsel in the trial court. *Snellman v. Ricoh Co.*, 836 F.2d 528, 5 USPQ2d 1341 (Fed. Cir. 1987).

[405]*Devices for Med., Inc. v. Boehl*, 822 F.2d 1062, 3 USPQ2d 1288, 1289 (Fed. Cir. 1987). The trial on the merits should be the main event rather than a tryout on the road. The Federal Circuit will not aid efforts of appellants to retry their cases on appeal. *Fromson v. Citiplate, Inc.*, 886 F.2d 1300, 12 USPQ2d 1299 (Fed. Cir. 1989).

[406]*Structural Rubber Prods. Co. v. Park Rubber Co.*, 749 F.2d 707, 223 USPQ 1264 (Fed. Cir. 1984). The court has disregarded an argument that sufficient trial time was not allowed for the appellant to present its case, because the objection was not voiced below. *Laitram Corp. v. Cambridge Wire Cloth Co.*, 863 F.2d 855, 9 USPQ2d 1289 (Fed. Cir. 1988).

[407]*Motorola, Inc. v. Interdigital Tech. Corp.*, 121 F.3d 1461, 43 USPQ2d 1481 (Fed. Cir. 1997).

[408]*Finch v. Hughes Aircraft Co.*, 926 F.2d 1574, 17 USPQ2d 1914 (Fed. Cir. 1991).

[409]*Glaros v. H.H. Robertson Co.*, 797 F.2d 1564, 230 USPQ 393 (Fed. Cir. 1986). See also *Orthokinetics, Inc. v. Safety Travel Chairs, Inc.*, 806 F.2d 1565, 1 USPQ2d 1081 (Fed. Cir. 1986). But see *Lummus Indus., Inc. v. D.M. & E. Corp.*, 862 F.2d 267, 8 USPQ2d 1983 (Fed.

cannot ask an appellate court, sitting with but a cold record, to do so.[410] The mere fact that a later position is inconsistent with an earlier one does not necessarily mean there was a waiver, however. In one case a party argued below that a provision in a contract was ambiguous. On appeal, it urged that the court below was correct in holding the provision unambiguous. There was no waiver; the issue of ambiguity was squarely presented and decided below, and the party can rely on that as a basis for further arguments.[411]

Ordinarily, appellate courts refuse to consider issues not raised before an administrative agency. Objections to the proceedings of an agency must be made while it has an opportunity for correction, in order to raise issues reviewable by courts. A corollary is that the issue must be raised with sufficient specificity and clarity that the tribunal is aware that it must decide the issue, and in sufficient time that the agency can do so.[412] Orderly procedure and good administration require that, in order to raise issues reviewable by the courts, objections to the proceedings of an administrative agency be made while it has the opportunity for correction. When a party to such a proceeding fails to assert an issue during that proceeding, other parties to the proceeding are not given notice and an opportunity to present arguments before the agency; moreover, the agency is not afforded the opportunity to consider the issue in the first instance. Thus, simple fairness to those who are engaged in the tasks of administration, and to litigants, requires as a general rule that courts should not overturn administrative decisions unless the administrative body not only has erred, but erred against objection made at the time appropriate under its practice.[413]

In appeals from the PTO, the court will not consider arguments presented by the Commissioner that were not relied upon by the Board. In the interest of an orderly and fair administrative process, it is inappropriate for the court to consider new grounds of rejection.[414]

Cir. 1988) (under Fourth Circuit law jury instructions not objected to may be reviewed on appeal if necessary to correct fundamental error of law or prevent a miscarriage of justice).

[410]*Weinar v. Rollform Inc.*, 744 F.2d 797, 223 USPQ 369 (Fed. Cir. 1984). Although the district court had indicated that a holding of summary judgment as to some claims might be reopened as a result of what transpired at trial, the party never actually requested a reopening of the matter, and the Federal Circuit refused to remand for that purpose. *Conservolite, Inc. v. Widmayer*, 21 F.3d 1098, 30 USPQ2d 1626 (Fed. Cir. 1994).

[411]*American Med. Sys., Inc. v. Medical Eng'g Corp.*, 6 F.3d 1523, 28 USPQ2d 1321 (Fed. Cir. 1993).

[412]*Wallace v. Department of Air Force*, 879 F.2d 829 (Fed. Cir. 1989). In *Texas Instr., Inc. v. United States ITC*, 988 F.2d 1165, 26 USPQ2d 1018 (Fed. Cir. 1993), a party made a reverse doctrine of equivalents argument to an administrative law judge, who made no findings on the subject. Although the party's petition for review to the ITC raised literal infringement as an issue, it did not specify reverse doctrine of equivalents as a defensive ground. The Federal Circuit held that the matter was not preserved for review on appeal.

[413]*Checkpoint Sys., Inc. v. United States ITC*, 54 F.3d 756, 35 USPQ2d 1042 (Fed. Cir. 1995). The issue here was the hearing examiner's treatment of a particular claim as representative of all the claims. Any objection to that should have been raised specifically in the petition to the ITC to review the examiner's initial determination.

[414]*In re Margolis*, 785 F.2d 1029, 228 USPQ 940 (Fed. Cir. 1986). The PTO Solicitor cannot raise a new ground of rejection or apply a new rationale to support a rejection in appeals from

Thus, the PTO cannot adopt a new theory of anticipation for the first time in its brief on appeal, for that would amount to a new ground of rejection.[415] On the other hand, where the PTO merely referred to new portions of the same prior art references to contravene a position taken by the applicant, the rule against presentation of a new ground of rejection on appeal was not violated.[416] Where an applicant argued on appeal that neither reference taught an invention, that was sufficient to permit him to appeal an examiner's rejection over a combination of the two references.[417] The court will consider only what the Board actually said, not what the PTO argues that it said. The argument may be so far removed from what the Board actually said that to adopt it would be to adopt a new ground of rejection.[418]

Federal Circuit review of PTO Board decisions is on the record before the PTO. When the Board affirms an examiner's rejection generally, without reviewing a particular ground the examiner relied on, that ground is assumed to be affirmed. Thus, in the absence of express reversal by the Board, it is appropriate for the reviewing court to consider such a ground.[419] Where a party failed to make certain arguments to the Board in justification of its position, it faces a well-nigh insurmountable appellate burden of convincing the court that the Board abused its discretion in not fathoming its mind. Prescience is not a required characteristic of the Board and the Board need not divine all possible afterthoughts of counsel that might be asserted for the first time on appeal.[420] It is not the practice of the court to review claims that an applicant has not separately argued at the Board level, because it lacks the benefit of the Board's reasoned decision on the separate patentability of those claims.[421]

The court may occasionally raise a matter sua sponte in an appropriate case. In one case the court vacated a treble damage award, despite the fact that the defendant did not raise the issue, on the

---

decisions of the Board. *In re Soni*, 54 F.3d 746, 34 USPQ2d 1684 (Fed. Cir. 1995). See also *In re Dembiczak*, 175 F.3d 994, 50 USPQ2d 1614 (Fed. Cir. 1999); *In re Robertson*, 169 F.3d 743, 49 USPQ2d 1949 (Fed. Cir. 1999).

[415]*Titanium Metals Corp. v. Banner*, 778 F.2d 775, 227 USPQ 773 (Fed. Cir. 1985).

[416]*In re Hedges*, 783 F.2d 1038, 228 USPQ 685 (Fed. Cir. 1986).

[417]*In re Evanega*, 829 F.2d 1110, 4 USPQ2d 1249 (Fed. Cir. 1987).

[418]*In re Hounsfield*, 699 F.2d 1320, 216 USPQ 1045 (Fed. Cir. 1983).

[419]*In re Nielson*, 816 F.2d 1562, 2 USPQ2d 1525 (Fed. Cir. 1987). However, where the examiner's final rejection does not clearly specify a particular issue, a general affirmance of the examiner by the PTO Board does not raise that issue for Federal Circuit review. *In re Webb*, 916 F.2d 1553, 16 USPQ2d 1433 (Fed. Cir. 1990).

[420]*Keebler Co. v. Murray Bakery Prods.*, 866 F.2d 1386, 9 USPQ2d 1736 (Fed. Cir. 1989). Where an applicant did not argue the merits of the examiner's rejections under §102 and §103, but instead argued that the particular documents being relied upon by the PTO were not prior art, the applicant is precluded on appeal from arguing the merits of the rejections. By the same logic, the court refused to consider alternative grounds (§102(a) prior knowledge and §102(g) prior invention) offered by the PTO in support of the Board decision, even though they were based on the same facts as the §102 and §103 rejections. *In re Epstein*, 32 F.3d 1559, 31 USPQ2d 1817 (Fed. Cir. 1994).

[421]*In re Dillon*, 919 F.2d 688, 16 USPQ2d 1897 (Fed. Cir. 1990). The court has approved the Board's practice under 37 CFR §1.197(b) in refusing to consider a second request for rehearing. Thus, the appellant is precluded from relying on the argument raised for the first

stated ground that it required explicit findings in order to review the decision of the district court.[422] The court will not, however, affirm sua sponte on grounds the PTO Board declined to accept.[423] While the court does not generally condone or entertain arguments raised for the first time on appeal, it may sua sponte consider all bases for the district court's jurisdiction,[424] or its own.[425]

(e) Need for Cross-Appeal

The general rule of appellate procedure is that the prevailing party may present any argument that supports the judgment in its favor, without filing a cross-appeal. The Federal Circuit applies the rule in this fashion: a party will not be permitted to argue an issue on which it has lost, and on which it has not taken an appeal, if the result of the acceptance of the argument would be a reversal or modification of the judgment rather than an affirmance.[426] A prevailing party may, without cross-appealing, defend a judgment on any ground that would not expand the relief it has been granted.[427] But that rule does not apply if acceptance of the rejected contention would result in a modification of the judgment.[428] It is improper to file a cross-appeal for the sole purpose of preserving a right to offer arguments in support of a judgment. Appellees always have the right to assert alternative grounds for affirming the judgment that are supported by the record.[429] This application of the rule may suggest that where a judgment holds a patent valid but not infringed, the accused infringer, as appellee, must cross-appeal on validity in order to preserve

---

time in that second request as a basis for overturning the Board's decision. *In re Hyatt*, 211 F.3d 1367, 54 USPQ2d 1664 (Fed. Cir. 2).

[422]*Paper Converting Mach. Co. v. Magna-Graphics Corp.*, 745 F.2d 11, 223 USPQ 591 (Fed. Cir. 1984). One suspects that the court was of the strong feeling that the award was ill-advised, or at least ill-considered.

[423]*In re Hounsfield*, 699 F.2d 1320, 216 USPQ 1045 (Fed. Cir. 1983).

[424]*Broughton Lumber Co. v. Yeutter*, 939 F.2d 1547 (Fed. Cir. 1991).

[425]*Registration Control Sys., Inc. v. Compusystems, Inc.*, 922 F.2d 805, 17 USPQ2d 1212 (Fed. Cir. 1990).

[426]*Radio Steel & Mfg. Co. v. MTD Prods., Inc.*, 731 F.2d 840, 221 USPQ 657, 660 (Fed. Cir. 1984).

[427]*Genentech, Inc. v. Wellcome Found. Ltd.*, 29 F.3d 1555, 31 USPQ2d 1161 (Fed. Cir. 1994); *Consolidated Alum Corp. v. Foseco Int'l Ltd.*, 910 F.2d 804, 15 USPQ2d 1481 (Fed. Cir. 1990); *Marsh-McBirney, Inc. v. Montedoro-Whitney Corp.*, 882 F.2d 498, 11 USPQ2d 1794 (Fed. Cir. 1989).

[428]*High Tech Med. Instr., Inc. v. New Image Indus., Inc.*, 49 F.3d 1551, 33 USPQ2d 2005 (Fed. Cir. 1995). The district court had granted a preliminary injunction on one claim but not another. The defendant appealed as to the enjoined claim but the plaintiff did not appeal as to the other, thus giving up its right to argue that claim on appeal. Because an injunction framed to grant relief from infringement of the nonenjoined claim would be different from and in some respects broader than one framed to grant relief from infringement of the first claim, a cross-appeal was required.

[429]*Mehl/Biophile Int'l Corp. v. Milgraum*, 192 F.3d 1365, 52 USPQ2d 1303 (Fed. Cir. 1999); *Datascope Corp. v. SMEC, Inc.*, 879 F.2d 820, 11 USPQ2d 1321 (Fed. Cir. 1989).

the issue.[430] It has resulted in a holding that where a patent is held invalid, the successful appellee cannot attack a finding of commercial success, or a refusal to admit evidence of prior use or sale, because those matters go to validity.[431]

Many important questions concerning the need for cross-appeal remain to be decided. The court has passed the question whether an appellee must cross-appeal a finding of equivalence, where the lower court found noninfringement for another reason.[432] The cases illustrate the difficulty of knowing whether a cross-appeal is necessary. In one, the district court excluded evidence that the patent challenger contended would invalidate the patent, and held the patent valid but not infringed. The challenger appealed the evidentiary ruling but failed to cross-appeal the portion of the judgment holding the patent valid. The Federal Circuit indicated that an evidentiary ruling cannot of itself be the subject of an appeal. Thus the challenger should have either cross-appealed the validity judgment or, in response to the patentee's appeal of the noninfringement judgment, argued that the excluded evidence would have so limited the claims as to reflect noninfringement.[433] In another case, the defendant failed to appeal a finding of infringement as to one device, while the plaintiff appealed a finding of noninfringement as to another device. The defendant was barred from contesting the presence of a claim element common to both devices and was limited to supporting the district court's conclusion as to a claim element relevant only to the device that had been held noninfringing.[434] One case was so complicated procedurally that the court figuratively threw up its hands and held that all rulings, to the extent they were appealable, were preserved for appeal upon final judgment.[435]

---

[430]But see *Hill-Rom Co. v. Kinetic Concepts Inc.*, 209 F.3d 1337, 54 USPQ2d 1437 (Fed. Cir. 2).

[431]*Kansas Jack, Inc. v. Kuhn*, 719 F.2d 1144, 219 USPQ 857 (Fed. Cir. 1983). See the discussion of mootness in §16.3(h).

[432]*Thomas & Betts Corp. v. Litton Sys., Inc.*, 720 F.2d 1572, 220 USPQ 1 (Fed. Cir. 1983). The court seems willing to pass direct infringement and decide equivalents as an alternative. See *Under Sea Indus., Inc. v. Dacor Corp.*, 833 F.2d 1551, 4 USPQ2d 1772 (Fed. Cir. 1987). The implications of this may be significant. Are the two routes of decision entirely different or part of a single continuum? What is the impact of this on the need to cross-appeal?

[433]*Wahpeton Canvas Co. v. Frontier, Inc.*, 870 F.2d 1546, 10 USPQ2d 1201 (Fed. Cir. 1989). The ironic aspect is that a challenger must, to be safe, cross-appeal a judgment that the patent is not invalid, and yet that appeal is moot unless and until the patentee is successful in reversing the judgment of noninfringement. See text accompanying notes 16:476–489.

[434]*Marsh-McBirney, Inc. v. Montedoro-Whitney Corp.*, 882 F.2d 498, 11 USPQ2d 1794 (Fed. Cir. 1989). In *U.S. Philips Corp. v. Windmere Corp.*, 971 F.2d 728, 23 USPQ2d 1709 (Fed. Cir. 1992), a company was a party below on some claims for relief but not others. There was no appeal from the claims to which it was a party. The other parties appealed other claims, but then settled and moved jointly to vacate the judgment below. The company sought at the appellate level to oppose the vacatur. The Federal Circuit held that there was not standing on the part of the company to oppose, despite these facts: (1) the company was included in the official appellate caption, (2) the company might have a financial interest (e.g., as an indemnitor), and (3) the company might wish to obtain a possible preclusive effect of the judgment for use in another suit. For the subsequent history of this case, see note 16:471.

[435]*Genentech, Inc. v. University of Calif.*, 143 F.3d 1446, 46 USPQ2d 1586 (Fed. Cir. 1998).

(f) *Standing*

Questions of standing can have significant impact. Article III of the Constitution limits the role of federal courts to adjudication of actual controversies. Standing is one element of the case or controversy requirement, and is a requirement for appellate jurisdiction.[436] In general, a nonparty has no standing to appeal a judgment that would not bind it by res judicata or collateral estoppel.[437] In *Boeing Co. v. Commissioner of Patents,*[438] the court discoursed at some length on the matter of appellate standing. When the standing of a litigant is placed in issue, the court must undertake a two-step analysis that involves both constitutional and prudential limitations. It must determine whether the litigant satisfied the requirements of Article III, and whether any prudential limitations restrain the court from exercising its judicial power.[439] Fundamentally, standing calls into question the power of the court to hear and decide a case, and it is therefore impossible for a party to waive that requirement. A court must dismiss an appeal whenever it becomes apparent that jurisdiction is lacking.[440]

The matter before the court in *Boeing* was the standing of an intervener to bring an independent appeal. The court made it clear that an intervener is required to establish its own independent standing to appeal where the parties to the action have not appealed. A party's status as an intervener, whether permissive or as of right, does not automatically confer on it standing to appeal. In order to establish standing to appeal, a party must show that it has suffered some actual or threatened injury. The injury alleged must be distinct and palpable. It must be fairly traceable to the challenged action and relief from the injury must be likely to follow from a favorable decision. The mere assertion of a right to have the government act in accordance with the law is not sufficient, in and of itself, to satisfy the injury requirement. Nor is the continued existence of a patent sufficient, without conduct creating a reasonable apprehension of a suit for infringement. Without such an apprehension, the alleged injury is indistinguishable from any injury that the issuance of a patent might cause the general public.[441]

---

[436]*Boeing Co. v. Commissioner of Patents,* 853 F.2d 878, 7 USPQ2d 1487 (Fed. Cir. 1988). The standing requirement is also discussed in §8.1(a)(iv).

[437]*Spindelfabrik S., S. & G. GmbH v. Schubert & Salzer Mas. Ak.,* 903 F.2d 1568, 14 USPQ2d 1913 (Fed. Cir. 1990).

[438]*Boeing Co. v. Commissioner of Patents,* 853 F.2d 878, 7 USPQ2d 1487 (Fed. Cir. 1988).

[439]*Boeing Co. v. Commissioner of Patents,* 853 F.2d 878, 7 USPQ2d 1487 (Fed. Cir. 1988). Prudential considerations are discussed in detail in §8.1(a)(iv).

[440]*Boeing Co. v. Commissioner of Patents,* 853 F.2d 878, 7 USPQ2d 1487 (Fed. Cir. 1988). The court rejected an intervener's argument that failure of the parties to object to intervention in the district court resulted in a waiver of any objection regarding standing of the intervener to bring an independent appeal.

[441]*Boeing Co. v. Commissioner of Patents,* 853 F.2d 878, 7 USPQ2d 1487 (Fed. Cir. 1988). Thus the court held that a nonpatentee requester for reexamination is neither an applicant entitled to appeal under 35 U.S.C. §145 nor a patent owner entitled to appeal under §306.

A party shows standing to appeal by demonstrating, among other things, that it suffered some actual or threatened injury as a result of the appealed action. The threat of an unfavorable determination in future litigation due to the res judicata effect of an adverse judicial determination may be such an injury.[442] A manufacturer who supplies and indemnifies the government, even where joined by the government as a third-party defendant, has no standing to appeal an adverse judgment of the Court of Federal Claims (after the government had dismissed its appeal from a judgment of noninfringement).[443]

Of course, appellate standing is not necessarily limited to parties only. A person who is within the zone of interest affected by an administrative determination may be able to appeal it.[444] Thus a nonparty supplier of components can appeal an ITC exclusion order where it is clear that the order would cover the components as incorporated into the excluded infringing products of the party respondent.[445] In another case, a nonparty purchased the infringer's facility after trial but before judgment. The trial court entered an injunction binding upon the infringer and its successors in interest. The Federal Circuit held that the purchaser had standing to appeal a refusal to modify the injunction, because it was bound by the injunction.[446]

But the court has refused intervention in a patentee's appeal from a PTO Board decision in a reexamination proceeding, where the proposed intervener was a party to stayed district court litigation involving the patent undergoing reexamination. It was expected that third persons would have an interest in the outcome of reexamination, and the existence of such interest does not change the congressional

---

Therefore such a requester, even one who has intervened in a §145 action, has no independent statutory right to bring a §145 action. Nor is any injury caused such a requester within the zone of interest protected by §§145 and 306 so as to give it standing to appeal in its role as an intervener.

[442]*National Presto Indus. v. Dazey Corp.*, 107 F.3d 1576, 42 USPQ2d 1070 (Fed. Cir. 1997). Here the trial court dismissed for lack of subject matter jurisdiction after making substantive findings. Such a decision both deprives the appellant of the benefit of its victory under those vacated findings and allows the appellee a second opportunity to litigate the issues. The appellant thus suffered a genuine adverse effect sufficient to establish its standing to appeal.

[443]*Penda Corp. v. United States*, 44 F.3d 967, 33 USPQ2d 1200 (Fed. Cir. 1994). The reasoning was that third-party status alone does not confer standing. Nor does potential liability as an indemnitor. Even if the manufacturer is ultimately held liable to the government under the indemnification agreement, its pecuniary interest in the case at hand is indirect and consequential rather than direct and immediate. The judgment would not preclude the manufacturer from raising the issue of patent invalidity in litigation either with the government or the patentee because, among other reasons, of the very fact that it cannot appeal alone.

[444]*LSI Computer Sys., Inc. v. United States ITC*, 832 F.2d 588, 4 USPQ2d 1705 (Fed. Cir. 1987).

[445]*LSI Computer Sys., Inc. v. United States ITC*, 832 F.2d 588, 4 USPQ2d 1705 (Fed. Cir. 1987). This result seems dictated by the statute, 19 U.S.C. §1337(c), which provides that "any person adversely affected by a final determination of the Commission" may appeal. In the absence of legislative history indicating that Congress intended to limit appeals to parties only, the plain meaning of "any person" controls. The court was quick to emphasize that a would-be appellant must be "adversely affected." It remains to be seen how adverse and how proximate the effect must be to provide standing.

[446]*Kloster Speedsteel AB v. Crucible Inc.*, 793 F.2d 1565, 230 USPQ 81 (Fed. Cir. 1986).

intent that the proceeding be limited in its inter partes attributes. Even though the district court will undoubtedly give great weight to the outcome of the reexamination, a mere interest in the outcome is not sufficient to justify intervention.[447] The PTO Board held that the counts in an interference were unpatentable and both applicants sought review, one in the district court under 35 U.S.C. §146 and the other by appeal to the Federal Circuit. The applicant who brought the §146 action moved the Federal Circuit to remand the appeal to the PTO. The court held that the moving applicant lacked standing in that it was not a party to the appeal; the actual appellee was the PTO itself.[448] The Commissioner has no right to appeal a Board decision to the Federal Circuit.[449]

(g) *Miscellaneous Matters*

Each claim of a patent is presumed valid independently of the validity of any other claim. For this reason, where a defendant does not counterclaim for invalidity of all claims, a judgment of invalidity encompassing all claims must be reversed where it appears that the validity of certain claims was not actually litigated at trial.[450] Nonetheless, the court will not consider separately claims that were not considered separately below.[451] Claims not separately argued will stand or fall together on appeal.[452]

Unless authorized by statute, appellate courts cannot consider evidence de novo.[453] Certainly the court may not base its decision on evidence that was properly excluded at trial.[454]

---

[447]*In re Opprecht*, 868 F.2d 1264 (Fed. Cir. 1989). This seems a particularly decisive holding, inasmuch as the proposed intervener was not the reexamination requester and thus never had a chance to get its "two cents worth" in before the PTO.

[448]*In re Van Geuns*, 946 F.2d 845, 20 USPQ2d 1291 (Fed. Cir. 1991). The court also refused to enjoin prosecution of the §146 action on the grounds that the parties and issues differed from those presented by the appeal; thus both routes of review were permitted to proceed simultaneously.

[449]*In re Alappat*, 33 F.3d 1526, 31 USPQ2d 1545 (Fed. Cir. 1994). The repeated reenactment of 35 U.S.C. §141 reflects the belief of Congress that the Commissioner does not need such right in view of his or her rule-making authority and limited control over the Board. *Id.*

[450]*Datascope Corp. v. SMEC, Inc.*, 776 F.2d 320, 227 USPQ 838 (Fed. Cir. 1985); *Gardner v. TEC Sys., Inc.*, 725 F.2d 1338, 220 USPQ 777 (Fed. Cir. 1984). See also *Valmet Paper Mach., Inc. v. Beloit Corp.*, 112 F.3d 1169 (Fed. Cir. 1997).

[451]*In re Corkill*, 771 F.2d 1496, 226 USPQ 1005 (Fed. Cir. 1985). A failure to argue the validity of dependent claims separately from the validity of an underlying independent claim precludes consideration of that matter on appeal. *Becton Dickinson & Co. v. C.R. Bard, Inc.*, 922 F.2d 792, 17 USPQ2d 1097 (Fed. Cir. 1990).

[452]*Sibia Neurosciences Inc. v. Cadus Pharm. Corp.*, 225 F.3d 1349, 55 USPQ2d 1927 (Fed. Cir. 2); *In re Kemps*, 97 F.3d 1427, 40 USPQ2d 1309 (Fed. Cir. 1996); *Amgen, Inc. v. Chugai Pharm. Co.*, 927 F.2d 1200, 18 USPQ2d 1016 (Fed. Cir. 1991); *In re Margolis*, 785 F.2d 1029, 228 USPQ 940 (Fed. Cir. 1986); *In re Kaslow*, 707 F.2d 1366, 217 USPQ 1089 (Fed. Cir. 1983).

[453]*Underwater Devices, Inc. v. Morrison-Knudsen Co.*, 717 F.2d 1380, 219 USPQ 569 (Fed. Cir. 1983). Initial consideration of evidence is not the appellate role. *H.H. Robertson Co. v. United Steel Deck, Inc.*, 820 F.2d 384, 2 USPQ2d 1926 (Fed. Cir. 1987).

[454]*Shatterproof Glass Corp. v. Libbey-Owens Ford Co.*, 758 F.2d 613, 225 USPQ 634 (Fed. Cir. 1985).

An appeal from a final judgment may include challenges to all rulings that produced the judgment.[455] Review under 28 U.S.C. §1292(d) is not limited to the question certified, and the appellate court can consider all questions material to the correctness of the interlocutory order.[456] Similarly, the court may review the entirety of an interlocutory order granting a preliminary injunction, including a portion establishing an escrow account for royalty payments.[457] On the other hand, substantive issues such as validity and infringement are not raised for final resolution by motions for preliminary injunction, and the Federal Circuit will decline to decide them on a review of such a motion.[458] Indeed, the decision whether, in connection with the review of an appealable interlocutory order, to review another interlocutory order that would ordinarily be unappealable standing alone, is an exercise of discretion. The major factor in deciding whether to exercise that discretion is whether review of the appealable order will involve questions relevant to the otherwise unappealable order.[459]

---

[455]*Scripps Clinic & Res. Found. v. Genentech, Inc.,* 927 F.2d 1565, 18 USPQ2d 1001 (Fed. Cir. 1991) (9th Circuit law).

[456]*Senza-Gel Corp. v. Seiffhart,* 803 F.2d 661, 231 USPQ 363 (Fed. Cir. 1986); *Minnesota Chippewa Tribe v. United States,* 768 F.2d 338 (Fed. Cir. 1985). But where plaintiff failed to raise in the district court the argument that a summary judgment of misuse would be inappropriate because the defendant had not established certain elements of misuse, that argument could not be raised on the appeal of a certified question relating to other elements of misuse. *Hodosh v. Block Drug. Co.,* 833 F.2d 1575, 4 USPQ2d 1935 (Fed. Cir. 1987).

[457]*Cordis Corp. v. Medtronic, Inc.,* 780 F.2d 991, 228 USPQ 189 (Fed. Cir. 1985). As a general matter, a reviewing court is not restricted in its review of the grant of an injunction to the merits. A departure from the basic procedural requirements for issuance of an injunction may also require that it be vacated. Similarly, the scope of injunctive relief is itself subject to review. *Digital Equip. Corp. v. Emulex Corp.,* 805 F.2d 380, 231 USPQ 779 (Fed. Cir. 1986).

[458]*Roper Corp. v. Litton Sys., Inc.,* 757 F.2d 1266, 225 USPQ 345 (Fed. Cir. 1985). On appeal from denial of a preliminary injunction, the court is not obliged to make a definitive claim construction. *International Comm. Materials, Inc. v. Ricoh Co.,* 108 F.3d 316, 41 USPQ2d 1957 (Fed. Cir. 1997). In *Genentech, Inc. v. Novo Nordisk, A/S,* 108 F.3d 1361, 42 USPQ2d 1001 (Fed. Cir. 1997), the court vacated a preliminary injunction and remanded with instructions to dismiss the complaint on the ground that the patent was invalid for lack of enablement. It should be noted that both parties appeared to agree that the record was full and complete enough to permit an ultimate decision on the issue, even at this stage.

[459]*Intermedics Infusaid, Inc. v. Regents of Univ. of Minn.,* 804 F.2d 129, 231 USPQ 653 (Fed. Cir. 1986). The court refers to this discretionary jurisdiction as "the doctrine of pendent jurisdiction at the appellate level." *Id.* It is not clear whether the court intends to engage in selective review of unappealable interlocutory orders under 28 U.S.C. §1292(c)(1) pursuant to a discretionary test, or not. In *Cordis Corp. v. Medtronic, Inc.,* 780 F.2d 991, 228 USPQ 189 (Fed. Cir. 1985), the court seemed to adopt a flat rule that it had jurisdiction over the entirety of an interlocutory order that contained a provision for injunctive relief. In *Intermedics Infusaid, Inc. v. Regents of Univ. of Minn.,* 804 F.2d 129, 231 USPQ 653 (Fed. Cir. 1986), it articulated a discretionary test involving the extent to which review of an appealable interlocutory order would involve consideration of factors relevant to an otherwise nonappealable interlocutory order. But in *King Instr. Corp. v. Otari Corp.,* 814 F.2d 1560, 2 USPQ2d 1201 (Fed. Cir. 1987), the court again seemed to take the view that the entire order, and not simply the propriety of the injunctive relief, is before the appellate court for review, regardless of any discretionary factors. In *Broyhill Furn. Indus. v. Craftmaster Furn. Corp.,* 12 F.3d 1080, 29 USPQ2d 1283 (Fed. Cir. 1993), the court decided that an otherwise unappealable order granting a party leave to file counterclaims was not sufficiently closely related to an appealable order denying a motion for relief from judgment under Rule 60(b) to warrant review.

Typically, the Federal Circuit will accept and dispose of an issue as it is presented.[460] An appellate court may consider only the record as it was made before the district court. Where documents are filed after entry of judgment in the district court, apparently for the purpose of including them in the appendix on appeal, such inclusion is improper.[461]

(h) Mootness

Article III, §2 of the Constitution limits the federal judicial power to enumerated cases and controversies. Moot cases do not present live controversies, and therefore federal courts have no jurisdiction to decide them.[462] If an event occurs while a case is pending on appeal that makes it impossible for the court to grant any effectual relief whatever to a prevailing party, the appeal must be dismissed as moot. The case ceases to present a case of actual controversy, thereby divesting the appellate court of jurisdiction.[463] The Federal Circuit seems inclined, by and large, to handle moot appeals in traditional fashion. Where a case becomes moot while on appeal, the proper disposition is to vacate the judgment and remand with instructions to dismiss the complaint; it is not proper simply to dismiss the appeal.[464] For example, where there is no claim for damages and the patent expires during the pendency of the appeal, the plaintiff is no longer entitled to an injunction and a judgment dealing with the patent's validity is moot; the judgment is therefore vacated and the case remanded for dismissal of the infringement claim.[465]

---

[460]*Connell v. Sears, Roebuck & Co.*, 722 F.2d 1542, 220 USPQ 193 (Fed. Cir. 1983).

[461]*Ballard Med. Prods. v. Wright*, 821 F.2d 642 (Fed. Cir. 1987). In *Beverly Hills Fan Co. v. Royal Sovereign Corp.*, 21 F.3d 1558, 30 USPQ2d 1001 (Fed. Cir. 1994), a party filed an affidavit in connection with a motion for reconsideration of a dismissal on jurisdictional grounds. The other party moved to strike the affidavit. The district court denied the motion for reconsideration and, presumably, the motion to strike, although there was no docket entry disposing of it. On appeal, the successful party moved to strike the affidavit on the grounds that it was not properly before the court. The Federal Circuit disagreed, addressing many complex factors, including the notion that under certain circumstances courts of appeal can exercise jurisdiction over a judgment or decision that is not expressly appealed.

[462]*Kimberly-Clark Corp. v. Procter & Gamble Distrib. Co.*, 973 F.2d 911, 23 USPQ2d 1921 (Fed. Cir. 1992). Indeed, when an issue becomes moot while being appealed, continuation of the appeal is frivolous. *Nasatka v. Delta Scientific Corp.*, 58 F.3d 1578, 35 USPQ2d 1374 (Fed. Cir. 1995).

[463]*Nasatka v. Delta Scientific Corp.*, 58 F.3d 1578, 35 USPQ2d 1374 (Fed. Cir. 1995).

[464]*Gibralter Indus., Inc. v. United States*, 726 F.2d 747 (Fed. Cir. 1984). Where the appeal is mooted by a settlement, and the effect of the settlement is permanent withdrawal of the claims below, a dismissal with prejudice is indicated. Since this disposes of the appeal, there is no need to dismiss the appeal with prejudice. *Smith Int'l, Inc. v. Hughes Tool Co.*, 839 F.2d 663, 5 USPQ2d 1686 (Fed. Cir. 1988). A case that becomes moot prior to appeal may be handled somewhat differently. In *Sun-Tek Indus., Inc. v. Kennedy Sky Lites, Inc.*, 856 F.2d 173, 8 USPQ2d 1154 (Fed. Cir. 1988), the court dismissed an appeal of a moot question, and awarded attorney fees and costs on the grounds that the appeal was frivolous.

[465]*Kinzenbaw v. Deere & Co.*, 741 F.2d 383, 222 USPQ 929 (Fed. Cir. 1984). Where the patent had expired, the patentee's appeal from a denial of a preliminary injunction was dis-

In an ITC proceeding the patent was held invalid, not infringed, and unenforceable for inequitable conduct. The patentee appealed only the unenforceability holding. Meanwhile the patent had expired. The Federal Circuit held the appeal moot on the ground that the ITC can issue orders touching only future conduct and neither exclusion orders nor cease-and-desist orders are applicable once the patent expires.[466] Although recognizing that ITC determinations are given no preclusive effect, the patentee evinced a definite and real concern that the determination of inequitable conduct would impair its future efforts to enforce its patent portfolio.[467] The Federal Circuit addressed that concern by pointing out that the established practice in dealing with civil cases that become moot while on their way through the appeal process is to reverse or vacate the judgment below and remand with direction to dismiss. That procedure clears the path for future relitigation of the issues between the parties and eliminates a judgment that was unreviewable by happenstance.[468]

There may be a distinction, however, between cases that become moot during the appellate process and cases that are mooted at the trial level. Settlement moots an action, although jurisdiction remains with the district court to enter a consent judgment. When the case between the parties has been settled, there is no actual matter in controversy. Thus a consent judgment that purports to dispose of everything except the trial court's ruling that held some claims invalid cannot create jurisdiction for an appeal of that ruling, for an agreement of the parties cannot confer jurisdiction on the court. But rather than vacate the consent judgment with respect to the invalidity ruling,

---

missed as moot. *Metaullics Sys. Co. v. Cooper,* 100 F.3d 938, 40 USPQ2d 1798 (Fed. Cir. 1996). Where two of three patents in suit are expired, one of those two invalid and the other not infringed, and the third not infringed, the question of enforceability of any of them is moot on appeal, even though inequitable conduct is relevant to a nonmoot attorney fee question, and "fraud" may be relevant to further proceedings on an antitrust count. *FMC Corp. v. Hennessy Indus., Inc.,* 836 F.2d 521, 5 USPQ2d 1272 (Fed. Cir. 1987). The reissue statute, 35 U.S.C. §251, provides for reissue "for the unexpired part of the term of the original patent." An applicant had filed a reissue application before expiration of the original patent, but the original expired during the pendency of an appeal from a decision of the PTO Board in the reissue. The Federal Circuit dismissed the appeal as moot. *In re Morgan,* 990 F.2d 1230, 26 USPQ2d 1392 (Fed. Cir. 1993). Where attorneys have already withdrawn, any question of whether they should have been disqualified is moot on appeal. *Thermocycle Int'l, Inc. v. A.F. Hinrichsen Sales Corp.,* 851 F.2d 339, 7 USPQ2d 1407 (Fed. Cir. 1988). During the pendency of an appeal from a Board decision rejecting computer program product claims on eligibility grounds, the Commissioner issued an order that "computer programs embodied in a tangible medium, such as floppy diskettes, are patentable subject matter." The PTO asked for dismissal of the appeal and the applicant asked for vacatur. The court concluded that there was no longer a case of actual controversy and vacated and remanded to the Board. *In re Beauregard,* 53 F.3d 1583, 35 USPQ2d 1383 (Fed. Cir. 1995).

[466]*Texas Instr., Inc. v. United States ITC,* 851 F.2d 342, 7 USPQ2d 1509 (Fed. Cir. 1988).

[467]Apparently the patentee was concerned that the unenforceability of one patent might render its entire portfolio unenforceable, under the reasoning of *Keystone Driller Co. v. General Excavator Co.,* 290 U.S. 240 (1933). There was also a concern about an antitrust claim based upon inequitable conduct.

[468]*Texas Instr., Inc. v. United States ITC,* 851 F.2d 342, 7 USPQ2d 1509 (Fed. Cir. 1988).

the Federal Circuit dismissed the appeal, on the ground that the case did not become moot during the appeal process.[469]

Generally, settlement of a dispute renders a case on appeal moot. However, there are situations in which one issue in a case has become moot, but the case as a whole remains alive because other issues have not become moot.[470] Thus, although vacatur of a judgment at trial is appropriate when settlement moots the action on appeal, there may be circumstances where vacating the judgment below is inappropriate.[471]

Unusual circumstances can dictate strange results in this area. In an ITC proceeding an order was entered barring import of devices infringing two patents that happened to expire on the same day. On review the court upheld validity and infringement of one patent, found it unnecessary to consider validity, infringement, and unenforceability as to the other, and vacated the ITC's determinations on the latter. Apparently the court was proceeding on the theory that one patent is enough to support such an order, and therefore all questions as to the other patent were rendered moot.[472] In the trial court certain claims of two patents were held not infringed. On appeal the Federal Circuit reversed the holding as to one claim of one of the patents. In

---

[469]*Gould v. Control Laser Corp.*, 866 F.2d 1391, 9 USPQ2d 1718 (Fed. Cir. 1989). The controversy was also rendered moot because pursuant to the settlement agreement the plaintiff acquired the defendant, thus becoming the dominus litis.

[470]*Kimberly-Clark Corp. v. Procter & Gamble Distrib. Co.*, 973 F.2d 911, 23 USPQ2d 1921 (Fed. Cir. 1992). In *Nasatka v. Delta Scientific Corp.*, 58 F.3d 1578, 35 USPQ2d 1374 (Fed. Cir. 1995), the district court dismissed a patent infringement claim without prejudice and awarded Rule 11 sanctions. Plaintiff appealed, but in the meantime the district court entered a new order rescinding the sanctions. The Federal Circuit found this to have mooted the appeal, inasmuch as the plaintiff could refile its infringement suit and dismissal could make no difference to its legal interest (but what if, for example, the statute of limitations was cutting off past damages each day?). Thus, the court dismissed the appeal; vacation and remand would have been inappropriate inasmuch as the whole case was not mooted (apparently there was still a §285 motion for attorney fees pending before the district court).

[471]*U.S. Philips Corp. v. Windmere Corp.*, 971 F.2d 728, 23 USPQ2d 1709 (Fed. Cir. 1992). The Supreme Court granted certiorari to review the Federal Circuit's practice of routinely vacating district court final judgments at the parties' request when cases are settled while on appeal. *Izumi Seimitsu K.K.K v. U.S. Philips Corp.*, 507 U.S. 907, 28 USPQ2d 1930 (1993). In a per curiam opinion, the Supreme Court later dismissed the writ as improvidently granted, because the petitioner, Izumi, had been denied leave to intervene in the Federal Circuit appeal on grounds of lack of standing, and the intervention question had not been raised in the petition for certiorari. Justice Stevens, joined by Justice Blackmun, dissented from the dismissal of the writ, and concluded that the Federal Circuit's vacatur practice was as objectionable as the practice that it had condemned in *Cardinal v. Morton* (see note 16:483 and accompanying text). The per curiam majority opinion observed that the Second Circuit, like the Federal Circuit, will generally grant motions to vacate when parties settle on appeal, while the Third, Seventh, and District of Columbia Circuits generally deny such motions. The Ninth Circuit requires the district court to conduct a balancing analysis. In a subsequent related case, the court indicated that it may have been wrong in vacating in view of the Supreme Court's later ruling in *U.S. Bancorp Mortgage Co. v. Bonner Mall Partnership*, 115 S.Ct. 386 (1994), which held that vacatur by an appellate court, absent extraordinary circumstances, is not justified by mootness due to settlement. *U.S. Philips Corp. v. Sears, Roebuck & Co.*, 55 F.3d 592, 34 USPQ2d 1699 (Fed. Cir. 1995).

[472]*Texas Instr. Inc. v. United States ITC*, 871 F.2d 1054, 10 USPQ2d 1257 (Fed. Cir. 1989). But how is the court to choose which patent to deal with? The court also vacated a determination that devices did not infringe one patent where the exclusion order also barred import of the same devices on the ground that they infringed a later expiring patent.

view of the patent owner's concession during oral argument that infringement of the remaining claims would not give it a basis for greater relief, the court vacated the judgment of noninfringement without considering them on the merits.[473]

A trial court held both product and process claims were infringed. After affirming on the product claims, the Federal Circuit declined to decide whether the process claims were infringed, justifying this jurisprudence on the ground that "a patent is infringed if any claim is infringed."[474] In another case the trial court found infringement under the doctrine of equivalents and the plaintiff cross-appealed a partial summary judgment of no literal infringement. The Federal Circuit found literal infringement and thus vacated the equivalents finding as moot.[475]

Mootness and noninfringement. For a period of several years, the Federal Circuit constructed and then embraced a doctrine that caused a fair bit of controversy in the patent litigation world. In its fullest flower, the doctrine simply held that the issue of patent validity was mooted when a finding of noninfringement of the patent was affirmed. Although the doctrine did not blossom immediately, the incipient signs were certainly there for the foresighted observer of Federal Circuit jurisprudence. In an early case the court passed the question of whether the existence of an actual controversy would survive a holding of noninfringement.[476] And in a talk delivered in March 1987 to a bar group, then Chief Judge Markey left no doubts about his own views:

> Courts have no roving commission to destroy every invalid patent. Assuming the patent would have been proven invalid, a trial required for its destruction, after a finding of no infringement and thus in the absence of a case or controversy, is not justified, by considerations of public policy or otherwise.[477]

Beginning in mid-1987, the court moved swiftly. In its first look at the matter it affirmed the noninfringement portion of a jury verdict finding a patent valid but not infringed. The defendant's separate appeal on validity was dismissed as moot, and the judgment that defendant had not proven the claims invalid or unenforceable was vacated.[478] In its next case, the court got straight to the heart of the

---

[473]*Stiftung v. Renishaw PLC*, 945 F.2d 1173, 20 USPQ2d 1094 (Fed. Cir. 1991).

[474]*Pall Corp. v. Micron Separations, Inc.*, 66 F.3d 1211, 36 USPQ2d 1225 (Fed. Cir. 1995).

[475]*Transmatic, Inc. v. Gulton Indus., Inc.*, 53 F.3d 1270, 35 USPQ2d 1035 (Fed. Cir. 1995).

[476]*Envirotech Corp. v. Al George, Inc.*, 730 F.2d 753, 221 USPQ 473 (Fed. Cir. 1984).

[477]H. Markey, *On Simplifying Patent Trials*, 116 F.R.D. 369, 377 n.15.

[478]*Fonar Corp. v. Johnson & Johnson*, 821 F.2d 627, 3 USPQ2d 1109 (Fed. Cir. 1987). See also *Environmental Instr., Inc. v. Sutron Corp.*, 877 F.2d 1561, 11 USPQ2d 1132 (Fed. Cir. 1989); *Julien v. Zeringue*, 864 F.2d 1569, 9 USPQ2d 1552 (Fed. Cir. 1989). Yet the court indicates that a challenger must cross-appeal a judgment that the patent is not invalid or lose its right to challenge validity on appeal. See *Wahpeton Canvas Co. v. Frontier, Inc.*, 870 F.2d 1546, 10 USPQ2d 1201 (Fed. Cir. 1989). Thus we have the strange situation of a cross-appeal

matter. After expressly recognizing that it had not squarely decided whether it should or must decide a cross-appeal seeking a declaratory judgment of invalidity where a companion appeal has been disposed of on grounds of noninfringement, it held that it may properly exercise its discretion to dismiss the cross-appeal as moot where there is no indication that the controversy extends beyond the accused devices found to be noninfringing.[479] The teaching of this decision was that the case or controversy must be extant at all stages of review, not merely at the time of the complaint. This requirement avoids having the court unnecessarily address what might turn out to be a hypothetical question. The burden is therefore on the party seeking the declaratory judgment to show the continued existence of a case or controversy that survives the holding of noninfringement. The net result was judgments of invalidity would normally be vacated if noninfringement was found.[480]

Even setting aside any fundamental jurisprudential objections to this approach, it was not without difficulty in practical application. Illustrative cases are discussed in the note.[481] Finally, one panel of the

---

that is moot when brought, and only becomes cognizable when and if the patentee is successful on its appeal of the noninfringement judgment.

[479]*Vieau v. Japax, Inc.*, 823 F.2d 1510, 3 USPQ2d 1094 (Fed. Cir. 1987). The court also indicated that the validity issue did not seem to be one in which invalidity was plainly evident. This seems to leave room for a positive exercise of discretion in an appropriate case.

[480]E.g., *Winner Int'l Corp. v. Wolo Mfg. Corp.*, 905 F.2d 375, 15 USPQ2d 1076 (Fed. Cir. 1990); *Advance Transformer Co. v. Levinson*, 837 F.2d 1081, 5 USPQ2d 1600 (Fed. Cir. 1988); *Perini Am., Inc. v. Paper Converting Mach. Co.*, 832 F.2d 581, 4 USPQ2d 1621 (Fed. Cir. 1987).

[481]In a declaratory judgment action four patents were declared unenforceable for fraud. Two of them were declared invalid and not infringed, and two invalid. The defendant patentee did not appeal the noninfringement holding on the first two, and did not appeal the invalidity holding on the second two. Its appeal as to enforceability and validity on the first two was therefore dismissed as moot because there remained no controversy requiring a decision on those issues. The appeal as to enforceability on the second two was likewise dismissed as moot, because they were invalid. But the judgment of unenforceability as to all four patents was vacated. *Sun-Tek Indus., Inc. v. Kennedy Sky Lites, Inc.*, 848 F.2d 179, 6 USPQ2d 2017 (Fed. Cir. 1988). Query: Was this case correctly decided? One of the first two patents was found invalid on obviousness grounds (as well as fraud), and the patentee seems to have been deprived of an opportunity for review on that issue. In another case, the plaintiff announced on the eve of trial that it was not pressing its claim for infringement of one of the patents in suit. However, it did not move to dismiss and no order was entered. Thus its claim for infringement remained technically in the case. The patent was held invalid and that judgment was affirmed on appeal, with the Federal Circuit reasoning that a continuing actual controversy remained with respect both to validity and infringement. *Environmental Instr., Inc. v. Sutron Corp.*, 877 F.2d 1561, 11 USPQ2d 1132 (Fed. Cir. 1989). Should not the court have found no infringement (for failure of any proof at all) and vacated the invalidity judgment? In yet another case, the district court found the claims infringed, but some valid and some invalid. The parties settled, and defendant took a license under the valid claims. The agreement explicitly reserved the issue of the invalid claims, and plaintiff appealed the consent judgment of invalidity. The Federal Circuit held that the settlement mooted the action, but instead of vacating the consent judgment it simply dismissed the appeal. A dissenting panel member felt that vacating the judgment would have been consistent with the court's practice of vacating invalidity determinations if, on appeal, the accused devices are found noninfringing. Here the defendant had taken a license as part of the settlement and thus no longer infringed any claims of the patent. *Gould v. Control Laser Corp.*, 866 F.2d 1391, 9 USPQ2d 1718 (Fed. Cir. 1989). The plaintiff, of course, was concerned with the collateral estoppel effect of the invalidity ruling. The majority justified its refusal to vacate on the ground that the case did not become moot during the appeal process, and reasoned that vacating the judgment would preclude a collateral estoppel defense and would decide the issue before it arises. The lessons in this case are that one must be very cautious in dealing

court, divided 2–1 on the question, vacated a judgment of invalidity for a second time, thus leaving the patentee free for a third bite at the apple.[482] This moved the Supreme Court to grant certiorari and, in May 1993, in *Cardinal v. Morton,* the high Court reversed, holding that it was an abuse of discretion not to consider validity.[483] On remand, the Federal Circuit ended the matter, at least as to the patents there involved, by affirming the district court's judgment of invalidity.[484]

One had hoped and expected that this fundamental question might now be regarded as settled. The court regards the Supreme Court holding as directing it to rule on validity issues even if the patent is not infringed.[485] By and large, it seems inclined to do so without controversy.[486] However, a pair of more recent cases, decided the same day by different panels, has injected a measure of uncertainty. In *Phonometrics v. Northern Telecom,*[487] the district court granted summary judgment of noninfringement and dismissed as moot a counterclaim for invalidity and unenforceability. The Federal Circuit concluded that the district court has the discretion to dismiss a counterclaim alleging that a patent is invalid as moot where it finds no infringement, and that *Cardinal* does not preclude this discretionary action. *Cardinal,* according to this panel, simply prohibits the Federal Circuit from vacating a judgment of invalidity when it concludes that a patent is not infringed. In *Multiform v. Medzam,*[488] there

---

with consent judgments in general, and some of the problems posed by partial consent judgments may be particularly troublesome.

[482]*Morton Int'l, Inc. v. Cardinal Chem. Co.,* 959 F.2d 948, 22 USPQ2d 1231 (Fed. Cir. 1992). The opinion of Chief Judge Nies, dissenting from an order declining suggestion for rehearing in banc, is reported at 967 F.2d 1571 (Fed. Cir. 1992).

[483]*Cardinal Chem. Co. v. Morton Int'l, Inc.,* 508 U.S. 83, 26 USPQ2d 1721 (1993).

[484]*Morton Int'l, Inc. v. Cardinal Chem. Co.,* 5 F.3d 1464, 28 USPQ2d 1190 (Fed. Cir. 1993).

[485]*Mendenhall v. Cedarapids, Inc.,* 5 F.3d 1556, 28 USPQ2d 1081 (Fed. Cir. 1993).

[486]*North Am. Vaccine, Inc. v. American Cyanamid Co.,* 7 F.3d 1571, 28 USPQ2d 1333 (Fed. Cir. 1993); *Carroll Touch, Inc. v. Electro Mechanical Sys., Inc.,* 3 F.3d 404, 27 USPQ2d 1836 (Fed. Cir. 1993). In *Carroll Touch,* the patentee had only asserted a single claim at trial, but the district court invalidated the entire patent while holding that there was no infringement. After affirming the judgment of noninfringement, the Federal Circuit did vacate the judgment as to the unasserted claims, inasmuch as there was no case of actual controversy as to those claims. In *General Electro Music Corp. v. Samick Music Corp.,* 19 F.3d 1405, 30 USPQ2d 1149 (Fed. Cir. 1994), the patent was held invalid and unenforceable for inequitable conduct. The Federal Circuit affirmed the inequitable conduct portion of the judgment and refused to review the invalidity judgment, holding that none of the *Cardinal* concerns were present. In *Sun Hill Indus., Inc. v. Easter Unlimited, Inc.,* 48 F.3d 1193, 33 USPQ2d 1925 (Fed. Cir. 1995), the lower court found the patent infringed and not invalid. At oral argument the defendant stated that it would waive its validity appeal if it prevailed on infringement. The Federal Circuit reversed on the infringement issue and properly concluded that it need not vacate the validity finding. However, in a dictum it remarked that the defendant could not compel it to revisit the finding of validity, which had become immaterial to the disposition of the case. One doubts the correctness of this dictum. In *Lamb-Weston, Inc. v. McCain Foods, Ltd.,* 78 F.3d 540, 37 USPQ2d 1856 (Fed. Cir. 1996), the court vacated a finding of inequitable conduct after affirming a finding of invalidity, distinguishing *Cardinal* on the ground that it is limited to its specific facts.

[487]*Phonometrics Inc. v. Northern Telecom Inc.,* 133 F.3d 1459, 45 USPQ2d 1421 (Fed. Cir. 1998).

[488]*Multiform Desiccants Inc. v. Medzam Ltd.,* 133 F.3d 1473, 45 USPQ2d 1429 (Fed. Cir. 1998). In *Hill-Rom Co. v. Kinetic Concepts Inc.,* 209 F.3d 1337, 54 USPQ2d 1437 (Fed. Cir. 2),

was no declaratory judgment counterclaim for invalidity, but simply an affirmative defense. The district court found the patent not infringed, and chose not to exercise its discretion to decide the invalidity defense. Despite stressing the useful general rule that trial courts should, in the interest of finality, decide all litigated issues, the Federal Circuit affirmed.

Cardinal is apparently not a two-way street. A holding that claims are invalid eliminates, as a practical matter, the need to consider on appeal whether those claims are infringed, even if the accused infringer has filed a counterclaim for a declaratory judgment of noninfringement. Due to the expense of litigating validity, the strong public interest in resolving validity questions, and the potential impact of the question beyond the immediate case, the Court in *Cardinal* advised that routinely refusing to address validity was improper. Refusing to address infringement does not raise these same problems. Whereas invalidity operates as a complete defense to infringement for any product, forever, a determination of infringement applies only to a specific accused product or process. Thus, a vacatur of a declaratory judgment of noninfringement is essentially of no import when accompanied by an affirmance of a declaratory judgment of invalidity. Of course, in appropriate cases the Federal Circuit may address infringement after a conclusion of invalidity for the same reason that a district court may elect to do so—to aid appellate review and avoid a remand. A declaration of unenforceability, as opposed to a declaration of noninfringement, can present a different story. Whereas a declaration of invalidity does not necessarily extend to all claims of a patent, a counterclaim for a declaration of unenforceability affects the entire patent. In those circumstances, the court must review the issue if it is properly raised on appeal.[489]

---

the district court held the patent not infringed and not invalid. On appeal the noninfringement judgment was affirmed, and the accused infringer asked the court to vacate the finding of no invalidity. The court held that there was no need to vacate the district court's validity ruling or address that ruling on the merits. The invalidity argument was raised only as an affirmative defense, not in the form of a counterclaim, and the district court therefore did not include in the judgment any reference to its ruling on the issue of invalidity. Moreover, the district court's resolution of the issue of invalidity was not necessary to the judgment. For that reason, the court's invalidity ruling will have no collateral estoppel effect in any possible future dispute between the parties involving the patent.

[489]*Weatherchem Corp. v. J.L. Clark Inc.*, 163 F.3d 1326, 49 USPQ2d 1001 (Fed. Cir. 1998).

17

Federal Circuit Practice

§17.1 Standards of Review

An appeal is not a second chance to try the case. That approach would be wasteful of judicial resources and therefore wrong.[1] Moreover, the appellate function is not to determine whether the findings and conclusions of the tribunal being reviewed were right or wrong, in the sense that the appellate judges would or would not reach the same result if they were to decide the matter in the first instance.[2] The Federal Circuit, like other courts of appeal, avoids both the temptation and the effort of appellate retrial by employing certain carefully defined review standards. And it insists that the issues be framed and addressed by parties to the appeal in the terms mandated by the applicable standard of review.[3]

The court's views on the standards of review, and the role of court and counsel in applying those standards, are as clear as words can make them:

---

[1] *Eaton Corp. v. Appliance Valves Corp.*, 790 F.2d 874, 229 USPQ 668 (Fed. Cir. 1986). Nor is an appeal a means for counsel to cure mistakes and omissions made at trial. *DMI, Inc. v. Deere & Co.*, 802 F.2d 421, 231 USPQ 276 (Fed. Cir. 1986). It is beyond cavil that a case is decided on and only on the evidence as presented in that case. *Datascope Corp. v. SMEC, Inc.*, 879 F.2d 820, 11 USPQ2d 1321 (Fed. Cir. 1989).

[2] *Corning Glass Works v. United States ITC*, 799 F.2d 1559, 230 USPQ 822 (Fed. Cir. 1986).

[3] *Corning Glass Works v. United States ITC*, 799 F.2d 1559, 230 USPQ 822 (Fed. Cir. 1986).

This is the eighty-fourth case in which the court has been forced, ad nauseam, to remind counsel that it is a court of review, i.e., that it will not find the facts de novo, that it is not a place for counsel to retry their cases, that its judges do not participate as advocates to fill gaps left by counsel at trial, and that the function of appellant's counsel in relation to the district court's findings is to show that those findings are clearly erroneous or, if correct, cannot support the district court's conclusion. Obviously, a finding not made cannot be reviewed; nor can a naked phrase for which no basis is set forth be deemed a reviewable finding. Nonetheless, the parties here argue strenuously and at length for what they should know is not available on appeal, i.e., original findings.[4]

The standard of review that governs the appeal in a particular case can depend on various factors. For example, different standards of review may apply depending upon the nature of the tribunal below: district court, administrative agency, ITC, Claims Court, PTO. The standard may vary according to the route by which the question reaches the appellate court: summary judgment, preliminary injunction or contempt hearing, plenary bench trial, jury trial.[5] And clearly, different standards will apply to different questions, depending upon whether they are legal or factual. This section will first examine the various standards available and then see how they are applied to specific issues and proceedings.

As a preliminary matter, it should be noted that the level of acceptance by appellate courts of determinations of fact by a trial tribunal is extremely high, and in cases involving dispositive motions neither court has much choice other than to determine whether a question of fact exists. Appellate courts must approach determinations of trial courts with all due respect. In the case of conclusions of law, however, the parties are entitled to a complete and independent appellate review.[6]

(a) Available Standards

The standards available to the reviewing court range over a wide spectrum. De novo review is the broadest: there the appeals court exercises independent judgment on the evidence of record and weighs it as a trial court, although the decision below need not be ignored. Next is the clearly erroneous standard: although there is evidence to support a finding, the reviewing court on the entire evidence is left with the definite and firm conviction that a mistake has been committed. The substantial evidence standard requires more than "a mere

---

[4]*Fromson v. Western Litho Plate & Supp. Co.,* 853 F.2d 1568, 7 USPQ2d 1606, 1609 (Fed. Cir. 1988).

[5]Indeed, the very vehicle for review can determine the standard. For example, the standard of review of denial of an extraordinary writ is abuse of discretion. *In re Innotron Diagnostics,* 800 F.2d 1077, 231 USPQ 178 (Fed. Cir. 1986).

[6]*Cohen v. United States,* 995 F.2d 205 (Fed. Cir. 1993).

scintilla" of proof—something that a reasonable mind would accept. Finally, the narrowest standard is abuse of discretion, or arbitrary and capricious action: no reliance on relevant factors and clear error of judgment.[7] And under any standard, the court disregards any error or defect in the proceeding that does not affect the substantial rights of the parties.[8]

(i) Clear Error

In reviewing findings of fact of district courts, the Federal Circuit is governed by Rule 52(a), FRCP, and must apply the "clearly erroneous" standard of review.[9] It is not the role of the Federal Circuit to review the proceedings below de novo. The appellant bears the burden of showing that the probative findings underlying the trial judge's legal conclusion were clearly erroneous in light of the record made at trial.[10] This standard is satisfied when the court is left with the firm conviction that error occurred.[11] The burden of overcoming the district court's factual findings is, as it should be, a heavy one. In reviewing a judgment based on those findings, the appellate judges do not sit as robed PTO examiners, nor do they repeat the role of the trial judge in finding their own facts.[12] Thus, the most effective strategy on appeal is to have won below. The deference to be accorded the firsthand fact finder requires more than mere second guessing.[13]

Where there are two permissible views of the evidence, the fact finder's choice between them cannot be clearly erroneous.[14] Indeed, it is commonplace that findings other than those of the trial judge might find some support in the record, or that reviewing judges if sitting at trial might have reached such other findings. It is thus ineffective on appeal merely to present a scenario in which the trial judge could have gone appellant's way.[15] An appellant cannot, by

---

[7]*SSIH Equip. S.A. v. United States ITC,* 718 F.2d 365 (Fed. Cir. 1983).

[8]*Sofamor Danek Group, Inc. v. DePuy-Motech, Inc.,* 74 F.3d 1216, 37 USPQ2d 1529 (Fed. Cir. 1996).

[9]*Heisig v. United States,* 719 F.2d 1153 (Fed. Cir. 1983).

[10]*Medtronic, Inc. v. Daig Corp.,* 789 F.2d 903, 229 USPQ 664 (Fed. Cir. 1986).

[11]*Medtronic, Inc. v. Daig Corp.,* 789 F.2d 903, 229 USPQ 664 (Fed. Cir. 1986); *Ralston Purina Co. v. Far-Mar-Co, Inc.,* 772 F.2d 1570, 227 USPQ 177 (Fed. Cir. 1985).

[12]*Polaroid Corp. v. Eastman Kodak Co.,* 789 F.2d 1556, 229 USPQ 561 (Fed. Cir. 1986). The role of the Federal Circuit is not that of an examiner considering a claim in an application in light of the prior art. *Kloster Speedsteel AB v. Crucible Inc.,* 793 F.2d 1565, 230 USPQ 81 (Fed. Cir. 1986). Initial consideration of evidence is not the appellate role. *H.H. Robertson Co. v. United Steel Deck, Inc.,* 820 F.2d 384, 2 USPQ2d 1926 (Fed. Cir. 1987). The court will not reweigh the evidence on appeal. *Ultradent Prods., Inc. v. Life-Like Cosmetics, Inc.,* 127 F.3d 1065, 44 USPQ2d 1336 (Fed. Cir. 1997).

[13]*Lear Siegler, Inc. v. Aeroquip Corp.,* 733 F.2d 881, 221 USPQ 1025 (Fed. Cir. 1984).

[14]*Hybritech Inc. v. Monoclonal Antibodies, Inc.,* 802 F.2d 1367, 231 USPQ 81 (Fed. Cir. 1986); *Rolls-Royce Ltd. v. GTE Valeron Corp.,* 800 F.2d 1101, 231 USPQ 185 (Fed. Cir. 1986); *Kloster Speedsteel AB v. Crucible Inc.,* 793 F.2d 1565, 230 USPQ 81 (Fed. Cir. 1986); *Ashland Oil, Inc. v. Delta Resins & Refracs., Inc.,* 776 F.2d 281, 227 USPQ 657 (Fed. Cir. 1985); *American Original Corp. v. Jenkins Food Corp.,* 774 F.2d 459, 227 USPQ 299 (Fed. Cir. 1985).

[15]*Polaroid Corp. v. Eastman Kodak Co.,* 789 F.2d 1556, 229 USPQ 561 (Fed. Cir. 1986).

citing only evidence favorable to it, create in the court of appeals a definite and firm conviction that a mistake has been committed.[16] The clearly erroneous standard of review plainly does not entitle a reviewing court to reverse the finding of the trier of fact simply because it is convinced that it would have decided the case differently.[17] If the district court's account of the evidence is plausible in light of the record viewed in its entirety, or where it chooses one of two permissible views of the evidence, there is no clear error.[18]

It does not matter that an appellant may be able to reconstruct its proofs to show that another factual conclusion could have been reached.[19] The appellant must establish not only that its view is permissible but that the view of the district court was clearly in error.[20] It wastes the time of all concerned when an appellant misstates the record and cites only its mere disagreement with findings as support for its burden of showing them clearly erroneous.[21] If an appellant could establish clear error in a district court's findings by merely citing a contrary view advocated at trial by the appellant's expert, the fact-finding role of the district court would be rendered meaningless.[22]

Adoption of findings. That the court below adopted the prevailing party's proposed findings of fact does not make the clearly erroneous standard any less applicable. But an apparent absence of personal attention by the trial court need not be disregarded. Particularly where the adopted findings are those proposed by a party before trial, there is a greater chance that they may be clearly erroneous.[23] Thus, adoption of a party's proposals may increase wariness on review.[24] The court has strongly criticized verbatim adoption of a prevailing party's pretrial findings or brief on this basis. Rule 52(a) ensures care in the preparation of an opinion and provides appellate courts with

---

[16]*Amstar Corp. v. Envirotech Corp.,* 823 F.2d 1538, 3 USPQ2d 1412 (Fed. Cir. 1987). It is a "frequent and foolish appellate ploy" to cite only such bits of evidence as may support one's own view. *Datascope Corp. v. SMEC, Inc.,* 879 F.2d 820, 11 USPQ2d 1321 (Fed. Cir. 1989).

[17]*Miles Labs., Inc. v. Shandon, Inc.,* 997 F.2d 870, 27 USPQ2d 1123 (Fed. Cir. 1993); *American Original Corp. v. Jenkins Food Corp.,* 774 F.2d 459, 227 USPQ 299 (Fed. Cir. 1985).

[18]*Miles Labs., Inc. v. Shandon, Inc.,* 997 F.2d 870, 27 USPQ2d 1123 (Fed. Cir. 1993). See also *Hybritech Inc. v. Monoclonal Antibodies, Inc.,* 802 F.2d 1367, 231 USPQ 81 (Fed. Cir. 1986).

[19]*Studiengesellschaft Kohle v. Dart Indus., Inc.,* 726 F.2d 724, 220 USPQ 841 (Fed. Cir. 1984).

[20]*Kloster Speedsteel AB v. Crucible Inc.,* 793 F.2d 1565, 230 USPQ 81 (Fed. Cir. 1986).

[21]*Mathis v. Spears,* 857 F.2d 749, 8 USPQ2d 1029 (Fed. Cir. 1988).

[22]*Rolls-Royce Ltd. v. GTE Valeron Corp.,* 800 F.2d 1101, 231 USPQ 185 (Fed. Cir. 1986).

[23]*Lindemann Maschinenfabrik v. American Hoist & Derrick Co.,* 730 F.2d 1452, 221 USPQ 481 (Fed. Cir. 1984). Where a trial court adopts a proposed but unaccepted settlement offer as its judgment, it has failed to perform its obligation to determine the case on the basis of the evidence, a clear violation of Rule 52(a), FRCP. *Cheyenne River Sioux Tribe v. United States,* 806 F.2d 1046 (Fed. Cir. 1986). The fact that some findings and conclusions adopted by the court are very like those proposed by the appellee is not so objectionable as to relieve the appellant of its appellate burden of establishing error. *FMC Corp. v. Manitowoc Co.,* 835 F.2d 1411, 5 USPQ2d 1112 (Fed. Cir. 1987).

[24]*Pentec, Inc. v. Graphic Controls Corp.,* 776 F.2d 309, 227 USPQ 766 (Fed. Cir. 1985).

the benefit of the district court's insights into a case, by requiring the district court to find the facts specially and state separately its conclusions of law thereon. Nonetheless, findings of fact, no matter how arrived at, are those of the district court and may be reversed only if clearly erroneous.[25] Even wholesale adoption does not alter the standard of review.[26]

Credibility. Where credibility determinations are involved, it is especially important to observe the rule of clear error. Determining the weight and credibility of the evidence is the special province of the trier of fact.[27] Where evidence is ambiguous and before the district court, the reviewing court cannot redetermine its weight and credibility.[28] In the face of an express finding of credibility, the reviewing court cannot substitute a contrary credibility determination based on a cold paper record.[29] Trial courts have and must continue to have the right to reject the testimony of a witness, a right that can be defeated only when clear error is shown. That a trial court's opinion does not contain language expressly discrediting the testimony of a witness does not license an appellate court to reweigh that testimony and make its own credibility determinations.[30] Where the evidence consists solely of competing expert opinions, the court of appeals has no basis for overturning the district court's credibility determinations.[31]

Nevertheless, a trial judge may not insulate his or her findings from review by denominating them credibility determinations; if documents or objective evidence contradict the witness's story, clear error may be found even in a finding purportedly based on a credibility determination.[32] Findings must be viewed in their entireties.[33]

---

[25]*Mathis v. Spears,* 857 F.2d 749, 8 USPQ2d 1029 (Fed. Cir. 1988); *Hybritech Inc. v. Monoclonal Antibodies, Inc.,* 802 F.2d 1367, 231 USPQ 81 (Fed. Cir. 1986).

[26]*Roton Barrier, Inc. v. Stanley Works,* 79 F.3d 1112, 37 USPQ2d 1816 (Fed. Cir. 1996).

[27]*Revlon, Inc. v. Carson Prods. Co.,* 803 F.2d 676, 231 USPQ 472 (Fed. Cir. 1986); *DMI, Inc. v. Deere & Co.,* 802 F.2d 421, 231 USPQ 276 (Fed. Cir. 1986); *Mainland Indus., Inc. v. Standal's Patents Ltd.,* 799 F.2d 746, 230 USPQ 772 (Fed. Cir. 1986); *Kloster Speedsteel AB v. Crucible Inc.,* 793 F.2d 1565, 230 USPQ 81 (Fed. Cir. 1986); *Gyromat Corp. v. Champion Spark Plug Co.,* 735 F.2d 549, 222 USPQ 4 (Fed. Cir. 1984). The Federal Circuit gives great deference to the trial court's decisions regarding credibility of witnesses. *Goodyear Tire & Rubber Co. v. Hercules Tire & Rubber Co.,* 48 USPQ2d 1767 (Fed. Cir. 1998); *Para-Ordnance Mfg. v. SGS Importers Int'l, Inc.,* 73 F.3d 1085, 37 USPQ2d 1237 (Fed. Cir. 1995).

[28]*Dow Chem. Co. v. American Cyanamid Co.,* 816 F.2d 617, 2 USPQ2d 1350 (Fed. Cir. 1987). Issues of credibility of witnesses are for the jury, and are not amenable to appellate review. *Brooktree Corp. v. Advanced Micro Devices, Inc.,* 977 F.2d 1555, 24 USPQ2d 1401 (Fed. Cir. 1992). As the finder of fact, the jury receives deference for its function of weighing witness demeanor, credibility, and meaning. *Al-Site Corp. v. VSI Int'l Inc.,* 174 F.3d 1308, 50 USPQ2d 1161 (Fed. Cir. 1999).

[29]*DeSarno v. Department of Commerce,* 761 F.2d 657 (Fed. Cir. 1985). Rejection of a special master's credibility determinations has been termed "highly unusual." *TWM Mfg. Co. v. Dura Corp.,* 789 F.2d 895, 229 USPQ 525 (Fed. Cir. 1986).

[30]*Polaroid Corp. v. Eastman Kodak Co.,* 789 F.2d 1556, 229 USPQ 561 (Fed. Cir. 1986).

[31]*Amstar Corp. v. Envirotech Corp.,* 823 F.2d 1538, 3 USPQ2d 1412 (Fed. Cir. 1987).

[32]*Hybritech Inc. v. Monoclonal Antibodies, Inc.,* 802 F.2d 1367, 231 USPQ 81 (Fed. Cir. 1986).

[33]*FMC Corp. v. Manitowoc Co.,* 835 F.2d 1411, 5 USPQ2d 1112 (Fed. Cir. 1987).

Documentary evidence. But should the clearly erroneous standard apply where a finding is based upon documentary evidence? The court has said that the rule applies not only to credibility determinations but to findings based on physical or documentary evidence or inferences from other facts.[34] Yet the court has not really had to decide that question in the context of purely documentary evidence. In one case, it refused to decide whether to adopt an exception to the clearly erroneous rule where all of the evidence is documentary, probably because the trial court there relied at least partially on witness testimony to support the finding.[35] In another case, it pointed out that an appellate court is not in as good a position as the trial court to judge the true significance of documentary and physical exhibits that are introduced through or testified about by live witnesses.[36]

The fact that ultimate findings are entered on a motion for judgment under Rule 41(b), FRCP, does not alter the standard of review. A trial judge in passing on a Rule 41(b) motion evaluates and resolves conflicts of evidence and credibility, and findings entered as a result of such a motion are therefore reviewed under the same clearly erroneous standard as are findings entered at the close of all the evidence.[37]

(ii) Legal Correctness

Questions of law are subject to full and independent review, sometimes referred to as "de novo" or "plenary" review.[38] The court regards the term "de novo" as something of a misnomer, inasmuch as de novo consideration is to determine a matter as if it had not been heard before and no decision had been rendered. What the court really means when it uses the term is that it does not defer to the lower court or agency ruling in question.[39]

Legal conclusions of district courts will not be reversed unless they are incorrect as a matter of law.[40] The Federal Circuit regards itself as largely unfettered in its review of legal questions. It sees its task as follows: to consider the facts, either as properly found by the fact finder or as stipulated to or otherwise uncontested by the parties, and reach its own conclusion on the ultimate legal question. It then either affirms if it agrees with the trial court, reverses if it does not, or vacates and remands if the record lacks facts essential to

---

[34]*Hybritech Inc. v. Monoclonal Antibodies, Inc.,* 802 F.2d 1367, 231 USPQ 81 (Fed. Cir. 1986); *Tyler Refrigeration v. Kysor Indus. Corp.,* 777 F.2d 687, 227 USPQ 845 (Fed. Cir. 1985). See also *TWM Mfg. Co. v. Dura Corp.,* 789 F.2d 895, 229 USPQ 525 (Fed. Cir. 1986).

[35]*Gardner v. TEC Sys., Inc.,* 725 F.2d 1338, 220 USPQ 777 (Fed. Cir. 1984).

[36]*Preemption Devices, Inc. v. Minnesota Min. & Mfg. Co.,* 732 F.2d 903, 221 USPQ 841 (Fed. Cir. 1984).

[37]*Lemelson v. United States,* 752 F.2d 1538, 224 USPQ 526 (Fed. Cir. 1985).

[38]*In re Asahi/Am. Inc.,* 48 F.3d 1204, 37 USPQ2d 1204 (Fed. Cir. 1995). The meaning or interpretation of precedent is a question of law, and a determination thereof is given de novo review by the Federal Circuit. *YBM Magnex Inc. v. United States ITC,* 145 F.3d 1317, 46 USPQ2d 1843 (Fed. Cir. 1998).

[39]*Litton Sys., Inc. v. Honeywell, Inc.,*87 F.3d 1559, 39 USPQ2d 1321 (Fed. Cir. 1996).

[40]*Heisig v. United States,* 719 F.2d 1153 (Fed. Cir. 1983).

formulating a conclusion.[41] It is suggested, with all respect, that this view may be overbroad, at least to the extent that it seems to admit of no respect whatever for the conclusion of the trial judge. Must an appellate court be convinced that the trial court was wrong, or is simple disagreement enough for reversal? While one can argue with some conviction that disagreement is alone sufficient in the case of a point of law, perhaps a greater degree of "wrongness" must be present in order to reverse on an ultimate legal question, such as obviousness or claim interpretation.

The court has said that a lower court is presumed to have applied the law correctly, absent a clear showing to the contrary.[42] One doubts that this statement signals any deliberate retreat from the Federal Circuit's broad view of its role in reviewing legal questions. For example, the court often says that, in reviewing claim interpretation—a question of law based upon intensely factual inquiries—it need not defer to the district court.[43]

It misperceives the roles of fact and law in the judicial process to suppose that because a finding cannot stand if reached through improper application of a legal standard governing the fact-finding function, a legal conclusion can exist in a vacuum. Established facts (undisputed or correctly found) lead to legal conclusions, not the other way round.[44]

In any event, it is clear that reversal requires more than a mere demonstration of error in analysis on questions of law. There must be a demonstration that if the errors were corrected, the application of the law to the facts would produce a different result. In short, such errors as may be demonstrated must further have been harmful.[45] Affirmance does not require that the appellate court and the trial court reach the same conclusion in precisely the same fashion.[46] But controlling misstatements of the legal criteria applicable to obviousness determinations confirm the certain presence of reversible legal error.[47]

(iii) Abuse of Discretion

On many matters, the lower court has a range of choice, and its decision will not be disturbed as long as it stays within that range and is not influenced by any mistake of law. The reviewing court

---

[41]*Gardner v. TEC Sys., Inc.*, 725 F.2d 1338, 220 USPQ 777 (Fed. Cir. 1984).

[42]*Lee v. Dayton-Hudson Corp.*, 838 F.2d 1186, 5 USPQ2d 1625 (Fed. Cir. 1988).

[43]*Specialty Composites v. Cabot Corp.*, 845 F.2d 981, 6 USPQ2d 1601 (Fed. Cir. 1988). See cases cited in and discussion accompanying notes 17:182–192.

[44]*FMC Corp. v. Manitowoc Co.*, 835 F.2d 1411, 5 USPQ2d 1112 (Fed. Cir. 1987).

[45]*Cable Elec. Prods., Inc. v. Genmark, Inc.*, 770 F.2d 1015, 226 USPQ 881 (Fed. Cir. 1985). See also *Carella v. Starlight Archery & Pro Line Co.*, 804 F.2d 135, 231 USPQ 644 (Fed. Cir. 1986).

[46]*Gardner v. TEC Sys., Inc.*, 725 F.2d 1338, 220 USPQ 777 (Fed. Cir. 1984).

[47]*Panduit Corp. v. Dennison Mfg. Co.*, 810 F.2d 1561, 1 USPQ2d 1593 (Fed. Cir. 1987).

must address a matter left to the discretion of the district court with hesitancy. Abuses must be unusual and exceptional; the reviewing court must not merely substitute its judgment for that of the trial judge.[48] The proper exercise of discretion should not be impeded by second guessing at the appellate level.[49] Abuse of discretion is reflected in a definite and firm conviction that the court below committed a clear error of judgment.[50]

The court seems to approve the concept that a clear error of judgment occurs only if the appellate court comes close to finding that the trial court has taken leave of its senses.[51] An abuse occurs only when (1) the decision is clearly unreasonable, arbitrary, or fanciful; (2) the decision is based on an erroneous conclusion of law; (3) the court's findings are clearly erroneous; or (4) the record contains no evidence on which the district court could rationally have based its decision.[52] Demonstrating abuse of discretion is a difficult task.[53] However, denial of relief without any justifying reason is not an exercise of discretion; it is merely abuse of discretion.[54]

(b) Tribunal or Proceeding

The standard of review employed by the Federal Circuit may often be dictated, or at least conditioned, by the nature or stage of the proceeding under review, or by the type of court or administrative body that conducted it in the first instance.

(i) Particular Tribunals

Courts and the ITC. As we have seen, review of district court fact findings is governed by Rule 52(a), FRCP.[55] The same is true for findings of fact of the Court of Federal Claims.[56] The Federal Circuit

---

[48]*Heat & Control, Inc. v. Hester Indus. Inc.*, 785 F.2d 1017, 228 USPQ 926 (Fed. Cir. 1986).

[49]*Rosemount, Inc. v. Beckman Instr., Inc.*, 727 F.2d 1540, 221 USPQ 1 (Fed. Cir. 1984).

[50]*Verdegaal Bros., Inc. v. Union Oil Co.*, 750 F.2d 947, 224 USPQ 249 (Fed. Cir. 1984).

[51]*Datascope Corp. v. SMEC, Inc.*, 879 F.2d 820, 11 USPQ2d 1321 (Fed. Cir. 1989). See Friendly, "Indiscretion about Discretion," 31 *Emory L.J.* 747, 763 (1982). Discretion, in this sense, is abused if the record contains no basis on which the district court rationally could have made its decision or if the judicial action is arbitrary, fanciful, or clearly unreasonable.

[52]*Heat & Control, Inc. v. Hester Indus. Inc.*, 785 F.2d 1017, 228 USPQ 926 (Fed. Cir. 1986). Certainly the second and third criteria must require, in addition, a definite and firm conviction of error; otherwise the standard would not seem to differ from clear error and legal correctness. See also *Abrutyn v. Giovanniello*, 15 F.3d 1048, 29 USPQ2d 1615 (Fed. Cir. 1994); *Haworth, Inc. v. Steelcase, Inc.*, 12 F.3d 1090, 29 USPQ2d 1368 (Fed. Cir. 1993).

[53]*J.P. Stevens Co. v. Lex Tex Ltd.*, 822 F.2d 1047, 3 USPQ2d 1235 (Fed. Cir. 1987). In an "additional views" opinion, Judge Bissell presented a useful discourse on appellate review of discretionary rulings. *PPG Indus., Inc. v. Celanese Polymer Spec. Co.*, 840 F.2d 1565, 6 USPQ2d 1010 (Fed. Cir. 1988).

[54]*Kalman v. Berlyn Corp.*, 914 F.2d 1473, 16 USPQ2d 1093, 1098 (Fed. Cir. 1990).

[55]*Heisig v. United States*, 719 F.2d 1153 (Fed. Cir. 1983).

[56]*Atlas Corp. v. United States*, 895 F.2d 745 (Fed. Cir. 1990); *Hankins Constr. Co. v. United States*, 838 F.2d 1194 (Fed. Cir. 1988); *Alger v. United States*, 741 F.2d 391 (Fed. Cir.

reviews judgments of the Court of Federal Claims to determine whether they are premised on clearly erroneous factual determinations or otherwise incorrect as a matter of law. It reviews in a plenary fashion whether the Court of Federal Claims properly grants summary judgment or properly dismisses for failure to state a claim upon which relief can be granted, as both are questions of law.[57] The Federal Circuit reviews a district court's review of a bankruptcy court decision involving patent issues independently, applying the clearly erroneous standard to the factual determinations of the bankruptcy court and de novo review to its conclusions of law.[58]

On the other hand, an ITC proceeding is not a civil action, and the clearly erroneous standard does not apply.[59] Rather, factual findings of the ITC are reviewed to determine whether they are supported by substantial evidence,[60] which is such relevant evidence as a reasonable mind might accept as adequate to support a conclusion[61]—the same stringent standard applicable to a trial court in taking a case from a jury or in reviewing a jury verdict on a motion for JNOV.[62] The ITC can issue an order only if it is in accordance with substantial evidence. This requires weighing the evidence with respect to reliability, materiality, relevance, probativeness, and quantity. But the Federal Circuit reviews the ITC determination to see whether it is unsupported by substantial evidence, a far different standard that requires no weighing.[63] There is a significant difference between this standard and the clearly erroneous standard, and in a close case the difference can be controlling. It was the intent of Congress that greater weight and finality be accorded to the ITC's findings than those of a trial court.[64]

1984); *Milmark Serv., Inc. v. United States,* 731 F.2d 855 (Fed. Cir. 1984). The de novo standard of review of Claims Court legal conclusions provides the court with substantial latitude. *Confederated Tribes v. United States,* 964 F.2d 1102 (Fed. Cir. 1992).

[57]*Dairyland Power Coop. v. United States,* 16 F.3d 1197 (Fed. Cir. 1994).

[58]*Institut Pasteur v. Cambridge Biotech Corp.,* 186 F.3d 1356, 51 USPQ2d 1321 (Fed. Cir. 1999).

[59]*SSIH Equip. S.A. v. United States ITC,* 713 F.2d 746, 218 USPQ 678 (Fed. Cir. 1983).

[60]*Tanabe Seiyaku Co. v. United States ITC,* 109 F.3d 726, 41 USPQ2d 1976 (Fed. Cir. 1997); *LaBounty Mfg., Inc. v. United States ITC,* 867 F.2d 1572, 9 USPQ2d 1995 (Fed. Cir. 1989); *Texas Instr., Inc. v. United States ITC,* 805 F.2d 1558, 231 USPQ 833 (Fed. Cir. 1986); *New England Butt Co. v. United States ITC,* 756 F.2d 874, 225 USPQ 260 (Fed. Cir. 1985); *American Hosp. Supply Corp. v. Travenol Labs., Inc.,* 745 F.2d 1, 223 USPQ 577 (Fed. Cir. 1984). Summary determinations by the ITC are reviewed as a matter of law. Because the ALJ has not made any factual determinations at that stage in the proceedings, the substantial evidence standard of review is not applicable. *Hazani v. United States ITC,* 126 F.3d 1473, 44 USPQ2d 1358 (Fed. Cir. 1997).

[61]*Checkpoint Sys., Inc. v. United States ITC,* 54 F.3d 756, 35 USPQ2d 1042 (Fed. Cir. 1995); *Akzo N.V. v. United States ITC,* 808 F.2d 1471, 1 USPQ2d 1241 (Fed. Cir. 1986); *DMI, Inc. v. Deere & Co.,* 802 F.2d 421, 231 USPQ 276 (Fed. Cir. 1986); *SSIH Equip. S.A. v. United States ITC,* 713 F.2d 746, 218 USPQ 678 (Fed. Cir. 1983).

[62]*Corning Glass Works v. United States ITC,* 799 F.2d 1559, 230 USPQ 822 (Fed. Cir. 1986).

[63]*Fischer & Porter Co. v. United States ITC,* 831 F.2d 1574, 4 USPQ2d 1700 (Fed. Cir. 1987).

[64]*Tandon Corp. v. United States ITC,* 831 F.2d 1017, 4 USPQ2d 1283 (Fed. Cir. 1987). At the same time, it is the primary responsibility of the ITC to administer the trade laws and not the patent laws. *Id.*

The Federal Circuit is not bound by the ITC's legal conclusions, however.[65] Under 19 U.S.C. §1337(c), the standard of review for ITC determinations is established by the more general provisions of 5 U.S.C. §706, which provides that the reviewing court shall decide all relevant questions of law.[66]

The matter of Federal Circuit review of ITC orders is treated in substantially more detail in §11.2.

Masters. The proper standard of review where the district court rejects the findings of a special master is simply whether the district court was correct. The clearly erroneous standard would apply, however, to any substitute or additional findings of the district court and to any of the master's original findings that are adopted by the court.[67] Rejection of a master's credibility determinations is regarded as "highly unusual."[68]

Administrative agencies. Review of findings of administrative agencies in general is governed by the substantial evidence standard.[69] Federal Circuit review of administrative action is discussed in detail in §18.1.

PTO tribunals. Similar considerations govern review of PTO rules and procedures. There the standard is whether they are within the statutory authority of the PTO and reasonably related to the purposes of the enabling legislation, and do no violence to due process.[70] On substantive matters, however, the PTO tribunals were not,

---

[65]*American Hosp. Supply Corp. v. Travenol Labs., Inc.*, 745 F.2d 1, 223 USPQ 577 (Fed. Cir. 1984); *SSIH Equip. S.A. v. United States ITC*, 713 F.2d 746, 218 USPQ 678 (Fed. Cir. 1983). Inasmuch as obviousness is a question of law, the Federal Circuit is not bound by the ITC's ultimate determination on that matter. *Akzo N.V. v. United States ITC*, 808 F.2d 1471, 1 USPQ2d 1241 (Fed. Cir. 1986). In an ITC case the underlying factual determinations are reviewed under the substantial evidence standard and the holding of obviousness is reviewed de novo. *Intel Corp. v. United States ITC*, 946 F.2d 821, 20 USPQ2d 1161 (Fed. Cir. 1991). The ITC's legal determinations are reviewed de novo, including those relating to claim interpretation and patent validity. *Checkpoint Sys., Inc. v. United States ITC*, 54 F.3d 756, 35 USPQ2d 1042 (Fed. Cir. 1995). Rulings of law by the ITC receive plenary review on appeal. The meaning or interpretation of precedent is a question of law, and an ITC determination thereof is given de novo review by the Federal Circuit. *YBM Magnex Inc. v. United States ITC*, 145 F.3d 1317, 46 USPQ2d 1843 (Fed. Cir. 1998).

[66]*Corning Glass Works v. United States ITC*, 799 F.2d 1559, 230 USPQ 822 (Fed. Cir. 1986). The Federal Circuit reviews final determinations of the ITC in accordance with Chapter 7 of the Administrative Procedure Act, 5 U.S.C. §§701–706. *Genentech, Inc. v. United States ITC*, 122 F.3d 1409, 43 USPQ2d 1722 (Fed. Cir. 1997).

[67]*Milliken Res. Corp. v. Dan River, Inc.*, 739 F.2d 587, 222 USPQ 571 (Fed. Cir. 1984). In *Riverwood Int'l Corp. v. Mead Corp.*, 212 F.3d 1365, 54 USPQ2d 1763 (Fed. Cir. 2), a special master heard the evidence, made findings of fact, and concluded that the claims would have been obvious. The district court accepted the findings in whole and without modification, but concluded that the claims would not have been obvious. The Federal Circuit reversed on the basis that the findings would support only the legal conclusion of obviousness.

[68]*TWM Mfg. Co. v. Dura Corp.*, 789 F.2d 895, 229 USPQ 525 (Fed. Cir. 1986).

[69]*SSIH Equip. S.A. v. United States ITC*, 718 F.2d 365 (Fed. Cir. 1983).

[70]*Patlex Corp. v. Mossinghoff*, 758 F.2d 594, 225 USPQ 243 (Fed. Cir. 1985).

until just recently, treated like other administrative agencies. With regard to questions of law, the review was without deference to the views of the PTO. With regard to questions of fact, the Federal Circuit deferred to the PTO unless its findings were clearly erroneous. With regard to questions that fall somewhere near the middle of the spectrum, it recognized the inappropriateness of the fact-law dichotomy, since the determination at issue, involving as it does the application of a general legal standard to particular facts, is probably most realistically described as neither of fact nor of law, but mixed. When it encountered such questions, the extent to which the court deferred to the PTO turned on the nature of the case and the nature of the judgment.[71]

Thus, facts found by PTO tribunals were reviewed under the clearly erroneous standard.[72] In the mid-1990s, the PTO began a campaign to force the court to apply the substantial evidence standard of the Administrative Procedure Act.[73] This culminated in the 1999 decision of the Supreme Court in *Dickinson v. Zurko*,[74] where the Court made it clear that the Federal Circuit is to review decisions of the PTO using the review framework of the Administrative Procedure

---

[71]*In re Brana*, 51 F.3d 1560, 34 USPQ2d 1437 (Fed. Cir. 1995). See also *In re McCarthy*, 763 F.2d 411, 226 USPQ 99 (Fed. Cir. 1985).

[72]*Gechter v. Davidson*, 116 F.3d 1454, 43 USPQ2d 1030 (Fed. Cir. 1997); *In re Alton*, 76 F.3d 1168, 37 USPQ2d 1578 (Fed. Cir. 1996); *In re Epstein*, 32 F.3d 1559, 31 USPQ2d 1817 (Fed. Cir. 1994); *In re Rijckaert*, 9 F.3d 1531, 28 USPQ2d 1955 (Fed. Cir. 1993); *In re Woodruff*, 919 F.2d 1575, 16 USPQ2d 1934 (Fed. Cir. 1990); *In re Kulling*, 897 F.2d 1147, 14 USPQ2d 1056 (Fed. Cir. 1990); *In re King*, 801 F.2d 1324, 231 USPQ 136 (Fed. Cir. 1986); *Denen v. Buss*, 801 F.2d 385, 231 USPQ 159 (Fed. Cir. 1986); *Coleman v. Dines*, 754 F.2d 353, 224 USPQ 857 (Fed. Cir. 1985). Cf. *Fregeau v. Mossinghoff*, 776 F.2d 1034, 227 USPQ 848 (Fed. Cir. 1985). Thus in appeals from PTO rejections the Federal Circuit did not find facts de novo but overturned PTO findings only when left with the definite and firm conviction that a mistake had been made. *In re Caveney*, 761 F.2d 671, 226 USPQ 1 (Fed. Cir. 1985). These same standards—correctness of legal analysis and clear error as to factual analysis—applied to cases reaching the court on requests for reexamination. *In re Andersen*, 743 F.2d 1578, 223 USPQ 378 (Fed. Cir. 1984).

[73]In the case of *In re Brana*, 51 F.3d 1560, 34 USPQ2d 1437 (Fed. Cir. 1995), the PTO asked the court to reconsider its long-time standards, to apply the Administrative Procedure Act, 5 U.S.C. §706, and use the abuse of discretion or substantial evidence standards, based upon the presumed expertise of the PTO. The court declined the invitation on the ground that adoption of the standard urged by the PTO would not have changed the result in the case. A similar request was declined in *In re Napier*, 55 F.3d 610, 34 USPQ2d 1782 (Fed. Cir. 1995) and again in *In re Kemps*, 97 F.3d 1427, 40 USPQ2d 1309 (Fed. Cir. 1996). In the latter case, the court showed a deal of impatience with the PTO because the entire appeal was briefed and argued by the PTO under the incorrect standard. See also *In re Mac Dermid, Inc.*, 111 F.3d 890, 42 USPQ2d 1479 (Fed. Cir. 1997). In *In re Zurko*, 111 F.3d 887, 42 USPQ2d 1476 (Fed. Cir. 1997), the court suggested that the PTO might want to seek in banc review of the question in an appropriate case. In *In re Lueders*, 111 F.3d 1569, 42 USPQ2d 1481 (Fed. Cir. 1997), a panel refused to refer the matter for in banc review. The *Lueders* panel traced the history of the standard of review of PTO decisions, looked at the legislative history of the APA and the Patent Act of 1952, and concluded that its current standards of de novo review of legal questions and clear error for factual questions remained the appropriate ones. The court finally sat in banc in rehearing of *In re Zurko*, 142 F.3d 1447, 46 USPQ2d 1691 (Fed. Cir. 1998), and adhered to its long-standing clearly erroneous standard of review.

[74]*Dickinson v. Zurko*, 527 U.S. 150, 50 USPQ2d 1930 (1999), *reversing In re Zurko*, 142 F.3d 1447, 46 USPQ2d 1691 (Fed. Cir. 1998).

Act, 5 U.S.C. §706. Thus, the less stringent APA court/agency standards (arbitrary, capricious, abuse of discretion, or unsupported by substantial evidence) must be applied, rather than the somewhat stricter court/court standard of clear error. Factual findings of the PTO Board must now be affirmed if they are supported by substantial evidence.[75]

For PTO Board legal conclusions, the standard of review is correctness or error as a matter of law.[76] For example, whether the Board possesses jurisdiction to continue an interference in order to decide patentability issues is a question of law that is reviewed de novo.[77] Board decisions may be in error even if there is a rational basis therefor, and it is the responsibility of all appellate courts to apply the law correctly. Review of Board decisions on legal conclusions such as obviousness will therefore be deeper than that required to determine a "rational basis."[78]

When a decision pursuant to a permissive statute concerns only PTO practice, the Federal Circuit reviews the decision for abuse of discretion. This standard likewise applies to decisions taken pursuant to a permissive regulation; this is a proper exercise of the authority granted under 35 U.S.C. §6(a). Thus, both a decision to sanction an interference party and the choice of sanction are reviewed for abuse of discretion.[79] A Board decision to resolve issues of patentability that are not placed in issue by the parties to an interference is reviewed for abuse of discretion.[80] The determination whether a party seeking to initiate an interference has shown good cause for its failure to present additional evidence at the time of its initial submission is also a matter within the discretion of the Board.[81] In either case, an abuse of that discretion may be found when the Board's decision is clearly unreasonable, based on an erroneous conclusion of law or a clearly erroneous finding, or the record is devoid of any evidence upon

---

[75]*In re Hyatt,* 211 F.3d 1367, 54 USPQ2d 1664 (Fed. Cir. 2); *In re Gartside,* 203 F.3d 1305, 53 USPQ2d 1769 (Fed. Cir. 2). This standard applies to interferences as well as ex parte determinations. *Singh v. Brake,* 222 F.3d 1362, 55 USPQ2d 1673 (Fed. Cir. 2). See *In re Kotzab,* 217 F.3d 1365, 55 USPQ2d 1313 (Fed. Cir. 2), as an example of how the court applies the substantial evidence standard in reviewing PTO determinations.

[76]*In re Caveney,* 761 F.2d 671, 226 USPQ 1 (Fed. Cir. 1985). The question of whether a party properly raised an issue is a question of law based on subsidiary factual findings. Where there is no factual dispute as to what statements were contained in a final hearing brief, but only the legal significance to be accorded the statements, the court reviews de novo the Board's conclusion that the statements did not adequately raise the issue. *Cooper v. Goldfarb,* 154 F.3d 1321, 47 USPQ2d 1896 (Fed. Cir. 1998).

[77]*In re Gartside,* 203 F.3d 1305, 53 USPQ2d 1769 (Fed. Cir. 2).

[78]*In re Raynes,* 7 F.3d 1037, 28 USPQ2d 1630 (Fed. Cir. 1993); *In re McCarthy,* 763 F.2d 411, 226 USPQ 99 (Fed. Cir. 1985). The court reviews Board determinations of obviousness for correctness or error. *In re Mills,* 916 F.2d 680, 16 USPQ2d 1430 (Fed. Cir. 1990).

[79]*Gerritsen v. Shirai,* 979 F.2d 1524, 24 USPQ2d 1912 (Fed. Cir. 1992). See also *Abrutyn v. Giovanniello,* 15 F.3d 1048, 29 USPQ2d 1615 (Fed. Cir. 1994).

[80]*In re Gartside,* 203 F.3d 1305, 53 USPQ2d 1769 (Fed. Cir. 2).

[81]*Huston v. Ladner,* 973 F.2d 1564, 23 USPQ2d 1910 (Fed. Cir. 1992).

which the Board rationally could have based its decision. The court will not simply substitute its judgment for that of the Board.[82]

While the evidentiary record before the Board serves as the evidentiary nucleus of the district court proceeding in an action under 35 U.S.C. §145, the parties are entitled to submit additional evidence. In such an action, the district court can set aside the Board's fact findings only if they are clearly erroneous, but if new evidence is presented on a disputed question of fact, a de novo fact finding is made by the district court. Thus, on a question of law, where extensive additional evidence directed to the factual underpinnings of that legal question was presented to the district court, Federal Circuit review will be as for any bench trial: clear error in fact findings and error in law.[83]

(ii) Nature or Stage of Proceeding

Jury trials. The role of a trial court should not be significantly different in a patent jury trial from its role in a patent bench trial with respect to legal issues, and the standard of appellate review is the same: it is the duty of the appellate court to be satisfied that the law has been correctly applied to the facts regardless of whether the facts were determined by judge or by jury.[84] But a different and stricter standard applies to findings of fact by a jury: they are reviewed only for reasonableness under the substantial evidence test.[85]

The matter of appellate review in jury cases is treated in detail in §10.3(g).

Trial management. Indeed, be the trial by jury or bench, the Federal Rules of Civil Procedure recognize the need for the exercise of discretion by the trial court in carrying out its duty of managing the judicial process, the business of the court, and the administration of justice. The proper exercise of that discretion should not be impeded by second guessing at the appellate level.[86] District judges are overburdened and need flexibility to operate efficiently. They deserve tolerance by reviewing courts so they can tailor procedures of adjudication

---

[82]*Gerritsen v. Shirai*, 979 F.2d 1524, 24 USPQ2d 1912 (Fed. Cir. 1992); *Huston v. Ladner*, 973 F.2d 1564, 23 USPQ2d 1910 (Fed. Cir. 1992).

[83]*Gould v. Quigg*, 822 F.2d 1074, 3 USPQ2d 1302 (Fed. Cir. 1987).

[84]*Structural Rubber Prods. Co. v. Park Rubber Co.*, 749 F.2d 707, 223 USPQ 1264 (Fed. Cir. 1984).

[85]*Orthokinetics, Inc. v. Safety Travel Chairs, Inc.*, 806 F.2d 1565, 1 USPQ2d 1081 (Fed. Cir. 1986); *Structural Rubber Prods. Co. v. Park Rubber Co.*, 749 F.2d 707, 223 USPQ 1264 (Fed. Cir. 1984). But where a jury is asked to decide a question of law that depends on underlying factual determinations, the jury's legal conclusion is subject to independent review by the court on appeal. *Sjolund v. Musland*, 847 F.2d 1573, 6 USPQ2d 2020 (Fed. Cir. 1988).

[86]*Rosemount, Inc. v. Beckman Instr., Inc.*, 727 F.2d 1540, 221 USPQ 1 (Fed. Cir. 1984). A district court's trial management should not be disturbed absent a clear abuse of judicial discretion. *Abbott Labs. v. Brennan*, 952 F.2d 1346, 21 USPQ2d 1192 (Fed. Cir. 1992).

to the case at hand.[87] Trial courts have substantial discretion in the management of their case load, including determination of when and how to discipline those who appear before them.[88] Thus the procedure and arrangements adopted by a district court for managing a trial and entering judgments are clearly within that court's discretion when exercised under the rules.[89]

For example, the standard of review from a trial court's decision to waive the 30-day notice requirement for a prior art statement under 35 U.S.C. §282 places a burden on the appellant to show abuse of discretion; the trial court is not even required to give reasons for the waiver.[90] Stay orders are reviewed for abuse of discretion as well.[91] The court reviews rulings under local court rules for abuse of discretion.[92]

The abuse of discretion standard is applied generally to review of evidentiary rulings in the federal system.[93] Evidentiary rulings are reviewed with extreme deference. In matters of trial management the district court has a limited right to be wrong without incurring appellate intrusion. Appellate review of evidentiary rulings is therefore extremely restricted; it must be shown that there was manifest error, such as a reasonable likelihood that the improper exclusion of evidence prejudiced the outcome.[94] When balancing probative value against possible prejudice, the trial court has broad discretion. A trial court's admission or exclusion of evidence on grounds of relevance is reviewed for abuse of discretion. Excluded evidence is viewed in the light most favorable to its proponent, giving the evidence its maximum reasonable probative force and its minimum reasonable prejudicial value. The reviewing court, in order to reverse such a decision made at trial, must be firmly convinced that a prejudicial mistake was made.[95] Admission of expert testimony is within the discretion of the

---

[87]*Reebok Int'l Ltd. v. J. Baker, Inc.*, 32 F.3d 1552, 31 USPQ2d 1781 (Fed. Cir. 1994).

[88]*Hendler v. United States*, 952 F.2d 1364 (Fed. Cir. 1991); *Thermocycle Int'l, Inc. v. A.F. Hinrichsen Sales Corp.*, 851 F.2d 339, 7 USPQ2d 1407 (Fed. Cir. 1988).

[89]*Atari, Inc. v. JS & A Group, Inc.*, 747 F.2d 1422, 223 USPQ 1074 (Fed. Cir. 1984). Procedural errors that do not unfairly affect the outcome are to be ignored. Trials must be fair not perfect. *Newell Cos. v. Kenney Mfg. Co.*, 864 F.2d 757, 9 USPQ2d 1417 (Fed. Cir. 1988). The court reviews a decision to forego a binding jury determination of factual issues common to a legal and equitable claim for abuse of discretion, recognizing that such discretion is narrowly limited in these circumstances and must, wherever possible, be exercised to preserve jury trial. *Cabinet Vision v. Cabnetware*, 129 F.3d 595, 44 USPQ2d 1683 (Fed. Cir. 1997).

[90]*Trans-World Mfg. Corp. v. Al Nyman & Sons*, 750 F.2d 1552, 224 USPQ 259 (Fed. Cir. 1984).

[91]*Intermedics Infusaid, Inc. v. Regents of Univ. of Minn.*, 804 F.2d 129, 231 USPQ 653 (Fed. Cir. 1986).

[92]*Serrano v. Telular Corp.*, 111 F.3d 1578, 42 USPQ2d 1538 (Fed. Cir. 1997).

[93]*ATD Corp. v. Lydall Inc.*, 159 F.3d 534, 48 USPQ2d 1321 (Fed. Cir. 1998).

[94]*National Presto Indus., Inc. v. West Bend Co.*, 76 F.3d 1185, 37 USPQ2d 1685 (Fed. Cir. 1996). Evidentiary rulings are reviewed for prejudicial legal error. *Eastman Kodak Co. v. Goodyear Tire & Rubber Co.*, 114 F.3d 1547, 42 USPQ2d 1737 (Fed. Cir. 1997).

[95]*Abbott Labs. v. Brennan*, 952 F.2d 1346, 21 USPQ2d 1192 (Fed. Cir. 1992). See also *Roton Barrier, Inc. v. Stanley Works*, 79 F.3d 1112, 37 USPQ2d 1816 (Fed. Cir. 1996); *Kearns v. Chrysler Corp.*, 32 F.3d 1541, 31 USPQ2d 1746 (Fed. Cir. 1994). Exclusions of evidence under

trial court. A decision on such a question will not be disturbed unless the court abuses its discretion.[96]

All aspects of Rule 11 determinations are reviewed under an abuse of discretion standard,[97] as are sanctions pursuant to 28 U.S.C. §1927.[98] In matters of sanctions particular deference is owed the trial court's discretion, for the trial judge has viewed the matter at first hand, has considered all the circumstances, and made assessments of credibility and other intangibles that escape the written record.[99] Sanctions pursuant to local court rules are also reviewed for abuse of discretion.[100]

There are limits, however. In one case a grant of summary judgment of noninfringement was reversed on grounds that the trial court had abused its discretion in refusing to permit testimony on claim interpretation.[101] A highly disproportionate penalty can constitute an abuse of discretion.[102] In order to show abuse of discretion in exclusion of evidence, the appealing party must show that its substantive rights have been affected.[103]

Proper interpretation of a pretrial stipulation, like any contract, presents a legal question that is addressed on appeal de novo.[104]

Summary judgment and Rule 12 motions. As a general rule, when a district court grants summary judgment, the Federal Circuit reviews without deference to the trial court whether there are disputed material facts, and independently whether the prevailing party is entitled to judgment as a matter of law. By contrast, when a district

---

Rule 403, FRE, are reviewed under an abuse of discretion standard. *Mendenhall v. Cedarapids, Inc.,* 5 F.3d 1556, 28 USPQ2d 1081 (Fed. Cir. 1993). It must be shown that the district court abused its discretion in admitting the challenged evidence and that such rulings prejudiced substantial rights and were thus not harmless error. *Kolmes v. World Fibers Corp.,* 107 F.3d 1534, 41 USPQ2d 1829 (Fed. Cir. 1997); *Munoz v. Strahm Farms, Inc.,* 69 F.3d 501, 36 USPQ2d 1499 (Fed. Cir. 1995).

[96]*Trilogy Comm., Inc. v. Times Fiber Comm., Inc.,* 109 F.3d 739, 42 USPQ2d 1129 (Fed. Cir. 1997); *General Electro Music Corp. v. Samick Music Corp.,* 19 F.3d 1405, 30 USPQ2d 1149 (Fed. Cir. 1994); *Abbott Labs. v. Brennan,* 952 F.2d 1346, 21 USPQ2d 1192 (Fed. Cir. 1992); *Acoustical Design, Inc. v. Control Elec. Co.,* 932 F.2d 939, 18 USPQ2d 939 (Fed. Cir. 1991).

[97]*S. Bravo Sys., Inc. v. Containment Tech. Corp.,* 96 F.3d 1372, 40 USPQ2d 1140 (Fed. Cir. 1996); *Refac Int'l, Ltd. v. Hitachi, Ltd.,* 921 F.2d 1247, 16 USPQ2d 1347 (Fed. Cir. 1990); *New Idea Farm Equip. Corp. v. Sperry Corp.,* 916 F.2d 1561, 16 USPQ2d 1424 (Fed. Cir. 1990).

[98]*Baldwin Hardware Corp. v. Franksu Enter. Corp.,* 78 F.3d 550, 37 USPQ2d 1829 (Fed. Cir. 1996). The abuse of discretion standard applies to both the decision to sanction, and the amount of the sanction. *View Eng'g Inc. v. Robotic Vision Sys. Inc.,* 208 F.3d 981, 54 USPQ2d 1179 (Fed. Cir. 2).

[99]*Abbott Labs. v. Brennan,* 952 F.2d 1346, 21 USPQ2d 1192 (Fed. Cir. 1992).

[100]*Baldwin Hardware Corp. v. Franksu Enter. Corp.,* 78 F.3d 550, 37 USPQ2d 1829 (Fed. Cir. 1996). The same standard applies to the terms of a disciplinary order issued under the trial court's inherent authority to sanction attorneys for unprofessional conduct. *Id.*

[101]*Moeller v. Ionetics, Inc.,* 794 F.2d 653, 229 USPQ 992 (Fed. Cir. 1986).

[102]*Thermocycle Int'l, Inc. v. A.F. Hinrichsen Sales Corp.,* 851 F.2d 339, 7 USPQ2d 1407 (Fed. Cir. 1988).

[103]*DMI, Inc. v. Deere & Co.,* 802 F.2d 421, 231 USPQ 276 (Fed. Cir. 1986).

[104]*Kearns v. Chrysler Corp.,* 32 F.3d 1541, 31 USPQ2d 1746, 1749 (Fed. Cir. 1994).

court denies summary judgment, that decision is reviewed with considerable deference to the trial court.[105] In an appeal of a grant of summary judgment, such factual inferences as are material to the grant are not reviewed under the clearly erroneous standard, as though they were findings of fact made following a trial of issues. Since a district court has no genuine discretion in determining whether to grant summary judgment, a reviewing court must determine de novo that the strict standard to be applied by the district court has been met. To affirm a grant of summary judgment, an appellate court must accordingly determine that the record demonstrates an absence of any actual dispute as to factual inferences that would have a material impact on the entitlement of the summary judgment movant to judgment as a matter of law.[106] Thus a reviewing court determines for itself whether the standards for summary judgment have been met and is not bound in any respect by the trial court's ruling that there was no material factual dispute present.[107] But the Federal Circuit will not retry a motion for summary judgment. Its review is based on the record—evidence actually presented—not on assorted evidentiary might-have-beens.[108] On appeal from a grant of summary judgment the record will be viewed in the light most favorable to the party against whom summary judgment was granted.[109] The Federal Circuit reviews a bankruptcy court's grant of summary judgment, a conclusion of law, de novo.[110]

A district court's ultimate conclusion as to whether it has in personam jurisdiction, and any subsidiary conclusions regarding the legal effect of particular jurisdictional facts, present questions of law subject to review de novo.[111]

---

[105]*SunTiger Inc. v. Scientific Res. Fund Group,* 189 F.3d 1327, 51 USPQ2d 1811 (Fed. Cir. 1999).

[106]*Avia Group Int'l, Inc. v. L.A. Gear Calif., Inc.,* 853 F.2d 1557, 7 USPQ2d 1548 (Fed. Cir. 1988); *Lemelson v. TRW, Inc.,* 760 F.2d 1254, 225 USPQ 697 (Fed. Cir. 1985). In reviewing a trial court's grant of summary judgment, an appellate court is not bound by the clearly erroneous rule because proper summary judgment is not based on debatable findings of fact. *Burlington Indus., Inc. v. Dayco Corp.,* 849 F.2d 1418, 7 USPQ2d 1158 (Fed. Cir. 1988).

[107]*Intellicall, Inc. v. Phonometrics, Inc.,* 952 F.2d 1384, 21 USPQ2d 1383 (Fed. Cir. 1992); *Vas-Cath Inc. v. Mahurkar,* 935 F.2d 1555, 19 USPQ2d 1111 (Fed. Cir. 1991); *C.R. Bard, Inc. v. Advanced Card. Sys., Inc.,* 911 F.2d 670, 15 USPQ2d 1540 (Fed. Cir. 1990); *Prineville Sawmill Co. v. United States,* 859 F.2d 905 (Fed. Cir. 1988); *A.B. Chance Co. v. RTE Corp.,* 854 F.2d 1307, 7 USPQ2d 1881 (Fed. Cir. 1988); *Armco, Inc. v. Cyclops Corp.,* 791 F.2d 147, 229 USPQ 721 (Fed. Cir. 1986). See also *Cohen v. United States,* 995 F.2d 205 (Fed. Cir. 1993). The court reviews the propriety of a summary judgment decision de novo. *Oddzon Prods., Inc. v. Just Toys, Inc.,* 122 F.3d 1396, 43 USPQ2d 1641 (Fed. Cir. 1997); *Conroy v. Reebok Int'l,* 14 F.3d 1570, 29 USPQ2d 1373 (Fed. Cir. 1994); *Dehne v. United States,* 970 F.2d 890 (Fed. Cir. 1992). A grant of summary judgment may be affirmed only if the judgment was the only one possible under controlling law. *Burroughs Wellcome Co. v. Barr Labs., Inc.,* 40 F.3d 1223, 32 USPQ2d 1915 (Fed. Cir. 1994).

[108]*Chemical Eng'g Corp. v. Essef Indus., Inc.,* 795 F.2d 1565, 230 USPQ 385 (Fed. Cir. 1986).

[109]*Confederated Tribes v. United States,* 964 F.2d 1102 (Fed. Cir. 1992).

[110]*Institut Pasteur v. Cambridge Biotech Corp.,* 186 F.3d 1356, 51 USPQ2d 1321 (Fed. Cir. 1999).

[111]*North Am. Philips Corp. v. American Vending Sales, Inc.,* 35 F.3d 1576, 32 USPQ2d 1203 (Fed. Cir. 1994). Where the jurisdictional facts are undisputed, the matter presents a

In determining whether to dismiss a claim pursuant to Rule 12(b)(6), FRCP, the district court accepts as true all of the factual allegations of the complaint, and appellate review is on the same basis.[112] Whether a complaint is properly dismissed for failure to state a claim upon which relief can be granted is a question of law that is reviewed de novo.[113] A dismissal without prejudice is reviewed only for abuse of discretion.[114]

Injunctions and contempt. The injunctive orders reviewed by the Federal Circuit are usually those granting or denying preliminary relief. Although the standard of review is sometimes simply characterized as abuse of discretion,[115] a somewhat broader formulation of the standard is that the appellant must show abuse of discretion, error of law, or serious misjudgment of the evidence.[116] The issuance of an injunction is clearly discretionary under 35 U.S.C. §283.[117] But the discretion is not absolute and must be measured against the legal standards for injunctive relief. Where the right to an injunction is

---

pure question of law, reviewable de novo. *Akro Corp. v. Luker*, 45 F.3d 1541, 33 USPQ2d 1505 (Fed. Cir. 1995).

[112]*Abbott Labs. v. Brennan*, 952 F.2d 1346, 21 USPQ2d 1192 (Fed. Cir. 1992).

[113]*Bristol-Myers Squibb Co. v. Royce Labs., Inc.*, 69 F.3d 1130, 36 USPQ2d 1641 (Fed. Cir. 1995); *Highland Falls-Fort Dist. v. United States*, 48 F.3d 1166 (Fed. Cir. 1995); *Dairyland Power Coop. v. United States*, 16 F.3d 1197 (Fed. Cir. 1994); *Advanced Cardiovascular Sys., Inc. v. Scimed Life Sys., Inc*, 988 F.2d 1157, 26 USPQ2d 1038 (Fed. Cir. 1993); *Dehne v. United States*, 970 F.2d 890 (Fed. Cir. 1992).

[114]*L.E.A. Dynatech, Inc. v. Allina*, 49 F.3d 1527, 33 USPQ2d 1839 (Fed. Cir. 1995).

[115]*Litton Sys., Inc. v. Sundstrand Corp.*, 750 F.2d 952, 224 USPQ 252 (Fed. Cir. 1984).

[116]*High Tech Med. Instr., Inc. v. New Image Indus., Inc.*, 49 F.3d 1551, 33 USPQ2d 2005 (Fed. Cir. 1995); *Xeta, Inc. v. Atex, Inc.*, 852 F.2d 1280, 7 USPQ2d 1471 (Fed. Cir. 1988); *Cordis Corp. v. Medtronic, Inc.*, 835 F.2d 859, 5 USPQ2d 1118 (Fed. Cir. 1987); *T.J. Smith & Nephew Ltd. v. Consolidated Med. Equip., Inc.*, 821 F.2d 646, 3 USPQ2d 1316 (Fed. Cir. 1987); *H.H. Robertson Co. v. United Steel Deck, Inc.*, 820 F.2d 384, 2 USPQ2d 1926 (Fed. Cir. 1987); *Datascope Corp. v. Kontron Inc.*, 786 F.2d 398, 229 USPQ 41 (Fed. Cir. 1986); *Cordis Corp. v. Medtronic, Inc.*, 780 F.2d 991, 228 USPQ 189 (Fed. Cir. 1985); *Stein Assoc., Inc. v. Heat & Control, Inc.*, 748 F.2d 653, 223 USPQ 1277 (Fed. Cir. 1984); *Smith Int'l, Inc. v. Hughes Tool Co.*, 718 F.2d 1573, 219 USPQ 686 (Fed. Cir. 1983). See also *Rosemount, Inc. v. United States ITC*, 910 F.2d 819, 15 USPQ2d 1569 (Fed. Cir. 1990) (ITC case). When a preliminary injunction is denied, to obtain reversal the movant must show not only that one or more of the findings relied on by the district court was clearly erroneous, but also that denial of the injunction amounts to an abuse of the court's discretion upon reversal of the erroneous findings. *Reebok Int'l Ltd. v. J. Baker, Inc.*, 32 F.3d 1552, 31 USPQ2d 1781 (Fed. Cir. 1994).

[117]*Odetics Inc. v. Storage Tech. Corp.*, 185 F.3d 1259, 51 USPQ2d 1225 (Fed. Cir. 1999); *T.J. Smith & Nephew Ltd. v. Consolidated Med. Equip., Inc.*, 821 F.2d 646, 3 USPQ2d 1316 (Fed. Cir. 1987); *Datascope Corp. v. Kontron Inc.*, 786 F.2d 398, 229 USPQ 41 (Fed. Cir. 1986). See also *Tieleman Food Equip., B.V. v. Stork Gamco, Inc.*, 56 F.3d 1373, 35 USPQ2d 1568 (Fed. Cir. 1995). Section 283 grants the district courts broad discretion in determining whether the facts of a case warrant an injunction and in determining the scope of the injunctive relief. The grant, denial, or modification of an injunction under 35 U.S.C. §283 is reviewable under an abuse of discretion standard. *Ortho Pharm Corp. v. Smith*, 959 F.2d 936, 22 USPQ2d 1119 (Fed. Cir. 1992). Although the standard of review for the issuance and scope of an injunction is abuse of discretion, whether the terms of the injunction fulfill the specificity mandates of Rule 65(d), FRCP, is a question of law that is reviewed de novo. *Signtech USA Ltd v. Vutek Inc.*, 174 F.3d 1352, 50 USPQ2d 1372 (Fed. Cir. 1999).

clearly made out, the trial court cannot deny the remedy.[118] An injunction staying concurrent litigation is reviewed on the standard of abuse of discretion.[119]

Whether or not to proceed by way of contempt rather than supplemental complaint for violation of an injunction against patent infringement is within the discretion of the court.[120] If the correct legal standards for contempt are employed, a finding of civil contempt invokes the clearly erroneous standard.[121]

Amended pleadings. The entire question of amendments to pleadings rests with the sound discretion of the trial court and may be overturned only if the court abuses that discretion.[122] Thus, a denial of a motion to amend the pleading to assert a different patent claim[123] or add a party[124] is subject to review under the abuse of discretion standard. Whether to permit amendment of pleadings after trial is also within the discretion of the district court[125] and reviewable on the same basis.

Discovery. Discovery rulings are reviewed for prejudicial legal error.[126] The scope and conduct of discovery are committed to the discretion of the trial court, and the standard of review is abuse of discretion,[127] although the Federal Circuit will typically apply regional

---

[118]*Smith Int'l, Inc. v. Hughes Tool Co.,* 718 F.2d 1573, 219 USPQ 686 (Fed. Cir. 1983).

[119]*Katz v. Lear Siegler, Inc.,* 909 F.2d 1459, 15 USPQ2d 1554 (Fed. Cir. 1990).

[120]*Additive Cont. & Meas. Sys. Inc. v. Flowdata Inc.,* 154 F.3d 1345, 47 USPQ2d 1906 (Fed. Cir. 1998); *KSM Fastening Sys., Inc. v. H.A. Jones Co.,* 776 F.2d 1522, 227 USPQ 676 (Fed. Cir. 1985).

[121]*Preemption Devices, Inc. v. Minnesota Min. & Mfg. Co.,* 803 F.2d 1170, 231 USPQ 297 (Fed. Cir. 1986). See also *Glaxo, Inc. v. Novopharm, Ltd.,* 110 F.3d 1562 (Fed. Cir. 1997) (protective order violation).

[122]*Datascope Corp. v. SMEC, Inc.,* 962 F.2d 1043, 22 USPQ2d 1573 (Fed. Cir. 1992); *Intrepid v. Pollock,* 907 F.2d 1125 (Fed. Cir. 1990); *Senza-Gel Corp. v. Seiffhart,* 803 F.2d 661, 231 USPQ 363 (Fed. Cir. 1986); *Tenneco Resins, Inc. v. Reeves Bros., Inc.,* 752 F.2d 630, 224 USPQ 536 (Fed. Cir. 1985).

[123]*Jervis B. Webb Co. v. Southern Sys., Inc.,* 742 F.2d 1388, 222 USPQ 943 (Fed. Cir. 1984).

[124]*Charles Greiner & Co. v. Mari-Med Mfg., Inc.,* 962 F.2d 1031, 22 USPQ2d 1526 (Fed. Cir. 1992); *Kalman v. Berlyn Corp.,* 914 F.2d 1473, 16 USPQ2d 1093 (Fed. Cir. 1990). In another case, however, the court appeared to select a de novo standard of review for a joinder issue. *Katz v. Lear Siegler, Inc.,* 909 F.2d 1459, 15 USPQ2d 1554 (Fed. Cir. 1990). Permissive intervention is a discretionary matter. *Chapman v. Manbeck,* 931 F.2d 46, 18 USPQ2d 1565 (Fed. Cir. 1991). The standard of review of an order denying a motion for permissive intervention is abuse of discretion. *Haworth, Inc. v. Steelcase, Inc.,* 12 F.3d 1090, 29 USPQ2d 1368 (Fed. Cir. 1993) (applying Sixth Circuit law).

[125]*Trans-World Mfg. Corp. v. Al Nyman & Sons,* 750 F.2d 1552, 224 USPQ 259 (Fed. Cir. 1984).

[126]*Eastman Kodak Co. v. Goodyear Tire & Rubber Co.,* 114 F.3d 1547, 42 USPQ2d 1737 (Fed. Cir. 1997).

[127]*Katz v. Batavia Mar. & Sporting Supp., Inc.,* 984 F.2d 422, 25 USPQ2d 1547 (Fed. Cir. 1993); *Keebler Co. v. Murray Bakery Prods.,* 866 F.2d 1386, 9 USPQ2d 1736 (Fed. Cir. 1989); *Truswal Sys. Corp v. Hydro-Air Eng'g, Inc.,* 813 F.2d 1207, 2 USPQ2d 1034 (Fed. Cir. 1987); *Florsheim Shoe Co. v. United States,* 744 F.2d 787 (Fed. Cir. 1984).

circuit law on these questions.[128] An abuse of discretion may be found when (1) the court's decision is clearly unreasonable, arbitrary, or fanciful; (2) the decision is based on an erroneous conclusion of law; (3) the district court's findings are clearly erroneous; or (4) the record contains no evidence upon which the district court rationally could have based its decision. A district court's determination of the law and the application thereof to the facts is not a matter within its discretion.[129]

A determination that a district court has the power to order discovery does not end the inquiry. It must also be determined whether an abuse of discretion occurred in exercising that power.[130] A trial judge, having presided over an action for several years, is in the best position to assess whether the party seeking discovery had shown some reasonable relationship between the claimed invention and the information sought.[131]

Review of the grant or denial of sanctions for failure to provide discovery[132] or for abuse of the discovery process[133] is governed by the abuse of discretion standard. A discovery sanction will not be disturbed unless upon a weighing of the relevant factors the reviewing court is left with a definite and firm conviction that the court below committed a clear error of judgment. The question is not whether the reviewing court as an original matter would have granted the sanction.[134]

Relief from judgment. The standard of review of a grant or denial of a motion for new trial is abuse of discretion.[135] The decision to grant

---

[128]*Dorf & Stanton Comm., Inc. v. Molson Breweries,* 100 F.3d 919, 40 USPQ2d 1761 (Fed. Cir. 1996); *Truswal Sys. Corp v. Hydro-Air Eng'g, Inc.,* 813 F.2d 1207, 2 USPQ2d 1034 (Fed. Cir. 1987); *Heat & Control, Inc. v. Hester Indus. Inc.,* 785 F.2d 1017, 228 USPQ 926 (Fed. Cir. 1986). Under Seventh Circuit law, the relevant inquiry is not how the reviewing judges would have ruled if they had been considering the case in the first place, but rather whether any reasonable person could agree with the district court. An abuse occurs when (1) the record contains no evidence on which the court could rationally have based its decision; (2) the decision is based on an erroneous conclusion of law; (3) the decision is based on clearly erroneous factual findings; or (4) the decision clearly appears arbitrary. *American Standard, Inc. v. Pfizer, Inc.,* 828 F.2d 734, 3 USPQ2d 1817 (Fed. Cir. 1987).

[129]*Badalamenti v. Dunham's, Inc.,* 896 F.2d 1359, 13 USPQ2d 1967 (Fed. Cir. 1990); *Western Elec. Co. v. Piezo Tech., Inc.,* 860 F.2d 428, 8 USPQ2d 1853 (Fed. Cir. 1988).

[130]*United States v. Cook,* 795 F.2d 987 (Fed. Cir. 1986).

[131]*American Standard, Inc. v. Pfizer, Inc.,* 828 F.2d 734, 3 USPQ2d 1817 (Fed. Cir. 1987).

[132]*Nike Inc. v. Wolverine World Wide, Inc.,* 43 F.3d 644, 33 USPQ2d 1038 (Fed. Cir. 1994); *Refac Int'l, Ltd. v. Hitachi, Ltd.,* 921 F.2d 1247, 16 USPQ2d 1347 (Fed. Cir. 1990); *Badalamenti v. Dunham's, Inc.,* 896 F.2d 1359, 13 USPQ2d 1967 (Fed. Cir. 1990); *Ingalls Shipbuilding, Inc. v. United States,* 857 F.2d 1448 (Fed. Cir. 1988); *Chemical Eng'g Corp. v. Essef Indus., Inc.,* 795 F.2d 1565, 230 USPQ 385 (Fed. Cir. 1986); *Minnesota Min. & Mfg. Co. v. Eco Chem, Inc.,* 757 F.2d 1256, 225 USPQ 350 (Fed. Cir. 1985); *Stock Pot Restaurant, Inc. v. Stockpot, Inc.,* 737 F.2d 1576, 222 USPQ 665 (Fed. Cir. 1984).

[133]*Bio-Rad Labs., Inc. v. Nicolet Instr. Corp.,* 739 F.2d 604, 222 USPQ 654 (Fed. Cir. 1984). An award of attorney fees under Rules 11 or 37 is subject to review under an abuse of discretion standard. *New Idea Farm Equip. Corp. v. Sperry Corp.,* 916 F.2d 1561, 16 USPQ2d 1424 (Fed. Cir. 1990).

[134]*Adkins v. United States,* 816 F.2d 1562 (Fed. Cir. 1987).

[135]*Orthokinetics, Inc. v. Safety Travel Chairs, Inc.,* 806 F.2d 1565, 1 USPQ2d 1081 (Fed. Cir. 1986); *Mainland Indus., Inc. v. Standal's Patents Ltd.,* 799 F.2d 746, 230 USPQ 772 (Fed.

or deny relief under Rule 60(b), FRCP, is also largely discretionary,[136] and the standard is abuse of discretion.[137] Nonetheless, the underlying fact findings by the district court in support of a denial of a Rule 60(b) motion must be upheld unless they are clearly erroneous.[138] Rule 60(b) is applied most liberally to judgments in default, and even a slight abuse of discretion may justify a reversal of a denial of a party's motion to be relieved from default judgment.[139]

The standard of review on appeal from a denial of a motion to vacate a recused judge's prior orders in the case is abuse of discretion.[140] A district court's denial of a motion to supplement the record after trial is reviewed under an abuse of discretion standard.[141]

Certification under Rule 54(b), FRCP, is within the discretion of the district court, and as a general proposition a refusal to certify will not be interfered with.[142] Orders whose review is by extraordinary writ may be overturned only when there has been a clear abuse of discretion or usurpation of judicial authority. The petitioner has the burden of establishing that its right to issuance of the writ is clear and indisputable.[143]

(c) *Specific Issues*

The applicable standard of review—legal correctness or clear error—depends upon whether the specific issue under review is regarded as a question of law or a question of fact. The resolution of this dichotomy has not seemed to present any particular difficulties, although some curious results have emerged. Perhaps the greatest danger here is that an activist court would succumb to the temptation of regarding too many questions as legal rather than factual, thereby to achieve a broader scope of review. The Federal Circuit has, with

---

Cir. 1986); *Medtronic Inc. v. Intermedics, Inc.*, 799 F.2d 734, 230 USPQ 641 (Fed. Cir. 1986); *Witco Chem. Corp. v. Peachtree Doors, Inc.*, 787 F.2d 1545, 229 USPQ 188 (Fed. Cir. 1986); *Perkin-Elmer Corp. v. Computervision Corp.*, 732 F.2d 888, 221 USPQ 669 (Fed. Cir. 1984); *Underwater Devices, Inc. v. Morrison-Knudsen Co.*, 717 F.2d 1380, 219 USPQ 569 (Fed. Cir. 1983).

[136]*Case v. BSAF Wyandotte*, 737 F.2d 1034, 222 USPQ 737 (Fed. Cir. 1984).

[137]*Rodime PLC v. Seagate Tech. Inc.*, 174 F.3d 1294, 50 USPQ2d 1429 (Fed. Cir. 1999); *Broyhill Furn. Indus. v. Craftmaster Furn. Corp.*, 12 F.3d 1080, 29 USPQ2d 1283 (Fed. Cir. 1993); *Fraige v. American-National Watermattress Corp.*, 996 F.2d 295, 27 USPQ2d 1149 (Fed. Cir. 1993); *Information Sys. & Net. Corp. v. United States*, 994 F.2d 792 (Fed. Cir. 1993); *Ashland Oil, Inc. v. Delta Oil Prods. Corp.*, 806 F.2d 1031, 1 USPQ2d 1073 (Fed. Cir. 1986); *United States v. Atkinson*, 748 F.2d 659 (Fed. Cir. 1984); *Case v. BSAF Wyandotte*, 737 F.2d 1034, 222 USPQ 737 (Fed. Cir. 1984); *CTS Corp. v. Piher Int'l Corp.*, 727 F.2d 1550, 221 USPQ 11 (Fed. Cir. 1984).

[138]*CTS Corp. v. Piher Int'l Corp.*, 727 F.2d 1550, 221 USPQ 11 (Fed. Cir. 1984).

[139]*Information Sys. & Net. Corp. v. United States*, 994 F.2d 792 (Fed. Cir. 1993).

[140]*Polaroid Corp. v. Eastman Kodak Co.*, 866 F.2d 1415, 9 USPQ2d 1877 (Fed. Cir. 1989).

[141]*Westvaco Corp. v. International Paper Co.*, 991 F.2d 735, 26 USPQ2d 1353 (Fed. Cir. 1993).

[142]*Jeannette Sheet Glass Corp. v. United States*, 803 F.2d 1576 (Fed. Cir. 1986).

[143]*In re Regents of the Univ. of Calif.*, 964 F.2d 1128 (Fed. Cir. 1992).

the notable exceptions of obviousness, claim construction, and prosecution history estoppel, pretty much resisted the temptation.

(i) Validity Issues

The ultimate question of patent validity is one of law.[144] Not unlike a determination of infringement, a determination of anticipation, as well as obviousness, involves two steps. First is construing the claim, a question of law for the court, followed by, in the case of anticipation or obviousness, a comparison of the construed claim to the prior art. This comparison process involves fact finding, and is for the fact finder in the first instance.[145]

Anticipation. Anticipation pursuant to 35 U.S.C. §102 is a factual determination, reviewable under the clearly erroneous standard.[146] Because anticipation is a factual determination, the critical question in the JNOV context is whether a reasonable juror could have found that the reference failed to anticipate; in the context of a motion for a new trial, it is whether the trial court abused its discretion in determining that a finding of no anticipation was not against the clear weight of the evidence.[147] The challenging party must demonstrate, among other things, identity of invention. Identity is likewise a factual question, and the challenger must ordinarily show that each element of the claim in issue is found in a prior patent or publication, either expressly or under principles of inherency.[148] Inherency, too, is a question of fact.[149] Although the ultimate questions of public use and on sale are legal conclusions,[150] the facts underlying those conclusions

---

[144]*Paragon Podiatry Lab., Inc. v. KLM Labs., Inc.*, 984 F.2d 1182, 25 USPQ2d 1561 (Fed. Cir. 1993).

[145]*Key Pharm. Inc. v. Hercon Labs. Corp.*, 161 F.3d 709, 48 USPQ2d 1911 (Fed. Cir. 1998).

[146]*Glaxo, Inc. v. Novopharm Ltd.*, 52 F.3d 1043, 34 USPQ2d 1565 (Fed. Cir. 1995); *Glaverbel S.A. v. Northlake Mkt'g & Supp., Inc.*, 45 F.3d 1550, 33 USPQ2d 1496 (Fed. Cir. 1995); *In re Paulsen*, 30 F.3d 1475, 31 USPQ2d 1671 (Fed. Cir. 1994); *In re Baxter Travenol Labs.*, 952 F.2d 388, 21 USPQ2d 1281 (Fed. Cir. 1991); *Allen Archery, Inc. v. Browning Mfg. Co.*, 819 F.2d 1087, 2 USPQ2d 1490 (Fed. Cir. 1987); *Akzo N.V. v. United States ITC*, 808 F.2d 1471, 1 USPQ2d 1241 (Fed. Cir. 1986); *In re King*, 801 F.2d 1324, 231 USPQ 136 (Fed. Cir. 1986); *Titanium Metals Corp. v. Banner*, 778 F.2d 775, 227 USPQ 773 (Fed. Cir. 1985); *Ralston Purina Co. v. Far-Mar-Co, Inc.*, 772 F.2d 1570, 227 USPQ 177 (Fed. Cir. 1985); *Lindemann Maschinenfabrik v. American Hoist & Derrick Co.*, 730 F.2d 1452, 221 USPQ 481 (Fed. Cir. 1984); *Carman Indus., Inc. v. Wahl*, 724 F.2d 932, 220 USPQ 481 (Fed. Cir. 1983). The standard of review for anticipation in a matter before the ITC is substantial evidence. *Texas Instr., Inc. v. United States ITC*, 988 F.2d 1165, 26 USPQ2d 1018 (Fed. Cir. 1993).

[147]*Standard Havens Prods., Inc. v. Gencor Indus., Inc.*, 953 F.2d 1360, 21 USPQ2d 1321 (Fed. Cir. 1992).

[148]*Tyler Refrigeration v. Kysor Indus. Corp.*, 777 F.2d 687, 227 USPQ 845 (Fed. Cir. 1985). As a question of fact, identity is subject to review under the clearly erroneous standard in a bench trial. *Minnesota Min. & Mfg. Co. v. Johnson & Johnson Orthopaedics, Inc.*, 976 F.2d 1559, 24 USPQ2d 1321 (Fed. Cir. 1992).

[149]*In re Grasselli*, 713 F.2d 731, 218 USPQ 769 (Fed. Cir. 1983). Whether a claim limitation is inherent in a prior art reference for purposes of anticipation is a question of fact. *Finnigan Corp. v. United States ITC*, 180 F.3d 1354, 51 USPQ2d 1001 (Fed. Cir. 1999).

[150]*Barmag Barmer Masch. AG v. Murata Mach., Ltd.*, 731 F.2d 831, 221 USPQ 561 (Fed. Cir. 1984). See also *In re Mahurkar Hemodialysis Catheter*, 71 F.3d 1573, 37 USPQ2d 1138

are subject to the clearly erroneous standard.[151] Appellate review of an on-sale bar proceeds as a question of law. The Federal Circuit reviews the trial court's conclusion de novo, with factual findings underlying that conclusion subject to review for clear error.[152] Priority of invention is a question of law to be determined based upon underlying factual findings. In reviewing a judgment of invalidity based on a conclusion of prior invention under 35 U.S.C. §102(g), the court must consider not only whether the underlying findings were clearly erroneous, but also whether there was legal error.[153]

Whether a patent or publication is in the prior art is a legal question, but whether something legally within the prior art is analogous is a factual question subsumed in the "content" of the prior art.[154] What a prior art reference teaches is likewise a question of fact.[155] An examination for unexpected results is a factual, evidentiary inquiry, which is reviewed for clear error.[156]

Obviousness. The ultimate conclusion on obviousness is one of law to be determined from the facts and is reviewed for correctness or error as a matter of law and not under the clearly erroneous

---

(Fed. Cir. 1995). Whether or not an invention was on sale or in public use is a question of law that the court reviews de novo. *Paragon Podiatry Lab., Inc. v. KLM Labs., Inc.*, 984 F.2d 1182, 25 USPQ2d 1561 (Fed. Cir. 1993); *Sonoscan, Inc. v. Sonotek, Inc.*, 936 F.2d 1261, 19 USPQ2d 1156 (Fed. Cir. 1991); *Manville Sales Corp. v. Paramount Sys., Inc.*, 917 F.2d 544, 16 USPQ2d 1587 (Fed. Cir. 1990).

[151]*Sonoscan, Inc. v. Sonotek, Inc.*, 936 F.2d 1261, 19 USPQ2d 1156 (Fed. Cir. 1991); *Manville Sales Corp. v. Paramount Sys., Inc.*, 917 F.2d 544, 16 USPQ2d 1587 (Fed. Cir. 1990); *U.S. Envtl. Prods., Inc. v. Westall*, 911 F.2d 713, 15 USPQ2d 1898 (Fed. Cir. 1990); *Hycor Corp. v. Schlueter Co.*, 740 F.2d 1529, 222 USPQ 553 (Fed. Cir. 1984). Adequacy of testing is a factual matter. *Biodex Corp. v. Loredan Biomedical, Inc.*, 946 F.2d 850, 20 USPQ2d 1252 (Fed. Cir. 1991).

[152]*Ferag AG v. Quipp, Inc.*, 45 F.3d 1562, 33 USPQ2d 1512 (Fed. Cir. 1995); *Atlantic Thermoplastics Co. v. Faytex Corp.*, 970 F.2d 834, 23 USPQ2d 1481 (Fed. Cir. 1992). Review of the factual determinations underlying the §§102/103 bar is for clear error in a bench trial. *Pfaff v. Wells Elec., Inc.*, 124 F.3d 1429, 43 USPQ2d 1928 (Fed. Cir. 1997), *aff'd*, 525 U.S. 55, 48 USPQ2d 1641 (1998).

[153]*Innovative Scuba Concepts, Inc. v. Feder Indus., Inc.*, 26 F.3d 1112, 31 USPQ2d 1132 (Fed. Cir. 1994).

[154]*In re Clay*, 966 F.2d 656, 23 USPQ2d 1058 (Fed. Cir. 1992); *Panduit Corp. v. Dennison Mfg. Co.*, 810 F.2d 1561, 1 USPQ2d 1593 (Fed. Cir. 1987). See also *Wang Labs., Inc. v. Toshiba Corp.*, 993 F.2d 858, 26 USPQ2d 1767 (Fed. Cir. 1993). Interpretation of statutory terms, including whether a German Geschmacksmuster is a foreign patent under 35 U.S.C. §102(a), is a question of law that the Federal Circuit reviews de novo. *In re Carlson*, 983 F.2d 1032, 25 USPQ2d 1207 (Fed. Cir. 1993). Whether a prior art reference is analogous is a fact question that is reviewed under the clearly erroneous standard. *In re GPAC, Inc.*, 57 F.3d 1573, 35 USPQ2d 1116 (Fed. Cir. 1995); *In re Paulsen*, 30 F.3d 1475, 31 USPQ2d 1671 (Fed. Cir. 1994); *Heidelberger Druckmaschinen AG v. Hantscho Comm. Prods., Inc.*, 21 F.3d 1068, 30 USPQ2d 1377 (Fed. Cir. 1994).

[155]*In re Baird*, 16 F.3d 380, 29 USPQ2d 1550 (Fed. Cir. 1994); *In re Beattie*, 974 F.2d 1309, 24 USPQ2d 1040 (Fed. Cir. 1992). Whether the prior art teaches toward or away from the claimed invention is a determination of fact. *Para-Ordnance Mfg. v. SGS Importers Int'l, Inc.*, 73 F.3d 1085, 37 USPQ2d 1237 (Fed. Cir. 1995). Prior art printed publications must be enabling, thus placing the allegedly disclosed matter in the possession of the public. This is a mixed question of law and fact. *In re Epstein*, 32 F.3d 1559, 31 USPQ2d 1817 (Fed. Cir. 1994).

[156]*In re Geisler*, 116 F.3d 1465, 43 USPQ2d 1362 (Fed. Cir. 1997).

standard.[157] The underlying factual determinations, on the other hand, are reviewed for clear error[158] or, in an ITC proceeding[159] or jury case,[160] substantial evidence.

It is important to observe the distinction between the ultimate legal conclusion and the underlying factual determinations. That the parties fervently dispute the ultimate conclusion on obviousness is not enough to raise a factual question.[161] Indeed, the Federal Circuit has observed that a de novo review of obviousness would amount to nothing different than that "the parties mail us the patent and prior art and ask whether we think the claimed invention would have been obvious."[162] That the question of obviousness is legal, therefore, does not mean that "to a judge" may be substituted for the statutory phrase "to one of ordinary skill in the art." The question is not answerable by a judge on the sole basis of what he or she thinks ought to be patentable under §103. The trial judge, eschewing all personal predilections, must decide on the totality of the evidence whether the accused infringer has carried its §282 burden by proving, by clear and convincing evidence, facts that require a conclusion that one of ordinary skill would have found the claimed invention obvious at the time it was made. The appellate judge, equally eschewing all personal predilections, must decide whether the trial judge's controlling fact

---

[157]E.g., *In re Geiger,* 815 F.2d 686, 2 USPQ2d 1276 (Fed. Cir. 1987); *In re De Blauwe,* 736 F.2d 699, 222 USPQ 191 (Fed. Cir. 1984). So too in a design case. *In re Klein,* 987 F.2d 1569, 26 USPQ2d 1133 (Fed. Cir. 1993). A PTO Board determination as to whether a claimed invention would have been obvious is reviewed de novo. *In re Raynes,* 7 F.3d 1037, 28 USPQ2d 1630 (Fed. Cir. 1993). Underlying factual inquiries are reviewed for clear error. *In re Rijckaert,* 9 F.3d 1531, 28 USPQ2d 1955 (Fed. Cir. 1993).

[158]E.g., *Smithkline Diagnostics, Inc. v. Helena Labs. Corp.,* 859 F.2d 878, 8 USPQ2d 1468 (Fed. Cir. 1988); *Specialty Composites v. Cabot Corp.,* 845 F.2d 981, 6 USPQ2d 1601 (Fed. Cir. 1988); *Allen Archery, Inc. v. Browning Mfg. Co.,* 819 F.2d 1087, 2 USPQ2d 1490 (Fed. Cir. 1987); *Panduit Corp. v. Dennison Mfg. Co.,* 810 F.2d 1561, 1 USPQ2d 1593 (Fed. Cir. 1987); *Revlon, Inc. v. Carson Prods. Co.,* 803 F.2d 676, 231 USPQ 472 (Fed. Cir. 1986); *Kloster Speedsteel AB v. Crucible Inc.,* 793 F.2d 1565, 230 USPQ 81 (Fed. Cir. 1986); *Polaroid Corp. v. Eastman Kodak Co.,* 789 F.2d 1556, 229 USPQ 561 (Fed. Cir. 1986). Underlying factual inquiries concerning the claimed invention and the prior art are binding upon the court unless they are shown to be clearly erroneous, even in appeals from the PTO Board. *In re Kulling,* 897 F.2d 1147, 14 USPQ2d 1056 (Fed. Cir. 1990). The degree to which the legal determination of obviousness involves facts, and is thus subject to the clearly erroneous standard of Rule 52(a), FRCP, is that degree required to erect a foundation of facts sufficient to support the legal conclusion. *Ryco, Inc. v. Ag-Bag Corp.,* 857 F.2d 1418, 8 USPQ2d 1323 (Fed. Cir. 1988). For example, the question whether an application made a showing of unexpected results is one of fact, subject to the clearly erroneous standard of review. *In re Mayne,* 104 F.3d 1339, 41 USPQ2d 1451 (Fed. Cir. 1997); *In re Soni,* 54 F.3d 746, 34 USPQ2d 1684 (Fed. Cir. 1995).

[159]*Checkpoint Sys., Inc. v. United States ITC,* 54 F.3d 756, 35 USPQ2d 1042 (Fed. Cir. 1995); *Texas Instr., Inc. v. United States ITC,* 988 F.2d 1165, 26 USPQ2d 1018 (Fed. Cir. 1993); *Surface Tech. v. United States ITC,* 801 F.2d 1336, 231 USPQ 192 (Fed. Cir. 1986); *Aktiebolaget Karlstads v. United States ITC,* 705 F.2d 1565, 217 USPQ 865 (Fed. Cir. 1983).

[160]*Railroad Dynamics, Inc. v. A. Stucki Co.,* 727 F.2d 1506, 220 USPQ 929 (Fed. Cir. 1984).

[161]*Structural Rubber Prods. Co. v. Park Rubber Co.,* 749 F.2d 707, 223 USPQ 1264 (Fed. Cir. 1984).

[162]*Railroad Dynamics, Inc. v. A. Stucki Co.,* 727 F.2d 1506, 220 USPQ 929 (Fed. Cir. 1984). Nonetheless, an obviousness determination per se is a question of law that is reviewed de novo by the Federal Circuit. *In re Kulling,* 897 F.2d 1147, 14 USPQ2d 1056 (Fed. Cir. 1990). In reaching its own conclusion regarding obviousness, the Federal Circuit need not give

findings are clearly erroneous or whether, on the controlling facts correctly found, the trial judge's legal conclusion can or cannot stand.[163] The appealing party bears the burden of showing either that the district court in deciding the question of obviousness committed reversible legal error, or that its probative findings underlying the conclusion on obviousness were clearly erroneous. The legal error must have been so fundamental as to require reversal or remand; the findings must have been so critically required to support the legal conclusion that their collapse would preclude arrival at that conclusion.[164]

Although obviousness is said to be freely reviewable,[165] this does not mean that the reviewing court may proceed on a paper record as though no trial had taken place. To prevail, the appellant must convince the court that the judgment cannot stand on the record created at trial.[166]

Section 112 issues. The question whether a disclosure satisfies the enablement requirement of §112 is one of law, but may involve subsidiary questions of fact or law.[167] Appellate review of a jury verdict on enablement requires review of whether a reasonable jury could have made the underlying factual findings necessary to provide substantial evidence in support of a conclusion of lack of enablement.[168] The description requirement of §112, on the other hand, presents a factual question, and the unsuccessful party must demonstrate that the district court erred in its application of the law to the facts, or that its findings of fact were clearly erroneous.[169] The other principal

---

deference to a particular analytical construct utilized in a district court's opinion. *Gillette Co. v. S.C. Johnson & Son,* 919 F.2d 720, 16 USPQ2d 1923 (Fed. Cir. 1990).

[163]*Polaroid Corp. v. Eastman Kodak Co.,* 789 F.2d 1556, 229 USPQ 561 (Fed. Cir. 1986).

[164]*Fromson v. Advance Offset Plate, Inc.,* 755 F.2d 1549, 225 USPQ 26 (Fed. Cir. 1985).

[165]*EWP Corp. v. Reliance Universal Inc.,* 755 F.2d 898, 225 USPQ 20 (Fed. Cir. 1985).

[166]*Polaroid Corp. v. Eastman Kodak Co.,* 789 F.2d 1556, 229 USPQ 561, 562 (Fed. Cir. 1986).

[167]*Utter v. Hiraga,* 845 F.2d 993, 6 USPQ2d 1709 (Fed. Cir. 1988); *Quaker City Gear Works, Inc. v. Skil Corp.,* 747 F.2d 1446, 223 USPQ 1161 (Fed. Cir. 1984). See also *Process Control Corp. v. HydReclaim Corp.,* 190 F.3d 1350, 52 USPQ2d 1029 (Fed. Cir. 1999). Whether making and using an invention would have required undue experimentation, and thus whether a disclosure is enabling under §112¶1, is a legal conclusion based upon underlying factual inquiries. *Enzo Biochem Inc. v. Calgene Inc.,* 188 F.3d 1362, 52 USPQ2d 1129 (Fed. Cir. 1999); *Johns Hopkins Univ. v. Cellpro Inc.,* 152 F.3d 1342, 47 USPQ2d 1705 (Fed. Cir. 1998). The issue of §112 support for claims is also legal, dependent upon underlying factual and legal findings. *Paperless Accounting, Inc. v. Bay Area Rapid Transit Sys.,* 804 F.2d 659, 231 USPQ 649 (Fed. Cir. 1986). Enablement is reviewed de novo. *Amgen, Inc. v. Chugai Pharm. Co.,* 927 F.2d 1200, 18 USPQ2d 1016 (Fed. Cir. 1991). The underlying fact findings are reviewed for clear error. *In re Goodman,* 11 F.3d 1046 (Fed. Cir. 1993).

[168]*Allen Organ Co. v. Kimball Int'l, Inc.,* 839 F.2d 1556, 5 USPQ2d 1769 (Fed. Cir. 1988).

[169]*Hyatt v. Boone,* 146 F.3d 1128, 47 USPQ2d 1128 (Fed. Cir. 1998); *Gentry Gallery, Inc. v. Berkline Corp.,* 134 F.3d 1473, 45 USPQ2d 1498 (Fed. Cir. 1998); *Kolmes v. World Fibers Corp.,* 107 F.3d 1534, 41 USPQ2d 1829 (Fed. Cir. 1997); *In re Alton,* 76 F.3d 1168, 37 USPQ2d 1578 (Fed. Cir. 1996); *Wang Labs., Inc. v. Toshiba Corp.,* 993 F.2d 858, 26 USPQ2d 1767 (Fed. Cir. 1993); *In re Spina,* 975 F.2d 854, 24 USPQ2d 1142 (Fed. Cir. 1992); *Vas-Cath Inc. v. Mahurkar,* 935 F.2d 1555, 19 USPQ2d 1111 (Fed. Cir. 1991); *Utter v. Hiraga,* 845 F.2d 993,

demand that §112 places upon the disclosure—best mode—is likewise factual and reviewable for clear error[170] or, in a jury case, substantial evidence.[171] Compliance with the definiteness standard for claims found in the second paragraph of §112 is a question of law.[172] Determination of whether a priority document contains sufficient disclosure under §112 is a question of law. However, compliance with the written description aspect of that requirement is a question of fact.[173]

Other validity issues. Utility is a question of fact in the context of both usefulness[174] and operativeness.[175] Whether a claim is directed to eligible subject matter is a question of law. Although determination of that question may require findings of underlying facts specific to the particular subject matter and its mode of claiming, if the material facts are undisputed, the court of appeals will undertake plenary review.[176]

Double patenting is a question of law that is reviewed de novo.[177] An obviousness-type double patenting defense or rejection is analogous to a defense or rejection under §103 and will be reviewed under the same guidelines: the clearly erroneous standard applies to the underlying factual determinations and the ultimate conclusion of obviousness is reviewed for legal correctness.[178] Derivation under 35

---

6 USPQ2d 1709 (Fed. Cir. 1988); *Ralston Purina Co. v. Far-Mar-Co, Inc.*, 772 F.2d 1570, 227 USPQ 177 (Fed. Cir. 1985); *In re Wilder*, 736 F.2d 1516, 222 USPQ 369 (Fed. Cir. 1984).

[170]*Minco, Inc. v. Combustion Eng'g, Inc.*, 95 F.3d 1109, 40 USPQ2d 1001 (Fed. Cir. 1996); *Northern Telecom, Inc. v. Datapoint Corp.*, 908 F.2d 931, 15 USPQ2d 1321 (Fed. Cir. 1990); *DeGeorge v. Bernier*, 768 F.2d 1318, 226 USPQ 758 (Fed. Cir. 1985).

[171]*Applied Med. Res. Corp. v. United States Surgical Corp.*, 147 F.3d 1374, 47 USPQ2d 1289 (Fed. Cir. 1998); *Great Northern Corp. v. Henry Molded Prods., Inc.*, 94 F.3d 1569, 39 USPQ2d 1997 (Fed. Cir. 1996); *McGill Inc. v. John Zink Co.*, 736 F.2d 666, 221 USPQ 944 (Fed. Cir. 1984).

[172]*Orthokinetics, Inc. v. Safety Travel Chairs, Inc.*, 806 F.2d 1565, 1 USPQ2d 1081 (Fed. Cir. 1986). Compliance with the definiteness requirement is reviewed de novo. *In re Warmerdam*, 33 F.3d 1354, 31 USPQ2d 1754 (Fed. Cir. 1994); *Credle v. Bond*, 25 F.3d 1566, 30 USPQ2d 1911 (Fed. Cir. 1994); *North Am. Vaccine, Inc. v. American Cyanamid Co.*, 7 F.3d 1571, 28 USPQ2d 1333 (Fed. Cir. 1993). Indefiniteness, under §112¶2, is not only a question of law, but part of the court's performance of its duty as the construer of patent claims. *Personalized Media Comm. LLC v. United States ITC*, 161 F.3d 696, 48 USPQ2d 1880 (Fed. Cir. 1998).

[173]*Waldemar Link v. Osteonics Corp.*, 32 F.3d 556, 31 USPQ2d 1855 (Fed. Cir. 1994).

[174]*Process Control Corp. v. HydReclaim Corp.*, 190 F.3d 1350, 52 USPQ2d 1029 (Fed. Cir. 1999); *Stiftung v. Renishaw PLC*, 945 F.2d 1173, 20 USPQ2d 1094 (Fed. Cir. 1991); *Raytheon Co. v. Roper Corp.*, 724 F.2d 951, 220 USPQ 592 (Fed. Cir. 1983).

[175]*Fregeau v. Mossinghoff*, 776 F.2d 1034, 227 USPQ 848 (Fed. Cir. 1985).

[176]*Arrhythmia Res. Tech., Inc. v. Corazonix Corp.*, 958 F.2d 1053, 22 USPQ2d 1033 (Fed. Cir. 1992). Invalidity for failure to claim statutory subject matter under 35 U.S.C. §101 is a question of law that the court reviews without deference. *AT&T Corp. v. Excel Comm Inc.*, 172 F.3d 1352, 50 USPQ2d 1447 (Fed. Cir. 1999).

[177]*In re Lonardo*, 119 F.3d 960, 43 USPQ2d 1262 (Fed. Cir. 1997); *In re Goodman*, 11 F.3d 1046 (Fed. Cir. 1993); *Texas Instr., Inc. v. United States ITC*, 988 F.2d 1165, 26 USPQ2d 1018 (Fed. Cir. 1993). De novo review of double patenting questions is appropriate because double patenting is a matter of what is claimed, and therefore is treated like claim construction upon appellate review. *Georgia-Pacific Corp. v. United States Gypsum Co.*, 195 F.3d 1322, 52 USPQ2d 1590 (Fed. Cir. 1999).

[178]*In re Longi*, 759 F.2d 887, 225 USPQ 645 (Fed. Cir. 1985). A rejection under the doctrine of double patenting is a legal conclusion to which the Federal Circuit gives complete and

U.S.C. §102(f) is a question of fact.[179] Functionality of a design is a determination that is reviewed for clear error in a bench trial.[180] Whether reexamined claims have been enlarged is a matter of claim construction, a question of law subject to complete and independent review on appeal.[181]

(ii) Claim Construction

The court feels that its standard of review of claim construction is now firmly established: it exercises independent review.[182] In *Cybor v. FAS*,[183] the court sat in banc to resolve a perceived conflict among its decisions. It held, unequivocally, that claim construction is a pure question of law. That being the case, it reviews claim construction de novo, including any allegedly fact-based questions relating to claim construction. In other words, the clearly erroneous rule does not apply to any findings or conclusions that the trial judge may have reached while construing the claims. Prior decisions touching on this subject are collected in the note.[184] Where the court's claim interpretation is not set forth in its instructions to the jury, it must perform its role

---

independent review. The ultimate determination of whether a one-way or two-way analysis is appropriate is also a question for the court. The underlying factual findings are reviewed for clear error. *In re Emert*, 124 F.3d 1458, 44 USPQ2d 1149 (Fed. Cir. 1997). See also *In re Berg*, 140 F.3d 1428, 46 USPQ2d 1226 (Fed. Cir. 1998).

[179]*Price v. Symsek*, 988 F.2d 1187, 26 USPQ2d 1031 (Fed. Cir. 1993). But prior conception, as an element of derivation, is reviewed as a question of law based on underlying factual findings. *Gambro Lundia AB v. Baxter Healthcare Corp.*, 110 F.3d 1573, 42 USPQ2d 1378 (Fed. Cir. 1997).

[180]*Best Lock Corp. v. Ilco Unican Corp.*, 94 F.3d 1563, 40 USPQ2d 1048 (Fed. Cir. 1996).

[181]*Hockerson-Halberstadt Inc. v. Converse Inc.*, 183 F.3d 1369, 51 USPQ2d 1518 (Fed. Cir. 1999); *Quantum Corp. v. Rodime, PLC*, 65 F.3d 1577, 36 USPQ2d 1162 (Fed. Cir. 1995).

[182]*Key Pharm. Inc. v. Hercon Labs. Corp.*, 161 F.3d 709, 48 USPQ2d 1911 (Fed. Cir. 1998). However, it does not start from scratch; rather it begins with and carefully considers the trial court's work. *Id.*

[183]*Cybor Corp. v. FAS Tech. Inc.*, 138 F.3d 1448, 46 USPQ2d 1169 (Fed. Cir. 1998).

[184]*Howes v. Medical Components, Inc.*, 814 F.2d 638, 2 USPQ2d 1271 (Fed. Cir. 1987); *George v. Honda Motor Co.*, 802 F.2d 432, 231 USPQ 382 (Fed. Cir. 1986); *Moleculon Res. Corp. v. CBS, Inc.*, 793 F.2d 1261 (Fed. Cir. 1986); *Windsurfing Int'l, Inc. v. AMF, Inc.*, 782 F.2d 995, 228 USPQ 562 (Fed. Cir. 1986); *Lemelson v. United States*, 752 F.2d 1538, 224 USPQ 526 (Fed. Cir. 1985); *Raytheon Co. v. Roper Corp.*, 724 F.2d 951, 220 USPQ 592 (Fed. Cir. 1983). Interpreting the scope of claims is a question of law, and review is therefore plenary. *Intervet Am., Inc. v. Kee-Vet Labs., Inc.*, 887 F.2d 1050, 12 USPQ2d 1474 (Fed. Cir. 1989). When the interpretation of claims requires findings of underlying fact, those factual findings are reviewed in accordance with the appropriate evidentiary standard. *Minnesota Min. & Mfg. Co. v. Johnson & Johnson Orthopaedics, Inc.*, 976 F.2d 1559, 24 USPQ2d 1321 (Fed. Cir. 1992) (in a bench case, clear error); *Tandon Corp. v. United States ITC*, 831 F.2d 1017, 4 USPQ2d 1283 (Fed. Cir. 1987) (in an ITC case, substantial evidence). Claim interpretation is subject to de novo review. *Carroll Touch, Inc. v. Electro Mechanical Sys., Inc.*, 3 F.3d 404, 27 USPQ2d 1836 (Fed. Cir. 1993); *Texas Instr., Inc. v. United States ITC*, 988 F.2d 1165, 26 USPQ2d 1018 (Fed. Cir. 1993); *Intel Corp. v. United States ITC*, 946 F.2d 821, 20 USPQ2d 1161 (Fed. Cir. 1991). The reviewing court need not defer to the district court either under a clearly erroneous standard or otherwise. *Smithkline Diagnostics, Inc. v. Helena Labs. Corp.*, 859 F.2d 878, 8 USPQ2d 1468 (Fed. Cir. 1988); *Specialty Composites v. Cabot Corp.*, 845 F.2d 981, 6 USPQ2d 1601 (Fed. Cir. 1988). But see the dissents in *Advanced Card. Sys., Inc. v. Scimed Life Sys., Inc.*, 887 F.2d 1070, 12 USPQ2d 1539 (Fed. Cir. 1989), and *Senmed, Inc. v. Richard-Allan Med. Indus., Inc.*, 888 F.2d 815, 12 USPQ2d 1508 (Fed. Cir. 1989).

of deciding this issue in ruling on a JNOV motion.[185] Claim interpretation is, most emphatically, a question of law to be reviewed de novo on appeal[186] without deference to the trial judge.[187]

Whether the language of a claim is to be interpreted according to 35 U.S.C. §112¶6, i.e., whether a claim limitation is in means-plus-function format, is a matter of claim construction and is thus a question of law, reviewed de novo.[188] Under §112¶6, a determination of the claimed function, being a matter of construction of specific terms in the claim, is also a question of law, reviewed de novo.[189] Likewise, the "means" term in a means-plus-function limitation is essentially a generic reference for the corresponding structure disclosed in the specification. Accordingly, a determination of corresponding structure is a determination of the meaning of the "means" term in the claim and is thus also a matter of claim construction.[190]

Surprisingly, the court has decided that, inasmuch as compliance with the All Elements Rule is a legal limitation on the application of the doctrine of equivalents, it will review such compliance as a question of law.[191] Likewise, the determination of whether the scope of equivalents accorded to a particular claim would encompass the prior art is an issue of law that is reviewed de novo.[192]

(iii) Infringement Issues

Literal infringement—whether properly interpreted claims read on an accused product or method—is a question of fact, and a finding on that question will not be disturbed unless clearly erroneous.[193]

---

[185]*Read Corp. v. Portec, Inc.*, 970 F.2d 816, 23 USPQ2d 1426 (Fed. Cir. 1992).

[186]*Markman v. Westview Instr., Inc.*, 52 F.3d 967, 34 USPQ2d 1321 (Fed. Cir. 1995).

[187]*Exxon Chem. Patents, Inc. v. Lubrizol Corp.*, 64 F.3d 1553, 35 USPQ2d 1801 (Fed. Cir. 1995).

[188]*Kemco Sales Inc. v. Control Papers Co.*, 208 F.3d 1352, 54 USPQ2d 1308 (Fed. Cir. 2).

[189]*Kemco Sales Inc. v. Control Papers Co.*, 208 F.3d 1352, 54 USPQ2d 1308 (Fed. Cir. 2); *Unidynamics Corp. v. Automatic Prods. Int'l Ltd.*, 157 F.3d 1311, 48 USPQ2d 1099 (Fed. Cir. 1998); *Chiuminatta Concrete Concepts Inc. v. Cardinal Indus. Inc.*, 145 F.3d 1303, 46 USPQ2d 1752 (Fed. Cir. 1998).

[190]*Kemco Sales Inc. v. Control Papers Co.*, 208 F.3d 1352, 54 USPQ2d 1308 (Fed. Cir. 2); *Mas-Hamilton Group Inc. v. LaGard Inc.*, 156 F.3d 1206, 48 USPQ2d 1010 (Fed. Cir. 1998); *Chiuminatta Concrete Concepts Inc. v. Cardinal Indus. Inc.*, 145 F.3d 1303, 46 USPQ2d 1752 (Fed. Cir. 1998).

[191]*Festo Corp. v. Shoketsu KKK Co.*, 172 F.3d 1361, 50 USPQ2d 1385 (Fed. Cir. 1999).

[192]*Streamfeeder LLC v. Sure-Feed Inc.*, 175 F.3d 974, 50 USPQ2d 1515 (Fed. Cir. 1999).

[193]*Miles Labs., Inc. v. Shandon, Inc.*, 997 F.2d 870, 27 USPQ2d 1123 (Fed. Cir. 1993); *Under Sea Indus., Inc. v. Dacor Corp.*, 833 F.2d 1551, 4 USPQ2d 1772 (Fed. Cir. 1987); *Perini Am., Inc. v. Paper Converting Mach. Co.*, 832 F.2d 581, 4 USPQ2d 1621 (Fed. Cir. 1987); *Moleculon Res. Corp. v. CBS, Inc.*, 793 F.2d 1261 (Fed. Cir. 1986); *Windsurfing Int'l, Inc. v. AMF, Inc.*, 782 F.2d 995, 228 USPQ 562 (Fed. Cir. 1986). A jury's finding of infringement must therefore be upheld if it is supported by substantial evidence. *Braun Inc. v. Dynamics Corp.*, 975 F.2d 815, 24 USPQ2d 1121 (Fed. Cir. 1992). In an ITC proceeding the factual determination of literal infringement is likewise reviewed on a substantial evidence standard. *LaBounty Mfg., Inc. v. United States ITC*, 867 F.2d 1572, 9 USPQ2d 1995 (Fed. Cir. 1989). Though infringement is a factual question, it was of no consequence that the district court put its finding on that question among its conclusions of law. *Fromson v. Western Litho Plate & Supp. Co.*, 853 F.2d

Nevertheless, a determination regarding literal infringement may be rendered clearly erroneous through an improper interpretation and application of the governing law. In such case, the factual finding would be overturned as having resulted from legal error.[194] Similarly, where the prior art is compared with erroneously interpreted claims, findings of differences between the prior art and the claims will necessarily be clearly erroneous.[195]

Whether an act is repair or reconstruction is a question of law that is reviewed de novo.[196] Design patent infringement is a question of fact.[197] Since the issue of willfulness not only raises issues of reasonableness and prudence, but is often accompanied by questions of intent, belief, and credibility, appellate review requires appropriate deference to the special role of the trial court in making such determinations. Thus a finding of willful infringement will be sustained unless the reviewing court has a definite and firm conviction that the trier of fact erred.[198]

A finding of equivalence, or a finding of infringement under the doctrine of equivalents, is a factual determination, reviewable for clear error.[199] If a district court is not clearly erroneous in finding

---

1568, 7 USPQ2d 1606 (Fed. Cir. 1988). Although claim interpretation is a question of law, subject to de novo review on appeal, the district court's ultimate finding on infringement, as well as subordinate findings relating to proper claim construction, are issues of fact, reviewed under a clearly erroneous standard. *Morton Int'l, Inc. v. Cardinal Chem. Co.,* 959 F.2d 948, 22 USPQ2d 1231 (Fed. Cir. 1992). When the meaning of a term in a patent claim is unclear, subject to varying interpretations, or ambiguous, the jury may interpret the term en route to deciding the issue of infringement. The jury's verdict on infringement is reviewed, in accordance with the rules governing review of jury determinations, to ascertain whether reasonable jurors could have interpreted the claim in a way that supports the verdict. *Tol-O-Matic, Inc. v. Proma Produckt-und Mktg. GmbH,* 945 F.2d 1546, 20 USPQ2d 1332 (Fed. Cir. 1991).

[194]*Amstar Corp. v. Envirotech Corp.,* 730 F.2d 1476, 221 USPQ 649 (Fed. Cir. 1984).

[195]*Panduit Corp. v. Dennison Mfg. Co.,* 810 F.2d 1561, 1 USPQ2d 1593 (Fed. Cir. 1987).

[196]*Aktiebolag v. E.J. Co.,* 121 F.3d 669, 43 USPQ2d 1620 (Fed. Cir. 1997).

[197]*Oddzon Prods., Inc. v. Just Toys, Inc.,* 122 F.3d 1396, 43 USPQ2d 1641 (Fed. Cir. 1997).

[198]*Georgia-Pacific Corp. v. United States Gypsum Co.,* 195 F.3d 1322, 52 USPQ2d 1590 (Fed. Cir. 1999); *SRI Int'l, Inc. v. Advanced Tech. Labs., Inc.,* 127 F.3d 1462, 44 USPQ2d 1422 (Fed. Cir. 1997). See also *American Med. Sys., Inc. v. Medical Eng'g Corp.,* 6 F.3d 1523, 28 USPQ2d 1321 (Fed. Cir. 1993); *Westvaco Corp. v. International Paper Co.,* 991 F.2d 735, 26 USPQ2d 1353 (Fed. Cir. 1993); *State Indus., Inc. v. Mor-Flo Indus., Inc.,* 883 F.2d 1573, 12 USPQ2d 1026 (Fed. Cir. 1989); *Paper Converting Mach. Co. v. Magna-Graphics Corp.,* 785 F.2d 1013, 228 USPQ 938 (Fed. Cir. 1986); *Ralston Purina Co. v. Far-Mar-Co, Inc.,* 772 F.2d 1570, 227 USPQ 177 (Fed. Cir. 1985); *Kori Corp. v. Wilco Marsh Buggies, Inc.,* 761 F.2d 649, 225 USPQ 985 (Fed. Cir. 1985); *Leinoff v. Louis Milona & Sons,* 726 F.2d 734, 220 USPQ 845 (Fed. Cir. 1984); *Underwater Devices, Inc. v. Morrison-Knudsen Co.,* 717 F.2d 1380, 219 USPQ 569 (Fed. Cir. 1983). In a jury case willfulness is therefore reviewed under the substantial evidence standard. *Hoechst Celanese Corp. v. BP Chem. Ltd.,* 78 F.3d 1575, 38 USPQ2d 1126 (Fed. Cir. 1996); *Braun Inc. v. Dynamics Corp.,* 975 F.2d 815, 24 USPQ2d 1121 (Fed. Cir. 1992). In a bench trial the judge's finding on that point should be sustained unless it is clearly in error. *L.A. Gear, Inc. v. Thom McAn Shoe Co.,* 988 F.2d 1117, 25 USPQ2d 1913 (Fed. Cir. 1993).

[199]*Insta-Foam Prods., Inc. v. Universal Foam Sys., Inc.,* 906 F.2d 698, 15 USPQ2d 1295 (Fed. Cir. 1990); *Ryco, Inc. v. Ag-Bag Corp.,* 857 F.2d 1418, 8 USPQ2d 1323 (Fed. Cir. 1988); *Perkin-Elmer Corp. v. Westinghouse Elec. Corp.,* 822 F.2d 1529, 3 USPQ2d 1321 (Fed. Cir. 1987); *Texas Instr., Inc. v. United States ITC,* 805 F.2d 1558, 231 USPQ 833 (Fed. Cir. 1986); *Great Northern Corp. v. Davis Core & Pad Co.,* 782 F.2d 159, 228 USPQ 356 (Fed. Cir. 1986); *American Hosp. Supply Corp. v. Travenol Labs., Inc.,* 745 F.2d 1, 223 USPQ 577 (Fed. Cir. 1984); *Envirotech Corp. v. Al George, Inc.,* 730 F.2d 753, 221 USPQ 473 (Fed. Cir. 1984); *Thomas

merely that a single function required by a claim, or an equivalent function, is not performed by the accused device, the court's finding of no infringement must be upheld.[200] The companion doctrine of prosecution history estoppel, on the other hand, is a question of law and is reviewed for legal correctness.[201] Because prosecution history estoppel is a question of law, the court regards itself as free to undertake a complete and independent analysis of the issue.[202] Section 112¶6 equivalence is a question of fact, as is regular equivalence and reverse equivalence.[203] The existence of an implied license, as a defense to an infringement action, presents a question of law,[204] and the Federal Circuit therefore undertakes plenary,[205] or de novo,[206] review.

(iv) Damages and Other Relief

The patent statute does not instruct a court on how to compute damages; the only congressional intent expressed ensures that a claimant receive adequate damages. The size of the award is left to the trial court's sound discretion and is reviewable only with respect to whether the court has abused its discretion in choosing a method with which to compute an award.[207] In the damages context, as in

---

& Betts Corp. v. Litton Sys., Inc., 720 F.2d 1572, 220 USPQ 1 (Fed. Cir. 1983). In proceedings before the ITC, equivalence is reviewed under the substantial evidence standard. *Texas Instr., Inc. v. United States ITC*, 988 F.2d 1165, 26 USPQ2d 1018 (Fed. Cir. 1993). The court has held that although the district court may have erred in placing the burden of showing noninfringement on the defendant, the error was harmless where the court's finding of equivalence is not clearly erroneous. *Under Sea Indus., Inc. v. Dacor Corp.*, 833 F.2d 1551, 4 USPQ2d 1772 (Fed. Cir. 1987). This seems to tilt the playing field against the accused infringer. It is wrongly saddled with the trial burden, and then is given the burden on appeal to show clear error.

[200]*Pennwalt Corp. v. Durand-Wayland, Inc.*, 833 F.2d 931, 4 USPQ2d 1737 (Fed. Cir. 1987).

[201]*Loral Fairchild Corp. v. Sony Corp.*, 181 F.3d 1313, 50 USPQ2d 1865 (Fed. Cir. 1999); *Cybor Corp. v. FAS Tech. Inc.*, 138 F.3d 1448, 46 USPQ2d 1169 (Fed. Cir. 1998); *Texas Instr., Inc. v. United States ITC*, 988 F.2d 1165, 26 USPQ2d 1018 (Fed. Cir. 1993); *LaBounty Mfg., Inc. v. United States ITC*, 867 F.2d 1572, 9 USPQ2d 1995 (Fed. Cir. 1989). Whether or not an amendment was made for reasons of patentability is a legal question. *K-2 Corp. v. Salomon S.A.*, 191 F.3d 1356, 52 USPQ2d 1001 (Fed. Cir. 1999). Estoppel based upon what occurred during prosecution is similar to the traditional doctrine of prosecution history estoppel and is likewise a question of law reviewed for legal correctness. *Waldemar Link v. Osteonics Corp.*, 32 F.3d 556, 31 USPQ2d 1855 (Fed. Cir. 1994).

[202]*Hoganas AB v. Dresser Indus., Inc.*, 9 F.3d 948, 28 USPQ2d 1936 (Fed. Cir. 1993).

[203]*Hartness Int'l, Inc. v. Simplimatic Eng'g Co.*, 819 F.2d 1100, 2 USPQ2d 1826 (Fed. Cir. 1987). See also *Odetics Inc. v. Storage Tech. Corp.*, 185 F.3d 1259, 51 USPQ2d 1225 (Fed. Cir. 1999). In order to meet a means-plus-function limitation, an accused device must perform the identical function recited in the means limitation using the structure disclosed in the specification or an equivalent structure. That factual determination is reviewed for clear error. *Carroll Touch, Inc. v. Electro Mechanical Sys., Inc.*, 3 F.3d 404, 27 USPQ2d 1836 (Fed. Cir. 1993).

[204]*Met-Coil Sys. Corp. v. Korners Unlimited, Inc.*, 803 F.2d 684, 231 USPQ 474 (Fed. Cir. 1986).

[205]*Carborundum Co. v. Molten Metal Equip. Innovations*, 72 F.3d 872, 37 USPQ2d 1169, 1172 (Fed. Cir. 1995).

[206]*Augustine Med. Inc. v. Progressive Dynamics Inc.*, 194 F.3d 1367, 52 USPQ2d 1515 (Fed. Cir. 1999); *Wang Labs., Inc. v. Mitsubishi Elec. Am., Inc.*, 103 F.3d 1571, 41 USPQ2d 1263 (Fed. Cir. 1997).

[207]*Minnesota Min. & Mfg. Co. v. Johnson & Johnson Orthopaedics, Inc.*, 976 F.2d 1559, 24 USPQ2d 1321 (Fed. Cir. 1992); *Paper Converting Mach. Co. v. Magna-Graphics Corp.*, 745

others, abuse of discretion may be established by showing that the district court made an error of law or a clear error of judgment, or made findings that were clearly erroneous.[208] Certainly the reviewing court may not exercise de novo review over a finding on the infringer's expected profit, and this is so whether the basis for the finding is testimony or physical or documentary evidence.[209]

In a recent decision the court undertook to clear up possible confusion over some of its previous statements with respect to the standard of review on damages issues. Thus, the amount of a prevailing party's damages is a finding of fact on which the plaintiff bears the burden of proof by a preponderance of the evidence. Where the amount is fixed by the court, review is in accordance with the clearly erroneous standard of Rule 52(a), FRCP; where the review is of a denial of a motion for JNOV, the more restrictive substantial evidence standard is employed. On the other hand, certain subsidiary decisions underlying a damage theory are discretionary with the court, such as the choice of an accounting method for determining profit margin or the methodology for arriving at a reasonable royalty. Such decisions are of course reviewed under the abuse standard. Finally, the principle that a judge has discretion to choose the methodology does not mean that he or she may choose between basing an award on lost profits or on a reasonable royalty. That is not choosing methodology. If a winning patentee seeks and proves lost profits, he or she is entitled to an award reflecting that amount. A judge may, however, choose between reasonable alternative accounting methods for determining the amount of lost profits or may adopt in his or her discretion a reasonable way to determine the number of infringing units.[210]

A jury's measurement of actual damages must be upheld unless the amount is grossly excessive or monstrous, clearly not supported by the evidence, or based only on speculation or guesswork.[211] The

---

F.2d 11, 223 USPQ 591 (Fed. Cir. 1984). See also *Yarway Corp. v. Eur-Control USA Inc.,* 775 F.2d 268, 227 USPQ 352 (Fed. Cir. 1985); Manville Sales Corp. v. Paramount Sys., Inc., 917 F.2d 544, 16 USPQ2d 1587 (Fed. Cir. 1990). A jury award of damages is reviewed on the reasonable jury/substantial evidence standard. *Richardson v. Suzuki Motor Co.,* 868 F.2d 1226, 9 USPQ2d 1913 (Fed. Cir. 1989).

[208]*Trell v. Marlee Elec. Corp.,* 912 F.2d 1443, 16 USPQ2d 1059 (Fed. Cir. 1990); *State Indus., Inc. v. Mor-Flo Indus., Inc.,* 883 F.2d 1573, 12 USPQ2d 1026 (Fed. Cir. 1989); *Mathis v. Spears,* 857 F.2d 749, 8 USPQ2d 1029 (Fed. Cir. 1988); *Fromson v. Western Litho Plate & Supp. Co.,* 853 F.2d 1568, 7 USPQ2d 1606 (Fed. Cir. 1988); *Nickson Indus., Inc. v. Rol Mfg. Co.,* 847 F.2d 795, 6 USPQ2d 1878 (Fed. Cir. 1988); *Hartness Int'l, Inc. v. Simplimatic Eng'g Co.,* 819 F.2d 1100, 2 USPQ2d 1826 (Fed. Cir. 1987); *TWM Mfg. Co. v. Dura Corp.,* 789 F.2d 895, 229 USPQ 525 (Fed. Cir. 1986).

[209]*TWM Mfg. Co. v. Dura Corp.,* 789 F.2d 895, 229 USPQ 525 (Fed. Cir. 1986).

[210]*Smithkline Diagnostics, Inc. v. Helena Labs. Corp.,* 926 F.2d 1161, 17 USPQ2d 1922 (Fed. Cir. 1991). The amount of damages is reviewed for clear error and the methodology employed to assess damages is reviewed for abuse of discretion. *Stryker Corp. v. Intermedics Orthopedics, Inc.,* 96 F.3d 1409, 40 USPQ2d 1065 (Fed. Cir. 1996).

[211]*Brooktree Corp. v. Advanced Micro Devices, Inc.,* 977 F.2d 1555, 24 USPQ2d 1401 (Fed. Cir. 1992). But the court reviews for abuse of discretion a grant of remittitur or a new trial because of an excessive damage award. *Oiness v. Walgreen Co.,*88 F.3d 1025, 39 USPQ2d 1304 (Fed. Cir. 1996).

existence of a noninfringing substitute is a question of fact, reviewable under the clearly erroneous standard.[212] Valuation determinations for purposes of eminent domain are viewed for clear error as are determinations of what constitutes a reasonable royalty.[213]

Awards of increased damages, costs, and attorney fees are all matters committed to the discretion of the district court and will not be overturned absent a clear showing of abuse.[214] The abuse of discretion standard governs review of decisions about sanctions and attorney fees under Rule 11 and 35 U.S.C. §285.[215] The grant or denial of prejudgment interest is reviewed to determine whether the district court abused the available range of discretion in so doing.[216]

Nonetheless, trial court discretion, at least as to attorney fees and increased damages, may be exercised only upon a specific finding of exceptional circumstances,[217] such as willfulness of infringement, which is a finding of fact reviewable under the clearly erroneous rule.[218] In a jury case, a finding of willful infringement is reviewed under the substantial evidence standard.[219] In order to permit meaningful review, the district court should not only make the ultimate

---

[212]*Zygo Corp. v. Wyko Corp.*, 79 F.3d 1563, 38 USPQ2d 1281 (Fed. Cir. 1996); *Minnesota Min. & Mfg. Co. v. Johnson & Johnson Orthopaedics, Inc.*, 976 F.2d 1559, 24 USPQ2d 1321 (Fed. Cir. 1992).

[213]*Hughes Aircraft Co. v. United States*, 86 F.3d 1566, 39 USPQ2d 1065 (Fed. Cir. 1996).

[214]*Cybor Corp. v. FAS Tech. Inc.*, 138 F.3d 1448, 46 USPQ2d 1169 (Fed. Cir. 1998); *State Indus., Inc. v. Mor-Flo Indus. Inc.*, 948 F.2d 1573, 20 USPQ2d 1738 (Fed. Cir. 1991); *Syntex Ophthalmics, Inc. v. Novicky*, 795 F.2d 983, 230 USPQ 427 (Fed. Cir. 1986); *Korody-Colyer Corp. v. General Motors Corp.*, 760 F.2d 1293, 225 USPQ 1099 (Fed. Cir. 1985); *Rosemount, Inc. v. Beckman Instr., Inc.*, 727 F.2d 1540, 221 USPQ 1 (Fed. Cir. 1984); *Hughes v. Novi Am., Inc.*, 724 F.2d 122, 220 USPQ 707 (Fed. Cir. 1984). Attorney fees decisions under the Copyright Act and the Semiconductor Chip Protection Act are reviewed for abuse of discretion. *Brooktree Corp. v. Advanced Micro Devices, Inc.*, 977 F.2d 1555, 24 USPQ2d 1401 (Fed. Cir. 1992). An award of attorney fees under Rules 11 or 37 is subject to review under an abuse of discretion standard. *New Idea Farm Equip. Corp. v. Sperry Corp.*, 916 F.2d 1561, 16 USPQ2d 1424 (Fed. Cir. 1990). The question of "how much" for costs is reviewed under an abuse of discretion standard. *Manildra Milling Corp. v. Ogilvie Mills, Inc.*, 76 F.3d 1178, 37 USPQ2d 1707 (Fed. Cir. 1996). An award of attorney fees and costs is reviewed under the highly deferential abuse of discretion standard. *L.E.A. Dynatech, Inc. v. Allina*, 49 F.3d 1527, 33 USPQ2d 1839 (Fed. Cir. 1995). In *Gardco Mfg., Inc. v. Herst Lighting Co.*, 820 F.2d 1209, 2 USPQ2d 2015 (Fed. Cir. 1987), there was no showing that the district court was clearly erroneous in finding an absence of exceptional circumstances, and thus no showing of an abuse of discretion in failure to award attorney fees, despite the fact that the Federal Circuit indicated that the patentee's appeal of the finding of inequitable conduct would have been deemed frivolous if not for the presence of a jury trial issue of first impression.

[215]*Cambridge Prods., Ltd. v. Penn Nutrients, Inc.*, 962 F.2d 1048, 22 USPQ2d 1577 (Fed. Cir. 1992).

[216]*Lummus Indus., Inc. v. D.M. & E. Corp.*, 862 F.2d 267, 8 USPQ2d 1983 (Fed. Cir. 1988).

[217]*Bayer Aktiengesellschaft v. Duphar Int'l Research B.V.*, 738 F.2d 1237, 222 USPQ 649 (Fed. Cir. 1984).

[218]*Bic Leisure Prods., Inc. v. Windsurfing Int'l, Inc.*, 1 F.3d 1214, 27 USPQ2d 1671 (Fed. Cir. 1993); *Gustafson, Inc. v. Intersystems Indus. Prods., Inc.*, 897 F.2d 508, 13 USPQ2d 1972 (Fed. Cir. 1990); *Avia Group Int'l, Inc. v. L.A. Gear Calif., Inc.*, 853 F.2d 1557, 7 USPQ2d 1548 (Fed. Cir. 1988); *Bott v. Four Star Corp.*, 807 F.2d 1567, 1 USPQ2d 1210 (Fed. Cir. 1986); *Kaufman Co. v. Lantech*, 807 F.2d 970, 1 USPQ2d 1202 (Fed. Cir. 1986).

[219]*Amsted Indus. v. Buckeye Steel Castings Co.*, 24 F.3d 178, 30 USPQ2d 1462 (Fed. Cir. 1994).

finding of exceptionality but should articulate the underlying findings on which it is based.[220] On appeal, the factual underpinnings are reviewed under the clearly erroneous standard, and the reviewing court must also be satisfied that the correct legal standard was applied in reaching the conclusion of exceptionality. Then, and only then, does the discretion of the district court come into play: once the case is found to be exceptional, the district court may, but need not, award fees, and its decision is subject to review only under the abuse of discretion standard (both as to fees, and if any, as to amount). Thus, it is incorrect to say, ever, that exceptionality is a matter within the discretion of the district court.[221] The Federal Circuit will not hesitate to set aside an award of attorney fees if it is unsupported by adequate findings as to the basis for the award.[222] Nonetheless, the fact that the Federal Circuit, had it been sitting at trial, might have differently appraised the suit as to its exceptionality is not a basis for holding that the district court's appraisal was error.[223]

The grant or denial of a preliminary injunction is reviewed under an abuse of discretion standard.[224] When a preliminary injunction is granted, to obtain reversal on appeal an alleged infringer need only convince the appellate court that one of the factual premises is clearly erroneous. In contrast, when a preliminary injunction is denied, the movant carries a heavier burden to obtain a reversal. The movant must show not only that one or more of the factors relied on by the district court was clearly erroneous, but also that a denial of the preliminary relief sought would amount to an abuse of the court's discretion upon reversal of the erroneous finding.[225]

---

[220]*Reactive Metals & Alloys Corp. v. ESM, Inc.*, 769 F.2d 1578, 226 USPQ 821 (Fed. Cir. 1985); *Hughes v. Novi Am., Inc.*, 724 F.2d 122, 220 USPQ 707 (Fed. Cir. 1984). Whether a case is exceptional is a factual determination reviewed for clear error. *Cybor Corp. v. FAS Tech. Inc.*, 138 F.3d 1448, 46 USPQ2d 1169 (Fed. Cir. 1998).

[221]*Reactive Metals & Alloys Corp. v. ESM, Inc.*, 769 F.2d 1578, 226 USPQ 821 (Fed. Cir. 1985). See *PPG Indus., Inc. v. Celanese Polymer Spec. Co.*, 840 F.2d 1565, 6 USPQ2d 1010 (Fed. Cir. 1988); *J.P. Stevens Co. v. Lex Tex Ltd.*, 822 F.2d 1047, 3 USPQ2d 1235 (Fed. Cir. 1987); *Porter v. Farmers Supply Serv., Inc.*, 790 F.2d 882, 229 USPQ 814 (Fed. Cir. 1986). See also *Beckman Instr., Inc. v. LKB Produkter AB*, 892 F.2d 1547, 13 USPQ2d 1301 (Fed. Cir. 1989).

[222]*Hycor Corp. v. Schlueter Co.*, 740 F.2d 1529, 222 USPQ 553 (Fed. Cir. 1984).

[223]*Porter v. Farmers Supply Serv., Inc.*, 790 F.2d 882, 229 USPQ 814 (Fed. Cir. 1986).

[224]*Oakley, Inc. v. International Tropic-Cal, Inc.*, 923 F.2d 167, 17 USPQ2d 1401 (Fed. Cir. 1991); *Black & Decker, Inc. v. Hoover Serv. Ctr.*, 886 F.2d 1285, 12 USPQ2d 1250 (Fed. Cir. 1989). Findings of fact are subject to the clearly erroneous standard of Rule 52(a), and conclusions of law are reviewed de novo. *Id.* As a basic proposition, the matter lies largely in the sound discretion of the trial judge. The standard of review is whether there was an abuse of discretion, an error of law, or a serious misjudgment of the evidence. *Chrysler Motors Corp. v. Auto Body Panels of Ohio, Inc.*, 908 F.2d 951, 15 USPQ2d 1469 (Fed. Cir. 1990); *Atari Games Corp. v. Nintendo of Am., Inc.*, 897 F.2d 1572, 14 USPQ2d 1034 (Fed. Cir. 1990). See also *Rosemount, Inc. v. United States ITC*, 910 F.2d 819, 15 USPQ2d 1569 (Fed. Cir. 1990) (ITC case). The appellant bears a heavy burden. E.g., *Payless Shoesource, Inc. v. Reebok Int'l Lts.*, 998 F.2d 985, 27 USPQ2d 1516 (Fed. Cir. 1993).

[225]*New England Braiding Co. v. A.W. Chesterton Co.*, 970 F.2d 878, 23 USPQ2d 1622 (Fed. Cir. 1992).

(v) Fraud and Inequitable Conduct

Judgments of a district court concerning good and bad faith are not easily overturned.[226] Inequitable conduct is reviewed on appeal under an abuse of discretion standard. The appellant must establish that the district court's ruling is based on clearly erroneous findings of fact or a misapplication or misinterpretation of applicable law, or that the district court ruling evidences a clear error of judgment.[227] The ultimate question of fraud or inequitable conduct is one of law, but the underlying elements are largely factual determinations.[228] To determine if the district court abused its discretion, the court asks whether the subsidiary factual findings of materiality and intent are clearly erroneous.[229] Thus, questions such as good faith, intent to deceive, scienter, and materiality are all factual, and the court of appeals must affirm findings on those questions unless it is left with a definite and firm conviction that error has occurred.[230] Of course, the clearly erroneous standard is applicable to factual determinations of the PTO Board in the fraud context.[231] The court gives de novo review to the question of whether the issue of prosecution irregularities is of consequence, inasmuch as the question of whether a party has stated a legally relevant defense on that basis is one of law, not a matter of trial management.[232]

(vi) Other Patent Issues

The ownership of patent property is a matter of law, the decision of which may entail underlying factual inquiries. The court gives

---

[226]*Spectra-Physics, Inc. v. Coherent, Inc.*, 827 F.2d 1524, 3 USPQ2d 1737 (Fed. Cir. 1987).

[227]*General Electro Music Corp. v. Samick Music Corp.*, 19 F.3d 1405, 30 USPQ2d 1149 (Fed. Cir. 1994); *Modine Mfg. Co. v. Allen Group, Inc.*, 917 F.2d 538, 16 USPQ2d 1622 (Fed. Cir. 1990); *Fox Indus., Inc. v. Structural Preservation Sys., Inc.*, 922 F.2d 801 (Fed. Cir. 1991); *Hoffman-La Roche Inc. v. Lemmon Co.*, 906 F.2d 684, 15 USPQ2d 1363 (Fed. Cir. 1990). See also *Minnesota Min. & Mfg. Co. v. Johnson & Johnson Orthopaedics, Inc.*, 976 F.2d 1559, 24 USPQ2d 1321 (Fed. Cir. 1992).

[228]*Amgen, Inc. v. Chugai Pharm. Co.*, 927 F.2d 1200, 18 USPQ2d 1016 (Fed. Cir. 1991); *Halliburton Co. v. Schlumberger Tech. Corp.*, 925 F.2d 1435, 17 USPQ2d 1834 (Fed. Cir. 1991); *In re Jerabek*, 789 F.2d 886, 229 USPQ 530 (Fed. Cir. 1986); *Argus Chem. Corp. v. Fibre Glass-Evercoat Co.*, 759 F.2d 10, 225 USPQ 1100 (Fed. Cir. 1985); *J.P. Stevens & Co. v. Lex Tex Ltd.*, 747 F.2d 1553, 223 USPQ 1089 (Fed. Cir. 1984); *American Hoist & Derrick Co. v. Sowa & Sons, Inc.*, 725 F.2d 1350, 220 USPQ 763 (Fed. Cir. 1984).

[229]*Molins PLC v. Textron, Inc.*, 48 F.3d 1172, 33 USPQ2d 1823 (Fed. Cir. 1995).

[230]*Allen Organ Co. v. Kimball Int'l, Inc.*, 839 F.2d 1556, 5 USPQ2d 1769 (Fed. Cir. 1988); *Carella v. Starlight Archery & Pro Line Co.*, 804 F.2d 135, 231 USPQ 644 (Fed. Cir. 1986); *Kangaroos U.S.A., Inc. v. Caldor, Inc.*, 778 F.2d 1571, 228 USPQ 32 (Fed. Cir. 1985); *J.P. Stevens & Co. v. Lex Tex Ltd.*, 747 F.2d 1553, 223 USPQ 1089 (Fed. Cir. 1984). The court has demonstrated caution, however, in according its usual deference to the fact finder's assessment of a witness's credibility and character in this context. Given the ease with which a relatively routine act of patent prosecution can be portrayed as intended to mislead or deceive, clear and convincing evidence of conduct sufficient to support an inference of culpable intent is required. *Molins PLC v. Textron, Inc.*, 48 F.3d 1172, 33 USPQ2d 1823 (Fed. Cir. 1995).

[231]*In re Jerabek*, 789 F.2d 886, 229 USPQ 530 (Fed. Cir. 1986).

[232]*Magnivision, Inc. v. Bonneau Co.*, 115 F.3d 956, 42 USPQ2d 1925 (Fed. Cir. 1997).

plenary review to the legal issue, and reviews for clear error any disputed findings of fact made below.[233] The existence of an implied-in-fact contract to assign inventive rights is a question of fact, reviewed for clear error.[234] The existence of an implied license is a question of law that is reviewed de novo.[235] The interpretation of 35 U.S.C. §116, dealing with inventorship, is a question of law freely reviewable on appeal.[236] Inventorship is a question of law that is reviewed without deference. However, the underlying findings of fact are reviewed for clear error.[237]

Priority is a question of law that is to be determined based upon underlying factual findings. As in any bench trial, the Federal Circuit reviews the district court's judgment for clearly erroneous findings of fact and errors of law.[238] Conception and reduction to practice are legal determinations subject to review free of the clearly erroneous standard, while findings supporting those conclusions are, of course, reviewed for clear error.[239] Suppression or concealment is a question of law that is reviewed de novo.[240] Interpretation of an interference count is a question of law to be reviewed de novo.[241] What is disclosed in an application involved in an interference, and whether an application supports the subject matter of a count, are questions of fact reviewed under the clearly erroneous standard.[242]

Determining whether an applicant has met the statutory requirements of 35 U.S.C. §251 for reissue is a question of law, which is

---

[233]*Kahn v. General Motors Corp.,* 77 F.3d 457, 38 USPQ2d 1063 (Fed. Cir. 1996).

[234]*Teets v. Chromalloy Gas Turbine Corp.,* 83 F.3d 403, 38 USPQ2d 1695 (Fed. Cir. 1996).

[235]*Glass Equip. Dev. Inc. v. Besten Inc.,* 174 F.3d 1337, 50 USPQ2d 1300 (Fed. Cir. 1999).

[236]*Kimberly-Clark Corp. v. Procter & Gamble Distrib. Co.,* 973 F.2d 911, 23 USPQ2d 1921 (Fed. Cir. 1992). Conception and inventorship are questions of law, reviewed de novo. *Fina Oil & Chem. Co. v. Ewen,* 123 F.3d 1466, 43 USPQ2d 1935 (Fed. Cir. 1997).

[237]*Ethicon Inc. v. United States Surgical Corp.,* 135 F.3d 1456, 45 USPQ2d 1545 (Fed. Cir. 1998).

[238]*Conservolite, Inc. v. Widmayer,* 21 F.3d 1098, 30 USPQ2d 1626 (Fed. Cir. 1994). Priority in general is a question of law. *Price v. Symsek,* 988 F.2d 1187, 26 USPQ2d 1031 (Fed. Cir. 1993). Priority is a question of law to be decided based upon underlying factual determinations. *Innovative Scuba Concepts, Inc. v. Feder Indus., Inc.,* 26 F.3d 1112, 31 USPQ2d 1132 (Fed. Cir. 1994). Entitlement to priority under 35 U.S.C. §120 is a matter of law, and receives plenary review on appeal. Any disputed factual questions are reviewed on the clearly erroneous standard. *In re Daniels,* 144 F.3d 1452, 46 USPQ2d 1788 (Fed. Cir. 1998).

[239]*Hybritech Inc. v. Monoclonal Antibodies, Inc.,* 802 F.2d 1367, 231 USPQ 81 (Fed. Cir. 1986). Conception is a legal determination that is reviewed by the Federal Circuit de novo. *Bosies v. Benedict,* 27 F.3d 539, 30 USPQ2d 1862 (Fed. Cir. 1994); *Filmtec Corp. v. Hydranautics,* 982 F.2d 1546, 25 USPQ2d 1283 (Fed. Cir. 1992). Reduction to practice is a question of law to be reviewed de novo. *Scott v. Finney,* 34 F.3d 1058, 32 USPQ2d 1115 (Fed. Cir. 1995); *DSL Dynamic Sciences Ltd. v. Union Switch & Signal, Inc.,* 928 F.2d 1122, 18 USPQ2d 1152 (Fed. Cir. 1991). But the underlying factual findings are reviewed under the clearly erroneous standard. *Fujikawa v. Wattanasin,* 93 F.3d 1559, 39 USPQ2d 1895 (Fed. Cir. 1996); *Schendel v. Curtis,* 83 F.3d 1399, 38 USPQ2d 1743 (Fed. Cir. 1996); *Holmwood v. Sugavanam,* 948 F.2d 1236, 20 USPQ2d 1712 (Fed. Cir. 1991).

[240]*Fujikawa v. Wattanasin,* 93 F.3d 1559, 39 USPQ2d 1895 (Fed. Cir. 1996).

[241]*Credle v. Bond,* 25 F.3d 1566, 30 USPQ2d 1911 (Fed. Cir. 1994); *Davis v. Loesch,* 998 F.2d 963, 27 USPQ2d 1440 (Fed. Cir. 1993).

[242]*Credle v. Bond,* 25 F.3d 1566, 30 USPQ2d 1911 (Fed. Cir. 1994).

reviewed de novo. This legal conclusion is based on underlying findings of fact, which are sustained unless they are clearly erroneous.[243] The question of claim scope before and after reexamination is a matter of claim construction, and thus is subject to de novo review on appeal.[244] Intervening rights, however, is reviewed under the abuse of discretion standard.[245]

A determination whether assignor estoppel applies in a particular case requires a balancing of the equities between the parties. That determination is a matter committed to the sound discretion of the trial court and is therefore reviewed for abuse of discretion.[246] Compliance with the patent statute governing marking and notice is a question of fact.[247] Application of the laches bar is reviewed under the abuse of discretion standard.[248]

(vii) Miscellaneous Issues

The court reviews subject matter jurisdiction, a question of law, de novo.[249] Likewise, personal jurisdiction is reviewed without deference to the view of the district court.[250] Disputed facts underlying this legal determination, however, are reviewed for clear error. Thus, although the determination whether the assertion of personal jurisdiction comports with due process is a question of law that is reviewed

---

[243]*In re Clement*, 131 F.3d 1464, 45 USPQ2d 1161 (Fed. Cir. 1997). The statutory reissue requirement of "error" is a question of law, reviewed de novo. *Mentor Corp. v. Coloplast, Inc.*, 998 F.2d 992, 27 USPQ2d 1521 (Fed. Cir. 1993). A determination of identity, for purposes of 35 U.S.C. §252, is one of law, reviewed de novo. *Westvaco Corp. v. International Paper Co.*, 991 F.2d 735, 26 USPQ2d 1353 (Fed. Cir. 1993). See also *Vectra Fitness Inc. v. TNWK Corp.*, 162 F.3d 1379, 49 USPQ2d 1144 (Fed. Cir. 1998).

[244]*Anderson v. International Eng'g & Mfg. Inc.*, 160 F.3d 1345, 48 USPQ2d 1631 (Fed. Cir. 1998). The court reviews without deference a conclusion that reexamined claims remained identical in scope. *Minco, Inc. v. Combustion Eng'g, Inc.*, 95 F.3d 1109, 40 USPQ2d 1001 (Fed. Cir. 1996).

[245]*Westvaco Corp. v. International Paper Co.*, 991 F.2d 735, 26 USPQ2d 1353 (Fed. Cir. 1993).

[246]*Carroll Touch, Inc. v. Electro Mechanical Sys., Inc.*, 3 F.3d 404, 27 USPQ2d 1836 (Fed. Cir. 1993).

[247]*Maxwell v. J. Baker, Inc.*, 86 F.3d 1098, 39 USPQ2d 1001 (Fed. Cir. 1996).

[248]*Hall v. Aqua Queen Mfg., Inc.*, 93 F.3d 1548, 39 USPQ2d 1925 (Fed. Cir. 1996).

[249]*Interspiro USA, Inc. v. Figgie Int'l, Inc.*, 18 F.3d 927, 30 USPQ2d 1070 (Fed. Cir. 1994); *Dehne v. United States*, 970 F.2d 890 (Fed. Cir. 1992). A dismissal under Rule 12(b)(1) for lack of subject matter jurisdiction is reviewed de novo. In the context of a ripeness determination, the underlying factual findings must be accepted unless clearly erroneous. *Cedars-Sinai Med. Ctr. v. Watkins*, 11 F.3d 1573, 29 USPQ2d 1188 (Fed. Cir. 1993) (applying Ninth Circuit law). The question of a party's standing to bring a case is a jurisdictional one that is reviewed de novo. *Textile Prods. Inc. v. Mead Corp.*, 134 F.3d 1481, 45 USPQ2d 1633 (Fed. Cir. 1998); *Enzo APA & Son v. Geapag A.G.*, 134 F.3d 1090, 45 USPQ2d 1368 (Fed. Cir. 1998); *GAIA Tech., Inc. v. Reconversion Tech., Inc.*, 93 F.3d 774, 39 USPQ2d 1826 (Fed. Cir. 1996). Whether or not an act constitutes the tort of unfair competition under 28 U.S.C. §1338(b) is a question of law that is reviewed de novo. *Mars, Inc. v. Kabushiki-Kaisha Nippon Conlux*, 24 F.3d 1368, 30 USPQ2d 1621 (Fed. Cir. 1994).

[250]*Graphic Controls Corp. v. Utah Med. Prods. Inc.*, 149 F.3d 1382, 47 USPQ2d 1622 (Fed. Cir. 1998); *Viam Corp. v. Iowa Export-Import Trading Co.*, 84 F.3d 424, 38 USPQ2d 1833 (Fed. Cir. 1996).

de novo, this determination is based on subordinate questions of fact that are reviewed for clear error.[251] A district court's decision not to exercise jurisdiction under the mandamus statute for federal officers (28 U.S.C. §1361) is a discretionary one that is reviewed for abuse.[252] The Federal Circuit reviews de novo a district court's determination of state law.[253]

An attorney disqualification order will not be disturbed if the record reveals any sound basis for the court's action. This means it will be reversed only where it is not based on articulable principles, or where the court either misperceives the relevant rule of law or abuses its discretion.[254] In a matter involving attorney disciplinary proceedings before the PTO, a reviewing body—district court or Federal Circuit—must decide whether a reasonable mind could have found the evidence of attorney misconduct clear and convincing.[255]

Whether the parties have entered into a contract is an issue of fact.[256] Contract interpretation is a matter of law, and the Federal Circuit reviews it de novo.[257] Unfair competition and trademark infringement, like patent infringement, involve questions of fact reviewed under the clearly erroneous standard.[258] A jury's determination of secondary meaning is one of fact and therefore warrants a substantial evidence standard of review. The determination of likelihood of confusion, however, is the ultimate conclusion of law to be

---

[251]*Dainippon Screen Mfg. Co. v. CFMT Inc.*, 142 F.3d 1266, 46 USPQ2d 1616 (Fed. Cir. 1998).

[252]*Franchi v. Manbeck*, 972 F.2d 1283, 23 USPQ2d 1847 (Fed. Cir. 1992).

[253]*Abbott Labs. v. Brennan*, 952 F.2d 1346, 21 USPQ2d 1192 (Fed. Cir. 1992).

[254]*Sun Studs, Inc. v. Applied Theory Assocs.*, 772 F.2d 1557, 227 USPQ 81 (Fed. Cir. 1985); *W.L. Gore & Assoc. v. International Med. P.R. Assoc.*, 745 F.2d 1463, 223 USPQ 884 (Fed. Cir. 1984). Under Second Circuit law, a motion to disqualify an attorney is addressed to the discretion of the district court, and a ruling thereon will not be overturned absent a determination of abuse of discretion. *Telectronics Prop., Ltd. v. Medtronic, Inc.*, 836 F.2d 1332, 5 USPQ2d 1424 (Fed. Cir. 1988). The standard of review is abuse of discretion (Sixth Circuit) unless the question of disqualification is purely legal (Tenth Circuit). *Picker Int'l, Inc. v. Varian Assoc., Inc.*, 869 F.2d 578, 10 USPQ2d 1122 (Fed. Cir. 1989).

[255]*Klein v. Peterson*, 866 F.2d 412, 9 USPQ2d 1558 (Fed. Cir. 1989). The court reviews a Commissioner's decision that an attorney violated his or her duty of candor for substantial evidence. *Lipman v. Dickinson*, 174 F.3d 1363, 50 USPQ2d 1490 (Fed. Cir. 1999).

[256]*S & T Mfg. Co. v. County of Hillsborough, Fla.*, 815 F.2d 676, 2 USPQ2d 1280 (Fed. Cir. 1987) (applying Eleventh Circuit law).

[257]*American Med. Sys., Inc. v. Medical Eng'g Corp.*, 6 F.3d 1523, 28 USPQ2d 1321 (Fed. Cir. 1993); *Texas Instr., Inc. v. United States ITC*, 988 F.2d 1165, 26 USPQ2d 1018 (Fed. Cir. 1993); *Craft Mach. Works, Inc. v. United States*, 926 F.2d 1110 (Fed. Cir. 1991). See also *Interspiro USA, Inc. v. Figgie Int'l, Inc.*, 18 F.3d 927, 30 USPQ2d 1070 (Fed. Cir. 1994). The interpretation of contractual language, including license agreements, is reviewed as a question of law. *Ethicon Inc. v. United States Surgical Corp.*, 135 F.3d 1456, 45 USPQ2d 1545 (Fed. Cir. 1998). The construction of a license agreement is a question of law that the court reviews de novo. *Heidelberg Harris Inc. v. Loebach*, 145 F.3d 1454, 46 USPQ2d 1948 (Fed. Cir. 1998). The interpretation of a settlement agreement, i.e., a contract, is a question of law that is reviewed de novo. *Augustine Med. Inc. v. Progressive Dynamics Inc.*, 194 F.3d 1367, 52 USPQ2d 1515 (Fed. Cir. 1999). Interpretation of the terms of a supersedeas bond, like those of any contract, is a matter of law and review is therefore de novo. *Beatrice Foods Co. v. New England Printing & Lith. Co.*, 930 F.2d 1572, 18 USPQ2d 1548 (Fed. Cir. 1991).

[258]*Charles Greiner & Co. v. Mari-Med Mfg., Inc.*, 962 F.2d 1031, 22 USPQ2d 1526 (Fed. Cir. 1992).

decided by the court and, as a result, a de novo standard of review is applicable.[259]

Where the only issue before the district court is one of statutory interpretation, a question of law, the appellate court independently determines the proper interpretation and need not defer to the district court[260] or the PTO.[261] Application of the attorney-client privilege is a question of fact.[262] Laches and estoppel both depend on the facts of the particular case and are matters within the trial court's discretion that will not be set aside absent a showing of abuse.[263] The decision whether to invoke judicial estoppel lies within the trial court's discretion, and a refusal to apply the doctrine is reviewed for abuse.[264] Whether a claim is barred by the doctrine of res judicata is a question of law that is reviewed de novo.[265]

In deciding declaratory judgment jurisdiction, the legal effect of the parties' conduct, and in particular whether it was sufficient to create an actual controversy, is a question of law that is reviewed de novo.[266] If jurisdictional facts are undisputed, the question of declaratory judgment jurisdiction is one of law, and the clearly erroneous

---

[259]*Braun Inc. v. Dynamics Corp.*, 975 F.2d 815, 24 USPQ2d 1121 (Fed. Cir. 1992). Under Eighth Circuit law, both actual confusion and likelihood of confusion are questions of fact reviewed under the clearly erroneous standard. *Conopco, Inc. v. May Dep't Stores Co.*, 46 F.3d 1556, 32 USPQ2d 1225 (Fed. Cir. 1994). Under Second Circuit law, a jury's fact findings on inherent distinctiveness or secondary meaning are reviewed for substantial evidence and its ultimate finding of likelihood of confusion is reviewed de novo. *Imagineering, Inc. v. Van Klassens, Inc.*, 53 F.3d 1260, 34 USPQ2d 1526 (Fed. Cir. 1995). Under Eleventh Circuit law, functionality of trade dress is a question of fact, subject to the substantial evidence standard of review. *Elmer v. ICC Fabricating, Inc.*, 67 F.3d 1571, 36 USPQ2d 1417 (Fed. Cir. 1995).

[260]*Gardner v. Brown*, 5 F.3d 1456 (Fed. Cir. 1993); *Glaxo Oper. UK Ltd. v. Quigg*, 894 F.2d 392, 13 USPQ2d 1628 (Fed. Cir. 1990); *Chula Vista Sch. Dist. v. Bennett*, 824 F.2d 1573 (Fed. Cir. 1987). Statutory construction is a question of law that is reviewed de novo. *Bristol-Myers Squibb Co. v. Royce Labs., Inc.*, 69 F.3d 1130, 36 USPQ2d 1641 (Fed. Cir. 1995). Whether equitable tolling is permitted under a statute of limitations raises a pure question of federal law involving statutory interpretation; such matters are reviewed de novo. *Weddel v. Secretary, Health & Hum. Serv.*, 100 F.3d 929 (Fed. Cir. 1996).

[261]*In re Portola Packaging, Inc.*, 110 F.3d 786, 42 USPQ2d 1295 (Fed. Cir. 1997).

[262]*American Standard, Inc. v. Pfizer, Inc.*, 828 F.2d 734, 3 USPQ2d 1817 (Fed. Cir. 1987).

[263]*Scholle Corp. v. Blackhawk Molding Co.*, 133 F.3d 1469, 45 USPQ2d 1468 (Fed. Cir. 1998); *A.C. Aukerman Co. v. R.L. Chaides Constr. Co.*, 960 F.2d 1020, 22 USPQ2d 1321 (Fed. Cir. 1992); *Vaupel Textilmaschinen KG v. Meccanical Euro Italia S.P.A.*, 944 F.2d 870, 20 USPQ2d 1045 (Fed. Cir. 1991); *Adelberg Labs., Inc. v. Miles, Inc.*, 921 F.2d 1267, 17 USPQ2d 1111 (Fed. Cir. 1990); *Jamesbury Corp. v. Litton Indus. Prods., Inc.*, 839 F.2d 1544, 5 USPQ2d 1779 (Fed. Cir. 1988). The court may reverse a discretionary decision if it rests on an erroneous interpretation of law or clearly erroneous factual underpinnings. Without such error, however, a laches determination stands unless it evinces unreasonable judgment in weighing relevant factors. *Eastman Kodak Co. v. Goodyear Tire & Rubber Co.*, 114 F.3d 1547, 42 USPQ2d 1737 (Fed. Cir. 1997).

[264]*Data Gen. Corp. v. Johnson*, 78 F.3d 1556 (Fed. Cir. 1996).

[265]*United Tech. Corp. v. Chromalloy Gas Turbine Corp.*, 189 F.3d 1338, 51 USPQ2d 1838 (Fed. Cir. 1999).

[266]*Shell Oil Co. v. Amoco Corp.*, 970 F.2d 885, 23 USPQ2d 1627 (Fed. Cir. 1992). Whether an actual controversy exists upon particular facts is a question of law subject to plenary review. The district court's factual findings pertinent thereto are reviewed for clear error under Rule 52(a), FRCP. *BP Chems. Ltd. v. Union Carbide Corp.*, 4 F.3d 975, 28 USPQ2d 1124 (Fed. Cir. 1993).

standard is not involved.[267] But there is no absolute right to a declaratory judgment; where there is a clear controversy and thus jurisdiction, a district court's decision on whether to exercise that jurisdiction is discretionary.[268] Thus the existence of an actual controversy is an absolute predicate for declaratory judgment jurisdiction. When there is no actual controversy, the court has no discretion to decide the case. When there is an actual controversy and thus jurisdiction, the exercise of the jurisdiction is discretionary. Dismissal for lack of jurisdiction is reviewed as a matter of law, keeping in mind that the district court's view of the legal effect of the fact pattern before it is not to be lightly disregarded.[269] Indeed, the Federal Circuit recognizes that the Supreme Court has recently made it clear that appellate courts should use a more deferential standard for reviewing decisions regarding the exercise of declaratory judgment jurisdiction.[270]

The mere recitation by a district court of finality and no just reason for delay pursuant to Rule 54(b), FRCP, does not automatically render a judgment appealable as a final decision. Instead, when an appeal is certified pursuant to Rule 54(b), an appellate court should review the finality of the judgment de novo in order to assure itself that it has jurisdiction. While the district court's determination that there is no just reason for delay is reviewed under an abuse of discretion standard, a district court cannot, in the exercise of its discretion, treat as final that which is not final.[271]

The court reviews the interpretation of its own mandate de novo.[272]

§17.2 Practice Before the Court

In many respects, the Federal Circuit is no different from the regional courts of appeals. But its limited jurisdiction has imposed certain constraints that make it unique among American appellate bodies. The full form and figure of this special body remain to be

---

[267]*Arrowhead Indus. Water, Inc. v. Ecolochem, Inc.*, 846 F.2d 731, 6 USPQ2d 1685 (Fed. Cir. 1988). The Federal Circuit reviews questions about subject matter jurisdiction de novo. *Manville Sales Corp. v. Paramount Sys., Inc.*, 917 F.2d 544, 16 USPQ2d 1587 (Fed. Cir. 1990); *Kunkel v. Topmaster Int'l, Inc.*, 906 F.2d 693, 15 USPQ2d 1367 (Fed. Cir. 1990).

[268]*Arrowhead Indus. Water, Inc. v. Ecolochem, Inc.*, 846 F.2d 731, 6 USPQ2d 1685 (Fed. Cir. 1988).

[269]*Spectronics Corp. v. H.B. Fuller Co.*, 940 F.2d 631, 19 USPQ2d 1545 (Fed. Cir. 1991). See also *Super Sack Mfg. Corp. v. Chase Packaging Corp.*, 57 F.3d 1054, 35 USPQ2d 1139 (Fed. Cir. 1995).

[270]*EMC Corp. v. Norand Corp.*, 89 F.3d 807, 39 USPQ2d 1451 (Fed. Cir. 1996). Compare *Minnesota Min. & Mfg. Co. v. Norton Co.*, 929 F.2d 670, 18 USPQ2d 1302 (Fed. Cir. 1991).

[271]*W.L. Gore & Assoc. v. International Med. Pros. Res. Assoc.*, 975 F.2d 858, 24 USPQ2d 1195 (Fed. Cir. 1992). See also *Spraytex, Inc. v. DJS&T*, 96 F.3d 1377, 40 USPQ2d 1145 (Fed. Cir. 1996).

[272]*Odetics Inc. v. Storage Tech. Corp.*, 185 F.3d 1259, 51 USPQ2d 1225 (Fed. Cir. 1999); *Engel Indus. Inc. v. Lockformer Co.*, 166 F.3d 1379, 49 USPQ2d 1618 (Fed. Cir. 1999).

shaped by years of work and experience. Nonetheless, some definite features—even some sharp edges—have already begun to emerge. This section will examine some of the unusual characteristics of the work of and practice before the court.

(a) Binding Precedent

In its first decision, *South Corp. v. United States*,[273] handed down October 28, 1982, the court dealt unequivocally with the matter of binding precedent. Sitting, appropriately, in banc, the court held that it would adhere to the body of law that existed in its predecessor courts, the CCPA and the Court of Claims, as of September 30, 1982. Overruling such precedent, or resolving a conflict between the two predecessors, would require in banc consideration.[274]

The court has faithfully observed the rule of *South*. Even where it is possible that a prior decision of the CCPA would be decided differently today, it still stands as binding precedent until overruled.[275] The Federal Circuit is also bound by decisions of the Court of Claims.[276] In one case the argument was made that the court should overrule controlling precedent in view of a bill pending in Congress that purported to do just that. The court pointed out that it is the province of Congress to make changes in the law based on public policy. The court should not act in anticipation of possible action by the legislature. It is inappropriate for the court to abandon long-standing precedent on the eve of congressional consideration.[277] On the other hand, what may have been traditional practice is not, without a clear holding of one of the Federal Circuit's predecessors, binding upon it.[278]

The Federal Circuit has adopted the rule that prior decisions of a panel of the court are binding precedent on subsequent panels unless and until overturned in banc. Where there is direct conflict,

---

[273]*South Corp. v. United States*, 690 F.2d 1368 (Fed. Cir. 1982).

[274]See also *UMC Elec. Co. v. United States*, 816 F.2d 647, 2 USPQ2d 1465 (Fed. Cir. 1987); *United States v. Rush*, 804 F.2d 645 (Fed. Cir. 1986); *Gindes v. United States*, 740 F.2d 947 (Fed. Cir. 1984); *Mother's Restaurant, Inc. v. Mama's Pizza, Inc.*, 723 F.2d 1566, 221 USPQ 394 (Fed. Cir. 1983).

[275]*In re Durden*, 763 F.2d 1406, 226 USPQ 359 (Fed. Cir. 1985). See also *Larry Harmon Pictures Corp. v. Williams Rest. Corp.*, 929 F.2d 662, 18 USPQ2d 1292 (Fed. Cir. 1991). The court has recognized that later CCPA decisions could resolve precedential inconsistencies sub silento; later CCPA decisions would control because that court always sat in banc. *In re Gosteli*, 872 F.2d 1008, 10 USPQ2d 1614 (Fed. Cir. 1989).

[276]*Johns-Manville Corp. v. United States*, 855 F.2d 1556 (Fed. Cir. 1988); *United States Steel Corp. v. United States*, 848 F.2d 1232 (Fed. Cir. 1988). Decisions of the predecessor Court of Claims that are on point with the facts and legal issue of an appeal bind the court unless overruled by an in banc decision. *Gargoyles, Inc. v. United States*, 113 F.3d 1572, 42 USPQ2d 1760 (Fed. Cir. 1997).

[277]*In re Thorpe*, 777 F.2d 695, 227 USPQ 964 (Fed. Cir. 1985).

[278]*Dynamics Corp. v. United States*, 766 F.2d 518, 226 USPQ 622 (Fed. Cir. 1985).

the first decision controls.[279] But the court need not overrule a prior case in order to clarify that case by stating a requirement that was met but not discussed. A court may refine holdings in its precedent that were stated or have been interpreted too broadly.[280] Where conflicting statements appear in the court's precedent, the panel is obligated to review the cases and reconcile or explain the statements, if possible. If not reconcilable and if not merely conflicting dicta, the earlier statements must be followed, or the panel may seek in banc consideration if it believes the later decision correctly states the law.[281] In *Atlantic v. Faytex,*[282] the court apparently found a way around the rule that a prior Federal Circuit panel decision controls subsequent panels unless overturned in banc: if the prior decision can be shown to have failed properly to consider Supreme Court precedent, it may be disregarded. In a fascinating display of internal disagreement, one judge called the panel decision in *Atlantic* "insulting," "mutiny," "heresy," and, somewhat redundantly, "illegal."[283] In another case, the court took what appears to be an unusual step when it sat in banc on a portion of the case only, to resolve its own perceived conflicts in precedent.[284]

The court is not bound by stipulations of law.[285]

(b) Regional Circuit Law

The court has said that it is required, absent manifest injustice, to apply the law as it exists at the time of its decision.[286] But what law? The answer was some time in coming. Not until the middle of 1984 did the Federal Circuit begin to grapple with this problem. In a case involving the appealability of an order disqualifying counsel, the court recognized that a district court should not be obliged to answer a procedural question one way when it will go to a regional court of appeals and another way when it will end up in the Federal

---

[279]*Newell Cos. v. Kenney Mfg. Co.,* 864 F.2d 757, 9 USPQ2d 1417 (Fed. Cir. 1988). Decisions of a three-judge panel cannot overturn prior precedential decisions of the court. *Vas-Cath Inc. v. Mahurkar,* 935 F.2d 1555, 19 USPQ2d 1111 (Fed. Cir. 1991). A reversal of such a holding would have to be through an in banc proceeding in the Federal Circuit, Supreme Court review, or a change in the patent statute by Congress. *Jacobs Wind Elec. Co. v. Florida Dep't of Transp.,* 919 F.2d 726, 16 USPQ2d 1972 (Fed. Cir. 1990).

[280]*Woodard v. Sage Prods., Inc.,* 818 F.2d 841, 2 USPQ2d 1649 (Fed. Cir. 1987).

[281]*Johnston v. IVAC Corp.,* 885 F.2d 1574, 12 USPQ2d 1382 (Fed. Cir. 1989).

[282]*Atlantic Thermoplastics Co. v. Faytex Corp.,* 970 F.2d 834, 23 USPQ2d 1481 (Fed. Cir. 1992).

[283]The opinion of Judge Rich, dissenting from a denial of rehearing in banc, is reported at 974 F.2d 1279, 23 USPQ2d 1801. Judge Rader's separate concurring opinion in support of the panel decision appears at 974 F.2d 1299, 24 USPQ2d 1138.

[284]*Kingsdown Med. Cons, Ltd. v. Hollister, Inc.,* 863 F.2d 867, 9 USPQ2d 1384 (Fed. Cir. 1988). With all respect, the questions here did not seem, in every instance at least, to be all that much in conflict.

[285]*Technicon Instr., Corp. v. Alpkem Corp.,* 866 F.2d 417, 9 USPQ2d 1540 (Fed. Cir. 1989).

[286]*Lindahl v. Office of Personnel Management,* 718 F.2d 391 (Fed. Cir. 1983).

Circuit. The court accordingly applied regional circuit law to the disqualification issues.[287] This has led to the general rule that the Federal Circuit reviews procedural matters that are not unique to patent issues under the law of the particular regional circuit where appeals from the district court would normally lie.[288]

Each case must be decided by reference to the core policy of not creating unnecessary conflicts and confusion in procedural matters. The court's practice is to defer to regional circuit law when the precise issue involves an interpretation of the Federal Rules of Civil Procedure[289] or the local rules of the district court. But where there is an essential relationship between the exclusive statutory mandate of the Federal Circuit, or its functions as an appellate court, and the relevant procedural issue, it will apply its own law, with due regard for established regional circuit law. Such issues include interpretation of the Federal Rules of Appellate Procedure.[290]

Thus the court applies regional circuit law to questions such as amendments to pleadings,[291] joinder of parties,[292] permissive intervention,[293] Rule 12(b)(6) motions,[294] application of the rules of evidence,[295]

---

[287]*In re International Med. P.R. Assoc.*, 739 F.2d 618 (Fed. Cir. 1984). See also *Picker Int'l, Inc. v. Varian Assoc., Inc.*, 869 F.2d 578, 10 USPQ2d 1122 (Fed. Cir. 1989); *Atasi Corp. v. Seagate Tech.*, 847 F.2d 826, 6 USPQ2d 1955 (Fed. Cir. 1988); *Telectronics Prop., Ltd. v. Medtronic, Inc.*, 836 F.2d 1332, 5 USPQ2d 1424 (Fed. Cir. 1988).

[288]*DMI, Inc. v. Deere & Co.*, 802 F.2d 421, 231 USPQ 276 (Fed. Cir. 1986). The court will also obtain nonbinding guidance from other circuits in uncharted areas. *U.S. Philips Corp. v. Windmere Corp.*, 861 F.2d 695, 8 USPQ2d 1885 (Fed. Cir. 1988). It should be noted that the court feels that it is improper to predict how a regional circuit would rule unless such a prediction is essential to disposition of the appeal. *Biodex Corp. v. Loredan Biomedical, Inc.*, 946 F.2d 850, 20 USPQ2d 1252 (Fed. Cir. 1991). Where the district court sits in the Eleventh Circuit, decisions from the Fifth Circuit rendered before October 1, 1981, are controlling. *Windmere*, supra.

[289]*Trilogy Comm., Inc. v. Times Fiber Comm., Inc.*, 109 F.3d 739, 42 USPQ2d 1129 (Fed. Cir. 1997).

[290]*Atasi Corp. v. Seagate Tech.*, 847 F.2d 826, 6 USPQ2d 1955 (Fed. Cir. 1988). Here the court found that the presumption of shared confidences among attorneys in the same firm had not been overcome, and therefore found it unnecessary to predict whether the Ninth Circuit, which had not yet spoken on the subject, would hold that the presumption is in any event rebuttable.

[291]*Datascope Corp. v. SMEC, Inc.*, 962 F.2d 1043, 22 USPQ2d 1573 (Fed. Cir. 1992); *Kalman v. Berlyn Corp.*, 914 F.2d 1473, 16 USPQ2d 1093 (Fed. Cir. 1990); *Senza-Gel Corp. v. Seiffhart*, 803 F.2d 661, 231 USPQ 363 (Fed. Cir. 1986).

[292]*Katz v. Lear Siegler, Inc.*, 909 F.2d 1459, 15 USPQ2d 1554 (Fed. Cir. 1990). Whether a party is indispensable under Rule 19(b) is a matter of regional circuit law. *Dainippon Screen Mfg. Co. v. CFMT Inc.*, 142 F.3d 1266, 46 USPQ2d 1616 (Fed. Cir. 1998). In reviewing an order denying a motion to amend a complaint to add a party, the court looks to the law of the regional circuit. *Kalman v. Berlyn Corp.*, 914 F.2d 1473, 16 USPQ2d 1093 (Fed. Cir. 1990). It would seem, however, that joinder questions may often raise issues that are squarely within the patent jurisprudence of the Federal Circuit; perhaps the court may wish to develop its own coherent body of precedent on the subject.

[293]*Haworth, Inc. v. Steelcase, Inc.*, 12 F.3d 1090, 29 USPQ2d 1368 (Fed. Cir. 1993).

[294]*C&F Packing Co. v. IBP Inc.*, 224 F.3d 1296, 55 USPQ2d 1865 (Fed. Cir. 2).

[295]*Rodime PLC v. Seagate Tech. Inc.*, 174 F.3d 1294, 50 USPQ2d 1429 (Fed. Cir. 1999); *Ethicon Inc. v. United States Surgical Corp.*, 135 F.3d 1456, 45 USPQ2d 1545 (Fed. Cir. 1998); *Abbott Labs. v. Brennan*, 952 F.2d 1346, 21 USPQ2d 1192 (Fed. Cir. 1992); *Mainland Indus., Inc. v. Standal's Patents Ltd.*, 799 F.2d 746, 230 USPQ 772 (Fed. Cir. 1986). In *Arthur A.*

subpoenas,[296] procedural requirements for the grant of an injunction,[297] relief from judgment under Rule 60(b),[298] and even jurisdictional questions involving the effect of a notice of appeal,[299] whether a judgment is final,[300] retention of jurisdiction to enforce a settlement agreement,[301] or the failure to exercise discretionary jurisdiction of a pendent claim.[302] Apparently the court will follow regional circuit law on the question of whether a motion for new trial is sufficiently particular under Rule 7, FRCP, to preserve the jurisdiction of the district court.[303] The question whether a district court retains jurisdiction to alter or amend its judgment under Rule 59, FRCP, is a procedural issue, not unique to patent law, to be decided under regional circuit law.[304] Other such issues are choice of law, mootness, and ripeness,[305] law of the case,[306] inconsistent jury verdicts or

---

Collins Inc. v. Northern Telecom Ltd., 216 F.3d 1042, 55 USPQ2d 1143 (Fed. Cir. 2), the court seemed to treat the issue of the sufficiency of support for an opinion of an expert expressed in an affidavit opposing summary judgment as one governed by regional circuit law.

[296]*Truswal Sys. Corp v. Hydro-Air Eng'g, Inc.*, 813 F.2d 1207, 2 USPQ2d 1034 (Fed. Cir. 1987); *Heat & Control, Inc. v. Hester Indus. Inc.*, 785 F.2d 1017, 228 USPQ 926 (Fed. Cir. 1986).

[297]*Xeta, Inc. v. Atex, Inc.*, 852 F.2d 1280, 7 USPQ2d 1471 (Fed. Cir. 1988); *Hybritech, Inc. v. Abbott Labs.*, 849 F.2d 1446, 7 USPQ2d 1191 (Fed. Cir. 1988); *Digital Equip. Corp. v. Emulex Corp.*, 805 F.2d 380, 231 USPQ 779 (Fed. Cir. 1986). An injunction staying concurrent litigation is reviewed on the abuse of discretion standard. *Katz v. Lear Siegler, Inc.*, 909 F.2d 1459, 15 USPQ2d 1554 (Fed. Cir. 1990).

[298]*Marquip Inc. v. Fosber Am. Inc.*, 198 F.3d 1363, 53 USPQ2d 1015 (Fed. Cir. 1999); *Rodime PLC v. Seagate Tech. Inc.*, 174 F.3d 1294, 50 USPQ2d 1429 (Fed. Cir. 1999); *W.L. Gore & Assoc. v. C.R. Bard, Inc.*, 977 F.2d 558, 24 USPQ2d 1451 (Fed. Cir. 1992); *Amstar Corp. v. Envirotech Corp.*, 823 F.2d 1538, 3 USPQ2d 1412 (Fed. Cir. 1987); *Ashland Oil, Inc. v. Delta Oil Prods. Corp.*, 806 F.2d 1031, 1 USPQ2d 1073 (Fed. Cir. 1986). A refusal to reopen the record to admit new evidence is reviewed under regional circuit law. *Enzo Biochem Inc. v. Calgene Inc.*, 188 F.3d 1362, 52 USPQ2d 1129 (Fed. Cir. 1999). However, where the district court's Rule 60(b) ruling turns on matter unique to patent law, the Federal Circuit applies its own law. One such issue is whether a consent judgment enjoining infringement should be set aside following a judicial determination that the patent was procured by inequitable conduct. Because the court perceives a clear need for uniformity and certainty in the way that question is treated, it is resolved as a matter of Federal Circuit law. *Broyhill Furn. Indus. v. Craftmaster Furn. Corp.*, 12 F.3d 1080, 29 USPQ2d 1283 (Fed. Cir. 1993).

[299]*Power Controls Corp. v. Hybrinetics, Inc.*, 806 F.2d 234, 231 USPQ 774 (Fed. Cir. 1986); *Chemical Eng'g Corp. v. Essef Indus., Inc.*, 795 F.2d 1565, 230 USPQ 385 (Fed. Cir. 1986).

[300]*CAE Screenplates Inc. v. Heinrich Fiedler GmbH*, 224 F.3d 1308, 55 USPQ2d 1804 (Fed. Cir. 2); *Phonometrics Inc. v. Hospitality Franchise Sys. Inc.*, 203 F.3d 790, 53 USPQ2d 1762 (Fed. Cir. 2).

[301]*Interspiro USA, Inc. v. Figgie Int'l, Inc.*, 18 F.3d 927, 30 USPQ2d 1070 (Fed. Cir. 1994).

[302]*Sun-Tek Indus., Inc. v. Kennedy Sky Lites, Inc.*, 848 F.2d 179, 6 USPQ2d 2017 (Fed. Cir. 1988).

[303]*Registration Control Sys., Inc. v. Compusystems, Inc.*, 922 F.2d 805, 17 USPQ2d 1212 (Fed. Cir. 1990). Because the denial of a motion for a new trial is a procedural issue not unique to patent law, the court applies the law of the regional circuit. *WMS Gaming Inc. v. International Game Tech.*, 184 F.3d 1339, 51 USPQ2d 1385 (Fed. Cir. 1999).

[304]*Verdegaal Bros., Inc. v. Union Oil Co.*, 750 F.2d 947, 224 USPQ 249 (Fed. Cir. 1984).

[305]*Molins PLC v. Quigg*, 837 F.2d 1064, 5 USPQ2d 1526 (Fed. Cir. 1988). When reviewing a district court's conclusion that the causes of action in a case are not ripe for adjudication, and therefore are beyond the Article III jurisdiction of the federal courts, the Federal Circuit applies regional circuit law. *Cedars-Sinai Med. Ctr. v. Watkins*, 11 F.3d 1573, 29 USPQ2d 1188 (Fed. Cir. 1993).

[306]*Jamesbury Corp. v. Litton Indus. Prods., Inc.*, 839 F.2d 1544, 5 USPQ2d 1779 (Fed. Cir. 1988). Of course, on matters coming from the Court of Federal Claims, where the Federal

findings,[307] waiver of jury trial,[308] timeliness of a motion for JNOV,[309] standard of appellate review on denial of motion for JNOV,[310] judicial estoppel and admission by pleadings,[311] sanctions for attorney misconduct,[312] including Rule 11 determinations,[313] dismissal without prejudice,[314] appropriateness of directed verdict,[315] effect of failure to move for directed verdict,[316] application of res judicata and collateral estoppel,[317] effect of consent judgment,[318]

Circuit is in effect a regional circuit, it will follow its own views as to law of the case. *Exxon Corp. v. United States,* 931 F.2d 874 (Fed. Cir. 1991).

[307]*Arachnid, Inc. v. Medalist Mktg. Corp.,* 972 F.2d 1300, 23 USPQ2d 1946 (Fed. Cir. 1992); *Beckman Instr., Inc. v. LKB Produkter AB,* 892 F.2d 1547, 13 USPQ2d 1301 (Fed. Cir. 1989); *Allen Organ Co. v. Kimball Int'l, Inc.,* 839 F.2d 1556, 5 USPQ2d 1769 (Fed. Cir. 1988).

[308]*Cabinet Vision v. Cabnetware,* 129 F.3d 595, 44 USPQ2d 1683 (Fed. Cir. 1997); *Transmatic, Inc. v. Gulton Indus., Inc.,* 53 F.3d 1270, 35 USPQ2d 1035 (Fed. Cir. 1995).

[309]*Wilson Sporting Goods Co. v. David Geoffrey & Assoc.,* 904 F.2d 677, 14 USPQ2d 1942 (Fed. Cir. 1990).

[310]*Moxness Prods., Inc. v. Xomed, Inc.,* 891 F.2d 890, 13 USPQ2d 1169 (Fed. Cir. 1989); *Wahpeton Canvas Co. v. Frontier, Inc.,* 870 F.2d 1546, 10 USPQ2d 1201 (Fed. Cir. 1989); *Sjolund v. Musland,* 847 F.2d 1573, 6 USPQ2d 2020 (Fed. Cir. 1988). In *Biodex Corp. v. Loredan Biomedical, Inc.,* 946 F.2d 850, 20 USPQ2d 1252 (Fed. Cir. 1991), the court noted an apparent conflict between its decisions in *Sjolund v. Musland,* supra, and *Perkin-Elmer Corp. v. Computervision Corp.,* 732 F.2d 888, 221 USPQ 669 (Fed. Cir. 1984), over whether regional circuit law applies to review of postverdict motions. It passed the question because no such motion had been filed, but did indicate that the conflict may be a distinction without a difference, because the law seems uniform in any event. *Biodex* does squarely hold, however, that regional circuit law will not govern the reviewability of fact findings made by a jury in a patent case in the absence of postverdict motions.

[311]*Wang Labs., Inc. v. Applied Computer Sci., Inc.,* 958 F.2d 355, 22 USPQ2d 1055 (Fed. Cir. 1992); *Water Techs. Corp. v. Calco, Ltd.,* 850 F.2d 660, 7 USPQ2d 1097 (Fed. Cir. 1988).

[312]*Baldwin Hardware Corp. v. Franksu Enter. Corp.,* 78 F.3d 550, 37 USPQ2d 1829 (Fed. Cir. 1996); *Thermocycle Int'l, Inc. v. A.F. Hinrichsen Sales Corp.,* 851 F.2d 339, 7 USPQ2d 1407 (Fed. Cir. 1988). Regional circuit law governs the appealability of efforts to expunge from a district court opinion statements chastising an attorney. *Fromson v. Citiplate, Inc.,* 886 F.2d 1300, 12 USPQ2d 1299 (Fed. Cir. 1989).

[313]*Abbott Labs. v. Brennan,* 952 F.2d 1346, 21 USPQ2d 1192 (Fed. Cir. 1992).

[314]*L.E.A. Dynatech, Inc. v. Allina,* 49 F.3d 1527, 33 USPQ2d 1839 (Fed. Cir. 1995).

[315]*Newell Cos. v. Kenney Mfg. Co.,* 864 F.2d 757, 9 USPQ2d 1417 (Fed. Cir. 1988); *U.S. Philips Corp. v. Windmere Corp.,* 861 F.2d 695, 8 USPQ2d 1885 (Fed. Cir. 1988).

[316]*Delta-X Corp. v. Baker Hughes Prod. Tools, Inc.,* 984 F.2d 410, 25 USPQ2d 1447 (Fed. Cir. 1993). The court applies the law of the regional circuit to the question whether a party waived its right to JMOL by not renewing its motion at the close of trial. *Zodiac Pool Care Inc. v. Hoffinger Indus. Inc.,* 206 F.3d 1408, 54 USPQ2d 1141 (Fed. Cir. 2).

[317]*Mars, Inc. v. Nippon Conlux K-K,* 58 F.3d 616, 35 USPQ2d 1311 (Fed. Cir. 1995); *Flowdata, Inc. v. Cotton,* 57 F.3d 1046 (Fed. Cir. 1995); *Hartley v. Mentor Corp.,* 869 F.2d 1469, 10 USPQ2d 1138 (Fed. Cir. 1989). Regional circuit law governs questions of res judicata arising under the compulsory counterclaim provisions of Rule 13(a), FRCP. *Beech Aircraft Corp. v. EDO Corp.,* 990 F.2d 1237 (Fed. Cir. 1993).

[318]*Foster v. Hallco Mfg. Co.,* 947 F.2d 469, 20 USPQ2d 1241 (Fed. Cir. 1991); *Epic Metals Corp. v. H.H. Robertson Co.,* 870 F.2d 1574, 10 USPQ2d 1296 (Fed. Cir. 1989).

discovery questions,[319] and discovery sanctions,[320] and recusal problems.[321]

One seemingly procedural issue that does not always implicate patent law is the question of the Federal Circuit's own jurisdiction. Here, however, the court feels, and quite correctly so, that deference to regional circuit law is inappropriate.[322] Similarly, it does not regard itself bound by regional circuit decisions regarding declaratory judgment jurisdiction in patent cases.[323] The question of whether a properly brought declaratory action to determine patent rights should yield to a later filed suit for patent infringement raises the issue of national uniformity in patent cases and invokes the special obligation of the Federal Circuit to avoid creating opportunities for dispositive differences among the regional circuits. Thus, although the Federal Circuit applies the procedural law of the regional circuit in matters that are not unique to patent law, and although matters of procedure do not always carry substantive weight, the regional circuit practice

---

[319]*Dorf & Stanton Comm., Inc. v. Molson Breweries,* 100 F.3d 919, 40 USPQ2d 1761 (Fed. Cir. 1996); *Haworth, Inc. v. Herman Miller, Inc.,* 998 F.2d 975, 27 USPQ2d 1469 (Fed. Cir. 1993); *Badalamenti v. Dunham's, Inc.,* 896 F.2d 1359, 13 USPQ2d 1967 (Fed. Cir. 1990); *Tennant Co. v. Hako Minuteman, Inc.,* 878 F.2d 1413, 11 USPQ2d 1303 (Fed. Cir. 1989); *Solarex Corp. v. Arco Solar, Inc.,* 870 F.2d 642, 10 USPQ2d 1247 (Fed. Cir. 1989). Entitlement to discovery under Rule 56(f), FRCP, is decided according to the law of the regional circuit. *Vivid Tech. Inc. v. American Sci. & Eng'g Inc.,* 200 F.3d 795, 53 USPQ2d 1289 (Fed. Cir. 1999).

[320]*Seal-Flex Inc. v. Athletic Track & Court Constr.,* 172 F.3d 836, 50 USPQ2d 1225 (Fed. Cir. 1999); *Nike Inc. v. Wolverine World Wide, Inc.,* 43 F.3d 644, 33 USPQ2d 1038 (Fed. Cir. 1994); *Wexell v. Komar Indus., Inc.,* 18 F.3d 916, 29 USPQ2d 2017 (Fed. Cir. 1994). Regional circuit law is applied in reviewing questions concerning violation of protective orders. *Glaxo, Inc. v. Novopharm, Ltd.,* 110 F.3d 1562 (Fed. Cir. 1997).

[321]*Baldwin Hardware Corp. v. Franksu Enter. Corp.,* 78 F.3d 550, 37 USPQ2d 1829 (Fed. Cir. 1996); *Hewlett-Packard Co. v. Bausch & Lomb, Inc.,* 882 F.2d 1556, 11 USPQ2d 1750 (Fed. Cir. 1989).

[322]*Enercon Indus. Corp. v. Pillar Corp.,* 105 F.3d 1437, 41 USPQ2d 1630 (Fed. Cir. 1997); *Sanders Assoc., Inc. v. Summagraphics Corp.,* 2 F.3d 394, 27 USPQ2d 1853 (Fed. Cir. 1993); *Wang Labs., Inc. v. Applied Computer Sci., Inc.,* 958 F.2d 355, 22 USPQ2d 1055 (Fed. Cir. 1992); *Sun-Tek Indus., Inc. v. Kennedy Sky Lites, Inc,* 856 F.2d 173, 8 USPQ2d 1154 (Fed. Cir. 1988). The court may, of course, look for guidance in the decisions of the regional circuit to which appeals from that court would normally lie, as well as those of other courts. However, its decision to follow another circuit's interpretation of a common jurisdictional statute results from the persuasiveness of its analysis, not any binding effect. *Woodard v. Sage Prods., Inc.,* 818 F.2d 841, 2 USPQ2d 1649 (Fed. Cir. 1987). The court has passed the question of whether to apply its own law or regional circuit law on the question of when a judgment is final for purposes of certification under Rule 54(b), FRCP. It found that the Supreme Court had spoken sufficiently on the subject. *W.L. Gore & Assoc. v. International Med. Pros. Res. Assoc.,* 975 F.2d 858, 24 USPQ2d 1195 (Fed. Cir. 1992). In a later case, however, it applied its own law to a question of appealability absent Rule 54(b) certification. *Spraytex, Inc. v. DJS&T,* 96 F.3d 1377, 40 USPQ2d 1145 (Fed. Cir. 1996). The court applies its own law in deciding whether a district court has jurisdiction to hear a claim of infringement of a foreign patent, but may look for guidance to the decisions of the regional circuits. *Mars, Inc. v. K.K. Nippon Conlux,* 24 F.3d 1368, 30 USPQ2d 1621 (Fed. Cir. 1994).

[323]*Shell Oil Co. v. Amoco Corp.,* 970 F.2d 885, 23 USPQ2d 1627 (Fed. Cir. 1992); *Minnesota Min. & Mfg. Co. v. Norton Co.,* 929 F.2d 670, 18 USPQ2d 1302 (Fed. Cir. 1991); *Goodyear Tire & Rubber Co. v. Releasomers, Inc.,* 824 F.2d 953, 3 USPQ2d 1310 (Fed. Cir. 1987). The right to file a counterclaim for patent infringement in response to a declaratory action for patent noninfringement is unique to patent law and warrants a uniform national rule. *Vivid Tech. Inc. v. American Sci. & Eng'g Inc.,* 200 F.3d 795, 53 USPQ2d 1289 (Fed. Cir. 1999).

need not control when the question is important to national uniformity in patent practice.[324] On the other hand, where its jurisdiction over trademark issues arises only because the district court's jurisdiction was based in part on 28 U.S.C. §1338(a), the court will look to the law of the regional circuit to determine the existence of a controversy for declaratory judgment purposes.[325]

In its seminal case on personal jurisdiction in patent cases, the court decided to apply its own law rather than that of the regional circuit. Although in one sense the due process issue is procedural, it is a critical determinant of whether and in what forum a patentee can seek redress for infringement of its rights. The regional circuits have not reached a uniform approach to the stream of commerce theory that governs the underlying jurisdictional issue. Thus, application of regional circuit law would not promote the court's mandate of achieving national uniformity in the field of patent law. Conversely, the creation and application of a uniform body of Federal Circuit law as to this question would clearly promote judicial efficiency, would not create undue conflict and confusion at the district court level, and would be consistent with its mandate. Moreover, it would further the elimination of forum shopping.[326] The court has since recognized that determining whether jurisdiction exists over an out-of-state defendant involves two inquiries: whether a forum state's long-arm statute permits the assertion of jurisdiction and whether assertion of personal jurisdiction violates federal due process. With regard to the federal constitutional due process analysis of the defendant's contacts with the forum state in patent cases, the court does not defer to the interpretations of other federal and state courts. However, in interpreting the meaning of state long-arm statutes, it elects to defer to the interpretations of the relevant state and federal courts, including their determinations regarding whether or not such statutes are intended to reach to the limit of federal due process.[327] The jurisdictional issues presented by an out-of-state patentee defending a declaratory judgment action are no less intimately involved with the substance of the patent laws than that of an out-of-state accused infringer. Accordingly, the court applies its own law to the question of in personam jurisdiction in such cases as well.[328] However, a motion to transfer

[324]*Genentech, Inc. v. Eli Lilly & Co.*, 998 F.2d 931, 27 USPQ2d 1241 (Fed. Cir. 1993). See also *Serco Servs. Co. v. Kelley Co.*, 51 F.3d 1037, 34 USPQ2d 1217 (Fed. Cir. 1995). The impact of forum shopping has been tempered by the creation of the Federal Circuit; the stakes of a race to the courthouse are less severe. *Id.*

[325]*Windsurfing Int'l, Inc. v. AMF Inc.*, 828 F.2d 755, 4 USPQ2d 1053 (Fed. Cir. 1987).

[326]*Beverly Hills Fan Co. v. Royal Sovereign Corp.*, 21 F.3d 1558, 30 USPQ2d 1001 (Fed. Cir. 1994).

[327]*Graphic Controls Corp. v. Utah Med. Prods. Inc.*, 149 F.3d 1382, 47 USPQ2d 1622 (Fed. Cir. 1998).

[328]*Akro Corp. v. Luker*, 45 F.3d 1541, 33 USPQ2d 1505 (Fed. Cir. 1995). See also *Red Wing Shoe Co. v. Hockerson-Halberstadt Inc.*, 148 F.3d 1355, 47 USPQ2d 1192 (Fed. Cir. 1998); *Dainippon Screen Mfg. Co. v. CFMT Inc.*, 142 F.3d 1266, 46 USPQ2d 1616 (Fed. Cir. 1998).

under 28 U.S.C. §1404(a) is governed by the law of the regional circuit.[329]

What about substantive nonpatent questions? It was not until two years after its creation that the court decided that it would apply regional circuit law, to the extent it can be discerned, on nonpatent, nonprocedural issues, such as trademark law. As the court rightly put it, "a district court judge should not be expected to look over his shoulder to the law in this circuit, save as to those claims over which our subject matter jurisdiction is exclusive."[330] Thus, as a general rule, the court defers to the law of the regional circuit when addressing substantive legal issues over which it does not have exclusive jurisdiction.[331] In practical effect, the court applies regional circuit law on all but the substantive issues reserved especially to it.[332] In deciding whether to apply its own law or the law of a regional circuit, the court must evaluate competing policy interests. On the one hand, it must remain mindful of the general policy of minimizing confusion and conflicts in the federal judicial system. On the other hand, it cannot forget that one of Congress's primary purposes in creating the court was to bring about uniformity in the area of patent law.[333]

The court regards the following matters as substantive and unique to its jurisprudential responsibilities, and thus not appropriate for application of regional circuit law: whether or not to grant a preliminary injunction against patent infringement,[334] assignor

---

Where a patent infringement claim is joined with state law claims, Federal Circuit law will apply to personal jurisdiction questions on both sets of claims. *3D Sys. Inc. v. Aarotech Labs. Inc.*, 160 F.3d 1373, 48 USPQ2d 1773 (Fed. Cir. 1998). However, where a claim for declaratory judgment of patent noninfringement was dismissed for lack of subject matter jurisdiction, leaving only state law trade libel and defamation claims, the court applied regional circuit law to the in personam jurisdiction question. *Amana Ref. Inc. v. Quadlux Inc.*, 172 F.3d 852, 50 USPQ2d 1304 (Fed. Cir. 1999).

[329]*Winner Int'l Royalty Corp. v. Wang*, 202 F.3d 1340, 53 USPQ2d 1580 (Fed. Cir. 2).

[330]*Imagineering, Inc. v. Van Klassens, Inc.*, 53 F.3d 1260, 34 USPQ2d 1526 (Fed. Cir. 1995) (Lanham Act); *Tone Bros., Inc. v. Sysco Corp.*, 28 F.3d 1192, 31 USPQ2d 1321 (Fed. Cir. 1994) (Lanham Act); *Bandag, Inc. v. Al Bolser's Tire Stores, Inc.*, 750 F.2d 903, 223 USPQ 982 (Fed. Cir. 1984). Regional circuit law governs the denial of a preliminary injunction against trademark infringement. *Black & Decker, Inc. v. Hoover Serv. Ctr.*, 886 F.2d 1285, 12 USPQ2d 1250 (Fed. Cir. 1989). In deciding trademark, trade dress, and other unfair competition questions under §43(a) of the Lanham Act, the court applies regional circuit law. *Al-Site Corp. v. VSI Int'l Inc.*, 174 F.3d 1308, 50 USPQ2d 1161 (Fed. Cir. 1999); *Elmer v. ICC Fabricating, Inc.*, 67 F.3d 1571, 36 USPQ2d 1417 (Fed. Cir. 1995); *Keystone Ret. Wall Sys., Inc. v. Westrock, Inc.*, 997 F.2d 1444, 27 USPQ2d 1297 (Fed. Cir. 1993); *L.A. Gear, Inc. v. Thom McAn Shoe Co.*, 988 F.2d 1117, 25 USPQ2d 1913 (Fed. Cir. 1993); *Braun Inc. v. Dynamics Corp.*, 975 F.2d 815, 24 USPQ2d 1121 (Fed. Cir. 1992); *Oakley, Inc. v. International Tropic-Cal, Inc.*, 923 F.2d 167, 17 USPQ2d 1401 (Fed. Cir. 1991).

[331]*Payless Shoesource, Inc. v. Reebok Int'l Ltd.*, 998 F.2d 985, 27 USPQ2d 1516 (Fed. Cir. 1993).

[332]*Sun Studs, Inc. v. Applied Theory Assocs.*, 772 F.2d 1557, 227 USPQ 81 (Fed. Cir. 1985).

[333]*Manildra Milling Corp. v. Ogilvie Mills, Inc.*, 76 F.3d 1178, 37 USPQ2d 1707 (Fed. Cir. 1996).

[334]*Reebok Int'l Ltd. v. J. Baker, Inc.*, 32 F.3d 1552, 31 USPQ2d 1781 (Fed. Cir. 1994); *Hybritech, Inc. v. Abbott Labs.*, 849 F.2d 1446, 7 USPQ2d 1191 (Fed. Cir. 1988). A denial of a preliminary injunction against trademark infringement is governed by regional circuit law. *Black & Decker, Inc. v. Hoover Serv. Ctr.*, 886 F.2d 1285, 12 USPQ2d 1250 (Fed. Cir. 1989).

estoppel,[335] and separation of inequitable conduct issues for nonjury trial.[336] The court applies its own substantive law to issues arising under the Plant Variety Protection Act.[337] It also applies its own law to the question of whether the public policies expressed in *Lear v. Adkins* override the general principles of res judicata that would otherwise apply to consent judgments.[338]

From the outset, the Federal Circuit was disposed to apply regional circuit law to federal antitrust issues, approaching antitrust claims as would a court of appeals in the circuit of the district court whose judgment is being reviewed.[339] In prior editions of this book the author surmised that this rule would nonetheless generate a coherent body of "Federal Circuit" patent antitrust and misuse law, inasmuch as the regional circuits would resolve any subsidiary patent issues by reference to Federal Circuit law. Apparently this hope was too tenuous for the court. In *Nobelpharma v. Implant Innovations*,[340] it sat in banc to repudiate the rule, and held that whether conduct in procuring or enforcing a patent is sufficient to strip a patentee of its immunity from the antitrust laws is to be decided as a question of Federal Circuit law. This conclusion applies equally to all antitrust claims premised on the bringing of a patent infringement suit. However, the court will continue to apply the law of the appropriate regional circuit to issues involving other elements of antitrust law such as relevant market, market power, damages, etc., as those issues are not unique to patent law.[341] Similarly, in *Midwest v. Karavan*,[342] the court overruled its prior decisions to the contrary,[343] and decided that it will henceforth apply its own law, rather than that of the

---

[335]*Diamond Scientific Co. v. Ambico, Inc.*, 848 F.2d 1220, 6 USPQ2d 2028 (Fed. Cir. 1988).

[336]*Gardco Mfg., Inc. v. Herst Lighting Co.*, 820 F.2d 1209, 2 USPQ2d 2015 (Fed. Cir. 1987).

[337]*Delta & Pine Land Co. v. Sinkers Corp.*, 177 F.3d 1343, 50 USPQ2d 1749 (Fed. Cir. 1999).

[338]*Foster v. Hallco Mfg. Co.*, 947 F.2d 469, 20 USPQ2d 1241 (Fed. Cir. 1991). But on the application of those general principles of res judicata to consent judgments, regional circuit law is applied. *Id.* See also *Mars, Inc. v. Nippon Conlux K-K*, 58 F.3d 616, 35 USPQ2d 1311 (Fed. Cir. 1995).

[339]*Eastman Kodak Co. v. Goodyear Tire & Rubber Co.*, 114 F.3d 1547, 42 USPQ2d 1737 (Fed. Cir. 1997); *Cygnus Therapeutics Sys. v. Alza Corp.*, 92 F.3d 1153, 39 USPQ2d 1666 (Fed Cir. 1996); *Atari Games Corp. v. Nintendo of Am., Inc.*, 897 F.2d 1572, 14 USPQ2d 1034 (Fed. Cir. 1990); *U.S. Philips Corp. v. Windmere Corp.*, 861 F.2d 695, 8 USPQ2d 1885 (Fed. Cir. 1988); *Loctite Corp. v. Ultraseal Ltd.*, 781 F.2d 861, 228 USPQ 90 (Fed. Cir. 1985).

[340]*Nobelpharma AB v. Implant Innovations Inc.*, 141 F.3d 1059, 46 USPQ2d 1097 (Fed. Cir. 1998).

[341]Thus, the court applies its own law in deciding whether a refusal to license or sell patented parts constitutes a violation of the antitrust laws; however, when evaluating that conduct with respect to copyrighted diagnostic software, it applies regional circuit law. *In re Independent Serv. Org. Antitrust Litig.*, 203 F.3d 1322, 53 USPQ2d 1852 (Fed. Cir. 2).

[342]*Midwest Indus. Inc. v. Karavan Trailers Inc.*, 175 F.3d 1356, 50 USPQ2d 1672 (Fed. Cir. 1999). The opinion provides a nice review of how the court goes about deciding whether it should apply its own law. See also *University of Colorado Found. v. American Cyanamid Co.*, 196 F.3d 1366, 52 USPQ2d 1801 (Fed. Cir. 1999).

[343]*Hunter Douglas, Inc. v. Harmonic Design, Inc.*, 153 F.3d 1318, 47 USPQ2d 1769 (Fed. Cir. 1998); *Interpart Corp. v. Italia*, 777 F.2d 678, 228 USPQ 124 (Fed. Cir. 1985); *Cable Elec. Prods., Inc. v. Genmark, Inc.*, 770 F.2d 1015, 226 USPQ 881 (Fed. Cir. 1985).

regional circuit, when determining whether patent law preempts particular state law causes of action or conflicts with rights created by other federal laws.[344] The court also applies its own law in determining whether inequitable conduct can qualify as a predicate act under the federal RICO statute.[345]

The court is on a similar tack regarding certain business tort claims arising under state law. The torts of interference with actual or prospective business relationships require that the purportedly interfering communications or other conduct not be legally justified. However, where the conduct was giving notice of patent rights and the intent to enforce them, the question of legal justification raises considerations of federal law governing the giving of notice of patent rights. To the extent that conflict arises in the interaction between state commercial law and federal patent law, federal law must be applied. National uniformity, in confluence with the national scope of the patent grant and the general federal exclusivity in patent causes, requires that determination of the propriety of a patentee's actions in giving notice of its patent rights is governed by federal statute and precedent and is not a matter of state tort law.[346]

Regional circuit law is applied to such substantive matters as copyright law,[347] bankruptcy issues,[348] issues arising under the Semiconductor Chip Protection Act,[349] unfair competition,[350] interpretation and enforcement of settlement agreements,[351] choice of law rules,[352]

---

[344]However, different considerations underlie federal preemption of state laws dealing with contracts. Most importantly, enforcement of a contract does not restrict the actions of nonparties. The Supreme Court in *Aronson v. Quick Point Pencil Co.,* 440 U.S. 257, 201 USPQ 1 (1979), spoke broadly on federal preemption of state contract laws, and that decision binds all regional circuits. Thus the Federal Circuit is guided by *Aronson* in such matters. *Power Lift, Inc. v. Weatherford Nipple-Up Sys., Inc.,* 871 F.2d 1082, 10 USPQ2d 1464 (Fed. Cir. 1989).

[345]*Semiconductor Energy Lab. Co. v. Samsung Elec. Co.,* 204 F.3d 1368, 54 USPQ2d 1001 (Fed. Cir. 2).

[346]*Mikohn Gaming Corp. v. Acres Gaming Inc.,* 165 F.3d 891, 49 USPQ2d 1308 (Fed. Cir. 1998).

[347]*Atari Games Corp. v. Nintendo of Am., Inc.,* 975 F.2d 832, 24 USPQ2d 1015 (Fed. Cir. 1992).

[348]*Institut Pasteur v. Cambridge Biotech Corp.,* 186 F.3d 1356, 51 USPQ2d 1321 (Fed. Cir. 1999).

[349]*Brooktree Corp. v. Advanced Micro Devices, Inc.,* 977 F.2d 1555, 24 USPQ2d 1401 (Fed. Cir. 1992).

[350]*Jurgens v. McKasy,* 927 F.2d 1552, 18 USPQ2d 1031 (Fed. Cir. 1991); *Cicena Ltd. v. Columbia Tel. Group,* 900 F.2d 1546, 14 USPQ2d 1401 (Fed. Cir. 1990); *Power Controls Corp. v. Hybrinetics, Inc.,* 806 F.2d 234, 231 USPQ 774 (Fed. Cir. 1986). See note 17:330. However, a question concerning whether alleged inequitable conduct in the prosecution of a patent constitutes unfair competition impacts the exclusive jurisdiction of the Federal Circuit, and it therefore does not defer to regional circuit law on that issue. *Pro-Mold & Tool Co. v. Great Lakes Plastics, Inc.,* 75 F.3d 1568, 37 USPQ2d 1626 (Fed. Cir. 1996).

[351]*Novamedix Ltd. v. NDM Acquisition Corp.,* 166 F.3d 1177, 49 USPQ2d 1613 (Fed. Cir. 1999); *Gjerlov v. Schuyler Labs., Inc.,* 131 F.3d 1016, 44 USPQ2d 1881 (Fed. Cir. 1997); *S & T Mfg. Co. v. County of Hillsborough, Fla.,* 815 F.2d 676, 2 USPQ2d 1280 (Fed Cir. 1987).

[352]*Bradley v. Chiron Corp.,* 136 F.3d 1370, 45 USPQ2d 1819 (Fed. Cir. 1998); *Sun Studs, Inc. v. Applied Theory Assocs.,* 772 F.2d 1557, 227 USPQ 81 (Fed. Cir. 1985).

and sovereign immunity.[353] The law of the regional circuit governs interpretation of supersedeas bonds[354] and questions regarding injunction bonds.[355] The court applies regional circuit law to the definitions of civil and criminal contempt.[356] Similarly, contempt damages in a patent infringement suit do not raise issues unique to patent law, and thus the court will apply the law of the regional circuit.[357] The amount of costs to be awarded is decided according to regional circuit law.[358] Determining the dividing line between pre- and post-judgment interest is a question that is not unique to patent law, and the court therefore looks to the law of the regional circuit.[359] On the other hand, Federal Circuit precedent governs the substantive interpretation of the attorney fee provision of 35 U.S.C. §285, which is unique to patent law.[360]

Sometimes procedural issues are so related to the substantive matters in question that it is difficult to decide the one without implicating the other. Thus, when the court considers questions involving substantive matters not exclusively assigned to it, its general practice is to apply to related procedural issues the appropriate regional circuit law. When the question on appeal is one involving substantive matters unique to the Federal Circuit, it applies its own law to related procedural issues.[361] For example, in a patent infringement action, a determination of relevance for discovery purposes implicates substantive patent law, and the Federal Circuit therefore applies its own law rather than that of the regional circuit.[362] The Federal Circuit applies its own law to the issue of whether the attorney-client privilege applies to an invention record prepared and submitted to house counsel.[363] In the absence of postverdict motions, the court will look to its own law to ascertain the reviewability of fact findings made by a jury in

---

[353]*College Sav. Bank v. Florida Prepaid Bd.*, 148 F.3d 1343, 47 USPQ2d 1161 (Fed. Cir. 1998).

[354]*Beatrice Foods Co. v. New England Printing & Lith. Co.*, 930 F.2d 1572, 18 USPQ2d 1548 (Fed. Cir. 1991).

[355]*Hupp v. Siroflex of Am., Inc.*, 122 F.3d 1456, 43 USPQ2d 1887 (Fed. Cir. 1997).

[356]*Spindelfabrik S., S. & G. GmbH v. Schubert & Salzer Mas. Ak.*, 903 F.2d 1568, 14 USPQ2d 1913 (Fed. Cir. 1990).

[357]*Graves v. Kemscop Group, Inc.*, 864 F.2d 754, 9 USPQ2d 1404 (Fed. Cir. 1988). Under Seventh Circuit law, damages in a civil contempt action need not be proved by clear and convincing evidence—only violation of the injunction itself. Damages for civil contempt are within the discretion of the district court. *Id.*

[358]*Manildra Milling Corp. v. Ogilvie Mills, Inc.*, 76 F.3d 1178, 37 USPQ2d 1707 (Fed. Cir. 1996). However, in the absence of uniformity in the circuits, the court applied its own law to the issue of whether the meaning of the statutory term "prevailing party" is a question of fact or law.

[359]*Transmatic Inc. v. Gulton Indus. Inc.*, 180 F.3d 1343, 50 USPQ2d 1591 (Fed. Cir. 1999).

[360]*Pharmacia & Upjohn Co. v. Mylan Pharm. Inc.*, 182 F.3d 1356, 51 USPQ2d 1466 (Fed. Cir. 1999).

[361]*Chrysler Motors Corp. v. Auto Body Panels of Ohio, Inc.*, 908 F.2d 951, 15 USPQ2d 1469 (Fed. Cir. 1990).

[362]*Micro Motion, Inc. v. Kane Steel Co.*, 894 F.2d 1318, 13 USPQ2d 1696 (Fed. Cir. 1990).

[363]*In re Spalding Sports Worldwide Inc.*, 203 F.3d 800, 53 USPQ2d 1747 (Fed. Cir. 2).

a patent case.[364] The question of whether a district court case should be stayed pending the outcome of PTO proceedings is governed by Federal Circuit law.[365] Quite surprisingly, however, the court applies regional circuit law to the question of whether a pleading states a claim upon which relief can be granted under Rule 12(b)(6), in the context of patent infringement.[366]

Strange as it may seem to any district judge not to be governed by the precedents of his or her own regional court of appeals, that is the situation created by Congress in the interest of promoting a uniform patent law by having only one court of appeals deciding questions of patent law.[367] Counsel practicing in the Federal Circuit are admonished that it is their duty and role to brief and argue the nonpatent counts just as if they were appearing before the regional court of appeals for the circuit in which the case originated.[368]

Thus, the Federal Circuit follows the guidance of the regional circuits in all but the substantive law fields assigned exclusively to it by Congress in order to promote the general policy of minimizing confusion and conflicts in the federal judicial system. Presumably those same concerns will prompt the regional federal circuit courts, when confronted with issues in those substantive fields, to look in turn to Federal Circuit precedents for guidance. Similarly, state courts confronted with federal law issues usually turn to the law of the appropriate federal court to aid in the resolution of those federal issues. While the prevailing view among the highest courts in the various states is that a state court is only bound as to the meaning of federal constitutional and statutory law by interpretations of the U.S. Supreme Court, the decisions of lower federal courts on issues of federal law are usually respected as persuasive, especially where uniform among the lower courts. Since Congress created the Federal Circuit in order to bring uniformity to the national law of patents, presumably the state courts confronted with issues of federal law relating to patents will therefore also look to the decisions of the Federal Circuit for guidance.[369] The Federal Circuit is a coequal member of a system of 13 appellate courts arranged in a single tier. It is not a superior member possessed of jurisdiction to review and reverse the judgments of the other 12. It has not been granted jurisdiction to engage in appellate review or rehearing of a final decision, or to recall or countermand a mandate, of a coordinate court of appeals.[370]

---

[364]*Biodex Corp. v. Loredan Biomedical, Inc.,* 946 F.2d 850, 20 USPQ2d 1252 (Fed. Cir. 1991).

[365]*Slip Track Sys. Inc. v. Metal Lite Inc.,* 159 F.3d 1337, 48 USPQ2d 1055 (Fed. Cir. 1998).

[366]*Phonometrics Inc. v. Hospitality Franchise Sys. Inc.,* 203 F.3d 790, 53 USPQ2d 1762 (Fed. Cir. 2).

[367]*Titanium Metals Corp. v. Banner,* 778 F.2d 775, 227 USPQ 773 (Fed. Cir. 1985).

[368]*Cable Elec. Prods., Inc. v. Genmark, Inc.,* 770 F.2d 1015, 226 USPQ 881 (Fed. Cir. 1985).

[369]*Speedco, Inc. v. Estes,* 853 F.2d 909, 7 USPQ2d 1637 (Fed. Cir. 1988).

[370]*In re Roberts,* 846 F.2d 1360, 6 USPQ2d 1772 (Fed. Cir. 1988).

(c) Attorney Conduct

The authority of a U.S. court of appeals over matters concerning the administration of its bar is well recognized. Membership in a state bar or admission to practice before the highest court of a state is a prerequisite to admission to the bar of a federal court. Absence or loss of state bar status may absolutely destroy the condition of fair private and professional character, without the possession of which there could be no possible right to continue to be a member of a federal bar.[371] Counsel's role as an officer of the court should not be subservient to his or her role as an advocate.[372] The court has chided counsel for "an inability or refusal . . . to understand the purpose and rules governing the appellate process," reminding us that "one does not persuade by insulting the intelligence of the persuadees."[373] It is the duty of counsel to explain, where necessary, esoterics of patent law to a district court.[374] Cases should not be cited for mere words. What counts is what the court did in a cited case.[375] Attacks on a trial judge as lacking in skill or understanding, or legal competence, are ineffective and counterproductive.[376] Distortion of the record, by deleting critical language in a quotation, reflects a lack of candor in violation of Rule 3.3 of the Model Rules of Professional Conduct, wastes the time of the court and opposing counsel, and imposes unnecessary costs on the parties and on the public.[377] The court regards it a "frequent and foolish appellate ploy" to cite only such bits of evidence as may support one's view, while ignoring a wealth of evidence that establishes the district court's findings to have been not clearly erroneous.[378] The court has not hesitated to award double costs as sanctions in such instances.[379]

---

[371]*In re Martin*, 120 F.3d 256 (Fed. Cir. 1997).

[372]*Crostic v. Veterans Admin.*, 730 F.2d 1464 (Fed. Cir. 1984).

[373]*Lindemann Maschinenfabrik v. American Hoist & Derrick Co.*, 895 F.2d 1403, 13 USPQ2d 1871, 1873 (Fed. Cir. 1990).

[374]*Senza-Gel Corp. v. Seiffhart*, 803 F.2d 661, 231 USPQ 363 (Fed. Cir. 1986). A deliberate mischaracterization of an appealed decision goes beyond the bounds of legitimate advocacy. *Octocom Sys., Inc. v. Houston Computer Serv., Inc.*, 918 F.2d 937, 16 USPQ2d 1783 (Fed. Cir. 1990).

[375]*Illinois Tool Works, Inc. v. Grip-Pak, Inc.*, 906 F.2d 679, 15 USPQ2d 1307 (Fed. Cir. 1990); *Fromson v. Western Litho Plate & Supp. Co.*, 853 F.2d 1568, 7 USPQ2d 1606 (Fed. Cir. 1988).

[376]*Preemption Devices, Inc. v. Minnesota Min. & Mfg. Co.*, 732 F.2d 903, 221 USPQ 841 (Fed. Cir. 1984).

[377]*Amstar Corp. v. Envirotech Corp.*, 730 F.2d 1476, 221 USPQ 649 (Fed. Cir. 1984). See also *McGill Inc. v. John Zink Co.*, 736 F.2d 666, 221 USPQ 944 (Fed. Cir. 1984). In one case, the dereliction was so easily checkable that the court refused to award sanctions to the opposing party, on the ground that a phone call to advise of the error would have saved everyone much time and trouble. *Glaros v. H.H. Robertson Co.*, 797 F.2d 1564, 230 USPQ 393 (Fed. Cir. 1986).

[378]*Datascope Corp. v. SMEC, Inc.*, 879 F.2d 820, 11 USPQ2d 1321 (Fed. Cir. 1989).

[379]*Paulik v. Rizkalla*, 796 F.2d 456, 230 USPQ 434 (Fed. Cir. 1986); *Panduit Corp. v. Dennison Mfg. Co.*, 774 F.2d 1082, 227 USPQ 337 (Fed. Cir. 1985); *Amstar Corp. v. Envirotech Corp.*, 730 F.2d 1476, 221 USPQ 649 (Fed. Cir. 1984).

In an air traffic controller case, the court for the first time exercised its disciplinary authority under Rule 46(c), FRAP. An attorney who filed more than 100 frivolous appeals was given a one-year suspension.[380] Personal sanctions against an attorney under 28 U.S.C. §1927 are appropriate for conduct that, viewed objectively, manifests either intentional or reckless disregard of the attorney's duties to the court.[381]

Yet perhaps the court has gone too far in some cases. It has taken the position that an attorney practicing before it should not file a motion simply on the ground that it will save the client money, if it appears the result will be to inconvenience the court.[382] Despite its recognition that the limit lines of lawyering are not always clear,[383] it has repeatedly and bitterly labeled briefs and arguments as disingenuous and lacking in candor.[384]

The Federal Circuit has been eloquently vocal in condemning what it perceives to be improper conduct. It believes that the law is not a sport where winning has been called everything, and neither a trial nor an appeal should be only an exercise in gamesmanship. Judges have much and many better things to do than to referee irrelevant cat-fights of counsel.[385] True enough. But one wonders whether some members of the court have not forgotten their own days as trial lawyers. In many cases it is not necessary that the court of appeals determine on which if either side the angels reside.[386] Nonetheless, the court quite properly insists upon civility as a guideline to litigation conduct.[387]

The court insists that it retains the ability to control its docket and dismiss cases where counsel fail to perform their duties.[388] The

---

[380]*In re Solerwitz,* 848 F.2d 1573 (Fed. Cir. 1988). The case was noteworthy in several respects. A hearing was actually held by Senior Judge Bennett, who recommended a two-year suspension with a two-year stay pending a demonstration of rehabilitation during probation. The full court modified Judge Bennett's recommendation. The court also dismissed out of hand the attorney's complaint that the hearing was defective because it was not "adversary," in that the court had no attorney appearing on its behalf at the hearing.

[381]*Julien v. Zeringue,* 864 F.2d 1572, 9 USPQ2d 1554 (Fed. Cir. 1989). Here the court awarded the excess costs, expenses, and attorney fees reasonably incurred in the appeal as a result of the attorney's improper conduct, which included missing deadlines, obtaining 10 extensions of time to file briefs, and filing an improper and late appendix.

[382]*Crostic v. Veterans Admin.,* 730 F.2d 1464 (Fed. Cir. 1984).

[383]*Railroad Dynamics, Inc. v. A. Stucki Co.,* 727 F.2d 1506, 220 USPQ 929 (Fed. Cir. 1984).

[384]E.g., *Brenner v. United States,* 773 F.2d 306, 227 USPQ 159 (Fed. Cir. 1985); *W.L. Gore & Assoc. v. Garlock, Inc.,* 721 F.2d 1540, 220 USPQ 303 (Fed. Cir. 1983). Cf. *Refac Int'l Ltd., v. IBM,* 798 F.2d 459, 230 USPQ 537 (Fed. Cir. 1986). See also *Pac-Tec, Inc. v. Amerace Corp.,* 903 F.2d 796, 14 USPQ2d 1871 (Fed. Cir. 1990).

[385]*Glaros v. H.H. Robertson Co.,* 797 F.2d 1564, 230 USPQ 393 (Fed. Cir. 1986).

[386]*FMC Corp. v. Manitowoc Co.,* 835 F.2d 1411, 5 USPQ2d 1112 (Fed. Cir. 1987).

[387]Failure to attempt to notify the opposing party by telephone of a motion to quash a deposition out of town, and reliance instead upon a mailing that was unlikely to be timely, resulted in an award of costs under Rule 39, FRAP, in *Katz v. Batavia Mar. & Sporting Supp., Inc.,* 984 F.2d 422, 25 USPQ2d 1547 (Fed. Cir. 1993).

[388]*Julien v. Zeringue,* 864 F.2d 1572, 9 USPQ2d 1554 (Fed. Cir. 1989).

court feels that it has inherent power to assess attorney fees against counsel who willfully abuse the judicial process.[389]

All former Federal Circuit law clerks should read *In re Violation of Rule 50*,[390] where the court served notice that it intends strict future enforcement of its rule prohibiting former court employees from working on any case pending there during employment.

(d) Frivolous Appeals

Unfortunately, the Federal Circuit has done harm in its treatment of what it regards as frivolous appeals. Some of its rulings will quite clearly have a chilling effect on legitimate advocacy.

The court served fair warning, early on, that it intended to be tough in this area. In its second reported decision it assessed costs and attorney fees against a party and its attorney for appealing from a settlement of an administrative claim. It remarked that the appeal had entailed a waste of the resources supplied by the public to the court and had impeded access to the court by those having at least an arguable basis for appeal.[391] In its next case on the subject, it refused to hold that an appeal from an order denying a disqualification motion was frivolous, despite the fact that there was a clear Supreme Court holding that such orders were not appealable.[392]

The handwriting was on the wall, however. In a remarkable case, the court awarded double costs and $500 damages on the ground that the appeal was frivolous. The reasons appeared to be that the appellant had a history of bringing nuisance suits and was asserting a clearly invalid patent that had been fraudulently procured. Nevertheless, it is important to note that there had been a jury verdict of patent validity and infringement that was set aside on motion for JNOV, and even the trial judge had not found fraud. With all respect, it is difficult in the extreme to justify a determination that the appeal was frivolous under such circumstances.[393]

In *Finch v. Hughes*,[394] the court undertook to explain that an appeal can be deemed frivolous in two distinct ways, either of which alone would support sanctions. In the first, the judgment by the tribunal below is so plainly correct and the legal authority contrary to appellant's position so clear that there really is no appealable issue. In such a case, the very filing of an appeal is frivolous and justifies

---

[389]*Cambridge Prods., Ltd. v. Penn Nutrients, Inc.*, 962 F.2d 1048, 22 USPQ2d 1577 (Fed. Cir. 1992). Here the court sanctioned defendant's attorney personally for misrepresenting the import and content of the record on appeal; it awarded reasonable attorney fees to plaintiff for having to defend the appeal.

[390]*In re Violation of Rule 50*, 78 F.3d 574 (Fed. Cir. 1996).

[391]*Asberry v. United States Postal Serv.*, 692 F.2d 1378 (Fed. Cir. 1982). The award was remitted because the Federal Circuit's predecessor courts did not operate under Rule 38, FRAP, which deals with frivolous appeals.

[392]*C.P.C. v. Nosco Plastics, Inc.*, 719 F.2d 400 (Fed. Cir. 1983).

[393]*Connell v. Sears, Roebuck & Co.*, 722 F.2d 1542, 220 USPQ 193 (Fed. Cir. 1983).

[394]*Finch v. Hughes Aircraft Co.*, 926 F.2d 1574, 17 USPQ2d 1914 (Fed. Cir. 1991).

the imposition of Rule 38 sanctions. In the second, while genuinely appealable issues may exist, the appellant's contentions in prosecuting the appeal are frivolous. Such appeals, though not necessarily frivolous as filed, are held to be frivolous as argued.[395] The court went on to observe that access to the appellate courts is an important value in our system of justice. Thus, in determining whether or not an appeal is frivolous, an appellate court must be mindful of the possibility that awarding damages and costs could have an undue chilling effect on the behavior of later litigants. An appeal having a small chance for success is not for that reason alone frivolous, and a questionable appeal may simply be due to the overzealousness or inexperience of counsel. The line between the tenuously arguable and the frivolous can be an uncertain one, and sanctions should not be imposed so freely as to make parties with legitimately appealable issues hesitant to come before an appellate court. At the same time, appellate courts must consider the importance of conserving scarce judicial resources. A frivolous appeal imposes costs not only upon the party forced to defend it, but also upon the public whose taxes supporting the court and its staff are wasted.[396]

In expanding upon the concept of an appeal that is frivolous as argued, the court identified other types of postfiling appellate litigation conduct that are considered sanctionable, such as seeking to relitigate issues already finally adjudicated, failing to explain how the trial court erred or to present clear or cogent arguments for reversal, rearguing frivolous positions for which sanctions had already been imposed in the trial forum, failing to cite authority and ignoring the opponent's cited authority, citing irrelevant or inapplicable authority, distorting cited authority by omitting language from quotations, making irrelevant and illogical arguments, and misrepresenting facts or law to the court.[397] It appears that when an appellant, by winning, removes the "as filed" possibility, it is more difficult to show frivolity "as argued." When an appellant's main arguments for reversal are both relevant and in fact meritorious, the court recognizes that it should guard against unduly chilling appellate advocacy.[398]

---

[395]The court went on to observe that an appeal that is frivolous as filed, in the sense that no nonfrivolous arguments could be made to support it, logically must also be frivolous as argued, since any arguments made are, by definition, frivolous. *Finch v. Hughes Aircraft Co.*, 926 F.2d 1574, 17 USPQ2d 1914 (Fed. Cir. 1991). However, in the case of a pro se litigant, the court is more reluctant to find that the case was frivolous as argued. See *Constant v. United States*, 929 F.2d 654, 18 USPQ2d 1298 (Fed. Cir. 1991). In *Munoz v. Strahm Farms, Inc.*, 69 F.3d 501, 36 USPQ2d 1499 (Fed. Cir. 1995), the appeal was found to be frivolous both as filed and as argued. Elimination of any of the challenged evidence would have served only to reduce the amount of cumulative evidence, thus meeting the harmless error standard for review.

[396]*Finch v. Hughes Aircraft Co.*, 926 F.2d 1574, 17 USPQ2d 1914 (Fed. Cir. 1991).

[397]*State Indus., Inc. v. Mor-Flo Indus. Inc.*, 948 F.2d 1573, 20 USPQ2d 1738 (Fed. Cir. 1991). In this case the appellant argued that certain findings had not been disturbed on a previous appeal when, in fact, the Federal Circuit had vacated the judgment and remanded for reconsideration. This argument was termed a very serious misrepresentation that, even standing alone, could be grounds for sanctions.

[398]*Olde Tyme Foods, Inc. v. Roundy's, Inc.*, 961 F.2d 200, 22 USPQ2d 1542 (Fed. Cir. 1992). Here the successful appellant had relied upon evidence that was, as a matter of law,

Certainly the court's generalized rules regarding frivolous appeals are difficult to fault. A losing case is not necessarily a frivolous one.[399] Lack of merit does not prove frivolity.[400] A frivolous appeal is one in which the appellant can set forth no basis, however tenuous, that might result in a reversal or undoing of the judgment or order appealed from.[401] An appeal clearly hopeless and unquestionably without any possible basis in fact or law wastes the time of the court and of opposing counsel and imposes unnecessary costs on the parties and on fellow citizens whose taxes support the court and its staff.[402] An appeal of a matter that is moot when the appeal is taken may well be frivolous.[403] When an issue becomes moot while being appealed, continuation of the appeal is frivolous.[404] Sanctions may be imposed in a summary judgment case as in any other. Where a party blindly disregards long-established authority and raises arguments with no factual foundation, the judicial process is abused.[405]

And yet the appeals that have been regarded as frivolous by the court have not always appeared, at least to this commentator, to be clearly hopeless and without any possible basis in fact or law. Some have involved complex legal situations[406] or constitutional arguments

---

immaterial. In *Haynes Int'l, Inc. v. Jessop Steel Co.*, 8 F.3d 1573, 28 USPQ2d 1652 (Fed. Cir. 1993), the court gave the patentee the benefit of the doubt and found the appeal not frivolous as argued, even though it felt the patentee had pressed only the weaker of its two infringement arguments. In *Haworth, Inc. v. Steelcase, Inc.*, 12 F.3d 1090, 29 USPQ2d 1368 (Fed. Cir. 1993), it refused to find that the appeal was frivolous where the lower court had indicated that the appellant's arguments were not without merit.

[399]*Tieleman Food Equip., B.V. v. Stork Gamco, Inc.*, 56 F.3d 1373, 35 USPQ2d 1568 (Fed. Cir. 1995). Here the court modified an injunction, which in itself indicated that the appeal was not frivolous.

[400]*American Med. Sys., Inc. v. Medical Eng'g Corp.*, 6 F.3d 1523, 28 USPQ2d 1321 (Fed. Cir. 1993).

[401]*United States v. Atkinson*, 748 F.2d 659 (Fed. Cir. 1984). See also, e.g., *Eltech Sys. Corp. v. PPG Indus, Inc.*, 903 F.2d 805, 14 USPQ2d 1965 (Fed. Cir. 1990); *Pac-Tec, Inc. v. Amerace Corp.*, 903 F.2d 796, 14 USPQ2d 1871 (Fed. Cir. 1990).

[402]*Porter v. Farmers Supply Serv., Inc.*, 790 F.2d 882, 229 USPQ 814 (Fed. Cir. 1986). For example, it is frivolous to attack a settlement agreement on appeal. *S & T Mfg. Co. v. County of Hillsborough, Fla.*, 815 F.2d 676, 2 USPQ2d 1280 (Fed Cir. 1987).

[403]*Sun-Tek Indus., Inc. v. Kennedy Sky Lites, Inc*, 856 F.2d 173, 8 USPQ2d 1154 (Fed. Cir. 1988).

[404]*Nasatka v. Delta Scientific Corp.*, 58 F.3d 1578, 35 USPQ2d 1374 (Fed. Cir. 1995).

[405]*Octocom Sys., Inc. v. Houston Computer Serv., Inc.*, 918 F.2d 937, 16 USPQ2d 1783 (Fed. Cir. 1990). In *S. Bravo Sys., Inc. v. Containment Tech. Corp.*, 96 F.3d 1372, 40 USPQ2d 1140 (Fed. Cir. 1996), the appeal of a grant of summary judgment of noninfringement was frivolous because there was no proffer of evidence that the accused device contained every claim element exactly or by a substantial equivalent.

[406]*In re Oximetrix, Inc.*, 748 F.2d 637, 223 USPQ 1068 (Fed. Cir. 1984); *Colt Indus. Oper. Corp. v. Index-Werke K.G.*, 739 F.2d 622 (Fed. Cir. 1984). In a truly egregious situation, a divided court found the appeal in large part frivolous, and awarded costs and attorney fees to the prevailing party for resisting the frivolous portion. *Mathis v. Spears*, 857 F.2d 749, 8 USPQ2d 1029 (Fed. Cir. 1988). But the dissenting panel member disagreed as to one of the issues that the majority felt was frivolous (whether expert witness fees are recoverable under 35 U.S.C. §285) and therefore would not have imposed any sanctions. In condemning recreational litigation in *Constant v. United States*, 929 F.2d 654, 18 USPQ2d 1298 (Fed. Cir. 1991), the court said: "Litigation is a serious business. This and other federal courts are funded by the

that had been made elsewhere.[407] Some have involved pro se litigants whom the court accused of engaging in "recreational litigation."[408] The court does take pains to warn pro se litigants that they are treading on thin ice.[409]

Interestingly, in the court's first reported recusal decision, the moving party was held to have been frivolous in filing the recusal motion.[410] With all respect, it is suggested that the court may, without meaning to, be placing undue restraints on ordinary advocacy.[411] In two such instances it has awarded sanctions for frivolous appeals in cases where questions were presented that needed deciding.[412] In one of these the dissenting judge observed:

> The eye of the bench falls upon many erroneous, inartful, specious, often exotic arguments, perhaps the last gasp of an appellant facing the awesome burden of an appeal, and set against the sweet reason with which the appellee supports the judgment appealed from. Appellant's counsel should not be personally impugned for taking an appeal, as of right, and presenting losing arguments, as here. . . . I do not think that appellant's request for our review, although admittedly a lost cause, was so villainous as to justify the level of castigation heaped upon it.[413]

The court has warned that, given the difficulty of showing reversible error in discretionary rulings, counsel should be particularly cautious about filing an appeal that challenges them.[414]

Refreshingly, the court has recently condemned appellee briefs that contain perfunctory allegations that the appeal is frivolous. It

---

taxpayers of this country to adjudicate genuine disputes, not to function as playgrounds for would-be lawyers or provide an emotional release for frustrated litigants."

[407]*D.L. Auld Co. v. Chroma Graphics Corp.,* 753 F.2d 1029, 224 USPQ 737 (Fed. Cir. 1985).

[408]*Beachboard v. United States,* 727 F.2d 1092 (Fed. Cir. 1984). The court did recognize, properly, that the fact that a small amount is involved does not alone require a finding that an appeal is frivolous. See also *Wright v. United States,* 728 F.2d 1459 (Fed. Cir. 1984).

[409]*In re Nilssen,* 851 F.2d 1401, 7 USPQ2d 1500 (Fed. Cir. 1988); *Constant v. Advanced Micro-Devices, Inc.,* 848 F.2d 1560, 7 USPQ2d 1057 (Fed. Cir. 1988). In *Constant v. United States,* 929 F.2d 654, 18 USPQ2d 1298 (Fed. Cir. 1991), the court awarded sanctions in view of the fact that the pro se plaintiff had twice been warned about his conduct and in view of his long litigation history and experience.

[410]*Maier v. Orr,* 758 F.2d 1578 (Fed. Cir. 1985). See also *Hodosh v. Block Drug Co.,* 790 F.2d 880, 229 USPQ 783 (Fed. Cir. 1986), where the court observed that the moving party should have known that there was not even an appearance of impropriety.

[411]See *Griessenauer v. Department of Energy,* 754 F.2d 361 (Fed. Cir. 1985). The court in this case may have come close to suggesting that appeals involving an abuse of discretion standard of review are more vulnerable to the frivolity label.

[412]In *Mathis v. Spears,* 857 F.2d 749, 8 USPQ2d 1029 (Fed. Cir. 1988), the question was whether expert witness fees are recoverable under 35 U.S.C. §285 (the court held that they were). In *Devices for Med., Inc. v. Boehl,* 822 F.2d 1062, 3 USPQ2d 1288 (Fed. Cir. 1987), the question was whether notice under 35 U.S.C. §287 was necessary where both method and apparatus claims were being asserted (the court held that it was). In both cases there was a dissenting panel member on the question of whether the appeal as a whole was frivolous. In neither case was the merits question clear, at least to this author; certainly neither question had been decided previously by the Federal Circuit.

[413]*Devices for Med., Inc. v. Boehl,* 822 F.2d 1062, 3 USPQ2d 1288, 1294 (Fed. Cir. 1987).

[414]*State Indus., Inc. v. Mor-Flo Indus. Inc.,* 948 F.2d 1573, 20 USPQ2d 1738 (Fed. Cir. 1991). Perhaps so, but it should not be forgotten that this court itself frequently reverses or vacates discretionary rulings.

likened such practice to "printing a ticket to what appellees may perceive as a frivolity lottery in hope of recouping the expenses of an appeal," and served notice that henceforth, an assertion by an appellee that an appeal is frivolous should be accompanied by citation to the opposing brief and the record below, and clear argument as to why those citations establish the allegedly frivolous nature of the appeal.[415] On the other hand, the court in another case indicated that a party's failure either to withdraw its appeal or reply in its brief to well-documented allegations of frivolity, and its failure at oral argument to justify its actions, strengthened the court's conviction that sanctions were warranted.[416] If the author may be permitted a modest proposal: Would it not be possible for a law clerk or technical advisor to circulate a bench memorandum, in banc fashion, to all actively sitting judges of the court, summarizing the issues and arguments presented by the appellant in any case where the panel majority is convinced that the appeal is frivolous? Let a straw vote be taken. If one of those judges feels, after reviewing the memorandum, that the appeal is *not* clearly hopeless or is *not* unquestionably without any possible basis in law or fact, then surely it is not frivolous.

Counsel, of course, can be and often are personally liable for sanctions under Rule 38, FRAP, for frivolous appeals.[417] It may be justifiable to refuse to hold counsel personally liable under Rule 11, FRCP, on the theory that he or she may have been misled by his or her client. But the appellate setting is different; counsel usually knows that there is no basis for appeal and thus should be held personally liable.[418] Unfortunately for attorneys, sanctions are usually imposed under Rule 38, FRAP, and not Rule 46(c), FRAP, which relates to disciplinary action for conduct unbecoming a member of the bar. Rule 46(c) provides for notice and an opportunity to be heard, while Rule 38 does not. The Federal Circuit has rejected an argument that

---

[415]*Biodex Corp. v. Loredan Biomedical, Inc.,* 946 F.2d 850, 20 USPQ2d 1252 (Fed. Cir. 1991). See also *Quad Envtl. Tech. Corp. v. Union Sanitary District,* 946 F.2d 870, 20 USPQ2d 1392 (Fed. Cir. 1991). Indeed, an assertion of frivolity that is nothing more than a mere incantation of Rule 38 can itself be frivolous. *Nasatka v. Delta Scientific Corp.,* 58 F.3d 1578, 35 USPQ2d 1374 (Fed. Cir. 1995). A baseless sanctions motion unfairly forces an opponent into satellite litigation while diverting attention away from the real issues in a case. It also unjustly challenges the integrity of the accused party and the professionalism of its counsel, and it wastes judicial resources. *Schendel v. Curtis,* 83 F.3d 1399, 38 USPQ2d 1743 (Fed. Cir. 1996).

[416]*State Indus., Inc. v. Mor-Flo Indus. Inc.,* 948 F.2d 1573, 20 USPQ2d 1738 (Fed. Cir. 1991).

[417]E.g., *S. Bravo Sys., Inc. v. Containment Tech. Corp.,* 96 F.3d 1372, 40 USPQ2d 1140 (Fed. Cir. 1996); *Sun-Tek Indus., Inc. v. Kennedy Sky Lites, Inc,* 856 F.2d 173, 8 USPQ2d 1154 (Fed. Cir. 1988); *In re Oximetrix, Inc.,* 748 F.2d 637, 223 USPQ 1068 (Fed. Cir. 1984); *Colt Indus. Oper. Corp. v. Index-Werke K.G.,* 739 F.2d 622 (Fed. Cir. 1984). See also *Pac-Tec, Inc. v. Amerace Corp.,* 903 F.2d 796, 14 USPQ2d 1871 (Fed. Cir. 1990); *Dreamlite Holdings Ltd. v. Kraser,* 890 F.2d 1147, 13 USPQ2d 1076 (Fed. Cir. 1989). Even if there are genuinely appealable issues, counsel's behavior in presenting them may be frivolous. *In re Perry,* 918 F.2d 931 (Fed. Cir. 1990).

[418]*Chemical Eng'g Corp. v. Marlo, Inc.,* 754 F.2d 331, 222 USPQ 738 (Fed. Cir. 1984). This would be especially so where the counsel is his or her own lawyer. *Finch v. Hughes Aircraft Co.,* 926 F.2d 1574, 17 USPQ2d 1914 (Fed. Cir. 1991). Despite criticism of plaintiff's inexperienced counsel, the court refused to award sanctions against him personally, because

Rule 38 sanctions awarded against an attorney for a frivolous appeal entitle the attorney to notice and a hearing, either by reference to Rule 46(c) or by virtue of due process.[419] Bad faith is not a requirement for imposition of Rule 38 sanctions. Thus good faith, if proved, would be irrelevant. The standard under Rule 38 is an objective one and has nothing to do with the mental state of the person sanctioned. The "empty head and pure heart" defense will not excuse objectively unreasonable conduct, and counsel's good faith beliefs that are unreasonable in light of dispositive authority will not immunize him or her from Rule 38 sanctions. Nor does an honest belief in the merits of a claim excuse an appellate brief that ignores significant issues and facts while deploying a smokescreen of irrelevant and tangential issues. Nor would the attorney's prior reputation have any bearing on the quality of his or her sanctionable conduct in a particular case.[420]

Affirmance of a trial court's denial of attorney fees does not preclude the appellate court from awarding costs and attorney fees resulting from opposing a frivolous appeal.[421] But fees cannot be awarded absent some activity in opposition to the frivolous action.[422]

An award of the attorney fees and cost incurred in defending a frivolous appeal, made pursuant to Rule 38, FRAP, is unlike an award of attorney fees under various fee-shifting statutes that call for "reasonable" attorney fees. It is intended to deter frivolous appeals and thus preserve the appellate calendar for cases worthy of consideration. Thus, in the absence of exceptional circumstances, the Federal Circuit will not stop to inquire whether the fees were reasonable, but merely whether they were actually expended.[423] It is abuse of the judicial process that is the cause for sanctions. It is therefore not necessary to await a determination of which side prevails on appeal before requesting a sanction. Such a request may and should when appropriate be stated in a brief.[424]

---

he had obtained a favorable jury verdict below and was appealing a JNOV. *Connell v. Sears, Roebuck & Co.*, 722 F.2d 1542, 220 USPQ 193 (Fed. Cir. 1983).

[419]*Sun-Tek Indus., Inc. v. Kennedy Sky Lites, Inc*, 856 F.2d 173, 8 USPQ2d 1154 (Fed. Cir. 1988); *Toepfer v. Department of Transp.*, 792 F.2d 1102 (Fed. Cir. 1986). The court may have retreated somewhat from the view that Rule 38 does not provide for any notice or opportunity to be heard. But if it does, a request for Rule 38 sanctions in the opposing party's brief is sufficient notice. The court's Practice Note to Rule 38 indicates that a party whose case has been challenged as frivolous is expected to respond in his or her reply brief or voluntarily dismiss the appeal. The opportunity to respond in the reply brief and at oral argument is a sufficient hearing; an adversarial, evidentiary hearing is not required. *In re Perry*, 918 F.2d 931 (Fed. Cir. 1990). See also *Finch v. Hughes Aircraft Co.*, 926 F.2d 1574, 17 USPQ2d 1914 (Fed. Cir. 1991).

[420]*In re Perry*, 918 F.2d 931 (Fed. Cir. 1990). Nor does the fact that the party's prior conduct of the litigation appeared to have been entirely proper have any bearing under Rule 38. *State Indus., Inc. v. Mor-Flo Indus. Inc.*, 948 F.2d 1573, 20 USPQ2d 1738 (Fed. Cir. 1991).

[421]*Porter v. Farmers Supply Serv., Inc.*, 790 F.2d 882, 229 USPQ 814 (Fed. Cir. 1986).

[422]*Maier v. Orr*, 758 F.2d 1578 (Fed. Cir. 1985).

[423]*Sun-Tek Indus., Inc. v. Kennedy Sky-Lites, Inc.*, 865 F.2d 1254, 9 USPQ2d 1574 (Fed. Cir. 1989). See also *Pac-Tec, Inc. v. Amerace Corp.*, 903 F.2d 796, 14 USPQ2d 1871 (Fed. Cir. 1990).

[424]*Korody-Colyer Corp. v. General Motors Corp.*, 828 F.2d 1572, 4 USPQ2d 1203 (Fed. Cir. 1987).

In addition to double or single costs, Rule 38 authorizes the court to award "just" damages, which it has interpreted as covering attorney fees.[425] An alternative mechanism to sanction frivolous appeals in patent cases is provided by 35 U.S.C. §285, which requires bad faith, in addition to the other more general provisions which, like Rule 38, do not require a showing of bad faith, such as 28 U.S.C. §§1912 and 1927 and the inherent power of Article III courts to impose sanctions.[426]

The amount of a damage award under Rule 38, FRAP, is within the discretion of an appellate court, and it is also possible to award a fixed amount reflecting an appropriate penalty rather than a precise sum based upon proof of the appellee's actual attorney fees. Sanctions are awarded to compensate the victimized party for the burden of continued litigation in what long ago should have been a settled matter, as well as to discourage frivolous appeals that unnecessarily clog the docket. It would be ironic were an adjudication of frivolity to impose on the opposing party and the court an even greater burden in forcing them to engage in proceedings over the actual amount of damages.[427]

The court has squarely held that attorney fees can be awarded for appellate activity pursuant to 35 U.S.C. §285 on grounds of exceptionality.[428] However, it is the appellate activity itself that must constitute the exceptional conduct.[429] The court has warned that negligence on the part of one's prior attorney does not justify appealing a weak case; however, it declined to sanction the losing party that was, in its view, doing its best to restore a case in which it perhaps failed to make its best showing in the PTO.[430] Clearly, an appeal is not frivolous if it is partially successful.[431] By the same token, the fact that a

---

[425]Compare *Shelcore, Inc. v. Durham Indus., Inc.,* 745 F.2d 621, 223 USPQ 584 (Fed. Cir. 1984), with *Porter v. Farmers Supply Serv., Inc.,* 790 F.2d 882, 229 USPQ 814 (Fed. Cir. 1986).

[426]*State Indus., Inc. v. Mor-Flo Indus. Inc.,* 948 F.2d 1573, 20 USPQ2d 1738 (Fed. Cir. 1991). Apparently §1927 does require bad faith, although knowing or reckless conduct meets this standard and the lack of an explicit finding of bad faith by the trial judge will not preclude sanctions when the record supports such a finding. *Baldwin Hardware Corp. v. Franksu Enter. Corp.,* 78 F.3d 550, 37 USPQ2d 1829 (Fed. Cir. 1996).

[427]*State Indus., Inc. v. Mor-Flo Indus. Inc.,* 948 F.2d 1573, 20 USPQ2d 1738 (Fed. Cir. 1991). Here the court awarded a fixed sum of $5, against the appellant and the attorney who prepared and signed the briefs.

[428]*PPG Indus., Inc. v. Celanese Polymer Spec. Co.,* 840 F.2d 1565, 6 USPQ2d 1010 (Fed. Cir. 1988); *Rohm & Haas Co. v. Crystal Chem. Co.,* 736 F.2d 688, 222 USPQ 97 (Fed. Cir. 1984).

[429]*Paper Converting Mach. Co. v. Magna-Graphics Corp.,* 788 F.2d 1536, 229 USPQ 480 (Fed. Cir. 1986).

[430]*Huston v. Ladner,* 973 F.2d 1564, 23 USPQ2d 1910 (Fed. Cir. 1992).

[431]*Vandenberg v. Dairy Equip. Co.,* 740 F.2d 1560, 224 USPQ 195 (Fed. Cir. 1984). But one nonfrivolous argument will not preclude Rule 38 sanctions. It would be strange if by the happenstance of including one colorable (though losing) claim amidst an ocean of frivolous ones, a litigant could ward off all sanctions. When an appeal is a complete loser, Rule 38 sanctions should be imposed. In that connection, the general rule is that it is not worthwhile to divide a suitor's claims or defenses into frivolous and nonfrivolous and to award attorney fees in respect to some but not others. *In re Perry,* 918 F.2d 931 (Fed. Cir. 1990).

dissenting opinion was filed tends to refute the idea that the appeal was unreasonable.[432]

(e) *Miscellaneous Substantive Matters*

Supersedeas. The purpose of requiring a supersedeas bond to be posted is to preserve the status quo while protecting the nonappealing party's rights pending appeal.[433]

Stay pending appeal. The court has set forth four factors that always guide its discretion to issue a stay of execution of the judgment pending appeal: (1) whether the stay applicant has made a strong showing that it is likely to succeed on the merits; (2) whether the applicant will be irreparably injured absent a stay; (3) whether issuance of the stay will substantially injure the other parties interested in the proceeding; and (4) where the public interest lies. Each factor need not be given equal weight, and likelihood of success in the appeal is not a rigid concept. The four stay factors can effectively merge to a sliding scale of likelihood of success versus balance of harm.[434]

Enjoining proceedings. In an interesting situation the PTO Board concluded that the counts of an interference were not patentable and entered judgment against both parties. One appealed ex parte to the Federal Circuit and the other filed suit in the district court under §146. The appellant in the Federal Circuit moved to enjoin the §146 action, but the court refused on the ground that the parties and issues were different.[435]

Counsel. The court's Rule 7(a) provides that except for an individual appearing pro se, a party to an appeal must be represented by a lawyer admitted to practice before the Federal Circuit. Thus the

---

[432]*Paper Converting Mach. Co. v. Magna-Graphics Corp.,* 788 F.2d 1536, 229 USPQ 480 (Fed. Cir. 1986). But see note 17:412.

[433]*Beatrice Foods Co. v. New England Printing & Lith. Co.,* 930 F.2d 1572, 18 USPQ2d 1548 (Fed. Cir. 1991). In this case, the court analyzed and interpreted the boilerplate provision that the surety's obligation would continue unless the appeal were prosecuted "to effect." The interpretation of a bond's terms, like any other contract, is a matter of law.

[434]*Standard Havens Prods., Inc. v. Gencor Indus., Inc.,* 897 F.2d 511, 13 USPQ2d 2029 (Fed. Cir. 1990). Here the success factor favored the infringer, on the ground that the PTO had granted a request for reexamination. The infringer also showed that it would suffer layoffs, immediate insolvency, and perhaps extinction if the injunction were allowed to continue and the money judgment were executed. On the other hand, the patentee would not be greatly harmed, because it appeared that there was serious doubt whether it would be able to collect the full judgment if it were allowed to throw the infringer into bankruptcy. The public interest did not appear to favor either party. On this basis the court granted a stay of execution pending appeal.

[435]*In re Van Geuns,* 946 F.2d 845, 20 USPQ2d 1291 (Fed. Cir. 1991). The PTO was ordered to file a brief in accordance with 35 U.S.C. §143; apparently the PTO must have concluded that the party that had sought review in the district court was also the appellee before the Federal Circuit.

nonlawyer president of a corporation cannot appear for the corporation; it must have a lawyer.[436] This is so even where the corporation's president is himself a pro se party.[437]

Recusal. Recusal is appropriate under 28 U.S.C. §455(a) when a judge's impartiality may reasonably be questioned, and under §455(b)(1) when the judge has a personal bias or prejudice concerning a party, or personal knowledge of disputed evidentiary facts concerning the proceeding. Absent a factual showing of a reasonable basis for questioning his or her impartiality, or allegations of facts establishing other disqualifying circumstances, a judge should participate in cases assigned.[438]

In its first published recusal decision, the court held that a decision disposing of an appeal on its merits is a decision of the panel, not that of the individual judge who set forth the panel's reasons. The authoring judge did not "decide" the case, the panel did. Accordingly, even if recusal of that judge had been appropriate, it would not form a basis for attack on the decision. If recusal had occurred, the two remaining judges from the original panel would have been at liberty to decide the appeal.[439] In a later case the court reconfirmed this rule: a unanimous decision rendered by a three-judge panel need not be vacated merely because one of the judges learns, after the decision is handed down, that there was reason for disqualification.[440] The court has also dismissed a proceeding as not in conformity with 28 U.S.C. §372 because it was not based upon facts supportive of an allegation that any judge of the court had engaged in conduct in any manner prejudicial to the effective and expeditious administration of the business of the court.[441]

Supreme Court orders. Supreme Court review of Federal Circuit decisions promises to be rare. In what was probably the first such instance, the Court vacated a Federal Circuit judgment and remanded

---

[436]*Richdel, Inc. v. Sunspool Corp.*, 699 F.2d 1366, 217 USPQ 8 (Fed. Cir. 1983).

[437]*Jones v. Hardy*, 727 F.2d 1524, 220 USPQ 1021 (Fed. Cir. 1984).

[438]*Maier v. Orr*, 758 F.2d 1578 (Fed. Cir. 1985). The assertion that a judge improperly participated in a case from which he or she should have recused constitutes a charge most grave. Counsel should not make such an assertion precipitously or recklessly, or on unsupported rumor, conjecture, and speculation. To do so is to trifle with the court and the administration of justice. *Id.*

[439]*Maier v. Orr*, 758 F.2d 1578 (Fed. Cir. 1985). This holding may not give enough credit to the undeniable reality that the views of the authoring judge can often influence those of his or her colleagues. Certainly the decision could have rested solely on the merits of the request for recusal.

[440]*Hodosh v. Block Drug Co.*, 790 F.2d 880, 229 USPQ 783 (Fed. Cir. 1986). In this case one of the judges recused himself after the three-judge panel handed down a decision, and the losing party moved to vacate the decision. The court quite properly denied the motion, but its criticism of the motion on the grounds that there was not even an appearance of impropriety was probably misplaced. See 28 U.S.C. §455.

[441]*In re Leighton*, 790 F.2d 78 (Fed. Cir. 1986). Apparently this attorney was unhappy with the way he supposed cases were being assigned in the Federal Circuit.

the case for further consideration. The Federal Circuit expressed doubt as to whether the Supreme Court intended to vacate the entire judgment, or only so much as could be affected by the reconsideration. In an abundance of caution, the court therefore reinstated the remaining, unaffected portions of the judgment.[442] In another case, the court vacated all previous injunctive orders in light of a Supreme Court decision and mandate.[443]

The Federal Circuit views the Supreme Court's GVR (grant, vacate, remand) procedure like this: a GVR occurs when intervening developments, or recent developments that there is reason to believe the lower court did not fully consider, reveal a reasonable probability that the decision below rests upon a premise that the lower court would reject if given the opportunity for further consideration, and where it appears that such a redetermination may determine the ultimate outcome of the litigation.[444] However, GVR does not create an implication that the lower court should change its prior determination. Moreover, it does not require that the Federal Circuit review the trial court's original decision anew, but rather that it merely reconsider its own prior decision.[445]

The law of the case cannot bind the Supreme Court in reviewing decisions below. A petition for writ of certiorari can expose the entire case to review. Just as a district court's adherence to law of the case cannot insulate an issue from appellate review, a court of appeals' adherence to the law of the case cannot insulate an issue from Supreme Court review.[446]

Amicus participation. The grant or denial of a request to intervene or to appear as amicus is discretionary with the court.[447]

(f) Formal Matters

Notice of appeal. Rule 3, FRAP, directs that an appeal permitted as of right shall be taken by filing a notice of appeal with the clerk of the court from which the appeal is taken.[448] Under Rule 4, FRAP, the time permitted is 30 days, except that 60 days are allowed in a case where the United States is a party.[449] The extra time allowed after service of pleadings by mail is not applicable here, inasmuch as the time begins to run upon entry of judgment, not service of

---

[442]*Syntex Ophthalmics, Inc. v. Novicky,* 767 F.2d 901, 226 USPQ 952 (Fed. Cir. 1985). See also the discussion of the *Panduit* decisions in §4.2(b)(iv).

[443]*Eli Lilly & Co. v. Medtronic, Inc.,* 915 F.2d 670 (Fed. Cir. 1990).

[444]*Festo Corp. v. Shoketsu KKK Co.,* 172 F.3d 1361, 50 USPQ2d 1385 (Fed. Cir. 1999).

[445]*Hughes Aircraft Co. v. United States,* 140 F.3d 1470, 46 USPQ2d 1285 (Fed. Cir. 1998).

[446]*Christianson v. Colt Indus. Oper. Corp.,* 486 U.S. 800, 7 USPQ2d 1109 (1988).

[447]*In re Opprecht,* 868 F.2d 1264 (Fed. Cir. 1989).

[448]*Armstrong Rubber Co. v. United States,* 781 F.2d 889 (Fed. Cir. 1986).

[449]*Sofarelli Assoc., Inc. v. United States,* 716 F.2d 1395 (Fed. Cir. 1983).

notice of its entry.[450] The timely filing of a notice is mandatory and jurisdictional,[451] and this is so for all appeals.[452] The Federal Circuit will take jurisdiction over an appeal on an untimely notice only under unusual circumstances.[453]

Rule 3(c), FRAP, which provides that a notice "shall designate the judgment, order or part appealed from," has been interpreted to permit an appeal that may be "technically defective." However, where an appellant clearly and specifically intends to confine its notice to only one of two patents, the notice is not technically defective with respect to the excluded patent, and the appellant cannot expand the scope of its specifically limited notice, by amendment or otherwise. Amendments are permitted only where the deficiency is a mere technicality.[454]

The court has dealt with several complex situations involving appeal formalities. In one case the district court granted summary judgment of noninfringement and the losing party filed a motion for reconsideration within 10 days. The same party filed a notice of appeal within 30 days after the grant of the summary judgment motion. The district court later denied the motion for reconsideration. Held: no jurisdiction over the appeal from the grant of the summary judgment or from the denial of the reconsideration motion. Under Rule 59(e), FRCP, the motion to reconsider was, because made within 10 days, a motion to alter or amend the judgment. Under Rule 4(a)(4), FRAP, a notice of appeal filed before the disposition of such a motion "shall have no effect." Because the party filed no new notice of appeal following the denial of the motion to reconsider, its position is the same as that which would exist if no notice of appeal had ever been filed. Without a timely notice, the Federal Circuit lacks jurisdiction.[455] Interesting complexities can even arise in the context of appeals from the PTO Board.[456]

In an action involving patent infringement and breach of contract claims, and a counterclaim for breach of contract, the defendant moved for a new trial on "all issues" but only specifically referred to the infringement and breach claims, and not the breach counterclaim. This is insufficient under Rule 7(b)(1), FRCP. Accordingly, the motion

---

[450]*Sofarelli Assoc., Inc. v. United States,* 716 F.2d 1395 (Fed. Cir. 1983).

[451]*Marsh-McBirney, Inc. v. Montedoro-Whitney Corp.,* 882 F.2d 498, 11 USPQ2d 1794 (Fed. Cir. 1989); *Sofarelli Assoc., Inc. v. United States,* 716 F.2d 1395 (Fed. Cir. 1983). A brief is not a substitute for a notice of appeal, even if it otherwise complies with the requirements of FRAP Rules 3 and 4. *Jurgens v. McKasy,* 905 F.2d 382 (Fed. Cir. 1990).

[452]*Armstrong Rubber Co. v. United States,* 781 F.2d 889 (Fed. Cir. 1986).

[453]*Sofarelli Assoc., Inc. v. United States,* 716 F.2d 1395 (Fed. Cir. 1983).

[454]*Durango Assoc., Inc. v. Reflange, Inc.,* 912 F.2d 1423, 15 USPQ2d 1910 (Fed. Cir. 1990).

[455]*Tylo Sauna, S.A. v. Amerec Corp.,* 826 F.2d 7, 3 USPQ2d 1792 (Fed. Cir. 1987). A second postjudgment motion of the type referred to in Rule 4(a)(4), FRAP, such as a motion to reconsider an order disposing of a Rule 59(e) motion, does not stay the period for appeal unless filed within the original 10-day period. *Durango Assoc., Inc. v. Reflange, Inc.,* 912 F.2d 1423, 15 USPQ2d 1910 (Fed. Cir. 1990).

[456]See *In re Graves,* 69 F.3d 1147, 36 USPQ2d 1697 (Fed. Cir. 1995).

did not satisfy Rule 59 as to the counterclaim, and defendant's appeal was dismissed. The fact that the motion was allowed as to the infringement and breach claims did not alter the result.[457]

An untimely postjudgment motion cannot toll the running of the time to appeal, and an appellate court therefore lacks jurisdiction to review a subsequent order.[458] Timing is important. The district court entered findings and conclusions on liability, but not a formal judgment. The defendant promptly appealed the infringement issue. The court later entered a judgment on liability and damages and defendant appealed the damages issue. The Federal Circuit held that the earlier appeal was premature and ineffective because Rule 4(a)(2), FRAP, applies only to decisions that would be final upon entry. Thus, the failure to appeal liability from the later judgment was fatal.[459]

Each party that seeks to act independently to overturn or modify a judgment must file a notice of appeal.[460] Rule 43(a), FRAP, provides that a cross-appeal must be filed within 14 days of an appeal. In consolidated cases a party won the first and lost the second. Its opponent appealed the first within 30 days of judgment, and the party appealed the second within 14 days of the opponent's appeal but more than 30 days after judgment. In a broad interpretation of Rule 43(a), the Federal Circuit denied a motion to dismiss the "cross-appeal" as untimely.[461]

Rehearing. When the court grants rehearing, its original decision is set aside and the appeal is revived. Thus, the case or controversy originally present has not disappeared.[462] Rehearing petitions are

---

[457]*Snellman v. Ricoh Co.,* 836 F.2d 528, 5 USPQ2d 1341 (Fed. Cir. 1987). The court rejected the argument (apparently based on Rule 54(b), FRCP) that a timely new trial motion enables the district court to retain jurisdiction to grant relief not requested by the motion. In *Davis v. Loesch,* 998 F.2d 963, 27 USPQ2d 1440 (Fed. Cir. 1993), the court assumed without deciding that the Supreme Court rule in *Torres v. Oakland Scavenger Co.,* 487 U.S. 312 (1988), applies to review of administrative agencies, boards, and commissions. *Torres* holds that the failure of a party to be specifically named in the notice of appeal from a judgment of a district court deprives the appellate court of jurisdiction over that party. The Federal Circuit avoided *Torres* by observing that, in an interference proceeding, joint inventors are deemed to be a single party. Thus, a notice of appeal captioned "Davis et al." meets the requirement of Rule 15(a), FRAP, that the notice of appeal "specify the parties seeking review."

[458]*Registration Control Sys., Inc. v. Compusystems, Inc.,* 922 F.2d 805, 17 USPQ2d 1212 (Fed. Cir. 1990).

[459]*Marsh-McBirney, Inc. v. Montedoro-Whitney Corp.,* 882 F.2d 498, 11 USPQ2d 1794 (Fed. Cir. 1989). This seemingly harsh result may be explainable on the basis that the first appeal appeared to have been taken almost in a willful manner; the district court had warned against it and threatened sanctions. In *Phonometrics Inc. v. Hospitality Franchise Sys. Inc.,* 203 F.3d 790, 53 USPQ2d 1762 (Fed. Cir. 2), the district court dismissed a claim with leave to amend, and the appeal was taken prior to the end of the period allowed for amendment. The court of appeals nonetheless had jurisdiction, even though the district court did not enter a final judgment until after the period for amendment has run. There was no prejudice to the appellee because of the premature notice of appeal, and a denial of jurisdiction would spin judicial wheels for no practical purpose.

[460]*Armstrong Rubber Co. v. United States,* 781 F.2d 889 (Fed. Cir. 1986).

[461]*Jackson Jordon, Inc. v. Plasser Am. Corp.,* 725 F.2d 1373, 220 USPQ 945 (Fed. Cir. 1984).

[462]*Bosco v. United States,* 976 F.2d 710 (Fed. Cir. 1992).

normally not a suitable vehicle for making new arguments to the appellate court.[463] No inferences can be drawn from the court's silence in response to a request for clarification. Courts normally do not respond to petitions for rehearing and it would be a mistake to conclude that a court's nonresponse to an argument made in a rehearing petition necessarily means that the court has rejected that argument on the merits. The court's failure to grant a request for clarification could well reflect the view that clarification was not required, rather than an intention to reject on the merits the legal argument on which clarification was sought.[464]

Briefs, appendix, and record. The court has put the bar on notice that failure to comply with its rules, including the requirements for preparing and filing briefs, appendices, and other papers, may result in dismissal of an appeal for failure to prosecute.[465] Where an appellant urges error in refusing to admit testimony, it must specifically refer to the page of the transcript at which the evidence was offered and rejected.[466] A failure to provide citations to the record to support an argument, as required under FRAP 28(e), may result in a refusal of the court to entertain the argument.[467] The Federal Circuit also expects that a party challenging findings will identify them by number, if they are in that form.[468]

The brief must include a certificate of interest to avoid judicial conflicts of interest. Counsel are admonished to keep abreast of the affairs of their clients and to amend the certificate if circumstances change.[469] It is inappropriate for appellants to discuss in reply briefs matters not raised in either of the principal briefs. Reply briefs are to be used to reply to matters raised in the brief of the appellee.[470] It is inappropriate to quote mere language from a court opinion, while

---

[463]*Exxon Chem. Patents Inc. v. Lubrizol Corp.,* 137 F.3d 1475, 45 USPQ2d 1865 (Fed. Cir. 1998).

[464]*Exxon Chem. Patents Inc. v. Lubrizol Corp.,* 137 F.3d 1475, 45 USPQ2d 1865 (Fed. Cir. 1998).

[465]*Julien v. Zeringue,* 864 F.2d 1572, 9 USPQ2d 1554 (Fed. Cir. 1989). In *Yukiyo, Ltd. v. Watanabe,* 111 F.3d 883, 42 USPQ2d 1474 (Fed. Cir. 1997), the court dealt with the requirements to obtain leave to file a cd rom brief with hypertext links to case and record citations.

[466]*Lemelson v. United States,* 752 F.2d 1538, 224 USPQ 526 (Fed. Cir. 1985). See Rule 28(e), FRAP.

[467]*Engdahl v. Department of Navy,* 900 F.2d 1572 (Fed. Cir. 1990).

[468]*Milmark Serv., Inc. v. United States,* 731 F.2d 855 (Fed. Cir. 1984).

[469]*Hodosh v. Block Drug Co.,* 790 F.2d 880, 229 USPQ 783 (Fed. Cir. 1986). In this case an acquisition took place during the pendency of the appeal, resulting in recusal of one of the judges, but only after the decision was handed down. A prompt amendment of the certificate would have avoided this problem. Nonetheless, the court refused to award sanctions against the derelict party, on the ground that sanctions are reserved for matters more serious than mere oversight having no effect on the administration of justice.

[470]*Kaufman Co. v. Lantech,* 807 F.2d 970, 1 USPQ2d 1202 (Fed. Cir. 1986). In *Allied Colloids, Inc. v. American Cyanamid Co.,* 64 F.3d 1570, 35 USPQ2d 1840 (Fed. Cir. 1995), the court denied a motion to strike where appellant in its reply brief referred to an order of the trial court that was received after it filed its opening brief. The order was properly raised because it could have affected consideration of the various issues presented on appeal.

disregarding the actual holding of the court and the factual pattern that gave rise to the quoted language.[471] The court has ordered both parties to rebrief the appeal because of "woefully inadequate and improper briefs" as an alternative to "struggling to make sense of this morass and imposing appropriate sanctions."[472] Under Rule 28(a)(6), FRAP, arguments may not be properly raised by incorporating them by reference from the appendix rather than discussing them in the brief.[473]

Failure to oppose an appeal by way of a brief does not automatically result in judgment for the appellant. In one case the PTO Board imposed sanctions against one party to an interference. That party appealed and the Commissioner filed an amicus brief, while the other party remained silent. The court refused to hold that the failure of the other party to respond or take a position regarding the appeal means that the court could not decide the appeal on the merits.[474] The purpose of the appendix is to provide each judge with pertinent portions of the record. It need not be printed or professionally bound and may in most cases be prepared in counsel's office by photocopying copies of the pertinent papers and binding with staples or tape. Many times all that is necessary is the decision under review (where the facts are not challenged). The appendix can always be challenged as inaccurate or inadequate, and the court may sua sponte order the entire record if it deems it necessary.[475]

The record on appeal includes all original papers filed in the district court, including pretrial orders.[476] The general rule on supplementing the record with new evidence is that appellate courts can act on no evidence that was not before the court below, nor receive any paper that was not used at the hearing below.[477] Submission of

---

[471]*Illinois Tool Works, Inc. v. Grip-Pak, Inc.,* 906 F.2d 679, 15 USPQ2d 1307 (Fed. Cir. 1990).

[472]*Laitram Corp. v. Cambridge Wire Cloth Co.,* 905 F.2d 386 (Fed. Cir. 1990). In *Laitram Corp. v. Cambridge Wire Cloth Co.,* 919 F.2d 1579, 16 USPQ2d 1929 (Fed. Cir. 1990), the court rejected the initial briefs of both parties and ordered the appeal rebriefed. Apparently the replacements were worse, prompting the court to characterize the proceedings as a kind of "Alice in Patentland" approach to the judicial process. Although the court recognized that both Rule 38, FRCP, and 28 U.S.C. §1927 call for payment of costs and attorney fees to the other side, the court called upon its inherent powers to discourage such conduct and resolved the quandary by ordering each attorney who had signed a brief to pay personally $1, to the Treasury of the United States.

[473]*Graphic Controls Corp. v. Utah Med. Prods. Inc.,* 149 F.3d 1382, 47 USPQ2d 1622 (Fed. Cir. 1998).

[474]*Gerritsen v. Shirai,* 979 F.2d 1524, 24 USPQ2d 1912 (Fed. Cir. 1992).

[475]*Crostic v. Veterans Admin.,* 730 F.2d 1464 (Fed. Cir. 1984). In *Baldwin Hardware Corp. v. Franksu Enter. Corp.,* 78 F.3d 550, 37 USPQ2d 1829 (Fed. Cir. 1996), the court refused to order a complete trial transcript, at government expense, to help appellant prove judicial bias below. And although it roundly condemned the appellant's behavior on numerous grounds, it also refused to award fees for the appeal to appellee, who was uncooperative with respect to compromising on the cost of a transcript.

[476]*Kori Corp. v. Wilco Marsh Buggies, Inc.,* 761 F.2d 649, 225 USPQ 985 (Fed. Cir. 1985).

[477]*Coplin v. United States,* 761 F.2d 688 (Fed. Cir. 1985). It does seem that judicial notice is an exception to this general rule, however. For example, in *Hoganas AB v. Dresser Indus.,*

newly discovered evidence to the court of appeals is improper where it was not before the district court.[478] Federal Circuit review is limited to the record of the case.[479]

Argument. The court commends waiver of oral argument and submission on the briefs, at least in a questionable appeal.[480] The court has had something to say about intemperate outbursts by counsel during argument.[481]

Costs. Normally, costs on appeal include costs of reproducing (e.g., printing, photocopying) briefs and record. If one uses a word processor to produce the multiple copies, as by printing several ribbon copies from an original stored in the word processor, then that would be reimbursable. But not so where the use of the word processor was simply as a fancy typewriter to produce a single ribbon copy from which multiple copies were made by another method.[482]

Where it appeared that the unsuccessful appellee had relied upon only a small fraction of the portions of the record that it had designated for printing, the court assessed appellee with the full cost of printing the appendix.[483] Where the unsuccessful appellant had filed a sparse appendix, while the PTO Commissioner filed a nine-volume supplemental appendix, including some improper materials, the court refused to tax the appellant with the costs of the Commissioner's appendix.[484]

Miscellaneous. The court explained its policy regarding publication of opinions on this basis: in general, the stress has been on nonpublication of judicial opinions or, rather, publication of only a selected few, as a means of conserving judicial resources and keeping channels clear and unobstructed, for legal opinions that really matter, to circulate in. A by-product of selective publication is avoiding needless invasion of the privacy of individuals. The significance of this must not be overstressed as the unpublished opinion is still, of course, a public record that normally anyone can consult and copy.[485]

Inc., 9 F.3d 948, 28 USPQ2d 1936 (Fed. Cir. 1993), the court was willing to take judicial notice of a patent that, although not part of the record on appeal, was referred to at argument and is publicly accessible.

[478]*Amstar Corp. v. Envirotech Corp.*, 823 F.2d 1538, 3 USPQ2d 1412 (Fed. Cir. 1987).

[479]*DMI, Inc. v. Deere & Co.*, 802 F.2d 421, 231 USPQ 276 (Fed. Cir. 1986). In *American Standard, Inc. v. Pfizer, Inc.*, 828 F.2d 734, 3 USPQ2d 1817 (Fed. Cir. 1987), the court struck portions of the brief that relied upon a file history that was not before the district court and that dealt with a motion filed in another case after the entry of the order appealed from.

[480]*Constant v. United States*, 929 F.2d 654, 18 USPQ2d 1298 (Fed. Cir. 1991).

[481]*Nordberg, Inc. v. Telsmith, Inc.*, 82 F.3d 394, 38 USPQ2d 1593, 1596 (Fed. Cir. 1996).

[482]*CTS Corp v. Piher Int'l Corp.*, 754 F.2d 972, 221 USPQ 954 (Fed. Cir. 1984).

[483]*Merck & Co. v. Biocraft Labs., Inc.*, 874 F.2d 804, 10 USPQ2d 1843 (Fed. Cir. 1989). The appellee fully reproduced a 700-page book that was mentioned once and not really relied upon at all.

[484]*Newman v. Quigg*, 886 F.2d 329 (Fed. Cir. 1989).

[485]*Seligson v. Office of Personnel Management*, 878 F.2d 369 (Fed. Cir. 1989).

Unpublished opinions are not to be taken as an adoption of the district court's reasoning for purposes of precedent. An affirmance could have been on any ground appropriate to the case.[486] The court continues to remind counsel and the lower courts that its nonprecedental opinions and orders are not citable to it, do not represent its considered view regarding aspects of a particular case beyond the decision itself, and are not intended to convey its view of law applicable in other cases. Nonprecedental orders and opinions are used in summary dispositions of cases in which a full precedential opinion is not considered necessary, but something more than a one-sentence Rule 36 affirmance is warranted or needed. They are not precedential for a reason: while the decision itself receives due care, the explanation given in the summary disposition does not necessarily contain a full recitation of all the relevant facts and legal authorities. The opinion or order is primarily for the benefit of the parties. It is error to assume that a nonprecedental order or opinion provides support for a particular position or reflects a new or changed view.[487] A nonprecedental opinion construing patent claims can, however, be relied upon in a later case involving the same patent.[488]

---

[486]*Quad Envtl. Tech. Corp. v. Union Sanitary District,* 946 F.2d 870, 20 USPQ2d 1392 (Fed. Cir. 1991).

[487]*Nike Inc. v. Wolverine World Wide, Inc.*, 43 F.3d 644, 33 USPQ2d 1038 (Fed. Cir. 1994). This seems to indicate that the court will disregard any discussion of a nonprecedental order by a lower court or in the parties' briefs and arguments. It is for this reason that this treatise makes no effort to analyze any nonprecedental decision of the Federal Circuit. See also *United States Surgical Corp. v. Ethicon, Inc.,* 103 F.3d 1554, 41 USPQ2d 1225 (Fed. Cir. 1997).

[488]*Burke Inc. v. Bruno Indep. Living Aids Inc.,* 183 F.3d 1334, 51 USPQ2d 1295 (Fed. Cir. 1999).

18

General Legal Principles

Owing to its limited subject matter jurisdiction, the Federal Circuit has not developed a broad body of law. Nonetheless, there is a fairly intensive focus in areas such as administrative law (due to its review of PTO, contract board, and other agency determinations), statutory interpretation (due to the high degree of codification of the patent law), and the preclusive effect of judgments (due to the very nature of patent litigation). This chapter will examine these and other areas of general jurisprudence, such as conflicts and constitutional law, with special emphasis on how the principles developed by the court may be applied in patent cases.

§18.1 Administrative Law

Some specific aspects of administrative law are covered in Chapter 15, which deals with patent prosecution and interference practice in the PTO. This section, then, concentrates on rules of administrative law that have more general applicability.

Administrative discretion. The grant of discretionary authority to an agency implies that the exercise of discretion be predicated upon a judgment anchored in the language and spirit of the relevant statutes and regulations.[1] As a general rule, a long-standing interpretation of a statute by an agency charged with its administration must be upheld if reasonable.[2] And an administrative determination pursuant to a broad congressional grant of discretion can only be set aside for abuse of discretion, or because it is so arbitrary as to be clearly wrong.[3] But the discretion of an administrative agency is not unlimited, and reasonableness cannot cover for arbitrary or capricious action.[4]

A court's inquiry into the validity of an administrative interpretation of a statute is limited to whether the interpretation at issue is reasonably related to the purpose of the enabling legislation. To sustain an agency's construction of its authority, it need not be found that its construction is the only reasonable one, or even that it is the result the court would have reached had the question arisen in the first instance in judicial proceedings. In other words, the court gives deference to the interpretation accorded a statute by the officers or agency charged with its administration.[5] But a court may reject an agency interpretation that contravenes clearly discernible legislative

---

[1]*Freeport Minerals Co. v. United States,* 776 F.2d 1029 (Fed. Cir. 1985).

[2]*Horner v. Andrzjewski,* 811 F.2d 571 (Fed. Cir. 1987).

[3]*Adams v. United States,* 810 F.2d 1142 (Fed. Cir. 1987).

[4]*Beardmore v. Department of Agric.,* 761 F.2d 677 (Fed. Cir. 1985).

[5]*Nutrition 21 v. United States,* 930 F.2d 862, 18 USPQ2d 1351 (Fed. Cir. 1991); *American Lamb Co. v. United States,* 785 F.2d 994 (Fed. Cir. 1986); *Kester v. Horner,* 778 F.2d 1565 (Fed. Cir. 1985). This deference is particularly appropriate when the administrative practice at stake involves a contemporaneous construction of a statute by the persons charged with the responsibility of setting its machinery in motion, of making the parts work efficiently and smoothly while they are yet untried and new. *Chula Vista Sch. Dist. v. Bennett,* 824 F.2d 1573 (Fed. Cir. 1987). On the other hand, the rule applies only where Congress has explicitly or implicitly delegated to an agency the making of such determinations. *Glaxo Oper. UK Ltd. v. Quigg,* 894 F.2d 392, 13 USPQ2d 1628 (Fed. Cir. 1990).

intent.[6] The courts are the final authorities on issues of statutory construction, and they must reject administrative constructions of the statute, whether reached by adjudication or by rule making, that are inconsistent with the statutory mandate or that frustrate the policy that Congress sought to implement.[7] In essence, the issue is whether the agency's interpretation is based on a permissible construction of the statute.[8]

An agency is obligated to follow precedent, and if it chooses to change, it must explain why.[9] An agency interpretation of a statute that conflicts with the same agency's earlier interpretation is entitled to considerably less deference than a consistently held view.[10] The meaning of a contract cannot change simply because the government changes its interpretation of the law.[11] Nonetheless, an agency need not exercise its discretion identically in every case.[12] Administrative actions taken in violation of statutory authorization are of no effect.[13]

There is a compelling difference between noncompliance with a statutory requirement and a mere technical defect. While the latter may often be remedied with discretionary benevolence, the former is another matter. Administrative discretion may enable correction of a technical defect nunc pro tunc, but failure to comply with a statutory provision offers far less flexibility to the administrator and the courts. The distinction has long been recognized between mandatory and directory provisions of a statute. The term "directory" describes provisions that partake more of formality than of substantive legal requirement; in such case, failure of strict compliance need not invalidate the underlying proceedings.[14]

Due process.　Congress in the performance of its legislative functions may leave it to administrative officials to establish rules within the prescribed limits of a statute. A statute valid on its face may nevertheless be administered in such a way that constitutional or statutory guarantees are violated. Although administrative convenience must be considered, neither convenience nor necessity can override the constitutional requirements of due process.[15] Due process

---

[6]*Ulmet v. United States,* 822 F.2d 1079 (Fed. Cir. 1987). But the court has indicated that the rules of deference apply only where the statutory language leaves a gap or is doubtful or ambiguous. *Glaxo Oper. UK Ltd. v. Quigg,* 894 F.2d 392, 13 USPQ2d 1628 (Fed. Cir. 1990).

[7]*Ethicon v. Quigg,* 849 F.2d 1422, 7 USPQ2d 1152 (Fed. Cir. 1988).

[8]*Ulmet v. United States,* 822 F.2d 1079 (Fed. Cir. 1987).

[9]*M.M.&.P. Maritime v. Department of Commerce,* 729 F.2d 748 (Fed. Cir. 1984).

[10]*Madison Galleries, Ltd. v. United States,* 870 F.2d 627 (Fed. Cir. 1989).

[11]*Craft Mach. Works, Inc. v. United States,* 926 F.2d 1110 (Fed. Cir. 1991).

[12]*Villela v. Department of Air Force,* 727 F.2d 1574 (Fed. Cir. 1984).

[13]*United States v. Amdahl Corp.,* 786 F.2d 387 (Fed. Cir. 1986).

[14]*In re Mother Tucker's Food Exp. (Canada) Inc.,* 925 F.2d 1402, 17 USPQ2d 1795 (Fed. Cir. 1991).

[15]*Patlex Corp. v. Mossinghoff,* 771 F.2d 480, 226 USPQ 985 (Fed. Cir. 1985); *Patlex Corp. v. Mossinghoff,* 758 F.2d 594, 225 USPQ 243 (Fed. Cir. 1985).

in administrative proceedings requires evaluation of three factors: (1) the private interest that will be affected by the official action; (2) the risk of an erroneous deprivation of such interest through the procedures used, and the probable value, if any, of additional or substitute procedural safeguards; and (3) the government's interests, including the function involved and the fiscal and administrative burdens that the additional or substitute procedural requirement would entail.[16]

Absent special considerations, the general rule is that due process does not require a hearing at the initial stage, at any particular point, or at more than one point in an administrative proceeding, so long as the requisite hearing is held before the final order becomes effective.[17] Likewise, in the absence of statute or regulation due process does not prohibit ex parte communications or contact between an agency's deciding official and persons having knowledge of the incidents upon which the matter will be decided.[18]

Specific holdings about agency due process are collected in the footnote.[19]

Regulations. It is well settled that regulations promulgated by an agency must be consistent with statutory provisions enacted by Congress.[20] An interpretative regulation is valid if it harmonizes with the statute's origin, purpose, and language.[21] An interpretative rule describes the agency's view of the meaning of the statute. A substantive rule grants rights or imposes obligations on those affected by it. Interpretative rules are not subject to the notice provisions of the Administrative Procedure Act.[22] A rule is substantive when it effects

---

[16]*Patlex Corp. v. Mossinghoff,* 771 F.2d 480, 226 USPQ 985 (Fed. Cir. 1985).

[17]*Patlex Corp. v. Mossinghoff,* 771 F.2d 480, 226 USPQ 985 (Fed. Cir. 1985). If an agency lacks jurisdiction, in that jurisdiction is not properly invoked, then it is not a denial of due process to preclude a statutory right of review of the agency action. *Rose v. Department of Health,* 721 F.2d 355 (Fed. Cir. 1983).

[18]*Brewer v. American Battle Mons. Comm'n,* 779 F.2d 663 (Fed. Cir. 1985).

[19]The procedural safeguards of Executive Order 10096, which deals with ownership of inventions made by government employees, and its accompanying regulations satisfy due process. *Heinemann v. United States,* 796 F.2d 451, 230 USPQ 430 (Fed. Cir. 1986). The initial three-month period of silence in reexamination proceedings does not offend due process. *Patlex Corp. v. Mossinghoff,* 771 F.2d 480, 226 USPQ 985 (Fed. Cir. 1985). Section 555(b) of the Administrative Procedure Act does not confer a blindly absolute right upon a party to appear in person in an administrative proceeding; due process is satisfied if the party's outside counsel has access to the information developed. *Akzo N.V. v. United States ITC,* 808 F.2d 1471, 1 USPQ2d 1241 (Fed. Cir. 1986). Section 720 of the Administrative Procedure Act gives standing to any person adversely affected or aggrieved by an agency action within the meaning of a relevant statute. But it is the patent statute (in a PTO matter), not the APA itself, that is the relevant statute. Thus, to have standing, a party must be deemed within the zone of interests protected by the patent laws, not the APA. *Animal Legal Defense Fund v. Quigg,* 932 F.2d 920, 18 USPQ2d 1677 (Fed. Cir. 1991).

[20]*Spears v. Merit Sys. Prot. Bd.,* 766 F.2d 520 (Fed. Cir. 1985). The rule-making powers of the PTO are limited to the conduct of proceedings in the PTO; it has no general substantive rule-making power. *Merck & Co. v. Kessler,* 80 F.3d 1543, 38 USPQ2d 1347 (Fed. Cir. 1996).

[21]*Thomas Int'l Ltd. v. United States,* 773 F.2d 300 (Fed. Cir. 1985).

[22]*Animal Legal Defense Fund v. Quigg,* 932 F.2d 920, 18 USPQ2d 1677 (Fed. Cir. 1991); *Chula Vista Sch. Dist. v. Bennett,* 824 F.2d 1573 (Fed. Cir. 1987). Interpretive rules, such as the

a change in existing law or policy that affects individual rights and obligations. In contrast, a rule that merely clarifies or explains existing law or regulations is interpretative. A limitation of discretion, by itself, does not make an agency action substantive. One must also look for the adverse effect of that limitation on an individual's rights and obligations.[23] Where a regulation does not clearly contradict or exceed the scope of the statute, the administrative interpretation is entitled to deference.[24] Indeed, in determining whether a regulation is reasonable, a court must give considerable deference to the expertise of the agency—"the masters of the subject."[25] A regulation that by its own definition is permissive, not precatory, cannot be viewed as a mandatory restriction.[26]

There is a general rule that courts should not topple administrative decisions unless the administrative body not only has erred but has erred against objection made at the time appropriate under its practice. But this rule cuts both ways. Practice before agencies is controlled by each agency's own regulations, and where the rights of individuals are affected, it is incumbent upon the agency to follow its own procedures. Weight should be given to the normal practices of the agency, as understood by practitioners before it.[27]

Review of administrative action. Judicial review is essential to the integrity of our system of government; it is the necessary premise of legal validity. Judicial review of administrative action also serves to protect and preserve the separation of powers, a function clarified early in our nation's history.[28] Thus, absent statutory provision to the contrary, judicial review of administrative action is favored.[29] But every perceived injury caused by improper agency action does not carry a right to immediate judicial redress. A right to judicial review must be granted or reasonably inferred from a particular statute. For example, a potential infringer may not sue the PTO seeking retraction of a patent issued to another by reason of its improper allowance by

---

General Requirements bulletin promulgated by the Commissioner to interpret the regulations dealing with the practice of patent agents before the PTO, are not subject to the notice and comment requirements of 5 U.S.C. §552. Interpretive rules enable agencies to explain ambiguous terms in legislative enactments without having to undertake cumbersome proceedings. *Premysler v. Lehman,* 71 F.3d 387, 37 USPQ2d 1057 (Fed. Cir. 1995).

[23]*Animal Legal Defense Fund v. Quigg,* 932 F.2d 920, 18 USPQ2d 1677 (Fed. Cir. 1991). The court held that the PTO Notice indicating that nonhuman animals can constitute patentable subject matter was interpretative and did not require notice of proposed rule making under §553 of the Administrative Procedure Act.

[24]*Sohio Trans. Co. v. United States,* 766 F.2d 499 (Fed. Cir. 1985).

[25]*Consumer Prod. Div., SCM Corp. v. Silver Reed Am., Inc.,* 753 F.2d 1033 (Fed. Cir. 1985).

[26]*Connolly v. Department of Justice,* 766 F.2d 507 (Fed. Cir. 1985).

[27]*In re Nielson,* 816 F.2d 1562, 2 USPQ2d 1525 (Fed. Cir. 1987).

[28]*Patlex Corp. v. Mossinghoff,* 771 F.2d 480, 226 USPQ 985 (Fed. Cir. 1985).

[29]*Alder v. United States,* 785 F.2d 1004 (Fed. Cir. 1986). However, where a procedural right of review is defined by statute, a party is entitled to it only if jurisdiction is properly invoked. *Rose v. Department of Health,* 721 F.2d 355 (Fed. Cir. 1983).

the PTO. A remedy must await confrontation with the patent owner.[30] The federal administrative process of examining and issuing patents, including proceedings before the PTO's boards, is not subject to collateral review in terms of the common law tort of abuse of process. The conduct of litigants in administrative proceedings is not remediable by state action in tort, at least unless it is shown that the entire federal agency action is a sham. A contrary rule would in effect create another forum for litigating issues arising from the administrative process, or a new system of judicial overview of actions before agencies.[31]

The finality concept of district court litigation, requiring both liability and damages to be resolved before an appeal, is not necessarily applicable to agency board proceedings. The agency's characterization of a decision is not determinative of the finality issue, and the relevant statutes outlining the required administrative procedures must be examined. Where an appeal would not disrupt the administrative process, in that there is nothing more for the agency board to do, the reviewing court has jurisdiction.[32] Ordinarily, appellate courts refuse to consider issues not raised before an administrative agency. Objections to the proceedings of an administrative agency must be made while it has an opportunity for correction in order to raise issues reviewable by the courts. A corollary is that the issue must be raised with sufficient specificity and clarity that the tribunal is aware that it must decide the issue, and in sufficient time that the agency can do so.[33] The court recognizes that an agency tribunal must have an opportunity to consider procedural deficiencies prior to an appeal to a court. However, that rule does not apply to substantive questions that are raised by the agency tribunal sua sponte. The party need not request reconsideration prior to seeking court review.[34]

Orderly procedure and good administration require that objections to the proceedings of an administrative agency be made while it has opportunity for correction in order to raise issues reviewable by the courts. When a party to such a proceeding fails to assert an issue during that proceeding, other parties to the proceeding are not given notice and an opportunity to present arguments before the agency; moreover, the agency is not afforded the opportunity to consider the issue in the first instance. Thus, simple fairness to those who are engaged in the tasks of administration, and to litigants, requires as a general rule that courts should not overturn administrative decisions unless the administrative body not only has erred but

---

[30]*Syntex (U.S.A.) Inc. v. United States PTO,* 882 F.2d 1570, 11 USPQ2d 1866 (Fed. Cir. 1989).

[31]*Abbott Labs. v. Brennan,* 952 F.2d 1346, 21 USPQ2d 1192 (Fed. Cir. 1992).

[32]*Dewey Elec. Corp. v. United States,* 803 F.2d 650 (Fed. Cir. 1986).

[33]*Wallace v. Department of Air Force,* 879 F.2d 829 (Fed. Cir. 1989).

[34]*In re Evanega,* 829 F.2d 1110, 4 USPQ2d 1249 (Fed. Cir. 1987).

erred against objection made at the time appropriate under its practice.[35]

When a court reviews an agency's construction of a statute that it administers, it is confronted with two questions. First, always, is the question whether Congress has directly spoken to the precise issue at hand. If the intent of Congress is clear, that is the end of the matter, for the court, as well as the agency, must give effect to the unambiguously expressed intent of Congress. If, however, the court determines Congress has not directly addressed the precise issue, the court does not simply impose its own construction on the statute, as would be necessary in the absence of an administrative interpretation. Rather, if the statute is silent or ambiguous with respect to the particularly issue, the question for the court to decide is whether the agency's view is based on a permissible construction of the statute.[36]

The scope of review of the validity of an administrative regulation is limited. As long as the regulation reasonably implements the purpose of the legislation and is not inconsistent with any constitutional or specific statutory provision, the court has no basis on which to overturn it. The court cannot substitute its judgment for that of the agency with respect to the determination of which particular requirement will best serve the statutory purpose.[37] For example, the PTO operates in accordance with detailed rules and regulations, including those set out in the *Manual of Patent Examining Procedure*, which is available to the public and describes procedures on which the public can rely. The standard for review is whether such rules or procedures are within the PTO's statutory authority, are reasonably related to the purposes of the enabling legislation, and do no violence to due process.[38] By the same token, an agency's interpretation of a statute need not be the only reasonable interpretation, or even the one that the court views as the most reasonable.[39]

Of course, where an agency undertakes administrative action without stating reasons therefor, a court may set aside such action.[40] District courts may direct an agency to perform its duty. Before a writ of mandamus may properly issue, however, three elements must exist: (1) a clear right in the plaintiff to the relief sought; (2) a clear duty on the part of the agency to do the act in question; and (3) no other adequate remedy available.[41]

---

[35]*Checkpoint Sys., Inc. v. United States ITC*, 54 F.3d 756, 35 USPQ2d 1042 (Fed. Cir. 1995).

[36]*Wassenaar v. Office of Personnel Management*, 21 F.3d 1090 (Fed. Cir. 1994).

[37]*Morgan v. Office of Personnel Management*, 773 F.2d 282 (Fed. Cir. 1985); *Melamine Chem., Inc. v. United States*, 732 F.2d 924 (Fed. Cir. 1984).

[38]*Patlex Corp. v. Mossinghoff*, 758 F.2d 594, 225 USPQ 243 (Fed. Cir. 1985).

[39]*Consumer Prod. Div., SCM Corp. v. Silver Reed Am., Inc.*, 753 F.2d 1033 (Fed. Cir. 1985). See also *Kelley v. Department of Labor*, 812 F.2d 1378 (Fed. Cir. 1987).

[40]*Bacon v. Department of HUD*, 757 F.2d 265 (Fed. Cir. 1985).

[41]*Maier v. Orr*, 754 F.2d 973 (Fed. Cir. 1985). A similar statutory procedure is contemplated by 35 U.S.C. §145, which provides for a civil action in the District Court for the District of

Appellate standing is not necessarily limited to parties. A person who is within the zone of interest affected by an administrative determination may be able to appeal it.[42]

The Supreme Court has now made it clear that the Federal Circuit is to review decisions of the PTO using the review framework of the Administrative Procedure Act, 5 U.S.C. §706. Thus, the less stringent APA court/agency standards (arbitrary, capricious, abuse of discretion, or unsupported by substantial evidence) must be applied, rather than the somewhat stricter court/court standard of clear error.[43]

Evidentiary rules. The general rule is that administrative agencies like the PTO are not bound by the rules of evidence that govern judicial proceedings. Agencies may provide for the application of evidence rules, as the PTO has done in patent interference and public use proceedings, both of which are inter partes in nature. However, the PTO has not made any special provision for evidence rules during ex parte examination.[44]

It has long been settled that hearsay may be used in administrative proceedings and may be treated as substantial evidence, even without corroboration, if to a reasonable mind, the circumstances are such as to lend it credence.[45] In administrative cases, circumstantial evidence can be used to prove the elements of a charge, including the element of intent.[46] Preponderance of the evidence, with respect to the burden of proof in administrative actions, means the greater weight of evidence—evidence that is more convincing than the evidence offered in opposition to it.[47] The determination of the credibility of witnesses is within the discretion of the presiding official who heard their testimony and saw their demeanor.[48] A statute setting rules or procedure and assigning burdens to litigants in a court trial does not automatically become applicable to proceedings before the PTO.[49]

Preclusion. The same principles of judicial efficiency that justify application of the doctrine of collateral estoppel in judicial proceedings

---

Columbia against the PTO Commissioner by a dissatisfied patent applicant. District court review of decisions of the PTO Commissioner relating to applications for patent term extension under 35 U.S.C. §156 is governed by the Administrative Procedure Act, 5 U.S.C. §706(2)(A). *Glaxo Oper. UK Ltd. v. Quigg,* 894 F.2d 392, 13 USPQ2d 1628 (Fed. Cir. 1990).

[42]*LSI Computer Sys., Inc. v. United States ITC,* 832 F.2d 588, 4 USPQ2d 1705 (Fed. Cir. 1987).

[43]*Dickinson v. Zurko,* 527 U.S. 150, 50 USPQ2d 1930 (1999).

[44]*In re Epstein,* 32 F.3d 1559, 31 USPQ2d 1817 (Fed. Cir. 1994). The court held in this case that it is not appropriate in ex parte prosecution to require a strict adherence to the rules of evidence regarding hearsay.

[45]*Hayes v. Department of Navy,* 727 F.2d 1535 (Fed. Cir. 1984).

[46]*DeWitt v. Department of Navy,* 747 F.2d 1442 (Fed. Cir. 1984).

[47]*Hale v. Department of Transp.,* 772 F.2d 882 (Fed. Cir. 1985).

[48]*Griessenauer v. Department of Energy,* 754 F.2d 361 (Fed. Cir. 1985). The appellant admitted that if the court accepted the presiding official's credibility determinations, there was no basis for reversal. In view of this, the appeal was frivolous.

[49]*In re Etter,* 756 F.2d 852, 225 USPQ 1 (Fed. Cir. 1985). Nor can it acquire an independent evidentiary role in any proceeding.

also justify its application in quasijudicial proceedings before administrative agencies.[50] Thus an administrative review board, like other quasijudicial tribunals deciding on the basis of an adversary, litigated record, can apply the doctrine of issue preclusion in appropriate circumstances[51] and perhaps judicial estoppel as well.[52]

Litigation and exhaustion of remedies. The doctrine of primary jurisdiction does not require a court to refer a question to an agency where the agency has declined to decide the precise question on a prior reference by the court. Primary jurisdiction is not a doctrine of futility.[53] Similarly, a party bringing a facial challenge to agency rules or regulations may not need, in certain instances, to await final agency action or to exhaust administrative remedies in order to mount the challenge. But the general rule is that the requirements of finality and exhaustion are not waived with respect to "as applied" challenges, where the litigant contests the application of the provision to its particular situation. This is in part due to judicial economy, and in part to the need for a well-developed record including appropriate findings of fact so that the court can determine how the challenged provision has been applied to specific facts.[54]

Legal conclusions of an agency tribunal having expertise are helpful to the court, even if not compelling.[55] On the other hand, the mental process of an agency official is not subject to inquiry in a judicial or administrative proceeding.[56] Of course, the policy of an administrative agency faced with specific tasks and deadlines cannot control a trial court's discretion in managing the litigation before it.[57]

There is no principle that precludes the government from settling, upon whatever terms it deems suitable, cases in which it determines that the likelihood of success is so low as to make continued litigation inappropriate. The decision whether to settle a particular case and upon what terms is a matter particularly within the discretion of the agency conducting the litigation.[58]

Spontaneous administrative duplication of the work of one agency by another, to avoid "mischief" if the first agency erred, should not

---

[50]*Graybill v. United States Postal Serv.,* 782 F.2d 1567 (Fed. Cir. 1986).

[51]*Thomas v. General Servs. Admin.,* 794 F.2d 661 (Fed. Cir. 1986).

[52]*Data Gen. Corp. v. Johnson,* 78 F.3d 1556 (Fed. Cir. 1996).

[53]*Skaw v. United States,* 740 F.2d 932 (Fed. Cir. 1984).

[54]*Patlex Corp. v. Mossinghoff,* 771 F.2d 480, 226 USPQ 985 (Fed. Cir. 1985). The fact that regulations may be held void does not necessarily require that the administrative proceeding be stayed pending the court litigation. Here, although the court held that the so-called rule of doubt reexamination regulations were void, it would not order a stay absent a showing that the PTO relied upon the rule of doubt in ordering reexamination.

[55]*Erickson Air Crane Co. v. United States,* 731 F.2d 810 (Fed. Cir. 1984).

[56]*Western Elec. Co. v. Piezo Tech., Inc.,* 860 F.2d 428, 8 USPQ2d 1853 (Fed. Cir. 1988); *Bacon v. Department of HUD,* 757 F.2d 265 (Fed. Cir. 1985).

[57]*U.S. Steel Corp. v. United States,* 730 F.2d 1465 (Fed. Cir. 1984).

[58]*Bergh v. Department of Transp.,* 794 F.2d 1575 (Fed. Cir. 1986).

be permitted. An authorization for such duplicative effort cannot be inferred or implied.[59]

§18.2 Statutory Interpretation

A statute is by definition the law to be followed—not disregarded, effectively repealed, rewritten, or overruled—in the federal courts. It is improper to diminish the effect of a statute by judicial legislation.[60] Judicial power is never exercised for the purpose of giving effect to the will of the judge; it is always for the purpose of giving effect to the will of the legislature or, in other words, to the will of the law.[61] If a law as it has been written by Congress creates anomalous situations, then it is for Congress to decide whether to change the law.[62] The remedy for any dissatisfaction with the results in particular cases lies with Congress and not the court. Congress may amend the statute; the court may not.[63] On the other hand, a law may be amended, superseded, or rescinded by another law, but not by subsequent legislative history. It is the function of the courts not the legislature to say what a previously enacted statute means.[64]

The starting point in interpreting any act of Congress is the text of the statute itself. The words of a statute are deemed to have their plain meaning in the lexicon of the subject matter of the legislation. When the statutory text is clear and when the legislative intent is implemented by the statute, that ends the inquiry. Should the statutory text be afflicted by ambiguity in meaning or in application to a particular case, the legislative history can often provide useful guidance. Only in the rare case, when the literal application of a statute will produce a result demonstrably at odds with the intention of its drafters, should a statute be construed in departure from its plain language.[65] Equitable considerations in a particular case are inappro-

---

[59]*Lannom Mfg. Co. v. United States ITC,* 799 F.2d 1572, 231 USPQ 32 (Fed. Cir. 1986). Thus there is no warrant for the ITC to ignore the presumption that the PTO properly did its job in granting a patent. *Id.*

[60]*In re Mark Indus.,* 751 F.2d 1219, 224 USPQ 521 (Fed. Cir. 1984).

[61]*Panduit Corp. v. Dennison Mfg. Co.,* 810 F.2d 1561, 1 USPQ2d 1593 (Fed. Cir. 1987).

[62]*Studiengesellschaft Kohle v. Northern Petrochem. Co.,* 784 F.2d 351, 228 USPQ 837 (Fed. Cir. 1986).

[63]*Reid v. Department of Commerce,* 793 F.2d 277 (Fed. Cir. 1986). Stare decisis has special force in the area of statutory interpretation, for here the legislative power is implicated, and Congress remains free to alter what a court has done. *In re Zurko,* 142 F.3d 1447, 46 USPQ2d 1691 (Fed. Cir. 1998), *rev'd on other grounds, Dickinson v. Zurko,* 527 U.S. 150, 50 USPQ2d 1930 (1999).

[64]*Madison Galleries, Ltd. v. United States,* 870 F.2d 627 (Fed. Cir. 1989).

[65]*Genentech, Inc. v. Eli Lilly & Co.,* 998 F.2d 931, 27 USPQ2d 1241 (Fed. Cir. 1993). The starting point in every case involving construction of a statute is the language itself. *VE Holding Corp. v. Johnson Gas Appliance Co.,* 917 F.2d 1574, 16 USPQ2d 1614 (Fed. Cir. 1990); *Madison Galleries, Ltd. v. United States,* 870 F.2d 627 (Fed. Cir. 1989).

priate in interpreting a statute.[66] Words will be interpreted as taking their ordinary, contemporary, common meaning.[67]

The court first looks to the statute for any express definitions of the key terms, and if none are found, then to see whether the terms can fairly be said to have a plain, nonambiguous meaning.[68]Congress may define terms in a statute, but is not required to define each and every word in a piece of legislation in order to express clearly its will. A phrase appearing in the context of a statute may be unambiguous where it has clearly accepted meaning in both legislative and judicial practice, even though it is not explicitly defined by the statutory text. Indeed, terms are defined in statutes often for the very reasons that they would be ambiguous without a statutory definition. That a term is not defined in a statute does not mean that the term is per se ambiguous.[69]

Where a statute states what a term means then all other meanings not stated are excluded.[70] Nonetheless, although there is a natural presumption that identical words used in different parts of the same act are intended to have the same meaning, it is not unusual for the same word to be used with different meanings in the same act, and there is no rule of statutory construction that precludes the courts from giving to the word the meaning that the legislature intended it should have in each instance.[71] The doctrine of noscitur a sociis permits the court to ascertain the meaning of ambiguous terms by reference to the terms with which they are associated in the statute or regulations.[72]

Statutory analysis requires first that the court look to the express language of the statute to determine its meaning. If, in a given case, the words of the statute do not provide an answer, then a court has no choice but to fill in the interstices.[73] But if it is plain and unequivocal on its face, there is usually no need to resort to the legislative history underlying the statute.[74] While legislative history may aid the court's

---

[66]*Unimed, Inc. v. Quigg,* 888 F.2d 826, 12 USPQ2d 1644 (Fed. Cir. 1989).

[67]*Hoechst-Roussel Pharm., Inc. v. Lehman,* 109 F.3d 756, 42 USPQ2d 1220 (Fed. Cir. 1997); *Ethicon v. Quigg,* 849 F.2d 1422, 7 USPQ2d 1152 (Fed. Cir. 1988). A court must give effect, if possible, to every word of the statute. *Unimed, Inc. v. Quigg,* 888 F.2d 826, 12 USPQ2d 1644 (Fed. Cir. 1989).

[68]*UNR Indus., Inc. v. United States,* 911 F.2d 654 (Fed. Cir. 1990). The court must refer to the definitions specifically provided in the statute itself. *Ulmet v. United States,* 822 F.2d 1079 (Fed. Cir. 1987).

[69]*Gardner v. Brown,* 5 F.3d 1456 (Fed. Cir. 1993).

[70]*Johns-Manville Corp. v. United States,* 855 F.2d 1556 (Fed. Cir. 1988).

[71]*Nike Inc. v. Walmart Stores Inc.,* 138 F.3d 1437, 46 USPQ2d 1001 (Fed. Cir. 1998).

[72]*Auto-Ordnance Corp. v. United States,* 822 F.2d 1566 (Fed. Cir. 1987).

[73]*VE Holding Corp. v. Johnson Gas Appliance Co.,* 917 F.2d 1574, 16 USPQ2d 1614 (Fed. Cir. 1990). Statutory interpretation begins with the language of the statute. If the statute clearly expresses Congress's intent, the court must give effect to that intent. But if it be determined that Congress has not directly addressed the issue, then it must be considered whether the proposed interpretation is permissible. *Texas Instr., Inc. v. United States ITC,* 988 F.2d 1165, 26 USPQ2d 1018 (Fed. Cir. 1993).

[74]*Reid v. Department of Commerce,* 793 F.2d 277 (Fed. Cir. 1986); *Darsigny v. Office of Personnel Management,* 787 F.2d 1555 (Fed. Cir. 1986). In the absence of persuasive reasons

understanding of the function and purposes of a statute, and in cases of doubt assist in interpretation of the language, when the legislature has clearly spoken the law the court's duty is to enforce it as written.[75]

Thus the Federal Circuit recognizes and applies the "plain meaning" rule for construing explicit statutory language. When the terms of the statute are unambiguous, judicial inquiry is complete except in rare and exceptional circumstances.[76] The plain meaning rule, although often lumped with other rules for statutory construction, also has important structural effect beyond its rhetorical value. Honestly applied, it tells a court what not to look at—legislative debates, committee reports, newspaper commentary, and other "aids" to policy development. The meaning of the law is what the words say it is.[77] Absent a very clear legislative intent, the plain meaning will prevail.[78]

The function of the court is then limited to enforcing the statute according to its terms, unless a literal interpretation would lead to an incongruous result. For example, if a literal reading of the statute would impute to Congress an irrational purpose or would thwart the obvious purposes of the statute or would lead to a result at variance with the policy of the legislation as a whole, then literal interpretation will be eschewed in favor of resort to the legislative history to ascertain

---

to the contrary, words in a statute are to be given their ordinary and common meaning. *In re Canadian Pac. Ltd.*, 754 F.2d 992, 224 USPQ 971 (Fed. Cir. 1985). The search for clarity is an integral part of statutory construction. *Lindahl v. Office of Personnel Management*, 718 F.2d 391 (Fed. Cir. 1983). Where the words of a statutory provision are clear and the provision is internally consistent with the remainder of the statute, preference must be given to the plain meaning of the statute. However, where other provisions of the statute raise significant questions about the plain meaning of a subsection, it is necessary to analyze the statute as a whole and to consult the legislative history. *Horner v. Merit Sys. Prot. Bd.*, 815 F.2d 668 (Fed. Cir. 1987). Indeed, even when the plain meaning of the statutory language in question would resolve the issue before the court, the legislative history should usually be examined at least to determine whether there is a clearly expressed legislative intention contrary to the statutory language. But this analysis is not conducted from a neutral viewpoint; rather, given the plain meaning, there must appear an extraordinary showing of contrary intention. *Glaxo Oper. UK Ltd. v. Quigg*, 894 F.2d 392, 13 USPQ2d 1628 (Fed. Cir. 1990). See also *Amgen, Inc. v. United States ITC*, 902 F.2d 1532, 14 USPQ2d 1734 (Fed. Cir. 1990). Although a statute clear on its face does not warrant resort to history, inquiry is proper to determine whether ambiguity has invaded an apparently clear text. *Nike Inc. v. Walmart Stores Inc.*, 138 F.3d 1437, 46 USPQ2d 1001 (Fed. Cir. 1998).

[75]*Telectronics Pacing Sys., Inc. v. Ventritex, Inc.*, 982 F.2d 1520, 25 USPQ2d 1196 (Fed. Cir. 1992).

[76]*Hoechst-Roussel Pharm., Inc. v. Lehman*, 109 F.3d 756, 42 USPQ2d 1220 (Fed. Cir. 1997); *Fisons PLC v. Quigg*, 876 F.2d 99, 10 USPQ2d 1869 (Fed. Cir. 1989); *LSI Computer Sys., Inc. v. United States ITC*, 832 F.2d 588, 4 USPQ2d 1705 (Fed. Cir. 1987).

[77]*UNR Indus., Inc. v. United States*, 911 F.2d 654 (Fed. Cir. 1990). Where the plain language of the statute would settle the question before the court, the legislative history is examined with hesitation to determine whether there is a clearly expressed legislative intention contrary to the statutory language. *Madison Galleries, Ltd. v. United States*, 870 F.2d 627 (Fed. Cir. 1989). See also *Hoechst Aktiengesellschaft v. Quigg*, 917 F.2d 522, 16 USPQ2d 1549 (Fed. Cir. 1990); *Unimed, Inc. v. Quigg*, 888 F.2d 826, 12 USPQ2d 1644 (Fed. Cir. 1989).

[78]*Johns-Manville Corp. v. United States*, 855 F.2d 1556 (Fed. Cir. 1988); *Martin J. Simko Constr., Inc. v. United States*, 852 F.2d 540 (Fed. Cir. 1988); *Ethicon v. Quigg*, 849 F.2d 1422, 7 USPQ2d 1152 (Fed. Cir. 1988); *Ulmet v. United States*, 822 F.2d 1079 (Fed. Cir. 1987). Indeed, the court has said only the most extraordinary showing of contrary intentions from the legislative history would justify a limitation on the plain meaning of the statutory language. *LSI Computer Sys., Inc. v. United States ITC*, 832 F.2d 588, 4 USPQ2d 1705 (Fed. Cir. 1987).

the intent of Congress.[79] Although recourse to the legislative history of a statute is unnecessary in light of the plain meaning of the text, the court may look to the history to determine whether there is a clearly expressed legislative intention contrary to the statutory language. But because the language is clear, the court cannot analyze the history from a neutral viewpoint; there must be an extraordinarily strong showing of clear legislative intent in order to convince it that Congress meant other than what it ultimately said.[80] An absurd construction of a statutory provision should be avoided. Where no one of conflicting interpretations completely harmonizes a statutory provision, the goal is to find that interpretation that can most fairly be said to be imbedded in the statute, in the sense of being most harmonious with its scheme and with the general purposes manifested by Congress.[81] Certainly, a statutory construction that would impute a useless act to Congress must be viewed as unsound and rejected.[82] Congress does not legislate unnecessarily and thus an interpretation that would render a statute redundant is to be avoided.[83]

Congressional intent is therefore the touchstone of statutory interpretation.[84] When Congress intends to grant a right of action, it does so clearly and unambiguously.[85] Similarly, when Congress wishes to change historic common law principles, it must "say so in explicit and even shameless language."[86] In interpreting a statute, the court should look to what Congress really did, and not to conflicting comments of a few congressmen.[87] Where Congress repeatedly revisits a

---

[79]*Reid v. Department of Commerce,* 793 F.2d 277 (Fed. Cir. 1986). See also *VE Holding Corp. v. Johnson Gas Appliance Co.,* 917 F.2d 1574, 16 USPQ2d 1614 (Fed. Cir. 1990).

[80]*Gardner v. Brown,* 5 F.3d 1456 (Fed. Cir. 1993).

[81]*Witco Chem. Corp. v. United States,* 742 F.2d 615 (Fed. Cir. 1984). Sometimes the literal language of some part of a statute may seemingly contradict the intent of the statute as a whole, but absent a clear-cut contrary legislative intent, the statutory language is ordinarily regarded as conclusive. *Madison Galleries, Ltd. v. United States,* 870 F.2d 627 (Fed. Cir. 1989). Headings are often helpful in interpreting an ambiguous text, but they cannot of themselves operate to take a significant portion of the textual subject matter out of a statute. They cannot limit or undo that which the text makes plain. *Genentech, Inc. v. Eli Lilly & Co.,* 998 F.2d 931, 27 USPQ2d 1241 (Fed. Cir. 1993).

[82]*South Corp. v. United States,* 690 F.2d 1368 (Fed. Cir. 1982).

[83]*Kimberly-Clark Corp. v. Procter & Gamble Distrib. Co.,* 973 F.2d 911, 23 USPQ2d 1921 (Fed. Cir. 1992).

[84]*Lindahl v. Office of Personnel Management,* 718 F.2d 391 (Fed. Cir. 1983). In an interesting case, the court found that both the statutory language and the legislative history were ambiguous. What was clear, however, was that Congress intended to overturn a previous Federal Circuit decision, and the court therefore construed the statutory language to give effect to that intention. *Eli Lilly & Co. v. Medtronic, Inc.,* 872 F.2d 402, 10 USPQ2d 1304 (Fed. Cir. 1989).

[85]*Lannom Mfg. Co. v. United States ITC,* 799 F.2d 1572, 231 USPQ 32 (Fed. Cir. 1986).

[86]*Roche Prods., Inc. v. Bolar Pharm. Co.,* 733 F.2d 858, 221 USPQ 937 (Fed. Cir. 1984). The issue at hand was whether injunctive relief under 35 U.S.C. §283 was mandatory rather than discretionary. When Congress borrows a common law term in a statute, absent a contrary instruction it is presumed to adopt the term's widely accepted common law meaning. *Mars, Inc. v. Kabushiki-Kaisha Nippon Conlux,* 24 F.3d 1368, 30 USPQ2d 1621 (Fed. Cir. 1994).

[87]*Lindahl v. Office of Personnel Management,* 718 F.2d 391 (Fed. Cir. 1983). Margin notes are generally not used in interpreting statutes, but they may be referred to as indicating the

statute, the courts should be slow to create additional exceptions.[88] The general rule is that retrospective operation will not be given to a statute unless such be the unequivocal and inflexible import of the terms, and the manifest intent of the legislature.[89]

A degree of deference is always due the interpretation of a statute by the agency or officer charged with its administration or enforcement.[90] This is so even though that interpretation of the statute is not the only one the court views as reasonable. Even so, the courts are the final authorities on issues of statutory construction and must reject an administrative construction inconsistent with a statutory mandate or a policy Congress has sought to implement.[91]

An agency's construction need not be the only reasonable interpretation or the one that the court views as the most reasonable. Rather, a court must give it deference so long as it is drawn from among alternative reasonable interpretations, even if the court might have preferred another. Giving deference, however, does not entirely dispense with meaningful review. To the contrary, an agency's interpretation should not stand if it is unreasonable. All statutes must be construed in light of their purpose and a reading of them that would lead to absurd results is to be avoided when they can be given a reasonable application consistent with their words and purpose.[92]

As a general rule, a long-standing interpretation of a statute by an agency charged with its administration must be upheld if reasonable.[93] An agency interpretation that conflicts with the same agency's earlier interpretation is entitled to considerably less deference than a consistently held agency view.[94]

Conflicting statutory provisions present special problems. A statute must be interpreted to give effect to each of its provisions.[95] The

---

intention of Congress. *Motorola, Inc. v. United States,* 729 F.2d 765, 221 USPQ 297 (Fed. Cir. 1984). Post hoc statements of a congressional committee are not given much weight in determining legislative intent. Letters written by individual committee members years after enactment shed no light. *Riggsbee v. Bell,* 787 F.2d 1564 (Fed. Cir. 1986).

[88]*Lindahl v. Office of Personnel Management,* 718 F.2d 391 (Fed. Cir. 1983).

[89]*Genentech, Inc. v. Eli Lilly & Co.,* 998 F.2d 931, 27 USPQ2d 1241 (Fed. Cir. 1993).

[90]*Nutrition 21 v. United States,* 930 F.2d 862, 18 USPQ2d 1351 (Fed. Cir. 1991) (considerable weight); *Kelley v. Department of Labor,* 812 F.2d 1378 (Fed. Cir. 1987) (substantial weight); *Wilson v. Turnage,* 791 F.2d 151 (Fed. Cir. 1986) (great deference); *Lisiecki v. Merit Sys. Prot. Bd.,* 769 F.2d 1558 (Fed. Cir. 1985) (some deference); *Burlington N. R.R. Co. v. United States,* 752 F.2d 627 (Fed. Cir. 1985) (great deference); *Smith-Corona Group v. United States,* 713 F.2d 1568 (Fed. Cir. 1983) (some deference). The court has indicated, however, that the rule applies only where the statutory language leaves a gap or is doubtful or ambiguous. *Glaxo Oper. UK Ltd. v. Quigg,* 894 F.2d 392, 13 USPQ2d 1628 (Fed. Cir. 1990).

[91]*Hoechst Aktiengesellschaft v. Quigg,* 917 F.2d 522, 16 USPQ2d 1549 (Fed. Cir. 1990); *Ethicon v. Quigg,* 849 F.2d 1422, 7 USPQ2d 1152 (Fed. Cir. 1988); *Chula Vista Sch. Dist. v. Bennett,* 824 F.2d 1573 (Fed. Cir. 1987); *Ulmet v. United States,* 822 F.2d 1079 (Fed. Cir. 1987); *Lisiecki v. Merit Sys. Prot. Bd.,* 769 F.2d 1558 (Fed. Cir. 1985). Compare *Fisons PLC v. Quigg,* 876 F.2d 99, 10 USPQ2d 1869 (Fed. Cir. 1989).

[92]*Wassenaar v. Office of Personnel Management,* 21 F.3d 1090 (Fed. Cir. 1994).

[93]*Horner v. Andrzjewski,* 811 F.2d 571 (Fed. Cir. 1987).

[94]*Madison Galleries, Ltd. v. United States,* 870 F.2d 627 (Fed. Cir. 1989).

[95]*Genentech, Inc. v. Eli Lilly & Co.,* 998 F.2d 931, 27 USPQ2d 1241 (Fed. Cir. 1993). Statutes in pari materia are to be construed together. *Imazio Nursery, Inc. v. Dania Greenhouses,* 69 F.3d 1560, 36 USPQ2d 1673 (Fed. Cir. 1995).

normal assumption, where Congress amends one part of a law, leaving another part unchanged, is that the two were designed to function as parts of an integrated whole, and each should be given as full a play as possible.[96] Simply because a later enacted statute affects in some way an earlier statute is poor reason to ask the court to rewrite the earlier one.[97] Congress is presumed to be aware of an administrative or judicial interpretation of a statute and to adopt that interpretation when it reenacts a statute without change.[98] In cases of doubt, prior definitions may be helpful in determining congressional intent, but they cannot replace the definitions set forth or codified in the current statute.[99]

Repeals by implication are not favored and are permitted only to the extent of clear repugnancy.[100] There is no obligation on the part of Congress to demonstrate that it is aware of the consequences of its action; rather, laws are presumed to be passed with deliberation and with full knowledge of all existing ones on the subject. When two statutes are capable of coexistence, it is the duty of the courts to regard each as effective, absent expression of contrary congressional intention.[101] Similarity of two statutory schemes in one respect does not warrant eradication of purposefully designed differences in another.[102]

Where the only issue before a district court is one of statutory interpretation—a question of law—the appellate court independently determines the proper interpretation and need not defer to the district court.[103]

In a fascinating foray into the complexities of statutory interpretation, the Federal Circuit decided that the 1984 amendments to 35 U.S.C. §116 were retroactive despite a nonretroactivity provision in the enacting legislation. Section 116 was amended to provide that

---

[96]*Lovshin v. Department of Navy,* 767 F.2d 826 (Fed. Cir. 1985).

[97]*Roche Prods., Inc. v. Bolar Pharm. Co.,* 733 F.2d 858, 221 USPQ 937 (Fed. Cir. 1984).

[98]*Johns-Manville Corp. v. United States,* 855 F.2d 1556 (Fed. Cir. 1988). See also *VE Holding Corp. v. Johnson Gas Appliance Co.,* 917 F.2d 1574, 16 USPQ2d 1614 (Fed. Cir. 1990).

[99]*Ulmet v. United States,* 822 F.2d 1079 (Fed. Cir. 1987).

[100]*Lovshin v. Department of Navy,* 767 F.2d 826 (Fed. Cir. 1985); *Roche Prods., Inc. v. Bolar Pharm. Co.,* 733 F.2d 858, 221 USPQ 937 (Fed. Cir. 1984); *Lindahl v. Office of Personnel Management,* 718 F.2d 391 (Fed. Cir. 1983).

[101]*Roche Prods., Inc. v. Bolar Pharm. Co.,* 733 F.2d 858, 221 USPQ 937 (Fed. Cir. 1984). This is particularly true where a specific statute is asserted to have been superceded by a more general one. *Southwest Marine, Inc. v. United States,* 896 F.2d 532 (Fed. Cir. 1990). A specific statute prevails over a general one. *Lindahl v. Office of Personnel Management,* 718 F.2d 391 (Fed. Cir. 1983).

[102]*Warner Bros., Inc. v. United States ITC,* 787 F.2d 562, 229 USPQ 126, 127 (Fed. Cir. 1986).

[103]*Hoechst Aktiengesellschaft v. Quigg,* 917 F.2d 522, 16 USPQ2d 1549 (Fed. Cir. 1990); *Chula Vista Sch. Dist. v. Bennett,* 824 F.2d 1573 (Fed. Cir. 1987); *Glaxo Oper. UK Ltd. v. Quigg,* 894 F.2d 392, 13 USPQ2d 1628 (Fed. Cir. 1990). Statutory interpretation is a question of law that the Federal Circuit reviews de novo. *In re Portola Packaging, Inc.,* 110 F.3d 786, 42 USPQ2d 1295 (Fed. Cir. 1997); *Bristol-Myers Squibb Co. v. Royce Labs., Inc.,* 69 F.3d 1130, 36 USPQ2d 1641 (Fed. Cir. 1995); *Gardner v. Brown,* 5 F.3d 1456 (Fed. Cir. 1993); *In re Carlson,* 983 F.2d 1032, 25 USPQ2d 1207 (Fed. Cir. 1993).

each joint inventor need not have made a contribution to the subject matter of every claim in a patent. The enacting legislation provided that the amendments would not apply to litigation pending as of the date of enactment. However, the court found that there was a split among the regional circuits prior to the date of enactment—the "all claims" rule was not uniformly accepted as the substantive law at that time. Reasoning that it was doubtful that Congress intended the nonretroactivity provision of the enabling act to give a litigant a right to invoke the law of a particular circuit where there was a division of views on an issue, the court held that the nonretroactivity provision did not negate the applicability of amended §116 in cases pending on the enactment date.[104]

§18.3 Choice of Law

The Federal Circuit is confronted with two basic types of choice of law problems. The more traditional of the two arises from the familiar principle that state law issues are controlled by state law, to the extent the state has spoken.[105] Inasmuch as a federal district court is obliged to apply the conflict of laws rules of the state in which it sits,[106] the Federal Circuit must, on state law questions, be satisfied that the district court has correctly applied the forum state's choice of law rules to select the law of the proper state, and has also correctly discerned that law. Thus, once the forum's conflict rules have identified the proper state, a state unfair competition claim must be decided by looking to the law of that state as declared by its legislature in a statute or by its highest court in a decision. If there is no decision by that state's highest court, proper regard should be given relevant rulings of other courts of that state. Where no court of the state has spoken, the question is whether the district court properly predicted the applicable state law.[107]

The court decides in personam jurisdiction questions in patent infringement cases purely as a matter of federal law. The tort of patent infringement exists solely by virtue of federal statute and

---

[104]*Smithkline Diagnostics, Inc. v. Helena Labs. Corp.*, 859 F.2d 878, 8 USPQ2d 1468 (Fed. Cir. 1988).

[105]*Eaton Corp. v. Appliance Valves Corp.*, 790 F.2d 874, 229 USPQ 668 (Fed. Cir. 1986). See also *Teets v. Chromalloy Gas Turbine Corp.*, 83 F.3d 403, 38 USPQ2d 1695 (Fed. Cir. 1996).

[106]*Bradley v. Chiron Corp.*, 136 F.3d 1370, 45 USPQ2d 1819 (Fed. Cir. 1998); *Eaton Corp. v. Appliance Valves Corp.*, 790 F.2d 874, 229 USPQ 668 (Fed. Cir. 1986); *Syntex Ophthalmics, Inc. v. Novicky*, 745 F.2d 1423, 223 USPQ 695 (Fed. Cir. 1984). Where a prior state court judgment is involved in a federal suit, the district court should apply the law of state with respect to the preclusive effect of the judgment. *Syntex Ophthalmics, Inc. v. Novicky*, 767 F.2d 901, 226 USPQ 952 (Fed. Cir. 1985).

[107]*Litton Indus. Prods., Inc. v. Solid State Sys. Corp.*, 755 F.2d 158, 225 USPQ 34 (Fed. Cir. 1985). For example, in applying a state antitrust law it is reasonable to assume that a state court would look to how the federal antitrust laws have been applied. *Id.*

defining its contours inevitably entails the construction of that statute—not a state long-arm statute. The latter simply creates a general, procedural rule that torts committed in the state give rise to jurisdiction over potential defendants. It is not the source of the substantive right and does not purport to affect its scope or nature. So while the federal choice of law rule concerning personal jurisdiction requires the court to look to state law in the first instance, the character of the particular tort alleged requires a look back to federal law on the conceptualization of the tort and its situs.[108]

Where an inventor creates, builds, and uses a device in a particular state, the trade secrets laws of that state apply.[109] State passing-off claims are decided under the law of the forum state.[110] However, the propriety of a patentee's actions in giving notice of its patent rights is governed by federal statute and precedent and is not a matter of state tort law.[111] State law controls in matters of contract law and interpretation,[112] including interpretation of the provisions of a patent license agreement,[113] interpretation of an agreement settling a patent infringement case,[114] construction of the terms of an insurance policy,[115] and evaluating damages for breach of contract.[116]

That federal courts are to afford full faith and credit to judgments reached in state court proceedings is made clear in 28 U.S.C. §1738. The full faith and credit statute does not permit federal courts to employ their own rules of res judicata in determining the effects of state judgments. Rather, a federal court is to accept the rules chosen by the state in which the judgment is rendered. This remains true even though that judgment turned on construction of subject matter within the exclusive jurisdiction of the federal courts.[117]

Foreign law may also be pertinent. For example, one who owns land in a foreign country looks to the laws of that country to determine

---

[108]*North Am. Philips Corp. v. American Vending Sales, Inc.*, 35 F.3d 1576, 32 USPQ2d 1203 (Fed. Cir. 1994).

[109]*Lariscey v. United States*, 949 F.2d 1137, 20 USPQ2d 1845 (Fed. Cir. 1991).

[110]*Braun Inc. v. Dynamics Corp.*, 975 F.2d 815, 24 USPQ2d 1121 (Fed. Cir. 1992).

[111]*Mikohn Gaming Corp. v. Acres Gaming Inc.*, 165 F.3d 891, 49 USPQ2d 1308 (Fed. Cir. 1998).

[112]*American Med. Sys., Inc. v. Medical Eng'g Corp.*, 6 F.3d 1523, 28 USPQ2d 1321 (Fed. Cir. 1993). In *Bradley v. Chiron Corp.*, 136 F.3d 1370, 45 USPQ2d 1819 (Fed. Cir. 1998), the court was not impressed by an appellate argument that "federal common law" applies to contracts to which the government is a party.

[113]*Interspiro USA, Inc. v. Figgie Int'l, Inc.*, 18 F.3d 927, 30 USPQ2d 1070 (Fed. Cir. 1994).

[114]*Augustine Med. Inc. v. Progressive Dynamics Inc.*, 194 F.3d 1367, 52 USPQ2d 1515 (Fed. Cir. 1999); *Gjerlov v. Schuyler Labs., Inc.*, 131 F.3d 1016, 44 USPQ2d 1881 (Fed. Cir. 1997).

[115]*U.S. Test Inc. v. NDE Envtl. Corp.*, 196 F.3d 1376, 52 USPQ2d 1845 (Fed. Cir. 1999).

[116]*U.S. Valves Inc. v. Dray*, 212 F.3d 1368, 54 USPQ2d 1834, 1838 (Fed. Cir. 2).

[117]*MGA, Inc. v. General Motors Corp.*, 827 F.2d 729, 3 USPQ2d 1762 (Fed. Cir. 1987). See also *United Tech. Corp. v. Chromalloy Gas Turbine Corp.*, 189 F.3d 1338, 51 USPQ2d 1838 (Fed. Cir. 1999).

the incidents of ownership.[118] Foreign law can certainly be relevant to discovery disputes in this country.[119] When evaluating statements of counsel, due regard should be given for differences in foreign law.[120] In federal courts foreign law is a question of law to be determined by expert evidence or any other relevant source.[121]

The second fundamental choice of law problem faced by the Federal Circuit arises from its limited subject matter jurisdiction. The court applies regional circuit law, to the extent it can be discerned, on all but the substantive issues reserved especially to it, on the theory that a district court judge should not be expected to look over her or his shoulder to the law of the Federal Circuit, save as to those claims within the exclusive subject matter jurisdiction of the Federal Circuit.[122] In resolving such choice of law questions, the Federal Circuit considers the general policy of minimizing confusion and conflicts in the federal judicial system. Consistent with that policy, it applies the law of that circuit to which district court appeals normally lie, unless the issue pertains to or is unique to patent law.[123] Presumably those same concerns will prompt the regional federal circuit courts, when confronted with patent law issues, to look in turn to Federal Circuit precedents for guidance. Similarly, state courts confronted with federal law issues usually turn to the law of the appropriate federal court to aid in the resolution of those federal issues. While the prevailing view among the highest courts in the various states is that a state court is only bound as to the meaning of federal constitutional law and federal statutory law by interpretations of the Supreme Court, decisions of lower federal courts on issues of federal law are usually respected as persuasive, especially where uniform among the lower courts. Since Congress created the Federal Circuit in order to bring uniformity to the national law of patents, presumably the state courts confronted with issues of federal law relating to patents will

---

[118]*Langenegger v. United States,* 756 F.2d 1565 (Fed. Cir. 1985).

[119]*Cochran Consulting, Inc. v. Uwatec USA, Inc.,* 102 F.3d 1224, 41 USPQ2d 1161 (Fed. Cir. 1996).

[120]*Lindemann Maschinenfabrik v. American Hoist & Derrick Co.,* 730 F.2d 1452, 221 USPQ 481 (Fed. Cir. 1984); *Caterpillar Tractor Co. v. Berco, S.P.A.,* 714 F.2d 1110, 219 USPQ 185 (Fed. Cir. 1983).

[121]*Merck & Co. v. United States ITC,* 774 F.2d 483, 227 USPQ 779 (Fed. Cir. 1985).

[122]E.g., *Sun Studs, Inc. v. Applied Theory Assocs.,* 772 F.2d 1557, 227 USPQ 81 (Fed. Cir. 1985); *Bandag, Inc. v. Al Bolser's Tire Stores, Inc.,* 750 F.2d 903, 223 USPQ 982 (Fed. Cir. 1984). The subject is considered in detail in §17.2(b). This general precedent path can also lead to the application of state law. In *Sun Studs, Inc. v. Applied Theory Assocs.,* 772 F.2d 1557, 227 USPQ 81 (Fed. Cir. 1985), the enforceability of a settlement agreement, although arising in the context of a patent infringement case, was to be determined by reference to regional circuit law. The choice of law rules of the regional circuit dictated that the question was to be resolved under state rather than federal law. The route ultimately led to application of the statute of frauds of a particular state. Similarly, a license agreement is a contract governed by ordinary principles of state contract law. *Power Lift, Inc. v. Weatherford Nipple-Up Sys., Inc.,* 871 F.2d 1082, 10 USPQ2d 1464 (Fed. Cir. 1989).

[123]*Molins PLC v. Quigg,* 837 F.2d 1064, 5 USPQ2d 1526 (Fed. Cir. 1988).

therefore also look to the decisions of the Federal Circuit for guidance.[124] In the end result, it is the nature of the legal issue, rather than the court's statutory basis for subject matter jurisdiction, that determines choice of law in this context.[125]

§18.4 Constitutional Law

The case or controversy requirement for federal jurisdiction, together with the other doctrines that cluster about Article III of the Constitution to further define that requirement, such as standing, have been considered in detail in §§8.1(a)(ii) and (iii).[126] Similarly, the constitutional status of other judicial and quasijudicial bodies, such as the Court of Federal Claims and the ITC, is considered in §§11.1 and 11.2.[127] Also, due process considerations arising in the context of administrative actions and procedures have been dealt with in this chapter, in §18.1. Federal preemption, as a constitutional topic, is the subject of §1.4(c).

The declaration that an act of Congress is unconstitutional is the gravest and most delicate duty that a court is called upon to perform.[128] The Federal Circuit apparently has not yet had to exercise this difficult responsibility.[129]

Equal protection. It is well settled that where a statute does not burden fundamental rights or create classifications predicated on "suspect" criteria, it will not be invalidated on equal protection grounds unless the varying treatment of different groups or persons is so unrelated to the achievement of any combination of legitimate purposes that the court can only conclude the legislature's actions were irrational.[130]

---

[124]*Speedco, Inc. v. Estes,* 853 F.2d 909, 7 USPQ2d 1637 (Fed. Cir. 1988).

[125]*Sun Studs, Inc. v. Applied Theory Assocs.,* 772 F.2d 1557, 227 USPQ 81 (Fed. Cir. 1985).

[126]One of these, the political question doctrine, is rooted in concern for separation of powers. Although foreign affairs questions may make the courts uncomfortable, the Constitution mandates the role of the judiciary without regard to its comfort. *Langenegger v. United States,* 756 F.2d 1565 (Fed. Cir. 1985).

[127]See *Akzo N.V. v. United States ITC,* 808 F.2d 1471, 1 USPQ2d 1241 (Fed. Cir. 1986) (ITC); *United States v. Rush,* 804 F.2d 645 (Fed. Cir. 1986) (Claims Court).

[128]*Patlex Corp. v. Mossinghoff,* 758 F.2d 594, 225 USPQ 243 (Fed. Cir. 1985).

[129]The court has held the Magistrates Act (28 U.S.C. §§631–639) constitutional. *D.L. Auld Co. v. Chroma Graphics Corp.,* 753 F.2d 1029, 224 USPQ 737 (Fed. Cir. 1985). Also, the reexamination statute is not invalid as a deprivation of the right to a jury trial, or of the right to have patent validity determined by an Article III court. *Patlex Corp. v. Mossinghoff,* 758 F.2d 594, 225 USPQ 243 (Fed. Cir. 1985). Executive Order 10096, which governs ownership of inventions made by government employees, does not result in a taking of property without due process and is therefore valid under the Fifth Amendment. *Heinemann v. United States,* 796 F.2d 451, 230 USPQ 430 (Fed. Cir. 1986).

[130]*Kester v. Horner,* 778 F.2d 1565 (Fed. Cir. 1985).

Seventh Amendment. A right to a jury trial in federal court must arise out of the Seventh Amendment or be granted by a federal statute. The Seventh Amendment preserves the right to a jury trial in those actions in which the right existed at common law when the amendment was adopted in 1791.[131] This topic is discussed in detail in §10.3(a).

Sovereign immunity. Sovereign immunity shields the United States from suit unless immunity is waived. When Congress waives immunity, a plaintiff has a right to trial by jury only where that right is one of the terms of the government's consent to be sued. Thus a party in an action against the United States has a right to trial by jury only where Congress has affirmatively and unambiguously granted that right by statute.[132] When Congress authorizes suit against the United States, the terms of the statute waiving sovereign immunity define the extent of the court's authority to consider claims for money against the government.[133] The government has waived immunity with respect to monetary sanctions for discovery abuses in cases over which the Court of Federal Claims has jurisdiction.[134]

The general rule is that when a government entity has waived its immunity from federal judicial authority by taking legal action in federal court, the person charged can raise all counterclaims that arise from the same transaction or events. A counterclaim must be compulsory in order to be raised as of right in an area of law in which the government is otherwise immune from suit. Also, it must be in recoupment of the government claim. Recoupment is an established remedy based on the principle that neither sovereign immunity nor principles of federalism prevents a private person from raising, in defense and setoff, claims that arise from the same transaction or occurrence on which the state is seeking to recover damages.[135]

---

[131]*Washington Int'l Ins. Co. v. United States,* 863 F.2d 877 (Fed. Cir. 1988).

[132]*Washington Int'l Ins. Co. v. United States,* 863 F.2d 877 (Fed. Cir. 1988). Litigants in the Court of International Trade are not granted a right to a jury trial under 28 U.S.C. §1876, which is an enabling statute that simply sets forth procedures to be followed when a Court of International Trade action is tried before a jury. *Id.* Under the doctrine of sovereign immunity, the United States cannot be held liable for costs without its consent. *Johns-Manville Corp. v. United States,* 893 F.2d 324 (Fed. Cir. 1989).

[133]*Hart v. United States,* 910 F.2d 814 (Fed. Cir. 1990). See also *Broughton Lumber Co. v. Yeutter,* 939 F.2d 1547 (Fed. Cir. 1991). In *Lariscey v. United States,* 949 F.2d 1137, 20 USPQ2d 1845 (Fed. Cir. 1991), the court entertained a Fifth Amendment "taking" claim by a federal prison inmate against the federal government for misappropriation of an invention made by the inmate in prison.

[134]*M.A. Mortenson Co. v. United States,* 996 F.2d 1177 (Fed. Cir. 1993).

[135]*Genentech, Inc. v. Eli Lilly & Co.,* 998 F.2d 931, 27 USPQ2d 1241 (Fed. Cir. 1993). Here, the plaintiff had sued the state for a declaration of patent invalidity and noninfringement, and also raised many other claims, some of which could be said to be compulsory counterclaims to a state claim of patent infringement. Although the state had not yet answered the complaint, the court reasoned that it must counterclaim for patent infringement or be forever barred. Thus, upon remand, if the state chooses to make its claim for infringement, the various antitrust and state law counts of plaintiff's complaint that meet the criteria of defenses and compulsory

State immunity from suit in federal court is founded upon the fundamental relationship and constitutional balance between the federal government and the states. In general, without the state's consent a federal court is without power to entertain a suit by a private person against the state. But there are qualifications to the reach of the Eleventh Amendment. Congress may abrogate state immunity in specific circumstances under the Fourteenth Amendment or the Commerce Clause.[136] A state may also waive its immunity, in its entirety or as to any specified agency, action, or event. This can be done by state statute, state constitution, or clear state action. But an authorization to an arm of the state to sue and be sued is not presumed to include suit in federal court.[137]

Thus, when a state maintains a claim in federal court it thereby consents to the exercise of federal judicial authority over that claim to the full extent required for its complete determination. The principles of federalism underlying the Eleventh Amendment do not prevent a person from defending against an action by a state. Defenses such as unenforceability based on antitrust violation, or contract-based estoppel, are available to an accused infringer in responding to a claim of infringement of a state-owned patent.[138]

The state action doctrine, although grounded on general principles of federalism, relates specifically to state sovereignty in state legislatively authorized activity. The doctrine provides immunity, or "exemption" as it is sometimes called, from federal competition laws when the state is performing official actions, whether or not such actions are anticompetitive in effect. To warrant such immunity, the anticompetitive acts must be taken in the state's "sovereign capacity" and not as a market participant in competition with commercial enterprise. If the acts are not explicitly ordered by a legislative arm of

---

counterclaims to such a claim would be proper and not subject to dismissal on grounds of sovereign immunity.

[136]*Genentech, Inc. v. Eli Lilly & Co.*, 998 F.2d 931, 27 USPQ2d 1241 (Fed. Cir. 1993). Such abrogation must be explicit and unambiguous and must show clearly that Congress intended to subject the states to suit in federal court. *Id.*

[137]*Genentech, Inc. v. Eli Lilly & Co.*, 998 F.2d 931, 27 USPQ2d 1241 (Fed. Cir. 1993). State officials may be sued as individuals in certain circumstances. *Id.*

[138]*Genentech, Inc. v. Eli Lilly & Co.*, 998 F.2d 931, 27 USPQ2d 1241 (Fed. Cir. 1993). In *In re Regents of the Univ. of Calif.*, 964 F.2d 1128 (Fed. Cir. 1992), it was held that the coordination by the Multidistrict Litigation Panel of pretrial procedures for several pending cases does not have the effect of requiring a state, in violation of Eleventh Amendment sovereign immunity, to appear in actions to which it is not a party or to defend against claims to which it is not otherwise subject. The state also argued that it had limited its waiver of immunity to the Northern District of California, where it brought an infringement action. But the Eleventh Amendment is not designed to give procedural advantage to state litigants; rather, it serves to shield states from unconsented actions against them. When the state filed the action in federal court in California, it requested adjudication of the claims that it put before the court. Upon entering the litigation arena, the state, like all litigants, became subject to the Federal Rules, including the procedural efficiencies administered by the Multidistrict Litigation Panel. Having invoked the jurisdiction of the federal court, the state litigant accepted the authority of the court.

state government, they must be conducted pursuant to legislative authorization that contemplates such acts.[139]

State immunity from patent infringement suits. The Supreme Court, in *Florida Prepaid Board v. College Savings Bank,*[140] decided that the states retain their sovereign immunity from patent infringement suits, despite the 1992 enactment of 35 U.S.C. §§271(h) and 296. This decision caps an interesting history of Federal Circuit and Supreme Court rulings and congressional intervention. The primary significance of this history is its illumination of the circumstances under which a state may waive that immunity.

In a pair of cases, *Chew v. California*[141] and *Jacobs v. Florida,*[142] the Federal Circuit held that Congress did not, in enacting the patent legislation, evidence any intent to subject the states to patent infringement suits in federal courts. Thus the immunity of the states under the Eleventh Amendment had not then been abrogated by the federal patent laws. Congress reacted swiftly by enacting 35 U.S.C. §271(h) and §296. In *Genentech I* the Federal Circuit held that these enactments not only overrule *Chew* and *Jacobs* by permitting states to be sued for infringement, but they abrogate state immunity in any suit involving a violation of the patent laws with respect to a patent owned by the state, including actions seeking a declaration of invalidity and noninfringement.[143]

In the meantime, while the *Genentech* litigation was working its way through the district court, the Supreme Court held in *Seminole*

---

[139]*Genentech, Inc. v. Eli Lilly & Co.*, 998 F.2d 931, 27 USPQ2d 1241 (Fed. Cir. 1993). Here the court was able to pass the question of whether a state university licensing activities establish a market participant exception to state action immunity because it found that the activities in question would not in any event amount to acts in restraint of trade.

[140]*Florida Prepaid Bd. v. College Sav. Bank,* 527 U.S. 627, 51 USPQ2d 1081 (1999).

[141]*Chew v. California,* 893 F.2d 331, 13 USPQ2d 1393 (Fed. Cir. 1990). One of the more interesting arguments advanced by the plaintiff was based on deprivation of property without due process: (1) interpreting the patent statute to preclude patentees from infringement remedies against a state in federal court violates procedural or substantive due process under the Fifth Amendment; and (2) a state's use of the patented invention without compensation deprives the patentee of property contrary to the Fourteenth Amendment. As to the first point, the proper party for a federal "taking" claim would be the United States, not the state. As to the second point, a patent infringement suit is not the appropriate legal remedy for vindicating a "taking" claim.

[142]*Jacobs Wind Elec. Co. v. Florida Dep't of Transp.,* 919 F.2d 726, 16 USPQ2d 1972 (Fed. Cir. 1990). Here the court refused to distinguish *Chew* on two proposed grounds: (1) that *Chew* involved a nonresident of the state, while in *Jacobs* the plaintiff was a Florida resident; and (2) that the Eleventh Amendment should preclude only suits for damages not an action to obtain a declaration of validity and infringement. The court also pointed out, in passing, that the plaintiff was not left without a remedy: it could seek relief in the state legislature through a claims bill, and it could assert a "taking" claim against the state under the Fifth and Fourteenth Amendments.

[143]*Genentech, Inc. v. Eli Lilly & Co.*, 998 F.2d 931, 27 USPQ2d 1241 (Fed. Cir. 1993). The court also held that §§271(h) and 296 apply to suits pending at the time of the enactment, even though the suits would have been subject to state immunity at the time they were filed. This is in keeping with the general rule that changes in law apply to cases that are pending before the courts, unless the interest of justice, or the law itself, requires otherwise.

Tribe v. Florida[144] that Article I of the Constitution did not empower Congress to abrogate a state's Eleventh Amendment immunity. In *Genentech II*,[145] the Federal Circuit had to agree that *Genentech I* could not stand, for that was the ground upon which it was premised. However, the court went on to find that the state had by its litigation-related actions waived its immunity and impliedly consented to suit. As it explained, the Eleventh Amendment is not directed to the competence of the federal courts, but enacts a sovereign immunity from suit, rather than a nonwaivable limit on the federal judiciary's subject matter jurisdiction. The Supreme Court consistently has held that a state may consent to suit against it in federal court. Thus, where a state creates a case of actual controversy by a charge of patent infringement and a threat of federally imposed and enforced remedial action, it in effect creates the federal cause of action. The declaratory judgment action by the accused infringer was enabled solely by the state's deliberate acts.[146]

In *Genentech II* the Federal Circuit was thus able to pass the question, which had been raised by the declaratory plaintiff, of whether the result in *Genentech I* could have been supported by broad property principles protected under the Fourteenth Amendment. However, the court was squarely confronted with this question when it took up the appeal in *College Savings Bank*.[147] It held that the intent of Congress to abrogate state immunity from suits for patent infringement was unmistakably clear in the language of §§271(h) and 296 and that, under the Fourteenth Amendment, which was expressly invoked in the legislative history of those sections, Congress had the power so to do.

The Supreme Court reversed, holding that those provisions could not be sustained as legislation enacted to enforce the guarantees of the Fourteenth Amendment's Due Process Clause. In order for Congress to invoke §5 of the Fourteenth Amendment, which gives it the power to enforce the amendment's provisions by appropriate legislation, it must identify conduct transgressing the Fourteenth Amendment's substantive provisions, and must tailor its legislative scheme to remedying or preventing such conduct. The Court reasoned that a state's infringement of a patent does not violate due process unless the state provides no remedy, or only inadequate remedies, to injured patent owners. The legislative record offered scant support for the conclusion that states were depriving patent owners of property

---

[144]*Seminole Tribe of Florida v. Florida*, 517 U.S. 44 (1996).

[145]*Genentech, Inc. v. University of Calif.*, 143 F.3d 1446, 46 USPQ2d 1586 (Fed. Cir. 1998).

[146]*Genentech, Inc. v. University of Calif.*, 143 F.3d 1446, 46 USPQ2d 1586 (Fed. Cir. 1998). The court made it clear that it was not holding that simply by the act of obtaining federal patents the state had waived its Eleventh Amendment immunity. See also *Regents of Univ. of Calif. v. Eli Lilly & Co.*, 119 F.3d 1559, 43 USPQ2d 1398 (Fed. Cir. 1997).

[147]*College Sav. Bank v. Florida Prepaid Bd.*, 148 F.3d 1343, 47 USPQ2d 1161 (Fed. Cir. 1998), *rev'd*, 527 U.S. 627, 51 USPQ2d 1081 (1999).

without due process of law by pleading sovereign immunity in federal court patent actions. Moreover, §§271(h) and 296 subjected the states to expansive liability without limiting its coverage to cases involving arguable constitutional violations, or to suits against states with questionable remedies or high incidence of infringement.[148]

Due process. Modern due process inquiry includes a determination of whether the legislature used a rational approach to achieve a legitimate end.[149] To have a property interest in a benefit protected by procedural due process, a person must have a legitimate claim of entitlement to the benefit.[150] Once a property interest is shown, all due process requires is notice and an opportunity to be heard.[151] Due process is a flexible concept and the particular procedural safeguards required will vary depending upon all the circumstances.[152] The demands of due process may be met with notice reasonably calculated, under all the circumstances, to apprise interested parties of the pendency of the action and afford them an opportunity to present their objections.[153]

Where subject matter jurisdiction over an action exists by virtue of a federal question, rather than diversity, the due process consideration is that of the Fifth Amendment. The jurisprudence of the Supreme Court has thus far largely dealt only with state claims and diversity cases. Nonetheless, the Federal Circuit applies that jurisprudence, including the minimum contacts standard, to personal jurisdiction issues in federal question cases, such as those arising under the patent laws. The most recent summarization of minimum contacts as a constitutional theory looks to whether the defendant has purposefully directed its activities at residents of the forum and whether the litigation results from alleged injuries that arise out of or relate to those activities.[154] The constitutional aspects of in personam jurisdiction are discussed in §8.1(c).

At a minimum, due process requires that an individual being deprived of his or her property interest be given an opportunity to be heard at a meaningful time and in a meaningful manner. Nonetheless, to determine exactly what process is due in any particular case, a more exacting analysis must be conducted that considers the particular circumstances and interests involved. Three factors are considered: (1) the individual's interests affected by the government's adverse action; (2) the government's interests; and (3) the risk of an

---

[148]*Florida Prepaid Bd. v. College Sav. Bank,* 527 U.S. 627, 51 USPQ2d 1081 (1999).

[149]*Patlex Corp. v. Mossinghoff,* 758 F.2d 594, 225 USPQ 243 (Fed. Cir. 985).

[150]*Zucker v. United States,* 758 F.2d 637 (Fed. Cir. 1985).

[151]*Alberico v. United States,* 783 F.2d 1024 (Fed. Cir. 1986).

[152]*Julien v. Zeringue,* 864 F.2d 1572, 9 USPQ2d 1554 (Fed. Cir. 1989).

[153]*Beatrice Foods Co. v. New England Printing & Lith. Co.,* 930 F.2d 1572, 18 USPQ2d 1548 (Fed. Cir. 1991).

[154]*Akro Corp. v. Luker,* 45 F.3d 1541, 33 USPQ2d 1505 (Fed. Cir. 1995). See also *Viam Corp. v. Iowa Export-Import Trading Co.,* 84 F.3d 424, 38 USPQ2d 1833 (Fed. Cir. 1996).

erroneous decision and whether more accurate procedures might not reduce that possibility.[155] Failure to provide a hearing before, rather than after, termination of a property interest is not in and of itself violative of due process.[156]

There may be debate as to the full meaning of "due process," and the courts have struggled to define its boundaries and requirements within the context of nonjudicial governmental action. However, it is unambiguously clear that federal judicial proceedings, with their extensive notice, opportunity to be heard, and procedural protections, satisfy the constitutional requirement of procedural due process required for the invalidation of a patent.[157] Ample due process safeguards are also available in the summary judgment procedures of Rule 56, FRCP. A litigant is not "deprived" of a trial upon grant of summary judgment where the evidence of record at the time of the motion supports its opponent on all key issues and the nonmovant fails to put in sufficient evidence to create a triable issue of any material fact.[158]

There are constitutional limitations upon the power of courts, even in aid of their own valid processes, to dismiss an action without affording a party the opportunity for a hearing on the merits of its

---

[155]*Engdahl v. Department of Navy,* 900 F.2d 1572 (Fed. Cir. 1990).

[156]*Alberico v. United States,* 783 F.2d 1024 (Fed. Cir. 1986). The apparent grant to a party of the right to appear in person bestowed by the Administrative Procedure Act (5 U.S.C. §555) is not blindly absolute; the fact that the party's outside counsel had full access to the information developed in an agency proceeding was sufficient to ensure due process. *Akzo N.V. v. United States ITC,* 808 F.2d 1471, 1 USPQ2d 1241 (Fed. Cir. 1986). In *Ohio Cellular Prods. Corp. v. Nelson,* 175 F.3d 1343, 50 USPQ2d 1481 (Fed. Cir. 1999), a patent owned by a corporation was found unenforceable for inequitable conduct. The trial court held the corporation liable for attorney fees. The inventor, who was also president and sole shareholder of the corporation, and who had prosecuted the application and committed the inequitable conduct, had his lawyer write the successful defendant, suggesting if it tried to collect the fees award, he would liquidate the company. The defendant moved to join the inventor, and the trial court added him as a party and immediately entered judgment against him as well. The Federal Circuit, over a vigorous dissent by Judge Newman, affirmed. Its decision was not based on piercing the corporate veil, but rather on the fact that the individual had adequate notice and would not be substantially prejudiced. His clear control over and participation in the litigation, and his central role in the wrongdoing, were the critical factors. The Supreme Court granted certiorari and, not surprisingly, reversed and remanded. *Nelson v. Adams USA Inc.,* 529 U.S. 460, 54 USPQ2d 1513 (2). The rationale was a failure of due process. The individual was never afforded a proper opportunity to respond to the claim, but was adjudged liable the very first moment his personal liability was legally at issue. The Federal Circuit felt that no basis had been advanced to believe anything different or additional would have been done in defense had the individual been a party from the outset. The Supreme Court firmly rejected this as speculation, and observed that judicial predictions about the outcome of hypothesized litigation cannot substitute for the actual opportunity to defend that due process affords every party against whom a claim is stated. See *Toepfer v. Department of Transp.,* 792 F.2d 1102 (Fed. Cir. 1986), where the court dismissed a no-hearing attack on Rule 38, FRAP. See *Broomall Indus. v. Data Design Logic Sys., Inc.,* 786 F.2d 401, 229 USPQ 38 (Fed. Cir. 1986), where the court indicated that a no-notice argument would prevail against a discharge in bankruptcy.

[157]*Constant v. Advanced Micro-Devices, Inc.,* 848 F.2d 1560, 7 USPQ2d 1057 (Fed. Cir. 1988).

[158]*Avia Group Int'l, Inc. v. L.A. Gear Calif., Inc.,* 853 F.2d 1557, 7 USPQ2d 1548 (Fed. Cir. 1988).

cause.[159] If a motion to dismiss challenges the truth of the jurisdictional facts alleged in the complaint, the plaintiff must be given an opportunity to be heard before dismissal is ordered.[160] A dismissal, even sua sponte, for failure to state a claim upon which relief can be granted does not violate due process. In such a case, the court is simply stating that, as a matter of law, the party's case is untenable, and no additional proceedings could have enabled the party to prove any set of facts entitling it to prevail.[161]

Before a state can grant preclusive effect to its own judgments, due process must be present. This requires a full and fair opportunity to litigate. But the very nature of due process negates any concept of inflexible procedures universally applicable to every imaginable situation.[162] Before sanctioning an attorney under 28 U.S.C. §1927, the court must give the attorney notice and an opportunity to be heard.[163] But under Rule 38, FRAP, the counsel against whom fees and costs for a frivolous appeal are assessed is not entitled to notice or a hearing.[164] It is well established that formal service is not required in a contempt proceeding. However, parties to a contempt proceeding are entitled to adequate notice and an opportunity to be heard.[165]

The Fifth Amendment reflects an historic hostility to retroactive legislation. The presumption of correctness that accompanies congressional action is subject to the important restraint that retrospective aspects of legislation, as well as prospective, must meet the test of due process, and the justifications for the latter may not suffice for the former.[166]

---

[159]*Ingalls Shipbuilding, Inc. v. United States,* 857 F.2d 1448 (Fed. Cir. 1988). But see *Claude E. Atkins Enter., Inc. v. United States,* 899 F.2d 1180 (Fed. Cir. 1990).

[160]*Reynolds v. Army & Air Force Exch. Serv.,* 846 F.2d 746 (Fed. Cir. 1988).

[161]*Constant v. United States,* 929 F.2d 654, 18 USPQ2d 1298 (Fed. Cir. 1991). But does this mean that it is unnecessary to afford a party a hearing on purely legal questions? One doubts it, but see *Beatrice Foods Co. v. New England Printing & Lith. Co.,* 930 F.2d 1572, 18 USPQ2d 1548 (Fed. Cir. 1991).

[162]*MGA, Inc. v. General Motors Corp.,* 827 F.2d 729, 3 USPQ2d 1762 (Fed. Cir. 1987). Due process is a flexible concept and the particular procedural safeguards required will vary depending upon all the circumstances. *Fromson v. Citiplate, Inc.,* 886 F.2d 1300, 12 USPQ2d 1299 (Fed. Cir. 1989).

[163]*Beatrice Foods Co. v. New England Printing & Lith. Co.,* 899 F.2d 1171, 14 USPQ2d 1020 (Fed. Cir. 1990); *Julien v. Zeringue,* 864 F.2d 1572, 9 USPQ2d 1554 (Fed. Cir. 1989). If the court intends to sanction an attorney sua sponte, due process is satisfied by issuance of an order to show cause why sanctions should not be imposed and by providing an opportunity to respond. *Julien v. Zeringue,* 864 F.2d 1572, 9 USPQ2d 1554 (Fed. Cir. 1989). A magistrate found attorney misconduct in responding to discovery. The district court held a hearing at which the magistrate testified. The Federal Circuit felt this satisfied due process. *Fromson v. Citiplate, Inc.,* 886 F.2d 1300, 12 USPQ2d 1299 (Fed. Cir. 1989).

[164]*Constant v. United States,* 929 F.2d 654, 18 USPQ2d 1298 (Fed. Cir. 1991); *In re Perry,* 918 F.2d 931 (Fed. Cir. 1990); *Sun-Tek Indus., Inc. v. Kennedy Sky-Lites, Inc.,* 865 F.2d 1254, 9 USPQ2d 1574 (Fed. Cir. 1989).

[165]*Additive Cont. & Meas. Sys. Inc. v. Flowdata Inc.,* 154 F.3d 1345, 47 USPQ2d 1906 (Fed. Cir. 1998).

[166]*Patlex Corp. v. Mossinghoff,* 758 F.2d 594, 225 USPQ 243 (Fed. Cir. 1985). Nonetheless, retrospective application of the reexamination statute does not violate Fifth Amendment due process. *Id.*

A person's decision, although apparently voluntary, cannot be binding as a matter of fundamental fairness and due process if it is based on misinformation or a lack of information. Thus a misinformed choice between options provided by the government may not satisfy due process.[167] The court was presented with an interesting issue of right to counsel in *Lariscey v. United States*.[168] An inmate of a federal prison made an invention working in the prison shop. He filed a pro se suit in the Claims Court, asking among other things that a patent attorney be assigned to prosecute a patent application for him. The Federal Circuit passed the question whether the Court of Federal Claims has power under any circumstances to appoint counsel and opted instead to decide that there was no right to counsel in these circumstances. In civil proceedings the right to counsel is highly circumscribed. A strong presumption that there is a right to appointed counsel exists only when an indigent may lose his or her personal freedom. Beyond that narrow framework, the Supreme Court has not recognized a constitutional right to appointed counsel in civil matters, and here there was no statutory provision for mandatory or discretionary appointment.

Due process may sometimes bar trial by judges who have no actual bias and who would do their very best to weigh the scales of justice equally between contending parties. To perform its high function in the best way, justice must satisfy the appearance of justice.[169]

Full faith and credit. The Full Faith and Credit Clause of the Constitution, as implemented by 28 U.S.C. §1738, requires that state court judgments be given the same preclusive effect in later federal actions that they would be given under the laws of the state in which the judgments were rendered.[170] The subject of preclusion by judgment is covered in §18.5.

Patent and copyright legislation. In *Constant v. Advanced Micro-Devices*,[171] the court took a fresh and careful look at some fundamental principles involving the constitutional and legislative underpinnings of our patent system. As an historical matter, the Patent and Copyright Clause of the Constitution, Article I, Section 8, Clause 8 says that Congress shall have the power to "promote the Progress of Science and useful Arts, by securing for limited Times to Authors and Inventors the exclusive Right to their respective Writings and Discoveries." The power to grant patents to inventors is for the promotion of the

---

[167]*Covington v. Department of Health*, 750 F.2d 937 (Fed. Cir. 1984).

[168]*Lariscey v. United States*, 861 F.2d 1267, 8 USPQ2d 2007 (Fed. Cir. 1988).

[169]*Hewlett-Packard Co. v. Bausch & Lomb, Inc.*, 882 F.2d 1556, 11 USPQ2d 1750 (Fed. Cir. 1989).

[170]*MGA, Inc. v. General Motors Corp.*, 827 F.2d 729, 3 USPQ2d 1762 (Fed. Cir. 1987); *Graybill v. United States Postal Serv.*, 782 F.2d 1567 (Fed. Cir. 1986).

[171]*Constant v. Advanced Micro-Devices, Inc.*, 848 F.2d 1560, 7 USPQ2d 1057 (Fed. Cir. 1988).

useful arts, while the power to grant copyrights to authors is for the promotion of "Science," which had a much broader meaning in the 18th century than it does today.

It is erroneous to argue that the word "securing" in the Patent Clause requires that a patent issued by the PTO be conclusively valid and unchallengeable. Since the adoption of the first Patent Act in 1790, Congress has permitted judicial review of the validity of patents. The courts, the interpreters of the meaning of the Constitution, have consistently construed the Patent Clause to permit judicial review of patents. Public policy requires that only inventions meeting the statutory standards are entitled to patents. This policy is furthered when the validity of a patent, originally obtained in ex parte proceedings in the PTO, can be challenged in court.[172]

Thus, 35 U.S.C. §282 permits federal courts to adjudicate the validity of patents when invalidity is raised as an affirmative defense in infringement suits. Congress was fully within its constitutional power when it delegated this authority to the courts. Similarly, Congress has the power to delegate to the courts the authority to review decisions of the PTO so that the courts may declare an invention to be patentable after it has been rejected by the PTO. Congress was also within its constitutional powers when it created a reexamination procedure as an additional mechanism for the review of patents. The creation of reexamination did not divest the courts of any power to review patent validity.[173] Retrospective application of the reexamination statute does not violate Fifth Amendment due process.[174] On the other hand, every perceived injury caused by improper agency action does not carry a right to immediate judicial redress. A right to judicial review must be granted or reasonably inferred from a particular statute. For example, a potential infringer may not sue the PTO seeking retraction of a patent issued to another by reason of its improper allowance by the PTO. A remedy must await confrontation with the patent owner.[175] Although a state court is without power to

---

[172]*Constant v. Advanced Micro-Devices, Inc.*, 848 F.2d 1560, 7 USPQ2d 1057 (Fed. Cir. 1988).

[173]*Constant v. Advanced Micro-Devices, Inc.*, 848 F.2d 1560, 7 USPQ2d 1057 (Fed. Cir. 1988). Federal judicial proceedings, with their built-in procedural protections, satisfy the constitutional requirement of procedural due process required for the invalidation of a patent. *Id.* The patentee also made the imaginative argument that it was unconstitutional for a court to invalidate his patent using prior art that was the result of government-funded research. His thesis was that the Patent Clause sets forth the only permissible means for the government to promote science. The court pointed out that the Constitution also authorizes Congress to spend money to promote the "general welfare" and government support for research and development is well within this discretionary power.

[174]*Patlex Corp. v. Mossinghoff*, 758 F.2d 594, 225 USPQ 243 (Fed. Cir. 1985). In *Joy Tech., Inc. v. Manbeck*, 959 F.2d 226, 22 USPQ2d 1153 (Fed. Cir. 1992), the court rejected an argument that inasmuch as there was no reexamination mechanism in existence when the particular patent issued, it would be an improper denial of the right to trial by jury for the PTO to hold certain claims unpatentable upon reexamination. The court was able (because some claims remained in the reexamined patent) to pass another interesting argument: in order to get a patent in the first place, the applicant had to make a public disclosure of proprietary information. Having done so, it was deprived of private rights and got nothing in return.

[175]*Syntex (U.S.A.) Inc. v. United States PTO*, 882 F.2d 1570, 11 USPQ2d 1866 (Fed. Cir. 1989).

invalidate an issued patent, there is no limitation on the ability of a state court to decide the question of validity when properly raised in a state court proceeding.[176]

Article I, Section 8, Clause 8 of the Constitution also gives Congress the authority to set the parameters of authors' exclusive rights. The Constitution sets forth the purpose of copyright protection as the promotion of "the Progress of Science," not the rewarding of authors. The Copyright Act thus balances the interests of authors in the control and exploitation of their writings on the one hand, and society's competing interests in the free flow of ideas and information on the other hand.[177]

§18.5 Res Judicata—Preclusion by Judgment

There is no support in law for repeated bites at the apple. On the contrary, the law whenever possible reaches for repose.[178] That is the policy that drives judicial respect for prior judgments and adjudications.

This section covers the traditional concepts of prior adjudication: res judicata and collateral estoppel, as well as the less rigorous doctrines of law of the case and stare decisis. Related topics such as interference estoppel and prosecution history estoppel are treated elsewhere.[179]

The Federal Circuit has signaled clearly[180] that it intends to adhere to the merger/bar/estoppel rules of the *Restatement,*[181] and to

---

[176]*Jacobs Wind Elec. Co. v. Florida Dep't of Transp.,* 919 F.2d 726, 16 USPQ2d 1972 (Fed. Cir. 1990).

[177]*Atari Games Corp. v. Nintendo of Am., Inc.,* 975 F.2d 832, 24 USPQ2d 1015 (Fed. Cir. 1992).

[178]*Burson v. Carmichael,* 731 F.2d 849, 221 USPQ 664 (Fed. Cir. 1984).

[179]See §15.2(e) for interference estoppel; see §6.3(b) for prosecution history estoppel. Assignor and licensee estoppel are treated in §7.2(d), and equitable, legal, and judicial estoppel and the doctrine of preclusion by inconsistent positions are treated in §7.2(e).

[180]See, e.g., *Chromalloy Am. Corp. v. Kenneth Gordon, Ltd.,* 736 F.2d 694, 222 USPQ 187 (Fed. Cir. 1984); *Mother's Restaurant, Inc. v. Mama's Pizza, Inc.,* 723 F.2d 1566, 221 USPQ 394 (Fed. Cir. 1983); *Young Eng'rs, Inc. v. United States ITC,* 721 F.2d 1305, 219 USPQ 1142 (Fed. Cir. 1983). The court seems to have come around to the view that the application of principles of res judicata and collateral estoppel is not a matter within its own exclusive jurisdiction, and it will therefore look to regional circuit law to resolve such questions. *Epic Metals Corp. v. H.H. Robertson Co.,* 870 F.2d 1574, 10 USPQ2d 1296 (Fed. Cir. 1989). Nonetheless, it is willing for purposes of convenience to employ *Restatement* terminology. *Hartley v. Mentor Corp.,* 869 F.2d 1469, 10 USPQ2d 1138 (Fed. Cir. 1989). The court will apply its own law to the question of whether the public policies expressed in *Lear, Inc. v. Adkins,* 395 U.S. 653, 162 USPQ 1 (1969), override the general principles of res judicata that would otherwise apply to consent judgments. On the application of those general principles of res judicata to consent judgments, regional circuit law—determined by reference to the *Restatement* and the issue preclusion/claim preclusion analytical framework—will be applied. *Foster v. Hallco Mfg. Co.,* 947 F.2d 469, 20 USPQ2d 1241 (Fed. Cir. 1991). However, the full faith and credit statute, 28 U.S.C. §1738, does not permit federal courts to employ their own rules of res judicata in determining the effects of state judgments. Rather, a federal court is to accept the rules chosen by the state in which the judgment is rendered. *United Tech. Corp. v. Chromalloy Gas Turbine Corp.,* 189 F.3d 1338, 51 USPQ2d 1838 (Fed. Cir. 1999).

[181]*Restatement (Second) of Judgments* 131 (1982).

apply those rules using the issue preclusion/claim preclusion analysis popularized by Professor Vestal.[182] That is the analysis employed here as well. The principles of direct estoppel by judgment—either by merger if the judgment favors the plaintiff, or by bar if for the defendant—that have traditionally been comprehended by the term "res judicata" are analyzed in terms of claim preclusion. The principles of collateral estoppel are analyzed by reference to issue preclusion.

The doctrines of res judicata (claim preclusion) and collateral estoppel (issue preclusion) relieve parties of the cost and vexation of multiple lawsuits, conserve judicial resources, and, by preventing inconsistent decisions, encourage reliance upon adjudication.[183]

(a) Issue Preclusion

The doctrine of res judicata applies to prevent repetitious litigation on the same cause of action. But where a second suit is brought upon a different cause of action, res judicata has no force or effect. In such cases, those matters actually presented and determined in the first suit serve as collateral estoppel or issue preclusion as to the same matters in the second suit.[184] Collateral estoppel is an umbrella term and can cover both an estoppel on a different claim between the same parties, or between parties who have not previously litigated on the subject (unilateral estoppel). Collateral estoppel may be based on the operative effect of a prior judgment or may be based on a reversal of a party's prior position, taken either in the context of prior litigation or by prior conduct wholly outside the courtroom. It may be used offensively or defensively. In accordance with the *Restatement,* the Federal Circuit calls the res judicata aspect of collateral estoppel "issue preclusion," while the other aspect of collateral estoppel is called "preclusion of inconsistent positions."[185] The Federal Circuit seems willing to adopt the doctrine of preclusion of inconsistent positions in an appropriate case, particularly if the application is defensive and not unilateral.[186]

A rationale for issue preclusion is that once a legal or factual issue has been settled by the court after a trial in which it was fully

---

[182]Vestal, *Res Judicata/Preclusion* (1969).

[183]*MGA, Inc. v. General Motors Corp.,* 827 F.2d 729, 3 USPQ2d 1762 (Fed. Cir. 1987).

[184]*Wilson v. Turnage,* 791 F.2d 151 (Fed. Cir. 1986).

[185]*Jackson Jordon, Inc. v. Plasser Am. Corp.,* 747 F.2d 1567, 224 USPQ 1 (Fed. Cir. 1984).

[186]*Jackson Jordon, Inc. v. Plasser Am. Corp.,* 747 F.2d 1567, 224 USPQ 1 (Fed. Cir. 1984). A narrow claim interpretation was adopted in a prior suit against a different accused infringer, resulting in a finding of validity and infringement. The successful patentee could not appeal that interpretation even if he felt it was narrower than necessary and so was not bound by it as a matter of issue preclusion in a later suit against a different infringer. Nor was he estopped by preclusion of inconsistent positions. The court felt a more sharply defined flip-flop would be required, rather than a mere shift from narrower to broader claim interpretation. Moreover, there was no evidence that the shift was any affront to the court who rendered the first decision, nor that the present defendant had in any manner relied upon the narrower interpretation to its prejudice. See §7.2(e) above.

and fairly litigated, that issue should enjoy repose. Such litigated issues may not be relitigated even in an action on a different claim.[187] Application of the more traditional aspect of collateral estoppel— issue preclusion—requires that (1) the issues to be concluded are identical to those involved in the prior action; (2) in that action those issues were raised and actually litigated; (3) the determination of those issues in the prior action was necessary and essential to the resulting judgment; and (4) the party precluded was fully represented and had a full and fair opportunity to litigate the issues in the first action.[188]

Issue preclusion in patent litigation may arise under the same conditions as in any litigation, the principal requirements being that the issue must have been actually litigated in the prior proceeding, the parties must have been given a full and fair opportunity to do so, and the issue must provide the basis for the final judgment entered therein.[189] Identity of issues can be a troublesome question, as will be seen in the discussion of the *Blonder-Tongue* doctrine, in §18.5(b).[190]

Difficulty sometimes arises in delineating the issue on which litigation is, or is not, foreclosed. The problem involves a balancing of important interests: on the one hand a desire not to deprive a litigant of an adequate day in court; on the other hand, a desire to prevent repetitious litigation of what is essentially the same dispute.[191]

Whether an issue was raised and actually litigated can also be difficult to know: the issues resolved by a court are defined by the facts in the case and the law applied; they are not necessarily limited to those briefed by the parties.[192] However, if the parties to the original suit disputed the issue and the trier of fact resolved it, it was actually litigated.[193] In the case of a consent judgment, no issues are litigated and there can be no issue preclusion.[194]

---

[187]*Foster v. Hallco Mfg. Co.*, 947 F.2d 469, 20 USPQ2d 1241 (Fed. Cir. 1991).

[188]*Comair Rotron, Inc. v. Nippon Densan Corp.*, 49 F.3d 1535, 33 USPQ2d 1929 (Fed. Cir. 1995); *In re Freeman*, 30 F.3d 1459, 31 USPQ2d 1444 (Fed. Cir. 1994); *McCandless v. Merit Sys. Prot. Bd.*, 996 F.2d 1193 (Fed. Cir. 1993); *Thomas v. General Servs. Admin.*, 794 F.2d 661 (Fed. Cir. 1986); *Mother's Restaurant, Inc. v. Mama's Pizza, Inc.*, 723 F.2d 1566, 221 USPQ 394 (Fed. Cir. 1983); *A.B. Dick Co. v. Burroughs Corp.*, 713 F.2d 700, 218 USPQ 965 (Fed. Cir. 1983). See *Flowdata, Inc. v. Cotton*, 57 F.3d 1046 (Fed. Cir. 1995) (Fifth Circuit law).

[189]*Hartley v. Mentor Corp.*, 869 F.2d 1469, 10 USPQ2d 1138 (Fed. Cir. 1989).

[190]The Federal Circuit uses a similar analysis to determine whether it is appropriate to adjudicate an allegedly infringing modified device by contempt proceeding or by new or supplemental complaint. *KSM Fastening Sys., Inc. v. H.A. Jones Co.*, 776 F.2d 1522, 227 USPQ 676 (Fed. Cir. 1985). The decision in *Arachnid, Inc. v. Merit Indus., Inc.*, 939 F.2d 1574, 19 USPQ2d 1513 (Fed. Cir. 1991), provides a good illustration of how difficult and confusing issue identity analyses can become.

[191]*In re Freeman*, 30 F.3d 1459, 31 USPQ2d 1444 (Fed. Cir. 1994).

[192]*Zenith Radio Corp. v. United States*, 783 F.2d 184 (Fed. Cir. 1986).

[193]*In re Freeman*, 30 F.3d 1459, 31 USPQ2d 1444 (Fed. Cir. 1994); *Mother's Restaurant, Inc. v. Mama's Pizza, Inc.*, 723 F.2d 1566, 221 USPQ 394 (Fed. Cir. 1983).

[194]*Chromalloy Am. Corp. v. Kenneth Gordon, Ltd.*, 736 F.2d 694, 222 USPQ 187 (Fed. Cir. 1984). If an issue was not litigated in a prior suit, obviously the doctrine of issue preclusion cannot apply. *Cordis Corp. v. Medtronic, Inc.*, 835 F.2d 859, 5 USPQ2d 1118 (Fed. Cir. 1987). It is therefore generally correct that a judgment entered pursuant to a stipulation will give

The court uses the *Restatement* view of the actual litigation requirement: an issue is not actually litigated if it is raised in an allegation by one party and is admitted by the other before evidence on the issue is adduced at trial; nor is it actually litigated if it is the subject of a stipulation between the parties. A stipulation may, however, be binding in a subsequent action between the parties if the parties have manifested an intention to that effect.[195]

Normally, where a judgment is entered by consent prior to trial on any issue, no issue may be said to have been fully, fairly, or actually litigated, and issue preclusion does not arise. There is, however, a form of issue preclusion that is not dependent upon actual litigation. Thus, if a consent judgment, by its terms, indicates that the parties thereto intend to preclude any challenge to the validity of a particular patent, even in subsequent litigation involving a new cause of action, then that issue can be precluded.[196]

In order to give preclusive effect to a particular finding in a prior case, that finding must have been necessary to the judgment rendered in the previous action. The purpose of this requirement is to prevent the incidental or collateral determination of a nonessential issue from precluding reconsideration of the issue in later litigation.[197] The court appears to be signaling a fairly strict view, for purposes of evaluating collateral estoppel issues, as to whether a finding in prior litigation was essential to the prior judgment. Thus, when a judgment may have been based upon alternative grounds, any of which would be sufficient to support the result, the judgment is not preclusive with respect to any ground standing alone. A less strict view would encourage litigants to appeal all peripheral findings for the sole purpose of avoiding the possible preclusive effect as to any one; this would unnecessarily increase the burdens of litigation on parties and courts.[198] Where the prior holding is one of patent invalidity, however, it is necessary to the judgment even if there was also a holding of noninfringement.[199]

---

rise only to claim preclusion not issue preclusion. *Hartley v. Mentor Corp.,* 869 F.2d 1469, 10 USPQ2d 1138 (Fed. Cir. 1989). But see text accompanying notes 260–267 below.

[195]*Flowdata, Inc. v. Cotton,* 57 F.3d 1046 (Fed. Cir. 1995). In a prior case the defendant had admitted validity and infringement but only for purposes of that action. In this case, brought by the patentee against the prior defendant company's president, there could be no issue preclusion (even if the president satisfied the alter ego or participation requirements) because the issues had not actually been litigated. The court below had also granted summary judgment against the president on some unfair competition issues that had been involved in the prior case. He argued that it was error to apply issue preclusion as to those issues because they had not been actually pleaded in the present case. The Federal Circuit agreed.

[196]*Foster v. Hallco Mfg. Co.,* 947 F.2d 469, 20 USPQ2d 1241 (Fed. Cir. 1991).

[197]*In re Freeman,* 30 F.3d 1459, 31 USPQ2d 1444 (Fed. Cir. 1994).

[198]*Comair Rotron, Inc. v. Nippon Densan Corp.,* 49 F.3d 1535, 33 USPQ2d 1929 (Fed. Cir. 1995). In a prior case against a different defendant, the present defendant's accused device, along with several others, was found to be an acceptable noninfringing substitute for purposes of a lost profits inquiry. The court's rationale for refusing to apply collateral estoppel to the infringement question presented here is not altogether clear.

[199]*Mendenhall v. Barber-Greene Co.,* 26 F.3d 1573, 31 USPQ2d 1001 (Fed. Cir. 1994). This is so because of the *Cardinal* doctrine; see text accompanying notes 16:476–489. Apparently

Whether the issue in question was essential to the judgment is highly dependent upon the facts of the particular case. For example, judicial statements regarding the scope of patent claims are entitled to collateral estoppel effect in a subsequent infringement suit only to the extent that determination of scope was essential to a final judgment on the question of validity or infringement. Further, such statements should be narrowly construed and should not be binding where they were made in the abstract and not related to the context of validity or infringement.[200] Nonetheless, the requirement that the issue have been essential to the judgment does not mean that the finding must have been so crucial that the judgment could not stand without it.[201]

Finally, the question of representation and opportunity to litigate must be approached with care. Summary proceedings on a documentary record do not always result in a full and fair adjudication.[202] A full and fair opportunity to litigate is required for a prior judgment to have preclusive effect.[203]

To apply issue preclusion, the party against whom the estoppel is being asserted must have been accorded a full and fair opportunity to litigate in the prior court proceeding the very issue it now seeks to relitigate. If there is reason to doubt the quality, extensiveness, or fairness of the procedures followed in the prior litigation, relitigation may be warranted.[204] Fairness is a key ingredient in the issue preclusion analysis. Where the situation is vitally altered between the time of the first judgment and the second, the prior determination may not be conclusive. For example, a judicial declaration intervening between the two proceedings may so change the legal atmosphere as to render the rule of collateral estoppel inapplicable.[205] Offensive use of collateral estoppel should not be allowed where its application

---

the converse is not true. The court has indicated that there is no need to vacate a finding of no invalidity where a noninfringement judgment is affirmed on appeal, because the ruling on validity would have no collateral estoppel effect in any possible future dispute between the parties involving the patent. *Hill-Rom Co. v. Kinetic Concepts Inc.*, 209 F.3d 1337, 54 USPQ2d 1437 (Fed. Cir. 2).

[200]*A.B. Dick Co. v. Burroughs Corp.*, 713 F.2d 700, 218 USPQ 965 (Fed. Cir. 1983). Indeed, in one case the court has said that claim construction litigated between the same parties on identical factual premises is law of the case. *Del Mar Avionics, Inc. v. Quinton Instr. Co.*, 836 F.2d 1320, 5 USPQ2d 1255 (Fed. Cir. 1987). See also *In re Freeman*, 30 F.3d 1459, 31 USPQ2d 1444 (Fed. Cir. 1994). But see the contrary dictum in *Markman v. Westview Instr., Inc.*, 517 U.S. 370, 38 USPQ2d 1461, 1471 (1996).

[201]*Mother's Restaurant, Inc. v. Mama's Pizza, Inc.*, 723 F.2d 1566, 221 USPQ 394 (Fed. Cir. 1983).

[202]*Interconnect Planning Corp. v. Feil*, 774 F.2d 1132, 227 USPQ 543 (Fed. Cir. 1985). With all respect, this is a very questionable basis for refusing to give collateral estoppel effect to a summary judgment. Either summary judgment was proper or it was not, and if it was, it should result in issue preclusion.

[203]*MGA, Inc. v. General Motors Corp.*, 827 F.2d 729, 3 USPQ2d 1762 (Fed. Cir. 1987).

[204]*In re Freeman*, 30 F.3d 1459, 31 USPQ2d 1444 (Fed. Cir. 1994).

[205]*Wilson v. Turnage*, 791 F.2d 151 (Fed. Cir. 1986).

would be unfair to the precluded party. The court has some discretion in the matter.[206]

Collateral estoppel is an affirmative defense that must be pleaded and is premised on principles of fairness.[207] When a party moves for summary judgment on res judicata or some other preclusive grounds, it must be shown that the claim or issue would be precluded even on the nonmovant's version of the case.[208]

Must the prior judgment relied upon as preclusive have been final? Certainly interlocutory orders are not automatically entitled to a conclusive effect under res judicata.[209] The court has said that a determination is conclusive only when the issue of fact or law is determined by a valid and final judgment.[210] Yet the court has indicated that finality for purposes of collateral estoppel is not necessarily the same as that for appeal and seems minded to follow the view that finality for collateral estoppel purposes requires only that the prior adjudication be sufficiently firm to be accorded conclusive effect.[211] This requires, in turn, that the party against whom the estoppel is asserted have had the right, even if not exercised, to challenge on appeal the correctness of the earlier decision.[212] The grant of a right to appeal does not in itself limit the decision-making mechanism available to the appellate tribunal, including collateral estoppel.[213] However, the law of collateral estoppel is not intended to penalize a party for declining to attempt to take a piecemeal appeal. Thus, a failure to seek certification for an interlocutory appeal will not result in a nonfinal judgment having preclusive effect.[214] No issue preclusion attaches to lost issues that cannot be appealed, e.g., where a party wins on its overall claim but loses on any issue. But a voluntary relinquishment of one's right to appeal, as by a stipulated judgment of dismissal, where one stands as an overall loser, does not fall within

---

[206]*A.B. Dick Co. v. Burroughs Corp.*, 713 F.2d 700, 218 USPQ 965 (Fed. Cir. 1983).

[207]*Jackson Jordon, Inc. v. Plasser Am. Corp.*, 747 F.2d 1567, 224 USPQ 1 (Fed. Cir. 1984).

[208]*Amgen, Inc. v. Genetics Inst., Inc.*, 98 F.3d 1328, 40 USPQ2d 1524 (Fed. Cir. 1996).

[209]*Yachts Am., Inc. v. United States*, 779 F.2d 656 (Fed. Cir. 1985). An interlocutory ruling that has not been subject to appeal normally cannot be given preclusive effect. *Genentech, Inc. v. United States ITC*, 122 F.3d 1409, 43 USPQ2d 1722 (Fed. Cir. 1997).

[210]*Block v. United States ITC*, 777 F.2d 1568, 228 USPQ 37 (Fed. Cir. 1985).

[211]*Interconnect Planning Corp. v. Feil*, 774 F.2d 1132, 227 USPQ 543 (Fed. Cir. 1985).

[212]*Interconnect Planning Corp. v. Feil*, 774 F.2d 1132, 227 USPQ 543 (Fed. Cir. 1985). See also *Block v. United States ITC*, 777 F.2d 1568, 228 USPQ 37 (Fed. Cir. 1985), where an ITC order terminating an investigation was not appealable and therefore the statements of the ITC in the opinion accompanying the order were not binding. Similarly, a denial of a request for reexamination is not appealable and therefore does not deprive the requesting party of the right to contest validity in later court proceedings. *In re Etter*, 756 F.2d 852, 225 USPQ 1 (Fed. Cir. 1985). Apparently the converse is true: a nonparty does not have standing to appeal a judgment that would not be binding upon it by res judicata or collateral estoppel. *Spindelfabrik S., S. & G. GmbH v. Schubert & Salzer Mas. Ak.*, 903 F.2d 1568, 14 USPQ2d 1913 (Fed. Cir. 1990).

[213]*Kroeger v. United States Postal Serv.*, 865 F.2d 235 (Fed. Cir. 1988).

[214]*Interconnect Planning Corp. v. Feil*, 774 F.2d 1132, 227 USPQ 543 (Fed. Cir. 1985).

that rationale.[215] Conversely, the fact that a judgment is on appeal probably does not alter its preclusive effect.[216]

Are the rules of issue preclusion dependent upon the tribunal involved? Certainly the same principles of judicial efficiency that justify application of the doctrine of collateral estoppel in judicial proceedings also justify its application in quasijudicial proceedings before administrative agencies.[217] Thus an administrative review board, like other quasijudicial tribunals deciding on the basis of an adversary, litigated record, can apply the doctrine of issue preclusion in appropriate circumstances.[218] For example, a court decision that a mark is incapable of indicating origin precludes relitigation of that issue in the PTO.[219] As another example, a decision of the Court of Customs and Patent Appeals in a multiparty interference was held to have collateral estoppel effect in a later ex parte PTO proceeding involving one of the interference parties.[220]

The doctrine of issue preclusion is premised on principles of fairness. Thus a court is not without some discretion to decide whether a particular case is appropriate for application of the doctrine. Preclusion will not be applied when the quality or effectiveness of the procedures followed in the two suits differs. For example, issue preclusion will not be applied if the scope of review of the first action is very narrow.[221] Another exception to issue preclusion arises where the forum in the second action affords procedural opportunities in the presentation and determination of the issues that were not available in the first action and could likely result in the issue being differently determined.[222]

In ex parte situations, such as judgments of the PTO Board of Appeals, only the collateral estoppel aspects of res judicata are

---

[215]*Hartley v. Mentor Corp.,* 869 F.2d 1469, 10 USPQ2d 1138 (Fed. Cir. 1989).

[216]*Rice v. Department of Treasury,* 998 F.2d 997 (Fed. Cir. 1993); *Syntex Ophthalmics, Inc. v. Novicky,* 745 F.2d 1423, 223 USPQ 695 (Fed. Cir. 1984). See also *SSIH Equip. S.A. v. United States ITC,* 713 F.2d 746, 218 USPQ 678 (Fed. Cir. 1983).

[217]*Graybill v. United States Postal Serv.,* 782 F.2d 1567 (Fed. Cir. 1986).

[218]*Thomas v. General Servs. Admin.,* 794 F.2d 661 (Fed. Cir. 1986).

[219]*International Order of Job's Daughters v. Lindeburg & Co.,* 727 F.2d 1087, 220 USPQ 1017 (Fed. Cir. 1984).

[220]*In re Ziegler,* 992 F.2d 1197, 26 USPQ2d 1600 (Fed. Cir. 1993).

[221]*In re Freeman,* 30 F.3d 1459, 31 USPQ2d 1444 (Fed. Cir. 1994). Here the issue in question, claim interpretation, was reviewed under the de novo standard, which is a broad scope of review.

[222]*In re Freeman,* 30 F.3d 1459, 31 USPQ2d 1444 (Fed. Cir. 1994). The first action was an infringement suit and the second was a reexamination; the issue was claim interpretation. The Federal Circuit held that while a patentee may amend claims during reexamination, the ability to do that must be seen in light of the fundamental purpose of reexamination—the determination of validity in the context of a substantial new question of patentability, which is the focal point of every reexamination. Here the amendments were not made in response to a substantial new question of patentability or to distinguish the claims from any prior art. Thus, the fact that the ability to amend was available to the patentee does not rise to a procedural difference that avoids issue preclusion.

applied.[223] A losing party in an interference is collaterally estopped from relitigating priority as to a more generic invention than that represented by the count.[224]

In general, a decision of an administrative agency may be given preclusive effect in a federal court when the agency acts in a judicial capacity.[225] However, an administrative agency decision, issued pursuant to a statute, cannot have preclusive effect when Congress, either expressly or impliedly, indicated that it intended otherwise.[226] The preclusive effect of prior arbitration awards is for individual resolution, absent a provision in the governing contract that requires earlier awards to bind subsequent arbitrators.[227] There are and will be cases in which application of collateral estoppel to an arbitrator's decision is justified. Though some courts have cited fairness as a criterion in deciding whether to apply collateral estoppel, it is not enough merely to label application unfair because it follows procedures that may be different from those used before another adjudicating body. Unfairness is not an abstract concept. Unfairness sufficient to bar application of collateral estoppel requires a specific showing that the precise dispute was not fairly litigated and resolved before the arbitrator.[228] On the other hand, the courts should be careful not to judicialize the arbitration process. Thus in order for collateral estoppel to apply, it must be shown that the issue previously arbitrated is identical to the one now under arbitration. Arbitration normally envisions that each case be decided on its own under the controlling contract without undue reliance on other arbitration awards, even if the facts and circumstances are close. It is one thing to bind the parties by estoppel when the same facts have already been resolved by an earlier forum of competent authority. It is quite another to bind them

---

[223]*Applied Materials, Inc. v. Gemini Research Corp.,* 835 F.2d 279, 15 USPQ2d 1816 (Fed. Cir. 1987). This case involved an unusual circumstance. The claims in a parent application had been rejected and the Board decision was affirmed by the Court of Customs and Patent Appeals. Applicants filed a continuation and introduced new evidence to overcome the finding of prima facie obviousness in the original application. A patent ultimately issued. The district court in the present case granted summary judgment, holding the claims invalid on the basis of collateral estoppel in view of the prior CCPA decision. The court on appeal vacated and remanded on the ground that the district court did not give proper weight to the presumption of validity. In order for the summary judgment to stand, the record would have to show conclusively that the new evidence was immaterial. One wonders how a res judicata or collateral estoppel analysis even applies to a situation where new evidence is permitted as a matter of course.

[224]*In re Zletz,* 893 F.2d 319, 13 USPQ2d 1320 (Fed. Cir. 1989). The disputed point must, however, have been actually litigated and essential to the judgment. *Schendel v. Curtis,* 83 F.3d 1399, 38 USPQ2d 1743 (Fed. Cir. 1996).

[225]*Bio-Technology Gen'l Corp. v. Genentech, Inc.,* 80 F.3d 1553, 38 USPQ2d 1321 (Fed. Cir. 1996).

[226]*Texas Instr., Inc. v. Cypress Semiconductor Corp.,* 90 F.3d 1558, 39 USPQ2d 1492 (Fed. Cir. 1996).

[227]*Gonce v. Veterans Admin.,* 872 F.2d 995 (Fed. Cir. 1989).

[228]*Kroeger v. United States Postal Serv.,* 865 F.2d 235 (Fed. Cir. 1988).

when there is not precise correspondence of facts, circumstances, and timing.[229]

The Full Faith and Credit Clause of the Constitution, as implemented by 28 U.S.C. §1738, requires that state court judgments be given the same preclusive effect in later federal actions as they would be given under the laws of the state in which the judgments were rendered.[230] Thus, where a prior state court judgment is involved in a federal suit, the federal court should apply the state's preclusion rules.[231]

Before a state can grant preclusive effect to its own judgment, due process must be present. This requires a full and fair opportunity to litigate. But the very nature of due process negates any concept of inflexible procedures universally applicable to every imaginable situation.[232] It is inappropriate to subject a state court judgment to collateral attack in federal court in an attempt to avoid, defeat, or evade the judgment, thus denying it force and effect.[233]

(b) The Blonder-Tongue *Doctrine*

In its celebrated *Blonder-Tongue* decision,[234] the Supreme Court announced a far-reaching principle of collateral estoppel. Inasmuch as that ruling came in the context of a patent infringement case, it has been of special significance to the Federal Circuit in developing its jurisprudence about issue preclusion. In brief, *Blonder-Tongue* held simply that, despite any lack of mutuality of estoppel, a prior determination of patent invalidity may be asserted as a defense to a subsequent attempt to enforce the patent unless the patentee demonstrates that it was somehow denied a full and fair opportunity to litigate in the first action. Factors to be considered in determining the fullness and fairness of the prior litigation are: (1) whether the patentee was the plaintiff in the prior suit and chose to litigate at that time and place; (2) whether the patentee was prepared to litigate and to litigate to the finish against the defendant there involved;

---

[229]*Gonce v. Veterans Admin.*, 872 F.2d 995 (Fed. Cir. 1989).

[230]*MGA, Inc. v. General Motors Corp.*, 827 F.2d 729, 3 USPQ2d 1762 (Fed. Cir. 1987); *Graybill v. United States Postal Serv.*, 782 F.2d 1567 (Fed. Cir. 1986).

[231]*Syntex Ophthalmics, Inc. v. Novicky*, 767 F.2d 901, 226 USPQ 952 (Fed. Cir. 1985). The full faith and credit statute, 28 U.S.C. §1738, does not permit federal courts to employ their own rules of res judicata in determining the effects of state judgments. Rather, a federal court is to accept the rules chosen by the state in which the judgment is rendered. This remains true even though that judgment turned on construction of subject matter within the exclusive jurisdiction of the federal courts. *MGA, Inc. v. General Motors Corp.*, 827 F.2d 729, 3 USPQ2d 1762 (Fed. Cir. 1987).

[232]*MGA, Inc. v. General Motors Corp.*, 827 F.2d 729, 3 USPQ2d 1762 (Fed. Cir. 1987).

[233]*MGA, Inc. v. General Motors Corp.*, 827 F.2d 729, 3 USPQ2d 1762 (Fed. Cir. 1987).

[234]*Blonder-Tongue Labs., Inc. v. University of Illinois Found.*, 402 U.S. 313, 169 USPQ 513 (1971).

(3) whether, if the issue was obviousness, the first validity determination purported to employ the proper standard under §103; (4) whether the prior case was one of those relatively rare instances where the courts wholly failed to grasp the technical subject matter and the issues in suit; and (5) whether without fault of its own the patentee was deprived of crucial evidence or witnesses in the first litigation.[235]

The *Blonder-Tongue* rule is of necessity a one-way street and does not bar someone charged with infringement from challenging the validity of patent claims that were upheld in a prior infringement suit to which it was not a party. Thus the fact that claims were held not invalid in another suit against another infringer does not prevent a defendant from challenging them. Nor is the prior adjudication to be given great weight. The statutory presumption of validity is not augmented by an earlier adjudication of patent validity.[236] However, in the context of a motion for preliminary injunction against infringement of a patent, the patent holder may use a prior adjudication of patent validity involving a different defendant as evidence supporting its burden of proving likelihood of success on the merits. The district court is not bound, as a matter of law, by the prior adjudication of validity, but it may, as an exercise of its discretion, give considerable weight to it.[237]

A court decision upholding a patent's validity does not ordinarily preclude another challenge to the patent's validity, and certainly collateral estoppel does not prevent the PTO from completing a reexamination in that situation. To the extent that MPEP §2286 stated that the PTO is bound by a court's decision upholding a patent's validity, it is incorrect. On the other hand, if a court finds a patent invalid, the PTO may discontinue its reexamination. This is consistent with *Blonder-Tongue*. Of course, in the end it is up to a court, not the PTO, to decide if the patentee had a full and fair chance to litigate the validity of the patent, but it is certainly permissible for the PTO to act on a standing judgment of invalidity unless and until a court has said it does not have res judicata effect.[238]

By and large the Federal Circuit has had little difficulty in its application of *Blonder-Tongue*. It has been faithful in its adherence to the notion that the sole question is whether the patentee had a full and fair chance to litigate the validity of its patent the first time. Even the fact of inconsistent prior adjudications does not transform the question into which was correct;[239] inconsistent rulings are no

---

[235]*Blonder-Tongue Labs., Inc. v. University of Illinois Found.*, 402 U.S. 313, 169 USPQ 513 (1971). See, e.g., *Stevenson v. Sears, Roebuck & Co.*, 713 F.2d 705, 218 USPQ 969 (Fed. Cir. 1983).

[236]*Allen Archery, Inc. v. Browning Mfg. Co.*, 819 F.2d 1087, 2 USPQ2d 1490 (Fed. Cir. 1987). The significance of a prior decision that finds the patent not invalid is discussed in the presumption of validity context at notes 1:198ff in light of *Mendenhall v. Cedarapids, Inc.*, 5 F.3d 1556, 28 USPQ2d 1081 (Fed. Cir. 1993).

[237]*Hybritech, Inc. v. Abbott Labs.*, 849 F.2d 1446, 7 USPQ2d 1191 (Fed. Cir. 1988).

[238]*Ethicon v. Quigg*, 849 F.2d 1422, 7 USPQ2d 1152 (Fed. Cir. 1988).

[239]*Stevenson v. Sears, Roebuck & Co.*, 713 F.2d 705, 218 USPQ 969 (Fed. Cir. 1983).

more than a "red flag" of caution.[240] Losing one's case is not evidence that the jury failed to grasp the technical subject matter.[241]

The court seems quite willing to hold that collateral estoppel in the *Blonder-Tongue* setting applies even to a prior summary judgment; although such a judgment is based on affidavits, the fact that depositions were available results in a full and fair opportunity to litigate.[242]

Under the Supreme Court's *Cardinal*[243] decision, a finding of invalidity is probably necessary to the judgment even where no infringement is found.[244]

The fact that the trial records in two cases may differ materially will not alone defeat the application of collateral estoppel. The party opposing a plea of estoppel must establish that it did not have a full and fair opportunity to litigate; it must demonstrate that without fault of its own it was deprived of crucial evidence or witnesses in the first litigation. The fact that the party now has evidence to rebut or counter the evidence upon which invalidity was based is not sufficient. It must also be shown that such evidence was not then in existence or was unavailable through no fault of the patentee.[245]

The court has extended *Blonder-Tongue* to cover infringement issues, on the theory that the scope of a claim as determined in prior litigation with other defendants can be determinative in a second case, if the defendant in the second case can show that its device is

---

[240]*Mississippi Chem. Corp. v. Swift Agric. Chem. Corp.*, 717 F.2d 1374, 219 USPQ 577 (Fed. Cir. 1983). In *Mendenhall v. Barber-Greene Co.*, 26 F.3d 1573, 31 USPQ2d 1001 (Fed. Cir. 1994), the court encountered a very complex situation involving its own prior appellate ruling. It had affirmed a holding that the patents were not invalid in an interlocutory appeal against a first defendant, and the case went back to the district court for a damages determination. Meanwhile, the Federal Circuit affirmed a judgment of invalidity of the patents in a suit against a second defendant. On appeal from the damages award against the first defendant, the court applied a *Blonder-Tongue* estoppel. The patentee's principal argument was that the Federal Circuit was thereby overturning its own prior decision in the first case. The court's response was (1) the issue is not validity but the viability of a collateral estoppel defense, (2) the first decision had held only that the first defendant had failed to establish the merits of its invalidity defenses, and (3) the first decision resulted in a remand for the damages proceedings and was not a final judgment. The court observed that the patentee was attempting to invoke a novel kind of res judicata "within" a case. This characterization seems apt. If anything, it would be law of the case principles that should apply. Another complicating factor in this case was the presence of yet another defendant in yet another case; the decision deserves careful study and review, particularly in light of the dissent.

[241]*Pharmacia & Upjohn Co. v. Mylan Pharm. Inc.*, 170 F.3d 1373, 50 USPQ2d 1033 (Fed. Cir. 1999).

[242]*Stevenson v. Sears, Roebuck & Co.*, 713 F.2d 705, 218 USPQ 969 (Fed. Cir. 1983). A nonparty who had been charged but not sued objected to a subpoena for sales information on the ground that it would be prejudiced if the patentee should win its suit, because the nonparty would have had no opportunity to participate. In rejecting this argument, the Federal Circuit pointed out that the nonparty would not be bound by an adverse result; on the other hand, if providing the requested information would assure the patentee of a full and fair opportunity to litigate, the nonparty could take advantage of a favorable judgment. *Truswal Sys. Corp v. Hydro-Air Eng'g, Inc.*, 813 F.2d 1207, 2 USPQ 1034 (Fed. Cir. 1987).

[243]See text accompanying notes 16:476–489.

[244]*Mendenhall v. Barber-Greene Co.*, 26 F.3d 1573, 31 USPQ2d 1001 (Fed. Cir. 1994).

[245]*Dana Corp. v. NOK, Inc.*, 882 F.2d 505, 11 USPQ2d 1883 (Fed. Cir. 1989).

so similar to those in the first that it falls outside that scope.[246] The issue of infringement provides a good illustration of the difference between issue preclusion, or collateral estoppel, and claim preclusion, or res judicata. When a previous judgment of noninfringement is offered with respect to a new accused device, there is no claim preclusion, because the original claim of infringement embraced no more than the specific device before the court in the first suit. However, inasmuch as the claim interpretation issue decided in the first case was necessary to the decision, the prior judgment has collateral estoppel effect and precludes the parties from relitigating that issue.[247] A patentee, once having sought and obtained a broad construction of its claim in an action against one accused infringer, is barred, in a subsequent action against a different accused infringer, from arguing a narrow construction of the claim so as to avoid anticipation.[248] But a device not previously before a court, and shown to differ from those structures previously litigated, requires determination on its own facts. Neither res judicata nor issue preclusion applies.[249]

The court has held[250] that judicial statements regarding the scope of patent claims are entitled to collateral estoppel effect in a subsequent infringement suit only to the extent that determination of scope was essential to a final judgment on the question of validity or infringement. It has warned that statements regarding the scope of patent claims made in a former adjudication should be narrowly construed. In addition, to apply issue preclusion to a claim interpretation issue, the interpretation of the claim had to be the reason for the loss in the prior case.[251]

The doctrine of *Kessler v. Eldred*[252] bars a patent infringement suit against a customer of a seller who has previously prevailed against the patentee because of invalidity or noninfringement. *Kessler* grants a limited trade right in such a seller to have that which it lawfully produces freely bought and sold without restraint or interference.

---

[246]*Molinaro v. Fannon/Courier Corp.*, 745 F.2d 651, 223 USPQ 706 (Fed. Cir. 1984). Somewhat surprisingly, issue preclusion was applied here in a summary judgment. It was not clear whether the question of sufficient similarity was disputed. See note 18:202.

[247]*Pfaff v. Wells Elec., Inc.*, 5 F.3d 514, 28 USPQ2d 1119 (Fed. Cir. 1993).

[248]*Dana Corp. v. NOK, Inc.*, 882 F.2d 505, 11 USPQ2d 1883 (Fed. Cir. 1989). This is the doctrine of *Smith v. Hall*, 301 U.S. 216 (1937), which the Federal Circuit regards as an example of collateral estoppel. *Id.* This seems consistent with *Blonder-Tongue.* Here the rule was not applied because the court in the first case did not adopt the sought-for construction.

[249]*Del Mar Avionics, Inc. v. Quinton Instr. Co.*, 836 F.2d 1320, 5 USPQ2d 1255 (Fed. Cir. 1987).

[250]See note 18:200 and accompanying text.

[251]In *In re Freeman*, 30 F.3d 1459, 31 USPQ2d 1444 (Fed. Cir. 1994), the court applied these rules to a later reexamination, giving preclusive effect to its own former ruling regarding claim interpretation in an infringement context. The court pointed out that this was not a situation where the later proceeding, the reexamination, involving the same issue, was unforeseen. The PTO proceedings on the reexamination had been stayed pending the outcome of the district court action. This scenario is no longer possible, of course, because the PTO cannot stay reexamination proceedings. See text accompanying notes 16:476–489.

[252]206 U.S. 285 (1907).

Thus, a state court judgment that a manufacturer's products were not covered by a license and therefore required no payment of royalty bars an infringement suit against a customer and precludes relitigation of whether the machines infringe.[253]

The court has also indicated that a judgment that adjudicates fewer than all claims of a patent may under certain circumstances operate as collateral estoppel to preclude the patentee from asserting the remaining claims.[254] In deciding whether to apply collateral estoppel to unadjudicated patent claims, the first step is to determine whether any new issues are raised by the unadjudicated claims, or whether the claims are substantially identical. Substantial identity for purposes of collateral estoppel is a matter of claim interpretation, and thus a question of law, and can be resolved by summary judgment.[255]

The *Blonder-Tongue* doctrine sometimes arises in an unusual factual setting. In one situation, the patent had been held valid in a first case and invalid in a second. In the third case, the district court refused to grant a summary judgment of collateral estoppel on grounds that the parties were about ready for trial. The Federal Circuit granted a writ of mandamus directing the district court to enter summary judgment. The *Blonder-Tongue* doctrine is not based solely on economy, so that being ready for trial and having done most of the work is not persuasive. Nor can relitigation be permitted because of equitable considerations.[256]

In another case, the ITC had issued an exclusion order on three patents. After the order but before presidential review, the district court in a copending infringement suit against a different defendant held two of the three patents invalid. The ITC promptly modified its order to apply only to the valid patent. This was held proper, despite the pendency of an appeal from the district court judgment.[257] In

---

[253]*MGA, Inc. v. General Motors Corp.*, 827 F.2d 729, 3 USPQ2d 1762 (Fed. Cir. 1987). Interestingly, the court was able to pass the question of whether *Kessler* is a matter of substantive federal patent law, or a long-recognized exception to the mutuality of estoppel requirement, because it found that Michigan courts would apply the *Kessler* doctrine, which in its effect may be compared to defensive collateral estoppel, to give preclusive effect to a judgment of noninfringement.

[254]*Jervis B. Webb Co. v. Southern Sys., Inc.*, 742 F.2d 1388, 222 USPQ 943 (Fed. Cir. 1984). In *Amgen, Inc. v. Genetics Inst., Inc.*, 98 F.3d 1328, 40 USPQ2d 1524 (Fed. Cir. 1996), the court went so far as to give preclusive effect to its own prior holding of nonenablement involving a different patent with different, albeit closely related claims.

[255]*Interconnect Planning Corp. v. Feil*, 774 F.2d 1132, 227 USPQ 543 (Fed. Cir. 1985).

[256]*Mississippi Chem. Corp. v. Swift Agric. Chem. Corp.*, 717 F.2d 1374, 219 USPQ 577 (Fed. Cir. 1983). The district court also felt that one of the claims had not been held invalid in the second case. But the judge in the second case had ruled that it was holding that claim invalid, and this ruling too was collateral estoppel and could not be relitigated even if erroneous.

[257]*SSIH Equip. S.A. v. United States ITC*, 713 F.2d 746, 218 USPQ 678 (Fed. Cir. 1983). Nor does the pendency of posttrial motions in the earlier case affect the situation. While it may be preferable in a particular case to permit some time to pass to allow for resolution of such motions, there is no compelling argument for treating such motions any differently than appeals for finality purposes. *Pharmacia & Upjohn Co. v. Mylan Pharm. Inc.*, 170 F.3d 1373, 50 USPQ2d 1033 (Fed. Cir. 1999).

another situation involving the ITC, a district court held a patent invalid on summary judgment. Three weeks later, the CCPA affirmed a prior ITC holding of validity. With classically correct reasoning, the Federal Circuit held that the CCPA decision did not bind the defendant in a third suit, because it was not a party to the ITC proceeding and therefore had no opportunity to litigate. But the patentee was precluded by the summary judgment of invalidity.[258]

In another unusual situation, two infringement cases were pending on the same patent. In the one at hand, the defendant, while not admitting validity, did not contest it, and the appeal was solely on the question of damages for infringement. While the appeal was pending, the Federal Circuit itself held, in the other case, that the patent had been procured by fraud. The court balanced public policy on fraud against the general proposition that conceded or unappealed issues are not reviewable and held that the present defendant could take advantage of the fraud holding.[259]

In another unusual situation, a manufacturer who had indemnified the government was joined as a third-party defendant in a suit against the government in the Court of Federal Claims. In holding that the third-party defendant had no standing to appeal alone, after the government had dismissed its appeal from a judgment of infringement, the Federal Circuit looked closely at the preclusive effect of the judgment. It concluded that the manufacturer would not be precluded on the issue of patent invalidity (1) as to the government, because they were allies, not adversaries, on all issues decided by the Court of Federal Claims; (2) as to the patentee, because the action did not involve an obligation of the manufacturer, but only the government; and (3) as to both, because, as the court ultimately held, the manufacturer had no standing to appeal.[260]

A plea of *Blonder-Tongue* estoppel may be timely made at any stage of the affected proceedings, including the appellate level.[261]

Consent judgments. The court has begun to grapple with the preclusive effect of consent judgments. If an issue was not litigated in a prior suit, obviously the doctrine of issue preclusion cannot apply.[262] It is therefore generally correct that a judgment entered pursuant to a stipulation will give rise only to claim preclusion, not

---

[258]*Stevenson v. Sears, Roebuck & Co.,* 713 F.2d 705, 218 USPQ 969 (Fed. Cir. 1983). Not surprisingly, the court rejected an argument that it should give stare decisis effect to the prior CCPA holding of validity.

[259]The court did not indicate what its result would have been if (1) validity and unenforceability had been admitted, or (2) if the other holding had been pure invalidity rather than fraud. *Thompson-Hayward Chem. Co. v. Rohm & Haas Co.,* 745 F.2d 27, 223 USPQ 690 (Fed. Cir. 1984). The rule of *Blonder-Tongue* applies to unenforceability for inequitable conduct. *General Electro Music Corp. v. Samick Music Corp.,* 19 F.3d 1405, 30 USPQ2d 1149 (Fed. Cir. 1994).

[260]*Penda Corp. v. United States,* 44 F.3d 967, 33 USPQ2d 1200 (Fed. Cir. 1994).

[261]*Mendenhall v. Barber-Greene Co.,* 26 F.3d 1573, 31 USPQ2d 1001 (Fed. Cir. 1994); *Dana Corp. v. NOK, Inc.,* 882 F.2d 505, 11 USPQ2d 1883 (Fed. Cir. 1989).

[262]*Cordis Corp. v. Medtronic, Inc.,* 835 F.2d 859, 5 USPQ2d 1118 (Fed. Cir. 1987).

issue preclusion. However, where rulings on a specific issue are made after a full and fair opportunity to litigate, and those rulings are firm and consistent with the subsequent settlement agreement and the judgment actually entered in the case, issue preclusion can be applied to the judgment. The stipulated judgment must, like a contract, be construed to determine its effect in light of all the circumstances, including the intent of the parties.[263]

In *Foster v. Hallco*,[264] the court cleared up a little of the confusion surrounding consent judgments and their binding effect. The court held unequivocally that *Lear*[265] does not permit challenges to validity where, under normal principles of res judicata applicable to a consent judgment, such challenges would be precluded.[266] Thus, if a consent judgment, by its terms, indicates that the parties thereto intended to preclude any challenge to the validity of a particular patent, even in subsequent litigation involving a new cause of action, then that issue can be precluded as between those parties. But such an intention should not be readily inferred; a narrow construction of the consent judgment strikes a reasonable balance between the policy considerations of *Lear* and those favoring voluntary settlement of litigation.[267]

In one case a defendant had agreed in a pretrial stipulation to be bound, as to validity and enforceability, by the judgment in a case against another defendant, "excluding a consent judgment." The other defendant vigorously contested validity and enforceability at trial, lost, and exhausted all available posttrial remedies. It then reached a settlement on the issue of damages that mooted its posttrial motions and forced it to forfeit its appellate rights. This was held not to be a consent judgment within the meaning of the stipulation by the present defendant.[268] However, where the trial court had held a patent invalid on the merits and the parties agreed to a stipulated dismissal of the infringement claim with prejudice, the judgment operates as an adverse adjudication on the merits of the claim; the holding of invalidity provides one possible ground to support the stipulated dismissal.[269]

[263]*Hartley v. Mentor Corp.*, 869 F.2d 1469, 10 USPQ2d 1138 (Fed. Cir. 1989).

[264]*Foster v. Hallco Mfg. Co.*, 947 F.2d 469, 20 USPQ2d 1241 (Fed. Cir. 1991).

[265]*Lear, Inc. v. Adkins*, 395 U.S. 653, 162 USPQ 1 (1969).

[266]The court explained that *Lear* did not involve a judgment but only a license. No court has ever suggested that *Lear* abrogates the application of res judicata to judgments imposed by the court after full litigation. Nor should it prohibit the application of res judicata in the consent judgment setting. A binding consent judgment encourages patent owners to agree to settlement, and to remove its force would have an adverse effect on settlement negotiations. *Foster v. Hallco Mfg. Co.*, 947 F.2d 469, 20 USPQ2d 1241 (Fed. Cir. 1991).

[267]*Foster v. Hallco Mfg. Co.*, 947 F.2d 469, 20 USPQ2d 1241 (Fed. Cir. 1991). The court remanded for a determination of the intent of the parties, noting that extrinsic evidence could be introduced where the consent judgment itself was ambiguous on the question.

[268]*Kearns v. Chrysler Corp.*, 32 F.3d 1541, 31 USPQ2d 1746 (Fed. Cir. 1994). The court made rather short work of the defendant's argument that public policy should rescue it from a decision that it later finds to have been imprudently made. To the contrary, public policy favors preventing it from reneging on an agreement into which it freely entered and upon which both the plaintiff and the district court relied.

[269]*Hartley v. Mentor Corp.*, 869 F.2d 1469, 10 USPQ2d 1138 (Fed. Cir. 1989). Here the patentee and its exclusive licensee had previously sued a third party for infringement, and the

A party may expressly reserve in a consent judgment the right to relitigate some or all issues that would have otherwise been barred as between the same parties. Any such reservation must be discerned within the four corners of the consent decree and cannot be expanded beyond the decree's express terms.[270]

The court seems inclined not to prejudge application of *Blonder-Tongue* to consent judgments. In a case where the trial court had found some claims valid and infringed, and some claims invalid, the defendant took a license under the valid claims and a consent judgment reflecting the trial court's holding was entered. The plaintiff then appealed the invalidity portion of the judgment. The Federal Circuit dismissed the appeal on the jurisdictional ground that the settlement had removed the controversy between the parties. It justified its refusal to vacate the consent judgment on the ground that the case did not become moot during the appeal process—rather, the consent decree mooted any possibility of the plaintiff pursuing an appeal and thereby foreclosed the court from obtaining jurisdiction. Consequently, vacating the consent judgment would preclude a collateral estoppel defense in a later case and thus effectively decide the *Blonder-Tongue* issue before it even arises.[271]

(c) Claim Preclusion

Res judicata embodies the public policy of putting an end to litigation. In its simplest construct, it precludes the relitigation of a

---

trial court found the patent invalid. Thereafter, the parties negotiated a settlement that provided, among other things, for a stipulated dismissal with prejudice of the infringement claim. The defendant in the present case purchased the license rights of the exclusive licensee who was party to the prior suit and refused to pay royalties to the patentee, citing a provision in the agreement that no royalties would be required if the patent were to be held invalid. The court first decided that the defendant in the prior suit would have been able to assert issue preclusion, and then went on to hold that the present defendant could as well under *Blonder-Tongue*. The court disposed of the patentee's argument based upon alleged inconsistent positions by the present defendant by pointing out that this is not a situation where the licensee won the first time around and is seeking to win here on the flip side of the same theory. In fact, the licensee lost the first time around.

[270]*Epic Metals Corp. v. H.H. Robertson Co.*, 870 F.2d 1574, 10 USPQ2d 1296 (Fed. Cir. 1989). Here the consent judgment provided that the patent was valid over the art before the PTO and the art considered in another litigation. It expressly left open whether a proposed structure was an infringement, and reserved the right to contest infringement on the basis that the structure was following the prior art or was an obvious modification of it. Two judges of the panel held that this express language nonetheless did not reserve the right to challenge validity on new prior art while the third panel member felt that the plain intent of the judgment was to permit a challenge to validity on new prior art.

[271]*Gould v. Control Laser Corp.*, 866 F.2d 1391, 9 USPQ2d 1718 (Fed. Cir. 1989). In view of this decision one must exercise extreme caution when negotiating and drafting consent judgments, especially partial consent judgments, so as not to foreclose the right to appellate review of a part of the underlying rulings of the trial court. Also, the decision may be at odds with the court's unwillingness to permit determinations of invalidity to stand absent a holding of infringement. See the discussion under "Mootness and noninfringement" in §16.3(h) above. Here the defendant took a license under the valid claims and therefore was no longer an infringer of the patent. Thus it would seem that a vacation of the judgment of invalidity was

claim, or cause or action, or any possible defense to the cause of action, that is ended by a judgment of a court. This aspect of res judicata, known as claim preclusion, applies whether the judgment is rendered after trial and imposed by the court or entered upon the consent of the parties.[272] Thus, where a complaint arises out of substantially the same subject matter as an earlier complaint, the dismissal of the earlier bars litigation of the later. Res judicata prevents litigation of all grounds for, or defenses to, recovery that were previously available to the parties, regardless of whether they were asserted or determined in the prior proceeding.[273]

Claim preclusion analysis raises a variety of issues, such as identity of claims (splitting a cause of action), identity of parties (privity), the nature of the judgment, and the jurisdiction of the tribunal that rendered it. The Federal Circuit has considered some of these questions.

It is clear that the court will follow the *Restatement* view on splitting a cause of action.[274] Thus, claim preclusion will bar or merge all rights with respect to all or any part of the transaction, or series of connected transactions, out of which the prior action arose.[275] A party may not split a cause of action into separate grounds of recovery and raise the separate grounds in successive lawsuits. Instead, a party must raise in a single lawsuit all the grounds of recovery that arise from a single transaction or series of transactions that can be brought together.[276] By the same token, a patent owner must plead

---

in order. Certainly the Federal Circuit would have jurisdiction to do that much, inasmuch as that is its normal procedure when it finds that the controversy has been mooted.

[272]*Foster v. Hallco Mfg. Co.*, 947 F.2d 469, 20 USPQ2d 1241 (Fed. Cir. 1991). See also *W.L. Gore & Assoc. v. C.R. Bard, Inc.*, 977 F.2d 558, 24 USPQ2d 1451 (Fed. Cir. 1992). The topic of consent judgments and their preclusive effect is discussed in detail in §10.6(c).

[273]*Finch v. Hughes Aircraft Co.*, 926 F.2d 1574, 17 USPQ2d 1914 (Fed. Cir. 1991). Under *Mercoid Corp. v. Mid-Continent Inv. Co.*, 320 U.S. 661 (1944), this may not hold true in the case of a misuse defense. See *Glitsch Inc. v. Koch Eng'g Co.*, 216 F.3d 1382, 55 USPQ2d 1374 (Fed. Cir. 2). Whether, based on the facts of the case, a claim is barred by res judicata is a question of law that is reviewed de novo. *United Tech. Corp. v. Chromalloy Gas Turbine Corp.*, 189 F.3d 1338, 51 USPQ2d 1838 (Fed. Cir. 1999).

[274]*Chromalloy Am. Corp. v. Kenneth Gordon, Ltd.*, 736 F.2d 694, 222 USPQ 187 (Fed. Cir. 1984). Under the "transactional" approach to res judicata, as discussed in the *Restatement (Second) of Judgments* §24, subsequent litigation of a claim is barred if it arises out of the same subject matter as a previous suit and, through the exercise of diligence, could have been litigated in a prior suit. What constitutes the subject matter of a suit depends on the factual basis of the complaint, and any cause of action that arises out of the same facts should be litigated in the same action. *United Tech. Corp. v. Chromalloy Gas Turbine Corp.*, 189 F.3d 1338, 51 USPQ2d 1838 (Fed. Cir. 1999).

[275]*Restatement (Second) of Judgments* 196 (1982). Claims are the same where they arise from the same operative facts even if the operative facts support different legal theories that cannot all be brought in one court. *Johns-Manville Corp. v. United States*, 855 F.2d 1556 (Fed. Cir. 1988).

[276]*Mars, Inc. v. Nippon Conlux K-K*, 58 F.3d 616, 35 USPQ2d 1311 (Fed. Cir. 1995). The patent owner first sued a U.S. subsidiary and later its Japanese parent. Both complaints alleged injury by infringement attributable to the same group of products, and the U.S. subsidiary was the sales representative in this country for the Japanese parent. The court found claim preclusion and rejected plaintiff's argument that the parent probably would have resisted any effort to obtain jurisdiction over it in the first action.

a charge of patent infringement in response to a claim for a declaratory judgment of noninfringement, or be forever barred by res judicata from doing so.[277] Under claim preclusion a plaintiff is barred from a subsequent assertion of the same transactional facts in the form of a different cause of action or theory of relief.[278]

In *Foster v. Hallco*,[279] the court explored what is meant by "same claim" in a claim preclusion context. "Claim" does not mean merely argument or assertion. Thus an assertion of invalidity of a patent by an alleged infringer is not a claim but a defense to the patent owner's claim. This is not altered by the fact that invalidity is raised in a declaratory judgment action, because the transactional foundation for such an action rests on the facts respecting the patent owner's claim for infringement. In order for a patent infringement claim in a later case to be the "same" as that in a subsequent case, the accused infringements must be essentially the same. Colorable changes in an infringing device or changes unrelated to the limitations of the patent claims would not present a new cause of action. Finally, the burden to show that the infringements are essentially the same in the two cases falls upon the party invoking claim preclusion.

Important questions regarding splitting causes of action remain to be decided. In one case a prior decision between the same parties in another court had held that device A infringed but device C did not. The defendant argued that plaintiff was barred from claiming here that device B infringes, on the basis that B could have been litigated in the first case. But apparently B was not then known to the plaintiff; indeed, the plaintiff asserted that it was within the scope of its discovery requests but was not identified. On this basis the court concluded there was no bar.[280] The implication is that a patent must be asserted against all known devices the first time around. Is it also true that all patents that might be infringed must be asserted against a particular device the first time around?[281]

Where a party withdraws from a litigation and suffers dismissal of its unfair competition claim with prejudice, that claim becomes barred by the judgment.[282] A summary judgment is a decision on the

---

[277]*Genentech, Inc. v. Eli Lilly & Co.*, 998 F.2d 931, 27 USPQ2d 1241 (Fed. Cir. 1993). Regional circuit law governs questions of res judicata arising under the compulsory counterclaim provisions of Rule 13(a), FRCP. *Beech Aircraft Corp. v. EDO Corp.*, 990 F.2d 1237 (Fed. Cir. 1993).

[278]*Vitaline Corp. v. General Mills, Inc.*, 891 F.2d 273, 13 USPQ2d 1172 (Fed. Cir. 1989).

[279]*Foster v. Hallco Mfg. Co.*, 947 F.2d 469, 20 USPQ2d 1241 (Fed. Cir. 1991).

[280]*Del Mar Avionics, Inc. v. Quinton Instr. Co.*, 836 F.2d 1320, 5 USPQ2d 1255 (Fed. Cir. 1987).

[281]The matter is far from clear. In *Kearns v. General Motors Corp.*, 94 F.3d 1553, 39 USPQ2d 1949 (Fed. Cir. 1996), the court refused to bar a second suit that included additional patents that apparently could have been but were not asserted in the first action. The two-judge panel seemed to rely heavily on the fact that the judgment against the patents in the first action was based on procedural rather than substantive ground. This decision raises more questions than it answers.

[282]*Water Techs. Corp. v. Calco, Ltd.*, 850 F.2d 660, 7 USPQ2d 1097 (Fed. Cir. 1988).

merits with res judicata effect, while a dismissal for lack of subject matter jurisdiction is not a disposition on the merits and thus permits a litigant to refile in an appropriate forum.[283] The presence of a valid defense does not oust a tribunal of jurisdiction unless, of course, the defense is jurisdictional. If it did, the only cases decided on the merits would hold for victorious plaintiffs, and no successful defense would generate a res judicata bar.[284]

A dismissal with prejudice, for whatever reason, cannot act as res judicata where the court did not have subject matter jurisdiction to decide the claim.[285] If a prior infringement suit is dismissed with prejudice, the burden is on the defendant infringer to show that the devices charged in the second suit are the same as those in the previous suit. Not every charge of infringement is precluded, and the defendant does not become an unfettered licensee by virtue of the prior dismissal.[286] A stipulated dismissal with prejudice of a declaratory judgment action does not resolve the merits of the underlying claim and thus has no preclusive effect.[287]

A nonparty may be bound by a judgment if one of the actual parties is so closely aligned with the nonparty's interests as to be its virtual representative. So, too, if the nonparty controls or substantially participates in the control of the presentation on behalf of a party. These are questions that must be decided, ultimately, by the court that is invoking preclusion, but they may well be questions that are themselves determined by issue preclusion, if they were actually litigated in the previous case.[288] A nonparty that acquires assets of

---

[283]*Vink v. Schijf*, 839 F.2d 676, 5 USPQ2d 1728 (Fed. Cir. 1988). The distinction between lack of jurisdiction and failure to state a claim upon which relief can be granted is an important one, for a dismissal on the merits carries res judicata effect and dismissal for want of jurisdiction does not. *Do-Well Mach. Shop, Inc. v. United States*, 870 F.2d 637 (Fed. Cir. 1989).

[284]*Do-Well Mach. Shop, Inc. v. United States*, 870 F.2d 637 (Fed. Cir. 1989).

[285]*Bundrick v. United States*, 785 F.2d 1009 (Fed. Cir. 1986). Even with jurisdiction, the claim may not be precluded if it is clear that the court did not intend, by dismissing, to adjudicate it on the merits. *Id.* A dismissal for lack of jurisdiction may be given res judicata effect as to the jurisdictional issue. *Amgen, Inc. v. United States ITC*, 902 F.2d 1532, 14 USPQ2d 1734 (Fed. Cir. 1990). But a dismissal without prejudice for want of jurisdiction is not res judicata as to a new complaint alleging additional jurisdictional facts. *Arrowhead Indus. Water, Inc. v. Ecolochem, Inc.*, 846 F.2d 731, 6 USPQ2d 1685 (Fed. Cir. 1988).

[286]*Young Eng'rs, Inc. v. United States ITC*, 721 F.2d 1305, 219 USPQ 1142 (Fed. Cir. 1983). See text accompanying note 18:249.

[287]*Hartley v. Mentor Corp.*, 869 F.2d 1469, 10 USPQ2d 1138 (Fed. Cir. 1989). The patentee had dismissed its infringement claim with prejudice after a partial adjudication that found the patent invalid. As part of the settlement the defendant likewise dismissed its declaratory judgment counterclaim with prejudice. The patentee argued that the dismissal of the counterclaim was inconsistent with the adjudication and thus should negate any issue preclusion resulting from dismissal of the infringement claim. The court properly rejected this argument. But consider whether a dismissal with prejudice of an unadjudicated declaratory judgment counterclaim for patent invalidity, albeit as part of a settlement, should not have at least claim preclusive effect. This author has litigated the question with precisely that result.

[288]*Mother's Restaurant, Inc. v. Mama's Pizza, Inc.*, 723 F.2d 1566, 221 USPQ 394 (Fed. Cir. 1983). Thus, where a state court finds likelihood of confusion, and for one reason or another also finds privity or virtual representation or control, the state court decision will be binding on the represented party in a cancellation proceeding before a PTO tribunal. *Id.*

a defendant-infringer after a suit begins is in privity and bound by a judgment.[289]

It is well settled that claim preclusion is not limited to cases involving identical parties. For example, claim preclusion may be invoked by and against those in privity with parties. The notion of privity is sometimes criticized as not aiding analysis but simply stating a conclusion that a particular nonparty should be treated the same as a party for claim preclusion purposes. For that reason, courts often focus directly on the question whether the relationship between the parties is such that one party should enjoy the benefit, or suffer the burden, of a judgment for or against another. A plaintiff who chooses to bring two separate actions against two tortfeasors who are jointly responsible for the same injury runs the risk that the court will find the parties sufficiently related that the second action is barred by claim preclusion.[290]

What if the prior judgment is reversed? A state court held that, as between A and B, A had title to several patents. In a second case, A settled by assigning all rights in the patents to C. In a federal suit, B and C were contesting title to the patents. During the pendency of the federal suit, the first state court judgment was reversed on appeal as to some but not all of the patents. The Federal Circuit held that B was precluded as to the patents unaffected by the reversal, but not as to the others.[291] In actions against the government in which the district courts and the Claims Court have concurrent jurisdiction, the doctrine of res judicata will protect the government from having to defend itself on the merits against a second claim brought by the same party sequentially on the same legal theories in both courts. Similarly, res judicata will protect the government against second suits in those actions over which the district courts and the Court of Federal Claims have exclusive jurisdiction because of different legal theories or causes of action, but where the actions, though theoretically different, involve the same set of operative facts.[292]

As in the case of issue preclusion, claim preclusion is an operative doctrine in quasijudicial and administrative proceedings. Thus the

---

[289]*Kloster Speedsteel AB v. Crucible Inc.,* 793 F.2d 1565, 230 USPQ 81 (Fed. Cir. 1986). See also *Arco Polymers, Inc. v. Studiengesellschaft Kohle,* 710 F.2d 798, 218 USPQ 481 (Fed. Cir. 1983).

[290]*Mars, Inc. v. Nippon Conlux K-K,* 58 F.3d 616, 35 USPQ2d 1311 (Fed. Cir. 1995). Here the court applied claim preclusion to a situation where the patent owner prosecuted a first action to judgment against a U.S. subsidiary of a Japanese parent corporation, and then sued the parent separately in a second action. It applied regional circuit law, reasoning that the question turned on general principles of claim preclusion, not on a rule of law having special application to patent cases. In *Speedplay Inc. v. Bebop Inc.,* 211 F.3d 1245, 53 USPQ2d 1984 (Fed. Cir. 2), the court indicated that where an individual patentee controls the operation of a closely-held corporate licensee, and actively participates in the conduct of a patent infringement action brought by the corporation, the judgment will have preclusive effect with respect to any parallel claim that might be brought by the patentee.

[291]*Syntex Ophthalmics, Inc. v. Novicky,* 745 F.2d 1423, 223 USPQ 695 (Fed. Cir. 1984).

[292]*UNR Indus., Inc. v. United States,* 911 F.2d 654 (Fed. Cir. 1990).

PTO can, in a proper case, reject claims on the basis of res judicata.[293] The mere fact that the remedy of total exclusion is not available in a district court infringement suit does not prevent claim preclusion by virtue of the district court judgment in a later ITC proceeding. The Federal Circuit is willing to adopt a pragmatic approach, and holds that if an infringement claim would be barred in a second district court action, the exclusion remedy may also be barred in an ITC proceeding.[294] The court has passed the question whether a failure of the licensee to raise patent invalidity as a defense to a state court suit for royalties would, in the event of a judgment in the state court action, be res judicata as to validity in a federal action.[295]

The ITC itself long was of the view that its determinations are not res judicata in court proceedings; the Federal Circuit initially passed this question.[296] More recently, it has sided unequivocally with the ITC, holding that ITC judgments cannot bar later court claims based on the same transactional facts.[297] However, a district court is still free to attribute whatever persuasive value to the prior ITC decision that it considers justified.[298]

(d) Law of the Case

Issues decided at an earlier stage of the same litigation, either explicitly or by necessary inference from the disposition, constitute the law of the case. The law of the case doctrine is that courts should generally refuse to reopen what has been decided.[299] The doctrine of

---

[293]*In re Donohue,* 766 F.2d 531, 226 USPQ 619 (Fed. Cir. 1985). Such a rejection is improper where the applicant in a continuing application makes a new record that presents a new issue of patentability. *Id.* But see note 18:223 and accompanying text.

[294]*Young Eng'rs, Inc. v. United States ITC,* 721 F.2d 1305, 219 USPQ 1142 (Fed. Cir. 1983).

[295]*Intermedics Infusaid, Inc. v. Regents of Univ. of Minn.,* 804 F.2d 129, 231 USPQ 653 (Fed. Cir. 1986). There is, of course, a strong public policy component to the argument that opposes preclusive effect. See *Lear, Inc. v. Adkins,* 395 U.S. 653, 162 USPQ 1 (1969). In *Hemstreet v. Spiegel, Inc.,* 851 F.2d 348, 7 USPQ2d 1502 (Fed. Cir. 1988), the court passed the question of whether, under Seventh Circuit law, a settlement order adjudicated validity and infringement and thus became res judicata as to enforceability.

[296]*Corning Glass Works v. United States ITC,* 799 F.2d 1559, 230 USPQ 822 (Fed. Cir. 1986). The court did appear to indicate some agreement with the ITC view, citing supportive legislative history. See also *Texas Instr., Inc. v. United States ITC,* 851 F.2d 342, 7 USPQ2d 1509 (Fed. Cir. 1988).

[297]*Bio-Technology Gen'l Corp. v. Genentech, Inc.,* 80 F.3d 1553, 38 USPQ2d 1321 (Fed. Cir. 1996). The reasoning is that the ITC does not have power to award damages for patent infringement.

[298]*Texas Instr., Inc. v. Cypress Semiconductor Corp.,* 90 F.3d 1558, 39 USPQ2d 1492 (Fed. Cir. 1996). This result was rather remarkable. The ITC had issued an exclusion order, finding two claims infringed, and the Federal Circuit had affirmed. A later district court proceeding against the same defendant resulted in a JMOL of noninfringement of those same claims. This time around, not only did the Federal Circuit refuse to give the affirmed ITC judgment preclusive effect, but it affirmed the JMOL!

[299]*Kori Corp. v. Wilco Marsh Buggies, Inc.,* 761 F.2d 649, 225 USPQ 985 (Fed. Cir. 1985). Of course, a district court is absolutely bound by a decision of the Federal Circuit on appeal. *King Instr. Corp. v. Otari Corp.,* 814 F.2d 1560, 2 USPQ2d 1201 (Fed. Cir. 1987).

law of the case posits that when a court decides upon a rule of law, that decision should continue to govern the same issues in subsequent stages in the same case. The rule promotes the finality and efficiency of the judicial process by protecting against the agitation of settled issues.[300] A prior ruling is entitled to great deference under the law of the case doctrine. That doctrine ensures judicial efficiency and prevents endless litigation. Its elementary logic is matched by elementary fairness—a litigant given one good bite at the apple should not have a second.[301]

Law of the case does not involve preclusion after final judgment; it regulates judicial affairs before final judgment. It is a doctrine resting on the need for judicial economy. But it merely expresses the practice of courts generally to refuse to reopen what has been decided, not a limit to their power. The difference is that law of the case directs discretion while res judicata supersedes it and compels judgment.[302]

Law of the case is a judicially created doctrine, the purposes of which are to prevent the relitigation of issues that have been decided and to ensure that trial courts follow the decisions of appellate courts. The doctrine requires a court to follow the decision on a question taken previously during the case. It is applied more or less strictly depending on the circumstances of the case. When a judgment of a trial court has been appealed, the decision of the appellate court determines the law of the case, and the trial court cannot depart from it on remand. At the trial level, however, the law of the case is little more than a management practice to permit logical progression toward judgment. Orderly and efficient case administration suggests that questions once decided not be subject to continued argument, but the court has the power to reconsider its decisions until a judgment is entered.[303]

Law of the case merely requires a trial court to follow the rulings of an appellate court. It does not constrain the trial court with respect to issues not actually considered by an appellate court and thus does not require the trial court to adhere to its own previous rulings if they have not been adopted, explicitly or implicitly, by the appellate court's judgment. While a mandate is controlling as to matters within its compass, on remand a lower court is free as to other issues. When a judgment comes before the Federal Circuit for review, and certain findings of fact are not examined in, relied on, or otherwise necessary to the appellate decision, law of the case does not prevent the trial court on remand from reexamining those findings, with no more deference than if the decision had never been appealed at all.[304]

---

[300]*Christianson v. Colt Indus. Operating Corp.*, 486 U.S. 800, 7 USPQ2d 1109 (1988).

[301]*W.L. Gore & Assoc., Inc. v. Garlock, Inc.*, 842 F.2d 1275, 6 USPQ2d 1277 (Fed. Cir. 1988); *Perkin-Elmer Corp. v. Computervision Corp.*, 732 F.2d 888, 221 USPQ 669 (Fed. Cir. 1984).

[302]*Mendenhall v. Barber-Greene Co.*, 26 F.3d 1573, 31 USPQ2d 1001 (Fed. Cir. 1994).

[303]*Jamesbury Corp. v. Litton Indus. Prods., Inc.*, 839 F.2d 1544, 5 USPQ2d 1779 (Fed. Cir. 1988).

[304]*Exxon Corp. v. United States*, 931 F.2d 874 (Fed. Cir. 1991). The Federal Circuit was not troubled by the fact that the district judge on remand was not the original judge. An

Thus, the law of the case doctrine is simply a matter of sound judicial practice, under which a court generally adheres to a prior decision unless one of three exceptional circumstances exists: (1) the evidence on a subsequent trial was substantially different, (2) controlling authority has since made a contrary decision of the law applicable to such issues, or (3) the earlier ruling was clearly erroneous and would work a manifest injustice.[305] The standard under the clearly erroneous exception to the law of the case doctrine is a stringent one and requires a strong showing of clear error.[306] Mere suspicion of error, no matter how well supported, does not warrant reopening an already decided point. Only if the court is convinced to a certainty that the prior decision was incorrect would it be warranted in reexamining it.[307]

Apart from the three exceptions noted above, there are several additional requirements for application of the law of the case doctrine. First, the doctrine extends only to issues that were decided earlier and not to questions that might have been decided but were not.[308] It may be appropriate to refuse to apply the law of the case doctrine where a previous proceeding, e.g., a denial of a motion for directed verdict or for summary judgment, did not conclusively address the opposing party's arguments.[309] Similarly, findings and conclusions made in connection with a motion for preliminary injunction are not binding at trial. There is always the possibility of new evidence

---

argument that the second judge was bound by the earlier findings unless they were shown to be clearly erroneous was also rejected; Rule 52(a), FRCP, applies only to appellate review of findings, not to a trial judge's reconsideration of his or her own or predecessor's findings. See also *State Indus., Inc. v. Mor-Flo Indus. Inc.*, 948 F.2d 1573, 20 USPQ2d 1738 (Fed. Cir. 1991).

[305]*Yachts Am., Inc. v. United States*, 779 F.2d 656 (Fed. Cir. 1985); *Kori Corp. v. Wilco Marsh Buggies, Inc.*, 761 F.2d 649, 225 USPQ 985 (Fed. Cir. 1985); *Smith Int'l, Inc. v. Hughes Tool Co.*, 759 F.2d 1572, 225 USPQ 889 (Fed. Cir. 1985); *Perkin-Elmer Corp. v. Computervision Corp.*, 732 F.2d 888, 221 USPQ 669 (Fed. Cir. 1984); *Central Soya Co. v. Geo. A. Hormel & Co.*, 723 F.2d 1573, 220 USPQ 490 (Fed. Cir. 1983). See also *J.E.T.S. v. United States*, 838 F.2d 1196 (Fed. Cir. 1988). Here the tribunal in the first appeal was unaware that the contract in question had been obtained by fraudulent representations. Thus, law of the case did not apply because it would have worked manifest injustice. In *Mendenhall v. Barber-Greene Co.*, 26 F.3d 1573, 31 USPQ2d 1001 (Fed. Cir. 1994), the court considered its own intervening judgment of invalidity in a case against another defendant as intervening controlling authority on the relevant issue of law, even where it had previously affirmed an interlocutory judgment of validity of the same patent against another defendant. This complex case is also discussed in §18.5(b).

[306]*Smith Int'l, Inc. v. Hughes Tool Co.*, 759 F.2d 1572, 225 USPQ 889 (Fed. Cir. 1985).

[307]*Yachts Am., Inc. v. United States*, 779 F.2d 656 (Fed. Cir. 1985).

[308]*Smith Int'l, Inc. v. Hughes Tool Co.*, 759 F.2d 1572, 225 USPQ 889 (Fed. Cir. 1985); *Stearns v. Beckman Instr., Inc.*, 737 F.2d 1565, 222 USPQ 457 (Fed. Cir. 1984).

[309]*Jamesbury Corp. v. Litton Indus. Prods., Inc.*, 839 F.2d 1544, 5 USPQ2d 1779 (Fed. Cir. 1988). There was no error in the district court refusing to apply law of the case to its previous determination that laches was not appropriate for summary judgment and in granting summary judgment the second time around. Much time, and a trial, had intervened and much was known later that was not known at the time of the original motion. Also, the party was not precluded on its laches defense by the denial of its motion for directed verdict, because no judgment was entered on that defense and it could not therefore have cross-appealed. But the court has hinted that it may possibly treat its determinations on a motion for preliminary injunction as law of the case. *Black & Decker, Inc. v. Hoover Serv. Ctr.*, 886 F.2d 1285, 12 USPQ2d 1250 (Fed. Cir. 1989).

changing the court's impression of the facts.[310] Nonetheless, the doctrine does comprehend things decided by necessary implication as well as those decided explicitly.[311] There is also a due diligence requirement.[312]

The law of the case cannot bind the Supreme Court in reviewing decisions below. A petition for writ of certiorari can expose the entire case to review. Just as a district court's adherence to law of the case cannot insulate an issue from appellate review, a court of appeals' adherence to the law of the case cannot insulate an issue from Supreme Court review.[313] The Federal Circuit is not bound by the law of the case as to its own decision in the same way a district court is. It can reconsider the decision if certain exceptional circumstances exist. One such is where the evidence on a subsequent trial is substantially different.[314] But the doctrine does apply as much to the decisions of a coordinate court in the same case as to a court's own decisions. Federal courts routinely apply law of the case principles to transfer decisions of coordinate courts.[315] It has also been said that revisions in the law of the case should occur very infrequently when an appellate court is asked to review the decision of a coordinate court.[316] Although a court has power to revisit prior decisions of its own or of a coordinate court in any circumstance, it should be loath to do so in the absence of extraordinary circumstances such as where the initial decision was clearly erroneous and would work a manifest injustice.[317] Whatever may be the basis for this rule, the Federal Circuit has applied it unhesitatingly. The court has given law of the case effect to prior

[310]*Illinois Tool Works, Inc. v. Grip-Pak, Inc.,* 906 F.2d 679, 15 USPQ2d 1307 (Fed. Cir. 1990).

[311]*W.L. Gore & Assoc., Inc. v. Garlock, Inc.,* 842 F.2d 1275, 6 USPQ2d 1277 (Fed. Cir. 1988); *Smith Int'l, Inc. v. Hughes Tool Co.,* 759 F.2d 1572, 225 USPQ 889 (Fed. Cir. 1985). Thus, where a court holds a patent valid, the necessary implication is that it rejected fraud and inequitable conduct defenses. *Id.* A jury instruction to which no timely objection is made was said to become law of the case in *Allen Organ Co. v. Kimball Int'l, Inc.,* 839 F.2d 1556, 5 USPQ2d 1769 (Fed. Cir. 1988). Would not waiver have sufficed?

[312]*Smith Int'l, Inc. v. Hughes Tool Co.,* 759 F.2d 1572, 225 USPQ 889 (Fed. Cir. 1985). The due diligence limitation of Rule 60(b)(2), FRCP, serves the salutary purpose of providing finality to judicial decisions and orders by preventing belated attempts to reopen judgment on the basis of facts that the moving party could have discovered at the time of trial. Since the law of the case doctrine is also designed to provide finality, it is not inappropriate to apply the same due diligence standard to the newly discovered evidence exception to that doctrine. *Id.*

[313]*Christianson v. Colt Indus. Operating Corp.,* 486 U.S. 800, 7 USPQ2d 1109 (1988). A denial of a petition for certiorari makes the legal conclusions in an earlier Federal Circuit decision final and law of the case and bars the parties from attempting to relitigate them. *Constant v. United States,* 929 F.2d 654, 18 USPQ2d 1298 (Fed. Cir. 1991).

[314]*W.L. Gore & Assoc., Inc. v. Garlock, Inc.,* 842 F.2d 1275, 6 USPQ2d 1277 (Fed. Cir. 1988).

[315]*Christianson v. Colt Indus. Operating Corp.,* 486 U.S. 800, 7 USPQ2d 1109 (1988). In a multidistrict matter, the court held that denial of a motion to transfer under 28 U.S.C. §1404(a) did not bar coordination of pretrial procedures under §1407. *In re Regents of the Univ. of Calif.,* 964 F.2d 1128 (Fed. Cir. 1992). However, the court did not discuss broader aspects of the law of the case doctrine as it might apply in multidistrict litigation proceedings.

[316]*Perkin-Elmer Corp. v. Computervision Corp.,* 732 F.2d 888, 221 USPQ 669 (Fed. Cir. 1984).

[317]*Christianson v. Colt Indus. Operating Corp.,* 486 U.S. 800, 7 USPQ2d 1109 (1988).

rulings of the Fifth Circuit,[318] the First Circuit,[319] the Tenth Circuit,[320] and the Court of Federal Claims.[321] The Supreme Court has instructed the Federal Circuit and its sister regional courts of appeals how to approach transfer matters to avoid a perpetual game of jurisdictional ping pong: adhere strictly to principles of law of the case.[322]

The court has, however, rejected an effort to engraft public policy limitations on the doctrine. Law of the case rests upon weighty considerations of sound judicial administration, and its application should not and cannot depend upon the nature of the issue that a party seeks to relitigate. Thus, the important public interest in protecting the integrity of the patent-issuing process and in preventing the enforcement of patents secured by fraud is nevertheless insufficient to justify an exception to the law of the case doctrine.[323]

The doctrine has been applied on such fundamental issues as anticipation,[324] validity in general,[325] infringement,[326] alter ego,[327] and willfulness and bad faith.[328] It is axiomatic that claims must be construed in the same way for infringement that they were for determining validity. Thus a district court is bound by law of the case to use

---

[318]*Kori Corp. v. Wilco Marsh Buggies, Inc.*, 761 F.2d 649, 225 USPQ 985 (Fed. Cir. 1985); *Stearns v. Beckman Instr., Inc.*, 737 F.2d 1565, 222 USPQ 457 (Fed. Cir. 1984).

[319]*Wang Labs., Inc. v. Applied Computer Sci., Inc.*, 958 F.2d 355, 22 USPQ2d 1055 (Fed. Cir. 1992).

[320]*Central Soya Co. v. Geo. A. Hormel & Co.*, 723 F.2d 1573, 220 USPQ 490 (Fed. Cir. 1983).

[321]*City of Fulton v. United States*, 751 F.2d 1255 (Fed. Cir. 1985); *Gindes v. United States*, 740 F.2d 947 (Fed. Cir. 1984). See *Hughes Aircraft Co. v. United States*, 717 F.2d 1351, 219 USPQ 473 (Fed. Cir. 1983).

[322]*Christianson v. Colt Indus. Operating Corp.*, 486 U.S. 800, 7 USPQ2d 1109 (1988). The Federal Circuit has faithfully observed these principles, e.g., *Xeta, Inc. v. Atex, Inc.*, 852 F.2d 1280, 7 USPQ2d 1471 (Fed. Cir. 1988), even though a transfer decision of a coordinate court may implicate Federal Circuit jurisdiction, *Smith v. Orr*, 855 F.2d 1544 (Fed. Cir. 1988). However, in *Rodriguez v. United States*, 862 F.2d 1558 (Fed. Cir. 1988), a district court concluded that it lacked jurisdiction and transferred to the Claims Court. The Claims Court and the parties agreed that the Claims Court lacked jurisdiction. But instead of retransferring, the Claims Court dismissed. The Federal Circuit reversed and remanded with instructions to retransfer to the district court. *Christianson v. Colt* says that law of the case does not control where the original transfer decision was clearly erroneous and would work a manifest injustice. Here, the original decision was clearly erroneous because it was based on the conclusion that the Claims Court had jurisdiction. A manifest injustice would result because dismissal would frustrate the plaintiff's right to appeal other aspects of the case. It would seem that *Rodriguez* does differ from *Christianson v. Colt* in that it was clear in the latter case that one of the courts would have jurisdiction in any event.

[323]*Smith Int'l, Inc. v. Hughes Tool Co.*, 759 F.2d 1572, 225 USPQ 889 (Fed. Cir. 1985). The law of the case doctrine applies in patent cases. *Jamesbury Corp. v. Litton Indus. Prods., Inc.*, 839 F.2d 1544, 5 USPQ2d 1779 (Fed. Cir. 1988).

[324]*Jones v. Hardy*, 727 F.2d 1524, 220 USPQ 1021 (Fed. Cir. 1984).

[325]*KSM Fastening Sys., Inc. v. H.A. Jones Co.*, 776 F.2d 1522, 227 USPQ 676 (Fed. Cir. 1985).

[326]*Hughes Aircraft Co. v. United States*, 86 F.3d 1566, 39 USPQ2d 1065 (Fed. Cir. 1996); *Trell v. Marlee Elec. Corp.*, 912 F.2d 1443, 16 USPQ2d 1059 (Fed. Cir. 1990).

[327]*Kori Corp. v. Wilco Marsh Buggies, Inc.*, 761 F.2d 649, 225 USPQ 985 (Fed. Cir. 1985).

[328]*Beatrice Foods Co. v. New England Printing & Lith. Co.*, 923 F.2d 1567, 17 USPQ2d 1553 (Fed. Cir. 1991).

the Federal Circuit's earlier validity interpretation of a claim element when later deciding infringement.[329]

The law of the case doctrine is determined by reference to regional circuit law because it is a procedural matter not unique to patent law.[330] On matters coming to it from the Court of Federal Claims, where it is in effect the regional circuit, the Federal Circuit must apply its own law. In the context of law of the case, the court regards what it said in its *Jamesbury*[331] decision as expressing its views on the subject, which are those commonly accepted in federal jurisprudence.[332]

(e) Stare Decisis

As the phrase is used here, stare decisis has two aspects. The first has to do with what legal precedent will be followed, and how faithfully. The second has to do with the persuasive weight that will be given to prior adjudications that are not binding under either law of the case or some aspect of res judicata.

From the outset, the Federal Circuit has been quite clear as to what it will regard as binding precedent. In its first case, *South Corp. v. United States,*[333] the court held that it would follow, as binding precedent, the body of law that existed in the CCPA and the Court of Claims as of September 30, 1982.[334] Conversely, what may have been traditional practice is not, without a clear holding of one of the Federal Circuit's predecessor courts, binding upon it.[335]

In light of the general policy of minimizing confusion and conflicts in the federal judicial system, the Federal Circuit follows the guidance of the regional circuits in all but substantive law fields assigned exclusively to it by Congress.[336] Presumably those same concerns will

---

[329]*W.L. Gore & Assoc., Inc. v. Garlock, Inc.,* 842 F.2d 1275, 6 USPQ2d 1277 (Fed. Cir. 1988). See also *Del Mar Avionics, Inc. v. Quinton Instr. Co.,* 836 F.2d 1320, 5 USPQ2d 1255 (Fed. Cir. 1987).

[330]*Exxon Corp. v. United States,* 931 F.2d 874 (Fed. Cir. 1991); *Jamesbury Corp. v. Litton Indus. Prods., Inc.,* 839 F.2d 1544, 5 USPQ2d 1779 (Fed. Cir. 1988).

[331]*Jamesbury Corp. v. Litton Indus. Prods., Inc.,* 839 F.2d 1544, 5 USPQ2d 1779 (Fed. Cir. 1988).

[332]*Exxon Corp. v. United States,* 931 F.2d 874 (Fed. Cir. 1991).

[333]690 F.2d 1368 (Fed. Cir. 1982).

[334]Such precedent can be overruled only by review in banc; in banc review is also required to resolve conflicts between the two predecessor courts. *Id.* Similarly, prior decisions of a panel of the court are binding precedent on subsequent appeals unless and until overturned in banc. *Newell Cos. v. Kenney Mfg. Co.,* 864 F.2d 757, 9 USPQ2d 1417 (Fed. Cir. 1988). In one case the court took the unusual step of sitting in banc on a portion of a case only, to resolve its own conflicting precedents. *Kingsdown Med. Cons, Ltd. v. Hollister, Inc.,* 863 F.2d 867, 9 USPQ2d 1384 (Fed. Cir. 1988). It explained this procedure on the basis that precedent may be overturned only by the entire court. With all respect, however, it would seem that there is a significant difference between overturning a clear prior precedent and resolving apparently conflicting precedents.

[335]*Dynamics Corp. v. United States,* 766 F.2d 518, 226 USPQ 622 (Fed. Cir. 1985).

[336]See §17.2(b) above.

prompt the regional federal circuit courts, when confronted with issues in those substantive fields, to look in turn to Federal Circuit precedents for guidance. Similarly, state courts confronted with federal law issues usually turn to the law of the appropriate federal court to aid in the resolution of those federal issues. While the prevailing view among the highest courts in the various states is that a state court is only bound as to the meaning of federal constitutional law and federal statutory law by interpretations of the U.S. Supreme Court, the decisions of lower federal courts on issues of federal law are usually respected as persuasive, especially where uniform among the lower courts. Since Congress created the Federal Circuit in order to bring uniformity to the national law of patents, presumably the state courts confronted with issues of federal law relating to patents will therefore also look to the decisions of the Federal Circuit for guidance.[337]

The court has cautioned that general rules should not be deduced from fact situations in one or two court cases, precluding the possibility that the same result may be attainable on quite different fact situations.[338] It misinterprets precedent to convert a fact finding that with others supported a decision into a universal requirement for all future cases. Most, if not all, "tests" employed in the art of judging arise in a particular factual milieu. Hence they must be read, applied, and perhaps modified in light of the facts of subsequent cases.[339] It is well established that a general expression in an opinion, not essential to the disposition of the case, does not control a judgment in a subsequent proceeding. Broad language in an opinion, unnecessary to the court's decision, cannot be considered binding authority.[340] The court has also rejected an argument that it should overrule controlling precedent in view of a bill pending in Congress that purports to do just that. It is the province of Congress to make changes in law based on public policy, and the court should not act in anticipation of possible action by the legislature.[341] Stare decisis has special force in the area of statutory interpretation.[342]

The other aspect of stare decisis usually arises in the context of a prior determination that a patent is not invalid. What weight should be given such a determination? In its first look at the question, the court indicated that stare decisis is generally inappropriate in patent litigation, at least as to validity. But the court quickly went on to say that a holding of validity should certainly be given weight, and if the record is similar in each case, perhaps the earlier judgment of validity

---

[337]*Speedco, Inc. v. Estes,* 853 F.2d 909, 7 USPQ2d 1637 (Fed. Cir. 1988).

[338]*In re N.A.D. Inc.,* 754 F.2d 996, 224 USPQ 969 (Fed. Cir. 1985).

[339]*Arrowhead Indus. Water, Inc. v. Ecolochem, Inc.,* 846 F.2d 731, 6 USPQ2d 1685 (Fed. Cir. 1988).

[340]*Smith v. Orr,* 855 F.2d 1544 (Fed. Cir. 1988).

[341]*In re Thorpe,* 777 F.2d 695, 227 USPQ 964 (Fed. Cir. 1985).

[342]*In re Zurko,* 142 F.3d 1447, 46 USPQ2d 1691 (Fed. Cir. 1998), *rev'd on other grounds, Dickinson v. Zurko,* 527 U.S. 150, 50 USPQ2d 1930 (1999).

could be given stare decisis effect.[343] In a later case, the court stated that the presumption of validity was not augmented by an earlier adjudication of validity.[344] The fact that the validity of claims has previously been upheld in an earlier litigation is to be given weight in determining validity, though not stare decisis effect.[345] The significance of a prior decision that finds the patent not invalid is discussed in more detail in the presumption of validity context.[346]

The court has indicated that it was appropriate to give weight to a PTO Board decision on an application related to the one that resulted in the patent in suit, where the PTO decision resolved issues pertinent to those at bar.[347] Certainly a PTO decision must be given appropriate consideration and due weight if it deals with the same application.[348]

In its decision[349] affirming the Federal Circuit's *Markman* holding that claim construction is a question of law exclusively within the province of the court, the Supreme Court made it clear that claim construction holdings as to a particular patent will not normally result in issue preclusion against new accused infringers, even within the same jurisdiction. However, it strongly signaled an expectation that stare decisis would play a significant role in promoting uniformity in claim construction as to a given patent. The Federal Circuit has since made it clear that its decisions on claim construction have a national stare decisis effect.[350]

There is a well-recognized exception to the doctrine of stare decisis: a court will reexamine and overrule a prior decision that was clearly erroneous.[351]

A court need not overrule a prior case in order to clarify that case by stating a requirement that was met but not discussed. A court may refine holdings in its precedent that were stated or have been interpreted too broadly.[352]

---

[343]*Stevenson v. Sears, Roebuck & Co.*, 713 F.2d 705, 218 USPQ 969 (Fed. Cir. 1983).

[344]*Shelcore, Inc. v. Durham Indus., Inc.*, 745 F.2d 621, 223 USPQ 584 (Fed. Cir. 1984).

[345]*Gillette Co. v. S.C. Johnson & Son*, 919 F.2d 720, 16 USPQ2d 1923 (Fed. Cir. 1990).

[346]See notes 1:190ff discussing *Mendenhall v. Cedarapids, Inc.*, 5 F.3d 1556, 28 USPQ2d 1081 (Fed. Cir. 1993).

[347]*Kloster Speedsteel AB v. Crucible Inc.*, 793 F.2d 1565, 230 USPQ 81 (Fed. Cir. 1986). It should be noted that the parties had apparently agreed at trial that the PTO decision was to be given great weight; perhaps this holding was simply a manifestation of impatience with an attempt by a party to renege on an agreement.

[348]*Interconnect Planning Corp. v. Feil*, 774 F.2d 1132, 227 USPQ 543 (Fed. Cir. 1985).

[349]*Markman v. Westview Instr., Inc.*, 517 U.S. 370, 38 USPQ2d 1461 (Fed. Cir. 1996).

[350]*Key Pharm. Inc. v. Hercon Labs. Corp.*, 161 F.3d 709, 48 USPQ2d 1911 (Fed. Cir. 1998). The citation of a nonprecedential decision to establish a prior claim construction does not violate the court's Rule 47.6(b). The interest of consistency in the construction of patent claims would be ill served by interpreting Rule 47.6(b) to preclude consideration of a prior claim construction rendered as a matter of law by the Federal Circuit. Because the second case concerns the identical issue of law decided in the first case, an exception to the noncitation rule should be applied. *Burke Inc. v. Bruno Indep. Living Aids Inc.*, 183 F.3d 1334, 51 USPQ2d 1295 (Fed. Cir. 1999).

[351]*Scott Optical Glass, Inc. v. United States*, 750 F.2d 62 (Fed. Cir. 1984).

[352]*Woodard v. Sage Prods., Inc.*, 818 F.2d 841, 2 USPQ2d 1649 (Fed. Cir. 1987).

Appendix

Validity and Infringement Statistics

The first question the trial lawyer will hear from a client who has litigated a patent to judgment in the district court is "What are my chances on appeal?" Another sure question, on the day of the oral argument, is "How does the makeup of this panel affect the chances you quoted me earlier?" The formulation of an answer to questions such as these is a complex and difficult business at best, involving assessments of strengths and weaknesses, evidence and equities, and sometimes plain old prejudice. Nonetheless, every appellate lawyer must undertake the analysis and must come up with an answer, his or her private view of the reliability of the analysis notwithstanding.

Such a lawyer is playing with less than a full deck if he or she relies on anecdotal wisdom rather than cold statistics in coming up with an answer. In the experience of this author, there are all too many court-watchers who fancy themselves able to predict what the Federal Circuit is likely to do in a given case, and yet do not really have a grasp of what the court has actually done in many given cases.

The following statistics from cases with full published opinions may provide some insight. V and NV stand for valid and not valid; I and NI for infringed and not infringed; How for whether the trial court was reversed (r) or affirmed (a) on the question; and the numeral is the number of individual patents involved:

Author	Panel	V	How	NV	How	I	How	NI	How
Archer	Bissell, Cowen	1	a			1	a		
Archer	Cowen, Mayer	3	a			3	a		
Archer	Davis, Newman	1	r			1	r		
Archer	Friedman, Plager			1	a			1	r
Archer	Friedman, Rader							1	a
Archer	In banc							1	a
Archer	In banc					1	a		
Archer	Lourie, Rader					1	r		
Archer	Lourie, Skelton					1	a		
Archer	Mayer, Skelton					1	a		
Archer	Michel, Lourie					1	r		
Archer	Michel, Plager							2	a
Archer	Michel, Senter	1	a			1	a		
Archer	Michel, Skelton			1	r				
Archer	Newman, Clevenger	1	r						
Archer	Newman, Mayer	1	a			1	r		

1125

Author	Panel	V	How	NV	How	I	How	NI	How
Archer	Nichols, Mayer							1	r
Archer	Plager, Schall			1	r				
Archer	Rich, Newman			1	r			1	r
Archer	Rich, Newman	1	a					1	r
Baldwin	Bennett, Archer							1	a
Baldwin	Bennett, Miller	1	a			1	a		
Baldwin	Friedman, Bissell	1	a			1	a		
Baldwin	Friedman, Nichols	1	a			1	a		
Baldwin	Markey, Miller							2	a
Baldwin	Markey, Miller			1	a				
Baldwin	Markey, Miller	1	a			1	a		
Baldwin	Miller, Kellam			1	a				
Baldwin	Miller, Smith	1	r						
Baldwin	Nies, Bissell	1	a			1	a		
Baldwin	Skelton, Archer					2	a		
Baldwin	Smith, Newman	1	a			1	a		
Bennett	5-judge panel			1	a				
Bennett	Markey, Davis			1	a				
Bennett	Markey, Friedman							1	a
Bennett	Miller, Smith			1	a				
Bennett	Skelton, Miller					1	r		
Bissell	Archer, Michel							1	a
Bissell	Archer, Re	1	a			1	a		
Bissell	In banc							1	a
Bissell	Markey, Friedman	2	a			2	a		
Bissel	Michel, Cowen	1	r						
Bissell	Miller (Archer recused)			1	r			1	r
Bissell	Nichols, Baldwin	4	a			4	a		
Bissell	Nichols, Mayer	1	r						
Bissell	Nies, Nichols							1	r
Bissell	Smith, Skelton			1	a				
Bryson	Archer, Newman			1	r			1	r
Bryson	Clevenger, Rader							1	a
Bryson	Michel, Plager							1	a
Bryson	Michel, Plager			1	a				
Bryson	Newman, Gajarsa							2	a
Bryson	Plager, Clevenger	1	a	2	r	2	a		
Bryson	Plager, Lourie							1	a
Bryson	Plager, Schall			1	a			1	a
Bryson	Plager, Smith			1	a				
Bryson	Schall	1	r						
Bryson	Skelton, Gajarsa							2	a
Clevenger	Lourie, Gajarsa	1	r						
Clevenger	Lourie, Schall					1	r		
Clevenger	Mayer, Archer							1	a
Clevenger	Mayer, Gajarsa					1	a		
Clevenger	Michel, Archer	1	r			1	a		
Clevenger	Michel, Plager							1	a
Clevenger	Michel, Smith			1	a			1	a
Clevenger	Newman, Michel	1	r						
Clevenger	Newman, Plager			3	a				
Clevenger	Nies, Kaufman	1	a			1	a		
Clevenger	Nies, Newman	2	a			2	a		
Clevenger	Plager, Gajarsa							1	a
Clevenger	Plager, Nies							1	r
Clevenger	Plager, Rader			2	a			2	a
Clevenger	Rader, Gajarsa							1	a
Clevenger	Rich, Rader							1	r

Author	Panel	V	How	NV	How	I	How	NI	How
Clevenger	Rich, Schall							1	a
Clevenger	Schall, Bryson							1	a
Clevenger	Skelton, Rader	1	r						
Clevinger	Rich, Michel			1	a			1	a
Cohn	Rich, Plager					1	a		
Davis	5-judge panel							1	a
Davis	Cowen, Newman	1	a	1	a	1	a	1	a
Davis	Friedman, Newman	1	a						
Davis	Markey, Bissell	1	a	3	a	1	a		
Davis	Markey, Nichols	1	a			1	r		
Davis	Markey, Nies			1	a				
Davis	Markey, Nies	1	a			1	a		
Davis	Markey, Skelton	1	a	1	a	1	a		
Davis	Smith, Cowen			2	a				
Friedman	5-judge panel			3	a			1	a
Friedman	Baldwin, Newman							1	a
Friedman	Bissell, Mayer	2	a			2	a & r		
Friedman	Cowen, Newman	1	a	1	a	1	a		
Friedman	Davis, Bennett	1	a						
Friedman	Davis, Cowen	1	a			1	a		
Friedman	Markey, Baldwin					1	a		
Friedman	Mayer, Michel							1	a
Friedman	Miller, Re	1	a			1	r		
Friedman	Nichols, Kashiwa							1	a
Friedman	Rich, Nies	1	a			1	a		
Friedman	Skelton, Smith							1	a
Gajarsa	Bryson, Friedman			1	r				
Gajarsa	Bryson, Linn							1	a
Gajarsa	Bryson, Skelton							1	a
Gajarsa	Clevenger, Bryson	1	a			1	a		
Gajarsa	Mayer, Clevenger							1	a
Gajarsa	Mayer, Friedman	1	a	1	r				
Gajarsa	Mayer, Michel			1	r				
Gajarsa	Michel, Bryson	2	r						
Gajarsa	Newman, Michel							1	a
Gajarsa	Newman, Rader	1	r					1	a
Gajarsa	Newman, Schall	1	a			1	a		
Gajarsa	Newman, Smith					1	a		
Gajarsa	Plager							2	r
Gajarsa	Plager, Rader			1	r				
Gajarsa	Rader, Schall			1	a				
Kashiwa	Bennett, Smith			1	a				
Kashiwa	Cowen, Bennett	1	a					1	r
Kashiwa	Friedman, Rich	1	a			1	a		
Kashiwa	Markey, Davis	1	r						
Kelly	Newman, Lourie	1	r						
Lifland	Nies, Miller			1	a				
Linn	Bryson, Gajarsa							2	a
Linn	Clevenger, Bryson			1	a				
Lourie	Archer, Bryson			1	r				
Lourie	Archer, Clevenger			1	a				
Lourie	Archer, Clevenger	2	a			2	a		
Lourie	Archer, Mayer							1	a
Lourie	Archer, Mayer	1	a					1	a
Lourie	Archer, Mayer	1	r					1	a
Lourie	Archer, Newman			1	a				
Lourie	Archer, Nies			1	a				
Lourie	Archer, Plager	1	a			1	a		

Author	Panel	V	How	NV	How	I	How	NI	How
Lourie	Archer, Rader					1	a		
Lourie	Archer, Rich	1	a			1	a		
Lourie	Archer, Schall							1	a
Lourie	Clevenger, Bryson	1	r						
Lourie	Clevenger, Rader	1	a						
Lourie	Clevenger, Rader	1	r						
Lourie	Clevenger, Rader			1	a				
Lourie	Clevenger, Schall							2	a
Lourie	Clevenger, Schall			1	a				
Lourie	Clevenger, Schall			1	r			1	r
Lourie	Friedman, Rader	1	a						
Lourie	Markey, Brown			1	a				
Lourie	Markey, Clevenger	1	a	1	r	1	a		
Lourie	Mayer, Black	1	r						
Lourie	Mayer, Clevenger					2	a		
Lourie	Mayer, Friedman							1	a
Lourie	Mayer, Michel			1	r				
Lourie	Mayer, Rader			2	a			3	a
Lourie	Mayer, Rader	3	a			3	a		
Lourie	Mayer, Schall	1	a					1	r
Lourie	Michel, Plager					1	a	1	r
Lourie	Michel, Plager			1	a				
Lourie	Michel, Rader	1	a					1	a
Lourie	Michel, Schall					1	a		
Lourie	Michel, Skelton	2	a					2	a
Lourie	Newman, Bryson					1	a		
Lourie	Newman, Bryson			1	a			1	a
Lourie	Newman, Plager							1	a
Lourie	Newman, Rader					1	a		
Lourie	Newman, Schall			1	a				
Lourie	Newman, Schall			1	a			1	a
Lourie	Nies, Clevenger			1	a				
Lourie	Nies, Clevenger	1	a					1	r
Lourie	Nies, Mayer							1	a
Lourie	Nies, Newman			1	a				
Lourie	Nies, Rich	1	r					1	a
Lourie	Plager, Bryson			1	a				
Lourie	Plager, Clevenger							1	a
Lourie	Plager, Clevenger			1	r				
Lourie	Plager, Rader	1	a			1	a		
Lourie	Plager, Rader	1	r						
Lourie	Plager, Schall							2	a
Lourie	Rader, Bryson							1	r
Lourie	Rader, Schall	1	a			1	a		
Lourie	Rich, Archer	2	a			2	a		
Lourie	Rich, Friedman			1	r			1	a
Lourie	Rich, Mayer							1	a a
Lourie	Rich, Mayer							1	a a
Lourie	Rich, Mayer							2	a
Lourie	Rich, Michel	1	r						
Lourie	Rich, Michel	1	r					1	a
Lourie	Rich, Michel	1	r			1	r		
Lourie	Rich, Plager			1	a				
Lourie	Rich, Plager			1	a			1	a
Lourie	Rich, Rader							1	a
Lourie	Schall, Bryson							1	r
Lourie	Skelton, Michel							1	a
Lourie	Skelton, Rader							2	a

Author	Panel	V	How	NV	How	I	How	NI	How
Lourie	Skelton, Rader	1	a			2	a,r		
Lourie	Skelton, Rader	1	r					1	a
Lourie	Skelton, Schall					1	a		
Lourie	Smith, Gajarsa							2	a
Lourie	Smith, Schall	1	a			2	a		
Lourie	Smith, Schall	1	a	2	a				
Markey	5-judge panel	2	a			2	a		
Markey	Archer							1	a
Markey	Baldwin, Nies							1	a
Markey	Baldwin, Nies							2	a
Markey	Bennett, Cowen			1	a				
Markey	Bennett, Harvey			1	a				
Markey	Bennett, Plager	2	a			2	a		
Markey	Bennett, Senter			1	a				
Markey	Bennett, Sharp			6	a				
Markey	Bennett, Smith							1	a
Markey	Bissell, Archer	2	a			2	a		
Markey	Cowen, Archer			1	a			1	a
Markey	Cowen, Bennett	1	a			1	a		
Markey	Cowen, Bennett	1	r						
Markey	Cowen, Newman	1	a			1	a		
Markey	Cowen, Newman	3	r						
Markey	Davis, Baldwin					1	a		
Markey	Davis, Baldwin			1	a				
Markey	Davis, Baldwin			1	a				
Markey	Davis, Baldwin	1	a			1	a		
Markey	Davis, Baldwin	1	a			1	r		
Markey	Davis, Bissell			1	a				
Markey	Davis, Harvey	1	a	1	a	1	a		
Markey	Davis, Kashiwa	2	r						
Markey	Davis, Kellam	1	r			1	a		
Markey	Davis, Miller	2	r						
Markey	Davis, Nichols	1	r			1	a		
Markey	Davis, Skelton			1	a				
Markey	Davis, Smith							1	a
Markey	Friedman, Baldwin							1	a
Markey	Friedman, Davis					1	r		
Markey	Friedman, Nichols	1	a			1	a		
Markey	Friedman, Nies							1	a
Markey	Friedman, Nies	1	a			1	a		
Markey	Friedman, Re	1	a			1	a		
Markey	Friedman, Rich			1	a				
Markey	Friedman, Rich	1	a			1	a		
Markey	Kashiwa, Smith							1	a
Markey	Mayer, Kelleher							1	a
Markey	Newman, Archer							1	a
Markey	Newman, Archer							1	r
Markey	Newman, Swygert	2	r			2	a		
Markey	Nichols, Bissell	1	a			1	a		
Markey	Nichols, Kashiwa	2	a	2	a	1	a	1	a
Markey	Nichols, Newman							1	a
Markey	Nichols, Newman	2	a			2	a		
Markey	Nies, Michel	1	a			1	a		
Markey	Re, Nichols					3	r		
Markey	Rich, Archer							1	a
Markey	Rich, Baldwin							1	a
Markey	Rich, Bennett			1	a				
Markey	Rich, Mayer			1	a			2	a

Author	Panel	V	How	NV	How	I	How	NI	How
Markey	Rich, Nies			1	a				
Markey	Rich, Plager					1	a		
Markey	Rich, Smith	1	a			1	a		
Markey	Smith, Bissell							1	a
Markey	Smith, Newman	1	a			1	a		
Markey	Smith, Newman	7	a			7	a		
Markey	Smith, Nichols			1	a				
Mayer	Archer, George			1	a				
Mayer	Archer, Michel			1	a				
Mayer	Archer, Plager	1	r						
Mayer	Archer, Rader			1	a				
Mayer	Bissell, Bennett			1	r				
Mayer	Friedman, Michel					1	r		
Mayer	Friedman, Skelton	1	a			1	a		
Mayer	Lourie, Schall			1	a				
Mayer	Michel, Bryson			1	a				
Mayer	Michel, Lourie			1	r				
Mayer	Michel, Lourie	2	a						
Mayer	Newman, Schall					1	a	2	a
Mayer	Newman, Schall					2	a		
Mayer	Plager, Schall	3	a			3	a		
Mayer	Rader, Bryson	1	r						
Mayer	Schall, Gajarsa			1	r				
Mayer	Skelton, Clevenger					1	r		
Michel	Archer, Clevinger	1	a			1	a		
Michel	Archer, Lourie			1	a				
Michel	Archer, Schall					1	a		
Michel	Archer, Skelton			1	a				
Michel	Clevenger, Bryson							1	a
Michel	Clevenger, Rader	1	a						
Michel	Friedman, Schall							2	r
Michel	Friedman, Skelton							1	r
Michel	Lourie, Bryson							1	a
Michel	Lourie, Friedman					1	r		
Michel	Markey, Miller	1	a						
Michel	Newman, Clevenger							3	a
Michel	Newman, Lourie	1	a						
Michel	Newman, Plager	1	r					3	a
Michel	Newman, Rader	2	r			2	a		
Michel	Nies, Skelton	1	r			1	r		
Michel	Plager, Gajarsa	1	a					1	a
Michel	Plager, Rader					1	r		
Michel	Plager, Rader	1	a			1	a		
Michel	Rader, Gajarsa	1	a						
Michel	Skelton, Schall			1	a				
Miller	Davis, Nichols			1	r				
Miller	Kashiwa, Bennett			1	a				
Miller	Skelton, Smith					1	r		
Mixed	Archer, Newman, Mayer	1	a					1	r
Newman	Archer	1	r			1	a		
Newman	Archer, Clevenger	1	a			1	a		
Newman	Archer, Lourie	1	r						
Newman	Archer, Michel	1	r						
Newman	Archer, Rader	1	r						
Newman	Baldwin, Cowen	1	a					1	a
Newman	Bennett, Bryson	1	a						
Newman	Bennett, Rader			1	a				
Newman	Bissell, Re							2	a

Author	Panel	V	How	NV	How	I	How	NI	How
Newman	Clevenger, Rader					1	a		
Newman	Clevenger, Schall							1	a
Newman	Cowen, Bissell							1	a
Newman	Davis, Bennett							1	a
Newman	Davis, Cowen							1	a
Newman	Davis, Smith	1	r						
Newman	Friedman, Archer							1	a
Newman	Friedman, Archer					1	a		
Newman	Friedman, Archer	1	r						
Newman	Friedman, Archer	1	r			1	a	1	a
Newman	Friedman, Bennett	3	a			3	r		
Newman	Friedman, Miller	1	a			1	a		
Newman	Friedman, Rader							1	a
Newman	Friedman, Rader							1	r
Newman	Friedman, Rader							2	a
Newman	Lourie, Clevenger							2	a
Newman	Lourie, Clevinger					1	r		
Newman	Lourie, Rader	1	a			1	a		
Newman	Lourie, Rader	1	r						
Newman	Lourie, Schall	1	r						
Newman	Markey, Bennett			1	a				
Newman	Mayer, Bryson	1	r	1	a			1	a
Newman	Mayer, Clevenger	1	a						
Newman	Mayer, Clevenger	2	a					2	a
Newman	Mayer, Friedman					1	a		
Newman	Mayer, Gajarsa							1	a
Newman	Mayer, Lourie	1	a						
Newman	Mayer, Lourie	1	a						
Newman	Mayer, Plager	1	a			1	a		
Newman	Mayer, Plager	1	r					1	a
Newman	Mayer, Plager	1	a			1	a		
Newman	Mayer, Schall							1	r
Newman	Michel, Clevenger	1	r						
Newman	Michel, Plager	1	r						
Newman	Michel, Rader	2	a			1	a		
Newman	Plager, Bryson							1	a
Newman	Plager, Bryson	5	r						
Newman	Plager, Schall							1	a
Newman	Rader, Schall	1	a			1	a		
Newman	Rader, Skelton	1	r					1	a
Newman	Rich, Clevenger	2	r					2	a
Newman	Rich, Lourie					1	r		
Newman	Rich, Mayer					1	a		
Newman	Rich, Michel					1	a		
Newman	Rich, Michel	2	a			2	a		
Newman	Skelton, Archer	1	r					1	a
Newman	Skelton, Lourie			2	a	1	a	1	a
Newman	Skelton, Michel			1	a				
Newman	Smith, Bissell	1	a			1	a		
Newman	Smith, Bryson							1	a
Newman	Smith, Clevenger	1	r					1	a
Newman	Smith, Cowen	2	a			2	a		
Newman	Smith, Miller	1	r					1	a
Newman	Smith, Rader	1	a			1	a		
Newman	Smith, Skelton	1	a			1	a		
Nichols	5-judge panel			1	a				
Nichols	Bennett, Nies					1	a		
Nichols	Davis, Baldwin	1	a			1	a		

Author	Panel	V	How	NV	How	I	How	NI	How
Nichols	Kashiwa, Bennett	1	a	1	r			1	r
Nichols	Kashiwa, Nies	1	a			1	a		
Nichols	Markey, Kashiwa					1	r		
Nichols	Rich, Nies					1	a		
Nies	5-judge panel	1	a						
Nies	5-judge panel	1	a					1	r
Nies	Archer, Michel					1	a	1	r
Nies	Baldwin, Bissell			1	a				
Nies	Bennett, Cowen			1	a				
Nies	Bissell, Archer	1	r						
Nies	Bissell, Baldwin							1	a
Nies	Cowen, Michel	1	a						
Nies	Davis, Kashiwa			1	r				
Nies	Friedman, Archer			1	a				
Nies	Friedman, Smith			1	a				
Nies	Lourie, Bryson	1	a			1	a		
Nies	Lourie, Rader			1	a				
Nies	Markey, Bennett			1	a				
Nies	Markey, Davis			1	r				
Nies	Markey, Kashiwa	1	r						
Nies	Markey, Skelton	1	r						
Nies	Marshall, Friedman							1	a
Nies	Mayer			1	a				
Nies	Mayer, Lourie			2	a	2	a		
Nies	Miller, Cowen			1	a				
Nies	Newman, Archer			1	a				
Nies	Newman, Bissell	1	r						
Nies	Nichols, Kashiwa					4	a		
Nies	Plager, Will							1	a
Nies	Rich, Bissell	2	a			1	a	1	a
Nies	Rich, Clevenger							1	r
Nies	Rich, Nichols	1	a			1	r		
Nies	Skelton, Archer	4	a			4	a		
Nies	Smith, Archer			1	r				
Nies	Smith, Kellam			2	a				
Nies	Smith, Mayer	2	a			2	a		
Per curiam	3-judge panel	1	r						
Per curiam	5-judge panel			1	a				
Per curiam	Bryson, Archer,Gajarsa					1	a		
Per curiam	En banc					1	a		
Per curiam	Lourie, Clevenger					1	a		
Per curiam	Markey, Newman, Archer	1	a			1	a		
Per curiam	Mayer, Lourie, Clevenger							2	a
Per curiam	Newman, Michel, Rader			1	a				
Per curiam	Newman, Michel, Schall	2	r						
Per curiam	Newman, Rader, Bryson					1	a		
Per curiam	Nids, Archer, Cohn			1	a				
Per curiam	Nies, Bissell, Archer					1	r		
Per curiam	Nies, Newman, Re					1	a		
Per curiam	Plager, Clevenger, Rader							1	a
Per curiam	Rader, Cowen, Schall	1	a			1	a		
Per curiam	Rich, Newman, Schall							2	a
Plager	Archer, Michel			1	a				
Plager	Clevenger, Gajarsa							1	a
Plager	Clevenger, Rader	1	r						
Plager	Clevenger, Schall							1	r
Plager	Clevenger, Schall			1	a				
Plager	Cowen, Lourie							3	r

Author	Panel	V	How	NV	How	I	How	NI	How
Plager	Cowen, Schall			1	a			1	a
Plager	Lourie, Bryson							1	a
Plager	Lourie, Clevenger			1	a				
Plager	Lourie, Rader			1	a				
Plager	Mayer, Clevenger	1	a						
Plager	Mayer, Michel							1	r
Plager	Michel, Meskill					1	r		
Plager	Michel, Rader			1	a				
Plager	Newman, Michel							1	r
Plager	Rader, Bryson							1	a
Plager	Rich, Clevenger					1	a		
Plager	Rich, Michel							1	a
Plager	Rich, Michel	1	a						
Plager	Rich, Newman							1	a
Plager	Rich, Newman							1	r
Plager	Schall	2	a						
Plager	Schall, Bryson							1	a
Plager	Skelton, Bryson					1	a		
Plager	Smith, Clevenger							1	a
Plager	Smith, Rader	1	a	1	a	1	a		
Plunkett	Newman, Schall					2	r		
Rader	Archer, Gajarsa							1	a
Rader	Archer, Lourie	1	r						
Rader	Archer, Michel	1	a						
Rader	Archer, Plager							1	r
Rader	Archer, Plager	2	a&r	4	a				
Rader	Archer, Skelton					1	a		
Rader	Friedman, Archer							1	a
Rader	Gajarsa	1	r						
Rader	Mayer, Gajarsa			1	a			4	3r,1a
Rader	Mayer, Lourie					1	a	1	a
Rader	Mayer, Lourie	1	a						
Rader	Mayer, Michel							3	a
Rader	Mayer, Michel			1	a				
Rader	Mayer, Michel			1	a				
Rader	Mayer, Michel			2	a				
Rader	Mayer, Newman							1	a
Rader	Mayer, Rich	4	a			4	a		
Rader	Mayer, Schall							3	a
Rader	Mayer, Schall					1	a		
Rader	Michel, Clevenger							1	a
Rader	Michel, Friedman							1	r
Rader	Michel, Gajarsa							1	a
Rader	Michel, Lourie							1	r
Rader	Michel, Lourie			1	a				
Rader	Michel, Schall							1	a
Rader	Newman, Alarcon	1	a						
Rader	Newman, Bryson	1	r			1	r		
Rader	Newman, Cowan					1	r		
Rader	Newman, Gajarsa	1	a						
Rader	Nies, Newman					1	a	2	a
Rader	Nies, Skelton			1	a				
Rader	Plager, Bryson					1	r		
Rader	Plager, Clevenger							1	a
Rader	Plager, Friedman							1	r
Rader	Plager, Smith							1	a
Rader	Rich, Bryson					3	a		
Rader	Rich, Schall			1	a				

Author	Panel	V	How	NV	How	I	How	NI	How
Re	Markey, Newman							2	a
Re	Rich, Smith					1	a		
Rich	5-judge panel			1	r				
Rich	5-judge panel			1	r			1	r
Rich	5-judge panel	1	a						
Rich	5-judge panel	1	a			1	a		
Rich	5-judge panel	1	a	1	r	1	a		
Rich	Archer, Clevenger							1	a
Rich	Archer, Friedman							1	a
Rich	Archer, Mayer	1	a						
Rich	Archer, Mayer	1	a	1	r				
Rich	Archer, Michel					1	a		
Rich	Baldwin, Kashiwa	1	a			1	a		
Rich	Bennett, Clevenger							1	r
Rich	Bennett, Miller					1	a		
Rich	Clevenger, Bryson	1	r						
Rich	Clevenger, Gajarsa					1	r		
Rich	Cowen, Kashiwa			1	a				
Rich	Cowen, Newman							1	r
Rich	Davis, Archer	1	a			1	a		
Rich	Davis, Baldwin			1	r				
Rich	Davis, Cowen			1	a				
Rich	Davis, Cowen			1	a			1	a
Rich	Davis, Skelton			1	a				
Rich	Davis, Smith	1	a						
Rich	Davis, Smith	1	r						
Rich	En banc			1	a				
Rich	Friedman, Cowen							1	a
Rich	Kashiwa, Smith			1	a				
Rich	Lourie, Bryson			1	r				
Rich	Markey, Cowen							1	r
Rich	Markey, Cowen			1	a				
Rich	Markey, Davis	1	a			1	a		
Rich	Markey, Davis	4	a						
Rich	Markey, Friedman			2	a				
Rich	Markey, Kashiwa	1	a			1	a		
Rich	Mayer, Bryson							1	r
Rich	Mayer, Lourie							1	r
Rich	Mayer, Newman			1	a				
Rich	Mayer, Schall	2	a			1	a	1	a
Rich	Michel, Clevenger							1	a
Rich	Michel, Schall							1	a
Rich	Michel, Senter							1	a
Rich	Miller, Archer	1	a			1	a		
Rich	Newman, Bryson							1	a
Rich	Newman, Clevenger	1	a						
Rich	Newman, Cowen	1	a			1	a		
Rich	Newman, Mayer							1	r
Rich	Newman, Michel							1	a
Rich	Newman, Rader							1	a
Rich	Nies, Mayer							1	a
Rich	Nies, Mayer	1	a			1	a		
Rich	Nies, Michel			1	a			1	a
Rich	Nies, Plager	1	a					1	r
Rich	Plager, Bryson	1	r						
Rich	Schall, Gajarsa			2	a				
Rich	Skelton, Archer			2	a				
Rich	Skelton, Clevenger	1	r						

Author	Panel	V	How	NV	How	I	How	NI	How
Rich	Skelton, Kashiwa	1	r					1	a
Rich	Smith, Nichols			1	r				
Rich	Smith, Nies			1	r				
Rich	Smith, Plager	1	a			1	a		
Rich	Smith, Rader	4	a			4	a		
Schall	Archer, Bryson	1	a			1	a		
Schall	Archer, Clevenger			1	a				
Schall	Clevenger, Bryson							1	a
Schall	Michel, Lourie							1	a
Schall	Plager, Clevenger	1	r						
Schall	Rader	1	a			1	a		
Schall	Rader, Plager			1	a				
Skelton	Davis, Miller			1	a				
Smith	Bennett, Nies	1	a			1	a		
Smith	Friedman, Davis	1	a	1	a	1	a		
Smith	Friedman, Skelton					1	a		
Smith	Markey, Baldwin			1	a			1	a
Smith	Miller, Re	1	r					1	a
Smith	Nichols, Nies							1	a
Smith	Nichols, Nies			1	a				
Smith	Rich, Newman			1	a				
Smith	Skelton, Bissell			1	a			1	a
Smith	Skelton, Nies	1	a					1	a

One can make much or little of these data. If this author may be permitted one inference, let it be that an accused infringer had better win below. And even then it is not out of the woods. The court had 256 opportunities to reverse holdings of validity, and did it only 40 times. It had 280 chances to reverse holdings of infringement and did it but 58 times. The accused infringer who loses below thus has a little better than 1 chance in 6 of turning things around on appeal. On the other hand, of the 492 chances the court had to affirm holdings of invalidity or noninfringement, the accused infringer lost out on appeal 130 times. The patent owner, then, has better than 1 chance in 4 when it appeals an unfavorable decision.

Perhaps a word of caution is in order. At least one former member of the court—an influential one by any measure—took vigorous exception to the use of statistics in analyzing the court's jurisprudence. In a talk delivered to the Section of Patent, Trademark and Copyright Law at the Annual Meeting of the American Bar Association in Honolulu, Hawaii on August 8, 1989 (reprinted in the Section's *PTC Newsletter,* Vol. 8, No. 1, Summer/Fall 1989), then Chief Judge Markey called upon the patent bar to defend the court against the assertion, based upon "silly and vicious" result-oriented statistics, that it is "biased in favor of patents." The major thesis of Judge Markey's talk was that each case is decided on its own special facts and circumstances, and the only bias in the court is in favor of a uniform application of the law itself. Nonetheless, a clear primary message in his talk was that he does not approve of conclusions based upon statistical analysis of results alone.

This author happens to agree that statistics do not tell the whole story, or even a large part of it. But I do not agree that the court needs defenders willing, as Judge Markey suggests, to produce "thousands of truthful letters from the bar." The Federal Circuit is perfectly capable of defending itself, if defense be required, simply by continuing to discharge its jurisprudential responsibilities with the same extraordinary competence and efficiency that the bar has come to expect and respect during the court's short life. Moreover, suggesting that statistics may lie or be unfair is a far cry from suggesting that a prudent lawyer should not take them into consideration, together with all other relevant factors, in advising clients.

In previous editions of this book, the author offered his own belief that the enforcement climate in the United States is one that strongly favors the patentee. Several additional years of observation of the Federal Circuit and its impact upon district court infringement litigation has modified that belief somewhat. At the present time, I feel comfortable in concluding that the patent enforcement pendulum is swinging toward a more neutral position, where it really ought to be.

Table of Cases

Cases are referenced to chapter and footnote numbers, e.g., 4: 12; 6: 15, 43 indicates the case is cited in chapter 4, footnote 12 and chapter 6, footnotes 15 and 43. Names of cases discussed in text are italicized; the corresponding footnote number indicating the location of the discussion in text also is italicized, to distinguish the discussion from other footnotes that merely cite the case. Alphabetization is letter-by-letter, e.g., "Airborne" precedes "Air Prods."

A

Abbott Labs.
—v. *Brennan*, 952 F.2d 1346, 21 USPQ2d 1192 (Fed. Cir. 1992) **1:** 112, 113, 118, 126, 134; **8:** 299, 487, 502; **9:** 279; **10:** 224–26, 228, 245; **11:** 128, 149, 169, *253;* **15:** 65; **16:** 46; **17:** 86, 95, 96, 99, 112, 253, 295, 313; *18:* 31
—v. Diamedix Corp., 47 F.3d 1128, 33 USPQ2d 1771 (Fed. Cir. 1995) **8:** 199, 204, 205, 353; *10:* 1
—v. Geneva Pharm. Inc., 182 F.3d 1315, 51 USPQ2d 1307 (Fed. Cir. 1999) **3:** 170, 212, 214

ABB Robotics, Inc. v. GMFanuc Robotics Corp., 52 F.3d 1062, 34 USPQ2d 1597 (Fed. Cir. 1995) **9:** 42, 45, 74

A.B. Chance Co. v. RTE Corp., 854 F.2d 1307, 7 USPQ2d 1881 (Fed. Cir. 1988) **3:** 168, 206; **8:** 318; **9:** 283, 310, 394; *14:* 112; *16:* 310; **17:** 107

A.B. Dick Co. v. Burroughs Corp.
—713 F.2d 700, 218 USPQ 965 (Fed. Cir. 1983) **5:** 113; **6:** 32, 75, 97; *18:* 188, 200, 206
—798 F.2d 1392, 230 USPQ 849 (Fed. Cir. 1986) **9:** 179; **10:** 239

Abele, In re, 684 F.2d 902, 214 USPQ 682 (CCPA 1982) **2:** 44

Abrutyn v. Giovanniello, 15 F.3d 1048, 29 USPQ2d 1615 (Fed. Cir. 1994) *15:* 80, 81; *17:* 52, 79

Abtox, Inc. v. Exitron Corp., 122 F.3d 1019, 43 USPQ2d 1545, *amended opinion,* 46 USPQ2d 1735 (Fed. Cir. 1997) **5:** 286, 331; **6:** 138

A.C. Aukerman Co. v. R.L. Chaides Constr. Co.
—935 F.2d 1262, 18 USPQ2d 2056 (1991) **9:** 6, 7
—960 F.2d 1020, 22 USPQ2d 1321 (Fed. Cir. 1992) **1:** 202; **9:** *5,* 9, 12, 13, 15, 18, 24, 25, 28, 32, 34, 36, 44, 50, 53, 61, 67, 70, 73; **10:** 231, 288; **17:** 263

Ackermann, In re, 444 F.2d 1172, 170 USPQ 340 (CCPA 1971) **4:** 199; **5:** 160

Acoustical Design, Inc. v. Control Elec. Co., 932 F.2d 939, 18 USPQ2d 939 (Fed. Cir. 1991) **7:** 167; **10:** 245; **17:** 96

ACS Hosp. Sys., Inc. v. Montefiore Hosp., 732 F.2d 1572, 221 USPQ 929 (Fed. Cir. 1984) **4:** 167; **5:** 489; **6:** 80; **16:** 279, 288

Adams
United States v., 383 U.S. 39, 148 USPQ 479 (1965) **4:** 14; **5:** 494
—v. United States, 810 F.2d 1142 (Fed. Cir. 1987) *18:* 3

Additive Controls & Measurement Sys., Inc. v. Flowdata, Inc.
—986 F.2d 476, 25 USPQ2d 1798 (Fed. Cir. 1993) **8:** 44, 229, 234; *11:* 250; **13:** 25, 29
—96 F.3d 1390, 40 USPQ2d 1106 (Fed. Cir. 1996) **8:** 482; **13:** 50, 57, 187
—154 F.3d 1345, 47 USPQ2d 1906 (Fed. Cir. 1998) **13:** 30, 51, 53, 55, 161, 166, 177; *17:* 120; *18:* 165

Bandag, Inc.
—v. Al Bolser's Tire Stores, Inc.
——719 F.2d 392, 219 USPQ 1049 (Fed.
    Cir. 1983) *16:* 27
——750 F.2d 903, 223 USPQ 982 (Fed.
    Cir. 1984) *1:* 43; *5:* 448; *6:* 181, 190,
    195, 197, 201; *14:* 43; *16:* 41, 44, 47;
    17: 330; *18:* 122
—v. Gerrard Tire Co., 704 F.2d 1578, 217
    USPQ 977 (Fed. Cir. 1983) *9:* 104; *12:*
    152, 166, 174
Barmag Barmer Masch. AG v. Murata
    Mach., Ltd., 731 F.2d 831, 221 USPQ
    561 (Fed. Cir. 1984) *1:* 203; *2:* 103; *3:*
    171, 179, 199, 202, 228; *9:* 334, 336; *15:*
    132; *17:* 150
Bartfeld, In re, 925 F.2d 1450, 17
    USPQ2d 1885 (Fed. Cir. 1991) *3:* 114;
    15: 339, 363
Barton v. Adang, 162 F.3d 1140, 49
    USPQ2d 1128 (Fed. Cir. 1998) *15:*
    179
Bausch & Lomb, Inc. v. Barnes-Hind,
    Inc., 796 F.2d 443, 230 USPQ 416 (Fed.
    Cir. 1986) *1:* 167, 171, 180, 208; *3:*
    152; *4:* 123, 127, 158, 180, 207, 231; *5:*
    236; *6:* 17; *7:* 40
Baxter Healthcare Corp. v. Spectramed,
    Inc., 49 F.3d 1575, 34 USPQ2d 1120
    (Fed. Cir. 1995) *1:* 221; *6:* 68; *10:* 57,
    121, 155, 161; *16:* 280
Baxter Int'l Inc.
—v. Cobe Labs., Inc., 88 F.3d 1054, 39
    USPQ2d 1437 (Fed. Cir. 1996) *3:* 218,
    238, 250
—v. McGaw Inc., 149 F.3d 1321, 47
    USPQ2d 1225 (Fed. Cir. 1998) *1:* 205;
    9: 181, 278; *15:* 15
Baxter Travenol Labs., In re, 952 F.2d
    388, 21 USPQ2d 1281 (Fed. Cir. 1991)
    3: 53, 62, 87; *4:* 107, 297, 367; *17:* 146
Bayer AG v. Elan Pharm. Research
    Corp., 212 F.3d 1241, 54 USPQ2d 1710
    (Fed. Cir. 2000) *6:* 136, 141, 409; *9:*
    355; *10:* 260
Bayer Aktiengesellschaft v. Duphar Int'l
    Research B.V., 738 F.2d 1237, 222
    USPQ 649 (Fed. Cir. 1984) *6:* 403,
    415; *14:* 109, 215, 233; *16:* 311, 371;
    17: 217
B. Braun Med., Inc. v. Abbott Labs., 124
    F.3d 1419, 43 USPQ2d 1896 (Fed. Cir.
    1997) *5:* 398; *9:* 21; *10:* 68; *11:* 161,
    163, 167
Beachboard v. United States, 727 F.2d
    1092 (Fed. Cir. 1984) *8:* 84, 127; *11:*
    4, 15; *17:* 408
Beachcombers v. Wildewood Creative
    Prods., Inc., 31 F.3d 1154, 31 USPQ2d

1653 (Fed. Cir. 1994) *3:* 156; *5:* 127,
    135, 274, 439; *10:* 214
Beardmore v. Department of Agricul-
    ture, 761 F.2d 677 (Fed. Cir. 1985)
    18: 4
Beatrice Foods Co. v. New England Print-
    ing & Lithographing Co.
—899 F.2d 1171, 14 USPQ2d 1020 (Fed.
    Cir. 1990) *8:* 488; *12:* 13, 18, 92; *18:*
    163
—923 F.2d 1567, 17 USPQ2d 1553 (Fed.
    Cir. 1991) *12:* 169, 204, 205; *14:* 22;
    18: 328
—930 F.2d 1572, 18 USPQ2d 1548 (Fed.
    Cir. 1991) *17:* 257, 354, 433; *18:*
    153, 161
Beattie, In re, 974 F.2d 1309, 24 USPQ2d
    1040 (Fed. Cir. 1992) *4:* 169, 345;
    17: 155
Beauregard, In re, 53 F.3d 1583, 35
    USPQ2d 1383 (Fed. Cir. 1995) *2:* 64;
    16: 465
Beaver, In re, 893 F.2d 329, 13 USPQ2d
    1409 (Fed. Cir. 1989) *15:* 59
Beckman Instruments, Inc. v. LKB Pro-
    dukter AB, 892 F.2d 1547, 13 USPQ2d
    1301 (Fed. Cir. 1989) *3:* 55; *4:* 188;
    10: 119, 174; *14:* 109, 133, 138, 161,
    169, 172, 173, 179, 208, 217; *17:* 221,
    307
Becton Dickinson & Co. v. C.R. Bard,
    Inc., 922 F.2d 792, 17 USPQ2d 1097
    (Fed. Cir. 1990) *5:* 315, 368, 375; *6:*
    15, 27, 34, 97, 238; *9:* 336, 358; *16:* 378,
    381, 451
Beech Aircraft Corp. v. EDO Corp., 990
    F.2d 1237 (Fed. Cir. 1993) *7:* 3, 5; *8:*
    324; *17:* 317; *18:* 277
Beghin-Say Int'l, Inc. v. Ole-Bendt
    Rasmussen, 733 F.2d 1568, 221 USPQ
    1121 (Fed. Cir. 1984) *7:* 54; *8:* 23, 42,
    52, 68; *16:* 11, 14
Bell, In re, 991 F.2d 781, 26 USPQ2d
    1529 (Fed. Cir. 1993) *4:* 362
Bell & Howell DMP Co. v. Altek Sys., 132
    F.3d 701, 45 USPQ2d 1033 (Fed. Cir.
    1997) *5:* 264, 351, 355; *13:* 112, 121,
    132
Bell Comm. Research v. Vitalink Comm.
    Corp., 55 F.3d 615, 34 USPQ2d 1816
    (Fed. Cir. 1995) *5:* 460, 463; *6:* 114
Beloit Corp. v. Valmet OY, 742 F.2d 1421
    (Fed. Cir. 1984) *11:* 98, 99
Belton Indus., Inc. v. United States, 6
    F.3d 756 (Fed. Cir. 1993) *8:* 470
Bennett
—In re, 766 F.2d 524, 226 USPQ 413
    (Fed. Cir. 1985) *15:* 21, 208, 230

Corning Glass Works
—v. Sumitomo Elec. U.S.A., Inc., 868 F.2d 1251, 9 USPQ2d 1962 (Fed. Cir. 1989) *1:* 87, 92; *3:* 34, 48; *5:* 116, 453, 456, 465, 467, 496; *6:* 35, 221, 238, 257, 271
—v. United States ITC, 799 F.2d 1559, 230 USPQ 822 (Fed. Cir. 1986) *11:* 44, 46, 56, 69, 71, 72, 75, 82, 87, 91, 101; *12:* 107; *13:* 60; *16:* 362; *17:* 2, 3, 62, 66; *18:* 296
Cornwall v. U.S. Constr. Mfg., Inc., 800 F.2d 250, 231 USPQ 64 (Fed. Cir. 1986) *8:* 291, 311, 334
Correge v. Murphy, 705 F.2d 1326, 217 USPQ 753 (Fed. Cir. 1983) *11:* 220; *15:* 98, 140, 155
Cortland Line Co. v. Orvis Co., 203 F.3d 1353, 53 USPQ2d 1734 (Fed. Cir. 2000) *6:* 331
Cortright, In re, 165 F.3d 1353, 49 USPQ2d 1464 (Fed. Cir. 1999) *2:* 107, 123; *5:* 33, 59, 62
Costello, In re, 717 F.2d 1346, 219 USPQ 389 (Fed. Cir. 1983) *3:* 113; *15:* 33, 58, 127
Cover v. Hydramatic Packing Co., 83 F.3d 1390, 38 USPQ2d 1783 (Fed. Cir. 1996) *1:* 58, 123, 125, 127; *7:* 146; *9:* 97
Covington v. Department of Health, 750 F.2d 937 (Fed. Cir. 1984) *18:* 167
C.P.C. v. Nosco Plastics, Inc., 719 F.2d 400 (Fed. Cir. 1983) *16:* 215, 239; *17:* 392
CPG Prods. Corp. v. Pegasus Luggage, Inc., 776 F.2d 1007, 227 USPQ 497 (Fed. Cir. 1985) *10:* 364, 365; *11:* 201; *12:* 29, 36; *14:* 89, 202; *16:* 389, 390, 403
Craft Mach. Works, Inc. v. United States, 926 F.2d 1110 (Fed. Cir. 1991) *7:* 107, 108, 120, 139; *11:* 37; *17:* 257; *18:* 11
Crane Co. v. Aeroquip Corp., 364 F. Supp. 547, 179 USPQ 596, *aff'd in part & rev'd in part,* 504 F.2d 1086, 183 USPQ 577 (7th Cir. 1974) *9:* 121
Crawford Fitting Co. v. J.T. Gibbons, Inc., 482 U.S. 437 (1987) *10:* 269; *14:* 180
C.R. Bard, Inc.
—v. Advanced Cardiovascular Sys., Inc., 911 F.2d 670, 15 USPQ2d 1540 (Fed. Cir. 1990) *5:* 239, 368; *6:* 454, 460; *9:* 334, 387; *10:* 270; *17:* 107
—v. M3 Sys. Inc., 157 F.3d 1340, 48 USPQ2d 1225 (Fed. Cir. 1998) *4:* 316; *5:* 315, 403, 464; *6:* 329; *7:* 6, 16, 22, 25, 38; *9:* 143; *11:* 127, 130, 147, 156, 161; *15:* 216

—v. Schwartz, 716 F.2d 874, 219 USPQ 197 (Fed. Cir. 1983) *7:* 70; *8:* 102, 119, 123, 129, 164; *10:* 416; *16:* 11
Credle v. Bond, 25 F.3d 1566, 30 USPQ2d 1911 (Fed. Cir. 1994) *5:* 124, 127; *15:* 32, 91, 173, 178, 182, 183, 189; *17:* 172, 241, 242
Critikon, Inc. v. Becton Dickinson Vascular Access, Inc., 120 F.3d 1253, 43 USPQ2d 1666 (Fed. Cir. 1997) *9:* 128; *14:* 43, 95; *15:* 10
Cronyn, In re, 890 F.2d 1158, 13 USPQ2d 1070 (Fed. Cir. 1989) *3:* 107, 142
Cross v. Iizuka, 753 F.2d 1040, 224 USPQ 739 (Fed. Cir. 1985) *2:* 99, 101, 106, 109, 134; *5:* 8, 54; *15:* 98
Crostic v. Veterans Admin., 730 F.2d 1464 (Fed. Cir. 1984) *8:* 491; *17:* 372, 382, 475
Crucible Materials Corp. v. United States ITC, 127 F.3d 1057 (Fed. Cir. 1997) *11:* 107, 113; *16:* 120, 129
CTS Corp. v. Piher Int'l Corp.
—727 F.2d 1550, 221 USPQ 11 (Fed. Cir. 1984) *10:* 374, 381, 382; *15:* 202; *17:* 137, 138
—754 F.2d 972, 221 USPQ 954 (Fed. Cir. 1984) *12:* 239; *17:* 482
Cuno Engineering Corp. v. Automatic Devices Corp., 314 U.S. 84, 51 USPQ 272 (1941) *4:* 4
Custom Accessories, Inc. v. Jeffrey-Allan Indus., Inc., 807 F.2d 955, 1 USPQ2d 1196 (Fed. Cir. 1986) *1:* 71, 208, 231; *2:* 103; *4:* 84, 87, 104, 105, 114, 127–29, 136, 241, 316, 381; *15:* 287, 288; *16:* 315
CVI/Beta Ventures, Inc. v. Tura LP, 112 F.3d 1146, 42 USPQ2d 1577 (Fed. Cir. 1997) *5:* 298, 327, 353; *16:* 340
Cybor Corp. v. FAS Tech. Inc., 138 F.3d 1448, 46 USPQ2d 1169 (Fed. Cir. 1998) *5: 376,* 390; *6:* 345, 346; *14:* 217, 226; *17:* 183, 201, 214, 220
Cygnus Therapeutics Sys. v. Alza Corp., 92 F.3d 1153, 39 USPQ2d 1666 (Fed. Cir. 1996) *8:* 161; *11:* 151; *16:* 75; *17:* 339
Cyrix Corp. v. SGS-Thompson Microelectronics, Inc., 77 F.3d 1381, 37 USPQ2d 1884 (Fed. Cir. 1996) *6:* 184

D

Dahl v. United States, 695 F.2d 1373 (Fed. Cir. 1982) *7:* 125
Dainippon Screen Mfg. Co. v. CFMT Inc., 142 F.3d 1266, 46 USPQ2d 1616 (Fed. Cir. 1998) *8:* 264, 267, 275, 276, 287, 355, 362; *17:* 251, 292, 328

F

396; *16:* 126, 149, 199, 202, 204; *17:* 48, 52, 128, 296

Hebert v. Lisle Corp., 99 F.3d 1109, 40 USPQ2d 1611 (Fed. Cir. 1996) *5:* 390; *6:* 213, 394; *9:* 146, 195, 198, 251; *10:* 52, 258, 268; *12:* 45, 88

Heck, In re, 699 F.2d 1331, 216 USPQ 1038 (Fed. Cir. 1983) *4:* 182

Hedges, In re, 783 F.2d 1038, 228 USPQ 685 (Fed. Cir. 1986) *4:* 180, 296; *16:* 416

Heidelberger Druckmaschinen AG v. Hantscho Commercial Prods., Inc., 21 F.3d 1068, 30 USPQ2d 1377 (Fed. Cir. 1994) *1:* 153; *2:* 130; *4:* 82, 157, 273, 286, 316; *9:* 241; *17:* 154

Heidelberg Harris Inc. v. Loebach, 145 F.3d 1454, 46 USPQ2d 1948 (Fed. Cir. 1998) *7:* 56, 58, 71, 77, 94; *8:* 214; *17:* 257

Heinemann v. United States, 796 F.2d 451, 230 USPQ 430 (Fed. Cir. 1986) *7:* 189; *9:* 289; *11:* 11; *18:* 19, 129

Heisig v. United States, 719 F.2d 1153 (Fed. Cir. 1983) *17:* 9, 40, 55

Helfgott & Karas P.C. v. Dickinson, 209 F.3d 1328, 54 USPQ2d 1425 (Fed. Cir. 2000) *15:* 5, 23; *16:* 107

Helifix Ltd. v. Blok-Lok Ltd., 208 F.3d 1339, 54 USPQ2d 1299 (Fed. Cir. 2000) *3:* 54, 215; *4:* 127; *15:* 353; *16:* 136, 221

Hemstreet

—v. Computer Entry Sys. Corp., 972 F.2d 1290, 23 USPQ2d 1860 (Fed. Cir. 1992) *9:* 16, 21, 25, 34, 36, 37, 56

—v. Spiegel, Inc., 851 F.2d 348, 7 USPQ2d 1502 (Fed. Cir. 1988) *10:* 393, 419; *18:* 295

Hendler v. United States, 952 F.2d 1364 (Fed. Cir. 1991) *8:* 371, 410, 419, 425; *10:* 1; *16:* 144; *17:* 88

Hess v. Advanced Cardiovascular Sys., Inc., 106 F.3d 976, 41 USPQ2d 1782 (Fed. Cir. 1997) *1:* 207, 236; *7:* 16, 37; *10:* 296

Hester, In re, 838 F.2d 1193, 5 USPQ2d 1832 (Fed. Cir. 1988) *16:* 356

Hester Indus. v. Stein Inc., 142 F.3d 1472, 46 USPQ2d 1641 (Fed. Cir. 1998) *15:* 213, 215, 216, 219, 222, 227, 238, 239

Hewlett-Packard Co.

—v. Bausch & Lomb, Inc.

——882 F.2d 1556, 11 USPQ2d 1750 (Fed. Cir. 1989) *9:* 223, 271–73; *10:* 28, 33; *11:* 157; *14:* 113; *15:* 205, 210, 213, 214, 252; *17:* 321; *18:* 169

——909 F.2d 1464, 15 USPQ2d 1525

(Fed. Cir. 1990) *1:* 167; *4:* 198; *6:* 434, 466

—v. Repeat-O-Type Stencil, 123 F.3d 1445, 43 USPQ2d 1650 (Fed. Cir. 1997) *5:* 282; *6:* 170, 178

H.F. Allen Orchards v. United States, 749 F.2d 1571 (Fed. Cir. 1984) *10:* 401, 403

H.H. Robertson Co. v. United Steel Deck, Inc., 820 F.2d 384, 2 USPQ2d 1926 (Fed. Cir. 1987) *5:* 239; *13:* 70, 75, 76, 78, 82, 85, 90, 97, 99, 120, 122, 123, 133; *16:* 453; *17:* 12, 116

Hibberd, Ex parte, 227 USPQ 443 (PTO Board 1985) *2:* 26

Highland Falls-Fort District v. United States, 48 F.3d 1166 (Fed. Cir. 1995) *8:* 296, 299; *17:* 113

High Tech Med. Instrumentation, Inc. v. New Image Indus., Inc., 49 F.3d 1551, 33 USPQ2d 2005 (Fed. Cir. 1995) *6:* 112; *13:* 1, 66, 80, 126, 127; *16:* 428; *17:* 116

Hilgraeve Corp. v. McAfee Assoc. Inc., 224 F.3d 1349, 55 USPQ2d 1656 (Fed. Cir. 2000) *5:* 430

Hi-Life Prods., Inc. v. American Nat'l Water-Mattress Corp., 842 F.2d 323, 6 USPQ2d 1132 (Fed. Cir. 1988) *6:* 40, 414, 420; *9:* 283

Hill-Rom Co. v. Kinetic Concepts Inc., 209 F.3d 1337, 54 USPQ2d 1437 (Fed. Cir. 2000) *5:* 319, 346; *16:* 430, 488; *18:* 199

Hills Materials Co. v. Rice, 982 F.2d 514 (Fed. Cir. 1992) *7:* 109, 110, 112

Hilton Davis Chem. Co. v. Warner-Jenkinson Co.

—62 F.3d 1512, 35 USPQ2d 1641 (Fed. Cir. 1995), *rev'd & rem'd,* 520 U.S. 17, 41 USPQ2d 1865 (1997) *1:* 57; *6:* 10, *240,* 246; *10: 103*

—114 F.3d 1161, 43 USPQ2d 1152 (Fed. Cir. 1997) *6:* 255, 408

Hiniker, In re, 150 F.3d 1362, 47 USPQ2d 1523 (Fed. Cir. 1998) *15:* 281, 309; *16:* 301

Hobbs v. Beach, 180 U.S. 383 (1900) *2:* 77

Hockerson-Halberstadt Inc.

—v. Avia Group Int'l Inc., 222 F.3d 951, 55 USPQ2d 1487 (Fed. Cir. 2000) *5:* 273, 317, 324

—v. Converse Inc., 183 F.3d 1369, 51 USPQ2d 1518 (Fed. Cir. 1999) *15:* 299, 300; *17:* 181

Hodosh v. Block Drug Co.

—786 F.2d 1136, 229 USPQ 182 (Fed.

Q

R

V

Index

References are to page numbers.

About the Author

Robert L. Harmon was a partner with the Chicago intellectual property law firm of Brinks Hofer Gilson & Lione for 33 years, where he specialized in patent litigation. He retired from the firm at the end of 1997 to devote his professional efforts largely to service as an expert witness and special master in patent infringement cases, although he continues to consult with the firm on special projects. He received a B.S.E. degree in electrical engineering in 1960 and a J.D. degree in 1963, both from the University of Michigan. Upon graduation from law school, he served for two years as law clerk to Judge Arthur M. Smith of the U.S. Court of Customs and Patent Appeals. He is a member of the Illinois, Wisconsin, and District of Columbia bars and is admitted to practice before the U.S. Supreme Court and numerous federal appellate and trial courts. He was coauthor, with the late Judge Smith, of the casebook Smith, *Patent Law* (2d ed. 1964), and has published articles in the intellectual property field both in the United States and Japan. Although he remains based in Chicago, he spends the winter months on the bonefish flats of the Florida Keys and the summer months on the trout streams of central Wisconsin, where he pursues his passion for flyfishing.